A
GENEVA
SERIES
COMMENTARY

EZEKIEL

AN EXPOSITION OF EZEKIEL

William Greenhill

THE BANNER OF TRUTH TRUST

THE BANNER OF TRUTH TRUST

Head Office
3 Murrayfield Road
Edinburgh, EH12 6EL
UK

North America Office
610 Alexander Spring Road
Carlisle, PA 17015
USA

banneroftruth.org

First published 1645-1667
First Banner of Truth Trust edition reprinted from
the 1863 Nichol edition 1994
Reprinted 2024

*

ISBN: 978 0 85151 669 1

*

Printed in the USA by
Versa Press Inc.,
East Peoria, IL.

ADVERTISEMENT.

THE Rev. William Greenhill, the learned and pious author of the following Exposition, was born in the year 1581, of humble parents residing in Oxfordshire. As early as the age of thirteen he entered a student of Magdalen College, Oxford, in the condition of Servitor, and when he had completed his twenty-first year, took his degree of Master of Arts. In 1643 he acted as one of the Assembly of Divines at Westminster, and about the same time was made afternoon lecturer at Stepney church. Mr. Jeremiah Burroughs preached there in the morning at seven o'clock, and Mr. Greenhill in the afternoon at three, and were hence styled "the Morning Star" and "the Evening Star" of Stepney. He was chosen to be chaplain to the dukes of York and Gloucester, and the Lady Henrietta Maria, and in the year 1656 had the living of Stepney presented to him. Calamy says, "He was a worthy man, and much valued for his great learning and unwearied labours." Howe styles him "that eminent servant of God, Mr. Greenhill, whose praise is still in the churches."

His Exposition of the Prophecy of Ezekiel was delivered in Lectures in the city of London, which were attended by many of the chief personages of his day, and have been long and deservedly valued. They were originally printed a volume at a time, as the lectures on a few chapters were concluded, till five small quarto volumes completed the Exposition. Happy that biblical student thought himself who could obtain a perfect copy, although it has been sold at the enormous price of from seven to ten pounds. The last volume is rarely to be obtained; and is supposed to have been destroyed in the calamitous fire of London.

No pains or expense have been spared to render this edition complete. It could hardly be expected that in a work of this magnitude no errors should inadvertently have been overlooked, but, from the most careful examination, it is confidently expected they will scarcely be found. Believing that the reader of Greenhill would not thank any editor who might attempt to beautify his style, the reviser has been anxious that he might appear again in his own garb of 1650, and not in the more polite dress of 1837. His style is abrupt, not always chaste, often imperfect, and full of singularities; yet searching, bold, striking, and effective. An attempt to improve it would most likely enfeeble it, and shear it of its point and power.

Like most writers of his day, he introduces Latin quotations very frequently in the margin, the substance of which generally appears in the exposition. As they encumber the page, and seldom illustrate the text, many of them have been omitted; but whenever they throw any fresh light on the scripture, not to be found in the Exposition, they have been either introduced into the body of the work, or retained as notes. He also frequently inserts a Hebrew, Greek, or Latin word not answering any critical purpose, nor even by way of illustration, but, apparently, because the original of a casual English word occurred to him while writing: in these cases it has been left out; but when such a word was essential to the elucidation of a passage, it has been invariably preserved.

The only alterations in this edition are, the occasional substitution of a more common for an obsolete word—the rectifying of numerous errors of the pen or press—and the omission of some coarse and indelicate expressions, not at all connected with the explication of the prophecy. The reviser has not felt himself at liberty to alter a single sentiment of Greenhill, or to soften any of his statements, for which no editor is accountable. Various remarks occur on the discipline and government of churches, and other matters, peculiar to the times, which may not agree with the sentiments of some readers; but the omission of them would have been unwarrantable, and any attempt to alter them to the taste of the reviser, criminal. Indeed no omissions or alterations have extended to a single word, but such as were essential more clearly to understand the author, and to render his general design more apparent.

As a practical expositor of Ezekiel, whose prophecy contains many things "hard to be understood," Greenhill will ever rank deservedly high. He fully explains the meaning of the prophet, and then applies the truth to the consciences of his auditory by many most pertinent and heart-searching observations. It is impossible that a prayerful mind can read this exposition, without growing "in grace and in the knowledge of our Lord and Saviour Jesus Christ."

The reviser trusts that the future readers of Greenhill will reap the fruits of much anxiety and care, to prepare for them an edition of this valuable work, in which the sentiments of the author should be faithfully retained, and the peculiar spirit of his style be uniformly manifest; while the translation of the Greek and Latin words and phrases—the beautiful typography—the condensation of five volumes into one of moderate size—one complete index and table of texts, instead of one to each volume, and the correctness, portability, and cheapness of this edition, he hopes will be considered real improvements to the Exposition. And he earnestly prays that by its more general circulation among theological students and private christians, the knowledge of salvation through Christ may be advanced, and the holiness of the christian character be promoted.

J. SHERMAN.

Surrey Chapel,
January 26th, 1837.

THE EPISTLES DEDICATORY.

[PREFIXED IN THE ORIGINAL EDITION TO THE PART CONTAINING CHAP. I.—V.]

TO

THE EXCELLENT PRINCESS,

AND MOST HOPEFUL LADY,

THE PRINCESS ELIZABETH,

HER HIGHNESS.

MAY IT PLEASE YOUR HIGHNESS,

SOLOMON, the wisest of princes, counsels us to remember our Creator in the days of our youth. It is a great virtue to be mindful of God timely. Timothy from a child knew the holy Scriptures. Josiah, that good prince, while he was yet young, or tender, (as the Hebrew bears it,) began to seek after the Lord; he did that which was right in his sight, 2 Chron. xxxiv. 3; he walked in the ways of David, he turned not aside to the right hand or left, 2 Kings xxii. 2. The Lord takes special notice when young ones are mindful of him. The children's crying "Hosanna" is recorded in the gospel, Matt. xxi. 15; children walking in the truth, is observed by John, 2 Epist. 4; and the Lord minded the good that was found in the child of Jeroboam, 1 Kings xiv. 13. Doubtless God's eye is upon your Highness, for that good which is found in you in these your tender years, and is well pleased that your sweetness of nature and choiceness of wit are joined with desire to know him, with love to his worship, affection to the godly, and delight in such sentences as these are, viz.

> Χαίρετε ἐν Κυρίῳ πάντοτε, πάλιν ἐρῶ, Χαίρετε.
> Deus meus et omnia.
> La mia Grandezza dal Eccelso.

All which, with these precious speeches of yours, "I had rather be a beggar here than not go to heaven," and, "How shall I be sure to go to heaven?" are acceptable to the Highest, and make strong impressions upon us inferiors. Your desire to know the original tongues, that you may understand the Scripture the better; your resolution to write them out with your own princely hand, and to come to the perfect knowledge of them, breed in us hopes that you will exceed all of your sex, and be without equal in Europe; as Drusius said of his son, who at five years learned Hebrew, and at twelve wrote it *extempore*, both in prose and verse. Encouraging instances your own sex will afford. Eustochium profited so much in the Latin, Hebrew, and Greek, that in her time she was called the wonder of the world. Istrina, queen of the Scythians, so excelled in Greek, that she taught her sons the Greek tongue. Zenobia, queen of the Palmyrenians, was skilled in the Latin, Egyptian, and Greek tongues; she read the Roman story in Greek, abridged the Alexandrian and all the oriental histories. Politian hath an epistle to Cassandra, a Venetian maid, whom he calls the glory of Italy. Her delight was not in wool, but books; not in the spindle or needle, but in the pen; not in paint, but in ink: she wrote epistles and orations to admiration; she excelled in logic and philosophy, and had such perfections, as caused the learned to admire, if not adore her. Queen Elizabeth was so learned, that she read every author in the original, and answered ambassadors of most nations in their own language: she went twice to Oxford, and once to Cambridge, purposely to hear the learned academical disputations, where herself made Latin orations: she translated Sallust, and wrote a century of sentences: she set apart some hours daily to read, or hear others read to her: she so excelled in learning and wisdom, that her teachers rather learned of her than brought learning to her. Your Highness seems to aim at all the excellences in the prementioned; for your writing out the Lord's Prayer in Greek, some texts of Scripture in Hebrew, your endeavour after the exact knowledge of those holy tongues, with other languages and learned accomplishments, your diligent hearing of the word, careful noting of sermons, understanding answers at the catechising, and frequent questioning about holy things, do promise great matters from you. If the harvest be answerable to the spring, your Highness will be the wonder of the learned, and glory of the godly. It is my unhappiness that I cannot be sufficiently adjuvant to such princely beginnings; yet because this following treatise is an exposition of Scripture, I take the boldness to present it to your Highness, and shall continue to pray to him who is All, and able to give all, that he would preserve your royal person, bless your hopeful endeavours, fill you with all divine perfections, make you a chief praise in Israel, and fit you for an eternal weight of glory.

Your Highness's most humble servant,

WILLIAM GREENHILL.

TO ALL WELL-WILLERS OF TRUTH;

ESPECIALLY TO THE AUTHORS AND FAUTORS OF THE EXPOSITORY LECTURES IN THIS CITY.

In most arts and sciences are difficulties; in divinity are depths. Plato, Aristotle, Euclid, have their *nodos*, and the Scriptures have their *δυσνόητα*. In them are dark sayings, Psal. lxxviii. 2; riddles, Ezek. xvii. 2; parables, Matt. xiii. 35; wonders, Psal. cxix. 18; great things, Hos. viii. 12; things hard to be uttered, Heb. v. 11; hard to be understood, 2 Pet. iii. 16; mysteries, Matt. iii. 11; hidden and manifold wisdom, 1 Cor. ii. 7; Eph. iii. 10; the deep things of God, 1 Cor. ii. 10. Much is in it that God hath intermixed the Holy Scriptures with some difficulties. Hereby we are led up to conceive there are infinite depths in God, which eternity must take us up to study. They convince us of our incapacity of high things, John xvi. 12; they prevent our undervaluing of divine truth. Flesh and blood is very apt, upon reading, and apprehension of easiness, to lay aside choice works; God hath therefore hid some truths under the rocks, laid them deep, that so there might be digging and searching, as for treasures, Prov. ii. 4. Difficulties quicken and whet endeavours. Sloth is a great gulf which hinders men from coming at the truth; and it made the Father fear* lest thereby the Lord's book should not only be shut, but also sealed up. Ingenuous spirits, when they hear of hard things, stir livelily; and what they get by sorest labour, is most precious. The rocky and knotty things in the prophets and apostles suffice to exercise the greatest abilities and graces which are seated in human nature;† they keep men's thoughts from swelling into a conceit of omnisciency; they make us long to be where we shall know as we are known, 1 Cor. xiii. 12; and, in the mean time, to pray with David, "Open thou our eyes, that we may see the wonders of thy law." Hard things drove David to the Lord; he knew that without God he could not understand the things of God,‡ whose glory it is both to conceal and reveal a thing, Prov. xxv. 2; Matt. xvi. 17. Many have sued to God for further discovery of his mind, and have attempted to help us in Scripture difficulties; but all dark things are not yet cleared, nor all depths yet sounded. To this day a veil is upon the heart of the Jews in reading the Old Testament, 2 Cor. iii. 14, 15; and surely, the veil is not fully removed from the hearts of us christians. We have seen very dimly into sundry things, not only of Paul, Peter, and John, but of Moses and the prophets, especially of this prophet Ezekiel; who hath, therefore, been passed over, both by writers and readers, as dark, difficult, and less useful. Robert Stephen § mentions one, and that a Sar-

* Ego vereor ne per nimiam negligentiam et stoliditatem cordis non solum velata sint nobis divina volumina, sed etiam signata. *Origen.*

† In verbo Dei abundat quod perfectus comedat, et quod parvulus fugat. *Fulg.*

‡ Sine Deo, impossibile est discere Deum. *Iren.*

§ Respons. ad censu. Theol. Paris. in præf.

bonist, who had lived above fifty years, and knew not what the New Testament meant: and have not sundry persons among us lived their fifty years, and not known what Ezekiel meant? hath he not been a book clasped and sealed unto them? If this hieroglyphical prophet have been a wonder to all for his visions, yet he hath been known to few, by reason of the abstruseness of his visions, which have kept off great rabbies from employing their talents to open them. If weakness and error be found in these poor labours of mine, I entreat you to remember, I have been among prophetical deeps and difficulties, which may plead for him who, knowing his own insufficiencies, came *invita Minerva* to this task. If any light appear for the better understanding of these enigmatical things, I must say with Daniel, there is a God in heaven which revealeth mysteries, to him be all the glory, Dan. ii. 28.

My prayers shall be to him who enlighteneth every man which cometh into the world, that he would anoint your eyes with eye-salve, whereby you may daily see more into the great and glorious truths of God, and those things which may strongly make for your eternal peace and comfort. So prayeth

Your friend and servant in the Lord,

W. G.

[PREFIXED IN THE ORIGINAL EDITION TO THE PART CONTAINING CHAP. VI.—XIII.]

TO ALL LOVERS OF DIVINE TRUTHS;

ESPECIALLY THE UNDERTAKERS FOR THE EXPOSITORY LECTURES IN THE CITY OF LONDON.

THE infinite and only wise God hath annexed to the ministry conversion, Acts xxvi. 18; regeneration, 1 Cor. iv. 15; the addition of sinners to the church and to himself, Acts ii. 41, 47; xi. 24; faith, Rom. x. 14; 1 Cor. iii. 5; the perfecting of the saints, and edification of the body of Christ, Eph. iv. 12; collation of the Spirit, Gal. iii. 2; Acts x. 44; yea, salvation, Acts xi. 14; 1 Cor. i. 21; 1 Tim. iv. 16. Now, notwithstanding the ministry be the great medium and appointment of God to effect and accomplish such needful and glorious things, yet some there be that thrust hard at it, and endeavour to throw it down. But were it removed, and the pernicious desires of men fulfilled herein, a sadder judgment could not befall the nation. Solomon, the firstborn of Wisdom, saith, "Where there is no vision the people perish," Prov. xxix. 18. Where the word of God is not expounded, preached, and applied to the several conditions of the people, there they perish. *Feriabitur populus,* saith Montanus, they will be idle, keep holiday, cease from doing the work of the Lord, and do the works of the flesh and darkness. Piscator reads it, *Nudatur populus,* The people is made naked: they are like men without clothing, without armour, exposed to wind and weather, to spiritual storms and temptations, having nothing to defend themselves. The Vulgate is, *dissipabitur populus;* lay aside preaching and expounding the Scriptures, the people will be scattered, run into errors, wander up and down as sheep without a shepherd. Pagnine hath it, *Rebellis erit,* The people will be rebellious, they will not be kept in order, obedience, and subjection to authority; for where means of knowledge are wanting, there must be ignorance, and ignorance is the mother of rebellion.

When queen Elizabeth, whose memory is precious, was instigated, by some ill-affected to the ministry, to abridge the number of preachers, Edmund Grindal, archbishop of Canterbury, was much troubled at it, and wrote her a learned and serious letter about it; out of which, having the manuscript by me, I have thought fit to transcribe and commend unto you what follows:

"I cannot marvel enough how this strange opinion should once enter into your mind, that it should be good for the church to have few preachers? Alas! Madam, is the Scripture more plain in any one thing, than that the gospel of Christ should be plentifully produced? and that plenty of labourers should be sent into the Lord's harvest, which being great and large, standeth in need of not a few but many workmen? There were appointed to the building of Solomon's material temple a hundred and fifteen thousand artificers and labourers, besides three hundred and thirty overseers, and shall we think that a few preachers may suffice to build and edify the spiritual temple of Christ, which is the church. Christ, when he sendeth forth his apostles, saith unto them, 'Go ye, preach the gospel to every creature.' But all God's creatures cannot be instructed in the gospel, unless all possible means be used to have a multitude of preachers and teachers to preach unto them. 'Let the word of Christ dwell in you richly,' saith Paul, Col. iii. 16. And to Timothy, 2 Epist. iv. 2, 'Preach the word, be instant in season, out of season; reprove, rebuke, exhort,' which thing cannot be done without often and much preaching. To this agreeth the practice of Christ's apostles, Acts xiv. 23, 'And when they had ordained them elders in every church.' Paul likewise to Titus, chap. i. 5, writeth, 'For this cause left I thee in Crete, that thou shouldest set in order the things that are wanting, and ordain elders in every city;' and afterward describeth how the presbytery should be qualified; not such as we are compelled to admit, by mere necessity, unless we should leave a great number of churches utterly desolate, but such indeed as were able to exhort, 'by sound doctrine convincing the gainsayers.' And in this place I beseech your Majesty to note one thing necessary to be noted, which is this; if the Holy Ghost prescribe expressly that preachers should be placed in every city, how can it well be thought that two or three preachers may suffice for a shire? Public and continual preaching of God's word is the ordinary means and instrument of the salvation of mankind. St. Paul calls it, The ministry of reconciliation of man unto God. By the preaching of God's word, the glory of God is enlarged, faith nourished, and charity increased; by it ignorance is instructed, the negligent exhorted and incited, the stubborn rebuked, the weak comforted, and to all those that sin of malicious wickedness, the wrath of God is threatened. By preaching also, due obedience to christian princes and magistrates is planted in the hearts of subjects; for obedience proceedeth of conscience, conscience is grounded upon the word of God, and the word of God worketh this effect by preaching, so as generally where preaching is neglected, obedience faileth. No prince ever had more lively experience hereof than your Majesty hath had in your time, and may have daily. If your Majesty come to the city of London never so often, what great gratulation, what joy, what concourse of people is there to be seen, yea, what acclamations and prayers to God for your long life, and other manifest significations of inward and unfeigned love, joined with most humble and hearty obedience, are there to be heard! Whereof cometh this, Madam, but of the continual preaching of God's word in the city, whereby that people hath been plenteously instructed in their duty towards God, and towards your Majesty? On the contrary, what bred the rebellion in the north? Was it not papistry, and the ignorance of God's holy word through want of preaching? And in the time of that rebellion, were not all men of all estates that made profession of the gospel, most ready to offer their lives for your defence? insomuch that one poor parish in Yorkshire, which by continual preaching had been better instructed than the rest, Halifax I mean, was ready to bring three or four thousand able men into the field, to serve you against the said rebels. How can your Majesty have a more lively trial and experience of the contrary effects of much preaching, and little or no preaching? the one working most unnatural disobedience and rebellion, the other most faithful obedience."

By this part of the letter you see how firm the archbishop was for preaching, and that he hath fully confirmed that sense of the words, Where there is no vision or preaching, the people will rebel; and if he would not yield to the abridging of preachers, why should any desire the abolishing of them, and so make way for the people to be idle, naked, scattered, rebellious, yea, for their perishing? It was one of the saddest times that ever Israel had, when Israel was without a teaching priest, 2 Chron. xv. 3; then they had no peace within nor without, but great vexations were upon all the inhabitants of the countries, even all the ten tribes. This being without a teaching priest was such an affliction, as that the Lord promised his people afterwards, that what affliction soever befell them, this should not; Isa. xxx. 20, "Though the Lord give you the bread of adversity, and water of affliction, yet shall not thy teachers be removed into a corner any more, but thine eyes shall see thy teachers." This is a gracious promise for the continuance of the ministry. They had the law, and should have teachers to instruct them therein; we have the gospel, and teachers to instruct us therein. The church and ministry may be hid, Rev. xii. 6, but not extinct. Christ is a King, the government is upon his shoulder, he has a kingdom, and it knows no end, Isa. ix. 6, 7; Luke i. 32, 33; his throne is for ever, Heb. i. 8. He, therefore, hath promised to be with his church, and the ministry thereof, unto the end of the world, *ἕως τῆς συντελείας τοῦ αἰῶνος*, Matt. xxviii. 20; not, to the end of that age, but of the world; for so the word *αιων* signifies: Matt. xiii. 39, 40, "The harvest is the end of the world;—and so shall it be in the end of the world;" *ὁ δὲ θερισμὸς συντέλεια τοῦ αἰῶνός ἐστιν.—οὕτως ἔσται ἐν τῇ συντελείᾳ τοῦ αἰῶνος τούτου.* Christ's kingdom, and officers of it, were not only for the apostolical and primitive times, but for all times and ages, Eph. iii. 21; iv. 11, 12; Rev. vii. 14, 15; xi. 19; otherwise what hope were there for Jews or gentiles? If one should leave the Jewish synagogue, and the other heathenism, whither should they come, if Christ have no true church, no visible kingdom? Herein himself hath satisfied us: John x. 16, "Other sheep I have, which are not of this fold; them also I must bring, and they shall hear my voice; and there shall be one fold, and one shepherd." The fold was the church, the sheep to be brought in, the gentiles, who were not brought in in Christ's days, nor all in the apostles' days, or primitive times. Some are yet to be brought in; and therefore there is yet a fold, and ministers to cause them to hear the voice of Christ, that they may come into this fold: for whom he predestinates he calls, Rom. viii. 30; and his calling is not immediate, but by the ministry of the word. And though the ministry now be not infallible, as the apostles were, but fallible, yet their fallibility doth not make void their calling, nor cause the churches to be reputed false, as not having the word of God taught in them infallibly; for those holy men who were prophets and apostles you may find sometimes failing. Nathan failed, when he bid David go and build the house of the Lord, 2 Sam. vii. 3. David was out, when he said he was cut off from before the Lord's eyes, Psal. xxxi. 22; and when he said, all men were liars, Psal. cxvi. 11. Jeremiah spake like a man, when he said, "I will not make mention of him, nor speak any more in his name;" and especially when he cursed the day of his nativity, and the man who brought tidings thereof, chap. xx. 9, 14—16. Jonah spake from himself, not from God, when he said, "Take my life from me; for it is better for me to die than to live;" and, "I do well to be angry even unto death," Jonah iv. 3, 9. And Paul professes he had no commandment of the Lord concerning virgins, but gave his judgment as one that had "obtained mercy of the Lord to be faithful," 1 Cor. vii. 25. Now, though these men had such failings, spake from their own spirits, yet were neither the churches falsified hereby, nor their callings frustrated. That which was needful to be the rule and standard, was given out by an infallible Spirit. The Spirit of truth took of Christ's, showed it to them, and led them into all truth. And while the ministers now do bring that truth unto you, they are infallible. If in their constructions, interpretations, and expositions of the same, they vary, or be out, you ought to "try the spirits," 1 John iv. 1; and to "hold fast what is good," 1 Thess. v. 21; not despising prophesyings, lest you quench the Spirit. It is ill when any destroy commands of God to maintain their opinions. Some would have the word only read, and that there should be no preaching or expounding of it. It was not the eunuch's reading, but Philip's preaching, that wrought faith in him, Acts viii. The spices of the Scripture send forth the strongest and sweetest smells when they are bruised and broken; the fire of the sanctuary yields most heat and light when stirred up and blown. It is neither fleshly, devilish, nor treason to the Father, to make constructions upon the prophets and apostles, and expound their meaning. If so, then Ezra and others, who read the law and gave the sense of it, Neh. viii. 8, sinned, were fleshly, devilish, and traitors to the Father: then Paul gave ill counsel to Timothy, to divide the word of truth aright, 2 Tim. ii. 15. How children should have their milk, young men their bread, old men their wine, and that only by reading, I see not. If that could be, surely Christ needed not have appointed a wise and faithful servant "over his household, to give them meat in due season," Matt. xxiv. 45. If we may not expound the word because we are fallible, then why should any translate the word out of the original tongue into others, seeing they are fallible, and may, yea have, mistaken therein, as well as others in expounding and preaching: and because it is so, some little regard the Scriptures, expecting *evangelium Spiritus Sancti et tertium Testamentum*, the gospel of the Holy Spirit and a third Testament.* The Jews look for Messias, the papists look for Enoch and Elias, but without warrant; and so do these men for another gospel, Gal. i. 8, 9, and extraordinary men, who may raise up churches, and declare what is truth. I beseech you, be content with, and thankful for, those precious, glorious truths the Lord hath given you in the law and gospel, studying to know them more fully; and endeavour to yield unto the Author of them the obedience of faith; acknowledging it an unspeakable gift, that you have them, with preachers and expositors amongst you, to further you in the knowledge and practice of them. If this ensuing work shall contribute aught that way, I shall be abundantly satisfied therein. In hopes whereof, I commend both it and you to the blessing of the Lord, subscribing myself,

Yours in this work of the Lord
to love and serve,

Septemb. 28, 1649. W. G.

* Vide Hornbeeck in Apolog. pro Eccles. Christiana.

[PREFIXED IN THE ORIGINAL EDITION TO THE PART CONTAINING CHAP. XIV.—XIX.]

TO THE UNDERTAKERS FOR AND HEARERS OF THE EXPOSITORY LECTURES IN THE CITY OF LONDON,

AND ALL WHO DESIRE UNDERSTANDING IN THE WORD OF GOD.

When I was expounding the 17th and 19th chapters of this Prophecy of Ezekiel, and saw an end put to kingly government in Judah, (for after Zedekiah there was "no strong rod to be a sceptre to rule,") my thoughts ran much upon that ancient prophecy, Gen. xlix. 10, "The sceptre shall not depart from Judah, nor a lawgiver from between his feet, until Shiloh come." Concerning which, though somewhat were then said, yet I shall now endeavour to satisfy both you and myself more fully. The words seem to imply a presence of the sceptre in the hand of Judah when they were given forth; because a thing cannot be said to depart from any who hath it not; but it was long after ere the tribe of Judah had any sceptre. Jacob's meaning was, that the sceptre should come in time to that tribe, and when it came, it should not depart; for Jacob prophesies of things to come. They were at that time in Egypt, few, poor, and low; and when they were increased, they had no sceptre amongst them, they were under the Egyptian sceptre, and had Egyptian task-masters over them. After the Lord had brought them out of Egypt by a strong hand, there was a sceptre and lawgiver amongst them; but it was Moses, who was of the tribe of Levi, Exod. ii. 1, 2, 10, and after him Joshua, who was of the tribe of Ephraim, Numb. xiii. 8, 16. All that Judah had was a little priority in pitching his standard and camp first, Numb. ii. 3; in sending the first prince to offer at the dedication of the tabernacle, Numb. vii. 12; in marching first from Sinai to Paran, Numb. x. 14; in having the first lot when the land of Canaan was divided, Josh. xv.; and in going up first to fight against the Canaanites, Judg. i. 2. And when account was taken of the genealogies, Judah carried the pre-eminence, being first numbered, 1 Chron. ii. 3. Afterwards in the days of the judges, who bare the sceptre three hundred and thirty-nine, or three hundred and sixty-two, or three hundred and seventy years, as the accounts of chronologers are, or about four hundred and fifty, as the apostles' account is, Acts xiii. 20, there were but two of the tribe of Judah; Othniel, Judg. iii. 9, who was of that tribe, as appears, Josh. xv. 17, 20; 1 Chron. iv. 1, 13; and Ibzan, who was of Bethlehem, Judg. xii. 8. The following judges were of other tribes. And when it came to kingly power, the first set up was Saul, who was a Benjamite, 1 Sam. ix. 1, 2. The next was David, of Jesse, the Bethlehemite, 1 Sam. xvi. 1. It was now between six and seven hundred years from the time of Jacob's giving out this prophecy, all which time it lay as dead and destitute of regal power; which now being settled in this tribe, continued but to the captivity of Zedekiah, four hundred and sixty-eight, as some do chronologize, four hundred and seventy-three years, as others. The first king the Jews had God gave them in his wrath, 1 Sam. viii.; and the last he took away in his fury. Judah, that had been his pleasant plant, "was plucked up in fury," Ezek. xix. 12, and all the branches of that vine plucked off, and not one left to hold the sceptre, Jer. xxii. 30. Therefore some Jews and others, deriving the word *Shiloh* from *Shalach*, render the words, until he who is to be sent shall come; and so interpret this prophecy of Nebuchadnezzar, who was sent of God to destroy Judea, and so the sceptre departed from Judah. But the next words in the prophecy confute this interpretation, "and unto him shall the gathering of the people be." Shiloh was he that the nations should desire, and unto whom the people should be gathered, which never was verified in Nebuchadnezzar. The Chaldee paraphrase hath it, *donec veniat Christus*, till Christ come: and the Targum hath it, until the time wherein Messiah the King shall come. Rabbi Moses Gerundensis saith, *donec veniat filius ejus qui est Messias*, till his son come who is the Messiah.

Helvicus.

Galatinus, l. 4. c. 4. cited by Amama. Lyra in locum.

Vatabl. in loc. Martinii Lexicon in verbo Silo. Manasseh Ben Israel, q. 65. in Genesim.

If we take the word "sceptre" for kingly power, which it certainly notes, as Psal. xlv. 6; Zech. x. 11, it may be granted that now the sceptre departed from Judah; for it is said, Ezek. xxi. 27, "It shall be no more, until he come whose right it is; and I will give it him;" and that was Christ: from the putting down of Zedekiah and the death of his sons, none had right to kingly power till Christ came. Now the crown was laid aside, and laid up for his head alone, and no others. But if we take *shebet*, or *shevet*, for a tribe, as it is Josh. iii. 12; vii. 14; Psal. cxxii. 4; Jacob's sense in the prophecy is, that the tribe of

Judah should not cease, however it fared with other tribes, till Shiloh or Christ came. Ten of the other tribes were carried away captive by Sennacherib, and never returned more; but as for that of Judah, though it were carried into Babylon, yet it was preserved there, and returned again to its own land, with few of any other tribe. It was that tribe chiefly, which made up the estate and church, and continued till Christ's coming.

This sense is true, but reaches not fully the scope of Jacob in this prophecy, which is not simply to show the duration of the tribes, but the peculiar benedictions they should have; and Judah's was, the sceptre, which doth not only note royal power, but any rule, dominion, or authority, as Isa. xiv. 5; Ezek. xix. 11. And so that tribe should have power, more or less, till Shiloh came; if not kings, yet lawgivers; if not supreme, yet subordinate power. Upon the captivity of the ten tribes, kingly power was only and eminently in it for one hundred and thirty years and upwards; and after Zedekiah's downfall, although it lost royal dignity, which was for a lamentation to the prophet, Ezek. xix. 14, yet it had other sceptrical power in it. Manasseh Ben Israel saith, that in Babylon it had its heads and rulers always of the seed of David.

When they returned from Babylon, Zerubbabel was governor of Judah, Hag. i. 1; *et ab illo usque ad Machabœos nunquam defuerunt duces de tribu Judæ, quanquam regio diademate propter persas nunquam uterentur:* from him to the days of the Maccabees, or Asmoneans, they had rulers and governors of that tribe, which was two hundred and seventy years, as Paræus observes; but Rivet makes the time shorter, affirming that the government was *pœnes sacerdotes levitici generis.* When Alexander the Great came into Judea, which he reckons to be but fifty-three years from the time of Zerubbabel, (chronologers make it much more,) at that time Josephus informs us, Jaddus was high priest, who being then the principal ruler, came out to meet Alexander, conducting him into the city and temple. Now the high priests were not of the tribe of Judah, Heb. vii. 13, 14, but of Levi; and so were the Asmoneans, or Maccabees, 1 Macc. ii. 1, 4; 1 Chron. xxiv. 7, among whom continued the chief government till Herod's days, divers of them assuming kingly power to themselves, as Aristobulus, Alexander, Hyrcanus, and Antigonus. Montague observes, that after the captivity they were under the Persians, Alexander, the Macedonian princes of the Lagidan and Seleucidan lines, till the Maccabees freed them for a time; and last of all they were under the Romans: yet during these troublesome times, they were governed by their own laws and country customs. They had their ethnarchs, toparchs, high priests, rulers, princes, and sometimes kings of their own; Jews and Israelites, though not of David, nor of Judah. To help in this strait, it is affirmed that the Asmoneans were by the mother's side of Judah, and so therein the dignity of the tribe was preserved; but it doth not appear by Scriptures, that the females were of that tribe, neither were they to marry out of their tribes, especially women inheritresses to their parents, they were tied to marry in their own tribe, *ne confunderentur hæreditates.* And ordinary women might not bear rule among the Jews, though Deborah a prophetess once did; besides, the mother's line amongst them was not reckoned; and the Talmud saith, he is the end of the family, who hath no masculine issue. We cannot then make it out this way, that the sceptre departed not from Judah, nor a lawgiver from between his feet, till Shiloh came.

Suarez, tom. 1. disput. 1. contra Judæos. Pareus in Gen. Rivet, ibid.

Joseph. Antiq. l. 11. c. ult.

Joseph. Antiq. l. 12. c. 8.

Acts and Monuments of the Church.

Rivet in Gen.

Some therefore, which is the better way, refer it to the sanhedrim, which was *quasi supremus senatus,* as the highest judicatory and royal council. This sanhedrim remained in the captivity, and continued to the days of Christ; and was either taken from them by Herod, or at least the power of judging and sentencing to death was taken out of it by him. Therefore said the Jews, John xviii. 31, "It is not lawful for us to put any man to death." In former times they might, but now they were deprived of that power. The difficulty here is to make it out, that those who made up the sanhedrim were of the tribe of Judah. It is not necessary that all should be of it; if the major part were, that sufficeth to pre-eminence the tribe.

Suarez, tom. 1. disp. 1. contra Judæos, Sect. 1. p. 6.

At first the men of the sanhedrim were chosen out of all the tribes; but when ten tribes fell off, it could not be, they being under Jeroboam and other kings who were against Judah; and much less could it be, when those ten tribes were carried away, and returned no more. The Babylonish captivity therefore being ended when the commonwealth of the Jews was restored, and consisted most of the tribe of Judah, it is more than probable, that the sanhedrim was most of that tribe, which in Scripture account was but one before; for the Lord told Solomon he would give one tribe to his son, 1 Kings xi. 13; and chap. xii. 20, "There was none that followed the house of David, but the tribe of Judah only;" and 2 Kings xvii. 18, "The Lord was very angry with Israel, and removed them out of his sight; there was none left but the tribe of Judah only." Benjamin did follow Rehoboam; but there is little or no mention made of it, *quia*

Suarez ubi ante. *non fuit integra sicut tribus Judæ*, it was not entire as the tribe of Judah, whose dignity and excellency was such as made that inconsiderable. The Levites also, say the Annotations upon 1 Kings xi. were no distinct tribe; when they were cast out by Jeroboam, they left their suburbs and possessions, and came to Judah and Jerusalem, 2 Chron. xi. 13, 14. When therefore the return came from captivity, it was Judah the Lord looked chiefly upon; the rest were either reduced to that tribe, or as inconsiderable then as before the captivity. Judah made up the bulk and body of their commonwealth, and the governing power, if not altogether, yet must needs be mostly in it. Manasseh Ben Israel saith, that in the times of the Asmoneans, *Princeps Jehudæ erat caput senatus Israelitici nuncupati sanhedrin*, A prince of Judah was chief in the great council called the sanhedrim, which continued till Herod's days; and such was the power of it, that Herod himself was called before it, for which, when he obtained the kingdom, he put them all to death, except one Sameas, as Josephus reports in his 14th book of the Antiquities of the Jews, chap. 17. In this sense not only were their rulers and governors of the Jewish nation till Christ came, as some do carry it, but even of the tribe of Judah; for now in Herod's days did Shiloh come, Christ was born, Matt. ii. 1. The sceptre was departing when Pompey brought Judea under the Romans, and the power of it more weakened when it was made a province afterward; but it fully departed not, till Titus overthrew the city, and ruined the whole commonwealth of the Jews; before which time Christ was to come and enter into his kingdom, taking the crown to himself, being his right, (which he did, and changed it into a spiritual kingdom, so raising up the tabernacle of David which was fallen,) and then shortly after was the tribe of Judah and Jewish state utterly ruined.

In this prophecy you see the faithfulness of the Lord, making good his truths notwithstanding all dark and contradictory appearances; his power also, in raising up kingdoms and pulling them down again, in changing forms of government at his pleasure, and bringing them to nothing. You may also see how blind the Jews are, who have many shifts to put off this prophecy from Christ; or being convinced that it is a clear prophecy of the Messiah, affirm it is not yet fulfilled, saying, there are rulers of the tribe of Judah to this day about Babylon, and that a prince was seen at Bagdad, riding in a chariot, where were a multitude of Jews crying, *Facite locum filio Davidis*, Make way for the son of David. It is true, there are Jews in the world, but they have no sceptre, no kingdom; there is no mention or vestigium of any such thing in the world, saith Suarez. Suppose it were so, that in Asia the greater, or beyond the mountains of Cordilliere in America, they had a kingdom and sceptre, yet this was nothing to Jacob's prophecy, which speaks of Canaan, where Judah should have rule and power till Shiloh came. Let those therefore who have seen this prophecy fulfilled, felt the power and enjoyed the blessings of the Messiah, pray that the face of the covering cast over all people, and the veil spread over all nations, may be destroyed; that so Jews and gentiles may behold him who is "the desire of nations," that unto him may be the gathering of the people, and that all saints, especially themselves, may be enabled, through his grace, to improve all mercies, and the ensuing truths, to his glory, which is the earnest desire of him who is

Manasseh Ben Israel. tom. I. Disp. 1.

Yours in the work of the Lord,

W. G.

The 11th month, the 27th day, 1650.

[PREFIXED IN THE ORIGINAL EDITION TO THE PART CONTAINING CHAP. XX.—XXIX.]

TO THOSE IN THE FAMOUS CITY OF LONDON,

WHO ARE THE UNDERTAKERS, PROMOTERS, AND MAINTAINERS OF THE EXPOSITORY LECTURES THEREIN, AND TO ALL OTHERS WHO LOVE TRUTH.

WE read in holy writ of many cities, which for their structures, situations, fortifications, trading, accommodations, and epithets, were famous; as, populous No, Nahum iii. 8; Nineveh the great, Jonah i. 2; Tarsus in Cilicia, Acts xxi. 39; golden Babylon, Isa. xiv. 4; renowned Tyrus, Ezek. xxvi. 17; righteous and faithful Jerusalem, Isa. i. 26, which exceeded them all; for as Canaan was the glory of all lands, flowing with milk and honey, so Jerusalem had its milk and honey, and was the glory of all cities. There was the Lord's presence, his worship, his oracles, his ordinances, and his prophets, which made it the glory of the world, and "perfection of beauty." Had other cities strong towers? Jerusalem had them, and the temple also. Had they gods of gold, silver, stones, and sticks in them? Jerusalem had Jehovah the true and living God in her. Had they wise counsellors in them? Jerusalem had the sanhedrim. Had they human laws which were good? Jerusalem had divine laws, such as no city or people ever had, Deut. iv. 8. Had they temporal excellencies and privileges? Jerusalem had spiritual. Had they the glory of the world, art, and nature? Jerusalem had the glory of heaven; there God shined, Psal. l. 2. But what now is become of these cities, and Jerusalem itself? are they not all laid waste, made heaps, dead and buried in the womb of the earth? Cities have their periods as well as men. Babylon had a time to be born, Gen. xi. 4, and a time to die, Isa. xiv. 4. Nineveh had her day to get up, Gen. x. 11, and her day to fall, Nahum iii. 7. Tyrus had her day of rising, and her day of ruining, and she is descended into the pit with others, Ezek. xxvi. 18, 20. Jerusalem had her day for building, and her day for burning, Jer. lii. 12, 13. This is matter of lamentation, that such cities, especially Jerusalem, should have such an end. The cause of such dismal ends, upon search, we shall find to be SIN, which is of so malignant a nature, that it destroys nations, and pulls down the strongest cities. Cruelty, falsehood, and robbery, with many other, were the sins which laid Nineveh waste, Nahum iii. Pride, fulness of bread, abundance of idleness, with neglect of the poor, were the sins which made the Lord take Sodom away, Ezek. vi. 49, 50. Pride, violence, unmercifulness, vain confidence, and treachery, were the sins which rent Babylon in pieces, Isa. xlvii.; Jer. l. What sins destroyed Ammon, Moab, Edom, Philistia, with their cities, and what sunk Tyrus into the sea, Ezekiel tells you, chap. xxv. and xxvi. A large catalogue of those sins which kindled the fire in Jerusalem, and turned her into ashes, you have in the 22nd of Ezekiel, and other chapters; most of which I fear are to be found in this city. Are there not in her those who set light by father and mother? are there not those who vex the fatherless and widow? are there not those who despise the holy things of God, and profane his sabbaths? are there not those who take usury and increase, are greedy of gain, and live by dishonest gain? Ezek. xxii. 12, 13; are there not those who devise mischief and give wicked counsel? are there not those who carry tales to shed blood? are there not those who exercise robbery, vex the poor, the needy, and oppress the stranger? are not her professors as dross, even the dross of silver? May not the Lord say of this city as he did of Jerusalem, Thou hast "been to me a provocation of mine anger and of my fury from the day that they built thee even unto this day, that I should remove thee from before my face," Jer. xxxii. 31: thou art the city I have been purging, but art not purged; "thou shalt not be purged from thy filthiness, till I have caused my fury to rest upon thee," Ezek. xxiv. 13. Surely London deserves not better at the hands of the Lord than other cities did, especially Jerusalem; and having her sins, may fear her end. Be instructed therefore, O London, lest the Lord's soul depart from thee, and thou be made desolate; for the Lord hath a day to reckon with sinful lands and cities. Isa. xvii. 4, "In that day the glory of Jacob shall be made thin, and the fatness of his flesh shall wax lean." The princes, counsellors, soldiers, prophets, priests, with their cities, the rarities and riches of them, were the glory and fatness of Jacob; these God had a day to take away, and so made Jacob thin and lean. God had a day for Tyre, and interrupted her great merchandizing for seventy years, by laying her in the deep, Isa. xxiii. 15. If it be demanded, How came Tyrus, so strong and stately, so fat and full, to so deplorable an end? the Spirit of God tells you, when it saith, "Thy rowers have brought thee into great waters," Ezek. xxvii. 26, that is, the princes and rulers, by their pride, policy, and profaneness, caused such storms as sunk the ship. Tyrus had as much to secure her as any city in the world; she was built upon a rock, her borders were in the midst of the seas, she had walls, and an army to watch them; she had towers, and Gammadims to keep them; she wanted not for ships, pilots, mariners, for soldiers, shields, and helmets; she had counsellors, merchants, and plenty of all things, so that she seemed invincible; but all these did not preserve her station, or make her impregnable; for though she endured a siege of thirteen years by Nebuchadrezzar and his forces, yet at last she fell into the midst of the sea in the day of her ruin, Ezek. xxvii. 27. Jerusalem was so well fortified by nature and art, being compassed about with mountains, Psal. cxxv. 2, having walls, bulwarks, and towers, Psal. xlviii. 12, 13, that it was thought incredible, and impossible, for an enemy to have entered her gates, Lam. iv. 12; but sin being found in her, and God against her, nothing secured her. She was oft warned by the prophets, and judiciary providences of God, to repent and reform, Isa. xxxvii.; Amos iv. She was as a pot over the fire, when besieged by Sennacherib, when famine and plague devoured her inhabitants, but her scum went not out, and that was her ruin. Let none think the poor to be the scum of the city; the Lord made the poor as well as the rich, Prov. xxii. 2, and despises not the work of his own hands. It is the sin of rich and poor, it is their wickedness, which is the scum.

Great cities have much sin in them, and so much scum ; unsound opinions, counsels, fashions, and practices. Thus was it with Jerusalem, and her scum boiled in, she was the worse for corrections and judgments, Isa. i. 5, her scum caused the cracking and bursting of the pot. These things the book of God holds forth for our instruction, "upon whom the ends of the world are come." Let our great city and citizens look to it, there is scum in the city, and not a little : is it gone out, or boiled in ? Was not the sword lately at your gates ? was there not yesterday great sickliness within your walls ? is not trading diminished ? have there not been strange murders amongst you ? have not many sad fires been kindled, broke out, and consumed your habitations ? was there not a plot (which hath cost some their lives) to fire your city ? God hath been warning you by these judiciary dispensations, and are you bettered by them ? have all you have seen, feared, or felt, caused your scum to depart from you ? If so, it is well ; well will it be with you, well with your city, and well with your undertakings, and well with your posterity ; but if it be boiled in, and you are the worse for all the boiling judgments and providences you have been in, and under, know that some dreadful calamity, if not destruction itself, hastens, and will certainly take hold of you and your city, without speedy repentance. Hitherto you have had sparing mercy and gentle corrections ; if these lead not to repentance, severity abides for you, and God will say, From the first to the last I have been provoked by this city, "I will break this people and this city," Jer. xix. 11. How sad would it be, should the Lord lay your city waste ! It is not the strong structures, great treasures, military or naval forces, wise counsels, which can protect you, if scum be found amongst you. If you are careful that the filth of the streets be carried out, will you not much more see that the filth of your hearts and houses be purged out ? Will not London be made clean ? when shall it once be ? let this be the time ; lest the plague, which hath been much feared, enter your borders, and cause sad cries in your streets and families. Now "wash you, make you clean, put away the evil of your doings, and learn to do well ; seek judgment, relieve the oppressed, judge the fatherless, and plead for the widow ;" now let holiness of life, execution of justice, speaking truth, doing righteousness, showing mercy, and promoting the good of one another in love, take place ; and they will not only secure you and the city, but make you and it glorious, and perfect in beauty, so that the Lord will take pleasure therein, and say of it and you, This is "the city of righteousness, the faithful city," and her citizens are like herself, righteous and faithful. Now her brass is become gold, her iron silver, her officers peace, and her exactors righteousness ; therefore now her walls shall be salvation, and her gates praise ; now shall she be my habitation, and her people my glory, and I will be to them a defence for evermore. That this may be the portion of this city, and yourselves, and that a blessing may go with this work, is the hearty prayer of him who is

Your servant in this expository
work of the Lord,
WILLIAM GREENHILL.

The 30*th of the* 5*th*
month, 1658.

[PREFIXED IN THE ORIGINAL EDITION TO THE PART CONTAINING THE NINETEEN LAST CHAPTERS.]

TO THE CHRISTIAN READER,

AND ESPECIALLY TO THOSE WHO COUNTENANCED THE EXPOSITORY WORK.

THIS is the fifth and last part upon Ezekiel; which was finished in the latter end of the year 1654, and hath been latent full seven years, like Josiah in the temple; but now, through the instigation of learned and godly ministers, some others, and considerations of mine own, cometh to public view. Ezekiel prophesied unto the Jews, who were then the only people God had in the world, and honoured with singular titles: "sons of the living God," Hos. i. 10, his "firstborn," Exod. iv. 22, his "inheritance," Isa. xix. 25, his "peculiar treasure," Psal. cxxxv. 4, his "pleasant portion," Jer. xii. 10, "a noble vine," chap. ii. 21, "the holy flock," Ezek. xxxvi. 38, "a chosen generation," Isa. xli. 8, 9; 1 Pet. ii. 9, the Lord's "glory," Psal. lxxviii. 61, "the dearly beloved of his soul," Jer xii. 7; and endued with great privileges, Rom. ix. 4, 5: yet were they not exempted from afflictive and severe sufferings; they were "a reproach unto the heathen, a mocking to all countries, and much vexed," Ezek. xxii. 4, 5; the pestilence, sword, and famine consumed them, so that the "pitiful women" did eat their "own children," Lam. iv. 10, and plucked off their own breasts, Ezek. xxiii. 34; the "priests and elders gave up the ghost, while they sought for meat to relieve their souls," Lam. i. 19; those brought up in scarlet embraced dunghills, chap. iv. 5; the women were ravished in Zion, the maids in the cities of Judah, and princes were hanged up by their hands, chap. v. 11, 12; they could not walk safely in the streets, chap. iv. 18; their necks were under persecution, chap. v. 5; lions, Tiglath-pileser and Shalmaneser, took away the ten tribes, and Nebuchadnezzar broke the bones of Judah and Benjamin, Jer. l. 17; he burned the temple and city, he ruined church and state, and carried the Jews into captivity, where they suffered unspeakable misery. The prophet tells us, that their punishment was greater than the Sodomites', Lam. iv. 6. That which chiefly provoked God to deal thus severely with them, as Ezekiel and others testify, was their leaving his pure worship, ordinances, and institutions, falling to false ways of worship, and compliance with the nations. They had "the image of jealousy," Ezek. viii. 3, the altar of Damascus, 2 Kings xvi. "the statutes of Omri," Mic. vi. 16, "high places," 2 Chron. x. 33, traditions and statutes of their fathers, Ezek. xx. 18; Jer. ix. 14, customs of the nations; they set their posts with God's posts; worshipped with their faces toward the east, Ezek. viii. 16; they would be as the heathens, Ezek. xx. 32, and walk after their own imaginations, Jer. xviii. 12, whereas they should have walked in God's laws and statutes, Ezek. xx. 19. When therefore the house of Israel degenerated into dross, God gathered them into the furnace, and poured out his fury upon them, Ezek. xxii. 19—22. Apostatizing from the pure worship of God, to the superstitious rites and ceremonies of men, provokes bitterly. It is a reproach to God, his worship, truth, and ordinances; it is a violation of former promises; it is high ingratitude and rebellion against God; it is a great scandal to all the godly, especially the weak; it encourages, justifies, and hardens the wicked; it ruins souls, gratifies Satan; it exposeth men to visible and unavoidable judgments. When the Jews purposed to leave the Lord's tents, and fall to Babylonish temples, then did he swear, that he would rule over them with fury, Ezek. xx. 32, 33. This should caution us to keep distance from inward approbation of, and outward compliance with, either Jewish ceremonies or Romish rites: the first are abrogated by the Lord, and it may be Jericho work to raise them up again; the other are the mark of the beast, and it is not safe to bear that mark, Rev. xiv. 9, 10; xvi. 2, God is a jealous God, and would not have his people to symbolize with idolatrous or superstitious practices; he forbad his people to take, or desire in their hearts, the silver and gold which was upon idols, Deut. vii. 25, they might not touch with their hearts or hands any thing which belonged to them; they might not do as other nations, Lev. xviii. 3, nor inquire after their gods, and mode of worship, Deut. xii. 30. They might not be like the nations in apparel and hair, saith Maymonie, much more not in the service and worship of God: we should not be as other nations, but keep God's ordinances, and walk therein, Lev. xvii. 4. Symbolizing with idolatrous worship, persons,

In Treatise of Idolatry, chap. 11. sect. 1.

or things, God allows not. In Babylon they might not touch any unclean thing, Isa. lii. 11; and shall we in Zion, where all is to be pure according to the mind of the Holy One of Zion? This made that great apostle Paul say, "Touch not the unclean thing," 2 Cor. vi. 17; (whatsoever is from man in the worship of God hath imperfection, like the man whence it comes, and is an unclean thing;) and if not touching do cause suffering, casting out or off, God will receive, be a Father, and recompense sufferings. God would not have his people touch or countenance any corruption in worship. When the Damascene altar was in the temple, and God's altar removed out of its place, 2 Kings xvi. 14, our Saviour, and those with him, did not appear at that altar, lest they should seem to countenance it, but at the brazen altar, Ezek. ix. 2, though deserted and despised. As Christ will own nothing but what is appointed of the Lord; so those who are with him will not own the superstitious appointments of men, but cleave to the institutions of God, though out of place, and despised. The papists say of the protestants, that in matters of religion, in praying, reading their books, hearing their sermons, presence at their service, partaking of their sacraments, and all other communicating with them in spiritual things, is a great, damnable sin. If they hold it so sinful to communicate with us in the institutions of Christ, shall we symbolize with them in the superstitions of antichrist. Judicious Calvin saith it is unlawful for believers to manifest by any rite that they symbolize with superstitious ones. Mr. Paget tells us, that temples wherein idols and idolatrous service are still retained, and daily practised, cannot lawfully be frequented, nor walked in, because of the woe, incurred by reason of scandal, Matt. xviii. 7. Marcus bishop of Arethusa, having pulled down an idolatrous temple, at the command of Constantine, and being put upon it by Julian either to build it up again, or pay for building of it, he denied both: a small sum was demanded; his answer was, It is as great wickedness to give a halfpenny towards such a work, as to give the whole: he suffered great tortures, rather than he would contribute one halfpenny to promote idolatry. And the forenamed Paget holds it to be the duty of a christian man rather to die than give any thing for the furtherance of idolatry, though it were but a halfpenny. Tertullian defends and commends the christian soldiers that would not wear a crown of laurel, like the heathens: and Rhenanus, in his argument, before that book of Tertullian, saith, it concerned the christians to take heed of complying with their rites. Another of the fathers saith, it were better to be starved to death than to eat things offered to idols. Those who take part in the ceremonies of idolaters offer to devils, and join themselves to the service of idols, 1 Cor. x. 20.

Rhemist, on 2 Epist. of John, ver. 10.

In his Arrow against Separat. pag. 319.

Theodor. l. 3. cap. 6. juxta finem.

Arrow against Separat. pag. 253.

De Corona Militis.

Reader, it is dangerous to symbolize with the superstitious rites and inventions of men. Do not judaize, do not gentilize, do not romanize, but see you christianize. Nothing in worship pleaseth God but what is his own; what man brings is spurious, pollutes his ordinances, and frustrates his commands, Matt. xv. 6. That which comes from God, is set up by him, carries to him, is pure, and approved of by him. False worship, and mixtures with the pure ordinances of God, are as smoke to his eyes, vinegar to his teeth, an abomination to his Spirit; and when they come into his sanctuary, he goeth out of it and far from it, Ezek. viii. 6. God had chosen Zion to dwell in, Psal. cxxxii. 13, 14, there was the glory; but when the people grew profane, the princes and priests corrupted his worship, then the glorious Lord, and glory of the Lord, left them, Ezek. ix. 3; xi. 23. God's worship is his name; and that is so dear unto him, that he will not endure any human mixtures therewith, but show vehement indignation against them; and had rather men's souls and bodies should perish, than his name be polluted. "Go ye, serve every man his idols; but pollute ye my holy name no more," &c. Ezek. xx. 39.

Keep off therefore from false worship, and mixtures of men; you are not to come there, you are not to hear those who teach such things, but to decline them as serpents in the way, and as poison in your meats; you are to feed on nothing but "the sincere milk of the word," and to worship God only with word service, Rom. xii. 1, such as is appointed and ordered by the word, not contrary to or beside it. The jealousy of the Lord about matters of his worship appeared eminently in Ezekiel's temple, (which represented the church under the gospel,) where nothing was to be of the priests' devising; but the rule was, "They shall keep my laws and my statutes in all mine assemblies; and they shall hallow my sabbaths," Ezek. xliv. 24. The assemblies are the Lord's; in them must be, not men's, but his laws and statutes; otherwise his assemblies are robbed and wronged, his sabbaths polluted and profaned. Some say the church follows the government: the false church may, but the true church follows Christ; his sheep hear his voice, and not strangers. They say, Christ we know, and Paul we know, but who are you? They will not comply with false ways and mixtures, but stand for pure worship and pure ordinances, saying,*

* Ut cœlum terræ misceri contingat, merito tutem pluris esse nobis debet sincerus Dei cultus et sacro sancta ejus veritas, in quo nobis reposita est eterna salus, quam centrum mundi. *Calv. Epist. Com. in Tor. Col.* 298.

Let heaven and earth be confounded, yet the sincere worship of God, and his holy truth, in which eternal life is laid up for us, deservedly ought to be and shall be more dear unto us than a hundred worlds. Happy are the souls who are so resolved! they will buy the truth, whatever it cost them, and it will be no simony: they shall find in God's pure ways, where nothing of man is, God's gracious presence, large discoveries of himself, transformation into his image, intimate communion with him, sensation of his goodness, strong consolations, and increasements with the increases of God, which will make up all losses and sufferings, and fit men for the new heavens, new earth, wherein shall dwell righteousness; which the Lord hasten, and for which let us believingly and patiently wait, giving diligence that we may be found of him in peace, without spot, and blameless.

Reader, if thou hast found any benefit by the four former parts upon Ezekiel, or shall gain any by this, give God all the glory, who hath led me through the difficulties and depths of this prophet; and vouchsafe him an interest in thy prayers, who hath spent his strength for thee; and be at some pains to read what he hath taken much and long pains to write. The faithful God, who makes good his promises, put his Spirit into thee, and cause thee to walk in his statutes, to keep his judgments, and do them. So prayeth,

He that affectionately desireth
the spiritual and eternal
good of souls,

The 1*st of the* 3*d month*, 1662.

W. G.

THE INTRODUCTION TO THE WORK.

All Scripture being the breath of God's Spirit, 2 Pet. i. 21; 2 Tim. iii. 16; none can be judge or expounder of it but the same Spirit. Men are only *indices veritatis*, they cannot bring a sense, but show you what is the sense of Scripture. Those who are called to be expositors, must not fetch senses *ab extra*, but take what is in the bowels of the text, and hold forth unto others; a work which requires ability, wisdom, diligence, and faithfulness; ability to inquire into the originals; wisdom to compare Scriptures, consider circumstances, and to discern the verity, spirituality, and propriety of texts and phrases; diligence to dig and search after truth, which lieth deep, and hid; faithfulness to give out truths, being found, with their own lustre, not human tincture. Whosoever doth thus, shall purchase favour in heaven and esteem on earth. Expository work is ancient and honourable: ancient as Nehemiah's time; chap. viii. 8, the Levites gave the sense of the law, they expounded it. In those days the Jews had their *perushim*, interpreters, which was above five hundred years before Christ. What ways they interpreted Scripture, you may read in Shindl. Pentagl. p. 1491; and in Weems's Christian Synagogue, book ii. chap. 1. p. 221. It is also honourable: for the Lord Christ was an expositor: Mark iv. 34, "He expounded all things;" Luke xxiv. 27, he interpreted; and ver. 32, "he opened the Scriptures." Paul also was an expositor: Acts xxviii. 23, "He expounded." * This work being so ancient and honourable, let it find the more acceptance with you.

Helvicus.

Some would have expositors only give the literal sense, without observation or application of any thing. If all people could prophesy, were skilful in Scriptures, as Ezra, mighty, as Apollos, I could like it; but because many truths lie so deep, and so closely couched, as all cannot easily discern or extract them, it is necessary to give the sense, and draw forth points observable, yet with a brevious perspicuity and a perspicuous brevity. The literal sense may be strong meat for some, when observations may be milk for others. That course shall I take, and so I come to the title.

* Ἐπέλυε. διηρμήνευε διήνοιγε ἐξετίθετο.

AN EXPOSITION

UPON

THE BOOK OF EZEKIEL.

THE ANTIQUITY, SCOPE AND OCCASION OF WRITING, NATURE, BENEFIT AND PARTS OF THIS PROPHECY HANDLED IN THE TITLE.

Few of the other sacred books have this title in the original prefixed. The word ספר *sephar*, a book, signifieth any writing, be it great or small, short or long. It hath this name in the Hebrew language. In Jer. iii. 8, a bill of divorce is mentioned; the word in the original is *sephar*, a book of divorce. It was the use of the Jews to call any writing, though it had but a few lines in it, *sephar*, a book. And so a catalogue that had not many names in it, is called a book, Matt. i. 1, "The book," or the catalogue, "of the generation of Jesus Christ."

This book of Ezekiel is large, having eight and forty chapters in it, and may rather be called a volume, than *sephar*, a book, a bill, a catalogue. Some books in the Scripture that are far less than this of Ezekiel have that title. Esther, which is not long, hath this title, *Megillath* Esther, the volume of Esther, or the book of Esther, so it is in your Bible. The word cometh from גלל *galal*, which signifieth to roll or fold up; for the use of the Jews was to fold up their writings, as being the best way to preserve them from dust and other dangers. These two words are sometimes found both together, as in this prophet, chap. ii. 9. There was sent unto the prophet a hand, and in it there was *megillath sephar*, a roll of a book.

The Jews had many *megillaths*, many such volumes or rolls, especially five, which they did use at several times.

There was the *megillath* of the Canticles, which they read at the feast of the passover, because it contained much of the love of God to the church, and in the passover they apprehended much of God's love towards them.

2. Then they had the *megillath* of Ruth, which was read at the feast of Pentecost, because it contained the genealogy and original of David their king, who was so beloved and dear unto them.

3. They had the *megillath* of Ecclesiastes, and that they read at the feast of tabernacles, in memory of God's protection of them forty years in the wilderness, because that volume contained many acts of God's providence, which watcheth over his people continually.

4. The fourth was the *megillath* of Esther, which was read in the month of Adar, because that discovered the plot of Haman, and the goodness of God that did deliver them from that imminent danger.

5. The last *megillath* was the book of the Lamentations, and this contained, as the sum, so the bewailing of the Babylonish captivity, which was grievous unto them. This book they read in the fifth month, which was answerable to the latter end of July.

These were all little books, little volumes. Ezekiel is rather a *megillath*, and Ezekiel must be our volume, a book written in the Babylonish captivity, some five hundred and fourscore years before Christ; so that it is above two thousand two hundred years since this book was written. From hence you may observe:

First, The wisdom of God in causing this and other books to be written. A book is a writing, the original word signifieth to write. Here is the wisdom and goodness of God, that the prophecies of Ezekiel and other prophets should be written. God will have his church furnished with and regulated by written truths, not unwritten traditions. The Jews had their *Cabala*, which they say were full of secret mysteries. The papists have their traditions; they call them unwritten verities, and we call them unwritten vanities. We have a sure word of prophecy to stick unto, and they uncertain fancies, which corrupt the worship of God, and endanger immortal souls. Bellarmine hath a whole book *De Verbo Dei non scripto*, of the word of God unwritten; such words of God we acknowledge not. It was the wisdom of God that the prophets should write, and that their writings should be extant. When the lawyer asked Christ what he should do to inherit eternal life, Christ doth not send him to unwritten traditions, or to Jewish Cabalas, but he sends him to a known and written law; "What is written in the law? how readest thou?" Luke x. 26. So we must look to what is written, and how we may read, not what they tell us was revealed to such a saint, and hath continued to so many generations, and is the truth of God, these are delusions. The writings of the prophets and apostles are sufficient for us, and we acknowledge the infinite goodness of God, in that these should be written for us to have resort unto. If this and other prophets' and apostles' works had not been written, there would have been great inconveniences, some things would have been forgotten; some neglected, many things corrupted, and all things in time questioned, and so the whole truth would have been without authority in the hearts of people.

Secondly, See here the providence of God likewise, in preserving this book of Ezekiel, which was written in Babylon, for there was the prophet, and there he had his visions. For a book to be preserved in Babylon, is a wonder. The law was lost in Sion, in Manasses' days, and found again in Josiah's time: if the law may be lost in Sion, much more may a prophecy be lost in Babylon; and if not lost in Babylon, yet it might have been left in Babylon; if not left there, it might have miscarried in their return; if not then, yet when Titus and Vespasian took and sacked Jerusalem, it might there have perished, and been utterly extinguished, and we never have heard of this prophecy of Ezekiel. But here is the hand of God manifested in it, that though this prophecy was revealed to Ezekiel in Babylon, and run through so many hazards, yet it should be preserved to this very day.

Again, See where is the true antiquity. This book was written five hundred and fourscore years before Christ, two thousand two hundred years ago; and is not this book now very ancient? Other prophets, and the whole Scripture, are the true antiquity. Papists, and many amongst us, stand upon antiquity; and what is their antiquity? The fathers, or some heathen writers, are their antiquity. But what is the true antiquity but the word of God? That is *prima veritas*, and *pura veritas*, the first truth, and the pure truth; that is the fountain, all other are but muddy channels. When any points are in controversy they fly to fathers and to antiquity, and what is found there they take for truth: but this is to desert God, and run to man. "My people have forsaken me the fountain of living waters, and hewed them out cisterns, broken cisterns, that can hold no water," Jer. ii. 13. I am the fountain, saith God, my Scriptures are the fountain of living waters, yet they run to their own pits and cisterns that hold no water. Some moth-eaten and old writings, some ancient copies that have lain hid some hundreds of years from the world, are brought forth, and obtruded upon people for truths, and they must be truths. But for your direction know, that if they be not in the King's records, whatever writings they be, never regard them: and if you will search, never search into inferior courts, search not books that are on this side the King's court, that are made of late; but go to the King of heaven's records, have recourse to his court, look into the law of God; "To the law and to the testimony, if they speak not according to this word, it is because there is no light in them," Isa. viii. 20. Throw them by; that truth which is found in any writings, and not to be drawn out of God's book, is not from antiquity. These are the true records, here is the true antiquity. And so much for this word book, "The Book of the prophet Ezekiel."

חזק אל
κράτος κυρίου.

Ezekiel, that is the name of our prophet. Among the Jews there were no surnames, but every man had only one name, as Samuel, David, Isaiah, Jeremiah, Ezekiel, &c. This name Ezekiel doth signify, the strength of God, or, one strengthened by God. He had a great work to do, he needed great strength for that work. He was to deal with wicked princes, and wretched people, such as were exceeding opposite, desperately wicked, impudent, hardhearted, rebellious. Therefore, chap. iii. 8, 9, "Behold," saith God, "I have made thy face strong against their faces, and thy forehead strong against their foreheads," &c. The Hebrew words here for strong, are חזקם *chazakim*, and חזק *chazak*, I have made thy faces *chazakim*, strong, I have given thee many faces, and I have given thee many strengths; strong both in the singular and plural number, all the strengths that is fit for a prophet that had such a great task to undertake and go about. He was to reprove them for their sins, to threaten God's judgments, to vindicate God's justice in bringing them into captivity, himself was to endure much hardship, and many conflicts, for which ordinary strength would not suffice: therefore he is fitly called Ezekiel, the strength of God, or a man strengthened of God.

Cingere, vincire.

Or thus: Ezekiel doth signify one girt of God; for *chazak* is to gird or bind, and Ezekiel is one whom God hath girt and bound up for some employment: answerable to that expression of Paul, "Behold," saith he, "I go bound in the Spirit to Jerusalem," Acts xx. 22, so you read it; but it may be, bound to the Spirit; the Spirit of God goes before me; and I being bound to the guidance of the Spirit, do follow the same whithersoever it leads me. So here, our prophet was girt up of God from the world, bound in or to the Spirit, and so followed that, which way soever it led him.

δεδεμένος τῷ πνεύματι.

Touching this name of Ezekiel, you may observe a note or two.

First, See the wisdom of God in giving names suitable to the events that do follow and fall out afterward. Ezekiel was to deal with a stubborn people, a rebellious house, that did oppose Heaven, that did stand it out against God to the uttermost. There was need therefore of a strong prophet to subdue their rebellious spirits. If an ordinary man had come, he would soon have been discouraged, his spirit would have sunk and fallen within him; therefore here the Lord ordereth it so, that a name shall be given unto him which shall be suitable to the event; he shall be a man of God, he shall be strong, strengthened, girt up of God, to deal with a proud, rebellious, obstinate people.

You may find in Scripture divers names that have been imposed through the wisdom and guidance of God upon parties before their birth, and the event hath answered afterward very fully: as Gen. xvii. "Thou shalt call his name Isaac." Isaac signifieth laughter, and Isaac proved matter of laughter to his father and mother, all their days. He was a dutiful son, you never read that Isaac fell into such sins as some other of the patriarchs and prophets fell into. He was a child of laughter to them. So 1 Chron. xxii. 9, "His name shall be Solomon, for I will give peace and quietness unto Israel in his days:" and the event was answerable to his name. So Josiah, 1 Kings xiii. 2, it signifies the fire of the Lord; and Josiah was the fire of God indeed to make a reformation, to pull down Jeroboam's altar, and to offer upon it the priests of the high places that had burnt incense upon it, to burn men's bones thereon, to throw out idolatry, and to destroy the high places. So the name of our blessed Saviour which was imposed before his birth, "Thou shalt call his name Jesus, They shall call his name Emanuel," he shall save his people, he shall be God with us, and it was so. Luke i. 13, "Call his name John." John noteth gracious, and he was gracious in the eyes of his very enemies, he had favour in the eyes of Herod, favour in the eyes of the people. God's wisdom is seen in ordering of names beforehand, suitably to events that follow afterward.

2. This should direct parents to impose encouraging names upon their children. What encouragement was it to Ezekiel to think of his name, the strength of God, a man girt up of God for some great design and employment! Names at first were imposed for distinction sake, and not only so, but to show the hopes and desires of parents touching their children for the time to come. Good names were prognostical; parents expected, and children were encouraged much by them. Leah nameth her son Judah, which is praise, that she might praise God for him, and he might do things worthy of praise all his days, and the tribe of Judah did worthily in Israel.

Ob virtutis auspicium imponuntur vocabula. *Jeron.*

Thus much from the name of Ezekiel.

The Book of the prophet Ezekiel.

This word prophet is not in the Hebrew: The book Ezekiel, or the book of Ezekiel: but it is in the body of the prophecy, chap. ii. 5, "They shall know that there hath been a prophet among them." Prophet is from the greek word, and it signifies one that foretells things to come. The Hebrew word נבא נביא *Nabi* of *Naba*, which signifies to foreknow, foretell, or discover things. Some derive it from a root, which signifieth to bud, to bring forth: for as a tree draws sap from the earth, sends forth that sap into leaves and fruit, and becomes profitable and serviceable unto man; so doth the prophet, he draws sap from the root, which is God, from him he hath many hidden, deep, and divine truths, which he reveals and sends forth for the delight and benefit of others.

Προφήτης.

Prophets were of two sorts, distinguished by the temples; some were *prophetæ priores*, and others *prophetæ posteriores*. The former prophets were those of the first temple, the latter prophets were those of the latter temple, and they were Haggai, Zechariah, Nehemiah, Ezra, and Malachi. These prophets continued but forty years after the second temple was built, and then did prophecy depart from Israel, which was one of the saddest blows that ever Israel had. All the rest were prophets of the first temple, and among them was our prophet Ezekiel and Daniel, though they were in the captivity; for the first temple was not yet destroyed, and they had lived at Jerusalem among the prophets: and the prophets of the former temple, it is observed, had the largest visions, and the fullest discoveries of the mind of God; more was discovered in the first temple than in the second, till Christ's coming; for the second temple had prophets but forty years after it was built, and the first temple had prophets for four hundred and thirty years.

Transit prophetia ab Israele. *Shind.*

The prophets (to speak for the honour of this our prophet) were all honourable men, men of great esteem and worth; they were men of God, as it is said, 1 Kings xvii. 24, "I know thou art a man of God," *Ish Elohim*, a man of Gods, a man of God the Father, a man of God the Son, a man of God the Holy Ghost. He had to do with all, a man of God's counsel, a man of God's protection, a man of God's countenancing, a man of God that stood for God, a man of God that would plead the cause of God in the corruptest times, against the desperatest enemies. A prophet was a man of God.

That they were very honourable, you shall find by that passage, 1 Sam. x. 11, "Is Saul also among the prophets?" It is a proverbial speech, and noteth a thing that is very rare and unusual. What! is Saul, that was a man of mean condition, Saul, that was erewhile seeking his father's asses, is Saul now come to so high and honourable a condition, as to be among the prophets? This was matter of wonder. The prophets were so honourable, and in so high an esteem, that it was counted a strange thing for any to come to that dignity and preferment, that were not of the prophetical race, the tribe of Levi, or such as were in order to those holy functions.

They were likewise men privileged. Psa. cv. 15, "Touch not mine anointed, and do my prophets no harm." Anointed is the same with prophet, as expositors observe, though it is carried otherwise, in the general apprehension of men, for kings, but anointed, here, is the same with prophet. They were anointed, when the Holy Ghost was given unto them, and they were called unto their office; this was their anointing of God, and they must not be touched nor harmed. Gen. xx. 7, saith God to Abimelech, "Give the man his wife, for he is a prophet," he is an honourable man, he is a man of high account in mine eyes. Princes must not wrong a prophet. God spake to a prince, "Give him his wife, for he is a prophet." The greatest person in the world should not dare to touch a prophet, that is, a man so honourable, a man of God, and so gifted, and sent of him to such great employments.

Further, a prophet was called in Scripture a seer. 1 Sam. ix. 9, "Let us go to the seer; for he is now called a Prophet that was beforetime called a Seer," that is, from the Hebrew word to see, and not barely to see, but to see exactly, curiously, throughly into things. The prophets saw through the clouds, they saw into the heavens, they saw into the very counsel of God. Isa. xxx. 10, "Which say to the seers, See not," you see too much; the meaning is, you see too accurately; why do you see so, and tell us such things? So Abraham, he was a prophet, you heard before, he was likewise a seer. John viii. 56, "Abraham rejoiced to see my day:" he saw it distinctly, he saw it so as it affected him, "he saw it and was glad."

עד·הראה ראה

There is, besides this word, another name in the Hebrew, which the prophets had, and that was חזה *chozeh*. Isa. xxx. 10, "That say to the prophets, Prophesy not;" the Hebrew is *la chozim*, to those that foresee, and foretell things. You have a conjuncture of these three in one verse, 1 Chron. xxix. 29, "They are written in the book of Samuel, *haroeh*, the seer, and in the book of Nathan, *hannabi*, the prophet, and in the book of Gad, *hachozeh*, the seer." The word cometh of *chazah*, to contemplate, to see; from which root comes our English word to gaze; and so it is interpreted, Isa. xlvii. 13, "star-gazers:" this only by the way.

Our prophet had the honour to be a seer as well as a prophet, therefore, ver. 1, it is said ואראה מראות "I saw visions," I had the honour to see visions, and visions of a God.

These titles of seer and prophet, as they set out the dignity, so likewise they point out the duty of the person. As they were seers, they were *oculi ecclesiæ*, the eyes of the church, to see good coming, or evil, that they might encourage them upon the one, and draw them to repentance upon the other. As they were prophets, they were *os Domini*, the mouth of the Lord, to speak to the people whatsoever the Lord himself did make known to them.

All this then doth but serve to breed in you an honourable esteem of this our prophet; he is a man of God, he is a man honourable among the rest of the prophets; he is a seer; he is the eye of the church; he is the mouth of God.

Having thus opened unto you the title, I shall now show to you;

I. The scope and occasion of this prophecy.

II. The nature and condition of it.

III. The seasonableness of this prophecy for this time.

IV. What benefit you are like to have by this prophet; and then divide the prophecy in general, and fall into the chapter.

I. For the scope and occasion of this prophecy. In general, it is to show the certainty of Jerusalem's destruction, and the seventy years' captivity, which were now in question; and so to confirm the prophecy of Jeremiah, being of the same argument.

Jeremiah having prophesied of the captivity of Jerusalem for seventy years, the utter ruin of the city and temple; many, both in Jerusalem and Babylon, (the captivity being begun, for now Ezekiel and divers were in Babylon,) murmured and complained of Jeremiah, that he was a false prophet; that he had not the Spirit of God; that he had misled the people; that he had brought them into bondage by his fair words, put them upon yielding unto the king of Babylon, and betrayed them. You shall find false prophets bestirred themselves, and opposed his prophecy both in Sion and in Babylon, as Jer. xxviii. 1—4. Hananiah being at Jerusalem, when Jeremiah was in the house of the Lord, in the presence of the priests and of all the people, saith he, "Thus speaketh the Lord of hosts, the God of Israel, saying, I have broken the yoke of the king of Babylon. Within two full years will I bring again into this place all the vessels of the Lord's house, that Nebuchadnezzar king of Babylon took away from this place, and carried them to Babylon: and I will bring again to this place Jeconiah the son of Jehoiakim king of Judah, with all the captives of Judah that went into Babylon." Here is a false prophet contradicts all that Jeremiah had spoken, touching the seventy years' captivity.

The false prophets likewise in Babylon were at work, and strengthened the hands of the false prophets at Jerusalem by their doctrine. Jer. xxix. 8, 9, "Thus saith the Lord of hosts, the God of Israel; Let not your prophets and your diviners, that be in the midst of you, deceive you, neither hearken to your dreams which ye cause to be dreamed. For they prophesy falsely unto you in my name: I have not sent them, saith the Lord." And in ver. 24—28 of the same chapter, you shall find, that Shemaiah the Nehelamite sent letters from Babylon to all the priests, and to all the people that were at Jerusalem, accusing Jeremiah for a madman, for making himself a prophet, for sending letters to them in Babylon, for lengthening out the captivity to seventy years, for encouraging them to build houses, to plant gardens, to eat the fruit of them; he would have Jeremiah imprisoned and set in the stocks.

Thus Jeremiah was accused, cried down at home and abroad, his prophesy was slighted, scorned by many, and most were troubled, at what Jeremiah had prophesied. This made such work, both at Jerusalem and at Babylon, that the people of God were much despondent, and their enemies mightily insultive. Now hereupon the Lord stirreth up Ezekiel, poureth out his Spirit upon him, calleth him forth to prophesy, setteth him a work to justify Jeremiah, and to ratify what he had foretold concerning the Babylonish captivity, threatening ruin to the city and temple, to kingdom and king, to their nobles, priests, and all the people.

Hereupon (saith Josephus) the prophecy of Ezekiel, as soon as ever it was written, (I conceive he meaneth not the whole prophecy, but some part of it,) was sent to Jerusalem, but little fruit came of it; for Zedekiah being then king, and having seen it, he would neither believe Jeremiah nor Ezekiel, but presently concludes, that both were liars and false prophets: and that upon this ground, Jeremiah had said, chap. xxi. 7, that Zedekiah should be carried captive into Babylon; and Ezekiel denied that he should see Babylon, chap. xii. 13. Hereupon, saith Zedekiah, they were both false, here is a contradiction, the one saith, I shall be carried into Babylon, the other saith, I shall not see Babylon. But God quickly made this good, for shortly after, Nebuchadnezzar came, besieged Jerusalem, took Zedekiah captive, put out both his eyes, bound him with fetters of brass, carried him to Babylon, which he never saw, 2 Kings xxv. 7.

From hence, by the way, you may observe; 1. Upon what slight and weak grounds princes and people will cast off prophecies and truths of God, even upon mistakes and misapprehensions. Zedekiah could not apprehend what truths there were in these two prophecies: had he compared one thing with another, he might easily have seen truth; but small matters will make princes and people turn off the truths of God, especially when they are not suitable to their own spirits; and in these days people can without much ado turn off any truths ministers bring, if they be not suitable to their apprehensions and fancies.

2. That God will make good the word of his ministers and prophets, though they seem contradictory to men's fancies and sense. Jeremiah saith, that Zedekiah shall go into Babylon, and Ezekiel saith, he shall not see Babylon. God makes it good notwithstanding the prophecy is thrown away. The word of God shall take hold upon princes, nobles, people, and slay them, if they have despised and stood out against it.

But from this general scope of Ezekiel's prophecy, that he is sent to strengthen and justify Jeremiah, take this observation, (1.) That it is good for ministers to strengthen the doctrine, works, hands, and hearts one of another. A prophet is questioned, trod under foot, his prophecy thrown out as false; an Ezekiel is stirred up to justify a Jeremiah. When ministers justify one another, the work goes on with more strength; when there is a double witness to a truth, it will seal it more strongly to the heart. God gave four evangelists: one had been a great mercy; but that things might be ratified in your hearts, sealed up in your consciences, you have four evangelists, each one strengtheneth the doctrine and things of another: so the consent of minister and prophets is a great matter to ratify truths in the hearts and consciences of people, and to establish the church. It is good therefore for an Ezekiel to strengthen a Jeremiah.

(2.) More specially the scope of the prophet is, to comfort the captives that were then in Babylon; for they began now to be troubled that they had hearkened to Jeremiah, yielded to the king of Babylon, because Jeremiah had prophesied that Jerusalem should be destroyed, the temple burnt, and that all should be laid waste; whereas Jerusalem stood still, and now five years were gone, and nothing done unto the city or temple (for it was in the fifth year of Jehoiachin's captivity that Ezekiel began his prophecy). They now began to be discouraged that they had left their habitations, that they had hearkened to Jeremiah so far, as to come to Babylon. They were likewise disheartened in Babylon, they met with much hardship there, being put upon building, planting, sowing, and other difficulties; yea, the Babylonians themselves scoffed at them, and said, Sing us one of your songs of Zion. This made them to droop, and to wish, O that we were at Jerusalem again, that we had never hearkened to Jeremiah. The Jews also at Jerusalem reproached them, and they said they were men of cowardly and base spirits, discouraged with the words of a timorous and lying prophet, one Jeremiah, and thereupon yielding themselves into the hands of Nebuchadnezzar, they wretchedly betrayed the city, religion, and their country. These things went to the very bowels and reins of the godly, and did greatly disturb them. Hereupon the Lord, to support their spirits, to comfort them in these their distresses, and to be an Ezekiel, even the strength of God, unto them, stirreth up Ezekiel, sets him on work.

Lastly, The scope of the prophet is the same with the rest of the prophets, viz. to lead unto Christ, as you may see by reading Luke xxiv. 44; Acts iii. 18, 21, 24. They spake of Christ, and led to him; but it is more especially aimed at by this our prophet, who begins with the law executed, a captivity, but ends with a temple, and restoration by Christ, thereby leading the people that were captives in Babylon to Christ the King of Jerusalem. In Eph. i. 10, you have this expression, "That he might gather together in one, all things in Christ." The word notes, to sum up, or to make a brief collection of the heads of all that was spoken before; implying, that much hath been said of Christ by others, and that the chief heads of all should be summed up, brought together, and be found in Christ. Much was spoken by David of Christ, much by Isaiah, much by Jeremiah, Zechariah, Ezekiel: now the sum of all that is in them, and in the rest, shall be gathered together as in one head, you shall meet it all in Jesus Christ. He is the Magazine and Treasury of all their strength and wealth, the chief things that ever have been spoken by the prophets formerly, are all concentred in him. He is the Alpha and Omega, the Alpha of Genesis, "The seed of the woman shall break the serpent's head;" and the Omega of the Revelation, "The grace of our Lord Jesus Christ be with you all." So that all between Genesis and the Revelation, leads either directly or collaterally unto Jesus Christ. 1 Pet. i. 10, "The prophets prophesied of grace that should come unto you, searching when, or what manner of time the Spirit of Christ which was in them did signify, when it testified beforehand the sufferings of Christ and the glory that should follow." See here, they showed you the grace that should come, the Spirit testified in them of the sufferings of Christ, and of the glory that should follow. They were seers, and they saw Christ, and the glory of Christ, and they lead the people up to Christ.

ἀνακεφαλαιώσασθαι.

Thus have you the scope and occasion of our prophet's prophesying and writing; it was to convince them of the heavy captivity of seventy years, to strengthen Jeremiah's prophecy, to encourage the church of God in Babylon, and to lead them unto Christ.

II. In the next place we are to show you the nature and condition of this prophecy, which is full of majesty, obscurity, and difficulty. Nazianzen saith, That Ezekiel is the chiefest of all the rest; for matter of admiration and acuteness he is the greatest of all the prophets, and the deepest: which made Jerome say, there was in this prophecy of Ezekiel a sea of scriptures, he is so deep; a labyrinth of the mysteries of God, he is so dark, so difficult; if he do but equalize other prophets in dignity and worth, yet he exceeds them in difficulty and darkness. It must be said of this prophet, as of Paul's epistles, 2 Pet. iii. "There are some things in them hard to be understood;" and so there are many things in this prophet which are hard to be understood. There are some strange words in him, such as are no where else in Scripture to be found. He hath dark visions in him, such as will exercise the greatest abilities in the world to find out the aim of God, and those truths that are wrapped up in them; he hath uncertain chronologies and chorographies, mystical parables, foreign histories, and many transcendent matters, which may awaken your attention, and do call for the uttermost of man's industry in the opening.

Orat. 23.

Hence it was counted rashness for any one to read this prophet till he was thirty years of age. And Jerome tells us, that it was prohibited among the Jews, that any should read the beginning of Genesis, the book of Canticles, the beginning or ending of this prophet, till he were thirty years of age. The rabbins think it not lawful to interpret this prophet, but only by touching some general things in it; particular things might not be descended into. One saith, Ezekiel is Jeremiah veiled, a hand shut up, and you know not what is in it; like a book sealed up, and none can open it, or knows what is written within. These expressions have been used to set forth the darkness and difficulty of our prophet.

Maldonat.

Ante ætatem sacerdotalem.

A. Lapid.

And I will appeal unto you all, this day, that if that question were put to you, when you shall read this prophet, which Philip once put to the eunuch, Acts viii. 30, 31, "Understand you what you read?" might you not all answer without blushing, How shall we understand without a guide? And who is sufficient to guide your understandings through this difficult and dark prophecy? For my own part I durst not have ventured to launch into this deep, unless I had been requested unto it: and being called unto it, I desire to go out in the strength of the Lord, and to be as a star in his hand, guided by his Spirit, to lead you through the difficulties of this hieroglyphical prophet.

III. But you will say, If this prophet be so difficult and dark, surely he is not seasonable, nor suitable to these times; some other scripture might have had the pre-eminence.

For this, take two or three answers: First, I find that many interpreters have fallen upon this prophet, in troublesome and tumultuous times. Gregory the Great wrote and preached upon this prophet, when the barbarians were almost at the gates of Rome, and when the sword was devouring multitudes. Jerome likewise studied and wrote upon this prophet, what time Alaricus king of the Goths took Rome and wasted all, and filled the christian world with tears and blood. Calvin, that great light of Europe, spent his last breath upon this prophet, and in times that were not very peaceable, but stirring and troublesome. Lavater's lectures upon this prophet were together with the commotions in France; and he professeth, that he did the more willingly give up himself to the study of this prophet, that so he might free his spirit from the sad thoughts of the public and private mischiefs which were in his days, and acknowledgeth this was a remedy to him against many evils.

Gallicis tumultibus.

Secondly, I answer, that compare our times a little with the times and state of the jews, and we shall see some seasonableness in handling this prophet at this time.

1. The sins the prophet cries out of amongst them, are rife amongst us. The sins then were idolatry, superstition, oppression, corruption in the worship of God, luxury, uncleanness, profaneness, scorning at goodness, hiding their eyes from the Lord's sabbaths, and the like. Now I ask, are not all these sins alive and too lusty in our kingdom at this time, and in this city wherein we live?

2. There was then a malignant party which

was active and at work, and did oppose and hinder the reformation (what lay in them) which was on foot by Jeremiah, by Ezekiel, by the three children, by Baruch, by the Rechabites. All these and many others opposed the corruptions of the times, and laboured to have a reformation in the worship of God, to bring the people back again from their corrupt ways to the Lord; but there was a great opposition by the malignant party, and the chief opposers then, were the priests, and the false prophets, who poisoned the judgments of the people, who suggested false things unto them, who fed them with vain hopes, with corrupt opinions, and deceivable doctrines. The chief of the priests were chiefest in malignancy and opposition: this you shall see, 2 Chron. xxxvi. 14—16, "All the chief of the priests and the people transgressed very much, they polluted the house of the Lord, they mocked the messengers of God, despised his words, and misused his prophets;" this was the practice of those times. Was there ever any great disorder, corruption in the church, or any sedition, or treason almost in the state, but some of the chief of the priests have had their hands in it? When the calf was set up in Moses's days, Aaron the priest had his head and hand in it. When David was dying, Adonijah makes the sedition and stir in the kingdom, but Abiathar the priest had a great hand in it. Both in the state and in the church you may well observe, that the chief of the priests have had their hands in the evil, in the trouble. And have not we now a malignant party that oppose the reformation intended and begun? Do they not set themselves with all their might against the Jeremiahs, Daniels, Ezekiels, and Rechabites of the land, that will not defile themselves? There is such a party, you all know, that do oppose godliness, that despise the prophets, scorn the saints, make sad the hearts of the righteous, and strengthen the hands of wickedness; therefore this prophecy may be seasonable enough in regard of that malignant party that doth oppose too openly.

3. They had lost their country, their choicest comforts; they were in captivity and constant jeopardy of their lives; if they provoked the Babylonians, they were ready to fall upon them, and root them out presently. And those at Jerusalem were in danger every day to have their liberties, estates, consciences, religion, and lives, taken from them. And are not we like unto them? and are not we, even in a land of liberty, in a state of captivity? Do not our estates, our liberties, our consciences, our religion, our lives, and all lie at the stake? We are even in Babylon in the midst of Sion; we are in a sad and heavy condition; therefore this prophecy may be seasonable now, considering our estate is so like to theirs.

4. The times then were such, that they loathed manna, ordinary and plain truths would not go down. Unless truths were new and transcendent, they were weary of them, and slighted them. Jeremiah was too plain a prophet for them, too low; and God gives them Ezekiel, a dark and hard prophet. And is it not so in these days? We have been fed with manna so long, that we loathe manna, as a wormy thing. If we have not something new, unheard of, transcendent, we are weary, we think it not worth our going out of doors. If so, then here is a prophet that may be suitable to these times, and your desires. God gave them this prophet in a time of affliction; and there was something in it; for afflictions open men's understandings, and enlarge their capacities. When people are under pressures, then their understandings are quickest, then they are most apprehensive: therefore God gave them such a prophet as might suit with their condition, in exercising their parts and graces to the full, when at the best. Now is a time of affliction: if your spirits be awakened, and the bent of them be after high and hard things, lo, here are difficulties and transcendencies for you; here are high things to draw up your thoughts, to exercise your spirits, be they never so choice and apprehensive.

Vexatio dat intellectum.

One thing more for the seasonableness of this prophet. It is said heaven was open, and Ezekiel saw visions of God. If ever God hath opened heaven since Christ, now he hath done it in these sad times. God hath now caused, and is causing you every day, to see visions out of the prophets, and out of the gospel. These expository lectures are openings of heaven, and let out clear and choice light unto you from heaven; therefore seeing heaven is opened, let visions of God be counted seasonable, and become acceptable unto you.

IV. But if this prophet be so dark and difficult, what is the benefit and fruit we shall have by him?

This is the next head we are to come unto, and the benefits of this prophet are these.

1. The darker the prophet is, the more of God you may look for from him. God dwelleth in darkness, as well as in light. Psal. xviii. 11, "He made darkness his secret place." And Exod. xix. 9, "God came to Moses in a thick cloud," and there Moses had the most of God. Here God is coming to you in a dark prophet, and questionless you shall find much of God in him. Here you shall see much of God's mercy in upholding and comforting the spirits of his people, and providing for them in a strange land; here you shall see much of God's justice in punishing sinners for their sins and iniquities; here you shall see much of God's truth in fulfilling of prophecies; here you shall find much of God's power in subverting of kings and kingdoms; here you shall find much of his manifold wisdom in these dark visions; here you shall find more of God than you expect.

Tenebræ sunt latibulum Dei.

2. This prophecy is an exact history of the time of the Jews being in captivity. In it you have many passages of Nebuchadnezzar's reign and government, of his acts abroad and at home, and of God's dealing with his people in the time of this their seventy years' captivity. Were not Daniel and Ezekiel extant, we should have such a great loss as the world could not tell how to repair it; the acts of God's dealing with his church and people in that seventy years, would be swallowed up in a chaos of darkness.

3. You shall see for what sins God subverteth and overthroweth kingdoms and states. In this prophet you shall find that the Lord doth ruin glorious churches, great cities, mighty kingdoms, men of great renown, families and posterities, and the particular sins for which he doth it; namely, for false worship, idolatry, injustice, uncleanness, profaning of his sabbaths, contempt of his word, abuse of his prophets, and sins of that nature. So that as it is, Prov. xxi. 30, "There is no wisdom, no counsel, nor understanding against the Lord." God will overthrow even kings, with their councils and kingdoms, with their nobility and gentry, with their magistrates and people. God will overthrow them when he once sets upon such a work, such a design: there is no standing out against him.

4. You shall see here also the different carriage between the godly and the wicked, in times of judgment. When judgments are abroad in the world, the inhabitants of the earth should learn righteous-

ness; but wicked men, they grow more active against God, more impudent, more desperate and hard-hearted. They combine and plot together to root out the righteous: this you shall see in this prophecy. And for the godly, you shall find that when judgments are near and upon them, they are mourning in secret, they get together, they that fear God speak often one to another; they fast, they pray, they redeem the time, they work out their salvation with fear and trembling, they give God no rest, they will be at it at midnight: in a word, you shall find the carriage of the godly to be exceeding contrary to the carriage of the wicked.

5. Here you shall find God's new covenant, wherein you shall see the riches of free grace, God doing all, both making the covenant and performing it, both commanding and giving what he doth command unto your souls.

6. You shall find that this prophet is an evangelical prophet, for he points at Christ; he will show you where he is, he will lead you to the temple, where you shall see Christ with his line in his hand, and measuring out a temple for the times of the gospel, measuring of his worship, his worshippers, and all that doth concern the new Jerusalem. Much of Christ will be found at least in the conclusion of this prophet.

7. You shall have a lively representation of the uncertainty of all things, and of all conditions in this world. In Lam. iv. 12, it is said, that the kings of the earth, and all the inhabitants of the world, would not have believed that the adversary and the enemy should have entered into the gates of Jerusalem. None thought, none of the kings of the earth, none of the kings of Israel, believed that ever Jerusalem, which was so fortified by mountains round about, should be taken by the enemy. But you shall see in this prophet, that even Jerusalem, the city of God, the temple, that was the glory of the world, and Sion, the perfection of beauty, are all laid waste. Neither prince, priest, prophet, nobles, nor any are spared, but all are destroyed, all are carried into captivity, all are brought under; the sons, the precious sons of Sion are carried away into Babylon. So that there is no place, no condition, no prerogative that can privilege any from the hand of God where once sin is come to a perfection. "Righteousness exalteth a nation: but sin is a reproach to any people," Prov. xiv. 34. Let them be Jews or gentiles, let them be kings, priests, or prophets, when sin is grown to a height, then the wrath of God comes to a perfection; and God will lay a Sion waste, God will raze a temple, God will carry a Jehoiakim, a Zedekiah, prince and prophet, priest and people into captivity. Is Sion gone? is the temple razed? is Jerusalem laid in the dust? What confidence then can any kingdom, can any city have? Let not England, let not London be secure. Fear and tremble. Repent of sin. Take heed of provoking God. Look beyond the kingdoms of the earth. Look up to heaven, and make sure of that kingdom which cannot be shaken, which cannot be taken from you. Thus you have some of the benefits that are to come by this prophet.

We are now to fall upon the general division of the prophecy.

In this prophet you have,

I. The preface; wherein is contained God's appearing to Ezekiel, his calling of him and strengthening of him in his office; and these are laid down in the three first chapters.

II. You have the prophecy itself; wherein you have these four things.

1. The destruction of the Jews by the Babylonish captivity, with the causes thereof, viz. their sins. This is laid down in the next 21 chapters.
2. Threatening of judgment and destruction to several nations that had insulted over the people of God, being carried away captive, and the hand of God being upon them; these were the Ammonites, the Moabites, the Edomites, the Philistines, the Assyrians, and Babylonians: and this he doth from the 25th to the 33rd chapter.
3. Sharp reproving of the Jews for their iniquity, for their hard-heartedness, for their not improving the hand of God upon them. And exhorting them to repentance, he tells them of freedom, some mercy and deliverance; and after that again of affliction and trouble that shall befall them: and this he doth from the 33rd to the 39th chapter.
4. A typical prophecy concerning Christ, and spiritual freedom through him; laid down in the vision of the new temple, and of the new Jerusalem, from the 39th chapter to the end; wherein there will be many glorious things made known in due time.

Thus have you the general division of the prophecy.

CHAPTER I.

In this Chapter you have :

I. Ezekiel's first vision, from the fourth verse to the end of the chapter.
II. In the three first verses you have :
  1. The time, what year, what month, what day this vision was, ver. 1, 2.
  2. The place, 1. General, the land of the Chaldeans ; 2. Particular, by the river of Chebar, ver. 3.
  3. Together with this, you have the occasion ; his being there among the captives.
III. The subject of this vision, Ezekiel ; described,
  1. From his office ; a priest.
  2. From his parentage ; the son of Buzi.
IV. The Author of this vision, God. "I saw visions of God ;" such visions as came from God.

Ver. 1—3. *Now it came to pass in the thirtieth year, in the fourth month, in the fifth day of the month, as I was among the captives by the river of Chebar, that the heavens were opened, and I saw visions of God. In the fifth day of the month, which was the fifth year of king Jehoiachin's captivity, the word of the Lord came expressly unto Ezekiel the priest, the son of Buzi, in the land of the Chaldeans by the river Chebar ; and the hand of the Lord was there upon him.*

"Now ;" the word in the original is, And ; "And it came to pass." It seems a strange beginning of a book ; especially when it refers to nothing said or wrote before. There are many of the books of sacred writ begin in this manner ; as Exodus, Leviticus, Numbers, Joshua, Ruth, Samuel, Kings, and divers others. In historical books, it may note the series, and connect things antecedent with things consequent ; but in prophetical books, it cannot note or make a connexion with things foregoing. Jonah begins his prophecy so ; and what was the antecedent to make up the connexion ? Here is the query, and difficulty, why the prophet should begin his book in this manner, "And it came to pass."

Some satisfy the doubt thus, they make it an idiom or propriety of the Hebrew tongue, to begin books with this particle, *and*, or *now ;* and so they make nothing of it. But surely this is not all ; there is something wrapped up in this *now*, or *and*, which may be of instruction and use to us.

"Now," or, "and it came to pass." The prophet doubtless was meditating upon the condition he was in ; meditating upon the condition he had been in. Time was that we were at Jerusalem, that we went with joy to the temple, to the solemn assemblies ; that we heard the voice of God, that we saw his glory, his beauty, his power, and his strength there. Time was that we had communion with the saints ; that we sung songs of Sion together with cheerfulness and with joy. We had precious ordinances, honourable sabbaths, sacrifices that did cheer our hearts, and seal up pardon of our sins to us, and intimate the good will of God in Christ to our souls ; we sat under our vines and under our fig-trees, and were in safety. But now, now we eat the bread of mourners, we drink our own tears. Now we are deprived of all ordinances, stript of all our comforts ; we are sold into the hands of enemies, we are become captives to a heathen prince ; our bondage is grievous, and must continue seventy years. It is the fruit of our sin. God is righteous in all his judgments, and if we willingly accept the punishment of our iniquity, he will in wrath remember mercy, regard us in our low estate ; he will sweeten and sanctify our captivity to us.

Such thoughts as these were in the breast of the prophet. And I incline the rather to think so, because it was upon the sabbath day (as I shall show you afterwards when I come to open some things that follow) when he was meditating in this manner. Also you shall find in Scripture relatives used without antecedents ; as Psal. lxxxvii. 1, "His foundation is in the holy mountains." Here is a relative without any antecedent, yet the antecedent is supposed, and easily found out. His foundation. Whose foundation ? The foundation of the temple, the foundation of the city, is in the holy mountains. The Scripture doth sometimes lay down things relatively and conjunctively, when the antecedent may be supposed and found out with a little inquiry. So here, And it was thus and thus with the prophet, he was meditating ; there was the word in his bosom, and the particle *and* connects that with this word of God revealed to him, and expressed by him.

Hence then take this note : That the hearts of the servants of God are exercised with thoughts of God's dealings with the church and themselves. Their thoughts are better exercised than the world thinks. Ezekiel here had his thoughts busied about his former and present condition, his heart was exercised that way. "I have other meat to eat," saith Christ, "than ye know of ;" so the saints, they have other meat, other thoughts to feed upon, than the world takes notice of. It is oft unknown how their thoughts are exercised. Eli thought Hannah mad when he saw her lips go ; but her heart was better employed then he fancied. Many think God's people melancholy, and not worthy of their company, they are but heavy pieces, when their hearts are in heaven, and they are at solid and serious converse with God. You have an expression to this purpose in Cant. i. 1, "Let him kiss me with the kisses of his mouth." The spouse had not spoke of her Beloved before. It is a strange speech to begin thus ; "Let him kiss me with," &c. Who should kiss her ; here is no mention of Christ, no mention of God, no mention of any before, but on a sudden, "Let him kiss me with," &c. Though Christ had not been mentioned by her lips, yet Christ was deep in her thoughts, and in her desires, she had meditated on Christ before, and so breaks out into this speech, "Let him kiss me with," &c. And Ezekiel having his heart meditating, and taken up with the thoughts of his former and present condition, of the church in general, of God's wrath to them, and God's mercy in the midst of his wrath, breaks out, "And," or "now," in the thirtieth year it was so and so.

This then instructs us what is the practice of the

choice worthies of God; their hearts are meditating and taken up with divers things that the world is not aware of. It is good for us to be in meditation this way. Isaac went out to meditate in the evening, and while he was meditating cometh Rebekah, the desire of his soul: and the prophet being in that posture, hath visions of God to cheer his soul, and the souls of his people. If you would be meditating, you may see heaven opened, and God coming down into your bosoms.

"In the thirtieth year." This time doth trouble interpreters very much; it is not said in the thirtieth year of what, or of whom, but barely in the thirtieth year. Here is an uncertain chronology, which makes a difficulty in the prophet.

1. "In the thirtieth year." Not the thirtieth year from the jubilee, as some make it, for the fifth year of Jehoiachin's captivity corresponds not with the thirtieth from the jubilee; for as Junius and some others (that take pains in searching out the truth herein) observe, that falls in but with the ninth year from the jubilee; therefore we let that pass.

2. "In the thirtieth year." Some make this to be the thirtieth year of his age; the prophet was thirty years old, and then he began to prophesy. But this is not the practice of the penmen of Scripture, to compute the prophecies from their own age and birth. And there is good reason for it, because prophecies, and things that concern the good of the church so nearly and so much, receive witness and strength from the time wherein they are extant; and those times must not be particular times, times of particular men that are not known, but the times must be such as are known to the world, that all may be convinced the thing was done at such a time. Now the birth of one that afterward was to be a prophet, is not like to be a time so noted in the world, that the world then should take notice that Ezekiel was born, and did begin the computation of his prophecy from thence. It is not like therefore that this should be the meaning of the thirtieth year. If so, he would have said, In the thirtieth year of my life.

3. "In the thirtieth year." That is, in the thirtieth year since the law was found in Josiah's days, and since that great passover which was kept by him. In 2 Kings xxii. there is mention of finding the book of the law; and in chap. xxiii. of the great passover, and this was in the eighteenth year of Josiah's reign, ver. 33.

Now if we compute the time from the eighteenth year of Josiah, it doth amount even to the thirtieth year, in which our prophet had his vision, and began his prophecy. For Josiah reigned thirteen years after this, (as you may observe in the story,) "he reigned thirty and one years" in all, 2 Kings xxii. 1; and then Jehoahaz his son reigned three months, chap. xxiii. 31; then Jehoiakim reigned eleven years, ver. 36; and Jehoiachin his son reigned three months before he was carried captive into Babylon, chap. xxiv. and five years of his captivity was past when Ezekiel began his prophecy. So then take the thirteen years of Josiah, and the eleven years of Jehoiakim, there are twenty-four; then add the five years of Jehoiachin's captivity, which make twenty-nine, and then take three months that Jehoahaz reigned, and the three months that Jehoiachin reigned before he was carried captive, they make up twenty-nine years and six months: therefore saith he in the thirtieth year; it was the thirtieth year current, and so expositors do for the generality put it.

And whereas some would have it to be the thirtieth year of the Chaldean account; it being, according to them, thirty years from the beginning of that monarchy from Nebuchadonosor, (as some call him,) who was the father of this Nebuchadnezzar the Great, that carried away Jehoiachin into captivity. If it were the thirtieth year of that monarchy, it falls in with the thirty years since the eighteenth of Josiah, wherein the law was found, and the passover kept, so that these two may stand together, and there need be no jarring between interpreters for this time.

"In the fourth month." It was not the month Tebet or Thebeth, (as some will have it,) which answers to that we call January; but the month Tamuz, or Tammuz, that which answereth to part of June and part of July; (about the time we are now in); for the Jews were to reckon their months from April, as Exod. xii. 2, "This shall be the beginning of months, it shall be the first month of the year to you;" that month was Abib, Nisan, or Nissan, and answereth to part of March, and part of April; now from thence this is the fourth month, and falleth in with the latter end of June and beginning of July.

"In the fifth day of the month." This I find some do make to be the sabbath day, and it is very probable that it should be so; for, chap. iii. 16, he saith, that at the "end of seven days the word of the Lord came unto him again." Hence they collect, that it is not likely that God would step over the sabbath day, and give Ezekiel visions upon another day, and not upon that; for if Ezekiel had had his visions upon another day, the people should have been destitute of all the benefit. They were so employed in their works of building and planting, and other accommodations for a captivity, that they had no leisure to resort unto Ezekiel upon a week day; therefore they strongly conclude, that it was upon a sabbath day, in the latter end of the week. From hence

Obs. 1. That that time is not considerable wherein the law of God is out of date; the time was reckoned here from the eighteenth year of Josiah, wherein the law was found. It was lost in Manasseh's and Amon's days, till the eighteenth year of Josiah, when being found, it was brought forth for the comfort and instruction of the people, for the worship and honour of God; and from that *punctum* the Spirit of God reckons the time, and begins the account. When God's law is out of the way, and his worship down, that is no considerable time at all in the eye of God. Parties that are in the dark, or dead, we do not reckon of their time. One converted in his old age said, I have been long in the world, I have lived but a little time, meaning, since he was converted, the time before was incomputable. The widow that liveth in pleasure, the apostle saith, "is dead while she lives," 1 Tim. v. 6. And the world is dead that hath not the law, the place is dead that hath not the ordinances of God. So long they have been, but they have not lived, they have not measured time; and therefore the Spirit of God fixeth the account at the finding of the law.

Obs. 2. The things here not being specified, but left undetermined, that God would have us observe the remarkable passages in churches and states when they fall out, not one or two, but many, or all the chief. As the eighteenth year of Josiah, when the law was found, when that great passover was kept, when he and the people of God entered into a solemn covenant with God, when the great reformation was made among them, such great acts were taken notice of; as also the changes in Babylon, when the Chaldean monarchy began, when Nebuchadnezzar was put into the throne, and his head lifted up above others. God would have us take notice of the chief acts of his mercy and providence at chief times; Hos. xiv. 8, "Ephraim shall say, What have I to do any more with idols?" There will be a great alteration; then it will be a remarkable time; said God, "I have heard him, and observed him;" and then followeth, "Whoso is wise, and he shall understand these things? prudent, and he shall know them?"

Now is a time of memorable emergencies, and they should be considered; the famous things of 1640 and 1641 ought to be had in everlasting remembrance: a triennial parliament, resurrection of religion, law and gospel were found again; reformation begun, protestation and covenants taken, the kingdoms united here, and foreign ones shaken in pieces.

Obs. 3. This makes for the truth and strength of our prophet's visions and prophecy; for when exact particular times and places are set down, that things were done in such a year of such a king, such a month, such a day of the month, it adds weight to an ordinary history; and when the Spirit of God shall so punctually determine the time to a year, a month, a day, it is a strong seal to the truth of the visions and prophecy.

Obs. 4. See here, (from "the fifth day,") that God hath a special care of his sabbaths, and of the spiritual good of his servants. Of his sabbaths, that they shall not lie in the dark, when they are in Babylon; God will open heaven and appear to a prophet, and give him visions, upon a sabbath day. God will do it too upon a sabbath day, that so the people, which were in a sad condition, that laboured now in brick and clay again, that were building, planting, taken up with secular affairs, might have a seasonable opportunity for the good of their souls. The sabbath was made for man, for the good of man, and they found it so. Though they be in Babylon, they shall have a prophet, they shall have visions, and visions upon a sabbath day, when they have liberty and opportunity to come to the prophet to be instructed in these visions, without prejudice to their callings.

"As I was among the captives by the river Chebar." Here is the place mentioned where the prophet was, and the occasion of his being in it.

"Among the captives." The original is, In the midst of the captivity; the abstract being put for the concrete, captivity for captives: and this is ordinary in the Scripture; as circumcision for circumcised, Phil. iii. 3; election for elected, Rom. xi. 7, "the election hath obtained," that is, the elected; and here, in the midst of the captivity, is, in the midst of the captives.

"In the midst," is not to be taken geometrically and strictly, as if he were exactly in the midst of them proportionably every way considered; but, in the midst is to be understood, "among the captives;" they were captives, and so was he: as Josh. vii. 13, "There is an accursed thing in the midst of you," that is, amongst you.

"By the river Chebar." This is the particular place. The notes upon your quarto Bibles, say that this river Chebar was part of Euphrates. Rabbins and others say it is Euphrates itself. But if it were Euphrates, why should the Spirit of God change that name which was known, and take a name which was unknown. Surely the Spirit of God would have said Euphrates, and not Chebar. If it be a part or channel of Euphrates, why kept it not one of those names that is mentioned, Gen. ii. Gihon, Pison, Hiddekel? Gihon it cannot be, for that river runneth toward Ethiopia. Hiddekel it is most likely to be, which lieth in those parts; but that river kept its name, and was not changed, as appeareth, Dan. x. 4, where it is said, "He was by the river Hiddekel." If Pison, some reason must be given of deserting that name, and imposing one new and unheard of. Interpreters therefore conceive this Chebar to be a river of itself, rising from the mountain Masius, (running through Mesopotamia,) and emptying itself into Euphrates, at a place where is a town called Chebar, whence the denomination probably may come; but rather, it is called Chebar, because of the plenty of waters that are in it, and for the plenty of grass that is upon the banks thereof.

Near this river had the Jews their habitation, and they were placed together. Chap. iii. 15, "I came to them of the captivity, that dwelt by the river Chebar." Here they were placed, because the Jews were odious to the Babylonians, as of old they were to the Egyptians, and dwelt distinct from them. In Salmanassars' time, when the ten tribes were carried into Assyria, they were put in Halah, and Habor, by the river of Gozan, 2 Kings xviii. The rabbins call this river Sabbation, the sabbatical river, because it flowed not, but desisted from its ordinary course, upon the sabbath day; and Josephus saith, that it was certain this river did constantly forsake its course upon the sabbath day; God thereby miraculously intimated to them, that he would have them keep a sabbath, though in a strange land. These captives were fixed by Gozan, or by Chebar, which is the particular place; the next is the general place, the land of the Chaldeans.

Chaldea was the country of Abraham, he went from Ur of the Chaldeans, Gen. xi. 31; and Stephen calls it Mesopotamia, Acts vii. 2; "Abraham was in Mesopotamia before he dwelt in Charran." It lay on the north of Chaldea, between Euphrates and Tygris. In ver. 4, it is said, "Abraham came out of the land of the Chaldeans, and dwelt in Charran." Chaldea and Mesopotamia were promiscuously taken, sometimes being near together, and sometimes distinctly. The chief city in Chaldea was Babylon, now called Bagdat, from Baga, which in Arabic signifieth a garden, because it stood in a pleasant place, and had many gardens in it. It was built by Nimrod, that mighty hunter, the first king that ever the world had. When the tower in it was built up nine thousand one hundred threescore and four paces from the ground, which is above nine of our miles, then it pleased God from heaven to confound their language, and of one made threescore and twelve; hence was it called Babel, Quia ibi בלל
Gen. xi. 9, because God there con- Quæ excussit.
founded the language of all the earth, and their work together.

This country was called the land of Nimrod, Mic. v. 6; and the land of Shinar, Gen. x. 10, which signify shaking, because it shook their language, and scattered the people that inhabited it out of the land. It is branded by Zechariah for the dwelling-place of wickedness, Zech. v. 11. Out of this land of Chaldea, it is conceived by some, came the three wise men, who offered the gifts to Christ; for the Chaldeans were the chiefest astrologers and exactest astronomers that were in the world, as you observe, Dan. ii.

These Chaldeans were a martial people, very cruel. Jer. vi. 22, 23, "A people cometh
from the north country, and a great Jer. l. 41, 42.
nation. They shall lay hold on bow and spear; they are cruel, and have no mercy; their voice roareth like the sea," &c. They were polluted with abominable idolatries, superstitions, sorceries, enchantments, and all manner of profaneness. Into this

land, and among this people, did God bring the Jews, who had been so dear to him.

Babylon was the seat of the chiefest and greatest monarch of the earth. Thither came a continual conflux of people from all parts of the world, to whose scorns and wrongs the Jews were daily exposed. They said, These are the holy people, these are they come out of the holy land, come and sing us one of the songs of Zion; and so profane was Belshazzar, as that he took the holy vessels to quaff and carouse in. Into this land were they brought, and the godly were constrained to hear and see the blasphemies and abominations that were amongst them, and to bear the scorns and frowns of all comers.

Thus have I opened to you the particular place, "by the river Chebar," and the general place, "the land of Chaldea."

Let us see now what observations will arise from hence.

Obs. 1. That God is not tied to places. Let the place be never so holy, let it be the holy land, the holy city, the holy temple, God is not tied unto either of them, but hath his liberty to work and manifest himself where he pleaseth, even in Babylon. The rabbins have a rule goeth for truth amongst them, and is firmly believed, that the Holy Ghost never spake unto the prophets out of the holy land; and therefore they say, Jonas fled to Tarshish from the face of the Lord, to avoid the inspiration of the Almighty. But here we see in Chaldea, by the river Chebar, is Ezekiel inspired; here heaven is opened unto him; here he seeth visions of God; here the word of the Lord cometh expressly unto him; and here the Spirit of God doth work mightily in him. One shift they have for this; they say Ezekiel was a prophet before he was carried out of the land of Canaan, before he came into Chaldea. But we have no proof in Jeremiah nor Ezekiel, nor in any other part of Scripture, that Ezekiel was a prophet, and moved to prophesy before he came into Chaldea: and therefore it is said, ver. 3, "That the hand of the Lord was upon me there," there first, in that polluted land; I never had the Spirit of the Lord before I came into Chaldea. When the inhabitants of Jerusalem had polluted the holy city, profaned the holy temple, and defiled the holy land with their idolatries, and other wickednesses, then God departs, pitcheth his tabernacle elsewhere, and poureth out his Spirit in Babylon. God is not tied to places, he can in a dungeon, in a prison, in a Babylon, let down his Spirit into the heart of any servant of his, and raise him to a prophetical height.

Nunquam Spiritum sanctum extra terram sanctam prophetis loqui.

שם

Obs. 2. That no place is so wicked, but God can raise up instruments to do him and the church service there. Babylon was a seat or land of wickedness, a sink of all sin, "the mother of harlots and abominations of the earth," Rev. xvii. 5. Yet here, even out of hell itself, doth God raise up a prophet for his people. It was said by Nathanael, John i. 46, "Can any good come out of Nazareth?" Much more may it be said, Can any good come out of Babylon? Can any good come out of Rome? What was answered there? "Come and see." So here, Come and see a prophet in Babylon, come and see the Spirit of God poured out upon Ezekiel, even there. And to this may the first word of the prophecy have some respect; as if the prophet had said, They have had prophets in Jerusalem a long time, but no prophets elsewhere: behold, now also is a prophet in Babylon. God can raise up to himself saints in Nero's court; he can raise up instruments ordinary and extraordinary to do him service, in Babylon, in Rome, in Egypt, in most profane and vile places, that are overspread with all idolatries and abominations whatsoever.

Quasi ab ipsis inferis?

Obs. 3. See here a door open for the enlargement of the church, a type of God's goodness toward the gentiles. The church had been shut up for 850 years in Judea, (for so long it was from Joshua's entering into Canaan to the captivity,) but now he openeth a door for the gentiles; here is a prophet, a church in Babylon; here is a way made for the bringing in of the gentiles, and enlarging the borders of Sion. God will not only have mercy upon Jews, but upon the Babylonians.

Obs. 4. That the godly are wrapped up in the same calamity with the wicked. Ezekiel is among the captives, and many others with him. They lost their country, friends, estates, liberties, ordinances. They were in great misery, brought very low, under a heathen king, amongst enemies, exposed to the scorns and wrongs of all; and Ezekiel, Daniel, the three children, Mordecai, and many others, were all in the same condition. The children of God are subject to the same outward public or private calamities that the wicked are. All things come alike unto all; if you look upon the outward face of things, there is no exception. Good Josiah was slain in the battle as well as wicked Ahab. Naboth was stoned as well as Achan. If David, a man after God's own heart, prosper in the wars, so doth Nebuchadnezzar, a heathen, a tyrant. Sicknesses, diseases, deaths, of what kind soever, are common to good as well as to bad. The sword, plague, famine, hath seized upon the carcasses of the godly as well as the wicked. If wicked women die in childbirth, so doth good Rachel. There is no condition but may befall the children of God; 1 Pet. v. 10, "The same afflictions are accomplished in your brethren, that are in the world;" and no temptation hath taken hold of you, but such as is common to the nature of man. Whatsoever affliction then you have, whether public or private, this may be some solace, it is no other than what befell Ezekiel, Daniel, and hath befallen the godly in all generations.

Obs. 5. That the godly are mingled in this world with the wicked and profane. Men of great worth, great grace, rare excellences, are not so privileged as to be exempted from the society of the wicked and ungodly. Here is Ezekiel amongst the Chaldeans: Joseph was amongst the Egyptians: and Job saith of himself, chap. xxx. 29, that he was a brother to dragons, and a companion to owls; and David cries out, Psa. cxx. 5. "Woe is me that I sojourn in Mesech, and that I dwell in the tents of Kedar," that is, with a barbarous and profane people, that were like to the posterity of Mesech and Kedar. The church of Smyrna, Rev. ii. 9, was pestered with the synagogue of Satan; and Pergamus, ver. 13, had her dwelling where Satan's seat was. In that city, if you observe the 14th and 15th verses, you shall find there was much idolatry and persecution; for there were those that held the doctrine of Balaam, "who taught Balak to cast a stumbling-block before the children of Israel, to eat things sacrificed to idols, and to commit fornication; and there Antipas my faithful martyr was slain." Where there is idolatry, there will be persecution and uncleanness; and where these be, is the seat of Satan. And the church of Pergamus was seated even where Satan had his seat and throne; therefore it is no strange thing for the people of God to dwell amongst the wicked. In Canticles the church of Christ is said to be a lily among thorns; a lily, and none growing near but thorns, that scratch, prick, and tear the church. Micah vii. 4, "The best of them is a brier, the most upright is sharper than a thorn-hedge;" the best of the wicked are briers and thorns one time or other. It is the lot of the godly to be among the Chaldeans while they live here in the world.

Obs. 6. See here, that God hath a special care of his church and people, when they are in the lowest and worst condition. What now is Jerusalem become? where is the glory of all the world? Now they are carried into captivity; now they are in a strange land, under a strange king and government; now they are deprived of all their sacrifices, and services of that nature; now they are imprisoned; now they are in danger of their liberties and lives every day. Yet, as the psalmist saith, "Thou rememberest us in our low estate;" in this low estate, when they are at the river Chebar, in the land of the Chaldeans, doth God remember them, and sends an Ezekiel to them; and unto him, even in Chaldea, in Babylon, were the heavens opened, and he saw visions of God. Where there are the greatest enemies, God will show himself a friend; where the church is exceedingly straitened, God will give enlargement. Now his people are in Babylon, in captivity, he sends a prophet to them, Ezekiel, the strength of God; such a prophet as shall be strong to keep them off from idolatry, though they were amongst idolaters; strong to comfort their hearts against all the strong discouragements they had; strong to lead them toward God and heaven, though they had false prophets to lead them down to hell; strong to oppose the false prophets, to reprove them stoutly, to encourage the people faithfully, and to make known the mind of God unto them without flattery. They shall have a prophet, though they be in Babylon. This should stay up the spirits of the godly, if they should be driven into wildernesses, God will provide Ezekiels for them.

Obs. 7. That we are to take heed of judging the condition of men by their outward afflictions. When great calamities come, people ordinarily grow great censurers, and condemn those parties that are under them to be the greatest sinners of all others. Take heed of this. If you will draw such conclusions as these, The hand of God is upon such; in such a place there is the plague, there is the sword cutting them off, there they are carried out of their country into captivity, there they are imprisoned, there they are held in great bondage; surely these are none of God's people, these are naught, vile persons, reprobates: if you will judge thus, you will condemn the generation of the righteous; for Ezekiel, Daniel, Mordecai, the three children, and many others very godly, were in the captivity, as well as those that were very wicked. Such conclusions must not be drawn from the sufferings of the saints. You know the prophets and apostles met with very hard measure; while they were in the world they were whipped, stocked, imprisoned, stoned, sawn asunder, tempted, tormented, slain with the sword, and evil entreated every where; and if you should measure their condition by their afflictions, condemnation must be their portion, and they must be in the catalogue of delinquents. Have not some in our days been flayed, roasted alive, cut in pieces, thrown into the river? have not their houses, and many in them, been burnt together in Ireland? Have there not been cruel and desperate things done? Ireland now is full of blood, skulls, and graves; shall we say they are the greatest sinners that have suffered such great things? When Pilate had mingled the blood of some of the Galileans with their sacrifices, there were those that presently thought them greater sinners than the rest: but Christ that taught them and us, what use to make of judgments upon others, not to censure them, but to repent ourselves; "Except ye repent, ye shall all likewise perish." Think not that they are greater sinners than others; think not now that the Jews in Babylon are greater sinners than all others; think not those in Ireland are greater sinners than yourselves. If he be a wicked man that meets with great afflictions, then Christ must be the wickedest man that ever was; for he was *vir doloris*, a man of sorrows, and had the greatest affliction that ever befell any. As it was no argument for Zedekiah's goodness, who at this time was in Jerusalem, that he drank wine in bowls, and had a great deal of felicity; so it was no argument for Ezekiel's guiltiness and sinfulness, that he was in a strange land, in Chaldea, among the captives, by the river Chebar. Paul, when he was at the bar with iron fetters about his heels, was a better man than Agrippa with his crown on his head, and his sceptre in his hand, and sitting in judgment to condemn him. Daniel in his captivity is said to be "a man of desires," Dan. ix. a man that God took great delight in; when Jeconiah a king, and dwelling at Jerusalem, "is a despised, broken idol, a vessel in which there is no pleasure," Jer. xxii. 28. Those that are in great affliction may be greatly beloved, when those who are in great prosperity may be greatly hated.

Luke xiii.

Obs. 8. That the wicked fare the better for the godly. There were many godly now in captivity, as well as there were many wicked ones; and because of the godly that were there, God poureth out the Spirit of prophecy upon Ezekiel, and by that means the very wicked come to have the benefit of this prophecy, and partake of his visions. Many wicked ones have a share in the public duties of God's worship, when the godly meet together in those exercises. Ezekiel, in chap. xxxiii. 32, is said to be unto them "as a sweet song of one that hath a pleasant voice, and can play well on an instrument;" he was a sweet song to sweeten their bitter captivity. Joseph being in Potiphar's house bringeth a blessing; and Jacob in Laban's family increaseth the stock of his Master; and Joseph in Egypt saveth the Egyptians, and almost the whole world. Godly men and women are great advantages to the wicked, however they hunch and punch at them. Were the godly once out of the world, God would soon put fire to the four quarters thereof, and the wicked should presently feel it.

"Which was the fifth year of king Jehoiachin's captivity." Touching Jehoiachin, there are many things remarkable: as,

1. In 2 Chron. xxxvi. 9, it is said, that "he was eight years old when he began to reign;" and in 2 Kings xxiv. 8, it is said, "he was eighteen years old when he began to reign." Here seems to be a great difference in the Scripture, hardly to be reconciled, and it hath puzzled many.

This difference is thus reconciled: the kings of Judah, when they were in imminent danger, did use to declare their sons to be their successors; and so Jehoiakim, the father of this Jehoiachin, being beset by Nebuchadnezzar about the second or third year of his reign, did declare his son Jehoiachin to be his successor. Now in the book of Chronicles he speaks of the time from the first declaration, which was about the eighth year of Jehoiachin's age; and the book of the Kings mentions the time when he came to reign alone, and reckons from thence: for

Jehoiakim reigned divers years after his son was declared to be king, and reigned with his father. So that the one book speaks of the time he reigned with his father, the other of the time that he reigned alone in the throne.

2. It is remarkable touching Jehoiachin, that he had other names; as 1 Chron. iii. 16, he is called Jeconiah, and Jer. xxii. 24, in disgrace, Coniah. He was a wicked king, and God cut off the first part of his name, a sad presage that ere long he would cut him off. Evil kings who have had God's name joined with theirs, when they have rent themselves from God's commands and worship, he hath cut off his name from theirs, and taken mercy and peace from them. This you shall see in Eliakim; he was a wicked king, and in 1 Chron. iii. 15, he is called Joakim: El, that signifieth God, and was joined to his name, is taken away. God would not suffer his name to be joined with the name of so wicked a king any longer. So here in Jeconiah, Jah, which is one of the names of God, is taken away, and in hatred and contempt he is called Coniah: God was taken from his name, and departed from him too. When God will honour a man, he adds letters of his own name to theirs. As Abram afterward was called Abraham, a letter out of God's name was put into his. And so Jacob, his name was changed to Israel, a prince of God, or one that prevails like a prince with God, Gen. xxxii. 28.

ה

When God changeth names in mercy, and makes an addition of letters of his own name unto men's, it is an argument of God's great love, of great esteem and great honour to the party; but it is an argument of disgrace, when God either brands them, or detracts from their names. Thus God branded Jeroboam, "Jeroboam the son of Nebat, that made Israel to sin," and "Judas the traitor." And sometimes he detracts from their names, as here Jeconiah is called Coniah; the beginning and glory of his name is taken away; and he was (as Coniah signifieth) prepared of God, prepared of God for vengeance, prepared of God for a captivity, for base services; prepared of God to be a broken idol, to be cast out and despised, as it is in that 22nd of Jeremiah.

Magnæ benevolentiæ pondus.

3. This Jehoiachin was written childless: Jer. xxii. 30, "Write this man childless." A heavy doom, to write a man childless, especially a noble, a royal family, when children are much desired by all, most by princes, that so the crown may not be alienated. Jeconiah is not written childless in regard he had not any child; for, ver. 28, it is said, "Wherefore have they cast out him and his seed?" He had seed, and yet was written childless. How is that? He was as one that had no seed; he was deprived of the benefit and comfort of his seed; in effect, he was a childless man, because his children were carried into captivity, and none of them did inherit the kingdom and succeed him in the throne; for it is said, ver. 30, "No man of his seed shall prosper, sitting upon the throne of David, and ruling any more in Judah;" they died in captivity, and none of them did sway the sceptre of that kingdom.

But there is some objection lying against this; for in 1 Chron. iii. 17, Salathiel is said to be his son, and his son begotten in captivity, Matt. i. 12. If Salathiel be his son, and his son begotten in captivity, how then is this true that he was written childless?

You must know (for answer) that this in 1 Chron. and Matt. i. is spoken after the legal account; for Jeconiah, or Jehoiachin, having been thirty-seven years in captivity, (as you shall read afterward,) he had seen the death of his sons and daughters, his uncles and kindred, so that he had none left of his own loins, or any that were very near unto him, to declare to be his successor, and to inherit the crown; therefore having neither son, brother, uncle, nor kindred that were near unto him, he was as a man childless every way. Now Salathiel being his nearest kinsman alive, he declareth him to be heir to the crown, and to succeed him in the royal dignity, according to the order set down by God in case of the want of issue, Numb. xxvii. 8, 9, &c. And now this kinsman, in the legal sense, is said to be the son of Jehoiachin, that is, the successor of Jehoiachin; not that he was his natural son, come out of his loins; for, Luke iii. 27, Salathiel was the son of Neri, according to the natural line. Be it then according to the legal account, that Jehoiachin was his father, yet still it holds good, Jehoiachin was a man childless.

4. In this king was ended the glory and royal dignity of the house of David. It is true that Zedekiah reigned some years after him, but Zedekiah died before Jehoiachin: and in the genealogy of Christ, Jehoiachin is mentioned, not Zedekiah, neither is there mention of any more kings of Judah after him: he was the period of the book of the Kings, and he finished the line of the house of David. None out of his loins, nor out of any other loins, did sit upon the throne till Christ came. As for Zerubbabel, who was thought to be king, and to sit upon the throne after the captivity, it will appear he was no king; for the learned observe that he was rather a captain, duke or leader of the people, and was stirred up of God to further and finish the work of the temple, after which (the rabbins say) Zerubbabel returned into Babylon, and there died.

But if that be not sufficient to clear that he was no king, you may observe in Zech. vi. 11, that when two crowns were made, neither of them was set upon the head of Zerubbabel, but both were set upon the head of Joshua, the son of Josedech the high priest; showing that all the power was invested in the high priest, and translated from regal to pontifical. So that Jehoiachin was an unprosperous man, to lay the glory of the house of David, and of his own, in the dust. And hence that name is conceived likewise to be given him, Jer. xxii. 11. The name of Shallum, which cometh of a word that signifies to perfect, finish, or put an end to a thing, because he finished the kingly government of the house of David. And although some put this name upon Jehoahaz the son of Josiah, making him that Shallum, yet others understand it of Jehoiachin, and it is most probable to be him, because (saith the text) he went forth out of his place, and was not to return thither any more; and so did none but Jehoiachin, who voluntarily yielded himself to Nebuchadnezzar, 2 Kings xxiv. 12. He was that Shallum that put an end to all the kings of Judah, and laid the royal glory in the dust, and turned the government to the priesthood, where it continued till Christ came and sat upon the throne himself.

שלם

5. His captivity was long and sore, thirty-seven years was he a prisoner in Babylon, as appears 2 Kings xxv. 27. Others had there more liberty, they were not imprisoned, they had the benefit of the prophets, and the advantage of all the ordinances which were amongst them. Those they had to sweeten their captivity, with many outward comforts; whereas Jehoiachin lay in prison, and was deprived of them; his crown, throne, sceptre, kingdom, country, all were gone, and he is a captive imprisoned. A king, and a king of Judah, one that had lived so high, and been in such glory and great pomp, for him to lie in a prison, and in a prison in Babylon, not a few, but twenty, almost forty years;

this is a thing observable in this king, and sets forth the constancy of his misery. He was one of Josiah's posterity, and it is observed that the posterity of Josiah, who were kings of Judah, in twenty-three years were carried four times into captivity, whereas Josiah himself enjoyed thirty-one years in peace. And it appears thus: Jehoahaz, his son, reigned three months, and then was carried away by Pharaoh-nechoh king of Egypt, 2 Kings xxiii. 34; after him Eliakim or Jehoiakim, another son of Josiah, being made king, was taken by Nebuchadnezzar, 2 Kings xxiv. 1, twice, (as some observe,) and carried to Babylon; and then, if it were so, they were five times in captivity; but, howsoever, sure we are that in the eleventh year of his reign, Nebuchadnezzar came up against Jerusalem, and took Jehoiakim, "and bound him in fetters to carry him to Babylon," 2 Chron. xxxvi. 5, 6. After him Jehoiachin, of whom we are speaking, is set up, and reigneth three months and ten days, who being young and fearful, yieldeth himself to Nebuchadnezzar that besieged Jerusalem, and was carried away, together with many thousand others, into Babylon, 2 Kings xxiv. 10—12. After him Zedekiah his uncle, who reigned eleven years, and having broken his promise, violated his oath, and denying tribute to Nebuchadnezzar, is taken, his sons slain before his eyes, himself carried away to Babylon, and there he dieth, 2 Kings xxv. 7, &c.; and all this was within twenty-three years; for this Zedekiah reigned eleven years, and Eliakim or Jehoiakim eleven more, and the other two, three months apiece. From all this

Obs. 1. The different proceeding of God with kings that are good, and kings that are evil. Good kings, as David, Hezekiah, Jehoshaphat, Josiah, how precious are their names! how sweet are they! like an ointment poured out. How do they keep up the glory of their houses! They are not written childless, they are not written men that shall not prosper. God doth not brand them with any note of infamy, nor detract from their names. They are not carried into captivity. But for kings that are wicked, how doth the Lord proceed in his anger against them, and make their names to rot! See it in Ahaz, 2 Chron. xxviii. 22. God sets an emphasis, a star upon him, brands him with a note of disgrace for all men to observe that read his story; "This is that king Ahaz." What king was he? Even that king that in the "time of his distress did trespass yet more against the Lord;" that king that ruined himself and all Israel with him; that king that shook the foundation of church and state; "This is that king Ahaz." So Jeroboam is branded; he is seldom or never mentioned but this is added to his name, "he made Israel to sin." So Eliakim, a wicked king, had part of his name taken away; and here this Jehoiachin is called Jeconiah and Coniah, a broken idol, a vessel in which there is no pleasure, a man that must be written childless, a man that must be carried into captivity, and be imprisoned thirty-seven years. Good kings are the glory of the world, the glory of that state where they live: but these evil kings in Judah and Israel, their memory stinks, their names rot, their posterity is cut off, their houses fall to the dust, and they have a foundation of wrath for their issue, if they have any. Four times within the compass of twenty-three years, were they carried into captivity. God proceedeth against wicked kings to the third and fourth generation, for their idolatry and oppression, for the evils they countenance and maintain in their kingdoms, and in his worship.

Obs. 2. That afflictions are invalid to subdue corruptions. Five years they had been now in captivity, and yet their corruptions were not mortified; all the hard things they had met withal, had not made them yield and stoop to God. Jeremiah had been God's hammer to batter them in Jerusalem, in Sion, and God had exercised them five years with his wrath in Babylon, and yet their iron, adamantine hearts were not broken; but Ezekiel must be stirred up now in the fifth year of Jehoiachin's captivity, a prophet that must be the strength of God to break them, that must lay on load and not spare. You see then that afflictions of themselves do not kill corruptions, they do not break the principle of stubbornness and strength of rebellion that is in the hearts of men and women. Nay, sometimes it proveth so, that afflictions make us the worse, 2 Chron. xxviii. 22; like waters, being restrained they swell higher, and threaten heaven itself; so corruptions, being restrained, they swell and threaten the ruin of states, families, of souls and bodies to all eternity. Isa. i. 5, "Why should ye be stricken any more? ye will revolt more and more." Let God come with a plague to a city, with a sword to a sinful nation; let God come with any judgment; the judgments themselves will never do us good, unless there be something added to the judgments, unless they be sanctified to us; our proud, stubborn hearts, our vile natures, will stand it out against God, even when the sword is in his hand.

"Ezekiel the priest, the son of Buzi." We are now to come to the subject of the vision, set down in the first verse indefinitely, "I," in the third specially, "Ezekiel," described from his office, "a priest," and from his parentage, "the son of Buzi." Josephus and some others, conceive the time of Ezekiel's transmigration to be in Jehoiakim's days, but others make it to be in the days of Jehoiachin the son of Jehoiakim, when he and so many thousands were carried away by Nebuchadnezzar into Babylon, 2 Kings xxiv. 10—12. Then was Daniel, Mordecai, the three children likewise, and Ezekiel, carried into captivity, as sundry affirm. And that he was then carried into captivity, is evident from the text itself; for in the 40th chapter of this prophecy, ver. 1, it is said, "In the twenty-fifth year of our captivity:" he joineth himself, and doth not say, their, but, our captivity, and therefore was then brought into Babylon, when Jeconiah was, and from that time began the captivity, and the reckoning of the seventy years. Now he began to prophesy in the fifth year of the captivity, thirty-four years after Jeremiah, who began in the thirteenth year of Josiah, Jer. i. 2, and had prophesied long, but done little good amongst them, they were so obstinate in his days. God stirreth up Ezekiel, and sets him to work, and he prophesieth twenty-two years, as we may gather out of his own prophecy, chap. xxix. 17, "In the twenty-seventh year the word of the Lord came unto me." It was five years before he began to prophesy, and twenty-two years after we hear of his prophesying. He might prophesy longer, but we find it not recorded in holy writ.

If it be demanded, What became of this prophet Ezekiel? Antiquity tells us that his end was very lamentable, and yet like a prophet's; for usually the prophets came to untimely deaths. Adrichomius saith, he was torn in pieces with horses. Athanasius tells us, he was killed for the people's sake. Epiphanius relates that he was slain by the ruler of the people for reproving his idolatry. Chrysostome, in his 46th Homily upon Matt. xxiii. and those words, "O Jerusalem, thou that slayest the prophets," &c. saith thus, "O Jerusalem, I have sent to thee Isaiah the prophet, and

Lib. de Incarn. Verbi.

thou hast sawn him asunder; I have sent thee Jeremiah, and thou hast stoned him to death; I have sent to thee Ezekiel, and by dragging him amongst the stones, thou hast dashed out his brains." All agree in this, that Ezekiel came to an untimely and bloody end, and so did most of the prophets and apostles. Whatever men's ends were in killing the prophets, God had other ends; that by their blood and death, the doctrine they delivered, being sealed, might pass the better; that none should look for great matters here in this world when such great worthies were so ill entreated; that men might be stirred up by their example, to stand for the truth unto the death; that it might be a demonstration of the judgment to come, seeing they were used so hardly here. Surely it follows then that there is a time wherein God will call over things again, and recompense the sufferings of his prophets, and be avenged on those that had done them such wrong. God had such ends as these. Hence,

Obs. 1. The wisdom of God, that touching the lives and deaths of the prophets and apostles, speaks little. There is not much said in the Scripture touching them; and why? Lest we should attribute too much to them, and too little to God. We are apt to look at the pen, rather than at him that made the pen, puts in the ink, and writes with it. We look at the instrument, and neglect the principal agent. Since the lives and deaths of martyrs and holy men came into request, God hath lost too much of the honour that hath been due unto him; creatures have had it.

Obs. 2. See here the ingratitude of the people, that do not only kick, but kill their prophets, not only mock, but murder their prophets. Isaiah is sawn asunder, Jeremiah stoned, Ezekiel's brains are dashed out. Oh the ingratitude of the sons of men, that do thus requite God for the prophets he sends to them, that break the earthen vessels for bringing them heavenly treasures in them!

"Ezekiel the priest." He was both of the prophetical and priestly dignity, which was not common, very few of the prophets had this honour.

כהן ἱερευς. The Hebrew word is, a Sacrificer; the Greek signifieth as much: one that meddleth with holy things, that offereth sacrifice for sin. Priests were of high account, both among the Jews and gentiles. Among the Jews, great was the honour the high priest had; and the inferior priests had their honour likewise; none might take this honour to himself, but he that was called of God, as was Aaron, Heb. v. 4. They had the charge and command of the sanctuary, and of all things that did appertain to the house of God. The Jews and their rabbins tell us, that there were twenty-four several sorts of gifts appointed of God for the priests, all which are set down in their law expressly, and are mentioned by Mr. Ainsworth, upon Numb. xviii. xix. Among the heathens also they were very honourable; Potipherah was a priest of On; the Chaldee saith, prince of On, because though a priest, yet he had princely dignity.

The priesthood, you know, was entailed upon the tribe of Levi, and it is very observable what was the occasion of it, Exod. xxxii. When the people had sinned in idolatry, and grew seditious and tumultuous, Moses stood in the gate of the camp, and said, "Who is on the Lord's side? Let him come unto me." Whereupon all the sons of Levi gathered themselves together unto him, with their swords by their sides, and presently executed the commands and counsel of Moses, and slew every man his brother, companion, neighbour, ver. 27. They were one of the least, if not the very least tribe of all the twelve; yet were they not fearful, or backward unto this work, but ventured themselves among the people, showing great faith and zeal to vindicate religion and the glory of God. This fact and forwardness of theirs was so well taken of God, that it brought a choice blessing upon them and theirs, God fully rewarded them for it: for whereas a curse was threatened against Levi, Gen. xlix. 7, "I will divide them in Jacob, and scatter them in Israel;" yet this curse was turned into a blessing, and they are exalted to be near the Lord in the holy things of the temple that did appertain to his worship and service. For after they had finished that execution upon the people, the text saith, ver. 29, that Moses said to them, "Consecrate yourselves to-day to the Lord, because every man hath been against his son, and against his brother, that the Lord may bestow upon you a blessing this day;" and thereupon they were taken into the place of the first-born, (that did all before,) and had the priesthood settled upon their tribe, together with a choice blessing, which is recorded, Deut. xxxiii. 8—11. "And of Levi he said, Let thy Thummim and thy Urim be with thy holy one.—Bless, Lord, his substance, and accept the work of his hands: smite through the loins of them that rise against him, and of them that hate him, that they rise not again." Here was the occasion of Levi's being taken into the priesthood, and to serve with God, and to serve for ever.

From hence take this note, which is very considerable: That it is good to appear in the cause of God, and to be forward to vindicate his honour and glory, to stand for him and his people. It is good to vindicate God when he suffereth in his worship, in his servants, in his cause any way. The tribe of Levi was forward to vindicate God, and God rewarded them, they had a blessing that day. So Phinehas was zealous for God; Numb. xxv. 11—13, "Phinehas," saith God, "hath turned away my wrath from the children of Israel, while he was zealous for my sake among them.—Wherefore say, Behold, I give unto him my covenant of peace: and he shall have it, and his seed after him, even the covenant of an everlasting priesthood; because he was zealous for his God." If we shall appear in God's cause, and venture ourselves in his quarrel, we shall never lose by it. Peter was a man forward, he put forth himself for Christ, he would be first speaking: when Christ had said, "Whom do you say that I am?" saith he, "Thou art Christ, the Son of the living God." And presently Christ fastened a blessing upon him, "Blessed art thou, Simon Bar-Jonas, flesh and blood hath not revealed this unto thee. Thou art Peter, and upon this rock will I build my church." Men that go upon good grounds, and will lift up God's sabbaths, worship, honour, out of the dust, though they do hazard lives, estates, or limbs, God will remember it, and they shall be recompensed. You shall find in Judges v. 18, that "Zebulun and Naphtali were a people that jeoparded their lives unto death in the high places of the field." They went forth, and stood for God and his people against Jabin and Sisera that came against Israel, and threatened ruin: and, in Matt. iv. 13—15, when Christ cometh, he preacheth the gospel first to them; God remembereth their kindness, and rewardeth it, though it were long before. So you may lay the foundation of a mercy for your posterities a hundred years hence. This should put us on to appear in the cause of God, whensoever we see idolaters, and the enemies of God, lift up their heads, and strike at truths, and God in his ordinances and servants. Put forth yourselves, God will remember you, though you jeopard your very lives.

"The son of Buzi." Ezekiel was neither the servant nor the son of Jeremiah, as some have fancied, but "the son of Buzi." This Buzi was a prophet, if the rule of Jerom and the rabbins be true. Jerom saith, when a prophet nameth his parentage in the beginning of his prophecy, it is to affirm that he was the son of a prophet; and so say the rabbins likewise, That man was a prophet, whom the Scriptures set down to be the father of a prophet. Then Buzi here, who was the father of Ezekiel a prophet, by these rules was a prophet himself. But this is the voice of men, not of Heaven.

Filium prophetæ se asserere.

His name signifieth contempt, disgrace, a man contemned, scorned, despised in the times and places where he liveth. You may hence

Obs. 1. That the prophets and ministers of God have always been subject to derision and scorn. Isa. viii. 18, "I and my children are for signs and wonders in Israel." If the vine do bear such ill fruit, what then doth the thorn bear! If there be mocking and scorning of the prophets in Israel, what reproaches, what taunts and bitter sarcasms will there be then in Babylon! 2 Chron. xxxvi. 16, "They mocked the messengers of God, and despised his words, and misused his prophets;" they counted them teachers of lies, false prophets, seditious, factious, such as delivered strange doctrines, plotted treasons, &c.; nothing was too vile, too bad to lay upon the prophets and the sons of the prophets. Zedekiah smote good Micaiah on the cheek, and saith he, "Which way went the Spirit of the Lord from me to speak unto thee?" 1 Kings xxii. 24. Thou fool, thou silly man, thou madman, thou false fellow, thou deceiver of the king and people, "which way went the Spirit of God from me to thee?" and so smites him on the cheek. Now to smite on the cheek was a proverbial speech among the Hebrews, and it was a sign of the greatest disgrace that could be done to any. This was the condition of the prophets, while they were here in the world; and also of the apostles, "We are made as the filth of the world, and off-scouring of all things to this day," 1 Cor. iv. 13. Paul, a great scholar, full of the Holy Ghost, called by an extraordinary way, yet he saith of himself, and the rest of the apostles, that they were counted as the off-scouring of all things; men get up all every where, on every side, so the word carries it. The men of the world were like unto a man that raked every where to get a basket of filth, dirt, and dung to throw in some one's face; so they scrape in the doctrines, lives, and passages of the servants of God, catch at all advantages, seek every where to pick up something, that they may have wherewithal to upbraid, reproach and revile them; and we are made as the very filth and dung upon the face of the earth. Was not Huss, that worthy of God, so counted? When the prelate (who had the power of ordering things) had put a paper crown on his head with three ugly-shaped devils upon it, and this title over their heads, *Hæresiarcha*, here is the diabolical heretic, that great heretic that hath three devils in him; and when they sent him away to the stake with this farewell, Go thy ways, we commit thy soul to the devil; was not here a man made the filth of the world? Even such mockings, such dealings, such doings must the servants of God look for while they are here. They are the sons of Buzi, they are Buzies indeed, men of contempt and scorn among wicked and vile men.

Signum maximæ ignominiæ.

ὡς περικαθάρματα.

Obs. 2. That whom the world contemneth, God will honour. Here is a Buzi, a man of contempt in the world, but God giveth him a son, and a son who is a prophet, and a son whose name is recorded in Scripture, together with his own, all honourable things. Hannah was scorned, reproached by Peninnah, but God giveth her a Samuel, and honoureth her with the motherhood of such a son. Joseph was thrown out by his brethren, cast into the pit, sold to Potiphar, put into prison, but God did lift him up in Egypt, and set him almost in the throne, made him the next man to the king himself. Christ was the stone disallowed and rejected by the builders, even the master-builders, the great ones, the rabbies, the pharisees; but God makes him the chief corner stone, God sets him up on high. This is for the comfort of those that are godly and thrown out by the world; God will take them up and put honour upon them in a way they know not of.

From the subject we come to the things which fell out, with the author of them, and they are these:

1. Heaven is opened.
2. Visions are presented.
3. They are seen of Ezekiel.
4. The author of them is specified, "Visions of God."

"The heavens were opened, and I saw visions of God." The word opening, among the Jews, denotes sometimes not the reality, but the effect of a thing. Gen. iii. 7, "Their eyes were opened;" they were not shut before, but now they saw that which they saw not before, and so their eyes are said to be opened. In the gospel, Christ is said to open the eyes of the blind, the ears and mouth of the deaf and dumb; not that their mouths were absolutely shut, or their ears absolutely stopped, or their eyes so closed that they could not stir their eye-lids; but Christ opened them so, as he made them to see, hear, and speak, to do that which they could not do before; so that in regard of the effect they are said to be opened. Sometimes again it denoteth the truth of a thing; and so Stephen saw heaven opened, and Christ standing at the right hand of God; and Peter saw heaven opened, and a sheet coming down to him.

The question is, whether of these ways it is to be taken here? Origen saith, That the heavens were open to the eyes of his body, there was a division of the heavens, and so in a literal sense he saw the visions, and the things presented to him; but Jerom saith, The heavens were opened, not by the rending of the firmament, but by the faith of the believer. You may take it in the literal sense, and according to the truth of the thing. The inconvenience objected against it is not considerable: for it is said, if the heavens were literally opened, how could Ezekiel see so far, as to see things in heaven? the strength of his eyes could not reach it; for if the sun, and fixed stars which are far above the sun, are greater bodies than the earth, and seem so little unto us, how little would any thing in heaven seem to the eye, when it is exceedingly beyond both these?

Non divisione firmamenti, sed fide credentis.

Answ. The heavens being opened, it doth not follow that Ezekiel must see the visions in heaven; the things he saw might be nearer than the stars or sun. The dove came down and lighted upon Christ, and the sheet was let down from heaven unto Peter; and so the visions might be nearer unto Ezekiel than the highest heavens. "The heavens were opened, and he saw visions of God;" it is not said that he saw visions in heaven. And grant it to be heaven, Stephen saw Christ there, and so might Ezekiel see the object of his vision there: yet neither did Stephen by his natural strength see Christ, nor Ezekiel these visions, but he that opened heaven did open their eyes, strengthened them to see at such a distance. Or, secondly, you may take it effectively, that it was done to the eye of faith; as if heaven had been opened. A thing is said to be opened when that is removed which hinders coming at the thing shut up. "The seven seals were loosed," Rev. v. then was the book opened. When the shutters of the window are turned aside, that the eye can come at the light, then the window is open, the impediments are taken away. And heaven is open, when all lets being set aside, God causeth the eyes of his to see divine visions, or reveals divine mysteries unto them, as if heaven were open; and this is the way most peculiar to the servants of God. "Hereafter," saith Christ, "you shall see heaven opened, and the angels ascending and descending upon the Son of man." The angels are not corporeal, they cleave not the heavens asunder in their descent or ascent, that is not the meaning; but the spirit of the text is this, the impediments should be taken away from their minds, they should be so enlightened with the glory of the gospel, they should see, as it were, even angels come down and minister unto Christ; they should, as the expression is, 2 Cor. iii. 18, "with open face behold as in a glass the glory of God," see heaven opened in Christ, and the angels descending upon the Son of man. And so did Ezekiel see heaven opened.

Ubi discussis omnibus obstaculis Deus facit ut fidelium oculi usque ad gloriam ipsius cœlestem penetrent.

Nova acie, apertis oculis.

Obs. 1. The key of heaven is in the hand of God; he openeth heaven at his pleasure, and letteth out and in what parties and things he pleaseth. Angels, visions, and other things he lets out; he openeth heaven, and letteth in your prayers, your tears, your souls at his season. The key of the grave, the key of the womb, the key of the clouds, the key of hell is in the hand of God, and he turns them at his pleasure; but above all, the key of heaven is in the hand of God. He is Lord Chamberlain, there is none goeth out, nor comes in, till God himself turns the key. If you would have mercies, you must look up to God for them, and desire him to turn the key. Rev. iii. 7, he is said to "have the key of David, he opens and none can shut, he shuts and none can open." A key denotes power, and the key of David, chief power in the house, in the kingdom: where that key is, there is the greatest power. God hath that key in his hand, the key of David, all power to open and shut heaven when he will; he can open your hearts at his pleasure, he can open texts at his pleasure, he can open dark things unto you; therefore seeing all power is in the hand of God, look up to him for mercies, and desire him to turn the key for your good and his glory.

Obs. 2. That God doth great things for those that are truly godly, that are true believers. Heaven is opened for them, and only for them.

We do not read in the book of God, that heaven was ever opened for any wicked man: wickedness shutteth up heaven; godliness hath the privilege; to the godly heaven is opened. To Christ it was opened, Matt. iii. 16. To Stephen, Acts vii. 56. To Peter it was opened, Acts x. 11. To John it was opened, Rev. iv. 1; xix. 11. And it is opened to Ezekiel here in the text; "I saw heaven opened." It is shut against others; wicked men shall never see it open in mercy; the judgment at last shall not be in heaven, but in the air, or on the earth. It is the privilege of believers to have choice mercies.

Great things God will do for them, that the world shall have no share in. It was the godly that saw Christ after the resurrection, and not any wicked man. It was for believers that Christ prayed, and not for the world, John xvii. It is for the heirs of salvation that the angels are sent forth to be ministering spirits unto, Heb. i. And it is for the faithful the heavens are opened, that they may see what the glory of their Father's house is, into what a family they shall ere long be received. This sets out the excellency of faith unto us; for as it is a hand to receive Christ and his benefits, a mouth to eat his flesh, and drink his blood; so it is an eye to see into heaven, and the eye for which heaven is opened.

"I saw visions of God." God hath manifested himself unto his prophets several ways.

1. By speaking immediately unto them without interposition of any medium, even mouth to mouth, and face to face. So he spake to Adam in paradise; to Moses, Exod. xxxiii. 11, "The Lord spake to Moses face to face, as a man speaks to his friend." This manner of God's manifesting himself was peculiar to Moses above any, or all the prophets besides, as you may read, Deut. xxxiv. 10.

2. God manifested himself to his people by dreams, which was in the night season: there was some representation of something unto them when they were asleep. Thus God manifested himself to Jacob, Gen. xxviii. 12. And Jacob saith, Gen. xxxi. 11, that "the Angel of God spake unto him in a dream."

3. God hath manifested himself to his people by visions; Psa. lxxxix. 19, "Thou spakest in vision to thy holy one." And Gen. xv. 1, "The word of the Lord came unto Abraham in a vision." These three you have together in two verses, Numb. xii. and part of the 8th, "If there be a prophet among you, I the Lord will make myself known to him in a vision, and speak to him in a dream; and to Moses will I speak mouth to mouth." Here in the text it is by way of vision that God speaks or appears unto Ezekiel; "I saw visions of God."

In a vision there are these things:

1. There is some species or similitude represented to the sight, whether it be to the eye of the body externally, or to the eye of the mind internally, always something is represented to the eye.

2. A vision of something that is future, whether at some little distance, or very remote. Hence it is that vision is put for prophecy, Isa. i. 1.

3. In a vision there is always such an irradiation of the mind, such divine, satisfying, overpowering, strong light, that the party who hath the vision is put out of all doubt and dispute concerning the truth of the thing he hath seen, or is represented.

4. There is in a vision a strong impulse upon the spirit of the party to do that which is the mind of God concerning that vision.

Moller, Psa. lxxxix. 20.

5. It is when they are awake. God speaks to men by dreams in the dark when they are asleep, but usually visions are when men are awake.

All these are found here in the prophet Ezekiel's vision:

1. There are representations of divers things to him: he was an hieroglyphical prophet, he had more things presented unto him of that nature than any prophet besides: all that followeth here in this chapter are representations of things to Ezekiel in this vision.

2. It is of things to come; for this prophecy being either of the ruin of Jerusalem, or of the state of the church, still it was of that which was not present but future.

3. The prophet he had strong enlightenings, he had such irradiations of his mind that he was satisfied touching the thing, therefore he saith, "The word of the Lord came expressly unto him," the hand of the Lord came upon him in a great deal of strength.

4. He had a mighty impulse; though he was backward, unwilling to go on in the work of God, yet the Spirit came upon him with power, and put him on.

And lastly, it was when he was awake, walking up and down by the river Chebar, there he had these visions.

Thus much for the nature of a vision. Now these visions were visions of God; "I saw visions of God." Not that he saw God oft, and so every sight of God made a new vision, (for no man can see God and live,) but visions revealed to him by God, which did in some measure set out the glory and majesty of God; and so they are called visions of God.

Or visions of God by way of opposition and exclusion, thus; "I saw visions of God," I had divine visions, not Satanical delusions, (for Satan hath his prophets, and they have their visions whereby they delude the world,) not dreams and conceits of mine own; no angel, no devil, no dream, no fancy of mine presented them unto me, but they were prophetical visions, such as God himself hath presented.

Or visions of God, lastly, in regard of the eminency of them. "I saw visions of God," that is, choice, rare, difficult, transcendent visions. Things that excel, in Scripture phrase, usually are said to be things of God; as, the mountains of God, the cedars of God, the city of God; as you may read, Psa. xxxvi. 6; lxxx. 10; Jonah iii. 3.

1. Observe here the certainty of the things contained in this prophet. He doth not say, I heard, but, "I saw visions of God." The sense of sight is the most certain, most active, most discerning, most evidential of all the senses. Therefore, 1 John i. 1, 3, "That which we have seen with our eyes, which we have looked upon,—we declare unto you." There was certainty in that which they saw. One eye-witness is more than ten hearsays, than ten ear-witnesses. Thales being asked the question, How much truth should differ from a lie? answered, As much as the eyes differ from the ears; intimating, that what you hear may be false, but what you see, that is certain. The prophet here saw "visions of God," to show the certainty of these visions, and so of the whole Scriptures, which are "visions of God."

Quantum oculi ab auribus.

Obs. 2. See here the dignity of these visions; they are "visions of God," such as are great, glorious, transcendent things. Men's words, works, things are mean, poor, and worthless; but the things, the "visions of God," are so high, so excellent, that few can reach them, they are beyond the apprehensions of ordinary men: yea, the prophets themselves did not see all that was in those visions God did vouchsafe unto them. This shows, the things of God have transcendency in them, are of great authority, and challenge answerable esteem. These are "visions of God," and must, with all Scripture, be valued accordingly. Hence the ancients have called the Scriptures, an epistle of God sent from heaven to the sons of men. Therefore in them is nothing impertinent, or empty, but all in them is glorious, full of sense, mysteries, and spirit. This strengthens the authority of Scripture, that our faith may not stagger at all, but be confident, and build upon them, as visions and truths of God.

Ne titubet fides.

Obs. 3. See here, that when God beginneth once to let out mercy to his servants, he stints not presently, but proceeds; I saw not one vision, but "I saw visions of God," he had many choice ones. It was kindness that Ezekiel had such a name, The strength of God; it was kindness that the Lord would open heaven to him; it had been great kindness if he had seen but one vision; but for Ezekiel to have heaven opened, and to see visions of God, many visions, one after another, this showeth the great kindness of God. When Rachel had her first son, she called his name Joseph, which signifieth adding, or increase; for she said, "The Lord shall add to me another son," Gen. xxx. 24; now God hath begun to show kindness, he shall not only give me this, but he shall give me another son also. When the Lord hath bestowed one mercy on you, you may name it Joseph, increase, addition, for God will bestow another upon you. Abraham had many mercies from God, one after another; and Moses, a multitude of mercies; he converseth with God face to face, he heareth God speak, he hath God's presence to go along with him; yea, he seeth all God's goodness and glory to pass before him. When mercies come forth, God will not presently shut the door of mercy again. Heaven is opened, visions are presented one after another. Psa. xxxvi. 10, "Continue thy loving-kindness;" the Hebrew is, draw forth, or draw out thy loving-kindness: a metaphor either taken from vessels of wine, which being set abroach once, yield not only one cup, but many cups; so when God setteth abroach the wine of his mercy, he will not fill your cup once, but twice and seven times: or, taken from a mother, who hath her breasts full of milk, draws them out for her child, not once, but often; the child shall have the breast many times in the day, and many times in the night; so when God beginneth to show mercy to you, he will draw out his breasts of consolation, and will bestow mercy after mercy upon you: or, from a line which is extended; for so God being in a way of mercy, will extend the line of mercy, and measure out mercy after mercy for you. Is not heaven opened? Do you not see visions of God this day? How often is heaven opened in this city in a week! How many visions have you from the prophets! What manifestations of truths are there! what discoveries of the mind and will of God to your souls are there in these days! "I saw visions of God," saith Ezekiel, and so may you.

"The word of the Lord came expressly." The Hebrew is emphatical, the word of the Lord by being, hath been, or, hath altogether been, had much being in me. Besides the visions I saw, there was a real communication of truths to my understanding; evident and express commands from God came unto me, and it came so, as it had entrance and abiding in me: *Accurate factum est*, there was an accurate and real work of it upon me, and in me. Prov. iii. 21, "Keep sound wisdom;" the word for sound wisdom in the original is, that which is essence or being; intimating, that all other things are nothing; and "the Word of God," that only hath substance and being in it, making substantial where it comes. And so here, it gave being, and was an ingrafted word in the soul and heart of the prophet; so that the meaning is, the word came with that evidence and clearness unto me, that I could not withstand it, it had such entity and substance in it, that it made me of a common man a prophet.

היה היה Essendo fuit, omnino fuit fiendo factum est.

תושיה

"And the hand of the Lord was there upon me." The hand of the Lord is taken in two senses, especially in Scripture:

1. For judgment, or punishment; so you have it, Acts xiii. 11. Speaking of Elymas the sorcerer, saith Paul, "The hand of the Lord shall be upon thee, and thou shalt be blind;" God's hand was upon Elymas, and he was stricken blind for perverting the deputy. In this sense it is not taken here.

2. The hand of the Lord is taken for prophecy. When the Lord doth come upon the sons of men, and

stirs up their spirits to prophesy, that is the hand of the Lord.

But yet this is not all: it denoteth the virtue and power of the Spirit of God which came upon the prophet, not shaking, disturbing, and throwing of him down, as some rabbies conceive, but changing, comforting, elevating, and exciting the spirit of the prophet to see divine mysteries; and denotes also, that efficacy and power which set on the word upon the heart and conscience of the prophet; that power which subdued all opposition and carnal reasonings, and removed all impediments, whatsoever stuck upon the heart of the prophet, and hindered him in that work which God would have him to undertake. It is this hand of the Lord that makes the word mighty, spiritual, lively, according to that in Heb. iv. 12. The prophet felt the intrinsical virtue of this hand, the Spirit of God in his own heart; it was a quick and lively word unto him. This intrinsical virtue of the Spirit, if it reached not the prophet's hearers, yet it abode in the prophecy, and it remains an efficacious prophecy to this day. It is worth inquisition, what the virtue of the Spirit is, expressed here by the hand of God.

There are three things in it: the hand is,

1. *Symbolum roboris.*
2. *Index veritatis.*
3. *Instrumentum operationis.*

1. The hand is *symbolum roboris*, the type or emblem of strength; therefore of a strong man we say, he is a man of his hands, that is the symbol of his strength. So the Spirit of God is a Spirit of strength: the hand of God notes the strength of God, and the Holy Ghost is the power and strength of God; Luke i. 35, "The Holy Ghost shall come upon thee, and the power of the Highest shall overshadow thee:" and, "Greater is he that is in you, than he that is in the world." The Spirit of God that is in the hearts of his children, he is of more strength then Beelzebub, the prince of devils, and god of this world.

2. The hand is *index veritatis*, the discoverer of truth. The hand or finger doth show a thing. If you would have a man go this way or that way, you show him or point him with the finger, you direct him with your hand. Solomon, Prov. vi. 13, speaking of the wicked man, saith, "He teacheth with his fingers;" that is, he shows others by his hand to do wickedly. The Spirit of God is *index veritatis*, this hand of God doth show you the truth: John xvi. 13, 14, "He shall show you," saith Christ, "things to come, he shall take of mine, and show it unto you." It is the Spirit of Christ, this hand of God, that showeth you all things. You will never know truths till this hand point to them, and teach you. You may have notions in your head, and guessings in your spirits and bosoms, but the reality and certainty of things will never be attained to, till the Spirit of God acquaint you with them.

3. The hand is *instrumentum operationis*, the instrument of action. Men do all by the hand, therefore it is called the organ of organs by the philosopher. So it is the Spirit of God that doth all; Zech. iv. 6, "Not by might, nor by power, but by my Spirit:" I will do all by that, saith God. It is the Spirit of God that doth convince; it is the Spirit that converts; it is the Spirit that dictates to and inspires godly men; it is the Spirit that sanctifies; it is the Spirit that leads into truth, that comforts; the Spirit is the great agent, the hand of God by which God doth all his works. It was the Spirit that moved upon the face of the waters at first; the Spirit of God was the agent in the work of creation, and the great agent in the work of redemption and salvation.

These phrases being thus opened, observe hence:

1. That the prophet received what he delivered to them from God; "The hand of the Lord was there upon me; and the word of the Lord came expressly." The prophets must deliver to the people what they receive from God, and not what they bring of themselves. They must not bring their own visions, their own conceits, what seemeth good in their own eyes; but they must bring the word of the Lord to the people. They must not speak according to the humours of the people, as they move them, as they would have them, but they must speak as the Spirit of God moves them, as God will have them. 2 Pet. i. 21, "The holy men spake as they were moved by the Holy Ghost." And Paul saith, 1 Cor. xi. 23, "What I have received of the Lord, that I deliver unto you;" he would not deliver any thing he had from the world, or from himself, but, "what I received from the Lord, that I deliver unto you." Ministers they are God's seedsmen, and they must have their seed from God, else they will sow tares.

Obs. 2. It is of much concernment for ministers to see they have a good and clear call to their ministry. Ezekiel here stands much upon it; "I saw heaven opened, I saw visions of God, and the word of the Lord came expressly to me, and the hand of the Lord was there upon me." Here were strong evidences of his call to the work he was to go about. Ministers are to be the mouth of God to the people, and the mouth of the people to God: both are weighty businesses; they deal about the eternal truths of the eternal God, your immortal souls, and the everlasting condition of them. The glory of God is concredited in a great measure unto them; the great things of the kingdom of Christ are put into their hands, to dispense as God shall move, and give them opportunity. Had they not need therefore to see to it, that their call be right, and to make it out strongly and clearly, that God hath sent them? If they can clear it up that God hath sent them, they may expect his assistance, his blessing, his protection, and success in their labours. However things prove, this will be their comfort in the midst of opposition, reproach, persecution, hazard of liberty and lives; I was called of God, I am in his work, in his way, he brought me into his vineyard, he will stand by me, I will go on, let him do with me what he pleaseth. The clearness of a man's call will add much comfort to a man's spirit in a black day: it makes him conscientious, pitiful, and painful. A minister's call being evident, the people's consciences will be satisfied, will receive his doctrine; then will they look upon him as their pastor and teacher, reverence him for his work's sake, and are likely to receive much good by him. Whereas otherwise, if the calling of ministers reach no higher than a patron or prelate, there is seldom any good comes either to ministers or people. Therefore it concerns them to look narrowly to it, that their calling be of God, clear and strong to themselves, else they cannot make it out to others; neither shall find that comfort, nor do that good which otherwise they might.

Obs. 3. That in corrupt times, when religion, the church, and God's glory are greatly endangered, God then takes care to raise up some extraordinary servants to vindicate his truth, his people, his glory. All was brought now to a desolate condition; false prophets prevailed, religion suffered, God's honour was low; and now God takes Ezekiel, that was one of the ordinary priests before, and bestows a larger measure of his Spirit upon him, and raiseth him up to be a prophet, and sets him awork, to do great things in Babylon. Though now men be not called immediately by the voice of God and Christ, as of old, yet by extraordinary instincts and motions of God's Spirit, they were heretofore, and are still put upon great services. Philip was a deacon by his ordinary calling, but by extraordinary instinct and hints of God's Spirit, he was raised up to be an evangelist, and to do greater service unto the church of God. So Luther, that was a friar at first, by extraordinary instinct of God's Spirit, was raised up to purge errors out of the church, and to glorify God, especially in clearing the doctrine of justification by free grace. So Zuinglius, Wickliffe, and others in our days. God hath not left himself without witness at this day, he hath stirred up the spirits of some to do him great and extraordinary services.

Obs. 4. That those ministers are fittest to speak to the people, that find the word of God to have being in them. "The word of the Lord came expressly to me;" the word of the Lord had being in him, was ingrafted in him. When the word is a word of being in our hearts, then it will be a word of power in your consciences. That which comes from our hearts, will reach to yours, and will be effectual in you; otherwise the word is but an empty sound, it cometh from the teeth outward, and reacheth but to your ears, and seldom goeth down into your souls.

Obs. 5. Take this note, That there are principles of opposition in the dearest servants of God to the work of his Spirit. It is said, "The hand of the Lord came upon me;" invaded me, so some render it. I stood out against God, I had my carnal reasonings, I had stubbornness and opposition in my will; I said there was a lion in the way, and I pleaded hard against this work and service. But the Spirit of God came upon me, came mightily upon me, came with a strong hand upon me, as he saith; came so upon me, that it subdued all my carnal reasonings, subdued the stubbornness of my will, removed all my shifts and pretences, and brought me off to go about the work of God. Is it not thus with most christians? when you would pray, when you would do good, is not evil present with you? But when the Spirit of God cometh upon you, it will overcome that indisposition, that sluggishness, that opposition; it will work down distempers, and frame you sweetly to go about the work of God, as it did Ezekiel.

Obs. 6. That the word and ordinances of it, that visions and revelations, do the heart of man real good, when divine virtue goes along with them, otherwise not. What if Ezekiel had seen never so many visions? what if God had spoken never so expressly unto him? unless the hand of God had been upon him too; unless the Spirit of God had improved those visions, and ingrafted those words in him, all had been as an empty sound, all had been as mere shadows and sights to him. But when the Spirit of God goes along, then there is efficacy and benefit in any ordinance. Take away the Spirit from the word and ordinances of God, and they will be but dry bones, without meat or marrow: take the gospel, which is called the ministration of the Spirit; if the Spirit be not in it, the choicest promises, the sweetest truths there, what are they? they are *literæ damnatoriæ*, and *leges mortis*, they are letters and laws of death to the soul. When the hand of the Lord is upon an ordinance, and upon a man in that ordinance, then is there good gotten, and then doth the soul gain; 2 Cor. x. 4, "Our weapons are mighty through God."

Obs. 7. That all spiritual good received and done by the saints, is from the operation of God's Spirit, which therefore is called God's hand. Luke xi. 20, "If I by the finger or hand of God cast out devils;" this finger, Matt. xii. 28, is called the Spirit of God; "If I by the Spirit of God cast out devils." That which is called finger in one, is called the Spirit in the other. Now do men receive any good? have you faith? have you love, patience, meekness, understanding, zeal, godliness, any, all graces? It is this hand of God that hath wrought them. Do you any divine good unto others? It is this Spirit of God that works by you, and enableth you to do that good. Acts vi. 10, "They were not able to resist the wisdom and spirit by which he spake." Stephen spake by the Spirit of God. If you hear, if any good be done, or received, it is from the Spirit, which is the hand of God. Therefore you should know to whom to give the glory and honour of all your receipts, and of all your actions.

Obs. 8. Note here, That the messengers of God should come not only with the word of God, but also with the hand of God; they should bring his truths and his Spirit. The word of the Lord came expressly to Ezekiel, and the hand of the Lord was upon him. It is needful that ministers come not only with law and gospel, with the word of God, but that they come with the very hand, even the Spirit and power of God; for all the efficacy and good done, is by the Spirit. If a minister come and bring the letter only without the Spirit, what evidence will there be to his own soul, of the certainty of those things whereof he speaks? How will he be able to see into the spiritualness of them, to know that they are of God, and that they are to be commended to the people in the name of God, when he wants the Spirit of God to discern them himself? What prevalency can there be in the hearts of hearers, when the minister comes not with demonstration of the Spirit? What bottom is there for the faith of men, where there is the wisdom of words, without the power of the Spirit? The hearers get most good when God's letters come to them with his seal, evidencing they are his letters. Hence saith Paul, 1 Cor. ii. 4, 5, "My preaching was not with enticing words of man's wisdom, but in demonstration of the spirit and of power, that your faith should not stand in the wisdom of men, but in the power of God." Then doth the faith of hearers stand in the power of God, when the ministers come with evidence and demonstration of the Spirit of God.

Last of all, From these three verses generally considered, observe, That when God's servants are in deep afflictions, then are usually brought in the sweetest consolations. Here is Ezekiel taken out of his own country, deprived of his estate and friends, of the temple, of God's ordinances and solemn assemblies, and of all the sweet and good that Jerusalem afforded: he is brought into Babylon, he is a captive there; he is solitary now by the river side; he was in a distressed and forlorn condition. What man here would be in Babylon now, and not think himself very miserable? When Ezekiel was in this condition, heaven is opened, visions are seen, God speaks expressly unto him, the hand of the Lord is there upon him. So that you may see, when we are in deep afflictions, many times God cometh in with his sweetest consolations. Gen. xv. 1, Abraham in the chapter before had gotten a victory, and rescued Lot his brother's son out of the hands of sundry kings; and being come home, he falleth into a shaking fit, and is filled with fear lest those kings should reinforce their strength, come upon him and his, and destroy all. While he is in this agony, God cometh to him; "Fear not, Abraham, I am thy shield and exceeding great reward." God came in his deep distress, and brought in a sweet refreshing to his soul. Elijah, that great prophet and worthy servant of God, after he made a sacrifice of Baal's priests, and Jezebel sought after him to slay him, and had vowed that he should die the death, if there were no more men in the world, he was forced to fly for his life, and he flieth into the wilderness, 1 Kings xix. And there was a great famine, neither bed nor bread he had there, and whither to go he knew not. He had many enemies, he hardly knew a godly man left, he was even weary of his life. Now he sitteth down under a juniper tree, and desireth that God would take away his life: "It is enough now, O Lord," saith he, "take away my life, for I am not better than my fathers;" I am even willing to die, the world is so wretched, and there is so much hatred of thee and thine. Ahab and Jezebel are against me, all the country and land cry out of me as the troubler of Israel, and to what purpose should I live any longer? While he is in this condition, God sendeth an angel unto him, and an angel with bread to feed him, and with glad tidings to comfort him. When John was banished by Domitian to Patmos, a place where the condemned parties belonging to the state of Rome, the most desperate and vile wretches, were sent, he had those revelations that were full of glory and excellency. The three children, when they were in the fiery furnace, the fire did them no hurt, but loose their bands and set them at liberty; and then one like the Son of God cometh and walketh amongst them, and comforteth them in those fiery flames. In deep distresses God doth often let out himself: he dwelleth in the darkness, and letteth out himself, and becometh light to those that are in darkness. You know that passage in the Book of Martyrs, of Glover and Austen. Mr. Glover was sad, and full of fears, some days before he was to suffer; his spirit was down, he quaked and trembled to think of the stake, and of that bitter cup he was to drink; he was afraid that he should deny his Saviour, and undo his soul. But the night before he was to suffer, he cried out unto Austen, "Oh Austen, he is come, he is come."

Mistress A. G. I knew a woman in travail, and in that travail whereof she died, who had been sometime in darkness, and having much sought God and waited for the revelation of his countenance, when she was almost spent in her travail and come near her end, upon a sudden she sprang up, and fixing her eyes toward heaven, said, "He is come, he is come; he hath kissed me with the kisses of his mouth; his love is better than wine. I will not exchange my condition with the greatest prince in the world. The Lord is infinitely good, he hath not deceived me; neither will he ever deceive any." She had these impressions upon her spirit, till the breath went out of her body. Thus God in great distresses, in deep afflictions, bringeth in seasonable and sweet consolations.

Ver. 4. *And I looked, and, behold, a whirlwind came out of the north, a great cloud, and a fire infolding itself, and a brightness was about it, and out of the midst thereof as the colour of amber, out of the midst of the fire.*

We are now come to the vision. Some make five visions in this chapter.

The first is a vision of a tempest, in this fourth verse.

The second is of the four living creatures, with their description, from this verse to the 15th.

The third is of the wheels, from the 15th verse to the 22nd.

The fourth is of the firmament, from the 22nd verse to the 26th.

The fifth is of a throne with one on it, from the 26th to the end.

Some others put them all together, and make them one vision; these being all parts of it.

Before I come to open this vision, or any parts thereof, it will be needful to show you the scope of this vision, which will help us in the understanding of the same.

The scope of this vision is to set forth the glory of God; and this appeareth from the last verse of the chapter, where it is said, "This was the appearance of the likeness of the glory of the Lord." The Spirit interprets all to be a manifestation of the glory of God.

This glory of God is evidenced two ways:

1. By his powerful providence in the administration and ruling of all the creatures in the world. For all creatures are under the command of God, and he doth dispose of them for what services he pleaseth. And not only in the world, but specially in the church, is his active providence manifest, preserving and destroying, as seemeth best in his own eyes; so that nothing is done there rashly, or without his will; nothing otherwise, sooner or later, than he hath decreed. All creatures, actions, events, come under his will, rule, and power.

2. By a representation of Jesus Christ, the Judge and Governor of this world, who is the brightness of the glory of God, and the express image of his person; and this from the 22nd verse to the end of the chapter; as the other is from the 4th verse to the 22nd.

This glory of God is presented to Ezekiel in this vision, for these ends:

1. To breed in him a high reverence of divine majesty. The sight of great and glorious things do awaken our dull, heavy, sensual spirits: naturally we are indifferent to the things of God, and unless something transcendent and glorious be presented to us, like Gallio, we care little for other things. Therefore in Exod. xix. 16, when the people saw the lightning, and heard the thunder, when God came down upon the mount in that glorious manner, this awakened them, and bred an awful reverence in them of divine majesty; "All the people that were in the camp trembled."

2. To prepare and fit him for entertainment of what God should speak unto him. We are not always in a frame to hear God speak; there are great distempers in our spirits: you have all experience enough of the truth of this: therefore it is said, Psal. xlvi. 10, "Be still, and know that I am God." Be still, let not your spirit be in a rage, taken up with the world, the cares, fears, pleasures, and businesses of it; be not parleying with a lust, but be still, and know that I am God.

3. It is to encourage him to his work, and to frame his spirit to a ready execution thereof. Ezekiel was to enter upon a heavy task, he was to deal with the stubborn Jews, a rebellious people. He knew that Jeremiah had preached thirty-five years, and other prophets in times better than he was in, and little or no good had been done upon this hard-hearted people. Therefore lest Ezekiel should be discouraged, that his heart might not faint, but be quickened to the work, the Lord doth show him his glory in these hieroglyphics, his glory in these creatures, his glory in his Son; that so seeing the glory of God, he might be warmed, oiled, and encouraged to run about this work. For the sight of glory is potent with a gracious heart, to make it active for God. "We cannot," say Peter and John, in Acts iv. 20, "but speak the things which we have seen and heard." Now they had seen his "glory as the glory of the only begotten Son of God," John i. 14. They had been in the mount, seen Christ

transfigured, and his face shine as the sun, Matt. xvii. 1, 2. And having seen his glory and heard his voice, this encouraged them, notwithstanding all difficulties, to be active for him. This was God's way to appear to his servants, to encourage them to the work he would set them about. God appeared to Moses in a burning bush, Exod. iii. To Joshua in a vision like a man with a sword in his hand, Josh. v. 13. To Elisha by horses and chariots of fire, 2 Kings vi. 17. Peter, being confirmed by a vision of a sheet let down from heaven, goes and preacheth to the Gentiles, Acts x. And Ezekiel here hath vision upon vision, that so being strongly confirmed, he might not fear the faces of Jews or Babylonians, but proceed with life and spirit about the work he was sent.

Note, The sight of God's glory is very efficacious upon the spirits of men. If God let out his glory, it will work strangely upon good and bad. When Christ said to those who came to apprehend him, "I am he," John xviii. 6, it is conceived that Christ let out some glimpse of his glory, which so astonished them, that presently they recoiled, and fell to the ground. Isaiah, when he saw the glory of the Lord, cried out, "Woe is me, I am undone, I am a man of unclean lips, and I dwell among a people of unclean lips," Isa. vi. 5, 6. And then God manifesting his glory so far for his good, that his lips were touched by an angel; "Now, Lord," saith he, "here am I, send me;" I am ready to go, though it be on a message of death, though it be to root up nations and kingdoms. So it was with Job; "I have heard of thee," saith he, "by the hearing of the ear, but now mine eye seeth thee," that is, thy glory. "Wherefore I abhor myself in dust and ashes," Job xlii. 5, 6; I will speak no more against God, I will do whatsoever thou shalt command or expect at my hands. So Isa. xl. 5, 6, "The glory of the Lord shall be revealed, and all flesh shall see it together." And what then? "All flesh is as grass, and all the goodliness thereof is as the flower of the field." There is no greater or more efficacious way, to take off your hearts from the creature, than to behold the glory of God. There was no man that ever saw the glory of God, but he looked upon the creature as nothing afterward.

Videnti Deum omnis creatura est angusta.

"I looked, and, behold, a whirlwind came," &c. In this verse we have the first part of the vision, and it is of a tempest. A whirlwind is a sudden wind, which takes up what is obvious, and carrieth it in a circular motion, wheeling it about, and hurling it here and there. Theodoret calls it the blast of a storm; the Septuagint, a wind which takes away trees, houses, lesser things, and disperseth them. Some have been eye-witnesses of whirlwinds in Italy, which have taken away *stabula cum equis*, stables with horses, carried them up into the air, and dashed them against the mountains; so mighty are these whirlwinds in some countries.

A Lapid.

"Out of the north." The northern winds are very piercing; and if we respect the prophet in this whirlwind, it was to purge the air, that the visions might be clearer and more conspicuous to his eyes, and himself better disposed to the reception of them: for southern winds make the humours fluid, and the body heavy, they relax the sinews, and prejudice the motions of the man; but northern winds shut up the humours, consolidate the parts of the body, intend the spirits, make man more lively, fit to receive and do.

Bacon's Natural History.

But there is something else in this north wind. Great difference there is among expositors concerning this vision, and no man almost knoweth where to fasten. What I conceive to be the truth you shall have.

By this whirlwind from the north, is meant Nebuchadnezzar, with his army that should come and besiege Jerusalem. Jer. i. 13, 14, this is set out under the representation of a seething pot; "I saw," saith he there, "a seething pot from the face of the north" (so the Hebrew is); and what is that? "Out of the north an evil shall break forth upon all the inhabitants of the land." The evil is, "The families of the kingdoms of the north shall come against Jerusalem," ver. 15. There is the evil; the Babylonians shall come to Jerusalem, and be a wind, a whirlwind, a tempest to it.

Nebuchadnezzar and his army are compared to a whirlwind, in the sudden rising, swift going, and terrible execution.

1. In the sudden rising. Winds (you know) rise suddenly. Acts ii. 2, "Suddenly there came a sound from heaven, as of a rushing mighty wind;" which showeth that winds do come unexpectedly. Jonah i. 4, No sooner was Jonah in the ship, but God sent out a great wind upon the sea. Such a wind should Nebuchadnezzar be, he should come suddenly upon them. Jer. vi. 26, "The spoiler shall come suddenly upon thee." Hab. ii. 7, "Shall they not rise up suddenly that shall bite thee? and awake that shall vex thee?" a metaphor taken from a dog, serpent, or wild beast: when a man passeth by the way, before ever he thinks of it, the dog, serpent, or wild beast starteth up, bites, or stings him. So should Nebuchadnezzar be, (for he speaks of him in that second of Habakkuk,) he should come suddenly and set upon Jerusalem, and overthrow it as a mighty storm and tempest doth a tree or house.

How could this be sudden, when the prophets had foretold them of it long before?

To this I answer, First, That because they did not believe what the prophets did foretell, touching Nebuchadnezzar and his destruction of Jerusalem, therefore it was sudden to them, though foretold. Lam. iv. 12, "The kings of the earth, and all the inhabitants of the world, would not have believed that the adversary and the enemy should have entered in at the gates of Jerusalem." Neither king nor people would believe the prophets, they would not be persuaded that ever an enemy should enter within the gates of Jerusalem, and lay it waste.

Secondly, Though they were foretold, though they did believe it, yet because they were not prepared for it when it did come, therefore it was sudden unto them. Luke xxi. 34, "Take heed, lest by any means your hearts be overcome with surfeiting and drunkenness, and that day come upon you unawares." Though men believe that evil shall come, if they be taken unawares, unprepared, it is sudden to them. So these either not believing, or not being prepared though they did believe, the coming of Nebuchadnezzar was to them as a whirlwind, very sudden.

2. In its swift going. The wind is said to have wings, 2 Sam. xxii. 11, because of its swiftness and speedy motion; and ships that are driven by it, are said to be swift, Job ix. 26. And so it is said of the Chaldean horses, that they are swifter than leopards, Hab. i. 8. Leopards are very swift creatures, so swift, that Claudian fastens this epithet upon them, *Pardi fulminei*. Leopards are as swift as lightning and thunder; and therefore, Dan. vii. 6, Alexander is compared to a leopard, because of his speedy conquering the world. Celerity in matters of war is of great moment: and it would do well, that those that are now interested in it, would make more speed; for speed doth great things. Alexander being asked the question how he overcame the world in so little

time, answered, By not delaying: every opportunity was taken. These Chaldeans and their horses were very swift, and they came with great speed upon Jerusalem, and therein resembled the wind.

3. In its terrible execution. A whirlwind, or any wind which bringeth a tempest, what dreadful work doth it make! Houses, mountains, trees, steeples, are shaken and torn in pieces. What can stand before a tempestuous wind? You may see the power thereof in 1 Kings xix. 11, "A great strong wind rent the mountains, and brake in pieces the rocks." The strength of rocks and mountains was weakness to the strength of the winds. Those great vessels at sea, viz. ships, when a storm cometh, how are they battered and shaken, sunk and split against the rocks! There is terrible execution done by the winds at sea and land, when they are in their strength. So Nebuchadnezzar and his forces were very terrible: Hab. i. 6, and so on, we may see the terribleness of them; "I will raise up the Chaldeans, a bitter and hasty nation;" and ver. 7, "They are terrible and dreadful:" and ver. 9, "They shall come all for violence, their faces shall sup up as the east wind:" that wind was most vehement and scorching in Judea, and devoured all that was green. So did the Chaldeans devour and destroy all their pleasant things. "They shall gather the captives as sand:" the wind drives great heaps of sand together, raiseth a mountain presently; so should they gather the captives as heaps of sands. Then afterward, ver. 10, "They shall scoff at the kings, and the princes shall be a scorn unto them; they shall deride every strong hold, for they shall heap dust and take it." No person, no hold can stand before them. In these respects Nebuchadnezzar and his army are compared to a whirlwind, and a whirlwind out of the north.

"A great cloud." Clouds are moist vapours exhaled from the earth and sea by the sun, and condensated by the cold in the middle region, and carried by the winds up and down, this way and that way: they are the bottles of heaven, which God doth fill with wine or vinegar, with mercy or wrath. This cloud here likewise doth represent the same thing again unto us, Jer. iv. 13, Nebuchadnezzar and his army, chiefly, his army. In the prophets Ezekiel and Jeremiah oftentimes his army and himself are compared to a cloud, and that in three respects.

1. Clouds cover the face of heaven; many vapours gathered together rise up and darken the sun, and keep from us the comfortable aspect thereof. Ezek. xxxii. 7, "I will cover the sun with a cloud." The same word that is used for a cloud, doth signify likewise a multitude, a great company. Livy speaks of a cloud of horsemen and foot-men; and Epiphanius speaks of a cloud of flies; another of a cloud of locusts; and the apostle speaks of a cloud of witnesses, Heb. xii. 1: and here you have *nubes militum*, a cloud of soldiers, and this cloud doth cover the face of the earth; this army of Nebuchadnezzar doth cover the land. 2 Kings xxv. 1, it is said, that he and all his host came against Jerusalem; all the militia of 127 provinces: and Hab. i. 8, "Their horsemen shall spread themselves," they spread themselves through the country. Ezek. xxxviii. 9, "Thou shalt ascend and come like a storm, thou shalt be like a cloud to cover the land, thou, and all thy bands, and many people with thee." It is expressly meant of Nebuchadnezzar's army, which should be so great, as that it should cover the earth. The Talmud expounds those words, they shall be like a cloud to cover the earth, of Nebuchadnezzar's covering the land with his army.

Peditum equitumque nubes.

2. A cloud is so swift, as that it is irresistible; it pours out the rain and none can let; it will keep its way, go on, or break itself into pieces. Isa. lx. 8, "Who are these that fly as a cloud?" clouds fly so swiftly, that there is no resisting of them. So this army of Nebuchadnezzar's went with that swiftness and irresistibleness, that it was not in the power of any to withstand them, neither Joakim, nor Jehoiachin, neither Zedekiah, nor Pharaoh king of Egypt; four kings could not withstand this Nebuchadnezzar, and many other heathen kings that he had to deal with, none of them could resist him and his forces. He went on invincibly, strong holds were nothing to him, he made heaps of dust, and took them at his pleasure, Hab. i. 10.

3. Lastly, clouds are emblems of misery and afflictions. The Hebrew word for a cloud ענן signifieth also calamity; for clouds are full of waters, hail, fire, lightning, and thunderbolts. They send down such things upon the sons of men, as fill all with darkness, fears, and troubles. It is natural for a cloud to be an emblem of misery, for clouds bring storms and tempests. The day of the Lord's wrath, in Scripture, is set out by clouds, frequently. Zeph. i. 15, "That day is a day of trouble and distress, a day of darkness and gloominess, a day of clouds and thick darkness: so Joel. ii. 1, 2; Ezek xxx. 3; and xxxiv. 12. So this army of Nebuchadnezzar is fitly compared to a cloud, because of the misery and calamity which came along with it. Great miseries have gone along with all armies, but specially with this. Hab. i. 6, They were a hasty and a bitter nation, they rained down their wrath upon Jerusalem; they had instruments of death, they sent out their thunder and lightning, and burnt the house of God, the king's house, and every great man's house in Jerusalem, 2 Kings xxv. 9. A terrible storm was now upon Jerusalem, when they shot their arrows into the city, slew multitudes, burnt down all, and carried the people into captivity; what a storm was it! Lo here God stormed Jerusalem with Nebuchadnezzar's army; and what are armies but clouds of blood and fire, the great ordnance of God, out of which he shoots thunderbolts of death, Isa. xxviii. 2, and by which he storms the strongest towns?

1. Observe here, That winds, clouds, and all vapours, are subject to the power of God. He calls them forth at his pleasure, and carries them which way he pleaseth, to execute his will. He sent the whirlwind, and the great cloud; these lawless creatures, over which no king, no nation ever had command; (for who can command the winds or the clouds?) yet God hath absolute power over winds. Prov. xxx. 4, "He gathereth the wind in his fist," he can open it, and let out a wind where and when he will, to shake the foundations of the earth. He hath the waters in a garment, covered up in a cloud; he only can pour them out, and make great floods. He is the father of the great rain. Amos v. 8, "He calleth for the waters of the sea," that is, the vapours whereof the clouds and rain are made, "and poureth them out upon the face of the earth." It is God that flieth upon the wings of the wind, Psal. xviii. 11. It is God that rideth upon the clouds, and makes them his chariot, and walketh upon the wings of the wind, Psal. civ. 3. It is God that rideth upon the swift clouds, Isa. xix. 1. God hath the use of the winds as a fowl of his wings, and can flutter and make a great or small wind as he pleaseth. God hath the command of the clouds as a prince of his chariot, to drive it which way he pleaseth.

If you have a wind at sea or land to do you good,

remember that it came out of God's hand; remember God rides upon that wind, and carried it that way you would have it. If the clouds, the bottles of heaven, be carried over your gardens, orchards, lands, habitations, cities, or countries, do water them and make them fruitful, remember that God rideth in those chariots, that he openeth those bottles of heaven, and lets down that which is sweet and comfortable to the sons of men. If they prove terrible unto you, if there be a storm and tempest, remember it is God that sends the storm and tempest. All is in his hand.

Obs. 2. That it is God's prerogative to impose higher significations upon things, than they have by nature. This whirlwind out of the north, this great cloud, naturally had no other signification than other clouds and winds. God lifts them up to a higher honour, and makes them to represent Nebuchadnezzar and his army, his own wrath and vengeance in that Nebuchadnezzar and in that army of his. It is God's privilege to put things into a higher condition than they have by nature. No man, no prince on earth could have put this signification upon that whirlwind. The rainbow was before the flood, but had not that honour to be a witness between God and man, that God would never drown the world any more, till God himself imposed it. The brazen serpent was no more than other brass, but by divine institution it was made a type of Christ. Where such institution is not, no creature can be translated to another or higher condition than that it was set in by the first creation, without sin. To make garments signify purity, crosses, Christ crucified, (besides the superstition and injury in thrusting them out of their rank,) it is a presumptuous stepping into the throne of God, and a bold usurpation of his prerogative; it belongeth unto him to impose significations of a higher nature upon the creature than ordinarily it hath.

Obs. 3. That the anger of God, which way soever venting itself, makes a storm and a terrible tempest. God was about to pour out his wrath by Nebuchadnezzar and his army; and this proved such a tempest as ruined Jerusalem: this verified Psal. xi. 6. "Upon the wicked he shall rain snares, fire and brimstone, and an horrible tempest: the portion of their cup." When God's wrath once breaks out, it will be terrible to all it falleth upon.

What therefore will wicked men do when God shall come out like a whirlwind, when God shall come out as a great cloud, thunder, lightning in the world, rain fire and brimstone and an horrible tempest? When God shall do this, what will become of them? Wicked men, in Ezek. xiii. 10, 11, are compared to a wall that is daubed up with untempered mortar. When God shall come with a tempest and shake that wall, can it stand? No; it is said it shall fall, a stormy wind shall rend it. The Jews daubed with untempered mortar, and when the storm came, they fell. Many christians daub up themselves with the untempered mortar of their own righteousness, of vain hopes, of doing this and that. But when this whirlwind blows, they will down. They are houses built upon the sand, and when the winds blow, the floods beat, and the rain falls, they will fall also, Matt. vii. 27, and fall from the hopes of heaven to the bottom of hell. Therefore look to your foundation, look that you be not built upon the sand, but upon a rock, and that you daub not with untempered mortar, for there is a tempest already begun.

Obs. 4. That God can bring adverse power from any quarter. He can raise wind and clouds from the north, from remote places, those we little think of. He can make use of a hasty, bitter, and merciless nation, and that suddenly, to awaken a secure people, to correct his own servants, and to plague his enemies. It is likely they had such thoughts at Jerusalem as these; Surely Babylon is a great way off, Nebuchadnezzar hath his hands full, none of the kings of the earth will or dare come near Jerusalem, Lam. iv. 12. We are in no such danger as these timorous prophets speak of. Why should we trouble ourselves with needless fears? we will on in our wonted ways. And are not such as these our thoughts? Do not we think that foreign enemies are so employed and taken up at home, that they have no leisure to come and trouble us? But God can from the north bring a tempest; God can from foreign nations bring in those that can pour out their wrath upon us, and make as grievous a storm as ever fell upon Jerusalem. We do not believe, and they did not believe. But what if God do not bring it from abroad, cannot he raise up a storm from within? Is there not already a wind out of the north, a whirlwind and a cloud raised? and how soon do any of us know but there may be blackness, darkness, and the day of the Lord round about us? we may be suddenly environed with winds and dreadful storms, such as our hearts never thought of, and our eyes never saw. Let us not be secure, a bloody tempest is amongst us already. The drunkard may be secure when he is at sea asleep upon the top of the mast, (though it may cost him his life for doing so,) but a sober man will look about him when he seeth the ship shaken, and heareth the winds blow, and perceives the waves rise; and if it be possible, save his own life, and the ship too. If you be sober men, look about you. Is not the storm begun? Do not the winds blow? Are not the clouds dark? Is not the day of the Lord upon us? If it be possible, save your own lives, and the ship that you are in, that now begins to shake, to sink. The heathen mariners had so much religion, that when there was a storm every one cried to his god; and so much charity, as not to suffer Jonah to lie asleep, but go to him and say, Awake, thou sleeper, what meanest thou? "arise, call upon thy God," that if it may be, he may save both thee and us. Be not you behind the heathen mariners, show so much religion and charity in you, as every one to go and call now upon his God. Cry to your God now, that he would still the winds; that he would rebuke the waves; that he would still this storm. Cry to God now with all your strength, and wrestle with him night and day, that he may show some mercy to his beloved, and not give her up to be a spoil to the hands of enemies. Awaken your Jonahs that are asleep in your houses. Call upon husband, wife, friends, minister, all and every one, to put to their hearts and hands, to secure this ship that is almost now split and falling in pieces. Now take your censers, for wrath is gone out from the Lord; put fire and incense in them, that, if it be possible, you may stop the wrath. When the disciples were at sea, and a storm arose, Matt. viii. 24, Christ being with them asleep in the ship, they awoke him, saying, "Lord, save us, we perish." So do you. Christ seems to be asleep; awake him with your prayers, and say, Lord, save us; we are called by thy name, we are christians, save us, else we perish. Christ you see presently arose, rebuked the winds, and the sea, and there was a great calm. Be not secure now of all times, but think with yourselves what you would do if all the nations of the world were come against England, if all the counties in England were in an uproar, if this city were besieged and fire thrown into it to burn the houses. Think what you would do then, do it now, fit and prepare yourselves for the stroke of God in the storm and tempest, that however it go with your bodies, estates, liberties, or lives, yet it may go well with your immortal souls.

Obs. 5. That God disposes of winds and clouds for what services he pleases. A whirlwind is made Elijah's chariot to heaven, 2 Kings ii. 11. The Lord hath his way in the winds, Nahum i. 3. He answered Job out of the whirlwind, chap. 40. 6. By a wind he conveys the Holy Ghost to the apostles, Acts ii. 2. So for the clouds, God sets his bow in them to witness the security of the world from drowning, Gen. ix. He created a cloud upon the assembly, Isa. iv. 5. He went before the Israelites in a pillar of a cloud, Exod. xiii. And the glory of the Lord appeared in the cloud, Exod. xvi. 10. The temple was filled with a cloud, 2 Chron. v. 13. A cloud received Christ and carried him to heaven, Acts i. 9. When we behold the clouds, and hear the winds, we should be carried higher in our thoughts, than to look at them philosophically in a natural way; we should mind them theologically, as instruments of choice services of God, as instruments of his power, wisdom, and glory.

אש מתלקחת Ignis se involvens. *Mont.*

"And a fire infolding itself:" or, as the Hebrew word is, a fire that doth put forth itself, and receive itself into itself; like unto a wave of the sea, that riseth high, and falleth into itself again; or as in a house on fire, the fire breaks forth strongly, and the flame returns into itself presently. The Septuagint render it, bright shining fire, which comes out of a cloud, viz. lightning; and, however some think it not to be meant of the lightning, because lightning goeth straight forth, and never returneth, according to Matt. xxiv. 27, "The lightning cometh out of the east, and shineth even unto the west," and so doth not infold itself; yet we have Scripture to confute this conceit. Exod. ix. 24, there was fire mingled with the hail; the same word is in the original, fire that doth infold itself. And they that curiously observe the lightning, may find that it doth oftentimes return into itself, and pass (as it were) as a ball in the air, or as wound up into a globe. But this reacheth not the meaning yet in the text, "a fire infolding itself." Sanctius thinks it rather a fiery globe which remained in the cloud, and like cabbage leaves grow up into themselves, and infolding, make a globe; so the flames of this fire turned into themselves and became a globe. And it is probable to be this, because it is said, there was a brightness round about it, the fiery globe within begat that circular brightness, which lightning, being transparent, could not do. And the rather it is thought to be this than lightning, because the colour is said to be as the colour of amber, whereas if it had been lightning, that is transient, and the colour hardly observable; therefore it should seem to be some fixed thing. I conceive it to be vapours in the clouds, kindling and burning into themselves, the flame turning inward, and making a globe; and thus I find it expounded, a fire kindling itself: and so it is most natural to the cloud to have vapours in it, which fire and kindle themselves, and burn into the form of a globe. Now what is meant by this fire infolding itself, or this fiery globe, is very doubtful; they that come nearest to the truth, take it to be the wrath of Nebuchadnezzar, or rather the wrath of God in using Nebuchadnezzar to burn the city and temple. But with submission to the judgment of the learned and godly, I take the fire to be meant of sin: the sins of prince and people, priests and prophets, did kindle and involve them in the fire, their own sins took hold of and consumed them.

Ignis fulgurans.

אש מתלקחת

Ignis se accendens. *Shind.*

Prov. v. 28, "His own iniquities shall take the wicked himself, and he shall be holden with the cords of his own sin." A man's sins will turn upon him, take hold of him and bind him; and so here Jerusalem's sins kindle upon herself, take hold of her and burn her. Sin, we find in Scripture, cometh up to the nature of fire; Prov. xvi. 27, "In the lips of the ungodly there is a burning fire." And it is likened to fire, because of the destructive nature. Whatsoever fire takes hold of, it consumeth; and so doth sin: Job v. 2, "Wrath killeth the foolish man, and envy slayeth the silly one;" and Prov. i. 32, "The turning away of the simple shall slay them." So then Jerusalem's sins, the sins of kings and nobles, the sins of prophet, priest, and people, are here to be understood by this fire infolding itself, which drew the wrath of God into Jerusalem, and so kindled, fired, and consumed them all.

From hence note, That the cause of the ruin of kingdoms, cities, princes, and people is in themselves, their own sins are the fire infolding. Hos. xiii. 9, "O Jerusalem, thou hast destroyed thyself," thou art the cause of thine own spoil and captivity; thou hast set up the calves, worshipped them, and they bleat so against thee, that they have undone thee. Israel's sin was Israel's destruction; and so Jerusalem. It was not the whirlwind, nor the cloud, not Nebuchadnezzar or his army, that could have made one breach upon Jerusalem, or led one soul into captivity, if there had not been sin amongst them. It was their own sin which kindled divine wrath, and brought in their destruction; otherwise they had been safe enough. Jerusalem might have stood to this day, and have been as great and glorious as ever. The principles of our ruin are in ourselves. Iron breeds the rust, garments the moths which devour them. The ill humours in a man's body fire and consume the house by a burning fever; children breed the worms which bring them to their graves; and states, the sins which bring them to their ends. Where sin is bred and countenanced, it proves *consumptio totius.* Families, cities, kingdoms go down where sin goes up. Let not kingdoms therefore blame God or others, but let them and all say, The root of the evil is in ourselves; we should never be laid waste, if we were true to God, faithful and close to the rule. If we did not sin, there would be no fire to consume us and ours.

"And a brightness was about it." There being a globe of fire within, it sent forth beams which produced an answerable brightness; which brightness (the cloud being thick and dark of itself) was a window to let in the prophet's eye to see what was in the cloud.

By this brightness is shadowed out unto us, the terrible majesty and glory of the divine presence, putting itself forth in the punishment of sinners. As fire begets a splendour round about where it is; so do the judgments of God set out to the world his glory, justice, holiness, Psal. ix. 16. The glory of his judgment in punishing ill-doers, is a solid, constant, spreading glory; as that brightness was not flashy in the cloud, occasioned by the lightning, but fixed, certain, and on every side.

The note hence is, That execution of justice upon delinquents makes God and magistrates glorious. There was a bright splendour in the cloud, Exod. xv. 6, upon the destruction of Pharaoh and his army in the Red sea. It is said, "Thy right hand, O God, is become glorious in power; thy right hand, O God, hath dashed in pieces the enemy, and in the greatness of thine excellency thou hast overthrown them that rose up against thee." This act of justice was a glorious and powerful work; so when God destroyed the Bethshemites, 1 Sam. vi. 20, "Who is able to stand before this holy God?" say they. The holiness of God's justice and power shine so clearly in the world, that they dazzle men's eyes and hearts, and make them tremble before God. When Phinehas executed justice, how honourable was he in the hearts of the godly! what a great and glorious reward did he get by it! Never was Solomon more honourable than when he executed justice between the two harlots, and called for the sword to decide the controversy. Our magistrates are clothed with scarlet, and they may think that makes them honourable, but their robes never bring true honour to them if justice be not done; one act of justice executed upon delinquents makes them more honourable than all the scarlet robes in the world. How glorious and dreadful was the parliament, when that great man fell in Israel! And if justice were executed upon delinquents, and they had their due, we should be glorious in power, dreadful to nations, terrible to our enemies; they would say, Who is able to stand before the God of this parliament? before the God of this kingdom?

Strafford.

"And out of the midst thereof as the colour of amber." That is, out of the midst of the fire, not out of the midst of the wind, or out of the midst of the cloud. The Hebrew word for amber, is a word that is found no where else in all the Scripture but in this prophet, and but twice more, viz. at the 27th verse of this chapter, and at the 2nd verse of the 8th chapter. Rabbi Iarchi confesseth he knoweth not what the meaning of this word is; another rabbi saith it was the name of an angel, who instructed Ezekiel. The Septuagint, Jerom, and divers others, translate it, *electrum*, amber; and because here is mention of the colour of amber, we must inquire what amber this was. There be divers kinds of amber; one sort of amber is called *succinum*, which is the juice of certain trees, the gum of pine trees, which being hardened by the air, is yellow and bright; that which is white and duskish is bastard amber.

החשמל

Succinum quarundam arborum succus.

A second sort of amber is a liquid substance which flows from the sea rock, and about the sea shores, and being hardened by the air, winds, and water, floats up and down upon the sea, especially about Florida, and other Indian shores; and it is of a honeyish and waxy colour.

The third kind of amber is metallical, made of metals, and those more precious than gold, as Jerom; inferior to it, as Zanchius saith. This amber is compounded of gold and shining silver, is very precious, and of great use. But besides this, there is yet another metallical amber, called *aurichalcum*, the choicest and purest brass, and this is thought to be the *chasmal* or amber here mentioned, according to that, Rev. i. 15, "His feet were like to fine brass, as if it had burned in a fiery furnace." Brass doth most nearly resemble fire. The colour of amber here is a fiery colour; and surely this is near the truth. But yet it cometh not up fully to the nature of the word here; for I do not find amongst those that search into the nature of words, that this word *chasmal* is interpreted amber: as the learned observe, it signifies a coal that is fired most intensively; a coal that hath the utmost heat it is capable of, so hot, that presently it burneth any thing it toucheth: such coals are more red and lively than others, and it comes nearest to the nature of the word to render it, as the colour of a burning coal. Hence Junius and Tremelius render the word, *color vividissimus*, the most lively colour; for nothing hath a more lively colour than hot coals, or fine brass burning in the fire; either of which you may take, but I rather cleave to that of burning coals, which being in the midst of the fire, might so sparkle and shine, as to dazzle the eyes: and whether *chasmal*, in this place, were not more fitly rendered, as the colour of burning brass, or of a burning coal, than as the colour of amber, I leave to consideration.

Prunam ardentissimam, or summe ignitam.

חשמל quasi חש מל festinanter excidens, consumens. Color insignis. *Calv.*

Now what is meant by this amber or coal, there is great dispute. Some understand by it Christ, because he is more precious than amber, more lively than any burning coal whatsoever. But we must lay this sense aside, because there is a vision of Christ in the latter end of the chapter. The soundest expositors by *chasmal* lead us to some inferior to Christ, viz. the angels, who are called seraphim, *animalea ignea*, as Kimchi hath it, of שרף to burn, and seraphims are fiery burning creatures. Isa. vi. 2, "About it stood the seraphims," that is, the fiery burning angels; answerable to the *chasmal* or burning coals here. So in Judg. xiii. 20, an angel went up to heaven in a flame of fire; that element was most suitable to a seraphical and angelical nature. 2 Kings vi. 17, there were horses and chariots of fire round about Elisha, and angels were in those chariots. They are likened to fire, because of their ardent and burning zeal to do the will of God, Psal. ciii. 20.

For the word colour, "the colour of amber," in the Hebrew it is, the eye of amber, the organ is put for the object: so you have it used, Numb. xi. 7, "The colour of it was as the colour of bdellium;" the Hebrew is, the eye of it was as the eye of bdellium.

Now having given you the meaning of *chasmal*, viz. that he saw angels of fiery colour, like to hot burning coals, so intense and zealous that they were ready to do and execute whatsoever God would have done; note hence:

1. That heavenly things are so transcendent, and we so weak, that we can comprehend or receive very little of them. They must be presented in things beneath their excellency, to make us capable of a little of them. God must manifest his mind here by winds, clouds, by brightness of a cloud, by a fire infolding, by burning coals, that so we may take up a little of the mind of God. John iii. 12, saith Christ to Nicodemus, "If I have spoken to thee of earthly things, and thou dost not understand them, how wilt thou understand if I speak unto thee of heavenly things?" Nicodemus, a doctor in Israel, did not apprehend the doctrine of regeneration, when expressed in his own dialect; had Christ spoken of the great things of the kingdom of heaven in their own nature, how could he or any of us have understood? Here we see darkly and as in a glass. God is pleased to go in the way of man with us, to condescend to our capacities, and to present heavenly things in hieroglyphics, winds, clouds, fire and coals, that so we may have a little apprehension of the nature of those things.

Per corporales ostensiones incorporearum percipimus notitiam. *Prad.*

Obs. 2. That heavenly spirits are most pure and lively. So much the word *chasmal* leads us unto; it noteth coals that have no darkness, no smoke in them, that are altogether fiery, and so lively as that they cannot be more lively. Such is God; he is light, and no darkness; he is more lively than all the world beside. He is *actus purissimus*, all his actions exceed our apprehensions. Such are angels, they are pure and lively creatures. Heb. i. 7, angels are spirits for their purity, and flames of fire for their activity and zeal. Rev. xv. 6, the seven angels are clothed in pure and white linen, and their breast

Sunt luminaria clarissima, specula pura, quantum possibile est summæ luci simillima. *Dionysius.*

girded with golden girdles: pure linen they have and golden girdles, no spot in the linen, no dross in the gold, to set out their purity; and girt they are, to show their readiness and zeal to do the will of God. They are as burning lively coals, that if God do but speak the word, they run, they fly. But of this more hereafter.

Ver. 5. *Also out of the midst thereof came the likeness of four living creatures. And this was their appearance; they had the likeness of a man.*

Now we come to that part of the vision which concerns the living creatures, from this 5th verse to the 15th; where God's glory and government of the world are set out from superior causes, viz. celestial things.

These four creatures are commended to us:

I. From their general nature, they are living creatures.

II. From their number, they are four.

III. From their form, they had the likeness of a man.

IV. From their several parts: as,

1. Their faces, and the number of them, ver. 6, 8, 10.
2. Their wings, the number, situation, and use of them, ver. 6, 8, 9, 11.
3. Their feet, set out by the figure and colour of them, ver. 7.
4. Their hands, set out by the figure and situation of them, ver. 8.
5. From their motion, which was forthright, ver. 9, 12. And this is illustrated from the quality of it; it was swift, ver. 14, they ran; it was as speedy as lightning: and from the cause of it, which was the Spirit, ver. 12, "whither the Spirit was to go."
6. From their colour, which was like burning coals and lamps, ver. 13.

What these living creatures are, is the great dispute among expositors. Some make them to be the four covenants of God: 1. That with Adam. 2. That with Noah. 3. That with Moses. 4. That with the apostles. Some make them to be all the creatures. Some, the four cardinal virtues, justice, wisdom, fortitude, temperance. Some, the four faculties in the soul; the rational, irascible, concupiscible, and conscience. Some, the four chief passions; joy, grief, hope, and fear. Some, the four monarchies; Assyrian, Persian, Grecian, and Roman. Some, the twelve tribes of Israel, in their stations, east, west, north, south, when in the wilderness. Some, the four elements, of which man's body doth consist. Some, the four evangelists, Matthew, Mark, Luke, John; and this being the opinion of Jerom and Gregory the great, prevailed much, but now is deserted. Others understand by these four creatures, those who are complete and more perfect in the church. Others expound them to be Christ; but Christ is brought in, in the latter end of the chapter, sitting upon the throne: these creatures are some distinct ones from him, and inferior to him. By them then we are to understand the angels, which have a great part under God in the government of the world. The word חיות living creatures, doth not only signify a creature that is corporeal, living, and sensible; but it denotes any living being or substance, whether corporeal or spiritual: and so Tully calls *intelligentias animales*, living intelligences, in Quest. Acad. l. 4.

The best interpreters go this way, and understand by the living creatures, *exercitus invisibiles*, principalities and powers, and we need not fetch light from men, where the Scripture gives interpretation itself. Ezek. x. there you have frequent mention of cherubims, which were these living creatures; for ver. 8, it is said, "There appeared the form of a man's hand under their wings." They had the same faces, one excepted, and as many, ver. 14, and Ezekiel saith, ver. 15, "This is the living creature that I saw by the river of Chebar." And more plain yet in ver. 20, "This is the living creature that I saw under the God of Israel by the river Chebar, and I knew that they were the cherubims." Although he called it before the living creature, in the singular number, yet here he changeth the number, and saith, they were the cherubims. We may trust Ezekiel's judgment, he was guided by the Spirit, and his cherubims do hold forth the same parties to us, that Isaiah's seraphims did to him.

The word cherub notes generally any figure of man or beast, say the Hebrews, but especially the figure of a young man or a child, with wings stretched out, Exod. xxv. Such were the two cherubims before the ark. The Chaldeans call a little child, *rabi* or *rabia;* whence some derive the word cherubim, *quasi cherabia,* as a little child; others fetch it from *caph,* which notes likeness, and *rob* or *rab,* which words signify, as, in general, quality and quantity, so multitude and magnitude; so that cherubims etymologized are *tanquam multi et magni,* as it were many and great.

The word cherub notes not only angels, but angels as they appeared and were figured with any external form of man or beast, and such figures were hieroglyphical, as here in this vision. The prophet saw not these cherubims, or angels, or living creatures, but the likeness of them. For the nature of spirits is invisible; no soul, no angel, neither God himself, can be seen. How then is their likeness presented to the prophet? It is no bodily likeness, but a likeness in life, quality, and motion. But the text saith, "They had the likeness of a man," that is, not in his nature and essence, but in some qualities; they had the face, hands, thighs, and legs of a man, all which set out some choice qualities in the angels. They had also something of the beast and bird. And if they were in nature like the living creatures, angels were strange monsters, and not spirits in compound.

They are ἄϋλοι, incorporeal, without flesh and bones, Luke xxiv. 39. They are pure as God is, *actus purissimus.*

By their likeness unto man is laid before us the rationality, knowledge, and understanding of angels. They are not ignorant creatures, but *ipsæ intelligentiæ,* the most understanding creatures in heaven or earth. 2 Sam. xiv. 20, the widow of Tekoah told David, he was wise according to the wisdom of an angel of God, to know all things that are in the earth; that is, he was very wise, as the angels are, to search out, understand, and discover things. Therefore Jerom thinks they are called cherubims from their much knowledge. Cherubims, as it were, rabbies, doctors, teachers of others; and this office some angels have had. Dan. viii. 16, "Gabriel, make this man to understand the vision;" and chap. x. 14, "I am come to make thee understand what shall befall thy people in the latter days." They have prophetical knowledge in them, and a treasury of things that are past and done long since. Rev. iv. 6, 8, there is mention of four beasts or living creatures, (the same with these in Ezekiel,) full of eyes before and behind, because they see and know what is past, and what is before them; their natural knowledge is great, being such excellent

A multitudine scientiæ: Cherubim quasi cherabbim.

spirits. But besides that, they have much revealed to them concerning God, Christ, the church, and things contingent. Hence it is said, 1 Pet. i. 12, "Which things," namely of Christ and the gospel, "the angels desire to look into." The word denotes bowing down, to pry heedfully into a thing, John xx. 5. The cherubims were made looking down towards the mercy-seat, Exod. xxv. and here the angels look into the things of Christ, in whom are hid the treasures of wisdom; and so they grow in this knowledge daily, as also in experimental knowledge, arising from things done daily in the world and in the church. Angels love to be at the congregation, to meet the saints, and learn of and amongst them. They understand partly by their essences, and partly by species communicated to their understandings as to ours. Angels are good philosophers, they know the principles, causes, effects, life, motions, death of natural things, Rev. vii. 1, 2, and xvi. 5. They are great statists, and know the affairs of kingdoms: Dan. x. 13, saith Gabriel, "I remained with the kings of Persia;" he became a courtier, and acquainted himself with the affairs of Persia.

παρακύψαι. παρακύψας βλέπει.

"Four living creatures." These were four angels in particular; some conceive, Michael, Gabriel, Raphael, and Uriel, which were chief over the rest of the whole host of angels. But that is not the sense, neither that God only uses four angels in his service; for many thousands are employed. Luke ii. 13, "There was a multitude of the heavenly host;" and 2 Kings vi. 17, there was an army with the prophet. But it relates to the object, viz. the world, which is distinguished into four parts, east, west, north, and south. The work of these angels laid in all those parts, and none of them were exempt from the presence, observation, and operation of the angels.

Obs. 1. That God employs not ignorant, silly ones in his service, but those that are intelligent, angels that are wise and very knowing. Such should the angels of the churches be; "The priest's lips should keep knowledge," Mal. ii. 7. And as God is termed, 1 Sam. ii. 3, "a God of knowledge;" so should he be a man of knowledges. The Pharisees were blind guides; and what a multitude of blind priests were there till within these few years in the christian world! and too many there are to this day that have their right eye darkened, Zech. xi. 17. But the man of God should have new and old in his treasury, and be throughly furnished unto every good word and work.

אל דעות איש דעות

Obs. 2. That the angels are in all quarters of the world, taking notice of men's words, works, and ways they go; I had almost said, of their very thoughts; and that they do, if discovered by some sign. Angels can be present at all times, know what devils or other men can know of us; any voice, any act they are privy to; yea, by outward expressions they may gather what is within; they, being spirits, can insinuate far into our hearts and natures, though not immediately know our thoughts. Therefore we should carry ourselves soberly, righteously, and holily, in this world, in regard of them. 1 Cor. xi. 10, the woman is "to have power on her head because of the angels," she is to be covered, and to carry herself modestly, reverently, because of the angels. Psa. cxxxviii. 1, "Before the gods will I sing to thee:" the Vulgate hath, *in conspectu angelorum*, before the angels; their presence should awe men and women, and keep them from all dishonesty; evil words, acts, gestures, secret grudging, all discontents and distempers. For as they are rejoiced to discern a good frame of spirit in you, to see you keep that order God hath set in the church and state, to walk as christians to the honour of God; so they are grieved to see the contrary, and you must answer for your sins against these great officers in the great family of heaven and earth. A thing that is little thought about; but if it be a sin to despise and grieve a believer, a brother that is inferior to an angel, is it not much more sin to dishonour their presence, and grieve their persons? Smoke drives away bees, and an ill savour doves; so do ill passages drive away the Spirit and angels of God. Eccl. v. 6, the angel that is of God's counsel, a witness of our ways, will not take it well; the angel may smite thee for neglect of duties, ill performances of them.

Si signo externo prodantur. *Less.*

Grata est angelis pia significatio. *Aug.*

Magna cura vigilanti studio adsunt nobis omnibus horis et locis succurrentes et providentes omnibus necessitatibus nostris, gemitus nostros, et suspiria referentes ad Deum. Ambulant nobiscum, in omnibus viis nostris, considerantes quam pié quam honesté in medio pravæ nationis conversemur, adjuvant laborantes, protegunt quiescentes, hortantur pugnantes, coronant vincentes; grandis eis cura de nobis. *Aug. Soliloq.* c. 27.

Obs. 3. That men should be ashamed to be ignorant, seeing angels are likened unto them for knowledge and understanding. Many men, yea, such as are called christians, are brutish in their knowledge, their souls serve only for salt to keep their bodies from putrefaction; Eph. ii. 12, "without God in the world;" that is, without the fear, authority, and sovereignty of God falling upon their hearts, and without the knowledge of God in their heads. And God may say of many christians, "My people is foolish, they have not known me; they are sottish children, they have none understanding: they are wise to do evil, but to do good they have no knowledge," Jer. iv. 22. The apostle bids us in understanding to be men; shall we be babes only? Let us now be angels in understanding. David was wise as an angel; and the saints shall judge the angels, 1 Cor. vi. The evil angels, they are very subtle, they have their depths, methods, wiles; and how shall we do it, if we be ignorant? They come to the assemblies to get advantage to accuse us; let us get knowledge to condemn them.

Obs. 4. That God doth interest angels, and use their service in the government of the world; not only men, magistrates and ministers, but angels also. The Jews made Jerusalem the prison of God and angels; they thought that neither God nor his angels did appear or rule any where else. To take off this conceit, God appears to Ezekiel in Babylon after this manner, to convince him, that he and his angels do govern there, and in all quarters of the world, as well as at Sion. That God rules in the world is granted, but that angels should help to sway the sceptre is not so credible. A little therefore to clear it. 2 Cor. iv. 4, "In whom the god of this world hath blinded their minds." Some understand it of the true God that created the world, but the best interpreters give us in Satan here, and make him the god of the world, and that by example, command, and suggestion; and Christ doth thrice call Satan the prince of the world, Job xii. 31; xiv. 30; xvi. 11: and Eph. ii. 2, "According to the prince of the power of the air, the spirit that now worketh." The devil hath great power in the air to raise winds, to cause storms, thunder, lightning, which is the power of the air; and the same power hath he in the spirits of the children of disobedience: and by that spirit, whereof he is lord, he can move them any way, as the winds and clouds, and carry them against Christ and his truths. Now hence I infer, that if Satan and ill angels be as gods,

Carcer Dei et angelorum.

Exemplo, imperio, et suggestione.

Unaquæque res visibilis habet angelicam potestatem sibi prepositam. *Aug.* in l. 83. qu. 79. q. In hoc mundo visibili nihil nisi per creaturam invisibilem disponi potest. *Thom.* 1. part qu. 110.

princes in this world, have power in the air and hearts of wicked men; then must it needs follow, that good angels are as gods, and princes, and have as much power in the world and hearts of good men as they; otherwise devils should gain by their fall more than ever they had by their standing; and it is not credible that wicked, damned spirits should have more honourable titles and larger power than the holy and glorious angels.

What are those services then good angels are employed in?

Answ. 1. To inform us of God's will, and God of our ways.

They acquaint us with God's mind. Angels told Abraham and Lot what God would do to Sodom, Gen. xviii. xix. An angel tells Elijah what to say to the messengers of the king of Samaria, 2 Kings i. 3. An angel tells the apostles, that Christ shall return in that manner they had seen him go up to heaven, Acts i. 11. Christ tells John, Rev. xxii. 16, that he had sent his angels to testify those things in the churches. The angel tells Daniel that he came forth to give him skill and understanding, chap. ix. 22. Matt. i. 20; ii. 13, an angel informs Joseph of the mind of God, touching Mary and Christ. So to inform God what is done here among men, the angels went up the ladder as well as came down. Zech. i. 11, the angel sent out by the Lord, certified the Angel Christ, that stood among the myrtle trees, that they had travelled up and down the world; "and behold," say they, "all the earth sitteth still, and is at rest." This God doth for honour and not necessity, he knoweth all things, but he will have them witnesses of his will.

Per ministros more potentissimi regis omnia facit. *Bonav.*

2. In opposing the great enemies of Christ and his church, whereupon they intermeddle with kings and kingdoms, and the great affairs thereof. Dan. x. 20, "Knowest thou wherefore I come unto thee? now will I return to fight with the king of Persia: and when I am gone forth, lo, the prince of Grecia shall come." This angel Gabriel opposed the cruel edicts of Cambyses king of Persia, who laboured to keep the Jews in captivity longer, and to oppress them sorer than others had done; but Gabriel kept them from execution, and brought his kingdom to ruin by degrees. And therefore he saith, The prince of Grecia shall come: I will leave Persia, and go into Greece, and stir up Alexander to come into Persia, and spoil the king of his kingdom. When princes are stirred up by flatterers and profane wretches to oppress the godly, to hinder the work of the temple, then angels do fight against them. Elesbaan king of the Ethiopians being in arms against Dunaan a tyrant, his army was much oppressed with famine and the power of the tyrant; whereupon he cried to God for help, and presently heard, Gabriel, Gabriel, Gabriel. Thrice he heard that voice from heaven, intimating, that Gabriel would help him; whereupon he joined battle with the tyrant, overcame, killed most, and took the tyrant king of the Homerites, and bound him in chains. At a great battle between Clotharius and Theodoricus was seen an angel with a drawn sword, and many were slain on both sides. Some understand these princes to be spirits; if good, there is no discord between them. Good angels are without sin, and so no opposition in their wills to God's, or one another. If of evil angels, it is that we aim at, the good angels oppose and contend against the evil with all their strength. Rev. xii. 7, "Michael and his angels fought against the dragon and his." There was a great battle in heaven, the devil and his angels were cast out, which is for the great comfort of Sion. Certainly devils and devilish men would overrun all, if there were not angels employed in the four quarters of the world, to keep the church and people of God. When Balaam and Balak would have cursed God's people, an angel cometh forth and fights against them, Numb. xxii. 22. This is one great office of the angels, to fight against princes, potentates, and men of the earth, that seek to oppress the people of God, and labour to hinder temple work, and the welfare of Sion.

Baron. anno. 523. Ammonius de gestis, Francorum, l. 3. c. 87, 88. Ubi non est contrarietas voluntatis, non est pugna.

3. To execute the judgments of God upon wicked men. The death of their first-born in Egypt (which was the chiefest of the plagues, and touched them nearest) was done by a destroying angel; who therefore is called Hammaschchit, Exod. xii. 23. The destroyer shall not come into their houses, but into the Egyptians' he did come; the singular number is put for the plural, a thing usual in Scripture; and so the sense is, that angels were the destroyers of the Egyptians. The psalmist, in Psa. lxxviii. 49, saith, God did this work by sending evil angels among them; not that these angels were wicked spirits, as some have thought, but angels or messengers of evil, of death unto them. The Egyptian sorcerers used the help of wicked angels to oppose Moses and harden the Egyptians, and God used the help of good angels to punish evil-doers; they have been, and are employed in such service. The angels that came to Lot's house, smote the Sodomites with blindness, great and small, which were at Lot's door, Gen. xix. 11. They fetched fire from heaven, and destroyed the place, ver. 13. When seventy thousand died of the plague, 2 Sam. xxiv. 17, in David's days, it is made the work of an angel, ver. 17; he saw the angel that smote the people. It was an angel that slew 185,000 Assyrians, Isa. xxxvii. 36. It is their work to chase and persecute wicked men, Psa. xxxv. 5, 6. Often angels of God do suddenly destroy them: "And immediately the angel of the Lord smote him," Acts xii. 23. Lorinus thinks it was the devil did it; but it was some good angel, that being zealous for God, he did vindicate his glory, which was given to a mortal, sinful man. Angels cannot endure this dishonour. Josephus, in his 19th book, and 8th chapter, sets out this story fully, how he came in, in cloth of silver, was saluted as a God, saw an owl over his head, felt a pain in his bowels, and said, I whom ye all call a god, am commanded to leave my godship, and by death to confute your lie of my immortality. Neither belongeth it to angels only to punish the wicked, but to exercise chastisement upon the godly. An angel meets Moses in the inn, and would have slain him, Exod. iv. 24; so the Greek and the Chaldee read it; and that because he neglected the circumcision of Moses. An angel smote Zacharias with dumbness, because of his unbelief, Luke i. So an angel corrected David for his sin of numbering his people.

Ego ille vestra appellatione Deus vitam relinquere jubeor fatali necessitate coarguente vestrum mendacium; et quem immortalem salutastis ad mortem rapior.

4. To defend the godly, to save and deliver them from harms. This is a constant office; they keep the saints from evil men, spirits, and things. Rev. vii. 1—3, four angels stood on the four corners of the earth, and held the four winds of the earth, that they should not blow on the sea, or any tree: and another angel cries to the four, "Hurt not the earth, sea, trees, till we have sealed the servants of our God in their foreheads." Psal. xxxiv. 7, "The angel of the Lord encampeth round about them that fear him, and delivereth them." Angels are like armies round about the general, and keep from

danger. When Jacob was to meet with his brother Esau, (who came with a band of four hundred men against him,) the angels of God met him, (they are forward to this service). And when he saw them, What, said he, "this is God's host;" what need I fear my brother's host? and he called the place Mahanaim, or Machanaim, Gen. xxxii. 1, 2. It is in the dual number, and notes two hosts, two camps: if my brother have one band, I have two; if he have men, I have angels; if four hundred men, I have twice four hundred angels. When Elisha was in Dothan, the king of Syria sent a great host with horses and chariots, and they came by night, compassed the city about, and now Elisha is a lost man; and Gehazi cries out, "Alas, master! what shall we do? Fear not," saith he, "they that be with us are more than they that be with them." And when the young man's eyes were opened, he saw the mountain full of horses and chariots of fire, and that round about Elisha, 2 Kings vi. 14—17. Was there an army against Elisha? here is an army for him: were they many? here are more: were there chariots and horses? here are chariots and horses of fire. When Daniel was in the den of lions, he had no fire to scare them, no weapon or strength to kill them, but an angel is sent to shut their mouth: so that here is a wonder, a lamb amongst lions, and not rent in pieces. Where angels are the lambs' keepers, there the lions are toothless and mouthless. The angels have a special charge of the godly; Psal. xci. 11, "He shall give his angels charge over thee." The angels stand charged with the custody of the godly; and when a guard is set about a person of quality, who dares come near to hurt such a one? It is said in ver. 7, "A thousand shall fall at thy side, and ten thousand at thy right hand: but it shall not come nigh thee." It is nigh, when at a man's side, at his right hand; but it shall not come nigh to hurt thee: and what is the reason? "For he shall give his angels charge," &c. They look well to their charge, they never slumber nor sleep. God's care of his church now, is greater than it was under the law, for the watch is double to what it was then, there are twelve angels at the gates of Jerusalem, Rev. xxi. 12; whereas in Ezekiel ix. 2, there were but six. The church being now enlarged, the enemies are enraged, and the guarding angels increased. No sooner were the apostles imprisoned, but an angel brings them forth, Acts v. 18, 19. And what great things the angel did for Peter, Acts xii. is known to all; his deliverance was so great, that they could not believe he was come forth and knocked at the door, but that it was his angel, ver. 15; whence the opinion of tutelar angels hath received great strength. Some affirm from hence, that every man hath his particular angel to keep him, Dan. vi. 22, which seems rather a Platonical conceit, than a Scripture truth, for Isidorus Clarius turns this place, his messenger, and so the word is used in Scripture. Judg. ii. 1, "The angel of the Lord came up," or messenger, as it is in the margin; and Mal. iii. 1, "I will send my messenger," the Hebrew is, my angel. And surely this party that knocked at the door they supposed was Peter's messenger, not his angel: and if this be well rendered angel, why is not that so rendered, Luke vii. 24, The angels of John being departed: it is, the messenger, and so it were better here, his messenger, than, his angel; for shall we suppose the faithful so ignorant, as to think an angel could not come in without knocking, and having doors opened? Besides, the apparition of an angel would have affrighted them greatly. Not to stick at this, although we find no warrant in the word for assignment of a particular angel to every man, yet we acknowledge many angels appointed to that work. Matt. xviii. 10, "Their angels" (not their angel) "behold the face of my Father."

Nuncius ejus.

ἀπελθόντων τῶν ἀγγέλων Ἰωάνου.

5. To guide and lead the godly in good and safe ways. Gen. xxiv. 7, "He shall send his angels before thee, and thou shalt take a wife unto my son from thence." So ver. 40, "He will send his angel with thee, and prosper thy way." The business of marriage is so weighty and honourable, that angels' presence and assistance is in it: angels are present and preside over that work. Psa. xci. 11, 12, they are charged to keep thee in all thy ways, to bear thee up in their arms; that is, their strength shall be employed to uphold and lead thee in a good way. God begets children to himself by the word and Spirit, and puts them forth to angels to nurse, to guide, and lead; it is a metaphor taken from nurses, that bear their children upon their arms, and lift them over thresholds. Exod. xxxii. 24, "Behold," saith God to Moses, "my angel shall go before thee:" he was to go to Canaan, and an angel was to lead him that way. Angels are well acquainted with the ways to heaven; if you will go that way, you are sure to meet with angels.

Angeli reges, et Domini eorum sunt quos regunt.

6. To comfort. Next to Christ and the Spirit, angels are the best comforters, because they stand nearest God always, before his face, and they are sent to comfort God's servants, when in straits, under pressures. Mary was a poor maid, of mean condition, and to her comes an angel. Luke i. 30, "Fear not, Mary; thou hast found favour with God." So Cornelius, "Thy prayers and alms are come up a memorial before God," Acts x. 4. When the ship was tossed, waves, winds, and darkness conspired their ruin, then saith Paul, An angel stood by me, and said, Fear not, Paul, God hath given thee thy life, and the lives of all with thee, wherefore be of good cheer, Acts xxvii. 23—25. He had drank a cup of angelical consolation, and knew well to comfort them with the same consolation. When Daniel fasted and prayed, and was much afflicted for his people, "O Daniel, a man greatly beloved, understand the words that I speak unto thee; for unto thee am I now sent.—Fear not, Daniel," Dan. x. 11, 12. Mary rises early, and meets with angels that comforted her, John xx. An angel appeared to Christ and strengthened him, Luke xxii. 43; the servant comforted the Master.

7. To look unto the souls of men, that they fall not into the hands of devils at their death; for if the devil durst contend with Michael for the body of Moses, much more for the souls of men. Luke xvi. 22, Lazarus's soul was carried by the angels into Abraham's bosom: men carry the body to the ground, but angels carry the soul to glory, they guard it through the clouds into the presence of the blessed God: before he had none but dogs to pity him, now he hath angels to attend him. The devil is mighty busy while we live, he goes about like a roaring lion, but at death then he is most busy, and presumes there is a tree cut down for his fire.

8. They are God's reapers at the end of the world. Matt. xxiv. 31, "He shall send his angels, and they shall gather together his elect from the four winds, from one end of the world to another;" they must blow that terrible trumpet, awaken the dead, and cite them to judgment; they must gather the ashes of saints together. Matt. xiii. 41, 42, "The Son of man shall send his angels, and they shall," &c. Basil, in his Homily of Forty Martyrs, tells of one that seeing them thrust in a winter's

night into a cold lake, he saw angels descend, and putting crowns upon all their heads, but one.

9. To declare kingdoms, cities, people cursed. Judg. v. 23, Curse ye Meroz bitterly, said the angel of the Lord, because they came not out to help, &c. Some think this angel was Michael, who was general in this war, but that is the opinion of men, not the warrant of Scripture.

A Lapid. in locum.

10. The angels have work and power in the church of God. Rev. xv. 6, "Seven angels came out of the temple;" and chap. xiv. 15, 17, "Another angel came out of the temple." Angels being in the temple is often spoken of, and notes some power that they have in the assemblies under the gospel. Zech. iii. The stone with seven eyes, some make to be Christ with his angels that are employed for the government of the church throughout the world; and surely Michael and his angels do contend daily in the assemblies against the dragon and his. In the assemblies devils are present and active; Satan stood at Joshua's right hand to resist him, to hinder all the temple work. When we are near God, devils are near us, intending mischief; but angels are at hand, and hinder their designs; they observe us, and our carriages in the congregation. Eccl. v. 6, make not vows, and then slight them, there is an angel present; and it will not be enough to say it was an error, God will be angry, and an angel may smite thee for it: this is spoken of us, when we are in the house of God, there the angels keep special watch. Josephus saith, that the voice of an angel was heard out of the temple, saying, Let us leave these seats; they had a place in the church as well as the others. And again, he saith, the angels were the keepers of the Jewish people, and that a little before the Romans' coming was heard a voice out of the temple, Let us go hence: and a heathen writer saith, that a voice greater than man's was heard, That the gods were departing.

Ribera.

Lib. 6. de Bello Judaico. Relinquamus has sedes.

L. 7. c. 12. Migremus hinc.

Audita major humana vox excedere deos. *Tacit.*

Ver. 6. *And every one had four faces, and every one had four wings.*

Now we come to their several parts; and first of their faces, which are mentioned here in the 8th and 10th verses. Every one had four faces, and the likeness of their faces were:

1. The face of a man.
2. Of a lion.
3. Of an ox.
4. Of an eagle.

In some pictures you may see several faces, so drawn they are, that which way soever you look, a several face is presented; so here, before was the face of a man, behind of an eagle, on the right side of a lion, and on the left side of an ox: here is not a face but is compared to the face of some principal creature; man is the chief of all the rest; a lion is the king of wild beasts; the ox is the chief of tame ones; and the eagle, of birds.

The face of a man represents to us the understandings of angels, and that their administrations are with knowledge and equity; of this we have already spoken.

This face is put, first, to show the excellency of reason, which must have the introduction into and managing of all actions, else they are neither human nor angelical.

By this face also is noted their love to mankind. Angels are of a loving nature, and most careful of men; therefore it is said, Heb. i. 14, They are ministering spirits sent out, &c.

The face of a lion signifies the strength of angels. A lion is a creature of great strength; Prov. xxx. 30, "The strongest among beasts, and turneth not away for any;" he never flies or fears: Isa. xxxi. 4, If a multitude of shepherds be called forth, he will not be afraid of them, nor abase himself at their noise; and Judg. xiv. 18, "What is stronger than a lion?" said the interpreter of Samson's riddle; and we may say, Among all creatures, what is stronger than an angel? The Scripture calls the devil, the strong one, Matt. xii. 29, and so it calls the angel, Rev. x. 1, "I saw a mighty angel;" and they are very mighty: an angel can hinder the blowing of the wind, Rev. vii. 1; stop the mouths of lions, Dan. vi. 22; break iron chains, open prison doors, and iron gates, Acts xii.; an angel can smite with blindness, Gen. xix. 11; 2 Kings vi. 18; both Sodomites and Syrians were so smitten. Angels work upon the fancy, Matt. ii. 13, 19, 20, suggest many things of great and good use to the mind; for if devils can take the word out of our minds, sow tares in the field, Luke viii. 12; Matt. xiii. 24, 25, put devilish thoughts into the heart, John xiii. 2, work powerfully in the heart of the disobedient, Eph. ii. 1, and trouble their spirits, 1 Sam. xvi. 15; I see not but good angels may do as much, being more potent than they. Rev. xii. Michael and his angels overcame the dragon and his; and Psal. ciii. 20, they excel in strength; they are called *exercitus cœlestis*, the heavenly host, Luke ii. 13; one can do more than a great army; one slew 185,000 in a night, 2 Kings xix. 35. They are *bellatores fortissimi*, and have appeared most valiant warriors. David saw an angel with a sword in his hand stretched over Jerusalem, 2 Chron. xxi. 16. Elisha saw them with horses and chariots of fire, 2 Kings vi. 17. As such, angels are God's militia; "The chariots of God are twenty thousand, even thousands of angels," Psal. lxviii. 17; they stand always before God, and can do whatever God wills and commands.

Arist. nunquam fugit aut metuit.

τὸν ἰσχυρὸν.

This consideration of the strength of angels should add to our comforts and God's praises. If a man be in danger, and have a strong convoy appointed by the king, he is secure, much comforted, and thankful too, that majesty hath appointed it. God hath given us the mighty angels, that are stronger than lions, to be our guard to convoy us through the wilderness of this world; let it multiply our comforts, and God's praises.

The next face is that of an ox; and it shows the willing obedience, faithfulness, patience, and usefulness of angels in their ministrations; for an ox accustomed to the yoke is very tractable, not stubborn, as untamed heifers are. Hos. x. 11, "Ephraim is as a heifer that is taught, and loves to tread out the corn;" a heifer taught, and delighting in her work, is willing to it; such are angels, Psal. ciii. 20. They hearken to the voice of his word, they look upon God as the great General, and if he give out the word, they give out their strength, and go about the work willingly. They are very attentive to his commands; if he says, Go smite Herod for his pride, Balaam for his covetousness, David for his vain-glory, Sennacherib for his blasphemy, and Sodom for its uncleanness, presently they go.

2. Faithfulness. An ox doth faithful service; horses do oft deceive in their service, but an ox seldom, in ploughing or carrying of burdens. So angels are faithful in their ministrations, they fail not in the least particular: the

Præstat fidum ministerium.

angel would not let John worship him; and the angels would not suffer Lot to linger in Sodom.

3. Patience. An ox is a patient creature; what burden soever is laid upon him, or what work soever he is employed in, the ox is not impatient: so the angels, they are patient in their ministration, though they meet with much opposition. The prince of Persia withstood Gabriel twenty-one days, Dan. x. 13. In the midst of oppositions and great services, they are without all impatience; though their work never end, Rev. iv. 8, yet they never complain.

4. Usefulness. Prov. xiv. 4, "Much increase is by the strength of the ox." No creature more useful to the support of a family than the ox; for of old, all the ploughing was by oxen. Elijah finds Elisha ploughing with twelve yoke of oxen, 1 Kings xix. 19. And Job had five hundred yoke of oxen; and it is said, they were ploughing, Job i. 3, 14; no mention of horses: and in some places of this kingdom they make greatest use of oxen. By their strength, kingdoms and families are maintained. Therefore, Moses, Deut. iii. 17, compares Joseph to the bullock or ox, because he sustained his father's family and Egypt with corn. Exod xxii. 1, if an ox or sheep were stolen, and so killed, or sold, the thief was to restore five for the ox, four for the sheep; and the reason was, because of the usefulness of those creatures; they served for sacrifice to God, to plough the earth, to feed and clothe the family; in other things they were to restore only double. David makes it one part of the happiness of a commonwealth, that the oxen be strong to labour, Psal. cxliv. 14. Oxen are needful and useful creatures; and angels herein resemble oxen, they are ministering spirits, sent out for the service of God's family, they live not to themselves, but to the public. In the Revelation you may read what great services the angels are employed in; they sound the trumpets, and pour out the vials of God's wrath; they preserve the saints from the violence of devils and devilish men.

This instructs man to be like angels in these qualities; if God command, call for any duty, to be obedient, yielding, and to say, with Samuel, Here I am, speak, Lord, thy servant is willing to hear, ready to obey. And when we are in the service, let us be faithful, do it conscionably; let us be patient, although we meet with delays, oppositions, reproaches, and loss; let us be serviceable and profitable to others. Angels have no benefit by their ministrations, God hath the glory, and man the good.

The last face is of an eagle, and in it, as in a glass, we may see the perspicaciousness, swiftness, and vivacity of the angels; for these three are in eagles observable.

1. They are quick-sighted; Job xxxix. 29, "Her eyes behold afar off," speaking of the eagle; from the top of the rocks, out of the clouds, they are said to behold fishes swimming in the seas; so strong is their sight, that they soar aloft, and can a long time behold the sun with open and stedfast eyes. Scaliger hath seen it in a tamed eagle. A man of acute parts, that can see quick and far into matters, we say he is eagle-eyed; the angels are not wanting in this particular, they are quick-sighted, 2 Sam. xiv. 20. And Rev. iv. 6, the four beasts there mentioned, being the same here in Ezekiel, are said to be "full of eyes before and behind;" and in the 8th verse, "full of eyes within;" they have much natural knowledge, much revealed knowledge, set out by their eyes within, and much experimental knowledge coming in by their observation and deep insight into things, noted by their eyes before and behind; they soar aloft, stand before God, behold the face of God always, Matt. xviii. 10.

In aquila cicurata. *Merlin in Jobum*, c. 39.

2. Eagles are swift in their flight; Lam. iv. 19. 2 Sam. i. 23, "Swifter than eagles;" and Job ix. 26, "The eagle maketh haste to the prey." Pindar calls the eagle the queen of birds, for her swiftness, no fowl flies more swiftly than the eagle; hence, when things were to be done suddenly, the Scripture mentioneth the eagle; Hos. viii. 1, "He shall come as an eagle against the house of the Lord;" that is, Nebuchadnezzar shall come suddenly. Angels are no dull creatures; in a night the destroying angel slew all the first-born in Egypt; in a night, 185,000 in the camp of Sennacherib; and Dan. ix. 21, Gabriel came flying swiftly to Daniel; "and suddenly there was with the angel a multitude of the heavenly host," Luke ii. 13.

3. Eagles are fresh and lively always, age and sickness works not upon them as upon other birds; the eagle in her age is youthful; how then doth she die? Pliny tells us, that it is neither age nor sickness that kills the eagle, but hunger; the upper bill groweth so over the under, that she cannot open her mouth to take in sustenance, and so dies. Psal. ciii. 5, "Thy youth is renewed like the eagle's;" the eagle is renewed by the oft change of her feathers. The cherubims before the mercy-seat (which represented the angels) were without beards, to show their vigour, vivacity, and eternity. Angels never grow old, they are always lusty and lively, their service doth not wear them out; it is man's sin that withers and consumes him more than his work. Adam should never have looked old, never have decayed, but retained an immortal vivacity, if he had not sinned. Angels are lively in their service, not dull.

Nec annis debilitatur, nec morbis obnoxia est.

Crebra mutatione pennarum. *Hieron.*

Imberbes ut juvenes.

Obs. 1. That angels are fit for public and great service; they have four faces, a man's, a lion's, an ox's, an eagle's, which tells us they have all that is requisite to great undertakings. They have wisdom to consult, to contrive and manage the affairs of the world prudentially; they have the strength of a lion to execute, they have the willingness and faithfulness of the ox to rejoice the heart of the commander, patience to undergo the difficulties of the work, and usefulness for the public. They are quick-sighted to discern and prevent the designs of enemies, and speedily to despatch much in a little time, and that with cheerfulness; this is meant by their four faces, which notes their perfection and fitness for service in all parts of the world; in regard of which, and the prophet to whom this vision was made, they are said to have one face before, another behind, and on each side one; and that God doth use their service in all creatures rational and irrational; they have the shapes of men, birds, and beasts.

Obs. 2. That suitable persons ought to be employed in public and great services. God employs angels in the government of the world, who are wise, trusty, strong, and speedy: and you know what men God calls for in the state and church. Exod. xviii. 21, "Provide thou out of the people able men, such as fear God, men of truth, hating covetousness, and place such over them to be rulers of thousands, hundreds, fifties, tens;" he must search amongst all the people for such, far and near, and if in one tribe he cannot find them, he must in another. The time hath been, that seniority, money, favour, friendship, have carried the great places in this city; but you have smarted for it; instead of good angels you have had ill spirits. Now I hope you will not look who hath most money, or best friends to support him, but most wisdom in his head, and zeal in his heart, and God on his side. Now I trust you will learn of God, and employ such as have the faces of men, lions, oxen, and eagles, men full of wisdom, courage, trust, serviceableness to the public, and of great despatch; such should be in the city, and in the army. So for the church, you know what men God points you to, 1 Tim. iii. and 1 Pet. v. God's bishops must not lord it over God's heritage, and exercise dominion over it; God's officers must not be prelatical; it is the fleece, and not the flock, that such men look after, unless it be to scatter, to wound their conscience, and suck their blood: some of that sect, instead of preaching to save souls, have only plotted to ruin kingdoms.

Obs. 3. That angels being noble and glorious creatures, disdain not to do service to them that are far beneath themselves. Man at first, when in his glory, was under the angels; but now, since he sinned, he is fallen lower, as low as hell. Man is now a miserable, mortal creature, he hath a vile body, a defiled conscience, and a polluted soul; yet angels, that are styled gods, Psal. viii. 5, so is the original, that are cherubims of glory, Heb. ix. 5, that are holy, Matt. xxv. 31, elect, 1 Tim. v. 21, that are of the privy council of heaven, and the life-guard of God himself, Matt. xviii. 10; even these blessed creatures are not ashamed to serve us; though we have the scent of the earth and hell about us, though we do oft grieve and offend them with our sinful carriages, and the great God their Lord and Master, yet they despise us not, but cheerfully minister unto us. Would any great prince attend a mean man full of sores and vermin? if so, it argues wonderful humility. It is more that angels do, in waiting upon us. It is monstrous pride then in men that have parts, place, honour, greatness, grace, whatever it be, not to stoop to those that are inferior: thou hast not more worth in thee any way than an angel hath; and angels condescend to serve us: therefore let us not mind high things, but condescend to men of low estate, and not be wise in our own conceit, Rom. xii. 16.

Obs. 4. That God desires speed in his service. Angels are swift as eagles, and despatch great things in a little time; they know a dull, lazy motion is not the motion Heaven approves; Zech. ii. 4, saith one angel to another, "Run, speak to this young man:" going is not sufficient, where running can be had: *Festina lente*, Hasten by slow degrees, is not a motto for heaven's gates. In the worst work that ever was in the world, Christ calls for speed, "That thou doest, do quickly," John xiii. 27, when Judas was about his treason. Speed and life in businesses is commendable and acceptable: Matt. v. 25, "Agree with thine adversary quickly." Darius would have his decree done speedily, Ezra vi. 12; and God would have his decrees and will fulfilled, done with speed. Zech. viii. 21, it is God's will now, that you should help him against the mighty. When the temple was to be built, the people came so fast, brought in so much, that they were bid to stay, and that work of theirs was pleasing to God and man. We have a Babel to pull down, as well as a temple to build; can you be employed better? Luke xvi. you are stewards, and may quickly be called to account, be speedy in what you do

In the 11th verse you have one thing more touching their faces, and that is, their faces were stretched upwards; "Thus were their faces." It is in your books, as if it had reference only to the former verse, and not to what follows in the eleventh; but Montanus and others, that render the Hebrew exactly, read it thus, But their faces and their wings were stretched upwards: it is true, they have the faces of men and beasts, but they are stretched upward, they looked up to him that sat upon the throne, which was Christ. The cherubims' faces, Exod. xxv. 20, 21, were towards the mercy-seat, and that was above upon the ark; so that there and here, the cherubims, these angels, look upward.

Obs. 1. That all creatures depend upon Christ; these angels have the faces of men, lions, oxen, eagles, and look up to him. If there were nothing in it but this, that angels in their own nature look up, it might convince us, that all inferior creatures do depend upon him, as well as those noble ones; but when they come in with the faces of other creatures looking up, it is clear evidence, that all depend upon Christ. Col. i. 16, 17, "By him were all things created, that are in heaven, and that are in earth, visible and invisible, whether thrones, or dominions, or principalities, or powers: all things were created by him, and for him,—and by him all things do consist." He holds all in his hand, heaven and earth, men and angels, they all consist and subsist in him. Heb. i. 3, "He upholds all things by the word of his power."

Obs. 2. That in all our ministrations, we are to have our instructions and directions from Christ. Angels look up to him; if he speak, they hear, they move and act; if not, they stir not. Moses and Aaron did nothing in the state or church, without direction from God. Princes must look into the law of God continually, Deut. xvii. that they may do things warrantably: the centurion's soldiers and servants did come, go, and do at his appointment, not their own; and angels run not of their own heads, they will hear a word of command, have a commission from Christ, before they go. It is not enough that we be knowing, full of courage, quick to despatch much; a commission, a warrant from God we must have, else all our doing is nothing: if we do the will of God without knowing we are warranted by God to do it, it is rather sin than service. Prov. iii. 5, 6, "Lean not to thine own understanding;" let it be never so great, acute, clear, it is not beyond angels'; they look up to God, and so must thou; "In all thy ways acknowledge him, and he shall direct thy paths." Christ is the great Counsellor, and we must not in one or two, or some great exigence of business consult with him; but in all our ways, whatever we attempt for ourselves, families, state, or church, we must consult with him that sits upon the throne, and he will direct our paths. Most miscarry in their ways, or make little progress, because they consult not at all, or very little, with Christ; whereas if men did consult with Christ, and do all upon his warrant, upon a divine ground, they should never miscarry in their ways, but proceed further in the paths of godliness in a few weeks, than they did before in many years. When David had consulted with God, he could say, God was at his right hand, so that he should not be moved, Psa. xvi.

Obs. 3. That the pleasure of Christ is worthy our waiting for. Angels look up and attend what he will say, and make known unto them; these holy, glorious, and mighty creatures think not much to wait upon Christ, and exercise their patience till he please to reveal his mind. Christ is a great King, the only Counsellor, and his counsel of infinite worth, and it is not state, but equity, that all creatures wait upon him. Angels do it, and shall we grudge at it? Psal. cxxiii. 1, 2, "Unto thee lift I up mine eyes, O thou that dwellest in the heavens. Behold, as the eyes of servants look to the hand of their master, and as the eyes of a maiden to the hands of her mistress, so our eyes wait upon the Lord our God." He interprets the meaning of looking up, which is waiting upon God, for manifestation of himself. Psal. v. 3, David would direct his prayer to God, and look up; not down to the world, down to corruption, but up to God, what he would speak. Psal. lxxxv. 8, "I will hear what God the Lord will speak." Let the resolution of the prophet be thine, "I will look unto the Lord; I will wait for the God of my salvation: my God will hear me," Mic. vii. 7.

Obs. 4. That Christ is an object of admiration and adoration. The looking upwards is *signum admirationis et typus reverentiæ*, a token of admiration and an example of reverence. The cherubims looked towards the mercy-seat, admiring and adoring him who was figured by it; and we lift up our faces towards heaven, when we admire and adore God: you have the phrase in Job xxii. 26, "Thou shalt have thy delight in the Almighty, and lift up thy face unto God;" that is, admire and adore that God thou delightest in. Where is most delight, there is most admiration and adoration. Christ is the delight of angels; when he was incarnate, they bowed down to pry into that mystery; and now he is glorified, they look up to admire him. There is still matter of admiration in Christ, all in him is not yet discovered; 2 Thess. i. 10, Christ shall come to be admired in all them that believe. As it is in a country when it is discovered, still new and new things are met with, so in Christ. The vision of Christ is compared to river water, and that is always new and fresh; and to a tree of life, with twelve manner of fruits every month, Rev. xxii. 1, 2. The vision and fruition of God is new, savoury, and pleasant unto them every month, day, and hour; and this is to angels as well as to any other. Christ also shall be adored; Heb. i. 6, "Let all the angels of God adore him:" they do look up, acknowledge him God, and tender to him that glory the Father hath, even adoration. He that was despised, rejected of men, the stone disallowed of the master builders, that we hid our faces from, and esteemed not, is the object of angels' adoration.

Obs. 5. That the service of Jesus Christ is honourable service. Angels do stretch up their faces and wait for it; and it is the glory of the angels, that they are ministering spirits sent out by Christ. Heb. i. 14, is a comparison between the glory of Christ and angels; and their glory is, that they are his servants. We think the service of great persons is an honour to us. Who is greater than Christ? All power in heaven and earth is given unto him, Matt. xxviii. And he is more honourable than all princes; he is King of kings, and must be honoured as the Father, John v. The apostles counted it their great honour to be servants of Christ; Paul, James, Jude, Peter, begin their epistles with it; they set it in the front, as the most honourable title. This service is liberty, not bondage; his Spirit is a Spirit of liberty, his law is a law of liberty; and, Rom. viii. 2, "The law of the spirit of life in Christ, hath made me free from the law of sin and death;" he that is not the servant of Christ, is the slave of Satan. This service is spiritual, profitable, honourable. David had rather be a door-keeper in Christ's house, than dwell in the tents of wickedness, Psal. lxxxiv. Luther said, he had rather fall with Christ than stand with Cæsar. John xii. 26, "If any man will serve me, him will my Father honour." If we serve Christ, angels are our fellow-servants, Rev. xxii. 9.

Servire Deo, est regnare. *Philo.*

Servitus Christianorum regia est libertas. *August. in Psal.* 99.

Obs. 6. That holy creatures have heavenly minds. Angels look up, and that in their employments, their eyes are fixed above upon the Lord Christ; and it is certain where there is holiness, it carries upward; water will rise as high as the spring, and so doth the water of the Spirit. Paul's conversation was in heaven, Phil. iii. 20. Rev. x. 2, an angel hath sea and earth under his feet; and Rev. xii. 1, the church hath the moon under her feet, all ceremonial worship, all mutables in the world; and saith, Cant. vii. 10, "I am my beloved's, and his desire is towards me." The church finding Christ's affection towards her, cannot but look out, and look up. Most men look downwards, and are neither like angels nor men, more like swine, worms, moles. Many are loth to come near God, lest he should say, "Put off thy shoes from thy feet," put off thy earthliness: if we would have God look down from heaven, we must look up to heaven. David said, "When I awake I am still with thee," Psal. cxxxix. 18. He was with God when he lay down, and with him when he awoke and rose.

ἄνθρωπος παρὰ τὸ ἄνω ἀθρεῖν, from looking upwards, or ἄνω ῥέπων, which is the same. Os homini sublime dedit.

The next thing is their wings, mentioned in the 6th verse, "every one had four wings;" and ver. 8, "under their wings on their four sides;" and in ver. 8, "they four had their faces and their wings;" and in ver. 9, "their wings were joined one to another;" ver. 11, "their wings were stretched upward, two of every one were joined one to another, and two covered their bodies."

Angels are set forth to us in Scripture with wings; here with four; in Isa. vi. and Rev. iv. with six wings each of them: and they are said to be winged, for the agility of their natures, and swift motion in executing their office. Tertullian saith, Every spirit is winged, they fly in a moment into any part of the world, to execute the commands of God. Gabriel came flying to Daniel, chap. ix. 21, and that swiftly.

Omnis spiritus ales est.

Their wings are four, but the seraphims, in Isa. vi. and the four beasts, in Rev. iv. are set out by six wings each of them. A question hereupon arises, Why, the visions being correspondent, the angels here are described only with four wings. *Answ.* That pair of wings which is wanting here did cover the face of Isaiah's seraphims, and John's four beasts; for they, standing before the throne and face of God, were not able to behold such majesty, brightness, and glory with open face, although they were most pure creatures. We cannot look upon the sun in its strength and glory, but we cover our eyes with our hand; so they their faces with their wings. Now here was something instead of these wings, and did the office of those wings, and that was the firmament: ver. 22, "The likeness of the firmament upon the heads of the living creatures;" and ver. 26, "Above the firmament was the throne." This firmament interposed between the lustre of divine glory and their eyes, as the wings did in the prophet's and apostle's vision, and therefore here was no need of that pair of wings; they were not before the throne, but *sub expanso*, under the firmament, and to do works beneath the world.

Obs. That the glory and majesty of God is such as no eye can fully behold; there wings, here the firmament, is interposed between God and angels. When God came down upon mount Sinai, and manifested his majesty and glory, what said the people? "Speak thou to us, and not the Lord, lest we die." They could not endure the shining of Moses's face, much less the lustre and majesty of the Lord's: something must intervene, else man dies for it.

Touching the wings of these angels, three things are laid down: 1. The conjunction of their wings; 2. The execution of them; 3. The use.

The conjunction is in the 9th verse, "Their wings were joined one to another;" and ver. 11, "Two wings of every one were joined one to another." The extremity of their wings, when stretched out and ready to fly, did touch one another; so as they seemed to have but one wing.

Obs. 1. That there is mutual love and much agreement between the angels. The connexion of their wings, notes the connexion of their hearts; and the Hebrew is, As sisters that love one another entirely, and work together most sweetly, so are the angels, they love and labour together most sweetly; there be no divisions or distractions among them, what business soever is appointed, they all agree in. We men can hardly agree in any one business; so many men, so many minds. Sallust told Tully, that his mind was very changeable concerning the commonwealth; and it is true of most of us, what we allow now in matters of the state or church, we condemn anon, and so are at agreement neither with others, nor with ourselves; but angelical concord parallels, yea exceeds our discord; angels are all love, peace, and unity.

אשה אל אחותה Fœmina ad sororem suam.

Aliud stans, aliud sedens de republica sentis. *Declam. in Ciceron.*

Obs. 2. That there is a blessed harmony in the works of God done by angels; their wings go evenly, jointly, not one before another, above another, divided any way, but there is unity and uniformity in all their actions and operations. Could we behold the actions and works of angels, we should see such glory and beauty, as never was seen in the works of men. If we look upon a building that is uniform, and every part proportionable, we are much taken with it: a garden that is drawn out exactly, and every thing in it set in order; an army that keepeth rank and posture, and proceeds in all things according to rule, how beautiful and comely are they! All the actions of angels are such; one runneth not before another, one is not divided from another, one disallows not what another doth; but their harmony and correspondency is such, that if a man could see the same, he would be ravished with the works of angels. Jam. iii. 16, "Where envying and strife is, there is confusion;" but among angels there is no envy, no strife, so no confusion.

Alæ æqualiter extentæ, elevatæ, conjunctæ.

Obs. 3. That we should join our helps for furtherance of the works of God. Angels join their wings, and afford help to each other to do the will of God; devils and wicked men join together against God and his ways; Psal. ii. 2, "The kings of the earth set themselves, and the rulers take counsel together against the Lord, and against his Anointed," &c. And good men should join together, their heads, their purses, and abilities whatsoever, to further God's work. If angels appear and put forth their wings to do the will of their God, let us appear and put forth our hands to do the work of our God.

Mutuas sibi invicem tradunt operas ad exequenda Dei decreta.

The second thing about their wings is, they were stretched upwards; not let down, drawn up, resting upon their bodies, but extended as ready for service as might be, ver. 11.

This notes unto us the readiness of angels to do the will of Christ; their faces look up, attend their commands, and their wings are stretched out to fly about them as soon as they are made known; as a hawk that is upon the wing, watches till the fowl rise, and then falls upon her, and flies after her immediately. Angels are upon the wing before the command goes out, and when it is out, God shall not need to use motives or arguments to put them on. The manifestation of his will, is the strongest motive unto them; and it should be so with us. We pray that God's will may be done on earth as it is done in heaven; the mere manifestation of God's will therefore should prevail with us, as with angels: but let God manifest his will, bring forth his strong arguments to move us, yet we have no wings, or if wings, not stretched forth, or if stretched forth, we rather flag than fly with them.

The third thing is the covering of the wings, ver. 11, two covered their bodies, their thighs, and feet, Isa. vi. 2; that is, their uncomely parts, which are in Scripture phrase called "the feet." One wing did cover the forepart of their body, another their hinder parts.

Femora.

Obs. 1. In this covering of their bodies, God propounds them as a pattern of chastity and modesty unto us: those parts are hid, which might, uncovered, argue disreverence of God, or concupiscence in them, or be offensive unto men. God loves chaste spirits, and chaste behaviours: the angels are very chaste, and would not have any indecent thing objected to divine view, whose authority and majesty they adore. No impure thing must come into the sight of God, therefore God ordered, Exod. xx. 26, that there must be no steps to his altar, lest the nakedness of the priests were discovered in their going up, and so offence given to God and man; and further, he appointed linen breeches to cover the priest's nakedness, Exod. xxviii. 42.

Nihil impurum in conspectum Dei veniat.

Obs. 2. It notes out to us that angelical nature is a thing hidden, and too high for us, while we are in our houses of clay, their natures are beyond the reach of man's brain; and that we are so far from the knowledge of God's face, nature, and ability to behold them, that we cannot know and behold the lowest parts, the very feet of angels, they are veiled up from us, as too transcendent for our capacities. We know not the natures of any creatures here below, not of a flower, a fly; we describe things, but do not, cannot define them. I would see the proudest of you all define the nature of a straw, as one preached in Cambridge to all the scholars: if we know not the nature of these visibles, of bodies, then much less of angels; and if not of angels, least of all of God.

Vitreum vas lambimus, pultem non attingimus.

Obs. 3. That men are apt to idolize choice instruments employed in God's service, and therefore the angels are covered with wings to prevent it. Such is the beauty, wisdom, strength, use, and celerity of angels in God's service, that man is apt to deify them. John falls down to worship before the feet of an angel, Rev. xxii. 8. And when Paul and Barnabas had healed a cripple, the Lycaonians said, "The gods are come down to us in the likeness of men," and they would have sacrificed to them, Acts xiv. And should the angels appear to us in their natures, without being covered up, we should take them to be gods; but they will not have that honour, they will hide their beauty and excellency, and desire the glory only be given to God.

The next thing we are to come unto, is their feet, in the seventh verse.

Ver. 7. *And their feet were straight feet; the sole of their feet was like the sole of a calf's foot: and they sparkled like the colour of burnished brass.*

"Straight feet." They were feet of men, and by a synecdoche, feet are put for legs and thighs. The Septuagint read it, Their thighs were right or straight; and therefore could not be the thighs or feet of beasts, which in the hams are with compass and not straight; they were neither bending inward nor outward, but straight as pillars. This shows to us,

Columnarum instar.

1. That the ways of angels are all straight and right. Feet in Scripture are put for ways; inward of the soul, outward of the whole man. Prov. iv. 26, "Ponder the path of thy feet;" Psal. cxix. 105, "Thy word is a lamp unto my feet;" that is, all my actions; and Eccles. v. 1, "Keep thy foot when thou goest to the house of God;" that is, thy thoughts, affections, will, reason, and all within. Take the feet of angels for their thoughts, desires, wills, reason, actions, they are all right; there is no act of theirs void of reason, as the acts of brutes are; none done by rash motion or sudden passion, as too many of men's are: they go not without warrant, and when they go, they go in the way appointed of God, never turn out, but are exact, keeping to his will.

2. They are firm, constant in their resolutions, and service for God: that is noted by feet in Scripture; for feet are the basis and foundation of things. Exod. xxx. 28, "The laver and his foot;" that is, his basis whereon he rested: men's feet or legs are the foundation whereon the body rests. In Eccl. xii. 3, they are called "the strong men;" and Cant. v. 15, Christ's legs are said to be as pillars of marble; and Scaliger saith, that men's firmness is in their feet, on which the burden of the whole body directly depends. Here then we have the firmness and constancy of angels to go on in God's work; no burden can make them bow, no act, no force can put them out of the way, no weariness can make them sit still: angels will meet and stop Balaam, and give him commands: the angels will have Lot out of Sodom.

Firmitas homini debebatur in pede ad quem pertinebat onus totius corporis quod per lineam rectam incumberet. *De Subtil.*

"The sole of their feet was like the sole of a calf's foot." As it were the sole of a round foot, so the Hebrew signifieth, both round, and a calf that is fat, and hath round feet, smooth, round, and movable to carry any way. The Septuagint hath it, winged feet. Mercury, the poet's god, was painted with shoes which had wings. This sets out to us, both the swiftness of angels, of which before, and also their usefulness to move any way to do service in any part of the world; like a bowl, or globe, which is equally disposed for motion into any of the four quarters of the world; so are the angels ready to move any way upon every occasion and hint from Heaven. Man cannot do so; one man is fit for one service, not for all; one is fit for counsel, another for war, a third for sea, a fourth for land, &c.

עגל Quasi planta pedis rotundi: pedos rotundos, like a globe.

οι πόδες πτερωτοι.

Cum talaribus. *Horat.*

Ad omnem occasionem et nutum Dei.

"They sparkled like the colour of burnished brass." Steel or brass being polished or burnished, shines very beautiful, and sends out eye-dazzling beams, such as have much glory in them: and by this colour of their feet, we are led into these observations.

Obs. 1. That the angels are unpolluted in all their ministrations; they contract no filth, no soil to their feet. When they are in motion they are pure spirits, act purely, and abide most pure; their feet are like polished, not polluted, burnished, not blemished, brass; and so hold forth to us an example of purity in our ministrations, that we should be conversant in them so as to be unblemished. 1 Tim. ii. 8, "Lifting up holy hands," &c. 2 Pet. iii. 11, "What manner of persons ought ye to be in all manner of holy conversation?" here it is answered, Like angels.

Obs. 2. That the works of God by angels or men done rightly, with a straight foot, that is, done according to God's will, have much glory and efficacy in them; they shine like the polished brass, there is their glory; and sparkle, there is their efficacy. When the angel destroyed Sennacherib's host, what glory and efficacy was in that work! When the angel came to Manoah, and went up from him in a flame of fire, how glorious was this sight, how efficacious was the work in the heart of Manoah! John preached the truth with a right foot, and without delay, when called to it; "and he was a burning and a shining light," John v. 35. Herod found him so: Mark vi. 20, He "feared John, knowing he was a just and holy man;" the glory of his justice and holiness shined into his head, and the power of them affected his heart; he knew, he feared. Actions done according to God's will, hold forth much of God in them. 1 Cor. xiv. 24, if any unbeliever come in and hear them prophesy, that is, according to the mind of God, carry the action as becomes the church and the presence of God, he is convinced, and almost converted, and saith, God is in you of a truth: he sees so much glory, feels so much power, that he can contain no longer, &c. Isa. lii. 7, their feet are beautiful to your eyes, and their actions are efficacious in your hearts. God's will is the standard and measure of all actions, and when they are done according to it, they are very glorious and beautiful.

Obs. 3. That they are cheerful in the ways and works of God: they go not dully about their service, their feet do shine; they have more delight in doing one act of God's will, than we have in doing all the natural acts of our lives. You shall find them in a sweet posture and frame always; Rev. iv. 9, they give glory, honour, and thanks to God; and Rev. v. they are brought in singing, and singing a new song, which notes their cheerfulness, and earnestness in it: so in Luke ii. 13, 14, angels are the choristers of heaven, they make heaven heavenly.

The last part they are described by, is, their hands.

Ver. 8. *They had the hands of a man under their wings.*

Some would make sixteen hands to each living creature or face, but that is not likely; we find no number set down, and therefore will be content to leave that undisputed, whether two, four, eight, or sixteen: hands they had, and hands of a man; and that under their wings, on their four sides.

The hand notes action; Eccl. ix. 10, "Whatsoever thy hand findeth to do, do it with thy might;" so Prov. iii. 27. The philosopher calls it, The instrument of instruments; and saith, God hath given to man two special organs, to the body the hand, to the soul reason: and look, what use reason is to the soul, the hand is of the like use to the body; yea, soul, reason, body, are all beholden to the hand for the service that it doth; the great things in families, cities, kingdoms are done by the hand. Scaliger saith, Nature hath armed man with three things, reason, speech, hands. Reason is the hand of the understanding; speech the hand of reason; and hand the executrix of speech, that doth the commands; all things would be as dead, if the hand did not quicken them by the spirit and motion of art.

ὄργανον ὀργάνων Arist. 3. de Anima.

Scal. Exercit. 259.

Obs. 1. That angels are fit for service; they have hands; and hands are not made in vain, they are for work: where there are no hands, no power, strength, or way to put forth that power, there is no fitness for service; but angels have power, and ways to execute that power; they have hands, not for ornament, but for action.

Obs. 2. That angels do their works rationally, they have the hands of a man. As men do manage the works of their hands judiciously and wisely, so do angels; there is nothing defective, superfluous, perverse, rash, indiscreet, or culpable in their ministrations, they know all circumstances, and miss not in any. How wisely did the angel manage the business with Mary! Luke i. 28; he salutes her, she fears; in the 30th verse he comforts her, and tells her, she should conceive, and have such a son as never woman had; and when she doubted of it, ver. 34, "How shall this be, seeing I know not man?" ver. 35, the angel tells her, "The Holy Ghost," &c. And further, see the wisdom of the angel; he tells her, ver. 36, that her cousin Elisabeth had conceived a son in her old age, and that was the sixth month with her, and however thou thinkest it impossible for thee that art young without man to conceive, and for her that is old with man to conceive, ver. 37, yet nothing is impossible with God.

Obs. 3. That knowledge must issue into actions. Angels are full of eyes, and full of hands too, their actions are answerable to their knowledge; Rev. iv. 8, "They are full of eyes within, and they rest not day and night;" if they have no service in the world beneath, they will be praising God above; they know much, and therefore act much. Knowledge without practice is little worth; if hid from others, it is as nothing, as not being, saith the poet. Unless knowledge be improved, it is of no account; the Egyptians painted a tongue, and a hand under it, to show that knowledge and speech is efficacious and good, when that which is known and said is done. What good doth the unpractical speech of golden-tongued men. Let men be Chrysostoms, golden-headed and golden-mouthed, if they be not golden-handed too, it is nothing. God would not have us all eye, and rest in knowledge: John xiii. 17, "If ye know these things, happy are ye if ye do them;" and Rev. xxii. 14, "Blessed are they that do his commands, that they may have right to the tree of life." Happiness is entailed to doing, not knowing; and the angels seem to find greater happiness in doing God's commands abroad in the world, than standing always in his presence. Psal. ciii. 20, they hearken unto the voice of his word, if he bid them go they are gone, and account it their greatest honour to be doing; they have hands, and would not be idle. Knowledge without action, is a man without arms; it is wine shut up in the vessel, that doth good to none, and will corrupt at last, and mar the vessel; such knowledge will be like the poison that lies long in the body, and at last kills without remedy.

Scire tuum nihil est nisi te scire hoc sciat alter. *Pers.*

Quid prodest χρύσον λαλούντων των ἄπρακτος λόγος. *Nazian.*

Obs. 4. That angels are great agents, and do much service. They have hands on their four sides, at least they had four hands, and they were able to do much and great service; some make more, and no hand of theirs is idle. One angel can do more than thousands of men, witness that great slaughter in a night, and other things formerly spoken of. Briareus, a great doer, is said to have a hundred hands.

Obs. 5. That God doth carry on his works here in the world by invisible virtue, by hands under wings, by ways and means not seen. There is *vis plastica*, forming power, in the womb, which shapes and perfects the birth, yet is not seen; and in the womb of the world, God hath the same, which forms and perfects his works, yet not seen: much is done by the power of angels, yet their power is not seen. Mighty things are done by God's Spirit in the ordinances, in the assembly, in our hearts, and yet God's Spirit is an invisible agent; the minister, the word, would not do it, unless some invisible virtue went along therewith. Zech. iv. 2, 3, though none were found to pour oil into the lamps, yet God had olive trees which were not thought of, nor seen. Zechariah saw not the candlestick, bowl, lamps, or two olive trees, till the angel awakened him, and made him see, that God had ways to communicate virtue unto the church he knew not of; and that though the church were poor, low, not able to make a considerable army to carry them to Jerusalem, and plant them there, yet he had his Spirit to work it out for them; and therefore saith, "Not by might, nor by power, but by my spirit." 2 Thess. ii. 8, the Lord shall consume antichrist by the spirit of his mouth: and so the two witnesses, fire goes out of their mouths and devours their adversaries, Rev. xi. 5, in an invisible way, by a secret work. It was a hand under the wing that made peace betwixt Scotland and us, that gathered this parliament, that hath, and doth keep it; it is invisible virtue that hath made them unanimous and magnanimous; invisible virtue that upholds this kingdom, that restrains the remainder of wrath, that daunts the adversary; that hath shaken the prelacy, and brought forth the great things in our days; it is the hand under the wing that hath opened the hearts and purses of many to further the great service in hand.

Obs. 6. That we are to do God's works without noise or notice of ourselves. Angels, that are agents for God, have their hands under their wings; their actions are seen, but not their hands. In Judg. xiii. when Manoah catechised the angel, and asked him, "What is thy name?" ver. 17; the angel would not tell him, but said, "Why askest thou thus after my name, seeing it is secret?" ver. 18. And you shall not find the names of above two angels in Scripture, Gabriel and Michael. Angels are jealous of God's glory, and had rather conceal their hands and names, than God should lose the least degree of his glory; for Manoah would therefore have known his name, that he might have honoured the angel afterward: and we are very apt to look at the instrument, and neglect the principal. It is wisdom to muffle up ourselves, and to hold forth God as much as may be: Matt. v. 16, "Let your light so shine before men, that they may see your good works," &c.; he doth not say, that they may see you, but see your good works, and glorify your Father, not you. As fishers, they would have the bait seen, not themselves; they would catch the fish with their bait, not scare them with their sight. Matt. vi. 1, "Take heed you do not your alms before men, to be seen of them:" alms must be given, but we and our hands must be hid. Paul exhorts the Philippians to hold forth the word of life, Phil. ii. 16; not themselves, but the word of God, which is the word of life.

Obs. 7. That their operations and presence are together. They are not in heaven, and so work on earth, or in one part of the world and work in another; but their hands are under their wings; whither their wings do carry them, there they act, and not elsewhere. The angel came down to stir the water in the pool, John v. 4, and cure the party that stepped in first; they have not that power to work at any distance.

Obs. 8. That angelical virtue and nature is hid from us, it is too high for our capacity; their hands, their operative virtue, we cannot discover, or see into. A little of the angels is presented to us by their faces, wings, feet, hands, &c.; but the distinct knowledge of angels as angels is reserved till we are like the angels in heaven. Therefore we must not intrude into those things which we have not seen, vainly puffed up with our fleshly minds, but be content to be ignorant of their natures, and many of their actions and excellences, till we come to glory.

Now from their parts we come to their motions; and it is said,

Ver. 9. *They turned not when they went; they went every one straight forward.*

Ver. 12. *And they went every one straight forward: whither the spirit was to go, they went; and they turned not when they went.*

Ver. 14. *And the living creatures ran and returned as the appearance of a flash of lightning.*

"They turned not when they went." Which way soever they moved, they turned neither face, wings, nor bodies, but went straight forward; there was no digression, regression, wandering, nor circulation, but their motion was straight, they moved in *linea recta*, in a straight line; they move, and move not impertinently, but directly. By this motion of angels, is set out God's government in the world; they are his agents. Our prophet seems to cross himself. In ver. 14, it is said, "they ran and returned," and ver. 17, "they returned not when they went;" here in this ver. 9, "they turned not when they went." This knot must be loosed, or else our prophet will suffer.

The solution of this doubt is, that the angels being in their work appointed of God, went on without turning or looking back till they came to the issue and end of it, till they came to the place appointed, and then they returned unto God to give account of their service, and to receive new instructions. They went not back after the work was begun, but after it was ended: whatever difficulties interposed in the way, none of them could drive back, or divert the angels, till their work was done, and then they presently returned.

Obs. 1. That the works of God in ordering the things of the world are straight. Angels are as God's hands, and in them is the agency of his work, and they go straight on, and there are no windings, no turnings in their operations: the works of God seem crooked to us, but there is nothing crooked in them. A carpenter that builds a house hath some pieces of timber long, some short, some bowing, some straight, of all which he builds a goodly house; but some rude, ignorant fellow understands not the reason of that diversity; and when the work is done there is nothing seen defective, but all is straight and perfect: so in the works of Providence and divine dispensations in the world, they seem crooked, (and therefore some have called providence crooked and winding,) but no such thing is in them. Psal. xviii. 30, "His ways are perfect." Deut. xxxii. 4, "His work is perfect." Examine the works of creation, providence, redemption, they are without obliquity, deformity, or defect; but men are not so: and the reason is given, "for all his ways are judgment," that is, all his administrations, all his doings, are judicious, right, and equal.

Constantia est in proposito, perseverantia in opere. Charles V. his motto was, *Plus ultra.*

Fælicitatis index ultimus dies. *Solon.*

Obs. 2. That angels persist in and carry on their work; they are constant and persevere, they turn not back, they give not over, but proceed to the end; they are not slothful, weary, unfaithful, but active, lively, holding on to the end. This may be useful to our thoughts. Angels go on, and are lively in their work; shall we be lazy? they persevere; shall we draw back, or turn aside? Lot's wife looked back, and she was turned into a pillar of salt, Gen. xix. 26; she looked to the things behind, which was unwarrantable, and God did severely punish her; she had part of Sodom's judgments, which were brimstone, salt, and burning, Deut. xxix. 23. And she was made a pillar of salt to season after-ages, with the fear not only of backsliding, but also of back-looking. Josephus saith, he saw the pillar in his days, which was near two thousand years after; but Borchardus, that lived some three hundred years since, saith, it was in his days. Adrichomius saith it is yet extant; and the Targum hath it, that it will endure to the day of judgment. Whether this material pillar be extant or not, is doubtful: Christ hath set up a spiritual pillar, that will endure to the end, to make us faithful to the end: "Remember Lot's wife," Luke xvii. 32. Look back, and die; go on in the ways and commands of God, and live. It was the reproach of the Israelites, that they would have gone back to Egypt; and they died for it in the wilderness. Matt. x. "He that endures to the end shall be saved;" and Luke ix. 62, "No man having put his hand to the plough, and looking back, is fit for the kingdom of heaven." A man ploughing, if he look back, endangers the oxen which plough, and must needs make crooked furrows, and mar all: so one that hath begun to plough in God's field, if he look back, he is unfit for heaven. Exod. xvii. 12, "Moses' hands were steady till the going down of the sun;" and so must ours, till the sun set, till our lives end. Gal. iv. 9, "How turn ye again to weak and beggarly elements?" Gal. v. 7, "Ye did run well." It is dangerous when either of these come in against a people; but the godly have a promise, Jer. xxxii. 40, "I will put my fear in their hearts, that they shall not depart from me."

Antiq. l. 1. c. 12.

Obs. 3. That they keep close to the work in hand, to what is enjoined, they divert neither one way nor other; as they give not over, so they turn not aside upon any pretence whatsoever, but hasten to the execution of what is commanded. How un-angelical are we, that have such roving spirits in all our employments! Though we look not back, yet we look aside. God complains, "This people draw nigh with their lips, but their heart is far from me;" they are in my house, and in my work, but their hearts are in neither; they look towards me, as if they were my people, but their hearts look another way, as if they were worldlings, hypocrites; like watermen, they row one way, and look another. Ezek. xxxiii. 31, "With their mouth they show much love, but their heart goeth after their covetousness:" we are too guilty of this evil, our hearts are seldom at home. What is said of the harlot's feet, Prov. vii. 11, "They abide not in her house;" the same may be said of our hearts, they abide not in the house. When you walk abroad and keep the path, the spaniel that is with you ranges over much ground, and seldom is in the path; so it is with our hearts, we may be in the path of duties, but our hearts ranging over the world, heaven, and hell. Jam. v. 15, "Elias prayed earnestly;" in the original it is, he prayed in prayer, intimating, a man may be at prayer, in prayer, and yet be a prayerless man, not pray, and that because the heart is not in it: so in hearing, you may hear and not hear, &c. What is the reason Christ knocks at the door so oft, and is not let in? the heart is dead asleep, or abroad.

לא יסבו They fetched no compass.

Obs. 4. That angels have the mark in their eye which they aim at. They went every one straight forward; the Hebrew is, to the way or passage of his face, that path which was before his face; that is, they went thither where their eyes or faces were fixed; as they look not back nor aside, so they always look

Ad transitum, faciei suæ aut tractum faciei suæ objectum. So *Piscat.*

upon the mark, each goeth forward to that which is before him; this keeps them on to the work, and in the work, they have the mark in their eye: Prov. iv. 25, "Let thine eyes look right on, and let thine eye-lids look straight before thee;" look to the charge appointed, to that which is right, to that which is set before thee of God, and this will quicken thy industry. Phil. iii. 13, 14, "Forgetting those things which are behind, and reaching forth unto those things which are before, I press towards the mark." Paul had not his eye upon what was done bygone, or on what was upon either side of him, but upon that which was before him, the mark: heaven, eternal life was the mark in his eye, and he pressed after them; he was as intent upon them, and as pursuant of them, as he was in the work of persecuting the saints; he reached after them as the one thing necessary. We set not the mark before us; instead of heaven, Christ, eternal life, we have the world, our pleasures, and a multitude of things in our eyes, and so we are divided, and do nothing.

κατὰ σκοπὸν διώκω.

Assequitur nulla qui sequitur multa; Is angelicus qui nec multus nec varius est.

Obs. 5. That angels mind and pursue every one his own work, not the work of others. They went forward to the work, object, mark, set before their faces; he that had his work designed him in the east, minded not his work which lay in the west; each acted his own part, and fell not upon any thing that concerned another, although their employments lay the same way; what was before their faces, that they did, and nothing else. Devils compass the earth, and meddle with all men, and with all matters: it is not so with the good angels; they kept their station, and do keep order, they intermeddle not with ought that concerns them not. The apostle would have christians to be angelical: 1 Thess. iv. 11, "Study to do your own business," those things which concern our general and particular calling: if men will with their wit and curiosity run out of their bounds, they are extravagant and busy-bodies. Some think because they are neighbours, they may meddle in all contentions; because subjects, they may interpose in all state affairs; because christians, deal with others' sins: but this is to break the hedge, to break out of our own callings into others; and such, though they seem great doers, do nothing. 2 Thess. iii. 11, "There are some among you that walk disorderly, working not at all, they are busy-bodies." What! busy and do nothing? Yes, because they do things impertinent unto them, unfruitful, unprofitable, out of place. When Peter meddled too far in John's matters; and said, "What shall this man do?" Christ takes him up sharply, "What is that to thee?" John xxi. 22. And some think this made Peter so sharp against that sin afterwards, and to look upon it as bad as theft and murder; 1 Pet. iv. 15, "Let none of you suffer as a murderer, or as a thief, or as an evil-doer, or as a busy-body in other men's matters."

πράττειν τὰ ἴδια.

μὴ ἐργαζομένυς, ἀλλά περιεργαζομένυς.

"They ran, and returned." Here is the quality of their motion; it was swift, they had wings to fly, and feet to run. Much hath been spoken of the angels' swiftness; I shall here therefore touch upon their return. When their work is done, they make no stay, they linger not at all, but return with all speed. When God sends them out, or calls them in, their motion is very speedy: it is set out here by a flash of lightning; that is the soonest into the world and out again of any sensible creature; in a moment it is in your houses; and out again, in a moment it shines from east to west, and is gone; it is very glorious and marvellously active. Angels are cherubims of glory, Heb. ix. 5, and the most active of all God's works; and when their work is finished they retire immediately: as lightning, when it is come to its period, doth reciprocate and fall back into itself without delay; so do the angels return to him who sent them out, to know his further pleasure, and to do him more service.

Obs. 1. That angels in their services are glorious and terrible; they are like the lightning, which shines, dazzles, and doth dreadful things. Judg. xiii. 20, when Manoah and his wife saw the angel go up to heaven in a flame of fire, they fell down on their faces to the ground, and thought they should die, ver. 22. It was a received opinion among the Jews, that if they saw God or an angel, they should die upon it. Judg. vi. 22, 23, Gideon, a mighty man of valour, cries out, "Alas, O Lord God! because I have seen an angel of the Lord face to face. And the Lord said, Fear not: thou shalt not die." If they had a vision being awake, they apprehended death; but they never had experience of any that died upon any such occasion; this rose rather from the apprehension of glory and majesty in God and angels, and consciousness of their own weakness and guilt, as not able to abide the presence of those glorious creatures, that came immediately from the presence of the glorious God; and we find that some have been much affrighted, and almost struck dead, at the presence of the holy angels. Matt. xxviii. 2—4. an angel comes from heaven, whose countenance was like lightning, and his raiment as the sun, and for fear of him the keepers of the sepulchre did shake, and became like dead men; there was no spirit left in them, the glory of the angel did exanimate them. They are glorious and terrible in their ministrations; and so should the ministers of the gospel, the angels of the church, be. Nazianzen saith of Basil, His speech was thunder, and his life lightning. Such were James and John, Boanerges, Sons of thunder, Mark iii. 17: they were terrible to sinners in their preaching, like thunder and lightning.

Βρόντη σεῖο λόγος ἀστεροπὴ δὲ βίος.

Obs. 2. That account is to be rendered to God of all our services. Whom God sets to work, he will reckon with. Angels return and become responsible to God their Lord and Master; those mighty and glorious creatures, when their work is finished, do willingly and cheerfully return, and give in their answer; God looks for it, and they delight to do it. And, account we must all give of our work in the world: Rom. xiv. 12, "Every one of us shall give account of himself unto God." God will say to us, Come, give account of your stewardships, Luke xvi. 2. Every one hath a talent, is a steward, hath some trust committed to him, and he must not think to run, and never return. Let men act how they will, return they shall, be they never so great, be they princes, magistrates, commanders, &c. Eccles. xii. "God shall bring every work into judgment, with every secret thing, whether it be good or evil;" both the work and the workman must be questioned. Matt. xii. 36, "Of every idle word that men shall speak, they shall give an account in the day of judgment."

Obs. 3. That angels are lively and unweariable in their negociations, they run and return as a flash of lightning; when they had done great service in the world, they were as lively at the end of it as at the beginning, they return back with as much life and speed as they went forth, and were ready for new employments; they returned, as to give account of what was done, so to receive new commands and work. This is a pattern for us all, that in the works of God, those employments he calls us to, we grow not weary. One sin fits for another, and men are unweariable in that trade; so one duty should fit for another, and we should never be tired in our spirits, though we be in our bodies. Gal. vi. 9, "Let us not be weary in well-doing." The wicked are weary of and in well-doing; What profit is it, say they, that we keep his commandments, and that we walk humbly before the Lord of hosts? Mal. iii. 14. "When will the new moon be gone, that we may sell corn? and the sabbath, that we may set forth wheat?" Amos viii. 5. "He hath left off to be wise, and to do good," Psal. xxxvi. 3. They said, What a weariness is it! and snuffed at it, and brought that which was torn, lame, sick, Mal. i. 13. But the godly are never weary of God's work, though sometimes they are weary in it, through the strength of the flesh, weakness of grace, and other discouragements; but they, having tasted how gracious the Lord is, are not, will not, cannot be weary of his service; his commandments are not grievous to them.

Ad lætitiam et animi pacem magnum pondus habent rectæ actiones.

Desidia, est mors superstes, vacua est vita.

Obs. 4. That they seek not themselves, but the honour and glory of their Master. They stay not when their work is done, upon pleasure, curiosity to see or know any thing, but immediately return, and are taken up wholly with the glorifying of God; they are attent, watching his commands, for they look up; they are intent upon his work, they turn not to either side, look not back, but go straight forward; they contend for his glory, they run, return, and give account, and would have new commissions, be at work again, and have God to be glorified to their utmost abilities. Isa. vi. 3, "Holy, holy, holy, is the Lord of hosts; the whole earth is full of his glory:" they see God so glorious, excellent, and holy in himself, so glorious in all his works, that they mind not themselves, but God, and make it their only and great design, to glorify God, Rev. iv. 8, 9. And this is our duty, and comfort if done. 1 Cor. x. 31, "Whether you eat or drink," &c. The glory of the infinite, holy, wise, and great God, should be precious to us; we should attend his commands, intend his work, contend against all lets, within or without, and promote his work and glory to our utmost. That work which is not referred to God's glory, but our gain, credit, or profit, is a dead work. The schoolmen call for a right intention in every work, as that which animates and enlivens the same; and though we cannot actually intend God's glory always in every thing, yet there should be a virtual intention of it. A bowl runs, an arrow flies, by virtue of that arm which first sent them forth; and all our actions should proceed in the strength of a primary intention of God's glory.

Omnibus operibus nostris cœlestis intentio adjungi debet. *Aquinas.*

One thing yet remains touching the motion of angels, namely, the efficient cause of their motion; and it is the Spirit, set down in these words:

Ver. 12. *Whither the spirit was to go, they went.*

Some doubt there is, what is meant by the spirit here. Not the counsel or will of the angels; and so the sense to be, that they went which way they had a mind, whither their own wills and spirit carried them; and my reason is, because they are brought in here as servants and officers: and therefore not to be left to their own wills, but to be under command, and at the will of another; soldiers go not where they please, but where their general pleaseth. By spirit, we are to understand, neither the will of angels, nor winds, nor the soul of man, (for spirit in Scripture doth signify all these,) but the essential and eternal Spirit of God: and this is evident by the 20th verse, "Whithersoever the spirit was to go, they went:" it is not said, whithersoever their spirit was to go, they went, but whithersoever the Spirit, that is, the Holy Ghost, co-essential and co-equal with the Father and the Son, whither that Spirit of wisdom and power led them, thither they went: when that Spirit bad them return, they returned; as that Spirit moved them, so they moved.

Object. The Spirit of God neither goes nor moves from place to place, being infinite; how then can this be meant of the Spirit?

Answ. This is spoken after the manner of men, in regard of the vision Ezekiel had, it seemed so to him; but the Spirit, being infinite, neither goes nor moves by real change of place or essence, but by declaration of its power and grace. When the Spirit, or God, doth that which is unusual, then they are said to come and be present. Again, the Spirit went in the angels, not simply in itself; there was in the angels *imperium et impetus Spiritus*, the imposition and impression of the Spirit, which carried them on.

Non mutatione loci, aut essentiæ, sed declaratione potentiæ et gratiæ.

Obs. 1. That angels, although exceeding wise, full of knowledge, active, and able to do great service, yet are not at their own disposal, they move not at their own pleasure, they went not where they listed. Let the abilities of the creature be never so excellent, they must be under the power of a superior, they must be ordered and directed by a higher cause. Angels themselves are not lords of themselves, they are not *sui juris*, at their own disposal; much less men, that are lower than angels. 1 Cor. vi. 19, men are bought, and they must be his servants, at his disposal, that hath bought them, and that is God; and therefore they must not abuse their bodies and souls to fornication, or any other sin, but glorify God with both.

Obs. 2. That it is the Spirit of God who is the great agent that sets angels to work; they perform nothing by their own virtue and strength, but at the command and impulse of the Spirit they act, they set out, proceed, finish, and return. As it is in a ship at sea, there are the winds without to drive it, and the pilot within to guide it to what place he pleaseth; so here is the command of the Spirit *ab extra*, externally, and the *impetus intra*, the inward influence, to carry out and order these. The great things angels have done, have been done by the Spirit of God: if they suggest good thoughts; if an angel strengthen Christ in his agony; if they reveal mysteries and things to come to Daniel and others; if they contend against princes, and agitate the great affairs of the kingdom; it is by virtue of the Spirit of God, that works efficaciously in them, and in good men, that are employed for the glory of God, and the public good of church or state. When choice garments were to be made for Aaron, Exod. xxviii. 3; xxxi. 3, cunning and carved work in gold, silver, and brass, was to be made for the tabernacle, it was the Spirit of God that enabled men for that service. When great things were to be done by the judges in Israel, it is said, The Spirit came upon them, and the Spirit moved them: Judg. iii. 10, the Spirit of the Lord came upon Othniel, and he judged Israel, and went out to war, and the Lord delivered the enemies into his hand, and his hand prevailed. So Jephthah, Judg. xi. 29, and Samson, chap. xiii. 25. The Spirit came upon them, and moved them, and they did great things; and this is set down to let us see, that it is the Spirit doth all in the magistracy, and in martial affairs, in city and camp; yea, and church too; Zech. iv. 6, "Not by might, nor by power, but by my spirit, saith the

Lord of hosts." Oft mention is made of the Lord of hosts, and truths that concern the temple are sealed up with it in this prophet more than others; because there needed to such a work as building the temple, the power of a mighty God, so many, so mighty were the enemies; yet God would not do it by the might and power Zerubbabel had, but by his Spirit.

Obs. 3. That angels are led, and easily led by the Spirit. "They went;" it notes their tractableness; they went without dispute, without delay, immediately, cheerfully; and they went whither the Spirit was to go, that is, whither the Spirit would have them go. The Spirit is so infinitely wise, holy, and good, that even angels do freely and fully submit to the conduct of it; and therefore it is that they go straight forward, that there is no crookedness in their works; that they do such speedy and honourable service; and if such glorious, able, and perfect creatures be willingly led by the Spirit, shall we, that are base and beggarly, refuse the manuduction of the Spirit? If so, we forsake the choicest mercy: for, Rom. viii. 14, "As many as are led by the Spirit of God, are the sons of God," be they angels or men. It seems there are but few that are led by the Spirit of God, because he saith, "As many as are led," intimating all are not, few are. There are other spirits that lead men; there is a spirit of envy, Jam. iv. 5; of the world, 1 Cor. ii. 12; of whoredoms, Hos. iv. 12; of security, Isa. xxix. 10; a spirit of error, 1 John iv. 6; of antichrist, ver. 3: and by these most men are not only led, but driven, quenching, grieving, vexing, and resisting the good Spirit of God; more like devils than angels: but let us, when we have *imperium*, the government, or *impetum monitum*, the suggested influence, or *motum Spiritus*, motion of the Spirit, let us say, whither the Spirit will have us go, we will go, what that will have us do, we will do. Offer up yourselves, freely and fully, to the conduct of the Spirit, and that will lead you into all truth, and into the land of uprightness. It is an argument you are of the world, if you receive not the Spirit of truth, and submit not to the guidance thereof, John xiv. 17.

Ver. 13. *As for the likeness of the living creatures, their appearance was like burning coals of fire, and like the appearance of lamps: it went up and down among the living creatures; and the fire was bright, and out of the fire went forth lightning.*

לפיד The Hebrew word notes a torch or burning wood, where the fire and flame are more tenacious and strong; fire-brands, that are lively and flaming, heating and lightening.

In this verse is set out, not the figure and shape of the living creatures, that was done in the 10th verse, but the colour of their faces; which is described,

First, by similitudes.

1. They are likened to burning coals of fire.
2. To lamps.

Secondly, by the motion of it, "It went up and down among the living creatures."

Thirdly, by the operation and efficacy of it, "Lightning went forth of it."

For the better understanding of this dark verse, we must consider, that the Lord Jesus Christ, being exceedingly offended with the wickedness of the Jews, is presented in the vision to the prophet sitting as an angry Judge upon the throne, ready to take vengeance on them for their sins. They were idolatrous, oppressive, profane, ungrateful, slighting and persecuting the prophets; therefore Christ comes armed against them with zeal and fury, and suffer they must: hereupon the angels being inflamed with the zeal and indignation of their Lord and Master, are said to be like burning coals and lamps. When men have a holy anger against sin and sinners, and are zealous for God, how do their faces burn and glow, and their eyes sparkle! So was it here; the angels were affected much to see the Lord Christ so wronged by a company of sinful, wretched men; whereupon their colour became fiery, their faces burned with zeal, and their eyes sparkled, and they were ready to execute the sentence of the Judge upon this delinquent people.

"It went up and down among the living creatures." The fire and flame that stood not still, but was in perpetual motion, *mithhallecheth*, it מתהלכת made itself to walk of its own accord and pleasure; it went up and down; it, that was fire, went up and down among those four formed creatures. Some make it the likeness and appearance itself that went up and down; but it is better to understand it of the fire, which is distinct from the likeness of the creatures, and it is the vigour of Christ's Spirit. Virtue came out from Christ, the King and Judge upon the throne, which was like fire and flame, to prepare, quicken, and actuate these spirits to a fuller execution of divine pleasure.

"It was light, and out of the fire went forth lightning." Here you have the operation of this fire. "It was light;" that is, it did enlighten the angels; they saw by this light what was to be done in this great design of Christ in saving the innocent and punishing the guilty. "Out of it went forth lightning;" that is, the effect of it was dreadful unto men, as lightning is: the judgments of Christ executed by angels in the world, work effectually for the benefit of the godly, and for the undoing of the wicked.

Obs. 1. That the Lord Christ doth use angels in the execution of his judgments upon sinners. An angel smote Herod, Sennacherib's host, Pharaoh's first-born, the Sodomites. Psal. xxxv. 5, 6, it is the angel of the Lord that chaseth and persecutes the wicked.

Obs. 2. That angels are zealous, forward, and effectual in executing judgments upon delinquents. They are burning coals; Heb. i. 7, they are called a "flame of fire." Fire is hot, and notes their zeal and forwardness; it is active and consuming, which notes their effectualness. Angels are like the fire that fell upon Elijah's sacrifice, which consumed the sacrifice, the wood, stones, dust, and licked up the water, 1 Kings xviii. 38. So effectual was that fire, that nothing could stand before it; and when the Lord Christ sends out angels, none can stand before them, they are so zealous of and effectual in the execution of his judgments. The wicked are but as the wood, stones, dust, and water; these flames of fire will consume them. This should quicken magistrates, and those that are armed with authority, to be zealous and forward in punishing malefactors, and executing judgment upon delinquents. Rom. xiii. 4, the sword is not given them in vain, they are revengers of God's quarrel, and it is angelical to execute wrath upon them that do evil. It was Saul's sin that he spared Agag, but Samuel's glory that he hewed him in pieces; he was zealous, forward, and effectual in it. So Asa, in removing his mother Maachah from being queen, because she had made an idol in a grove, which he cut down, 2 Chron. xv. 16, and brake her idol in pieces, and burnt it. Those that are appointed of God to see justice done, if they do it not, become guilty themselves. Old Eli, a judge in Israel, because he was too partial towards his sons, God was angry, and his end was sad. Lewis XI. king of France, having pardoned a murderer twice, and suing again for his life, said, "What! dost thou ask pardon again? this is the third murder thou art guilty of." His fool standing by, said, "The other two are thine, who didst pardon them, this is his first; had justice been executed then upon him, he would never have fallen into this." So another Lewis having pardoned a murderer, and afterward reading that in Psal. cvi. 3, "Blessed are they that keep judgment, and he that doth righteousness at all times;" presently recalled the pardon, and said, "That prince which doth not punish delinquents when he may, is no less guilty before the Lord, than if he himself had done the fact." Let those therefore that it concerns, be zealous of, ready to, and effectual in the execution of justice upon delinquents.

Jam tertium homicidium perpetrasti.

Non minus coram Deo reus est quam si ipse perpetrasset.

Obs. 3. That angels have new influence from Christ, suitable to the ministration they are to be employed in. Though angels be creatures of much knowledge, wisdom, strength, speed, and usefulness, yet when Christ is to employ them, they must have new virtue and influence. "It went up and down among the living creatures." Let them be as burning coals, they have need of more heat; let them be as lamps, they have need of more light; their services are great, and Christ contributes unto them continually: as they have new instructions, so new accessions and additions of virtue, which are needful to their callings and operations. If they have need of divine virtue to further them in their operations, much more have we need of fresh supplies. John xv. 5, "Without me ye can do nothing:" he saith not, You may do something, or, You can do little, but plainly, "Without me ye can do nothing." It is the virtue and influence of Christ which enables angels and men to do the duties of their places and callings. Phil. iv. 13. "I can do all things through Christ that strengthens me:" when he that sits upon the throne sends out fire and flame, light and heat, to strengthen us, then can we do all things. 1 Cor. xii. 5, "There are differences of administrations, but the same Lord." It is the Lord Christ that points the administration of men and angels, that gives direction about them, with supplies of grace and strength, to exercise them. When we go about any employments of our general and particular callings, we should consider our own impotency, and look up to Christ, who hath all fulness, and is ready to send out virtue to supply all our wants: therefore Paul tells the Philippians, chap. iv. 19, "My God shall supply all your need according to his riches in glory by Christ Jesus."

Quæ ad singulares vocationes et effectiones eorum, sunt necessariæ.

Obs. 4. That the divine virtue which comes from Christ, is an active thing, it went up and down, it rested not. Men have sought after the perpetual motion, and lo, here it is. This virtue acted continually in the angels; it went not by a transitive motion, from one angel to another, but the motion was immanent, continually acting in them; and therefore it is called fire, which is a living, active thing. The word of God was as fire. Jer. xx. 9, "His word was within mine heart as a burning fire shut up in my bones, and I was weary with forbearing, and I could not stay;" it overcame him, and quickened him up to his work when he thought to preach no more. Many a christian thinks to hear, pray, read, meditate, receive no more; but there is virtue gone out from Christ, that will walk up and down in them, and cause them to fall to it again. That virtue which comes forth from Christ, is no dull thing. 1 Cor. xv. 10, Paul had fire from Christ, and it set him awork; "I laboured more abundantly than they all." See how active he was, he exceeded all the rest of the apostles. And how came that about? what metal was he made off? He had fire from Christ; "It was not I, but the grace of God that was with me," that went up and down in him, and fired his affections and spirit. David, Psal. xxxix. thought to be silent, and not to speak any more before the wicked, even from good conference he refrained; but what was the issue? "My heart was hot within me;" the virtue and fire he had from Christ began to work; "while I was musing, the fire burned" and flamed out: "then I spake;" he could hold no longer. So Acts iv. 20, "We cannot but speak the things which we have seen and heard."

Obs. 5. That actions done by divine virtue, afford light and lightning. The fire went up and down among the angels, put them upon execution of judgment; and from hence (these actions being so done) prove light and lightning to the world; they are seen, and seen far. They are light to the godly. When angels execute God's judgments upon sinners, the saints see much in it; they see matter of fear and praise: of fear, in that God's power, wrath, and hatred are manifested in them against sin and sinners; of praise, in that themselves are delivered, and justice is performed. Psal. lviii. 10, 11, "The righteous shall rejoice when he seeth the vengeance; he shall wash his feet in the blood of the wicked." When the wicked are taken away by a divine stroke, by the hand of justice, and God hath the glory of his justice, the righteous rejoice at it: but is that all? no, "he washeth his feet in the blood of the wicked;" that is, by this judgment he fears and reforms. It is a metaphor taken from the practice of those parts, where they went barefoot, or with sandals, and so contracted much filth, and used to wash and cleanse their feet when they came in: so here, the godly, seeing the hand of God upon the wicked, fears, and judges himself for his sins, purges his conscience and affections, and stands now in awe of that God who hath stricken the wicked for those sins which he himself in part is guilty of. Waldus, a man of note in Lyons, seeing one struck dead in his presence, he washed his hands in his blood; for presently he gave alms to the poor, instructed his family in the true knowledge of God, and exhorted all that came unto him to repentance and holiness of life.

They are lightning to the wicked, that is, dreadful and confounding. In this work of executing judgment, as they are lamps to light the godly, so they are burning coals and lightning to destroy the wicked. How terrible was the destroying angel when the plague was in David's days! Rev. xvi. when the angels poured out their vials of wrath, how dreadful were they! Men blasphemed, and repented not, to give glory to God.

Ver. 15. *Now as I beheld the living creatures, behold one wheel upon the earth by the living creatures, with his four faces.*

We have done, through divine aid, two parts of the vision, and now are coming to the third, that of the wheels, which hath its darkness and difficulties; and here the glory of God in his providence is considerable from earthly things and second causes.

In the vision of the wheels, two things I shall present unto you.

First, the signification.

Secondly, the description of these wheels.

What these wheels may signify, there is great variety of opinions; with all which I will not trouble you. Wheels, by a synecdoche, some think, is put for a chariot, in which God is presented to the prophet, guarded with angels on every side, who stand with great reverence and readiness to do his will: and by this chariot they understand the majesty, glory, providence, and kingdom of God, in which he rules all things at his pleasure, as a waggoner or pilot; and by the wheels, the immensity, eternity, celerity, perspicacity, and efficacy of God in his operations. Some think by chariots is meant the church, and by the wheels, the apostles. These are thoughts of men; we will therefore labour to give you the thoughts and intention of God's Spirit, so near as we can. By the wheels we are to understand this visible world, with all things in it, the kingdoms of the earth, and the church of God, and condition of all human things, which are all in motion and uncertain: and that this is the sense of the wheels may be gathered from the prophet in chap. x. 13, where it is said, "As for the wheels, it was cried unto them in my hearing, O wheel," O world. Their name is, The or this world: the word in the Hebrew is *haggalgal*, and not the same with the usual word for wheel; and it is both substantively and distinctively used, and notes out this world in which we live, in which Ezekiel was; it is not *galgal*, but *haggalgal*, which is demonstrative and distinguishing. Psal. lxxvii. 18, there is the same word, and it is not rendered, in the wheel, but in the heaven, or in the round, that is, the air; and the Vulgate translates it, "The lightnings have shined in the world;" and so the Septuagint. Seeing it is evident, that by the wheels is meant the world and things therein; it is needful to examine the fitness of this comparison, and so to see the wisdom of God's Spirit in it.

Quasi auriga.

Ipsis nomen vocatum est hic orbis, or, Ipsæ vocatæ sunt orbis. *Jun.*

הגלגל

Illuxerunt coruscationes orbi terræ, φωνὴ τῆς βροντῆς σῆ ἐν τῳ τροχῳ, that is, ἐν τῳ κόσμω; for the Greeks do absolutely take τροχὸς for the world. *Heins. in Jacob.* 3. 6.

Obs. 1. The wheel or wheels are round; such is the form of the world, it is called *orbis, globus,* an orb, a globe, from the roundness.

Orbe rotundato sidera quæque micant.

Obs. 2. A wheel is movable, and mutable, that part which is on high is presently at the bottom, and that which is at the bottom is quickly again at the top: and this informs us in the mobility and mutability of all human and mundane things, and is principally intended by this vision of the wheels: kingdoms, churches, families, *volvuntur, revolvuntur,* are daily wheeled about, moved, changed, and never long permanent in any condition. The four great monarchies, the Babylonian, Persian, Grecian, Roman, how were they kicked like foot-balls, and tossed like tennis-balls from one to another, and at last devoured by each other! After that great rent made in the house of David by Jeroboam, what changes, what wars and famines, were in the kingdoms of Judah and Israel, you find in the books of the Kings and Chronicles. You may see the relation of these wheels in one chapter. 1 Kings xvi. you will find, that in twelve or thirteen years of Asa's reign, king of Judah, there was the death of Baasha, Elah, Zimri, Tibni, Omri, that were wretched kings, and made fearful stirs and murders in Israel: and beside, wicked Ahab in that time began his reign, and troubled all Israel. The church, what a low ebb was it at in Elijah's days, when he complains, God's covenant is forsaken, his altars thrown down, his prophets slain, himself left alone, and his life also sought for! 1 Kings xix. 14. The church now, when Ezekiel had this vision, was in captivity, without a temple, altar, sacrifice; and the church is never long in any settled condition. Rev. viii. 1, "There was silence in heaven about the space of half an hour." Under the ten fiery persecutions, the church had no rest, but in Constantine's times it had a little; but presently the Arian heresy brake out, and did more mischief the church than all the persecutions before. The church is wheeled about from condition to condition; sometimes it is in Egypt, sometimes in the wilderness, sometimes in Canaan, and sometimes in Babylon; it is Noah's ark, that rides upon rough waters, and is not like to take harbour before Christ comes. So for families and persons, they are in a movable condition: Eccles. i. 4, "One generation passeth away, and another cometh;" that goes, and a third hastens after them to the grave. 1 Cor. iv. 9, "We are made a spectacle to the world," a theatre; that is, we come into the world, and act here a little while upon the stage of it, and presently we are gone; kings, princes, and all conditions of men do so; Noah and his generations are gone, David and his. If we come nearer ourselves, the Merovignian family was driven out by Pepin, son of Martel, and that family by Hugh Capet; so that there have been three races of the royal line in France. The Plantagenets' race here is wholly gone, or lies in obscurity. Great is the uncertainty, motion, and mutation of the things in this world; the wheels are up and down, and not consistent: Job is very rich and poor in one day; Haman in great favour and under great displeasure in a wheel of time. There is a story very suitable to this vision of the wheels, and brought in by expositors to give light unto it, which I may not omit; and it is of Sesostris a king of Egypt, who had a golden chariot, bedecked with many precious stones; and when he rode in it, no meaner persons must draw it than four kings that he had conquered. One of the four cast his eye altogether upon the wheel, and being demanded the reason of it by Sesostris, said, I see in this wheel the mutability of all conditions; that part of the wheel which is nearest heaven, is by and by upon the earth; and the contrary, that which is upon the earth is presently again nearest heaven. This wrought so upon Sesostris, that he thought his condition might change, and therefore freed those kings from that servitude, and would not have his chariot drawn any more by them. Belisarius, general of Justinian's forces, overcame the Persians in the east, the Vandals in Africa, the Goths in Italy, and did extraordinary service, at last had his eyes put out, his whole estate taken away, and forced to beg of passengers without the gates of Rome: *Da obolum Belisario, quem extulit virtus, cæcavit invidia,* O give one farthing to Belisarius, whom his own virtue advanced, and others' envy hath blinded. Adonibezek, who sat upon the top of this wheel, was soon brought under: he had seventy kings with their thumbs and toes cut off, and put like dogs under his table to eat scraps; and himself was made acquainted with that condition, Judg. i. 7. In the present affairs of Ireland, we may see the mystery of Ezekiel's wheel; all things are running, moving, and working to a change. Jam. iii. 6, he calls it the wheel of nature, or rather of this generation, showing, that the present generation is hastening out of the world.

Ætas parentum pejor avis mox datura progeniem vitiosiorem. *Horat.* θέατρον.

Baron.

τὸν τροχὸν τῆς γενέσεως.

Obs. 3. Wheels make in their motion a great noise and rattling. Joel ii. 5, "Like the noise of chariots on the tops of mountains;" so the things in the world move not silently, but make a great stir and mighty noise. Rev. vi. 1, when the first seal was opened, and Christ rode abroad upon his white horse of the gospel, conquering the nations, there was as the noise of thunder, and stirs and tumults were raised in kingdoms, and mighty oppositions were made in the world. When Christ shall judge the great whore, and avenge the blood of the saints, it will not be without noise: chap. xix. 6, "I heard as it were the voice of a great multitude, and as the voice of many waters, and as the voice of mighty thunderings, saying, Alleluia: for the Lord God omnipotent reigneth." There is the voice of the people like waters, a low and less noise; and there is the voice of parliament and armies, a greater, a thundering voice. The things now in motion in this kingdom and others, make a great thundering in the world; as in former days, between the houses of York and Lancaster were fought seventeen pitched fields, in which eight kings and princes perished, forty dukes, marquises, and earls, 200,000 of the people, besides barons and gentlemen; which things were not done without a great noise.

Obs. 4. Wheels are moved by some hand, and set on running, else they stir not: so this world is moved, acted, and governed by divine virtue. Things are carried in this world like wheels, up and down, backwards and forwards, as if all were left at six and seven, and hurried up and down by some blind chance or fortune; which we exclude, and only acknowledge all to be moved, ordered, and effected by Divine Providence. It is God that, by his providence and the ministry of his angels, sets all the wheels in the world in motion: a sparrow falls not to the ground, nor a hair off our heads, without his will.

Obs. 5. By the motion of the wheel many works are done. The potters of old made their vessels by the motion of the wheel, Jer. xviii. 3. By it the corn was ground, and justice was done: Prov. xxii. 26, "He bringeth the wheel over them;" that notes the punishment of evil doers: it is a metaphor from husbandmen, that, in hot countries, did by the help of a wheel break the ears of corn, Isa. xxviii. 28, and so get it out; and justice is the wheel that breaks men, and gets out the truth, and separates the chaff from the wheat. In some places a wheel hath been used to break the bones of sinners. Hence Tully saith, That an innocent life had nothing to do with the wheel. So that by the motion of the wheel much hath been done; and God, by the rotations and strange motions in the world, brings about great works. Dan. ix. 25, the walls of Jerusalem should be built in a troublous time. In the 8th, 9th, and 16th chapters of the Revelation, mention is made of trumpets and vials, which note great stirs and changes in the world, and notable effects follow thereupon. We hope that the stirs of our time are the preparation to the most glorious work of antichrist's ruining, our reforming, Christ reigning, and the Jews' raising; old things are passing away, and all things are becoming new; old religion, viz. popery, old prelacy, old service and ceremonies, are going downwards, and they that led into captivity, are themselves a leading into captivity, Rev. xiii. 10.

5. Tuscul. Beatam vitam in rotam non ascendere.

Remark. The world and the things in it are not fit for us to fix our hearts upon. The world itself, and all in it, are of a wheeling nature, uncertain, movable, and running away: and the word גלגל a wheel, and the world, signifies also a mote, chaff, straw, any thing driven before the wind; and so it is used, Isa. xvii. 13, כגלגל as a wheeling thing before the whirlwind; the margin renders it, as a thistle, or thorn; the one shows the vanity of the world, the other the vexation of it. Shall we let out our hearts to that which runs from us like a rolling thing, and if we overtake it, runs into us like a thorn? They that will be rich, catch the world, pierce themselves through with many sorrows, 1 Tim. vi. 9, 10, and break upon this wheel. Because it runs smoothly sometimes, men are taken with the motions of the world; but at length you shall find its motion rough, swift, ready to overthrow and break you all in pieces. They are broken in Ireland, and we are breaking here. Now let the apostle's counsel be acceptable: 1 Cor. vii. 29—31, "Brethren, the time is short: let them that have wives, be as if they had none; let them that weep, be as if they wept not; and them that rejoice, as if they rejoiced not; and them that buy, as if they possessed not; and them that use this world, as not abusing it." And why all this? "For the fashion," or show, "of this world passeth away." It acts otherwise than you expect; if you affect the world, wives, children, or any part of it, it will deceive you: you think to hold it, and it is but a shadow, no substance; and a shadow, a show, going away. Let us therefore not look at this wheel, but at him that moves the wheel; who is unchangeable, unmovable, of infinite being; in comparison of whom the world is a drop, a little dust. Let us with David say, "Whom have we in heaven but thee? and there is none in earth we desire in comparison of thee;" let us let go our hold of the world, draw in our affections from it, hopes after it, and look only after that city, Heb. xi. 10.

παράγει præterit, decipit.

Having given you the signification of the wheels, the next thing premised, is the description of them. And now I come to the particular handling of the wheels, where we shall meet with difficulties and excellences.

Ver. 15, 16. *Now as I beheld the living creatures, behold one wheel upon the earth by the living creatures, with his four faces. The appearance of the wheels and their work was like unto the colour of a beryl: and they four had one likeness: and their appearance and their work was as it were a wheel in the middle of a wheel.*

In these verses they are described:

1. From their number, implied in the 15th, expressed in the 16th verse, "four."

2 The place where they were, and that is "the earth."

3. Their colour; they were "like a beryl."

4. Their likeness between themselves; "they four had one likeness."

5. Their form was, "as it were, a wheel in a wheel."

Touching the first, viz. the number of the wheels, they were four. Mention is made of one in the 15th verse, but it is one with four faces; not the faces of the four cherubims, but of four wheels; which wheels were so like, that they are said to be one wheel; he that saw one saw all. As in some picture of a prince, when we have seen the same in divers places, or oft in the same, we say, This is one and the same picture; so here, our prophet saith he saw all the wheels, but they were so like, that they might well be called one and the same; for the prophet mentions in the 16th verse, wheels, and four wheels, and one likeness of them. Here, by a figure called hypallage, we may make the sense more easy thus; there appeared one face in the four wheels, for, one wheel having four faces. In chap.

x. it is out of all dispute that there were four wheels. Ver. 9, "When I looked, behold the four wheels by the cherubims, one wheel by one cherub, and another wheel by another cherub."

These wheels being four, represent to us the four parts of the world, eastern, western, northern, southern; that in them are great stirs and changes.

The next thing in this verse, is the place; "I saw one wheel upon the earth." How could that be, when Ezekiel saw the vision in heaven?

Answ. This is a vision, and it appeared to him to be on the earth; not the true earth, but the earth in a vision: as in pictures, if a wheel, a chariot, a city, be drawn, and presented to the eye, they are presented as being upon the earth.

Obs. 1. That all inferior causes, wheels, instruments, agents whatsoever, are but as one wheel before the Lord. All things in the four quarters of the world were presented by God to the prophet as one wheel; to us they are many, mighty, divers, contrary, infinite, but unto God they are otherwise; all the armies, parliaments, kingdoms, crowns, agents in this world, are but one cause, one wheel, before the great God, they are a small thing to him. Isa. xl. 15—17, "Behold, the nations are as a drop of a bucket, and are counted as the small dust of the balance: behold, he taketh up the isles as a very little thing. Lebanon is not sufficient to burn, nor the beasts thereof sufficient for a burnt-offering. All nations before him are as nothing; and they are counted to him less than nothing, and vanity."

Obs. 2. That changes, stirs, and tumults, are here on the earth, not in heaven. The prophet saw the wheels on earth, not in heaven; there be no wheelings, no turnings, no troubles, no wars, no deaths, no diseases, no sins, no fears, no tears, no wicked men, no wicked thing, and so no changes. It is only the prerogative of Heaven, to say, "I am the Lord, I change not," Mal. iii. 6; the world cannot say it. Jam. i. 17, "With him is no variableness, or shadow of turning:" in God and heaven, there is nothing of the wheel, all is constant, immutable; but on earth it is contrary, the things under the sun are vanity, inconstancy, and change itself.

Obs. 3. That all the inferior agents and causes are at the disposal of the superior, of angels. They have a great interest in the government of the world; the wheel is by the living creatures, at their feet, to move and turn it which way they please; if they will bespeak wars in the north, or south, if they will have the world in an uproar, it is done. Angels are God's hands and deputies in the administration of all things here below: in the world God supports and subverts kingdoms by them. Dan. x. Gabriel tells Daniel, that he withstood the prince of Persia twenty-one days, and his counsellors that sought to oppress the people of God, and that he would go again and fight with him. Kingdoms, and the affairs of them, yea, the quarters of the world, under God, are ordered by angels; and while angelical and divine protection are over kingdoms, they prosper; but when God is provoked by the sins of a people, he leaves the wheels of that kingdom to men and devils, it runs to ruin. Then the princes and potentates are deluded with strong delusions, grow tyrannical, idolatrous, false, hostile, &c.; then the kingdom grows weak, without spirit, counsel, strength, success, and is infinitely entangled with difficulties, internal, and external; good counsels are slighted or opposed, opportunities of doing that kingdom good not discerned, dangers not foreseen, or put off without due consideration; blasphemers, traitors, oppressors, and enemies to public good, are set up; divisions, seditions, domestic wars, (if not foreign,) are made and maintained, and all things work strongly to ruin. It is observed by some, that there are more wars and desolations among christians than others; and the reason is given; their sins are greater than others, and provoke God to take away his own and angelical protection; they leave the wheels of kingdoms to men of corrupt minds, that move them wholly for private interests. This informs us of the honour and greatness of angels, that have the wheels of the world in their hands. We look upon them as great men, which have the command of some province or country; what then are angels, that have the rule of the whole world under God? Know, though their place be great, yet they are under command, and move not but as they are moved by the Spirit of God. Let us also take heed how we offend persons employed in such great services as they are.

Obs. 4. That there are turnings and wheelings in all estates and parts of the world. The four living creatures noted the four parts of the world, and their agencies in them and by them: now are presented the wheels; every living creature had a wheel by it: and this strongly implies that there are wheelings, turnings, and changes in all parts; yea, the very same that are in one part are at one time or other in another part. The wheels are alike. Are wars, plagues, famine in one country? they are, or will be, in another. Do men die here? so in all parts. Are men unfaithful now? so they were of old; in David's days he said, "Men of high degree are a lie, and men of low degree vanity," Psal. lxii. 9. Are there unseasonable times here? such are abroad. Are things carried by violence, oppression, injustice here? so they are elsewhere. Are there designs, plots upon our kingdom and church? so there are upon others. Whatever befalls one state, befalls another, internally and externally. The wheels are the same, and move alike, though sometimes backward in one part of the world, and forward in another; there is no stability any where, but all things are changing. In vain then do men travel the world to find certainty and content in it; in vain do we go up and down, here and there, thinking to find settledness, and something satisfactory. The world is like itself every where; go east or west, and there is nothing but a wheel, and a wheel running. Solomon had tried all conditions; he had wealth, wisdom, and opportunities, for he saith, "Who shall come after the king?" intimating, that none can travel further than he did, to search and know the world and creatures, and all conditions: and what doth he conclude, but "Vanity of vanities?" that is, all is extreme and superlative vanity; and because men will not believe it, he doubles and trebles it, "Vanity of vanities, all is vanity," Eccles. i. Take any place, or any thing in that place, it is vanity, empty, fruitless, inconstant; so far from satisfying, that it vexeth. Hence some have pictured Solomon upon a high hill, and all the world coming towards it, and climbing up, thinking to find happiness there; but he beats them down with a rod, saying, It is not here, it is not here. We must not look for stability, content, certainty, among the wheels, but above them: now it is not time to look about and abroad, but to look above the world and the wheels of it. Christ hath told us what is to be had in this world; and it is certain: "In the world," saith he, "you shall have tribulation." And do you not find it? surely now it is eminent and pungent. And he hath told us what is to be had in himself: "In me you shall have peace." If we have tribulation in the world, we may have peace in Christ.

Ver. 16. *The appearance of the wheels and their work was like unto the colour of a beryl: and they four had one likeness: and their appearance and their work was as it were a wheel in the middle of a wheel.*

Here we have the colour, likeness, and form of the wheels to examine. First, their colour, (as for the work, that is, the matter whereof they were made, or the artificial form of them;) "Their colour and work was like the beryl:" the Hebrew is, as the eye, or colour, of תרשיש. The word *Tarshish* in Scripture sometimes notes a city, Jonah i. 3, sometimes a precious stone, Exod. xxviii. 20, it is the same word; and interpreters observe there is a sea also called Tarshish, Isa. ii. 16, and it is like to be that where the city Tarshish was; for Tarshish that Jonah fled to, was a sea town. When our prophet saith, "The colour was like the colour of *Tarshish*," he means not the city. The dispute is between the sea or a stone: some render it, as the colour or visions of the sea; others, as the colour of a precious stone: and then the query grows, what stone, whether of a chrysolite, a hyacinth, a crystal, or a beryl. That here is meant a stone, is determined by infallible testimony, even Scripture itself. Ezek. x. 9, "The appearance of the wheels was as the colour of a *Tarshish* stone;" and it is well rendered by our interpreters, a beryl stone; for neither the chrysolite nor hyacinth do discover a sea colour, the one being yellow, the other sky colour; and the scope of the wheels and description of them, is to possess us with the uncertainty and fluctuation of all things, which is livelily set out by the sea: we are therefore to hold to the crystal or beryl. It is true, the crystal hath a watery colour, and its original from the water; yet it doth not so fully set out the sea colour as the beryl, which is a green stone, and they are counted best that have the sea-greens. The best rendering of this word *Tarshish*, is the sea beryl, because it hath altogether a sea colour, and reminds us of the sea, by whose floating condition the uncertainty of all things is laid before us.

Rureus de gemmis. Beryllus Thalassius.

Obs. 1. That the things here in this visible world are like unto the sea, uncertain and unstable as the waters of the sea; they are never quiet, but always rolling up and down from shore to shore, even in the greatest calm. These waters are in motion, and suddenly in a rage by virtue of the winds, which lift up the waves to heaven, and make all stormy and outrageous: there is no stability at all in these waters; and the world is as unstable as any sea, as Euripus itself, that ebbs and flows seven times a day. All creatures are in motion, and tending to corruption; all conditions are full of changes and inconstancy. Who can tell how many inhabitants have been in some one street, in some one house, what wares have been brought in and sold out of some one shop? Men bless and curse, love and hate, in one day, in one hour: Amnon is sick for Tamar till his lust be satisfied, and then immediately hates her: Ahasuerus turns off Vashti, and entertains Esther: Reuben, Gen. xlix. 4, unstable as water: Pharaoh on the throne, anon in the bottom of the sea: Hezekiah healthy now, and hears by and by, "Set thy house in order, for thou shalt die:" Jerusalem besieged and freed in one night. In youth we are altogether for pleasure, in manhood for credit, in age for riches, as if thick clay must be our *viaticum* for heaven. We are fixed in nothing, and nothing is firm to us. What certainty is there in honours, riches, pleasures? What constancy in health, wealth, worship? What Seneca said of a great city burnt, There is a day's difference between a great city and none; the like may be said of most things and conditions.

Una dies interest inter maximam civitatem et nullam.

Obs. 2. Deceitful. The sea hath a pleasant colour to allure, it is greenish, which is most suitable unto the senses; and yet it deceives many, if not most: it fills with fears, it impoverisheth many, shipwrecks them, promiseth safety, and drowns thousands; oft it looks calm, and invites to come on, and being on, it becomes rough and ruinous. Hence the poet calls it, *fallax profundum*, the deceitful deep. A merchant carrying figs at sea, suffered shipwreck; and sitting by the sea-shore, beholding it pleasant and calm, said, *Novi quid velis, ficus vis,* You would have me again to venture through the deeps, but I will trust you no more: he spake wittily, and did wisely. We should prove as wise for this world. Trust it not, it is a deceitful thing; it promiseth content, but that cluster never grew on the world's thorns. The devil ever disquiets whom he possesses, and so doth the world: it promises pleasure, but pays with smart; *Breve est quod delectat, æternum quod cruciat,* An hour's pleasure and eternal torture. Dives' dainties now bite like a serpent, and sting like a cockatrice. The world promiseth much good, even to make them, its friends, happy; but it is otherwise. Achan's wedge of gold purchased the stones that beat out his brains; Judas's thirty pieces bought the halter that strangled him; Shechem's lust brought the sword upon himself and the city. It promises help in time of trouble; it rather sinks than helps; like a man in the sea with his pockets full of gold; it hastens his drowning, it helps him not to the shore. Prov. xi. 4, "Riches profit not." It tells us of continuance and abode with us; but here it gulls us greatly: the best thing the world hath, deals with us like false friends, they leave us in the lurch, and say, as the ten tribes to Rehoboam, "Look to thine house, David," 1 Kings xii. 16. Health saith, I must leave you, now look to yourselves. Riches take wings and fly away, eagles' wings, and fly with strength, Prov. xxiii. 5. Are not men's estates, liberties, honours, privileges now upon the wing? If Nebuchadnezzar be in the palace among his nobles, anon he is in the park among the beasts all night. As Jacob said of Laban, Gen. xxxi. 7, "Your father hath deceived me, and changed my wages ten times;" so may we say of the world, it hath, it will deceive us: we look for honour, it will change our wages, and give us disgrace; we look for riches, and it gives us poverty. Adonijah you may find in one day upon the throne and at the horns of the altar, 1 Kings i. 5, 50; he will be king, and have the lives of all in his hand, and before night he runs to secure his own life. It tells us of happiness, success, victory, life; but Zedekiah sees Jerusalem taken, his sons slain before his own face; then his eyes being put out, he is bound in fetters, and carried to Babylon. Good Josiah goes forth to battle, and he is slain: Ahab goes forth against the Assyrians, victory is promised him, but he is wounded, and dies of his wounds: Richard the third, after his cruelties, is slain in Bosworth field; and at the battle of Edge-hill, were not some taken, many wounded, and more slain? Joab pretended kindness to Amasa, but it proved cruelty; he kissed him, and killed him, 2 Sam. xx. Agag is hewn in pieces like an ox; Jezebel eaten by dogs, like a piece of carrion; Bajazet carried in an iron cage up and down the world by great Tamerlane. Trust it not, it is like Jael; she began with milk and butter, but ended with a nail and hammer. An emperor of Turkey married his daughter to a bashaw, and after one night's pleasure, sent for his head the next morning.

"They four had one likeness." All the wheels were equal, none higher than other, greater, lesser, but an even and suitable proportion between them all; no difference was to be seen at all.

1. This informs us that there is no stability in any part of the world, but changes every where, and such in other parts as they find with us. But of this before.

2. That God's administration of the world, and all the wheels of it, is equal and harmonious. This is set out to us by the likeness of the wheels: although in the world and things of it there be disparities, inconstancies, strange motions, and mutations; yet the wisdom and providence of God moves and turns the wheels, so that there is an admirable equability and harmony in all things; and if our eyes were opened, we should see and say, that no wheel could be moved better. To us the wheels seem all out of course, and to run with crooked motions, and to be hurried contrary ways by men and devils; but all things are in their right course, and move that way God would have them; and whatever the appearance be, all things agree well among themselves. We oft condemn the sentence the judge hath given, and blame a man for going about when he may go a nearer way; but when the reasons are made known, then we are satisfied.

Nulla linea possit melius dirigi; Rectissime omnia inter se consentiunt.

"Their appearance and their work was as it were a wheel in the midst of a wheel." Here you have the form of the wheels, a wheel in a wheel. This is hard to explain unto you. The words may be taken either transverse, or comprehensive.

1. Transverse. The wheels were crosswise, entangled in one another; as the lines or circles in a globe cut and cross one another, they were so entangled, they were in one another crosswise. And hereby is laid before us the several cross, entangled, and difficult motions of things in the world: all things do not go one way, nor evenly, in our sight and apprehension, but there are cross motions, great intricateness and knottiness in the affairs of the world.

Ut duo circuli ad rectos angulos se intersecantes.

2. Comprehensive. A wheel in a wheel; not the nave stock in the midst of the wheel, to which the spokes are fastened, for that hath not the form of a wheel: but there was one wheel in another; as the orbs of the heavens comprehend one another; as in some water-works, and watches, there be wheels one in another: and then the meaning is, that there is a secret hidden motion or wheel, that moves the wheels which way soever they run.

Obs. 1. That the motions of the world, and the kingdoms, are perplexed and cross motions, like a wheel in a wheel. Saul moved with all his strength to settle the kingdom upon his own son; but he met with a contrary motion. David is anointed to be king, and the men of war "came to David to Hebron, to turn the kingdom of Saul to him," 1 Chron. xii. 23. And so Adonijah said to Bathsheba, The kingdom that was mine is turned about and become my brothers, 1 Kings ii. 15; he met with a cross wheel, that carried the kingdom from him. How perplexed, and entangled, were the motions of the Jewish affairs, both in Babylon and at Jerusalem, when the prophet saw this vision! Nebuchadnezzar's wheel was in theirs, and entangled them much in both places. What cross motions were in France, when the king of Navarre, prince of Conde, the admiral, and all that were of the protestant religion, looked for peace, and met with a massacre! Are not there Romish, Spanish, French, and popish wheels moving in our kingdom, armies, and councils? Look at this instant upon the motions of this kingdom, in parliament, or out of it, and they are exceeding intricate. Never was skein of silk or thread so knotty or involved, as the affairs of the kingdom and world are; never bird so entangled in the lime-twigs or nets, as things are at this time.

The papists do erect *regnum in regno*, an ecclesiastical monarchy in the temporal, exempt from temporal jurisdiction, only subject *ob pacem*, for peace' sake, or *bonum commune*, on account of the common good, if subject at all; and so they give monarchs a broken right in some things, but defeasible in other things, by their spiritual monarchy.

Obs. 2. The motions to mutations and ruins are very swift. Things move faster then we conceive to their ends. The Jews hasted out of Egypt, and destruction hasted on the Egyptians. A wheel in a wheel, notes intention of motion. As Elias prayed in prayer, Jam. v. 17; that is, he was intense; so a wheel in a wheel, intimates intenseness of the motion. All things make speed to their own ruin.

Obs. 3. There is a secret motion which carries on the wheels, and moves them that way they go. There is a wheel in a wheel, and that sets the other moving; as a spring in a watch sets all the wheels going. Some latent engine stirs the wheels of the world. In some places you shall see the waters suddenly fly all about you: the cause of that motion is hidden. So in all the motions, turns, and stirs of the world, there is a secret wheel, Divine Providence, that sets on work and carries on. That was a great wheel and turn, when ten tribes at once fell from Rehoboam, and ran to Jeroboam. Politicians and statesmen could see sedition, rebellion, and treason in that motion; the outward wheel was obvious, but the wheel in the wheel was not seen by every eye: "Behold, I will rend the kingdom out of Solomon's hands, and give ten tribes to thee," 1 Kings xi. 31. If there be divisions, ruins, plunderings in a kingdom, there is a wheel in those wheels, a Providence that acts and orders. Job vi. 5, "Afflictions come not forth of the dust, nor trouble out of the ground;" they come out of the wheel: God turns that upon kingdoms and families; as Micah i. 12, "Evil came down from the Lord to the gates of Jerusalem;" God hath a wheel in all the wheeling businesses of the world. Anastasius the emperor being informed of a conspiracy against him and the state, commanded Justinian and Justinus, with many others, to be executed. By a voice in the night he was bid to spare Justinian and Justinus, for they were to do good service; and they both afterward were emperors: the motion of the wheel in the wheel saved their lives, and advanced them to honour. At the battle of Keinton was a wheel in a wheel: the wheel at first ran for the adverse party, but the wheel in the wheel turned it on our side. At Brainford there was a wheel in a wheel. When the enemies' plots have been their plagues, and their doings their undoings, the wheel in the wheel both moved and turned their own works upon them, Psal. ix. 16.

An internal mystery in an external appearance or dispensation; the spirit of life within keeps the wheels in motion.

Zonar.

Obs. 4. The motions of Divine Providence in the things of the world, are beyond the reach of the wisest. Providence walks and works so darkly, deeply, changeably, wheels about, so that mortals cannot tell what conclusions to make. When the issues of things are extant, we can see what the antecedent motions carried in their womb, otherwise not, unless we have it by vision; as here Ezekiel had; or some extraordinary way. Providence hath such intricacies, as puzzle the thoughts and hearts of the ablest and best. When the children of Israel were at the borders of Canaan, they were carried back again to Ezion-gaber, Numb. xxxiii. Exod. xiii. 18, it is said, "God led them about through the way of the wilderness, by the Red sea:" and so Providence leads affairs about, they go backwards and forwards, so that we cannot make sense of God's motions in the world; as in characters, till a man learn, and be instructed in them, he can make no sense of them; and men now of rare abilities, cannot tell what sense to make of the motions of the wheels. Monsieur Chastileon, admiral of France, at the match of Charles IX. his sister with the king of Navarre, was invited with chief of the protestants by the king to celebrate the marriage at Paris, and to confirm peace: the protestants at Rochelle advised him not to go, but importunity of others prevailed with him, he went, and was massacred for it. Although he was of great wisdom, he could not discern what way the wheels would move. The wisest man is too weak to spell out the meaning of the wheels and mysteries of Providence. Once before he had refused to come to court at the king's sending, who sent Monsieur Du Tore his cousin to advertise him of important affairs he had to communicate: he suspecting, answered, The king means me no good; and tell him, there be no Count Egmonds in France: I will not suffer my head so easily to be cut off, as he did in Flanders. Roderick king of Spain, to insure himself against the children and friends of king Vitiza, whom he had deposed, dismounted all the strong-holds, and disarmed the people: this strengthened him against domestic enemies, not foreign attempts; for the Moors invading him, shortly after overthrew him, and finding little resistance, in seven or eight months conquered almost all Spain. The Britons, molested by the Picts and Scots, called in the Saxons, who for some time served them to purpose, but in the end conquered them and their country. These could not foresee what would be the issues of things. The motions of Providence are so secret and various, that it lies not within the compass of man's power to make certain conclusions therefrom.

Obs. 5. There is a connexion of causes and things together in the world. Hosea ii. 21, 22, "I will hear the heavens, and they shall hear the earth; that shall hear the corn, wine, and oil; and they shall hear Jezreel:" as in architecture, there is a dependence and connexion.

Ver. 17. *When they went, they went upon their four sides: and they turned not when they went:* and so on to the end of the 21st verse.

In these verses we have two things:

I. We have the effect of the wheels, which is motion, laid down in ver. 17, 19, 20, 21. And,

II. The adjuncts of them, which are two, 1. Height, 2. Eyes, in the 18th verse.

The commodiousness of their motion for all parts, and the form of it, are both in this 17th verse. The Hebrew is, In going, they went to their four sides, to the four parts which were next to their sides, or through the four parts; and so the sense is, they went to, into, or through the four parts of the world. If you read it according to our translation, upon them; the sense is, when the four living creatures moved, the wheels moved upon their sides. It is our phrase, when we ask one, which side went he of such a man? we answer, Upon, or on his right or left side: but the better sense to me is, they went according to their four sides. Look what side, what part of the world was appointed them, that the wheels went to, and moved in.

"And turned not." They came not back, but went forward: there might be variety of motions, but no back motions, no retrogradations; being once gone forth, they returned not.

The observation first is this: That in all parts, human things move to their appointed period, and there is no return of them being once there. Pharaoh and his host came to their period in the bottom of the sea, and never saw Egypt more. The patriarchs, prophets, apostles, martyrs, have taken up their lodgings in the dust, and return no more. What David said of the child, "I shall go to it, it shall not return to me," is a fit motto to all creatures; they must go to those who are gone before, not they return to these: cities, people, families, silver, gold, fine linen, they must see that corruption those saw in former days.

Obs. 2. That inferior causes move constantly in their motions, to do the will of God. The wheels turned not when they went, nothing could turn them back; nor the angels in their administrations, but they go on. We think it is the creature makes stops, lets, in the affairs of the world; but it is God's hand, his providence doth it: the wheels, all inferior causes, proceed in their motions, till God check them, and cause a stand: Isa. xliii. 13, "I will work, and who shall let it?"

Ver. 18—21. *As for their rings, they were so high that they were dreadful; and their rings were full of eyes round about them four. And when the living creatures went, the wheels went by them: and when the living creatures were lifted up from the earth, the wheels were lifted up. Whithersoever the spirit was to go, they went, thither was their spirit to go; and the wheels were lifted up over against them: for the spirit of the living creature was in the wheels. When those went, these went; and when those stood, these stood; and when those were lifted up from the earth, the wheels were lifted up over against them: for the spirit of the living creature was in the wheels.*

In the 18th verse, we have the rings of the wheels described, from their height, and from their eyes. They were so high, they caused terror; so full of eyes, they caused wonder. The Hebrew reading is somewhat different, it runs thus, And the rings of them, both height to them, and fear to them, or by reason of them; that is, the wheels were so high, that they bred terror, struck fear into the prophet. The word rings in the Hebrew is, backs, their backs were high, dreadful; that is, their circumferences or rings were so, of such breadth and altitude, (for there is no difference between those in rings and circles,) that they caused fear to those who looked upon them. Propter eas.

Now what is meant by this height and greatness of the wheels, must be opened unto you; and it is this: the motions of second causes and changes of things here in this world, are so great, so incomprehensible by man, that they produce fears and terrors to the sons of men. Men are troubled that they cannot fathom the depths, and measure the height and breadth of the wheels. When men see times and seasons changed, kingdoms dashed in pieces, the godly brought into bondage, the wicked advanced, truth persecuted, errors in credit, justice trodden down, and all things moving by contrary motions, they stand amazed; and not able to reach the causes of things, to measure the wheels, and see into the exact motions of them, they become sensible of their own weakness, and say, O the height of the wheels! O the shallowness of our spirits!

Obs. 1. That the causes, and motions, and changes in the world, are unknown to the sons of men. The wheels are too high for them to measure: man is so purblind, that the dim sight of his soul pierceth not into the secrets and knowledge of causes; it only comes at the outside and extremities of things, the superficies of the wheel, but not the height and depth of it, not the true nature and causes of things; so that admiration, and opinion, not science, is begotten in man. This Agrippa knew, that wrote a book of the vanity of sciences; and Zanchez, that wrote a tractate, *Quod nihil scitur*, That nothing is certainly known: and Socrates was judged the most learned man, for that he said, This I know, that I know nothing: and above all these, the apostle saith, 1 Cor. viii. 2, "If any man think he knoweth any thing, he knoweth nothing yet as he ought to know;" and 1 Cor. xiii. 12, "We see through a glass darkly," things are a riddle to us, we know not what to make of them. Look into the world, and what can we make of it? The wheels in every quarter have such a height as none can reach; second causes move so suddenly, as none can spy them out. Cast your eye upon physical wheels, and they are too high for physicians to measure. What reason can they give of antipathies; or that some trees should have a venomous root on the one side, and a remedy on the other? They meet with diseases and difficulties that are *ludibria medicorum*, defiances of the skill of physicians, and must refer you to occult qualities. Cast your eye upon political wheels, and there you will find such heights and depths, as neither Ahithophel can measure, nor Machiavel can sound. Look at theological wheels and motions, and there are such heights that none of the prophets nor apostles have been able to measure. I will give you an instance in two or three. Jer. xii. 1, 2, "Righteous art thou, O Lord: yet let me talk with thee of thy judgments: Wherefore doth the way of the wicked prosper? wherefore are all they happy that deal very treacherously?" Jeremiah, a great prophet, is puzzled at this height of the wheel: "Thou hast planted them, yea, they have taken root: they grow, yea, they bring forth fruit: thou art near in their mouth, and far from their reins." Job is at a stand in this case, chap. xxi. 7, "Wherefore do the wicked live, become old, yea, are mighty in power?" God puts Job to it in chap. xxxviii.—xli. So Asaph, Psal. lxxiii. and Habakkuk, chap. i. 3, were troubled at the prosperity of the wicked, and could not take the altitude of the wheels in their days; nature nor grace could do it. If Solomon knew not the way of an eagle in the air, of a serpent upon the rock, of a ship in the midst of the sea, of a man with a maid, Prov. xxx. 19; how shall we know the motions of the wheels in the world?

Eccles. iii. 11.

Deorum crimen. Sylla tam felix. *Sen.*

Obs. 2. That the consideration of the unsearchableness of God's ways should beget fear and trembling in us: the wheels had a height, and dreadfulness upon that height. When a man comes to the sea-shore, beholds the vastness and strange motion of it, and finds he is puzzled, fear creeps upon him from the apprehension of the greatness and majesty of God, who sits upon the floods, and commands the deeps: so here, when we think of the wheels, how high they are, that we cannot search out the cause of their motions, this way or that way, our souls should tremble at the majesty of that God which sets such mighty wheels at work. Psal. xxxvi. 6, "Thy judgments are a great deep." Men's sins are a great deep, and Satan's ways are called a depth; but God's judgments, his ways in the wheels, are the greatest deep of all, they are unsearchable.

That christian kingdoms are shaken in pieces with wars, when heathen kingdoms are spared; that there is such unequal dispensation of the means of grace in the world; that the greatest part are without the knowledge of God and Christ to this day; that many able men are laid by, or cast into corners, where are but handfuls of people, and great towns, where are multitudes, have no ministers, or such as preach holiness, and the power of godliness, out of their parishes; that people are most hardened under the most powerful means of grace; that there be such unequal distributions of riches, talents of nature and grace; that precious young ministers and others are taken away in a time of great need, when others that are vile and base are spared; that wicked pirates prosper at sea, when honest men are shipwrecked; that those who have little or no means thrive, that those have the best who are barren; God's working in sinful actions, his fitting vessels for destruction, his leaving his ancient people the Jews sixteen hundred years under a curse; O the depth! how unsearchable are his ways? Rom. xi. 33.

The next thing in the verse to be touched, is, the eyes in these rings.

"And the rings were full of eyes round about them four;" or, on every side to them four. Every wheel had eyes; they were *stellatæ oculis*, bedecked with eyes, as the heaven with stars: there were eyes within, and eyes without, and not a few, but many; every ring, every wheel, was full of eyes.

By eyes, we are to understand the active and infinite providence of God, which runs through all things. 2 Chron. xvi. 9, "The eyes of the Lord run to and fro throughout the whole earth;" that is, Divine Providence is active every where.

The Scripture, by eyes, referring to God, intends, first, his knowledge and notice of things; Prov. xv. 3, "The eyes of the Lord are in every place, beholding the evil and the good." Secondly, his care; Psal. xxxiv. 15, "The eyes of the Lord are upon the righteous;" that is, he careth for them. Thirdly, his direction; Psal. xxxii. 8, "I will guide thee with mine eye." And these eyes show God's inspection, care, and ordering the wheels in all their motions, and that in all quarters. The rings were full of eyes, and whatever the thoughts of men were, they moved according to direction of Divine Providence.

Obs. 1. That however the wheels and motions of them be too high for men, and dreadful unto them, yet they are not so to God; he sees into all the wheels, they have eyes on every side; God knows them throughly, their essences, qualities, operations. We cannot pry into the state of kingdoms, councils, armies, cities: there are as secrets of states, so secrets of wheels in those states, which none know but God, and God knows them perfectly. Let wheels be never so great, terrible, move never such strange and cross ways; as kings, armies, parliaments, are great wheels, and have unknown motions; yet they are subject to the Lord's eyes, he sees into all their secrets, and sees more in their motions than they themselves.

Arcana imperii et arcana rotarum.

Obs. 2. The motions of the wheels are considerable and judicious. They are not carried on blindly; however they seem to be carried, yet they are carried by reason and counsel: there are eyes in the wheels. When men do things rashly, injudiciously, we say, Have you no eyes in your heads? Here are eyes in

Non cæco impetu voluntur rotæ.

the rings, and they move not casually. Those motions in the world that seem most confused, are composed and ordered motions. Are rich men made poor; honourable men base? are conquerors made captives? do servants ride, and princes go on foot? are the wicked oppressors in the seats of justice? are the godly beneath, and the vile above? are the counsels of Jesuits, foreigners, and desperate malignants, entertained, and others rejected? are there civil wars in a land, great plundering, spoiling of ministers, christians, parliament, men themselves? These things are not done without considerate and judicious motions of the wheels. Acts iv. 27, 28, when Herod, Pilate, gentiles, Jews, were gathered together against Christ, were not the motions then (though inhuman, bloody, and murderous) considerate and providential motions? The text saith, they did "whatsoever the hand and counsel of the Lord determined before to be done:" it was no blind business; the wheels of it were full of eyes, and moved by the motions of Heaven. God's own eye, heart, and head were in it. And now, when the Herods, Pilates, and malignants of the world do stir against Christ and his members, the wheels move considerately.

Obs. 3. The motions of the rings, wheels, and all second causes, are certain, arriving at the end appointed. They are full of eyes, which direct them to their journey's end, so that they miss not the mark they aim at. What if many second causes be ignorant, blind, know not their own motions; yet if they have guides infallible to lead them, it is sufficient to conduct them to the intended end. If a seeing dog can lead a blind beggar from place to place, direct his motion to the desired end; shall not the eye of Providence lead any, all second causes to their end? Providence is an unerring thing, and disappoints not God of his expectation. The pilot carries a great ship from harbour to harbour, over the seas, through the storms, and fulfils the mind of the master; and so Providence carries the great wheels up and down, to the very place appointed.

Obs. 4. The least motions of the wheels are not without Providence. Some think that the great things in kingdoms and the world are transacted by Providence; but for the less, they pass in a casual manner, Providence reaches them not: but the eyes were every where, the wheels were full of eyes; not a few eyes, here and there one, but in every part, that so man's mind might be freed from such sinister thoughts, as that there should be any motion of any wheel without the direction and influence of Providence. God hath made the least and greatest creatures, and he causeth the least and greatest motions. Let us pitch our thoughts upon some lesser motion, the dispensation of a lot, the fall of a hair from the head, the preparations of the heart, the answer of the tongue, these are all of the Lord, and directed by Providence; the earth loseth not a pile of grass, the trees not a leaf, the water not a fish, the air not a bird, without an ordinance of Providence.

Providentia ita curat omnia, ut unum aliquid, ita singula, ut si illud curaret unicum. *August. in Confess.* And the schoolmen say, that Providence is infinita in omnibus, infinita in singulis.

Obs. 5. Providence orders the motion of the rings and wheels in all parts, all the world over: not one, two, or three wheels had eyes, but all four had eyes round about them. God, by his divine providence, ordered things as well in Babylon as in Sion. Providence wrought in Egypt, and the Red sea. As there are wheels in all parts of the world, in all kingdoms of the earth; so there are eyes in all those wheels.

Obs. 6. The works of God in disposing and governing second causes, are admirable, glorious, and beautiful works. The wheels were full of eyes, fitly disposed, wisely carried on, certainly attaining their ends. Could we see the eyes in the wheels, we should never fault the works of God in the world, but stand and admire their glory and beauty. When the heavens are veiled with clouds, we have sour and discontented thoughts of the heavens themselves; but when the clouds are gone, that we can see the stars, those eyes of heaven, then we admire their beauty and glory: and certainly it is a most glorious sight to see the heavens full of stars in a clear night; and it is no less glorious to see the eyes in the wheels, and the choice acts of Providence in all their turnings and windings. Caussin saith, the world in all its parts is ruled like a paper with music lines, and if we could see those lines, they would be as glorious as lines of gold.

Obs. 7. The motions of the wheels are such as that they hold out a providence to all. There is something in the wheels that none can reach, and something that any may see; they are full of eyes, and the weakest may see one providence or other; if not all the eyes, yet some of them: there are mysteries in the wheels to exercise the greatest, and eyes to satisfy the weakest. As no man but sees the stars in the heaven at one time or other, so no man but may see the eyes in the wheels. That evil doth not overrun all, and the wicked devour the good, argues a Providence. In one of the Canary Islands, Johannes Metellus saith, there is a tree which drops water at every leaf, and sufficeth the inhabitants and their flocks, being a dry island without water. Mithridates, when in his cradle, had his clothes consumed with lightning, and his body not touched. A father and a son shipwrecked at sea, the son sailed to shore upon the back of his dead father. In these particulars and such like Providence doth eminently appear.

Ver. 19. *And when the living creatures went, the wheels went by them: and when the living creatures were lifted up from the earth, the wheels were lifted up.*

Ver. 21. *When those went, these went; and when those stood, these stood; and when those were lifted up from the earth, the wheels were lifted up over against them.*

Here we have,

1. The motion of the wheels further commended unto us.
2. Their station.
3. The time of both.

The motion was forwards, upwards, and downwards; and for the time of their motion and station, it was when the creatures moved or stood: as the cherubims moved, so moved the wheels, forward, upward, downward; and when they stood still, the wheels stood. The kind and manner of their motions, with their rest, depending on the living creatures, they moved equally at their motion. What is meant by the lifting up of the wheels must be inquired. For angels to be lifted up is not strange, they are heavenly creatures, and heaven is their habitation; but for the wheels to be lifted up, that is very strange: we must search out the sense; for into heaven they were not lifted. Expositors leave us in the dark; all except one that I have met with pass over this difficulty; and what I find in that one is this: The lifting up of the angels and the wheels, refers to the Supreme Cause, and seems to tell us, that inferior and superior causes, wheels and angels, are under the regiment of the First Cause. And if we take the words actively, as Montanus doth render them, viz. the living creatures in lifting up themselves from the earth, the wheels lift up themselves also; and that is, they looked up to heaven for direction and assistance, which may well be called a lifting up themselves. Psal. xxv. 1, "Unto thee, O Lord, do I lift up my soul;" that is, to thee do I look for counsel, comfort, and strength.

If we take the words passively, "when the living creatures were lifted up from the earth, the wheels were lifted up," then I will give you my thoughts what the sense may be: and it is this; the lifting up is not meant of lifting up to heaven, but to service. When God should more than in an ordinary way let out himself to the angels, give them new light, new strength, and so lift them up to great service, then the wheels also were lifted up proportionably to do their parts: and the words in the text invite me to conceive it to be the sense; because it is said, "the spirit of the living creature was in the wheels:" when God by his Spirit lifted up the angels to great employments, then the Spirit lifted up the wheels, the second causes, to more than ordinary service. And the word lifting up notes service, a higher degree of it than before. 2 Kings xix. 4, "Lift up thy prayer for the remnant that are left." Hezekiah sends to Isaiah when Rabshakeh blasphemed, and Jerusalem was besieged, and saith, Isaiah, thou art a prophet, and hast more than an ordinary measure of the Spirit; lift up thy prayer, let it be extraordinary, such as may lift up the spirits of all to join with thee, higher than ever; such as may lift up Jerusalem out of misery. So Jehoiachin, when he was set up upon the throne to govern and to do great service, it is said, his head was lifted up, Jer. lii.; and so in Psal. x. 12, the lifting up of God's hand notes doing of some great matter.

The next object of inquiry, is, the standing of the living creatures and the wheels; when the one stood, the other stood. Do the angels stand still at any time? they are active spirits, and always in motion. Two things this standing implies:

1. A cessation from any service in hand, at the will and pleasure of God, if he would call off the angels from their employments before they were finished. In this sense the angels are said to stand, and so the second causes they used, although they were both employed in some other service: or,

2. When they had perfected any work in hand, then they were said to stand, not idle, but in expectation of a new commission. Like as faithful servants, when their work is done, present themselves before their master, and demand his pleasure; so the angels, and second causes, hearken what God will say more, and what is the next word and work to be done; they wait upon God for new instructions.

Obs. 1. The motions of this inferior world, and the second causes in it, do depend upon higher causes, even heavenly motions, the ministry of angels. The observation is plain from the words, "When the living creatures went, the wheels went by them." If the angels move, the wheels move also. They are great things the angels have in their hands; the wheels of nature, of states and kingdoms, yea, of the church itself.

Obs. 2. Nothing in the world is casual. Many things seem so to us, but in reality are not so. All things here below move at the motions of others; and that which is ordered by the motion of angels, or God himself, cannot be casual. The wheels are moved by angels, and angels by God himself. God directs all; nothing happens wherein the hand of God or angels is not. Things are not accidental: if a thing could drop from the heavens, or be done on earth, without God and his angels, that were casual and accidental indeed. And because men see not the immediate or remote causes of things, who they be that move the wheels on earth, therefore they attribute effects, events, and accidental things to chance, to good or bad days and hours, which proclaims men's ignorance and forgetfulness of God. Isa. lxv. 11, "Those that forget God, prepare a table for that troop;" for fortune, some read it: but those who know God, acknowledge his eye and hand, seeing and ordering all.

Qui paratis mensam fortunæ. *Hier.* Qui ponitis mensam fortunæ, *Vulg.*

Austin misses his way, and so escapes the danger of death that was intended. Another being in a despairing humour, seeks a knife, a halter, to undo himself, and finds a great treasure. A third hath his ring drop off his finger into the sea, and afterwards finds it in the bowels of a fish. God so directs all these accidental things, that there is nothing done but by a secret instinct and hint from himself; and in all such passages we should mind something of God.

Absconditum quid?

Obs. 3. That nothing can hinder the motion of the wheels when angels and Providence would have them stir. When the living creatures moved, the wheels went presently. It is not in the power of second causes, of men or devils, to hinder the work of God in the hand of angels. The king of Persia may withstand Gabriel twenty-one days together, Dan. x. 13, but the wheels moved all the time; Gabriel prevailed, and God's work prospered in his hand. Wicked men make head against God, providence, and angels, and think to stop the wheels when they move not on their side; but all is in vain. If a man should catch hold of a chariot, running to stop or turn the course of it, were it not folly or madness in him? and because he would be the chariot's hinderance, that may prove his ruin: so here, men and devils do ruin themselves in opposing the wheels, which, notwithstanding all oppositions, proceed and keep their course. And let me tell you a riddle: God's words go on through the hearts, heads, and hands of his greatest enemies; Providence fetches them in, and makes them subservient to the work; they oil the wheels, although they know it not, and forward the work, though against their wills. God in this kind makes use of kine and cart, men and devils, yea, any creature, to carry his ark to its place.

Obs. 4. That God doth sometimes raise the spirit of the creature to more than an ordinary height, and enables it to unwonted service; "the living creatures and wheels were lifted up." So Moses, when called up to the mount, his spirit was raised much, else the service had been too hot and hard for him. Joshua was advanced when it was told him, that there should not any man stand before him all the days of his life, Josh. i. 5. Jeremiah tells the Jews, that the Chaldeans, whom they thought would depart, and not meddle with their city, he tells them, that though they had smitten the whole army of the Chaldeans, and that there remained but wounded men, yet they should rise up every man in his tent, and burn the city with fire, Jer. xxxvii. 10. When men are wounded, thrust through, as the Hebrew is, they can have but little strength; how should they be able to do it? God would lift them up to that service; as David, when he grappled with the bear and lion, encountered with Goliath, had his spirit lifted up to a great height. Hence that in Zech. xii. 8, "He that is feeble among them at that day, shall be as David," that is, such a warrior as David, who, though a young stripling, slew a bear, a lion, and Goliath; "and the house of

מדקרים

David shall be as God, and as the angel of the Lord." The godly, though weak, yet shall be lifted up to divine and angelical strength. This was made good in the time of the Maccabees; when the people of God were weak, Antiochus fierce and vile, then God raised up the spirit of Judas, Jonathan, and Simeon, to do extraordinary things. This was also made good in the time of the apostles. What great things did they do! and Paul saith, "I can do all things through Christ that strengtheneth me." What bitter things did they and others suffer! and it was not common strength, but special influence: Phil. i. 29, "To you it is given, not only to believe, but also to suffer." Blandina's spirit was heightened above the malice and torments of men; for having animated her children to suffer, and sent them as conquerors to Christ their King, she comes forth to suffer before the tormentors cheerfully, as called to supper with Christ her Husband, as one comes to a marriage supper; and after stripes, tearing with wild beasts, burnings, putting into a net, and tossings by a bull, being without sense of torment by reason of her faith and conference she had with Christ, at last they killed her with the sword; and the enemies confessed, they never saw such a woman, suffering such things so courageously and constantly. As sometimes God suspends the ordinary operation of the creature; the lions' mouths are shut, they touch not Daniel; the fire burns not the three children; so, sometimes he lifts up and extends the operation and strength of the creature to an extraordinary height. The winds, what virtue doth God put into them! how doth he raise them! what terrible work do they make at sea and land; tear navies in pieces, sink them in the deeps, and toss ships out of the water upon the dry land! Ravens fed Elijah morning and evening, he goes in the strength of a cake and a cruse of water forty days, 1 Kings xix. God hath lifted up many in these days to do more then ordinary service. Ezra i. 5, God had raised their spirits to go up to build the house of the Lord; so Hag. i. 14.

ὡς ἔις νυμφικὸν δεῖπνον κεκλημένη, *Euseb.* lib. 5.

Obs. 5. That God at his pleasure puts stands to the motions of the second causes; the angels stood, and the wheels stood, and this was the overruling hand of God, that can stop the course of nature, any wheels or agents whatsoever. Josh. x. 12, 13, God stayed the course of the sun and moon, and made them stand still the space of a whole day; and hereupon some gather, that the ebbings and flowings of all seas ceased. In Hezekiah's days the sun went backward ten degrees. God stopped the course of the waters, and made them as steady as walls and mountains, when the Israelites were to go through the Red sea; did not he take off the wheels of Pharaoh's chariot? God can put a stand to the greatest wheels. 1 Kings xii. 21, when an army of 180,000 chosen men was brought into the field, to fight and fetch back the kingdom that was wheeled over to Jeroboam, see what a stand God put to that army; ver. 24, "Ye shall not fight against your brethren: return every man to his habitation:" they did so, and presently that mighty army was disarmed. The buying in of impropriations, a work of great and good concernment, God put a stand to it. The undertaking for Ireland hath the wheel stopped, if not taken off. The motion of the wheels to the isle of Providence are stayed by the eye of Providence. Are there not stands in our consultations, and doth not God oft take wisdom from the wise, and understanding from the prudent? Are there not stands in our military affairs? the mighty men do not always find their arms. Hath not God oft put a stand to the enterprise of our adversaries? It is the Lord that hath hedged up their way with thorns, that they have not found their paths; and God hath hedged up our ways, that we have not found our paths to a full and thorough reformation. This great wheel hath great stops; the children are come to the birth, but there is no strength to bring forth: neither doth God's work cease, when he makes stops. A man who is printing a book, defers the edition, because he will make an addition; if it be delayed it is enlarged, and that is no loss. Stops of Providence in the wheels of the world are God's parentheses, and while they are writing, the work goes on.

Ver. 20. *Whithersoever the spirit was to go, they went, thither was their spirit to go; and the wheels were lifted up over against them: for the spirit of the living creature was in the wheels.*

In this verse is laid before us the immediate cause of the wheels' motion; and that is the Spirit, which is the first and highest agent, and moves both superior and inferior causes. This Spirit is set out emphatically; "the spirit," or, that spirit; not the spirit of the angels, but the eternal Spirit of God which was in the angels, or the living creatures: that Spirit was in the wheels; and with what motion it moved the living creatures, with the same it moved the wheels. This is the scope, to show that the four living creatures and four wheels were moved by the same Spirit of God.

הרוח

Touching this Spirit, I spake in the 12th verse, where I also showed you how the Spirit is said to go, and move from place to place.

This answers a secret objection; How could the wheels move at the motion of the living creatures? they are dead and senseless things, without any motive virtue in them. And this objection is fully answered in these words, the spirit of life was in the wheels.

That which is rendered, "the spirit of the living creature," is in the Hebrew, *spiritus vitæ*, the spirit of life, the enlivening, quickening spirit, the lively, active spirit; or the spirit of the living creatures, and by a change of the singular number into the plural, the spirit of the living creatures; and so the sense runs, that spirit that was in them, the same was in the wheels.

רוח החיה Spiritus vitalis, or, spiritus animalis.

Object. If the same Spirit be in the wheels, are not they also living creatures, having the same spirit and motion?

Answ. If I should say they were moved, as if they had the Spirit in them, this might help the difficulty, but doth not satisfy the text; which saith, the spirit was in the wheels. Therefore know, that as the living God is in every thing, moving and acting them according to their several natures, and yet doth not make all to be living creatures; so the Spirit of God was in these wheels, not animating, enlivening, but moving them to those services that were commanded and appointed.

Obs. 1. That second causes move not of themselves, neither superior, nor inferior. Not the wheels which are weaker here beneath, nor the angels which are stronger and above, they move not, but at the motion of the Spirit; whither that was to go, they went. Earth, water, winds, beasts, fowls, men, their counsels, wars, peace, trades, they all move *ad motum Spiritus*, according to the influence of the Spirit; it is the Spirit of God that moves all the wheels. All motions, all wheels, are subject to the Spirit, and regulated by it. When the devil accused, tempted, smote Job, he and all his motions were ordered by a higher power. So when the devils entered into the swine, they did what, and moved whither, the Spirit would have them to do, to go.

Obs. 2. No creatures, wheels, nor angels, no causes inferior or superior, can go otherwhere, or act otherwise, than the Spirit would have them. Whither the Spirit went, thither they went; they moved not before the Spirit moved them; and when they moved, they moved that way the Spirit moved. Devils and wicked men cannot be any where but where the Spirit would have them to be, nor do anything but what the Spirit would have done. Pilate, with the gentiles and people of Israel, were gathered together to do whatsoever the hand and counsel of God had determined before to be done, Acts iv. 27, 28. For the Spirit is the supreme, most potent, and efficacious agent, overruling all motions, so that no creature can move any other way than it doth. Prov. xxi. 1, "The heart of the king is in the hand of the Lord; he turneth it whithersoever he will." Kings cannot turn them whithersoever they will; ill counsellors cannot draw them which way they will; but they move which way the Spirit and providence of God will have them move. This turning or inclination, saith Luther, is that strong operation of God which the king cannot shun or change. If kings' hearts go after outlandish women, as Solomon's; if carried to ill counsellors, as Rehoboam's; if to idolatry, as Jeroboam's; if to root out the godly and godliness itself, as Ahab's; if to ruin their kingdom, as Ahaz's did; if to shed innocent blood, as Manasses' did; the hearts of kings are in the hands of the Lord, he turns them whithersoever he will: in all those motions he acts in just judgment, not changing their wills, but making use of them to bring about his own designs.

Est actuosissima illa operatio Dei quam vitare et mutare non possit. Sive sinat, sive inclinet Deus, ipsum sinere vel inclinare, non sit nisi volente et operante Deo; quid voluntas regis non potest effugere actionem Dei omnipotentis, quia rapitur omnium voluntas, ut velit et faciat, sive sit bona, sive sit mala.

Obs. 3. The motions of the wheels are not unseasonable. When the living creatures went, then the wheels went: and what is the cause of their motion? the Spirit was in the wheels, and the Spirit was in the living creatures. If we condemn their motions and changes as untimely, we shall question and condemn the work and wisdom of the Spirit, which is infinitely wise and uncontrollable in all its operations. Men, even the best of them, are apt to fault the motions of the wheels, and to censure the acts of Providence as unseasonable. "The counsel is not good at this time that Ahithophel hath given," 2 Sam. xvii. 7. Did the Spirit then move that wheel seasonably? Yes; because the counsel, though not good for David, whose destruction it tended unto, yet it was good for the ruin of Ahithophel and Absalom, and that was the intent of the Spirit in moving that wheel: ver. 14, "The Lord had appointed to defeat the good counsel of Ahithophel, to the intent to bring evil upon Absalom," and Ahithophel too. What! civil wars in England, when Ireland lies a bleeding to death? when such a time to vindicate the Palatinate, and wrongs sustained at the hands of the emperor? when such a time to help the protestants in France? what! now to have king and parliament divided? now to be embroiled in a bloody civil war? is not this most unseasonable? Stay thy thoughts and censures, O vain man; the Spirit of God is a Spirit of wisdom, and knows when it is best to move the wheels. No musician tunes it better than the Spirit of God. Had these changes and motions been, and our enemies abroad at peace, they would have taken the advantage of our divisions and wars, and made a prey of us. Seeing therefore we must be let blood, or die, this great and wise Physician, the Spirit in the wheels, hath done it seasonably. Are great towns plundered, counties disturbed, families impoverished, or churches dissolved, the righteous smitten, the wicked spared, and kingdoms shaken into pieces? these motions, changes, are not unseasonable; they are all in their appointed time: this war is in its appointed time. Ezra iv. 17, there is mention of "Peace, and at such a time," the time is observed; so now, the war, and at such a time, such a time as is appointed, as the Spirit of God judges fittest. Eccles. iii. 8, there is "a time of war and a time of peace;" ver. 3, "a time to kill, and a time to heal; a time to break down, and a time to build up." The Spirit knows and observes those times punctually, and moves not a wheel but in its due time, and so the motions of all are beautiful in God's eye, and should be free from man's blame. "Man knows not his time," Eccles. ix. 12. But it is not so with the Spirit; it knows times and seasons, and never misses to move the wheels in their due season. If the tree, Psal. i. bring forth her fruit in due season, and the Spirit moves the wheels in due season, none are too early, none too late.

Obs. 4. The consent which is between heaven and earth. The angels and wheels are from the Spirit of God which moves in them. When the living creatures went, the wheels went; when they stood, these stood; when they were lifted up, these were lifted up. And what is the ground of this harmony? The Spirit was in them, that acted them, and ordered their motions; having the same Spirit, they went the same way, and did the same work, without difference, without contentions. The Spirit of God is a Spirit of union; where that moves it moves not to discord, but to mind the same things, and to move the same ways. Numb. xi. 16, 17, when the same Spirit which was upon Moses, was put upon the seventy elders, then they judged as he judged, then they moved the same way, and did bear the burden of the people together with Moses; and, ver. 25, then they prophesied, and it being told Moses, that Eldad and Medad prophesied, he will make no breach upon it, but finding the same Spirit in them that was in himself, said, "Would God all the people were prophets, and that the Lord would put his spirit upon them," ver. 29: he knew the same Spirit would move them the same way that he went. So Elisha, when he had received the Spirit of God which Elijah had, he moved his way, carried on that work he did, 2 Kings ii. Wicked Balaam, when acted by God's Spirit, consents with the true prophets, and prophesieth the happiness of Israel; and cannot curse the people of God, though tempted and hired to it, Numb. xxiv.

Obs. 5. That the wheels readily do the will of God, and follow the Spirit; wherever it goes, thither their spirit was to go, the Spirit was in the motion. And therefore they are said to have eyes, and the Spirit in them, and to move at the motion of the Spirit. Wheels have roundness, and so readiness to move, but not God's way: full of eyes they are, and look at God's ends; but if they had not the Spirit in them, they would not move that way; or if they did, it would not be without dispute, sloth, murmuring: it is the Spirit makes them move the right way, and readily in that way. Where the Spirit is in any, there the motion is right and ready. Air, sea, land, have no vigour in them, but what the Spirit puts in, and they move as the Spirit will have them: Psal. cxlviii. 8, "Fire and hail, snow and vapour, stormy wind fulfilling his word," they all do the will of God, fulfil his word readily; they have the vigour of God's Spirit in them: Gen. i. 2, "The Spirit moved upon the face of the waters;" not an angel, not the wind, but the eternal Spirit of God; and so they move by virtue of the Spirit into their place. The Spirit createth, cherisheth, and sustains all things; and they are all obedient to the call of the Spirit, and tread in the paths of it, all creatures move after the Spirit: Psal. civ. 30, "Thou sendest forth thy spirit: they are created, and thou renewest the face of the earth." Herbs, plants, trees, beasts, fowls, all living creatures, are created and formed by the Spirit, and move according to those principles and instincts the Spirit puts into them; their motions and services are no other than what the Spirit leads them unto, and those motions they readily perform.

Obs. 6. The wheels and second causes do go on and move incessantly, and without weariness, in the way the Spirit puts them. They went whither the Spirit went: neither the Spirit nor the wheels do faint or fail in their motions.

Obs. 7. The Spirit of God is a living and lively Spirit. It is "the Spirit of the living God," 2 Cor. iii. 3; and the living God cannot have a dead and lifeless Spirit. It is a Spirit of life; Rom. viii. 2, "The law of the Spirit of life in Christ Jesus." The Spirit hath life in itself, it gives life to all; Job xxxiii. 4, "The Spirit of God hath made me, and the breath of the Almighty hath given me life:" all life comes from this Fountain and Author of life. Eve was called the mother of all living, that is, of all men and women; but the Spirit is the Father of all living, men, women, and other creatures. It is the Spirit that maintains life, Acts xvii. 28. Job xxvii. 3, "All the while my breath is in me, and the Spirit is in my nostrils;" the Spirit of God is in that breath, and maintains life by it. The Spirit quickens and improves life, 2 Cor. iii. 6. The Spirit quickens, not only makes life, but makes lively: it is the Spirit that quickeneth, not only from death, but from deadness and dulness. Cant. iv. 16, "Awake, O north wind; and come, thou south; blow upon my garden, that the spices thereof might flow out:" the meaning is, Let the Spirit breathe in the ordinances, and quicken up the saints, and then they will be lively, active, and fragrant as spicery. The Spirit rested upon Christ, Isa. xi. and he was quick in understanding, and quick in operation; Acts x. 38, he was anointed with the Holy Ghost, and with power, and went about doing good. The Spirit made him lively: and so it is the work of the Spirit that makes the saints lively and active; it is the Spirit that leads unto life.

ζωοποιεῖ.

Obs. 8. It is the Spirit of God that worketh all in all things; the Spirit is in the wheels, and works in them and by them. We speak not now of the choice operations of the Spirit in the elect, but the common operations of the Spirit in all creatures. There are admirable qualities, instincts, and excellent operations in plants, birds, and beasts: whatever they are, it is the Spirit that wrought them there; the Spirit is in the wheels. The instincts in the bees and birds to build so curiously; in the locusts, to go out by bands; in the ants, to gather their meat in summer; in the conies, to make their houses in the rocks; in the spider, to weave so fine a web, is put in by the Spirit of God. 1 Sam. x. 6, "The Spirit of the Lord will come upon thee, and thou shalt prophesy, and be turned into another man;" that is, thou shalt have gifts fit for government; the Spirit will instruct and enable thee to rule this people.

The consideration of this point should be a stay to our spirits; which way soever the wheels move, the Spirit of God is in them. When we look abroad, behold the cross and confused motions of the world, our hearts repine, murmur, sink in us, shift, and we are ready to start aside out of our places to unwarrantable practices; but let us remember the Spirit of God is in the wheels, and stirs them at its own pleasure. If Shimei curse, David sees God in that motion, and saith, Let him alone, God hath bid him. So Job, when all was taken away by the Chaldeans and Sabeans, he was so far from impatience, that he falls to praising and blessing God. There is no just ground of impatience in the world; it is the Spirit in the wheels which moves them.

It should also help our faith, because in all the designs of men, the motions of the wheels, God hath his design going on: the Spirit is in the wheels, which is an invisible, but a strong agent, and doth invisible work, carry on the Lord's design, however the motions of the wheels seem to us; let the wheel be entangled, run, stand still, or move contrary ways, yet God's work goes on, and our faith should get up.

Ver. 22—25. *And the likeness of the firmament upon the heads of the living creature was as the colour of the terrible crystal, stretched forth over their heads above. And under the firmament were their wings straight, the one toward the other: every one had two, which covered on this side, and every one had two, which covered on that side, their bodies. And when they went, I heard the noise of their wings, like the noise of great waters, as the voice of the Almighty, the voice of speech, as the noise of an host: when they stood, they let down their wings. And there was a voice from the firmament, that was over their heads when they stood, and had let down their wings.*

In these verses we have the fourth vision, or fourth part of the general vision, which is concerning the firmament. This vision, as formerly hath been shown, holds forth unto us the glory of God: and of that glory which lies in his providence and government of the world, we have spoken in the precedent parts of this vision. There is yet more and higher glory to be spoken of, and that is, the glory of God in the person of Christ. This vision of the firmament is preparatory to the vision of Christ upon the throne. It is described,

1. From the place of it: it was "upon the heads of the living creature."

2. From the colour: it was like crystal, and "terrible crystal."

3. From the noise which came thence, ver. 25.

In the 23rd and 24th verses, we have a renewed and intermixed description of the living creatures, from their wings, the situation, the number, the office, and noise of them.

To begin with the firmament. The hebrew word is *rachiah*, from a word which signifies to draw out and make thin, as metals are, and wool, to stretch out, as curtains and tents are, Isa. xl. 22: whence heaven is called *expansum*, because it is stretched out over the whole earth. The Greeks call it στερέωμα, because of the firmness and permanency: hereupon we call it the firmament, not from the hardness or solidity, as if it were like iron, or stone, but from the firmness of it, that it hath endured many thousand years, and is not melted by its motion, nor at all changed. It is taken sometimes for the air, sometimes for the clouds, and sometimes for heaven itself; and so we may take it here, even the starry firmament.

רקיע distendere, expandere.

This firmament was over the heads of the living creatures, the wheels and angels were under it; and it was between the Lord Christ and these creatures, and did the office of that pair of wings which did cover the faces of the seraphims in Isa. vi. 2. Great was the glory of Christ, and through this veil of the firmament presented to them.

"The colour and likeness of it was as the terrible crystal." We must a little explain these words. It was the likeness of the firmament, not the firmament itself. The Hebrew words run thus, the ice, the terrible, or the terrible ice, קרח is ice, water hardened by cold, whence crystal hath its birth; for, though ice be not crystal, yet crystal is from ice. When ice is hardened into the nature of a stone, it becomes crystal: more degrees of coldness, hardness, and clearness, give ice the denomination of crystal; and the name crystal imports so much, that is, water by cold contracted into ice; and Pliny saith, the birth of it is from ice vehemently frozen: and so you see the original of crystal.

הקרח הנורא

ακρώος καὶ στέλλομαι, quasi ἀπὸ τȣ͂ κρύȣς στελλόμενον ὕδωρ.

Nat. Hist. l. 37. c. 2.

The epithet here added, "terrible," hath some difficulty in it. That heaven, a visional firmament, should be terrible, seems strange. Terribleness ariseth from newness, greatness, or the glory of a thing. Things new and strange do cause fear: as when the earth opened, and swallowed up Corah, Dathan, and Abiram, there was great fear, it was a terrible thing; and this is called a new thing, Numb. xvi. 30, "If the Lord make a new thing:" so when new sights are seen in the heavens, they cause astonishment to the beholders; as comets, the standing of the sun, and the like.

2. Things great are dreadful; great waters, great mountains, great armies. Deut. i. 19, he calls the wilderness a "great and terrible wilderness." Joel ii. 11, "The day of the Lord is great and terrible:" and so, "the Lord great and terrible," Nehem. iv. 14. From the greatness of it, therefore, might this crystal be terrible.

3. The glory of it, that might make it terrible; for glorious things are so. Lightning is glorious and dreadful. When God's glory appeared in the mount, it was terrible unto Moses, and made him to quake, Heb. xii. 21. At Paul's conversion there was a glorious light, which struck fear into all that were with him, Acts ix. And this crystalline firmament was full of glory. Crystal is a clear thing, receives the light, so as to affect the eyes much: in like manner this firmament had a great clearness and transparency, being the footstool of Christ sitting upon the throne. The Septuagint sometimes translate the Hebrew word for terrible, "glorious;" Deut. x. 21, "Who hath done for thee these great and terrible things;" great and glorious things, say they: so Isa. lxiv. 3, "Thou didst terrible things;" they render it, glorious things; for they are terrible. And here, from the gloriousness of this crystal or crystalline visional firmament, it may be called terrible; and this I conceive to be the true cause of its terribleness; it was so glorious, that none could behold it without being dazzled, astonished, and put into a trembling.

Suppendaneum Christi sedentis in throno. ἔνδοξον.

Tam vehementer nitebat ut formidinem aspicienti afferret. *Pol.* Divinitatem quandam præ se ferebat. *Mald.*

Obs. 1. That all creatures are under Christ, even angels themselves. They and the wheels are under the firmament where Christ is; he walks above; his feet are where creatures' heads are: all are subject to the power of Christ, and he sits above, and he rules them, and overrules their actions. Angels and all wheels stoop to him. The prophet saw the wheel on the earth, the angels under the firmament, but Christ was above. 1 Cor. xv. 27, "All things are put under him," all angels, all men, and all devils. "God hath highly exalted him, and given him a name which is above every name," Phil. ii. 9.

Obs. 2. That heavenly things are pure and glorious, and hold forth the glory of God; they have the clearness, splendour, and lively colour of the crystal. The higher we ascend, the more purity, beauty, and glory. There is more in the air than in the earth and waters; more in the sun, more in the stars and firmament, than in the inferior things. God's glory is every where, the earth is full of it; if we look downwards we may see it, but if we look upwards we shall see more excellency and glory. How much glory is in the sun! who can tell how many wonderful things it hath in it? And so the firmament; Psal. xix. 1, "The heavens declare the glory of God, and the firmament showeth his handywork." The outspread firmament, that is so vast, so transparent, so beset with stars, that darts down such sweet influences, it holds forth God's glory exceedingly; the glory of his wisdom, power, goodness; there is much of God's glory seen in it. The sky, or firmament, is compared to a looking-glass, Job xxxvii. 18; not because you may see several species of things, as we see several faces in the water, and birds in the air; but chiefly, because in it we see so much of the glory of God, even most of his attributes. We should be oft looking in this glass, and observe the glory of God.

Rev. xxii. 1.

Obs. 3. That the things above are dreadfully glorious, so glorious, that our weak eyes cannot behold them. The glory of the firmament was as the terrible crystal, such as caused dread in a prophet. What eye can look upon the sun in its glory and strength? Could we see an angel in his glory, it would terribly affright us. When angels veiled up their glory in human shapes, it made great worthies of God to quake; as Gideon, Judg. vi. Manoah, chap. xiii. and others. Glorious objects work strongly upon our spirits, and quickly scatter them. And if the glory of creatures be such, what is the glory of God himself? 1 Tim. vi. 16, God "dwells in the light, which no man can approach unto:" it is such exceeding glorious light, that no created eye can endure it: that light or glory is God's habitation, and so glorious a one it is, that we cannot look upon it. Paul could not behold that glorious light which shined about him, Acts xxii. 11. The earth, heavens, and world, which are God's out-house, we may behold; but his glory, which is himself, his inmost room, we may not, we cannot eye. This light is darkness unto us; there is so much brightness in it, that it will put out our eyes: and whether this glory be accessible by the saints or angels, may be disputable; because God is invisible, and his glory inaccessible; and besides, the angels, they had wings to cover their faces, Isa. vi. And here they are presented to Ezekiel under the firmament, with that upon their heads; which shows, that they, and all creatures, are distanced from God, and capable of seeing his glory only in that way he thinks good to propound it. That in Matt. xviii. 10, seems to speak the contrary, where it is said, "That in heaven their angels do always behold the face of my Father." It is true, they are in the special presence of God, have sweet and satisfactory communion with God, stand ready to do his will; but God hath no face in heaven, and whether they see his essential glory, I leave to further inquiry.

Incutians sacrum quendam honorem.

Sensibile excellens destruit sensorium.

Obs. 4. That all things here below are exposed to the eye and view of Christ. The firmament is so clear that Christ sees through it. It is the window of heaven, and through it he looks into the world. It is a molten looking-glass, Job xxxvii. 18; and as we may see God's attributes and glory in it, so Christ sees our shapes, thoughts, distempers, and motions. He saw Saul when he got the letters to Damascus, to persecute the saints; the Lord Christ saw him, and knew the bloodiness of his mind, and said unto him, "Saul, Saul," Acts ix. Many are atheistical, and say in their hearts, as he in Job xxii. 13, "How doth God know? can he judge through the dark cloud?" They do evil in the dark, and say, "Who seeth us? and who knoweth us?" Isa. xxix. 15. There is one in the heavens that seeth through the clouds, and darkness itself, they are as the sun and firmament to him; darkness is no darkness, the firmament is as light itself: all things done in armies, councils, markets, shops, families, closets, beds, hearts, "are naked and open to the eyes of Him with whom we have to do," Heb. iv. 13.

I come now to ver. 23, where the glory of Christ is set out from his ministers, or officers; and they are the living creatures.

Ver. 23. *And under the firmament were their wings straight, the one toward the other: every one had two, which covered on this side, and every one had two, which covered on that side, their bodies.*

I have spoken before of the wings, yet somewhat I shall add. Four wings they had, and more we may not give them, though it may seem in this verse they had more: for it is said, "their wings were straight," that is, stretched out; and then, that they had two on this side, and two on that side; but the meaning is, when they did fly, those wings that did cover upward were stretched out, and the other did still cover their bodies or feet.

The scope of the verse is, to show that the ministry of the angels doth refer to and set out the glory of Christ; and that may be seen in the observations to be given.

Obs. 1. That where Christ is, there the angels are near unto him. He was above the firmament, and they just under it; the firmament was upon their heads; there was only a glorious transparent firmament between Christ and them: distanced from Christ they are, but not far.

Obs. 2. The angels, wise, strong, serviceable, swift, and glorious creatures, attend Christ's throne, and are subject unto him; they were under the firmament about his throne. Is it not for the honour and great glory of a king, to have nobles, potentates, and princes under him, attending in his court? It was much for Ahasuerus's glory and honour, when he had the nobles and princes of the provinces before him, and under him, Esth. i. 3. And so it is much for the honour of Christ, that he hath angels, which are greater than the kings of the earth, attending him.

Obs. 3. They are ready to exercise the will and pleasure of Christ. This further advances the honour of Christ: their wings were stretched out, and they willing to move in any service, if their Lord gave out the word. When the centurion's servants were so willing to go and come at his bidding, it made much for his honour, Matt. viii. 9. Ready, cheerly, active servants are an ease and honour to their masters: unreadiness and unwillingness in inferiors, do disparage authority, and stain the glory of it. Angels that serve at Christ's throne are never unready or unwilling for any service.

Obs. 4. They are unanimous in their ministrations. They fall not out by the way, their wings are straight the one towards the other; they carry on the work put into their hands with love, sweet agreement, peace, and content. At the birth of Christ they sung all one song, and sung without division, "Glory to God on high, on earth peace, good will towards men:" as they sung, so they act, there is no disagreement amongst them. "Can two walk together, except they be agreed?" Angels do fly together, and act together; they are so agreed, that no devil, no creature can divide them; they have all but one mind, and serve the Lord Christ with one consent: and what honour is this to Christ, that hath so great, so many servants, and all minding the same thing!

Obs. 5. They reverence the greatness and majesty of Christ. Though they be high and glorious, yet they see so vast a distance between Christ and themselves, that they cover their faces, Isa. vi. and their bodies, here; they come not into his presence rudely, but with great respect and reverence. As God is to be had in reverence of all that are about him, Psal. lxxxix. 7, so Christ is reverenced by all the angels that are about him. Women are to be veiled in the assemblies, because of the angels, 1 Cor. xi. 10, to show their reverence and subjection to them being present; and angels are covered, to show their reverence and subjection unto Christ. It is an honour to the angels, that in reverence to them the women are to be veiled; and it is a great honour to Christ, that angels reverence and adore him.

Obs. 6. They are careful to prevent all offence in their ministrations, either of God or man, of Christ or any creature. They cover up their bodies, their feet, that nothing improper may be seen and give distaste; nothing excellent be seen, and draw to an overvaluing and idolizing of them; so wise and cautious they are. And this adds much to the glory of Christ, that his servants the angels never give advantage to men or devils to reproach their Lord and Master. Alas, how much doth Christ suffer by us, even by ministers and others, in their ministrations! Men see our weakness, our pride, our vain-glory, miscarriages many ways, and rejoice in our flesh, even when Christ is reproached. But angels pass through all their employments, so that they are blameless, and Christ made beautiful, whom they serve.

Obs. 7. That angels are furnished for their ministrations; they have wings to fly, and wings to cover their bodies; whatever may make them and their services acceptable, speedy, successful, they have it. And this is for the honour of Christ: those he employs in his work he enables and accommodates, they go not forth empty, unqualified: he sent apostles, and filled them with his Spirit; he gives gifts to men, and wings to angels.

Ver. 24. *And when they went, I heard the noise of their wings, like the noise of great waters, as the voice of the Almighty, the voice of speech, as the noise of an host: when they stood, they let down their wings.*

Here is a further description of the angels, by their going, their noise, their standing, and letting down their wings. The principal is the noise of their wings; and that I shall make most inquiry into. A difficulty encounters us in the beginning of the verse, "when they went, I heard the noise of their wings;" rather when they did fly was the noise of their wings, than when they went. The original will help us something in this strait; it is otherwise there: thus the words are read, And I heard the noise of their wings, like the noise of great waters, as the voice of the Almighty when they went; so that there the original brings it in, and so we may take it, thus;

The noise of their flying was as the noise of great waters, and the noise of their going as the voice of the Almighty; or, rather thus: by going we may understand their motion, the execution of their office; and that made a great noise, which is amplified and set out by divers similitudes.

The first similitude is of "great waters." Waters that run among the stony and rocky mountains, make a terrible noise, gulling into the earth, and threatening the foundations of the mountains: hence, Job xiv. 19, the waters are said to wear the stones; they eat into them, making concaves and chambers therein: and for their noise, in Psal. xlvi. 3, there it is no gentle murmuring, but a roaring: the sea roars, so that it is heard in some places many miles.

The second similitude is, "as the voice of the Almighty," or, the voice of God. Some understand hereby, a great voice, because it is the usual dialect of the Hebrew tongue, to express great things, by saying, they are things of God: as, cedars of God, for tall and great ones, Psal. lxxx. 10, 11; rivers of God, for great rivers, and full of waters, Psal. lxv. 9; mountains of God, for high ones, Psal. xxxvi. 6; so a trembling of God, 1 Sam. xiv. 15, for a very great trembling: and in like propriety of speech, "the voice of the Almighty," for a great voice. Some truth in this may be granted, but somewhat more than a great voice in general is to be looked at, it being a vision, and hieroglyphical things presented to the prophet therein: we must therefore refer it to that in Psal. xxix. even the thunder, which is called the voice of the Lord: ver. 4, 5, "The voice of the Lord is powerful; the voice of the Lord is full of majesty: it breaks the cedars, yea, the cedars of Lebanon;" and so to that, Psal. xviii. 13.

Psal. xviii. 13.

The third similitude is, "the voice of speech." Some mystery lies in this, that their noise should be like an articulate voice, the speech of man. And two things may be intended in it; either the speech of man that is upon some terrible design, and so speaks grievous words, even words of death; and so it holds analogy with the other similitude of waters, and of thunder. Or else, by "voice of speech," the noise of their wings, the judgments they executed did speak and proclaim God's commands, his wrath, and the people's sins. If the judgments seemed terrible, as they were indeed; the cutting down of a kingdom, the ruin of the chiefest city and people in the world; the voice of speech was, God commands, God is angry; you are guilty, and we must proceed.

The fourth and last similitude is, "as the noise of an host." This is a dreadful noise; there is beating of drums, sound of trumpets, clattering of armour, jumping of chariots, rattling of wheels, neighing, stamping, prancing, and rushing of horses, the roaring of cannons, the clamours of men wounded, groans of men dying. "Carry me out of the host, for I am wounded," saith Ahab. O the doleful complaints that are there! such as would astonish a man of spirit to hear. The noise of the angels was such a noise.

Obs. 1. That the judgments of God executed upon kingdoms, cities, persons, are very dreadful: they are like roarings of the sea, when great storms are, and mighty navies are dashed in pieces, and sunk into the deeps; they are formidable as the noise of an army, marching or fighting. How dreadful were the plagues of Egypt! That in Exod. ix. 23, 24, when hail, thunder, and fire were mingled together, was very grievous, such as never was. The burning of Sodom was dreadful; yet Jerusalem's judgment was sorer, Lam. iv. 6. All their pleasant things were spoiled; women and maids ravished in the streets; their mighty men trodden under feet; young men and virgins crushed, trodden down as grapes in the wine-press; priests and elders died for famine; children swooned in the streets, poured out their souls in their mothers' bosoms for want of bread and water; pitiful women sod their children of a span long, and made meals of them; they were slain in the sanctuary, terrors were round about, and no way to escape left; if they looked for comfort, there was none to give it; princes were hanged up by the hands, those did wear scarlet, embraced dunghills; sabbaths, sanctuary, law, vision, all failed; prevailing fire was in their bones; death they longed for, and found it not; God was against them; their enemies prospered, and mocked at them and their sabbaths, Where is your God? what is become of all your worship, sacrifice, prayers, fastings? they clapped their hands, hissed, wagged their heads, and said of Jerusalem, Is this the perfection of beauty, the joy of the whole earth? this is the day that we looked for. These expressions you have in the book of Lamentations. David, a king, a prophet, a man of a warlike spirit, that feared not the bear, the lion, Goliath, saith, "My flesh trembleth for fear of thee; I am afraid of thy judgments," Psal. cxix. 120. When other things did not daunt him at all, God's judgments did; there was daunting terror in them; and no marvel, there is wrath in them; such rage, wrath, fury, as is in wild beasts: Hos. v. 14, "I will be unto Ephraim as a lion, and as a young lion to the house of Judah: I, even I, will tear and go away; I will take away, and none shall rescue." Such terror as is in an earthquake, that shakes the foundations of all, Isa. xxix. 6; such as in a strong wind, and an overflowing shower, Ezek. xiii. 13; such as in a flail that beats out the corn, and breaks the straw in pieces, Hab. iii. 12; such as in the sea or earth swallowing up, Psal. xxi. 9. What a dreadful cry, when Korah and his company sunk alive into the earth, when Pharaoh and his host were overwhelmed in the sea! Such terror is in God's judgments; yea, more dreadful yet, such as in thunder, lightning, and devouring fire, Isa. xxix. 6; yea, such as is in fire and brimstone, Psal. xi. 6. God is *Baal-chemah*, Nahum i. 2, A Lord of wrath, so the original is, a possessor of wrath; and in his judgments doth distribute terrors and sorrows: him therefore should the sons of men reverence.

בעל חמה

Obs. 2. God's judgments have the voice of speech in them, they speak unto sinners. Mic. vi. 9, "The Lord's voice crieth unto the city, and the man of wisdom shall see thy name: hear ye the rod, and who hath appointed it." If the first voice be the cry of the prophets and ministers, the second is the cry of the judgments of God. The rod speaks aloud; it proclaims God's anger, wrath, fury, jealousy, revenge, his omniscience, holiness, justice, the terror of the Almighty; it proclaims our folly, shame and ingratitude, treachery and great guiltiness before God. It cries to us for repentance: when destruction lay at the gates of Nineveh, they understood the language thereof, and repented in dust and ashes, Jonah iii. It cries to us for righteousness: "When God's judgments are in the earth, the inhabitants of the world will learn righteousness," Isa. xxvi. 9. They cannot learn unless they be taught. And do they not teach, and teach many lessons to fear God, whom men have forgotten in their prosperity; to make restitution to men whom they have wronged in the day of their wills; to be charitable in censuring others, and rigid in censuring themselves?

Obs. 3. Angels are not only swift, but efficacious in their motions and administrations. The great waters, mighty thunders, and numerous armies make way before them, and nothing can withstand their force: and so it is with angels when they are upon service, none can stand before them; they destroy armies, shake kingdoms, move all the wheels in the quarters of the world, and their motions are not faint, but forcible.

Obs. 4. It is not every ear that hears the noise of angels' wings; though their noise be great, efficacious, like waters, thunder, the voice of speech, as an host, yet all hear them not. It is the prophet hears them, and such as have divine spirits. The operations of angels are unperceivable to most of the world. All eyes see not visions, neither do all ears hear the things that visions do speak: few are capable of divine mysteries; "To you it is given to know the mysteries of the kingdom," Matt. xiii. 11. There be mysteries in the government of the world, as well as in the kingdom of heaven, and it is a special gift to be acquainted with them. God's secrets are made known to them that fear him, Psa. xxv. 14. Some choice, precious, excellent spirits, they hear, they see what others do not. Such as turn from iniquity, Dan. ix. 13; such as are wise, Hos. xiv. 9, they understand: such as are deeply interested in the truth and church's cause, as have suffered much, and have their dross purged out by the fire of afflictions; they hear, they see more and greater things than the men of the world. Nehemiah, Isaiah, Daniel, Ezekiel, John, that were men of great sufferings, they heard voices which others heard not. In the Revelation it is said oft, "He that hath an ear to hear, let him hear." Every man hath an outward ear, but not the inward, the ear of the heart, whereby to perceive the meaning of the Spirit. Men hear not the voice of the Spirit in the churches; they hear men, but not the Spirit, what that speaks in the ordinances; and as they hear it not in them, so they hear not the Spirit in the wheels, nor the voice of it in the great judgments of God.

Ver. 25. *And there was a voice from the firmament that was over their heads, when they stood, and had let down their wings.*

Here we have a description of the firmament, from the noise that came from it; and that is the cause of the angels making their appearance before the Lord; and the manner of their appearance is, they stood with their wings let down.

Whose voice this was comes now into question. It was not a voice of the firmament, but from above, which is in the original, besides from the firmament: so that it was not the noise or voice of the firmament, neither of any angel; for they are here present under the firmament; but it was the voice of Christ, of him that was above upon the throne; and it hath much in it.

מעל לרקיע De-super firmamenta.

1. It sets out the majesty and state of Christ, who, like a mighty emperor, sits upon his throne, and speaks unto his nobles and people at a distance.

2. His authority, calling in the angels, his great agents in the world, from their services, to appear before him. They upon this voice come from the quarters of the world, and stand about his throne, to give account of their administrations, to receive new instructions, and are sent out by him to great services.

3. To awaken, quicken, and prepare the prophet, who had hard things to meet with, harsh people to deal with; but when he saw angels come and go at the voice of Christ, it hushed all objections, and set his spirit to attend to the voice of Christ, to receive instructions from him, and to do his will. Thought he, shall those glorious angels, those great agents in the world, hearken to Christ, be informed by him, execute his will; and shall I, a poor captive, dispute the case with him? No, I will be like to these angels, hear, receive, and obey.

Of the standing of the angels I have spoken formerly in the 21st verse, to which I refer you.

The letting down their wings, notes their cessation from employment; as birds or fowls, when they fall upon their feet on trees or ground, let down their wings, and rest from flying.

Obs. 1. The voice of Christ is mighty and efficacious, a voice that shook the firmament, that commanded the angels; there is majesty, authority, efficacy in it. Rev. i. 15, it is said to be "as the sound of many waters," which notes the terribleness and efficaciousness of it, being strong, piercing, powerful as water, that breaks into the great ships, and eats into the hard rocks, and makes a dreadful noise. What an efficacy and majesty was in that voice of Christ, Acts ix. 4, "Saul, Saul, why persecutest thou me?" it struck Saul (who was a stout and stiff Pharisee) to the ground: so that in Matt. xxii. 12, "Friend, how camest thou in hither not having a wedding garment? And he was speechless." When Christ spake these few words, "I am he, they went backward, and fell to the ground," John xviii. 6: three words overthrew a great multitude; and it is observable they went backward and fell. The majesty and power of Christ's speech was such, as if stricken with thunder and lightning in their faces, they fell backward. When he rebuked the winds and seas, those fierce and senseless creatures heard his voice and obeyed it. When he preached, his hearers said, he spake with authority, and not as the Scribes and Pharisees. There is a mighty operation in the voice of Christ; it enters into the heart of the wicked, into the graves, and makes the dead to hear. "Now is the hour," saith Christ, "that the dead shall hear the voice of the Son of God," John v. 25: he means the dead in sins. Ver. 28, "The hour is coming, in which all that are in the graves shall hear his voice." His voice was so powerful, it fetched Lazarus out of the earth, John xi. "There is power in the word of a king," Eccles. viii. 4. Christ is the greatest King, and in his word is the greatest power, power over the living and dead. Hence the word of Christ is compared to piercing and efficacious things; to "goads and nails fastened," Eccl. xii. 11; to "a hammer and fire," Jer. xxiii. 29; to "a burning fire," Jer. xx. 9; to "mighty weapons," 2 Cor. x. 4; to "arrows in the heart of kings," Psal. xlv. 5; to "a sword," Ephes. vi. 17; "a two-edged sword," Rev. i. 16; "sharper than a two-edged sword," Heb. iv. 12: it is also like to the voice of "a trumpet," Rev. i. 10, that awakened men at midnight, and summoned them to the battle.

Obs. 2. When we are out of business, in a quiet posture, then are we fittest to hear the voice of Christ. When they stood and had let down their wings, then was the voice from the firmament, then were they fit to hear *magnalia Christi*, the wonderful things of Christ, the oracles and commands of Christ. When our hands and hearts are filled, entangled with earthly employments, how unapt are we to spiritual things! and if our hearts be turbulent, stirred in passion, they are fitter to hear Satan's voice than Christ's. A sedate, quiet mind, free from passion, and all entanglements, is most capable of divine things. Eccl. ix. 17, the words of wise men are heard in quiet spirits, well-composed minds. When there are great winds and tempests, we hear not others speaking: when the wind blows in the soul, and there is a tempest, we cannot hear God speaking: Job iv. 16, "There was silence, and I heard a voice;" then God spake when the silence was; he delights in a calm and meek spirit, that is of great price with him, 1 Pet. iii. 4. When spirits are in such a frame, sequestered from the world, free from distempers, God loves to communicate himself to them. In the night oft God appeared unto our forefathers, because then they were in a manner out of the world, and had tranquillity in their bosoms. When John was in Patmos, he heard Christ's voice; when Ezekiel was by the river side, he saw heaven opened, and heard a voice from above: that in Cant. ii. 12, "The voice of the turtle is heard in our land:" it is observable, the turtle sings not in winter, when the winds and storms are, but when it is spring and summer, all quiet and serene, then her voice is heard; so Christ's voice is heard, when winter is over, when the tumults and stirs are laid.

Obs. 3. As his voice refers to Ezekiel, it affords this instruction; that there must be a voice from above, before we are fit to hear or do any service for God. There are no preparations or qualifications in men by virtue of man; Ezekiel himself is not fitted to preach the word unto this captive people, till he hear Christ's voice. Christ doth not only give the word to be preached, but prepares the organ to receive and communicate it. Preparatory works in man by man, are popish conceits: the chemists, by all their art and labour, cannot bring any material nearer gold than at the first; it differs specifically from gold, and so it doth when they leave it. Counterfeit gold is no gold. It is not man that can prepare himself for God and his service. "The preparations of the heart and answer of the tongue are of the Lord," Prov. xvi. 1. And Paul saith, we are not sufficient of ourselves to think a good thought, 2 Cor. iii. 5. You may hear Paul telling of his preparatory works, 1 Tim. i. 13, "I was a blasphemer, a persecutor, and injurious!" what preparations were these to grace an apostleship! Dead men have no preparation to life, or motion, and living men ofttimes are lifeless, unfit for divine mysteries and employments, till a voice from above prepare, quicken, and encourage them.

Ver. 26—28. *And above the firmament that was over their heads was the likeness of a throne, as the appearance of a sapphire stone: and upon the likeness of the throne was the likeness as the appearance of a man above upon it. And I saw as the colour of amber, as the appearance of fire round about within it, from the appearance of his loins even upward, and from the appearance of his loins even downward, I saw as it were the appearance of fire, and it had brightness round about. As the appearance of the bow that is in the cloud in the day of rain, so was the appearance of the brightness round about. This was the appearance of the likeness of the glory of the Lord. And when I saw it, I fell upon my face, and I heard a voice of one that spake.*

In these words we have the last and best part of the vision, being of Christ in his throne. In the 26th verse we have the throne described:

1. From the situation of it; it was "above the firmament."

2. From the colour or likeness of it; it was "a sapphire stone."

3. From the party in it; and that was one who had "the appearance of a man."

The word "throne" sometimes signifies kingdoms and dominions: Dan. vii. 9, "I beheld till the thrones were cast down;" that is, the kingdoms of the earth were ruined. Sometimes it notes a choice seat, fit for kings and judges to sit in: 1 Kings x. 18—20, "The king made a great throne of ivory, and overlaid it with the best gold;" there were six steps and twelve lions; and there was not the like in any kingdom. In this last sense we are here to take it, a seat for Christ to sit in: and so the temple or sanctuary is called the throne of God, Jer. xvii. 12, "A glorious high throne from the beginning is the place of our sanctuary." A throne here holds out unto us sundry things:

1. Divine majesty and highness of Christ.
2. Kingly dignity.
3. Triumphant glory.
4. Judiciary power: Psal. ix. 4, "Thou satest in the throne judging right." Kingly and judiciary power are chiefly meant: 2 Chron. xviii. 18, "I saw the Lord sitting upon his throne, and all the host of heaven standing on his right hand and on his left:" and Rev. xx. 11, 12, "I saw a great white throne, and him that sat on it:—and the dead, small and great, stood before God; and the books were opened." Here Christ sat in judgment over the Jews, and exercised his power, pronouncing sentence against them.

The next thing is the likeness; "as the appearance of a sapphire stone." The glory of this throne was great: Solomon's was of ivory and gold, but Christ's is of sapphire. The Scripture mentions palaces, Psal. xlv. 8, towers, Cant. vii. 4, beds, Amos vi. 4, houses, chap. iii. 15, vessels, Rev. xviii. 12, and thrones of ivory, 2 Chron. ix. 17; but none of sapphires. The sapphire is a stone of admirable worth and splendour, the chiefest of pearls; and Pererius saith, it was among the ancients always of great esteem; the empire and high priesthood were signified by it. Among the Egyptians, the chief priests, being judges, also wore a sapphire about their necks; and at that time when cardinals are newly created, the pope sends to each of them a sapphire, which sets out dignity and greatness.

Gemma gemmarum. *Abulens. Hieroglyph.* 41.

Ælianus.

Deorum munera et opima beneficia invitare conciliareque fertur, ut vel hinc Ecclesiasticis præsulibus omnium maxime dignam rude vulgus profiteatur. *Ruen. de Gemmis.*

For the colour of the stone. Pliny saith, in his lib. 37. c. 9. that it is of an airy colour: he should have said, of a sky or blue colour; for when the heavens are most clear, and have a transparent, pleasant blue, then the sapphire doth most resemble them; very fair and beautiful. Jerom will have sapphire to be from *saphar, pulcher*, because these stones are very fair and delightful. Pliny, in the place before cited, saith, they do flame and sparkle with purple veins, much like the colour of brimstone when it is first fired; there is a pleasant blue, with a little purple in it: and so oft it is in the heavens when they are clear. The sapphire, and heaven's clearness, are brought in together by Moses: Exod. xxiv. 10, "They saw the God of Israel; and there was under his feet as it were a paved work of a sapphire stone, and as it were the body of heaven in its clearness;" the pavement was sapphire, and the colour of it, as the clearness of heaven. We must inquire what the sapphire represents unto us; for surely there is something, yea, much in it. Should we tell you what virtue is given to this stone by men of great note, it would take up much time. Avicen, Albertus, and Mathiolus, affirm this stone to be good against melancholy, and the quartan ague. Galen and Dioscorides,

Cœlesti colore conspicui sunt. *Ruen. ibid.*

ספיר
Aureis punctis lucere.

that it helps against poisoning, ruptures, and exulcerations. But I will pass by such things, and come to that which is nearer our purpose. The sapphire is an emblem,

Symbolum libertatis. 1. Of liberty. So you shall find it to speak in Exod. xxiv. 10. The Israelites were come from their pavement of bricks to one of sapphire; now the God of Israel was exalting them to precious liberty from their vile bondage.

Puritatis et soliditatis. 2. Of purity and solidity. It hath the colour and clearness of heaven; it hath no impurity in it. Things impure are the ruin of themselves, and so are unsolid; but that which is pure is firm; as the firmament, it is pure and solid. Hence the sapphire is a foundation stone of the new and heavenly Jerusalem, Rev. xxi. 19. . .

Sublimitatis cœlestium mysteriorum. Sapphirum cœlestiale quid portendere significat ipsius color. *Sanct.* 3. Of the incomprehensibleness of divine mysteries. It hath a sky colour, the colour of the firmament itself: and that blueness we see in the heavens is intense light, and sets out the incomprehensibility of God's ways.

Castitatis, venereos compescit affectus. *Rivet.* 4. Of chastity. It is an enemy to wanton lusts: hence, Cant. v. 14, Christ's belly is said to be overlaid with sapphires: and his throne being sapphirine, it tells us, that Christ expects chastity in the spiritual marriage between him and his church.

Vigoris et letitiæ vultus eorum sapphirus. 5. Of vigour and cheerfulness. Lam. iv. 7, "Their polishing was of sapphire;" Their faces were sapphirine, so the Chaldee reads it. Their countenances before were full of vigour, cheerful, like those which are well polished; but now, through famine, black they were, withered, and like a stick, without all cheerfulness.

Gloriæ. 6. Of glory. And here in this vision, Christ's glory is likened to sapphire; the glory of his throne was sapphirine.

From the likeness of the throne, we come to the party, whose the throne is, and that is, one who had "the appearance of a man." Who this is, must be cleared. It was not God the Father, or God the Holy Ghost; for the learned observe, that neither the Father nor the Holy Ghost have ever appeared in man's shape: but that will not hold; for the Ancient of days, God the Father, appeared to Daniel, chap. vii. 9, in the form of a man. Expositors do mostly agree it was the Lord Christ: and of that judgment shall we be, not because they say so, this was a blind ground for a rational man to be led by, but because we find in Scripture, that Christ hath oft appeared in visions like unto man; Dan. vii. 13, "I saw in the night visions, and, behold, one like the Son of man." The Jews acknowledge this to be meant of Messiah. So in Rev. i. 13, one like the Son of man appeared in the midst of the seven candlesticks; and Rev. xiv. 14, "I looked, and behold a white cloud, and upon the cloud one sat like unto the Son of man." By these places we have good warrant to conceive, that it was Christ that did appear unto Ezekiel in this vision.

Quest. But seeing Christ was not yet incarnate, why is he here presented in the likeness of man?

Answ. 1. Because in his divine nature he is invisible, and being to manifest himself, he appeared in the form of man, as being most suitable to the nature of man.

2. It was a prefiguration of his incarnation, that in the fulness of time his divine nature should assume our flesh into the unity of his person.

3. That according to his human nature, he should sit upon the throne of God, and judge the sons of men: he was the great Agent of his Father.

Whether Christ in this vision sat or stood, is doubted, because it is said, "above upon it," neither standing nor sitting being expressed; but my inclinations are to conceive, that the Lord Christ sat, and stood not.

1. Because thrones are not for standing, but sitting; and we never find in Scripture, that any stood in thrones, but sat they have. Sitting in thrones is the usual phrase in Scripture: 1 Kings ii. 12, "Solomon sat upon the throne of David his father;" and in chap. xxii. 10, "The king of Israel and the king of Judah sat each on his throne;" and Isa. vi. 1, Isaiah "saw the Lord sitting upon a throne;" Rev. iv. 10, "The twenty-four elders fall down before him that sat on the throne."

2. Kings and judges here on earth do not use to stand, but sit, which doth more fully set out their state and majesty; and if kings on earth do so, how much more this King in heaven! Besides, standing is a servant's posture, Deut. xvii. 12, and chap. x. 8; but sitting is not, Luke xvii. 7, 8; that is the master's, the lord's posture.

Obs. 1. The wisdom of God's Spirit in laying down things to prevent the corruptions and mistakes of man. We are apt to think grossly of the divine nature, that God is visible, corporeal, contained in place, sitting as man; but see how the Spirit of God here speaks, and takes off from all such conceits. Here is mention of likeness, appearance of things, not that they were materially so; it is the likeness of a throne, the appearance of a sapphire, and upon the likeness of the throne was the appearance of a man, no true body. The anthropomorphites thought God to be like unto us, to have his throne in heaven, and sit in it; and so far did these men proceed in this opinion, of God's corporeity and circumscription, that they assembled into troops, and threatened to stone all who opposed it: so tenacious of and violent for errors are men, even the deluded sons of men.

Obs. 2. That man is not capable of immediate access to and converse with God. Here are many steps and degrees before the prophet comes to see Christ, and then it is not in his divine nature, but in the appearance of a man. Here are the living creatures in the way, a firmament over their heads, and then a throne, and that of sapphirine colour; and afterward a sight of Christ in the form of a man, and then converse. If the Lord should not condescend to our weakness, and mantle up his majesty, there could be no communion between him and us.

Obs. 3. That the Lord Christ, who appeared like man, hath kingly majesty. Here is a throne, and a throne set before him. Thrones represent royal majesty unto us, and this throne representeth Christ's: when on earth he was in the form of a servant, but in heaven he appeared to the prophet in the form of a king. Neither hath he a throne only, but whatever appertains to kings. Unction he had, and such as other kings had not; he was anointed with the Holy Ghost, and with power, Acts x. 38. Promulgation; Zech. ix. 9, "O daughter of Jerusalem, behold thy King cometh unto thee." A crown; Heb. ii. 9, "We see Jesus, crowned with glory and honour:" the Jews crowned him with thorns, the Lord with glory. A sceptre he hath also, and better than of gold; Heb. i. 8, "A sceptre of righteousness is the sceptre of thy kingdom." A royal guard of angels; they are under the firmament, stand ready at his footstool. He hath his agents and ambassadors in the kingdom of the world, to declare his pleasure, to transact his appointments; Eph. iv. 11, "Apostles, prophets, evangelists, pastors, teachers;" these negociate the great affairs of this King, they dispense the mysteries of this kingdom. He is not a titular king, but hath large dominions: Dan. vii. 14, "There was given him dominion, and glory, and a kingdom, that all people, nations, and languages, should serve him;" and Psal. ii. 8, the heathen are his inheritance, and the ends of the earth his possession. He hath a legislative power, he makes and abrogates laws at his pleasure. He came of the princely tribe that made laws. Judah bare the sceptre, and gave the laws, and therefore by David is called the lawgiver, Psal. lx. 7; and Christ descending thence, and being typified by the king of Judah, he is the true Lawgiver; Jam. iv. 12, "There is one lawgiver," and therefore, Matt. xxviii. 20, "Teach them to observe all things whatsoever I have commanded you." He hath a pardoning and punishing power; he pardoned Mary Magdalene, and punished him that had not on his wedding garment.

Gen. xlix. 10.

Obs. 4. That Christ is not only King, but the chiefest of kings. His throne is not on earth, but in heaven; it is above the firmament; that was over angels' heads, and Christ's throne is above them both; so that all power in heaven and earth are under Christ; his throne is exalted above them all: Heb. i. 6, "Let all the angels of God worship him;" the greatest archangel must do it. Those thrones, for so they are termed, Col. i. 16, must stoop to this throne. Eph. i. 20—22, God hath "set Christ in heavenly places," among the heavenly thrones, yea, in supercelestial places; for it follows, he hath set him "far above all principality, and power, and might, and dominion, and every name that is named, not only in this world, but also in that which is to come: and hath put all things under his feet." Even angels are under the firmament, where his feet stand; and all the princes of the earth are under him, Rev. i. 5, he is "the Prince of the kings of the earth." The inscription on his vesture and thigh is "King of kings, and Lord of lords." This title is not Xerxes's, Nebuchadnezzar's, nor Alexander's, but Christ's alone. The kings of the world, when they sit upon their thrones, have their firmament over their heads, some cloth of state, made of the richest stuff that the skill of men can reach unto, bedecked with diamonds and pearls that are most costly; but this over their throne intimates their subjection to some higher power. But it is not so with Christ; he is above the firmament; nothing is over his head; angels, kings, devils, are under his feet, and unto him must every knee bow.

ἐν τοῖς ἐπουρανίοις. ἐν τοῖς ὑπερουρανίοις.

Obs. 5. That the Lord Christ, who hath such a glorious throne, is exceedingly glorious himself. His throne is like sapphires, of a sapphirine colour, which is very beautiful; it is like the glory of the heavens. If an earthly throne be a throne of glory, as Hannah styles it, 1 Sam. ii. 8, what is this throne! a resemblance of the throne of his glory, which he speaks of in Matt. xix. 28, and chap. xxv. 31. The clothing of the king's daughter, Psal. xlv. 13, was wrought gold, a glorious outside; but there was more glory within, she was "all glorious within:" so if Christ's throne, the outside of it, be so glorious, what is he in the throne! all glorious, all glory. John i. 14, "We beheld his glory, the glory as of the only begotten." If apostles saw glory in him, being on earth, in his low condition, what did our prophet see in him, being above the firmament, in his throne and glorious condition! The Scriptures set him out, not only to be glorious, but glory: Psal. xxiv. 8, "King of glory:" Jam. ii. 1, "Have not the faith of our Lord Jesus Christ, the Lord of glory, with respect of persons." The word Lord in the second place is not in the original, but thus it stands there, have not the faith of our Lord Jesus Christ, the glory; so that Christ is glory, and the glory; the glory of heaven, the glory of the world, the glory of Sion, the glory of the soul. And not only is Christ glorious and glory, but he is "the brightness of glory," Heb. i. 3; that is, spotless, perfect, intense, exceeding glory. He is the brightness of the glory of the Father, or the Father's glory shines out most brightly and intensely in the Son. The Father's glory in the whole creation is but darkness to his glory in Christ; and therefore he is brightness of glory, and every thing that comes from Christ hath some beams of glory in it. His works are called glorious; Luke xiii. 17, they "rejoiced for all the glorious things done by him:" the liberty he purchased is glorious liberty, Rom. viii. 21; his church is glorious, Eph. v. 27; his gospel is glorious, 1 Tim. i. 11.

τῆς δόξης.

ἀπαύγασμα τῆς δόξης.

Obs. 6. That Christ's throne must not be of common stone, but precious ones, of sapphires. The pavement of God was of stones or bricks of sapphire, Exod. xxiv. 10; and Christ's throne must be of sapphires. The church is Christ's throne, visible and conspicuous as the heavens, Jer. iii. 17. Jerusalem is called "the throne of the Lord;" and the churches under the gospel are the throne of Christ; he sits in the congregations, and bears rule in them: Rev. ii. 13, "I know where thou dwellest, where Satan's seat" or throne "is." There was a congregation of persecutors, idolaters, and unclean parties; for such sinners are mentioned in ver. 13, 14; and this company was the seat and throne of Satan. Many congregations are thrones of iniquity; and "shall the throne of iniquity have fellowship with thee?" Psal. xciv. 20; but godly congregations are the seat and throne of Christ. Now as the conscience, which is the invisible seat of Christ, must be pure, 1 Tim. iii. 9, "Holding the mystery of the faith in a pure conscience;" so must the visible seat of Christ be pure, the congregation where he will sit and reign. Therefore the promise is, Isa. liv. 11, 12, that the state of the church under the gospel shall be better than it was under the law. There all stones were laid in the building; but here should be a difference made; God will lay stones with fair colours, sapphires, agates, carbuncles, and precious stones. And that it is meant of gospel times and churches, the words following in the 13th verse show, "All thy children shall be taught of the Lord," which Christ applies to these times, John vi. 45. So then the churches now are to be of sapphires, such as have a heavenly virtue and purity in them; not of sand-stones, toad-stones, or any highway-stones; they are fitter to make Satan a seat than Christ a throne. They are called "lively stones," 1 Pet. ii. 5; not dead stones, that have no true grace in them, but lively ones they must be, that make a house, a throne for Christ: stones, that it may be a solid building; lively, that it may be a useful, profitable building; and sapphire, that it may be a pure and glorious building.

Obs. 7. Judiciary power is put into the hand of Christ, not only as God, but as man. There was the appearance of a man above upon the throne; there sat the Son of man, and sitting upon the throne imports power, and power judicial. Therefore when Christ tells his disciples of sitting upon the twelve thrones, he tells them also of judging the twelve tribes of Israel, Matt. xix. 28. And that Christ had such power, and that as Son of man, appears, John v. 27, The Father hath given the Son "authority to execute judgment, because he is the Son of man;" ver. 22, "he hath committed all judgment to the Son," both judgment of actions, things, and persons. God "will judge the world in

Acts xxiii. 3.

righteousness by that man he hath ordained," Acts xvii. 31: the last judgment shall be by Christ, even that great judgment. So particular judgments here; as now Christ sat in judgment upon Jerusalem, and sentenced them to death and captivity. And because judgment is *opus potestatis*, an act of power, therefore Christ himself tells us, that all power in heaven and earth is given unto him, Matt. xxviii. 18.

Obs. 8. The Lord Christ actually ruleth the world, and all things in it; he sits upon the throne, and exerciseth his power and authority. "Solomon sat upon the throne of David his father," 1 Kings ii. 12; that is, he ruled the kingdom, and all the affairs of it: so Christ sitting upon the throne, presents to us his active ruling. The prophet might see he held the globe of the world in his hand; that he raised tempests out of the north, sent abroad the four living creatures in the several parts of the world; that he orders the wheels, and causes them to stand or go at his pleasure. The Lord Christ is not out of office, or idle now in heaven, though he sits upon a throne of glory at his Father's right hand. He is not neglective of the world, he upholds it by his power, Heb. 1. 3, he sends out his angels to minister unto his, ver. 14; he still gives gifts to men, and provides for his church, Eph. iv., and makes the word the savour of life or death to men. He restrains the wrath of enemies, and hedges up their ways, he makes use of them as rods to drive his straggling sheep into the fold; he subdues hearts and spirits to himself, and protects them being subdued; he discovers and confounds the enemies' plots and persons.

Obs. 9. The Lord Christ doth govern all with great tranquillity and with great facility. He sits upon the throne, and doth all in a sedate temper; there is no passion or perturbation in him: he is a Lion for his power, and a Lamb for his meekness; he rules by counsel and wisdom in much quietness, he judgeth in righteousness, Acts xvii. 31, and what he doth is done without difficulty. Let him speak the word, and presently it is done. If he bids Nebuchadnezzar go and sack Jerusalem, and carry them away to Babylon, he goes, he accomplisheth his will fully.

Obs. 10. That Christ is ready ever to hear the causes and complaints of his church; he sits upon the throne. Other judges are of the bench and throne, and parties aggrieved may come unseasonably to them; but it is not so here: Christ sits upon the throne, and that constantly, to assure us, that he is always willing and ready to hear the motions his servants shall make, and to execute judgments upon their enemies; which is matter of great comfort to poor afflicted souls, that they may at any time find this Judge sitting, and open their grievances unto him, and have audience. Other judges are absent from their seats, or not at leisure; or stately, and will not give way to poor oppressed ones to ease themselves, and acquaint them with their suits: none of these things are to be feared here.

Obs. 11. Christ sitting on the throne shows to us, that Christ should accomplish the whole work of man's redemption, which the Father hath appointed him, and so sit down in glory upon the throne. He appeared as man in that nature, he did and suffered the will of God on earth, and in that nature he sat down at the right hand of God. Had not Christ been to fulfil all righteousness, he had not appeared as man sitting on the throne; and had he not done it, he should never have returned to heaven and sat down in glory. He hath satisfied the law, is freed from the guilt of our sins, and hath presently finished the work undertaken; and therefore told his Father, he had glorified him on earth, he had finished the work he had given him to do; and thereupon desired him to glorify him, and set him upon the throne, John xvii. 4, 5, which is done: and this may be of singular comfort against all our imperfections, corruptions, temptations, and death itself.

Ver. 27. ***And I saw as the colour of amber, as the appearance of fire round about within it, from the appearance of his loins even upward, and from the appearance of his loins even downward, I saw as it were the appearance of fire, and it had brightness round about.***

Here the man that sat upon the throne is described unto us: 1. In general. 2. More particularly.

1. In general; "I saw as the colour of amber."

2. Particularly, upwards and downwards. Upwards, "as the appearance of fire round about within it: from the appearance of his loins upward;" so that this fire was more latent. And then downwards the fire was more visible, and had brightness about it. Touching the word *hashmal*, or *chasmal*, I have spoken largely in the 4th verse; and it signifies a coal intensely hot, and, as it were, presently consuming whatever it touches: such coals are most fiery and lively; and they that render the word *color vividissimus*, a most lively colour, or as the colour of a burning coal, give the truest sense of the word. Before it referred to the angels, here to Christ. The word *chasmal* read backward, is *lammashach*, or *lammashiach*, which is interpreted, the Messiah; it is the Cabalist's observation, and the sum in general is this; "I saw as the colour of amber;" I saw Christ that sat upon the throne, all of an intense fiery colour, like the most hot burning coals. And so the Lord Christ is set forth, Rev. i. 14, 15, "His eyes were as a flame of fire, his feet like unto fine brass, as if they burned in a furnace;" so here, from head to feet, Christ is presented in a fiery colour. It is frequent in Scripture, when acts of power and judgment are to be executed against kingdoms or churches, to have Christ presented in a fiery way. So Rev. x. 1, the mighty Angel, Christ, is brought in there with his face shining as the sun, and his feet as pillars of fire; and presently there were great thunders, and dreadful things. So Rev. ii. 18, he is brought in with eyes like fire and feet like brass; and then tells Thyatira he hath a few things against her. So Rev. xix. 11—13, "In righteousness he doth judge and make war," and then his eyes were as a flame of fire, and his vesture dipt in blood. Thus is he described, when some great designs are afoot, as sentencing a church, warring against his enemies, &c.

Quasi חשמל festinanter consumens.

The particular description is next, which falls into further inquiry. From his loins upward, was as the appearance of fire within it. There is a difference between the fire in the upward parts of Christ, and that in his lower; the one is external, the other internal. Within it. Within what? Within the colour of the amber; or, according to the word as we have interpreted it, within that fire of burning hot coals, there was as the appearance of fire in the concave of it round about; so that there was a fire in a fire, a secret hidden fire burning inwardly: this fire doth not put forth its virtue so apparently as the other did, but burnt inwardly, and reflected upon itself. What this fire was, is our work to open unto you. By fire within, Gregory, in his seventh Homily, understands Christ before his incarnation, he was *ignis in Judea tantum*, a fire in Judea only; there only he shined, the gentiles knew him not; but after his incarnation he shined from his loins downward, and was made

Ignis latens, et igniens intrinsecus. *Sanct.*

known unto all. But by it we understand the divine nature of Christ, which being full of perfection, too bright for human eyes, was more inward and remote from sense; and it is likened unto fire in regard of the lustre and efficacy of it, which none can endure. By the burning hot coals, we may understand the burning zeal of Christ to the glory of God in executing judgment upon the wicked; and at this time he sat in judgment upon Jerusalem.

"From his loins downward, there was as the appearance of fire, and it had brightness round about it." This fire and brightness was more apparent, visible, and enlightening than the other, and it represents to us the great glory and majesty of the Lord Christ, as it is exhibitive to and comprehensive by creatures. It is the glory of human nature, which was the lower part of Christ, less glorious; the strength of the divine nature's glory shining through it, and giving out itself in that way and degree as man is capable of. The sun in a cloud may be beheld by the weakest eye; in itself, not by the strongest. The glory of both Christ's natures are shadowed out unto us in this verse.

"And it had brightness round about." That fire produced a brightness, and a brightness on every side. It sets out the glory of Christ in execution of justice upon those that are delinquents; or the glory of his presence and actions: he dwells in light, and all his actions are lightsome.

Obs. 1. That the Lord Christ, as man, is very glorious; he was here in the appearance of man, and the prophet saw him, having the colour of *chasmal*, that is, like unto the most burning and hottest coal or coals; not those in common fires, but those that are in a furnace, which glow and shine most. In his transfiguration, which was a prelude to his glorious condition in heaven, Christ's face shined as the sun, Matt. xvii. 2. What a glorious creature is the sun! and Christ's face as glorious as that is. In Dan. xii. 3, it is said, "The wise shall shine as the brightness of the firmament, and they that turn many to righteousness as the stars for ever;" but Christ as the sun, which is the great glory of the heavens: the godly may have firmament and star-brightness, but Christ sun-brightness; neither doth that reach the glory of Christ's human nature, it goes beyond it. Acts xxvi. 13, when Christ appeared to Paul at his conversion, what saith he? "I saw a light from heaven, above the brightness of the sun, shining round about me;" this was the light of the glory of Christ glorified, and it was beyond the brightness of the sun. The star that led the wise men to Christ, Ignatius thinks did exceed all the rest in light and brightness, that none ever was like it. Be it so, yet the glory of Christ's human nature is far above it; no creature is so glorious, as fully to represent the glory of it. Therefore saith the apostle, Phil. iii. 21, "He shall change our vile bodies, and make them like," not the stars or sun, that were too low, but like "his glorious body;" the original is, his body of glory; that is, his body which is exceeding glorious, above the glory of all creatures.

Dan. x. 6.

Rev. i. 16.

Epist. ad Eph.

Obs. 2. That the Lord Christ sitting upon the throne in judgment, is very dreadful; he is *ignis vividissimus*, the brightest fire, as hot burning coals. The prophet Malachi tells you of his coming, and when he comes "who may abide the day of his coming? and who shall stand when he appeareth? for he is like a refiner's fire; and he shall sit as a refiner and purifier of silver, chap. iii. 2, 3. A refiner's fire is the hottest, it melts, purges, consumes, and is terrible: such a fire is Christ in his judgments; Jerusalem could not stand before him, but he destroys them by the strength of Babylon, and afterward is terrible to Babylon itself: Jer. li. 25, "I am against thee, O destroying mountain," speaking of Babylon, "which destroyest all the earth; I will stretch out my hand upon thee, and roll thee down from the rocks, and will make thee a burnt mountain." This burning coal, Christ, will fire and burn down that great mountain; and what then? they shall not take of thee a stone for a corner, nor a stone for foundations, but thou shalt be desolate for ever. Severe was the spirit of Christ against Babylon in the letter, and as severe is he now against Babylon in the mystery: he shall "destroy them that destroy the earth," Rev. xi. 18. He makes "Jerusalem a burdensome stone" to all that meddle with it, Zech. xii. 3. There is mention made in our prophet, chap. xxviii. 14, of stones of fire: Christ is the stone of fire that breaks and burns the kingdoms of the earth. Many kingdoms in Europe are on fire at this day, and almost broken in pieces, and burnt to ashes. We may see that Christ is terrible in his judgments; he is riding now upon his red horse, taking peace from the earth, dipping his garments in blood, and causing his great sword to eat flesh and drink blood: he is upon his black horse, bringing in famine and pestilence: the pale horse is saddled, and death is on the back of him, and intends to ride through our cities, countries, towns, families, and make a great slaughter, Rev. vi. and will yet be more terrible; ver. 17, "The great day of his wrath is at hand, and who shall be able to stand?" Neither kings, great men, captains, mighty ones, nor any other sort can do it. They will call on rocks and mountains to fall upon them, and hide them from the face of him that sits on the throne, and from the wrath of the Lamb. His eyes sparkled with fire, his feet are like burning brass, and out of his mouth issue flames of fire. And to set out the dreadfulness of this Judge, Paul tells us, he shall come in flames of fire, 2 Thess. i. 8. And as his appearance, so his name will be dreadful, for he hath an unknown name belongs to him in his way of ruling and judgment, Rev. xix. 12; and this will be known when he sets up his kingdom among the Jews, saith Brightman.

Obs. 3. That he is zealous in sentencing and punishing malefactors. He is *pruna summe ignita*, a coal brightly burning; and not only so, but here is a fire within, zeal in his breast, a spirit of burning within. You may see the zeal of Christ in John ii. 14—17. The temple being a type of Christ, and by divine appointment set apart for worship, should not have been made a place for merchandise; but Christ coming and finding in the temple those that sold oxen, sheep, doves, and changers of money, sitting, made a scourge of small cords, and whipped them out of the temple like a company of rogues; drove out the sheep and oxen, poured out the changers' money, overthrew the tables, bid them take away their doves, and not make his Father's house a house of merchandise. They might have said, All these are brought for sacrificing, for public service and the worship of God; and what! dost thou pretend God's glory, and take away his sacrifice? we will whip thee out of the temple, and use thee as an enemy to God and his worship. And it was a wonder they did not, Christ being a poor man, having no countenance from the rulers, and meddling with rude fellows, and dealing with them so sharply and shamefully as to whip them out; it was wonder they tore him not in pieces, or stoned him to death for it. Christ's zeal was hot, and carried him on to punish and disgrace those delinquents, not fearing their rage or malice, so God's glory might be repaired. This zeal in Christ was so intense that it warmed the hearts of his disciples, who upon it remembered what was written of him, "The zeal of thine house hath eaten me up." How zealous was Christ in his carriage towards the Asian churches! He tells Ephesus, that except she repent, recover her first love, and do her first works, he will come quickly, remove her candlestick out of its place, and unchurch her, Rev. ii. 5. To Pergamus also he saith, "Repent; for I come quickly, and will fight against thee with the sword of my mouth," ver. 16. So for Thyatira, wherein Jezebel lived and did much hurt, "Behold," saith Christ, "I will cast her into a bed, and them that commit adultery with her into great tribulation, except they repent of their deeds: and I will kill her children with death," &c. ver. 22, 23. So for Laodicea, how zealous is Christ against that zealless church! "I know thou art neither cold nor hot: I would thou wert cold or hot. So then because thou art lukewarm, I will spue thee out of my mouth," chap. iii. 15, 16. His proceeding with the churches answers his appearance to John in the vision, which was with eyes as a flame of fire, and feet like burning brass, chap. i. 14, 15.

Obs. 4. That the divine nature of Christ is too glorious for man's eyes to behold; and therefore is presented here more remote and hidden from the prophet's sight. There was the appearance of fire in the colour of amber, or within the outward fire; this was glorious, that exceeding glorious, the fire in the fire: here is infinite glory shut up, obscured by that which is less glorious. You heard before of Christ's human nature, that it is very glorious; much more the divine that communicates the lustre and glory to the human: 2 Pet. i. 17, "A voice came from the excellent glory, glory that excelled all the glory of the creature, that excelled all the apprehensions of creatures; from the glory greatly becoming, or great becoming glory: it is glory that greatly becomes the great God. And such is the glory of the divine nature of Christ, it is excellent glory; and if it were let out a little, in the strength and fulness of it, we should be sunk by it: for glory is a weighty thing; the Hebrew word for glory signifies *gravitas, pondus, onus*, heaviness, weight, burden; intimating that glory, as it is a bright, so a heavy thing; brightness and weightiness are in it; 2 Cor. iv. 17, it is called a weight of glory, and the glory of Christ's divine nature would oppress us, if fully opened to our view. Moses made a request to God, which if he had granted, would have been his death: Exod. xxxiii. 18, "I beseech thee," saith he, "show me thy glory." God tells him in the 20th verse, "No man can see me and live," my glory will be a consuming fire unto thee; yet God is pleased to communicate the glory of his divine nature here to Moses in that way which might do him good, and not destroy him: he puts him into the cleft of a rock, and shows him his back parts, ver. 23, which was some glorious body, as Tostatus thinks; some human shape, as others conceive: and not unlikely to be Christ, as he appeared in his transfiguration, full of glory and majesty. Thus God condescended to Moses, and so here to the prophet; he sees the glory of the divine nature in the human, which in itself is not subject to man's sense, but through divine dispensation is made visible according to man's capacity. If we cannot behold the sun for its brightness, nor one creature behold another; without prejudice to itself; how can we behold the exceeding glory of the Creator, of the divine nature, without great danger, without death? The glory of such majesty would turn us into nothing.

ὑπό τῆς μεγαλοπρεποῦς δόξης.

כבוד

βάρος δόξης.

Oleaster. Osiander.

Non cadit sub sensum corporis.

Juxta possibilitatem humanam.

Fulgor ille tantæ majestatis nos in nihilum redigerer.

Obs. 5. That Christ's actions, even judiciary ones, are glorious. There was brightness round about his presence, sitting in judgment; and his actual punishing of the Jews with war, famine, captivity, are all full of glory. This supreme Majesty executing judgment, fills all with brightness and glory. When the angel came with power to judge Babylon, Rev. xviii. 1, 2, it is said, "the earth was lightened with his glory." Acts of judgment and justice are glorious and shining. Ribera saith, this is meant of judgment upon Rome, which shall be evident to all, and fill the world with the glory of it, when it shall be fulfilled. God was glorious as well in destroying the Egyptians as in delivering the Israelites. There is so much beauty and brightness in works of justice and judgment, that they are called "the glory of the Lord," Numb. xiv. 21. The people, upon the ill report brought upon the land of Canaan, murmured, thought to make a captain, and go back to Egypt; whereupon God threatened to smite them with the pestilence, and to disinherit them. Moses interposes, intercedes for them. God answers him, and saith, At thy request I have pardoned them; "but as truly as I live, all the earth shall be filled with the glory of the Lord." What is that? The glory of his just judgments upon them in the wilderness. And shortly after, Corah and his confederates were swallowed alive by the earth; Zimri and Cosbi were run through for their wickedness; and in these and other particulars was the glory of the Lord seen evidently. Would magistrates, and those who have power in their hands, shine and be glorious? let them execute judgment, and see justice done. Solomon by that act of judgment between the two harlots, touching the dead and the living child, became renowned. What a glorious act was in it, when Darius set Daniel at liberty, and caused his accusers to be cast into the den of lions! If men in place would punish delinquents, executing justice in the fear of God, without respect of persons, distemper of affections, or any sinister respects, they would be like angels, and enlighten the city and kingdom with glory: such a one is *sol justitiæ*, the sun of justice, and fills the world with the beams of righteousness; he is *dextra Dei*, the right hand of God, and relieves kingdoms, cities, families, with equity.

Rev. xvi. 11, the fire and brimstone they are tormented with, is, vindicta Dei ex qua quasi sumus prodiit Dei laus et gloria, *Alcazar*.

Ver. 28. *As the appearance of the bow that is in the cloud in the day of rain, so was the appearance of the brightness round about.*

Here is a description of that brightness or glory which compassed him that sat upon the throne. Himself was glorious, the brightness of glory, and he had circumferential brightness; and this is resembled unto the bow in the cloud, that which we call the rainbow. First mention of it is in the 9th of Genesis, ver. 13, where God puts double honour upon it.

1. He owns it for his; "I do set my bow in the cloud:" and,

2. Makes it federal, a token of the covenant between him and the earth; and so by divine institution is exalted to a supernatural work, a sacramental sign.

I shall speak something of this bow philosophically, and something theologically.

1. Philosophically. The generation of it is in the womb of a cloud, and the cause natural, viz. the reverberation of the sun-beams in a moist cloud; for when there is a moist cloud opposite to the sun,

fitly disposed to receive the sunbeams, and to reflect them, then is the rainbow's birth and appearance. The figure of it is a semicircle, sometimes less, but never greater. Sometimes there had been a rain-bow in the night from the beams of the moon, which is weak, and like a white cloud.

In lib. 2 Plin.

Mylichius observes, that from the sun hath sometimes been a white rainbow; but constantly the rainbow is of divers colours, especially blue, green, and red; all very glorious, and wonderful, drawing the eyes of the world to behold it; whereupon Plato thinks it is called the daughter of wonder, it is so admired.

Thaumantis filiam propter admirationem. *In Theæteto.*

Exercitat. 80.

The natural signification of it is, rain, and moist weather. Scaliger saith, if it be in the morning, it betokens rain, if in the evening, fair weather; but we may find by observation, that evening rainbows in our horizons have been messengers of rain, as oft as morning ones. The Grecians call it Iris, which Eustathius saith is from εἴρω, *nuntio*, because it doth foretell rain. Some derive it from ἔρις, contention, because it presageth stormy and wet weather. Homer constantly calleth it ἄγγελος, and θεῶν ἄγγελος, a divine messenger, to tell the world there should be rain and storm. This is the observation of some learned, that if the colours of the bow appear thick, and end in blackness of a cloud, rain follows certainly; but if they grow clearer, and so vanish, a serene time follows.

Lib. 12. c. 22.

Besides this signification, Pliny attributes a special operation to it; where the horns of the bow do light, plants and herbs are made more fragrant and pleasant: and Scaliger is of the same opinion, who saith, the incubation of the rainbow upon plants, makes them more odoriferous: and Aristotle tells us, Hist. Animal. lib. 5. cap. 22, that it doth much conduce to the generation of honey-dew.

Iridis incubatu plantæ fiunt odoratiores. *Exercit.* 80.

Ad generationem mannæ et mellis aerii.

2. For the theological consideration of this bow, it is to put us in mind of the great flood that drowned the world, and to assure us that God will never more do so. Gen. ix. 14, 15, "When I bring a cloud over the earth, and the bow shall be seen in the cloud, I will remember my covenant between me and you and every living creature; and the water shall no more become a flood to destroy all flesh." When we see the bow therefore in the heavens, we should,

1. Be led to consideration of divine justice against the iniquities of the world, which he punished most severely, so as to destroy all flesh: and,

2. To mind the rich mercy of God to our forefathers and ourselves, to whom he hath bound himself by covenant, and the bow being the sign of it, that he will never destroy the world again in that kind: and whereas some make the red colour in the bow a sign of the world's destruction by fire at last, it hath foundation in man's brain, not in any institution of God.

Qui infra lumbos imaginis apparebat. *Maldon. A Lapid.*

But I come to the words of our prophet. Here is "a bow in a cloud in the day of rain," &c. Some make the brightness here to be that which is downward from his loins, and to be like unto the bow in the cloud; and so they exclude all the parts from his loins upward, from having reference to this bow; understanding by his upper parts, the divine nature, by his lower, the human. And something there is in it, because the text saith, ver. 27, "I saw from the appearance of his loins downward, as the appearance of fire, and it had brightness round about it." That fire had not the other; but it seems to me more suitable to the text and truth, that this brightness, being in circuit round about it, did compass, not the lower parts only, but the whole throne and person of Christ; and so we find in Rev. iv. 3, where Christ is upon the throne, that there is a rainbow round about it, and therefore conceive, that here also the rainbow was round about the throne.

We will not stand upon that longer, but come to see what the bow points at. And,

1. It is an emblem of glory. God's glory is much seen in the heavens always; but when the bow is set in the cloud, *Habet accessionem aliquam non spernendam, ac si Deus adderet aliquid ad nudum cœli aspectum*, Cal. It has an addition which is not to be neglected, as if God would add somewhat to the bare appearance of the heavens. It is a glorious creature, and hath glorious colours in it; various, and yet beautiful; affecting the eye for the present, more than all the glory of the heavens besides: and I find among interpreters, that it signifies,

First, the glory and beauty of Divine Providence in its various proceedings with the wicked and the godly; it punisheth the one, it rewards the other; and when these are done, there is so much glory in it, that angels and men are affected with it.

Secondly, the glory which is conveyed and communicated to the creatures; for in the heavens the glory of God doth shine. You know the rainbow's original and being is from the beams of the sun, communicated, received, and reflected; and though it be glorious, yet it is a borrowed glory, and so informs us that the glory in all creatures is from another, from Christ; "By him kings reign, He gives gifts to the sons of men, He enlightens every man that comes into the world."

2. It is a token of mercy and favour. It is a bow without arrows. The back (saith Ramban) of it being towards the heavens, and ends downward, it is a sign of mercy; for when one shooteth arrows, he holds the back from him. And that it is a sign of grace and mercy, we will make out by Scripture unto you. That covenant made by Noah about the waters in Isa. liv. 8—10. is applied to the covenant of grace, stricken with man in Christ; "In a little wrath," saith God, "I hid my face from thee for a moment; but with everlasting kindness will I have mercy on thee. For this is as the waters of Noah unto me: for as I have sworn that the waters of Noah should no more go over the earth, so have I sworn I would not be wroth with thee. For the mountains shall depart, and the hills be removed; but my kindness shall not depart from thee, neither shall the covenant of my peace be removed, saith the Lord that hath mercy on thee." Here you see the covenant of waters applied to the covenant of grace; and in the Revelation you shall see the same sign, even the rainbow applied for a sign of grace, Rev. iv. 3. There is Christ sitting upon the throne, and a rainbow round about it, which shows, that the throne of Christ is compassed about with mercy: and Rev. x. 1, "A rainbow was upon his head;" Christ is presented in visions, crowned with the rainbow, as a messenger of grace and peace; for he is the Prince of peace, Isa. ix. 6, and his crown is the rainbow, a certain emblem of peace, Gen. ix. 13, 14. The rainbow hath variety of colours, and all glorious, and so doth the more fitly resemble the mercies of Christ, which are various and glorious.

Symbolum clementiæ, gratiæ, et misericordiæ.

This brightness, then, in the figure of a rainbow, signifies grace and mercy, held out to those that were godly, or should repent of their wickedness. The brightness before noted the glory of his judiciary proceeding, and here being formed into a bow, it betokens mercy.

Obs. 1. That mercy and grace come to us

through the human nature of Christ, from thence goeth out the brightness and the beams that make the bow. When the Word was made flesh, then went out glory, John i. 14, and grace, ver. 16; then was the most glorious rainbow that ever was or shall be in the world. He was not a sign of peace, but our peace; Eph. ii. 14, by his blood we are brought nigh, "for he is our peace."

Obs. 2. God hath his days of rain. When the flood was, then there was rain to purpose forty days together. If God hath rained bread, Exod. xvi. he hath rained wrath, Job xx. 23; snares, storms, fire, brimstone, Psal. xi. God rains blood upon kingdoms; Ezek. xxxviii. 22, "I will plead against him with pestilence and with blood; and I will rain upon him, and his bands, and the many people with him, overflowing rain, great hailstones, fire and brimstone."

Obs. 3. That the Lord Christ in wrath remembers mercy, he mingles mercy with judgment. He sits as Judge upon the throne, he pronounces sentence against a sinful kingdom, executing the vengeance written against sinners; and yet here he is compassed with the rainbow; showing that he will not utterly destroy the Jews, a remnant should be spared. When the great deluge of water was drowning the world, yet Noah and his family were saved; there was mercy in the midst of judgment: and here is a Judge with a rainbow over his head, to assure the godly they should not perish in this flood of wrath, now pouring out upon the Jews. Jerom saith of the bow, it is a sign of mercy, and the covenant which God made with man, that when it appeared in the cloud, we might know we should not perish by a flood: and much more, when Christ sits in judgment with the rainbow about him, may the godly know, that they shall not perish by the wrath of God. If the glory of his majesty, stateliness of his throne, terror of his justice, and the greatness of his power, do at any time discourage us, we must look at the rainbow round about him, and remember his throne is compassed with mercy. It is said of the Jews, when they see the rainbow, they go forth, confess their sins, but will not look upon it. Confession of sins, or any duty whatsoever, will do us no good, unless we look upon the bow, the mercy of Christ. Now was a storm, and in it a rainbow, for the prophet and godly to look at. It is said in the text, "the bow in the cloud in the day of rain." Then it is a rainy day, when God rains snares, fire and brimstone, and horrible tempest, upon the wicked; even then the bow is in the cloud, and the righteous should look for it, and look to it; they should remember the covenant and mercy of it. Is it not a rainy and stormy time now? is not this great Prince angry with the kings and kingdoms of the earth? doth he not frown, chide, and smite, and that with deadly strokes in many places? Let us look at the rainbow now, and know, if there should come an overflowing scourge, a deluge of wrath upon the world, yet the Noahs shall be arked and safe, the righteous shall be hid, Christ will manifest mercy to them. Saith John, Rev. iv. 2, "I was in the spirit: and, behold, a throne was set in heaven; and there was a rainbow round about the throne." No sooner was John in the Spirit, but he saw the throne and the rainbow. Let us now be in the Spirit, look with eyes of faith, and we shall see the throne, him that sits on it, and the bow round about him; and then, though kingdoms lie under the floods of errors, superstition, and ungodliness, though drowned in troubles and blood, yet we shall see God and Christ in a way of love and mercy towards us.

Obs. 4. That justice and mercy do compass the throne of Christ; there was brightness round about, and the bow was round about. Go to Christ's throne any way, there is nothing but justice for the sinner, unless penitent and believing, and if such, nothing but mercy.

Ver. 28. *This was the appearance of the likeness of the glory of the Lord. And when I saw it, I fell upon my face, and I heard a voice of one that spake.*

Here is the conclusion of the vision, and in it we have the scope of all that was presented to the prophet's view, and it is to manifest the infinite glory of God; and then follows a double effect:

First, upon the sight of it, he fell upon his face; and,

Secondly, he hears a voice; and so a fit passage is made to that which follows.

The first thing is the manifestation of God's glory: and the glory of God is considerable,

1. In God himself, in the divine nature; and there it is infinitely glorious, exceeding glory.

2. In the creation, as it is expressed and opened in the volume of the creatures, there God's glory is greatly seen: Isa. vi. 3, "The earth is full of his glory;" the Hebrew is, the fulness of the earth is his glory: the world is glorious, and filled with God's glory; it is nothing else but God's glory interpreted and opened unto us in the creatures, and Divine Providence about them.

Quid est mundus nisi Deus explicatus?

3. In divine dispensations towards his church and people. God's glory is in the firmament, in all the creatures, but more specially and fully in the church: Psal. xxix. 9, "In his temple doth every one speak of his glory;" there it is most visible, affecting, and provoking of every one to speak. In the world few take notice of it, but in the temple every one sees it, and speaks of it. The world is God opened, and so glorious; the church is Christ opened, and so very glorious. This made David long to be in the sanctuary, when he was in the wilderness; and why so? "To see thy power and thy glory," Psal. lxiii. 2. Could not David see them in the heavens, in the mountains, in the goodly cedars, and other works of God? Yes, but not as in the sanctuary; and therefore he saith, "To see thy power and glory, as I have seen thee in the sanctuary;" there I have seen thee otherwise than ever elsewhere; there he saw the King upon his throne and in his glory.

The glory of God in each of these, is held forth in this vision, in some measure. There was the Spirit in the wheels, a fire within, by which the glory of the divine nature appeared. There was a whirlwind, a cloud, fire, brightness, living creatures, and wheels moving several ways, which represent the glory of God in the world and government of it. There was a firmament and a throne, and one sitting upon it, surrounded with a rainbow; which sets out the glory of God in his several dispensations towards his church, both in his judgments, mercies, and government thereof.

A question is moved, whether our prophet sa the glory of God?

The answer is, It "was the appearance of the likeness of the glory of the Lord." He doth not say, he saw God in his essence: it is acknowledged by most, that we cannot see God's essence while we are pilgrims on earth, and absent in the flesh. Augustine and Aquinas are of opinion, that Moses and Paul saw God in his essence: but they were men, and not without their errors; for had they seen God's essence, their faith had ceased, being swallowed up in vision.

In vid. Lib. de viden. Deum. Hom. 2. Tho. 2. q. 174, 175.

The schoolmen would help it thus; the light of glory in them had not a permanent being, but was given them transitively. But this answer will not bear up the opinion; for faith and vision of glory cannot consist in a larger tract, or in the least instant of time: as in one man there cannot be a perfect and obscure light together; the full light of the sun, and least degree of darkness, cannot at once be in the eye. And further, if they saw the essence of God, they had not the act of faith, but evidence; for if a man had seen Rome, and after remembers it, he saith not he believes there is such a city, but he hath seen it: and so of God's essence. It must not be granted, that ever any saw God's essence; you have uncontrollable authority for it, John i. 18, "No man hath seen God at any time." Durand. saith, these words are to be understood exclusively,

Esse permanens per modum transeuntis.

Non habet fidem, sed evidentiam de eo quod vidit.

1. Of corporeal vision; for with a bodily eye none ever did or shall see God.

2. Of intellectual, natural vision; because a natural understanding cannot attain unto the clear vision of God.

3. Of the vision of comprehension, from all created understandings. Though angels and saints in heaven see God, yet not comprehensively: and 1 Tim. vi. 16, "Whom no man hath seen, nor can see;" there is a denial both of the fact and the possibility. Austin himself confesseth, in l. 2. de Trin., that the substance of God is not *ullo modo corporaliter visibilem*, not to be seen at all with the eyes of flesh. And the rule of the schoolmen touching visions and apparitions is infallible, that the nature of God is not seen with the eyes of the body, but only some corporeal thing is exhibited, which being visibly seen, or sensibly perceived, God is invisibly represented to the understanding.

C. 16, 17, 18.

Al. Halens.

But Moses saw God face to face, Exod. xxxiii. 11. So Jacob saw God face to face, Gen. xxxii.

Answ. Those patriarchs and prophets that are said to see God, saw him in divers resemblances; and this is an unanswerable argument, that they never saw God's essence; for that is pure, unmixed, always alike, neither standing nor sitting, having no parts, no shape, or likeness to any thing. Therefore saith Athanasius, those fathers saw God in some creature, not in his own nature, for it is invisible.

Deum non fuisse ab antiquis patribus visum: nisi in assumptione creaturæ, secundum dietatem vero esse invisibilem.

Again, this phrase of seeing God face to face, in the Hebrew dialect, imports two things:

First, Familiarity.

Secondly, Perspicuity.

1. Familiarity. They had familiar converse with God: Deut. v. 4, "The Lord talked with you face to face;" you asked him questions, and he gave you answers: and it is evident that this is intended in the phrase, Exod. xxxiii. 11, "The Lord spake to Moses face to face, as a man speaks with his friend:" Moses questioned it with God, and God most friendly answered him. So in Numb. xii. 8, "Mouth to mouth will I speak with him;" it notes the familiarity of God with Moses.

2. Perspicuity. They saw God face to face; that is, comparatively. Others saw God in dreams and visions, which were most obscure, but these saw God more clearly, had more illustrious visions of God; they saw God's back parts, these saw God's face. And the phrase is used in the New Testament: 1 Cor. xiii. 12, "Then shall we see face to face;" that is, more fully and perfectly than here; but whether we shall see the divine essence in heaven, is questionable. Chrysostom, Hom. 14. on John, saith, that before the incarnation, the Son of God was *angelis invisibilis*, invisible to the angels; and if they in their glory saw not the divine nature of Christ, it is like we shall not. Whether Christ saw the Father or Holy Ghost with the eyes of his body, is questionable; if some doubt it, others deny it. Halensius grants, that the soul of Christ saw God perfectly from his conception; but he saith not, the eye of his body saw him. Aquinas saith, that glorified eyes shall see God in that manner, as now our eyes do see the life of man; life not seen with a bodily eye, as a thing visible by itself, but by the intervention of something else, and so accidentally become sensible; it is our understanding, not the eye, reacheth life: and so in God.

But, in 1 John iii. "We shall see him as he is."

Answ. He speaks of a new and unutterable way of seeing God. We shall see him as he is to be seen, *mediante lumine gloriæ*, the light of glory intervening. The beams of the sun so fill the eye, but we cannot behold the nature of it; and whether it be so in heaven, we shall not know till we come there. Let us get holiness, and then we shall see Him who will resolve this doubt.

Obs. 1. That all the glory which is seen of God in this life any ways, is but the appearance and likeness of the glory of God. There was much and great glory in this vision: there is more in the world, in the creatures, more in the church; and yet all this is only a shadow, and a small appearance of the glory of God. If we should see ten thousand torches lighted up in a dark night, they make a glorious light; yet they are nothing to the light of the sun: when that comes, torch-light, star-light, seem appearances of light, rather than light itself. So when the glory of God shall be revealed, it will darken all other glory: and there was not so great a difference between the light in Goshen, and darkness in Egypt, as there will be between the glory of God, and that glory which now appears in the world. The glory of God is neither expressible, nor comprehensible, by any, or all the creatures. The glory that Isaiah saw on earth, and that Ezekiel saw in the heavens, did not express the thousandth part of this glory; and neither heaven nor earth are able to comprehend the same.

Obs. 2. See the infinite goodness of the Lord, that will expose that to the eyes of his servants which is so dear unto him, his own glory. Precious things of princes and great ones, are not common for the view of all, but choice friends, favourites, shall see them. God hath nothing more precious than his glory; yet this shall his choice friends and favourites see; and, because they cannot see it in the perfection of it, God will draw a picture of it with his own hand, and hold forth to the eyes of his people here. Ezekiel had an appearance of the glory of the Lord; but it is the greater mercy, that God will put forth creating power in a vision, and present the likeness of his glory in variety of things, according to the capacity and for the advantage of his servants. So Moses saw the glory of the Lord in the mount; so Christ showed unto Peter, James, and John, his glory in his transfiguration, Matt. xvii. Isaiah, he had a glorious vision, chap. vi. and so glorious it was, that it is called the glory of the Lord; and this did the prophet Isaiah see in the likeness and appearance of it, not in its own nature, for no man yet ever could see the glory of God and live.

Jehovah: this name by the learned Jews is called,

1. *Hashem*, that name emphatically, as the chiefest of all the rest.

2. The name of four letters. τετραγραμματον.

3. The great name.

4. The blessed name; for the high priest did pronounce it only once a year, and that in the temple, at the feast of propitiation, at the solemn blessing, Numb. vi. 24, 25.

5. The glorious name.

6. The name separate, *shem Hammephorash;* because separate from ambiguity, saith Maimonides, from our knowledge, saith the son of Maimonides.

7. The name appropriated to God, because it is most proper to him.

8. The name of remembering, because it brings to mind the being of God.

9. The name of essence or being, *Shemhaetzem*, a name of substance.

Plebi sub pœnâ mortis ejus pronuntiatio vetita fuit. *Buxtorf.* Qui pronuntiat nomen Tetragrammatum, non habet partem in futuro seculo. *Gerard. in loc.*

The Jews are exceedingly superstitious about this name, and say it must not be pronounced; they term it the inexpressible name; themselves never utter it, but *Adonai*, or *Elohim*, instead of it. They tell us, that the woman's son in Lev. xxiv. was accused of blasphemy, and stoned to death, because he pronounced this name Jehovah. And there is a relation of the priests of the sanctuary, that not knowing how to read this name, being written by Moses, they laughed, and were smitten to death of God for it. It is strange to think what miracles the Jews attribute to this name. Moses had it written in a rod or staff; Christ got it, and put it in his thigh; and so by virtue of it they both did all their miracles. They tell of one David a magician, that by virtue of this name went in one day a journey of ten days. But to leave rabbinical conceits; this name Jehovah imports essence, being, existence; and by it, the eternity, independency, efficacy, and truth of God are laid before us, together with his being: and here it is attributed to Christ, and tells us, that he hath his being of himself; he is complete in himself, and an infinite sea of being: eternal, Rev. i. 8; independent, Rev. i. 5; efficacious, giving being, life, and perfection to all creatures, Heb. i. 2, 3; Col. i. 16, 17: he is true, yea, truth; fulfilling the promises, 2 Cor. i. 20.

Spasmo correpti interierint. *Shindl.*

Ab הוה fuit, est.

ἕλος ἐν ἑαυτῷ πέλαγος ὀυσιεις ἄπυρον.

Obs. 1. Jesus Christ, who sat upon the throne here, is Jehovah, of the same essence with the Father and the Holy Ghost. He is not consimilar, but substantial with them; not like the Father, or like the Spirit, but the same: the one differs from the other personally, but not essentially. 1 John v. 7, "There are three that bear record in heaven, the Father, the Word, and the Holy Ghost: and these three are one," one in essence, one in propriety, one Jehovah. The prophet speaking of Christ, tells us what his name shall be called, *Jehovah-tsidkenu*, "The Lord our righteousness," Jer. xxiii. 6; and in Mal. iii. 1, "Jehovah, whom ye seek, shall suddenly come to his temple:" by the name Jehovah, is meant Christ, who is God. And this is of great concernment; it is the foundation of our faith in Christ, of our worshipping of Christ, of our salvation by Christ, and of all good from Christ. If he were not Jehovah, the gospel would be a lie, our faith a fancy, our worship false, the church a fable, all men lost, and that for ever.

ὁμοιόυσιος but ὁμόυσιος. Alius Pater, alius Filius, alius Spiritus; but not aliud Pater, aliud Filius, aliud Spiritus.

Obs. 2. Again, that the glory here represented in this vision, was not the glory of a creature, but of Jehovah; there was a man presented to his eye, but Jehovah to his faith. It was the appearance of the glory of the Lord; not only of Christ as man, but as God-man, and so the glory was glorious glory.

"And when I saw it, I fell upon my face." Here is the first effect of it; when he had this vision, beheld this glory, he was amazed, so smitten with the lustre of it, that he could stand no longer, but he falls down, and that upon his face. There is frequent mention in Scripture, that upon visions, and appearances of divine majesty, the servants of God have fallen down. Daniel, chap. viii. 17, he fell upon his face; and Saul, Acts ix. 4, he fell to the earth. Abraham, Gen. xvii. 3, he fell on his face when God appeared to him. The three disciples Christ took up into the mount, when they saw the glory, and heard the voice, they fell on their faces. There was a great difference between falling on the face, and falling on the back. To fall forward notes respect and humility; but to fall backward is a note of sin and guilt. Abraham fell twice upon his face; the prophets oft: the godly, when they are to deal with God, fall forward, the wicked backward. Except old Eli, we read not of any good man that fell backward: but all those that came to take Christ, John xviii. 6, "went backward, and fell to the ground:" so Isa. xxviii. 13, "Precept upon precept,—that they might go, and fall backward."

Cadere in faciem, observantiæ est, et humilitatem semper olet; sed retro cadere peccatum supponit, aut indicat. *Jer.*

There be divers reasons or grounds of men's falling upon their faces, in visions and apparitions of God.

1. The majesty of God that is present in these visions, and some way or other represented to those that have the visions: so Dan. x. 9.

2. The lustre of divine glory that accompanies the same: this made Paul and his company fall to the ground, Acts xxvi. 13, 14.

3. Some new and dreadful thing that appears in the vision, as here; creatures with four faces and four wings, wheels, rings full of eyes, and so high that they are dreadful.

4. Sense of their own frailty and weakness. Visions having divine majesty, glory, and some terribleness in them, have wrought strange effects upon infirm men; they have locked up their senses, and put them in a deep sleep, Dan. viii. 18; x. 9; made them sick and faint many days, chap. viii. 27; much grieved and troubled their spirits, chap. vii. 15; taken away their strength and comeliness, chap. x. 8; smitten dumb, ver. 15, breathless, ver. 17.

5. To testify two things: First, thankfulness for some mercy received or promised. Upon this ground Abraham fell on his face, Gen. xvii. 17; when God appeared to him, and told him that he would make a covenant with him, and multiply him exceedingly, he fell on his face, to manifest, as his humility, so especially the grateful frame of his spirit toward God for such a mercy. Second, reverence, worship, and respect unto divine Majesty. Falling upon the face notes so much in the language of Canaan: 2 Chron. xx. 18, "Jehoshaphat bowed his head with his face to the ground: and all Judah and the inhabitants of Jerusalem fell before the Lord, and worshipped him." So bowing, in Psal. lxxii. 9, is to note reverence and worship, "They that dwell in the wilderness shall bow before him; and his enemies shall lick the dust;" they shall come in to Christ, and by bowing their faces to the ground, and licking the dust of his feet, shall testify their reverence and subjection unto him. So Isa. xlix. 23.

That which made our prophet fall down on his face here, was, fear and amazement at the apprehension of the majesty of Christ, the great glory that appeared, newness and dreadfulness of things in the vision.

Obs. 1. See what mischief sin hath done unto us; it hath disabled us from partaking of our greatest good. The sight of glory is the happiness of the creature. When Peter saw Christ's transfiguration but dimly, he said, O Master, it is good being here! but sin hath made us incapable of the sight of glory: Peter and the rest fell upon their faces, and could not behold it as otherwise they might.

Cum magno mœrore pensare et considerare cum lacrymis debemus in quantam miseriam et infirmitatem cecidimus, qui et ipsum bonum ferre non possumus ad quod videndum creati sumus.

Gregory in his 8th Homily saith, it is matter of great mourning, to consider we are fallen into such an estate, as that we cannot behold what would make us happy; we cannot endure that good, that glory, which God created us to behold; yea, such weakness hath sin brought us to, that we cannot bear the sight of the appearance of the likeness of glory. They are weak eyes that cannot endure the sunbeams, they more weak that cannot endure the light which is more remote from the brightness and glory of the sun; and so here, man cannot endure the glory of the Lord, nor the likeness of it, nor the appearance of the likeness.

Obs. 2. That the sight of glory is an humbling thing. When the prophet saw the appearance of the glory of the Lord, he falls upon his face; then he is conscious of his own weakness and worthlessness; then he trembles, and sees the great disproportion between majesty and nothingness. Isa. xl. 5, "The glory of the Lord shall be revealed, and all flesh shall see it;" and then follows, "All flesh is grass." Glory will convince us that we are but grass. It is not hearing will do it, at least, not so effectually: seeing, and seeing of glory, doth humble mightily. Seeing of misery causeth grief, "Mine eye affecteth mine heart;" but seeing of glory causeth godly sorrow. Job xlii. 5, 6, "Now mine eye seeth thee, I abhor myself, and repent in dust and ashes." When he saw the Lord and his glory, then he abhorred himself, his own righteousness, all his confidences, duties, and whatever the heart and wit of man catcheth hold of, and repented, and said, What am I unto God, the great, the glorious God! He is so infinitely glorious and distanced from me, that I am no better than dust and ashes, and worthy to be buried under them out of his sight. And so Isaiah, when he saw the glory of the Lord, then was he sensible of his own vileness, and cries out, "Woe is me! I am undone, because I am a man of unclean lips;" though a prophet, yet a man of unclean lips; "for mine eyes have seen the King, the Lord of hosts." He had heard the seraphims cry, "Holy, holy, holy, is the Lord of hosts; the whole earth is full of his glory;" but this wrought not so powerfully as the sight of his glory: now he saw his sin, what a great and foul sinner he was, and therefore saith he, "Woe is me," &c.

Nisi aliquid de æternitate in mente videremus, nunquam in facie nostra pœnitendo caderemus. *Gre.*

Obs. 3. That those that are thoroughly humbled with the sense of their own vileness and weakness, are fittest to hear divine truths, and to receive divine mysteries. Ezekiel falls on his face, and then hears a voice; so was it with Daniel. Flesh and blood is apt to be lifted up, to trust in something of its own; men look at, and like their own parts, their graces; some confidence or other we are apt to catch hold of; but we must let all go, be low in our own eyes, if we will be fit auditors of Christ; we must fall down at the feet of his throne, if we will hear him speak from his throne. He giveth grace to the humble, they find the choicest favours at his hands, James iv. 6. Moses, a meek man, yea, the meekest of all living, and God showed himself the most to him, and so to him as not to others. Numb. xii. 8, he spake to him "mouth to mouth." Deut. xxxiv. 10, "There arose not a prophet since in Israel like to Moses, whom the Lord knew face to face." See Isa. lxvi. 2.

"And I heard a voice of one that spake." This is the second effect following his sight of the glory of God; he first falls upon his face, and then hears a voice. This was the voice of him that sat upon the throne, and was so glorious, that the prophet could not behold him. It was not the voice of the heavens, Psal. xix. 3, nor of the thunder, Psal. xxix. 3, but of Christ: and the voice of Christ is taken in the Scripture,

First, for an extraordinary voice, having extraordinary power with it: John v. 28, "All that are in the graves shall hear his voice;" that is, the power of his voice shall fetch them out of their graves.

Secondly, for the doctrine of Christ: John x. 27, "My sheep hear my voice," that is, my doctrine; they do not hear Christ immediately speaking, but they hear his gospel, his ministers opening it unto them.

Thirdly, for the speech of Christ, speaking unto others: Acts ix. 4, "He heard a voice, saying, Saul, Saul," &c.; such is the voice here, Christ speaking himself unto Ezekiel.

This vision and voice was,

First, to affect the prophet, that he might be humbled, awakened, quickened up, and prepared to the work the Lord Christ intended him.

Secondly, to confirm him,

1. In his call to his ministry. He was to be a prophet to this people in a strange land, and therefore hath an extraordinary call to it; Christ from heaven appears,

2. In the truth of his prophecy. He should utter nothing but what he had from Christ, the author of all truth; he would put words into his mouth.

3. In the whole race and work of his ministry, that he might not be discouraged; seeing that he had seen such a vision, heard such a voice.

Thirdly, to confirm the jews, and gentiles, all to whom this prophecy should come, of the majesty, reality, and truth of it.

Note, 1. God sets one sense to work after another: his eye was taken up before with the sight of great and glorious things; now his ears come to be exercised and filled with as choice truths as the eye had objects; and afterwards there is a roll for his taste and touching. God lets in mercy and goodness to us through every window and door.

2. That great fear doth astonish, and hinder judgment: he heard a voice, but knew not whose it was; fear doth disturb and surprise.

CHAPTER II.

Ver. 1. *And he said unto me, Son of man, stand upon thy feet, and I will speak unto thee.*

In the former chapter we met with great deeps and difficulties, mysteries of a high nature; and if any light have appeared in the opening of them, let him that sits upon the throne have the glory of it. By his assistance we have gone over sundry rocks, and through some depths; and we desire by the same assistance to proceed: and now we are come from the mountains to the plains, where we may walk with more safety.

In quibus liberis gressibus locutionis nostræ intrepidum pedem ponamus. *Greg. Hom.* 9. *in Ezek.*

The glory of the Lord being set out in his government of the world, in his dispensations towards his church, in the antecedent chapter; the scope of this chapter is, to corroborate Ezekiel smitten down with the sight of glory, and to show his call unto his prophetical office. The parts are, the confirming, sending, and instructing of the prophet.

1. His confirmation and comforting is laid down in the two first verses.

2. His sending in the three next to the sixth verse.

3. His instructing from the sixth to the ninth. After that, mention is made of a roll in the two last verses, and in the beginning of the next chapter, which is of much concernment, as in its place may appear.

The confirming of the prophet is,

1. By the word of God, in the first verse.

2. By his Spirit, in the second verse.

In the first verse are two things considerable:

1. The party speaking.

2. The matter spoken; where you have,

1. The appellation; "Son of man."

2. The command; "Stand upon thy feet."

3. The ground of it, which is a gracious promise; "And I will speak unto thee."

It is Christ who speaks, and unto Ezekiel, whom he calls "the son of man;" the original is, the son of Adam, that is, of earthly man: for, as the apostle saith, 1 Cor. xv. 47, "The first Adam was of the earth, earthy;" and Adam signifies earth, or red earth, whereof his body was made: and when we read in Scripture this phrase, it notes out to us,

1. Our base beginning, that we are of the earth. There is no man, be he never so excellent, high, wise, honourable, but he is the son of Adam, *terræ filius*, a son of the earth: Psal. xlix. 2, "Both low and high," both the sons of Adam and the sons of Jacob, are so; they have all one father, and all one mother, and that is the earth.

2. Our frailty, that we are earthen vessels and soon broken in pieces. Psal. ix. 20, "Put them in fear, O Lord, that the nations may know themselves to be but men;" they think themselves gods, but show them thy power, thine iron rod and sceptre, bring a war, a plague, a famine amongst them, and then they will know that they are frail, weak men.

3. Our worthlessness and fitness to be rejected. Who amongst us regards a clod of earth, an earthen vessel? Silver or golden ones some prize, and prize too much, but earthly ones are contemptible. Nations are as the drops of the bucket, and small dust of the balance, Isa. xl.; and are not they contemptible things? This made David to wonder, and say, "Lord, what is man, that thou takest knowledge of him! or the son of man," the son of earth, "that thou makest account of him!" Psal. cxliv. 3; "that thou visitest him!" Psal. viii. 4: and Job vii. 17, "What is man, that thou shouldest magnify him? and that thou shouldest set thine heart upon him?" These are high and great expressions to be bestowed upon so poor a thing as man is; to take knowledge of him; and such knowledge, as to make account of him, as to mind him, visit him, magnify him, to set the heart upon him; this is exceeding much from an infinite, great, and glorious God towards worthless men, and not credible, if the Spirit of God had not revealed it.

4. Our end, that we are earth; thence we came, and thither we must go; Gen. iii. 19, "Dust thou art, and unto dust thou must return."

This title of "Son of man" I do not find given to any but three, in the book of God: once to Daniel, chap. viii. 17, "Understand, O son of man;" forty times and upwards to Christ; and above eighty times to this our prophet; but with this difference, Ezekiel is called the "son of man" by another, Christ always calls himself so. Ezekiel is four times in this chapter so called, and it is given him,

1. To prevent pride, say some expositors. He had a glorious vision, was among angels, saw the Lord Christ, and was to enter upon the prophetical function; the least of which might stir corruption, and make pride blossom. When Paul had his rapture into the third heavens, and heard things unutterable, what saith he? 2 Cor. xii. 7, "Lest I should be exalted above measure through the abundance of revelations, there was given to me a thorn in the flesh, the messenger of Satan to buffet me," &c. Paul was in danger of being lifted up, but God preventeth it; and so here, Ezekiel is reminded of his mean original, his frailty, worthlessness, and end, that he might not be exalted with his vision or office. We are exceeding apt, upon the receipt of great mercies, to grow proud and confident, which are evil in any, but worst in a prophet; and therefore, to prevent these, he calls him "son of man."

2. To frame his spirit to a right estimate of himself, throughout the whole course of his office; that whatever good was done he should still remember he was the son of man, and it was God, not he, that did it. It is a hard thing to keep the heart in an humble frame and fitness, to give unto God the glory of what he doth by us. God helps our prophet by this title, which runs through the whole prophecy, and took such interest in his heart, that whatsoever was seen, heard, said, or done by him, the son of man, the glory of all was given to Christ, the Son of God. He could say, I am an earthen vessel; if there be heavenly treasure in it, he that sat upon the throne put it in: for mine own part, I am the son of man, like all the children of Adam; and if there be any difference, he made it, and if there be any glory, he shall have it. So Paul, 1 Cor. xv. 10, "I laboured more abundantly than they all;" that seems a derogating speech, but he corrects himself for it; "yet not I, but the grace of God that was with me."

Nihil supra naturæ humanæ vires sibi assumeret.

3. To let Ezekiel and others see the rich bounty and goodness of God, in that he would take a son of man, who is earth, frail, and worthless, and exalt him to so high and honourable a condition; and specially at such a time as this was, when God was wroth with his inheritance, laid them waste, had brought them into Babylon, and was stripping them naked of all comforts, yet now to give them a prophet, to call out Ezekiel, this could not but put his spirit, and all their spirits, into admiration of God's goodness.

"Stand upon thy feet." Here is the command of Christ. Ezekiel, I see thou art a frail man, stricken with great fear, and canst not endure my glory and presence; stand up, this is not for thy hurt, but good; I appear not to confound thee, but to comfort thee, not to cast thee down, but to exalt thee.

Why doth the Lord command standing?

1. It is a fitter posture for hearing than lying on the ground was. Stand, that thou mayst recover thy spirits, and hear the better what I shall say unto thee. So the angel bid Daniel stand upright, Dan. x. 11. Oracles are for standers, not prostrate ones; therefore, when Balaam came with the oracles of God to Balak, he said, "Rise up, Balak, and hear," Numb. xxiii. 18; show thou reverence and respect to the word of God; for kings were wont to stand when messengers from God were brought unto them. So Eglon rose out of his seat when Ehud told him

Stantis est divinorum auditio, non resupini. *Apollin.*

he had a message from God unto him, Judg. iii. 20. Eusebius tells us of Constantine the Great, that he did hear the word standing; and being requested to rest himself in his royal throne, which was set there for that purpose, he refused; and being pressed, after long time of hearing, to sit down, with a stern countenance he answered, "It were a great sin in me not to hear attentively when God is spoken of."

Nefas esse institutis de Deo disputationibus negligentes aures præbere. *Euseb. de Vita Constans.*

2. To show that all mundane things should be beneath us; when we deal with God, we must not lie down and embrace them, but stand up, and have them under our feet. Jerom saith, the saints stand and tread all down, but sinners they fall and embrace the earth and furniture of it. Rev. xii. 1, the church hath the moon under her feet: all sublunary things are under the saints' feet, not in their hearts, or over their heads.

Sanctorum est stare.

3. That he might be in a posture for service; Ephes. vi. 14, "Stand, having your loins girt." Prostration on the earth is no posture for employment, but standing is; and the Lord Christ would not have his so affected with his greatness and glory, so reverential, as to be hindered or disabled from his service. Holy reverence doth not make idle or inept to service. Stand on thy feet, therefore, saith Christ, and be in a readiness to execute what I command.

The words being opened, now take the observations.

Obs. 1. That the Lord Christ is full of bowels and compassions. Ezekiel was fallen down upon his face; the glory of the vision, and greatness of him that sat upon the throne, had conquered, and felled this our prophet to the earth, and there he lay as a man wounded, and without strength; but Christ leaves him not in this condition, but speaks, and that kindly to him, "Son of man, stand upon thy feet;" he is affected with his infirmity, sensible of his fears and troubles. The man that fell among thieves going from Jerusalem to Jericho, being plundered and wounded, found no pity from the priest and Levite, but much from the good Samaritan: when he saw him, he had compassion on him, he went to him, bound up his wounds, put in oil and wine, set him upon his own beast, was content to go on foot by him, brought him to an inn, and took care of him, and paid for his cure, Luke x. 33—35. This Samaritan was Christ, who pitied Adam, and in him mankind, that went from Jerusalem, the state of perfection, to Jericho, a state of change. For, as Chemnitius observes, Jericho signifies the moon, and so a changeable condition; the priest and Levite notes the law, with all its additaments, they passed by, and never reached or healed the wounded soul of man; but Christ the Samaritan, with the grace of the gospel and blood of the covenant, with that oil and wine, cured man, brought him upon his own shoulders to the church, to Jerusalem again, and there took care for him. We have not a legal high priest which is without bowels, and can do little for us; but we have an evangelical High Priest, full of bowels and mercy, such a one as is touched with our infirmities, Heb. iv. 15; which should encourage us with boldness to come unto his throne, which is a throne of grace and compassion.

Obs. 2. That those who are humble, and smitten down with sense of their own vileness, weakness, or worthlessness, through the sight of glory and greatness, Christ quickly raises to comfort again. Our prophet was down in the end of the former chapter, and in the beginning of this he is up again. The humbling from the sight of God, his glory and greatness, is the most effectual humbling; and the most speedy, effectual, and sweetest comfort doth follow it. Job, after he had seen God, and humbled himself, thereupon his captivity is turned, his comforts multiplied, Job xlii. 5, 6, 10, 12. So Isaiah, being humbled upon the sight of glory, presently a seraphim comforts him, touches his lips with a coal from the altar, and saith, "Thine iniquity is taken away, and thy sin is purged." Daniel was humbled for his own sins, the sins of his forefathers, and the afflictions of the church, Dan. ix.; and the Lord sent Gabriel to comfort him, who told him he was a man greatly beloved, and that he came to give him skill and understanding, ver. 22, 23. God doth not humble and throw down his to leave them, but reaches out a hand to raise them.

Obs. 3. That man carries about him principles of humiliation; he is the son of man, the son of the earth. Isa. xxxi. 3, "The Egyptians are men, and not God," they are weak and worthless things; and so are not only Egyptians, but Israelites, all men; and so have no cause to be puffed up at all, but great cause to be humbled. Job called corruption his father, and the worm his mother, Job xvii. 14. You see what stock and kindred Job came of, and we are all of the same house. Therefore afterward, in chap. xxv. 6, it is said, man, and the son of man, is a worm; and so David, "I am a worm, and no man," Psal. xxii. 6: he was a sorry, sinful, miserable man; he was *Adam*, an earthly man, but not *Ish*, a man of worth, strength; a worm, son of the earth, weak, contemptible. Coniah, Jer. xxii. 28, in the Vulgate is called, *vas fictile*, an earthen vessel, a broken idol, or a vessel in which is no pleasure; and then follows, "O earth, earth, earth, hear the word of the Lord." Princes, priests, and people, he calls them all earth, to mind them of their mean original, to bring down their spirits, to make them sensible of their weakness, and condition they were hastening unto. Isa. xl. 6, 7, "All flesh is grass, and all the goodliness thereof is as the flower of the field: the grass withereth, the flower fadeth: because the spirit of the Lord bloweth upon it: surely the people is grass."

Obs. 4. That the command of Christ is powerful. "Stand upon thy feet," saith he, and it proved efficacious; let Christ speak and the thing is done. "By him were all things made," John i. 3. He said, "Let there be light, and there was light;" he said, "Let there be an earth, and let it bring forth, and it was so;" he called forth things that were not, and gave them a being. Under the gospel, how powerful were his commands: he bade devils depart the possessed, and they did so; he bade the winds and waves be still, and they were so; he called Lazarus out of the grave, and he came forth presently. There is infinite power in Christ, and great, yea, oft exceeding great virtue goes forth with his commands: he said to the fishermen that were strangers to him, "Follow me, and they left all, and followed him."

Obs. 5. That the Lord loves to encourage man to his duty. He saith not here, "Stand upon thy feet" only, which might have sufficed; but he makes him a promise, "and I will speak with thee;" I that am upon the throne, compassed with glory, that have the rule of all the world in my hand, I will speak with thee. Here was singular encouragement to this duty, and so to other duties. It is man's duty to walk uprightly, and to encourage unto it, the word saith, "No good thing will he withhold from them that walk uprightly," Psal. lxxxiv. 11. It is our duty to believe. And did not Christ tell Martha, in a particular case, that if she would believe, she should see the glory of God? John xi. 40. And told he not another, that all things are possible to him that believeth? Mark ix. 23. So Christ is lifted up, "that whosoever believeth in him, shall not perish, but have everlasting life," John iii. 14, 15. So for prayer, it is our duty; but see what encouragement, "Open thy mouth wide and I will fill it," Psal. lxxxi. 10, and, "Whatsoever you shall ask the Father in my name, he will give it you," John xvi. 23. To persevere and overcome is our duty; and see Rev. xxi. 7, "He that overcometh shall inherit all things; and I will be his God, and he shall be my son." To give alms is man's duty; as Luke vi. 38, "Give, and it shall be given unto you; good measure, pressed down, and shaken together, and running over, shall men give into your bosom."

Obs. 6. That the word of Christ is a sweet comfort to a soul troubled. "Stand upon thy feet, and I will speak to thee;" thou art amazed, cast down, but my word will revive thee, put life and spirits into thee. What a comforting word is that of Christ's, Matt. xi. "Come unto me, ye that are weary and heavy laden, and I will refresh you:" and John vi. 37, "Him that cometh unto me I will in no wise cast out." Christ had "the words of eternal life," ver. 68, and those must needs be sweet and acceptable to afflicted spirits; and these words he hath given us in the gospel, which is glad tidings, the savour of life, the power of God to salvation.

Ver. 2. *And the spirit entered into me when he spake unto me, and set me upon my feet, that I heard him that spake unto me.*

The prophet being confirmed by the word of Christ in the foregoing verse, here he is comforted and confirmed by the Spirit also. What is meant by the Spirit, must be opened. Some have conceived, that when our prophet fell upon his face at the sight of him and his glory that sat upon the throne, his spirit left him, and he lay for dead; and so here, by spirit, to be understood his soul, or spirit, returned, entered, revived him, and set him upon his feet; but this interpretation we cannot admit for three reasons.

1. We never read that any were stricken dead when God appeared unto them in visions; the utmost we find is that of Daniel, chap. x. ver. 17, "Neither was there breath left in me:" through fear, he was as a man out of breath, but not without a soul; he had a deadly fear, but was not dead.

2. The text itself confutes that opinion; for, in the last words of the former chapter, it is said, "I heard a voice of one that spake." If Ezekiel had been spiritless, soulless, when he fell upon his face, it had been impossible for him to have heard a voice.

3. Had it been the return of his own spirit, the words would not have been, he "set me upon my feet," but, I arose; we must therefore leave that interpretation.

2. By spirit, some understand an angel; and their reason for it is, because it is said, he "set me upon my feet;" the prophet being among angels, and they seeing him down, one lifted him up, and set him upon his feet; but this interpretation, although it be Piscator's, I cannot commend unto you: for,

First, how could any of these angels that had faces, bodies, wings, and feet, enter into the prophet? for here it is said, "The spirit entered into me."

Secondly, if it had been an angel, the words must have run thus, rather than as they do; one of the spirits, one of the angels, entered into me, and not, the spirit.

By spirit then understand, that spirit which was in the living creatures, and in the wheels, chap. i. 20, even the eternal Spirit of God; and of this judgment is Jerom, Gregory, Calvin, Junius, Maldonate, &c. If their testimonies suffice not, take the testimony of Scripture, chap. iii. 24, "Then the spirit entered into me, and set me upon my feet, and spake with me, and said, Go, shut thyself within thy house," &c. Here the prophet, repeating the same words, showeth that it was the Spirit of God he spake of, and neither angel, nor his own spirit. The meaning is this: when Christ spake unto me, and I heard his voice, presently I felt divine virtue, the Spirit seized upon, entered into me, comforted and confirmed me, set me upon my feet, and fitted me to hear the voice of that glorious person that sat upon the throne.

Two things fall into consideration here, touching the Spirit:

The first is, the Spirit's entrance into him.

The second, the Spirit's setting him upon his feet.

1. It entered into him. There are phrases in Scripture concerning the Spirit, which import motion of it from place to place, but must not be so understood. 1. The sending of the Spirit, Gal. iv. 6. 2. The coming of the Spirit, John xv. 26. 3. The descending of the Spirit, John i. 32. 4. Receiving of it, John xx. 22. 5. The entering of the Spirit. These all seem to imply the moving of the Spirit from one place to another; but the Spirit of God is infinite in essence, filling heaven and earth, and changes not place. The thing aimed at in them is, 1. Operation. 2. Manifestation. 3. Impletion. When the Spirit works effectually in any, manifests itself by any, fills the heart of any with divine graces and influences; when it doth either of these, or all these, then it is sent, descended, come, received, entered. But for the phrase here, "The spirit entered into me," a like one is in Hab. iii. 16, "Rottenness entered into my bones;" that is, it came not *ab extra*, from without, but there was a disposition and principle in him before to rottenness; but now it wrought, it manifested itself, and filled him with it. So here, the Spirit was in the prophet before, but now there was a more lively operation and manifestation of it. Yea, further, this entrance of the Spirit notes out his filling with the Spirit; it possessed him fully, there was abundance of the Spirit in him, to fit him for and confirm him in his prophetical function. The Spirit entered into him, took him up, and singled him out for divine service.

2. It set him upon his feet. Here the efficacious operation of the Spirit appears; that which nature could not do, the Spirit did; it chased away all distempering fears, enabled him to stand up, to behold glory, to hear the King speak from his throne of glory, and to be ready to do his will, whatever he should say: this was a great work of the Spirit in our prophet.

Obs. 1. From the prophet's being down, and set up by the Spirit, that the Spirit is the chief comforter. The words of Christ, "Stand up, and I will speak unto thee," were good and comfortable words; but the Spirit wrought the solid and lively comfort, which scattered the clouds of fear, confirmed him, and set him up. To speak good words to one sick in prison, is a comfortable thing; but to heal the sick party, to bring out the prisoner, is real comfort. Thus did the Spirit; it healed the sick heart of the prophet, and freed him, being imprisoned with fears: the real and choice comfort is from the Spirit. Hence the Spirit is called the Comforter in John four times, John xiv. 16, 26; xv. 26; and xvi. 7; and not only the Comforter, but the Comforter that testifies of Christ, that teacheth all things, that abides with you for ever, as appears in the places before mentioned. Men comfort, the word comforts, and angels comfort; it was an angel comforted Christ in his agony

Luke xxii. 43; but none comfort like the Spirit. Ezekiel had the Spirit of God, the great and solid Comforter, to raise, confirm, and comfort him.

Obs. 2. That those the Lord Christ intends to set up for officers in his church, he gives his Spirit unto. The Spirit enters into Ezekiel before he is called; he is filled with the Spirit, the gifts and graces of it. When officers of an inferior nature were to be made in the apostles' days, even officers to serve tables, what men must be looked out? Men of honest report, full of the Holy Ghost and wisdom; they must be such as the Holy Ghost hath entered into and filled, else they were unfit for that service, Acts vi. 3. Much more then should they be filled with the Spirit, that are for the highest place in the church of God. Acts ix. 17, Saul was filled with the Holy Ghost: Acts xi. 24, it is said of Barnabas, he was full of the Holy Ghost: the Spirit entered into them and they preached; Acts xiii. 2, they must be separated for the work whereunto the Lord had called them, even for the chief places in the church of God. The offices in the church are for men that have the Spirit of Christ in them, in some fulness of it. Those places are not for others, such as are filled with wine, with the world, with a spirit of envy, error, contention, and antichristianism, but have not the Spirit of Christ in them: the false and lying prophets had no entrance of the Spirit into them, and therefore the Lord saith, he sent them not, Jer. xiv. 14. They flattered themselves they were called and sent of God, and had the Spirit, as Zedekiah said to Micaiah, "Which way went the Spirit from me to thee?" 1 Kings xxii. 24; but they neither had it, nor were sent of God, but ran, and were not sent, Jer. xxiii. 21. And unless men have the Spirit enter into them, they are neither fit for that function, nor satisfyingly know they are called to it. Many among us are called of men, that were never called of God.

Obs. 3. That man by his natural abilities cannot reach or receive the things of God. Ezekiel must have the Spirit enter into him, before he can hear or understand any thing to purpose. Reason and discourse is not more above the capacity of a beast, than the things of Christ and his Spirit are above the capacity of man: 1 Cor. ii. 14, "The natural man receives not the things of the Spirit of God, for they are foolishness unto him." The preaching of the gospel and Christ crucified was a stumbling-block to the Jews, and foolishness to the Greeks. The Jews were skilled in the law, and the Greeks in philosophy; and neither of them entertain Christ or his gospel: their knowledge and abilities served them to take offence at Christ, and to condemn the gospel for foolishness. And it is all that natural abilities do, not only not reach the things of the Spirit, but they cannot do it: "neither can he know them," saith the text, "for they are spiritually discerned." Tell a natural man, that God hath begotten a Son, that God is man, that a virgin hath brought forth, that God hath purchased a church by his blood, that men are reconciled unto God, and justified by the death of Christ, they are riddles unto him; such truths are like a sealed book, the spirit and life of them he is incapable of: tell him that a man must deny himself, mourn for his sins, walk in the Spirit, believe in another for salvation, and these things are foolishness unto him.

Verba audit, spiritualem sensum non assequitur.

Obs. 4. That the word without the Spirit is inefficacious. When he spake the Spirit entered: had not there been entrance of the Spirit, the word had not prevailed, the prophet had not been raised. The word is of little moment and power, unless the efficacy of the Spirit be in it; if it be not quickened by the Spirit, it is a dead letter. Many thousands hear the word, who are fallen by Adam's and their own sin, but they are not set upon their feet, as our prophet was; and the principal reason is, the Spirit enters not into them; it may stand and knock at the door, but hath not entrance; and therefore they are not lifted up out of their unbelief, and other corruptions; they are not removed from the wilderness to Canaan, from the state of nature to the state of grace. When therefore you find such expressions in Scripture, as that the word is incorruptible seed, 1 Pet. i. 23, a burning fire, Jer. xx. 9, the power of God to salvation, Rom. i. 16, the word of life, Phil. ii. 16; that it is quick, powerful, sharper than any two-edged sword, piercing to the dividing asunder of the soul and spirit, &c., Heb. iv.; that it is converting the soul, Psal. xix. 7, the grace of God that brings salvation, Tit. ii. 11. These, and such like phrases you must understand, not exclusively, as if the word were and did so without the Spirit; but conjunctively, when the Spirit enters together with the word, then it is so: the efficacy is not *in sonitu ipso*, in the word itself, but proceeds *ab arcano Spiritus instinctu*, from the secret power of the Spirit, all the virtue and operation is in the power of the Spirit; neither is the word useless, it is the medium by which the Spirit works. God is the Father of lights, yet is not the sun useless, by it he enlightens us.

Obs. 5. That the word is the chariot of the Spirit. When he spake the Spirit entered into me, together with the word of Christ went the Spirit; that is *vehiculum Spiritus*, the chariot of the Spirit. John xx. 22, Christ breathed upon them, and that breath conveyed the Holy Ghost unto the disciples. So it is the word that carries the Spirit to men; by the dispensation of the word, the Spirit is conveyed to our souls: hence the gospel is called the ministration of the Spirit, 2 Cor. iii. 8, and the ministers of the gospel, the ministers of the Spirit, ver. 6. The law, which was from mount Sinai, the apostle calls a dead, a killing letter; but the gospel, which came out of mount Sion, he calls the Spirit, or ministration of it: and therefore more fully in Gal. iii. 2, he saith, "Received ye the Spirit by the works of the law, or by the hearing of faith?" not by the works of the law, that was the ministration of death, but by the gospel, that was the ministration of the Spirit. So that the word of Christ transports the Spirit over to the hearts of those that believe; and if search should be made, whether the Spirit do always accompany the word of Christ, preached unto the sons of men, some inferior degrees and works of it may be allowed to go along with the word. Acts vii. 51, "Ye stiff-necked and uncircumcised in heart and ears, ye do always resist the Holy Ghost;" and Heb. vi. 4, they "were made partakers of the Holy Ghost." There was something of the Spirit in the word, when it was preached unto these two sorts of hearers; the one resisted the Spirit in the ordinance, the other received the common gifts of it. Some weak operations of the Spirit may be yielded always, to attend the word, but effectual and powerful do not. The beams of the sun are oblique and direct; where oblique, they produce weak effects, where direct, strong ones: and so the operations of the Spirit are oblique towards all reprobates, and the work is ineffectual on them, but direct upon the elect, and so strong and efficacious: 1 Thess. i. 5, "Our gospel came not to you in word only, but also in power, and in the Holy Ghost;" chap. ii. 13, it wrought effectually in them.

John vii. 37–39. Acts x. 44–46.

Obs. 6. What God commands his people, he gives them strength to do it. "Stand upon thy feet," saith Christ, ver. 1, there is the command; and the Spirit entered, and set him upon his feet, there is the strength given to fulfil the command. Commands import power and free-will in us, say the adversaries of free grace; we say no, let them stand upon free-will and their own strength, we will stand to free grace. Ezekiel cannot stand upon his feet till the Spirit set him up, much less can he tread in the ways of holiness, and walk in them, being commanded: the word of Christ did it not, his own will did it not, natural reason and strength did it not, but the Spirit given did it. "Without me you can do nothing," John xv.; not much, not something, not a little, doth he say, but nothing. When Christ commands, therefore, he gives power to do. He bids Lazarus come forth of the grave; he had neither will nor power to do it, but Christ gave spirit and power to do it. When he bids sinners believe, repent, walk in the Spirit, &c. he gives power to do so; he doth it for them: Deut. x. 16, they are commanded to circumcise the fore-skin of their hearts, and, Deut. vi. 5, to love the Lord with all their hearts; these they could not do, but God promises to do them for them: Deut. xxx. 6, "The Lord thy God will circumcise thine heart, and the heart of thy seed, to love him with all thine heart, and all thy soul." We are commanded to fear the Lord; Psal. xxii. 23, "Fear him, all the seed of Israel;" and Jer. xxxii. 40, "I will put my fear in their hearts, that they shall not depart from me." We are bid to make us new hearts, and new spirits, Ezek. xviii. 31; and, Isa. i. 16, to wash us, and make us clean: and see what sweet promises are made, Ezek. xxxvi. 25, 26, "I will sprinkle clean water upon you, and ye shall be clean: from all your filthiness, and from all your idols, will I cleanse you. A new heart also will I give you, and a new spirit will I put within you:" yea, "I will put my Spirit within you, and cause you to walk in my statutes, and ye shall keep my judgments and do them," ver. 27. We are bid to believe and trust in God oft in Scripture: and, Eph. ii. 8, we find faith is the gift of God; and, Matt. xii. 21, "In his name shall the gentiles trust;" and, Phil. i. 29, "To you it is given to believe." Christ bid the apostles to go and preach the gospel to all nations, Matt. xxviii. 19. How could they, not knowing languages, do it? They might have said, it is an impossible thing; but, Acts ii. 4, they were filled with the Spirit, and every man heard them speak in his own language. When God commands, therefore, we must not look at abilities, as Arminians and papists do, nor disabilities, as sundry christians do, but look out some promises made of such things as are commanded; see free grace, and draw strength from thence, through the promise, to enable us to stand upon our feet, being down, to walk, being up, and to persevere in the walking.

Divina vox jacenti prophetæ jussit, ut resurgeret; sed surgere omnino non possit, nisi in hunc omnipotentis Dei spiritus intrasset, quia ex omnipotentis Dei gratia ad bona opera conari quidem possumus, sed hæc implere non possumus, si ipse non adjuvet, qui jubet. *Greg. Hom.* 9. *in Ezek.*

Obs. 7. It is the Spirit of God that enables to discern the things of God, and assures our spirits of the truth and reality of them. The Spirit entered into the prophet, set him upon his feet, that he heard him that spake unto him; now, having the Spirit, he was fitted to hear Christ, enabled to judge of what he spake, to satisfy his soul concerning the truth, reality, and excellency of his doctrine. John x. 27, "My sheep hear my voice," and "a stranger will they not follow," ver. 5; they can distinguish between the voice of Christ, and all others; and how come they to do it? They are sheep; not goats, not wolves, not foxes. And how come they to be sheep? Christ pours out his Spirit upon them; that enters into them, and brings them into the fold, and enables them to hear and know the Shepherd's voice, and the Shepherd himself. "We have received, not the spirit of the world, but the spirit which is of God, that we might know the things that are freely given to us of God," 1 Cor. ii. 12. If the apostle had not had the Spirit, and the Spirit of God, he could not have apprehended the things of Christ and the gospel; they are such deep and spiritual things, that none but the Spirit of God can search out, or discover, being searched out. Into whom the Spirit enters, spiritualizing his heart and head, he is a man fit to trade with Christ, and to hear him speak; for, ver. 15, the spiritual man judgeth all things, he hath a principle within, to taste and discern the nature of them; he only hath a fitness, though not a fulness to judge; he hath a discerning faculty, and according to the measure of that he judgeth.

δυναμις διακριτικὴ.

Ver. 3—5. *And he said unto me, Son of man, I send thee to the children of Israel, to a rebellious nation that hath rebelled against me: they and their fathers have transgressed against me, even unto this very day. For they are impudent children and stiff-hearted. I do send thee unto them; and thou shalt say unto them, Thus saith the Lord God. And they, whether they will hear, or whether they will forbear, (for they are a rebellious house,) yet shall know that there hath been a prophet among them.*

Ezekiel being raised, comforted, and filled with the Spirit, fitted to hear the Lord Christ, and to do him service;

In these verses we have his call to his office, and the parties specified he is sent unto, and the reason of his sending to them.

His call, in these words, "I send thee."

The parties he is sent unto, are "the children of Israel;" who are described to be,

First, "a rebellious nation;" and this their sin is amplified three ways:

1. It is "against me."

2. It is the same evil their fathers have done; they "transgressed against me," and so have their children.

3. It is continued; "to this day."

Secondly, "impudent children."

Thirdly, "stiff-hearted."

Fourthly, "a rebellious house."

The reason of his sending is; that they might "know there hath been a prophet among them."

I shall first open the words of this third verse; and after give you the observations.

"I send thee." In the Hebrew it is, I am sending thee, or, about to send thee. The present tense in the Scripture noteth the purpose and firm resolution of the mind: Luke xix. 8, saith Zaccheus, "The half of my goods I give to the poor;" that is, I purpose and decree to give them, it is the firm resolution of my mind. But it notes more here: "I send thee," I intend and am resolved to make thee a prophet; that is not all, I ordain, constitute thee to be a prophet, for such is the meaning of send in this verse; and that will appear from Jer. xiv. 14, "The prophets prophesy lies in my name;" they pretend, saith God, that they have commission and countenance from me, but I sent them not, I never intended or constituted them to be prophets. They never had authority from me, I commanded them not, neither spake unto them, they went of their own heads, for their own ends; and if they be prophets, they are lying ones; my authority did never establish them, but it shall punish them.

שׁולח mittens.

"Children of Israel." That is, the Jews, that were brought into Babylon, who were called the children of Israel, from Jacob, who wrestling with God, and prevailing, had his name changed from Jacob to Israel; Gen. xxxii. 28, "Thy name shall be no more Jacob, but Israel; for as a prince hast thou power with God and with men, and hast prevailed." Not Israel because he hath seen God, as some interpret it; nor Israel because he was a man right with God; but Israel is of a word which signifies to rule, with the addition of *el* to it; and so it follows in the verse, because thou hast prevailed with God. Here was a good root, but the branches were degenerate, the sons of Israel were not like their father Israel, a praying and prevailing people: sons of Israel, according to the flesh, external shows, and in opinion, so the most of them were; but they did not follow the faith and purity of their father Israel: Rom. ix. 6, "They are not all Israel that are of Israel."

איש רואה אל / ישר אל

שרה dominari, instar principis se gerere, et אל Deus.

כי שרית עם־אלהים

"A rebellious nation." The word for nation is in the plural number, גוים which word is mostly in Scripture applied to the unbelieving gentiles, those that were without God, and strangers to the commonwealth of Israel: as Hab. i. 5, "the heathen," and Psal. cvi. 41, "He gave them into the hand of the heathen," it is *goiim:* the Septuagint renders it, "Into the hands of their enemies:" so the Jews accounted the gentiles, and in disgrace called them *goiim*, an abominable nation; and at this day they call the christians so, and make that name which was common before to all gentiles, now, since Christ, to be special to christians. The Turks they call Ishmaelites; and Ethiopians, Cushites; but the christians, *goiim*, an abominable nation; and here the Spirit of God calls them *goiim*, a rebellious nation, by way of contempt. The prophet prophesied against the Syrians, Egyptians, Babylonians, and others, which, in common sense of the word, were the nations; but here it is put upon the Jews, who were as vile in the eyes of God, as the gentiles were in theirs; for they had forsaken the truth, entertained their idolatries and corruptions, and turned aside to notorious wickednesses. Something of most nations about them they had taken in, and so are called *goiim*, nations, as if they had had the wickedness of all the nations. Or, because they were divided in their false and idolatrous worship; some were for the Ammonitish way, some the Moabitish, some for other ways, most for wrong ways; and this made them like the nations, who had their several ways, and to deserve the brand of *goiim.*

εἰς χεῖρας ἐχθρῶν.

Ad nefaria scelera.

"Rebellious." המורדים the rebellious ones of Marod, which signifies to fall off, to apostatize, to rebel and resist. It is like the practice of men against states and princes; when they have made laws for their subjects to live by, and they have accepted of those laws, and then fall off, withdraw from their subjection, obedience, and shake off their yoke, it is called rebellion: Gen. xiv. 4, the kings served Chedorlaomer twelve years, and in the thirteenth rebelled; that is, shook off those laws and yokes they were under.

In the law sense, rebellion is a traitorous taking up arms against the state, be it by the natural subjects, or by others formerly subdued, or by whomsoever. When arms are taken up to overthrow the settled laws of a kingdom, and religion settled by those laws, this is rebellion against that state; and that state may preserve itself, the law of nature, reason, and religion warranting the same. I am not to speak of rebellion in this sense, but theologically. When men will not be under the laws and government of Christ, but go a whoring after their own lusts and inventions, or others', then they rebel: so the other tribes told Reuben, Gad, and Manasseh, Josh. xxii. 16, "What trespass is this ye have committed against the God of Israel, to turn away this day from following the Lord, in that ye have builded you an altar, that ye might rebel this day against the Lord?" Turning from God, and taking up our own or other inventions, is rebelling against God.

The Vulgate hath it, to the apostatizing nations; and the Septuagint renders the word rebel, in Nehem. vi. 6, to apostatize, Thou and the Jews think to apostatize. And apostasy is a wicked departing from God and his truth, acknowledged and confessed, to false ways of worship. And such were the Israelites at this time; they had left the God of Israel, and chosen other gods, and served idols, which made the Lord to say, Jer. ii. 11, "Hath a nation changed their gods, which yet are no gods? but my people have changed their glory." Such is the apostasy of antichrist and his followers, they have departed from the true God and his worship, and set up false gods and false worship; so that he and all his children are *goiim hammordim*, a rebellious, an apostatizing nation.

Ad gentes apostatrices.

λογίζεσθε ἀποστῆσαι.

"Against me." It is not against their king, their high priest, but against me, against my covenant, saith Jerom. God had made a covenant with them, not only a spousal covenant, "I will betroth thee to me for ever," Hos. ii. 19, but a matrimonial covenant, "I am the Lord thy God; thou shalt have no other gods before me," Exod. xx. 2, 3. God said, he would have them, and no other people, to be his. God kept the covenant on his part, he took not in any other nation; but they brake with him, and took in other gods, and brought them not into the city only, but into the temple, and provoked their God to jealousy.

In pactum meum. *Jerom.*

"Even to this day." The Hebrew is, to the body, strength, essence of this day, even this self-same day: these very words you have in Lev. xxiii. 14, "until the self-same day." Had not this people been brutish, they might have seen what an unprofitable thing it was to bestow honour upon altars, idols, to set up corrupt, invented worship; they might have seen what truth and force was in prophetical threats, how powerful God was to save and to destroy: for now they were carried out of their own country, they were in Babylon, a most idolatrous place, subject to the nations they so disdained, and had been some years in bondage; yet even here, to that present time, they were addicted to their old ways, and served false gods night and day, Jer. xvi. 13.

שר־עצם היום הזה

"Transgress." The Hebrew word signifies, to sin, not ignorantly, or of infirmity, but wilfully, *ex superbia*, from pride. Isa. i. 2, "I have brought up children, and they have rebelled;" it is the same word is in the text, They have proudly, voluntarily sinned against me. The Septuagint therefore render it, They have prevaricated with me, rejected me, they have taken me out of the way, who was established to be their God, and have willingly brought in other gods. And this word *pashang* is of larger extent than *marad*, say rabbies; but in Scripture they are promiscuously used: Hos. xiv. 9, "The transgressors shall fall therein;" those who go from under the command of God, and oppose him.

פשע

αὐτοὶ δέ με ἠθέτησαν.

Obs. 1. That it is Christ's prerogative to set up and send officers unto the church. I send thee, I that sit upon the throne, that am Jehovah, that know things to come, that have all power in my hand, that can save and destroy, that am the great Prophet of my people, I send thee. So Matt. xxviii. 18, 19, Christ is invested with all power, and therefore sends officers to all nations: Eph. iv. 11, "He gave some, apostles; and some, prophets; and some, evangelists; and some, pastors and teachers:" it was Christ gave them, and set them up in the church. Hence saith the apostle, 1 Cor. iv. 1, "Let a man so account of us, as the ministers of Christ;" we are set up and sent by him, who is the Head of the church, the Author of all offices, and Lord of all officers. Hence follows:

(1.) That those offices and officers are holy and warrantable, which depend upon the will and authority of Christ; not those which are of the wills and authority of men, as are all in the Romish synagogue, and too many are amongst us. Apostles, prophets, evangelists, they were of Christ; but being extraordinary, are ceased. Pastors, teachers, elders, deacons, Christ hath given to be standing officers in the church, and their callings we acknowledge holy and lawful; but all others are of human institution, and so unholy, and unwholesome for the church. The papists deny the calling of pastors and teachers in the reformed churches to be lawful, because they are not sent by the pope, and ordained by his bishops, and so in succession from Christ; but it is clear that pastors and teachers were given of Christ, before ever popes or prelates were thought on, Eph. iv. 11. And as for them, the pope and his clergy, we may safely say, that neither himself, nor any of his hierarchy, ever had any lawful calling; because none of them are sent of Christ, he will never own it that he sent any of them, neither were they ordained according to the will of Christ and his apostles.

(2.) That men unable and dishonest, in the offices of the church, if set up by him, were never sent by him. He gives gifts and graces to men, and then sends them; the Spirit entered into Ezekiel, and then, "I send thee." He hath the power of sending, it depends on his will, and that is sacred; he would not put in an insufficient or corrupt man upon any terms, and therefore he hath set rules and laws to show what men he would have in those holy functions. He hath given precedents of his own choosing: Rom. i. 5, "By whom we received grace and apostleship," first grace, and then apostleship. 2 Cor. iii. 6, "Who hath made us able ministers of the new testament." The Lord Christ's ministers are able, not only in parts, but chiefly in the Spirit, that is light and life in them; such he sends, such he approves. And as for ignorant and evil ones, see what the Lord saith, Hos. iv. 6, "Because thou hast rejected knowledge, I will also reject thee, that thou shalt be no priest to me:" Christ would not have a profane, ignorant man to be in that calling.

(3.) That those that are sent of Christ may not delegate their power, and execute the office by others, but must do it themselves. The prophet might not appoint another, being sent of Christ to the children of Israel; "I send thee," and thou shalt say unto them, Thus saith the Lord. Ambassadors are themselves to deliver their messages, and not others for them, or in their stead. Ministers are ambassadors, and, 2 Cor. v. 20, for Christ, and do preach and pray in Christ's stead, who is their Head and Lord; whereupon saith Paul, "Woe unto me, if I preach not the gospel," 1 Cor. ix. 16. And what is the ground of it? Ver. 17, "The dispensation of the gospel is committed unto me;" I am commanded to do it, I may not, I dare not commit or delegate this trust, this power, to others. Delegation is *actus imperii*, an act of power, and all the officers of the church must be obsequious, not imperious; therefore hierarchists, and those that substitute others to preach in their stead, usurp the power of Christ, to whom it belongs to delegate men to preach in his stead, and over thousands of churches, if he please.

(4.) That those Christ sends, and sets over people, are by divine institution. "I send thee to the children of Israel;" he was not a prophet to others, but unto them, and that by divine authority. Acts xx. 28, "Take heed unto all the flock, over which the Holy Ghost hath made you overseers;" this was the church of Ephesus, and the elders of it were set there by no less authority than that of the Holy Ghost: the office, power, jurisdiction over such a people is not human, arbitrary, but of divine institution.

Obs. 2. That many are called, and seem to be Israelites, which in truth are not. The Jews were called the children of Israel here, and were so according to the flesh, but they were not so in the Spirit; they had not the principles of Jacob in them; they walked not in his steps; they had his name, but not his faith. They were called Israelites, but were not true Israelites: Rom. ix. 6, "They are not all Israel that are of Israel;" in the true sense of the Scripture, they are not all Israel; that is, spiritual, such as Jacob was, men of prayer, wrestling with God, prevailing like princes; but they are of Israel according to the flesh, and fleshly Israelites, to whom the promises pertained not. In Matt. viii. 12, they are called children of the kingdom, but yet such as should be cast out into utter darkness: they thought themselves safe in being called so, and conceited themselves such, but they were deluded. And so now many thousands think themselves christians, saints, when in truth they are nothing less, the very contrary, enemies to true christians and saints. The papists boast that they are catholics, christians, the church of God; but it is in no better sense than these rebellious Jews are termed the children of Israel. What are titles, when truth is wanting? No other than a kind of blaspheming: Rev. ii. 9, "I know the blasphemy of them that say they are Jews, and are not:" they were jews by name, and did reproach the christians, and the Lord Christ, but were not Jews in truth: Rom. ii. 28, 29, "He is not a Jew which is one outwardly," in circumcision of the flesh; "but he is a Jew which is one inwardly," whose heart is circumcised, and is one in the Spirit. Now these men, saying they are Jews, and were not, did blaspheme, much prejudice and wound the honourable name of being a Jew; and what were they? a synagogue of Satan. And now these that think, call themselves christians, and are not, they blaspheme and wound that honourable name of christians; and so they that call themselves churches, and are not, they blaspheme and wrong that honourable name of church. Papists say they are the church. Be it so; it is the church of Satan, not of Christ; they worship idols, not Christ; they are Babel, not Bethel; they have title, not the substance.

Obs. 3. That when God's people degenerate, and fall to sinful practices, then they lose their glory, and contract reproach. Before the Israelites fell to idolatrous courses, and violation of divine law, they were God's inheritance, Deut. iv. 20, his portion, Deut. xxxii. 9, his peculiar treasure, Exod. xix. 5, his strength and his glory, Psal. lxxviii. 61, his anointed ones, Psal. cv. 15; they were so honourable in his account, and precious in his eye, that he suffered none to do them harm; he rebuked kings for their sakes, and he gave Egypt a ransom for them, men and people for their life, Isa. xliii. 3, 4. God thought nothing too dear for them, no titles too good, "a kingdom of priests, a holy nation," Exod. xix. 6; but when they fell from him to sinful and base courses, then their honourable titles are turned into reproachful and bitter ones. They are called here *goïim*, profane, rejected, pollution; so the Jews accounted of the gentiles, and so God accounts of them here; they judged so of the Babylonians, and God metes out the same measure unto them. In Prov. xiv. 34, it is said, "Righteousness exalteth a nation: but sin is a reproach to any people," even to God's own people; it makes them vile, hateful, abominable to God and man, and brings such terms as proclaims their shame. God calls them rulers of Sodom, and people of Gomorrah, Isa. i. 10; sons of the sorceress, the seed of the adulterer and whore, Isa. lvii. 3; an hypocritical nation, Isa. x. 6; a nation not desired, Zeph. ii. 1; a thievish nation, Mal. iii. 9; the generation of his wrath, Jer. vii. 29; Lo-ammi, none of my people, Hos. i.

Viles facit. *Syr.*

Obs. 4. See here the great evil which is in sin. It is rebellion against God, 1 Sam. xii. 15; not only great sins, idolatry, murder, &c. but even all sin. It is a casting off God, a withdrawing from his laws, commands, authority: as Hos. iv. 12, "They have gone a whoring from under their God;" as a wife that is false to her husband will not be kept in, be under the guidance, counsel, and power of her husband, but will out, follow her lovers, and satisfy her lusts. And so is it with the soul's sinning with God, it will go from under the guidance, counsel, command, and authority of God. It saith of God, in effect, as they in the gospel said of God, "We will not have this man to reign over us," we will not be under him; and sinners will not be under God. God commanded Saul to smite Amalek, to destroy all, and neither spare man nor beast; but Saul spared Agag, the goodly things, and fat of the beast, and this by entreaty of the people. This might seem no great matter, especially the cattle being spared to sacrifice to the Lord, as they pretended. But see what God saith of it, 1 Sam. xv. 11, "It repenteth me that I have set up Saul to be king, for he is turned back from following me;" he is apostatized from me. God calls this sin apostasy, and Samuel, ver. 23, calls it rebellion: Saul, thou hast rebelled against God; and will you know what a sin rebellion is? it "is as the sin of witchcraft," and you all know it is abominable, and worthy of death: thy sin is of that malignity, as that by it thou hast rejected God, and for it God hath rejected thee, and thou art a man of death for it. Rebel is an ill name, and here is a king a rebel against God; and so is every sinner, for he not only withdraws from under God, but takes up arms against God. Bitter lying, swearing, reproaching words, are called arrows and swords, in Psal. lvii. 4; and Psal. lxxiii. 9, it is said of wicked men, "They set their mouth against the heavens," that is, against God in the heavens: and of a proud man it is said, Jam. iv. 6, God resists him: he is in rebellion against God, hath taken up arms against him, and God takes up arms to meet him; it is a military word, God sets himself in a military posture against him; Acts v. 39, those who opposed the apostle, were fighters against God. But there is no hope for sinners to do good this way; God will prevail, and wound the hairy scalps of his enemies, whatever they be, that go on still in their wickedness. Let us therefore cast down our weapons, and submit to God. Rebellion is an odious thing against a state, much more against God. Let us all say, we will not be rebels but subjects of the Most High; we will be governed by his laws, we will be under his authority: and as they said to Joshua, chap. i. 18, let us say to God, "Whosoever he be that doth rebel against thy commandment, and will not hearken to thy words in all that thou commandest him, he shall be put to death."

ἀντιτάσσεται.

θεόμαχοι.

Obs. 5. That sins about worship are rebellious against Christ, and he takes it heinously; they have "rebelled against me." It was Christ who sat upon the sapphirine throne, that spake to the prophet, that said, They rebel against me; and wherein was the rebellion? in casting off his worship, and in corrupting it. When people fall to idolatrous and false worship, or corrupt the true and pure worship of Christ by detraction of any part of it, or by additionals and mixtures of their own, then they sin. So about worship, as it is rebellion against Christ; sometimes they fell to flat idolatry, forsaking the true worship of God, and joined to Baal-Peor, Psal. cvi. 28; sometimes they set up their posts with God's posts, and brought in their own inventions, and mingled their water with God's wine, and the wisdom of their flesh with the wisdom of Christ. And this he complains of as rebellion against him; and the ground of it is, because Christ was the Head of the church then as well as now, and the Lawgiver unto them as well as unto us. There was never but one Head and one Lawgiver to the church; and when he, out of his infinite wisdom, hath set a way of worship that will delight the Father, himself, and his Spirit, for mortal worms of the earth to leave it, to pervert it, to mix their own devices with it, provokes bitterly, and mounts up to the nature of rebellion, and that against Christ. "Blessed are the undefiled in the way," Psal. cxix. 1. What way? In the way of worship especially; that admit not unwarranted worship, nor worship in a wrong manner, but walk in the law of the Lord.

Indebitum cultum, indebito modo.

Obs. 6. That children usually tread in the paths of their fathers: "They and their fathers have transgressed against me." Do the fathers sin knowingly, wilfully? the children will do so; do they fall off from the true worship of God, embrace lies, superstition, oppression, whoredom? it is a miracle if their children do not. Adam ate the forbidden fruit, and all mankind have followed his steps to that tree. The name of a father, and his example, are strong traces, to draw the children into their way. We read of some kings in Judah, that left the way of their fathers; but not one of Israel, they all followed the steps of Jeroboam, the son of Nebat, that made Israel to sin. Let the parents be never so vile, if grace prevent not, the children will walk in their ways. Ahab was bad enough, that sold himself to commit wickedness; and yet Ahaziah his son is said to walk in his way, in his mother's way, who was Jezebel, and in Jeroboam's, 1 Kings xxii. 52. And if it be possible, they will go beyond their fathers in wickedness: Judg. ii. 19, "They corrupted themselves more than their fathers." Jer. vii. 26, "They did worse than their fathers." Iniquity improves in the going; like a river, the farther it runs, the broader and deeper it grows. In John viii. 44, Christ tells the Jews they were of their father the devil, and his lusts they will do; they were such wilful sinners, sinning against such clear and strong light, that their sin was devilish. Let parents take heed what they do, how they sin before their children: when they do so, they pave a way to hell for them, and dig the pit for their destruction. Raboldus, a duke of Friezeland, about the year of Christ 900, being persuaded to turn christian, and going to be baptized, asked the bishop if all his forefathers were damned; who indiscreetly affirming it, saith the duke, Then will I be damned with them, rather than be baptized by thee.

Obs. 7. Antiquity is not the rule for worship. You and your fathers have transgressed against me. The traditions and examples of forefathers will not warrant the children in point of worship. Here they could plead, We did what our forefathers did many hundred years together, and have faithfully walked in their steps, and hope we are unblamable. No, saith Christ, you and your fathers have transgressed; you should not have made their examples, but my word, the rule of worship. The Samaritans could plead antiquity for their worship in mount Gerizim, above two hundred years, where they had a temple, and many things according to Moses. And hence was it, that the woman of Samaria said to Christ, "Our fathers worshipped in this mountain," John iv. 20. But Christ told her, ver. 22, "You worship you know not what." You have the wills, inventions, and examples of men for the warrant of your worship, and good intentions in the execution of your worship; but because you have not my word, that is not a light, a law, and rule unto you in point of your worship, "you worship you know not what;" and your good intentions neither make it acceptable unto God, nor profitable to you. In Hos. xi. 12, it is said, "Ephraim compasseth me about with lies, and the house of Israel with deceit:" they had their fathers and antiquity to plead, even from Jeroboam's days; but because they had corrupted the worship of God with their own inventions, the Lord calls all lies and deceit. In point of worship, you must look at divine laws, not human examples; the rust of antiquity will not go for pay with God. Men's traditions make ineffectual his commands, Matt. xv. 6; and can they be effectual ordinances unto us? If so, we had not been redeemed from them by the blood of Christ. 1 Pet. i. 18, 19, he tells them they were redeemed from their vain conversation by tradition from their fathers, by the precious blood of Christ. And what was that vain conversation? A Jesuit tells us, it was *in lege Mosis, et gentilismo*, in the law and in gentilism. And are they freed from Moses's law given by God, and gentilism, the traditions of men? Are not we freed from that vain conversation which is in the laws of popery and prelates, and traditions of fathers? Yea, we are freed, and that by the blood of Christ; he must be our antiquity, our rule, our law; and what is not after Christ, but after the traditions of men, must be thrown out and trodden down as beggarly elements and worldly rudiments. Therefore hear Christ, (who speaks in this prophecy,) in Ezek. xx. 18, 19, saying, "Walk ye not in the statutes of your fathers, neither observe their judgments, nor defile yourselves with their idols: I am the Lord your God, walk in my statutes, and keep my judgments, and do them."

Legibus, non exemplis judicandum, vivendum est.

A Lapid. in locum.

Obs. 8. A sinful nation is not changed by afflictions. They were now in captivity amongst Babylonians, that were bitter, scoffing enemies, that said, "Sing us one of the songs of Sion;" they were under the wrath of God, put hard to it for all their necessaries; and yet they ceased not their rebellious transgressions against God, "even to this very day:" they had been five years also in this hard condition, and yet continued. Afflictions are invalid to subdue corruptions, or change dispositions. Put a stone into the fire, it neither softens it, nor changes it: neither cold nor hot water will make a blackamoor white: empty vinegar from vessel to vessel, it will never become wine; and empty a wicked heart from condition to condition, it will never become gracious. Afflictions may cause restraint of corruption, hinder execution of it, stir up natural principles and common gifts to act, but never alter a man; but usually wicked men are worse for afflictions. Here they sinned against God rebelliously in the land of their captivity. Wicked men grow worse and worse every day: Isa. i. 5, "Why should you be smitten any more? you will revolt more and more: the whole head is sick, and the heart is faint," &c. When sinners are in an ill way through their own corrupt natures, strengthened in it by example of their fathers and their own practice, the more blows they have, the harder they grow, and sin more desperately.

Ver. 4. *For they are impudent children and stiff-hearted.*

The words, "impudent children," are in the Hebrew, hard of face; their faces were so hard, that reproof and reproach would not make them blush; and therefore it is rendered impudent, without shame, without blushing. The face is the seat of shame; and when men sin, and are told of it, or conceive others know it, their faces are oft filled with shame: and it is hard for one guilty to keep shame out of his face; it is hard not to be a traitor to himself. But these were past shame, they had the forehead of a harlot; they sinned, and were not ashamed. Jer. vi. 15, "Were they ashamed when they had committed abomination? nay, they were not at all ashamed, neither could they blush."

"Stiff-hearted." Strong in heart, or of heart; strong with a sinful strength, with stubbornness against God. There is a natural stiffness in men, which they inherit from their forefathers, and bring into the world; and there is a contracted stiffness, gotten by continuance in sin. Both these were in this people, and the principle of stubbornness was not broken, but strengthened; so that no threatenings did make them fear, no blows did make them yield; but being stubborn they rebelled all; no promises or kindnesses did melt them. This sin had been in them even from Moses's time; Matt. xix. 8, "Moses, because of the hardness of your hearts, suffered you to put away your wives:" the tender love of a wife could not prevail with them.

Obs. 1. That progress in sin makes impudent. The original is, and are impudent; they sin to this day, and are impudent, or hard of face. The beginnings of sin are modest, but progress in sin is shameless. In a harlot are first wanton thoughts, then wanton looks, after waiting for opportunities, and here yet may be blushing; but when it comes to that in Prov. vii. 13, "She caught him, and kissed him," then it is come to shamelessness; and therefore it follows, "with an impudent face she said, I have peace-offerings, I have paid my vows;" God hath had his due, and now my flesh must have its due; "I have decked my bed, come, let us take our fill of love." The Hebrew for impudent is, she strengthened her face; it was strengthened against modesty and shame; for progress in sin had made her shameless of sin: and so the prophet speaks of the Jews, Jer. iii. 3, "Thou hast a whore's forehead, thou refusest to be ashamed;" Judah was so impudent, that she scorned to blush: Jer. viii. 12, "Were they ashamed when they committed abomination?" I looked for it, but "they were not ashamed at all, neither could they blush." O what a condition doth

Erubescentia est fuga rei indecentis. Impudence is the contrary: sin is the most indecent thing, et maxime erubescibile; we blush at the nakedness of our bodies, not at sin, which made the nakedness of the body shameful. Quantum displicet Deo immunditia peccati, in tantum placet Deo erubescentia pœnitentis. *Bernard.*

sin bring to! Monica, the mother of Austin, at first sipped a little wine, after drank off a little more, in time whole cups, and at last it came to drunkenness, and so to impudency. When the calves were first mentioned in Israel, the people trembled at it; but afterwards they could kiss calves, and sacrifice to Baal, Hos. xiii. 1, and outstand the threats of the prophet. Sin banisheth shame from its habitation; so that the sinner and shame are not acquainted. Psal. lii. 1, "Why boastest thou thyself in mischief, O mighty man?" Doeg boasted of his bloodiness, that he had killed the priests at the command of Saul. Zeph. iii. 5, "The unjust knoweth no shame." Though men foam out their shame, Jude 13, and glory in their shame, Phil. iii. 19, yet they will know no shame. It is an exceeding evil to be past shame, to be impudent in sinning; if ever God show mercy to such sinners, they must be ashamed. "What fruit had you in those things, whereof now ye are ashamed?" Rom. vi. 21: ye were impudent in committing, but now ye are ashamed in confessing and remembering of them.

Obs. 2. That where there is an impudent face, there is a hard, stiff heart. If the heart were not stony before God, the face would not be impudent before man: Acts vii. 51, "Ye stiff-necked, and uncircumcised in heart;" there was brawnishness within, and impudency without. And a hard heart is one of the greatest evils. Mercies prevail not: what mercies had they in the wilderness, and in Canaan, and yet they did not move them! Miracles will not do it: when they took Christ, he said, "I am he," and they all fell backward to the ground: after this, Peter cuts off Malchus's ear; Christ heals it: here were two miracles, yet they did no good upon their hard hearts; they went on, laid hands on Christ, who wrought the miracles, bound him as a malefactor, and thought to make him sure for doing any more miracles. Pharaoh saw ten miracles; the Israelites wore a miracle about them; forty years their clothes and shoes wore not out; they were new at forty years' end; yet these wrought not upon their hard hearts. It is not fasting and prayer will do it; many are hardened in them. There are waters, that whatever is cast in, they turn into stone; and some men's hearts grow stony in whatever ordinances they are. A hard heart is a grievous disease, worse than the stone in the reins or bladder. It was Nabal's disease and death; and most men are sick and die of that disease.

Pliny tells of a river in Lucania, that turns leaves and sticks into stones.

Obs. 3. That God sends his prophets and ministers about hard services, such as are full of discouragements, when they are looked upon with a carnal eye. Ezekiel had presently to object, Lord, wilt thou send me to a people that is impudent? I shall never make them blush; to a people hard-hearted? I shall never make impression on their spirits, by any truths I shall preach unto them; my labour will be in vain. Are they a rebellious nation? do they rebel against thee? and will they not much more rebel against me? This is a hard task; if thou regardest not me, yet regard thy truths. What! shall they be cast away about such a people as this? O spare me, and spare thy truths! No, saith God, I send thee unto them, and thou shalt speak unto them. They are hard tasks that God puts his servants upon. Isaiah was called to a hard service, chap. vi. 9, 10, to preach ruin and destruction to a people; and so unwelcome he was, that he saith, chap. viii. 18, "I am for a sign and wonder in Israel." Jeremiah is set over nations and kingdoms, "to root out, to pull down, and to destroy," chap. i. 10: the kings of Judah, the princes, priests, and people, he was to deal with; and ver. 19, it is said, "They shall fight against thee." Preaching provokes all sorts of men: and so hard did Jeremiah find his work, although God promised to be with him; he was so derided, saw so little good come of his labours; that he resolved to lay down his calling, and to speak no more in the name of the Lord, Jer. xx. 9. Knox, when called to preach, he burst forth into an abundance of tears; and so withdrew himself to his chamber, and was full of grief, and troubled, till he was compelled to preach. Preaching is a warring, 2 Tim. ii. 4, and preachers are soldiers. Hence Paul calls Timothy "a good soldier of Christ." And when we come to spoil and plunder people of their goods, their lusts, wills, humours, opinions, and to take away their strong holds, their carnal reasoning against Christ in the gospel, and ways of God; they are in a rage, take up arms against us. Paul fought with beasts at Ephesus, 1 Cor. xv. 32, and they gored him, and sought his death. The Galatians, that would have at first pulled out their eyes for Paul, thrust out their tongues against Paul; he was their enemy, because he told them the truth. Those who cried Hosannah a little before, were ready to cry, Crucify, crucify. Hardly a prophet or an apostle, but suffered by the hands of their hearers.

Quid est prædicare, nisi furorem populi in se derivare? *Luth.*

Obs. 4. Ministers should not so much look at the persons they are sent to, or the event of their ministry, as at their call. "I send thee," saith God, look thou to that; trouble not thyself at the persons that are so wicked, nor at the success of thy ministry, but consider I have called and sent thee. God's will and command must content us, support us. What if we be scoffed at, reviled, made the offscouring and filth of the world; yet here is the comfort of a true prophet, of a true minister, Christ sent him; and he that set him to work will pay him his wages, whether they hear or hear not to whom he is sent. The nurse hath her wages, whether the child live or die; and "we are a sweet-savour of Christ unto God in them that are saved, and in them that perish," 2 Cor. ii. 15. The soldier hath his respect and reward, whether he kill men or take them alive; and we are acceptable unto God as well in the deaths as the lives of men. This consideration comforted Isaiah: chap. xlix. 4, 5, "I have laboured in vain, I have spent my strength for nought: yet surely my judgment is with the Lord, and my work with my God. And though Israel be not gathered, yet shall I be glorious in the eyes of the Lord, and my God shall be my strength." He would look at God, and not at the difficulty of the work, or discouragements from men, and want of success. Sometimes God gives large encouragement, promises, hope, success, providing for our infirmities; at other times a bare commission and command must suffice, to do that which would make one's heart ache: it is his prerogative to send whom he will, and upon what service he will. Let us lay aside all discouraging thoughts, look to our call, rest in God's will, and know it is honour to be in his service, though nothing come of it; we are acceptable to him, if not to men, and shall find a reward in heaven, if none on earth.

Obs. 5. That those who are sent of God must deliver, not their own, but God's message: "And thou shalt say unto them, Thus saith the Lord God." A prophet is *os Dei*, the mouth of God; and it is great honour to him, that the great God will speak by his tongue; "Thou shalt be as my mouth," Jer. xv. 19. So Jeremiah had God's words put in his mouth, chap. i. 9; and those he must speak, not his own words; what God commanded, that he must speak, and not what himself fancied. When a man comes furnished with the word of God, then he comes as a man of God, with authority and power. This made the apostle say, "Our weapons are not carnal," not the words of man's wisdom, but the oracles of God, "which are mighty through God:" Acts xx. 27, he delivered the whole counsel of God, and not his own.

Ver. 5. *And they, whether they will hear, or whether they will forbear, (for they are a rebellious house,) yet shall know that there hath been a prophet among them.*

Here the end or reason of the prophet's sending is given. I send thee to this people: to take away all pleas and pretences of theirs, thou shalt prophesy unto them, and tell them of their sins, what I require at thy hands; and if they will not hear, I have not left myself without witnesses; "they shall know," &c. They would otherwise have had to object against thee, and said, If we had had a prophet in our captivity to have reproved us for our sins, to have showed us God's displeasure, our danger, and the way to escape, we would have ceased from our evil ways, have learned righteousness, and laid hold of offers of mercy and grace; but we had not any to reprove or instruct us, we perished for want of visions. It is true, we had prophets in our country, but there they were common, and we did not much regard them; but had one been given us now in this desolate, afflicted condition, we would have hearkened, obeyed, &c. This objection God takes away, and tells them, whether they will hear or no, a prophet they shall have; he will not be wanting to them, they shall have no cause to object against or complain of him.

בית מרי

Domus exasperans.

Irritans. *Sept.* Domus amaricans. In amaritudinem me convertunt.

"A rebellious house." The original is, a house of rebellion. It is in the abstract, and notes the strength and provocation of their sin. The Vulgate hath it, the exasperating house, the house that provokes and vexes the Lord, or, the embittering house, that embitters God; and so the Septuagint renders that in the third verse, which have rebelled against me, which have turned me into bitterness, and made me deal bitterly with them. A house, not because God dwelt amongst them, and was now driven out by their rebellions; but a house, because they were the family and seed of Israel. And this parenthesis is inserted to arm the prophet against their obstinacy, that he, understanding beforehand what they were, might not be despondent, but proceed cheerfully in his work, whatever he met with.

Obs. 1. That there be few that hear and receive the word savingly. I send thee to this people, and there be not many among them that will entertain thy message, or believe the word that I put into thy mouth. "Whether they will hear, or forbear, for they are a rebellious house." This strongly imports they would not hear, not savingly, but rather oppose the truth. There was a great number of them in Babylon, yet very few hearkened to the prophet; and so was it before they went into Babylon: Isa. liii. "Who hath believed our report?" We have preached, and made report of God and Christ, in the temple, in the synagogues, in the gates and streets; but, who hath believed us? Isaiah was a princely prophet, had a princely language, and yet neither among the great ones at court, nor inferior sort, was there any considerable number; for, Isa. viii. 18, he saith, "I and the children the Lord hath given me, are for signs and wonders in Israel." If they had been many, they would not have been for wonders: that is a wonder which is rare, and it is a rare thing for men and women to believe the word of God. Multitudes flock to the gates and posts of Wisdom, but few lay up sound wisdom in their hearts: many hearers, few believers. "We preach Christ crucified, unto the Jews a stumbling-block, and unto the Greeks foolishness," 1 Cor. i. 24; the generality of both reject Christ and his doctrine. Of those that hear the gospel, scarce the hundredth man is a believing man, saith Calvin. And Chrysostome exceeds him in his 40th Homily Ad Pop. Antioch. He thinks that scarce the thousandth man that hears the word will be saved. It is conceived by some expositors, that in Antioch were above a hundred thousand people; and yet this father feared that hardly a hundred of them were right. Noah preached unto the old world, and few or none hearkened. When the Jews were in the wilderness, how few hearkened unto the voice of the Lord! Of six hundred thousand only Caleb and Joshua hearkened, obeyed, and entered into Canaan. Set aside all profane hearers, all negligent ones, all forgetful, all unbelieving and unpractical hearers, and you shall find the number very few of saving hearers. Many come to hear, but few get into heaven. And you know what Christ hath said, That narrow is the way to life, and few there be that find it; but broad is the way to destruction, and many there be that go in thereat. Let Christ speak, he is not heard, not received; let Satan or antichrist do it, they are heard and followed. John v. 43, "I come in my Father's name, and ye receive me not; if another shall come in his own name, him ye will receive." When antichrist came he was received; Rev. xiii. 3, "And all the world wondered after the beast and worshipped the beast, saying, Who is like unto the beast?" The doctrine and worship of the beast was easy, suitable to carnal spirits; but the doctrine of Christ is spiritual, deep, contrary to our fleshly and sinful principles. And herein the greatness of the mystery of the gospel is set out, that few do hear and believe.

Vix centesimum quemque fore fidelem. *Calv. in Isa.* li.

Quot esse putatis qui in civitate nostra salventur? infestum quidem est quod dicturus sum, dicam tamen, non possunt in tot millibus centum inveniri qui salventur, quin et de his dubito. Quanta enim est, in juvenibus malitia? quantus in senibus torpor? nemo zelum habet, multitudo sumus fœni, inordinatum mare. *Chrys.*

Ad fidem plures veniunt, sed ad cœlestia regna pauci perducuntur. *Greg. Hom.* 19. *in Evang.*

Obs. 2. See the infinite goodness of God, that will give a prophet to such a people as this. They were rebellious, had slighted, rejected, abused all the prophets in Canaan: 2 Chron. xxxvi. 15, 16, "The Lord God sent to them by his messengers, because he had compassion on them; but they mocked the messengers of God, despised his word, and misused his prophets, until the wrath of the Lord arose, and there was no remedy" or healing. God saw nothing would do them good, but that they must be ruined by war, be thrown into captivity, and buried in Babylon; yet such was the compassion and goodness of God, that he gives them a prophet here to try them what they will do, whether they would hear and learn righteousness: God will not be overcome with man's evil, but will overcome evil with good. When the Jews had taken Christ the heir, and put him to death, yet he being risen, pours out his Spirit upon the apostles, and gives them both to Jews and gentiles; and Peter, at a sermon, converted some of those that had washed their hands in his blood. When God will, nothing shall hinder his kindness; he will give the choicest ministers to the most corrupt people.

Obs. 3. That sinners in time come to a height and perfection of sinning. They were not only a rebellious house, but a house of rebellion: when it comes to the abstract once, it is at the height. As there is a going on in God's ways to perfection, Heb. vi. 1, so there is in sin's ways. James tells us of sin finished, perfected, chap. i. 15. Hence, Eccles. viii. 11, mention is made of hearts fully set to do evil; and, Jer. iii. 5, Judah is said to speak and do evil, as she could: and Israel's sins are called mighty sins, Amos v. 12; the original is, bony sins: as men when their bones are come to their full growth, are strong, and men of might; so is it in sinning, when sins are come to their full growth, then are they mighty sins. The like is that in Jer. xliv. 16, 17, "As for the word thou hast spoken unto us in the name of the Lord, we will not hearken unto thee. But we will certainly do whatsoever thing goeth out of our own mouth; to burn incense to the queen of heaven, and to pour out drink-offerings unto her, as we have done, we, and our fathers, our kings, and our princes," &c. This was the sin of Judah, her whole heart and will was in it; and Israel was not behind: Hos. ii. 5, "I will go after my lovers, that give me my bread and my water, my wool and my flax, mine oil and my drink." They sinned with greediness, as they in Ephes. iv. 19, which sets out the greatness of their sin. The Scripture calls such sinners, sons of Belial; Judg. xix. 22, "Sons of Belial beset the house round about," where the Levite and his concubine were, in the old man's house at Gibeah; they got her and forced her to death. These were sons of Belial indeed, without profit, as some interpret the word, without yoke, as others; that is, lawless, rebellious men, men of wickedness, given to wickedness; as Hophni and Phinehas, 1 Sam. ii. 12; such as Christ will have nothing to do with, 2 Cor. vi. 15, unless it be to destroy them.

ἁμαρτία ἀποτελεσθεῖσα.

Fortia peccata. עצמים חטאתיכם

Obs. 4. That sin is an embittering thing. The house of rebellion may be termed the house of bitterness, that deals bitterly with me, and embitters my Spirit against them: Hos. xii. 14, "Ephraim provoked him to anger most bitterly," with bitternesses. Ephraim's sins were sins full of bitterness; they turn God's sweetness into bitterness, his patience into wrath, his bowels into wormwood. If any thing can sadden divine nature, and embitter the same, it is sin. What a bitter thing is it, that God should be thrust out of his throne and temple, and an idol set up! What a bitter thing, that the heart and conscience, which is the seat of God, should be the habitation of lusts and devils! When God sees this, it doth much embitter his spirit. When Christ hung upon the cross, they gave him gall and vinegar to drink, which was a bitter provocation; and when we sin, we give God and Christ pure gall to drink. Lam. i. 18, the words there are, "The Lord is righteous, for I have rebelled against his commandment;" the Hebrew is otherwise, because I have made bitter his mouth, I have given him gall and wormwood to drink, a cup of rebellion and disobedience; he is righteous in these bitter afflictions, because I have embittered his mouth and Spirit with my bitter sins. God is all love, sweetness, mercy, and would not afflict and deal bitterly with us, if we did not drink to him in gall, provoke him by our sins to it. Hos. xiii. 16, "Samaria shall become desolate, for she hath rebelled against God;" the Vulgate is, because she hath stirred up God to bitterness: and he will deal as bitterly by her; "They shall fall by the sword," saith God, "their infants shall be dashed in pieces, and their women with child shall be ripped up." Here was great bitterness, we think, but it is nothing to the bitterness of our sins: our sins cross God's will, darken his glory, murdered his Son, grieve and vex his Spirit, deface his work, and burden him daily. There is a double bitterness considerable about sin, the bitterness in sin, and that for sin: this last God never tastes, but all mankind hath, and shall taste; fears, sorrows, troubles, sickness, death, &c.; but the other bitterness in sin, God always tastes it. Deut. xxxii. 32, "Their grapes are grapes of gall, their clusters are bitter;" both their works and worship are bitter, there is hypocrisy and superstition in them. There cannot be the least dram of gall in any thing his people do, especially in worship, but the Lord tastes it, and distastes it. Our mouths are so out of relish, that we find sweet in sin, which is gall, wormwood, yea, bitterness itself. Job xx. 12—14, "Though wickedness be sweet in his mouth, he hide it under his tongue; keep it, and will not forsake it: yet his meat in his bowels is turned, it is the gall of asps within him." It is a metaphor from a man given to his appetite, who meeting with some sweet, pleasing morsel, keeps it long in his mouth, sucks out the sweet, delights his sense with it, and lets it not go down too quickly; but when it is down it proves a poisoned bit; and though it pleased his palate, yet it torments his bowels. So sin in most men's mouths, in their fancies and to their senses, is sweet, and they roll it up and down in their thoughts, and delight themselves in a conceited pleasure of it; but there is the gall of asps in it, the bitterness of death. And Solomon, who had found sweetness in the ways of the flesh, at last felt and acknowledged the bitterness in sin, and in that sin, Eccles. vii. 26, "I find more bitter than death the woman whose heart is snares and nets." Prov. v. 4, "Her end is bitter as wormwood." The bitterness in sin will be tasted at one time or other: Jer. ii. 19, "It is an evil thing and bitter, that thou hast forsaken the Lord thy God."

תמרורים Peccata sunt amaritudines Dei. O iniquitas peccati quæ suavitatem Dei in amaritudinem convertit.

כי פיהו מריתי

Felle et amaritudine propinare Deo.

Quoniam ad amaritudinem concitavit Deum suum.

Quod palatum oblectavit viscera disrumpit.

Obs. 5. A rebellious people grow worse by the means of grace. Let them hear the word, or have it tendered to them, they are more obstinate, opposite than before. The point rises thus: "whether they will hear or no; for they are a rebellious house." They will not hear, they will not receive thee nor thy message; but out of their old malice and rebellious dispositions, they will be the worse for a prophet sent unto them; more hardened they will be against thee, thy person, thy doctrine, thy conversation, and thy calling; they will quarrel and question all. Jer. xliv. 16, 17, "As for the word that thou hast spoken unto us in the name of the Lord, we will not hearken unto thee: but we will certainly do whatever thing goeth out of our own mouth." They were the worse for the prophet, more obstinate and set against him, and the truths he delivered: In doing we will do; since thou hast spoken to the contrary, we are more resolved and set upon it. When Christ the great Prophet was sent unto the Jews, did they not grow more hard, vile, and opposite to him and his doctrine? did they not question his calling, and quarrel at his conversation? When Christ had told them that the Spirit was upon him, and that he was sent to preach the gospel, deliverance, liberty, the acceptable year, Luke iv. 18, 19; and spake so, as that they wondered at the gracious words which proceeded out of his mouth; yet, in ver. 28, 29, it is said, "All they that were in the synagogue, when they heard these things, were filled with wrath, and rose up, and

Faciendo faciemus, is the Hebr.

thrust him out of the city, and led him unto the brow of the hill, that they might cast him down headlong." Christ was a Nazarene; and yet thus would the Nazarenes have served their Prophet, their Messiah, their own citizen; they would have thrown him down, and broke his neck and bones together: which made Ambrose say, that these men were worse than the devil; because when he had Christ upon the top of the pinnacle, he offered not to throw him down, but said, "Throw thyself down;" but these would have thrown him down with their own hands. Wicked men storm and rage against Christ, his doctrine and doings: Luke vi. 11, when he had confuted their corrupt opinions about the sabbath, and healed the man with the withered hand, it is said, "They were filled with madness, and communed one with another what they might do to Jesus." You may see how the words of Christ ripened their corruptions. The gospel is like the sun, which ripens weeds as well as corn, crabs as well as good fruit; the vine of Sodom, Deut. xxxii. 32, as well as the vine of Sibmah, Isa. xvi. 8; and the vineyards of Timnath among the Philistines, Judg. xiv. 5, as the vineyards of Engedi among the Israelites, Cant. i. 14. And so the word of God and gospel of Christ ripen the corruptions of the rebellious, as well as the graces of the regenerate: Judas's treason, the Pharisees' hypocrisy, are ripened by the word, as well as John's love, and Nathanael's sincerity. In the hottest countries are the rankest poisons, the most venomous serpents; and in England, which is *zona torrida* for the means of grace, is the bitterest enmity to godliness, here are the rankest serpents that ever lived.

Est pejor magistro discipulorum hæreditas. *Ambr.*

Obs. 6. That God will leave wicked men without excuse. It is God's intention; they shall never be able to challenge me, nor to justify themselves. God's primary intentions, where he sends prophets and means of grace, are the good of his elect, their comfort, sanctification, and salvation; but his secondary intentions, are the inexcusableness of the wicked, and their just damnation. Hence is it that the apostle saith, "We are the savour of life unto life, and the savour of death unto death," 2 Cor. ii. 16. There is a sort of men that the gospel is a sweet savour unto, they smell life in it, and it revives them, it works unto life; and these are the elect ones. But there is another sort, that the gospel is a savour of death unto; they smell death in it, and find deadly effects from it; they are hardened, made worse, embittered, and so it works unto death; it is like a strong scent, that kills immediately: and those it proves so unto, are the reprobate, the lost, whose minds the god of this world hath blinded, 2 Cor. iv. 4. Christ also tells us, John ix. 39, "For judgment I am come into this world, that they which see not might see; and that they which see might be made blind." His first aim was at those under election, to do them good, to make them see; the secondary end and aim was, to make others blind, that is, such as were in a reprobate condition. When God sends his word to any place, it shall and must prosper in the thing whereunto he sends it, Isa. lv. 11; be it to win and draw, or to harden and make inexcusable. See Isa. vi. 9, 10, "Go and tell this people, Hear ye indeed, but understand not; see ye, but perceive not. Make the heart of this people fat, make their ears heavy, and shut their eyes," &c. And this scripture is six times in the New Testament repeated; intimating, that as people are hardened under the means, so they are inexcusable having had the means; and it is a dreadful condition, to have law or gospel, prophets or apostles, and not to thrive by them. Christ pronounces a woe to the cities, Matt. xi. that had the means of grace, and mighty works done in them, and repented not; he tells them, it shall be more tolerable for Sodom than for them, at the day of judgment. Cursed Sodomites, that were destroyed with so dreadful a judgment from Heaven, shall find more favour at the day of judgment, and more ease in hell after that day, than any that have had the gospel and means of grace, and not profited by them. Let us learn to tremble at the word of God, hear it as the word of God, as that word that shall judge us, and receive the truths of God with love; lest otherwise God send us strong delusions, and we be damned for not believing the truth.

Obs. 7. Wicked men shall one day be awakened, and see what mercy, what means, offers of grace, they have refused and slighted. "They shall know that there hath been a prophet amongst them." The time shall come, that they shall see and feel that I was near, that my word was among them, that salvation was at their doors. They shall find me a severe Judge, that would not accept of me a tender Father. Men go on a long time in a careless, sleepy, or scorning way; but when sickness comes, death is before them, and they ready to take possession of an eternal condition, then their conscience stings them, and they feel what an evil it is, that they have opposed, neglected, undervalued the prophets, and sons of the prophets. The adulterer will be roused out of his pleasing dream and soft bed at last, "And say, How have I hated instruction, and my heart despised reproof; and have not obeyed the voice of my teachers, nor inclined mine ear to them that instructed me!" Prov. v. 12, 13. There will be strong convictions in the bosom of such a sinner, and conscience will sound in his ears, and set upon his spirit those truths of his teachers that formerly have been despised. When Pharaoh and the Egyptians were in the Red sea, and the old world had the flood about its ears, what language did their consciences speak? Did they not tell them, they had had Moses and Noah, prophets and preachers of righteousness, and gave no ear to them? did they not sting them to death, and make them cry out, and say, O that we had hearkened to those servants of the living God? Whilst wicked men are hearing, sometimes their consciences are nettled and galled. "The high priest, and all with him," when they heard and saw what was done by the apostles, they "were filled with indignation:" Acts v. 17; and John viii. 59, the Jews were so vexed at Christ, that they took up stones to cast at him: and those that heard Stephen, Acts vii. 54, "They were cut to the heart, and gnashed on him with their teeth;" with the saw of anger, malice, and envy, they were even sawn in sunder, and gnashed on him with their teeth. And if the word were so terrible, while they had shifts to evade the stroke of it, and comforts to allay the power of it, what would it be to them at last, when all shifts and comforts should fail them! Some have confessed their consciences have been so affected at the hearing of some men, as they never were in all their days before; others, that truths have been so darted into them, they could not get them out in a week or month after; they have stuck like arrows in their livers, and have been half-deaths unto them. What will the word be at last unto rebellious sinners? It will arrest them, and be most terrible unto them: Zech. i. 6, "Did not my words take hold of your fathers?" It did, and will do in these days; John xii. 48, the word of Christ will judge and condemn sin-

διεπρίοντο, disserrabantur. Super Martyrem, Stephanum, dentibus colubrinis stridebant quem quasi serpentem in corde habebant. *Aug. Serm.* 6. *de sanct.*

Mortes dimidiatæ.

ners, be an Anathema Maranatha unto them, and they shall know it.

Obs. 8. That the prophets shall be witnesses at last, for or against their hearers. "They shall know there hath been a prophet amongst them;" his person, his pains, his truths, his life, his sufferings, his death, will all come in for witnesses one day. Every prophet, every preacher that Christ sends, is a witness, as well as an officer or a minister; Acts xxvi. 16, I have made "thee a minister and a witness." All faithful ministers are Christ's witnesses, Acts i. 8. They bear witness of Christ and his doctrine; and if we receive not him and his doctrine, they will be Christ's witnesses against us. When the Lord Christ shall say to a people, I have knocked at your doors many years together, but ye would not open unto me; I tendered life and salvation, grace and glory, in my gospel and ordinances, but you would none of them; you had your farms, oxen, and wives to take up your thoughts, mammon to serve, honour and praise to seek of one another, examples of men to follow, &c. As for me and my prophets, my ministers, you despised, or only gave the hearing, and that was all: and my charge is not false; here are my witnesses. What say you to it? Speak, you ministers of such a city, and such a place. What, did you not preach many a sermon, shed many a tear, sweat many a drop, make many a prayer for them? did ye not early and late watch for the good of their souls? &c. Yea, Lord, but they would not receive us, they would not believe our report we made of thee, they would not take thy yoke upon them, &c.; we shook off the dust of our feet against them. This will be dreadful, when such witness of the prophets comes in against hearers.

Ver. 6. *And thou, son of man, be not afraid of them, neither be afraid of their words, though briers and thorns be with thee, and thou dost dwell among scorpions: be not afraid of their words, nor be dismayed at their looks, though they be a rebellious house.*

The prophet being struck down with the sight of his glory which sat upon the throne, in the former chapter, is lifted up and comforted by the Spirit, in the two first verses, and called to public service, in the three next, and that among a wretched, rebellious people. In this and the two next verses, the Lord Christ gives him instruction concerning his office.

First, negatively, in the 6th verse, "Be not afraid of them;" I have made thee a prophet, and it is not for a prophet to fear the face of man.

Secondly, positively, in the 7th verse, where he informs him, whose words he must speak unto them; "Thou shalt speak my words unto them:" it is not for a prophet to speak his own words, but the words of him that sends him.

Thirdly, both negatively and positively, in the 8th verse; "Be not thou rebellious, like that rebellious house:" they will not hear me, submit to my laws, walk in my ways, they go after their own counsels, wills, lusts; but be not thou like them. And then positively, "Open thy mouth, and eat that I give thee."

In the 6th verse you have,

1. The appellation, "Son of man."

2. The instruction, prohibition, or duty, "Be not afraid," which is often repeated in the verse.

3. The causes and grounds of fear are specified, which are divers:

First, the quality of their persons. Thou mayst pretend they are great, princes and nobles, but "be not afraid," *mehem*, from them. מהם

The second cause is their words. They will reproach thee, and seek by evil speeches to discourage thee, but, "Be not thou afraid of their words."

The third is their looks. They will look strangely, frown bitterly, swell against thee, and brow-beat thee; "Be not dismayed at their looks."

The fourth is their disposition:

1. Metaphorically, by briers, thorns, and scorpions; they will scratch and tear, sting and kill.

2. Literally, "They are a rebellious house."

"Fear not, be not afraid, be not dismayed," &c. These words are four times mentioned in the verse, to show our aptness unto fear, and to show the forwardness of the Lord Christ to cure our fear. The word dismayed (there is no difficulty in the other) comes from a word that signifies to bruise or beat in pieces. Be not thou so affected with fear, as to have thy spirit faint, broken, sink, and discouraged within thee: "be not dismayed," let not thy spirit yield at all, stand it out; show thyself a man of courage, a man of God, carrying thyself in thy place befitting the Son of God that put thee in that place.

The greater difficulty lies in the other words; briers, thorns, and scorpions.

"Briers," סרבים This Hebrew word is no where found in holy writ, except in this place. ἅπαξ λεγόμενον. The rabbies speak of twenty kinds of thorns in Scripture, whereof this is one, and notes briers with sharp pricks, which do fret and burn in the pricking, much like unto a nettle; and therefore Kircker thinks the word here to signify nettles: the Jews would be as nettles unto the prophet; and nettles are stinging, burning things. Urtica, ab urendo. The Septuagint expresses it by a word which notes a kind of madness: as cattle that are bit with flies which suck blood, and make them run as if they were mad; so they should, like wild beasts, grow cruel and outrageous against the prophet. παροιστρήσουσι, insanientes quasi boves æstro agitati. Pertinaciter resistentes *Buxt.* Shindler interprets it, rebellious, contumacious; others, refractory, drawing back, and stubbornly resisting. Retractantes. *Mont.*

"Thorns," *sallonim. Spinæ aculeatæ*, sharp-pointed thorns. Ezek. xxviii. 24, *Spina dolorifica*, "a pricking brier, a grieving thorn." סלון ממאיר The Septuagint, an offence of bitterness, or, a bitter offence. σκόλοψ πικρίας. The word here in our text is in the Vulgate, subverters, because thorns in a man's way do hinder and subvert him; Subversores. therefore Kircker thinks *sillon* is from *salal*, which is, properly, to lay heaps of earth and stones in the way; and so here heaps of thorns, which may prick and offend passengers.

There is one word more to open, and that is scorpion.

"Scorpion," עקרבים It signifies sometimes *spinosam herbam*, a plant that grows in the form of a scorpion, whereof instruments were made to scourge malefactors. 1 Kings xii. 14, Rehoboam would chastise them with scorpions, that is, with whips that had hooks in them, resembling the claws and stings of scorpions. It is also a living creature, venomous, hurtful, and stinging with its tail; Deut. viii. 15, "God led them through the great and terrible wilderness, where were fiery serpents and scorpions." Mercer thinks the word to be from עקב the heel or hoof, because this serpent doth bite those parts, and the name scorpion is from its scattering and throwing its poison up and down. Scorpion à σκορπιζειν τὸν ἴον.

Now the great business we have to do, is to open

unto you who are meant by these thorns, briers, and scorpions. And by these are meant wicked and ungodly men. I shall make that out unto you from two places of Scripture: Josh. xxiii. 13, "They shall be scourges in your sides, and thorns in your eyes;" he speaks of the nations that were wicked and among them. And Luke x. 19, Christ tells the Seventy, they should "tread upon serpents and scorpions," that is, wicked men, which are like unto those venomous creatures; and thrice in Matthew are wicked men called "a generation of vipers," Matt. iii. 7; xii. 34; xxiii. 33.

I will show you,

I. Wherein they resemble thorns; and,

II. Scorpions: and then draw some conclusions.

I. Ungodly men are like unto thorns in these respects:

First, they are worthless things, of little use; they serve to make a hedge, to stop a gap, and that is all; they are not for great use and service. And wicked men are worthless things: Prov. x. 20, "The heart of the wicked is little worth;" the best part of a wicked man, his heart, is of little or no value. His lands may be worth somewhat; his shop, his clothes, his jewels may be of great value; but himself is a worthless thing. Jer. xxii. 28, Coniah, king of Judah, because wicked, is called "a despised broken idol, a vessel wherein is no pleasure." "An idol," saith the apostle, 1 Cor. viii. 4, "is nothing in the world;" that is, a thing of no moment, of no use. What then is a broken idol? That is altogether inconsiderable. But may there not be some beauty, some engraving, some gilding upon it, that may delight? No; he is "a vessel wherein is no pleasure;" he is so far from delighting at all, that he is a vessel loathsome, to be cast on the dunghill, and trod under-foot. Hence in Daniel, Antiochus Epiphanes is called "a vile person," Dan. xi. 21; one so little worth, as to be scorned and rejected as a vile thing. And Job, speaking of such men, tells us they are "viler than the earth," men to be trod and spit upon as the vilest earth, Job xxx. 8.

Secondly, they are vexing and grieving things. Ezek. xxviii. 24, there is mention made of the pricking brier and grieving thorn; and wicked men are full of prickles and grievances. "If you will not drive out the inhabitants of the land from before you, then those you let remain of them shall be pricks in your eyes, and thorns in your sides, and shall vex you in the land wherein you dwell," Numb. xxxiii. 55.

Wherein lies this grieving and thorny disposition of the wicked?

1. In their words: and that appears,

(1.) In their misconstruing the words and ways of the godly. Matt. xxvi. 61, said the witnesses against Christ, "This fellow said, I am able to destroy the temple of God, and build it in three days." They mistook Christ, who "spake of the temple of his body," John ii. 21. Jer. xxvi. 4, 6, "Thou shalt say unto them, Thus saith the Lord; If ye will not hearken to me, to walk in my law, then will I make this house like Shiloh, and this city a curse." Now in the 9th verse see how they mistook his words, and perverted his meaning; "Why hast thou prophesied in the name of the Lord, saying, This house shall be like Shiloh, and this city desolate?" He had told them it should be so, if they did not hearken, repent, and amend; but they left out that, and pretend he had absolutely said, "This house shall be like Shiloh." So many people mistake the ministers, and say they preach damnation, when it is conditionally; if they repent not and believe, they must then certainly look for damnation.

(2.) In their calumniations. They forge lies and falsehoods. Job's friends charged him with lies, hypocrisy, pride, &c.; but he tells them they are "forgers of lies," Job xiii. 4; you come to comfort me, but you wound me with your lies and slanders. And David found this, Psal. cxix. 69, "The proud have forged a lie." They trim up lies with shadows of truth and neat language; they have mints to frame their lies curiously in, and presses to print their lies withal. Sanballat calumniates Nehemiah, that zealous and faithful servant of God, and tells him, It is reported among the heathen, and Gashmu saith it, that thou and the Jews think to rebel; that thou wilt be king, and hast appointed preachers at Jerusalem to say, There is a king in Judah, Neh. vi. 6. Here was a malicious forgery, a trim lie, and no less reproach than rebel, traitor, must be laid upon this great worthy and reformer in Israel. Nehemiah returns an answer, ver. 8, "There are no such things done as thou sayest, but thou feignest them out of thine own heart." The devil is the father of lies, John viii. 44, and all his children are like him, forgers of lies. Jer. xx. 10, "Report," said Jeremiah's back friends, "and we will report it;" invent some slanders, some lie against the prophet, and we will report it, spread it, carry it to the king's court and ear, and cause him to smart for his boldness. Jeremiah heard the defaming of many; it was their daily work. They said, "Let us smite him with the tongue," Jer. xviii. 18. No man can have a beautiful and well-favoured name for these briers; they will scratch it, and make it very bloody: it was their daily work. The christians in the primitive time were accused of all the evils that fell out: if there were great floods, famines, wars, earthquakes, plagues, in the Roman commonwealth, they cried, Away with the christians to the lions; and Austin observeth, that they made it a proverb, The rain failed, because the christian name was suffered.

Concinnarunt mendacia. Vatablus.

Christiani ad leones.

Pluvia defecit christiani nominis gratia.

(3.) Daring, provoking words. Neh. vi. 2, Sanballat and Geshem dared Nehemiah to meet them; "Come, let us meet together in one of the villages." Four times they sent unto him in that manner, thinking by this way to have drawn out Nehemiah, and done him mischief. Daring provocation comes from the wicked, and herein they are thorns and briers.

(4.) Scorning, scoffing speeches. Neh. iv. 2, when the walls of Jerusalem were building, Sanballat scoffs, and says, "What do these feeble Jews? will they fortify themselves? will they sacrifice? will they make an end in a day? will they revive the stones out of the heaps of the rubbish which are burned?" And so Tobiah, "If a fox go up, he shall even break down their stone wall." These scoffs and jeers went to the heart of Nehemiah, and made him pierce the heavens for help; "Hear, O our God; for we are despised:" the Hebrew is, despight; we are not only despised, but we and our work are despight, in the abstract. Mockings are biting things, therefore they are called cruel mockings, Heb. xi. 36. Ishmael's mocking of Isaac, Gen. xxi. 9, is called a persecution, Gal. iv. 29. The servants of God have been mocked and reproached in all ages.

Luther was called Germana illa bestia.

(5.) Threatenings. Acts iv. 17, "Let us straitly threaten them, that they speak no more in Christ's name;" and ver. 21, "When they had further threatened them." Their tongues were tipt with threats; they were thorny tongues, *minæ sunt spinæ*, threats are thorns, and pricked them on to the throne of grace, and made them pray as men pierced to the quick: for, ver. 29, "Now, Lord, behold their threatenings," let not them wound and weaken us, but "grant unto thy servants, that with all boldness they may speak thy word." Saul, Acts ix. 1, breathed out threatenings against the saints. He was Benoni, a son of affliction to the church: so are all wicked men, and their tongues are thorns. Hence they are said in Scripture to be "whet," Psal. lxiv. 3; to be "a sharp sword," Psal. lvii. 4, "a sharp razor," Psal. lii. 2; and the words of it are called "arrows, bitter words, devouring words," Psal. lii. 4, "deadly words," Prov. xviii. 21. Death and life are in the power of the tongue; it comforts, it destroys. Take the tongue of an evil man that slanders and backbites, it is a great murderer. We read of some double-tongued, 1 Tim. iii. 8; but such a one is treble-tongued, and kills, as Bernard saith, three at once; himself that speaks, the person he speaks to, and him he speaks of: and the worst is, he murders his own soul. Therefore Chrysostom observes well, and saith, The tongue is almost the very gate of death, it is the death and ruin of most men in the world.

Lingua ejus est gladius triceps. *Bernard.* Felo de se: Mortis fere unicum ostium lingua est. *Chrys.*

(6.) "Their tongues are briers and thorns," in regard of their slighting and undervaluing of God's servants; as Paul is called a babbler, Christ, a fellow, the carpenter's son. And many of God's servants are slighted in these days; such words they meet with as are thorns and pricks in their sides and eyes. Because I will not multiply, take their blasphemies, O what thorns are those! thorns to God, and thorns to man. When the French had got some victory in Scotland against the reforming party there, the queen regent brake out into these speeches, "Where is now Knox's God? Now my God is better than Knox's God." Here was a blasphemous passage. And have we not such blasphemies in our days? Where is now your God of prayer and fasting? What is become of all your hearing, preaching, and seeking of your God? I might add another particular, which is the thorny counsels that wicked men do give. 1 Kings xxi. 9, what counsel Jezebel gave against Naboth! "Proclaim a fast, set him up on high among the people, and set two sons of Belial before him, to bear witness against him, that he blasphemed God and the king;" here were words of death, here was counsel from hell. It is not unknown what ill counsel hath been given his Majesty of late, and likewise to many others.

2. In their looks; that is in the text also. There is much in the faces of men to daunt and trouble; men's spirits are much discerned by their faces: Gen. xxxi. 5, I see your father's countenance is not towards me as before, by his face I find a difference in his spirit, saith Jacob to his wives; he found no favour in it. The face is the seat of favour or frowns. There is some majesty in the face and looks of man; and when he is angry, frowns, there is majestical terror in it. In Prov. xxv. 23, there is mention of an angry countenance, and it is likened to a north wind, which is cold and scattering; it drives away the clouds that have the rain in them: and ofttimes wicked men have such northern countenances, that they discourage, if not drive away, the prophets, who come with the dews of heaven. When men frown, knit their brows, look angrily, they have put on vizards, and they be scaring things: Job xxiv. 15, "He disguiseth his face;" he is like a man that hath on some terrible vizard, which affrights those that behold it. One of the Nevils, earl of Warwick, had so terrible a look when moved a little, that it was said of him, every wrinkle in his forehead was a sepulchre to bury a prince in: he was of kin to that nation, Deut. xxviii. 50, that had fierce countenances. And Antiochus, a wicked king, is described in Dan. viii. 23, to be of a fierce countenance; his very aspect was terrible. And some have been blasted by the frowns of mortals. When some men frown, look sour, and sparkle with their eyes, they prove basilisks, and kill those they look upon.

3. Like thorns in their catching nature; they catch hold of a man when he thinks he is rid of them, and entangle him more: so wicked men, when you think you have satisfied them, and done with them, they catch hold again, they seek new advantages. Jer. xx. 10, "All my familiars watched for my halting, saying, Peradventure he will be enticed, and we shall prevail against him, and we shall take our revenge on him." The words, "all my familiars," in the Hebrew are, every man of my peace. I thought I had satisfied all their cavils, slanders, and objections, that they had aimed at my peace and good; but they watched for my halting, they sought to entice me, and get advantage. This is the nature of wicked men. Christ, when he had to do with any sort of them, he convinced them, stopped their mouths, they went away and left him, and yet they were not satisfied, but sent, and set men to catch him in his words, Mark xii. 13. When the godly fall into the courts and prisons where wicked men have some power, what advantages do they seek against them. And when nothing can be proved, no reason but they should be dismissed, fees are multiplied, oaths and protestations tendered; and unless these thorns may scratch them, and draw blood from their purses and consciences, they will hold them fast, and liberty must not be had.

4. A thorn will never alter its nature; set it in the garden or orchard, water it with milk or wine, do what you will to the thorn, when you have done all, a thorn is a thorn: so is the nature of wicked and ungodly men. Transplant them whither you will, bring them from the country to the city, from the city to the court, put them in high or low places, bring them to the water's side, to the rivers of God, plant them in the orchards of God, in paradise itself, under the means of grace, let them have the dew of heaven, the shining of the sun;—a wicked man, he abides wicked still, he will not alter his nature, he will be no more a changeling; he is a blackamoor, he will be a blackamoor; he will live and die in his way, though he perish in that way.

5. Thorns are for the fire, Psal. lviii. 9, "Before your pots can feel the thorns," the heat of the fire made with thorns: they are for burning; and that is the end of wicked ones, Isa. x. 17, "The light of Israel shall be for a fire; and it shall burn and devour his thorns and his briers in one day." In fire is light and heat; God would be light to Israel, comfort and joy, but heat and burning to the Assyrian; he sent down fire to burn the sacrifice, and he would send a fire to burn the Assyrians, which were briers and thorns to the Jews, and that in one day. And when was this? When he sent an angel, and slew 185,000. Here was fire from heaven, a seraphim, a coal of juniper, that burnt up such a thicket of briers and thorns; and after this fire they fell into a worse, even the fire of hell, which is the place prepared for all the wicked: Psal. ix. 17. "The wicked shall be turned into hell, and all the nations that forget God;" there is their end. Hell is large enough to hold all; Isa. xxx. 33, it is "deep and large, the pile thereof is fire and much wood;" it is *silva execrabilis*, an accursed wood; such wood the earth brought forth upon the curse, briers and thorns, Gen. iii. 18, and the wicked are the fruit of the curse. This phrase "much wood," some expositors think, hath reference to the fact of the Jews, when the 185,000 Assyrians

Musc.

were slain in the valley of Tophet, they made great piles of wood, and burnt those bodies. So God hath piles of wood, thousands and millions of wicked ones, briers and brambles heaped together; and his breath like a stream of brimstone, kindles those heaps.

II. In what hath been said you see wherein wicked men are thorns and briers; now I must present to you wherein they are scorpions. You may by briers and thorns understand wicked men of a lower condition, and by scorpions those of a higher, that have more power, means, and opportunity to do mischief; and the analogy between the scorpion and them, lies in these particulars.

1. The scorpion is *animal insidiosum*, an insidious creature, it lies lurking under thorns and briers, hides itself in holes. Serpents also are subtle. "The serpent was more subtle than any beast of the field," Gen. iii. 1; and stops his ear against the voice of the charmer, Psa. lviii.; and bites the horse by the heel, so that the rider may fall, Gen. xlix. 17. And there is one word that signifies simplicity and subtilty, that signifies plainness and double-dealing: when Adam and Eve were both naked, they were plain and simple; but the serpent was *gnarum* in a contrary sense, crafty, full of folds and windings. And wicked men are subtle: "Come let us deal wisely with them," Exod. i. 10. The Septuagint is, Let us deal cunningly against them. And in Psal. cv. 25, it is said, they dealt subtilly with his servants. How cunningly did the adversaries carry their plot in the days of Nehemiah! chap. iv. 11, "They shall not know nor see, till we come in the midst of them and slay them." The gunpowder treason was, and some since have been, carried on with dark lanthorns, with secrecy and craft. Had not the enemies a close and crafty design to make a conjunction between papists and protestants in doctrine, discipline, and ceremony? And had not the only wise God interposed, turned wise men backward, and made their knowledge foolish, England and Rome had met, and we had been in conjunction with antichristian planets. And we may fear conjunctions still, more than open violence. Are not things carried with that subtilty at this present, as makes the world to wonder? Men against us pretend religion, king, parliament, the liberty of the subject, to be their quarrel. Here is much of the serpent, and little of the dove.

When they will sting, Terga vertunt, ut à nobis declinare videantur. *Conrad. in Apocal.*

ערוּמִים

κατασοφισώμεθα αὐτȣς.

2. The scorpion is vigilant, watching opportunity of mischief. Pliny saith, some serpents sleep not all the summer, but are always thrusting out their stings, and waking, lest they should miss their opportunity. And wicked men are very wakeful, and watching their opportunity to do mischief: Prov. iv. 16, "They sleep not, unless they have done mischief, or caused some to fall." Ahab is sick, and cannot sleep, unless he have Naboth's vineyard. Amnon must have Tamar to satisfy his lust, else he must lay awake all night. Wicked men cannot be in quiet unless they sleep in wickedness. When Christ came to his disciples, they were asleep; but the wicked rout were awake, and coming to take him. They are restless like the sea: Isa. lvii. 20, "The wicked are like the troubled sea, when it cannot rest;" not when it is calm, but in its working, boiling, restless condition; when it threatens storms, to swallow up ships, to break over the banks, &c. Such are wicked ones, they storm, they swell, and watch where to break out to empty themselves of their estates, to drown a country in the blood of a civil war. Mic. vii. 2, 3, "They all lie in wait for blood; they hunt every man his brother with a net; that they may do evil with both hands earnestly," &c. They have their net set, they hunt, they watch, and will not lose an opportunity; if one hand will not serve, both shall, and in the intention of their spirits also they are earnest in the work. And as they are wise to watch their season, so their feet are swift in running to the accomplishment of them, Prov. vi. 18. Were not our enemies watchful and active to break parliaments, to make canons, to search pockets, to fetch men into their courts?

Tota æstate insomnes sunt quamdiu venenum viget. *Plin.* l. 8. c. 29.

Semper in ictu est, nulloque momento meditari cessat, ne quando desit occasioni. *Idem.*

3. They are exceeding troublesome to the countries where they are. They will get up their walls, into their chambers and beds, as some expositors observe; and therefore to prevent such evils, they set their beds remote from the wall, and the feet of their beds in pots full of water; and for fear of them, they lie in the highest rooms: they molest them much, and multiply their fears. In this they are not unlike them. Ahab was a troubler of Israel. Wicked men are the incendiaries in church and state. I must not name any; you know more than enough that are not nick-named when they are so termed; they have troubled this state and this city.

Eglinus in Apocal.

4. They join to do mischief. One will stick fast to the roof or wall, a second unto him, a third unto the second, and so make a chain, till they reach the party asleep; and the last stings him, and returns, and so every one back in order. This I find of the scorpion in Eglinus upon the Revelation. Here is both their craft and malice unto man, that they are subservient one to another, and so linked together for such a purpose. Herein are wicked men truly scorpions: Prov. i. 14, "Come, let us all have one purse." Nahum i. 10, the wicked are as thorns folded together, stick together as the scales of leviathan. Acts iv. 5, 6, rulers, elders, scribes, high priest, Caiaphas, John, Alexander, and as many as were of the kindred of the high priest, were gathered together against Christ and his apostles.

5. The scorpion feeds upon the dust of the earth. It feeds upon base and low things, upon vile and venomous things; so do wicked and ungodly men. As the serpent licks the dust of the earth, so do they lick the dust of the earth; they feed upon malice, they feed upon blood, they feed upon that which is not their own: Amos ii. 7, "They pant after the very dust of the earth;" they pant after the estates and means that poor men have in any place where they come, and they feed upon it, and satisfy their malice and revenge to the full, in sucking the estates, and crushing the bones of the saints of God.

6. They kill *lenta morte*, by a slow death, but *gravi supplicio*, with severe torment. When they set upon a man, they lick him, they prick him, they poison him, which quickly torments, and within a few days kills: Rev. ix. 5, "Their torment was as the torment of a scorpion, when he striketh a man." Some scorpions have double stings, and that they may be sure to kill, they strike with both. Wicked men deceive us with their treaties, and kill us with their treacheries: Psal. lv. 21, their words are softer than oil, but they are drawn swords. In the treaties and flatteries of wicked men, if we were not blind, we might see drawn swords, death at the throat of our estate, of our religion, laws and liberties. Haman flattered Esther, that sought the destruction of the Jews; the decree is sealed for the death of young and old, Esth. iii.: here was a scorpion. And Jer. xxxviii. 4, the princes beseech the king to put Jeremiah to death. Such a scorpion was Jezebel and Ahab, which stung Naboth to death, and got his vineyard. Hence

Lambunt, pungunt, venenum infundunt.

that law in Ezek. xlvi. 18, "The prince shall not take of the people's inheritance by oppression, to thrust them out of their possession."

Si aliqui eorum in medio domus exurantur, say *Palladius* and *Virga*.

7. Scorpions are driven away, if any of them be burnt in the house where they haunt. When Joab and Shimei were put to death by the sword of Solomon, then the other scorpions in Israel were afraid, and hid themselves; "and the kingdom was established in the hand of Solomon," 1 Kings ii. 46. If we shake not our vipers into the fire, they will do us harm. Thus you see wherein the resemblance lies between the wicked, in regard that they are called briers, thorns, and scorpions in the text.

The observations that do arise from the text are:

Obs. 1. That he is the fittest man for public employment, who is sensible of his own weakness, and insufficiency for place or service. "Son of man, be not afraid." I see, Ezekiel, that thou art sensible of thy own insufficiency; be not thou afraid, thou art the fitter man for my service. Moses pretended that he was a man slow of speech, and unfit for the great work of delivering God's people, and leading them out of Egypt into Canaan; but he was the fitter man for God. So those ministers or magistrates that are sensible of their own weaknesses, they are fittest for Christ and church service, and the Lord Christ will show his power most in their weakness.

Obs. 2. Those that are in God's work, and do intend heaven, they must look for afflictions, they must look for trouble. Ezekiel, saith Christ, I will put thee into my service; but know, thou must not go a smooth way, thou must meet with thorns and briers; thou shalt meet with scorpions and serpents. There is a scorpion in heaven, and scorpions on earth too: let a man be in a heavenly calling, a prophet; let a man be in a worldly calling, a magistrate; he shall meet with scorpions and serpents Through many afflictions we must enter into heaven, and it is well we enter through many afflictions.

Obs. 3. The way and method of the Lord Christ is, to propound unto us the hardest things at first. He deals so with Ezekiel here. He hears of thorns, scorpions, a rebellious house, and hears of that which might have discouraged him; but Christ's way is to let you know what you must look for: Matt. x. "You shall be hated of all men for my name's sake;" you shall be carried to the court; you shall be scourged; you shall be brought before governors; you shall be put to death. He tells them of all these things,

First, because it was the way to arm them against those evils. We say, *præmoniti, præmuniti*, men forewarned are forearmed.

Secondly, that they may have no cause to complain they met with worse things than ever they heard of.

Thirdly, to strengthen their faith. When they should see such things fall out; they might say, These are the things which were foretold, and are tokens that we are in Christ's way. God began the world with this method: Gen. i. "The evening and the morning were the first day." It is not the morning and the evening, but you must have night before day, a winter before a spring, and thunder and lightning before a calm: and this is Christ's way. Therefore, if you intend heaven, think not to meet only with ease.

These things are all general; we come now to more particular observations.

Obs. 1. Then we must walk warily. Though wicked men be not to be feared, yet they are to be heeded. When Christ sent out his apostles, he tells them what thorns and scorpions they must be amongst; men as cruel as wolves, that would persecute unto death; and what saith he? Be wise as serpents, innocent as doves, Matt. x.; keep yourselves from their teeth, do not you inconsiderately run into their harms; give them no just cause or occasion of injuring you. "Be innocent as doves;" without horns, without pushing, goring, wronging any; only be wary, and defend yourselves, as the next verse is. "Beware of men;" look to them, they are dangerous creatures; wolves, thorns, serpents are not so dangerous as they. Be exact, therefore, circumspect; yet not so cautelous as to prejudice duty, or multiply fears; for, ver. 26, it is said, "Fear them not." He had told them they should be hated, ver. 22, scourged, ver. 17, persecuted from place to place, ver. 23, put to death, ver. 21; yet they must not fear, but they must beware of men. He saith not, beware of devils, they were subject unto the disciples through Christ's name; but men would not be subject, therefore beware of them. Ælian tells us, in Libya men slept with their boots on, because of the scorpions, that they might not sting them. Let us not sleep, but walk, booted; I mean, let us be "shod with the preparation of the gospel of peace," Eph. vi. 15, be shod with a disposition unto peace: let us be peaceable, harmless, innocent, and careful of our conversation, that they do neither scratch nor sting us.

ἀκέραιοι.

Ocreatos dormire solere.

Obs. 2. Public and great designs cannot be carried on with ease and speed; there be thorns and briers in the way, yea, scorpions, some difficulty or other. Sluggards pretend lions in the way; but public, active spirits, when they are upon weighty affairs, find lions in the way. Joshua, when about a great work, to take Ai, there was an Achan in the way to make a great demur, and had almost overthrown the design, Josh. vii. Nehemiah had a great work in hand; and were there no obstacles to hinder? Tobiah and Sanballat were in the way, they scoffed, they complied, they armed, threatened; yea, the nobles of Judah give intelligence to Tobiah, Neh. vi. 17. The work of reformation now is a great and good work; and are there no obstacles in the way? Yea, there are thorns, and heaps of them, which have pricked and lamed some; scorpions, which have bit and stung others, that they move not, or very slowly, in this great work: some are unwilling, some unfaithful, some insufficient, some deeply guilty of foul sins, which puts the work more back in one day, than they can forward with their hearts, heads, hands, purses, and lives in many days. There are men employed that are Achans, Sanballats, Judases. We have much policy and carnal wisdom, and think by that to speed great works to their period; but this is, I will not say, the only, but a principal hinderance. While we will convey the ark, and carry on things, upon the shoulders of policy, we are in danger to lose the ark; yea, in danger to lose all. We will not yet see, lay the finger upon the right sore, and go to the root of evils. Things of weight in state or church have their obstacles, and come not to birth in the day of expectation. This should keep our hearts from sinking, and our tongues from censuring, when great designs stick, and come not to perfection. Let us remember there be thorns, scorpions in the way. Pity and pray for the parliament, armies, magistrates, and ministers, who have difficult and dangerous work.

Molestum et impeditum cursum.

Obs. 3. Wonder not that men in place are injured in their credits, and wounded in their estates; they dwell among thorns and scorpions; the fleece and flesh suffer by them many times. Nehemiah is a rebel, Elijah a troubler of Israel, Christ an enemy to Cæsar, and Paul a seditious and pestilent fellow.

The Israelites could not go through the wilderness, without being stung with the fiery serpents. Daniel escaped the teeth of the lions in the den, but not the sting of the scorpions in the court. Men that go into the war, must not think to escape all bullets and blows. Magistrates and ministers are God's soldiers, they both bear the sword; Jer. i. 19, "They shall fight against thee," and it must not seem strange if they get wounds. When Adam and Manasses are among the bushes, can less be expected than wounds? It is the nature of wicked men to blast the name of others; they have learned and do practise the devil's or the Jesuits' doctrine, Reproach to purpose, and something will fasten. But let the wicked black, God will white, wash the names of his servants. Daniel's innocency was cleared up to the king himself, Dan. vi. 22. Christ saith, "Woe to you, when all speak well of you!" Luke vi. He never saith, Woe to you when men speak ill of you! he is so far from that, that he fastens a blessing upon it; Matt. v. 11, "Blessed are you, when men speak all manner of evil of you falsely, for my sake." Basil saith, When men defame us we are sorry for them; else I should almost have said, we acknowledge thanks to them for their blasphemies, as procurers of our bliss. It is honour to be reviled of the wicked, their calumniation is our commendation: then a man shows himself a man of God and for God, when he displeases those who please not God. Seneca could see on which side right was, when he said, *Argumentum est recti malis displicere*, The displeasure of the wicked is a testimony to the truth.

Calumniare fortiter, et aliquid hærebit.

Eorum detractatio est vitæ tuæ approbatio.

Obs. 4. Seek not the acquaintance of wicked men. The prophet Micah will give you reason for it, chap. vii. 4, "The best of them is a brier; the most upright is sharper than a thorn hedge." You think some of them are fair men, have good natures, good parts, great places; and you may be intimate with them, lean upon them, and get good by them, if not do good to them: but you are deceived; saith he, "the best of them," for wit, parts, birth, breeding, place, "is a brier;" yea, "the most upright," those that are civil, that have a form of godliness, and walk according to their light, even they "are sharper than a thorn hedge." And because it is incident to the nature of man to mind great ones, and seek their acquaintance; he speaks, in the verse before, of princes, judges, and great men, and beats men off from looking after and leaning upon them. The sheep run to the hedge for shade in the heat, and shelter in the storm; but what is the issue? If they escape with their lives, yet they go off with rent garments. And if the best of them be briers, what are the worst of them? When David was become a courtier, he met with a spear, and found Saul sharper than a thorn hedge. His spirit was vexed with him, and no marvel; wicked men vex the Spirit of God, who hath more patience and wisdom than men, who is without all corruption, and altogether holy, yet his Spirit is vexed with them, Isa. lxiii. 10. Therefore the Spirit of God counsels us what acquaintance to seek: Job xxii. 21, "Acquaint thyself with God, and be at peace; and thereby good shall come unto thee:" he will not be a brier or thorn to run into thy hand; he will not vex thy spirit; trust him, he will not deceive or disappoint thee.

What shall you, what can you have from a scorpion, but aculeum, vulnus, venenum clam et palam insidiabuntur. Semper lanam, sæpe vitam perdunt. When one commended Julian the cardinal to Sigismund the emperor, he answered, Tamen Romanus est. And so when any wicked man is commended to you, answer, Tamen sentis est.

Obs. 5. See what fruit to look for from them; fruits suitable to their nature. 1 Sam. xxiv. 13, "Wickedness proceedeth from the wicked;" it is a proverb, and they have much truth and strength in them; and it was ancient then, and in all ages hath been made good, observed, that wickedness comes from the wicked. By it David clears himself, taxes his malicious enemies, and confutes Saul himself. As for me, I am accused to be a seditious and traitorous fellow, a man that seeks thy life, O Saul; thou hast followers and flatterers about thee to exasperate thee against me, that put thee on to hunt me as a partridge on the mountain, and to spill my blood; but I am no such man as they pretend, and thou conceivest. I had thee at advantage, was counselled to take away thy life, and could have done it; but wickedness was not in me; I cut off the lap of thy coat when I could have cut off thy head. I will make thee judge who is the wicked man, those that accuse me, thou that pursuest the soul of an innocent man, or myself, that have spared thee, having such advantage. Wickedness proceeds from the wicked: if I had been a wicked subject, as thou and others thought, thy life had gone: but thy courtiers, thy counsellors, are wicked; yea, and thou art wicked, and nothing but wickedness comes from you; and that proceeds as light from the sun, water from the fountain, breath from the nostrils. Christ tells us; we must not look for good from them, Matt. vii. 16, "Do men gather grapes of thorns, or figs of thistles?" If you look for such fruit, you will be deceived; they may grow green as the vine and fig tree, but their fruit is different. What fruit have papists and prelatical ones brought forth in church or state these many years? Corrupt trees cannot bear good fruit: briers, thorns, brambles, may bring fruit for Gadarenes and swine, not for Christ and his disciples. Judg. ix. the olive tree had its fatness, the fig tree its sweetness and good fruit, the vine its pleasant wine; (they would not leave their places for promotion: for usually when men are promoted, they lose of their excellency; the olive trees, fig trees, vines, they lose of their fatness, if not all their fatness, of their sweetness, if not all their sweetness;) but what had the bramble? Fire, and fire to consume the cedars of Lebanon. Brambles are of an aspiring nature, and when they are got up, they fire states and kingdoms.

Obs. 6. Then it is no great loss when wicked men are taken away. When briers and thorns are cut down, and scorpions killed, who is a sufferer by it? Wicked men are the very plagues of the earth, they suck away the sweet from the vine, the fat from the olive. It was said of Nero, that he was *venenum terræ*, the poison of the earth; and when that pitcher was broken, it was gain, not loss, matter for praise, not mourning. The husbandman is not grieved when the grieving thorn and pricking thistle are cut out of his corn. Prov. xi. 10, "When the wicked perish, there is shouting;" shouting on earth, that justice is done, his wickedness at an end, the church and state eased of such a burden, rid of such a thorn; and shouting in hell, Isa. xiv. 9. When Jehoiakim died, there was no lamentation made for him; he was a wicked and worthless king, his carcass was no better than the body of an ass, and he had the burial of an ass, drawn and cast out in the highway or ditches, Jer. xxii. 18, 19; he had an infamous burial. And such, saith Olympiodorus, is the end of every magistrate or minister that teaches and governs well, but lives ill, his end is infamous, he is buried in infamy. But godly men are of great worth: Heb. xi. 38, "The world was not worthy of them;" those precious ones mentioned there, and those who are living now, God valued, and values above the world. Godly men are

Spinæ sunt pestes terræ et frugum morbi. *Plin.*

the pillars of the earth; they are the marrow, blood, and soul of the world; the world languishes and lies dying when they are pulled away. Moses held God's hands, Exod. xxxii. 10. Moses is a man that hath power in earth and in heaven; he is a man that, when there is a danger, can go up to the heavens, and so put the Lord to it, that he saith, Let me alone, that I may destroy this wicked people, and I will make thee a great nation; he would have hired him to come to an accommodation. Men are now upon accommodating, but a Moses will not accommodate; no, not with God himself, when his people are in danger; but he will have a blessing upon good terms, he will have God's wrath removed, and a reconciliation between heaven and earth, or else Moses will never be quiet with God. What a loss is such a man! After his death, if God had not raised up a Joshua, what had become of Israel? When Elijah was taken away, the horsemen and chariots of Israel went.

Obs. 7. See here a ground why we are so wary in having peace with our adversaries. There is much ado about peace; we all say, Peace, but give us leave to be wary when we make a peace, when we dwell among thorns and scorpions. Thorns have their prickles and grievances, scorpions have their stings, and we are unwilling to be stung; we would not have our consciences, our liberties stung; we would not have our privileges plucked from us, and all be in danger; we are unwilling to come to this. When Scotland had made peace with England, Flanders, and the Easterlings, it was said, they had peace with the world: but their prelates made war with God; so we may have peace with men, but there are those amongst us, who, if we look not to it, will make war with God, with the Lamb, and those that follow him. It is reported of the Spaniards, that they had peace with all the world, but were out with God. If we make such a peace, as to have peace with men, and to be out with God, this would be a cursed peace. If wicked men will lay aside their stings and subtilties; be Nathanaels, and not Ahithophels; doves, and not serpents, we would willingly embrace a peace. We have on the shoes of the gospel of the preparation of peace.

Obs. 8. Seeing wicked men are thorns and scorpions, let those in authority look to it, and do their duty, that the briers and thorns grow not too high, nor too great; that scorpions do not abound. It is said there were nine kinds of scorpions about Jerusalem and Syria, and very great ones; and twenty kinds of thorns also. I fear we have all those kinds of thorns and scorpions amongst us. The Greeks have a proverb, There is a scorpion under every stone. And where almost can a man go among us, but there are scorpions, thorns and briers, scratching, catching, and doing a mischief? Let magistrates tread upon those scorpions, and ministers hew those thorns, Psal. xci. 13; Hos. vi. 5. Let ministers do as Chrysostom did, who would have his hand cut off, before he would suffer scorpions and thorns to come to the table of the Lord, to poison that wine and bread, and to prick the sheep that came to feed there. Magistrates likewise should do what lies in them, that neither the scorpions nor briers do mischief the sheep. You may find scorpions in more places than one; in your courts, markets, shops, fields, ale-houses. If you drive them not out of their holes, they will be "pricks in your eyes, and thorns in your sides, and vex you in the land wherein you dwell," Numb. xxxiii. 55. You may make oil of these scorpions, and meat of these leviathans. Pliny and others observe, that if you burn one scorpion in the midst of the house, all the rest will fly away. If authority would execute justice upon some of our scorpions, cut down some of our thorns, the rest would fly away. We are so fearful and backward herein, that we let scorpions multiply, thorns and brambles increase, not only till our fleeces be scratched from us, but our flesh stung about us, our liberties and lives endangered. We will not see where our sore is, nor search to the bottom of it; and because we will not do it, God may justly send fiery serpents to sting us, and afford no brazen serpent to cure us. For your encouragement to deal with these, consider Psal. cxviii. 12; 2 Sam. xxiii. 6; and Ezek. xxviii. 24, where it is said, "There shall be no more a pricking brier, or grieving thorn unto the house of Israel; and they shall know that I am the Lord God."

ὑπο παντί λίθῳ σκορπιος εὕδει.

Another principal observation is, That we must not be afraid of men, whatever they be; especially those who are called to public place, as ministers and magistrates. Christ calls Ezekiel to public service, and four times he is forbidden to fear in this verse. "Be not afraid of them," that is, their frowns, be they great ones, kings, princes, nobles, or whomsoever; be not "afraid of their words," though stormy, grievous, stout, contradictory, &c.; because words do stick and strike deep ofttimes, it is repeated again, "Be not afraid of their words," let them not affect thee, "nor be dismayed at their looks." The Hebrew word חתת signifies to be amazed, dejected, discouraged, and hindered in one's way; but the prophet must not be amazed, or discouraged, with whatever he hears, sees, or meets with.

To give some few reasons concerning this, and some helps whereby to fortify our spirits, that we may not be fearful, having to do with scorpions and thorns:

1. Fears are prejudicial; they take away our liberty; they put halters about our necks, and strangle our comforts; they multiply and prolong our miseries; they wound and disable us. The work is to be done *bene, libere, intrepide,* well, freely, boldly; if we fear, that will fetter, enfeeble, and make us bungle. Isa. xxii. 2, they were slain, not with the sword, but with fears. Fear slays a man while he is alive; fear buries a man before he is dead; fears are prejudicial to those that are in public place.

Tuus timor tibi est Nero, tua tentatio tibi est Julianus.

2. They are to be men of courage who are in public place. Exod. xviii. 21, Moses was to provide able men to be magistrates and rulers; the original is, men of strength and courage. The word signifies virtue, strength, a bulwark, riches, an army, all which do increase courage: so that a magistrate should have the courage of all these; of the virtuous, of the strong, of one in a bulwark, of the rich, of an army. He is to be a man of might: Dan. iii. 20, "He commanded the most mighty men;" it is the same word; the men of most courage, that were of mighty courage, "to bind Shadrach, Meshach, and Abednego." Those God puts into public places are to be such. Josh. i. 9, "Be strong and of a good courage; be not afraid, neither be thou dismayed." Where courage is required, fear is prohibited; and where fear is prohibited, as in our text, there courage is employed. "Should such a man as I flee?" fear? said Nehemiah, chap. vi. 11. No, I will not fear ncr flee, but be courageous, and stand it out against Sanballat and the rest, their power, their scoffs, their threats, their plots. Magistrates, ministers, and all God's people, should be men of courage, when reformation and temple work are in hand. Hag. ii. 4, "Be strong, O Zerubbabel; and be strong, O Joshua; and be strong, all ye people of the land, saith the Lord, and work." The work of reformation, and of

the temple, will not go on if you faint and flag. Samuel was a man of courage, when he told Saul, entreating him to return with him, that he might worship, but he would not return with him, For, thou hast rejected God, and God hath rejected thee from being king; and thinkest thou that I will countenance thee? 1 Sam. xv. 25, 26. So Elijah was no timid prophet, but a man of courage: 1 Kings xviii. 15—19, "As the Lord of hosts liveth, before whom I stand," speaking to Obadiah, "I will surely show myself to Ahab this day." But Jezebel hath vowed thy death, and Ahab makes search for thee all the land over, and if thou be found, thou art a dead man. Well, saith Elijah, I will show myself. And when he came into his presence, what a salute had he! "Art thou he that troubleth Israel?" I will have thee despatched one way or other. Is the prophet daunted now? No, but replies, I am not he, but it is thou and thy father's house. Send and gather to me all Israel: (what a commanding, what a suspicious word was this! he might have thought that this man would get power about him, and offer violence to him and his house:) thou thinkest to have my blood, but I will have the blood of all the false prophets, &c. Who might not think that Elijah rather was king than Ahab? 2 Chron. xxvi. 17, 18, when king Uzziah would have burnt incense to the Lord, the priest resisted Uzziah, and thrust him out of the temple. They that are in public place, are to be men of courage, and therefore they must not fear.

3. God is with his, those he calls and employs in public service. Josh. i. 9, why should he be strong, and of good courage? "for the Lord thy God is with thee." Jer. i. 8, "Be not afraid of their faces; for I am with thee to deliver thee." God's presence should put life into us. When inferior natures are backed with a superior, they are full of courage: when the master is by, the dog will venture upon creatures greater than himself, and fear not; at another time he will not do it, when his master is absent. When God is with us, who is the supreme, it should make us fearless. It did David; Psal. cxviii. 6, "The Lord is on my side," my help; "I will not fear: what can man do unto me." Let him do his worst, frown, threat, plot, arm, strike; the Lord is on my side, he hath a special care of me, he is a shield unto me, I will not fear, but hope: as it is in the next verse, "I shall see my desire on them that hate me," I shall see them changed or ruined. Our help is in the name of the Lord, but our fears are in the name of man. God takes special care of men in public place. The angels of the church are as the stars in his right hand, Rev. i. 16, he holds them fast; and it is said of Christ, Isa. xlix. 2, that he was hid "in the shadow of his hand;" in the protection of his hand, is the Septuagint. *Umbra est symbolum protectionis*, The shadow is the symbol of protection, it defends from the heat of the sun, that was in Judea exceeding hot: God hides Christ, yea, all that are eminent, and under, who belong to him, in a special manner, and delivers them from danger. Zech. ii. 5, I will be unto Jerusalem "a wall of fire round about;" who shall dare to come near it then, to hurt the magistrates, ministers, or people there? Some think it alludes to the cherubim, that with a fiery flaming sword kept paradise; others, to the fiery chariots round about Dothan, 2 Kings vi. 17, where Elisha was: either of these is good, and notes protection. But there is another, and it may be a more suitable interpretation; and it is this: When they travelled in the wilderness, oft wild beasts would be assaulting them, especially in the night, when they laid down to rest; then they made a circular fire about them, and so no beast, lion, wolf, or leopard dare meddle with them, the fire was a wall to them: and hence the expression seems to be taken, that God, when wild beasts, wicked men, should offer violence to Jerusalem, he would be a wall of fire round about it.

Jer. i. 19.

4. Those who are in public place, are in God's place; "I have said, Ye are gods," Psal. lxxxii. 6. Moses was to Aaron instead of God, Exod. iv. 16. And so ministers, they are in Christ's stead, 2 Cor. v. 20; and they must be like unto God, fearless of men, but dreadful unto men. It is an ill thing to see a drunken god, to hear a swearing god; and it is as ill to see a trembling, fearful god, a magistrate, a minister, afraid of man, whenas they, having the image and authority of God stamped upon them, are to make others, especially sinners, to quake. Rom. xiii. 4, the apostle bids evil-doers, not the powers, be afraid. Why? they are the ministers of God, and bear not the sword in vain; they must not fear, but make others do it. So did the apostles and prophets; John made Herod quake, and Paul made Felix tremble: here were lambs scaring lions.

5. They that are godly, true christians, their godliness, their cause suffers by their fearfulness. They have received another spirit than that of the world, 1 Cor. ii. 12, even the Spirit of God, which is no timorous, cowardly Spirit: the apostle denies that, 2 Tim. i. 7, "God hath not given us the spirit of fear; but of power, of love, and a sound mind." Where there is a base fear, there is sickness of mind, no soundness; and there is little love, and less power. Those that have the Spirit of Christ, and the Spirit of God, it is not for them to fear. Have you the Spirit of the Lord of hosts in you? have you the Spirit of Jesus Christ in you? and will you fear and tremble before men, that have the spirit of devils in them? The Spirit of the Lord of hosts is like himself, and the Spirit of Jesus Christ is like Christ himself: he was not afraid of any. If therefore men in place have this Spirit, they must not fear, for they do dishonour christianity, and the Spirit they have received from their Lord and Master Jesus Christ.

6. There is not that in wicked men, that should make us to fear them, if we consider they are briers, thorns, scorpions, contemptible things, rather to be despised than feared. If they had truth, grace, and God with them, then they might be feared: they have not God with them, they are a rebellious house, and he is against them. They cannot pray to fetch in might to make them dreadful: if they say a prayer, "the prayer of the wicked is abomination to the Lord." They are full of fears themselves, and have no true valour in them; that arises from other and better principles than they have. If they had truth of grace, God with them, then we might fear them; but their guilt, their wickedness doth weaken them, and multiply their fears. Can wicked men be without fears? Isa. viii. 12, "Fear ye not their fear:" they have a slavish, distracting, heart-smiting, tormenting, hellish fear. Saul feared the people, 1 Sam. xv. 24. Is there not a spirit of fear upon many in Ireland and England too? Have not judges feared the courts they have sat in?

7. God will dismay and confound us, if we fear men. Jer. i. 17, "Be not dismayed at their faces, lest I confound thee before them," or break thee in pieces. Jeremiah, saith God, if thou dost fear them, and betray the truth I have committed to thee, I will forsake thee, leave thee to their hands, malice, cruelty, and break thee to pieces before their faces. Fearfulness doth much provoke God. He that sees not sufficiency in God to support him, shall find enough

to daunt and confound him; but if we go on with courage, discharge the place and trust committed to us, if we should fall into the hands of wicked men, and suffer, God will own us, let out himself unto us, support us, sympathize with us, deliver us, or make us and our sufferings glorious. Stars shine in the night; they are obscured in the day. When Vincentius was tormented by the tyrant, he said, Thou shalt see me more courageous in suffering, than thyself in tormenting.

Stellæ in nocte lucent, in die latent. *Bern. in Cant.* Videbis me plus posse dum torqueor quam ipse dum torques.

Some helps against fear.

1. Let your fear be exercised about God; he is an object fit to be feared. All flesh is grass, all nations are a drop of the bucket, and the small dust of the balance; inhabitants of the earth are as a swarm of flies, a troop of grasshoppers; and shall we fear these little things? The world is nothing unto God; there is no greatness beside God himself. He hath made the world, he hath dried up the seas, he sends out the mighty winds, he changes times and seasons; he brings princes to nothing, makes judges vanity; he tumbles nations into hell, and can destroy the soul and body eternally. Him fear, saith Christ, Luke xii. 4, 5, not men, that can but kill the body; but fear him, who, after the body is dead, can kill the soul, and cast into hell; I say unto you, fear him. And Isa. viii. 13, "Sanctify the Lord of hosts himself; and let him be your fear, let him be your dread:" let there be such a frame of spirit in you as becomes the Lord of hosts, suitable to his greatness, his sovereignty and authority over you and all creatures; then you will not fear. When the fear of God is strong in your heart, then the fear of man ceaseth. When the dictator ruled at Rome, then all other officers ceased; and when this fear of God rules, all other fears will be hushed: and that is not all, if God be sanctified by us, he will be a sanctuary unto us.

Nihil magnum, nisi magnus Deus.

Psal. cxix. 120.

2. Set faith to work. Men in public places should have their hands at work on earth, and their faith in heaven. The just live by faith, and will not die by fear. Hezekiah, 2 Chron. xxxii. 7, 8, when Sennacherib was coming against Jerusalem, and troubled the whole land, he set his hands to work to fortify the city, and his faith to fortify himself: "Be strong and courageous, be not afraid nor dismayed for the king of Assyria and his multitude; for there be more with us than be with him: with him is an arm of flesh; but with us is the Lord our God to help us, and to fight our battles." Here was an army of 185,000 to affright him; but here was faith in the Lord of hosts to establish him. Moses feared not "the wrath of the king: for he endured, as seeing him who is invisible," Heb. xi. 27: by faith he saw the invisible God, and that made him hold out against the king, though his wrath was hot, his looks fierce, his words terrible, his face cruel. Moses knew, that whatever he lost for God, he should find in God. Prov. xxix. 25, "The fear of man bringeth a snare: but whoso putteth his trust in the Lord shall be safe." Man's fear brings a snare, and so death. Had Moses feared Pharaoh, he had compounded with him, and so ruined himself and others: but he that puts his trust in the Lord shall be safe; the Hebrew is, set on high, like a bird upon the wing, that is, out of the reach of every snare and fowler, though never so cunning. Cardinal Borromæus being told of great danger from some who lay in wait for him, said, *An Deus est in mundo pro nihilo?* Is God idle in the world? and Johannes Silentiarius, being in the like case, said, If God take not care of me, why do I live?

Si Deus mei curam non habet, quid vivo?

3. Labour for purity and holiness. The most holy men are the least fearing men. Paul was of great courage, he had much holiness, 1 Thess. ii. 10, and when the viper leaped upon his hand, he feared not; it could not kill him, but he could kill it; he shook it into the fire. Adam, at first no creature could harm him, because holy. In the lives of the fathers, mention is made of one Abbas Paulus, who handled serpents and scorpions, and cut them in pieces, without any hurt; and being asked how he came to this condition, said, If a man be holy, all things are subject to him, as to Adam before his sin in paradise. If our hearts and consciences be polluted, we shall fear, if not flee. 1 Sam. xviii. 12, Saul was afraid of David: he had great riches, many forces, yet fears David, a poor man, a banished, reproached man. And Herod feared John: he was a holy man: piety has great weight. Job xvii. 9, "The righteous shall hold on his way, and he that hath clean hands shall be stronger and stronger." "The righteous are bold as a lion," Prov. xxviii. 1. A man that is truly and thoroughly godly, that knows nothing by himself, that hath purged out every spot, and gotten off all guilt, and needs not blush at any thing, past or present, he is a lion, he is a brazen wall, nothing shall daunt him; but the wicked flee when none pursue. Nehemiah was a holy man, and he would not flee; but Manasseh, a wicked king, hides himself among the thorns, and Adam runs to the thickets; they had prickings without, and worse prickles within.

4. Value not life too much. Let us be willing to lay out our lives in God's service, to spend and be spent for God. Paul said, "I am ready not to be bound only, but to die at Jerusalem for the name of the Lord Jesus," Acts xxi. 13: he prized the name of Christ above his life; and if we would prize something above our lives, we should not so overrate them, as, through fear of man, to lose better things to keep them. The devil tells us, "Skin for skin, yea, all that a man hath will he give for his life," Job ii. 4: true, all to save life. But there are some things of more worth than man's life; as, the glory of God, the favour of God, the peace of God, the truth of God, the name of Christ, &c.; and we should so account of them, and be ready to sacrifice our lives for them. Nehemiah would not go into the temple to save his life; he knew the glory of God, the cause, work, and people of God, should suffer by it, and therefore he would venture his life. So Basil, when threatened with cruel usage and death, said to him who had the power in his hand, This body thou art lord of only, not of our faith, or the cause we stand for; and whereas swords, wild beasts, cutting of our flesh, &c. are threatened, these things are rather pleasures than terrors to us; we look at better things than the world hath, for which we are not unwilling to lay out our lives. The worthies of those times "loved not their lives unto the death," they stood, bled, died for Christ and his cause, who had stood, bled, died for them, Rev. xii. 11. Another observation is, that it is the lot of the righteous to dwell amongst the wicked. The prophet here dwelt amongst scorpions, and was amidst briers and thorns, a sad habitation, yet such as is common to the saints. Lot dwelt in Sodom, and his righteous soul was vexed, 2 Pet. ii. 8; it was pained, tormented, as a man upon the rack. And David dwelt among those who were enemies to peace, and it made him cry out, "Woe is me, that I sojourn in Mesech, that I dwell in the tents of Kedar!" Psal. cxx. 5; that is, with ungodly and barbarous people. And it is not the condition of some few, but the church itself.

Potius nobis deliciæ quam tormenta sunt.

which is "as a lily among thorns," Cant. ii. 2. So was the church in Egypt, in Babylon, in the primitive times, amongst the persecuting emperors and their officers; so in the time of antichrist, and at this day, it is among thorns and scorpions: but here is the comfort of it, God takes notice thereof. The church of Pergamus dwelt where Satan's throne was; where he bare most sway, had most honour, a multitude of servants; where was great uncleanness, hot persecution, Rev. ii. 13: there did the church of Pergamus dwell: and what saith the text, "I know thy works, and where thou dwellest;" I know, that is, I take special notice of all thy works, wrongs, how the thorns do scratch, the scorpions sting thee, and I will reward thee for all. After mention being made of Lot's being vexed with the Sodomites, it is said, "The Lord knoweth how to deliver the godly out of temptations;" he observes who they are among, how they are tempted, and knows ways of deliverance for them, and appears amongst them, 2 Pet. ii. 9.

Ver. 7. *And thou shalt speak my words unto them, whether they will hear, or whether they will forbear: for they are most rebellious.*

There is nothing difficult in this verse; the words, "they are most rebellious," in the original are, they are rebellion, in the abstract; noting the strength and growth of their sin, of which hath been spoken in the 5th verse; only observe from hence:

1. That the messengers of God must speak the word of God. "Thou shalt speak my words unto them;" not thine own, not other men's, but my words. God's words are divine, *verba vitæ et mortis*, words of life and of death, and they must be spoken unto the people; not our chaffy, powerless words. Matt. xxviii. 20, "Teaching them to observe whatsoever I have commanded you;" they must speak only that, and all that, nothing must they dissemble or hide away.

2. That God cares not whether wicked, vile sinners hear or not. It is sufficient to him that they refuse offers of grace; that is enough to justify him, and condemn them; "whether they will hear or forbear," it matters not, I shall have my glory, and thou thy reward, whatever becomes of them. And God deals roundly with them. So Christ, in Mark xvi. 16, "He that believeth shall be saved, and he that believeth not shall be damned;" yea, John iii. 18, "He that believeth not is condemned already." And when Christ sent out his disciples, see how quick and round he is with those who should not receive them and their word: "Whosoever shall not receive you and your words, when ye depart out of that house or city, shake off the dust of your feet," as a testimony against them, Matt. x. 14. "It shall be more easy for Sodom and Gomorrah than for that house or city," Mark vi. 11.

Ver. 8—10. *But thou, son of man, hear what I say unto thee; Be not thou rebellious like that rebellious house: open thy mouth, and eat that I give thee. And when I looked, behold, an hand was sent unto me; and, lo, a roll of a book was therein; and he spread it before me: and it was written within and without: and there was written therein lamentations, and mourning, and woe.*

In these verses, besides Christ instructing of the prophet, you have his further confirmation in his prophetical office, and that by a visible sign, by which he conveys the gift of prophesying unto Ezekiel; and it is by "a roll of a book," concerning which we have these things considerable:

1. The efficient cause, or whence it came, "an hand was sent unto me."

2. The material cause, "a roll of a book."

3. The opening of it, it was "spread before me."

4. The contents of it, "lamentations, mourning, and woe."

But before we come to this roll, and the particulars of it, we must speak of Christ's instructions to the prophet, in the 8th verse, where we have,

First, an exhortation, "Son of man, hear what I say unto thee."

Secondly, a prohibition, "Be not thou rebellious like that rebellious house."

Thirdly, a command, "Open thy mouth, and eat that I give thee."

The sum of the verse is this: Ezekiel, saith Christ, see thou hearken unto my voice; whatsoever I say to thee, let that be acceptable: regard not what men, what thy heart and carnal reason, say to thee; but remember I am God and King, I sit upon the throne, my counsels and words must stand. Be not thou rebellious as the Jews are; let not their example, power, relation to thee, make thee refuse to hear what I say, or to eat this visible and sacramental sign which I give thee.

There is nothing difficult in the verse to clear up unto you; only these words, "open thy mouth," you may think superfluous, and that the word "eat" had been enough: but there is nothing idle in the Scripture, all is of weight, and such weight, that heaven and earth shall pass away before one iota of God's word. It is a rule among the learned, *Vox quæ videtur otiosa plurimum facit ad effectum*, The word which seems least important gives the greatest force. It notes the ardent desire of Christ, that the prophet should have the benefit of this sacramental sign, and that he should be forward and ready unto it, do any thing that conduced that way.

Obs. 1. That those who are to teach others, must first hear and be taught themselves; they must hear Christ, and learn of him. Ezekiel must hear what Christ saith unto him, and then he would be fit to speak unto others. When the Lord Christ sent out his disciples, he instructed them first, Matt. x. So the apostles were taught forty days together in the things pertaining to the kingdom of God, Acts i. 3; the institution of churches, the laws, government, ordinances, offices, and officers of them, they were instructed in. And John, in his first epistle, chap. i. 3, saith, "That which we have seen and heard declare we unto you." And so it was of the prophets, what they heard, that they spake: Heb. i. 1, "God spake unto the fathers by the prophets;" he first spake to the prophets, and in them to the fathers. The ministers and messengers of God must hear Christ first, and then declare his mind; be obedient unto his commands, and then mention and publish his will.

Obs. 2. God looks for more from them he calls to any service than from others. And "thou, son of man, be not thou rebellious;" I expect other things at thy hand; I look thou shouldst be as tractable as they have been untractable, as dutiful as they have been rebellious: you see who have been most active among them against me, I look thou shouldst be as active in thy place for me. Those God doth put honour upon, and set in public places, it is equal he should have much from, yea, more than from others. Paul says, The Lord Christ enabled me, counted me faithful, put me into the ministry, 1 Tim. i. 12; and, 1 Cor. xv. 10, "His grace which was bestowed upon me was not in vain; but I laboured more abundantly than they all." God, who had done much for him, expected it at his hands; and he deceived not expectation.

Obs. 3. See here what God accounts rebellion. We think it must be some great, notorious thing that makes a rebel or rebellious; but there is great difference between the judgment of men and judgment of God. If Ezekiel should be difficult and backward to his work he called him unto, he would count it rebellion; if he would not hear and do what God bid him, he should be numbered among the rebellious. If he did not hear every thing that Christ spake, *Quæcunque ad te loquar audi*, Whatsoever things I shall speak to thee, hear thou; so the words are read by Calvin, and the original bears it; if there should be a crossing of God's will in any thing, in the least thing, in refusing to hear or do, it should be before him rebellion. Isa. i. 20, "If ye refuse and rebel:" refusing to hear God's will, and to do it, being heard, is rebellion against God. So in 1 Sam. xii. 15, "If ye will not obey the voice of the Lord, but rebel against the commandment:" not obeying God, whatever pretence we have, is rebellion.

Obs. 4. That we must not follow the examples and ways of sinful men. "Be not thou rebellious like that rebellious house;" they have set an ill example before thee, do not thou imitate them; they have written a foul copy, write not after them; they have walked in wrong paths, do not trace their steps. Men usually are such as those they live with. It is easy to grow naught, if we live among those that are naught. Joseph learned to swear in Pharaoh's court, and Peter to judaize among the Jews. Consent and example of others, is like a mighty torrent that carries down all before it. Example is a potent thing; Gal. ii. 14, "Why compellest thou the gentiles to judaize?" Paul tells Peter, that there was a compulsory virtue and force in his example, to draw the gentiles into evil. And it is certain, the customs, traditions, persuasions, and examples of friends, are of much prevalency. That Christ foresaw, and arms the prophet against them: "Hear what I say," not what they say; let them say what they will, regard it not; only let my words have place in thee, and power with thee. But thou wilt object and say, They are my friends that persuade me; my kindred, my own flesh and blood, that counsel me; they are great ones, yea, all, prince and people, that go that way; they are my parents that command me to do so, and I may sin in refusing to hearken unto them. The Lord Christ takes off all these and other objections: Be not rebellious, as they have been, and are; but consider, are they friends, kindred, great, parents? and have they and theirs long been in that way? know, that I that speak to thee am thy Friend, and best Friend thou hast. I am thy Kinsman; I am here in the form of the Son of man, and to suffer in thy nature hereafter, that thou mayst be the son of God. I am thy Brother, who hath redeemed thee from sin, death, and hell. If others be great, I am greater than they, and my throne is above all thrones; if they be thy parents, I am thy "everlasting Father," Isa. ix. 6; and as I have had everlasting care of thee, so do give thee everlasting laws and rules of worship and godliness, in comparison of whose light and wisdom all men are darkness and folly. And what! will you prefer friends, kindred, great ones, parents, any before me? Be not rebellious like them, but hearken unto me, and let them go. Make no league with them that are wicked and rebellious, Exod. xxxiv. 12; do not imitate their worship, match not into their families, feast not at their tables, choose none of their ways, Prov. iii. 31; and, Rom. xii. 2, "Be not conformed to this world, but be ye transformed by the renewing of your mind;" that is, do not make the manners of the world the rule of your life, nor the worship of the world the rule of your worship, but look higher. Let not your corrupt minds, that will carry you after a corrupt world, a corrupt worship, and corrupt manners, prevail with you; but receive new light from Christ and the gospel into your minds, and then you will be transformed, you will reject all old ways, old traditions and examples of men, and will be led by Christ, and live by his rules and laws. And thus we may be wiser than our forefathers and teachers. Psal. cxix. 99, 100, "I have more understanding than all my teachers," saith David, and "I understand more than the ancients." And what was the ground of it? He made God's law and word his meditation and his rule. And those in these latter days, that have done so, have got more understanding than their teachers, and are wiser than the ancients that are for human inventions. It is laws, not examples, we must look to; and the lawyers have a rule very useful, Men must consider, not what is done, but what ought to be done.

Præcepta ducunt, exempla trahunt.

Pro fæcibus humanis.

Non tam spectandum quid Romæ fiat, quam quid fieri debeat.

Obs. 5. That it is the Lord's prerogative to appoint significant typical and sacramental signs. "Eat that I give thee:" that was the roll, which was sacramental, and signified the gift of prophecy. No man may lift up a creature to a higher spiritual excellency than what God has set it in by nature. What mortal had power to have put upon the brazen serpent a typicalness to represent Christ? who had power to make the rainbow a sign of the covenant between God and man? who could make the temple a type of Christ, but he that filled the temple with glory? and who can institute sacraments, ordinary or extraordinary, but God and Christ? In them always is a command and a promise of grace, which falls not within the compass of man's power.

Obs. 6. That the Lord Christ provides meat for his servants: "Eat that I give thee." Christ had prophetical meat for him, a roll to give him. It is from Christ that truths come. As a nurse prepares meat for the child, and puts it into the mouth of the child, so doth Christ here; he ever gives seed to his sowers; he furnisheth his servants with abilities; if they want books he will provide them.

Ver. 9. *And when I looked, behold, an hand was sent unto me; and, lo, a roll of a book was therein.*

Here we have the efficient instrumental and material cause to treat of. "A hand was sent unto me," sent from Christ. There could not be a hand without some author. He that sat upon the throne, and made all, he made, he sent this hand. No mention is made of any arm or body: a hand might write it, and reach it forth. In Belshazzar's sad vision, the fingers of a hand came forth, and wrote upon the plaster of the wall, Dan. v. 5; nothing but a hand appeared. Had there been no hand, the prophet might have doubted whence it came, taken it for some casual thing; but being reached out by a hand, it was evident to him it came from Heaven, even him that he saw so glorious, fell down before, and was comforted by.

The material cause is, "a roll of a book," מגלת־ ספר The ancients at first wrote in barks of trees, afterwards in skins of beasts, which they call *Pergamena*, vellum, or parchment, supposing them to be invented at Pergamus, by king Attalus, where was a famous library of parchments and manuscripts; but rolls of vellum or parchment were before that time. Ezekiel's vision was long before the Roman monarchy; Attalus lived when that flourished, and having no issue, made the Roman state heir to his crown; but rolls were in Isaiah's days, chap. viii. 1, "Take thee a great roll;" yea, in David's days, Psal. xl. 7, "In the volume of thy book," במגלת־ספר in the roll of thy book. They are very ancient, and called rolls from the rolling them up about cedar, or some precious wood, that they might be the better preserved. The law and prophets were written in such rolls, and when they unrolled them, the Jewish doctors used to expound them, as is gathered from that place, Luke iv. 17. These rolls are in practice to this day in the Jewish synagogue; and they have their תורה or law written in one volume, and rolled up, as Paræus observes on the 5th of the Revelation. Kings have their courts of rolls. And there is nothing ancient in the courts and libraries of princes, in their treasury of monuments, but is written in rolls or volumes.

Nihil est vetustum in principum archivis quod non sit scriptum in voluminibus. *Calv.*

For the signification of this roll, some make it to signify the secret counsels of God. It is true, they were written in it, but not signified by it. The roll here is *symbolum prophetiæ*, a typical sign of the gift of prophecy to be given to the prophet, and in that sense we are to take it.

Obs. 1. That the Lord Christ doth at his pleasure put forth creative and infinite virtue to effect what he speaks. "Eat that I give thee;" and presently a hand is created, a roll is presented unto the prophet, which none could have done being destitute of divine power. Christ hath a hand in readiness always to do what he will have done. He hath sometimes a visible hand to do it, as here; sometimes an invisible. When he called Lazarus forth from the grave, he had a hand invisible to effect it; when he bid the dead to hear, the dumb to speak, the lame to walk, devils to depart their habitation, he had an invisible hand that effected those things. So in Acts xi. 20, 21, when some of the brethren had preached the Lord Christ, and faith in him, it is said presently, "The hand of the Lord was with them, and a great number believed;" there was a secret hand of divine power effecting that in their hearts, which the disciples preached in their ears. And Acts iv. 30, Christ hath a hand to stretch forth, and to heal; to heal soul diseases, and bodily too; to heal state and church diseases. The leper said to Christ, "Lord, if thou wilt, thou canst make me clean. And Jesus put forth his hand, and touched him, saying, I will; be thou clean. And immediately his leprosy was cleansed," Matt. viii. 2, 3. If we would look to Christ as this leper did, we might find and feel the hand of Christ.

Obs. 2. That the Lord doth oftentimes extraordinary things for the encouragement and confirmation of his servants in their function. Here is a hand and a roll reached out to Ezekiel. Jeremiah is fearful and backward to the work of God, and God, to encourage and establish him, puts forth his hand, and toucheth his mouth, Jer. i. 9. Moses is doubting, and pleading with God to dismiss him; but by the miracles of the rod, and of the leprous hand, he is confirmed in his call to that great and hard service, Exod. iv. Isaiah's lips are touched with a coal from the altar in the hand of a seraphim, his iniquity is purged, and so he is heartened to his work, Isa. vi. Christ breathed upon his apostles, and said, "Receive the Holy Ghost," John xx. 22; by these extraordinary things they were consecrated to and confirmed in their offices.

Obs. 3. That there is a near conjunction and sweet analogy between the symbols the Lord Christ useth, and the things intended. Christ intends here the gift of prophecy, to confirm that upon Ezekiel. Now what is the external sign or symbol? It is a book written full of prophetical things, and so did fitly resemble the thing intended. In all the symbols that God had used in the Old and New Testament in a sacramental way, there have been fit analogies between them and the thing signified by them. Circumcision, the paschal lamb, water in baptism, bread and wine in the supper of the Lord, do set out the manifold wisdom of God and Christ in accommodating symbols so near to the truth, and holding it forth so lively; and the wisdom of Christ appeared in conveying the gift of prophecy by "a roll of a book." From this example of Christ, giving a roll to Ezekiel, some conceive, springs that custom in the universities, at the creation of doctors,—it is done by reaching them out a book; but how warrantable, I leave to judgment. They that do it, may give them *volumen*, but not *rem voluminis*, the volume, but not its power. If they had given them the gift of prophecy, we should never have had so many unpreaching doctors and prelates.

Obs. 4. That the gift of prophecy is from Christ. He reached out a hand, and gave the roll of a book. He is the great Prophet, and hath all prophecy and prophetical power in himself; and whom he pleaseth he can make a prophet, and inspire with prophetical virtue, and where he pleases, even in Babylon as well as in Canaan.

Ver. 10. *And he spread it before me: and it was written within and without: and there was written therein lamentations, and mourning, and woe.*

In this verse you have the opening of the roll, the fulness and contents of it. "He spread it before me," that is, unrolled it, and laid it open before me. The word in the original signifies to expound and interpret; and we may conceive that Christ did not only spread the roll before his eyes, but caused him to understand it: by this spreading, he saw it was written within and without; but by Christ's interpretation of it, he knew that there were written in it, "lamentations, mourning, and woe."

Expanditur quando hoc quod obscure prolatum fuerat per latitudinem intellectus aperitur. *Greg.*

"It was written within and without." The Hebrew is, in the face and in the back; that is, on both sides. Lavater thinks, that on one side were written their sins, and on the other God's judgments. This fulness of the roll intimates, either the length of the prophecy, as Vatablus conceives, or a multitude of evils hanging over the heads of the Jews, as Maldonate thinks, or the abundance of revelations committed to the prophet, as Junius; not what Jerom and Bellarmine conceit, that the writing within and without should note the literal and mystical sense of the Scripture.

"Lamentations, mourning, and woe." Here are the contents of the roll, bitter and sad things; the burning of the temple, the overthrow of Jerusalem, the captivity of the Jewish nation, and all the evil which should befall them. The word *kinim*, lamentation, noteth a plain complaint, a sad speech, testifying the sorrows of mind; as David in the case of Absalom, "O Absalom, Absalom," &c.; this was a natural complaint, and simple lamentation, suddenly breaking forth, without all premeditation.

Amara et mœsta.

Mourning is more, it is deeper, and upon consideration. The word in the Hebrew is from הגה to meditate, and noteth the deepest sigh. When one hath mused much and seriously upon the cause and matter of grief, and then fetcheth deep sighs, such as are indicative of intense and bitter sorrows, that is the mourning here. Isa. xxxviii. 14, "I did mourn like a dove;" the Hebrew is, I will meditate, noting mourning that comes from meditation; the dove's mourning is inward. Cranes chatter and lament, doves mourn.

"Woe." This word הי noteth not only the voice in lamentations and groans in mourning, but knocking of the breast, and clapping of the hands together, as is used in great afflictions: thus some interpreters understand it; but I conceive by "woe" here, is meant the threatenings of judgment, or judgments threatened, according to those woes in Matt. xxiii. and the fruit of them, as it is, Lam. v. 16.

Obs. 1. That divine mysteries are unknown to men, though very easy and familiar, till they be unfolded. This roll could the prophet never have comprehended the meaning of, if Christ had not opened it. Take all the types and ceremonies of the law, there were mysteries wrapped up in them, which neither Aaron nor Moses had known, if they had been left to their own abilities. Those elements used in baptism and the supper of the Lord, we should never have known the mysteries of them, if Heaven had not helped us. Would we think the rainbow an emblem of mercy, if Scripture had not held it out to us? Indians, heathens, do not, cannot so apprehend it. Take any divine mysteries, they are too transcendent for our capacities, there are depths in them that we cannot fathom: 2 Cor. ii. 14, the natural man cannot know the things of God, they are spiritually discerned; there must be a great mystery wrought in him before he can discern mysteries.

Obs. 2. It is the Lord Christ that opens and interprets mystical things efficaciously unto the faithful. He spread the roll before Ezekiel, and made him to understand the mysteries of it. What are the Scriptures but a roll folded up, a book sealed till Christ open it? We may all say as the eunuch, being demanded if he understood what he read, said, "How can I, except some man guide me?" Acts viii. 30, 31. So, unless Christ guide us, and lead us into the mysteries of the word, we cannot understand them. When none could open the book sealed up, "the Lion of the tribe of Judah" could do it, Rev. v. 5. He hath strength to untie all knots, and a Spirit to search all deeps. Christ himself is the greatest mystery, and he is the great opener of mysteries: "All things are delivered to me of my Father; and no man knoweth the Father, save the Son, and he to whom the Son will reveal him," Matt. xi. 27. If ever God be made known savingly to the soul, it must be by the Lord Christ; and he doth not reveal unto all, but to whomsoever he will, to his elect ones; from others he conceals him; they have the letter, the roll, but not the mystery thereof; their light is darkness. But there are some in the world, that Christ doth interpret the riddles and dark things of the Scripture unto: see that place in John xv. 15, "Henceforth," saith Christ, "I call you not servants; for the servant knoweth not what his lord doeth: but I have called you friends; for all things that I have heard of my Father I have made known unto you." These were Christ's friends, Christ revealed all to them, but from others all was kept. It was Christ revealed unto the prophets what they had, and to the apostles what they had. The Scripture may well be called the Revelation of Christ. You have one book called so; Rev. i. 1, "The Revelation of Jesus Christ, which God gave unto him, to show unto his servants," that is, his faithful ones. If we would therefore understand the roll of the book, the mysteries in the Scripture, we must look up to Christ, and entreat him to spread them before our eyes, and to interpret them to our hearts.

Obs. 3. That the servants of God must not refuse to receive and propound large and sad messages to the people. Here is a "roll, written within and without," and filled with "lamentation, and mourning, and woe." Here was *liber mortis*, a book of death, and deadly things; this the prophet must receive, and declare to the people, however they take it. People would gladly hear from the men of God good tidings; they would have a law of kindness in our lips, our mouths to drop honey; they would have us sons of consolation: but we must speak what our great Lord and Master puts into the roll; if he bid us preach "lamentation, mourning, and woe," we must do it.

Obs. 4. That the Lord gives to his prophets truths suitable to his providence. Here is a roll, full of "lamentation, mourning, and woe;" sad things, and such things the Lord was bringing upon them. There is a sweet analogy between God's word and works; his works are his word fulfilled: Psal. cxlviii. 8, "Fire and hail, snow and vapours, stormy wind; fulfilling his word." When there is thunder and lightning, snows, rains, and winds, these are fulfillings of God's word: no providences do cross his word, but all perform it. God's works are the best commentaries upon his word; and had we the wisdom to bring his word and works together, we should see a sweet harmony between them. This roll given to the prophet, and God's proceedings with the Jews after, were proportionable, they felt what here was written. All that is done in the world now, is the fulfilling of what was written. When God gave John his Revelation, he laid in truths to suit with his providence and works to the end of the world. It is *liber Providentialis*, the book of Providence, and many things in it are acting in our days, and before our eyes, though we discern it not: there are truths for these times, and it is their advantage that can take them up.

Obs. 5. That dreadful things hang over the head of a sinful, guilty nation.

CHAPTER III.

Ver. 1—3. *Moreover he said unto me, Son of man, eat that thou findest; eat this roll, and go speak unto the house of Israel. So I opened my mouth, and he caused me to eat that roll. And he said unto me, Son of man, cause thy belly to eat, and fill thy bowels with this roll that I give thee. Then did I eat it; and it was in my mouth as honey for sweetness.*

THESE words, and to the end of the 15th verse, by some expositors, are made part of the second chapter; and when the division of chapters was made, (about four hundred and fifty-seven years since,) it had been more suitable to have ended the second chapter at the 4th or 15th verse of this chapter, than where it is; but we will take it as we find it. In the chapter you have,

I. A further narration of Ezekiel's call, to the 12th verse.

II. A declaration of what befell him thereupon, from the 12th to the 16th.

III. A new revelation, with the events following it, unto the end of the chapter.

In the first part of the chapter you have two things:

The first is the continuance of Christ's speech, and the prophet's actions about the sacramental sign, viz. the roll.

Secondly, a renewal of his sending to prophesy, which is from the 4th verse to the 11th.

In these verses there is little that needs explaining. That which hath most difficulty in it, is the "eating of the roll." What eating is here meant? How could the prophet eat a great roll (a thing not credible) without prejudice of his health, life, or both?

Answ. He that commanded him to eat, could have prevented all danger and prejudice, if the eating had been corporal and literal. But it is conceived here, that the eating was not literal, but spiritual, or in vision; and that in the 10th verse of the chapter confirms us in it, where it is said, "All my words that I shall speak unto thee, receive in thine heart, and hear with thine ears:" this was the eating, to hear, meditate, and believe. His journey was spiritual, his work was spiritual; he was to go and prophesy, and such was his meat, spiritual meat, and spiritually eaten.

But why is he bid to eat the roll? had not seeing and reading been more suitable? Look on it, read it; why is the mouth brought in rather than the eye or ear?

Answ. The Scripture doth attribute excellency to, and place natural and supernatural virtue in, that organ or sense by which it is exercised. Gen. ii. 7, "God breathed into his nostrils the breath of life;" the meaning is, he put a soul into him. The nostrils are not the seat of the soul; but because the breath in the nostrils doth manifest the presence of the soul in man, and discovers it, therefore it is said, "He breathed into his nostrils the breath of life." And so here, Ezekiel is said to "eat the roll;" not to see or hear it, because by the mouth the gift of prophecy which was given him by the roll was to be manifested and discovered to the people.

"Cause thy belly to eat." Could his, or can any man's belly eat? This seems a strange speech: but take it thus; eating is taken in Scripture, not only for chewing, but for all the actions belonging to meat, as concoction and consumption of it; and the Hebrew word אכל signifies to eat, to dissolve, to consume; and so the sword and fire in Scripture are said to eat, that is, to dissolve, and to destroy. The meaning then is, do thou by this roll, as the stomach and belly do by meat, when they get good thereby: the one doth not presently reject, nor the other transmit, but they retain the meat, draw out all the virtue, concoct it, live and work in the strength of it: so here, "let thy belly eat," that is, concoct, digest the truths thou hearest, by serious meditation, and by faith: do not like those that have weak and sickly stomachs, that quickly return what they receive, and get no benefit thereby; but do thou take in all the arguments and truths of this roll; do thou so concoct and consume them by the stomach and belly of meditation and faith, that they may become thy nutriment, and thou mayst feel the power and efficacy of them in thy heart, and act accordingly.

"And fill thy bowels." Satisfy thyself, take enough, be not content with a little.

Obs. 1. That our obedience unto Christ must be absolute and simple. "Eat that thou findest," saith Christ, whatever thou findest. There might something unsavoury, bitter, have been tendered to the prophet, even that which nature abhors; however, he must eat it, not dispute the case, but yield obedience. When Christ commands, entire obedience is the best, to do it upon that ground, and no other; here the commander's will is warrant for the fact. Luke v. 5, this prevailed with Peter, "Master, we have toiled all the night, and have taken nothing; nevertheless at thy word I will let down the net." Christ's word was all unto him; he looked not at his labour lost, at his gain to come, but at the word of Christ, and that was warrant enough to him. So other apostles, when Christ called them, and bid them follow him, "they left all, and straightway followed him;" they consulted not with flesh and blood, they made no objections, chose not what they would themselves, but submitted to Christ's will. Abraham left his country at God's call, and knew not whither he should go, and this was true obedience. With men we must not be so tractable, as to do things merely upon their wills and commands: they are no gods, their wills and power are no rules. They may sin; we must give account; and therefore may and must examine, "prove all things, and hold fast that which is good." Human things it is our duty, it is wisdom and safety, to question, and search into; but divine things are without dispute to be believed and obeyed. Therefore saith Christ, "Ye are my friends, if ye do whatsoever I command you," John xv. 14; then we show the greatest love to Christ, when we give him absolute obedience.

Autheritas præcipientis est ratio præcepti.

Obs. 2. That the symbols and truths which Christ gives, are the meat that the souls of prophets and ministers must feed upon. "Eat what thou findest;" "eat this roll." It is *this*, emphatically; other rolls and books they may look into, but this they must eat. The book of Christ is the book of their studies. Many scholars study other books more than the Scriptures, than the rolls of Christ; they are *heluones librorum*, book-eaters; fathers, schoolmen, historians, poets, and pamphlets, they devour, and are least acquainted with the Scriptures; but Christ's command is to eat this roll, search the Scriptures, meditate in the law night and day; he sends us to no other. A young disciple asking an old rabbi whether he might not have time to learn the Greek tongue, he said, if he would do it neither by night nor by day he might, because by night and day he was to study the law: hereby he intimated that scholars' greatest study should be in the word of God. Paul therefore exhorts Timothy to give attendance to reading, to exhortation, to doctrine; he bids him "meditate upon these things, give himself wholly to them," 1 Tim. iv. 15; his whole strength and time should be in them. Man's life is short; and if it were never so long, it should be spent in the knowledge of the holy Scriptures. When Paul was at the gates of death, 2 Tim. iv. 6, 13, you find he sends for the books and parchments: Paul would study them over again. It is said of Ambrose, that to his death he ceased not to write commentaries, and expound Scriptures, and died at that in the psalm, "Great is the Lord, and greatly to be praised." This book they must eat, read, study, with great diligence, and make it their own. Alphonsus, king of Aragon, read over the Scriptures some twelve or fourteen times, notwithstanding his great public employments; and one of note read over the New Testament with Beza's larger notes, sixteen times in three years. The Scriptures are Heaven's epistles sent to men; they cannot be read too often, being full of divine mysteries.

Epistola Dei ad homines missa. *Aug. 2 Serm. in Psal.* xc.

Obs. 3. That when ministers and messengers of God have eaten and digested the truths of God, then they are fit to go and preach them to the people of God. "Eat this roll, and go;" first eat, then

Omnia etiam minima plena sunt sensu, mysterio et spiritu. *Bas. Hom.* 6.

go. Elijah must eat, and then take his journey; and so ministers must first eat themselves, then feed others. If the nurse herself do not eat, she will have no milk for her child; if she eat and do not digest, turn it into blood and milk, all is in vain; so the messengers of God must turn what they eat, what they read, *in succum et sanguinem*, into nourishment; and then, being their own, in their hearts and bowels, they will speak from the heart.

Obs. 4. That faith is requisite to the receipt of spiritual things: he opened his mouth, and ate the roll, he received the truths and believed. Look, how necessary a mouth is to take in the meat of the body, to chew it, and send it down to the other parts, else there is no benefit comes to a man by it; so necessary is faith to take in the spiritual food of the soul. Faith is the mouth and stomach of the soul; if that receive in truths, digest and send them to the organs of actions, benefit accrues to the man; if not, prejudice. John vi. 35, 36, Christ tells them that he is the "bread of life," that he that comes to him shall "never hunger," and that he that believes on him shall "never thirst," but "ye have seen me and believe not." Though Christ were bread and water of life, because they had no faith, no mouth to eat and drink thereof, therefore they had no benefit; and as a man that can receive no food must die: so here, John viii. 24, "If ye believe not that I am he, ye shall die in your sins:" here is prejudice irreparable, death eternal, for want of faith. Our prophet received the fruits Christ tendered, and got by them. All believers are or may be gainers by the truths of Christ: 1 Thess. ii. 13, "The word wrought effectually in them that believed." Faith makes good concoction of that meat, and answerable operation; but, Heb. iv. 2, "The word preached did not profit them, not being mixed with faith in them that heard it." Where there is no faith to receive into the soul, there is no profit: the ear may set it into the head, but faith must bring it into the heart, and keep it there, till it be spirit and life to the man. The original is, the word of hearing did not profit them, being not united by faith to them that heard.

Obs. 5. The godly must act and put forth their graces towards further reception of spiritual things. When Christ will give Ezekiel *donum prophetiæ*, the gift of prophecy, a roll to eat, he opens his mouth, he employs his faith to receive this gift of prophecy. Faith in the habit is like the mouth shut up, nothing enters; but in exercise it is like the mouth open and ready to receive. It is infinite mercy that God at any time will offer us spiritual favours and excellences; we should therefore be forward, and stir up our souls and graces to the receipt of such mercies. It is a lazy and ill excuse for godly ones to say they can do nothing. Grace is an active and an enabling thing, and where there is a principle of life, (as all godly men have,) there is a special difference between that man and another that hath it not: a man without it, cannot act and stir up himself to a further reception of spiritual things, because he is dead; but a man that hath it, can and ought to quicken up his own soul to spiritual things. The prophet had received the Spirit that entered into him, and he opened his mouth, exercised his faith, to take what the Lord should give. The apostle Paul bids Timothy stir up the gift of God that was in him, 2 Tim. i. 6; he would have men deal with their gifts and graces, as they do with fire under the ashes, they blow them off, and blow the fire up, and there is a flame fit for service. Sloth, fear, infirmity, carnal reason, are ashes that do often cover divine fire, that it seems dead; but we must stir up

ἀναζωπυρεῖν.

ourselves, blow off those ashes, and blow up the fire of grace, that it may burn and shine, be useful to ourselves and others. The prophet complains in Isa. lxiv. 7, "There is none that stirreth up himself to take hold of thee;" they are like men asleep, that sit still and do nothing. The Vulgate is, *Non est qui surgat*, There is no one who will arise.

Obs. 6. When man hath done all he can, the efficacy and fruit is from God. Ezekiel opened his mouth, but the Lord Christ caused him to eat the roll; he makes it effectual. It is not our stirring up our graces, opening our hearts, putting forth ourselves to the utmost, that will make an ordinance effectual, without Christ; it is he must do the deed: John xv. 5, "Without me ye can do nothing." Ezekiel could not eat the roll; nor digest it, being eaten; nor act, being digested: and so the apostles, though branches in the vine, could draw no sap from the root, unless that sent it up; when sent up, they could not send it forth without him; if sent forth into clusters, they could not ripen it without him. All is from him; he gives grace, exercises and strengthens grace: Paul may plant, but there is no rooting of those plants but by Christ; Apollos may water, but there is no growth, no increase, but by Christ, 1 Cor. iii. 6.

Obs. 7. Ministers and all should feed liberally upon the word. "Fill thy bowels with this roll;" not taste of it a little, but feed and fill themselves. There is great variety in the rolls of God, and we may feed upon them all, and fill ourselves with divine truth. Matt. xiii. 52, Every scribe instructed to the kingdom of heaven hath a treasury of things new and old. As a householder hath all meats, wines, household-stuff, and furniture that are needful, both old and new; so should a servant of God have old and new truths, those of Moses and the prophets, and the mysteries of the gospel also. "Let the word of God dwell in you richly," Col. iii. 16; he means not some part of it, but the whole word of God; it is not limited to any part, but spoken indefinitely, and so includes all; and it must not be in the assemblies, in the houses only, but it must be in you, and dwell in you; you must know it, and have it in readiness, as you know those who dwell in the house with you, and are ready to do any service for you. The Corinthians were enriched in all knowledge; and we should so abound with divine knowledge, that there should be no place for errors in us: the word of God should be in our hearts, in our heads, in our lips, in our lives; we all should be like Ezekiel's roll, written within and without.

Obs. 8. The word of God is sweet and delightful to the soul. It was "as honey for sweetness." There is nothing more sweet than honey. The word is as sweet as it; yea, Psal. xix. 10, "sweeter than honey and the honeycomb:" the greatest sweetness is in the word of any thing in the world. The sweetness is in the revelation of the counsels and mysteries of God and Christ, which is sweet to know; for "knowledge is pleasant," Prov. ii. 10; and the more excellent the knowledge, the more pleasant it is. It is a "word of life," Phil. ii. 16; and life is sweet, and the more spiritual the life is, the more sweet still. It converts the soul, Psal. xix. 7. It is *pabulum animæ*, the food of the soul, called by Peter, ἄδολον γάλα, 1 Pet. ii. 2, sincere milk; and that is sweet, nourishing unto eternal life. It is "the grace of God that bringeth salvation," Tit. ii. 11; and "the power of God to salvation," Rom. i. 16; and herein is sweetness. It sanctifies, Job xvii. 17. It comforts the soul in all straits and afflictions; Psal. cxix. 92, "Unless thy law had been my delights, I should then have perished in mine affliction." It satisfies the conscience, which nothing else can do. It shows the equity of God's judgments and dealings with wicked men; and so the sharpest threats, and most dreadful judgments, are sweet to a gracious heart. Here was a roll full of "lamentation, mourning, and woe;" and yet when the Lord commends it to Ezekiel, he finds sweetness in it: not that he was not sensible and affected with the miseries coming upon him, for he was not ἄϛοργος, without natural affection; but seeing the righteousness of God in his judgments towards them, he could not but be affected with a spiritual joy, and find sweetness therein, his will being revealed, and that which a gracious heart rests in.

Ver. 4—11. *And he said unto me, Son of man, go, get thee unto the house of Israel, and speak with my words unto them. For thou art not sent to a people of a strange speech and of an hard language, but to the house of Israel; not to many people of a strange speech and of an hard language, whose words thou canst not understand. Surely, had I sent thee to them, they would have hearkened unto thee. But the house of Israel will not hearken unto thee; for they will not hearken unto me: for all the house of Israel are impudent and hardhearted. Behold, I have made thy face strong against their faces, and thy forehead strong against their foreheads. As an adamant harder than flint have I made thy forehead: fear them not, neither be dismayed at their looks, though they be a rebellious house. Moreover he said unto me, Son of man, all my words that I shall speak unto thee receive in thine heart, and hear with thine ears. And go, get thee to them of the captivity, unto the children of thy people, and speak unto them, and tell them, Thus saith the Lord God; whether they will hear, or whether they will forbear.*

In these verses is a renewal of the prophet's sending to his prophetical function, and they have in them matter of encouragement, and manifestation what he must expect.

1. Matter of encouragement; and,

(1.) In that he was not sent to "a people of a strange language," that understood him not, ver. 5, 6; that would be discouragement, to preach to a people that should not know what a man said. This was not the prophet's case, but he was to go "to the house of Israel," whom he knew, whose language he understood, who also understood his.

(2.) In that Christ had strengthened and fitted him for that service, ver. 8, 9, and would yet do more for him, give him more truths, reveal more prophetical things unto him, ver. 10.

(3.) That it should be all one to him, whether they heard the prophet or not, ver. 11.

2. There is manifestation what he must expect.

(1.) More from heathens than from them; ver. 6, end, "Surely, had I sent thee to them, they would have hearkened."

(2.) Obstinate refusal of him and his prophecy; ver. 7, "The house of Israel will not hearken unto thee:" and it is proved by a double argument.

First, "they will not hearken unto me," is an argument from the greater. If they will not hear me their God, they will not hear thee my servant, their prophet.

The second is an argument from their disposition, and the universality of it; "for all the house of Israel are impudent and hardhearted." And then a repetition of his mission, in the 11th verse.

I shall open what is difficult in the verses, and then give you some observations out of them.

The words in the 5th verse, "of a strange speech and hard language," and the same in the 6th verse, are expounded in that place in Isa. xxxiii. 19. In the original the words are עִמְקֵי שפה וכבדי לשון deep of lip, and heavy of tongue, or rather, a people of depths of lip, and heaviness of tongue. In the word depths, there is a metalepsis; depths are dark and difficult, hard to be understood. It is not so here; thou art not sent to such a people, a people of a hard and heavy language, of an unknown tongue. The Septuagint hath it thus, οὐ προς λαὸν βαθύχειλον καὶ βαρυγλωσσον, not to a people of a deep lip, or heavy tongue; thou art sent to a people that understand thee, and what thou sayest, and whom thou dost understand also. It is not with thee as it was with Jonah; he was sent to a people of a strange speech and hard language. I send thee not to Egyptians, to Chaldeans, but to Israelites, not Parthians, Scythians, &c.; but though thou art in Babylon, where was the confusion of tongues, yet thou art to go to the house of Israel, and speak to them, that have heard Moses and other prophets before, and me in them.

In the 7th verse it is said, "the house of Israel are impudent and hardhearted." The Hebrew is, strong of face, and hard of heart, the same with those words in the second chapter, ver. 4; only the difference is, that in chap. ii. it is *duri faciebus*, strong of face, and here it is *duri corde*, hard of heart; there it is *robusti corde*, strong in heart, and here it is *robusti fronte*, bold in countenance.

In the 9th verse it is, כשמיר "as an adamant harder than flint have I made thy forehead;" *keshamir*. The word *shamir* signifies a brier: Isa. v. 6, "There shall come up briers," שמיר a brier; and it is from שמר *custodire, servare*, to keep, to preserve, because a brier by its prickles doth preserve itself. It signifies also a hard and flinty stone, such as an adamant is, which is *lapis servabilis*, because it keeps itself by its hardness from all injuries; no weather, no violence of hammer or fire will conquer it: so much the name adamant imports, being *lapis indomabilis*: Zech. vii. 12, "They have made their hearts as an adamant." There are four sorts, the Arabic, Macedonian, Cyprian, and Indian, which is the chiefest.

Ab α et δαμάζω. Plin. lib. 37.

"Harder than a flint;" חזק מצר strong above a rock. By these expressions are set out the invincible courage and constancy that God would give the prophet; such as neither shame nor fear should prevail against.

Nec pudore vinceretur, nec metu taceret aut pallesceret.

In the 10th verse, "All my words receive in thine heart, and hear with thine ears;" it is ὕστερον πρότερον, the last first, and first last, hear with thine ears, and receive into thine heart.

Obs. That those that are sent of God must speak with or in God's words. Saith Paul, 1 Cor. xi. 23, "For I have received of the Lord that which also I delivered unto you:" not what I have received of men, of learned heathens and Jews; not what I had of my own; but what I received of the Lord, his words, his institutions. God's words are weighty, and have divine authority in them, but man's are weak like himself.

From the 5th and 6th verses,

Obs. 1. That it is God determines and disposes of his prophets and ministers, for their places and people; what places they shall be in, what number they shall be over: "Thou art not sent to a people of a strange language, not to many people, but to the house of Israel." God had the power in his hand to have sent him to other nations, great, mighty, of an unknown language, but he sent him among Israelites: Acts xx. 28, it is a divine constitution.

Obs. 2. That men called of God to do him service in the church, should not be discouraged, whatever difficulties are before them. "Thou art not sent unto a people of a strange speech, not to many:" this implies, that if he were sent to these, he should go willingly, cheerfully; and much more, being upon easier service, the call of God should be encouragement enough. And if our eyes be much upon that, it will prevent much sin, many distempers. Oft the servants of God (when they come amongst their own friends, acquaintance, countrymen) are slighted, and meet with hard measure and coarse usage; but they must remember who called, who sent them.

Obs. 3. That God's ways and judgments are unsearchable. The means of grace are denied to those that would embrace them, and given to those that refused them. "Surely, had I sent thee to them, they would have hearkened;" although thou hadst preached in a tongue unknown, by one means or other they would have been brought to repentance; they would not have been so perverse and ungrateful as the Jews were. Jonah, and Nahum too, as Pradus conceives, preached to Nineveh, and they repented; and it is likely many nations now, if they had the gospel preached unto them, would embrace it, and bring forth better fruits than christians do. Matt. xi. 21, 23, Christ saith, if the works he had done in Chorazin, Bethsaida, and Capernaum, had been done in Tyre, Sidon, and Sodom, "they would have repented, and remained to this day;" but God, in his infinite wisdom and justice, denied both the words and works of Christ to those places. We cannot sound this depth; yet let us say, God is righteous, and take heed it be not verified of us, that Turkey, Persia, and Tartary, would have repented, if they had had the means we have.

Per interpretes, per nutus, per gestus commoverentur ad pœnitentiam.

From the 7th verse,

Obs. 1. Men's wills do harden them and ruin them: "They will not hearken unto thee." There is obstinacy and malice in the wills of men, that they reject the word of God, and what is for their good: "Ye will not come to me, that ye might have life," saith Christ, John v. 40. I will give you life for fetching, and you will none of it. And when he came to them, what said they to him? "We will not have this man to reign over us." Let Christ come, a King of righteousness, seeking the good, the salvation of sinners, they will not submit to him; their own wills shall stand between them and salvation. Bernard saith, A man's will is his hell; it carries a man against heaven, and swiftly to hell.

Voluntas tua est infernus tuus.

Obs. 2. There is such corruption and strength of stubbornness in men, that they will not hear God himself: "They will not hearken unto me." Though there be infinite equity in it, that they should give me their ears, hearts, all their strength and intentions; for I have created them of nothing; redeemed them, being worse than nothing; I have prepared eternal mansions in the heavens for them that do hear me; I speak the words of wisdom and life; I aim at their good and comfort in all that I speak; yet they will not hear me. Here is the strength and perfection of stubbornness. A child not to hear its parents, a people not to hear their minister, subjects not to hear their prince, is thought bad enough; but children, people, subjects, not to hear their God, is the height of iniquity. And because they will not hear Christ, therefore they will not hear his messengers, but despise, persecute, and murder them, and that because he sends them; John xv. 21, "All these things will they do unto you for my name's sake."

Obs. 3. Corruption lies not only hid in the heart of sinners, but breaks out in an impudent manner: they "are impudent and hardhearted;" there is stoniness within, and impudence without.

Obs. 4. Sin is of a spreading, infectious nature: the whole "house of Israel are impudent and hardhearted," the one corrupted another. As it is in a bunch of grapes, if one be corrupt, it will corrupt its neighbour, and that another, till they be all alike; so was it here, one infected another, till the whole house was so; it is like the leprosy in a garment or house, that spreads through all. Gen. vi. 12, "All flesh had corrupted his way upon the earth."

From the 8th and 9th verses,

Obs. 1. That the ministers of God must look for opposition in their way. Their face and foreheads were against the prophet; they would be like beasts, that use to push with their horns and heads. 1 Cor. xvi. 9, "There is an effectual door opened unto me, and there are many adversaries." When God opens to his ministers a door of hope to do good, there presently appear many adversaries to shut that door again, and so to take away the hope and opportunity of doing good. It was at Ephesus, and there he met and fought with beasts. In the course of his ministry he met with Hymeneus, Alexander, and Demetrius, that opposed him. John met with a Diotrephes, and we must look for many such.

Obs. 2. Divine virtue and assistance doth accompany a divine call. "I have made thy face strong against their faces:" I called thee, and strengthened thee. The Hebrew is, give thee a face strong; I do and will enable thee with spirit and audacity to outface them. In Matt. xxviii. 20, Go preach, "and lo, I am with you alway to the end of the world." He sends them, and seconds them; he calls them, and encourages them; "I am with you," by my grace, strength, comfort, direction, Spirit. Those that are called of Christ, and sent of him, therefore may with comfort expect the help of Christ to go through the work he hath put them in. Paul, when sent to the Corinthians, he came "in demonstration of the Spirit and power," 1 Cor. ii. 4. And in Col. i. 29, he saith, the working of grace was mighty in him, in power and efficacy. We are oft discouraged at the greatness and difficulty of the work: "Who is sufficient for these things?" said Paul; but when he looked at Christ, he said, "I can do all things through Christ which strengtheneth me," Phil. iv. 13. And if we would look more at him, and lean upon him, we should do more, and do better. If thoughts of our weakness, of the work, of our oppositions and enemies, sink us, Christ gives balm, spirit, and a face to bear all. A minister doth not warfare in his own strength, but is armed from above.

Non militat propriis viribus, sed armatur cœlesti virtute.

Obs. 3. Whatever ministers have, it is given; if they be endued with the Spirit, wisdom, liberty of speech, courage, or any other excellency, it is that the Lord Christ bestows upon them; I have made thee so and so. Let not us be lift up; our Master, Christ, had in him all the treasures of wisdom, the Spirit above measure; he was full of grace and truth, did more than all; his fame was great, and yet he was humble, and bad us learn of him. He did not slight or despise men of mean talents, and infinitely beneath himself, but acknowledged the least good which was in any, and encouraged it. His steps should we follow, and not swell with a conceit of worth, nor with reality of parts and excellences. It is the practice of too many to slight others, and build up themselves by their ruins; but this is a worldly and wicked practice, never taught by Christ. His doctrine is, "Let each esteem other better than themselves. Look not every man on his own things, but every man also on the things of others," Phil. ii. 3, 4: it is injury and indignity to Christ, not to reverence and esteem his graces and gifts in others. Bernard tells of one, who, bewailing his own condition, said, he saw thirty virtues in another, whereof he had not one in himself. And perhaps, saith Bernard, of all his thirty, he had not one like this man's humility. This grace is the glory of a christian, and especially of a minister: pride is for prelates, and humility for prophets. God brooks not pride in any, least of all in his messengers. Christ's disciples had a tincture of it; their thoughts were aspiring, who should be greatest; but he sets a child before them, and tells them who is greatest; not he that hath the strongest head, the best notions, doth the most service, but he that is the most humble, he is the most high. Humility is so valued of God, that he likes it in *malefactis*, those that have done ill, rather than pride in *recte factis*, those that have done well. A man that is innocent and proud, is less in God's eye than he that is guilty and humble. Let us rather mind the good in others, to honour them, and maintain love, than that which is in ourselves, to lift us up, and make us slight others.

Obs. 4. Christ puts insuperable virtue and strength into his servants, such as the powers of darkness and the world cannot prevail against. "I have made thy face strong against their faces, as an adamant," as a rock. Let the winds, waters, floods, blow, wash, beat, they prevail not against the adamant, the rock; they are things which cannot be conquered. So is the power, virtue, and grace of Christ in the heart and head of a faithful minister. Reproach and derision put Jeremiah to it, had almost silenced him: I will preach no more, Jer. xx. 9, "but his word was as a burning fire, shut up in my bones, and I was weary with forbearing, and I could not stay;" there was virtue within which would out and act. God had told them, that they should fight against him, but not prevail, Jer. xv. 20. Christ tells his disciples, he will give them "a mouth and wisdom which all their adversaries shall not be able to resist," Luke xxi. 15. And could that great council, in the 4th of the Acts, prevail against Peter and John? "We cannot but speak the things which we have seen and heard," ver. 20. So Stephen was too stout for all his adversaries, Acts vi. 10. Such virtue was put into Basil the great. You know how he answered the ruler, and stood impregnable against his threats, who went and told the emperor, saying, *Victi sumus, rex, in ecclesiæ hujus negotio; vir ille minis est superior, verbis robustior, et persuasionibus fortior*, We have been vanquished, O ruler, in this affair of the church; that man is superior to our threats, more powerful than words, and one who will not yield to persuasions. This made Nazianzen say of him, that he was *percutientibus adamas, et dissidentibus magnes*, an adamant to those striking him, and a loadstone to those differing from him. Could all the policy of the conclave, and power of antichrist, conquer that divine virtue which was put into Luther? The wicked may drive the godly from their standings, not from their stedfastness.

Obs. 5. That the messengers of God, being called and strengthened by Christ, are to go on *animo intrepido*, with an intrepid mind. "Fear them not, neither be dismayed at their looks, though they be rebellious," &c. If they be strong, or against thee, I am stronger that am with thee; if they frown, I smile; if they watch to do thee hurt, I watch to do thee good; if thy doctrine provoke them, yet it pleases me.

From the 10th verse,

Obs. 1. That the heart is the treasury where the truth should be laid up. "Receive my words in thine heart." He must hear with his ear, but that is not enough, he must also admit the word into his heart, and lay it up there. What is in the head may soon be lost, but what is in the heart abides. Books locked up in the closet are safe, and truths laid up in the heart are secure. Jam. i. 21, "Lay apart all filthiness and superfluity of" malice, or "naughtiness, and receive with meekness the ingrafted word," *τὸν ἔμφυτον λόγον*. They must first put out of their hearts filthiness, malice, wrath, whatever had possession of the heart, and kept out the word, and open their hearts to entertain the word; that as it is with a graft put into a stock, so it might be with the word in their hearts, even be an ingrafted word, a word to root and grow there, and bear fruit in the life. The seed on the good ground, are they which in an honest and good heart, having heard the word, keep it, and bring forth fruit, Luke viii. 15. The heart is the ground this seed will grow in. David knew this, and therefore hid the word of God in his heart, Psal. cxix. 11: and why there? "that I might not sin against thee." This corn will not let the weeds grow: when the word is in the heart, it keeps under all corruptions, it makes them languish and come to nothing. Many do by the word as by their jewels, they hang them at their ears, that is the place for them: and so the word is only in their ears; they hear, and that is all; it enters not into their hearts, and therefore is subject to casualty, the devil, world, pleasures, one thing or other, steal it away, or make it unfruitful; but the heart is the right and best place for that treasure. A godly man's treasure is in the heart, within; and theirs in the ear, and without; many hear the word with the ear, but receive it not into the heart, and that is a worthless hearing: John viii. 47, the Jews heard Christ preach, yet he tells them their hearing was no hearing; "Ye hear not God's words, because ye are not of God." They heard, but not with the heart; the truth entered not, abode not with them. Let us look to our hearing, and lay up the truths of Christ in our heart: Luke ii. 19, "Mary kept all these things, and pondered them in her heart."

Obs. 2. All the truths of Christ must have interest in the heart. Psal. xl. 8, "Thy law is within my heart:" he doth not say, a precept or two, a part, or half the law is within my heart, but thy law, the whole law. Some truth is with most persons. None is so bad, but he would give entertainment unto truths of mercy, truths of liberty, truths of ease and comfort, truths in credit: so men might pick and choose what truths they listed, they would embrace them; but when truths are reproached, will subject to danger, loss, difficulties, when they strike at our lusts, call for mortification, self-denial, conformity to Christ, &c. then men will scarcely afford truth their ears, much less their hearts. Hence those expressions in Scripture, of men's perverting the ways of God, Acts xiii. 10; of being contentious against the truth, Rom. ii. 8; speaking evil of it, 2 Pet. ii. 2; of resisting it, 2 Tim. iii. 8; yea, persecuting it, Acts xxii. 4. There are many truths that flesh and blood cannot endure. Some have torn out parts of Scripture, because cross to their lusts and lives. It is known what hath been done to the word of God in Ireland, and England too of late days. Some are enemies to the whole truth, most to some parts of it, but we must receive all the words of Christ. If the least tittle of the

Matt. v. 18. law and gospel be more durable and excellent than heaven and earth, there is sufficient reason it should have interest in our hearts. Let the truths be what they will, so they be the words and truths of Christ, we should receive them; and that which makes us receive one, should make us receive all. Do I receive one, because it is from Christ? then I should receive all, because they are from Christ. If I do not receive all, I may miscarry for refusing of one truth: Psal. cxix. 6, "Then shall I not be ashamed, when I have respect unto all thy commandments."

From the 12th verse,

Obs. 1. That affliction is a fit time for instruction. "Get thee to them of the captivity." They were in Babylon, stript of all, captives under Nebuchadnezzar, and now the Lord judged it a fit season for a prophet to be sent unto them. When people are in misery, they see the uncertainty of life, the insufficiency of all creatures, the sinfulness of sin, that the wrath of God is a dreadful thing; thoughts of death and eternity are upon them; and now is a good season to bring the truths of the eternal God unto them. *Vexatio dat intellectum*, affliction quickens consideration; it makes men thoughtful, look about, inquire how they may be delivered, where to get safety. When a kingdom is in danger, a parliament is seasonable; when there is war in the gates, then counsel and instruction are welcome; and when people are in captivity, a prophet amongst them will do well.

Obs. 2. When God's people degenerate, he owns them not for his. "Get thee to the captivity, and to thy people." God owned them not; now his care of them, and affection towards them, is much abated. God doth look upon things and persons, that he formerly took delight in, being corrupt, as not his own. Isa. i. 14, "Your new moons and appointed feasts my soul hateth:" they were the Lord's people, he appointed the new moons and feasts, but because they had corrupted them, he owns them not, but calls them theirs. So in Exod. xxxii. 7, God bids Moses get him down from the mount. What was the matter? "Thy people, which thou broughtest out of the land of Egypt, have corrupted themselves:" their corrupting themselves with idolatry, made God disclaim them: They are thy people, go look after them, or I will destroy them. He calls them Moses's people there, and here he calls them Ezekiel's, to let them see how his heart was estranged from them. While they were faithful to God, he counted highly of them, they were precious in his sight, honourable, Isa. xliii. 4. beloved; but when they went a whoring from God, he accounts not of them, he calls them not his, owns them not: they had shamefully dishonoured God by their sins, and he will not honour them with the title of his people.

Obs. 3. The servants of Christ must execute their functions without respect of persons, or regard to success. "Speak to them," whatever they be, "and tell them, Thus saith the Lord," that one greater than themselves hath sent thee, and will call them to account; and "whether they will hear or forbear," let not that trouble thee, do thy duty, be not troubled at the oppositions of men, or successlessness of thy labours.

Ver. 12—15. *Then the spirit took me up, and I heard behind me a voice of a great rushing, saying, Blessed be the glory of the Lord from his place. I heard also the noise of the wings of the living creatures that touched one another, and the noise of the wheels over against them, and a noise of a great rushing. So the spirit lifted me up, and took me away, and I went in bitterness, in the heat of my spirit; but the hand of the Lord was strong upon me. Then I came to them of the captivity at Tel-abib, that dwelt by the river of Chebar, and I sat where they sat, and remained there astonished among them seven days.*

These words are the second part of the chapter, and contain in them a declaration of what befell the prophet, being so called; and the particulars are these:

I. The work of the Spirit in taking and lifting him up, ver. 12.

II. The voice he heard, ver. 12, and what it was, "Blessed," &c.

III. The noise of wings and wheels, ver. 13.

IV. The ablation of the prophet, ver. 14. In the 12th was a sublation, in this an ablation.

V. The journey he went, in ver. 14, 15. And,

VI. His condition; he was in bitterness of spirit, he sat and mourned seven days, ver. 14, 15.

"The spirit took me up." By spirit here we understand, not the wind, as if some great wind should take up the prophet; nor an angel, as if he had been lift up by angelical virtue; nor his own spirit, as Jerom would have it: but that Spirit which was in the living creatures and wheels, chap. i. 12, 20, and led them; that Spirit which entered into Ezekiel, and set him upon his feet, chap. ii. 2; that Spirit which led Christ into the wilderness, Matt. iv. 1; even the eternal Spirit of God.

This taking up of Ezekiel by the Spirit of God was:

1. To perfect and ratify his call to the prophetical office. The Lord Christ had spoken much unto him about it, and now the Spirit lifts him up, and seals the same unto his soul, strengthening him in the full assurance thereof. When he had heard Christ's voice, and found his Spirit working so extraordinarily, as to lift him up; this could not but mightily prevail with and satisfy the soul of the prophet.

2. That he might have a more clear and full view of the glory of him that sat upon the throne. When we would have one see things distinctly and fully, we set or lift him up on high. The devil carried Christ unto an exceeding high mountain, and showed him the glory of the kingdoms of the world, Matt. iv. 8.

3. To put honour upon him, in letting him see that he was to be an organ of the Spirit for the future; he was to be employed in great service by the Spirit, and that was a great honour. He was to be the mouth of the Spirit unto that people; to be wholly at the disposal of the Spirit.

4. To call away his thoughts from things below, and to settle them upon the contemplation of things divine. A prophet is not to look downward, his heart should be lifted up to heaven and heavenly things.

"And I heard behind me a voice of a great rushing." It was not the voice of thunder, or of an earthquake, but of "the living creatures;" and the voice some make to be the words, "Blessed be the glory of the Lord from his place;" which words are in the original, the blessed glory of the Lord from his place; that is, the glory of God is now going out of his place, and it troubles the angels, that they lament, and make a great noise, to behold so dreadful a judgment to befall Jerusalem and the Jews; and so the voice to be differing from these words. If it be granted, that these words were the voice uttered, yet may they be taken in that sense which is expressed, to show their sorrow for the ruin of the church. The blessed glory of the Lord is departing from its place, God is leaving his habitation and people, and all is hastening to spoil and desolation; this affected the very angels. When some great man, that hath been a great patron and friend to a place, is going away, what lamentation is made! what a noise and stir is there at it! As in these days, when some ministers, magistrates, and other eminent christians, are forced from their place by the enemy, what complaint doth it cause! what a noise doth it make! And so when God leaves a people, that were beloved and dear unto him, it fetches sighs and complaints, not only from men, but even from angels also: the soul finds it a sad thing when God departs from it, and oft mourns bitterly. Some take the words for a doxology, and make the sense this; Blessed be the glory of God, which is seen in punishing the wicked, and delivering the church. God shows himself just and righteous, that he will no longer stay among a sinful people, but be gone from them, and render to them according to their ways. The query will be, in what sense we may take the words? Both senses may without prejudice be admitted. While the angels looked upon the great loss the Jews should have by God's departure, the great evils which would follow thereupon; they sympathized, and were so affected with it, that they brake out into these expressions. The blessed glory of God is going out of its place; and so it was *vox lamentationis*, an expression of grief. But when they looked at God's justice and holiness, "Blessed is" or be "the glory of the Lord." Though men be ruined, cities and nations destroyed, and God driven from his habitation, yet let his name be glorious. And so it is *vox laudis*, an expression of praise, and brought in to answer the objections and cavils the people might make. They might say, What! will God leave us? expose us to the spoil of foreign enemies? shall we and ours be cut off? will he thus deal with his people? is it come to this? What equity is in it? The angels, to prevent such murmurings, and vile speech, said, "Blessed," &c.; even when he is in a way of judgment, he is to be honoured and made glorious.

"Blessed be the glory of the Lord from his place." We must make some search into these words, and inquire after the person, the place, and the glory. The person here is taken to be Christ, who appeared unto the prophet in the vision; the place, the throne where Christ sat; and the glory, that is mentioned in the end of the first chapter. And Christ now being about to go off his throne, and put an end to the vision, the angels cried, "Blessed be the glory of the Lord from his place." This is not all we must expect from the words, they type out unto us the departure of the Lord from the temple; that God would be gone, and take away that which was the chief glory of it.

"From his place." God is without place, and the rabbins use that word to signify it. *Makom* is a space, or place, because all things subsist in it; *Hammakom, per antiphrasin*, is *illocalis, infinitus*, one that subsists, or is comprehended in no place, and so is an attribute of God. How then is God here said to have place, ממקומו, from his place? God properly hath no place; in a metaphorical sense that place is given to him; where he in any special manner doth manifest his glory, power, grace, and goodness, that is said to be his place.

And three places God is said to have in the Scripture:

1. The heavens: Isa. lxvi. 1, "Heaven is my throne;" and 1 Kings viii. 30, "Hear in heaven thy dwelling-place."

2. The humble heart, Isa. lvii. 15, that is God's dwelling place. And,

3. The temple in Sion. Psal. cxxxii. 13, 14, Sion was his habitation, there was his rest and abode; that is, in the temple, being in Sion. In the temple and sanctuary were his voice, his way, Psal. xviii. 6; lxxvii. 13. That was the place where his honour dwelt, Psal. xxvi. 8, the habitation of his glory. The words are in the original, the place of the habitation or tabernacle of his glory, alluding to that in Exod. xl. 34, 35, where it is said, "The glory of the Lord filled the tabernacle." So the glory of the Lord filled the temple; there was the presence of God; there were manifestations of his glory; there he heard prayers, and there he gave out many gracious answers; there he accepted of their sacrifices, and communicated himself unto them; there were the ark and sign of God's presence, and the cherubims, from between which God gave out the answers. In these things lay the glory of the temple; but now God would be gone, and all the glory of the temple should depart. God moved not from place to place, being infinite, without place, immovable; but he is said to depart, when he ceases to do as formerly he did in the soul; when you find not God acting and manifesting himself, you say he is gone. Here now God would answer them no more, not accept their sacrifice, nor hear their prayers, &c.; he would not do as formerly he had done; he would not protect them any longer, but look upon them as being unworthy of his presence, glory, protection, and help, and in his wrath leave them to ruin and the spoil of their adversaries: and this was God departing, according to that in Hos. v. 15, "I will go and return to my place, till they acknowledge their offence." That phrase, "Blessed be the glory of the Lord," you may, for your better understanding, conceive thus, Blessed be the glorious Lord, or, the glory, the Lord; or, if you will take it as it is read, the meaning is, that the glory of the Lord is to be celebrated.

Obs. 1. That those that are called to employment in the church of Christ, have need not only of Christ's word, but Christ's Spirit also. Christ had spoken largely unto Ezekiel, and here the Spirit lifts him up, and doth in an especial manner animate and arm him to the work. When the apostles had been long with Christ, heard his sermons, seen his miracles and life, joined with him in prayer, all this would not do it, though Christ had forty days spoken to them in particular of the things of the kingdom, Acts i. 3, till they had the Spirit, and were filled with that; therefore Christ bid them wait for it, ver. 4. He knew they had need of it, and that it would do more in them, than all he had said unto them. The Spirit would be *Doctor intus*, an inward Teacher, and acquaint them with all truth. The Spirit would purge out their fears and distempers; it would warm, heat, seal, ratify, and make them resolute in the work.

Obs. 2. That the angels do sympathize with the church and people of God in their miseries. This voice was, as I showed in the opening, the voice of the living creatures; and they made a noise, lamenting the state of Jerusalem, God being upon the leaving of it, and exposing it to great misery. Ah, said they, the blessed and glorious Lord is going from his place, and all miseries are now stepping in upon his people: this affected them. We know that the angels rejoice at the conversion of sinners, and by the law of contraries we infer they are saddened at the destruction of sinners, of states and churches. They have been employed to comfort in trouble; and where there is no sympathy, there is little solace. Do you not think, that the angel seeing Christ his Lord and Master in his agony, that he did sympathize first with him, and then strengthen him? Angels being without sin, are as full of pity as the devils are of cruelty. God, Christ, and the Spirit, are full of pity; and it cannot be that angels, which are so near them, should be void of it. No, they have a holy sympathy with us: in God's departure from a place is sad news, even to angels.

Obs. 3. The happiness of a people is to have the Lord and his glory amongst them, and their greatest misery is to have God depart from them. Most think the happiness of a people to lie in liberty, honour, plenty of all things. David once subscribed to it, Psal. cxliv. 15, "Happy is that people that is in such a case;" but he quickly crossed out that subscription, and said, "yea, happy is that people whose God is the Lord:" there is the happiness, to have God among them. He is the glory of a people: Zech. ii. 5, he was the glory in the midst of Jerusalem; there God dwelt, as his worship, laws, oracles, miracles, testified, and so he made Jerusalem glorious among all nations. Where true religion is, pure worship and ordinances, and God working for the good of a people, defending them, that is the glory and excellency of a kingdom. 2 Chron. xiii. 12, saith Abijah, "God is with us for our captain;" this was more than all the strength of Judah beside, when Jeroboam came against him with 800,000 chosen men. With you are the golden calves, ver. 8, "ye be a great multitude;" but God is not with you to be your glory and defence: you have the calves, which is your shame and nakedness, but God is with us, who is our glory and defence. And when Jerusalem fell to idolatry, God tells them, that they had "changed their glory for that which did not profit," Jer. ii. 11, they had driven away their glory; and here was the beginning of their woe. That is the misery of a kingdom, to have God depart from it: then public enterprises prosper not, Josh. vii. 12: then counsel fails, 1 Sam. xxviii. 15, protection is gone, Isa. v. 5; then peace, loving-kindness, and mercies go, Jer. xvi. 5. This is as taking the sun out of the firmament, the eyes out of the head, or soul out of the body. Now a kingdom and people lie exposed to all evils and mischiefs: Hos. ix. 12, "Woe to them when I depart from them." All mischiefs presently crowd in upon a people left of God: famine, wars, captivity, a perverse spirit, and treacherousness one to another, came upon this people, when God left his place. And so after Christ's days, when God left them, and that voice was heard in the temple, *Migremus hinc*, Let us depart hence: which Tacitus in his Annals also mentions, *Audita major humana vox, excedere deos, simul ingens motus excedentium*, A greater than a human voice was heard, that the gods had departed, and at the same time a prodigious motion as of those departing: after this, dreadful misery befell them, war, famine, dispersion was their portion; they are without God, Christ, and mercy to this day; an undone and most unhappy people. We had almost driven away God by our sins, specially by our idolatry and superstitions; but God and his glory are not quite gone: Jer. xiv. 9, "Yet thou, O Lord, art in the midst of us, and we are called by thy name; leave us not."

Joseph. de Bel. Jud. l. 7. c. 2.

Lib. 21.

Obs. 4. God is glory, or glorious. There is nothing in God inglorious. As in the sun is only light, so God is light, and in him is no darkness. He is all light, all glory; his attributes are glory, his essence is glory, his life is glory, God is only glory. Blessed be the glory, the Lord.

Obs. 5. Under the law, God confined himself to a particular place, to the temple; there he dwelt, appeared, received sacrifices, gave answers, &c. So that the temple was not only *locus*, the place, but *medium divini cultus*, the medium of divine worship: the Jews were bound to set their faces towards it when they prayed, 1 Kings viii. 48; Dan. vi. 10; it being also a type of the body of Christ, John ii. 19, that sanctified their assemblies and sacrifices, Matt. xxiii. 19. But it is otherwise now under the gospel; neither Jerusalem nor Samaria is the place where God is fixed, John iv. 21, but God's habitation is in all places where he hath saints. Matt. xviii. 20, "Where two or three are gathered together in my name, there am I in the midst of them." 2 Cor. vi. 16, "Ye are the temple of the living God:" and what saith God? I will dwell in them, and walk about in them; that is, in the church of Corinth; and so in all congregations. Now the congregations are God's habitation; he walks amongst the golden candlesticks; there is the glorious God seen, the glorious God heard. But the place now where the meetings are held, are neither means nor parts of worship, no types of Christ, nor do they sanctify the people or service done in them: rather do the people and ordinances, while they are there, sanctify them; and yet when the ordinances are ended, and people gone, no holiness abides in them, but they are as other places.

ενοικήσω ἐν αὐτοῖς, καὶ ἐμπεριπατήσω.

Obs. 6. The Lord is worthy of praise, when he is in a way of judgment. "Blessed be the glory of the Lord from his place." Now he was departing from Jerusalem, all woes and miseries taking hold of them, yet was he a God deserving praises. God's judgments are deep; we oft know not the reasons of them, see not the equity of God's proceedings in them, yet we should be so far from murmuring, that we should count him worthy of honour and praise, when he deserts churches and kingdoms: Exod. xv. 11, "God is fearful in praises."

Obs. 7. It is the work and office of angels to praise God. The living creatures here said, "Blessed be the glory of the Lord from his place." And Rev. v. 11, 12, there were many angels about the throne; and what did they? They sang, "Worthy is the Lamb that was slain to receive power, and riches, and wisdom, and strength, and honour, and glory, and blessing." So the seraphims in Isa. vi. 3, their song was, "Holy, holy, holy, is the Lord of hosts: the whole earth is full of his glory." Angels are musical creatures, and make the best melody. Arias thinks it was an angel dictated the song of Deborah unto her. Luke ii. 13, 14, there was a heavenly chorus, and sang a heavenly song, "Glory to God in the highest, on the earth peace, and good-will towards men:" this was a short, but a sweet song. When great things have been done by God, the angels have been brought in praising God, as when God created the world; Job xxxviii. 4, 7, "Where wast thou," saith God to Job, "when I laid the foundations of the earth?—when the morning stars sang together, and all the sons of God shouted for joy?" that is, the angels, as interpreters observe, who, at the sight of that great and glorious work, were much affected, and sang the praises of God. So at the birth of Christ, and here at the departure of God out of the temple, the great God, doing great works, must have great praises, even the praises of angels. Praise is an angelical work, and the office of angels, and the Spirit calls for it at their hands; Psal. cxlviii. 2, "Praise ye him, all his angels;" and they do it when he is in his judgments. The Jews thought God dealt hardly in punishing them; but angels saw cause to praise God for his departure from them, and vindicating his glory in the punishment of hypocrites.

A. Lapid. on Judg. v. 23.

τῶν ἀγγέλων λειτουργία ἐστι ψαλμωδία. Theod.

Obs. 8. God doth his works without motion or mutation. Here it is said, "from his place;" there is a show of motion and change, but no such thing befalls God; his works make motions and changes in the creature, not in himself. He is infinite, fills heaven and earth, and never removes from one place to another; he is immutable, and not subject to changes.

From the 13th verse of the wings, wheels, and noise of them, I have spoken in the first chapter largely; yet a little I shall speak of this verse. It is said, that the living creatures "touched one another:" the Hebrew is from נשק to kiss; and each other, in the Hebrew, is a woman to her sister.

Obs. 1. God makes use of angels and second causes in the government of the world, and execution of his judgments. All creatures have being from and dependence on God, and he may employ them to what service he will.

Obs. 2. God's judgments do often come suddenly and swiftly. Wings make a noise, and wheels do rattle in a moment, and judgments come in an instant: Hos. x. 15, "In a morning shall the king of Israel be cut off utterly;" Belshazzar, in a night, Dan. v. 30; Nebuchadnezzar in an hour driven from his palace and pride, Dan. iv. 33.

Obs. 3. There is much harmony and love between the angels. Their wings touch, kiss, they go lovingly together in the execution of their offices; they have like affections, as a woman to her sister. They sang sweetly together at the birth of Christ. There is no contention, envy, or division among them, but much love; they are near God, and the nearer any are to God, the more love is in them. If we could agree better, and love more, we should be angelical.

In the 14th verse is laid down, what the Spirit did with the prophet, after it had lift him up. It took him away; after the sublation, there was an ablation. The prophet was carried by the power of the Spirit to Tel-abib. This was not a visional thing, but real; for being lifted up, he was taken away from the place where he saw the vision; he was not set down, and so left to go to Tel-abib, but he was carried in the arms of the Spirit, as Philip was caught up by the Spirit, and carried to Azotus, Acts viii. 39, 40. The Spirit was the fiery chariot that carried Philip and our prophet through the air to their several places.

"And I went in bitterness, in the heat of my spirit." The Hebrew is, I went bitter in the hot anger of my spirit. Here the infirmity of our prophet appears much, in that after he had seen and heard such great and glorious things, had found such favour in the eyes of Christ, as to have his Spirit enter into him, comfort him, confirm him, and to bestow prophetical gifts upon him, yet now he should be unwilling to obey Christ's call, be in bitterness and opposition to his will; this is a great infirmity. If I go and preach of the glory departing from the temple, I shall stir up the people against me, they will stone me; if not, I shall offend God. The prophet now thought upon God's anger against his people; his departure out of the temple, the ruin of the city, the stubbornness and impudence of the house of Israel. Now the weightiness of the work enjoined him by Christ seized upon him; and now, like Jonah, he thought to decline the service. His spirit was bitter, he in a great heat, that he was so pressed to a work so little affected, and overpowered by the Spirit of God, that, willing or unwilling, on he must; for the next words are,

"But the hand of the Lord was strong upon me." Which words do declare, that had not God's hand overpowered him, he would not have set upon that hard work of the prophetical office; fears, difficulties, dangers, carnal reason, unbelief, self-love, one or all of these, would have turned him back, if the hand of God had not strongly prevailed with him.

By "hand of the Lord," some understand the spirit of prophecy, as if that did mightily urge him; so the Chaldee exposition is. Others understand by it, *divinum auxilium*, divine aid, or, *virtus Spiritus*, the influence of the Spirit, which is as a hand to help. We may safely understand the Spirit by it, which put forth its mighty power upon and in the prophet. Why the Spirit is resembled to a hand, I showed in chap. i. 3. A hand is *symbolum energiæ, index rei, et instrumentum operationis*, the symbol of power, a director, and the instrument of operation. There is strength in the hand; it shows what is to be done, and effects it: so here, the Spirit took hold of the prophet, which notes his power, showed him his duty, and caused him to do it.

"Was strong." The Hebrew root חזק signifies, *fortiter apprehendere, tenere*, to lay hold of firmly, to retain; as one that holds loose joints and nerves of the body, to strengthen and confirm them, that so the man may be more compact and able to do any thing: it notes laying hold with strength, as men in danger of drowning; and the Septuagint frequently renders it by a word that notes so much; as Ezek. vii. 13; κρατεῖν, et ὑπερκρατεῖν. xxii. 14, which is to hold by strength. And this sense suits with the hand of the Lord that took hold of the prophet, whose spirit was remiss, infirm, like a member out of joint, and strengthened it, and enabled it to do what was intended and appointed: the Spirit held the prophet by its mighty power, that he could not wrest from it by any means, but like a man conquered, must yield, and do what was required.

Obs. 1. The prophets were put on to and carried on in their works of prophecy, and giving the Scriptures, by extraordinary acts of the Spirit; that enters into Ezekiel, takes him up, takes him away with mighty power, comes upon him, and constrains him to prophesy. Here was inspiration and impulsion of the Spirit. 2 Pet. i. 20, 21, "Prophecy came not by the will of man, but holy ἰδίας ἐπιλύσεως. men of God spake as they were moved by the Holy Ghost:" it was not their own spirit moved, that is private; but it was the Spirit of God, which is divine and public, and carried them on with might: so that the Scriptures are not *inventum humanum*, but *oracula Dei*, they are not of man, but of God. Therefore Philo saith, *Propheta est interpres Dei dictantis oracula*, A prophet is an interpreter of God declaring his will. The Spirit dictates all, and man only utters or writes what is dictated. And as the Scriptures are not of man, but of the Spirit, so their interpretation is not of man, but of the Spirit likewise. Let councils, fathers, churches, give their sense of Scripture; it is private, if it be not the sense and interpretation of the Spirit. Let a private man give the true sense of the Scripture; it is not private, because it is divine. The sense of the Holy Ghost, and private, in this place of Peter, is not opposed to public, but to divine; and the words are to be read, no Scripture is of a man's own interpretation; that is, private, contrary to divine.

Obs. 2. The Holy Ghost is God, and a person distinct from the Son. The Spirit was in the living creatures, in the wheels, and in Ezekiel. How could this be, if the Spirit were not God? None but God can be at the same time in many places; it is his peculiar prerogative and nature to be every where. The beams of the sun are in several places, but not the essence or body of the sun, that is in one place only;

but the Holy Ghost was in its essence, in the angels, in the wheels, in Ezekiel; it was in Jeremiah, who lived then at Jerusalem; it was in all the saints there, in Daniel, and the rest of the saints in Babylon: so that the Spirit is co-essential with the Father and the Son, and it is a person; otherwise how could it have taken up the prophet, and carried him? And it is distinct from the Son, who is described to be upon the throne, and to give commands unto the prophet. And that the Spirit here is brought in distinct from him, is most clear in that place in Matt. iii. 16, 17, where the Spirit is distinguished from the Son, baptized, and from the Father, acknowledging Christ his Son, in whom he was well pleased.

Obs. 3. Great saints have great infirmities. Ezekiel goes in bitterness, in the heat of his spirit; he was in a froward humour, in a great distemper; the Vulgate hath it, *in indignatione spiritus*, there was indignation in his spirit to the work. Some have thought this affection of the prophet not altogether sinful, yet some sinfulness to be in it, which cannot be denied. It is granted by Calvin, that it did differ from the grace of the Spirit; and for him, after so clear and strong a call, to refuse, to be in a chafe, to withstand, was an infirmity, if not a sin. He had rather have been out of service than in it, lien hid among the people, than have been an ambassador of Christ unto them; he had rather they should have perished without vision, than that himself should be a seer amongst them: here was the weakness of this good man. I could tell you of Abraham's, Jacob's, Moses's, David's, Paul's, and John's failings. There never was since sin entered any perfect saint: in many things we sin all, Jam. iii. 2. And yet the apostles were filled with the Spirit, there was a fulness of grace in them, and in the prophets; yet neither the one nor the other were altogether free from carnal influence, notwithstanding all their graces and excellences, they did still breathe something earthly. And now, wherever the Spirit comes, it neither extinguishes nature nor corruption wholly in this life. The best wine hath its dregs and its lees, and the best of saints hath his spots and weaknesses; there is no perfection in any.

Obs. 4. Holy men set down their own infirmities, which is an argument of the truth of the word, and the divine nature of it. Men that are mere men, seek their own glory, and will not shame themselves in their writings; but the penmen of Scripture, having received another spirit, are content to shame themselves, so God may have glory, his truth credit, his people caution and comfort: all these are in the setting down of their own sins. When holy men confess their weaknesses, set them down, as Moses, Exod. iv. 10; as David, Psal. li. 3—5; as Jonah, chap. i. 3; as Paul, 1 Tim. i. 13; as John, Rev. xxii. 8; God is glorified by their shame. It is evidenced what God did for, and by, these men, notwithstanding their sins. Men are persuaded of the truth of the word, seeing they spared not themselves, and would not bury their own thoughts in silence. Others, that see the slips of such men of God, are admonished thereby to look to their standings, and to be watchful; and those who are beaten down with the sense of their failings, see it is the common sickness of the saints, and not their case alone, which is some ease unto them.

Obs. 5. That some truths of God, sweet in the reception, oft prove bitter in the operation. The roll that Ezekiel did eat, ver. 3, was sweet as honey at first unto him; but now he was to go and put it in practice, he found it bitter, and sought to decline that service; it was like pills sugared over, sweet in the mouth, but being dissolved in his bowels, produced distressing pain. He was upon the rack, and sick of the business, and perplexed that he had eaten such a roll. The stony-ground hearers heard the word with joy, it was sweet to the taste, but afterwards it was bitter: when persecution and temptation came, those hearers were offended and fell away, Matt. xiii. 20, 21. The word of joy proved a word of bitterness unto them, and it is so to most men at one time or other; they find it a sad and difficult thing to act those truths which are sweet to the understanding. John ate the little book, it was sweet in his mouth, bitter in his belly, Rev. x. 9, 10; that is, in the operation of it; John saw that those truths written in it would beget hatreds, persecutions, imprisonments, banishments, martyrdom, &c. When we come to find the operations of truths, that they will cost us dear, dear friends, dear liberties, dear lusts, dear limbs, dear lives; we find a bitterness in truths, though formerly they have been like Ezekiel's roll and John's little book to our mouths.

Obs. 6. Man's wisdom and spirit is opposite to the wisdom and spirit of the Lord Christ. Christ calls, sends Ezekiel in his infinite wisdom; he thinks it best for him to go to these captive Jews, this rebellious house. The Spirit enters into Ezekiel, assures him of his call, strengthens him, assists him; and yet he is averse, in bitterness, in the heat of his spirit; he shows the antipathy between his wisdom and Christ's, his spirit and the Spirit of Christ, they closed not. There are principles of opposition in godly men to the ways of Christ and his Spirit; so far as they are unregenerate, so far they are opposite. Rom. viii. 7, "The carnal mind is enmity against God;" it is in the original, the wisdom of the flesh is enmity against God. There is flesh in the best men; that flesh hath wisdom, it hath a spirit; (the flesh is the old man, a whole man, and must have a spirit in it to act it, such a one as it is;) and both the wisdom and spirit of the flesh are enmity to God, not subject to his law and will; and enmity to man, they work death, and end in death. Jonah had such wisdom, and such a spirit in him, when he ran from God; but it had cost him his life, if God had not been more gracious than he dutiful. Paul complains, he found a law in his members warring against the law of his mind, Rom. vii. 23. Gal. v. 17, "The flesh lusteth against the Spirit;" the work of the flesh is lusting and warring against the Spirit. It is with a godly man, as it was with Rebekah, Gen. xxv. 22, 23; she had great strugglings in her womb, and what was the cause of it? there were two nations in her womb, one contrary to the other: and there is heaven and earth in a godly man's heart, which are contrary, and make great struggings. The same soul that commands obedience, opposeth obedience; the same will that delights in the law of God, hath a cross motion to the law of sin; the heart that trusteth God, doubts of his favour; while we are believing, unbelief is opposing; Mark ix. 24, "Lord, I believe; help thou mine unbelief."

Obs. 7. Saints may do the will of God unwillingly, if not against their will. Ezekiel was in bitterness, in the heat of his spirit, unwilling to be a prophet to this people, yet he went—"I went." Jonah goes to Nineveh, but his heart is not full on the work, there was not a thoroughness in it: he saw there was a necessity for it; God had power to punish disobedience, and could quickly crush him; and therefore now, in a prudential way, he would go and prophesy to Nineveh: there was in him an unwilling willingness, his spirit was not totally willing, as you may gather from chap. iv. 1—3. He was against the sparing of Nineveh; it stuck upon his spirit, that he should lie under the imputation of a false prophet; he wishes death upon it, which shows that his spirit was not wholly in the service. We do the work and will of God ofttimes with great unwillingness, as women part with their jointures, or children; as merchants throw their goods overboard in a storm; as many, now assessed, part with their goods to the public service; necessity is too strong for them, and prudence puts them on, and there is a willing unwillingness: so it is with the godly, they pray and hear unwillingly, they give unwillingly, &c. This is from the imbecility of grace, the power of corruption, misapprehension of God and his ways, violence of temptations, entanglements with the world, pressures of guilt, and unsuccessfulness of service. Let us be sensible of our unwillingnesses in God's ways, be humbled for them, and strive to do all *animo prompto*, with a ready mind. Deut. xxviii. 47, 48, "Because thou servedst not the Lord thy God with joyfulness, and with gladness of heart, for the abundance of all things; therefore shalt thou serve thine enemies." It is good for us to have our wills and whole hearts in the work of God.

Obs. 8. The infirmities of God's people do not interrupt his love and grace. Ezekiel went in bitterness, in heat of spirit, "but the hand of the Lord was strong upon me." This great distemper in the prophet did not distemper God, it did not cause him to retract or divert his love; but he takes hold of him by his hand, and upholds him, as a parent would do to a child, falling, or down: the weakness or sickness of a child doth not estrange the heart of the parent, it rather enlarges and draws out the bowels more fully. And so it is with God: Psal. ciii. 13, 14, "As a father pitieth his children, so the Lord pitieth them that fear him;" and why so? "he knoweth our frame; he remembereth we are but dust;" the Lord knows what weak and frail things we are. The word for frame, notes a formed vessel of earth, and the Chaldee expounds it, of our evil concupiscence, which carrieth us into error: God knows that we are earthen vessels, full of lusts and infirmities, which lead us from him, which disable us to serve him. Now here is the love, bowels, goodness of a God; because we are so, therefore he pitieth us: so Psal. lxxviii. 37, 38, their hearts were not right nor stedfast with God, but God was right and stedfast with them; "he, being full of compassion, forgave their iniquity, and destroyed them not." Infirmities may bring crosses, but cannot cut off from mercies: this should strengthen our faith, comfort our hearts, and encourage us with a holy boldness to go to the throne of grace. Heb. iv. 15, 16, Christ, saith the apostle, is a merciful "High Priest, touched with the feeling of our infirmities;" and what infers he upon it? "Let us go boldly to the throne of grace, that we may obtain mercy, and find grace in time of need."

Obs. 9. The Spirit of Christ is the healer and helper of our infirmities. Ezekiel was distempered and sick of the business, and the hand, the Spirit of the Lord, was strong upon him, that helped, that healed him: Psal. cvii. 20, "He sent his word and healed them;" the Spirit in that word did the cure. And here he sent his Spirit to seize upon Ezekiel, to work out the ill humour, to settle his thoughts, and sweeten his spirit that was so embittered. The Spirit is compared to oil, Psal. xlv. 7; 1 John ii. 27, and that is of a mollifying, cleansing, healing, and quickening nature. When Christ was anointed, then he healed the broken-hearted, Luke iv. 18, he dropped that oil into their hearts, and that did soften, purge, heal, and quicken them. Gifts of healing are attributed to the Spirit, 1 Cor. xii. 9; and helping our infirmities in prayer is the work of it, Rom. viii. 26. The Spirit brings the strength: we are infirm, and can do nothing; but the Spirit, together with us, and for us, takes up the work, that we faint not. It answers to the word here, "was strong, took hold on me," bound up my spirit together, and strengthened me, not suffering my spirit to run out.

συναντιλαμβάνεται.

Lastly, the Spirit works invincibly. Ezekiel may struggle, but the Spirit will overcome; that was strong upon him. Men would not come in to Christ, and do his work, unless a Spirit mightier than their own come upon them. God's Spirit is a Spirit of power: Luke i. 35, "The Holy Ghost shall come upon thee, and the power of the Highest shall overshadow thee;" the Holy Ghost is the power of the Highest. And when Paul preached, it was "in demonstration of the Spirit and of power," 1 Cor. ii. 4; and his ministry was able to beat down strong-holds, 2 Cor. x. 4, 5, to cast down all high things, and to captivate thoughts and spirits to the obedience of Christ. The Spirit works invisibly, it is a hand under a wing; and it works invincibly, it is a strong hand, there is none can stand before the strength of it: antichrist shall be consumed by the Spirit of the Lord, 2 Thess. ii. 8. This Spirit is fire to consume enemies; it is a hand, powerful to fetch in the friends under election. The Jews are now stiff enemies of Christ; but when the Spirit of grace is poured out upon them, when this hand takes hold of them, then they will mourn, come in, submit to Christ. No violence doth the Spirit offer to the wills of men, notwithstanding it works invincibly; it files off the enmity and averseness of our wills to God, and inclines them to yield, *omnipotenti suavitate, et suavi omnipotentia*, by an omnipotent sweetness, and a sweet omnipotence.

Oportet non tantum moveri, sed novum fieri. *Prosp.*

Ver. 15. *Then I came to them of the captivity at Tel-abib, that dwelt by the river of Chebar, and I sat where they sat, and remained there astonished among them seven days.*

In this verse is the *terminus*, or end, of his journey, and his condition then, mourning and sadness.

The word Tel-abib signifies a heap of new fruits, or green ears of corn; of תל *acervus*, and אביב, *spica maturescens*. Jerom and the Vulgate translate it, a heap of new fruit or corn; and Jerom thinks the Jews were placed there, to plough, sow, reap, thrash, and that now they were beating out the new corn. But this opinion we cannot admit, for it was in the fourth month, chap. i. 1, that Ezekiel had his vision, and their harvests in those hot countries were not in the fourth month, but rather in the first or second. The Israelites came out of Egypt in the month Abib, Exod. xiii. 4; and that was their first month, Exod. xii. 2, and answered to the latter end of that month which is called January, and to the beginning of the other called February. And in Exod. ix. 31, it is said, "the barley was in the ear;" the word is *abib*, an ear of corn, and denominates the month, because in it the barley eared. So then it could not be harvest when Ezekiel came to them at Tel-abib, it was rather over. We take the word for the name of a place, as Tel-melah, Tel-harsa, Ezra ii. 59; in their etymology, the one signifies a heap of wood, the other a heap of salt; yet by Ezra they are called places; "These were they which went up from Tel-melah, Tel-harsa," &c. so "Tel-abib" here. And

Acervum novarum frugum.

Ad opera rusticana exercenda.

it was in the middle part of Mesopotamia, between two rivers, Chebar and Saocorah; and here they were placed, as Junius thinks, both to secure them, that they might not think of getting away, being shut up between two rivers, or if they did, not easily accomplish it; and secondly, to secure the place, which was subject to inundations, and so uninhabited, and opened to enemies, but now by their labour, art, and strength, might be made useful and defensive.

"By the river of Chebar:" of that river, was spoken in chap. i. 1.

"I sat where they sat, and remained there astonished among them seven days." Sitting notes a quiet posture of the body, abiding in a place; Exod. xvi. 3, "When we sat by the flesh pots," that is, abode, dwelt where we had them. Also great grief; Lam. ii. 10, "The elders of the daughter of Zion sit upon the ground, and keep silence." And so in that place in Isa. xlvii. 8, "I shall not sit as a widow," solitary, mourning in deep sorrow; to which alludes that in Lam. i. 1, "How doth the city sit solitary! how is she become as a widow!" Great grief silenceth the whole man; the tongue speaks not, the body moves not. Job ii. 13, Job's friends "sat down with him upon the ground seven days and nights, and none spake a word to him; for they saw that his grief was very great;" so great, it made them all quiet and hushed: and seven days he sat in that doleful posture, because they were used to mourn seven days in cases of great grief; as Joseph mourned seven days for his father, Gen. l. 10; and seven days' mourning is an argument of great grief, and a testimony of much love. If we refer our prophet's mourning to the condition which the Jews were coming to, it might be lawful; he saw their death and funeral was at hand, and so, being sensible, laid it deeply to heart, and bewailed it seven days, testifying his good will and affection to them; but if we refer it to his unwillingness to go in the service Christ called him to, it is not excusable, but a further argument of his great weakness. The cause of the prophet's sitting there seven days, might be to know the state of the people more exactly, to whom he was to prophesy; it might be upon divine command; it might also be for further direction from God when to begin his prophecy. A prophet he was made, but had no time appointed to begin his hard work. It might also be to prepare and awaken the people, that seeing him sit still, sad, amazed, they might inquire what this strange sadness meant, and so his word take the deeper impression when he should speak unto them.

Septemdialis luctus est quoddam acerbi doloris indicium et benevolentis animi legitimum argumentum.

"Astonished." The Hebrew word משמים *masmim*, from *shamam*, notes great astonishment, even to wonder; Isa. lix. 16, "He wondered that there was no intercessor." It notes also desolation, and may here be rendered, I sat desolate seven days; the Spirit left me in that place, and men regarded me not, being full of grief, and telling them I had sad news; so the word is used, Lam. v. 18, "The mountain of Zion is desolate;" and thus we may take it. The vision being ended, the prophet, set down there by the Spirit, and neither seeing, hearing, or having to do now with Christ, the living creatures, wheels, or the Spirit, found himself desolate, and was astonished at that great change. The Septuagint renders it *αναςρεφόμενος*, intimating the prophet's meditating, and inward discoursing of the miseries and woes that were written in the roll, and coming upon the people; the hard task he had to perform among this people.

Obs. 1. That in the place and condition God sets his people, they must abide in the same. The Spirit brings Ezekiel to Tel-abib, there he continues, till the Spirit adviseth his departure: let him be among captives, between overflowing rivers, he continues and stirs not. It must not be any slight thing that removes men from the calling God hath set them in. Ministers may not at pleasure go from place to place, as if there were no tie upon them. Neither captivity, incorrigibleness of persons, nor discommodity of place, are weighty enough to take off Ezekiel from that place and people the Spirit had set him over. When the Holy Ghost hath set men over a flock, they must take heed to that flock, and not seek occasion to be gone upon discontents, &c. The worst are forwardest to remove. The bramble will leave his place to be king, when the olive, fig-tree, and vine will not stir. Christ will not be made a king by entreaty, nor by force.

Obs. 2. The men of this world are politic for their own ends. The captivity were placed at Tel-abib, between two rivers, that they might not get away, that they might make that part of the country strong and useful. Worldly men are wiser in their generation than the children of light. How cunningly did Pharaoh deal with the Israelites! Exod. i. 10, "Let us work wisely with them," saith he; they multiply, and we are in danger, lest upon any occasion they take part with our enemies, or make a head of themselves, or attempt an escape: come, let us set taskmasters over them, wear them out with much work, and employ them to build cities for us. Here was the cunning to avoid the name of tyranny: he will not destroy them with sword, fire, open violence, but work they must in brick and clay, and fall by hard labour; so he covers up his cruelty under a fair pretence, and provides for his own security and profit in the Israelites' service. Wicked and worldly men are all self, and all their actions draw homewards, they are their own centres; the wisdom of the flesh, of the serpent, of the world is theirs, and they must needs be crafty for themselves.

Obs. 3. The condition of the saints and servants of God is very changeable here. Ezekiel hath a glorious vision, sight of, and converse with Christ, the company of angels, sees the course and motion of things in the world, had the Spirit enter into him, comforting him, strengthening and assisting him; and now he is a desolate, an astonished man, he sits as one forsaken of all. Here was a great change, and it was not Ezekiel's case alone; others, even all the worthies of God, have found the like. David was strong through divine favour, and quickly troubled for the want of God's face; he had his singings and his sorrowings, Psal. xxx.; he was oft in the valleys: Psal. xxv. 16, 17, "I am desolate and afflicted; the troubles of my heart are enlarged;" and Psal. cxliii. 4, "My spirit is overwhelmed, my heart within me is desolate." Paul is one day rapt up into the third heavens, and another day he hath a thorn in the flesh; if he have the revelation of the Spirit to exalt him, he hath the buffetings of Satan to humble him. Paul himself knew changes.

Obs. 4. Distempers of spirit fasten and continue oft with the servants of God. Ezekiel was in his distemper of bitterness and heat of spirit seven days. It is not easy to shake off distempers when they have taken hold of us. Jonah was in an ill humour and frame of spirit many days together; he must be drenched, buried, and boiled in the whale's belly, ere he will be pliable to the will of God. When Uzzah was smitten for his error, David was displeased, and in a pet with God himself, and would not bring the ark in three months to Sion, 2 Sam. vi.

Obs. 5. Distemperedness of spirit unfits for the service of God: he sits seven days, and nothing is done. The apostle James knew this, and therefore said, "Be slow to wrath; for the wrath of man worketh not the righteousness of God," Jam. i. 19, 20. Wrath darkens the mind, and puts all out of frame. Wise men in their wrath see not their ways nor work: when the light of reason, truth, and the Spirit is gone, what can a man do befitting God? Wrath makes men err in their own business, much more in the Lord's; it works not the righteousness of God, but its own righteousness; that which seems right in its own eyes, that shall be done. Ezekiel thought it right not to prophesy, not to submit to the will of Christ and work of the Spirit; but his passion was prejudice to him and to the work of God. It is evil when wrath prevents reason, and forceth it to action; then whatever is done, is the work of anger, not of reason, not of righteousness. When wrath hath the kingdom, when that is in the head and heart, there is no place for the righteousness of God. This made Clement say, Where wrath dwells, God dwells not. Wrath is a special friend of Satan's, many of his counsels and designs are effected by it: the more of this humour, the more service hath hell; the less of it, the more serviceable for heaven. Moses was the meekest man upon the earth, and he did most work for heaven. Christ was meeker than all other, and he did work the righteousness of God effectually, he did work for heaven and earth.

Per iram sapientia perditur ut quid quove ordine agendum sit omnino nesciatur. *Greg.* 5. *Moral.* c. 30.

Per iram lux veritatis amittitur, Spiritus sancti splendor excluditur. *Ibid.*

Aquin. 3. p. q. 15. art. 9.

Ubi est ira, ibi non est Dominus, sed amica Satanæ. l. 2. *Const.*

Obs. 6. That the prophets could not prophesy at their pleasure. Ezekiel sits seven days, and there is no prophesying. Aquinas hath a question, whether prophecy be a habit; if it were so, it is in the power of man to use it any time, but so could not the prophet. When the Shunammite's son was dead, and she came to Elisha, what said he? "Her soul is vexed within her; and the Lord hath hid it from me, and hath not told me," 2 Kings iv. 27. Unless the Lord reveal himself unto them afresh, the prophets could not tell things; the schoolmen therefore conclude, that prophecy is not in the prophet as a habit, but as a transient impression. Habits are permanent things, but prophecy is a transient thing, a light in the air; for as the air doth always need a new illumination, so the mind of a prophet doth always need a new revelation, else the prophet sits in darkness, and knows not more than other men: Lam. ii. 9, "Her prophets find no vision from the Lord;" and so in Psal. lxxiv. 9, "There is no more any prophet, neither is there among us any that knoweth how long." It was night oft with the prophets. Nathan spake not from heaven, when he bid David go and do all that was in his heart touching the building of God a house; for it is said, "that night came the word of the Lord unto Nathan," 2 Sam. vii. 3, 4: before he had not a word, and when it came, it was not for David, but Solomon, to build the house. So that it is true which Gregory saith, Sometimes the spirit of prophecy is wanting to the prophets, and their minds are dark. Samuel mistook, when he said, "Surely the Lord's anointed is before him," 1 Sam. xvi, 6, 7.

Aliquando prophetiæ spiritus deest prophetis, nec semper eorum mentibus præsto est. *Hom.* 1. *in Ezek.*

Ver. 16—19. *And it came to pass at the end of seven days, that the word of the Lord came unto me, saying, Son of man, I have made thee a watchman unto the house of Israel: therefore hear the word at my mouth, and give them warning from me. When I say unto the wicked, Thou shalt surely die; and thou givest him not warning, nor speakest to warn the wicked from his wicked way, to save his life; the same wicked man shall die in his iniquity; but his blood will I require at thine hand. Yet if thou warn the wicked, and he turn not from his wickedness, nor from his wicked way, he shall die in his iniquity; but thou hast delivered thy soul.*

In these words, and the rest to the end of the chapter, is a new revelation made to the prophet, together with the events following thereupon; or thus:

I. You have the call of the prophet to his office renewed, and that is in the words read, and on to the end of the 21st verse.

II. Special directions and events laid down from the 21st verse to the end of the chapter.

In the words read, you have,

First, the circumstance of time, when this repetition of his call or new revelation was made, and that was after "seven days," ver. 16.

Secondly, his office specified, which is to be "a watchman," ver. 17.

Thirdly, the parties he is to watch over and admonish:

1. In general laid down, and that is, "the house of Israel," ver. 17.

2. More particularly:

(1.) "The wicked," ver. 18, 19.

(2.) "The righteous," ver. 20, 21.

Fourthly, the reasons of it, why he must admonish both sorts:

The first is, the danger and mischief of it; both they and he shall die if it be not done.

The second, it may be they will turn upon admonition, and so be saved; if not, yet the prophet delivers his own soul, and there is advantage by it.

The words in the 16th verse have little difficulty in them.

"At the end of seven days." It is probable the sitting still and silence of the prophet was from sabbath to sabbath; on that day he had his glorious vision, and seven days after he had a new revelation, the word of the Lord came to him. All the six days he was solitary, mourning, meditating, and silent, but on the seventh the Lord appeared again unto him; and so after, he had upon sabbaths revelations from God.

Junius.

Obs. 1. That God bears with the weaknesses and distempers of his servants. Ezekiel declines the call of Christ, shows his great ingratitude; having had such great favours from Christ, seen so much glory, and being commanded once, twice, to go and preach to the house of Israel, yet he sits down, is silent, and that seven days together. This might have provoked the Lord to great wrath, to have refused him, as a stubborn, self-willed man, and made him to say, he would never admit him to be his prophet, put such honour upon him, intrust him with such great matters; but the Lord bears with his weakness, yea, his continued weakness. Sometimes God's anger kindles, and breaks out quickly, and that for little things in our eyes and opinions; as the man that gathered a few sticks on the sabbath, he must be stoned to death; those who peeped irreverently into the ark, the Lord smote fifty thousand and upward dead for it presently, 1 Sam. vi. 19. Ananias and Sapphira, a small matter in our conceits, it was to keep back a portion of their goods, and to excuse it with a lie; for this God was wroth, and they died, Acts v.: but the weaknesses of his children he bears with and those great ones.

Obs. 2. Man's will and weakness cannot hinder the efficacy and execution of God's decree. The prophet's spirit was against this work; he refused, sat still seven days together, and would have frustrated God's intentions if he could, but it was decreed in heaven: that decree was efficacious, his will must be brought off, and he must be the man to execute God's pleasure in a prophetical way to the house of Israel. Jonah departs, will prejudice God's design concerning Nineveh; but the Lord knew how to humble him, to fetch him back, being fled, and to make him instrumental to his ends, notwithstanding his wilfulness and weakness. Psal. xxxiii. 9, "He commanded, and it stood fast;" and ver. 11, "The counsel of the Lord standeth for ever." Let there be contrary counsels, wills, commands; they stand not. God brings them to nought, he makes them of none effect: Prov. xix. 21, "There are many devices in a man's heart;" he thinks not to do this, and not to do that, and it shall be so and so; "nevertheless the counsel of the Lord shall stand;" he will perfect the work he hath begun in men, and by men, notwithstanding their infirmities.

Obs. 3. Spiritual employments must have sedate, quiet, well composed affections and spirits. The Spirit of prophecy came not upon Ezekiel all the time he was distempered and discontented; but when time had wrought off the distemper, and the ill humour was digested, then was he stirred by the Spirit of prophecy: when the minstrel was tuned, then the hand of the Lord came upon Elisha, 2 Kings iii. 15. Men's hearts and spirits are like minstrels, out of order quickly, and long in tuning, and right setting; but the music is sweetest when the instrument is best set, then God delights to communicate his Spirit to us, to employ us. In the night oft God appeared to the patriarchs; then were they most quiet, and fittest to receive instruction. In Augustus's days, when there was peace throughout the world, then was Christ given, then was he born. When there is peace throughout the little world, then are we aptest for reception of Christ's instructions, and readiest for his service; God will not commit weighty and great things to men, without due fitness for them. The prophet had this time deeply to consider of the business, and to get himself into such a frame, as might best sort with the function he was to be in.

Obs. 4. The Lord doth not leave his people long, although they be in distempers; at the end of seven days the word of the Lord came unto him. We may by our failings and distempers drive away God from us, but he will visit us again; he may be gone all the week, but come again at the end of it. God's anger is for a moment; our weeping for a night, and joy in the morning, Psal. xxx. 5. It is not long this good Physician will be absent from his patient, and when he comes, he will comfort and cure.

Obs. 5. Our prophet brought not his own, but the word of the Lord unto the people. It is his word must be commended unto them; prophets, apostles, ministers, are his ambassadors, and must speak what is given them in commission. If they go or speak of their own heads, they provoke God and wrong the people. Jer. xxiii. 30, "I am against the prophets, saith the Lord, that steal my words, every one from his neighbour:" the false prophets would take some sayings of the true prophets, and mingle them with their own lies and errors, to get the more credit unto them; and sometimes by false interpretations they would wrest the word to establish their own phantasies. They would prophesy for their own glory and profit, and this was stealing of the word: they did handle the word *alieno sensu, spiritu, et fine*, in another sense and spirit, and for another end, than God or the true prophets intended; so that their word was not conceived to be the word of God, but their own. And yet they would fasten it upon God; ver. 31, "I am against the prophets that use their tongues, and say, He saith." The word is הלקחים which signifies, *lenire*, to mitigate. They flattered and smoothed up the people, speaking things pleasing, and said, "He saith." They made God the author of their dreams, which the Lord reproves, ver. 32, and saith, "Behold, I am against them that prophesy false dreams, and do tell them, and cause my people to err by their lies, and by their lightness; yet I sent them not, nor commanded them: therefore they shall not profit this people at all, saith the Lord." People had need look to their teachers, what they are, whether sent of God, and such as speak the truths of God; otherwise they can look for no blessing, no profit; but when men come in God's name, and with God's word, you may look for great benefit; you must expect reality: for in the Hebrew are two words, which note reality and being. ויהי דבר God's words are things of great weight and worth.

Ver. 17. *I have made thee a watchman unto the house of Israel: therefore hear the word at my mouth, and give them warning from me.*

In this verse is the office of Ezekiel laid down:
First, generally, "a watchman."
Secondly, more peculiarly:
1. He must learn of Christ.
2. Warn the people.

"A watchman." צופה is from צפה to watch, to see from a high place, to look about on every side, to observe accurately; as in Prov. xv. 3, "The eyes of the Lord are in every place, beholding the evil and the good." The word for beholding, is *tzophoth*, the same with that in the verse, and notes God's exact and accurate eyeing of things; and it is metaphorically taken from those that are set in watch-towers, whose office is to observe with the eye, and intention of mind, what danger is in preparation, approach, or execution, and to inform the city, town, or army, to which he is a watchman, that all may timously look to themselves. If any fire, robbery, treachery, invasion, or danger whatsoever, appeared, the watchmen were wont to give notice by signs or voice, both in the night and day, and that constantly. Such was the prophet to be here unto the house of Israel, he was to foresee and foretell the dangers that were threatened, prepared, approaching, in execution; and this he was to do constantly, according to that in Isa. xxi. 8, "I stand continually upon the watch-tower in the day time; and I am set in my ward whole nights:" so Gen. xxxi. 40.

There were two sorts of watchmen God set in his church; extraordinary, prophets, apostles, evangelists; and ordinary, pastors and teachers; these continue to this day, and these watch for the good of souls, Heb. xiii. 17, and their office is, as the prophets', to learn of Christ, and to warn the people: the other are ceased.

Obs. 1. The goodness and bounty of Christ, that converseth with, and communicates unto the sons of men his precious truths and counsels. "Son of man," saith Christ, "I have made thee," &c. It had been honour to Ezekiel to have had an angel confer with him, and impart secrets to him; it is a great matter to have a prince talk kindly to his subject, tell him his counsels and purposes; what was it then for our prophet, to have Christ, the Lord of angels, and King of kings, to speak lovingly to him, to tell him of heavenly mysteries! And thus he doth to us in his word, that yet never saw his face; there he opens himself sweetly to us, all things being written for our instruction.

Obs. 2. It is Christ's prerogative to appoint watchmen in the church. "I have made thee a watchman;" he might not make himself one; others, without Christ's commission and directions, might not have made him one. Men should not come into the watch-tower, except called, Heb. v. 4; if they do, they will prove neither good watchmen nor good workmen. Christ himself is the great Watchman of the church, he is the Head, and appoints who shall be in his stead. 2 Cor. v. 20, the apostles were in his stead; so the prophet here; so are all the faithful ministers of the gospel, who are called mediately by the church according to his will.

Obs. 3. The ministers of Christ must be men of knowledge. They are watchmen, and watchmen must have eyes in their heads, they must not be blind. In 1 Sam. ix. 9, they are called seers; if they have no eyes, they cannot be seers, and if not seers, not watchmen; and then mischief may befall the church suddenly, and that without remedy: if the blind lead the blind they may both fall into the ditch. Isa. ix. 16, "The leaders of this people cause them to err; and they that are led of them are destroyed." Ignorance causeth error, and error destruction; therefore said the apostle to the elders of Ephesus, "Take heed to the flock over which the Holy Ghost hath made you overseers," ἐπισκόπȣς, Acts xx. 28, unto which, and over which you are overseers, or watchmen. The Septuagint renders it here in our prophet, σκόπον; and Origen calls a bishop or watchman, *oculum ecclesiæ*, the eye of the church. And Psal. cix. 8, "Let another take his office;" the word office is from *pacad*, which is, to visit; and visiting cannot be without eyes, without knowledge. If a watchman want eyes and knowledge, how can he discern danger, instruct the ignorant, heal the wounded, reduce the straying, lift up the fallen, feed the hungry, comfort the feeble, resolve conscience, and compare things past with things present and future: a watchman, a minister, should be like Argus, who, the poets say, had a hundred eyes; they should be full of eyes. The beasts about Christ's throne were full of eyes, before and behind, Rev. iv. 6; they saw things gone, and things to come; they saw every way. Ignorance is blamable in any, but chiefly in a watchman. Papists say, Ignorance is the mother of devotion, but the Toletan council tells them otherwise. Ignorance is the mother of all errors, and chiefly to be avoided in the ministers of God, who have taken upon them the office to instruct the people of God. "The priest's lips should keep knowledge," not ignorance, Mal. ii. 7. Let antichrist have ignorant priests, blind watchmen; Christ must have knowing, judicious, seeing watchmen; they are men of God, "throughly furnished," 2 Tim. iii. 17.

Si in laicis videtur intolerabilis inscitia, quanto magis in his qui præsunt, nec excusatione est digna, nec venia? *Leo Ep. Const.*

Dist. 38. c. Ig.

Obs. 4. Ministers must not be sleepy, drowsy persons. They are watchmen, and it is not enough to have eyes in their heads, but their eyes must be open; not sufficient to have knowledge, but that must be improved: the wakeful geese did better service than the sleepy watchmen. Matt. xiii. 25, "While men slept, the enemy came and sowed tares." By men Jerom and Augustine understand the officers of the church; and by their sleeping, their carelessness and negligence in their place; wicked ones took advantage to sow tares, errors, and heresy, while they were remiss. The same word that is for a seer, is for a sleeper, *chosim;* because if men see not to purpose, they are no better than sleepers. Such watchmen Isaiah speaks of, chap. lvi. 10, "His watchmen are blind, sleeping; lying down, loving to slumber." When the shepherds sleep, then the wolves watch, walk, and devour. Acts xx. 29, "I know, that after my departing shall grievous wolves enter in among you, not sparing the flock. Therefore watch," saith he, ver. 31; intimating, that if there be not watching of the shepherds, there will be fearful spoiling of the sheep: the sleepiness of the shepherds is the joy of the wolves. Luke xii. 37, "Blessed are those," &c.

Somnolentia pastorum est gaudium luporum. *Ephrem tract. De Timore Dei.*

Obs. 5. If watchmen, then they must endure hardships, all winds and weathers, the cold of the night, and heat of the day. They must look for succession of good and bad. Isa. xxi. 11, 12. "Watchman, what of the night? The watchman said, The morning cometh, and also the night." It was now night with the watchmen, there were troubles, afflictions, saddening things; but there was a morning of hope, and after that an evening of sorrows; changeable conditions, which the watchman must endure. 2 Tim. ii. 3, Paul counsels Timothy to endure hardness as a good soldier of Christ. Soldiers must not only stand sentinel in the night and day, but go upon desperate services. Such a watchman was Paul; 2 Cor. xi. 23—30, he saith, in stripes he was above measure, in prisons frequent, in deaths oft, five times he had forty stripes save one, thrice was he beaten with rods, once stoned, thrice he suffered shipwreck, a night and a day in the deeps, in perils every where, in weariness, painfulness, watchings, fastings, cold, nakedness, &c. The scouts and sentinels are exposed to the greatest hazards, they are taken first. You know the ministers are the men stricken at in these days, they are likeliest to meet with the first and greatest dangers. When the people were to go through the waters of Jordan, Josh. iii. 13, the Levites and priests were first to go in, and to stand therein till all the people passed over. It is the watchmen who are to meet with the waters of affliction, and to stand in them.

Obs. 6. That the church and people of God, the house of Israel, are subject to dangers and enemies; otherwise what should a watchman need? Cities and armies do not send out scouts and watchmen, if there are no enemies: where there is watching and warding, you may be sure of it there is danger. The church is like a ship, tossed at sea among rocks and sands, with winds and waves, and needs the most skilful pilot to direct and steer it; it is like a lamb among lions, and needs the most watchful shepherd. They were in much danger in Babylon amidst scoffing enemies, and the church is not safe in Zion; her children are the wheat, and the world thrasheth them; they are the vine, the clusters, and the wicked rend, press, tear them. What is the colour of the church but black? Schisms have so divided her, errors so shaken her, heresies so tossed her, and persecutions so battered her, that she is black and blue, and hardly a sound part left in her. The church is besieged with devils and wicked men, open enemies, secret hypocrites, endangered daily; out of its own bosom and bowels do those arise that threaten the ruin of it daily, Acts xx. 30. The church hath bred Eutychians, Nestorians, Pelagians, antitrinitarians, and a generation of vipers in our days, that under pretence of the church, would eat up the true church; and certainly it had been done, if we had not had a better watchman than Ezekiel. Isa. xxvii. 3, "I the Lord do keep it; lest any hurt it, I will keep it night and day."

Obs. 7. That watchmen are not for themselves, but for the flock, for the whole. " I have made thee a watchman to the house of Israel," not some particular person, not some part, not to half, but to the house of Israel. When one is become a watchman, he hath a great trust committed to him, and must look to that, the welfare of the whole depends on him: as a man, as a christian, he may foresee danger, and hide himself; but as a watchman he may not foresee it, run away, and leave the flock to spoil; he must discover it, discharge the trust reposed in him, and see to the safety of the whole, with the hazard of himself; if he do not so he will show himself a treacherous watchman, a false, fearful, self-seeking prophet: the good of Zion, and not of self, should be aimed at in every prophet, in every minister. But we may take up the apostle's complaint in Phil. ii. 21, " All seek their own, not the things which are Jesus Christ's," not his gospel, his church, his government. Paul had the care of all the churches upon him, 2 Cor. xi. 28. And for Corinth, he sought not theirs, but them, chap. xii. 14, their safety, their peace, comfort, growth in knowledge, in faith, in all spiritual excellences; and why? he looked upon them as his children, his bowels, his heirs, and therefore would communicate all he could to them, and do what was in his power for them.

ἐκδαπανηθήσομαι ὑπὲρ τῶν ψυχῶν ὑμῶν.

Hence he saith in ver. 15, " I will very gladly spend and be spent for you:" the former word, δαπανήσω, notes to be at cost with them, to take some pains; he would pray for them, preach to them, write to them, do much: but the other word notes the spending of all; so that he would keep back nothing at all, his estate, his strength should go, so that he would empty himself wholly; and when that was done, then his spirit, his blood, his life should go. Besides that that false apostles or teachers will do, I will do more: if they will give you of their estates, you shall have all mine; if they will take pains, I will take more; if they will venture their liberties to do you good, I will venture my life and all for you; let them go far, I will go beyond them, gladly will I be spent for you; it is for your souls, not for your estates. And though he should get nothing by it, he would do it, though they should love him the less. Here is a great apostle, of a greater spirit, and of the greatest charity; he was careful of all those he was a watchman unto, faithful in seeking their good, and should be a precedent unto us.

Now I come to the two particular duties of the watchman, laid down in the verse:

" Therefore hear the word at my mouth," there is the first;

" And give them warning from me," there is the second.

Obs. 1. That none have such a sufficiency of light, knowledge, grace, but they must depend upon Christ for more. Ezekiel had seen and heard much, the Spirit entered into him, he had eaten the roll, yet he must attend upon Christ, and hear the word at his mouth. No prophet, no apostle, no minister hath a perfection of knowledge, or knoweth the whole mind of Christ. Paul studied to know Christ more and more; and so did other apostles: if they had not received daily, they could not have given daily.

Obs. 2. That ministers must learn as well as teach, hear before they speak; and it is Christ they must hear, of him they must learn. Thou shalt " hear the word at my mouth:" they must hear a word, but it must be a word of Christ; he spake immediately to Ezekiel, he speaks in his word to us: Matt. xvii. 5, " Hear him," saith the Father; and why? " He is my beloved Son, in whom I am well pleased;" what he saith is truth, he had it from my bosom, out of my counsels, and it is pleasing unto me; therefore hear him. And Matt. xxiii. 8, " One is your Master," καθηγητὴς, " even Christ;" he is the only teacher, according to the mind of God; he is the leader in the way, in the right and good way. Then prophets and ministers must learn, and be learned; but their learning is not to be fetched from Aristotle, Justinian, Machiavel, from traditions, fathers, or councils, but from Christ. Ministers are watchmen, and therefore they must hear the word at Christ's mouth; they must inform the church and people of God in nothing he speaks not and warrants not. You have an excellent place in Hab. ii. 1, " I will stand upon my watch, and set me upon the tower, and will watch to see what he will say unto me." The prophet's eye and ear were towards God, he cared not what the people and false prophets said, desired, determined, expected, but he only looked at God; he would see what he did, hear what he said, which way he moved, and take all his light from him, and then he knew he should not err, he should not wrong any. And it follows, " The Lord answered me, and said;" the prophet durst not give out any thing to the church, till the Lord first gave out to him; and when ought was revealed to him, he durst not keep it back. If prophets might not bring what they had not from the mouth of God, how shall we dare to do it? They sin greatly, who obtrude upon the church the wills and decrees of men, as authentical.

Qui patrum placita, conciliorum decreta, et visiones hominum pro verbo Dei ecclesiæ obtrudunt.

Obs. 3. That it is the office of prophets and ministers, to premonish their people, to foresee danger, and foretell them. The word *sahaz* properly signifies to shine, enlighten, to make clear as the sun; and metaphorically, to admonish, because he who is admonished is enlightened. Ministers must deal plainly and clearly with sinners; convince them of their sins, and the punishments which are threatened against them. Ministers must not daub and sew pillows under men's elbows; but, as it is in Isa. lviii. 1, they must " cry aloud," and " not spare," they must " lift up their voice like trumpets, and show the people their transgressions, and the house of Jacob their sins." The word "show them" notes a setting of them before their faces; so that they must see and take notice of them, and the danger they are subject unto. The ministers must not spare any, not great ones, not the greatest, the house of Jacob must be told of them; and Ezekiel is a watchman to the house of Israel, to the kings, princes, nobles, great, small, to all; therefore all must be warned. Chrysostom told Eudoxia the empress of her sins, and spared not for her greatness: she had set up a silver statue, about which the people exercised vain and needless sports, which tended to the disgrace of the church, and for this he dealt roundly with her. It is the prophets' fault, that princes and great ones are so bad; they seldom hear of their own sins, or God's truths.

Qui admonetur, illustratur et de rebus futuris edocetur.

Obs. 4. The prophets and ministers of Christ are to do their office in the name of Christ. Thou shalt " give them warning from me," not from thyself, not in thine own name. Christ, when he was upon the great work of redeeming man, and revealing the gospel, said he came in his Father's name, John v. 43, and did his work in his Father's name, John x. 25. God sent the Son, and he did all in his name. Christ sends prophets, apostles, ministers, and they must preach and work in his name; because what they ask in his name, they receive, it is done for them; and what they do in his name abides, is blessed, John xv. 16. This should prevail with people to receive the messengers of Christ as his messengers, as those who come in his name, whatever their message be, conviction of sin, denouncing of judgment. Saith Paul, 2 Cor. v. 20, "We pray you in Christ's stead;" and here Ezekiel must warn them from Christ: be it matter of comfort or terror, all must be done in Christ's name and stead, and they entertained as those that are sent of Christ, and come from him. It is good for us so to do, for in receiving them, we receive Christ; and that is not all, we receive the Father also, that sent Christ, Matt. x. 40. A minister is good company when he brings God and Christ with him; and there is nothing lost by receiving any messenger of Christ the right way; ver. 41, "He that receives a prophet in the name of a prophet, shall receive a prophet's reward." You must not receive a man because he is learned, witty, of note, akin unto you, because he is engaged to you, or you to him, because you have some design upon him; but you must receive him in the name of a prophet, because he belongs to Christ, is sent out by him, and comes in his name; and then you shall have a prophet's reward, you shall profit by his doctrine, he shall bless you in the name of Christ, his prayer shall be available for you. The widow of Sarepta lost nothing by entertaining Elijah, nor the Shunammite by receiving Elisha; their presence and prayers did much advantage them. But you may take the words thus: "A prophet's reward," that is, the prophets have a great, hard, and glorious work in hand, and they shall have an eminent reward in heaven; and seeing you receive them as prophets in my name, notwithstanding all the reproach and discouragements they meet with, and danger their doctrine brings; seeing you encourage them, and help on their work, you shall have such reward as they have, be received into the same mansion I receive them.

Non quia dives, potens, amicus.

1 Kings xvii. 2 Kings iv.

Ver. 18, 19. *When I say unto the wicked, Thou shalt surely die; and thou givest him not warning, nor speakest to warn the wicked from his wicked way, to save his life; the same wicked man shall die in his iniquity; but his blood will I require at thine hand. Yet if thou warn the wicked, and he turn not from his wickedness, nor from his wicked way, he shall die in his iniquity; but thou hast delivered thy soul.*

In these verses is a more particular object of his office, viz. "the wicked," whom he must tell of his sin, or die for it. Here was the operation of the roll, sad and bitter work in the thoughts and apprehensions of the prophet.

"When I say unto the wicked." God speaks not immediately unto the wicked, how then is it here said, "When I say?" &c. God sometimes speaks to them by their conscience, which tells them from God, that they are guilty, and shall die. But this reaches not the sense of the words; it may be thus taken: "When I say to the wicked," that is, in my word; God speaks to all wicked men in his word, and there it is evidenced what is the portion of every sinner: but yet there is somewhat more in this phrase, "When I say to the wicked," that is, of the wicked, "Thou shalt die, and thou givest him not warning," &c. That in Heb. i. 7, "Of the angels he saith," in the original is, πρὸς τȣς ἀγγέλȣς λέγει, to the angels, but the sense is, "of the angels he saith;" and so here, "to the wicked," is, of the wicked: or, if this be not full enough, you may take it thus; When I suggest to thee by my Spirit, that the wicked shall die, and thou dost not give him notice thereof, &c.

"Thou shalt surely die." מות תמות in dying thou shalt die, that is, thou shalt certainly die. Amongst the Hebrews, where there is repetition of the word by an adverb, gerund, participle, or the verb itself, it ever increaseth the signification of the first word; as in 1 Kings viii. 13, "I have surely built thee an house;" it is in the Hebrew, In building I have built thee an house: so in 1 Sam. xxvi. 25, "Thou shalt both do great things, and also shalt still prevail;" the Hebrew is, in doing thou shalt do, in prevailing thou shalt prevail: by such duplication of the words, the signification is intended; and so in these words, "thou shalt surely die."

"In his iniquity." That is, for his iniquity; so the preposition ב *beth* must be understood. If he would take notice of his sin, repent and leave it, he should not die; but because he goes on in it, he shall die for it. Hosea xii. 12, there you find "Israel served for a wife;" the Hebrew is באשה in a wife, but the sense enforceth it to be rendered "for a wife," and so here, "for his iniquity."

"His blood will I require at thine hand." His death shall be imputed unto thee, and thou shalt answer for it, I will charge it upon thy head, and deal with thee as a murderer; thou hast shed his blood, and I will avenge it on thee; so the word "require" imports, Gen. ix. 5, "Surely your blood of your lives will I require," &c. "Require" is thrice in that verse; and what is meant by requiring the blood or life of man, is fully expressed in the next verse, "Whoso sheddeth man's blood, by man shall his blood be shed;" so then when blood is shed, and life is lost, God's requiring of it is to have blood for blood, and life for life; he that sheds blood, or suffers blood to be shed, when he may prevent it, he shall be responsible for it. God is wronged by shedding of blood, and will have satisfaction for it; therefore he is said to make inquisition for blood, Psal. ix. 12. God's requiring, mentioned Deut. xviii. 19, is expounded by Peter, of destruction, Acts iii. 23.

What death is meant in this verse is doubted among interpreters; whether the death of the body, or of the soul, or of both. The ancients interpret it of the death of the soul; the soul of the wicked going on in his sin, and of the prophet neglecting his duty, shall die for it. Some later expositors would have it meant of the death of the body, some temporal judgment to cut them off by; but we see many ill prophets, that neglect to warn the wicked of their evil ways, and many wicked men, go on in their sinful courses, and neither taken away by temporal judgments. The young prophet was slain by a lion, 1 Kings xiii. because he was less faithful than he should have been; and Jonah was cast into the deep, buried in the belly of a whale, because he declined the service of the Lord; but these were extraordinary acts and chastisements, not *vindictæ*, true, real punishments. I conceive therefore by death is meant all calamities leading unto death, and the death of soul and body at last, if faith and repentance did not intervene. If eternal death be due to the sinner dying in his sins, it is threatened to the prophet for not telling him of his sin; otherwise a temporal punishment for an immortal soul lost eternally by the negligence of the prophet, should be all the recompence made, and that is not *compensatio sufficiens*, an ample compensation; nay, frequently there should not be any, for ill and idle prophets do live as long, as healthfully and happily

Hoc loco accipitur sanguis pro animæ damnatione, licet etiam pro corporis cæde et pernicie possit intelligi. *Pint. in loc.*

as others, and die without any hand of God observable upon them.

Obs. 1. The Lord Christ knows who are wicked and vile. We guess at men, and presume oft wrongfully they are such, but the Lord knows who are such in truth, and is not deceived; he knows the goats and swine as really as the sheep and lambs; he can distinguish between the vile and precious, between his jewels and the reprobate silver. He never mistitles or miscalls any; he knew the scribes and Pharisees were hypocrites, and therefore called them so; he knew that Judas was a traitor, and therefore branded him with that name; he called Herod a fox, Nathanael a true Israelite, and in neither was he mistaken; 2 Tim. ii. 9, "The Lord knoweth them that are his," yea, and those that are not his. Christ could tell Ezekiel what the people of Israel were, better than himself that dwelt amongst them; he told him they were briers, thorns, scorpions, a rebellious house. If all the world besides had said so, and not Christ, it had been no great matter; the world is full of error, it mistakes; but when the Lord himself, who is infallible, shall pronounce a man wicked, then is he wicked indeed. There is great weight in it, let us look to it; what he saith in his word of us, if he call us wicked, proud, froward, &c. we are so.

Non eadem est sententia tribunalis Christi et anguli susurronum. *Jer. Ep.* 1. 39.

Obs. 2. The power of life and death is in Christ's hand. "When I say to the wicked, Thou shalt die;" he hath authority over their lives, and can at his pleasure pronounce them dead men: Acts iii. 15, he is "the Prince of life;" and Rev. i. 18, he hath "the keys of hell and death," he can let out the soul from the body, and let it into hell, when he will. The life of man, which is most dear to him, is at the will of another. He spake with authority, when he said, "Bring those mine enemies that will not have me to reign over them, and slay them before me," Luke xix. 27. When men are armed with power over our lives, they are much feared. Judges, when they go forth to keep assizes, make counties to quake; and princes, when they go forth to war, make kingdoms tremble. Now, Psal. ii. 10—12, kings and judges are commanded to serve him with fear, to kiss him with subjection, lest he be angry, and command them to be slain, or tell them they shall die. If kings and judges, that make others fear, must fear the Lord Christ, and submit unto him, how should all under them do it then! Christ knows us, what we are, how we have sinned, what we deserve, and can in a moment destroy us, or proclaim in our consciences that we shall die in our iniquities, and eternally suffer for them. It was he awakened Judas's conscience, and set it on fire, let out his life, and sent his soul to perdition. Be you great or small, he is the Lord, he is Ruler of the princes of the earth, all power is in his hand; and though he be the Lamb of God, yet he is also the Lion of the tribe of Judah, and can shake kingdoms and consciences with his voice: let us fear before him.

Obs. 3. When Christ sends prophets and ministers, he doth not deprive himself of his power, and authorize them to condemn or absolve at their pleasure; they must depend upon Christ, hear him speak, and say of the wicked, "Thou shalt surely die," before they pronounce a man a dead man, a wicked man. Their power is declaratory, and if Christ do not declare to them, they must not declare against others; Jam. iv. 12, "There is one Lawgiver, who is able to save and to destroy: who art thou that judgest another?" None have power to make or impose laws upon the good or the bad, but Christ; all others must have warrant from him, be they princes or prophets; and why? it is he that hath the power to save and to destroy, not they; and therefore it follows; "Who art thou that judgest another?" It is arrogancy and boldness in any to step into Christ's place, and impose any laws, decrees, or inventions of men upon the consciences of others, or to judge the conditions of men, without warrant from Christ, and his word; prophets may not do it, much less others. Hence, what the prophets and all ministers say, must be examined: Isa. viii. 20, "To the law and to the testimony: if they speak not according to this word, it is because there is no light in them;" no morning, saith the Hebrew; because Christ hath not appeared unto them, warranted them, and then their impositions and censures have no weight in them, and we may prudentially refuse them.

Obs. 4. The fruit of sin is death. If wickedness be found in men, death will be threatened from God; wickedness calls for its pay, and that is death: "If I say to the wicked, Thou shalt surely die." When man's wickedness clamours in heaven, Christ will cause the sound of death to be heard on earth: Rom. vi. 23, "The wages of sin is death;" the word is ὀψώνια, and properly signifies whatever is edible with bread, and synecdochically, the wages or salary of soldiers, and it suits in both senses with our purpose. Sin is a work, and a work of darkness, Eph. v. 11, a work of the flesh, Gal. v. 19, and they who commit it are workers of iniquity, Psal. liii. 4; and it is equity that workmen should have meat and wages, and here is both; death is the delicacy that the sinner hath to feed upon, and death the wages that the sinner earns; such meat and wages he is sure to have. Others may miss of both, work and have no meat, work and go without wages; but this workman, the wicked man, he shall never miss of either of these, "he shall surely die," his meat and wages shall not be withheld; man's own sin will slay him, Prov. v. 22.

Obs. 5. The prophets and ministers of Christ must not only warn the people, but warn them oft, warn them themselves, and speak to warn, put on others also to do it; they must not be slack, remiss in this business, they must do it earnestly and constantly, use all means to regain the wicked; the repetition of the words imports so much; if thou givest him not warning, nor speak to warn; he must be solicitous and frequent in the work. Paul knew it, and therefore counsels Timothy, not only to preach the word, but to be instant, in season and out of season, 2 Tim. iv. 2. Carnal reason counts preaching unseasonable, that is, upon week days and occasional; but the servants of God must take all opportunities to warn sinners of their evil courses, and to win souls. Christ forbore his meat and drink, and Paul his sleep, Acts xx. 7, to preach unto the people. Flesh and blood judges night preaching unseasonable, if not unlawful; but Paul thought it not unseasonable to preach even till midnight to do them good: he was a night preacher and a day preacher; ver. 31, saith he, "By the space of three years I ceased not to warn every one night and day." Such was his vigilance and diligence; he was exceeding careful to prevent evil, and to do them good; Phil. iii. 18, he told them often of the same thing, and warned them to take heed of the same men.

Obs. 6. There is hope of wicked men, that live in dissolute ways. Before, the Lord termed them "a rebellious nation, impudent children, stiff-hearted, briers, thorns, scorpions, most rebellious, that rebellious house;" and here he calls them "wicked ones;" and yet they must be warned, that they may return from their wicked ways and live. Some are hopeful and curable, where wickedness prevails generally, and all seems desperate. Manasses was as wicked a king as lived, a great idolater, a great dealer with enchanters, wizards, and familiar spirits, a great seducer of the people, to make them do worse than the nations did, a great shedder of innocent blood: so that the text saith, he did "wickedly above all that the Amorites did," 2 Kings xxi. 11: yet this great sinner found mercy, greater than all his sins; 2 Chron. xxxiii. 12, 13, "he humbled himself greatly," he prayed, and God was entreated of him. He who is wicked one day, may turn another day; he may become penitent and believing the next day, that is cursing, blaspheming this day, as in Saul. Some come in early, at the third, sixth, ninth hour; others late, at the eleventh and twelfth; the thief came in at the last hour. Let times be never so corrupt, persons desperately wicked, yet there is hope, and God may have a seed amongst them. Let us throw the net oft, we may catch fish in *mari mortuo*, the dead sea.

Obs. 7. The end and scope of a prophet's and minister's labours must be to save life. He must warn the wicked, that so he may save his life, preserve his soul. Paul tells Timothy, that by preaching and continuing in the word, he should save himself, and those that heard him, 1 Tim. iv. 16. Men's lives and souls are in great danger daily; errors, heresies, lusts, temptations, threaten ruin and destruction to men continually; the work and care of the prophets is, to secure them from these, and to recall them from their sinful practices. Jam. v. 20, "He that converteth the sinner from the error of his way, shall save a soul from death, and hide a multitude of sins." That which Ezekiel calls the sinner's wicked way, James calls "the error of his way," his sinful manners, actions, courses, opinions, humours, affections, and principles; from these must the servant of God labour to deliver him. It is ministers' work, and the end of the ministry, to save souls; therefore,

(1.) Their scope must not be to show learning, wit, eloquence. The apostle preached, "but not with wisdom of words," 1 Cor. i. 17; "not with excellency of speech," chap. ii. 1; "not with enticing words of man's wisdom," ver. 4: and he gives the reason of it; "lest the cross of Christ should be made of none effect;" that is, lest men should think they are saved rather by virtue of man's wisdom than Christ's passion. Or as it is more fully in chap. ii. 5, that their "faith should not stand in the wisdom of men." It will go off from one to another, as men are more witty, and hold out the truth in finer and more enticing expressions, which will prove evil. Therefore he declined the wisdom of men, and preached in demonstration of the Spirit, that their faith might stand in the power of God, in such conviction and operation of the Spirit, as might breed invincible stedfastness in them.

Regnum Dei non in eloquentia, sed in fide constat.

(2.) Not to please men. Gal. i. 10, "Do I seek to please men?" if that were my end, "I should not be the servant of Christ;" but he must serve Christ in saving of souls, not in pleasing of men. When that is propounded unto men, they will subject truth to men's humour, and become flatterers; but ministers must not do so, not frame their sermons according to men's humours and minds. Jer. xv. 19, "Let them return unto thee, but return not thou unto them;" do not thou comply, debase the truth, to please them, but speak as the oracles of God, and let them please or provoke, it matters not; the provoking of them may be the nearest way to their salvation, and that is thy end.

(3.) Not to get a living; that is not the end of a prophet's office; it is to make men living men, to save their lives and souls. Paul preached the gospel without charge to any, and told the Corinthians he sought them, not theirs, their souls, not their substance. Yet he denies not but "that they that preach the gospel should live of it," 1 Cor. ix. 14. It is fit preachers should have maintenance, and sufficient; but the end of preaching is not a living, but life, the life of sinners, to save, to deliver them. Seeing this is the end of their calling, how should it quicken them to their work! If a sheep were in a pit, a child in a fire, what haste would we make to pull them forth! And shall we see souls rushing into the eternal pit, the eternal fire, and not move our feet, our tongues to help them!

Cadit asina, et est qui sublevet eam, perit anima et nemo est qui reparet. *Bern.*

Obs. 8. The office of a prophet and minister is honourable. It is to save life, to save souls; their calling is conversant about the lives and souls of men. The soul is the immediate work of God, the image of God, of more worth than all the world. It was for the soul's sake that Christ came down from heaven, prayed, preached, wrought miracles, suffered death, and gave his heart's blood. This made the father say, Precious is the soul, being redeemed with Christ's blood. And being a thing of such worth and consequence, the minister's work is to save it, that very work which is the Lord's and Christ's. Therefore in 1 Cor. iii. 9, the apostle saith of himself, and all ministers, "We are labourers together with God," co-workers, concurrent with God in the salvation of sinners. This is great honour, and made Jerom say, *Ipse Salvator apostolos suos mundi esse voluit salvatores*, Christ hath made apostles saviours of the world. He calls them the light and salt of the world, they enlighten the blind, and season the unsavoury souls of men, and so save them from corruption and perdition. It is a hard, but an honourable work; therefore saith James, Let him know that hath converted a sinner, that he hath saved a soul from death, Jam. v. 20; let him know it, it is a great and glorious work which is done, that he may be encouraged, and God be praised.

Magna res anima quæ Christi sanguine redempta est. *Bern. Ep.*

συνεργος.

In Obad.

Obs. 9. Ignorance will be no plea for wicked men. If they be not warned, not told of their sins, they shall die. Men are apt to excuse themselves; they are ignorant, they know not this or that to be sins, their teachers were insufficient or negligent; and this may be truth; but neither their fault nor thy ignorance will be a sufficient plea before God: warned or unwarned, the wicked shall die. Isa. xxvii. 11, "It is a people of no understanding: therefore he that made them will not have mercy on them, and he that formed them will show them no favour." Nescience may excuse in part, but ignorance hardly at all. That which men produce in favour of themselves, God produces against them. You are an ignorant people, saith God, of no understanding; you know not *prima principia*, first principles, neither God nor yourselves, and think because you are ignorant, therefore to find mercy and favour at my hands; but you are deceived, your ignorance aggravates your woe ever; therefore will I show you no mercy, no favour. Those that are ignorant of God and his ways, God will be ignorant of them in their greatest straits: "Depart from me; I never knew you," Matt. vii. 23. Ignorance is a great evil; it makes men brutish, like Nebuchadnezzar, who had an ox's heart in a man's shape. Ignorance is part of the devil's image, as knowledge is of God's; we should labour therefore to get knowledge, savoury and saving; for it is not good that the heart be without knowledge, Prov. xix. 2.

Obs. 10. See here who are the most cruel, bloody, and damning ministers; even those that are silent, that warn not the people of their sins, that preach flattering things, or to no purpose. Let men be dumb, and not speak at all, or preach so as not to warn them of their sins and dangers; they are, whoever they be, whether the greater or lesser clergy, as they use to distinguish themselves, they are the bloody, damning, soul-murdering ministers. You cry out of those ministers that tell you most of your sins, that set judgment, hell, and damnation before you, they are bitter, harsh men, cried out of on all sides; whereas they are the faithfullest friends that sinners have; they would fain save your souls, pull you out of the pit, keep you out of hell, and help you into heaven; and are they censurable for this? Should one see a company of travellers going in a way they should fall into the hands of cavaliers or thieves, and tell them the danger of it with great affection and compassion; should another see them, and say nothing, or bid them go on, and they do so, are taken, stripped, imprisoned, starved to death; you can easily tell which of these dealt most faithfully and friendly, which treacherously and cruelly. Too many of the ministers in England have been faulty this way, and guilty of murdering multitudes, if not millions of souls; it is one of the crying sins of the land, that we have had such a dumb, insufficient, and consequently such a bloody, soul-damning ministry; and many amongst them having slain souls, now, by putting on these wars, seek to slay bodies also.

Obs. 11. There is a great necessity lieth upon the prophets and ministers of Christ, to preach, and to preach home to the conscience. Warn them they must, and so warn them that they may take notice; else it is in vain, and shall be before the Lord as no warning. This they must do, and do it oft; and why? else the blood of the wicked will be required at their hand. Their blood, their lives, lie at the stake for sinners' souls, they have a hard task, a dangerous calling; and therefore had need preach, and tell them of their sins, that, if it be possible, they may save their souls, if not, their own. People wonder many times at some preachers, they are so fiery, so particular, so terrible, so long. You may cease to wonder; their lives, their souls, go for it, if they do it not; the hazard of souls and lives will make dumb men speak. Crœsus' son being dumb, and seeing one ready to strike and endanger the life of his father, cried out, "What! will you kill my father?" and if our dumb ministers had any faith, if they did believe that sin was slaying the souls of their people, they would lift up their voice, they would speak. Psal. cxvi. 10, "I believed," said David, "therefore have I spoken;" and godly ministers believe men's souls are in danger, that their own do lie at the stake, and therefore they have spoken, do speak, and will speak. You that have *curam animarum*, the charge of souls, look about you; if you discharge not your duty, you undo them, and undo yourselves; let not fear, favour, credits, gifts, hopes, bias you; let not difficulties, mistakes of people, or any other thing, discourage you; but remember your own danger, warn sinners, else their blood will be upon you, and that is a dreadful thing. Did men well consider this, they would not be so greedy of livings, and pawn their souls for pelf. If the death of the body were only here meant, as it is not, we have great cause to fear silence; for if we be liable to death for the death of that which is perishable and must die, what guilt then doth a prophet contract for the death of a soul, which might have lived for ever if he had done his duty! David knew the weight of blood-guiltiness; Psal. li. 14, when he cried out so, "Deliver me from blood-guiltiness," &c. That was but the blood of the body; what then is the blood of souls! it is a mountainous, sinking thing. We have sins sufficient of our own, we had not need to draw the guilt of others upon us. So many we kill, as we see to sin, and silently suffer to go on in their sins. Paul knew it, and therefore said, "Woe is unto me, if I preach not the gospel," 1 Cor. ix. 16. And there is a woe to all that have charges, that preach not unto them; it is needful for us all, but especially for non-residents, dumb ministers, those who are negligent in their preaching, or impertinent, to meditate oft on these words, "his blood will I require at thy hands;" which words are *fulmina, non verba*, thunderbolts, not words, saith Erasmus. When the bell rings for a wicked man, fear, lest there be blood to be required at thy hand. Euenius, a shepherd, that had the sheep belonging to a city committed to him, through his negligence, a wolf entered, and devoured sixty of them; upon this he was condemned, and lost his eyes. Not only ministers, but parents and masters, their souls are engaged for their children and servants, and they must be responsible for them, if they warn them not, if they perish through their default.

Alienas mortes addimus, quia tot occidimus, quot ad mortem ire quotidie tepidi et tacentes videmus. *Greg. in loc.*

The world is full of priests, sed tamen in messe Dei rarus valde invenitur operator. We take upon us the office, but opus officii non implemus. *Greg. Hom.* 17.

Herod. l. 9.

Obs. 12. It is the duty of people to hear their ministers, and willingly to receive instructions, and take warning from them; especially people of their ministers, because they watch for their souls, they work for them, and they venture for them, even their own lives and souls; it is mercy God will send any to admonish us. If we hearken to admonitions we shall live, if we do not, we grieve the servants of God; if they be silent, our sins are not the less.

From ver. 19,

Obs. 1. That men may be warned from their wicked ways, and yet be never the better, they may go on still; this is too evident amongst us daily.

Obs. 2. It is not fruitless, if wicked men return not from their evil ways upon warning. The prophet hath warned the wicked, and hath freed his own soul; and this was a great comfort unto Paul, Acts xx. 26, when he appeals to the people themselves, "I take you to record this day, that I am pure from the blood of all men;" and how doth he prove it? thus, "for I have not shunned to declare unto you all the counsel of God." He left none unwarned of sin and danger, untaught their duty towards God and man; and therefore he had this testimony, yielding sound comfort, "I am pure from the blood of all." So when he had preached Christ to the Jews, and they opposed, blasphemed, "he shook his raiment, and said, Your blood be upon your own heads; I am clean," Acts xviii. 5, 6; much like that of David, 2 Sam. iii. 28, 29, "I and my kingdom are guiltless before the Lord for ever from the blood of Abner; let it rest on the head of Joab." That which Paul calls clean, David calls guiltless; when a man is guiltless, he is clean, he hath solid comfort. A minister having conscionably warned the wicked, and nothing comes of it in regard of them, yet somewhat comes of it in regard of himself; he is a free man, a clear man; the blood of souls shall not be charged upon him. A minister that is faithful shall not need to complain of the want of success; if he save not others he shall save himself.

Ver. 20, 21. *Again, when a righteous man doth turn from his righteousness, and commit iniquity, and I lay a stumblingblock before him, he shall die: because thou hast not given him warning, he shall die in his sin, and his righteousness which he hath done shall not be remembered; but his blood will I require at thine hand. Nevertheless if thou warn the righteous man that the righteous sin not, and he doth sin, he shall surely live, because he is warned; also thou hast delivered thy soul.*

In these words is laid down the other part of the prophet's charge. It is not only "the wicked," but "the righteous" also fall under his care; and if he sin, and be not warned, that effect will be dangerous and deadly to the prophet. He is not only to deal with the wicked, to get them into the way of God; but also with the righteous, to see that he go not out of the way; and if he do, to reduce him. Guilt will lie upon a prophet, if he do not call upon the wicked for repentance; and likewise, if he keep not the righteous in the right way, them must not he suffer to run out into errors, into loose courses; but he must inform them of the danger, bring them to a sound mind, into the right way, and confirm them in the truth, otherwise their blood will be required at his hand.

There is difficulty in these words, and they must be opened unto you. In Prov. x. 25, "The righteous is an everlasting foundation;" and chap. xii. 3, "The root of the righteous shall not be moved;" ver. 7, "The house of the righteous shall stand;" Matt. xxv. 46, "They go into life eternal:" if so, how saith our prophet here, "When a righteous man turns from his righteousness?" it seems that righteousness is not an incorruptible seed, a man may leave it, fall into sin, and die in it. I must therefore bestow some time in opening these words.

"When a righteous man doth turn from his righteousness," &c. You shall find in Scripture a double righteousness, and so, suitably, "righteous men." There is,

1. "A righteousness of faith," Rom. ix. 30; and this is in Phil. iii. 9, "The righteousness of God by faith;" this is evangelical righteousness.

2. There is "the righteousness of the law," Rom. ii. 26; x. 5; and this is called a man's "own righteousness," Rom. x. 3. Phil. iii. 9, "Not having mine own righteousness, which is of the law." When a man's actions are suitable unto the law, that is legal righteousness, and so his own.

According to these two, are two sorts of righteous men:

(1.) The man that is righteous by faith, who hath the pardon of his sins, union with Christ, and communion with God. Such a one is he Peter speaks of, 1 Pet. iv. 18, "If the righteous scarcely be saved;" such a one John mentions, 1 Epist. ii. 29; and Paul pointeth at such, Rom. v. 19; and their "righteousness remaineth for ever," 2 Cor. ix. 9. Of a man righteous in this sense, I conceive the words are not meant: this righteousness makes a man's person righteous, and righteous before God.

(2.) There is a righteous man according to the law. Paul was such a man before his conversion; Phil. iii. 6, "Touching the righteousness which is in the law," saith he, "I was blameless." And men righteous in this sense, are either seeming, or real: seeming, Matt. xxiii. 28, "Ye outwardly appear righteous unto men, but within ye are full of hypocrisy and iniquity;" men thought them to be righteous, but God knew them to be wicked; and such legalists think themselves righteous, Luke xviii. 9, they "trusted in themselves that they were righteous;" in others' and their own eyes they seemed so, but in truth were not so. Zacharias and Elisabeth were righteous before God, Luke i. 6.

But there is, [1.] An outside actional righteousness before men, without reality within, and from this it is no difficult thing to turn aside; and of such "a righteous man" we may understand this place. The Chaldee expounds it so; *Eos qui justi videri volunt, permittam in publicum peccatum labi,* Those that seem to be righteous, I will suffer to fall into open sins. And the scholiast refers a righteous man to the priest, who hath doctoral dignity, and seems to love virtue, but doth not; and the soundest interpreters agree in it. Calvin calls it a righteousness which hath *externam speciem tantum, non radicem,* an outward show but no reality. Many have been zealous in the service and cause of God, and gone beyond others in promoting his glory, but have had no true root within. Such were those who promoted lately with much intention the prelatical ways and innovations, but now are turned from their righteousness, and are become parliament converts; their righteousness lay in opinion, not in reality, and such is this here; and the Scripture speaks frequently after the opinions and conceits of men; "I came not to call the righteous, but sinners to repentance." The Pharisees were conceived by this world and themselves to be righteous, when in truth they had none; and Matt. viii. 12, "The children of the kingdom shall be cast out into outer darkness;" they were not so really, but in opinion, and externally.

[2.] If it be here meant a real righteous man, whose inside and outside is suitable to the law, blameless, as Paul and Zacharias; yet he that stands upon that foundation, viz. the law, he will slide from his righteousness. Witness Adam, who had a fuller righteousness than any of his sons since, and yet he turned away from it. The law required two things, to depart from evil, and to do good; and he did the contrary, depart from good, and do evil; and in this he hath too many followers; all his children have traced those steps; and men that not only seem, but are legally righteous, may still do it; the 18th chapter of this prophecy is clear for it.

[3.] If it should be granted that here is meant man justified, righteous with the righteousness of faith, it follows not that he must necessarily turn from his righteousness, lose his faith, and be in an unjustified condition. Gal. i. 8, "Though we, or an angel from heaven, preach any other gospel unto you than that which we have preached, let him be accursed." It cannot be inferred hence that an angel will, or ever shall preach another gospel; it is one thousand five hundred years since this was written, and no angels have attempted any such thing, nor ever will. Hypothetical propositions, according to logicians, produce no effects, but they prove the necessity of a consequent; as thus, 1 Cor. xv. 14. "If Christ be not risen, then is our preaching vain, and your faith is also vain;" the supposition doth not enforce that Christ is not risen, but it strongly proves, that if Christ be not risen, preaching and believing in Christ are in vain. And so here, if a righteous man could turn from his righteousness he should die; but he that is once righteous with the righteousness of faith, is ever righteous; because God's decree is unchangeable, 2 Tim. ii. 19; his love is permanent, John xiii. 1; his promises are faithful, 1 Cor. i. 8. 2 Cor. i. 20; he forgets not his covenant, Psal. lxxxix. 34; Christ's prayers are efficacious, John xi. 41, 42; xvii. 15; because he is

Quod gratia semel fecit, perpetuo manet. *Thom.* 3. p. q. 88.

united to Christ, and that union is indissoluble, 1 Cor. xii. 13; because the Spirit abides in them, 1 John ii. 27; and lastly, because he is "kept by the power of God through faith unto salvation," 1 Pet. i. 5.

"Commit iniquity." The Hebrew is, עשה עול to do evil, and answereth to that phrase in the New Testament, *ὁ ποιῶν τὴν ἁμαρτίαν*, 1 John iii. 4, he that committeth sin. And this phrase of committing sin, hath more in it than *ἁμαρτανειν*, which is, to sin, to miss the mark; for 1 John ii. 1, *ἐάν τις ἁμάρτῃ*, "If any man sin, we have an advocate with the Father," Christ pleads and intercedes for such a sinner; but "he that commits sin is of the devil," 1 John iii. 8; he is his son, he is of his seed, family, kingdom, acted by his counsel and spirit; it is his trade to sin as it is the devil's, and this trade he delights in and follows: a godly man hath given it over; 1 John iii. 3, "He that hath this hope purifies himself;" and then follows, "He that commits sin;" and it is in opposition to him that purifies himself from sin, he is a man that minds not holiness. Besides this, John viii. 34, "He that commits sin is the servant of sin;" where sin reigns, and its counsels, laws, commands are obeyed by men, there is the commission of sin: it is a ready, a willing obedience; to commit sin is, *magnopere delectari peccato*, to have a man's will and heart in it; when a man's thoughts, counsels, meditations, purposes, lie that way, and he is given to that work, *ὁ ποιῶν ἁμαρτίαν*, is a sin maker, one that is an artist, a workman. Such the prophet speaks of, Jer. iv. 22, "They are wise to do evil;" Ezek. xxi. 31, "skilful to destroy:" some are bunglers in that work, others take pleasure in it, and set it off better. That in Rom. xiii. 14, "Make not provision for the flesh, to fulfil the lusts thereof:" men love to provide for their families, their wives and little ones, and when they do so, they make provision; and so men love to provide for the flesh and lusts of it, and then they make sin, or commit sin. There be three expressions in Scripture about sin, which give us light in this point.

Rollock in John.

1. *Νόμος ἁμαρτίας*, the law of sin, Rom. vii. 23.
2. Ὁδὸς, the way of sin, Matt. vii. 13.
3. Ἀποτέλεσμα, the perfection of sin, James i. 15.

When a man subjects himself to the law of sin, chooses and walks in the way of sin, and brings sin to a perfection, then doth he commit sin.

"And I lay a stumblingblock before him." The Hebrew is, and I give a stumblingblock before his face; מכשול comes of כשל to dash against, to offend, to fall; and a stumblingblock is that a man dasheth his foot against, is offended at, and falls by; the same with *scandalum*, the bridge in a trap, which when vermin or wild beasts touch, they are taken: so that to lay a stumblingblock in a man's way, is to trap him, destroy him. This phrase of God's laying "a stumblingblock before him," seems very harsh; therefore some fathers think the word stumblingblock is not here put in an ill sense, as tending to his destruction, that "turns from his righteousness," but that it proceeds from favour, not hatred. When a just man goeth out from God, God will cross him in his sinful way, not let him thrive in it, but cast in something contrary to his expectation and intention, whereby he may come to see his error, and be reduced, according to that in Hos. ii. 6, 7. Theodotus thinks God will set hell before him, and therefore he renders it *barathrum*, I will lay hell before him; as if God would present the terrors of hell and state of the damned to him, to make him consider and return to his former righteousness. But this sense of the fathers coheres not with what follows, "he shall die;" this stumblingblock is in order unto his death: it was the watchman's part to propound heaven and hell, all arguments possible to do him good, else he should die. Some other expositors would have it to be meant of punishment, that God would punish such a sinner by some act of his, make him smart, repent, and so to live; therefore the Septuagint render it *βάσανον*, torment, God would afflict his body or conscience; and if it be taken in this sense, then you must carry it further, God would punish him, not in a saving, but a destroying way; and therefore this stumblingblock comes not from love, but revenging justice. I conceive God's laying a stumblingblock, is to be taken for the punishment of sin past, and an occasion of sin future. The righteous man having turned from his righteousness, God might lay aside that peculiar care and providence which he exercised formerly towards that man; he may take away those means and helps which should preserve from stumbling, let him go on in just judgment for his deserting him, and not recall him, but turn all things into snares and stumblings unto him, whereby corruptions are ripened, and destruction is hastened: Psal. lxix. 22, "Let their table become a snare before them; and that which should have been for their welfare, let it become a trap." When God in his justice once orders it so, that men's tables (that is, all their comforts) do turn to their ruin, then he lays stumblingblocks before them. Neither is God the author of sin, but the avenger of it, by denying assistance, propounding objects, and exciting affections. God may be said to lay stumblingblocks, but he never infuses any corruption; and so that in James, "God tempts no man," chap. i. 13, is to be understood. Gregory saith, this laying a stumblingblock is by no means to lead men to sin; he is not the cause of any man's sin. A man may lay money to try his servant. God takes away estates from men, gives peace to the wicked: true; he lays before them outward occasions, 2 Sam. xvi. 21, 22; he gives Satan leave to tempt and seduce them, 1 Kings xxii. 22; when they are out of his way, he carries them forward in their own evil way, Psal. cvi. 15; and this he doth in justice, punishing one sin with the occasion or commission of another. Hence he is said to "add iniquity unto their iniquity," Psal. lxix. 27; to "send them strong delusion," or, as the words are, the efficacy or activity of error, 2 Thess. ii. 11; to give up to uncleanness, to vile affections, to a reprobate sense, Rom. i. 24, 26, 28. God finds sin in man, and may draw it out without sin. There is *suavitas in rosa, fœtor in cadavere*, sweetness in the rose, offensiveness in the dead body; the sun by his beams draws forth the one and the other, and without fault.

"His righteousness shall not be remembered." Men may remember it, but God will not, he will have no regard to what is done to reward it; his righteousness shall not be set against his iniquities to keep off punishments; his righteousness shall be as filthy rags, Isa. lxiv. 6, in the eyes of God. When God pardons the sins of his people, he blots them out and remembers them no more, Isa. xliii. 25. So when God deals with a man who degenerates, he blots out his righteousness, and remembereth it no more, it is as if it had never been; it neither profits him unto life, nor frees him from death. Ezek. xviii. 22, when a wicked man turns away from his sins, "they shall not be mentioned unto him," that is, they shall no way hurt him, he shall not hear of them, nor see them any more; and the righteous man that leaves his righteousness, shall neither hear nor see it any more. Aquinas hath a question,

Part. 3. q. 89. *Utrum opera virtutum in charitate facta possint mortificari?* Whether good works done in love can perish? And he affirms it from that in Ezek. xviii. 24, "All his righteousness which he hath done shall not be mentioned."

Obs. 1. It concerns every man to look narrowly to his righteousness. Some righteousness or other every man looks at, fixes his heart upon; and there is deceivable righteousnesses. If our righteousness be legal, a duty righteousness, and not evangelical, a righteousness of faith, it will deceive us. Matt. v. 20, "Except your righteousness exceed the righteousness of the scribes and Pharisees, ye shall in no case enter into the kingdom of heaven." Let that righteousness be what it will, a man is in an ill case that cannot enter into heaven with it; yet the scribes and Pharisees were exact keepers of the law, but the righteousness of the law and of duties will never send or help a man into heaven. Paul laboured to win Christ, to be found in him, not having his own righteousness, but "the righteousness which is of God by faith," Phil. iii. 8, 9. Paul durst not stick to a legal and duty righteousness, he knew it was too short to satisfy divine justice, to cover man's nakedness, or comfort his conscience; it was a higher, a better righteousness he minded, even the righteousness of Christ; and that is the righteousness God will accept, and he that is righteous with that righteousness, shall not fall away, but shall enter into heaven. 2 Pet. i. 10, 11, "Brethren, give diligence to make your calling and election sure;" that is, their calling to Christ, and election in him. And what follows? "If ye do these things, ye shall never fall; for so an entrance shall be ministered unto you abundantly into the everlasting kingdom."

Obs. 2. No man should boast of or confide in his own righteousness. There were some who "trusted in themselves that they were righteous, and despised others;" but this neither pleased God, nor profited them, as the parable ensuing shows, Luke xviii. 9. If men have excellences, they should be humble and fearing, not boasting and confident, especially when their excellences are in the number of movables and changeables. 1 Cor. i. 30, Christ is made unto us wisdom and righteousness, that no flesh should glory in itself, but in the Lord; and so that no flesh should have confidence in itself, but in the Lord. Phil. iii. 3, "We rejoice in Christ," saith Paul, "and have no confidence in the flesh." Whatever we have or do, let us not repose upon it: we are apt to do it, but there are apostolical rules to help us: Gal. vi. 3, "If a man think himself any thing, when he is nothing, he deceiveth himself." We are nothing, and it is nothing we do; and shall we glory in nothing, or confide in nothing? Christ is something, and God is something; in them we may, we must glory and confide; the more we do it the better; we cannot sin in going too far that way. Another rule is, Phil. ii. 3, "Let each esteem others better than themselves," their righteousness may be a lasting righteousness, when thine is a perishing one. Another rule is, Rom. xi. 20, "Be not high-minded, but fear." Let men's righteousness be legal or evangelical, they should not swell, but fear, lest they fall; and besides, they should watch, pray, and persevere in prayer; remembering what our blessed Saviour hath said, "He that shall endure to the end, the same shall be saved," Matt. xxiv. 13. Let none be secure, but "serve the Lord with fear," Psal. ii. 11.

Obs. 3. Apostasy from God and his ways is a dreadful condition. When men fall from their righteousness, great mischief is done; they stain the society they were of, they blast the church, they make their friends mourn, and enemies laugh; they wrong God much, yea, more than infidels and heretics. *Plura vincula conjunctionis violantur, et Deus ipse tacite accusatur quasi iniquus.* Many bonds of union are broken, and God himself is tacitly accused as unjust; which causeth God to complain, O my people, what have I done unto thee? wherein have I wearied thee? testify against me; You are withdrawn, fallen to idolatrous passages; I brought you out of Egypt, and sent before you Moses and Aaron, I delivered you from Balak, &c.; many ties are upon you to keep close to me, and to cause you to honour me; but you have forgotten all my kindnesses, are gone away, and do slight me, as if idol gods and ways were better than Jehovah and his ways. This made God to say, Heb. x. 38, "If any draw back, my soul shall have no pleasure in him;" and what an ill condition is that man in, in whom God hath no pleasure!

There be four great evils in the words of our prophet:

(1.) He will "commit iniquity." When a man turns from righteousness he turns to sin, embraces it, serves it, walks in the ways of it, and fulfils the ends of it, and this is a sad condition; for such a man is a worker of iniquity, and so hated of God. Psal. v. 5, "Thou hatest all workers of iniquity;" it is more than having no pleasure, and notes God is against them, and will pursue them as enemies.

(2.) God will "lay a stumblingblock before him;" one thing or other, at which he shall fall. God denies him assistance, gives Satan leave to tempt and seduce, propounds objects to draw out his corruptions to the full. Demas forsook Paul and the truth, and loved the present world; there was an object sufficient to draw out his covetous disposition. 2 Tim. iv. 10. Sometimes the afflictions of the godly are a stumblingblock unto the wicked; sometimes the prosperity of the wicked is a stumbling unto them, &c. It is a dreadful thing when God shall make any thing a stumbling unto a man, but more dreadful when he makes every thing so.

(3.) He shall die in that condition. Julian apostatized, and by the stroke of God he died in his apostasy; and what heavier judgment than to die in a man's sinful condition! Therefore Christ told the Pharisees they should die in their sins, John viii. 21; they would not receive him, believe in him, therefore they should die in their unbelief, and no place is left unto them for repentance.

(4.) "His righteousness which he hath done shall not be remembered." If a man die, yet if his righteousness might follow him and help him, it were some comfort; but that shall not be thought upon, he loseth all he hath done and suffered. Suppose he have done much for the church, for poor ministers, prisoners, and other christians, for truth itself, and for the glory of God, no good shall come of it unto him now. All Adam's righteousness would not advantage him; whatever he had done before, when he comes to eat of the forbidden fruit, he must surely die, Gen. ii. 17, his former righteousness is forgotten. Jam. ii. 10, "Whosoever shall keep the whole law, and yet offend in one point, is guilty of all." Antecedent righteousness will not make up the present breach, nor prevent future wrath. When the Galatians began to fall off, Paul intimates to them, that all their sufferings would be lost; "Have ye suffered so many things in vain?" Gal. iii. 4. When men in war forsake their colours, and run to the other side, all the good services they have done are forgotten, and they are accounted traitors to their country and cause; and so it is when men run from God and his truth, to the world's and Satan's service; *Inanis est pœnitentia quam sequens culpa coinquinat,* The repentance is fruitless which is polluted by succeeding crime. But this is not all; that his righteousness shall not be remembered for him, but it will be remembered against him. 2 Pet. ii. 21, "It had been better for them not to have known the way of righteousness, than, after they have known it, to turn from it;" and why better? because they now sin against righteousness, and that way they have affected and professed, and their righteousness will be a witness against them. Let us all take heed, lest there be an evil heart in any of us, to depart from the living God, Heb. iii. 12.

Lumb. l. 4. d. 14.

Obs. 4. Man's ruin is from himself. He departs from his righteousness, commits iniquity, and God lays a stumblingblock; this in justice he doth, because man hath sinned: but who causes him to fall? not God; that is man's own act, he looks not to his way, it is his own lust draws him aside, enticeth him, Jam. i. 14; the cause is from within, only the occasion is from without. Riches, honour, friends, peace, credit, parts, beauty, truths, Christ, are the good and great blessings of God; and God, in his wise disposition of things, may lay these as occasion of stumbling before us; but if we do stumble, that is man's, not God's fault. Hos. xiii. 9, "O Israel, thou hast destroyed thyself; but in me is thy help;" destruction is man's, salvation is the Lord's. Man fell by his own free will, but if ever he be raised, it is by God's free grace; and if God will not have mercy, he will turn their iniquity upon them: Psal. xciv. 23, "He shall bring upon them their own iniquity, and shall cut them off in their own wickedness;" yet, Prov. i. 32, it is said, "The turning away of the simple shall slay them, and the prosperity of fools shall destroy them."

Obs. 5. God's proceedings with the wicked and godly are divers. Here he speaks of laying a stumblingblock before the wicked man; and in Jer. vi. 21, "Behold, I will lay stumblingblocks before this people, the fathers and the sons together shall fall upon them; the neighbour and his friend shall perish;" yea, Isa. viii. 14, God himself will be "a stone of stumbling, a rock of offence to both the houses of Israel, for a gin and for a snare to the inhabitants of Jerusalem;" and Jer. xlvi. 6, "They shall stumble and fall." But it is otherwise with the godly; touching them he saith, "Take up the stumblingblock out of the way of my people," Isa. lvii. 14, he will remove what offends and endangers them: and Isa. lxiii. 13, lest they should stumble he leads them;" and Prov. iv. 12, "When thou runnest, thou shalt not stumble;" and Psal. cxix. 165, "Great peace have they which love thy law, and nothing shall offend them." God is careful of the godly, that they be not offended. If they should be so offended, as to stumble and fall at any time, Psal. xxxvii. 24, "He shall not be utterly cast down, for the Lord upholdeth him with his hand," and keepeth them that they dash not their feet against the stones. If God do lay stumblingblocks at any time before his people, it is in the ways of sin, as Hos. ii. 6, "I will hedge up thy way;" but for the wicked he lays stumbling blocks in the way of mercies; they stumble at the word, 1 Pet. ii. 8; it is the savour of death to them, 2 Cor. ii. 16; they stumble at the Lord's supper, they eat and drink damnation there, 1 Cor. xi. 29; they stumble at Christ himself, 1 Cor. i. 23.

Obs. 6. An unfaithful minister is perfidious to God and man. "Because thou gavest him not warning, he shall die in his sin, and his blood will I require at thy hands." God hath put honour upon the minister, set him in a great place, made him a watchman, trusted him with souls, and he now, through sloth, fear, inconsiderateness, entanglements in the world, neglects to warn the sinner; hereby souls are lost, Satan robs God of them, is diligent to get and keep them; this will be treachery and sacrilege too at last, and fall heavy upon him that is guilty. If a band of men be slain through the captain's fault, or taken through falsehood, all cry out of it; and when souls perish through the fault and falsehood of the prophet, it is dreadful. Zeph. iii. 4, "Her prophets are light and treacherous persons;" the word treacherous in Hebrew, is, *viri prævaricationum, qui debitam Deo et populo fidem pariter violaverint,* such as falsify their faith to God and man; and it is the highest treachery that can be, to be false to God, and to rob him of the souls of men.

Mont. in loc.

Obs. 7. That if a minister may perish for not warning of sinners, much more for encouraging them by corrupt doctrine, and by a lewd life. If death be in an omission, much more in positive evils; corrupt doctrine, and a corrupt life, are strong traces to draw men to perdition, 2 Pet. ii. 1; he speaks of false teachers, that bring in damnable heresies, and withal, that bring upon themselves swift destruction; but their damnable heresies and opinions prevail with the people, they follow their pernicious ways, and meet with their destructive ends: Isa. ix. 16, "The leaders of this people cause them to err; and they that are led of them are destroyed."

Ver. 21. *Nevertheless if thou warn the righteous man, that the righteous sin not, and he doth not sin, he shall surely live, because he is warned; also thou hast delivered thy soul.*

The words need little opening. "He shall surely live;" in living he shall live; he shall have his life for a prey in time of danger, or shall live comfortably, that persists in this righteousness, he shall be secure from fear of death.

Obs. 1. A minister's or prophet's care must extend to all sorts of people. Before he had said, the wicked must be warned; here he saith, the righteous also must be warned. Good and bad fall under admonition and circumspection of the prophets; both are committed to their charge, and they must warn them, give account of them, and if they fail of their duty, die for it: the best and worst they must tell of their sins.

Obs. 2. The ministry of the word is very needful. Wicked and righteous must be warned that they may not sin, return when they have sinned, escape death and be saved. The warnings of the prophets are, *salutaria remedia adversus mortem animarum,* salutary remedies against the death of souls; not only the ministry of the word in general, but admonitions and reproofs are means through God to prevent the death of souls. Prov. xv. 31, it is called "the reproof of life;" there is life in reproof, as death in sin; *increpationes sunt salutares, et vivificatrices,* censures are profitable to souls, they teach the way to live, and lead to eternal life. Hence you have such expressions, as that, "he that hateth reproof is brutish," Prov. xii. 1, he is void of understanding, a sensual, brutish creature; "he that regardeth it shall be honoured," Prov. xiii. 18, honoured with comfort, safety, and life. Noah was warned of God, and made an ark to the salvation of himself and his house, Heb. xi. 7; and when sinners take warning, it is life, sal-

Prov. xv. 10.

vation to them. Ezek. xxxiii. 5, "He that taketh warning shall deliver his soul." How needful then is warning! how profitable, if souls be saved by it! 2 Tim. iii. 16, "All Scripture is given by inspiration, and is profitable for instruction, for reproof," &c.; it is so profitable that the salvation of souls depends upon it. When David was reproved by Nathan for his sin, it reduced him from the error of his way, and was salvation to him. Let us bless God for his word, and reproofs tendered to us out of it; and subject ourselves unto them, as tending to our present and eternal good. Be not offended with the reprovers, but affected with the reproofs.

Ver. 22—24. *And the hand of the Lord was there upon me; and he said unto me, Arise, go forth into the plain, and I will there talk with thee. Then I arose, and went forth into the plain: and, behold, the glory of the Lord stood there, as the glory which I saw by the river of Chebar: and I fell on my face. Then the spirit entered into me, and set me upon my feet, and spake with me, and said unto me, Go, shut thyself within thine house.*

In these and the following verses to the end, you have directions for the prophet, and events that fell out.

The hand of the Lord coming upon him, he is directed to go to the plain, where the Lord Christ promised to speak with him; and he going thither,

I. He saw the glory of the Lord standing there, ver. 23.

II. He is amazed and falls down at it, which is implied in ver. 24.

III. He hath the Spirit entering into him, and is strengthened by it, set upon his feet, which is expressed in ver. 24.

Then here is a further direction, that he should go and shut up himself, ver. 24. And here his silence is declared,

1. By this inclusion of himself in his house.

2. By the bands imposed upon him, ver. 25, "They shall put bands upon thee."

3. By the impediments Christ himself infers, ver. 26, "I will make thy tongue to cleave to the roof of thy mouth, and thou shalt be dumb."

4. The time of his prophesyings mentioned, ver. 27, which is, when Christ should speak unto him.

I come to open the words:

"The hand of the Lord was there upon me." In the 14th verse of this chapter, and in the 3rd verse of the first chapter, you have had these words opened already. This "hand of the Lord" was the Spirit of the Lord, which acted the prophet, and showed him and others, that he was not moved in a human way, or by inconsiderate motions, but divinely; the power and efficacy of the Spirit.

"There." That is, at Tel-abib, in ver. 15; he came thither, and sat down there seven days. And being in his habitation, sad, and backward unto the work he was called unto, the word of the Lord came to him, ver. 16, and the hand of the Lord was there upon him. He thought, being shut up in his house, that the business would fall, and that he should be excused from prophetical service; but he was mistaken. God's hand finds him out, and he is bidden to go forth into the plain, not to stay any longer within his doors, but to go into the plain, or valley; so the word in Hebrew signifies, being בקעה בקע from a word which is to cut, divide, break. This plain, or valley, was divided from the mountains, and a solitary place, free from company and disturbances, delightful, fit to refresh and quiet the spirits of men.

Obs. 1. The Spirit is the great agent in divine things. It is the hand of the Lord that doth all; it beautifies with gifts and graces, calls to office, directs whither to go, what to do; it assists and enables to all divine operations. Christ had the chiefest work to do that concerned the church, and the hand of the Lord was upon him: Isa. lxi. 1, "The Spirit of the Lord God is upon me;" and Isa. xi. 2, it is a "Spirit of might," and, Luke xxiv. 19, enabled him to do mighty things. And so Stephen, Acts vi. 10, "They were not able to resist the Spirit by which he spake." It is the Spirit doth the great things in religion; sanctification and mortification are the works of this hand of the Spirit of God, 1 Cor. vi. 11; Acts xiii. 2, "Separate me Barnabas and Saul for the work whereunto I have called them."

Obs. 2. The servants of Christ have daily need of new influences of the Spirit to encourage them to and strengthen them in their work. Ezekiel was full of fears, had many discouragements, sat in a doubtful condition what to do, and the hand of the Lord was upon him. He had formerly felt divine virtue, seen Christ, and heard him; yet all this doth not suffice, the hand must work again and help him, else nothing will be done. The apostles had been much with Christ, seen his miracles, heard his doctrine, and yet they must stay at Jerusalem till the Spirit fall upon them, Acts i. 4. Paul saith of himself and others, "We are not sufficient of ourselves to think any thing as of ourselves; but our sufficiency is of God," 2 Cor. iii. 5; that is, all our strength and help lies in him; we daily find a want in ourselves, and God, as it pleases him, lets out from his sufficiency unto us, now a little, and then a little, and we are ever receiving from him, and enabled by his grace and Spirit to do what is done. In ἐπιχορηγίας τοῦ πνεύματος. Phil. i. 19, is mentioned the supply of the Spirit; it is the administration, subministration, under-supplying, underpropping of the Spirit; all which words note the saints' infirmities, and need of the Spirit. Those things which befell Paul, would not turn to his good without the Philippians' prayers, and further supply of the Spirit: as a weak house must be underpropped, a sickly man have daily help, an army constant supply; so must the servants of God be underpropped, helped, and supplied by the Spirit. Therefore we should daily pray, as it is in Psal. lxviii. 28, "Strengthen, O God, that which thou hast wrought for us," and that which thou hast wrought in us.

Obs. 3. No place can keep off the hand of God from coming upon us. There at Tel-abib, shut up in his house, divine virtue seized upon him. He thought now to hear no more of prophesying, and doing public service of that nature to the Jews; but the Spirit of God found him out; that cannot be excluded from any place, or limited to any time; it is like the wind, that blows where and when it listeth. When the apostles were shut up in a room, Acts ii. 2, 4, there was a rushing mighty wind, that filled all the house, and the Spirit with it, that filled all them. So when Cornelius and his company heard Peter preach in a private room, "the Holy Ghost fell on them all," Acts x. 44. As no place can include the Spirit of God, so can none exclude it. There were saints in Nero's court, and this hand of God had been working there. It is not a dungeon, any prison, can keep out the Spirit of God from coming to and comforting of his servants. Glover found the truth of it when he said, O Austin, he is come!

Obs. 4. The more separate from the world, the

more fit for communion with God. Ezekiel must go into the plain, and there the Lord would talk with him. He could have conversed with him at Tel-abib, among the people in his own habitation; but the Lord declines that, intimating that while we are conversant with worldly and wicked men, we are incapable of divine mysteries; but when we are remote from them, solitary and sedate, we are fitter to hear God speak. When the church was allured into the wilderness, Hos. ii. 14, then God would speak, and that comfortably, unto her. It was by the river Chebar he had his former visions; when he was absent from popular noise, domestic troubles, his mind serene and contemplative, then the Lord opened himself unto him. Christ oft left the multitude; and when he was gotten aside into the mount, then was his transfiguration, and the voice, "This is my beloved Son, in whom I am well pleased; hear ye him," Matt. xvii. 5.

Ver. 23. *Then I arose, and went forth into the plain: and, behold, the glory of the Lord stood there, as the glory which I saw by the river of Chebar: and I fell on my face.*

If aught have need of opening in this verse, it is "the glory of the Lord;" and there is no cloud upon this. The verse expounds itself, it is the glory he saw before by the river Chebar; that glorious vision he had there, is represented again here unto the prophet. The vision was not like the temple, fixed to a place; but it was movable; it was first presented to him at Chebar, and now again in this plain.

The reasons of this second apparition of the glory of God, are,

First, to possess the heart of the prophet with greater reverence of divine Majesty. He was unwilling to the service called to by God, sought excuses, thought to decline it, which argued neglect of divine Majesty. To strike out such distempers, and to strike in a deeper impression of fear and respect to God, this glorious vision is set before his eyes, and frames him to a fitness for that employment. He might now see Christ sitting as judge, compassed about with glory, having angels ready to execute his pleasure and power in and over all parts of the world; and if he should refuse the employment appointed, he ran a manifest hazard of his life.

Secondly, to confirm the truth of the prophecy, and him in it.

Thirdly, to prepare the church in all ages to a high esteem of this prophecy, that was ushered into the world with such glorious visions.

Obs. 1. Divine virtue makes men obedient unto the command of God. The hand of the Lord was upon him, he bids him go forth; and presently he arose and went forth into the plain. If things enjoined suit not with our wills, opinions, and humours, we deny them, excuse and take off ourselves from the doing of them, or defer them; but let God enjoin what he will, be it harsh to flesh and blood, contrary to our wills, carnal reason, &c. if divine virtue once come upon us, and the Spirit move in us, we will do it. God bid Abraham take his son, his only son Isaac whom he loved, and go and sacrifice him upon a mountain in the land of Moriah, Gen. xxii. Flesh and blood had much to object here; but because he was acted by divine virtue, therefore he obeyed presently; he rose early, took his son, went to the place, stretched out his hand to slay him, and to make him a sacrifice. We stick oft at small things when nature only works; not at any thing when the Spirit of God works in us.

Obs. 2. They who are obedient to God simply upon his command, meet with mercies unexpected. Ezekiel goes forth upon command, not knowing what was to come, what was to be done, and he meets with an extraordinary mercy; he saw the glory of the Lord, a ravishing, a satisfying mercy. Abraham, obeying the command of God, hears the voice of an angel twice, and meets with a multitude of blessings: Gen. xxii. 17, "In blessing I will bless thee, and in multiplying I will multiply thy seed as the stars of heaven, and as the sand which is upon the sea-shore; and thy seed shall possess the gate of his enemies; and in thy seed shall all the nations of the earth be blessed; because thou hast obeyed my voice." So Jacob returned from Laban to his father's house upon divine command, and he meets with angels, Gen. xxxii. 1; he met with God, and, like a prince, prevailed with him for a blessing, ver. 28. No man ever lost by his obedience unto God. Though we see no reason for things, yet if we have the will of God that is reason enough. Let us be tractable and forward to do the will of God, and we shall not lose our labour; we may meet with mercies unexpected, as some by coming to the ordinances have done.

Obs. 3. See the goodness of the Lord in two things:

First, in that he will manifest his glory to the view of mortal, sinful creatures. His glory is precious, a hidden thing, and not obvious to creatures; yet here, as before, he is pleased in a vision to present it to the sight of Ezekiel. It was to the ambassador of a prince that "Hezekiah showed the house of his precious things," Isa. xxxix. 2, and it was a favour to let them see such rarities: it was a greater favour from God to let Ezekiel see this rarity of rarities, his glory.

Secondly, that God should act over the same thing again, present the same vision in living creatures, wheels, eyes, firmament, a throne, and one sitting upon it, and give a sight of his glory the second time; this sets out God's goodness abundantly. Men are unwilling to do the same thing twice, whenas they may do it better the second time than the first, and advantage themselves by it; but God hath no advantage, doth it perfectly at first; yet, simply for man's good, he condescends to do the same thing again. So, that Ezekiel may be brought to a fitness for divine dispensations, encouraged to, and in his work, he shall have a sight of glory, and a glorious vision presented to him the second time by God's own hand. We think repetitions of things in vain; a sermon twice over is stale, unwelcome, oft neither minister nor people find any savour in it; and so other things; but God repeats the vision without prejudice to himself, or damage to the prophet.

Obs. 4. Sin makes us incapable of happiness. It is man's happiness to see the glorious God, and have communion with him. While Adam stood, he could behold God, converse with him in his glorious appearances unto him; but after his fall, he fled from his presence, was disabled, and incapable of the sight of him and his glory: so here, Ezekiel cannot abide the sight of this glorious vision, but falls down upon his face, and hides himself from his own happiness. Till sin be purged out of us, it will be so; therefore God hath appointed purging ordinances, that we, being purified, might at last see him, and have fruition of him. Two things especially are required to the sight of glory; holiness and strength, to both which sin is opposite: it defiles, it enfeebles, so that we dare not, we cannot behold glory. See what mischief sin hath done us.

Obs. 5. Apprehensions and sight of glory do much humble gracious hearts. When Ezekiel saw the glory of the Lord, he fell upon his face: the glory of a creature raises a carnal heart, but the glory of the Creator humbles a gracious heart. John i. 14, "We beheld his glory, as the only begotten of the Father;" and this made John, the greatest prophet that ever was born of a woman, to be so low in his own eyes, that he professed himself unworthy to loose the latchet of his shoe, ver. 27. There be some things in the sight of divine glory, that work strongly to humble the soul.

(1.) It is of that lustre and excellency, as that it darkens all the glory of the world, and makes it seem no more than the lustre of a glowworm to the sun.

(2.) It sets out the shamefulness and blackness of sin.

(3.) It discovers the insufficiency of all human motions and duties to attain unto it.

(4.) It shows the infinite distance between God and the creature.

All which are humbling things, and concurring do humble more thoroughly. Ezekiel was not only amazed, doth not only fall down, but falls upon his face, and that after a second sight of the same glory; so that it is in the nature of glory to humble. Other things may humble a little, but glory most of all: that which comes by the ear doth something, but that which is seen by the eye affects most. Isaiah had heard the seraphims crying, "Holy, holy, holy,—the earth is full of his glory;" but this struck not so deeply into his heart, as the sight of glory. When he saw the King, the Lord of hosts in his glory, then he cried out, "Woe is me! I am undone:" his holiness was nothing, his prophetical office was nothing, all was nothing to him, he was an undone man, he saw so much sin in himself; "I am a man of unclean lips," &c.

Ver. 24. *Then the spirit entered into me, and set me upon my feet, and spake with me, and said unto me, Go, shut thyself within thine house.*

Being in a dejected condition, the Spirit entered. It was said before, "the hand of the Lord came upon him," which was the Spirit; and here, "the Spirit entered into me." What difference is there between these two phrases? You may observe this difference: the hand of the Lord upon the prophet, notes the efficacy and work of the Spirit in general, the common gifts and graces of it, which may fit a man for public employment. The entering of the Spirit notes, not only those, but the sanctifying of a man, so that he shall employ his gifts and graces to the glory of God, and eternal good of his own soul. Of the Spirit's entering and setting the prophet upon his feet I spake in the 2nd chapter, ver. 2. It was not the air, his own spirit returning, nor an angel, but the Holy Spirit of God. This entrance of the Spirit notes, not motion from place to place, for the Spirit is infinite and fills heaven and earth; but it notes operation, manifestation, impletion. When the Spirit doth work efficaciously, manifest itself, (for there may be invisible operations,) fill the heart of any with divine virtue; when it doth any one of these, or all these, it is said to be sent, to come, to enter. It comforted the prophet, being amazed, sunk in apprehension of his own unworthiness, and manifested its operation by setting him upon his feet, giving new strength to go and prophesy when time should serve.

"Go, shut thyself within thine house." These words are not ironically spoken, or by way of sarcasm, because he had formerly shut up himself; but they are a command from God to the prophet. It is true, by reason of the rebellious disposition of the people, the weightiness of the calling he was to be in, and the infirmity of the flesh, he had withdrawn from his duty; and God bears with him, bids him withdraw from the public view. Jerom thinks this shutting up was a type of the besieging of the city, that as he should be shut up in his house, so the Jews at Jerusalem. Others think more probably, that it was to receive instructions from God, and to hear from him, before he should speak aught to the people; therefore some observe that our prophet heard and saw much, and spake not till the end of the 11th chapter, ver. 25, where he saith, "Then I spake unto them of the captivity," &c. This shutting up made way for the credit and authority of the prophet and his prophecy.

Obs. 1. The Spirit affects and visits an humble soul. When the prophet was humbled with the sense of his own unworthiness, trembled at the sight of glory and majesty, was destitute of strength, then it pleased the Spirit of God to enter. Humiliations upon sight of glory and greatness are deepest, and the Spirit loves to visit them speedily. God doth not long leave humble souls without operations and manifestations of his Spirit: Jam. iv. 6, "He resisteth the proud, but giveth grace unto the humble;" he sends the Spirit into their hearts to comfort and strengthen them, because they are low, vile in their own eyes; but destruction is for the proud, God is in battle-array against them. The Spirit appeared like a dove, and is a dove of the valleys, not of the mountains. While Paul was a mountain in his own eyes, the Spirit never came near him; but when he was humbled with the sight of glory, Acts ix., even the glory of Christ, and became a valley, then quickly the spiritual Dove took her flight to him; for, ver. 17, saith Ananias, "Brother Saul, the Lord hath sent me that thou mightest receive thy sight, and be filled with the Holy Ghost:" the Lord Jesus would not let him want his Spirit to revive him, that was so effectually humbled at the sight of his glory.

Obs. 2. The godly before Christ had the same Spirit, grace, and comforts that we have since Christ. Ezekiel had the Spirit enter into him. What Spirit? Even the Spirit of God and Christ, the third Person in the sacred Trinity. Neither doth that in John cross this truth, "The Holy Ghost was not yet given, because that Jesus was not yet glorified," chap. vii. 39. Not given at all is not the meaning, but was not given so plentifully, so visibly, till Christ was glorified. You know that kings, when they enter their kingdoms first, or ride in triumph after great victories, then they scatter gold and silver plentifully, and give the greatest honours and gifts unto men; so Christ reserved the pouring out of his Spirit in such plenty and visible signs, till his glorifying. Therefore Austin saith, The prophets had not another Spirit who foretold Christ to come. But this is meant of that manner of giving, which appeared not at all before. They under the law had not the Spirit given in that way and so largely, but they had the same Spirit, 2 Pet. i. 21, and Luke i. 41, 67.

Obs. 3. The Spirit of Christ which the godly receive, is not a spirit of bondage, but of comfort, of grace and freedom. This Spirit did not straiten the prophet, but enlarge him. He was imprisoned with his own fears, beat down under a sense of his own worthlessness; but this Spirit of Christ did set him at liberty, and lifts him up again, and works graciously in him. This Spirit is oft called the Comforter, and that emphatically, because no man, no angel, no ordinance, do or can comfort like the Spirit; it helps against fears, sins, guilt, temptations, straitness of heart: this made the apostle say, "Where the Spirit of the Lord is, there is liberty," 2 Cor. iii. 17. It knocks off bolts, locks, shackles; it makes way for his own graces to act, and act with liveliness; and if there be strong-holds within, strong lusts that oppose, it is a Spirit of power, and will carry all before it: 2 Tim. i. 7. "God hath not given us the spirit of fear, but of power;" such power as will conquer all the rebellions of a man's will, bring all into order, captivate every thought unto Christ, and make a man able to do the whole will of God, an Ezekiel to prophesy to a rebellious people, and to venture his life amongst them.

Obs. 4. Those Christ sends unto the church, he gives his Spirit unto. Ezekiel hath the Spirit enter into him before he enters upon his office. Men void of the Spirit, are not meet to be church officers. All things in the church come under spiritual consideration; the people are to be professors of holiness, ordinances are holy, and what should unholy officers do there? If they have not the Spirit of Christ, they are none of his; and what should they do in the church of Christ? He will ask them one day, Friend's how came you in hither? I sent you not.

Obs. 5. The Spirit performs what Christ promiseth. In the 22nd verse, Christ bids the prophet go forth into the plain, and tells him he will there talk with him; but being come thither, the Spirit entered into him, and spake with him. Christ and the Spirit are one in essence, one in will, and one in operation; so that the prophet was not deceived, but it was the same as if Christ had spoken to him. I will be with you to the end of the world, saith Christ. His Spirit was with them, and so in that it was made good that he was with them. The Spirit makes good whatever the Lord Jesus hath promised, when it comes; and it cannot be otherwise, for these three, Father, Word, and Holy Ghost, are one, and agree in one, 1 John v. 7.

Obs. 6. There is a language of the Spirit within a man. "The Spirit entered into me, and spake with me." How it speaks is hard to make out unto you. We have heard that the devil hath spoken in parties bewitched and possessed, and you have text of Scripture for it; Acts xix. 13—15, when the sons of Sceva adjured the evil spirit in the name of Jesus, "the evil spirit answered, Jesus I know, and Paul I know, but who are ye?" Thus did the devil express himself in the possessed. And surely the Spirit of God can speak vocally in those where it dwells; but that is not the ordinary language of the Spirit. A man speaks to another, *quando conceptum mentis alteri manifestat*, when he makes known to another that which he has conceived in his mind; and as the schools say of angels, they speak *manifestando suum volitum*, in the manifestation of their will, so we may say, the Spirit speaks unto us by manifestation of its mind unto us. John xvi. 13, "Whatsoever the Spirit shall hear, that shall he speak; and he will show you things to come:" and ver. 14, "He shall receive of mine, and shall show it unto you."

Halens.

Obs. 7. The proceedings of God with his own servants are various and darksome. The prophet was bid to preach oft before. In the 22nd verse, he is called forth into the plain; and when he is there the Lord bids him go and shut himself up in his house, as it is in this 24th verse. Now he will have him prophesy, and presently he suspends him from his office and liberty; neither is there any change in God, but he by these various dispensations fulfils his eternal counsels.

Obs. 8. God considers the weaknesses of his servants, bears with and provides well against them. Ezekiel was timorous, the house of Israel rebellious, and like enough to offer violence to the prophet, if he should have presently propounded the dreadful judgments of God that were at hand against Jerusalem; and therefore he takes care of him, and commands him to shut up himself, that so he might be safe, and not at first be discouraged at the wickedness of the people, or weightiness of his work. God is full of bowels, and tenders his servants, when put upon difficult employments.

Ver. 25. *But thou, O Son of man, behold, they shall put bands upon thee, and shall bind thee with them, and thou shalt not go out among them.*

This verse speaks of the bands imposed upon the prophet, and what these were we must inquire. The word is עבותים which the Syriac renders *catenæ*, chains; the Vulgate, *vincula*, bands; Montanus, *funes*, ropes; and not any ropes, but *funes contorti adeoque densi*, thick twisted ropes, as the original signifies. Now these ropes or bands are taken literally by some, and metaphorically by others.

Literally thus: They seeing the prophet sad seven days, and now astonished at what he had seen and heard, and observing some strange looks and carriages from him, they thought he was or would be beside himself, and therefore they bound him. It was a conceit among Jews and gentiles, that prophets were a kind of madmen. Hos. ix. 7, "The spiritual man," or, as the Hebrew is, the man of the Spirit, "is mad;" they thought him out of his wits. Our prophet had received the Spirit of Christ, and that wrought in him, and the people might be apt enough to judge him a madman. When a prophet came to anoint Jehu, his companions said, "Wherefore came this mad fellow?" 2 Kings ix. 11, Prophets were reputed mad fellows, and that not only by the Jews, but by gentiles also. Plato in Phædro saith, *Quidam divino beneficio sunt insani, ut prophetæ et sibyllæ*, Some are mad by a divine influence, as prophets and the sibyls; and Tully, in his 2nd book De Divinationibus, *Quid habet authoritatis furor iste quem divinum vocatis, ut quæ sapiens non videt ea videat insanus; et is qui humanos sensus amiserit, divinos assecut us sit; et vaticinari idem sit quod insanire*, What authority has that madness which you call divine, that what things a wise man does not perceive, are seen by an insane person; and he who has lost the natural senses, has obtained those which are divine; and to prophesy is the same thing as to be mad. This opinion was also in the apostles' time: Acts xxvi. 24, Festus the governor of Syria tells Paul, that he was beside himself; that much learning had made him mad.

Martyr in 2 Kings ix. 11. Kimchi thinks that the prophets were so called quod dum vaticinarentur speciem præferrent hominis alienati cum à mente, tum à sensibus.

In the metaphorical sense take it thus: The Jews cannot endure thee, nor thy prophecy; they are so bitter, so rebellious, obstinate, and set against thee, that they will not suffer thee to look out of doors, and come among them; they decline thee and thy prophecy, they will not endure either of them; and so thou art as a prisoner and man in bands. Not that he had any material bands upon him, but was bound up in this sense; their sins were the prophet's bonds. And we may take up this observation from it, that people's sins do imprison and imbondage the spirits of the prophets, and so hinder the course of the word. This Paul knew, and therefore requests the Colossians to pray, that God would open to him and others a door of utterance, Col. iv. 3, that they might not be straitened in the work of their ministry. Men's sins do silence the ministers, and send them to prisons. If you look not well to it, your sins may quickly make this good.

I incline to the literal sense, and then it is doubtful who bound the prophet. "They shall put bands," &c. Not the angels; though God use them in the government of the world, yet we find not that God uses them to bind his prophets. Some conceive it to be his friends and familiar acquaintance, and that it was done in love. If others had done it, they would have left him in custody other where than in his own house; but without prejudice to any, I conceive it came from the people, who either bound him, or bespoke his binding. And my ground for it is this: he is made a watchman to the house of Israel; in that capacity and relation the Lord speaks unto him. Here is no mention of any domestic friends, but of the people; it was they without, not they within; as is clear from the words, "They shall put bands upon thee, and thou shalt not go out among them."

Obs. 1. Christ deals fairly, not fraudulently with his; he tells them at first what they must expect; not gold and silver, but bands and chains, "They shall bind thee." He told Jeremiah, they shall fight against him, Jer. i. 19. So Paul no sooner is called to preaching, but he hears of suffering: Acts ix. 16, "I will show him how great things he must suffer." And Matt. xxiv. 9, Christ tells all the apostles that they must be afflicted, hated, killed; and this he doth in faithfulness, love, and wisdom, that they might not be deceived in looking for other kind of entertainment in the world; that they might not have hard thoughts of him for hiding away such things from them; that they might be confirmed against such evils when they fell out, and remember it was no more than the Lord foretold them of: John xvi. 2, "They shall put you out of the synagogues: yea, they shall kill you, and think they do God good service;" and ver. 4, "These things have I told you, that you may remember I told you of them when the time comes."

Obs. 2. No excellency exempts a prophet from the malice of men's tongues and hands. Ezekiel is immediately called and sent by Christ, sees extraordinary visions, hath much converse with Christ, is filled with the Spirit; yet all this keeps him not out of bonds; they spake evil of him, and bound him. Christ himself was all excellency, beauty, goodness, yet these preserved him not out of the hands of malice. There is nothing will satisfy it, but men's liberties and lives; malice feeds on such dainties.

Obs. 3. The generality of people are enemies to their own good, and active to their own ruin. The house of Israel, they are against the prophet; they fetter and chain him up, and think they have done well, to make him secure from coming amongst them. And alas, what have they done! thrust away the physician that should cure them; shut out mercy by shutting up a prophet; put out the light. And now are there not droves and multitudes of people that would think it a happiness to get all the prophets silenced, imprisoned, banished, if not more? they would live in darkness, and die in darkness, and so undo themselves for ever. Christ the great Prophet, the people, after all his precious sermons and glorious miracles, cry, "Away with this man, Crucify him, crucify him," Luke xxiii. 18, 21. They had cried Hosanna formerly, but now the time being turned, they turn against Christ. There be many that show some kindness outwardly to the prophets, but inwardly they are against them.

Obs. 4. Wicked ones deal severely, cruelly with the prophets, when they fall into their hands. They put bands, not one or two, but many bands upon Ezekiel; and they were wreathed, twisted, heavy, thick bands, such as might not only hold, but hurt and pain the prophet. When Ahab had got Micaiah into his hands, he sends him to prison, and commands him to be fed with bread and water of affliction; that is, with so little and so unsavoury, *ut longam potius mortem trahat, quam vitam sustentet,* that it would rather bring on a lingering death than support life; he would kill him, *non brevi morte, sed lenta fame,* not by a speedy death, but by slow famine. Jeremiah, the princes are wroth with him, smite him, put him in the prison, Jer. xxxvii. 15; yea, into the dungeon, where he sunk into deep mire, and had perished, if Ebed-melech, an Ethiopian, had not been more propitious to him than his own countrymen the Jews were, Jer. xxxviii. 6, 7. Josephus saith, they put him
into a muddy pit, *ut ibi præfocatus* Antiq. 10.
moreretur, that there suffocated he might die, which might easily have been, for he was *usque ad collum mersus,* plunged even to the neck. Others think they aimed not at his present death, but thought, *pædore et fame,* by filth and by famine, lingeringly to consume him. Peter, when he fell into Herod's hands, was bound with two chains, Acts xii. 6. You may observe something in that verse; there is a prison, chains, soldiers, keepers, all these mentioned in it; which show the severity of Herod. A bare prison had been too much for such an apostle, but he must be chained, and with two chains; and for fear he should get out of his chains, he must be between two soldiers, which probably were more afflictive to his spirit with their oaths, &c. than the iron was to his body. And lest he should get from these, there was also the keepers at the door, watching. Paul tells you how he was handled by wicked men: 2 Cor. xi. 23, 24, "In stripes above measure, in prisons more frequent, in deaths oft. Of the Jews five times received I forty stripes save one. Thrice beaten with rods, once was I stoned, thrice I suffered shipwreck."

Obs. 5. Afflictive conditions seldom better men's spirits. They were in Babylon under captivity, and five years passed in that condition, chap. i. 2; yet were their proud hearts not humbled, their old enmity to the prophets not worn out. 2 Chron. xxxvi. 15—17, God sent them messengers, prophets, and they mocked them, misused them, till the wrath came, and there was no remedy; and therefore he brought upon them the Chaldeans, who led them into captivity, where they were servants and slaves. Their wronging of the prophets was the cause of their suffering, and yet all their sufferings did not subdue their spirits, and work them to entertain the truth, and walk peaceably towards the prophet; they bind him in the land of bondage. The plough breaks the earth in many places, but doth not better it, but leaves it as it was; nothing is put in by the plough. If the master dung it, and sow good seed in it, when the plough hath broken it, then there is like to be a harvest; but if nothing be sown, weeds, nettles, thorns will grow where the plough hath been. And so afflictions may break our estates, our bodies, our sleep; yet if nothing be added, if God do not sanctify them, the harvest will be tares, and not wheat.

Obs. 6. It is no new thing for prophets and ministers to be roughly entreated, and laid by as useless things. Ezekiel, four hundred years before Christ, is shut up, bound, kept from coming among the people; and this misery hath befallen the prophets in several ages. Jezebel cut off the prophets, and then they were hid by fifties in caves, 1 Kings xviii. 4.

Jeremiah was shut up in the prison in the king's court, Jer. xxxii. 2. Most of the prophets and apostles were restrained from their public employments, shut up in prisons, banished or driven into corners; and that proves oft a great saddening to ingenuous spirits, not so much in that they suffer, but because they are out of employment. But let those that are in such conditions, or may shortly be, consider it is no strange, unwonted thing; such afflictions have been formerly; 1 Pet. v. 9, "The same afflictions are accomplished in your brethren that are in the world;" besides, God hath need of no men, nor any of their parts.

Ver. 26. *And I will make thy tongue cleave to the roof of thy mouth, that thou shalt be dumb, and shalt not be to them a reprover: for they are a rebellious house.*

Here is a further and full manifestation of his silence, but there is doubt concerning the meaning of the words. The Septuagint hath it, I will bind thy tongue; and this bond, it is conceived, was a divine precept; God commanding him to be silent, and thereupon it was that he forbore to speak unto them. Others take the words literally, and hold that the use of his tongue was taken away; so that neither in public nor in private he might speak unto them, but be a wordless and tongueless man amongst them; whereupon they being troubled, and wondering at what had befallen Ezekiel, might search out the cause, and become more willing to hear those sad messages he had to deliver. But I conceive the words are not to be taken in their literal sense:

1. Because the prophet is bid in the next chapter, ver. 9, to prepare him meat, and to eat thereof, which he could not do, if his tongue had cleaved to the roof of his mouth; the motion of the tongue is needful to that action.

2. It is plain from the 14th verse of that 4th chapter, that it cannot be meant literally; for there the prophet speaks, "Then said I, Ah Lord God! behold, my soul hath not been polluted," &c. We are then to take the words figuratively, thus: Thou shalt be as a man whose tongue cleaves to his mouth, as a man that is dumb; such a one shalt thou be amongst them. And this sense the words following infer, "Thou shalt not be to them a reprover;" they would not have thee to tell them of their sins, of my judgments, and the danger thereupon; "and thou shalt not be a reprover unto them:" and it is the Scripture language to call them dumb that are in the place of ministers and prophets, and preach not, Isa. lvi. 10.

Obs. 1. The Lord hath the power over prophets' lips, to shut and open them at his pleasure: "I will make thy tongue cleave to the roof of thy mouth," &c. If God forbid the prophets to speak, they must be dumb; on the contrary, if he command, they cannot be silent: Amos iii. 8, "The Lord hath spoken, who can but prophesy?" The Jews objected against the prophets, that they prophesied no good unto them, only sad things, and were messengers of death. The prophet answers, It is true, but God hath commanded; he hath spoken, and who can be silent? Who shall dare not to deliver and hear his message? he is a roaring lion, will tear in pieces disobedient prophets and people. He was to speak, and to be silent, when God would have it so. Balaam knew this, Numb. xxii. 38, "Lo, I am come unto thee, O Balak; have I now any power at all to say any thing?" can I with canning do any thing? so is the Hebrew; "the word that God putteth in my mouth, that shall I speak." It was in God to open or shut his mouth; he could not with all his canning do ought. Prov. xvi. 1, "The preparations of the heart in man, and the answer of the tongue, is from the Lord;" and so the silence of the tongue, and cessation of the spirit in man, is from the Lord. Prophets are to be silenced and suspended, not when prelates or people will, but when the Lord will.

Obs. 2. People are impatient of reproofs. "Thou shalt not be a reprover unto them; for they are rebellious;" they would not endure him to deal roughly with them, to convince them of their sins. Many affect the prophets being shining lights, but when they are burning lights they hate them; when they scorch men with thorough reproofs and evident convictions of their guiltiness, then they hate them, and seek to mischief them: Isa. xxix. 21, he that reproved in the gate had a snare laid for him; and Micaiah is a hateful man to Ahab, 1 Kings xxii. 8, because he prophesied not good to him. Reproofs are *veritates mordaces*, biting truths; they have salt and fire in them, which few men can endure, especially being sore; and therefore they will imprison and murder the prophets: "Put this fellow into prison," saith Ahab, ver. 27. Let John reprove Herod, and he is presently clapped into a prison, Luke iii. 19. proofs evidence to men that their sins are known, awaken guilt, and cross them in the things they love, and therefore they cannot endure them. Like Moses's rod, in hand it was without hurt, but thrown down it became a serpent; so reproofs thrown forth prove serpents to men, they molest and sting them.

Obs. 3. The people's sins do cause God to cut them short of spiritual mercies. Here was a prophet furnished with the treasure of heaven, and the Lord shuts up his mouth and makes him a dumb prophet unto them. And why so? "for they are a rebellious house;" they did not profit under their judgments; they still undervalued their prophets; they went on stubbornly in their ways against God; and this made God deny them the benefit of the prophet's labours. Unbelief, neglect of reformation, and ingratitude are provoking sins, and God punishes people for them, and such like, with the removal of his word and prophets. In Amos viii. the Lord tells them, there shall be howlings in the temple, dead bodies in all places, ver. 3; that their sun should go down at noon, their feasts be turned into mournings, and such mournings as are for an only son, deep and lasting, ver. 8, 9. And why so? they had sinned greatly in slighting and being weary of God's sabbaths and ordinances; they were covetous, they oppressed the poor, &c.; and now God would send a famine of the word, ver. 11, and there would be howlings, darkness, and death above measure. It is a dreadful thing when people provoke God to take away his prophets by death, to command them silence, or to remove them into corners. The prophets and ministers are the light and salt of the earth; if God take them away, people will be unsavoury, full of worms, noisome lusts, and corruptions, they will be in darkness, and hasten to eternal darkness. It is the word that makes all sweet and comfortable; if that go, God's face is hid, his presence departed, and all lies open to ruin. It is the sins of the people that introduce such a judgment. God takes away his word, and the preachers of it, because the people's lives are exasperating, not conformable to what is taught. This judgment we may fear in this land. because the distance is exceeding great between God's word and our lives. I will not prophesy, but pray. The Lord prevent and divert such a judgment from England. If it should come, it would be the most dreadful that befell the land these fourscore years. Afflictions you are like to

meet withal, and pressing ones; but that I may not discourage your hearts, cast your eyes and thoughts upon that promise in Isa. xxx. 19, 20, "He will be very gracious unto thee at the voice of thy cry; when he shall hear it, he will answer thee. And though the Lord give you the bread of adversity, and the water of affliction, yet shall not thy teachers be removed into a corner any more." The word in Hebrew literally is, Thy teachers shall not be winged, and fly from thee when danger is, but thine eyes shall see thy teachers, and thou shalt hear a voice behind thee, &c. This is spoken of the church under the gospel, as well as before. If you can therefore take hold of this promise, and cry earnestly unto God, you shall not lose your teachers, and the truth, though you lose your estates and outward comforts. If God should take away your teachers from you, it would be an argument of much wrath, and that this people is unworthy
Lam. ii. 9. of spiritual mercies.

Ver. 27. *But when I speak with thee, I will open thy mouth, and thou shalt say unto them, Thus saith the Lord God; He that heareth, let him hear; and he that forbeareth, let him forbear: for they are a rebellious house.*

The greatest part of this verse hath been spoken of in the 11th verse of this chapter, and 5th verse of the second chapter, and therefore shall not need now to be opened unto you.

Obs. 1. All times are not times for the prophets to speak in. Thy mouth is now shut, and it is not seasonable for thee to prophesy; but hereafter when I shall speak with thee, I will open thy mouth. Prophets must therefore wait upon God, as for warrant to speak, so for liberty and opportunity of speaking: Amos v. 13, "The prudent shall keep silence in that time." There are times when God, in judgment to a people, would not have them speak: Eccl. iii. 7, "There is a time to keep silence, and a time to speak;" and both these the Lord will show his servants.

Obs. 2. Neither the prophets' infirmities, nor the people's sins, shall always keep the prophets' mouths shut: "When I speak with thee, I will open thy mouth, and thou shalt say unto them," &c.

Obs. 3. God tries many ways with a sinful, wretched people to gain them; he sends them into captivity, gives them a prophet there, shuts up his mouth, opens it again, and all to see what this people will do: "I will open thy mouth, and thou shalt say, Thus saith the Lord; He that heareth, let him hear," &c. There are but few amongst you who will hear, I am afraid; but if any will hear, "let him hear," &c. God will try men whether they are curable or no.

CHAPTER IV.

Ver. 1—3. *Thou also, son of man, take thee a tile, and lay it before thee, and pourtray upon it the city, even Jerusalem: and lay siege against it, and build a fort against it, and cast a mount against it; set the camp also against it, and set battering-rams against it round about. Moreover take thou unto thee an iron pan, and set it for a wall of iron between thee and the city: and set thy face against it, and it shall be besieged, and thou shalt lay siege against it. This shall be a sign to the house of Israel.*

In the three former chapters you have had the preface, now we are to come to the prophecy itself. In this chapter and the next is a prophecy against Jerusalem, the chief city of the Jews; the besieging of it, and miseries which attend that condition are laid down therein.

This chapter hath in it these parts:

I. A typical besieging of Jerusalem, in the first eight verses.

II. A great famine during this siege, and that is in ver. 9—11, 16, 17; and this is aggravated from the eating of polluted bread baked in dung, ver. 12—15.

I shall begin with the typical besieging of the city. The Jews that yet lived at Jerusalem trusted in their strength and privileges, were secure, fearing no dangers; they accounted them fools and weak ones, who had yielded themselves into the hands of the Babylonians; and because Jeremiah had counselled them to do it, and prophesied hard things against Jerusalem, they dealt roughly with him, and got him imprisoned. Here, therefore, the Lord set our prophet to work to lay siege against Jerusalem, to batter it with warlike instruments, that so the captives with him might not repent them of what they had done, nor those at Jerusalem put off any longer the evil day, cry, Peace, peace, when destruction was at hand.

In the first verse the prophet is commanded to draw the picture of Jerusalem, and that upon a tile; in the other two to represent the actions of men besieging a city.

"Take thee a tile." The Hebrew word לבנה is, a brick, or a tile. It is questioned whether one green or one dried; and if dried, whether in the sun or fire; and whether white or red: which I will pass over as not being of any great moment. It signifies also any figure that is foursquare, and so any table or thing that may be engraven upon; and because it is from a root in Hebrew that is, to be white, it is conceived to be a table of chalk, or some other whitish stone, in the form of a brick or tile, whereon incision might easily be made. Bricks and tiles are neither white, nor easily admit engravement.

"Pourtray upon it the city, even Jerusalem." That is, express the picture of it by incision and engraving in the same. It is more than describing with the pen or pencil.

The city being pictured upon the tile or table, he is commanded in the next verse to lay siege to it; and so builds a fort, casts a mount, sets a camp and battering-rams against it, and hereby shows what the Chaldeans should shortly do against Jerusalem.

"A fort." The Hebrew word is דיק, and diversely expounded by the learned. Rabbi Solomon thinks it to be an engine to throw stones within the walls, which might annoy them; the Chaldee renders it, *machinas*, engines; the Vulgate, *munitiones*, defences for the soldiers, and such as might prevent the flight of adversaries. Some other rabbies think it to be a wooden tower, out of which they threw stones and weapons to batter the walls and kill the citizens.
Vitruvius saith, that some of them were Lib. 10.
120 cubits high, some 60, some less, Vid. Joseph. lib. 10. Antiq.
and 20 cubits broad at least. The cap. 11. et 6. de
Septuagint hath it, προμαχῶνας, strong- Bel. Jud.
holds, block-houses, fortresses; and so it agrees with our translation, "forts:" 2 Kings xxv. 1, when "Nebuchadnezzar" came "against Jerusalem with his forces, they built forts against it."

"Cast a mount against it," סללה. It is, *per enallagen numeri*, a singular number for a plural, "cast mounts against it." The word is from סלל which is, to raise up the way, when stones, turfs, and other earth are heaped up together, that make a mount: Job xix. 12, "His troops come together, and raise up their way against me;" it is the same word. When they besieged towns, it was their manner to raise mounts before them, that they might come without hurt to the walls.

"Set the camp;" or pitch tents against it, draw out forces, and let them sit down before the city.

כרים. "Set battering-rams against it." The word *carim* signifies rams, living creatures; and here it is put for a warlike instrument, which was made with an iron head and horns like a ram, to batter and break down the walls of cities. It was drawn back by a great number of men, and then driven on with violence against the walls, and so made breaches in them; and hence it had its name, because in form it was like a ram, *et adversa fronte in muros incurrebat*, and with adverse forehead ran against the walls. Some understand here the chief leaders in the army, that like as rams are the leaders in the flocks, so princes, nobles, generals, colonels, and captains, are leaders in armies. 2 Kings xi. 4, 19, the word captain there is the same in Hebrew with that here for rams, and notes the chief leaders; but in this place we are to take it for military instruments, which at the command of the chief ones were employed.

"Take thee an iron pan, and set it for a wall of iron between thee and the city." The Hebrew is, מחבת ברזל "a pan of iron." By this it describes the hard-heartedness of the Jews; they were as iron or brass, inflexible before God. Others set out by it the great wrath of God against Jerusalem, which now was come to that height, that no sacrifice, no prayers or tears, could divert or abate it: Lam. iii. 44, "Thou hast covered thyself with a cloud, that our prayer should not pass through." This pan stood as a wall between the city and the prophet; a great impediment between God and them; so that neither their prayers or miseries should come up to God, nor his mercies descend upon them; according to that in Isa. lix. 2, "Your iniquities have separated between you and your God, and your sins have hid his face from you, that he will not hear." Others think it notes out miseries and tortures the Jews should suffer from the king of Babylon, when he besieged and took Jerusalem. This pan was such a one as they used to fry things in; and Jer. xxix. 22, it is said, that Ahab and Zedekiah were "roasted in the fire" by the king of Babylon; they suffered hard things, they were fried in the pan of afflictions. And this sense agrees with that of Jeremiah, chap. i. 13, who saw a seething pot from the north, which set out the terrible afflictions Nebuchadnezzar should boil the Jews in. There may be some truth in these several senses, but we may, I conceive, understand by this "iron pan" set between the prophet and the city, the firm resolution of Nebuchadnezzar to besiege this city, and to continue it till he had obtained his design; he would not be moved from it, but be as inflexible as iron, and as unmovable in it as a settled wall. Or to go a little higher; the resolution of God himself by Nebuchadnezzar to besiege and destroy this city, and that without remedy; for the prophet besieging the city acted God's part, and this iron pan sets out his firm purpose to besiege them, and his implacable displeasure against them; which is also noted in these words;

"Set thy face against it;" which, as Pradus saith, is *severitatis signum gestusque judicis constantis in decreto, qui nullius auctoritate, precibus, aut fletibus commoveatur ad veniam*, a token of the firm adherence of the judge to the law, who by no authority, entreaties, or tears can be induced to pardon. And this noted out God's setting his face against them, of which he told them, Jer. xxi. 10, "I have set my face against this city for evil, and not for good, saith the Lord: it shall be given into the hand of the king of Babylon, and he shall burn it with fire."

"This shall be a sign to the house of Israel." Here was the end of all, that the Jews at Jerusalem might no longer trust in the lying words of false prophets, which promised safety to them and their city, whereupon they derided those who were gone into Babylon, and insulted over them; and likewise that those in captivity with the prophets might lay aside all thoughts of returning again into their country, and see it mercy that they were from Jerusalem, which was to undergo the greatest wrath of the Lord.

Obs. 1. The Lord deals with his people not only by his word, but also by signs and types. Here is a tile, and Jerusalem portrayed upon it; here are forts, mounts, tents, rams, iron bands, all which typed out God's dealing with Jerusalem; and in this language God had oft expressed himself. By the rainbow in the heavens God speaks to the world. Circumcision, the paschal lamb, the high priest's garments, the stones in Aaron's breast, the sprinkling things with blood, did all signify and type out something to the people. So Jeremiah's seething pot, chap. i.; his linen girdle, and bottles with wine, chap. xiii.; the potter's vessel, chap. xix.; the basket of figs, chap. xxiv.; and yoke of iron, chap. xxviii. And so all the parables in the Old and New Testament, they utter forth the mind of God. God hath throughout his word abundantly expressed himself this way; and the Lord doth it, because types and figures make truth more evident and efficacious. The word affects the ear; types and figures affect the eye, and carry a greater efficacy with them than simple and plain speech. The parable of the barren fig-tree, lost sheep, prodigal son, ten virgins, &c. had much life and efficacy in them. So when Christ took a little child and set before his disciples, Matt. xviii. it wrought more effectually upon them than many words, and left deeper impression in them. We may therefore see the goodness of the Lord in it, that affords us such helps in his word as may affect our hearts most.

Obs. 2. That the Lord knows things to come, and reveals them at his pleasure. He knew that Jerusalem should be besieged by Nebuchadnezzar, and discovers it unto the prophet, and causes him to make a draught of it; which shows a difference between the true God and all others. They that cannot foresee and foretell things to come, are not gods; but the God of Israel can foresee things, though afar off; Psal. cxxxix. 2, "Thou understandest my thoughts afar off, even from all eternity;" and he only foretells things that fall not within the reach of created abilities. He foretold the Messiah, the Egyptian and Babylonian captivity, and times of both; there is nothing future hid from God. We know not what shall be to-morrow, Jam. iv. 14, but God knows what shall be to-morrow, next year, yea, hundreds and thousands of years hence, if time be so long; and this proclaims him to be God, even the only true God. Isa. xli. 21—23, God calls there to other gods, to bring forth their reasons whereby to prove their divinity; let them show what is past, and things that are to come, and then he will take them for strong reasons, and acknowledge them gods with himself; but to tell things past and things to come, can none but the Lord himself, and they to whom he reveals them.

Obs. 3. God's appointment and authority makes things and actions mean and ridiculous in the eyes of the world to be weighty and of great use. It seems to carnal reason a childish thing, that the prophet should take a tile, draw the city upon it, make forts, mounts, warlike engines to batter it, yea, to take "a pan of iron" and set between him and the city; these men of the world are apt to look at as ridiculous, much like the practice of boys in a snow, that make forts, mounts, &c. in sport. But be not deceived; what the infinitely wise God commands, is of great concernment, how mean soever the things and actions about those things appear. The legal worship, if you look upon it in itself, seems strange; that they should kill so many beasts, and burn them to ashes; that the tabernacle, and things belonging to it, should be sprinkled with blood; that they must refrain from such meats, be unclean if they touch such things; be circumcised, eat a paschal lamb, &c.; I say, if we look at them externally, they seem irrational things, but if we eye God commanding them, they had an excellency, and were of great use to them, and instruments of much good. Now bread, wine, water, in baptism and the supper of the Lord, seem mean things, and such they are as are common to the world; but Christ's appointment to use these makes the difference; that gives *dignitatem et pondus*, dignity and weight, so that they are of great virtue to them that rightly partake of them. The pope and his prelates have commanded and brought much into the worship of God, *quicquid poterat desiderari ad eximium splendorem*, whatever could be desired for imposing splendour; but it is foolish, unsavoury, unprofitable, and efficacious only to make void the ordinances and commands of God. And why? because the Lord never commanded such things. That is contemptible in the eye of man, which being commanded of God, is honourable and efficacious; when that which is pompous, decent, honourable in the eye of the world, being not commanded of God, is despicable, fruitless, and frivolous.

Obs. 4. God is an enemy to sinful cities. He bids the prophet lay siege to Jerusalem, and to batter it; he who commands the ruin of a city is an enemy to that city; Ezek. v. 8, "Behold, I, even I, am against thee, saith the Lord." Jerusalem was once beloved; it was God's rest and desire, Psal. cxxxii. 13, 14; a faithful city, Isa. i. 21; a holy city, Isa. lii. 1; the city of the Lord, Isa. lx. 14; but now it was become a harlot, full of murders; the princes of it were rebellious, and companions of thieves, Isa. i. 21, 23. The sins of Jerusalem were very great; you may read largely of them in the 16th of Ezekiel, where you may find, that Jerusalem's sins and provocations exceeded Sodom's and Samaria's; she justified them in their abominations, they were little, not the half of Jerusalem's; and therefore this made the Lord to say, Jer. xxxii. 31, "This city hath been to me as a provocation of mine anger," or, for a provocation of mine anger, "and of my fury from the day that they built it even unto this day; that I should remove it from before my face." There was no rank of men but had greatly provoked him, kings, princes, priests, prophets, men of Judah, and inhabitants of Jerusalem, ver. 32; and therefore God was resolved to destroy it, and to make it a curse to all nations, Jer. xxvi. 6, and pronounced a woe to it in Zeph. iii. 1—4, where you further see what a city Jerusalem was now become, and what her citizens were: "Woe to her that is filthy and polluted, to the oppressing city! She obeyed not the voice; she received not correction; she trusted not in the Lord; she drew not near to her God. Her princes within her are roaring lions; her judges are evening wolves; they gnaw not the bones till the morrow. Her prophets are light and treacherous persons: her priests have polluted the sanctuary, they have done violence to the law. The just Lord is in the midst thereof," &c. And in the 6th verse, "their cities are destroyed, so that there is no man, no inhabitant." Sin makes God to lay waste great cities; Tyre, Sidon, Sodom, Gomorrah, Babylon, Jerusalem, felt the stroke and strength of God's wrath.

Obs. 5. Nothing secures a sinful city from ruin. Let it be strongly built, well fortified, abound with soldiers and munition, have great privileges, yet all these protect it not from invasion, from destruction. Jerusalem is besieged, ruined, burnt with fire; this Jerusalem was the city of David, 1 Kings ix. 24; and God did great things for David's sake, Isa. xxxvii. 35; it was the holy city, Neh. xi. 18; a strong city, Psal. xxxi. 21; the joyous city, Isa. xxxii. 13; the city of solemnities, Isa. xxxiii. 20; the perfection of beauty, and joy of the whole earth, Lam. ii. 15. It was the city which had the temple, the oracles, and ordinances of God, and greatest privileges that ever city had; therefore it is said, kings should bring presents thither, Psal. lxviii. 29. It was the city that God himself chose above all others, to put his name there, 1 Kings xiv. 21; and hereupon it was called oft the city of God, Psal. xlvi. 4; the city of the great King, Psal. xlviii. 2; the city of the Lord of hosts, ver. 8. And for her situation, it was among mountains, Psal. cxxv. 2; had towers and bulwarks, Psal. xlviii. 12, 13; and was accounted impregnable: Lam. iv. 12, "The kings of the earth, and all the inhabitants of the world, would not have believed that the enemy should have entered into the gates of Jerusalem." It was conceived to be of invincible strength; therefore the Jebusites, when David came to take it, placed the lame and blind to defend it, thinking them sufficient to keep out David and all his strength, 2 Sam. v. 6, 7, 8. But notwithstanding all these particulars, this was the city to be visited, Jer. vi. 6: and why? she was wholly oppression in the midst of her; she cast out wickedness as a fountain waters, ver. 7. This was the city to be besieged and made desolate, Jer. xix. 8; yea a curse, Jer. xxvi. 6. Nineveh was the great city, Jonah i. 2, but its greatness preserved it not, Neh. iii. Babylon was the golden city, and yet it ceased, Isa. xiv. 4. Jerusalem exceeded all in favours, in privileges, in promises of safety, yet this city is invaded, taken, and laid even with the ground. Let none therefore confide in cities, in any created strength, in any arm of flesh: men are exceeding apt to do it; some trust in chariots, some in horses, some in cities, some in princes and great men; but you will find horses, and chariots, and cities vain things; and for men, that there is no trusting in them at any time; therefore saith David, Psal. lxii. 8, "Trust in the Lord at all times; ye people pour out your heart before him: God is a refuge for us;" other things are not: and because you will think men are considerable, he adds, "Surely men of low degree are vanity, and men of high degree are a lie," they will deceive if you confide in them.

Obs. 6. The sins of a people and city may be so provoking, at such a height, that neither God nor man will show mercy to them. God bids him set an iron pan between him and them; showing, that both himself, and the army that he should bring, would be as iron to them. They had iron hearts and necks, Isa. xlviii. 4, and would not yield to God; and now he would be so to them, and cause their enemies also to be such; God would set his face against them, and the faces of their adversaries.

Great sins make God inexorable, severe: Ezek. xiv. 13, 14, "When the land sins grievously, I will stretch out my hand, and cut off man and beast; and though Noah, Job, and Daniel were in it, they should deliver but their own souls;" all their prayers, tears, righteousness, interest in God, should extend no further than themselves. God now had shut his eyes, and would not look upon them; he had stopped his ears, and would not hear them praying, nor others for them. He was set against them, resolved to punish them; therefore no miseries, no complaints, no sufferings of the living, or groans of the dying, could prevail with him; and when the army came, it used them severely enough.

Obs. 7. The Lord sends out his declarations before he causes destructions. "This shall be a sign to the house of Israel." God steals not upon men by public judgments before they hear of them, but tells them of their coming while they are at some distance; the prophets hear of them, and they proclaim and discover them some way or other. This fact of the prophet's would quickly spread and be at Jerusalem, and so might be a warning unto them. God sends out the lightning before he thunders, he frowns before he smites, and gives tokens of his coming in wrath before he executes it.

Ver. 4—8. *Lie thou also upon thy left side, and lay the iniquity of the house of Israel upon it: according to the number of the days that thou shalt lie upon it thou shalt bear their iniquity. For I have laid upon thee the years of their iniquity, according to the number of the days, three hundred and ninety days: so shalt thou bear the iniquity of the house of Israel. And when thou hast accomplished them, lie again on thy right side, and thou shalt bear the iniquity of the house of Judah forty days: I have appointed thee each day for a year. Therefore thou shalt set thy face toward the siege of Jerusalem, and thine arm shall be uncovered, and thou shalt prophesy against it. And, behold, I will lay bands upon thee, and thou shalt not turn thee from one side to another, till thou hast ended the days of thy siege.*

In these verses the prophet proceeds in the typical besieging of Jerusalem; and the words declare to us the duration of the siege, which was to be many days; and the cause of it, their iniquity.

The word "iniquity" notes here, not sin, but the punishment of sin, and in that sense it is oft used in sacred language: Isa. liii. 6, "The Lord hath laid on him the iniquity of us all," that is, the punishment of our sin; and Psal. lxix. 27, "Add iniquity unto their iniquity," that is, punish their iniquity; punishment is an inseparable companion of sin, and therefore it hath the name of sin. And the prophet was to bear their iniquity; that is, the punishment of it. This he did representatively, by this act of lying upon his side so long; setting out the long-suffering of God, who had borne with the sins of this people, and not punished them as they deserved. Our prophet did not here represent Christ, who bare our iniquities; but at the command of God he sustained the person of the ten tribes and kingdom of Judah; and therefore it is said, ver. 5, "I have laid upon thee the years of their iniquity," I have appointed thee, by lying on thy side so many days, to represent the time they have offended me by their idolatries and sins attending the same, and so to set out my patience, and aggravate the punishment of their sin. Christ bare the sin of men to take away the punishment of it; the prophet, to increase the same.

For our better understanding of these hieroglyphical passages in the verses read, we shall make inquiry into sundry things.

1. Whether our prophet did in the literal sense lie so many days upon his side, or was it only in vision?

Some make it real, and say, Ezekiel did lie upon his side all the days that are mentioned; although he slept not all the time, yet he lay in that posture; and that it was by special help of God, if nature could not of itself reach unto it. Yet it is related of a noble man of Louvain, who lay sixteen years in one posture, viz. with his face upwards; and Pradus saith, he saw a madman which had lain upon one side fifteen years. Theodoret thinks he lay bound all this time, and felt most grievous pain, that so he might represent the great miseries of Jerusalem's siege, which suffered great famine.

This opinion hath many and great authors; yet I must join with those who are for the prophet's visional lying on his side. For besides that nature could not bear it, how shall we clear the justice of God, that should for the idolatries and sins of others, which former prophets had reproved, so greatly afflict and punish one innocent.

Again, he was to prepare himself bread, ver. 15 of this chapter; he was to set his face against the mountains of Israel, chap. vi. 2; and if he lay still all these days on his sides, how could either of these be done? It is also said in the 8th chapter, ver. 1, "In the sixth year, in the sixth month, in the fifth day of the month, as I sat in mine house, and the elders of Judah sat before me, that the hand of the Lord God fell there upon me." If Ezekiel did in the letter lie so many days, the time was not expired; for the prophet had his first vision in the fifth year of the captivity, the fourth month, and the fifth day, chap. i. 2; and seven days after this vision he had another, chap. iii. 15, which made it the twelfth day of that month; and on that day he was commanded to lie on his side; and if you reckon from thence, you will find not above 413, as Pradus reckons it, or 418; and then if you join the days the prophet lay on his side, they amount to 430. So it will then appear the prophet had twelve or seventeen days to lie on his side, when the text saith, "he sat before the elders." This lying therefore is to be taken visionally, not really.

2. What the lying on the left side points out unto us; and why the iniquity of Israel is laid upon that side. There is some mystery in it, and the opinions of men are different. Some make the reason of it to be the situation of Samaria, which was the head city of the ten tribes, Isa. vii. 9, and this city was on the left hand of Jerusalem, Ezek. xvi. 46; and thereupon the prophet lay on his left side, to represent them and their sins, and on his right to represent the house of Judah and their sins. But beyond this, there is something to be taken hold of, and it is this; the left side, or hand, notes disrespect; the right side, or hand, dignity or favour; Matt. xxv. 34, 41, the good were on the right hand, the bad on the left. By this posture of the prophet, is typed out to us the different respect of God to the house of Israel and Judah. The ten tribes were less dear to God than the other; they had grievous sins, and God would show them less mercy, deal with them as those at his left side. But for Judah, whose sins were as great as theirs, yet God would chastise with less severity; he would not take away his lovingkindness from Judah, though he did from Israel;

Judah was at his right side, and God would in his distribution of sorrow and wrath remember mercy.

3. Whom we are to understand here by the house of Israel. The ten tribes, which are usually so called in the Scripture, were carried into captivity 130 years before by Shalmaneser, in the sixth year of Hezekiah, 2 Kings xviii. 9, 10. To what end, therefore, should they be brought in here, under a typical siege of Jerusalem, when they sinned not at Jerusalem; and if they had, were now gone, and under the severity of God?

Some take "the house of Israel" to be meant distinctly of the ten tribes; and this lying of the prophet on his left side not to refer to Jerusalem's siege, but to the sins of the tribes, and the patience of God towards them. Others include the house of Israel in the house of Judah, and so make not the prophet's literal lying to look at the ten tribes in captivity, but at those of them who were joined to the house of Judah. For when the great rent was by Jeroboam, all of the ten tribes did not cleave to him; and many that at first did, afterwards seeing the evil of his idolatrous ways, withdrew from him, and closed with the house of Judah; 2 Chron. xi. 16, 17, when they saw what Jeroboam intended those that "set their hearts to seek God came to Jerusalem to sacrifice, and strengthened the kingdom of Judah." And in Asa's days, many fell to him out of Ephraim, Manasseh, and Simeon, 2 Chron. xv. 9; yea, in abundance: Asa being a good king, they came flocking to him, and willingly sat down under his shade. It is more than probable also, that when Shalmaneser came out against Samaria, and carried away the tribes, that many fled to Jerusalem, and the parts there about; for it is said in 2 Chron. xxx. 6, "That they escaped out of the hand of the kings of Assyria;" and in the 11th verse, that divers of "Asher, Manasseh, and Zebulun humbled themselves, and came to Jerusalem;" this was to receive the passover, and then they returned to their possessions in their own cities, chap. xxxi. 1. So that there were some of the other tribes left, which did partly mingle with them of Judah and Benjamin, and partly dwell by themselves; these, I conceive, our prophet means by "the house of Israel," and together with these their predecessors, which were dead, and in captivity; and that because the three hundred and ninety days, which import so many years, as it is expressed in the 6th verse of this chapter, must needs fetch the house of Israel into this consideration from before the time of their captivity; and that is the next thing we are to examine, namely, where these three hundred and ninety days, typing out so many years, begin.

Various and intricate are the thoughts of men about the beginning and ending of these years; and it would take up much time to present them unto you, and perplex your thoughts much.

I will give you on this point, not what myself, but the soundest interpreters and chronologers, do judge the truth.

Funccius and Bibliander, two famous chronologers, begin this account at the falling off of the ten tribes, 1 Kings xii.; and so do interpreters of much worth.

Lavater, Polanus, Pradus, A Lapide, and Sanctius, begin it at the beginning of the Jewish monarchy, between Rehoboam and Jeroboam; then were the calves set up at Dan and Bethel, and the ten tribes became idolatrous, and not only Jeroboam and his subjects, but Rehoboam and his likewise, forsook the Lord, 2 Chron. xii. 1.

From this time to the destruction of Jerusalem, were three hundred and ninety years; which will thus appear:

Rehoboam reigned well	3	years	2 Chr. xi. 17.
After his rent	13		2 Chr. xii. 12.
Abijah his son,	3		2 Chr. xiii. 1.
Asa	41		1 Kin. xv. 10.
Jehoshaphat	25		1 Kin. xxii. 42.
Jehoram	8		2 Chr. xxi. 5.
Ahaziah	1		2 Chr. xxii. 2.
Athaliah	7		2 Kin. xi. 4.
Jehoash	40		2 Kin. xii. 1.
Amaziah	29		2 Kin. xiv. 2.
Azariah	52		2 Kin. xv. 2.
Jotham	16		2 Kin. xv. 33.
Ahaz	16		2 Kin. xvi. 2.
Hezekiah	29		2 Kin. xviii. 2.
Manasseh	55		2 Kin. xxi. 1.
Amon	2		2 Kin. xxi. 19.
Josiah	31		2 Kin. xxii. 1.
Jehoahaz	3	months	2 Kin. xxiii. 31.
Jehoiakim	11		2 Kin. xxiii. 36.
Jehoiachin	3	months	2 Kin. xxiv. 8.
Zedekiah	11		2 Kin. xxiv. 18.

These summed, being added together, make up 390 years. Junius begins this account at the 27th year of Solomon's reign, when he and the people fell to idolatry, and extends it to the 5th year after Zedekiah's captivity; but according to the account formerly given, this amounts to a greater sum; besides, Solomon did not by any public edict set up idolatry, nor abolish the true worship of God.

The next thing to be opened, is the forty days, referring to the house of Judah, in the 6th verse; and here it is questioned whether these years are to be taken inclusively in the three hundred and ninety, or exclusively and distinct from them. Some comprehend them in the three hundred and ninety days, because otherwise they would not be finished before the vision in the 8th chapter, ver. 1, as hath formerly been showed; but the prophet's lying on his sides, being visional, not real, it makes not against a distinct exception of these forty years from the three hundred and ninety; for he might in a vision see that he must bear the iniquity of the house of Israel three hundred and ninety days, and the iniquity of the house of Judah forty days, and this vision be over long before either number of days were accomplished. Neither is that in the 9th verse sufficient to prove these forty years are to be taken inclusively from the words, "three hundred and ninety days shalt thou eat thereof." Some collect that the prophet was to lie no longer on his sides than he was to eat of the meat prepared; if it had been said in the verse, Make thee bread according to the number of the days that thou shalt lie upon thy sides, this argument had been strong; but it is, "according to the number of the days that thou shalt lie upon thy side," that was his left side, and so the argument is invalid. I conceive the forty years to be taken distinct from the other number, because in the 5th verse you have the three hundred and ninety laid upon the prophet to bear for the house of Israel; if forty be excepted out of them, then there remains three hundred and fifty; and it could not be said, "So shalt thou bear the iniquity of the house of Israel;" neither could it be said, "When thou hast accomplished them, lie again on thy right side;" he could not reach that number if forty years were cut off: and here is also a distinct command, "Lie again on thy right side," that is, after those three hundred and ninety be finished, then turn thee to the other side, and lie on it forty days. These forty days for so many years, are not additional to the three hundred and ninety, but he is to begin again; and that forty years within the three hundred and ninety, yet not as part of them, or included in them, but as a new account, a day for a year, to represent God's patience toward the house of Judah.

These forty years some make to be the tyrannical, bloody, and idolatrous reign of Manasseh, 2 Chron. xxxiii.; who having forty years opposed Judah, was carried into captivity, and after ten years' suffering returned, purged out idolatry, and for fifteen years served the Lord: these forty provoking years God bare with Judah. Others begin the time of these forty years from the thirteenth of Josiah unto the end of Zedekiah, the space between these is forty years; God now looked for a reformation, but they became worse and worse, as by 2 Chron. xxxvi. 16 doth evidently appear. Whether we pitch these forty years upon Manasseh's ill reign, or the time after, is not much material; so many years did the Lord bear with Judah in a special manner; only take notice, that some reckon these forty years not from the thirteenth of Josiah, but from the eighteenth, wherein was the covenant renewed between God and the people, and then they reckon five years after the captivity of Zedekiah, to make up the forty years, for it is the opinion of learned men, that it was five years after his carrying away, that Nebuzaradan came and burnt both temple and city.

Some make the three hundred and ninety days not only to set out God's patience, but to demonstrate the time of Jerusalem's siege, and God's just hand in it; which, upon due observation, will be found to be just so many days, although there be a great difficulty to make it evident. For in Jer. lii. 4, 5, 6, you may read that in the ninth year of Zedekiah's reign, the tenth month, and tenth day, Nebuchadnezzar besieged Jerusalem, and that his siege lasted to the eleventh year of Zedekiah, the fourth month, and ninth day. Now the time between comes up towards eighteen months, and makes five hundred
Sanctius saith, 550. thirty and nine days, which sum contains a hundred forty and nine days more than our prophet's three hundred and ninety, which make but thirteen months precisely, thirty days the month: so that here are five months more in this siege, according to Jeremiah, than we have in this type of Ezekiel. To clear this difficulty we must take notice, that in time of this siege Pharaoh king of Egypt came to help Zedekiah, and raised the siege: Jer. xxxvii. 5, "Then Pharaoh's army was come forth out of Egypt: and when the Chaldeans that besieged Jerusalem heard tidings of them, they departed from Jerusalem:" and so, ver. 11, it is thought they brake up the siege to go and meet Pharaoh's army, which being discomfited, turned back to Egypt, and the Chaldeans to Jerusalem, ver, 7, 8. Five months were spent this way, which Jeremiah reckons in to the siege of Jerusalem. These our prophet leaves out, and looks precisely at the time they were about Jerusalem, which was three hundred and ninety days, or thirteen months. And so you have this difficulty resolved.

Ver. 7. "Set thy face toward the siege of Jerusalem." That is, strengthen, harden thy face against them, be inexorable. And this notes out the obstinacy of the Chaldeans that should besiege them; they were a resolute people, and would not be wearied out with difficulties, or easily hearken to entreaties; herein the prophet takes on him the person of the enemy, and shows he should be stern against them.

"Thine arm shall be uncovered." Soldiers of old were wont to have their arms naked in fight; the pictures of the ancient warriors and worthies are so
Gellius, l. 7. c. 12. painted; and P. Africanus upbraided Sulpicius Galbus, *quod tunicis uteretur manicatis uti fœminæ*, because he made use of robes with sleeves after the fashion of women; and some interpreters say, that the Indians and Africans do it to this day, they fight with their arms naked. Here it shows the readiness and diligence of the Chaldeans, whom our prophet doth personate, to execute their resolution, and shortly to fight against Jerusalem. They would not come with faint hearts, or feeble hands; but as their faces were set against the city, so their arms were naked and prepared against it; not in their bosoms, in their pockets; not folded up, but naked and stretched out, ready to do service: and so the Vulgate reads the word *extentum*, not uncovered, but stretched out, which implies the uncovering, and more. A like phrase to this you have in Isa. lii. 10, "The Lord hath made bare his holy arm:" as servants strip up their sleeves, make their arms bare, and ready for service; so the Lord made bare his arms, and put forth his power to do some choice service for his people. In this manner was the prophet to prophesy unto the people.

Ver. 8. "I will lay bands upon thee, and thou shalt not turn from one side to another," &c. Some make the bands real, and take the words in a literal sense; but we are to look at all herein as visional. And here is commended the cause of the Chaldeans' obstinacy and resoluteness in this siege and ruin of Jerusalem, and that is, the authority and command of God. He commanded the prophet to lay siege to Jerusalem, to lie on his side till he had ended the days of his siege; and by the band of his power he held him so to it in the vision, that he could not do otherwise; and this typed out the authority and power of God in the king of Babylon towards his soldiers, who should hold them so to the siege of Jerusalem, that they should not depart till they had accomplished it. Their going away to meet the Egyptian army, and drive that back, was in order to the siege of Jerusalem; and these military forces were as bands upon Jerusalem, whose condition the prophet here sustained, and when the Chaldeans compassed the city about, they could not turn aside any way till the firm decree of the Lord was accomplished.

Obs. 1. That God bears with the sins of his people, though great, a long time, and forbears the punishment due to them. Three hundred and ninety years did he suffer them, which marvellously commends to us the patience of God. They provoked him daily, most bitterly, and did evil as they could, Hos. xii. 1, 14; Jer. iii. 5; yet God held his peace and his hands for hundreds of years; and therefore saith, in Isa. xlii. 14, "I have long time holden my peace; I have been still, and refrained myself." If God had not power in him to punish, his suffering with sinners so long were not so much; but God hath power enough to be avenged on all the sinners of the earth; he could crush them as a moth in his hand, every moment; he hates sin with a perfect hatred, and yet he bears with notorious sinners, with all sinners and sins, deferring the punishment of them sometimes a long season; so that he is not only patient, but long-suffering: 1 Pet. iii. 20, "The long-suffering of God waited in the days of Noah, while the ark was a preparing." What did it wait for? even their repentance. Noah preached unto them of the flood, warned them by preparing of an ark, and God expected they should amend and turn to him; and it was a hundred years at least he waited upon that generation; and now, "the Lord is long-suffering to us-ward, not willing that any should perish, but that all should come to repentance," 2 Pet. iii. 9. If we will not repent of our sin, God will repent of his long-suffering; his wrath will kindle, and we shall perish, be inexcusable, and have the deeper condemnation for abuse of his long-suffering.

Obs. 2. Though the Lord bear long with sinners, yet he forgets not their sins; they are in his book, sealed up in his bag, Job xiv. 17, among his treasures, Deut. xxxii. 34. It is a speech borrowed from men that count up their money, look over their writings, and put them into bags, and seal them up, that they may be safe, and reserved for a long time: so God keeps men's sins safe by him, and that a long season, and then at length, when they have forgot them, he unseals the bag, and brings them forth, and shows them how their sins have abounded, what a treasury of sin they have, and what a treasury of wrath he hath, Rom. ii. 5. God remembered the defection of Israel, which was almost three hundred and ninety years before; and however men think of their sins past, God will rub their memories, revive their consciences, and indict them for old sins: Job xiii. 26, "Thou makest me to possess the iniquities of my youth." Job xx. 11, "His bones are full of the sin of his youth." Psal. xxv. 7, "Remember not the sins of my youth." God presented before them their youthful sins that had been committed many years before. 2 Sam. xxi. 1, Saul was dead, but his sin was alive; there was a triennial famine, and for whose sake was it? "for Saul's, and his bloody house, because he slew the Gibeonites," which was done many years before; but here God remembers the sin, and visits it upon the heads of his sons; seven of them suffer for that sin. Nah. 1, 2, "The Lord reserveth wrath;" he doth not presently punish sinners, but twenty, thirty, forty years after he reckons with them, and pours out the wrath reserved: when he hath had the glory of his patience, then God visits for old sins. Isa. xlii. 4, God had been silent a long time; "Now will I cry like a travailing woman; I will destroy and devour at once:" patience being ended, God's wrath begins, and revives the guilt and sin that hath lain asleep so long. Joseph's brethren being in affliction, their sins came to mind, Gen. xlii. 21, "We are verily guilty concerning our brother:" they had sold him long before, above twenty years, and thought they should never hear of him, or their sins in the sale of him; but now in a strait God brings that sin to memory: sin is not over when it is acted, but may be heard of many years after. It is likely now in these afflictive times, that many meet with their old sins, and they lie hard upon them; let that be the prayer of such, which you find, Psal. lxxix. 8, "O remember not against us former iniquities: let thy tender mercies speedily prevent us, for we are brought very low." And take heed of sinning for the future against God; for be "sure your sin will find you out," Numb. xxxii. 23, and be thorns, not in your flesh, but in your consciences; old sins will be old serpents, sting unto death: Isa. x. 3, "What will ye do in the day of visitation?" Ezek. xxii. 14, "Can thine heart endure, or can thine hands be strong, in the days that I shall deal with thee?"

Obs. 3. Such is the nature of states and churches, that falling into sinful ways, they seldom return, but proceed, adding sin to sin, filling up the measure of their iniquities. Jeroboam makes a rent, lays a foundation in idolatrous practices, and the house of Israel continue in that way three hundred and ninety years, not one king of Israel right. Solomon goes out by the enticing of his wives to false worship, he corrupts Judah, leavens it with idolatry, and not all the good kings in Judah could get out that leaven again perfectly; if there were a stop of idolatrous passages made in one king's reign, there was liberty granted in another's. Idolatry and other sins so abounded in Ahaz's, Manasseh's, and Zedekiah's days, that the Lord was weary of them, and not quiet till he had rejected them. And this is not only so in states and churches, but also in particular cases; if men fall into any way of wickedness, so corrupt is nature, so prone unto sin, that it persists unto its own perdition, rather than returns to its own salvation: it must be a merciful and powerful hand of God that reduceth a straying sinner, much more a straying state.

Obs. 4. That length of time is no good plea for errors, false worship, sinful customs and practices. They could plead hundreds of years for their high places, calves, Samaritan rites, altars, priests, &c. yet antiquity would not exempt them from guilt and punishment. He "must bear the iniquity of the house of Israel;" they had sinned in the erection, use, and retention of these, and God had visited, and would yet visit more for them. What if we have had prelacy and popery, ceremonies and superstitious rites among us hundreds of years? they are plants not of God's planting, and through age so rotten, that they need plucking up, and it will be his honour whose shoulder and strength is employed that way.

Obs. 5. The Lord shows more favour to his people, sinning great sins, than he doth to others that are not his. The house of Israel hath the left side, is *Lo-ammi*, none of God's people, and therefore utterly rejected, sent into captivity, and return not; the house of Judah hath the right side, God would show them favour in their captivity, and return them after seventy years' correction in Babylon. God's carriage towards his servants is different from that towards others: Psal. lxxxix. 30—33, "If his children forsake my law, and walk not in my judgments; if they break my statutes, and keep not my commandments; then will I visit their transgression with the rod, and their iniquity with stripes. Nevertheless my loving-kindness will I not utterly take from him." Here God took not away loving-kindness utterly from Judah, sending her into captivity, but it was utterly taken from Israel; if the one be whipped with rods, the other is whipped with scorpions. Saul sins in offering sacrifice, 1 Sam. xiii. in sparing Agag, 1 Sam. xv. David sins in the defilement of Bathsheba, in the murdering of Uriah, 2 Sam. xi. in numbering of the people, 2 Sam. xxiv. Solomon sins in hearkening to his wives, in falling to idolatry. Yet God dealt not with David or Solomon, whose sins were greater than Saul's, as he did with Saul: Thy kingdom shall not continue, saith Samuel, and the Lord hath rejected thee from being king: and it repented God that he had set up Saul to be king, 1 Sam. xv. 11, and he dealt severely with him, he would not answer him in his straits, but cut him off by the Philistines' and his own sword. So that he and his were broken in pieces, and rooted out by the wrath of God; but David and Solomon were chastised with the rods of men, 2 Sam. vii. 14: and see what followeth in the next verse, "My mercy shall not depart away from him," (meaning Solomon, when he committed iniquity,) "as I took it from Saul, whom I put away before thee." God proceeds otherwise with wicked men than he doth with his children; there is much love in all their afflictions, and mere wrath in all the wicked's sufferings. Peter's sin in denying Christ was greater than Ananias's and Sapphira's in denying a portion of their goods, and almost parallel with Judah's; yet he hath a gracious aspect from Christ, fetching penitent tears from his heart, when the others are smitten with strokes of death.

Obs. 6. The instruments God uses in the execution

of his judgments shall be resolute, ready, and active. "Set thy face toward the siege, and thine arm shall be uncovered, and thou shalt prophesy." The Chaldeans were resolute upon the siege, came fitted every way to it, and were active in the work: Hab. i. 8—10, "They shall fly as the eagle that hasteth to eat;—they shall gather the captivity as the sand;—they shall deride every strong-hold, for they shall heap dust and take it." When God will have any notable work done, he raiseth up instruments for it.

Obs. 7. God's power and providence overrules secondary agents so, that they shall execute his pleasure, and not disappoint it. God laid bands upon the prophet, and he could turn no way till he had accomplished the days of the siege; and when the king of Babylon and his forces were come to the work, God held them to it, and executed his judgments by them. Pilate would have quit his hands of Christ's death, but he was to be an instrument, together with Judas and others, and they did what the hand and counsel of God determined to be done, Acts iv. 28. Moses would have declined the work of bringing out the Israelites from Egypt, and bringing in of judgments upon the Egyptians, but God ordered and overruled his spirit.

Ver. 9—17. *Take thou also unto thee wheat, and barley, and beans, and lentiles, and millet, and fitches, and put them in one vessel, and make thee bread thereof, according to the number of the days that thou shalt lie upon thy side, three hundred and ninety days shalt thou eat thereof. And thy meat which thou shalt eat shall be by weight, twenty shekels a day: from time to time shalt thou eat it. Thou shalt drink also water by measure, the sixth part of an hin: from time to time shalt thou drink. And thou shalt eat it as barley cakes, and thou shalt bake it with dung that cometh out of man, in their sight. And the Lord said, Even thus shall the children of Israel eat their defiled bread among the Gentiles, whither I will drive them. Then said I, Ah Lord God! behold, my soul hath not been polluted: for from my youth up even till now have I not eaten of that which dieth of itself, or is torn in pieces; neither came there abominable flesh into my mouth. Then he said unto me, Lo, I have given thee cow's dung for man's dung, and thou shalt prepare thy bread therewith. Moreover he said unto me, Son of man, behold, I will break the staff of bread in Jerusalem: and they shall eat bread by weight, and with care; and they shall drink water by measure, and with astonishment: that they may want bread and water, and be astonied one with another, and consume away for their iniquity.*

The time of Jerusalem's siege being typed out by the prophet's side-lying, he comes here to type out the grievous famine that should be in that siege; and this he doth,

1. From the coarse materials they should make their bread of, in ver. 9, "Wheat, barley, beans, lentiles, millet, and fitches."

2. From the quantity they should eat, ver. 10, 11, they must eat and drink by measure.

3. From the quality of it, ver. 12, it should be bread baked with dung, defiled bread; this was to type out the Israelites' eating polluted bread among the gentiles, where they were to be captives.

4. From the prophet's deprecation against eating polluted bread, ver. 14, "Ah Lord! my soul hath not been polluted," &c.

5. From God's answer, yielding to the prophet's request, in ver. 15, giving him "cow's dung for man's;" and then declaring his intention in ver. 16, 17, that he would "break the staff of bread," bring them to extreme want, and cause them to pine away.

Something I must open before I come to the instructions arising out of the words.

Ver. 10, "Twenty shekels a day." There were shekels of gold, 2 Chron. iii. 9, shekels of silver, 2 Kings xv. 20, shekels of brass, 1 Sam. xvii. 5, of iron also, ver. 7. Some of these shekels are yet to be found amongst antiquaries; on one side they have stamped the homer of manna, which God commanded Moses to lay up in the sanctuary, and in Samaritan letters written *Sekel Israel;* and on the other side is stamped Aaron's rod flourishing, with these words, *Jerusalem Kedoshah*, because the Scripture mentions the shekel of the sanctuary, as Exod. xxx. 13, and Numb. iii. 50. The rabbies, and many others, make a difference between shekels, and say, that of the sanctuary was holy, and of twenty gerahs; others were common, and of ten gerahs, half the weight of the other; and this opinion hath prevailed much amongst authors; but I find it by later writers opposed, and especially by Vilalpandus. It is called the shekel of the sanctuary, not because it differed from others, but for that it was kept there to be a standard and measure for all the rest, that there might not be great and small shekels at the pleasure of men, and mischief accrue that way. They hold that the shekels were all of one weight, though not of one substance; and that,

Vid. Waserum de Nummis Hebra. Pradum in Ezek. Rivet. in Exod.

Shekel is a weight, from *shakal*, to weigh, from whence our word scale, or scoal, is taken.

First, because no just reason can be given why they should differ, and so doubts be multiplied of what shekel it was meant, when mention is made of shekels and half shekels, as Exod. xxx. 13, and the third part of a shekel, Neh. x. 32.

Secondly, because the shekels that are now extant in the world, are of the same weight.

Thirdly, the Scriptures make the shekels that were in common use, the same for weight with those of the sanctuary. Observe two places, and it is evident: Ezek. xlv. 9—12, he blames princes there for violence and fraud, and exhorts them to use just weights and measures, and then mentions the shekel, which shall be twenty gerahs; this was the shekel in common use: now see Exod. xxx. 13, where he speaks of the shekel in the sanctuary, and saith there a shekel is twenty gerahs, and so the same with that in public use. A gerah weighed sixteen barleycorns, and twenty gerahs came to three hundred and twenty barleycorns, which made the weight of the shekel of the sanctuary and others. Some render the word gerah by *obolus*, for farthings; some by stivers, and was the value of two shillings, or two shillings and four pence. For the weight, which is the thing we are here chiefly to look at, a shekel was the same with the stater among the Grecians and Romans; and Eusebius calls shekels, *ϛατῆρας*, and a stater was four drachms, called *τετραδράχμον*, which was half an ounce, and so accordingly the twenty shekels' weight was ten ounces; so that the loaf or weight of bread here allowed to the prophet, day by day, was of ten ounces only. Others, that follow the opinion of the common shekel, which was the fourth part of an ounce, make the weight of his

See Lev. xxvii. 15. Numb. iii. 47.

Vide Ainsw. upon Exod. xxx. 13.

Lib. 10. ἀποδειξ-εως.

meat or bread, only five ounces, for so much do twenty shekels amount unto; and this is so little, that hardly life can be maintained by it. I incline to the former opinion, and leave it to your judgment.

Ver. 11. "The sixth part of an hin." From the bread he descends to the drink, which was no better than fair water, and not overmuch of that. A hin was a measure of liquid things, as of oil, wine, and water, and it contained twelve of those measures which are called logs, of which you read in Lev. xiv. 10, "One log of oil," which Ainsworth saith, is half a pint, the rabbies, as much as six eggs; but Pradus observes that the eggs in Palestine were greater than elsewhere, and that six of them would fill the Roman sextarius. And he clears a common error about those eggs: they are not to be taken for the eggs of fowls, which are sometimes greater, sometimes lesser; but an egg was a certain standing measure among the Jews, in the form of an egg, and the least measure they had; six of these made a log, and seventy-two an hin. So that the sixth part of an hin was two logs, that is, so much as twelve eggs would contain; for their measure of an egg was after the proportion of ordinary eggs, and came to no more then one pint, or six ounces, as some conceive; but a pint of water weighed comes to sixteen ounces, which was very little for four and twenty hours; *vires non tribuit, sed mortem tantum prohibuit*, it did not strengthen but only prevented death; bread and water was so little, that their hunger and thirst were rather increased then diminished thereby.

Maimon. in his Tract of Sacrifice, ch. 2. § 7.

Ver. 12. "Thou shalt bake it with dung that cometh out of man, in their sight." Poor people in many places use mean things for firing; some burn straw, some brakes, some turf, some thorns, some dung, but it is the dung of beasts, which being dried by the wind and sun, burns well, and supplies the necessity of the needy; but the dung of man for firing hath scarce been heard of. This he should take, and in the embers and ashes thereof bake his miscellany bread, to set out the great scarcity of fuel, both in their siege, and in their captivity. This was a very irksome business for a prophet, to gather the dung of men, to dry it, make fires with it, and prepare his diet with such unsavoury fire, and that in their sight, not privately; this did much trouble him; but especially to eat such bread: and this sets out also the great haste and hunger they should be in; they should not stay till the bread was baked in an oven, but presently hastened their dough to the fire, though never so unwholesome.

Ver. 13. "Defiled bread." Because, in Lev. xix. 19, they were forbid to sow their fields with mingled seed, it hath been conceived thence, that this was called defiled bread, because of the mixture of grain, wheat, barley, beans, &c.; but mingling of seeds neither made the ground nor the bread polluted; for he is not afterwards bid to change the seeds, but the dung; it was that made it polluted bread, the baking of it in so noisome a fire: and this set out the coarse and polluted diet they should eat, not only when they were besieged in Jerusalem, but when they should be in Babylon.

Ver. 14. "I have not eaten of that which dieth of itself, or is torn in pieces; neither came there abominable flesh in my mouth." Whosoever toucheth or eateth of these was unclean, Lev. xi. 39, 40; xxii. 8; Deut. xiv. 21; and so for their excrements, the Lord is careful they should not be defiled with them, Deut. xxiii. 10—14; Lev. v. 3; vii. 21. It doth not appear any where in Scripture, that bread prepared thus is defiled, only here in the former verse God calls it so; and the Jews had tender, delicate stomachs, which did abhor all unclean things, and therefore they used much washing, and oft washed their hands before meat. The strength of the prophet's argument lieth thus: Lord, I have never eaten any abominable polluting flesh, and how shall I now eat defiled bread? I have ever kept myself from what thy law hath forbidden, and how shall I now defile myself with that which nature itself abhors.

Ver. 15. "Cow's dung for man's dung." This was less terrible to nature. This relaxation was of advantage to the prophet, not to the people; for when the siege came, they did more horrid and unnatural things than eat bread baked in cow's or man's dung, as you may read, Lam. iv. 10.

Ver. 16. "I will break the staff of bread." The staff of bread is a metaphorical expression, borrowed from staves, used by those who are weak, sickly, and aged; by their staves they help and support themselves: such a staff is bread to the frail nature of man, and man that hath it blessed unto him, finds it as a staff to stay up his fainting spirit. This phrase imports two things:

First, the virtue and nourishment which comes by bread; and hence it is said to strengthen man's heart, Psal. civ. 15.

Secondly, the bread itself. There may be much bread, and little virtue in it; and, on the contrary, little bread and much virtue in it, as in the widow's meal and oil, 1 Kings xvii. 14. But when God will break the staff of bread, he ever takes away the one, if not the other, the plenty of bread, if not the virtue of it: Lev. xxvi. 26, "When I have broken the staff of your bread, ten women shall bake your bread in one oven, and they shall deliver you your bread again by weight: and ye shall eat, and not be satisfied." The Greek for breaking the staff of bread, renders it, afflicting with penury of bread. As breaking of bread, Acts ii. 46, notes plenty and communicating of food; so breaking the staff of bread implies want and scarcity: Psal. cv. 16, "He called for a famine upon the land, he brake the whole staff of bread," so that the land could not sustain them; and Isa. iii. 1, "The Lord of hosts doth take away from Jerusalem and from Judah the stay and the staff, the whole stay of bread, and the whole stay of water." God would take away the plenty and the virtue, he would not bless either unto them: hence it is said, "They shall eat, and not have enough," Hos. iv. 10; "not be satisfied," Mic. vi. 14. "Ye drink, but ye are not filled with drink; ye clothe you, but there is none warm," Hag. i. 6. Some would here understand by breaking the staff of bread, to be meant only a deficiency, not an insufficiency; but I conceive God would take away both their bread and the blessing of that which remained, according to that in Deut. xxviii. 17, "Cursed shall be thy basket and thy store:" God would take away both the bread and the blessing; that, the blessing being removed, they might be weakened, and the bread being removed, they might be consumed.

The word מקק ver. 17, signifies to pine away, as a man in a consumption, and not only so, but to become noisome and loathsome; and so it is used, Psal. xxxviii. 5, "My wounds stink and are corrupt." So they should not only consume, but grow loathsome and unsavoury, as it is usual with those who are almost famished.

Obs. 1. That God's judgments upon a sinful people are seldom single, but one succeeds in the neck of another. Before the prophet had been put upon a siege, and now he must express a famine, and mind them of eating polluted bread in another land. In Deut. xxviii. and Lev. xxvi. God threatens judgment after judgment, till he hath consumed them. It is long before God begins to strike, but when he once strikes, he will go on and despatch his work, and make an end of an impenitent people; and so recompense his slackness to punishment with severity and succession of judgments. Amos iv. God had judgments, which like fish-hooks should snatch them away, cleanness of teeth, droughts, blastings, pestilence, &c. Ezek. xiv. God hath sword, famine, pestilence, and noisome beasts, to send one after another, and what one leaves the other shall devour. God smote them with the sword in Ireland, and hath not the famine followed it? We are under the edge of the one, and shall be, I fear, under the teeth of the other.

Obs. 2. That a famine upon any is a distressing judgment. If God send it upon Jerusalem, they shall find it very heavy. When David was put to that hard choice, 2 Sam. xxiv. he would not have the sword or famine to come upon him or his. Curtius reports of Alexander, that warring against the Bactrians, he and his were besieged with such a famine, as they were forced to eat up their horses that carried their necessaries. When the Carthaginians besieged Saguntus in Spain, they were brought to such miseries with a famine, that they made a fire in the midst of the market-place, and first burned that they had left, and could not eat, and then cast in themselves and children, to put an end to their miseries; whence arose that speech or proverb, *Saguntina fames*, a Saguntine famine, noting extreme want. It is also related of Cambyses, son of Cyrus, that seeking to subdue the revolted Ethiopians, his army was in such a strait for victuals, that they were forced to tithe out every tenth man, and to live upon them; and that this continued so long, that Cambyses feared himself, and thereupon returned. It is known what a grievous famine was at Sanserre in France, when Charles IX. besieged it in the year 1573, and shot against it in three days' space 3500 great shot of ordnance, and killed not one by them; yet almost all the people were consumed by the famine in the siege thereof, having eaten up all things living, and the leather off trunks and saddles. In the days of Edward II. there was such a famine, as a parliament was called to moderate the prices of things. Such was the dearth, that bread could scarce be gotten to serve the king's own family. The famine grew so terrible, that horses, dogs, yea, men and children, were stolen for food, and thieves newly brought into the gaols were torn in pieces, and eaten presently half alive, by such who had been longer there. The Scripture tells us of as great famine as we can read of: the Samaritan famine was such, as that, like vultures, dogs, and swine, they fed upon carcasses and dung itself; 2 Kings vi. 25, the Assyrians besieged Samaria, until "an ass's head was sold for fourscore pieces of silver," that is, shekels, and that came to above eight pounds of our money, "and the fourth part of a kab of doves' dung for five pieces of silver;" a kab contained four pounds and five ounces, and the fourth part was thirteen ounces, and for this they gave ten shillings and upward. Some think it was the corn in the crop of the dove, which did fly abroad, and came home full; but the text is plain, it was the dung of doves, which whether they used for salt, having an acrimonious humour in it, or for food, their distress was very great. But this of Jerusalem was the sorest that ever was. They had coarse fare, the food of beasts, beans, lentiles, millet, fitches, and little of this; bread and water were measured out unto them; their bread was defiled, dressed with dung; their firing failed, having burnt up all things combustible; God's curse was upon what they had, he brake the staff of bread; no nourishment came from that they had; they went up and down distressed, and died for hunger. Read Lam. iv. 4, 5, &c. The tongues of the sucking children did cleave to the roofs of their mouth; other children asked bread, and none brake it unto them: the scarlet men of the city embraced dunghills, the beautiful Nazarites were blacker than coals, the slain with the sword were preferred before the slain with famine, the pitiful women sod their children, they were their daily meat. Thus God brought down Jerusalem, and quickly can do any. Let us acknowledge God's mercy that we are not under such a judgment; let us be humbled for abuse of his good creatures, no more pamper the flesh with them; let us not be proud of what we have, hoard up God's blessings, but communicate and distribute to the necessities of others, and use all to God's honour.

Lib. 6.

Speed's History, Lib. 9. c. 11.

A. Lapid. in loc. When Hannibal besieged Cassilinum, a mouse was sold for 200 groats. *Val. Max.* l. 7.

Deut. xxviii. 53, 55.

Obs. 3. That hunger makes coarse and loathsome things pleasant. Bread polluted will be acceptable in a famine; bread made of that which horses and swine eat, of beans, lentiles, fitches, &c. and be as barley cakes: barley of itself is a sweet grain, but being made into cakes, it was more pleasant; and such is ill diet in time of famine. Prov. xxvii. 7, "To the hungry soul every bitter thing is sweet;" the sweetest thing is bitter to the full, the bitterest is sweet unto the empty. When Esau was faint, then red pottage was worth a birthright, Gen. xxv. 32. Artaxerxes being put to flight, his provisions taken away, and he had only a few dry figs, and a little barley bread, said, Hunger is the best cook, and the best sauce. When Darius drank puddle-water, and that defiled with dead carcasses, he said, he never drank more pleasant drink. As it is with women in their longings, any thing longed for is pleasant, not other things, whatever they be; so in famine, any thing edible is longed for, and that makes it pleasant, even an ass's head, doves' dung, polluted bread, man's flesh.

Cicer. 5. Tusc.

Obs. 4. The conformity of the punishment to their sin. They had sinned in excess, and God would take away their plenty. Hos. xiii. 6, "According to their pasture, so were they filled;" they had full pastures, fed largely, exalted their hearts, and thought they should never want; they forgot God in their fulness, and he made them to remember him in a famine. Fulness of bread was the sin of Sodom, and the sin of Jerusalem also. God brake the staff of bread. They sinned in defiling themselves with idols, and offered meal and oil, honey and flour, for a sweet savour to their idols, Ezek. xvi. and now they must eat polluted bread among the gentiles; they had worshipped dunghill gods, and should shortly eat dunghill bread; they had been proud of their ornaments, and those in scarlet should embrace the dunghills. Hab. ii. 8, "Because thou hast spoiled many nations, all the remnant of the people shall spoil thee:" it is spoken of the Chaldeans. Pharaoh drowned the Israelites' children; he and his were drowned in the Red sea for it. Solomon, to please his idolatrous wives, divided the worship of God between God, himself, and idols; and God divided his kingdom between his son and his servant. Socrates tells of Severianus a bishop, that called Chrysostom a kneeless fellow, because he would not bow and crouch to good causes: one trod upon his toe, which rankled, and he was forced to cut off that leg, and the other, and so became kneeless himself. Charles IX. who had been bloody in his life, died of a bloody

Comment of Civil Wars of France.

flux; and the blood issued out of the several parts of his body, who in the bloody massacre had caused and suffered blood to be shed in the several parts of his kingdom: he used to blaspheme in his life, and died blasphemously at his death. A Romish zealot repined at the fuel burnt at the king's return from Spain, and said, There was such waste of wood, as shortly there would not be a faggot left to burn heretics: this party being at Blackfriars when the downfal was, received a mark of remembrance by a piece of wood. See Doctor Goad in his relation of that accident.

Obs. 5. The afflictions and judgments which befall God's people, are not casual, but providential. If the Jews be besieged, famished, taken, carried away into other lands, and eat polluted bread there; God's eye hath directed, his hand hath acted, and therefore he saith, Whither shall I drive them? What Nebuchadnezzar and his army did, was the work of God. So Joseph said of the dealing of his brethren in selling him into Egypt, Gen. xlv. 5, that it was God sent him thither. It is the power and providence of God that acts in all troubles, and circumstantiates them for time, place, measure.

On ver. 14, *Obs.* 1. That the saints of old were careful to walk according to the prescriptions of the law. The law forbad eating of those things which died of themselves, whatever was torn in pieces, every abominable thing; and our prophet was careful to observe such and other prescriptions. It was the saints' duty to live after the directions of the law; what God had written to them therein, they were bound to observe, and did exactly. David had respect unto all the commands of God, Psal. cxix. Moses was faithful in all the house of God.

Obs. 2. A gracious heart will deprecate that which is contrary to its sanctification. "Ah Lord, my soul hath not been polluted;" thou art the author of holiness, and I have walked holily hitherto, and now must I defile myself? ah Lord, let it not be. The words are very pathetical; he saith not *Jehovah* in the original, but *Jehovi*, which the servants of God have used in their most pathetical prayers and speeches: as Abraham, Gen. xv. 2—8. Deut. iii. 24; ix. 26, "I prayed unto the Lord," saith Moses, "and said, O Lord God, destroy not thy people and thine inheritance." Moses's spirit was exceedingly affected; and in such cases, he and others called God *Jehovi;* and so doth Ezekiel here, he was intense in deprecating defilements. So Peter, Acts x. when the sheet was let down with all beasts, fowls, and creeping things in it, and the voice said, "Rise, Peter; kill, and eat," his heart was stirred: What! shall I eat that which is common, unclean, and pollute my soul? "not so, Lord," ver. 14; *μηδαμῶς, Κύριε*, in nowise, Lord; whatever becomes of me, though I starve, I will not eat any thing that shall defile me.

Obs. 3. The godly are careful not only to abstain from great sins, but from little ones also. It was no great matter to eat bread baked with a fire made of man's dung, and that in time of necessity, but even this would not Ezekiel yield unto; there was evil in it. So Daniel would not defile himself with the portion of the king's meat, chap. i. 8; Moses would not leave a hoof in Egypt; Job made a covenant with his eyes not to look upon a maid, and therefore gave not sway to his mind to think upon one, Job xxxi. 1; thinking is less than looking, and this he would not allow himself; Joseph abhorred the act, and Job the thought of uncleanness. Paul would not be subject one hour unto false brethren, Gal. ii. 5; and he bids the Thessalonians to "abstain from all appearance of evil," not only evil, but the appearances of it. This made Paul to blame Peter for yielding to Jewish ceremonies, when they carried a face of evil, Gal. ii. 14; and to say, rather than he would offend his weak brother by eating, he would "eat no flesh while the world standeth," 1 Cor. viii. 13. The primitive christians would not throw a little frankincense into the fire, nor bow before an idol, though their lives lay at stake upon the refusal.

Obs. 4. That the saints, through darkness and doubts, do stick at that which is lawful and warrantable. God bids Ezekiel bake his bread with man's dung, and eat it; here was warrant sufficient for him; God's command makes a thing holy. Acts x. 13, "Kill, and eat," said the voice to Peter; No, saith Peter; and why? the creatures in the sheet are common and unclean; but it was replied, "What God hath cleansed, that call not thou common or unclean." How came all to be clean in the sheet, when by the judgment of the law there were creatures unclean in it? It was the command of God made all so, "Kill, and eat." Peter, without doubting or questioning, might have killed and eaten any creature there, without polluting his spirit; and so Ezekiel might have eaten such bread without defilement. God's command legitimates any thing: Abraham's sacrificing of his son, Gen. xxii. 2; Hosea's marrying a wife of whoredom, Hos. i. 2; the brother marrying with the brother's wife, Deut. xxv. 5; and carrying of the bed on the sabbath day, John v. 11. Where there is a word from Heaven for any thing, we need not fear defiling ourselves. The saints of God stuck at things when they had a word; no marvel if saints now stick at things when they have no word.

On ver. 15, Note, that God doth condescend to the weakness of his servants, and mitigates what seems grievous unto them. Man's dung was very irksome to the spirit of the prophet; the Lord dispenseth with his command, and gives him cow's dung for man's. The saints are precious in God's eye, and rather than grieve and displease them, he will oft, upon their petitioning to him, dispense with his own will; but take it up warily, when the dispensation is in things that are not prejudicial to his glory, his wisdom, his truth, or his justice, and here it was not. God suffered no way in mitigating the sentence, and giving cow's dung for man's; it rather magnified God, that he will yield to the desires of his people, when he is in a way of judgment. Joshua, when Israel had sinned, and God smote them, he falls down, he weeps, and laments, beseeches God in behalf of the people; and what saith God to him? Josh. vii. 10, "Get thee up; wherefore liest thou thus upon thy face;" I will have thee mourn no longer; I will not destroy Israel. So that in Amos vii; there is a sore judgment of grasshoppers, that eat up all the grass of the land; the prophet is grieved, and prays, "O Lord God, forgive, I beseech thee: by whom shall Jacob arise? for he is small;" and ver. 3, it is said, "The Lord repented for this," and said, "it shall not be;" and so a second time, after he yielded to the request of the prophet. This should encourage us to sue to God in these times of distress, without doubting, for a mitigation of our miseries, if not a removal; he is a God hearing prayer, a God that will mitigate his own judgment, rather than exasperate the spirits of his people. Let it also teach us a condescension one to another; let us not be rigid and stick to our wills, and think it disparagement to abate of our wills and right, and yield to others, when God, who is infinitely above us, can yield to us, and doth so daily, bearing our infirmities: remember that place, Rom. xv. 1,—3, where the strong are bid to bear the infirmities of the weak, and not to please themselves, but to please and edify their neighbour: and what is the ground of it? Christ pleased not himself, but for our sakes he bare reproach,

On ver. 16, 17, *Obs.* 1. It is in God's power to blast the comforts of this life. "Behold, I will break the staff of bread." God gives bread, drink, clothes, whatever sweetens the lives of sinful, sorry men here on earth; and when he pleases he can take them or the blessing of them from us. What are clothes if they keep not warm? What is bread if it do not nourish? it is the same as if you had none. God can break the staff of bread, so that all your comforts shall be broken comforts; and he can take away the staff of bread, so that your comforts shall be no more. Amos iv. 8, "Two or three cities wandered unto one city, to drink water; but they were not satisfied;" the waters quenched not their thirst, they were broken comforts: and Hos. iv. 10, they did eat, but had not enough, they were not filled and satisfied; the staff of bread was broken, and the comfort of it too short for them. But that is not all; sometimes there is no water, no bread left; Lam. i. 11; iv. 4, 5, there was not a little, but none. God can take away all the comforts of this life, and leave us as naked as we came into the world. Neither is it only in his power to break the staff of natural bread, but of the spiritual also: "Behold, I will send a famine, not of bread, nor a thirst for water, but of hearing the words of the Lord: and they shall wander, and shall not find it," Amos viii. 11, 12. This is the sorest famine; and such a famine is in many places. Let us take heed we provoke not God to plague us with such a famine.

Obs. 2. The end of God in his judgments, is to perplex and ruin wicked, impenitent sinners. God sends a famine, that they may eat and drink with care, with astonishment, and consume away in a loathsome manner. What a miserable sight is it to see a man pined, even to death, for want of bread! Many in time of plenty are filled with care and fear about their backs and bellies, what they shall eat, and what they shall drink, and how live the next day; how much more men in the depth of a famine! See what Isaiah saith, chap. ix. 19—21; there was a civil war to be amongst them, famine accompanying that, and the wrath of God to consume them, as fire doth fuel; and what then? "No man shall spare his brother. And he shall snatch on the right hand, and be hungry; and he shall eat on the left hand, and they shall not be satisfied: they shall eat every man the flesh of his own arm: Manasseh, Ephraim; and Ephraim, Manasseh." When they could not consume one another fast enough, they would consume themselves; eat their own arms to save life, and that eating was death.

Obs. 3. It is men's iniquities which bring such consumptive judgments upon them. "They shall consume away for their iniquity." Sin is poison, and that makes languishing; it eats up the strength of a man, wears out all his comforts, and brings him to the pit: Lev. xxvi. 39, "They shall pine away in their iniquity;" their flesh, their spirits, their hopes, their lives may leave them, but their iniquities will not.

CHAPTER V.

Ver. 1—4. *And thou, son of man, take thee a sharp knife, take thee a barber's razor, and cause it to pass upon thine head and upon thy beard: then take thee balances to weigh, and divide the hair. Thou shalt burn with fire a third part in the midst of the city, when the days of the siege are fulfilled: and thou shalt take a third part, and smite about it with a knife: and a third part thou shalt scatter in the wind; and I will draw out a sword after them. Thou shalt also take thereof a few in number, and bind them in thy skirts. Then take of them again, and cast them into the midst of the fire, and burn them in the fire; for thereof shall a fire come forth into all the house of Israel.*

THIS chapter carries on the argument of the former. Jerusalem's misery in that was presented to you under single types, a siege and famine; in this also, under a complex type, is set forth the judgments of God against Jerusalem. I call it a complex type, because it contains many judgments of God. It is generally propounded in the first verse, particularly in the three next. The matter of this type is here, and, touching it, he is commanded,

1. To take a knife or razor, and to cut off the hair of his head and beard.
2. To weigh it, being cut off; and,
3. To divide it.

Something I must open in the words; give you the sense of them, and then the observations.

"Take thee a sharp knife." In the Hebrew it is, a sword, חרב which signifies any instrument that cuts and divides, of iron or stone: in Josh. v. 2, "Make thee sharp knives;" knives of flint is the original. What knife our prophet meant is expressed, "a barber's razor," Hebrew, a razor of barbers, such as they use when they trim men; and they are very sharp, most commodious, and fit for that service. This razor here sets out the will and judiciary power of God in punishing the Jews by Nebuchadnezzar, who, in Isa. vii. 20, is called a razor; and that is sharp, strong, and fit for shaving.

This razor must pass upon the prophet's head and beard, and take away the hair of both, even close to the skin.

"Head." It types out unto us Jerusalem, which had the regions round about subject unto it, and now the chief city of Judah. God would shave the head and beard of this city off.

The citizens are resembled to hair of a man's head and beard:

1. For their multitudes; they are numberless, and Jerusalem had multitudes in it of her own, and thither was a conflux of all sorts, from most parts.

2. Hair is an ornament, 1 Pet. iii. 3; not only to women, but also to men; their hair doth become them, Cant. v. 11; and people are a great ornament to a city: a city unpeopled is a head without hair; people are the beauty and glory of a city. Solomon saith, Prov. xx. 29, grey hairs are the beauty of old men; and grey-headed counsellors are the beauty of cities. Some by the hair of the head think the wise men of the city are figured out, and by the hair of the beard, are the strong men; the beard is a token of manhood.

3. Hair is a weak thing, blown this way and that way with every wind; and so it is with the people; they are weak, inconstant things: Heb. xiii. 9, they were "carried about with divers and strange doctrines;" 2 Pet. ii. 2, "Many follow their pernicious ways." People are truly in this sense hair; they move forward and backward, every way, there is no stedfastness in them: hence they are compared to waters, in the holy writ, which are ever ebbing

and flowing; to clouds carried about of winds, Jude 12.

By the hair of the beard we may understand those in the country towns and villages that were near unto Jerusalem.

The shaving off this hair points to us three things:

(1.) Great mourning. Shaving off the hair was used in that case, Job i. 20; when all the sad accidents were reported to Job, he "rent his mantle, and shaved his head," which was a sign of great mourning. So Ezra, chap. ix. 3, when the Jews had defiled themselves with strange women, he plucked off the hair of his head and beard, and sat down astonished. See Isa. xv. 2; Jer. xlviii. 37.

(2.) Great disgrace. So when Hanun suspected the messengers David had sent unto him, he shaved off half their beards, which was a great reproach, and vindicated with the sword, 2 Sam. x. When men are without hair on their heads or faces, it is a reproach to them; hence the boys mocked the prophet, and called him "bald head," 2 Kings ii. 23.

(3.) Destruction. When hair is cut off it falls to the earth, and perisheth; and when people are cut off from God, they perish. God would separate them from Jerusalem, from his worship, from his presence, and so they should fall to the earth, be as filth, and come to nothing.

The next thing considerable, is the weighing of the hair.

Balances are an emblem of justice, and set out here the great equity of God in dispensing of his judgments; he is exact in them, even to a hair's weight; his judgments are not too light or too heavy, but have their just weight and measure.

The division of the hair follows; and that notes out the diversity of their conditions; they should not all fare alike, but the judiciary providence of God would proceed, with some in one kind, with some in another.

Ver. 2. A third part was to be burnt in the midst of the city. It may be questioned what city, he being now in Babylon: it was the city portrayed upon the tile, chap. iv. 1, which was Jerusalem. What is meant by fire is doubted. Fire in Scripture often notes out great calamities, as in Psal. lxvi. 12, "We went through fire and through water;" 1 Pet. iv. 12, "Think it not strange concerning the fiery trial:" and here some understand fire in a metaphorical sense, for famine and plague, whereby a third part of the citizens died; others take it literally, and conceive hereby is represented the burning of Jerusalem, of which you may read 2 Kings xxv. 9, and in the last of Jeremiah. And this sense Junius favours, because it was to be done at the end of the siege; when his visional siege was expired, then he was to burn the hair; and when the siege of Jerusalem was out, and it taken, then was it burnt with fire.

Another part was to be smitten with a knife; that sets out those who were to be cut off by the sword, either in the siege, or after it, as 2 Kings xxv. 4—7; and not only those in the city, but all in the regions about it.

After this, a third part was scattered into the wind; which notes their dispersion into several parts. As hair before the wind is carried some one way, some another; so were these Jews scattered, some into Moab, some into Ammon, some into Egypt; and Johanan carried divers thither, Jer. xliii.; but God threatened them with a sword, Jer. xlii. 16, and xliv. 27, and made it good when Nebuchadnezzar conquered Egypt; which is prophesied of in the 46th of Jeremiah: God drew out a sword, and sent it after them.

Ver. 3. The binding up a few in his skirts, typifies the exemption and preservation of some few from the common calamities. It is a metaphorical speech, taken from gardeners, that pick up the good fruit in their laps and skirts, and throw aside the other. This little number were the poor which Nebuzaradan left for the vine-dressers and husbandmen, over whom Gedaliah was made ruler, 2 Kings xxv. 12, 23; and those that escaped out of Egypt when the judgment fell there, Jer. xliv. 28, it is said, a small number should escape, and return to Judah.

Ver. 4. "Take of them again, and cast into the fire." Of that remnant which was preserved he must take a parcel and burn; this was to represent to the world the death of Gedaliah, who was left governor of the little number remaining in Judea. You have the story of his death, by Ishmael, in the 41st of Jeremiah, who conspired against him, and slew him and fourscore more. After this he took those who were left by Nebuzaradan that were under Gedaliah, and attempted to carry them captives into the land of Ammon; but Johanan and the captains withstood him, recovered the people, and after carried them into Egypt; and so from that treachery against Gedaliah, a fire went forth into all the house of Israel. Some refer the fire going out of this remnant preserved, to the Jews returning out of Babylon, a great part of whom were slain by Antiochus Epiphanes; some put it upon their destruction by Titus. Gallatinus extends it to Hadrian's time, who slew at one time 50,000 of them in India in the city Bitter, and so ruined the whole nation. These opinions I leave, as having less truth and suitableness to the text, than that which was first mentioned. Euseb. l. 4. Hist.

Obs. 1. That wicked men are of little worth; take a whole city of them, they are of no more account with God than a little hair of the head or beard. Hair in itself is an ornament, but when it groweth burdensome, off it goes, and is rejected as a thing of nought; so inhabitants are a glory to a city, but when they become wicked, they are a burden to it, and to God, he will cut them off, and value them no more than a little hair. Absalom cut off his hair when it was heavy, but he prized it very high, at two hundred shekels, 2 Sam. xiv. 26. God cut off the hair of the head of Jerusalem, it was very heavy, but he prized it not: wicked men, multitudes, millions of them, are not worth a hair, they are inconsiderable, worthless things; all the wicked of the world are but excrements in it, which must be cut off and thrown unto the dunghills: Psal. ix. 17, "The wicked shall be turned into hell, and all the nations that forget God." Take the best thing of the wicked, it is of small price, some farthing matter: Prov. x. 20, "The heart of the wicked is little worth;" his clothes, his ornaments, and jewels, his estate, and house, and land, may be of great worth; but himself, his very heart, is of little worth, not accounted of in heaven. But now take the meanest thing of a godly man, it is valued, regarded; "the very hairs of his head are all numbered," Matt. x. 30.

Obs. 2. It is the privilege of Christ to appoint whom and what instruments he pleases to execute his pleasure upon sinners. "Take thee a sharp knife, a razor, and cause it to pass upon thine head and beard." The prophet might not take what instrument he pleaseth, but what Christ appointeth; it was he set apart Nebuchadnezzar, Nebuzaradan, and the Chaldeans, to shave Jerusalem; and therefore the whole work is given to God: Isa. vii. 20, "The Lord shall shave with a razor that is hired by them beyond the river, by the king of Assyria, the head, and the hair of the feet: and it shall also consume the beard:" this is spoken of Sennacherib, and verified also in Nebuchadnezzar. Both these were razors in the hand of God, by which he shaved "the head," the princes and nobles, counsellors were cut off by him; "the beard," the priests and strong men; "the feet," the common people. It is the Lord appoints and sets instruments on work to afflict churches and states: Amos iii. 6, "Shall there be evil in a city, and the Lord hath not done it?" there is no razor shaving in a city, but the Lord hath set it on work there. Micah i. 12, "Evil came down from the Lord, unto the gate of Jerusalem;" it came from above, and it came to Jerusalem. Hereupon the prophet, in chap. vi. 9, said to them, "The Lord's voice crieth unto the city, and the man of wisdom shall see thy name; hear ye the rod, and who hath appointed it."

Obs. 3. When God hath been long provoked by a people, he comes with sharp and sweeping judgments amongst them; and that is set out by the razor. He had waited much upon them, they went on in their sins, but now God calls for a razor, and that should go to the quick. God would not reap them or lop them; in those cases the stubble and trunk are left; he would shave them, not leave a politic body or church state. That place in Isa. vii. 20 holds out the truth fully; he would spare neither head, beard, nor feet; every condition of people, the honourable, the mean, the lowest, should be shaven. He would not only strip them of their clothes, but shave them, and take away their native beauty; he would fill them with mourning, make them a scorn, cut off their limbs, and destroy their lives; there should be no city, no temple, no king, no priest, no sabbath, no God left them. But hath not God shaven them in Germany, in Ireland? and is he not shaving us now?

Obs. 4. That there is no standing out against God; whatever our number or strength is, his judgments are irresistible. Men here are compared to hairs, his judgment to a razor; can the softest or harshest hair withstand the razor? can any one or all the hairs of the head or beard do it? no, the razor will easily pass through all, as a scythe through grass or corn: hairs are weak things, razors sharp and strong. Pharaoh was the strength of Egypt, but God by the Red sea did shave him, and many thousands more, from off the face of the earth. The great men of the world are no more to God than hairs before the razor; he cuts off the spirit of princes, Psal. lxxvi. 12, he challengeth the briers and thorns of the earth, "Who would set them against me in battle? I would go through them, I would burn them together," Isa. xxvii. 4.

Obs. 5. The judgments and proceedings of God with sinners are not rash, but most carefully weighed. He weighs out the hair, and proportions suitable judgments unto those that were represented by it; the infinitely wise God is exact in his proceedings. Hence you have it in Scripture, that God doth weigh actions, Psal. i. 2, 3; the paths of men, Isa. xxvi. 7; their spirits, Prov. xvi. 2, he examines how they are clogged with sin and guilt. God measured the covetousness of Babylon, which was exceeding great, and he brought answerable judgments upon her; Jer. li. 13, 14, God would send caterpillars to eat up all her wealth. Let God deal with Babylon or Zion, he observes a proportion in his judgments; Jer. xlvi. 28, speaking of Jacob's seed, he tells them he will correct them in measure. The afflictions of the church seem great, and oft are great, yet never are they without measure: Psal. lxxx. 5, "Thou feedest them with the bread of tears, and givest them tears to drink in great measure."

Obs. 6. There is no escaping of God's judgments for hard-hearted sinners. Here are diversity of judgments; fire, sword, dispersion: if one did not take, then another would overtake them; if the fire did not scorch them, the sword should cut them off; if not, that they should be scattered. 1 Kings xix. 15—17, God bids Elijah anoint Hazael king of Syria, Jehu king of Israel, and Elisha prophet in his room; and tells him there should be no escaping for sinners: if they escaped Hazael's sword, they should die by Jehu's; if not by his, they should by Elisha's; not that he used the sword, but by his prayers, and by his prophecies. In Jer. i. 10, he was set over kingdoms, to root out, pull down, and to destroy: many escape the swords of princes, and are smitten by the swords of prophets. Let not sinners think to delude God; he will meet with them one way, one time or other. Amos ix. 1—3, God comes there in judgment, he stands upon the altar, and bids them smite the lintel of the door, that the posts may shake; this was spoken of Jerusalem, not of Dan and Bethel; God would not at all appear there. And what follows? God would destroy them; there would be fleeing presently. And what saith he? "He that fleeth of them shall not flee away, and he that escapeth of them shall not be delivered:" let them dig to hell, climb up to heaven, hide themselves in Carmel, in the bottom of the sea, God will follow them, find them out, and make them smart; if enemies should carry them away, and show favour to them, God will send a sword, and it shall slay them, ver. 4. See Amos ii. 13—16. Nothing will privilege; not speed, strength, courage, bow, horse, these are good, but in time of judgment they will not secure; not a great house, though of stone, Amos iii. 15; not gods of gold and silver, Isa. ii. 20, 21; not heaps of such treasure, Ezek. vii. 19, "They shall cast their silver in the streets, and their gold shall be removed: their silver and their gold shall not be able to deliver them in the day of the wrath of the Lord:" not horns of the altar, 1 Kings ii. 28, 30, 31; not prayer, Jer. xi. 14; not fasting and sacrifice, Jer. xiv. 12.

Obs. 7. That in great judgments and general destructions, God of his infinite mercy spares some few. Ezekiel must take a few and bind up in his skirts, all must not be destroyed; the fire and sword devoureth many, but the dispersion preserved some, and some few are left in Judah. God is just, and yet when he is in the way of his judgments, he forgets not mercy: a little of the hair shall be preserved, when the rest goes to the fire, sword, and wind. When all flesh had corrupted their ways, and a general flood was brought in, Noah and his family were saved: when Sodom was burnt with fire and brimstone, Lot was bound up in the skirt of God: when Athaliah slew all the seed royal, Joash was hid, and escaped that treachery, that butchery, 2 Kings xi. 1, 2. No storm sinks all ships; no plague, famine, war, eat up all particulars; God will have a number exempt: Isa. i. 9, God left them a small remnant, a few clusters after the vintage. When the cities were to be laid waste, the houses unpeopled, a great forsaking to be in the midst of the land, Isa. vi. 11, 12; in the 13th verse it is said, "but yet in it shall be a tenth:" God would spare a number, though small; he is merciful, hath tender bowels, remembers his covenant, his name; and therefore in his hottest wrath shows some mercy. This made Jeremiah say, Lam. iii. 22, "It is of the Lord's mercies that we are not consumed." He and some few more were hid from the common calamities; they met with mercy in the midst of fire and sword. This made Habakkuk pray, Hab. iii. 2, "In wrath remember mercy."

Obs. 8. That the paucity preserved in common

calamities are not all precious, truly godly. Here was hair bound up in their skirt, kept from fire, sword, destruction; yet some of that hair, of that number, must be thrown into another fire. Reprobates for the present escape as well as elect vessels; some choice ones may be cut off, and some vile ones may be kept. In the flood all were not naught that were destroyed, nor all good that were saved; there was a wicked Ham in the ark: and Lot's daughters that escaped the fire of Sodom were none of the best; that fire had not purged out their lust: and those who were set at liberty from the brick and clay of Egypt, afterward were destroyed for their unbelief, Jude 5; they were patient in their bondage, preserved in the Red sea, tempted God, murmured in the wilderness, and there were destroyed of serpents, 1 Cor. x. 9. They were murmurers, fornicators, idolaters, unbelievers, that God delivered from the tyranny of Pharaoh, and after perished by the stroke of God. In a storm cedars and oaks are smitten, when bushes and briers are spared; and yet after they are cut up and cast into the fire. Sinners may escape present wrath, but there is wrath to come, Luke iii. 7.

Obs. 9. God may take occasion, from the sin of some, to bring in judgment upon all. He must take of the remnant preserved, and throw into the fire, and out of that fire went forth fire into all the house of Israel. Shechem ravisheth Dinah; from thence the Lord took occasion to bring the sword, by Jacob's sons, upon the Shechemites, who slew their males, spoiled the city, and took their sons and daughters captives, Gen. xxxiv. David sins in numbering the people, and God sent in a plague amongst them for his sin, which slew seventy thousand of them, 2 Sam. xxiv. The people were not innocent; if so, God would not have destroyed them; they were defiled with the contagion of his sin, or under the guilt of others. God may let in a judgment into a family, city, kingdom, upon the sin of some one or few, and when it is in, it may extend to all or most in them: when one house is on fire, all the rest are in danger that are near, and ofttimes do suffer. Hanun's discourtesy to David's messengers, his sin against the law of nations, provoked God, and cost the Ammonites and Syrians dear; for God stirred up David's spirit, who warred upon them, and slew many thousands of them, 2 Sam. x.

Ver. 5, 6. *Thus saith the Lord God; This is Jerusalem: I have set it in the midst of the nations and countries that are round about her. And she hath changed my judgments into wickedness more than the nations, and my statutes more than the countries that are round about her: for they have refused my judgments and my statutes, they have not walked in them.*

In the ensuing part of the chapter is the explanation of the types, and in this explanation you have:

I. The subject, or head to be shaven, opened unto you, and that is Jerusalem, ver. 5.

II. God's dealing with Jerusalem, in the same verse.

III. The motives that made him proceed in such a judicial way, ver. 6, 7.

IV. Threatening of judgments, answerable to the types, from ver. 8, to the end.

"This is Jerusalem." It was not Jerusalem literally, but represented Jerusalem; it was a sign of the city that was to be shaven. This head to be shaven is here by the Lord's own mouth pronounced to be Jerusalem, which was not only the head city of Judah, but of the whole world. Things and persons that are eminent among others, are called the heads or chief of them: 1 Sam. xv. 21, they took the chief or head of the things which should have been destroyed; and chap. ix. 22, "He made them sit in the chiefest place:" and for persons, Deut. i. 15, "I took the chief of your tribes," that is, the heads of them; Psal. cx. 6, "the heads over many countries." And so here Jerusalem was the head and principal of all other cities, built upon mount Zion, and had the temple, the prophets, the true worship and presence of God: so Jerusalem, as the head, gave light, influence, and motion to the whole body. "The law shall go forth of Zion, and the word of the Lord from Jerusalem," Isa. ii. 3; from thence all parts of the body hath instruction and direction.

"I have set it in the midst of the nations and countries that are round about her." These words have occasioned some to think, that Jerusalem was the heart and centre of the earth, lying in the midst of it; on the south was Africa, on the north Scythia, Armenia, and Pontus, on the east Asia, and on the west Europe; and with these great parts of the world it was compassed about. Hence the Spirit of God also affirms it to be "in the midst of the earth," Psal. lxxiv. 12, and Ezek. xxxviii. 12. And infinite wisdom appeared in it, that so the sound of law and gospel might disperse the better into all parts of the world. But this opinion must not be taken in a mathematical sense, as if it were so in the midst of the earth, as that all other parts should be equidistant from it in their extremes, as the line from the centre; for so it will hardly admit of truth, some quarters of the world being of larger extent than others. "In the midst of the nations and countries" we need not to extend to the whole world, but only to those that were neighbouring thereunto; or if we will have an eye to all nations and countries of the earth, we must expound, in "the midst," among, or in, and the sense then is safe; I have set thee in, or, among, the nations, as head and chief: thus the phrase is used oft in Scripture: Psal. ci. 7, "He that worketh deceit shall not dwell within my house;" the Hebrew is, in the midst of my house: so Gen. xviii. 24, if there be fifty righteous in the midst of the city, that is, in the city; and Ezek. i. 1, "As I was among the captives;" the Hebrew word is, in the midst of them: so that it frequently signifies, in, or, among. And so in this verse we may take it; or thus, Thou hast chief nations and cities about thee, very rich and noble, as Asia Minor, Egypt, Babylon, &c.; and I have set thee chief in the midst of these chief ones, thy prerogatives exceed theirs, and whatever they can pretend unto, thou canst pretend to more; are they fruitful, rich, honourable, populous, strong? thou goest beyond them even in all these: I have set thee in the midst of them, that they may all behold thy beauty and excellences. Heathens called this city famous, and chief of the eastern cities, well fortified, &c. The psalmist sets it out best, Psal. xlviii. and lxxxvii. where are many eulogies of it; as, "The city of our God," "The mountain of his holiness," "The joy of the whole earth," "The city of the great King," that kings saw and marvelled at; "Founded in the mountains," "Loved of God in a special manner," "Glorious things were spoken thereof;" and that which is above the rest, "God was known in her palaces," not in the palaces of other cities, and "known for a refuge." Jerusalem was exalted and privileged above all cities and nations, and set on a high hill, that so the truth and worship of the true God might have been held forth to all round about her: but Jerusalem was ungrateful; she honoured not that God who had so honoured her;

and therefore, being "set in the midst of the nations," is brought in here, not for Jerusalem's praise, but for a reproach and aggravation of her ingratitude.

This ingratitude is illustrated in the 6th verse two ways:

1. God gave them his judgments, and they changed them into wickedness.

2. They did it more than the nations and countries about them.

"Changed." The word is from מור and it is feminine, noting Jerusalem's act, which had caused God's judgments to be changed; she made a great and thorough change. The word signifies to exchange one thing for another, and to do it thoroughly: Jer. ii. 11, "My people have changed their glory for that which doth not profit." A great change they had made, in exchanging glory for unprofitables.

"My judgments." The word משפט notes commands, precepts, laws, rules, ways of God and his worship. These had Jerusalem changed, especially the rites and ordinances of his worship. So the word is taken, Psal. lxxxi. 5; the blowing of the trumpet in the new moon was a *mishphat*, a rite, an ordinance due to the God of Jacob.

The word statutes is much of the same nature, noting rules, decrees, and ordinances about the worship of God. See Ainsworth on Psal. ii. 7, and Leigh, in his Critica Sacra, of the word חק It is mentioned in the 119th Psalm twenty-two times, and notes the constancy of divine decrees and laws; and therefore is applied to the heavens and waters, which keep their place and course unchangeably, Psal. cxlviii. 6.

"Into wickedness." This is a high expression, I think not in the whole Scripture again: Ezek. vii. 11, "Violence is risen up into a rod of wickedness." It is far short of this you have in Rom. i. 23, 25, expressions suitable to this; they changed the glory of the incorruptible God into an image, and the truth of God into a lie. And so in Jude, "The grace of our God into wantonness," ver. 4. And Jerusalem changed God's judgments, which are his glory, his truth, his grace, into wickedness; the inventions, superstitions, ceremonies, laws, worship, idols of the gentiles, were taken in, set up, countenanced, and God's judgments, statutes, and worship, thrust out, laid aside.

This they did more than the nations and countries round about them; they dealt worse with God than heathens; and wherein was that? in the refusal of him and his ways: for, "they have refused my judgments and my statutes." The Hebrew word to refuse notes not a bare refusal, but a rejecting, and that with disdain; Hos. iv. 6, they rejected knowledge, and loathed the means of grace; they dealt with God's ordinances and worship contumeliously: Prov. iii. 11, the word is expressed by despising; they made no account of God's statutes and judgments, and so despised and rejected them; they did neither for their worship nor their lives regard his will. Jerusalem having God's statutes, should have so prized them, stuck to and practised them, that thereby she might have drawn the gentiles round about her to the knowledge and worship of the true God, but she sinned more than the gentiles, and justified them in their wickedness. They sinned not out of ignorance and weakness, but wilfully, maliciously.

Obs. 1. That the Lord gives to the sign the name of the thing signified. "This is Jerusalem:" it was only a sign, and not Jerusalem itself; yet God was pleased to call it so; and the Scripture doth frequently speak in that manner. Gen. xli. 26, "The seven good kine are seven years, and the seven good ears are seven years;" they were not the years, though so called, but signs of years: 1 Cor. x. 4, "That Rock was Christ," a sign of Christ, not Christ himself; and chap. xi. 24, "This is my body," not his flesh and blood, as papists would have it, but a sign of it.

Obs. 2. It is an honour for cities to be the head and chief of the regions where they are, especially where the covenant, truth, and church of God is in them. Jerusalem was the head, and God had made good his promise in Deut. xxviii. 13, "The Lord shall make thee the head and not the tail; and thou shalt be above only, and thou shalt not be beneath, if that thou hearken unto the commandments of the Lord thy God." The way for cities to be honourable, only above, and always above, is to hearken unto God, to cleave close to his ways, to exalt him in his worship; but if they will go aside from his word and worship, God will shave them, their honour shall quickly be laid in the dust, they shall be made the tail instead of the head: ver. 43, "The stranger that is within thee shall get up above thee very high; and thou shalt come down very low;" and ver. 44, "He shall be the head, and thou shalt be the tail:" and this you may see fulfilled, Lam. i. 5, "Her adversaries are the chief." The Babylonians had shaved Jerusalem, and brought her low, which made Jeremiah say, "How doth the city sit solitary, that was full of people! how is she become as a widow! she that was great among the nations, and princess among the provinces, how is she become tributary!" ver. 1.

Obs. 3. The Lord sets his church and people among the wicked, and that for special ends. "I have set thee in the midst of the nations;" and God had peculiar ends in it. The nations and country about were full of ignorance, idolatry, and profaneness; God recorded his name at Jerusalem, set his worship there, and them in the midst of the nations, that they might make known the true God, the true religion, the true way of worship; that they might by their holy lives win those that were without, bring them in to serve the God of Israel. And had the Jews been conscientious of their ways, faithful and spiritual in their worship, they might have prevailed much with the nations to have turned from their idols, and other sins, to the living God; at least have convinced them of the evil of their own ways, and the excellency of God's ways. Therefore Moses used this argument to persuade the Jews to keep God's statutes; Deut. iv. 6, "Keep therefore and do them," saith he, "for this is your wisdom and your understanding in the sight of the nations, which shall hear all these statutes, and say, Surely this great nation is a wise and understanding people." Examples of cities and nations are convincing and persuasive orators, if they be godly; beacons on a hill, whose light extends far. Great cities have influence into all the counties and countries round about. They came from all places to Jerusalem, from Sheba, 1 Kings x. 1; from Æthiopia, Acts viii. 27; from Parthia, Mesopotamia, Libya, Rome, and many other parts, Acts ii. 9, 10; and what they saw and heard at Jerusalem, that fastened upon them. What is done in great cities is much observed, and goes forth to the ends of the earth; Rev. xvii. 5, "Babylon, the mother of harlots, and abominations of the earth."

Obs. 4. Ingratitude is a sin that provokes Heaven itself; it caused God the giver to upbraid Jerusalem the receiver. "I set thee in the midst of the nations;" I made thee the head, put honour upon thee, called thee my city, was thy defence, glory, strength; I gave thee my judgments and statutes; and what hast thou done? Corrupted thyself, corrupted the nation; changed my judgments into wickedness, and rejected them. This troubled the Lord greatly in all ages: Deut. xxxii. 6, "Do ye thus requite the Lord, O foolish people and unwise? is not he thy father that hath bought thee? hath he not made thee?" &c. And notwithstanding all that God had done for them, and was to them, yet they corrupted, bespotted themselves, dealt perversely and crookedly with God: so Isa. i. 2, "Hear, O heavens, and give ear, O earth: I have brought up children, and they have rebelled against me;" oxen and asses were more respective of their owners, than they were of their God, and therefore God upbraids them with it. God had done much for that people; his law, prophets, temple, worship, miracles, choicest blessings of heaven and earth, were for them, and yet they were ungrateful; therefore God calls heaven and earth to witness against them how unreasonable they were in their carriage towards the Lord. So in Jer. ii. 12, he puts it higher, "Be astonished, O ye heavens, at this, be horribly afraid, very desolate." And why should there be such a change in the heavens? because God's people had made a dreadful change on earth. God had been a fountain of living waters unto them, filled them with comforts of all sorts, made them green and flourishing, and now they had forsaken him for puddle and broken cisterns of their own. Ingratitude troubles heaven and earth. Bernard saith, man's ingratitude troubled Christ more than his cross, nails, whippings, reproaches, yea, his death; for Christ to become man, to suffer all for man, and he to be unthankful, this pierced him to the heart most. And when God doth much for kingdoms and cities, and they prove ungrateful, it puts God into an upbraiding way: Isa. v. 4, I did so and so for my vineyard, oh, "what could have been done more?—I will take away the hedge thereof, and it shall be eaten up," trod down, laid waste; it shall have briers, and no rain shall fall upon it.

Obs. 5. Those who have the name and face of God's people may become worse than heathens. Jerusalem changed God's statutes into wickedness, that was ill; but she did it more than the nations, which was exceeding ill. Hence you find, Ezek. xvi. 46—48, that the sins of Jerusalem exceeded the Samaritans' and Sodomites', "Thou hast not walked after their ways, nor done after their abominations: but, as if that were a very little thing, thou wast corrupted more than they in all thy ways:" their sins were inconsiderable to Jerusalem's. And because Sodom's sins being so great, notorious, as that they fetched fire from heaven, and God could not forbear them any longer, it would hardly be received that Jerusalem's sins were worse than Sodom's; the Lord swears to it: "As I live, saith the Lord God, Sodom and her daughters have not done as thou and thy daughters have done." The nations and countries about never sinned so desperately against God, as those who professed his name, and went for his people; and you have the sentence of Heaven for it, Jer. ii. 10, 11, "Pass over the isles of Chittim, and see; and send unto Kedar, and consider diligently, and see if there be such a thing. Hath a nation changed their gods, which are yet no gods? but my people have changed their glory for that which doth not profit." The turpitude of their fact is fully set out; it was such as could not be paralleled among heathens. Inquiry was made, the report given in, that the gentiles changed not their gods, they would not alter their laws and worship they had from men; but the Jews parted with their glory, when they would not part with their
Hos. ix. 10. shame; they let go their religion, which was divine; and, without any just cause, changed God's judgments and statutes into wickedness, into that which neither did nor could profit; they were changelings, chopped away heaven for earth, God for idols, and his worship for men's inventions. This made the Lord say of them, Jer. iii. 5, "Behold, thou hast spoken and done evil things as thou couldest." What could they do worse, than let the infinite, glorious, wise, most holy, and blessed God, go for idols and idolatrous worship; when the heathens would not let their gods go, that were of base and corruptible materials, made by the hands and art of men, that could neither see, hear, or help them? What could Manasseh do worse than he did? 2 Kings xxi. 11.

Ver. 7, 8. *Therefore thus saith the Lord God; Because ye multiplied more than the nations that are round about you, and have not walked in my statutes, neither have kept my judgments, neither have done according to the judgments of the nations that are round about you; therefore thus saith the Lord God; Behold, I, even I, am against thee, and will execute judgments in the midst of thee in the sight of the nations.*

The 7th verse is of the nature of the 6th, and hath in it motives unto God to proceed in judgment with Jerusalem. First, they observed not the laws of God. Secondly, not the laws of the nations, but multiplied more than they. And, Thirdly, before them unto whom they should have been patterns of piety.

"Because ye multiplied more than the nations." Some expositors refer these words to their mercies, not their sins; and make the sense thus: Because thou hast multiplied in number, in riches, in honour and strength, in victory, in profits, in ordinances, in all blessings; for which ye ought to have been thankful, fruitful, and obedient unto that God who blessed you thus above the nations; but instead of this hast dishonoured God, grown loose, idolatrous, &c.; therefore will I deal accordingly with thee. Take it thus, and you have this note; That prosperity rather renders a people worse than better; they had more mercies than the nations, and more sins than they; as they abounded in God's blessings, so they abounded in ingratitude: Deut. xxxii. 15, "Jeshurun waxed fat, and kicked," &c. Hos. xiii. 6.

But others refer this multiplying to their sins; and the sense is this: Because thou hast not satisfied thyself with a little wickedness, but multiplied sins, iniquities, transgressions, and that more than the heathens, that had not thy mercies, nor thy light, therefore will I judge thee. And that they multiplied sin is evident: Ezek. xvi. 25, "Thou hast built thy high place at every head of the way, and hast opened thy feet to every one that passed by, and multiplied thy whoredoms;" she sinned with the Egyptians, Assyrians, Chaldeans, ver. 26, 28, 29.

"The judgments of the nations." The gentiles have their judgments, their laws, rules, and ways of living and worshipping. Some understand here the laws of nature, what men have written in their hearts naturally, according to what you find, Rom. ii. 14, 15; and the Jews that had the laws of God superadded to the law of nature, did not abstain from those sins the nations did; they observed the law the Jews brake.

Others refer it to their laws, decrees, and practice, touching their gods, and the worship of them; they were tenacious of both, and would not alter their worship, nor exchange their gods. It was a maxim among heathens, That no novelty should be indulged in the affairs of religion; and thus they thought it impious to depart from what they had received. When Paul came to Athens, they did and would worship their unknown God; Paul could not prevail with them to exchange a lie for a truth. Not all the miracles Moses did in Egypt prevailed with Pharaoh and the Egyptians to forsake their false gods. So that these words are a reproach to the Jews, who were not so constant as the nations to their gods.

Obs. 1. That God walks not in the way of judgments till men do walk out of the way of his statutes. Because ye have not walked in my statutes, neither have kept my judgments, therefore I will do so and so by you. God's delights are in ways and works of mercy; judgments are his strange works, and strange acts, Isa. xxviii. 21; he is provoked unto them as a bee unto stinging; it is the child's wantonness causes the father to use the rod. David's sin brought the sword to his own house, the plague to the people. When the wickedness of the earth was great, then the windows of heaven were open, and the flood came, Gen. vi.

Obs. 2. When God intends judgments, he usually convinces sinners. Judgments and convictions are not far asunder. God sets their sins before them; they walked not in his statutes, they sinned more than the nations, therefore he would proceed in judgment with them; he convinces them of their sin, to make way for a further conviction, namely, of the equity of his judgments. When the Lord shall convince a sinful people to be guilty, and that of great sins, it stops their mouths, and proclaims the equity of his judgments, which are ever short of the merit of men's iniquities; Ezra ix. 13, "Our God has punished us less than our iniquities."

Obs. 3. That heathens are oft more true to their principles than the people of God. The nations kept their judgments, their gods, their worship; they would not suffer aught to be spoken against their gods. Demetrius and others were in a rage against Paul and his companions for it, Acts xix. They were free from many of those sins which were practised and countenanced among the Jews, who kept neither to the true God, nor to his statutes and judgments. Ahaz is better pleased with an altar from Damascus, than that the Lord had appointed, 2 Kings xvi. Solomon, that excelled in wisdom, showed his folly in this, that he built high places for Chemosh and Molech. And not only a particular man, but the body of the people turned aside from the true God: Judg. ii. 12, "They forsook God, that brought them out of Egypt, and followed the gods of the people that were round about them, they bowed to them, and served Baal and Ashtaroth:" and chap. x. 6, it was an ordinary thing with them: "The children of Israel did evil again in the sight of the Lord, and served Baalim, and Ashtaroth, and the gods of Syria, the gods of Zidon, and the gods of Moab, and the gods of the Philistines;" they were not satisfied with one or two false gods, but fetched in the gods of the nations round about. Hence this people are said to go "a whoring from under their God," Hos. iv. 12; his laws, statutes, worship, government would not suffice them, but they would wander, and have strange gods, and strange laws. 2 Chron. xii. 1, "Rehoboam forsook the law of the Lord, and all Israel with him." God's law was exchanged for the laws of men. They kept the statutes of Omri, and brake the statutes of Jehovah, Mic. vi. 16. The Jews were as inconstant to their God, and in his worship, as any nation under heaven. God upbraids them for it, Jer. ii. 36, "Why gaddest thou about so much to change thy way?" God had given them a good way, a way of life, and they would not abide in it, but hasten into ways of sin and death; they loved to wander, Jer. xiv. Hath not England been weary of God's ways, wandered to Rome, and other parts, to fetch in somewhat of theirs? Have we not been upon conjunctures of protestants and papists, in doctrine, discipline, and ceremony?

Ver. 8. In the 8th verse is laid down a dreadful threatening; "Behold, I, even I, am against thee;" and the denunciation of judgment runs on to the end of the chapter, with many aggravations. Here the Lord is brought in a just and severe judge, and the chief author of all the judgments which were to come upon them; "I, even I, am," &c. It is doubled, and notes,

1. Evidence, that so they might be persuaded of it. The Jews thought that God would never be against Jerusalem; but to convince them, he tells them, "I, even I, am against thee."

2. Certainty, that whether they believed it or no, they should find it so.

3. Earnestness, to set out the intensiveness of God in this thing. He was serious and real, his heart was in it, he was not words, but weight; "I, even I," &c. that so they might be the more affected.

The Vulgate reads it, to thee, instead of "against thee;" the Hebrew bears both, and the sense abides the same: I, even I, to thee; that is, coming to thee with my judgments; I am hastening towards thee for thy ruin and destruction; and so coming to Jerusalem, is being against it. That phrase in Lev. xxvi. 24, of walking contrary to them, and punishing them, is the expository of this here; God would come to them, come against them, and destroy them; and this should be not in a private way, but in the sight of the nations. It is a sad thing to have God secretly out with one, much worse to have him an open enemy, as God professes he would be unto them all who should see his dealings with them.

"Judgments." Here it is not taken as in the 6th and 7th verses, but notes wrath, vengeance, and punishment to be inflicted upon evil-doers. It is the same word in the Hebrew that notes laws and punishments, and both are called judgments, being from the infinite wisdom, counsel, and judgment of God.

Obs. 1. That it is God who is the great agent in all judgments which befall cities and kingdoms. Nebuchadnezzar, Nebuzaradan, and many thousand fierce bloody soldiers came against Jerusalem, but God was in them, acted and ordered them; they were the rod and staff in his hand, with which he beat Jerusalem; the axe with which he hewed them; the razor wherewith he shaved them; and might have said, It is not we but your God who is against you; he hath commanded us to come forth, to plunder your country, to besiege, take, and burn your city. Though you yielded not obedience to his commands to prevent the judgment, yet we must and will, to execute the judgment appointed by him. Sufferers are apt to look at the next and second causes; not at God, but armies, plagues, famines. Whatever judgments are extant, they are in God's hand, he is the principal actor in them. 2 Chron. xii. 7, God calls the wrath his wrath, and Shishak was to pour it out upon Jerusalem: Shishak was the vial, God put in the wrath, and poured it out at his pleasure. Amos iv. 6, 10, God tells them it was he gave them cleanness of teeth, and sent the pestilence; and it is he breaks out like fire in the house of Joseph, chap. v. 6; and Isa. lxiii. 10, "He fought against them;" it was God in their enemies did it.

Obs. 2. It is a dreadful thing to have God against a city or kingdom. "Behold, I, even I, am against you;" I that have loved you so dearly, that have done so much for you, that have been a friend, a father, a husband, a deliverer, a counsellor, a God of salvation, even I am against you. The word, "Behold," imports so much; where that is prefixed, usually some great, strange, and dreadful thing follows: and so here, could a greater, stranger, or more dreadful thing befall God's people, than to have God against them?

(1.) All in God is against them; all his attributes, his wisdom, holiness, mercy, justice, patience, power, &c. working for their ruin. Jer. xviii. 11, "Behold, saith the Lord, I frame evil against you, and devise a device against you;" God's head and hand was at work against them: and so in Micah ii. 3, "Behold, against this family do I devise an evil;" it was ill with the family of Jacob, when God set his thoughts to work to devise judgments for them. The infinite, wise, and powerful God, when he is once against a people, improves his attributes for their ruin: hence you have it in the word, that God's face is against the wicked, Psal. xxxiv. 16; and set against them, Lev. xxvi. 17; and so his hand is against them, Lam. iii. 3.

(2.) All from God; as, [1.] All the creatures. When the king himself is out with any, all his officers and servants frown; also angels are against a people, when God is against them. When two states fall out they call away their ambassadors; and God calls away his angels when he is wroth with a nation; and because their Lord and Master is wronged by that nation, they take part with him against it, and stand ready to execute his judgments upon it. When Christ was injuriously dealt with, Peter drew in his Master's behalf presently; when God was against Egypt, the destroying angel was quickly felt there. Not only angels, but all inferior creatures, act answerably unto their Lord; when he moves against a people, they do it also. The stars fought against Sisera, Judg. v. 20; the waters against Pharoah, Exod. xiv. 26; the earth against Corah, Dathan, and Abiram, Numb. xvi. 32; fiery serpents stung the Israelites, Numb. xxi. 6: see Lev. xxvi. 22; Ezek. xxxiv. 28; chap. xiv. 15. Wild beasts God would send amidst them, and he did it; 2 Kings xvii. 24, 25, there were lions, and 2 Kings ii. 24, there were bears, which did devour. Herod was eaten up by worms, Pherecides with vermin. Pliny tells that in Spain they were constrained to forsake their cities, because undermined with conies; one in Thessaly, with moles; and in France many towns were left, because annoyed with frogs, locusts, mice, and wasps. God is the Lord of hosts, and can quickly muster up an army of the creatures against his enemies.

[2.] All ordinances. The word is the savour of death, 2 Cor. ii. 16; the gospel is hid to them, chap. iv. 3; prayer and fasting witness against them, Isa. lviii. 5; Zech. vii. 5; passover, circumcision, sacrifices, temple, sabbaths, new moons, &c. did them no good, but increased their woes, Isa. i. 11—15; and chap. vi. 9—11, "Hear ye indeed, but understand not; and see ye indeed, but perceive not: make the heart of this people fat, and make their ears heavy, and shut their eyes; lest they should see, hear, understand, be converted, and healed." And why thus? God was against them, he would waste their cities, and make their land desolate. God was against the Jews, his purpose was to root them out; and what did Christ's glorious gospel and treasures of it profit them? As Ahab said of Micaiah, 1 Kings xxii. 8, He prophesied no good unto us; so these proved no ways good unto them.

[3.] When God sets a people he is against, against itself, he divides them. Ephraim is against Manasseh, and Manasseh against Ephraim and both against Judah, Isa. ix. 21. When people will divide from God, God will multiply their divisions; he can and doth mingle a perverse spirit in the midst of a people he is against, Isa. xix. 14; there shall be no agreement, but in the ruin one of another, ver. 2, "I will set the Egyptians against the Egyptians; and they shall fight, brother, neighbour, city, kingdom, each against another."

[4.] All miseries, plagues, judgments, curses, break in quickly upon that people. Levit. xxvi. when God is in march against a people, he will appoint over them terrors, consumptions, burning agues, &c.; and if these do not humble them, he will have seven more judgments for them, ver. 18; and after them seven more, ver. 21; and if they prevailed not, seven more, ver. 24; and seven more after those three sevens, ver. 28: God would multiply their judgments by sevens. And they found it truth what God said, Judg. ii. 15, "Whithersoever they went out, the hand of the Lord was against them for evil, as the Lord had said: and they were greatly distressed;" they met with variety of evils on every side; and that which is worse than all these, spiritual judgments seize upon their hearts, so that either they see not evils coming to fear and prevent them, or profit not by them being come and felt; their great distresses and gracious deliverances did them no good, their hearts were still idolatrous, and "they went a whoring after other gods," ver. 17. Hos. vii. 9, strangers devoured Ephraim's strength, and he knew it not; grey hairs were here and there, and not discerned.

[5.] No refuge is left when God is against a people. Riches will not profit, Prov. xi. 4. Zeph. i. 18, "Neither their silver nor their gold shall be able to deliver them in the day of the Lord's wrath: but the whole land shall be devoured." Then may they say with David, Psal. cxlii. 4, "Refuge failed me." Will ye flee to cities and sanctuaries? Lev. xxvi. 31, "I will make your cities waste, and bring your sanctuaries unto desolation." Will ye flee to your own hearts? Ezek. xxii. 14, "Can thine heart endure, or can thine hands be strong, in the days that I shall deal with thee?" Will ye return, weep, and pray unto God? Deut. i. 45.

The evidences or discoveries of God's being against a people are these:

First, when God is against a people, they are unspirited, their hearts are despondent within them. Hos. iv. 1, God had a controversy with the land; and chap. vii. 11, "Ephraim also is like a silly dove without heart;" they call to Egypt, they go to Assyria, they had no courage, but were fearful and faint-hearted like doves. When enemies and dangers were at hand, when Jehu's letter came to Samaria, the men of the city "were exceedingly afraid, and said, Two kings were not able to stand before him: how then shall we stand?" 2 Kings x. 4. Their hearts failed them, when man was in apprehension against them; what will men's hearts do when God is against them? His being with men, puts courage and life into them; Josh. i. 9, "Be strong, and of a good courage; be not dismayed, for the Lord thy God is with thee:" and his being against them, daunts and damps all; Isa. xix. 13, when God came against Egypt, the heart of it melted, and the spirits of it failed in the midst thereof.

Second, they are not successful in their great and public undertakings. Deut. xxviii. 29, "Thou shalt not prosper in thy ways: and thou shalt be only oppressed and spoiled evermore;" God blasts their enterprises. Jehoram comes out with a great army against Abijah, he had 800,000 chosen and mighty men of valour; Abijah had only 400,000, half so many, 2 Chron. xiii. 3: and what argument did he use? ver. 12, "Behold, God himself is with us for a captain;" he is not with you, and you shall not prosper; and they did not, but fell in the battle, 500,000 of them; a strange victory, that they should slay 100,000 more than themselves were in number. God was with the one, and against the other, therefore was the success so glorious and great to Judah, and so bloody and shameful to Israel. When God is against a people, he works wonders to ruin them, there is a secret curse upon their counsel, Isa. xix. 3, "I will destroy the counsel of Egypt;" upon their goings out, and whatever they put their hands to, Deut. xxviii. 19, 20. Moses knew that it is God's presence and countenance that makes things successful; God would send an angel with him to drive out the Canaanites, and to plant them in Canaan, but that sufficed not him, he must have God go with him, Exod. xxxiii. 2, 15.

Third, he sets over them such as prove their ruin. Lev. xxvi. 17, "I will set my face against you: and they that hate you shall reign over you;" διώξονται, shall persecute you, intimating, that when God is against a people, he gives them persecuting rulers. Rehoboam whipped them with scorpions, 1 Kings xii. 14; Ahaz made Judah naked and distressed the land, 2 Chron. xxviii. 19, 20; Manasseh filled Jerusalem with innocent blood, 2 Kings xxi. 16; and made the people do worse than heathens, 2 Chron. xxxiii. 9: all the kings of Israel were naught, and many of them sore plagues unto the people, and especially Ahab, whom his wife Jezebel stirred up to do wickedly, more than any before him, 1 Kings xxi. 25. When God's face was hid from and against a people, he set such rulers over them as proved roaring lions and ranging bears, Prov. xxviii. 15. And I fear God is in controversy with the christian world at this time, because most princes in it are haters of their people, bringing them under, and tyrannizing over them. But if God will return in mercy, he will give his people favour, "and they shall rule over their oppressors," Isa. xiv. 1, 2.

Fourth, judgments awaken not, prevail not to reform, to return to God: Isa. xxvi. 11, "When thy hand is lifted up, they will not see." They saw in a general way that God was angry, but not so as to humble themselves under his mighty hand; they were rather hardened than humbled under the judgments of God: Jer. ii. 30, "In vain have I smitten your children; they received no correction;" Isa. i. 5, "Why should you be stricken any more? ye will revolt more and more." God multiplied judgments, and they multiplied revolts; God tried them with plagues, famine, wars, and bondage, but they were stiff-necked, hard-hearted, judgment-proof, and daily worse and worse, and walked contrary to God; they were stubborn, and set light by his judgments. When God is against a people, his judgments are not sanctified, they work not out the filth and mud that is in kingdoms and cities, a wrong construction is made of them.

Fifth, there is a spirit of envy and bitterness against those who are dear to God, and stand most for his ways and worship. They envied God's people, Isa. xxvi. 11; they mocked his messengers, misused his prophets, 2 Chron. xxxvi. 16. There was a malignant spirit in them in times of the gospel, when they went off from the old way of jewish worship, and were formed into gospel fellowship; there was bitterness of spirit against them: Acts viii. 1, there was a great persecution of the church which was at Jerusalem, and they were all scattered abroad, except the apostles; and quickly after, Herod laid hands upon, and killed James. Chrysostom and Theophylact tell you the reason; because he was a son of thunder, opposed the Jews, the old national way of worship, therefore he was *postulatus ad necem*, doomed to execution. The Jews petitioned Herod to do it; and the more christianity spread, and churches multiplied in Judea, the more bitter were the Jews against that way; and that was antecedent to the destruction of Jerusalem by Titus.

In Matt. xvii. A Lapid. in Act.

Sixth, he makes that people base and contemptible in the eyes of others; they lose their honour and glory; they were the head whilst God was with them, but they became the tail when he was against them.

Obs. 3. That the Lord will be known by executing of judgments. He will not smite in secret, in a corner of the land or city, but in the midst of them; and so, as his judgments should come abroad, be seen and heard of the nations. The Jews thought God like themselves, Psal. l. 21; because he was silent, they felt him not a revenger, and therefore would make him a partaker in their sins; God would vindicate himself, and execute judgment in the midst of them. The gentiles were blind, deeming judgments to be casual, but God would so deal with Jerusalem, inflict such punishment, as that they should see and say, they were not accidental, but from the God of heaven. So that here the equity and greatness of judgments are held out; they sinned, and grievously, in the midst of the nations, and are punished accordingly in the sight of the nations. This was an addition to the Jews' misery, that their enemies should be witnesses of what they suffered. Tertullian tells of Claudius Hermianus, who persecuted the christians bitterly, and the rather, because his wife was turned to that sect, as he called it; he being smitten with the just hand of God, said, Keep it secret, lest the christians rejoice.

Ad Scapul. c. 3.

Nemo sciat, ne gaudeant christiani.

Ver. 9, 10. *And I will do in thee that which I have not done, and whereunto I will not do any more the like, because of all thine abominations. Therefore the fathers shall eat the sons in the midst of thee, and the sons shall eat their fathers; and I will execute judgments in thee, and the whole remnant of thee will I scatter into all the winds.*

These verses contain further aggravations of Jerusalem's miseries: the 9th verse tells you they should be such as the world had not seen, nor should see; the 10th verse specifies some particulars.

The 9th verse extends to the time past, and to the time future, and falls into examination, whether true in either part.

First, "I will do in thee that which I have not done." Had not God dealt severely with the old world, with Sodom and Gomorrah, with the Egyptians whom he drowned? Yes, he had; but their sins being not so grievous as the Jews', their judgments were not so great. The sorest was that of Sodom, and, Lam. iv. 6, "The punishment of the iniquity of the daughter of my people is greater than the punishment of the sin of Sodom:" that was overthrown in a moment, it was a sharp but short punishment; Jerusalem had severity and length of time, therefore it is added, ver. 9, "They that be slain with the sword are better than they that be slain with hunger," their judgment is easy.

But was not the siege of Samaria as sad a judgment as this executed against Jerusalem? 2 Kings

vi. 28, 29, there the women ate their own children, and suffered great distress through famine.

Ans. The women ate their children, but it came not to that extremity, as that the fathers should eat their sons, and the sons the fathers, as here it was. And,

Secondly, that was not taken as Jerusalem was, and burned, many put to the sword, many carried into captivity.

This part of the verse you see cleared; that which respects the time to come is more difficult: "I will not do any more the like." Did God do his utmost now? did he not do as much or more against Jerusalem and its inhabitants, for putting Christ to death? When Titus besieged Jerusalem, did they not eat their children, one another, die with famine? did not the plague and sword destroy? ran not their blood down the streets, out at the gates, and affected their very enemies? came not the wrath of God upon them to the utmost? 1 Thess. ii. 16; and said not the Lord Christ, Matt. xxiv. 21, that there should be at that time such "tribulation as was not from the beginning of the world, nor ever should be?" how then is it truth in our prophet, that God saith, "I will not do any more the like?"

1. The Hebrew word עוד no more, doth not always signify perpetuity, but some time, a long tract of time, or a considerable space. 2 Kings vi. 23, the heads of Syria came no more into the land of Israel; that was, for a certain time they did not, but yet afterward they came again, as appears in the next verse. So Isa. ii. 4, "Nation shall not lift up sword against nation, neither shall they learn war any more;" it is spoken of Christ's time; and for some years there was quietness in the world, but after the gospel spread wars were learned and practised again. One place more in Gen. xlvi. 29, Joseph fell on his father's neck, and wept on it a good while; it is the same word. So then God would not do so any more, that is, for a good while, a long season, for that age and generation.

2. We do not find that ever there was such a hand of God upon a people, that the fathers should eat their sons in an open, visible way, and the sons the fathers, as there it was. The Scripture mentions not the like again, scarcely any story in the world; and in this particular it may exceed all that ever God had done, or would do. God never would do like that again. No such precedent should be after it; and so that they should be scattered into all parts of the world.

3. Some interpreters conceive the words, "that which I have not done, and whereunto I will do no more the like," to be a usual phrase amongst the Hebrews to set out the greatness of the judgment.

"Because of all thine abominations." The Hebrew word תועבת signifies a hateful thing, such as is loathsome and dangerous. The Septuagint do frequently render it by Βδέλυγμα, which is a thing so detestable, as *propter fœditatem nemo non adversatur*, on account of its vileness, every one is opposed to it, a wickedness of which *ne fari liceat*, it is not lawful to speak, it is so offensive; it is such a thing as a man *omnibus sensibus*, with all his faculties, abhorreth, that a man endures not patiently to hear, see, or speak of: it points out notorious sins, of all kinds. I shall name some unto you: the counterfeiting of the sexes, men by wearing the women's, and women the men's apparel; this was an abomination unto the Lord, Deut. xxii. 5; incestuous marriages, adulteries, sodomy, Lev. xviii. 26, 27, he had mentioned the sins, and then calls them abominations; falsehood in weights and measures, Deut. xxv. 14—16; idolatry, as 1 Pet. iv. 3; abominable idolatries, and so odious are idols, that they are called abominations, 2 Chron. xv. 8, Asa put away the abominable idols; the Hebrew is, abominations. Idols are mere abominations; Milcom was the abomination of the Ammonites, Chemosh of Moab, and Molech of Ammon, 1 Kings xi. 5, 7. Idols make nations abominations to God and man; they are a shame, Hos. ix. 10, an accursed thing, Deut. vii. 26. Such abominations as these mentioned, and others, they were guilty of.

Ver. 10. "Therefore the fathers shall eat the sons in the midst of thee," &c. Here the dreadfulness of God's judgments is in part expressed: fathers should eat their sons, and sons their fathers; not as Pradus would have it, they ate the food of one another, that should have preserved life, and so became the death of each other. It was a real eating: Lam. iv. 10, "The pitiful women have sodden their own children: they were their meat;" and may it be thought their hungry husbands shared not with them in those viands? What was threatened was made good, and certainly the fathers did eat their own children at that time, and the children the parents. If tender mothers did this, much more fathers, *qui solent esse teneriores in filios*, who are not so tender towards their offspring. So extreme was the famine, that it made them do acts against piety, honesty, humanity, light of nature: necessity breaks all bands. In the Samaritan famine they did eat their children, 2 Kings vi. 29. You may read a lamentable discourse of a mother killing and eating her child for hunger in Joseph. l. 7. Bel. Judaic. c. 8, when Titus besieged Jerusalem; it was Mary the daughter of Eleazar, a noble woman: she boiled one part, and kept the other; some smelling flesh, asked, What was done? she tells the fact, and they went away amazed. In Honorius's time there was such a famine at Rome, that there was a public cry, Set the price of man's flesh.

Obs. 1. When God is become an enemy to a people, he doth unheard-of things, such severity is in his judgments as is not ordinary. Their abominations had made the Lord against them, and therefore he would do as he had not done, send a sharper sword and famine than ever: Lev. xxvi. 30—32, "My soul shall abhor you. And I will make your cities waste, bring your sanctuaries and land into desolation: and your enemies that dwell therein shall be astonished at it." They shall wonder at the severity of God towards his people, and not only inmates, but foreigners shall wonder. Jer. xix. 3, "Behold, I will bring evil upon this place, the which whosoever heareth, his ears shall tingle:" and Jer. xxii. 8, 9, "Nations shall say, wherefore hath the Lord done thus unto this great city? Then they shall answer, Because they have forsaken the covenant of the Lord their God," &c. God's judgments would be so hard and heavy, that the nations should marvel, and be unsatisfied at them, till they should hear how they had dealt with God. Hath not God of late been against Germany, and executed extraordinary judgments there, such as cause astonishment? Have not men's eyes been twisted out with cords, their skins flayed off alive, their faces planed with chisels, their noses and ears cut off to make hatbands, their mouths gagged, and filthy liquids poured down? have not men been hung up by the hands in the smoke? put into hot ovens, roasted with straw fires? have not divines been cut in pieces, and their limbs thrown to dogs? have not many fed and lived upon the flesh of dead men and women, eaten their own children, killed one another for relief against hunger? Strange judgments God brought upon Germany, and as strange upon Ireland. Hath it not been the land of

Lament of Germany.

God's ire, and the people the generation of his wrath; and felt more for so short a time, than Germany or other nations? have not women with child been ravished, then ripped open, the bed of conception viewed, the child taken out, and thrown into the fire? have not the protestant ministers been stripped, bound to trees or posts, their wives and daughters ravished before their faces, then hanged up before them so ravished, cut down half dead, quartered and dismembered? have not many been turned out naked, forced into waters, famished to death under hedges? some have been mortally wounded, their bellies ripped, bowels let out, and left upon dunghills, that they might not be soon out of their misery.

Ver. 11. *Wherefore, as I live, saith the Lord God; Surely, because thou hast defiled my sanctuary with all thy detestable things, and with all thine abominations, therefore will I also diminish thee; neither shall mine eye spare, neither will I have any pity.*

In this verse are two further aggravations of Jerusalem's judgments, and the cause of them.

The first aggravation is the inevitableness of them, "Surely I will diminish thee;" and that confirmed by an oath, "As I live, saith the Lord, I will do it."

The second is the disposition of God punishing them, and that is dreadful, "he will neither spare nor pity them;" and then the cause is, their defilement of his sanctuary with their "detestable things and abominations."

"As I live." It is the form of an oath, and is much used in the Old Testament; as in Zeph. ii. 9; Jer. xlvi. 18; xxii. 24; Isa. xlix. 18; Deut. xxxii. 40; Numb. xiv. 21, 28; but it is more in our prophet than in all the Scripture besides, fourteen times I find it. Men are hardly persuaded to believe God in his way of judgments, and therefore being in that way in this prophecy, he swears oft. You have this oath, chap. xiv. 16, 18; xvi. 48; xvii. 19; xviii. 3; xx. 3, 31, 33; xxxiii. 11, 27; xxxiv. 8; xxxv. 6, 11. It is a weighty oath, and imports that which follows is not comminatory, but absolute, without evasion, without revocation; As sure as I live, and am God, it shall be done: Psal. cx. 4, "The Lord hath sworn, and will not repent." A thing is ratified and cannot be altered when it is confirmed by an oath, which is an immutable thing, Heb. vi. Let me not live, let me not be God, if I do not diminish you, but be an idol god, without sense, understanding, or life. The sign of an oath, anciently, was the lifting up the hand to heaven; and this is given to God when he swears: also Deut. xxxii. 40, "I lift up my hand to heaven, and say, I live for ever." This way of swearing hath lately been renewed at our taking the covenant; and it is to be wished that it may be used when there is just occasion of swearing, rather than laying the hand upon a book, and kissing it afterwards. Such a way of taking an oath the Scripture holds not out; and the lawfulness thereof is questioned by many.

"Thou hast defiled my sanctuary." The word מקדש notes sometimes a holy place for refuge, and refers to God himself; Isa. viii. 14, "He shall be for a sanctuary:" here it notes the temple, the place of God's worship, from *kadash*, to separate and consecrate to divine use. (Schindl.) The sanctuary or temple was consecrated, *ad doctrinam, ad precationem, et ad cultum divinum*, for teaching, for prayer, for the general worship of God; it was only for holy uses. Some divide the temple into the porch, palace, and place of the oracle; others into the court of Israel, (Weems.) the court of the priests, and the court of God, where the ark and cherubims were, and this they make the sanctuary or place of (Jun. Maldon.) holiness; for *mikdashi* is, my holiness, as well as, my sanctuary; there the glory of God appeared between the cherubims, and this place they desired.

I shall speak a little of the holiness of places, because there is an opinion in the world, that some places are holy, and that duties done in them are better than done elsewhere. It was the saying of a great prelate, That God heard prayer, because the prayers were in such a place.

Two ways places become holy:

First, by divine presence.

Secondly, by divine institution.

For the first, when God did in a visible extraordinary way manifest himself and his glory in any place, this made it holy; as Matt. xvii. when Christ was transfigured in the mount, and excellent glory appeared; this made the place holy, and the apostle called it "The holy mount," 2 Pet. i. 18. So God's appearing to Moses in the bush, Exod. iii. 5, made that place holy. Such appearances of God are not now.

The second way is, by institution and appointment from God. When the Lord doth depute and consecrate places to holy uses, then are they holy, as the temple was; God appointed the place, the building of the temple, the dedication and consecration thereof. It is only God can make any thing holy; none but he that made the creature, can lift it up to a higher condition than it was set in at first; no man can make persons, things, times, places holy, besides the Lord. Now the temple was by the institution of God so sanctified, that it was a type of Christ, a part of worship, a powerful means of grace, giving acceptation to the persons, and all the duties of worship there done; so that it was a sin for them to worship elsewhere, or to divert the temple to any other use. We have no extraordinary appearance of God to make places holy, nor any consecrated by divine institution to type out Christ, or any spiritual thing, to be a part of worship, a means of grace, making the worshippers and worship more acceptable; and therefore I conceive we have no place holy. It was not the temple, but the synagogues, that resembled our public places of worship, and they were not holy: Matt. x. 17, they scourged in their synagogues; and that was no holy act: it is the judgment of learned ones, that Paul had his five whippings, of which he (A Lapid. Brugens.) speaks in 2 Cor. xi. 24, in the synagogues. They had the word preached in them, John xviii. 20; Acts xv. 21, as it is in these public places, yet that did not make them holy, and privilege them from common acts of justice. The holiness of places under the law was ceremonial, and Christ hath put an end to such holiness; the difference of places he hath taken away, and no one is more holy than others. John iv. 21, "The hour cometh," saith Christ to the woman, "when ye shall neither in this mountain, nor yet at Jerusalem, worship the Father:" it is true, now there is holiness in these places, the men and their services are more accepted here than any where else; but the hour is at hand, that all such respects shall be taken away, and all places made alike, and you and your services shall be as acceptable in every place of the world, as at Jerusalem. Hence is it that Paul puts men upon praying every where, 1 Tim. ii. 8. Many think their prayers better in such a meeting-place as this, than in their closets, than in the fields; but they are deceived, places now add no efficacy or acceptation to men's prayers. It is rather prayer, ordinances, and so the spiritual presence of God in them, that make places holy; and this is the argument that some stick upon; but upon examination, this will not make the public place of meeting more holy than others; for, Matt. xviii. 20, it is said, "Where two or three are gathered," &c. be it in a ship, a private house, a field, if gathered together in his name, he "is in the midst of them," he is there not for the place but the people's sake; yet no judicious man accounts all places holy where spiritual duties are doing, or after they are done; and why public places of worship should be so accounted of in time of worship or after, is not discernible to a religious and judicious eye: of old the altar sanctified the gift; it is not so now.

"Hast defiled." In the Vulgate it is, *violasti*, hast violated, wronged; but the Hebrew word notes more, it is, to render impure; and it is the same word with that which sets out the defilement of Dinah, Gen. xxxiv. 5: a woman may be wronged, and not be defiled; the sanctuary was defiled, polluted, profaned. Sometimes you read of the land's being defiled, as Numb. xxxv. 34; sometimes of the priesthood, Neh. xiii. 29; sometimes of the Lord's holy name being defiled, Ezek. xliii. 7; and here of his sanctuary. We must inquire what it is that defiles the same.

1. Sacrificing otherwhere than God commanded. Lev. xvii. 3, 4, if an ox, lamb, or goat were killed in the camp, or out of it, and not brought to the door of the tabernacle to offer, it was accounted of God bloodshed: they would offer in the fields, and not where God appointed; and this was a defilement, and as great as shedding of blood.

2. When they brought things or persons prohibited; as,

(1.) Unwarrantable sacrifices, any thing corrupt, and not according to rule. Mal. i. 7, 8, "Ye offer polluted bread upon mine altar;" it was not unleavened, of fine flour and oil, according to prescription, Lev. vii. 12; it was of rye, barley, or coarse wheat; and this bread, this *mincha*, polluted God's altar: and so when they offered the blind, sick, and lame for sacrifice, they were corrupt things, Mal. i. 14, and defiled the altar and temple of the Lord.

(2.) Idols. God would not have any idol come in his house; 2 Cor. vi. 16, "What agreement hath the temple of God with idols?" God and Dagon cannot dwell in one house. This was the quarrel here, Jer. vii. 30, "They have set their abominations in the house which is called by my name, to pollute it." The same words you have again in Jer. xxxii. 34. And you shall find there were strange altars set up in God's house: Ahaz brought in the altar of Damascus, 2 Kings xvi. 10, &c; and there were the altars of Manasseh in the court of the Lord's house, 2 Kings xxiii. 12; and the high places on the right hand of the mount of corruption, ver. 13: they did defile also, as the carcasses mentioned in Ezek. xliii. 9, which were the carcasses of Manasseh and Amon, buried in the king's garden close by the wall of the temple.

Mead.

(3.) When persons were brought in legally unclean: Ezek. xliv. 7, "Ye have brought into my sanctuary strangers, uncircumcised in heart and in flesh, to pollute it."

"With all thy detestable things." The original word notes not offensive things simply, but so offensive as to offend the senses and the mind, and so to offend them, as it causeth an abhorring with execration; and such things are images and idols. 2 Kings xxiii. 24, those that had "familiar spirits, the wizards, the images, the idols, and all the abominations," the word is *shikkutzim*, all the detestable and execrable things, "did Josiah put away." The Spirit of God speaks of them with detestation: Jer. xi. 13, "Ye have set up altars to that shameful thing, even Baal;" Acts xv. 20, "Pollutions of idols," dunghill gods, so the word *gillulim* signifies, Ezek. xxii. 3. They are a terror to them that worship them: 1 Kings xv. 13, Maachah "made an idol," a thing to terrify, the word is; and Psal. cxxxv. 15, "The idols of the nations," it is the grief and torment of the nations. These names express the detestation of God against idols, and should quicken us to the detestation of them; according to that in Deut. vii. 26, "Thou shalt utterly detest and utterly abhor an idol," or any part of it: the original is, in detesting thou shalt detest, and in abhorring thou shalt abhor; noting the great detestation and abhorrence which should be in God's people to idolatry; for it defiles men's consciences, God's worship and sanctuary; therefore the Septuagint renders the word abominations or detestations, in Jer. xxxii. 34, *μίασματα*, pollutions.

"Therefore will I also diminish thee." The Hebrew word is גרע which the Vulgate renders, *confringere*, I will break thee; and then the sense runs thus: My purpose was to have preserved the temple safe from all violation, if so be you had kept it unpolluted; but now, seeing you have defiled it with your detestable things, I must and will break it down, as being no better than a common, profane house. It signifies also to shave, as in Jer. xlviii. 37, "Every beard shall be clipped," or shaven. The Nazarites were holy to the Lord, and if by the sudden death of any they were defiled, their cleansing was by shaving of their heads, Numb. vi. 9. So also was the leper to be cleansed by shaving off his hair, Lev. xiii. 33; xiv. 8. And so here they were defiled, and God would cleanse them by shaving; and so it corresponds with the razor mentioned in the first verse; and both these senses fall in with the word "diminish," which the Hebrew word also denotes, *diminuere detrahendo*, to diminish by taking from, and so is contrary to *jasaph*, which is to add to a thing. God would not add any more mercies, but take away their mercies, and diminish them: they had diminished his honour, he would diminish their comforts; they had stained his glory, and he would take away their glory, the temple and city. Some render it *succidam*, I will cut down; God would deal with Jerusalem as an husbandman doth with a barren or rotten tree.

"Neither shall mine eye spare." This kind of expression is much used in this prophecy, more seldom in others. The eye is the index of the mind, the disposition whereof is seen, discerned there as in a looking-glass; anger, joy, love, grief, are inmates, yet visible in the eye, that is the casement they look out at; the hidden things of the heart are revealed by the eye. Pity, sparing, compassion, are affections of the heart and mind, and God, speaking after the manner of men, saith, Mine eye shall not spare; as it is in Isa. xiii. 18, "Their eye shall not spare children," there should be no sign of pity or remorse in them: sparing is given to the eye as the sign of it. From the eye is intelligence given of mercy or severity within. You shall not have the least hint of mercy from mine eye, but evidence of wrath only; and whereas others were wont to be affected with the miseries they behold, their eye affects their heart, Lam. iii. 51, I will not be at all affected with their miseries: let a great army sit down before them, let famine, plague, sword devour, let all mischiefs be upon them, mine eye shall not affect mine heart, I will not repent.

"I will not have any pity." What could have been said more dreadful? The Hebrew word חמל signifies to be of a prone, pitiful affection towards any, though they deserve ill. Joel ii. 17, 18, God's people had sinned greatly, were under sore judgments, deserved utter destruction; but let them fast, pray, and turn, then will the Lord pity them; though they deserve no mercy, yet will he show them mercy. So in 2 Chron. xxxvi. 15, they were exceeding ill, yet God had compassion on them; it is the same word, and hath a contrary signification to קטל which is, to destroy without mercy; and so the word in this place, when it hath לא joined unto it, signifieth as much as, I will not have pity, that is, I will destroy without mercy. 1 Sam. xv. 3, "Smite Amalek, utterly destroy all that they have, and spare them not," that is, have no pity on them; and when God ceaseth to pity a people, it is sad, then no redemption for them, Isa. lxiii. 9; God will deliver them into the hands of their enemies, Zech. xi. 6, he will harden others against them. When God pities not, yet if men will, it is some comfort; but men shall not do it: Jer. xxi. 7, when in Nebuchadnezzar's hands, he shall not spare, pity, or show mercy; when they should fall down, beg for their lives at the hands of Babylonians, they should find no mercy, only bitter words and bloody deeds. In Amos i. 11, it is said, "Edom cast off all pity, and his anger did tear;" and so God, he cast off all pity, and destruction followed: Jer. xiii. 14, "I will dash them one against another, even the fathers and the sons together: I will not pity, nor spare, nor have mercy, but destroy them;" and you may see this fulfilled in the Lamentations, chap. ii. 2, "The Lord hath swallowed up all the habitations of Jacob, and hath not pitied;" as a wild beast doth his prey, as a sea doth ships, God left not one, no pity at all: see ver. 17, 21.

Obs. 1. That sin defiles the holy things of God. They defiled not only themselves, but the sanctuary, and worship of God in it. The land of Canaan was holy, and sin defiled that, Jer. xvi. 18; the temple was holy, and sin defiled that, Ezek. xxiii. 38; the altar was holy, and sin polluted that, Mal. i. 7; the sabbaths were holy, and sin profaned them, Neh. xiii. 17; the priesthood and covenant were holy, and sin defiled them, ver. 29; God's name is holy, and sin pollutes that, Ezek. xx. 39.

Obs. 2. That defilement of God's worship brings certain and severe judgments. They had defiled his sanctuary with idols, superstitions, polluted bread, blind, lame, corrupt sacrifice, by suffering unclean and uncircumcised persons to come there; and the prophet brings in the Lord swearing, "As I live, saith the Lord, surely, because thou hast done so, I will therefore diminish thee;" here is the certainty of judgment: "neither shall mine eye spare, neither will I have any pity;" here is the severity of it. God's worship and the ordinances of it, are his name, Mal. i. 11, 12. Exod. xx. 24, "In all places where I record my name," that is, where God puts his worship. 1 Kings xiv. 21, Jerusalem is the city that God chose out of all the tribes to put his name in; 1 Kings viii. 29, "My name shall be there." Hence saith David, Psal. lxxvi. 1, "In Judah is God known; his name is great in Israel." The gentiles knew not God, they had not his name amongst them, nothing of his worship; no true prayer, and that is his name, Gen. iv. 26; not the seals of the covenant, Matt. xxviii. 19, not the censures of the church, 1 Cor. v. 4, 5, and these are his name. Now God's name is very precious, and the profaning of it is forbidden in a special manner; Lev. xxii. 31, 32, "Ye shall keep my commandments and do them: I am the Lord. Neither shall ye profane my holy name:" when they presumptuously break any command of God, say the rabbies, then they profane God's name. It is the greatest presumption and violation of God's commands, to corrupt his worship, to mingle our inventions with it; the spirit and the strength of the second command is against all invented worship and idolatry, which is a hating of God, and provokes to jealousy and wrath more than other sins. Ezek. xxiii. 37, 38, they had sinned in murder, adultery, and idolatry, but what went nearest to the heart of God? even the corrupting of his worship, and that is set out with a special emphasis, "This they have done unto me, they have defiled my sanctuary:" to defile it with blood is bad, but with false worship, with idols, and superstitions, is abominable. What makes God reject a people, and count them "the generation of his wrath?" Jer. vii. 29, 30, "They have set their abominations in the house which is called by my name, to pollute it." Read the 8th of Ezekiel, and see the conclusion, "Therefore will I also deal in fury: mine eye shall not spare, neither will I have pity: and though they cry in mine ears with a loud voice, yet will I not hear them."

Ver. 12. *A third part of thee shall die with the pestilence, and with famine shall they be consumed in the midst of thee: and a third part shall fall by the sword round about thee; and I will scatter a third part into all the winds, and I will draw out a sword after them.*

Here is an explication of the type in the first and second verses, with a further aggravation of Jerusalem's misery, from the variety of punishments:

1. Pestilence.
2. Famine.
3. Sword.
4. Dispersion. Four sore judgments.

"Pestilence." It is from a word דבר
that signifies to speak, and speak out; the pestilence is a speaking thing, it proclaims the wrath of God amongst a people. Drusius fetches it from the same root, but in *piel*, which is, to decree; showing that the pestilence is a thing decreed in heaven, not casual. Kirker thinks it
is called *dever*, because it keeps order, In Hab. iii. 5. דבר
and spares neither great nor small. The Hebrew root signifies, to destroy, to cut off, and hence may the plague or pestilence have its name. The Septuagint renders it *θάνατος*, death, for ordinarily it is death; and it is expressed by death, Rev. vi. 8, he sat on the pale horse, killed with sword, hunger, death, and beasts of the earth; it refers to Ezek. xiv. 21, where the pesti- פשט
lence is mentioned. Pestilence may be from a word which signifies to spread, spoil, rush upon, for it doth so; 2 Sam. xxiv. 15, seventy thousand slain in three days; and plague, *a πλήγη* from *πλησσω*, to smite, to wound, for it smites suddenly, and wounds mortally; hence it is in Numb. xiv. 12, "I will smite them with the pestilence." This judgment is very grievous; Psal. xci. 3, it is called "the noisome pestilence," because it is infectious, contagious; and therefore the French read it, *de la peste dangereuse*, from the dangerous pestilence, it doth endanger those that come near it: and Musc. hath it, *a peste omnium pessima*, from the worst pestilence of all: and others, the woful pestilence; it brings a multitude of woes with it to any place or person it comes unto, it is a messenger of woful fears, sorrows, distractions, terrors, and death itself.

"With famine." Of this sore judgment hath been spoken in the fourth chapter. רעב is, *exardere fame*, consume with hunger; and the famine here is such a one as burns, withers, dries up a man: when the *calor nativus*, natural heat, hath nothing able to feed upon, it consumes the *humidum radicale*, radical moisture, and man quickly perisheth. The Scripture speaks of a three years' famine, 2 Sam. xxi. 1, a seven years' famine, Gen. xlv. 6; what numbers perished then! when famines are mighty, Luke xv. 14, terrible, Lam. v. 10, prevailing, 2 Kings xxv. 3, and destroy not only the branches, but the root, Isa. xiv. 30.

חרב "By the sword round about thee." *Charab* signifies to dry up, to lay waste, to destroy; whence *chereb*, a sword, is derived, for it draws out the blood, dries up the body, lays waste and destroys: Deut. xxxii. 42, it is said to eat flesh; Isa. xxxiv. 6, to drink and be filled with blood. Here it is put for wars, the wars of the Babylonians against Jerusalem, which are called "The sword of the king of Babylon," Ezek. xxi. 19; xxxii. 11. What a judgment the sword of war is, we begin to know and feel; it dries up the blood of kingdoms, it makes them wildernesses, and destroys round about: hence the sword is said to be hurtful, Psal. cxliv. 10, powerful, Job v. 20, oppressive, Jer. xlvi. 16, bereaving, Lam. i. 20, to reach to the soul, Jer. iv. 10, to "devour from one end of the land to the other," so that "no flesh shall have peace," Jer. xii. 12.

"I will scatter a third part into all the winds." It is such a scattering as is of dust or chaff before the winds, a fanning of them; God would bring a wind out of the north that should fan them, as corn is fanned, and scatter them abroad, Jer. iv. 12, 13. "I will fan them with a fan," Jer. xv. 7; it is the same word which is here, and notes a great fanning, scattering of them; and complaint is made of such scattering, Psal. xliv. 11, "Thou hast scattered us among the heathen," that was, into the several winds and countries round about; and Zech. vii. 14, "I scattered them with a whirlwind among all the nations whom they knew not." This was a heavy judgment; to be removed from their own country, friends to be scattered several ways, to be with them whose language and manners they knew not, that were cruel, barbarous, haters of God, his worship, people, to be servants and slaves to them, this was a judgment sorer than pestilence, famine, sword, and they had better been cut off in their own land, or in their journey to those places; neither were they in safety there, for God would draw out a sword after them, they should be captives, undergo great hardship, and be daily in jeopardy of their lives; the sword should pursue them, as the phrase is, Jer. xlviii. 2. These judgments were contrary to the blessing of plenty, safety, and peace, promised in Lev. xxvi. 4—6.

Ver. 13. ***Thus shall mine anger be accomplished, and I will cause my fury to rest upon them, and I will be comforted: and they shall know that I the Lord have spoken it in my zeal, when I have accomplished my fury in them.***

In this verse two ends of divine judgments are held forth:

1. The satisfaction of his own justice; when judgments are fully executed, he "will be comforted."

2. The conviction of his adversaries, "They shall know that I the Lord have spoken."

"Thus shall mine anger be accomplished." Here is mention of anger and fury, which you oft find given to God. But neither these nor other passions are in God, he is not carried by affections as men are; they are neither materially nor formally in God, whose essence is unmixed and immutable. Anger and fury are given to God, when he manifests by his actions that something displeases him, and especially when he punisheth the creature; they are effects from God, not affections in God; Isa. xxvii. 4, "Fury is not in me."

"Be accomplished." The Hebrew is, to finish, to perfect; as in Gen. ii. 2, "God ended his work," he accomplished what he was about; so here, the Septuagint hath it, συντελεσθήσεται, shall be perfected: it notes a progress in God's wrath, which shall not cease in the mid-way, but go on to the highest degree; as men, when they are much incensed, proceed in punishment of delinquents till they be satisfied, they let out their wrath to the full, and so God would do. Formerly God had kept in his wrath, not let it have the reins, nor break over the banks; and if it did get loose at any time, and break out, he quickly called it back, and turned it away, Psal. lxxviii. 38; but now he would stir up all his wrath, and let it out to the full, and accomplish it among them; now plague, famine, sword, dispersion should have their will and power over them, God would inflict what he had conceived and threatened against them.

"I will cause my fury to rest upon them." That is, God would terminate, fasten, settle his wrath upon them, not cease it from them, it should not fleet or move, but abide; they should be a people under fury, a "generation of his wrath," Jer. vii. 29, a "people of his wrath," Isa. x. 6. God would shoot his arrows into them, and they should stick in their sides; whithersoever they went, God's fury should be still upon them. It notes out the continuation of God's anger, which Jeremiah expresseth to the full, chap. vii. 20, "Behold, mine anger and my fury shall be poured out upon this place, upon man, and upon beast, and upon the trees of the field, and upon the fruit of the ground; and it shall burn and not be quenched:" neither their tears nor their blood shall put out the fire of divine wrath kindled against them; it should still burn, notwithstanding all means used to quench the same. God would make his wrath abiding wrath; such is that speech in Isa. xxx. 32, "In every place where the grounded staff shall pass, which the Lord shall lay upon him," which the Lord shall cause to rest upon him, is the Hebrew. What is the grounded staff? the wrath of God intended to be fixed, laid in, and laid down for a foundation of ruin, that wrath would God cause to rest upon him, that is, the Assyrian; the mark of the staff should be in their flesh and state for ever.

"I will be comforted." God is "the God of all comfort," 2 Cor. i. 3, yet he saith, he will be comforted; not that God was enfeebled through discomfort, and needed addition of comfort and strength from any creature, but it is spoken after the manner of men: God had mourned over them a long time, expressed his grief by the prophet's threatenings, by lesser judgments inflicted; they had done no good, and now he would ease himself of them and be comforted. Wicked men are a burden to God, and when a burden is taken off, it is ease, it is comfort. Isa. i. you have God brought in much grieved, and complaining of this people, ver. 2—4, &c.; and in ver. 24, he saith, "Ah, I will ease me of mine adversaries, and avenge me of mine enemies." Ah! the time is now come, and I am glad of it, that I shall be eased of this great burden, bearing with this rebellious people; I will cast them off, and revenge myself upon them. Revenge is sweet, it is an ease to reproached, provoked spirits; for where is anger, there is

Æstuantem animam vindicta levat.

grief and desire of revenge, which obtaining, takes away grief and anger, whereby the mind is comforted: therefore God would ease himself by avengement on them. So here, God would accomplish his anger, settle his fury upon them, and be comforted in it; he would execute severe judgments, and approve, yea applaud them being executed.

"In my zeal." These words are oft in the prophet: the Hebrew signifies sometimes zeal, sometimes jealousy; the Septuagint renders it ἐν ζήλῳ μοῦ, in my zeal, not, in my jealousy. Zeal is the intention of all affections; it notes,

1. The earnest love of God for the good of his church and his own glory, Isa. ix. 7.

2. Jealousy, which is with great indignation and grief, Numb. xxv. 11, such as amounts to hatred and enmity, Isa. lix. 17. God was very zealous of the good of his people, and therefore gave them zealous prophets, by whom his zeal was made known. The prophets spake in God's name, delivered their message with authority, power, life; they lifted up their voices, told the people of their sins, reproved them sharply, were very zealous in their prophecies. Hence they were counted factious and fiery spirits, men venting their own opinions and humour; hence their labours were slighted; they were looked upon as contemptible men, not worthy to live, they did so trouble both church and state with the things they delivered: but they shall know, that not men, but God spake; that it was not their zeal, but my zeal; that they have opposed and rejected me in my prophets. If you refer it to jealousy, it notes God's taking them into covenant to be his people; their revolt by idolatry and other sins, and God's jealousy upon it; who growing hot with displeasure, spake sharp and dreadful things against this people, as a jealous husband would do against an adulterous wife.

Obs. 1. That God goes on by degrees in his wrath against a people. He did not accomplish his anger and fury at first, he began with lesser judgments, but at last came up to a perfection. Before he had whipped them with scourges, now he would do it with scorpions; he had formerly done much, vexed them with wars, famine, plague, but never laid waste their city, ruined their temple, scattered them to the four winds, as now he would do: he had in times past corrected them like a father, he would now execute them like a judge; the drops of his wrath had done no good, now they should have the full vials, all the wrath conceived against them should be inflicted, accomplished.

Obs. 2. That wrath let out against a sinful people, ofttimes lies long upon them. "I will cause my fury to rest upon them." They were seventy years under God's displeasure in Babylon. God's wrath hath been upon the Jews that rejected the gospel these 1600 years; they would not be under the blessing of Christ, and they are under the curse of God, his wrath abides upon them. God's anger hath rested upon Germany above twenty years. These kingdoms of Ireland and England are under it: fervent prayer is requisite, that God would remove his wrath, and not let it rest upon us. It is a dreadful thing to have settled plague or war amongst us. The barons' wars in king John's, Henry the third's, and Edward the second's days, made sad times; God's wrath rested then for a long season upon this kingdom, the choicest blood of it was let out, and it brought a deplorable condition. Let us repent and reform, that wrath may not rest upon the kingdom; and let us believe, that wrath may not abide upon us; John iii. 36, "He that believeth not, the wrath of God abideth on him." Man came into the world a child of wrath, an heir of wrath; Christ is a remedy propounded for removal of that wrath; if men believe not, the wrath of God abides still on them, goes along with them, and will eternally sink them.

Obs. 3. God takes pleasure in executing judgment, in accomplishing his wrath, and causing his fury to rest upon impenitent and incurable sinners, he will be comforted in it. Prov. i. 26, "I will laugh at your calamity;" God would bring calamities upon them, just judgments for the setting at nought his counsels, refusing his reproofs, and rejoice in them; for as judgments are satisfaction to divine justice, they are delightful unto God. Isa. xxx. 32, "In every place where the grounded staff shall pass, which the Lord shall lay upon him, it shall be with tabrets and harps." When God should destroy the Babylonians and Assyrians, it should be with delight, which the tabrets and harps express, which were musical instruments, used in wars and victories, Exod. xv. 20. And when God executed judgment upon spiritual Babylon, it was with joy; therefore the Spirit of God calls for it, Rev. xviii. 20, "Rejoice over her, thou heaven, and ye holy apostles and prophets; for God hath avenged you and himself on her also;" which was a comfort and ease, a delight to God. Hence judgments in Scripture are termed his pleasure; Isa. xlvi. 10, 11, "I will do all my pleasure: calling a ravenous bird from the east;" and chap. xlviii. 14, "He will do his pleasure on Babylon."

Obs. 4. The word of God may be preached among a people, and they, through ignorance and malice, not know it, nor entertain it. "They shall know that I the Lord have spoken it." They conceived not that it was the word of God which the prophets delivered; they thought them to be no more than other men, and their word human, and therefore slighted it. There was much affected ignorance in them: Isa. xxvii. 11, "It is a people of no understanding;" Jer. iv. 22, "My people is foolish, they have not known me." And as many were blind, so many were malicious against the prophets, and their messages they brought from God: Jer. xliv. 16, 17, "As for the word that thou hast spoken unto us in the name of the Lord, we will not hearken unto thee. But we will certainly do whatsoever thing goeth forth out of our own mouth." Christ came and preached to his own, and they received him not, they neither knew him nor his doctrine, or if they did, they maliciously rejected both.

Obs. 5. That wicked men shall be convinced, and left without excuse. "They shall know that I the Lord have spoken:" they eyed men and not me, they deemed it man's voice, not Heaven's; but they shall find that it was the voice of God amongst them. And what can men say, when God hath spoken, and hath not been hearkened unto? every mouth will then be stopped. They would not know, but they shall know; they would not own my truths, but they shall feel my judgments, and when they are upon them, then will they remember the prophets and their words, which will be as burning coals in their bosoms; then they will see what desperate revolts they have made from God; how they are besieged with his power, and cannot escape the stroke thereof. When men shall see it is the infinite, great, and glorious God that they have slighted, in the prophets, in the ordinances, then they will be struck dumb, and fall under the wrath of that God.

Obs. 6. God will justify his servants in their zealous labours for him. "They shall know that I have spoken it in my zeal." It is God speaks in the prophets; it is his zeal they express. Let men be zealous against sin, the iniquities of the times, they are counted mad, fiery fellows, troublers of Israel, seditious, factious, &c. Paul was a zealous man, and not only Festus a heathen counted him mad, Acts xxvi. 24, but even the christian Corinthians, 2 Cor. v. 13, thought him beside himself. And such conceits had the people about Christ, who was a man of zeal: they thought him too hot, that his zeal was beyond his judgment; Mark iii. 21, they plainly said he was beside himself. Michal scoffed at David as one of the fools for his zeal. Let the world pass what censure it will upon God's ministers, God will justify those who are sincerely zealous, and count their zeal his zeal.

Obs. 7. That the Lord is intense, and will not recall his indignation, when he deals with unfaithful, covenant-breaking persons. As in God's zeal there is intense love towards his church, (when God promises mercy to his people, it is sealed with this, "The zeal of the Lord of hosts shall do it," 2 Kings xix. 31,) so here is intense hatred, wrath against his enemies. Therefore God beats them off from their own inventions in the second command by this consideration, that he is a jealous God, and his jealousy extensive to the fourth generation. And Deut. xxxii. 22, saith God, "A fire is kindled in mine anger, and shall burn unto the lowest hell, and shall consume the earth with her increase, and set on fire the foundations of the mountains;" and what is the reason of this indignation? it is given in ver. 21, "They have moved me to jealousy with that which is not God:" when God is in his jealousy, he speaks dreadful things, and doth answerably. To speak in zeal, is to decree an irrevocable and bloody sentence: hence, Josh. xxiv. 19, "He is a jealous God;" and then follows, "he will not forgive your transgressions:" and Deut. xxix. 20, "The Lord will not spare, his jealousy shall smoke against that man, and all the curses in this book shall lie upon him." What man? the man that breaks covenant with God, going out to false worship, and thereby putting him into jealousy; which, as it is the rage of a man, and makes him cruel in the day of vengeance, so it is the rage of God, and makes him without pity, or mercy: when he executes vengeance, he will then accomplish his wrath, and not spare, pour out all his wrath and vengeance.

Ver. 14, 15. *Moreover I will make thee waste, and a reproach among the nations that are round about thee, in the sight of all that pass by. So it shall be a reproach and a taunt, an instruction and an astonishment unto the nations that are round about thee, when I shall execute judgments in thee in anger and in fury and in furious rebukes. I the Lord have spoken it.*

In ver. 14, are two judgments more laid down, desolation and reproach; this last is aggravated from the extent of it, "to the nations round about," and "all that pass by."

In the 15th you have the repetition of the last judgment, and the ends of both annexed; which are,

First, for information.

Secondly, for astonishment.

"I will make thee waste." That is, Jerusalem, with the villages and all the land adjacent. Judah was a fruitful land, Isa. v. 1, "the glory of all lands, flowing with milk and honey," Ezek. xx. 6. Moses calls it a good land, a land of brooks, waters, fountains, deeps that spring out of valleys and hills; a land of wheat and barley, vines, fig-trees, pomegranates; a land of oil, olives, and honey; a land where nothing was lacking, the stones of it were iron, and in the hills were brass, Deut. viii. 7—9. It was the Lord's land Hos. ix. 3, Immanuel's, Isa. viii. 8, a land that God cared for, and watched over all the year long, Deut. xi. 12. Egypt was an inconsiderable land to this, ver. 10; that was profane, this was the holy land, Zech. ii. 12, the pleasant land, chap. vii. 14; it was well built, well tilled, and greatly peopled. Yet this land must be laid waste; they should be *in ariditatem*, a state of drought, like a river dried up, that if you look for water in it, there is none; so if you look for a temple, worship, or ordinance, &c. in Jerusalem, there is none: their cities and habitations are burnt, their gardens unfenced, their trees cut down, their vines undressed, their fields untilled, and all made a wilderness, a land of briers and thorns, Isa. vii. 24. And this was fulfilled, as you may see in Neh. ii. 17. Lam. i. 4, "The ways of Zion do mourn, because none come to the solemn feasts;" see chap. ii. 2, 3; v. 18; and the adversary's hand was upon all her pleasant things, chap. i. 10. Hence the church complains, Isa. lxiv. 10, 11, "Thy holy cities are a wilderness, Zion is a wilderness, Jerusalem a desolation. Our holy and beautiful house, where our fathers praised thee, is burned up with fire, and all our pleasant things are laid waste." See here the truth of divine threats, and the mischief of sin; it so exasperates God, that he turns a fruitful land, even his own land, into barrenness, saltness, "for the wickedness of them that dwell therein," Psal. cvii. 34.

"A reproach among the nations." God would make them not only for a waste, but also for a reproach. חרף is simply to reproach, to disgrace; and that is not all they should have, but they should be for a taunt also, and that is more, גרופה from *giddeph*, to blaspheme, revile; and so it is used, Matt. xxvii. 39, for Matthew wrote his Gospel in Hebrew, where it is said, they reviled Christ and wagged their heads: so should this people be reproached and reviled, have bitter taunts and sarcasms thrown at them; Jer. xxiv. 9, they shall be "removed into all the kingdoms of the earth for their hurt, to be a reproach and a proverb, a taunt and a curse." Hence grew those reproaches and imprecations, Let it be with thee, as it was with Zedekiah, his family and followers; and Jer. xxix. 22, the curse in the captivity was, "The Lord make thee like Zedekiah, and like Ahab, whom the king of Babylon roasted in the fire." This judgment was very sore; reproaches and taunts are bitter things, piercing deep, scarce any thing afflicts an ingenuous spirit more than they do. Zedekiah feared nothing more than reproach and mocking; Jer. xxxviii. 19, "I am afraid of the Jews, that are fallen to the Chaldeans, lest they deliver me into their hand, and they mock me:" it was a sad thing to be stripped of all their cities, the land to be laid waste, but much more to be exposed to scorn, yea, publicly of all; and that by the appointment of the Judge, even God, whom they took to be their friend; and that to the nations they had hated, and held tributary many years; this was exceedingly pungent, especially they being the top and glory of all nations. It was fulfilled, Lam. ii. 15—17, "All that pass by clap their hands at thee; they hiss and wag their head at the daughter of Jerusalem, saying, Is this the city that men call The perfection of beauty, The joy of the whole earth? All thine enemies have opened their mouth against thee: they hiss and gnash their teeth: they say, We have swallowed her up: certainly this is the day that we looked for; we have found, we have seen it. The Lord hath done that which he had devised; he hath fulfilled his word."

Vide de Dieu. in Matt. xxviii.

"An instruction." The Vulgate is, *exemplum*, example; this act of God upon Jerusalem exposed so to reproach, should be an example to the heathen. The Hebrew is מוסר from יסר to bind, to discipline, to instruct. The judgments of God upon his people are bonds, to bind up heathens from their sins; they are reproofs unto them, being guilty of great sins; they are instructions, to teach them to repent of their sins: because the Jews by their holy lives did not excite the nations to inquire after and serve the true God, therefore their judgments shall be their instructions, teach them to fear and forsake their idolatry. They could reason thus: If God spared not the holy city, the holy people, the holy land, when they fell to idolatry, uncleanness, and other vile sins, how will he spare us, if we be found in the same ways? His judgments are exceeding dreadful; we will take warning; their sufferings shall be our safety. If judgments were to be instructions to heathens, and wrought upon them, shall they not much more be so to christians? The ruins of Germany, the blood of Ireland, the breaches of England, let them be instructions unto us. Let us all say with Isaiah, chap. xxvi. 8, 9, "In the way of thy judgments, O Lord, have we waited for thee; the desire of our soul is to thy name, and to the remembrance of thee: with my soul have I desired thee in the night, yea, with my spirit within me will I seek thee early: for when thy judgments are in the earth, the inhabitants of the world will learn righteousness." Heathen inhabitants will do it, and shall not christians? It is seasonable wisdom to learn by the blows of others.

"An astonishment." Not for stupifying and hardening, which sometimes is the end and fruit of judgments, but for admiration. God would so deal with Jerusalem and her inhabitants, that the nations round about should be astonished at his dealings; God would "make them an astonishment, and an hissing, and perpetual desolations," Jer. xxv. 9; yea, the plagues of the city should be such, that "every one that passeth thereby shall be astonished, and hiss," chap. xix. 9; yea, many nations should say, "Wherefore hath the Lord done thus unto this great city?" Jer. xxii. 8. Deut. xxix. 22—24, God saith, the plagues of that land should be such, as that it should be like Sodom and Gomorrah; so great, so strange, that all nations should say, "Wherefore hath the Lord done thus unto this land? what meaneth the heat of this great anger?" God might have done thus with this great city, with this pleasant land; but he hath spared us, and we have cause to be as much astonished at his mercies, as they were at his judgments. Let us fear and reform, lest our sweet mercies be turned into astonishing judgments.

"When I shall execute judgments in thee in anger and in fury and in furious rebukes." There is mention of executing judgment in ver. 8, 10, and here in this verse with addition of "anger, fury, and furious rebukes." The prophet may seem too repetitious and verbose, but it is otherwise; repetitions of the same thing serve to confirm the truth of the matter, to show the speed of the event, and to excite the minds of those the things concern; all which fall in here. The prophet prophesying against the Jews at Jerusalem, their city and state, and threatening destruction to all, himself keeping in Babylon, conceived that they would not believe what he said, and fear what he threatened, neither be affected with what he delivered; to prevent these evils, he repeats the thing oft, and strengthens it with variety of words, that so his doctrine might be the more weighty, the sooner believed, they awakened, and the judgment that was at hand feared.

"In furious rebukes." The Hebrew is, in rebukes of heat. Pradus observes, that *jacach* notes rebuking before witness; and God would do it before the nations; and these rebukes were not to cure, but to destroy.

"I the Lord have spoken it." Lest they might think the prophet and his prophecy might die together, and come to nothing, the Lord tells them, it was himself spake, and that the prophecy should take place, whatever became of the prophet; because it was from him who was the living God, and would see it fulfilled at Jerusalem, though uttered in Babylon.

Ver. 16. *When I shall send upon them the evil arrows of famine, which shall be for their destruction, and which I will send to destroy you: and I will increase the famine upon you, and will break your staff of bread.*

I have spoken of "famine" and "breaking the staff of bread" in chap. iv. 16. Only I shall open unto you that expression, "The arrows of famine:" they are either the arrows that bring famine, or the arrows that famine brings. The arrows that bring famine, are great droughts, palmer-worms, locusts, canker-worms, caterpillars, thunder, lightning, winds, storms, immoderate rains, great hails, long frosts, murrains, transportations of commodities, monopolizing, hoarding up of creatures, wars, &c. Many of these are shot down from heaven by God, and all are sent from God, and cause famine; and they are called arrows, for that they do to the corn, cattle, fruits, and state where they are, what arrows do to the bodies of man or beast, wound, disquiet, consume; hence, when mention is made of a famine in Habakkuk's days, ch. iii. the Lord is said "to march through the land in indignation," ver. 12, and his bow to be made quite naked, ver. 9; then did God shoot amongst them the arrows of famine.

The arrows famine brings, are leanness, faintness, sickness, loathsomeness, frettings, fears of death, longings for death, gnawings of the stomach, pinching of the wind got into the bowels, eating of their own flesh, thirsting and burning heat, &c.; these are arrows that famine brings, and kill like arrows shot into the liver, which wounding deeply, pain greatly, and kill quickly. And in this sense I rather take it here, because the judgment spoken of concerning the Jews, who were to be besieged, if it be taken in the other sense, would have been a judgment to the besiegers, who lay in the field, and were not so well fortified against those arrows as they within; it is therefore meant of the arrows famine brought upon them chiefly, not excluding the arrows which brought that famine, namely, war. And these arrows were prepared in Moses's days: Deut. xxxii. 23, "I will heap mischiefs upon them; I will spend mine arrows upon them;" and what arrows? "They shall be burnt with hunger, and devoured with burning heat, and with bitter destruction," ver. 24. Famine is like a multitude of hot coals in a man's bowels and bones, that cause grievous pain, even "bitter destruction;" and therefore they are called here, "the evil arrows of famine," because they bring many evils, and at last a miserable death. This Jeremiah acknowledges made good, Lam. iii. 12, 13, speaking in the person of the church and state; "He hath bent his bow, and set me as a mark for the arrow. He hath caused the arrows of his quiver to enter into my reins."

Ver. 17. *So will I send upon you famine and evil beasts, and they shall bereave thee; and pes-*

tilence and blood shall pass through thee; and I will bring the sword upon thee. I the Lord have spoken it.

Here is a repetition of the former judgment, only one is new, and that is, "evil beasts." Some would have it meant of the Chaldeans, that were like evil beasts, that with their horns, teeth, heels, and hoofs, should toss, gore, rend, and devour them: others understand it literally, for evil and wild beasts, lions, bears, &c. which were threatened, Deut. xxxii. 24, "I will send the teeth of beasts upon them, with the poison of serpents of the dust;" Lev. xxvi. 22, "I will send wild beasts which shall rob you of your children, destroy your cattle, and make you few in number; and your high ways shall be desolate." See the truth of it, 2 Kings xvii. 25; lions were sent that slew them, they feared not God. But this was past, and our prophet speaks of that which was to come. Know then, that as God sent lions to destroy them there, so he could send lions to destroy them in Babylon. Besides, those eastern countries were not without lions; Daniel was put into the lions' den; and certainly there were lions, and other evil beasts, to make good what was threatened, whensoever divine pleasure would.

"I the Lord have spoken it." They looked at Ezekiel as a mere man, and whatever he threatened, yet it could do little, and therefore were like to regard neither him nor his prophecy. To prevent this, and to add the greater weight to the prophecy, the Lord takes all upon himself, and saith, It is not Ezekiel, but I that am Jehovah, who gave being to all creatures, and will give being to my word, it is "I the Lord have spoken it." Here the Lord subscribes his own name, acknowledges all his, and that is enough to make all authentic. This Lord, who is dreadful in threatenings, mighty and faithful in execution of threats, let all the world fear and give glory unto, before he cause darkness.

CHAPTER VI.

Ver. 1—7. *And the word of the Lord came unto me, saying, Son of man, set thy face toward the mountains of Israel, and prophesy against them, and say, Ye mountains of Israel, hear the word of the Lord God; Thus saith the Lord God to the mountains, and to the hills, to the rivers, and to the valleys; Behold, I, even I, will bring a sword upon you, and I will destroy your high places. And your altars shall be desolate, and your images shall be broken: and I will cast down your slain men before your idols. And I will lay the dead carcases of the children of Israel before their idols; and I will scatter your bones round about your altars. In all your dwelling-places the cities shall be laid waste, and the high places shall be desolate; that your altars may be laid waste and made desolate, and your idols may be broken and cease, and your images may be cut down, and your works may be abolished. And the slain shall fall in the midst of you, and ye shall know that I am the Lord.*

IN this chapter you have,

I. A command to prophesy, in the two first verses.

II. The prophecy itself; in which are three things:

1. A threatening of desolation to the land of Judea, the idols, altars, and men thereof, in ver. 3—7.

2. A promise of mercy unto them in their scattered condition, ver. 8—10. Some should escape the judgments, repent of their evil ways, and know the Lord.

3. A prefiguration of the grief they should have for the judgments to come upon them; which are repeated, ver. 11—14.

Junius observes this prophecy to have been on the sabbath day, the one and twentieth of the fifth month, in the sixth year of their captivity; and on the twenty-eighth day of the same month, the prophecy in the next chapter; and on the fifth day of the sixth month, the vision in the eighth chapter.

God honoured his own day, with giving out his word by revelations and visions; that day they rested from their labour, and were fittest to hear, see, and receive divine things. It was now above a year since Ezekiel had his first vision; for that was in the fifth day of the fourth month, and fifth year of the captivity, this in the sixth year and fifth month.

The prophets had not all communicated to them at once, but by degrees, as infinite wisdom saw best; and the church understands not all at once what they wrote, but now a little, and then a little, as it pleases God to let in light.

Ver. 2. "Set thy face toward the mountains of Israel." Turn thee unto them, speak boldly and freely, prophesy their destruction. The mountains of Israel were divers: there was mount Ebal, and mount Gerizim, Deut. xxvii. 12, 13; mount Carmel, 1 Kings xviii. 19; mount Horeb, 1 Kings xix. 8; mount Zemaraim, 2 Chron. xiii. 4; mount Gilead, Cant. iv. 1; mount Ephraim, Josh. xvii. 15; mount Naphtali, and mount Judah, Josh. xx. 7; mount Hermon, 1 Chron. v. 23; mount Lebanon, Judg. iii. 3; mount Tabor, Judg. iv. 6; mount Bethel, Josh. xvi. 1; mount Moriah, 2 Chron. iii. 1; mount Zion, Psal. cxxv. 1; mount Olivet, Luke xix. 37, which is called the mount of corruption, 2 Kings xxiii. 13, because Solomon had built there high places for Ashtoreth, Chemosh, and Milcom; and not only in that, but divers other of these mountains, were altars and images, which provoked the Lord; and therefore he bids the prophet to prophesy against them.

He speaks to the mountains, hills, rivers, and valleys, to hear the word of the Lord. This kind of speaking sets out the weightiness of the prophecy, the vehemency of affection, and seemed to convince the Jews of their insensibleness and incurableness; they were so hardened in sin, that there was as much hope of doing good to these creatures, as to them by the word.

Here is a prosopopeia, attribution of sense to dumb creatures, which is frequent in the Scriptures: Deut. xxxii. 1, "Give ear, O ye heavens, and I will speak; and hear, O earth, the words of my mouth." So Jer. ii. 12; Isa. i. 2. Hence the earth is said to tremble, the hills to move at the wrath of God, Psal. xviii. 7; lxxvi. 8; cxiv. 7; winds and seas to obey, Matt. viii. 27. All creatures are more ready to obey the will of their Creator, than man is. Apostrophes are therefore oft made from the sensible and rational creatures, to those that are void of both; to set out the stupidity of man, and his unworthiness of the word. The Lord passes by the masters, and looks to the servants, neglects men, and speaks to the mountains, that so he might provoke them to consider.

"To the rivers." The Vulgate is, *rupibus*, to the rocks. אפיק in the Hebrew doth signify channels·

Isa. viii. 7, "The king of Assyria shall come up over all his channels, and go over all his banks:" 2 Sam. xxii. 16, "The channels of the sea appeared." (Psal. xviii. 15.) It signifies also the waters that run in the channels: Job vi. 15, "As the stream of brooks they pass away;" and Psal. cxxvi. 4, "As the streams in the south." Hence it is rendered rivers, Joel iii. 18; Ezek. xxxv. 8, from אפק which signifies to contain and corroborate, and both these the channels do; they contain the waters, keep them within their banks, and strengthen them being kept together, so that they run with force, and bear burdens.

The Septuagint hath it *νάπαις*, which notes thickets and woody places which use to be about waters.

"Valleys." By the water-sides, and in the valleys, they provoked God. Jer. xlix. 4, "Wherefore gloriest thou in the valleys?" they trusted in their flowing and fat valleys. Isa. lvii. 5, they inflamed themselves "with idols under every green tree, slaying the children in the valleys, under the clifts of the rocks." And Jer. xxxii. 35, "They built the high places of Baal, which are in the valley of the son of Hinnom, to cause their sons and their daughters to pass through the fire unto Molech;" and this valley was afterward called, "The valley of slaughter," Jer. xix. 6; and the reason is given, Jer. vii. 32, 33: they had slain their children there, and God punished them with a great slaughter there, and defiled the place with their blood, which they had formerly defiled with their sin.

"A sword upon you." That is, the Assyrians, armed with instruments of war; they should come and lay all waste, break down altars, cut down groves, dig down hills, dry up their channels, and let out their waters.

"The high places." They are first mentioned in Leviticus, chap. xxvi. 30. They were mountains or hills where the people worshipped, (2 Chron. i. 3.) taken from the practice of heathens, who chose out pleasant places, woody hills and recesses, where they built chapels, temples, and altars to their gods. Numb. xxii. 41, "Balak brought Balaam into the high places of Baal," where there was a temple or chapel for the worship of Baal; and therefore, in the next chapter, he bids him make seven altars, that they might worship their god Baal there. Heathens had many such places; Deut. xii. 2, 3, "Ye shall utterly destroy all the places, wherein the nations served their gods, upon the high mountains, the hills, and under every green tree: ye shall overthrow their altars, break their pillars, burn their groves with fire, hew down the graven images of their gods, and destroy the names of them out of that place." God would not have his people to worship him in any heathenish ways, or with heathenish rites; but they built themselves "high places, images, and groves, on every high hill, and under every green tree," 1 Kings xiv. 23. Jeroboam "made an house of high places," 1 Kings xii. 13. They were to sacrifice in the tabernacle: when they had special and prophetical warrant, they might sacrifice any where; and after the ark was taken, which had stood at Shiloh three hundred and forty three years, and was movable from place to place, then it was lawful for the people to offer in the high places. Before the temple was built, notwithstanding the destruction of the high places threatened by Moses, Lev. xxvi. 30; by Amos, chap. vii. 9; by Hosea, chap. x. 8, and other prophets; many of God's people sacrificed in the high places, under trees, and elsewhere: as Gideon, Judg. vi. 19; Samuel, 1 Sam. ix. 19; David, 2 Sam. xxiv. 25; Solomon, 1 Kings iii. 4; Manoah, Judg. xiii. 19; Elijah, 1 Kings xviii. 31, 32, &c. God accepted their sacrifices, and winked at this error; but their sacrificing afterward in the high places, did bitterly provoke God, and the complaint was, that the high places were not taken away, 1 Kings xxii. 43; xv. 14. They continued till Hezekiah's days, who removed them, 2 Kings xviii. 4; but Josiah utterly destroyed them out of the land, 2 Chron. xxxiv. 3. Yet those kings that came after, restored them again. It is said of Jehoahaz, "He did evil in the sight of the Lord, according to all that his fathers had done," 2 Kings xxiii. 22.

Ver. 4. "Your images shall be broken." Hebrew חמניכם the sun images. חמה is a name given to the sun, Job xxx. 28, from חמם *calere*, to be hot, because of the great heat thereof, and *chammanim* is sun images. Hence Jupiter Ammon, who had a famous temple in Africa, wherein was the image of the sun, as A. Lapid. in Lev. xxvi. 30, hath it; and Macrobius shows, that Jupiter and the sun were the same. (Macrobius, lib. 1. Saturn. c. 23.) The idolatrous Jews were accustomed to worship the sun; 2 Kings xxiii. 5, they "burned incense to the sun:" and because the heathens were wont to worship the sun under (Ovid. l. 2. Metam.) the figure of a chariot and four horses, it is said, the kings of Judah gave horses and chariots to the sun, ver. 11. The rabbies think these were living horses, which drew a chariot daily toward the east, and some sitting in it did salute the sun in the king's name; others more probably conceive these horses and chariots were portrayed effigies, set up at the entering in at the house of the Lord, in honour of the sun, and so set above their altars, 2 Chron. xxxiv. 4. Buxtorf and Junius call them, *subdiales statuæ*, statues that stood abroad, and were exposed to the sun. Aben Ezra thinks they were houses or chapels, made for the worship of the sun. I conceive they were images set up for that purpose; you have mention made of them in Isa. xxvii. 9; xvii. 8. Some think they were little courts wherein were altars and fire preserved upon them, in honour to the sun. Calvin thinks them so called from their warmth, *ab æstu*, because idolaters run after them, as adulterers do after whores: others from *chemah, furor*, madness, because they (Deod. on Lev. xxvi. 30.) are carried with fury to that service. Vid. Buxtorf in *Chamam*. Isa. lvii. 5, "Inflaming yourselves with idols."

"I will cast down the slain men." This seemeth a strange speech; slain men are not standing, need not casting down. The Hebrew is חלליכם which the Vulgate renders, *interfectos vestros*, your slain men; (It is also to profane, pollute.) they are slain men that fall down to idols, that serve other gods, men appointed to be slain; or *confossos vestros*, your wounded men; for *shalal* is *perforare*, to stab through, and it is probable that many being wounded by the Chaldeans, would flee out of Jerusalem to the hills, altars, groves, and idols, for safety, and there the Lord would destroy them before the idols; their enemies should find them out, and make an end of them: Hos. x. 8, "They shall say to the mountains, Cover us, and to the hills, Fall on us;" they were in great fear, distress, and hid themselves, yet that prevented not their death. Jer. xii. 12, "The spoilers are come up upon all high places through the wilderness: for the sword of the Lord shall devour from the one end of the land even to the other end of the land, and no flesh shall have peace;" they should find no favour at their altars, in sight of their idols. Idolaters conceit, that the gods, in honour of whom they set up their altars and images, will relieve them in distresses, and turn aside evil from them; but it should not be, they should find no mercy:

Sennacherib was slain before Nisroch his god, Isa. xxxvii. 38.

It is also in the 5th and 6th verses.

"Before their idols." גִּלּוּלִים dung-hill gods, excrementitious deities, from גלל dung; so it is rendered in 1 Kings xiv. 10, even man's dung, which is most loathsome.

This name is put upon idols, to show how they do stink in the nostrils of God, and make the worshippers of them filthy, stinking creatures; they are like swine, that feed upon, and wallow in dung. Idols defile the soul and body both; for usually spiritual uncleanness and bodily do go together. Idolatry and adultery are companions, Jer. v. 7, 8, they worship other gods, and neigh after their neighbours' wives. Idols do defile and cause defilement, Ezek. xxii. 3, "The city maketh idols against herself, to defile herself."

Ver. 5. "I will lay the dead carcasses of the children of Israel," &c. They should want burial, be exposed to open shame, their altars be defiled with blood and bones. Josiah polluted the altar with the bones and carcasses of dead men, 2 Kings xxiii. 16, 20; and Jeremiah tells of the bones of kings, princes, priests, prophets, and inhabitants of Jerusalem, that should be taken out of their graves, be spread before the sun, moon, and host of heaven, whom they worshipped, and not to be buried; but should be for dung upon the face of the earth. They had served dung-hill idols, and God would make them dung; yea, in the place where they had so sinned, should they suffer this heavy judgment, even before the idols. The Jews used to bury the bones of their kings with gold, silver, costly garments, crowns, sceptres, and arms: prophets, and other chief men, had some precious things buried with them. Josephus tells that Hyrcanus took out of David's sepulchre six thousand talents. Curtius tells of Alexander the Great, that hearing there was much wealth in Cyrus's sepulchre, he commanded it to be opened, but found none. The Chaldeans, being covetous, would search their sepulchres for wealth, scatter the bones of the dead in disgrace, and leave them as dung upon the face of the earth. This judgment Moses had foretold them of, Lev. xxvi. 30, "I will cut down your images, and cast your carcasses upon the carcasses of your idols:" their worship seemed holy to themselves, but God would pollute it with their own carcasses. That which is of great account among men, is an abomination unto God.

Altare polluitur contactu cadaveris. *Calv.*

Lib. 13. Antiquit.

Lib. 10.

Ver. 6. "In all your dwelling-places the cities shall be laid waste," &c. Here is the extent of the judgment, to all their cities, wherever they dwelt; all their cities were defiled with idols and idolatrous worship: Jer. xi. 13, "According to the number of thy cities were thy gods, O Judah; and according to the number of the streets of Jerusalem have ye set up altars to that shameful thing, even altars to burn incense unto Baal."

Superstition and idolatry are spreading things, they quickly get into all the cities of a kingdom, and streets of cities, and head of every high way, Ezek. xvi. 25. Therefore all the cities of Judah are threatened, Jer. i. 15; and ix. 11, "I will make Jerusalem heaps, a den of dragons; and the cities of Judah desolate, without an inhabitant."

Isa. ii. 8, "Their land is full of idols."

Obs. 1. The first observation is, That where idols and false worship are got into a church or state, they are not easily got out again. Their cities must be destroyed, that their altars and idols may be broken and cease. After the calves were up at Dan and Bethel, the prophets could never get them down till the sword came: the high places stood many hundred years, and were not fully put down till Josiah's days, and quickly after they were up again. Hath not antichrist and his abettors brought in false worship, tyrannical government, into the church, and held it in many hundred years? What ado hath there been among us, to pluck up popery and prelacy, which are not yet fully done!

Obs. 2. See what it is that ruins cities; altars, idols, false worship, mixtures of man's inventions with the Lord's pure ordinances. These are great cannon, that batter cities; these are gunpowder, that blow them up; these bring the Lord of hosts to war against them. It was the calves that wounded Israel, and laid the cities thereof waste. Hos. x. 5, "The inhabitants of Samaria shall fear because of the calves of Beth-aven." Hos. xiii. 2, 3, they had images and idols, kissed the calves; therefore they should be as the morning cloud, the early dew, as chaff and smoke: ver. 9, "O Israel, thou hast destroyed thyself," thine own idols have wrought and brought thy destruction. Isa. x. 11, Samaria and her idols were destroyed, and such destruction is threatened to Jerusalem and her idols. And Abijah knew that the calves would ruin Jeroboam and his great army; and therefore saith, 2 Chron. xiii. 8, "With you are the golden calves."

Obs. 3. Idolatry and false worship do so provoke God, that he will destroy cities, kingdoms, churches, but he will have them out. Their cities and high places must be laid waste, that their altars and idols, their corrupt worship, might be taken away. Sins of this nature make God jealous, furious, clothe himself with vengeance, and do terrible things: Jer. ii. 11, Israel had taken in other gods, and it follows in the 15th verse, "The young lions roared upon him, and made his land waste: his cities are burned without inhabitant;" God looked upon them as already burned. You have the indignation of God against idolaters and idolatrous places fully set out in the 13th of Deuteronomy, from the 12th verse to the end. If the men of a city did fall to idolatry, the men and cattle must be all destroyed with the edge of the sword, the city and all in it burned with fire, and never be built again; and they must not meddle with any accursed thing: when this is done, God will turn from the fierceness of his anger. Nothing kindles God's wrath more than forsaking of and corrupting his worship. Hath not popery and popish inventions cost the christian world much blood, and the ruin of many places? Babylon must be destroyed for her whoredom; and, Rev. xiv. 9, 10, "If any man worship the beast and his image, and receive his mark in his forehead, or hand, the same shall drink of the wine of the wrath of God, which is poured out without mixture into the cup of his indignation; and he shall be tormented with fire and brimstone," &c. God is severe against false worship and worshippers. God will lay waste all places and persons rather than not have men's works out of his worship.

Obs. 4. That men love to have somewhat of their own in worship; they are not content with what the infinitely wise God commends unto them, but will be adding. Here is much of man's mentioned; your high places, your altars, your idols, your images, and works. The second commandment, Exod. xx. 4, shows that man is prone to be meddling and making something in worship, till he mar all. The people quickly forgot God and made a calf, when Moses was in the mount; and their hearts ever hankered after heathenish gods, rites, and cere-

Ahaz would have in altare Damascenum, and we altare Romanum.

Service Book was patched together by additions of men.

monies. Psal. cvi. 29, "They provoked him to anger with their inventions:" they were given to changing, and adding of their own, and their additions provoked God: and why so? they were taken more with their own, than with the Lord's; "they went a whoring with their own inventions," ver. 39, they pleased and delighted them, as adulterers are more delighted with their whores than their wives; but they are defiling delights, they were defiled with their own works.

Obs. 5. God is not pleased with any thing in worship which is not his own; he must prescribe what way and wherewith he will be worshipped. It is not altars, high places, appointed and made by men, not any of their works, that are acceptable to him, not the works of their hands, nor of their heads; no devices of man, nor his vestures, gestures, ceremonies, services; they all have in them *aliquid fæcis et terræ*, something of dross and earth, they are like their authors. That which pleases God must come from God, be set up by him and carry unto him. That which he appoints, he approves, it is pure; that which man brings, he abhors, it is spurious, pollutes his ordinances, frustrates his commands, Matt. xv. 6; therefore such plants God will pluck up, such works he will break down.

Obs. 6. That judgments cause idolaters to know the true God from the false. When God's hand is upon the mountains, hills, valleys, cities, high places, altars, and their slain fallen, then shall they know that I am the Lord, Jehovah; not an idol god, but the true, the living God, that have being of myself, that give being to my promises and threats, that take being from others: you would not believe my prophets, but you shall know there was truth in their threats, and power in me to make them good.

Ver. 8—10. *Yet will I leave a remnant, that ye may have some that shall escape the sword among the nations, when ye shall be scattered through the countries. And they that escape of you shall remember me among the nations whither they shall be carried captives, because I am broken with their whorish heart, which hath departed from me, and with their eyes, which go a whoring after their idols: and they shall loathe themselves for the evils which they have committed in all their abominations. And they shall know that I am the Lord, and that I have not said in vain that I would do this evil unto them.*

Here is the second part of the prophecy, viz. A promise of mercy.

The eighth verse is of the nature of the third verse in the fifth chapter, where the prophet was bid to bind up a few hairs in his skirts; and here God would leave a remnant, the sword and dispersion should not devour all.

Obs. God's wrath is never so hot against his people, but he will show mercy to some. God would bring a sweeping judgment, lay mountains, hills, rivers, valleys, cities, high places, altars, idols, images, waste and desolate; yet he would leave a remnant, preserve some, when in the midst of their enemies, amongst Babylonians and other nations.

In the fifth chapter, ver. 12, God would "scatter them, and draw out a sword after them." It was great wrath to be driven out of their country, to be in banishment, which lawyers call a civil death, because men in it are divided from their friends, liberties, and comforts, which sweeten their lives; but to have the sword at their heels, added to the weight of wrath, threatens all their lives; yet notwithstanding this condition, God reserved some from the sword in their banishment. They might upon this severe prophecy think, What will become of the church, shall all perish, and God's faithfulness fail? No, God would have a care of that, a remnant he would save. Storms may be so terrible and lasting, that the church may be brought low, not be visible, yet it shall never be extinct. When the prophets were cut off by Jezebel, there were a hundred hid in caves by Obadiah, 1 Kings xviii. 4. When Elijah thought himself alone, and his life at the stake too, the Lord told him there were seven thousand in Israel lay dormant, "which had not bowed their knees to Baal," 1 Kings xix. 18. When Herod "slew all the children in Bethlehem, and all the coasts thereof, from two years old and under," yet Christ escaped, he was preserved: and as in that storm God preserved the Head, so in every storm he will preserve the body. At the massacre in France, all the protestants were not cut off, and the wars of Ireland have not devoured all. The church shall never cease being, the gates of hell shall never prevail against it.

Ver. 9. "And they that escape of you shall remember me," &c. In this verse is the fruit of divine mercy towards them:

First, "They shall remember me."

Secondly, "Loathe themselves for the evils they have committed."

Thirdly, the ground of both these, "Because I am broken with their whorish heart and whorish eyes."

Fourthly, the place where they should do it, "Among the nations."

"Remember me." They shall know then that I am God, infinitely differing from the gods that they have chosen; that my worship is spiritual, and admits not mixtures of men: they shall remember my holiness, that I hate all false ways of worship; my justice, that I have not done any wrong to them in ruining their country and temple, and scattering them in all quarters; they shall remember my bounty and love to them, and how they forgot me and abused all; they shall remember my mercy in preserving them from the pestilence, the famine, the sword, and their taunting adversaries; and say, We all deserved to have been destroyed and rooted out for ever; but the Lord is gracious, hath had compassion on us and spared our lives; we will therefore repent of our ways, return to him, trust in him, and give glory to his name: all which are implied in the word "remember." So it is used, Psal. cxxxvii. 1, there are remembrance and weeping joined together; Psal. xxii. 27, there are remembrance and turning; Psal. xx. 7, remembrance is there for trusting; Psal. lxiii. 5, 6, praising and remembering go together: and when men fall to idolatry, they are said to forget God, Judg. iii. 7; implying that remembering of God is to worship him his own way, and so to glorify his name.

"Broken with their whorish heart." The Vulgate reads it actively, I have broken their heart. The word is passive נשברתי I am broken. Here is great difference, and the Vulgate is corrupt; and the Greek mistakes, which reads it, ὀμωμοκά τῃ καρδία αὐτῶν, I have sworn to their hearts; the ground of which error is, they took it to be נשבעתי for נשברתי Some would have it, I have bought their whorish hearts, that were for idols and any thing but me; because the word is twice or thrice in the Scripture used in that sense: Gen. xli. 57, "All countries came into Egypt to Joseph for to buy corn," *Hishbar, ad frangendum*, Montanus reads it: and chap. xlii. 6, Joseph "sold to all the people of the land,"

Hammashbir faciebat, frangere. *Montanus.*

and so in the 5th verse: but the common sense of the word is, to break, and it is truly rendered, "I am broken with their whorish heart."

God had taken this people to be his, as a man takes a woman to be his wife; but they had whorish hearts, and went out from God to idols; they had a "spirit of whoredoms" in them, that "caused them to err, and go a whoring from under their God," Hos. iv. 12; ix. 1. They were not content with God's love, his ordinances, his worship; but they would try what the gods of the heathen were, what their way and worship was, prostitute themselves to them; and this troubled the sight of God, afflicted his soul, brake his heart, as a man's is by the whorish acts of his wife. We say, a man or woman break much, that have much trouble, jealousy, care, sorrow. God was troubled with, jealous of, careful and sorrowful for, his people above all others, and this even brake the heart of God. Their courses grieved him exceedingly. Great grief vexeth the heart, and lieth like a mighty weight upon it: hence that in Amos ii. 13, "Behold, I am pressed under you, as a cart is pressed that is full of sheaves;" the grief God took at their courses was as a great load upon his spirit. God's eye beheld their courses, and his eye affected, yea, afflicted his heart, Lam. iii. 51: the Vulgate reads it, *Oculus meus deprædatus est animam meam*, Hath taken away the virtue, spirit, and life of my heart.

"Whorish heart." A heart hankering after idols, pleading for them, delighting in them, and prostituting itself unto them. This people was much addicted unto this sin, which is oft expressed by the name of whoredoms and whoring, Lev. xx. 5; xvii. 7; Judg. ii. 17. This sin is so called,

First, because it is a breach of covenant, as whoredom is. God marries his people to himself, he is for them, and they should be for him only, Exod. xx. 23. He is a husband to them, Jer. ii. 2; Hos. ii. 19; and now to leave him for idols, is to deal treacherously with him, Jer. iii. 9, 20; Deut. xxxi. 16.

Secondly, it is a pleasing sin, as whoredom is. Hence all Israel is said to go a whoring after Gideon's ephod, Judg. viii. 27; and Isa. lxvi. 3, "Their soul delighteth in their abominations;" they please their senses, give some satisfaction to blind consciences, help on their devotions, as they conceit, which affects much.

Thirdly, it is a defiling sin. Whoredom is a defiling sin, and so is idolatry, and all false worship: Ezek. xxii. 3, Jerusalem "maketh idols against herself to defile herself." Acts xv. 20, they are called ἀλισγήματα, pollutions; and they pollute the persons and places where they are, Jer. iii. 9. As pure worship sanctifies, so false worship pollutes: Rev. xiv. 4, "They were not defiled with women," not with false worship, with the whore of Babylon, or any of her inventions; but were virgins that kept themselves chaste, not going out from God to the corruptions of any.

Fourthly, it hardens, stupifies, makes impudent, Prov. vii. 13; and so idolatry produces such effects. Hence the Jews which were given to it are called "impudent children," Ezek. ii. 4, "hard-hearted," Ezek. iii. 7; "sottish children," Jer. iv. 22. Jezebel stirred up Ahab to idolatry, 1 Kings xxi. 25, 26; they were both idolaters, they were hard-hearted, impudently wicked, bloody and cruel; Naboth and the prophets were slain by them.

Jer. ii. 20, it is called playing the harlot.

Fifthly, it inflames, and idolatry doth so; Isa. lvii. 5, "Inflaming yourselves with idols, slaying the children in the valleys."

"With their eyes, which go a whoring after their idols." It is evil when the heart follows the eye, worse when the eye follows the heart; this notes habitual evil, the other but occasional. Their eyes, as well as their hearts, went a whoring; they looked, and lusted; their eyes were "eyes full of adultery," 2 Pet. ii. 14. Ahaz saw the altar at Damascus, and he must presently have such a one up at Jerusalem, 2 Kings xvi. 10. Men follow "the sight of their eyes," Eccl. xi. 9; "the lust of their eyes," as John calls it, 1 John ii. 16; and sensual men are led by the eye in point of worship, as in point of women; Ahaz was; but men's eyes and hearts are ill factors for worship: Numb. xv. 39, "Remember all the commandments of the Lord, and do them; and that ye seek not after your own heart, and your own eyes, after which ye use to go a whoring." The eyes are the spies of the body, they give information to the heart, that lusts, whoredom is committed, and God is provoked to jealousy. The eyes are called whorish, because they are *internuncii adulterii et idololatriæ*, the assistants of adultery and idolatry; they dislike, forsake the beauty of God's worship, truth, ordinances, and spy beauty in corruption, in false worship, superstition, idolatry, men's additions; they see a decorum in them, are pleased with them, and draw the heart to them.

It is bad when eyes are in *amore duces*, worse when in *religione duces*.

"They shall loathe themselves." The Vulgate reads it, *displicebunt sibimet*, they shall displease themselves; Calvin, *pudefient*, they shall be ashamed; Junius, *fastidium erunt sibi ipsis*, they shall be a loathing to themselves. The Hebrew hath more in it: *Nakottu, ingemiscent*, saith Montanus; they shall so sigh and groan, that you shall see it in their faces: Shindler, *offensi sunt in faciebus suis ad mala*, when they saw what they had done, it was offensive to them, and they smote themselves upon the face for grief. The word notes a cutting; when a man is so ashamed that he dares not behold God or man, he is like a man cut down. So it is used, Job x. 1, "My soul is weary of my life;" it is the same word, and rendered in the margin, cut off: his sorrow was piercing, and cutting. Such should be the condition of those here, their idolatry and other evils should be *carnifices qui corda eorum discerperent*, executioners which rend their hearts. The meaning is, they shall have much shame, sorrow, and breaking of heart, for their sins.

קמט נקמו vel קוט ingemiscere.

Septuag. is Κόψονται.

Ver. 10. "And they shall know that I am the Lord," &c. They shall know experimentally, that I speak and threaten not in vain, punish not unjustly, but order all things for my glory and their good.

Obs. 1. God's people escaping destruction in common calamities, are mindful of God, though they suffer much hardship. As here, they had lost all, their very liberty, and were captives; yet being preserved by God among the gentiles, they should remember God; that is, repent, return, and trust in God, honour him, praise him, and worship him the right way. Psal. lxxviii. 34, 35, "When he slew them, then they sought him: and they returned and inquired early after God; and remembered that God was their rock, and the high God their redeemer:" when death devoured some, and mercy delivered others, then their hearts were affected, and God seriously thought upon. Never is the heart in a better frame towards God, than when it hath been in the jaws of death, and is set at liberty from the king of terrors. David made the sweetest psalms when he had the greatest deliverances, Psal. xviii. xlvi. ciii. and many others; which made him say, "Thou liftest me up from the gates of death, that I may show forth all thy praise in the gates of the daughter of Zion," Psal. ix. 13, 14. God brings his people into trouble, that he may deliver them, and that they may remember him. Psal. l. 15, "I will deliver thee, and thou shalt glorify me;" that is, effectually, not in a low, faint, formal degree. Such great deliverances as give life, should cause those they concern to look strongly and live wholly unto God, to glorify him in all things, to remember him at all times, and to show forth all his praises.

Obs. 2. That God is not tied to any persons, places, or times, to show mercy; but on whom he will, where he will, and when he will, he showeth mercy. These persons were idolaters in the holy land, met with sore judgments there, were driven forth into Babylon, a polluted, idolatrous, heathenish place; there the lives of some of them are preserved, they being under heavy pressures from God and man; yet they are brought to know God, to loathe themselves and their former ways. These were times wherein they had no sacrificing, little or no help for their souls, but lay in darkness, and notwithstanding all this, God showed mercy: neither their sins, nor the sins of the place, both which were great, nor the time of wrath they were under, (for so it is called, Isa. liv. 8,) could obstruct the free grace of God; but some he spares, some he touches with the lively sense of their sins, and puts into a state of grace in the midst of enemies, of sins, and of judgments. God could show mercy in Babylon as well as Zion. Let the holy land, holy city, holy temple, holy altar, holy sacrifices, and all the holy things be laid waste, and persons be brought to the greatest improbabilities of finding mercy, be as great sinners as any living, as these were, and in Babylon; yet God is free, can, will, doth show mercy even to such, in such a place, and at such a time, when his wrath is pouring out. Manasseh was a great sinner, a murderer, an idolater, a sorcerer, carried into Babylon, and, in the eye of all, in a hopeless condition; yet there God visits him, his Spirit breathes and blows upon him, he humbles his soul greatly, prays effectually, is returned to Jerusalem, and knows the God of his fathers, 2 Chron. xxxiii. 11—13. Nothing could keep off God from showing mercy. God took Abraham, the father of the faithful, from Ur of Chaldea; he found favour among idolaters, and God showed mercy to his posterity, even in that land. When "all flesh had corrupted its ways," yet mercy was shown to Noah, Gen. vi. Yea, those that put Christ to death had their hearts pricked, Acts ii. 37. To the gentiles that had lived in abominable idolatries, God "granted repentance unto life," Acts xi. 18. There is nothing in man, in any place or time, that can impede God from showing mercy; that is an act of his will, nothing in us moves him to it, nothing in us hinders him from it: "I will have mercy on whom I will have mercy, and I will have compassion on whom I will have compassion," Rom. ix. 15.

Obs. 3. That often God shows the choicest mercy, when he hath cause to execute the sharpest judgment. "They shall remember me, because I am broken with their whorish hearts." Had they broken God's heart, he had cause to have broken their bones, and destroyed them utterly; but the Lord would deal graciously with them, and instead of destruction, cause them to remember him, to loathe themselves, and to come in to fear and serve him. They would not fear, remember, and honour God in Zion, where they had the prophets, the ordinances of God, and mercies of all sorts, but provoked God to plague them; and when they were ripe for destruction, and nothing to be expected but severity, even then doth God deal graciously with them. Isa. lvii. 17, 18, saith God, "For the iniquity of his covetousness was I wroth, and smote him: I hid me, and was wroth, and he went on frowardly in the way of his heart;" he adds sin to sin, in a presumptuous manner; and what could be looked for now but destruction? Doth the great and glorious God smite, and doth man sin more? Yes, he doth, and God sees it; and what then? "I have seen his ways, and will heal him;" not wound him more, not destroy him, but "I will heal him: I will lead him also, and restore comforts unto him and to his mourners." Isa. xliii. 24, 25, "Thou hast made me to serve with thy sins, thou hast wearied me with thine iniquities;" and what then? "I, even I, am he that blotteth out thy transgressions for mine own sake, and will not remember thy sins." God's thoughts are not as man's; that which is argument of death in man's apprehension, is argument of mercy and life in God's. David knew it, and therefore presseth God with an argument, which might have undone him in the judgment of reason; "O Lord, pardon mine iniquity; for it is great," Psal. xxv. 11. God might have said, Therefore will I not pardon thee, because thy sin is great. I have suffered much by thee, by thy murder and adultery, and thinkest thou that I will pardon such great sins? Is this an argument to come to me withal? I have as great wrath as thou hast sins. Thou art a man of death for what thou hast done; thou shouldst die by the law for thy murder, and die for thy adultery, and thou hast given the sentence thyself, "The man that hath done this shall surely die," and bound it thou hast with an oath, "as the Lord liveth," 2 Sam. xii. 5; and therefore die thou must, thou shalt. Such language as this might David have looked for; but he hears of pardon, and that from the mouth of a prophet: and when he moved God with the argument of the greatness of his sins, he did it in the judgment of faith, knowing it would be much for the honour of God, to pardon great sins; that he was as ready to show mercy, as his sins had made him ripe for judgment. Hos. ii. 13, 14, Israel followed Baalim, and forgot God. Had he not now cause to destroy her? It was God's way to destroy such, Psal. lxxiii. 27. Yet it follows, "Therefore, behold, I will allure her, and bring her into the wilderness, and speak comfortably unto her." Because she had forgotten God, God would remember her; because she had been drawn away by idols, God would allure her from idols; because she had vexed God, he would comfort her: here God lets out choice mercy, when he had cause to execute severe wrath. When Peter had denied Christ thrice, and forswore him and the knowledge of him, Matt. xxvi. 72, 74, was there not cause that Christ should have renounced him, smitten him with some great judgment, and made him an example for self-confiders and Christ-deniers to the end of the world? Surely Christ had cause enough, and the opportunity for it was fair before him; but Christ turned and looked upon Peter, and instead of ruining him, raises him.

Obs. 4. False worship doth most afflict God. "I am broken with their whorish heart." Their idolatries, superstitions, and corruptions did not simply displease or grieve God; but oppressed, afflicted, broke the heart of God. Great injuries enter deep, work strongly, eat up the spirits of any they are done unto; and what greater wrong can be done to God, than to set at nought his counsels, to forsake his worship, to withdraw from his government, and to proclaim to the world, that there are better ways than his, and better gods than himself? Those that are idolatrous, and worship God a false way, they do so by God; therefore, Jer. iii. 5, it is said of them, that they did speak and do evil as they could. Men cannot do more to break God, than to worship idols, wrong gods, or the true God a wrong way. Such sins break God's covenant; Deut. xxxi. 16, "This people will go a whoring after other gods, forsake me, and break my covenant;" they break God's silence, Jer. ii. 12, "Be astonished, O ye heavens," &c.; they break God's patience, Isa. xliii. 24, "Thou hast wearied me with thine iniquities;" and here they break even God himself, "I am broken with," &c. The heart should be only for God and his ways, as the wife should be for the husband and his commands; and when God sees the heart, which is his by creation, by command, by purchase, and by desert, to be after false ways, base inventions, and giving that honour to them which is only due unto himself, this pricks him at the heart, and is taken extremely evil; it makes God's soul to abhor a people, Lev. xxvi. 30, to loathe Zion, Jer. xiv. 19. Bring any thing to one that hath an antipathy against it, and that thing afflicts him grievously, it makes him fear, sweat, faint, and sometimes swoon away. God hath a true antipathy, and great, against all false ways of worship; when any therefore is brought near him, it is that puts the Lord more to it than any thing. Lev. xxvi. 11, "I will set my tabernacle among you; and my soul shall not abhor you;" that is, I will delight in you, while my tabernacle and ordinances are with you: Amos v. 26, 27, but when the "tabernacle of Moloch" is amongst them, when they set up ways of their own, then God abhors them, and will send judgments upon them. Let not us retain any thing that tends that way, no names, no ceremonies, no gestures.

Obs. 5. The works of men in God's worship steal away the hearts of the worshippers. They had idols, altars, groves, images, and high places; and whatever pretences they had to colour over things with, their hearts went a whoring after these, and departed from God. There is much, yea all in false worship, that suits with carnal hearts; therefore that which is of God, being spiritual, above the reach of flesh, yea contrary to corruption, it is burdensome and neglected; and that which is of men, being suitable unto man, is closed with. In popery you see how their hearts are taken with that which is from popes, prelates, councils; their music, vestments, perfumes, pictures, images, &c. have their hearts: and let them pretend they do help their devotion with these, help up their hearts more to God; it is not so, these steal away their hearts from God; they are more delighted with these, than with the pure worship of God. Be they idols or images made use of in worship, it is all one; that distinction will not heal a papist's idolatry, nor fetch back his whorish heart to God; for the Hebrew word פסל is in Scripture used promiscuously for both, and put for an image, Isa. xliv. 9, 10: and imagery superstition draws away the heart from God as well as idolatry.

Were not men affected lately with innovations, and that so much, that the ordinances of God were laid by? What the heart affects, that goes up, what it slights, that goes down; as in Isa. xxix. 13, when their hearts were removed far from God, then the precepts of men had interest in God's worship, and what men commended to them their hearts advanced.

Obs. 6. That being in pure worship, is being with God. While they kept to God's ordinances, and were hearty in them, they were with God; but when they corrupted them, then they departed from God.

Obs. 7. That men's eyes are instruments of great evil. They had whorish eyes, they were the inlets of idolatrous and sinful motions, which firing, inflamed the heart after idols. No sense doth more mischief to the soul than the eye; it is an imperial ranging sense, and fetches in, far and near, matter of danger into the bosom: Prov. xvii. 24, "The eyes of a fool are at the end of the earth." The Scripture makes mention of "a mocking eye," Prov. xxx. 17; "an offensive eye," Matt. v. 29; "a beamish eye," Matt. vii. 3; "an evil eye," Prov. xxiii. 6; "a lofty eye," Psal. cxxxi. 1; "a wanton eye," Isa. iii. 16; "a painted eye," Ezek. xxiii. 40; "adulterous eyes," 2 Pet. ii. 14; and here, "whorish eyes:" they are the windows at which sin creeps in. The prince of darkness conveys many works of darkness by the eyes. The serpent deceived Eve by the eye, Gen. iii. 6. Achan saw a goodly Babylonish garment, and a wedge of gold, and so was snared, Josh. vii. 21. Samson saw a harlot, and was taken with her, Judg. xvi. 1. It is the colour of the wine invites the drunkard to excess, Prov. xxiii. 31. Ahab saw Naboth's vineyard laid commodiously for him, and so was set on work to covet it, 1 Kings xxi. 2.

The eyes open the doors first and soonest to let idols into the heart; and when they are in, the heart sets the eyes on work to delight in them; Ezek. xviii. 6, they lift up their eyes to behold idols; they were delectable things to them, Isa. xliv. 9. Great use doth Satan make of the eye, by corruption that is within us, and the creature that is without. Job knew it, and therefore makes a covenant with his eyes, and would not only not see, but not think of a maid, Job xxxi. 1; and if he did see any object that pleased and stirred corruption, he would not let his heart walk after his eye, ver. 7. David would not "set any wicked thing before his eyes," Psal. ci. 3; he prays unto God to "turn away his eyes from beholding vanity," Psal. cxix. 37; and, "Mine eyes are ever towards the Lord," Psal. xxv. 15. And not only should we have care of our eyes, but of our hearts also; for such as our hearts are, such will our eyes and other senses be: if the heart be whorish, the eyes will be whorish; if the heart be covetous, the hand will be covetous; if the heart be froward, the tongue will be froward: therefore Solomon adviseth to "keep the heart with all diligence," Prov. iv. 23.

Obs. 8. That true penitents have their hearts affected for their sins, and loathe themselves for the evils of their ways. "They shall remember me," whom they have broken with their sins, be affected with it, "and loathe themselves for the evils they have committed in all their abominations." Repentance is not a sudden or slight sorrow, but that which goes deep and enters into the heart, as the word here imports; such sorrow as should make them loathe themselves, sigh and groan, smite, yea cut their faces. The Scripture expressions touching repentance and godly sorrow are of like nature, and show the heart is deeply wounded therein, Zech. xii. 10.

It is set out by mourning as for an only son, and being in bitterness as for the loss of a first-born. It is drawing of water and pouring it out before the Lord, 1 Sam. vii. 6; it is the breaking of the heart, contrition of the spirit, Psal. xxxiv. 18; the rending of the heart, Joel ii. 13; ploughing up of the fallow ground, Jer. iv. 3; travailing in child-birth, Isa. xxvi. 17; pricking of the heart, Acts ii. 37.

All which evidences that repentance is a heart business; it works strongly upon that, and brings it up to loathing. When the heart is truly penitent, what it before loved and delighted in, it loathes and abhors. The voice of Ephraim repenting, is, Hos. xiv. 8, "What have I to do any more with idols;" I now loathe them, will not lift mine eyes or hands unto them, nor speak a word for them, nor think of them. Jer. xxxi. 19, "After that I was turned, I repented; I smote upon my thigh: I was ashamed, yea, even confounded, because I did bear the reproach of my youth:" I had sinned in my former days with idols, false worship, satisfied my lusts, but I am now confounded with the shame and reproach of them; now I loathe them, and cannot endure them. Isa. xxxi. 7, when they are turned unto God, "in that day every man shall cast away his idols of silver, and his idols of gold:" they cannot stand before repentance, no more than Dagon before the ark. After God had scourged and purged them with the Babylonish captivity, it is observed that they could never abide idols more, nor would suffer any to come up unto the temple. When Caius Caligula sent his statue to Petronius, president of Judea, to honour it with a place in the temple, the Jews professed they would die rather than behold that abomination in the temple; if that came there, they would not come there; if that lived, they would die. This is the nature of true repentance, that whatever errors, false worship, ways, lusts, things it delighted in before, now it loathes as dung, as filth, and abhors as pestilential and deadly. The Jews repenting, cursed their idols, and their own madness in running a whoring after them.

Here are three evidences of the reality and truth of this repentance.

First, their loathing themselves. It is a hard thing to bring a man to self-loathing; every man loves, exalts himself, and labours to be somebody in the world. Diotrephes affects pre-eminence, but true repentance will make the greatest loathe himself. Repentance sees what black, defiled creatures they are: Ezek. xx. 43, "Ye shall remember your ways, wherein ye have been defiled; and ye shall loathe yourselves in your own sight." A repentant eye sees matter enough of self-abhorrence. When Job, chap. vii. 5, saw his sores, filth, and worms in his flesh, he loathed himself; but not so much as when he saw the sins of his heart, chap. xlii. 6; then he abhorred himself, and all which had excellency in it before, he thought fit to be buried under dust and ashes.

Secondly, "For the evils which they have committed." Not for the evils which their sins had deserved, or God had inflicted, did they loathe themselves, but for the evil of their own ways; so that they did mourn for sin as sin; not for the evil *of* sin, but for the evil *in* sin; which is the contrariety of it to God's will, the offence of divine Majesty, its burdening God himself, breach of union between him and their souls, its violation of his law: it pollutes the soul, hardens the heart, turns the gospel of Christ, all mercies, and means of grace, to our hurt, and is a foundation of eternal ruin. It was the evil of sin, and not of punishment, that David prayed against, 2 Sam. xxiv. 10—17; Psal. li. 2.

Thirdly, it is impartial and universal: "They shall loathe themselves for the evils which they have committed in all their abominations." It is not one or two, but all, comes into question when the heart is in a penitent way: Ezek. xx. 43, "Then shall ye remember your ways, and all your doings, wherein ye have been defiled; and ye shall loathe yourselves in your own sight, for all your evils that ye have committed." Sins, great or small, in any place, with any person, or thing, but especially of worship, come into, fall under, censure, and are abhorred. Manasseh, when he was humbled in Babylon, he loathed his practices in Zion, and took away all the altars that he had built in the mount of the house of the Lord, and in Jerusalem, and cast them out of the city, 2 Chron. xxxiii. 15.

Let us look back, see the evil of our ways, especially in worship, and loathe ourselves for the evil of them all; that we have defiled God's name, ordinances, ourselves, with altars, crucifixes, cringings, conformity to the impositions, innovations of men, subscriptions, oaths of canonical obedience, supporting of a false and tyrannical government in the church of Christ, have been contented under a dull, formal way of worship, &c. Ezek. xliii. 11, "If they be ashamed of all that they have done, show them the form of the house, and the fashion thereof." Shame for false, corrupt worship opens a door for sight, and entrance, of true and pure worship.

On ver. 10, *Obs.* 1. That before men are afflicted and humbled for their sin, they refuse and slight the word of God. Let his prophets come and preach powerfully and terribly unto them, lay God's judgments before them, they mind it not, at least tremble not; but they shall know they have refused my word and messengers: the time is coming they shall be in Babylon, be sorely afflicted, and then they shall know, as for the precedent time, their hearts were stout against God, his truth, his servants, and they were secure. "Who hath believed our report?" saith Isaiah, chap. liii. 1; and chap. xlix. 4, "I have laboured in vain, I have spent my strength for nought;" his hearers slighted his prophecies. So in Zech. vii. 11, 12, "They refused to hearken, and pulled away the shoulder, and stopped their ears, that they should not hear. Yea, they made their hearts as an adamant stone, lest they should hear the law, and the words which the Lord of hosts hath sent in his spirit by the former prophets."

Obs. 2. That a heart under affliction, broken for sin, and loathing itself for its own sins, will give due honour to the word of God, submit to it, acknowledge him and his prophets. "Then shall they know," &c. That is, when they have smarted in the captivity, been cut to the heart for their sins, loathed themselves for all the evils of them, even then shall they know. Afflictions opens men's eyes, blows beget brains, and men come to see their ingratitude towards God, their abuse, neglect, contempt of means, what great loss they have made thereby; and so mourn for each, prize the word, tremble at threatenings, close with promises, subject to commands, honour the Lord and his prophets.

The truest penitent doth most abhor himself, his lusts, his errors, his own ways; and the more abhorrence of these, the more complacency in truth, and the God of truth. Such a one understands the dealings of God, acknowledges the majesty of God in his ordinances, the equity of God in his judgments, the mercies of God in his deliverances, the faithfulness of God in his word, and his infinite love in Christ.

What God doth in the world he doth to fulfil his word. The providences now extant, are accomplishments of the word of God in prophecies and promises.

Obs. 3. The Lord will not leave his word (whatever it be) unaccomplished. "They shall know that I have not said in vain I would do this evil," that I would afflict them. A word is in vain when it is not fulfilled, inefficaciously fulfilled, or unseasonably fulfilled: none of all these befall the word of God, threats or promises. Isa. lv. 11, "The word that is gone forth of my mouth shall not return to me void, but it shall accomplish that which I please, and it shall prosper in the thing whereto I sent it:" if God give out a word for wars, for destruction of cities, kingdoms, churches, for carrying into captivity, that word shall take place, and be effectual. Zech. i. 6, "My words and my statutes, did they not take hold of your fathers?" they overtook them, and arrested them.

Ver. 11—14. *Thus saith the Lord God; Smite with thine hand, and stamp with thy foot, and say, Alas for all the evil abominations of the house of*

Israel! for they shall fall by the sword, by the famine, and by the pestilence. He that is far off shall die of the pestilence; and he that is near shall fall by the sword; and he that remaineth and is besieged shall die by the famine: thus will I accomplish my fury upon them. Then shall ye know that I am the Lord, when their slain men shall be among their idols round about their altars, upon every high hill, in all the tops of the mountains, and under every green tree, and under every thick oak, the place where they did offer sweet savour to all their idols. So will I stretch out my hand upon them, and make the land desolate, yea, more desolate than the wilderness toward Diblath, in all their habitations: and they shall know that I am the Lord.

Here is the third part of the prophecy, which sets out the great grief they should have for the sore judgments of God upon them; which judgments are again mentioned, "sword, famine, pestilence, desolation."

In the 11th verse their grief is set out by symbolical expressions, as, smiting with the hand, stamping with the foot, and crying, Alas. And the cause of these:

First, their sins.

Secondly, their punishments.

"Smite with thine hand, and stamp with thy foot." Such gestures have been used in contrary cases; as well in great joy, as in great grief: Ezek. xxv. 6, "Because thou hast clapped thine hands, and stamped with the feet, and rejoiced in heart with all thy despite against the land of Israel." It is spoken of Ammon, who used those gestures in an insulting way against the Jews; but in this place, these gestures declare their unspeakable grief for their sins and judgments, and were usual in case of sorrow. Jer. xxxi. 19, the prophet brings in Ephraim repenting, and that is a declaration of it, "I smote upon my thigh, and was ashamed;" and when God would bring terror upon his people he bids the prophet smite upon his thigh, Ezek. xxi. 12. Sometimes in their grief they did smite upon their thigh, sometimes the breast, sometimes the other hand; so Balak did, Numb. xxiv. 10, "smote his hands together;" sometimes the head. Homer hath it often, *πεπλήγετο μηρῷ*, He smote on his thigh. And Tully mentions, among other kinds of mourning, their smiting of the cheeks, their breast, their thigh, their head.

Lib. 3. Tuscul.

"Stamp with thy foot." In cases of great and sudden grief, men use to stamp upon the earth. Homer, speaking of Irus, about drawing of teeth, saith, *λακτίζων ποδὶ γαῖαν*, He stamped the earth with his foot. And Cicero in Bruto saith, *Nulla pedum supplosio*, There was no stamping with the feet.

Odyss. l. 6.

"Alas." In Hebrew, אח The Septuagint and Theodotian render it *Euge*, Well done! and make it a note of rejoicing and exulting, because idols were destroyed, and God's judgments executed. But it is upon mistake of *Ach* for *Heach*, which is *Euge*, but *Ach* is always a note of grief; and that exposition of theirs suits not with the subject matter, which is sin and judgment. It is well rendered by Jerom, *Heu*, and by our translation, "Alas," a word constantly used to note grief. Josh. vii. 7, Israel fell before Ai; Joshua rent his clothes, fell on the earth, and cried, "Alas, O Lord God," &c. Joel i. 15; Amos v. 16; Rev. xviii. 10; in cases of great sorrow, they used this word.

These outward signs of sorrow are commended, that the people might be awakened out of their security, that they might be more affected with the calamities that were coming, and their sins that hastened such calamities upon them. Words are transient, and leave little impression, but visible signs work more strongly, affect more deeply, and draw the spirits of beholders into a sympathy.

Obs. God would have those who are his to mourn for the sins and judgments that are coming upon a land and people for them. The prophet must "smite with the hand, stamp with the foot, and say, Alas for all the evil abominations of the house of Israel," and for their calamities! Some do mourn for calamities, few for the sins of the people; but here their sins come in first, and afflict the prophet's spirit most, the judgments afterwards: Psal. cxix. 136, "Rivers of water run down mine eyes, because they keep not thy law." And ver. 158, "I beheld the transgressors, and was grieved." It is safe to do it: Ezek. ix. 4, "Go through Jerusalem, and set a mark upon the foreheads of the men that sigh and cry for all the abominations." 1 Cor. v. 2, the apostle blamed them, that they did not mourn for the incestuous Corinthians.

Ver. 12. Of these sore judgments hath been formerly spoken in the fifth chapter, that there is no escaping them, and of God's accomplishing his fury; he would bear no longer, but utterly destroy them.

On ver. 13, *Obs.* 1. That God doth often punish men where they sin. Their slain should be among their altars, idols, in the place where they offered their sweet savour. Sennacherib was slain in the house of his god Nisroch, as he was worshipping, Isa. xxxvii. 38.

Obs. 2. That idolatry and false worship is costly. They offer sweet savour every where to all their idols; they think nothing too much for their false way. The sweet incense was very costly, and only for God's use, not their own houses; yet their idols shall have it. Men will part with much this way; Isa. xlvi. 6, "They lavish gold out of the bag," &c.

Ver. 14. "Wilderness toward Diblath." Some make it to be the same with Riblah, in 2 Kings xxv. 6, and Jer. xxxix. 5; mentioned also in Numb. xxxiv. 11. This may well be, because of the likeness of ר and ד in the Hebrew tongue. And Jerom conceives it is the same with Riblah, which was a city in the land of Hamath, where Pharaoh put Jehoahaz in bonds, 2 Kings xxiii. 33; in the borders of the Moabites near the wilderness, spoken of in Deut. viii. 15; a great and fearful wilderness, full of fiery serpents and scorpions, where was drought and no water. God would make their land not only desolate, and desolate like this wilderness, but more desolate.

"I will stretch out my hand upon them." There is difference between God's stretching out his hand to a people, and upon a people. The first notes invitation to repentance; Isa. lxv. 2, "I have spread out my hands all the day unto a rebellious people." The second notes smiting, punishing, destroying; Isa. v. 25, "The anger of the Lord is kindled against his people, and he hath stretched forth his hand against them, and hath smitten them;" Jer. li. 25, "Behold, I am against thee, O destroying mountain; and I will stretch out mine hand upon thee," &c. "Upon" and "against" notes the same thing; when God's hand is upon a land or people, it is against them, and so the phrase oft runs; Jer. xv. 6, "Thou art gone backward: therefore will I stretch out my hand against thee, and destroy thee:" see Exod. iii. 20.

The sins of the people lay waste the land; they

fell to idolatry, and so God stretched out his hand upon the land and laid it waste.

This people were so degenerate, corrupted, besotted with their own ways, that they understood little of God's; they fell to the sins of the nations, and those sins in a special manner stupify. All sin doth it, but idolatry and false worship most; hence, Jer. x. 14, speaking of such sinners, he saith, "Every man is brutish in his knowledge." Idolaters know not God, how he is provoked by their ways, what foolish doing it is to go out from God; therefore in this chapter it is four times, "They shall know that I am the Lord," ver. 7. 10. 13. 14.

CHAPTER VII.

Ver. 1—4. *Moreover the word of the Lord came unto me, saying, Also, thou son of man, thus saith the Lord God unto the land of Israel; An end, the end is come upon the four corners of the land. Now is the end come upon thee, and I will send mine anger upon thee, and will judge thee according to thy ways, and will recompense upon thee all thine abominations. And mine eye shall not spare thee, neither will I have pity: but I will recompense thy ways upon thee, and thine abominations shall be in the midst of thee: and ye shall know that I am the Lord.*

This chapter, as the former, is prophetical of the destruction of the Jews, and of their land.

I. In it is a denunciation of their total ruin, in ver. 2, 3, 5—7, 10—13.

II. In the rest of the chapter is a declaration of their calamities, and the causes thereof.

Of the first verse hath been formerly spoken, and likewise of "the son of man;" and most things in these verses. In the second verse, the prophet is in general acquainted with the mind of God towards Israel, and in the two next more specially.

Ver. 2. "Also, thou son of man." The Hebrew is, ואתה And thou, O son of man: here is a nominative case absolute, without reference to any thing. The like you have Psal. xli. 12, "As for me, thou upholdest me in mine integrity." The Hebrew is, And I, in the nominative, thou upholdest me: *Ego in integritate supportasti me.* Zech. vii. 5, "Did ye at all fast unto me, even to me?" this last me is *ego: Jejunasti mihi ego,* saith the original. Eccles. ii. 15, "As it happeneth to the fool, so it happeneth even to me," *Secundum eventum stulti etiam ego eveniet mihi.* Such hebraisms you have, 1 Sam. xxv. 24; Gen. xxvii. 24; and in Isa. xi. 10; Psal. xi. 4, you have nominative cases put absolute, as "thou" here in the text; and it serves to quicken up the prophet's spirit, and to put him into a readiness of prophesying; And thou, Ezekiel, attend, prophesy.

"Unto the land of Israel," or, concerning the land of Israel. It is not spoken of all the tribes; ten were gone long before into captivity; but, by a synecdoche, of the tribe of Judah, which yet remained undestroyed.

"An end, the end is come." The word end is doubled, and mentioned again in the third verse, "Now is the end," repeated in ver. 6, "An end is come, the end is come." These repetitions are not in vain; they set out, first, the zeal, intention, and speed of the speaker: secondly, the evidence, certainty, and weight of the thing spoken of: thirdly, they serve to make the deeper impression.

End notes destruction, yea, a general destruction: Gen. vi. 13, "The end of all flesh is come;" God would bring a flood upon the whole earth, take away all flesh; and this is called the end of all. So here, God had dealt mercifully with them formerly, but now he would be severe, and make an end of them.

"Upon the four corners of the land." Hebrew is, wings, which metaphorically expresses the parts of the land. Wings are extensive things, and the parts of Judea that extended from Jerusalem, east, west, north, south, are called the wings or corners thereof; and the end should come, not only upon the extreme parts of the land, but the whole land; upon all their cities, habitations, and quarters, from one end to the other. What our prophet calls here the four corners or wings of the land, Christ calls, Matt. xxiv. 31, "the four winds;" they shall gather his elect from the four winds or quarters of the world.

Obs. 1. That kingdoms and churches have their periods. They may continue for some hundreds of years, but at length they expire. The kingdom and church of Judah flourished many years; from Saul their first king to Zedekiah their last, were 480 years; but then you see an end is come, the end is come; an end of the state, an end of their church, an end of all comforts, of all glory and greatness. The Assyrian, Persian, Grecian, and Roman monarchies had their ends, their glory was laid in the dust, after it had dazzled the world's eyes a few years. Wisdom, strength, greatness, riches, were found in them; but neither any, nor all of these, preserved them from seeing corruption. The seven famous churches in Asia are gone, and since that time many other churches and kingdoms have been ruined. Is not an end coming, if not come, upon many kingdoms at this day? let Germany, Denmark, Ireland, speak. No state, no church, no condition under the sun, is everlasting; all have their changes and their ends: Psal. cxix. 96, "I have seen an end of all perfection: but thy commandment is exceeding broad." There is nothing in the world so firm, perfect, lasting, but it is subject to corruption. Kingdoms are subject to wars, plagues, famines, treacheries, which ruin them; churches are subject to errors, heresies, schisms, corruptions, profaneness, which ruin them. And all other things have principles of destruction in themselves, which bring them to an end within the compass of a few years. "But thy commandment is exceeding broad," it goeth beyond the term of these perishing things; it is not for a hundred or thousand years, and so to expire, but it abides for ever.

Obs. 2. God will premonish before he doth punish a sinful people; he comes not upon them unwarned; he tells them beforehand what they must look for. If a general destruction be decreed, ready to be executed, he will hint it to his prophets, they shall declare it to the people; that those that are the Lord's may be awakened, brought to repentance, be secured from eternal ruin, if not the temporal, and that the rest may be convinced of their own evil ways, and may justify the proceedings of the Lord.

Ver. 3. "Now is the end come upon thee." They having the common sickness of mankind in them, to put off judgments, and the day of evil, when threatened, as if there were no such thing, or at a great distance; the Lord brings the judgment home to them, and cuts off all their shifts. Now is the end upon thee, now is the final destruction; and for thee, not for others that live among the nations; not for thy posterity that comes after thee; not for the tribes who are carried away; but for thee that art secure and fearest not. "Now is the end," it is very nigh: some years were to pass before the end came; it was now the sixth year of their captivity, and Zedekiah, that succeeded Jehoiachin, was upon the sixth year of his reign at Jerusalem; and the ninth year, the tenth month, began this final destruction, 2 Kings xxv. 1. Then came Nebuchadnezzar with all his forces into the land, and besieged Jerusalem, and in the eleventh year, the fourth and fifth months, it was accomplished, ver. 2—4, 8—10. So that here were three or four years before this end came, five and upwards before it was fulfilled, yet it is said, "Now is the end come upon thee."

Things future in Scripture are spoken of as present or past. Isa. i. 8, "The daughter of Zion is left as a cottage in a vineyard;" chap. xxiv. 10, 11, "The city of confusion is broken down: every house is shut up, that no man may come in. There is a crying for wine in the streets:" this is spoken as present, and it was yet to come. Chap. xlii. 22, "This is a people robbed and spoiled;" Rev. xviii. 2, "Babylon the great is fallen, is fallen, and is become the habitation of devils;" John iii. 18, "He that believeth not is condemned already:" these scriptures speak of things as past, and were then to come. The Lord useth to speak so in his word, of things future sometimes as present, sometimes as past, because with him is no difference of times, and for that they are as certainly to take place, as if they were doing, or done.

God looks not upon time as we do. That which is future we think to be at a great distance; that which is to come, two, three, seven, twenty, or a hundred years hence, that we apprehend very remote, and it hath little influence upon us; but God looks upon things at little and great distances as present. "Now is the end come upon thee." Seventy years he calls a present little moment, Isa. liv. 7, 8. And 1 Pet. iv. 7, "The end of all things is at hand;" 1 John ii. 18, "It is the last time:" it is about one thousand six hundred years since the Spirit of God spake thus by Peter and John, and yet the end of all things is not come, the last hour is not out. Times future are present with God, and so propounded to us that they might work the more strongly upon us, cause us to fear God more, to be sober and watch unto prayer.

"I will send mine anger upon thee." God had formerly dealt sparingly with them, now and then chastised them with rods; now he would be more severe, and chasten them with scorpions: he had kept in his wrath formerly, but now he would send it forth in strength; they should not have gentle corrections, but terrible judgments; he would send out wrath and not mercy. Anger here is put for the effects of anger, punishments, judgments, by a metonymy of the efficient.

"Will judge thee according to thy ways." Judging is sometimes put for sentencing of persons or things; Rom. ii. 16, "In the day when God shall judge the secrets of men," that is, pass a sentence upon them: sometimes for punishing; Heb. xiii. 4, "Whoremongers and adulterers God will judge," that is, punish. And so here, "I will judge thee;" first, I will punish, and lest it may be thought God in his anger should exceed measure in punishing, it is added,

"According to thy ways;" not according to my ways, but thine, which in the judgment of any, or all, must be equal; look, what thou hast done and deserved by it, that thou shalt have. The word "ways" is metaphorical, and notes men's manners, actions, courses of life: Prov. xxi. 2, "Every way of a man is right in his own eyes; so Psal. i. 1, 6. Men's own devices, Judg. ii. 19, custom, Jer. x. 2, and in this place, their actions and conversations, are called ways; because their affections, the feet of the soul, are in them, and they lead unto some place, as ways do; all actions have a tendency to heaven or hell. This phrase is expounded by that in Hos. iv. 9, "I will punish them for their ways;" they have done evil and shall suffer for it.

"And will recompense upon thee all thine abominations." The Hebrew is, I will give, or put upon thee, &c. The Vulgate is, I will put against thee all; and others have it, I will repose or turn back upon thee all thine abominations: hitherto thou hast put them upon me, and I have borne them; now I will return them, and lay them upon thyself. God would now reward them for their abominations: Hos. iv. 9, "I will punish them for their ways, and reward them their doings;" their reward should return upon their own head, Obad. 15.

Obs. 1. God's judgments prevent sinners' expectations, they are nearer men than they conceive. "Now is the end come;" the prophet in Babylon sees it, but they at Jerusalem apprehended it not, none would believe that destruction should come upon Jerusalem, Lam. iv. 12. "Ye put far away the evil day," Amos vi. 3; they put it far from their thoughts, and hearts; if it came at all, they looked upon it as coming in after-generations, and not in theirs. Ezek. xii. 22, it was come to a proverb in Israel, "The days are prolonged, and every vision faileth;" ver. 27, "The vision that he seeth is for many days to come, and he prophesieth of the times that are far off." They grew secure, feared not the threatenings put upon them at a great distance, and, what lay in them, nulled the prophecies; and therefore, in ver. 28, God saith, "There shall none of my words be prolonged any more;" God would hasten the punishment of them, and they should suddenly overtake them. Isa. xxix. 1, "Woe to Ariel, to Ariel, the city where David dwelt!" Ariel is Jerusalem, so called, because there was the mountain, temple, and altar of God: so it is Ezek. xliii. 15, "The altar shall be four cubits;" the Hebrew is, Harel, the mountain of God, where the temple and altar was; but the word is Ariel, not Harel, and signifies the lion of God, not because Jerusalem was in the form of a lion, but for that it was a strong city, thought to be impregnable, and God threatens ruin against it. And Isa. xxix. 5, "It shall be at an instant suddenly," when men have no thoughts thereof; it should be as sudden as thunder, earthquakes, and tempests are, ver. 6; Hab. ii. 7, "Shall they not rise up suddenly that shall bite thee?" yes, they should, the northern army was upon them before they looked for them; they cried, Peace, peace, and when it is so, then "sudden destruction" is at hand, 1 Thess. v. 3. The old world was secure "until the day that Noe entered into the ark," Luke xvii. 27, and then the flood came presently and destroyed them all; they believed neither Noah's preaching, nor his preparations for himself and children. So in Sodom, they were not awakened out of their security till the fire and brimstone was felt, Gen. xix. 28, 29. Agag thought the bitterness of death past, when he was going to execution, 1 Sam. xv. 32. While Belshazzar is drinking healths, God sends a hand to write a sentence of death against him and his kingdom, Dan. v. 4, 5, 30. "In a morning shall the king of Israel utterly be cut off;" ere he can get out of his bed God would let out his blood, Hos. x. 15. Whatever men think, the Judge and judgment is at the door, it is near. Germany, Denmark, Ireland, England, did not think that such sad, bloody, destroying judgments were so near as now they find them. Let us not be secure, but fear, pass the time of our sojourning here in fear, remembering Solomon's happiness, Prov. xxviii. 14, "Happy is the man that feareth alway;" and Job's practice, "The thing which I greatly feared is come upon me," Job iii. 25. Let God's judgments come sooner or later, it is duty, wisdom in us to fear, to prepare for them: it is folly to sleep when thieves are about the house, and may prove death to do it when a fire is kindled in the habitation.

Obs. 2. No people sinning grievously against God are exempted from desolating judgments. This people was God's people more peculiarly than any people in the world besides, Deut. vii. 6; "A people near unto God," Psal. cxlviii. 14; "Wise and understanding," Deut. iv. 6. They were "the redeemed" ones, Isa. lxii. 12; "the holy people," Dan. viii. 24; that knew God's name, Isa. lii. 6; that had God's law in their hearts, Isa. li. 7; that were "blessed above all," Deut. vii. 14. They had the holy land, the temple, worship, ordinance, oracles of God, the prophets, and presence of God, only. All the world besides lay in darkness, were without God; but these were "his strength, his glory," Psal. lxxviii. 61; as dear to him as "the apple of his eye," Zech. ii. 8. Yet when these people sinned and rebelled against God, destructive judgments came upon them; "An end is come upon thee;" upon thee Jerusalem, upon thee my people. They were honoured with many titles, were God's church; yet when they sinned against God, cast off his yoke, none of them, not all their privileges, would protect them from desolation.

Obs. 3. God's judgments are God's messengers sent forth at his pleasure. "I will send mine anger upon thee." God hath the command of judgments, as any man hath of his servants: the centurion had not so much power over his soldiers, as the Lord hath over punishments, calamities, and ruins of kingdoms; be they public or private judgments, they are at the beck of the Lord. What was the anger and judgment here? the sending of Nebuchadnezzar with his hasty and bitter Chaldeans to destroy the Jewish nation. God had that king and all his forces at command, to send out of Babylon about his service, to make war upon his people that were idolatrous. God hath his "four sore judgments" to send upon a land when he pleases, Ezek. xiv. 21. He can send hornets among people to sting them to death, Deut. vii. 20. If he do but "hiss for the fly of Egypt, and for the bee of Assyria, they shall come," and do their office, Isa. vii. 18, 19. If God call for any evil upon kingdoms, cities, churches, families, persons, they come presently, and accomplish the message they are sent for. When God spake by Moses, and said, Let there be frogs, flies, lice, murrain, hail, locusts, blood, darkness, death, they came immediately. God hath called for a sword upon most part of the christian world; and is it not at work? Doth it not eat flesh and drink blood? May we not say, "O thou sword of the Lord, how long will it be ere thou be quiet? put up thyself into thy scabbard, rest, and be still. How can it be quiet, seeing the Lord hath given it a charge against Ashkelon, and against the sea-shore? there hath he appointed it," Jer. xlvii. 6, 7.

God hath command of wars, gives charge to the sword against Ireland, England, other places, there hath he appointed it; and how can it be quiet? no, till God's will and work be accomplished, there is no quiet.

Obs. 4. God's proceedings with a guilty nation are just and equal, his judgments are without reproof. "I will judge thee according to thy ways;" not as I will, but as thou hast done; not after my ways, or the ways of other people, but after thine own ways. How just is it that a man should reap what he sows! If men have the law pass upon them according to the nature and merit of their facts, what wrong is done to any? who hath cause to complain of the judge? God knows the nature and merits of a nation's sins, and proceeds in his judgments accordingly. He is a righteous Judge, and no man hath just cause to complain; he stops the mouth of iniquity: Lam. iii. 39, "Wherefore doth a living man complain, a man for the punishment of his sins?" he should not do it. It is just and equal, that if a man sin against God, he should suffer from God; if God bear his sins, he must bear God's punishments. Let kingdoms suffer dreadful things from heaven, wars, famine, pestilence, whatever is destructive, God is to be justified by all; he deals with you according to your ways: let the severest critic, let Satan himself, God's greatest enemy, examine his judgments upon kingdoms, churches, together with their sins, and he shall justify God, and pronounce him clear, equal, righteous. In his ways, God deals not otherwise with men than their ways require; Zech. i. 6, "According to our ways, and according to our doings, so hath the Lord dealt with us:" therefore justify God and be patient.

Obs. 5. It is men's own ways which bring ruin upon them. "I will judge thee according to thy ways," thy ways bring my judgments. Prov. i. 31, "They shall eat of the fruit of their own ways, and be filled with their own devices." What fruit do men's sinful ways bring forth? even sour and bitter fruit, guilt, fears, sorrows, afflictions, ruin; upon such fruit they must feed, with such fruit they shall be filled. Hos. xiii. 9, "O Israel, thou hast destroyed thyself:" Israel's sins were her wounds, they were the plague, famine, and sword, that ruined them. The iniquities of a kingdom are the deaths of a kingdom, their sins will find them out, Numb. xxxii. 23; they are like blood-hounds, that hunt out the authors of them, and seize upon them· hence, Isa. lix. 12, it is said, "Our transgressions are with us," to weary us, to wound us, to destroy us: men cannot shake off the sins they have committed, they will follow them, seize upon them, hold them fast; Prov. v. 22, "His own iniquities shall take the wicked himself, and he shall be holden with the cords of his sins;" he shall die without instruction. Wicked men's sins may take others, and sometimes do, but they certainly take themselves; they twist cords to bind, but it is themselves; it is to make themselves burnt sacrifices for hell.

Obs. 6. When God comes in judgment upon a nation, he will deal thoroughly with it, visit for all sins. "I will recompense upon thee all thine abominations." God took notice of what was done in the dark, in the light, upon mountains, in valleys, under every green tree; no idols, false worship, inventions of theirs, but the Lord observed them, reserved them in mind, and rendered unto them answerable for them. Before, he had dealt with them for some, now he would deal with them for all their abominations, and bring them as an insupportable burden upon them.

Ver. 4. "And mine eye shall not spare," &c. Much is said in the sacred Scriptures of the great and tender mercies of the Lord, and many patterns of his mercies are to be found therein; and the sinners in Zion conceited God to be all mercy, sinned securely, and feared no judgments. Upon this great abuse of divine mercy, saith the Lord, "Mine eye shall not spare, neither will I have pity;" you shall find me all justice, consuming fire, without any sparing or pitying; judgment after judgment shall come upon you, till you are destroyed: you think to go on in your sinful ways, and find me merciful, but I am provoked, and you shall feel me dreadful; nothing shall prevail to draw me to any remorse or pity, the consideration you are my people, not reproach of heathens round about you, not your prayers, tears, sufferings, blood, not that you are Abraham's and David's posterity, not the dishonour my name shall have by you: I am now hardened against you, and will punish you openly according to your abominations; you shalt have great punishments in the midst of you, which will evidence the greatness of your sins, and cause you to acknowledge me to be a just God. Of the words in this verse have been spoken, chap. v. 11, and ver. 8, and chap. vi. 7, and in the preceding verse of this chapter.

Ver. 5—9. *Thus saith the Lord God; An evil, an only evil, behold, is come. An end is come, the end is come: it watcheth for thee; behold, it is come. The morning is come unto thee, O thou that dwellest in the land: the time is come, the day of trouble is near, and not the sounding again of the mountains. Now will I shortly pour out my fury upon thee, and accomplish mine anger upon thee: and I will judge thee according to thy ways, and will recompense thee for all thine abominations. And mine eye shall not spare, neither will I have pity: I will recompense thee according to thy ways and thine abominations that are in the midst of thee; and ye shall know that I am the Lord that smiteth.*

Something I shall open in these verses, not much.

In the 5th, "An only evil." Evil befell them before, but none like this, none so great, so destructive to the Jewish church and state. It hath reference to that in chap. v. 9, "I will do in thee that which I have not done, and whereunto I will not do any more the like:" no such extreme and deadly destruction shall befall thee; I have one evil now left for thee, which shall be without all comparison; there shall need none after this to make a full ruin of thee. God hath evils to do his will at once, and so it may be called "an only evil." 1 Sam. xxvi. 8, saith Abishai to David, "Let me smite Saul with the spear even to the earth at once, and I will not smite him the second time."

אחת At once; it is the same word with only in this verse: he would utterly slay Saul at one stroke, and God with one judgment would utterly destroy the Jews. Such a phrase you have in Nahum i. 9, "He will make an utter end; affliction shall not rise up the second time." God would bring such a judgment upon Nineveh, that at once it should be destroyed, a second affliction should not be needful, the evil of that day should be sufficient. The Chaldee reads it otherwise, evil after evil; אחר showing the succession of evils that should follow one after another, till they were destroyed; as wave follows wave, one cloud another, &c. so affliction should come after affliction. Sins go linked together, and so do afflictions; Lev. xxvi. 18, 21, 24, 28, they go by sevens. God can at one judgment at once destroy sinners, kingdoms, cities; he can at pleasure bring many, one after another, destroy by degrees, be a moth, rottenness, a lion to Israel and Judah, Hosea v. We should take heed how we offend such a God.

Ver. 6. "It watcheth for thee." Thou thoughtest judgment slept, but it is awake, and waits for, or against thee. Thou thoughtest it a dead thing, but it is alive, and making haste towards thee. The Hebrew word signifies to be weary, as קיץ if judgment were weary with staying so long, or God weary with deferring it: now there should be no more delay. It notes also to excite a man asleep, one dead, as in 2 Kings iv. 31, "The child is not awaked," that is, not raised from the dead. So here, God had threatened them by his prophets, Isaiah, Jeremiah, others, many years, and they thought the prophets' words wind, because nothing was done; at least that such a judgment would not befall them in these days, as they had foretold, Ezek. xii. 22, 27; as if the judgment they spake of was asleep, or as a thing dead: therefore it is said, it lives, is awake, and watcheth as a thief to spoil, as a lion for a prey. And hereby is pointed out the suddenness of its coming, and intention of God to destroy them.

This verse, the former, and that which follows, are full of divine rhetoric; asyneton, anadiplosis, epanalepsis, metaphoraes, paronomasia, apostrophe, and others, are evident in them. The Scripture hath as great elegance as any authors whatsoever.

Obs. 1. In case of people's security, repetition of the same thing is necessary. They were fearless of judgments, secure of their estates, put far off the evil day, and see how the Lord doubles and trebles his threats, "An evil, an only evil, an end, the end is come, is come, is come, is come, is come, is come," six times; and further, "behold, behold it is come;" the several expressions of the season, the morning, the time, the day of trouble, and then it watcheth, is come, is near. Why doth the Spirit of God repeat all these? even to awaken them out of their security, to convince them, as of the certainty, so the suddenness, of the judgment, and to make the greater and deeper impression upon them. Things once spoken pass away, but being iterated, are like to take some hold of men's ears and affections. This prophet is very repetitious of threats and judgments, and presseth them frequently; they were near final destruction, and therefore the Spirit of God urgeth such things oft in the mouth of this prophet, that so no means being left unattempted, he might awaken all and gain some. Christ pronounces the same words eight times in one chapter, "Woe unto you," scribes, Pharisees, hypocrites," Matt. xxiii. 13, 14, 15, 16, 23, 25, 27, 29, to affect them with the imminency of their danger, and others with the evil of their ways.

Obs. 2. God's judgments may seem to linger, but they do not slumber. Wicked men God bears with, and forbears long, even so long, that they think his judgments are laid to sleep, or dead; as in 2 Pet. iii. 4, "Where is the promise of his coming? for since the fathers fell asleep, all things continue as they were from the beginning of the creation;" there is no Christ to reign or judge; the flood is dried up, and the fire to consume the world is not yet kindled; but, ver. 10, "The day of the Lord will come as a thief in the night; in the which the heavens shall pass away with a great noise, and the elements shall melt with fervent heat:" chap. ii. 3, "Whose judgment lingereth not, and their damnation slumbereth not." God's judgments, whatever sinners think, are awake, and hastening to their ruin. That which the wicked call a lingering and slumbering judgment, God's Spirit calls, in ver. 1, "Swift destruction;" it will be upon them before they see their doings, or repent of their sin: Rev. vi. 2, 4, 8, you shall find that judgments come riding in, they make haste.

Obs. 3. That God keeps judgment quiet till he please. It may watch, but cannot walk, or work, till he seal a commission. God hath variety of judgments, creatures in a readiness to do him service; he hath angels, stars, winds, waters, sword, famine, pestilence, &c. but no one stirs till he say, Go; they watch to hear his voice, to do his will; they move not at the call of man, their motion is only at the appointment of their great Creator. If he bid Nebuchadnezzar, Nebuzaradan, with thousands of Babylonians, to arise, and hasten to the ruin of Jerusalem, they are watchful, swift, and active to execute his commands. All creatures are God's army, and have cause sufficient to watch for the ruin of man, because man's sin hath subjected them to ruin, and imbondaged them to corruption. But here is the wisdom, power, and mercy of God, he keeps all in their banks, and without warrant from the great General, the Lord of hosts, no attempt is made against any.

"The morning is come unto thee." That they might be affected, he tells them, the day is broke, the morning is come, and the day of trouble beginneth. He would have them be no longer in the dark, but to look abroad to see how providences were working to fulfil prophecies. The original word is diversely rendered, it comes from צפר *maturare, mane surgere*, and signifies *matutinum quid*, some morning, some early thing. Ex usu Chaldæo, and A Lapide, interpret it *primum germen*, the first bud that is upon any tree, the early, the morning bud: and so the sense is, Judgments are budding, breaking forth, appearing, and as near as spring and summer are when a tree buds and blossoms; or, as the word is, The morning is come; you have thought judgment slept, that it was still evening, not past midnight, but the morning is come; judgment not only watcheth, but is rising, risen, coming forth, and it will be early upon thee.

Some think he alludes to the practice of the Jews, who executed delinquents in the morning, according to that in Jer. xxi. 12, and Ps. ci. 8, God would early bring the sword upon them; and there is an emphasis in the word הצפירה that morning, which was the most observable and deplorable morning that ever they had. Such a morning was Sodom's, when fire and brimstone rained upon it, Gen. xix. 23, 24; such a morning was the king of Israel's, Hos. x. 15.

The Septuagint implies there was a connexion and series of evils coming upon them: Aquila hath it *προσκόπησιν, prospectionem*, as if the evil they had foreseen and feared were now coming upon them: the Chaldee, *coronam, diadema*, so the word is used in Isa. xxviii. 5; and because it notes royal power, it is thought the king of Babylon is here meant: the Vulgate is, *contritio*, breaking into pieces, grinding to dust, is come upon thee: Maldonat, *contractio*, besieging is come, and thou must be in a narrow compass: Shindler, *revolutio ad te*, Nebuchadnezzar shall return, compass thee about as a crown, and carry thee into captivity.

πλοκη.

La sentence du matin, in the margin of the French.

"The day of trouble is near." The Hebrew word notes great trouble, vexation, with tumult and destruction; היום מהומה or a day of sore trouble. You may hear the prophet Isaiah describing such a day, chap. xxii. 5, "It is a day of trouble, and of treading down, and of perplexity by the Lord God of hosts in the valley of vision, breaking down the walls, and of crying to the mountains." God hath days of trouble for kingdoms, and when they come there is great distress and great destruction: 2 Chron. xv. 5, 6, "In those times there was no peace to him that went out, nor to him that came in, but great vexations were upon all the inhabitants of the countries. And nation was destroyed of nation, and city of city; for God did vex them with all adversity:" this was a time or day of trouble for Israel. In Scripture is mentioned a day of calamity, Psal. xviii. 18; a day of wrath, Job xx. 28; a day of battle, Psal. cxl. 7; a day of vengeance, Jer. xlvi. 10; a day of evil, Prov. xvi. 4; of rebuke, Hos. v. 9; of slaughter, Jer. xii. 3; of burning, Mal. iv. 1; of destruction, Job xxi. 30: and all these may be in a day of trouble.

You shall find many of them together in Zeph. i. 14—17, where he speaks of the day that Ezekiel doth: "The great day of the Lord is near, it is near, and hasteth greatly, even the voice of the day of the Lord: the mighty man shall cry there bitterly. That day is a day of wrath, a day of trouble and distress, a day of wasteness and desolation, a day of darkness and gloominess, a day of clouds and thick darkness, a day of the trumpet and alarm against the fenced cities, and against the high towers. And I will bring distress upon men, that they shall walk like blind men," &c.

"Not the sounding again of the mountains." The land of Israel was full of mountains; Psal. cxxv. 2, "As the mountains are round about Jerusalem;" and Judah was a "hill country," Luke i. 35. About these hills were their vines planted, and it was a land of vines, Deut. viii. 8; Isa. vii. 23; and at their vintage, when they gathered their grapes, they had many labourers, who to sweeten and facilitate their pains, made great shoutings, Isa. xvi. 10, which made the mountains to echo and resound; but now there should be no joyful sound, but the rattling of arms, noise of chariots, neighing of horses, cry of soldiers, these should be heard in the mountains. Or thus: upon the hills and mountains they had their idols and altars, chap. vi. 13; and where idolaters sacrificed, there they had their music, songs, and dances, which made the mountains to ring, and were as the glory of them; but now, there should be a day of slaughter, and dreadful clamour of enemies should be in the mountains; the glory of them stained with the blood of men slain; there should be groaning, mourning, howling, shrieking of men and women wounded and wronged. Or thus: You think all threats empty sounds, as an echo from a mountain, which presently vanisheth; but you shall find the day of trouble no echo work, it will be real, and make you in the bitterness of your spirits cry to rocks and mountains, and seek to hide yourselves in the clifts of them.

Non gloriæ montium. *Vulgate.* Non repercussio montium. *Montan.* Non Echus montium. *Jun.*

Ver. 8. The 8th verse hath formerly been opened, only you have pouring out of fury, for accomplishing fury, chap. v. 13; and it is the same for substance. God would not hold in his fury any longer, he would give full scope unto it, freely, fully, strongly would he proceed in his fury against them, all which are included in the word "pour out."

So for the ninth verse, "I am the Lord that smiteth." You think it is the Chaldeans, the second cause, but ye shall know that it is the Lord himself.

Ver. 10, 11. *Behold the day, behold, it is come: the morning is gone forth; the rod hath blossomed, pride hath budded. Violence is risen up into a rod of wickedness: none of them shall remain, nor of their multitude, nor of any of theirs: neither shall there be wailing for them.*

In these verses he goes on to show the approach and extent of their ruin; it was at hand, and none of them should remain; and likewise the causes thereof, pride and violence. Of "morning" was spoken in ver. 7, but I must open something here, for the words are difficult.

"The rod hath blossomed." By rod, sundry interpreters understand Nebuchadnezzar, whom they conceive so called, Jer. i. 11; and that in Isa. x. 5, "O Assyrian, the rod of mine anger," refers not only to Sennacherib, but also to Nebuchadnezzar.

A rod in the Scripture sense denotes,

First, power, strength; Psal. ii. 9, "A rod of iron."

Secondly, afflictions, heavy judgments; Psal. lxxxix. 32, "I will visit their transgression with the rod."

Thirdly, rigid and harsh government; Isa. xiv. 5, "The Lord hath broken the staff," or rod, "of the wicked," that is, their rigorous and cruel government. Nebuchadnezzar had great strength, sorely afflicted the land of Judah, he was an iron rod that brake them in pieces, and ruled them rigidly in Babylon; Jehoiakim was kept thirty-seven years in prison, Jer. lii. 31. "The rod blossometh;" that is, was in a readiness to come and smite Jerusalem. After blossoming comes fruit, and the fruit that this rod bare was fruit unto death.

Vir superbiæ. Vatablus turns it and means it of Nebuchadnezzar.

"Pride hath budded." This king and people lifted up themselves above others, and prided themselves in their greatness, strength, riches, and victories. Jer. l. 31, God saith of Babylon, "I am against thee, O thou most proud." The Hebrew is, I am against thee, pride. These Babylonians were pride itself. In Dan. iv. 30, you may hear the king priding himself in this language, "Is not this great Babylon, that I have built for the house of the kingdom by the might of my power, and for the honour of my majesty?"

Both king and people were proud, and their pride budded forth and appeared to all when they put out Zedekiah's eyes, slew his sons before his face, and said, "Sing us one of the songs of Zion," Psal. cxxxvii. 3.

Others by rod understand the state of Judah and Jerusalem. So the word rod is used in Scripture; Jer. xlviii. 17, "How is the strong staff broken, and the beautiful rod!" that is, the state and dignity of Moab; and thus we may understand it.

מטה

The word for rod signifies a tribe, as in Numb. i. 4, 16, 21; either because they grew out of the stock of Jacob, as branches do out of a tree, or because the names of the twelve tribes were written upon rods, Numb. xvii. 2. And the word being *hammatteh*, the tribe, "the rod" carries me to conceive it is meant of Judah rather than of Nebuchadnezzar. And the sense runs in a continued allegory: Judah is compared to a tree that blossoms, buds, and brings forth its fruit; it had blossomed or flourished; so the word is, Psal. xc. 6; and now the fruit was growing ripe, their sins were great, the measure of them almost full, and punishment grew near and weighty.

The sins mentioned are, 1. "Pride." That pride, so the Hebrew is; there was eminency in it, Judah was grown very proud: Jer. xiii. 9, "I will mar the pride of Judah, and the great pride of Jerusalem." And wherein appeared this great pride? ver. 10. "They refuse to hear God's words, they walk in the imagination of their heart, and walk after other gods, to serve them and to worship them." The proud men told Jeremiah he spake falsely, Jer. xliii. 25.

הזדון

The rulers were scornful, Isa. xxviii. 14.

This sin reigned among men and women also: Isa. iii. 16, "The daughters of Zion are haughty, and walk with stretched forth necks and wanton eyes, walking and mincing as they go, and making a tinkling with their feet." They had great bravery, tinkling ornaments, cauls, round moon tires, chains, bracelets, mufflers, bonnets, leg-ornaments, headbands, rings, ear-rings, nose-jewels, changeable suits of apparel, mantles, crisping pins, glasses, fine linen, hoods, and veils. They were clothed with pride; their children carried themselves proudly against the ancients, and the base against the honourable. So great and general was the pride of Jerusalem, that it made the prophet weep in secret places, Jer. xiii. 17. Their pride budded and blossomed, so that the prophet's eye seeing it, affected his heart, fetched rivers of tears from him, seeing their destruction now at hand.

The Septuagint renders this place of our prophet thus, Injury hath risen up. Pride is an injurious thing to God and man, it rises up against him, and thrusts him out of his worship, ordinances, and ways; it disquiets kingdoms, and the meek of the earth; it is injury itself.

ἐξανέστηκεν ὕβρις.

"Buds;" that is, puts forth, is green and growing. As a tree, Cant. vii. 12, puts out buds in every part of it in the spring, so as a fowl puts out feathers all over; so did Judah's pride bud forth in all ranks and conditions of people.

פרח

2. The other sin is "violence." The Vulgate translates it, iniquity; the Greeks, unrighteousness; others, rapine, injury: but the Hebrew is emphatical, that violence, that iniquity, &c. It signifies open wrong; as Mercer observes upon Gen. vi. 11. This sin was in strength among this people. Isa. lix. 6, "Their works are works of iniquity, and the act of violence is in their hands;" they oppress the poor, they rob and spoil them, and that openly; the act, even the things they have taken from them are in their hands. Amos iii. 10, "They know not to do right, who store up violence and robbery in their palaces:" the rulers and great men that dwelt in palaces, they oppressed, they robbed, and stored up what they got in their palaces, that it was known to all, and cried out of by the prophet. Micah iii. 1—3, he tells you of the heads' and princes' doings, who above others should have seen to the execution of justice; and they were the men who plucked off the skin from the people, and their flesh from their bones; they flayed, brake, chopped them in pieces as for the pot. The peoples' estates and livelihoods were as their skin, flesh, bones unto them; but the great ones wrung them from the people, and did live upon the spoil; "They ate the bread of wickedness, and drank the wine of violence," Prov. iv. 17. And this sin staid not in the heads, but descended to the body, the people generally; they that were rich oppressed the poor: Amos viii. 4, they swallowed up the needy; they made the ephah small, and the shekel great; they falsified the balances; sold the poor for silver, and the needy for shoes, ver. 5, 6; men endued with immortal souls worth all the world, they sold for old shoes; and filled the land with violence, Ezek. viii. 17.

החמס

ἀδικία.

"Risen up into a rod of wickedness." The phrase imports thus much, That their injustice and oppression had prepared and brought forth judgment.

A rod of wickedness, that is, a rod, the fruit of wickedness; out of their great sins hath sprung up this rod: or thus, a rod of wickedness; that is, a rod to correct and punish wickedness withal. In both senses it may be called a rod of wickedness, both because it buds from wickedness, and serves to beat wickedness. If we refer violence to Nebuchadnezzar, then the meaning is, God will raise up him to be the rod of his anger, to beat the Jews for their iniquity; he shall rise up into a rod of wickedness. If we refer it to the Jews, then the meaning is, their own wickedness is risen up into a rod, into judgment, and that rod will be their ruin. Such a phrase there is in Prov. xiv. 3, "In the mouth of the foolish is a rod of pride;" that is, the proud speeches in the mouths of fools offend others, provoke God, produce shame, trouble, danger to themselves, and so their own sin is a rod to themselves.

Obs. 1. That pride is a forerunner of destruction. Judgment, utter ruin, was coming upon them; but pride had budded; they were grown exceeding proud and haughty, their pride testified to their faces, as the phrase is; Hos. v. 5, "Therefore shall Israel and Ephraim fall in their iniquity, Judah also shall fall with them."

Is Israel proud? so is Judah; must Israel fall? so must Judah. Pride struts before, and ruin follows at the heels; Prov. xvi. 18, "Pride goeth before destruction, and an haughty spirit before a fall." Haman was haughty, he thought scorn to lay hands on Mordecai alone, he will have the blood and bones of all the Jews to satisfy his pride, Esth. iii. 6; and quickly after he was hanged, chap. vii. 10. Before the worms did eat Herod, his heart was swoln with pride, Acts xii. 23. Nebuchadnezzar, Dan. iv. 30, 31. David in the pride of his heart numbers the people, and the plague sweeps away seventy thousand of them presently after. Absalom, Adonijah, aspire, but destruction was their end. Pride affects to go before, but it is before a fall, before destruction. If you find pride in the premises, you shall certainly find destruction in the conclusion. Pride preceded the grand fall of our first parents; they would "be as gods, knowing good and evil," Gen. iii. 5. And pride preceded the angels' fall in heaven, some gather from that in 1 Tim. iii. 6. It was so from the beginning, and will be a truth to the end, Luke xiv. 11, "Whosoever exalteth himself shall be abased, and he that humbleth himself shall be exalted:" be they particular persons, cities, or kingdoms, if they exalt themselves through pride, God will throw them down. Jer. l. 29, 30, "Babylon hath been proud against the Lord, against the Holy One of Israel," and therefore she should be ruined. I believe the kingdoms that are ruining now, have been proud against the Lord and his worship; they have provoked God with that sin, and he will plague them with his judgments. God threatened Jerusalem for this sin; Jer. xiii. 9, "I will mar the pride of Judah, and the great pride of Jerusalem." And how, you may see in Isa. iii. 24, "Instead of sweet smell there shall be stink; and instead of a girdle a rent; and instead of well set hair baldness; and instead of a stomacher a girding of sackcloth; and burning instead of beauty:" thus God would mar it, Isa. xxiii. 9, "The Lord of hosts hath purposed to stain the pride of all glory, and to bring into contempt all the honourable of the earth;" he hath purposed, and is powerful to do it.

Obs. 2. The ruin of persons and kingdoms is from themselves. "Violence is risen up into a rod of wickedness;" their own injustice, oppression, and iniquities brought forth that which was their destruction, a rod of wickedness. David's sin was a rod to himself, 2 Sam. xii. 9—11, Thou hast killed Uriah, defiled Bathsheba; now therefore the sword shall never depart from thine house; I will raise up evil against thee out of thine own bowels: the sin and rod grew out of one stock. Men's sins prove their rods. Joseph's brethren sinned in Canaan, and their sin was a rod to them in Egypt, Gen. xlii. 21. Judas's treason became the halter that hanged him, Matt. xxvii. 5. Adam's eating the forbidden fruit prepared birch for his own back, and all ours; the world is whipped with the rod of his sin. Sin in the Scripture is called a burden, weight, Gal. vi. 5. it is that which sinks into misery, thorns, briers, Heb. vi. 8; it pricks and scratches, Nahum i. 10; it is a sting, 1 Cor. xv. 56, it is that brings terrible pangs and pains to all; a snare, Psal. ix. 16, and that will take him who makes and sets it; and here a rod, that caused fear, smart, wounds, death. The tree bears a helve for the axe that cuts itself down; the garment breeds the moth that devours it; and Judah planted the rod which brake itself in pieces: while Judah is sinning, God's wrath is growing, Nebuchadnezzar is coming, the rod of his indignation. It was Israel's idolatry that ruined her, Hos. xiii. 1; and Judah's injustice, oppression, that ruined her, Jer. v. 1; Isa. v. 7.

"None of them shall remain." God would make a general destruction, yet not so general as not any to escape. We know divers did, and some returned, who had seen the glory of the former temple. "Shall remain" is not in the original, it is only, none of them; a defective speech, and refers to the rod of wickedness, and may thus be supplied: None of them shall go unpunished; they have all sinned, and shall one way or other smart, all of them. And so they did, though all of them were not carried away, or cut off.

"Nor of their multitude." The Hebrew is, tumult, sound, or company making a noise; where there is a great number, there is tumultuousness. Let their number be never so great, none of them shall escape the rod; if it destroy them not, it shall wound them; if not wound them, it shall affright them. המון

Others interpret it of their wealth. None of their wealth; that is, none of it shall do them good, or go unpunished.

"Nor of any of theirs." The Hebrew is considerable two ways; either from *hem*, and that doubled, *mehemehem*, of them, of them; and then the sense is, None of them, I say, none of them that have thus sinned, dishonoured me before the nations, shall go unpunished. Or thus, None of them, of them, none of their seed, none come from such a race, shall escape the smart of that rod which is now growing up. All their posterity were not quite ruined, but they all smarted. מהמהם

Or the Hebrew may be considerable from המה which is, to make a noise. And then the meaning is, None of those men that make a noise shall go unbeaten with this rod; none of the great men that, with their honour, wealth, train, make such stirs in the city and land; none of them that think themselves through their greatness exempt from all courts, all accounts, all corrections, shall be free from the strokes of this rod; be they never so great; be they priests, prophets, nobles, princes, kings, they shall come under the lash. Neither multitude, riches, nor greatness, will privilege sinners when the rod comes. The old world's multitude, Damascus' riches, Jerusalem's sons of pride, men of noise, could not protect them from the wrath of God or man.

"Neither shall there be wailing for them." Though men of quality, yet shall not their friends bewail them in any solemn manner. The destructions, miseries, fears, through power and insolency of the enemy, shall be such, that they shall not dare to lament the dead openly, nor much mind their death. Jeremiah speaks of this evil, chap. xvi. 4; xxv. 33. Their slain should be so many, death so common, that they should lie unburied, unbemoaned.

Ver. 12, 13. *The time is come, the day draweth near: let not the buyer rejoice, nor the seller mourn: for wrath is upon all the multitude thereof. For the seller shall not return to that which is sold, although they were yet alive: for the vision is touching the whole multitude thereof, which shall not return; neither shall any strengthen himself in the iniquity of his life.*

In these two verses our prophet sets down what the condition of their temporal estates should be, subject to spoil and loss. If the buyer bought a great pennyworth, he should have little cause to rejoice; it should be suddenly taken from him, house, land, cattle, goods; the time was even at hand. And so if the seller had sold his estate not for half the worth, and parted with his inheritance which was dear to him, he should not mourn; had he not taken a little for the present, within a few days, he should have had nothing, all should have been taken from him, and he separated from his inheritance. Judgment is coming, and so dreadful, that there shall be no leisure to look at what is sold or bought.

"For wrath is upon all the multitude thereof." The Hebrew word will bear it, upon all the wealth thereof; and some interpreters so read it: *hamon* signifies plenty of riches, and also of other things.

המונה

Jerusalem and Judah were rich, wealthy places: Psalm lxvi. 12, "Thou broughtest us into a wealthy place;" and there they became great, waxed rich, Jer. v. 27; and gloried in their riches, Jer. ix. 23. But God's wrath was upon their riches; he would bring the Chaldeans upon them, plunder and spoil them of all, and neither buyer or seller should have any advantage.

"Upon all the multitude thereof." Upon all; not any one condition singled out, but upon all; upon sellers, upon buyers, upon poor, upon rich; all that are in Jerusalem and Judea, of what condition soever, wrath is come upon them, they shall be spoiled and carried captive.

"For the seller shall not return to that which is sold." To understand these words, we must have recourse to the year of jubilee:

Wherein first they were to sound trumpets, Lev. xxv. 10, 13.

Secondly, to proclaim and give liberty to all that were restrained.

Thirdly, to release all lands and tenements; and those that had sold or mortgaged them, were to return and enjoy them. To this last our prophet speaks, and certifies them, that their condition should be such, that when the joyful year of jubilee should come for releasing of lands, and reinhabiting of what was sold, the seller should have no benefit by that year; they should be carried into a strange land, and lose that privilege; they should die there, or be detained that they could not come; or if they did get away, they should find their possession in their hands that would not regard the jubilean law. This was great comfort to poor men, and those who were necessitated to sell their estates, that at such a time they would come in freely again; but this hope is here taken away.

"Although they were yet alive." Though their life were yet in the living, so is the Hebrew. If sorrow, exile, miseries did not consume them, but they should live to the year of jubilee, it should be no advantage to them.

Quest. But why did Jeremiah purchase land after this time? In Jer. xxxii. you shall find he bought land. In the tenth year of Zedekiah, when Jerusalem was besieged, when himself was in prison, ver. 2, he bought, Hanameel sold; subscribed and sealed the evidences, which Baruch put into an earthen vessel, and hid for many days.

Answ. 1. The right of redemption belonged to him; he being the nearest kinsman, was to do it; see Lev. xxv. 24; Ruth iv. 4. But there were wars in the gate; and when wars are awake, the laws do sleep.

Inter arma silent leges.

2. He had special warrant for it, ver. 8: he saith, "Then I knew that this was the word of the Lord," that Hanameel came to him, and bade him buy his field. He knew that it came from God, and it had been sin in him not to have done it.

3. He purchased this land by faith, knowing that the captivity should not exceed seventy years, and that there should be a repossession of houses, fields, and vineyards after the captivity, ver. 15, and believed that the holy seed should return. Ezekiel spake of those present in Jerusalem that should be carried away, perish, and not return.

"For the vision is touching the multitude thereof, which shall not return." These words must be cautiously observed. The multitude's returning must not here be understood; but, the vision shall not return. The Hebrew is, The vision to the multitude thereof shall not return, or, the vision shall not return to the multitude thereof. There is no "which" in the Hebrew, which makes the doubt in the English, and alters the sense. The vision shall not return; that is, the prophetical threatening I have had touching the besieging and destroying of Jerusalem, and the whole land, shall not be in vain; the prophecy denounced against them shall not return void, be without success; it shall not be recalled, but stand firm; not be reiterated, once shall suffice. By that time the truth of this prophecy is executed, and weight of it fallen upon you, there will be no thought of possessions, or place of inheriting lands.

Some read it, The vision to all the wealth, making the sense to be a threatening of their estates to be plundered and spoiled, which they trusted so much unto. This is supposed in the other; for the prophecy taking hold upon them, their estates could not be safe.

"Neither shall any strengthen himself in the iniquity of his life." The Hebrew is, A man in his iniquity of his life shall not strengthen; or thus, A man shall not strengthen himself whose life is in his iniquity; it is so in the margin. Not comfort, saith the Vulgate; where there is comfort, there is some strengthening. Men have thoughts to strengthen themselves in their wicked ways; but it shall not be; not their counsels, not their multitudes, not their riches, not their privileges, not their confederacies with others, not their military preparations, not their serving of false gods, nothing shall strengthen them against the Chaldeans, to withstand them. The iniquity of their lives is stronger to ruin them, than all the strength they have besides can make to defend them. It is not their art, policy, power, that shall deliver them from the judgment decreed and threatened. Sometimes men's iniquities, their malice, violence, blasphemies, stubbornness, make others forbear them, and lose their right rather than they will meddle with them. But here it shall not be so; the greater their iniquities, the rather, the sooner would God punish them. Or thus: You have heard many threats and heavy judgments against the city and land, but you are secure, you repent not, you go on justifying your ways, thinking all well, that we the prophets are liars, that there is no danger of fear; but you shall know that your ways are sinful, and will not afford comfort or strength to stand it out in the evil day. No man ever got strength by, or in, iniquity.

Obs. 1. That the things of this life are little to be valued. We should not be solicitous about them; for the time may come that wrath may be upon them, and what are they then? worthless, comfortless, vexing things. It vexed many of them that their estates should fall into Chaldeans' hands; and the price of desirable things was abated; the buyer was not to rejoice, nor the seller to mourn, for neither the one nor the other had got or lost much; and whatever they had should come to nothing. If men magnify temporals, and exalt the price of them, God will vilify them, and make them at a low rate. All the wealth of Judah and Jerusalem was now to be a prey to the adversary; yea, their gardens, orchards, vineyards, lands, houses, wives, children, and whatever was considerable amongst them, should be taken from them. Now there was no *terra firma* in that kingdom; all things were movable and upon the wing, and little cause had they to laugh or weep for those things. The like is our condition at this present time, all uncertain, much in the enemy's hand; therefore, as the apostle, 1 Cor. vii. 29, "Let them that have wives be as though they had none; they that weep, as though they wept not; they that rejoice, as though they rejoiced not; and they that buy, as though they possessed not." Now let men's hearts be off from all; so look upon all conditions, all possessions, as uncertain, as nothing; as taken from you, as departing from them. Let your thoughts be upon "the inheritance that is incorruptible, and undefiled, and that fadeth not away, which is reserved in heaven," 1 Pet. i. 4.

Obs. 2. Covetous men are glad of good bargains. Though wrath be upon them, they look at the gains, not the wrath. Necessity, danger, made men sell all, and covetousness made others buy all; and because they had much for a little, they rejoiced; but little cause had they, for the wrath of God was upon all they bought. Covetousness is watchful for advantages of gain, but blind in discerning wrath accompanying that gain. Achan's covetousness caused him to take the garment, the shekels of silver, and wedge of gold, Josh. vii.; but it blinded him so, that he saw not the cursedness of them, nor the stony death that followed them. In Lot's days there was buying and selling, till the fire consumed what was bought and sold, together with the buyer and seller, Luke xvii. 28, 29. Covetousness is greedy of its prey, even when death is in it: it will buy houses when fire is kindled in them, and land when the curse of God is upon it. Beware, therefore, of this sin, saith he, Luke xii. 15, "for a man's life consisteth not in the abundance of the things which he possesseth;" his death and his destruction may be in them; they cannot add to his life, or the true comfort of it, but they may take away from it; Jam. v. 3, the rust of their gold and silver shall witness against them, and eat their flesh as fire.

Obs. 3. God's wrath sometimes is so hot, that it takes away not only the present comfort, but even the future hope of temporal things: they should have no benefit of the year of jubilee when it came, they should not return again, although they should suffer much, and long; be alive at a time when men's hopes were wont to be fully answered for their lands and houses, yet they should be without hope. They dealt hypocritically with God, they were "an hypocritical nation," Isa. x. 6; "And the hypocrite's hope shall perish, be cut off, be a spider's web," Job viii. 13, 14. They grow great and green, but God hath judgments to cut them down; they are fastened to the walls of the house, as the spider's web, but God hath a besom of destruction to sweep them away. Whatever wicked men's hopes are of greatness here, and happiness hereafter, yet God in his wrath can, and oft doth, blast them altogether; Job xiv. 19, "Thou washest away the things which grow out of the dust of the earth; and thou destroyest the hope of man."

Obs. 4. The judgments decreed, and given forth by the ministers of God, shall certainly take place. The vision shall not return without its accomplishment, efficacy, and fruit. God foreknows all emergencies, oppositions, events, and nothing can withstand, or finally impede the execution of his decrees and threats; he is wise in appointing them, faithful to perform them, and mighty in the execution of them: Isa. lxiii. 13, "I will work, and who shall let it." When God hath not promised, or threatened, none can let his working; much less when the word is gone forth of his mouth, and himself is engaged to make it good. See Isa. lv. 11, "My word shall not return unto me void, but it shall accomplish that which I please." God will see to it constantly, that it be so: and seeing it is so, and God now working in his judgments, "let all the earth fear the Lord; let all the inhabitants of the world stand in awe of him, for he spake, and it was done," Psal. xxxiii. 8, 9.

Obs. 5. Men's sins do not strengthen them, but weaken them. "No man shall strengthen himself in the iniquity of his life." There is no strength comes in by sin; it deprives us of our strength, it blinds the mind, prejudices the strength of reason, it wounds the spirit, brings guilt on the conscience, which accusing, causeth despondency, and makes ashamed; it adds weight to all afflictions, fills with fears, and so produceth discouragements; it keeps out the comfort and benefit of the ordinances, makes God out with us, all creatures against us, brings a curse upon our undertakings, subjects us to the curse of the law, and sentence of condemnation: any of these will weaken the heart of a sinner, much more all. In Ezek. xvi. 8, Jerus lem's sins are reckoned up; and ver. 30, "How weak is thine heart, seeing thou doest all these things!" They do not strengthen, but sink thee: innocency, righteousness, strengthens, Prov. xxviii. 1.

Obs. 6. Sin is the life of a wicked man, as blood is the life of all flesh, Lev. xvii. 14. It maintains and strengthens the life. So iniquity is the life of all sinful flesh; wicked men live upon wicked ways; it is pastime to a fool to do wickedly, Prov. x. 23. There is a life of sin in the soul, and things of iniquity maintain that life. Christ lives in and by the Father, John vi. 57; a godly man lives in Christ, 2 Tim. iii. 12; and a wicked man lives in sin, delights in it, feeds upon it: 1 Tim. v. 6, "She that liveth in pleasure is dead."

Obs. 7. When God comes in judgment, there is nothing can strengthen or secure a sinful people against the punishment of their iniquity; no power, no policy, no privilege, no wealth. Jerusalem had as much to plead as any place in the world, and those people had the choicest privileges of all others. Amos iii. 2, "You only have I known of all the families of the earth: therefore I will punish you for all your iniquities." They were known above others; none had so many miracles, special providences, blessings, truths, prophets, ordinances; none were seated better, oftener delivered, honoured with such titles, as they were; and no people sinned as they sinned: their sins exceeded the heathen's, Ezek. v. 6. And now neither their privileges nor their sins could exempt them from, or relieve them under, their sufferings. Their iniquities hastened the enemies; sharpened their swords, and armed them with severity to their utter destruction. There is nothing in creatures in the ways of wickedness to help in the day of wrath, Amos ii. 13—16.

VER. 14. *They have blown the trumpet, even to make all ready; but none goeth to the battle: for my wrath is upon all the multitude thereof.*

In this verse is set down one of the most grievous calamities that could befall them, namely, despondency of mind. They were called upon to battle, but none had a heart to go forth to it; and the cause is given, "My wrath is upon them all."

Some conceive these words to be spoken ironically, and read them thus: Blow the trumpet, let all be in a readiness; O ye Jews, call forth, call together your strong soldiers, let all arm, and hasten to meet the enemy; he is come into your quarters, ready to assault you in your cities. Where are you? Why do you not appear in the open fields, or stand upon your guard to defend your country and cities? you are cowardly, spiritless men.

"There is none goeth to the battle." Such ironies and sarcasms the Scripture sometimes hath; Isa. viii. 9, "Associate yourselves, O ye people, and ye shall be broken in pieces;" Isa. xxi. 5, "Arise, ye princes, and anoint the shield."

Belshazzar and his nobles were voluptuous; the Medes were coming to his destruction, undermining the walls of Babylon, and here the Spirit of God upbraided him and his princes for their effeminacy and cowardliness.

We may take them literally, "They have blown the trumpet," given public notice to city and country to make ready for war; but none stirs, none goes forth, they are without spirit. The first mention of trumpets we find in Scripture, is Exod. xix. 16, and there they were used at the giving and promulgation of the law; and to this day in many places laws are proclaimed with the sound of trumpets. They were also used to proclaim fasts, and convocate solemn assemblies; Joel ii. 15, "Blow the trumpet in Zion, sanctify a fast, call a solemn assembly;" and solemn feasts, Psal. lxxxi. 3; in worship, 2 Chron. v. 12, 13; in the journeying of their camps, Numb. x. 2, for then the cloud that used to be over them removed, Numb. ix. 22; then Moses prayed, Numb. x. 35, and then the trumpet sounded, ver. 5, 6. It was also used to warn the people against the danger of war, Ezek. xxxiii. 3; and in their wars, Josh. vi. 9. Here they blow the trumpet to warn them of the danger, to quicken them up to prepare against it; there was loud sounding, and vehement crying, Arm, arm, arm, and none went out to the battle: they wanted not men, means, munition, horses, chariots, spears; shields they had, but hearts they had not; no courage to fight with their adversaries, to stand for religion, their country, liberty, or lives.

Obs. 1. That when God is wroth, all preparations and attempts are in vain. They blow the trumpet, make ready for war, and none stirs to go forth; and what is the reason? the wrath of God is upon the whole multitude. God was not with them to counsel, to encourage them, to prosper their attempts, and so nothing came of all.

Obs. 2. Human endeavours sink, when they are not seconded by God. Economical and political affairs fall to the earth, when they are not upheld by Heaven; Psal. cxxvii. 1, "Except the Lord build the house, they labour in vain that build it." It is not man and wife can build up a family without God; this the elders knew that said to Boaz, Ruth iv. 11, "The Lord make the woman that is come into thine house like Rachel and like Leah, which two did build the house of Israel." So, "except the Lord keep the city, the watchman waketh but in vain." Let cities, states, kingdoms have many watchmen, let them be faithful and industrious, yet if God watch not more than they do, more than they, all is lost. Cities have been suddenly surprised, kingdoms overrun, notwithstanding all the art, vigilance, and industry of men. It is not the counsel, militia, magistracy, ministry of a city or kingdom that can secure them, if God's wrath be upon them.

2. That it is a dreadful evil when the heart and spirit of a people is taken away. Here was danger calling to arm and go forth; but none went forth, they were heartless, unspirited men.

It is a great mercy, among other necessaries to war, to have men of valour; if there be money, arms, skill, men, and not courage, all is nothing. When Goliath defied the armies of Israel, 1 Sam. xvii. 10, 11, they were dismayed, their hearts failed within them; and had not God put courage into David, all Israel had lain under the reproach of one Philistine.

It is observable in Scripture, that in Judah were many valiant men, 2 Sam. xxiv. 9. There were five hundred thousand such in David's days; in Abijah's days there was an army of four hundred thousand valiant chosen men, 2 Chron. xiii. 3; in Asa's days was an army of five hundred and eighty thousand out of Judah and Benjamin, and "all these were mighty men of valour," 2 Chron. xiv. 2; in Ahaz' days were a hundred and twenty thousand valiant men of Judah slain in one day, 2 Chron. xxviii. 6. The men of Judah were famous for their valour, yet now there were no valiant men left, there were none had hearts to go forth and give the enemy battle. The promise was, that one of them "should chase a thousand, and two put ten thousand to flight," Deut. xxxii. 30. The meaning is, they should mightily prevail in battle; this was in case they provoked not God against them. And therefore it follows; "except their Rock had sold them, and the Lord had shut them up;" if it were come to that, then they should be faint-hearted and feeble. And so was it now, God their Rock was against them; he had sold them into the hands of the Chaldeans, and shut up their spirits, and the strong were become as tow, Isa. i. 31. They were heartless, headless, armless, none durst oppose the stout and proud adversary. God hath variety of ways to frustrate the endeavours of men; and one among other, and of the saddest nature, is, to unspirit men. It is a wonderful judgment, when the wisdom of the wise doth perish, when the understanding of the prudent is hid, Isa. xxix. 14. And it is as heavy, strange a judgment, when the mettle and courage of valiant soldiers in time of need is not to be found.

The Germans were a warlike people, and Lavat observes, that after the council of Constance their spirits failed them; there they dealt unfaithfully with Husse, and after, cruelly and shamefully they put him to death; and attempting to bring the Bohemians to the old way of worship, they were easily overcome, and sometimes fled at the sight of their enemies.

Obs. 3. Apprehension of divine wrath discerned and approaching, dispirits strong men. There were without doubt many strong men in Judah as at other times, but they were without spirit. Their sins had stirred up God to bring the northern force upon them, Nebuchadnezzar with all his forces. They were now entering their land, ready to sit down before Jerusalem, and they saw now the sad threats of the prophet's fulfilling, God even fighting against them, and this sunk their guilty hearts: Deut. xxxii. 25, "Terror within shall destroy the young man;" the young men that are full of blood, spirits, lively, even terror within shall destroy them. Their guilt will not only dispirit them, but take away their life: Job xv. 20, "The wicked man travaileth with pain all his days;" he hath prickings, stingings within: and ver. 24, "Trouble and anguish shall make him afraid; they shall prevail against him, as a king ready to the battle." There is power in these to destroy a sinner, as in a king armed, attended with a multitude of soldiers, to ruin his wounded, his flying adversaries. Jeremiah knew the power of divine wrath, and therefore prays, chap. xvii. 17, "Be not a terror unto me; thou art my hope in the day of evil:" he feared lest he that was his hope should be his terror. The day of evil awakens sleepy, guilty, dead works, and then God, before trusted in, becomes dreadful. Look well to your hearts and consciences, get off the guilt upon them, and get out the filth in them: Heb. ix. 14, "The blood of Christ doth purge the conscience from dead works;" that is, all sins, and all guilt which works death, and binds over to death. But that is not all, they lie as dead things in the soul, and upon occasion revive, have their resurrection, and slay us anew.

Ver. 15. *The sword is without, and the pestilence and the famine within: he that is in the field shall die with the sword; and he that is in the city, famine and pestilence shall devour him.*

Of sword, famine, pestilence I have formerly spoken. God hath these judgments in his hand, and can let them out when and where he pleases; and when God's public judgments are abroad, there is no safety for sinners in their cities, or in the fields; God will pursue them though they flee, and slay them though they be never so stout. He will not only scare them with these, but he will destroy them by these.

Ver. 16—19. *But they that escape of them shall escape, and shall be on the mountains like doves of the valleys, all of them mourning, every one for his iniquity. All hands shall be feeble, and all knees shall be weak as water. They shall also gird themselves with sackcloth, and horror shall cover them; and shame shall be upon all faces, and baldness upon all their heads. They shall cast their silver in the streets, and their gold shall be removed: their silver and their gold shall not be able to deliver them in the day of the wrath of the Lord: they shall not satisfy their souls, neither fill their bowels: because it is the stumblingblock of their iniquity.*

Sundry calamities are set down before, he persists in the addition of more; every verse hath its peculiar calamity. In ver. 16, is contained their flight; in ver. 17, their feebleness; in ver. 18, their sorrow and shame, and in ver. 19, the insufficiency of the creature to help in the time of trouble.

I begin with ver. 16. It is misery to be in danger, especially of life, and to be put to flee for it, as these were, when the enemy came to their walls and gates. Some fled and escaped "to the mountains." The original is, their escapers shall escape: those I have appointed to famine, sword, pestilence, shall be consumed by them; but those I have appointed to escape, they shall escape, and get to the mountains, where they "shall be like doves of the valleys."

יונה כיוני The Hebrew root, whence doves comes, signifies to prey upon, to oppress, circumvent, make sad; and the dove is subject to prey, oppression, circumvention, and mourning, as much as any fowl.

Hence two things in the dove are aimed at, fearfulness and mourning.

First, the dove is a trembling, fearful creature, any little noise makes it fly; Hos. xi. 11, "They shall tremble as a dove." The sight of the hawk, the noise of her bells, or wings, doth multiply fears in a dove: and so should those Jews that escaped be full of fears, fly to rocks and mountains as doves, for fear of hawks, and dare not stir. They should hide themselves there, and be afraid to speak, to groan out their grief, lest they should be discovered, and die for it.

Second, it is a mourning creature; Isa. xxxviii. 14, "I did mourn as a dove," saith Hezekiah. And Isa. lix. 11, "We mourn sore like doves."

Doves sit solitary, and mourn when they have lost their young, their mates, or are wounded by any means; yea, it is their nature as to tremble, so to mourn. And so should these Jews sit and mourn; they should have no joy of their lives; their losses, the place they should be in, yea, the thought of life, should be matter of mourning unto them.

"Of the valleys." There were not doves of mountains, and doves of valleys; but they are so called, either because they did oft feed and appear there; as fowls of the air are so called, because they are oft in the air, or for that being pursued by fowlers, they fled to the valleys and hid themselves there, not enduring to be in open places; or because they did breed in the holes of rocks, which were towards the valleys. In Job you have mention of "cliffs of the valleys," Job xxx. 6. Or because they mourned in the valleys, there they made a mourning or doleful noise.

"All of them mourning, every man for his iniquity." Here is the cause of their calamity, viz. "their iniquity;" this was a serpent in the bosom, and gave them no rest. Had there been no enemies at their gates, at their heels, their own sins besieged, pursued them.

Obs. 1. In common calamities, when danger is abroad, those that have escaped, and got hiding places, think not themselves secure. These were in the mountains, in the holes of the rocks, and yet as fearful as doves, trembling that the Babylonians were so nigh, fearing discovery and death every moment. A spirit of fear seizes upon sinners at such times, that imprisons reason, and holds them in bondage.

They are fallen into the hands of divine judgments, which are dreadful; those who were like lions before, were as silly doves, Jer. xlviii. 28.

Obs. 2. That the fruit of sin is sorrow: "all of them mourning, every one for his iniquity." Before they sported in their sins, now they should sigh for them; their consciences were asleep through custom of sinning, God's judgments had now awakened them, and they brought their sins so to mind, that they wept and sorrowed sorely for them. They had gone on in their idolatrous, oppressing, and provoking ways long; they saw no cause to be sorry, all was well with them; but when trouble came, their sins appeared, their souls were sad and filled with apprehensions, that drew bitter tears from them.

What is the fruit of wantonness, whoredom? Prov. v. 11, Solomon tells you that such a sinner "shall mourn at the last, when his flesh and his body are consumed." That of Job is suitable for him; "his flesh upon him shall have pain, and his soul within him shall mourn," chap. xiv. 22. Eve's sin had sorrow, and sorrow multiplied, greatly multiplied, Gen. iii. 16. God told them, Lev. xxvi. 14, 16, that if they sinned they should have "sorrow of heart," and Deut. xxviii. 65, "sorrow of mind." And they had that plentifully; Isa. lxv. 14, "Ye shall cry for sorrow of heart, and shall howl for vexation of spirit." Sin causes howling and mourning; David, when he had sinned, it made him to roar, Psal. xxxii. 3: only his terrors were penitential, these unprofitable; showed their misery, but made no way to mercy.

This sorrow was the fruit of sin; godly sorrow is the fruit of the Spirit: that looks at the punishment, which removed, the guilt and filth of sin still abides;

this at the sin, and would have that destroyed, though the judgments never be taken away, Hos. xiv. 2.

This changes the mind, not that it is godly sorrow; the prophet's sermons could not draw tears from them while there was hope, God's judgments did it when it was too late.

Ver. 17. "All hands shall be feeble." Fear made them flee, and fear made them feeble. Where great fear falls upon any, there the hands grow weak, and are not able to do their office; the spirits retire to the heart, to relieve that, lest life should fail, and thereupon the hands become weak. The trumpet was blown, all called upon to make ready, but none went out to battle: and why? their hands were feeble, they could not hold and handle their weapons to defend themselves; their knees were feeble, they could not flee to save themselves.

There is a treble feebleness of hands: one natural, as when a man hath naturally a weakness, lameness in his hands. There is one accidental, as when a man's hands are by some stroke, fall, wound, made feeble; but such feebleness is not here meant. And there is a metaphorical weakness, which ariseth from despondency of mind through fear and fearful apprehensions.

In this sense we are to take it, and so it is oft used in the Scripture. Jer. vi. 24, the report of the northern forces was come to them, and what then? "Our hands wax feeble: anguish hath taken hold of us." Jer. l. 43; 2 Sam. iv. 1; Job iv. 3; Ezek. xxi. 7; Isa. xiii. 7; Jer. xlvii. 3; in all these places is mention of weakness, feebleness of hands, which is to be taken in the metaphorical sense: their hands were not able to do what they should, and formerly could have done, and here, when they had most need of their hands, they had least use of them,

"All knees shall be weak as water." These words are in chap. xxi. 7. The same they are here; and the original is, shall go into water, or flow with water.

Some interpret it of sweating; but in great pains, not in fears, do the lower parts of the body sweat. I take the sense to lie in this, That their knees should be as water, which is a fluid and weak thing; their legs should not be serviceable unto them. It is a proverbial kind of speech, "weak as water," and when applying to any thing, or part of man, sets out great feebleness; they would attempt to flee, and fear would loosen the joints of their knees, so that they should have no strength, nor stand them in any stead: and it was not the knees of some few or aged, but all knees, even of youth, and the stoutest ones; Isa. xl. 30, "Even the youths shall faint and be weary, and the young men shall utterly fall." Their knees and legs should fail them; as waters are driven this way and that way with the winds, so should they with their fears.

Obs. 1. That human strength is not to be confided in. Let a state have multitudes of men, and all those men of arms, men of legs, of great strength; in a time of most need and use of such, their hands may become feeble, and their knees be weak as water, they may prove unserviceable altogether to the state where they are. Strong men have fainted in the day of adversity, been without hearts when they have come to battle; Isa. xxxiii. 7, "Their valiant ones shall cry without: the ambassadors of peace shall weep bitterly." When Sennacherib was before Jerusalem, their valiant ones were so afraid that they cried: the Hebrew word some interpret, their seers, that is, their prophets; others, their soldiers that were their watchmen; their hearts melted, and tears flowed from them: and those that were sent to treat with Sennacherib, now when they should have been fullest of courage, they had none; they made good what Abishai said, 2 Sam. xvii. 10, "He that is valiant, whose heart is as the heart of a lion, shall utterly melt;" their hearts melted away, and their hands became feeble, and knees weak. God cares not for the arms or legs of men, Psal. xxxvii. 17; cxlvii. 10. He brake the arms of Pharaoh, and caused "the sword to fall out of his hands," Ezek. xxx. 22. He loosed the joints of Belshazzar's loins, and made his knees war one against the other, Dan. v. 6. So Nineveh's heart melted, and knees knocked together, Nah. ii. 10. Let none confide in an arm of flesh; see Jer. xvii. 5: and Isa. xxxi. 1—3, they sent to Egypt for help, and relied too much upon horses, men, chariots, because they were many and strong, and looked not to the Holy One of Israel; whereupon the Lord tells them, that "the Egyptians are men, and not God, and their horses flesh, and not spirit;" and when he should stretch out his hand, both the helper and helped should fall and fail together.

Prov. xxiv. 10.

Obs. 2. That true valour lies not in a natural boldness, or habits gotten by man's industry. We conceive that if men have spirits, and, by their actions and experience in the world, have acquired strength to their spirits, so that they are resolute, fearless, we conceive they are the valiant men; but we are mistaken. Natural abilities, and habits purchased with our endeavours, are quickly separated. Their hands were feeble, their knees weak, because their hearts and all in them failed. Kings, chief captains, great, rich, mighty men, feared and hid themselves in dens and rocks, Rev. vi. 15. True valour is the gift of God; that greatens men's spirits, and lifts them up above fears. Moses feared not the wrath of the king, Heb. xi. 27; he had more than his natural courage, or acquired habits, he had a principle of grace given, continued, preserved, and that made him truly valorous.

The truest valour is ever in a gracious heart that fears God, and so all other fears are swallowed up; that enjoys God, and hath divine influence to uphold it in all conditions. Josh. i. 5, 6, 9, "I will be with thee; be strong and of a good courage, be not afraid nor dismayed, for the Lord thy God is with thee whithersoever thou goest:" his courage and strength, was upon divine promise and presence.

Ver. 18. "They shall also gird themselves with sackcloth." The first mention we have of sackcloth is in Gen. xxxvii. 34, where Jacob, upon the misapprehension of Joseph's death, put sackcloth upon his loins. This was a mark of great misery and sorrow. When the famine was in Samaria, and death ready to eat up them that had nothing to eat, "the king had sackcloth within upon his flesh;" under his royal garments, next his skin, was coarse rough sackcloth, 2 Kings vi. 30. When Ahab, king of Israel, had beaten and sore distressed the Assyrians, they put on sackcloth, and sued to him for pardon and the life of Benhadad, 1 Kings xx. 32; testifying hereby their misery, sorrow, humility. And it is sometimes joined with other signs of sorrow: as Esth. iv. 1, when the writings were sealed and sent out by Haman for destruction of the Jews, "Mordecai rent his clothes, and put on sackcloth with ashes," that is, he sprinkled the sackcloth with ashes, and then put it on. So in Neh. ix. 1, you have sackcloth and earth joined together; this was at a fast, and they were tokens of godly sorrow: they professed they were not worthy of any good clothes, sackcloth was too good for them, only somewhat they must have to cover their nakedness; and they had earth upon them, intimating they deserved to be buried alive. But frequently sackcloth set out their common sorrow for calamities, and so it is here; they should be miserable, mourning people, not for a few days, but many years. If they escaped death, they should be girt with sackcloth. Job xvi. 15, "I have sewed sackcloth upon my skin:" there was now no removing of it, he continued in his doleful condition; God's hand was upon him, and his sackcloth abode with him as a thing sewed to him.

"Horror shall cover them." The word for "horror" notes great trembling that comes from fear; Job xxi. 6, "I am afraid, and trembling taketh hold of my flesh." It is such trembling as in earthquakes; Job ix. 6, "Which shaketh the earth out of her place, and the pillars thereof tremble." Such a horror or trembling should be upon them as should hazard their beings, lives, wits. Isa. xxi. 4, "Fearfulness affrighted me;" it is the same word with our prophet's; and affrightments are dangerous, and sometimes deadly, and probably the meaning here for it was such horror as should cover them, oppress them, and hide them from the living.

פלצות

But there is another sense of the word "cover." "Horror shall cover them," that is, compass them about; so the word "cover" is used, Job xxi. 26, "The worms shall cover them;" and Psal. cix. 29, "Let them cover themselves with their own confusion." Psal. xliv. 19; Lam. iii. 43, in these places covering notes compassing: and Jonah ii. 5, compassing is the same with covering; "The waters compassed me about," they did compass and cover him. And here horror did cover them as a garment, and beset, compass every part of them; neither hands, arms, body, nor legs were free.

"Shame shall be upon all faces." Shame is the blushing of the face upon the sight, hearing, apprehension, or doing of something unseemly, dishonest, or filthy, as Rom. vi. 21; Luke xiv. 9; 2 Cor. iv. 2; Phil. iii. 19. Shame notes two things:

1. Disappointment. Psal. cxix. 116, "Let me not be ashamed of my hope."

2. Confusion, Psalm xxxv. 4. Job vi. 20, "They were confounded because they had hoped; they came thither, and were ashamed." And here disappointment and confusion were upon their faces, their expectations were disappointed, and hopes confounded.

Shame was upon their faces, that they could not look up to God whom they had provoked against them. This shaming of sinners is expressed in the word divers ways: "They shall be clothed with shame," Job viii. 22; that is the garment they shall wear: be put to shame, Psal. xliv. 7; brought to shame, Psal. lxxi. 24; have their faces filled with shame, Psal. lxxxiii. 16; lie down in shame, Jer. iii. 25; be covered with shame, Obad. 10; bear it, Ezek. xvi. 52; be consumed with it, Jer. xx. 18. All these were made good upon these Jews; they were clothed, put to, and filled with shame; they bare their shame upon their faces, lay down in it, were covered and consumed with it.

"Baldness upon all their heads." Their miseries and griefs should be so great, that they should pluck off the hair of their heads and beards, though it were against rule, Deut. xiv. 1. God provided for the comeliness of their heads and faces, yet in their sorrows they would disfigure themselves as the heathens did, and add to their own misery.

They deformed themselves, Jer. xlvii. 5; xlviii. 37; Micah i. 16; Amos viii. 10; Isa. xv. 2. Hair was an ornament, and baldness a reproach; 2 Kings ii. 23, "Go up, thou bald head."

It was said in the 11th verse, there should be no wailing for them, and here is mention of sackcloth and baldness, signs of common and great sorrow. There was no public wailing and solemn mourning at their burials; but privately they bewailed their friends, mourned for the evils upon them; or some few did appear that were not considerable.

It is questionable whether baldness were upon all their heads; did all tear off their hair, and make themselves unsightly? Doubtless many of them did, and all had cause to do it. The prophet speaks not what every one should do, but what their condition required; their calamity was such as called for all signs of sorrow, sackcloth, horror, shame, baldness.

Obs. The equity of God's dealing with sinners. He punisheth them in the thing wherein they have sinned: they had ruffled it in their silks, scarlets, and fine linen; now God brought them to sackcloth made of hair and coarse materials, that was as harsh to their flesh as the other was delightful. The scarlet men were brought to dunghills, Lam. iv. 5; they that were confident themselves of their strength, now trembled; they that were proud of their beauty, had haughty eyes, painted faces, &c. now were filled with shame; and they that gloried in their hair, now were made bald: here was the just hand of God. Isa. iii. 24, "Instead of sweet smell there shall be stink; and instead of a girdle a rent; and instead of well-set hair baldness; and instead of a stomacher a girding of sackcloth; and burning instead of beauty." Wherein they sinned, there God smote them. Psal. lxviii. 21, "God shall wound the hairy scalp of such an one as goeth on still in his trespasses." They gloried in their hair then, as too many do now, and God would wound them in that, their hairy scalps should suffer; the Hebrew is, the crowns of hair walking in its own wickedness. The hair holds forth the pride and vanity of the master thereof, and God would wound it, and the head that bare it. The word for wound, Muscu. and Moller. interpret, shall make bloody, or dip in blood; they have oft powdered their hair, to dry and sweeten it, and God would dye it in their own blood.

Ver. 19. "They shall cast their silver in the streets." That which had been much desired, was gotten with great pains, they should throw into the open streets for any to take up. They were flying for their lives, and their bags of silver were burdensome; or they were faint with famine, so that silver would not relieve, or purchase relief for them; and therefore they must throw it into the streets as dung and filth: there was an insufficiency in the creature to advantage them in this great distress, and thereupon despairing, they threw away that they had formerly so prized, so laboured for, and safely kept a long time. When seamen are in storms and hazard of their lives, they will throw overboard things precious; and this was the case here. By silver and gold understand not only coin, but plate, and all things made thereof.

"Their gold shall be removed." The Hebrew is, for a removal, the Chaldeans shall take it away and carry it into Babylon, afar off; so much the original root signifies, to carry it far from the place where it was: they had hoarded it up in Zion, and now it should be carried to Babylon. The Vulgate reads it, their gold shall be for a dunghill, their great heaps of gold made dunghills; and the word doth something countenance it, which signifies separation on account of pollution. Their gold was the gold of their covetousness and oppression, polluted with idolatry, and so matter fit to be separated from them to the dunghill: that which had lain so long by them, and was thought should never be stirred, that shall be for removal; either themselves shall throw it out upon, or hide it in the earth, or dunghill, or the barbarous enemies shall carry it into far countries.

לנדה נדה

In sterquilinium.

"Their silver and their gold shall not be able to deliver them." They had conceits of and confidence in their riches, that they would benefit them one way or other: if Chaldeans came, they would hire them to be gone; if they took the city, they would buy out their lives and liberties; they dreamed that money could do any thing with any sort of men, but it was otherwise. If by gold and silver we understand their gold and silver gods, they hoped for help from them; but they being without life, had neither counsel, power, nor any blessing for them.

"They shall not satisfy their souls, neither fill their bowels." Such shall be the famine and want of bread, that all their wealth shall not purchase bread enough to relieve and satisfy them; though they have houses full of all wealth, yet their bellies shall have want, and souls faint for hunger. Soul here is put for the appetitive virtue, as in Matt. vi. 25, "Take no care for the life, what ye shall eat or drink;" the word is, for the soul, that is, for the appetite, God will provide. Here they took care for their bellies and appetites, and had little or nothing.

"Because it is the stumblingblock of their iniquity." They had no use or benefit of their estates, when they had most need of them; and why? here is the cause, they were the stumblingblocks of their iniquity. By iniquity, some expositors understand punishment; and then the sense is, that their silver and gold were the occasion of these sad judgments which fell upon them; their wars, firing of the city and temple, and their leading into captivity. The former translation hath it, "For this ruin is for their iniquity;" it renders stumblingblock ruin, and shows the cause, "it is for their iniquity," and so iniquity is taken properly for sin, not punishment. They had sinned, and this ruin or judgment of casting away their silver and gold, of finding no help, of being hungry and unsatisfied, was upon them for their sin.

This sense is truth; but the Hebrew being thus, because it hath been the stumblingblock of your iniquity, it leads to this sense, that their wealth was the matter and occasion of their sin; their silver, gold, and great estates occasioned them to sin more fully and more foully, and therefore these judgments came upon them; their estates bred their sins, and brought their judgments.

That wealth is the occasion and fuel of sin appears thus: Rich men in Scripture are set out as apt to trust in their estates, to be high-minded, 1 Tim. vi. 17; to glory in what they have, Jer. ix. 23. They are liberal to their own backs and bellies, but hard-hearted to the poor, Luke xvi. 19, 20, &c. They answer roughly, Prov. xviii. 23. They scorn others, Psal. cxxiii. 4. They are covetous, deceitful, having treasures of wickedness in their houses, Micah vi. 10. They oppress the poor, corrupt justice, and fill all with violence, ver. 12. They keep back the wages of servants and labourers; they live in pleasures, wantonly, securely, James v. 4, 5. They little mind Christ and his ways, John vii. 48; Matt. xix. 23, 24; when Christ calls, they have their yokes of oxen, which draw them so fast from Christ, that all his sweet invitations prevail not. They are prone to, and prodigal in, false, idolatrous worship, Isa. xlvi. 6. What wickedness doth not wealth prompt men unto? Jer. v. 27, 28, "They are waxen rich," and what then? "they are waxen fat, and shine," their faces, their apparel glitters; but it follows, "they overpass the deeds of the wicked;" the richer they are, the worse they do; their riches are fuel to their lusts, and cause them to act with more heat and strength. Hence Christ calls them unrighteous mammon, Luke xvi. 9, 13. Riches are men's mammons, gods that open the door wide for, and strongly entice to, unrighteous and wicked things; therefore wealth is called wickedness, Psal. lii. 7; speaking of a wicked rich man, "he strengthened himself in his wickedness." In the margin, it is substance, and notes wealth gotten by a man's labour. Wealth gotten most honestly hath somewhat in it, which, through our weakness and corruption, may draw us to wickedness, and therefore here it falls under that notion.

Obs. 1. That the creatures which promise the most help, and raise expectation highest in times of trouble, can do little or nothing for us. "Their silver and their gold shall not be able to deliver them in the day of the wrath of the Lord;" things precious and powerful can do nothing for the owners in the day of distress, Zeph. i. 18; Prov. xi. 4. They cannot deliver, they cannot profit in the day of man's jealousy; wealth will not profit then, much less in the day of God's wrath.

But it is said, Eccles. vii. 12, "Money is a defence;" and chap. x. 19, "Money answereth all things." Money may defend from poverty, human wrongs, but not from sickness, death, or the wrath of God; and it may answer for all our debts to men, but not for our debts to Heaven. It is not the fruit of your body can answer for the sin of your soul, Micah vi. 7, much less the fruit of your purse.

The profit men labour for in their health, will not profit in the days of God's wrath. Judas's thirty pieces could not still one throb of his conscience. Herod's royal robes, sceptre, crown, greatness, could not protect him from the teeth of a few feeble worms; nor all Jerusalem's gold and silver, the Jews from the fury of the Medes, Isa. xiii. 17, 18. It is not all your wealth can keep the plague out of the city, or secure your lives when it is come.

In a famine, is not one loaf of bread more satisfying than all the gold of the earth? Silver and gold are not eatable; green herbs are more serviceable in such a case than they are. Let the counsel of God's Spirit therefore prevail with you, Prov. xxiii. 4, 5, "Labour not to be rich: cease from thine own wisdom. Wilt thou set thine eyes upon that which is not? for riches certainly make themselves wings, they fly away as an eagle toward heaven." Here are three arguments against it.

(1.) It is human wisdom, not divine, to do so.

(2.) They are inconsiderable things, they have no being in them, they are not sufficient to help and deliver you in your straits.

(3.) They are uncertain things, they make wings to themselves and fly away; they are like birds in the nest, that seem to dwell there, but presently their feathers grow, and they are gone; and their wings are eagle's wings, they fly swiftly, strongly from you—a fire in a night, &c. Therefore set not your hearts to get riches; or if they be gotten, set not your hearts upon them.

Obs. 2. That wealth in the day of God's wrath, when he deals with sinners, is so far from advantaging, that it prejudiceth and wounds. "They shall cast their silver in the streets," &c.; they found it did them hurt. In prosperity they plead prerogative, and must have their will; and in adversity they have their prerogative above others, but it is a prerogative of woes. If any suffer, go into captivity, they do it first, Amos vi. 7. Nebuzaradan took the rich and fat ones with him, and left the poor that had nothing, to dress the vineyards, and possess the land, Jer. xxxix. 10; these had the privilege of safety, when others had a prerogative of misery. The wealth of these men did multiply their woes.

(1.) One wound to them was, that they had not believed the prophet's threatening the ruin of their estates.

(2.) That they had gotten their estates by unlawful means.

(3.) That they had done little good, but much hurt by them.

(4.) That they were disappointed now, and could not bribe the Chaldeans with all their estates to spare them; they regarded not gold, Isa. xiii. 17. Hence the Chaldee renders that in Prov. xi. 4, "Riches profit not," a lie profits not. Riches are lying and deceitful things, they disappoint, and this wounded them.

(5.) They were so smitten with fear, distraction, and blindness, that they saw not what to do with their wealth, but threw it away; they do not carry it away.

(6.) That what they had laboured hard for, kept with difficulty, prized so high, must now in a moment be parted with and thrown away.

(7.) That all opportunities were now lost of doing good to their friends or others with their estates.

(8.) That they should be exposed to more shame, scorn, misery, and be more sensible of the same, than those that never had any estates; like one that hath warm clothes, and being stripped of them, is more affected with the cold than beggars that feel it every day.

(9.) That they had not sought the eternal good of their souls with their estates, but sinned with them, and made way for a dreadful account.

(10.) And lastly, that their lives were in the greater danger the more wealthy they were. Riches invite enemies to plunder, Jer. xlix. 31. Fat cattle are nearest the slaughter: wealthy men are called fat men, they are filled and fatted with their great estates, and the wrath of God came first upon them, Psa. lxxviii. 31; Judg. iii. 29. It was their gold that caused the Jews' bellies to be ripped, when the Romans took Jerusalem.

Obs. 3. Note here the folly of covetousness; men tainted with that sin lay up wealth for they know not whom, for their enemies. The Jews were a covetous people, Micah ii. 2; Isa. lvii. 17. They were generally given to covetousness, even great and small, Jer. vi. 13; viii. 10. Their eyes and hearts were for nought but covetousness, Jer. xxii. 17; wealth was the only object of their eyes, and idol of their hearts. They had treasures, but God could give them away to spoilers, Jer. xv. 13; yea, "all their treasures," Jer. xvii. 3. Little did these covetous Jews think that the Babylonians should be enriched with their labours, wealth, and treasures: they had vexed their heads, hearts, and hands to get houses and vineyards, banks of silver and gold, and now mere strangers, men their souls hated, must possess their desirable things, and fill their pockets with their treasures. This misery is upon all men, that they cannot foresee who shall enjoy what they get; and therefore it should prevail with men to labour less for the creature, seeing they work for they know not whom; it may be a Babylonian, some bloody cavalier, idolatrous papist, or bitter enemy to God and his saints, some one he never saw, exchanged a word with, had any reference unto; and what thou hast been twenty or thirty years in gathering, he shall possess in one hour. David, Psal. xxxix. 6, brands this practice with vanity and disquietment of spirit: "Surely every man disquiets himself in vain;" and why? "He heapeth up riches, and knoweth not who shall gather them," who shall be owner and take them into his custody. Solomon upon this ground hated his labour in pursuit of the creature, because he knew not whether the man that came after him should be a wise man or a fool, Eccl. ii. 18, 19. You know neither the man nor his qualities who shall come after you, and why will you disquiet yourselves for you know not whom, wise men or fools, saints or devils? You will say it is for your children. If so, they are either godly or ungodly; if godly, they have wealth enough, God is their portion, he will bless their endeavours, and provide sufficiencies; if ungodly, a little is enough, if not too much for them. But you are not sure to leave your estates to your children, nor to keep them yourselves; remember thieves and robbers are in the land, and if you labour all day for thieves at night, what folly will this be!

Obs. 4. Abuse of our estates defiles them, and brings the wrath of God upon them. Their silver and gold they had hoarded up and confided in, maintained their pride, lusts, and idolatry with, that must be separated as an unclean thing. Lev. xiv. 55, the leprosy defiled garments, houses; and sin defiles persons, whole estates. When men divert their estates otherwise and to other ends than God hath appointed them, they wrong the creature, imbondage it to their own lusts; they defile it, and bring the curse of God upon it. Isa. xxiv. 5, 6, "The earth also is defiled under the inhabitants thereof; because they have transgressed the laws, changed the ordinances, broken the everlasting covenant. Therefore hath the curse devoured the earth, and they that dwell therein are desolate:" their sin defiled the land and fruit of it, and brought the curse of God upon all. When Adam and Eve put the fruit of the tree to another use than God appointed, they then brought the curse upon themselves and the whole earth. Jer. xv. 13, "Thy substance and thy treasures will I give to the spoil, and that for all thy sins." If you would not have your substance defiled and cursed, take heed of abusing it.

(1.) Acknowledge all you have to be the Lord's. You are stewards, not owners; Hos. ii. 9, God calls it his corn and wine, &c. Not only receive them as from God, but acknowledge them to be the Lord's.

(2.) Labour to see much of God in your estates. Most look at the outside, the glass, the galley-pot, not at what is within. God is in the creatures, Rom. i. 20.

(3.) Make use of all truths you hear about the insufficiency and emptiness of the creatures: say, Here is much silver, gold, bread, but I live not by these, but the blessing of God; these are nothing without him.

(4.) Work up your hearts nearer to God by them. Estates should be as ladders and mountains; when you are on them you go up towards heaven, and when at the top you are nearest heaven.

(5.) Have your eyes ever upon something better than your estates, unto which make your estates serviceable.

(6.) Lay out your estates for God, his worship, cause, the public, the spiritual good of your families and friends, and relief of the poor. It is Christ's direction, Lay not up treasures, but lay out; give and it shall be given you, &c.

(7.) Meditate oft upon that scripture, Come, "give account of thy stewardship," Luke xvi. 2, as you do of your silver and gold.

Ver. 20—22. *As for the beauty of his ornament, he set it in majesty: but they made the images of their abominations and of their detestable things therein: therefore have I set it far from them. And I will give it into the hands of the strangers for a prey, and to the wicked of the earth for a spoil; and they shall pollute it. My face will I turn also from them, and they shall pollute my secret place: for the robbers shall enter into it, and defile it.*

In these verses comes the temple into consideration, and the calamity which befell them in regard thereof, with the cause of it. The temple here is described,

I. By its appellation; it is "his ornament."

II. By its qualification; it is beautiful.

III. From its end, set for majesty; or from the manner, set in majesty.

IV. The author; "He set it."

V. The calamities which befell it; and these are,

1. Rejection, or separation of it; "I have set it far from them."

2. Tradition of it into hands of others: and they are set out to be,

(1.) "Strangers."

(2.) "The wicked of the earth," ver. 21.

3. Depredation; it shall be "for a prey," and "for a spoil," ver. 21.

4. Profanation; "they shall pollute it," ver. 21.

5. Aversion, and that of the face of God; ver. 22, "My face will I turn also from them."

6. Contamination of the holy of holies; "They shall pollute my secret place."

The cause of all these evils is set down in ver. 20, "They made the images of their abominations and of their detestable things therein."

"As for the beauty of his ornament, he set it in majesty." Some expositors interpret these words, not of the temple, but of their silver, gold, jewels, and such like precious things, with which they were decked as a bride, for which they should have been dutiful and thankful; but they abused all to idolatry, pride, and service of their lusts, and so provoked God to take all from them.

Jonathas, et Rabbi David de templo interpretantur. *Maldonat.*

Others expound them only of the temple, to whose judgment I incline, and that upon these considerations:

First, it is said, "He set it," which takes off the connexion of this verse with the former. Had it been meant of their gold, silver, &c. it should have run plurally, They cast their silver in the streets, they shall not be satisfied; and so, they set the beauty of their ornament for pride; whereas it is "he set," not the people, but God.

בו in eo Montan. Piscat. Jun. Polan.

And if it be urged, He set their gold, silver, the beauty and ornament of his people, in majesty, or for excellency, it suits not with what follows, "they made images of their abominations and detestable things therein;" it should have been *thereof*, if that had been the sense; but it is *therein*, agreeable with the original, and so choice expositors render it.

חלל

Secondly, those words in the 21st verse refer more properly to the temple, than to their silver and gold; holy things are subject to pollution more than common. Some, to help this, interpret the word for pollute, to kill, and make the sense, they shall kill their captives; and so refer it to the men, not their wealth; or if to wealth, then they render it vilify, they shall vilify their silver and gold which they have made their beauty and ornament. But I see no cause why the sense of the word should be changed in this verse, when it is taken for polluting in the next verse, "they shall pollute my secret place."

Thirdly, in this 22nd verse, he speaks of the secret place, the holy of holies, which was in the temple; and hence to me is an argument that he spake of the temple.

"The beauty of his ornament." These words are a metaphorical description of the temple, whereby it is likened to a beautiful garment which becomes the party that wears it, or to any precious thing that adorns the body. Exod. xxxiii. 4, "No man did put on him his ornaments;" that is, his chief apparel, and other precious things which might adorn the body. Ornaments were choice things, 2 Sam. i. 24; Judg. viii. 26; the Hebrew word signifies choice robes, silken veils, costly chains, crowns, &c. Whatever excellency may be fastened to the body or garments of a man, such an ornament was the temple, to God, and to the Jews.

First, to God. It was his "dwelling-place," Psal. lxxiv. 7, and no mean one. Isa. lx. 7, he calls it the "house of his glory:" so great was the glory of it, that in comparison thereof the second temple was nothing, Hag. ii. 3. There multitudes of his people met, prayed; whence it is named "an house of prayer," Isa. lvi. 7. There they sang praises, Psal. cl. 1; and God there "inhabited the praises of Israel," Psal. xxii. 3. There they sacrificed, 2 Chron. xi. 16, and it was an house of sacrifice. Thither did kings bring presents unto the Lord, Psal. lxviii. 29; kings did honour the place, and garnished the temple with great gifts: Seleucus king of Asia, of his own revenues, bare all the costs belonging to the service of the sacrifice, 2 Macc. iii. 2, 3. By his worship there he was distinguished and made known from all false gods. There the saints desired to dwell, to behold the Lord's beauty, Psal. xxvii. 4, and see his power, Psal. lxiii. 2. There "every one speaks of his glory," Psal. xxix. 9. The earth is full of the glory of God, but the temple is fuller; there is the chief and brightest glory, glory that affects every eye, heart, and tongue. All these are ornaments and honour to God.

Secondly, to the Jews. If we should look at the structure only, it was one of the stateliest and most magnificent buildings that ever the world had; there were one hundred and fifty thousand workmen employed about it, 1 Kings v. 15, 16, and seven years in building, chap. vi. 37, 38. The apostles wondered at the goodly stones and glory of the second temple, Luke xxi. 5, which were inconsiderable to those of the first, Hag. ii. 3. In this respect it was a great ornament to Jerusalem and the Jewish nation. But it was "the house of the great God," Ezra v. 8; the house "called by his name," Jer. vii. 11. There he made his people joyful, and accepted their offerings, Isa. lvi. 7. There they had "fatness," Psal. xxxvi. 8, "loving-kindness," Psal. xlviii. 9, help in their distresses, Psal. xx. 2. In Ezek. xxiv. 21, 25, you have these expressions: it is called "their strength," "the excellency of their strength," "the desire of their eyes," "that which their souls pitied," (lest it should be destroyed,) "their glory," "the joy of their glory;" all which show the temple was an ornament to them.

"The beauty of his ornament." The temple was beautiful, Isa. lxiv. 11, "Our holy and beautiful house is burned up with fire." There was a material beauty in it, as you may read, 1 Kings vi. and 2 Chron. iii. 6, 8, "He garnished the house with precious stones for beauty; and the gold was gold of Parvaim: and he overlaid it with fine gold," which made it glorious. There was a spiritual beauty in it; Psal. xcvi. 6, "Strength and beauty are in his sanctuary:" there was "the beauty of holiness," Psal. xxix. 2; there was beautiful order, beautiful worship, beautiful ordinances, and a most beauteous God, Psal. xxvii. 4, whose glorious presence and lovely truths drew the eyes and hearts of the godly there: Isa. ii. 3, "Come ye, and let us go up to the mountain of the Lord, and he will teach us of his ways." Hence Zion the mount, where the temple was, is called "the perfection," or universality, "of beauty," Psal. l. 2: there was all beauty.

"He set it in majesty." In magnificent pomp; or for majesty, glory, and excellency. God set the temple among the Jews, that it might be their glory, excellency, and make them glorious and excellent among all nations. Isa. lx. 15, is the same word, and it is rendered "an excellency;" it might well be, for so ל is rendered thrice in one verse, Exod. xxviii. 2, "Thou shalt make holy garments for Aaron, for glory and for beauty."

Or, he set it into majesty, into excellency. The majesty and excellency of the temple was not only the stateliness of the structure, the strength, and situation of it on a hill; but in that it was sanctified and bare God's name, 1 Kings ix. 7; viii. 29. It was a type of Christ and the church, a part of their worship; in it their gifts and sacrifices were sanctified and accepted, Matt. xxiii. 19; "Fire came down from heaven, and consumed the burnt offering and the sacrifice," 2 Chron. vii. 1. There was the "ark of the covenant," a sign of God's presence, 1 Kings viii. 6. In it were glorious visions of God, Isa. vi. 1. It was filled with glory, 2 Chron. vii. 1. The people prayed towards the same, 1 Kings viii. 38. The eye and heart of God was there perpetually, 1 Kings ix. 3. It was "exceeding magnifical, of fame and of glory throughout all countries," 1 Chron. xxii. 5. In these and such things consisted the majesty, glory, and excellency of the temple; and therefore it is called "their excellency," Ezek. xxiv. 21; "the excellency of Jacob," Amos vi. 8.

Vide Drus. in locum. Some refer it to the holy land, to their own habitations, to the city. If these, any, or all of them were "the excellency of Jacob," much more the temple, Psal. xlvii. 4. The temple and worship of it distinguished them from and made them excel all others.

"But they made the images of their abominations and of their detestable things therein." Here is the cause of all their miseries: God had dealt bountifully with them, set his ornaments amongst them, put glory upon them, and distinguished them from all nations; but they forgot God, proved ungrateful, and polluted their glory, even the temple, with superstition and idolatry. These words, "abominations and detestable things," have been opened before.

"Therefore have I set it far from them." Here is one part of their calamity. God had set the temple amongst them, a divine ornament, for his own honour, their good and glory; but they corrupted themselves, dishonoured God, and defiled his worship, his holy place, with their own inventions, abominations, and detestable things; and "therefore have I set it far from them;" or, as the Hebrew is, I have made it to them an unclean thing, or given it to them for separation; it shall now be for their reproach, rejection, and destruction; it shall be taken from them, and destroyed out of my sight as a polluted thing.

Obs. 1. The chief ornaments and glory of a people are, the ordinances of God, and his presence. The temple where God manifested himself, and the divine ordinances that were to be performed, were their beauty, their glory; Zech. ii. 5, "I will be the glory in the midst of her," meaning Jerusalem. Other things may be some ornament to a people, as riches, peace, liberty; cities well built, peopled, and fortified; arts and sciences, wise counsellors, strong soldiers, just judges, good laws, prudent governors, these adorn a people; but their chief ornament is true religion and the divine presence. The gentiles had those fore-mentioned ornaments; yet, because they had not the true God, and true worship of his, amongst them, they were unlovely, accounted of as dogs, Matt. xv. 26; an unhappy, a hopeless people; Eph. ii. 12, "Without Christ, without God." David tells you what people is happy; even "that people whose God is the Lord." Not those that have a false god and false worship among them; but they who have Jehovah, his temple and ordinances, with them. Moses knew that the presence of God and his ordinances were the honour and chief ornament of a nation, and therefore makes a challenge, Deut. iv. 7, "What nation is there so great, who hath God so nigh unto them as the Lord our God is." God was nigh them in the pillar of fire, in the cloud, in the tabernacle, in the ark, and other ordinances, and no nation under heaven had God so near them, and gloriously amongst them, as the Jews had. No nation, though ever so wise, wealthy, or honourable, had such statutes and righteous judgments as they had. Moses tells God that his presence would be an argument they had found favour in his sight, and were a people "separated from all people on the earth," Exod. xxxiii. 16.

Divine ordinances and God in them is the glory of any people, Jer. ii. 11; Psal. cvi. 20. Therefore when the ark was taken, which was a symbol of God's being amongst them, and before which they worshipped, Phinehas's wife said, "The glory is departed from Israel," 1 Sam. iv. 22. But when God manifests his presence with a people, then are they glorious, Isa. lix. 21: he speaks of his covenant with them, and Spirit upon them; and chap. lx. 1, 2, he saith, "Arise, shine; for thy light is come, and the glory of the Lord is risen upon thee. Darkness shall cover the earth, and gross darkness the people; but the Lord shall arise upon thee, and his glory shall be seen upon thee:" others had darkness, but the people where God and his ways were, had light and glory. When the new Jerusalem comes down from heaven, she is said to have the glory of God, Rev. xxi. 10, 11. Pray that the new Jerusalem may come among us, that so "glory may dwell in our land," Psal. lxxxv. 9.

Obs. 2. It belongs to God to appoint worship, and the beauty of it. He set the ornament and beauty of it; not Moses in the tabernacle, nor Solomon in the temple, might prescribe any substantial or ceremonial worship. Exod. xxxv. 10, "Every wise-hearted among you shall come, and make all that the Lord hath commanded; not what I have commanded, but what the Lord hath commanded: though they were wise, yet they might not do aught after their own hearts or heads, no, not Solomon, the wisest of men: 2 Chron. iii. 3, "He was instructed for the building of the house of God;" the Hebrew is, founded; he had a foundation laid in him by the Spirit of God, before he laid the foundation of the temple, or did any of the work thereof. הוסד

What God appoints is an ornament, hath beauty, is for glory; but let men set up aught in the worship of God, it hath no beauty, but blackness, no holiness, but iniquity; and God must be worshipped "in the beauty of holiness," 1 Chron. xvi. 29, not in the blackness of iniquity. Men think that ceremonies do become the worship of God, that pictures, altars, golden vessels do make it glorious; but all is deformity which God hath not set up, and set up for glory.

Obs. 3. The people to whom God vouchsafeth his presence, his ordinances, they are his glory above all others. In 1 Cor. xi. 7, it is said "the woman is the glory of the man," especially when she is adorned with many jewels, and more virtues. The church is compared to a bride, Isa. lxi. 10; lxii. 5; and when she is decked with God's ordinances, and beautified with the graces of his Spirit, how doth he rejoice over her, delight in her, what a glory is she unto him! The church is God's glory, Isa. iv. 5, as the wife is man's; and being under covert-baron, he will protect her, and esteem her as his glory. Hence he calls his people his peculiar treasure, Exod. xix. 5; his portion, Deut. xxxii. 9; his jewels, Mal. iii. 17; his anointed, Psal. cv. 15; a holy temple, the habitation of God, Eph. ii. 21, 22; the fulness of God, the body of Christ, chap. i. 23. And Christ calls the church his love, his sister, his spouse, a garden enclosed, a spring shut up, a fountain sealed, Cant. iv. 10, 12; the fairest among women, chap. v. 9; fair as the moon, clear as the sun, chap. vi. 10; and pleasant for delights, chap. vii. 6. The church is very beautiful and glorious, "a crown of glory in the hand of the Lord, and a royal diadem in the hand of her God," Isa. lxii. 3. The world hath base and low thoughts of the church and people of God, but they are his glory, and glory in his hand.

Obs. 4. That images in the places of God's worship are unwarrantable and sinful. Here God complains, that they made images, and set them in the temple; the Hebrew signifies an image, shape of things corporeal, or incorporeal, and it is the same with that in Gen. i. 27, "God created man in his own image;" and this word includes all images; 2 Kings xi. 18, they brake Baal's images: be they images of creatures, or Creator, they may not come into the place where God hath set his name, and meets his people. The cherubims were by divine appointment, Exod. xxv. 18, others were forbidden, Exod. xx. 4, "Thou shalt not make unto thee any graven image." The Targum hath the same word which is here; and if no images may be made for holy places and uses, they may not be brought into them, being made. Clemens Alexandrinus calls it a deceitful art to make pictures, and saith we are forbidden to exercise it. The emperor Adrian commanded temples to be made in all cities without images, bare temples without such ornaments; whence came the proverb, *Adriani templum*, The temple of Adrian. When the gentiles built them bare temples, and when Adrian made such temples, it was conceived they were for Christ: the gentiles demanding of the christians why they had no known images, it was answered, What image shall be made to God, when man himself is God's image. Ambrose saith, Our church knoweth no such thing as pictures. Jerom, upon Ezek. iv. saith, We worship one image only, and that is Christ, the express image of the Father; no other image ought to be in the assemblies but Christ, and what he appoints. It was a canon of the Eliberine council about the time of Constantine the Great, It is our mind that pictures ought not to be in the church, lest that which is worshipped should be painted on the walls. There is great danger in them, as you may read at large in the homily of the Peril of Idolatry; and bitter contention they caused among the eastern and western christians heretofore, and still great strife and offence is between papists, Lutherans, and others, about them. The Lord convince all of their unlawfulness, throw out all such abominations and detestable things.

[Margin notes: צלם — Protrept. ad Gent. — Lamprid. in vita Adriani. Idem in vita Alexand. Seu. — Minut. Fælix, in vit Octa. De fug. seculi. — Concil. Elib. c. 36.]

Obs. 5. Such is the corruption of man, that he is ungrateful for, and abusive of, the choicest of mercies. God had set his temple and pure worship amongst them in much beauty, for glory to them, and to himself; but they, forgetting what a high favour this was, instead of honouring God in his temple, and preserving his worship entire and pure, bring in the images of their abominations, their detestable things, and so blemish their beauty, defile their ornament, and stain their glory. It was wicked to corrupt themselves with strange marriages, Ezra. x. 2; by dealing treacherously with their lawful wives, Mal. ii. 15, 16; by making a calf to worship, Exod. xxxii. 7, 8; but worse to bring their detestable things into the temple, into God's presence and ordinances. When they made the calf, Moses was in the mount receiving instructions for worship, yet they had no place fixed for worship, nor the way of worship clearly opened unto them; but when God had set his temple in Zion, they had a fixed place, a settled way of worship, and the most glorious beautiful worship in the world; yet they corrupt themselves herein. The majesty of God's presence there, his glory, his commands did not awe them, they were not content with what his infinite wisdom had prescribed, the abomination and detestableness of their images was not seen; but they being blinded with their own conceits, and hardened with their sins, proceeded to corrupt God's worship. Zephaniah saith of them, that they "corrupted all their doings," chap. iii. 7. Even when they had to do with God in matters of religion and their salvation, even there they were corrupters, "a corrupt spring," Prov. xxv. 26.

Obs. 6. The church's unthankfulness for choice mercies, causeth upbraiding "buts" from God. He set his temple, the greatest ornament and blessing they could have, but they made the images, &c. Nothing exasperates God more than wretched unkindness after great mercies. Psal. cvi. he reckons up God's great mercies to them, and they being ungrateful, ever and anon comes in a "but," ver. 7, 14, 25, 43. He did deliver them, do great things for them; but they provoked him, lusted, murmured. Ingratitude is a kicking the benefactor; Deut. xxxii. 15, "Jeshurun waxed fat, and kicked." The Scripture hath observable expressions touching this sin; Deut. xxxii. 6, 7, "Do you thus requite the Lord, O foolish people and unwise? Is not he thy Father that hath bought thee? hath he not made thee and established thee?" How did they requite the Lord? they corrupted and spotted themselves with the sins of the times and places. They were a perverse people towards God, and therefore saith Moses, "Do ye thus requite?" &c. It is folly and madness in you. Isa. v. 2, God repeats the kindnesses vouchsafed the house of Israel; and ver. 3, he calls the "inhabitants of Jerusalem, and men of Judah," to judge between him and his vineyard. God refers it to men to judge how kind and bountiful he had been, how base and ungrateful they; and therefore he would break down the wall thereof, and lay it waste. In such a case as this he was willing to be judged by men; they could not but see the great wrong done to God, and justify him in righting himself. Ingratitude makes the author worse, and the Benefactor angry and wary.

Angry; for God denounces six woes against them in the chapter afterwards.

Wary; he would take heed how he bestowed his choice mercies upon such people; others that would be more fruitful and thankful should have them: Matt. xxi. 43, "The kingdom of God shall be taken from you, and given to a nation bringing forth the fruits thereof;" not their own fruits, but such as Christ and the gospel appointed.

This sin was so prodigious, that Lycurgus would make no law against it; but God hath made a law; Psal. ix. 17, "The wicked shall be turned into hell, and all the nations that forget God." Ingratitude is the greatest and worst forgetfulness: Judas forgot the kindness and bounty of Christ, he betrayed him, and therefore was turned into hell.

Ver. 21. "And I will give it into the hands of strangers for a prey," &c. They had sinned shamefully, and God would punish them severely. Strangers, that is, Chaldeans, should come and have temple, city, them, and all they had in their hands; and God, whom they flattered themselves in, thought still to be their friend, their help, even he would give all into their hands.

These Chaldeans he calls the "wicked of the earth." David calls such, "men of the world," Psal. xvii. 14; "men of the earth," Psal. x. 18; that is, base and vile men, as it is in Job: children of base men, viler than the earth, fit for any cruel and bloody designs. The Septuagint hath it, τοῖς λοιμοῖς τῆς γῆς, the plagues of the earth.

The king of Babylon and his cursed crew went up and down in the world plundering nations, shaking kingdoms, and laying all waste, Isa. xiv. 16, 17. They were the pests and vipers of the earth, and into their hands must the Jews, God's own people, fall; they must spoil the temple, have all the ornaments, vessels, and treasures in it, all the pictures of silver and gold.

"They shall pollute it." The temple was a holy place, the habitation of the holy God, had in much reverence by all sorts of people; but now they should see it not regarded as a thing consecrated to God; now heathens, uncircumcised ones, should enter it, which was against law, Ezek. xliv. 7. Now their blood should be spilt in it, now it should be made a prison, a stews, a stable; the Jews had polluted it with images, and these barbarians should pollute it many other ways.

Obs. 1. The abuse of spiritual mercies causeth God to take them away. Jer. xi. 15, their lewdness caused the holy flesh to pass from them: they had the temple, the beauty and worship of it for their glory, to make them glorious within, as well as glorious without; but they abused their mercies, polluted God's ordinances, and therefore he removed the temple far from them.

He took it away. The Lord had set his name at Shiloh, pitched his tabernacle there, Josh. xviii. 1; and they abused his name and worship, as you may see, Psal. lxxviii. 58; then "he was wroth, and greatly abhorred Israel: he forsook the tabernacle of Shiloh, and delivered his strength into captivity, and his glory into the enemy's hand," ver. 59—61; which some interpret of the ark taken by the Philistines, 1 Sam. iv. 11. And in Jer. vii: when they lived loosely, and blessed themselves with their carnal confidence in the temple, and worship of it, ver. 4, 9—11, God sends them to Shiloh, and bids them search and see what he did there for the wickedness of his people, and threatens to do so by them, even destroy their temple, worship, them and their seed. They sinned in special things, and God punished them in that wherein they sinned: they pollute the temple, and God causes the Chaldeans to pollute it; they confide in the temple, and God lays it waste; they make an idol of it, and set it near their hearts, and God removes it far off; they look upon it as clean, as their glory, and God removes it as vomit, as a polluted, loathsome thing.

Obs. 2. It is a dreadful thing when God gives up a church, a state, either or both, to the wills of wicked men.

Ver. 21. "I will give it into the hands," &c. I have set it far from them. If evil come to the gates of Jerusalem, and doors of the temple, it is from the Lord, Micah i. 12; and it is very grievous when God judges kingdoms and churches.

1. They fall into the hands of men, strangers they know not, the wicked of the earth, such as neither fear God nor regard men, bulls, lions, dogs, Psal. xxii. 12, 13, 16.

2. They are for a prey and spoil; their names, estates, habitations, chastity, children, limbs, consciences, lives, are preyed upon. They "eat up God's people as they eat bread," Psal. xiv. 4; they make them "meat unto the fowls of heaven, and beasts of the earth;" they crush their bones, and shed their blood like water, Psal. lxxix. 2, 3.

3. Profaning and polluting of holy things. "They shall pollute it." God's holy name is blasphemed; Psal. lxxix. 10, "Where is their God?" why doth he not now help them? they have prayed, fasted, hoped in him, made their boast of him, why comes he not to help them? All holy things are defiled, and therefore Asaph, in Psal. lxxix. 1, made upon the destruction of Jerusalem, cries out, "O God, the heathen are come into thine inheritance; thy holy temple have they defiled." This came first, and struck deepest into the heart of this holy man, that heathenish, idolatrous, bloody, profane persons should come and pollute the holy ordinances of God. The church laments this as a dreadful evil; Lam. i. 10, "The adversary hath spread out his hand upon all her pleasant things; for she hath seen that the heathen entered into her sanctuary, whom thou didst command that they should not enter into thy congregation."

4. Removal of all true worship, divine ordinances. "I will set it far from them." Now they should be without God, the means to know him, and way to worship him; now God would have no oblation, incense, new moons, sabbaths, solemn feasts, or any worship at Jerusalem; there only was he known, worshipped; and now temple, ordinances, and all must down, be taken away, and God be unknown, unworshipped in the world; no public place for him left. Isaiah, foreseeing this, saith, chap. xlii. 22, "This is a people robbed and spoiled;" and hereupon having a special query to make, he calls for attention; "Who among you will give ear to this, and hearken for the time to come," ver. 23, and make use of it? will any of you do it? Then thus, Jacob is spoiled; but "who gave Jacob for a spoil, and Israel to the robbers?" was not Jacob the beloved of God, his excellency, his glory? &c. "did not the Lord, he against whom we have sinned? for they would not walk in his ways, neither were they obedient unto his law. Therefore he hath poured upon him the fury of his anger, and the strength of battle: and it hath set him on fire round about, yet he knew not; and it burned him, yet he laid it not to heart," ver. 24, 25. And is it not so with England? We had need to cry with David, Psal. lxxix. 8, 9, "O remember not against us former iniquities: let thy tender mercies speedily prevent us: for we are brought very low. Help us, O God of our salvation, for the glory of thy name: and deliver us, and purge away our sins, for thy name's sake."

Ver. 22. "My face will I turn also from them, and they shall pollute my secret place," &c. This verse is a continuation of their calamities, and hath in it two grievous ones.

1. The aversion of God's face.

2. The pollution of the secret place.

Concerning the first, it is questionable from whom he would turn his face, from the Chaldeans, or from the Jews. Some carry it, from the Chaldeans, and so the sense is this; though they be a barbarous people, and do unheard-of things, pollute my holy place, sack my holy city, burn all to the ground, slay and carry captive my people; yet I will turn my face from them, I will not restrain them at all, but let them go on freely and fully in such ways, and take no notice of any thing done against me or my worship.

Others, to whom I incline, expound it of the Jews, that God would turn his face from them: and then the meaning is, that God would afford them neither his presence, counsel, comfort, nor deliverance; but he would leave them to shift for themselves, and take no further care of them. God's face in the Scripture signifies,

1. His presence. Psal. li. 11, "Cast me not away from thy presence;" the Hebrew is, from thy face.

2. Counsel. 2 Sam. xxi. 1, "David inquired of the Lord;" Hebrew, sought the face of the Lord, that is, sought counsel of him.

3. Comfort. Psal. lxix. 17, "Hide not thy face from thy servant, for I am in trouble;" shine upon me, and comfort me. So Psal. xxxi. 16, "Make thy face to shine upon thy servant;" that is, favour, comfort, make him glad.

4. Deliverance. Psal. xiii. 1, "How long wilt thou hide thy face from me?" that is, deny to deliver me.

There is mention of hiding his face, turning away his face, and setting his face against. The first befals the godly, Psal. lxxxviii. 14, and xxx. 7. The other two the wicked, as here in our prophet: they were a wicked generation, and God turned his face away from them, and set his "face against them," Ezek. xv. 7.

"They shall pollute my secret place." That is, the *sanctum sanctorum*, the most holy place, where the ark was, which had the two tables of stone, 1 Kings viii. 9. Into this only came the high priest, and but once in the year, and that upon the day of expiation; in which day he expiated the sins of the whole year by blood, for blood and incense he carried in with him, Heb. ix. 7. And some think the smoke of the incense darkened the holy place, because no man can see God and live.

At first it was filled with a cloud, and God was in that cloud, 1 Kings viii. 10, 12. God's nature is invisible, and inaccessible; but in the cloud and smoke he did manifest his glorious presence to the high priest, who consulted with the Lord for the good of the people. The Septuagint renders it, my visitation, because there God and the high priest visited one another. It is observed in histories, that Pompey went into this secret place, and being asked what he saw, said, a cloud, and hereupon it was given out, that the Jews were cloud worshippers. One Heliodorus also thrust into this holiest of places, who afterwards was struck with madness.

The place was called χρηματιστηριον.

Cunæus de Republ. Jud. Weems.

"Robbers shall enter into it." The Septuagint hath it, they shall enter without restraint, without any keeping them back: Theodotus, plagues shall enter, men that will be a plague, infecting and destroying all. The Hebrew notes such robbers as do make a violent entrance into the houses and possessions of others.

Your margins express it, "burglars;" and burglary, in the acceptance of law, is a felonious entering into another man's house wherein some person is, or into a church in the night time, with intent to steal, or do some felonious act there, albeit the act be not done. But in the natural signification of the word, burglary is a robbing of a house, whether by night or day; and these Chaldeans were burglars, men that should break into the sanctuary, and secret place. Ezek. xviii. 10, there is the same word, and it is joined with blood; "If he beget a son that is a robber, a shedder of blood," a house-breaker, a murderer, which shows there is violence joined with it, which regards not laws and rights.

Obs. That judgments succeed one another upon a guilty people. "Also I will turn away my face." He had spoken of sad judgments, some, eleven or twelve, and yet he comes in with more: there was a succession of sins, and answerably, a succession of judgments.

Obs. 2. They are a miserable people from whom God turns his face. Where his face is, there is happiness. When Aaron and the priest prayed for a blessing upon the people, Numb. vi. 25, 26, this was the chief petition of it, "The Lord make his face shine upon thee: The Lord lift up his countenance upon thee;" intimating that if they had these, no comforts or blessings would be wanting; Psal. xliv. 2, 3, the destruction of the Canaanites, the implantation of the Israelites, and their salvation, is attributed to the "light of God's countenance," as well as to his "right hand and arm;" because if they have God's face and favour, they shall have his hand and arm to do any thing for them. Therefore Asaph, in Psal. lxxx. three times prays thus; "Cause thy face to shine, and we shall be saved," ver. 3, 7, 19. He knew if God's face were towards them, God's power would work for them, and they should have salvation of all sorts; salvation from enemies, which there he speaks of, and from errors; Psal. lxvii. 1, 2, if God's face did but shine upon them, then his way would be known upon earth; if not, they should mistake and fall into errors and foul ways. Prov. xvi. 15, "In the light of the king's countenance is life;" much more in the light of God's countenance is life, the life of kingdoms, churches, families; which Daniel knew, and therefore prayed, chap. ix. 17, that God would make his face to shine upon the sanctuary which was desolate; the turning his face to them would quickly reedify it, as the turning it from them had made it desolate. When the Lord doth turn away his face, nothing but misery attends a people. Gen. iv. 14, saith Cain, "From thy face shall I be hid;" thy favour will not be towards me, no shine shall I have, but all shade: and what then? "I shall be a vagabond in the earth," and fear death by every one that meeteth me. When God takes away his face from any, the face of calamity and destruction is towards them, nay, destruction is upon them. No sooner doth God turn away from a nation, but destruction steps into that nation: Deut. xxxi. 17, "I will hide my face from them, and they shall be devoured, and many evils and troubles shall befall them; so that they will say in that day, Are not these evils come upon us, because our God is not among us?" where you may see that God's hiding his face is departing from them, and his departing lets in all miseries. When God is gone, nothing is left but sin and judgment, and they make fearful work in all places.

If God would pity people under destruction, it were something; but he will not pity them then, not hear their groans, receive their prayers, nor mind their tears, wounds, blood, death. Jer. xviii. 17, "I will show them the back, and not the face." And when? "in the day of their calamity," when they are in their greatest distresses, necessities, without council, help, comfort, even at the height of misery, I will not vouchsafe them one look, but go away from them in fury, leave them without hope, my back shall be toward them, and not my face. See Jer. xiv. 12.

Obs. 3. When the holy God goes away from his holy places, then profane, polluting wretches come into them. I will turn away my face, and robbers shall pollute my secret place. Thither should they come, whither none but the holy God and high priest were to come. And whereas before it was filled with a cloud, with incense, with glory, and the presence of God; now it should be filled with burglars, idolaters, oaths, and all profaneness, which could not but affect the Jews, that were so zealous of preserving the temple unpolluted by strangers. Acts xxi. 27, 28, a great stir was made against Paul by the Jews, because he had brought Greeks into the temple, and polluted it. And when the Jews were under the Roman emperors, they obtained of them, that none, no not a Roman, should enter into the temple under pain of death; yet themselves polluted it with false worship, drave God out of it, and of the holiest of holies, and made way for the worst of men to come in and defile the same.

Joseph. l. 7. de Bell. c. 4. and in his 5th book of Antiq. c. 14, he saith, "Capitale erat Gentili ingredi Templum.

Ver. 23. *Make a chain: for the land is full of bloody crimes, and the city is full of violence.*

In this verse is another calamity, and the cause of it laid down. The calamity is a chain; the cause, blood, or violence.

"Make a chain." "Trouble," saith the Septuagint; "a conclusion," the Vulgate; the Hebrew is, הרתוק and so it is rendered in 1 Kings vi. 21, chains, and so the rabbies take it here. We may extend it to a rope, a withe, a chain, any thing that a man may be bound with.

A chain is an emblem of bondage; Nahum iii. 10, "Her great ones shall be bound in chains." See Psal. cvii. 10; Acts xii. 6. And Jer. xxviii. 13, 14, the yoke of iron that the prophet was to make, noted the imbandaging of the nations unto Nebuchadnezzar, king of Babylon.

Whether by the "chain" be prefigured the siege of Jerusalem, as some interpret it, or leading into captivity, as others will have it, bondage is included in both. Some think the Lord here alludes to malefactors, that in chains answered at the bar of justice, as Paul did, Acts xxvi. 29. They had freely and fully run out in vicious courses, but now they were to answer it to God, who was set in judgment, and sentencing them to suffer heavy things. This also notes bondage, which is the sense of the prophet.

In a chain four things are considerable.

1. It is burdensome, heavy. 1 Kings xii. 10, "Thy father made our yoke heavy." And yokes, chains, fetters about necks, arms, legs, are grievous: when Peter was bound with two chains, Acts xii. 6, it was troublesome unto him; and so was the condition of these Jews, the siege, their captivity was very burdensome; therefore, Lam. iii. 7, the church saith, "He hath made my chain heavy." She calls her bondage a chain, and a heavy one.

2. It is restrictive; a man's liberty of going and doing is taken away by a chain. Acts xxi. 33, when Paul was bound with chains, whither could he go, what could he do; and bondage by a siege, captivity, imprisonment, sickness, or otherwise, is a restraint of a man, which are threatened here. "Jehoahaz was put in bands at Riblah, that he might not reign in Jerusalem," 2 Kings xxiii. 33.

3. Reproachful. 2 Tim. i. 16, "Onesiphorus was not ashamed of my chain." There is shame and reproach attending chains, and therefore Paul at the bar, when he wished Agrippa and others were such as he was, excepted his bonds, as reproachful things, Acts xxvi. 29. This is threatened here, and was made good; Jer. xxxix. 7, Zedekiah had his eyes put out, and was bound with two brasen chains; and so the thing he feared came upon him, mocking and reproach, Jer. xxxviii. 19. And not only he, but all of them should be for "a curse, and an astonishment, and an hissing, and a reproach, among all the nations," Jer. xxix. 19.

4. Tendency to further punishment. Paul was bound, Acts xxi. 33, "with two chains;" and Acts xxiv. 27, two years he lay in bonds; and to what end? that he might come to judgment, and have further punishment; and he was to that purpose brought before Agrippa and Festus, Acts xxvi. 29; and that in bonds: they tend to other and sorer judgments. Hence the devils are said to be "in chains of darkness reserved unto judgment," 2 Pet. ii. 4; Jude 6; they have not their full damnation, they are *semi-damnati*, half condemned, and kept in chains for the rest. And here God would chain up these Jews with bondage, and reserve them in bondage to further punishment, even eternal destruction: Job xxi. 30, "The wicked is reserved to the day of destruction, they shall be brought forth to the day of wrath."

"The land is full of bloody crimes." The Hebrew is, the judgment of bloods; they gave out unjust sentences that had power, and condemned the innocent; guilty men were spared, and the good suffered. 2 Kings xxi. 16, Manasseh filled Jerusalem with innocent blood; Athaliah slew all the royal seed, 2 Kings xi. 1; Naboth is falsely condemned and stoned to death, 1 Kings xxi. 13; Zechariah is slain by an unjust sentence, 2 Chron. xxiv. 21; Joash the king was slain by his servants, ver. 25. Hence it is said, Isa. lix. 3, that their "hands are defiled with blood;" that they are "full of blood," Isa. i. 15; and here, that "the land is full of bloody crimes;" Ezek. xxii. 6, every prince in Israel to his power did shed blood.

By "bloody crimes" some understand heinous sins, capital offences, such as deserved death, and the shedding of men's blood; as, idolatry, Deut. xiii. 6, 9; blasphemy, Lev. xxiv. 16; witchery, sorcery, Lev. xx. 27; bestiality, Lev. xx. 15, 16; sodomy, ver. 13; adultery, ver. 10; rapes, Deut. xxii. 25; false witnessing, to take away a man's life, Deut. xix. 16, 18, 19, 21; stealing any man, woman, or child, Exod. xxi. 16. These, with murder and treason, were bloody sins. So that the meaning may be, the land was so full of these crimes, that it could not escape severe punishment: Hosea iv. 2, "By swearing, and lying, and killing, and stealing, and committing adultery, they break out, and blood toucheth blood. Therefore shall the land mourn," &c.

"The city is full of violence." This holy city was now so corrupted, that whereas God and men expected justice and righteousness at Jerusalem above all places in the world, there was violence; yea, a fulness of violence.

By violence, understand whatever was contrary to justice and equity; as fraud in bargaining, thefts, oppression, usury, withholding of rights and wages from the owners thereof, pillaging men of their estates, &c.: Ezek. xxii. 7, "In thee," that is, Jerusalem, "have they set light by father and mother; oppressed the stranger; vexed the fatherless and the widow."

That blood and violence, the sparing of the guilty, and condemning of the innocent, do bring lands and cities into bondage; such sins put them into chains, which are burdensome, reproachful, restrictive, and tending to further miseries: Ezek. xii. 19, "They shall eat their bread with carefulness, and drink their water with astonishment, that her land may be desolate from all that is therein, because of the violence of all them that dwell therein." It is spoken of

Jerusalem, Ezek. xxii. 4, "Thou art become guilty in thy blood that thou hast shed; and hast defiled thyself in thine idols which thou hast made; and thou hast caused thy days to draw near, and art come even unto thy years: therefore have I made thee a reproach unto the heathen, and a mocking to all countries." Jerusalem's sins brought reproaching chains upon her, which grieved and much vexed her, ver. 5. Zeph. iii. 1, "Woe to her that is filthy and polluted, to the oppressing city!" And why woe to her? which includes all miseries, all judgments; "her princes within her are roaring lions; her judges are evening wolves," ver. 3; they suck the blood, eat the flesh, and gnaw the bones of the people, and therefore woe to them! Jer. vi. 6—8, "Hew ye down trees, and cast a mount against Jerusalem: this is the city to be visited; she is wholly oppression in the midst of her. As a fountain casteth out her waters, so she casteth out her wickedness: violence and spoil is heard in her; before me continually is grief and wounds. Be thou instructed, O Jerusalem, lest my soul depart from thee; lest I make thee desolate, a land not inhabited." She refused instruction, and was made desolate. Let us be instructed, now we look to have our chains broken, &c. Jer. xxii. 15, 16, when Josiah "judged the cause of the poor and needy, then it was well with him" and the land; but when Jehoiakim's eyes and heart were for covetousness, blood, oppression, violence, then God threatened that he should be cast out, and "buried with the burial of an ass," ver. 17, 19. Isa. x. 1—3, "Woe unto them that decree unrighteous decrees, and that write grievousness which they have prescribed; to turn aside the needy from judgment, and to take away the right from the poor of my people, that widows may be their prey, and that they may rob the fatherless! And what will ye do in the day of visitation? to whom will ye flee for help? and where will ye leave your glory?" Let magistrates, judges, men in place, take heed what decrees they make, what sentences they pronounce in judgment; they may make our chain heavy, &c. Let people pray earnestly that God would assist them, guide them by his Spirit, that they may judge righteous judgment, execute justice upon delinquents, and keep the land from blood and violence. Of Edom it is said, "For thy violence against thy brother Jacob shame shall cover thee, and thou shalt be cut off for ever," Obad. 10.

24. *Wherefore I will bring the worst of the heathen, and they shall possess their houses: I will also make the pomp of the strong to cease; and their holy places shall be defiled.*

In this verse he shows what instruments God would use, and they were the Chaldeans, whose title is, "The worst of the heathen;" and they should,

1. Possess their houses.
2. Destroy the pomp of the Jews, &c.
3. Defile the holy places, and so lay waste both civil and ecclesiastical state.

רעע malum vel malignum esse.

"Worst of the heathen." The root whence the word "worst" comes, signifies to be wicked, to be a malignant, to do evil; Jer. iv. 22, "They are wise to do evil." The Septuagint renders it here, The wicked of the heathen: and it is the same word which is given to the devil, 1 John iii. 12, "Of that wicked one," the great malignant of heaven and earth. The Chaldeans are here called the worst of nations, or heathens, as the Hebrew is. Their wickedness appears in these things: they were a peevish people, they robbed Job of his camels, and slew his servants, Job i. 17; they were great sorcerers, Dan. ii. 2, 10; great oppressors, Isa. xiv. 4, 17; very cruel, therefore compared to lions, Isa. v. 29; to a razor, Isa. vii. 20; to cockatrices and serpents, Jer. viii. 17; they were idolatrous, Ezek. xxiii. 14; a bitter and hasty nation, Hab. i. 6; terrible and dreadful, ver. 7; all for violence and spoil, ver. 9; they were drunkards, Hab. ii. 15; proud and unsufferably covetous, ver. 5. And Ezek. xxiii. 25, it is said, they shall deal furiously with thee; they shall take away thy nose, and thine ears, and deal hatefully with thee, ver. 29; they shall stone them, despatch them with swords, and burn up their houses with fire, ver. 47. These were the worst of nations, or the worst of that nation should come.

πονηρούς.

ἐκ τοῦ πονηροῦ, Les plus mauvais, in the French.

See Deut. xxviii. 49—51.

"They shall possess their houses." These wicked and merciless wretches, sparing neither man, woman, nor child, should take all into their possession.

ירש

The word for "possess" hath a contrary signification: to inherit, possess, Deut. iv. 1, and to disinherit, dispossess, Zech. ix. 4, "The Lord will cast her out," it is the same root; and you have both significations in one verse, Josh. xxiii. 5, "The Lord shall drive them from out of your sight; and ye shall possess the land;" it is the same root for driving out and for possessing. This is rare, and for the learned to observe, that a word signifies contrary things.

יורשנה

Its frequent signification is to possess by hereditary right, to succeed; but it is used sometimes more largely, to possess any way, as in 1 Kings xxi. 15; Deut. ii. 24, Ahab took possession of Naboth's vineyard, and Moses of the king of Heshbon's land, which was not by succession. And so it is to be taken in this place; they should come in by force, and possess their habitations. And there is something more in this phrase; possessing notes continuance of habitation in their hands, as being their own: 1 Cor. vii. 30, Let them that buy be as if they possessed not. Possessors look upon things as their own, and to continue with them. Here by the Chaldeans' possessing their houses, is closely pointed out the seventy years' captivity, all which time the land and habitations left should be in the Chaldeans' power.

"I will also make the pomp of the strong to cease." Whatever lifts up, and causes the spirits of men to swell, it is pomp; so the word is used, Jer. xii. 5, "In the swelling of Jordan," when the waters increased, and made the river swell over its banks, which Jordan always did in harvest time, Josh. iii. 15.

"Strong," or potent, men; whence great ones are called potentates. Their riches, attendance, honours, places, alliances, and the like, do make them proud, stately, self-confident; but their pomp, power, magnificence, excellency, shall all cease and come to nothing. It is not their arms or armour, their big looks, insolent speeches, rich attire, honourable titles, or any thing wherein they glory, that shall advantage them; be it their soldiery, their strong and stout men, their pomp shall cease, I will crush their crests, and bring them low. Pintus understands it of Zedekiah and the nobles of Jerusalem.

"Their holy places shall be defiled." The holy places were the court, the temple, and the holiest of all. Some refer these words to persons, and not to places, and read them thus: They shall see profaned, defiled, that which sanctify them; noting, the priests who sanctified the people by their offerings and prayers for them, they should not be regarded as priests of the highest God; but because they had dealt deceitfully with the people, corrupted the covenant of Levi, therefore they should be slain as other persons, or led into captivity with them.

Others read the words thus: They shall inherit their holy places, the Chaldeans shall come and take possession of them, because it is said here, "their holy places," and not mine. It is conceived by some that these were chapels, or oratories, which they had made in several places in or near to their houses, and consecrated to God.

Theod. Lavat.

Obs. 1. That God can use the worst of men to accomplish his holy designs, and execute his righteous judgments. The Chaldeans he brings to afflict, chain, and take captive the Jews. Wicked men have wicked ends, answerable principles, and mediums to attain those ends, Isa. x. 7; but they are as staves and rods in the hand of God, with which he corrects hypocritical nations, ver. 5, 6. They are God's sword, God's hand, Psal. xvii. 13, 14; and he knows how to use both to effect his own pleasure, and to execute judgments upon sinners, and that without sin. Hath not God brought in, and set on work the worst men among us? What miscreants, blasphemers, plagues, vermin, what Egyptians, Chaldeans, and bloody, merciless wretches, have we doing mischief in this land! men that justify Chaldeans, that are skilful to shed blood, to cheat a nation of its God and religion, to betray and undo kingdoms. Many wonder such vile wretches should live and have a being upon the earth; many are troubled that God uses such filth and scum to do him any service; but we must know that there is use of thistles, scorpions, and serpents, and God would not use such men if there were not good to be done by them: Isa. x. 12, "It shall come to pass, that when the Lord hath performed his whole work upon mount Zion and on Jerusalem, I will punish the fruit of the stout heart of the king of Assyria, and the glory of his high looks."

Obs. 2. That houses, lands, and good things of this world, we should not much seek after, seeing they may fall into the hands of the worst men. "I will bring the worst of the heathen, and they shall possess their houses." All they had gotten fell into the hands of the Chaldeans.

Obs. 3. That no external excellency or pomp is to be confided in. God will make the pomp of the strong to cease; policy, power, riches, honours, strength of armies, are not pillars of brass to confide in; they are glass, metal, soon broken, and blown away by the breath of the Lord, when he is in a way of wrath. Nebuchadnezzar was a proud tyrant, that with his plundering "made the world as a wilderness," Isa. xiv. 17; that exceeded most princes of the world in greatness, in kingdoms, tributary princes, honour, strength of soldiers, &c. See, in ver. 11, what is said of him, "Thy pomp is brought down to the grave;" ver. 12, "How art thou fallen from heaven, O Lucifer, son of the morning! how art thou cut down to the ground, which didst weaken the nations!" So for Egypt, that abounded in horses, Isa. xxxi. 1, and trusted in their strength; Ezek. xxx. 18, "The pomp of her strength shall cease in her:" and chap. xxxii. 12, "By the swords of the mighty will I cause thy multitude to fall." They shall spoil the pomp of Egypt, and all the multitude thereof shall be destroyed; God would destroy them with a great destruction, and then mercy should come in; then "neither the foot of man nor beast should trouble them any more;" then would the Lord "make their waters deep, and make their rivers run like oil," ver. 13, 14. Neither Babylonish nor Egyptian pomp endure long. God makes "the arrogancy of the proud to cease, and lays low the haughtiness of the terrible," Isa. xiii. 11.

This God hath done lately before our eyes, he hath made the pomp of the strong to cease. There were the potentates of the earth; honours, riches, strength, arms, horses, and whatever might make them pompous, was with them; great hopes and hearts they had; they looked for the day, and thought not only the north but the south should be theirs; not York, but London, yea England, to be theirs: but they are disappointed, their honour is laid in the dust, their pomp ceaseth. We may say, according to that in Zech. xi. 2, 3, "Howl, fir tree; for the cedar is fallen; because the mighty is spoiled: howl, O ye oaks of Bashan; for the forest of the vintage is come down;" their strength and comforts are abated. "There is a voice of the howling of the shepherds," (that is, princes which should feed and seek the good of the people,) "for their glory is spoiled, a voice of the roaring of young lions: for the pride of Jordan is spoiled."

Victory at York, 2nd July, 1644.

The ceasing of their pomp should be the beginning of our praise: Psal. xcviii. 1, "O sing unto the Lord a new song; for he hath done marvellous things: his right hand, and his holy arm, hath gotten him the victory." We may sing with Moses, Exod. xv. 6, 7, "Thy right hand, O Lord, is become glorious in power: thy right hand, O Lord, hath dashed in pieces the enemy. And in the greatness of thine excellency thou hast overthrown them that rose up against thee: thou sentest forth thy wrath, which consumed them as stubble:" and with David, Psal. cxxxvi. 1—4, "O give thanks unto the Lord; for he is good: for his mercy endureth for ever," &c.: and Psal. cvii. 8, "Oh that men would praise the Lord for his goodness, and for his wonderful works to the children of men!"

Obs. 4. Unspiritual worship pleases not God, neither profits the worshippers. They had the temple, ordinances of it, appeared oft before God, brought their sacrifices; but God threatens them, and all their worship; their civil estate, and ecclesiastical also, should be ruined. God in worship looks at the hearts and spirits of men; if they be absent from, but half or in part, in the worship, God regards it not. Their oblations are vain oblations, Isa. i. 13. Their fasts and prayers are a trouble, a weariness to God, ver. 14. And he tells them that he had mouth-nearness and heart-farness, lip-labour and heart-dishonour, Isa. xxix. 13; yea, Ezek. xxxiii. 31, he had mouth-love, mouth-worship, when their silver and gold had heart-love, heart-worship. It is the heart is the principal thing in God's eye; "My son, give me thine heart," Prov. xxiii. 26. If that be not given him in worship, nothing is given, nothing is accepted that we think given. David therefore prays, Psal. cxix. 80, "Let my heart be sound in thy statutes; that I be not ashamed." If a man have a deceitful spirit, a rotten heart, he will be ashamed when he shall find that all his prayers, fasts, services, shall be thrown back as dung in his face. Cain gave the fruit of the earth, not the fruit of his heart, and it was not accepted; neither do they gain ought at God's hands who worship him carnally; 1 Tim. iv. 8, "Bodily exercise profiteth little."

Cor est principium vitæ, cogitationis omnis voluntatis et actionis.

Obs. 5. Men are apt to rest in outside worship, and bless themselves for it. They cried, "The temple of the Lord, The temple of the Lord," &c. Jer. vii. 4. They looked at the temple and worship of it, and hence concluded safety to themselves; they thought it not probable that ever destruction should come to them, their city, state, and church; they looked upon their temple as a glorious thing, and that worship therein would secure them from all; but God oft threatens the defilement, removal, and destruction of it, from this 20th verse to the 25th. The Pharisee went up to the temple, he fasted, prayed, gave tithes of all, and in such outside services did he rest. Men now have their chapels and chaplains, and think that by the prayers of the one, and holiness of the other, they shall be fitted for heaven.

Ver. 25. *Destruction cometh; and they shall seek peace, and there shall be none.*

He told them before, that the worst of the heathen should come, and now, that destruction was coming; and annexeth a new calamity, their vain expectation, and real disappointment of peace.

"Destruction." The Septuagint is quite out in rendering it mercy, propitiation cometh. Others read it thus, a strait grief cometh. The Hebrew signifies more, a breaking, a cutting off: so the word is used, Isa. xxxviii. 12. The Chaldee hath it, precision or forecutting. Piscator, *excisor*, the cutter up, the destroyer, or man of destruction, cometh; and he proves it must be taken so, because it is joined with a verb masculine: and so the sense is, Nebuchadnezzar the destroyer, the man that cuts down nations, that breaks kingdoms in pieces, is coming upon you, even Nebuchadnezzar, who is destruction itself.

ἐξιλασμὸς ἥκει
קפרה

"They shall seek peace." God had threatened by his prophets the utter ruin of Jerusalem, which they would not believe. The false prophets suggested the contrary, they cried "Peace, peace," Jer. viii. 11; Ezek. xiii. 10; seduced the people, so that they feared not: they considered the strength of their situation, tower, temple, soldiers, and what these prophets had said, and would not believe that enemies should come within their gates, Lam. iv. 12; but when the enemy was come, they sought for peace and safety, but found it not. They excused Zedekiah that he brake with Nebuchadnezzar in the point of tribute: they tendered silver and gold to buy a peace, and that would not do it, Isa. xiii. 17; Ezek. vii. 19. They conceived that men come far could not lie long before their walls and gates, but that they would be consumed, or glad to retire with shame, so they should be safe; or if things came to the worst, that the city must be yielded, yet it should be upon good and honourable terms, at least with security of life and liberty. But neither their money, their policy, their prayers, or aught else, could prevail for peace or safety; they had found them perfidious, and would hearken to no terms of peace; the Chaldeans were cockatrices, and would not be charmed, Jer. viii. 17. Therefore it is said, ver. 15, "We looked for peace, but no good came; and for a time of health, and behold, trouble!"

Ezek. xxxviii. 22.

Some refer this seeking of peace, to God; they should in their straits, at the destruction by Nebuchadnezzar, cry to God, make many fasts and prayers in the time of the siege, and seek for peace with God, whom they had offended with their grievous sins, and he would not hear them, peace they should not find, Jer. xiv. 12; Ezek. xiv. 17, 18.

Obs. 1. That wicked men in time of divine judgments, when they come upon them, are peaceless. Destruction cometh, and they should seek peace. They had neither peace within, nor peace without; wars were in their gates, and wars in their hearts; their own consciences did accuse, smite, condemn them. Common calamities roused their sleepy consciences; they saw themselves in ill case from Nebuchadnezzar, in worse by reason of God; the one threatening their lives, the other their souls; so that which way soever they looked, peace they saw none, the winds of affliction stirred the waves of their corruption; Isa. lvii. 20, "The wicked are like the troubled sea, when it cannot rest, whose waters cast up mire and dirt." When the great winds are abroad, the sea hath no rest, it cannot rest, it rages, and throws up and out mire and dirt: so when great and death-threatening calamities are abroad, wicked men rest not, they cannot rest, they are "mire," Isa. x. 6; and their expressions are miry; and what is the conclusion? "There is no peace to the wicked, saith the Lord." They may say they have peace, others may confirm their assertion, but God saith they have none; nothing of that which is included within the sweet name of peace is to be found in them. You may find Satan there, a hellish conscience there, sinful lusts there, fears, sorrows, terrors there, but no peace there. "The way of peace they know not; and there is no judgment in their goings: they have made them crooked paths: whosoever goeth therein shall not know peace," Isa. lix. 8.

Obs. 2. Great necessities and straits cause sinners to seek for that they formerly neglected, violated, viz. peace with God, and peace with man. Zedekiah, these Jews, had broken the covenant made with Nebuchadnezzar, they provoked God, 2 Chron. xxxvi. 12, 13; and now when destruction was upon them, they seek peace from heaven and earth: in their prosperity they regarded neither God nor man, but when both were against them, then they sue, they seek for peace at their hands. When Herod's displeasure was upon the Tyrians and Sidonians, they sought for peace at his hands, Acts xii. 20; and Hos. v. 15, "In their affliction they will seek me early," and earnestly too; Jer. xi. 14, they cry in their trouble; and, saith the Lord, "I will not hear them in the time that they cry unto me for their trouble."

Obs. 3. That states may seek too late for peace with God and man; they may defer so long, that their seeking may be in vain, their endeavours frustrated, and hopes disappointed. "They shall seek peace, and there shall be none;" neither God nor man will give in any peace.

The date of mercy was out, and the door of hope shut, therefore, Jer. xii. 12, God tells them the spoilers were come, the sword devouring, and no flesh should have peace, neither young nor old, though they sought it earnestly. Instead of peace, they should be in travail as one with child; their hands should be upon their loins, their faces pale, and cry out, "Alas! for that day," Jer. xxx. 5, 6. The time was come, that God had taken peace from the land; Jer. xvi. 5, "I have taken away my peace from this people, even loving-kindness and mercies." God had taken it away, and now it was too late for them to seek after it, too hard for them to bring back, or any friend they had. If they looked that Jeremiah, who was a prophet, acquainted with and interested in God, should do it, he was forbidden to pray for them; Jer. xiv. 11, "Pray not for this people for their good." If he prayed against them, God would hear him, but not if for them; it would be sin in him so to do. If they looked for others, that they had better thoughts of than Jeremiah, God tells them that if they had as good men as Noah, Daniel, and Job, who were acquainted with great afflictions, could pray very powerfully, and being precious men, righteous, perfect, desirable, as God's testimony is of them, yet they should not help them with their prayers at all, Ezek. xiv. 14. Nay, if they should set upon fasting and praying themselves, God would not hear, or give in any peace; Jer. xiv. 12, "When they fast, I will not hear their cry; and when they offer burnt-offering and an oblation, I will not accept them: but I will consume them." They beg peace, I will send the sword; they ask bread, I will send a famine; they desire health, I will bring the pestilence: and these shall consume them.

It is dreadful when any come too late unto God; then instead of mercy they meet with judgments. Hence Jer. viii. 15, "We looked for peace, but no good came; and for a time of health, and behold trouble!" When it will be thus with a land, see Ezek. xiv. 13; Prov. i. 24, &c.; Matt. xxiii. 37, 38.

Ver. 26. *Mischief shall come upon mischief, and rumour shall be upon rumour; then shall they seek a vision of the prophet; but the law shall perish from the priest, and counsel from the ancients.*

Here is more woe yet discovered, not single, but multiplied woes, one mischief at the heels of another; no sooner shall one be over, but they shall hear of another; one mischief in the morning, and presently news of another before noontide or evening, and after that, another by midnight, and so they were never free from feeling and fearing miseries.

News they should have of the Chaldeans coming with fury and for spoil, beset they should be with mischiefs, and when they looked for comfort and counsel from the prophets, priests, and ancients, there should be no vision, no law, no counsel. Those who had holpen them in former times should now fail them.

"Mischief." Contrition, trouble, woe. This word mischief sometimes notes sin, as Psal. xxxvi. 4; cxl. 2; Acts xiii. 10; sometimes an ill accident befalling one, 2 Kings vii. 9, "If we tarry till the morning light, some mischief will come upon us;" sometimes judgment, Isa. xlvii. 11, "Mischief shall fall upon thee; and thou shalt not be able to put it off;" the stroke of God shall come unavoidably. They were a people "set on mischief," Exod. xxxii. 22, set upon sinning, and God told them he would be set upon punishing; Deut. xxxii. 23, "I will heap mischiefs upon them;" which here, in the text, were coming one after another, and crowding in upon them.

Mischief upon mischief notes multiplicity and coherence of judgments, sword, plague, famine, and those evils which attend them, which are not a few. Job xix. 12, you have a like phrase, "His troops came together:" there was a multiplicity of calamities, troops and coherency, they came together.

"Rumour shall be upon rumour." The news shall be brought them of the Chaldeans' coming from several quarters, and by several messengers, to their city; their ears shall be filled with tidings and reports of their drawing near. It is conceived the Jews had their scouts and spies abroad that watched on the tops of the mountains, and places suspected, and when any danger appeared, they gave notice thereof, and so rumour was upon rumour. One brought news that the king of Babylon was in arms such a day with so many thousands; a second, that he had marched so far; a third, that he had invaded the borders of their land; a fourth, that he had taken some towns, put most to the sword, and burnt the towns, &c.; another, that they would presently be at the gates of Jerusalem.

"Then shall they seek a vision of the prophet." Finding no peace, seeing mischiefs multiply, and hearing sad rumours from all parts, they had one refuge left, and that they make use of, viz. they seek to the prophet for a vision. Surely, thought they, we shall have some good tidings from heaven when we have none from earth; the prophet will help us, when all others fail us; in our great straits we shall have some counsel or comfort.

But either there was no vision, or such as was in no stead to them. The false prophets had nothing to say, the true they hated, and what they said would not be believed, or practised: Jer. xxxviii. 14, &c. Zedekiah speaks to Jeremiah for a vision; he makes known the mind of the Lord, tells him what he must do to save himself and the city, yield up himself into the hand of the king of Babylon's princes, and then he should live, and the city be unburnt; this vision was sad, not entertained, and so as none. Zedekiah and the rest would have had a vision, ver. 27, that is, a word of God by the prophet to have freed them from the misery and straits they were in, and there was no such vision.

"But the law shall perish from the priest." And the law shall perish, many read it so, noting out a further degree of their misery. Prophecy shall not only fail them, which is extraordinary, but even that which was ordinary, the preaching and expounding of the law, the priests should have no sound or true knowledge of it.

Read it, But the law, &c. the sense will not much differ. They look for visions from prophets, but they shall not have the law from priests, vision and preaching both shall fail them.

This phrase, To perish from, is a hebraism, and noteth not abolition, but absence; the law should not be dissolved, lost, but taken from those priests, they should be without the law. Take some places where you have the like speeches: Psal. cxlii. 4, "Refuge failed me;" the Hebrew is, perished from me, I was without refuge. Amos ii. 14, "Flight shall perish from the swift;" power of flying shall be absent. And Joel i. 5, "Howl, all ye drinkers of wine, because of the new wine: for it is cut off from your mouth;" that is, there is none for you. And so here, "The law shall perish from the priest;" that is, the sound knowledge and true interpretation of the law shall be absent from them, their lips shall preserve no knowledge.

"Counsel from the ancients." Elders: some refer these to church officers; the prophets were to teach them, the priests, to offer sacrifices, and the elders to order and discipline them, which required wisdom and counsel.

מִזְקֵנִים Isa. xxxvii. 2, "Elders of the priests."

Others refer them to state elders, in which sense the word is frequently used, Gen. l. 7; Exod. xvii. 5; Psal. cv. 22, and is there translated "senators." Take it in which sense you will, counsel should perish from them, they should not be able to advise for the welfare of church or state.

Obs. 1. When a people is under divine displeasure, there is a succession of evils for them, mischief after mischief; they may not expect a few, but many. Saul, after he had sinned in sacrificing, rejected God: Samuel tells him that his kingdom should not continue, 1 Sam. xiii. 14. Then three companies of spoilers came, mischief from the Philistines, ver. 17, 18. Then had they no smith in all Israel, ver. 19. After, chap. xv. 23, he hears God had rejected him from being king, that he had rent the kingdom from him, ver. 28. After this he was troubled with "an evil spirit from the Lord," chap. xvi. 14. In chap. xvii. 10, Goliath defies the armies of Israel. Chap. xviii. 7, 8, David is magnified above Saul, which vexed him to the heart, and filled him with fear, ver. 29. He is disappointed of David, whom he attempts to kill, chap. xix. He distrusts his servants, and complains of their unfaithfulness, chap. xxii. The Philistines invade his land, being in pursuit of David, chap. xxiii. David and Abishai came upon Saul sleeping, and could have killed him, chap. xxvi. Being sore distressed, he seeketh to the witch of Endor; when God was departed, no answer by prophets, and the Philistines were upon him; the witch raises the devil, who tells him of nothing but his own and Israel's ruin, chap. xxviii. 19. These tidings struck him half dead, ver. 20. After this, his sons are slain, his army is routed, and he and his armour-bearer kill themselves, chap. xxxi. Here mischief followed upon mischief.

Pharaoh had ten plagues one after another: and in the Revelation you read of seven trumpets, seven vials; they came not single, but by sevens, and brought in mischief after mischief, and judgment after judgment. Jer. li. 31, 32, "One post shall run to meet another, and one messenger to meet another, to show the king of Babylon that his city is taken at one end, and that the passages are stopped, and the reeds they have burned with fire, and the men of war are affrighted."

Many evils and troubles do befall states and churches when they are under God's wrath. Deut. xxxi. 17, "Then my anger shall be kindled against them in that day, and I will forsake them, and I will hide my face from them, and they shall be devoured, and many evils and troubles shall befall them; so that they will say in that day, Are not these evils come upon us, because our God is not among us."

When God is in a way of revenge, he is continually at his work, so that one misery is but the messenger of another: and here is the misery of the wicked, they shall perish rather a hundred times over, than go unpunished.

Obs. 2. God proceeds by degrees and steps to severity of judgments. Though people be exceeding guilty, deserve as much wrath as is in all the vials of God, yet he pours not out all his wrath at once, mischief comes after mischief, and rumour after rumour. First, some drops of a vial, then some little streams, after that the strength. God hath clemency in him, moderating his punishments; if little ones will prevail with sinners, he will withhold the greater; sometimes, though he see no amendment in the creature, his own goodness, bowels, and compassion do cause him to forbear. Psal. lxxviii. 38, "He did not stir up all his wrath:" he had cause to have done it; they flattered with him, lied unto him, their heart was not right, they brake covenant, ver. 36, 37, and yet he stirred not up all his wrath; he kindled not the fire so hot as utterly to consume them. Nay, that wrath which was up, and coming out, he turned away; and why? he was full of compassion, and remembered they were but flesh. Yet, because they were a stubborn people, profited neither by mercies nor judgments, but fell to idolatry, it is said, ver. 59, "he greatly abhorred Israel;" and then the consuming fire was kindled, ver. 63. At first God's wrath is little, Psal. ii. 12; "I was but a little displeased," Zech. i. 15: but if sin grow, God's wrath grows; as Ahab's cloud, at first little as a hand, but quickly it covered the face of heaven, it was black with clouds and winds, and there was a great rain. How little soever God's wrath be in the rise, it can suddenly cover the face of heaven, and cause a great rain, a rain of "fire and brimstone, an horrible tempest," Psal. xi. 6. God hath great wrath, and fierceness of wrath, 2 Kings xxiii. 26. He hath a little finger, a hand, an arm, and loins to be heavy upon sinners. He begins with the little finger; if that do good he will stop, if not, you shall feel his hand, his arm, and weight of his loins. He hath wrath reserved, Nahum i. 2; "wrath to come," 1 Thess. i. 10.

Obs. 3. Wicked men in great straits will sue to them for help, whom before they hated. They could seek for a vision from the prophet now they were in extremities, and they run from prophet to prophet to get some counsel and comfort. The false prophets, who had been countenanced by them, had deceived them, the true were hateful to them; Jeremiah, Zephaniah, Baruch were left, and now they sue unto them for visions. See Jer. xxxvii. 17, and xxxviii. 14, 27, and xlii. 1—3. There the king, princes, and people, being distressed, seek to Jeremiah; yet he was cursed by them, chap. xv. 10, beaten and put into prison, chap. xxxvii. 15. Ahab sends for and consults with Micaiah, whom he hated, when he was to go out to war, and in a strait what would be the issue of it, 1 Kings xxii. 8. When the plagues were upon Pharaoh, then he sends for Moses and Aaron, Exod. viii. 8, 25, and ix. 27, and x. 8, 16, 24; he sends for them in haste, and in the night, chap. xii. 31; seven times he did it. Prophets are precious in times of trouble; when men's liberties, estates, and lives are in question, then they are glad to have help from prophets; their counsel, prayers, holiness, they think may do them good. Abimelech took away Abraham's wife; but what said God to him? Gen. xx. 7, "Restore the man his wife; for he is a prophet, and he shall pray for thee, and thou shalt live: if not, thou shalt surely die, and all that are thine."

Take heed how you abuse and ill-treat the prophets; the time may come you may have need of them, and be glad to hide yourselves under their wings, ask their counsels, importune their prayers.

Obs. 4. They that will not hear God's servants when they are at ease, shall not have help from them in time of their distress. They refused to hearken to Jeremiah, chap. xliv. 16, "As for the word that thou hast spoken unto us in the name of the Lord, we will not hearken unto thee;" and now they seek unto him for a vision, and there is none for them, or that which afflicted them more than if they had none. It is just with God to withhold visions from the prophets, when people desire them who slighted them when God gave them. If people stop their ears, and will not hear, God will stop the prophets' mouths, they shall not speak. Lam. ii. 9, "Her prophets find no vision from the Lord:" they sought to the prophets, the prophets to the Lord, but neither found any vision, night and darkness was upon them, and there was "no answer of God," Micah iii. 6, 7.

Obs. 5. That it is a dreadful evil when God takes away the signs of his presence. Visions among the prophets, the law soundly interpreted by the priests, and seasonable counsel from the elders, were evident tokens of God's presence amongst them; when these failed, they were demonstrations of his absence. Here they should all perish, from the prophet, the priest, and the ancient; now they should neither have extraordinary nor ordinary help, as it was with Saul, 1 Sam. xxviii. 15, God answered him neither by prophets nor by dreams, which was an argument he was departed, and hereupon he was in great distress. Micah was troubled greatly when the Danites took away his idols, Judg. xviii. 23, 24; he thought that a great evil, that the signs of his gods' presence were gone; but how much greater evil is it, when the signs of the true God's presence are taken away! 1 Sam. iv. when the Philistines had routed the Israelites, and taken the ark, and a Benjamite brought news of it to the city, "and all the city cried out," ver. 13; great and small were afflicted at this, that the ark, the pledge of divine presence, was gone; and Eli was not so much affected at the death of his two sons, as at the taking of the ark; when he heard that was gone, he could live no longer, he fell backward, ver. 18, brake his neck, and died. So Phinehas's wife upon this occasion falls into travail, and names her child Ichabod, ver. 21, which is, Where is the glory? the ark is gone, God is gone, Israel hath now no more glory. So here, the tokens of God's being among them were removing, vision failing, the law perishing, &c.; and where these go away, it is night; ignorance comes in, errors increase, and all woes are at hand. While God is present by his word and ministers, what evils soever fall out, there is relief in the word and ordinances against them, thence arguments are fetched patiently to bear them; but if they be gone, that evil may sink the heart without others; and when seas of vinegar, and floods of bitter water, compass you about, you have no oil to allay them, nor sugar to sweeten them.

Obs. 6. That truths are not confined to any sort of men, not to prophets, priests, or ministers, in these or any days; the prophets should be without vision, the law should perish from the priests, and counsel from the elders. It was a conceit of old that this rank of men should not be without knowledge and truth: Jer. xviii. 18, "Come, and let us devise devices against Jeremiah; for the law shall not perish from the priest, nor counsel from the wise, nor the word from the prophet. Come, and let us smite him with the tongue," &c.; let us accuse him to be a false prophet, get him silenced, imprisoned, put to death. All in authority in the church, the prophets, the priests, the elders, are against him, and you need not fear if he be taken out of the way; though a priest, a prophet, full of wisdom and counsel, there will be others as good as he, more mild and sweet; it will be no considerable loss, for the law shall not perish from the priest.

They were possessed with this apprehension, that truth, knowledge, counsel, and the Spirit of God, were peculiar to them, and should not be removed from them; but the Lord confutes them, and confounds their conceit; there shall be no vision, no law, no counsel. Aaron had neither vision nor law when he said, "These be thy gods, O Israel," Exod. xxxii. 4. Ahab had four hundred prophets, but no vision amongst them. Had there been a council of these priests and prophets gathered to counsel and determine for the good of the church, what canons and conclusions would they have made! The papists and some others stick much to councils, and challenge knowledge, truth, and God's Spirit to be amongst them; they are the representative church, and where should light and counsel be, if not amongst them? Let them and all consider that the Lord is not tied to men, that truth is not the inheritance of priests, prophets, popes, councils, more than others: "The law shall perish from the priests." And Mark xiv. 53, there was a grand council, "the high priest: and with him were assembled all the chief priests, and the elders, and the scribes;" and, ver. 64, you have the result of this council; they all vote Christ to be a blasphemer, and condemn him to be guilty of death, whereupon he was spit on, buffeted, and greatly abused. If a whole council have condemned Christ the Head, it is like they have condemned many of the members since.

The great council of Nice had erred in point of ministers' marriage, if Paphnutius had not prevented. That of Arminum held rebaptization of those heretics had baptized. That of Constance denied one of the elements in the supper of the Lord to the people. God is not tied to counsels, to prophets, or priests, but is free to be where he please, and to impart truth to whom he please, and to as few as he please: *Ubi tres, sunt ecclesia est, licet laici fuerint,* Where there are three persons they constitute a church, though they be of the laity, said Tertullian long since: and if they be a church, they may have truth amongst them, and more given in unto them, as well as others. (Tertul. in Exhort. ad Castitatem.)

Obs. 7. God gives vision, law, counsel, and takes them away at his pleasure; he creates light and darkness. They shall seek vision of the prophets, and there shall be none. Prophets could not prophesy at pleasure; but when God gave in visions, then they gave out light. Nathan had no vision, no word from heaven, to encourage David to build; he had one to take him off, 2 Sam. vii. Neither had the priests the knowledge of the law always, Hos. iv. 6; Mal. ii. 8; neither is counsel always with the ancient, Isa. xxix. 14. You that have vision, the law and gospel, the counsel of the ancient, how soon God may remove it is a secret; the light was extinguishing lately, there were many extinguishers, jesuitical, prelatical, and others. Be not unthankful for the light you have, sin not against light by disgracing that as new light which suits not with your spirits; it was in the womb of the Scriptures, though not brought forth till of late. If you spurn at any light, any truths of God, you may lose what you have; if you receive not the truth with love, "God will send you strong delusions." If you hate those that bring you light, you are in darkness, notwithstanding all the light that shines amongst you; 1 John ii. 9, 10, "He that saith he is in the light, and hates his brother, is in darkness even until now. He that loveth his brother abideth in the light, and there is none occasion of stumbling in him." Let me say to you as Isaiah, chap. ii. 5, "O house of Jacob, come ye, and let us walk in the light of the Lord;" and as Christ to the people, "Yet a little while is the light with you. Walk while ye have the light, lest darkness come upon you," John xii. 35. Acts xxvi. 19, Paul was not disobedient to the heavenly visions he had; be not you, but walk in the light and warmth of them, and then see what a blessing you shall have: 1 John i. 7, "If we walk in the light, as he is in the light, we have fellowship one with another, and the blood of Jesus Christ his Son cleanseth us from all sin."

Obs. 8. Those who will not do what they know, shall not know what to do. Zedekiah and the rest would not do what they knew; Jeremiah bade them go forth, yield themselves, and it should be well with them and the city; but they did it not, and quickly after they knew not what to do, no vision, no law, no counsel; in a strait, and knew not which way to turn them. Adam knew what to do, but did it not, and presently after his head is in the thicket, and he knows not what to do. Saul knew that he should not offer sacrifice, that he should have slain Agag, spared neither man nor beast, he did it not; and how oft he was in straits, and knew not what to do, you may observe in the story, especially in that famous place, 1 Sam. xxviii. 15, when the witch had raised the devil in Samuel's likeness and mantle, he tells him why he had called him; I know not what to do, but

"I have called thee, that thou mayest make known unto me what I shall do."

Ver. 27. *The king shall mourn, and the prince shall be clothed with desolation, and the hands of the people of the land shall be troubled: I will do unto them after their way, and according to their deserts will I judge them; and they shall know that I am the Lord.*

Having spoken of the ecclesiastical estate in the former verse, in this he comes to the civil estate, and shows that the judgments should light upon all sorts, king, prince, and people; mourning, desolation, and trouble shall be upon them. He names the subjects of misery, and the miseries: then he lays down the causes; the efficient, God; the material and meritorious, their ways, deserts: then the end of all these judgments, That they may know, &c.

"The king shall mourn." Hebrew is יתאבל, the word being in *hithpael*, notes continuation of mourning; some therefore render it, He shall pine away, or kill himself with mourning; it is mourning with sighing, and sighs are wasting: and surely Zedekiah had cause of constant mourning, even to his death; he lost the kingdom, his sons, and his eyes at once, which were dear things unto him; and some observe, when the word is referred to men, it notes mourning for dear things.

The Septuagint is ὁ βασιλεὺς πενθήσει, which denotes a great measure of sorrow, and expressions of it outwardly.

"The prince;" that is, princes, the singular number for the plural, as prophet for prophets.

"Shall be clothed with desolation." It is metaphorical, from garments, which do cover and compass about; so desolation should compass the princes and nobles on every side. The word notes such desolation as breeds amazement in the beholders; which was here when they saw the city, the temple, the kingdom laid waste, all things in them desolated; they were clothed with desolation, and amazed at so strange a garment upon them.

"The hands of the people of the land shall be troubled." When the people should see their king mourning, their nobles desolate, no heart or spirit in them for the church and state, for their liberties or lives, their hearts and hands were troubled.

But he expresses it by their "hands," because it was more visible by them, and set out the greatness of their misery: they had no hands, through fear and faintness, to follow their callings; no hands to take up arms to defend themselves; no hands to lift up in prayer.

"According to their deserts." The Hebrew is, According to their judgments; they have made ill judgments of persons and things, and deserve my judgments for them, and answerably I will deal with them. They have oppressed, they shall be oppressed; they have not heard the cry of others, they shall not be heard crying; they have rejected me, and they shall be rejected by me; they have killed, and they shall be killed; they have spoiled, and they shall be spoiled. And so that of Christ, in Matt. vii. 2, is made good, "With what judgment ye judge, ye shall be judged; and with what measure ye mete, it shall be measured to you again." In the 3rd, 4th, 8th, and 9th verses of this chapter hath been spoken of judging and recompensing them according to their ways.

Obs. 1. That God hath times for kings and courtiers to mourn in. Greatness exempts not from God's hand; if great ones sin, they shall smart for their sins: "the king shall mourn," &c. God takes off royal robes and puts sackcloth upon kings' loins that sin against him; heavy judgments he brings upon kings. Zedekiah's sins were great:

First, he was false, a thing too incident to kings; 2 Chron. xxxvi. 13, he violated the oath he had taken.

Secondly, idolatrous. Heathenish idolatry was practised in his days; ver. 14, the temple and worship of it were polluted.

Thirdly, trusted to and sent for Egyptians to help him, Jer. xxxvii. 7; he would not hearken to God's counsel, to the true prophets, to those who advised him well, Jer. xxxvi. 25; xxxvii. 2, but to false prophets and wicked counsellors.

Fourthly, he hated, imprisoned, and persecuted the prophets, 2 Chron. xxxvi. 16; Jer. xxxvii. 21.

Fifthly, unjust and cruel. "Let Jeremiah be put to death," say the princes, Jer. xxxviii. 4. "Then Zedekiah said, Behold, he is in your hand; the king is not he that can do any thing against you," &c. ver. 5. He was overpowered by the princes, and durst not displease them, but it cost dear at last.

Look upon other kings, they had their sins and their sorrows. Rehoboam hearkens to ill counsel, oppresses his people, and loses ten tribes at once for it. Jeroboam, upon wicked advice, sets up calves, restrains the people from the true worship at Jerusalem, and God sends him a dreadful message by Ahijah, 1 Kings xiv. 6, &c. Ahab did not execute justice upon Benhadad, a man appointed to death; and therefore saith the prophet, "Thy life shall go for his life, and thy people for his people," 1 Kings xx. 42. The court was very wicked then; Jezebel had the greatest power in it; she stirred up Ahab to work wickedness, she set the elders and nobles to work, to accuse and stone Naboth to death; but there was a time of mourning for them, 1 Kings xxi. 23, 24, 27. Ahaz was wicked, and the worse for his afflictions; but God had a sad day for him, when he lost one hundred and twenty thousand valiant men in one day, and had two hundred thousand women carried away captives, 2 Chron. xxviii. Asa, who was a good king, yet is branded with trusting in an arm of flesh, 2 Chron. xvi. 7, with oppression of some of the people, ver. 10; and therefore Hanani tells him he should have wars; and besides he was greatly diseased in his feet, ver. 9, 12. Manasseh was the great oppressing king, he shed and filled Jerusalem with innocent blood, 2 Kings xxi. 16; and as he found times to shed blood, so God found times to have him in the thorns, in fetters, in captivity, in mourning and humbling himself. Oppression is the common sin of princes; because they have greatness and power in their hands, they think it is warrantable for them to do what they list, "Ephraim loveth to oppress," Hos. xii. 7. The kine of Bashan, the great ones that were strong and fat, that had horns and hoofs, they oppressed the poor, and crushed the needy, "a man and his house, a man and his heritage," Micah ii. 2: Naboth and his vineyard went both at once. Hence the princes of Jerusalem are called, "roaring lions," Zeph. iii. 3; they are greedy of their prey, they scare, scatter, and devour the flock: but God will hunt these lions, and judge these men of the earth, Psal. x. 18, whose trade is oppression, and hath promised a time when his princes shall oppress no more; Ezek. xlv. 8, "My princes shall no more oppress." Either this prophecy is not fulfilled, or the oppressed in these days are not God's people, or the princes who oppress are not God's princes; and if so, say to the oppressing kings and queens of the earth, "Humble yourselves, sit down: for your principalities shall come down, even the crown of your glory," Jer. xiii. 18. See Acts xii. 23; Rev. vi. 15.

Obs. 2. That God hath apparel for princes and

nobles; and what is it? desolation, "The prince shall be clothed with desolation." God had an eye to the clothing of the great ones, and their sin about the same, and fits garments for them, such as they were not formerly used to. Great ones sin in their variety of garments; they have many lie spoiling by them, when the nakedness of others is seen for want of clothes; therefore God threatens to take away their changeable suits of apparel, Isa. iii. 22. They sin in the strangeness of them, they will have strange fashions; therefore, Zeph. i. 8, God threatens to "punish the princes, and the king's children, and all such as are clothed with strange apparel." The Jews had peculiar garments appointed them, Numb. xv. 38; Deut. xxii. 12; but they fetched in foreign garments, made after the manner of the heathens and nations about them. The courtiers and great ones then, as now, affected strange and costly apparel, were prodigal of their estates that way, had their chests and wardrobes filled with rich garments, which at pleasure they put on, to draw respect from men, but wrath from God; who clothed himself with vengeance, Isa. lix. 17, that he might clothe them with desolation; which was a strange garment, never put upon their backs before; an unchangeable garment, which lasted to their death. God stripped them by the Chaldeans of their proud attire, rich suits, yea of all they had, and clothed them with desolation: hence, Lam. iv. 5, "They that did feed delicately are desolate in the streets; they that were brought up in scarlet embrace dunghills."

Obs. 3. Wheresoever is a generality of sinning, there shall be a generality of suffering. "The king shall mourn, and the prince shall be clothed with desolation, and the hands of the people of the land shall be troubled." The whole nation was rebellious, Ezek. ii. 3; from the greatest to the least they were guilty, Jer. vi. 13, and therefore they should die from the least to the greatest, Jer. xliv. 12. God is impartial in his judgments; he will not spare kings, princes, nobles, people; but if their hearts, heads, hands be joined in wickedness, they shall be joined in punishment. All flesh had corrupted its ways, Gen. vi. 12, and all flesh was drowned in the floods of God's wrath, Gen. vii. 21. The Sodomites were all guilty, and none escaped the vengeance of eternal fire, Jude 7. And here, having all sinned, the wrath of God seized upon them all. Isa. lxv. 12, Ye shall all bow down to the slaughter: because when I called, ye did not answer; when I spake, ye did not hear; but did evil before mine eyes, and did choose that wherein I delighted not."

Obs. 4. That God smites sinners in that they have much offended with, and should stand them in most stead in times of affliction. "The hands of the people," &c. They had sinned with their hands several ways; in making idols, Isa. ii. 8; Hos. xiv. 3; in shedding blood, Isa. lix. 3; in acts of violence, ver. 6; they did evil "with both hands earnestly," Micah vii. 3; even princes and judges had covetous hands. God therefore smites them in their hands; and whereas they should have been serviceable unto them, now in their distress they were troubled, faint, useless. Before they had hands for the queen of heaven, Jer. xliv. 25; but now they had none for the God of heaven. They had hands for the service of Egyptians and Assyrians, Lam. v. 6; but now they had none to serve themselves in their personal callings, or military affairs.

Obs. 5. The Lord observes the ways and works of all. No church, no state, no person, but whatever they do comes under divine cognizance; their ways and deserts are known to the Lord. Some are so profane and atheistical, that they think God sees, regards not the things done here below: Psal. xciv. 5—7, they break in pieces God's people, afflict his heritage, slay, murder widows and fatherless ones; yet say, The Lord shall neither see nor regard it. And in Psal. x. 11, he saith, "God hath forgotten, he hideth his face, he will never see it." And not only God's actual seeing, but his power of seeing and knowing things here is denied; Job xxii. 13, "How doth God know? can he judge through the dark cloud?" Some have confidence to say God sees no sin in his children, and others blush not to say he sees not the sins of and in the wicked; and so God shall see no sin at all, they make him an unseeing and unknowing God. David calls this brutishness: Psal. xciv. 8—11, "He that formed the eye, shall he not see? He that teacheth man knowledge, shall not he know?" Yes, saith he, "the Lord knoweth the thoughts of men," and that their thoughts are vanity. What is most remote from man's eye and knowledge, that God knows exactly and afar off, Psal. cxxxix. 2; and denounceth a woe to men of such thoughts and practices, Isa. xxix. 15, "Woe unto them that seek deep to hide their counsel from the Lord, and their works are in the dark, and they say, Who seeth us? and who knoweth us?" God seeth them, God knoweth them, and pronounceth a dreadful woe against them. Because men's lives do proclaim that they believe not God's omnisciency, therefore God professeth it openly, Isa. lxvi. 18, "I know their works and their thoughts." He had observed all within and without, and therefore they should be consumed. God's eye is upon all our ways and works: let us every day do as God did, review them, and see that they be good.

Obs. 6. God in his judgments will proceed with sinners according to their ways and deserts. Job xxxiv. 10—12, Elihu proves there that God will not do wickedly, nor pervert judgment; and why? "For the work of a man shall he render unto him, and cause every man to find according to his ways." God is most just, and therefore takes notice of all thoughts, counsels, projects, attempts, and actions, that so he may deal answerably with men; Jer. xxxii. 19, "His eyes are open upon all the ways of the sons of men, to give every one according to his ways."

That in Rev. xviii. 6, seems to cross this truth; when God will judge Babylon, she must have double punishment, her cup must be doubled. God doth not command here that Babylon should be twice punished for the same sin; that were not according to the rules of divine justice. Double here hath reference to Babylon's dealings with the church: she did greatly afflict Zion, and now God would have Babylon to have double affliction to that: Babylon did unjustly in oppressing Zion; Zion should do righteously in destroying Babylon. And observe the word double, "double unto her double according to her works." If she had twice as many strokes and judgments, twice as much blood shed, as Zion had, it is according to her works, she deserves it, and nothing can be too much for her: therefore, Jer. li. 49, "As Babylon hath caused the slain of Israel to fall, so at Babylon shall fall the slain of all the earth." The Babylonian empire was a little world to Israel, and called itself the universal empire; and Babylon said she was the queen and the only city of all others, Isa. xlvii. 7, 8, the golden city, Isa. xiv. 4; but now when God would punish Babylon for her bloodiness against Zion, not only should Babylon's children that dwelt in her be destroyed, but all her subjects in her great territories should be

A Lapid. understands it of Rome heathenish.

slain for her sake, or together with her; which sets out the greatness of her punishment suitable to her deserts, and is well called double, for the death of one Israelite deserves the death of two Babylonians.

Obs. 7. They that will not know God in the way of his mercies, shall know him in the way of his judgments. God had walked in paths of mercy amongst this people many years, and they minded not God, honoured him not in the midst of mercies, but fed according to their pastures, and forgot God; therefore he brought heavy judgments upon them, and saith, "They shall know that I am the Lord." This phrase is used above fifty times in this prophet, and assures us that God will be known, and that amidst his enemies; and with an experimental knowledge, for that is the meaning of the words, not a literal and brain knowledge. Isa. xxvi. 11, "When thy hand is lifted up, they will not see: but they shall see:" they will not see to fear, to repent; but they shall see; that is, have experience of the strength of his hand to their shame and destruction.

The phrase of, knowing I am the Lord, sometimes refers to mercies, as Exod. vi. 6, 7; God would bring them out from the burdens and bondage of Egypt, take them for his people, and then they should know him to be the Lord. So in Exod. xvi. 12; 1 Kings xx. 28, God would give them manna, deliver up enemies into their hands, and they should know, &c. that is, have experience of his mercy, truth, and loving-kindness. Sometimes, and mostly, it refers to divine judgment, especially in this our prophet. God would bring in the Chaldeans with the sword, and those grievous calamities which attend it, and they should know that he was the Lord; that is, they should have real experience of his authority, and power over them, they should feel the bitter fruits of his displeasure in them.

CHAPTER VIII.

Ver. 1. *And it came to pass in the sixth year, in the sixth month, in the fifth day of the month, as I sat in mine house, and the elders of Judah sat before me, that the hand of the Lord God fell there upon me.*

In this and the three next chapters you have the grievous sins, and answerable punishments, of the Jews at Jerusalem laid down, with some other things considerable.

This eighth chapter hath three things in it:

I. An introduction to a new vision, ver. 1.

II. The vision itself, from ver. 2—17.

III. A declaration of God's severe dealings with them, ver. 18.

In the introduction to this vision you have these particulars.

1. The time exactly set down when it was, in the sixth year, the sixth month, the fifth day.

2. The place where it was, as he sat in his house.

3. The persons before whom it was, "The elders of Judah sat before me."

4. The cause of it, "The hand of the Lord God fell there upon me."

For the time, it was now the sixth year of Jehoiachin's captivity, and in the sixth month.

The Jews' first month is Nisan, the second Jiar, the third Sivan, the fourth Thamuz, the fifth Ab, and the sixth Elul, and answereth to that which is called August. The fifth day of this month had he this vision, which Junius saith was the sabbath day, which was a day fitting for visions of God. It was now a year, two months, and upwards, since he had his first vision.

"As I sat in mine house." Having been now six years in captivity, the prophet and others had hired, or builded themselves, houses. This was a house of some capaciousness, the elders of Judah sat before him in it; that is, the chief of those that were brought with Jehoiachin into Babylon, 2 Kings xxiv. 12. And why they should come and sit there is inquirable. It was not to catch advantages against the prophet, as some fancy; not to consult of their civil affairs in Babylon, others were more fit for such things than prophets; but it was to hear of the prophet what the Lord intended to do with Jerusalem and the Jews there, what the meaning of the types and visions he had was, whether he had any word of their returning from that condition they were in. Or they came to see if he had any word to speak unto them, being the sabbath day; for on those days it was ordinary for the people to go to the prophets, 2 Kings iv. 23; and Ezekiel sat composed, and disposed to speak the word of God to those who came to him.

"The hand of the Lord God fell there upon me." The powerful operation of the Spirit of Christ seized upon him, and was as a hand carrying him on to that work he was appointed unto; he had a mighty impulse of the Spirit, and was as a man rapt out of himself, wholly acted by the Spirit. See chap. i. 3, where hath been spoken of the hand of the Lord.

Obs. 1. That the Lord takes special notice of the times in which he gives out truths and visions to prophets and people, he keeps an exact account of those years, months, and days. "In the sixth year, the sixth month, and fifth day," &c. So in the first chapter, "In the thirtieth year, the fourth month, the fifth day," the word of the Lord came unto him. You have the time mentioned in chap. xx. 1, "The seventh year, in the fifth month, the tenth day of the month." So in chap. xxvi. 1; xxix. 1; xxxi. 1; xxxii. 1; xl. 1; in these places, there is special notice and account set down of the time wherein God gave out his truth and visions to the prophet, and by him to the people. In chap xxiv. 1—3, the year, month, day, and name of the day, are written down when Jerusalem was besieged, and a parable put into the prophet's mouth. And not only was it thus in Ezekiel's, but also in other prophets' days, Zech. i. 1; vii. 1; Hag. i. 1; ii. 1, 10. Whatever men's thoughts are of truths, when they are tendered unto them, the Lord looks upon it as a work of great concernment, and registers the time when it is done: In such a year, the city, land, had fasts every month, and the prophets preached such truths and texts unto them; such a month they had a thanksgiving day, and the text was, &c.

Especially in times of affliction, God takes notice what truths are commended by the prophets unto men, and therefore the time in Ezekiel is more particularized than any where else, because many were now in captivity, the rest were coming; and of all truths, those will cost dearest that are preached unto us in our afflictions and not improved.

Obs. 2. That great ones in times of affliction will seek unto the prophets, and prize vision when it is rare. The elders came to his house, sat there expecting some word from him. Ezekiel was a priest and a prophet, chap. i. 3; and priests did teach as well as sacrifice: 2 Chron. xv. 3, "Israel was without a teaching priest;" see Lev. x. 8—11. And Mal. ii. 7, "The priest's lips should keep knowledge, and they should seek the law at his mouth."

These elders, the princes and chief ones, were come to seek it at Ezekiel's mouth. Now they were in captivity, now priests and prophets were scarce; and now great ones, that before little regarded the prophets and priests, that mocked them, despised and misused them, 2 Chron. xxxvi. 16, now they get to Ezekiel's house, wait upon him, and long to hear a word from him.

Afflictions abate the pride of great men's spirits, remove prejudice, awaken conscience, convince of sin, God's greatness and authority over the highest, the shortness of life, of judgment, and that eternal condition which is coming: and when it is so with great ones, they will be glad to go to a poor prophet's house, and hear a word from him. Jeroboam, when his son was sick, sends to Ahijah the prophet, to know what should become of him, 1 Kings xiv. 2, 3. Naaman in his leprosy goeth to the prophet Elisha for help, 2 Kings v. See Isa. xxxvii. 2; Jer. xxxvii. 3; there you shall find great ones, even the greatest, seeking to the prophets in their troubles.

Obs. 3. Meeting in private houses to enjoy God's ordinances, is ancient and warrantable. The elders came to the prophet's house, sat there to hear the word of the Lord; this was above two thousand years ago, therefore ancient; and the prophet taught them in private: they worshipped God in a house, they kept the sabbath there, and therefore not unlawful. This was frequent in Christ's and the apostles' days. Luke x. 38, 39, in Martha's house Christ preached. Acts xx. 7, the disciples met every first day, in houses and chambers; and when they were so met, Paul preached to them. And Acts ii. 46, they brake bread from house to house; that is, privately, in opposition to the public, saith De Dieu. And Acts v. 42, "In every house they ceased not to teach and preach Jesus Christ;" in Cornelius's house they did it, Acts x. 33, 34; in the jailor's house they did it, Acts xvi. 32. The high priests cried out of such meetings, and thought the temple and synagogues, which were allowed by authority, were sufficient. But this would not suffice the apostles, they preached in public to convert the Jews, in private to strengthen the christians; they would not be tied to places, when Christ by his doctrine and practice had warranted them to preach and worship any where.

John iv. 20, 21. 1 Tim. ii. 8.

In Tertullian's time such meetings were counted factious and schismatical: but he vindicates the same, saying, We are the same congregated, and together, as we are asunder, we hurt, we grieve none. When good and godly men meet together, it is no conventicle, but a court. They are a conventicle, a faction, that, in hatred of good men, meet and plot against them, pretending they are the cause of all evils and disturbances.

Tertull. in Apologet.

In the prelates' days there was much rigour and severity used against godly meetings of this nature, more than ever we read of formerly. It can hardly be shown in Scripture, that ever any met together in private to worship the Lord, were surprised, molested, taken, or imprisoned. For their public preaching they were frequently questioned, and suffered; it is not so evident that they did for their private meetings. These they had in Babylon without imputation or molestation; and shall not Zion be as indulgent to her children as Babylon was to her enemies? If not, Babylon will rise up in judgment against such sons of Zion.

Obs. 4. God honours holy meetings, though they be private. The hand of the Lord fell there, and then, upon the prophet. Where two or three meet together in a sacred manner, God will be in the midst of them, Matt. xviii. 20; he will be president of that meeting, and powerful in it, not only show his presence and power in an ordinary way, but many times extraordinarily, as at this time. John xx. 19, when the disciples were assembled in private, "Jesus stood in the midst of them, and said, Peace be unto you;" and so in ver. 26, when they were met in private Christ came amongst them; he honoured their meetings in a special manner with his presence, blessing, and miracles. The world hath prejudice against such meetings, speaks ill and attempts the ruin of them; but Christ thinks honourably of them, puts honour upon, and manifests his acceptance of them. Acts ii. 1—4, when the apostles were got together in a house, the cloven tongues of fire sat upon each of them, and they were filled with the Holy Spirit. Acts x. 44, while Peter was preaching in Cornelius's house, the Holy Ghost fell upon them. And you will scarcely find such visible signs of God's presence in public as were then in private.

I speak not this to disparage public meetings, God is in the solemn assemblies, there his glory and power is seen; but to take off that odium which is in the hearts of many against all private meetings.

Obs. 5. Those who wait upon God in the ways of his worship are not losers by it. The elders came to the prophet, sat there, expected something from him, and they had more than ordinary; they beheld the hand of God upon the prophet, and were made witnesses of that vision he had, and partakers of the same.

The people that flocked after Christ into the field, had the word, and besides that, the loaves and fishes, John vi. When the disciples were met together to worship the Lord the first day of the week, Christ came to them, breathed upon, and gave them the Holy Ghost, John xx. 19, 22. Paul seeks God in prayer, Acts ix. 11, and continued in it, "Behold he prayeth," he was at it night and day; and Ananias was sent to him to help him to his sight, and to the Holy Ghost, so that he might see men, and how to save men. Old Simeon, and old Anna the prophetess, they came into the temple to serve the Lord, and at that time Christ is brought in, whom they see, and magnify God for, Luke ii. In Acts xvi. 13, you read how Paul left the city and went to a river-side, where women did usually meet to pray; thither many were come, and to them Paul preaches; Lydia's heart is opened, and Christ let in, who was before a stranger unto her; and besides this, she was baptized, and gained the company of the choicest apostles, ver. 14, 15. Cornelius, Acts x. fasts and prays, and he hath an angel sent to him, to assure him that all was accepted in heaven; and to help him to the speech of an apostle, whom hearing, he received the Holy Ghost, ver. 44. Men lose not, but gain greatly, by waiting upon God in his ordinances. If they have not what they expect sometimes, they have more than they look for at other times. "Blessed is the man that heareth me," saith Christ, Prov. viii. 34, "watching daily at my gates, waiting at the posts of my doors." They are blessed already, and unexpected blessings are waiting for them.

Obs. 6. That former operations and impressions of the Spirit suffice not the holiest of men, when new services are to be done. Ezekiel was a holy prophet, he had the hand of God, the virtue of the Spirit, falling upon him before, chap. i. 3, entering into him, chap. ii. 2, strongly upon him, chap. iii. 14; and yet all this was not sufficient; there was new work for him, new visions to be seen and given out, and the hand of the Lord fell anew upon him.

New employments must have new influences; new trials must have new strength; if we trust to antecedent receipts, we shall miscarry. Peter failed when he came to encounter with a new trial; he leaned upon what he had, and looked not up for more. Paul stood, when buffeted by a messenger of Satan; and why? being conscious of his own weakness, and insufficiency of what he had received, he sought to God, who told him, "My grace is sufficient for thee;" not the graces I have given thee, but the grace I have to give thee. If a messenger of Satan molest thee, be too strong for thee, I have a messenger, even my Spirit of grace, that shall come and comfort thee, that is stronger than all, and shall uphold thee. Paul had experience of this, and therefore counsels Timothy, 2 Tim. ii. 1, to "be strong in the grace that is in Christ Jesus." Though he had unfeigned faith, knew the Scripture from a child, had a gift given him by the laying on of Paul's hands; yet he must not be strong in these, but in the grace of Christ, see his strength lie there. Former impressions of Christ's Spirit wear out, and received virtue is soon spent: we must look for new influences, impressions, and operations of the hand of Christ, else all will be too little. Cant. iv. 16, "Awake, O north wind; and come, thou south; blow upon my garden, that the spices thereof may flow out." "And Samson called unto the Lord, and said, O Lord God, remember me, I pray thee, and strengthen me, I pray thee, only this once," Judg. xvi. 28.

Ver. 2. *Then I beheld, and lo a likeness as the appearance of fire: from the appearance of his loins even downward, fire; and from his loins even upward, as the appearance of brightness, as the colour of amber.*

Our prophet being in an ecstasy, the Lord Jesus Christ appears unto him as a man, and is described,

I. Generally, and that is by a likeness of fire; he seemed to him to be a man of fire, or as the appearance of fire.

II. More particularly; and,

1. From his loins downward, and the appearance thereof was as fire.

2. From his loins upward, the appearance whereof was,

(1.) As brightness;

(2.) As the colour of amber.

Christ being presented here as a man of fire, it is worthy consideration to examine the grounds of it.

The Jews had sinned exceedingly, provoked God by their idolatry to great jealousy, and being now resolved upon their destruction, he gives out a fiery vision of Christ unto the prophet, which appearance was suitable to the work now intended.

Appearances in fire have been formerly. Christ appeared to Moses in a flame of fire, Exod. iii. 2; the angel there, interpreters make to be Christ: and God led the Jews in the wilderness by a pillar of fire, Exod. xiii. 21; and he was in that pillar, Exod. xiv. 24.

Christ is likened to fire.

1. It is a shining, glorious thing; so Christ is glorious: John i. 14, "We beheld his glory, the glory as," &c. And, Titus ii. 13, his appearing will be glorious, and so glorious as to lighten the world. When men come to judgment, they come with some glory and majesty.

2. He is likened to fire, to set out his knowledge and discovery of things. Fire is of a discovering nature, and makes manifest; Rev. i. 14, Christ's eyes are like a flame of fire, they see into every place; and here Christ discovers to the prophet the sins of Jerusalem, the hidden abominations there.

3. To show the active virtue which is in Christ. Fire is a lively and purging thing, separating dross from the precious metals; and Christ is of infinite virtue, he distinguisheth between the precious and the vile: Mal. iii. 2, "He is like a refiner's fire," exceeding active and discretive, he burns with zeal and jealousy.

4. The severe punishment he would inflict upon this people. Fire notes revenge, destruction: Psal. xviii. 8, "Fire out of his mouth devoured." Isa. lxvi. 15, 16, fire there notes severe punishment and utter destruction; and Christ now would make a final end of this sinful people, he would be a fire unquenchable. If they looked to him upwards, they should find him a fire, he would plead with his Father for their destruction. If they looked downwards, they should see him kindling a consuming fire amongst them. The law was given in fire, Deut. iv. 33; v. 4, and therefore called a fiery law; and Christ appears in fire when he comes to revenge the breaches of the law.

In chap. i. 27, Christ's appearance from his loins upward and downward is the same; here, downwards he appears as fire, upwards, as brightness; fire noting his anger, brightness his clemency, as some conceive.

The word for brightness notes such brightness as is from the morning, זהר the firmament, the sun; therefore some render it, As the appearance of the bright sun. Take the sun when in it's greatest lustre and glory, such was the appearance of Christ upward, and may note the glory of Christ in execution of judgment, in giving out his threatenings to the prophets against sinners.

"As the colour of amber." Of this hath been spoken, chap. i. 4, 27. The Hebrew, *chasmal*, signifies a coal intensely hot; and such as a coal is, at the height of its heat, in a fiery furnace, such was the appearance of Christ: at this time he was in a way of wrath, and giving out threats against this people, and filled with the fire of zeal and jealousy for the Lord.

Obs. If the appearance of Christ be fiery and glorious, the presence of him will be so much more: Appearances are not perfect expressions of that they resemble. The appearance of fire upon the tabernacle, Numb. ix. 15, had not that virtue and glory in it which real fire had; if real, it would have consumed the tabernacle. The appearance of lightning, Dan. x. 6, is not so glorious as lightning itself; and what the prophet saw here of Christ was appearance only, little to that which is in Christ.

When Christ shall really be seen, not in visions, but as he is, he will be very glorious. Mark xiii. 26, when Christ comes, it will be "with great power and glory," great, refers to glory as well as power: Matt. xxiv. 30, there it is "with power and great glory." And if you demand how great, even so great as cannot be greater; Matt. xvi. 27, "He shall come in the glory of his Father," and no glory can exceed that.

Ver. 3. *And he put forth the form of an hand, and took me by a lock of mine head; and the spirit lifted me up between the earth and the heaven, and brought me in the visions of God to Jerusalem, to the door of the inner gate that looketh toward the north; where was the seat of the image of jealousy, which provoketh to jealousy.*

In the former verse you had Christ's person described; in this are his actions commended to us, which are these:

I. The putting forth of his hand.

II. The employment thereof, by it he took our prophet by a lock.

III. The lifting him up between heaven and earth by his Spirit.

IV. The bringing him to Jerusalem; where is considerable,

1. The manner of his bringing; "in the visions of God."

2. The special place; he was brought "to the door of the inner gate that looketh toward the north."

3. The nature of this place; it was the seat of an image, which is described,

(1.) From its name; an "image of jealousy."

(2.) From the effect; it "provoketh to jealousy."

"He put forth the form of an hand." He that appeared like fire, that had such brightness, and was so glorious, he put forth his hand; sent out his hand, is the original. Not a real hand, but the form or likeness of a hand. It was the likeness and appearance of a man that he saw, and such was the hand here; not a substantial, fleshy hand.

"And took me by a lock of mine head." By the hair, the word signifies, that which grows out of the head and flourisheth there, as grass out of the ground, or boughs out of a tree. בציצת

"The spirit lifted me up between," &c. It was said the hand took hold of him; did not the hand lift him up? if not, to what end took it hold? That hand was the Holy Spirit of Christ, which in these visions of Ezekiel is oft called a hand, chap. i. 3, and iii. 14. The Spirit that lifted him up is called "the hand of the Lord," because Christ by his Spirit doth whatever the hand of man can do.

"And brought me in the visions of God to Jerusalem." The prophet thought himself like a bird or an angel flying through the air, and carried to Jerusalem. This was no real elevation or corporeal transportation of the prophet to Jerusalem, as will appear thus:

1. It is said it was "the form of a hand," the likeness of one, not a hand itself.

2. Had he been really taken up by a lock, it would have been exceeding grievous and tormenting to him, if not deadly.

3. He saith he was brought "in the visions of God to Jerusalem," not in the reality of his person; all was done as he sat in his house, and the elders of Judah before him. The ancients say, it was in his spirit, not in his body, that he was translated, a mental, not an ocular vision.

Our prophet being in a rapture, or ecstasy, seemed as a man dead, and had secret things revealed unto him, which he calls "visions of God." Whether these were to his spirit in the body, or called out of it, is uncertain. 2 Cor. xii. 1, 2, when Paul had his revelation and visions, whether it was in the body or out of it himself could not tell. Visions they both had, and they were visions of God, not delusions of Satan, who can be a lying spirit in the hearts and mouths of false prophets, 1 Kings xxii. 22. Nor were they fancies of their own; for when men are in divine raptures, there is a cessation of all sensible and natural actions; nature contributes nothing thereunto. In some diseases there is a stilling of all nature's organs and operations, as when *deliquium animæ*, a fainting, seizeth upon any; but there is nothing then offered to the soul, as here. Such visions had our prophet as were clear, and without all doubt he knew them to be visions of God.

"The door of the inner gate." The temple was yet standing, and had two courts; one called the outer court, Rev. xi. 2, which was the place whither the Israelites assembled for divine exercise; and an inner court, 1 Kings vi. 36, which was the priests' court, 2 Chron. iv. 9. The other was the great court, and called Solomon's porch, saith Maldonat. Into this court was Ezekiel brought, and set at the door going into the inner court. Mead on Rev.

"That looketh toward the north." In the courts about the temple there were gates and doors towards the four quarters of the world; which included this mystery, that in due time the partition-wall should be broken down, that stood between Jews and gentiles, and all sorts from all parts should come in to the true worship of the true God; came they from east or west, south or north, there should be a door open to let them in. At this north gate was the image seated that the prophet did first see.

"Image of jealousy." Two things are to be opened here:

1. What this image was.

2. Why called an image of jealousy.

1. It is doubted amongst the learned what image this should be. The most agree it was the image of Baal. It is true that Josiah had taken away Baal and his altars, 2 Chron. xxxiv. 4; but Jehoiakim, and Jehoiachin, and Zedekiah had restored them again, as is gathered from 2 Kings xxiii. 37; xxiv. 9, 19; 2 Chron. xxxvi. 14.

2. Why called the image of jealousy. The heathens had no idols or gods of that name, nor is it so called in reference unto them; but,

(1.) From the wicked zeal of Ahaz, who, as you read, 2 Kings xvi. 10, sent the pattern of an altar at Damascus to Urijah, who set it up for the honour of Baal at the north gate of the inner court; and to this altar did Ahaz bring the altar of the Lord, ver. 14: here was his zeal for Baal.

(2.) Because it provoked God to jealousy. When God saw his own altar and word to be so abused, subjected to Baal, that his people went a whoring from him to that shameful thing, he would bear no longer, but was jealous for his honour, discovers to the prophet their great sin, and his jealousy burning now against them.

This image made the people forsake their God, commit spiritual adultery, Jer. vii. 30, and God would recompense it now unto them.

It was seated at the gate northward; because that way was the most frequent passage to the temple, the ascent being not so steep and difficult as other sides of the hill, on which the temple stood, and for that sacrifices came mostly from that side.

Obs. 1. The Spirit is the agent of Christ, by which he doth his works. He put forth his hand, and took hold of me. The hand of a man is that which doth immediately take hold of a thing; so the Spirit being the immediate agent which Christ useth, is called a hand, and doth whatever the Lord Christ will have done. If he would have men walk in his statutes, keep his judgments, he puts his Spirit into men, and by it causeth them to do so, Ezek. xxxvi. 27; that is the hand which overacts them. If he would have young or old prophesy, it is done by his Spirit, Joel ii. 28. And the prophets gave out what the Spirit gave in to them, Zech. vii. 12. If the Lord Christ would not have Paul preach in Asia, the Holy Ghost forbids him; if he would go into Bithynia, the Spirit suffers him not, Acts xvi. 6, 7; if he should preach, the Spirit presseth him in his spirit, Acts xviii. 5. It is Christ's Spirit that mortifies our corruptions, Rom. viii. 13, that helps us to pray, ver. 26. It is the Spirit works all graces in us, Gal. v. 22, 23. It is not by might nor power, but by the Spirit, Christ doth all, Zech. iv. 6.

Obs. 2. That holy men must be lifted up out of themselves, and above themselves, if they would participate of divine things. The Spirit lifted up the prophet between earth and heaven. Paul, 2 Cor. xii. 4, was caught up into paradise, where he heard the unspeakable words; the Spirit of God had lifted him up above himself and all worldly things, and then God spake such things to him as he never heard. Rev. i. 10, John was in the Spirit when he had those great and glorious revelations; he was in the Spirit, that is, in the hand of the Spirit, and by the power thereof lifted up, and carried above and out of himself. There was not only a pressure of the Spirit, but a comprehension; the Spirit comprehended him; he was in a manner all Spirit; and the more spiritual any is, the more fit for converse with God, and to have visions of God. "The natural man receiveth not the things of God," 1 Cor. ii. 14; it is not flesh and blood that reveals, receives, and judges of them: men must be lifted up by the Spirit from the earth, their earthly dispositions and affections, before they are fit for divine excellency. Those who have left the earth as Paul did, and have their conversations in heaven as he had, they are fitted to know and partake of the great mysteries of Christ. Self is the great let to divine things; therefore apostles were usually rapt out of themselves when they had their visions.

Obs. 3. Christ by his Spirit makes known to the prophet the sins of men; the Spirit showed him the image of jealousy, and the abominations the people committed at Jerusalem. Ezekiel was in Babylon, and yet by the help of the Spirit he comes to see and know the doings of sinners at Jerusalem. When they should hear Ezekiel had prophesied or preached of their sins particularly, they would wonder who had informed him of them; as now, when ministers preach conscientiously, and meet with the particular sins of men and women, they think some or other have informed them, told tales of them, when it is only the Spirit of God hath directed them. A godly minister was charged to be a conjurer, because he told men in his preaching of the particular things they did. It is the Spirit helps in studying, and in preaching. The Spirit convinces the world of sin, John xvi. 9; and the ministers of the sins of the world, that so they may abhor those sins, and denounce the judgments of God against them.

Obs. 4. Wicked men are wise, and take their advantages to promote their superstitions. They set their image of jealousy at the inner gate northward; that way was the greatest concourse of people, and so the advantage great for their worshipping of or before this image. Men are "wise to do evil," Jer. iv. 22; they set up altars in all the streets of Jerusalem, to burn incense to Baal, that shameful thing, Jer. xi. 13; they could not suffer any street to be without an altar; they were wise and zealous to promote sin. Jeroboam feared lest the people should go from him, and therefore, in his witty wickedness to prevent it, sets up the calves at Dan and Bethel, 1 Kings xii. 29. The papists have had repute for such wisdom; they had their crosses in highways, and in public places where people most frequented.

Obs. 5. When images go up, then the worship of God goes down. Ahaz set up Baal, and brought the altar of the Lord to it; Baal was regarded, and the true God and his worship neglected, 2 Kings xvi. 14. Men are zealous for their own inventions, and jealous lest they should suffer.

Obs. 6. Superstition and idolatry are provoking sins, they provoke God, who is a God of patience, to jealousy: Deut. xxxii. 16, "They provoked him to jealousy with strange gods," strange invertions. Sins of this nature are called "provocations," Nen. ix. 18, great provocations. No sins provoke God more than idolatry and false worship.

(1.) It is a breaking of covenant with God, who had taken people in to be his, as a husband doth a wife; and when she breaks covenant, forsakes the guide of her youth, and is for others, this provokes the husband more than any thing besides.

(2.) Because it is a giving God's honour and glory to idols. Aquinas saith, We adore the image of Christ with divine worship. Bellarmine with many others acknowledge that the image of Christ may in some kind be honoured *cultu latriæ*. When God's glory is given to creatures, this provokes "the eyes of his glory," as it is Isa. iii. 8; and he will not endure that his glory and praise be given to another, Isa. xlii. 8.

Nos adoramus adoratione latriæ imaginem Christi. Parte 3. q. 25. a. 3. Tom. 1. Controv. 7. l. 2. c. 23.

(3.) They that are guilty this way hate God, Exod. xx. 5. Being provoked therefore, and the spirit of jealousy kindled in him, he will not put it up, he will not spare; according to that in Prov. vi. 34, "Jealousy is the rage of a man; therefore he will not spare in the day of vengeance;" and Cant. viii. 6, "Jealousy is cruel as the grave," no mercy will be shown. God will "stir up jealousy, and prevail against his enemies," Isa. xlii. 13, devour whole lands by the fire of his jealousy, Zeph. iii. 8.

Ver. 4. *And, behold, the glory of the God of Israel was there, according to the vision that I saw in the plain.*

Our prophet being visionally brought to Jerusalem, Christ by his Spirit shows him glory, which is set forth,

The glory of God, that is, the glorious God, was there manifesting his glory to him in some visible way.

I. Absolutely; the glory of God.

II. Relatively; the God of Israel.

III. The place; there at the inner gate.

IV. The manner; according to the vision he had seen.

In chap. iii. 23, the prophet saith, he "arose and went forth into the plain; and, behold, the glory of the Lord stood there, as the glory which I saw by the river of Chebar." He had twice before seen the glory of God, and now here again he sees it.

There is nothing difficult in the words; one thing is considerable in them, why the prophet had now a third time the glory of God presented to him.

1. To keep his heart in an humble and reverential frame, that whatever God revealed to him about the utter ruin of the Jewish nation, he should not stick at it, decline the revealing of it, because he saw that God was a glorious and dreadful God.

2. To let him see what unspeakable wrong the Jews had done him, to forsake the glorious God, to serve base, shameful, dunghill idols; this made God complain, Jer. ii. 11, "They have changed their glory for that which doth not profit," the God of Israel for the gods of the nations.

3. To kindle the zeal of the prophet. When he had seen God so glorious once, twice, or thrice, and also what they had done to this God; this could not but fire his spirit, and make him burning with zeal, in justifying God, and denouncing threatenings against such idolaters.

4. To let the prophet see that he was going away from his sanctuary, and from his people; and therefore it is said, "the glory of the God of Israel was there," there at the inner gate looking northward,

where the image which provoked so much was; not that the glorious God would have communion with the image; but to evidence, that seeing they had brought in a false god, the true God would leave them.

5. To confirm the prophet in the truth of this prophecy, and make way for the high esteem of it in after-ages, being brought in with so many glorious visions.

"God of Israel." Jacob's name being changed to "Israel," Gen. xxxii. 28, in time the Jews came to be called "Israelites," Exod. ix. 7, "The children of Israel," Exod. xix. 3. And God taking them for his people, is frequently styled "the God of Israel," Exod. v. 1; Josh. vii. 19. And he is so styled here to put them in mind of two things:

1. The covenant that he made with their fathers, Abraham, Isaac, Jacob, and Moses, Deut. xxix. 12, 13. God took them to be his people, and became their God.

2. The great things he had done for Israel above all other people. None of the nations had such a God as their God was. The nations' gods were impotent, impure, perishing gods, but the God of Israel was the Lord of hosts; Jer. vii. 3, "Thus saith the Lord of hosts, the God of Israel." He had all power, command of all creatures, and could do enough for them. He was "the Holy One of Israel," Isa. v. 19, and would not endure iniquity in Jacob and Israel; "the Strength of Israel," 1 Sam. xv. 29, and never failed, and did wonderful things for them; he brought them out of Egypt, &c. Micah vi. 4; he had known them above all families of the earth, Amos iii. 2.

Obs. 1. That the true God, the God of Israel, is a glorious God; he is a glorious essence, and essential glory. Psal. xxix. 3, he is "the God of glory," and Psal. xxiv. 7, 9, 10, he is thrice called "the King of glory." Not only hath he glory to dispose of to others, but he is a King all of glory, and glorious excellences; his attributes are glory, his omnipotence, omniscience, eternity, immutability, wisdom, justice, mercy, holiness, are his glory; Exod. xv. 11, he is "glorious in holiness." It is said of Aaron, he had garments for glory, Exod. xxviii. 2. God's attributes are his garments for glory; and how glorious is God, who hath so many glorious garments on him! There is nothing in God, or about him, but it is glorious; his eyes are eyes of glory, Isa. iii. 8; his right hand is glorious, Exod. xv. 6; his arm is glorious, Isa. lxiii. 12; his majesty is glorious, Psal. cxlv. 5; his work is glorious, cxi. 3; his works of creation, providence, redemption are so; his name is glorious, 1 Chron. xxix. 13; his glory is so bright, so great, that it fills the earth, Isa. vi. 3; his Spirit is glory, 1 Pet. iv. 14; his Son is the Lord of glory, 1 Cor. ii. 8. God is not only glorious, or glory, but excellent glory, 2 Pet. i. 17; it excels the glory of the sun, the glory of all kings, of all angels and glorious ones, of the whole creation, yea, the comprehensions of all intelligent creatures; it is so excelling, that none but God himself can measure it.

Let us give glory to the God of Israel who is so glorious, acknowledge what he hath done, magnify his name, multiply his praises: where praises dwell, God dwells; Psal. xxii. 3, "He inhabits the praises of Israel." He is the God of Israel, dwells there, to counsel, comfort, deliver, sanctify, and save them; they praise him, and he is there to give in daily new matter of praise.

Obs. 2. Sight of the glory of God is a great privilege, it is not for every one to see. Ezekiel saw it; not all in Babylon, not all the elders who were in the house with him. Ungracious, unbelieving spirits see not divine glory; John i. 14, "We beheld his glory," not others; we that received of his fulness, of his graces, we had the favour and the power to behold his glory. Many saw Christ's miracles, but not his glory held out by them, John ii. 11. When the water was turned into wine, Christ manifested his glory, which the disciples saw, not others: they believed; and Christ told Martha, if she believed, she should "see the glory of God," John xi. 40. Faith is the eye of the soul, and God shows his glory in Christ to that eye.

Obs. 3. That whithersoever God calls a man, he can show him his glory. At the river Chebar he had seen it, in the plain also, and now at Jerusalem, which abounded with idolatry.

Ver. 5, 6. *Then said he unto me, Son of man, lift up thine eyes now the way toward the north. So I lifted up mine eyes the way toward the north, and behold northward at the gate of the altar this image of jealousy in the entry. He said furthermore unto me, Son of man, seest thou what they do? even the great abominations that the house of Israel committeth here, that I should go far off from my sanctuary? but turn thee yet again, and thou shalt see greater abominations.*

In these and the following verses are gradually set out the great abominations of the Jews at Jerusalem. Their wickedness was not positive only, but superlative, of the highest nature. Besides the appellation, "son of man," the fifth verse hath in it,

I. Christ's commandment, "Lift up thine eyes."

II. The prophet's obedience, "So I lifted up min eyes."

III. The thing seen, "The image of jealousy."

IV. The place where, "At the gate of the altar in the entry."

"Lift up thine eyes." This phrase imports a thorough view, an exact notice of things. Gen. xiii. 10, "Lot lifted up his eyes, and beheld all the plain of Jordan, that it was well watered every where:" he diligently considered the place and commodities of it. Isa. xlix. 18, "Lift up thine eyes round about, and behold;" that is, consider well how all that gather against thee shall be for thy good. The lifting up of the eyes notes a distinct and fuller observation of things: and so here, Ezekiel, be not remiss and careless in the viewing of things, but lift up thine eyes, open them fully, observe exactly what is before thee. This you must take to be meant of the eyes of his mind, not his body; for he was in an ecstasy in the spirit at Jerusalem, not in the flesh.

"At the gate of the altar." No gate was so called originally; but after Ahaz had corrupted the worship of God by his altar from Damascus, fixed an altar by that gate, and brought the Lord's altar thither, 2 Kings xvi. 14, it is conceived hereupon this gate was called the altar-gate; there was an altar for Baal, and a misplaced altar for God.

Obs. 1. If we will rightly discern the corruption in worship, distinguish between what is human and what is divine, we must set the eyes of our minds to work, they must be lift up, be open, and intent to the thing. There is great difference between the external view and judgment of the flesh, and between the internal view and judgment of the spirit. This Baalitical altar, doubtless, was glorious outwardly, as false worship is, (Jeroboam's calves were golden ones, 1 Kings xii. 28,) and affected the eyes, stole away the hearts, of many; but it was loathsome to the eye of a judicious, considering mind; God's worship was hindered, defiled by it, his jealousy provoked, and their ruin procured by it.

The popish religion is pompous, and to carnal eyes hath beauty in it; but to those that lift up the eyes of their mind, and well consider, it is superstitious, idolatrous, and abominable. Some have called the ceremonies used lately in our worship innocent; but those who examined them well, found them injurious, the seed of contention, snares to conscience, and flies in our precious ointment. John vii. 24, "Judge not according to the appearance, but judge righteous judgment;" see exactly into things, let the eyes be lift up, and so shall you pass a more judicious sentence.

How pompous was our worship become lately, but since eyes have been lift up, the vanity, corruption, and superstition thereof have appeared.

Obs. 2. They may safely observe, examine, the nature and sinfulness of false worship, who have a call unto it. The Lord Christ bids Ezekiel "behold the image of jealousy," see what the people did there. The prophet did not willingly lift up his eyes, but at command, and being lawfully called to it, there was no danger of being seduced, of bowing to Baal, of countenancing false worship: God keeps those who are in the way he sets them. Had the prophet, out of curiosity and desire to see this altar, this image, gone to Jerusalem, he might have been insnared; as too many of our nation by going to Rome, having no better ground than an itching desire to see and know what is done there. Romish worship hath inveigled them, jesuitical charms bewitched them, and lost they have both truth and innocency; their consciences have been defiled, and their judgments prejudiced against those ways they were formerly acquainted with. If the spirits of some have been heightened against those abominations by the sight of them, this is matter for wonder, not for imitation. It is not safe entering into the lions' den because one Daniel was kept safe there; where one hath been preserved, scores have been corrupted, and many of them insensibly. Philosophers say, an egg wrapped up in salt loses the good meat which was in it, the shell remaining whole; and so when young ones travel into those brackish countries, and live amongst those who are salted with popery, they lose the good savour they had of true religion, and only the shell remains whole.

Obs. 3. See here the tractableness, the obediential frame of the prophet's spirit. Christ commands him to lift up his eyes, and so he lift up his eyes, he doubted not, disputed not, he lingered not; but the word being given out, immediately he obeys, his spirit was set towards, and suitable to, the will of Christ. He might have stuck and said, It is an abominable idol, an accursed thing that provokes thee to jealousy, mine eyes shall never see that which so pollutes thy worship, and is so contrary to thy glory; but he presently submits, and fulfils the will of Christ, which is very acceptable unto him. Moses's delays made God angry, Exod. iv. 14; and it is the great shift of Satan to keep men off from obeying the will and voice of God by delays. He doth not tell men the commands in Scripture are not the commands of God, but he causeth delays, and so impedes, retards the execution of divine commands; so that God is hearkened unto months and years after the command is gone forth: such obedience is not so precious and acceptable. David knew it, and therefore saith, Psal. cxix. 60, "I made haste, and delayed not to keep thy commandments." A lazy, lingering spirit is a provoking spirit. David made haste and ran when God commanded, which greatly pleased God. Abraham is bidden to leave his country, and go to an uncertain place he knew not whither; he did it presently, and it is twice recorded in Scripture, Gen. xii. 1, 4; Acts vii. 3, 4.

Ver. 6. *He said furthermore unto me, Son of man, seest thou what they do? even the great abominations that the house of Israel committeth here, that I should go far off from my sanctuary? but turn thee yet again, and thou shalt see greater abominations.*

This verse needs little opening. It is probable that some of the Jews were worshipping before that idol Baal, whereupon the Lord being moved, asketh our prophet whether he did not see what they did, even such things as would cause him to depart from them, and to leave them to the spoil of enemies. They intended not to drive God out of the sanctuary, but that was the sequel and fruit of their abominations.

"That I should go far off from my sanctuary." The Hebrew runs thus; To go far from the sanctuary; not, I should go: and so some refer it to the people that worshipped Baal; and so those who pervert, corrupt the worship of God, go from the sanctuary; they go from God, and have nothing to do with him. But I conceive it refers to God, who would leave the sanctuary, because of the pollutions and corruptions in it.

Obs. 1. That where God's pure worship is, there is his presence. God had given them pure ordinances in the temple, and there he was; 2 Kings xix. 15, he dwelt "between the cherubims." They were upon the ark of the covenant in the sanctuary, where God manifested himself, and gave out oracles to those who sought him; hereupon David, Psal. xxvii. 4, desired to "dwell in the house of the Lord, to behold the beauty of the Lord, and to inquire in his temple;" there he saw the beautiful face of God, and heard his sweet voice. God is in his own ordinances, when the temple is measured out, and the holy city built, according to God's mind; and then the name shall be Jehovah-shammah, "The Lord is there," Ezek. xlviii. 35; and the churches, whilst golden candlesticks, Christ is in the midst of them.

Obs. 2. Corruptions, abominations in worship, cause the Lord to leave his people, to depart from his sanctuary. They brought in heathenish altars, set up Baal, and removed God's altar out of its place; and hereupon God forsakes his dwelling-place, his presence, protection, counsel, countenance, blessings, are all withdrawn from them. And woe is to that people when God goeth out of the sanctuary! if outward calamities do not ruin them, spiritual judgments undo them. But see the mischief of false worship, men's additions and mixtures with the pure ordinances of the Lord; they are as smoke to God's eyes, vinegar and gall to his taste, abominations to his Spirit; if they must go into his house, he will go out of it: when the ark comes in, Dagon goes down; and when Dagon comes in, the ark goes out. In Christ's time the temple was a den of thieves, and Jehovah was not amongst them. It is needful therefore to stand, contend for pure ordinances and divine worship.

Obs. 3. Men may have ordinances, and forms of worship, without God in them. They had the sanctuary, altars, sacrifices, when God was gone from them, yea, far from them; as they had corrupt ordinances, so powerless ordinances, there was nothing of God, Christ, or his Spirit in them. When God is out of the sanctuary, it matters not who is there, or what is done there, all is to little purpose: 1 Kings xix. 11, 12, there was a wind, an earthquake, a fire, but God was in neither of them; and let there be priests and Levites, sacrifice and incense, preaching and praying, God is not in them.

Obs. 4. There are degrees of sins; abominations

great, and greater; sins of ignorance are of a low nature, sins of knowledge higher; the more of the head and heart is in a sin, the worse, the greater, it is; knowledge and will do edify sin much. David's murder, Peter's denial of Christ, were sins more heinous than others which they committed.

Obs. 5. God discovers sins by degrees, not all at once; he had shown him great abominations, and Christ bids him turn, and he should see greater abominations. Sins are not all committed at once, nor all discovered at once, they grow by degrees, and are discovered by degrees. Abominations in kingdoms and churches lie wrapt up in the mantle of secrecy and darkness, but God hath his times to discover and make them known to the sons of men. Hosea ii. 10, "Now will I discover her lewdness." Ephraim had sinned, added abomination to abomination, lewdness to lewdness, and they had been covered up for a season, but now the discovering time was come, several murders and adulteries were brought to light. Ephraim and Samaria's sins were made known when Israel was to be healed, Hosea vii. 1. When God would come and cover the wounds of his own people, then the wickedness of their enemies is laid open. It is evident in our days God hath been upon healing England, and the sins of many have been discovered.

Estates and churches are like bodies full of gross and noxious humours, stir them a little, and they appear, to the danger of the whole.

Ver. 7—12. *And he brought me to the door of the court; and when I looked, behold a hole in the wall. Then said he unto me, Son of man, dig now in the wall: and when I had digged in the wall, behold a door. And he said unto me, Go in, and behold the wicked abominations that they do here. So I went in and saw; and behold every form of creeping things, and abominable beasts, and all the idols of the house of Israel, pourtrayed upon the wall round about. And there stood before them seventy men of the ancients of the house of Israel, and in the midst of them stood Jaazaniah the son of Shaphan, with every man his censer in his hand; and a thick cloud of incense went up. Then said he unto me, Son of man, hast thou seen what the ancients of the house of Israel do in the dark, every man in the chambers of his imagery? for they say, The Lord seeth us not; the Lord hath forsaken the earth.*

These verses contain the second part of the prophet's new vision: where,

I. You have a new discovery of more idolatry in ver. 7, 8, 9, and beginning of ver. 10.

II. A description of it, in ver. 10, 11.

III. The ground of all their vile practices, ver. 12, "They say, The Lord seeth not."

I shall open what hath any difficulty, and so give you the observations.

"The door of the court." Another door than that in ver. 3. It was the door of the Levites' or priests' court, into which none might come that were not of the tribe of Levi; and herein the sin of the priests and people is aggravated, that the priests suffered any to come in there who should not, and that the people durst venture into that holy place, or bring their abominations so near the Lord.

"Dig in the wall, and, behold, a door." The door of the court being shut, he spies a hole, and upon command, digging in that, finds another door about the gates of the wall, "chambers," Ezek. xl. 10, for the door-keepers and Levites, who had their weekly courses of administration, 1 Chron. xxiii. 28; Luke i. 8. And it is likely this door in the wall was a back-door, by which the priests, Levites, and others, entered into their chambers and chapels of imagery, secretly; and our prophet entering in at this door, sees their gross and brutish idolatry.

There they had pictured upon the walls the forms of all things which creep, and of beasts. God had forbidden the Jews to make themselves any images, but now they not only had images, set them in private, but also in public and holy places, and those of the basest sort; crocodiles, cats, moles, beetles, which creatures the Egyptians worshipped, they had portrayed there.

"Abominable beasts." The Hebrew is, of animal abomination. No creatures of God are abominable in themselves; some prohibited by the law were unclean for such and such uses, but yet good in themselves; the picturing of them and others made them abominable. And I conceive abomination refers rather to the form of the creature which they worshipped, than to the creature itself, and may be read thus, Every form of creeping thing, and of beast, is abomination; and secondarily, the creatures abominable, for their form's sake, which were worshipped.

"Seventy men of the ancients of the house of Israel." In Numb. xi. 16, God bids Moses gather seventy of the elders together; which done, he joined them with Moses, to help him to bear the burden of the people; these seventy made a standing senate, or their sanhedrim. There were six out of every tribe, which amounted to seventy-two, but were called the seventy; as in Luke x. 1, they are called the seventy disciples, but in the Syriac it is seventy-two. These met in a great court near the sanctuary, called *Synedrion*, from their sitting there; and this was the great council, to which were admitted those that were wise, afraid to sin, meek and able. Their qualifications are set down, Exod. xviii. 21; Deut. i. 13. And to these, hard and weighty matters were brought to judge of, as defection of tribes, false prophets, war, and such like. Now this council, these seventy, were so degenerate, that they were become idolaters, and offered incense to idols.

Some think they were all priests, because every man was with his censer in his hand; but then it should have been seventy men of the tribe of Levi, not of the ancients of Israel; and besides, it is known that the sanhedrim consisted not all of priests, but some out of every tribe.

"In the midst of them stood Jaazaniah the son of Shaphan." Who this Jaazaniah was is uncertain. Deodate, in his notes upon the place, is mistaken; he saith the name is no where else mentioned, whereas you shall find it twice more, in 2 Kings xxv. 23; Jer. xxxv. 3. There were divers Jaazaniahs; this in the prophet is said to be the son of Shaphan, who, it is probable, was that Shaphan the scribe in Josiah's days, 2 Kings xxii. 12, grandfather or uncle to Gedaliah, whom the king of Babylon left governor in Judea, Jer. xl. 5, 11: so that Gedaliah and Jaazaniah were near of kin, of great place, whether a priest, or some chief ruler. He stood in the midst of the seventy, as being principal; for the chief in wisdom they set over the rest of the sanhedrim, and called him *nasi*, the prince, they sitting in the form of a half moon before him, or about him. His name signifies hearkening of, or to, the Lord, whom, had he remembered, he would not have been found in such service.

"A thick cloud of incense went up." Hebrew is, abundance of a cloud of in- עתר

cense; that is, the smoke of the incense was so thick, that it seemed a cloud.

Incense or perfume was made of sweet and costly things, and was a token of worship, yea, chief worship, saith Calvin. Anciently they burnt sweet wood, and with the smoke thereof worshipped their gods. It is like the heathens learned it from Moses, who was appointed of God to burn incense to him, Exod. xxv. 6; xxx. 7, 8. The entrails of beasts boiled, or roasted, the heathens did burn unto their gods at first, but afterwards used incense. Tully saith, that to the statues set up for Caius Marius they burned frankincense or incense, and wax candles, which were in honour thereof. In the primitive times, when they forced the christians to idolatry, they would have them throw a little frankincense into the fire, which was a token of worship.

Obs. 1. That idolaters ofttimes act closely, and cover up their works from the eyes of the world. They had their imagery in chambers and secret places, it was walled up, and unobvious to most eyes. Some covers and pretences such persons always have for their superstitions and idolatries: they cover them with their good intentions, great devotion, religion of their forefathers, such as have some pomp and state; there are in them such objects as help their memories and affections. There is, say they, some truth, some good, and the rest may be borne with; those that worship so, prosper, and are at ease in their way, they meet not with those temptations and troubles others do.

Obs. 2. Such ways of wickedness cannot be carried so close, but there will be some espial of them. Let them make walls to cover them up, yet Providence will order it so, that there will be a hole in the wall, some crevice to look through at and discern their doings; the mystery of iniquity could not work so closely, but it was discerned.

Peter Soave found a hole in the walls of Rome, and discovered the pope's practices to hinder reformation of errors in the council of Trent. The secret plottings and conveyances to bring in popery amongst us by Jesuits and others, were espied, detected, and in due time disappointed.

Obs. 3. To find out exactly the great evils and abominations in states and churches, much pains must be taken. The prophet must dig, and dig in the wall. Their idolatry was fortified and walled up, and clear knowledge of it could not be attained without great toil.

The popish idolatry hath been so walled up by Romish champions, that it cost our worthies and prophets, Whitaker, Reynolds, Perkins, Amess, and others, much digging to discover the ill-favouredness of their imagery. Their strong arguments are answered, and popery hath a black face. And not only in this particular must there be digging to find out the mischief thereof, but also in others. It hath cost this parliament digging to find out the evil in prelacy and malignancy in the land.

Obs. 4. Such is the force of superstition and idolatry, that men engaged therein go further, and grow worse. They were not content with the image of jealousy, but they had forms of creeping things and abominable beasts to worship: they multiplied abominations, Ezek. xvi. 51, and had painted gods upon the wall round about, or, as the Hebrew is, about and about, double ranks of gods; superstition knows no end. We were of late in this kingdom got into the paths of superstition, and walked daily further and further therein; they had gotten all gods but the true God.

Obs. 5. Idolatry is a grievous sin, it is abomination, and the Lord therefore calls the prophet to see what they did, that he might be a witness of so great and grievous a sin as that was: and the grievousness of it lies in this;

(1.) That they had forsaken the true God.

(2.) Had changed the glory of the uncorruptible God into the forms of creeping things, beasts abominable.

(3.) That they had brought them into the holy place, even where God's holy ordinances ought to be.

(4.) That they had driven God out of his holy place.

(5.) That the chief men were drawn away, and offered incense to those dunghill gods.

(6.) That they said, "The Lord seeth us not."

(7.) That they looked for help from those helpless gods.

Obs. 6. Note here, that idolatry infatuates wise men. The ancients of Israel were become idolaters; those that were the counsellors and judges, that should have maintained the true worship of God, encouraged others by their counsel and example not to cleave to false worship, but to the true and living God, that should have punished idolaters with death according to the law of Moses, even they become brutish, they worship forms of creeping things; they disclaim the infinite, glorious, great, holy, and wise God, even the God of Israel, and adore bats, moles, &c.: a just hand of God upon men, to whom, because they receive not the truth with the love of it, or the love of the truth, God sends strong delusions, that they believe lies.

Obs. 7. There is consent in wickedness and false worship. Seventy of them are of one mind; they take censers, and offer incense to base dunghill gods; all the people break off their ear-rings to make a calf. Psal. lxxxiii. 5, "They have consulted together with one consent;" the Hebrew is, with one heart; "and are confederate against thee;" hearty consultation, and hearty confederation against God and his worship. Rev. xiii. 3, "And all the world wondered after the beast, and worshipped the dragon."

Obs. 8. See the cunning of idolaters. The priests, that most usually are first in such ways, they draw in the great ones to countenance their ways, they let them offer incense with their own hands, which was a violence to the priesthood; and they do all in darkness, that so objections may be prevented, some great mysticalness be conceited to be in those ways, which may breed reverence and esteem of them in the hearts of lower persons.

Obs. 9. Idolatrous and superstitious persons are expensive to maintain their worship. Here was much incense burnt to their idols, "a thick cloud went up." In Exod. xxxii. 3, where their idolatry first began after their coming out of Egypt, how prodigal were they of their jewels and ear-rings to make a false god! Egyptian jewels given them for adornation, they make an object of adoration. And when they had made them golden and silver gods, of which God complains, Ezek. xvi. 17, their prodigality ceased not there, but they were at daily charges to honour and maintain them: they decked the high places with garments of divers colours, they covered the gods with broidered garments, they bestowed oil, incense, fine flower, and honey, upon them; yea, they sacrificed their sons and daughters unto them, Ezek. xvi. 18—20.

The papists are profuse in their superstitious worship; the churches of some saints are so stuffed with vowed presents and memories, that they are fain to hang their cloisters and churchyards with them.

It is the nature of idolatry and adultery to be prodigal. If adulterers think nothing too much for their harlots, idolaters think nothing too much for their false worship.

Obs. 10. God appeals to man in a case of great ingratitude and wrong done unto him. They were unthankful for all the great things God had done, they gave that honour which was due unto the Divine Majesty unto images and idols, whereupon saith God to Ezekiel, "Son of man, hast thou seen what the ancients of Israel do?" Judge thou of it; should not they, being aged, lifted up to honour, invested with power, prevent and punish such sins in a church and state as here are committed? should not they counsel and lead others by their example to serve me, the only true and living God? should it not be so? I appeal to thee to make judgment of it. But they do otherwise; are not the ancients become idolaters? have they not chambers of imagery? are there not censers in their hands? seest thou not the smoke of the incense going up? What thinkest thou, are not these worthy of death themselves for these sins, who should put others to death for the like? Speak thy mind, I appeal to thee in this case; the injury is so notorious, thou canst not but condemn them, and justify me. It is frequent in Scripture for God in such cases to appeal to man and other creatures, Isa. v. 3; Jer. ii. 12; Deut. xxxii. 1. Appeals are relief to the hearts of those that are wronged and grieved, and God in this case deals after the manner of men.

Obs. 11. False worship is a work of darkness. Idolaters have corners, chambers, dark places; these seventy were in the dark, and did the works of darkness. Idolatry is called a "work of the flesh," Gal. v. 19, 20, and all works of the flesh are darkness.

The heathens had their *opertanea et tenebrosa sacra*, occult and dark worship.

Truth loves the light, but error and iniquity, darkness; John iii. 20, evil-doers hate the light, they hide up themselves and their ways. These seventy had power in their hand, yet durst not justify their works openly, but carried all closely; but how close soever sinners are, God sees them. Those words, "In the chambers of his imagery," some render it, in the secret of their own imaginations; which shows, that whatever are the thoughts, workings, and imaginations of men's hearts, the Lord sees them, and can discover them.

Lavater.
Calvin.

Idolaters have strong thoughts in their hearts of the ways they are in, of some mystery and excellency in them, which the vulgar know not; but let men be ignorant of them, the Lord sees them. Isa. xxix. 15, men think to hide their counsels, thoughts, practices from the Lord, but he sees the deceitfulness of their hearts, the wickedness in them; and because they carry things close, he searches, he tries them what they are, Jer. xvii. 9, 10.

They had idols in their chambers, and idols in their hearts.

Obs. 12. That atheism, unbelief, and pride, are the causes of men's going out from God, and falling to idolatrous and other sinful, vile practices; for they say, "The Lord seeth us not, he hath forsaken the earth." Atheism denies his presence, infidelity his assistance, and pride carries them out for help elsewhere, and tacitly lays the blame upon God: He hath left the caring of us, we are in the midst of dangers, and must seek for protection from some deity or other. And if it be a sin, he may thank himself; if he had not forsaken us we would not have forsaken him, chosen any other; but we are necessitated to it. Here is the pride of idolaters; and in Jer. xviii. 15, all these are included in one word, "Because my people hath forgotten me, they have burned incense to vanity." They forgot God, and hereupon became atheistical, unbelieving, and proud.

Ver. 13, 14. *He said also unto me, Turn thee yet again, and thou shalt see greater abominations that they do. Then he brought me to the door of the gate of the Lord's house which was toward the north; and, behold, there sat women weeping for Tammuz.*

Here you have a third part of the prophet's new vision, containing yet greater abominations than before; which is set out,

I. From the place, "The door of the gate of the Lord's house." It was the priests' court, and at the entrance into the Lord's house, and the nearer they sinned to the Lord's house, the greater was the wickedness.

II. The nature of the abomination, "Women sat there weeping for Tammuz." It was not according to law for any to be in that court, at that gate, but priests only. Now here were women, and women sitting and weeping, and that for Tammuz; which were greater abominations than what were before.

What or who this Tammuz was, must be opened unto you; the word is not mentioned elsewhere.

Some rabbies say this Tammuz was a hollow idol, with eyes of lead under which they used to put fire, and the heat melting the leaden eyes, the idol seemed to weep, and so moving compassion in the women, they became co-weepers with it; but the text saith not the idol wept, but that the women wept. Shindler saith the idols had their prophets, and this Tammuz was one of the idolatrous prophets, whom the king slew. In honour of him was set up an idol, so called from his name, or because on the first day of the month Thamuz they did celebrate his festivity: the seventeenth day of this month they fasted for the breach of the tables of the law, and on the first, feasted, and brake the law itself most abominably.

R. David.
R. Solomon.

The Vulgate translation reads it, Adonis, and many interpreters so carry it. Adonis was son of Cinara, king of Cyprus, a great lover of pleasures, chiefly of garden delights; whence arose the proverb, *Adonidis horti*, the gardens of Adonis, which were curious and choice, but soon fading away.

This Adonis was a great lover of Venus, and being unhappily slain by a boar, great lamentation was made for him; and the rather because he had a sweet voice, and delighted men and women with his singing, from whence his name seems to be given him; and by the lovers of music amongst them he was accounted for a god, and yearly solemnities instituted for him, in which were the weepings of women.

Adonis ἀπο τῦ ἀδειν, a Canendo.

Lucian in his Dialogues saith, that yearly in memory of Adonis's death by a boar, they did beat themselves and weep; after which, they sacrificed to Adonis as dead; and a day after, they, thinking him alive, shaved their heads, and those women who would not do it, were to prostitute their bodies to all strangers for a day, and the gain gotten was given in sacrifice to Venus.

De dea Syria.

Plutarch saith, women did bring to the solemnities of Adonis images like dead bodies, and, wailing, sang funeral verses.

In vita Alcibiad.

Maternus Firmicus tells us that an image was put in a bed, bewailed by many; and they having satisfied themselves with weeping, a light was brought in, and the faces of all that wept were anointed, and these words softly pronounced, Trust in the god, he will deliver us from our miseries; and so they unbed the idol with much joy.

Others make Tammuz to be Osiris, husband, brother, or son of Isis, (for authors vary about it,) and king of

Theod. Scalig. de emendat temp. Lactant. divin. instit. l. 1. c. 21.

Poeticum Dictionarium. In verbo Apis. Plut. lib. de Isid. et Osirid.

Egypt, the same with Apis or Serapis, who, coming into Egypt, and teaching them civility, and how to dress vines, was chosen their king; and having governed them well, at his death was honoured as a god under the form of a black ox. Suidas saith, he was an Egyptian god, worshipped for the moon's sake. The Egyptians called this god Tammuz, or Ammuz, which signifieth in their language, hidden, because the sacred things of this idol were covered and secret.

Ludovicus Vives, in his notes upon August. de Civ. Dei, l. 6. c. 10, tells us, that Osiris was torn in pieces by his brother Typhon; (which some say was for his whoredom with Isis, wife of Typhon, and all his members thrown into Nilus;) this fact greatly afflicted Isis, who with much search and labour got the dispersed members of Osiris again, which caused great joy in her. Hereupon she appointed a set time for seeking of Osiris, with weeping and howling.

Some affirm, Isis buried Osiris's members, being found, in a fenny island near Memphis, which she called Stix, whither went certain mitred persons at set times to mourn and weep: and a goodly ox appearing unto them, they thought it Osiris, whereupon the Egyptians adore an ox for their god, and call it Apis Osiris: this idol being brought to the temple, was their Tammuz. Junius fetches it from a root which signifies to burn, inflame, and thinks thereby is meant the god of the Phœnicians, which is the god of harvest and hot weather; but we may add also, that his worshippers were inflamed with lust and heat, with the fire of concupiscence, they forgot all bounds of modesty. He conceives it to be the same with Osiris (which signifies blessed, or enlightening all things) and with Adonis.

מוא

"Women sat there." These women were the she-priests of Isis, and did wear linen garments, and performed many of their wretched rites in woven houses, of which you read, 2 Kings xxiii. 7; the word "hangings" in the Hebrew is houses; women that lived in filthy houses, did weave those houses, or tents, to cover the lewdness of other women when they came to honour Tammuz. There dwelt near to this idol, youths, the servants of Tammuz, which were for all naughtiness; and now at the temple was practised sodomy and all uncleanness; there were houses of sodomites by the house of the Lord.

"Weeping for Tammuz." For his death, many tears were bestowed upon this idol; and being the same with Adonis, is etymologized thus, The lord or god of sorrow. And Theocritus calls him the god honoured with tears; and also the god worthy of threefold love, which they expressed not only in their tears, but in the vilest adoration.

Obs. 1. That when men leave the true God and his worship, they fall upon, and fetch in, any gods; inventions and abominations are increased. If they have gods of their own making, that sufficeth not, but they will have gods other nations have made; therefore it is said, "Turn thee yet again, and thou shalt see greater abominations."

Judg. v. 8, "They chose new gods." Micah had a house of gods, Judg. xvii. 5. Judah had as many gods as cities, Jer. ii. 28.

The Jews, after once they fell to idolatry, were not contented with one or two gods, but had a multiplicity of gods. Baal-peor, of the Moabites, Numb. xxv. 3. Ashtoreth, the goddess of the Zidonians, 1 Kings xi. 5. Chemosh, the god of the Moabites, 1 Kings xi. 33. Milcom, the abomination of the Ammonites, 2 Kings xxiii. 13. Molech, the abomination of Ammon, 1 Kings xi. 7. Baal-zebub, the god of Ekron, 2 Kings i. 2. Baal, 1 Kings xvi. 31. The gods of Syria, and the gods of the Philistines, Judg. x. 6. The gods of the children of Seir, 2 Chron. xxv. 14. The gods of Damascus, 2 Chron. xxviii. 23. These, with other gods, they had, yet were not content with them, but sought after more, the gods of Edom, 2 Chron. xxv. 20.

The Romans had a temple called Pantheon, wherein they worshipped all gods; only the God of Israel they had not, neither would have, because he must be worshipped alone, and they would not reject all their other gods for one.

Thus is it with Rome; they are not satisfied and settled in their old way, but still multiply saints, orders of friars, Jesuits, articles of faith, and an infinity of intricate dumb ceremonies.

Obs. 2. That false worship and filthiness do usually go together, spiritual and corporal whoredom, idolatry and adultery. These she-servants of Isis wept for Tammuz, but were wanton, lewd with the men that looked to this idol. Houses for all uncleanness were near the temple, and this idol.

Obs. 3. Idolatry spreads unto both sexes; not only men are drawn away to that sin, but the women also, they sat before Tammuz. Idolaters fetch in many gods, he-gods and she-gods; Ashtoreth was a goddess, and the Grecians think Tammuz or Osiris was not a man, but their goddess Ceres; and these gods or goddesses draw persons of all sorts and sexes unto them: Jer. xliv. 9, their wives are taxed for their idolatry.

Obs. 4. Women could weep for Tammuz, Osiris, who for his filthiness justly suffered; they supposed him wronged, and therefore laid out their hearts for him. How much more should we weep for the great and glorious God, who unjustly suffers by all sinners in the world! They wept for an idol, for remembrance of a wicked wretch, when their tears did neither themselves nor the idol good: if we weep for God and his wrong, it will please him, profit us. David did so, Psal. cxix. 136, "Rivers of waters run down mine eyes, because they keep not thy law."

Obs. 5. Idolatry, which is a shameful thing, makes persons shameless. These persons discovered their nakedness to the idol, and offered themselves to commit filthiness with Tammuz. Who could have believed that the Jews, instructed in the law of Moses, would have fetched in such an idol, so beastly, from the Egyptians; and that Jewish women should so far forget the law of God, and the law of nature, as to prostitute themselves in so obscene a manner to so filthy an idol as this was? but idolatry besots, and God in justice gives up to a reprobate sense, Rom. i. 25, 26, 28.

Dominus apertionis.

Idolatry is shameful; Hosea ix. 10, "They went to Baal-Peor, and separated themselves unto that shame." It was a shameful idol, and made them shameless; for it is judged they did also before this idol discover their nakedness.

Sands in his Europæ Speculum, p. 19.

Among papists, where idolatry is in countenance, modesty is in disgrace; priests and friars strive to exceed each other in impudence, and what elsewhere would not be tolerated, in Italy is in high honour; and what in other places a loose person would be ashamed to confess, that priests and friars there refrain not openly to practise.

Ver. 15, 16. *Then said he unto me, Hast thou seen this, O son of man? turn thee yet again, and thou shalt see greater abominations than these. And he brought me into the inner court of the Lord's house, and, behold, at the door of the temple of the Lord, between the porch and the altar, were about five and twenty men, with their backs toward the temple of the Lord, and their faces toward the east; and they worshipped the sun toward the east.*

In ver. 15 is a transition to the last part of the vision, lying in ver. 16. And this abomination, yet greater than the former of the image of jealousy, the mixed forms of beasts, and creeping things, than Tammuz, is described,

I. From the place in general, "The inner court." More particularly, "The door of the temple." And yet more specially, "Between the porch and the altar."

II. The persons with their number, "Five and twenty men."

III. Their posture, "With their backs toward the temple of the Lord, and their faces toward the east."

IV. Their act, "They worshipped the sun."

This idolatry was in the temple itself, and acted by the chiefest persons. It is conceived these twenty-five were the king and his council; there were two tribes left, and twelve out of each, with the king, made up that number. It is thought these twenty-five are mentioned again in chap. xi. 1, where two princes are named, and therefore probable to be the king and his nobles, the chief and heads of the people. These stood "between the porch and the altar," which was near to the *sanctum sanctorum*, and where the priests used to weep and pray, especially in times of common calamities, Joel ii. 17.

"With their backs toward the temple of the Lord," &c. The temple was so built that the *sanctum sanctorum* was in the western part of it, the entrance into it in the eastern part, and when any service was done by the people or priests, in prayer or sacrifice, they did it with their faces westward towards the ark and holiest of holies, and their backs were eastward; which the Lord in wisdom ordered to be so, that he might prevent eastern and sun-worship, which was the practice of the gentiles; whereupon saith Job, chap. xxxi. 26, "If I beheld the sun when it shined," if I looked upon it to adore it as others did; it was the practice then. Of it speaks Mercurius Trismegistus, (In fine Asclepii.) when the sun rose they minded the east, but when it set they would not look westward, lest seeing their God dying, *in cultu ejus tepescerent*, they should become remiss in his worship. And Vitruvius saith, (Lib. de Arch. 4.) their temples were so built, that they might pray looking to the sun rising. The learned observe, that the Sidonians, Grecians, Romans, Assyrians, Egyptians, and Persians, did all worship the sun, each giving a several name to this god of theirs. The Persians, especially, honoured and stood for this god, whom they called Mithra, that is, Lord or mighty; for in the year 612, when Heraclius the emperor sent to Cosroe king of the Persians for peace, his answer was, he would not lay down arms till he had brought him to worship the sun; but Heraclius prevailed in the wars, and burned his idol temples of the sun. From whomsoever the Jews learned this custom, God had forbad them expressly to worship the sun, moon, and stars, Deut. xvii. 3, and appointed them to worship with their faces westward; yet they turn their backs upon God, as if he were unworthy of any respect from them, and looking towards the east, adore a creature which God had made to serve them.

Obs. 1. It is wisdom not to give way to any sin, but to stop sin in the birth, crush it in the conception. You see what abominations after abominations, greater and greater, come in here. Lesser sins make way for greater, superstition for idolatry, yea, the worst of idolatry, and other sins.

Obs. 2. That the nearer destruction, the worse they grow in church and state. All was out of order, great confusion amongst them; the land was filled with corruptions, the image of jealousy, chambers of imagery, houses for stews, were about the temple; Tammuz, a most abominable idol, set up, adored in it, women suffered to come there and do shameful things; the ancients offer incense to those who were no gods; the king and nobles come into the priests' court, turn their backs upon God; no priest had any zeal for God to reprove these things, but were deeply in themselves; the land filled with violence, their abominations greater and greater, and judgment at the door.

Obs. 3. That in corrupt times great persons are generally very profane. The twenty-five turn their backs upon God, slight him and his worship, disgrace, reproach the same. What greater indignity could they do to God, than to come into his temple, to the holy place, and there turn their backs upon him, and worship the sun in his presence: it is as if a woman should cast off her husband, and commit lewdness with another man before him.

When Jeremiah's roll was read, the king cut and cast it into the fire, which others consented unto, Jer. xxxvi. 23, 24. After, he and his agents cut in pieces the vessels of the house of God, shut up the doors of the temple, and would suffer the Lord to have no sacrifice, no incense, no priest; and when God distressed him for his wickedness, he sinned more and more, 2 Chron. xxvi. 22, 24. Belshazzar and his princes drank wine in the sacred bowls of the temple, and praised their idol gods, Dan. v. 2—3, 4. And not only in corrupt times are great ones profane, but even in reforming times; Neh. xiii. 17, the nobles of Judah profaned the sabbath, and increased wrath. Such profane acts God takes very ill, and will requite in their kind. "They have turned unto me the back, and not the face," Jer. xxxii. 33; and therefore "I will show them the back and not the face, in the day of their calamity," Jer. xviii. 17.

Obs. 4. That kings and princes are not to be patterns to us in point of religion and worship. If we will follow them, we may suddenly be led into idolatry. Here be twenty-five, the chief of the city and land, and they turn their backs upon the true God and his worship, and choose heathenish religion, and heathenish practices: the people were not bound to follow them. Great ones soonest go out of God's way. 2 Chron. xxiv. 19, 20, after Jehoiada's death, the princes came and bowed to Joash, gave ill counsel; and with them he hearkened, and they together leave the house of the Lord, his worship, and fell to false worship. Jeroboam, and all the kings and princes in Israel after him, went the wrong way, and never pleased or truly served God for hundreds of years together. We must not follow great ones in matters of religion, and say we will be of that religion the king or parliament are of. Great ones do greatly mistake in the things of God and religion. The princes of this world neither knew the wisdom of God, nor the Lord Christ, 1 Cor. ii. 7, 8; and to this day few of them do know the truth, "for not many wise, mighty, or noble are called," 1 Cor. i. 26. Therefore fetch your religion from Christ and the apostles, who gave out truths which came down from heaven, which embraced, will sanctify you, and fit you for heaven.

Obs. 5. That adoration towards the east was taken up from the heathens, the jews had it from them, and it was displeasing to God; and that practice crept in amongst christians. Tertullian saith, it was a known thing that the christians prayed with their faces toward the east; but the heathens stumbled at it, and said the christians' god was the sun. Some fathers held it an apostolical tradition, that christians should pray with their faces that way; but traditions of fathers are no warrant for worship, or postures in it: we have nothing from Christ or apostles leading us to do so, and from others we may not take up such a practice, though ancient, holy, and learned. Christ and the apostles were before them, more holy, more able than they, and in their writings and practices we find no such thing.

In Apolog.

Justin Mart. Basil. Greg.

The papists, and some among us, do yet plead for eastern worship; and would have christians look that way, because paradise is that way, because Christ was crucified with his face westward, because he who is the light of the world ascended to heaven there, and shall come again there. These are weak grounds to draw us from that liberty the word gives us, to a superstitious, jewish, heathenish practice, (for deliberately and determinately to do it, in reference to paradise or Christ, is no better;) 1 Tim. ii. 8, we have liberty to pray any where, and any way, so it be without wrath and doubting.

As this facing the east sprung from them, so it is as likely that the building of temples east and west, that the people may sit with their faces eastward, and burying of the dead with their heads unto the west, that they may rise with their faces eastward, came from them; however, it savours strongly of superstition, if not of heathenism, to do so.

Ver. 17. *Then he said unto me, Hast thou seen this, O son of man? Is it a light thing to the house of Judah that they commit the abominations which they commit here? for they have filled the land with violence, and have returned to provoke me to anger: and, lo, they put the branch to their nose.*

This verse hath in it the sum of all the evils before spoken of, and an addition of somewhat else; an appeal to the prophet for to be judge in it: Hast thou seen the image of jealousy, &c.? Is it a light thing? Give thy sentence *supra totam materiam*, upon the whole matter, that all these abominations are done in and about the temple: and besides, they have oppressed every where, wronged all sorts, "filled the whole land with violence:" and as if that were nothing, to provoke, to wrong, men, they return to the temple, and provoke me, "they put the branch to their nose."

זמורה

"The branch to their nose." The Hebrew word for a branch is rendered by some a sound, or song, as if they sung, and made a noise with their nose, in disgrace or contempt of God. Some render it a stink or ill savour, noting how unclean and loathsome idolaters are, that delight in impure sacrifices and corrupt worship, which are a stink in the nostrils of God and good men. We have it a "branch," pulled or cut from the tree, which is the proper sense of the word; it comes from that Hebrew root which signifies to cut, lop off: and so it is expressed, Numb. xiii. 24, the cluster or branch of grapes cut down.

זמר

For the better understanding of this expression, we must know that the heathens honoured their gods by dedicating certain trees unto them; and when they sacrificed, they adorned their altars and themselves with some boughs of those trees which were so dedicated unto them. To Jupiter the beech tree was sacred, to Minerva the olive, to Venus the myrtle tree, to Hercules the poplar, to Bacchus the ivy and vine, to Apollo the laurel.

Among the Thracians it was a law to wear garlands of ivy when they sacrificed. The Egyptians wore garlands of ivy and bays; and the Israelites here learned from them, had branches in their hands, which they took either from the altars or heads of the sacrifices or sacrificers; and after they had put them to the idol, or sprinkled them with the blood of these vile sacrifices, or sweetened them with some idolatrous perfume, they put them to their nostrils, and kissed them, in honour of the sun. It is conceived they were branches of the laurel which were dedicated to the sun; and that they carried these branches to their houses, and often they put them to their nose in memory and honour of the sun, by virtue of whose influence the laurel did grow and receive its sweet savour.

Some take it to be a proverbial speech, noting out they were authors of their own punishment and destruction; they sin, and put the branch to their nose, and this will be their destruction.

Obs. 1. The greatness or littleness of sin is to be measured, not by man's, but God's account of it. "Is it a light thing to the house of Judah?" They think it so, but it is otherwise. The interrogation sets out the greatness of it. Is it so? no, it is not light, but grievous. This expression sets out the weightiness of a thing; 1 Sam. xviii. 23, "Seemeth it to you a light thing to be a king's son in law?" no; it is a great matter for a poor man to be so advanced, whatever your thoughts are. And let men think sin a light matter, it is far otherwise, there is lead in it, and will weigh them down: 1 Kings xvi. 31, speaking of Ahab, the scripture saith, "And it came to pass, as if it had been a light thing for him to walk in the sins of Jeroboam the son of Nebat, that he took to wife Jezebel." The Hebrew is, Was it a light thing for him to commit the sins of Jeroboam? Yes, he thought so, esteemed them light, and went to serve Baal; but they were notorious, weighty sins, kingdom and church-destroying sins. Men pare and lessen their sins, they make little account of them: Prov. xiv. 9, "Fools make a mock at sin," as an inconsiderable matter; and chap. x. 23, "It is as sport to a fool to do mischief;" it is no heavy thing to his conscience, but a light thing like a feather, with which he can sport and play. Job xv. 16, "Man drinketh iniquity like water," he delights himself with sin like a fish, that draws in the water, and spouts it out again in a sporting way; so doth man, to him sin is sweet, delightsome, Job xx. 12, not burdensome. Matt. xxii. 5, when they refused Christ and his offers of grace, mercy, and salvation, when they sinned with a high hand, yet they made light of it, and went their ways. And in Isaiah, when they committed idolatry, fell to other gods, they looked upon it as a sporting business; Isa. lvii. 4, "Against whom do ye sport yourselves? against whom make ye a wide mouth, and draw out the tongue?" What men's thoughts are of their sins, you see; they weigh them in false balances, and make them light, but when they come to the balance of the sanctuary, they will be found heavy. Is it a light thing such abominations are in our land?

Obs. 2. To sin where God manifests his presence, and vouchsafes the means of grace and choice mercies, is a great aggravation of sin, and grievous provocation of divine majesty. Is it light that ye commit the abomination which ye commit "here," in the temple, the place of my presence, where I have given them mine ordinances, and do meet them for my worship; to set their idol of jealousy near that place, have their chambers of imagery, their Tammuz brought into the temple, and women weeping about that filthy idol, and men standing with their backs towards God, and worshipping the sun? This aggravated their sin, and provoked bitterly; here, here they do such things. Psal. cvi. 19, "They made a calf in Horeb." Was this more than if they had made it in Egypt, or some other place? Yes; Horeb was the same with mount Sinai; if you compare Deut. iv. 10, 11, with Exod. xix. 18, it is evident; and there God appeared, gave out the law, and made a covenant with them, Deut. v. 2; and it was called "the mount of God," 1 Kings xix. 8. Now here they made a calf, here they sinned, and this was a great aggravation of their sin; insomuch, that, Deut. ix. 8, Moses saith, "In Horeb ye provoked the Lord to wrath," even destroying wrath. So touching Gilgal, the Scripture speaks of Gilgal's wickedness, Hos. ix. 15, of sacrificing bullocks there, chap. xii. 11, and multiplying transgression there, Amos iv. 4. The Lord took their sins at Gilgal very heinously, and cause he had for it; at Gilgal were the twelve memorial stones of their passing over Jordan pitched, Josh. iv. 20; at Gilgal they were circumcised, and God rolled away the reproach of Egypt from them, Josh. v. 8, 9; there they had the passover, ver. 10: Gilgal being a place famous for these things, their sins at Gilgal did increase their reproach, and aggravate their villany. Where God hath manifested himself, and done remarkable things, sin there is double sin. Psal. cvi. 7, they "provoked him at the sea, even at the Red sea." Where God pitied them being in a great strait, where God showed his mighty power in dividing the seas, in leading the Israelites safely through, and in drowning the proud, cruel, bloody adversaries, yet there they provoked him, "at the sea, even the Red sea." So for Canaan, which was the holy land, "the land of uprightness," the land where God had shown and done great things for them, sin there hath an emphasis set upon it, Isa. xxvi. 10, there they deal unjustly. Ezek. xx. 28, "When I had brought them into the land, for the which I lifted up mine hand to give it to them;" (four times he accents their sins;) "there" they offer their sacrifices, "there" they present the provocation of their offerings, "there" they made their sweet savour, "there" they poured out their drink-offerings. God hath given us in this land, in this city, many choice mercies, done wonderful things for us; shall it be said, Here they commit sin, where the gospel and means of grace are, where they have lately entered into covenant with me, where they have seen my hand stretched out to do many great things? if it be so, there will be an accent upon our sins.

Obs. 3. Violence is a spreading sin. "They have filled the land with violence," with wrong, injustice, oppression. The princes had violent hands, they oppressed and exacted of the people, Ezek. xlv. 8, 9. "The rich men, they are full of violence," Micah vi. 12, and wronged the poorer sort. Servants were infected with this sin, and "filled their masters' houses with violence and deceit," Zeph. i. 9. The priests, they violated the law, Zeph. iii. 4; Ezek. xxii. 26; they corrupted it with their glosses, forced interpretations, constructions such as God never put into it; they set by the law, and set up their own inventions, wills, traditions, by which the law was made void. Thus violence had filled the land, the city, the sanctuary, and ran through all sorts of men. If freedom from this sin had been any where, it is probable in Jerusalem some should have been found free; but, Zeph. iii. 1, "Woe to the oppressing city;" and, Jer. vi. 6, "She is wholly oppression in the midst of her." Not only oppressing, but oppression, she was thoroughly grown and perfect in that sin; and not only oppression, but wholly oppression, nothing remaining in her but oppression, and this evident, visible; in the midst of her, princes, priests, rich, servants, poor, oppress, wrong, offer violence one to another: Jer. v. 1, "Run, see, seek, if there be any that executeth judgment;" all were for violence, none for justice.

Obs. 4. Injustice is abomination unto God, and the more it spreads, the greater abomination it is. The Lord calls them abominations, for they have filled the land with violence. Violence in the princes was abomination, violence in the priests was abomination, oppression in the rich was abomination, injustice in their judges was abomination, injury and wrong in their servants and officers was abomination, and all these amounted to abominations.

Injustice and violence are crying sins; Isa. v. 7, "The Lord looked for judgment, but behold oppression; for righteousness, but behold a cry;" there were hundreds and thousands crying, because their orchards and vineyards were taken from them, their wages detained, and themselves and their houses ready to be swallowed up by the mouths of the violent. The word for oppression, "Behold oppression," in Hebrew, is a scab, a wound, למשפט
a leprosy; when a body is free from והנה משפח
these, it is beautiful, but when overrun with these, it is loathsome. Injustice was a scab, adherent to the Jews, and made them abominable; oppression was a wound, and made them incurable; violence a leprosy, and caused them to be separated from the sight of God.

Is our state free from this sin? may we not fear God looked for "judgment, but behold oppression," a scab, a wound, a leprosy? Is not truth oppressed? are not the righteous and innocent oppressed? and may not many of us take up that of Job, chap. xix. 7, "Behold, I cry out of wrong, but I am not heard?" Let oppressors of others, be it in their names, liberties, estates, consciences, know, their sin is abomination to the Lord, and that there is a cry in heaven against them: the oppressed cry, "Break in pieces the oppressor," Psal. lxxii. 4, and judge the fatherless and oppressed, that the man of the earth may no more oppress.

Obs. 5. State oppression and church corruption go together; in the temple were pollutions, and in the land violence. The princes and judges they wronged men, the priests and prophets they wronged God; Zeph. iii. 3, 4, there you find them linked together; princes and judges oppressed the state, removed the bounds, the prophets and priests polluted the sanctuary, and violated the law; they break both tables. When one is eminently violated, breaches are quickly made upon the other. If there be violence in a land, there will be corruptions, pollutions, abominations in the sanctuary; if there be superstition, idolatry in the church state, there will be oppression, injustice, and spoil in the civil state: when the temple is a den of thieves, the land will be a den of oppressors and murderers, Jer. vii. 9, 11.

Obs. 6. Men's intentions to please God oft prove provocations of God. They intended not to provoke God, but returned in their apprehensions to worship God in the temple, and to please him; not their purpose, but the event was the provocation. So in ver. 6, their abominations drave God far from the sanctuary. They did not purpose and intend to drive God away, but that was the event and issue of their actions, with which they thought they pleased God.

Jer. vii. 9, 10, "Will ye steal, murder, and commit adultery, and swear falsely, and burn incense unto Baal, and walk after other gods whom ye know not; and come and stand before me in this house, and say, We are delivered?" They returned from their vile and sinful practices to God's house, and thought by their sacrifices and prayers to please the Lord, when-as in truth they provoked him greatly, as you may see in ver. 12, 14, 15, where he tells them he will destroy the temple as he did Shiloh, cast them out as he did their brethren, the whole seed of Ephraim, and forbids the prophet to lift up a cry or prayer for them, ver. 16. So in Isa. i. 13, 14, that which they did to please God was vain, abomination, iniquity, trouble, hateful, such as he could not away with. Nadab and Abihu thought not to provoke God with their strange fire, but did to their own ruin, Numb. iii. 4. John xvi. 2, They shall put you out of the synagogues, and think they do God good service when they kill you, saith Christ; but they provoke God against their own souls. Isa. vii. 12, Ahaz thought it would please God not to ask a sign, but it was otherwise. Matt. xxiii. 29—31, they thought they did well in building the tombs of the prophets, and garnishing them, but thereby they provoked God more against themselves.

Obs. 7. God sets a special mark upon those that do put the branch to their nose; "Lo, they put the branch to their nose." Such are,

(1.) Those who adorn idols and images. Isa. xxx. 22, they covered their images, and put ornaments upon them, but they were no better than a menstruous cloth; and Ezek. xvi. 16—18, they decked their high places with colours, jewels, and broidered garments. This provoked the Lord, and is branded with fornication, ver. 15, and abomination, ver. 22. Have not many among us gilded and adorned crosses, altars, crucifixes, &c.?

(2.) Those who find any content and delight in superstitious and idolatrous practices. Ezek. xvi. 18, 19, God tells them they had set his oil and incense before the image for a sweet savour; the Hebrew is, for a savour of rest; they were pleased, and rested in what they had done, thinking also that the idol was delighted therewith. Exod. xxxii. 6, they took pleasure in their new god, and danced about the golden calf. And such expressions as these you have, "Their heart went after their idols," Ezek. xx. 16; "Their eyes go a whoring after their idols," Ezek. vi. 9; "Inflamed with idols," Isa. lvii. 5; "Mad upon idols," Jer. l. 38: which do show the pleasure they had in these evils, and how God brands them for the same.

(3.) Those that acknowledge any blessings to be from saints and images. They here adored the sun as author of trees and fruits; and Jer. xliv. 17, 18, they burned "incense to the queen of heaven," and acknowledged their welfare and plenty to be from her. Papists at this day acknowledge the cure of many diseases to be from such and such saints.

(4.) Such as preserve relics in memorial of their images and gods. They touched the image with it, and put it to their noses in memorial of the sun. Deut. vii. 26, the silver and gold that was on the images they might not desire, or take unto them, lest they should be snared therein; no relics, though never so precious, were permitted them to take, they were abomination to God, and would be snares to them. Whence the rabbins observe, that the idol, and things which serve it, are offered to it, and made for it, are unlawful for any use. The papists abound with relics, and so with abominations.

(5.) Those who give divine honour to creatures. Psal. cvi. 19, "They worshipped the molten image." Jeroboam "sacrificed unto the calves that he had made," 1 Kings xii. 32, and said to the people, "Behold thy gods, O Israel, which brought thee up out of the land of Egypt," ver. 28. Here was divine honour given to dumb idols; but he is branded for this frequently, "Jeroboam, that made Israel to sin;" and 1 Kings xiii. 34, it is said, "this thing became sin unto the house of Jeroboam, even to cut it off, and to destroy it from off the face of the earth."

Obs. 8. Idolatrous worship is stinking, and brings destruction to the authors. Ver. 10, "All the idols," (in the Hebrew is, all the dunghill images) and image-worship, are dunghill, stinking, loathsome things to God and man, and they brought destruction upon the whole seed of Ephraim, even the ten tribes. Psal. xvi. 4, "Their sorrows shall be multiplied that hasten after another god." Jeroboam did so, 1 Kings xii.; and, chap. xiii. a prophet prophesieth against his altar and calvish gods, his hand was dried up; and, chap. xiv. 10, 11, most grievous things are threatened against him and his. Jer. vii. 18, 19, when they had sacrificed to the queen of heaven, "Do they provoke me to anger? saith the Lord: do they not provoke themselves to the confusion of their own faces?"

Ver. 18. *Therefore will I also deal in fury: mine eye shall not spare, neither will I have pity: and though they cry in mine ears with a loud voice, yet will I not hear them.*

Here is a sad epiphonema or conclusion; he had oft in the chapter called upon Ezekiel to see the doings, which being shown unto him, the Lord sounds in his ears what dreadful things he will do.

"Deal in fury," &c. The Scripture mentions God's anger, Psal. xxx. 5; his indignation, Psal. lxix. 24; his wrath, Isa. liv. 8; and his fury, Jer. x. 25: and these exceed each the other. Anger is the displeasure of God against sin; indignation is anger more intense, therefore, Isa. xxx. 30, it is called "indignation of his anger;" wrath is yet higher and permanent, according to that in Nahum i. 2, "He reserveth wrath for his enemies;" and fury is highest, Job xx. 23, "The fury of his wrath." In Jer. xxi. 5, fury and great wrath go together, and when God is in his fury, he rests not till he is revenged: Jer. vii. 20, "My fury shall be poured out upon this place, upon man, and upon beast, and upon the trees, fruit, and ground, and burn unquenchably." Ezek. xvi. 41, 42, When Jerusalem should be destroyed, then God would make his fury to be at rest.

"Mine eye shall not spare, neither will I have pity." Of these words hath been spoken before.

Obs. 1. There is a time when God, who is patient, gracious, and slow to wrath, will deal in fury; he that delights in exercising mercy, hath a time for fury, and trading in it; he that is patient and long-suffering, hath times of being furious.

When is it that God will deal in fury?

(1.) When lesser judgments will not serve turn. If he threaten in anger, smite in his indignation and wrath, and there be no good use made of those strokes, then will the Lord appear in fury. Lev. xxvi. God threatens them with sundry inferior judgments, and if they do not work, but still walk contrary to God, ver. 28, then saith God, "I will walk contrary unto you also in fury;" if they grew worse, God would be more violent and furious.

(2.) When a reformation is offered and refused. Jer. li. 9, "We would have healed Babylon, but she is not healed: forsake her, for her judgment reacheth unto heaven, and is lifted up even to the skies." So much fury should be poured out upon Babylon, that heaven, air, and earth should wonder at it: Ezek. xxiv. 13, 14, "Because I have purged thee, and thou wast not purged, thou shalt not be purged from thy filthiness any more, till I have caused my fury to rest upon thee. I the Lord have spoken it," &c. When God tenders a reformation to a people, it is great love, rich mercy; and mercy refused, is mercy abused, and that turns into fury: and God's fury shall not only be poured out against such a people, but rest upon them, which is much more.

(3.) When men are furious against God, his servants, and ways, when they cannot endure his prophets, saints, and ordinances, then is a time for God's fury to break out. When the husbandmen in the parable would not endure Christ's servants, nor himself, but beat and stoned them, then fury came forth, and miserable destruction was the portion of those men, Matt. xxi. 35, 36, 38, 41. When righteous Lot, being abused, was got out of Sodom, then God sent fire and brimstone upon it, and poured out his fury like fire, as it is in Nahum i. 6; and, 2 Chron. xxxvi. 16—18, they mocked the messengers of God, despised his words, misused his prophets, until the wrath of the Lord arose; and it rose very high, even to the height of fury, for he brought the king of Babylon in fury upon them, who slew their young men in the sanctuary, who had no compassion upon man or maiden, young or old; all men and things were given into his hand, all their glorious things were burned and laid waste.

(4.) When there is a general corruption in state and church, then the fury of the Lord will appear, then will he deal in fury, Gen. vi. 5, 6, 7, 13. This will appear more fully in the next observation.

Obs. 2. Oppressions in a state, superstition and idolatry in the church, do cause God to deal in fury. There was violence in the land, and the branch at their nose, and therefore God would deal in fury; Jer. xxi. 12, "O house of David, thus saith the Lord; Execute judgment in the morning, and deliver him that is spoiled out of the hand of the oppressor, lest my fury go out like fire, and burn that none can quench it." Where there is want of justice, there will be plenty of oppression; and where that is, the door is open for God's fury; it is kindled, and will break out against such a state, whatever it be. And for idolatry, see Ezek. xvi. 36, "Because thy filthiness was poured out, and thy nakedness discovered through thy whoredoms with thy lovers, and with all the idols of thy abominations;" ver. 38, "I will judge thee," saith God, "as women that break wedlock and shed blood are judged." And how is that? Lev. xx. 10; Gen. ix. 6, they were without mercy to be put to death; and so God would do: "I will give thee blood in fury and jealousy."

If these sins be amongst us, we have cause to tremble, for they will cause God to deal in fury, to cast upon us the fury of his wrath, as it is, Job xx. 23. They will cause fury to be upon our armies, Isa. xxxiv. 2; and Jer. xxi. 4—6, "Behold," saith the Lord, "I will turn back the weapons of war that are in your hands, wherewith ye fight against the king of Babylon, and against the Chaldeans, which besiege you without the walls, and I will assemble them into the midst of this city. And I myself will fight against you with an outstretched hand and with a strong arm, even in anger, and in fury, and in great wrath. And I will smite the inhabitants of this city, both man and beast; they shall die of a great pestilence." And those that die not, shall be mad, when they are made to drink of the cup of God's fury, Jer. xxv. 15, 16. God's fury is a trampling thing, Isa. lxiii. 3; a bloody thing, Ezek. xvi. 38; fiery and plentiful, he pours it out like fire, Lam. ii. 4. Therefore let us tremble, and prevent God's fury, which is so terrible; and do as is written, Jer. iv. 3, 4, "Break up your fallow ground, and sow not among thorns. Circumcise yourselves to the Lord, and take away the foreskins of your heart, ye men of Judah and inhabitants of Jerusalem: lest my fury come forth like fire, and burn that none can quench it, because of the evil of your doings."

Obs. 3. God's dealing in fury is dreadful, he will not spare, not pity, nor be moved to mercy: and is not this dreadful? You may think it is never so with God, but the Scripture saith it here, and in other places; Ezek. xxiv. 13, 14, "Thou shalt not be purged, till I have caused my fury to rest upon thee;" and whatever you commit, "I the Lord have spoken it: it shall come to pass, and I will do it; I will not go back, neither will I spare, neither will I repent; according to thy ways, and according to thy doings, shall they judge thee, saith the Lord God." Men are apt to think God is all mercy, but they will find it otherwise.

His eye that spared them in Egypt, that looked upon them and pitied them there, his eye will not spare, himself will not pity them in Zion. Their provocations were great; he that spared Ninevites will not spare Israelites.

When God deals in fury, there is no dealing with him then; he is a consuming fire, and nothing will prevail with him.

What if they cry, will not that prevail? Is not God a God hearing prayer, doth he not hear the cry of ravens? Jer. xi. 11, "Though they shall cry unto me, I will not hearken unto them." See Isa. i. 15; Micah iii. 8; Deut. i. 45.

What if Noah, Job, and Daniel should pray, would not God be entreated, pity, and spare them? see Ezek. xiv. 14, 18, 20. God forbade Jeremiah, chap. vii. 16, to pray for them; "Pray not thou for this people, neither lift up cry nor prayer for them, neither make intercession to me: for I will not hear thee." His ear is deaf, his heart is hardened, when he is in fury, and deals in it: fury lies in severity, where there is no sparing; in implacability, where is no hearing.

Obs. 4. That wicked men in their straits will cry to God, and cry aloud. When Nebuchadnezzar came, besieged the city, when plague and famine increased, then they fell upon their knees and cried to God for help; as malefactors, when the judge is ready to give sentence, cry out, and importune him to spare their lives. Such prayers are the voice of the flesh, not of the spirit, forced, not free, faithless and unseasonable prayers, coming too late, and therefore unacceptable. Let men therefore not defer seeking of God till necessity puts them upon it.

CHAPTER IX.

Ver. 1. ***He cried also in mine ears with a loud voice, saying, Cause them that have charge over the city to draw near, even every man with his destroying weapon in his hand.***

In the eighth chapter Ezekiel saw in a vision the sins of the city Jerusalem; here the vision proceeding, he sees the judgments of God to be executed upon them for those sins, and by whom.

The chapter contains,

I. A narration of judgment to be executed upon Jerusalem in the first seven verses.

II. The prophet's intercession for Israel, ver. 8.

III. An answer thereunto, ver. 9, 10.

IV. A report of what was done, ver. 11.

In the narration you have,

1. A commission given to the prophet to cause military men to appear, ver. 1.

2. Their number and manner of appearing, ver. 2.

3. A mandate given,

(1.) To mark the mourners, ver. 4.

(2.) To slay the rest, ver. 5—7.

4. Mention of the glory of God departing, ver. 3.

The first verse hath in it,

1. The author of this commission, "He."

2. The manner of giving it out, by way of cry, and that "with a loud voice."

3. The witness before whom it was done, and that was Ezekiel, "In mine ears."

4. The commission itself, "Cause them that have," &c.

Where we have,

(1.) The persons specified, and they are such as "have charge over the city."

(2.) What they are to do, "To draw near."

(3. The manner, "With a destroying weapon in each hand."

"He cried." Not an angel, but the Lord, whose glory he had seen at the temple, who had shown him the several abominations of the people, and who had authority to call for executioners of his fury upon these notorious delinquents.

"He cried." Crying in man is intense or loud speaking, when it is expressed by a loud voice; but God crieth not as man. His crying is the efficacy of his Spirit, or force of his providence, strongly moving the creature to the execution of his will. Zech. vii. 7, the Lord cried by the prophets, his Spirit moved them to cry unto the people: and 2 Sam. xvi. 10, God said unto Shimei, "Curse David;" that is, Divine Providence moved him to do so. God cries to the ministers of justice, when he moves their wills to come and do execution upon a sinful people. Here God spake to the prophet, not providentially, but by the inward language of his Spirit, and visionally.

The reasons of his calling or crying aloud were,

1. To declare the weightiness of the thing he was now about; namely, to bring a final destruction upon church and state, according to that, chap. vii. 6, "An end is come;" and this was a business of high concernment, that that people which had been so beloved, so honoured, so delivered, so observed in the world, should now be utterly ruined. So when the seven thunders were to be, the angel, Rev. x. 3, "cried with a loud voice."

2. God's serious intentions to destroy them. He was impatient now of bearing any longer with them, he was burdened, wearied with their iniquities, therefore cried out of them, and called for destroyers; Isa. i. 24, "Ah, I will ease me of mine adversaries."

3. To quicken and hasten the instruments he should use in that service. When great persons are intense in their voices and commands, it edges their spirits who are employed, and makes them quick, active: loud cries leave deep impressions.

4. In reference to the wicked's sins, and mourners' prayers. The sins of the one, and prayers of the other, cried aloud in God's ears, and now God cries too, and adds cry to cry; they cried for vengeance, and vengeance they shall have. Come, Ezekiel, send for such and such men, which may destroy the wicked, and deliver the mourners.

"In mine ears." That is, I hearing; the Lord spake aloud, and the prophet heard him. So the like phrase in Gen. iii. 8; xliv. 18, is to be understood. God honoured Ezekiel here with the knowledge of what he was about, and singled him out to be a witness of his proceedings.

"Cause them that have charge over the city to draw near." The Hebrew is, The visitations of the city have drawn near; or, Let the visitations of the city draw near. Here is the abstract put for the concrete, visitation for visitors, which is frequent in Scripture; as Col. i. 16, thrones are put for kings, dominions for lords, rulers, principalities, and powers for them that are in chief places. Isa. lx. 17, "I will also make thy officers peace;" the Hebrew is, thy visitation, in the abstract, and rendered in the concrete, officers, or visitors, and so here. Some read it, the men of visitation; others, the visitors of the city; our translation, those that have charge over the city, especially the military affairs.

Who these were is to be examined. Not the ancients of Israel, mentioned in the former chapter, who were to be destroyed, and not to destroy; but they were certain angels or archangels, to whom the Lord had committed the custody of Jerusalem; for angels have the care of kingdoms, provinces, and cities, and these God calls for, and employs, to fetch in the Chaldeans for destruction of the city, and inhabitants of it. Angels are defenders and destroyers of cities.

"Every man with his destroying weapon in his hand." A man, in the Hebrew, it is not every man; but the meaning is, that not any should appear without his weapon, every one that came should bring it in his hand.

"Destroying weapon." Hebrew, instrument of his destruction; that is, not with an instrument to destroy himself, but with an instrument to destroy others, a deadly instrument.

Obs. 1. The Lord will not always be silent, and bear with sinners, he will cry out against them; the longer he hath been silent, the louder he will cry at last. Here God held his peace long, or spake in secret to the prophet, showing him the sins of this city, how grievous they were, what abominations they had committed; and that being done, he cries out of them, calls for executioners to be avenged on them. Isa. xlii. 14, "I have long time holden my peace; I have been still, and refrained myself: now will I cry like a travailing woman; I will destroy and devour at once." A travailing woman feels pain, but keeps as long as she can from discovering the same; but when her throes and pangs come strongly upon her, she cries out of her pains, and calls for help. So God had borne with their sins, restrained his fury and vengeance; but being overcome with the greatness of their sins, wearied with their iniquities, he cries out, and calls for help of angels and men to avenge him of his adversaries. Micah vi. 9, "The Lord's voice crieth unto the city;" he called aloud unto them, his patience was expired, Spirit exasperated; his voice was now intended, as being in a strait, and necessitated to proceed to judgment. Amos ii. 13, "Behold, I am pressed under you, as a cart is pressed that is full of sheaves." A cart is long a loading, and when it is greatly loaded, oft it breaks, and all is laid in the dust: so God, being pressed, breaks silence, brings in dreadful and inevitable judgments; "Therefore the flight shall perish from the swift," &c.

Obs. 2. The Lord usually makes known his judgments before he executes them: "He cried also in mine ears."

Ezekiel shall know the Lord's intendments before he doth any thing against the city and people. Before notable judgments come upon men, God's method is to reveal them. God told Noah of the flood, Gen. vi. 13, 17; the captivity of the ten tribes was not hid from the prophets, 2 Kings xvii. 14—16; this Babylonish captivity was known to Isaiah, Jeremiah, Ezekiel, and others, 2 Chron. xxxvi. 15—17. Christ told the apostles of the destruction of the temple, and miseries that should befall the city, before they fell out, Matt. xxiv. 1, 2; Luke xix. 41—44. Upon this ground Amos is bold, and saith, "Surely the Lord God will do nothing, but he revealeth his secret unto his servants the prophets," chap. iii. 7. There is no necessity upon God for revealing his judgments, he doth execute many secretly, and openly, which were never heard of till felt; but God's ordinary way with his people was, to let them hear of his judgments before-hand; he made them known to the prophets and prophetical men. Joseph had the seven years' famine revealed to him, Gen. xli.; and God would not hide his purpose of ruining Sodom from Abraham; Gen. xviii. 17, "Shall I hide from Abraham that thing which I do?" no, I will not; Abraham is my friend, he shall know my thoughts. Jonah is acquainted with God's intentions touching Nineveh, that great city. And the judgments now upon us were not unforeseen, the servants of the Lord had notice of them many years since, and spake of these tempestuous days. This God doth to stop the mouth of iniquity, that wicked men may not object God came upon them without warning. This Lion roars before he devours the prey; the Lord of hosts sounds the trumpet before he comes to battle: he tells his prophets and ministers of justice, that they may give warning unto others, that they may prepare to meet the Lord, that they may tremble at his judgments, repent, reform, return to God, or else perish most justly; and that the godly, seeing his care herein, for ye might work out your salvation with fear and trembling, draw others out of their dangerous conditions, exercise their graces more fully, and intercede earnestly with God for averting, mitigating, removing, or sanctifying of his judgments. Abraham entreated for Sodom, and Jeremiah for the Jews, when they knew God's mind was to destroy them.

Obs. 3. No judgments, no afflictions, come upon any states or churches but at the Lord's call and appointment. Let the visitation of the city draw near; or, cause the visitors to come. God hath sovereign authority over all creatures, he is Lord of hosts, and when he gives out the word, then judgments step forth, and the executioners of them appear. 2 Kings viii. 1, there was a seven years' famine in the land, and how came this? Elisha tells the Shunammite woman, that the Lord had called for it, he commanded it to come forth of his treasury of judgments. When David had sinned in numbering the people, God sent him a message by Gad his seer, which was this: "Shall seven years of famine come unto thee in thy land? or wilt thou flee three months before thine enemies, while they pursue thee? or that there be three days' pestilence in thy land." One of these David was to choose; and the pestilence he chooseth, which God sent amongst them, 2 Sam. xxiv. 12—15. Judgments are in God's hand, and let out at his pleasure; he calls for the sword, and gives it commission to go up and down; Ezek. xiv. 17, he saith, "Sword, go through the land;" Hos. xi. 6, "Abide on his cities:" he causeth his "sword to devour flesh," and his "arrows to be drunk with blood," Deut. xxxii. 42. Judgments come not till God call them, they go not but where he directs them, they hurt not any, or more than he appoints, nor cease till he commands. There is nothing casual, accidental in them, but they are by the determinate counsel and will of God.

Obs. 4. When the Lord is in his fury, he is not only intense upon, but hastening of judgments. "He cried with a loud voice," which sets out his intention; he would have executioners of his judgments draw near. Polan. renders the word, to make speed and hasten: Zeph. i. 14, "The great day of the Lord is near, it is near, and hasteth greatly." The time was near, and all things in heaven and earth making haste to their destruction, yea great haste. God brings on judgments sooner than they are expected. Did not the Chaldeans come with speed and haste upon them? "his horses were swifter than eagles," Jer. iv. 13; than "leopards," Hab. i. 8. And are any creatures swifter for wing or foot than the eagle or leopard? yet the Chaldeans' judgment was swifter than they; Lam. iv. 19, "Our persecutors are swifter than the eagles of the heaven;" they made great haste. Sinners are secure, and think judgments slumber, when they are upon their march, upon the wing: Jer. xlviii. 16, Moab's affliction hasted fast, it came flying; and Isa. v. 26, God hissed for the Chaldeans, and they came with speed swiftly. God hasteneth judgment, and no marvel, he is provoked to it, as an army is provoked sometimes to fight, when there was no intention; or if intention, being stirred, falls to fight immediately. Isa. v. 19, wicked men say, "Let him make speed, and hasten his work, that we may see it; and let the counsel of the Holy One of Israel draw nigh and come, that we may know it." They mocked the prophet that told them of judgment, captivity, and destruction. You say such things are decreed in heaven, and must take place; let us see them, let them come; Jerusalem is strong, well fortified, &c. As these provoke him by their sins, so the godly importune him by their prayers; Luke xviii. 8, "He will avenge them speedily."

Obs. 5. That angels have the care of cities, kingdoms, and communities committed to them. "Cause them that have charge over the city." That was the angels, say interpreters; and in the opening of the first chapter, I showed you, that angels were employed in the government of the world. Deut. xxxii. 8, "He set bounds according to the number of the children of Israel:" the Septuagint hath it, according to the number of the angels of God, as if they had the land divided first among them, and then the people were settled according to those divisions. That in Dan. x. 20, is more clear and full, where the angel tells Daniel, that he would fight with the prince of Persia, he would prevent his hindering their return to Jerusalem; and when he should go forth and leave the care of that country, the prince of Greece should come, namely, Alexander the Great, and overthrow that monarchy. Clemens saith, the charge of angels was divided by nations and cities; and Epiphanius, Heres. 51, *Regna et gentes sub angelis positæ sunt*, Kingdoms and nations are placed under the angels.

Obs. 6. When God calls angels, or any creatures, at his command they come, and are willing to contribute any power or strength they have, to damnify and destroy God's enemies, Psal. lxxviii. 49; 2 Chron. xxxii. 21; 2 Sam. xxiv. 16. It was at God's command that the waters drowned the world, that fire and brimstone consumed Sodom, that the stars fought against Sisera, and that the earth opened her mouth and swallowed up Corah, Dathan, and Abiram.

Ver. 2. *And, behold, six men came from the way of the higher gate, which lieth toward the north, and every man a slaughter weapon in his hand; and one man among them was clothed with linen, with a writer's inkhorn by his side: and they went in, and stood beside the brasen altar.*

In this verse you have the effect of the former command, those who had the charge of the city being called, appear: and here is considerable,

I. How they are called, "men."

II. Their number, "six men."

III. Whence they came, "from the way of the higher gate," &c.

IV. The manner of their appearance, "every man with a slaughter weapon in his hand."

V. Another man added, and described,

1. From his place, "among them."

2. From a double adjunct:

(1.) Of his clothing, he "was clothed with linen."

(2.) Of an inkhorn, he had "a writer's inkhorn by his side."

VI. What they did, "they went in, and stood beside the brasen altar."

"Men." They were angels, but are called men, because they appeared in human shape, which was ordinary in ancient times: Gen. xviii. 2, 3, angels like three men appeared to Abraham; the angels that came to Lot were like men, Gen. xix. 5; and Gabriel, that came to Daniel, is called "the man Gabriel," Dan. ix. 21. They have not the true bodies of men, but are real bodies formed into the likeness of men's bodies, which are easily assumed and easily deposed; for the union between the angel assuming the body, and the body assumed, is not substantial, like the union between man's soul and body, nor hypostatical, like the union between Christ's human and divine nature, nor accidental, but it is assistential; the angel is in the body by an inward real presence, as the mover to that which is moved, with a particular regard to its direct use. As the body holds out something of the soul, so doth the body assumed hold out somewhat of an angel; and therefore when angels appeared, they feared, they knew them to be more than men.

"Six men." Six devils, saith Jerom; six angels, saith Theodoret, and most interpreters go that way.

Some think by these six were represented the principal leaders of the Chaldean army, mentioned Jer. xxxix. 3, Nergal-sharezer, Samgar-nebo, Sarsechim, Rab-saris, Nergal-sharezer, Rabmag; but here were seven or eight, as the original runs, and other princes beside.

Others interpret these six of the kingdoms that helped Nebuchadnezzar in this service, as the Edomites, Ammonites, Idumeans, Moabites, Midianites, and some of Palestine. Others, to whom the chief care of the war was committed. More probable it is, that six are named in reference to the three parts of Jerusalem, and the chief gates therein. 2 Kings xiv. 13, there you have the gate of Ephraim, and the corner gate, and these were in *oppido Benjaminis*, in the part of Benjamin; Neh. xii. 39, you have the old gate, and the fish gate, and those were in the city of David; Neh. iii. 14, the dung gate, and the sheep gate, and they were in *oppido Judæ*, in the part of Judah: these were the chief gates, and led into the chief streets. To these it is likely do the six angels refer, intimating that a destroyer should come in at every chief gate of Jerusalem; these six angels should bring in the chief leaders of the Chaldean forces with their regiments at these gates. Or by these six you may understand the whole army of Nebuchadnezzar, a part being put for the whole.

Zech. xiv. 10.

Jer. i. 16.

"Came from the way of the higher gate which lieth toward the north." This gate was a temple gate, not a city gate; 2 Chron xxvii. 3, "Jotham built the high gate of the house of the Lord;" and this was called the new gate also, Jer. xxvi. 10, "The princes sat down in the entry of the new gate of the Lord's house." This gate looked northward toward Chaldea; and that way these six men came, pointing out whence their misery should come, and where it should begin; Jer. vi. 1, "Evil appeareth out of the north, and great destruction." On the north side Nebuchadnezzar made his entrance, and not only he, but Antiochus and Titus, as Josephus observes.

Jer. xx. 2.

Pradus in loc.

"Every man a slaughter weapon in his hand." The Hebrew is, an instrument of contrition or dissipation. Prov. xxv. 18, it is translated a maul, an instrument to beat out a man's brains. The Septuagint renders the word here an axe. It may be interpreted a sword, or any weapon that sufficeth to kill a man with.

מפיץ

Obs. 1. That there is power and efficacy in the calls and commands of God. When he said, "Cause them that have charge over the city to draw near," you see it here fulfilled, "Behold, six men came." Ezekiel called, told them the mind of God, but there was not power in him to bring these slaughter angels before the Lord; Divine Providence acted, the secret virtue of the Lord did it. There is power in the commands of God, and when that goeth along with his word it produceth any effects; his word and power brought the flood upon the world at first, and will bring the fire on it at last.

Obs. 2. When God is against a city, he sets angels against it also. Here were six angels that appeared at his call for the destruction of the city; those who before he had appointed to preserve it, now he calls forth to destroy it. Sin makes God our enemy, and when he is out with us, who can be friends to us? If the king frown, the nobles and courtiers will do it also. While God is our friend, angels are, and all other creatures: 1 Cor. iii. 21, Paul saith to the Corinthians, "All things are yours," your servants, your friends for your good; and why? "ye are Christ's," his friends, his servants; if they had been enemies to Christ, all things had been enemies to them. What the wise man saith of any man, Prov. xvi. 7, "When a man's ways please the Lord, he maketh even his enemies to be at peace with him," is true of any city; when they please God, he makes their enemies to be at peace with them. Babylon was ever an enemy to Zion, but never harmed Zion till Zion had offended or lost her God; and when cities have provoked God against them, he makes their friends their enemies, and their enemies enmity unto them. Have not we kindled divine wrath by our sins, caused him to deal in fury, to set angels and men against us; are they not abroad with slaughter weapons? Jerusalem improved not the sword of justice, the magistrates were neglective of punishing delinquents, of righting the wrongs of the oppressed; and therefore God put a sword into the hands of angels and Chaldeans to destroy both magistrate and subject. Let us take heed how we make God our enemy; by all means make him your friend; Job v. 23, stones and beasts will be at league, at peace with you: compare it with Deut. xxxii. 13; Isa. xi. 6—8.

Obs. 3. At what gate men drive God away, at the same gate they let judgment in; at what door men let in sin, at the same door they let in wrath. The destroying angels came from the north to the north gate, there was the idol of jealousy, chap. viii. 3; by the brazen altar: this way came in idolatry, this way God was driven from them, and this way came the angels, came the Chaldeans, to be avenged on them; they sinned northward, and from thence came their judgment. At that gate was the great concourse of people, there they worshipped the image of jealousy, and that way came in the greatest evil they ever had. The prophets often mention the northern evil: Jer. i. 14,

עון Iniquity and judgment.

"Out of the north an evil shall break forth upon all the land." Chap. iv. 6, "I will bring evil from the north, and a great destruction;" see chap. vi. 1, 22, 23. Chap. x. 22, "A great commotion out of the north, to make the cities of Judah desolate, and a den of dragons." Judgment came to that gate they sinned at; sin lay behind the door, called for, and let in the enemy. Gen. iv. 7, God told Cain if he did not well, sin lay at the door, that is, punishment, judgment, lay at the door, and would quickly come in at that door sin had opened. Rom. v. 12, "By sin death entered;" sin opened a door, it brake open God's command, and so let in death, and all judgments beneath death.

Ahaziah sends to Baal-zebub the god of Ekron about his recovery, being sick; this so offended God, that an answer was returned him, that therefore he should not come down from his bed, but should surely die, 2 Kings i. 4. Gideon's ephod was a snare to him and his house, Judg. viii. 27.

Obs. 4. When God comes against a people, he will surround them with judgments. At all the chief gates there should be angels, Chaldean forces; so that if they would flee to the gates of any of the streets, to the gate of Ephraim, to the corner gate, the old gate, or fish gate, the dung gate, or common gate, or other gates whatsoever, they should find angels with destroying weapons in their hands; and see themselves so beset with judgments, that there should be no escaping: they might run from street to street, from gate to gate, and hope to get away; but, Jer. xi. 11, "I will bring evil upon them, which they shall not be able to escape;" their hearts, heads, hands, heels, shall not avail them to an escape; if they fight or flee, if they entreat God or man, seek secretly to steal away, it is in vain, they shall not be able to escape.

Obs. 5. When God is upon acts of justice, and calls for angels or any creatures, at his command, they come, and willingly contribute what power they have to damnify and destroy his enemies: every one came here with a slaughter weapon in his hand. The creatures are ready to execute vengeance upon their fellow-creatures, when the glorious Creator, being offended, calls for it: Isa. xxxvii. 36, an angel, at God's appointment, went forth and slew one hundred and eighty-five thousand; he had his slaughter weapon ready, and acted like an angel, slaying so many in one night. It is said of angels, Psal. ciii. 20, that they excel in strength, that they do the commandments of the Lord, hearkening unto the voice of his word; if he do once speak, they hear, yea, they put forth their great strength, and do that strongly they are sent about.

"One man among them was clothed with linen." Who this one man should be, is questionable. Some make him to be an angel, and the grounds they go upon are these:

1. He is "clothed with linen," in which kind of garment angels were wont to appear, Acts i. 10; Luke xxiv. 4; John xx. 12.

2. In the end of this chapter this man saith, "I have done as thou hast commanded me," which respect an angel rather than Christ, who being equal with the Father, receives not commands from him; angels being his servants, and ministering spirits, are fittest to receive commands.

For the first of these arguments, it is true, that angels have appeared oft in white linen and shining garments, but not they alone. Rev. iv. 4, the twenty-four elders were clothed with white linen. And chap. vii. 9, a great multitude stood before the throne, and the Lamb, clothed in white robes. And Christ in his transfiguration had his raiment white as the light, Matt. xvii. 2. It is not sufficient therefore to say, this man was clothed with linen, a white garment, and therefore was an angel.

To the second, that commands are unsuitable to Christ; hear what Christ saith, John xiv. 31, "As the Father gave me commandment, even so I do." Chap. xv. 10, "I have kept my Father's commandments." So chap. xii. 49; x. 18, he received commands from his Father, and kept them. This was no disparagement to Christ; as God, he was equal with his Father; as man, himself saith, "My Father is greater than I," John xiv. 28.

Others by this one man understand the Lord Christ, the Angel of the covenant; and those contend that in the letter here is meant an angel, and makes that angel representative of Christ; so that the difference is not much: but I join with them that make this one man to be Christ, and that,

1. Because he is brought in as mediator here with an adjunct of oneness, as in 1 Tim. ii. 5, "One mediator," &c.; the godly Jews had no other mediator.

2. Here are implied the three offices of Christ.

(1.) His kingly office, whereby he rules and commands all creatures; and that is couched up in those words, "among them," or in the midst of them: as King and Commander, he appears in the midst of those angels which had the destroying weapons in their hands; he was their General, and showed himself in the midst of them. Josh. v. 13—15, he appeared to Joshua with a drawn sword, and told him he was Captain of the Lord's host; whereupon Joshua fell down and worshipped, which had been sinful if it had been an angel, not the Lord General of men and angels.

(2.) His priestly office, implied in his linen clothing; the Hebrew signifies flax, especially white flax or silk, which was used in holy vestures. 1 Sam. ii. 18, Samuel ministered to the Lord girded with a linen ephod; that is, with an ephod of fine flax, or silk, which grew in Egypt, and was called *shesh*, Ezek. xxvii. 7; *gossipium*, by Pliny, whereof he affirms were made garments for the Egyptian priests, who doubtless took it up from the Jewish priests, who were appointed by God to wear such garments, Exod. xxviii. 42, 43; Lev. vi. 10; xvi. 4; whereby was set out the innocency and purity which should be in the priests, who were to intercede with God for the people. In such a garment doth Christ appear, a sacerdotal garment, pointing out his holiness, innocency, and priestly office, whereby he intercedes for sinners.

Nat. Hist. l. 19. c. 1. Vestes inde sacerdotibus Ægypti gratissimæ.

(3.) His prophetical office, shadowed out by the inkhorn he had by his side. Prophets were to declare the mind of God by speaking and writing, to discover who were good, who bad, whose names were in the book of life, whose not; and so Christ here would make known the mind of God, and mark out those who were for deliverance, and those who were for destruction.

"A writer's inkhorn." The Septuagint reads it, a sapphirine girdle about his loins, mistaking ספר for ספיר. Some have it, the tables of a writer, or table-book. Others term it a case for pens; we, an inkhorn, that which contains the ink, and hath the pen-case joined with it. Some taking it for a book, conceive Christ wrote in it the names of those who should be spared, or made known whose names were written already in this book. The Scripture mentions a book of life, Exod. xxxii. 32; Psal. lxix. 28. But that Christ declared out of this book the names of the inwritten, is groundless. We are to take it for an inkhorn, which notes Christ giving instructions to these agents, his observing, recording of all things, and his distinguishing between the precious and the vile, and his readiness to seal and instruct those that are the Lord's. Or it notes a manifesting the decrees of God touching Jerusalem.

Quest. It was Christ sat upon the throne, who spake to Ezekiel, and how could this one man among the angels be Christ? This is the only difficulty against this interpretation, that the same person in the same vision should be represented diversely.

Answ. Christ having divers offices, which cannot be typified or shadowed out by any one thing, it pleaseth him to represent himself variously to us in the same vision; as in Rev. v. 1, there is one sits upon a throne, and this was Christ, (as appears, chap. i. 18; xxi. 6,) he had a book in his hand sealed, which none being able to open caused great weeping; and ver. 6, there is Christ represented as a Lamb, who, ver. 7, came and took the book out of the hand of him that sat upon the throne: here Christ is variously represented, he sat in the throne as God, and held the book in his hand, he took it as mediator, and opened it unto men. Christ is the priest, the sacrifice, and altar, but under a diverse consideration. And so in this vision, sometimes Christ is represented as God sitting in his throne; sometimes as a prophet, instructing Ezekiel; sometimes as mediator, interceding for the elect. It is not incongruous therefore to see the same person, having several offices, and conveying several benefits to his church, represented in a vision several ways at the same time.

"They went in, and stood beside the brazen altar." The Scripture speaks of a golden altar, 1 Kings vii. 48, 49, and this was before the oracle. There was also a brazen altar, 1 Kings viii. 64, which was for holocaust, as the other for incense, and stood in the midst of the court before the temple; but at this time it was removed, and the Damascene altar set in the place of it, where the idol of jealousy was honoured.

Now these men came not to this idolatrous altar, but went to the brazen altar which was near, though out of its place. There they stood to receive answers: they would not go to the other, where false worship was, lest they should seem to countenance it; but to the other deserted, despised altar, to which the sacrifices belonged, and where God gave them true answers.

There they stood; which phrase implies a readiness in whomsoever, to hear, receive, and execute the commands of those they stand before. If Levites stand before the Lord, it imports a promptness in them to minister unto the Lord, Deut. x. 8. If servants, 2 Kings v. 25, if great ones, 2 Kings viii. 9, stand before others, it argues a proneness in them to hearken to what shall be given out and imposed upon them: so here.

Obs. 1. Elect Jews under the law were saved by the mediatorial work of Christ incarnate, as we are under the gospel. Christ frequently appeared as man, intimating thereby his future incarnation, and that that nature must concur to the making up of his mediatorship: he did not mediate for them as God, for us as man; but he mediated then *ut homo promissus*, as man promised, now he mediates *ut homo exhibitus*, as man manifested. Isa. liii. 5, the prophet speaking of Christ, saith, "He was wounded for our transgressions, he was bruised for our iniquities; the chastisement of our peace was upon him, and with his stripes we are healed." The prophet's faith, and in his, the faith of the Jewish church, looked upon Christ as already wounded, slain, and fetched healing virtue from his stripes: Christ's death was their life, his cross their crown.

Obs. 2. That the Lord Christ is the chief commander of all angelical and human forces. He was in the midst of these six military angels that were to bring in the Chaldean forces at the several gates of the city; he was their General, from him they had their commissions, and without a word from him they could not stir. All power in heaven and earth was given him, Matt. xxviii. 18. His prerogative it was, and is, to call forth angels, and send out armies: Rev. xix. 14, "The armies which were in heaven followed him," that is, Christ, he was their Leader; and his name is "King of kings, and Lord of lords," ver. 16. And certainly where Christ goes at the head of armies, there will be great slaughter.

Obs. 3. When judgments are abroad, and the godly are in danger, Christ mediates and intercedes for them. Now the Jewish church and state were at the door of destruction, and public calamities ready to involve all; Christ appears like a priest with linen clothes, to offer sacrifice on their behalf, and to mediate for them. When imminent dangers were at hand, or judgments upon the people, the priests were to appear, to stand between the Lord and them, making intercession for them, Numb. xvi. 47, 48. And so in Joel ii. 17, "Let the priests, the ministers of the Lord, weep between the porch and the altar, and say, Spare thy people, O Lord." And here Christ being a merciful High Priest, shows himself, and interposeth for the saints, who were to meet with a terrible tempest. The like did Christ when he was in the flesh on earth; he saw what a storm was coming upon Jerusalem, what persecution upon the saints, and therefore, John xvii. he intercedes with his Father for apostles and believers, ver. 11, 20. When Stephen was questioned, and in jeopardy of his life, heaven was opened, and he saw Christ stand at the right hand of God: Christ pleaded his cause, propitiated for his sins, and encouraged him in his sufferings.

Obs. 4. Christ hath a special care of his in times of trouble; he appears with an inkhorn to write down what is said and done against them, to make known the mind of God to them, to seal and discriminate them from others, to give commissions to those he employs to cut off the enemies of his people. Rev. vii. 2, 3, there were four angels had power given them to hurt the earth and sea; but there was "another angel ascending from the east, having the seal of the living God," viz. Christ, for so expositors understand it; and this Angel, the Lord Christ, "cried with a loud voice, saying, Hurt not the earth, neither the sea, nor the trees, till we have sealed the servants of our God in their foreheads." Christ had great care of his churches; for by earth, sea, trees, some of the learned understand the church in several places: by earth, the inland churches; by sea, the maritime; and by trees, the mountain and woodland churches; Christ would not have these hurt till all the godly in them were sealed. It is prophesied in Mal. iv. 1, 2, that when it is a fiery day of the Lord, the Sun of righteousness shall arise with healing in his wings to them that fear the Lord. Rev. ix. 4, when the locusts came out of the bottomless pit, and had power like scorpions given them to sting and do hurt, there was a command, "that they should not hurt the grass of the earth, nor any green thing, nor any tree," that is, no christian that had life in him, weak or strong; but only those who had not the seal of God in their foreheads, that is, those who had no life, no greenness in them, and they were subject to hurt others. Mark iv. 37—40, when the disciples were in a grievous storm, the waves beat so into the ship that they filled it, they were afraid, and suspected the care of Christ, and therefore said, "Master, carest thou not that we perish?" Yes, saith Christ, I have a special care of you, and presently you shall see it; "he rebuked the wind, and said unto the sea, Peace, be still. And immediately the wind ceased, and there was a calm." And from rebuking the winds and seas, he falls to rebuke them for their fear and faithfulness: they perceived not yet that he cared for them as well sleeping as waking; though his body slept, yet his spirit was awake; his care for his servants is constant and intense. When he was to leave the world, how full of trouble were the hearts of his apostles, and how full of care and compassion was Christ towards them, laying down several grounds of comfort for them in the 14th, 15th, 16th, and 17th chapters of John.

Obs. 5. Those who are upon great and public designs, should begin with God and consult with him. These seven here go in and stand by the altar, inquire of God what his pleasure is, whither he will send them, what he had to do for them, and whatever it was, that he would counsel and prosper them. So have the worthies of God done. Ezra, chap. viii. 21, when he was to come from Babylon about the great work of the temple, he sought God extraordinarily for direction, assistance, and protection; which he obtained of God, ver. 23. Jehoshaphat, when the Moabites, Ammonites, and others came out to war against him, he began with the Lord in prayer and fasting, and from him had encouragement and success, 2 Chron. 20. So Asa, he began with God, when Zerah had a thousand thousand in the field against him; he knew that the Lord was the Lord of hosts, and that these uncircumcised ones came against him; therefore looks up to him, and saith, "O Lord, thou art our God; let not man prevail against thee;" and hereupon the Lord smote the Ethiopians, 2 Chron. xiv. 11, 12. One reason why armies miscarry is, because they confide in their own strength and policy, and lean not wholly upon the Lord, seeking to him in the first place. Joshua miscarried in a great business in making peace with the Gibeonites, Josh. ix.; and the reason is given; "they asked not counsel at the mouth of the Lord," ver. 14. All businesses, for right managing and success of them, depend upon the Lord, it is he blesses or curses; therefore it is wisdom, it is necessary, to look up to him at the beginning, lest through neglect of Divine Majesty we lay the foundation of our enterprises in wrath. Christ being to choose apostles, which was a great work, he prayed all night before, Luke vi. 12, 13. And the angels that were to pour out the vials of wrath, are said to come out of the temple; they had been there before the Lord.

Obs. 6. Those who are employed by the Lord, must be careful that they countenance no corruptions in worship. Neither Christ nor the angels would come at the false altar, which Ahaz had caused to be set up; but they go to God's altar, the brazen altar; by this they stood, not the other. Symbolizing with idolatrous worship, persons, and things, God allows not: Deut. xii. 30, they must not inquire after the nations' gods; Lev. xviii. 3, they must not do after the doings of Egyptians or Canaanites. When God's people were in Babylon, (of their condition there the prophet speaks,) they must not touch any unclean thing, Isa. lii. 11; much less may they touch any in Zion: therefore Paul presseth that phrase, 2 Cor. vi. 17, upon the Corinthians, who were too forward to symbolize with corruptions, "Touch not the unclean thing;" marry not with unbelievers, be not at their feast eating that which is sacrificed to idols, go not to law before the judges, use none of their rites, countenance nothing of their worship; you will be defiled, offend your weak brethren: let all those things go, and, whatever you lose or suffer, I will be your Father, receive you, if you be cast off or out, and make good all your losses. God would not have his people touch or countenance any corruptions in worship. The primitive christians would not cast a little incense into the fire to countenance an idol. You know in Tertullian's days it was counted unlawful for christians to wear a garland, because it conformed them unto heathens; and what warrantableness hath been in our surplicing, crossing, kneeling, cringing, altaring, observation of days, consecration of places? These have conformed us to papists, and brought an imputation upon us, that we have romanized, rather than evangelized. The Rhemists condemn the heathenish names of the week days, Sunday, Monday, &c. because it is a countenancing of heathen corruptions; it were well that we let fall all holy days, because the keeping of them is a countenancing of their corrupt observations of them. And Calvin saith, *Fidelibus fas non est ullo symbolo ostendere sibi cum superstitiosis esse consensum*, It is not right for faithful persons to give any token of approbation of those who are superstitious. By our ceremonies and service we hardened the papists, begat hopes in them of our return to them, and grieved, if not stumbled and wounded, the godly and weak amongst us.

On Rev. i. 10.

In Psal. xvi. 4.

Obs. 7. In times of judgment, as God discountenances false worship, so he discovers and countenances his own way of worship. Christ and the six angels here came not at the altar and idol of jealousy which was now in credit, but to the brazen altar which they had set by; and now the false worship must down, the true and good way be countenanced. Ahab maintaining Baalitish worship and prophets, God sent a famine, 1 Kings xviii. which brought them all low; and God now stirred up the spirit of Elijah to ruin the false prophets and worship, and raise up his own; therefore by sacrificing he discovers the false and true worship, the false and true God: and therefore after sacrificing, the people halted not any longer between two opinions, but their hearts were turned back to the Lord, and they cried, "The Lord, he is the God; the Lord, he is the God," ver. 39. In Josiah's days God's wrath was abroad, 2 Kings xxii. 13; and then was the law found, and idolatry rooted out, chap. xxiii. 4.

When God visits for errors and corruptions in worship, then he opens a door for truth, which was shut up; and there is great reason for it, that he may clear and vindicate his proceedings. When truth and God's ways are discovered and countenanced, then sinners see they have been out, acknowledge the equity of God's judgments, if not repent of their follies.

The axe was at the root of the tree when the gospel came in; their corruptions of the law, false interpretations and traditions, were discovered, condemned, and the glorious truths of the gospel by degrees were let in. When Christ had the whip in his hand, and was purging the temple, he had the truth in his mouth; "My house shall be called the house of prayer; but ye have made it a den of thieves," Matt. xxi. 12, 13; John ii. 15, 16.

Ver. 3. *And the glory of the God of Israel was gone up from the cherub, whereupon he was, to the threshold of the house. And he called to the man clothed with linen, which had the writer's inkhorn by his side.*

Here our prophet had a sad sight, he sees the glory removed from its place, and going away, which presaged no good to Jerusalem.

The parts of the verse are these :

I. The subject of this glory, "the God of Israel."

II. The motion of this glory, or glorious God, he "was gone :" and in his going you have,

1. From whence he went, "from the cherub," &c.

2. Whither he went, "to the threshold of the house."

3. What he did, "he called."

4. To whom, "to the man clothed with linen," &c.

"The glory of the God of Israel." For the glorious God of Israel, some take it, *per hypallagen.* I have spoken of these words before, chap. viii. 4. We may hold to the words, and understand thereby some visible sign of the gracious presence of God. It is thought our prophet alludes to that in Exod. xxv. 22, upon the ark were two cherubims, between those the mercy-seat was, where God appeared, and from whence he gave out his mind to Moses and others; Numb. vii. 89, Moses heard God speak from the mercy-seat. And that God now had left his place which he had dwelt and sat in so long; for those expressions you have, 2 Kings xix. 15; Psal. xcix. i. Now he was withdrawing his presence, and denying them assistance.

Others think by the glory of God here, to be meant that glory which the prophet had formerly seen, chap. i. 28; iii. 23; viii. 4. This visional glory, the sign of God's presence, went away, according to that, chap. x. 4, "The glory of the Lord went up from the cherub;" cherub being put for cherubims, which is usual in Scripture to put one number for another. We may safely take either of these senses; because this vision Ezekiel had of Christ was a sign of divine presence, as the mercy-seat was, the going away of it, or this glory, do both clearly evidence to us that God was departing; which is the scope of the Spirit here.

"Gone up from the cherub." Pradus denies that the Lord left the cherubims, and went without them to the threshold, but together with them; and Deodate seems to be of that opinion, in his notes upon the place: but the text itself leads us to think otherwise; for chap. x. 18, "The glory of the Lord departed from off the threshold of the house, and stood over the cherubims," which shows that the glorious Lord returned to the cherubims he had left.

"To the threshold of the house." The Septuagint has it, *εἰς τὸ αἴθριον τοῦ οἴκου, in serenum, sub dio,* they say the Lord went out of the temple into the open air; but it is said, the glory of the Lord went to the threshold, not over it, or beyond it; and it is conceived to be the threshold of the priests' court. The Lord went thither,

1. To show he was now going from the temple, where was such impure worship, and leaving his "glorious high throne," as it is called, Jer. xvii. 12. The Jews thought the Lord was confined to the temple, and the prophets to the holy land.

2. Because he was to pronounce sentence against this wicked, idolatrous, oppressing people, which he would not do in *sancto sanctorum,* or in the temple, which was the place of his gracious presence, and a type of Christ, and mercy by him. In the gates of the city they sat in judgment, Amos v. 15; and God here at the threshold gives sentence against them.

3. To treat with the men who stood at the brazen altar, and to give them commissions and instructions touching those who were to be spared and destroyed.

Obs. 1. The Lord's way of manifesting his gracious presence in his church, was by some notable sign or other. "The glory was gone up;" it was there before. When God was pleased with his people, he evidenced his presence by some special sign. Exod. xiii. 21, 22, when the church came out of Egypt, "the Lord went before them by day in a pillar of a cloud, to lead them the way; and by night in a pillar of fire, to give them light." They had guidance and protection from the Lord Christ, whose presence was evidenced by these visible signs, out of which the Lord also spake sometimes, Psal. xcix. 7. Afterward they had the tabernacle, ark, and mercy-seat, where God met them, and communed with them, Exod. xxv. 22. They had the Urim and Thummim, to inquire of God, and receive answers by, Numb. xxvii. 21; 1 Sam. xxviii. 6. In Solomon's days God manifested his gracious presence in the temple by a cloud, 1 Kings viii. 10. God answered Elijah by fire, and manifested with whom his presence was, 1 Kings xviii. 38. And so under the gospel, Christ the Lord manifested his presence with his church by visible signs: Acts ii. 3, cloven tongues like fire sat upon each of the apostles; and chap. iv. 31, the place was shaken where they were, and they were filled with the Holy Ghost. And Christ hath left his word and sacraments as signs of his presence in the christian church.

Obs. 2. The signs of God's presence are the glory of God. So the text calls them, "The glory of the God of Israel was gone up." All those visible signs before mentioned were the glory of the Lord; so the Spirit is pleased to call the sign of God's gracious presence. 1 Kings viii. 10, 11, the cloud that filled the temple is called "the glory of the Lord." Psal. xxix. 9, "In his temple doth every one speak of his glory." The ordinances there have much of God's glory in them, and they are his glory.

Obs. 3. God's withdrawing the signs of his gracious presence from his church and people, is a forerunner of heavy judgments. Here the glory of the God of Israel went up from the cherub, and shortly after the men with their slaughter weapons are set on work to destroy. It is God's method to take away the special tokens of his presence and love from a people, and then to bring in sad judgments: people sin, and hereupon the glory removes, and judgments draw near. Exod. xxxii. the people made a calf; upon which God denies to go with them as he had done, chap. xxxiii. 3; now they should not have visible signs of his presence; and of them it is said, chap. xxxii. 35, "The Lord plagued the people, because they made the calf," &c. When God would not answer Saul by dreams, by Urim, or prophets, then his destruction was near at hand.

Among other signs of God's presence, there are these:

(1.) Efficacy of the word, that it works mightily in the hearts of people. The Lord was with the apostles, and how mightily did the word work! but when the word is inefficacious and powerless, it is evident the glory of the Lord is departing, and judgments dreadful enough at hand. The prophet prophesied to the people, but the word wrought not; Isa. vi. 9, 10, hearing they understand not, seeing they perceive not; their hearts were fat, their ears heavy, and their eyes shut: now the word was inefficacious to them. And how long shall this be? saith Isaiah; "Until the cities be wasted without inhabitant, the houses without man, and the land be utterly desolate." Six times is this scripture quoted in the New Testament.

(2.) Unity and love of saints. Psal. cxxxiii. 1, where brethren dwelt together in unity, there the Lord commanded the blessing, ver. 3, and showed his gracious presence. Where love is, God dwells, 1 John iv. 16; but where bitterness and division increase, Satan hath much interest; hearts, heads, tongues, hands, are divided every where; Isa. ix. 21, Manasseh is against Ephraim, Ephraim against Manasseh, and both against Judah; Matt. xxiv. 12, love is grown cold. Instead of fervent love, are fervent contentions; instead of love without dissimulation, are crafty underminings; instead of covering infirmities, are rakings in one another's hearts.

When the breaches were stopped in the walls of Jerusalem, the enemies were very wroth, Neh. iv. 7. God hath promised to close breaches, Amos ix. 11; let us improve the promise, and importune him to fulfil it, for rich mercy depends upon it, Isa. xxx. 26. Unity is a human saviour of kingdoms and churches; division is Abaddon, Apollyon, a hellish destroyer: Matt. xii. 25, a kingdom divided cannot stand, God is departed from it.

Division hath turned religion into disputation, driven God from the heart to the head; and now men are polemical, rather than practical, in divinity.

(3.) Activity of men in place for God. Where God is present, there is courage, Josh. i. 9; 2 Chron. xiii. 12; but when he withdraws, men are without spirit, divine influences cease, a numbness seizeth upon them, and they act faintly, be it in church or state. Hos. vii. 11, God was departing from Ephraim, if not departed, and Ephraim was a silly dove without heart, void of counsel and courage, and so fit for prey and spoil; Ephraim was quickly spoiled after the Lord left them.

(4.) Safety, protection, Jer. i. 19; Psal. xlvi. 5. Isa. xxvii. 3, "Lest any hurt it, I will keep it night and day." Where there is keeping, watching, there is presence. But is not our safety almost, if not altogether, gone? can we challenge safety of any thing, estates, liberties, lives, religion? have not our armies smarted, had blows and breaches? is not our land spoiled, and under grievous pressures? are we not for a prey, and none delivereth, Isa. xlii. 22.

Obs. 4. The Lord doth not willingly depart from his people when they have provoked him. He goes from the cherub to the threshold of the house, and there stands, as loth to go any further; he had rather stay with them, than depart from them, if there were any hope of amendment. Hos. xi. 8, "How shall I give thee up, Ephraim? how shall I deliver thee, Israel? how shall I make thee as Admah? how shall I set thee as Zeboim? mine heart is turned within me, my repentings are kindled together." Ephraim had deeply corrupted herself; swearing, lying, killing, stealing, adultery, idolatry, oppression, were found in Ephraim; and yet God saith, "How shall I give," &c. And further, that God is unwilling to leave his people, is evident:

(1.) He desires they should prevent it, Isa. i. 2—4, 16, 18.

(2.) Doth upon easy terms offer favour; Jer. iii. 13, 14, "Only acknowledge thine iniquity, for I am married unto thee."

(3.) Useth strong arguments to persuade his people to turn to him; Ezek. xxxiii. 11, "As I live, saith the Lord, I have no pleasure in the death of the wicked. Turn ye, turn ye," &c. See chap. xviii. 32.

(4.) He is troubled when it cometh to departing.

(5.) When the Lord goes from a people, it is not suddenly, but by degrees. He did not here in a moment leave the temple, but moved first to the threshold; afterwards it went up over the threshold, chap. x. 4; then higher, towards heaven, ver. 19; then to the midst of the city, and from thence to the mountain on the east side of the city, chap. xi. 23; and so went wholly from them: thus God step by step left them.

Ver. 4. *And the Lord said unto him, Go through the midst of the city, through the midst of Jerusalem, and set a mark upon the foreheads of the men that sigh and that cry for all the abominations that be done in the midst thereof.*

In this verse divine pleasure is made known to him who had the inkhorn by his side, and it consists in a double command:

1. He is commanded to "go through the midst of the city," and find out who sighed and cried for the abominations therein.

2. He must "set a mark upon the foreheads" of them who sighed and cried.

"Set a mark." What this was is much disputed. Popish expositors say it was the letter *tau*, which prefigured the cross of Christ. Some Hebrews by that mark *tau* understand those who have perfect knowledge of the law; some, those who kept the law, *tau* standing for *thorah*, signifying the law. Others understand believers in the Messiah, *tau* noting a cross. Jerom and some with him think the Hebrew ת was originally like the Greek τ, representing a cross; and that Ezra returning from the captivity, found out new characters, which are those we use; and Pradus saith, Arius Montanus had a silver shekel, in which the Hebrew letters were not unlike the Greek, and this shekel himself had seen; but it is not evident, saith Sanctius, that the moneys or shekels which were before the captivity had any letters upon them, they were not known by any stamp, but by their weight; and it is not probable Ezra should reject the original characters of the sacred tongue, and devise new himself. Some that will have the mark *tau* meant here, make it a sign of life, as θετα was of death. Judges marked those who were condemned with a θετα, and those who were to be freed with *tau*. If conjectures might take place, thus *tau* is the basis of the Hebrew alphabet, and marking by Christ is the basis of all true comfort and sound profession. But to leave conjectures, and to feed you with truth, "Set a mark," refers no more to one letter than another, not to the Greek τ, or Latin *t*, because the Lord spoke not in those languages, but in the Hebrew; and he means not the letter ת there, but a sign in general, as the word תו not the letter ת signifies; for the original is sign, a sign; תו *signum*, from תוה *signare*. And so it is used in Job xxxi. 35, "Behold, my desire is, that the Almighty would answer me;" the Hebrew is תוי Behold, my sign is, that the Almighty would answer me. So it is rendered in the margin; in this sense also the Septuagint renders it, give or put a sign; and so Symmachus and Aquila.

Asconius Pedianus, cited by A Lapid.

This sign was no corporal sign, as if the Lord had made some impression in their foreheads, whereby to distinguish them from others; for this was a vision, not to be taken really, but in a spiritual sense. The Lord Christ took special notice of these, and did distinguish them by special providence from those who were to perish in the destruction of the city: he did not go up and down from house to house, and set a mark in their foreheads, he applied his blood and merits, and sealed them by his Spirit; not that they were not washed in the blood of Christ before, but now there was a new and special evidence of it.

"Upon the foreheads." Not on their backs, breasts, arms, but on their foreheads. Some think the prophet alludes to a practice of marking servants in the forehead, who had their masters' names fixed therein, whence they were called *inscripti literati servi;* and it is the use among us to brand some delinquents

Rhodigin, l. 5. c. 31. Vid. Sen. l. 4. de Benefic. c. 37, 38.

with a T in the shoulder, hand, or forehead; and, as before was said, judges marked those who were questioned, and to be freed, with *tau*. Here was nothing written upon their foreheads, but something is held out by these words unto us; Christ having intimated their election, effectual calling, justification by his blood, intercession for them, providential care over them in the dreadful judgments coming upon them, doth by this phrase declare his public owning and caring for them. The forehead is an open place, exposed to view of all, and whatever is there, is visible: Rev. xiii. 16, the mark of the beast was in the hand and forehead; one was secret, more private, the other more open. Christ would so deal by these persons, and so deliver them, that it should openly appear he had distinguished them from others.

Upon their foreheads is specified, to let us see here was a personal, not a family deliverance intended.

Quest. Were all delivered who were marked?

Answ. It is believed that some godly ones suffered by the sword and famine, that some also were carried away captive. Jeremiah himself was not free from sufferings.

Quest. For what end were they then marked?

Answ. 1. To secure them of their eternal condition, that their sins were pardoned, and persons accepted.

2. To assure them that he was with them, and would work all things for their good, and increase of their glory.

3. To encourage their hearts against all opposition and hardship whatsoever.

"The men that sigh." The word notes sighing for grief of mind: grief is a heavy burden, and causes men to sigh as those that are burdened. Exod. ii. 23, "The children of Israel sighed by reason of bondage:" the heavy bondage they were under made them groan and sigh; and so these here had the burden of Jerusalem's abominations upon them, and that made them sigh. Prov. xxix. 2, "When the wicked beareth rule, the people mourn:" it is the same word; they meet with heavy pressures which make them sigh.

"That cry." This notes such sorrow as exceeds sighing, and must vent itself in a more full way, viz. with crying vehemently, as wounded men use to do when they breathe out their souls. Ezek. xxvi. 15, "The wounded cry when the slaughter is made;" and Jer. li. 52, "Through all the land the wounded shall groan," or cry; it is the same word: so that the meaning is, they did sigh greatly, and cry out bitterly, for the abominations which were in Jerusalem.

Obs. 1. The Lord looks upon the world with a discriminating eye; some he looks upon to be marked, and some to be left unmarked. All are not equal in God's thoughts or eye; some from eternity he predestinated, some he passed over; and now in time some he eyes for salvation, some he sets by for perdition; his eye distinguisheth between the precious and the vile. Psal. xxxiv. 15, 16, "The eyes of the Lord are upon the righteous, and the face of the Lord is against them that do evil:" he beholds both, but with a different aspect; one sort he beholds to do good to, the other to cut off. Psal. xi. 4, "His eyelids try the children of men;" he looks fixedly upon them, and as they are, so he deals with them. Job xxxvi. 7, it is said, "He withdraweth not his eyes from the righteous:" they are the delight of his eyes, but the wicked are thorns, provocations to his eyes, Isa. iii. 8.

Obs. 2. When the Lord proceeds to judgment of cities, churches, people, kingdoms, he doth it judiciously, considerately. He doth not pour out wrath from heaven at all adventures, let it light where and upon whom it will; but he makes inquiry who are fit to be punished, and who are to be spared. Psal. ix. 7, "The Lord hath prepared his throne for judgment;" and then, ver. 8, "He shall judge the world in righteousness;" and, ver. 12, "He maketh inquisition for blood:" the oppressed he will relieve, the oppressors he will cut off. When judgments are abroad, especially wars, all things seem to move confusedly, and wicked men to do what they list; they will destroy all before them: but they cannot; the judgments are the Lord's, and he carries them on judiciously; there are eyes in the wheels, and a divine Spirit in them, and they do not move, they cannot move otherwise than the wise God will have them.

Obs. 3. In the worst times God hath some who are faithful, and serve him. Violence had filled the land, the idol of jealousy was set at the altar gate, chambers of imagery in the walls of the temple, the ancients of Israel worshipped the forms of creeping things and abominable beasts, the women wept for that shameful idol Tammuz, corruptions abounded in church and state; yet some faithful ones the Lord had, that were undefiled. The church of God did never totally fail, nor ever shall. When all flesh had corrupted its way, the wickedness of man was grown great; when the earth was filled with violence, Gen. vi. 5, 11, 12, yet then, even then was Noah untainted, "he was just and perfect in his generations, and walked with God," ver. 9. In Ahab's days, when Jezebel cut off the prophets of the Lord, and he vexed the righteous with his will-worship and abominable idolatries, and forced them to flee to Jerusalem; and things were so extremely ill, the righteous so wasted, that Elijah, a prophet, thought there was none left in Israel but himself; even then the Lord tells him there were seven thousand, which had not bowed their knees to Baal, nor kissed him, 1 Kings xix. 18; they have showed that false god no reverence, contracted no pollution by doing as the rest did. When Ahaz, who is stigmatized for his wickedness, 2 Chron. xxviii. 22, when he reigned, cut in pieces the vessels of the temple, and shut up the doors of the temple, and made altars in every corner of Jerusalem, ver. 24; yet his own son Hezekiah was godly at that time, and hated the ways of his father. When Christ came, there was a Joseph and Mary, a Zacharias and Elisabeth, a Simeon and Anna, with some few others; and the times were exceeding bad then. In the depths of popery were *pauperes Lugdunenses*, of whom Reinerus a popish inquisitor writes, that they had a great show of godliness, because they lived justly before men, believed all things well concerning God and all the articles of faith, only they blasphemed and hated the church of Rome. God had his Huss, Jerom of Prague, and Luther, in times bad enough.

Obs. 4. The number of men to be saved in Jerusalem is few. Commission is given to the man with the inkhorn by his side, to go and search through Jerusalem, and where he found any mourning, sighing, to mark them; and surely this number was very few: he is not to mark streets, families, but particular persons, which notes the paucity of those that were truly godly, and to be saved. In Egypt the blood was upon the lintel and side-posts of the door, and so whole families there escaped; but here in Jerusalem the mark is not upon the door, but the forehead; many doors, whole families, were passed over, here and there one found and marked. Take a place or two to this purpose: Jer. v. 1, "Run ye to and fro through the streets of Jerusalem, and see now, and know, and seek in the broad places thereof, if ye can find a man, if there be any that executeth judgment, that seeketh the truth; and I will pardon it. Here God bids them search and see if they could find a man and bring forth, so that the city might be spared, but they could not find one. This satisfied not God, they might be careless in that work, overlook some man that did it; God therefore will search himself: Ezek. xxii. 30, "I sought for a man among them, that should make up the hedge, and stand in the gap before me for the land, that I should not destroy it; but I found none." Neither man nor God could find any. These expressions show that the number of the godly was very few; that those who were so durst not appear in public, because the times were so profane and perilous, but hid themselves and mourned in secret. Few is the number of true believers and true mourners; there were two prophets, Jeremiah and Uriah, the Rechabites, Baruch the scribe, Ebedmelech the Ethiopian, with some few beside. The thought of the scant number of the good ones made sad the heart of the prophet Micah, chap. vii. 1, "Woe is me! for I am as when they have gathered the summer fruits, as the grape-gleanings of the vintage: there is no cluster to eat."

Obs. 5. The Lord hath a special care of his saints when dreadful and destroying judgments are coming upon others. "Go, set a mark upon them that sigh," &c. provide that they be secured, distinguish them from all the rest, and let them have mercy in the common calamity. It appears,

(1.) From the person employed to do it, and that is the Lord Christ, who was the man with the inkhorn by his side. When God shall employ not a prophet, not an angel, but his own dear Son to do this work, to mark the godly, it is argument of tender care towards them.

(2.) He must "go through the midst of the city," and look into every place, make an exact search, and find them out wherever they were hid; God would not have him neglect any place, lest he should pass by any saint. Matt. ii. 8, Herod would have the wise men make diligent search for the young child; and God would have Christ here make diligent search for mourning saints; they are his treasure, and Christ would search for them as for hid treasure.

(3.) He must surely mark them. You shall sign them with a sign, that is, certainly sign them; the doubling of the word in the original notes God's intention and care to have it done: it might have sufficed to have said, You shall sign them; but he adds, with a sign, to put it out of doubt.

(4.) From the persons sealed:

[1.] Men. It is put indefinitely, not confined to noble, wise, rich, learned, but any condition of men that were godly; any poor man, any servant, any child, any little one, let their grace be never so mean, if they had any grace at all, they should have the seal as well as the best.

[2.] Mourners. When filled with sorrow for the sins of the land, with fears for the judgments which were coming upon the land, all in a confusion, every one at a loss, not knowing what to do, which way to turn themselves; liberties, ordinances, city, sanctuary, all comforts, all friends, being upon departure; now to be marked out for life eternal, now to have the conscience sprinkled with the blood of Christ, the Spirit to bear witness and seal up the soul, with assurance of God's love; this shows God hath a great care of his people in time of dangers.

Not only at this time, but in all times of judgments God hath been careful of his people. Lot's righteous soul was vexed at the unclean conversation of the Sodomites; and when fire and brimstone scorched, consumed Sodom, God sent his angels to find, hasten, and force Lot out of that wicked place, Gen. xix. The flood that drowned all the world, could not hurt Noah; God put him into the ark, shut him in, and kept him safe there, Gen. vii. When the destroying angel comes forth to destroy the first-born of Egypt, the Israelites' posts were sprinkled with blood, Exod. xii. 22, and no blood must be shed there; they were marked for deliverance. When Jericho was taken and destroyed, the scarlet thread in the window was a sign of deliverance to Rahab and her house, Josh. ii. 18; vi. 23. Rev. vii. 2—5, Christ the Angel of the east, who had the seal of the living God, viz. the Spirit, forbids the angels to hurt any, till the one hundred and forty-four thousand were sealed in their foreheads. When Paul was brought before Nero, and all left him in the jaws of that roaring lion, the Lord stood by him and strengthened him: the more careless others were of Paul, the more careful was God of him. A little before Jerusalem was taken by the Romans, a voice was heard, *Ite Pellam;* Mal. iii. 16, 17.
the faithful no sooner escape thither, but the city was ruined, and all the foretold woes accomplished in it.

Obs. 6. It is the Lord Christ who is the marker of the saints. All power in heaven and earth is given to him; sealing and saving power, as well as rejecting and destroying power. He is said to have the seal of the living God, Rev. vii. and to take order for the sealing the servants of the Lord. Rev. iii. 12, "Him that overcometh will I make a pillar in the temple of my God, and he shall go no more out: and I will write upon him the name of my God, and the name of the city of my God, which is new Jerusalem, which cometh down out of heaven from my God: and I will write upon him my new name." Christ makes him a pillar in the temple, that is great honour; but that is not all, Christ writes three names upon that man; the name of his God, of new Jerusalem, and his own name; he causeth him to know he is the son of God, a citizen of the heavenly city, and should have interest in the glory and dignity of Phil. ii. 9.
Christ, which divines call the new Heb. ii. 7.
name given him after his passion and ascension: such marking have the saints and faithful servants of Christ. The Scripture tells us of another marker besides Christ, and it is the beast mentioned Rev. xiii. 16, 17, who causeth all to receive a mark in their right hand and forehead. Christ had sealed his, Rev. vii. to separate them from the world and danger; and the beast seals his, to separate them from Christ's sealed ones, and for the world, that they might buy and sell: this sealing was not for deliverance, but for destruction; Rev. xiv. 9, 10, "If any man receive the beast's mark in his hand or forehead, the same shall drink of the wine of the wrath of God, and be tormented with fire and brimstone." Here was a dangerous mark, whether it was the mass, sign of the cross, profession of popish worship, subjection to the pope as head of the church, obedience to his canons and decrees, observation of his fasts, days, rites; whether auricular confession, popish orders, or any vows or oaths to maintain the pope and his power, such as Otho took in the year 960.

Obs. 7. God and Christ are not ashamed of theirs in the worst times and greatest dangers; God will have them marked, and Christ doth mark them in the forehead. In Sodom God owned Lot; in Rome he stood by Paul, 2 Tim. iv. 17. When four destroying angels were come abroad, the Lord Christ seals twelve thousand of every tribe in their foreheads, Rev. vii. 3, 5—8. Christ owns his people

Rev. xxii. 4, "His name shall be in their foreheads." The beast had marked and owned those that were here, and Christ would do so by his; it was *vindicationis nota.*

here and hereafter; see John x. 3, 14, 27. He calls them his sheep, his friends, chap. xv. 15, his brethren: "I ascend unto my Father, and your Father; to my God, and your God," John xx. 17. When Christ was in heaven, he owned Stephen being amidst his enemies, Acts vii. 55, 56; and he promises, Matt. x. 32, to confess and own the man before his Father in heaven, who shall confess and own him here on earth. It is a great privilege to be owned by the Lord; Heb. xi. 16, "God is not ashamed to be called their God:" notwithstanding all the saints' sins and infirmities, God is not ashamed of them. When they were in Egypt, God owned them; Exod. iii. 6, 7, he tells Moses he was the God of Abraham, Isaac, and Jacob, and that he had surely seen the affliction of his people.

Victoria, a holy virgin, under Dioclesian, being asked by the proconsul if she would go with her brother Fortunatianus, a heathen; answered, No, because I am a christian, and they are my brethren which keep the commands of God.

Let not us be ashamed of God and his cause, but openly and truly profess him and his ways: we shall lose nothing by it; 1 Sam. ii. 30, "Them that honour me I will honour, and they that despise me shall be lightly esteemed." If we have shame with men and honour with God, vilified on earth and be accepted in heaven, we have no cause to be discouraged. It is likely the godly here were reproached, threatened, hardly used; but because they honoured God, God owned them; and who ever honoured God, and was not honoured by him? The three children would not obey Nebuchadnezzar's command, nor worship his image, Dan. iii. but honour the God of Israel, trust in him for help; rather die in his cause than dishonour him at all; and did not the Lord honour them with his presence, with safety and deliverance. When Peter and John were bold in the cause of Christ, and would preach the truth notwithstanding the command of rulers to the contrary; presently after God honoured them miraculously, shaking the house, and filling them all with the Holy Ghost, Acts iii. 18—20, 31. And if you ask how you shall honour God; it is answered, by purging yourselves from the corruptions of the times, 2 Tim. ii. 21, "If a man purge himself, he shall be a vessel unto honour," and by standing for the truths of the times.

Obs. 8. Another observation is, that the faithful are so far from complying with the wickedness of the times, that they sigh and cry for the abominations thereof.

(1.) They comply not. Wickedness is powerful, and hath its arguments of pleasure, profit, countenance, to draw good men to side with her; but they are things intractable. "How can I do this wickedness, and sin against God?" Gen. xxxix. 9. David would not sit with the wicked, he hated the congregation of evil-doers, Psal. xxvi. 5; and see what he resolved upon, Psal. ci. 4—8; he would rather cut them off than countenance them. Grace is as strong in the saints, as corruption is in the wicked. The vigour of faith, 1 John v. 4, the power of the Spirit, chap. iv. 4, and the efficacy of Christ's prayer, John xvii. 15, 20, do keep the servants of God from complying with the wicked. When all flesh had corrupted its ways, yet Noah was uncorrupt; Gen. vi. 9, "Noah was a just man and perfect in his generations." Ahab could not get Micaiah to comply with the court, and suit with the humour of the times. The godly are like fish in salt waters, they grow not brackish, they lose not of their sweetness. Zacharias and Elisabeth, in the great corruptions at Christ's coming, in the great scarcity of good men, yet they walked in all the commandments of the Lord blameless, not in the commands of the high priests and pharisees. God hath spoken to the righteous with a strong hand, and instructed them that they should not walk in the ways of the wicked, Isa. viii. 11. Here the godly did not bow to the image of jealousy, join with the seventy elders in offering incense; they wept not for Tammuz, they put not the branch to their nose.

(2.) They sigh and cry for the abominations which are in their times, they bewail the sins of others: Psal. cxix. 53, "Horror hath taken hold upon me because of the wicked that forsake thy law." Ver. 158, "I beheld the transgressors, and was grieved; because they kept not thy word." Lot, 2 Pet. ii. 7, was vexed with the filthy conversation of the Sodomites; yea, vexed from day to day; what he saw and heard was a continual vexation unto him. The Lord Christ, when they honoured him with their garments cast in the way, when they acknowledged him King, and magnified him, Luke xix. 36, 38, even then he weeps over Jerusalem for her impenitency, others' sins, and the judgments of God coming upon her, ver. 41. The two witnesses, Rev. xi. 3, prophesy in sackcloth, which was the habit of mourners: Mordecai, Daniel, the Ninevites, and others, when they mourned, wore sackcloth; so did these witnesses bewailing the abominations and tyranny of antichrist, the desolations of the church, and delusions of the people. 2 Cor. xii. 21, "When I come again I fear my God will humble me among you, and that I shall bewail many which have sinned already, and have not repented of the uncleanness and fornication and lasciviousness which they have committed."

This mourning is, [1.] hearty, real; they sigh, they groan; it is not a light matter, the abominations were weighty, and pressing upon their spirits. 2 Pet. ii. 7, the word there for vexed is, *καταπονούμενον ὑπὸ τῆς τῶν ἀθεσμων εν ἀσελγείᾳ ἀναστροφης*, and it is then to be rendered word for word, oppressed under the conversation of the ungodly in wantonness. The ungodly's wanton, wicked conversation is an oppressing evil unto the godly, and afflicts their hearts, as the Egyptians afflicted the Israelites: Acts vii. 24, Moses avenged the oppressed. Lot's soul was vexed, ver. 8, he tormented, racked his soul; a metaphor taken from engines they did torment with, his soul was troubled as a man upon the rack. Jer. iv. 19, "My bowels, my bowels! I am pained at my very heart:" what was the matter? there was "the sound of the trumpet, the alarm of war."

[2.] As it was cordial, so it was constant and great grief; they sighed and cried, a little sufficed not, it continued. Jer. ix. 1, "Oh that my head were waters, and mine eyes a fountain of tears, that I might weep day and night." The prophet wished himself turned into waters, into a fountain, that, weeping day and night, he might with a flood of tears carry down the floods of iniquity which he saw. So Ezra, chap. ix. 3, when he saw the holy seed match with strangers, the princes and rulers to be chief in the trespasses, he rent his garments, plucked off the hair of his head and beard, and sat down astonished; his grief was such as made him astonished.

[3.] It is inward and outward; they sigh, they cry, there are expressions of their grief, it was not hidden, but evident; they declared how their souls were oppressed, how they were filled with grief, and could not forbear. Christ wept over Jerusalem. Micah, when he considered the sins of Samaria and Jerusalem, with the heavy judgments which were coming, chap. i. 8, saith, "I will wail and howl, I will go stripped and naked" (as if sorrow had bereft him of his wits); "I will make a wailing like the dragons, and mourning as the owls." *Vid.* A Lapide and Sanctius, what they say of the dragons' and owls' mourning: great mourning with outward expressions are set out thereby; Job xxx. 29, "I am a brother to dragons, and a companion to owls" or ostriches.

[4.] Universal; not for some few or great abominations, but for all the abominations, church, state, city, family abominations; they laid all to heart, and left none unbewailed.

Inquire, I. Why do the godly sigh and cry?

1. God is dishonoured by the sins of others, as well as by our own, and the godly are grieved when God is dishonoured by any. Psal. cxix. 136, "Rivers of waters run down mine eyes, because they keep not thy law." David's afflictions drew not so many tears from him, as the sins of others; not his banishment by his son, as the breach of God's law by the wicked. Nothing went so to his heart as the dishonour of God, whose glory shining in his word and ordinances, is dearer to the godly than their lives. Elijah desired to die when he saw God so dishonoured by Ahab and Jezebel. The eye is for two things, for sight and tears: if we see God dishonoured, presently our eyes should be filled with tears.

2. If we mourn not for the sins of others, we draw them upon us, we make them ours. They mourned here for all their abominations, lest they should be found guilty of any: and 1 Cor. v. the Corinthians were defiled with the sin of the incestuous person, because they did not mourn and do their duty to affect his heart, or remove him from their body. Bradford prayed the Lord to forgive him his other men's sins.

3. It is argument we mourn for sin as sin when we mourn for it in others. Sin is the breach of the law any where, and if I grieve, sigh, cry for it in myself, and not in others, it is some selfish respect, not the nature of sin, which causeth that mourning. He who hates poison as poison, hates it every where, in whose hand soever it be; and he who mourns for sin as sin, would neither himself, nor have others, violate the law of God.

4. The sins of others are of a destroying nature, as well as our own; they may destroy armies, states, churches, counsels. Eccles. ix. 18, "One sinner destroyeth much good." One Achan, one murderer may undo a land; he defiles it, brings peril upon it. God appointed a special sacrifice to expiate murder, Deut. xxi.; and no satisfaction was to be taken for a murderer's life, Numb. xxxv. 31. Saul slays the Gibeonites unjustly, and the three years' famine is upon David and his people, 2 Sam. xxi. 1—3. The death of the Levite's concubine, and Benjamin's refusal to deliver up the delinquents to justice, caused a bloody war, and the death of above sixty-five thousand men.

5. It argues strength of grace to mourn for others' sins. Censuring and reproaching of others for their sins argues strength of corruption; and mourning for them argues strength of grace, a sound spiritual constitution: such a one was in Christ, he prayed for the hardness of others' hearts, Mark iii. 5.

6. They who mourn for abominations, do great service for the places where they live; they stand in the gap, they keep off God's judgments. When the people had sinned in making a calf, and God's judgments were breaking in upon them, did not Moses mourn, weep, pray before the Lord, and keep off the sad things that were hastening towards them? Psal. cvi. 23, "He said that he would destroy them, had not Moses his chosen stood before him in the breach, to turn away his wrath, lest he should destroy them." The mourner's tears oft quench the fire of God's wrath, divert judgments; if not, but destruction comes, as here, yet the mourners have this testimony in their breast, that they drew not down the vengeance on the church or state.

7. They are blessed that mourn, Matt. v. 4. These here were marked, had testimonies of God's good will towards them. Jeremiah was a mourner, chap. ix. 1; and chap. xv. 11, saith God there, "I will cause the enemy to entreat thee well in the time of evil." Here was a blessing promised, and the faithful God could not but perform it. When the earth is watered by the heavens, it is blessed; but when the earth waters the heavens, when we put tears into the Lord's bottle, when we mourn and weep for the abominations of the earth, there is a greater blessing: Psal. xii. 5, "For the sighing of the needy, I will arise and set," &c. Isa. lvii. 18, "I will restore comforts unto him and to his mourners."

8. Others mourn for the sins of men that are not men: "Because of swearing the land mourneth," Jer. xxiii. 10. "The whole creation groaneth and travaileth in pain," Rom. viii. 22.

Inquire, II. For what should we mourn?

1. For effusion of so much blood in the kingdom, and spoiling so many towns. When Ziklag was burned, it is said, David and those with him wept till they had no more power to weep, 1 Sam. xxx. 4. What would David do, if he were now alive and amongst us, to see countries and kingdoms consumed with civil wars? Isa. xxii. 4, 5, "Look away from me; I will weep bitterly, labour not to comfort me, because of the spoiling of the daughter of my people. For it is a day of trouble, and of treading down, and of perplexity by the Lord God of hosts in the valley of vision, breaking down the walls, and of crying to the mountains." Jer. xxxi. 15, "A voice was heard in Ramah, lamentation and bitter weeping; Rachel weeping for her children, refused to be comforted, because they were not." Rachel was buried in Bethlehem, Gen. xxxv. 19, and Ramah was not far from it; she is put for the Bethlemitical women, who wept bitterly for their children who were slain, and carried that way into captivity. And should not England weep because thousands of her children are not; many precious ones are gone, the sword hath drunk their blood? If Martha and Mary wept for one Lazarus, the friend of Christ, why should not all our Marthas and Marys weep, when so many Lazaruses, so many friends of Christ, have been cut off? Isa. lvii. 1, "The righteous perisheth, and no man layeth it to heart."

2. That justice takes not place, but rather injustice and oppression. Isa. lix. 11, "We roar all like bears, and mourn sore like doves: we look for judgment, but there is none:" and ver. 14, 15, "Justice standeth afar off, equity cannot enter; he that departeth from evil makes himself a prey: and the Lord saw it, and it displeased him that there was no judgment." The oppressed cry.

3. For the sinful, selfish policy which hath been in the great businesses of the kingdom which are to carry on reformation. They carted the ark, when their own shoulders should have carried it; their prudence in the things of God made way for Uzzah's sin and suffering, and hindered the progress of the work. There hath been too much of man seen in our undertakings. Oh the policy, falsehood, treachery, that hath been among us! What was it made Jeremiah weep and mourn so? chap. ix. 1, 2; it was because they were "adulterers, an assembly of treacherous men."

4. For the great and bitter divisions which are among us, not only among those who are wicked or indifferent, but even among those who are godly; they shoot their arrows one at another, even bitter words and bitter actions. Is it not sad when Christ's

disciples and apostles fall out? Matt. xx. 24, "The ten were moved with indignation against the two brethren." It troubled Christ to see such variance between them, and had he not wisely and speedily taken up the matter, the issue might have been very ill. When brethren wrong one another, it will affect a Moses, Acts vii. 26. Is it not to be lamented when our fountains run salt water? when brethren speak evil one of another, and so speak evil of the law and gospel also? Gal. v. 15, it troubled Paul's spirit to see such biting and devouring of one another. Certainly if we should see two or three dogs biting of a man, it would much work upon us, and move us to rate and beat them off; and can we see men biting men, and not be affected with it? To see men destroyed with a spirit of bitterness, when they should be restored with a spirit of meekness, is mourning to some, however it be music to others.

5. That God's judgments have been so long upon us, and done us so little good. God hath given us much physic, and it doth not work; we may be a dying people, as those Jews were, Ezra x. 9; it is said there that all the people sat in the street of the house of God trembling, because some were carried away captive, and for the great rain, the great showers which beat down their fruit and corn. We have had many taken prisoners, carried away captive, used barbarously; we have had great rains of blood; and have we yet trembled? have we learned righteousness, and beheld the majesty of the Lord? Isa. xxvi. 9, 10. May it not be said, as it is Jer. v. 3, "Thou hast stricken them, but they have not grieved; thou hast consumed them, but they have refused to receive correction: they have made their faces harder than a rock?"

Amos vi. 6, we "drink wine in bowls, and anoint," &c. *Intus vino, extus oleo.*

6. That so many thousands have perished in their sins, and multitudes are in a perishing way: Rom. ix. 2, "I have great heaviness and continual sorrow in my heart. For I could wish myself separated from Christ for my brethren, my kinsmen according to the flesh:" he feared they would perish eternally, and therefore mourned continually. Granctensis tells of a woman that was so affected with souls' miscarryings, that she besought God to stop up the passage into hell with her soul and body, that none might have entrance. Do not people perish for want of vision, and few lay it to heart?

7. That God's name suffers so much amongst us. God's name should be dear to us; the Scripture tells us it is glorious and fearful, Deut. xxviii. 58; great and terrible, Psal. xcix. 3; holy and reverend, Psal. cxi. 9; honourable, Psal. lxvi. 2: and that this name of God should suffer by sinful, wretched men is matter of sighing and crying. Some despise his name, Mal. i. 6, some profane his name, Lev. xxi. 6, some blaspheme his name, Isa. lii. 5, and most darken the glory of his name; and as it was to Joshua a great grief, bitter affliction, when his name suffered, Josh. vii. 9, so it should be to us.

Ver. 5—7. *And to the others he said in mine hearing, Go ye after him through the city, and smite: let not your eye spare, neither have ye pity: slay utterly old and young, both maids, and little children, and women: but come not near any man upon whom is the mark; and begin at my sanctuary. Then they began at the ancient men which were before the house. And he said unto them, Defile the house, and fill the courts with the slain: go ye forth. And they went forth, and slew in the city.*

The Lord Christ having marked some for mercy, in these verses is declared what was to be done with the rest.

I. Here is a command to execute them.

II. The execution itself.

In the command you have these particulars:

1. The party commanding; "he said."

2. The parties commanded; "the others."

3. The witness of what was commanded, and that is Ezekiel; "in mine hearing."

4. The things commanded, which are these:

(1.) To "go;" they must go after him who marked the mourners.

(2.) To "smite," ver. 5, to "slay," ver. 6, to "defile," to "fill the courts" of the sanctuary "with the slain," ver. 7.

III. A double prohibition.

1. Of mercy to the wicked; "Let not your eye spare, neither have ye pity," ver. 6.

2. Of meddling with the marked; "Come not near any upon whom the mark is," ver. 6.

IV. Whom they must smite, slay; "old, young, maids, children, women."

V. The place where they must begin, and that is the "sanctuary," ver. 6.

VI. Then the execution itself; "They went forth," &c.

I shall open the words wherein any thing seems difficult, and then give you the observation.

"The others." They were the six angels who had the slaughter weapons in their hands; they must now go and make use of them; they were not called for in vain.

"Let not your eye spare." This phrase is sometimes referred to things without life; as Gen. xlv. 20, "Regard not your stuff:" the Hebrew is, Let not your eye spare your stuff. It is Joseph's speech to his brethren, when he was inviting them to come to Egypt, and his meaning is this; When you shall look upon the furniture of my father's house, and see what goodly, rich, and useful stuff it is, you will be loth to leave it behind you, your eyes will be affected with it, you will say you cannot be without it, though you know not how to bring it; but let not your eyes spare it, look on it as a needless thing, regard it not, Egypt is before you, and there is enough to supply and suffice you.

Sometimes it is referred to things with life, as men and beasts, and notes thus much, that there should be no sign of mercy in their eyes, not a look, not a favourable aspect towards those they were to execute; their eyes must be terrible, and not spare from vengeance, they must show no pity; and the word in Scripture is so rendered; Deut. xiii. 8, "Thine eye shall not pity him, neither shalt thou spare;" that which is "pity" here is "spare" in my text, and that which is "spare" in my text, is "pity" here. And Deut. vii. 16, "Thine eye shall have no pity upon them:" the Hebrew is the same word; thou shalt not spare upon them, spare to execute vengeance upon them: so that they are used promiscuously, and one interprets the other; an eye not sparing, is to show no mercy, no pity. That in 1 Sam. xxiv. 10 clears it; when some bade David kill Saul when he cut off the skirt of his garment, saith he, "But mine eye spared thee," that is, had pity" on thee, and I killed thee not; if mine eye had not spared thee, I had killed thee without pity, without mercy. Jer. xxi. 7, "He shall not spare them, neither have pity, nor have mercy;" the two first words are in my text, and they are both interpreted by the last, not to spare. Not to pity is to have no mercy, whatever motives be thereunto.

"Slay utterly old and young." In the Hebrew it

is, the old man, the young man, the maiden, and little child, all in the singular number, which is put for the plural.

Quest. Here a great question is movable, How it stands with the justicè of God to give charge for the destruction of little children which were innocent?

Answ. The word טף for little children some take to be meant of such as could play in the streets, and were under twenty years. Gen. xlvii. 12, "Joseph nourished his father, and his brethren, and all his father's household, with bread, according to their families," לפי הטף according to the little ones; they were not sucking children, but such as could run up and down, that Joseph nourished: now if the little children be taken for such, they might be guilty of great sins, as the children that mocked the prophet, and so deserve death.

Ad os parvuli.

But take little children for such as have not committed actual sin, even babes new born, in the womb, of which sort many perished in the flood, and many in Sodom, such God may cut off without impeachment of his justice.

1. He hath an absolute dominion over his creatures; he is the potter, and we are the clay; if he make the vessel, he may break the vessel; shall he not do with his own as he please? He gives life to babes, and he may take it from them when and how he pleases.

2. They were defiled with original sin, and deserved death. "The wages of sin," be it original or actual, "is death," and it matters not whether a natural or a violent death: therefore he forbade Jeremiah to take a wife, to have sons and daughters in Jerusalem; and as for those sons and daughters which should be born there, they and their fathers and mothers should be consumed by the sword, and by famine, Jer. xvi. 2—4.

3. They are parts of their parents, part of their family, part of their substance, and God may punish the sinning parent in his child, as well as in his stock.

4. Had they lived, it is likely they would have trod in their fathers' steps, and sinned those great sins they did, like them in Jer. vii. 18, "Children gather wood, and the fathers kindle the fire, and the women knead their dough." Neither doth God punish upon prevision of future sin, but takes them away from present and future pollution.

5. God might, notwithstanding this outward temporal judgment, have mercy on their souls. Questionless many children die more terrible deaths than by the sword, and yet perish not eternally.

"Come not near any man upon whom is the mark."

Quest. If this mark were not a visible mark, how should they know them, and spare them?

Answ. The Lord knew who were his, though men knew them not; and it is probable such is the rage of the wicked against the godly, that if they had a little distinguishing character from others, they would the rather have fallen upon them, and cut them off; but the Lord ordered the judgment so, and their spirits so, that they came not near them. The mark was inward in the foreheads of their consciences, and Providence watched and wrought for them without. God might dart a fear into them, disable them from doing the marked ones any hurt, divert them to other families and persons: and this manner of speech is more than if he had said, Do not kill them; they might do much hurt to them, yet not kill them; but when he saith, Come not near them, God doth make a fence about them, and compasseth them with this command and his favour in it, as with a shield against all evil and wrong.

This deliverance of the marked ones from the slaughter men, is a type of God's preserving his people in all great and general calamities, and especially of freeing his elect ones from hell and the furies thereof. The Chaldeans must not come near the marked ones to destroy them, and devils must not come near those Christ hath sprinkled with his blood, to ruin and destroy them; they are freed from the power of Satan and eternal death.

"Begin at my sanctuary." This was the holy place, the habitation of God, where his worship was, where he gave out gracious answers unto them, yet here they must begin.

Why here?

1. They trusted in the holiness of this place: Jer. vii. 4, 10, when they had sinned grievously, they thought that if they came and worshipped there, all was well, they were delivered, and cried out, "The temple of the Lord." God would begin with their confidence.

2. They had greatly polluted that holy place: there was the idol of jealousy; there was the form of every creeping thing and abominable beast portrayed upon the walls; there were men offering incense to those idols; there was the filthy idol Tammuz, and women weeping for it; there were men with their backs towards God, the ark, and worshipping the sun eastward; there they put the branch to their nose. Great abominations were gotten into the temple, they must therefore begin there.

3. The sins of the priests and prophets who belonged to the temple were exceeding great. They were messengers of God to the people, and mouths of the people to God, and above others should have been clean, holy, gracious, free from the sins of the times; they should have been exemplary unto others; but if you observe the Scripture a little, you shall find they were patterns of all impiety to the people: they were ignorant, blind, dumb, drunken, Isa. xxviii. 7; lvi. 10, 12; unclean, filthy, strengthening the hands of the wicked, Jer. xxiii. 14; covetous and cruel, Isa. lvi. 11; Micah iii. 5; conceited of their own abilities, Jer. viii. 8; flatterers, and dealt falsely with the people, Jer. vi. 13, 14; xxvii. 15; they perverted the word of the Lord, Jer. xxiii. 36; they rejected his word, Jer. viii. 9; they prophesied their own dreams, Jer. xxiii. 2, 7, and put it upon God, saying, "He saith," ver. 31; they ruled with rigour, Ezek. xxxiv. 4; they reproached, slandered, and complained of the true prophets, stirring up enemies against them, and seeking their liberties and lives, Jer. xxvi. 8, 9, 11; Amos vii. 10. This made Jeremiah conclude, Lam. iv. 13, that Jerusalem was destroyed chiefly "for the sins of her prophets, and the iniquities of her priests, that shed the blood of the just in the midst of her."

Obs. 1. When God is upon executing judgment, he first manifests, yea, vouchsafes mercy to his friends, before he lets out wrath upon his enemies. "Go ye after him:" one was sent to mark the mourners, before those with the slaughter weapons had commission to destroy the rest. His mercy acts before his justice, he separates the righteous before he destroys the wicked; he makes up his jewels before the day comes that burns like an oven, Mal. iii. 17; iv. 1; he prepares an ark for Noah, before he sends a flood upon the world. God sends an angel to fetch Lot out of Sodom, before he rains fire and brimstone upon them; and at the last great judgment, the sheep shall have mercy before the goats shall have judgment: "Come, ye blessed;" that joyful sound shall be heard first, and after, "Depart, ye cursed," Matt. xxv. 34, 41. Mercy is God's firstborn, and visits the saints ere judgments break out.

Obs. 2. When the godly are secured, then judgment delays not. When the mourners are near marking, then the six men follow him presently that marks them, and they do their office. When Lot is out of Sodom, fire and brimstone come into Sodom; God could do nothing while he was there, Gen. xix. 22, but when he was gone, he consumed them with the vengeance of eternal fire. Judgments sometimes do linger, and what is the cause? some servants of God are not marked, secured, got into their chambers of safety; if they were, judgment would quickly be upon the backs of the wicked. Isa. xxvi. 20, 21, "Come, my people, enter thou into thy chambers, and shut thy doors about thee: hide thyself as it were for a little moment, until the indignation be overpast. For, behold, the Lord cometh out of his place to punish the inhabitants of the earth for their iniquity:" when once they were got into safe places, then would indignation come upon the wicked. When swallows and other birds fly from us, it is a sign of winter approaching; and when good men are removed out of places, are driven into corners, it is a sign of judgment upon that place.

Obs. 3. Sinners may so provoke God, that he will neither show them mercy himself, nor let others do it. No pity, no mercy should they have from God or man. Go through the city, from one street to another, from gate to gate, and smite, smite every one of them, slay utterly, do not wound or weaken, but slay to perdition; and though they fall upon their knees, beg hard for their lives, promise you great matters, yet spare them not, neither have pity, be not affected with ought they say, do, or suffer. God hardened them here against them; but might they not find some sparing and pitying from God, if none with man? Ezek. v. 11, "Mine eye shall not spare, neither will I have any pity," and he ratifies it with an oath there.

What were their sins which made the Lord deal thus severely with them?

(1.) Their defilement of the temple with such abominations as they had done provoked desperately, they despited God therein to his face: there he vouchsafed his presence, heard their prayers, accepted their sacrifices, bestowed choice mercies upon them, and yet to defile that with their abominations, this greatly provoked.

(2.) Their abuse of the true and faithful prophets: Jeremiah forbid to prophesy lest he die for it, Jer. xi. 21. They laid hands on him, and said he should die, Jer. xxvi. 8. And 2 Chron. xxxvi. 16, "They mocked the messengers of God, despised his words, and misused his prophets, until the wrath of the Lord arose against his people." These sins made it rise a great height, even such a height, that all pity and mercy were laid aside.

(3.) Their great unfruitfulness under means and mercies. They reproached and derided the word, Jer. xx. 8, 9, and those that believed and obeyed it, Isa. viii. 18. You know what pains God took with his vineyard, he gathered out the stones, planted it with the choicest vine, built a tower in it, made a wine-press, did all which could be done for it; and now he looked for grapes, and it brought forth wild grapes: this kindled God's wrath, and banished pity, mercy from his heart: I will take away the hedge, break down the wall, lay it waste, it shall have no digging, pruning, clouds, or rain, but it shall be trodden down, and eaten up; by whom? by Chaldeans; those briers and thorns should scratch and tear it in pieces. Man's unfruitfulness makes God merciless: Luke xiii. 7, when the Lord came to the fig-tree planted in his vineyard, and found no fruit on it, what saith he? "Cut it down: why cumbereth it the ground?"

(4.) Pitilessness to one another. Micah iii. 2, 3, the princes and rulers did pluck off the skins and flesh from the bones of the people; they brake their bones, and chopped them in pieces. In their skirts was found the blood of the souls of poor innocents, Jer. ii. 34; and Manasseh had filled Jerusalem with innocent blood, which made the Lord to say, Jer. xv. 5, "Who shall have pity upon thee, O Jerusalem?" neither God nor man.

Obs. 4. Nothing will privilege sinners in the day of God's wrath; when he gives out commission to destroy, there will be a general destruction: old, young, maids, children, and women, they must all suffer, all die. In their military oath this was one branch, *Ne quis lædat fœminas, pueros, senes, ægrotos,* That no one should injure women, youths, the aged men, or the sick: even nature pleads strongly for such who are fearful and feeble, and not able to help themselves. Deut. xx. 14, when the Jews took a city, they were to spare the women and the little ones; and when they took Midian, they spared the maids and the little ones, Numb. xxxi. 9, 18. But here neither oath nor nature should take place, neither age, sex, or condition should advantage or secure them; not the hoary head of the aged, not the beauty of the virgins, not the tears of the mothers, nor the tenderness of the babes; but all must die. So 1 Sam. xv. 3, Samuel saith to Saul, "Go and smite Amalek, and utterly destroy all that they have, and spare them not; but slay both man and woman, infant and suckling, ox and sheep, camel and ass." Amalek sought the ruin of Israel, therefore God would have him utterly ruined: when judgments are general, sins are grievous.

Obs. 5. Open sins involve not only themselves, but those who are dearest to them, into open destruction. The ancients offered incense to idols, the women wept for Tammuz, others worshipped the sun; and these brought famine and sword not only upon themselves, but upon the young maids and little children which were free from those sins; the parents' sins ruined the children, and wrapped them up in an open and public calamity. Korah, Dathan, and Abiram rebel against Moses, and the earth swallowed up them, their houses, and all that belonged to them, Numb. xvi. 31, 32. The Sodomites' sins caused themselves and their little ones to be roasted in fire and brimstone. So princes, their sins bring down vengeance upon themselves, their posterity, and subjects. All sorts should therefore take heed of sinning against Divine Majesty, who is so dreadful in his judgments; if they will not pity themselves, yet they should pity those who are theirs, and dear to them.

Obs. 6. The lives and comforts of all God's marked ones are dear unto him. He gives order that they should not only not take away their lives, but also that they should not endanger their comforts: "Come not near any man upon whom is the mark;" do not fright them with your stern looks, bitter words, rough handling, keep your distance, they are very dear to me, and I am very tender of them. The marked ones are a people near to God, Psal. cxlviii. 14, and he will not suffer them to be wronged; Psal. cv. 14, 15, "He suffered no man to do them wrong; yea, he reproved kings for their sakes; saying, Touch not mine anointed." God's anointed ones are his marked ones, and they must not be touched, which is as much as, Come not near them. God doth not only keep the wicked from harming them, keep off judgments and blows from them, which is called sparing them, Mal. iii. 17, but he makes them up as his jewels: they lie scattered as common stones here and there, but God hath his days to make them up, to set them in ranks and orders, that they may shine more gloriously, and live more comfortably. Or thus, when a house is on fire, the owners will be sure then to look after their jewels, and to take and make them up, above all the rest; so God, when judgments are upon cities, towns, kingdoms, will have special care of his jewels and peculiar treasure; Luke xvii. 34, 35, "Two men shall be in one bed; the one shall be taken, and the other shall be left."

Obs. 7. See the order of divine judgment here. Those who were ringleaders to others, and drew them to sin by their place, authority, counsel, example, they must first be slain; "Begin at my sanctuary:" there were the seventy ancients of the house of Israel, mentioned chap. viii. 11; there were the priests, who had the charge of the holy things, and should not have suffered such corruptions, pollutions, to have come near the temple; but both the princes and priests were foremost in iniquity; they should have preserved the worship of God pure, kept the people from idolatrous practices, into which they drew them, and made Isaiah say twice, that their leaders caused them to err, Isa. iii. 12; ix. 16: there was enforcing virtue in them, constraining the people to err, and run upon their destruction; and therefore now, seeing they were first and deepest in sinning, they should be first and depeest in punishment. The slaughter men, representing the Chaldeans, must begin there, while they were fresh, strong; they must bathe their swords in the bowels and blood of princes and priests. Many times it is so, that those who are great are first in wickedness, and are first smitten; Numb. xxv. 4, "Take all the heads of the people, and hang them up before the Lord against the sun." They had been principal actors in whoredom and idolatry, led others to those sins, and their heads must off first. So Korah, Dathan and Abiram, Numb. xvi. they were prime rebels, made seditious work amongst the people; and went not they down first alive into the earth? and did not fire from heaven consume the two hundred and fifty princes that offered incense? It is too well known that men eminent in place are eminent in sin, be they in the state or in the church; and it is just they should be eminent in punishment.

Our prelates, who were sanctuary men, and pretended divine institution for their standing, declared by their fruits that they were not from above, but from beneath; an earthly generation, that hath been eminent in treasons, conspiracies, rebellions, seditious innovations, and corruptions of religion, as ever was; but God hath found them out, poured contempt upon them, plucked them up by the roots. Strafford and Canterbury were heads of wickedness in the church and state, and God hath lopped off their heads. Great ones make great breaches for others to perish in, and God begins with them to stop those breaches, and prevent open ruin. The devil carried Christ to the temple, and the pinnacle of it, and tempted him from thence to cast himself down, knowing that the sins of those who belong to the temple are most conspicuous, and beneficial to him and his kingdom.

Obs. 8. It is not the holiness of any place can mitigate or avert the wrath of God, when those who belong to it have defiled the place with their abominations. The temple was the holiest place in the world; 2 Chron. xxxvi. 14, "All the chief of the priests, and the people, transgressed very much;" and what was their transgression? "They polluted the house of the Lord which he had hallowed;" not which men had hallowed, but "which he had hallowed in Jerusalem:" no where else had he hallowed any place, yet that holy place they polluted, and the Lord therefore bids the slaughter men begin there, and defile it. They had defiled it with sin, and now God would have it defiled with the coming of heathens into it, with blood, with dead corpses, &c.; which made Jeremiah to sigh and say, "The Lord hath cast off his altar, he hath abhorred his sanctuary, he hath given up into the hand of the enemy the walls of her palaces; they have made a noise in the house of the Lord, as in the day of a solemn feast," Lam. ii. 7. It was music to the enemy to slay them in the temple itself, to dash out their brains against the ark and altar; 2 Chron. xxxvi. 17, "They slew their young men with the sword in the house of their sanctuary, and had no compassion upon young man or maiden, old man, or him that stooped for age." As they regarded not sex or condition of men, so not the place, though holy. Holy places were wont to be refuges unto those that fled to them, even heathens would spare those who betook themselves to the temples of their gods when they took the city; but in this destruction of Jerusalem, those who fled to the temple found no favour from God or man: "Slay them utterly," said God, defile the temple with their blood; and they did it, and filled the temple with such sacrifices as it never had.

Obs. 9. Divine justice oft smites sinners in the place where they have sinned. They had defiled the temple with their abominations, with idolatry, false worship, hypocrisy, and vain confidence in it, and there God commands them to be put to death. God had manifested great love, bestowed great mercies, imparted much light to them, heard their prayers, accepted their sacrifices in the temple, and now seeing there they sinned against him, there he would have them punished. When Ahab had murdered Naboth, 1 Kings xxi. this message was sent unto him, "In the place where dogs licked the blood of Naboth shall dogs lick thy blood, even thine," ver. 19; and it was made good, chap. xxii. 38; 2 Kings ix. 26.

Obs. 10. God's judgments are as extensive as sinners' sins. They must slay not only sanctuary sinners, but city sinners. They had sinned every where, the land was full of violence, and now the land, city, sanctuary, were full of bloody men and bloody judgments; and as they had filled all with sin, so they must fill all with slain ones. When sins are general, judgments are answerable: Isa. viii. 8, speaking of the king of Assyria, it is said, "He shall pass through Judah; he shall overflow and go over, he shall reach even to the neck; and the stretching out of his wings shall fill the breadth of thy land." This is spoken of Sennacherib, who, like a flood over all the land, came up to the neck, viz. Jerusalem; but Nebuchadnezzar came not only up to the neck, to Jerusalem, but into it, and overflowed the head, he drowned all in blood: where there was no mark, there was no mercy to be showed.

Obs. 11. God, after long forbearing, is intent upon, and speedy in his judgments. Observe the phrases in these verses which show it; "go ye through the city," "spare none," "slay utterly," "begin at my sanctuary," "defile the house," "fill the courts with the slain," "go ye forth." These expressions set out the bent and intensiveness of God's Spirit in this work; he would have his executioners hasten about it, and despatch all out of hand.

Obs. 12. God's instruments do readily obey his commands, of what nature soever they be. Here they are appointed to harsh and bloody services, to destroy utterly all sorts and conditions of men, women, children, without pity; and they went forth, and slew in the city. God commanded, and they presently obeyed; not the holiness of the place, the multitude of persons to be destroyed, or danger of mistaking the marked ones, did retard them.

Ver. 8. ***And it came to pass, while they were slaying them, and I was left, that I fell upon my face, and cried, and said, Ah Lord God! wilt thou destroy all the residue of Israel in thy pouring out of thy fury upon Jerusalem?***

This verse is the second general head of the chapter, and contains the prophet's intercession for Israel. When he saw what bloody doings were in the temple and city by the slaughter angels, he is affected therewith, he cannot hold, but falls down, and cries out, "Ah Lord God!" &c.

In the verse you may consider,

I. The occasion of the prophet's interceding, or moving cause thereof, which is double;

1. The people's slaughter.

2. His own solitariness, "I was left."

II. The circumstances or adjuncts thereof; which are,

1. Falling upon his face.

2. Crying.

III. The intercession itself; where you have,

1. A pathetical invocation of God, "Ah Lord God!"

2. An efficacious deprecation of judgment, "Wilt thou destroy all the residue?" &c.

For opening of the words,

1. We must inquire how the prophet here saith, "I was left." There were many sealed and spared, which makes the difficulty. Some think the Septuagint passed by these words, and left them out, lest they should seem contrary to what went before. Theodoret adds μονος, I was left alone; but the Hebrew is, I was left. For understanding of this phrase, you may take notice, that it is usual in Scripture, when great destructions are, to say few or none are left: Judg. iv. 16, "All the host of Sisera fell upon the edge of the sword; and there was not a man left;" yet Sisera, if no others, was fled. So, in 1 Kings xix. 14, Elijah saith, they have "slain thy prophets with the sword; and I, even I only, am left," when there were seven thousand that bowed not their knees to Baal. If this satisfy not,

ונאשאר אני

2. "I was left." That is, left with the sealed ones, all were destroyed besides: or,

3. Of those in the temple, or belonging to it, "I was left." Our prophet saw them all slain, and the slaughter men were gone out into the city, and there they were destroying; and as they had spared none in the temple, so he might fear there would be few spared in the city, and so safely say, "I am left."

That they in the temple were not spared appears thus; they were not sealed, and all such were to suffer. The destroyers' commission was, not to come near the marked ones, but to slay without pity all others; and, besides, the man that marked them was bid to go through the city and mark there, not to come at the temple at all, there were none to be marked, there they practised and justified abominations, they did not mourn for them. Those who had to do with the holy things were most unholy, and suffered in the temple; yet it is not safe to think, or say, that all the Levitical race were cut off at this time, and in this place; for, Jer. lii. 24, "Seraiah the chief priest, and Zephaniah the second priest, and the three keepers of the door," with others, were carried to the king of Babylon, and put to death in Riblah.

"I fell upon my face." Falling upon the face in order to prayer, notes great sorrow and humiliation. Numb. xiv. 5, when the people would make a captain, and return to Egypt, "Moses and Aaron fell on their faces before all the assembly;" they were deeply affected with that evil. So Moses, when he heard what Korah and those of his faction said, "he fell upon his face," Numb. xvi. 4. And Joshua, when Israel fell through Achan's sin, he falls to the earth upon his face, and prays, chap. vii. 6. Sometimes they stood and prayed, 1 Kings viii. 22; sometimes sitting, Neh. i. 4; so Christ sitteth at the right hand of God, and makes intercession for us; sometimes kneeling, Dan. vi. 10; sometimes prostrate upon their faces, as here; and when it comes to this posture, it argues great grief and sorrow, as in Christ; Matt. xxvi. 38, "My soul is exceeding sorrowful;" and ver. 39, "He fell on his face, and prayed." So Ezekiel, being filled with sorrow that all sorts were now slaying, that no mercy must be showed, he falls upon his face and cries out,

"Ah Lord God!" The Hebrew, אהה is a token of grief, and used in such cases; as, they cried out for grief, Jer. i. 6; iv. 10; and is sometimes expressed by alas, Josh. vii. 7; Judg. vi. 22; Joel i. 15; sometimes by woe, as Ezek. xxx. 2, "Woe worth the day!" where it is הה for אהה.

"Lord God," ארני יהוה. These be two chief names of the Most High, the one noting his dominion, the other his essence. The prophet had an eye to these, seeing God about to destroy, as if he should have said, Thou hast being of thyself, and hast given being to these; thou that art Sovereign over all, and canst call back the destroyers, "Ah Lord God!" do it.

It is *Jehovih*, not *Jehovah;* and some observe that it is used so when the servants of God were most intense and affected in prayer, as in Deut. iii. 24; ix. 26, and Gen. xv. 2, 8; in which places it is *Jehovih;* and both Abraham and Moses were exceeding earnest with God.

"Wilt thou destroy all the residue of Israel," &c. This deprecation is very argumentative, and hath many considerations to divert God from destroying them.

The first lieth in the word "thou:" Wilt thou who hast chosen Zion, and said it should be thy "rest for ever," Psal. cxxxii. 13, 14; wilt thou, who hast made a covenant with the people, and swearedst by thy holiness to David, that his seed should endure for ever as the sun and moon, Psal. lxxxix. 35—37; wilt thou, who promisedst Abraham that in his "seed all the nations of the earth should be blessed," wilt thou now disannul thy promises, break covenant, and show thyself forgetful of all, yea unfaithful?

2. In the word "destroy:" What! will nothing suffice but destruction? Thou saidst, "If they break my statutes, and keep not my commandments; then will I visit their transgression with the rod, and their iniquity with stripes. Nevertheless my loving-kindness will I not utterly take from them, nor suffer my faithfulness to fail," Psal. lxxxix. 31—33: but if thou destroy, and that without pity, mercy, where is thy loving-kindness, where is thy faithfulness?

3. In the word "Israel," which was a moving word, and put God in mind how dear they had been unto him. Israel was his son, his "first-born," Exod. iv. 22; his chosen one, Isa. xliv. 1; his glory, Isa. xlvi. 13. Israel he had "brought out of Egypt," and done great things for, Exod. xviii. 1, 8, 9. It is Israel who is so dear to thee, whom thou hast done so much for; and wilt thou destroy Israel? Israel here is put for Judah, by a synecdoche.

4. In the "residue of Israel." There are ten

tribes gone already into captivity, yea, a great part of the other two tribes are now in Babylon, and wilt not thou have compassion on the little remnant that is remaining?

5. "All the residue." What! shall all of them be destroyed, and utterly? man, woman, child, they are all slain in the temple, most in the city? didst not thou bid me bind up a few hairs in my skirts, chap. v. 3; thereby typifying out that some should be saved? didst not thou tell me, chap. vi. 8, "Yet will I leave a remnant?" and what now, Lord, must "all the residue" be cut off, I be a lying prophet, and thou false in thy word? O do it not, do it not.

6. "In pouring out of thy fury." It notes emptying of himself, as clouds, vials, buckets, when all that is in them is poured out, and the argument runs thus; Lord, must all thy fury be poured out at once? where are thy bowels, thy mercies? thou sayest thou reservest "wrath for thine enemies," Nahum i. 2; wilt thou pour it all out upon thy people, and reserve none for heathens, for thine adversaries, for whom properly thy fury is? Isa. lix. 18. O reserve thy wrath for them, and pour it not out upon us!

7. "Upon Jerusalem." This is the place thou chosest, and where thou didst set thy name, 2 Kings xxiii. 27. This city was "The perfection of beauty, The joy of the whole earth," Lam. ii. 15; "The city of God, the great King, and Lord of hosts," Psal. xlviii. 1, 2, 8; "The holy city," Isa. lii. 1. It had the holy temple, the holy ark, the holy sacrifices and ordinances, the holy priests and prophets, the holy law; here only was God known, and his name great. Lord, wilt thou pour out thy wrath upon Jerusalem? thou wilt then have no place left thee in the world to be worshipped in: what will become of thy name, thy glory, all thy holy things? thou wilt have no church, no people, no praise in the earth: nay, the adversary will mock and blaspheme; and what will the marked ones think and say, when Jerusalem is laid waste, the pledge of their hope? may they not say, We looked for light, but behold darkness; we expected a Messiah, but our hopes are cut off; we have our lives for a prey, and that is all.

Obs. 1. The godly do sympathize with the miseries of others. The prophet here is affected greatly with the judgments of God upon this people. When the prophets told them of God's judgments coming upon them, they thought hardly of the prophets, they could not hear them, 2 Chron. xxxvi. 16; they conceived the prophets hated them, and meant them no good, but when the things they foretold came to pass, they pitied them and mourned for them. Ezekiel, through deep sense of their slaughter, falls down, and sheds tears as they shed blood; their bodies were wounded, and his heart was wounded; wounded for their sins, wounded for God's wrath and heavy judgments that were now upon them; Jer. ix. 1, "Oh that my head were waters, and mine eyes a fountain of tears, that I might weep day and night for the slain of the daughter of my people!" Jeremiah so sympathized with them, that he had a mind neither to eat, drink, or sleep, but only to weep night and day; tears should be his meat, drink, and sleep. Such a sympathizing man was Moses; Deut. ix. 12, 13, when the people had sinned in making them a calvish god, and God's wrath was coming out to their destruction, what did Moses? ver. 18, he "fell down before the Lord forty days and forty nights, and did neither eat bread, nor drink water, because the people had sinned, and provoked God to anger." Here was a man affected with their miseries; (I was afraid, saith he, of the anger and hot displeasure wherewith the Lord was wroth against you to destroy you;) forty days did Moses mourn for them, and humble himself: and this kind of mourning forty days in case of judgment, some think, riseth from God's raining upon the world forty days and forty nights. Answerable to which, Moses, Elijah, and Christ, fasted, mourned, and prayed; and so to Nineveh forty days were given them to prevent their destruction.

This duty of sympathizing with others in their misery was David's practice. Though they were wicked, and rewarded him evil, yet if they were in misery, Psal. xxxv. 13, he would share in it; when they were sick, his clothing was sackcloth, he humbled his soul with fasting. Wicked men laugh and are glad at the miseries of the godly, but the godly sigh and mourn at, and for, the miseries of the wicked; they remember the apostolical command, Rom. xii. 15, "Weep with them that weep," that will be some ease to them to see others sensible of their condition. This makes them like to Christ himself; Heb. iv. 15, he is "touched with our infirmities." Judgments are upon the kingdom; many of God's dear servants, as well as others, suffer hard things.

(1.) Take notice of their grievances, burdens, dangers.

(2.) Mind them.

(3.) Be tenderly affectioned towards them. And,

(4.) Help them what you can; and this is true sympathy.

Obs. 2. The servants of God, that draw near him in time of his judgments, are conscious to themselves of their own weakness, sinfulness, and unworthiness. Ezekiel falls down upon his face, as unworthy to look upon the great and glorious God, his own sins and infirmities made him hide his face, and the great wrath of God against his people made him tremble. When Abraham parleyed with the Lord, being about to destroy Sodom, he remembered that he was "dust and ashes," Gen. xviii. 27. God is terrible in judgment, and humility is the best posture an angry God can find any in; when we lie prostrate at his feet he will not destroy us.

Obs. 3. Those who are faithful messengers of God will deprecate judgments when they are coming upon the people: "Ah Lord God! wilt thou," &c. So did Moses, that was faithful in God's house, Exod. xxxii. 11—13, 32, where he uses strong arguments to press the Lord to forgive their sins, to divert his wrath, and to spare their lives, or else to blot him out of his book. Joshua and the elders of Israel lie upon their faces, put dust upon their heads, and pray earnestly to God not to deliver them into the hands of the Amorites, and to remember his great name, Josh. vii. 6, 7, 9. Samuel thought it a sin for him not to pray for the people when they were in danger of destruction; 1 Sam. xii. 19, 23, "God forbid that I should sin in ceasing to pray for you." He had done it, and would still do it, and, if possible, turn away the displeasure of the Most High. Jehoshaphat, when a great army was coming upon them, and ready to overrun all, he makes an effectual prayer, produceth strong arguments, which you may read, 2 Chron. xx. 6—12, from God's power in heaven and earth; from the experience they had of him in driving out enemies, and giving them the land; from the sanctuary built for honour of his name, and his promise to hear prayer there; from the spring of the enemies when they came out of Egypt, and their intentions now to cast them out of God's possession; and then concludes with a conquering argument of faith: "O our God, wilt thou not judge them? for we have not might against this great company that cometh against us; neither know we what to do: but our eyes are upon thee." He first overcame God by his mighty prayer, and then overcame the enemies. Jeremiah seeing a great famine upon the people, he sets upon God, chap. xiv. 7—9, "O Lord, though our iniquities testify against us, do thou it for thy name's sake. O the hope of Israel, the saviour thereof in time of trouble, why shouldest thou be as a stranger in the land, and as a wayfaring man that turneth aside to tarry for a night? Why shouldest thou be as a man astonied, as a mighty man that cannot save? yet thou, O Lord, art in the midst of us, and we are called by thy name; leave us not:" do not according to our sins, but thy name; thou art the hope of Israel, and it hath been thy office, work, to save Israel; why shouldst thou be a stranger, as if thou hadst nothing to do, no right in us?

Obs. 4. God's judgments puzzle even prophets, they see not into the equity and depths of them. Now that all were slain in the temple, the city, and all in it ruining, the prophet is astonished, and knows not what to make of it: that wrath should be so fully poured upon Jerusalem, that God would leave himself no people, no place to be worshipped in, frustrate the hopes of his people touching the promised Seed, and make void all promises thereabout, and give up the holy land to profane, uncircumcised wretches; this puzzled him.

There is something ever in God's judgments which we cannot reach, and then, because they proceed cross to our wills, expectations, and desires, we are ready to think hardly of them, and boil in our spirits against Heaven; but we must remember God's ways are not ours; he is ever righteous in his judgments, though we see not the reason thereof. Psal. xxxvi. 6, "Thy judgments are a great deep." Some refer it to providence, thus, Men's sins are a deep sea of wickedness, yet God's providence is a greater deep, which orders them, sinners, and all things. Others take it literally; God's judgments in punishing sins is such a depth, that no human understanding can sound. Our prophet could not do it, neither the apostles, and therefore cries out, How unsearchable are his judgments!

When states, churches, or persons suffer hard things, let us not think them wronged; they suffer not more than they deserve, no, nor so much; Ezra ix. 13, "Thou hast punished us less than our iniquities."

Ver. 9, 10. *Then said he unto me, The iniquity of the house of Israel and Judah is exceeding great, and the land is full of blood, and the city full of perverseness: for they say, The Lord hath forsaken the earth, and the Lord seeth not. And as for me also, mine eye shall not spare, neither will I have pity, but I will recompense their way upon their head.*

The prophet having pressed the Lord with many strong arguments to spare Jerusalem, in these verses he hath an answer from God, and the reasons thereof.

The answer is negative, ver. 10, "Mine eye shall not spare, neither," &c.

The reasons of this answer are in the ninth verse, which are strong and weighty.

I. A general reason; "The iniquity of the house of Israel," &c.

II. Particular ones, which are three.

1. "The land is full of blood."
2. "The city is full of perverseness."
3. Atheism, a ground of all the former reasons; "For they say, The Lord hath forsaken the earth."

"The iniquity of the house of Israel." By "house of Israel," some understand those that had betaken themselves from the ten tribes to those of Judah, whereof was spoken, chap. iv. 4; but I conceive we may interpret it of the ten tribes, whose sins contributed much to the final destruction of all. Though they were gone into captivity, yet their sins stayed behind them, and had defiled the whole land.

"Is exceeding great." The Hebrews, when they would make a thing superlative, express it by gemination of the word, and so it is here, their iniquity is great; and the Vulgate hath it, *nimis valde*, it is come to the height, and scarcely admits of more degrees. A like phrase you have in Gen. xxvi. 13, he "grew until he became very great." So Matt. ii. 10, and 2 Cor. iv. 17, there is duplication of the word to set out the greatness of the thing.

"The land is full of blood." Hebrew is, bloods, bloody sins. Isa. i. 15, their "hands are full of blood;" and Manasseh filled Jerusalem with blood, 2 Kings xxi. 16. And not only kings did it, but the prophets and priests shed the blood of the just in the midst of Jerusalem; their preaching, prophesying, counsels, and discourses, tended that way, and therefore they are said to shed their blood: so Athaliah slew all the royal seed, 2 Kings xi. 1; Naboth is stoned to death for his vineyard, 1 Kings xxi. 13; and Hos. iv. 2, "Blood toucheth blood." There were continual and daily slaughters, so that blood streamed every where.

Blood notes also heinous sins, as oppression, cruelty; Hab. ii. 12, "Woe to him that buildeth a town with blood;" that is, by oppressing the hireling and labourer, by grinding the faces of the poor. In Zeph. iii. 1, Jerusalem is called "the oppressing city," her princes were "roaring lions," and her judges "evening wolves," ver. 3: see Micah iii. 2, 3; ii. 2. They did not "strengthen the hand of the poor and needy," Ezek. xvi. 49.

Bloody intentions against the prophets, and others who were godly; Ezek. xxii. 6, "Behold, the princes of Israel, every one were in thee to their power to shed blood." They hated the prophet Jeremiah, smote him, "put him in the stocks," Jer. xx. 2; "into the dungeon," chap. xxxvii. 16; they judged him worthy of death, chap. xxvi. 11.

Soul-murder; Ezek. xxxiii. 8, "If thou dost not speak to warn the wicked from his way, he shall die in his iniquity; but his blood will I require at thine hand." Here the destruction of souls is expressed by blood, as also in Ezek. iii. 18; and Hos. iv. 6, "My people are destroyed for lack of knowledge."

"The city full of perverseness." The Hebrew word for perverseness is מטה and may be rendered, perverse, a perverse thing, the city is full of that which is perverse; it comes from נטה which signifieth, to decline, withdraw, pervert. The Vulgate reads it, *aversione*, the city is full of turning from God.

This city, that was once called the faithful city, was now become a harlot. Jerusalem had left God, his worship, his laws, his ordinances, and taken in other gods, other laws, and other ways of worship. Not only Israel is branded for backsliding, Jer. iii. 6, 8, 11, but Judah was treacherous, ver. 7, 11, and her backslidings many, Jer. xiv. 7; and being once fallen from God, she loved to wander, ver. 10, after the gods and ways of other nations. They grew worse and worse, and were perverse in their judgment of things; Isa. v. 20, they called light darkness, and darkness light; they were perverse in their practice, walked "after their own thoughts," Isa. lxv. 2; they chose "their own ways, and their soul delighted in their abominations," Isa. lxvi. 3. Here was perverseness, to leave what God had chosen for them, which was their glory, and to choose that which was abominable, and delight in

Jer. ii. 36, "Why gaddest thou about so much to change thy way?"

it. And when God corrected them for such perverseness, they grew more perverse: Isa. i. 5, "Why should ye be stricken any more? ye will revolt more and more."

There is another exposition of the word. It is referred by some to law cases, and when saints were brought before them, they perverted judgment; Micah iii. 9, the heads of Jacob, and princes of Israel, abhorred judgment, and perverted all equity. So, in Amos v. 12, "They afflict the just, they take a bribe, and they turn aside the poor in the gate:" their cause could not be heard, or, if heard, it was to their grief and prejudice. Mal. iii. 5, They "turn aside the stranger from his right, and fear not me, saith the Lord of hosts:" no, they were turned from God, and turned away all equity.

"The Lord hath forsaken the earth." This phrase you find not elsewhere than in our prophet, and only twice, chap. viii. 12, and here. It sets out the rank atheisticalness of those times, denying God's presence, counsel, blessing, and assistance; they thought God was gone out of the world, that there was no God in Israel, that God left men to think, speak, and do what they listed.

"The Lord seeth not." This is a higher degree of impiety, blasting divine omnisciency; before, his omnipresence suffered, now, his omni-vision: he is a blind God, say they, or sees not at such a distance; he is shut up in heaven, and takes no notice of our temple, city, or country affairs. Such an expression you have in Psal. x. 11, "He will never see:" they did wickedly, and boasted that God neither did, nor would, take any notice of it. In Psal. xciv. 7, they proceed higher in their profaneness: "The Lord shall not see, neither shall the God of Jacob regard it;" as if they had power to restrain God, and shut the eye of providence; Isa. xxix. 15, "Who seeth us? and who knoweth us?" Men entertain atheistical thoughts of God, that they may go on more securely and fully in sinful courses. They filled the temple with idolatry, the city with perverseness, the land with blood, and say, "The Lord seeth not." When atheism hath got possession of a people, that people runs riot into wickedness, fear of a Deity ceaseth, and the door is open to all profaneness. Atheism is worse than idolatry; this robs God of his worship, that of his attributes and being.

Obs. 1. The Lord's readiness to give account of his judiciary proceedings unto the prophet. "Then said he unto me." The prophet had questioned God about the destruction of Jerusalem; "Wilt thou destroy the residue," &c.: he brake in upon God, and interrupted him in his way he was in; but because it was in prayer, out of respect to his glory, and tenderness to the people, the Lord doth not reject him, but condescends and gives him an answer. And this he doth,

(1.) To clear the equity of his proceedings, which lie in the dark, and are not apprehended by all, no, not by prophets. God will make it out that he is righteous and just in his judgments, whatever thoughts men have of them. When Abraham moved the question to God, Gen. xviii. 23, "Wilt thou also destroy the righteous with the wicked? shall not the Judge of all the earth do right?" What if there be fifty, forty, thirty, twenty, ten righteous in it? Saith God, If there be but ten righteous I will not destroy it. It is true their cry is great, and their sin grievous, yet I am so just in my judgments, that while righteous Lot is in it I will not destroy it; but when he is gone, and none but filthy Sodomites left in Sodom, I will rain down fire and brimstone upon them.

(2.) To quiet the minds of his servants, which are troubled, yea perplexed, at the severity of God's judgments. When our prophet saw all slain in the temple, and the slaughter men gone forth, utterly to slay, without pity, old and young, maids, little children, and women, he was greatly distressed and perplexed in his spirit, and knew not what to think of such dreadful dealings; therefore the Lord tells him the ground of his proceeding.

Obs. 2. Sins of people may be such as God will not hear their prayers, or others for them. Many amongst them prayed, and the prophet prayed for them, but God had no ear to hear them.

(1.) For their own prayers: Jer. xi. 11, "I will bring evil upon them which they shall not be able to escape;" but they will cry to God when they are in affliction, and he is merciful. What follows then? "Though they shall cry unto me, I will not hearken unto them." But what if they cry aloud, will not God hearken then? Ezek. viii. 18, "Though they cry in mine ears with a loud voice, yet will I not hear them." But what if they fast and pray, will not the Lord hear them then? Jer. xiv. 12, "When they fast, I will not hear their cry." But what if they spread their hands to heaven, and make many prayers? "Isa. i. 15, When ye spread forth your hands, I will hide mine eyes from you: yea, when ye make many prayers, I will not hear." But what if they weep before God? Deut. i. 45, "Ye returned and wept before the Lord; but the Lord would not hearken to your voice, nor give ear unto you."

(2.) For others': Ezek. xiv. 14, "Though these three men, Noah, Daniel, and Job were in it, they should deliver but their own souls." These were holy and choice men; Gen. vi. 9, "Noah was a just man and perfect in his generations, and walked with God." Daniel was the wisest of men, Ezek. xxviii. 3; it was a proverb, As wise as Daniel; and he was innocent, Dan. vi. 22; "a man greatly beloved," Dan. ix. 23. Job was "a perfect and upright man, and one that feared God, and eschewed evil," Job i. 1. There lay no exception against these men, they were acquainted with God and his ways, they were great sufferers, and men of prayer. Noah had prevailed for his family; Daniel for the wise men of Babylon, when they should have died for not discovering Nebuchadnezzar's dream; and Job for his three friends.

Try two more, Moses and Samuel. They were heads of the people, holy men, full of bowels, mighty in prayer, interceded with God for the people, and prevailed: Exod. xxxii. 10, "Let me alone," saith God, "that my wrath may wax hot against them, and that I may consume them, and I will make of thee a great nation." But Moses would not let God alone; ver. 11—13, he presseth him with strong arguments, and told God, if he would not forgive their sins, he should blot him out of his book, ver. 32. So Samuel, 1 Sam. vii. 9, when the Philistines came up against Israel, prays, and fetches thunder from heaven, and ruins a whole army of the enemies; and chap. xii. 17, 18, he prayed, and thunder and rain came in harvest, so that they were in danger of death, and sued to him to pray for them. Now, Jer. xv. 1, notwithstanding these two were such powerful praying men, yet saith God there, "Though Moses and Samuel stood before me, yet my mind could not be toward this people;" all their prayers could do no good.

What if Jeremiah, who lived in those times, and was acquainted with their condition, should pray for them, he was a praying and weeping man, Jer. ix. 1; yet see Jer. vii. 16; xi. 14; xiv. 11; and you shall hear God in those three places forbidding him to pray for them.

God will not hear,

[1.] Because people are incurable: they reject God; Jer. ii. 13, "They have forsaken me the fountain of living waters;" and ver. 31, "We are lords, we will come no more to thee." They reject his word; Jer. viii. 9, "Ye reject the word of the Lord, and what wisdom is in you:" and you may hear them doing it, Jer. xliv. 16, "As for the word that thou hast spoken unto us in the name of the Lord, we will not hearken unto thee. But we will certainly do whatsoever thing goeth forth out of our own mouth." And 2 Chron. xxxvi. 16, their sins were such, as that there was no remedy but destruction.

[2.] God's heart is gone from such a people: Jer. xv. 1, "Though Moses and Samuel stood before me, yet my mind could not be toward this people;" they are turned from me, and I am turned from them, and it is not the prayers of men and angels can reconcile us. I am against them: Ezek. v. 8, "Behold, I, even I, am against thee;" I, that have heard so many prayers, been so oft for thee, I, that have done so great things, destroyed such mighty enemies of thine, I am against thee.

[3.] If God should hear prayer for them and spare them, it would encourage them to go on in their sinful ways; they would presume, grow more confident and corrupt, if possible: Jer. vii. 9, 10, "Will ye steal, murder, and commit adultery, and swear falsely, and burn incense unto Baal, and walk after other gods, whom ye know not; and come and stand before me in this house, which is called by my name, and say, We are delivered to do all these abominations?" When they were smitten they grew worse; much more would they if spared.

[4.] The condition of the church requires it, that is in imminent danger of being ruined. When the weeds overtop the corn, briers and thorns are grown great, thick, high above the vine, the Lord must cut them down, else there will be no harvest, no vintage. When all flesh had corrupted its ways, the flood must come in, lest the corruption should infect Noah.

[5.] To vindicate his name, providence, honour. When God is silent in a wicked time, and spares sinners, they think him like themselves; Psal. l. 21, altogether such as they are; but, Ezek. vi. 14, "I will stretch out my hand upon them, and make the land desolate, yea, more desolate than the wilderness toward Diblath, in all their habitations: and they shall know that I am the Lord;" now, my name is not feared, my providence is denied, and my honour is laid in the dust; but they shall know what a God I am. So in Ezek. xxviii. 22, "Behold, I am against thee, O Zidon; and I will be glorified in the midst of thee: and they shall know that I am the Lord, when I shall have executed judgments in her."

Obs. 3. God's judgments, though great, yet do not exceed men's sins. That temple, city, land, and those in them, should be destroyed, was grievous, but their iniquity was exceeding great. If there be national judgments, there are national sins; "The land is full of blood, and the city full of perverseness." If judgment was in every place, sin was in every place; if there were fulness of wrath, fulness of sin preceded. Job's sufferings were great, and just punishments for his sins, as Zophar thought, and therefore prays, chap. xi. 5, 6, "Oh that God would speak, and open his lips against thee; and that he would show thee the secrets of wisdom, that they are double to that which is," &c. His meaning is this: Job, thou justifiest thyself, thou sayest thy doctrine is pure, and thyself clean in his eyes, and that thy sufferings are greater than thy sins; but thou art deceived. If God would be pleased to speak, and open the secrets of wisdom which are shut up from thee, thou shouldst see God just in his judgments, and merciful towards thee; for there is double to that which is, double wrath, double punishment due to thee; thou hast but a little inflicted upon thee, and there is a double portion yet behind due to thy sin; therefore do not complain of God, or justify thyself any more; for "know, that God exacteth of thee less than thine iniquity deserveth." Though thou hast great affliction, yet he may justly afflict thee with more: thy doctrine is not pure, thy person is not clean; that thou thinkest is acceptable with God, that provokes him; and where thou expectest favour, there wrath is due. You shall find in sacred writ that God punishes less than men's sins deserve, but never above; "according to their sins" is the usual phrase. Psal. xxviii. 4, "Give them according to their deeds, and according to the wickedness of their endeavours; give them after the work of their hands; render to them their desert:" all these phrases evidence, that God in the punishment of sinners exceeds not the merit of them; if he come up to that, it is all.

The judgments now upon Germany, Ireland, England, do not exceed the sins of the places; the iniquities of them are exceeding great.

Obs. 4. God's patience is exceeding great, he bears long, till sins be excessive. The iniquity of the house of Israel and Judah is exceeding great; God might have prevented the greatness of it, cut them off many years before, but he let their sins grow great, to manifest the greatness of his patience. He is oftentimes in the Scripture said to be long-suffering. When he was provoked much by his people, and they deserved that his patience should end, and wrath begin, what saith the text, 2 Kings xiii. 23? he "would not destroy them, neither cast them from his presence as yet;" yet there was more patience in God, yet it was long-suffering. So chap. viii. 19, Jehoram, king of Judah, walked in the ways of Ahab, and "did evil in the sight of the Lord; yet the Lord would not destroy Judah:" his compassion would not suffer him to grow into passion; rather than destroy them for their sins, he would yet bear the burden of their sins. So Jer. xxxiv. 4, "Yet hear the word of the Lord, O Zedekiah, king of Judah:" God's patience is not yet worn out, it will be very shortly; oh yet hear the word of the Lord, and ye shall not die by the sword! God bears long with sinners, but he will not always forbear; Psal. xxxvii. 10, "Yet a little while, and the wicked shall not be; yea, thou shalt diligently consider his place, and it shall not be."

Obs. 5. That churches and states degenerating from God's ways, go on to a height of sinning. "Their iniquity is exceeding great, the land is full of blood, the city full of perverseness." When they fell to idolatry, they were idolatrous to purpose; they multiplied God's altars, sinned more than the nations round about them, Ezek. v. 7; they fetched in the gods of all nations to them, they had the image of jealousy, every form of creeping things and abominable beasts, and all the idols of the house of Israel, Ezek. viii. 5, 10; they wept for Tammuz, and worshipped the sun: and when they began to shed blood, they made progress in bloody passages, till the whole land was filled with blood; and when they began to be perverse, the city was filled with perverseness of spirit, perverseness in opinions, perverting of judgment. It is not easy to make stay in the ways of sin, it is going downhill; wicked men, wicked states and churches, grow worse and worse: Ezek. xvi. 25, "Thou hast built thy high places at every head of the way, and hast made thy beauty to be abhorred, and hast opened thy feet to every one that passed by, and multiplied thy whoredoms."

Jerusalem abounded in idolatry, and was insatiable in wickedness, ver. 28, 29.

When it is ill in the church, it is not well with the state; if there be corruptions in the one, there will be confusion in the other. Idolatry, denial of providence and divine presence, was in the one; and shedding of blood, and perverting of justice, was in the other. When the first table is violated, the second table will not be preserved. If men make not conscience of sins against God, they will not make conscience of sins against men; if there be atheism in the church, there will be tyranny in the state; if idolatry in the sanctuary, there will be perverting of equity in the city.

Ver. 10. *And as for me also, mine eye shall not spare, neither will I have pity, but I will recompense their way upon their head.*

In this verse is presented to us,

I. God's severity, He will not spare, he will not pity.

II. The equity of his dealing, "I will recompense their way upon their head."

These words have been spoken of chap. v. 11; vii. 4. God's not sparing, not pitying, intimates a contrary disposition, severity, cruelty; Isa. xiii. 18, they should have no pity, they should not spare, but dash the young men to pieces, they should be cruel to all sorts. When God handled Job so sharply, chap. xvi. 13, what said he? "His archers compass me round about, he cleaveth my reins asunder, and doth not spare; he poureth out my gall upon the ground:" here was a contrary disposition to pity and sparing; and Job xxx. 21, he tells God that he is become cruel to him. And God professes, Jer. xxx. 14, that he had "wounded them with the wound of an enemy, with the chastisement of a cruel one."

"Upon their heads," that is, upon themselves. The head is put for the whole man: 2 Kings ii. 3, "Knowest thou that the Lord will take away thy master from thy head to day?" that is, from thee. Prov. x. 6, The blessing of the Lord is upon the head of the just; that is, upon the just. Psal. lxvi. 12, "Thou hast caused men to ride over our heads;" that is, us. Head here may be mentioned, because they devised mischief therewith.

Obs. 1. The sins of God's own people fetch the greatest severity from him. "The iniquity of the house of Israel and Judah is exceeding great; and as for me, mine eye shall not spare," &c. No people under heaven were so dear to God as the Israelites; hence Israel is put for God's elect ones, both Jews and gentiles, Rom. xi. 26; Gal. vi. 16; and a Jew for a true worshipper of God, Rom. ii. 29. Yet when these sinned, God became more severe against them than others; Ezek. v. 8, 9, "Behold, I, even I, am against thee, and will execute judgments in the midst of thee. I will do in thee that which I have not done, and whereunto I will not do any more the like." No such dreadful judgments ever befell any city as Jerusalem, no such wrath poured out upon any as upon the Jews. As they had more love and favour from God than others whilst they were faithful to him, so they had more wrath and fury from him when they forsook him: Amos iii. 2, "You only have I known of all the families of the earth: therefore I will punish you for all your iniquities;" they only were the family of his love, and they only were punished above others. They were made as evident a pattern of justice as ever they were of mercy, for God executed judgment among them in anger, in fury, and furious rebukes, Ezek. v. 15: yea, he set his jealousy against them, and dealt furiously with them; he delivered them up to those that dealt hatefully with them, Ezek. xxiii. 25, 29. There is one passage very observable in 2 Kings xxiii. when Josiah had done great things, caused the people to enter into a covenant with God, destroyed idolatry and sodomy out of the land, kept a solemn passover, such a one as had not been from the judges' time, not in four hundred years before, when he turned to the Lord with all his soul and might, and none like him rose up afterwards; would you not look now that God should be propitious to his people, and to Jerusalem? But hearken what is said in ver. 26, 27, "Notwithstanding the Lord turned not from the fierceness of his great wrath, wherewith his anger was kindled against Judah, because of all the provocations that Manasseh had provoked him withal. And the Lord said, I will remove Judah also out of my sight, as I have removed Israel, and will cast off this city Jerusalem which I have chosen." We have done something in way of reformation; kept fasts, taken a solemn covenant, &c; but may not the Lord, for the blood shed in queen Mary's days, and of later days, say, I will remove England or London out of my sight.

Obs. 2. God deals equally with sinners; he recompenseth their own ways upon their own heads, he sets their sins in order before them, lays the burden of them upon them, and causes them to eat the fruit of their own works, and what can be more equal? Obad. 15, "As thou hast done, it shall be done unto thee: thy reward shall return upon thine own head." Edom had afflicted and spoiled God's people, and the like should befall Edom; Ezek. xxxv. 15, "As thou didst rejoice at the inheritance of the house of Israel, because it was desolate, so will I do unto thee: thou shalt be desolate, O mount Seir, and all Idumea."

Ver. 11. *And, behold, the man clothed with linen, which had the inkhorn by his side, reported the matter, saying, I have done as thou hast commanded me.*

These words are the fourth and last part of the chapter, in which you have,

I. A reporter.

II. His report.

I. The reporter is Christ, who was sent to seal the mourners, and is here described by two adjuncts:

1. He is clothed with linen.

2. Hath an inkhorn by his side; of which hath been spoken in ver. 2.

II. The report is in these words, "I have done as thou hast commanded."

"Reported the matter." Hebrew, returned the word, or caused the word to return; that is, gave in an answer.

Quest. Why doth only Christ report what he had done, and not the other six who had commission also to slay those who were unmarked?

Answ. 1. To let us understand that the Lord is more solicitous about the welfare of the godly than the ruin of the wicked. He had a tender care of his mourners and marked ones, he was desirous to hear of their safety, and acceptance of his love, and therefore Christ hastens to make report of what was done; they are all sealed, and so secured.

2. To revive the drooping spirit of Ezekiel, who was perplexed and greatly cast down at the bloody slaughter of his people. He was yet in the temple, and the report was made in his presence, that so he, hearing it was well with all the godly, mourning party, might be comforted. Had the other six come in and told how many thousands they had slain, this would have added affliction to him that was afflicted.

Obs. 1. That Christ is a faithful and forward executioner of God's will. God bade him go and seal those who mourned in Jerusalem, and presently he did it, comes and informs his Father of it, "I have done as thou hast commanded me;" both what was commanded, and as it was commanded: John xiv. 31, "As the Father gave me commandment, even so I do." He doth the will of his Father, and no otherwise than he would have it done; he minded what was to be done, and the manner of doing it. Here is a precious pattern of obedience for us. Doth Christ do the will of his Father, not his own; and shall we do our wills, and not the Lord's? It is argument then that we are neither of Christ, nor of God, but of ourselves. Most men, when God commands, they either neglect, or do it not speedily, or not in that manner they ought to do.

Obs. 2. Those that faithfully and conscientiously execute the commission given them of God, may boldly give up their accounts to God. The man here clothed with linen had done his duty, executed his commission to the full, and he could with cheerfulness and confidence come before the Lord, and say, "I have done as thou hast commanded me." When Christ was on earth, and had many commands from his Father, and great work to do, he did perform what was imposed, and so exactly, that he could at the end of the day, when his work was done, with confidence give up his account, give in his report, and say, "I have glorified thee on the earth: I have finished the work which thou gavest me to do. And now, O Father, glorify thou me with thine own self." He did not his own will, but his Father's will, not his own works, but his Father's works. If we do the will and work of God, we shall be able to lift up our heads, and comfortably to make report of what we have done.

The unjust steward, when called to give account, could not do it with comfort or confidence. Those who abide in the doctrine and work of Christ, shall have confidence before Christ at his coming. You who are in place, look to your charge; can you say with him in the gospel, Luke xiv. 22, "Lord, it is done as thou hast commanded?"

Obs. 3. Christ delights in doing good to, and securing of, those his Father affects. Mourners here pleased God; he sends Christ to seal them and comfort them, and he quickly returns to satisfy the mind of his Father, and to show what delightful work that is unto him. Christ was as careful afterwards as now; John vi. 39, "This is the Father's will which hath sent me, that of all which he hath given me I should lose nothing, but should raise it up again at the last day."

CHAPTER X.

Ver. 1—3. *Then I looked, and, behold, in the firmament that was above the head of the cherubims there appeared over them as it were a sapphire stone, as the appearance of the likeness of a throne. And he spake unto the man clothed with linen, and said, Go in between the wheels, even under the cherub, and fill thine hand with coals of fire from between the cherubims, and scatter them over the city. And he went in in my sight. Now the cherubims stood on the right side of the house, when the man went in; and the cloud filled the inner court.*

OUR prophet had already seen many visions; and being by the Spirit in a vision, yet at Jerusalem, chap. viii. 3, he hath in this tenth chapter a vision much like that mentioned in the first chapter, yet with some difference, as will appear in the opening. Their sins being great, as you heard, chap. viii. and slaughter men being sent out utterly to destroy, here likewise the Lord manifests his purpose to go on in judgments; he would leave them and burn their city.

Three things chiefly are observable in this chapter.

I. The scattering of burning coals over the city Jerusalem, which some call the vision of coals, ver. 2, 3, 6, 7.

II. The Lord's change of his place, ver. 4, 18, 19.

III. A description of the cherubims, in ver. 5, 8, 9, 10, &c.

The scattering of the coals is specified in ver. 2, and prefigured the burning of Jerusalem; and this is set out to us,

1. From the author commanding, who is the Lord in the throne, ver. 1.

2. From the instrument acting, "the man clothed with linen," ver. 2.

3. From the command itself: where we have,

(1.) The place whither he was to go, "in between," &c.

(2.) What to do:

[1.] "Fill his hand with coals of fire."

[2.] "Scatter them over the city."

4. The execution of the command, ver. 2, 6, 7, "he went;" and this is illustrated,

(1.) From the witness thereof, Ezekiel, "in my sight."

(2.) From the place where the cherubims stood, "on the right side of the house," ver. 3.

(3.) From the event, "the cloud filled the inner court," ver. 3.

(4.) From the manner of conveying of the fire, ver. 7, "A cherub put forth his hand, took fire, and put into the hands of him clothed with linen."

In ver. 1, the majesty and greatness of him who commands is set out,

1. By the firmament above.

2. By the cherubims underneath.

3. By a throne which was of sapphire.

In chap. i. 22, hath been spoken of the firmament, רקיע from רקע to extend, expand; *expansum*, because stretched out over the whole earth. The Greek is *στερέωμα*, because of its strength and firmness, not melted or changed by its motion. This firmament, the footstool of the Lord, was over the head of the cherubims.

"Cherubims." This word is not in the first vision, chap. i. There they are called the living creatures, here cherubims; which is evidence that they are the same, and may strengthen the interpretation given to be of the angels.

There is a difference between the words, chap. i. 22, where it is said, "the firmament upon the heads of the living creature," and the words here, which are, "the firmament that was above the head of the cherubims." There it is, living creature and heads; here it is, cherubims and head; which may mind us of their oneness and consent in judgment and operations. If there be heads, it is but as one living creature acts from those heads; if there be cherubims, they have all but as one head.

Why are they called cherubims here, and not living creatures, as before?

I suppose the reason is this: 1. The former vision was at Chebar, in the open field by a river's side; this was in the temple, where the cherubims were,

1 Kings viii. 6, 7, and so that notion suited with them there.

2. In Babylon, a profane land, the prophet sees living creatures, he had a general and confused apprehension of them; but when he is in the temple, he hath a more clear and distinct knowledge of them. Hence you have this note, the Lord did more clearly make known himself and mysteries in the holy land than in other places; Psal. lxxvi. 1, "In Judah is God known" more fully and familiarly than elsewhere: a vision in Babylon is not so clear as a vision in Zion; Psal. xxix. 9, "In his temple doth every one speak of his glory."

"A sapphire stone." Jerom derives it from שפר *pulcher*, because these stones are fair and pleasant to the eyes. The sapphire notes,

1. Liberty. Exod. xxiv. 10, God appeared to them with a paved work of sapphire under his feet, when the Israelites were going from bondage to liberty.

2. Purity. Therefore it is brought in a foundation stone of the new Jerusalem, Rev. xxi. 19.

3. Of chastity. Cant. v. 14, Christ's belly is overlaid with sapphires, and his spouse must be chaste.

4. Glory, greatness. Among the Egyptians the chief priests, being judges, wore a sapphire about their necks. These, and some other particulars, were spoken of in chap. i. 26.

"Throne." A throne is a seat of majesty, and belonging to kings and great governors, Jonah iii. 6; 2 Kings xi. 19; Neh. iii. 7; and therefore,

1. Are called kingly, Dan. v. 20; and put for kingdom, Prov. xx. 28; for government, Heb. i. 8.

2. Glorious, Isa. xxii. 23; and hence are put for angels, Col. i. 16; for heaven, Acts vii. 49; for great dignity, Job xxxvi. 7. Here it notes a seat of judgment, according to that in Psal. cxxii. 5, "There are set thrones of judgment." Here was a throne of judgment set, and that of sapphire, holding out the majesty, power, and greatness of him that sat in it, who was in a readiness to give out sentence against Jerusalem.

The firmament, cherubims, sapphire, throne, are mentioned, but not he that sat in it. That one was in it, is evident from the next verse, "He spake unto the man clothed," &c. that was he in the throne. In the first vision, one like the appearance of the Son of man was in the throne, and because no such appearance is here, it is conceived to be Jehovah.

Obs. 1. The Lord is King, and hath kingly power, he hath a throne: and Isa. lxvi. 1, "Heaven is my throne;" and, he "sitteth King for ever," Psal. xxix. 10.

He hath a double throne:

(1.) A throne of justice; Psal. ix. 7, "He hath prepared his throne for judgment:" and his throne is terrible; Dan. vii. 9, 10, it is like a fiery flame, and sends out a fiery stream to scorch and consume delinquents. The law is called a fiery law, Deut. xxxiii. 2, and the breath of him who sits in this throne; it is fire, and kindles upon those who appear before it unquenchably.

(2.) A throne of mercy and grace, Heb. iv. 16. No sinners die before this throne, they may come boldly to it, and find, yea, obtain mercy and grace to help in time of need. Jerusalem was at the throne of justice, and coals of fire were giving out to burn her to ashes.

Obs. 2. His throne is the chiefest of thrones, it is in the firmament; Psal. xi. 4, "The Lord's throne is in heaven," it is above all thrones; he hath angels, men, and devils under his command; the cherubims' heads were under the firmament whereon his throne was, those immortal and glorious spirits. He is "King of nations," Jer. x. 7; "of all the earth," Psal. xlvii. 2; "A great King above all gods," Psal. xcv. 3. They have their expanses over their heads, of some rich stuff, which shows their subjection to some other; but it is otherwise with God, he is above the expanse; "He is the blessed and only Potentate, the King of kings, and Lord of lords," 1 Tim. vi. 15.

Obs. 3. The Lord, who hath so glorious a throne, is much more glorious himself; his throne is sapphirine, very beautiful, like the colour of the heavens. If an earthly throne be a throne of glory, as Hannah styles it, 1 Sam. ii. 8, what is this visional throne? a more perfect pattern of the throne of his glory. Surely if such thrones be glorious, he who is in them exceeds in glory. The glory of heavenly things is far beyond the glory of terrene things, and the glory of God is infinitely beyond them both: he is not only glorious, and that in holiness, Exod. xv. 11; in name, Deut. xxviii. 58; Isa. xxxiii. 21; in majesty, Psal. cxlv. 12; but he is glory itself: and therefore, Acts vii. 2, is called "The God of glory;" Psal. xxiv. 7, "The King of glory;" Eph. i. 17, "The Father of glory." He that creates, begets, disposeth of glory, must needs be glory itself, and not only glory, but "excellent glory," 2 Pet. i. 17.

Obs. 4. Note what stones God takes pleasure in; not any stones, but in precious ones, such as sapphires are; Exod. xxiv. 10, "Under his feet was a paved work of a sapphire stone." He walks among sapphires, sits in a sapphirine throne. Stones which are beautiful, and of a heavenly colour, he affects, of such he makes his throne. Now the church in Scripture is called the throne of God, Jer. iii. 17; and Isa. liv. 11—13, speaking of the churches of the gospel, which are the thrones of God and Christ, he saith, "I will lay thy stones with fair colours, and lay thy foundations with sapphires. And I will make thy windows of agates, and thy gates of carbuncles, and all thy borders of pleasant stones. And all thy children shall be taught of the Lord."

The temple was made of stones, "glistering stones, all manner of precious stones, and marble stones in abundance," 1 Chron. xxix. 2.

You see what stones God would have in his temples, in his thrones; not ordinary, common, highway stones. 1 Pet. ii. 5, "As lively stones, be ye built up a spiritual house." Here is a house, a spiritual one, to be made; and whereof? of lively stones; there must be not only life in them, but liveliness, dead and dull stones are not so fit for that service: stones they must be, that it may be a solid building; lively, that it may be a spiritual and useful building; and sapphirine, that it may be a pure and glorious building.

Obs. 5. Holy and good men are not able to bear divine excellences in their own nature, not capable of immediateness to God. Here is a firmament, a sapphire stone, a throne, and these but in appearance; and then a voice heard, none seen. Had the Lord showed himself as he is, Ezekiel could not have endured it, the glory and majesty of God would have confounded him. If God should not regard man's weakness, and muffle up his excellences some way or other, we could have no communion or converse with God. Moses himself is not able to behold the glory of God.

Obs. 6. Angels and all creatures are in a readiness to do the will of God when he is upon judiciary designs. The cherubims were under the firmament near to the throne, and if the Lord did but speak the word, presently they were ready to execute his pleasure; Psal. ciii. 20, "They do his commandment, hearkening unto the voice of his word:" as soon as the sound comes to them, they do it; if he bid them go and stir up Nebuchadnezzar and the Babylonian soldiers to côme, they do it.

Obs. 7. The Lord is not forward to the execution of judgment. Here is the Lord sitting in judgment, but yet they were not destroyed. The prophet hath vision after vision; eats a roll full of lamentations, mourning, and woe; sits seven days at Tel-abib, then is carried into the plain, bound, dumb; must portray Jerusalem upon a tile, lay siege to it; lie upon his side three hundred and ninety days; then take a razor, shave his head, beard, burn, smite, scatter, bind up a third part of the hair; after, hath a type of a chain; then is led by the Spirit to see Jerusalem's sins; after this, sees the six slaughter-like men sent out to destroy; and here, the Lord is sitting in his throne, and giving out judgment still against Jerusalem, and all this time nothing is done.

Ver. 2. *And he spake unto the man clothed with linen, and said, Go in between the wheels, even under the cherub, and fill thine hand with coals of fire from between the cherubims, and scatter them over the city. And he went in in my sight.*

In this verse you have,

I. The speaker, "He;" that is, the Lord, Jehovah, who was in the throne; some make it Christ.

II. The party spoken to, "the man clothed with linen;" and who this was, you heard opened in chap. ix. ver. 2, namely, Christ, who in regard of his offices is the Servant of his Father; Isa. xlii. 1, "Behold my servant, whom I uphold." He had done service in marking the mourners, and now was to do it another way.

III. The thing spoken or commanded.

"Go in between the wheels, even under the cherub." The wheels have been largely opened in the first chapter: the world and the motions of it are set out thereby. There were four wheels, by each cherub one, as appears by ver. 9. Some take it thus: Conceive the form of a waggon in the midst, on each side two wheels, the cherubims riding in it, or carrying of it, two in the former part, two in the hinder, the ark in the midst of it, the foot-stool of Divine Majesty, and before this the altar where the fire was; and you may apprehend how the man was to go between the wheels, under the cherub, that is, under the cherubims, and so to reach up his hand to the altar, and take coals. This way it is easily comprehended; but if we come up close to the examination of the wheels, we shall find they were not at such a distance as here is made; but one in another, ver. 10, a wheel seemed to be in the midst of a wheel; and how the man clothed with linen went between them I cannot express; but that he did the text affirms, and notes Christ's interest in the wheels and angels.

"Fill thine hand with coals of fire from between the cherubims." The fire was between the cherubims, and the cherubims above, between the wheels, and the man must come between both to fill his hand with coals of fire.

The altar was near the oracle before the cherubims, 1 Kings vi. 22.

There was fire you know in the temple on the altar, and it never went out; Lev. vi. 13, "The fire shall ever be burning upon the altar; it shall never go out." The Jews say of this fire, that it was the angels' ladder to go up to heaven by; Ezek. ix. 2, the six men, six angels stood by the brazen altar; and Judg. xiii. 20, the angel who appeared to Manoah and his wife, ascended in the flame of the altar. Whether it was a ladder for angels may be questioned; but certainly it was a ladder to carry up their incense and sacrifices unto God, whereby God was propitious unto them, and so was a reconciling fire. But this fire here is mentioned in opposition to such an effect, and was a destructive fire, like that which went out from the Lord, and destroyed Nadab and Abihu. It sets out God's wrath, which is frequently in Scripture expressed by fire.

"Fill thy hand." He must not take a coal or two, but his hand full: neither one hand, but both; for the word is in the dual number, and notes the hollow of the hands, the most capacious parts, those he must fill. חפניך

"And scatter them over the city." He must take his hands full of coals; and what then? not keep them in his hands, but scatter them; not upon a house or two, one street or two, but over the whole city. God's intention was to destroy the city by fire; and here it is represented to Ezekiel by coals, and those scattered over the city; the Hebrew is emphatical. העיר

This part of the vision, with that in Ezek. ix. 4, 11, where Christ is brought in marking the mourners, and here scattering the coals of fire over Jerusalem, seems to represent the double coming of Christ:

1. That coming of his in mercy, when he took our nature upon him, and sought out that which was lost, healed the broken-hearted, preached deliverance to the captives, set them at liberty who were bruised, and refreshed those who were weary and heavy laden.

2. His coming in judgment, which will be in flames of fire, to take vengeance on them that know not God; then Christ will come with both his hands full of fire, and scatter those coals all the world over, and set it on fire, and sentence the reprobate to eternal fire. 2 Pet. iii. 10, 12.

Obs. 1. God looks upon and after the things of the world, the ways of men, whatever the thoughts of men are concerning him. In chap. ix. 9, they said, "The Lord hath forsaken the earth, the Lord seeth not;" but here you may see he saw the wheels, all the motions of things in the world, and especially at Jerusalem, where they thought themselves secure; the Lord saw into their hearts, knew their thoughts, and heard their atheistical speeches.

Obs. 2. Christ receives authority and commission from the Father for what he doth. He in the throne said to the man clothed, "Go." John v. 19, "The Son can do nothing of himself;" and ver. 22, "The Father hath committed all judgment unto the Son." He hath the keys of hell and death in his hand, Rev. i. 18, and they were put into his hand; Matt. xxviii. 18, "All power is given unto me in heaven and earth."

Obs. 3. The cherubims or angels have power over the wheels; they move not of themselves, they are under the cherubims, under their command, at their disposing. Angels have great interest in the affairs of the world; there are scarce any natural motions, but they have influence into them, winds, tempests, thunders, earthquakes, plagues, famines: so for other wheels, in kingdoms and churches, which have voluntary motions, as wars, tumults, divisions, changes, &c. these are not accidental, casual, but have superior agents.

Obs. 4. The Lord doth use the ministry of angels in the execution of his judgments, especially his fiery judgments. The fire was between the cherubims; God had given them charge of the fire, and they were to kindle a fire in Jerusalem. You heard in chap. ix. of the six angels that had their slaughter weapons, and were sent out of God to destroy utterly man, woman, maid, and child. They are ready to execute his judgments; they are flames of fire, Heb. i. 7, and it is suitable to them to be employed in fiery judgments.

Obs. 5. The Lord Christ hath power over the angels and all inferior creatures. The cherubims are over the wheels, and Christ is over them and the wheels too; he goes in between the wheels, and takes fire that is between the cherubims. Let services of what nature soever be in the hands of the creatures, men or angels, Christ can step in and do what the Father hath appointed, overrule the motions of the highest and lowest wheels, of the noblest or meanest creatures.

Obs. 6. Christ hath variety of dispensations, he is a dispenser of judgment as well as mercy; he dispenseth the favours of the Father, and the wrath of the Father. In chap. ix. he marks the mourners, and here he scatters coals of fire. He represents several persons. Sometimes the same man hath sat in parliament, hath been a warrior in the field, a father in the family, and acted answerably. A steward provides for those in the family, and punisheth those who are delinquents in it. So Christ is sometimes upon the throne, doing acts of mercy, sometimes acts of justice; and sometimes he is off the throne, and acts as a servant.

Obs. 7. When the Lord is wroth with a people, and intends judgments, he turns those creatures who have been very comfortable and useful unto them, into a terror unto them. Fire, what a necessary, what a refreshing creature is it! and now fire must be taken to fire their city, to burn down all that through the help of fire was built. They had abused fire to maintain their gluttony, for fulness of bread was one of their sins; they burned incense to idols, and abused the altar fire, which had been the greatest refreshing to their souls; their sacrifices were by fire, and were consumed by fire, they had acceptance with God, atonement was made; and now even this fire kindled upon them.

Obs. 8. Terrible judgments are in the hand of Christ, and come out from him. "Fill thy hand with coals, and scatter them over the city." This is spoken after the manner of men, not that Christ took coals, but he hath that which is analogous unto coals, fiery virtue, creative power of any dreadful judgments. When Christ said to the man who had not on the wedding garment, Friend, how, &c.; take him, bind him hand and foot, cast him into utter darkness, this was dreadful. In chap. i. 27, and viii. 2, Christ appeared like a man of fire; and Rev. i. 14, 15, Christ's eyes and feet were like unto fire: in the two first places he was in a way of judgment against Jerusalem; in the last against the churches, and had fiery judgments in his hand. They are in his power to produce, to increase, to order, and moderate; he can make a judgment terrible and fiery, continue it as long as he pleases. He hath fire in his hand, and can scatter it when and where he pleases: he scattered it upon Jerusalem here, upon it afterward, when Titus besieged it. He scattered fire upon the Jews, which consumes and wastes them to this day; he scattered fire upon the seven churches, which dissolved them: and hath he not scattered coals of contention and war among us, which burn and consume us daily, and threaten the foundations of church and state? We may think it is this man and that man that throws the coals, but it is Christ doth it: Luke xii. 49, "I am come to send fire on the earth;" and Matt. x. 34—36, "Think not that I am come to send peace on earth: I came not to send peace, but a sword. For I am come to set a man at variance against his father, and the daughter against her mother, and the daughter-in-law against her mother-in-law, and a man's foes shall be they of his own household." The coals are scattered, the fire is kindled, and who can put it out? It is Christ who hath power over fire; you must sue earnestly to him to quench the violence of that fire which burns amongst us.

Obs. 9. None can destroy or fire a city, unless God give command and commission for it. Go, take coals, and scatter them upon the city. The Chaldeans could never have burnt Jerusalem, if the Lord had not bid them. Hence saith the prophet, "Evil came down from the Lord unto the gate of Jerusalem," Micah i. 12. It is an evil that Jerusalem shall be burned; but this evil was determined in heaven, a commission for it came from thence, and it is the Lord sends the fire to the gates thereof. Till God give out the word, it cannot be done, how sinful soever cities be. Jerusalem was full of pride, gluttony, oppression, blood, atheism, idolatry, &c.; yet none could fire it, till God said, Scatter coals upon the city: and when he saith so, nothing can privilege a city from burning. Jerusalem was the city he had chosen, 2 Kings xxiii. 27; there was the temple, and all the chief worship, 1 Kings viii.; so famous was it for vision, that it was called "the valley of vision," Isa. xxii. 1; "the city of solemnities," Isa. xxxiii. 20; "the city of God," Psal. xlvi. 4: and the inhabitants of this city were Abraham's seed, Matt. iii. 9; God's firstborn, Exod. iv. 22. In Rom. ix. 4, 5, you have eight privileges of theirs set down together; the adoption, the glory, the covenant, the law, the service, the promises, the fathers, and descent of Christ, were all theirs. Yet notwithstanding the city was such, and inhabitants so privileged, God would have Jerusalem burned; he destroys the people, and their chief glory with them. Let no cities stand upon their privileges after Jerusalem. Rome thinks she hath much to glory in; but, Rev. xviii. 8, "she shall be utterly burned with fire;" and kings who have served her, shall see and bewail the smoke of her burning, ver. 9. The coals may be now scattering in Italy, which may burn Rome; and it is sure, and so comfort to us, she shall be burned. Let us repent, else we may perish, Luke xiii. 3.

Obs. 10. Christ is obedient to the commands of his Father, even in execution of severe judgments. When the Lord bade him seal the mourners, he did it; and now he bade him take and scatter coals over the city, he went about it; he did not dispute, delay, but immediately did what his Father commanded. This should beget in us such a tractableness and conformity to Christ, that whatever our heavenly Father counsels or commands us, we should presently hearken thereunto, and yield obedience.

Obs. 11. God makes known to his prophets what he will do. All was said and done in Ezekiel's presence, he was privy to and witness of all. It is a great honour to be near, to see and hear the transactions of God and Christ. Such honour had our prophet, other prophets; and such honour have many of the saints.

Ver. 3. *Now the cherubims stood on the right side of the house, when the man went in; and the cloud filled the inner court.*

Before the accomplishment of what was commanded, some circumstantial things are promised, Christ being to go in between the wheels, and to take coals.

I. "The cherubims stood."

II. A "cloud filled the inner court."

I. "The cherubims stood." When Christ, "the man clothed with linen," came upon that great service of his Father, the angels stood either to receive commands from him, being supreme, and over them, or to adore him, being come into the temple; both which are testimonies of divine majesty.

"On the right side of the house." Which side this was is doubtful; some make it the north side, and so to note the Babylonians coming from the northern parts to burn and destroy all; others make it the south side; but when they came in at the eastern gate or door, the south was on their left hand, and north on their right. We have a place of Scripture which will help us in this strait, 1 Kings vii. 39, "He put five bases on the right side of the house, and five on the left side of the house; and he set the sea on the right side of the house eastward, over against the south." Hence it appears, that the north part was the right side; therefore they are out, that make the north part the left side, and say the cherubims stood not there, because that side was defiled with idols. The whole house was polluted wherever they stood, and on the right side they did stand; which might intimate the Lord of the temple was there, and if any side were more honourable than another, he ought to have it.

"The cloud filled the inner court." God hath often appeared in a cloud; he went before the Israelites in a cloud, Exod. xiii. 21; he gave the law in a cloud, Exod. xix. 16; Deut. iv. 12; Christ was transfigured in a cloud, Matt. xvii.; and clouds have been symbols of divine presence; as Exod. xl. 34, "A cloud covered the tent of the congregation, and the glory of the Lord filled the tabernacle." By this cloud God took possession of the tabernacle, manifested his good pleasure towards them, in his intention to dwell among them; so, Numb. ix. 15, and 1 Kings viii. 10, 12, by a cloud God manifested his gracious presence. That here was the presence of Christ is not doubted, but whether the gracious presence was questioned. Christ came to take fire, and scatter over the city; and the cloud here is rather a testimony of his displeasure and departure from the temple, than of his favour and purpose graciously to be with them. The Scripture signifies God's angry presence by a cloud or smoke, for they in Scripture language are one; Ezek. viii. 11, "A thick cloud of incense went up." Isa. vi. 4, when God manifested his presence, "the house was filled with smoke;" but this presence of God was to send out Isaiah a messenger of death unto them. Rev. xv. 8, "The temple was filled with smoke from the glory of God, and from his power; and no man was able to enter into the temple, till the seven plagues of the seven angels were fulfilled:" there was wrath going out from the temple. And now Christ appeared here, the inward court, the priest's court, was filled with a cloud, intimating divine majesty, the Lord's departure, and darkness following thereupon.

Obs. 1. Heavenly creatures attend upon Christ. The cherubims stood, and tendered their service, they acknowledge and adore his majesty, and expect his commands. No creatures are too great, too good, or glorious, to wait upon Christ in any ministrations of his; Heb. i. 6, angels, and all of them, wait upon and worship him, and are sent forth at his pleasure to minister to whom he pleases, ver. 4.

Obs. 2. The angels are desirous to know the things of God and Christ in the church. They stood; but where? in the house of God, in the temple. They are knowing creatures, but they know not all things, there be mysteries in the ways of Christ that they "desire to look into," 1 Pet. i. 12; and Paul tells us there is wisdom made known by the church to "principalities and powers in heavenly places," Eph. iii. 10.

Obs. 3. The Lord manifests his pleasure by signs and actions, as well as by speech. They "stood on the right side of the house;" that side was northward, toward Babylon, and this signified that thence should come their destruction: they had seated the image of jealousy there, which provoked God to jealousy, and he stirred up the Babylonians to come out of the north and lay them waste.

Obs. 4. Christ he is Lord of the temple. He went in, and then the cherubims stood, then the court was filled with a cloud, which notes a glorious majesty and royal presence; 2 Chron. v. 13, 14, "The house was filled with a cloud; so that the priests could not stand to minister by reason of the cloud; for the glory of the Lord had filled the house of God." It is Christ who hath all to do in the temple; when he in the days of his flesh came into it, he thrust out all corrupters and corruptions; he walks in the midst of the seven golden candlesticks.

Obs. 5. When Christ is in the temple, doing the will of his Father, any part of his office, then doth his glory appear. Now he went into the temple about judiciary service, and it was filled with a cloud, which sets out the majesty and glory of Christ. When he preached in the temple or synagogues, his glory appeared; "Never man spake like this man;" all his ministrations were beautiful and glorious: John i. 14, "We beheld his glory;" his glory appeared in all his works.

Obs. 6. Divine glory is usually hidden up in cloudy darkness. When Christ came into the temple, here was a glorious majesty, but a cloud presently filled the court, covered up the glory. When God came into the temple in Solomon's days, a cloud filled and covered all: so Numb. xvi. 42, a cloud covered the tabernacle, and the glory of the Lord appeared in the cloud.

Ver. 4. *Then the glory of the Lord went up from the cherub, and stood over the threshold of the house; and the house was filled with the cloud, and the court was full of the brightness of the Lord's glory.*

This verse mentions the first removal of glory; where we have,

I. Whence the removal was, "from the cherub."

II. Whither it was, to the threshold, "it stood over," &c.

III. The events thereupon; and they are,

1. The filling of the "house with a cloud."

2. The court "with glory."

3. "The sound of the cherubims' wings," which is in the next verse.

God had his temple at Jerusalem, in the most holy place of it was the ark, and the cherubims covering it; between these God was said to dwell, or sit, because he gave out answers thence in difficult cases, and there he would be worshipped. The Jews grew proud of God's presence; and because they did not glorify him as God, but set up idols, and provoked him many ways, therefore the Lord resolved to leaed them, and ruin them; and that is the scope of the vision here.

"The glory of the Lord." This was Christ, say expositors, who was in his glorious apparition, and now in the temple, but going out of it. He had once before done thus, gone off from the cherub to the threshold, chap. ix. 3, but was returned again, and here the second time doth it. He was now in a judiciary way, and would leave the temple, if they did not presently prevent it by repentance.

Christ standing thus upon the threshold, and being upon terms of departure, behind him was the cloud that filled the house, there was darkness; but before the Lord Christ was light and brightness, the court, which he stood looking into, was full of brightness of the Lord's glory: the glory was now gone out of the sanctuary into the court.

Observations suitable to this verse see upon Ezek. ix. 3, yet take here these following.

Obs. 1. When God is about to visit his church with some sharp judgments, he gives out some evident signs and tokens thereof. He was now bringing in a sad judgment upon the Jews, and their glory goes up from the cherub to the threshold, which showed God was about some great change. God testified by the ark which Noah made, that he was about some great judgment, and alteration of things in the state.

Obs. 2. That Christ, with the signs of his presence, is the glory of the temple. Where Christ is, there is glory. Hag. ii. 9, "The glory of this latter house shall be greater than of the former." How was that? When, as ver. 3, the glory of the latter temple in comparison of the former was as nothing, Christ should personally come into it, teach in it; this was more than all typical or visional glory, and external beauty, the other had. Where Christ is, there is glory, and where his ordinances are, there is glory.

Obs. 3. When Christ leaves the temple, nothing but darkness remains. When he was upon the threshold, there was a cloud behind him; when he goes out of the church, glory, light, truth go, but night and darkness come in. Isa. vi. 4, that which he calls here a "cloud," there he calls "smoke;" and when God leaves the church, then smoke, and little else, is to be found in it; smoke of ignorance, smoke of errors, smoke of divisions, smoky and false worship, and quickly after, smoking judgments. The churches of Asia, when Christ left walking among them, darkness overspread them, and smoky judgments consumed them.

Obs. 4. The way Christ goeth, is glory or glorious. He goeth out of the temple, and now before his face, as he stands upon the threshold in the court, is brightness of glory; his glory goeth with him, before him; he leaves darkness behind him, but hath brightness before him. His departure from his people is glorious, his ways and works of judgment are glorious.

Ver. 5. *And the sound of the cherubims' wings was heard even to the outer court, as the voice of the Almighty God when he speaketh.*

Here is the third event upon the Lord's coming to the threshold, and hastening to give judgment against this city. The angels do rejoice at it, and applaud the act of Christ, which the sound of their wings imports. Of this verse was spoken, chap. i. 24.

This sound of their wings is described two ways:

I. From the extent; "It was heard even to the outer court," which was a great distance.

II. From the resemblance of it to the Lord's voice, "as the voice of the Almighty God when he speaketh;" that is, like a mighty voice, even the voice of thunder.

Obs. The angels do applaud the righteous judgment of God and Christ against sinful cities, churches, states, or persons.

Here Christ was leaving the temple, the city, this people, and ready to scatter fire among them, and the angels made a joyful sound at it; the temple, the inward and outward court, rang of it. Their voice (which is meant by the sound of their wings) was a mighty voice like thunder; it is music to them that God hath the glory of his judgments as well as of his mercies, that obstinate sinners be destroyed as well as mourners be marked. The angel was glad when Babylon was fallen, and God's judgments executed upon her; Rev. xviii. 2, "He cried mightily with a strong voice, saying, Babylon the great is fallen, is fallen."

Ver. 6, 7. *And it came to pass, that when he had commanded the man clothed with linen, saying, Take fire from between the wheels, from between the cherubims; then he went in, and stood beside the wheels. And one cherub stretched forth his hand from between the cherubims unto the fire that was between the cherubims, and took thereof, and put it into the hands of him that was clothed with linen; who took it, and went out.*

In ver. 6 is a repetition of what was said in ver. 2. There God spake to the man clothed with linen, here he "commanded the man," &c.; there it is, "Go in between the wheels, and fill thine hand with coals of fire from between the cherubims," and here it is, "Take fire from between the wheels, from between the cherubims." Then the obedience of the man clothed with linen is set down, "he went;" so here, "he went in;" only there is this addition, "and stood beside the wheels."

This repetition of the same matter argues not backwardness in Christ to do the commands of his Father, but sets out the earnest intention of God to have this fiery judgment accomplished; now he would not have it delayed, but hastened.

"Stood beside the wheels." I find not any interpreter to touch at all upon this, Christ's standing beside the wheels, and yet surely there was something in it. The Lord had bid him go in between the wheels, and take fire from between them, but Christ stood beside them; he did not neglect or cross any thing his Father commanded; he was between the wheels, when he stood beside them, or near them. This might be,

1. To acquaint the cherubims with the command the Father had given him. They were at some distance from him who sat in the throne, and from the man clothed in linen; it is said, "he went."

2. To try their spirits, how they affected this judgment.

3. To consider the mutability and uncertainty of all things.

Obs. 1. Christ, being in the form of man, is under the command of his Father, "he commanded the man clothed with linen." Hence he calls him his servant; Matt. xii. 18, "Behold my servant, whom I have chosen:" he was the most able, diligent, and faithful servant that ever God or man had, therefore the Lord saith of him, "My Beloved, in whom my soul is well pleased." God was not only contented with Christ, and what he did, but satisfied, well pleased; he being under his commands, performed them fully. John xii. 49, saith Christ of his Father, "He gave me a commandment, what I should say;" and chap. xiv. 31, "As the Father gave me commandment, even so I do;" and chap. xv. 10, "I have kept my Father's commandments." If Christ, when he appeared in the form of man, and when he was man, was under the commands of God, let not us think much to be under his commands.

Obs. 2. That judgments are in God's power, and at his disposal; he saith, "Go, take fire." It is the Lord that creates the fire, keeps, and gives it out, when, by whom, and where he pleaseth; he had fire in store, he bids the man clothed with linen take of it, and scatter it over the city. No judgments but are at the Lord's command. Jer. xxv. 29, "I will call for a sword upon all the inhabitants of the earth."

It is at God's call, and only his call doth it; if he say the word, there shall be wars in all kingdoms. He brings diseases and plagues upon people when he will, Deut. xxviii. 22; he sends enemies to tread down his people like mire in the streets, Isa. x. 6; he stirs up the scourge when it comes, ver. 26; he throws down, Mal. i. 4; he pours out wrath like water, Hos. v. 10; he kindles fire to burn the green and dry tree, yea, such fire as none can quench, Ezek. xx. 47. All judgments, lesser or greater, are at his command, and therefore he takes it to himself; Isa. xlv. 7, "I form the light, and create darkness; I make peace, and create evil. I the Lord do all these things." Let us fear, and not provoke, this God, who can command fire to burn cities at his pleasure.

Obs. 3. Christ proceeds in execution of his Father's will considerately. He stood by the wheels, informs the angels, tries their spirits, and observes the motions of all things, and sees what equity there is to take fire and throw upon the city.

Ver. 7. ***And one cherub stretched forth his hand from between the cherubims unto the fire that was between the cherubims, and took thereof, and put it into the hands of him that was clothed with linen: who took it, and went out.***

This verse presents to us the way how the fire was conveyed to Christ. He being come to the side of the wheels, one of the cherubims stretcheth out his hand, takes fire, and puts it into the hand of Christ, the man clothed with linen.

Angels have no hands, they are spirits without human parts; visionally they had hands, they appeared so to the prophet.

The fire they took of we must a little inquire into. If we will refer it to material fire, it was that of the altar, of which I spake before, ver. 2; but we may understand by fire that active virtue and power which is in the angels; they are glorious creatures, likened to flames of fire, Heb. i. 7, and the taking fire here, and putting it into the hands of Christ, is their yielding up their strength, power, and activity to further the design, and do the will of Christ, in executing of the judgments intended. Fire hath light, heat, and activity in it; and the angels have much knowledge, zeal, and active virtue in them, all which they tender to Christ.

"Who took it, and went out." Here is no mention made what the man clothed with linen did with this fire, viz. their resignation of themselves, and their active virtue, to be at his disposal.

Some think that Christ presently executed the command of his Father, though it be not specified. In ver. 2, he was bid to scatter the coals over the city, and now it was needless to re-mention it.

Others are of judgment, to whom I consent, that Christ did not presently set fire to Jerusalem, or employ the angels to the destruction of it; and the reason given is this, and hath weight in it: our prophet was now in a vision at Jerusalem, and as he had had many things offered to his sight, so many things were yet offering, and to be offered to his view; all which had been disturbed and prevented, if there had been present execution of the command; he could not have seen what follows here in the vision, nor that in the next chapter. Further, I conceive some time was allotted between the command and execution for repentance.

Obs. 1. Angels watch, and take opportunities to serve Christ. He comes unto them to take fire, and presently one of them takes the fire and puts it in his hand, being glad of such an opportunity to do him service. Angels are vigilant creatures, and wait for opportunities, and when they come they will not lose them. Psal. ciii. 20, they hearken to the voice of his word; they neither slumber nor sleep, but hearken constantly what the Lord will say, what opportunity there will be for action; so, in Ezek. i. 11, they are described with their wings stretched upward, manifesting their watchfulness and readiness for service. When Christ was born, a multitude of them appeared and celebrated his nativity, Luke ii. 13. When Christ was taken by Judas and his train, Peter drew his sword in his Master's defence; but what saith Christ? "Put up thy sword," it is not a time now to fight, but to suffer; "thinkest thou that I cannot now pray to my Father, and he shall presently give me more than twelve legions of angels?" It is not a time now to pray for help, I must die, and Scripture must be fulfilled; but if I would, my Father would bid the angels to aid me, and they presently would come, whole legions of them, yea, all the angels in heaven. Let us learn of angels, watch opportunities, and take them. There are nicks of time wherein to do the work of Christ; Eccl. iii. 1, "To every thing there is a season, and a time to every purpose under the heaven." It is wisdom to observe those seasons and times, Rom. xii. 11. Τῳ κυρίῳ δȣλέυοντες.

Obs. 2. Angels do honour the Lord Christ exceedingly, to their utmost; they resign up themselves and all they have to the will and command of Christ; their wings, hands, feet, faces, their natures, their knowledge, zeal, active virtue, shall be all for Christ. One took fire and put into his hand. This is great honour to Christ, when any creature gives up what it is, what it hath, and what it can do, unto him fully. More cannot be required or expected by any superior and divine power, more cannot be performed by any creature; they are angelical who can resign up all into the hand of Christ: let us learn this duty. The scribe, Matt. viii. 19, said well, "Master, I will follow thee whithersoever thou goest;" I will trace thy steps, learn thy doctrine, do thy will, be at thy disposal: and Isaiah, chap. vi. 8, "Here am I," send me, Lord; I give up myself unto thee; all the fire in me, all my knowledge, zeal, active virtue are at thy disposal. So Paul, Acts ix. 6, "Lord, what wilt thou have me to do?" I have been against thee, I will now be for thee, I give up myself to thee wholly. If angels did it, whose nature Christ took not, for whom he died not, how much more should we do it, whose nature he took, for whom he did and suffered all!

Obs. 3. Things done seasonably are acceptable to Christ. The angel observed Christ coming for fire, to demand their service, and he takes fire and puts into Christ's hand, and Christ took it; which notes his acceptance: he neither reproved nor rejected the angel or his service, but was well pleased, the putting fire into his hand was seasonable, and so acceptable. There be seasons, which, if taken, sweeten actions, and open the door for their better entertainment: Prov. xxv. 11, "A word fitly spoken is like apples of gold in pictures of silver;" the Hebrew is, A word spoken upon its wheels: fit times and seasons are wheels to carry words with great advantage. And so for actions; when things are done in the due time, they are beautiful, acceptable. When God gives rain to a land in season, how acceptable is it! when a tree bears fruit in its season, it is grateful; so when angels or men do things seasonably, it is pleasing to the Lord Christ: there are fit times, which, if we miss, actions are unlovely, and miss of their aims. Psal. xxxii. 6, "For this shall every one that is godly pray unto thee in a time when thou mayest be found:" there are times, if we have the wisdom to discern them, when prayer will be seasonable, acceptable, effectual.

Ver. 8. *And there appeared in the cherubims the form of a man's hand under their wings.*

Our prophet having seen the cherub stretch out a hand, take fire, and put it into the hand of the man clothed with linen, here he describes what kind of hand it was, and where it was: for the kind, it was a man's hand, "there appeared the form of a man's hand;" for the place, it was "under their wings." I have spoken hereof, chap. i. 8. There, is mention of "hands," here, of a "hand;" not that they had only one hand, but under every wing was a hand; they had wings, and under them he saw the form of a hand. Their wings set out not only their swiftness in motion, but also their divine instinct and secret guidance of God, which carries them as wings this or that way, to this or that action; and hand imports both vigour to act, and action; active virtue, and the activity itself.

Obs. 1. Angels are furnished with abilities, and are fitted for employments; they have hands and wings. Whatever the Lord calls them to do, they want not aught tending to the accomplishment thereof. If speed be required, they have wings to fly; if work be to be done, they have hands, and can do much in a little time.

Obs. 2. They do not things rashly, but advisedly, judiciously; they have the hands of a man. Men's hands are ordered by judgment in their operations, and so are angels'; they do all things wisely, understandingly; they observe the best seasons, and all circumstances which may add beauty and advantage to their actions; and therefore, ver. 12, it is said, "their hands were full of eyes," they see into all the intrinsicals or extrinsicals of any business.

Obs. 3. The works of God are done by hidden and secret means, by ways unthought of, by hands under wings. Here a cherub stretches out a hand from under a wing, takes fire, and puts into the hand of Christ.

God hath secret hands to do his work; sometimes angels' hands, sometimes the hand of providence, sometimes the hand of his Spirit. Angels are invisible agents, and we have unknown mercies from their hands. An angel rolled away the great stone from the sepulchre; and they remove many difficulties out of our way. It was the hand of an angel that brought the apostles out of prison, Acts v. 19; xii. 9. Angels encamp round about them that fear the Lord, Psal. xxxiv. 7. They are invisible guards, and do invisible things for us, their hands work when we feel them not; so the hand of Providence is doing when we slumber, and discern it not. Joseph is sold into Egypt, and it was not discerned by the sellers or the sold, what work God was about: the hand of Providence was secret, but wrought strongly for the raising of Joseph, and safety of Jacob, and many thousands besides. Mordecai will not bow to Haman; was the hand discerned here which was working Haman's ruin? I believe not. Haman goes on, plots the death of all the Jews, had almost accomplished his desire, but Providence acts in an unexpected way, and cuts off this bloody man. A secret hand of Heaven hath done the great things in all ages; invisible virtue hath done more than all visible instruments. In our counsels, armies, undertakings, had not God's hand of providence wrought, we had been ruined. Was it not a strange hand of providence that began the work in Scotland? If ought be done in the work of reformation amongst us, is it not the hand of God rather than the hand of man? Isa. i. 25, "I will turn my hand upon thee, and purely purge away thy dross." Matt. viii. 3, Jesus put forth his hand, and healed the leper. If our leprosy be healed, or healing, it is by the hand of Christ put forth: the safety of this nation is from a secret hand; we are held and hid in the hollow and shadow of an invisible hand. So the hand of the Spirit doth secret work in Zion. Christ, by the finger of God, Luke xi. 20, by the Spirit of God, Matt. xii. 28, cast out devils. It is this hand that mortifies and kills the lusts, Rom. viii. 13; it is this hand which quickens and brings life, John vi. 63; it is this hand works holiness in you, that comforts and supports you, that guides and seals you; it is this hand that brings you out of the ways of sin, error, death, into the ways of Christ, truth, and life; it is this hand which makes all ordinances effectual. 2 Cor. x. 4, "Our weapons are mighty, through God, to the pulling down of strong holds:" through God, that is, through the Spirit of God. Weapons must be in some hand or other; these were spiritual weapons, and in the hand of the Spirit, as well as in the apostle's hand, else had they not been able to pull down strong holds.

Obs. 4. When God's work is done, we should hide up our hands that do it. The cherub stretched out his hand, took fire, put it into Christ's hand; and what then? the hand is hid under the wing. Angels are not vain-glorious, they seek not themselves, but the honour of him they serve; they say not, This have I done, hath my hand wrought; they hold not forth their hand for mortals to admire or adore, but rejoice that the work is done, and hide up their hands. This is a good precedent for us, who are apt to be puffed up with what we do, and to expose not only the work, but the hand also too much to view. If actions be done, and others reap the good thereof, without selfish respects of ours, it is angelical. Paul was of this judgment, and practised answerably; 1 Cor. xv. 10, "I laboured more abundantly than they all: yet not I." See here how he hides up himself, and puts all upon God; "not I, but the grace of God which was with me." It was not Paul, but God's grace that did all the work. So Isa. xxvi. 12, "Thou hast wrought all our works in us;" we have done nothing, but thou hast done all.

Ver. 9—13. *And when I looked, behold the four wheels by the cherubims, one wheel by one cherub, and another wheel by another cherub: and the appearance of the wheels was as the colour of a beryl stone. And as for their appearances, they four had one likeness, as if a wheel had been in the midst of a wheel. When they went, they went upon their four sides; they turned not as they went, but to the place whither the head looked they followed it; they turned not as they went. And their whole body, and their backs, and their hands, and their wings, and the wheels, were full of eyes round about, even the wheels that they four had. As for the wheels, it was cried unto them in my hearing, O wheel.*

In these verses, and most of the rest to the end, is a description of the wheels and cherubims, which represent things earthly and heavenly, and both under the command and disposal of Divine Majesty. Take things below in states or churches, they pass not without the interposure of Providence, the hand of Heaven acts in them; take things above, they are not absolute, there is one in the throne overrules them.

For the wheels, which are the principal subject of these verses, and note out inferior things and causes unto us, they are,

I. Described,

II. Explained.

I. They are described,

1. From their number, "four wheels."

2. By their reference, dependence, or situation, they were "by the cherubims."

3. By a particular and special distribution of one to another; the four wheels were not all together by the four cherubims, but "one wheel by one cherub, and another wheel by another cherub."

4. From their appearance or likeness, which "was as the colour of a beryl stone;" and those four are in the 9th verse.

5. From their likeness and coherence among themselves, "they four had one likeness," &c. ver. 9.

6. From their motion, ver. 11, "They went:" which is set out,

(1.) From the way they went to those parts, which was upon their sides; into those quarters of the world which were next them, "whither the head looked."

(2.) Their progress; they turned not back, but went on.

7. From their eyeness; ver. 12, "Their whole body, backs, hands, wings, were full of eyes."

II. The explication of the wheels, and that is in ver. 13; it was cried, "O wheel!" O world!

I have spoken largely of the wheels in the first chapter, and therefore now shall say little of them; the most will be of those particulars wherein there is difference from what is there set down.

In chap. i. mention is made, first, of the living creatures, and then, of the wheels; here, the wheels are first set down, and after them the cherubims, or living creatures. Why there is a great inversion and change made in the vision, I find no reason given, neither do I conceive any satisfactory reason can be given, but the will of the Lord; it pleased him to represent the vision in that way to the prophet, and that may suffice us. Yet if we may conjecture, the wheels are set first here, for that changes and motions of second causes in the world are more obvious unto our eyes, we observe them first, and that virtue which acts them is more out of sight.

In chap. i. 15, there is one wheel upon the earth by the living creatures; here, in ver. 9, are four wheels by the cherubims, and the assignment of one wheel to one cherub, which makes this part of the vision more distinct and clear.

Wheels set out all the motions and changes of things here below; and the four wheels, all that are in the four parts of the world; and a wheel is a fit instance to resemble them by, as hath been shown: and whatever appears casual, accidental, confused, and contrary, comes under the notion of the wheel.

Obs. 1. That all things in this world have dependence upon higher causes. The wheels consist not of themselves, but are by the cherubims, they have reference unto and dependence upon them. The creatures are servants, not masters, or lords; and however things seem to be carried in the world confusedly, without any respect to any superior causes, yet the wheels are regulated, they are by the cherubims, they have influence into them, and order them.

Obs. 2. The Lord is methodical in disposing the things of the world. Each one of the angels hath his wheel; they were not all by one angel, or all four promiscuously by the four cherubims, but the wheels were methodically disposed of, to each angel one; and so they acted methodically, and looked to their wheels in their several quarters. God hath set a wheel by every one of us; something he hath committed to our care and government: let us look to our wheels.

The 10th verse you have in chap. i. 16, only a little alteration of the words. In the first place it is, "They four had one likeness, and their appearance was as it were a wheel in a wheel:" in this place it is, "As for their appearances, they four had one likeness, as if a wheel had been in the midst of a wheel." They were like in figure, in colour, and equal in quantity, as if one had been made by another.

Quest. But if the wheels prefigure the motions and changes of things in the world, as is affirmed, are the motions and events of things alike every where, in all quarters of the world?

Answ. We see that, otherwise, there be wars in one kingdom, and peace in another; riches in one city, and poverty in another; the gospel leaving one place, and going to another: yet are they alike in that they represent.

(1.) There are changes every where, good and bad; one generation goes, another comes.

(2.) There are great difficulties, perplexities in all mundane affairs; not only in one place, but in all places.

(3.) In that they all work, and further God's great designs in the world; they go on in one kingdom as well as another.

(4.) In that they are all ordered to produce that great end, God's glory; not any wheel but is productive of it.

"As if a wheel had been in the midst of a wheel." Some think there were in every wheel four semicircles, or half-wheels, which appeared as a wheel in the midst of a wheel; but we find no warrant for that: the text speaks of a wheel in a wheel; it may be transverse, one crossing and cutting another; it may be comprehensive, as one orb in another.

Obs. 1. That the wheels in all places are alike, they are not the same, but they are alike. Such is man's nature, that it is not long contented with its condition, but thinks that all things move better elsewhere than at home; and hereupon many have made trial of foreign nations, remote parts of the world, and found the wheels there like the wheels in their own country, full of changes and intricacies: so they were in Ezekiel's days, so they will be in our days; so they were in Babylon, in Zion, so they are in England, and will be. We should learn to make the best of our condition; if the wheels be alike in changes and perplexities, then they are alike in furthering God's designs, and producing God's glory, and this they may do as strongly and speedily at home as they do abroad.

Obs. 2. Man is not able to judge of God's works and ways in his administration of the world. They are so intricate and perplexed, that Ezekiel knew not what to make of them; he saw as it were a wheel in the midst of a wheel, one wheel entangled in another. The acts of Providence at this day in churches and states are so various and dubious, that created abilities cannot comprehend God's intentions. It is said, Zech. xiv. 6, "In that day the light shall not be clear nor dark;" men shall be puzzled, not knowing what to judge. This day is come upon us; can you tell what to judge of the wheels and their motions amongst us? they are much entangled; we have cross motions from without, and from within. Is there any great or public business in the kingdom, but is perplexed, and the issue of it uncertain? our counsels are entangled, our military affairs at sea and land, our city and domestic businesses, are not without wheels in them.

Obs. 3. There is a coherence of the second causes

and motions which are from them, they are knit and linked together. Our prophet saw a "wheel in the midst of a wheel," one change follows upon another, and there is a concatenation of causes and their operations. The cherubims were by the wheels, and wheels in the wheels. Satan, Chaldeans, Sabeans, the winds, and humours in Job's body, did all conspire to humble and afflict him; after these, his three friends tread in the same path, and add to his affliction. Night and day, winter and summer, have not a nearer coherence than the wheels. They so run among us, that we are necessitated to sit in council, and counsel begets actions, actions make alterations, alterations make strange impressions in men's spirits. It is easy to see the puzzling intricacies of the wheels, how crossly, perversely things move every where, but the coherence and harmonious part of them is not so quickly discerned; the lines in a globe, the ropes in a ship, cross one another, which every eye seeth, but their harmony and use is not so discernible. The bees, when they swarm without and work within, make a thousand cross motions, and yet there is sweet harmony in their commonwealth.

The 11th verse, which speaks of their motion, agrees in part with ver. 17, of the first chapter, where it is said, "when they went, they went upon their four sides," and so the words are here; "and they turned not when they went," here it is, "they turned not as they went;" and it is twice so; then here is an addition which is not there, "but to the place whither the head looked they followed it."

The meaning of the words is, that they went to those parts of the world which were upon their sides, and their motions in those ways were like and uniform, none went backward when others went forward.

Jerom refers it to the wheels, whither the head wheel went; but the wheels were equal.

"Whither the head looked." What is intended by the word "head" we must inquire. The Hebrew is הראש Some render it, the first, and so make the sense this, whither the first cherub went, thither went all the rest; but the text will not indulge this interpretation, for it is said, "they went upon their four sides;" that is, into the several ways their sides were towards, and so could not follow one another. Others understand by "head" the cherub designed to each wheel; as ver. 9, the four wheels were by the cherubims, "one wheel by one cherub, and another wheel by another cherub," so that every wheel had his head, that is, his cherub; and whither that head looked, thither went that wheel. But we may ascend somewhat higher, and make the head, either he who sat in the throne and spake to the man clothed with linen, or the Spirit who guided the motions both in the living creatures and the wheels: chap. i. 12, 20, "Whither the spirit was to go, they went;" here the Spirit was הראש the head or first mover, and I conceive there is no danger in putting it higher than the cherubims.

Caput cujusque; so Pisc. renders the word.

Obs. 1. The motions of all inferior things are directed by a superior head which is over them; they move not when and whither they list, but as their head will have them, be the head the cherubims, the Spirit, or Jehovah. It is the head regulates and orders them, they cannot move of themselves, they go whither the head looks, whither the Spirit will have them go, and when the Lord commands. The body of man goes that way, and then, when the head will have it; and so it is with all wheels, all creatures, their motions are as the Lord will have them. If angels move the wheels, the Spirit and the Lord move the angels, and they cannot but make such motions and commotions in the world; if there be great winds, tempests, wars, bitter divisions, falsehood and treachery, plundering, burning, oppression, &c. the wheels move that way their head looks, and follow their head, a superior guide leads them; if they break some, raise others, if their motions are swift, dangerous, bloody, they are moved by one which is over them.

Obs. 2. That the wheels are constant in, and intent to, their motions appointed. They turn not as they go, they keep on their way; and it is twice mentioned, "they turned not as they went," they followed their head, "they turned not as they went." Which double mentioning of their not turning sets out their intentness upon their way and work, and that we should take special notice of it, because we think the wheels may move otherwise and other ways; but they cannot, the Lord sits in the chariot commanding the wheels, what way, and how to move; the Spirit is in them, and carries them on, the cherubims are by, and help forward the motions; so that the wheels must oppose the angels, and God himself, if they move otherwise than they do; they cannot stop their motions, much less turn their motions.

The 12th verse tells you of their eyeness, body, backs, hands, wings, wheels.

Vulg. corpus earum.

"Body." In the Hebrew it is, flesh. Some expound all said here of the wheels, both Jerom and others: by body or flesh they understand the bulk of the wheels; by backs, the rings about the wheels; so they are called, chap. i. 18, and the Hebrew word וגבתם is, backs; by hand and wings they mean the spokes of the wheels, which extend themselves like hands and feathers from the navestock to the circumference. By the wheel some intend the globe or navestock in the midst, in which is the axletree; others, the whole chariot, and the only reason I find given is this, he had spoken immediately before of the wheels, and after in this verse is mention of them. And why the cherubims should be brought in here, seemeth not so reasonable; but it is not so harsh as to expound flesh, hands, and wings of the wheels; and we know that he had spoken not long before of the cherubims, ver. 9; and if head refer to the cherubims, as some make it, then they are spoken of in the 11th verse, immediately before this: and if because eyes were given to the wheels in chap. i. and not to the cherubims, therefore here they must be confined to the wheels; upon the same ground, their hands and wings, because they are given to the cherubims in chap. i. and not to the wheels, must here be confined to the cherubims. I do therefore fall in with them who refer body, backs, hands, wings unto the cherubims, which in these visions do more properly belong to the cherubims than to the wheels.

"Full of eyes round about." Here is a difference from that in chap. i. 18. It is said there the rings were full of eyes; here, that all, even wheels and cherubims, were full of eyes, and he that sat in the throne, even the Lord, he is full of eyes.

Obs. 1. That the motions of causes and creatures here below, are not casual or disorderly. The wheels and cherubims are full of eyes, they see and know their way, the work they have to do, the place they are to go unto: the eye of Providence is in every creature and every motion. Things appear to us very casual and disorderly; but there are eyes in the wheels, no motion of them is injudicious or out of course. If these eyes were blind, sleepy, vitiated, or shut, then there would be strange motions, just ground of complaint; but the eyes of Providence are ever open, they slumber not, they are not corrupted with any vicious humours, they see clearly and distinctly; and in whatever they are, as they are in all wheels, public or private, little or great, they make the motions judicious and orderly. When things fall out contrary, or beside our expectations, you say they are mischances; but you are mistaken: in sea or land affairs, in martial, magisterial, or ministerial, yea domestic affairs, whatever falls out is an act of Providence; surprising or sinking of ships, disappointment of counsels, defeating of armies, escape of prisoners, interception of letters, firing of towns, drownings, self-murderings, divisions of brethren, clandestine marriages, abortions, divorces, the eyes of Providence are in them all, and Heaven's intentions are accomplished in them.

Obs. 2. There is much glory and beauty in the works of Divine Providence. All the wheels and cherubims are full of eyes; the wheels have eyes round about, not in one place, but in every place; the cherubims, their bodies, backs, hands, and wings are full of eyes; and, Rev. iv. 8, they are full of eyes within, they are inwardly and outwardly glorious, beautiful. Man's eyes add not so much beauty and glory to his face, as these eyes do to the works of God in the world. The peacock's train, which is full of eyes, how beautiful and glorious is it! yet far short of the beauty and glory which is in God's government of the world. When the queen of Sheba saw so much wisdom in a man, so much glory and beauty in the order of his house, she admired, and had no spirit left in her, 1 Kings x. 4, 5. And could we see the wisdom which is in God, the glory and beauty which is in his ordering the wheels, we would be so far from complaining of any wheel's motion, that we would admire every wheel, the order and motion of it; but oh how blind are we, who hardly have an eye to see any of these eyes! David's eye was open and observant in the 104th Psalm, where he declares and delights himself in the wonderful providence of God ordering all things; and hear what he saith, ver. 31, "The glory of the Lord shall endure for ever:" he saw glory in them. There is glory in all the works of Providence, and such glory as abides for ever to all generations: there is glory now in them, as well as in David's days; there were changes, breaches, troubles then, as you may see, ver. 29, yet they hindered not, but rather added to the glory of providential works; and so do our changes, breaches, differences. When a man is on a high hill, there are many hedges, ditches, and separations of one piece of land from another; there are low shrubs and higher trees, here a hill and there a river; yet all contribute something to make a beautiful and glorious prospect to the eye: and so it is in the works of Providence. If we were lifted up by the Spirit, to view the wheels and their motions, we should find that all those things that seem grievous to us, our wars, divisions, taxes, burdens, and such like, do contribute much towards a glorious prospect.

Ver. 13. *As for the wheels, it was cried unto them in my hearing, O wheel.*

This verse is an expository verse, and gives light to the vision of the wheels, yet it hath need of exposition itself. In the words you have,

I. One crying, which is implied; "It was cried."

II. The cry itself; "O wheel."

III. Unto whom or what the cry was made; it was unto the wheels.

IV. In whose presence this cry was; in Ezekiel's, "in my hearing."

Who cried is not set down: some think one of the cherubims. That cherub which stretched out his hand, and reached the fire to the man clothed in linen, he cried, "O wheel," and commanded it to hasten to the destruction of Jerusalem. But that any cherubim should cry out so, unless he had command from above, is not probable, and the text affords us no encouragement so to conceive. Others therefore affirm it was the Lord, who sat in the throne, who commanded the man clothed in linen to take fire, he cried unto the wheel, and his cry was,

"O wheel." The Hebrew is, הגלגל *Hic orbis:* this name doth the Lord give to the wheels, to instruct the prophet, and us by him, what he meant by the wheels, viz. the world and motions in it. The Vulgate renders the word *volubiles*, and so makes it an adjective, agreeing with the substantive, wheels, *rotas istas, vocabit volubiles;* this will hold in the Latin, but not in the Hebrew, for it is לאופנים להם קורא הגלגל *laophannim* is plural, and *Haggalgal* is singular, a substantive, not an adjective, and is set down by way of distinction and demonstration; thus, As for these wheels, would you know what they are, it was cried in mine ears, *Haggalgal*, their name is, This world; I the Lord call them so. And here you may observe how the Spirit of God leaves the word *ophannim*, by which only he expressed the wheels in chap. i. and here also till now, and takes another word, *Haggalgal*. *Ophannim* is a more common and doubtful word, *Haggalgal* more distinct and certain; and so the prophet by it came to know what the vision of the wheels held out to him.

Why the Lord should cry out thus, "O wheel," is doubted: it was not the greatness, work, or use of it, which could beget admiration in God. It is thought somewhat is concealed which the Lord said: probably he gave out some command to the wheels, touching the motions and work of it; or rather it may be a complaint, O world! how unstable and changeable art thou!

"Unto them." He cried unto the wheels, "O wheel!" There were four wheels, ver. 9, and they went into those parts of the world which were upon their four sides, ver. 11; and these wheels represented the world, which is one, and therefore it is cried unto them, "O wheel!" O world!

"In my hearing." There was a voice, and such as came to Ezekiel's ears, and informed him in this difficult vision. He was an eye and ear-witness of it; his eye bred admiration in him, but his ear let in the information what it was.

Obs. 1. The Lord speaks to all creatures, and they are under his command, they hear his voice. We think angels and men only are capable of hearing God speak. There is not a creature God hath made, but hearkens to the voice of its Creator: he saith, "O wheel!" O world! and nothing in it acts or moves without him. If he speak, the wheels move what way he pleases: when there is thundering, lightning, earthquakes, storms, war, peace, famine, plenty, divisions, &c. God's voice hath been there. Psal. cxix. 91, the creatures are called God's servants; they hear and obey his voice as servants do their masters. Psal. cxlvii. 18, when there is ice and snow, "he sendeth out his word and melteth them:" they come not without his word, they melt not away without it; the creatures hear and obey. Mark iv. 37—41, when a great storm was at sea, and all in danger of their lives, Christ "rebuked the wind, and said unto the sea, Peace, be still;" and those uncontrollable creatures heard his voice, "the wind ceased, and there was a great calm;" which made them relent, wonder, and say, "What manner of man is this, that even the wind and the sea obey him?"

Obs. 2. It is the Lord who hath his times to make known distinct things. In the 1st chapter the prophet had this vision, without any hint or light what was meant by it: here the Lord doth speak, and instruct the prophet something concerning the meaning thereof. He crieth in the ears of Ezekiel, "O wheel!" O world! and by this he came to understand part of God's mind in it. Samson had a time to unfold his riddle, Christ, his parables, and God, his difficult visions. Pharaoh and Nebuchadnezzar had dark, difficult dreams, and God by Joseph and Daniel interpreted them. Yea, Daniel had visions, and God sent Gabriel to him to make him to understand those visions. The Revelation hath many things beyond our reach, but God hath his times to expound the same unto us.

Ver. 14—17. *And every one had four faces: the first face was the face of a cherub, and the second face was the face of a man, and the third the face of a lion, and the fourth the face of an eagle. And the cherubims were lifted up. This is the living creature that I saw by the river of Chebar. And when the cherubims went, the wheels went by them: and when the cherubims lifted up their wings to mount up from the earth, the same wheels also turned not from beside them. When they stood, these stood; and when they were lifted up, these lifted up themselves also: for the spirit of the living creature was in them.*

In these verses, and those after the 18th, you have a description of the cherubims:

I. From their faces, ver. 14.

II. From their actions and motions, ver. 14, 15.

III. From the harmony between them and the wheels, ver. 16, 17.

Of these hath been spoken in the first chapter: what I find differing from the vision there, I shall most insist upon.

In ver. 14 it is said, "every one had four faces;" this is the same with that in chap. i. 6; and their faces agree with those, ver. 10, only one face is otherwise presented here than it is there; instead of the face of an ox, you have here the face of a cherub, which is set first in order, whereas the other was the third. This alteration hath occasioned diversity of opinions among interpreters. Some affirm, that anciently they pictured the cherubims with the face of an ox, and that there is no difference between their faces; but we find no proof of this, and it is as easily denied as affirmed. Others think the vision was so, that the prophet first saw an ox's face, which he knowing, calls the face of a cherub. Flavius Josephus affirms the face of a cherub to be the face of a bird, whose likeness God showed to Moses in mount Horeb, but was never seen of men. Some think, that further off this face appeared as the face of an ox, and nearer, as the face of a cherub. Some make this face of a cherub to be the face of a child, and the common form of picturing cherubims hath been like a young man or boy; therefore a rabbi saith, *Cherub esse puerum elegantem*, that a cherub is a beautiful boy, and many are of that judgment. Even Lavater makes the face of a cherub to be the face *pueri alati*, of a winged boy. Cherub sounds like *recheb*, a chariot, and the cherubims are called so, 1 Chron. xxviii. 18. And the angels are the Lord's chariots; Psal. lxviii. 17, "The chariots of God are twenty thousand, even thousands of angels;" Psal. xviii. 10, "He rode upon a cherub." But if we should grant that the face of a cherub is the face of a child, or young man, it would be the same with the face following, viz. the face of a man, whereas the vision holds out distinct faces. Some expositors render it the face of an ox, and their reason is this, כרוב by a metathesis of the letters is from רכב, which signifieth to ride, to be carried in a chariot; and so they will have the word cherub to note out *agens currum;* and it being proper to an ox or bullock to draw, they conceive here, by cherub, is meant an ox, by face of a cherub, the face of an ox. But I find no warrant given us to transpose letters in the words of sacred writ, and thereupon to make expositions. The text saith, it was the face of a cherub; and if the Spirit of God had meant the face of an ox, he could have as easily said here פני-שור as פני כרוב I conceive therefore that here is some differing thing intended from the face of an ox. The former vision was in Babylon, near unto the river Chebar, this was in the temple; and that he might more fully understand the vision, that by the living creatures were meant the angels, here he seeth the face of a cherub, which had more glory and majesty in it than the other faces; and is therefore set first in order, as before man's face was set first, which was the principal: what manner of face it was is not expressed, only in general the face of a cherub; and doubtless some special thing is in it, not only the making known the living creatures he saw before to be angels, but to note they had a heavenly ministration, an ardent desire to do the will of God, and were restless till it were done.

Rabbi David. Pagn. in lexico.

Solom.

One thing lieth in our way as an objection, and must be removed; it is this, ver. 15, 20, 22, it is said it was the living creature he saw before at Chebar, and that the likeness of their faces was the same; if this face of a cherub differs from the face of an ox, how is it the same living creature? how are the faces said to be like, or the same?

The Scripture calls that sometimes the same, which is near or like unto it, and tends to the same end; as 1 Cor. x. 3, 4, "The fathers did all eat the same spiritual meat, and drink the same spiritual drink." Manna was their meat, and water out of the rock was their drink; these differ from the bread and wine in the supper of the Lord; yet because they tended to the same end, and had some likeness, he calls them the same. So here, there was much likeness, and they tended to the same end which the former faces and living creatures did, and therefore he saith it was the living creature he saw before, and the faces the same; three differed not at all from those he saw before, only one, which made it not another creature, nor the faces other faces.

There are divers questions movable about this face of a cherub, as, why it is put off, and the face of the ox left out? whether the prophet had in this vision only the appearance of the face of a cherub, or of an ox also? why not some other face left out, rather than that of the ox? which are curious and needless. I shall pass them by; only one question I shall answer:

Quest. Why are they called cherubims rather then men, lions, eagles, seeing they had one face of a man, one of a lion, and one of an eagle, as well as of a cherub?

Answ. 1. Every one had four faces, and the face of a cherub was the chief, something divine and more excellent appeared in it than in the others, and denominations are *a præstantiori.*

2. It was God's Spirit directed our prophet to call them cherubims, whatever their faces were, ver. 20.

The 15th verse hath the cherubims' action, and the prophet's declaration of his judgment touching the cherub.

Their action is in these words, "were lifted up." The English is passive; but וירמו is interpreted by Montanus and others actively, *exaltaverunt se*, they lift up themselves. If the English words be taken

As it is in the 16th verse. in this sense, "they were lifted up," namely, by their wings, it is in effect thus much, they lifted up themselves by their wings, and seeing their Lord going away, they would follow and attend him.

"This is the living creature." The singular number here is put for the plural, creature for creatures, These are the living creatures which I saw at, &c. This sets out the certainty of the vision: had not the prophet seen it again, he might have doubted whether such strange things had been real or not; but now seeing all again, he was assured of the reality of them, and therefore, ver. 20, he saith, "This is the living creature that I saw by the river of Chebar and I knew that they were the cherubims."

Obs. 1. To see and hear the same things again, is not damage, but advantage to the servants of God. Ezekiel seeth the same vision he saw before, the same wheels and same cherubims, and cometh thereby to more distinct knowledge of them, to fuller certainties of particulars. All things are not seen or understood at first, therefore a second sight and second hearing of the same thing may be needful. Man is apt to doubt, ready to mistake things, backward to practise; and therefore God gives in truths and visions double ofttimes, that so he may help our weakness, prevent mistakes, provoke us to practise. You have the same truths oft in the Psalms, in the prophets, in the gospels, which serve to strengthen and comfort. Paul tells the Philippians, chap. iii. 1, that to write the same things, as it was not grievous to him, so it was safe for them. It is likely they affected variety and novelty, slighting wholesome and ordinary truths, a common disease of all times; when they had manna, they loathed it, they would have had change, and something new; but Paul intimates there was danger in that novellous humour, and therefore saith it was safer for the Philippians to hear the same things again and again, to hear them preached, to have them written. And Peter tells those he wrote to, that he would not be negligent to put them always in remembrance of those things they knew, 2 Pet. i. 12.

The 16th verse hath been spoken of, chap. i. 19—21; where the going, lifting up, and standing of the creatures and wheels, was handled. Here is a little difference from what is there, and that in two things:

The first is of the cherubims. There it is said, "when they were lifted up from the earth;" here it is, "the cherubims lifted up their wings to mount up from the earth," and so by their wings were lifted up.

The second difference is concerning the wheels. In chap. i. it is said, "they were lifted up over against them;" here it is, "the same wheels also turned not from beside them." It is the same thing in diverse phrases; when the cherubims were lifted up, the wheels that were against their sides were also lifted up, and turned not any way, but went along beside them, which way soever they went. The cherubims had their free motions, and did the will of God readily, and the wheels followed their ducture, and went no other way than they would have them.

Inferior causes are acted and led by the superior; when the cherubims went, the wheels went; when they were lifted up, these attended them. No creature moves here below without a guide.

The 17th verse, which you have in a manner word for word, chap. i. 21, shows there is a dependence and convenience of causes, one upon and with another; the motions and stations of inferior things, of all the wheels, depend upon the higher, viz. the angels; when they stand or move, so do these.

"The spirit of the living creature," Hebrew, the spirit of life, "was in them."

Obs. 1. The Spirit of God is in all creatures, and acts in and by them; it doth not only support all by divine virtue, but is present in all, sets all wheels a running, stops all at its pleasure, orders and moderates all their motions and operations. The Spirit of life was in the wheels, and in the cherubims. There is no public or private agent, rational or irrational creatures, used in the motions of the world, but the Spirit is in them all. The Spirit was at the creation of all, Gen. i. 2; Job xxvi. 13; and the Spirit is in the operations of all, 1 Cor. xii. 11. Whatever gifts men have, it is the Spirit works them, and works in and by them: and so in the other creatures, whatever virtues, qualities, instincts, dispositions, operations they have, the Spirit of life wrought them in them, and works by them. This may quiet our spirits; whatever is done in the world by the creatures, however the wheels move, they move not of themselves, but the Spirit which is in them moves them.

Obs. 2. The stands and motions of cherubims and wheels are neither disorderly nor unseasonable; they stop, they stir at the dictates of the Spirit of life which is in them, and that Spirit is a Spirit of wisdom, appointing nothing to be done disorderly or unseasonably. When great stops are made in public or more private businesses, when they seem to us to go backward, cross, to be untimely, it is the Spirit of life that is in and acteth by the second causes; and who may with safety blame the Spirit of God for stopping or turning the wheels. The times of the Spirit in all providential things are most seasonable, and act most orderly.

Obs. 3. We should not terminate our thoughts upon second causes, but look up to the supreme overruling Cause. Here the prophet is led up to the Spirit; he doth not look at the cherubims' and wheels' standing or moving only, but his eye is higher, it is upon the Spirit of life that was in them. We are apt to look at that instrument or cause which is next us, in present view, and there to terminate. This is a great evil, to eye the creature, and forget God: it is his Spirit that acts in the wheels, and if we take not notice of it, how can we be thankful when the creature is instrumentive of good to us, how patient when it is instrumentive of hurt to us? If the creature smite and damnify you, it is the Spirit of life in that creature which set it on work; and if it profit and please you, it was the same Spirit moved it to do so. Many are so blind that they see nothing of the Spirit in any wheel or in any motion.

Ver. 18, 19. *Then the glory of the Lord departed from off the threshold of the house, and stood over the cherubims. And the cherubims lifted up their wings, and mounted up from the earth in my sight: when they went out, the wheels also were beside them, and every one stood at the door of the east gate of the Lord's house; and the glory of the God of Israel was over them above.*

These verses contain a further removal of the glory. In chap. ix. 3, there was one removal, from the cherub to the threshold. A second is in this chapter, ver. 4, where it is said, the glory went up, and stood over the threshold. A third in this verse; where we have,

I. From whence it departed, "from the threshold of the house."

II. Whither it went, it "stood over the cherubims."

The Jews thought themselves safe; while the temple stood, God dwelt there, and would preserve it and the city from all evils, and all enemies: what could other nations do to them, being without God?

and what should they fear, seeing they had God shut up in their temple, and were persuaded that he would never leave them? This foolish conceit undid them, for they observed not the Lord to worship him purely, and only according to his will and rules given them; but defiled the temple with all abominations, and constrained the Lord to leave them; therefore saith the prophet, "Then the glory of the Lord departed from off the threshold." When he saw their vain confidence, notwithstanding all their pollutions, that they took no warning by his prophets, observed not his judiciary threatenings and proceedings, repented not of their evil ways, continued still the same, having told them of his departure from them, he begun it.

I have spoken before oft concerning the glory of the Lord, chap. viii. 4; ix. 3; in the 4th verse of this 10th chapter; and therefore now shall not need to enlarge. Sanctius thinks that the glory had not left the cherubims, but only was hid from the eyes of the prophet by the cloud, and that he makes the departure of the glory from the cherub; but this is clouding of the text, which saith, "The glory of the Lord went up from the cherub, and stood over the threshold;" the cherubims were not at the threshold, but at the right side of the house, ver. 3; and here in this 18th verse, "The glory departed from off the threshold of the house, and stood over the cherubims."

In Isa. vi. 2, it is said, the seraphims there stood above the throne; and here, the glory and throne were over the cherubims. Some make these distinct visions, the one being of seraphims, the other of cherubims; they having six wings, these four, and then they being above, and the cherubims under, here is no opposition. Others think it the same vision; and then here is a difficulty, the seraphims are above, the cherubims under the throne of glory.

ממעל לו The words in Isaiah, "above it," by the Septuagint are turned *κυκλῳ αὐτοῦ, in circuitu ejus*, they compassed the throne about. Rabbi Kimchi hath it, near him, before his

Musc. face: they were not above their Lord and Master, but seemed to stand above to the prophet's eye, who represents them as they appeared to him. Some render the Hebrew word *juxta*, by or nigh; as Exod. xvi. 3, "When we sat by the flesh-pots," not above, or upon them: so Psal. xxiv. 2, "He hath founded the earth upon the seas;" it is a hard speech, nigh the seas is better: and Psal. cxxxvii. 1, "By the rivers of Babylon we sat down;" the Hebrew word is the same, *juxta*, not *supra*, they sat, not upon, but by, them; so here, the seraphims were not above, but by, about the throne.

The glory departed from the threshold of the house, the threshold of the priests' court, to the door of the east gate, where the cherubims stood. The east gate was the gate of the court where the people met, the outward gate at which they came in, and prayed with their faces westward.

Obs. 1. How unwilling the Lord is to depart, and leave that people he hath dwelt amongst, and been engaged unto! He had taken in this people to be his, and now, though they had provoked him bitterly by their idolatry in his worship, and by oppression in the state, and he had great cause to have left them utterly at once, yet see how he goes away in a gradual manner, step by step; this was the third or fourth step he had taken. He was before removed to the side of the temple, and then from within the temple to the threshold, and now he steps to the east gate; expecting that upon every step they should have been affected, and used means to have kept the Lord from departing from them. He looked that they should have repented of their evil ways, purged their temple from false gods and worship, have executed justice, and showed mercy to the afflicted, and walked in his ways; and then he would not have left them.

Obs. 2. There is no visible church but may fall, and cease to be. Here was the only visible church in the world, and the glory departed from it, and quickly it became no church. The seven churches of Asia were famous visible churches, and is not their glory long since departed from them? No visible church but may cease its being; all the churches in Judea are dead and buried in obscurity; meetings of God's people may cease, ordinances, ministers, and administrations may all be taken away, and so the visibility of the church. I do not say visible saints shall all fail, but visible churches may; the glory may depart from them, the signs of his presence and grace may leave them. God is not tied to any place, to any people; but if they corrupt his worship, he may withdraw: he did depart from Jerusalem, from the temple, and they were unchurched.

Obs. 3. When the Lord goes from a people, then the protection and benefits they have by the angels go away. When the glory departed, then the cherubims mounted up from the earth; they would not stay to comfort, guide, protect that people which had driven away their Lord and Master; seeing he left them, they would leave them also. One evil followed another. When the sun is in *apogæo*, gone from us, we have short days and long nights, little light but much darkness; and when God departs, you have much night, and little day left, your comforts fade suddenly, and miseries come upon you swiftly. When God and his angels go from a church, the dragon and his angels get in; when men's inventions prevail, they are subject to all woes and miseries; Hos. ix. 12, "Woe to them when I depart from them." Let us take heed we cause not the glory to depart from us; then the angels that are present at our solemn and public meetings will leave us, they will not pitch their tents about us any longer: Jer. vi. 7, 8, "As a fountain casteth out her waters, so she casteth out her wickedness: violence and spoil is heard in her; before me continually is grief and wounds. Be thou instructed, O Jerusalem, lest my soul depart from thee, lest I make thee desolate, a land not inhabited." Let us be instructed to cease from wickedness, violence, spoil, else God will depart from us, angels leave us, and both be against us.

Obs. 4. God would have men take notice of his departure. The cherubims stood at the door of the east gate, and there the glory stood over them; that gate was so seated in mount Zion, that they might see the entrance by it from most parts of the city, and here the glory now stood; it was come forth from the temple, and now exposed to public view, that they might inquire what was the matter, use all means to recover the glory which was going.

Ver. 20—22. *This is the living creature that I saw under the God of Israel by the river of Chebar; and I knew that they were the cherubims. Every one had four faces apiece, and every one four wings; and the likeness of the hands of a man was under their wings. And the likeness of their faces was the same faces which I saw by the river of Chebar, their appearances and themselves: they went every one straight forward.*

For the 20th verse, you have heard of it in the 15th. He called them living creatures in the 1st chapter, not knowing them so fully at first view as afterwards. Now beholding them in the temple, he had there more distinct and clear knowledge of them, he knew what they were, viz. cherubims, glorious creatures, of great wisdom, strength, and agility, subservient unto the Lord, and therefore are said to be "under the God of Israel." He hath cherubims and seraphims at his command; be creatures what they will, they are under God,

"The God of Israel." Because he appeared to Jacob, changed his name to Israel, whence his posterity were called Israelites, and God having made a covenant with him and his seed, Gen. xxviii. and xxxii. hence he was called the God of Israel.

Some have thought here were not four living creatures, but one, which in divers respects represented those four. By face they understand not the countenance, but any figure, form, aspect, or habit of the body, and thus they make it out: the creature had the face of a man, in regard of his mouth, hands, thighs, and straight body; he had the face of a lion, in respect of his neck, shoulders, and breast; of an eagle, in respect of his wings; and of an ox, in respect of his cloven hoofs; but why the word face should be so interpreted, there is no reason: besides, ver. 9, it is said, by each cherub there was a wheel, noting they were several creatures, not one; and in this 20th verse, the prophet saith, he knew they were the cherubims, not one cherub; and, ver. 7, he distinguished that cherub from the rest, which took fire and put into the hands of Christ; and in ver. 21 it is said, every one had four faces and four wings, therefore this could not be one living creature. It is called the living creature, *per enallagen numeri*, the singular number is put for the plural.

"Every one had four faces apiece." The Hebrew is, four, four faces to one, which repetition expresses the force of the cardinal number among the Hebrews; when that number is repeated, it stands for the ordinal or distributive, which they want. It notes thus much, there were four faces to each of them.

Ver. 22. Of this verse was spoken in the 1st chapter, and thither I refer the reader.

CHAPTER XI.

Ver. 1—3. *Moreover the spirit lifted me up, and brought me unto the east gate of the Lord's house, which looketh eastward: and behold at the door of the gate five and twenty men; among whom I saw Jaazaniah the son of Azur, and Pelatiah the son of Benaiah, princes of the people. Then said he unto me, Son of man, these are the men that devise mischief, and give wicked counsel in this city: which say, It is not near; let us build houses: this city is the caldron, and we be the flesh.*

EZEKIEL, as you have heard, was in a vision at Jerusalem, chap. viii. 3; the 9th and 10th chapters were parts of that vision, and so also is this chapter. In it you have two parts:

I. A further addition to the vision our prophet had, to the 24th verse.

II. The conclusion of the vision, from the beginning of the 24th verse to the end.

In the first part you have these things:

1. A manifestation unto Ezekiel of those who gave ill counsel, and seduced the people, in the three first verses.

2. Denunciation of judgment against those evil counsellors and seducers, from the 3rd verse to the 13th, wherein the death of one of the chief of them is laid down.

3. The prophet's complaint, ver. 13.

4. The Lord's answer to his complaint, ver. 14, 15.

5. Comfort for the captives, from ver. 15 to 22.

6. The departure of the glory out of the city, ver. 22, 23.

In the verses read we have the manifestation of the ill counsellors and seducers to our prophet, where these several particulars fall into consideration:

I. The efficient cause showing the prophet these ill counsellors, "the spirit."

II. The place where he saw them, at "the east gate," &c.

III. The number of these men, "five and twenty."

IV. The names of two of them, described also from their parents, "Jaazaniah," &c. and "Pelatiah," &c.

V. Their dignity, "princes of the people:" and all these in the 1st verse.

VI. The complaint made against them, which is set down,

1. In general, ver. 2.

2. Specially, ver. 3.

"The spirit lifted me up." It pleased the Spirit of God to take Ezekiel and carry him to Jerusalem, and there to remove him from place to place; he did nothing of his own head, but as the Spirit ordered him. The Spirit moved the wheels, the living creatures, and our prophet also; it was not an angel nor his own spirit moved him, but the Spirit of God.

"And brought me unto the east gate of the Lord's house, which looketh eastward." The Hebrew is קדימה Polanus renders it *ad ortum solis;* Piscator, *orientalem ventum versus;* towards the sun-rising, saith one, towards the east wind, saith the other. Sanctius thinks this gate was in the inner court, and therefore it is called "the gate of the Lord's house" to which the prophet was brought; not as being out of the temple, but removed from another place thither. But our prophet was in the inner court before, chap. viii. 16, and we find not that he was removed from that place till now. It is not evident therefore that this east gate should be in the inner court; and other gates were called the gates of the Lord's house; chap. viii. 14, the north gate was called "the gate of the Lord's house;" that is therefore no argument to prove it to be in the inner court. Others therefore more judiciously conceive, that our prophet having seen the slaughter of all in the temple by the six men, chap. ix. and heard the sentence of burning the city, by scattering of coals, chap. x. and that in the inner court; he was now removed out of the temple to the east gate of the outward court, whither the glory was gone, chap. x. 19. This gate was famous, and very obvious to view eastward, north-east, and south-east; here stood the glory of the Lord now, here were the cherubims under the glory, here were the wheels under the cherubims, and hither was the prophet brought; there he seeing God going away, might shortly declare the mind of God against the Jews at Jerusalem.

"Behold at the door of the gate five and twenty men." Here is the number of them. In chap. viii. 16, were twenty-five men mentioned, and the query is, whether these be the same. Some affirm they were the same, but I incline to think otherwise;

1. Because our prophet had seen them formerly; and why should he see them again?

2. They were in the temple, worshipping the sun with their faces toward the east, and these were out of the temple at the east gate: and if it be said they might return from their idolatrous sun-worship within

to this eastern gate where the prophet now saw them, we must remember that the prophet saw those in the sanctuary slain; chap. ix. 6, the destroying angels were to begin at the sanctuary, and they began at the ancient men which were before the house; and though they were but visionally slain, yet that was sufficient to keep them from being presented to the prophet's view the second time.

The ground for their opinion is this: it is conceived by some of the learned, that the prophet had the vision of this 11th chapter before the 9th and 10th; and therefore they read the first verse thus, The spirit had lifted me up, and had brought me: but this is not sufficient to persuade us to be of that judgment; for,

(1.) In the vision is set out to the prophet the order of God's departure from them. Chap. viii. 4, "The glory of the God of Israel was there;" chap. ix. 3, it went "to the threshold of the house;" chap. x. 4, it went up "over the threshold;" then, ver. 19, it departed to "the east gate;" after this it went to the midst of the city, and from thence to the mountain out of the city, chap. xi. 23. So that the gradual departure of the glory doth evince that this chapter was not before the 9th and 10th, but following, as in order it lies.

(2.) The conclusion of the vision confutes that opinion; for, ver. 24, 25, it is said that the vision went up from him, that he was carried into Chaldea, and that he spake to the captives what he had seen. If this chapter were to succeed the 8th, and precede the 9th and 10th, he had been excluded from a great part of the vision, and in Chaldea before those parts had been given in to him.

These twenty-five men were principal men; and Pradus informs us from the Jewish writings, that Jerusalem had twenty-four divisions or wards, which were governed by twenty-four choice men, who are in the verse called "princes of the people:" they, with the governor of the city, who is thought to be a prince of the house of Judah, and for the king, considered of the city and state affairs; and these twenty-five were at the east gate. The magistrates and governors were wont to sit in the gates, and hear causes, and consult of their weighty affairs; Jer. xxvi. 10, "When the princes of Judah heard these things, then they came up from the king's house unto the house of the Lord, and sat down in the entry of the new gate of the Lord's house;" and there they heard the accusation of Jeremiah.

Others think they were principal men chosen out of the two remaining tribes, twelve out of each, and a president amongst them, who was ruler of the city.

"Jaazaniah." This Jaazaniah differs from him in chap. viii. 11, who was the son of Shaphan, and this was the son of Azur; whether it was that Azur mentioned Jer. xxviii. 1, is not known; that Azur was a prophet, and if a true one, a helper, as his name signifies.

"Pelatiah the son of Benaiah." The French hath it, *Pheltias fils de Benaias:* the Tigurine reads it, *Pelatiahn* the son of *Benaiahn*, most near the Hebrew. This Benaiah might be him mentioned in 2 Chron. xxxi. 13, who was one of the overseers for the things dedicated to the house of the Lord; and so, according to his name, was a builder of the Lord's. It is like our prophet knew not any of the rest, and therefore mentions these only; and this last he names, because presently he was made an example of the just judgment of God, ver. 13.

"Princes of the people." That is, chief rulers; Numb. vii. 2, "The princes of Israel, heads of the house of their fathers, who were the princes of the tribes, and were over them that were numbered." And this was a great honour, to be a prince of the people: when God will honour a man in this life, he is said to "set him with princes, even with the princes of his people," Psal. cxiii. 8.

Ver. 2. "These are the men that devise mischief." Here begins the complaint against these men; in the first part of it they devise mischief; and secondly, they give ill counsel.

"Devise mischief." The Hebrew word חשב is not simply to think, but *excogitare*, to set the head and heart on work to find out something; it carries the intention of the mind with it. Jer. xviii. 18, "Come, let us devise devices against Jeremiah." It is the same Hebrew word; and they would set themselves wholly, fully to devise devices, they would be solicitous in it, and to find out some way to mischief Jeremiah. So the word is used, Ezek. xxxviii. 10, "Thou shalt think an evil thought:" the other translation hath it, evil thoughts: it is spoken of Gog, who should have many evil thoughts against the people of God, and be set upon devising evil. It notes intention and solicitousness: 1 Cor. vii. 32, μεριμνᾶ, careth for; the Vulgate hath it, *sollicitus est*, and Cyprian, *cogitat*, to think of a thing with care, and with intention: this is the word here.

"Mischief." Junius hath it, vanity; the Septuagint hath it, μάταια, vain things; the Vulgate, iniquity; and so the French, *qui present iniquitie:* so the Tigurine, *qui cogitant iniquitatem;* Castalio, *qui nefas cogitant.* The Hebrew is און which includes all these, and is well rendered "mischief," which is such evil as tends to the ruin and destruction of a state or church: such was the device of Haman against the Jews.

"And give wicked counsel." They do not only devise mischief, but give it out being devised; the Hebrew runs thus, and counselling ill counsel.

Ver. 3. "Which say, It is not near; let us build houses." These words are variously rendered and interpreted. Some expound them thus, many are carried into captivity, the wrath of God is overpast, not near, let us therefore build houses. The Vulgate is, *Nonne dudum ædificatæ sunt domus?* Were not houses built long since? and their meaning is this; Why are you troubled about the ruin of the city, as if it should suddenly be, as Jeremiah that false prophet hath said? the city is so far from being ruined, that you see long since it hath been increased, the old houses stand, new have been added, and Jeremiah is proved a liar; therefore fear not, no such evil shall come upon us; Nebuchadnezzar destroyed not the houses heretofore, and can he do it now? But this Vulgate translation suits not with the text.

The Tigurine translation is, *Non est in propinquo contritio, ædificemus igitur domus:* and so Vatablus, only *igitur* he leaves out; Contrition, destruction is not near, let us therefore build houses: this interpretation we condemn not. Montanus goeth that way, and adds *contritio* in the margin; *Nonne noviter edificatæ sunt domus?* Are not houses lately or newly built?

The Septuagint has it οὐχὶ προσφάτως ᾠκοδόμηνται αἱ οἰκίαι.

The Hebrew is, לא בקרוב בנות בתים it is not near to build houses; here is an infinitive put for an imperative, to build, for let us build, or let houses be built.

"It is not near." What is not near? the desolation threatened, that they said was not near. Jeremiah had told them of the Lord's wrath, and that a sore captivity was at hand; and because God had forbade him to marry and beget children, because they should be destroyed, as you have it, Jer. xvi. 2—4, "Thou shalt not take thee a wife, neither shalt thou have sons or daughters in this place. For thus saith the Lord concerning the sons and concerning the daughters that are born in this place, and concerning their mothers that bare them, and concerning their fathers that begat them in this land; They shall die of grievous deaths; they shall not be lamented; neither shall they be buried; but they shall be as dung upon the face of the earth: and they shall be consumed by the sword, and by famine; and their carcasses shall be meat for the fowls of heaven, and for the beasts of the earth." These sad tidings had Jeremiah made known as being given not only for himself, but others; and hereupon he wrote to the captives in Babylon, that they should build houses, plant gardens, take wives to themselves, and sons, that they might increase, and not diminish, as they were like to do at Jerusalem, Jer. xxix. 5, 6. Because of these things the people were full of fears, refused to build and plant: hereupon these princes of the people counselled things contrary to God and the prophet, and said, " It is not near;" what Jeremiah threatens, or any other prophet, those things they speak of are far off; according to that in Ezek. xii. 22, " The days are prolonged, and every vision faileth;" and ver. 27, " He prophesieth of the times that are afar off;" therefore fall a building, plant, multiply, and increase, there is no such danger as you dream of.

Some carry it thus, houses are not to be built in nearness to the city; and so make it military counsel, as if these princes would not have any suburbs, or neighbouring villages, which might advantage the enemy, if he should come and take them, and so shut up the city: therefore they conceive these words import thus much, houses are not to be built near; that is, they are to be pulled down, and the rubbish removed.

" This city is the caldron, and we be the flesh." These words have their difficulty in them. If you take the last sense of the former words, then you may understand these thus: We are threatened to be boiled in the siege of this city by the Chaldeans, as flesh is boiled in a caldron; but we will take a course to prevent that; we will pull down all the houses without the walls of the city, and near hand, so that the enemy shall not come near us, and then we shall see what truth is in it, that this city is the caldron, and we the flesh. Had they such an opportunity to sit down in the houses, they would besiege us straitly, press us with famine, be as a fire to this city, and consume us to nothing.

Others think these words spoken scoffingly against Jeremiah, who, chap. i. 13, had said, " I see a seething pot;" it is the same word which is here סיר and here it is הסיר the caldron, the seething pot. Jeremiah had prophesied that the enemy should come from the north, and besiege them in the city; that they should be as flesh in a caldron, boiled with the Chaldean fire till they were consumed: this they mock at; "This city is the caldron, and we be the flesh," saith that false and lying prophet; for you see we are as before, we need not fear Chaldeans.

A caldron, 1. Is made of strong materials, as brass, or the like. 2. It will endure the fire many years before it be consumed. 3. It contains the flesh put into it, and that is not to be taken out till it be thoroughly boiled. Hence upon these grounds they scoffed at Jeremiah: If the city be the caldron, it is a strong city, and hath brazen walls, it will endure the fire. Let the Chaldeans come as thou sayest, if we be a caldron, their fire will not melt us; and though they do boil us, yet we shall not be taken out of this caldron to be eaten before we are thoroughly boiled, till old age and death itself take us out of it. Thus did these princes profane that prophecy, and bred security in the hearts of the people, and fed them with hopes of liberty and long life. Or thus you may take it, If this city be the caldron. and we the flesh, we will rather be boiled in it, than be destroyed by the sword; we will rather die in the fire, be boiled to death, than fall into the hands of our enemies; we will rather die here, than yield ourselves into their hands, be slain out of the city, or be carried into Babylon: but we fear no such thing. Thus these princes eluded the prophetical threats, hardened the people in their ill ways, and ripened them for destruction.

Obs. 1. Our prophet was acted in these visions by the Spirit; sometimes it entered into him, sometimes it fell upon him, and sometimes it lifted him up: chap. ii. 2; iii. 24, "The spirit entered into me;" chap. i. 3; viii. 1, "The hand of the Lord" (that is, the Spirit) " came upon me, fell upon me;" and chap. iii. 12, "The spirit took me up;" and here, "The spirit lifted me up." The Spirit had much to do with our prophet, and so with all the prophets; they were acted by the Spirit in all their visions and prophecies, they were lifted up above themselves, and out of themselves, when they were to have cognizance of divine things.

Obs. 2. The Spirit is God, it knows men and their ways, it discovered them unto the prophet. Here the Spirit took notice of these men, what devices they had in their heads, what counsel they gave, and acquainted the prophet with them; so before in chap. viii. the Spirit showed him the image of jealousy, the seventy men that were offering incense to the idols, the women that wept for Tammuz, the twenty-five men that worshipped the sun, and put the branch to their nose. As it is said of the sun, Psal. xix. 6, "there is nothing hid from the heat thereof;" so much more of the Spirit, there is nothing hid from his knowledge: 1 Cor. ii. 10, "The Spirit searcheth all things;" all in heaven, and all in earth, all things in the closets, in the heart: Psal. cxxxix. 7, "Whither shall I go from thy Spirit." David could not hide himself from the sight and presence of God's Spirit, neither can we. Let us look well therefore unto our ways, the Spirit may make them known to the prophets and servants of God.

Obs. 3. That men chief in dignity and place are for the most part corrupt. Here were the twenty-five who bare the sway in the city, and had great power, all confederate in wickedness. Isa. i. 10, he calls their rulers " rulers of Sodom," because of their extreme wickedness; and he excepts none, they were generally such. So Neh. xiii. 11, " I contended with the rulers, and said, Why is the house of God forsaken?" they kept away the portions of the Levites, and therefore they left the house of God: so ver. 17, the nobles of Judah they profaned the sabbath day, and brought wrath upon Israel. 2 Chron. xxiv. 17, 18, the princes of Judah were all idolatrous, and led Joash into idolatrous practices, but they were quickly after all slain for it, ver. 23. John vii. 48, " Have any of the rulers believed on him:" they were so wicked, even all of them, that they could make their boast, " Have any of them believed on him?" No, no, they are not for Christ and his ways. Jer. v. 5, " I will get me unto the great men, and will speak unto them; for they have known the way of the Lord, and the judgment of their God: but these have altogether broken the yoke, and burst the bonds." The prophet thought the great ones, who had great obligations upon them to honour God, who knew what pertained to worship and justice, that they would hearken to him; but they cast off all respect, subjection, and obedience to the law of God; they followed their own wills, lusts, humours; they regarded neither equity nor honesty; they were far worse than the poorer sort, whom the prophet had tried also. Luke mentions but one judge, and he was an unjust one. Are not too many of the great ones among us corrupt, loose, and enemies to Christ and his kingdom?

Obs. 4. It is matter of mourning when those who are set over others to be punishers of the wicked, countenancers of the godly, examples of piety and virtue, and should seek the good of the public, prove clean otherwise, and are actors and patrons of wickedness. The Spirit here is affected with it, and affects the prophet: Son of man, these are the men that do so; these pervert, obstruct justice, these encourage evil-doers, these sadden the hearts of the godly, these hinder good designs; these are the men that seek themselves, that cry, Give, give, and love to have it so; these are the men that pretend the good of the state and people, but are the ruin of both. This was matter of grief to heaven and earth. Isa. i. 10, when the prophet had termed them "rulers of Sodom," he complains, ver. 23, saying, "Thy princes are rebellious, and companions of thieves: every one loveth gifts, and followeth after rewards; they judge not the fatherless, neither doth the cause of the widow come unto them:" they sought themselves, not the good of particulars, or the public, and this troubled the prophet; and not only him, but the Lord also; for it follows in the next verse, "Therefore saith the Lord, the Lord of hosts, the mighty One of Israel, Ah, I will ease me of mine adversaries, and avenge me of mine enemies." God had been wearied and grieved with them a long time, and though they were many, and mighty, yet he was the Lord of hosts, &c. This argument did affect God much, and he was oft upon it: Isa. iii. 12, "As for my people, children are their oppressors, and women rule over them. O my people, they which lead thee cause thee to err, and destroy the way of thy paths;" they destroyed justice and religion.

Obs. 5. There will never be wanting in any place men to devise mischief. In Jerusalem there were men whose hearts, heads, and tongues were at work. In chap. viii. he tells you of the seventy ancients, and of the twenty-five, who had all devised and were practising mischief. In Shushan was not wanting a Haman to devise mischief against the Jews, Esth. viii. 3. Pharaoh and his courtiers devised mischief against the Jews, Exod. i. There were those who devised to take away David's life, Psal. xxxi. 13. "They imagined a mischievous device," Psal. xxi. 11. No city, no kingdom was ever free from men of deceitful, wicked, and mischievous devices, and no time ever abounded more with such men, and such devices, than our times; and if I should say, no place more than this kingdom, I should not much fail. Who can reckon up the mischievous devices which have been against the estates, laws, liberties, religion, and consciences of the people of this kingdom? Ship-money was a cunning device to dry up their estates; prerogative was cried up to bring the laws and liberties of the subject down; innovations and new canons were prelatical devices to rid you of your religion and consciences, to make way for popery. What wicked devices have been against the parliament, against this city, against this kingdom! whatever hath been devised for the good of all, hath met with anti-cross devices. There are those who devise as strongly and speedily to ruin us, as any do to relieve us. The device against Ireland was a bloody and mischievous device, and bloody devices are in men's heads against us; but here is the comfort, Job v. 12, "God disappointeth the devices of the crafty, so that their hands cannot perform their enterprise." They devise to undo all, but they cannot. Micah ii. 1, "Woe to them that devise iniquity." God hath threatened, and though they cannot accomplish their devices, yet he will accomplish his threats. Prov. xii. 2, "A man of wicked devices will he condemn." Many of wicked devices have been amongst us, and hath not the Lord condemned them?

Dan. vi. 7, all the presidents of the kingdom, governors, princes, counsellors, captains, devised a plot against Daniel.

Obs. 6. Men in place being evil, they make others evil; they do not only devise mischief, but communicate mischief, they give and obtrude ill counsel upon others. These that were in place, especially Jaazaniah and Pelatiah the princes, they gave out ill counsel to the people. They and such men do the greatest hurt; their power, honour, estates, examples, are prevalent with the people, and when they counsel corruptly, their counsel takes and infects a multitude quickly. Jeroboam tells the people it was too much for them to go up to Jerusalem, that was a long journey, would be very chargeable, and might prove dangerous; therefore he had taken a better course for them, he had made calves, set them up for gods at Dan and Bethel, and now they should need to go no further for to worship: this counsel took. Balak being advised by Balaam, counsels the Midianitish women to entice the Israelites to folly, which took; and they drew them both to whoredom and idolatry, Numb. xxv. 1, 2, with chap. xxxi. 16. Ill counsel from great ones doth great mischief: Nah. i. 11, "There is one come out of thee, that imagineth evil against the Lord, a wicked counsellor;" it is spoken of Nineveh concerning Sennacherib. We have many come out of us that are wicked counsellors, and prevail with the people to do what they counsel. Did not prelates, judges, nobles, princes, lately give ill counsels, and were not the people too forward to hearken? All counsels that seem good are not always safe; men should therefore examine others' counsels, whether they be such as agree with the word of God, are really for the good of church or state, before they approve or entertain them.

Take heed what counsels you take from great ones that are corrupt; this hath endangered cities, churches, whole kingdoms. Take counsel of the great God, who dasheth all wicked counsels, and establisheth his own; Psal. xxxiii. 10, 11, he brings the counsels of men to nought, but the counsel of God endures for ever.

Obs. 7. That great ones are greatly secure, they put the evil day far from them; "It is not near." They are lavish to entertain thoughts that may disquiet their hearts, or shake their foundations. Honours, pleasures, secular affairs take them up so, that they fear not changes, they consider not the evil day, they are as quiet as men that are in covenant one with another. Isa. xxviii. 14, 15, those who ruled the people, they said, "We have made a covenant with death, and with hell are we at agreement; when the overflowing scourge shall pass through, it shall not come unto us." The great ones were covenanters, such as ruled the city; but with whom did they covenant? with death and hell, and now feared not any threatenings of them by the prophets. Although the prophets threatened death and hell to them, it was as nothing, they feared not. Some think they, being idolatrous, sacrificed to Pluto, *fatum Atropos*, those gods they conceived had power over death and hell, and so had them their friends, and lived without fear. Amos vi. 3, he tells you of some that "put far away the evil day;" but who were they? men of place and power; they were such as caused the seat of violence to come near, that lay upon beds of ivory, that stretched themselves upon their couches, and did eat the lambs out of the flocks, and calves out of the midst of the stall; they were dancers, drinkers, and such as anointed themselves with the chiefest ointments. These are men "settled on their lees," as Zephaniah speaks, chap. i. 12; they were like wine in vessels, not emptied from vessel to vessel, but settled in their sinful security. And not only great ones are secure, but, Zech. i. 11, the angel told the man among the myrtle trees, that all the earth sat still and was at rest. Security is an epidemical disease.

Obs. 8. See the impiety and profaneness of these men:

(1.) They oppose God, and give contrary counsel to what he had given by Jeremiah, that they should not build houses in that place, but in Babylon, Jer. xxix. 5, 6, and that because of the great judgment which was coming upon them; but they say, "It is not near; let us build houses," there is no danger; or if the enemy should come, we had need build and strengthen ourselves: thus they counsel contrary to the prophet, and to God.

(2.) Their profaneness; they scoff at the word of God: "This city is the caldron, and we be the flesh." Jeremiah had told them that God would bring the Chaldeans upon them, and boil them in that city like flesh in a caldron. This they scoff at, strengthening their malice and profaneness from abuse of the word of God. There is such corruption in the heart of man, that it turns the best things of all into bitterness.

This made Jeremiah say, "I am in derision daily, every one mocketh me;" and, "The word of the Lord was made a reproach unto me, and a derision daily," Jer. xx. 7, 8.

Isa. xxviii. 14, 15, "Hear the word of the Lord, ye scornful men." They mocked and scoffed at what was prophesied; whatever the prophet threatened they derided it; therefore, ver. 22, "Be not mockers, lest your bands be made strong," lest you have double fetters, double judgments. 2 Chron. xxxvi. 16, "They mocked the messengers of God, and despised his words," all his threatenings; and Peter, 2 Pet. iii. 3, 4, tells us, "there shall come scoffers, walking after their own lusts, saying, Where is the promise of his coming." Those under the law scoffed at the threatenings; these under the times of the gospel scoff at the promises, those of Christ's coming, of the resurrection, last judgment, the end of all, and life eternal: such as these walk after their own lusts, "they bring a city into a snare," Prov. xxix.

לֵצִים

8. The Septuagint translates the word "scornful," Psal. i. 1, λοιμοὺς, *pestes*, because such men are pestilent men, the very plagues of church and state, contemners of God and men. Jude said it long since, that there should be mockers in the last time, and we have found it true; there are as profane, bitter scoffers amongst us, as ever were; even the truths of God are scorned and scoffed at.

Obs. 9. No devices, counsels, attempts of men can null or frustrate the purposes of God. They devise mischief, give ill counsel, scoff at the truths of God, put the people upon contrary designs; yet all this would not do, desolation was near, the Chaldeans came, they were besieged in that city, boiled in it as flesh in a caldron, and God's counsels, truths, threats took place, notwithstanding all their counsels and endeavours to the contrary. Balaam was hired by Balak to cross God's design, in cursing of his people; he attempted to do it, but God overpowered him, he could not do or speak ought to their prejudice, Numb. xxiii. 3, 8; therefore he professed, ver. 23, "Surely there is no enchantment against Jacob, neither is there any divination against Israel: according to this time it shall be said of Jacob and of Israel, What hath God wrought?" Man would have wrought mischief, but could not; what hath God wrought? he hath wrought, and none could hinder; therefore, Isa. xiv. 27, it is said, "The Lord of hosts hath purposed, and who shall disannul it? not Balak or Balaam, not Jaazaniah or Pelatiah, not the twenty-five rulers in Jerusalem; his hand is stretched out, and who shall turn it back? It is not in the power of princes, no not the prince of darkness, to let his work, to alter his counsels: what God hath determined, shall so come to pass as he hath determined; ver. 24, "Surely as I have thought, so shall it come to pass; and as I have purposed, so it shall stand;" and all his pleasure shall be done, Isa. xlvi. 10: so that "there is no wisdom, nor understanding, nor counsel against the Lord," Prov. xxi. 30.

Ver. 4—12. *Therefore prophesy against them, prophesy, O son of man. And the Spirit of the Lord fell upon me, and said unto me, Speak; Thus saith the Lord; Thus have ye said, O house of Israel: for I know the things that come into your mind, every one of them. Ye have multiplied your slain in this city, and ye have filled the streets thereof with the slain. Therefore thus saith the Lord God; Your slain whom ye have laid in the midst of it, they are the flesh, and this city is the caldron: but I will bring you forth out of the midst of it. Ye have feared the sword; and I will bring a sword upon you, saith the Lord God. And I will bring you out of the midst thereof, and deliver you into the hands of strangers, and will execute judgments among you. Ye shall fall by the sword; I will judge you in the border of Israel; and ye shall know that I am the Lord. This city shall not be your caldron, neither shall ye be the flesh in the midst thereof; but I will judge you in the border of Israel: and ye shall know that I am the Lord: for ye have not walked in my statutes, neither executed my judgments, but have done after the manners of the heathen that are round about you.*

In these verses is contained the denunciation of judgments against these devisers of mischief and wicked counsellors. The parts are these:

I. A command, "Prophesy against them," ver. 4.

II. A discovery of their thoughts and counsels, ver. 5.

III. Demonstration of their wickedness, ver. 6; those who hearkened not to their counsels, they slew.

IV. The death of these counsellors, and the place where it should be; not in Jerusalem, but "in the border of Israel," ver. 8—11.

V. The end of God in it, ver. 11, 12.

VI. The ground of God's proceeding thus with them, ver. 12, "For ye have not walked," &c.

Ver. 4. "Therefore prophesy against them," &c. The word prophesy is twice mentioned, to set out the intention of God, which was set against them, the certainty of the thing, and to prevent delay in the prophet; he must go and tell them of heavy and sad things. God was greatly displeased with them, and therefore will have the prophet without any delay to make known his pleasure against them; he must speak freely and boldly, and foretell them of their destruction.

Obs. 1. That profane scoffing at the truths and threats of God provokes him greatly. They had scoffed at Jeremiah's words, "This city is the caldron, and we be the flesh," and made constructions of them to please themselves; therefore saith God, "Prophesy against them." His Spirit was stirred, and he stirs up the prophet to declare his wrath against such scoffers. God's threats and judgments should make men tremble; Job xli. 10, "Who is able to stand before me?" At his presence the mountains melt, Isa. lxiv. 3; when he threatened, the great city Nineveh repented, Jonah iii.; and devils tremble, Jam. ii. 19. Mountains, Ninevites, devils, melt, repent, tremble, and yet Israelites scoff at the threats and judgments of God; but the Lord will not endure it, the prophet must declare dreadful things against them.

Men that have scoffed at the truths and ways of God, have been lashed with the judgments of God. John Apowel scoffing at one for praying, was presently surprised with fear, and the next day found mad,' crying out night and day, "Oh the devil, the devil!" Another hearing a godly minister preaching from that text, Prov. x. 7, "The memory of the just is blessed: but the name of the wicked shall rot," scoffed at the minister, and said, he made a rotten sermon: presently after hurting his tongue with a little wood which he held at his mouth, his tongue swelled, rotted, and he died of it.

Fox in Acts and Monuments.

Obs. 2. That servants of God having divine warrant, are forthwith to do their office, although they be messengers of sad tidings. "Prophesy, prophesy against them." He hath command from God, and he must not stick now, and say, They are great men, the chief of the city, such as sought Jeremiah's death, and if I shall prophesy against them, they will use means to crush me; God, by doubling the word, takes him off from all such reasonings, from all delays, and expected immediate performance of his commands. Let men fret at the messages of God's servants; they must respect God, and not man, they must give out what the Lord hath given in. If men be great, God is greater; we must be faithful to him, whoever suffers by it.

Ver. 5. "And the Spirit of the Lord fell upon me." The Hebrew word נפל notes the falling of a thing from a high place, *cum vi et impetu*, with force and violence; and so here the Spirit coming from above, offered not violence to the prophet, but came upon him with might and power, and provoked him to prophesy.

"Thus have ye said." Whether the Spirit or prophet repeated their words, is not evident, they are not expressed; where the sense is evident from former expressions, the Scripture is frequently silent, and repeats not the words. 2 Kings v. 4, "Thus and thus said the maid that is of the land of Israel." So 2 Sam. xvii. 15, "Thus and thus did Ahithophel counsel," saith Hushai, "and thus and thus have I counselled;" the sense was known by what was before, and therefore the words are not repeated: the Scripture shuns the multiplying of words needlessly.

"O house of Israel." That is, the house of Judah, the whole being put for a part; and this is frequent.

"I know the things that come into your mind." The Hebrew is, מעלות which notes those things that rise up out of men's hearts, as weeds out of the earth, or leaves upon trees; עלה is a leaf; *quia sursum crescit*, whatever goes out and up from the heart or spirit of a man, that is understood by *maaloth*. Matt. xv. 19, ill thoughts go out from the heart, go up to the tongue, to the eyes. Luke xxiv. 38, Why do evil thoughts or reasonings arise in your hearts?

Ascensiones spiritus vestri. *Calv.*

Obs. 1. Whom the Lord sends about his work, he enables to do it. Go, prophesy, prophesy; and presently the Spirit fell upon him, whereby he was furnished with prophetical matter, and enabled to deliver it. When God sent Moses, he furnished him for the great work he appointed him to: Moses pleaded his ineloquence and slowness of speech; but God said, Exod. iv. 12, "Go, and I will be with thy mouth, and teach thee," &c.

Obs. 2. To new acts of prophecy, new access of the Spirit is requisite. He had received the Spirit before divers times, chap. i. 3; ii. 2; iii. 14, 22, 24; viii. 1; and here again, before he prophesies, the Spirit falls upon him; which shows that to spiritual work antecedent receptions of the Spirit suffice not, there must be new influxes of the Spirit for new acts of prophecy. If the Spirit therefore did not reveal new things unto the prophets, they could not prophesy; for prophecy is no habit which men might stir up, and use at their pleasure. Prophets know not secret and future things, but as the Spirit reveals them. Elisha knew not the death of the Shunammite's son, 2 Kings iv. 27, "The Lord hath hid it from me, and hath not told me;" and Nathan knew not the mind of God about building the temple, 2 Sam. vii. 3. There must be new acts of the Spirit revealing unto the prophets when they give out prophetical things; but Numb. xi. 26, "The Spirit rested upon Eldad and Medad, and they prophesied in the camp." Some think they continued constantly prophesying, and ceased not, but that is an opinion only. The Spirit resting upon them, argues not that they did always prophesy, or had a habit of prophesying, but that they were numbered amongst the prophets, and at what times it pleased the Spirit, had new revelations, which they declared; suitable to that in Isa. l. 4, "He wakeneth morning by morning, he wakeneth mine ear to hear as the learned;" the prophet could not speak a word in season if God had not wakened him, and spake to him every morning.

Obs. 3. Supernatural things commanded are not in vain. God bid Ezekiel prophesy: he was not able to do it; the Philistines might more easily have interpreted Samson's riddle: Job might as well have answered God's great questions, in chap. xxxviii.—xli. as our prophet have prophesied; but God commanded, and he caused the Spirit to fall upon him. As the Lord calls upon us to repent, to believe, these are supernatural works, and men may as soon remove mountains, pluck the sun out of heaven, as do these; but God that commands them, gives power and grace to do them, Phil. i. 29; 2 Tim. ii. 25.

Obs. 4. The prophets had warrant to deal particularly, even with the greatest sinners. "Speak; Thus have ye said;" how? thus, "It is not near; let us build houses; this city is the caldron, and we be the flesh." The prophet may go and tell them what they have said, though they were the chiefest men of the city. When great ones sin, they must be told of their sins in a special manner. David defiles his body with adultery, and the land with blood; Nathan comes to him, and tells him a parable that was so general as David took it not home to himself; thereupon the prophet deals roundly with him, and tells him, "Thou art the man," 2 Sam. xii. 7; and ver. 9, "Thou hast killed Uriah the Hittite with the sword of Ammon, and taken his wife; now therefore the sword shall never depart from thy house." So Elijah spake home to Ahab, and told him that it was he and his father's house that troubled Israel, because they had forsaken the commandments of the Lord, and followed Baalim, 1 Kings xviii. 18. Isaiah flattered not great nor small when he said, chap. i. 10, "Hear the word of the Lord, ye rulers of Sodom and people of Gomorrah;" and Jeremiah must "say unto the king and to the queen, Humble yourselves, sit down: for your principalities shall come down, even the crown of your glory," Jer. xiii. 18. John told Herod it was not lawful for him to have his brother's wife, Mark vi. 18; Luke iii. 19; it is said he was *ἔλεγχόμενος επ' αὐτοῦ*, he showed him the greatness, foulness, and danger of his sin, and laboured to convince him by strong arguments; so Paul dealt with Peter, and John with Diotrephes. And there is great reason that ministers should tell men of their sins; Ezek. iii. 18, "If thou speakest not to warn the wicked from his wicked way, to save his life; the same wicked man shall die in his iniquity; but his blood will I require at thine hand."

Obs. 5. That whatever risings, thoughts, workings, are in men's spirits, the Lord knows them, and that exactly. "I know the things that come into your mind, every one." There is nothing in man hid from God; a thought is a small thing, yet thoughts escape not the eye of God. Jer. xvii. 9, 10, "The heart is deceitful above all things, and desperately wicked: who can know it?" not a man's self, not Satan, not angels; who then? "I the Lord search the heart, I try the reins." Man may know it conjecturally, Prov. xx. 5, he may by his art pump out much; man may know it by revelation, 1 Sam. ix. 19, so Samuel the seer could tell Saul all that was in his heart: but to know what is in the heart of man, immediately, exactly, and certainly, can none but God; he only is *καρδιογνῶϛα*, therefore the apostles prayed to him under that notion, Acts i. 24, "Thou, Lord, which knowest the hearts of all men, show whether of these two thou hast chosen." There is no juggling with God, his eye beholds all; and if there could be doubt of any thing with him, he searcheth the heart, he tries the reins: this is spoken to our capacity, God needs no searching, no trying; for, Psal. cxxxix. 2, "Thou understandest my thought afar off:" not that God is at a distance from us, or our thoughts; but he understands them while they are far off from us, from our knowledge, while they are potential, as gardeners know what weeds such ground will bring forth, when nothing appears. Deut. xxxi. 21, "I know their imagination which they go about, even now, before I have brought them into the land which I sware:" God knew their thoughts before they came into Canaan, what they would be there. And how can it be, but that God should know all our thoughts, seeing he made the heart, and it is in his hand, Prov. xxi. 1; seeing "we live, move, and have our being" in God, Acts xvii. 28; seeing he is through us all, and in us all, Eph. iv. 6. Look well to your hearts, thoughts, risings, whatever comes into your mind; let no secret sins, corruptions, lodge there; think not to conceal any thing from the eye of God. Psal. xc. 8, "Thou hast set our iniquities before thee;" and not only them, but "our secret sins in the light of thy countenance;" thou lookest upon them fully, seest, knowest them exactly; therefore remember that. Eccl. xii. 13, 14, "Fear God, and keep his commandments;" and why? "for God shall bring every work into judgment, with every secret thing, whether it be good, or whether it be evil." There is no shuffling with God, men in great place, or of great parts, cannot elude or evade him.

Ver. 6. "Ye have multiplied your slain in this city," &c. Before they had been profane, now their injustice appears. Some think the men were not actually slain, but oppressed and cruelly dealt with; violence and oppression being counted, in the Scripture sense, murder: but it is not probable that our prophet would use such expressions, as, to multiply the slain, and fill the streets with slain, if none were slain. Chap. vii. 23, "The land is full of bloody crimes;" and chap. ix. 9, "The land is full of blood;" and chap. xxii. 2, it is called the "bloody city;" so in chap xxiv. 6, 9; the Hebrew is, the city of bloods. These great men who gave the ill counsel, it is likely that they crushed those who opposed them, and dealt with them as seditious, as rebellious, as enemies to the city and state. Jeremiah, you know, they sought his life, petitioned to the king that he might be put to death, Jer. xxxviii. 4; and it is probable, that many which would not conform to their idolatrous practices, were cut off.

Obs. When the Lord is about to proceed in judgment against evil doers, he declares the cause of his proceeding in such a way. When God intended to destroy the world, he made known the cause thereof, Gen. vi. 5, 6, 11, 12; when he was about to fire Sodom, he discovered to Abraham the ground of it, Gen. xviii. 20.

Ver. 7. "Your slain whom ye have laid in the midst of it, they are the flesh, and this city is the caldron." Here the Lord shows them who are the flesh in the caldron; not in that sense they took it; for they thought themselves should be the flesh, live till old age in the city: but the Lord tells them here that those they had slain unjustly, whose carcasses lay in the streets, and consumed away, they were the flesh boiled in the caldron. Manasseh had been bloody, and Zedekiah was bloody, and the slain were the flesh, and so the city was a caldron to them, but not to the others.

"I will bring you forth out of the midst of it." God tells them they shall neither live nor die in it, he would order things so, that they should be carried out of Jerusalem; and for certainty of it, the words are repeated in the beginning of the 9th verse.

Obs. Judgments of God cannot be waved by men's wit or power. They jeered, and made a construction of flesh and caldron suitable to their own minds, and conceited they should die in the city in peace; but the Lord tells them no, he would bring them forth out of the midst of it.

Ver. 8. "Ye have feared the sword; and I will bring a sword upon you," &c. Jeremiah had counselled them to yield themselves, chap. xxxviii. 17: the king and the rest through fear would not hearken. They feared the sword, and therefore sent to Egypt for help, Jer. ii. 18. They feared the sword, but not the Babylonish captivity: the Lord brought both upon them.

Obs. 1. Where guilt is, there is fear. They were deeply guilty of impiety and injustice; they had sinned against God by their idolatry, against their brethren by their bloodiness, against the king of Babylon by breaking oath and covenant with him, Ezek. xvii. 15; and now whatever they said, "It is not near," yet they were full of fear; God saw what timorous spirits they had. If the horror of their wicked acts did not seize upon them, yet fear of wrath and judgment possessed them. Psal. xiv. 5, speaking of workers of iniquity, he saith, "There were they in great fear;" Hebrew is, they feared a fear: but where was it, in their consciences? when the light of nature did convince them of their wickedness, there where the conviction was they feared greatly. Prov. xxviii. 1, "The wicked flee when no man pursueth:" they fear, and so fear, that they flee to secure themselves from imaginary dangers. Lev. xxvi. 36, "The sound of a shaken leaf shall chase them." And Job xv. 21, Eliphaz, speaking of the wicked, saith, "A dreadful sound is in his ears;" the Hebrew is, a sound of fears: such was in Richard the third, whose hand was ever upon his dagger. "The wicked are like the troubled sea," Isa. lvii. 20.

Obs. 2. That which sinners fear, the Lord brings upon them. Saul feared the devolution of the kingdom to another, and it fell to David. The Jews feared lest the "Romans should come, and take away their place and nation," John xi. 48, and they did do it. Prov. x. 24, "The fear of the wicked, it shall come upon him;" it is coming towards him every day, and will be upon him ere he die.

After the flood the people feared scattering, and therefore said, "Let us build a tower, whose top may reach unto heaven," Gen. xi. 4; and ver. 8, "The Lord scattered them abroad from thence upon the face of all the earth." Men that fear evils usually take surer courses to prevent them, which justly brings the thing feared upon them. Richard the third feared the kingdom would not be firm to him, his nephews he murders for security, and this kindled a fire in the kingdom, which quickly consumed him. The prelates feared their standing; to establish themselves, they remove from *jus regium* to *jus divinum;* they frame a new oath, with an &c. in it, to swear all men to put to their shoulders for support of their tottering kingdom; but it is fallen, it is fallen.

Ver. 9. "I will bring you out of the midst thereof." Of these words before in the 7th verse.

"And deliver you into the hands of strangers." Not of the neighbour nations; for had they come against them, because of commerce, consultation, language, and some references to them, the nobles and great ones might have found favour; therefore God would put them into the hands of strangers that understood not their language, that had no inducements to show favour to them, that regarded neither great nor small. They had destroyed their friends, now strangers should destroy them.

"And will execute judgments among you." Of these words I spoke, chap. v. 8.

Obs. The Lord can use any instruments to accomplish his judgments: strangers, heathens, profane ones, it matters not what the instruments are, if the holy God use them; his use of them is holy, and he orders all their thoughts, counsels, operations, to accomplish his own ends.

Ver. 10. "I will judge you in the border of Israel." The same words are in the 11th verse. Where this was must be inquired. It is generally thought to be at Riblah, and the scripture is for it, 2 Kings xxv. 6. Some have thought it to be in Babylon, but without warrant; 2 Kings xxiii. 33, Riblah was in the land of Hamath, which lay on the north part of Canaan on the east side: and Bonfrerius observes in his Onomasticon of cities and places, that Jerom thinks it to be Antiochia, Adrichomius, some city of Syria or Judea, in the tribe of Naphtali, and this the scripture gives countenance unto, Numb. xxxiv. 11, 12. Others think it to be a province in Syria, afterwards called Epiphania, from Antiochus Epiphanes. This Riblah or Epiphania was at the border of Israel, where Nebuchadnezzar was, whither Zedekiah was brought, and there God judged him and the rest. 2 Kings xxv. 6, "They took the king, and brought him up to the king of Babylon to Riblah; and they gave judgment upon him;" Hebrew is, spake judgment; they expostulated with him and the rest about their treachery, in breaking the oath, and revolting from the king of Babylon. And their judgment was executed; Zedekiah sees his sons slain, his eyes are put out, all the nobles are put to death, Jer. xxxix. 5—7; lii. 10.

Obs. God punisheth sinners in places and by persons they think not of. These men thought they should die in Jerusalem, never fall into the hands of strangers; but God carried them to Riblah, to the borders of the land, delivered them into the hands of strangers, from whom they found no pity, no mercy. It is some comfort to men to die in their own country among their friends, that will take care of their dead corpse, see the same interred honourably after death. Hence was it that Æneas counted them happy who died before the walls of Troy, when he was floating upon the seas, and in danger of death among the waves. Something is in it that the prophet saith, Jer. xxii. 10, "Weep ye not for the dead, neither bemoan him; but weep sore for him that goeth away: for he shall return no more, nor see his native country." They must not weep for the dead, but must weep, and that sorely, for those who lost their country: the Jews would rather die than lose their land, and be taken from Jerusalem. Ver. 26, it is laid as a great judgment upon Jeconiah and his mother, to be carried to another land, where they should die.

Ver. 12. "And ye shall know that I am the Lord," &c. In this verse is the end and ground of God's judgments. You have the first words of the verse oft before, especially in chap. vi. 7, 10, 13, 14; and those words, "Ye have not walked in my statutes, neither executed my judgments," you had opened, chap. v. 6. One thing in this verse must be spoke unto: it is said, chap. v. 7, "Neither have done according to the judgments" of the nations that are round about you;" and here it is, "but have done after the manners of the heathen that are round about you." The difficulty is not great; in the 5th chapter they were not so righteous and just as the heathens were, and here, they followed the manners of the heathen; what corrupt manners they had, those the Jews took up, their manners of worship and of life.

Obs. 1. The scope and end of God's judgments is to convince the wicked that he is the Lord. "Ye shall know that I am the Lord." You have cast me off, taken in other gods, worshipped the sun, and forms of creeping things; but I will bring heavy judgments upon you, carry you out of this city to the borders of Israel, slay you with the sword. And when you are in the hands of your enemies, you shall know experimentally that I am the Lord, that all other gods were false and idol gods, that they were not able to save you in time of trouble, that you have done exceeding ill to provoke me, who am Jehovah, the true and only God, who have all power in my hands, and will now make good my threats upon their heads and carcasses; your consciences shall tell you, whether you be willing or unwilling, that I am righteous in my proceedings, and that themselves die justly by my strokes.

Obs. 2. God therefore punisheth, because men do wickedly. "I will judge you in the border of Israel; and ye shall know that I am the Lord; for ye have not walked in my statutes, neither executed my judgments," &c. God hath a special eye to his own statutes and judgments; when they are kept and performed, he prospers, but when they are violated, he judgeth, he destroys. God's statutes and judgments come from infinite wisdom and holiness, they are good, equal, profitable; and for the sons of men, that depend upon God every moment for their lives and beings, to neglect the Lord's statutes, to transgress them, and do after their own wills, humours, fancies, or others', this is unspeakable wrong to God, and he hath, doth, and will visit for such wrongs. If men would not be broken with his judgments, let them not break his statutes; if they would secure their lives, let them walk in his laws.

Obs. 3. The Lord's own people are prone to take up the manners and customs of other nations. "Ye have done after the manners of the heathen;" and not one heathenish nation only, but of all round about you. They observed their manners of life, and manners of worship, liked, fetched them in, and practised the same: 2 Chron. xiii. 9, they made them "priests after the manner of the nations of other lands:" Psal. cvi. 35, they "mingled among the heathen, and learned their works" and ways: 2 Kings xvi. 3, Ahaz caused "his son to pass through the fire, according to the abominations of the heathen:" they would have a king to judge them, like all the nations, 1 Sam. viii. 5, 20.

Ezek. xx. 32, "We will be as the heathen, as the families of the countries." Such conformity had they with the heathen, that Moab and Seir could say, Ezek. xxv. 8, "Behold, the house of Judah is like unto all the heathen."

Obs. 4. When God's people take up the manners of heathens, and nations hateful to God, it provokes him greatly, and aggravates the evil much.

In this case, (1.) They reject God's statutes and ways, they laid them by and walked not in them; yet, Deut. iv. 8, no nation under heaven had statutes and judgments so righteous as they. 2 Kings xvii. 15, "They rejected his statutes," and his commandments, "and his testimonies; they followed vanity, and went after the heathen that were round about them." It was as if men should lay aside the Bible, and take the Turkish Alcoran, or popish mass-book.

(2.) There was a prohibition, that they should not do after the ways of the heathens: Deut. xii. 30, "Take heed thou be not snared by following them, and that thou inquire not after their gods, saying, How did these nations serve their gods? even so will I do;" ver. 31, "Thou shalt not do so," &c.; and 2 Kings xvii. 15, the Lord had charged them that they should not do like the heathen.

Jer. x. 2, "Learn not the way of the heathen."

(3.) God punished the heathens for those practices they took up; see Lev. xviii. 24—26, 28; Deut. xii. 29, 30; he cast them out before their eyes, 2 Kings xvi. 3.

Ver. 13. *And it came to pass, when I prophesied, that Pelatiah the son of Benaiah died. Then fell I down upon my face, and cried with a loud voice, and said, Ah Lord God! wilt thou make a full end of the remnant of Israel?*

This verse presents unto us,

I. The death of "Pelatiah."

II. The time of it, "when I prophesied."

III. The consequences of this judgment upon Pelatiah; which are,

1. The prophet's falling upon his face.

2. His exclamation; he "cried with a loud," &c.

3. What he cried out, "Ah Lord God!" &c.

Some doubts lie wrapt up in this verse, and must be cleared. Our prophet was, in body, amongst the captives in Babylon; in spirit, he was in the temple, at the east gate of the Lord's house, ver. 1.

Quest. 1. How Ezekiel saith here, "When I prophesied, Pelatiah died?" whenas he had yet prophesied nothing, he was now in a vision; and ver. 24, 25, after this he was returned "by the spirit into Chaldea," and then he spake all the things the Lord had showed him.

Answ. 1. Some think that by prophesying here is not meant actual prophesying, as if our prophet did prophesy, and give out what the Lord said, but the hearing of prophecy; and that place is brought to justify it, 1 Cor. xi. 5, "Every woman that prayeth or prophesieth;" that is, say they, which heareth prophecy: and so they will have our prophet only to hear prophetical truths which the Lord gave out, and that Pelatiah should die. But this sense of the words seems harsh, and the text saith, he prophesied, he did not hear prophecy, hear Pelatiah should die; why, at the hearing of these things, should he fall down upon his face, and cry out as he did?

2. The Lord had great indignation against these men that gave ill counsel, and bids Ezekiel prophesy, ver. 4, and doubles the command, "Prophesy, prophesy against them;" and then the Spirit fell upon him, ver. 5, and bade him speak, "Thus saith the Lord," &c.; therefore it might well be that he prophesied (while he was in the vision) visionally, and so had a visional sight of Pelatiah's death. And then after, when he came to them in the captivity, he spake to the captivity all the things that the Lord had showed him, and there the real death of Pelatiah was.

3. The prophet wrote this story after he had prophesied in Babylon, and so might insert these words here, being upon the storyof these twenty-five men; for it is usual in Scripture to set that before which was done after.

Quest. 2. But then a second doubt arises; if Ezekiel were in Babylon, and prophesied there, how could this prophecy reach the men that were at Jerusalem; to them it belonged, and the prophet's voice could not extend to their ears?

Answ. 1. Be it granted that the prophet was at a distance from them at Jerusalem, yet the virtue of the prophecy, though not the words, might, and did, extend to Jerusalem. When Ezekiel fell really to prophesy against these men, then Pelatiah died. When Isaiah prophesied against Babylon, Moab, Damascus, Ethiopia, and Egypt, Isa. xiii. xv. xvii. —xx. he was at a great distance from them, yet the prophecies were fulfilled upon them.

2. There was intercourse between those at Jerusalem and those in Babylon; Jer. xxix. 1, 3, Zedekiah sent Elasah and Gemariah to Babylon, and Jeremiah sent letters to them, to acquaint them with his prophecy concerning them, and by those men, or others, might Ezekiel's prophecy be made known to them at Jerusalem.

Quest. 3. How knew Ezekiel that Pelatiah died at that time when he prophesied?

Answ. 1. This he might know by comparing the tidings of his death by messengers brought unto him, and certifying the time, day, and hour thereof, comparing the same with the time of his prophesying; for Pelatiah being a prince of the people, great notice would be taken of his death, and the hour of it fly abroad swiftly, and that to Babylon. Ezek. xxxiii. 21, when the city was besieged, one got away, and brought tidings thereof to Ezekiel; much more easily might they do it before.

2. The spirit of prophecy might certify our prophet hereof, that when he did prophesy, Pelatiah should die at that time. Elijah could tell Ahaziah that he should never come off the bed he lay sick upon, 2 Kings i. 4; and Ahijah could tell Jeroboam's wife, that when her feet entered into the city, the child should die, 1 Kings xiv. 12; and, ver. 17, "when she came to the threshold of the door, the child died."

Quest. 4. How comes it to pass that these twenty-five men, not being of the number of marked ones, chap. ix. escaped the sword of the six slaughter-men, when they slew all unmarked ones in the sanctuary, and in the city?

Answ. They were visionally slain; not really, till the siege and taking of Jerusalem by Nebuchadnezzar, when also the other twenty-four perished, being carried thence to the borders of Israel. And whereas some think Pelatiah here died only visionally, they detract much from the words of the prophet, who saith, he died. You know he prophesied against them all, the twenty-five, and they were all cut off afterward; and if Pelatiah's death were visional, why saw he not visionally the death of all the rest.

The truth is, Pelatiah was made an example, to show the reality and efficacy of this prophecy; for when the captives understood that the thing was so at Jerusalem as Ezekiel prophesied in Babylon, that Pelatiah, a prince, was struck dead by the hand of the Lord, they began to change their thoughts of them at Jerusalem, that they had done wisely to stay it out there, and that themselves were improvident in coming into Babylon; but now they saw God was going on with his judgments against them, and that safety was on their own side.

Of falling upon the face, and crying out, "Ah Lord God!" see chap. ix. 8, where those expressions have been opened.

"Wilt thou make a full end of the remnant of Israel."

Quest. 5. What moved the prophet to use these words? Here was only the death of one man, and that a wicked man; had he seen thousands cut off, smitten dead by the hand of God, he might have feared all the remnant of Israel: he knew there were many marked ones, commission given to spare them, and therefore why doth he conceive the Lord would make a full end of the remnant of Israel?

Answ. 1. Some think Pelatiah, being the chief of the princes, and bearing great sway (for Zedekiah stood in awe of them, Jer. xxxviii. 5) among the people, that our prophet speaks in their person, rather than his own, and thus it is carried: Pelatiah hath been our counsellor, hath great interest in us, we confide more in him than others, and now thou hast cut him off who was our support: "Ah Lord! wilt thou make a full end of the remnant of Israel?" That the prophet should speak in their person, I see nothing to induce it; it is not like so wicked a people would make so gracious a use of this judgment, but rather encourage themselves in Jaazaniah and the rest.

2. I conceive the words refer only to the prophet, who seeing this stroke of God upon Pelatiah, cried out so,

(1.) From his love to that people in general; they were Israelites, and love is full of fears.

(2.) He remembered, chap. ix. 5, 6, the commission given to the slaughtering angels, to be without pity, to slay old and young, maids, women, children: and now seeing the judgment begun upon Pelatiah, he knew not but that it might proceed to the destruction of all, and he therefore saith, "Ah Lord God," &c. He had received in this vision much matter for prophecy, which was not yet given out, and hereupon seeing Pelatiah smitten, he cried out so.

Quest. 6. Should not Ezekiel have rejoiced in the death of Pelatiah? Psal. lviii. 10, "The righteous shall rejoice when he seeth the vengeance." Did not he neglect a duty, and so offend, seeing he wept and mourned?

Answ. We are to rejoice at the ruin of the wicked. Exod. xv. when Pharaoh and his host were drowned in the Red sea, and Egypt howling for their loss, then Moses and the Israelites sang unto the Lord; when Sisera was slain, Baruch and Deborah sang to the Lord, Judg. v.; and Solomon layeth it down for a maxim, Prov. xi. 10, "When the wicked perish, there is shouting" and great joy. The saints may rejoice at the deaths of wicked ones, be they natural or violent;

1. As it sets out the glory of his justice. He hath threatened sinners in his word, and when he executes his threats upon them, gives them according to the nature of their sin, then his justice is glorious.

2. As way hereby is made for the spreading of truth, enlargement of the gospel and kingdom of Christ.

3. As their death tends to the clearing of the godly. David was suspected, yea, accused, by Nabal, to be some runagate, 1 Sam. xxv. 10. God smites Nabal with death, ver. 38; when David heard it, he blesseth God for it, that he had pleaded the cause of his reproach from the hand of Nabal, and returned his wickedness upon his head, ver. 39.

4. As by their death the godly gain liberty. So when Haman was hanged, and his ten sons and other enemies of the Jews put to death, they feasted and rejoiced, Esth. ix. 19; they were freed from their vexations, oppressions, cruelties, plots.

5. As there is a stop made to wickedness. Prov. xxi. 11, "When the scorner is punished, the simple is made wise;" sin ceaseth in the scorner, being cut off, and others cease their wickedness, and grow wise by their stroke. Now Pelatiah's ill counsel, example, power, and whatever he had to promote iniquity with, ceased. So then we may rejoice upon those grounds, but not out of any private respect or revengeful apprehension.

But there is also matter of grief and mourning. God delights not in the death of a sinner, neither should any godly man; as, therefore, Pelatiah was a wicked man, died in his sins, was suddenly cut off, ran a hazard of his eternal condition, so it was matter of mourning. Our prophet, therefore, might rejoice upon the grounds first mentioned, and mourn upon these last named; but, as I hinted in the former question, he looked beyond this one man to the state of Israel.

Obs. 1. How dreadful God's judgments are upon evil counsellors, and scoffers though never so great! Pelatiah, a prince of the people, gave ill counsel in the city, scoffed at the prophecy of Jeremiah, "This city is the caldron, and we be the flesh," and here God smites him. The dreadfulness of the judgment is seen in four things.

(1.) In that he smites his life; not his estate, not his liberty, not his near friends, not any limb, but his life: he smote him in that which was dearest of all, his life; with that which was most feared of all, death, the king of fears.

(2.) It was sudden. When judgments are sudden, they note severity: Deut. vii. 4, when God's wrath is kindled, and kindled very hot against idolatry, he expresses the heat and severity of it this way, he will "destroy thee suddenly:" and Prov. vi. 14, 15, a wicked man "deviseth mischief continually; he soweth discord. Therefore shall his calamity come suddenly; suddenly shall he be broken without remedy." Sudden judgments are unthought of, such, men are unprepared for; and therefore, Isa. xxix. 5, God tells Jerusalem that her judgments should be "at an instant suddenly," yea, as sudden as thunder and lightning, ver. 6: and, chap. xxx. 12, 13, because they despised the word of God, he tells them their judgment should be as a "swelling out in a high wall, whose breaking cometh suddenly at an instant." When judgments are gradual, they are admonitory, and there is hope; but when they are so sudden, all hope is cut off, and remedy prevented.

(3.) Immediate from God's hand; it was the immediate hand of God upon him. Whatever is immediate from God, mercy or judgment, hath the more comfort or terror in it. In hell is immediate wrath from God, and therefore it is more dreadful; so when fire and brimstone came upon Sodom and Gomorrah, this made it so terrible, that it was immediately from the Lord, Gen. xix. 24. When judgments come immediately from God, they come with a greater weight of wrath upon them than others.

(4.) It is exemplary; a great man, a prince of the people. Great men have great sins, and great judgments: some men are not only hanged, or beheaded, but they are also quartered, their heads and quarters are set up on the gates of cities, and made spectacles to all that pass by; so here Pelatiah is made a spectacle of divine vengeance.

Solomon told us long since, that "judgments are prepared for scorners, and stripes for the back of fools," Prov. xix. 29; the word for stripes imports such blows as shiver and break a thing. Ahithophel caused Absalom to go in to his father's concubines, he gave him ill counsel against David, 1 Sam. xvi. xvii. and you know what a sad and dreadful judgment befell him. The captains with their fifties scoffed at Elijah, when they said, 2 Kings i. 9, "Thou man of God;" thou sayest thou art a man of God, and the foolish people think so of thee, but we know thou art a deceiver, and the king hath sent for thee: come down, or we well fetch thee down: but before they could fetch him down, he fetches down fire from heaven which consumed these scoffers to ashes. The children that mocked the prophet, 2 Kings ii. 24, forty-two of them were torn in pieces by two she-bears. Lucian, falling off from christianity, grew a scoffer, and said that he received no other benefit from christianity, than that since before he was called Lucius, now he was called Lucianus; but Suidas tells us he was eaten up of dogs. Julian would take away the christians' wealth, and say that he took this that they might receive a hundredfold, according to the doctrine of their Saviour; but the Lord struck him from heaven, and he died blaspheming. The story of Nightingale is known, which Mr. Fox relates, how abusing that scripture, He that saith he hath no sin is a liar, and the truth is not in him, he fell out of the pulpit and brake his neck. Another making mouths at a godly minister preaching, had his mouth drawn greatly awry, and so died. One present in this congregation was an eye witness of a woman scoffing at another for purity, and walking holily, who had her tongue struck immediately with the palsy, and died thereof within two days. Take heed of jeering and scoffing; the penitent thief was admitted into paradise, when the scoffing one was sent to hell.

Obs. 2. Princely and high conditions are quickly laid in the dust. Pelatiah, a prince of the people, in great honour, all things about him as heart could wish, likely to have continued long here, is brought in a dead corpse. There is no certainty in any condition; how suddenly was Herod eaten of worms, Acts xii. 23; Nebuchadnezzar driven from his palace, Dan. v. 21; and Pharaoh drowned in the bottom of the sea! Exod. xiv. 28.

1 Thess. v. 3, "When they shall say, Peace and safety; then sudden destruction," &c. And Christ said, Ye know not what hour the Lord will come, watch; so we know not what hour death will come, therefore let us watch. The papists call upon St. Christopher to keep them from sudden death; let us call upon Christ to prepare us for, and preserve us in death.

Obs. 3. God sometimes meets with wicked men when his ordinances are dispensing. "When I prophesied, then Pelatiah died;" it was at the time of prophesying. When the word is preached, other ordinances administered, then doth God smite sinners, sometimes present at the ordinance, and sometimes absent, as Pelatiah was. Ezek. xxxvii. 7, "As I prophesied, there was a noise, and behold a shaking, and the bones came together." This was done as he prophesied; there was great virtue and efficacy in his words: so here, when he prophesied, a noise was heard, "and behold, a shaking;" Pelatiah shakes, and shakes to pieces; the power of Ezekiel's prophecy in Babylon slays Pelatiah at Jerusalem. There is a converting power in the word, which converts when men are present; but there is a wounding and confounding power in it also, when men are absent or present. When the apostles preached, sometimes the Holy Ghost fell upon men, Acts x. 44, and sometimes heavy judgments. Elimas the sorcerer is smitten blind, Ananias and Sapphira are struck dead, if not in the time of the ordinance, yet immediately thereupon. Jeroboam thrusts out his hand to take hold of the prophet who prophesied against the altar at Bethel, and his hand was "dried up," 1 Kings xiii. 4. When Paul was preaching, Eutychus sleeps, falls down, and is "taken up dead," Acts xx. 9; at that time he fell down when the ordinance was dispensing. And certainly, when the servants of God do preach and prophesy against sinners, present or absent, sometimes God smites them: Hos. vi. 5, "I have hewed them by the prophets;" the word was an axe in their mouths, and every time they prophesied judgment, they hewed the state, and particular persons; 1 Kings xix. 17, they that escape the sword of Hazael and Jehu, shall Elisha slay; how? by his prophesying and preaching. This God doth to put honour upon his word, that so men may fear, respect his ordinances, and take heed how they hear.

Obs. 4. Not only judgments themselves are to be observed, but the circumstances of them also. "When I prophesied, then Pelatiah died;" he notes the time in a special manner. Circumstances of time, place, and person, do add much weight to the judgments of God, and truth of a story: here you have all; the time when Ezekiel prophesied; the place, the door of the eastern gate of the temple at Jerusalem, ver. 1; the name, "Pelatiah:" these add strength to the judgments and prophecy. Circumstances commend mercies and aggravate judgments; to be smitten when the prophet was prophesying against him, sets out the judgment with life and terror. Circumstances help to screw the thing into the heart, and to fasten it upon the memory. The time of things is much mentioned in the word, be it of sins, Jer. xi. 15, "When thou doest evil, then thou rejoicest;" or of mercies, when Manasseh was brought back to Jerusalem, "then Manasseh knew that the Lord he was God," 2 Chron. xxxiii. 13; or of judgments, Judg. v. 8, "They chose new gods; then was war in the gates;" Numb. xi. 33, "While the flesh was yet between their teeth, ere it was chewed, the wrath of the Lord was kindled against the people, and the Lord smote the people with a very great plague:" so Dan. iv. 13, "While the word was in the king's mouth" the voice was heard, "The kingdom is departed from thee;" and Dan. ii. 5, while Belshazzar tasted wine in the bowls of the temple, in the same hour came forth fingers that wrote letters of death upon the wall: and of Uzziah it is said, then he "was wroth," and while he was so, "the leprosy even rose up in his forehead," 2 Chron. xxvi. 19. The prophets observed the times of God's giving out the threatenings, and the times of execution.

Obs. 5. Holy and good men fear when the judgments of God fall heavily and suddenly upon wicked men. Psal. lii. 6, when God's hand should fall upon Doeg, saith David, "The righteous shall see and fear;" what shall they see to make them fear? the glory and power of God in executing justice, in cutting off delinquents: Psal. ix. 16, "The Lord is known by the judgments which he executeth," known to be most powerful, glorious, dreadful; he is present in them, and the godly have eyes to see much of him. When angels appeared, Gideon, a man of valour, and others, feared; much more when God appears in thunder and lightning, in sudden and grievous judgments, there is cause of fear. When Uzzah was smitten with a sudden stroke, David was afraid of the Lord, 2 Sam. vi. 9; this might occasion that in Psal. cxix. 120, "My flesh trembleth for fear of thee; and I am afraid of thy judgments." God's judgments are now abroad, and not only wicked men, but good also, are cut down suddenly. Let us fear, and not only that, but do as the prophet and other holy men did at such a time; Isa. xxvi. 8, 9, let us wait for God, let the desire of our souls be to his name, let us desire him in the night, seek him early with our spirits, for now is the time that the inhabitants of the world should learn righteousness.

Obs. 6. Sudden or great judgments do put the saints and servants of God upon humble, earnest, and argumentative prayer. Humble, "Then fell I down upon my face;" earnest, "and cried with a loud voice;" argumentative, "Ah Lord God! wilt thou make a full end of the remnant of Israel?" Judgments looked upon by the saints are of an humbling nature, prompt them with arguments to wrestle with God, and that earnestly, Josh. vii. 5—9.

Obs. 7. When God begins judgments with some who are wicked among them, the godly look upon it as an inlet to public misery: "Wilt thou make a full end of the remnant of Israel?" Joshua, when the men fell before Ai, and Israel fled, looked not only at the loss of those men who fell, but at the hazard of all; chap. vii. 7, "Hast thou brought this people over Jordan, to deliver us into the hand of the Amorites, to destroy us? So when God's wrath brake in a little upon the people in Moses's days, he feared lest the sea of God's wrath should come in at once upon them; therefore he stood in the briers, Psal. cvi. 23, to turn away his wrath, lest he should destroy them. When a cloud riseth, droppeth a little, they fear a great storm, a deluge, and therefore look at the public; they know what God hath said, "When I begin, I will also make an end."

Ver. 14, 15. *Again the word of the Lord came unto me, saying, Son of man, thy brethren, even thy brethren, the men of thy kindred, and all the house of Israel wholly, are they unto whom the inhabitants of Jerusalem hath said, Get you far from the Lord: unto us is this land given in possession.*

These words are an answer to the prophet's deprecation of judgment. He had pleaded with God to spare the residue of Israel; the Lord tells him that the inhabitants of Jerusalem looked upon them as none of the Lord's people, upon the land, city, temple, ordinances, as theirs only; they thought the captives had nothing to do with God, but were an abject people like the Babylonians and heathens, cut off from God, the holy land, and holy things. Now, saith God, see whom thou hast interceded for! Are these fit to be spared? wilt thou have those that hate thee and the rest of the captives to lie at peace in Jerusalem? The Lord sets them out before the prophet, what kind of persons they were, and leaves it upon his thoughts to consider of them, and gives not in the complete answer till after, in ver. 21.

Or thus: the prophet feared lest God would now destroy all, and so his church perish altogether; but God here intimates to him that the residue of Israel lay not in the twenty-five mentioned before, nor in them that were in Jerusalem, but rather in those who were gone into captivity, "thy brethren, even thy brethren, the men of thy kindred," &c. He calls his thoughts to them, and would rather have him look at them, as the seed of the church, the persons to whom the promises belonged, of whom should come the Messiah, than the others.

"Thy brethren." The word "brethren" hath divers acceptations in Scripture:

1. It notes the common nature of man, as in Gen. xxix. 4, saith Jacob, "Whence are ye, my brethren."

2. Those who are born of the same parents, one or both, Gen. xxxvii. 11, 23; Matt. xx. 24.

3. Such as are of kindred by consanguinity or affinity; so Christ's kinsmen were called his brethren, 1 Cor. ix. 5.

4. Those who agree together, and are partners in any business, as Simeon and Levi were brethren in iniquity, in murdering the Shechemites, Gen. xlix. 5.

5. Those who are godly true believers, that do the will of God, Matt. xii. 49; Heb. ii. 11; 1 Tim. iv. 6; 1 Thess. v. 27.

6. Them that are of the same calling, Numb. xviii. 2; Ezra vi. 20; 2 Cor. viii. 23.

Lastly, Those who are of the same country and nation; Rom. ix. 3, Paul could wish himself accursed for his brethren, who were Israelites of the Jewish nation. In what sense to take "brethren" is doubtful, because the verse speaks afterwards of the men of his kindred, and all the house of Israel, so that hereby two acceptations of the word seem to be excluded, and the first, second, and fourth are not intended. We may take brethren here for those of the same calling, such as were priests and prophets, and the Levites; but because these were few, we may take in also the kindred of the prophet, for the words are not, thy brethren, and the men of thy kindred, as making a difference between these; but thus are the words, "thy brethren, even thy brethren, the men of thy kindred."

"Men of thy kindred." Hebrew is, the men of thy redemption. The law of redemption was, that if a man were waxen poor, and had sold his house, land, or any person, some kinsman was to redeem it, as you may see, Lev. xxv. 25, and usually the nearest kinsman was to do it: he that was near to him, it lay upon him who was nearest of blood, to redeem house, land, or persons, and also to revenge the blood of persons if slain, Numb. xxxv. 12; and therefore is rendered by some, the men of thy avengements. Both these do set out near kinsmen, and therefore it is likely here are meant some special kindred of the prophet's.

"All the house of Israel." All that were in Babylon, carried away with Jeconiah; it is spoken synecdochically, Israel for Judah.

"Are they." These words are not in the original; but here are many nominative cases absolute, without any verb to refer to, or depend upon; "Thy brethren, even thy brethren, the men of thy kindred, and all the house of Israel wholly:" this is usual in the holy writ: Psal. xi. 4, "The Lord is in his holy temple, the Lord's throne is in heaven:" so Eph. iii. 1, "For this cause I Paul, the prisoner of Jesus Christ for you gentiles." It is so in many places, which may be to make us heed the more what we read.

"Unto whom the inhabitants of Jerusalem have said, Get ye far from the Lord," &c. In this part of the verse is laid down the unjust proceedings of the men at Jerusalem against those in Babylon; and it appears in these things:

1. They judge them not the Lord's people, and so deny them communion with God and his worship, and therefore say, "Get you far from the Lord."

II. They arrogate God's temple, and the worship of it, to themselves, which is implied.

III. They challenge the land and all in it to be theirs: "Unto us is this land given in possession."

IV. They spake those words with disdain and scorn against the captives; they said, "Get you far from the Lord;" ye are none of our brethren, none of the church, ye are of Babylon, we are of Zion; ye were a foolish and timorous company, void of counsel and spirit in leaving your own country, this city, and temple.

"Get you far from the Lord." They deemed God was no where but in the temple; and, chap. viii. 6, their abominations had caused God to go far from his sanctuary. It is probable that from this phrase the heathens took up that passage of theirs, *Procul este prophani*, Ye profane, be afar off. The Jews at Jerusalem thought the Jews in Babylon to be cut off from their body, they had unworthily left them, and were not now worthy to have any interest in their God or land.

Schotti adagia Sacra, p. 19. Lavat.

Obs. 1. God deals gently with his servants, notwithstanding their infirmities. Ezekiel showed some weakness in saying, "Wilt thou make a full end of the residue of Israel?" when God in his hearing had appointed the mourners to be marked, and had answered him this question before, chap. ix.; yet God bears with his weakness, and speaks to him in a loving manner, and saith, "Son of man;" and he upbraids him not for any forgetfulness of what was done, for any jealousy he had of God's failing in making good his promise. He saith not, What troublest thou me any more? thou hast had an answer, be gone, be silent! No, the Lord knows our weakness; Psal. ciii. 13, 14, "As a father pitieth his children, so the Lord pitieth them that fear him: for he knoweth our frame;" because we have weaknesses, therefore doth God pity; he doth not punish, but pity the weakness of his people. Deut. i. 31, "In the wilderness, the Lord thy God did bear thee, as a man doth bear his son, in all the way that ye went:" sometimes the father carries the child in his arms, sets it upon his knee, and dandles it; the crying, peevishness, half-services, cost, trouble in its education, he bears with all; and so whatever is burdensome in God's children, he suffers it. Acts xiii. 18, he suffered their manners, as a nurse beareth her child in her womb, in her arms, feedeth it with her breasts, so God suffered them; Isa. lxiii. 9, "He bare them, and carried them all the days of old," and doth so still. The Lord Christ bears our infirmities, and puts up many a hard thing from us; Peter's denial, Paul and Barnabas's contention, Thomas's unbelief; and not only the infirmities of one or two, but of all saints; Heb. iv. 15, he is touched, and touched to the quick, with the feeling of our infirmities.

Obs. 2. Those have the name and show of a church who are rigid, cruel, against those who are the true church. They of Jerusalem say to the others, "Get you far from the Lord;" they were in captivity, suffered hard and sore things there, yet these add afflictions to their affliction; they tell them they are none of God's people, have nothing to do with his worship, and so cut them off from all hope. Isa. x. 6, they were "a hypocritical nation," and they persecute, excommunicate those who were faithful and obedient to the will of God; for those Jews who were in Babylon, at the command of God, and the counsel of Jeremiah, yielded themselves to Nebuchadnezzar, and were carried away; hereupon they at Jerusalem reject them, and thrust them from God and his worship. False worshippers ever hate the true. The Samaritans, and those who worshipped the calves, hated the Jews that differed in their worship from them. 1 Thess. ii. 14—16, "Ye, brethren, became followers of the churches of God which in Judea are in Christ Jesus: for ye also have suffered like things of your own countrymen, even as they have of the Jews; who both killed the Lord Jesus, and their own prophets, and have persecuted us; forbidding us to speak to the gentiles." Thus the papists and others deal with us; because they have the name of church, and some corrupt ordinances, can plead succession of their priests from Peter, therefore they reproach us, who are justly gone from them, with the terms of heretics, schismatics, synagogue of Satan, the malignant church; that we have torn Christ's coat, rent ourselves from his body; that we have shaken the church, and troubled the whole world: thus with their virulent tongues do they asperse us. Thus Ishmael dealt with Isaac, Gal. iv. 29. Long ago, the worse persecuted the better; thus is it now.

Obs. 3. Men of rigid and bitter spirits are puffed up and conceited of their ways and privileges. See it here: they separate the other far from God, bid them get them far off, which amounts to this, You have nothing to do with God or his ways; God is not with you, he is with us, his ordinances are for us; you are false, erroneous, but we are orthodox, sound, and the possession and privileges of the temple are ours: they justified and preferred themselves above, and before, those who were in Babylon, and boasted closely of their own worth and advantages; their malice blinded them, and made them boast foolishly. Paul had a persecuting spirit at first, and how conceited was he of his own ways! Acts xxvi. 9—11, "I verily thought with myself, that I ought to do many things contrary to the name of Jesus of Nazareth;" and therefore he complained of the saints, got power from authority to punish them, to imprison them, to put them to death; therefore he compelled them to blaspheme, and persecuted them to strange cities, and fulfilled that which Christ had said, John xvi. 2, "They shall put you out of the synagogues; yea, the time cometh, that whosoever killeth you will think that he doeth God service." They, the scribes and Pharisees, they would not suffer the christians to meet in their synagogues, and their teachers to preach unto them, but stirred up those who had power in their hand to persecute and put them to death. The scribes and Pharisees were opinionated of their own ways, and could not endure others better than themselves. Luke xviii. 11, 12, saith the Pharisee, "I am not as other men are," true, for he was more conceited of his own righteousness, and further from mercy, than the publican.

Obs. 4. Men in false and corrupt ways are glad they are rid of those who are conscientious, bound up by divine truths, and obedient to the will of God. Ezekiel, Daniel, and others, knew that if they had staid in Jerusalem, and not yielded themselves to Nebuchadnezzar, they had died for it; they were acquainted with Jeremiah's prophecy and counsel, which doubtless he had delivered in Jehoiachin's days, as well as in Zedekiah's, chap. xxi. 9; xxxviii. 2; that if they yielded themselves to the king of Babylon, they should live, which they durst not disobey; and therefore it is said, 2 Kings xxiv. 12, that "Jehoiachin the king of Judah went out to the king of Babylon;" which act of his Josephus magnifies, saying, he was so good and just, that he would not see the city to perish for his sake; that the city and citizens might be the safer, he hearkened to Jeremiah's counsel. Now these men that were left at Jerusalem were glad they were gone, even

Ezekiel and his brethren, that were of his judgment, and differed from them; and Jeremiah they were weary of, and those who thought as he thought, Jer. xxxviii. 4; so that men in false ways are desirous and glad to be rid of those who conform not to themselves. Isa. lxvi. 5, "Your brethren that hated you, that cast you out for my name's sake, said, Let the Lord be glorified;" those who were the godly opposed the false ways of the rest, and laboured to reduce them to the truth, therefore they hated them, and cast them out, as they pretended, for the Lord's name's sake; they said they had the true way and worship, that the others were erroneous, factious, proud, censorious, troublers of church and state, and therefore in reference to God's name they cast them out, excommunicated them; the word is, מנדיכם *elongantes vos*, Get ye far off out of our coasts and quarters, get ye into Babylon, or to the ten tribes; we may not, we cannot, we will not bear you. And how did they rejoice in it! Let God be glorified; it is no fault of ours, thank yourselves; you are so tenacious of your opinions, so differing from us, and so burdensome to us, that we shall do God and the church good service to cast you out; God shall have glory, and we shall have ease, we shall go on quietly in our way. So the Jews and Pharisees cast out the blind man, when once he came to see more than themselves, John ix. 34; and made an order to cast any man out that should confess Christ, and so differ from them in judgment or practice, ver. 22. This is the nature of falsehood; whereas truth is so far from drawing men from God, that it invites them to come to God. Truth and true godliness is full of love, which beareth, hopeth, and endureth all things, 1 Cor. xiii. 7; and therefore the servants of God are described, 2 Tim. ii. 24, 25, to be gentle unto all men, patient, in meekness instructing those that oppose μήποτε, if at any time God, &c. They will not drive men from God, from truth, but bear and forbear, that, if it be possible, they may draw men to the truth. How was Ezekiel affected with their condition, how did he intercede for them!

Obs. 5. The Lord considers and takes notice of the words and ways of those which have ill will to his people, though far off from them. There were some faithful ones in Babylon, and they at Jerusalem spake hardly of them, dealt unkindly with them; they said, Get ye far off from the Lord, ye are neither our brethren, nor the Lord's children; ye have no right to this land, nor interest in us. This the Lord laid to heart, and took notice of, and acquaints the prophet with it. There is nothing thought, said, or done in the world against any of the Lord's, but he hath cognizance of it, and, as seems good to him, discovers the same; any bitter passages towards his he observes. Obad. 11, God tells Edom there of her dealing with his people; When strangers carried away my people captive, thou stoodest on the other side, and wast as one of the enemies; but thou shouldst not have looked on, rejoiced, and spoken proudly in the day of their distress, thou shouldst not have laid hands on their substance, nor have cut off those that escaped: ver. 15, "As thou hast done, it shall be done unto thee: thy reward shall return upon thine own head." They spoke proudly, and did cruelly against their brethren, but God observed it, and rewarded it. Psal. l. 20, "Thou sittest and speakest against thy brother; thou slanderest thine own mother's son: but I will reprove thee:" so in Jer. xlviii. 30, "I know his wrath, saith the Lord; but it shall not be so; his lies shall not so effect it:" Moab was proud and wrathful against the people of God, threatened them, plotted against them, and thought by lies and crafty carriages of things to ruin them; the Lord regarded it, and said, "His lies shall not so effect it." The word for lies is בדיו and rendered bars in the margin: lies were their refuge, their strength, the bars they trusted to, and leaned on; but lies should not effect it, God would break those bars, and frustrate their lies. Zeph. ii. 8, 9, "I have heard the reproach of Moab, and the revilings of the children of Ammon, whereby they have reproached my people, and magnified themselves against their border. Therefore as I live, saith the Lord of hosts, the God of Israel, Surely Moab shall be as Sodom, and the children of Ammon as Gomorrah, even the breeding of nettles, and salt pits, and a perpetual desolation." Let men speak and plot against the servants of God, in due time Christ will come, with ten thousand of his saints, to convince men of all their hard speeches which ungodly sinners have spoken against him and his.

Obs. 6. Men deeply guilty are deeply secure. They were idolatrous in the highest degree; so oppressive, that they filled the land with bloody crimes and cries; they were profane, and scoffed at the prophets and their prophecies: they had seen a sudden hand of God upon Pelatiah, and yet they were secure, and promised safety to themselves; The land is ours, it is given us in possession, we shall quietly enjoy it: we fear no captivity, loss of country, temple, or city. Their king was under disgrace, he had violated the oath, perjured himself; and shortly after mothers did eat their children, and men in scarlet embraced the dunghill; all was laid waste, and yet they feared not. Sometimes when their consciences were awakened, and guilt stirred, they did fear, but generally they were secure, and dreamed of liberty and long life. The Egyptians feared not till the waters came upon them and drowned them. God plucked away the ten tribes for their sins, and sent them into captivity; yet, Jer. iii. 8, "treacherous Judah feared not," but went on in her ways of wickedness; and when the sword was at the door, they looked still for peace, Jer. viii. 15, 16. Some creatures sleep most in winter, and many are drowsy against rainy weather: wicked men are sleepy when storms are coming.

Obs. 7. Those who go out from the brethren upon just grounds, and meet with unjust censures for it, God will justify and vindicate. These captives in Babylon went forth from Jerusalem, which only was the place of God's worship, where only he had a people, and that upon Jeremiah's counsel and exhortation, they went forth to save the city and their lives. For this they are censured deeply of the inhabitants of Jerusalem; but the Lord pleads for them, and saith to the prophet, Thy brethren, thy brethren are the men spoken against. This pathetical repetition of the word "brethren," notes God's indignation against their censure they gave of them; and his calling of them the prophet's brethren, argues his clearing of the prophet and them in what they had done. And the next verse clears it further; they did nothing but what God would have done, and therefore owns as his own act, "I have cast them far off among the heathen," &c. If God's people do withdraw from others upon good grounds, whatever men object against them, yet they shall have approbation in heaven, and in their own hearts. These were justified for going out of Zion into Babylon; surely, then, God will not condemn men for coming out of Babylon into Zion. When we left Rome and Romish trash, we had good warrant for it; and so Luther, who took the first step thence; for indulgences troubled Luther, and when he preached against them, the Romish priests did with great pride disdain his preaching. He heard the way of truth blasphemed, saw men were forced to new articles of faith, and himself was compelled to submit to satanical doctrine; these were just causes to induce Luther to leave the Romish Babylon. And therefore he was unjustly excommunicated by Pope Leo, in whose bull this is made the cause, Because he denied the church to have power to create new articles of faith. But the Lord hath justified his separation from them, and ours since him. Their idolatrous mass, their corrupt doctrines, denying of the cup to the people, &c. are just grounds for us and others to leave them; for if Rome be a church, it is not only subject to errors as other churches are, but more subject to erring than any other church christian, and the most schismatical of all christian churches, and the only church against which there is a prophecy in the gospel of falling from the faith; which three last things that learned man Morton shows: and he hath a section (it is the seventh of his fifteenth chapter) to show what may be judged necessary causes of separation from any particular churches; as obstinacy of error in teachers, affected ignorance, obduration of people, idolatry in God's worship, tyranny and persecution against the true and sincere professors. To which I conceive this may further be added, That if a church be so defiled that the members of it cannot partake of the ordinances without sin, having used all means for redress, they may justly depart, so it be in a peaceable manner, and God will justify them.

Mort. Grand Impost. p. 335.

We have not left the word of God, the apostles of Christ, or churches they instituted; but we are gone from the contagion of hypocrites. *Alsted.*

Obs. 8. Where much may be pretended for truth of churchship, there may be no church. Some make notes of the true church:

(1.) Succession. Those at Jerusalem in Ezekiel's days, priests and people, succeeded Aaron, Eli, and other priests and Levites, that were faithful; but at this time, they were, both priests and people, become fearfully idolatrous. *Frustra allegatur successio personarum ubi non est successio formæ*, In vain is succession of persons alleged where there is not a succession of resemblance.

There can be no true succession without true doctrine. *Stapleton.*

(2.) Carnal seed. They were of kin to Jeremiah, Ezekiel, Daniel, and other godly ones in Babylon, they were Abraham's, David's seed; yet this made them not a true church; therefore Jeremiah calls Judah a harlot, chap. iii. 8.

The Saracens are from Hagar and Abraham, though for honour they choose to be called from Sarah; yet these are not the true church.

(3.) Multitudes. Here were a greater multitude at Jerusalem than in Babylon; but what were they? a multitude of idolaters, oppressors, scoffers, persecutors; and such materials are fitter to make a tower of Babel, than a temple in Zion.

(4.) They dwell at Jerusalem, in Judea, the holy city, the holy land, but they had defiled both with their abominations, and neither of those added any holiness to them. Men at Jerusalem, and of Jerusalem, were worse than those in Babylon. It is not Jerusalem, or the local bounds of Judea, can make these the true church.

(5.) Prosperity, outward pomp, greatness, glory. These men at Jerusalem had what the world and creatures could afford them, plenty, honour, liberty; and they in Babylon were poor captives, despised, vilified, scorned ones: the glory of the church is internal, not external; and that glory had the mourners in Jerusalem.

(6.) The temple, and worship of it, had these men at Jerusalem. The captives had no temple, no sacrifices, no prosperity, no holy land or city, no multitudes, no succession, yet they were the church of God, and not those; for God is wroth with them of Jerusalem for thinking themselves the church, whenas they were none, and unchurching the other, whenas they were the true church, and are called by God "the house of Israel." And it further appears that those of Jerusalem were not the true church, because they were destined to destruction, and as sore judgments as ever people were, chap. v. 9, 10, and six slaughtermen designed to slay them utterly, chap. ix. The truth of churchship is to be fetched from other things. It is *cœtus fidelium*, a congregation of faithful men, saith our Article; such as profess Christ and his gospel, and practise answerably; such as are orderly united, and observe divine order in the things of God: Ephes. iv. 12, the apostles and other officers in the church were given *προσκαταρτισμον των ἁγίων*, for the joining together of the saints, and putting them as members of the body in their right places: see Col. ii. 5, 6.

The word may be truly preached to those who are no church, and the seals administered to those who are a false church, as at this time circumcision and the passover. Ordinances are food and maintenance of the church rather than marks of it.

Obs. 9. It is God's mind and will, that those who are strong, highly favoured of God, should look at those beneath them as brethren. There were many in Babylon, questionless, who were mean in knowledge, low in abilities, weak in faith, tainted with some errors and corruptions of Jerusalem, if not of Babylon; yet saith God, "Thy brethren, thy brethren." Where there is any thing of God or Christ, though many and great infirmities accompany and cloud the same, we should look upon them as brethren. When Christ saw a little moral good in the young man, he looked upon him, and loved him, Mark x. 21; and shall we see any spiritual good in any, and not love them and use them as brethren? Look only at the good and graces which are in one another, and not at the weaknesses; you can eye a little gold in much earth, and why not a little grace? Gal. vi. 2, "Bear ye one another's burdens, and so fulfil the law of Christ."

We must answer for stumbling at the infirmities of the godly, and also for neglect of their graces; if their corruptions do alienate, their graces should allure. It is more honourable and christian, to love them for bearing Christ's image, than for being of our judgment.

Ver. 16. *Therefore say, Thus saith the Lord God; Although I have cast them far off among the heathen, and although I have scattered them among the countries, yet will I be to them as a little sanctuary in the countries where they shall come.*

At this verse begins comfort for the captives. They were cast out, rejected, and insulted over by their brethren, filled with sad thoughts of their condition; but here heaven opens, and light breaks out in sweet promises; and they are these:

I. A promise of mercy to them in Babylon, ver. 16.

II. Of returning thence, from Babylon to Zion, ver. 17.

III. Of purifying them from their pollutions in the land of Canaan, ver. 18.

IV. Of regeneration or conversion, ver. 19, 20.

V. A threat to those whose hearts should cleave to their detestable things, which is comfortable to the godly.

For the 16th verse, the sum is this: They at Jerusalem look upon you in Babylon as a forlorn and forsaken people, without God and his worship; they exclude you from all fellowship and communion with them, yea from the land of Canaan, and condemn your act of leaving them as illegitimate; but go, Ezekiel, and tell them that it was my doing to remove and scatter you, and that howsoever they look upon this act of mine, as a certain token of my vengeance upon you, and tending to your utter destruction, yet let them know that they are mistaken, and that I am a Father of mercies, and will be a sanctuary unto you in Babylon, and have deserted them at Jerusalem, that the glory is departed thence and come to you. Go, declare this for their terror, and the comfort of you captives.

The words in the verse are most of them plain and easy, only those must be opened, "I will be a little sanctuary," for there is some difficulty about them, being variously interpreted. Sanctuary, למקדש the word whence *mikdas* comes, is sometimes used in Scripture for cleansing and sanctifying, as 2 Sam. xi. 4, "She was purified from her uncleanness," והיא מתקדשת hence some render the word here *in sanctificationem;* thus, I will be to you for a little sanctification; I will purge and cleanse them, this captivity shall be *ignis expurgatorius* unto them, seventy years they shall be in the fire, and after that they shall come forth, as a refiner's vessel well purified from its dross, be restored to their land, have a new temple, and pure worship. So the Vulgate hath it, *in sanctificationem modicam;* Jerom also takes it in this sense. In Babylon I will sanctify them, divorce them from their idols, turn them from their idolatry, that they may worship me purely; and it is observed, they never fell to idolatry more, after their return from the Babylonish captivity.

In this sense it affords us this note, The Lord doth sanctify and purge his people by sharp and long afflictions. They had greatly defiled themselves with the sins of the nations, and especially with idolatry, and now he threw them into the furnace of affliction, to melt and separate the dross and tin from them. Some conceive that in Isa. i. 25, refers to this Babylonish captivity, "I will turn my hand upon thee, and purely purge away thy dross, and take away all thy tin." Sennacherib's coming did only scare them; Nebuchadnezzar's carrying them away and keeping them so many years in Babylon was the means, through God's blessing, to sanctify them. God's hottest and fiery trials are to purge, Dan. xi. 35; God purges the iniquity of Jacob by affliction, Isa. xxvii. 9; and it is all the fruit he gives in it, to take away his sin, not to take away his limbs, or life, but his sin. When the seraphim touch Isaiah's lips with a burning coal, it was terrible to him; but then he said, "Thy iniquity is taken away, thy sin is purged." Others take the word as here it is rendered, "sanctuary," and so it is frequently used in the Scripture, as Jer. xvii. 12; Lam. ii. 7; Ezek. ix. 6. The Septuagint reads it, ἔσομαι αὐτοῖς εἰς ἁγίασμα, *in sanctuarium,* so Kerker, not *in sanctificationem;* and Suidas interprets ἁγίασμα, *templum:* and so Vatablus renders it, *mikdas,* and Montanus, *sanctuarium;* so Junius, Piscator, and Polanius. Castalio hath it thus, *Ero eis fanum,* I will be to them a temple, a sanctuary; and this sense fits the condition of the captives: for,

A Lapid.

1. The inhabitants of Jerusalem reproached them for going into Babylon, and looked on them as having nothing to do with the temple, God, or his worship, "Get you far from the Lord;" against this evil God comforts them, and saith, "I will be a sanctuary unto you," whatever your brethren think or say.

2. The captives wept to think of their condition. Psal. cxxxvii. 1, "By the rivers of Babylon there we sat down; yea, we wept, when we remembered Zion." When they called to mind what a glorious temple they had, what solemn assemblies there, what precious ordinances, and comforts they found therein, and now saw themselves destitute of all, they wept. For their consolation, saith God, "I will be a sanctuary unto you;" and whatever benefit you found by the saints at Jerusalem, you shall find in me.

(1.) The sanctuary was a place of refuge and defence, *quasi sancta tueri,* a place to defend holy things, for such things were laid up in sanctuaries. The Greeks call it ασυλον, from αλφα, a particle privative, and συλάω, to spoil, rob, take away; for a sanctuary was deemed a privileged place, from whence no thing, or person, might be taken away without sacrilege. Upon this ground Joab fled to the tabernacle of the Lord, 1 Kings ii. 28, and took hold of the horns of the altar. Moses had his cities of refuge; and in reference to these, many princes appointed sanctuaries to be privileged places, that those who fled to them might be secure. And this land heretofore abounded with such places; churches, churchyards, and other places were privileged, so that if felons or traitors did flee to them, they were sheltered for forty days, in which time they were to confess their fault, and to submit to banishment, taking an oath of abjuration; and during these forty days no man might take them thence, without danger of excommunication, or irregularity: in this time any might feed them; after the forty days, if their wives fed them, or gave them any sustenance, it was felony. This law was made by king Edward the Confessor, grounded upon the law of mercy, and reverence he bare to holy places. God would be a sanctuary to him in this sense; Isa. viii. 13, 14, "Sanctify the Lord of hosts himself; let him be your fear, and your dread. And he shall be for a sanctuary," that is, for a defence unto you. Jer. xlii. 11, "Be not afraid of the king of Babylon, of whom ye are afraid; be not afraid of him, saith the Lord: for I am with you to save you, and to deliver you from his hand:" here God was a sanctuary unto them. The three children, when the fiery furnace was heated so hot, and cast into it, found God a sanctuary unto them.

Exposition of Terms of Law. Stamf.

(2.) In it they had God's special presence. Hence Zion, where the temple stood, was called the habitation and rest of God, Psal. cxxxii. 13, 14. Hence God's goings and ways are said to be in the sanctuary, Psal. lxxvii. 13; lxviii. 24; and David professeth he had seen God in the sanctuary, Psal. lxiii. 2. God would be a sanctuary to them in this sense, they should have his special presence; he had left the temple at Jerusalem, the glory was gone, and now he was with them in Babylon. Ezekiel had the heavens opened to him by the river Chebar, saw visions of God, God did manifest himself in a special manner to him, and to Daniel even in Babylon. God had no church elsewhere, and now he was with his people there, and calls them his flock four times in one verse, Ezek. xxxiv. 8, and twelve times his flock in the whole chapter.

(3.) Acceptance in the temple and sanctuary. Their persons and prayers were accepted there; hence was it that they frequented the temple so much for prayer, Acts iii. 1; Luke xviii. 10; and that David intimates, Psal. xx. 3, that the offerings and sacrifices in the temple were accepted; "He heard my voice out of his temple," Psal. xviii. 6. So Jer. vi. 20, when they had corrupted the worship of God, he tells them there, burnt-offerings were not acceptable, nor their sacrifices sweet; before they were; and the prophecy is, Isa. lx. 7, that they shall come with acceptance to God's altar: where his altar was settled, there was the acceptance. This they had likewise in Babylon: when Daniel made his prayer to God for himself and his people, chap. ix. Gabriel comes and tells him, he was greatly beloved of God, a man of desires. So when Mordecai and Esther fasted, their persons and prayers were regarded, accepted in Babylon.

(4.) Encouragement and help. Psal. xx. 2, help came from the sanctuary, and strength from Zion; "Strength and beauty are in his sanctuary," Psal. xcvi. 6; there they had counsel to direct them, ordinances to sanctify them, and promises to comfort them. These they should not want in Babylon, God would be to them such a sanctuary as should afford them help; therefore he stirred up the spirit of Jeremiah to write to the captives, and to counsel them what to do: Jer. xxix. 5—7, "Build ye houses, and dwell in them; and plant gardens, and eat the fruit of them; take ye wives, and beget sons and daughters; and take wives for your sons, and give your daughters to husbands, that they may bear sons and daughters; that ye may be increased there, and not diminished. And seek the peace of the city whither I have caused you to be carried away captives, and pray unto the Lord for it: for in the peace thereof shall ye have peace." And God gave them prophets in Babylon, Ezekiel, and Daniel, by whom he counselled them from time to time; some ordinances they had; what they wanted, God made up himself, being a special sanctuary unto them. He also made Babylon an ordinance to cleanse them; and for promises they had many, divers in this chapter and others, as xxxiv. xxxvi.; which is full of sweet, gracious, and comforting promises.

Though they had no material temple to worship God in, yet God would sanctify them, and give them grace to worship him with an inward fear.

"A little sanctuary." מעט Some take this word adverbially, and render it *paulisper:* so Polanus, Junius, and Castalio; God would be a sanctuary to them a little time: and so to point out the shortness of the time they should be in Babylon, and thereby to comfort them against their captivity; seventy years was not long, and all that time they should have God a sanctuary.

Others take the word adjectively, *sanctuarium parvum*, or *modicum;* so Montanus, Piscator, the Vulgate, and the French. Why this expression is laid down, "a little sanctuary," we must inquire.

1. In opposition to that they had at Jerusalem. That was very beautiful, rich, and glorious, set in ivory, Ezek. vii. 20, eyed of all, resorted unto by all the Jews, and famous throughout the earth; God would be a temple to them, but not such a material, conspicuous temple. You think upon that great glorious temple, are troubled for it; I will be a little temple to you.

2. Little, in regard of the paucity that were there: You are but a few, and a little temple will suffice you; Vatablus hath it, *templum paucorum*, and Calvin, *sanctuarium paucitatis*. Many fell to the ways of the heathens; being mingled with them, they learned their ways, and served their gods; few were godly.

3. In regard of the hidden virtue, power, and goodness conveyed unto them, which Babylonish eyes saw not. They thought their God had wholly forsaken them, did nothing for them; but he was an invisible, spiritual, wonderful, and strange sanctuary unto them, all which was little to that they had in their own land, there they had mercy more openly and more plentifully.

"Will I be." ואהי *Et fui*, I have been a little sanctuary, and will be. Psal. lxix. 11, "I became a proverb unto them;" the word is *Vaehi*, I have been; it is future, yet rendered in the preter tense: and so much it showeth here, that God had been, and would be, a sanctuary to his people in Babylon.

Obs. 1. The harsh dealing of wicked and corrupt men with the godly, occasions God to give out comfortable truths and promises unto them. They at Jerusalem, that were very evil, said, "Get you far from the Lord: unto us is this land given in possession. Therefore say, Thus saith the Lord," &c. Because they spake so bitter, therefore God speaks so comfortably; because they rejected them, denied them to have to do with God, or the land, therefore God receives them, tells them he will be a sanctuary unto them. When others beat the child, the parents' bowels yearn, especially if unjustly, and show the more kindness. When Rabshakeh railed against Hezekiah, God's people, and blasphemed, from thence did the Lord take occasion to signify by Isaiah, to Hezekiah and the rest, things very comfortable: 2 Kings xix. 6, "Thus saith the Lord, Be not afraid of the words which thou hast heard, with which the servants of the king of Assyria have blasphemed me. Behold, I will send a blast upon him, and he shall hear a rumour, and shall return to his own land; and I will cause him to fall by the sword in his own land." God took a rise from the enemies' blasphemies, and rough proceedings against his people, to give in promises of mercy to his, and of destruction to them. When the enemy had dealt barbarously with Rachel, slain and captived her children, and she refused to be comforted, because they were not, hereupon the Lord steps in, and saith, "Refrain thy voice from weeping, and thine eyes from tears: for thy work shall be rewarded; and they shall come again from the land of the enemy:" because they have destroyed thy children, therefore will I give thee children, because they are scattered abroad, therefore they shall return. When the Pharisees had cast out the blind man, Jesus sought him out, found him, and told him who he was, John ix. 35; and Isa. lxvi. 5, when their brethren that hated them cast them out, then was the gracious promise given in; "He shall appear to your joy, and they shall be ashamed." Ill manners occasion good laws, and rough dealings have drawn forth sweet promises.

Obs. 2. Afflictions, be they of what nature soever, are the acts of God. They were deprived of their country, all their comforts there, they were in a sad captivity, mingled among the heathen; but who did this? was it their own act? the Babylonians or any others? No, the Lord takes it upon himself; I have cast them afar off, I have scattered them: it was his counsel, power, and providence did it, whoever were the instruments. The Scripture denies afflictions to be from beneath, they spring not out of the dust, the root of them is not in the earth, Job v. 6, but in heaven; it therefore attributes all of them to God: Micah i. 12, "Evil came down from the Lord unto the gate of Jerusalem." It is evil indefinitely, whatever evil came nigh that city, it came from the Lord, he created it, he sent it: and not only what was without the city, but all in the city; Amos iii. 6, "Shall there be evil in a city, and the Lord hath not done it? It is an interrogation, and vehemently affirms that all is the work of God. Men take not notice of the hand of God in affliction, and therefore the Lord is oft brought in and presented as the true and only author of them. The instruments are eyed by us, and we are vexed at them, and greatly perplex ourselves, that creatures of the same rank and condition we are in should harm us and afflict us; but did we see the Lord in all, it would quiet and still our spirits; whatever the agents were, God would have us to take notice of this: Isa. xlv. 6, 7, "That they may know from the rising of the sun, and from the west, that there is none beside me. I am the Lord, and there is none else. I form the light, and create darkness: I make peace, and create evil: I the Lord do all these things;" man doth none of them.

Obs. 3. God is mindful of his threats, and faithful in performing of them. He had long before, in the days of Moses, told them, that if they sinned against him, they should be plucked off the land they possessed, and be scattered among the heathen, Deut. xxviii. 63, 64; Lev. xxvi. 33; and see it here performed, "I have cast them out, I have scattered them among the countries." God is not forgetful of what he hath threatened against sinners, he hath his times to fulfil his threats, though some thousand years after. There is a prophetical threat in Hag. ii. 22, which it is probable that the Lord is now thinking of, and fulfilling; "I will overthrow the throne of kingdoms, and I will destroy the strength of the kingdoms of the heathen; and I will overthrow the chariots, and those that ride in them; and the horses and their riders shall come down, every one by the sword of his brother." Some interpret this place of Zerubbabel literally, and some shaking of heaven and earth was then, some great changes were made; but the most interpret it of Zerubbabel mystical, of Christ and his kingdom; so Deodate takes it. God, for the advance of his church under the gospel, will overthrow the throne of kingdoms, all power and greatness that is against the kingdom of his Son; and how shall it be done? by wars, mostly by civil wars, "Every one by the sword of his brother." God, in his wise providence, shall stir up kingdoms and kings one against another, and they shall break themselves and each other in pieces, that his truth and faithfulness may be seen.

Obs. 4. Afflictions are not always arguments of divine hatred. God had cast them afar off, and scattered them among the countries; this the inhabitants of Jerusalem took to be an argument of God's hatred, that he had forsaken them, that now they were none of his people; they conceived such great judgments upon them could not stand with God's love: but the Lord's thoughts differ from man's; he looked upon them as his people, as the true church, as dearer to him than they at Jerusalem, as those he would be a sanctuary unto. If great afflictions were arguments of the Lord's hatred and wrath, then Noah, Job, and Daniel were hated of God, they had exceeding great affliction. Noah saw a world drowned; Job had all plucked from him, his friends and wife against him, yea God also in appearance; Daniel was a captive, cast into the lions' den; yet how dear were these to the Lord! Noah, God accepted his sacrifice, Gen. viii. 21; blessed him, chap. ix. 1; made a covenant with him, ver. 8, 9. So Job, how doth God justify him; chap. xlii. 7, "Ye have not spoken of me the thing that is right, as my servant Job hath:" Job was God's servant, spoke what was right of God; Job must pray for his three friends, him God will accept; God gave Job twice as much as he had before. And Daniel was a man greatly beloved, Dan. ix. 23. Christ was a man of sorrows, yet the man in whom God's soul delighted, Isa. xlii. 1. Afflictions are arguments of love; Prov. iii. 12, "Whom the Lord loveth he correcteth, even as a father the son in whom he delighteth." God loves not affliction, but he loves his children, and his bowels cause him to correct: it were cruelty, not love, in a father, that would suffer his child to die for want of a little physic: if physic will do a child good, a loving parent will be at any cost that way. Take heed how you censure those that suffer; afflictions are not always wounds of an enemy, but arguments of love, especially when they break the stubbornness and pride of our hearts, purge out our pollutions, cause us to seek the face of God, quicken our endeavours after more holiness, cause us to mind the things of eternity more, make the word and Christ more sweet and precious to the soul, really and seriously.

Obs. 5. Whatever others think or say of God's people, whithersoever they are driven, whatsoever they lose or suffer, God will be a little sanctuary unto them. These men were hardly thought of, yea rejected and condemned of those at Jerusalem, carried captive into Babylon, they had lost all country comforts, city privileges, temple-ordinances, estates, and liberties; they had hard bondage. When they were yet now in this case, God was a sanctuary unto them, he preserved them, vouchsafed them his presence, accepted their persons and prayers, gave them counsel, sanctified and comforted them; he was a special sanctuary unto them, and instead of all ordinances. Take "sanctuary" for the land of Canaan, as some think it is taken, Exod. xv. 17, God would be a land of Canaan to them; or take it for sanctification, as some do here and in Psal. cxiv. 2, God would be their sanctification; or take it for heaven, as it is Psal. cii. 19, God would be a heaven unto them. However the Jews in Babylon appeared in the world, either to them in Zion or Babylon, they were glorious in the eye of God, and he calls them his glory, and would be a sanctuary unto them. This should afford comfort unto those who are deprived of ordinances, estates, liberties, friends, countries, and suffer very hard and sharp things; if they be godly, God will be a sanctuary unto them. Our brethren that were driven out into other parts of the world, hath not God been a sanctuary unto them? and hath he not always been a sanctuary unto us, and a stone of stumbling unto others, and for a rock of offence? If God hath been a sanctuary to defend us, to afford us his presence, to accept of our persons and prayers, to send us help, counsel, comfort, deliverance, let us sanctify this God himself in our heart, make him our dread and fear, and he will still be a sanctuary unto us: Psal. cxxxiv. 2, "Lift up your hands in the sanctuary, and bless the Lord."

This was the lecture presently after Nazeby fight.

Obs. 6. There is no place can hinder God from taking care of, and showing kindness unto, his people. They were in Babylon, a profane, polluted land, they were scattered up and down in the countries thereof, and yet God was a sanctuary unto them, and said he would be so in the countries where they should come. When they were in Egypt, God was a sanctuary to them there, and now in Babylon. Acts x. 34, 35, "God is no respecter of persons" or places; "but in every nation he that feareth him, and worketh righteousness, is accepted with him." God's people fear him, and work righteousness: wherever they are cast, if into strange nations, as these Jews; if into the dungeon, as Jeremiah; into the bottom of the sea, as Jonah; if into the fiery furnace, as the three children; lions' den, as Daniel, God is a sanctuary to them. Let a man be godly, and he shall have not only protection, but praise of God, Rom. ii. 29.

Ver. 17. *Therefore say, Thus saith the Lord God; I will even gather you from the people, and assemble you out of the countries where ye have been scattered, and I will give you the land of Israel.*

They at Jerusalem had vindicated the land to themselves, "To us is this land given," and so cut off the captives from hope of having any part in that land. This was questionless a great affliction to their spirits, and therefore the Lord bids the prophet tell them that, as he would be a sanctuary to them in Babylon, so he would gather them out of Babylon, bring them back to Canaan, and give them that land in possession, which the others unjustly challenged to themselves. In the former verse he spake to them at Jerusalem, in this he speaks to the captives.

"I will even gather you." Castalio, *convocabo;* the Septuagint, *εἰσδέξομαι αὐτοὺς ἐκ των ἐθνῶν*, I will receive, or undertake, to bring them out of the nations; the Hebrew word וקבצתי *congregabo vos*, from קבץ which is properly spoken, *de redispersa*, to gather that which is dispersed, men or other things; and these being dispersed among the nations, God saith he will congregate them. The Jews' prayer was in the time of their dispersion, *Congrega nos de populis quo dispersisti nos*, We are now no body, we have no face of a state or church, gather us into a body, make us a commonwealth, a church again. This is the thing God hath promised them.

"Assemble you out of," &c. TheHebrew is ואספתי I will add you out of those countries; and here it is spoken of those who were scattered; which I observe, because Buxtorf, showing the difference between *kabats* and *asaph*, saith, *asaph* is, *de re non dispersa;* and so doth Leigh out of him, in his Critica Sacra: but both *kabats*, and *asaph* here, refer to the Jews, who were scattered amongst the Babylonians; and the Vulgate renders it, *adunabo*, I will unite you and make you one body.

"I will give you the land of Israel." "The land of Israel" is not oft mentioned save in this prophecy, only nine times before it, and not after it at all, in the Old Testament, and but twice in the New, Matt. ii. 20, 21. In Ezekiel it is mentioned twenty times; in wrath, when it refers to those who were yet in it; in mercy, when it refers to those who were captives, or enemies insulting at the ruin of it, as you may see, Ezek. xii. 19; xxxvi. 6; xxv. 3, 6.

Why it is said, "the land of Israel," rather than the land of Judah, whenas it was called the land of Judah before it was called the land of Israel, (for we read in Moses's days it was called the land of Judah, Deut. xxxiv. 2, and the land of Israel first in Samuel's days, 1 Sam. xiii. 19,) is inquirable. The land of Judah is a restrictive term, and includes only what belonged to the tribe of Judah, of which you may read, Josh. xv. 1—4. But the land of Israel is a comprehensive term, containing all the tribes which came out of the loins of Israel; so that hereby he gives them to understand, that they should not enjoy a piece of the holy land again, but the whole, all that the twelve tribes had.

The land of Israel was a choice land, "A land that flowed with milk and honey," Deut. xxvi. 15; "a land of corn and wine, bread and vineyards," Isa. xxxvi. 17; a land of brooks, fountains, springs, vines, fig trees, pomegranates, oil, and honey, a land of plenty, wherein they should want nothing, Deut. viii. 7—9; a land given of God, Deut. iv. 1; the desire and glory of all lands, Ezek. xx. 6, because it was the land of Immanuel, Isa. viii. 8; God's holy habitation, Exod. xv. 13; the type of heaven, and therefore called the land of the living, Psal. xxvii. 13. This land of Israel God puts them in mind of, the loss of which, as it begat deep sighing in their souls, so the hope of repossessing it revived them not a little. God had given them this land once before; through their sin they had lost it, but now God would give it them again, and doubly engage them by a second deed of gift. This people were now captives, and their sins had oft captived them, after they had kings. Of their first captivity you may read, 2 Kings xv. 29, which was by Tiglath-pileser; a second by Shalmaneser, 2 Kings xvii. 6; a third by Sennacherib, 2 Kings xviii. 13; a fourth by the captains of the host of the king of Assyria, who carried Manasseh into Babylon, 2 Chron. xxxiii. 11; a fifth by Pharaoh-nechoh, 2 Kings xxiii. 33, 34; a sixth and seventh, by Nebuchadnezzar, 2 Chron. xxxvi. 5, 6; 2 Kings xxiv. 10—12; 2 Kings xxv. 7. Thus was this people oft brought low, carried into other lands from that "good land" of Israel, as it is called, Deut. iv. 21. And you shall hardly find that any of the preceding captivities had a promise of returning them again before this; but here God graciously tells them, he would gather them out of the countries and bring them back to Jerusalem.

Quest. 1. By whom did the Lord gather them, bring them to this land again?

Answ. By three men especially, whose names are very observable, Ezra, Nehemiah, and Zerubbabel. Ezra signifieth a helper, and he was a special helper of them, under God, out of Babylon, Ezra vii. 6. Nehemiah is, The consolation of the Lord, and he brought divine consolation unto them, Nehem. ii. 18; and was as a god amongst them in conveying and comforting them many ways, as you may observe in the book which bears his name. Zerubbabel is, as Jerom will have it, זהרב בבל *Iste princeps in Babylone;* and he that could bring this people out of such a country and condition they were in, had need to be a mighty prince, and so was he; therefore Zech. iv. 7, no mountainous strength of devils or wicked men could stand before him: others interpret it, one repugnant to confusion; and so he was, he led the people orderly out of that confused place and condition they were in, even unto the holy land, and divine order they had formerly enjoyed there; and thus *Ventilator babel*, The fanner of confusion, or זרב בבל *Fluxus Babylonis*, he brake down the bank of captivity, and made way for the stream to flow from Babylon to Zion.

Quest. 2. The promise here being made to the captives in Babylon that were brought thither with Jeconiah, whether had they any benefit of it that were now at Jerusalem, and afterwards carried captive with Zedekiah into Babylon?

Answ. Some think none of the captives with Zedekiah returned, or had any benefit of this promise; and the reason I find given is, because few returned; but there may more be said for it.

1. The promise was not made to them at Jerusalem, but to the captives in Babylon at that time.

2. We find many excepted from entering into the land of Israel after the captivity. Ezek. xiii. 9, the false prophets are excluded the land of Israel; and Ezek. xx. 38, "The rebels," God saith, "shall not enter into the land of Israel;" and who were the rebels, but those who refused to go with Jeconiah, who stayed at Jerusalem, and sinned greatly against God, and therefore are oft called the "rebellious house," the "rebellious nation," chap. ii. God saith, he would plead with them as he did with their fathers in the wilderness when they came out of Egypt, and there they died, only two of them entered into Canaan.

3. That chapter in Jeremiah of the good and bad figs, speaks to this business: it is the 24th of Jeremiah; where the good figs are interpreted of Jeconiah and his captives; God saith, he will acknowledge them, set his eyes upon them for good, bring them again to the land, and plant them in it, &c. ver. 5—7. The evil figs are interpreted of Zedekiah and his captives, and them God will deliver into all the kingdoms of the earth for hurt, to be a reproach, a proverb, a taunt, and a curse in all places.

Others conceive, that some of Zedekiah's captives returned to the land of Israel, and the grounds given are these:

(1.) In the 9th chapter some were marked that were godly, and these being preserved and carried away, it is not probable they should be shut out from interest in that gracious promise, "I will gather you, and give you the land of Israel:" whoever were denied the land, not the godly.

(2.) Cyrus's decree was not restrictive, but any Jew might return; 2 Chron. xxxvi. 23, "Who is there among you of all the Lord's people? The Lord his God be with him, and let him go up:" Cyrus gave liberty to any or all to go.

(3.) I shall add one thing, and it is that in Jer. xxxi. 8, "A great company shall return thither;" above forty thousand, as you may read, Neh. vii. 66, 67. And it is probable that some of them were of those that Nebuchadnezzar brought with Zedekiah into Babylon.

Quest. 3. Whether the gathering and deliverance of the church out of Babylon be typical, and a resemblance of the spiritual gathering and deliverance of the church in time of the gospel; whether they refer to Christ or not?

Answ. Those great deliverances out of Egypt and Babylon had something in them representative of the church's deliverance by Christ. Pharaoh and Nebuchadnezzar point out Satan, that held the gentiles, and antichrist, that held the christians in bondage, till Christ, as Moses and Zerubbabel, did deliver them. Their coming out of Egypt refers to the time of Christ and the gospel, if you compare Hos. xi. 1, with Matt. ii. 15. And for the Babylonish deliverance referring to Christ, consider Ezek. xxxiv. 12—14, where the Lord speaks of gathering and bringing his people from the countries where they have been scattered, to the mountains of Israel; and then in ver. 23, 24, "I will set up one shepherd over them, and he shall feed them, even my servant David; he shall feed them, and be their shepherd. I the Lord will be their God, and my servant David a prince among them." This one Shepherd, this David, this Prince, was Christ, as is generally agreed upon by interpreters; and John x. 11, Christ tells them he is "the good Shepherd," namely, that one and only Shepherd spoken of in Ezekiel. That of Rachel weeping for her children, when they went into captivity, Jer. xxxi. 15, referred to the time of the gospel, and had its fulfilling then, Matt. ii. 17, 18, and why their coming out should not also have reference to deliverances under the gospel by Christ, I see not. Some interpret those words of Isa. lxi. 1, 2, "The Spirit of the Lord God is upon me; because the Lord hath anointed me to preach good tidings unto the meek; he hath sent me to bind up the broken-hearted, to proclaim liberty to the captives," &c. to be meant literally of the Babylonish captivity; and you know how the Lord Christ, Luke iv. 21, saith, "This day is this scripture fulfilled in your ears."

Maldon. Tollet.

Obs. 1. The Lord's eye is upon his people, he takes notice of them wherever they are; let them be in Babylon, in the several countries thereof, he observes them. Fathers, when their children are scattered here and there, cannot take any notice of them, they are out of their sight: it is not so with God; let his children be among heathens, as now the Jews were, among lions, as Daniel was, among waters and fishes, as Jonah was; let them be where or in what condition soever, he sees them, observes, considers them: Prov. xv. 3, "The eyes of the Lord are in every place;" not of some one country, as Judea, Egypt, Babylon, but in every place of the world; 2 Chron. xvi. 9, "His eyes run to and fro throughout the whole earth, to show himself strong in the behalf of them whose heart is perfect toward him:" God's eyeing of his people is not a bare intuition, but in order to their assistance, to do them good, to put out strength from them.

Obs. 2. In low and miserable conditions, God sends in hope and help. They were now stripped naked of all their comforts, amidst barbarians, in a servile, sinking condition, saw no likelihood of bettering their condition, being under the hand of a potent and severe adversary; yet now hope and help comes in; I will gather you, you that are captives, desolate, more low and miserable than ever you were, even you will I gather: thus God lets in comfort to them in their comfortless estate; and it is God's way to do so. When the Israelites cried in Egypt by reason of their bondage; when they were sorely afflicted, saith the text, God heard them, remembered them, looked upon them, and had respect unto them, Exod. ii. 24, 25: and in the next chapter, he appears to Moses, tells him he had seen their affliction, knew their sorrows, and was come to deliver them, ver. 7, 8. When people are outwardly or inwardly low, it is God's method frequently, if not constantly, to afford relief: Psal. cxvi. 6, "I was brought low, and he helped me:" he was low in Saul's days, low in Absalom's, but the Lord helped him. When power is gone from a people, and none to be found, in public or private, to help a people, then are they in an afflicted, miserable condition; yet then God affords help, Deut. xxxii. 36. So Neh. ix. 27, "In the time of their trouble, when they cried unto thee, thou heardest them from heaven; and according to thy manifold mercies thou gavest them saviours." When the Jews were brought low by Haman, and at the borders of death all of them, God appeared in Esther, Ahasuerus, turned the storm upon Haman himself, and helped the Jews in that strait.

Obs. 3. Things which are hard and seem impossible to flesh and blood, are easy unto God. How difficult was it to the judgment of those captives to conceive a return! they were far from Jerusalem, the journey long and dangerous; they at Jerusalem had rejected them; they were under a mighty tyrant, the terror of nations; they were scattered in several places, employed to servile work, for the profit, pleasure of the Chaldeans, as digging in their mines, ploughing of their fields, dressing of their vines; if they should stir to get away, the king had command of a hundred and twenty-seven provinces, and could presently raise forces to fetch them back, or cut them off, &c. These and such like thoughts made it seem difficult, if not impossible to them, that they should ever return again to Jerusalem; but the Lord would gather them; it was an easy act to him, no more than a shepherd gathering of his flock into the fold: he whistles or sends out his dog, and presently they all run into his fold; so when God spake the word, moved the heart of Cyrus, he made a proclamation for the Jews to go up to Jerusalem, and presently it was done. In Ezek. xxxvii. 11, you may read the Jews' apprehensions of their condition; they say, "Our bones are dried, and our hope is lost; we are cut off for our parts." They thought themselves like dead and dry bones that lie in the bowels or on the face of the earth, without hope of life, or ever returning into their own land; but by the parable of the dry bones, which at a word of prophecy were enlivened, raised, and made a great army, God showed what he could easily do, in things seeming to man impossible; and he applies it to them, ver. 12, "Behold, O my people, I will open your graves, and cause you to come up out of your graves, and bring you into the land of Israel:" they conceived it as impossible for them to repossess their country, as for a dead man to live; but it was easy with God. There is nothing too hard for God; he could bring a great nation out of Sarah's dead womb, Gen. xviii. 14; and Jer. xxxii. 27, God tells them that he is "the Lord, the God of all flesh;" and then asks them this question, "Is there any thing too hard for me?" Did I not bring you out of Egypt, led you through the Red sea, through the wilderness, set you in the pleasant land, and can I not bring you back into it, though scattered up and down in Babylon? Ver. 37, "Behold, I will gather them out of all countries, whither I have driven them in mine anger; and will bring them again to this place, and cause them to dwell safely." Luke xviii. 27, "Things impossible with men are possible with God."

Obs. 4. Lands and countries are the Lord's, to dispose of to whom he pleases. "I will give you the land of Israel." "The earth is the Lord's, and the fulness thereof; the world, and they that dwell therein," Psal. xxiv. 1; and he disposes of the kingdoms thereof, Psal. cxv. 16, "The earth hath he given to the children of men;" there is not a son of man which hath any spot of earth, or kingdom in the world, but the Lord gave it him. He rules in the kingdoms of men; he takes them away, and gives them to whom he will, Dan. iv. 31, 32. He is God of all the kingdoms of the earth, Isa. xxxvii. 16; and Cyrus acknowledged that God had given them all to him, Ezra i. 2: being the Lord's, he may justly dispose of them as seems good to himself. This land of Israel was possessed by Canaan, the son of Ham, and called the land of Canaan; but his posterity, for their wickedness, were cast out of it, Lev. xviii. 25; and then God gave it to the seed of Abraham, Isaac, and Jacob, whose name was changed to Israel, and thence his posterity were called Israelites, and so this the land of Israel; but they, through their idolatry and oppression, forfeited this land, and now God had given it into the hands of Nebuchadnezzar, after they had possessed it eight hundred and fifty years. Sin thrusts people out of their country, and robs them of their rights and privileges; and had not God given them this land again, they had had little or no right to it. God gave it to Abraham when the Canaanites had it, and he gives it to the Israelites when the Chaldeans had it.

Obs. 5. The afflictions of the church, though great and grievous, yet have their period. Now Israel was in Babylon, their country, city, temple, ordinances, public worship, were gone; they were amidst idolaters, profane, blasphemous persons, in a polluted place, which was very sad; yet this condition should have an end, God would gather them out from Babylon, into the holy and pleasant land, where they should enjoy choice mercies again. "God will not always chide, neither keep his anger for ever," Psal. ciii. 9. Here, at the beginning of their captivity, God's heart was relenting, and he laid in this gracious promise, to refresh them. Man, when he is offended, is not only angry, but bears grudges in his heart, seeks revenge, and the ruin of them who have wronged him, as Haman, Mordecai and the Jews; but it is not so with God, he may be angry for seventy years, but that is not always, for ever. Isa. liv. 7, 8, it was but a moment, a small moment, and the wrath was but a little, as he calls it there; because God was a sanctuary unto them all the time, and made them gracious promises at the beginning. So then you may answer the question made, Jer. iii. 5, "Will he reserve his anger for ever? will he keep it to the end?" No; God is gracious, and will not always be wrath.

Ver. 18. *And they shall come thither, and they shall take away all the detestable things thereof and all the abominations thereof from thence.*

God doth not only promise them that they shall return to their own land, but also tells them what they shall do there, "take away the detestable things and abominations thereof."

"Detestable things." The Septuagint renders it, and so the word for abomination, *βδελύγματα*. Vulgate, *omnes offensiones:* Calvin, *omnia idola;* and idols are detestable things, as I showed when I opened chap. v. 11. One thing I shall add, and that is, שקוציה here rendered "detestable" by our translators, is the same word in Dan. ix. 27; xii. 11, where it is translated "abominations:" and Matt. xxiv. 15, *βδελυγμα τῆς ἐρημώσεως*, which some interpret of the Roman soldiers, profaning the temple with blood and brutish actions; others of antichrist, sitting in the temple, and worshipped as God; and others of idols, brought in and set up there.

"Abominations." *Flagitia;* Castalio. This word was largely opened in chap. v. 9. Notorious sins of all kinds are called in the Scripture sense, abominations, things to be abhorred: so Rom. ii. 22, *ὁ βδελυσσομενος τὰ εἴδωλα*, "Thou that abhorrest idols." Idols and idolatries are abominable, 1 Pet. iv. 3.

Obs. 1. What the Lord promises, that shall be performed. He had said in the former verse, "I will give them the land of Israel," and here he saith, "They shall come thither:" what obstructions soever may be in the way, what power soever opposes, yet the Lord having promised it, he would make it good. God is gracious in promising, faithful in keeping promise, and powerful in performing his promises. You may see it made good, Ezra i. 1, 3; God stirred up the spirit of Cyrus to make a proclamation for the Jews to go to their own land, and then he stirred up the spirits of the people to go, ver. 5; their spirits were down, they were heartless and hopeless, many of them, but God raised their spirits, to go up to Jerusalem; the word is העיר *evigilavit, suscitavit,* they were asleep, and God deals with them as we with sleepy men; they had their objections, but God took them all away, and raised their spirits above all difficulties, and caused them to hasten to their country, and the work he had for them. God hath promised a new Jerusalem, that he will dwell with men, and be their God, wipe away all tears from their eyes, that there shall be no more death, sorrow, crying, pain, Rev. xxi. 2—4; that the nations of those who are saved shall walk in the light of that city; that kings shall bring the glory and honour of the nations into it; that only those which are written in the Lamb's book shall enter: this will be a glorious time, God hath promised it, he is faithful and able to perform it.

Obs. 2. When judgments and mercies are sanctified to a people, they will produce answerable effects. They had sore judgments in Babylon, for seventy years; and when they were brought out of that furnace into this pleasant land, which was a great deliverance, when they were come thither, what should they do? "Take away the detestable things, the abominations thereof." The fruit of that affliction, and the deliverance out of it, evidenced that their judgments and mercies were sanctified.

(1.) They repented of their idolatry and sinful practices, which had laid the land waste; which is supposed in the words. They would never have taken away the detestable things, had not their hearts been broken for them.

(2.) They reform when they come into the land, they "take away the detestable things;" they are bitter against their master-sin, and serve it as it served them. Their detestable things had taken them away out of the land, Jer. xliv. 22, and they fall upon the detestable things presently, and take them away, and what else they apprehended offended God; not only idols did they take away, but reformed also the marriage of strange wives, Ezra x. in point of usury, Neh. v. and profaning of the sabbath, Neh. xiii.

(3.) They show themselves sincere in it; they spare none, but take away all detestable things, all abominations, Josh. xxiv. 14. It is sincerity to put away false gods, and especially all of them.

(4.) They endeavour to worship God purely, without any corruptions or mixtures of their own. They put away all detestable things, all abominations, they laboured to have only what was divine, and so what was pleasing to God. They would not come to God with any impieties, but in pure worship. As Jacob, Gen. xxxv. 2—4, when he was to go up to Bethel, he took all their strange gods, their earrings, and what might be occasion of sinning that way, and buried them under the oak out of sight, and cleansed himself and family, and would serve God, not with any mongrel but with pure worship; so was it here. When it is thus, it is an argument that judgments and deliverances are sanctified, that mercies are well bestowed, and well enjoyed. When corrections and mercies stir us up to repent, reform, to deal sincerely with God, and to worship him purely, it is evident they came from God's love, and are sanctified unto us.

Ver. 19. *And I will give them one heart, and I will put a new spirit within you; and I will take the stony heart out of their flesh, and will give them an heart of flesh.*

In the former verses you heard opened sundry sweet promises of God, made to his people; he would be a sanctuary to them in Babylon, bring them thence to Zion, purify them from the pollutions in their own land, all which were gracious; but here he exceeds all given in before: those promises concerned their outward conditions chiefly, but these their inward and spiritual estate only. Some make this verse to contain the covenant of grace which God made with his people Israel, whom he had chosen above any people in the world, but they forsook him, fell to idolatry, and were now justly made captive for their sin, suffered much among their enemies; and here God enters into a gracious covenant with them, and promises great things unto them. In the words consider.

1. The party promising; "I, I, I."

2. The things promised; (1.) "One heart." (2.) "A new spirit." (3.) Taking away the "stony heart." (4.) "Heart of flesh."

3. The persons to whom; "them."

4. The manner of conveying these, and it is expressed by giving, putting, taking.

"One heart." The Septuagint is ἑτεραν καρδιαν, another heart: they mistaking the Hebrew ר for ד take the word אחר for אחד and so fell into that error, which is not great; for one heart was another heart than that they had. The Hebrew is לב אחד one heart.

"Heart." By it here we may understand,

1. The judgment or understanding; so it is taken, Eph. iv. 18; heart and understanding are the same there.

2. For the will and affections; so Prov. xxiii. 26; Matt. xxii. 37.

3. For the conscience; so it is taken, 1 John iii. 20.

"One," is taken in the word,

1. For likeness: 1 Sam. vi. 4, "One plague was on you all;" that is, a like plague.

2. For sameness: 2 Cor. xi. 2, "I have espoused you to one husband;" Heb. x. 14, "By one offering he hath perfected for ever them that are sanctified." One is put for the same in both places.

3. For that which is united and makes one: Gen. xi. 6, "Behold, the people is one;" they were united together as one man, in the building of Babel. We may understand all here, that God would unite them together as one man, give them likeness and sameness of heart.

Some think, by one heart is meant the mutual consent to hasten to Jerusalem to build the temple. As they were one people, of one language and spirit, in building Babel; so these should be one people, of one mind and language, in rebuilding Jerusalem. But if it should be confined to this sense, it were no spiritual mercy, and here God is promising spiritual mercies. This sense may be included, but there is something beyond it. We will inquire what heart was antecedently in this people, which will give us light for the better understanding of this oneness of heart.

(1.) They had a backsliding, apostatizing heart in them. 1 Kings xviii. 37, Elijah prays that their hearts may be turned back again. Jer. v. 23, "This people hath a revolting and a rebellious heart." Ezek. ii. 3, they are called "a rebellious nation;" and Ezek vi. 9, God saith he was "broken with their whorish heart," which departed from him. They went out from God to idols, and to false ways of worship; they walked after the imaginations of their hearts, after other gods, to serve and worship them, Jer. xiii. 10.

(2.) They had a slippery, unfaithful heart. Psal. lxxviii. 8, their "spirit was not stedfast with God," they were off and on, no certainty in them, but full of changes. Hence they are said to gad much about to change their way, Jer. ii. 36; and in Isa. xxiv. 5, to change the ordinances; and in Ezek. v. 6, to change God's "judgments into wickedness, more than the nations."

(3.) They had a deceitful, hypocritical heart. Isa. xliv. 20, "A deceived heart hath turned him aside;" and chap. x. 6, God calls them "an hypocritical nation:" they pretended love and obedience to God; but, Jer. iii. 10, Judah served God "feignedly," in falsehood, is the Hebrew; their hearts were deceitful, false.

(4.) They had a divided, froward, bitter heart. Hos. x. 2, "Their heart is divided;" God had a piece of it, and the world a piece, Ezek. xxxiii. 31, and their idols a piece, Ezek. xiv. 3. And it was contentious and froward; Isa. lvii. 17, "He went on frowardly in the way of his heart." They had divided hearts, divided tongues, and divided ways; Manasseh was against Ephraim, Ephraim against Manasseh, and both against Judah.

Now this one heart here mentioned, is opposite to all these.

[1.] God would give them "one heart," and that is, a heart which should be for himself, and not for idols; a heart which should not withdraw or turn back to any false ways, but cleave to himself only. After they came out of Babylon, they never could endure idols more, God had separated their hearts from them; and therefore upon their return, God promised they should take away all detestable things, ver. 18.

[2.] A heart faithful and stedfast, that should hold fast the things of God, and not be given to change. Hence, Jer. xxxii. 39, God saith, "I will give them one heart, and one way, that they may fear me for ever:" their heart shall be settled, fixed in my way, and never look out and wander after other ways.

[3.] An honest, sincere heart, free from hypocrisy, guile, and lying. Zech. viii. 3, "Jerusalem shall be called a city of truth:" the inside and outside should be the same; intentions, words, and actions should be correspondent.

[4.] A united, loving, peaceable heart. As they shall have one God, be firm to his way, and sincere in that way; so they shall have sweet communion together; strife, bitterness, division, shall not be found amongst them; Isa. lx. 18, "Violence shall no more be heard in the land." There should be much unity, much love, and mutual agreement between them; they should have but "one heart;" that is, one which is *indivisum a se*, and *divisum ab omni alio;* such a heart they should have, a heart undivided in itself, and divided from all things heterogeneal, and of a dividing nature: as God, he is one simply, absolutely, undivided in himself, and mostly divided from every thing differing from himself; Gal. iii. 20, "God is one," and one is opposed to many; so that they shall have "one heart," not many hearts.

Isa. xi. 9, "They shall not hurt nor destroy in all my holy mountain."

This oneness of heart may be considered,

1. As respecting themselves: and so,

(1.) As it includes the judgment and affections; they shall not dissent and cross one the other, but when truth is in the understanding, the affections shall close with it. Ofttimes there is much truth in the heads of men, but no love to truth in their hearts; 2 Thess. ii. 10, "They received not the love of the truth;" the truth was revealed, made love to their souls, appeared very lovely and beautiful, but they had no love to it. John iii. 19, "Light is come into the world, and men loved darkness rather than light;" their affections closed with their own lusts and errors; but it should be otherwise here, they should have a heart towards truth, not divided from truth.

(2.) As it comprehends the will and conscience; they shall not be one against another. Sometimes conscience dictates and tells men they must do or not do such things; and their wills carry them a wrong way: Rom. i. 32, their hearts told them that they who did such things as are there mentioned, were worthy of death, yet their wills carried them to do those things, and to delight in them. So in ver. 18, they who held the truth in unrighteousness, their consciences told them it was truth, and to be obeyed, but their wills were against obeying that truth; so that here was not one heart in them. Here the promise is, will and conscience shall be one.

(3.) As it looks at the intention and practice. Many men have one heart within, and another without, fair pretences, but foul intentions; their actions and hearts laid together, would confute one another; Herod pretends to worship Christ, but intends to murder him: but these should have "one heart" within and without; the same they should be, inwardly and outwardly, as Nathanael; no guile was in his spirit, in his lips, in his actions, but the same heart was in all: Col. iii. 23, "Whatsoever ye do, do it heartily."

2. As respecting God. They should look at God as the only and adequate object of their heart, they should be content with him alone; they should not ask counsel, confide in, fetch comfort from, or worship any other; he only had made covenant with that people, and they should own him only for their God. Moses told them long before, that the Lord their God was one Lord, Deut. vi. 4; and Samuel told them they must serve him only, 1 Sam. vii. 3; and this could not be, unless their heart was one. David, who was a one-hearted man, said, Psal. lxii. 5, "My soul, wait thou only upon God."

One heart in regard of his worship; that should be pure, unmixed, and one. Zech. xiv. 9, "In that day shall there be one Lord, and his name one:" by name, interpreters understand worship, and that shall be one, and answerable shall be their hearts, Jer. xxxii. 39.

3. In respect of others.

(1.) Their judgment shall be one; they shall agree together in fundamentals, and substantial points of faith, though there be differences in circumstantials, inferences, consequences, and points of inferior alloy; Phil. iv. 2, they should τὸ αυτὸ φρονεῖν, think the same thing, "be of the same mind."

(2.) Their affections towards one another. Acts iv. 32, "The multitude of them that believed were of one heart and of one soul;" by these words, "one heart and one soul," Beza understands, *summa tum in doctrina tum in voluntatibus consensio*, an agreement in sentiment as well as a union in will; and he tells us, that in the old copy he had, there were these words more added, καὶ οὐκ ἦν εν ἀυτοῖς διακρισις οὐδεμία, there was no difference or controversy amongst them, they were united in judgment and affections, they had common faith, and common affections; they believed the gospel, and loved Christ's truth, and one another dearly.

(3.) In their converse and practice together, they should be one-hearted. Acts ii. 46, "They continuing daily with one accord in the temple, and breaking bread from house to house, did eat their meat with gladness and singleness of heart;" ἀφελότητι καρδίας. ἀφελως, Budæus interprets of men, *sine livore*, their hearts were without envy, or other evils; they were single. In this sense, chiefly, I conceive this one-heartedness is to be taken, the union and harmony of their judgments, affections, and practices in spiritual things.

Quest. 1. When was this performed?

Answ. Some think at their return from Babylon they were one-hearted, and united in their judgments, affections, and practices; and some phrases in Scripture import it: Ezra i. 5, "Then rose up the chief of the fathers of Judah and Benjamin, and the priests, and the Levites, with all them whose spirit God had raised, to go up to build the house of the Lord in Jerusalem;" they had the same mind and affection to that good work, to build the house of the Lord: and chap. ii. 1, they came "every one unto his city." Chap. iii. 11, "All the people shouted with a great shout, when they praised the Lord, because the foundation of the house of the Lord was laid:" and chap. vi. 16, "The children of Israel, the priests, and the Levites, and the rest of the children of the captivity, kept the dedication of the house of God with joy." These and such like passages give occasion to think that there was a fulfilling of this truth at that time. Others conclude it made good in the apostles' days, when the believers were so united as you read of, Acts ii. 42, 44, 46; chap. iv. 32, the believers, yea, the multitude of them, "were of one heart and one soul." Some are of judgment that it is not yet accomplished, because there were great divisions and contentions among the churches in the apostles' times; and therefore refer it to the calling of the Jews, when the two prophetical mystical sticks, mentioned Ezek. xxxvii. 19—23, are united and made one nation, and have David their king ruling over them; then shall there be this one-heartedness amongst them. If we should put it upon the times wherein those great and glorious things spoken of, Isa. lx. shall be given into the church, we shall not much mistake: there God saith, "I will make thine officers peace, and thine exactors righteousness. Violence shall no more be heard in thy land, the Lord shall be unto thee an everlasting light, and thy God thy glory; thy people also shall be all righteous:" which time I suppose may fall in with the new Jerusalem, Rev. xxi. in which should be no leanness, death, sorrow, crying, or pain; all things in it should be new, having the glory of God, ver. 4, 5.

Quest. 2. Whether this union, this one-heartedness be attainable in this life? Some judge it impossible that there should be one-heartedness in judgment, affections, and practice, because of the difference of constitutions, natural abilities, corruptions, and temptations of men, and unequal dispensations of grace; and therefore refer it to our condition after this life.

Answ. We must distinguish this one-heartedness. It is either incomplete, and inchoative, which is to be had in this life, or complete and consummative, which is a piece of our happiness in heaven: the angels and saints above enjoy the same perfectly; we who are here beneath, have it only in part. Though there be differences in the lesser things of religion, yet we agree in the weighty things thereof, and are one-hearted in them; and were there no possibility of being so, and being more and more so, the Lord would not here have promised it, nor the apostle exhorted to it, 1 Pet. iii. 8, "Be ye all of one mind," πάντες ὁμόφρονες, *idem sentientes et consentientes:* ὁμόφρονες, are they, *qui* τὰ ὅμοια φρονοῦσι, which think the same things; yea, ὁμοφρόνησις comprehends, as Gerard observes upon the place, *consensionem in fidei veritate et vitæ sanctitate*, a harmony in faith and holiness. Paul, 1 Cor. i. 10, prays, ἵνα τὸ αὐτὸ λέγητε παντες, and to "be perfectly joined together in the same mind, and in the same judgment;" let there be no deficiency, no redundancy, but a sweet coherency, as in the members of the body. So Phil. ii. 2, "That ye be like-minded, having the same love, being of one accord, of one mind:" he would not only have them, τὸ αὐτὸ φρονεῖν, but τὸ ἓν φρονεῖν, not only ὁμόψυχοι, but σύμψυχοι. In sundry other places the apostle exhorts unto it; 2 Cor. xiii. 11; Rom. xii. 16; xv. 5. And the text saith, Acts iv. 32, that the believers "were of one heart and one soul;" they were so united, that the heathens were affected with their union, and said ordinarily of the christians,
Tertul. in Apol. *Vide ut se diligant, ut alter pro altero mori sunt parati*, See how they love each other, so much so that they are ready to die for each other. There were many bodies, not many souls nor many hearts amongst them.

There have been great differences and contentions amongst the worthies of God, Paul, with Peter and Barnabas; Basil, with Eusebius; Chrysostom, with Epiphanius; and Jerom, with Ruffinus: but their differences have been rather in judgment than affection; and differences there may be without breach of friendship. Paul differed in judgment from the Jews, and other men, yet he became all things to all, he was wonderful loving to all. Or if the difference came to their wills and affections; yet it provoked to love rather than abated love, παροξυσμὸς, *pro salute animarum*, Heb. x. 24. Neither did they differ in the great things of religion; and had they, yet there might have been harmony in their affections and practice. The Thomists and Scotists, the Dominicans and Jesuits, have their controversies and differences; so the churches of Spain and Italy have a great controversy with those of France, about the infallible judgment in matters of faith: the Italians and Spaniards affirm the pope is that judge; the French deny it, and look upon him as liable to error with other men; and subject to schism, heresy, and deposure by a general council; and yet they hold together, in brotherly love and communion.

Obs. 1. Men's hearts of themselves are divided, multiplied, not one. Physically, men have but one heart; morally, they have many, according to the number of their lusts in the number of their hearts; men have proud hearts, froward hearts, unclean hearts, covetous hearts, malicious hearts, bloody hearts, &c. Pliny saith, the partridges
of Paphlagonia have double hearts; L. 11. 37.
and men have double and treble hearts. Psal. xii. 2, "With a double heart do they speak;" the Hebrew is, with a heart and a heart; they had diversity of hearts. When the heart is separated from God, it falls upon the creatures, and multiplies according to the objects it affects; so that no man in his natural condition, taken in a moral consideration, can have one heart, but many hearts; his heart is divided, and as he hath no agreement with God, so none with man, or himself.

Obs. 2. Oneness of heart is a great blessing, it is the fruit of the covenant of grace. It is the first blessing here mentioned; it is joined with other great blessings. I will show you the good of it in some particulars.

(1.) One-heartedness in christians rejoiceth the Spirit of Christ, which is a Spirit of love, peace, union, and is grieved with what is opposite to them. Therefore, Eph. iv. 30, 31, saith the apostle, "Grieve not the holy Spirit of God." And how should that be prevented? "Let all bitterness, and wrath, and anger, and clamour, and evil speaking, be put away from you, with all malice." Where these are, there are divisions, and the Spirit is grieved; where these are not, there is one-heartedness, and that rejoiceth the Spirit. *Spiritus res delicata*, the mind is tender: where tender hearts are, little breaches offend them: Isa. lxiii. 10, "They rebelled, and vexed his holy Spirit."

(2.) It greatly sweetens and contents the heart of man, when the will, affections, judgment, and conscience, are friendly and united the right way. It is heaven in the soul: Rom. xiv. 17, "The kingdom of God is righteousness, peace, and joy;" and Luke xvii. 21, "The kingdom of God is within you. When the heart is divided, then appear storms and troubles in the soul. When christians are at variance, divided, and not united in their judgments, affections, and practice, they have not that heavenly sweetness in them which otherwise they would have: James iii. 16, "Where envying and strife is, there is confusion," unquietness, unheavenliness.

(3.) It makes the communion one with another delightful and acceptable: Psal. cxxxiii. 1, "Behold, how good and how pleasant it is for brethren to dwell together in unity!" Where there is union of hearts, there is sweet communion; when the union is strongest, the communion is sweetest, as in the sacred Trinity. Acts iv. 32, the believers "were of one heart and of one soul;" and chap. ii. 42, "They continued stedfastly in the apostles' doctrine and fellowship, and in breaking of bread, and in prayer." Communion of those who are one-hearted, is a box of precious and sweet ointment, without flies.

(4.) It prevents all the evil which comes by divisions and contentions, which are great and many. I will name some few.

[1.] Much time is lost, where contentions are, in janglings, brawlings, and bitter expressions; we have woful experience of it in these days, both in men's preaching, printing, reading, conversing, and disputings. Time is precious, and the apostle bids us redeem the time, Eph. v. 16. Where one-heartedness is, there is prevention of this great loss; Acts ii. 46, 47, the christians there continued "daily with one accord in the temple, praising God."

[2.] Where divisions are, there is seeking the disgrace and damage, if not the ruin, of one another; there is plotting and practising to root out each other. Scribes, Pharisees, high priests, did not only disgrace Christ, and damage him several ways, but were restless till they had his blood. Gal. v. 15, where strife is, there is biting and devouring one another; but one-heartedness prevents all these things, it never disgraceth, damnifieth, or destroyeth any; 1 Cor. xiii. it is full of love, and is kind, not envying, it doth not unseemly, it thinketh no evil, but beareth all things.

[3.] They weaken much, and hinder the doing of much good; therefore it is the policy of Satan and his instruments, to make divisions in kingdoms, armies, councils, cities, families, that so the good intended may not be accomplished. When hearts and heads are divided, hands are weakened, and the good can never be done in a contentious way, which may be done in a peaceable and loving way. When men are divided, their councils, their motions, are oft destructive one to another. When a great river is divided into many channels, her waters cannot carry such great vessels as before, nor be so serviceable. Where union is, there is strength; this made Antisthenes say, *Fratrum inter se concordiam quovis muro firmius esse munimentum*, That unity among brethren is a defence more firm than any wall. Agesilaus being asked why Lacedemon had no walls, answered, pointing at the citizens who were unanimous and one-hearted, *Hi sunt Spartæ mœnia*, These are the walls of Sparta; intimating, that the agreement of citizens is the greatest strength to a city. And

In Apophtheg. regum.

Plutarch tells of old Scylurus who had eighty sons, and he on his death-bed gave them a bundle of arrows, and bade them break them, &c.; If you agree you will be invincible, and do great things; if not, you will be weak and do nothing. Therefore Solomon, Eccl. iv. 9, saith, "Two are better than one," there is more strength; and twenty are better than two, when they agree. Gen. xi. 6, "The people is one; and nothing will be restrained from them, which they have imagined to do;" being united, they were so strong to carry on that great work of building Babel, that none could hinder them but God himself.

[4.] Divisions grieve the weak, and harden the wicked, as you may observe, Rom. xiv.; but where one-heartedness is, there is no grieving of the one, nor hardening of the other; that were a strange spirit, which should be offended at union, peace, and love of brethren. Psal. cxxxiii. 2, the unity of brethren "is like precious ointment," which is pleasing to the weak, and softening to the hard heart; hence, Prov. xxv. 15, "A soft tongue breaketh the bone."

(5.) One-heartedness invites others unto that way where it is found. It is a pleasant and comely thing to see brethren dwell in unity; men are affected with it, there is much beauty and mirth in the harmony of hearts. The sweet peace and union which were amongst the christians in the primitive times, allured many to them: love unites and draws strongly. An Indian passing by the house of a christian, where they were brawling and contending, said, Habbomach dwells there, that was Satan, and would not turn in: but where love, union, and peace is, there God dwells; 1 John iv. 16, "God is love," and dwells where love is. And that society which hath God in it hath the strongest argument to draw others to it: Zech. viii. 23, "Ten shall take hold of the skirt of a Jew, saying, We will go with you, for we have heard that God is with you."

(6.) It improves grace, and makes christians thrive much; whereas jars, divisions, vain disputes, and wranglings, prejudice the lustre and growth of grace, if not the life. It is observed by some, that the power of godliness is greatly abated in many places, and among many christians, in these divided times we live in; these waters of Marah have imbittered their spirits, and quenched the graces of the Spirit; so that the wholesome words of our Lord Jesus Christ, and the doctrine which is according to godliness, are not so minded as formerly. In winter the trees put not forth, neither do the fruits of the earth grow in stormy weather; in times of war things are greatly defaced: but when winter is gone, sun shines, then do all things flourish; and in days of peace things prosper. Where one-heartedness is, this unity we speak of, there doth grace thrive among christians. Where envyings, grudges, jealousies, strifes, oppositions, and rising of spirits are among christians, they are as northern and eastern winds to the corn and fruits, they cause them to dwindle away, or to prove little and lank. 1 Cor. viii. 1, if love edifieth, and builds up christians, divisions pull down: when men are divided they seldom speak the truth in love, and then it doth little good; when it is spoken in love, then christians grow, and grow up into Christ in all things, Eph. iv. 15.

Acts ix. 31.

(7.) It furthers their prayers; when men are all of one heart, there is much sweetness and strength in their prayers. Acts iv. 24, "They lifted up their voice to God with one accord;" all their hearts were as one heart; and ver. 31, "When they had prayed, the place was shaken, and they were all filled with the Holy Ghost:" here was a sweet and efficacious prayer, all their hearts were in the prayer, and all were filled with the Holy Spirit. Matt. v. 23, 24, "If thou bring thy gift to the altar, and there rememberest that thy brother hath aught against thee; leave thy gift, go, and first be reconciled to thy brother, and then come and offer thy gift." Whilst divisions are amongst brethren, a prohibition lies against our sacrificing, but when there is peace and unity, then heaven is open for acceptance of our prayers. 1 Cor. vii. 5, Paul knew what an enemy contention was to divine duties; and therefore would not have married parties refrain the use of the marriage-bed, without consent of each other; if it were upon will and humour, it would not further, but hinder their prayers. So in 1 Pet. iii. 7, husbands must dwell as men of knowledge with their wives, honour them, though the weaker vessels, look at them as coheirs of the grace of life; and why? that their prayers be not hindered: if there be dissensions, their prayers will suffer; but if there be love, oneness of heart, their prayers will be more spiritual, fervent, and prevalent.

(8.) It is an honour to the Lord Christ, that christians do agree; they are members of his body, and it is a disparagement to the Head to have the members fall out, rend and tear one another: this makes strangers speak and think evil of the way of Christ; hereby he is dishonoured; but when there is one heart among his disciples, when they love one another, and are peaceable, it is a glory to Christ. John xiii. 35, "By this shall all men know that ye are my disciples, if ye love one another." Christ would be known in the world, and have his disciples known from all others; and how? by love. Chrysostom observes, He saith not, by miracles and wonders men shall know you to be my disciples; no, they are laid by; but by love. That is a glorious grace, it shows forth Christ, and who are his; it is not greatness of power, but greatness of love, which declares who are the disciples of Christ, and which honours Christ, 1 John iii. 10.

(9.) Sympathy with each other. If there be one-heartedness among men, what is the burden and comfort of the one, is the burden and comfort of the rest. As in marriage, the sorrows are divided and joys doubled which fall out to persons in that condition, and the reason is, because they are one flesh, and have *quasi animam unam*, as it were one soul: so where there is oneness of heart, there is a choice sympathy, the blows, wounds, losses, griefs, infirmities of one, are the blows, &c. of all the rest. When Peter and John had been imprisoned, brought before the council, threatened, they went to their own company, and told them how they had been used, and they were affected with their sufferings, and fell to prayer with them, Acts iv. 23, 24. How sensible were the rich christians of the burdens of the poor, pitying and relieving them! ver. 32. And when Peter was in prison, the church sympathized, Acts xii. 4. But where this is wanting, I mean sameness or likeness of spirit, there will be a rejoicing at their sufferings and wrongs, and mourning or envying at their good. They that are divided from others too oft glory in the infirmities of others; and if God's hand be upon them or theirs, they say it is a just judgment of God upon them for their judgments, opinions; and so add affliction to the afflicted.

(10.) What evidence of being in the covenant of grace, if there be not union of the heart within itself, union of it to God, and others? what satisfaction can a man have of his being in covenant with God? Here this one-heartedness is prefixed as the first thing we should look at; and so in Jer. xxxii. 39, "I will give them one heart and one way." Men that want this one-heartedness, cannot but suspect themselves, be jealous of their condition; if it be not in some measure in us, inchoatively and tending to increase, we are not the Lord's, 1 John iii. 18, 19.

(11.) It makes willing to do one for another. How forward was Jonathan to speak and do! &c. *Amantibus facile fit omne difficile*, Things difficult become easy where love exists; and the ground of it is, *Cor est ubi amat, non ubi animat*, The heart is where it loves, not where it lives.

I. Helps to unite our hearts.

1. Consider many things are darkly laid down in the Scriptures, and the scope of God and Christ therein is not to cause contention, difference, and censuring, but to unite us more strongly in those things which are clear, and to cause a forbearance of one another in things which are dark and doubtful: Phil. iii. 15, 16, "If in any thing ye be otherwise minded, God shall reveal even this unto you. Nevertheless, whereto we have already attained, let us walk by the same rule, let us mind the same thing." Saith Paul, I confide not in my own works or righteousness, but look at Christ alone; I labour to win Christ, and be found in him; I press after him, and none but him, and mind nothing else as a means of salvation. If any be otherwise minded, through ignorance, or weakness of faith, (as many were, who affected mosaical rites and ceremonies,) God shall reveal even this unto you; he will make known the truth unto you. Nevertheless, though there be differences, let us forbear one another therein; and whereto we have attained, let us walk harmoniously and peaceably together, minding the same things. What is clearly held out unto us in the gospel let us consent in, and walk answerably; in what is dark, doubtful, let us forbear each other, and stay till God reveal more. If we cannot unite in all, let us unite in what is clear. Things fundamental, and absolutely necessary, are most clearly laid down in the word; they are expressly commanded, or held forth in Scripture, whether they be matters of faith or practice; they are not things drawn out by remote consequences, and strength of men's parts, but immediately from, or in, the word; and in these most may or do agree, not being many in number: so far as we have attained in these, let us walk; and, as king James saith, in other things place may be given to christian liberty: and let us take heed how we charge men to hold fundamental errors; when fundamentals are few, Rom. x. 9; 1 John iv. 2, and men's errors are extra-fundamentals.

2. Divine Providence hath ordered it so, that there should be difference and inequality in the naturals and spirituals of christians, that so they may have a greater tendency and fitness for union. As in a ship, or house, all pieces of timber must not be of the same length, height, and breadth, but differing; that so they may fit their several places, and conduce to make up a more goodly fabric: so among men, some have great natural and spiritual abilities, some lower degrees of both, some lesser than they; and this is the will and wisdom of Divine Providence, so to dispense and dispose, that all may fitly fall in together, and make the more glorious structures for heaven. John tells you, 1 Epist. ii. 13, of fathers, young men, and little children, who differed in their naturals and spirituals, yet lived lovingly and peaceably together, and made up a church for Christ. If we quarrel because there be differences of judgment amongst us, we cross the intent of Divine Providence, and quarrel with that, which hath so dispensed his gifts and grace, and given them out unequally. When we see one man white, another black, one tall, another low; shall we quarrel because both are not white, both of one equal height: one hath sore eyes, another sound, the veil is fully drawn off one's heart, half way off another's; and this is the Lord's doing, it is that we may the better join together.

3. Seek the good one of another, and that indifferently. Selfishness and partiality undo and divide, they have private ends, ways, means, and move upon sinister respects; whereas if we had more self-denying, impartial, and public spirits, to mind the welfare of others, we should quickly attain to some good degree of this oneness of heart. 1 Cor. x. 24, "Let no man seek his own, but every man another's wealth:" it is not a flat prohibition from seeking a man's own good, but he should rather seek the good of others than of himself; as Paul did, ver. 33, "I seek not mine own profit, but the profit of many." If this were in practice, it would let in our hearts and spirits into the bosoms of others, and make us one-hearted with them. Phil. ii. 20, Paul speaking of Timothy, who sought the good of the Philippians, saith, "I have no man like-minded:" the word is ἰσόψυχον, of equal mind; so that Timothy and the Philippians were *æquanimes*, of equal mind; his heart, his soul was in theirs, and equal, yea, one with theirs; and what then? "who will naturally care for your estate;" the workings of his soul for their good were like the workings of a father towards his children natural, which are most strong, constant, and delightful. When men's hearts are equal, too, one with the hearts of others, they act naturally for their benefit; but when men seek the hurt of others, black their names, greaten their infirmities, catch advantages against them, they are unnatural, men of other and bitter spirits.

Rom. xv. 2, "Let every one of us please his neighbour for his good."

4. Lay aside the wisdom of the flesh, and exalt the wisdom of the Spirit. Fleshly wisdom makes and maintains divisions; Rom. viii. 7, Φρόνημα τῆς σαρκὸς ἔχθρα εἰς Θεόν, it is "enmity against God," and all the ways of God; it subjects not to them, neither can do it, but opposes continually. And as it hinders union with God and his ways, so it doth with the children of God; it keeps them from one-hearted-

ness, it makes breaches, and maintains them when made. It was such wisdom separated Paul and Barnabas, and kept them, being separated, at a distance. The fleshly mind puffs up, Col. ii. 18, and so the heart cannot lie even with another's; but spiritual wisdom is of another nature: Prov. xii. 18, "The tongue of the wise is health;" others' tongues are "like the piercings of a sword," they wound; but the spiritually wise they heal wounds, make up breaches, they pacify wrath, even the wrath of great ones, Prov. xvi. 14, Men think themselves wise in these days, but what is the wisdom of most? is it not such James speaks of, "earthly, sensual, devilish," because it is joined with bitterness, envying, strife? see James iii. 14, 15. And then he tells you the nature of spiritual wisdom, ver. 17, "That is from above, first pure, then peaceable, gentle, and easy to be entreated, full of mercy and good fruits, without partiality, and without hypocrisy." There is nothing in it but what tends to oneness of heart; it is "pure," there is no mixture of fleshly wisdom in it; it is "peaceable," averse from contention, studious of peace; "gentle, and easy to be entreated," not harsh and self-willed, but pliable to that which is good; "full of mercy and good fruits," it is ready to help and do for others in their necessities; "without partiality," without wrangling, judging; "without hypocrisy," it is real in what it doth.

5. Humility; where that is it draws the heart of God to it, Isa. lvii. 15, God dwells with the humble spirit; and surely it will gain the hearts of men to it: Prov. xxix. 23, "A man's pride shall bring him low," it will make God and man against him; "but honour shall uphold the humble in spirit," both God and man will support, speak well of, do good to and close with him. It is pride only, chiefly, that makes contentions, Prov. xiii. 10; men's lusts lift them up, divide themselves, and cause divisions amongst others; therefore, James iv. 1, "From whence come wars and fightings amongst you? come they not hence, even of your lusts that war in your members?" Proud men have many lusts and much war, and when they agree not with themselves, how can they agree with others? we should therefore purify our hearts from such lusts, and humble ourselves in the sight of the Lord, ver. 8, 10, and then our hearts would close better. It is men's proud lusts that dissolve union, that make war and breed confusion, blind men's eyes, and engage them in errors; but the humble man that hath had his heart broken, and hath let them out, he is readiest to unite with others; he stands not upon his will, his credit, he hath low thoughts of himself, and high of others. Hence Paul bids the Colossians "put on humbleness of mind," chap. iii. 12; and 1 Pet. v. 5, Peter bids them "be clothed with humility," that is the most becoming garment and least offensive of any. The man who walks with that garment on will not wrong any man in thought, word, or deed; he judges not others, but himself; he bears the burden and infirmities of men, and so gains upon and gets interest in the hearts of others.

6. Consider we are brethren, called and pressed unto peace and mutual agreement in the gospel. Moses thought the name brethren sufficient to reconcile the two struggling Hebrews; Acts vii. 26, "Sirs, ye are brethren;" what! your hearts, heads, and hands divided? think how near you are and dear you should be one to another. The word brethren should draw our hearts together, and make us desirous of peace. 1 Tim. vi. 1, 2, servants must not despise their masters, but count them worthy of all honour, because they are brethren; and we should not despise and contend one with another, because we are brethren, endued with divine nature, and brethren of Christ, Heb. ii. 12, "The Prince of peace," Isa. ix. 6; Partakers of "the gospel of peace," Eph. vi. 15; and are called of God to peace, 1 Cor. vii. 15; Col. iii. 15; and it is peace that we are pressed unto, Rom. xiv. 19, "Let us follow after the things that make for peace;" see 2 Tim. ii. 22; Heb. xii. 14. We should pursue peace with all men, but especially with those who are our brethren in Christ; they make up the body of Christ, in which the Spirit of Christ lives; therefore, Eph. iv. 3, Paul counsels them to "keep the unity of the Spirit in the bond of peace;" the Spirit hath united men to Christ, and peace is the bond which keeps the Spirit among them. When the Corinthians brake the bond of peace, saying, "I am of Paul," &c. the apostle told them they were carnal, not spiritual, 1 Cor. iii. 1. There should be no strife among brethren, but this, viz. who should be most loving and peaceable.

II. Preservatives of one-heartedness.

1. Look much at the gifts, graces, and excellences which are in others, not at their weaknesses and imperfections; let the bright side of the cloud be in your eyes, not the black side; and this will keep your hearts united. Peter eyed the "like precious faith" which was in the christians, with his and other apostles', 2 Pet. i. 1; and John takes special notice of the graces which were in the fathers, young men, little children, in the elect lady, and Gaius, and that kept his heart united to them. When men's persons, parts, or graces are slighted, it breaks the bond of peace, divides hearts and spirits. The apostle bids us "honour all men," 1 Pet. ii. 17; esteem them if there be any worth in them, take notice of it, and honour them answerably: if there be great sins and weaknesses in them, are they greater than thine own? if they be or be not, grieve for them, be not angry with them.

2. Lay aside all provoking, dividing names, terms, and speeches. Those names of Petrians, Paulians, Johannites, in the primitive times, did hurt; which Epiphanius observing, would not give way that there should be any name added to the christian name. Those names of Lutheran, Zwinglian, Calvinist, bred divisions among the protestants; and surely discriminating names have made divided hearts among us. So reproaching and bitter words have kindled a fire which might be put out, if all men had such spirits as Calvin had, who professed if Luther should call him devil, yet would he have a reverend esteem of him, and acknowledge him a worthy servant of the Lord's. If we would have our hearts kept in firm union, we must use soft tongues and gentle words, Prov. xv. 1; xii. 25.

3. Ever make the best construction of men's words and actions; that will preserve peace and oneness of heart. When other interpretations are put upon the words and actions of men than were intended, this sows the seed ofttimes of bitter contentions and great evils. John ii. 19, 20, with Matt. xxvi. 61, Christ speaks there of the temple of his body, the Jews interpret it of the temple that was forty-six years a building, and bring it in against Christ, as matter worthy of death. If we shall force the words or acts of others, and fetch senses, intentions out of them, which the authors aimed not at, we shall never maintain peace with any.

4. Get much love and exercise it; that makes hearts one, and preserves them being one. 1 Sam. xviii. 1, Jonathan loved David as his own soul; so, ver. 3, David loved Jonathan as his own soul; they two had as it were one heart and one soul. If there were love among us, it would cover a multitude of sins, and not discover one; it would make up

breaches past, and prevent breaches for the future. The very nature of love consists in union; *Amans est in amato*, He that loves lives in the loved, the heart of the loved is his habitation; and love is very forward to do any kindness for those it relates to. That chapter, 1 Cor. xiii. had need be new studied in these divided times. Whatever the knowledge of faith be, if we have not love, the text saith, we are nothing. He saith not, we are little, but plainly, we are nothing. Many among us are very bitter, uncharitable, and go among men for some things, and some bodies, but in the judgment of God they are nothing: if you have little love, you are little ones; if great love, great ones; if no love, nothing. It is love that Christ specially looked at, and called for, in Peter; "Peter, lovest thou me more than these," &c. Christ measures men by their love; and no marvel, love is the fulfilling of the law, Gal. v. 14; and if we serve one another by love and fulfil the law, where can the breach be made, how can the offence come in? "Love behaves not itself unseemly, seeketh not her own, is not easily provoked, thinketh no evil;" this grace binds a man to his good behaviour, and will keep peace with all men: hence is it, that whereas once we are bid above all things to take the shield of faith, Eph. vi. 16, we are twice bid above all things to put on love, 1 Pet. iv. 8; Col. iii. 14, "which is the bond of perfectness;" that is, both in regard of man and God: love knits the members of Christ together, and so perfects his body; it unites us to God, and so causeth the perfecting of divine love in us; 1 John iv. 12, "If we love one another, God dwelleth in us, and his love is perfected in us;" see ver. 17.

5. Be willing to learn one of another; that will endear our hearts each to other, and keep them in oneness. The scribes and Pharisees thought they knew the law better than Christ; they would not learn of him, and so never heartily closed with him, but were peremptory in their own opinions, and tenacious of traditions, and by this means were enemies to truth, and those who were one-hearted in the truth. Col. iii. 16, they were to teach and admonish one another; yea, chap. iv. 17, they must "say to Archippus, Take heed to the ministry which thou hast received in the Lord, that thou fulfil it." Their willingness to learn one of another, preserved them in order. And those that do teach, should willingly and meekly instruct "those that do oppose, if God peradventure will give them repentance to the acknowledging of the truth," 2 Tim. ii. 24, 25; for the promise is, Isa. xxix. 24, that those who have "erred in spirit shall come to understanding, and they that murmured shall learn doctrine."

6. See God's presence and nearness to us; that is a means to preserve us in a one-hearted condition. When the Master is present the servants are quiet, and keep so. James v. 9, "Grudge not one against another, brethren, lest ye be condemned;" and what should prevent this, and keep them in brotherly love? "Behold, the Judge standeth before the door," he is ready to come in, to examine you thoroughly, what the differences are, what the words, acts, thoughts are; he is in you all, through you all, observes every rising of the spirit, all workings there; and above you all, and will reckon with you.

III. Inducements to one-heartedness are these:

1. That great apostle Paul saith to the Ephesians, chap. iv. 3—6, "Endeavour to keep the unity of the Spirit:" and why? "There is one body, one Spirit, one hope, one Lord, one faith, one baptism, one God and Father of all." Here are seven ones, and every one a strong argument to move to unity and one-heartedness: one body, orderly united: one Spirit, which enlivens, enlightens, strengthens, sanctifies, comforts; and this Spirit is not contrary to itself, but one and the same, a Spirit of love and peace: one hope among you of immortality, glory, and eternal excellences: one Lord Christ, who rules over you, whose servants you are: one faith, one Christ that you believe in, one rule that you walk by: one baptism; you are all baptized in the name of the Father, Son, and Holy Ghost: one God and Father; there is but one God whom ye serve, and he is the Father, you are his children in his family; will you fall out? if you were of diverse families, had diverse fathers, diverse gods, that might be excusable.

2. Christ hath taken our nature upon him, and as to unite man and God together, so to unite man and man together in himself: hence, Gal. iii. 28, "Ye are all one in Christ Jesus;" and Rom. viii. 17, "Joint-heirs with Christ;" and Eph. ii. 6, said to "sit together in heavenly places in Christ Jesus." This should move us to live and love, as those who have such high privileges by Christ: and it is observed, Christ being united to us, bears with more in us than we can with one another; when we are in that condition as we can endure one another no longer, I mean dead, and must be buried out of the sight of the living, Christ then is united to our corrupt bodies; when Lazarus lay stinking in the grave, Christ loved him.

3. If you love them who are of your own opinion only, and love you, what do you more than others, than Pharisees, than publicans? Matt. v. 46, "If ye love them which love you, what reward have ye? do not even publicans," the worst of men, "the same?" "And if ye salute your brethren only, what do ye more than others?" publicans do it, all sorts will do that; and know, if you be one with men, and love them because they are of your opinion, it is the opinion, and not the men, you love; if of another opinion, then you cannot close with them and love them. But Christ would have you do more than others, more than publicans, he would have you "love your enemies, bless them that curse you, do good to them that hate you, and pray for them that despitefully use you, and persecute you." Why can you not love men who have the same graces with you, as well as those who have the same opinions with you.

4. It is the fulfilling of a prophecy, Isa. xi. 6—9. By wolf, leopard, lion, bear, and asp, are meant frenzied, choleric, strong, rigid, and hurtful men; by lamb, kid, calf, cow, and ox, the weak, meek, laborious, and useful; and these should dwell together, eat together, and lie down together. Their natures should be so altered by the gospel and Spirit of Christ, that the fiercest should be as meek as a lamb, and live in peace with the rest of the believers; they should come to the state of innocency, in which no creature should have preyed upon another, but all have lived harmoniously and sweetly together. So should it be under Christ; ver. 9, "They shall not hurt nor destroy in all my holy mountain," there shall be no hurting nor destroying in the whole church. The Jews, because they see not this fulfilled among us christians, take offence, and say, that therefore Christ is not yet come; that our Christ was not the true Christ; for yet the lion tears, the wolf devours, &c. A sad thing to cause Jews to deny Christ, and to blaspheme, because we are like lions, bears, wolves to one another. Let us remember the prophecy in Zeph. iii. 9.

5. Consider what oneness of spirit is amongst the enemies of God.

(1.) Devils. Seven devils dwelt together peaceably in Mary Magdalene, Mark xvi. 9; a legion in another, Luke viii. 30; the man was unquiet, but the devils were very quiet in him; though hundreds, yet there was no dissension. The devil's kingdom is an undivided kingdom, Matt. xii. 26; and all the devils in the world drive on the same design unanimously, they all seek to hinder the conversion, comfort, and salvation of sinners, they all labour to draw men to perdition.

(2.) Wicked men. Mahometans are of one heart in their Mahometanism. Papists, what a multitude of orders and differences among them, and yet all are one-hearted in popery and superstition; Rev. xiii. 3, 4, "All the world wondered after the beast, and worshipped the dragon and the beast." Herod, Pilate, the gentiles, and people of Israel, were gathered together against Christ, Acts iv. 27. And when they built Babel the people were one, Gen. xi. 6. Read Psal. lxxxiii. 3—9. Shall wicked men and devils be one-hearted, one-spirited in sinful practices, in false ways, and shall not those who are godly?

6. Where oneness is not, there will be divisions and offences; as amongst the Corinthians, they were the most divided church we read of, and their offences did most abound: and how sad it is to offend any who belong to Christ, hear Christ himself telling you, Matt. xviii. 6, "Whoso shall offend one of these little ones which believe in me, it were better for him that a millstone were hanged about his neck, and that he were drowned in the depth of the sea." So heinous a thing is it in the eye of God, that a man were better die any death than offend the godly, the meanest of the godly; what then if he offend the greatest and most of the godly? it were better a great millstone were hanged about his neck, and that he were drowned in the depths of the sea.

7. The Lord Christ may own them at the last day for sheep, whom you look upon and carry yourselves towards like goats, and those he may judge sound sheep, you have judged infected; and what shame will that be to those who have so foully mistaken! The Pharisees thought themselves skilful in the law, and judged the people cursed that followed Christ closest, John vii. 49; but those people were dear to Christ. When the blind man saw, and saw more than the Pharisees, they cast him out, but Christ received him, John ix.: so, many that now are cast out, as factious, seditious, erroneous, schismatical, ere long Christ will own; and then how will they blush who have reproached them, persecuted them, judged them unworthy of any liberty or being amongst them! God takes the foolish to confound the wise, the weak to confound the mighty, the base, despised, and things which are not, to bring to nought things which are, 1 Cor. i. 27, 28.

8. Where unity is amongst the saints, there the presence of the Lord Christ is. Matt. xviii. 20, "Where two or three are gathered together in my name, there am I in the midst of them:" where there is most unity, there God delights most to be. Jerusalem was as a city compact together, Psal. cxxii. 3, had God's presence in a special manner; and it represented the church under the gospel, which when it is fitly framed together, then it is an habitation for God, Eph. ii. 21, 22. The curtains of the tabernacle where God was present must be coupled together, Exod. xxvi. 3: the hearts of men must be knit together, if they would have God and Christ among them. The Jews affirm, that where two sit together, (that is, agreed, having one heart,) and speak of the law, *Divinitas habitat inter ipsos*, the Divinity dwells among them.

I shall end this point with that of Paul, Phil. ii. 1, 2, "If there be therefore any consolation in Christ, if any comfort of love, if any fellowship of the Spirit, if any bowels and mercies, fulfil ye my joy, that ye be like-minded, having the same love, being of one accord, of one mind."

Obs. 3. This one-heartedness is the gift of God, not the work of man. "I will give them one heart;" they cannot make their hearts one, but I can; it is a work not to be accomplished by force of man, but by the free grace of God: Jer. xxxii. 38, 39, "They shall be my people, and I will be their God: and I will give them one heart, and one way." When God is God in covenant with a people, then will he freely give and work this one-heartedness; he doth not force it, but freely work it. Men attempt, by compulsory acts, to make men differing in principles and practices to be one-hearted, and to go one way; but such attempts seldom take any good effect; men's judgments and consciences will not be forced. Bodinus in his fourth book of his commonwealth, saith judiciously, if a prince, persuaded of the truth of his religion, would draw his subjects thereunto, being divided into sects and factions, he must not therein use force, (for the minds of men, the more they are forced, the more froward and stubborn they are, and the greater punishments that shall be inflicted upon them, the less good is to be done; the nature of man being commonly such, as may of itself be led to like of any thing, but never be enforced so to do,) but without fainting, to profess his religion, devoutly serving the Almighty God, whereby he shall turn the wills and minds of his subjects unto the imitation and admiration of himself. Theodosius the elder, who found all the provinces of his empire at the beginning of his reign full of Arians, whose strength and power was so grown and increased under three or four Arian emperors their favourers, as that their doctrine was not only by eight councils confirmed, held at Tyre, Sardis, Syrme, Milan, Seleucia, Nice, Tarsis, Ariminum, (where six hundred bishops were of their opinion, and but three, of name, which held the contrary,) but that they punished also others their adversaries, of opinion contrary to themselves, with confiscations, proscriptions, and other most grievous punishments; yet would not this good emperor either force or punish the Arians, though he deadly hated them; but granted unto both the Arians, and other the catholics, their churches, and suffered them in every town to have two bishops, of either religion one: and though at the importunate suit of the catholic bishops, he commanded certain edicts to be published against the Arians, yet he was contented to have the same held in suspense, and not to be put in execution, as his letters to Ambrose declare. Theodoric king of the Goths, though favouring the Arians, would not yet enforce the consciences of his subjects, nor have them tormented for their religion, lest under the pretence of impiety, he should have seemed to have taken the spoil of their goods to bend their minds, which could by no threats or commands be constrained to bend; for thus he writes unto the senate of Rome, *Religionem imperare non possumus quia nemo cogitur ut credat invitus*, We cannot control religion, because no one can be compelled to believe against his will. He saith also, No man is to be forced; the private exercise of his religion is to be yielded, if it cannot be publicly professed without sedition; otherwise men will become atheists, and so, having lost the fear of God, and trod underfoot laws and magistrates, will practise all impieties and villanies. Mr. Forbes being sent for to the king of Sweden, when he was victorious, and asked by him what government he should set over Lutherans, Calvinists, papists, whom he had conquered; his answer was, You have conquered their bodies with ease, but you will find it a hard work to conquer men's judgments and consciences. What ill effects the forcing of men's spirits brought forth, you may read in that learned and judicious treatise of Sir Simon D'Ewes, entitled, The Primitive Practice for preserving Truth.

You know who said it, In things of the mind, we look for no compulsion, but that of light and reason.

He is not a loving father, but rather a step-father, who will compel his children to eat of that meat which is against their stomachs, when there are variety of dishes to feed upon which are suitable to them. Wise physicians persuade, do not force their patients to take physic. It is good to cure errors which are in men's minds, and to save their souls, but in God's way, James v. 19, by conversion, not by compulsion, by the power of the word, not the edge of the sword; this makes hypocrites, that saints. That conscience is not obstinate, which useth means to know truth. If God hide it from, it liveth under the power of conscience, and is not turbulent.

These things I speak, not to make way for licentiousness, that whatever opinions men hold, think, say, or practise, they may be free; but merely, that consciences truly tender, may not be forced. It is one thing to restrain men's practices which are idolatrous, blasphemous, against pure worship, the power of godliness, and peace of the state; another, to force men to that their judgment and consciences are against. I pleaded not ever for a toleration of all, neither do, but only that those whose lives are holy, peaceable, and differ in judgment from others in some things, may not be forced to conform or depart.

"I will put a new spirit within you." The word spirit notes sometimes the soul: Acts vii. 59, saith Stephen, "Lord Jesus, receive my spirit;" 2 Cor. vii. 1, "Let us cleanse ourselves from all filthiness of flesh and spirit." Sometimes for the heart and affections: 1 Kings xxi. 5, "Why is thy spirit so sad?" said Jezebel to Ahab; that is, why is thy heart so heavy? Acts xvii. 16, Paul, "his spirit was stirred within him," when he saw their idolatry, his affections moved him to speak and dispute with them. Sometimes for the faculties of the soul, viz. understanding, will, and conscience: 1 Thess. v. 23, "I pray God your whole spirit, and soul, and body be preserved blameless;" by "whole spirit," the understanding, will, and conscience may be meant: Prov. xviii. 14, "A wounded spirit who can bear?" that is, a wounded conscience. Sometimes for the gifts and graces of the Spirit; Gal. iii. 2, "Received ye the Spirit by the works of the law, or by the hearing of faith?"

"New," is in Scripture sometimes that which is totally new for matter; Deut. xx. 5, a new house; Judg. xv. 13, new ways; 1 Sam. vi. 7, a new cart; 1 Kings xi. 29, a new garment: sometimes for that which is renewed; 2 Chron. xx. 5, "Jehoshaphat stood before the new court," that is judged to be the priests' court, renewed in its building, or use, after some public profanation; so it is called a new ship or garment, that is altered and changed: sometimes for that which is excellent and admirable; Mark i. 27, "What new doctrine is this?" it is admirable and excellent doctrine; so the "new name," Rev. ii. 17; iii. 12; that is, an excellent and admirable name: sometimes for that which is diverse from what it was before, especially in regard of qualities; Mark xvi. 17, "They shall speak with new tongues," which, Acts ii. 4, are called "other tongues," tongues which had other gifts and graces in them.

By "new spirit" here is not meant a new soul, or faculties, for substance, or the inward form of it, but the same soul altered in the frame, renewed in the qualities, thereof. It hath other excellent qualities in it, which it had not before, even the gifts and graces of the Spirit; hence it is called the new birth, or birth of the Spirit, John iii. 6; "the new man," Eph. iv. 24; the "new creature," Gal. vi. 15. Not only faith and love, mentioned Gal. v. 6, but all divine qualities man is capable of, are included in this "new spirit."

1. The understanding is enlightened with divine light, which it had not before. Acts xxvi. 18, "To open the eyes, and to turn them from darkness to light:" The gentiles were blind before God gave them this new spirit, which brought new lights unto their minds. Eph. iv. 18, "Having the understanding darkened, being alienated from the life of God through the ignorance that is in them, because of the blindness of their heart;" but when they had put on "the new man," ver. 24, in the next chapter, ver. 8, Paul saith of them, "Ye were sometimes darkness, but now are ye light in the Lord;" the Lord by his Spirit had brought in marvellous light into their understandings, and scattered their darknesses. This Paul calls God's shining into the heart, 2 Cor. iv. 6; John, Christ's giving an understanding, 1 John v. 20; and Luke, an opening of the understanding, Luke xxiv. 45. All which phrases, as they suppose oldness of darkness, so a renewing of the understanding with newness of light; and this light is "the light of life," John viii. 12, brought into the soul by "the spirit of wisdom and revelation," Eph. i. 17, 18.

2. This "new spirit" hath influence into the will, and alters that which in itself is corrupt, and carryeth the soul the wrong way. Eph. ii. 3, "Fulfilling the desires of the flesh," τα ϑελήματα της σαρκὸς, the will of the flesh. Paul acknowledgeth nothing to be in the wills of men naturally, but fleshly corruption; and whatsoever that put them upon, that they did, and with delight, fulfilling the wills of the flesh; but when this "new spirit" comes, it alters the will, breaks the principle of stubbornness in it, purges the pollution and corruption out of it, and makes it pliable unto the will of God. "Ezek. xxxvi. 27, "I will put my spirit within you, and cause you to walk in my statutes." God's Spirit will so alter our spirits, so transform and renew them, that they shall be inclined to, and carried on in, the obeying of divine statutes. Before, they went on in the ways of sin, with strength, constancy, and delight; now they move with new strength, constancy, and delight in that which is good. This "new spirit" bows the will to the law of righteousness, so that it obeys and commands well.

3. The affections are renewed. Ezek. xxxvi. 26, "A new heart also will I give you;" that is, your affections, which are now corrupt and inordinate, shall be changed and regulated; they shall of sinful be made holy, of earthly be made heavenly, of unrighteous become righteous. Eph. v. 9, "The fruit of the Spirit is in all goodness, righteousness, and truth:" When the Spirit of Christ comes and makes our spirits new, there is truth for the understanding, goodness for the will, and righteousness for the affections; and Gal. v. 22, 23, the fruits of the Spirit refer most to the affections, as, "love, joy, long-suffering, gentleness, meekness, temperance." Now the old affections and lusts of the flesh are crucified, Gal. v. 24, and the new affections are set "on things above," Col. iii. 2.

4. The conscience is renewed. Before it is defiled, and acts according to that false or dim light which is in the understanding; but when this "new spirit"

comes in, the conscience is awakened, purged, and acts upon divine grounds. Heb. x. 22, "Having our hearts sprinkled from an evil conscience." The Holy Ghost, like water which washeth away the filth of the body, cleanseth the conscience from the blindness, impurity, and deadness which are in it, so that it, being endued with new qualities, becomes a pure, 2 Tim. i. 3, and good conscience, 1 Tim. i. 5, and acts new, not in a natural, but sanctified manner.

5. The memory is renewed and made able to retain good things. Before, like a strainer, it let the milk go, and kept the hairs and draff; like a boulter, it let the fine flour go, and kept the bran; but having a new quality in it, it is retentive of good: 1 Cor. xv. 2, Ye are saved by the gospel, "if you keep in memory what I have preached;" they had memories enabled to do it. Many a poor soul that is converted, when it comes to practise, remembers truths better than those of able memories.

These renewing and refining qualities make up the new man, and here are called a "new spirit."

"Spirit." 1. Because they are from the Spirit, that is the Author of them: John iii. 6, "That which is born of the Spirit is spirit;" it hath the qualities and graces of the Spirit, the Spirit begets its own likeness in the soul, as a father doth in the body.

2. In opposition to the flesh. These new qualities are contrary to those of corrupt nature, which the Scripture calls "flesh," and therefore fitly called Spirit, Gal. v. 17, "The flesh lusteth against the Spirit, and the Spirit against the flesh."

3. For that they make us spiritual. They have such operations in us, and honour us with such a denomination; 1 Cor. ii. 15, "He that is spiritual judgeth all things."

4. Because they are chiefly seated in the most spiritual part of a man, the soul and faculties of it are the subject thereof.

"New." 1. In opposition to the old corruptions which were in man before, which the Scripture calls "the old man;" Eph. v. 22, "Put off the old man, which is corrupt;" and ver. 23, 24, "Be renewed in the spirit of your mind; and put on the new man, which after God is created in righteousness and true holiness." Here it is called "the new man," (which is the same with the "new spirit,") in opposition to "old man."

2. For that it comes a new way into man. Had not Adam sinned, we should not have needed such ordinances as now we have, to work this "new spirit" in us; it is not by generation, but regeneration; it is not from nature, art, afflictions, ordinances, but the Spirit in ordinances.

3. Because it is wrought anew in us. No man hath aught of this "new spirit" in him naturally, but an old and contrary spirit; Rom. viii. 7, the wisdom of the flesh is enmity to God. This is totally new wrought, and therefore is called a creation, Eph. iv. 24.

4. From the effect. It makes us new; 2 Cor. v. 17, "If any man be in Christ, he is a new creature;" 1 Pet ii. 2, those endued with this "new spirit" are called "new-born babes."

5. Because it is ever vigorous, fresh, and lively, not decaying. So I find the words new interpreted by a late divine, and applied to the "new man;" and he thinks the new heavens and the new earth spoken of, Isa. lxv. 17; lxvi. 22; Rev. xxi. 1, (whatsoever is meant by them,) that the title "new" seems to import the admirable excellency and continuance thereof, never to alter or decay, but to remain before the Lord.

Mr. Balls, in his Covenant of Grace, p. 195.

Quest. 1. Whether was this promise fulfilled among the Jews, or in times of the gospel?

Answ. Many of the fathers refer the fulfilling of it unto the times of the gospel; but it being primarily made unto the Jews, we have just cause to think that it was in part fulfilled amongst them after their return from Babylon. So gracious a promise being given out by God, made known by Ezekiel, it is not likely they would neglect, having been so sorely afflicted in Babylon; but would improve, and press the Lord for the accomplishment of it: and, without dispute, many of them had this "new spirit," for after they came again to Jerusalem, they had such a hatred of idols, and love to truth, that they stood out to death for the law and religion of their God, as is recorded in the Maccabees.

Quest. 2. Whether is this "new spirit" given or wrought all at once?

Answ. This "new spirit" consists in those new qualities which are put into man, and the several qualities are wrought in at once, but they are wrought up by degrees; a man hath all graces at once *in semine, radice, habitu*, the seed, root, and habit: and this grace is called the law in the mind, Rom. vii. 22; the law written in the heart, Heb. viii. 10; the divine nature, 2 Pet. i. 4; Christ formed in us, Gal. iv. 19; the inward man, Rom. vii. 22; seed, 1 John iii. 9. Now this seed, this inward man, this Christ, this divine nature, are growing, this law receives addition; 2 Pet. iii. 18, "Grow in grace, and in the knowledge of our Lord and Saviour Jesus Christ;" 2 Cor. iv. 16, "The inward man is renewed day by day;" there is an addition of more strength, more degrees are added to those new qualities, the inward man grows stronger and better: so chap. iii. 18, we "are changed into the same image from glory to glory." When men are changed, and this "new spirit" is put into them, it is glory; and there is a progress in this glory, they go from one degree of glory to another.

Obs. 1. This "new spirit" is a great mercy, it is a renewal of the image of God in a man, knowledge, righteousness, and true holiness, Col. iii. 10; Eph. iv. 24. It is that makes a man good, and acceptable to God; it was the Holy Ghost and faith made Barnabas "a good man," Acts xi. 24. Till a man have some new qualities in him, this "new spirit," he is flesh, displeasing unto God; John iii. 6, "That which is born of the flesh is flesh; and that which is born of the Spirit is spirit," and so acceptable to God; then the tree is good, and the fruit good also, Matt. vii. 17, 18. It is that weakens and wastes sin in us; 2 Cor. v. 17, "If any man be in Christ, he is a new creature: old things are passed away;" old customs, practices, principles, corruptions, they are decaying, the old leaven is purging out. It is an argument of God's love in the covenant of grace towards a sinner, and evidence that thou art in that covenant; it is the promise of the new covenant, to give this "new spirit;" it is that makes us honourable and glorious. When we have this "new spirit," we are partakers of the divine nature, and "born of God," 1 John iii. 9; and that is honourable, ver. 1, and glorious, 2 Cor. iii. 18. It is a choice comfort to the man that hath it, more than thousands of silver and gold, more than a world to him; no such comfort to him as this. It is life; Luke xv. 24, "This my son was dead, and is alive again." The dead prodigal, when he had this "new spirit," had a new life, and this was a sweet, a great comfort to him, to his father, to others. It is that gives you title to the kingdom of heaven; John iii. 5, "Verily, verily, I say unto thee, Except a man be born of water," &c.

Quest. How doth this "new spirit" act and discover itself in that man where it is?

Answ. 1. It begets a noble ingenuity in the soul, to maintain the condition it puts into; it will shun whatever is contrary to it, or offensive to the Lord who gave it: 1 John v. 18, "Whosoever is born of God sinneth not, but keepeth himself, and that wicked one toucheth him not," he hath a nobleness of spirit, and keeps himself from sin and Satan; the things they propound are too low for him, too base. Joseph said, "How can I do this great wickedness, and sin against God?" Gen. xxxix. 9. Neh. vi. 11, "Should such a man as I flee." So saith the man endued with this "new spirit," Should such a man as I sin? God hath made me spiritual, and I will not embase myself to carnal things: 1 Pet. i. 14, "Not fashioning yourselves according to the former lusts."

2. A strong impression made upon the soul, so that it cannot but follow after Christ. Before, the heart could not but look downwards, pursue the creature, but now it doth the contrary. Acts xxvi. 18, "To open their eyes, and to turn them from darkness to light, and from the power of Satan unto God." When the turn is once made, they cannot but mind the light, and follow after God and Christ. When Elijah threw his mantle upon Elisha, he had such an impress made upon his spirit, that he must leave all, and follow him. The needle is unquiet till it come to the northern point; so a soul, till it come to Christ, when it is anointed with these new qualities, &c.

3. Seeth every thing with a new eye; there is divine light, the light of life in the soul, John viii. 12; and "the life of God," Eph. iv. 18. Before, they are alienated from it, but now, having this "new spirit," they partake of it, and not only live the life of God, but look upon things as God doth; they see sin exceeding sinful, Rom. vii. 13; grace to be free, glorious, exceeding rich, and abundant, Eph. i. 6; ii. 7, 8; 1 Tim. i. 14: they behold Christ in another manner than ever before; 2 Cor. v. 16, "Henceforth know we no man after the flesh; yea, though we have known Christ after the flesh, yet now henceforth know we him no more." Since we have had an eye to see spiritually, and the eye renewed to see more spiritually into the death of Christ, what satisfaction, peace, life, grace, salvation, glory, it hath wrought and brought! We know no man after the flesh, for their present honour, external excellences, no, not Christ; we look not upon him as poor, mean, afflicted, contemptible, but we see and judge spiritually, we look at what is divine in him, in others, in all. So for God himself; Jer. xxxi. 34, when he should put his law in their inward parts, then they should all know him, that is, in another manner than ever; they should see not only what an infinite Excellency he was in himself, but what a Father of mercies and God of consolations he was in Christ.

4. It makes a spiritual war in the soul. This "new spirit" sets upon the old man, the old spirit, and maintains a mighty war against the same, bringing under and captivating the flesh, with its lusts, members, wisdom, and strong holds. There was a natural war in the man before, between sin and the conscience, but this is a spiritual war; and it is known thus:

(1.) The whole frame of the soul is against sin, not the conscience alone, the understanding, will, affections, conscience. A drunken man may speak against drunkenness, and yet the frame of his heart be towards it; a covetous man may condemn covetousness, yet the frame of his spirit may be to it. Col. i. 21, "Enemies in your mind by wicked works:" a man being without this "new spirit," is an enemy to God, Christ, truth in his mind, by wicked works, the frame of his mind is against them; but being endued with this "new spirit," he is reconciled to God, and so an enemy in his mind to wicked works. So for his will, Rom. vii. 19, "The evil which I would not, that I do;" his will was against evil: so for his affection, ver. 15, "What I hate, that I do:" so for conscience, while it is natural, it restrains a man, and makes him say, I dare not do it; but when sanctified, it causes a man to fight against sin, and to say, I cannot do it; Gal. v. 17, "Ye cannot do the things that ye would:" the new nature is universally through a man, and where it is, it opposes. When Lot was in Sodom, he was vexed with all the sinful ways of the Sodomites; and when this "new spirit" is in a man, it is vexed with all the ways of the flesh.

(2.) This "new spirit" wars against sin as sin. The unsanctified conscience never doth so, therefore is carried against sin upon consideration it is a great sin, it brings damage, &c.; Darius, when Daniel was in the lions' den, Dan. vi. 18, his conscience troubled him; but if the sins be lesser, as omission of duties, vain thoughts, lusts, those beginnings of sin, they are dispensed with: but this "new spirit" is against every sin, be it little or great; it knows it is a breach of the law against the holy God, defiles, cost the blood of Christ.

(3.) By the weapons which are used. This "new spirit," where it is, useth spiritual arguments against sin, as God's love, God's dishonour, Christ's death, sense of pardon, the sealings and comforts of the Spirit, communion with God and Christ, love of holiness, the nature of grace, and scope of the gospel: see Col. iii. 4, 5; 1 John iii. 3; 2 Cor. vii. 1; Tit. ii. 11, 12. But an unregenerate heart, a natural conscience, uses arguments fetched from the curses of the law, terrors of death, fear of hell and damnation, shame of men, loss of friends, estate, the sovereignty of God over them.

(4.) By the continuance of this war, a hypocrite, that hath only a natural conscience, may go on skirmishing against sin a long time, but not for ever. An unenlightened, unsanctified conscience will either grow weary, or be bribed, or extenuate sin, or grow hard, seared, and commit sin without reluctance; but a man possessed with this "new spirit" will hold out the war to the end of his life; he grows not faint, he will not be bribed with aught, or all the world, flesh, and Satan have, to make a truce with sin; sin is sin to him, and shall not be lessened, he will fight it out, and die in the fight, rather than yield: Rom. vii. 24, "O wretched man!" saith Paul, "who shall deliver me?" &c.; 2 Tim. iv. 6, 7 "I am now ready to be offered, I have fought a good fight."

(5.) By the event. The man without this "new spirit," by all his combating against sin, gets it more restrained, and so more quiet, but not mortified; but where this "new spirit" is, there sin is wounded, crucified; Gal. v. 24, "They that are Christ's have crucified the flesh with the affections and lusts" thereof.

(5.) It works and acts in a new manner. Rom. vii. 6, Paul speaks of serving them in the "newness of the spirit, not in the oldness of the letter:" when you were under the law, that showed you your duty, provoked corruption, gave you no power to subdue the one, or do the other, and all the service then was after the old man, with much earthliness, difficulty, dulness, untowardly, inconstantly, and no better than dead works; but now you are under the gospel, the spirit hath begotten a new life in you, beautified you with new qualities and principles, laid in new strength, therefore now serve the Lord in newness of the spirit. And that is,

(1.) In a spiritual manner. The apostle speaks

of a "spiritual understanding," Col. i. 9; of "a spiritual house, a holy priesthood, to offer up spiritual sacrifices," 1 Pet. ii. 5. They being spiritualized, served the Lord in a spiritual manner, they had more spiritual conceptions of God and his worship, and put out more spiritual acts.

(2.) More readily. When this "new spirit" is in a man, he is like a ship which hath all its tacklings and sails up, and is ready to sail immediately; such a man is "prepared unto every good work," 2 Tim. ii. 21. Rom. i. 15, Paul was ready to preach the gospel; and ready to be bound and suffer, Acts xxi. 13; and the Corinthians had a ready mind, 2 Cor. viii. 19. Where this spirit is, there the wheels are oiled.

(3.) More delightfully. Rom. vii. 22, "I delight in the law of God after the inward man." Christ's yoke is easy, his commands are not grievous, the ways his wisdom prescribes "are ways of pleasantness," Prov. iii. 17: and Paul counted all the pains he took, hard things he suffered, but a recreation, Phil. iii. 8, "That I may win Christ;" he had as much pleasure and delight in them as men have in any games.

(4.) More beautifully. Before, they bungled, but now, they act more comelily, they pray and sing with the Spirit, and with understanding, 1 Cor. xiv. 15. Rom. xii. 8, he gives with simplicity, rules with diligence, shows mercy with cheerfulness; and, Cant. vii. 1, "How beautiful are thy feet with shoes, O prince's daughter!" the ways of the church are beautiful, actions comely.

(5.) More evenly and constantly. 2 Pet. i. 4, this "new spirit" is called "the divine nature," both because it is from God our Father, because all the children have it, because it cannot be altered, and also because it acts like nature, constantly, strongly; the eye is not weary with seeing, nor the ear with hearing.

(6.) It propounds new ends to itself, viz. God's glory. Before, a man's self was his centre and end: this "new spirit" came out from God, and works for God and to God; now it sees the nature of divine grace, beholds glory in that grace, and answers God's end; it doth act to the praise of the glory of his grace.

(7.) Makes cheerful and thankful. Col. iii. 10, after he had spoken of the new man, ver. 16, he tells them of singing with "grace in their hearts to the Lord." 2 Cor. v. 17, when old things are gone, and all new, &c. as in a house, when all is renewed in it, beautifully trimmed, &c., it cheers.

You have mention of "a new song" six times in the Psalms, xxxiii. 3; xl. 3; xlvi. 1; xcviii. 1; cxliv. 9; cxlix. 1: once in Isaiah xlii. 10: twice in the Revelation, v. 9; xiv. 3; sung with new fervency, as new things use to affect most; sung with the motions of the new spirit of grace, which mindeth more the new benefits by Christ, and the new covenant, than those by creation.

The twenty-four elders sang this new song, Rev. v. 9; the hundred and forty-four thousand redeemed from the earth learned it; it was a song of the new mercies given in redemption, justification, sanctification.

A new song, that is, an excellent song, with singular cheerfulness, made upon the giving in of some new mercy. [1.] New, because the singers were new, they had a "new spirit," a spirit of grace and glory in them. [2.] The matter of it was new, Christ's incarnation, passion, doctrine, miracles, ordinances, promises, church, kingdom, but especially the opening the book and redemption by his blood.

Non vulgare sed eximium. *Bez.*

Obs. 2. This "new spirit" is the work of God, and not of man; the Lord alone is the author and cause of it, man's will contributes nothing to it. "I will put a new spirit within you;" you oppose, resist, but I will overcome all that opposition and resistance, and plant new qualities, put a "new spirit" within you; I will work powerfully, efficaciously, so that the work shall proceed. The Arminians hold that the operation of God in the conversion of a sinner, or putting in this "new spirit," is *moralis suasio*, not *realis efficientia*, moral persuasion, not a real efficiency; that he doth not work immediately upon the mind and will, causing us to believe, to come to Christ, to live holily, but only propounds truths, which is sufficient that the understanding and affections are renewed with such power of God, and his grace, as cannot be withstood, but the will is quickened *resistibili modo*, in a manner which may be resisted; that, however it is sometimes renewed in the affectionate part of it, yet it continues unrenewed in the willing and nilling part thereof, *secundum modum libertatis*, according to the measure of liberty; that the grace of God doth nothing but accompany the will, consenting that all things supposed on God's part needful to the co-working this "new spirit," and regenerating the heart, yet a man may go without it, and still be as he was; that this "new spirit," and work of conversion, depends not upon any necessary causation or infallible event, from the intention or operation of God, but merely upon the will of man, and so is wholly contingent, and uncertain: all which are erroneous.

The papists also hold that there is free will in man before he hath this "new spirit," which doth concur and co-operate with God in the putting in this "new spirit" as an efficient cause thereof; and they pronounce him anathema, in the council of Trent, that says the will is merely passive in this work. Our divines hold it, and not only they, but the Lord himself; and if it be his judgment, how impious is that canon which puts an anathema upon the Lord. We cannot make our spirits new, nor any part of them; *Deus est causa totius entis*, God is the cause of all being, of this new spirit, of every quality in it, and every degree of every quality; Phil. ii. 13, "It is God which worketh in you, both to will and to do of his good pleasure." The will to have this "new spirit" is not from man's will, but from the grace of God; and that grace, when it is working and entering into the will, though the will of itself oppose it and reject it, yet because of the mighty power of God in the work, and strong intention of God to effect such a work, it cannot impede the introduction and forming of this "new spirit." It is called the circumcision of the heart, and is attributed to God, Deut. xxx. 6. It is not in the power of man to circumcise his own heart, God only doth it; and that he acts powerfully in this work of a "new spirit," see Ezek. xxxvi. 27, "I will put my spirit within you, and cause you to walk in my statutes, and ye shall keep my judgments, and do them." Though Satan, the god of this world, have got possession of a man, fortified himself in the strong holds which are in man; yet the Lord will bring in his Spirit, throw out Satan, throw down his holds, and cause a man, by the power of his Spirit and grace, to walk in contrary ways to what he did. Man in Scripture is said to be dead, and dead men neither desire, nor work their own resurrection; John v. 25, "The dead shall hear the voice of the Son of God." It must be a mighty and powerful voice which reacheth to a dead soul, and fetcheth it out of that condition; and when God speaks and

Sess. 6. de Justif. Can. 4.

John xv. 5, "Without me ye can do nothing," therefore all is from Christ.

works efficaciously to that purpose, the soul can no more withstand it than Lazarus could the call and power of Christ. Therefore saith Christ, John vi. 37, "All that the Father giveth me shall come to me;" they shall not prevent it by the liberty of their wills, the event is infallible, the causation necessary: otherwise God's election should be frustrate; for if man by his free will could keep out this "new spirit," and null all the operations of God about the working of it, what should become of his elect? his giving of men to Christ would be to no purpose.

Quest. Whereas they say, Propound suitable objects, and men will take them; as, propound honey to a bee, grass or a green bough to a sheep, and they will receive them; so let man have fit objects propounded to his understanding and will, and he will then close with them: and this is all which is done in the work of grace.

Answ. 1. See how derogatory this is to the Lord, that no more is given to his Spirit in working than is given to Satan. He propounds objects suitable to the sons of men, and if the Spirit propound divine objects, so doth Satan; Gen. iii. 5, "Ye shall be as gods, knowing good and evil." If the devil's objects be received or refused at the pleasure of man's will, so shall the Spirit's.

2. What suitableness is there between our carnal heart, and the spiritual high things of God? 1 Cor. ii. 14, "The natural man receiveth not the things of the Spirit of God; for they are foolishness unto him;" men must be made spiritual before they can discern or close with spiritual things. Honey is the proper food of a bee, and grass of a sheep, but spiritual things are not the proper food of a carnal heart: new wine is not for old bottles.

3. If suitable objects would do it, Christ propounded as suitable truths as ever any did, yet the Jews were not taken with them, John vi. 44; not any man, be he never so rational, have he never such rational objects propounded, that will hear, or can come.

Quest. Is it not in man's power to do aught towards the working this "new spirit" in himself? it seems otherwise, for the Lord saith, Ezek. xviii. 31, "Make you a new heart and a new spirit."

Answ. 1. Such phrases in Scripture import not liberty and power in man to do such things, but show his duty, and misery that he cannot do them. Man, having fallen, should set himself in the condition God placed him first in, he should cast away his sins, regain that image of God he hath lost, yet all his endeavours will not reach it: a man may with as much facility make a new sun, a new heaven, a new earth, a new world, as a new heart and "new spirit" within himself. David knew it, and therefore prayed, Psal. li. 10, "Create in me a clean heart," &c.

2. Neither is this command of God in vain, for the Lord gives what he commands; "Make you a new heart and a new spirit," saith God, here is his command; and in the verse we are on it is said, "I will put a new spirit within you;" so that, when a thing is commanded us to do which we cannot do, we are to look at the Lord to do it, who hath therefore made gracious promises to his people for that purpose. Man is commanded to fear God, Eccles. xii. 13; Isa. viii. 13; 1 Pet. ii. 17; and God hath promised to put his fear in his people's hearts; Jer. xxxii. 40, "I will put my fear in their hearts, and they shall not depart from me;" Hos. iii. 5, "They shall fear the Lord and his goodness." Prov. iv. 5, 7, we are bid to "get wisdom and understanding;" Isa. i. 17, "Learn to do well;" and the promise is, Isa. liv. 13, "All thy children shall be taught of the Lord." 2 Pet. iii. 18, we are commanded to "grow in grace;" but we can no more make grace to grow in our hearts, than the gardener can make the tree to grow in the orchard; therefore the promise is, Psal. xcii. 12—15, "The righteous shall flourish like the palm tree: he shall grow like a cedar in Lebanon. Those that be planted in the house of the Lord shall flourish in the courts of our God. They shall still bring forth fruit in old age; they shall be fat and flourishing; to show that the Lord is upright." Col. iii. 5. "Mortify your members which are upon the earth," that is the command, and, Micah vii. 19, "He will subdue our iniquities."

3. "Make you a new heart," that is, declare you have a new heart wrought in you. Saith Junius, God makes the new heart ἐνεργείᾳ, by effectual working, man doth it φανερώσει, by manifestation.

"I will take the stony heart out of their flesh." לב האבן *cor lapidis.* The word "heart" hath been opened formerly, and by it we comprehend and mean the understanding, will, affections, and conscience.

"Stony," or stone heart, or stoniness of heart. It is a metaphorical expression, taken from the nature of a stone, and notes out the spiritual stoniness and hardness which is in the heart.

1. A stone is senseless, and stirs not; Exod. xv. 16, "They shall be as still as a stone:" such is a stony heart; it is *cor sine sensu*, a heart without feeling, as in Nabal, 1 Sam. xxv. 37, "His heart died within him, and he became as a stone," senseless.

A stone feels no weight; lay the heaviest burden upon it, smite the hardest strokes, it is not sensible of any. Let a stony heart have a world of sin, and guilt in it, lying upon it, yet no feeling of it; Eph. iv. 19, "Who being past feeling have given themselves over unto lasciviousness, to work all uncleanness with greediness:" they had lost all sense of evil in sin, and went on without any check. Let men swear, lie, deceive, whore, &c. they feel no evil in it; let them be upon the pikes, like the young man in Proverbs chap. vii. going as "an ox to the slaughter, as a bird to the snare, they know not that it is for their lives;" tell such of danger, they are not sensible.

The Jews had stony hearts, and see how senseless they were, Matt. xiii. 15, "This people's heart is waxed gross, and their ears are dull of hearing, and their eyes they have closed; lest at any time they should see with," &c. This is five times more mentioned in the New Testament, Mark iv. 12; Luke viii. 10; John xii. 40; Acts xxviii. 26; Rom. xi. 8, fetched all from Isa. vi. 9.

Hence those expressions, "The unjust knoweth no shame," Zeph. iii. 5; they cannot blush, Jer. vi. 15; "they are impudent children," Ezek. ii. 4; their "brow brass," Isa. xlviii. 4.

2. It is hard and yields not; strike a stone oft, it yields not to the stroke. In Job xli. 24, speaking of the leviathan, he saith, "His heart is as firm as a stone; yea, as hard as a piece of the nether millstone;" brass, arrows, darts, and spears, are as stubble and straw to him, they will not enter. So is it with a stony heart, nothing enters; Zech. vii. 11, "They refused to hearken, and pulled away the shoulder, and stopped their ears, that they should not hear. Yea, they made their hearts as an adamant stone;" and that is *lapis indomabilis*, it will not yield at all. No reproofs, threatenings, afflictions, judgments, did prevail with their stony hearts; therefore, Isa. i. 5, saith God, "Why should ye be stricken any more? ye will revolt more and more." Man's natural heart is an unteachable, intractable heart; no prayers, no tears, no truths, no arguments, no mercies, no judg-

ments will conquer it; it is inexorable: Isa. xxvi. 10, "Let favour be showed to the wicked, yet will he not learn righteousness."

Hence two things:

(1.) Tenacity of opinions, principles, and conclusions, though never so false and corrupt. Jer. viii. 5, "They hold fast deceit;" chap. iv. 14, "O Jerusalem, how long shall thy vain thoughts lodge within thee?" They thought their worship was right, that God was pleased with their inventions and additions, that the Lord would not depart from the temple, &c.

(2.) Obstinacy in their ways, continuance in their old practices. Jer. xvii. 23, "They obeyed not, neither inclined their ear, but made their neck stiff, that they might not hear, nor receive instruction;" chap. v. 3, "They have made their faces harder than a rock, they have refused to return;" Judg. ii. 19, "They ceased not from their own doings, nor from their stubborn way."

3. Man's heart resists. Lam. iii. 16, "He hath also broken my teeth with gravel stones:" while a man thinks to break the stones with his teeth, they conquer by their hardness, and break the teeth. Adamants and other stones repel the force of the stroke, and oft break the instrument which strikes them; so do stony and hard hearts; Matt. xxiii. 37, "O Jerusalem, Jerusalem, thou that killest the prophets, and stonest them which are sent unto thee, how often would I," &c. When Christ preached unto them, they yielded not to his doctrine, but resisted, and sought the ruin of his person; Luke iv. 28, 29, "All they in the synagogue, when they heard these things, were filled with wrath, and rose up, and thrust him out of the city, and led him unto the brow of the hill, that they might cast him down headlong." Here was the stoniness of their hearts made evident fully, they would not receive Christ, but kill him. Such hearts make men possessed with them.

(1.) Contradictory to the truth; their tongues are busy. Rom. x. 21, the Jews are called "a disobedient and gainsaying people," they contradicted the prophets: 2 Chron. xxxvi. 16, "They mocked the messengers of God:" so Jer. xliv. 16, "As for the word which thou hast spoken unto us in the name of the Lord, we will not hearken unto thee. But we will certainly do whatsoever," &c.

(2.) Contentious. Rom. ii. 8, "Unto them that are contentious, and do not obey the truth:" hard hearts yield not to the truth, but contend against the truth. The Pharisees and others did not only cavil at Christ's doctrine, but plotted, acted, and contended against it and him: John xi. 47, 48, the chief priests and Pharisees gathered "a council, and said, What do we? If we let him thus alone, all men will believe on him," &c.; ver. 53, "From that day forth they took counsel together for to put him to death." God told Jeremiah that the Jews should fight against him, Jer. i. 19; and xxvi. 8, 9, you shall find it made good; when he had prophesied against their carnal confidence in the temple, they were gathered together against him, laid hands upon him, and threatened him with death.

4. A stone hath a strong tendency downwards. Exod. xv. 5, "They sank into the bottom as a stone:" stones hasten downward to the bottom, and they move not upwards at all; if by force you throw a stone upwards, it falls down again with swiftness. Such is the nature of a stony heart, it moves not God or Christ-ward, but sin and hell-ward; that is the proper motion of it, being weighty, and cannot but move downward: Prov. vii. 27, speaking of the adulteress, whose heart is hardened in wickedness, he saith, "Her house is the way to hell, going down to the chambers of death. Eph. iv. 19, "Being past feeling, they work all uncleanness with greediness:" there is a strong inclination to, and greediness of, committing sin, and every sin is a step to hell; Prov. ii. 18, "Her house inclineth unto death, and her paths unto the dead." Ezek. iii. 7, it is said, "All the house of Israel are impudent and hard-hearted:" and Ezek. vi. 9, their heart is said to be whorish; and why whorish? because it leads to death and hell, as the whorish woman's house doth. A stony heart is an earthly heart, and so an enemy to the cross of Christ, Phil. iii. 18, 19; that is, to all of Christ, it looks not upwards.

Prov. ii. 18.

Obj. It is said, a stony heart is not yieldable, teachable, receives not impression of any thing: Did not the stony ground receive the word? Matt. xiii. 20; if so, how is it true which hath been affirmed?

Answ. 1. It is said by Matthew, the seed "fell upon stony places," chap. xiii. 5, and "upon a rock," Luke viii. 6; it fell not into the stones, or into the rock: but some fell not only on the good ground, as Luke hath it, but into the good ground, as Matthew relates it, chap. xiii. 8.

2. There is a double reception of the word. First, a superficial, and secondly, a solid, reception of the word, which the place holds out; for that seed which fell upon stony places "lacked moisture," saith Luke, had "no deepness, no root," saith Matthew. It affected the natural fleshiness of the heart, but the spiritual hardness in it suffered it not to root, to enter, abide: the novelty and rationalness of the word caused them to rejoice, but the spiritualness of it was opposed by their stony hearts. Secondly, the solid reception is, when there is a deep impression made upon the heart, a thorough entrance into it, so that it roots, abides, and brings forth fruit: James i. 21, he calls it "the ingrafted word;" now it cannot be ingrafted into a stony stock, there is no life, no tenderness in such a stock; it may be propounded to such a heart, it cannot enter, unite, and grow.

"Out of their flesh." Flesh is sometimes put for corruption, or corrupt nature; Rom. vii. 18, "In my flesh dwelleth no good thing;" so it is not taken here: sometimes for the body of man; Psal. xxxvii. 3, "There is no soundness in my flesh," that is, in my body: sometimes for the whole man; Rom. iii. 20, "By the law shall no flesh be justified in his sight;" and so in Luke iii. 6, "All flesh shall see the salvation of God;" and thus it is taken here, "out of their flesh, it is out of them, out of the whole man.

Obs. 1. Men's hearts naturally are stony and hard. Some diseases are hereditary, even the stone in many persons. This stoniness is so in all, not a man born but hath a stony heart, a stony spirit; Ezek. iii. 7, "All the house of Israel are hard-hearted," young and old.

There is a natural hardness of the heart, and a contracted. Original sin, which is common to all, and comes with all, makes the heart hard; and actual sins make the heart stony, very hard; every sin contracts more stoniness, and where sin abounds, there stoniness abounds: hence the Scripture speaks of hearts like adamants; Zech. vii. 12, "They have made their hearts as an adamant" by their sins, they have brought their hearts to such a high degree of stoniness; Isa. xlviii. 4, "I knew that thou art obstinate, and thy neck is an iron sinew, and thy brow brass;" which sets out the great hardness they had contracted by their sin. Is there any thing harder than stone, iron, and brass? unto these are their hardened hearts, necks, and brows compared.

(1.) The spiritual hardness spreads itself into the understanding. Rom. xi. 7, "The rest were blinded."

Blindness respects the mind, the understanding, and it is such a blinding as burdens; their ignorance and unbelief blinded and hardened them. In the night we have the hardest frosts, &c.

Heb. v. 11, the apostle tells the Hebrews, they were "dull of hearing;" they had been long taught, yet scarcely understood the principles of religion: Luke xxiv. 25, "O fools, and slow of heart to believe."

(2.) Into the will and affection. Saith Christ, "Ye will not come to me, that ye might have life," John v. 40; there was a stone, stubbornness and obstinacy, in their wills. Did not Christ preach powerfully and spiritually? did he not command, threaten, promise, present strong arguments, tender the greatest mercies, bear with the greatest patience, weep over Jerusalem with the most pathetical and sacred tears, saying most compassionately, "O Jerusalem, Jerusalem," yet Jerusalem would not? Do not the ministers of Christ now beseech you, in his stead, to leave your sinful courses, and to come in, yet, &c.?

(3.) Into the conscience. Paul tells you of "conscience seared with a hot iron," 1 Tim. iv. 2. When any part of the body is seared with a hot iron, it grows hard, and feels nothing; such were the consciences of men then, and are now; they are so brawny and stony, that tell them of danger, judgments, death, hell, eternal damnation, that their sins are great, grievous, subjecting them every moment to all the vengeance of an infinite Deity, they are not troubled at it; tell them that all the curses in God's book due to sinners will come upon them, their hearts fail them not, their consciences are still, &c.

Now this stoniness of heart is a great evil; it is unthankful, what mercies soever it hath given in, insensible of all spiritual good, it is unyieldable to any ordinance, it resists the truth, and Spirit of truth; Acts vii. 51, "Ye stiff-necked and uncircumcised in heart and ears, ye do always resist the Holy Ghost: as your fathers did, so do ye." It is contradicting, and contending against the Lord and his ways; it is tending swiftly to destruction, for it is impenitent, it neither will nor can repent.

Obs. 1. It is the Lord that takes away the stony heart out of men; I will do it. It is not in the power of man to remove the stone out of the heart; he may get the stone out of the kidneys, out of the bladder, but not out of the heart. We may all say, "Who shall roll away this stone?" as they said, Mark xvi. 3; and the answer must be, Not an angel, not any creature, but only the Lord. God tells them that they should take away all the detestable things out of the land; but he would take away the stone out of their heart, and the stony heart out of them.

It is the work of free grace. Nothing is in a stony heart to move God to take it away, but enough to move God to destroy it, and him that hath it; it is merely good will puts him on to do it.

It is the work of omnipotent power to do it. Some read it, *auferam*, I will take away; some, *removebo*, I will remove; some, *extraham*, I will draw out of you, intimating, there must be a mighty power to do it; when you would remove a great stone, you bring a strong team, and tacklings, to draw it out of its place, so here.

It is a great mercy to have this stone removed. The stone in the heart is a great plague, yea, greater than all the plagues of Egypt; Pharaoh's hard heart was worse than all them; the removal, therefore, of it, is a greater mercy than the removal of all those judgments.

It is a heart incapable of reproof; that profits not by any means of grace whatsoever, that is not kindly affected with the greatest mercies or judgments. It is a heart that hates holiness, and the power of godliness, a heart that pleaseth itself in the ways of wickedness; it is a heart the devil lives in, and works his will by.

Quest. Whether doth God remove the stone totally out of the hearts of his people at first conversion, or while they are in this life?

Answ. God doth this work gradually, it is not all done at once. The apostles were converted, yet all hardness was not out of their hearts, Mark vi. 52; viii. 17. Stones are digged out of the quarries by degrees, and rocks hewn in pieces in time: so is it here, God breaks and separates the stoniness of the heart, some one day, some another day, and it is doing all a man's life: as a man subject to the stone and gravel, voids some one day, some another, and is not perfectly cured till death, so in this spiritual stoniness. Neither let any say, Then the heart is stony still, and in the same condition it was before. Not so; for though there be some stoniness in it, yet is it not stony; there is softness introduced, and the denomination is from that, "I will give them an heart of flesh."

Quest. If there be stoniness in the hearts of those that are in covenant with God, how shall I know the difference between the stoniness in the godly and that in the wicked?

Answ. 1. The stoniness of the wicked grows greater and greater, every day they are more stony, they grow "worse and worse," 2 Tim. iii. 13; but the stoniness in the godly grows less and less, they use all means to abate it; in the one it is incurable, in the other it is curing. 2 Chron. xxviii. 22.

2. That in the saints is rather accidental than essential, an external crustiness rather than an intrinsical hardness. It is an iciness, not a true stoniness: water may become ice, but not stone; it will thaw and melt again, it freezes and thaws oft; not so with a stone, or iron, they have intrinsical, essential hardness.

3. The godly feel the stone in their hearts, complain and cry out of it as a grievous evil; but the wicked feel it not, in them it reigns, is in full power and strength; Eph. iv. 19, they are "past feeling."

4. The stoniness in the godly is rather a stoniness against sin, than a stoniness of sin; he is facile to good, but obstinate to evil; Gen. xxxix. 9, "How then can I do this great wickedness, and sin against God?" Psal. cxix. 115, "Depart from me, ye evildoers; for I will keep the commandments of my God:" he had strong temptations to sin from the wicked, but he would not be drawn by them. But it is otherwise with the wicked, they are obstinate to good, and prone to evil; "they work all uncleanness with greediness," Eph. iv. 19; and cease not "from their stubborn way," Judg. ii. 19. So the Samaritans, who were fallen to false worship, said, in the stoutness and pride of their hearts, "The bricks are fallen down, but we will build with hewn stones," Isa. ix. 9, 10; and Mal. iii. 13, their words were stout against God. And Saul, a wicked king, it is said, he "rejected the word of the Lord," 1 Sam. xv. 23. The builders who had stony hearts rejected Christ the Corner-stone, Matt. xxi. 42; "lawyers rejected the counsel of God," Luke vii. 30.

"And will give them an heart of flesh." We have opened the word "heart" before, at the beginning of the verse, and showed it comprehended understanding, will, affections, and conscience.

"Flesh." Here it is set in opposition to stony, and differs from the word "flesh" mentioned immediately before; there "flesh" implied substance, their persons; here it implies a quality, tenderness, softness. Flesh is in itself a tender thing; sin hardens it, and makes it stony, but God would take out the stoniness, the hardness thereof, and make it tender and soft.

There is a double tenderness spoken of in Scripture:

1. A natural tenderness. 2 Chron. xiii. 7, "When Rehoboam was young and tender-hearted, and could not withstand them;" he was not hardened in wickedness, but being young, had a natural tenderness, which made him facile and yieldable to the onsets of others: but this is not the tenderness we are to speak of.

2. A spiritual tenderness. Eph. iv. 32, "Be ye kind one to another, tender-hearted." A mother hath natural tenderness to her child; have you answerable spiritual tenderness, such as is in the Lord, who is said to be full of pity and tenderness, Jam. v. 11; and this is the tenderness here meant.

This spiritual tenderness is a gracious disposition of the heart, wrought by the Spirit, easily admitting or receiving whatever spirituals are propounded unto it.

It is a gracious disposition, not natural, nor moral; neither parents nor education convey aught unto it. Grace is a tender thing, and makes tender; Luke i. 78, it is called "tender mercy of our God," and that makes a tender heart, a gracious disposition in it like itself.

Wrought by the Spirit. It is not the law works it; that may break the heart into pieces, as a hammer doth a stone, but not melt it and make it tender; it is the gospel and fire of the Spirit in it which produceth that effect; not the plough, but rain, which softens the ground: David saith, Psal. lxv. 13, "Thou makest it soft with showers." The Corinthians' hearts were not tables of stone, but fleshy tables; the Spirit had made them such, and written the gospel in them, 2 Cor. iii. 3. The Galatians received the Spirit, not by the preaching of the law, but by the preaching of faith, Gal. iii. 2, and that Spirit made their hearts tender. When Job was in his great afflictions, they softened not his heart, but he saith, God made soft his heart, Job xxiii. 16; that was, by his Spirit.

Easily admitting or receiving. This is the formal, intrinsical nature of this tenderness, that it is like wax taking in impressions. The stony heart yields not, but resists; this resists not, but yields; like Gideon's fleece, it drunk in the dew as fast as it fell, Judges vi.; like the soft earth, which drinks in the rain, not like the rocks and mountains, which shoot it off, Heb. vi. 7. Hence saith Moses, Deut. xxxiii. 3, speaking of saints who have tender hearts, and sit at God's feet, "Every one shall receive of thy words." And Paul, speaking of a natural man, 1 Cor. ii. 14, he saith, "The natural man receiveth not the things of the Spirit;" his heart is stony, not tender, and so without a capacity of receiving whatever spiritual things are propounded. It is ready to say, as Samuel, "Speak; for thy servant heareth," 1 Sam. iii. 10. Let God, or any from God, offer any spiritual things unto a tender heart, it is ready to receive them; Acts ix. 6, saith Saul, "Lord, what wilt thou have me to do?" propound what thou pleasest unto me.

Discoveries of this tenderness:

1. It is affected with, and mourns for, that hardness which remains in it, that it is not more tender and wrought upon by the mercies, ordinances, judgments of God. David was sensible of his hardness and deadness, and therefore cries oft to God for quickening; Psal. cxix. 154, "Quicken me according to thy word;" "Quicken me according to thy judgments," ver. 156; "Quicken me according to thy loving-kindness," ver. 159.

2. It feels the least sins and risings of corruption; as some bodies are so tender, that they discern any distempers stir in them presently, others are hardy, and discern little, till it come to some dangerous disease. It is not so here, a heart spiritually tender is sensible of the least sin: the least mote in the eye, crumb in the windpipe, are troublesome to them; and so the rising of corruption, the very being of sin in the heart, is troublesome to a tender heart; Paul saw and felt the "law in his members, warring against," &c.

3. It hearkens and yields to reproofs. Salt will not enter into a stone, but into flesh, seasons it, and makes it savoury. Reproofs are salt, they enter into fleshy and tender hearts: Prov. xvii. 10, "A reproof entereth more into a wise man than an hundred stripes into a fool;" his heart is tender, and a reproof presently makes impression, the door opens and it goes in: whereas the heart of a fool will not be beat open with many stripes; *nec credit, nec cedit*, neither does it believe nor yield; but the tender-hearted, wise, and godly, believe, and yield: David, Psal. cxli. 5, "Let the righteous smite me; it shall be a kindness: and let him reprove me; it shall be an excellent oil." Reproofs soften tender hearts, harden stony ones, Prov. xxix. 1.

4. It hath a lively sense of God's dishonour, and the saints' wrong.

(1.) Of God's dishonour. Psal. cxix. 136, "Rivers of waters run down mine eyes, because they keep not thy law." When David saw God's worship corrupted, heard his name blasphemed, beheld his law openly violated, his tender heart bled within him, melted into tears, and wept abundantly, that the infinite, holy, glorious, great God should be so dishonoured by sinful dust and ashes. And Psal. lxix. 9, "The reproaches of them that reproached thee are fallen upon me;" David reproved men that reproached God by their lips and lives, and they reproached him for it. Lot's righteous soul was "vexed with the filthy conversation of the wicked," 2 Pet. ii. 7.

(2.) It much feels the saints' wrong, and church's suffering. 2 Cor. xi. 29, "Who is offended, and I burn not?" When any member of the church suffered, Paul was afflicted, grieved, as a man burnt with fire, and the more tender the flesh is, the greater is the pain; and so in the heart, the tenderer that is, the greater sense and pain hath it of others' sufferings, especially the church's. Read Psal. lxxix. and lxxx. and you shall see how greatly Asaph was afflicted for the miseries of the church; the saints suffered much without, and he suffered much within; they were broken in their states and comforts, and he was broken in his heart and spirit: so Jer. ix. 1, "Oh that my head were waters, and mine eyes a fountain of tears, that I might weep day and night for the slain of the daughter of my people!" Acts xii. 5, when Peter, &c. As Christ was tender of the saints when persecuted by Saul, Acts ix. so every member of Christ, participating of his tenderness, feels in his degree the injuries done to the rest.

5. It trembles at the word of God. Isa. lxvi. 2, contrition of spirit, and trembling at the word, do go together; there is such majesty, authority, holiness, severity, and glory, in the word, that a tender heart trembleth at it. 2 Chron. xxxiv. 27, Josiah's heart was tender, he trembled and humbled himself before the Lord when the law was read before him. And those in Ezra "trembled at the words of the God of Israel," chap. ix. 4.

6. It is obedient unto the call and will of God. Let the Lord call, it saith, Here I am, what wilt thou have me to do? whither shall I go? I am

ready for it. Abraham had a tender heart, and when God called for his Isaac, and bade him go and offer him upon mount Moriah, Gen. xxii. he had a tractable heart, he yielded presently to the Lord, without any dispute or delay. A tender heart is an obediential heart: Josiah was tender-hearted, and he did the will of God most thoroughly of any of the kings of Judah, none of them did reform so as he did, 2 Chron. xxxv. 18. David was a man of a tender spirit, and he fulfilled all the will of God, Acts xiii. 22.

7. It is tender towards others. A tender heart hath a tender tongue and a tender hand; the man that hath such a heart speaks evil of none, doth harm to none; such a one is merciful to his beast, much more to men; he pities those who are in a perishing way, and would pull them out of the fire; the law of kindness is in his lips, and actions of love are in his hands. Job's heart was soft, Job xxiii. 16; and you may find what his words and actions were, chap. xxix. 11—13, 15, 16; "When the ear heard me, then it blessed me;" he spake such comfortable words to them, gave them such good counsel, that they blessed him for it; and his actions were, delivering the poor and fatherless, helping the blind and lame, and making the widow's heart to rejoice. Tenderness of heart breeds tenderness towards others. It is said of Esau, he was red, "all over like a hairy garment," Gen. xxv. 25; he was red and rough, bloody and bitter. It were well there were no sons of Esau in our days, men bloody and bitter, seeking the ruin of plain-hearted Jacobs. If others, by their rough speeches and dealings, do show the hardness of their hearts, let us, by the softness of our tongues, and bounty of our hands, show the tenderness of our hearts. Eph. iv. 32, "Be ye kind one to another, tender-hearted, forgiving one another, even as God for Christ's sake hath forgiven you."

8. It entertains and retains the motions and truths of God's Spirit. A tender heart will not suffer the Spirit to knock long at the door, and then go away grieved, but it opens quickly, and receives the message. When the Spirit came to Peter, Acts x. 19, 20, and bade him go to Cornelius, and preach Christ unto him, he went immediately. When the gospel was preached to the Thessalonians, in demonstration of the Spirit, it is said, they received it "with joy of the Holy Ghost;" that joy of the Holy Ghost may as well refer to the Holy Ghost itself, who rejoiced at their speedy receiving the word and Spirit in it, as to the Thessalonians, who had joy wrought in them by receiving of the word. 2 Cor. iii. 3, the Corinthians had fleshy hearts, and they are called "the epistle of Christ;" and why? because the Spirit had wrote the gospel in them with ease. Moses had much ado to write the law in the tables of stone, but the Spirit did it easily in the fleshy tables of their hearts. Those truths which are written in the heart, are held so fast, that men will rather lose their lives than lose them.

Obs. 1. A tender heart is a choice and great mercy; where this is, the understanding is apprehensive of divine things. The Lord Christ, who was without sin, and so nothing but tenderness, was quick of understanding, Isa. xi. 3; and the more free from sin our hearts are, the quicker our understandings will be. Matt. xiii. 15, where there is a gross and hard heart, there is an un-understanding heart, an unperceiving heart, Mark viii. 17; on the contrary, where a tender heart is, there is the clearest understanding.

The will is pliable to the truth of the gospel. Rom. vi. 17, "Ye have obeyed from the heart that form of doctrine which was delivered you," and into which ye were delivered.

The conscience is awake, and will not endure the guilt of any sin to lie upon it. Peter had sinned, but he goes out and weeps bitterly.

The affections are lively, and stir much towards God. David had a tender heart, and how strongly did his affections stir after God! Psal. xlii. 1, 2, "As the hart panteth after the water brooks, so panteth my soul after thee, O God. My soul thirsteth for God, for the living God; when shall I come and appear before God?" lxiii. 8, "My soul followeth hard after thee;" and lxix. 9, "The zeal of thy house hath eaten me up." It is that the Lord intends to write his whole will in; Jer. xxxi. 33, "I will put my law in their inward parts, and write it in their hearts;" first he will make them soft, and then write in the law and gospel. It receives discipline, correction; Jer. v. 3, "Thou hast stricken them, but they have refused to receive correction: they have made their faces harder," &c. A hard heart doth not receive correction, but a tender one doth.

Obs. 2. It is the gift of God, he gives this tender heart unto us. We can harden our hearts through sinning, but we cannot soften them, being once hardened, by any means we use. Tenderness of heart is a special grace, so is oneness of heart, newness of spirit, and all these are from God, who is styled "The God of all grace," 1 Pet. v. 10: there is not any grace but what is from God, he is the author of it. In this case of a heart of flesh, he puts his hand into the heart and pulls out the stone, and puts in tenderness. He that can turn stones into children, Matt. iii. 9, is he that turns stony hearts into flesh; and this he doth freely, there is no motive of his will; Phil. ii. 13, his working is of his good pleasure; James i. 18, "Of his own will begat he us." Not the pleasure of man, or his will, appears in this work, God consults not with man about it, but doth the work himself, "I will take away the stone," &c.; it is exclusive, and shuts out all: hence those sweet promises, Isa. xli. 18—20, "I will open rivers in high places, and fountains in the midst of the valleys: I will make the wilderness a pool of water, and the dry land springs of water. I will plant in the wilderness the cedar, the shittah tree, and the myrtle, and the oil tree; I will set in the desert the fir tree, and the pine, and the box tree together: that they may see, and know, and consider, and understand together, that the hand of the Lord hath done this, and the Holy One of Israel hath created it."

Isa. xliv. 3, "I will pour floods upon the dry ground."

God softens the heart by dropping his word upon it; Deut. xxxii. 2, "My doctrine shall drop as the rain," &c.; by the blood of Christ, by revealing his free grace, &c.

Ver. 20. *That they may walk in my statutes, and keep mine ordinances, and do them: and they shall be my people, and I will be their God.*

Here is the end of God's grace and goodness towards them, with an asserting of such to be his people, and his promise to be their God.

Obs. God multiplies mercies when he is in a way of mercy; when he is giving out promises, he gives not one, or two, but many. Jer. xxxi. 33, 34, there is a heap of promises: so in Ezek. xxxvi. 25—29, there are eight or nine promises together. Hos. xiv. 4—7, promise after promise is given out. Isa. lx. is full of sweet promises, one after another. This is a sweet subject to meditate upon, but I come to open the words.

"That they may walk." Walking here is metaphorical, taken from the motion of the body, moving by steps from place to place; and is applied to the conversation and life of man, in a spiritual sense, and imports progress in the way of God, Psal. cxix. 1.

בחקתי "In my statutes." The Hebrew word *chukkim*, notes rites pertaining to the ceremonial law, called also δικαιωματα; and not only so, but *chukkim* includes the whole ceremonial law. The Seventy do sometimes translate it ἐντολαι, commandments, which *mitzuoth* properly signifies, containing the moral law, or ten commandments, and not δικαιωματα; but, Deut. iv. 40, they render מצות by δικαιωματα, and חקים by ἐντολας. Eph. ii. 15, Paul calls *chukkim*, νόμον τῶν ἐντολῶν ἐν δόγμασι, The law of commandments in ordinances.

משפטי "Mine ordinances." *Mishphatim*, κρίματα, judgments. These some refer to the outward policy of Israel, their civil estate, but statutes and ordinances are used promiscuously; and here by them I conceive is meant the whole law of God revealed.

This walking in his statutes is set out in holy writ by such expressions as these, viz. walking after the Lord, Deut. xiii. 4; walking before God, 1 Kings ix. 4; walking in the light of the Lord, Isa. ii. 5; walking in the truth, 3 John 4; walking in the name of the Lord, Micah iv. 5; walking according to rule, Gal. vi. 16; and, walking with God, Gen. vi. 9.

"Keep mine ordinances." Keeping imports,

1. Remembering: Luke ii. 51, Mary "kept all these sayings in her heart."

2. Holding fast: 2 Tim. i. 14, "The good thing committed unto thee keep," that is, hold fast. Here we must take in both remembering and holding fast but in order to doing; men may know, remember, and hold fast the mind of God, but not do the same: Deut. v. 1, "Hear, O Israel, the statutes and judgments which I speak in your ears this day, and keep, and do them;" the Hebrew is, keep to do them.

"Do them." Doing implies,

1. The performing and practice of them: Psal. xv. 5, "He that doeth these things shall never be moved."

2. Fulfilling of things required: 1 Kings v. 8, saith Hiram to Solomon, "I will do all thy desire," that is, fulfil thy desire. Both may be understood here, not simply to do, but to do exactly.

Obs. 1. The end of God's giving us temporal and spiritual mercies is, that we should be obedient unto him. He gathered them out of Babylon, planted them in Canaan, gives them oneness of heart, newness of spirit, &c.; and why? that they might walk in his statutes, and keep his ordinances. God hireth us with mercies to do his will: Psal. cv. 43—45, "He brought forth his people with joy, and his chosen with gladness; and gave them the lands of the heathen: and they inherited the labour of the people; that they might observe his statutes, and keep his law." 2 Sam. xii. 7—9, David was obliged by God's bounty to obedience. Why did God so much for his vineyard, Isa. v. 2, but that it might bring forth grapes? the end of all mercies and means afforded us, was to make it fruitful in obedience; all in God's works and in his word are so many inducements to obedience. God hath given us the earth, and fulness of it, and the end is to provoke us thereby to walk in his statutes; he hath given us his good word, choice ordinances, heavenly counsels, precious promises, profitable commands, holy examples, and his end in all these is to quicken us up to obedience. It is the end of election, 1 Pet. i. 2; it is the end of redemption, Luke i. 74, 75; it is the end of our new creation, Eph. ii. 10. Paul beseeches the Romans by the mercies of God, to present their bodies a living sacrifice, holy and acceptable unto God. Our mercies should prevail with us; we are planted in a good land, we have the dews of heaven, and fatness of the earth. God hath done great things amongst us, and for us, we have had wonderful deliverances, and shall not we be encouraged thereby to walk in the statutes of our God? Deut. xi. 7, 8, "Your eyes have seen all the great acts of the Lord which he did; therefore shall ye keep all the commandments which I command you this day." Let the great things we have seen and heard put us upon obeying the Lord, and so obeying him that our obedience may be, (1.) General; God requires you should "walk in all his ways," Deut. x. 12. (2.) Hearty, yea, with the whole heart, Deut. xxvi. 16. (3.) Constant, Deut. iv. 9; Gal. vi. 9. (4.) Willing, cheerful, Phil. ii. 14; Deut. xxviii. 47. (5.) With strength and courage, Josh. xxiii. 6. If we do not walk in the statutes of the Lord, and keep his commands, we know not God, 1 John ii. 3, 4; we do not love God, 1 John v. 3, nor Christ, John xiv. 15; our prayers will be unfruitful and successless, 1 John iii. 22.

Obs. 2. Note, that walking in God's statutes, keeping his ordinances, and doing his will, do evidence the work of grace in the heart, and what the man is. God would give them oneness of heart, newness and tenderness of spirit, that they might walk, keep, do, &c. If then they did so, this declared what was within. Luke i. 6, "Zacharias and Elisabeth were both righteous before God, walking in all the commandments and ordinances of the Lord blameless;" their walking witnessed their righteousness: see 1 John iii. 10; ii. 29. Luke vi. 44, whatever the fruit is, such is the tree; figs do not grow upon thorns, nor grapes upon brambles, where you find grapes it is a vine: and not only doth God and Christ know them, but, Matt. vii. 16, "Ye shall know them by their fruits;" not by their leaves, but their fruits; not some few actions, but by a daily observation of them. Sometimes delay and time, and always attention, is required to discern them: 2 Tim. iii. 5, "Having a form of godliness," &c. this may be discerned, for, ver. 9, "Their folly shall be manifest to all men." James ii. 18, works are the glass, picture, child of faith: Adam begat a son after his image, and faith begets children after its own image: Abraham's offering of his son declared his faith, Heb. xi. 17. Works justify faith, and faith justifies the man. Some doubt whether works will prove grace, whether sanctification will evidence justification; but John tells us there is a witness of water, as well as of blood, and of the Spirit, 1 John v. 8. If the law written in books may be known, and the sense of it evidenced by commentaries, surely the law written in the heart may be known and evidenced by works.

Obs. 3. Grace in the heart will appear in the life. If there be a new spirit, a tender heart, there will be walking in the statutes. A new spirit cannot be imprisoned within, but it will break out into action; when the seed is sown in good ground, it will not lie long under-ground, but spring forth, Mark iv. 20; grace is light, and that will manifest itself, ver. 21, 22. God hath determined that hidden things shall be manifested; grace cannot always be hid, 1 Pet. ii. 9; such virtue will out, 1 Thess. i. 5—7. The Corinthians were the epistle of Paul written in his heart, read and known of all men. The Romans' faith was spoken of throughout the world, Rom. i. 8; that was, in all the churches of the world: so their obedience, chap. xvi. 19. There be divers things cannot be hidden, as the light, fire, life, the wind, a spring; and of this nature is grace, which is all those: it is light, and fire; John was a burning and shining light: it is life, Luke xv. 24; it is the wind of the Spirit, Cant. iv. 16; John iii. 8; it is a spring, John vii. 38. A good tree cannot bring forth evil fruit, and it cannot but bring forth good fruit; Acts iv. 20, "We cannot but speak the things we have seen and heard." Paul, when converted, presently said, "Lord, what wilt thou have me to do?" he would not be idle, but doing the will of the Lord Christ.

Obs. 4. It is not from man's strength but God's grace, that any walk in his statutes, keep his ordinances, and do them. I will take away the stony heart, give them an heart of flesh, and put a new spirit within them, that they may walk, keep, and do. Man is a feeble, impotent creature, he cannot think a good thought, make a hair white or black; and how then can he walk in the statutes of the Lord? Satan is powerful and politic, he makes strong assaults, and such, as that, if God did not assist by his grace, we should fall every moment; hence those expressions of David, Psal. cxix. 5, 35, 36. Moses and the covenant of works called for obedience, contributed no strength; but God in Christ gives strength to do what is called for: Ezek. xxxvi. 27, "I will put my spirit within you, and cause you to walk in my statutes, and ye shall keep my judgments, and do them." See Heb. xiii. 20, 21.

Obs. 5. God's statutes and ordinances are to be the saints' way to walk in, and rule to walk by. Statutes, ordinances, are called ways, paths, Jer. vi. 16. Young men must cleanse their ways according to the word, Psal. cxix. 9. David would have his steps ordered by the word, ver. 133. The word is the way to walk in, and a rule to walk by; we must try all spirits and doctrines by it, Isa. viii. 20; 1 Thess. v. 21; 1 John iv. 6; Acts xvii. 11: all things we believe, Acts xxvi. 27; Eph. ii. 20; John xx. 31; Gal. i. 8: all things we practise, 2 Tim. iii. 15, 17; Eccles. xii. 13. Matt. xxviii. 20, what God and Christ command must we observe, not what others direct. Isa. viii. 11, walk not in the ways of this people; not in the light of our own fire, Isa. l. 11; not after customs of men, Acts xxi. 21.

Obs. 6. Those whom God reneweth by grace, giveth newness and tenderness of spirit unto, he looks they should make progress in his ways, keep in mind his ordinances, and do them exactly, fulfil them. Deut. vi. 17, "Ye shall diligently keep the commandments of the Lord, and his testimonies and statutes." Psal. cxix. 4, "Thou hast commanded to keep thy precepts diligently." The Hebrew is, *valde*, greatly; the Septuagint, vehemently; and the Vulgate, *nimis*, too much; which expressions show, that we should endeavour to the utmost to keep them. God expected they should keep the sabbath exactly, Isa. lviii. 13; and so the rest of his commands.

מאד

"They shall be my people, and I will be their God." These words have two things in them:

I. God's asserting them to be his people.

II. A gracious promise to be their God.

You have these words often mentioned in the book of God; once in Leviticus, chap. xxvi. 12; seven times in Jeremiah, chap. vii. 23; xi. 4; xxiv. 7; xxx. 22; xxxi. 1, 33; xxxii. 38; four times in our prophet Ezekiel, chap. xxxvi. 28; xxxvii. 23, 27, and here in this verse; once in Zechariah, chap. viii. 8; twice in the New Testament, 2 Cor. vi. 16, and Rev. xxi. 3: in all there are fifteen times set down; which intimates to us that there is great weight in them, that they are of great consideration and use.

"They shall be my people." Hebrew is, they shall be to me for a people. And so, I will be to them *Lelohim*, for a God. I will show you,

והיו-לי לעם

I. What is implied in these words, "They shall be my people."

II. What in the other, "I will be their God."

I. "They shall be my people."

1. They shall acknowledge me to be their God, they shall not own any other god. There is difference between knowing and acknowledging; you may know such a one to be a child, but not acknowledge him to be your child; you may know such towns, countries, kingdoms, but not acknowledge them yours. This phrase, "my people," imports acknowledging God to be theirs: Psal. xlviii. 14, "This God," that dwells at Jerusalem, that breaks the ships of Tarshish, this God "is our God for ever and ever." Psal. lxxvii. 13, "Who is so great a God as our God?" Here is acknowledgment of God, not only to be great, but to be their God. Isa. xxv. 9, "This is our God; we have waited for him." Exod. xxix. 45, 56, "I will be their God; and they shall know that I am the Lord their God;" that is, they shall acknowledge me to be so; it is called vouching God to be their God, Deut. xxvi. 17.

2. They shall worship me only: Exod. v. 8, "Let us go and sacrifice to our God;" not to other gods. When a people is God's people, they are possessed with apprehensions of his glory, greatness, authority over them, and infinite worthiness to be honoured, adored, admired, and magnified by them; and will say, as it is Psal. xcv. 6, "O come, let us worship," &c.; and as it is Hos. xiv. 8, "What have I to do any more with idols?" They would not meddle with the worship of the nations, their own inventions, but they would worship God, and him only, Joel ii. 27; 1 Sam. xii. 24; Psal. cxlvii. 1; Rev. xix. 1.

3. They shall trust and rely upon me, and not on any other gods, or arms of flesh: Hos. xiv. 3, "Asshur shall not save us; we will not ride upon horses: neither will we say any more to the work of our hands, Ye are our gods: for in thee the fatherless findeth mercy." See Zeph. iii. 12; Psal. ix. 10.

4. They shall be a people unto me. When God takes a people to be his, they are holy unto him: Deut. vii. 6, "Thou art an holy people unto the Lord thy God;" God separated them from the world and other nations, to be holy unto himself; therefore it follows, "The Lord thy God hath chosen thee to be a special people unto himself;" see Lev. xix. 2. Hence they were called "an holy nation," Exod. xix. 6.

5. They shall hearken unto my voice, and do my will, and yield obedience unto me: Jer. vii. 23, "Obey my voice, and I will be your God, and ye shall be my people:" Josh. xxiv. 18, "We will serve the Lord, for he is our God." See Deut. vi. 17; Psal. l. 7; lxxxi. 8, 13.

6. They shall love me, and lay out their strength for me: Deut. vi. 5, "Thou shalt love the Lord thy God with all thine heart, and with all thy soul, and with all thy might;" Mark xii. 30, is added, "with all thy mind:" if God be ours he must have all. See Psal. lxviii. 28.

7. They shall stand for my glory, and make my name honourable: Isa. xliii. 21, "This people have I formed for myself; they shall show forth my praise."

II. "I will be their God." These are gracious words, and they do import much.

1. The free grace of God in pardoning their sins. Jer. xxxi. 33, 34, when he speaks of being their God, he tells them he "will forgive their iniquity, and will remember their sin no more." Psal. lxxxv. 2, "Thou hast forgiven the iniquity of thy people,

thou hast covered all their sin." The word "forgiven," signifieth to lift up, and take away. Sin is a great burden; when God becometh a God in mercy to a people, then he takes off that great burden, he lifts it up, carries it quite away, and it is hid out of sight and remembrance, Hos. xiv. 4.

2. The presence of God amongst them. Lev. xxvi. 11, 12, the Jews were God's people, and he saith, "I will set my tabernacle among you, and will walk among you, and be your God, and ye shall be my people:" the tabernacle and walking were arguments of his presence, and evidenced him to be their God. God is essentially present every where, but especially present with his people; Rev. xxi. 3, no creature, no angel, no representation of God, but God himself shall be with them; as a father with his children, as a husband with his wife, God will not only be with them, but in them, 2 Cor. vi. 16, he "will dwell in them, and walk in them."

3. The peculiar and special care of God over them. Deut. xxxii. 10—12, the Lord was as tender to them, as any creature could be to her young: the eagle is very careful of her young, carrying them not in her talons, but on her wings; so God deals by his people, he preventeth harms that might befall them. He went forth before his people, and did march in the front of them through the wilderness, Psal. lxviii. 7; lxxvii. 20. God doth provide for, and protect his people, Isa. xxvi. 20; Deut. xxxiii. 27; Psal. cxxv. 2. "Upon all the glory shall be a defence," Isa. iv. 5.

4. Deliverance, if in straits, dangers, misery. Exod. iii. 9, 10, "I have seen the oppression; come now therefore, and I will send thee unto Pharaoh, that thou mayest bring forth my people out of Egypt." Ezek. xxxvii. 12, "Behold, O my people, I will open your graves, and cause you to come up out of your graves." Where God is a God to any, he is a delivering God, he is affected with their condition and sufferings, Exod. iii. 7; Isa. lxiii. 9; 1 Sam. ix. 16; Isa. iii. 15.

5. Singular comfort. Rev. xxi. 3, 4, they shall be his people, and God himself shall be with them, be their God, and he shall wipe away all tears from their eyes, and there shall be no more death, nor sorrow, nor crying, nor pain. See Isa. xl. 1; xlix. 13; xxx. 26; li. 3. He doth encourage and hearten them, Isa. xli. 10.

6. Speaking and pleading for them. Isa. li. 22, "Thus saith thy Lord the Lord, and thy God that pleadeth the cause of his people." Their cause is many times like to suffer, men are unwise, unfaithful, manage it strangely, but God will plead the cause of his people; and he will not do it faintly, as if he cared not whether his people should have the day or no; but to purpose will he do it: Jer. l. 34, "Their Redeemer is strong; the Lord of hosts is his name: he shall thoroughly plead their cause, that he may give rest to the land, and disquiet the inhabitants of Babylon." See Micah vii. 9; Joel iii. 2.

7. Exalting and honouring of them. Deut. xxvi. 18, 19, "The Lord hath avouched thee to be his peculiar people;" and what then? "to make thee high above all nations, in praise, in name, in honour." God makes his people renewed: Isa. xxviii. 5, he is "a crown of glory" unto them; Isa. lx. 19, "Thy God thy glory:" see Jer. ii. 11; Isa. xliii. 7.

8. Teaching and instructing of them. Isa. xxviii. 26, "His God doth instruct him to discretion." Isa. li. 4, "Hearken unto me, my people; and give ear unto me, O my nation: for a law shall proceed from me, and I will make my judgment to rest for a light of the people." See Deut. iv. 36; Isa. xlviii. 17.

9. Delight in them. Isa. lxv. 19, "I will joy in my people:" no friends can rejoice more in one another, no bridegroom more in his bride, than God in his people; them he calls "his strength," and "his glory," Psal. lxxviii. 61; yea, "a crown of glory," Isa. lxii. 3, "Thou shalt be a crown of glory in the hand of the Lord, and a royal diadem in the hand of thy God." No king can delight more in a crown than the Lord doth in his people, which are his crown. God's people are near unto him, Psal. cxlviii. 14; they are his jewels, Mal. iii. 17; his portion, Deut. xxxii. 9; his heritage, Joel ii. 17; his peculiar treasure, Exod. xix. 5. The Hebrew word סגלה noteth an exquisite treasure, a thing very desirable, singular, and peculiar. Eccl. ii. 8, "The peculiar treasure of kings;" Aquila hath it, substance; Vatablus, a treasure entirely beloved: God's people are his choice treasure, dearly beloved. Things we delight in, we oft think upon, and speak of; and you may find this expression oft, viz. his treasure, or peculiar people; it is in Deut. vii. 6, "special people," it is the same word; so in Deut. xiv. 2; xxvi. 18; Psal. cxxxv. 4; Titus ii. 14; 1 Pet. ii. 9.

10. Blessing and communicating choice and satisfying mercies; where a people are his he will crown and load them with variety of blessings. Psal. iii. 8, "Thy blessing is upon thy people;" thy people are distinguished from all others, and thy blessings are distinct from all others. God's blessings note a plentiful bestowing of all good things, as appears, Gen. xxiv. 35; Eph. i. 3. Among his people are all his springs, the lower and upper ones. He blessed them with choice mercies: with his secrets, Psal. xxv. 14: with his name, Dan. ix. 19; Isa. lxiii. 19; the Shulamite was so called from Solomon, Cant. vi. 13; when God takes a people to himself, that people is married unto him, and it hath his name; the church is called Christ, 1 Cor. xii. 12: with his holiness, Heb. xii. 10: with the divine nature, 2 Pet. i. 4: with grace and glory, Psal. lxxxiv. 11; yea, with satisfying mercies, Psal. lxv. 4; xxxvi. 8; he will satisfy them with goodness, Jer. xxxi. 14, with himself, Gen. xv. 1.

Obs. 1. God prepares a people for himself, and then marries that people unto himself; he gives them oneness, newness, tenderness of heart and spirit, and then they shall be his people, and he will be their God. Ezek. xvi. 6, 8, "When thou wast in thy blood, I said unto thee, Live. I spread my skirt over thee, and covered thy nakedness, and thou becamest mine." When Abraham was come out of his country, had left his idolatrous ways, walked uprightly before God, then he hears, I am thy God and the God of thy seed, Gen. xvii. 7. This is the way of Christ; Eph. v. 26, 27, he is sanctifying and cleansing of his church, that he may present it to himself a glorious church without spot.

Obs. 2. It is great happiness to have God to be our God. Many think happiness to lie in other things, but in nothing else, only in this, it consists. Psal. xxxiii. 12, "Blessed is the nation whose God is the Lord; and the people whom he hath chosen for his own inheritance;" they are the blessed people. Psal. cxliv. 15, it is not thousands of cattle, full barns, laughter in the streets, peace and plenty, which make a people happy; the happiness of a people is, in having God to be theirs. Great parts, honours, friends, estates, do not make a man happy; but "happy is he that hath the God of Jacob for his help, whose hope is in the Lord his God," Psal. cxlvi. 5. When God is the God of a people he will do great things for them, 2 Sam. vii. 23; he will show them the power of his works, Psal. cxi. 6; he will not leave his people, 1 Sam. xii. 22. When heaven and earth shake, "the Lord will be the hope of his people," Joel iv. 16; the Hebrew מחסה is, the place of repair, or harbour.

Obs. 3. It is free grace and favour that God doth take any people to be his, and becometh a God unto. People choose not God; he saith, "They shall be my people, and I will be their God." We are vile in our natures, wicked in our works, no loveliness or profitableness is in us, or by us; Ezek. xvi. 5, 6, when thy person was loathed, and thou wast polluted in thy blood, I said unto thee, Live. There is nothing in a nation that sets his heart to work to do a people good; it was not their greatness moved him, Deut. vii. 7, they "were the fewest of all people;" nor their goodness, for what was their father Abraham? Josh. xxiv. 2, 3, Terah, Abraham, and Nachor, were idolaters, "they served other gods," saith the text, "and I took your father Abraham:" so when God took his seed in Egypt, they were idolatrous, Ezek. xx. 5—7. There is no righteousness in people to move God, neither can any sin in them hinder God from putting forth acts of his free grace. Deut. xxxii. 10, speaking of Israel, "he found him in a desert land, and in the waste howling wilderness;" to which some allusion may be, Cant. viii. 5. God found out and took this people in a wicked, lost, distressed condition, and brought them out by his power, and made them his people by his grace; 1 Sam. xii. 22, it pleased the Lord to make them his people.

Obs. 4. God doth not equally dispense his grace and favour, some are his people and he is their God, others are not. Many nations were left, when the Jews were taken, yea, all other nations: Amos iii. 2, "You only have I known of all the families of the earth;" the Lord's favour fell upon the Jews, and not others. Some infer, from Gen. xxii. 18, "In thy seed shall all the nations of the earth be blessed," that God loves all equally; at that time he did not. The words are a promise of what should be, not of what was, neither is it so now; for if he loves all alike, why doth he deny the means of grace to many nations? why doth he not bless and make the same effectual equally to all where they are? Besides, such an opinion overthrows election, God's dominion over the creatures, and his freedom in dispensation of grace and mercy, John x. 26; Acts xiii. 48.

Obs. 5. Those who are the Lord's have a strong ground to plead with God in prayer for any mercy. Where there is relation and interest, there is encouragement to ask; if God be ours and we his, surely we may plead with him for great things in our prayers. The people of God did so of old, Jer. xiv. 9; Psal. lxxx. 4; Isa. lxiv. 9; Deut. ix. 26; 2 Chron. xx. 12; xiv. 11.

Ver. 21. *But as for them whose heart walketh after the heart of their detestable things and their abominations, I will recompense their way upon their own heads, saith the Lord God.*

This verse is a threatening to those who should persist in their evil ways, yet a comfort to the godly, that the Lord would judge them and ease them of them.

"Detestable things and abominations." These words have been opened in ver. 18; and chap. v. 11; vii. 20.

"Heart of their detestable things." Hebrew is, Their heart going to the heart of their detestable things. Heart is sometimes put for the midst of a thing: Exod. xv. 8, "The heart of the sea;" which is called, Ezek. xxvi. 5, "The midst of the sea;" so their heart was in the midst of their idols, or amongst their idols; what was delightful in them, that was as the heart of the idol, and their hearts were carried thereunto. Or thus you may take the words, They conceived some deity to be in their idols, and they laboured to please and do those things that delighted the heart of that deity.

Those rites, ceremonies, ways, whereby they worshipped their idols, may be called the heart of their detestable things. It was a law among the heathens, that every god should be worshipped as he thought good, and the way prescribed by him of worshipping was as the heart and life of the idol and the idolatry.

"I will recompense their way upon their own heads." Of these words see what hath been said, chap. ix. 10; vii. 3, 4, 8.

Obs. 1. That when the Lord makes gracious promises to a people, they do not refer to and fetch in all. This observation rises from the two former verses and this laid together. God promises to give them oneness, newness, tenderness of heart, he promiseth that he will be their God, and they shall be his people. These promises were absolute, yet made good unto some of the captives, not unto all; "But as for them whose heart walketh after," &c. they should not come within the compass of them. Many promises of the Lord are delivered indefinitely, without restriction, and absolutely, without condition; and yet are made good only to some, even those who are given of the Father unto Christ. Many of these, after the captivity, never had these promises made good unto them, yet God was faithful in that some had the fruit and comfort of them.

Obs. 2. Tares, hypocrites, and naughty ones will be in the church always. Some had new spirits, tender hearts, and walked in God's statutes; others had old spirits, hard hearts, and walked after detestable things; some threw away all abominable things, and others their hearts went after them. They, coming out of Babylon, and laying the foundation of a new church, it was probable that none but choice ones should have been of it, or in it; but there were usurers, sabbath-breakers, and such as had mingled themselves with strange wives, Neh. v. and xiii. Ham was in the ark, Judas among the apostles, the church abounded with hypocrites in Christ's days; Matt. xiii. 30, there will be tares among the wheat to the end of the world.

Obs. 3. Afflictions, great and long, do not sanctify. They were to be in captivity, and that seventy years, yet, after their return, the hearts of many would be carried to their detestable things. It is granted, that after they came out of Babylon they never fell to idolatry, that is, the body of them did not, but doubtless some particulars did; their hearts went to the heart of their detestable things; when they saw some of the old idols, or relics of them, they were affected with them. Afflictions of themselves purge not out corruption, nor take the heart off from evil things.

Obs. 4. Men's hearts are in false ways and worship, they take pleasure in superstitious and idolatrous practices. Things invented by men, and brought into the worship of God, are pleasing to human senses, to carnal reason, men's corruptions, and so take their hearts. When the calf was made, Exod. xxxii. 19, they were greatly affected with it, and danced about it. 1 Pet. iv. 3, lasciviousness, lust, wine, revelling, banqueting, and idolatries, are joined together. False worship, and false ways of worship, are set out by such expressions as show their hearts were taken therewith, Numb. xv. 39; Isa. lvii. 5; lxvi. 3; Acts xvii. 16; 2 Kings xxi. 21; Psal. xcvii. 7; Ezek. xvi. 17—20.

Obs. 5. That which is an object of hatred to the godly, is an object of delight unto the wicked. In ver. 18, when the godly should come to the land again, they would take away all the detestable things, but the wicked, their hearts would go after them; the hearts of the one sort were for them, of the other were against them.

Obs. 6. God takes notice which way the heart looks, how it stands affected. "As for them whose heart walketh after," &c. see Ezek. xx. 16; xxxiii. 31. In chap. xiv. 3, 4, 7, thrice God observes, they had set up idols in their hearts. The heart is the principal thing in man that God calls for, Prov. xxiii. 26, and therefore he looks after it; Rev. ii. 23, "All the churches shall know that I am he which searcheth the reins and the hearts."

Obs. 7. Things men are much taken with, are detestable in the sight of God. They affected detestable things; Luke xvi. 15, that which is highly esteemed amongst men is abomination with God. When men bring into his worship things of their own, he accounts it iniquity, Exod. xx. 5; and the authors thereof, haters of him.

Obs. 8. Superstitious and idolatrous persons shall not go unpunished. "I will recompense their way upon their own heads." When they had made a calf, quickly after three thousand were slain for it; and though Moses mediated for them, yet God tells Moses that in the day he visits, he will visit their sin upon them, Exod. xxxii. 34; and ver. 35, "The Lord plagued the people, because they made the calf, which Aaron made." God is jealous, and cannot endure his glory should be given to another.

Obs. 9. Whenever God punisheth, or whomsoever he punisheth, he is just in his punishment. "I will recompense their way upon their own heads;" they shall have the fruit of their own labours, and it is certain: Thus saith the Lord, You think yourselves safe if you can avoid my stroke, that your false gods shall secure you; but it shall not be, "I will recompense your way upon your own heads." God may punish men sometimes less than they deserve, but never more; he is just, and returns their own doing upon them, Psal. vii. 16.

Ver. 22. *Then did the cherubims lift up their wings, and the wheels beside them; and the glory of the God of Israel was over them above.*

Here begins the fifth part of the chapter, which is a further description of the Lord's leaving the city.

The cherubims' wheels and glory were at the east gate of the temple, chap. x. 19, where you have the very words of this verse. Cherubims note out angels, and superior causes; wheels, inferior things, with the motions of them; and by "the glory of the God of Israel," is meant either the glorious Lord himself, or some visible sign of his glorious presence.

Obs. All things are under the God of Israel; he hath the eminence, he is above, wheels and angels are under him at his disposal; if he give out the word, the cherubims move, lift up their wings, and order the wheels.

Ver. 23. *And the glory of the Lord went up from the midst of the city, and stood upon the mountain which is on the east side of the city.*

Here you have God's departure from the city. To leave the temple was grievous; had he stayed at the gates of it, or in the city itself, any where within the walls, it had been mercy; but he leaves the east gate, (which he calls the midst of the city,) and goeth forth unto the mountain, which showed God would now expose the city to the fury and spoil of the Babylonians.

"The glory of the Lord." Of this see before, chap. x. 4, 18, 19; ix. 3; viii. 4; iii. 23.

"And stood upon the mountain." There were many mountains about Jerusalem, Psal. cxxv. 2, it was compassed about with them. The mountain which the "glory" went to, and stood upon, was mount Olivet, or mount of Olives; Zech. xiv. 4, this mountain was before Jerusalem, on the east, and the glory of the Lord stood before at the east gate, whence it removed, and went up this mountain; for it was high and had ascents, 2 Sam. xv. 30.

The standing of the "glory" upon this mountain may be either to see the ruin and destruction of the city, and so to weep over it, as Christ did upon, or near, the same mount, Luke xix; or, secondly, to upbraid them for their wickedness there, because they did abominable things in that mount, whence it was called the mount of corruption, 2 Kings xxiii. 13; or, thirdly, to make it typical to represent the ascending of Christ to heaven, which was from that place, Acts i. 12.

These things being granted, yet I conceive there was somewhat else in it. The "glory" of God had made several stands before, which they had not much minded; now it goeth from the temple and city, to a high conspicuous mountain, that they might take notice of God's departure, repent of their sins, and use all possible means for recalling, recovering, and keeping the glory with them; and, Zech. xiv. 4, the promise is of returning and standing upon the same mount.

Obs. 1. God is unwilling to forsake that people he hath vouchsafed his presence and communicated his favour unto. No people in the world had God so nigh them as this people, Deut. iv. 7. Here God goeth out of the city, but not quite away, nor quite out of sight, he steps to the mountain over against the city: before, he had removed to the side of the temple, then from within the temple to the threshold, after that to the east gate, and from thence to the mount of Olives; and God paused at every stand, whether he should go any further. The Lord is loth to leave his people, they put him upon it; Ezek. viii. 6, "Seest thou the great abominations that the house of Israel committeth here, that I should go far off from my sanctuary?" they forced God out of all; whereas seeing him upon the leaving them, they should have purged the sanctuary from all idols and false worship, and have importuned the Lord to stay among them. When a friend is leaving his friends, what entreaties, what tears many times are used to stay him! Acts xxi. 12, 13; Jer. xiv. 7—9.

Obs. 2. God is not tied so to any place, or people, but when they grow wicked, and defile his worship, he may leave them, and the place where he hath recorded his name. Mount Zion God had chosen above all places to dwell there: Psal. cxxxii. 14, "This is my rest for ever: here will I dwell; for I have desired it." For ever, is a long time, in Scripture sense, and God had dwelt a long time with them; but now the time was come of his departure, now the holy temple, holy city, holy people, were all profaneness unto him, they had corrupted his worship, polluted themselves, and therefore he would leave them. The Jews thought because they had the temple and God amongst them, that therefore they were well and happy, though their worship were mixed and their lives wicked; but they were deceived. No particular visible church hath assurance of God's abiding longer with it than it keeps his worship pure, walks holily and humbly with him; when any corrupt his glory, his worship, then the glorious Lord and the glory of the Lord doth leave them.

Obs. 3. When God leaves a people, then protection

of angels and comfort of creatures leave them also. The cherubims and wheels, together with the glory, left them, and went to the mountain. When the king goeth, the court removes, and the servants follow: when God is gone, we are left naked, lie open to all temptations and miseries; we have no God to counsel, comfort, protect, or save; and what a case is such a people in! Jer. vi. 8, "Be thou instructed, O Jerusalem, lest my soul depart from thee;" and what then? "lest I make thee desolate, a land not inhabited."

Ver. 24. *Afterwards the spirit took me up, and brought me in a vision by the Spirit of God into Chaldea, to them of the captivity. So the vision that I had seen went up from me.*

Here is the conclusion of this glorious vision our prophet had seen. The Spirit had carried him, not in body, but in spirit, unto Jerusalem, chap. viii. 3, and showed him how things were there, what God was purposed to do; and now having seen and heard glorious and terrible things, the vision went up to heaven, he saw it no more.

Obs. 1. The Spirit can show us things at a great distance, as if we were present. The Spirit caused Ezekiel to see things at Jerusalem, when his body was in Chaldea. Our senses cannot discern far, but the Spirit knoweth all things, in all places, and can satisfy us with the knowledge of them, give us spiritual and prophetical eyes. Paul saith, 2 Cor. xii. 2, 3, that he "was caught up to the third heaven," but "whether in the body, or out of the body," he knoweth not, and being there, he "heard unspeakable words." The Spirit took him up, caused him to hear such things; so did the Spirit here take up our prophet, and caused him to see such things.

Obs. 2. This vision was real, divine, no imaginary, feigned thing, not from his brain, but from the Spirit itself; therefore it is said, to put all out of doubt, "The spirit took me up, and brought me in a vision," and, "the vision that I had seen went up," which shows it was no human thing, but divine.

Obs. 3. The servants of God have glorious sights here sometimes, but they soon expire and come to an end. "So the vision that I had seen went up from me." He had seen the glory of God, the cherubims and wheels, and the man clothed with linen, viz. Christ, but here was no continuance of this glorious sight. Jacob seeth a ladder reaching up to heaven, angels ascending and descending, and the Lord at the top of the ladder, but this was only for a night, and then it ceased, Gen. xxviii. 12, 13, 16. Moses saw the Lord in the burning bush, Exod. iii. 2, but the sight lasted not. Isaiah saw the Lord sitting upon a throne, Isa. vi. 1. Peter James, and John, saw the transfiguration of Christ, Matt. xvii.; and all the apostles "saw his glory, as the glory of the only begotten;" but the vision went up from them.

Ver. 25. *Then I spake unto them of the captivity all the things that the Lord had showed me.*

Here you have what the prophet did after the vision: he had been in an ecstasy some time, and now being brought to his ordinary and pristine condition, he relates to the captives what he had seen and heard. Many of those in the captivity, and probably some of those elders which sat in the prophet's house, chap. viii. 1, thought them happy which were at Jerusalem, condemned their own act in coming to Babylon, judged their counsels foolish and weak, which they had about their coming thither, and blamed Jeremiah for exhorting them thereunto; hereupon Ezekiel being returned, as he thought, from Jerusalem to Chaldea, speaks unto them what he had received concerning the destruction of the temple, city, land, and the miseries of the inhabitants, and thereby convinceth them that they were in a far better condition than those they had left behind.

"All the things." Things in Hebrew is, words; now words are not shown but heard, how then doth he say, which he "had showed me?" They were not mere words, but words *vestita externo symbolo*, clothed with an outward symbol. He had many types, viz. of a siege, of a razor and hair, of a chain, of six men with slaughter weapons in their hands, and of a caldron, which were visible words.

Obs. 1. When men have been in the hand and power of the Spirit, acted thereby, then are they fit to speak unto the people, "Then I spake unto them." When Moses had been in the mount, then was he fit to speak to those at the foot of the mount; when the Spirit has irradiated the minds of men with divine light and truths, then are they meetest to communicate to others; the apostles being filled with the Spirit, spake freely, boldly, Acts iv.

Obs. 2. God's prophets and messengers must speak unto those they are intended for. Ezekiel had his vision, and all the types in it, for the Jews, those of the captivity, not the Babylonians. God had a care of the captivity, that they might be instructed concerning his mind, and be undeceived in their apprehensions about the things of Jerusalem: "Then I spake unto the captivity."

Obs. 3. They must declare what they have heard and seen, not what is their own. What is man's is uncertain, unsatisfying, unsanctifying; but that which is the Lord's is infallible, will satisfy and sanctify. Christ told the apostles the Spirit should take of his and show unto them, John xvi. 14; and Matt. xxviii. 20, they must teach the people to observe what he commanded them. 1 Cor. xi. 23, Paul received what he delivered; thus did Ezekiel, he spake what the Lord showed unto him.

Obs. 4. They must be faithful, speak all the things which are showed unto them. Thus did our prophet, he delivered unto them all the Lord had shown unto him, whatever he had seen or heard, that he faithfully giveth out. There must be no adding to the things of God, no detracting from them, no changing any of them, but what is the Lord's, that must be dispensed. Christ, who was sent of the Father, saith, "All things that I have heard of my Father I have made known unto you," John xv. 15; and Paul kept back nothing, but delivered all the counsel of God unto them, Acts xx. 20, 27.

CHAPTER XII.

Ver. 1—7. *The word of the Lord also came unto me, saying, Son of man, thou dwellest in the midst of a rebellious house, which have eyes to see, and see not; they have ears to hear, and hear not: for they are a rebellious house. Therefore, thou son of man, prepare thee stuff for removing, and remove by day in their sight; and thou shalt remove from thy place to another place in their sight: it may be they will consider, though they be a rebellious house. Then shalt thou bring forth thy stuff by day in their sight, as stuff for removing: and thou shalt go forth at even in their sight, as they that go forth into captivity. Dig thou through the wall in their sight, and carry out thereby. In their sight shalt thou bear it upon thy shoulders, and carry it forth in the twilight: thou shalt cover thy face, that thou see not the ground: for I have set thee for a sign unto the house of Israel. And I did so as I was commanded: I brought forth my stuff by day, as stuff for captivity, and in the even I digged through the wall with mine hand; I brought it forth in the twilight, and I bare it upon my shoulder in their sight.*

EZEKIEL, having been in a vision at Jerusalem, seen and heard many remarkable things, which he declared to them of the captivity, here the word of the Lord came afresh unto him, and he is put upon doing those things which might convince Zedekiah and others of the sad judgments coming upon them.

In the chapter are three things in general observable.

I. A prophecy of Zedekiah's carrying into captivity, with the citizens of Jerusalem, ver. 1—17.

II. The miserable condition of the people preceding and following the captivity of the king and people, ver. 17—21.

III. A confutation of those who mocked at the judgments of God threatened by the prophet, ver. 21, to the end.

In the first part you have,

1. A type set out in the first six verses.

2. The application of the type, from thence to ver. 17.

It is a question to whom these words of the Lord do refer, "Thou dwellest in the midst of a rebellious house," &c. Our prophet was in Babylon, and before the captives there; he was to remove in their sight, and this was not to give them hopes of any speedy return out of Babylon, but to quiet their disturbed minds; for these typical actions of the prophet in carrying out his stuff and digging through the wall, &c. have a double aspect, one towards them at Jerusalem, to evidence to them that their captivity was at hand, another towards these already in captivity, which was to comfort them, in letting them see what heavy judgments they had escaped, being safe there in Babylon, though burdened with some difficulties.

The scope is to show the certainty of their suffering and destruction at Jerusalem, and their advantage who were come to Babylon, and freed from the judgments which were coming upon the other.

"Thou dwellest in the midst of a rebellious house." Hebrew is, a house of rebellion; family, nation, people, who are rebellious, embittering, exasperating.

"Which have eyes to see, and see not; they have ears to hear, and hear not." Some take the sight for the understanding, the ear for the will, for these two senses are the servants of those faculties, and as the eye and ear are delighted with light and sweetness, so the understanding and will; but these men were spiritually blind and deaf, they neither heard nor saw as they might have done. They might have seen God's goodness to them, in bringing them from Jerusalem, in causing them to hearken to Jeremiah's counsel, in planting them in Babylon, in procuring more favour from the Babylonians than the condition of captives did require; they might have understood by the prophet's visions, and words spoken to them, what the Chaldeans should speedily do to them in Canaan, what bloody and fiery judgments they were bringing upon the city, temple, people, and whole land. They did not see inwardly, they considered not what God did, said, nor what they were to do.

Obs. 1. Wicked men neither see nor hear the things of God, neither mercies nor judgments are rightly discerned by them. They saw not the mercy they had in a strange land, nor the judgments they escaped in their own land. Mercies and judgments have much of God in them, they speak, and speak aloud; but wicked men neither see God, nor hear his voice, in his works, they are blind and deaf. When men see, hear, and do not profit by their seeing or hearing, then they neither see nor hear in Scripture sense; the more signs, threatenings, and judgments, the harder-hearted they grow, the blinder and deafer they are. We had need pray unto the Lord to open our eyes, that we may see what judgments, what mercies, we have had; that he would bore our ears, that we may hear his voice and repent of our wickedness.

Obs. 2. The cause of sinners' not seeing and not hearing is in themselves. "For they are a rebellious house:" their rebellion was the cause they neither saw nor heard; they did contrary to what God required, and so blinded their own eyes, hardened their own hearts: Isa. xxvi. 10, 11, "Let favour be showed to the wicked, yet will he not learn righteousness; when the Lord's hand is lifted up, yet will he not see." I fear this is the case of many amongst us. God hath given men senses to observe his works and ways, but they either do not, or will not, observe them: they have eyes to see mercies and judgments, but they consider them not; they have ears to hear the voice of his rod and word, but they hear not; their eyes, ears, and hearts are taken up and exercised about other things, which is a dreadful evil.

"Prepare thee stuff for removing." Hebrew is, instruments; what instruments? such were seen in Matt. x. 10, a scrip, a coat, shoes, a staff, some add a girdle; but whether these were the instruments Ezekiel was to prepare, I make some doubt: this might suffice for his own travelling, but he was to remove his household stuff, ver. 5, 6; he was to carry it out through the hole of the wall, and bear it upon his shoulder.

This he was to do for trial of their spirits. They had not been affected with his prophesying, and therefore now a visible sign is added; and what then? "It may be they will consider." When they should see the prophet removing from place to place, dig through the wall, go out in the night, cover his face, &c. these things were likely to affect them: actions are more observable than words, they make deeper impressions. If some chief man in a city should pack up all his stuff, break through the walls of the city in the night, carry all he had away, what strange effects would it cause in the hearts of men!

Obs. 1. The Lord is very patient towards a sinful and rebellious people; he trieth variety of ways to do them good. Visions, prophecies, signs, they had before; here again the prophet must do strange things, to see if they will be apprehensive of danger, repent, and prevent judgments. This is the way of God with sinners, he waits, is bountiful, and would with his goodness and long-suffering draw sinners to repentance. Let others be like God; a minister should be patient, not strive, be gentle towards all men, not bitter, nor cursing, in meekness instructing, &c.

Obs. 2. Prophets must venture, though the success of their endeavours be uncertain. Go, prepare stuff for removing, remove, and from place to place, "it may be they will consider." Prophets and others should look at God's will, not success. Divine pleasure is warrant sufficient for any to act; let the issue be what it will, ministers, magistrates, parents, must do their duty: it may be good will come of it, "it may be they will consider;" it is not a word of doubting, but of hope and encouragement.

"Thou shall bring forth thy stuff by day in their sight." The reason of this was, that so all might see, princes, nobles, and people, and be inexcusable if they did not take warning.

"Go forth at even." This was to show the stealing away of the king, nobles, and men of war by night, as it is 2 Kings xxv. 4, "The city was broken up, and all the men of war fled by night, by the way of the gate, between two walls, which is by the king's garden: and the king went the way toward the plain:" Jer. xxxix. 4, "They fled, and went forth out of the city by night," even Zedekiah with the rest.

"Dig through the wall," &c. To show what great straits they should be in, all gates should be beset, all known passages stopped, and they necessitated to break through the wall; and, ver. 7, Ezekiel saith, he did it with his own hand, "I digged through the wall with mine hand." In imminent danger any shift will men make, pull stones out of walls, &c.

"Thou shalt bear it upon thy shoulders." To show that the people and princes should carry away their precious things upon their shoulders.

"Thou shalt cover thy face, that thou see not the ground." Covering of the face was in use among the Jews and others.

1. In case of disappointment and shame they did it: Jer. xiv. 3, "Their nobles have sent their little ones to the waters; they came to the pits, and found no water; they returned with the vessels empty; they were ashamed and confounded, and covered their heads."

2. In case of sorrow and mourning: 2 Sam. xix. 4, when Absalom was slain, David covered his face, and cried, "O Absalom, my son!" so, in chap. xv. 30, David and the people had their heads covered, and wept when they went up mount Olivet.

3. In case of guilt and punishment for it: Esth. vii. 8, when Haman was accused by Esther, and to suffer for his villanous plot against the Jews, they covered his face, as not worthy to see the sun or earth. Here the prophet's covering was typical, and was to show not only what a dark, moonless night Zedekiah should choose to flee in, but what a dark condition he should be in when his eyes should be put out; therefore those words, "that thou see not the ground," are added, intimating, that though he were carried into Babylon, yet he should not see that land.

"For I have set thee for a sign unto the house of Israel." And, in ver. 11, I "am your sign." The word in Hebrew is מופת *portentum*, from יפה which signifieth something beautiful, specious, drawing to admiration; here it is put for a strange or wonderful thing, and is the same with oath, and is rendered "a sign," in this place and others; as in 2 Chron. xxxii. 24; Isa. viii. 18, "I, and the children whom the Lord hath given me, are for signs and for wonders;" there are both the words, and point out the same thing, and that is, a sign or token by which a future event of things is marked out. Isa. xx. 3, 4, his going naked and barefoot, was a sign and wonder upon Egypt and Ethiopia; and our prophet's digging the wall, carrying out his stuff, and covering of his face, made him a sign to the house of Israel; they would not believe that they should go into captivity, but this was a lively sign to convince them of it.

Obs. The Lord carrieth on his design in the world, ofttimes, by foolish, weak, and ridiculous means. The prophet must dig through the wall, carry out his stuff upon his shoulder, remove from place to place, and cover his face, that he see not the ground; these things seemed childish and foolish unto the Jews, they thought him a silly or mad man. So chap. iv. he must take a tile, picture Jerusalem upon it, he must build a fort, cast a mount, set a camp and battering-rams against it, he must also set an iron pan for a wall between him and the city, lie upon his left side, and then upon his right side, drink water by measure, and bake his bread in dung, &c.; all which seemed poor, ridiculous things in the eyes of the people, but there was weight in them.

"And I did so as I was commanded: I brought forth my stuff by day, as stuff for captivity," &c. In this verse is the obedience of the prophet to the type commanded, and in the two next, preparation to the application of the type.

Obs. from the 6th verse, It is man's duty readily to obey the Lord in whatsoever he commands; be they things of such nature as to seem ridiculous, unworthy a man, such as will expose him to scorn, disgrace, &c. yet he is bound to do them. Our prophet did as he was commanded, he stuck not at the doing those things which would make him a sign and fable in all Israel.

Ver. 8, 9. *And in the morning came the word of the Lord unto me, saying, Son of man, hath not the house of Israel, the rebellious house, said unto thee, What doest thou?*

God had appointed the prophet to do those typical things in their sight, and now he comes to inquire what the people did or said upon his so doing; and such was the blindness and stupidity of this people, that they did not so much as inquire of the prophet what these typical passages meant. The words in ver. 9, are an interrogation, and import a negative, not an affirmative; thus, "Hath not the rebellious house said unto thee, What doest thou?" No, I know it hath not; they dreamt rather of their own return out of captivity, than thought of their brethren's coming into captivity who were at Jerusalem; they rather derided the prophet for those strange acts, than consulted what they meant.

Obs. The Lord looks after his messengers, and messages sent by them, and will have an account what entertainment they have. The Lord commanded Ezekiel to go and do such things, which he did; and here he comes and inquires what was the effect of those typical actions, whether the people apprehended his meaning in them, or made inquiry after them; Have they come to thee, have they said, "What doest thou?" God minds the servants he employs, their words and actions shall not be in vain. He makes speedy inquiry here after all: "In the morning came the word of the Lord unto me, saying, Son of man, hath not the house of Israel said unto thee," &c. If they understood them not, it was their duty to come to the prophet for resolution, and his duty to resolve them.

Ver. 10—14. *Say thou unto them, Thus saith the Lord God; This burden concerneth the prince in Jerusalem, and all the house of Israel that are among them. Say, I am your sign: like as I have done, so shall it be done unto them: they shall remove and go into captivity. And the prince that is among them shall bear upon his shoulder in the twilight, and shall go forth: they shall dig through the wall to carry out thereby: he shall cover his face, that he see not the ground with his eyes. My net also will I spread upon him, and he shall be taken in my snare: and I will bring him to Babylon to the land of the Chaldeans; yet shall he not see it, though he shall die there. And I will scatter toward every wind all that are about him to help him, and all his bands; and I will draw out the sword after them.*

In these verses you have the application of the type to the prince, and all the house of Israel, which is in general laid down in ver. 10; then the common calamity of both, in ver. 11, "They shall go into captivity;" then a more special application of it to the king, in ver. 12, 13, where his bearing stuff upon his shoulder, his flight, digging through the wall, and covering his face, are set down, together with his apprehension, excæcation, deportation into Babylon, and death there.

"This burden." המשא from נשא to lift up, a word so rich in signification and efficacy, *ut vix centum aliarum linguarum verbis explicentur ejus divitiæ*, that scarcely can its riches be unfolded in a hundred words of other languages; it may be rendered, This burdensome doctrine, or prophecy, which these types do speak. By "burden," is meant the typical sign of captivity, which was a burden to the prophet to act, to open unto them, a burden to them to hear, and especially to bear. Grievous prophecies are called burdens in Scripture, Nahum i. 1; Hab. i. 1; so Isa. xv. 1; xvii. 1; xix. 1.

"The prince." It was Zedekiah, a wicked and timorous king. The Hebrew is, הנשיא from נשא to lift up; either because he is lift up above the people, or should *populi onera levare*, ease and lighten the grievances of the people, as they in Exod. xviii. 22. But if they grow tyrannical, and impose heavy burdens upon the people, the Lord hath a burden for them; as here Zedekiah must dig through the wall, carry forth on his shoulder, flee, &c. This you may see fulfilled, Jer. lii. 7—11, where you have his flight mentioned, the Chaldeans' pursuit and apprehension of him, his carrying to Riblath, where his eyes were put out, and after to Babylon, where he died.

"Say, I am your sign," &c. This relates to the few in Babylon; they conceived there should no judgment befall Jerusalem, nor the men there. By this typical work of the prophet, the Lord shows them their error, that it should not be well with them at Jerusalem: It is true they condemn you for removing into Babylon, and justify themselves, that they are the only people, righteous and acceptable unto me, and therefore are safe in Jerusalem. But you shall see, and they shall know, how vain and foolish their thoughts and reasonings are; as I have dealt with you, so will I do by them, they shall be made captives very speedily, and meet with sorer judgments than you did.

"My net also will I spread upon him, and he shall be taken in my snare." These words you have again in chap. xvii. 20. The Chaldeans here are likened unto fishermen, who usually dwell by the water-sides; now Babylon was among the waters, Euphrates and Tigris running by it, or through it; hence, Jer. li. 13, "O thou that dwellest upon many waters." Therefore fitly are they compared to fishermen, and the army was the net; a net spreads abroad, compasses, and catches; by this net was Zedekiah, the princes, city, and all precious things therein, taken.

"In my snare." Snares are for the land, and it is thought to be a hunter's snare, such as is set for wild beasts, which being hunted and chased hard, are driven into snares, and so taken; they are set secretly, catch suddenly, hold certainly. The Hebrew word *metzudah*, as Junius observes, signifies also a strong hold; and in this sense it may represent to us Riblath, whither Zedekiah was carried, where he received judgment, and had his eyes put out, or that hold he was put into in Babylon.

Obs. 1. The great mercy and goodness of God, who takes occasion from their sin to afford them this mercy, the exposition of this type. They were stupid, and minded not the prophet and his actions, or, if they did, they derided him as a foolish or mad man, to do such things; hence the Lord is pleased to take an advantage to acquaint them with it: Have they not asked thee, "What doest thou? Say thou unto them, Thus saith the Lord; This burden concerneth the prince," &c. Hos. ii. 13, 14; Isa. lvii. 17, 18; Gen. viii. 21, in those places God takes occasion from man's sin to show mercy. So in John xx. 25, 27, from Thomas's unbelief, &c. takes an opportunity to come and show his wounds, &c.

Obs. 2. To secure and confident sinners God will render judgment most certainly and impartially. Say to them, As I have done, so shall it be done unto them; whatever their thoughts are at Jerusalem, or yours here, their condition shall be like yours; have you been afflicted with war, famine, plague? have you lost the temple, city, your country and estates, are you brought into a heathenish land? so shall it be with them.

Obs. 3. The Lord hath burdens for princes; if they be wicked, there are burdensome prophecies against them, and burdensome judgments for them. Zedekiah did evil in the sight of the Lord, 2 Kings xxiv. 19, and you may see what burdens he had.

(1.) A burden of fear; he durst stay no longer; and, Jer. xxxviii. 19, "I am afraid of the Jews that are fallen to the Chaldeans, lest they deliver me into their hand."

(2.) A burden of shame; he covers his face, he will see none, nor be seen of any; he leaves Jerusalem in a shameful manner, carrying some burden upon his shoulder, as if he were some vulgar man; he is disguised, as being ashamed of a princely title.

(3.) A burden of flight; he is put to it to flee for his life.

(4.) A burden of darkness; in the evening, or night, he steals away.

(5.) A burden of difficulties; he must dig through a wall, go in by-ways.

(6.) A burden of sad judgments.

[1.] He is taken by the enemies.

[2.] His sons are slain before his face.

[3.] His eyes are put out.

[4.] He is led into captivity.

[5.] He is imprisoned till his death.

And why all these burdens? Because he had a burden of guilt in his conscience which was worse than all the rest, and that burden brings the burdens of judgment, for so it is called, 2 Kings ix. 25, when Jehu shot an arrow into the heart of Joram, a wicked king, he saith, "The Lord laid this burden upon him." Such a burden laid the Lord upon Jezebel for her whoredoms and witchcrafts; she is thrown out at a window, her blood sprinkled upon the wall, trod under foot by horses, and eaten up all by dogs, except her skull, feet, and palms of her hands.

Obs. 4. Sinful princes cannot escape the judgments of God, he hath nets and snares to surprise them, to hold them. Zedekiah thought by flight to get away, but the Lord spread out his net upon him, and took him in his snare. The Chaldeans' army was God's net and snare to catch sinners; Hab. i. 13, God makes men, yea takes them, as the fishes of the sea; and, ver. 15, "They catch them in their net;" meaning the Chaldeans, which troubled the prophet that such wicked men should catch and spoil the Jews: but the Lord knows how to make use of the worst men to execute his judgments. So the Goths and Vandals of old, Turks now, to scourge the christian world, &c. What base spirits hath God set on work to correct us! &c. If God will catch men, he hath nets; if he will hunt them, he hath snares.

Obs. 5. The Lord makes sinners' helps helpless. Zedekiah had some nobles, counsellors, friends, about him, a life or person-guard, bands of soldiers, but "I will scatter all that are about him to help him, and all his bands;" God would put him into a helpless condition, they should none of them be able to relieve him. Men are apt, in times of trouble, to look unto some helps and hopes, but they are vain things, soon blasted, scattered. Take heed of making flesh your arm, of creature-confidences. Wicked men expect help from things beneath, from those about them, but they are frequently disappointed, and so perplexed. Take David's counsel, Psal. cxlvi. 3, "Put not your trust in princes, nor in the son of man, in whom there is no help;" ver. 5, "Happy is he that hath the God of Jacob for his help."

Ver. 15, 16. *And they shall know that I am the Lord, when I shall scatter them among the nations, and disperse them in the countries. But I will leave a few men of them from the sword, from the famine, and from the pestilence; that they may declare all their abominations among the heathen whither they come; and they shall know that I am the Lord.*

In these two verses you have two great ends of God's judgments. The first is, that the wicked may be convinced, from what they have felt and seen, that it was the word of the Lord which they despised; that he spake by Jeremiah and Ezekiel; that they were his threatenings, and now made good by him, and this is in ver. 15. The second is, confession of their sin, and God's righteousness in their judgments, and this is in ver. 16.

Obs. 1. That sinners are of as little account with God as dust and chaff. This is held out to us in the words "scatter," and "disperse;" men are no more before God than a little dust before the wind, or chaff in a fan. The original word for disperse is, זריתי *ventilavero;* Jer. xv. 7, God said he would "fan them with a fan;" and, Isa. xl. 15, God counts the nations "as the small dust of the balance;" and, Isa. xli. 2, "gave them as the dust to his sword."

Obs. 2. Judgments produce those effects which mercies do not. They had great means and mercies at Jerusalem, in the land, city, temple, but under those they did not know, not confess, their sins, and give glory to his name; but when they were deprived of their mercies under sad and sharp judgments, they should do so: Isa. xxvi. 9, "When thy judgments are in the earth, the inhabitants of the world will learn righteousness;" ver. 16, "In trouble have they visited thee."

Obs. 3. The Lord in the midst of his judgments shows some mercy. "I will leave a few men." Hebrew is, men of number, that may quickly be numbered. Though many were destroyed by the sword, famine, pestilence, yet some would the Lord leave.

Ver. 17—20. *Moreover the word of the Lord came to me, saying, Son of man, eat thy bread with quaking, and drink thy water with trembling and with carefulness; and say unto the people of the land, Thus saith the Lord God of the inhabitants of Jerusalem, and of the land of Israel; They shall eat their bread with carefulness, and drink their water with astonishment, that her land may be desolate from all that is therein, because of the violence of all them that dwell therein. And the cities that are inhabited shall be laid waste, and the land shall be desolate; and ye shall know that I am the Lord.*

These words contain the second general part of the chapter, viz. the sad condition of the people, both before and after the captivity of the king. In ver. 18, a new type is commanded; in ver. 19, it is applied; and there you have the end of its application, which is desolation and devastation, and the procreant cause of both, viz. the violence which was amongst them. And in ver. 20, the end of God's putting them into such an afflictive condition, that they may know him to be the Lord.

"Eat thy bread with quaking." Fear and perplexity of spirit makes men tremble, and takes away the sweetness of any comfort present. The Hebrew is ברעש *in commotione: cum tremore corporis,* such quaking as the earth quakes with, or like unto corn and leaves; so should the prophet tremble, quake, in eating, looking this way and that way, as one affrighted.

"Drink thy water with trembling," &c. ברגזה the Septuagint, *μετα βασάνȣ καὶ θλίψεως,* with torment, affliction; the Vulgate is, *in festinatione,* in haste, as they did eat the passover. This eating and drinking with quaking and trembling, was to set out, either the great fear which should be upon them when the Babylonish army should besiege them, so that they should not enjoy the comfort of those creatures without great trouble; or the great famine which should be in the earth, which should cause great fear and trembling lest they should want, and die for hunger and thirst, lest others should snatch out of their hands, or pull out of their mouths, that little they had, and so they were full of care in their eating and drinking.

"Say unto the people of the land;" that is, those Jews who were in the land of Chaldea: he must tell the captives what should befall the Jews at Jerusalem, and in the land of Israel.

"They shall eat their bread with carefulness." בראגה it notes care, grief, fear, which commonly attend one the other. The Septuagint, *μετα ἐνδείας,* with want; before, they rendered this word *μετα θλίψεως,* want is a great affliction.

"And drink their water with astonishment." בשמּמון from שמם *stupescere, admirari.* The Septuagint hath it, *μετὰ ἀφανισμȣ̃, cum interitu,* despairing of deliverance and life; Chaldee, *cum stupore;* the French, *en desolation.*

"That her land may be desolate." Judea was the choicest of lands, a paradise to other countries; it abounded with milk, honey, corn, oil, wine, cattle, silver, gold, and other precious things; but now it was to be laid waste; now it should be stripped of its inhabitants, of its plenty and treasure: the Hebrew is, *a plenitudine sua.*

"Because of the violence of them that dwell therein." חמס notes injury, tyranny, spoil. The Septuagint renders it, *ἐν ἀσεβείᾳ,* because of the wickedness of them, &c.

Obs. 1. The Lord puts his servants oft upon troublesome service, and sad actions, for the conviction and benefit of others. Here Ezekiel must eat his bread with quaking, and drink his drink with trembling; he must dig through the wall, and bear his stuff upon his shoulder, go out at even, cover his face, remove his stuff, which were burdensome actions; and, chap. iv. he must lie upon his left side three hundred and ninety days, and then upon his right side forty days; he must eat bread baked with cows' dung; and, chap. v. he must shave his head and his beard, make himself bald and unsightly. So Hosea, he must marry a wife of whoredoms, chap. i. 2; and Jeremiah, chap. xxvii. 2, he must make yokes and bands, and put upon his neck. These things were to signify what God would do unto the nations, bring them into subjection to Nebuchadnezzar.

Obs. 2. It is divine pleasure, that when typical and dark things are given out to the prophets, that they should make them known to the people. Ezekiel must tell the people what was in it, that he ate his bread and drank his drink in such a manner; so for his digging, and removing, he must tell them what mystery was wrapt up in it: "Say unto them, This burden concerneth the prince," ver. 10; and here, ver. 19, "Say unto the people," &c. It is the duty of those that are teachers in the church, to open things which are mysterious, what they mean and signify.

Obs. 3. God can mingle sorrows with our comforts, and make our choice comforts comfortless comforts. "They shall eat their bread with carefulness, and drink their drink with astonishment." God would bring an enemy to the gates of Jerusalem, and put them to such straits, that they should neither eat nor drink with any comfort; fear, carefulness, and astonishment would be gravel in their bread, and gall in their drink. Adam's comforts in paradise were soon damped; Gen. iii. 17, "In sorrow shalt thou eat;" bread of sorrows was his bread, and is his children's bread to this day, only sometimes God puts in more sorrow than at others: there is "bread of affliction," 1 Kings xxii. 27; "bread of mourners," Hos. ix. 4. Here God would put in much sorrow, affliction, and mourning; quaking, trembling, care, and astonishment, should possess them; their plenty should be turned into scarcity; for wine they should have water, and very little of that too; for the finest of the wheat flour, they should have bran, and not their bellies full of that.

Obs. 4. It is sin, the sin of injustice, oppression, which causes God to lay waste a plentiful land. "That her land may be desolate from all that is therein, because of the violence of them that dwell therein." It is observed, that the Jews were, and still are, a covetous people: it was their covetousness put them upon unjust acts of oppression and violence, and God upon just judgments of famine and desolation: Psal. cvii. 34, he turns "a fruitful land into barrenness for the wickedness of them that dwell therein." Man's wickedness moves the Lord to lay plentiful and pleasant lands waste, yet it is made their act; Zech. vii. 14, "They laid the pleasant land waste;" they were the procreant cause, they begat sin, sin begat judgment, and judgment begat desolation.

Ver. 21—28. *And the word of the Lord came unto me, saying, Son of man, what is that proverb that ye have in the land of Israel, saying, The days are prolonged, and every vision faileth? Tell them therefore, Thus saith the Lord God; I will make this proverb to cease, and they shall no more use it as a proverb in Israel; but say unto them, The days are at hand, and the effect of every vision. For there shall be no more any vain vision nor flattering divination within the house of Israel. For I am the Lord: I will speak, and the word that I shall speak shall come to pass; it shall be no more prolonged: for in your days, O rebellious house, will I say the word, and will perform it, saith the Lord God. Again the word of the Lord came to me, saying, Son of man, behold, they of the house of Israel say, The vision that he seeth is for many days to come, and he prophesieth of the times that are far off. Therefore say unto them, Thus saith the Lord God; There shall none of my words be prolonged any more, but the word which I have spoken shall be done, saith the Lord God.*

In these verses you have the third part of the chapter, a confutation of those who made an ill construction of the prophet's prophecies. One kind of men gave no credence at all to what was prophesied, but derided the prophets, saying, When were you in heaven, or who told you the mind of God? You are deceivers; if any such thing had been as you speak of, it had taken place ere this, but nothing is done, therefore we will not believe you. Another kind of men were persuaded the prophets spoke truth, but it was at a great distance, long ere it was to take place; and therefore grew secure. Hence the Lord commands the prophet to let them know that his words should certainly and shortly come to pass. In the words consider,

I. A complaint of a proverb; "What is that proverb that ye have in the land of Israel?" ver. 22.

II. The mention of the proverb; "The days are," &c. ver. 22, 23.

III. The confutation of it; "I will make this proverb to cease, and they shall no more use it as a proverb in Israel," &c. ver. 23.

IV. A confirmation of that confutation,

1. From the Lord's proceeding with the false prophets, and their vain visions and flattering divinations; they should cease, ver. 24. And,

2. From the promise of making good his word, and that speedily, ver. 25, 28.

I. A complaint of a proverb; "What is that proverb that ye have in the land of Israel?"

I shall open the word "proverb" unto you, המשל which is from משל signifying to bear rule, to reign, to excel; and so a proverb is some notable speech, which excels others, and bears rule amongst men: "New wine is not for old bottles." "Do men gather grapes of thorns." "A little leaven leavens the whole lump." *Mashal* signifies κυρίαν γνώμην, a lordly, authentic sentence; as the Proverbs of Solomon, and such as these, viz. "The axe is laid to the root of the tree." "Where the treasure is, the heart will be also." "No man can serve two masters," &c. Or it is from the same root signifying to speak similes, or parables, adagies, or witty sayings. Hence the Septuagint renders it παραβολὴ, What is the parable which you have in the land? The gospel expresses a proverb by the word παροιμία, John xvi. 25; 2 Pet. ii. 22. And the learned think παροιμίαν, to be ἀπο τοῦ διμον. And Scaliger, l. 3. Poet. *censet* παροιμίαν *dici* παρα τὸν οἶμον, because it is a sentence that goes up and down by the way, it is common amongst men; or thus, it may rather be so called, because it is *præter viam*, beside the common way of speaking; having something mysterious, dark, and difficult in it. The Grecians say it is λόγος ὠφέλιμος ἐν τῷ βίῳ ἐπικρύψει μετριᾳ πολυ το χρησιμον ἐχων ἐν ἑαυτῳ, a speech useful for this life, having much good, and moderate darkness in it: they say also it is λόγος ἐπικαλύπτων το σαφει ἀσαφεὶᾳ, a speech veiled; light in a dark lanthorn. Some proverbs are obscure, and signify somewhat else than the words seem to express, as, "The dog is turned to his own vomit again; and the sow that was washed to her wallowing in the mire,"

2 Pet. ii. 22. So that in Ezek. xviii. 2, "The fathers have eaten sour grapes, and the children's teeth are set on edge." Some are more plain and easy, as 1 Sam. xxiv. 13, "Wickedness proceedeth from the wicked;" so that among us, "Truth begets hatred; flattery, friends." Some were wicked and false, and such had this people among them: that in Ezek. xviii. 2, "The fathers," &c. and that in this place, are wicked proverbs.

II. The mention of the proverb; "The days are prolonged, and every vision faileth."

Herein lies the evil of this proverb: when the prophets at the command of God prophesied sad things, threatened destruction to Jerusalem, captivity to the people, &c. they, not willing to hear of such things, put off all by this proverb thus; If that the prophet's prophecy be true, it is not for our days, but the days of those who are long after, for the next, the second, or third generation after, as "the days are prolonged," say they; or if they be false, as it is likely, what need we fear, or care, "every vision faileth," they come to nothing, they are words, wind; and thus wickedly they put off prophetical threats, and deluded their own souls; they laid not to heart their sins, they used not any means to divert divine wrath, or to secure their own souls; and that because sinfully they prolonged or disannulled the prophecies.

Obs. 1. That men very wicked are very secure; they look for peace, liberty, and long life, even when they have greatly provoked the wrath of God against them. What if we have sinned by violence in the land, by corruptions and false worship in the church, and the prophets have thundered against us with threatening judgments; yet "The days are prolonged," we shall have peace, walk at liberty, and fill up the number of our days. So in chap. xi. 3, "It is not near:" desolation is threatened by the prophets from Chaldea, but is not near; "let us build houses" for our delight, and dwell in them securely, and take a course with Jeremiah, and those of his strain, which think to trouble us. Jer. vii. 9, 10, they did "steal, murder, commit adultery, swear falsely, burn incense to Baal;" yet came and stood in the house of God, and said, "We are delivered to do all these abominations:" the meaning is, Though we have done such things, and have been grievously threatened for them by the prophets, yet we are delivered from their threats, and are well, safe, without fear or danger, and shall go on in our old ways: when God's threatenings are deferred, out of mercy, that men may consider, repent, and prevent them, they think they will never come, and so grow more secure and more sinful. Eccl. viii. 11, "Because sentence against an evil work is not executed speedily, therefore the heart of the sons of men is fully set in them to do evil;" they go on more freely, with more delight; this makes the Lord oft to remind sinners of the days of his wrath. Amos iv. 1, 2, "Hear this word, ye kine of Bashan, that are in the mountain of Samaria, which oppress the poor, which crush the needy, which say to their masters, Bring, and let us drink." They were secure, and, like kine, gored, trod under the poorer sort; and what must they hear? this, "The Lord God hath sworn by his holiness, that, lo, the days shall come upon you, that he will take you away with hooks, and your posterity with fishhooks." So Zeph. i. 14, "The great day of the Lord is near, it is near, and hasteth greatly."

Obs. 2. Such is the corruption of man, that, being opposed, it swells higher, and vents itself ofttimes blasphemously. The prophets reproved them for their sins, threatened the sorest judgments for them, and how did they entertain those threatenings? their hearts boiled against the prophets and their messages; and they uttered it with their tongues, "Every vision faileth," there is no truth in the prophets, nor in their visions, they are liars, and their visions lies. This was not only contumelious to the prophets, but blasphemous against the majesty of God, and the truth of his word. Men that live under the word, if their corruptions and lusts be not weakened and mortified, they are ripened, strengthened, and grow to an insufferable height. Jer. xvii. 15, "They say unto me, Where is the word of the Lord? let it come now:" thou tellest us of the word of the Lord, but it is thine own dream; if it be the Lord's, let it come now and we will believe it; but if not, it is thine, and thou art a deceiver to tell us so. 2 Pet. iii. 3, 4, "In the last days shall be scoffers, walking after their own lusts, saying, Where is the promise of his coming."

Obs. 3. That sinful words are of a spreading nature. They said, "The days are prolonged, and every vision faileth;" this wicked speech was become a proverb; it passed through the mouths of all sorts, young, old, great, small, learned, ignorant; it was in the city and country, a proverb in the land of Israel. The words of the prophet stuck not by them, they mocked at him, and made jests at what he said: Ezek. xxxiii. 31, "With their mouth they show much love;" in the Hebrew it is, they make jests; they made sport with the prophet and his threatenings; but this blasphemous proverb they took up, and conveyed from one to another all the land over, and made use of to disparage whatever he said. So that in Matt. xxviii. 13, when it was known that Christ was risen, money was given to the soldiers to say, "His disciples came by night, and stole him away while we slept;" this saying went abroad, "and is commonly reported among the Jews until this day," ver. 15.

Obs. 4. God takes notice of the ungodly speeches which are in men's mouths. They said, "The days are prolonged," &c.; God heard and observed what they said. Isa. lix. 3, "Your lips have spoken lies, your tongue hath muttered perverseness:" many think a lie nothing, and secret muttering against others nothing, but God observes every lie which is told, all whispering and muttering against others. Jer. xxxiii. 24, "Considerest thou not what this people have spoken?" if thou dost not, I do; they have said, "The two families which the Lord hath chosen, he hath even cast them off." Jer. xliv. 25, God regards what men and their wives say, yea, what every one saith; and will come ere long in judgment to convince sinners of the hard speeches spoken against him, Jude 15, and to call men to an account for every idle word which they have spoken, Matt. xii. 36; therefore, Eph. iv. 29, "Let no corrupt communication proceed out of your mouth, but that which is good to the use of edifying, that it may minister grace unto the hearers," and comfort to the speakers.

Obs. 5. The Lord hath an admiring indignation at the wickedness of his people. "What is that proverb that ye have in the land of Israel?" This interrogation implies admiration, and indignation. Admiration, that a people brought up in his house, which had had the law and prophets from the begining, so many hundred years, should be so stupid, wicked, profane, blasphemous, as to think and say, divine threatenings were in vain, the prophets liars, and their prophecies lies. And it shows indignation: What proverb is this which you have taken up? What! a proverb which strikes at me, which makes me a false and lying God, which overthrows all religion? O detestable and vile proverb! What! shall all that I say by my prophets fail, and come to nothing, vanish into the air?

III. The confutation of the proverb; "Tell them therefore, Thus saith the Lord God, I will make this proverb to cease," &c.

This verse is a confutation of their sinful proverb, which the Lord tells them should cease, and that the days they thought prolonged were at hand.

"They shall no more use it as a proverb in Israel." ולא-ימשלו which is, they shall no more proverb it, not with this proverb; others they might use; acute and wise sentences concerning man's life and manners, &c. of which nature proverbs are, God would not abridge them of; but this was a destructive proverb.

"The days are at hand;" Hebrew, have drawn near. That is at hand, or draws near, which is either presently to be done, or not far off. The time was not far now from Jerusalem's besieging, Zedekiah's taking, and the ruin of all; God's net was made, and his snare ready for them.

"The effect of every vision." Hebrew is דבר the French, *la parole*, the word or thing of every vision; *res omnis visionis*, so Piscator; whatsoever the vision did present to the prophet, and he to the people, that should be.

Obs. 1. The thoughts and words of the wicked are differing and contrary to the thoughts and words of God. They thought of peace, God of war; they thought of liberty, God of captivity; they of long life, God of cutting them off; they said the days of judgment were prolonged afar off, God saith, "They are at hand;" they said, "Every vision faileth," God said, every vision should take effect; they thought and said, this proverb should continue, but God thought and said, it should cease and be used no more; 1 Thess. v. 3, men cry, Peace, safety, and God cries, Destruction.

Obs. 2. When sinners are exceeding wicked, and have provoked God grievously, as they did here by this blasphemous proverb, yet even then God shows mercy. They had provoked him into the field, &c.; God might immediately have slain them, but he forbears them still, admonishes them of judgment near at hand; Go, say to them, "The days are at hand, and the effect of every vision." God tries them yet longer, and labours to awaken them with consideration of the nearness of danger.

Obs. 3. Length of time doth not frustrate and null the threatenings of God against sinners. Jeremiah had prophesied above thirty years, had threatened sad judgments, and because they came not to pass in so long time, they conceived they would come to nothing; but whatever be the distance of time between a threatening going forth, and the execution of it, yet it shall not fall to the ground, but have its time of fulfilling, if repentance intervene not.

IV. The confirmation of the confutation; "For there shall be no more any vain vision," &c.

Here begins the confirmation of the confutation. False prophets, who had vain visions, told them it should not be as Jeremiah had prophesied; Jerusalem should not be destroyed, they should not go into captivity, but dwell safely there, and enjoy that good land; but what saith God? "There shall be no more any vain vision:" the Hebrew runs thus, There shall not be any more all vision of vanity. Some refer these words to the true prophets and their vision, but they are put hard to it how to make it out, how some of their visions have been vain, for that is implied when it is said, There shall not be any more all, or any, vain vision; as when God saith, I will smite you no more, it argues, God hath smitten. But thus I conceive it may be taken: if it refer to the true prophets, There shall not be any more all vision of vanity; that is, hitherto you have looked upon all the vision of Jeremiah as a vision of vanity; but it shall be so no more; you shall have visions that shall be real, and quickly take place: but I incline to those who judge the words meant of the false prophets who had filled the people with vain visions, but they should be no more; God would make good the visions he had given touching the king and people, temple, city, and land, and this would put an end to all the vain visions of the false prophets.

"Nor flattering divination." מקסם חלק *divinatio blandientis; miksam* is from קסם *futura prædicere*, to foretell things to come, to divine good or evil; it is taken both ways, and when in the evil sense, it comprehends whatever is done by witchery, sorcery, astrology, or the like. 1 Sam. xxviii. 8, Saul comes to the witch, and saith, קסומי נא לי באוב *Divina quæso mihi in Pythone*, "I pray thee divine unto me by the familiar spirit." So 2 Kings xvii. 17, "They used divinations," ויקסמו קסמים They divined divinations that were wicked ones. Hence קסם is put for a soothsayer, Josh. xiii. 22, "Balaam the son of Beor," הקסם *illum magum;* and Numb. xxiii. 23, Balaam saith, כי לא-נחש ביעקב ולא-קסם בישראל "Surely there is no enchantment against Jacob, nor any divination against Israel:" no soothsaying, charming, prognostication, had power against Israel. The false prophets being addicted to magic, astrology, and such wicked arts, told them that whatever was prophesied by the other prophets of the king of Babylon's coming and taking Jerusalem, yet all should be well; which they gathered from the stars and planets.

Divinations were sometimes from the entrails of beasts or birds; as Ezek. xxi. 21, "The king of Babylon stood at the parting of the way, at the head of the two ways, to use divination; he consulted with images, he looked in the liver."

Lavater thinks their divinations were astrological, and that they had taken up the practice of heathens, who looked at and consulted much with the stars. Isa. xlvii. 13, "Let now the astrologers, the stargazers, the monthly prognosticators, stand up, and save thee from these things that shall come upon thee:" these things were spoken of Babylon, who made use of such artists, but in vain; and it was the use of the Jews to do so likewise; 2 Kings xvii. 16, 17, "They worshipped all the host of heaven, and used divination and enchantments:" to these the people hearkened; therefore, Jer. xxix. 8, "Let not your prophets and diviners, that be in the midst of you, deceive you."

Hence I might take a hint to speak against that part of astrology as unlawful, yea damnable, which is judicial and prognosticative. From the conjunction of planets, the benign and oblique aspects of them, men gather and foretell things to come; yea, some think that all material contingent accidents which concern man, are written in the face of heaven; and that God sets the stars in heaven to signify such things. If Deodate goes too far in his annotations that way, our learned divines in their annotations on the place, correct Gen. i. 14. that error, and give no allowance to judicial astrology; they say the place giveth no warrant to the presumption of prognosticators or judiciary astrologers, to foretell the fortunes of men, or fates of civil estates, by the stars; or to make any prediction of any other supernatural events from the face of the heavens, or the impression of the planets, or from the temperature, figure, colour, or posture of the celestial bodies; for such arts of divination are condemned by the word of God: Deut. xviii. 10, "There shall not be found among you any one that useth divinations, or an observer of times;" such men are bad; for, ver. 12, "all that do these things are abomination unto the Lord." Listen not therefore to their lying observations; it matters not what the conjunctions and aspects of planets and stars are, reason and religion will qualify them. If holy men have shut and opened heaven with their prayers, if they have cast out devils, they may stop the influence of stars. Stars are made for man, not man for stars. If the Lord be with us, let Saturn, Jupiter, Mars, &c. be against us. One of note saith of the astrologers and time observers, Either they tell you of things adverse or prosperous; if prosperous, and deceive you, you are miserable by expecting; if adverse things, and false, you are miserable by fearing: if they tell you true things, and not good, you are presently miserable before they come; if they foretell good things to come, your expectation will weary your hope, and your hope will deflour, yea devour the future fruit of your joy. No regard therefore ought ever to be paid to those persons who pretend to impart a knowledge of future events.

"Flattering." חלק *blandientis*, nor divination of a flatterer; the Hebrew word originally signifies, smooth, plain, even, and properly refers to things which concern the touching, as any thin plate, butter, oil; and metaphorically is transferred to the speech, and instruments of it, noting out the sweetness, smoothness, and flattery thereof. Psal. v. 9, "They flatter with their tongues," Hebrew is the same, and may be rendered, they smooth with their tongue, and make smooth their tongue, that is, they give flattering and deceitful words: so the apostle hath it, Rom. iii. 13, "With their tongues they have used deceit. So Psal. lv. 21, "The words of his mouth were smoother than butter, but war was in his heart;" that is, his words were flattering and deceitful; the singular number is put here for the plural, flatterer for flatterers, they promised the people a happy condition of things, and fed them with smooth words: the Septuagint hath it τὰ πρὸς χάριν, those things which seem gracious, which are acceptable and make way for favour, which please: the Vulgate reads it, *neque divinatio ambigua*, no more doubtful divination, such as the oracles were, which might be taken divers, yea contrary ways.

Obs. 1. False prophets have pretences and cunning ways to prevail with the people. The verse points out the practice of such; and what is that? they had visions and divinations, and when they came to the people and told them of these, they were taken therewith; Jer. xiv. 14, they prophesied lies in the Lord's name, they said he sent them, he commanded them, and so by these pretences made way for their lies. 1 Kings xxii. 24, Zedekiah smites Micaiah on the cheek, and saith, "Which way went the Spirit of the Lord from me unto thee." He pretended he had the Spirit, spake by it, and so gained upon those who heard him. Matt. vii. 17, "Beware of false prophets, which come to you in sheep's clothing;" they seem harmless, their countenance, words, and carriage do plead for them, and usher in their false opinions; no false teachers but have some pretences to ingratiate themselves with the people. Eph. iv. 14, Paul speaks of the condition of the people, how they were "carried about with every wind of doctrine, by the sleight of men, and cunning craftiness, whereby they lie in wait to deceive;" by mutual opinions and subtle sophisms, they cheated the people, as cunning gamesters at dice lie in wait to cheat young novices.

Obs. 2. That their visions and divinations are false and flattering.

(1.) False. They are called here, visions of vanity, there is no truth in them, no trust to be given unto them; the false prophets had their names from the falsehoods which they presented to the people. Sometimes they are said to "prophesy lies, false vision and divination, a thing of nought, the deceit of their heart," Jer. xiv. 14. Sometimes they are said to "make vain, and speak a vision of their own heart," chap. xxiii. 16; to "cause dreams to be dreamed," chap. xxix. 8. They are called "foolish prophets, that follow their own spirit, and have seen nothing," Ezek. xiii. 3; that "have seen vanity, and lying divination," ver. 6, which is as nothing. There were many such prophets amongst them; and this is the way that antichrist worketh, now in times of the gospel; 2 Thess. ii. 9, 10, his "coming is after the working of Satan with all power and signs and lying wonders, and with all deceivableness of unrighteousness." When Satan comes into a man, it is with efficacy, and there he works strangely and deceitfully; so antichrist, when he comes into the church or state, it is with efficacy; he pretends that all ecclesiastical power is his, he sits in the temple as God, and exalts himself above all that is called God, even above the civil powers, therefore, in ver. 9, is said to come "with all power." Of his "signs and lying wonders," you may see, Rev. xiii. 3, 13, 15. "And with all deceivableness of unrighteousness;" that is, with all the art and cunning to deceive, which an unrighteous heart, spirit, state, and policy, can afford.

(2.) Flattering. Jer. xxviii. 2—4, Hananiah, a false prophet, flatters them, and feeds them with vain hopes, saying, "Thus saith the Lord of hosts, I have broken the yoke of the king of Babylon: within two full years will I bring again into this place all the vessels of the Lord's house, and Jeconiah the son of Jehoiakim king of Judah, with all the captives of Judah, that went into Babylon." Here were pleasing words, which lulled them in security. When Ahab had a mind to go up to Ramoth-gilead and fight, what said the prophets to him? 1 Kings xxii. 12, "Go up to Ramoth-gilead, and prosper; for the Lord shall deliver it into the king's hand:" and when Micaiah a true prophet was called to speak, they would have corrupted him; say the messengers, "The words of the prophets declare good unto the king with one mouth: let thy word, I pray thee, be like unto the word of one of them, and speak that which is good." Foolish people think those words good which flatter and please them; but such words undo them. Ezek. xiii. 10, "Because they have seduced my people, saying, Peace; and there was no peace; and one built up a wall, and, lo, others daubed it with untempered mortar:" the true prophets threw down Jerusalem by their prophecies, but the false built up a wall, prophesied safety, deliverance, and others agreed with them, but this was flattery and their destruction; Prov. xxvi. 28, "A flattering mouth worketh ruin." This Paul knew, and therefore justifies himself, that at no time he used "flattering words," 1 Thess. ii. 5. If he should have pleased men, he should not have been the servant of Christ.

Obs. 3. Vain visions and flattering divinations of false prophets do cause people to be secure and fearless of divine threats. They regarded not what Jeremiah prophesied against Jerusalem, so long as Hananiah and such men prophesied the contrary; Ahab feared not scattering and falling at Ramoth-gilead, whilst the false prophets said, "Go, and prosper." Man's nature is apter to be secure than to fear, because pleasing things are sooner taken in than such as are averse to them.

Obs. 4. God hath his time to confute and confound visions of vanity, and divinations of flattery. "There shall be no more any vain vision," &c. When the Lord made good his word, brought Nebuchadnezzar to the walls of Jerusalem, gave it up into his hands, then were all the lying prophets confuted, and confounded with shame. Events discover visions, and distinguish prophets: Jer. xxviii. 9, "The prophet which prophesieth of peace, when the word of the prophet shall come to pass, then shall the prophet be known, that the Lord hath truly sent him." If it proved true that was prophesied, then was it a vision of God, if not, a vision of vanity, and this was the way for them to try the prophets by. Deut. xviii. 21, 22, the question is there, How shall we know whether a prophet speak of himself or from God? the answer is, Look to the event; if the thing he speaks come not to pass, it is not of God, it is a lie; shame and confusion to the prophet: when Ahab was wounded and fell at Ramoth-gilead, then the false prophets were confuted, and Zedekiah confounded, running into an inner chamber to hide himself, 2 Kings xxii. 25. Hence the Lord is said to frustrate the tokens of liars, to make diviners mad, to turn wise men backward, and to make their knowledge foolish, Isa. xliv. 25.

"For I am the Lord: I will speak, and the word that I shall speak shall come to pass," &c. In this and the last verse, the Lord promiseth to make good his word, and that without delay; it should not be prolonged as they imagined, but quickly take effect, and accomplish those ends it was intended for: I will confound the false prophets and justify the true; they speak and it never comes to pass, I will speak by my prophets, and it shall come.

In the words of this verse you have,

I. A reason, which first looks back to what was said in ver. 24. Vain vision and flattering divination shall cease; why? "I am the Lord;" and power is in my hand to discover vain and flattering prophets, to confound them and their visions. Secondly, forward to what God should say: "I will speak, it shall come to pass, it shall not be prolonged;" and why? "I am the Lord," Jehovah, and will give being to my word.

II. A general promise, of speaking what he pleases, and making it good: "I will speak, and it shall come to pass;" there shall not be any delay.

III. A special application of it to the house of Israel, and their time: "In your days, O ye rebellious house, will I say and perform."

Quest. Whether do the sins of people cause judgments threatened to come sooner than the time appointed, because it is said here "it shall be no more prolonged;" as if he should say, I thought yet to have prolonged, deferred my judgments, but they shall come speedily?

Answ. As men's repentance may prevent judgments threatened, so their sins may hasten them. Jer. xlviii. 16, "The calamity of Moab is near to come, and his affliction hasteth fast:" Moab's sins hastened Moab's afflictions. When men sin with a high hand after judgments given out, those sins add wings to judgment. Mal. iii. 5, "I will be a swift witness," saith God, "against sorcerers, adulterers, false swearers, those that oppress the hireling, widow, fatherless, and turn aside the stranger from his right;" he will come flying to judgment against them. 2 Pet. ii. 1, sinners are said to "bring upon themselves swift destruction," destruction makes haste to them. When men shall scoff at divine threats and jest at judgments, this provokes God to hasten them. Isa. v. 19, "Let him make speed, and hasten his work, that we may see it." They were so far from fearing and believing the threats of God, that they made a mock at them; hence saith the Lord, Jer. i. 12, "I will hasten my word to perform it," I will take the first opportunity to make it good. God will shorten the day of affliction for the elect's sake, and hasten the days of judgment for the wicked's sake.

Obs. 1. The thoughts and hopes of wicked men about the threatenings of judgment are foolish and vain; they think and hope, that either they will not come at all, or if they do, it will be a long time after. "It shall be no more prolonged." You conceit, because the time is long, that there is no such thing, or that it will not be in your days; but you are deceived, such threats are groundless, and hopes are vain: Jer. v. 12, "They have belied the Lord, and said, It is not he (that speaks by these prophets); neither shall evil come upon us, neither shall we see sword nor famine; and the prophets shall become wind, and the word is not in them:" they are deceived, not we; they look for a black and sad day, which will not come, and we look for good days, good things: therefore the prophet, impersonating them, saith, chap. viii. 15, "We looked for peace, but no good came; and for a time of health, and behold trouble!" They would not believe that ever an adversary should have entered within the gates of Jerusalem, Lam. iv. 12.

Obs. 2. That whatever word the Lord speaks, he will make it good. "I will speak, and it shall come to pass." Whatever God hath spoken by the prophets or apostles, yea, whatever is spoken warrantably from the word by any faithful minister of his, he will accomplish the same. He doth not possess his servants with vain visions, or flattering divinations; whatever he utters by them is divine and infallible; he is Jehovah, a God of power and faithfulness, sufficient every way to fulfil his promises and perform his threatenings. Some take these words, "I am the Lord," to be an asseveration, or an oath, and the sense to lie thus, As sure as I am God, Jehovah, that have being of myself, and give being to all others, so sure will I give being to my promises and threatenings; so that not only heaven and earth must pass away, before any tittle of any truth of the Lord's shall fall to the ground, but even God himself must cease to be, before his word shall be without effect. Isa. xliv. 24, "I am the Lord that maketh all things:" that "I am" doth frustrate and confound liars, diviners, wizards, and all impostors, as it is ver. 25: "that confirmeth the word of his servant, and performeth the counsel of his messengers," ver. 26. What word soever Isaiah gave out, the Lord confirmed and performed it. He gave out the word touching Cyrus, that he should be a shepherd to God's people, that he should further the Jews' return out of Babylon, and building of the temple: and this was above two hundred years before his birth, as Deodate saith in his notes upon the place, and about two hundred, as our late annotations have it: but if we reckon by Scripture account, you will find it not so much; for this prophecy of Cyrus was delivered by Isaiah after Hezekiah's sickness, chap. xxxviii. in which fifteen years were added to his days; and from thence it was but a hundred and twenty-five years and six months to Zedekiah's carrying into captivity, which was eleven years after the captivity began, for chronologers reckon the beginning of the captivity from the time of Jehoiachin's carrying away, and the Scripture countenances it, Ezek. i. 2: so then, reckon the captivity from Jehoiachin, seventy years, and there are but a hundred and fourteen before, and these make one hundred and eighty-four; and this person, prophesied of so long before, did God in due time give to the world, and stirred up to be helpful to his people, Ezra i. 1—3, and so made good both what Isaiah said here, and Jer. xxix. 10. God's word must take place, whoever gains or loses by it; Isa. lv. 11, "The word that goeth out of my mouth, it shall not return unto me void, but it shall accomplish that which I please, and it shall prosper in the thing whereto I sent it." Zech. i. 6, "My words and my statutes, which I commanded my servants the prophets, did they not take hold of your fathers?" God appointed them to do so, and they did accordingly; God's words overtook them, thinking to escape. Daniel bears witness to this truth, chap. ix. 12, "He hath confirmed his words, which he spake against us."

Obs. 5. The corrupt heads and hearts of men are subtle, and prone to elude and put off those truths which are presented unto them by the servants of God. The Lord sent his prophets unto them early and late; they being faithful, laid open the judgments of God, told them of their danger, invited them to repentance, mourned for the slight entertainment they found, &c. And what then? they either mocked at them, as it is in 2 Chron. xxxvi. 16, or charged them with falsehoods and lies, Jer. v. 12, 13, or resolved not to hearken to them, Jer. xliv. 16, or put it off, as not concerning them at all, or if it did, not for a long time, for those that were after them, not the present generation; ver. 27 of this chapter, "The vision is for many days, and he prophesieth of the times that are far off." Thus were they witty and wicked against themselves, to turn aside the stroke of God's word, which having been entertained, might have done their souls good. This was the practice in Christ's and the apostles' times, one thing or other still was pretended to wave the doctrine of Christ; as the meanness of his person, Matt. xiii. 55, 56; John vii. 27; his breaking of the sabbath, John v. 16; ix. 10, 16, "This man is not of God," &c. They said he blasphemed, Matt. ix. 3, that he deceived the people, John vii. 12, made himself a king and spake against Cæsar, John xix. 12; they pretended his doctrine to be new, Acts xvii. 19, to be hard and severe, John vi. 60, to be against Moses, Acts vi. 11; that it was heretical, Acts xxiv. 14, that he spake too particularly to them, Luke xi. 45, that the rulers and great ones received it not, John vii. 48, "Have any of the rulers," &c.; that his doctrine, and the followers of it, made great stirs wherever it came, caused sects and schisms, Acts xix. 23; xxviii. 22.

CHAPTER XIII.

Ver. 1—7. *And the word of the Lord came unto me, saying, Son of man, prophesy against the prophets of Israel that prophesy, and say thou unto them that prophesy out of their own hearts, Hear ye the word of the Lord; Thus saith the Lord God; Woe unto the foolish prophets, that follow their own spirit, and have seen nothing! O Israel, thy prophets are like the foxes in the deserts. Ye have not gone up into the gaps, neither made up the hedge for the house of Israel to stand in the battle in the day of the Lord. They have seen vanity and lying divination, saying, The Lord saith: and the Lord hath not sent them: and they have made others to hope that they would confirm the word. Have ye not seen a vain vision, and have ye not spoken a lying divination, whereas ye say, The Lord saith it: albeit I have not spoken?*

The former chapter concerned the king and the people; this concerns only the false prophets and prophetesses, who taking upon them that office, were led by their own spirits, and deceived the people with vain visions and lying divinations, to accomplish their own ends: against these doth the Lord set our prophet Ezekiel on work to prophesy severely.

In the chapter you have two general parts.

I. A prophecy against false prophets, in the first sixteen verses.

II. A prophecy against women prophets, from the 17th verse to the end.

In the first part you have the judgments and sins of the false prophets declared and laid down.

1. The judgments threatened against them, which are in ver. 2, 3, 8, 9, 11, 13—16.

2. The sins causing those judgments threatened, and they are expressed in ver. 2—10, 16. God's threatenings and their sins are promiscuously delivered by our prophet, and we shall handle them as they lie.

Ver. 1, 2, and 17, do show the author of this prophecy; and that was the Lord, who bade Ezekiel prophesy, and set his face against them. Our prophet had divine warrant for what he said, and wisely prefixes it, when he was to deal with false prophets, who had neither word nor warrant from God for what they said or did: true prophets have their commission and instruction from God.

In ver. 2, you have,

1. The appellation, "Son of man."

2. A command, and that is twofold:

(1.) Is to Ezekiel, "Prophesy."

(2.) Is to the false prophets, "Hear ye the word," &c.

3. The kind of prophecy, and that is comminatory; "Prophesy against the prophets of Israel."

4. The sin that moves God to set the prophet against them, and that is, They "prophesy out of their own heart."

"Against the prophets of Israel." Whether the prophets in Babylon or in Zion, you may demand; for there were false prophets in Babylon, who were the prophets of Israel, because they prophesied to the captive Jews, Jer. xxix. 8, 9; and there were false prophets at Jerusalem, Jer. xxvii. 14, and they were the prophets of Israel also? We may understand this prophecy of the false prophets in both places.

"That prophesy out of their own hearts." Hebrew, them that are prophets out of their own hearts. To prophesy out of their own hearts, is,

1. To prophesy upon their own mere motion. They are prophets because themselves will be prophets, and they prophesy because they will prophesy; they have no call to this office but their wills, they thrust themselves upon it.

2. The things they prophesy are their own; what their fancies, lusts, affections, carnal reason, suggest unto them, those things they deliver; their prophecies came by the will of man. 2 Pet. i. 21, "For the prophecy in old time came not by the will of man." The true prophets did not prophecy out of their own hearts, after their own wills, but they spake as they were moved by the Holy Spirit, what that brought in they gave out; divine truths were presented to them, and those they commended to the people: but false prophets had nothing of or from the Spirit; they had all out of their own hearts; yet pretended

they were inspired and had the Spirit. 1 Kings xxii. 24, "Which way went the Spirit of the Lord from me unto thee?" Zedekiah and all the rest of the false prophets thought they had the Spirit of the Lord, but it was the spirit of Satan, a lying spirit, they had; ver. 22, "I will go forth, and be a lying spirit in the mouth of all his prophets."

Quest. If they speak out of their own hearts, why are they called prophets? they are prophets that speak from God, and not themselves.

Answ. The word prophet is taken largely, for any one that foretells things true or false, and is common to good and bad; the Scripture speaks according to the use of words. Titus i. 12, "One of themselves, even a prophet of their own." That was Epimenides a poet; for poets were commonly called prophets: and so the Scripture gives the name to any foretelling things; 1 Kings xviii. 19, "Baal's prophets, and the prophets of the groves;" 2 Pet. ii. 1, "There were false prophets among the people."

"Thus saith the Lord God; Woe unto the foolish prophets," &c. Here the prophet proceeds in denouncing judgment, and describing those false prophets.

1. The judgment denounced is in this word, "Woe," a little word, but very comprehensive; all evils are contained in it. They promise all happiness to the people, but, woe to themselves! woe to their bodies, woe to their souls, woe to their names, woe to them here, woe to them hereafter! The dreadful judgments mentioned in the Revelation, are called woes; chap. ix. 12, "One woe is past; and, behold, there come two woes more hereafter."

2. The description of the prophets; they are foolish, and this foolishness of theirs is evidenced two ways:

(1.) They follow their own spirits.

(2.) They have seen nothing.

"Foolish." הנבלים from נבל which signifies vile, foolish, frail. These prophets were subtle and crafty, abounding with carnal and worldly prudence, but in the things of God they were blind and foolish; they called light darkness, and darkness light; they were lifted up with their pretended visions and divinations; they despised and insulted over the true prophets; they boasted themselves to be the men of God's counsel, and laboured to be had in admiration of all; they foresaw no danger, but spake pleasing things to the people, prophesying safety and good days, and this was their foolishness: there was no divine wisdom or truth in them.

"That follow their own spirit." These words are answerable to those in ver. 2, "That prophesy out of their own heart:" the Hebrew is, who walk after their own spirit: their own spirits led them, not the Spirit of God. In chap. i. it is said, The Spirit was in the wheels, and they went whither the Spirit led them, ver. 20; but these prophets had not the Spirit in them, neither went after it, but after their own spirit; whatever their own spirits dictated to them, that they embraced, magnified, and gave out to the people.

"Have seen nothing." The true prophets had visions of God, divine revelation; their understandings were in an extraordinary manner irradiated by the Spirit of God, and they saw, that is, understood, the mind of God. Hence prophets were called seers; Amos vii. 12, "O thou seer, flee away;" 2 Kings xvii. 13, God testified against them by all the seers. They foresaw judgments to come, and other things which God revealed unto them: Numb. xii. 6, "If there be a prophet among you, I will make myself known unto him in a vision." But these false prophets had seen nothing; they had no vision, no discovery of God's mind unto them any way.

Obs. 1. It is no new thing that there is in the church of God false prophets, corrupt opinions, great opposition to the truth, differences and divisions. In Ezekiel's days there were false prophets, which deluded the people, which opposed the true prophets with much insolence, which caused great stirs, contentions, and divisions amongst the captives in Babylon and people at Jerusalem; see for both these the 28th and 29th chapters of Jeremiah, where Hanan opposes Jeremiah, and Jeremiah writes letters into Babylon to quiet them there. In Ahab's days you may find false prophets, and their number very great: 1 Kings xviii. 19, "The prophets of Baal were four hundred and fifty, and the prophets of the groves four hundred." They exceeded the number of the true prophets eight to one, for they were but one hundred, hid by Obadiah in caves, ver. 4. And these false prophets drew many of the people from the worship of the true God; others they staggered, and made to halt between two opinions; and so caused great division, opposition, and persecution in Israel. There have always been and ever will be false teachers and prophets among the people of God. In the gospel you read of false Christs, Mark xiii. 22, false apostles, 2 Cor. xi. 13, false teachers, 2 Pet. ii. 1, and many false prophets that should arise, Matt. xxiv. 11. The churches in the apostles' days were much troubled with those who vented corrupt opinions and caused great contentions. The church of Galatia had those among them who preached another gospel, and justification by the law, and so troubled them, that the apostle wished them cut off, chap. v. 12. There were lying apostles in the church of Ephesus; the doctrine of Balaam and the Nicolaitanes in the church of Pergamos, &c. Such men, with their opinions, errors, and consequences of them, God suffers, to clear up truth, to make it more precious, to try the godly, to discover hypocrites, to show his power and wisdom, that can work good out of evil, and preserve his people in the midst of contentions.

Obs. 2. See here who are true prophets, and who are false. The word of the Lord came to Ezekiel, it came not to them; the true prophets saw visions, the false saw nothing; they were moved by the Spirit of God, these by their own spirits; out of their own hearts came what they delivered, out of heaven what the other delivered; God spake by the true prophets, Satan by the false, he is a lying spirit in the mouth of all the false prophets, 1 Kings xxii. 22. Either Satan's or their own they speak: Jer. xxiii, 16, "They speak a vision of their own heart, and not out of the mouth of the Lord;" ver. 26, "They are prophets of the deceit of their own hearts;" ver. 27, 28, they tell dreams; they feed the people with chaff, and not wheat, and make them to err and forget the name of God. But the true prophets ever spoke what they received from the Lord: therefore Micaiah, 1 Kings xxii. 14, told some desiring him to speak somewhat of his own, that as the Lord lived he would speak nothing but what the Lord should say unto him. Christ saith, John vii. 16, 18, "My doctrine is not mine, but his that sent me. He that speaketh of himself seeketh his own glory; but he that seeketh his glory that sent him, the same is true," &c.

Obs. 3. That what comes from man, however esteemed or magnified by men, is worthless in God's account. They prophesied out of their own hearts, followed their own spirits, which they set a price upon; but this the Lord blames, condemns, he calls foolish, mentions their own hearts and spirits in opposition to the revelations and inspirations of his Spirit, which only are of weight and worth; therefore whatever prophets or ministers do bring of their own, it is a wicked forgery. It is the office of the Spirit of truth to give out truth; he leads into all truth, he takes of Christ's and shows unto those who are Christ's prophets, apostles, and ministers, John xvi. 13, 14. If men preach or prophesy any thing which is not from the Spirit, but from themselves, it is not acceptable unto God, neither should be entertained by us. Hence you shall find, that what men have brought of their own is called lies, Jer. xxvii. 10, dreams, chap. xxiii. 32, untempered mortar, Ezek. xxii. 28, a thing of nought, Jer. xiv. 14, deceit, chap. xxiii. 26, perverse things, Acts xx. 30, commandments of men, Mark vii. 7, wisdom of this world, 1 Cor. ii. 6, another Jesus, another spirit, another gospel, 2 Cor. xi. 4. What is man's, is opposite to God and Christ; therefore Paul saith expressly, 2 Cor. iv. 5, "We preach not ourselves, but Christ Jesus the Lord;" only what we have from him by his Spirit, that we preach unto you. Paul was a man of great parts, a great scholar, and yet durst not vent any thing of his own.

Obs. 4. The folly and madness of false prophets, who pretend they have all from God, yet follow their own spirits. Those words "have seen nothing," import, that they pretended they had seen something, that they told the people they had visions from God. It is frequent in Scripture to hear of their visions: Isa. xxviii. 7, "They err in vision;" Jer. xiv. 14, "They prophesy a false vision;" chap. xxiii. 16, "They speak a vision of their own heart;" Zech. xiii. 4, "They shall be ashamed every one of his vision;" and ver. 7, of this chapter, it was a vain vision and a lying divination which they had, but the pretence was they had all from God; "The Lord saith it," albeit he spake not. Thus they made him author of all their lying, vain, and false prophecies, which was extreme madness and folly in them. Herein was a dreadful hand of God upon them; because they were malicious against the true prophets, and received not the truth with the love of it, God left them to blindness, hardness, to believe lies, so that they thought that to be from God, which was from their own spirits, or from Satan the spirit of errors.

Obs. 5. That wicked prophets are in a dreadful condition, woe is their portion. "Woe unto the foolish prophets!" they are men set out for judgment, under malediction, appointed to condemnation and utter destruction. Jer. xxiii. 15, God tells such prophets that he "will feed them with wormwood, and make them drink the water of gall:" God will deal bitterly with them; Jer. xiv. 15, "By sword and famine shall those prophets be consumed." Rev. xx. 10, the devil, the beast, and the false prophet are in the same lake of fire and brimstone, tormented continually and eternally: by the prophet some understand the pope, some his clergy; we may take in all false prophets and teachers, who "bring upon themselves swift destruction," 2 Pet. ii. 1; they should be thrust through by their own friends when they prophesied, Zech. xiii. 3.

"O Israel, thy prophets are like the foxes in the deserts." The words hold forth,

1. A pathetical exclamation, "O Israel."

2. A description of these prophets, they "are like foxes;" and that we must make out unto you.

The land of Israel abounded with foxes; Judg. xv. 4, Samson caught three hundred at once; Neh. iv. 3, the enemies told the Jews that if a fox went up the wall they built, he would break it down; Cant. ii. 15, "Take us the foxes," which shows their land had store of them. Now the prophets of Ezekiel's days are likened to foxes.

(1.) A fox is a subtle, crafty creature; the serpent and the fox exceed therein. The fox's craft is known in deceiving and catching fish, poultry, lambs, and fowls; when he is hungry he will lie as dead, and so the fowls coming to prey upon him as a dead carcass, he snaps them, and preys upon them; for hares, he counterfeits a sporting with them, till at last he seizeth upon them: he hath many dens to flee unto, and some of them have many entrances, that he may more easily deceive the hunters; Luke ix. 48, "Foxes have holes." False prophets are subtle to deceive the people; they say they are sent of the Lord, have seen visions, and make use of his name, Jer. xiv. 14; Zech. xiii. 3. Sometimes they did wear rough garments to deceive, Zech. xiii. 4. The true prophets had such garments, Isa. xx. 2, sackcloth and hairy vestments, and the false prophets would imitate them, that they might without jealousy the better deceive the people. Sometimes they came in sheep's clothing, Matt. vii. 15, and spake fair, smooth, pleasing words; they are full of insinuations, windings, turnings, rhetoric, language, to gain upon people; they are deep and politic to carry on designs to promote their own ends; they can conform to men, and transform themselves into variety of shapes, 2 Cor. xi. 13, "False apostles, deceitful workers, transforming themselves into the apostles of Christ," and by this means they had advantage to do what they aimed at. How foxish was the old prophet when he set upon the young prophet, 1 Kings xiii. 18, saying, "I am a prophet also as thou art; and an angel spake unto me by the word of the Lord, saying, Bring him back with thee into thine house, that he may eat bread and drink water. But he lied unto him," and so prevailed. False prophets and teachers have cunning carriage, cunning arguments and speech, to beguile others with: 2 Pet. i. 16, "We have not followed cunningly devised fables;" there were such as did. Arius was one of these foxes, who counterfeited that he was of the same mind with the orthodox; and that he might be received into communion of the church again, he subscribed the Nicene creed, and decrees, *Sicut subscripsi, ita quoque credo,* I believe as I have subscribed. Now he had in his bosom his own wicked confession, which he had written at home, and subscribed with his own name. The popish priests and Jesuits, what foxes have they been in churches and states to advance the catholic cause! In the eastern parts they show once a year their converts, in white, with palms in their hands, which is a great policy to draw others to their way. Contzin hath laid down subtle ways to cheat a state of its religion. The prelates had consulted with the fox when they made the *et cætera* oath, to support their tottering kingdom. It were to be wished that there were less of the fox now among the prophets, and more of the lamb.

(2.) The fox is cruel and malicious, the object of all his policy is the destruction of the other animals; when he gets amongst the poultry, the learned observe, he does not eat of the fowls till first he has killed them all. False teachers and prophets are foxes in their cruelty and maliciousness. Zedekiah smites Micaiah on the cheek, 1 Kings xxii. 24; he dealt injuriously and rigidly with him. Shemaiah stirred up authority against Jeremiah the true prophet, whom he would have put in the stocks and prison, Jer. xxix. 24, 26. (Jer. xxvi. 8.) And this would not suffice, they proceed to blood; Ezek. xxii. 25, "There is a conspiracy of her prophets in the midst thereof," not only like foxes, but even "like lions ravening the prey." They have devoured souls; the prophets laid their heads together to suck the blood of innocents: Lam. iv. 13, it was the prophets and the priests which shed the blood of the just in the midst of Jerusalem; they were not to meddle in matters of blood, but they incensed authority to do it, they preached against them, told those who had the power in their hand, that they should do God good service in sacrificing such persons. So great hath been the malice of wicked prophets and priests ever against the saints, that they have never rested till they have gotten their blood shed. The pope and his priests filled christendom with blood. It was the prelates and priests in queen Mary's days that brought so many to the fire, and caused that queen to imbrue her hands in innocent blood.

(3.) The fox is greedy of prey; so false prophets, they are greedy enough. Mic. iii. 5, "He that putteth not into their mouths, they even prepare war against him;" if they were not fed with the finest and fattest there was no peace, no safety. Ver. 11, "The priests teach for hire, and the prophets divine for money:" it was not the good of souls that they sought, they made merchandise of them, but gain was in their eyes; Ezek. xxii. 25, "They have taken the treasure and precious things," those they would be sure to lay hands on. Isa. lvi. 11, "They are greedy dogs, which can never have enough, and they are shepherds that cannot understand: they all look to their own way, every one for his gain, from his quarter;" the words for "greedy" in the Hebrew are עזי־נפש strong of soul, appetite, stomach, they presently concoct, digest whatever they take in; souls, Ezek. xxii. 25, widows' houses, Matt. xxiii. 14. It is known what great revenues the popish priests and prophets have had in the kingdoms under the popish jurisdiction; in king John's days, his revenues were sixty thousand marks, and theirs seventy thousand. Balaam was a false prophet, and he loved the wages of unrighteousness; he would have cursed the people of God for reward, if God himself had not withheld, Numb. xxii. A cardinal coming to Rome, and seeing nothing but offering of moneys at the election of a pope, said, In this way the roman pontiffs are made.

(4.) Foxes are timorous creatures, and when danger comes, they run to their holes, and shift for themselves; so are false prophets and teachers: 1 Kings xxii. 25, when trouble came, Zedekiah fled into his holes, he went from chamber to chamber, to hide himself. John x. 12, "He that is an hireling, and not the shepherd, whose own the sheep are not, seeth the wolf coming, and leaveth the sheep, and fleeth:" by wolf you may understand persecution, danger, when these approach and look sternly upon the man, he fleeth. Wickedness always renders men fearful.

(5.) The fox runs up and down from place to place doing mischief night and day. Cant. ii. 15, "Take us the foxes, the little foxes, that spoil the vines:" they ran from vineyard to vineyard, they spoiled the grapes and vines themselves. So false prophets and teachers are like them in this, they went up and down in Israel; they were at Samaria, at Jerusalem, Jer. xxiii. 13, 14, in Babylon, Jer. xxix. 25. In Paul's days there were such who went up and down from house to house, and "subverted whole houses, teaching things which they ought not for filthy lucre's sake," Tit. i. 11; and Christ tells us of such who compass sea and land to make one proselyte. Are not Jesuits and priests sent into most parts of the world to make proselytes, and to spoil the tender vines and grapes where they are.

(6.) The fox keeps his nature, whatever you do to him, or do with him; you may chain him up, but you cannot change him, it is questioned whether he can be tamed, if he get loose he is the same again that ever he was; so false prophets.

"In the deserts." In the breaches of the hedges, through which the foxes and other beasts entered into the vineyards. Some think there is nothing peculiar in these words; it is ordinary to say, the beasts of the field, the birds of heaven, and so, the foxes of the desert; but desert notes places neglected, without any fence, in those places the foxes abounded, were most hungry and ravening.

Obs. 1. It is a sad judgment to a people, when the prophets degenerate, and become foxes. Foxes, you know, are a cumber, a plague to the country where they live; and so are false prophets, wherever they come. They caused the people to err, and destroyed the way of their paths, Isa. iii. 12, they perverted and gainsaid what the true prophets gave in. They flattered the people, and concealed their sins and judgments due to them; Lam. ii. 14, "Thy prophets have seen vain and foolish things for thee: and they have not discovered thine iniquity, to turn away thy captivity; but have seen for thee false burdens and causes of banishment." Jer. l. 6, "Their shepherds have caused them to go astray," and so brought destruction upon them; Isa. ix. 16, "The leaders of this people," that is, prophets and priests, "cause them to err;" and what then? "they that are led of them are destroyed." Jer. xii. 10, "Many pastors have destroyed my vineyard, they have trodden my portion under foot:" foxes destroy lambs, poultry, vines, but those destroy souls. Bernard sets down many qualities of false prophets and teachers: they love to bear rule; they think pride and profit to be piety; they think themselves happy if they may enlarge their borders; they build stately houses, love full tables, exact of the poor, look strangely or big upon the inferior sort, and honour great ones; they either teach not, or teach for their bellies. Such prophets are a burden, if not destruction, to those they are among: and when the prophets are foxes, the princes are lions, and judges wolves, Zeph. iii. 3, 4.

Obs. 2. It is matter of grief and complaint to heaven itself, when the prophets are subtle, covetous, cruel. "O Israel, thy prophets are like unto foxes." God laid it to heart to see such prophets amongst them, as sought themselves, and preyed upon the people. Isa. iii. 12, "O my people, they which lead thee," or call thee blessed, "cause thee to err, and destroy the way of thy paths." Their leaders, the priests, prophets, princes, did that which affected Heaven, and provoked the Lord to cry out, "O my people."

"Ye have not gone up into the gaps," &c. Here the Lord proceeds in accusing these prophets; and this accusation respects,

1. Their duty.
2. The end of their duty.

1. They are accused, first, not to do their duty, and that is set down in two metaphorical expressions:

(1.) They went not up into the gaps.
(2.) They made not up the hedge.

2. Not to have minded the end of their duty, which was, that the people might stand in battle in the day of the Lord.

"Into the gaps." בפרצות into the breaches. It is judged by divers of the learned, that this metaphor is taken from a siege, where the siegers labour to make breaches in the fortifications and walls of the place or city besieged; and it is their duty within, who have the command and power, to make up those breaches, and stand for the defence of the people and place where they are; but the prophets did not this, when judgments came in upon the people, they stood not in the breaches to divert them. Had he spoken before of military men, I should have rested in this sense of the word; but having spoken of false prophets, and here by an apostrophe turning to them, we may consider a metaphorical war. God was out with them and against them; Ezek. v. 8, he was the enemy bringing judgments upon them, the people, the city; religion and their laws were the walls, their sins the gaps which let in wrath upon them.

These prophets did not oppose the sins of the people, convince them of their idolatry, oppression, security, hypocrisy, profaneness, &c.; but either sinned with them, or winked at their sins; and so went not up into the gap to keep out the severe judgments of God from crowding in upon them. They should have called the people to repentance, declared the judgments of God to have been at hand, interceded mightily with the Lord for them, and if possible have prevented judgment; but these things they did not: Ezek. xxxiv. 4, "The diseased have ye not strengthened, neither have ye healed that which was sick, neither have ye bound up that which was broken, nor brought again that which was driven away, nor sought that which was lost." When the people made a calf and worshipped it, there was a great gap made in the law, in the true worship of God; and now wrath was coming out, and God would have destroyed them, had not "Moses stood in the breach, to turn away his wrath," Psal. cvi. 23. Gaps therefore are the breaches which sins make.

"Neither made up the hedge." The Hebrew is, ye have not hedged a hedge. This is a metaphor taken from gardens, orchards, vineyards, and enclosures, which having hedges made about them, are secure from swine and beasts breaking into them: these prophets, instead of making hedges for their defence, they made gaps for their enemy. The hedge about a church and state is, divine protection, sound doctrine, pure worship, holiness of life, and execution of justice; and when there is a violation of either of these, the hedge is broken down; and the way to make up the hedge again, is by fasting, prayer, and hearty repentance: these prophets minded neither sound doctrine, pure worship, holiness of life, nor called upon authority for execution of justice; there was a general violation of all things in the church and state, and they laid it not to heart, they neither fasted, prayed, nor repented, but increased the violations, trod down the hedge more, and made the gaps wider. Ezek. xxii. 30, "I sought for a man among them, that should make up the hedge, and stand in the gap before me for the land, that I should not destroy it: but I found none."

"To stand in the battle in the day of the Lord." Their care should have been for the people's good, that when the day of the Lord's fury and judgments came that he should war against his people, they might have been able to stand. By "battle" understand not only the siege they endured by the Babylonians, but all afflictions and miseries which befell them; and had the prophets been faithful to them, the day of the Lord's wrath would have been their day of repentance, and so they might have stood, and not fallen.

Obs. 1. That people's sins make way for judgments to come in upon them; they break down the wall and the hedge, they make gaps and breaches, they unfortify a city, unhedge the vineyard, and unarm a state. Exod. xxxii. 25, when the people had sinned, Moses saw that they were naked, a city now without walls, an army without arms, they lay open to the winds and storms of divine wrath. 2 Chron. xxviii. 19, Ahaz "made Judah naked;" and how? "he transgressed sore against the Lord" by his sinful courses, he brake down the hedges and walls of protection, and so made them a naked people. God's people have their hedges and fences about them; Job i. 10, "Hast thou not made an hedge about him and his house;" Isa. v. 2, 5, his vineyard was fenced and walled; and if they were careful to flee sin, their hedges would be without gaps, their walls without holes, but when they sin, they make gaps and holes, and the greater their sins, the greater breaches still are made in them. When David sinned in numbering the people, what a wide gap made he for the pestilence to come in and destroy seventy thousand! 2 Sam. xxiv. When Uzzah made a breach in God's law by his sin, he made a gap for judgment to come in upon himself. Sin is a breach, Isa. xxx. 13, and ever makes way for judgments to enter. Psal. lxxxix. 31, 32, "If they break my statutes, and keep not my commandments; then will I visit their transgression with a rod, and their iniquity with stripes:" when they break God's laws, he will break them with his rods. Micah vii. 13, "The land shall be desolate because of them that dwell therein, for the fruit of their doings;" by their sinful actions they break the bounds, and by my just judgments I will make them desolate. Hos. xii. 1, "Ephraim daily increaseth lies and desolation;" how desolation? by his lies, his lying pretences and practices, he makes breaches for desolation to come in. Isa. xlii. 24, "Who gave Jacob for a spoil, and Israel to the robbers? did not the Lord, he against whom we have sinned? for they would not walk in his ways, neither were they obedient to his laws."

Obs. 2. It is the duty of the prophets and servants of the Lord, when gaps and breaches are made, to go up into them, and make them up; they are to stand between the people and God's judgments. When the people had sinned greatly, and made way for sore judgments to come in upon them, Exod. xxxii. Moses ascends into the gap, and makes up the breach, he sets upon God by prayer, and uses strong arguments to divert his wrath; he "besought the Lord his God, and said, Lord, why doth thy wrath wax hot against thy people, which thou hast brought forth out of the land of Egypt with great power, and with a mighty hand? wherefore should the Egyptians speak, and say, For mischief did he bring them out, to slay them in the mountains, and to consume them from the face of the earth? Turn from thy fierce wrath, and repent of this evil against thy people. Remember Abraham, Isaac, and Israel, thy servants, to whom thou swarest by thine own self, and saidst unto them, I will multiply your seed as the stars of heaven, and all this land that I have spoken of will I give unto your seed, and they shall inherit it for ever. And the Lord repented of the evil which he thought to do unto his people," ver. 11—14. Here was a true prophet, that stood in the breach and turned away wrath. It was the practice of the good priests and prophets to do so. Numb. xvi. 41—48, when the people murmured, made a breach for the plague to come in upon them, Aaron took his censer, fire from the altar, put in incense, hasted into the congregation and made an atonement for the people, and stood between the dead and the living, and stayed the plague. See Deut. ix. 24—26. When Ezekiel saw the slaughter men sent out to slay young and old, without pity, he steps into the gap and saith, Ezek. ix. 8, "Ah Lord God! wilt thou destroy all the residue of Israel in thy pouring out of thy fury upon Jerusalem?" Jeremiah was so frequent in the gap, deprecating judgments, interceding for mercy, that the Lord forbids him to pray for that people, chap. xiv. 11; and chap. vii. 16, "Pray not thou for this people, neither lift up cry nor prayer for them, neither make intercession to me." He used to pray, to cry, to intercede, and keep off wrath from them. Samuel, when Israel had sinned, and the Philistines were coming upon them, he gets up into the gap, offers sacrifice, and cries to the Lord, and he heard him, discomfits the Philistines, and delivers the Israelites, 1 Sam. vii. 9, 10. This is that which God looks for, when people have sinned, that some man of God or other should thrust into the breach, and prevent wrath. Ezek. xxii. 29, 30, "The people of the land have used oppression, and exercised robbery, and have vexed the poor and needy: yea, they have oppressed the stranger wrongfully." Here was the hedge broken down, and breadth enough for judgments to come in upon them; and what then? "I sought for a man among them that should make up the hedge, and stand in the gap before me for the land, that I should not destroy it: but I found none." These false prophets trod down the hedge more and more, made the gaps wider, increased and hastened the judgments of God upon them.

Obs. 3. The Lord hath days of battle with his people appointed; what times he comes forth to punish them with his judgments, those are his days of battle. God hath decreed times to deal with the sons of men for their iniquities, and if they persist in sinning, the Lord will take his days of warring against them. You read in 2 Sam. xi. 1, that kings had a time to go forth to battle; it was at the return of the year, when it was spring or summer, then they went out to war against their enemies, not in the winter; but all times are alike to God to go out to war with his enemies, he can bring judgments upon sinners in winter, spring, summer; yea, he hath his peculiar times and days appointed to meet with wicked ones. This day of the Lord in Scripture is called a "day of darkness," Joel ii. 2, a "day of evil," Jer. xvii. 17, a "day of calamity," Jer. xlvi. 21, a "day of indignation," Ezek. xxii. 24, a "day of visitation," Isa. x. 3, a "day of fierce anger," Lam. i. 12, a "day of ruin," Ezek. xxvii. 27, a "day of great slaughter," Isa. xxx. 25, a "day of grief, and desperate sorrow," Isa. xvii. 11, a "day of vengeance," Isa. lxi. 2, a "day of battle," Zech. xiv. 3. What time soever God enters into a controversy with the sons of men, walks contrary to them, avenges the quarrel of his covenant, executes any judgments upon them, it is the day of the Lord: hence the day of judgment is called "the day of Christ," Phil. i. 10; 2 Thess. ii. 2, because then he shall execute wrath upon sinners.

Obs. 4. Those the Lord finds in their sins in the day of battle, they cannot stand before him, they fall by the strength of his judgments. When Uzzah sinned, God made a breach upon him in the day of battle, and smote him dead, 2 Sam. vi. 6, 7. When he smote Egypt, he made it desolate; the fulness of it could not stand before him, Ezek. xxxii. 15. Israel is no more to God than a reed shaken in the waters, 1 Kings xiv. 15; one stroke of his will cut it down. Ephraim is no more than a tree to the axe; if God smite, the root dries up, and no more fruit grows thereon, Hos. ix. 16. If God smite habitations, be they never so costly, stately, great, of what materials soever, they quickly fall, Amos iii. 15. When God reckons with kings and queens, they cannot stand in judgment: Jehoram God smites with sickness till his bowels fall out, 2 Chron. xxi. 18, 19; Uzziah sins, and is smitten with leprosy; Jezebel and Athaliah are cut off by just judgment of his, 2 Kings ix. xi.; he cuts off the spirit of princes, and is terrible to the kings of the earth, Psal. lxxvi. 12. Great armies cannot stand in the day of the Lord's anger: 2 Chron. xiii. Jeroboam had an army of eight hundred thousand, and, ver. 15, God smote him and all Israel, "so that there fell down slain of Israel five hundred thousand chosen men," ver. 17. David asks the question, Psal. cxlvii. 17, "Who can stand before his cold?" If God can intend the cold, so that men cannot endure it, he can intend the heat also, so that there is no abiding of it; his wrath is hot, fierce, a consuming fire: this made Ezra cry out, chap. ix. 15, "Behold, we are before thee in our trespasses, but we cannot stand before thee, because of this;" *chi* is rendered here, for, but, under correction, it may be rendered, but; as in Gen. xlv. 8, "It was not you sent me hither," *chi haelohim*, "but God." 1 Sam. vi. 19, 20, when the Lord had smote fifty thousand and seventy men of Bethshemesh, for their irreverent meddling with the ark, what said the rest? "Who is able to stand before this holy Lord God?" No man in his sin can do it. Nahum i. 5, 6, "The mountains quake at him, the hills melt, the earth is burned at his presence, yea, the world, and all that dwell therein. Who can stand before his indignation? and who can abide in the fierceness of his anger? his fury is poured out like fire, and the rocks are thrown down by him." Let sinners be never so great, stout, when God comes in battle, he will overcome; and therefore saith, Ezek. xxii. 14, "Can thine heart endure, or can thine hands be strong, in the days that I shall deal with thee?" Jerusalem thought so, but she found it otherwise.

Obs. 5. The prophets' failing in their duty, is one great cause of the people's falling in the day of the Lord's battles. They went not up into the gaps, they made not up the hedge for the house of Israel, that they might stand, &c. therefore they fell. The prophets here are implied to be builders and husbandmen; builders, to make a wall about the people, who are the city of God; husbandmen, to make hedges and fences about them, being the garden, orchard, and vineyard of God: now when they neglect to do these, they expose them to spoil and ruin, and provoke God to destroy all. Samuel knew this, and therefore said, 1 Sam. xii. 23, "God forbid that I should sin against the Lord in ceasing to pray for you:" had he failed in his duty, sin would have increased, wrath broken out, and all have been overthrown. You have an observable place in Jer. xxiii. 22, "Had the prophets stood in my counsel, and had caused my people to hear my words, then they should have turned them from their evil way, and from the evil of their doings;" which had it been done, they had prevented the battle, and the people's falling therein.

"They have seen vanity and lying divination, saying," &c. Here is a further manifestation of the iniquity of these prophets.

I. You have the nature of their visions discovered; they were vanity and lies.

II. Their lying pretence for what they saw; and said, "The Lord saith, and the Lord hath not sent them."

III. The fruit and effect of their prophecy; they made the people to hope that they would confirm what they said; they gave it out that God had revealed it unto them, that they should not go into captivity, that those in Babylon should return to Jerusalem within a few years; and by this means they begat vain hopes in the hearts of the people with their vain visions.

What these prophets had was out of their own hearts, and from their own spirits, not from God; for nothing from him is vain or lying, but because it was from themselves, it was "vanity and lying divination."

"Lying divination." Hebrew, divinations of a lie, that had no truth in them.

"The Lord hath not sent them." True prophets

had two things: 1. The gift of prophecy. 2. A call to exercise that gift. Both these were wanting in these prophets, and therefore the Lord sent them not.

"That they would confirm the word." They opposed the true prophets, told the people God was merciful, and would never bring such a long judgment upon them, that ere long they should see who spake truth; and so the people were brought to a hope and persuasion that their word should be accomplished, and this they waited for. The Septuagint reads it, they began to stir up or revive the word: many times the people's hearts were fainting, misgiving them that it might prove otherwise than they said; hereupon they stirred up their words, bid them not doubt, but be confident they had all from God, and were sent of him.

Obs. 1. The impudence and arrogance of false prophets and teachers. They said they had visions, and had none, ver. 3, they saw nothing. They pretended they had visions and divinations from God, real and true, and they saw nothing but vanity and lying divinations: they said, "The Lord saith," and he said not so; that the Lord sent them, and he sent them not, but they ran of themselves: they engaged the name and faith of God in their lying prophecies, and would have had them to be thought as good Scripture as what any of the true prophets delivered; they condemned the true prophets for liars, and justified themselves. False teachers are very arrogant and self-justifying; Zedekiah said to Micaiah, "Which way went the Spirit from me to thee?" have not I the Spirit, do not I understand the mind of God as well as thee, or any of thy rank? 1 Kings xxii. 24. Are not Jesuits and many others of this strain? they pretend miracles, scriptures, councils, fathers for their traditions, new articles, faith, seven sacraments, &c. when there is hardly any such thing. And do not many among us wrest Scripture, and force it into other senses, to weaken truth, maintain error, and to obtrude their own terms upon others?

Obs. 2. People are easily misled, seduced by false prophets. When they come with pretence of divine revelations and mission, and say, "The Lord saith," they listen, they hope, especially when they shall bring things suitable to their nature and desires, as here. They persuaded them that Jeremiah had prophesied falsely in telling them they should be carried into Babylon, be seventy years there. No, no, we have truer visions than he, the Lord will never forsake you who are his people, he will never leave Jerusalem, your brethren shall return to you, you shall never go to them; and this the people hoped would be. Prov. xiv. 15, "The simple believeth every word." Jer. v. 31, "The prophets prophesy falsely, and the priests bear rule by their means; and my people love to have it so:" they affect the lies and flatteries of these false prophets, and what will they do in the end thereof? Let Paul's advice be acceptable to you, 1 Thess. v. 21, "Prove all things; hold fast that which is good;" believe neither one prophet nor other, but prove what they say, and what is truth, good, hold that fast.

Ver. 8, 9. *Therefore thus saith the Lord God; Because ye have spoken vanity, and seen lies, therefore, behold, I am against you, saith the Lord God. And mine hand shall be upon the prophets that see vanity, and that divine lies: they shall not be in the assembly of my people, neither shall they be written in the writing of the house of Israel, neither shall they enter into the land of Israel; and ye shall know that I am the Lord God.*

In these words are several judgments laid down against the false prophets.

I. General.

II. Particular.

I. The general are two:

1. God is against them; "Behold, I am against you."

2. His hand shall be upon them.

II. Particular ones are three:

1. Exclusion from God's people; "They shall not be in the assembly of my people."

2. Exclusion from having their names written amongst the Israelites; "Neither shall they be written in the writing of the house of Israel."

3. Exclusion from return from captivity: "Neither shall they enter into the land of Israel."

(1.) The reason of all, because they spake vanity, and divined lies; "Therefore, because ye have spoken vanity," &c.

(2.) The authority and certainty of all; "Thus saith the Lord God."

(3.) The event; "Ye shall know that I am the Lord."

"Spoken vanity." Hebrew is, for that ye speak a vain thing. These prophets, pretending they had visions and divinations, spake them to the people; and what were they? vanity and lies, there was no truth or reality in ought they delivered. The word שוא notes vanity of words, and falsehood, Psal. cxliv. 8. Deut. v. 20, "Thou shalt not bear false witness;" Hebrew is, witness of vanity. Zech. x. 2 "The idols have spoken vanity, the diviners have seen a lie, and have told false dreams:" vanity, lies, and dreams, are joined together here; these idol prophets spake vanity, saw lies, told dreams. Peter saith, the false prophets spake "great swelling words of vanity," 2 Pet. ii. 18.

"I am against you." Hebrew is, Behold, I am against you; it is an aposiopesis, something is concealed which may easily be apprehended; as, I come to you, to punish you, or, I come against you: Chaldee is, I am about to send my anger against you. This phrase you have again, Ezek. xxi. 3, "Behold, I am against thee;" and in chap. xxvi. 3. And it is used when the Lord is greatly offended, and destruction of persons and things near at hand: Rev. ii. 5, "Repent, and do thy first works; else will I come unto thee quickly, and remove thy candlestick." It is of sad importance when the Lord saith, I come to you, or am against you. They thought it was but a few men opposed, who were weak, inconsiderable things, but the great and glorious God tells them that he is against them.

"My hand shall be upon the prophets," &c. Hand notes God's power and stroke; he being against them himself, he would put forth his power and smite them with some judgment or other. The Septuagint reads it, I will stretch out mine hand to, or upon, the prophets: and the Chaldee, for, my hands, have, my stroke; thus hand is taken Psal. xxi. 8, 9, "Thine hand shall find out all thine enemies; thy right hand shall find out those that hate thee. Thou shalt make them as a fiery oven in the time of thine anger." 1 Sam. v. 7, "His hand is sore upon us;" chap. vi. 3, "It shall be known why his hand is not removed from you." God had smitten them with the emerods, and that they call the hand of God. The phrase here implies that God will in some special manner punish these prophets.

"They shall not be in the assembly of my people." Hebrew is, בסוד which Montanus interprets, in the secret; the Septuagint, ἐν παιδεία, in the instructing of my people; they shall not prophesy or preach unto them; their liberty and power of speaking shall be taken from them. The difference of interpreting the word, arises from the several significations of the Hebrew word סוד which signifies a secret council, and the company of those who consult or counsel. If we take it here for secret, they shall not be in the secret of my people, then the sense is, they shall not know those secrets, nor partake of that good, which I reserve for to make known and communicate to my people. The Targum hath it thus, *In occultis bonis quæ reposita sunt populo non habebuntur*, They shall not be accounted among those secret good things which are laid up for my people. Prophets were great mercies for people, and God gave them out upon occasion; but these should not be numbered amongst them, they should be detected and have their reward.

This secret of God's people is some choice knowledge of God and his will, beyond what is vulgarly known by men of the world. Psal. xxv. 14, "The secret of the Lord is with them that fear him." Prov. iii. 32, "His secret is with the righteous." Micaiah knew the secret of the Lord, touching Ahab, 1 Kings xxiv. which neither Zedekiah nor any other of the false prophets knew. Amos iii. 7, "The Lord revealeth his secret unto his servants the prophets," not to those who are false and against him.

If we take it for "assembly," as the word is sometimes used in holy writ, as Jer. vi. 11, "I will pour out my fury upon the assemblies of young men," על סוד בחורים then we must inquire what assemblies are meant. There were two kinds of assemblies among the Jews:

First, an assembly of elders; Psal. cvii. 32, "And praise him in the assembly of elders:" these were the magistrates and senators that had authority, and bare rule over the people; it might be the seventy or sanhedrim.

Secondly, an assembly of saints; Psal. lxxxix. 7, "God is greatly to be feared in the assembly of the saints:" the Jews were a holy people, and when there were public congregations of them, they were an assembly of saints. You may understand it of both assemblies, that these false prophets should neither come amongst the senators, to sit in council, there to consult about any matters of state or church; nor amongst the saints, they should have no communion with God's people: and this sense I like best; for the prophets came to ecclesiastic meetings, as appears, 2 Kings xxiii. 2, the prophets were present when Josiah read the book of the covenant; Jer. xxvi. 7, the priests and prophets heard Jeremiah in the house of the Lord.

"Neither shall they be written in the writing of the house of Israel." What this writing of the house of Israel was, search must be made. The Septuagint reads, In the Scripture of the house of Israel they shall not be written. By Scripture some understand the canonical books of Moses and the prophets, and will have the sense to be, that the prophecies of these false prophets should not be written in or among those books; but surely it was never in the thoughts of any true prophet, that the lies and vanities of false prophets should be joined to sacred writ: what hath the chaff to do with the wheat? We must look out some other meaning of these words. When it pleased the Lord to bring his people out of Egypt, he commanded them to be numbered, Numb. i. 2, 3. The names and number of all from twenty years old and upwards were to be taken, and when they were numbered they were to "give every man a ransom for his soul unto the Lord," Exod. xxx. 12. In like manner, when they came out of Babylon they were numbered, as appears, Ezra ii. viii.; and Neh. vii. where you have the number set down; ver. 66, 67, "The whole congregation together was forty and two thousand three hundred and threescore, beside man and maid servants seven thousand three hundred thirty and seven, and two hundred forty and five singing men and women." The catalogues in which the names of these were written, are judged to be the writings of the house of Israel; by these the tribes were known, preserved distinct, and those who were not found in the writing were displaced: Neh. vii. 64, "These sought their register among those that were reckoned by genealogy, but it was not found: therefore were they, as polluted, put from the priesthood." Isa. iv. 3, "Every one that is written among the living in Jerusalem shall be called holy." He speaks of great calamity, a destruction which should be upon the Jews, and few should escape, but he that was left, and written among the living, &c. All those who came to Jerusalem from the captivity, and were citizens thereof, were written in some book, catalogue, or register, which was the writing of the house of Israel; and was called also The book of life, or of the living; for upon the death of a man, his name was rased out of this book, or if he did any thing unworthy the name and right of a citizen; and then he was counted as a dead man. The sense of these words you may hence then take up thus, viz. These false prophets shall be reckoned amongst the dead, not the living; they shall not be written in the writing of the house of Israel, when they come back to Jerusalem; they shall be like trees pulled up and never planted again; they shall be cut off and destroyed by some judgment. In this sense some take those words of Moses, Exod. xxxii. 32, "Blot me out of thy book which thou hast written," take away my life; thou art now wroth with thy people, about to slay them; Lord, forgive them, spare them, else destroy me, and blot my name out of the book thou hast written, as our practice is.

This sense I condemn not, but something more some interpreters find in the words. This writing of the house of Israel they interpret the book of life, in which the names of all true Israelites were written; Phil. iv. 3, "Whose names are in the book of life;" Dan. xii. 1, "Every one that shall be found written in the book;" Luke x. 20, there is mention of names written in heaven; Rev. xiii. 8, it is called the Lamb's book of life; so Rev. xxi. 27. Contrary to this is writing their names in the earth; Jer. xvii. 13, "They that depart from the Lord, shall be written in the earth." The meaning then of the words must be of this nature: These false prophets think themselves to be my servants, that their names are in my book; they say, the Lord hath sent them, that they have my Spirit, do declare my will, and honour me much among my people; and you think them also happy men, that their names are written in heaven, that if any be saved they shall: but they neither are, nor shall be ever written in any book, accounted among my faithful ones; they are hypocrites, shall be discovered, and discarded for ever. In Psal. lxix. 28, you have such an expression, "Let them be blotted out of the book of the living, and not be written with the righteous:" there were many who appeared to others to be written in the book of life, but the prophet prays that the Lord would make it evident some way or other, that they were not there. Here the Scripture speaks according to the opinion of men, not according to the reality of things. God blots men out of the book of life, when he declares by some dealings of his with them, that they are not accepted of him. Here God's hand should be upon them, they should not be among his people, have communion with them or him in any ordinance of his, and this was evidence they were not in his book, in that they should not come into the land of Canaan, that they should not be written in the writing of the house of Israel.

"Neither shall they enter into the land of Israel." This is the third particular judgment. The land of Israel hath many eulogies in Scripture; it is called "The land of the living," Psal. xxvii. 13; David had fainted, but that he hoped "to see the goodness of the Lord in the land of the living." People that lived in other lands were dead men, they had deaf, dumb, dead gods, and deadly worship; but the Jews had the living God their God, and lively worship, Acts vii. 38. A "land of uprightness," Psal. cxliii. 10; where were the best laws that ever nation had. A land of delight, for so the Hebrew is, Dan. xi. 41, בארץ הצבי A land which was "the glory of all lands," Ezek. xx. 6. The land of Immanuel, Isa. viii. 8; where Immanuel was promised, born, lived, preached, wrought his miracles, and showed his glory. Into this land must not they come. They prophesied, that within a few years all should return into this land; but Ezekiel from the Lord tells them, that after seventy years they shall not return into their country, nor enter into heaven, whereof this was a type. Captivity was a little death, and to be in a land of dead ones was another death; and never to enjoy the land of the living, nor the living God, this was the sting of death. It was lawful for strangers to come into the land of Israel, 2 Chron. ii. 17, there were a hundred and fiftythree thousand six hundred at once in the land, and yet these prophets might not come in.

Obs. 1. The Lord is against evil prophets, and that is a dreadful thing. There are several things which makes God to be against them:

(1.) They abuse his name and authority, saying, the Lord sent them, ver. 6. If any man should abuse the name of a prince, or of parliament, and say, they sent them to speak or do any thing, and they did not, what injury were this unto them! how would they take it! much more is it a wrong to the Lord, who is greater than they.

(2.) Their prophecies are lies, vanity, the thoughts of their own heads, and conceptions of their own hearts, ver. 2, 3, 7, and so contrary to the truths of God.

(3.) They prejudice the design of God by the true prophets. By them the Lord made known his displeasure against the ways of sinners, convinced them of the evil of their doings, and drew them to repentance; Jer. xxv. 5, the prophets said, "Turn from the evil of your doings, and dwell in the land;" but the false prophets discredited them, disparaged their prophecies, and cried Peace.

(4.) They deceived the people with their falsehoods, filled them with vain hopes, ver. 6; and so strengthened them in their evil ways, and encouraged them to their own destruction.

(5.) They grieved the spirits of the godly, they made their hearts ache, as the false prophetesses did, ver. 22, they "made the hearts of the righteous sad."

(6.) They were evil themselves; Jer. xxiii. 11, "Both prophet and priest are profane; yea, in my house have I found their wickedness, saith the Lord:" they corrupted the worship of God with their inventions; God had cause enough to be against them. It is very sad, yea dreadful, to have God against one. I that know the secrets of all hearts, I that am holy and hate all sin, I that keep an exact account of all their ways, I that am infinitely just, and must punish all wicked ones, I that am infinitely powerful, and can destroy with an everlasting destruction, I, even I am against you. Rom. viii. 31, "If God be for us, who can be against us?" When God is for a man, all is safe, whoever attempts to hurt. David had many against him; Psal. cxviii. 10, "All nations compassed me about;" ver. 12, "they compassed me about like bees;" they swarmed about him, and had their stings ready, thrust out to sting him to death, but he had God with him, for him; and therefore saith, ver. 14, "The Lord is my strength and song, and is become my salvation;" but had God been against David, one of those bees would have been his death. Whoever the Lord is against, hath many enemies and few friends, all in heaven, all in earth, are against that man.

Obs. 2. Those prophets or people the Lord is against, he puts forth his power to punish. "Behold, I am against you, and my hand shall be upon you." Jer. xxviii. 15—17, God was against that false prophet Hananiah, and his hand was quickly upon him; "Hear," saith Jeremiah unto him; "The Lord hath not sent thee; but thou makest this people trust in a lie. Therefore thus saith the Lord; Behold, I will cast thee from off the face of the earth: this year thou shalt die, because thou hast taught rebellion against the Lord. So Hananiah the prophet died the same year." God was against Ahab, and spake against him, 2 Chron. xviii. 22, and the next tidings you hear of him, is his death by the hand of the Lord, ver. 33, 34. So Lev. xx. 3, "I will set my face against that man, and will cut him off;" if God's face be against a man, he will put forth his hand to destroy that man from before his face; and chap. xxvi. 17, "I will set my face against you, and ye shall be slain before your enemies." Ananias and Sapphira had God against them for their wilful lying, and presently his hand was upon them, Acts v. God's judgments are called his hand, 1 Pet. v, 6, his mighty hand; and if that fall upon any, it will break them to pieces.

Obs. 3. The fruits of God's displeasure are very grievous. First, they are shut out from the assemblies of God's people, they shall have no communion with the saints, those who are dear to God. All David's delight was in them, Psal. xvi. 3; and when he was a little put by coming at the assemblies of God's people, how did it trouble and afflict him! Psal. xlii. 1—4, "As the hart panteth after the water brooks, so panteth my soul after thee, O God. My soul thirsteth for God, for the living God: when shall I come and appear before God? My tears have been my meat day and night; while they continually say unto me, Where is thy God? When I remember these things, I pour out my soul in me: for I had gone with the multitude, I went with them to the house of God." So in the 84th Psalm, how did he long for communion with God and his people in the sanctuary! his soul longed and fainted for the courts of the Lord, his heart and flesh cried out for the living God, ver. 2; he counted a day in the Lord's courts better than a thousand, he had rather be a door-keeper there, than a favourite in Saul's house, ver. 10. David knew there was much good to be had in the assemblies of God's people, and therefore he prized them so, and was impatient of absence from them. In the assemblies men have communion with God; there his glory is seen; Psal. xxix. 9, "In his temple doth every one speak of his glory;" Psal. lxviii. 24, "They have seen thy goings, O God, in the sanctuary." There his wisdom, his power, his mercy, his truth, his glory, are evidenced, the treasures of his grace opened and dispensed, spiritual life begotten and maintained, drooping souls are comforted, raised, ravished; there we admire, adore, magnify, and glorify God; there we hear of our duty towards God and man; there we have fellowship with the saints, interest in their affections, gifts, graces, counsels, comforts, admonitions, exhortations, and prayers. In the assemblies of God's people, you have the presence of God, of Christ, the Spirit, and the angels, 1 Cor. xi. 10; and what a sore judgment is it to be shut out from these assemblies! Bless God for your liberties, be thankful for all the good you have in the assemblies, and walk so that you may honour truth and the God of assemblies.

Obs. 4. Many that in their own and the world's esteem go for true prophets and saints, will be in God's time discovered to be liars, hypocrites, false; themselves think, and others also, that they are written in the writing of the house of Israel, in the book of life, but their names were never there. The Jews said they were Abraham's seed, God was their Father, but they were found false, they were of their father the devil.

Ver. 10—16. *Because, even because they have seduced my people, saying, Peace; and there was no peace; and one built up a wall, and, lo, others daubed it with untempered morter: say unto them which daub it with untempered morter, that it shall fall: there shall be an overflowing shower; and ye, O great hailstones, shall fall; and a stormy wind shall rend it. Lo, when the wall is fallen, shall it not be said unto you, Where is the daubing wherewith ye have daubed it? Therefore thus saith the Lord God; I will even rend it with a stormy wind in my fury; and there shall be an overflowing shower in mine anger, and great hailstones in my fury to consume it. So will I break down the wall that ye have daubed with untempered morter, and bring it down to the ground, so that the foundation thereof shall be discovered, and it shall fall, and ye shall be consumed in the midst thereof: and ye shall know that I am the Lord. Thus will I accomplish my wrath upon the wall, and upon them that have daubed it with untempered morter, and will say unto you, The wall is no more, neither they that daubed it; to wit, the prophets of Israel which prophesy concerning Jerusalem, and which see visions of peace for her, and there is no peace, saith the Lord God.*

The words before you present to us two things:

I. The sin of the false prophets, viz. seduction, "They have seduced my people;" and the manner how, by "saying, Peace;" by building and daubing a wall with untempered mortar, ver. 10.

II. God's proceedings with them, and their wall; he will send a storm, overthrow their wall, shame and confound them, in the following verses.

"Because, even because." Hebrew is, For that, even for that; the words are doubled, and so emphatical: the like you have in Lev. xxvi. 43, "Because, even because they despised my judgments."

"Seduced." Hebrew is הטעו have caused to err; Vulgate is, *deceperint*, have deceived; but, causing to err, sets out the sense of the word more fully. 2 Chron. xxxiii. 9, "Manasseh made Judah and the inhabitants of Jerusalem to err;" the false prophets seduced him, and he seduced them. Seduction is when men are led aside from the right way, and upon false suggestions are carried into a wrong way, believe lies, and practise answerably; Amos ii. 4, "Their lies caused them to err, after the which their fathers have walked."

"Saying, Peace." שלום from שלם entire, perfect, because it preserves things, places, persons entire; whereas war wastes and consumes all. Peace among the Hebrews notes freedom from war, tumults, a quiet condition of life, and all kind of outward happiness; therefore the Jews when they wish happiness to a man, they wish him peace. These prophets told them in Babylon that they should have liberty and quick return, and their hearts' desire in the land of Judea; they told those there, that they should not need to fear Nebuchadnezzar or any forces of his, they should live in safety, be fat and flourishing, wanting nothing.

"One built up a wall." The word for "one" is והוא and he or himself: Junius, *hic*, he, or this man: Jerom will have this he, or one, to be meant of God, who by his law and prophets built them a wall; but had God built the wall, he would not have spoken against it, as here he doth. Some understand the people, but there is no sufficient ground for that. The Lord here is reproving the false prophets for seducing the people, not the people for seducing the prophets; it is unlikely therefore that the people should build a wall. By "one," or he, we conceive is meant some chief one amongst the false prophets. Zedekiah was a chief one among Ahab's false prophets; such was Hananiah, Jer. xxviii. and Shemaiah, Jer. xxix. 31, whom our prophet may intend; for this Shemaiah was in Babylon, he prophesied false things, sent letters to all the people at Jerusalem, and caused them to trust in a lie. Or "one" may be taken indefinitely.

"Built up a wall." This is a metaphorical expression borrowed from builders, who make walls about their houses, to secure and strengthen them from danger. Jerusalem had a wall about it, which was a great defence unto it. This wall was some false prophecy or doctrine given out unto the people, which caused them to be secure. Jeremiah had prophesied of the coming of Nebuchadnezzar, the destruction of the temple and city, seventy years' captivity, that so he might awaken this people, bring them to repentance, and prevent such judgments; but some one or other of the false prophets prophesied the contrary. Jer. xxix. 8, 9, they had some in Babylon who built a wall there, telling them that they should shortly return again to Jerusalem, and quieted the spirits of those in captivity; they had some at Jerusalem who built a wall there, and caused them to trust in vain things; ver. 21, there was Ahab the son of Kolaiah, and Zedekiah the son of Maaseiah, which prophesied a lie unto them in the name of the Lord: Either Nebuchadnezzar will not come, or if he do, you will have help from Egypt. Their false and lying prophecies, wherein the people trusted, was the wall they built; the prophecy of peace was the foundation of this wall, and the arguments they used, the brick to build it up. So that hereupon the people feared not any danger, humbled not themselves for their sins, but became secure and confident that all should be well; which made Jeremiah say, chap. vi. 14, "They have healed the hurt of the daughter of my people slightly, saying, Peace, peace." Jeremiah had threatened judgments to them for their sins, wounded them by his prophecies, but they healed the wounds by crying, Peace, peace.

"And, lo, others daubed it." Other prophets, with their fair words and false pretences, justified what the former had said; when some chief false prophet had prophesied of peace, the rest, who were inferior, would second him. The word for "daubed" is טחים from טוח to cover, plaster over, or anoint; and so the Septuagint reads it, καὶ αὐτοὶ ἀλείφουσιν αὐτὸν, and they anoint it. These false prophets were like masons and carpenters, who build deceitfully, and use their art and utmost skill to make such work seem goodly and beautiful.

"With untempered mortar." Hebrew is תפל which Montanus renders *insulso*, with that which is unsavoury; Piscator, Polanus, Junius, *inepto*, with that which is foolish; the Vulgate, *luto absque paleis*, with mortar which hath no straw, chaff, hair, or binding thing mixed with it. You know there must be something mingled with loam, or lime, which men use in buildings, if they will build to purpose; but these built with untempered mortar; and this mortar was their flattering, false, weak reasons and pretences with which they used to keep the people in security. Ezek. xxii. 28, "Her prophets have daubed them with untempered mortar, seeing vanity, and divining lies unto them, saying, Thus saith the Lord God, when the Lord hath not spoken." There was no truth, and so no strength in what they said; all was their own, and so *lutum sine firmitate*, loam without strength.

The word תפל may be rendered *casuro*, with that which is about to fall, from נפל and in ver. 11, it is said ויפל and it shall fall.

"An overflowing shower." גשם שוטף Great showers will try buildings, especially walls that are of untempered mortar. This overflowing shower was the Chaldean army: Isa. lix. 19, "The enemy shall come in like a flood;" Isa. viii. 7, 8, "The Lord bringeth up upon them the waters of the river, strong and many, even the king of Assyria, and all his glory: he shall overflow and go over, he shall reach even to the neck;" Jer. xlvii. 2, "Behold, waters rise up out of the north, and shall be an overflowing flood, and shall overflow the land, and all that is therein; the city, and them that dwell therein."

"Great hailstones." Hebrew is, אבני אלגביש stones of the hail. This word *elgabis* is only mentioned in this prophet, and but thrice, in this verse, ver. 13, and chap. xxxviii. 22, and it is great hail. The Septuagint is *δώσω λίθυς πετροβόλυς*, stones to throw against a rock; and these may note out the chief men in the army, or the whole army, who should be as stones of great hail, to shake this mud wall of theirs.

The word is a compound word of אל *potens*, and גביש *crystallus*. Job xxviii. 18, "No mention shall be made of coral, or of pearls;" the word in Hebrew for pearls is גביש which Shindler interprets a crystal. Now, because hailstones are like unto crystal and pearl, therefore the word is here used, and *el* added to it, to show what strong hailstones God would send.

"A stormy wind shall rend it." Hebrew is, ורוח סערות *ventus turbinum*. These words you have in chap. i. 4, rendered "a whirlwind," where they were opened unto you: such an expression you have in Isa. xxv. 4, "The blast of the terrible ones is as a storm against the wall." By these metaphorical words he sets out the wrath of God by the Chaldean army, which should be as tempestuous rain, hail, and wind; and the Scripture is frequent in this metaphor when it would make known to us the indignation of the Lord; as you may observe, Isa. xxi. 1; xxix. 6; Jer. xxiii. 19; xxx. 19; Isa. xvii. 13.

"The foundations thereof shall be revealed." There shall not a stone be left upon a stone of this building; the foundation of this wall built up and daubed with untempered mortar shall be discovered. God would detect the falsehood of their prophecies, the vanity of all their arguments, wiles, and ways, they used to seduce and secure this people, whatever they promised of help from Egypt, whatever they prophesied of the Chaldeans' not coming, whatever they said of the people's safety, of God's mercy and favour and good will towards them, whatever they pretended of being sent from God, of speaking his words, of having his Spirit, &c. God would discover all their imposturings, and lay them open to the world, so that nothing shall be left them but disgrace.

Some make the temple and city to be the foundation. Because they had the holy city and holy place where God had recorded his name, therefore they cried, Peace, peace, flattered the people into a good condition, and surrounded them with a wall of security; therefore God would destroy both, and discover their foundation.

"They shall be consumed in the midst thereof." You promise great matters to others, that they shall within few years return from Babylon, come and dwell safely in Jerusalem; but there is no safety in Jerusalem for yourselves, you shall be consumed in it, that are so confident of the safety of it. When a wall falls, and foundations are discovered, likely some do suffer by it, and so should these false prophets here.

Quest. In Jer. iv. 10, you have these words uttered by the prophet, "Ah, Lord God! surely thou hast greatly deceived this people and Jerusalem, saying, Ye shall have peace; whereas the sword reacheth unto the soul." If God promised them peace and deceived them, doth he not herein resemble the false prophets, and so lessen their sin?

Answ. 1. God did not promise them peace, but threatened severe judgments against them by Isaiah, Jeremiah, and Ezekiel, as you may see, Isa. xxix. 3—6; Jer. ix. 9—11; Ezek. v. 8—10.

2. Some make the prophets here to speak in the name of the people, and to personate them. They thought the peace which was promised them by the false prophets was from God, and therefore, finding the contrary, do charge God, as wicked men in their distresses are wont to do.

3. The words may be taken by way of interrogation, thus; Hast thou in deceiving deceived this people, hast thou promised them peace, and brought the sword upon them? Is this thy manner of proceeding with thy people? surely it cannot be, thou art faithful, and canst not deny thyself, 2 Tim. ii. 13; and Numb. xxiii. 19, "God is not a man that he should lie; neither the son of man, that he should repent: hath he said, and shall he not do it? or hath he spoken, and shall he not make it good?"

4. If God promised them peace, it was after their return from captivity, not at the present; and so, Jer. iii. 17, 18, you shall find it, "At that time they shall call Jerusalem the throne of the Lord; and all the nations shall be gathered unto it, to the name of the Lord, to Jerusalem: neither shall they walk any more after the imagination of their evil heart. In those days the house of Judah shall walk with the house of Israel, and they shall come together out of the land of the north," &c.

5. The prophet might thus speak and say, God had deceived them, because he suffered the false prophets to propound their dreams, lies, divinations, visions, and things of their own hearts and spirits, unto the people, whereby they were greatly deceived. A man that suffers a thing to be done, in ordinary speech, is said to be the author of it: if a physician will not give physic to cure a sick man, if he die of his sickness, it is vulgarly said he is the cause of his death; if the owner will not preserve a ruinous house from falling, when it is fallen he is said to be the author of its fall; so here, God is said to deceive them, because he hindered not those false prophets from deceiving them. God saw how averse they were to truth, how they slighted and mocked his prophets, 2 Chron.

xxxvi. 16, and despised his words, therefore in just judgment he gave them up to believe lies, falsehoods, and deceivable things.

Obs. 1. That false prophets and teachers seduce the people, feeding them with vain hopes. They cried, Peace, peace, all things shall be prosperous, comfortable, we shall have no wars in our gates, no famine or plague in our cities; they gave out pleasing prophecies, and so beguiled the unstable and credulous people, and swelled them with vast hopes. They hoped to see their brethren return from Babylon, to buy and sell, to marry and build, to grow great, and see many good days. The false prophets filled Ahab with great hopes of victory at Ramoth-gilead; "Go up, and prosper," said they, "for the Lord shall deliver it into the king's hand," 1 Kings xxii. 12. These prophets begat and maintained hopes in the hearts of the people, they made them trust in the temple, and corrupt worship which was in it; therefore Jer. vii. 4, Jeremiah sent to command them not to trust in lying words, "saying, The temple of the Lord," &c. Whatever wickedness they committed, yet if they appeared in the temple, and stood before the Lord, they said they were delivered, no threatenings of Jeremiah or others should take hold of them. They made them trust in their strong holds, and look to the hills and mountains about them; therefore, Jer. iii. 23, he tells them, that in vain they hoped for salvation from the hills, and from the multitude of mountains; they thought because Jerusalem was so well fortified with high hills and great mountains, that it could not be taken; Jer. xxi. 13, "Who shall come down against us; or who shall enter into our habitations?" and chap. xlix. 4, Jerusalem said, "Who shall come unto me?" Hananiah, a false prophet, told the people that within the space of two full years Nebuchadnezzar's yoke should be broken from off the neck of all nations, Jer. xxviii. 11; and ver. 15, Jeremiah saith, he made the people trust in a lie.

Obs. 2. It is a clear argument of a blind and false teacher, to speak things answerable to the humours and corruptions of men. This people could not endure Jeremiah prophesying truth, threatening judgment against them for their sins, see Jer. xxxviii. 2—5; they desired to hear of pleasing things. It was good tidings to them to hear that Nebuchadnezzar should not come against them, nor make them tributary unto him, therefore the prophets prophesied it; Jer. xxvii. 14, they told them they should not serve the king of Babylon. It was pleasing to them to hear of bringing back again the vessels of the temple; and, ver. 16, these prophets prophesied, saying, "Behold, the vessels of the Lord's house shall now shortly be brought again from Babylon." Wherein could they have humoured these people more? You have a notable place in Jer. xxiii. 16, "The prophets that prophesy unto you make you vain: they speak a vision of their own heart, and not out of the mouth of the Lord." Now that which comes not from God's holy mouth, but man's carnal heart, will be pleasing to other carnal hearts; and lest you may think I deceive you, observe ver. 17, "They say still unto them that despise me, The Lord hath said, Ye shall have peace; and they say unto every one that walketh after the imagination of his own heart, No evil shall come upon you." What is more pleasing to man, than to have his own mind, do his own will, walk after the imaginations of his own heart? and what softer words more suitable to him can be said, than no evil shall come upon him? False prophets speak *verba lactis*, milky, oily words, such as please men, and battle their humours, and so have a great advantage with men, who love to be humoured; but true prophets speak *verba veritatis*, words of truth, which have salt and fire in them, and so cross, fret, provoke men's lusts, and stir up their hatred against them: and as the other, with their lies and flatteries, find favour with men, so these, for their truths, with God, who loves truth. Paul durst not preach to please men, but Christ, Gal. i. 10. John would not please Herod.

Obs. 3. The prophecies and doctrines of false teachers seem unto them, and those who cleave to them, to have much strength. They "built up a wall;" walls are things of strength, be they earth, timber, or stone walls. They prophesied peace, that Nebuchadnezzar should not come against them, or depart, if he came, without prejudice to them; they said that the vessels and people should speedily return from Babylon, &c.; these doctrines of theirs were as walls unto them of strength and defence. Solomon tells us, that a rich man's riches are a high wall in his own conceit, Prov. xviii. 11; and so the opinions and tenets of false teachers are a high wall in their own conceits; they think the people are strengthened and secured by them. There are scarcely any opinions abroad, be they never so erroneous, heretical, blasphemous, tending to licentiousness, but the authors of them judge them to have strength in them, and look upon them as walls to advantage the people; and those who are deceived by them, think the like of them.

Obs. 4. That false prophets and teachers do concur and mutually endeavour to countenance and strengthen each other's doctrines and tenets. "One built up a wall, and, lo, others daubed it." The true prophets oft prophesied the same things, and so strengthened the hands each of other; and so did the false prophets, they improved their art and parts to strengthen one another: they brought their visions, divinations, dreams, lies, and whatever they had, to plaster and daub up this wall; they told them of God's mercy, covenant, promise to dwell at Jerusalem for ever, how greatly God was delighted with that place, that they were a holy people, had the law, ordinances, sacrifices, which none else in the world had, that God had no church but them, and therefore unlikely that ever he would destroy them, that his heart was towards them; thus they agreed all in falsehood, and strengthened themselves and the people in wickedness. So all the false prophets concurred in deceiving Ahab; Zedekiah, the chief, makes horns, and saith, "With these shalt thou push the Syrians, until thou have consumed them."

Obs. 5. Whatever prophets give out of their own unto the people, it is weak, unsolid, and unserviceable. These prophets prophesied of their own heads, out of their own spirits, they had nothing from God; and what was all, but untempered mortar, a thing unsavoury and foolish? did any of their visions, divinations, or prophecies, strengthen the hearts or hands of this people? were they not altogether seduced by them? They filled them with vain hopes, flattered them in their sinful ways, prophesied of peace and plenty, and so healed the hurt of God's people slightly; they skinned it over with fair words, but did not search it to the bottom, and lance it with sound and wholesome truths; they brought of their own, not of the Lord's, and therefore it was unserviceable; they brought lies, Jer. xxvii. 10; false dreams, chap. xxiii. 32; the deceit of their own hearts, ver. 26; false visions, divinations, and things of nought, chap. xiv. 14. Can lies, dreams, deceits, false, and things of nought, strengthen or build up? The truths and doctrines of God are solid, savoury, strengthening, well tem-

Jer. viii. 11.

pered mortar; they are tempered with the glory, wisdom, mercy, and love of God, with the blood of Christ, with the power of the Spirit, and they will build up a wall, be strength unto us; Zech. i. 13, his words are good and comfortable; Micah ii. 7, they do good; Psal. xci. 4, his truth is a shield and buckler; it is sure and will not deceive, 2 Pet. i. 19; the doctrines of the apostles confirmed the brethren and the churches, Acts xiv. 22; xv. 32. The doctrines and opinions of men are windy deceitful things, and hinder growth and strength, Eph. iv. 14, but the truths of God cause growth in all things, and so strengthen, making us firm as walls. What men bring of their own, are πλάστοι λόγοι, feigned words, untempered mortar, but what they have from God are wholesome words and doctrines, "according to godliness," 1 Tim. vi. 3.

2 Pet. ii. 3.

Obs. 6. Seducing of people by false, flattering, unsound doctrines doth greatly provoke God. "Because, even because they have seduced my people, saying, Peace; and one built," &c. Prophets' work is to make known truth, and to bring men out of their by and base ways into the way of truth; but if they turn men out of that way into the ways of error, they work, but their work is not pleasing unto God, it exasperates his Spirit against them, and no marvel they undo souls, which are precious things. James v. 20, he that converts a sinner from the error of his way saves a soul from death, and hides a multitude of sins, that would appear by his going on in an erroneous way. If, on the contrary, a man seduce a man from the truth, and lead him into ways of error, he destroys a soul, discovers and multiplies sin; and so did these false prophets, and so do all false teachers. Peter tells you of false teachers, 2 Epist. ii. 1, who bring in damnable heresies, and draw away many thereby. And is that all? no, they bring upon themselves swift destruction, they so provoke God by their corrupt and damnable doctrines, that he intends and hastens their destruction; and let the seduced look to it lest destruction be their portion: Isa. ix. 16, "The leaders of this people cause them to err; and they that are led of them are destroyed."

Obs. 7. Whatsoever works men work, God will try them. If the prophets build walls, daub with untempered mortar, preach visions of their own heads, &c.; God will prove their walls, what strength is in them, examine their mortar, whether tempered or not, whether aught of God be in it, or all be human: ver. 11, "There shall be an overflowing shower; great hailstones, and a stormy wind." When men build, the wind and weather tries their buildings; the prophets here go under the notion of builders, and they had made their building, and God would try it. Nebuchadnezzar, with all his forces, should come like an overflowing shower, great strong hailstones, a stormy wind, and if their wall could stand then, and their mortar endure, it would be evident that they were wise builders, had made a firm wall. 1 Cor. iii. 13, "Every man's work shall be made manifest; and the fire shall try every man's work of what sort it is." The work here is interpreted of doctrines and opinions, taught and held; they shall be tried by fire, either of affliction or of the Spirit, the word of God.

Obs. 8. God hath variety of ways and means to try men's works, he hath "showers, hailstones, winds."

Obs. 9. It is impossible for false prophets to avoid the judgments of God, they and their works must suffer. See what is said in ver. 15, 16, "I will accomplish my wrath upon the wall, and upon them that have daubed it; to wit, the prophets of Israel." God's judgments against them are sudden, irresistible, and unavoidable, they are likened to showers, hailstones, and stormy winds, which come suddenly, assault strongly, and cannot be avoided; and God saith, in ver. 13, he will rend their wall, and work in anger and fury: if he will rend, who can preserve? if he will tear in pieces, who shall deliver? Psal. l. 22.

Obs. 10. Whatever doctrines, opinions, tenets, false teachers and prophets do deliver, to scatter among the people, shall come to nought. They "built a wall, daubed it with untempered mortar;" but, ver. 11, "Say unto them, It shall fall." God had determined the ruin of this wall, of all the false prophecies they had delivered: the doctrines of men are windy, unstable, and vanishing things. Acts v. 36—38, Gamaliel tells of one Theudas, who boasted that he was somebody, a prophet, and vented his own opinions amongst them, and drew four hundred men after him; and this false prophet, with his prophecies and followers, were scattered, ruined, and brought to nought. After him Judas of Galilee drew away much people with his persuasions and pretences, and he perished, and those who obeyed him were dispersed. And then presents to the council where he was speaking the apostles and their doctrine, saying, "Refrain from these men, and let them alone: for if this counsel or this work be of men, it will come to nought." You have seen the end of Theudas and Judas, of their counsels, opinions, and works; they being from men, are fallen with the men, but if they had been of God, they would have stood; as he speaks of the apostle's doctrine, "if it be of God, ye cannot overthrow it." Men may venture who build upon divine truths, they have a divine arm to support them, but human opinions, doctrines, if we confide in, we shall greatly be deceived, they and we shall fall together. Babylon, you know, was supported by false doctrines, false worship, false government, false miracles, and lying wonders, as you may observe in the Revelation; chap. xviii. 2, you hear, "Babylon the great is fallen, is fallen;" and chap. xix. 20, "The beast was taken, and with him the false prophet;" that is, the pope and his clergy: they desired and endeavoured the standing of their kingdom, but being upon a false foundation, it fell. Psa. cxii. 10, "The desire of the wicked shall perish;" not only their desires, but doctrines, prophecies, endeavours, shall perish.

Obs. 11. False prophets and teachers shall be discovered, and they and their worship exposed to laughter and scorn. "When the wall is fallen, shall it not be said unto you, where is the daubing wherewith ye have daubed it?" you have made a goodly wall, such a one as could not endure a shower; ye are impostors, have deceived us and others; thus should they be detected and derided. There were many false prophets in Ahab's days, they were great with Jezebel and Ahab, and made use of their power to cut off the true prophets; but Elijah calls them forth to a sacrifice, some eight hundred and fifty of them, where they were discovered to be liars, seducers, and laughed to scorn before all the people. Those prophets that bade Ahab go up to Ramoth-gilead and prosper, 2 Chron. xviii. 11, how ashamed were they when Ahab was slain, and the soldiers returned with loss of their king and the day! What cause had these prophets to blush, when God brought Nebuchadnezzar to besiege the city, when the walls were broken down, and they discovered to be false prophets, and their foundation, with which they upheld the hope of this people, to be lies, flatteries, and false divinations!

Ver. 17—23. *Likewise, thou son of man, set thy face against the daughters of thy people, which prophesy out of their own heart; and prophesy thou against them, and say, Thus saith the Lord God; Woe to the women that sew pillows to all armholes, and make kerchiefs upon the head of every stature to hunt souls! Will ye hunt the souls of my people, and will ye save the souls alive that come unto you? And will ye pollute me among my people for handfuls of barley and for pieces of bread, to slay the souls that should not die, and to save the souls alive that should not live, by your lying to my people that hear your lies? Wherefore thus saith the Lord God; Behold, I am against your pillows, wherewith ye there hunt the souls to make them fly, and I will tear them from your arms, and will let the souls go, even the souls that ye hunt to make them fly. Your kerchiefs also will I tear, and deliver my people out of your hand, and they shall be no more in your hand to be hunted; and ye shall know that I am the Lord. Because with lies ye have made the heart of the righteous sad, whom I have not made sad; and strengthened the hands of the wicked, that he should not return from his wicked way, by promising him life: therefore ye shall see no more vanity, nor divine divinations: for I will deliver my people out of your hand: and ye shall know that I am the Lord.*

We are now come to the second part of the chapter, which is a prophecy against women prophetesses; and here, as before, you have their judgments, and the sins laid down causing those judgments.

The judgments are in verses 17, 18, 20, 21, 23; the sins moving God to be against them, and to proceed so with them, are in verses 17, 18, 19, 22, 23; the judgments and sins are intermingled in the several verses.

In Israel had been some true prophetesses, as Deborah and Huldah; now there were many false prophetesses, and the prophet is commanded to turn his speech against them.

"Set thy face against." Once before you had this phrase, chap. iv. 3, where the prophet was to set his face against Jerusalem; here it is against the women; be thou an adversary unto them, and prophesy against them. Enemies, when they are to encounter each other, they set their faces one against another; and so here, when the prophet should denounce judgment against them for their lying prophecies, he was as an adversary to them; and to "set the face," in Scripture sense, against any one, is to proclaim war against them. The Hebrew is, thy faces; speak boldly, freely, and be severe against them in thy prophesying.

"The daughters of thy people." Some would understand by these women, men prophets, who were weak and womanish, without courage, constancy, and prudence; but we have no cause to take the words in that sense. Our prophet had spoken of men prophets before, and now is directed of God to another distinct subject, and that is, the women prophets, who are called daughters of his people; this cannot belong unto the men.

"Which prophesy out of their own heart." As the false prophets did, ver. 2; that is, of their own accord, and their own imaginations. There were women of old who did prophesy without blame, it was lawful for them. Miriam was a prophetess, Exod. xv. 20, and went before the people, Micah vi. 4; so Huldah, 2 Kings xxii. 14; Anna also was a prophetess, Luke ii. 36; and the promise of the spirit of prophecy was to women as well as men; Acts ii. 17, "I will pour out my Spirit upon all flesh; and your sons and your daughters shall prophesy;" and Philip the evangelist had four daughters who did prophesy, Acts xxi. 8, 9, and, doubtless, the church and people of God received much good by their prophesying: but these were false prophetesses, which did deceive the people, and came not behind the false prophets in doing mischief. It is probable they exceeded men, for women, by reason of the tenderness of their nature, sweetness of their voices, respect amongst men, have the advantage to insinuate their opinions, and persuade more powerfully, especially when they have a repute for holiness, and are esteemed prophetical, as these were.

"Prophesy thou against them." They arrogated to themselves the call and authority of God, when there was no such thing; and for women to pretend this that they might deceive the people, was grievous; therefore Ezekiel is commanded to prophesy against them.

One thing here especially is observable, that the Lord calls the people not his, but the prophet's, "Set thy face against the daughters of thy people." When some heinous thing was committed dishonourable to God, reproachful to the people, and the Lord would object it against them, then the Lord would not own them for his people that did such things, that they might be convinced of the greatness of the evil they had done, which made them unworthy to be the people or children of the Lord any longer: Exod. xxxii. 7, 8, when the people corrupted themselves in making a calf and worshipping it, then God calls them Moses's people, "Get thee down, for thy people," &c.; hence that in Deut. xxxii. 5, "They have corrupted themselves, their spot is not the spot of his children."

"Woe to the women that sew pillows," &c. Here is a general judgment denounced against those women; "Woe," which includes evils of all sorts, and special sins set down:

1. Sewing of pillows to all armholes.

2. Making kerchiefs upon the head of every stature, which are typical actions; and then the end of these, hunting of souls.

"Sewing of pillows." למתפרות כסתות Septuagint is *συῤῥαπτούσαις προς κεφάλαια*, sewing things for the head; this is an obscure phrase. Pillows are soft things, filled with feathers, for the head to repose upon; some thereby understand, an easy and pleasurable life; others think these prophetic women were sorceresses, and did use these pillows and kerchiefs in their enchantments; they appointed those who consulted with them to have these on them, or about them, and hereby they were made fit to receive their oracles or prophecies; as those who went to the oracle in the den of Tryphonius, they had strange vestures and rites, they were clad with a linen coat, that was girt to them with a fillet, or hairlace, and they had slippers tied to their feet peculiar to that place; these things were to procure the great reverence to their religion, oracles, and prophecies.

The word is from כסה to cover, hide, and the nouns derived thence signify *operimentum, velamen, prætextum, quicquid obtenditur, ut aliquid abscondas vel dissimules;* hence Pradus interprets the word here, *chesathoth, rete, quod obtendunt aucupes ad capiendas aviculas.*

We must take the words in a metaphorical sense. A man that lies upon the hard ground, among stones or thorns, will sleep little, and very uneasily, unquietly; but a man that hath soft pillows to lie upon, he sleeps much, with great ease and quiet, he hath nothing to trouble or interrupt his sleep: when men are full of fears, cares, distractions, they sleep among stones and thorns. These prophetesses by their prophecies took away those fears, cares, and distractions, which were caused in the hearts of the people by the true prophets, who told them of Nebuchadnezzar's coming, and threatened the ruin of city and temple, and their going into captivity; they flattered them, and fed them with fair words, they promised them peace, safety, liberty, &c.; and so put pillows under their heads and armholes, and strengthened them in their security.

"Make kerchiefs upon the head," &c. המספחות Veils wherewith women did cover their faces. Hereby is meant the flatteries and false prophecies whereby they veiled and covered up the people in security, that they might sleep securely, and not be troubled with any apprehensions of danger; though they sinned grievously, they persuaded them the Lord was not angry with them, and they fitted their words and prophecies to the condition of every one. They had that which fitted the humours of the ancient, of the middle age, of youth; they, through their craft and lying prophecies, applied themselves to the head of every stature, and so pleased all, and lulled them in a general security. Junius thinks these kerchiefs were *triumphales pilei*, triumphal caps, made up into the form of crowns of hats, and set upon the heads of the statues, thereby presaging they should have not only safety from, but victory over, their enemies, which they learned from the practice of Egyptians and Babylonians. And to this purpose is Deodate, who expounds veils of the mourning and calamity of others. Now, if the Jews had been conquerors of the Babylonians, the Babylonians had had cause of covering their faces, and mourning for their loss.

"To hunt souls." לצודד which the Septuagint renders thus, *διαστρέφειν ψυχάς*, to pervert souls: Vulgate, *ad capiendas animas;* those that hunt, set their nets, and then drive what is hunted into their nets, and so make a prey of it. The like do these, the prophets, they seduce souls, that is, men and women, with a false hope of peace and good days, and so the evil day comes upon them unthought of, and they are made a prey.

"Will you hunt the souls of my people?" By this interrogation the Lord manifests his displeasure. They thought it was free for them to deceive the people with their pillows and kerchiefs, with their flattering words, false promises, and to make gain of them; but the Lord would not let things pass so. Will you hunt their souls, spoil and prey upon them? you shall be hunted yourselves, and taken in your lying prophecies.

"Will you save the souls alive, that come unto you?" The Hebrew, Will you make alive souls unto you? These words may refer either to the false prophetesses, or to others; if to the false prophetesses, the sense is this, Will you delude my people with vain hopes, with promises of life and happy days, that you may get from them meat and drink, that so you may quicken and keep alive your own souls? what! will you destroy their souls with your errors, to feed your own with bread? And so Piscator reads the words, Do you hunt the souls of my people? *Ut animas vobis vivas conservetis.* If to others, the sense is thus; You hunt the souls of the people, you insnare them with your lies, divinations, and feigned visions, and will ye save them alive that come to you, and believe what you say? No, while you persuade them they shall live, you take away their life from them; the very taking of them with your falsehoods is their death; you serve them as hunters their game, when it is taken, they kill it.

"And will ye pollute me among my people?" &c. This verse contains several sins also of these wicked prophetesses.

1. Their pollution of God's name.
2. Their covetousness, "Handfuls of barley, and pieces of bread."
3. Their cruelty, slaying of souls.
4. Their partiality; they slew those which should have lived, and spared those which should have died.

Then the manner how all these things were done, by their lies.

"Will ye pollute me," &c. They pretended they were sent and authorized of God to prophesy, that they had the Spirit of God, and were true prophetesses, that whatever they delivered should come to pass; they crossed the true prophets, they strengthened the people in their sinful practices, they made prophecy contemptible, and so profaned the name of the Lord, caused many to fall to atheism and apostasy. This God would not bear at their hands, therefore saith, "Will ye."

"For handfuls of barley and pieces of bread." This is a kind of proverbial speech, setting out the meanness of that work which is so cheap. Prophecy with them was at a vile and low price; if any brought never so mean a reward, as a little barley in his hand, or a crust of bread with him, to these deluding prophetesses, presently they had a pleasing answer. Had these women set their lying prophecies at the highest rate, it had not been warrantable to have profaned God's glorious name for great rewards, but for such petty gain to expose his name to scorn was extremely wicked.

"To slay the souls that should not die," &c. By "souls" you must understand persons; for souls are not to be slain, Matt. x. 28. They prophesied against the godly that they should die, and so deprived them of their peace, comfort, and apprehensions they had of God's favour; filled them with fears, griefs, and sad thoughts, if they hearkened to Jeremiah, and submitted to Nebuchadnezzar. Or thus, They stirred up the people against them who were godly, and would not adhere to them, believing their prophecies, and provoked the magistrates to restrain them, yea to cut them off, and so slew them before their time. They should have lived longer by the course of nature, had not these blood-thirsty prophetesses hastened their death.

"To save the souls alive that should not live." They promised life, peace, happiness, to those they should have threatened war, misery, death. Zedekiah, and many with him, had broken the oath made with Nebuchadnezzar to be tributaries to him, and so deserved death upon that ground; others oppressed, filled the land with bloody crimes, were notoriously idolatrous, and not worthy to live; yet these were justified, pleaded for, and protected against the power of any that would have had justice executed.

It is not against the judgment of some learned ones to understand death and life here, of eternal death and life. These women teachers threatened the righteous with eternal death, shut heaven upon them, and opened hell wide enough upon them, and what lay in them slew their souls; and for the others, they promised heaven and all joys of it to them, and so saved them alive they should not.

Obs. 1. That is an old practice of Satan, to trouble the church, as with false prophets, so with false prophetesses. God raised up women prophets to honour that sex, and to help his people; and the devil raises up women to spread lies, to deceive and damnify the people, and to gain by that sex the more to his kingdom. Satan imitates God; if he will have he or she prophets, the like will he have. In the church of Thyatira was a Jezebel, which called herself a prophetess, to teach and seduce the servants of Christ to commit fornication, and to eat things sacrificed to idols, Rev. ii. 20. Jezebel disturbed Israel, opposed and sought the death of the true prophets, maintained idolatry; so did this other Jezebel, &c. Neh. vi. 14, there is mention of one Noadiah, a prophetess; she with other false prophets prophesied against the building of the temple, encouraged Sanballat, Tobias, and others, to hinder it, laboured to possess Nehemiah and the builders with fear. Such there have been in former days, and such will be, women that take upon them to teach and deceive unwary people; such were Prisca and Maximilla, the companions of Montanus the heretic; such are the Jesuitesses.

Obs. 2. It is the character of false teachers of what kind soever, women or men, to flatter, soothe, insinuate, and speak pleasing things. The false prophets cried "Peace," &c.; these false prophetesses "sew pillows to all armholes," &c.; yea, their scope is to please all sorts, they observe the humours o. men, and so apply themselves to please answerably; Isa. xxx. 10, this was the disposition of the people, "Prophesy not unto us right things; speak unto us smooth things, prophesy deceits;" 2 Tim. iv. 3, people would have teachers after their own lusts.

Obs. 3. False prophecies, flattering and erroneous doctrines, are the snares and nets with which false teachers do hunt souls. Prov. vi. 26, an adulteress hunts for the precious life, and these for the precious souls. Eph. iv. 14, "They lie in wait to deceive." Rev. xx. 8, it is the devil's work "to deceive the nations in the four quarters of the earth."

Obs. 4. Whatever false teachers promise, they cannot perform. "Will ye save alive the souls that come unto you?" will you keep off war, plague, famine, when Nebuchadnezzar shall come about the walls? &c.

Obs. 5. False teachers profane God's name, and he takes it very ill at their hands. "Will ye pollute me among my people?" to make God the author of their dreams, lies, &c.; to pretend they are sent of him, and cause his people to conceive he deludes them, and tells them contraries, one thing by Jeremiah, other things by them, and that for such poor things as barley?

Obs. 6. Covetousness, and baseness of spirit, make merchandise of God's name, truth, and the souls of persons.

Micah iii. 5, "He that putteth not into their mouths," the prophets' he means, "they even prepare war against him." Judas sold Christ, &c. A woman to prostitute her chastity for handfuls of barley is base, much more to serve souls so; 2 Pet. ii. 3, "With feigned words make merchandise of you."

Obs. 7. That they kill whom God would not have killed, and spare those whom God would not have spared, they curse whom God blesses, and bless whom God curses.

In ver. 20, 21, 23, he sets down God's proceeding with these false prophetesses; he will be against them, tear their pillows and kerchiefs, deliver his people out of their hands, and destroy them and their divinations.

"To make them flee." לפרחות Piscator hath it, *in floribus hortis*, flower-gardens; they were wont to sacrifice in gardens, Isa. i. 29; lxv. 3; lxvi. 17. These prophetesses, with their flatteries, drew in young maids, to prophesy smooth and pleasing things, and they drew in the men, and so great lewdness and filthiness was amongst them, and they were charmed with their divinations. We may take it thus: They hunted them, they used seducing ways by their prophecies, promises, and flatteries, to make them flee from the truth, and true prophets, to take them off from Jeremiah and Ezekiel, and so should be like birds that fly from bough to bough, or beasts that run from place to place, and abide no where.

"I will let the souls go, even the souls that ye hunt." The meaning is, I will free them from the delusion of their false prophecies, they shall go captive into Babylon, and be no longer in their hands.

"With lies ye have made the heart of the righteous sad." The Hebrew is, to wear, to make contrite; the Septuagint, Ye have perverted the hearts of the righteous. There were some among them who hearkened to the true prophets, and it was in their hearts to yield to the Chaldeans, as Jeremiah counselled; but when they heard the false prophets and prophetesses encouraging the people not to fear Nebuchadnezzar, but promised safety to them that should stay in the city, they were troubled, and knew not what to do; and by this means also they "strengthened the hands of the wicked," who gave heed to their lying prophecies, and slighted whatever Jeremiah said.

"You shall see no more vanity, nor divine divinations." There was no weight, no truth, in what they said, whoever received their prophecies were deceived; the time was approaching which would discover the vanity of their visions, and cut them off from seeing any more, for they should perish.

Obs. 1. The Lord is against false prophetesses, and will destroy their prophecies, ceremonies they use, and them too. "Behold, I am against your pillows, I will tear them from your arms, and the kerchiefs from your heads, and ye shall see no more vanity, nor divine divinations." God will not let such persons and practices go unpunished as intrude into the prophetical office, abuse his name, authority, truth, and people.

Obs. 2. Women teachers and men teachers also are very subtle to seduce the people. They had their pillows and kerchiefs, their flatteries, pleasing prophecies and promises, to keep them in security, to hunt them into the gardens, to commit spiritual and corporal whoredom. Calvin judges that they pretended *altas speculationes*, some transcendent matters, thereby to excite the expectations of the people, who were weary of Jeremiah's prophecy, being of a lower strain than Isaiah's and some others, and were tainted with curiosity and itching ears; they were not content with wholesome and plain doctrine, but would be wise beyond sobriety, and God suffered subtle and false teachers to hunt and snare them. Sometimes fowls are snared in flying, where no danger is suspected; and these were deluded by those speculations which were given out by false prophetesses. How were the popish spirits taken with the tenet of Dionysius touching the heavenly hierarchy! so with the Jesuits' Dalilah, *de media scientia:* and at this day are not multitudes taken with speculations and novelties, do they not despise wholesome doctrine, and listen to erroneous teachers, both men and women?

Obs. 3. God's people may be taken with some errors of the times, and of false teachers. "I will deliver my people out of their hand, and they shall be no more in their hand." They were then in their hands, they had hunted them into their nets, and caught them with their enticing prophecies, and brought them over to be of their mind. Jezebel did seduce the servants of Christ, Rev. ii. 20; you know

Peter and Barnabas were drawn into an error, Gal. ii. 12—14; and Christ hath told you, Matt. xxiv. 11, that many "false prophets shall arise, and deceive many;" they rise from the earth, or out of the bottomless pit, and do much hurt with their smoky doctrines; they darken the heavens, so that the saints mistake their way. There were those who constrained the Galatians to be circumcised, chap. vi. 12; and Acts xx. 30, "Of your own selves shall men arise, speaking perverse things, to draw away disciples after them." The old lying prophet deceived and drew the young prophet into a snare, which cost him his life, a lion devoured him, 1 Kings xiii. I fear there are young prophets drawn away into dangerous errors, and many others about this city, whom I hope God will keep from the roaring lion, and deliver in due time from the error of their ways. Let the counsel of Solomon to his son, Prov. xix. 27, be welcome to you, "Cease to hear the instruction that causeth to err from the words of knowledge;" and hearken to Peter, 2 Epist. iii. 17, 18, "Seeing ye know these things before, beware lest ye also, being led away with the error of the wicked, fall from your own stedfastness. But grow in grace, and in the knowledge of our Lord and Saviour Jesus Christ."

Obs. 4. The doctrines of false teachers do prejudice both the godly and the wicked, they sadden the hearts of those who should not be made sad, and they strengthen the hands of the wicked which should be weakened. When false teachers give out their lies, corrupt truths, and opinions, they weaken the authority of the true prophets' doctrine, they fill the godly with fears, scruples, grief, and discouragement. What saddening doctrines are among the papists, from their false teachers; as that of auricular confession, all sins must be confessed to a priest; justification by works, satisfaction, purgatory, transubstantiation, that of the death of infants before baptism, falling away from grace, keeping of the law, traditions, &c. These, with others, are doctrines which wound the hearts of the godly, and much perplex them. And are there not as saddening and heart-perplexing doctrines among us? viz. denial of the sacred Trinity, Christ's divine nature, authority of the holy Scripture; that God is the Author, Creator, and Inventor of all sin; that it is the same spirit which is in the godly and the wicked; that there is no election, but a universal redemption; that God sees no sin in his people; that the law is of no use to believers; that Christ himself may sin as well as a child of God; that all days are alike, the Lord's day having no pre-eminence; that women may preach; that there is no power or rule in the church, but all in the civil magistrate: as these opinions sadden the hearts of the godly, so they strengthen the hands of those who are wicked, they go on in their ways, and never think of returning to the Lord. False teachers, which speak pleasing things, undo the souls of sinners; they promise life when they should threaten death, open to them their danger, show them the evil of their ways, and use the strongest arguments they can to awaken and reduce them; Jer. xxiii. 22, had they "caused my people to hear my words, then they should have turned them from their evil way, and from the evil of their doings."

Obs. 5. God hath his times to deliver his people from the flattery, tyranny, and policy of false teachers. "I will deliver them out of your hand." There was a day when the people were delivered from the tyranny and flattery of Ahab's false prophets, 1 Kings xviii; and, Rev. xix. 20, the beast with the false prophet, &c. were thrown into the lake.

CHAPTER XIV.

Ver. 1—5. *Then came certain of the elders of Israel unto me, and sat before me, And the word of the Lord came unto me, saying, Son of man, these men have set up their idols in their heart, and put the stumblingblock of their iniquity before their face: should I be enquired of at all by them? Therefore speak unto them, and say unto them, Thus saith the Lord God; Every man of the house of Israel that setteth up his idols in his heart, and putteth the stumblingblock of his iniquity before his face, and cometh to the prophet, I the Lord will answer him that cometh according to the multitude of his idols; that I may take the house of Israel in their own heart, because they are all estranged from me through their idols.*

In chap. xii. our prophet treated of the king and his nobles, their sins and judgments; in chap. xiii. of false prophets and prophetesses, and how the Lord would punish them; here of the elders and body of the people, and what sore plagues should befall them. There be three parts of this chapter:

I. A conference of God with hypocritical elders, and false prophets, ver. 1—12.

II. A threatening of sore judgments against a sinning land, ver. 12—22.

III. A respiting of some from those judgments, ver. 22, to the end.

In the first part, viz. that of it which concerns the elders, you have,

1. The occasion of it, that is, the coming of these elders to the prophet, ver. 1.

2. God's complaint of them, ver. 3.

3. A charge to the prophet what answer to give unto these men, ver. 3—8.

"Then came certain of the elders of Israel." After Ezekiel had declared the mind of God against Zedekiah, the princes, the false prophets and prophetesses, who drew many to sinful practices, and especially to trust in vain divinations, some of the elders of Israel thought in themselves to go to Ezekiel, and hear what he would say: He hath cried down all other prophets, and thinks himself the only true prophet; come, let us go to his house, and hearken what he will prophesy unto us.

"Elders of Israel." These men are called elders, not only because they were aged, but because they were in some place of authority, which required men grave in age and counsel: Jer. xxvi. 17, "Then rose up certain of the elders of the land, and spake to all the assembly of the people:" these were such elders. It is questioned whether these elders were elders of those in Babylon, or of those in Jerusalem; the most interpreters agree that they were of the elders of Judah in Babylon: chap. viii. 1, it is said, the elders of Judah sat before the prophet, and Jer. xxix. 1, tells you that there were elders carried away captive. But the judicious and learned Junius is of another mind, who thinks these elders were ambassadors sent from Zedekiah into Babylon to treat of state affairs between him and Nebuchadnezzar; as Jer. li. 59, Seraiah went with Zedekiah into Babylon in the fourth year of his reign. It is no where extant that Zedekiah ever went into Babylon till he was carried thither, and that was in the eleventh year. The meaning, then, of the words is, he went in the behalf of Zedekiah, so it is in the margin, and being a quiet prince, endeavoured to keep a peaceable correspondence between Zedekiah and Nebuchadnezzar. So, in Jer. xxix. 3, Elasah and Gemariah were sent by Zedekiah unto Nebuchadnezzar king of Babylon. It is ordinary for kings to send ambassadors to other states, and especially when a part of their people live in that state, as here; and when they send, it is some, or divers, of the elders and nobles that are sent; and of these, certain came to the prophet. It is likely some of those who were formerly brought hither, might accompany them, and the judgments spoken of in the chapter concerned those who belonged to Judea rather than those captives in Babylon.

"Sat before me." To converse with the prophet about the great affairs of the king and kingdom. They were in straits, full of doubts and fears, and came to feel the prophet, to inquire of him what would be the event of things; it is like they had no good tidings from Nebuchadnezzar, they would try what was to be had from God: or thus, They had heard what the false prophets and prophetesses had said, how they concurred in their prophecies, and now they would try Ezekiel, whether he prophesied the same, or differing things; and so came not to him with an upright mind, but fallaciously. If what he had said had liked them, then they would have affirmed he was of the same judgment the false prophets were; if otherwise, that he was a lying and false prophet, that he and Jeremiah were singular, dissenting in their prophecies from all the other prophets.

Obs. 1. When the true prophets detect and disparage those who are false, then those who adhere to them are offended at it, and seek advantages against them. As here, the elders of Israel came to Ezekiel; they could not bear it that he had said their prophets were foolish, followed their own spirits, played the foxes, were liars, seducers, daubed with untempered mortar, that they and their prophecies should perish, for the Lord was against them. Great persons will take part with false prophets, and appear for them, and seek to entrap those who have discovered them. When Micaiah discovered the false prophets, 1 Kings xxii. 22, 23, then Ahab appeared for them, and commands Micaiah to be imprisoned, fed with bread and water of affliction, ver. 26, 27.

Obs. 2. Many profess love to the true prophets, and to religion, yet are false-hearted to both. These elders of Israel came to the prophet, sat before him, pretended to learn and obey, but their intentions looked another way. Not all who seem religious, frequent the solemn assemblies, and hear the word from the mouths of the prophets, are truly godly: Ezek. xxxiii. 31, 32, saith God of the people, "They sit before thee as my people, and they hear thy words, but they will not do them; for with their mouth they show much love, but their heart goeth after their covetousness. And, lo, thou art unto them as a very lovely song of one that hath a pleasant voice, and can play well on an instrument; for they hear thy words, but they do them not." This people were as glad to hear Ezekiel prophesy, as men to hear music and songs, at marriages or feasts, and yet their hearts were unsound: see Isa. xxix. 13; lviii. 2—5; Jer. vii. 9—11, where you may find their professions were pious, but their spirits and practices impious. Profession is easy in all sorts, elders, and elders of Israel, can do that, but the practice of what men profess is difficult; men rest in forms of godliness, and deny the power, 2 Tim. iii. 5.

On ver. 2, *Obs.* That much of the Scripture hath been given out upon sinful occasions. When these elders came to the prophet, the word of the Lord came unto him, and he gave it out to them and us. Men's sins have opened the windows of heaven for much divine light to shine into the world; the prophecy of Haggai was occasioned by the neglect to build God's house, as you may read in chap. i. 2—4, &c.; Nineveh's sin drew out the prophecy of Jonah, chap. i. 1, 2; David's murder and adultery were occasions of some, if not of all, the penitential psalms; the Levite cutting his concubine, who was forced to death, into twelve pieces, and sending her into all the coast of Israel, occasioned some part of the book of Judges to be written; the Gospel of John, it is conceived by the learned, was written on the occasion of Cerinthus, Ebion, and some others, who did deny the divine nature of Christ, therefore in the beginning, viz. chap. i. he speaks much of his Godhead, sonship, and eternal generation; it was the disorders, divisions, scandals, and corruptions, which set Paul on work to write his two epistles to the Corinthians, as you may observe throughout the epistle; the doctrine of false teachers amongst the Galatians gave birth to that epistle, chap. i. 6, and in several parts of the epistle it clearly appears; the danger of the Jews forsaking their professing of christianity, and revolting to mosaical ceremonies, opened the doors for the epistle to the Hebrews to enter into the world; the faultiness of the angels in the churches, made way for the several epistles to be written and sent unto them.

Ver. 3. "Son of man, these men have set up their idols in their heart," &c. Here is,

I. God's complaint of them; and that,

1. Of their hypocrisy.

2. Of their idolatry; which is the argument he proves their hypocrisy by. Thus, those that "set up idols in their heart, and put the stumbling-block of their iniquity before their face," and come to inquire of me, they deal hypocritically with me; but these men do so.

II. God's indignation against them for these sins; "Should I be inquired of at all by them?"

"Have set up their idols in their heart." The Hebrew is, Have made their idols to ascend upon their heart; the Septuagint is, They have put their thoughts upon their hearts; Castalio, Their dunghill gods are for a delight to these men. The word for idols means that which defiles, and which is odious; so idols are offensive unto God: this word you had before, chap. viii. 18, where it was opened unto you. If one should now, for the sense of these words, tell you they had the pictures of their idols at their hearts, it may be you would not altogether condemn it, for it suits with the Hebrew, They made their idols to ascend upon their hearts: and such a practice the Scripture seems to hold forth; Hos. ii. 2, "Let her put away her adulteries from between her breasts;" that is, such pictures she had of her idols hanging at her breast: so that, in Jer. xvii. 1, may be understood, "The sin of Judah is graven upon the table of their heart;" they had a table, in the form of a heart, hanging at their breast, in which was engraven the effigies of their idol god; and that which adds some strength to this is ver. 20, of the former chapter, "Shall a man make gods unto himself?" If this be part of the meaning, yet, I conceive, not all.

"They set up their idols in their heart;" that is,

1. They gave them entertainment in their hearts, and made them the temples and altars for them. Before, they set them in God's house, Jer. vii. 30, to pollute that; now they set them in their own hearts, to pollute them; they minded and affected them, they were much in their thoughts and affec-

tions, and had the strength and supremacy of them; and so judicious Calvin interprets the place; he saith, They were so addicted to superstition, that their idols and rites about them had made deep impressions upon their hearts, and had the command of their thoughts and affections: Psal. lxii. 10, "If riches increase, set not your heart upon them;" that is, do not mind and affect them, let not them sway, command your thoughts or affections; but here their idols were set up in their hearts, and their hearts were set upon their idols.

2. They purposed to honour them with *dulia* and *latria*, service and worship, and to continue in their idolatry. When the calves were set up at Dan and Bethel, it was for to worship them; when Amaziah set up the Edomites' gods, he bowed down to them, 2 Chron. xxv. 14; and the setting these up in their hearts, notes their intention to persist in their way of worship.

3. They resolved not to part with them. What men set up in their hearts, they count as their gods, they will be at any cost to maintain them, venture their credit, limbs, lives, souls, in defence of them. You know how Micah was affected when the Danites took away his idol gods, Judg. xviii.; you must remember they were set up in his heart as well as in his house, and therefore he gets men together, pursues the Danites, and ventures his life to recover them. When any thing becomes an idol in the heart, as covetousness, wantonness, ceremony, any way of false worship, any foolish or blasphemous opinion, it is no easy matter to get down that idol.

"And put the stumblingblock of their iniquity before their face." The Hebrew for stumblingblock is from a word which signifies to fall, to dash against any thing, or person, so as to receive hurt, or do hurt; the Septuagint is, They have set the torment or punishment of their iniquity before them; Castalio, their detrimental evil. This stumblingblock of their iniquity was their idols, which while they affected, respected, reverenced, they fell into idolatry, caused many others to do so, and therefore are called "the stumblingblock of their iniquity;" they stumbled at these, fell from God upon these, and so wounded themselves: Zeph. i. 3, idols are called "stumblingblocks."

The putting them before their faces or eyes notes,

1. Delight in them; for usually we set such things before our eyes as are pleasing: Psal. xxvi. 3, "Thy loving-kindness is before mine eyes." So wives and children are called "the desire of men's eyes," Ezek. xxiv. 16, 25, because they are pleasing and delightful. Such were their idols unto these elders of Israel, and divers others; hence is that phrase, Ezek. vi. 9, "Your eyes go a whoring after your idols."

2. Insatiableness in that practice; they intend to look constantly upon them, as not being satisfied with one, two, or some few acts, but they must have them ever in their eyes: Prov. xxvii. 20, "The eyes of man are never satisfied:" the eyes and hearts of idolaters are never satisfied; Ezek. xvi. 28, Jerusalem is said to be insatiable; and chap. xxiii. 11, Aholibah, which was Jerusalem, was corrupt and inordinate in her love; that was, to idols.

"Should I be inquired of at all by them?" Hebrew is, Am I inquired by inquiring? or, Am I asked by asking? do they not dissemble? Ezekiel, dost thou think they are in good earnest now they are come, sit before thee, and make as if they would hearken to what counsel should be given? No, no, be not deceived, they have idols in their hearts, and before their eyes, and whatever pretences they have, all is fancied and false. The words are an interrogation, discovering and reproving their hypocrisy and impudency, that dare come to the Lord to inquire of him: "Should I be inquired," &c.? do they think I will mind them, give them any comfortable answer? far be it from me.

Obs. 1. That God takes notice of heart-idolatry; not only what idols are in temples, in his worship, what innovations, corruptions, superstitions are there, but also what idols are in men's bosoms.

Obs. 2. Where superstition and idolatry once get interest, they are not easily removed. These elders of Israel had turned aside from the true God, and fell to idolatry in Jerusalem, chap. viii. 11, and now being come into Babylon, they brought their idols with them in their hearts. Neither change of country, nor company, did prevail with their hearts to let go their idols; they saw many of their brethren in captivity for that sin, they heard Ezekiel prophesy against their practices and those who upheld them in it, they understood Nebuchadnezzar had no good will to them, yet the idols remain firm, and settled in their hearts. When idols get into Bethel, God's house, it is a great difficulty to get them out; but when gotten into the heart, they become immovable, you may as soon pluck out their hearts, as pluck out their idols. The papists hold fast their images and idolatrous practices to this day, notwithstanding all the judgments of God which have been upon them. Acts of authority may take down monuments of superstition, remove out of the public worship ceremonies, pictures, idols, but can they remove them out of men's hearts? it is not the power of man, change of place, company, or duties, will do it; till the Lord speak to the heart with a strong hand, the idol got in, will stand; men's affections and corruptions are very tenacious of them.

Obs. 3. Idols set up in the heart, or elsewhere, prove ruin to the authors and supporters of them. The text calls them "stumblingblocks," by them they fell into sin, and that brought ruin upon them. Idolatry hath snared and ruined many. When Gideon made and set up an ephod in the city, and in his heart, it became a snare to him and to his house, Judg. viii. 27; so Psal. cvi. 36, they served idols, and they were a snare unto them; it was their idolatry which brought their captivity. And there is no idol, in secret or public, but is cause of ruin; idols in worship bring destruction upon churches and states, idols in heart bring destruction upon souls.

Obs. 4. Men are active to their own destruction, they set up their idols in their own hearts. "And put the stumblingblock of their iniquity before their face." Men's destructions are from themselves: Jeroboam set the calves in Dan and Bethel, 1 Kings xii. 29; he "made priests of the lowest of the people;" and what saith the text, "This thing became sin unto the house of Jeroboam, even to cut it off, and to destroy it from the face of the earth," chap. xiii. 34. Hence God told them, Hos. xiii. 9, that they had destroyed themselves; they set up the calves at Dan and Bethel, and practised such things as brought total destruction upon them. Prov. v. 22, "His own iniquities shall take the wicked himself, and he shall be holden with the cords of his sins."

Obs. 5. However hypocrisy may escape the eyes of men, yet it cannot escape the eye of God. These elders carried it fair with the prophet, but the Lord saw their hypocritical and deceitful hearts, and discovered them unto the prophet: God's eye is a piercing eye, and can discern hypocrisy, how deeply soever it be hid. The scribes and Pharisees had their hypocrisy hid under long garments, long prayers, much zeal, and yet Christ saw it, and made it known; Matt. xxiii. "Woe unto you, scribes," &c. Whatever pretences men make, whatever they practise outwardly, if the heart be not clear, if they go after covetousness, &c. it is hypocrisy, seen of God, and shall be detected: Prov. xv. 3, "The eyes of the Lord are in every place, beholding the evil and the good;" he knows the secret counsels and plottings of men.

Obs. 6. When hypocrites fly unto God, they may rather expect wrath then mercy. These men came for counsel and comfort, but what saith the Lord, "Should I be inquired of at all by them?" They have no warrant to come to me with hypocritical hearts, with idolatrous spirits; and if they do, should I grant their requests? No, I will manifest my dislike of them, answer them in wrath, "according to the multitude of their idols;" for bread I will give them stones, for fish serpents. Would they have counsel from me? I will give them up to their own devices, and leave them to seduction by their own thoughts and lusts: Hos. viii. 13, "They sacrifice flesh for the sacrifices of mine offerings; but the Lord accepteth them not; now will he remember their iniquity, and visit their sins." They came hypocritically to God, expected acceptation when they sacrificed, but the Lord at that time remembered their sins, and instead of a gracious answer, they had a grievous judgment. Hence saith the Lord, in Isa. lxvi. 3, "He that killeth an ox is as if he slew a man; he that sacrificeth a lamb, as if he cut off a dog's neck; he that offereth an oblation, as if he offered swine's blood; he that burneth incense, as if he blessed an idol." What is the reason of this? why, "they have chosen their own ways, and their soul delighteth in their abominations;" they have their idols in their hearts, they are hypocrites, and come to me, thinking to have favour of me, and mercy from me. They shall hear such things as they would not hear: Ahab consulted with Micaiah about regaining Ramoth-gilead, not out of conscience to obey, but that he might have him speak things suitable to his heart; but he heard that which displeased him.

Obs. 7. God will give such answer to hypocritical heart-idolaters, as shall snare them. "I will answer" them that come to inquire of me "according to the multitude of their idols, that I may take the house of Israel in their own heart," in their own thoughts and devices: their tongues ask for mercy, but their hearts call for judgment; there is hypocrisy and idolatry in their hearts, and suitable thereunto shall be my answer. God answers such in justice, and sends them strong delusions to believe lies, 2 Thess. ii. 11; and to ripen their damnation, they bring matter of damnation in their hearts, and God seals it up.

Quest. How are they said to be taken in their hearts when God doth not answer their desires or hopes, but gives out what is contrary thereunto?

Answ. 1. When God answers not such men after their desires and expectations, they fret and rage against God, as if he dealt not well with them, and so God takes them in their heart, and discovers them to the world.

2. God threatening judgments takes the hearts of sinners with fear, which holds them in dreadful bondage night and day; famine, plague, sword, and noisome beasts, captivity, were threatened; and, chap. xii. 13, God calls his judgments, nets, snares.

3. He convinces them that they do not honour him by their false worship, but are guilty of those things which do greatly offend him; they think he sees not their idols, because shut up within in their hearts.

Obs. 8. Idolatry of what kind soever is a grievous sin, it estranges from God; "They are estranged from me through their idols." Man's happiness lies in his nearness to God, union with him, and fruition of him; now idolatry, though only heart-idolatry, estranges, divides, separates from God, and that is the great misery of the creature. They left the infinite, all-sufficient, living, only good and wise God, for dunghill gods that had nothing in them, that could do nothing for them, that brought a curse upon them and theirs: Jer. xix. 3, 4, "Behold, I will bring evil upon this place, the which whosoever heareth, his ears shall tingle. Because they have forsaken me, and have estranged this place, and have burned incense in it unto other gods." They first estranged themselves from God, then estranged the place of his worship; and then God dealt strangely by them, he brought destruction upon them. People may think themselves happy that they have communion with God in sacrifice and worship; but if there be any idols within or without, they are strangers unto God, and God is a stranger unto them, and strange judgments are in readiness for them.

Obs. 9. Note here, the right way of coming unto God to inquire of him. If you would have a gracious answer, you must come with hearts free from idols, with pure hearts: Psal. lxvi. 18, "If I regard iniquity in my heart, the Lord will not hear me;" if we come with sin in our hearts, (sin approved, countenanced, delighted in,) God will meet us with wrath in his hand; therefore the Scripture oft tells us of this duty, how we should come to God; Heb. x. 22, "Let us draw near with a true heart;" 1 Tim. ii. 8, Let us lift "up holy hands, without wrath and doubting;" there must be no wrath nor doubting in your hearts; James iv. 8, "Draw nigh to God;" but how? "cleanse your hands, ye sinners; and purify your hearts, ye double-minded:" inwardly they must be cleansed, and outwardly reformed; lives and spirits must be suitable unto God.

Ver. 6. *Therefore say unto the house of Israel, Thus saith the Lord God; Repent, and turn yourselves from your idols; and turn away your faces from all your abominations.*

This verse is part of the charge given the prophet, which he was to deliver to the house of Israel, and in it is a command, or an exhortation, to repentance, which is laid down,

I. In general; "Repent."

II. More specially.

1. "Turn yourselves from your idols."

2. "Turn away your faces from all your abominations."

"Repent." שׁובו from שוב to return, implying a going back from what a man had done. The Greeks have two words by which they express the nature of repentance: one is μεταμελεῖν, which is to be careful, anxious, solicitous after a thing done; this we term penitence. The other word is μετανοεῖν, *mentem et consilium in melius mutare, ab* ἀνοία, *dementia, et* μετά, *post*, it being the correction of men's folly, and returning *ad sanam mentem;* and μετάνοια is that which we term *resipiscentia*, a growing wise again; some express it by an after-mind, an amendment of the mind: one of these respects the change of the will, the other, the change of the mind. The Hebrew word for repentance is תשובה from the word in my text, and notes a returning from one thing to another, from sin to God: 1 Kings viii. 35, "If they pray towards this place, and confess thy name, and turn from their sin, when thou afflictest them: then hear thou in heaven."

Quest. Is not repentance the work and gift of God? if so, how is it that man is commanded to repent?

Answ. Repentance is of the Lord; Acts xi. 18, "God granted repentance to the gentiles unto life;" 2 Tim. ii. 25, ministers must meekly instruct those that oppose, if God peradventure will give them repentance. It is also the gift of Christ; Acts v. 31, he is "exalted to be a Prince and Saviour, to give repentance to Israel. Yet God commands man to repent,

1. Because man may do something that he may repent; as, first, seriously consider the nature of his sin, what circumstances it is clothed with, what aggravations it admits, how crimson and scarlet it is, against what light, mercies, means, engagements, &c.: apprehension of sin under false notions of profit or pleasure, induceth to it, and consideration of sin in its own nature, helps to repent of it, and abhor it. Did men lay to heart what wrong the infinite, holy, blessed God hath by sin, what mercies it keeps from them, how greatly it doth defile them, what miseries and mischiefs it brings upon them, what a weight of divine wrath hangs over their heads, it would have some operation upon their hearts. Secondly, they may confess them before God: Josh. vii. 19, "Give glory to God, and make confession unto him;" Prov. xxviii. 13, "Whoso confesseth and forsaketh them shall have mercy;" 1 John i. 9, "If we confess our sins," &c.

2. God gives what he commands. Chap. xi. 19, he had promised to "take the stony heart out of their flesh, and to give them an heart of flesh," and therefore here might command them to repent. Mark i. 15, "Repent ye, and believe the gospel:" neither of these were in their power; they might as well create new heavens and new earths, as do these acts; but God gives and works them both in the hearts of whom he pleases, 2 Tim. ii. 25; Phil. i. 29. Neither repentance nor faith are natural or any acquired habits by the industry and acts of men, but they are the efficacious work of the Spirit in and upon the heart; God and Christ do work repentance by the Spirit, and therefore it is attributed unto them, and denied to be in the power of man: 2 Cor. iii. 5, "We are not sufficient of ourselves to think any thing as of ourselves;" Phil. ii. 13, "It is God which worketh in you both to will and to do of his good pleasure." Commands argue not power and free will in man to repent.

There is a use of these,

(1.) In regard of God.

(2.) Of man.

(1.) In regard of God.

[1.] To manifest what the Lord may justly require at the hands of men; if they sin unjustly, he may justly call for repentance.

[2.] To clear himself, that it is not his fault if men cannot do what they are called upon for. The creditor may call for his debt of that man, who is fallen into extreme poverty through his own sin.

[3.] To set before us the corruption and impotency of our nature: by the law we come to the knowledge, not of our power, but our impotency; Rom. iii. 20, "By the law is the knowledge of sin."

[4.] To advise us to look out for help elsewhere: therefore where you have commands in one place of Scripture, you have promises in some other part.

(2.) In regard of man.

[1.] That he may be more thoroughly sensible of the wretched corruption of his nature, and bewail it more fully.

[2.] That he may be stirred up more effectually to beg of God that which he commands, for God commands nothing but that which is of great weight and advantage for man.

[3.] That wicked men may be inexcusable: John xv. 22, "If I had not come and spoken unto them, they had not had sin; but now they have no cloak for their sin."

Obs. 1. Repentance is a turning from sin to God. Sin turns men from God, draws the soul into ways that lead unto death; James i. 4, a man "is drawn away of his own lust," drawn away from God, from his worship, truths, rules; but when repentance comes, he turns back again, he changes his thoughts, his mind, his will, he befools, abhors himself for what he hath done, and so comes to God again from whom he departed. The prodigal was drawn away from his father's house through his own lust, and laid a long time in looseness and wantonness; at last he changed his judgment, counsels, purposes, and returning to himself, returns to his father; Luke xv. 17, 18, "When he came to himself, he said, I will arise and go to my father, and say, Father, I have sinned against heaven and before thee." Sinners are said to be mad, Psal. cii. 8, "They that are mad against me;" and Paul, when he was in his course of sinning, saith, he was "exceedingly mad," Acts xxvi. 11; and Baalam's sin is called "madness," 2 Pet. ii. 16: repentance brings a man to his right wits, he becomes wise, and turns from his folly and madness. It is called a turning of men "from darkness to light, and from the power of Satan unto God," Acts xxvi. 18. Sin is darkness, and when men sin, they know not what they do; it is the power of Satan holds them under his government; but repentance enlightens and sets at liberty, so that men see and walk from under Satan unto God. Ver. 20, repentance and turning to God are put together, they are the same; but it is not any turning, but a turning of the judgment, so that men judge otherwise of God, of his laws, ways, of sin, of themselves, than before; a turning of the will and affections, so that they are carried wholly and fully unto God: Joel ii. 12, "Turn ye even to me with all your heart;" if it be with a piece, it is partial, hypocritical, and deceitful.

Obs. 2. Repentance is a continued act; the word "repent" implies the continuation of it. Some have thought it one act, and that is sufficient for a man's sin, but repentance is a grace, and must have its daily operation as well as other graces; if faith, love, patience, humility, must continue, repentance must do so likewise: where a spring breaks forth, it is always flowing; this is the spring of the soul, when God once smites the rocky heart, the water will flow; sincere repentants can no more content themselves with one act of repentance, than with one act of faith, they oft renew their repentance. Hence is it that the Lord would not have us forget our old sins, but to think of them and mourn for them: Deut. ix. 7, "Remember and forget not, how thou provokedst the Lord thy God to wrath in the wilderness;" Psal. xxv. 7, "Remember not the sins of my youth, nor my transgressions;" 1 Cor. xv. 9, "I am the least of the apostles, that am not meet to be called an apostle, because I persecuted the church of God;" Ezek. xvi. 62, 63, "I will establish my covenant with thee; and thou shalt know that I am the Lord; that thou mayest remember, and be confounded, and never open thy mouth any more because of thy shame, when I am pacified toward thee for all that thou hast done."

Obs. 3. Sinners should stir up themselves, and do the utmost which lies in their power, to further their turning unto God. "Turn yourselves from your idols;" use all arguments you can to cause your hearts to turn from idols, and from other sinful ways. Consider,

(1.) That they are separated from the Lord; Isa. lix. 2, "Your iniquities have separated between you and your God, and your sins have hid his face from you, that he will not hear." For a woman to be separated from her husband, that is gracious, loving, and to join herself to some rogue, is grievous; so here are too sad effects of it, they have nothing of God's face, nor of God's ear.

(2.) That man's life is short, and the pleasures of sin but for a season. Let a man all his life enjoy them, yet they end then, and man may be cut off before he is aware of it: Matt. xxv. 13, "Watch therefore, for ye know neither the day nor the hour wherein the Son of man cometh."

(3.) The daily treasuring up of wrath, and danger of final impenitency: Rom. ii. 5, Thou "treasurest up unto thyself wrath against the day of wrath." It is a seal of condemnation.

(4.) The condemnings of a man's own heart and conscience: "There is no peace to the wicked," but they "are like the troubled sea, when it cannot rest," Isa. lvii. 20, 21.

(5.) Absolute necessity of repenting and turning unto God: Luke xiii. 3, "Except ye repent, ye shall all likewise perish."

(6.) The love of Christ, in laying down his life, shedding his blood, suffering such hard things as he did: Zech. xii. 10, "They shall look upon me whom they have pierced," &c.

(7.) That it is acceptable unto the Lord: he would not else call for it, as here; nor make such promises unto it, as 1 Kings viii. 48—50, if they will return to God with all their heart and soul, he will hear their prayers, maintain their cause, forgive their sins, and have compassion on them. It is acceptable to the angels, repentance makes them rejoice.

Obs. 4. True repentance and turning to the Lord, doth manifest itself in the effects and fruits of it: it hath meet fruit, Matt. iii. 8; worthy fruit, Luke iii. 8. Now here are three effects thereof in these words:

(1.) When the soul is truly turned to God, it seeks to turn others; it is not content that itself is come to God, but would have many come to him.

(2.) It dispenses with no sin, it saith not, Lord, be merciful to me in this, but turns from "all abominations," from every idol, the most darling sin shall then go to it: Hos. xiv. 8, "Ephraim shall say, What have I to do any more with idols?"

(3.) It avoids the occasions of sin, and appearances of evil. "Turn away your faces from all your abominations;" if you should look upon idols, they will endanger you, stir up the old corruptions. Hence Solomon counsels men not to "look upon the wine when it is red, and giveth his colour in the cup," Prov. xxiii. 31; not to enter "into the path of the wicked," chap. iv. 14.

Ver. 7, 8. *For every one of the house of Israel, or of the stranger that sojourneth in Israel, which separateth himself from me, and setteth up his idols in his heart, and putteth the stumblingblock of his iniquity before his face, and cometh to a prophet to enquire of him concerning me; I the Lord will answer him by myself: and I will set my face against that man, and will make him a sign and a proverb, and I will cut him off from the midst of my people: and ye shall know that I am the Lord.*

In the foregoing verse he exhorted them to repentance, and to turn from their idols and abominations, and here, in these verses, he backs it with reasons; thus, If ye will not repent, but persist in your idolatry and sinful practices, "I will answer you by myself, and I will set my face against you," &c.

"Every one of the house of Israel." The Hebrew is, *ish, ish*, man, man of the house of Israel; that is, every man of Israel that forsakes me to follow idols, I will do so and so by.

"The stranger that sojourns in Israel." Hebrew יגור which the Septuagint renders proselyte, of the proselytes that sojourn. Those who came from the gentiles, and embraced the Jewish religion, they were proselytes. There were two sorts of proselytes; one sort was called the proselyte of the covenant, and these were to be circumcised, and to keep the law: another sort was called the proselyte of the gate, from Deut. xiv. 29, these were not circumcised, neither received the law of Moses, but the seven precepts of Noah; one of which was, that they should not worship idols; if therefore they should come with idols in their hearts, God would answer them.

"And separateth himself from me." God had taken the Jews to be his people, and some of the gentiles came in to join with them, yet these separated themselves from God to go to idols; like a woman that leaves her husband, and follows other men, Hos. ix. 10. When men leave the law of God, and his pure worship, then they separate from God.

Of setting up idols in the heart, and putting the stumblingblock of iniquity before their face, we have spoken in ver. 4.

"And cometh to a prophet to inquire of him concerning me." In ver. 4, it is said, "and cometh to the prophet," then he adds, "to inquire of him." It was an ordinary thing for this people, upon occasions, to go to the prophets; Exod. xviii. 15, the people came to Moses, who was a prophet, to inquire of God; they went to the seer to inquire, 1 Sam. ix. 9; so 2 Kings viii. 8, Benhadad sends to Elisha the prophet, to inquire of him; Zedekiah sent again and again to Jeremiah, to inquire of the Lord for him, Jer. xxi. 2; xxxvii. 7. When they came to the prophets, or sent to them, it was to know the mind of the Lord in their straits, undertakings, desires, and doubts.

"I the Lord will answer him by myself." The Hebrew runs thus, I the Lord, it shall be answered to him in me, I will not let any answer him but myself. God spake himself to Moses, Numb. xii. 7, 8, which was an argument of great love and good will: and sometimes it is an argument of wrath and displeasure when he will not speak by others, but by himself; as here, I will not answer him by the prophet, whom he entreats to inquire for him, but by myself, whom he despises, by setting up idols in his heart; I will answer him, not with words, but deeds, not with mercies, but with judgments, as the next verse imports. God would not vouchsafe their questions they propounded any answer at all, but he would go on in his judgments, not be inquired of by them, but answer them according to the multitude of their idols.

Ver. 8. "I will set my face against that man." The Hebrew is, faces, the plural for the singular; this phrase is frequent in Scripture. The Targum expounds it, anger, which appears in the face, and face is oft put for the wrath and anger of God: Jer. iii. 12, "I will not cause mine anger to fall upon you;" Hebrew is, my faces פני Lam. iv. 16, "The anger of the Lord hath divided them;" Hebrew is, the face of the Lord: Psal. xxi. 9, "Thou shalt make them as a fiery oven in the time of thine anger;" Hebrew is, in time of thy face; that is, when the wrath is in thy face, thou wilt consume them as stubble in an oven: so 1 Pet. iii. 12, "The face of the Lord is against them that do evil;" that is, the anger of God is against such. So then, to set the face against a man is to manifest himself to be an enemy to that man, to persist in that enmity, and to act accordingly. You may see it in those scriptures where this phrase is mentioned: Lev. xvii. 10, " I will set my face against that soul that eateth blood, and will cut him off from among his people;" chap. xxvi. 17, " I will set my face against you, and ye shall be slain before your enemies;" Jer. xxi. 10, " I have set my face against this city for evil; it shall be given into the hand of the king of Babylon, and he shall burn it with fire." You see when God sets his face against any person or thing, he is an enemy unto them, and gives not over his enmity till he hath ruined them; and therefore it follows here,

" I will make him a sign." His punishment shall not be easy or common, but exemplary; the Vulgate is, *in exemplum;* such judgments would God bring upon them, as that others should be astonished at them: Deut. xxviii. 37, " Thou shalt become an astonishment, a proverb, and a by-word, among all nations."

" A proverb." God would so deal with these men, as that they should be talked of every where. Jer. xxiv. 9, Zedekiah, the princes, and residue of Jerusalem, God would remove them " into all kingdoms of the earth for their hurt, to be a reproach and a proverb, a taunt and a curse, in all places;" their punishment should be proverbial. Calvin observes, that משל signifieth disgrace, so that they shall not only be matter of talk to the people, but their names shall be infamous.

" And I will cut him off from the midst of my people." God would not only make him a sign and talk to others, that were no great matter, but destroy him, " cut him off." The Scripture oft speaks of cutting off men; it is not always meant by death, but thought to be some censure whereby they were deprived of the privileges of God's people; but sundry times it is spoken of God's cutting men off by death, Lev. xvii. 10; xx. 3—6, and it is certain, where God is said to set his face against any, and then speaks of cutting off from his people, that there it is to be understood of cutting off by death; as in this place, they should be cut off from his people, both by temporal and eternal death.

" And ye shall know that I am the Lord." Hypocrites pretend they are godly, they converse with the prophets, ask counsel of God, but yet they contemn the true prophets, and the power of godliness, they will choose their own ways; therefore saith God, " Ye shall know that I am the Lord;" you set up idols in your hearts, make gods of them, but I will myself deal with you for them, and punish you severely.

Obs. 1. That when men leave God, and his ways, then they fall to idolatrous and other sinful practices. They separated themselves from God, and set up idols in their hearts. When once corruption hath taken off the heart from the Lord, who is an Infinite good, then it cleaves to any creature, any dunghill god, and deifies that: Hos. ix. 10, " They went to Baal-peor, and separated themselves unto that shame;" it was a shameful idol, yet, having left God, they could embrace it: and Hos. iv. 10—12, " They have left off to take heed to the Lord. Whoredom, and wine, and new wine, take away the heart. They ask counsel at their stocks, and their staff declareth unto them." Jer. ii. 13, they forsook God, the fountain of living waters, and then hewed themselves cisterns that could hold no water: it was therefore good counsel the apostle gave, Heb. iii. 12. " Take heed lest there be in any of you an evil heart of unbelief, in departing from the living God." Through unbelief men separate from God, and that is the principle of all disobedience, and lets the heart loose unto any creature, to every sin.

Obs. 2. Men exceeding sinful may put on a face of holiness. These men, who were idolaters, come to the prophet, inquire of God by him, as if they were pious men, intended to know the mind of God, and do what he would have done; this was counterfeit holiness, they had idols in their hearts, and meant to keep them there. Saul was sometimes among the prophets; the devil seems an angel of light, and wicked, vile men appear saints; 2 Tim. iii. 5, " Having a form of godliness." The worst of men may make a cloak of religion; antichrist sits in the temple, 2 Thess. ii. 4; Simon Magus, believing, is baptized, and wonders at the miracles Philip wrought, Acts viii. 13.

Obs. 3. Look what men are in coming unto God, the like shall they find him unto them. They came to the prophet fallaciously, and God would not answer them by the prophet, but by himself; he knew how to deal with them, he knew their hearts, and so what was fittest to be said or done unto them: Psal. xviii. 25, 26, " With the merciful thou wilt show thyself merciful; with an upright man thou wilt show thyself upright; with the pure thou will show thyself pure; and with the froward thou wilt show thyself froward," or wrestle with them: so Lev. xxvi. 23, 24, if ye will walk contrary to me, I will walk contrary to you. If a people come humbly unto God, and sue for mercy, he will save them, but if their hearts swell, rise within them, he will bring down their high looks, Psal. xviii. 27. As God finds men, so he will proceed with them; so he dealt with Pharaoh.

Obs. 4. God will proceed impartially with every man; be he Jew or gentile, all is one to God. " Every one of the house of Israel, or of the stranger that sojourneth in Israel," &c. God neither accepts nor respects persons, Gal. ii. 6; Acts x. 34. If a Jew be guilty he shall have an answer suitable; so if a gentile be faulty, his gentilism shall not excuse him. Let men's conditions, nations, qualities, degrees, be what they will, it matters not, if they come to God with idols in their hearts, the greatest shall speed no better than the meanest, the Jew no better than the stranger.

Obs. 5. Men set up idols in their hearts, and God sets his face against them, he becomes an adversary unto them, looks severely upon them, speaks terribly unto them, and works powerfully against them. They had set their faces and hearts upon idols for evil, and God sets his face and heart against them for evil, and is resolved to ruin them: Jer. xliv. 11, " Behold, I will set my face against you for evil, and to cut off all Judah." To have God set his face against a people is very sad.

There are several sins mentioned in Scripture for which God sets his face against men; offering their seed to Molech, Lev. xx. 2, 3; despising of his statutes, and breaking his covenant, Lev. xxvi. 15, 17; idolatry and hypocrisy here in the text.

Obs. 6. When God's face is against a people, his judgments upon them will be exemplary, he will make them signs and proverbs in the world. Jer. xix. 8, " I will make this city desolate, and an hissing: every one that passeth thereby shall be astonished and hiss, because of all the plagues thereof;" chap. xviii. 16, " Every one that passeth thereby shall wag his head;" chap. xlii. 18, " Ye shall be an execration, and an astonishment, and a curse, and a reproach." Men's names are dear unto them, but God will blast their names, make them to be a taunt and proverb: Jer. xxix. 22, it was a proverb among them, "The Lord make thee like Zedekiah and like Ahab, whom the king of Babylon roasted in the fire." And when they wished hurt to any, they used this speech, God make them a reproach among all nations, Ezek. v. 14, 15; and when this is done, God cuts them off from the land of the living in that condition.

Obs. The end of God's setting his face against sinners, and proceeding severely with them, is, that they may acknowledge his justice and power over them.

Ver. 9. *And if the prophet be deceived when he hath spoken a thing, I the Lord have deceived that prophet, and I will stretch out my hand upon him, and will destroy him from the midst of my people Israel.*

False prophets were both in Judea and in Babylon, and the people had often recourse unto them; they spake pleasing things, they told them who were in Judea that Nebuchadnezzar should never subdue and carry them captives, as he had done Jeconiah, and some others with him; yea, they told them that those in Babylon should shortly return. These were vain, false, and deceitful prophecies, and Divine Providence ordered it so, and therefore God saith here, "If the prophet be deceived when he hath spoken a thing, I the Lord have deceived that prophet," &c.

In the verse you have,

I. A supposition.

II. An assertion.

III. A threatening.

I. For the supposition, the false prophets (for of them he speaks) were deceived in what they spake to the people. Zedekiah, and the rest of the prophets which bade Ahab to go up to Ramoth-gilead, and prosper, were deceived, 1 Kings xxii. Hananiah and Shelemiah made that people trust in a lie, Jer. xxviii. 15; xxix. 31. They were deceived in their prophets, and deceive others; the things they spake came not to pass.

"If the prophet be deceived." Hebrew original word is פתה which being taken in the ill part, as here, notes a turning of the heart to that. A man may be deceived by others, or by his own corruption, for a man may be seduced in himself by himself: James i. 14, "Every man is tempted, when he is drawn away of his own lust;" his lust is in him; by
Jer. xiv. 14. his lust he is enticed, seduced, and this seduction is voluntary, by his own act and will; so that in himself is the true efficient cause of his seduction.

II. "I the Lord have deceived that prophet." Here is the assertion. These words sound very harsh, and no man durst have attributed them unto the Lord, had not he himself said so. We must inquire into the sense of these, how God is said to deceive a prophet that speaks falsely.

To say God declared him to be deceived, or permitted him to be deceived, comes not up to the expression here; "I have deceived that," &c. פתיתי it is active and notes action. This we must lay down, that God neither is nor can be the author of sin; for then he must act against some rule. God's will, which is ever most holy, just, and wise, is his rule; and it is unreasonable and impious, to think that God should work or do any thing against his own will; yet God wills sin, not as good, but so far as he intends and is able to work good out of it, and bring about his glory by it. Mr. Baynes and some others hold, there is an efficacy of God reaching to the beginning of sin, though not to the essence of sin; and it is no more than some Jesuits acknowledge, who maintain a deadly quarrel against Calvin, for making God the author of sin, when he saith for substance no more than they. A Lapide saith, God's permission of sin is an action, otherwise no sin could be. He saith further, this permission is efficacious. He instanceth in a greyhound which a man lets loose to pursue the hare, and sets the dog upon the hare; so God lets Satan loose upon men, and so is active to the beginning of sin. 1 Kings xxii. 20, "The Lord said, Who shall persuade Ahab that he may go up and fall at Ramoth-gilead? And one said on this manner, another on that manner." Ver. 21, "There came forth a spirit, and said, I will persuade him." And ver. 22, "The Lord said unto him, Wherewith? I will go forth and be a lying spirit in the mouth of all his prophets. And he said, Thou shalt persuade him, and prevail also: go forth, and do so." Here is some concurrence of God to the deception of these prophets; and God might have said of them as here, I have deceived these prophets.

The words "I have deceived," are to be taken as a judicial act of God, who dealing with them as delinquents, punisheth them with this special judgment of seduction; they were idolatrous and hypocritical, and God punished those sins with others, and so accidentally was the efficient cause of their deception. God finding those men false and forward to deceive, hearkening to their own hearts, and following their own spirits, Ezek. xiii. 2, 3, he gave them up and over to vain visions and lying divinations, which was one punishment, and to perdition, which was another punishment following thereupon. Have you a mind to be prophets, to prophesy lies? ye shall be so.

Quest. Jer. xx. 7, saith Jeremiah a true prophet, "O Lord, thou hast deceived me, and I was deceived; thou art stronger than I, and hast prevailed." What! doth God deceive true prophets?

Answ. 1. The deception here is no sinful deception, he had no vain visions, no lying divinations, whatever he prophesied was truth, from the God of truth, and came to pass. The meaning here is this; Jeremiah was discontented that he saw so little fruit of his ministry, that he found such opposition, that he was daily in derision and mocked of every one; and therefore saith. "O Lord, thou hast deceived me," in making me a prophet; I looked for other things than I find, but I am deceived, and thou hast done it: I was unwilling to be a prophet, objected against it, chap. i. 6, but thou laidest thy charge upon me, overpoweredst me, and prevailedst against me, making me great promises, which yet I see not performed, ver. 7, 8, 18, 19.

2. The words may be read thus, Thou hast persuaded me, and I was persuaded; for when it is taken in the better sense, it notes to persuade.

Quest. Isa. lxiii. 17, "O Lord, why hast thou made us to err from thy ways? and hardened our heart from thy fear?" Did God make the prophet and people to err? did he harden their hearts?

Answ. 1. The prophet speaks in the name of the people, not of himself; he did not err from the way of God, but reproved the people for it.

2. God did this in judgment to the people, who affected false prophets, and chose their own ways, Isa. lxvi. 3, and delighted in their abominations; therefore God denied them his Spirit, and left them to their own spirits; he in judgment gave them up to their own ways, and to hardness of heart; and this was not sinful in the Lord. Psal. lxxxi. 11, 12, "My people would not hearken unto my voice, and Israel would none of me. So I gave them up unto their own hearts' lust: and they walked in their own counsels."

III. "I will stretch out my hand upon him." Here is the threatening. God hath no hand to stretch out, he is without all parts; the words are metaphorical, taken from the practice of men, who stretch out their hands to do this or that. Gen. xxii. 10, "Abraham stretched forth his hand to slay his son;" Jeroboam put forth his hand to lay hold upon the prophet that had prophesied against his altar, 1 Kings xiii. 4; so God would put forth his power to punish such a prophet.

Quest. If God deceived him, how can he in justice punish or destroy that prophet.

Answ. 1. The false prophet did whatever he did freely, he was not forced by any power or act of God, his seduction was principally from himself; and it was his own fault that he was deceived, that he deceived others.

2. A man may serve providence, and yet sin against the law of God. The secret providence of God had ordered it that this people should be seduced by false prophets, yet God in his word had forbid false prophets and prophecies, Deut. xiii.; and because men are to look at what is written, not what is secret and hidden, therefore if they violate the law, God may justly punish thereupon. Acts iv. 27, 28, Herod, Pilate, Judas, and the Jews, they did to Christ whatsoever God had determined to be done, yet were they not without sin, nor without punishment, because they transgressed the rule given them.

Obs. 1. The Lord, in his infinite wisdom and justice, doth make a punishment of sin, and punish one sin with another. Besides corporal judgments he hath spiritual; if the prophet be deceived, "I the Lord have deceived him," I have laid this judgment upon him, that he should be deceived, led into errors, and deceive others; this he hath deserved at my hands, and this punishment in just judgment I inflict upon him. The Scriptures hold out frequently this way of God's proceedings with sinners, his punishing of one sin with another; 2 Chron. xxv. 17—20, Amaziah provokes Joash to war, he dissuades him from it; but Amaziah would not hear; "for it came of God, that he might deliver them into the hands of their enemies, because they sought after the gods of Edom." Jer. iv. 10, "Then said I, Ah, Lord God! thou hast greatly deceived this people and Jerusalem, saying, Ye shall have peace, whereas the sword reacheth unto the soul." They were desirous of prophets that might speak pleasing things unto them; they regarded not Jeremiah and Ezekiel; and God in judgment lets them have such prophets which cried, Peace, peace, and gave them over to believe their lies; and this made Jeremiah say; "Thou hast greatly deceived," &c. Rom. i. 25, 26, "They changed the truth of God into a lie; worshipped and served the creature more than the Creator: for this cause God gave them up unto vile affections;" and ver. 28, "over to a reprobate mind." 2 Thess. ii. 10, 11, "Because they received not the love of the truth, that they might be saved; for this cause God shall send them strong delusion, that they should believe a lie."

Obs. 2. God will deal severely with false prophets. "I will stretch out my hand upon him, and will destroy him from the midst of my people Israel;" he would make him exemplary to all. Hananiah was a false prophet, and deceived many; therefore said God, "Behold, I will cast thee from off the face of the earth," and that quickly; "this year thou shalt die," Jer. xxviii. 15, 16: God would not stay long from cutting him off. Shemaiah was another false prophet, and God would destroy him and his seed; he should not have a man to dwell among that people, chap. xxix. 31, 32.

Ver. 10. *And they shall bear the punishment of their iniquity: the punishment of the prophet shall be even as the punishment of him that seeketh unto him.*

There being false prophets among this people, they gave ear to them, resorted unto them, took counsel of them; and here God tells Ezekiel, that not only the false prophets should be punished for deceiving the people, but even they that by seeking to those prophets were deceived by them.

The Hebrew is thus, they shall bear their iniquity; as the iniquity of him that seeks is, so shall be the iniquity of the prophet. Where you have "punishment," the original is, iniquity. This phrase is much in holy writ, "to bear iniquity," and is put for bearing of punishment, which iniquity doth cause, Lev. v. 1, 17. They that uncover the nakedness of their kin, "shall bear their iniquity," that is, their punishment for it, chap. xx. 17, 19. This phrase is applied to Christ, Isa. liii. 11, "He shall bear their iniquity;" which the 5th verse calls, wounding, bruising, chastisement, stripes. Paul hath the like phrase, Gal. v. 10, "He that troubleth you shall bear his judgment;" he shall have his punishment, whatever he be.

"The punishment of the prophet shall be even as the punishment of him that seeketh unto him." It may seem hence, that there is an equality in their sin, and in the punishment; but sins and punishment do differ in Scripture. Matt. v. 22, "Whosoever is angry with his brother without a cause shall be in danger of the judgment: and whosoever shall say, Raca, shall be in danger of the council: but whosoever shall say, Thou fool, shall be in danger of hell fire:" here are divers degrees of sin, and divers degrees of punishment. Matt. xii. 45, "The last state of that man is worse than the first;" worse for sin, worse for punishment. John xix. 11, "He that delivered me unto thee hath the greater sin;" his sin that betrayed Christ was greater than Pilate's, and answerable should be his punishment. Jer. vii. 26, "They did worse than their fathers;" so should have worse punishment than they. God appointed punishment to be inflicted according to the nature of the sin: Deut. xxv. 2, "If the wicked man be worthy to be beaten, the judge shall cause him to lie down, and to be beaten before his face, according to his fault." Rev. xviii. 7, "How much she hath glorified herself, and lived deliciously, so much torment and sorrow give her." By these scriptures you see that all sins are not equal, neither all punishment, and that God doth proportion punishments to the nature of sins. We are not here to conclude an equality of punishments upon the false prophet and those that came unto him; for certainly his sin in deceiving the people, pretending visions and divinations from heaven, that he was sent of God, &c. was greater than the people's: "even as," notes the quality and reality of the punishment, not the degree.

Obs. 1. The fruit or reward of sin is burdensome. "They shall bear their iniquity;" that is, the fruit and effect of it; it lights and lies heavy upon the authors of it. Guilt is a heavy burden for a soul to bear; it made a prophet cry out, Psal. li. 14, "Deliver me from blood-guiltiness, O God, thou God of my salvation." Guilt lay like a mountain of lead upon him; so any punishment for sin is weighty. If God send a plague, a famine, or sword, are they not heavy? when God brought tidings to David that one of those judgments must be upon him for numbering the people, he was in a great strait, 2 Sam. xxiv. 14. And Psal. xxxviii. 2—5, "Thine arrows stick fast in me, and thy hand presseth me sore.

There is no soundness in my flesh because of thine anger; neither is there any rest in my bones because of my sin: for mine iniquities are gone over my head; as an heavy burden they are too heavy for me: my wounds stink and are corrupt because of my foolishness." He had sinned, and found the burden of sin wonderful grievous. The church saith, Lam. iii. 7, "He hath made my chain heavy;" sin had brought an iron heavy chain upon her. Sin brings shame, and that is a burden; Ezek. xvi. 54, "That thou mayest bear thine own shame:" it brings sorrows, fears, pains, loss, death, damnation, and all these are grievous. Ezek. xviii, 20, it is said, "The wickedness of the wicked shall be upon him;" it shall be a burden upon him.

Obs. 2. To seek unto false prophets is a thing punishable before God. "The punishment of the prophet shall be even as the punishment of him that seeketh unto him." Men think it is nothing to consult with a wicked prophet, but God will not so pass it over; he counts it a great sin, and will lay upon him a proportionable burden. If prophets be not sent of God, if they give out erroneous and false things, if they be wicked in their lives, it is a dangerous thing to have recourse to them; God is against those prophets, and those that depend upon them. Jer. xxiii. 32, "I am against such prophets," saith God there, and "they shall not profit this people at all;" they thought by consulting with them, that they should gain much, and it is true they gained the displeasure of God, they brought exemplary judgments upon themselves. God had commanded them not to hearken to such prophets, ver. 16, as spake a vision out of their own heart, and not out of the mouth of the Lord; yea, he had commanded such prophets to be put to death, Deut. xiii. 5; for them, therefore, to consult with these prophets, to follow their counsels, and do what they appointed, leaving the true prophets, discountenancing and discouraging them, was a high provocation of God, and punished answerably. Ahab sought unto the false prophets, but God remembered it, and visited it upon his head. If God will punish those that seek to false prophets, surely he will not spare those that seek unto witches, sorcerers, astrologers, and star-gazers; nor those that seek unto another god; Psal. xvi. 4, "Their sorrows shall be multiplied."

Ver. 11. *That the house of Israel may go no more astray from me, neither be polluted any more with all their transgressions; but that they may be my people, and I may be their God, saith the Lord God.*

This verse shows the end why the Lord would punish the false prophets, and those that consulted with them, viz. to prevent the people's sinning against him by idolatry and other unlawful practices. When they should see God cutting off their prophets, and those who had hearkened to them, this would breed fear in them, and put a stand to their sinful ways, cause them to return, and continue in the ways of God.

"House of Israel." By these we are to understand the godly, those who were elected, the spiritual Israelites; not all after the flesh, for the false prophets, and those who clave to them, were so of the house of Israel. When God visited with great judgments, he ever reserved some, that so his covenant which he had made with Abraham might not fail; and they were the spiritual Israelites, not the carnal, who went no more astray.

"May go no more astray." לא יתעו from תעה to err, to wander; it is a metaphor borrowed from cattle which wander out of the right way, as Matt. xviii. 12, "If a man have an hundred sheep, and one of them be gone astray;" Exod. xxiii. 4, "If thou meet thine enemy's ox or ass going astray;" and is applied unto man, 2 Pet. ii. 15, "Which have forsaken the right way, and are gone astray, following the way of Balaam." Here they had left the way of God, and followed lying prophets.

"No more."

Quest. Do the godly being once redeemed go astray no more? David went astray oft; and the apostle saith, "In many things we sin all," James iii. 2.

Answ. 1. God's end in punishing the wicked, is to keep his people from straying at all; as a parent, when he corrects the child for lying, would have it lie no more, though through that corruption which is in it, it lie often.

2. That they go no more astray from him in that way and manner they did before, no more to false gods and false worship; they go not astray in any dangerous wandering.

"From me." The Hebrew is מאחרי from after me. God's people are to follow him; but by hearkening to false prophets, and the enticement of their own hearts, they are turned aside from following God.

"Neither be polluted any more." The original word טמא is to pollute, defile, be unclean; and it is contrary to טהר which is to be clean and innocent.

"With all their transgressions." Or prevarications; the word פשע notes not any transgression, but such a one as hath much of the will in it, joined with pride and malice, and therefore is rendered rebellion, Psal. v. 10, "Cast them out in the multitude of their transgressions; for they have rebelled against thee:" they were transgressions which had sedition and rebellion in them. Job xxxiv. 37, "He addeth rebellion unto his sin:" חטאתו פשע the Vulgate hath it, blasphemy.

"But that they may be my people, and I," &c. Hebrew is, and they shall be to me for a people, and I will be to them for a God. They were God's people before, in covenant, circumcised, had the temple, sacrifices, &c. God speaks thus, to show they had made a defection from him, forfeited all, deserved to be rejected, and had by their sins bred a great strangeness between him and themselves; for they had corrupted his worship, violated his laws, rejected his prophets, polluted his name and temple, forsaken him, and followed after strange gods, and so done what was in them to be none of God's people: but if they would awaken out of their spiritual slumber, consider, repent, and turn to him, he would manifest his faithfulness and loving-kindness unto them, they should be his people, &c. The like words you had in chap. xi. 20, "They shall be my people, and I will be their God."

Obs. 1. From the coherence with the two former verses, That God makes use of ill means to accomplish good ends; he lets errors, and strange opinions, seducing doctrines, prevail with false prophets and people, that so they suffering proportionably for their evil, his people may be kept from such ways and ends. He in judgment sent strong delusions to the prophets and people, which they venting and embracing, he punished them, that so the house of Israel might not go any more astray from him.

There is no creature so poisonous, but God makes use of it to some good end; and there is no prophet or teacher so corrupt, no opinions so damnable or blasphemous, but the Lord, by his infinite power, orders and works it to some good end. 1 Cor. xi. 19, "There must be heresies among you, that they which are approved may be made manifest among you:" God makes use of heresies, sects, and schisms, to discover who are sound, who are not: when it is a time of war, men of valour and counsel are made known. Deut. xiii. 3, when a false prophet rose up amongst them, the Lord tells them it was to prove them, whether they did love the Lord, and his truths, would hold them fast and follow him; or whether they would be led aside with erroneous doctrines, and follow seducing teachers.

Obs. 2. By judgments upon the wicked, God intends the good of his people. He will destroy the seducing prophet and seduced people, that the house of Israel may go no more astray from him; that those who were godly people might awake out of their secure slumber, consider what they had done, repent of it, and never do the like. When the prophets of Baal were slain, then the people were freed from their haltings between God and Baal, and clave to the Lord. Psal. ix. 16, "The Lord is known by the judgment he executeth;" when he lays his hand upon sinners, saints tremble, consider his power, majesty, greatness, the nature of his judgments, and so judge themselves, and remove out of the way whatever may provoke. Psal. cxix. 119, 120, "Thou puttest away all the wicked of the earth like dross: therefore I love thy testimonies. My flesh trembleth for fear of thee; and I am afraid of thy judgments." When God, by his fiery judgments, separated the dross from the gold, the wicked from the ungodly, David trembled, considered the law of God more thoroughly, and loved his testimonies. So Isa. xxvi. 9, "When thy judgments are in the earth, the inhabitants of the world will learn righteousness:" Isaiah knew that it was the mind of God, in his judgments, to advantage his people by them, and therefore saith, "the inhabitants of the world," that is, the godly inhabitants, "will learn righteousness," they will see the evil of sin and hate it.

Obs. 3. God's own people are apt to go astray. "That the house of Israel may go no more astray." They had gone astray, and were in danger to do it again. They are like sheep, and no creature apter to wander out of the right way than that: Psal. cxix. 176, David confesseth he had gone astray like a lost sheep, a sheep that hath lost the fold, and lost the way. Adam, who was the ram in the head of the flock, he went astray in eating the forbidden fruit, and the whole flock of mankind have ever since followed him. Psal. lviii. 3, "The wicked go astray as soon as they be born," even from the belly, as the Hebrew is; and Isaiah speaking in the name of the better sort, saith, chap. liii. 6, "All we like sheep have gone astray; we have turned every one to his own way:" one hath a way of pride; another of wantonness; a third hath a way of covetousness, &c. "Ye were as sheep going astray; but are now returned," &c. 1 Pet. ii. 25. A sheep is,

(1.) A foolish creature.

(2.) Subject to many diseases.

(3.) Obvious to much danger.

(4.) Aptest to leave the good paths and good pastures. The foolish Galatians were ready to embrace another gospel, and to admit circumcision. Peter and Barnabas stepped awry, when they dissembled with the Jews. David it is said turned aside "in the matter of Uriah the Hittite," 1 Kings xv. 5. And the people quickly turned aside out of the way of God, Deut. ix. 12.

Obs. 4. When God's people are once gone astray, they would never return of themselves, if God should let them alone in their wrong ways; he must reduce them by his own hand, and keep them in the right way by his own power. A sheep wanders further and further, and thinks not of returning: David when he had left the way of God, and turned aside to Bathsheba, he goes further, he makes Uriah drunk, plots his death, rejoices at it, takes the widow to be his wife, and never considers all this time that he is out of the way of God; and had not Nathan been sent to him, to tell him how he had wandered, he had not returned: so Peter denies his Master once, twice, thrice; and had not Christ looked upon him, he might have denied him for ever. This appears in the parable of the lost sheep, Matt. xviii. 12; the shepherd stays not for the sheep's returning, but goes into the mountains, and seeks that which is gone astray.

Obs. 5. God would have his people to keep close to him, to follow him, to walk with him, that they may no more go astray from after him. To go after God, is to worship him in his own way, to have him in our eye, to do things in order to him, to follow his directions, commands, to observe his operations in the world, to lean upon him for counsel, comfort, assistance, safety, and blessings, to submit to his will, to receive what he reveals, following on to know God, and to get further communion with him. God would have his people to do thus. Hosea xi. 10, "They shall walk after the Lord:" he would go before them, and they should follow him; they should not go after other gods, after their own eyes, hearts, inventions, but after him. God commends David for his following him, 1 Kings xiv. 8; he sets him there before Jeroboam, and condemns him by his example: "Thou hast not been as my servant David, who kept my commandments, and who followed me with all his heart, to do that only which was right in mine eyes." He went not from after God, but followed him closely; and it is very pleasing to God when his people do so. Elijah knew it well, and therefore said to the people, 1 Kings xviii. 21, "If the Lord be God, follow him," do not leave him to go after any other.

Obs. 6. God showeth mercy not only to little sinners, but great ones. They were polluted with all their transgressions, with all their rebellious seditions; yet being the house of Israel, his select ones, he would pardon their sins, though of a high nature. God is rich and great in mercy, and no sins can exceed his mercy; he would pass by their pollutions and transgressions, account them his people, and be their God, their sins should not obstruct his grace. Isa. i. 18, "Though their sins be as scarlet, they shall be as white as snow; though they be red like crimson, they shall be as wool." Scarlet and crimson are of a deep dye; silk and wool do hold those colours firmly, you cannot wash nor wear them out, neither nature nor art can reduce them to their pristine condition; but let souls be dyed and stained with sins most deeply, with the deepest and vilest sins, yet God can take out that hellish dye and tincture, he can make them white as snow, pure as wool undyed. The wool in those countries was exceeding white; Psal. cxlvii. 16, "He giveth snow like wool;" and Dan. vii. 9, it is called "pure wool," in regard of the whiteness; Rev. i. 14, the whiteness of wool and snow are put together, "His hairs were white like wool, as white as snow." Now let a man's sin be wilful murder, which is very great, and his soul be dipped in blood, yet God can and doth take away such sins, and make white again. Psal. li. 7, "Wash me," saith David, whose soul had a double dye, one of uncleanness, another of murder, "and I shall be whiter than snow." Manasseh's sins were exceeding great, yet the grace of God surmounted them all, and they were swallowed up in a sea of mercy. Luke vii. 37, it is said, a woman that was a sinner came to Christ. Was this such a matter to be recorded in holy writ? are not all men and women sinners? Yes; but the word sinner notes a notorious sinner; she was such a great and known sinner, that the Pharisee wondered at Christ, that he should suffer her to touch him, ver. 39. Her sins were many, ver. 47; yet mercy was reached out to her, ver. 48, "Thy sins are forgiven thee."

Obs. 7. Sin is a polluting thing. "Neither be polluted any more." Matt. xv. 19, 20, Christ reckons up sins there, and saith, "These are they which defile a man;" τα κοινοῦντα τον ἀνθρωπον, they make common, which in Scripture sense is, to defile, to profane, to make unclean; so Peter expounds it, Acts x. 14, "I have never eaten any thing common or unclean," κοινὸν ἤ ἀκάθαρτον, and Erasmus renders the word κοινοῖ, Matt. xv. 11, *impurum reddere*. It is sin, and sin only, which makes impure creatures; therefore in Scripture it is compared to blood, Ezek. xvi. 6, to mire and dirt, Isa. lvii. 20, to vomit, 2 Pet. ii. 22, to filth, Isa. iv. 4; yea more, it is put in the abstract, and called "filthiness," Prov. xxx. 12; 2 Cor. vii. 1, μολυσμος, that defiles both flesh and spirit; 2 Pet. ii. 20, τα μιάσματα τοῦ κόσμου. Physicians say, that *miasmata* are those spreadings or seminaries of the pestilence in a corrupt air: you know in a pestilence the air is infected, and that infection in the air spreads, and falling upon subjects capable of it, infects and kills them; so pollutions in the world are pestilential, they spread, infect, and kill many. Seeing sin is such a polluting thing, let us hasten to the fountain set open for sin and uncleanness, let us get our souls washed in the blood of Christ; Heb. ix. 14, that blood will purge, yea, purge out any spots, all defilements, 1 John i. 7. Rev. vii. 14, they had "washed their robes, and made them white in the blood of the Lamb." Blood makes red, but the blood of the Lamb makes white, takes away all sin, and makes innocent.

Ver. 12—21. *The word of the Lord came again to me, saying, Son of man, when the land sinneth against me by trespassing grievously, then will I stretch out mine hand upon it, and will break the staff of the bread thereof, and will send famine upon it, and will cut off man and beast from it: though these three men, Noah, Daniel, and Job, were in it, they should deliver but their own souls by their righteousness, saith the Lord God. If I cause noisome beasts to pass through the land, and they spoil it, so that it be desolate, that no man may pass through because of the beasts: though these three men were in it, as I live, saith the Lord God, they shall deliver neither sons nor daughters: they only shall be delivered, but the land shall be desolate. Or if I bring a sword upon that land, and say, Sword, go through the land; so that I cut off man and beast from it: though these three men were in it, as I live, saith the Lord God, they shall deliver neither sons nor daughters, but they only shall be delivered themselves. Or if I send a pestilence into that land, and pour out my fury upon it in blood, to cut off from it man and beast: though Noah, Daniel, and Job, were in it, as I live, saith the Lord God, they shall deliver neither son nor daughter; they shall but deliver their own souls by their righteousness. For thus saith the Lord God; How much more when I send my four sore judgments upon Jerusalem, the sword, and the famine, and the noisome beast, and the pestilence, to cut off from it man and beast?*

These words are the second part of the chapter, wherein,

I. The Lord shows what he will do with a sinning people, he will send judgment after judgment; and here are four laid down.

1. "Famine," in ver. 13.
2. "Noisome beasts," in ver. 15.
3. "A sword," in ver. 17.
4. "A pestilence," in ver. 19.

And all these are threatened against Jerusalem, ver. 21.

II. That he will not hearken unto the intercession of any, be they never so righteous, powerful in prayer, in the behalf of such a people.

Ver. 13. "By trespassing grievously." למעל מעל *Maal* signifieth in general, any disloyalty of inferiors toward superiors; yet especially it notes those sins which are against the Lord, his covenant, and holy things; as here, they had forsaken God, broken the covenant, set up idols in the temple, worshipped the sun, &c. These were grievous sins, and therefore Piscator renders the word, *prevaricando perfide*, by sinning treacherously; the doubling of the word notes the affection to, delight, and continuance in sin, they were obstinate.

Of breaking the staff of bread, and famine, hath been spoken in the 4th and 5th chapters. God breaks the staff of bread, when he either takes away the virtue of it, that it doth not nourish, but men pine away and come to nothing; or when he takes away the bread itself, so that there is not sufficient to nourish. This the Lord doth, by sending unseasonable weather, by too much drought, too much rain, by frosts, hail, mildews, blastings, caterpillars, locusts, &c. And these are the hand of God stretched out, to break the staff of bread.

Ver. 15. "Noisome beasts to pass through the land." Some would understand by these beasts, the Babylonians, who spoiled the land, and laid all desolate; and if we should do so, it were not much amiss; for we do not find that any wild beasts were sent as a judgment upon the Jews, before their going into captivity; yet because he speaks here of distinct judgments, and that which is to be exemplary for all, we shall take it literally as the rest are. It was threatened in Moses's law, that evil beasts should be sent amongst them; Lev. xxvi. 22, "I will send wild beasts among you, which shall rob you of your children, and destroy your cattle, and make you few in number; and your high ways shall be desolate." And it was made good; "The Lord sent fiery serpents amongst them," which stung and destroyed many of them, Numb. xxi. 6; bears, which slew their children, 2 Kings ii. 24; lions, which slew the men, chap. xvii. 25, 26; and Josh. xxiv. 12, by the hornet God drove out the two kings of the Amorites. And it is probable, that when the Chaldeans came, many who fled into woods, mountains, and by-ways, were wounded and slain by wild beasts.

Ver. 17. "If I bring a sword upon that land." Sword is put for war. Jer. iv. 10, "The sword reacheth unto the soul;" chap. xxv. 29, "I will call for a sword upon all the inhabitants of the earth," that is, a war; and so in this place, God would bring in an enemy, armed with the sword, and other military instruments, and they should make grievous work amongst them. Of the misery of war, formerly hath been spoken.

Ver. 19. "If I send a pestilence into that land." Hebrew is, דבר from דבר to speak; because in this judgment the Lord speaks aloud. It is a sore judgment, and because it is amongst us, I shall speak something of it. Philibertus Marchinus calls it *bellum divinum*, a divine war: this judgment is more immediately from God, and hath less of man and second causes in it, than others; and therefore when the murrain and plague was upon the cattle, Exod. ix. 3, there was no hand of Moses or Aaron in bringing it in, as in other judgments; and Psal. xci. 5, it is called an arrow, not of man's, but God's shooting; God shoots it into cities and families, by ways undiscernible unto us.

That there are second causes of it we do not wholly deny, but assert they are few, and hard to be found out. It puzzles the learned physicians to express clearly what are the causes of it; some refer it to the indisposition of the air, by dryness and heat; some to malignant and occult qualities in the air, or in the body, or in the diet men feed upon; some to corruption in the blood; some to hunger; some to surfeit.

God's hand is seen much in this noisome disease. Some pestilences kill cattle, and not men; some kill men, and not cattle; some kill one sort of men, and not others; some kill women, and not men; and some men, and not women; some kill young, and not old people; some the strong and healthful, and not the weak and sickly; some the rich, not the poor; some the poor, and not the rich, as the learned have observed.

This judgment, the plague, and pestilence, spreads far; it flies up and down by night and day, it devours multitudes suddenly. In David's time seventy thousand were consumed by it in three days, 2 Sam. xxiv. 15. In Vespasian's days, at Rome, there died ten thousand a day, for many days together; and in the year 1345, it was so general through the christian world, that it destroyed half mankind; and in this city, thousands have died in one week: and how suddenly men die of it, is known unto many of you; some within few days, yea, some within few hours.

The great cause of this judgment is sin. You may observe in Scripture some sins, which brought in the plague or pestilence. 2 Sam. xxiv. David's heart was lifted up, and he confided in the number of his people, and hereupon was the plague sent: when persons in place have lofty spirits, and pride themselves in what they have, they make way for this judgment. So oppression of God's people; Pharaoh would not let the Israelites have liberty, but held them under; therefore the murrain and plague of boils came upon the cattle and people, Exod. ix. When people sin grievously, then God is ready to send in the arrows of pestilence. Do not many sin greatly, by pride in their apparel, by excess in their feastings, and pomp in the funerals of their friends, by their bitterness against those who differ from them? When the plague was much in France, especially at Lyons, about 1629, the propapists judged Calvinism to be the cause; those sectaries and heretics were tolerated; therefore Marchinus, a Florentine, in his book De Bello Divino, tells his Italian friends, that the Lord's end in that plague was to root out Calvinism.

"And pour out my fury upon it in blood." To put this for blood corrupted in the body by the plague, sounds harsh; we may take it for death; Ezek. iii. 18, "He shall die in his iniquity, but his blood will I require at thine hand," that is, his death.

Ver. 14. "Though these three men, Noah, Daniel, and Job, were in it, they," &c. To speak something of each of these: "Noah," Gen. vi. 9, "was a just man, and perfect in his generations," there was none like unto him in the world in his days; "and he walked with God," he had great familiarity with him; his justice, sincerity, and piety were eminent. His name signifies, rest, or comfort; Gen. v. 29, "Lamech called his name Noah, saying, This same shall comfort us concerning our work and toil of our hands, because of the ground which the Lord hath cursed:" surely he was a great comfort both to God and man, being so holy as he was. It is conceived Lamech was a prophet, or at least uttered these words by a prophetical strain, intimating thereby, that Noah should be a type of Christ; and so he was in building the ark, and offering sacrifice, which was a sweet savour in the nostrils of God, and made him say, he would curse the earth no more for man's sake, Gen. viii. 21, 22. He was also "a preacher of righteousness," 2 Pet. ii. 5; and the man with whom God made a special covenant, and gave the rainbow for a sign thereof, Gen. ix. 9, 13: yet if this man should pray for them, God would not hear.

"Daniel." He was a holy man, and "would not defile himself with the portion of the king's meat" and drink, Dan. i. 8. And he was a man of great wisdom; Ezek. xxviii. 3, "Wiser than Daniel:" men that had great insight into things, who knew secrets and mysteries, were paralleled with Daniel, or preferred before him, but Daniel was the standard. Daniel was alive at this time, and young, as will appear, if you consider this time. Ezekiel spake these words in the sixth year of Jehoiachin's captivity, if you compare chap. i. 2, with chap. xx. 1, where he speaks of the fifth and seventh year; so that this was the time between; and Dan. i. 1, 6, it is evident that Daniel was carried into captivity the third year of the reign of Jehoiakim, father to Jehoiachin; so that now Daniel had been fourteen years in Babylon, eight years of Jehoiakim's reign, for he reigned eleven years, 2 Chron. xxxvi. 5, and six of Jehoiachin's captivity. So that the learned think Daniel was not above thirteen years of age when he came into Babylon; therefore is it that the king spake unto Ashpenaz to bring of the children of Israel, and of the king's seed, and of the princes, whereof Daniel was one; and now at this time, when Ezekiel ranked him with Noah and Job, about twenty-seven. Surely Daniel was a choice man, of singular wisdom and holiness, whom the Spirit of God would thus join with Noah and Job, such great worthies in their days. He was a man much given to prayer; Dan. vi. 10, three times a day he prayed in his chamber, with his face towards Jerusalem, and that when it lay upon the hazard of his life. His prayer and fasting are mentioned, chap. ix. 3; x. 2, 3.

"Job." The Lord gives him this testimony, that he was "perfect and upright, one that feared God, and eschewed evil;" he was much in offering sacrifice for himself and family, Job i. 1, 5; he was a man of much faith, great patience, chap. xiii. 15; xiv. 14; James v. 11; he was acceptable with God, and prevailed for his friends in prayer, ch. xlii. 8, 9. If these three men were in a land that hath grievously sinned, they should not deliver it.

Some make great inquiry why these three men should be mentioned, rather than others, and they give in their answer:

1. It is thought they are named, for that they could not divert God's wrath by their holiness and prayers from the people of their times. Noah could not keep off the flood, nor Job the sad things which befell himself and his, nor Daniel the captivity.

2. Others think they are named, because they freed others in imminent danger in their times; Noah saved his family from the flood; Job prayed for his friends, and they were spared; Daniel preserved the magicians and wise men. But rather they

are named, because they were men of great holiness, exercised with great trials, and so the more fervent in prayer. And what if these men, who were so acceptable to me, had so much interest in me, and often prevailed with me, should pray for you, yet they should do nothing for your deliverance by their prayers.

These were men in great afflictions, and affliction is the whetstone of prayer, the bellows to blow up that fire. David when he fled from Absalom, then he cried unto the Lord, and he heard him, Psal. iii. 4. Jonah, when he was in the whale's belly, prayed fervently; Jonah ii. 2, "I cried by reason of mine affliction unto the Lord, and he heard me." Surely Noah, when the flood came, poured out a flood of tears in prayer; and Job, when God's hand was so hard upon him, cried aloud unto God; and Daniel, among the lions; yet such was the case here, that if these three men were amongst them, they should do them no good.

Ver. 16, 18, 20. "They shall deliver neither sons nor daughters." Children are very dear to parents, they come out of their loins, are part of them, even the bowels; and holy parents would strive hard in prayer with God for them, they are so dear unto them, they would invent arguments (for love is inventive) to move the Lord to spare them; yet if they should bring the strongest arguments that nature, reason, or grace could find out, saith God, "They should deliver neither sons nor daughters" from any one of the judgments.

Ver. 14, 20. "They should deliver but their own souls by their righteousness." You must not think hence, that their holiness or righteousness merited deliverance of themselves. Man's goodness is nothing to God; all he can do is debt, and the best he doth is imperfect, no motive of God's will. Deliverance, salvation, are acts of grace and favour; Eph. ii. 8, 9, "By grace are ye saved; and that not of yourselves: it is the gift of God: not of works, lest any should boast." God hath out of his free grace promised to do great things for his elect, for the godly: and when he doth aught for them, it is not because they deserve it, or because they are godly, but because he hath promised. Many promises are made to godliness; 1 Tim. iv. 8, "Bodily exercise profiteth little: but godliness is profitable unto all things, having promise of the life that now is, and of that which is to come." Psal. l. 15, "Call upon me in the day of trouble: I will deliver thee;" not without calling, yet not for calling, but for his promise' sake.

Quest. If these three men, Noah, Daniel, and Job, who were so eminent in holiness, so fervent in prayer, should not by their prayers and piety deliver any, to what end should we desire the prayers of any in our days, when they are neither so holy nor effectual in prayer as these men were? is it not altogether in vain to crave the prayers of others, whatever our condition be?

Answ. 1. If God revealed our estate to be desperate, and that he would not hear any praying for us here, then it were in vain for us to request any to solicit the Lord on our behalf. 1 John v. 16, If a man have sinned a sin unto death, any prayer made for him by whomsoever, is to no purpose; I say not that you should pray for it, for the pardon of it, whoever should entreat you to do it.

2. We have divine warrant for the practice of it. 1 Sam. xii. 19, "All the people said unto Samuel, Pray for thy servants unto the Lord thy God, that we die not;" and 1 Thess. v. 25, "Brethren," (saith Paul,) "pray for us." Eph. vi. 18, 19, he entreats them to pray for all the saints, and for him. James v 14, "Is any sick among you? let him call for the elders of the church; and let them pray over him;" and then ver. 15, "The prayer of faith shall save the sick, and the Lord shall raise him up." Esth. iv. 16, she would have all the Jews gathered together that were in Shushan, to fast and pray for her.

Quest. 2. Had these three men met together, and agreed to pray for this people, would God have denied them? Doth not Christ say, Matt. xviii. 19, "If two of you shall agree on earth as touching any thing that they shall ask, it shall be done for them of my Father which is in heaven?"

Answ. If two, three, or more agree to ask any thing, it must be in faith, Matt. xxi. 22, according to God's will, 1 John v. 14; which could not here have been, for God had declared his mind otherwise, and so they could neither in faith, nor according to his will, have prayed; they would never have agreed together to ask a thing contrary to his mind.

Obs. 1. That lands may sin grievously against God, provoke him greatly. So did the Jews; Ezek. vii. 23, their land was full of bloody crimes, their city full of blackness, they had variety of abominations, chap. viii. 10. Hos. xii. 14, "Ephraim provoked him to anger most bitterly;" Isa. lxiii. 10, "They rebelled, and vexed his holy Spirit;" hereupon you find, Lam. i. 8, "Jerusalem hath grievously sinned;" and Amos v. 12, "I know your mighty sins;" they did mightily provoke, press, and weary God. See one place, in Jer. ii. 10—12, "Pass over the isles of Chittim and see; and send unto Kedar, and consider diligently, and see if there be such a thing. Hath a nation changed their gods, which are yet no gods? but my people have changed their glory for that which doth not profit. Be astonished, O ye heavens, at this, and be horribly afraid, be ye very desolate, saith the Lord."

Obs. 2. God hath variety of judgments to punish a sinning people; he can stretch out his hand, bring in a famine, the noisome beasts, the sword, and pestilence. When men have grievous sins, God hath sore judgments for them: read Deut. xxviii. and Lev. xxvi. Let lands be never so full of people and cattle, let their towns and cities be never so well fortified, God can quickly cut off man and beast, and lay all desolate. Cardanus in his eighth book De Varietate, ch. xlv. reckons up seven judgments of a grievous nature, that do befall the sons of men, three more besides those here in our prophet. (1.) Earthquakes, which sometimes are very grievous, and shake down whole towns. (2.) Inundations, when waters break out and drown up whole countries. (3.) Winds, which do great mischief, both at sea and land. And those we have here mentioned, how grievous are they! In famines, parties have ate their own flesh, and mothers their own children. Wild beasts fill all full of fears, that none dare look out of doors, or travel the highways. The sword hath made sore work in Germany, Ireland, and England of late days. The plague is amongst us, and what it will do ere it leave us, is unknown; we that have escaped the sword, it may be are numbered out for the plague. O let us repent of our former and present sins, pride in apparel, excess in diet, pomp in funerals, bitter divisions, unchristian carriages one towards another, unthankfulness for mercies, our unworthy walking of the gospel, and take heed of all sin for the future.

Obs. 3. Whatever the judgment be upon a sinning land and people, God is the author of it, acts in, and orders it. "I will stretch out my hand, and break the staff of bread," ver. 13; "If I cause noisome beasts to pass through the land," ver. 15; "If I bring a sword upon that land," ver. 17; "If I send a pestilence," ver. 19. These judgments come not casually, they are by divine power and providence; if man or beast fall by them, it is God cuts them off; if the wild beasts come here and there, it is God causes them to go those ways; he gives commission to the sword, and saith, Go through the land; it could not enter without God, much less go through a kingdom without warrant from him; if the plague wander up and down in a land, skip from street to street, from family to family, if it slay thousands and ten thousands, the Lord bids it, orders it to do so: therefore we should look at God's hand in all judgments, quietly submit to his stroke, and humble ourselves under his mighty hand. "I will stretch out my hand and break," &c. Shall God's hand be stretched out, and we not take notice of it? it is argument of a profane spirit not to do it. Isa. xxvi. 11, "Lord, when thy hand is lifted up, they will not see; but they shall see," and feel to their destruction.

Obs. 4. The sins of a land or people may be so great and grievous, that the Lord will show them no mercy, but proceed irrevocably to their destruction, what means soever be used for their help. You have sinned so against me, saith the Lord, that though Noah, Daniel, and Job were here, men of renown for their piety and prayers, though they should singly or jointly pour out their hearts before me, use all their interest in me for you, yet should they do no good; they should not change my thoughts, my heart, in the least degree, they should not obtain at my hands to abate aught of my fury; all the judgments intended should come, not one of them should be withheld. Jer. xv. 1—3, "Though Moses and Samuel stood before me, yet my mind could not be toward this people." Moses was "the man of God," Psal. xc. title; the man of God's choice, love, honouring, the man of his counsel, that did his work, that ruled his people; the man that was so potent in prayer, that he held God's hands, and kept him from destroying the progenitors of this people here spoken of, and brought God to repent of the evil he thought to do unto them, Exod. xxxii. 14; and Samuel was a man who had the ear and heart of God very much, when he cried for Israel God heard him, 1 Sam. vii. 9: yet if these two men stood before him, and, mediating for these people, should produce their strong arguments as of old, God's mind could not be towards them, but he would say, as it there follows, "Cast them out of my sight, and let them go forth;—such as are for death, to death; such as are for the sword, to the sword; such as are for the famine, to the famine; such as are for the captivity, to the captivity. And I will appoint over them four kinds, saith the Lord; the sword to slay, the dogs to tear, and the fowls of the heaven, and the beasts of the earth, to devour." Their sin was so high, that the prayers of the holy, yea the holiest men, would do them no good. Jeremiah was a praying and a weeping man, much affected with the condition of this people, Jer. ix. 1, 2; xiv. 7—9, and was much in prayer for them; but God was so far from hearing him for them, that he forbade him to pray for them, chap. vii. 16, "Pray not thou for this people, neither lift up cry nor prayer for them, neither make intercession to me; for I will not hear thee." So in chap. xiv. 11, "Pray not for this people for their good;" as if the Lord had said, Jeremiah, I know thou wilt be praying, weary and wear out thyself, but pray not for their good; if thou wilt pray for their destruction, that I would hasten in my judgments upon them, I will hear thee so praying, otherwise not.

Quest. But what if they prayed themselves?

Answ. It follows in the next verse, "When they fast, I will not hear their cry; and when they offer burnt offering and an oblation, I will not accept them; but I will consume them by the sword, famine, and pestilence." In James v. 16, you find "the effectual fervent prayer of a righteous man availeth much;" if of one righteous man, surely the working prayers of many righteous men should do more. You have six mentioned in Ezekiel and Jeremiah, Noah, Daniel, Job, Moses, Samuel, and Jeremiah himself; yet if all these should make the most fervent prayers that ever were made, God would not hear, but proceed in his intended judgments against this people. Their sins had such malignity in them, as that they outcried the prayers of all the righteous, yea, the very mercies of God.

Obs. 5. Righteousness is advantage to men in times of common calamity. Noah, Daniel, Job were righteous persons, and if they had been in the land or city when these sore judgments were come upon it, they should have been delivered, ver. 14, 16, 18, 20; though their righteousness could not profit others, yet it should profit themselves. Prov. xi. 4, "Riches profit not in the day of wrath; but righteousness delivereth from death;" and ver. 6, "The righteousness of the upright shall deliver them." When men are holy, praying, upright men, God hath a special care of them in times of danger: Noah, when the flood came, he had an ark to be secure in; when Sodom was destroyed, Lot was pulled out by an angel.

Ver. 22, 23. *Yet, behold, therein shall be left a remnant that shall be brought forth, both sons and daughters: behold, they shall come forth unto you, and ye shall see their way and their doings: and ye shall be comforted concerning the evil that I have brought upon Jerusalem, even concerning all that I have brought upon it. And they shall comfort you, when ye see their ways and their doings: and ye shall know that I have not done without cause all that I have done in it, saith the Lord God.*

These two verses are the third part of the chapter, and contain a respiting of some from the judgments there mentioned. You have here,

I. A gracious promise of preserving a remnant; "Therein shall be left a remnant."

II. A declaration what should be done with that remnant; "They shall be brought forth," and come to Babylon.

III. The events following hereupon; and they are these:

1. They should see their ways and doings, what the judgments upon Jerusalem, and their deliverance from them, wrought in them.

2. Be comforted,

(1.) Touching God's dealings with Jerusalem; "And ye shall be comforted concerning the evil," &c.

(2.) Enlargement of their comfort from the sight of their brethren's ways and practices; "And they shall comfort you, when ye see," &c.

(3.) Acknowledgment of the equity of God's dealing so with Jerusalem.

There were sundry things which saddened the hearts of the captives in Babylon much.

[1.] That God should so forget his covenant made with Abraham, Isaac, and Jacob, and his oath to David, Psal. lxxxix. 28—36, as to root out their seed from the land of the living.

[2.] That they had hearkened to the voice of Jeremiah and yielded themselves up into the hands of Nebuchadnezzar, who had brought them thither;

whereas their brethren still inhabited Jerusalem, had the benefit of the temple, and possessed their lands and habitations in Judea, themselves being destitute of all.

[3.] That the temple, city, and pleasant land should be laid waste, by such sore judgments brought upon them at once, as famine, wild beast, sword, and pestilence.

Against these sad apprehensions the Lord here lays in comfort. And,

For the first, he tells them there shall be left a remnant, that God will be mindful of his covenant and oath, that he will preserve a seed from the loins of their fathers, have a church and number to worship him.

For the second, he certifies them that those who escaped should be brought forth unto them in Babylon; and so they should not have cause any more to complain that they had listened to Jeremiah, and were brought into Babylon, for by this means they had escaped the sore judgments their brethren met with, and by this time were well accommodated in Babylon, and fitted in some measure to entertain their desolate brethren; and should see the judgments threatened by Jeremiah accomplished fully, and what mercy it was they were brought hither beforehand.

For the third, that all should be laid waste, he assures them that he hath had just cause for it, that he hath not in his fury done ought unadvisedly, to be repented of, but considered the cause thoroughly, viz. the grievousness of their sins, which deserved to the full all that he had done, and more; therefore saith, "Ye shall know that I have not done without cause all that I have done in it;" whatever I have done against the temple, city, land, and people, I had such cause for it, as will stop your mouths for ever. What if my judgments have been sore upon them? yet there is this good come by them, they acknowledge me just and righteous, are ashamed of and mourn for their ways, and will tell you, when they come amongst you, that in the midst of wrath they have met with mercy; for "they shall comfort you, when ye see their ways and their doings."

"Their ways." Some understand hereby, their former course of life at Jerusalem, which they should still walk in, which when the others should see, they should be comforted in the heavy hand of God upon them. Others understand by their ways, that sad course of life they should lead in Babylon. The primitive captives thought them happy who were at Jerusalem, and themselves the most miserable; but now when they should see them in captivity with themselves, and suffering as hard, if not harder things than themselves, the Babylonish yoke would seem easier. Consorts in misery are comforts to each other.

Junius interprets their ways and doings of the confession of their sins, and repentance; the sore and heavy judgments of God convinced them of the greatness of their sins, caused them, being now stripped of all, and in the hands of a potent and barbarous enemy, to confess their iniquity, and repent of their former ways and doings; and that induceth me to close with this exposition in those words, "They shall comfort you, when ye see their ways and their doings," thus: Though we have met with grievous judgments, have lost city, temple, country, all, are become captives like yourselves, yet God is just in all he hath done; he hath made good the word of his servants Jeremiah and Ezekiel, brought us to you, but withal, he hath broken our hearts for our sins, made us to abhor and loathe our former ways and doings, so that we must say, in wrath he hath remembered mercy, and recompensed all our temporal losses with spiritual advantages: and this was a comfort to the hearts of the former captives, when they saw their ways changed. Doubtless the first captives were a great comfort unto them, when they came into Babylon naked, and spoiled of all; and when they had told them of the severe judgments which befell them, how that some did eat their own children, &c. certainly they were astonished at it; but when they told them what good they had gotten by the dealings of God with them, they were comforted again.

Obs. 1. When God's judgments are sorest, yet then he shows mercy to some. When God brought his four sore judgments upon Jerusalem, viz. the sword, famine, noisome beast, and pestilence, yet a remnant is preserved; each judgment devoured its number, hundreds, thousands, and ten thousands, but all those judgments destroyed not all the people; God had some elect ones amongst them, and the election obtains mercy, and, together with them, some others. The Lord never poured out his wrath so fully, as that no drams of mercy were mingled with it. In the flood of wrath which drowned the world, were drops of mercy which saved Noah. In the brimstone and fire which burned up Sodom and Gomorrah, were sparks of divine love, to deliver Lot. He ever hath in wrath remembered mercy, and will do it to the end, the world shall not have advantage to charge him with cruelty; had none been spared, they might have said so; a remnant is left, and the mouth of iniquity is stopped.

Obs. 2. The Lord will satisfy and comfort the hearts of his people against the evil and scandal that comes by any of his judgments. When Jerusalem was destroyed, the Jews rooted out and carried to Babylon, what joy was there in the nations! what reproachings of the Jews! Where now is their God? what now is become of their holy city and temple, are not all laid waste, &c.? At these things the Jews' hearts in Babylon were grieved, offended; therefore the Lord tells them, they "shall be comforted concerning all the evil he hath brought upon Jerusalem;" they shall know the greatness of their sins, which moved him to do so, they shall know the fruit of his judgments, how they have caused those brought unto them to confess their sins, to repent of their ways, and turn to the Lord.

Obs. 3. That the Lord is righteous and just in his judgments. "I have not done without cause all that I have done in Jerusalem;" he cut not off man or beast without cause: it is the devil's design to do so; therefore saith God, Job ii. 3, "Thou movedst me against him, to destroy him without cause," but God would not do it; whatever he doth, he hath great cause for; he is the only and infinitely wise God, and doth all things upon the height of reason. Their sins were such as impeached his honour, corrupted his worship, brake the covenant, questioned his providence, violated justice, and conformed them to the heathen; he had cause enough therefore to destroy them, and do what he did, namely, to vindicate his honour, worship, covenant, providence, justice, and to show that his people, if they will sin with the world, must suffer grievous things for it. Jer. xxii. 8, 9, when the nations should pass by the city and say, "Wherefore hath the Lord done thus unto this great city?" God will have the cause known; "then they shall answer, Because they have forsaken the covenant of the Lord their God, and worshipped other gods, and served them:" and chap. xix. 13, God said he would make Jerusalem as Tophet (that is, fill it with blood, and the bodies of slain men); and why would he do so? "Because of all the houses upon whose roofs they have burned incense unto all the host of heaven, and have poured out drink offerings unto other gods."

Obs. 4. Men shall know in due time the equity of God's judgments. "And ye shall know that I have not done aught without cause." God's "judgments are a great depth," Psal. xxxvi. 6, men cannot sound or measure them; the nature of them, the suddenness and severity of them, the frequency and continuance of them, do puzzle men, and especially the causes of them, which are hidden from the eyes of most. Job's friends mistook the cause of God's dealing so sharply with Job, but afterwards they understood it; they in Babylon, and others, were astonished at the sore judgments of God, but God let them know the cause of it, and so they were brought to justify God. 1 Kings ix. 7—9, "I will cut off Israel out of the land which I have given them; and this house, which I have hallowed for my name, will I cast out of my sight; and Israel shall be a proverb and a by-word among all people; and at this house, which is high, every one that passeth by it shall be astonished, and shall hiss; and they shall say, Why hath the Lord done thus unto this land, and to this house? and they shall answer, Because they forsook the Lord their God, and have taken hold upon other gods, and have worshipped and served them; therefore hath the Lord brought upon them all this evil." God proclaims the cause of his severe judgments, that so men may see the equity of them, that he is "righteous in all his ways, and holy in all his works," Psal. cxlv. 17. When we hear of the bloody doings which have been in Germany so long, and of those in Ireland, we are amazed, wonder what is the cause that God proceeds so severely with them; there is cause sufficient for it, and if we know it not, God will in his time clear himself, and make it known to us.

CHAPTER XV.

And the word of the Lord came unto me, saying, Son of man, What is the vine tree more than any tree, or than a branch which is among the trees of the forest? Shall wood be taken thereof to do any work? or will men take a pin of it to hang any vessel thereon? Behold, it is cast into the fire for fuel; the fire devoureth both the ends of it, and the midst of it is burned. Is it meet for any work? Behold, when it was whole, it was meet for no work: how much less shall it be meet yet for any work, when the fire hath devoured it, and it is burned? Therefore thus saith the Lord God; As the vine tree among the trees of the forest, which I have given to the fire for fuel, so will I give the inhabitants of Jerusalem. And I will set my face against them; they shall go out from one fire, and another fire shall devour them; and ye shall know that I am the Lord, when I set my face against them. And I will make the land desolate, because they have committed a trespass, saith the Lord God.

In this short chapter, under the similitude of a useless and fruitless vine tree, is set forth the condition of the inhabitants of Jerusalem; that is fit for nothing but the fire, and so are they fit only for judgment.

I. The similitude is propounded in ver. 2, and illustrated in ver. 3—5.

II. The apodosis and application of it, to the men of Jerusalem, is in ver. 6—8.

III. The authority of this prophecy, in the first verse, "And the word of the Lord came unto me, saying." The prophet did not form this parable, or take it up from others, or by observation, but he had it from the Lord.

God often in Scripture calls Israel a vine, and his vineyard, Psal. lxxx. 8, 14, 15; Isa. iii. 14; xxvii. 2; Jer. xii. 10; Ezek. xvii. 6. And they were "a noble vine," Jer. ii. 21; "a choice vine," Isa. v. 2; "a goodly vine," Ezek. xvii. 8: but because it was now become a "degenerate plant of a strange vine," Jer. ii. 21; "an empty vine," Hos. x. 1, or brought forth wild grapes; therefore the Lord likens the Jews here to the wood of a fruitless vine.

We shall a little show you wherein the Jews, who were the church of God, resembled the vine.

1. Vines are few in respect of other trees, so were the Jews in respect of other people; Deut. vii. 7, they "were the fewest of all people."

2. Vines are planted by hill-sides, by houses, in gardens, orchards, &c.; and the Jews were planted in the choicest land; Hos. ix. 13, "In a pleasant place;" Isa. v. 1, "In a very fruitful hill." The vine was brought out of Egypt, it was a chosen vine, and was planted, Psal. lxxx. 8; but where? in "a good land," Deut. viii. 7, even a land of brooks, fountains, springs, valleys, hills; in a land "flowing with milk and honey, the glory of all lands," Ezek. xx. 6; therefore called a branch of his own planting, Isa. lx. 21, planted with his right hand, Psal. lxxx. 15.

3. Vines are weak, must have props and supports to uphold them; God dealt so by the Jews; Deut. i. 31, "In the wilderness the Lord thy God bare thee, as a man doth bear his son, in all the way that ye went." Children are weak, and must be carried in the arms; and so God did carry them; Deut. xxxiii. 27, "The eternal God is thy refuge, and underneath are the everlasting arms."

4. Fruitful; no tree so fruitful as the vine; Psal. cxxviii. 3, it is called the "fruitful vine;" it is fruitful in branches, and fruitful in clusters. The Jews were as fruitful a nation as any; Deut. x. 22, "Thy fathers went down into Egypt with threescore and ten persons, and now the Lord thy God hath made thee as the stars of heaven for multitude:" in a natural way they were very fruitful.

5. It spreads much; so the Jews, who were God's vine: Psal. lxxx. 9—11, the psalmist saith there of this vine, that it filled the land, covered the hills with its shadow, sent out her boughs unto the sea, and her branches unto the river, and they spread far.

6. It is pleasant and delightful; such were the Jews; Isa. v. 7, "The vineyard of the Lord of hosts is the house of Israel, and the men of Judah his pleasant plant;" the Hebrew is, his plant of pleasures.

7. Most pains required about vines of any plants or trees; much digging, dressing, pruning, supporting, fencing is needful: the Jews had much pains or cost bestowed upon them; Isa. v. 4, "What could have been done more to my vineyard, that I have not done in it?" Other trees are little looked after, but the vine must have special care; John xv. 2, the husbandman observes every branch, the fruitful and unfruitful: Amos iii. 2, "You have I known of all the families," &c.

Ver. 2. "What is the vine tree more than any tree?" The Hebrew is, עץ הגפן the wood of the vine; the word עץ signifies mostly a living tree, as Gen. i. 11, "Let the earth bring forth the fruit tree;" Psal. i. 3, "Like a tree planted by the rivers of water;" yet sometimes it notes the trunk and body of a tree cut down, as in Deut. iv. 28, "Ye shall serve gods, the work of men's hands, wood and stone." Some would understand it here of the vine tree dead and cut down, but that needs not; it is more suitable to Scripture, to take it for a fruitless vine tree, neither dead nor cut down, but as if dead and cut down: and what is such a vine more than other trees? it is not only lower, weaker, more bunched, wreathed, unsightly than they, but it is of less use than any of the trees of the forest; they serve to make temples, palaces, houses, ships, musical and martial instruments, and tools for many uses, but for the vine tree, it serves not for any such use. By the interrogation, he sets out the unusefulness of it; it is so far from being equal to the trees of the forest, as that it is not comparable to a branch of one of those trees. Take one arm or branch of an oak, elm, or ash, it would be of more use to the joiner or carpenter, than the wood of a thousand vines.

Therefore it follows,

Ver. 3. "Shall wood be taken thereof to do any work?" This is a great derogation from the vine, the wood of it is not fit for any work; the wood of other trees is fit for variety of services within doors and without, this for none. The Hebrew is, to make it into work. It is not fit to make a pin of, which is a small thing, and for small uses, as to hang a cloak, hat, or band on: "Will men take a pin of it to hang any vessel thereon?" no, they will not, they know it is unfit to hang the least thing on it.

Ver. 4. "Behold, it is cast into the fire for fuel." Here he showeth what it is fittest for, viz. "the fire;" neither is it the best fuel for that, for the branches of vines, cut and bound up, if they be reserved any considerable time, will not burn well.

"The fire devoureth both the ends of it, and the midst of it is burned." The roots and tops, namely, the branches, they are only for the fire, and quickly consumed in it; and whereas you may think the body, which is the middle part, may be good for somewhat, it is otherwise; the midst of it, that you think strongest, soundest, most useful, burns like the rest, and you cannot make aught of it. Other trees, when the roots and tops are burned, their bodies are improved to several great and good purposes: the vine tree is wholly combustible matter, and only for the fire. Some refer the ends to the ten tribes, and those carried away under Jehoiachin; the midst to those that remained at Jerusalem.

"Is it meet for any work?" The Hebrew is, היצלח Will it prosper to work? it will break in pieces, deceive a man's expectation, come to nought, and his labour will be in vain.

Ver. 5. "When it was whole, it was meet for no work: how much less shall it be meet yet for any work when the fire hath devoured it?" Sanctius thinks that their vines at this time were much wasted, for the Chaldeans had been twice there, in Jehoiakim's and Jehoiachin's time; and where armies come, they spoil the countries, pull down buildings, cut up trees, tear the vines in pieces, and lay the vineyards open to waste; they had almost ruined the metaphorical vine the Jews. As therefore the vine, neither whole nor burned, was meet for any domestic or state service; so this jewish people, neither in their prosperity nor adversity, neither before the Chaldeans afflicted them nor since, have been serviceable to God or his church.

Ver. 7. "Set my face against them." See chap. xiv. 8, concerning these words.

"They shall go out from one fire, and another fire shall devour them." By fire is meant affliction, judgments, Psal. lxvi. 12, "We went through fire and water," and there be sundry resemblances between them.

1. Fire is dreadful to men's thoughts; fire of Sodom, and fire of hell; how terrible! if you see a ship on fire, &c. So judgments, afflictions are exceeding terrible to the apprehensions of many; the sword, how sad did it make the hearts of many before it was drawn! the plague now is terrible to your thoughts.

2. It is painful; and so are the judgments of God; they put a land into travail. Isa. xxvi. when the judgments of God were abroad, what saith the prophet? ver. 17, "Like as a woman with child, that draweth near the time of her delivery, is in pain, and crieth out in her pangs; so have we been in thy sight, O Lord." God's judgments breed terrible pangs in those who are under them.

3. Fire enlightens the eyes, and judgments enlighten men's understandings: Hos. v. 15, "In their affliction they will seek me early;" then they will see the nature of their sins, the danger of their lives, the great need they have of mercy, and therefore will seek me early: hence it is that God saith so oft after judgments threatened, "They shall know that I am the Lord."

4. It refines; so do the judgments of the Lord: Zech. xiii. 9, "I will bring them through the fire, and refine them as silver is refined:" the Babylonish furnace purged out their idolatry. Isa. i. 25, "I will turn my hand upon thee, and purely purge away thy dross, and take away all thy tin:" when God takes away his hand of mercy from a nation, and turns his hand of judgment upon it, then he purges, &c.

5. It consumes; and so do his judgments: Psal. xxi. 9, "Thou shalt make them as a fiery oven in the time of thine anger: the Lord shall swallow them up in his wrath, and the fire shall devour them." Famine devoured its thousands, &c.

The scope of the words is, that they should have judgment after judgment; if they escaped one, they should fall into another, until they were consumed.

Ver. 8. "Because they have committed a trespass." Hebrew is, מעלו מעל, he means not one trespass only, but it is a singular put for a plural, and is cleared by that, chap. xiv. 13, "When the land sinneth against me by trespassing grievously," למעל מעל there is little difference in the words, and those here might have been so rendered, they have trespassed grievously.

Obs. 1. The ministers of God have warrant to use similitudes in their teaching of the people. God himself doth it here, he brings in a parable of the vine tree, and allegorizeth upon it; and the Scripture is frequent in parables and allegories. Christ was much in parables; they help memory, if familiar and known; they convince more fully than plain speeches.

Obs. 2. That men are apt to glory and confide in the privileges they have. "What is the vine tree more than any tree?" The Jews, because they were God's vine, God's people, thought themselves better than any, than all other, that they should never be cut down and destroyed: What! are not we God's vine, his pleasant plant? hath he not made a hedge about us, done much for us? will he pluck up the hedge and lay us waste? No man would ever destroy his own vine and vineyard, and shall we think God will deal so by his? The Jews doted upon their privileges, that they were Abraham's seed, they had the temple, that they were a plant of God's planting; and it is incident to most, to adhere to and confide in some privileges they have: but whence had they, or any, their privileges? if they were the people of God, his vine, the Lord chose them, they chose not him; he planted them, and was pleased to call them his vine, and vineyard; whatever excellency or privilege they had, it was from his free grace and good pleasure; neither they nor we can merit or purchase aught at the hands of God. Let us not glory in privileges, in carnal excellences, have any confidence in the flesh; but remember, the more privileges we have, the stronger obligation is upon us to admire free grace, and to honour the God of our mercies.

Obs. 3. The Lord knows what all trees are, the vine tree in the vineyard and the trees of the forest, the cedars of Lebanon, the oaks of Bashan, and shrubs of the wilderness; he knows the goodliness or meanness, the tallness or lowness, the weakness or strength, the fruitfulness or unfruitfulness, the usefulness or unusefulness of every tree. He knew what trees the Jews were, and what trees the gentiles were; which tree was fit for the fire, and which fit for other services; he knows every man's nature, qualities, operations, uses, and ends.

Obs. 4. Trees in the forest and wilderness may be of better use than trees in the orchard and vineyard, wild trees may exceed those which are planted. "What is the vine tree, to a branch among the trees of the forest? shall wood be taken thereof to do any work?" Will it serve for a pin to hang a hat on? no; other trees you may take the wood and timber of, and employ many ways. The heathens, that were trees of the forest, had more good in them than the Jews, who were his vine; they did more service to the world, they were more just, diligent, faithful, bountiful, pitiful than the Jews; they were fitter for temple work than the other: and is it not so now? are not many forest trees better than us christians?

Obs. 5. People degenerating from the condition they were set in, lose their esteem and favour. This people of the Jews was a noble vine, a choice vine, a good vine; but now it was become a degenerate plant of a strange vine. Jer. ii. 21, "I had planted thee a noble vine, wholly a right seed: how then art thou turned into the degenerate plant of a strange vine unto me?" They were become like Sodom and Gomorrah; Isa. i. 10, "Hear the word of the Lord, ye rulers of Sodom; give ear unto the law of our God, ye people of Gomorrah:" now their vine was of the vine of Sodom and of the fields of Gomorrah, now their grapes were of gall, and their clusters were bitter, Deut. xxxii. 32; and why so? Isa. i. 4, they were a sinful nation, a people laden with iniquity, a seed of evil-doers, children that were corrupters; they had forsaken the Lord, his ordinances, truths, worship; they had changed their glory, and wandered after idols, Jer. ii. 11, 20; they oppressed in the gates, the city and land were full of violence and bloody crimes, Ezek. vii. 23; and hereupon they lost their favour with God, and esteem they had of him, so that he came to abhor them; Psal. lxxviii. 59, he greatly abhorred Israel, forsook them, delivered them into captivity, and into the enemy's hand, ver. 61. Because they degenerated so, God branded them with disgraceful titles, as "a rebellious nation, impudent children," Ezek. ii. 3, 4; "hypocritical," Isa. x. 6; "lying," Isa. xxx. 9; "reprobate silver," Jer. vi. 30; "sons of the sorceress, seed of the adulterer," Isa. lvii. 3; "soothsayers," Isa. ii. 6; "supplanters, slanderers," Jer. ix. 4; "an assembly of treacherous men," ver. 2; "a homeborn slave," Jer. ii. 14; thorns and briers, Isa. x. 17; "naughty figs," Jer. xxiv. 8; "a garden without water," Isa. i. 30; "scorpions," Ezek. ii. 6; "a generation of vipers," Matt. iii. 7. When this vine lost its sweetness, it lost the interest it had in the heart of God, and the more it degenerated, the more distasteful and reproachful it became. Degeneracy from God and his ways is a provoking sin. God had done more for his people than any people in the world, he had given them such a land, such ordinances, laws, privileges, as none else had; and now for them to forsake God was a grievous trespass, they violated many bands of love, they brake the covenant of their God, and did secretly accuse God, as not being so good as he had promised to be unto them; therefore, Micah vi. 3, 4, "O my people, what have I done unto thee, and wherein have I wearied thee? testify against me. I brought thee up out of the land of Egypt, and redeemed thee out of the house of servants," &c.

Exod. xv. 17. Psal. xliv. 2.

It is good for us therefore to keep close to God, not to admit of any undervaluing or discouraging thoughts of God and his ways. Let not your hearts draw you back from God; Heb. x. 38, "If any man draw back, my soul shall have no pleasure in him." Drawing back is the way to perdition; Heb. iii. 12, Take heed, therefore, lest there be at any time, in any of you, a heart of unbelief, to depart from the living God. If you would be honourable and fruitful, you must cleave fully to God, and keep close to him and his ways; John xv. 4, "The branch cannot bear fruit of itself, except it abide in the vine; no more can ye, except ye abide in me."

Obs. 6. That people which is fruitless and useless, is determined of God to destruction. The vine tree being barren and of no use, was given and cast into the fire; and so should the inhabitants of Jerusalem, for they were neither fruitful nor useful.

(1.) Not fruitful. Hos. x. 1, "Israel is an empty vine, he bringeth forth fruit unto himself;" this seemeth a contradiction, that Israel should be called an empty vine, and yet bring forth fruit, but it is not, the fruit was selfish fruit, and that is as no fruit in God's account; it brought forth branches, leaves, and wild grapes, but God reckoned not these for fruit; their idolatry, superstition, oppression, violence, and injustice, were wild grapes; their hypocrisy, formal professions, carnal confidences, their fastings and sacrificings, were leafy things; they had no fruit unto holiness and righteousness, their worship was not pure, laws were not executed; so that they were unfruitful towards God and man.

The evil of fruitlessness lies in this:

[1.] A vine or people that are fruitless, deceive God's expectation: Isa. v. 2, "He looked that it should bring forth grapes, and it brought forth wild grapes:" God had taken great pains, been at great cost with his people, waited long for grapes, and when all came to all, there were only wild grapes; ver. 7, "He looked for judgment, but behold oppression; for righteousness, but behold a cry."

[2.] It offends God to have such trees in his vineyard, people that bring forth nothing but wild grapes, cursed fruit. How grievous was it to God, that there was no justice in the land! Jer. v. 1, "Run to and fro through the streets of Jerusalem, and see if there be any that executeth judgment, that seeketh the truth; and I will pardon it:" Isa. v. 3, "Judge between me and my vineyard;" it argues God was troubled. Though they had no good fruit, yet they had evil fruit too much, such as offended his eyes, his ears, his taste; therefore, Isa. i. 15, "I will hide mine eyes from you; yea, when ye make many prayers, I will not hear;" and the grapes they bare, were sour grapes, distasteful unto the Lord.

[3.] Fruitlessness is a reproach to God, who is the Husbandman of the vineyard, as if he were not skilful, or negligent, and did not what was fitting to make the vine to bear; and therefore, Isa. v. 3, 4, "Judge between me and my vineyard, what could have been done more;" I have done all which is fitting for a prudent and in-

Matt. vii. 16.

dustrious vine-dresser to do, and my vine is a reproach to me. When men till their land, sow it with the best seed, and it brings forth nothing but thistles, nettles, or weeds, it is a reproach to the owner. If other people had had that pains taken with them, those pains and mercies bestowed upon them, which the Jews had, they would have brought forth fruit unto repentance.

[4.] Fruitless ones are a burden to God, to the godly, and to the place where they grow.

First, to God, who, speaking of this people, Isa. i. 24, saith, "Ah, I will ease me of mine adversaries." They were a mighty burden unto him; Amos ii. 13, "Behold, I am pressed under you, as a cart is pressed that is full of sheaves."

Secondly, to the godly: Lot's righteous soul was vexed with the Sodomites, 2 Pet. ii. 7; they were a vine that brought forth nothing good. David sighed and said, "Woe is me," &c. Such hinder the liberties and sadden the spirits of those who are truly good.

Thirdly, to the place where they grow: Luke xiii. 7, the barren fig tree must be cut down; and why? it cumbers the ground, keeps out others which might be set up in the place, sucks up the moisture and fatness of the earth, overshadows and prejudiceth the plants which are near.

[5.] Such are slighted, looked upon as worthless, inconsiderable. Take a vine or tree which hath no fruit, it is not regarded: it is not the leaves or branches, but the fruit makes it esteemed: it is not a leafy profession, but a fruitful conversation, makes people to be esteemed. Mark xiv. 3, a woman bestows a box of precious ointment upon Christ's head; some envied at it, but Christ said she had wrought a good work, and this begat such a high esteem for her in the heart of Christ, that to honour her, he said, the fact should never be forgotten, but wherever the gospel should be preached in the world, that she had done should be spoken of for a memorial of her, ver. 9: she was a tree that bare good fruit, and was honoured for it, but fruitless trees are not minded, not valued; take a man that doth no good, we say he is an idle, an empty man.

[6.] Fruitlessness declares a man to be an evil man. A tree is known by its fruit: if it have good fruit it is a good tree, if ill, it is an ill tree; but what if it have no fruit? you cannot say, it is neither good nor bad, God hath no such trees in his garden: in that it hath no fruit, it is an ill tree; a barren tree cannot be good; when Christ found no fruit upon the tree, he dealt with it as with an evil tree.

[7.] That which is fruitless, is near to a curse. Matt. xxi. 19, when Christ saw a fig tree without figs, what said he to it? "Let no fruit grow on thee henceforward for ever. And presently the fig tree withered away." Heb. vi. 8, the ground that brings forth briers and thorns, not herbs meet for the dressers, "is rejected, and nigh unto cursing." Prov. x. 7, "The name of the wicked shall rot;" wicked men are fruitless, and God will curse their names; Esau, Jeroboam, Judas.

If a vine be fruitless, God will take away what he hath bestowed, and undo what he hath done. Isa. v. 5, "I will tell you what I will do to my vineyard; I will take away the hedge thereof, and it shall be eaten up; and break down the wall thereof, and it shall be trodden down." The hedge and wall were God's protection and defence of them; now because the vine had no good fruit, was an empty vine, the Lord would preserve them no longer, but expose them to spoil and ruin. God made a law concerning fruitful trees, that they should be preserved, Deut. xx. 19; and God himself is careful of fruitful trees, and vines that bring forth good grapes; Isa. lxv. 8, "As the new wine is found in the cluster, and one saith, Destroy it not, for a blessing is in it; so will I do for my servants' sakes." If God's trees, vines, be fruitful, God will preserve them, prohibit others to wrong them; Psal. cv. 15, "Touch not mine anointed, and do my prophets no harm." Cant. ii. 15, "Take us the foxes, the little foxes, that spoil the vines; for our vines have tender grapes." When the vines do bear good clusters and wine, the Lord is careful to preserve them, he is a hedge and wall unto them; but when they are barren, or bring forth sour grapes, he will protect and bless no longer, he will undo what he hath done, take away what he hath bestowed: Matt. xxi. 43, "The kingdom of God shall be taken from you, and given to a nation bringing forth the fruits thereof." The Jews had the title to be God's people, the gospel was presented to them; both should be taken away, and be bestowed upon the gentiles, who would bring forth the fruits thereof. Several kingdoms have several fruits, and the fruits of God's kingdom are the fruits of the Spirit.

[9.] Fruitless trees must be cut down or plucked up; Luke xiii. 7, "Cut it down." Matt. iii. 10, "Now the axe is laid unto the root of the trees:" the Jews were a fruitless vine tree, and when Christ came, he laid the axe to the root, and quickly they were cut down. And sometimes he pulls them up by the roots; Jude 12, "Trees whose fruit withereth, without fruit, twice dead, plucked up by the roots:" fruitless trees are twice dead, dead in the body and branches, and dead in the root, dead by nature, and dead by their apostasy from that profession they made; and these God plucks up by the roots, there shall nothing of them remain.

(2.) They were not useful. As the vine tree, if fruitless, it must be cut down, or plucked up, it is unserviceable for any work, to make a pin of, other trees, when they are growing or cut down, serve for divers uses at sea and land; this people were come to such a pass, as that they were unfit for any use; Jeremiah tells you they were like naughty figs, that could not be eaten, chap. xxiv. 8, and like the girdle he hid in the bank of Euphrates, chap. xiii. 7, which was marred and profitable for nothing. You know what Christ saith of salt, when it hath lost its savour, "it is good for nothing, but to be cast out and trodden under foot," Matt. v. 13; so the vine tree, when it hath lost its fruitfulness, its clusters, and wine, with which it cheered God and man, it is good for nothing but to be cast into the fire: such a vine tree were the Jews; Jer. iv. 22, "My people is foolish, they have not known me; they are sottish children, and they have none understanding: they are wise to do evil, but to do good they have no knowledge."

Let England, London look to it: we have been the vine and vineyard of the Lord, he hath made a hedge and wall about us, he hath of late digged us and pruned us; he looks for fruit, good fruit, the power of godliness, not the form, thorough reformation, not a half one, justice, not oppression, love, not bitterness, taking off burdens, not laying them on, countenancing of the saints, not reproaching, &c.: if we be found without such fruit, the axe is sharpening, we shall be cut down, and cast into the fire, like the inhabitants of Jerusalem. Let us now, then, after such warnings, such mercies and deliverances from the wild beasts and boars, bring forth fruit meet for repentance, meet for the gospel, meet for all that God hath done for us.

Reflection 1. We have been near cutting down, like the fig tree. Luke xiii. 6—9, a man had a fig tree, planted in his vineyard, and came three years to see what fruit it had, and there was none, either no figs, or naughty figs; and then he said to the dresser, Cut it down; but the dresser interceding, prevailed for another year, Lord, let it alone this year also; if it bear fruit, well, if not, then cut it down: so here, &c.

Reflection 2. God hath bestowed upon and done great things for us: he hath taken us out of the Romish Egypt, and planted us in Canaan, a land that flows with milk and honey; he hath given us the glorious and everlasting gospel, which many other nations have not; in it he hath given us exceeding great and precious promises, with it pardon of sin, the Spirit, Christ himself, all; to us heaven is opened, we have visions of God, dews, showers, and sunshine, to make us fruitful. He hath done for us wonderful things: Hath he not fenced and walled us about with his protection, defending us from enemies without and within, so that neither lion nor leopard, boar nor bear, wolf nor fox, jesuits, papists, malignants, have been able to devour us? hath he not delivered us from the greatest dangers, most devilish devices and plots, and out of many deaths? hath he not destroyed the serpents and scorpions that stung us, or driven them into holes, made their hosts to fall, "as the leaf falleth from the vine, and as a falling fig from the fig tree," Isa. xxxiv. 4? hath he not plucked up most of the thorns and briers that grew in his vineyard, and removed the stones of stumbling out of the ecclesiastical and civil estate? hath he not turned curses into blessings, wise counsels into foolish results, and by weak hands wrought glorious effects for us? hath he not disappointed the expectations of our enemies, when they have been high, puzzling the wit of hell, nonplussing the powers of darkness, causing their designs to dash out their own brains, and to promote those they were intended to ruin?

Reflection 3. God blesses and prospers a people that is fruitful in good. Gen. xlix. 22, "Joseph is a fruitful bough, even a fruitful bough by a well, whose branches run over the wall;" of him came two tribes, Ephraim and Manasseh; and how did he prosper in Egypt! to what a height and greatness did he grow! he was the only man in all the land, Gen. xli. 44. It is said of the man who is fruitful, that "whatsoever he doth shall prosper," Psal. i. 3. Moses exhorted the people to obedience upon this ground, Deut. xxix. 9, "Keep the words of this covenant, and do them, that ye may prosper in all that ye do." When men are obedient unto the will of God, and so fruitful, it pleases the Lord to bless them. The Jews were the terror of nations whilst they worshipped God in his own ways, and executed justice in their gates: 2 Chron. xxxii. 30, "Hezekiah prospered in all his works;" he abounded in doing good, and prospered accordingly. If you bring forth sweet grapes and pleasant fruit, you shall prosper in your families, shops, journeys, worship, &c.

Reflection 4. All creatures are fruitful one way or other. The earth is so plentiful in fruit-bearing, that as it is the mother of all living, so it is the maintainer of them. What is there grows upon the face of the earth, which is altogether fruitless, and doth not contribute something to the good of man, and glory of its Creator? Clouds are the bottles of heaven, and being carried over the quarters of the earth, they empty their silver drops to enrich the earth. The heavens yield us their light and influence, and move constantly to do us service; that old servant of the world the sun, is not yet weary of sending down his beams to warm us, and all other creatures. Hath God made the heavens and earth useful and fruitful for man, and all the fish, fowl, beasts, birds, plants in them? and shall man be barren? surely for a christian it is a great reproach to be so.

Reflection 5. It is the appointment of the Lord Christ, that those who are his servants should be fruitful. John xv. 16, "I have chosen you, and ordained you, that you should go and bring forth fruit;" that they should preach, pray, convert souls, work miracles, plant churches, set up his kingdom, &c. And now if Christ hath chosen you to any places, in the family, city, church, or state, he hath ordained that you should bring forth fruit; he would not have a parent fruitless in the family, nor a magistrate in the city.

Reflection 6. It is an honour to God to be fruitful. When a vine is full of goodly clusters, what a credit, what a cheering is it to the vine-dresser! When the ground yields great increase, it is an honour to the husbandman; when trees are loaden with fruit, the gardener glories in it, Come, look upon this tree! when the ewes bear twins, it is the shepherd's honour: and so when christians are fruitful, it is the honour and glory of God; John xv. 8, "Herein is my Father glorified, that ye bear much fruit." When christians are fruitful, it provokes others to praise the name of the Lord; Matt. v. 16, "Let your light so shine before men, that they may see your good works, and glorify your Father which is in heaven."

Reflection 7. Fruitfulness is delightful to God and man. Hos. xiv. 5, 6, God would be dew to Israel, he should grow, his beauty should be as the olive tree, (the beauty of the olive tree is to be full of olives,) and his smell as Lebanon; Lebanon was full of sweet trees and fragrant flowers, and filled all the parts thereabouts with a sweet smell; so should Israel be fruitful, and yield a sweet savour to God in heaven, and men on earth. Judg. ix. 13, the vine cheered God and man with its pleasant and sweet-smelling wine: God, in that it was offered in the freewill offering, for a sweet savour unto God, Numb. xv. 3, 5; man, Psal. civ. 15, wine makes glad his heart: so fruitfulness in christians hath a sweet savour, delights heaven and earth. The Philippians' fruitfulness was "an odour of a sweet smell, a sacrifice acceptable to God," Phil. iv. 18; so prayers and praise are as incense and music unto him, Psal. cxli. 2; Heb. xiii. 15. The Corinthians' bounty and fruitfulness so delighted Paul, that he boasted of them, 2 Cor. ix. 2; the savour of it extended far, and made many to glorify God on their behalf, ver. 13. Be fruitful, then, that you may please, delight, God and man, and leave a good savour behind you.

Reflection 8. It is the glory of any to be fruitful.

Reflection 9. Christ is coming to see what fruit is upon his vine trees: Heb. x. 37, "Yet a little while, and he that shall come will come, and will not tarry;" and when he comes, if there be ill fruit or no fruit upon them, he will not only curse those trees, but burn those trees, for his coming will be in flames of fire, 2 Thess. i. 8. The inhabitants of Jerusalem were not spared because barren; and the inhabitants of London will not be spared if found barren: if you be fruitful he will transplant you, and you shall be trees of righteousness in the heavenly paradise for ever.

Obs. 7. When God's face is against a people, he will follow that people with judgment after judgment, till they be consumed. "I will set my face against them, they shall go out from one fire, and another fire shall devour them:" if they escaped the famine, the plague should take hold of them; if that did not, the sword should; if that failed, the wild beasts should devour them; if by them they died not, captivity should be their ruin. When God is wroth, he hath fiery judgments for the wicked, and if he scorch them in one fire a little, pull them out like brands, he will throw them into another fire; if he burn them a little more in that, and pull them out again, at last he will throw them into a devouring, consuming fire. "The wrath of a king is as messengers of death," Prov. xvi. 14; but the wrath of God is as death itself, it pursues sinners till they are burnt to ashes. Wicked men are apt to think, that when they are got out of some one fiery affliction they are safe, but another is preparing for them. Nebuchadnezzar had twice before been in their land, carried away Jehoiakim and Jehoiachin at several times, and now he was ready to come again; and after a long siege, he took the city, and carried away many to Babylon: those who were left, he set Gedaliah over them, whom, with many others, Ishmael slew; this Ishmael presently after was put to flight by Johanan, who also going into Egypt, contrary to the counsel of Jeremiah, is slain there with divers others by the Babylonians, as Jer. xli. xlii. xliii. xliv. relates.

Obs. 8. The sins of the inhabitants bring desolation upon a land. "I will make the land desolate, because they have committed a trespass." Canaan was a pleasant and fruitful land, a very paradise, but because they committed a trespass, corrupted God's worship and oppressed the people, therefore God laid waste the land, even his own vineyard; he plucked away the fence, broke down the wall, and let in those wild beasts, bears, boars, and foxes, the Babylonians, who tore the vine in pieces, and rooted it wholly up, and laid all desolate; before they came, the land was as the garden of Eden, but they left it a desolate wilderness; and where the vines grew, there were briers and thorns, Isa. vii. 23; yea, "all the land should become briers and thorns," ver. 24. So chap. xxxii. 13, "Upon the land of my people shall come up thorns and briers; yea, upon all the houses of joy in the joyous city." Psal. cvii. 3, 4, the Lord turns "a fruitful land into barrenness, for the wickedness of them that dwell therein." If we would therefore prevent this, let us hearken to what is said, Jer. vii. 5—7, "If ye thoroughly amend your ways and doings; if ye thoroughly execute judgment between a man and his neighbour; if ye oppress not the stranger, the fatherless, and the widow, and shed not innocent blood in this place, neither walk after other gods to your hurt: then will I cause you to dwell in this place."

CHAPTER XVI.

Ver. 1—5. *Again the word of the Lord came unto me, saying, Son of man, cause Jerusalem to know her abominations, and say, Thus saith the Lord God unto Jerusalem; Thy birth and thy nativity is of the land of Canaan; thy father was an Amorite, and thy mother an Hittite. And as for thy nativity, in the day thou wast born thy navel was not cut, neither wast thou washed in water to supple thee; thou wast not salted at all, nor swaddled at all. None eye pitied thee, to do any of these unto thee, to have compassion upon thee; but thou wast cast out in the open field, to the lothing of thy person, in the day that thou wast born.*

WE are now come to the longest chapter in the whole prophecy, and it is against the Jews who were at Jerusalem.

The parts of it are these:

I. The principal scope of the chapter laid down in ver. 2.

II. The natural state of the Jews represented under a parable of an infant left and neglected of all, ver. 3—6.

III. A commemoration of God's dealing with them, ver. 6—15.

IV. An exprobration of their great ingratitude in running out from God, and sinning above other nations, ver. 15—35.

V. A commination of grievous judgments, ver. 35—60, wherein also the aggravation of their sins are laid down.

VI. A promise of mercy to restore and establish them, ver. 60, to the end.

Ver. 1. "Again the word of the Lord came unto me, saying." These words are frequent, they show whence he had what he spake, and with what authority he spake, viz. divine authority; and serve for attention, to provoke the sons of men to heed what the prophet delivered.

Ver. 2. "Cause Jerusalem to know her abominations." By Jerusalem, he means the men of Jerusalem; and by abominations, those sins of idolatry, adultery, injustice, &c. which were abominable.

The prophet being in Babylon, how could he cause Jerusalem to know her abominations, his voice would not reach thither?

He might by letters send to Jerusalem, to Jeremiah, or some of the faithful, to make known what a message, what a prophecy he had received from the Lord. Or else, he might give it out in Babylon, where were some that would quickly carry or send tidings thereof unto Jerusalem.

Obs. 1. That a people may be guilty of abominations, and not know nor acknowledge them. Jerusalem was so, and did not know nor acknowledge it; "Cause Jerusalem to know her abominations." Amos iii. 10, "They know not to do right." When men know not what is right, how can they know what is wrong?

They stored up violence and robbery in their palaces, they got wealth by injustice, oppression, laid it up, and thought it well gotten.

They know not God. Jer. ix. 3, "They proceed from evil to evil, and know not me, saith the Lord;" when people know not God, they do evil after evil, and know not that they do evil. "They know not the way of the Lord," Jer. v. 4; therefore their own ways seem good in their eyes. John xvi. 2, "The time cometh, that whosoever killeth you will think he doeth God service:" when men shall murder the saints of Christ, (a crying sin, a great abomination,) they will be so far from knowing or acknowledging it, that they will justify the fact. In Isa. v. 20, you may read what the Jews said of evil; they called "evil good, and good evil; they put darkness for light, and light for darkness; they put bitter for sweet, and sweet for bitter." They set up idols, worshipped the queen of heaven, oppressed in the gates, filled the land with bloody crimes, and yet justified themselves: Jer. vii. 9, "Will ye steal, murder, and commit adultery, and swear falsely, and burn incense unto Baal, and walk after other gods, whom ye know not; and come and stand before me in this house, and say, We are delivered?" we are in no danger, whatever is threatened. They were blinded, and as they knew not their abominations, so they acknowledged them not: Hos. v. 15, "I will go and return to my place, till they acknowledge their offence;" if they did know their doings to be evil, yet they did not acknowledge them to be such evils as in truth they were, they did not profess themselves to be guilty; the Lord therefore puts them upon it, Jer. iii. 13, "Only acknowledge thine iniquity, that thou hast transgressed against the Lord thy God," lay it to heart, and confess it.

Obs. 2. Note, there is an unwillingness, an averseness in sinners to hear of their sins. "Cause Jerusalem to know her abominations;" she is against it, but make her to know them. Jer. xliv. 16, "We will not hearken unto thee;" thou tellest us of sinning, and judgment for sins, but say what thou wilt, "we will not hearken:" Zech. vii. 11, 12, "They refused to hearken, and pulled away the shoulder, and stopped their ears, that they should not hear. Yea, they made their hearts as an adamant stone, lest they should hear the law, and the words which the Lord of hosts hath sent in his Spirit by the former prophets." What averseness was here in this people, to hear of their sins or duty! 2 Chron. xxxvi. 16, "They mocked the messengers of God, and despised his words, and misused his prophets;" they were not only unwilling to hear of their sins, but wilfully add to the heap of their sins, they mock, despise, misuse the prophets, that told them of their mocking, despising, misusing. When Stephen told them of their practices, Acts vii. 51, 52, what followed upon it? "They were cut to the heart, and they gnashed upon him with their teeth; they cried out with a loud voice, and stopped their ears, and ran upon him with one accord, and cast him out of the city, and stoned him," ver. 54, 57, 58: so when Christ told them of their sins, they derided him, Luke xvi. 14; told him he had "a devil," John viii. 48; they "were filled with wrath, and rose up, and thrust him out of the city, and led him unto the brow of the hill, that they might cast him down headlong," Luke iv. 28, 29. And not only wicked men are unwilling to hear of their sins, but even good men also. When God reproved Jonah, "Doest thou well to be angry?" his reply was, "I do well to be angry, even to death;" he thought God did evil in reproving him, that he had more cause to be angry than God had to chide him for his anger. When Hanani the seer came to Asa the king, (who was a godly king,) and told him he had done foolishly in relying upon the king of Assyria, and not upon the Lord, and that therefore he should have wars, "Then Asa was wroth with the seer, and put him in a prison house; for he was in a rage with him because of this thing." Paul was become the Galatians' enemy, because he told them the truth, he told them of their sins. Good men do not easily endure to hear of their faults, and this is that which discourages friends from telling them what they hear, observe, and know, and so through fear they become unfaithful.

Obs. 3. What God commands the prophets and ministers to do, it matters not how it is taken by the people, they are to do it.

Here God commands Ezekiel to cause the people to know the abominations; it was not for him to excuse himself from this service, to object against it, to say they will mock me, despise me, misuse me, hate me, seek my hurt, ruin me; God commanded, and it was his duty to do it, carefully, conscientiously, and faithfully; he must make known their sins to the world, to themselves, let the event be what it will. Isa. lviii. 1, "Cry aloud, spare not, lift up thy voice like a trumpet, and show my people their transgression, and the house of Jacob their sins:" the prophet must not whisper, but cry, and that aloud; it matters not who hears, he must lift up his voice like a trumpet. When men blow trumpets, they do it with all their strength, and the sound of it goeth far; so must the prophets, with extension of their voice, utter the sins of the people, and show them their transgressions, they must represent them fully and earnestly before their eyes, and to their ears. This they must do,

(1.) That others may take warning, and not do as they have done; 1 Tim. v. 20, "Them that sin rebuke before all;" them that sin openly, must be rebuked openly. And why? That others also may fear.

(2.) That they may bring the parties to repentance: Jer. xxiii. 22, "If they had stood in my counsel, and caused my people to hear my words, then they should have turned them from their evil way, and from the evil of their doings."

How shall sinners come to repentance, if they hear not of their sins, if they be not convinced of the sinfulness of them, by the prophets and ministers of God? This was the fault of the false prophets, they hid their sins from them; but the faithful ones must tell them of them.

(3.) That they may deliver their own souls: Ezek. xxxiii. 8, 9, "When I say unto the wicked, O wicked man, thou shalt surely die; if thou dost not speak to warn the wicked from his way, that wicked man shall die in his iniquity; but his blood will I require at thine hand. Nevertheless, if thou warn the wicked to turn from his way, if he turn not, he shall die in his iniquity; but thou hast delivered thy soul."

Obs. 4. The sins of people are abominations in God's account. He calls the sins of Jerusalem "abominations," what his soul loathed and abhorred: Psal. xiv. 1, "They have done abominable works;" Psal. liii. 1, "They have done abominable iniquity." Sins are works, but works of iniquity, abominable works, and abominable iniquity; now, Psal. v. 5, it is said of God, "Thou hatest all workers of iniquity;" if God's hatred be against the workers of iniquity, how great is it against iniquity itself! if a man hate a poisonous creature, he hates poison much more. The strength of God's hatred is against sin, and so should we hate sin, and hate it with strength; it is abomination unto God, let it be so unto us: Prov. vi. 16—19, "These six things doth the Lord hate; yea, seven are an abomination unto him: a proud look, a lying tongue, and hands that shed innocent blood, an heart that deviseth wicked imaginations, feet that be swift in running to mischief, a false witness that speaketh lies, and he that soweth discord among brethren."

Ver. 3. "And say, Thus saith the Lord God unto Jerusalem; Thy birth and thy nativity is of the land of Canaan." The Jews stood much upon their progenitors, and gloried in it that they were descended from Abraham; but they were so degenerated at this time, that the Lord sends the prophet to upbraid them, and tell them, that their birth and nativity was rather of the Canaanites, Amorites, and Hittites, than of Abraham; your ways and doings are such, that you seem rather to be the seed of any impious stock than of Abraham, who was so upright, faithful, and honourable; your works are contrary to his, they are such as the nations' are, and so testify that you are rather of them, than of him.

"Thy birth." The Hebrew is, מכורתיך which Montanus interprets *mansiones tuæ;* the Septuagint is, ἡ ῥίζα σοῦ, thy root; so the Vulgate, *radix tua;* Junius, Piscator, Polanus, have it, *commercia tua,* thy commerce, and trafficking in matters of religion is of Canaan; we have it "birth," which implies, beginning, rise; and all these may stand: Thy birth, habitation, commerce, whatever thou thinkest of thyself, do all declare that thou art of Canaan, of the Amorites and Hittites; thy worship and practices are such, that if any inquire whence thou art, where thou dwellest, whom thou resemblest, they would conclude thou art of, dwellest among, and most like unto, Canaanites, Hittites, Amorites.

This is truth, but some further thing the prophet seems to aim at here, viz. their condition before the Lord took them to be his people. And what were they then? no better than other nations, barbarous, idolatrous, like the Canaanites, &c.; and so the word מכורתיך may import, for some of the learned derive it from כור which is to dig and cut out; Isa. li. 1, "Look unto the rock whence ye are hewn, and to the hole of the pit whence ye are digged."

"Thy nativity." Hebrew is, מולדותיך *natales tui*, thy nativities or birth-days. It is plural, to signify their descent of both parents, that they were by father and mother of the Canaanites. They drew their pedigree from Abraham and Sarah, who were Chaldeans, Gen. xi. 31, but no better than the rest of other nations, till God pleased to call them, and distinguish them from others: Josh. xxiv. 2, "They served other gods," they and their fathers.

"Of the land of Canaan." Some understand Egypt here the land of Canaan, because the Jews had long lived in Egypt, which is called the land of Ham, or Cham, Psal. cv. 27; but Egypt was not Canaan. Canaan was a country in Asia the Less, so called from Canaan, the son of Ham, Gen. x. 6, 18, 19, possessed by him and his sons.

Now Canaan was cursed by Noah; Gen. ix. 25, "Cursed be Canaan; a servant of servants shall he be;" that is, extremely vile and base: from him came the Canaanites, a cursed race; they were so wicked, that Abraham caused his servant to swear he would not take a wife unto his son of the daughters of the Canaanites, Gen. xxiv. 3. They were given to such abominable sins, as that the land vomited them out, Lev. xviii. 25; and when the Israelites came to possess Canaan, they were so hateful to God, that he charged his people utterly to destroy them; Deut. vii. 2, "Thou shalt smite them, and utterly destroy them; thou shalt make no covenant with them, nor show mercy unto them;" ver. 16, "Thine eye shall have no pity upon them:" they had all abominations amongst them.

"Thy father was an Amorite." The Amorites were of Canaan, the son of Ham, Gen. x. 15, 16, and they were as wicked as the Canaanites. Gen. xv. 16, "The iniquity of the Amorites is not yet full." Their iniquities were very great, only God waited for the completing thereof, before he would destroy them; they were great idolaters, oppressors, made incestuous marriages, and Ahab, one of the most wicked kings that ever was, is compared to the Amorites; 1 Kings xxi. 26, "He did very abominably in following idols, according to all things as did the Amorites, whom the Lord cast out before the children of Israel." They were bitter enemies unto the Israelites, and would not let them pass through their country, Numb. xxi. 23, but fought with them; they forced the children of Dan into the mountain, Judg. i. 34. They were a people potent, and dreadful to the Jews, for, Amos ii. 9, it is said of them, that their "height was like the height of the cedars, and they were strong as the oaks;" they were a giant-like people, and as they exceeded in height and strength, so they exceeded in wickedness, and therefore God destroyed his fruit from above, and his root from beneath.

"Thy mother an Hittite." חתית *Chittith.* The Cethites, or Hittites, were of the same stock the Amorites were, viz. from Ham and Canaan; Gen. x. 15, Heth is said to be the son of Canaan, and from him sprung up the Cethites, or Hittites, as they are called, Gen. xv. 20. What kind of people these were, you may judge by profane Esau, who took two wives from among the Hittites, which were a continual grief to Isaac and Rebekah, Gen. xxvi. 34, 35; yea, such an affliction to Rebekah, that she said, "I am weary of my life, because of the daughters of Heth," chap. xxvii. 46. They were contentious, stubborn, and idolatrous, as the Greek, Chaldee, and the Targum observe; and when the charge is given to the Israelites to destroy the nations, the Hittites are mentioned first, Deut. xx. 17.

You see what the Canaanites, Amorites, and Hittites were, exceeding wicked; and the Jews which were at Jerusalem were so degenerate, that they were as if they dwelt amidst Canaanites, and were the offspring of cursed Amorites and Hittites: 2 Kings xxi. 9, it is said of them, that they did "more evil than the nations whom the Lord destroyed;" he means the Canaanites, Amorites, and Hittites, as appears by what follows, ver. 11, Manasseh did "wickedly above all that the Amorites did, which were before him."

Obs. 1. The Lord judges and pronounces otherwise of sinners than they do of themselves. The Jews thought themselves better than other nations, they called them *goijm*, nations, gentiles, by way of disgrace; they thought themselves the holy seed, the children of Abraham, an honourable and blessed people, but God thought and pronounced otherwise: he tells them they are Canaanites: What! you Abrahamites? no, you are Amorites; what! you Israelites? you are Hittites, as bad as the worst of nations. They thought themselves children of God, in high favour with him, the true church, whereas they were abhorred of God, and an apostatized church; Rev. ii. 9, they said they were Jews, when they were the synagogue of Satan. Ephraim said, "In all my labours they shall find none iniquity in me that were sin;" but God found "the balances of deceit in his hand," Hosea xii. 7, 8.

Obs. 2. Men are their children, whose ways, manners, and example, they follow. Jerusalem imitated the nations in their worship, fashions, practices, and she is the child of an Amorite, of an Hittite, and her citizens imitated their impiety, they contracted kindred with them, and obtained inheritance with them, as the fathers comment on the words. Orig. Jerom, Theodor.

When men live according to the courses, natures, manners of others, they are styled their sons, or children, and they be their fathers: John viii. 44, "Ye are of your father the devil, and the lusts of your father ye will do. He was a murderer from the beginning, and abode not in the truth;" so you abide not in the truth, you seek to kill me; and herein you resemble the devil, and he is your father. If Abraham were your father, as you pretend, "ye would do the works of Abraham," ver. 39; "If God were your Father, you would love me," ver. 42. The Father loves me, honours me, and, if you were his children, you would do so too; but you hate me and my doctrine, lie in wait to murder me, "ye are of your father the devil." Christ calls the scribes and Pharisees "a generation of vipers," they were so bitter, cruel, of such a bloody and persecuting nature.

When Elymas the sorcerer would have hindered the conversion of Sergius Paulus, the apostle told him he was "the child of the devil," Acts xiii. 10; his works, ways, were such as the devil's were, and therefore the devil was his father. In Isa. lvii. 3, God calls the Jews "sons of the sorceress, the seed of the adulterer and the whore," because they did such things as sorceresses, adulterers, and whores use to do: chap. i. 10, he calls them "rulers of Sodom," and "people of Gomorrah;" they so livelily represented their natures and practices, that they seemed to be of them, and justly deserved those titles.

Let us look to it whose ways we take up. If we imitate the world, we are children of the world; if Rome, Babylon, we are their children. The church of Rome boasts that her birth is from the apostle, that Peter, Paul laid her foundation; but doth she embrace their doctrine, imitate their examples? no, she is like the nations for her idolatry, superstition, whoredom, deceit, pomp, pride, &c. therefore her father is an Amorite, and her mother an Hittite. We say we are of Christ, but are we like unto Christ in our worship and lives?

Obs. 3. All are not godly who spring from godly parents, families, and have a name to be godly. The Jews, they came out of the loins of Abraham, Isaac, and Jacob, the best families that were then in the world, they of all people were counted the holy and godly people; but grace is not hereditary. You see here they were so wicked, that God reckons them among Canaanites, Amorites, &c.; they were as bad as any of the nations, yea worse; Ezek. v. 6, Jerusalem "hath changed my judgments into wickedness more than the nations, and my statutes more than the countries that are round about her." You see it made good, what Paul said, Rom. ix. 6, 7, "They are not all Israel, which are of Israel; neither, because they are the seed of Abraham, are they all children:" they were all Israelites, and the seed of Abraham, after the flesh, but they were not the children of God, they were of the land of Canaan, &c. Judge not thou from such external things, for, Rom. ii. 28, 29, "He is not a Jew, which is one outwardly; neither is that circumcision, which is outward in the flesh: but he is a Jew, which is one inwardly; and circumcision is that of the heart, in the spirit, and not in the letter; whose praise is not of men, but of God."

Obs. 4. When the Lord takes in any to be his people, they were like others, no better than they.

Ver. 4, 5. *And as for thy nativity, in the day thou wast born thy navel was not cut, neither wast thou washed in water to supple thee; thou wast not salted at all, nor swaddled at all. None eye pitied thee, to do any of these unto thee, to have compassion upon thee; but thou wast cast out in the open field, to the lothing of thy person, in the day that thou wast born.*

This chapter is a continued allegory, setting forth the state of the Jewish church, under the consideration of a woman in her birth, education, marriage, adultery, repudiation, and re-entertainment.

Something in the last exercise was said touching the nativity of the Jews, that they were of the Amorites and Hittites. Now to go on:

"In the day thou wast born." When to begin the birth of the Israelitish nation is inquirable; our prophet speaks of it in the person of a woman, and saith, "In the day thou wast born."

Some make her birth-day to be, the calling of Abraham out of Chaldea, and entering into covenant with him, to bless him, to be a God to him, and his seed.

The infancy and youth of this woman, or Jewish estate, was from the time of Jacob's going into Egypt, till they were led out by Moses; her grown estate, the time of the judges and kings; and her old age, from the time of the Babylonish captivity to Christ.

Others make the birth-day of this nation to be their going out of Egypt, when they were freed from their rigorous bondage there; but to this opinion I cannot cast in my approbation, because it was the time of this woman's youth, not her birth, and so the Scripture sets it out; Jer. ii. 2, "I remember thee, the kindness of thy youth, the love of thine espousals, when thou wentest after me in the wilderness;" and, Hosea ii. 15, the days of her youth, and of her coming up out of the land of Egypt, are the same; and presently after, God espoused this people unto himself.

Some take this birth-day to be the time of Jacob's going into Egypt with seventy souls. But this is forced, and suits not with what follows in ver. 5, where it is said, "none eye pitied thee, but thou wast cast out," &c. Jacob and his were received honourably by Pharaoh and the Egyptians, and greatly regarded for Joseph's sake.

Pradus makes the birth-day to be the time after Joseph's death, when another king rose up which knew not Joseph, but oppressed the Jews; from which time it is said, Exod. i. 7, "The children of Israel were fruitful, and increased abundantly, and multiplied, and waxed exceeding mighty; and the land was filled with them:" but to me their birth-day must needs be long before, take it literally or spiritually. A people must be born, have their being, before they can increase and multiply, and they were the Lord's people before this day. This birth-day I know not how we can begin it at any other time, than when the Lord called Abraham: Gen. xii. 1, 2, the Lord said unto him, "Get thee out of thy country, and from thy kindred, and from thy father's house, unto a land that I will show thee; and I will make of thee a great nation, and I will bless thee, and make thy name great;" and afterwards he told him his seed should be as the stars of heaven, Gen. xv. 5; as the dust upon the earth, chap. xiii. 16; "and as the sand which is upon the sea-shore," chap. xxii. 17. Hence is it that Abraham is called their father, Josh. xxiv. 3, "I took your father Abraham from the other side of the flood." We may include all the time, from God's calling Abraham to their going out of Egypt, to be their birth-time.

"Thy navel was not cut." Hebrew is, שרך from שרר with a double *resh*, which Aben Esra saith is so called *a firmitate*, for שריר is *firmum*, and the navel is that which gives strength to the child, from שורה *principale*, because it is the principal thing whereby the child is supported in the womb.

As a tree by the roots is fastened to the earth, and by the fibres, the little strings upon them, draws nourishment and spirits from the earth, so is it with a child in the womb; the navel fastens it to the mother, and by the veins and arteries in the navel, it fetches in nourishment and spirits.

For the meaning of the words,

1. It may be this: look as a child by the navel draws life, spirits, and nourishment from the mother, so did the Israelitish estate draw from the nations, that were her parents, Amorites, Hittites, Chaldeans, Egyptians, the life, spirit, and nourishment of several impieties. Rachel had her father's idols, and in Egypt they learned the manners, fashions, and worship of the Egyptians, they were not separate from idols, but drew thence the grounds of their idolatry.

2. It points out the miserable condition of this people at first. A child whose navel is not cut, must needs perish, be a dead child; so here, Thy navel was not cut, thou wast in a lost and desperate condition. Abraham was an idolater when the Lord took him; Psal. cvi. 7, "Our fathers understood not thy wonders in Egypt;" they were an ignorant, perverse, superstitious people.

"Neither wast thou washed in water to supple thee." When an infant is born, first the navel is cut, and then they use to wash it with warm water,

1. To cleanse it from that filth which adheres to the body of it.

2. For safety, that sickness may be prevented.

3. For sightliness, that its appearance may be more agreeable.

We have it, "to supple thee," למשעי that thou shouldst be lenified. The joints and parts may have some stiffness in them, it is usual, therefore, to mix butter, or oil, with the water they wash them in, that so their limbs may be tractable: but surely the flesh of infants, their bodies and bones, are very tender things, and do rather stand in need of consolidating than of suppling. I conceive, therefore, it were better translated, Thou wast not washed in water to my sight, or when I looked upon thee; thou hadst those pollutions, corruptions adhering to thee, which made thee unlovely, unsightly. Acts ix. 37, they washed the body of Dorcas, and laid it in an upper chamber. It was their use to wash at deaths and births.

"Thou wast not salted at all." It seems, in ancient days, it was the custom, after washing, to salt their infants, or to mingle salt with the water in which they washed them. We read nothing of this practice but only in this place.

That which the prophet hereby leads us unto, is, that this people had no heavenly wisdom, no fear of God, no true grace, no salt to cure their wounds, to keep them from putrefying, but abounded in noisome humours, were altogether weak and feeble.

"Nor swaddled at all." Hebrew is, החתל לא חתלת In swaddling thou wast not swaddled. Children are swaddled to strengthen their bodies, and to keep their limbs straight: Luke ii. 7, Christ was wrapped in swaddling clothes; and it is given as a reason why the bodies of barbarians were straighter than the bodies of the Romans, because they kept their children swaddled two or three years. Hereby is set out how destitute of all help this people were.

Ver. 5. "None eye pitied thee, to do any of these unto thee." Here the contemptible condition of this metaphorical infant is set out in three things:

1. That none eye pitied, or had compassion on her, to do aught for her. It is something, in misery, to be pitied, but to have none to pity, all to be without compassion, is sad.

2. That she was "cast out," not into some by or secret place, but into "the open field."

3. Her person was loathed.

"None eye pitied thee." Hebrew is, לא חסה, Eye hath not spared upon thee, the eye of man hath not looked after thee, hath not had pity on thee, no human eye; and the word חוס signifies, to pity, as well as, to spare; and this must be the sense, as these following words do show:

"To do any of these things unto thee." What things? To cut her navel, to wash her, to salt her, or swaddle her; these seemed no great things, of small moment, yet there was none found to do any of these. If some one had cut her navel, another washed her, a third salted her, &c. it had been some comfort; but she was so vile, sordid, contemptible, that none eye minded her, was moved to do aught for her, or show her the least compassion or kindness.

The words for pity and compassion were opened, chap. v. 11.

"But thou wast cast into the open field." It was a custom among the heathens, if they were poor, and could not bring up their children, or if the children were deformed, to carry them forth and lay them in the fields, if they did not otherwise make them away; and these children were called, *Liberi expositii*. This was so common a practice, that the Thebans made a severe law against it, that whoever exposed their infants in the woods or fields, should suffer for it. It is reported of the Japonians, that those of them who are not able to maintain their children, do usually make them away, especially if they be females, looking upon them as burdensome, and less useful. There is provision in some countries to prevent the untimely death of feeble children; they are looked after, and taken into houses appointed for their preservation. The Jews were free from this sin above all others, for it is said of them, never was an infant born among the Jews exposed; yet the Jewish state was as an infant cast out.

Now you know, when a little infant is cast out into the woods, or fields, it must needs perish, either by hunger, injury of weather, fowls of heaven, beasts of the field, or some vermin, if it be not taken up. Moses was cast out, and had perished in the ark among flags, if he had not been taken up.

Some divine this to be meant of the casting out of the Hebrew children to their destruction; others put it upon the time of their making brick and clay in the fields.

"In the open field." Hebrew is, In the faces of the field. The Hebrew call the outside or superficies of things, their faces, as, "the face of the deep," "face of the waters," Gen. i. 2; so here, the face of the field, and here rendered "open."

"To the loathing of thy person." Hebrew is, בגעל נפשך In the casting away of thy person.

The task-masters oppressed the Jews, their children were cast into the rivers, Pharaoh and others plotted their ruin, and there was none to pity, to help; but they were as a child cast out, to the loathing of their persons.

Obs. The miserable estate of man by nature, both Jew and gentile; for what is said here of the Israelites is true of all mankind, and is here implied; for if the Jew had no privilege, what must the gentile have? Man's condition by nature is very deplorable.

I shall give you it out, as it lies couched in this similitude of an infant new-born.

1. Man naturally is not cut off from the old stock, (as the infant's navel was not cut,) but draws life, spirits, nutriment from it; every man's father naturally is an Amorite and his mother an Hittite, and look what way they walk in, the same doth the child. Adam was of the earth, earthy, and savoured of the earth; so do all his children. Thou hast a navel about thee, carnal desire, which sucks nutriment from the womb and paps of the creature; their navels are fastened to the earth, which is their mother, thence they suck their nutriment; hence the church, Psal. xlv. 10, is bid to forget her own people, and her father's house.

2. Naturally, man is filthy, void of all beauty and comeliness. "Thou wast not washed with water." Washing supposes defilement; Psa. li. 5, "I was shapen in iniquity; and in sin did my mother conceive me," warm me; John iii. 6, "That which is born of the flesh is flesh;" Psal. xiv. 3, "They are altogether become filthy." There is some natural defilement adheres to a child newly born, but there is much spiritual defilement.

3. He is stiff in wickedness, he hath nothing to supple him; Psal. lxxviii. 8, "A stubborn and rebellious generation."

4. Man corrupts in his natural condition more and more. He abounds in ill humours, his thoughts are evil only and continually, his affections are inordinate, Col. iii. 5; wicked men grow "worse and worse," 2 Tim. iii. 13, they putrefy in that state. "Thou wast not salted at all." It is salt that preserves from

putrefaction; now man, by nature, having no salt, must needs grow more and more unsavoury. Naturally, men are not salted with the fire of the Spirit, or any spark of that fire, with any grace, with any divine truth.

5. Man is naked in his natural estate. "Thou wast not swaddled." An infant not swaddled, lies naked, sprawling, and is a miserable object. Man, since the fall, is naked, without God, and is not ashamed of his condition; Jer. iii. 3, "Thou hast a whore's forehead, thou refusest to be ashamed:" he is not clothed with humility, hath not put on the armour of God, the robe of righteousness, but is impotent, weak, and cannot help himself. A child new-born, how feeble is it! it cannot think of aught for its own good, it cannot speak a word for itself, it cannot go or do any thing that may advantage it: such is man in his natural condition; 2 Cor. iii. 5, we are not "sufficient of ourselves to think any thing," that is good, "as of ourselves;" Matt. xii. 34, "How can ye, being evil, speak good things?"

Nor can he do good; Rom. iii. 12, "There is none that doeth good, no, not one;" Matt. vii. 16, grapes do not grow upon thorns, nor figs upon thistles; he that is flesh, in the flesh, cannot please God, Rom. viii. 8. Here is his misery, he that was made at the first to serve God and please him, cannot now serve or please him at all; he is so impotent, that he is not able to receive good when it is presented unto him; 1 Cor. ii. 14, "The natural man receiveth not the things of the Spirit of God;" no, he is so far from entertaining of them, that he refuses them. Luke xiv. 16, when the great supper was made, many invited, and all things ready, what did they? they all made excuses, and refused to come, ver. 18—20.

An infant kicks, sprawls, and opposes its own good; so doth man naturally; Rom. i. 30, they hated God; John xv. 24, they hated Christ and his Father; Acts vii. 51, they do always resist the Holy Spirit.

6. Man in his natural estate is in a helpless condition, there is none can do him good. "None eye pitied thee, to do any of these unto thee, to have compassion upon thee;" none had any bowels to pity, or power to do for this child. And who pities, or hath power to do for men in their natural estates? All men are in the same condition, they cannot help themselves; other creatures are enemies to man since his fall. Angels have not power to cut the navel of a natural man, to wash him, salt him, swaddle him. Did either priest or Levite pity or help the man that went from Jerusalem to Jericho, when he fell amongst thieves, and was left half dead? Who pitied Abraham when he was in Ur of Chaldea?

7. Man in his natural estate is cast out, an exposed infant. "Thou wast cast out in the open field." Adam, and all in him, were cast out of paradise, a type of heaven, into the open field of the world; so that he hath no habitation, but is a vagabond upon the face of the earth, an excommunicate person. Moses could say, Psal. xc. 1, "Lord, thou hast been our dwelling-place in all generations."

8. He lies senseless in that condition, and perishes in it. The infant cast out is not sensible of that estate, lies obvious to a thousand dangers, and perishes, if not taken up.

9. Man in his natural estate is loathsome. This infant was cast out to the loathing of her person; when men saw her, they were so far from pitying her, they loathed her: and a man, in his natural estate, is so full of sin that he is abominable; his prayers and sacrifice are abomination, and what then is himself?

Lastly, this was in the day of birth, no sooner born but miserable, extremely miserable, either still-born, or devoted to death immediately. It is reported of the Indians and Brahmins, that after birth about two months, some are appointed to view their children, and if they be not likely to prove sound, strong, useful to the state, they make them away; so that these children were of all unhappy, because they were born, not to live, but to be murdered, according to that in Hosea ix. 13, Ephraim brought forth children to the murderer. And it was once an order amongst the Romans, to put children, supposed to become a burden to the commonwealth rather than advantage, to death the same day and hour they were born; a great misery. Jerusalem, in the day of her birth, was cast out, exposed to all misery.

Ver. 6. *And when I passed by thee, and saw thee polluted in thine own blood, I said unto thee when thou wast in thy blood, Live; yea, I said unto thee when thou wast in thy blood, Live.*

We are now at the third general part of the chapter, the commemoration of God's dealing with this Israelitish metaphorical infant. When none pitied her, but she was cast out, loathed, in a perishing condition, the Lord himself had compassion, and bestowed choice mercies on her, which are expressed in the ensuing verse to the 15th.

I. Is life, in ver. 6.

II. Is increase, growth, in ver. 7.

III. Is spiritual marriage, ver. 8.

IV. Spiritual washing, and cleansing and anointing, ver. 9.

V. Costly provisions of divers sorts for ornament, clothing, and delight for back and belly, ver. 10—13.

VI. Royal dignity, ver. 13.

VII. Great fame and glory, ver. 14.

"When I passed by thee." God is immutable, and immovable, he goes not from place to place. It is spoken after the manner of men, as if God, like some great man, were upon a journey, and in the way should spy a poor infant thrown out naked under a hedge, ready to perish, and should take pity on it; so did God towards this Israelitish infant. This passing by refers to the time of God's calling Abraham out of Ur of Chaldea; Gen. xii. 1, "The Lord said unto Abraham, Get thee out of my country;" and to their condition in Egypt; Exod. xii. 12, "I will pass through the land of Egypt this night."

This act of God's passing by this Israelitish infant, seems casual and accidental, but it was nothing so; for known unto God are all his works and creatures, and he doth nothing but upon foreknowledge and counsel; he knew in what case this infant was, where and how she lay. The expression of it in that manner, is to set out the extreme misery she lay in, that there was none she could look for in heaven or earth to show pity, and do for her.

"And saw thee polluted in thine own blood." We must let you understand what is meant by "blood." Some judge it to be the red earth, whereof they made their brick, which looked like blood; and that God pitied them when they were so put to it by their task-masters, and were near ruin by their hard labour, God passed by them, and beheld them in that condition.

But others by "blood" do understand that inbred corruption which is in man, and estate it hath put him into; he is without all spiritual good, full of all sin, in a miserable, helpless condition. A Lapide expounds it mystically of original sin, which is that innate and inherent corruption which is in man.

"Blood" doth in Scripture set out the corrupt

nature of man; as Matt. xvi. 17, "Flesh and blood hath not revealed it unto thee;" corrupt nature was never able to attain unto it; so Gal. i. 16; 1 Cor. xv. 50. Sin being set out by "blood" in Scripture, we must consider the resemblances.

1. Blood is natural; so sin; Psal. li. 5, "I was shapen in iniquity, and in sin did my mother conceive me." Corruption is hereditary, as chaff with wheat, bark with the tree; sense is not more natural than sin.

2. Blood diffuseth itself through the whole man; so doth sin; it is not in some one part, but in every part. As in the sea, all parts of it are brackish; in wormwood, every part is bitter; so in man there is sin in every part: in the heart, Matt. xv. 19; in the mind, Eph. iv. 17, they "walked in the vanity of their mind;" in the will, Matt. xxiii. 37, How oft would I have gathered you, and you would not; in the understanding, Eph. iv. 18, "Having the understanding darkened;" in the conscience, Heb. ix. 14; in the memory, Heb. ii. 1, that is unfaithful, and let things slip; in the eyes, 2 Pet. ii. 14, they had eyes full of adultery; in the tongue, James iii. 6, "It defileth the whole body, and setteth on fire the course of nature;" in the throat, Rom. iii. 13, "It is an open sepulchre;" in the hands, Isa. i. 15, they "are full of blood;" in the feet, Rom. iii. 15, they "are swift to shed blood."

3. Blood defileth; Psal. cvi. 38, "The land was polluted with blood;" and sin pollutes, yea, it is pollution: 2 Cor. vii. 1, let us cleanse ourselves from all pollution of flesh and spirit: 1 Thess. v. 23, he prays that they may be sanctified wholly: Psal. xiv. 3, man is altogether become filthy.

4. Loathsome. Sin is such; Prov. xiii. 5, a wicked man is loathsome, his sin makes him to be loathed; Job xlii. 6, "I abhor myself." See ver. 5, "To the loathing of thy person."

"I said unto thee when thou wast in thy blood, Live." There is some difference about the reading of these words. The Hebrew runs thus, I said unto thee, (and there makes the stop,) In thy blood live; "when thou wast" is not in the original. Others read it thus, I said unto thee in thy blood, (and there make the stop,) Live, I saw thee in thy blood, and said unto thee in that condition, Live.

The most interpreters do follow the Hebrew, and render it, *in sanguine tuo vive*, or, *in sanguinibus tuis vive;* not as if so be God would leave this infant in her sinful or afflicted condition still, Thou art cast into a miserable condition, and that thou shalt continue in; the scope of the place prohibits credit to such a sense of the words. We may take the words therefore strictly according to the Hebrew, in thy blood live; in thy blood live; that is, Thou art now in thy blood, in a polluted, loathsome condition thou shalt live, I will give thee life.

In the Hebrew, an imperative is put for a future sometimes, and notes power, efficacy: Deut. xxxii. 49, 50, Get thee up into the mount, and die in the mount; there is an imperative put for a future, and it notes power, I will cause thee to die in the mount; so in this place, "Live," I will cause thee to live: and so it hath the nature of a promise, and carries thus much with it, Though thou be in great affliction, yet thou shalt live, I will uphold thee in thy afflictions, they shall not sink thee; though thou be in thy natural and sinful condition, dead, yet thou shalt live, thy sins shall not undo thee.

"Live." What life is here meant? Some look no further than a natural or political life, that God preserved them, and made then prosper into a kingdom; and the ground of this interpretation is, their referring of the words to their being in Egypt, under sad afflictions, in which God preserved them, out of which he brought them, and caused them to grow into a political body. They were there in bondage, (which was a kind of death, as the Jews were said to be in their graves in Babylon,) and yet, by the hand of God, preserved and freed, which is called life.

But surely we are to look further than a natural, metaphorical, political life. We must take in a spiritual life here; and that will not be forced, if we refer the words to Abraham's call, when their birth-day began; God found him in his blood, and the life he bestowed on him was spiritual; a life of faith, for he was the father of the faithful; a life of holiness, for he walked before God, and was upright.

Obs. 1. God lets men lie in their blood as long as he pleases. Take blood for affliction, or man's natural condition; in either of these, men lie the Lord's pleasure. God passed not by presently; they lay in an afflicted condition in Egypt two hundred years and more, before the Lord appeared, and led them forth; they lay seventy years in Babylon before deliverance came; the two witnesses must prophesy twelve hundred and sixty days in sackcloth, Rev. xi. 3; the Jews have been now sixteen hundred years in an afflicted, tossed condition, and the Lord hath not appeared unto them. So for man's natural condition: Abraham was seventy-five years old when God spake to him, called him out of his country, and sinful condition, Gen. xii. 4; the gentiles laid in their blood, in their blindness, unbelief, impenitence, idolatries, profaneness, some thousands of years, before the Lord granted them repentance unto life, ere he passed by them, and called them; Nicodemus was a doctor in Israel, before the Lord let him know the nature of regeneration.

Obs. 2. The Lord takes notice of men in what condition they are, and lie in. "I saw thee polluted in thine own blood." He saw Abraham in his idolatry, heathenism; he saw the Jews making brick of red earth, in the house of bondage; there is no sinful, afflicted condition that any are in, but the Lord takes notice of it. When Adam hid himself in the bush, the eye of the Lord was upon him, and he saw in what a condition he was, and all mankind in him, all sinful and sinners, all blood and bloody: Gen. vi. 5, "God saw that the wickedness of man was great in the earth, and that every imagination of the thoughts of his heart was only evil continually;" he knew what a race came out of Adam's loins. Christ knew Jerusalem's condition, that she lay in her blood, when he said, "O Jerusalem, Jerusalem, how oft would I," &c. Matt. xxiii.; Luke xiii. So for Israel in her affliction; 2 Kings xiv. 26, "The Lord saw the affliction of Israel, that it was very bitter." God takes special notice of the conditions men are in, and not only so, but visits them in those conditions; "I passed by thee, and saw thee polluted in thine own blood," &c.

Obs. 3. Jerusalem, the church of God, in its primitive and natural consideration, was in a state of death. "I said unto thee, Live." Neither Abraham, nor any of his seed by nature, had any spiritual life in them, he and all his were dead in sins and trespasses; they were idolaters, unbelievers, under the power of sin; "guilty before God," Rom. iii. 19; "concluded under sin," Gal. iii. 22; they lay in their blood without life. And this is the condition of every man by nature, though he hath a natural life, yet he is morally dead. Matt. viii. 22, "Let the dead bury their dead;" let those who were dead morally, bury those who were dead naturally.

The whole world is dead. John vi. 51, Christ saith, he will give his flesh "for the life of the world;" it was dead before, and he brought life to it, therefore he is said to abolish death, to bring "life and immortality to light," 2 Tim. i. 10. But the world is not quickened, it hath not received life, it lies in wickedness, 1 John v. 19, and the members of it are dead; 1 Tim. v. 6, the widow "that liveth in pleasure is dead while she liveth;" and Luke xv. 24, "This my son was dead, and is alive;" whilst he lived in sinful courses, he was dead.

Obs. 4. God is the Author of life. He is the living God, and gives life, all life is in him and from him: he breathed into Adam the breath of life; he caused the spirit of life to enter into the witnesses after they were slain; he gave life to this dying infant; Abraham had his spiritual life from him; so hath the true church, and every member thereof.

(1.) There is a life of righteousness or justification, which lies in the remission of sin, the removal of the guilt, and deliverance from the curse of the law due to it, and acceptation of our persons unto favour; and this life is from God, and is called the life of faith, Hab. ii. 4; Heb. x. 38; "justification of life," Rom. v. 18, and this is of God; Col. ii. 13, "You, being dead in your sins and the uncircumcision of your flesh, hath he quickened together with him, having forgiven you all trespasses;" and Eph. i. 6, "He hath made us accepted in the beloved."

(2.) There is a life of holiness; 1 John iii. 3, he "that hath this hope purifieth himself, even as he is pure;" see Rom. vi. 11, 13, 19; Eph. iv. 24; which lies in conformity to the will of God, and walking as Christ walked; and this life is of God, "for we are his workmanship, created in Christ Jesus unto good works," Eph. ii. 10.

(3.) The life of glory, which consists in that happiness the saints have in the enjoyment of God in the heavens; and this God is author of, therefore is called "the Father of glory," Eph. i. 17; and is said to bring many sons to glory, Heb. ii. 10; and to call "us unto his eternal glory," 1 Pet. v. 10.

Obs. 5. There is nothing in the creature to move God to show mercy. "When thou wast in thy blood," in thy sin, "I said unto thee, Live." God saw nothing to incline or move him to do aught, or bestow aught, upon this infant. He saw no dispositions or qualifications in Adam or Abraham, when he spake to them and called them. Adam was the greatest malefactor that ever was amongst men, he destroyed the whole world at once; Abraham was amongst idolaters and idolatrous; yet God set his heart upon them, showed them mercy, said unto them, Live. Adam had no repentance, Abraham no holiness; there were no previous dispositions, neither could they, being "flesh," John iii. 6, being "dead," Eph. ii. 1, prepare themselves for mercy. If men could by themselves, or others, be fitted for mercy, then they should be in a middle condition, between a dead man and a living man, a natural man and a spiritual man, an ungodly man and a godly; but the Scripture acknowledgeth no such middle condition; whatever men have in them, they are one of those two, and if they be dead men, they are not nearer life by all they can do; Rom. ix. 16, "It is not of him that willeth," &c. There is nothing can have influence into the will of God; whatever he doth, is free.

There are several things which move men.

(1.) Birth and progeny. Royal and noble births have affected many; David was taken with Saul's daughter, 1 Sam. xviii. 17, 18; this moves not God, he "poureth contempt upon princes," Job xii. 21; he chooseth the poor to be rich in faith, James ii. 5. Believers are said to be "born, not of blood," John i. 13, which some refer to families of noble and royal blood; and, 1 Cor. i. 26, "Not many noble."

(2.) Beauty. Jacob was affected with the beauty of Rachel; Ahasuerus with the beauty of Vashti, Esth. i. 11. God is not moved with beauty; if we had it, there is nothing in man to affect his eye; Psal. xiv. 3, we are altogether filthy; and God saw them in their blood.

(3.) Natural parts prevail much with men. Ahithophel his counsel took much with David and Absalom; Joseph, Daniel, had excellent spirits, great wisdom, and they were advanced thereupon. Learning is persuasive, and conquers many, but parts and learning can do nothing with God: 1 Cor. i. 26, "Not many wise men after the flesh;" ver. 20, "Where is the wise? where is the scribe? where is the disputer of this world? hath not God made foolish the wisdom of this world? for after that in the wisdom of God the world by wisdom knew," &c.; Matt. xi. 25, "I thank thee, O Father, Lord of heaven and earth, because thou hast hid these things from the wise and prudent, and hast revealed them unto babes."

(4.) Profitableness, serviceableness. So Paul persuades Philemon to take Onesimus, because he would be profitable unto him. Men are taken with men, because they bring in gain unto them; it is not so with the Lord, he is not profited by the righteousness of men, Job xxxv. 7; he receives nothing at any man's hands, and when we have done all, we are unprofitable servants, we have meat, drink, wages, from him, and do all for ourselves.

(5.) Necessity moves mightily. It caused Abiathar to give the shew-bread to David, 1 Sam. xxi. 6; the necessity of the church moved the rich to sell their lands and goods to distribute unto every man as they had need, Acts ii. 45. This is no motive unto divine Majesty: the greatest part of the world lie in blindness, darkness, and they must perish without the means of grace, and God doth not vouchsafe it unto them.

(6.) Entreaty, that hath a great prevalency. Luke xi. 5, 8, when a man came to his friend to borrow bread of him at midnight, and used entreaties, importunity, he got what he desired; but let men pray that are in their blood, and it moves not God: Prov. xv. 8, "The sacrifice of the wicked is an abomination unto the Lord; Jer. xi. 14, and xiv. 12, God tells them that, when they pray, fast, cry, offer sacrifice, he will not hear, nor accept them; "The desire of the wicked shall perish," Psal. cxii. 10.

(7.) Hope of proving well draws forth men to do much; parents for children, and men for others; they conjecture that they may become instrumental to church, state, and to God's glory in both. The Lord that knows all, sees nothing that will make him prove well; he knows every man will run the wrong way, if he do not prevent, infuse, change and alter nature; Jer. iii. 5, they spake and did evil things as they could. There is nothing in the creature to move God to do for it; not foreseen works, faith, use of free will, perseverance. God doth bestow his favour where there is nothing to invite: "When I saw thee polluted in thy blood, I said unto thee, Live;" not when I saw thee washed out of thy blood, cleansed and well qualified; not when I saw thee penitent, believing, obedient; but when I saw thee in thy blood, in the worst condition of all. As nothing can incline God, so nothing can hinder God, from showing mercy; Rom. ix. 15, "I will have mercy on whom I will have mercy," &c. God will give gifts to Christ for the rebellious, and dwell among them, Psal. lxviii. 18. How rebellious was Manasseh! how did he sin against heaven and earth! yet God had a gift for him, life for him. Mary Magdalene,

Zaccheus, Christ said to them, Live, when they were in their blood. Paul, when he was a blasphemer, persecutor, an injurious person, he showed mercy to him, and bade him live. These were his preparations to grace and mercy; he knew that legal acts could not dispose him or others to receive grace, and therefore concludes, Rom. iii. 28, that a man is justified without the deeds of the law.

(8.) Nothing in the godly moves God, all they do is debt; Luke xvii. 10, when they had done all, it was but their duty. Besides, the will and deed are of the Lord; Phil. ii. 13, he works in us "to will and to do of his good pleasure," and his dispensations of grace and mercy are not according to our wills, dispositions, qualifications, but according to the good pleasure of his own will; 2 Tim. i. 9, he saves and calls, "not according to our works, but according to his own purpose."

Obs. 6. God doth all freely, and nothing can hinder the work of free grace. "When I passed by thee, and saw thee in thine own blood, I said unto thee, Live;" when there was nothing to move in the creature, there was much in God to move him to show compassion. The principle that sets him on work, is in himself, and that is his *εὐδοκία*, Matt. xi. 26, his good pleasure; *προθεσὶς*, Rom. ix. 11, his purpose; *βουλη του θελήματος αὐτοῦ*, Eph. i. 11, "the counsel of his will." The motive being within God, all he doth is free favour, mere mercy; if you will search from God's beginning with man, to his end, you shall find all to be of free grace and favour. Predestination and election are so, Rom. xi. 5; God hath chosen the foolish, weak, and base things of the world, 1 Cor. i. 27, 28; and these are called "vessels of mercy," Rom. ix. 23. Calling is of free grace, 2 Tim. i. 9; Gal. i. 15, "Who called me by his grace." Justification is so; Rom. iii. 24, "Being justified freely by his grace." Adoption; Eph. i. 5, it is "according to the good pleasure of his will." Christ himself is free grace, John iii. 16; iv. 10. Faith in him; Acts xviii. 27, they believed through grace. Repentance; 2 Tim. ii. 25, "If God peradventure will give them repentance." Love; 1 Thess. iv. 9, "Ye are taught of God to love." Change of heart and spirit, Ezek. xxxvi. 26. Good works, Eph. ii. 10; John xv. 5, "Without me ye can do nothing." Sanctification; 1 Thess. v. 23, "The very God of peace sanctify," &c. Perseverance; 1 Cor. i. 8, "Who shall confirm you unto the end;" and Ezek. xxxvi. 27, "I will put my Spirit within you, and cause you to walk in my statutes." Salvation; Eph. ii. 8, "By grace are ye saved through faith; not of yourselves: it is the gift of God;" Titus iii. 5, "According to his mercy he saved us." Eternal life; Rom. vi. 23, it is "the gift of God."

Let the consideration hereof draw your hearts to believe, cheer you against all doubts, fears, distempers, and cause you to give glory to God for what he hath done.

Obs. 7. The Lord shows mercy to men when they are in desperate conditions. When this infant was cast out, loathed, lay polluted in her blood, (for her navel was not cut, nor healed, but she lay bleeding to death,) ready to be devoured by the beasts of the field, the fowls of heaven, &c. then God said, "Live." Take life for preservation, freedom, and prosperity, it is true therein: when Moses, and other Hebrew children, were to be drowned, and so the male Jews to have been ruined, when their lives were grievous to them under their task-masters, the Lord preserved them, delivered them; when, in Babylon, all their necks were upon the block, by Haman's plot and power, the Lord showed them mercy, and said, "Live;" so Daniel in the lions' den, the three children in the fiery furnace, &c. God preserved them, freed them from their dangers, enemies, and caused them to live. Take life for spiritual life, and you shall find that the Lord hath said, "Live," when men have been in desperate cases, and at the brink of eternal destruction. The thief upon the cross met with life in the gates of death; and so the jailer, Acts xvi. One, having a fish-bone sticking in his throat, and ready to be strangled, being reproved for swearing and cursing, at that time was so wrought upon, that the life of sin was turned into the life of grace. Another, being in a wood, and going to hang himself, the Lord, in his providence, caused one going by the wood to hear a noise, who came in, counselled the man, so as that he was wrought upon at that time, and lived. You have heard of some that have come to godly ministers, who crossed them in their preaching, with resolution to murder them, but ere they parted, God said to them, "Live."

Obs. 8. When sinners look not after God, he is pleased to look after and find out them. This infant minded not God, inquired not after him, came not towards him; but God passed by, and seeing her in a bloody and sinful condition, he said unto her, "Live."

God found out and called the Jews, when they neither sought nor called; so was it with the gentiles, Isa. lxv. 1, "I am sought of them that asked not for me, I am found of them that sought me not." These words are paradoxical; how could they seek, that asked not? and how could they find, that sought not? in them therefore is held out the preventive mercy of God; God came to them, sought them, found them, before they asked or sought after him. Eph. ii. 17, Christ "came and preached peace to you which were afar off;" that was, the gentiles. And Paul was to bear the name of the Lord before them, Acts ix. 15; by him salvation was sent to them, Acts xxviii. 28; and he was the "apostle of the gentiles," Rom. xi. 13. Being prevented and converted by the grace of God, they sought him whom before they knew not, nor asked for, and now they found him they had not formerly sought. Rom. x. 20, the words run thus, "I was found of them that sought me not; I was made manifest unto them that asked not after me:" when they were worshipping false gods, blaspheming and dishonouring my name, I unexpectedly came to them, offered them mercy and salvation, which they neither thought of, or sought for; like men that dig in the earth for stones, and coals, and find a great treasure.

Muscul. reads the words in future, I will be sought of them that asked not for me, I will be found of them who sought me not; and so they are a gracious promise of God's looking after, finding out, and manifesting of himself unto them, before they had a thought thereof. All their learning, wisdom, morality, led them not to look after God and salvation by Christ; by those, they were carried the wrong way, and whilst they were in the way to destruction, God met them, revealed and tendered salvation unto them. Both gentile and Jew had preventing grace, and were sought out of God, before ever they sought God; hence Jerusalem had that promise or title, Isa. lxii. 12, "Thou shalt be called, Sought out;" God had called her children, and sought them out of many nations.

Obs. 9. God hath no need of any people. Whatever he did to this people, was not because he wanted them to do him service, to praise his name, to promote any of his designs, to suffer for his sake. He passed by, like some great man, that, riding forth, finds a poor distressed infant, and out of compassion takes it up, and into his family, and doth much for it; not because he needs it, but will show kindness to it of his own good pleasure: so dealt the Lord here, he passing by, and seeing so miserable a creature, said, "Live," not because he had need, but because he would show mercy. Deut. vii. 7, 8, the Lord chose them, not for their number, but because he loved them; and he loved them, not because he needed them, but because he would communicate good unto them. He is all-sufficient of himself, not depending on or beholden to any creature; if he needed people or nations, he could create them, raise them up from the stones. Isaiah saith, chap. xl. 15, "The nations are as a drop of a bucket, and are counted as the small dust of the balance;" and surely God, who is an infinite ocean, an infinite Being, needs not a little drop or a little dust. The Samaritan had no need of the wounded man, Luke x. but he needed the Samaritan's wine and oil. God hath no need of England.

Obs. 10. The Lord bestows great mercies in a transient way. "When I passed by and saw thee, I said, Live;" he took this occasion to do good to this bloody, helpless, sinful infant. The Samaritan, as he passed by the man wounded, took occasion to bind up his wounds, and save his life; Christ, in chap. ix. of John, going by, saw a blind man, and thereupon anointed his eyes, and caused him to see; so in Joel ii. 14, you read of leaving a blessing behind him. God passes through kingdoms, families, and uses to leave blessings where he goes; he takes occasion from what he sees, and finds, to distribute mercies. Christ, when he was going out of the world, said, "Peace I leave with you," John xiv. 27; he would not leave them without a blessing. We should labour to be like unto God and Christ, take occasions and advantages to do good.

Obs. 11. In bestowing mercies, God is serious and real. This appears from the ingemination of the words, "Live," "Live." When there is a doubling of the same word, there the intention, reality, and earnestness of the author speaking is held out, be it in matter of judgment, or matter of mercy: Ezek. v. 8, "I, even I, am against thee;" God was seriously and earnestly against them. Ezek. xxxvii. 5, 6, "Ye shall live," "Ye shall live;" God was set upon it, viz. the giving life to dry bones. Isa. xl. 1, "Comfort ye, comfort ye my people;" the duplication of the words imports God's seriousness to comfort them. Hos. ii. 19, "I will betroth thee unto me, yea, I will betroth thee unto me;" yea, a third time, "I will betroth thee unto me;" the more iteration, the more affection, intention, and reality. Isa. lv. 1, "Come," "Come," "Come," saith God thrice, and this sets out the real and vehement desire of the Lord to do sinners good. And how should this make sinners hearken unto the Lord when he speaks, and entertain any offers of mercy from him!

Obs. 12. When God hath done much for a people, and they are degenerate, ungrateful, disobedient, the Lord's way of dealing with them is to set before them their original condition, and his kindness unto them. "When thou wast in thy blood I said unto thee, Live," &c. So in Micah vi. 2—5, God had a controversy with them for their unkindness towards him, and saith, "O my people, what have I done unto thee? and wherein have I wearied thee? testify against me. For I brought thee up out of the land of Egypt, and redeemed thee out of the house of servants; and I sent before thee Moses, Aaron, and Miriam. O my people, remember now what Balak king of Moab consulted, and what Balaam the son of Beor answered him from Shittim unto Gilgal, that ye may know the righteousness of the Lord;" that I kept covenant, performed all I promised to Abraham, Isaac, Jacob, &c. I gave you prophets and prophetesses, choice deliverers, I turned curses into blessings, I led you by a pillar of fire in the night, and a cloud in the day. So in Jer. ii. 5—9, "Thus saith the Lord, What iniquity have your fathers found in me, that they are gone far from me, and have walked after vanity, and are become vain? neither said they, Where is the Lord that brought us up out of the land of Egypt, that led us through the wilderness, through a land of deserts and of pits, through a land of drought, and of the shadow of death, through a land that no man passed through, and where no man dwelt? And I brought you into a plentiful country, to eat the fruit thereof and the goodness thereof; but when ye entered, ye defiled my land, and made mine heritage an abomination. The priests said not, Where is the Lord? and they that handle the law knew not me: the pastors also transgressed against me, and the prophets prophesied by Baal, and walked after things that do not profit. Wherefore I will yet plead with you, saith the Lord, and with your children's children will I plead." God had done great things for them, and they had greatly corrupted their ways, degenerated fearfully from the worship of God, therefore God reduceth them to consider of their pristine condition, and what a bountiful, merciful, gracious God he was to them. He had done such and such things for them, and they forgot him and all his kindness, and made him say, Deut. xxxii. 6, "Do ye thus requite the Lord, O foolish people and unwise? Is not he thy father that hath bought thee? hath he not made thee, and established thee?"

Ver. 7. *I have caused thee to multiply as the bud of the field, and thou hast increased and waxen great, and thou art come to excellent ornaments: thy breasts are fashioned, and thine hair is grown, whereas thou wast naked and bare.*

This verse contains the second benefit which the Lord vouchsafed this infant, viz. growth, increase; after life granted, he caused her to multiply.

This multiplication is set out by a double comparison:

1. Is "the bud of the field."

2. Is of a young maid, growing up to a marriageable condition; "thy breasts are fashioned," &c.

"I have caused thee to multiply." The Hebrew word for multiply is, רבבה and Montanus renders the word thus, *Decem millia veluti germen agri dedi te*, I have given thee ten thousand as the grass of the field, I have increased thee exceedingly. The Hebrews use to put thousands for great numbers: Psal. lxviii. 17, "The chariots of God are twenty thousand, even thousands of angels;" that is, an innumerable, or exceeding great, company. Exod. i. 7, "The children of Israel were fruitful, and increased abundantly, and multiplied, and waxed exceeding mighty; and the land was filled with them:" God had made a promise to Abraham that he would make of him a great nation, Gen. xii. 2; that his seed should be as the stars of heaven, chap. xv. 5; "as the dust of the earth," chap. xiii. 16; "as the sand which is on the sea-shore," chap. xxii. 17; and here you see it made good; his posterity increased so abundantly, multiplied and waxed so mightily, that they filled the land.

Some observe that it was but fifty years from the death of Joseph to this time, or thereabouts, and in those few years they came to such a number as did fill the land, and exceed the number of the Egyptians, in their apprehensions; Exod. i. 9, "Behold, the people of the children of Israel are more and mightier than we." When they came into Egypt, they were not above seventy or seventy-five souls, but when they went out, they were six hundred thousand men: neither women, children, nor aged men were here reckoned; for in the second year after they were gone out of Egypt, and the second month of that year, they were reckoned again, and only those were reckoned who were twenty years old and upwards, and able for the war, and they were found to be six hundred and three thousand five hundred and fifty, Numb. i. 45, 46; here were neither Levites, aged women, or children numbered, which had they been, would have doubled the number. This made David say, Psal. cv. 24, "He increased his people greatly."

"As the bud of the field." Hebrew is, כצמח השדה *sicut germen agri*, as the grass of the field, or whatever grows in the field; the Septuagint is, *καθὼς ἡ ἀνατολὴ τοῦ ἀγροῦ*, as the rising or spring of the field. You know, every thing which hath life in it puts forth in the spring-time, corn, grass, flowers, weeds, trees, bushes, every thing buds and springs forth; and what a multitude of buds are upon some one tree, some one hedge, in one field, and the Jews multiplied not as some one of them, but as the bud of the field in general. Here our prophet seems to allude to Isaac's blessing of Jacob; Gen. xxvii. 27, "The smell of my son is as the smell of a field which the Lord hath blessed."

"Thou hast increased and waxen great." God gave out the blessing, and presently increase and greatness followed, both multitude and magnitude. Their multitude is set out in Numb. x. 36, "Return, O Lord, unto the many thousands of Israel;" the Hebrew is, ten thousands. Their greatness you have, Deut. iv. 6—8, where thrice they are called a great nation, yea, greater than others; and Joshua intimates the greatness of his people, when he saith to those that came out of Joseph's loins only, chap. xvii. 17, "Thou art a great people," hast great power: how great were they all, and all their power!

"Thou art come to excellent ornaments." Hebrew is, בעדי עריים to the ornament of ornaments. The Septuagint showed themselves here like other men, subject to error, for they, mistaking ד for ר read instead of *ade, adim, are, arim*, and so make the sense this, Thou art come to cities of cities, to chief and excellent cities; but the original is, ornament of ornaments. What those ornaments were, men's thoughts are divers; some have thought them to be the law, tabernacles, but that is too curious; others refer these ornaments to those jewels of gold and silver which they borrowed of the Egyptians, Exod. xi.; and this people, both men and women, had bedecked themselves with golden earrings, which they pulled off, and brake in pieces, to make the molten calf with, Exod. xxxii. 23. And not only these, but some take in all artificial ornaments that virgins marriageable, and near marriage, are wont to adorn themselves with, that they may be more amiable and delightful; but the words in ver. 11 and 12, forbid us to close with this opinion, for here the Lord speaks of such things; "I decked thee also with ornaments, and I put bracelets upon thy hands, and a chain on thy neck. And I put a jewel on thy forehead, and earrings in thine ears."

We are, therefore, to refer the words to natural ornaments, and beauty of the body; for when virgins are grown up and fit for marriage, then they have natural ornaments, which do greatly become them. And that this is the genuine sense, the words following do confirm, "Thy breasts are fashioned, and thine hair is grown;" these are natural ornaments, and in these he specifies what ornaments he meant.

"Thy breasts are fashioned." Now by this fashioning of the breasts, is held out the fitness of this metaphorical maid (the Israelitish state) for marriage.

"Whereas thou wast naked and bare." Hebrew is, And thou wast naked and bare. This nakedness may refer to the words before, in the fourth and fifth verses, "Thou wast not swaddled at all, but wast cast out in the open field, to the loathing of thy person, in the day that thou wast born;" and some are persuaded to it upon this ground: because now was the time of her youth, and it is improbable that God, who had taken care of her, (being born of an Amorite and an Hittite,) who had brought her up all this time, should let her be naked and lie exposed to shame, reproach, and contempt. But the Hebrew invites us to put it upon her present, not her past, condition, thus: I have caused thee to multiply, increase, grow great, brought thee to excellent natural ornaments, fashioned thy breasts, made thine hair grow, and yet thou art but naked and bare, thou art poor and hast nothing.

In what this nakedness lay, is needful a little to inquire. Some place it in her being void of the law, Theodoret saith of this person, *Nondum acceperat legis tegumentum:* the law was the chief honour and ornament of the Jewish people, and where that is not, there is a great nakedness. Some place it in their poverty; the rabbins say, that Israel was clad with vile garments, their nakedness was much seen.

It is probable their poverty was great in Egypt. When they were to go out of it, they borrowed raiment of the Egyptians, and jewels of gold and silver, Exod. xii. 35. Others put it in this, that they were destitute of all help, they were in great bondage, suffered great hardship, a politic plot was upon them to drown their male children, and so to ruin them; and being in this case, none pitied them, came in to their counsel or help, and so in this sense they were truly naked and bare.

Obs. 1. The Lord is mindful of his promises, and makes them good by degrees, and in due time. He had promised Abraham that he would make of him a great nation, Gen. xii. 2; that his seed should be as the stars, dust, sand; and here you see it made out, "I have caused thee to multiply as the bud of the field." It was very unlikely that it should ever be so. God promised Abraham a son, but he stayed near twenty years for him after the promise; some think it was forty years, if not more, before Isaac married, and when married, his wife was barren all Abraham's days; after, he had two sons, Jacob and Esau; then Jacob had twelve sons, and went down into Egypt with seventy souls, and from them proceeded multitudes without number. So God, by degrees, accomplished what he promised, and made Abraham's posterity innumerable.

Obs. 2. From mean beginnings God sometimes raises to much greatness, he brings from a low, despicable estate, to great excellence. This Israelitish state was at first as *infans expositus*, like a child thrown out by the friends, as not able to maintain it, left in the fields to perish; this child the Lord took up, and brought forth a great nation out of the loins of it. Abraham was the man, and from him came the populous nation of the Jews, &c. He brought those green buds out of a dry tree. It is God's method ofttimes to raise glorious buildings out of rubbish; he made the world out of nothing; from the little drops he makes great floods; from a little dust enlivened, he hath brought forth all mankind.

What is all the world but Adam? and all the Jews but Abraham?

At the first-fruit offering, they were to say, "A

Syrian was my father; he went down into Egypt, and sojourned there with a few, and became there a nation, great, mighty, and populous," Deut. xxvi. 5.

The Roman state grew up from Romulus a bastard. The Turkish had low beginnings. What was England once? The Britons went naked, they painted their bodies blue, were called Picti, and sky-coloured Britons; they wore their hair long; their towns were their woods; they had ten or twelve wives apiece, and those common to brothers and parents; they tilled no ground, did eat no flesh, but lived much upon roots and barks of trees; they were exceeding superstitious, and paralleled, if not exceeded, the Egyptian idols and idolatry; they were given much to magic; they held that the soul passed from one to another; they were hardly known to other nations, and had little or no commerce with any; the keels and ribs of their ships were of light wood, covered over with leather; their coin, of brass and iron rings. From these we came, and our beginning was mean.

Brit. signifies painted, *Taine*, a nation.

Obs. 3. The work of nature is the work of God. Multiplying, increasing, waxing great, fashioning of breasts, growing of hair, are all natural things; but, "I caused thee to," &c. It was the hand of God to bring that green sprig, Isaac, out of dry roots; and it is also the work of God to bring branches out of green roots. Children are the gift of God, Gen. xxxiii. 5, he forms them in the womb, brings them into the world, and bestows them upon the parents; Deut. xxxii. 6, "Hath not he made thee, and established thee?"

Obs. 4. The natural beauty, excellency that any person or kingdom hath, is of the Lord's good pleasure, and mere mercy. "Thou art come to excellent ornaments;" but who brought her to them? was it not the Lord took her in, being cast out, that gave her breasts, that fashioned them, &c. In ver. 14, the Lord saith, he puts comeliness upon her. Whatever excellences, ornaments of nature, kingdoms or people have, they had them from the Lord.

Obs. 5. Man in himself, or naked of himself, hath no excellency. "Thou was naked and bare;" no free will, no merits.

Ver. 8. *Now when I passed by thee, and looked upon thee, behold, thy time was the time of love; and I spread my skirt over thee, and covered thy nakedness: yea, I sware unto thee, and entered into a covenant with thee, saith the Lord God, and thou becamest mine.*

Here you have laid before you the third choice mercy which the Lord bestowed upon this metaphorical infant, grown up to woman's estate, viz. spiritual marriage; the Lord brought her to excellent ornaments, fashioned her breasts, made her hair to grow, and then married her unto himself.

In the verse you have,

I. The preparatories to this marriage; which are,

1. God's access to her, and observation of her; "When I passed by thee."

2. His acknowledgment of her time; "thy time was the time of love."

3. His manifestation of his love to her; "I spread my skirt over thee."

II. The marriage itself; "I sware unto thee, and entered into a covenant with thee."

III. The effect of it; special obligation between, and mutual relation to, each other, in these words, "thou becamest mine."

The parts of the verse being propounded, the next thing is to open the words unto you.

"Now when I passed by thee." Of God's passing by, I spake in ver. 6; it notes not local motion, but is spoken after the manner of men. God is resembled to a traveller, going from place to place, observing or doing several things in several places.

The former passing by referred to Abraham in his Chaldeeish estate. This is a second passing by, and refers to their estate in Egypt, Exod. ii. 24; xii. 12.

"And looked upon thee." Hebrew is, I saw thee, or, have seen thee. Not that God was ignorant of them and their condition, or that they were out of his sight, for he is present every where, seeth all things at all times; but it is to note, that God intended some special mercy towards them, to do some remarkable thing for them, and that was the calling and sending of Moses to be a deliverer unto them: Exod. iii. 7, 8, 10, God appeared to Moses in the burning bush, and said, "I have surely seen the affliction of my people, and am come down to deliver them. Come now therefore, and I will send thee unto Pharaoh," &c. The Lord's seeing notes his pitying and merciful regarding them.

"Behold, thy time was the time of love." Thy time, what time was this?

1. The time when she was in Egypt, and suffered hard things. The Israelites, you know, were hated of Pharaoh, Psal. cvi. 10; therefore he set taskmasters over them, and commanded their children to be murdered by the midwives, to be drowned by the people; they were made to serve with rigour in all their services, their bondage and oppression was such as made them cry out, and filled them with anguish of spirit, Exod. ii. 23; chap. vi. and ix.

2. The time of youth. She was now grown up to woman's estate, and was fit for marriage. When a maid hath her breasts fashioned, and her hair grown, then lovers and suitors frequent the places where she lives, labour to gain her affections, and to bring her into the honourable estate of marriage; and for that purpose they employ some faithful friends to speak for them, to make way for the accomplishment of their desires: thus dealt the Lord with the Israelitish state, being much multiplied, in Egypt, Exod. iv. 14—16; and chap. v. 1, they went in unto Pharaoh and said, "Thus saith the Lord God of Israel, Let my people go, that they may hold a feast unto me in the wilderness."

"The time of love." The Hebrew is, עת דרים the time of loves, or lovers; the Septuagint is, *καιρὸς καταλύοντων*, which Kirker interprets, *tempus divertentium*, which you may refer to the wooers, or to the wooed. If to the wooers, thus: it was a time for the wooers to leave their own houses, and to turn in to the house of their desired, to suit and solicit her their hearts and thoughts were upon; as Samson did the woman in Timnah. If to the wooed, thus: it was a time for the wooed to divert and pass from the state of virginity to the state of marriage, and to be ranked in the order of the married. But *καταλύοντων* signifies rather *dissolventium*, it was a time of dissolving or dissolvers, a time for the wooers and wooed to let out their affections one to another, and to declare their mutual delights in each other. Aquila, in his second edition, hath it, *tempus συναλλαγῆς*, a time of espousals and marriage, as Pradus renders the word; of commerce and exchange, as Sanctius gives it, because they have sweet commerce together, and do buy each the other, the man gives himself to and for the woman, and the woman herself to and for the man; they exchange persons, liberties, estates. Castalio, *cum esses ejus ætatis, quæ est amoribus idonea;* others, *καιρος τοῦ δια παρθενευθῆναι*, the time of departing out of their virginity. The words are expressive of God's love, he was the Lover; you must not take them in a carnal manner; love, in such a sense, is unsuitable to his nature, he is without all passions and perturbations. When God doth such acts as argue love, in the judgment of man, he is said in Scripture phrase "to love." When the time promised of their deliverance was come, (which was to be at the end of four hundred years, as you may see, Gen. xv. 13, 14; Acts vii. 6, 7,) when God began the work of deliverance, then he loved them, then was a time of loves. God loved them before; Abraham was the friend of God, 2 Chron. xx. 7; so Isaac and Jacob were beloved of him, with the rest of their forefathers; Deut. iv. 37, "He loved thy fathers," saith Moses: yet here it is called "the time of love," because the Lord manifested singular love unto them, in redeeming them from the house of bondage, in taking them, in a peculiar manner, to be his people, &c.; and therefore it is said to be a "time of love;" love in pitying them, love in remembering his promise, love in causing the midwives to spare their children, love in making them grow and increase, love in sending Moses and Aaron, love in working such wonders for them, love in giving them the Egyptians' jewels and raiment, love in bringing them out of the house of bondage, love in leading them through the Red sea, and drowning their enemies in it.

"I spread my skirt over thee." ואפרש כנפי עליך Septuagint, *τας πτερυγας μȣ*. The Vulgate is, *amictum meum*, I spread my clothing over thee. The word כנף properly signifies, the wing of a bird; Gen. vii. 14, that is, there every bird of every sort is כל־צפור, כל־כנף every bird, every winged thing. Metaphorically it is applied to the extremity or utmost part of things, as the outward parts of an army are called the wings of it: Isa. viii. 8, "The stretching out of his wings shall fill the breadth of thy land, O Immanuel;" the wings, that is, the utmost part of Sennacherib's army, when he lay before Jerusalem in Hezekiah's days. The ends of the earth are called so, Isa. xxiv. 16, "From the uttermost part of the earth have we heard songs;" so chap. xi. 12, he shall "gather together the dispersed of Judah from the four corners of the earth," כנפות הארץ from the wings of the earth. So it is put for the uttermost part of a garment, 1 Sam. xxiv. 4, David "cut off the skirt of Saul's robe privily," כנף המעיל the wing of thy robe. The like is Jer. ii. 34, "In thy skirts is found the blood of innocents," original, in thy wings.

Now what this spreading of the wing or skirt means, falls into consideration. It seems to import a marriage rite. When they were to be espoused or married among the Jews, it was a custom to spread their garment over them; hence it was that Ruth said to Boaz, Ruth iii. 9, "Spread therefore thy skirt over thine handmaid; for thou art a near kinsman," that is, betroth thee unto me, and marry me. The law was, that when a man died without issue, some near kinsman should marry the widow, enjoy the inheritance, and raise up seed to him who was dead, and the ceremony used was spreading the skirt over them. Deut. xxii. 30, a man must not discover his father's skirt; that is, he must not have to do with his step-mother, whom his father hath spread his skirt over, and married; defiling of her is uncovering of his father's skirt, Deut. xxvii. 20. Maldonate saith it was a rite of marriage, or certainly a promise of marriage, if a man did cover a woman with his skirt or garment.

Besides, this rite implies protection, defence, safety. The wing of any fowl, spread over its young, is a safety unto it. Isa. xxxi. 5, "As birds flying, so will the Lord of hosts defend Jerusalem:" when birds see their young in danger, they fly, make haste unto them, spread their wings over them, and so defend them; in like manner would the Lord do, spread his wing of protection over Jerusalem, and preserve it: hence that phrase in Scripture, of trusting in the shadow and covert of his wings, Psal. xxxvi. 7; lvii. 1; lxi. 4; lxiii. 7; xci. 4. But this protection we speak of is not protection in general, but *maritalis protectio*, as Abraham was to Sarah, Gen. xx. 16, "A covering of the eyes;" God was a covering to them; Isa. iv. 5, "Upon all the glory shall be a defence." So then by this expression is held out, God taking his people into his custody, his special care, provision, and defence of them.

Calvin thinks that by this spreading of their skirt, is meant all that power and goodness of God which he put forth in delivering of them out of Egypt; the Lord brought them out with a strong hand, and stretched-out arm, his power, mercy, wisdom, goodness, appeared marvellously in that work. He tells them, Exod. xix. 4, what he had done for them; "Ye have seen what I did unto the Egyptians," (I have sent plague after plague upon them, till I had utterly consumed them, and in the midst of all, you were preserved,) "and how I bare you on eagles' wings, and brought you unto myself." The eagle, when her young ones are in danger, or ready to go from the nest, she takes them upon her wings, and carries them away with strength, speed, safety, and that in open view: so did the Lord by this people, he carried them from their nest, the house of bondage, being in danger to be devoured by Pharaoh, that dragon, upon the wings of his power and goodness; and that with strength, all the power of Egypt could not detain them; speed, they hasted out of the land, Exod. xii. 33; safety, not a dog moved his tongue against them, Exod. xi. 7; in open view, they hired them to go with gold, silver, and with raiment, Exod. xii. 33, 35. This is more fully expressed, Deut. xxxii. 11, 12, "As an eagle stirreth up her nest, fluttereth over her young, spreadeth abroad her wings, taketh them, beareth them on her wings: so the Lord alone did lead him." Moses and Aaron were as the wings or hands of God, but God led them.

"And covered thy nakedness." The Hebrew is, ערותך *ignominiam tuam*: so the Septuagint, *ἐκάλυψα ἀισχημοσύνην σȣ*, thy shame; Vulgate, *ignominiam tuam*, thy shame.

1. This nakedness may be taken literally, and so God covered it, when he gave them the Egyptian garments; they might leave their ragged, tattered garments behind them; and it is likely they were poor, whenas the Lord preserved their garments and shoes from wearing out, or old, forty years together; Deut. xxix. 5, "I have led you forty years in the wilderness; your clothes are not waxen old upon you, and thy shoe is not waxen old upon thy foot." Had they had variety of garments, this miracle had not been so needful.

2. You may take it metaphorically, for that reproach, Gen. xxx. 23, which, under the law, was upon unmarried, fruitless, barren women: Isa. iv. 1, "Seven women shall take hold of one man, saying, Let us be called by thy name, to take away our reproach." It was a reproach for maidens not to be married; Psal. lxxviii. 63, "Their maidens were not given to marriage;" and Luke i. 25, when Elisabeth had conceived, she said, The Lord hath "looked on me, to take away my reproach among men." Want of marriage, and want of issue, were both matters of reproach in Israel; and if parents kept their virgins beyond the flower of their age, it was a reproach to them, 1 Cor. vii. 36. God's covering of

her nakedness and shame, was his entering into covenant with this people, and taking them to be his; so that they were not without God, without a husband, to love, to protect, to provide for them; which made Moses to say, Deut. iv. 7, "What nation is there so great, who hath God so nigh unto them, as the Lord our God is in all things?"

3. For that reproach and shame the Jews were under in Egypt. They were servants to the Egyptians, an idolatrous and heathenish people, who used them hardly, and held them under cruel bondage, Deut. xxvi. 6; they were under a king of another nation, that was cruel as a dragon; Ezek. xxiii. 3, Pharaoh is called "the great dragon," unnatural, wilful, hated them, sought their death: the Egyptians evil-entreated them, afflicted them, and laid upon them hard bondage; when they moved to go and worship the Lord their God, they were charged to be idle, and their task increased.

Now this was a great reproach to Abraham's posterity, that they were servants, and held in bondage generation after generation. This reproach God covered, and took away, when he brought them out of Egypt, and drowned the Egyptians (who had lorded it so over them) in the bottom of the sea.

No sooner were they come out of Egypt, but the Lord told them they were come "out of the house of bondage," Exod. xiii. 3; which is often mentioned in holy writ: and they were to remember that condition, that so they might consider how God had covered their shame; Deut. xv. 15, "Thou shalt remember that thou wast a bondman in the land of Egypt, and the Lord thy God redeemed thee;" so chap. xvi. 12; xxiv. 18. God redeeming and bringing them out thence, was the covering of their nakedness, and removing of their shame.

Obs. 1. The Lord doth wait and watch, to do good unto his people. Before, in ver. 6, he passed by, beheld this Israelitish maiden in her blood, said unto her, "Live;" and now again he passed by her, looked upon, and said it was a "time of love."

God observes times to be gracious; Isa. xxx. 18, "Therefore will the Lord wait, that he may be gracious unto you." God waits for fit opportunities and seasons to do for his people: Psal. lxxxi. 13, 14, "Oh that my people had hearkened unto me, and Israel had walked in my ways;" I looked for such a season; "I should soon have subdued their enemies, and turned my hand against their adversaries." Jer. viii. 6, "I hearkened and heard, but they spake not aright: no man repented him of his wickedness, saying, What have I done?" the Lord waited, expected, and longed for repentance, a time wherein to show them kindness; Jer. xxxi. 28, "I will watch over them, to build, and to plant, saith the Lord:" he would watch a time to do them great good, to build them up again into a civil estate, and to plant them a noble vine. That in Rev. iii. 20, "Behold, I stand at the door, and knock: if any man hear my voice, and open the door, I will come in to him." God waits and watches opportunities to show mercy to sinners; hence it is that David saith, Psal. lxxxv. 8, "I will hear what the Lord will speak: for he will speak peace unto his people, and to his saints:" and Wisdom invites her children to hearken; Prov. viii. 32, "Now hearken unto me, O ye children."

Obs. 2. There are special times wherein God makes and manifests love unto his people. "Thy time was the time of love." Solomon tells us, there is a time for every thing; Eccl. iii. 8, "A time to love," and that for God as well as man; he hath his times of wooing people, of making and manifesting love unto them.

I shall show you some of those times:

(1.) The time of affliction. This woman was in great distress in Egypt, hated, persecuted, oppressed, held under bondage, not suffered to go and worship her God, all liberty that way was denied her, new burdens imposed, her life imbittered and endangered, Exod. v. 7, 21; no friend to be found in court or country, no help or comfort appearing any where; and now was the time of God's love, he hears her cries, comes down into the bush, converses with Moses, sends him to this woman, to tell her that God had good thoughts towards her, intended love to her, and would suddenly bring her out of that condition, and put her in a new and nearer relation to himself; and when she heard this, she bowed her head and worshipped, Exod. iv. 31.

When this woman was in Babylon, and her neck upon the block, through the malice, power, and policy of Haman, then was a "time of love;" the Lord visited, delivered, and showed marvellous loving-kindness to her, he chose her to himself in that condition; Isa. xlviii. 10, "I have chosen thee in the furnace of affliction." Elective love is prime, strong, fundamental.

You may see also God's love to this woman, under the name of Rachel; Jer. xxxi. 15, 16, "A voice was heard in Ramah, lamentation and bitter weeping; Rachel weeping for her children refused to be comforted, because they were not." Here was a sad affliction, captivity hath bereft her of her children; but see, now was a "time of love," for presently the Lord visited her, and said, "Refrain thy voice from weeping, and thine eyes from tears: for thy work shall be rewarded; they shall come again from the land of the enemy to their own border," ver. 16, 17.

God visits his people in afflictions. When the high priests, rulers, elders, and scribes, threatened Peter and John, charged them not to preach, which was a sad thing; but they went to their own company and prayed, and presently God appeared, shaked the room where they were, and filled them with his Spirit. Rev. xii. when the dragon persecuted the woman, she had eagle's wings, &c.

Times of affliction are times of love, also, in this respect, because then, as it is Job xxxvi. 8—10, he shows men the nature and greatness of their sins, he opens their ears to disciplines and commands, that they return from their iniquities; chap. xxxiii. 16, he opens men's ears, and seals up their instruction.

(2.) The time of fulfilling promises is a "time of love." God had promised that his seed should serve four hundred years, and in the fourth generation should return to Canaan; this time being expired, now was the "time of love," that God should put forth his hand, lead them out with great substance of jewels and cattle, and so make good his promise. When God makes a promise, it is a "time of love," and when he fulfils it, it is a "time of love," many receive benefit thereby.

God had promised Adam, the seed of the woman should break the serpent's head; to Abraham, that in him all the nations of the earth should be blessed; now when this promise was fulfilled, Christ given out into the world, it was a "time of love," yea, of loves: Luke ii. 14, "Glory to God in the highest, and on earth peace, good will toward men." When the promise of the Spirit was made good, then was a time of loves; a "time of love" to the nations that heard them speak such excellent things in their own tongues.

God promised that, at the end of seventy years, they should return from Babylon. When that time was out, then was the "time of love," God fulfilled his promise, and brought them to Jerusalem again, which Isaiah, chap. liv. 7, calls, a gathering with great mercies.

(3.) The young time of a people is the "time of love;" God doth not only manifest, but make love known, to young ones. This infant was come to those years virgins are at when marriageable, and being so, God made love to her, he gave her love tokens, jewels of gold and silver, and raiment, Exod. iii. 21, 22; quails and manna from heaven, Exod. xvi. This time the Lord points at in Jer. ii. 2, "I remember thee, the kindness of thy youth," not of her kindness unto God, but his own kindness, love, or mercy, unto her. The Lord doth sue and woo young ones to come in unto him; Eccl. xii. 1, "Remember now thy Creator in the days of thy youth;" look upon me, how beautiful, glorious, great, rich, honourable I am, how suitable for thee, what a contented happy life thou mayst lead with me, remember and mind me for thy husband. God sent Samuel to call David, the youngest of the brethren, before him, and when he was come, "Arise, anoint him: for this is he," 1 Sam. xvi. 11, 12. Prov. i. 4, Solomon's Proverbs were written to give the young man knowledge and discretion. Zech. ii. 4, "Run, speak to this young man." Not only youth, but any, when God offers them grace, calls upon them for repentance, believing, that is a "time of love."

(4.) Calling of people into the church state, is a "time of love." They were in Egypt without mercy, they had not church-order and ordinances, but now the Lord was bringing them into such a condition.

Obs. 3. God's love is the foundation and fountain of all the good his people receive and have. It was love caused him to look upon this infant, to say to it, "Live;" that caused her to multiply and grow great, that brought her to excellent ornaments; it was his love, that made him spread his skirt over her, and cover her nakedness, to enter into a covenant with her, to take her to be his, and do all those things he did for her.

When Balak and Balaam would have cursed this woman, the Lord prevented it, and turned the curse into a blessing, because he loved her, Deut. xxiii. 4, 5. It was love which caused and moved God to choose this people to be his, nothing in them, Deut. vii. 7, 8; it was his love to give them favour in the sight of the Egyptians, Exod. xi. 3; it was his love to bring them out of Egypt with a mighty hand, Deut. iv. 37; his love to drive out the nations, to bring them into their land, and to give it them for an inheritance, ver. 38. It was from his love to give them the tabernacle, the temple, his laws, statutes, oracles, ordinances, priests, prophets, sabbaths, solemn feasts, &c.; all spiritual mercies are blessings from his love. Hos. xiv. 4, when he heals backslidings of a people it is because he loves them freely. Election, adoption, justification, sanctification, glorification, are the issues of his love; Christ is so, John iii. 16, "God so loved the world, that he gave his only begotten Son," &c. If divine love be the bottom and fountain of that gift, it is so of all others; Rom. viii. 32, "He that spared not his own Son, but delivered him up for us all, how shall he not with him also freely give us all things?" It was his great love that caused him to quicken us being dead, Eph. ii. 4, 5. God's love is the womb which conceives and sends forth all the good things we enjoy.

Obs. 4. When God takes a people to be his, he will protect them in a special manner, and cover their nakedness and shame. He took this Israelitish woman, spread his skirt over her, and covered her nakedness; he protected her forty years in the wilderness, against enemies and evils that threatened her ruin; he took away her reproach of barrenness and servitude in the house of bondage, he made her fruitful and free. When uncircumcision was a reproach unto this people, the Lord took that away, Josh. v. 9. When Goliath defied the host of Israel, God took him away by David, 1 Sam. xvii. And when the Lord took in the gentiles, did he not spread his skirt over them, and cover their nakedness? Isa. liv. 1—5, "Sing, O barren, thou that didst not bear; break forth into singing, and cry aloud, thou that didst not travail with child: for more are the children of the desolate than of the married wife. Enlarge the place of thy tent, and let them stretch forth the curtains of thine habitations: spare not, lengthen thy cords, and strengthen thy stakes; for thou shalt break forth on the right hand and on the left; and thy seed shall inherit the gentiles, and make the desolate cities to be inhabited. Fear not; thou shalt not be ashamed, for thou shalt forget the shame of thy youth, and shalt not remember the reproach of thy widowhood any more:" and what is the ground of all this? "Thy Maker is thine husband;" therefore God would have a special care of her, turn her barrenness into fruitfulness, and cover her shame, her idolatry and profaneness.

"Sin is the reproach of any people," Prov. xiv. 34, and makes naked, Exod. xxxii. 25; and when God loves a people, and takes them to be his, he covers their sins. Zech. iii. 4, God had good will to Joshua the high priest, and then said, "I have caused thine iniquity to pass from thee, and will clothe thee with change of raiment:" God took away his sins, by the satisfaction of Christ, and clothed him with his righteousness, that covers our spots, shame, nakedness. Rev. iii. 18, "I counsel thee to buy of me white raiment, that thou mayest be clothed, and that the shame of thy nakedness do not appear."

"I sware unto thee." Hebrew is, ואשבע לך. The meaning is, I have given thee assurance of marriage, conjugal faith.

Touching the Lord's swearing, I shall speak a little.

That the Lord did swear, is upon record, but what kind of oath it was, is not here specified.

Some conceive that "I am the Lord," these words do carry in them the force of an oath; and that this was the oath made to Abraham and Jacob, to which the Lord refers, Gen. xv. 7, "I am the Lord that brought thee out of Ur of the Chaldees, to give thee this land to inherit;" Exod. vi. 6—8, "Say unto the children of Israel, I am the Lord, and I will bring you out from under the burdens of the Egyptians; and I will take you to me for a people, and I will be to you a God," &c.

It is thought these words, "I the Lord," or, "I am the Lord," do hold out the nature of an oath, because, Exod. xiii. 5, it is said, "The Lord sware unto thy fathers, to give thee a land flowing with milk and honey;" but this will not hold, because no more is expressed than "I the Lord," and he is said to swear, that therefore no more was in this oath; if we consult well with the word, we may find there was more in it, for, Exod. xxxii. 13, it is plain he sware by himself; "Remember Abraham, Isaac, and Israel, thy servants, to whom thou swarest by thine own self, and saidst, I will multiply your seed as the stars of heaven, and all this land that I have spoken of will I give unto them." The word of God tells us that he hath sworn, sometimes, by his holiness, Amos iv. 2, by his life, Ezek. xiv. 16, by his great name, Jer. xliv. 26, by his soul, Jer. li. 14, by his right hand, and the arm of his strength, Isa. lxii. 8.

Now the oath God sware to Abraham, was by

himself, as you have heard, and may read, Gen. xxii. 16; therefore we may not rest in those words, "I the Lord," as being the oath, but look at God's swearing by himself.

The manner of God's swearing is set down in Deut. xxxii. 40, "I lift up my hand to heaven, and say, I live for ever:" the Lord imitated the practice of men in swearing, for it was their way to lift up their hands to heaven when they took an oath, Gen. xiv. 22; Dan. xii. 7; so the angel, Rev. x. 5, 6. This was done at the covenant-taking.

"And entered into a covenant with thee." ואבוא בברית אתך A covenant imports two parties consenting together, which a testament doth not: a man may make his will or testament, and give what he please to any specified therein, without consents; it is not so in a covenant, there mutual consent is required, especially in a marriage covenant. ברית some derive from ברה to eat, because at the making of covenants they were wont to have sacrifices and feasts, or to eat and drink. Obad. 7, "The men that were at peace with thee have deceived thee, and prevailed against thee; they that eat thy bread," or, the men of thy bread, "have laid a wound under thee:" they were the Egyptians, who drew them into a covenant against the Chaldeans, by eating bread, that is, by eating and drinking, which was a rite accompanied covenants. You find in the word mention made of "a covenant of salt," Numb. xviii. 19; 2 Chron. xiii. 5; which though some think to be so called for the firmness and everlastingness of the covenant, (because salt is a lasting and preserving thing,) yet somewhat else may be found in it, viz. because they did eat and drink at the making of covenants, and used salt which made all savoury, therefore also it may be called "a covenant of salt." To this sense that in Ezra giveth some light, chap. iv. 14, "Now because we have maintenance from the king's palace, and it was not meet for us to see the king's dishonour, therefore have we sent and certified the king:" these words, "maintenance from the king's palace," are in the original thus, Now seeing we are salted with salt of the palace; that is, we have obliged ourselves to him in a covenant, by eating and drinking with him, therefore, &c.: so that place in Lev. ii. 13, "Thou shalt not suffer the salt of the covenant of thy God to be lacking from thy meat offering."

Some derive the word *berith* from בתר *dissecare*, because then when they made covenants, there was some beast killed and cut in the midst; as Gen. xv. 9, 10, 18, when God made a covenant with Abraham, there a heifer, a she goat, and a ram were divided in the midst, and laid each piece one against another orderly, that so the covenanters might pass between them; according to what is in Jer. xxxiv. 18, "They cut the calf in twain, and passed between the parts thereof," and so cut out a covenant, and manifested thereby, that if they brake the covenant, they deserved to be cut in pieces.

Others derive it from ברה *eligere*, because it is that which two or more do choose out and agree upon. Abimelech and his people chose to make a covenant with Isaac, Gen. xxvi. 28; so the Gibeonites chose to make a league with Joshua and the Israelites, Josh. ix. 6: both persons and conditions are chosen and agreed upon, in making of covenants.

Again, some fetch it from ברא to create, order, dispose: for when they cut the beast in pieces, they did divide, order, and dispose of them equally on both sides; and so in a covenant, there is disposing and ordering of things, to the content of both.

Lastly, some draw it from ברר to purify and בר purity, because when covenants are making, the parties ought to be holy, and to deal holily, without all guile, hypocrisy, and overreaching of one another; and in this sense, among others, the covenant was called holy, Dan. xi. 28; Luke i. 72. The Gibeonites dealt fraudulently, when they came with their old sacks, bottles, shoes, garments, and mouldy bread, to make a covenant with Joshua, chap. ix. 4—6.

This covenant which the Lord entered into, was that at mount Sinai; Exod. xix. 5, 6, Moses being called up unto the mount, the Lord said to him, "If ye will obey my voice, and keep my covenant, then ye shall be a peculiar treasure unto me above all people: ye shall be unto me a kingdom of priests and an holy nation." Moses goeth with these words unto the people, to see if they would give their consent, which they presently did; ver. 8, "All the people answered together, and said, All that the Lord hath spoken we will do:" when the Lord heard this, he said, "Lo, I come," ver. 9; there was mutual consent and a solemn covenant made. So chap. xxiv. 3—8, there the consent on both sides is manifested, beasts are slain and sacrificed, both the altar and people sprinkled with the blood of the covenant, and the covenant was written, and read in the audience of all.

This covenant which God made at mount Sinai with this people, was a covenant of grace and mercy; take in all which was delivered by God to Moses being in the mount, and it was so. For,

1. It was a marriage covenant; God took this people to be his spouse, church; Exod. xix. 4—6, he brought them to himself, made them his peculiar treasure, a kingdom of priests, a holy nation; which words are appropriated by Peter unto the church under the gospel, 1 Pet. ii. 9. See Rev. i. 6.

2. It was given in the hands of a mediator, Gal. iii. 19: if it were Moses he typed out Christ, who was the only Mediator between God and man; and Acts vii. 38, he is said to receive "lively oracles to give unto us;" and therefore it is thought by some, that Christ himself was the Mediator, who led them through the wilderness, and gave out those lively oracles.

3. It was made with sacrifice, shedding and sprinkling of blood, Exod. xxiv. 5—8; and the blood was called "the blood of the covenant," which represented the sacrifice and blood of Christ, which is called, Heb. xiii. 20, "The blood of the everlasting covenant:" the covenant of works hath no sacrifices.

4. The ceremonial law was all instituted worship, types, figures, sacrifices, garments, washings, ointments; and what that law had led unto Christ, Gal. iii. 24; Heb. ix. 10, 11, and was evangelical. Now all instituted worship is contained and comprehended in the second command, they were bound to the observation thereof by that command, therefore this covenant must needs have grace and mercy.

5. If it were a covenant of works, not of mercy, what argument were here in the words, "I entered into a covenant with thee?" God was in a covenant of works with them and all the world before, and so it would be of no validity to tell them of it; he did no more for them than for others, and if they had broken covenant, it was but what all the world had done: here lieth a strong convincing argument in the words, I entered into a *gracious* covenant with thee, I knew thee above all the families of the earth, Amos iii. 2; and yet you have done thus, &c.

6. The covenant of grace was given out long before to Abraham, Isaac, and Jacob; therefore it is called "the covenant and mercy" he sware unto them, Deut. vii. 12. And Moses was under this covenant; Heb. xi. 24, "By faith he refused to be called, &c. when come to years;" he had Christ

with him, Exod. xxiii. 20, the Angel there was Christ: 1 Cor. x. 9, they tempted Christ in the wilderness. The scope of Moses's writings was Christ; John v. 46, "Moses wrote of me." Heb. iv. 2, it is said the gospel was preached unto them, viz. that were in the wilderness.

Now if Moses was under a covenant of grace before, God would not reduce him back to a covenant of works. It is conceived, that after the breach of the first covenant of works, God did never make any more such a covenant with man, but that after covenants were of grace and mercy: now it was the same covenant that God made with the people and Moses; Exod. xxxiv. 27, "Write thou these words: for after the tenour of these words I have made a covenant with thee and with Israel."

7. If a covenant of works, it should be to all, seeing that covenant at first was made with Adam, the root of mankind; but this is to some few, the seed of Abraham only, those who were brought out of Egypt; Deut. v. 1, "Hear, O Israel;" ver. 6, "I am the Lord thy God, which brought thee out of the land of Egypt."

"And thou becamest mine." These words note God's actual taking of this people to be his. Ruth iv. 13, "Boaz took Ruth, and she was his wife." Hos. iii. 3, "Thou shalt not be for another man, so will I be for thee:" here was a nuptial conjunction between the Lord and this Israelitish woman, she became his wife, his possession. This was the joyful day; Deut. xxvi. 18, "The Lord hath avouched thee this day to be his peculiar people," his church, his spouse.

In marriage, 1. There is a special union. "They two shall be one flesh;" two that were mere strangers before, by marriage become one: so here, God passed by this people, cast his eye upon them, the time of love was come, he betroths and marries them to himself, and so makes a near and dear union between himself and them.

2. Special communion with and delight in each other. Cant. ii. 16, "My beloved is mine, and I am his;" chap. vii. 10, "I am my beloved's, and his desire is toward me:" this woman called the Lord "Ishi," Hos. ii. 16, My husband; and the Lord called her "Hephzi-bah," Isa. lxii. 4, My delight in her. The wife is the glory of the husband, 1 Cor. xi. 7, and the husband the glory of the wife; so God looked upon this people as his glory; Isa. iv. 5, "Upon all the glory shall be a defence;" Isa. lxii. 3, they were "a crown of glory in the hand of the Lord;" and God was their "glory," Jer. ii. 11. There was mutual delight in each other; God looked upon them as his jewels, as his peculiar treasure.

3. Communication of what they have each to other, especially of the husband to the wife; he communicates himself, his name, his estate, his secrets to his beloved; and so did God unto this woman, and doth unto his church: Psal. lxxvii. 1, 2, "In Judah is God known; his name is great in Israel. In Salem also is his tabernacle, and his dwelling-place in Zion." They had God amongst them.

For his name; he imparts it to his church, Jer. xxxiii. 16, "She shall be called Jehovah our Righteousness," which is the Lord's name, chap. xxiii. 6; and the church is called Christ, 1 Cor. xii. 12; Jer. xiv. 9, "We are called by thy name."

Estate; she had the land of Canaan given her, which was the land of Immanuel, Isa. viii. 8.

God communicated to his people his wisdom, power, secrets, truths, Spirit, merits and righteousness of his Son.

By virtue of this covenant they had mercies temporal and spiritual promised them and given in.

1. Temporal; and they were many.

(1.) Canaan was promised them. Abraham had the first promise of it, and often to them it was renewed, Deut. vi. 10, 11; xi. 23, 24. This land hath divers encomiums in the word:

[1.] It is called the desire and "glory of all lands," Ezek. xx. 6.

[2.] The land of Immanuel, Isa. viii. 8.

[3.] It was a type of heaven, and therefore is called "the land of the living," Psal. xxvii. 13, the "rest and inheritance" of the people, Deut. xii. 9; and it was given them of free grace, through the covenant, Deut. ix. 6.

(2.) Great increase in that land, Deut. vii. 12—14; Psal. lxvii. 6, "The earth shall yield her increase, and God, even our own God, shall bless us."

(3.) Healthfulness, Deut. vii. 15; Exod. xxiii. 25, with Exod. xv. 26, God would be a physician amongst them, and heal them.

(4.) Length of days, if they kept covenant with God, Deut. iv. 40. This is made an argument to move children to honour their parents, Exod. xx. 12; Deut. v. 16; and people are pressed by this argument to love God, and obey him, Deut. xxx. 20; xxxii. 46, 47.

(5.) Honour and esteem in the world, Deut. xxvi. 18, 19; xxviii. 13; Psal. cxlviii. 14. This Balaam prophesied of, Numb. xxiv. 7.

(6.) Power against and victory over their enemies, Deut. xi. 25; Lev. xxvi. 7, 8; Deut. xxxiii. 27; Josh. x. 42; Psal. lxviii. 35; Numb. xxiii. 23.

(7.) Peace, Lev. xxvi. 6, "I will give peace in the land," &c. Hence they said, Isa. xxvi. 12, "Lord, thou wilt ordain peace for us."

(8.) Protection, Deut. xxxiii. 29; 2 Sam. xxiii. 3; 1 Chron. xvii. 24, "The Lord of hosts is the God of Israel," &c.; Psal. lxviii. 34, and xc. 1.

(9.) Deliverance, Lev. xxvi. 44, 45. Zech. ix. 11, they were delivered out of Babylon, through the blood of the covenant, when in danger by Zerah, 2 Chron. xiv. 9, 12; God by virtue of the covenant delivered them, Psal. xliv. 4.

(10.) By virtue thereof God made strangers and heathens serviceable unto his people, Isa. xlv. 3, 4; Ezra vii. 11, and turned the plots and curses of enemies into blessings, Deut. xxiii. 5.

2. Spiritual mercies; and they were divers.

(1.) They had God to be their God in a special manner. God was God of all creatures, and of the heathens, but not as of this people; in respect of them they were "without God," Eph. ii. 12; but the Jews had God to be theirs in a most peculiar manner, 2 Sam. vii. 24; 1 Chron. xvii. 22; therefore happy in the judgment of the Lord, Psal. cxliv. 15. All in God was theirs; as all the man is, and hath, is the woman's, when married unto him, Isa. liv. 5. Exod. xxxiii. 19, he let Moses see what he had in God; and not only Moses, but that people also saw his glory, Deut. v. 24. They owned one another, Exod. xv. 2; Deut. xxxii. 3; Psal. l. 7; Heb. xi. 16.

(2.) He recorded his name amongst them, and dwelt with them, Lev. xxvi. 11, 12; Psal. cxxxii. 13, 14; Numb. xxiii. 21. When God was with them, none could hurt them, but when he was absent, then evil came upon them, Deut. xxxi. 17. It is worth much to have God amongst a people, Psal. lxxvi. 1, 2.

(3.) The law was theirs, which was holy, just, and good. Deut. iv. 8, "What nation is there so great, that hath statutes and judgments so righteous," &c.; they made men wiser than their enemies, than all their teachers, Psal. cxix. 98, 99. They were "lively oracles," Acts vii. 38; Psal. cxlvii. 19, 20.

(4.) He made his mind and secrets known unto that people, 2 Sam. vii. 27. Moses had familiar converse with God; Abraham was his friend; God gave them Urim and Thummim, they were taught of God, whereas the nations were deluded by the devil and his oracles. The Lord appeared to Jacob, Joshua, Solomon, and others, and made known his will to them.

(5.) They had forgiveness of sins; Exod. xx. 6, that is a pardoning mercy, because visiting iniquity is contrary to it, and noteth punishment, Exod. xxxiv. 6, 7; Isa. lv. 7; Micah vii. 18; Dan. ix. 9.

(6.) This covenant was the ground of their being heard in prayer; 1 Sam. i. 17, "The God of Israel grant thee thy petition;" Dan. ix. 17; 1 Sam. xxiii. 10, 11; 1 Kings viii. 23; 2 Kings xix. 15; 1 Kings xvii. 21; Jer. xiv. 8. From hence they had,

[1.] A ground of expostulation with God; Psal. xxii. 1, "My God, my God, why hast thou forsaken me?" &c.; 2 Chron. xx. 12; Exod. xxxii. 11.

[2.] Of challenging God for help; Psal. iii. 7, "Arise, O Lord; save me, O my God;" Psal. xxxv. 23; xl. 17.

[3.] Of confidence; Micah vii. 7, "I will look unto the Lord; I will wait for the God of my salvation; my God will hear me;" Isa. xxv. 9.

(7.) They had many privileges by virtue of this covenant.

[1.] They were a holy people, Exod. xix. 6; Deut. vii. 6; Isa. lxii. 12; Dan. xii. 7. God called them his "anointed," Psal. cv. 15; his "saints," l. 5.

[2.] They were dear unto God, Deut. vii. 6; Exod. xix. 5, "a peculiar treasure;" they were his "jewels," Mal. iii. 17; as "the apple of his eye" unto him, Deut. xxxii. 10; "a people near unto him," Psal. cxlviii. 14; in his "arms," Deut. xxxiii. 27; his "glory," Isa. iv. 5; Psal. lxxviii. 61.

[3.] The Messiah was to come of them, Luke i. 72; Gen. xxii. 18.

[4.] Amongst them did the Lord choose out materials for the heavenly Canaan; Rom. ix. 4, the adoption appertained to them.

(8.) Eternal life and salvation; Acts xv. 11, "We believe that through the grace of our Lord Jesus Christ we shall be saved, even as they." They had sacrifices which typified Christ, and the brazen serpent.

Obs. 1. That we are backward to believe what the Lord saith and propounds unto us. He came to this woman, pitied her in her bloody, sinful, afflicted condition, said unto her, "Live," promised to do much for her; but she feared, doubted, apprehended not God's intentions by Moses, Exod. ii. 11, 12, compared with Acts vii. 25: she was like other women, that believe not their suitors too easily, when they tell them of great estates, honours, advantages they shall have by them, and so put them to it to make things out clear and evident, whereupon they vow and swear to them it is so. This was the case here, the Israelitish woman was not forward to believe, the Lord he swears by himself unto her, and you know an oath is for confirmation, Heb. vi. 16; so then that she might have her scruples, fears, doubts, jealousies removed, and be confirmed in the reality of things, the Lord is pleased to swear. She had seen the great plagues upon the Egyptians, the signs, wonders, and mighty hand of God, in bringing her out of Egypt, yet this satisfied her not; her spirit was unbelieving, and God swears, to cure and take away that unbelief.

Happy we, for whose sakes the Lord will vouchsafe to swear! but O most miserable we, if we believe not the Lord swearing! He hath sworn that he hath not pleasure in the death of the wicked, Ezek. xxxiii. 11: Isa. xlv. 23, "I have sworn, That unto me every knee shall bow."

Obs. 2. See the infinite kindness and condescension of God towards poor sinners, that he will enter into covenant with them. He is a God of infinite glory, excellency, majesty, holiness, greatness; to him all the nations of the earth are but as the drop of a bucket, and as the small dust of the balance, Isa. xl. 15; and what was this nation of the Jews? "The fewest of all people," Deut. vii. 7; and yet the Lord is pleased to make a covenant with this people, this Israelitish woman. What was there in it to move the Lord thereto; was she of great birth? No; "Thy father was an Amorite, thy mother an Hittite." Had she any breeding? any great portion? any beauty? No; she was an exposed infant, brought up in brick and clay, a bond-servant, not having a rag to cover her nakedness; she lay in her blood, and was without all beauty, under great scorn and reproach; yet the Lord is pleased to enter into a covenant of mercy with her. But it may be the Lord foresaw that she would prove well, be loving, obedient, dutiful. No; the Lord foresaw she would be a contentious wife, a continual dropping, that she would be murmuring, ungrateful, whorish, rebellious, and idolatrous; yet he strikes a covenant with her, &c. God might have dealt with her and us in an absolute way, commanded us, and immediately destroyed us if we had not obeyed; but he condescends to deal with us in a way of covenant, a way of mercy, with us worms. This should,

(1.) Put us into a rapture of admiration, and make us say with David, Psal. viii. 4, "O Lord! what is man, that thou art mindful of him? and the son of man, that thou visitest him?" Psal. cxliv. 3, "Lord, what is man, that thou takest knowledge of him! or the son of man, that thou makest account of him!" Job vii. 16, "What is man, that thou shouldest magnify him? and that thou shouldest set thine heart upon him?"

(2.) Endear the Lord unto us abundantly. When great ones stoop to weak unworthy ones, it is a great endearing of them unto those they stoop to. When Boaz condescended to Ruth, it drew her heart strongly towards him.

(3.) Make us faithful unto God, not to let our hearts run out a whoring after other things. "I am my beloved's," said the spouse; she was not for others. Job made a covenant with his eyes, and would not think of a maid; he was faithful to God. It was an imputation to Solomon, that "his heart was not perfect with the Lord," 1 Kings xi. 4.

(4.) Make us free and cheerful in our obedience, yielding such as springs from covenant rather than command, from love rather than fear.

Ver. 9. *Then washed I thee with water; yea, I throughly washed away thy blood from thee, and I anointed thee with oil.*

This verse lays before you the recital of former mercies God vouchsafed this people, and they are two:

I. Washing.

II. Anointing.

No sooner had the Lord taken this woman into covenant with him, made her his, but he washeth and anoints her.

"I washed thee with water." Some refer this washing to their passing through the Red sea, Exod. xiv. 21, 22, of which the apostle saith, 1 Cor. x. 1, 2, "All our fathers were under the cloud, and all passed through the sea; and were all baptized unto Moses in the cloud and in the sea." Their bringing out of Egypt was a type of redemption by Christ, and their passage through the Red sea, a figure of baptism, or washing in the blood of Christ.

Some here make the water to be heavenly doctrine, which the Lord gave them; Deut. xxxii. 2, "My doctrine shall drop as the rain:" when the rain falls, it washeth away the filth of places; so did the law, the corruptions and pollutions of this people.

Others think here to be meant those legal washings, spoken of in several places, begun in Exod. xix. 10, "The Lord said unto Moses, Go unto the people, and sanctify them to day and to morrow, and let them wash their clothes;" and Numb. xix. you may read of a water made of the ashes of a red heifer, to purify and cleanse those who were defiled. Heb. ix. 10, they had "divers washings." One was *ἁγνισμὸς*, John xi. 55, they went up to Jerusalem, "to purify themselves." A second, *καθαρισμὸς*, which was a more thorough washing; John iii. 25, there was "a question between some of John's disciples and the Jews," *περι καθαρισμοῦ*. You know they had their water-pots, which held two or three firkins apiece, in which they washed their clothes, hands, feet, when they were defiled by touching any unclean thing.

Others put it upon God's freeing them from their misery and sordid condition, through their poverty and meanness, raising them up to a considerable estate.

We may step over the second and fourth, and take the first and third; I washed thee in the Red sea, and with legal washings. Now because these were typical, and leading unto Christ, we must pass from the ceremony to the substance, viz. the blood of Christ, and remission of sins; I led thee by those washings and baptisms, to the fountain set open for uncleanness, Zech. xiii. 1. Sin defiles, and the blood of Christ cleanseth from that defilement. I find interpreters do understand by this washing with water, forgiveness of sins, which in the New Testament is oft expressed by the metaphor of washing, sprinkling, cleansing, purging, 1 John i. 7; 2 Pet. i. 9; Rev. i. 5; Heb. ix. 14; 1 Pet. i. 2. Water cleanses, cools, comforts; and so doth forgiveness of sin through the blood of Christ, Eph. i. 7; Heb. x. 22; Matt. ix. 2; Heb. xii. 24.

"I throughly washed away thy blood." The Hebrew is, I have flooded thy bloods from thee.

By bloods (so it is in the Hebrew) is meant sins, the analogy between which I spoke of in the 6th verse. Blood is natural, diffuseth itself through the whole man, defileth, makes loathsome; and so doth sin: I may add this, it abounds in man; and so doth sin; but God washed away their bloods, their sins, thoroughly.

Quest. How appears it their sins were washed away?

Answ. Some scriptures give in evidence: Psal. lxxviii. 38, "He being full of compassion, forgave their iniquity;" the word in the original, כפר is, to cover or cleanse; God cleansed the elect by the blood of his Son, as Deodate upon the place saith. Psal. xcix. 8, "Thou wast a God that forgavest them;" God did forgive them their manifold and great provocations of his majesty. That place in Numb. xiv. 19, 20, is very remarkable; saith Moses, "Pardon, I beseech thee, the iniquity of this people according unto the greatness of thy mercy, and as thou hast forgiven this people, from Egypt even until now." They had often and much provoked God after their departure out of Egypt, yet God had forgiven them, and this argument he pressed to move God to pardon them still; and ver. 20, "The Lord said, I have pardoned according to thy word;" thou hast desired me to pardon, and I have done it: hence in Neh. ix. 17, he is called a God of pardons; "ready to pardon," is the translation in our hands, but the original is, אלוה סליחות A God of propitiations of pardons.

"And I anointed thee with oil." The Hebrew is, ואסכך בשמן I anointed thee in oil. We must inquire in what sense these words are to be taken.

Some put this construction upon them, that God refreshed them after their great and long afflictions in Egypt. They had suffered long and much in the house of bondage, and when God brought them forth, freed them from their tasks and task-masters, gave them liberty and ease, this was a kind of anointing of them.

Others refer this to the holy oil, with which Aaron and his sons were anointed; Exod. xxx. 30, they were anointed and consecrated, to "minister unto the Lord in the priest's office," and so virtually in them the people were anointed; and you know that in Exod. xix. 6, they are called "A kingdom of priests, an holy nation;" and in Ezra ix. 2, "The holy seed;" Dan. viii. 24, "The holy people."

You may take the words in this sense: For the abundance of oil that God gave them, Deut. viii. 8, their land is called "A land of oil olive," or, as the original is, A land of olive tree of oil; that is, a land of such olive trees as yielded much oil. This land did not only abound with milk and honey, but also with oil; Joel ii. 24, their fats did "overflow with wine and oil;" they had it in such abundance that they sold it to other nations; Hos. xii. 1, "Oil is carried into Egypt."

Artaxerxes appointed his officers to allow Ezra upon his return one hundred baths of oil, Ezra vii. 22.

Now there were two sorts of baths; one called the lesser bath, which contained seventy-two quarts, another called the greater bath, which contained one hundred and eighty sextaruses or quarts; and this distinction is founded upon 1 Kings vii. 26, where the brazen sea is said to contain two thousand baths, which must be understood of the greater baths, and 2 Chron. iv. 5, where it is said it held three thousand baths, which you must interpret of the lesser baths. Ezra was allowed one hundred of them, which shows they had plenty of oil amongst them; and hence it is likely the prophet gave out the expression of "rivers of oil," Micah vi. 7, for they had olive yards in abundance, Neh. ix. 25.

For a more full understanding of these words, you must know that in the oriental parts they used much to wash and anoint themselves; Amos vi. 6, "They anoint themselves with the chief ointments:" it was ordinary at their feasts to do it; Matt. xxvi. 7, a woman came and poured a box of precious ointment upon Christ's head as he sat at meat; Luke vii. 38, a woman anointed his feet with ointment as he sat at meat; ver. 46, saith Christ to Simon, "My head with oil thou didst not anoint; but this woman hath anointed my feet:" Eccles. ix. 8, "Let thy head lack no ointment." They anointed not only at their feastings, but also upon their fastings; Matt. vi. 17, "When thou fastest, anoint thine head, and wash thy face."

Lavater saith, that among the eastern people the use of oil was the same with them, as the use of baths amongst those where he lived. Husbands had baths in their houses for themselves and wives to cleanse their bodies and strengthen their spirits. And so upon the marriage of women, they used to wash and bathe; Ruth iii. 3, when a match was intended between Ruth and Boaz, what said Naomi to her? "Wash thyself therefore and anoint thee, and put thy raiment upon thee, and get thee down to the floor:" so Esth. ii. 12, the wives of the Persian kings had twelve months for the time of their purification, six months with oil of myrrh, and six months with other sweet odours, that so they might be the more pleasing and delightful to the king; this was their custom. Now unto this, it seems to me, the Lord here alludes, who proceeding in the allegory of this metaphorical woman, the Jewish state, was now upon the marriage and enjoyment of her; and having washed away her blood and filth with water, he also anoints her with oil, that so she may be the more acceptable and delightful unto him. Now this anointing leads us to a spiritual consideration.

The stream of later interpreters runs that way. So Polanus, "I have anointed thee with oil," that is, I have regenerated thee by my Holy Spirit. Piscator, By this unction seems to be signified regeneration by the Holy Spirit. Œcolampadius, After washing comes the anointing of the Spirit. Pintus, "I have anointed thee with oil," that is, with the oil of my grace. Deodate, I have endowed thee with the graces of my Spirit, signified by the anointing. Of the same judgment are they who set out the Annotations upon the Bible. So Bernard, in his Thesaurus Biblicus, in the word Oil, referring to this place, saith, It is put for the grace of regeneration.

Now it is clear from the holy writ, that spiritual things are held forth by oil and anointing with it. Exod. xl. 13, 15, Aaron and his sons must be anointed with the anointing oil, which represented the anointing of Christ and his servants with the Spirit. Psal. xlv. 7, "Thy God hath anointed thee with the oil of gladness above thy fellows;" it is spoken of God's anointing Christ with his Spirit, and so likewise of his anointing the saints with the graces of his Spirit. 2 Cor. i. 21, "He who hath anointed us is God." The Spirit and graces of it are here represented by oil. We must inquire further what is meant by this anointing, for it is certain all of them had not the Spirit and graces of it.

1. By this anointing we may understand the consecration of this people unto the Lord; he separated them from the Egyptians and the rest of the world, who were profane, and made them a holy people to himself. Exod. xl. 9—11, the tabernacle, altar, and vessels of both were anointed with oil, that so they might be holy to the Lord, they were consecrated by that oil to the Lord: so when God by his Spirit in Moses told this people, Exod. xix. 6, that they should be "a kingdom of priests, an holy nation," then did he anoint them and consecrate them unto himself; and Psal. cv. 15, they are called the Lord's anointed ones, "Touch not mine anointed."

2. God's bringing them to a gladsome condition after their sore bondage in Egypt, and forty years' travel in the wilderness. Oil in holy Scripture sets out joy and cheerfulness; Psal. civ. 15, "Oil to make his face to shine." Oil when they anointed with it, and when they did eat it, much refreshed them; it is called "oil of gladness," Psal. xlv. 7, and "oil of joy," Isa. lxi. 3; and in that God made them a gladsome and a joyous people, he is said to anoint them. Psal. cv. 43, "He brought forth his people with joy, and his chosen with gladness;" the Hebrew is, with singing. When they saw themselves through the Red sea, and the Egyptians drowned, they sang for joy, Psal. cvi. 12, "They sang his praise;" and you have the song, Exod. xv. Before, they were filled with anguish of spirit, Exod. vi. 9; but God gave them for mourning the oil of joy by his Spirit, he put gladness into their hearts, they were the people that knew the joyful sound, Psal. lxxxix. 15.

3. God's teaching of them in the ways of his worship. Never before had any people such laws given them for divine worship, for regulation of their lives and ways towards God and man, as they had. Now teaching is set out by oil and unction, 1 John ii. 20, 27, "Ye have an unction, and the anointing teacheth you all things;" that was the Spirit: God anointed Moses and the prophets which were amongst this people with the Spirit, and so taught them all things needful for their condition. What saith Moses, Deut. iv. 5? "I have taught you statutes and judgments, even as the Lord my God commanded me:" Moses and the prophets spake as the Holy Spirit moved them, and having the spirit of prophecy amongst them, they may be said to be anointed. Origen saith, The anointing is the indwelling of the Holy Spirit in the knowledge of the truth.

4. God's working of grace in their hearts, and making of them truly holy. The giving of the Spirit and graces of it unto Christ, is called an anointing of him, Acts x. 38, "God anointed Jesus of Nazareth with the Holy Spirit;" and Cant. i. 3, "Because of the savour of thy good ointments the virgins love thee." Christ communicated the graces of his Spirit, and anointed the virgins therewith, which were sweet and savoury as a precious ointment; and here God saith he anointed the Jews with oil, and did give unto many of them his Spirit and saving grace. Abraham their father was eminent for faith, Rom. iv. 18—20; so Isaac, Jacob, Joseph, Moses, Caleb, Joshua, Gideon, Baruch, Jephthah, David, Samuel, the prophets, and multitudes of others, they had not only true grace, but much grace; Heb. xi. 39, "These all obtained a good report through faith."

This people was the church of God, he had no other people which he owned as his; the Jewish nation alone was his peculiar people, and if there was any true grace in the world it was amongst them: they were called the "holy people," Deut. vii. 6, the "holy nation," Exod. xix. 6, "holy seed," Isa. vi. 13, "the generation of the righteous," Psal. xiv. 5, "saints," l. 5; not only because they were separated from the rest of the world, came of Abraham, made a profession of the true God and his worship, but also because they had true grace. Isa. li. 7, God gives this testimony of them, "The people in whose heart is my law;" if there had not been many of them truly gracious, God would never have given them such a commendation.

Thus you see what is meant by this anointing, and though all had not true grace, yet how all may be in one respect or other said to be anointed.

Obs. 1. Those whom it pleaseth the Lord to enter into covenant with, and take to be his people, them he pleaseth to wash: this ariseth clearly from the coherence; "I entered into a covenant with thee, and thou becamest mine;" what then? "Then washed I thee with water."

There is a double washing to be considered: one external, which was in the Red sea, and in the legal washings, and so they were all washed, good and bad. There is another washing which is internal, viz. by the blood of Christ, signified by the outward washings, and this is the principal washing; and with this washing they were not all washed, only those who were elect and vessels of grace, they were washed in the blood of Christ, and had the forgiveness of sins. In Jer. xxxi. 33, 34, where God speaks of entering into covenant with the house of Israel, he tells them he will forgive iniquity; and chap. xxxiii. 8, "I will cleanse them from all their iniquity," טהרתים that cleansing is washing them away in the blood of Christ, and pardoning them for his sake, for it follows in the original וסלחתי "and I will pardon all their iniquities." Now in the times of the gospel, those who live under the sound of it, and do profess the same, they are washed with the water of baptism, but not all with the blood of Christ. Simon Magus had the outward washing, Acts viii. 13, but wanted the inward washing; so John baptized many with water, whom Christ never baptized with his blood; but all the Father gave him, and were covenanted for, those he washed with his blood; Rev. i. 5, "He loved us," that is, being in covenant with the Father, "and washed us from our sins in his own blood," which is therefore called "the blood of the covenant," Heb. xiii. 20. And whereas it is said, Heb. x. 29, that some which proved apostates were sanctified with that blood, you must understand it of those who by profession of the faith, and participation of the seals, baptism and the supper, were separated from judaism and paganism, and in the judgment of charity such: not that they were internally washed from their sins by the blood of Christ, for it is impossible that any man sanctified and pardoned through the blood of Christ, should tread under foot the Son of God, and count that blood an unholy thing; to such a soul nothing is more precious than Christ and his blood.

Obs. 2. Those whose sin God forgives, he fully forgives. "I throughly washed away thy blood," I suffered no sin, no guilt to stick upon thee. Ezek. xxxvi. 25, "I will sprinkle clean water upon you, and ye shall be clean; from all your filthiness, and from all your idols, will I cleanse you:" sprinkling of them with clean water imports the sprinkling of them with the blood of Christ, whereby sins are purged and done away. 1 John i. 7, "The blood of Christ cleanseth from all sin," not some few, some little, some great, some old, some new sins, but from all sin; when God pardons he pardons thoroughly, Jer. xxxiii. 8, "I will cleanse them from all their iniquity, whereby they have sinned against me; and I will pardon all their iniquities whereby they have sinned against me:" let the sins, iniquities, be what they will, when the Lord is upon the work of forgiving, he will forgive them all. David blesseth God upon this ground, because God was a God forgiving all iniquities, Psal. ciii. 3. That place in Isa. lv. 7, is to our purpose, "He will abundantly pardon;" not ten, twenty, a hundred, or a thousand sins, but ten thousand sins, all wicked ways, all evil thoughts. The Vulgate reads it, *Multus est ad ignoscendum*, He is much inclined to pardon, much in pardoning, he takes delight in it, as a thing natural to him. Micah vii. 18, "He pardoneth iniquity and passeth by transgression;" and why? "because he delighteth in mercy;" it is his will, his nature to be merciful, nothing pleases him more than to show mercy. The Hebrew is, He will multiply to pardon; if man have multiplied sins, he will multiply means to pardon those sins; the sins of the creature shall not be supernumerary to the mercies of the Creator. Man is a father of sins, and God is a "Father of mercies," 2 Cor. i. 3. Doth man beget and bring forth thousands of sins in a day? God begets and brings forth more mercies in an hour; where sin abounds, he makes grace much more to abound, Rom. v. 20.

Obs. 3. Those whose sins God washes away, them he separates from the world, makes glad, teaches his ways, and beautifies with the graces of his Spirit. "I throughly washed thee from blood, and anointed thee with oil;" all these are comprehended in that anointing; when God washeth away the sins of any, then he anoints them with oil. When Aaron was washed, then was he anointed, Exod. xl. 12, 13. And Peter tells them that had put the Lord Christ to death, that they were washed, and they should be anointed; they must first be baptized for remission of sins, and then they should receive the gift of the Holy Spirit, Acts ii. 38. When God pardons any, he purges them; after the remission comes the unction: and then,

(1.) They are off from the world, they are the Lord's, his beloved, they have sweet peace and fellowship with him; they are vessels anointed for the Lord's use, and dare not profane themselves with the world, knowing "that the friendship of the world is enmity with God," Jam. iv. 4. In 1 John i. he speaks of their cleansing from sin by the blood of Christ; in chap. ii. of their receiving the anointing; and in chap. iii. 13, of the world's hatred of them: they were now not of the world, the unction had severed them from the world, and they were consecrated to the Lord.

(2.) They are joyous and cheerful ones who are anointed. The apostles, after they received the Holy Spirit, their sorrows for the departure of Christ fled away, their troubles in the flesh were nothing. So Paul and Silas sang praises at midnight, after whipping, imprisoning, and thrusting into the stocks, Acts xvi. 24, 25. And the Hebrews "took joyfully the spoiling of their goods," Heb. x. 34; and why? they "were made partakers of the Holy Spirit," chap. vi. 4, they were anointed, and that made them joyful.

(3.) They are taught the ways of God. Heb. viii. 10—12, "I will put my laws into their mind, and write them in their hearts. They shall all know me, from the least to the greatest. For I will be merciful to their unrighteousness, and their sins and iniquities will I remember no more." When God should forgive them, and wash away their sins in the blood of Christ, then he would anoint them, he would teach them, little and great, the knowledge of himself and his ways.

(4.) They are sanctified and beautified with the graces of his Spirit. When sins are washed away in the blood of the Lamb, then God anoints with the graces of his Spirit. Tit. iii. 5, 6, upon "the washing of regeneration" (that is, upon the effectual washing of the soul by the blood of Christ in the use of baptism) followed the "renewing of the Holy Spirit; which he shed on us abundantly," poured out like oil, so that they were replenished, sanctified, and beautified with all the graces of his Spirit.

Ver. 10—13. *I clothed thee also with broidered work, and shod thee with badgers' skin, and I girded thee about with fine linen, and I covered thee with silk. I decked thee also with ornaments, and I put bracelets upon thy hands, and a chain on thy neck. And I put a jewel on thy forehead, and earrings in thine ears, and a beautiful crown upon thine head. Thus wast thou decked with gold and silver; and thy raiment was of fine linen, and silk, and broidered work; thou didst eat fine flour, and honey, and oil: and thou wast exceeding beautiful, and thou didst prosper into a kingdom.*

These verses hold out more of God's bounty towards this woman; like a loving husband newly married, he makes great provision for her.

I. Clothing, and that not common, but costly, ver. 10, and part of 13.

II. Ornaments, ver. 11, 12, bracelets, a chain, a jewel, earrings, a crown.

III. Diet, fine flour, honey, and oil.

"I clothed thee also with broidered work." אלבשך

רקמה I clothed thee with that which is drawn, painted, or embroidered with a needle. The word is from רקם to embroider with the needle, or by weaving, to work in divers colours, figures and pictures in cloths; they made the pictures of men, beasts, and other living creatures in them; sometimes they intermixed gold and silk of divers colours, and so the work was very curious and costly. Pradus conceives that the word *rickmah* doth properly signify work done by the needle; and Psal. xlv. 14, where it is said, "She shall be brought unto the king in raiment of needlework," לרקמות it sets out what broidery the word imports, viz. that which is done with the needle, and such embroidery is called *opus Phrygionicum*, because the Phrygians first invented it. Some refer this clothing with broidery to Aaron; Exod. xxviii. 4, there a "broidered coat" was to be made for him, in which they affirm was embroidered the whole world, heaven, earth, sea, with the fulness and furniture of them, as birds, fishes, beasts, meadows, and those living creatures which were *dos uxoris*, the dowry of the wife, these were intertext, woven in; also with the needle was embroidered most livelily the glory of their progenitors, according to that in Wisd. xviii. 24, "In the long garment was all the ornament, and in the four rows of the stones was the glory of the fathers graven." Theodoret refers the broidery, and what follows in the words, to the curtains, coverings, and ornaments of the tabernacle, which were costly and wrought with needlework, some of them, Exod. xxvi. 36. But both these are too narrow; the people were clothed with broidered work, as well as the priests and tabernacle; Isa. iii. 18, they had their bravery and their broidery too. Judg. v. 30, when Sisera was gone forth to fight with the Israelites, did not his mother and the ladies say, "Have they not divided the prey? to Sisera a prey of divers colours, a prey of divers colours of needlework on both sides, meet for the neck of them that take the spoil?" The Hebrew for needlework is *richmah* and *rickmathaim*, broidery made with the needle, which the Jews had plenty of; the repetition of the words import it; had they conquered and spoiled the Jews, they looked for a prey of divers-coloured needlework.

"And shod thee with badgers' skin." The Hebrew is, ואנעלך תחש That this *tachash* was some living creature all agree, but what creature, is doubtful; some rabbies say it was a beast, which only at that time had been found, having many spots, which the Chaldeans called *sasgona*, as delighting in colours, for some of the Hebrews say it had six colours; we have it "badgers' skins;" so it is rendered, Exod. xxv. 5; xxvi. 14; xxxv. 7, 23; xxxvi. 19; xxxix. 34; Numb. iv. 6, 8, 10, 11, 12, 14, 25; but whether so warrantable I leave to consideration, for the Jews held the *tachasch* to be a clean beast, which the badger is not, by Moses's law, as Ainsworth observes. How could they handle the badger, if it were an unclean creature, flay it, and make shoes of the skin, and not be defiled therewith? the wearing of such shoes was a defilement and abomination. Besides, it is not probable that God would have the tabernacle covered with the skins of unclean beasts, that being holy. Gesner also saith that the skins of badgers have no preciousness in them; he would have inquiry made whether it be not the Thos lynx, some such creature, whose skin is precious and spotted. Further, it appears not that badgers' skins were of use to make shoes, as here the *tachash* is said to be. It is most likely to be some living creature peculiar to those parts, having sundry blue spots in it, which occasioned the Septuagint and Vulgate to translate it as they have done, "I shod thee with skins of a *blue* colour." The Jews did wear their garments short, because their feet were seen; they had their shoes exquisitely made and much adorned; Isa. iii. 18, "Ornaments about their feet." This shoeing of them held out, saith Prado,

1. Liberty; for as to be unshod noted captivity, Isa. xx. 3, 4, so being shod the contrary, Exod. xii. 11.

2. Taking possession; for loosing the shoe was an emblem of man's parting with his right, Ruth iv. 7; Deut. xxv. 9, 10.

3. Joy: Ezek. xxiv. 17, in time of mourning they put off their shoes, and therefore the prophet being forbid to mourn, is commanded to put on his shoes.

4. Constancy and resolution. The word here for shoeing is from נעל to shut, because when a man is shod, his feet are shut up from danger of stones and thorns, and so he goes on boldly, constantly, resolutely: Eph. vi. 15, "Having your feet shod with the preparation of the gospel;" let the gospel be to the affections as shoes to the feet, have that in readiness, it will make you go on undauntedly.

"I girded thee about with fine linen." Hebrew is thus, ואחבשך בשש I covered thee with fine linen. Exod. xxv. 4, it is שש there, which Tremellius and Junius render *linum, xilinum*, not *byssum*, and upon this reason, because bysse or fine linen hath another name among the Hebrews, viz. בוץ as in 1 Chron. xv. 27; but this argument is not convincing, because both in the Hebrew tongue and in others, one thing may have divers names; and Boetius in his Sacred Animadversions saith that if שש be cotton, it hath also another name in the Hebrew, namely, פשתה and so he interprets that place in Josh. ii. 6, בפשתי העץ to be understood of cotton and not of flax, which is Masius's opinion. It appears to me that *shesh* was some choice material, whereof they made precious garments and girdles, such as were for kings and great persons. Gen. xli. 42, when Pharaoh would exalt Joseph, set him over all the land next to himself, he arrays him in vestures of *shesh*, bysse or fine linen. So in Prov. xxxi. 22, speaking of the virtuous wife, he saith, her clothing is *shesh*: in the verse before, it is said of her household, they were all clothed with scarlet; if they were clad with that, this *shesh* must be something more precious, otherwise her servants should be better clad than herself: I conceive the marginal reading were fitter, they were all clothed with double garments; so the Hebrew word will bear it, and the former words of the verse seem to infer it, "She is not afraid of the snow," that is, the greatest cold of all, because her household is clothed with double garments, and she herself with *shesh*, fine linen and purple, which were more costly than the others. Luke xvi. 19, the rich man is brought in clothed with purple and fine linen, *bysso;* and it is reckoned amongst precious things, Rev. xviii. 12, 16, as gold, silver, precious stones, pearls, fine linen or bysse; purple, silk, scarlet, &c.; fine linen here, or bysse, is distinguished from silk, and so is שש in my text; there is another word for silk משי they have mistaken therefore who have rendered שש silk, whereas it is the common consent of interpreters, that משי is silk; this *shesh* or *byssus* was a kind of flax greatly esteemed and desired of women, and of no less value than gold. The rabbies say, what place soever in the law speaketh of *shesh* or *butz*, it is flax, or bysse, maymony. Mercer saith it is a kind of flax most fine, white, and precious, and so divers others, only some doubt is made of the colour. Pausanias and Boëtius do conceive it was of a yellowish or reddish colour, but the Scripture itself may determine that doubt; Rev. xix. 14, it is called *βύσσινον λεὺκον*, white linen; and the word *shesh* is put for white marble, Cant. v. 15; and if the Scripture calls it white, we need not make inquiry after any colour: for the origin of it, Del. tells us that *byssum non vermiculi pratum esse sed terræ ceu plantæ.*

"I girded thee." The Hebrew חבש signifies, to bind and to cover. Isa. i. 6, Thy wounds have not been "bound up;" Gen. xxii. 3, "Abraham rose, and saddled his ass;" the Hebrew is, covered; in this place, the word is, to girt; now which sense of the word is fittest must be inquired after. Whenas some render it, I covered, I clothed thee; others, I girded, or bound thee; to me girding is most peculiar here, because he spake of clothing before, and speaks of covering in the next words: it is well rendered by our translators, "I girded thee," &c. that is, with a girdle made of fine linen, I girt thee and thy children. Aaron's girdle was of fine twined linen, Exod. xxxix. 29. Girdles usually were of costly things, needlework, Exod. xxviii. 39, of gold, Rev. xv. 6; Dan. x. 5; and girdles were for gifts, 2 Sam. xviii. 11, saith Joab to the young man, "I would have given thee ten shekels of silver and a girdle." Girdles amongst the attire and dressing of women, were of some account: Jer. ii. 32, "Can a maid forget her ornaments, or a bride her attire;" their hearts and thoughts are much taken up with them, and because they sinned so about them the Lord told them, Isa. iii. 24, "That instead of a girdle there should be a rent, and instead of a stomacher a girding with sackcloth:" this girding some make to note out chastity, and conjugal fidelity; others, fitness and preparedness for employment.

"Covered thee with silk." Hebrew is אכסך משי This covering was not any inward garment, but some outward veil, a covering, not a clothing. The Hebrew women did wear their veils and coverings over their outward garments: Gen. xxxviii. 14, Tamar covered herself with a veil; so did Rebekah, Gen. xxiv. 65; and Cant. v. 7, the spouse had her veil; so Isa. iii. 23, the daughters of Zion had their hoods and veils. Whether these veils did cover the whole bodies, like hukes in some countries, or their half bodies, whether their heads or faces, is doubtful amongst interpreters. That they were not only for the head, but larger, is clear from Ruth iii. 15. How big or little soever, it was of silk, so do expositors in general render it; only the Septuagint and Jerom read it otherwise: the one hath it *τρίχαπτον*, which Suidas affirms to be a silken cloth, or precious vesture; Theodoret, a net or caul made of fine hair, and put upon the heads of woman; Hesychius expounds it to be *βομβύκιον ὕφασμα ὑπερ τῶν τριχῶν κεφαλῆς ἁπτόμενον*, a silken covering, woven, knit, or made for the hairs of the head; and Stephanus in Thes. *τρίχαπτον*, is *textum quoddam tenue et bombycinum magni pretii quod crinibus obducebatur.* Jerom hath it, *subtilibus*, I covered thee with curious and fine coverings; it was of that fineness saith he, *ut capillorum tenuitatem habere credatur*, that it equalled small hair. Our prophet saith משי with silk, which may be drawn out into very curious threads; the word from whence *meshi* comes is משה signifying to draw out. 2 Sam. xxii. 17, "He drew me out of many waters;" and Moses had his name hence, Exod. ii. 10, because drawn out of the water; so silk is called *meshi* in Hebrew, because it is drawn out of the bowels of a worm, and afterwards being put into the water, is drawn out into the finest threads.

The use of veils in Scripture was twofold:

1. For declaration and preservation of modesty: Gen. xxiv. 65, when Isaac was coming, Rebekah puts on her veil, and covers her beauty from the sight of man, and manifests her modesty, 1 Cor. xi. 5, a woman prophesying was to have her head covered, she must not do it without her veil on; that was a shame to her, argued boldness and impudence, and was as disgraceful as being shorn; when therefore a woman prophesied, either in an extraordinary way, as Deborah, Huldah, Anna, the daughters of Philip, or in an ordinary way, that is, sung in public, (for so prophesying is taken, 1 Chron. xxv. 1, where the singers are said to prophesy with harps,) they were for modesty's sake to put on their veils; and God here gave a silken veil or covering to the Jewish church his spouse, that she might carry herself modestly towards him.

2. A veil notes subjection; 1 Cor. xi. 10, "A woman ought to have power on her head," that is, to cover it, that so it may appear she is under the dominion of her husband. Man being God's deputy on earth, lord of the world, he ought not to cover his head, lest he wrong the power put into his hand; but the woman being of man and for man, she ought to cover and veil herself, to declare her subjection to her husband, and reverence the power in him. God therefore giving a covering to this Jewish state, would have her to know, that she was not to live as she listed, but to be in subjection unto him, and to be ruled by his laws, that she was not at her own disposal, but at the pleasure and disposure of the Lord.

Ver. 11. "I decked thee also with ornaments." In the former verse you heard of the rich clothing of this Israelitish woman; in this and the next verse you have her ornaments, which are for comeliness and sight, rather than any necessity.

"I put bracelets upon thy hands." Hebrew is, צמדים *armillas*, from צמד to couple, join, unite together; and bracelets are made of such materials as are stringed and united together. This practice was very ancient; Gen. xxiv. 22, you have mention of golden bracelets for the hands of Rebekah; and these were worn sometimes by men also, as Gen. xxxviii. 18, Tamar asked Judah for his signet and his bracelets; and 2 Sam. i. 10, Saul had a bracelet upon his arm; these persons of note did use to wear, and they were a great ornament unto them, signifying, saith Origen, that the hands should do no uncomely thing.

"A chain on thy neck." Hebrew is, על רביד גרונך it is from רבד which was a chain of divers gems, or precious things, hanging down from the neck to the breast. This wearing of chains about the neck we find to be first in Egypt; Gen. xli. 42, Pharaoh put a gold chain about Joseph's neck, which was a great honouring of him; it is like the Egyptian kings and nobles did wear chains for ornaments. Dan. v. 16, Belshazzar said to Daniel, "If thou canst read the writing and make it known to me, thou shalt be clothed with scarlet, and have a chain of gold about thy neck." It was used as for honour, so for reward; Solomon saith, his beloved's neck was comely with chains of gold, Cant. i. 10; so obedience to parents is reckoned as a chain about the neck, Prov. i. 9. Here by chain, saith Bernard in his Bibl. Thes. is meant the laws and ordinances of God, which would be a chain to her neck.

Ver. 12. "I put a jewel on thy forehead." The Hebrew word for jewel is, נזם which notes a jewel for the forehead. In the original it is, on thy nose or nostrils; and Isa. iii. 21, you read of "nose jewels," נזמי האף the rings of the nose or jewels of the nostrils: so in Gen. xxiv. 47, "I put the earring upon her face," it is in the original, I put the jewel on her nose or nostrils. Some think it was a ring fastened in the cartilage, or partition between the nostrils, which is a place fit enough for such a purpose, and from thence hung down to the lips; Theodoret is of that judgment: and the Lord seems to allude unto Isa. xxxvii. 29, "I will put my hook in thy nose," or nostrils; and historians tell us, that there are Indians and others in the world who wear jewels in their noses. Others hold it was a jewel fastened on their foreheads, and so hung down to their noses. Castalio hath it, *frontale*, as if it were a forehead jewel. The author of this opinion was Jerom, who affirms that among their ornaments they were wont to have golden rings hang down from their foreheads to their mouths; and he renders Isa. iii. 21, *Gemmas ex fronte pendentes*. I shall not contend in this point, but when the Scripture calls them jewels for the nose, I should think it safest to rest there.

"Earrings in thine ears." Hebrew is, עגילים *circulos*, it is from עגול *rotundum*, because they are round. They were of gold usually: Exod. xxxii. 2, "Break off the golden earrings, which are in the ears of your wives;" Job xlii. 11, every one of Job's friends brought him an earring of gold; Judg. viii. 24, "They had golden earrings;" the word here signifies any round thing, and so rings in general.

I shall speak a word or two of rings. I find in Scripture that they were ancient, and their use to be,

1. Honorary: so when Joseph had told Pharaoh his dream, he honoured him with putting a ring upon his finger; Gen. xli. 42, "He took off the ring from his hand, and put it upon Joseph's."

2. Signatory: Ahasuerus bids Esther write in the king's name for the Jews, and seal it with the king's ring. Sealing rings were called signets; Gen. xxxviii. 18, Tamar demands of Judah his signet; Dan. vi. 17, "The king sealed it with his own signet, and the signets of his lords:" and they did wear their signets upon their right hands; Jer. xxii. 24, "Though Coniah were the signet," &c.

3. Decorary, or for ornament, either of the hands, Esth. viii. 2, or of the nose, as before, or of the ears, as in this place. By this earring, Theodoret understands the hearing of the word of God.

4. Testificatory:

(1.) Of joy: Luke xv. 22, said the father of the prodigal upon his return, "Put a ring on his hand."

(2.) Of estate: James ii. 2, "If there come unto your assembly a man with a gold ring," &c.; that shows him to be a man of estate. Crassus, that rich Roman, wore two rings, thereby intimating the great increase of his wealth.

(3.) Of power: Esth. iii. 10, when Haman had traduced the Jews, persuaded the king it was not for his profit to suffer them, and had offered a great sum of money for their destruction, the king took the ring from his hand, and gave it unto Haman, which testified the king thereby gave him power to do it: so Alexander, when sick unto death, was asked who should be his successor, answered, The best amongst them; and shortly after, his speech failing, he pulled off his ring, and gave it to Perdiccas.

Curt. lib. 6. de Gest. Alex.

Their earrings that entered their ears, had the names of their gods in them: Gen. xxxv. 4, they gave to Jacob all their strange gods, and their earrings, which he buried under the oak. Why should he bury the earrings, if they had not the names, effigies, or memorial of their gods in them?

Also they were tokens of reconciliation: Job xlii. 11, they brought to Job an earring of gold: so God had given them his word, that it might enter into their ears, carry the name and memorial of God to their hearts, and be a pledge of his friendship and good will towards them.

Obs. 1. That whatever wealth you have, clothing, ornaments, jewels, it is the Lord who gives you them. "I clothed thee, I girded thee, I covered thee, I decked thee, I put bracelets upon thy hands, I put a jewel on thy forehead;" here are six things. If we have clothes, we consider not who clothed us, therefore saith God, "I clothed thee;" if we be girded, &c. we are very apt to forget God's bounty, and to attribute what he gives to our own industry, prudence, providence, or some second cause: Hos. ii. 5, she thought her lovers, not God, gave her bread, water, wool, flax, &c.; ver. 8, "She did not know that I gave her." We all live upon the alms of God; no man hath a coat, a shoe, a girdle, no woman a veil, a hood, a jewel, but it is the gift of God. Cant. iv. 1, the church is said to have doves' eyes, because she looks much upward: others have swine's, they look downward.

"A beautiful crown upon thine head." Hebrew is, עטרת תפארת, a crown of glory, that is, a crown which made thee glorious and beautiful.

What this crown was we must inquire. A crown is somewhat that compasseth about; so the word עטר whence it comes, signifies, viz. to surround; and the learned conceive this crown was some ornament upon the head, made of fine linen, silk or gold intermixed with the same. In Isa. iii. 18, you read of round tires like the moon, which Deodate saith they wore on their shoes, but others, on their heads, that were made of costly materials, and round like the moon, and may be that which the Lord calls here the beautiful crown. Women in our days do tie up their hair in a round, which shows like a crown upon their heads.

Aaron you know was crowned; Lev. viii. 9, Moses put upon his head the holy crown, and so in him crowned the people, who are called a royal priesthood, "a kingdom of priests," Exod. xix. 6: to this crowning, some think, the Lord respects here. Others judge the Lord alludes to a custom among the Jews, and others, of putting crowns upon the heads of those who were to be married, and receive princely power and dignity; Cant. iii. 11, Solomon's mother crowned him with a crown "in the day of his espousals;" and Isa. lxi. 10, "As a bridegroom decketh himself with ornaments;" the Hebrew is, that decketh himself as a priest, who had choice ornaments, and among the rest a crown; and so the Vulgate reads it, As a bridegroom adorned with a crown: and so the brides had crowns, or peculiar dressings like crowns. The Vulgate reads the words, Cant. iv. 8, "Come with me from Lebanon, my spouse, with me from Lebanon," *et coronaberis*, and thou shalt be crowned. When Ahasuerus took Esther to be his spouse, he "set the royal crown upon her head," Esth. ii. 17; so God here, speaking of the marrying of this woman to him, tells you, that he put a crown upon her head; it was an honourable, a princely marriage, and God would have the world know, that his spouse should not be inferior to any, but have her crown and the honour of a kingdom: and by this crown I conceive is meant, not the cloud which covered and compassed them by day, nor the law which God gave them at mount Sinai, but princely dignity, dominion, and power; so it is used, Psal. cxxxii. 18, "His enemies will I clothe with shame; but upon himself shall his crown flourish," that is, his dignity and power shall flourish. Rev. vi. 2, he that sat on the white horse "had a crown given unto him, and he went forth conquering and to conquer:" the crown given was an emblem of dignity and dominion; and here it notes that honour and power God gave this people. Numb. i. 16, there were princes of the tribes, twelve are named in the verses before, and chap. xvi. 2, you have mentioned two hundred and fifty princes: they had store of princes amongst them, which shows they were an honourable and potent people; Joshua, Barak, Jephthah, &c. their dignity and dominion was the crown of glory the Lord had put upon their head. Jer. xiii. 18, "Say unto the king and to the queen, Humble yourselves; for your principalities shall come down, even the crown of your glory;" the word principalities is rendered in the margin, head tires, those ornaments on their heads which noted their principalities, as their crowns, which imported greatness, power, and sovereignty; these being crowns of their glory, should come down: or we may take the word as it stands, The principalities, what you count the principal things, as the royal dignity, and sovereign power, these shall come down, these are the crowns of glory, and they shall be laid in the dust.

Ver. 13. "Thus wast thou decked with gold and silver." The Hebrew is, and thou wast decked with, noting their riches and wealth they had, rather than their golden and silver apparel. Gold is the chiefest of metals, and hath the precedency in Scripture, it is first spoken of, Gen. ii. 11, 12; and this woman had much gold, she had jewels of gold from the Egyptians, Exod. xii. 35. You may read in Exod. xxv. what golden things were in the tabernacle, and in 1 Kings vi. vii. what gold and golden vessels were in the temple; and Solomon abounded with gold, he had yearly coming in 666 talents of gold, chap. x. 14; and the common talent was 1875 li. and the sacred was 3750 li.; now after the rate of the common talent, it was 1,248,450 li. and after the rate of the sacred, 2,496,900 li. David in his time prepared 100,000 talents of gold, and 1,000,000 of silver, for the house of the Lord. Solomon had targets and shields of gold, and all his drinking vessels, and silver was as plentiful as stones, and nothing accounted of in his days, 1 Kings x. 16, 17, 21, 27; yea, gold was so plentiful, that they made them gods of gold, 1 Kings xii. 28, and lavished out gold, Isa. xlvi. 6.

Obs. 1. The Lord doth not only give apparel, ornaments unto his people, but he gives rich and costly apparel, precious ornaments. He gave them broidered work, fine linen, and silk, bracelets, chains, jewels, and earrings of gold; Jer. xx. 5, there were precious things in the city; 2 Sam. i. 24, the daughters of Israel were clothed in scarlet, and had ornaments of gold upon their apparel, they had choice ornaments; Lam. iv. 5, they were "brought up in scarlet;" they were clothed with crimson, and decked with ornaments of gold, Jer. iv. 30. Now seeing the Lord gave them such raiment, and such ornament, there is a lawful use of such things. The apostle Paul seems to be against the use of them, 1 Tim. ii. 9, "I will that women adorn themselves in modest apparel, with shamefacedness and sobriety; not with broidered hair, or gold, or pearls, or costly array." Rev. i. 13, Christ was girt about with a golden girdle; it was no sin for Rebekah to wear the jewels and bracelets that Abraham's servant brought and gave her, Gen. xxiv. 47; it was not sinful for the virtuous wife to wear silk and purple, Prov. xxxi. 22: God would never have given materials at all to work them, if it were simply unlawful to wear them. Let us consider for what ends the Lord hath given apparel and ornaments, and hereby we shall come to discern more clearly of the lawful use or sinful abuse of these things.

There are several ends:

(1.) To cover man's nakedness. God set man and woman naked in the world at first, that they might see they had nothing of their own, that all was the Lord's who created them; but when they sinned in eating the forbidden fruit, they were ashamed of their nakedness, and sought to cover it, Gen. iii. 7; yea, God made them "coats of skins, and clothed them," ver. 21, that so their nakedness and shame might not be seen, that so modesty and chastity might be preserved: Hos. ii. 9, "I will recover my wool and my flax given to cover her nakedness."

(2.) To arm and defend them against the injury of the air, the violence of wind and weather, heat and cold: Prov. xxxi. 21, "She is not afraid of the snow, for all her household are clothed with" double garments, they keep off the harm that would come by snow and frost to the body if not clothed: therefore saith Solomon, it is unseasonable to take away a man's garment in cold weather, Prov. xxv. 20; and Job judgeth it an act of wickedness in them that cause men to want coverings in the cold, Job xxiv. 7.

(3.) To distinguish one sex from another. God would not have men and women dressed and adorned alike; Deut. xxii. 5, "The woman shall not wear that which pertaineth unto a man, neither shall a man put on a woman's garment:" God would not have men to be effeminate, nor women to be mannish. Some therefore judge it unlawful for women to put on any arms, because armour is the furniture or covering of man; the Hebrew word *cheli* signifieth an instrument or ornament that a man puts on him in time of peace or war.

(4.) To preserve the healthiness of our bodies. "Man is born to labour, as the sparks fly upward," Job v. 7; and man labouring, his body sweats, and sends forth those humours which would breed sicknesses, diseases, &c. which our vestures receiving are to be changed, and so health preserved: so in time of sickness, Job xxx. 18, "By the great force of my disease is my garment changed; it bindeth me about as the collar of my coat."

(5.) To notify the conditions, ranks, and places of men. Gen. xli. 42, when Joseph was exalted, he was "arrayed in vestures of fine linen," which was a mark that he was a man of great place; so Esth. vi. 8, the man the king would honour, must have the "royal apparel;" and Herod, Acts xii. 21, had on "royal apparel." Psal. xlv. 13, 14, the king's daughter was in clothing of wrought gold, and raiment of needlework; 2 Sam. xiii. 18, Tamar had a garment on of divers colours, for with such robes were kings' daughters apparelled; Lam. iv. 5, by scarlet they were differenced from others; Matt. xi. 8, soft silken raiment was for those who were in kings' houses, that were virgins; and because Christ was a King, and a pretended king, as the Jews thought, therefore they clothed him in scarlet, Matt. xxvii. 28.

(6.) To adorn the body. Gen. xxvii. 15, Esau had goodly, the Hebrew is, desirable raiment, that became him so, as made him lovely, desirable; Isa. lii. 1, Zion had "beautiful garments," was to put on such as made her beautiful; Hos. ii. 13, "She decked herself with earrings and jewels;" Jer. ii. 32, "Can a maid forget her ornaments?" Exod. xxviii. 40, Aaron's sons must have coats, girdles, bonnets, "for glory and beauty."

(7.) To testify grief or joy. Mordecai put on sackcloth in a time of mourning: Joel i. 13, "Come, lie in sackcloth;" there was a sore judgment upon them. So for joy, Luke xv. 22, "Bring forth the best robe, and put upon him:" Isa. lxi. 10, "A bridegroom decketh himself with ornaments, and a bride adorneth herself with jewels." Marriage is a time of rejoicing; garments and jewels do testify it: when joy and mirth are in the heart of a man, then, saith Solomon, "Let thy garments be white," Eccl. ix. 8.

Wherein persons sin about apparel and ornaments.

[1.] When it is not modest, but carries with it provocation to wantonness. Prov. vii. 10, there met the young man "a woman in the attire of an harlot," with naked breasts, with curled and powdered hair, with costly garments, which were incentives of evil. Rev. xvii. 1—4, the whore with whom the kings of the earth committed fornication, was arrayed with purple and scarlet colour, decked with gold, precious stones, and pearls, such things as might entice them to folly. Hos. ii. 2, he speaks of adultery between the breasts; they either had naked breasts, or hung enticing ornaments about their breasts: when the habit, hair, or adorning of the breasts are such as draw the eyes, this is the fault of her who sets her chastity to sale. Hierom saith, if a man or woman adorn themselves so as they provoke others to look after them, though no evil follow upon it, yet the party shall suffer eternal damnation, because they offered poison to others, though none would drink of it. 1 Tim. ii. 9, women should "adorn themselves in modest apparel, with shamefacedness and sobriety."

[2.] When persons exceed their degree and rank in costly apparel and ornaments. Gold, pearls, and costly array is forbidden by the apostle, 1 Tim. ii. 9, and 1 Pet. iii. 3. The Lord doth not simply forbid all adorning, as Pelagius would have it, but their adorning themselves beyond their degrees; it is not for the lower rank of people to be arrayed like unto the middle sort, nor for the middle sort like unto the highest.

[3.] When it proclaims and maintains pride, haughtiness, and contempt of others. Rich apparel and precious ornaments puff up the hearts of those who wear them: Isa. iii. 16, 18—23, "The daughters of Zion are haughty, and walk with stretched forth necks, wanton eyes," &c.; and what was the occasion and cause of this? they had their bravery, tinkling ornaments, cauls, and tires like the moon, chains, bracelets, earrings, rings, nose-jewels, changeable suits of apparel, fine linen, hoods and veils, and these they were proud of, and contemned those who wanted them. It is said of the leviathan, "his scales are his pride," Job xli. 15; so many, their clothing is their pride, and being proud they become contemptuous; Psal. cxxiii. 4, "Our soul is exceedingly filled with the scorning of those that are at ease, and with the contempt of the proud:" proud ones contemn others; the devil is a proud creature, and he accused, contemned Joshua, who was clothed with filthy garments; and when persons are puffed up with their apparel, they will contemn those who are clad with mean or filthy garments.

[4.] When it is so expensive as that it hindereth works of mercy. 1 Tim. ii. 9, 10, "Let women adorn themselves in modest apparel, not with broidered hair, gold, pearls, or costly array, but with good works;" now when they wear such costly apparel and ornaments, that they are disabled to do good to the poor, proportionable to their rank, their clothing and ornaments become sinful. Hence it is that many of note are very miserable in their houses, defrauding their bellies to lay the more upon their backs; yea, become not only covetous, but griping exactors upon their tenants, racking their rents to so high a rate, that their pride is maintained by the sweat, loss, and undoing ofttimes of others; yea, ofttimes so profuse this way, that they undo their own families.

[5.] When strange and foreign fashions are taken up, which is one of the great sins of England. You read in Zeph. i. 8, a terrible sentence, which is this, 'I will punish all such as are clothed with strange apparel;" that is, those which did follow and imitate the strange apparel of other nations. Some aped themselves into the Chaldean habits, some into the Egyptian, some into the Tyrian, some into the Philistian, and some into other gentilish habits; as it is amongst us, some take up the French, some the Spanish, some Italian habits. That we may conceive to be strange apparel, which is not peculiar to the nation where men live, nor found in the churches of God there.

[6.] When too much time is laid out about curious and costly apparelling of the body, and adorning it with ornaments. Our furniture and dressings therewith should be such as should take up little time, for time is more precious than all thy rich robes, than all thy precious jewels and ornaments: Eph. v. 16, "Redeeming the time, because the days are evil." Many men and women squander away the time in minding new fashions, and in tricking up their vile bodies with gorgeous apparel and ornaments, and spend so many hours therein, as that they have scarce one hour for God, or the good of their souls: if more time be not spent about that most noble part of man, the clothing and trimming up of it for the Bridegroom, viz. the Lord Jesus Christ, than upon the body, you sin greatly. It is a crying and provoking sin in this land, that many not only among the great and gallant ones, but even of inferior rank, do spend a third part, if not half of their day, in dressing up their bodies with their ornaments, whereas a divine prohibition lieth against these comparatively; 1 Pet. iii. 3, speaking of women, he saith, Let not their adorning be outward, of plaiting the hair, wearing of gold, putting on of apparel, but let it be the hidden man of the heart, in the ornament of a meek and quiet spirit; rather this than the other. Hence those scriptures: "Put on the Lord Jesus Christ," Rom. xiii. 14; "Put on the new man, which, after God, is created in righteousness and true holiness," Eph. iv. 24; "Put on bowels of mercies, kindness, humbleness of mind, meekness, long-suffering, charity," Col. iii. 12, 14; "Be clothed with humility," 1 Pet. v. 5.

[7.] When it is worn unseasonably. Costly apparel and ornaments are sometimes as unseasonable as snow in summer. When it is a time of mourning, when God calls either privately or publicly to it, then we sin if we put on rich attire, our chief robes and ornaments: Exod. xxxiii. 4, 5, there were evil tidings, "they mourned, and no man put on him his ornaments;" God had bid them put off their ornaments, and told them he would not go with them, which was a sore judgment. David, when the child lay sick, had not on his royal apparel, for the text saith, When the child was dead, he rose from the earth, and changed his garments, 2 Sam. xii. 20. When Haman had got power against the Jews, and their lives were in danger, Mordecai and many of the Jews fasted, but it was in sackcloth and ashes; and when Esther sent other raiment for Mordecai to put on, he would none of it; God called to mourning, and he would testify the sorrow of his heart, by the sackcloth on his loins, and ashes on his head. Judgments and afflictions had better effects in their days than ours. God hath a long time called upon us to put on sackcloth, to testify our sorrows, we have had many days of mourning, God hath spoken to us to put off our vain fashions, our gorgeous apparel, our costly ornaments, but we have not done it. When God hath looked for our coarsest and worst garments at a fast, we have come in silk and satin, plush and crimson, bespangled with pearls, diamonds, with curled locks, powdered heads, naked necks and breasts, fitter for pageants and play-houses, than the presence of a provoked God. Do you think it meet in their own consciences, that men and women should take pleasure in adorning their bodies, and manifest it at a fast, when God is so far displeased that he threatens our lives and liberties.

So when they may draw away the minds of those that wear them, or those that behold them, from the worship of God: therefore it is questionable whether such apparel and ornaments should be worn on the Lord's days, and at such times when people meet in the congregation to worship the Lord; if they take not up their own hearts, they draw away the eyes of others, and when they come home, they can tell you more of men and women's habits, and fashions, and ornaments, than of the preacher's sermon, &c.

It is inquirable why people should so dress up themselves when they are to come before God, especially put on rich attire, and costly ornaments. Do these make you more acceptable to God? upon consideration you may fear it is otherwise; for,

First, you come before God in an open breach of his will, 1 Tim. ii.; 1 Pet. iii.

Secondly, do you not come to the Lord in a petitionary way, that he would teach you, pardon, sanctify, comfort you; and should beggars come with badges of pride upon them? Should a beggar come to you adorned with pearls and diamonds, with silk, satin, scarlet, you would have little heart to give unto him. 1 Tim. ii. he puts them upon praying every where, and then tells them that they must not be adorned in costly array.

[8.] When the callings of men are hindered by their apparel, that they cannot do what is fitting in them, or with that activity they should. Sometimes garments are too long, sometimes so little, sometimes so wide, that they cannot walk in them, nor put forth themselves with such life, as in other garments. David, when he had Saul's armour on, he could not go in it, 1 Sam. xvii. 39; it hindered the natural actions and motions of his body. That apparel which doth impede, and not promote the actions of the body, be they natural, vital, or animal, is sinful. God never set up art to prejudice but to perfect nature; therefore all garments and ornaments should be to make you act more lively; they should not retard your walking, but further it. When the sheep's fleece is heavy and cumbersome, you take it away. Sailors will have clothes to further, not hinder, their motion.

[9.] When you multiply garments and ornaments, and have them to satisfy your eye, new-fangled humour, curiosity, to fill trunks and wardrobes, yea, to breed and feed moths, rather than for any necessity or good use. Isa. iii. 22, God threatens to take away the "changeable suits of apparel:" they had variety of suits, and shifted out of one into another, like many vain giddy spirits in our days, that change their habits twice, yea thrice sometimes in a day; they have such plenty, that though they do change oft, yet they cannot keep them from the moth: Jam. v. 1, 2, "Go to, ye rich men, weep and howl for your miseries that shall come upon you: your riches are corrupted, your garments are moth-eaten." Besides, they breed moths in you, they make you solicitous and careful how to keep them, which of them to put on, how to change them into the next fashion, &c. Matt. vi. 28, "Why take ye thought for raiment?" See 1 Tim. vi. 8.

[10.] When health is endangered by them, as when huffles, slits, and windows are made in garments, so that they let in the cold, &c.; when too short above or beneath; when sluttish. Christ's dead body was "wrapped in a clean linen cloth," Matt. xxvii. 59; our living bodies should not be covered with unclean linen or woollen.

[11.] When it doth misbecome the body. Apparel is for the adorning of the body; but there are many fashions now in the world, and dresses, that do disparage that natural beauty and comeliness, which God hath put upon the body, and ought to be maintained. Paul saith, women should adorn themselves with modest apparel, with becoming apparel, such as becomes nature, such as becomes women that profess godliness. If you put honour upon those parts which are less honourable, will you dishonour those parts which are more honourable?

[12.] When apparel is made use of to deceive. Zech. xiii. 4, the false prophets did wear rough garments to deceive; such were the garments of the true prophets, as you may see from Isa. xx. 2; 2 Kings i. 8, and they put on such garments, that they might be thought such prophets, and thereby deceive the people. Many put on rich apparel, that they may be thought wealthy men, of good families, that they may get rich matches, insinuate themselves into the society of rich and great ones, to make advantage of them: many cover their crookedness, deformities, to deceive the world.

[13.] When it is scandalous to others; either actively, by drawing them to do the like, or infecting the minds of others, and their own children, with sinful thoughts and lusts; or passively, when godly ones are made sad thereby.

We should not be proud of our clothing and ornaments,

First, because they are the fruit of sin, or consequents of it. Adam's sin brought in garments: they are the tokens of sin; had there been no sin there had been no need of them.

Secondly, they mind you of your great loss: you lost better garments and better ornaments than these.

Thirdly, all from the beasts or bowels of the earth; it is weakness, if not foolishness, to affect such things.

Fourthly, your bodies are better than your clothes; Matt. vi. 25, "Is not the body more than raiment?" yet, Phil. iii. 21, "Who shall change our vile body, that it may be fashioned like unto his glorious body, according to the working whereby he is able even to subdue all things unto himself." Our bodies are made of the earth, full of sin, subject to all diseases, are oft in base employments.

Fifthly, you must give account unto God of every mercy, garment, &c. James v. 9, The judge is at the door. 1 Pet. iv. 5, "Who shall give account to him that is ready to judge the quick and the dead."

Sixthly, because they are under condemnation, and are passing: 1 John ii. 15—17, "Love not the world, neither the things that are in the world. If any man love the world, the love of the Father is not in him. For all that is in the world, the lust of the flesh, the lust of the eyes, and the pride of life, is not of the Father, but is of the world. And the world passeth away, and the lust thereof: but he that doeth the will of God abideth for ever."

Seventhly, usually they have been wicked who have affected those things: Jezebel; those in Isa. iii.; the whore, Rev. xvii.; Herod, Acts xii.; Dives, Luke xvi.

Eighthly, Christ hath set us an example of humility, Matt. xi. 29; he wore no fine clothes, no jewels or ornaments, he was crucified naked for the sin of our apparel: and it was the practice of holy women to look at the inward adorning, "the adorning of a meek and quiet spirit;" 1 Pet. i. 5, "After this manner in the old time the holy women also, who trusted in God, adorned themselves."

Obs. 2. The Lord gives variety of blessings unto his people. Not only apparel, costly apparel, but variety of it; not only ornaments, and precious ones, but variety of them; they had broidered work, fine linen, silk, bracelets, chains, nose-jewels, earrings, gold, silver, in abundance: Deut. xxviii. 12, "Thou shalt lend unto many nations, and thou shalt not borrow;" whatever they lent, clothes, jewels, or money, they had variety. When the people offered so largely, gold, silver, precious stones, and other things, 1 Chron. xxix. it argues that God had given them abundance of each; which made David say, ver. 14, "All things come of thee, and of thine own have we given thee;" God had first given, else there had been no giving unto him. It is said, Deut. xxviii. 47, they had "abundance of all things;" yea, all things at land or sea; Deut. xxxiii. 19, "They shall suck of the abundance of the seas, and of treasures hid in the sand," of gold and silver, and apparel in great abundance.

Obs. 3. The Lord minds and provides for his people, from top to toe. Clothed her with broidered work, he covered her head with silk, he girded her with fine linen, and shod her with skins of תחש; her ears, nose, neck, hands, had their ornaments; God's eye was upon every part, and his hand gave coverings and adornments for them. God doth not only mind the honourable and highest parts, but the lowest, the very feet of his people; Isa. iii. 20, they had ornaments upon their legs; Deut. viii. 4, "Thy raiment waxed not old upon thee, neither did thy foot swell, these forty years;" chap. xxix. 5, "Thy shoe is not waxen old upon thy foot." God minded the tip of Aaron's and his sons' right ears, the thumbs of their right hands, the great toe of their right foot, Exod. xxix. 20. God hath put honour, and abundance of honour, upon the uncomely parts, 1 Cor. xii. 23, 24. Seeing God minds all, and provides for all, we should honour him with all, with our heads, hands, legs, feet, even the whole body. Thou hast adorned us, we will adore thee; thou hast clothed, girded, shod, and decked us from the head to the feet, we will see to it that the whole and every part may be serviceable unto thee, that our inward man may be clothed with the righteousness of Christ, and adorned from the top to the toe with the graces of the Spirit.

Ver. 13. "Thou didst eat fine flour, and honey, and oil." You have heard before what were this woman's clothing and ornaments, now you may hear of her diet. At marriages, as they had costly garments, precious ornaments, so they had suitable dainties. The Lord provided for this woman, not acorns, or the onions and leeks of Egypt, but diet answerable to her condition; for under these expressions is held out unto us all provisions which God gave into this Israelitish estate, to feed upon all things for nourishment.

"Fine flour." Hebrew is, סלת which Kirker renders *flos seu deliciæ; farinæ triticiæ*, the flour and delicacies of wheaten meal, being ground most finely; this was offerable in sacrifices, Lev. v. 11; but קמח was common flour or meal, and not used in sacrifice, but only in the offering of jealousy, Numb. v. 15. It was very fine, such as made bread or cakes for kings, 1 Kings iv. 22; such as Abraham entertained angels with, Gen. xviii. 6. This people had manna in the wilderness, and fine flour abundantly in Canaan; it is called the fat of wheat in Psal. lxxxi. 16. Solomon spent in a day thirty measures of fine flour, in that 1 Kings iv. 22; and it was cheap, "A measure of fine flour was sold for a shekel," 2 Kings vii. 16, which was about two shillings; and their land was "a land of wheat," Deut. viii. 8, and so abounded therein, that Solomon gave twenty thousand measures of wheat unto Hiram, 1 Kings v. 11: the word for measure is, כר core; now a core is the same with the homer, eight or ten bushels, so that he gave him twenty thousand quarters at the least.

"Honey." Hebrew is, דבש which notes all sweet things, honey, sugar, dates, figs, grapes, &c. 2 Chron. xxxi. 5, there the people brought for offerings, the first-fruit of corn, wine, oil, and honey, דבש Now it is not well translated honey in this place, because honey was forbid in offerings; Lev. ii. 11, no honey was to be in any offering made with fire. It is better in the margin, where you find it rendered dates. Junius and Tremellius have it *palmæ*, that is, dates, or the fruit of the palm tree. The law speaks not at all of the first-fruits of honey, but of other things it doth. דבש may there in Chronicles be translated, sweet things, or sweet fruits; and here in Ezekiel you may understand not only honey, but all honeyish and sweet things. You have that phrase oft, "A land flowing with milk and honey," Exod. iii. 8; xiii. 5; Deut. vi. 3; Josh. v. 6; Jer. xi. 5; Ezek. xx. 6; which comprehend all other blessings, and declare what sweet and delicate things they had to feed upon. When you read of honey in the word of God, you must not always confine it to that we strictly call honey, but you must extend it to any pleasant or sweet things edible. Deut. xxxii. 13, "He made him to suck honey out of the rock:" the rocks do not yield honey; but God gave them water out of rocks, which was as sweet as honey, and God made rocks, barren places, fruitful, which was as pleasant and delightful to them as honey. It is true, they had much honey itself in the land, as you may see from 1 Sam. xiv. 26, and they did eat it, Isa. vii. 22; yet honey comprehended other things also.

"Oil." Hebrew is, שמן from שמן to make fat. Oil is very nourishing, it makes plump and fat; Neh. ix. 25, "They took strong cities, and a fat land, and possessed houses full of all goods, wells digged, vineyards, and oliveyards, and fruit trees in abundance: so they did eat, were filled, and became fat, and delighted themselves in thy great goodness." Canaan was called a fat land, it abounded with oil and other choice things, which they fed upon and became fat with. Now oil here is comprehensive, and notes also plenty of mercies belonging to the belly: Deut. xxxiii. 24, "Let Asher dip his foot in oil;" that is, let him enjoy a country that abounds with fatness. Job xxix. 6, "I washed my steps with butter, and the rock poured me out rivers of oil:" these expressions show the plenty and prosperity he had; the rock did not send out rivers of oil, but rocky places became fruitful through God's blessing; and this was as if he had been anointed with or eaten oil. Isa. xxv. 6, "the word is put there for fat things, "In this mountain shall the Lord make a feast of fat things," משתה שמנים a feast of oils. By these three, flour, honey, and oil, are set out the delicate and abundant provision of the holy land.

"Thou wast exceeding beautiful." Hebrew is emphatical, ותיפי במאד מאד The doubling of the word sets a weight upon the sense, and imports that she was come to exceeding great beauty, her silken garments and costly ornaments made her beautiful; her feeding delicately, and feasting with the choicest dainties, made her have a fresh and lively colour, and to be very beautiful. But I conceive the beautifulness of the Jews' persons is not the thing so much aimed at here, as the beauty of her state, viz. that spiritual beauty this people had, which none of the nations had; they had the temple, which was called the "beautiful house," Isa. lxiv. 11; and because it was upon "mount Zion," Psal. xlviii. 2, that is said to be beautiful, yea, "the perfection of beauty," Psal. l. 2. "Strength and beauty are in his sanctuary," Psal. xcvi. 6; before that they had the sanctuary, which was called "the beauty of holiness," Psal. xxix. 2; xcvi. 9; 1 Chron. xvi. 29.

They had the priests, who had garments glorious and beautiful, Exod. xxviii. 2, 4; when Aaron had on his robes, the twelve stones in his breastplate representing the twelve tribes, how beautiful did he appear and they in him! They had the covenant, and seals of it, circumcision and the passover; they had the law, the prophets, Urim and Thummim, sabbaths, new moons, solemn feasts and assemblies; they had the sanhedrim, and other judicatories: all which were their great glory and beauty.

"Thou didst prosper into a kingdom." This is the sixth choice mercy that the Lord did bestow upon her. In ver. 7, it is said, she had multiplied "as the bud of the field, had increased and waxen great," and so great, as that she attained and came to the honour of a kingdom; not into the place of other kings, that were of the hills and valleys in Canaan and at Jerusalem, of which you may read, Josh. ix. x. xi. and xii; but this state itself grew up to a kingly state. At first it was governed by judges, it was a free estate, and they chose whom they pleased to rule over them; afterwards they mounted to royal dignity, and out of their own loins sprang kings, Saul, David, Solomon, and many others. And in Solomon's days did this kingdom most flourish, as you may see, Psal. lxxii. and 1 Kings iv. 24—26, &c.; he reigned over all kingdoms, from the river (that was, Euphrates) unto the Philistines, and unto the border of Egypt; they brought presents, and served Solomon all the days of his life; "Judah and Israel dwelt safely, every man under his vine, and under his fig-tree, from Dan even to Beersheba. And Solomon had forty thousand stalls of horses for his chariots, and twelve thousand horsemen."

Or thus, if we will follow the metaphorical allusion: God entered into covenant with this Jewish state, took it to be his, and married himself to it, being a great King, and so it became, or passed into, a kingdom, for the word צלח signifies, to pass over, as well as, to be in a prosperous state. God therefore becoming the King of Israel, the Israelitish state became a kingdom; Exod. xix. 6, "Ye shall be unto me a kingdom." King and people are like husband and wife; Isa. lvi. 5, "Thy Maker is thine husband;" God, who was the King of this people, was their Husband; Lam. i. 1, "How doth the city sit solitary, that was full of people! how is she become as a widow! she that was great among the nations, and princess among the provinces, how is she become tributary!" while God was in her, with her, she was a princess, but now having left her, she sat as a widow, her King and Husband was gone. This exposition suits with what you had in ver. 12, "I put a beautiful crown upon thine head;" I married thee, and gave thee princely dignity, dominion, and power.

Obs. 1. The Lord allows his people dainty and delicious fare. "Thou didst eat fine flour, and honey, and oil;" under these are comprehended all the choice edibles, and the pleasant meats, the land of Canaan brought forth. At first green herbs and fruit were their meats, Gen. i. 29, but afterwards, when sin had gotten into the world, and men's desires were enlarged after the creatures, God gave them license to eat of all creatures; Gen. ix. 3, "Every moving thing that liveth shall be meat for you; even as the green herb have I given you all things." Old Isaac must have savoury meat provided for him, Gen. xxvii. 4; and Job speaks of dainty meats, chap. xxxiii. 20, Hebrew is, meat of desire; and Lam. iv. 5, they fed delicately; Psal. lxxviii. 25, "man did eat angels' food;" ver. 27, "He rained flesh also upon them as dust, and feathered fowls like as the sand of the sea." God gave them the best and choicest of meats, and so still doth unto his people.

Now, that we may not abuse that liberty which God gives us, to eat and drink, and that of the best, we must consider these cautions and rules:

(1.) We must not eat to the offence of others: Rom. xiv. 21, "It is good neither to eat flesh, nor to drink wine, nor any thing whereby thy brother stumbleth, or is offended, or is made weak." God allows us not meat to be offensive therewith; 1 Cor. viii. 13, "If meat make my brother to offend, I will eat no flesh while the world standeth, lest I make my brother to offend:" much less doth he allow us dainties.

(2.) You must not be too expensive in diet, nor go beyond the place you are set in, and abilities God hath given you. Some waste all they have upon their backs and bellies, so that they have nothing for the cause of God, public occasions, for their poor friends, or the poor in general. It will be a sad complaint, if you shall hear Christ say at last, "I was an hungred, and you gave me no meat," Matt. xxv. 42.

(3.) You must not fare deliciously in times of public calamity: Isa. xxii. 12, 13, "In that day did the Lord God of hosts call to mourning, and to baldness, and to girding with sackcloth: and, behold, joy and gladness, slaying oxen and killing sheep, eating flesh and drinking wine." When God's judgments are abroad, he would have us lay aside our dainties, and drink our own tears, to eat the bread of mourners; and because they did not, God threatens them grievously; Amos vi. 1, 4, 6, 7, "Woe to them that are at ease in Zion, that eat the lambs out of the flock, and the calves out of the midst of the stall; that drink wine in bowls, and anoint themselves with the chief ointments; but they are not grieved for the affliction of Joseph. Therefore now shall they go captive with the first that go captive, and the banquet of them that stretched themselves shall be removed:" ver. 8, "The Lord God hath sworn by himself, saith the Lord, the God of hosts, I abhor the excellency of Jacob;" what is that? the pomp and riches; pomp in feasting, pomp in apparel, &c.; "and hate his palaces: therefore will I deliver up the city, with all that is therein."

(4.) Dainties must not be too frequent. It is a brand upon the rich man, Luke xvi. 19, that "he fared sumptuously every day," he feasted daily; so the kings of the earth are censured, Rev. xviii. 9, for that they "lived deliciously" with the whore. The choice and best of the creatures should be used sparingly.

(5.) In the use of them, you must not forget those who want necessaries: Neh. viii. 10, "Go your way, eat the fat, and drink the sweet, and send portions unto them for whom nothing is prepared." Christ bids you, when you make a feast, and have dainties, to call the poor; he counsels you to make them your guests; Luke xiv. 13, "When thou makest a feast, call the poor, the maimed, the lame, the blind." There may be maimed soldiers, poor widows, and orphans, did you ever invite any of these? if you mind them not to make them your guests, and eat your dainties, yet so far mind them, as to give them your scraps: Dives would not give Lazarus the crumbs which fell from his table.

(6.) Your dishes and dainties must not be too many, excessive. Some are so pompous, that they must have mess upon mess, course upon course, exceeding in quality and quantity: Sodom had fulness of bread; 1 Pet. iv. 3, the gentiles had excess of wine, and banquetings.

(7.) We must so eat and drink as to maintain health and strength, not impair them. Eccl. x. 17, Solomon tells you, that land is happy, where "princes eat in due season, for strength, and not for drunkenness." Meat was appointed of God to nourish and strengthen; Psal. civ. 15, "Bread," that is, all things given to eat, "strengtheneth man's heart." When princes and others eat for that end, to strengthen them to do service to the public, then they use the creature comfortably. Many sin in eating too much, few on the other hand: large and delicate diet breed abundance of humours, diseases, &c.

(8.) So must we partake of them, as to further us in the operations of body and mind, to make us more active and lively in the duties of our callings. A man hath not eat and drunk warrantably, when, as Terence saith, *nec pes, nec manus, nec lingua officium suum fungi possit,* neither foot, nor hand, nor tongue, can discharge its duty. You give horses provender, that they may more freely do their work. Tertullian saith of the primitive christians, that they were wont so to feed and feast, as to remember they were to pray: Luke xxi. 34, 36, "Take heed, lest at any time your hearts be overcharged with surfeiting. Watch ye therefore, and pray always;" so eat and drink should a man, as that he should ever be fit to watch and pray: 1 Pet. v. 8, "Be sober, be vigilant; because your adversary the devil, as a roaring lion, walketh about seeking whom he may devour."

(9.) You must feed and feast with fear. It is a charge upon some in Jude, ver. 12, that they did feed and feast without fear; they sinned in eating and drinking too liberally, they did not consider the nature of the meats, nor of their appetites, but inconsiderately ventured upon what was before them, and so gluttonized; whereas, Prov. xxiii. 1, 2, he bids a man, when he is at a ruler's table, where dainties and delicacies usually are, to consider diligently what is before him, and to put a knife to his throat, if he be a man given to appetite; what is that? put thyself into a condition as if thou wert to die: when the knife was at Isaac's throat, he was near death; so putting of the knife to the throat, is serious minding of death, account, judgment, eternity, which will keep thee from surfeiting. Paul tells you of some with a sad heart, that they make their bellies their gods, Phil. iii. 19; and they are dunghill gods; how do they make these their gods? by over-minding and over-pampering them. The rabbies say, he is a glutton, or a belly-god, that eats a pound of flesh, and that he is a drunkard who drinks a quart of wine. I know there is a difference in men's constitutions and inclinations, but whosoever eats too much, he is guilty of gluttonizing. 2 Pet. ii. 13, 14, they "riot in the day time, while they feast with you; having eyes full of adultery;" they maintain and strengthen their lusts by the dainties they feed upon: James v. 5, "Ye have lived in pleasure on the earth, and been wanton:" now the rule is, "Make no provision for the flesh, to fulfil the lusts thereof." Men should rather look at, and choose, that which is wholesome, than what is delicious.

(10.) There must be spiritual care had of the time. Too much time must not be spent about dressing or eating of meats, whole nights spent in preparing for feasts, and making provision for lusts; and do not multitudes in this city sit more hours at feasting their bodies, than ever they have done at feasting their souls? Here, an hour or two is enough, or too much, there, half days, half nights: Isa. v. 11, they rose early, and continued till night in following strong drink, and other dainties, to please their lusts: and 1 Thess. v. 7, "They that be drunken, are drunken in the night;" they spent that time which was allotted by God for rest in eating and drinking; and too many spend that time which is allotted for labour, Psal. civ. 22, 23, in pampering their flesh, yea, that time which should be for prayer.

(11.) You must have God's glory in your eye. When you are eating fine flour, honey, and oil, when you eat your daily dainties, that must not be forgotten, 1 Cor. x. 31, "Whether therefore ye eat or drink, or whatsoever ye do, do all to the glory of God." This is done,

[1.] When we acknowledge God to be the Author: Hos. ii. 8, "She did not know," that is, acknowledge, "that I gave her corn, and wine, and oil."

[2.] When we look for the sweet blessings and comfort to come from the Lord, rather than from the creature: Matt. iv. 4, "Man shall not live by bread alone, but by every word that proceedeth out of the mouth of God."

[3.] When we season our tables with heavenly and gracious discourse. Many vent corrupt, filthy, and lewd speeches, they fill their bellies, and foam out their shame; but Christ, when he was at meat with his disciples or strangers, he took occasion to speak some gracious things, to reprove misdemeanours, Luke xxii. 15; xi. 38; Matt. ix. 10, 12, 13.

[4.] When we see somewhat of God in the creature, and pass speedily through the creature unto God. Many stick in the creature.

[5.] When we take these as pledges of God's love in Christ, as coming through the covenant of grace, and are thankful for them: Eph. v. 20, "Giving thanks always for all things unto God, and the Father, in the name of our Lord Jesus Christ."

Obs. 2. The Lord bestows beautifying mercies upon his people, and not only so, but such mercies as make them very beautiful. "Thou wast exceeding beautiful," thou wast made beautiful very much. God made her so; he gave her such vestments and ornaments as made her beauteous; he gave her "fine flour, honey, and oil," the choicest diet, which added to her lustre, and made her look lovely. If we put the beauty of this Israelitish woman, or state, in temporals, she had the choicest of them; her land was, Deut. viii. 7—9, "A good land; a land of brooks, fountains, depths, springs; a land of wheat, barley, vines, fig-trees, pomegranates; a land of oil-olive, and honey:" she had goodly mountains: Deut. iii. 25, Tabor, Hermon, Olives, Lebanon; she had great and goodly cities, Deut. vi. 10; goodly houses, Deut. viii. 12; multitudes of gardens, Amos iv. 9; pleasant fields, Isa. xxxii. 12; goodly cedars, Psal. lxxx. 10; great and thick oaks, 2 Sam. xviii. 9; Ezek. vi. 13; her pastures were clothed with flocks, and her valleys were covered over with corn, Psal. lxv. 13; she had her navy of ships at sea, 1 Kings ix. 26, and thirteen hundred thousand fighting men on land at once, 2 Sam. xxiv. 9.

But if you place her beauty in spirituals, all nations of the earth were in ignorance when compared to her, they were without God and his worship: Psal. lxxvi. 1, 2, "In Judah is God known; his name is great in Israel. In Salem also is his tabernacle, and his dwelling-place in Zion;" there he gave more special testimonies of his presence than in any parts of the world besides; there he conversed with and converted sinners; there he poured out his Spirit, inspired the prophets, gave out divine truths; there he wrought miracles; there were all his ordinances and worship, the sanctuary, the temple, priests, sacrifices, altars, the covenant, seals, promises, the election, adoption, the law, the glory, salvation; Isa. xlvi. 13, "I will place salvation in Zion for Israel my glory." This Jewish state was the glory of the Lord, and the Lord was her glory; he was her God, her Husband, her Counsellor, her Strength. Spiritual mercies are the beauty, the glory, of any people, therefore Phinehas's wife did rightly call the ark the glory of Israel, 1 Sam. iv. 21. Jerusalem is said to be comely; it was the spiritual mercies which were there that made her comely, and this caused David to say, Psal. lxxxiv. 1, "How amiable are thy tabernacles, O Lord of hosts!"

Obs. 3. From low and mean conditions God raises up a people to greatness. "Thou didst prosper into a kingdom." A little before, you may remember, this woman's birth and condition are set out; her father was an Amorite, her mother an Hittite, she was cast out into the open field, lay in her blood, had none to pity her; only the Lord himself did pity her, caused her to multiply, as the bud of the field, to become great, and prosper into a kingdom. From Adam and Eve, God raised up the old world, which was very populous; from Noah and seven more, the world is come to that populousness you now find it in; from Abraham and Sarah, which were even dry roots, came the whole race of the Jews: Isa. li. 1, 2, "Look unto the rock whence ye are hewn, and to the hole of the pit, whence ye are digged. Look unto Abraham your father, and unto Sarah that bare you: for I called him alone, and blessed him, and increased him." Ruth iv. 11, Rachel and Leah are said to build the house of Israel; two weak women were the pillars of the Israelitish state, they bare many children, multiplied the posterity of Jacob, and so reared up the building of Israel. That in Deut. xxvi. 5, is remarkable: "Thou shalt say, A Syrian ready to perish was my father; and he went down into Egypt, and sojourned there with a few, and became there a nation, great, mighty, and populous." Jacob fled from Esau (who sought his death) into Syria, to his uncle Laban, and therefore is called a Syrian; and after went down into Egypt, when Joseph sent for him, and there he grew to a great nation. Great cities began with single houses, great woods with single trees, great armies with single men, and great floods with little drops; how low was the state of christianity at first, in Christ, and some few!

Obs. 4. It is the Lord that forms people into a kingdom, that gives them kingly power and dignity. Ver. 12, "I put a beautiful crown upon thine head;" and, ver. 13, "thou didst prosper into a kingdom;" I followed thee so with blessings and increase, as that thou becamest a kingdom: this caused David to say, 1 Chron. xxix. 11, "Thine is the kingdom, O Lord, and thou art exalted as head above all." God hath made Israel a kingdom, and given it to David to reign over under himself, and this he acknowledged. If any people in the world have grown great, had a crown set upon their heads, and prospered into a kingdom, the Lord did it, his hand brought it to pass; hence saith Hezekiah, 2 Kings xix. 15, "O Lord God of Israel, thou art the God, even thou alone, of all the kingdoms of the earth." There is not a heathen or christian kingdom, but the Lord is the Author of; the prosperity and welfare of them is of the Lord, so long as he pleases. When Saul sinned, God took the kingdom from him, 1 Sam. xv. 8, yea, slew him, and turned the kingdom to David, 1 Chron. x. 14; he stablisheth kingdoms, 2 Chron. xvii. 5, he shakes kingdoms, Isa. xxiii. 11: he rent the kingdom from Rehoboam, and bestowed it upon Jeroboam; 1 Kings xiv. 7—10, "Go tell Jeroboam," saith God to Abijah, "Forasmuch as I exalted thee among the people, and made thee prince over my people Israel, and rent the kingdom away from the house of David, and gave it thee: and yet thou hast not been as my servant David, who kept my commandments, and who followed me with all his heart, to do that only which was right in mine eyes; but hast done evil above all that were before thee; and hast cast me behind thy back; therefore, behold, I will bring evil upon the house of Jeroboam, and will take away the remnant of the house of Jeroboam, as a man taketh away dung till it be all gone." He grew base, and God destroyed him and his, and devolved the kingdom upon others. So that it is frequently made good which Daniel told Nebuchadnezzar, chap. ii. 21, "He changeth the times and the seasons; he removeth kings, and setteth up kings:" yea, he makes kingdoms to cease, Hos. i. 4; and it is terrible what God saith, Amos ix. 8, "Behold, the eyes of the Lord God are upon the sinful kingdom, and I will destroy it from off the face of the earth;" and he did so, when they were all carried away captives; but after that great destruction, he brought them back again, built them up, prospered them into a kingdom, and set a crown upon their head.

To speak a little of the nature and state of this kingdom: Jacob, prophesying of it, Gen. xlix. 9, compares it to a lion, which in strength and majesty exceeds all other beasts, and therefore is called the king of beasts; so this kingdom of Israel exceeded other kingdoms, and was above them. God was the King of this kingdom; Psal. lxxxix. 18, "The Holy One of Israel is our King; 1 Sam. viii. 7, They have rejected me, that I should not reign over them." They were the Lord's people, and he ruled them, he gave them laws, judicial and ceremonial, which other nations had not.

He chose their kings for them, Saul, David, Solomon; therefore, Deut. xvii. 15, "Thou shalt in any wise set him king over thee, whom the Lord thy God shall choose." God chose the house of David, and settled upon his posterity the kingdom itself, which was a glorious monarchy; "And Solomon reigned over all kingdoms from the river unto the land of the Philistines, and unto the border of Egypt," 1 Kings iv. 21. The church and state were so composed, that they made but one body. This kingdom brought forth Messiah, King of the Jews, and the land was called the land of Immanuel, Isa. viii. 1; this kingdom, and the kings of it, were representative of Christ and his kingdom, and standeth still in Christ; Luke i. 32, 33, "He shall be great, and shall be called the Son of the Highest; and the Lord God shall give unto him the throne of his father David: and he shall reign over the house of Jacob for ever, and of his kingdom there shall be no end." This kingdom was at the height in Solomon's days, then the glory of it was very glorious; and in Jehoshaphat's days it flourished, 2 Chron. xviii. 1, "Jehoshaphat had riches and honour in abundance:" so in Hezekiah's days; 2 Chron. xxxii. 27—29, he "had exceeding much riches and honour."

Ver. 14. *And thy renown went forth among the heathen for thy beauty: for it was perfect through my comeliness, which I had put upon thee, saith the Lord God.*

This verse holds out the last benefit which here the Lord tells this Israelitish state he had bestowed upon her, and that was great fame; concerning which you have,

I. The extent of it; "went forth."

II. Ground of it.

1. Beauty.
2. Perfection of it.
3. The cause of all; the comeliness God put upon her.

"Thy renown." Hebrew is, שם thy name. It is

put in Scripture for renown and fame; Gen. xi. 4, "Let us build us a city and a tower, whose top may reach unto heaven; and let us make us a name;" let us thereby get renown and fame in the world: so in chap. xii. 2, I will "make thy name great," that is, thou shalt be renowned in the world. Ezek. xxxiv. 29, Christ is called "A plant of renown," מטע לשם a plant for a name.

"Went forth." Hebrew is, ויצא thy fame, or renown, spread, and was known among heathens. There were sundry things which made this state renowned.

1. The temple. When Solomon went about the building of it, he sent to Hiram king of Tyre for cedars to build it, 1 Kings v.; and the letters which Solomon wrote to that heathen king were so greatly esteemed, that they were preserved by the Tyrians till the time of Flavius Josephus, as himself affirms, in his first book against Apio the Grammarian.

There were a hundred and fifty-three thousand three hundred men employed about the work of the temple, 1 Kings v. 15, 16; the glory and stateliness of it you may read in the sixth chapter. In the holy of holies the Lord did show himself in a special manner unto the high priest once in the year. This temple was exceeding famous, it was called the house of God, Eccl. v. 1; the temple of the Lord, Jer. vii. 4; the place where God's name should be, 1 Kings viii. 29; the holy and beautiful house, Isa. lxiv. 11; God's resting-place, 2 Chron. vi. 41; the mountain of the Lord, Isa. ii. 3; the desire of their eyes, Ezek. xxiv. 21. David had told Solomon, the house he "builded for the Lord must be exceeding magnifical, of fame and of glory through all countries," 1 Chron. xxii. 5. It was known far and near; hence it was prophesied, Psal. lxviii. 29, "Because of thy temple at Jerusalem shall kings bring presents unto thee."

2. Solomon's wisdom, house, and justice were such, as caused the name of this state to go out among the heathens: 1 Kings iv. 29, "God gave Solomon wisdom and understanding. And Solomon's wisdom excelled the wisdom of all the children of the east country, and all the wisdom of Egypt. For he was wiser than all men: and his fame was in all nations round about;" and ver. 34, "There came of all people to hear the wisdom of Solomon, from all kings of the earth, which had heard of his wisdom." Among others came the queen of Sheba, to prove him with hard questions, which he satisfied her in; and when she had seen his wisdom, his house, and the order of it, she said to the king, "It was a true report that I heard in mine own land of thy acts and of thy wisdom. Howbeit I believed not the words, until I came, and mine eyes had seen it: and, behold, the half was not told me: thy wisdom and prosperity exceedeth the fame which I heard," 1 Kings x. 1, 3, 4, 6, 7. His justice was foretold; Psal. lxxii. 4, "He shall judge the poor of the people, he shall save the children of the needy, and shall break in pieces the oppressor."

3. Their battles and victories. They had many choice warriors, and fighting men, among them; Joshua, Othniel, Ehud, Shamgar, Deborah, Barak, Gideon, Jephthah, Samson, David, &c. Asa had an army of five hundred and eighty thousand, and he ruined Zerah's army of a thousand thousand, 2 Chron. xiv. 8, 9, 12, 13; so Jehoshaphat vanquished the army of the Ammonites, Moabites, and those of mount Seir, 2 Chron. xx. The Lord of hosts was with them, and fought their battles for them, which filled the nations with the fame and fear of them.

4. The prophets, and the miraculous things they did, caused the fame of this Israelitish state to go forth. Elijah opened and shut heaven, James v. 17, 18; he raised the widow of Zarephath's son, 1 Kings xvii.; he sacrificed the prophets of Baal and of the groves, chap. xviii. So Elisha, what great things did he! he multiplied the widow's oil, 2 Kings iv.; he gave a son to the good Shunammite, which went childless, and restored him to life when he was dead; his fame spread into Syria, whereupon Naaman came to him, to be cured of his leprosy, 2 Kings v.; he disclosed the secrets of the king of Syria's counsel, chap. vi.

5. Their being in covenant with God, and walking according to his laws, rules, and commands, made them renowned. Hos. xi. 12, "Ephraim compasseth me about with lies, and the house of Israel with deceit;" they went out from God to false and idolatrous worship, they brake the covenant, the law, clave to their own inventions; "but Judah yet ruleth with God," he goeth along with God in his ways, and is faithful with the saints, he keeps covenant and touch with the Lord, and this is his wisdom, glory, renown. Deut. iv. 6, "Keep God's statutes and do them; for this is your wisdom and your understanding in the sight of the nations, which shall hear all these statutes, and say, Surely this great nation is a wise and understanding people;" their obedience to God's laws was that which made them honourable abroad, and to be counted wise and understanding. So Deut. xxvi. 18, 19, "The Lord hath avouched thee this day to be his peculiar people, and that thou shouldest keep all his commandments; and to make thee high above all nations which he hath made, in praise, in name, and in honour:" the way to be exalted in all these, is to walk in the ways of the Lord. It is "righteousness exalteth a nation: but sin is a reproach to any people," Prov. xiv. 34.

"For thy beauty." I have spoken of this woman's beauty before in ver. 13. Beauty consists in the symmetry or due proportion of all the parts well coloured; here it was so: there was a symmetry between church and state, a fit proportion between princes, prophets, priests, and the people, and they were all well-coloured with temporals and spirituals.

"It was perfect." The Hebrew word כליל signifies, entire, perfect. You must not take "perfect," for that which wants nothing absolutely, but for that which is complete or perfect in its kind; it is joined to peace, Isa. xxvi. 3; to love, 1 John iv. 18; to faith, James ii. 22: it notes the muchness or entireness of them.

"My comeliness." Hebrew is, בהדרי in my comeliness, הדר notes all honourable comeliness and adorning decency; Psal. viii. 5, thou "hast crowned him with glory," with honour, comeliness. Whatever this kingdom and people had which was excellent, majestical, honourable, beautiful, glorious, that is comprehended in this word "comeliness."

Obs. 1. That whatever comeliness any kingdoms, states, or persons have, it is not from themselves, but from the Lord. "Through my comeliness, which I had put upon thee." This Jewish state was without beauty, glory, honour, she lay in her blood, filth, was naked and loathsome; but God spread his skirt over her, covered her nakedness, washed away her blood, anointed her with oil, clothed her with broidered work, shod her with skins of *tachasch*, girded her with fine linen, covered her with silk, decked her with ornaments. Whatever external or internal comeliness is in any, the Lord hath put it upon them. Is a state decked with cities, people, trading, with mountains, woods, rivers, flocks of cattle, &c.? hath it good laws, good magistrates, justice duly executed, the righteous countenanced, the wicked awed?

it is the Lord's doing. Have any spiritual mercies, the word, other ordinances? 1 Cor. iv. 7, who makes thee differ? or what hast thou thou didst not receive? if you receive any thing, you receive it from God. The spouse was comely, Cant. i. 5; her countenance was comely, chap. ii. 14; her speech was comely, chap. iv. 3; this comeliness the Lord put upon her.

Obs. 2. That which we have is the Lord's. "Through my comeliness." God had bestowed many ornaments and excellences upon this woman, which made her comely, and here he calls all his "comeliness." 1 Kings xx. 3, Benhadad said to Ahab, "Thy silver and thy gold is mine; thy wives also and thy children, even the goodliest, are mine." He challenged all injuriously, but God most justly; Hos. ii. 9, "My corn, my wine, my wool, my flax." This woman was the Lord's, ver. 8, "Thou becamest mine," and so all she had was his.

Obs. 3. That renown and fame is a choice mercy, which God gives to his people "Thy renown went forth among the heathen;" God made her beautiful, and caused her renown to go abroad, and reckons it up amongst the mercies he bestowed upon her. Prov. xxii. 1, "A good name is rather to be chosen than great riches;" if man might have mountains of gold, the wealth of the Indies, it is nothing to a good name. Eccles. vii. 1, "A good name is better than precious ointment," it pleases, refresheth, is profitable; Prov. xv. 30, "A good report maketh the bones fat." God gives this name; 1 Chron. xvii. 8, speaking of David, "I have made thee a name like the name of the great men that are in the earth:" ver. 21, "What one nation in the earth is like thy people Israel, whom God went to redeem to be his own people, to make thee a name of greatness and terribleness." While they clave to the Lord, as a girdle to the loins, they were to the Lord for a name, for a praise, for a glory, Jer. xiii.; but when they degenerated from God and his ways, they became base. Prov. x. 7, "The memory of the just is blessed: but the name of the wicked shall rot:" Isa. lxv. 15, "Ye shall leave your name for a curse unto my chosen:" Isa. lxii. 7, "Give him no rest, till he make Jerusalem a praise in the earth."

Ver. 15—19. *But thou didst trust in thine own beauty, and playedst the harlot because of thy renown, and pouredst out thy fornications on every one that passed by; his it was. And of thy garments thou didst take, and deckedst thy high places with divers colours, and playedst the harlot thereupon: the like things shall not come, neither shall it be so. Thou hast also taken thy fair jewels of my gold and of my silver, which I had given thee, and madest to thyself images of men, and didst commit whoredom with them, and tookest thy broidered garments, and coveredst them: and thou hast set mine oil and my incense before them. My meat also which I gave thee, fine flour, and oil, and honey, wherewith I fed thee, thou hast even set it before them for a sweet savour: and thus it was, saith the Lord God.*

From the beginning of the 6th verse unto the 15th, you have heard of the choice mercies the Lord bestowed upon this Jewish state, even such mercies as should have engaged her heart and strength to God for ever. In these verses, and the fifteen following, you have the fourth general part of the chapter, viz. The Lord's exprobration of this Israelitish woman for her ingratitude; he was exceeding kind and merciful unto her, and she was exceeding unkind and unthankful unto him.

This ingratitude is set out,

I. By her defection from God to idolatrous practices, laid down ver. 15—35.

II. By her inhumaneness, in slaying and sacrificing her own children, ver. 20, 21.

III. The cause of these, ver. 22.

In ver. 15, you have,

1. Her sinful confidence, "Thou didst trust in thine own beauty."

2. Her whoredom, "and playedst the harlot."

3. The motive thereunto, her "renown."

4. The greatness and extent of her whoredoms, "and pouredst out thy fornications on every one that passed by."

5. The manner of her whorish and idolatrous practices; she took her garments, jewels, oil, incense, fine flour, and honey, and bestowed them all upon her images, ver. 16—19.

"Thou didst trust." Hebrew is, תבטחי thou hast trusted. Having received many mercies from God, both temporal and spiritual, she grew proud, confident, and trusted in what the Lord had given her to make her beautiful; she grew secure, presumptuous, and loose, leaving God, who gave her all, and resting in his gifts.

"And playedst the harlot." Hebrew is, ותזני the word זנה signifies, to be impure in body or mind, when one leaves her husband, and wantonizeth with others in mind or body. When it is spoken of the state of the Jews, (as here, and frequently in other places of Scripture,) it notes leaving of God, cleaving to idols, worshipping of them, which is called fornication, whoredom; Hos. i. 2, "The land hath committed great whoredom, departing from the Lord;" Judg. ii. 17, "They went a whoring after other gods, and bowed themselves unto them;" chap. viii. 27, when Gideon set up his ephod, "all Israel went thither a whoring after it." There is spiritual whoredom as well as corporal whoredom; the setting up idols or images, using any reverential gestures in honour of them, the worshipping of them, or God by them, is spiritual whoredom.

I shall show you wherefore idolatry is called fornication and whoredom, and that is, from the resemblances which are between them.

1. A whorish woman leaves and goes out from her husband to another; Prov. ii. 17, "She forsaketh the guide of her youth," that is, her husband; she pleads she had not that content, delight, satisfaction in him as she looked for: so here, this Israelitish woman forsook her Husband, and went out to other gods; Jer. ii. 11, 13, "Hath a nation changed their gods, which are yet no gods? but my people have changed their glory; they have forsaken me the fountain of living waters." Hos. ix. 1, "Thou hast gone a whoring from thy God;" and what was that whoring? Jer. iii. 9, committing adultery with stocks and stones; that was, idolatrous worshipping of them.

2. Whoredom is a breach of that covenant which was made between husband and wife at marriage. Prov. ii. 17, she "forgetteth the covenant of her God," that is, the covenant made with her husband, in the presence of God; so a people in covenant with God, going out to idolatrous practices, they break covenant with him; ver. 8, "I entered into covenant with thee, and thou becamest mine;" but this woman, falling into idolatry, brake covenant, therefore, Jer. iii. 20, "As a wife treacherously departeth from her husband, so have ye dealt treacherously with me, O house of Israel, saith the Lord:" this God foresaw, and foretold long before; Deut.

xxxi. 16, they will go a whoring after other gods, they "will forsake me, and break my covenant which I have made with them."

3. Whoredom is pleasing and delightful to men and women, but it is abominable and loathsome in the account of God: Prov. vii. 18, saith the harlot there, "Come, let us take our fill of love until the morning: let us solace ourselves with loves." They had pleasure and delight in their sin, but it was abominable in the sight of God, and therefore it is called uncleanness in a special manner, Rom. i. 24; Eph. iv. 19; so in idolatrizing, and superstitionizing, there is that which pleaseth man, but provokes God greatly. They went a whoring after idols, they saw beauty in them, found pleasure in letting out their hearts unto them; Ezek. xviii. 6, they lifted up their eyes to their idols, they took as much pleasure in beholding them as a man in beholding the beauty of a woman, their idolatry was delightful to them. Isa. xliv. 9, images are called their "delectable things," or desirable, as the Hebrew is; but however they were delightful to them, they were not so to God; Isa. lxv. 12, they "did choose that wherein I delighted not." God was so far from delighting in them that he abhorred them, and therefore calls them defiling abominations, Jer. xxxii. 34; devils, Deut. xxxii. 17; confusion, Isa. xli. 29; detestable things, Ezek. v. 11.

4. Whoredom darkens men's understandings, infatuates the spirits of men, and steals away their hearts; Hos. iv. 11, "Whoredom and wine and new wine take away the heart." Solomon, that was exceeding wise, had his spirit so besotted with women, that he was not able to see the sinfulness of idolatry, but had his heart turned after other gods, 1 Kings xi. Such is idolatry, it blinds men's understanding, and clouds their judgments; Rom. i. 21, "They became vain in their imaginations, and their foolish heart was darkened," and they, "professing themselves to be wise, they became fools," in making images of God, ver. 22, 23: see their folly, "They worshipped the works of their own hands," Jer. i. 16; they trusted in that which could neither hear, see, speak, smell, nor go, Psal. cxv. 5—8; they asked counsel of stocks, Hos. iv. 12; they said "to a stock, Thou art my father; and to a stone, Thou hast brought me forth," Jer. ii. 27.

5. Whoredom is a reproaching sin; Prov. vi. 33, speaking of a man committing adultery, he tells you, "A wound and dishonour shall he get; and his reproach shall not be wiped away:" so idolatry brings reproach upon men; 1 Pet. iv. 3, they are called "abominable idolatries," they make the names of men abominable, as well as their persons and actions. They are termed haters of God, Exod. xx. 5; blasphemers, Isa. lxv. 7; adulterers, Jer. iii. 9; worshippers of devils, Rev. ix. 20.

6. It is an inflaming sin. Job xxxi. 12, it is called "a fire," and kindles such a flame in the house, as ofttimes consumes it. Idolatry is of the same nature: Isa. lvii. 5, "Inflaming yourselves with idols;" there was a spirit of whoredoms in them, which kindled strong, burning, inflaming lusts after their idols: Jer. l. 38, "They are mad upon their idols:" where there is madness, there is a great inflammation of the blood and spirits.

7. Uncleanness is a sin destructive to body and soul: Prov. v. 11, it consumes the body; it destroys the soul, chap. vi. 32; and the harlot's house is the way to hell, going down to the chambers of death, chap. vii. 27. So idolatry is a dangerous sin, it threatens destruction of body and soul; Baal's prophets lost their lives for their idolatry, 1 Kings xviii.; Gideon's ephod was a ruin to him and to his household, Judg. viii.; and, in 1 Cor. vi. 9, 10, there is a dreadful place against fornicators and idolaters;" "Know ye not that the unrighteous shall not inherit the kingdom of God? Be not deceived; neither fornicators, nor idolaters, nor adulterers," &c. "shall inherit the kingdom of God."

8. Whoredom is a costly sin; much is wasted in vestments, much in ornaments, much in meats, drinks, junketings, and perfumes. Prov. vii. 16, 17, "I have decked my bed with coverings of tapestry, with carved works, with fine linen of Egypt. I have perfumed my bed with myrrh, aloes, and cinnamon:" the dressings, deckings, banquetings, perfumings which attend that vice, are very costly. Idolatry, likewise, is a chargeable thing; Isa. xlvi. 6, "They lavish gold out of the bag." When nothing else could fetch the gold out of it, idolatry could, and that in abundance; "they lavish it out," to maintain and adorn an idol-god; see Isa. xl. 19; Jer. x. 4, 9. So here, they decked their high places with broidered garments, with jewels of gold and silver, they bestowed upon them oil and incense, fine flour and honey.

9. It is an impudent sin, it makes bold and brazenfaced: Prov. vii. 13, the harlot had an impudent face, and spake impudent things. Idolatry begets impudence also: Ezek. iii. 7, "All the house of Israel are impudent;" and how impudently did they speak, when they offered incense in the chambers of their imagery, to creeping things, and abominable beasts, portrayed upon the walls! they said, "The Lord seeth us not; the Lord hath forsaken the earth," chap. viii. 10—12.

"Because of thy renown." Hebrew is, על שמך Thou hadst a great name, wast become famous abroad, and this invited the nations to come and visit thee, and brought in the gods of their countries, which thou receivedst, and playedst the harlot with: or thus you may read the words, against thy name; Thou hast played the harlot against thy name; whereas, before, thou hadst an honourable and precious name, now by thy sinful and base practices, thou hast polluted it, and made thy name to stink.

The Vulgate reads it, in thy name; and I find interpreters carry the sense to be this, That this woman having left her husband, under whose authority and power she formerly was, did all now in her own name; she pretended now she was *sui juris*, and would live as she list, and converse with whom she pleased: Hos. iv. 12, "They have gone a whoring from under their God;" they would not be under the authority and command of God, as a chaste spouse should be, but left him as a whore doth her husband, and so did all in their own name: Jer. ii. 31, "We are lords; we will come no more unto thee;" we are at liberty, are lords over ourselves and our own actions, we will have what gods we please.

"And pouredst out thy fornications." Hebrew is, ותשפכי like a whore that prostitutes herself to all comers; so did this Jewish state prostitute itself to the idolatrous practices of all nations that came to her. It is sinful for a woman to be taken with the desire of another man, worse to commit folly with him, though one of the same house, but it is far worse to be taken with strangers, and to prostitute herself to all comers, and to be a common strumpet; this Israelitish woman was so, if any had any new gods, or new devices in worship, she entertained them. The word pouring out sets forth the vehement and insatiable desire she had to sin. Or thus: "Pouredst out thy fornications;" thou didst communicate and impart thy idolatrous and false ways of worship to all that passed by, thou infectedst them therewith; thou was not content alone to be naught thyself, but drewest in many others to partake of thy sins: she was full of spiritual whoredoms, and taught all nations to be more idolatrous.

"His it was." Hebrew is, לו יהי to him it was. In ver. 8, saith God, "Thou becamest mine;" and in ver. 14, "Thy beauty was perfect through my comeliness, which I put upon thee;" but here it was another's, her comeliness, her beauty, her desire, her body, her estate, were all another's. Vulgate is, that thou shouldst become his; thou wast weary of my love, and hast sought out other lovers, that thou mightest mingle with them, and satisfy thy lust; and not only hast thou left, cast off, me, but thou hast embraced others; whoever passed by thee had thy heart and affection as much as ever I had, for him thou wast, and his was all thou hadst.

Obs. 1. Where God bestows choice mercies upon a people, he looks for answerable returns from them. He gave life to the Israelitish state, ver. 6; he multiplied it as the bud of the field, ver. 7; he loved this people, entered into covenant with them, married them unto himself, ver. 8; he washed away their blood, and anointed them with oil, ver. 9; he gave them costly apparel, precious ointments, fine flour, honey, and oil, royal dignity, special beauty and comeliness, great fame and glory, ver. 10—14; and now expected that they should have lived to him, loved, feared, obeyed, served him, and improved all for the honour of his name. "But thou didst trust in thine own beauty, and playedst the harlot," &c. I looked not for this at thy hands; of all the people in the world, I looked that thou shouldst have been faithful and fruitful in all good works, and been as exemplary for holiness and justice to other nations, as I was exemplary in my mercies towards thee above other nations. Isa. v. 2, there God fenced his vineyard, gathered out the stones thereof, planted it with the choicest vine, built a tower in the midst of it, made a wine-press in it, digged it, caused the clouds to rain upon it, and did all that could be done for the good of it; and what then? "I looked that it should bring forth grapes," ver. 4; I looked for judgment and righteousness, ver. 7: where God multiplies mercies, he expects suitable returns. See one place more, Deut. xxxii. 6—16, he shows there that God was their Father, had bought them, made them a great people from low beginnings, set them their bounds, chosen them to be his portion and inheritance, how he had led, instructed, and kept them as the apple of his eye, and what variety of other mercies he had bestowed upon them; "but Jeshurun waxed fat, and kicked." This people, that should have been righteous and upright, obeying the laws of their God and Father, rebelled and kicked like a fatted ox; which made Moses say, ver. 6, "Do you thus requite the Lord?" do you corrupt and spot yourselves with the courses of the world? The Lord looked for other things at their hands.

Obs. 2. Ingratitude in God's people is a provoking sin, and causes God to upbraid them for it. I gave thee life, increase, took thee to be mine, cleansed thee from thy filth and blood, anointed thee with oil, I clothed, decked, covered thee, fed thee, I made thee exceeding beautiful and comely, gave thee great renown, set a crown upon thy head, prospered thee into a kingdom; "but thou didst trust in thine own beauty, and playedst the harlot." From the beginning of ver. 6, to the end of ver. 14, which are but nine verses, there is "I" seventeen times, and every mention of it is matter of upbraiding unto them; there is hardly the like in all the book of God. When men will not mind God's mercies, to be thankful, he will remember them, to upbraid their unthankfulness for them.

When God had made Adam after his image, planted him in paradise, given him dominion over all the creatures, for him not to obey one little command, this was great ingratitude; provoked the Lord to come down from heaven, to upbraid him, and punish him for it, Gen. iii.; "Adam, where art thou?" what! hast thou forgotten me, and all the mercies so lately heaped upon thee, and eaten the forbidden fruit? "Cursed is the ground for thy sake; in sorrow shalt thou eat of it all the days of thy life," ver. 17. In Isa. xxxvii. you read of Sennacherib's great army before Jerusalem, which filled them with fears, and caused sadnesses in many families; God destroyed this army by an angel in a night. In the next chapter, you find Hezekiah was sick unto death: Jerom delivers it to be the judgment of the learned Jews, that therefore he was struck with sickness, because he was not thankful to God for this great deliverance; and this was a real upbraiding of him for his ingratitude. Isa. i. 2, 3, God was so troubled at the ingratitude of this people, that he could hold no longer, but must call forth a prophet, and cause him to begin his prophecy in this manner, "Hear, O heavens, and give ear, O earth: for the Lord hath spoken, I have nourished and brought up children, and they have rebelled against me. The ox knoweth his owner, and the ass his master's crib;" they give them a little hay, straw, grass, water, and the brute creatures are thankful for them; "but Israel doth not know, my people do not consider;" I give them their oxes, and asses, all that belongs to them, and greater things than so, yet they know not me.

Matt. xi. Christ upbraids Chorazin, Bethsaida, and Capernaum, where his mighty works were done, because they brought not forth fruits answerable, but were impenitent and ungrateful; he tells Capernaum, it shall be more easy for Sodom than for her in the day of judgment.

Judg. viii. 34, 35, "The children of Israel remembered not the Lord their God, who had delivered them out of the hands of all their enemies on every side: neither showed they kindness to the house of Gideon, according to all the goodness he had showed unto Israel." Socrates, saith the Athenians, admitted no ungrateful man into the republic.

What ingratitude was it in the men of Keilah, when the Philistines fought against them, robbed them, endangered their liberties and lives, and David with his men smote the Philistines with a great slaughter, and saved the inhabitants of Keilah, 1 Sam. xxiii. 15; and quickly afterwards, they would have delivered David, who had saved them, into the hands of Saul, his enemy! ver. 12.

Obs. 3. We are very apt to trust in, and be proud of, the mercies God bestows upon us. "Thou didst trust in thine own beauty;" those things I gave to make thee beautiful, those thou hast abused, been proud of, put too much confidence in. Such is the heart of man, that it is ready to idolize every mercy God gives.

There are several mercies we are apt to trust in.

(1.) In riches. Prov. x. 15, "The rich man's wealth is his strong city," he confides as much in it as citizens do in a walled, well fortified, and well built city: Psal. lii. 7, "This is the man that made not God his strength; but trusted in the abundance of his riches:" 1 Tim. vi. 17, "Charge them that are rich in this world, that they be not high minded, nor trust in uncertain riches;" he that doth it shall fall, Prov. xi. 28.

(2.) In princes and great ones. Psal. cxlvi. 3, "Put not your trust in princes, nor in the son of man, in whom there is no help," no salvation: Isa. ii. 22, "Cease ye from man, whose breath is in his nostrils; for wherein is he to be accounted of?" Jer. xvii. 5, "Cursed be the man that trusteth in man, and maketh flesh his arm." The Jews put confidence in Egypt, and the king of it; Isa. xxx. 3, "Therefore shall the strength of Pharaoh be your shame, and the trust in the shadow of Egypt your confusion."

(3.) In your own natural excellences. Jer. ix. 23, "Let not the wise man glory in his wisdom, neither let the mighty man glory in his might;" it shows there is a great propensity in the hearts of men to do it. Prov. xxviii. 26, "He that trusteth in his own heart is a fool;" the heart is the most excellent part of man: Prov. iii. 5, "Trust in the Lord with all thine heart; and lean not unto thine own understanding."

(4.) In the ordinances and means of grace. Jer. vii. 4, "Trust ye not in lying words, saying, The temple of the Lord," &c.: ver. 14, 15, "Therefore will I do unto this house, which is called by my name, wherein ye trust, as I have done to Shiloh. And I will cast you out of my sight, as I have cast out all your brethren, even the whole seed of Ephraim."

Obs. 4. Great renown, through man's corruption, oft proves a snare, occasions great sins. "Thou playedst the harlot because of thy renown;" thou wast grown great, famous abroad, exceededst other nations, who, coming to see thy beauty, and behold thy glory, which they heard of, thou dotedst upon them, and drewest them to fornication: her renown was the bait to allure them, and to induce them, being allured, to spiritual whoredoms. Renown is a great mercy of the Lord, and should be a special motive to make us honour God, and to improve it for his glory, and others' good; but usually estates and persons abuse that renown and esteem they have in the world, making advantage thereof only to serve their own turns and lust. God made this people above all nations, in praise, in name, in honour, that they might be a holy people unto him, Deut. xxvi. 19; their renown should have encouraged them to holiness, and it was an incentive unto looseness. Solomon had great renown abroad in the nations, 1 Kings iv. 31; that drew the princes to bestow their daughters upon him; chap. xi. 3, he had seven hundred wives, princesses; his name made way for unlawful marriages, and they made way for unlawful gods. You read of rooting up Israel, 1 Kings xiv. 15; of blotting out their name from under heaven, Deut. ix. 14; of cutting it off, Isa. xlviii. 19: the reason was, they abused that name God had given them to idolatry, and other sinful practices. Many of great credit take up money and break.

Obs. 5. Going out from God to false gods and ways of worship, is a grievous sin. "Thou playedst the harlot," that is, thou didst leave me, thy God and Husband, and wentest after others; thy body, thy beauty, thy heart and affections were theirs, and with them thou didst commit whoredoms; Psal. cvi. 28, "They joined themselves also unto Baal-peor." This was apostasy in this people, to forsake God, break covenant, all engagements, to go out to others, as if there were more good, content, sweetness to be had in them, than in the Lord; Micah vi. 3, "O my people, what have I done unto thee? and wherein have I wearied thee? testify against me." They made their nations think their gods better than the God of Israel, and their way of worship better than his, which was a great reproach to the Lord, and made him to complain. The Hebrew calls the winter חרף because it is a reproach to the earth; and such is an apostate people; they are חרף a reproach to God and his ordinances, they bring up an ill report upon Canaan, the grapes and God thereof. When the Samaritans worshipped strange gods, the Jews counted and called them bastards for it; but when they practised it themselves, they were blind, and discerned not the evil of it: John viii. 41, "We be not born of fornication;" they meant they were not the children of idolaters, and such as had apostatized from God; whereas their predecessors had been the greatest apostates and idolaters of the world. This sin kindles the jealousy of God, Exod. xx. 5; Prov. vi. 34; and made the Lord say, Heb. x. 38, "If any man draw back, my soul shall have no pleasure in him;" no, his soul should be exceedingly against them. Hence saith God of the Levites, that fell to idolatry, that they should "bear their iniquity. And they shall not come near unto me to do the office of a priest unto me," Ezek. xliv. 10, 13.

Some of the ancients have thought that a man falling away from the truth once, or twice especially, there is no mercy for him.

Obs. 6. The most beautiful and renowned church may degenerate, apostatize, and become so corrupt, that it may be questionable whether there be the face of a true visible church in all the world. This Israelitish woman was the only spouse of God, he entered into a covenant with her, she became his, ver. 8; he did great things for her, he put more spiritual beauty and comeliness upon her than upon all the nations, and made her renowned throughout the world; yet she forsook God, played the harlot, multiplied fornications, prostituted herself to every idol and idolater; and now where was the church of God? She "played the harlot with many lovers," Jer. iii. 1; here was visible apostasy, visible idolatry, but no true visible church in joining communion with God in his own way. Neither was God without a true church at this time. There were some godly ones in secret, which kept themselves from those idolatrous pollutions, who mourned in secret for the abominations done in the temple, city, and every where, Ezek. ix. 4; but these lay hid, and durst not appear in the ways of worship then amongst them. So in Elijah's days, Ahab, Jezebel, the false prophets and priests of Baal, had so corrupted the worship of God, and the people so apostatized, that there was no visible face of a church left in the view of Elijah himself; for he saith, "The children of Israel have forsaken thy covenant, thrown down thine altars, and slain thy prophets; and I, even I only, am left; and they seek my life, to take it away," 1 Kings xix. 10; but God had then seven thousand in secret, ver. 18.

The true church may be brought to such a paucity, such a lowness, as that there may be no public meetings, or view thereof. Whilst this church hearkened to her Husband, obeyed his voice, followed the rules of the word, she was chaste, and free from errors; but when she grew proud of her fame, and trusted in her beauty, then she fell into errors, defiled herself with idols, and sinned shamefully.

The papists say, their church cannot err, especially in things necessary to salvation; and why? because it is the spouse of Christ. Was not this Israelitish church the spouse of God? and did it not err in the great and weighty things of salvation? did it not leave God, and fall to idolatry, such practices as exclude the kingdom of heaven? What privilege hath the Roman church more than this had? Whatever papists say or write, their church hath trusted in her beauty, been proud of her renown, and played the harlot, as notoriously as ever Jerusalem did.

Ver. 16. "And deckedst thy high places with divers colours." The Hebrew is, And hast made to thyself spotted high places. In their high places were altars made for the honour of their idols, those they decked with tapestry, and clothes bespotted with divers colours, that so they might affect and allure more strongly the worshippers, and those that came to see them worshipping.

Ver. 17. "Thou hast also taken thy fair jewels." The Hebrew is, כלי תפארתך the vessels or instruments of thy glory. Some refer these instruments of glory to the golden or silver vessels of the temple, which were glorious vessels, and vessels of their glory. It is said that Ahaz, 2 Chron. xxviii. 24, "gathered together the vessels of the house of God, and cut them in pieces, and made him altars in every corner of Jerusalem." It is like he might convert the gold and silver of the temple to idolatrous uses; or you may interpret it of their plate, those vessels of glory they had for their domestic use, not excluding the golden and silver ornaments they had for their own adorning.

"And madest to thyself images of men." The Hebrew is, צלמי זכר images of man; not images of God, who was her Husband and beloved, but images of man. The nations had their gods and goddesses, he-gods and she-gods; Baal, Milchom, Chamos, Molech, were masculine gods; Ashtoreth, Isis, Derceto, were feminine gods. The Jewish state being here compared unto a woman, a whorish woman, who loves and affects the presence, beauty, and embracings of men, that is fitly said to make unto herself images of men, with which she might adulterize and idolize, and satiate her lusts both fleshly and spiritual. The Hebrew word for masculine, or of a man, is from זכר to remember; these images were memorials and remembrancers of their idol gods, of pleasures they had in accompanying with or worshipping of them.

Ver. 19. "My meat also which I gave thee." The Hebrew is, ולחמי my bread. Though לחם ordinarily signifies bread, yet here it must be taken comprehensively for any thing edible; the enumeration following shows it, as "fine flour, and oil, and honey;" and the word is so to be understood in Luke xiv. 1; Christ went into one of the Pharisees' houses to eat bread; by "bread" is meant whatever should be set before him: so Gen. xxxix. 6, Potiphar left all in Joseph's hand, he knew not aught he had, save the bread which he did eat; "bread," that is, all things he did eat: so Matt. vi. 11, daily bread comprehends all edible things, and more too.

"Thou hast even set it before them for a sweet savour." The Hebrew is, לריח ניחח That which is sweet and pleasing to the smell, we rest in as delightful to us. She set these things before the images of men, and the false gods, to practise them if they were offended, and to endear them more unto herself hereby, as if she had merited their favours and embraces. The offering of incense and sweet odours was a part of divine worship, and when sacrifice was made to him by Noah, he smelled a sweet savour; the Hebrew is the same with what was here, he was well pleased therewith. It is taken from the practice of men, who used sweet smells, Isa. iii. 24.

Obs. 1. The making of high places, altars, images for religious uses, the adorning of them, and offering unto them, is idolatrous and provoking. Here God upbraids and condemns this woman in ver. 16; in ver. 17, for making of images; in ver. 18, for covering of them with broidered garments; and in this verse and ver. 19, for offering oil, incense, flour, honey unto them. God calls these things playing the harlot, committing whoredom.

This practice of theirs hath many aggravations in it.

(1.) That they made high places the places of their idolatry, which were open to view; they would worship false gods in the sight of heaven and earth.

(2.) That they made masculine images, which showed their filthy lust, and filthy idolatry, and set them up in the stead of God.

(3.) That they covered them with divers colours, and broidered garments: those of one colour, of worse materials, might have sufficed them, but these pleased their eyes, and inveigled others.

(4.) That they offered the Lord's oil, incense, and meat unto them.

(5.) That they thought these made them acceptable to the idols, and the idols propitious unto them, and put some divineness in them.

Obs. 2. Idolaters and false worshippers think no expenses, no charges, too much, to accomplish their devices, and maintain their way. If they want a god, or an image, to mind them of the true God, they will take their vessels of glory, the gold and silver of the temple, their plate, their fair jewels and ornaments of their bodies, and have gods and images made with them; if these gods and images seem naked, they will bestow their own clothes, their broidered and best garments, their coloured hangings, yea, they will spare their meat out of their own bellies, and set it before them. When Moses was in the mount, the people were set upon it to have a new visible god to go before them, and they call upon Aaron to make them such a god; he thought they would not have been at any great cost for an idol-god, and therefore saith, If you will have a god, you must break the golden earrings out of the ears of your wives, sons, and daughters; if you will part with them which are your glory and ornament, which will put you to much pain before you get them out, for you must break them; if you will do so, you shall have a golden god, Exod. xxxii. 1, 2. Did they stick at this? no, no; ver. 3, "All the people brake off the golden earrings which were in their ears, and brought them unto Aaron:" here was no compulsion, no delay, they brake and brought. Hos. ii. 8, God "multiplied her silver and gold, which they prepared for Baal," or therewith made Baal; they freely bestowed it upon idols, and idolatrous worship. Should we come to people now, and say, You would gladly have the true God to be your God, his ways and ordinances to walk in, and serve him by, but it must cost you your vessels of glory, your plate, jewels, ornaments, embroidery; what could they think of it?

Obs. 3. It is a detestable sin to abuse the mercies God gives us, for our necessities, ornaments, or delights, to the dishonour of his name. I gave thee gold and silver, and thou madest images of them; I clothed thee with broidered work, and thou coveredst thine images with them; I gave thee oil, incense, honey, and fine flour, and thou hast set them before thine images. Here was abominable ingratitude; as if God should say here, Consider and commiserate my case, all ye my friends and faithful servants, men and angels, I have showed great kindness, and dealt bountifully with this people, honoured them above others, given them the choicest blessings the world hath, and they turn all against me, and bestow my blessings upon false gods; they take their vestments and ornaments, clothe, adorn, and beautify their abominable idols with them. Suppose a prince, most amiable and virtuous, should take a poor, beggarly maid, having nothing, sick unto death, be at great cost to cure her, clothe, adorn her, and make her his wife, and she should bestow her embroideries and jewels upon whore-masters, and prostitute her body unto common rogues, leaving the prince who had done so much for her, were it not horrible ingratitude? would not every one who heard of it commiserate the prince, and condemn her. Absalom turned all against his father, and it was intolerable ingratitude.

If a man should set up his child with a great stock, give him house and land, and he should spend it in sueing and vexing of his father, who would not cry out of such a child? Many men take the blessings God bestows upon them, and spend them wholly in the service of their lusts; their bellies are their gods, their honours, their pleasures are so, and all is wasted about them, to the grief and dishonour of that God who gave them all.

It was never the intent or end of God that we should pervert his blessings, and bestow them upon idols, or any of our base lusts; he aimed at our good and his own glory, and we cross both when we abuse his mercies, we wound his honour, darken his glory, and destroy ourselves.

Ver. 20, 21. *Moreover thou hast taken thy sons and thy daughters, whom thou hast borne unto me, and these hast thou sacrificed unto them to be devoured. Is this of thy whoredoms a small matter, that thou hast slain my children, and delivered them to cause them to pass through the fire for them?*

These words do set out the ingratitude of this woman yet more fully, viz. from her unnaturalness; God gave her children, and she slew and sacrificed them unto false gods.

"Whom thou hast borne unto me." Not brought forth that they should be the Lord's, but they were his; for in ver. 21 he calls them his children: though this Israelitish woman had forsaken God, and was become a notorious idolatress, yet the children she brought forth were the Lord's,

1. By the right of the Lord. He is the God of nature, having sovereign authority over all creatures, and so both the parents and children were the Lord's, as well as other creatures; he calls it his gold, his silver, his oil, his incense, &c.

2. By the right of the covenant. God had made a covenant with them, and promised to be their God, and the God of their seed, Gen. xvii. 7. He speaks of his being in covenant with his people, ver. 8 of this chapter; he took this Israelitish woman to be his, and though she played the whore, yet the children she bore were the Lord's, because God had not given her a bill of divorce, but her children had circumcision, which was a token of the covenant between God and them, Gen. xvii. 11; and it is called the covenant of circumcision, Acts vii. 8. In themselves considered, they were worthy rather the name of bastards, than to be honoured with the title of sons.

"These hast thou sacrificed." The Hebrew word זבח is, to kill, slay, as you do beasts, either for eating or sacrificing. Thou hast slain; so you have it in the next verse, "Thou hast slain my children," ותשחטי from שחט to kill, or extend, because, when the beast was killed, they extended the parts of it; here they killed their children, either before they put them into the fire and sacrificed them to idols, or by casting them alive into the fire. Jer. vii. 31, there is mention made of "Tophet in the valley of the son of Hinnom," and it was to burn their sons and daughters in the fire. Expositors say, this Tophet was a chapel, or altar, where Molech was, and here they offered their children to that idol. This idol Molech, the Hebrews tell us, was made of brass, hollow and capacious in the concave of it; they put their children either in it, or under it, there being a great fire; they burned them in honour to the idol. Others think they were put in the arms of the idol, being red hot, and so roasted to death; and because the lamentable shrieks and cries of the children in the fire should not be heard, they played upon tabrets, beat on drums or pans, whence it was called Tophet, for תף is a tabret, or drum.

This inhuman practice was frequent among the Jews, as you may observe from 2 Kings xvi. 3; xvii. 17; and xxi. 6; Jer. xix. 5; xxxii. 35. Ahaz "walked in the way of the kings of Israel, and made his son to pass through the fire," (that was their ordinary practice,) "according to the abominations of the heathen." And, 2 Kings xvii. 31, "The Sepharvites burnt their children in fire to Adrammelech and Anammelech, the gods of Sepharvaim."

This custom of sacrificing their children, it is judged, by the learned, that the heathens took up from the example of Abraham, who would have offered his son in sacrifice to God; they thought (though this was not done) surely such sacrifices were acceptable to God; if God took it well at Abraham's hands, who did but attempt it, he would much more take it well at their hands, who should do it: their children were dear to them, and when they should thus part with them for the honour of their God, as they conceived, how could it be but he should take it well at their hands: they considered not that Abraham did it upon special command. Besides, it is probable that the heathens had learned the meaning of their sacrifices, which typed out Christ, who should take man's nature upon him, and be a sacrifice to pacify the wrath of God. They thought, hereupon, that the sacrificing of children and men would do the like with their gods, and make them acceptable to them. Micah vi. 7, "Shall I give my firstborn for my transgression, the fruit of my body for the sin of my soul?" These words import, that both the heathens and idolatrous Jews did imagine, that the sacrificing of their children did make atonement for their sins, which the prophet confutes and condemns.

"To be devoured." The Hebrew is, to eat or to be eaten; they put their children into the fire, which did eat them up, and consume them. In Isa. v. 24, you have the same word, "as the fire devoureth;" the original is, eateth the stubble; and the word fire, in the Hebrew, is, לשון אש the tongue of the fire: the tongue licks in the meat, and eats it; so the flame catches hold of combustible matter, and consumes it.

"To pass through the fire." The Hebrew is, in causing them to pass through. Some children they burned wholly in the fire; others, as it is usually conceived, they caused to pass through the fire, which was a purging of them from the filth and defilements, as also a consecrating of them to the idol and his service: they placed much efficacy in fire, for the hallowing of those who passed through it.

The Tartars, saith Abuiensis, think all strangers, such as are not of their own race, unclean; and before they can see or speak with their king, they must pass between two fires, by which being purged, they are deemed worthy of his presence. We must pass through the fire of the law and gospel, before we come to the sight of the Lord.

Whether authors have not mistaken in this, thinking that some children only were drawn through the fire, and not burnt, I desire one thing may be taken into consideration, and that is, what the Scripture calls passing through the fire in one place, it calls burning in another: 2 Kings xvi. 3, it is said, Ahaz "made his son to pass through the fire;" 2 Chron. xxviii. 3, it is said, "He burnt his children in the fire:" so here in our prophet, that which is called devouring in ver. 20, is termed passing through the fire in ver. 21; not under correction, that they passed through the fire and so lived, but passed through it to the honour of the idol.

Obs. 1. When men leave God and his word, they fall into wicked practices, and proceed further and further daily. This Jewish state left God and his word, fell to idolatry, the idolatry of all the nations, yea, more than that, to the sacrificing of her children; "Moreover, thou hast taken thy sons," &c. Jehoram slew his brethren, divers princes of Israel, wrought evil in the eyes of the Lord, 2 Chron. xxi. 4, 6; ver. 11, "Moreover he made high places in the mountains of Judah, and caused the inhabitants of Jerusalem to commit fornication, and compelled Judah thereto." So Ahaz, besides his walking in the ways of the kings of Israel, and making molten images for Baalim, it is said, "Moreover he burnt incense in the valley of the son of Hinnom." See chap. xxxvi. 14; this 16th of Ezekiel, ver. 29, sinners have their moreovers, they add sin to sin. Herod had done much evil, yet he added more to it; Luke iii. 19, 20, he shut up John in prison. As sinners have their moreovers, so God hath his moreovers: Deut. xxviii. 45, after the Lord had threatened them with judgments and curses, ver. 15—45, there he saith, "Moreover all these curses shall come upon thee, and shall pursue thee, and overtake thee, till thou be destroyed;" so Ezek. v. 14, "Moreover I will make thee waste, and a reproach among the nations that are round about thee."

Obs. 2. Sinners may come to such a height of sinning, as to violate all bonds and bounds of restraint. "Thou hast taken thy sons and thy daughters, whom thou hast borne unto me, and these hast thou sacrificed unto them to be devoured. Is this of thy whoredoms a small matter?"

There were many bonds and considerations to have kept them off from this bloody work.

(1.) It was against the light of nature. The light which is in the souls of men, naturally tells them they should not murder, especially innocents, such as children; they should do as they would be done by: it was an unreasonable act.

(2.) It was against the law of nature, which Ulpian thus defines, It is that which nature hath taught all creatures living. You know nature hath put a law or instinct into all creatures to preserve their young, and if they be endangered by any, they will contend and venture much for them, even timorous creatures, as birds for their young, hens for their chickens, and all creatures more or less. The law and impulse of nature is strong in them, but here the law of nature had no force, "Thou hast taken thy sons," &c.: they came out of their loins, were parts and pieces of themselves, and nature should have moved, wrought strongly in them, for the preservation of their little ones; but they were unnatural, beneath the brute creatures in this act, they are so far from destroying their young, that they hazard themselves to preserve them.

(3.) Those were children consecrated unto the Lord, yet being circumcised, and having the token of the covenant, were the Lord's; therefore it is said, "Which thou hast borne unto me." This should have restrained them from so sacrilegious an act, as to take them from God and sacrifice them unto devils, for, Psal. cvi. 37, "They sacrificed their sons and daughters unto devils:" to take them from an infinite, gracious, blessed, holy God, and give them unto idols and devils, what an accursed and horrible thing was this! as if a mother should take the child out of the father's arms, who is loving, tender over it, and throw it to lions, bears, or any other ravenous creatures.

(4.) They had a full command to the contrary; Lev. xviii. 21, "Thou shalt not let any of thy seed pass through the fire to Molech:" yea, this was backed with no less penalty than death; Lev. xx. 2, 3, 5, "Whosoever he be of the children of Israel, or of the strangers that sojourn in Israel, that giveth any of his seed unto Molech; he shall surely be put to death: the people of the land shall stone him with stones. And I will set my face against that man, and against his family, and will cut him off."

(5.) The manner of the death should have prevailed with them not to have yielded to it. It was the most terrible death of all deaths, to be burnt in the fire; oh the shrieks, cries, and lamentations of poor innocents! but see the hand of God upon them for it, Lam. iv. 10, "They sod their own children."

Obs. 3. A whorish, idolatrous church may bring forth children unto God. This Jewish church was fallen to as gross idolatry and practices as were to be found among heathen, and yet the children she brought forth are termed to be the Lord's; in what sense, I showed you in opening of the words. A church may have ordinances which may entitle its children to be the Lord's, and yet not prove itself to be a true church. The Jews had circumcision, which the children partaking of, were counted the Lord's, but themselves were so corrupt, whorish, idolatrous, bloody in offering their children to idols, that the Lord did not own them for a lawful spouse and true church, as you may see, ver. 38, "I will judge thee, as women that break wedlock and shed blood are judged." So the tribes brought forth children unto God, but the Lord said of them, Hos. i. 9, "Loammi; ye are not my people." The Romish church may bring forth some children unto God, because she hath baptism and other ordinances in her; yet she is so corrupt, idolatrous, bloody in persecuting the saints, that she is rather the whore of antichrist, the synagogue of Satan, than the true spouse of Christ.

Obs. 4. In matters of worship, it is not men's zeal and good intentions will justify their actions. They sacrifice their children with zeal as hot as fire, they thought to pacify and please their idol-gods, that they did acceptable service in parting with their dearest comforts, their tender babes, for the honour of their god; but this was so far from acceptation, that it fearfully provoked God; "Is this of thy whoredoms a small matter?" the more zealous thou art in this, the worse; thy good intentions are abominations; who required this at thy hands? Gideon, in making an ephod, Jeroboam, in setting up the golden calves, the Galatians, in observing of days, the Colossians, in subjecting to ordinances, had their zeal and good intentions, but not one of them were justifiable by the word of God. Will-worship hath no acceptance in divine worship; men's inventions are nothing the better for their good intentions. The papists pretend good intentions for all their additions to baptism, and other parts of the worship of God, but, notwithstanding their intentions, they are no better than superstitious.

Obs. 5. In pretended ways of worship, men grow cruel and bloody. "Thou hast slain my children, and delivered them to cause them to pass through the fire for them;" they pretended this was a right and good way of worship, and, in honour of their false gods and ways, they become cruel, and murder their own children. False ways of worship have this grand evil intrinsical unto them, they have cruelty and bloodiness attending them; whereas true religion only, and the ways of it, hath this honour, to be mild and merciful, bearing and forbearing, James iii. 17. The Pharisees pretended they knew the law, were only in the right way, but they were deceived; and how bitter, bloody, and persecuting were they against Christ's apostles, and those who embraced the truths they delivered! John xvi. 2, 3, Christ tells them what would be the practice of men in false ways, they would kill them, and think they did God good service in it; and why? they knew not the Father, nor Christ, they were strangers unto their ways, which were full of love, meekness, kindness, and had ways of their own, which made them zealous, bitter, plot, and to break out into open violence: Rev. xvi. 5, 6, the Babylonish whore slew the children of the Lord, and was drunk with the blood of saints and martyrs; in her was found the blood of all the slain upon the earth, all that suffered for the truth: she succeeded the former, justified their ways, filled up what was wanting in them.

Ver. 22. *And in all thine abominations and thy whoredoms thou hast not remembered the days of thy youth, when thou wast naked and bare, and wast polluted in thy blood.*

This verse contains the ground and cause of this woman's sinful departure from God, of her idolatry and cruelty, viz. she forgot in what a poor, forlorn, and miserable condition she had been in, and what God had done for her; she neither remembered her own misery, nor God's mercies: she was naked, bare, and he clothed her; she was polluted in her blood, and he washed her; she was very deformed, and he put beauty upon her; she was base, contemptible, and he made her renowned in the world; but these things were not thought on. Had she kept in her heart what a low estate she once was in, and how the Lord dealt by her in that estate, she would never have left him, broken out into, and proceeded on in, such wicked ways as she did.

Obs. 1. When God's people are raised, they are apt to forget God and themselves, and to break out into sinful courses. This Israelitish woman being exalted by God, thought not upon her former low estate, nor what God had been unto her in that estate: Psal. cvi. 21, "They forgat God their saviour;" he saved them from the plagues in Egypt, from the Egyptians, from the Red sea, the fiery serpents, and other evils; and what! did they forget him? yea, they soon forgat him; ver. 13, they "soon forgat his works;" the Hebrew is, they made haste, they forgat. Man at first was called Adam, earth, or red earth, but after the fall, Enosh, which some render, forgetful, because through sin he was so cracked, that he could not hold or remember any thing. God had done great and many wonderful things for this people, Deut. iv. 32—34, and charged them they should not forget them or him, chap. iv. 9; xxiii. 12; viii. 11, 14; yet look into chap. xxxii. 18, where it is said, "Of the Rock that begat thee thou art unmindful, and hast forgotten God that formed thee:" God begot them, and formed them into a people, kingdom, did all for them, yet they forgot him. And is it not so among us, whom he hath begotten into families, and formed into cities, counties, and a kingdom? may we not say, with David, Psal. viii. 4, Lord, "what is man, that thou art mindful of him?" what is Enosh? he is a sorry, miserable, wretched, forgetful creature; do what thou wilt for him, be what thou wilt to him, he will soon forget thee, and all thou hast done.

Obs. 2. Consideration of men's misery, and God's mercy to them in that misery, is a special help to prevent sin. "In all thy whoredoms thou hast not remembered the days of thy youth, when thou wast naked and bare, and polluted in thy blood:" their forgetfulness of them opened the door unto sin; the remembrance of them would have shut it against, and kept them from, sin. When the heart is seriously exercised about a low, miserable, lost, perishing condition, and what undeserved kindness God showed in it, ingratitude, pride, carnal confidence, bud not out, grow not up, bring not forth; and as it is a curb to keep us from sin, so it is a strong trace to draw us out of sin: "In all thine abominations and thy whoredoms thou hast not remembered," &c. intimating, that if this woman had laid to heart her former condition, and the great kindnesses of God to her, she would have repented her of her ways, and turned to the Lord; thoughts thereof would have begot such thoughts, workings of spirit, as these: What! did God pity me when none would pity? did he take me in when I was cast out? did he bestow life upon me, make me grow and increase? hath he washed, anointed me, covered, adorned, beautified me? and have I gone out from him, left him, sinned against him, requited him ill for all his kindness? I am ashamed of it; I will turn to him and ask him forgiveness. When David had sinned, and lay in it, the prophet minds him of his former condition, and what God had done for him: 2 Sam. xii. 7, "I anointed thee king over Israel," thee who wast at the sheepfold, low, mean, despised; "I delivered thee out of the hand of Saul," he sought thy life; "I gave thee thy master's house," wives, the houses of Judah and Israel: these he sets before him, that upon the due minding of them he might be affected, and led to repentance for his sinful practices. If you would think what low estates you were lately in, what God did for you then, it would be a special means to keep you from sin.

Ver. 23—29. *And it came to pass after all thy wickedness, (woe, woe unto thee! saith the Lord God;) that thou hast also built unto thee an eminent place, and hast made thee an high place in every street. Thou hast built thy high place at every head of the way, and hast made thy beauty to be abhorred, and hast opened thy feet to every one that passed by, and multiplied thy whoredoms. Thou hast also committed fornication with the Egyptians thy neighbours, great of flesh; and hast increased thy whoredoms, to provoke me to anger. Behold, therefore I have stretched out my hand over thee, and have diminished thine ordinary food, and delivered thee unto the will of them that hate thee, the daughters of the Philistines, which are ashamed of thy lewd way. Thou hast played the whore also with the Assyrians, because thou wast unsatiable; yea, thou hast played the harlot with them, and yet couldest not be satisfied. Thou hast moreover multiplied thy fornication in the land of Canaan unto Chaldea; and yet thou wast not satisfied herewith.*

In these verses the Lord doth further accuse and charge this woman, that she made no stop nor stand in her wickedness, but proceeded further and further; "after all thy wickedness, thou hast also built unto thee an eminent place, and hast made thee an high place in every street."

This is set out unto us,

I. By the eminency of the place. She built not

some little, low place, obscure, unnoted, but one eminent, great, glorious, high.

II. From the multitude of high places and altars. She made not here and there one, but "in every street, at every head of the way," where was the most concourse of people.

III. From her impudence; "Thou hast opened thy feet to every one that passed by." Thou didst not, through frailty of nature, violence of temptation, transgress with one, two, or a few, but like an arrant whore past shame, "thou hast opened thy feet to every one."

IV. From the several nations she committed folly with. She was not content to be idolatrous herself, but made covenants and leagues with others, and drew them in; as,

1. The Egyptians, who are described to be,

(1.) Her "neighbours."

(2.) "Great of flesh," ver. 26.

2. The "Assyrians," ver. 28.

V. From the extent of her whoredoms, which was from "Canaan unto Chaldea," ver. 29. Not only in Canaan, but in Chaldea, she was idolatrous.

VI. From her insatiableness, ver. 28, 29.

VII. From the effects; which are,

1. Threatening from God; ver. 23, "Woe, woe unto thee!"

2. Abhorrence of her beauty; ver. 25, "And hast made thy beauty to be abhorred."

3. Punishment, ver. 27:

(1.) Set down in general, under this expression, "I have stretched out my hand over thee."

(2.) In particular, and that in two things,

[1.] In diminution of their comforts; "I have diminished thine ordinary food."

[2.] In putting them into the power of their enemies; "I delivered thee unto the will of them that hate thee."

4. Shame; so lewd and vile were her ways, that even her enemies were ashamed of her, ver. 27.

In ver. 23 there is nothing to open.

Obs. 1. That when God's own people go on in sinful ways, it is grievous unto him, it affects, yea afflicts, his heart. Here God, taking notice and speaking of this Israelitish woman's sinful practices, and proceeding on in them, breaks out in the midst of a sentence, saying, "Woe, woe unto thee!" he was so full with thoughts of her ingratitude, unkindness, rebellion, idolatry, &c. that he opens, empties, and eases himself in these expressions. Gen. vi. 5, 6, when God saw the wickedness of man to be great, it repented him that he had made man on the earth, and grieved him at the heart; Psal. lxxviii. 40, they did oft grieve him in the desert; Psal. xcv. 10, God saith, "Forty years long was I grieved with this generation;" Isa. lxiii. 10, they "vexed his holy Spirit," therefore, Isa. i. 24, "Ah, I will ease me of mine adversaries, and avenge me of mine enemies." Christ wept over Jerusalem.

Obs. 2. The end of wickedness is woe. She had been notoriously wicked, and what followed upon it? "woe, woe," it is double, and notes intenseness; she had been intense in sinning, and God was intense in threatening: Woe to thee, thou hast left me, woe to thee, thou hast embraced other gods; woe to thy estate and body, Assyrians shall come and destroy them, and woe to thy soul, I will destroy that. God was greatly exasperated, and therefore pours out a double woe against her, one temporal, another eternal. Let who will be wicked, be it Judah and Jerusalem, woe and woe must be their portion; let it be the Lord's own people, he will not spare; if they repent not, if they turn not from their evil ways, he will denounce woes against them, and bring woes upon them. "The wages of sin is death;" a temporal death, there is one woe; an eternal death, there is another woe.

Ver. 25. "Thou hast made thy beauty to be abhorred." This woman was very lovely, through her state and church beauty, she was renowned among the nations for it; but when she became idolatrous, she spotted her beauty, so as it became abominable. Take the fairest woman, that is most desirable and prized, if once she come to be common, and open her feet to all comers, as the phrase here is, she grows loathsome, abominable. Such was the Jewish state of our prophet's metaphorical woman, who multiplied altars, idolatries, and committed fornication with the nations far and near. The Lord had said long before, when they fell to idolatry, that their spot was not the spot of his children, Deut. xxxii. 5; when they were free from this sin they were beautiful and glorious; Numb. xxiv. 5, "How goodly are thy tents, O Jacob, and thy tabernacles, O Israel!" chap. xxiii. 21, "He hath not beheld iniquity in Jacob, neither hath he seen perverseness in Israel." The Vulgate reads it thus; There is not an idol in Jacob, nor is an image seen in Israel. Idolatry makes the most glorious nation abominable: Prov. xiv. 34, "Sin is a reproach to any people," and especially this sin; 1 Pet. iv. 3, they are called "abominable idolatries;" they are so in themselves, and they make so. Whatever a woman's beauty is, if she be mad and frantic, you despise her and her beauty, you will not have to do with her: idolatry is a madness; Jer. l. 38, "They are mad upon their idols;" and such madness makes the beauty of a state or church loathsome.

Ver. 27. "And have diminished thine ordinary food." The Hebrew for ordinary food is, חקך Jerom interprets it of their ceremonies, sabbaths, and solemnities; Theodoret of the law itself; others of their holy things. But God, dealing here with this Jewish state as a husband with an expensive and adulterous wife, saith, I have cut thee short of thy allowance, I have diminished thy portion. Prov. xxxi. 15, "She riseth also while it is yet night, and giveth meat to her household, and a portion to her maidens:" it is חק and it is taken for a portion of meat and drink; and it is not amiss to take it so here; Thou hast abused thy fine flour, honey, and oil, but I will lessen them, thou shalt have little of these hereafter, thy portion shall be smaller. The confining it to things edible I like not; let us extend it to other things also, and the sense will be more full, viz. to her garments, ornaments, silver, gold, incense, &c.; Hos. ii. 9, I will "take away my corn, my wine, recover my wool and my flax;" and so it suits with the Chaldee interpretation, I will take away thy good. It is our sin that causes God to diminish our comforts.

"Delivered thee unto the will of them that hate thee." The Hebrew for will is בנפש to the soul. It is a hebraism, the soul put for the will, lust or desire in it, and so it is frequently used; Exod. xv. 9, "My lust shall be satisfied upon them;" Psal. lxxviii. 18, "They asked meat for their lust;" the Hebrew is, soul; Psal. cv. 22, "To bind his princes at his pleasure," according to the lust and pleasure of his soul; Psal. xli. 2, Give him not "to the will of his enemies," Hebrew, soul of his enemies; Luke xxiii. 25, "He delivered Jesus to their will."

"The daughters of the Philistines." In Scripture sense, villages and towns are counted daughters, as chief cities were called mothers; 2 Sam. xx. 19, "Thou seekest to destroy a city and a mother in Israel," that was Abel, where they asked counsel. And because cities had towns and villages belonging to them, as you may read, 1 Chron. vii. 28, "Bethel, and the towns thereof; Gezer, with the towns thereof; Shechem, Gaza, and the towns thereof;" so, ver. 29, "Bethshean and her towns, Taanach and her towns," &c.; these towns were accounted the daughters of those cities, because they were either made, governed by, or some ways belonging to those cities and the citizens thereof. And so divers expositors do take the daughters of the Philistines here to be the towns and villages of Palestina; and so the daughters of Jerusalem, oft mentioned in the Canticles, to be the villages adjacent. But it is better to interpret the words of the persons than of the places, and to understand by daughters of Philistines, the Philistines themselves: 2 Sam. i. 20, "Tell it not in Gath; lest the daughters of the Philistines rejoice;" that is, not the villages, but the Philistines themselves. So, Psal. xlviii. 11, "Let the daughters of Judah be glad," that is, the people of Judah. In ver. 23, that which is "Egyptians," in the original is, sons of Egypt; and ver. 28, "with the Assyrians," in the Hebrew is, the sons of Ashur; and here, by "daughters of the Philistines," is meant the Philistines; and daughters are mentioned rather than sons, because the Lord had spoken of the Jewish state as a woman, and so continues the allegory in the same sex. The Philistines hated the Jews much, often warred against them, and brought them under, as you may observe in the book of Judges, chap. x. and xiii; they were glad when mischief befell them, therefore, when Saul and Jonathan were slain, David would not have it told in Gath or Askelon, lest the Philistines should triumph, 2 Sam. i. 20.

Obs. 1. To be delivered up to the wills of men that hate us is a sad judgment. To be given up to the wills and lusts of men is sad, but especially to the wills and lusts of those that hate us. David, when God propounded the three sad things to him, 2 Sam. xxiv. one whereof was to flee before his enemies, he chose rather famine or plague, than to fall into the hands of man, ver. 14; he knew that the hands and hearts of men were merciless: Psal. xxvii. 12, "Deliver me not over unto the will of mine enemies;" why? they bear false witness, they breathe out cruelty. Lev. xxvi. 17, "They that hate you shall reign over you;" the Philistines and Babylonians hated them, and they were lords over them, and very sad was their bondage under them. 2 Chron. xxviii. 18, "The Philistines invaded the cities of the low country, and of the south of Judah, and had taken Beth-shemesh, Ajalon, Gederoth, Shocho, Timnah, Gimzo, with the villages thereof: for the Lord brought Judah low because of Ahaz king of Israel; who made Judah naked, and transgressed sore against the Lord."

Obs. 2. Those who are accounted God's people may so exceed in sin, as that God's enemies may be ashamed of them. The Philistines, who hated God and the Jews, were ashamed of their lewd ways, they blushed at the sins the Jews gloried in: they gloried in their idolatry, they made high places every where; they committed spiritual whoredom with greediness; other nations kept their gods, but they changed their God and glory for that which did not profit, Jer. ii. 11. This levity and idolatry of theirs made the heavens astonished, and the Philistines ashamed: they saw more filth and loathsomeness in this sin than the Jews; such abominable idolatry affected their hearts. The word in Hebrew for lewd is זמה wickedness, yea, some notable and emphatical wickedness. The abusing and forcing the Levite's concubine unto death, Judg. xix. is called, chap. xx. 6, זמה lewdness, wickedness, abomination; and Hierom, upon the 24th of Ezekiel, interprets it, an execrable and villanous filthiness. The impudence of this Jewish woman was such in her accursed idolatry, that the daughters of the Philistines were ashamed at it, durst not do the like, and were chaste in comparison of Jerusalem and her daughters, who lusted after the gods and worship of the nations on every side. The Egyptians deified onions, leeks, cats, beetles, oxen, sheep, dogs, apes, hawks, crocodiles, serpents, bats, moles, &c.; and with Egyptian idolatry did the Jews entangle themselves, as also with the Assyrian and Chaldean. If they had any new gods, the Jewish hearts were on fire for them, and unquiet till they enjoyed them; the nations were content with their own gods, but Jerusalem must have all.

Obs. 3. Wicked and wanton lusts are insatiable. This metaphorical woman had vile lusts in her, she lusted after the Egyptians, Assyrians, Chaldeans, committed fornication with them, opened her feet to all passengers, yet she was not satisfied therewith, ver. 29; and in ver. 28, it is said, she was insatiable, and could not be satisfied. Eccles. i. 8, "The eye is not satisfied with seeing, nor the ear filled with hearing;" the one would see more, the other hear more; and so it is with the lusts of men and women, they would see, hear, and have more. "There are four things that are never satisfied, that say not, It is enough: the grave, the barren womb, the earth, the fire," Prov. xxx. 15, 16. And I may add, there are four evils, or lusts, that will never be satisfied.

(1.) Is the covetous lust; it would have more when it hath most: Eccles. iv. 8, the covetous man's eye is not satisfied with riches: chap. v. 10, "He that loveth silver shall not be satisfied with silver."

(2.) Is revenge: he that is haunted with this lust, be he great or small, will not be satisfied; Prov. vi. 34, 35, "He will not spare in the day of vengeance. He will not regard any ransom; neither will he rest content, though thou givest many gifts."

(3.) Frowardness of spirit: Prov. xvii. 20, "A froward heart findeth no good;" do what you will to him or for him who hath it, he finds no satisfying good in it.

(4.) Is the lust of the flesh, which is the most insatiable: Eph. iv. 19, they gave "themselves over unto lasciviousness, to work all uncleanness with greediness." Rom. i. 26, 27, they "burned in their lust one towards another," not in a natural way, but in that which was against nature, men with men and women with women. To this lust idolatry is compared, and called fornication, because idolaters are as insatiable in their way, as men and women in the lusts of the flesh. Hos. ii. 5, "I will go after my lovers," I will have more idols and more idolatrous practices, Ephraim was not satisfied with what she had; so Jerusalem had the Egyptian, Assyrian, and Chaldean gods, and they did not quench, but increase, her thirst after more still. Thus it is with any lust whatsoever, if you give way to it, it grows strong, insatiable, like water breaking over the banks, and will not be stopped, like fire getting strength, and cannot be quenched; it is wisdom therefore to deal with our lusts betimes, to keep them in, under, yea, to crucify and mortify them.

Some interpreters understand the fornication and whoredom committed with the Egyptians, Assyrians, and Chaldeans, in ver. 26, 28, 29, to be meant of those sinful leagues the Jews made with them, Isa. xx. 5, 6; xxx. 1—3; 2 Kings xviii. 21, 24; Isa. xxxi. 1; 2 Kings xvi. 7, 8; 2 Chron. xxviii. 16. They had little cause to confederate with any of the nations, especially the Egyptians, who had kept them under hard bondage many years, drowned their children, were the grossest idolaters under heaven, and pursued them to the Red sea, to bring them back to their tasks of brick, clay, and straw, or to destroy them; and God had forbid them to seek help from the nations; and therefore, Jer. ii. 18, "What hast thou to do in the way of Egypt, to drink the water of Sihor? or what hast thou to do in the way of Assyria, to drink the waters of the river?" What hast thou to do to treat and covenant with, or to fetch help from them, to drink of Nilus and Euphrates, those muddy rivers, and forsake the fountain of living waters, the Lord God of Israel? Ver. 19, "Thine own wickedness shall correct thee," &c. thou shalt fall by them, and suffer. It was a wicked thing, an evil and bitter thing, a forsaking of God, and casting him off, who had taken the protection of that land and people to himself in a peculiar manner.

It is questioned whether a nation or prince may covenant and confederate with them that are of a false religion; it should seem to be negative, because here the Jews' confederating with the Egyptians and Assyrians is called fornication, whoredom; and God was twice wroth with Jehoshaphat for entering into league with the kings of Israel, who had set up false worship; once for joining with Ahab, 2 Chron. xix. 2, and after for joining with Ahaziah, 2 Chron. xx. 36, 37. But notwithstanding these instances, it is not unlawful for those of the true religion to make leagues and covenants with foreigners that are of a another religion. Abraham was in confederacy with Eshcol and Aner, who were Amorites, Gen. xiv. 13, with Abimelech, chap. xxi. 27; Jacob with Laban, Gen. xxxi. 44, 45; Solomon with Hiram, 1 Kings v. 12; Joshua with the Gibeonites, Josh. ix. 15. If they were unlawful, these men must all lie under censure. Those leagues that are for defence against violence of wicked men, for preservation of peace, without prejudice to the true religion, tending to the propagation of it, they are warrantable. But when distrust of divine assistance, covetousness, compliance with idolaters, unjust war with and oppression of others, and hazard of corrupting the worship of God, are the grounds and ends of making leagues with them, they are unlawful. The Jews distrusted God, and sought to Egypt and Assyria for help, complied with idolaters, corrupted the pure worship of God thereby; therefore their leagues were unlawful. As for that of Jehoshaphat with Ahab and Ahaziah, besides his compliance and covetousness, there was a special consideration in it, viz. that they being revolters from God, (for the ten tribes fell from the true God, and set up the calves,) he should join in covenant with them; he helped Ahab in his war against Ramoth-gilead, which the prophet Micaiah had told them they should not prosper in; there being a law against revolters, Deut. xiii. 13—15.

Howbeit leagues be lawful with others, yet they are dangerous, and should cautiously be made.

Ver. 30. *How weak is thine heart, saith the Lord God, seeing thou doest all these things, the work of an imperious whorish woman.*

This verse is another effect of this woman's wickedness, and that is, weakness of heart; set out,

I. By way of admiration; "How weak," &c.

II. By way of comparison, viz. of an imperious whorish woman; she doth those things which enfeeble her heart, enervate her spirits, and thou doest the like, thy heart must therefore be weak.

"Weak." Hebrew אמלה The word *amlah* signifies a thing which hath no virtue, power, efficacy in it. Jer. xv. 9, "She that hath borne seven languisheth; she hath given up the ghost;" it is the same word; she was so without strength that her soul was ready to leave her. It notes not any weakness, but extreme weakness, and therefore sometimes it is put for a thing withered or dried up; Isa. xxiv. 7, "The vine languisheth," it was withered and dried up; so Joel i. 10, 12; Nah. i. 4; Lam. ii. 8. Pradus saith, the word signifieth, cut off, destroyed, corrupted, perverse, and makes the sense thus, How perverse, depraved, and corrupt is thy heart, when thou doest such things as declare that thou hast not only banished the fear of God from thy heart, but also all modesty from thy face! Jerom, What shall I do to thy heart? She was unstable, desired society with the gods of other nations; she could not contain, but used all means to accomplish her wicked desires.

"Imperious." Hebrew שלטת a woman that hath a domineering spirit; from שלט to domineer and exercise lordliness over others, to usurp authority. Septuagint παῤῥησιαζομένης, of one that is at liberty, that hath no husband, but runs up and down according to her own lust and will. The Vulgate is, wanton, impudent; when the mask of modesty and bridle of continency are laid aside, and a bold forwardness to filthiness is manifested, when a woman doth not only expect and wait for her lovers, but desires, invites, and constrains them to satisfy her lusts, and will have no nay. Such a shameless, saucy, imperious whore was she in Prov. vii. who, ver. 21, caused the young man to yield; so here Jerusalem was like a queen of whores, daring and doing any thing.

Procax idem quod petax.

"The work." What is that work?

1. To slight and leave her husband, or parents, friends, if she have no husband; so did this woman, Jer. ii. 13; Ezek. vi. 9.

2. To seek out, invite, follow, fetch in others, and to communicate herself to them; so did this woman, Ezek. xxiii. 16, 17, she sent to the Chaldeans and Babylonians, and they "came to her into the bed of love."

3. To waste her husband's estate; so here, Thou hast taken my gold and silver, made images, set mine oil, &c.

4. To neglect, deal harshly with the children of her husband; so here, Thou hast taken the sons and daughters thou didst bear unto me, and hast sacrificed them unto idols.

5. To excuse, clear, and justify herself: Prov. xxx. 20, "The adulterous woman eateth, wipeth her mouth, and saith, I have done no evil;" so this Jewish woman; Jer. ii. 23, "How canst thou say, I am not polluted, I have not gone after Baalim?" ver. 29, "Wherefore will ye plead with me? ye all have transgressed against me."

6. To be excessive in feasting and filthiness: Prov. vii. 18, "Come, let us take our fill of love;" 2 Pet. ii. 13, 14, they feast and have eyes full of adultery: so here, ver. 15, "Thou pouredst out thy fornications on every one that passeth by;" ver. 29, she multiplied her fornications in Canaan and Chaldea.

Obs. 1. That sin, especially whoredom and idolatry, do effeminate and enfeeble the hearts of people. Hos. iv. 11, whoredom is one of the things which takes away the heart, that is, the reason, understanding, judgment, so that a man becomes unstable, weak, and foolish. Corporal whoredom subjects men to the wild and insatiable lusts of the flesh; spiritual, to an idol, which is the work of man's hands; and what folly is this! Such sins weaken men's credit, consciences, hearts, and spirits. Adultery is the destruction of the soul, it wounds; Prov. vii. 26, "She hath cast down many wounded," and the more wound the more weakness. Delilah weakened Samson's hands and heart, and wounded him deeply. Gen. xlix. 4, Reuben, unstable as water, he went up to his father's bed. Prov. x. 29, "The way of the Lord is strength."

Obs. 2. Adulterers and idolaters are imperious. The Jewish state was guilty of those sins, and is compared here to an imperious whorish woman. All lusts are masterly and domineering. James iv. 1, "Whence come wars and fightings among you? come they not hence, even of your lusts that war in your members?" The word for lusts is ἡδοναι, pleasures, they are pleasing things, and must be pleased; they must have the heads, hearts, and hands of men to do them service, else they will make war in you; if they cannot win consent, they will force it, they are imperious things. Ver. 12, "There is one lawgiver, who is able to save and to destroy; who art thou that judgest another?" Here he shows the imperiousness of men's lusts, when they are rigid and censorious; they sit in judgment upon others, they thrust themselves into the throne of God, they take his prerogative upon them, and will be judges of the law, save and destroy at their pleasure. Psal. xii. 4, "With our tongue will we prevail; our lips are our own: who is Lord over us?" Their lusts were so imperious, they lorded it in their hearts and tongues. Exod. xv. 9, what said Pharaoh? "I will pursue, I will overtake, I will divide the spoil; my lust shall be satisfied upon them; I will draw my sword, my hand shall destroy them." Pharaoh was a great king, yet his lusts were above him. 2 Pet. ii. 14, "Having eyes full of adultery, and that cannot cease from sin;" their fleshly lusts commanded their hearts and eyes, and carried them with greediness to uncleanness. So for idolaters, Jer. xliv. 16, 17, "As for the word that thou hast spoken unto us in the name of the Lord, we will not hearken unto thee. But we will certainly do whatsoever thing goeth forth out of our own mouth, to burn incense unto the queen of heaven, and to pour out drink offerings unto her, as we have done, we, and our fathers, our kings, and our princes, in the cities of Judah, and in the streets of Jerusalem."

Obs. 3. Imperiousness argues weakness. "How weak is thine heart, seeing thou doest the work of an imperious whorish woman." The more weak the more imperious, and the more imperious the more evidence of weakness. Prov. xxix. 8, "Scornful men;" the Hebrew is, men of derision and scorn; the Septuagint, men without law, that are imperious, and make their wills and lusts their laws, they "bring a city into a snare," or set it on fire, which shows their weakness; "but wise men turn away wrath," which shows their strength. When men are hasty, violent, and imperious, they exalt folly, Prov. xiv. 29, and proclaim their weakness. The apostle saith, that women are the weaker vessels, 1 Pet. iii. 7, and being weak they are prone to be imperious; which Paul observing, gave out that rule, 1 Tim. ii. 12, "I suffer not a woman to teach, nor to usurp authority over the man." Many think that greatness and strength of spirit consists in imperiousness and stoutness; but it is otherwise, they who are the weakest are most imperious.

Ver. 31—34. *In that thou buildest thine eminent place in the head of every way, and makest thine high place in every street; and hast not been as an harlot, in that thou scornest hire; but as a wife that committeth adultery, which taketh strangers instead of her husband! They give gifts to all whores: but thou givest thy gifts to all thy lovers, and hirest them, that they may come unto thee on every side for thy whoredom. And the contrary is in thee from other women in thy whoredoms, whereas none followeth thee to commit whoredoms: and in that thou givest a reward, and no reward is given unto thee, therefore thou art contrary.*

These verses contain a repetition of what this whorish woman did, and also a further amplification and aggravation of her lewd and abominable practices.

The repetition is in ver. 31, which falls in with what you have in ver. 24, and beginning of ver. 25.

The amplification and aggravation of her lewd ways is set out,

I. From a dissimilitude, in the end of ver. 31; "And hast not been as an harlot, in that thou scornest hire;" other harlots took hire, but thou wouldst none.

II. From a similitude, in ver. 32; "as a wife," &c.: for a wife that hath a husband to take in strangers, that is great lewdness.

III. From the contrariety of her practice to other whores, ver. 33, 34. They had those who followed them, gave gifts unto them which they received; but Jerusalem had no followers, no gifts, but she gave gifts, and hired men to come unto her.

"Eminent place." Hebrew is גב which signifies whatsoever excels or appears above another; here it is an "eminent place," (a place raised above others,) it is so rendered in ver. 24. Septuagint translates it, οἴκημα πορνικὸν, there and here; πορνεῖον is a stews or house of fornication. These eminent places were for commission of those sins which drowned them in perdition. From this word גב it is more than probable that that word *Gabbatha*, in John xix. 13, doth proceed: the words are thus, "Pilate sat down in the judgment seat in a place that is called the Pavement, but in the Hebrew, Gabbatha," which signifies βῆμα, *locum* Grot. in loc.
excelsum, a lofty place, such a place as judges sit in to pronounce sentence against malefactors; it is called the Pavement, or λιθόςρωτον, because it was covered or paved with stones.

"Thine high place." Hebrew רמה רמתך is a place higher than others, from רום to lift up; they made altars and places for false worship higher than all the rest. Septuagint renders it by two words; in ver. 24, by ἔκθεμα, *prostibulum*, a place where they did prostitute themselves to whoredom, or to idolatry, or both; in this verse they render it βάσα, it being the foundation of the false worship offered up there.

"In that thou scornest hire." Hebrew is לקלס from קלס or קלס which hath a double, yea, contrary signification; sometimes it signifies to praise, and so the Jews used it in their prayers; Psal. lxviii. 5, what there is סלו extol, the Targum Pagn. in Thesauro.
hath it, קלסו praise him who rides upon the heavens; hence Shindler renders the word לקלס to be praised: and so the meaning must be, that Jerusalem was not like other whores, who did praise and magnify the gifts and hire they had from their lovers, that so they might draw more; no, she did not value or praise them. Sometimes, and most frequently, the word signifies to mock, despise, dispraise, and vilify; in this verse it is generally taken by interpreters so: the meaning then Meretrices a mercendo.
is, that Jerusalem was so far from praising, that she scorned hire; not in policy, to increase the hire, as common harlots do, who make advantage of their sin; but in way of opposition, to manifest that she was not for profit, but for pleasure; not for the purses of her lovers, but for their persons.

"Hire." Hebrew אתנן hire that belongs to a whore, from תנה, to hire, and properly it is, to give

Pagn. in Thes. a reward. Deut. xxiii. 18, *Ethnan zonah*, the hire of a whore: so Hos. ix. 1; Micah i. 7. Tamar, when Judah came in to her, would have hire, "What wilt thou give me," Gen. xxxviii. 16; and Hos. ii. 12, "These are my rewards that my lovers have given me."

Ver. 32. "As a wife that commits adultery." Hebrew is האשה המנאפת a woman an adulteress. A single woman that plays the harlot doth very ill; but a woman that hath a husband, to leave him, and receive others in his stead, that is exceeding grievous; especially when she wants nothing, hath abundance, and her husband is most loving, meek, delightful, wise, and faithful: this was the case of Jerusalem, yet she plays the adulteress, takes in strangers in the room of her husband.

Ver. 33. "They give gifts, but thou givest gifts." The word for gift is נדה and נדניך which is *merces meretricia*, from נדה which signifies to separate, and remove a thing as unclean. The hire of a whore was not to be brought into the temple, because gotten from that which was sinful, and therefore was to be kept, and separated from the temple, Deut. xxiii. 18.

Ver. 34. "The contrary is in thee." Hebrew is הפך *oppositum*, from הפך to invert, change, alter. This Jewish woman did invert, change, and alter the way that other women went in, for satisfaction of their lusts, in the abuse of their bodies; they had gifts given them, but this woman gave gifts; they were hired, this woman did hire. Septuagint is *διεςραμμένον*, *perversum quid;* Vulgate, *contra consuetudinem mulierum.* "Whereas none followeth thee to commit whoredoms:" the Hebrew runs thus, after thee it hath not been whored. So the Septuagint, *μετα σε οὐ πεπορνεύκασιν*, they have not gone a whoring after thee. The meaning is, Jerusalem sought after the idol gods of other nations, was at expenses, gave gifts to them to get and fetch in their idolatry; but no nation did so by them. Hos. viii. 9, "Ephraim hath hired lovers." 2 Kings xvi. 8, 10, Ahaz sent the silver and gold of the temple to the king of Assyria, and was at no small charges for the altar of Damascus. Isa. lvii. 7, "Upon a lofty and high mountain hast thou set thy bed;" that is, altars, chapels, temples, which he calls beds, because there they committed spiritual adultery: and they were upon the eminent and high places, because the more might see them, turn in, and worship their idol gods, and so commit folly with them; for it follows, "even thither wentest thou up to offer sacrifice." And in ver. 8, "Thou hast discovered thyself to another than me, and art gone up; thou hast enlarged thy bed, and made thee a covenant with them; thou lovedst their bed when thou sawest it." (2 Kings xxi. 4. Jer. xxxii. 34.) The sense is this, the Jewish state was not content with God alone to be her husband, but like a whorish wife left her husband, and went up to the bed of others: and not only so, but enlarged her own bed, made more room, built more altars, high places, and temples, for the gods of other nations to be taken in to her, and made covenant with them to worship and honour them; and whatever bed, that is, altar, temple, idol, she saw among the nations, she fell in love with it, and must have it, cost it never so dear.

Obs. 1. That the worship of God is not to be modelled according to the wisdom of states or churches. This Jewish state and church built high places, altars, fetched in the worship and ways of it, which other nations had, were at much cost and charges to accomplish the same, and thought herein they did acceptable service; but God was provoked sorely: and the more expensive any state or church is that way, the more they exasperate the Lord against them; as a husband, the more prodigal his wife is to entertain others, the more offended is he. God is a jealous God, and it is dangerous to alter in, or add any thing to his worship, especially to corrupt it with idolatrous inventions. Ahaz did so; but what saith the text, 2 Chron. xxviii. 22, "This is that king Ahaz" that spent the gold and silver found in the house of the Lord, that was affected with and brought into the temple the altar of Damascus, that sacrificed to the gods of Damascus, that shut up the doors of the temple, that made altars in every corner of Jerusalem, that burned incense to other gods, and provoked the Lord to anger, ver. 25.

Obs. 2. A pure virgin church may in process of time become whorish, adulterous, idolatrous, and worse than others. This church of Jerusalem was at first chaste, holy, glorious; but when she had left the Lord, and those ways and rules of worship which he had given her, then she became a strumpet, a common whore, did worse, yea, contrary to all whores; she sought for and hired lovers to come in to her. If churches would therefore not degenerate, let them "hold fast the form of wholesome words," 2 Tim. i. 13. Let them be content with the way of worship which God hath prescribed them, and lead such lives as may not blemish the religion they profess; and then they shall never provoke God to complain of them.

Ver. 35—38. *Wherefore, O harlot, hear the word of the Lord: thus saith the Lord God; Because thy filthiness was poured out, and thy nakedness discovered through thy whoredoms with thy lovers, and with all the idols of thy abominations, and by the blood of thy children, which thou didst give unto them; behold, therefore I will gather all thy lovers, with whom thou hast taken pleasure, and all them that thou hast loved, with all them that thou hast hated; I will even gather them round about against thee, and will discover thy nakedness unto them, that they may see all thy nakedness. And I will judge thee, as women that break wedlock and shed blood are judged; and I will give thee blood in fury and jealousy.*

Here begins the fifth general part of the chapter, viz. a commination of grievous judgments, together with the aggravation of their sins, the cause of those judgments, and this extends to ver. 60.

In the words from ver. 35, to ver. 44, you shall find,

I. An introduction to the judgments threatened, ver. 35.

II. A specification of the causes moving God to bring such judgments upon this woman, namely, her idolatry, murdering of her children, and forgetfulness of her low condition, and God's dealing with her in it, ver. 36, 43.

III. The enumeration of the judgments threatened; which are,

1. The gathering together of her lovers and enemies, and setting them against her, ver. 37.
2. Publication of her nakedness and shame, ver. 37.
3. Condemnation to die, ver. 38.
4. Rendition into the hands of her enemies, ver. 39.
5. Plundering, spoiling, and laying all waste, ver. 39.
6. Death itself by stones and swords, ver. 40.
7. Burning their houses, ver. 41.

IV. The consequents hereupon, which are two:

1. The cessation of this woman from her idolatries, ver. 41, last part of it.
2. Cessation of God's anger, ver. 42.

Ver. 35. "O harlot." The Lord calls her not wife, but harlot; he would not vouchsafe her that name, it carries honour in it; but gives her a disgraceful name, "harlot," the Jewish nation he calls a harlot.

Obs. 1. Sin brings reproachful names and terms upon people and persons; Isa. i. 10, "Rulers of Sodom, and people of Gomorrah." It causes God to fasten disgracing titles and epithets upon them: Deut. xxxii. 5, "A perverse and crooked generation;" Isa. lvii. 4, "Children of transgression, a seed of falsehood;" Jer. vi. 28, "Grievous revolters, corrupters;" chap. ii. 21, "Degenerate plants;" Isa. x. 6, "An hypocritical nation;" chap. lxv. 2, "A rebellious people;" chap. xvi. 3, "Outcasts;" chap. i. 4, "A people laden with iniquities;" Jer. vi. 30, "Reprobate silver;" Isa. lvii. 3, "Sons of the sorceress, the seed of the adulterer and the whore;" chap. xxi. 2, Treacherous dealers.

Formerly this people were very dear to God, and he gave them honourable titles: Exod. iv. 22, "Israel my son, my first born;" chap. xix. 6, "A kingdom of priests, an holy nation;" Deut. xxxii. 9, "The Lord's portion, and inheritance;" Psal. cxxxv. 4, "His peculiar treasure;" Isa. v. 7, "The Lord's vineyard;" Jer. ii. 21, "A noble vine;" Isa. iv. 5, "The glory;" chap. vi. 13, "The holy seed;" Jer. xviii. 13, "The virgin of Israel."

It is true you see what Solomon gave out long since; "Righteousness exalts a nation; but sin is a reproach to any people."

Obs. 2. From these words, "hear the word of the Lord;" They who will not hear the word of the Lord for their consolation, shall hear it for their condemnation. God had often spoken to this metaphorical woman, this Jewish state, by his prophets, and she would not hear: Isa. lxv. 2, "I have spread out my hands all the day unto a rebellious people;" God had sent prophets at the third, sixth, and ninth hour, and yet she would not hear: he had dealt like a loving husband by her, invited her to repent and turn, as you may read, Jer. iii. and iv. and in divers other places promised mercy and forgiveness, and nothing would prevail; here therefore the Lord speaks like a just judge, giving out a sentence of death; "Hear the word of the Lord, O harlot:" seeing that thou wouldst not hearken to my loving entreaties, gracious invitations, wholesome counsels, the word of grace and mercy; now thou must hear and hearken to my threats, my words of wrath, of condemnation, and destruction.

Ver. 36. "Thy filthiness." Hebrew נחשתך which Montanus renders, thy money; showing how lavish and profuse she was in spending her estate to hire lovers to come in unto her.

"Thy lovers." These lovers were the Assyrians, Babylonians, Chaldeans: Ezek. xxiii. 12, "She doted upon the Assyrians;" ver. 16, "She sent messengers unto them into Chaldea;" ver. 17, "The Babylonians came to her into the bed of love;" and in ver. 19—21, you shall find that the Egyptians were her lovers. So Jer. ii. 36; and iii. 1, "Thou hast played the harlot with many lovers;" she had lovers out of most nations.

Ver. 37. "Thou hast taken pleasure." Hebrew is ערבת *dulcuisti*, or *jocundata es;* the word ערב is of the largest signification amongst the Hebrew words; the primitive and chief signification of it is, to mingle; and so here notes that pleasure, delight, which comes upon mixture: this woman mingled herself with strangers, all comers, especially Assyrians, Babylonians, Egyptians, in bodily and spiritual whoredoms. God would gather together her lovers, and those she hated, having fallen off from her loves, and they should be against her, and besiege her.

Obs. 1. When God threatens, or brings judgments upon a people, it is upon considerable and just grounds. "Because thy filthiness was poured out," &c.: "behold, therefore I will," &c.

Obs. 2. That when God by the sin of man is provoked, he will set his friends and lovers against him. The Assyrians and Chaldeans had been Jerusalem's lovers; but because she sinned against God, he turns them to be her enemies: Lam. i. 2, "All her friends have dealt treacherously with her, they are become her enemies." Ahithophel was a choice friend and counsellor to David; and because he offended the Lord in the matter of Uriah and Bathsheba, therefore he turned the heart and head of Ahithophel against David, which went very near to him, and troubled his heart sorely: he speaks of it twice in the Psalms: once in Psal. xli. 9, "Mine own familiar friend, in whom I trusted, who did eat of my bread, hath lifted up his heel against me," i. e. hath dealt injuriously with me, and like a brute creature, kicked at his master who feeds him; or thus, he hath looked at me as one down, and lift up his heel to tread me under. Again he mentions it in Psal. lv. 12—14. Vashti refused to come at the king's call, and God set Ahasuerus and all the princes against her, Esth. i. So Obad. 7, "The men that were at peace with thee have deceived thee; they that eat thy bread have laid a wound under thee." See Matt. x. 36.

Obs. 3. God in his infinite wisdom and justice doth ofttimes make them instruments of his wrath, to punish us, with whom we have sinned. The Jews had pleased themselves in making covenants with the Assyrians, Chaldeans, and Egyptians, in fetching in their gods, forms of worship, in following their manners and practices; and what saith the Lord here? "I will even gather them round about against thee," they shall besiege thee, and lay thee waste. Rev. xvii. 16, "The ten horns which thou sawest upon the beast," and so did sin by the counsel and power of the beast; those horns, being so many kings, "shall hate the whore" with whom they had committed fornication; ver. 2, "and shall make her desolate and naked, and shall eat her flesh, and burn her with fire." As they had sinned with her, so God would use them to execute his wrath upon her. Martia, the concubine of Commodus the emperor, having espied her own name in a catalogue of chief persons, intended to be made away by him, consulting with others, she poisoned him in a cup of wine.

Obs. 4. In what kind people sin, in that kind sometimes God doth punish them. Jerusalem sinned in discovering her nakedness to others, ver. 36, and God doth punish her by discovering her nakedness to others, ver. 37, "I will discover thy nakedness unto them, that they may see all thy nakedness." Lam. i. 8, "All that honoured her despise her, because they have seen her nakedness." She committed sin in a shameful manner, and God would punish her shamefully. Adoni-bezek cut off thumbs and toes of seventy kings, and his thumbs and toes were cut off, Judg. i. 6, 7. Agag he had slain many by the sword, and himself suffers by it; 1 Sam. xv. 33, "As thy sword hath made women childless, so shall thy mother be childless among women." Obad. 15, "As thou hast done, it shall be done unto thee." Rev. xiii. 10, "He that leadeth into captivity shall go into captivity; he that killeth with the sword must be killed with the sword." Isa. xxxiii. 1, "When thou shalt cease to spoil, thou shalt be spoiled; and when thou shalt make an end to deal treacherously, they shall deal treacherously with thee."

This discovering of nakedness which was the punishment here threatened, was a grievous judgment, and should have caused this woman to have given over her whoredom and filthiness, as once it did the Milesian virgins their murders; for they being troubled and perplexed in their minds, were set upon it to make away themselves, no tears or entreaties of friends could prevail with them; many did make away themselves, notwithstanding all means used to prevent the same: at the last, one amongst them, wiser than the rest, made a law, that if they did make away themselves, they should be drawn naked through the market; this so prevailed with them, that they gave over that wretched practice; the thought of the shame of having their nakedness discovered, kept them from that bloody sin of self-murder.

Ver. 38. "I will judge thee as women that break wedlock." The Hebrew is, I will judge thee with the judgment of adulteresses. What the judgments of whores and adulteresses were, we shall find in Lev. xx. 10; Deut. xxii. 22. The adulterer and adulteress were both to be put to death, but what death is not specified. The Jews had four capital punishments or deaths.

1. *Chenek*, strangling: and this was the death they affirm that the adulterer and the adulteress were to suffer; for where the kind of death is not expressed, their rule is, it is strangling, because that is the easiest.

2. Is *hereg*, beheading.

3. *Sheriphah*, burning: so Judah judged Tamar, when she had played the whore, to be burnt, Gen. xxxviii. 24. The priest's daughter, if she played the whore, was to be burnt with fire, Lev. xxi. 9.

4. *Sekilah*, stoning: so the Pharisees tell Christ, John viii. 5, adulteresses should be stoned by the law of Moses; yet there is no express law in him for it, only those who committed sins of like nature were to be stoned, as Deut. xxii. 24; and it is evident from our prophet, who, in ver. 40, tells this adulteress woman she shall be stoned with stones.

The manner of stoning was, to lead the offender bound to a place without the gates, where one of the witnesses struck him behind upon the loins; then they took a very great and heavy stone and threw upon him; and if that did not kill him, then all the people threw stones upon him, according to Deut. xvii. 7. This death was counted the most grievous.

Among the Romans, adulteresses were beheaded by the Julian law. Tacitus relates, that among the old Germans, the adulteress being found out by her husband, she was stripped and set naked in the sight of her kindred; and afterward, her hair being cut off, her husband with rods drove her through the street so. Diodorus Siculus tells that the Egyptians did cut off and maim the nostrils of the adulteress, that so they might deform the face which had pleased: and the adulterer had a thousand stripes, with which he was almost beaten to death. *Vid.* Pet. Mart. upon 2 Sam. xii.

"And shed blood." Their judgment was to have their blood shed, Gen. ix. 6; Exod. xxi. 12. No satisfaction was to be taken for the life of a murderer, but he was absolutely to be put to death, Num. xxxv. 31, 32; whatever friends he could make, whatever ransom he could give, whatever quality he were of, these were not to be respected, but die he must. So here, Jerusalem had shed blood, even the blood of her infants, ver. 20, 21; and now her blood should be shed, she should be thrust through with swords, ver. 40.

"In fury and jealousy." Hebrew runs thus, I will give thee the blood of wrath and jealousy. The words show how severely the Lord will deal with her, even like a husband whose rage and jealousy is up, and nothing will pacify it but the blood of the adulterer and adulteress: Prov. vi. 34, "Jealousy is the rage of a man;" nothing exasperates him more than the falsehood of his wife; and so nothing exasperates God more than the falsehood and whoredom of his spouse. Psal. lxxix. 5, "Shall thy jealousy burn like fire?" yea, it burns like the hottest fire, and cannot be quenched. His fury and jealousy consumed Jerusalem before they ceased. These words agree with those in chap. v. 11, "Mine eye shall not spare, neither will I have any pity." God would give her blood without any mercy; no sacrifices, no tears, no prayers, no means should prevail with him.

Obs. 1. Adultery and bloodshed are sins which the Lord punisheth severely. He propounds the punishment of these sins to be the pattern of Jerusalem's punishment; I will judge thee with the judgments of adulteresses, and of those that shed blood. Their punishments are exemplary. Jer. xxix. 22, Zedekiah and Ahab are said to be roasted in the fire, which was a terrible judgment, a grievous torture: and what was the reason of it? "Because they have committed villany in Israel, and have committed adultery with their neighbours' wives." Mal. iii. 5, "I will be a swift witness against the adulterers:" that is so provoking a sin, and deserves such heavy judgment, that God will make haste to punish them. Heb. xiii. 4, "Whoremongers and adulterers God will judge;" that is, punish with emphatical punishments. Sodom's great sin was uncleanness, and God judged and punished them with fire and brimstone from heaven. The forcing of the Levite's concubine cost the blood of sixty thousand men, Judg. xx.; there uncleanness and murder were punished with severity. Psal. ix. 12, God "makes inquisition for blood;" he is so stirred at this sin, that he will up, search out the authors, contrivers, and commissioners of this scarlet sin; he will avenge for blood. Hos. i. 4, "I will avenge the blood of Jezreel upon the house of Jehu." Ezek. xxxv. 5, 6, because mount Seir had shed blood, "Therefore, as I live, saith the Lord God, I will prepare thee unto blood, and blood shall pursue thee. See how the Spirit of the Lord is up, he swears to it, that he would prepare them unto blood, and that blood should pursue them. Chap. xxxvi. 18, "I poured my fury upon them for the blood that they had shed upon the land, and for their idols wherewith they had polluted it.

Obs. 2. Note, there is difference of sin and punishments. Women that break wedlock and shed blood, they sin more grievously than others do, and their punishments are greater than others; their sins are scarlet and crying sins, abominations; and their punishments are answerable; they are judged otherwise than liars, slanderers, drunkards, thieves, &c. God punisheth some sins without blood; but these sins, adultery, murder, idolatry, with blood, and not only with blood, but with blood in fury and jealousy.

Ver. 39—43. *And I will also give thee into their hand, and they shall throw down thine eminent place, and shall break down thy high places: they shall strip thee also of thy clothes, and shall take thy fair jewels, and leave thee naked and bare. They shall also bring up a company against thee, and they shall stone thee with stones, and thrust thee through with their swords. And they shall burn thine houses with fire, and execute judgments upon thee in the sight of many women: and I will cause thee to cease from playing the harlot, and thou also shalt give no hire any more. So will I make my fury toward thee to rest, and my jealousy shall depart from thee, and I will be quiet, and will be no more angry. Because thou hast not remembered the days of thy youth, but hast fretted me in all these things; behold, therefore I also will recompense thy way upon thine head, saith the Lord God: and thou shalt not commit this lewdness above all thine abominations.*

The analysis of these words is before; I shall open some things in them, and then give you the observation.

Ver. 39. "Give thee into their hand." This phrase is sometimes expressed by delivering into the hand, 2 Chron. xxv. 20; sometimes by leaving in the hand, Neh. ix. 28; sometimes by giving up, 1 Kings xiv. 16. States, churches, cities, families, persons, come not into the hands of wicked men without the providence of God. They may all say as Christ did to Pilate, John xix. 11, "Thou couldest have no power at all against me, except it were given thee from above." So neither Chaldeans, Babylonians, nor any other could have had power against Jerusalem and the Jews, unless it had been given them from above. Psal. cvi. 41, "He gave them into the hand of the heathen;" he brought the heathen upon them, and delivered them up into their hands; see Jer. xx. 5; xxi. 7. Till God puts a people out of his own hands, and into the hands of others, they cannot hurt them.

"They shall throw down." Hebrew והרסו from הרס to pull down, subvert, demolish.

"Eminent place." Not the temple, or city, but some eminent place they had built, as it is in ver. 24 and 31, and with it all other high places where they had been idolatrous.

Obs. God's hatred is so great against idolatry and idolaters, that he will not endure the places where they have used idolatrous worship; the places where they sinned must be destroyed, broken, utterly razed and ruined. 2 Kings xviii. 4, Hezekiah is commended for four things; and the first is, for removing the high places; then for breaking the images, cutting down the groves, and breaking the brazen serpent. Amos v. 5, "Bethel shall come to nought." What was the matter that that place should come to nought? 1 Kings xii. 28, 29, Jeroboam had set up a golden calf there, made an altar, and brought the people to worship God in a false way, and in a false place. God's anger was so kindled against this, that presently he sent a prophet to cry against that altar in that place, and to threaten the ruin of it, chap. xiii. 2, 3; and in 2 Kings xxiii. 15, it is made good; Josiah breaks down the altar, the high place, stamps it to powder, and burns them and the grove to ashes: and afterwards God laid waste both city and temple, because they had filled them with altars and idols. They would not hear the prophets crying out against those things; God raised up means, &c. And so here against altars, crosses, &c.

"They shall strip thee also of thy clothes, and shall take thy fair jewels." Hebrew for fair jewels is, thy instruments of ornament, or vessels of glory; those things that did adorn, make thee glorious, as in ver. 17.

Obs. When we abuse the mercies of God, we give him cause to take them away. They decked their high places with their garments, ver. 16; they made images of their jewels, ver. 17, &c.; here God threatens to take away both the one and the other; he would give them into their hands who should rob them of their fair jewels, and strip them of all their clothes. Isa. xlii. 22, "This is a people robbed and spoiled." Ver. 24, 25, "Who gave Jacob for a spoil, and Israel to the robbers? did not the Lord, he against whom we have sinned? for they would not walk in his ways, neither were they obedient unto his law. Therefore he hath poured out upon him the fury of his anger," &c. Ofttimes you are robbed of your clothes and goods, because you have abused them to the dishonour of God.

"And leave thee naked and bare." Before, in ver. 8, it is said, that God covered her nakedness; he found her naked, and now he would leave her naked and bare.

Obs. When God hath showed much kindness to a people, and they have been ungrateful, he will reduce them to their former condition. He found this woman naked, and he would leave her naked. God did much for Ephraim, yet Ephraim was ungrateful, forgot God, went out to other lovers; and what saith the Lord? Hos. ii. 2, 3, "Plead with your mother: let her put away her whoredoms and adulteries, lest I strip her naked, and set her as in the day when she was born." God was upon the doing of it, and therefore put her upon a course of preventing it; but because she took not his counsel, in ver. 9, he saith, "I will return, and take away my corn in the time thereof, and my wine in the season thereof, and will recover my wool and my flax given to cover her nakedness," and then her condition would be as at the first. God had spread his skirt over this Jewish woman, clothed her with embroidered silk and fine linen, decked her with choice ornaments and jewels, put his comeliness upon her; but she abused all his bounty and love, proved ungrateful and whorish, and therefore he would put her into her first condition, strip her of all, and leave her naked: she came out of captivity, she should go into captivity; she was cast out, and now she should be cast out again; she was poor, beggarly, and had nothing, and should be made so again.

Ver. 40, 41. From the 40th verse, and beginning of the 41st,

Note, when God intends the ruin of a people, he will bring sore judgments upon them one after another, till they be consumed. "They shall bring up a company against thee." What company this was you may see, Hab. i. 6, "The Chaldeans, that hasty and bitter nation:" and what should they do?

1. They should stone her like a harlot, with stones; great stones should they sling in, which should kill many of her children.

2. They should thrust her through with swords; they should cut in pieces her sons and daughters.

3. They should burn her houses with fire. Each of these judgments was very dreadful. What sad apprehensions had the Jews, when they saw the Chaldeans before the walls and gates of Jerusalem, and called to mind what the prophets had foretold they should do to Jerusalem! In 2 Kings xxv. 8—10; 2 Chron. xxxvi. 17—20; Jer. lii. 12—14, &c. you may find these judgments executed, when the army came up; and that in Micah made good, where it is said, that for the judges', priests', and prophets' sins, Zion should be ploughed as a field, Jerusalem become as heaps, and the mountain of the house as the high places of the forest.

"In the sight of many women." By "women" I find expositors understand other nations, cities, and towns, and it suits well with the matter in hand; for here the Jewish state and nation is treated of under the notion of a woman: and therefore other nations and cities may be meant by the name of women, and so some interpret the word "women" in Isa. xxxii. 9, 11. The Jews say, these women were kingdoms and provinces: yet some

Vatab. Prad. Sanct. Pol. Pisc. Lavat.

R. David. Chald. Paraphr.

think by "women" here are to be understood the women in the Chaldean army, which were of divers nations. Maldonate thinks here is an allusion to the punishment of adulteresses, who were to be stoned or burned in the sight of other women, for the greater shaming of the sufferers, and for admonition of the spectators, that they beholding adulteresses brought to so shameful and dreadful an end, might learn to be faithful both to God and man; and such was the case here with Jerusalem, she was punished as a whore in the sight of nations, for the learning of the nations. When the Lord punisheth a nation with sharp and heavy judgments, other nations should take notice thereof, and be instructed thereby to take heed of those sins that nation is judged for; else God is provoked more, and the judgment will be heavier. Jer. iii. 8, "I put Israel away, and gave her a bill of divorce; yet her treacherous sister Judah feared not, but went and played the harlot also." God looked that Judah should have learned by Israel's judgments to have taken heed of such sins she was guilty of; but she did not, and that exasperated him the more. So Edom, Obad. 10—14, because she made no good use of Jerusalem's sufferings, but was glad at it; therefore the Lord threatens her, that shame should cover her, and that she should be cut off for ever.

Ver. 41. "And I will cause thee to cease from playing the harlot, and thou also shalt give no hire any more." These words afford us this observation.

Obs. That by great judgments God causeth a people to give over their great sins, to cease and rest from them. God would take away Jerusalem's wealth, her jewels, her gold and silver, her change of raiment; diminish her portion, cast her into captivity; and then she should not have to give to lovers, or spend upon idols, then she should not have leisure nor opportunity to seek or serve them. Isa. xxvii. 9, the fruit of God's judgments is to take away sin; by these sore judgments God cured them of their idolatry for ever.

Thus God hath dealt of late with Germany, Ireland, England; by his sore judgments he hath taken away the matter and occasion of sinning from thousands, they have not wherewithal to sin as formerly.

Poverty, sickness, imprisonment, loss of places, make men cease from sin, though their hearts be still the same.

Ver. 42. In this verse is mentioned God's fury, jealousy, anger. Fury is the excess of anger; Isa. xlii. 25, "He hath poured upon him the fury of his anger:" when anger is boiled up to the height, that is the fury of it. Jealousy is hot displeasure, Psal. lxxix. 5; 1 Cor. x. 22. Anger is a desire of punishing that which hath wronged us. Now these are given to God as becomes God; he is not as man, to become furious, jealous, angry, with perturbation, distemper, and imperfection; but he doth such acts as do entitle him to fury, jealousy, anger, yet without any change or weakness.

"So will I make my fury toward thee to rest." Some read it, I will make my fury to rest upon thee; and so it may refer to the whole time of their being in Babylon. Chap. v. 13, the Lord said, he would cause his fury to rest upon them. It is very dreadful when God's fury is out against a people, but it is most dreadful when his fury rests upon them. Hebrew is thus, I will make to rest my fury towards thee, that is, I will be furious no longer: when I have judged thee as adulteresses and murderers are judged, when I have stoned thee with stones, thrust thee through with swords, and burned thee with fire, there will be no more materials for my fury to feed upon, it shall rest and end. Septuagint, ἐπαφήσω τὸν θυμόν μȣ ἐπὶ σέ, I will dismiss mine anger upon thee, there shall be an end of it: this sense the words following do evince; "and my jealousy shall depart from thee," &c.

Obs. 1. When God's people sin against him, especially in ways of false worship and idolatry, they disquiet and trouble him, they cause his anger to kindle, his jealousy to burn, and provoke him to fury. A man, when his wife goes to other men, is enraged, so divided and perplexed, that he knows not what to do. The Septuagint reads it, for I will be no more angry: I will not be solicitous any longer; I will not be divided and distracted with cares and thoughts about thee. The heart and spirit of God was much troubled about his people when they left him, and went out to sinful practices. Hos. vi. 4, "O Ephraim, what shall I do unto thee?" O Judah, what shall I do unto thee?" God was even at a stand with them. Hos. xi. 8, "How shall I give thee up, Ephraim? how shall I deliver thee, Israel?" He was divided in himself; he considered this people were his wife, and so his mercy led him to spare them; yet a whorish wife, and so his anger, jealousy, and fury provoked him to punish them. Hence saith he, Ezek. vi. 9, "I am broken with their whorish heart, which hath departed from me." Jer. v. 7, "How shall I pardon thee for this? thy children have forsaken me." God had a fire and strife within himself; fain he would have pardoned Jerusalem, but he knew not how to accomplish it without prejudice to his justice, truth, and glory.

Obs. 2. When judgments are thoroughly executed upon a whorish and backsliding people, then God is at rest, and satisfied. When this woman, this Jewish state, fell into the hands of enemies, was plundered and spoiled, had her children stoned and thrust through, her city burnt to ashes, and all her glory laid in the dust; then God caused his fury to rest, his jealousy to depart, then he was quiet, and angry no more. Before judgment be thoroughly executed, God is troubled, and restless; but when it is done, he is pacified, comforted, as it is Ezek. v. 13. Before Jonah had judgment passed upon him, there was a great wind, and a mighty tempest in the sea, the Lord's anger, jealousy, and fury were up, and let out: but when Jonah was sent, and cast into the sea, justice done, it is said the sea ceased from her raging, it was so presently; and what was the reason of it? the Lord first ceased from his fury, he was pacified, and manifested it by stilling of the seas. The mariners did it not so much out of love to justice, as love to save themselves: they saw all like to perish, a common shipwreck at hand, Jonah was detected to be the delinquent; and so to secure themselves, they threw him over, and had their desire. When justice was executed upon Saul's bloody house for slaying the Gibeonites, the three years' famine ceased: till that was done, there was nothing but fury, jealousy, and anger from God; but being done, the Lord caused his displeasure to cease, and was at rest, 2 Sam. xxi. God would bring the Assyrians upon the Jews; and what then? "the indignation shall cease, and mine anger in their destruction," Isa. x. 25: when I have laid all waste, and destroyed them, then shall I be angry, jealous, furious no more. Esth. vii. 10, "They hanged Haman on the gallows, and then was the king's wrath pacified."

Ver. 43. "Because thou hast not remembered the days of thy youth, but hast fretted me in all these things." This verse contains two of the principal causes moving God to bring such dreadful judgments upon Jerusalem.

I. Her forgetfulness of her youth.

II. Her fretting of God by her lewd courses.

Of her not remembering the days of her youth was spoken in ver. 22.

"Hast fretted me." Hebrew ותרגזי from רגז to move, stir up, provoke. Septuagint, ἐλύπεις, hast grieved me.

"This lewdness." Hebrew, את-הזמה Something I said of *zimmah* in ver. 27; it signifies properly a premeditated evil or villany, which is shameful and abominable, as Lev. xviii. 17, the uncovering a woman's nakedness and her daughter's, it is *zimmah*, a wickedness; chap. xix. 29, whoredom is *zimmah*. Now what is this lewdness here spoken of? Piscator saith, it was the murdering of her children, ver. 20, 21, upon which act God sets an emphasis, "Is this of thy whoredoms a small matter?" Some read the words otherwise, thus; Neither hast thou made a thought upon all thine abominations, taking *zimmah* in a good sense, viz. thou hast never thought of thy wicked ways and abominations to repent thee of them, but gone on securely.

Obs. 1. The Lord expects we should be mindful of our primitive condition and estate he began with us in. "Thou hast not remembered the days of thy youth:" so in ver. 22. Psal. lxxviii. 42, "They remembered not his hand, nor the day when he delivered them from the enemy:" their poverty and bondage in Egypt they thought not of, and what God did for them in bringing them out of that land, and drowning their enemies in the Red sea; ver. 11, "They forgat his works, and his wonders he had showed them." It is often put upon them to mind their former estate. Deut. xv. 15, "Thou shalt remember that thou wast a bondman in the land of Egypt, and the Lord thy God redeemed thee." So chap. xvi. 12; xxiv. 18, 22. And that they might not forget their first condition, the Lord appointed the offering of the first-fruits, at which they were to profess before the Lord, that a Syrian ready to perish was their father, who went down into Egypt, sojourned there with a few, and became a nation, great, mighty, and populous. It is the way to keep us humble, make us thankful, and to walk answerably.

Obs. 2. When man is advanced, he is apt to forget the low, poor, and miserable condition he was in. "Thou hast not remembered the days of thy youth." There was a time, saith God, wherein thou wast inconsiderable: when Jacob served Laban, was in Egypt with seventy souls, how mean, how low was thy condition! but this thou hast forgotten. When Pharaoh's butler was brought out of prison, he forgot the prison, and Joseph who had been his companion there, Gen. xl. Saul was taken from seeking his father's asses, and set upon the throne of Israel, where he quickly forgot God and himself. When men or states are become great oaks and mountains, they forget what little acorns and hillocks once they were; when arrived to the height of cedars, they are loth to look what rushes once they were, growing in the mire. Deut. viii. 12—14, beware lest when thou art full, hast built goodly houses, and art multiplied with herds, flocks, silver, gold, &c. thine heart be lifted up, and thou forget the Lord, and the condition he brought thee out of, viz. Egypt, the house of bondage: and notwithstanding this caution, Israel did forget her first condition, and God's first and great kindness unto her, Deut. xxxii. 15; Hos. xiii. 6.

Obs. 3. When men forget the low, poor, and miserable estate they were once in, and God's loving-kindness and bounty in exalting them to a rich, high, or honourable condition, they exasperate the Lord greatly. "Because thou hast not remembered the days of thy youth, but hast fretted me." This sin frets and provokes God, that he should pity a nation when it is low, at the door of death, brink of despair, do great things for it, and then prove ungrateful and forgetful! Thus was it with the Jewish state. God did much for Jeroboam, preserved his life, called him out of Egypt, bestowed ten tribes upon him; and he forgot what he had been, what he was at the present through God's mercy, and therefore see what a message the Lord sent him; 1 Kings xiv. 7—10, "Go, tell Jeroboam, Forasmuch as I exalted thee from among the people," he was as low as others, "and made thee prince over my people Israel, and rent the kingdom away from the house of David, and gave it to thee; and yet thou hast not been as David, but hast done evil above all that were before thee, &c., therefore I will bring evil upon the house of Jeroboam," &c. God would utterly destroy it. So chap. xvi. 2, concerning Baasha; "Forasmuch as I exalted thee out of the dust, and made thee prince over my people Israel; and thou hast walked in the ways of Jeroboam, and made my people sin to provoke me to anger; behold, I will take away thy posterity, and make thy house like Jeroboam's," dogs and fowls shall devour those that die thereof. This was the sin which made the Lord to be as a lion, as a leopard, and as a bear bereaved of whelps, unto Ephraim, Hos. xiii. 6—8.

Obs. 4. God will deal with sinners according to their ways. "I will recompense thy way upon thine head;" if thy ways be sinful, thou shalt have the fruit and reward of them upon thy head. Prov. x. 6, "Blessings are upon the head of the just." God recompenseth to the just according to their way, and to the wicked according to their way. If men shed blood, God will return that blood upon their heads. Joab he slew Abner and Amasa, and see what is recorded, 1 Kings ii. 31—34; Benaiah falls upon him, and slays him at the horns of the altar; so their blood, which is called "his blood," returned upon his own head: this blood rested upon Joab's head all David's reign, 2 Sam. iii. 29, and was recompensed upon his head in Solomon's days: whatever a man's ways be, God will return them upon his head. Hence saith Solomon to Shimei, "Thou knowest all the wickedness which thine heart is privy to, that thou didst to David my father; therefore the Lord shall return thy wickedness upon thine own head," 1 Kings ii. 44. Solomon knew God was so just and exact in this point, that he prays God would distinguish between the wicked and the just, by recompensing their ways upon their heads, 2 Chron. vi. 23; and so Nehemiah, "Turn their reproach upon their own head," chap. iv. 4. Edria had slain Edmund the king for the sake of Chute, who after put him to death, saying, His blood be upon thy head. Canald. Rem. p. 252.

Obs. 5. Some sins God eyes, and brands, and beats off from above others. "Thou shalt not commit this lewdness above all thine abominations;" the slaying of her children: God took special notice of that wickedness, set a mark upon it, "this lewdness," and tells her that he would so punish her, as that she should not commit it any more. Deut. xvii. 5, the serving other gods is called there the committing "that wicked thing." When the Jews married the daughters of the nations, God was much displeased at it, and brands it with "this trespass," Ezra ix. 2, "this thing," ver. 3. So their sin in Jer. xliv. 4, is called an "abominable thing;" "Do not this abominable thing that I hate." Jer. ii. 10, 11, "Consider diligently, and see if there be such a thing: hath a nation changed their gods?" &c. So Judg. xix. 30, "There was no such deed done nor seen." Deut. xiii. 11, they should stone the seducer, and then all Israel should fear.

Ver. 44—46. *Behold, every one that useth proverbs shall use this proverb against thee, saying, As is the mother, so is her daughter. Thou art thy mother's daughter, that lotheth her husband and her children; and thou art the sister of thy sisters, which lothed their husbands and their children: your mother was an Hittite, and your father an Amorite. And thine elder sister is Samaria, she and her daughters that dwell at thy left hand: and thy younger sister, that dwelleth at thy right hand, is Sodom and her daughters.*

In these words you have,

I. Another judgment threatened, which is common reproach, ver. 44.

II. A comparison of her for wickedness with her parents and sisters; her parents were the Hittites and Amorites, ver. 45, her sisters Samaria and Sodom, ver. 46.

"That useth proverbs." Upon chap. xii. ver. 22, I opened the word proverb, and showed you the nature and meaning of it. All nations have their proverbs, which they much account of. Every one that can jeer and scoff shall disgrace thee.

"As is the mother, so is her daughter." The mother is lewd, idolatrous, bloody, rebellious, and the daughter is such; look therefore what befell the mother for her sins, what punishment was inflicted upon her, the like shall befall and be inflicted upon thee. Proverbs suitable unto this are these: "Ill birds lay ill eggs;" "Roses grow not out of shrimps;" "From the wicked proceeds wickedness;" "Ill seed, ill corn;" "By the children you may know the parents." Now these are not always true; but sometimes it falls out, that wicked parents have good children, and good parents wicked ones. Noah had a Ham, Isaac an Esau, David an Absalom, Hezekiah a Manasseh: and so contrary, Ahaz that wicked king had good Hezekiah for his son; Amon, Josiah; Lamech, Noah.

Ver. 45. "Thou art thy mother's daughter," &c. We must inquire who was her mother, and wherein the likeness between them lieth.

Her mother is said here to be an Hittite, and her father an Amorite, *vid. supra* in ver. 3. She was so unlike to Sarah and Abraham, out of whose loins by nature she came, and so like to the Amorites and Hittites, as that the Lord calls her the daughter of them.

Her sisters were, 1. Samaria: that was the chief city of the ten tribes, the royal city; it was upon a hill, built by Omri king of Israel, who bought the hill of one Shemer, so from him called it Samaria, 1 Kings xvi. 24, afterwards called Sebaste.

2. Sodom: this was the city were Lot dwelt, given so to filthiness and uncleanness, that one sin of that kind hath its name from hence; and was one of the five cities, yea the chief, that God consumed with fire and brimstone from heaven.

The daughters of these were the lesser cities, towns, and villages which depended on them for protection, counsel, maintenance, and were under the government of their kings.

The likeness between them is set out in these words, "which lothed their husbands and their children." The word געל signifieth, to cast out, to loathe with contempt, and spitting at. These nations forsook Jehovah the true God, who was their Creator, Lawgiver, and Benefactor, and served idols, murdered their children, and walked in all lewd ways, not regarding the light or laws of nature: see Deut. xviii. 9, 10, they made their children pass through the fire. They were so unclean, idolatrous, and profane, that the land vomited them out, Lev. xviii. 25, spewed out those nations, ver. 28.

Jerusalem was come to that pass, that she rejected God her Husband, and loathed his worship, violated all bonds of religion and humanity, sacrificing her children unto devils. She was exceeding like the Sodomites; Deut. xxxii. 32, "Their vine is the vine of Sodom;" Isa. i. 10, "Rulers of Sodom, and people of Gomorrah." The Jews were transformed into their natures, dispositions, customs. Samaria was at her left hand, that was the north part, and Sodom at her right hand, which was the south part.

It seems strange that Samaria here is called the elder sister, whenas Sodom was many years before her, and destroyed ere she had her birth. The original therefore consulted, and rightly interpreted, will help us in this; for the word for elder is הגדולה *magna*, thy sister, the great Samaria; הקטנה *parva*, or *minor*, thy sister, the little one in comparison of thee; or Samaria had more power, cities, and citizens belonging to her than Sodom had.

Obs. 1. When states, churches, cities, persons dishonour God by sinful and lewd ways, God will dishonour them, and set men to work that are skilful at and exercised in jeering, scoffing, and reviling, to disgrace them. This woman had brought up an ill report upon the land of Canaan and God of Israel; and therefore saith God, Those who are used to proverbs, yea, every one that is skilled that way, "shall use this proverb against thee, As is the mother, so is her daughter;" thy mother was a whore, an idolatress, a murderess, and so art thou. Jer. xxiv. 9, "I will deliver them to be removed into all kingdoms of the earth for their hurt, to be a reproach and a proverb, a taunt and a curse, in all places whither I shall drive them." 2 Chron. vii. 20, if they dishonoured God, he tells them he would pull them up by the roots out of the land, make them and their temple a proverb and by-word among all nations. Jer. xxiii. 40, "I will bring an everlasting reproach upon you, and a perpetual shame, which shall not be forgotten." Ezek. xxii. 5, "Those that be near, and those that be far, shall mock thee, which art infamous." Lam. v. 1, "Consider, and behold our reproach:" their princes, prophets, people, city, temple, land, were all reproached. Job xii. 21, "He poureth contempt upon princes."

Obs. 2. Children usually tread in the steps of their parents. "As is the mother, so is her daughter," of the same disposition, spirit, practice. Drunken parents have drunken children; unclean, covetous, proud, froward, contentious parents have had such children, they have learned of them to be and do as they were and did. 1 Kings xxii. 52, Ahaziah did evil in the sight of the Lord, and walked in the way of his father, who was Ahab, and of his mother, who was Jezebel. Jehoram the son of Jehoshaphat, it is said, "he walked in the way of the kings of Israel, for the daughter of Ahab was his wife," 2 Kings viii. 18. Take heed whom you marry, for the children will resemble the parent; and take heed what you do before your children, for your examples have great influence into them; they are strong traces to draw your children into your ways, especially if bad.

Obs. 3. Cities, states, churches, people, are their children in the account of the Scripture, whose manners, ways, and examples they follow. Jerusalem took up the ways, worship, manners, and customs of the nations and cities near to her; hence her mother is said to be an Hittite, her father an Amorite, her sisters Sodom and Samaria; according to their ways she fashioned herself. Those that follow the faith and steps of Abraham, are the children of Abraham, Gal. iii. 7; Rom. iv. 16. Those who are peaceable, and labour to make peace, they are children of God, Matt. v. 9. Men that mind the world are provident, frugal, and saving; they following courses of the world, are called children of the world, Luke xvi. 8. So those that do wickedly, they are the children of the devil, 1 John iii. 8, 10, 12; Matt. xiii. 38. "Ye are of your father the devil, and the lusts of your father ye will do," John viii. 44; they did imitate him: and here Jerusalem declared her sin as Sodom, Isa. iii. 9, and as the nations, and therefore is styled the daughter and sister of them.

Obs. 4. Those who are in near relation to God, and think well of themselves, may be hateful to him, and as bad as any. Jerusalem was in covenant with God, his spouse, the Jews his peculiar people, and thought themselves more holy, righteous, in a better condition than any of all the nations; and thought the prophets wronged them when they compared them to the nations, to Sodom and Samaria; but what saith the Lord here? "Thy mother is an Hittite, and thy father an Amorite:" whatever thou thinkest of thyself, that thou art of the stock of Abraham and Sarah, Isaac and Jacob, a true Israelite; yet it is otherwise, thou art of the seed of the nations, and worst of the nations, viz. the Hittites and Amorites: thou thinkest thou art holy, but art profane; that thou art dear to me above them, but thou art as odious and hateful as any.

The priests were near the Lord, stood before him, offered sacrifice, thought themselves to be somebodies. Mal. ii. 1, 2, they thought they did glorify God, and should be glorified by God; but, ver. 8, 9, "Ye are departed out of the way; ye have caused many to stumble at the law; ye have corrupted the covenant of Levi, saith the Lord of hosts. Therefore have I also made you contemptible and base before all the people, according as ye have not kept my ways, but have been partial in the law." Matt. vii. 22, 23, "Many will say to me in that day, Lord, Lord, have we not prophesied in thy name? and in thy name have cast out devils? and in thy name done many wonderful works?" You see they stood in near relation to God, pretend they did all in his name, thought themselves in a good condition, looked for some good and great reward; but what follows? "Then will I profess, I never knew you; depart from me, ye that work iniquity." There is vast difference between man's and God's judgment.

Ver. 47—50. *Yet hast thou not walked after their ways, nor done after their abominations: but, as if that were a very little thing, thou wast corrupted more than they in all thy ways. As I live, saith the Lord God, Sodom thy sister hath not done, she nor her daughters, as thou hast done, thou and thy daughters. Behold, this was the iniquity of thy sister Sodom, pride, fulness of bread, and abundance of idleness was in her and in her daughters, neither did she strengthen the hand of the poor and needy. And they were haughty, and committed abomination before me: therefore I took them away as I saw good.*

In these verses, and the two next, the comparison is still carried on between Jerusalem, the nations, Sodom, and Samaria, wherein the sins of Jerusalem are declared to exceed their sins.

I. This is laid down in general, ver. 47.

II. In special, in ver. 48, where the sin of Jerusalem is not only asserted to exceed the sin of Sodom, but ratified with an oath, "As I live," &c.

Now concerning Sodom you have,

1. The catalogue of her sins, ver. 49, and beginning of ver. 50.

2. God's dealing with the Sodomites for their sins, ver. 50, "Therefore I took them away," &c.

Ver. 47. "Yet hast thou not walked after their ways," &c. Before he had said, "As is the mother, so is her daughter," and, "Thou art thy mother's daughter, that loatheth her husband," &c. and here, "Yet hast thou not walked after their ways, nor done after their abominations;" how do these cohere?

The prophet doth not acquit Jerusalem from imitation of the Hittites, Amorites, Sodomites, and Samaritans, he grants she had done that; but by a figure called epanorthosis, correcting himself, he carries it on further, Thou hast not walked after their ways, nor done, &c. but thou hast gone beyond them all in thy wickedness. Thou thoughtest to be like unto them a small matter, a very little thing, this contented not thee, but thou hast done more abominably than they, and corrupted thyself more deeply.

Some take the words thus, Thou hast not walked after their ways, nor done after their abominations for a little and a little time; and so refer the time to the reign of Hezekiah, wherein Jerusalem having sinned greatly in Ahaz's days, after Samaria was taken by Sennacherib, repented, and abstained from idolatry; but presently after, in Manasseh's days, returned more fully to it, and exceeded Samaria, Sodom, and the nations: which hints this unto us, that state repentance and reformation are seldom sound or long-lived; it is fear of authority, not hatred of sin, conscience of duty, love of truth, virtue, justice, holiness, that set them on work; and when the bridle of fear is lax or removed, they return to their old ways, which cannot be otherwise, having their old natures.

Obs. 1. The Lord takes notice of the ways of a people even from their beginning to their end. This observation arises from ver. 45, 46, and this verse, laid together; there the Lord said their mother is an Hittite, their father an Amorite, their sisters, Samaria and Sodom; and here, "Thou wast corrupted more than they in all thy ways:" I have observed thee from the first to the last, from thy birth to thy end. God eyes the infancy, youth, growth, and age of a state, and what the ways of it are; whose tenets, manners, customs, and ways it follows. 2 Chron. xxviii. 26, of Ahaz, a wicked king, it is said, "The rest of his acts and of all his ways, first and last, behold they are written," &c.; there was nothing escaped the eye of Heaven. Jer. xxxii. 19, "Thine eyes are open upon all the ways of the sons of men;" even from the beginning to the end it is so. God doth not chop in like man, and observe here a passage and there a passage; but he is a constant observer of every thing, of every way: Prov. v. 21, "The ways of man are before the eyes of the Lord, and he pondereth all his goings."

Obs. 2. Sinful republics and states think it no great matter to be like their neighbour nations and cities in wickedness and villanies. The Lord told this commonwealth of Israel that she was like the Canaanites, Hittites, Amorites, Sodomites, Samaritans, in idolatry, uncleanness, and other sins; and she thought this no great matter, a little, yea a very little thing. Ver. 20, "Is this of thy whoredom a small matter?" she thought it so. 1 Kings xvi. 31, Ahab's walking in the sins of Jeroboam was reputed but a light thing; and Jehu saith of him, that he "served Baal a little," 2 Kings x. 18; yet, 1 Kings

xxi. 25, 26, "There was none like unto Ahab, which did sell himself to work wickedness in the sight of the Lord; and he did very abominably in following idols, according to all things as did the Amorites:" though he equalled the Amorites, yet this was a little thing. Ezek. viii. 17, "Is it a light thing to the house of Judah that they commit the abominations which they commit here?" they thought it so. Take any nation, even this nation, is it not like other nations for injustice, oppression, drunkenness, whoredom, swearing, falsehood, excess, fantasticalness, &c.? yet we say it is no great matter; sin, the greatest evil, is made nothing.

Obs. 3. Those God hath done much for, taken very near to himself, may degenerate so far, as to prove worse than others, than any. Thou whom I exalted from so low an estate, and took into my special favour, even thou hast corrupted thyself more than they in all thy ways. So notorious was Jerusalem in her abominable practices, that, ver. 27, the Philistines were ashamed of her lewd ways. Chap. v. 7, she multiplied sin more than the nations round about her. How desperately did this state sin in the days of Ahaz and Manasseh! is not Jerusalem called the filthy, polluted, oppressing city? Zeph. iii. 1. And is it not thus at this day? are not many christian states, which God hath done great things for, and blessed with choice means and mercies, are they not worse than heathenish nations? those sins found amongst us which are unknown to them? I fear Rome, Madrid, Paris, &c. with Italy, Spain, France, England, will be found to exceed the heathens.

Ver. 48. "As I live." Hebrew is חי־אני I living, or I live. Septuagint, ζῶ ἐγῶ, I do live. When God swears, most usually it is by his life; and Glassius tells us, that by the life of God is meant his eternal glory, majesty, power, and truth; so that all these are impawned in God's oath, and he had rather not be, than be found false and unfaithful. Of this oath of God was spoken in chap. v. 1. The Lord swears thus,

Philologia Sacra, l. 5. Tractat. 2. p. 540.

1. To let them know he did not hyperbolize: he had been in an allegory before, and spoken allegorically of this Jewish state; and that they might not think he did now allegorize or hyperbolize, he swears plainly that their sins were greater than Sodom's. This assertion was both odious and incredible; to take away both the odiousness and incredibility thereof, he binds it with an oath, and the greatest oath of all, by his life, by himself, as sure as he was God, as he lived, it was so.

2. To affect them, as with the greatness of their sins, so with the heinousness of their punishments; if they exceeded Sodom in sinning, surely they deserved more dreadful punishments and judgments than Sodom.

Obs. 1. That those who profess God, and are in common account God's people, may come to such a height of sinning, as exceeds belief. Who would, who could have thought that any city or nation should have been worse than Sodom; especially that Jerusalem, the holy city, the habitation of the Lord, and that the Jews, who were the Lord's first-born, his treasure and peculiar people, that these should outgo Sodom and the Sodomites in wickedness? It is matter of wonder; what! a Jew worse than a Sodomite? who can believe it; Jerusalem and her daughters worse than Sodom and her daughters?

Obs. 2. What great cities are, usually such are the lesser cities. The bordering towns and villages, which are called daughters, they imitate their mothers, learn their ways, receive their opinions, follow their counsels, practices, manners. Samaria and her daughters were alike, Sodom and her daughters, ver. 45, 46; and so Jerusalem and her daughters. Great cities have great influence into the adjacent towns and villages; if they be idolatrous, unjust, bitter, contentious, proud, excessive in diet and apparel, so will all about them be: Rev. xvii. 3, "Babylon the great, the mother of harlots and abominations of the earth."

Obs. 3. To assure us of the truth of things, God is pleased to take an oath. The Lord knew this would not easily be entertained, that Jerusalem and her daughters were greater sinners than Sodom and her daughters; to put it out of doubt, therefore, the Lord swears a great oath, "As I live" it is so, as sure as I am the living God it is truth: so God swears, Ezek. xxxiii. 11, to assure man. O happy they in whose cause God swears! but great their misery who do not believe a God giving such confirmation!

Ver. 49. *Behold, this was the iniquity of thy sister Sodom, pride, fulness of bread, and abundance of idleness was in her and in her daughters, neither did she strengthen the hand of the poor and needy.*

In this 49th verse he tells us the sins of Sodom; and the first was,

"Pride." Hebrew גאון pride, or lifting up of the mind against a precept, or an inordinate desire of excellency in any thing. It is a tumour and swelling of the mind, and lieth principally in contemning and slighting of God himself, his word, promises, threats, ordinances, worship, works; in self-esteem and admiration; in a swelling for gifts and graces, successfulness of endeavours, for birth, breeding, wealth, honour, place, relation, and in despising of others.

It is either inward in the heart, Hab. ii. 4; Prov. xvi. 5; or outward, and that,

1. In the speech: Dan. iv. 30, "Is not this great Babylon, that I have built for the house of the kingdom?" So chap. iii. 15, "Who is that God that shall deliver you out of my hands?" Here was a tongue that spake proud things, Psal. xii. 3; 1 Sam. ii. 3.

2. In the looks: Prov. vi. 17, "A proud look." Psal. cxxxi. 1, "My heart is not haughty, nor mine eyes lofty."

3. In the habit of the body: so Herod's pride appeared, Acts xii. 21; so the rich man's, Luke xvi. 19.

4. In the gesture and carriage of the body: Isa. iii. 16, "The daughters of Zion are haughty, and walk with stretched forth necks, wanton eyes, mincing and tinkling with their feet."

5. In actions: Isa. iii. 5, "The child shall behave himself proudly against the ancient." Neh. ix. 16, 29, "They and our fathers dealt proudly, and hearkened not to thy commandments." So in feasting and furniture, and in tenacity of opinions.

The evil and sinfulness of this sin will appear in several particulars:

(1.) It blinds and hardens the mind and heart of man. Dan. v. 20, Nebuchadnezzar's mind was "hardened in pride," and reason so blinded, that he became brutish.

(2.) Pride sets a man in opposition to God. Other sins are aversions from God, this sin is coming against God; in other sins they fly from God, in this sin they fly upon God. James iv. 6, "God resisteth the proud." Men do not resist till they are set upon: when thieves set upon travellers, if able they make resistance; when the devil sets upon a christian with his temptations, then he resists: so here, proud men set upon God, his truths, his church, and then he resists them. Psal. lxxiii. 9, "They set their mouth against the heavens."

(3.) It is the root of other sins. Absalom's pride carried him on to rebellion and other vile practices: it was Athaliah's pride which put her upon slaying the seed royal, that so she might reign, 2 Kings xi. Prov. xiii. 10, "Only by pride cometh contention:" all the contention in families, in suits of law, in trading, in the pulpits, in the wars, have sprung from pride. Ezek. vii. 10, "Pride hath budded." It is the nurse of covetousness: it was Haman's pride put him upon seeking and plotting the death of all the Jews in Babylon.

(4.) It is that makes us like the devil. 1 Tim. iii. 6, "Not a novice, lest being lifted up with pride he fall into the condemnation of the devil." God therefore sets Satan upon his servants sometimes to prevent this evil. 2 Cor. xii. 7, God had rather see him buffeted by Satan, then swell with pride.

(5.) It is that sin which makes God abhor man. Prov. xvi. 5, "Every one that is proud in heart is an abomination to the Lord." "A proud look" is one of the things God hates, Prov. vi. 16, 17. His hatred is great against proud men; Psal. cxix. 21, Proud men are cursed. God delights in nothing more than his glory, and he hates nothing more than pride, which would rob him of his glory.

(6.) It is a grand enemy to the spiritual good and salvation of man. The gospel saith, He that thinks he knows any thing, knows nothing as he ought to know; a proud man thinks he knows something, if not all things. The gospel saith, A man must become a fool, that he may be wise, deny himself, and go to Christ for wisdom, righteousness, redemption, grace, salvation; but a proud heart will not, he will be his own alpha and omega, the efficient and end of his own actions: "Ye will not come to me that ye might have life," John v. 40. Therefore it is twice upon record, Jam. iv. 6; 1 Pet. v. 5, "God resisteth the proud, and giveth grace to the humble." Full stomachs loathe the honey-comb. Matt. xi. 25, Christ thanketh his Father that he had hid the things of the gospel from the wise and prudent, from the proud men of the world.

(7.) It brings sad calamities and sore judgments upon men and places. Pride hath blasted many a man's parts. Prov. xv. 25, "The Lord will destroy the house of the proud." Haman, Ahithophel, were proud persons, and God destroyed them and their houses. Herod was presently smitten, and eaten of worms, Acts xii. 23. Isa. ii. 12—17, "The day of the Lord of hosts shall be upon every one that is proud, and he shall be brought low; upon all the cedars of Lebanon, all the oaks of Bashan, high mountains and hills; upon every high tower and fenced wall; upon all the ships of Tarshish, and all pleasant pictures: and the loftiness of man shall be bowed down, and the haughtiness of men shall be made low." The Jews would not have Christ to reign over them, and they were quickly after scattered and destroyed, and Jerusalem laid waste. So Moab, Ammon, Assyria, and Nineveh are threatened for their pride, Zeph. ii.; Tyre, Ezek. xxviii. And here pride was the first firebrand that set Sodom on fire.

Pride must down; as Christ said of the buildings of the temple, not a stone shall be left upon a stone. 2 Sam. xxii. 28, God's eyes are upon the haughty that he may bring them down; he watches his opportunities to do it. He commands us not to be proud; Prov. iii. 7, "Be not wise in thine own eyes." Godly men have prayed against it: Psal. xxxvi. 11, "Let not the foot of pride come against me." Psal. xix. 12, 13, "Cleanse me from secret faults; keep back thy servant also from presumptuous sins." Paul beat down his body lest he should be a reprobate; let us beat down our spirits, lest, &c.

We have spoken of the first sin, viz. pride, now we are come to the second,

"Fulness of bread." Hebrew, שבעת־לחם.

"Bread" is sometimes used in holy language for all things needful for the support and comfort of this life, as Luke xi. 3, "Give us this day our daily bread:" sometimes only for what is edible and potable, and tends to the nourishment of man; 2 Sam. ix. 7, saith David to Mephibosheth, "Thou shalt eat bread at my table continually." In this sense we are to take it here, for whatsoever men eat or drink.

"Fulness." Sodom was seated in a most fertile place, in the plain of Jordan, which was "well watered every where, even as the garden of the Lord, like the land of Egypt," Gen. xiii. 10. It was like Paradise and Egypt for fruitfulness; one was watered with Euphrates, the other with Nilus, and this plain with Jordan, so that it abounded with grass, corn, cattle, fruit, and other pleasant things. It was so fertile, that Luther thinks it was the place where Paradise was: that is disputable, but we are sure it was the place Lot chose for its fruitfulness when he left his brother Abraham; and it yielded such abundance, that the Sodomites had great plenty. You may demand whether a plentiful estate in corn, cattle, oil, wine, fowl, fish, fruit, &c. be sinful, because fulness of bread, which imports these things, is reckoned up among Sodom's iniquities? The answer is, that plentifulness of such things is not evil, but a great blessing, and men thereby have occasion to do much good. The sin lieth not in having much meat and drink, but in their excessive eating and drinking; they were intemperate, feeding and drinking so fully, that instead of satisfying, they surfeited nature: and here by fulness of bread is meant both gluttony and drunkenness; of both which something is to be spoken.

Gluttony may seem to be no sin upon a double ground:

1. From Matt. xv. 11, "Not that which goeth into the mouth defileth the man," saith Christ; "that goeth into the belly, and is cast out into the draught," ver. 17: that which is a sin doth defile, but nothing eaten doth so. It is true, that the meat eaten in its own nature doth not defile: the meats forbidden to the Jews, if any did eat of them at any time, the defilement lay not simply in the meat, but in the breach of the command, viz. eating forbidden meat; for if any meat did defile, *ratione sui*, of its own substance and nature, it were never lawful to eat that meat; but so doth no meat: it is therefore not the meat, but the inordinate desire of meat, which makes the sin, and causeth the defilement.

2. In whatsoever is sinful, the first motion thereunto is so; the first motion to anger, to idolatry, to uncleanness is so: but now the principle or first motion to eating is hunger, and it is most certain that is not sinful; for then the more hungry any should be, the greater sinner he is.

For clearing this doubt you must know there is a double desire of meat: one natural, simply tending to the nourishment of the creature, and subservient to the vegetative power of the soul; and this rises not from any apprehension of this or that in the meat, but only from want in nature; and this is truly called hunger, and so far from being sinful, that the greater it is, the more it excuseth liberal eating. There is another desire of meat, which is sensitive, and tendeth to the pleasing of the sensual part in man, and falls under the power of reason; which the other did not, being merely natural: and here the first motion or desire of meat beyond what sound reason approves, is inordinate in the sensitive appetite, and so sinful.

Gluttony, the nature of it lies in an inordinate desire of eating, and men are said to gluttonize several ways:

1. When they desire delicacies, not being content with those meats Providence hath given in. Numb. xi. 4, the children of Israel being discontented with their manna, "fell a lusting, and said, Who shall give us flesh to eat?" Manna, heavenly and angelical food, was loathed by them, and now they must have some dainties to satisfy their lusts.

2. When they are too solicitous about the cooking and dressing of their meats. 1 Sam. ii. 15, "The priest's servant came, and said to the man that sacrificed, Give flesh to roast for the priest; for he will not have sodden flesh of thee, but raw." Why would he have raw flesh? that he might prepare and cook it more curiously.

3. When men eat unseasonably, and prevent the due time. Eccles. x. 16, 17, there is a woe threatened when "princes eat in the morning," and the land is blessed when they "eat in due season." The morning is the time for them to do justice, Jer. xxi. 12, "Execute judgment in the morning;" and now for them to eat, drink, feast, when neither nature requires it nor the time is seasonable for it, this argues an inordinate desire of the creature. Isa. v. 11, "Woe unto them that rise up early in the morning to follow strong drink!" that is not a time to have the heart and thoughts taken up about pots and dishes. So when men are set upon eating, before there be a half or full concoction of what they took in before.

4. When men are greedy of meat, not observing such a decorum as becomes men. Swine are greedy and hasty of their meat, and ravenous in eating, but it ill becomes men to be so. The schoolmen say this was Esau's sin, who slighting his birth-right, sold it for pottage, and greedily devoured it.

5. When men eat too much, exceeding in the quantity; and this is most properly gluttony: and this was Sodom's sin, "fulness of bread" and drink. Now too much is eaten and drunk,

(1.) When the health or strength of the party eating and drinking is impaired thereby. Some overcharge nature with surfeiting and drunkenness, Luke xxi. 34, and so bring sickness and weakness upon themselves. Hence, Eccles. x. 17, "Blessed is the land, when princes eat for strength, and not for drunkenness."

(2.) When made heavy and dull, so that the operations of body and mind are hindered thereby, and men unfitted for the duties of their callings in public or private. Prov. xxiii. 21, speaking of the drunkard and glutton, he presently mentions drowsiness; because too much eating and drinking makes drowsy, and unfits for all action.

(3.) When men sit much at meat and drink, and through custom or strength can bear away much: though no prejudice come to their health, though they be not retarded and dulled in the operations of body or mind; yet if men are given to eating and drinking, this falls within the compass of sin, and under the notion of gluttony and drunkenness. When a man is "given to covetousness," as Jer. vi. 13, he is a covetous man; when one is "given to pleasures," as Isa. xlvii. 8, he is a man of pleasure: so when one is given to eat and drink, he is a man of eating, a man of drinking, "a man given to appetite," Prov. xxiii. 2; a man that lives to eat, and doth not eat to live.

I shall next come to show you the evil of intemperate eating and drinking, 1. As it respects God; 2. Others; 3. Themselves.

1. In respect of God; and so,

(1.) It makes men forget God and his laws: Hos. xiii. 6, "According to their pasture, so were they filled; they were filled, and their heart was exalted; therefore have they forgotten me." Prov. xxxi. 4, 5, drinking wine and strong drink will make men forget the law of God and man.

(2.) It is setting up another god, which is a notorious sin. Phil. iii. 19, "Whose god is their belly." The Babylonians had Bel for their god, a god of brass; but these men make their bellies their god, a god of flesh; their thoughts, care, endeavours are more to please their bellies, their idol-god, than the true God; they do all things for the indulgence of appetite. Their end is delight in edibles and potables. They are *ventricolæ*, belly-gods, which love good liquor and good cheer. They serve their bellies, Rom. xvi. 18. The rabbies say, he is a glutton or belly-god that eats a pound of flesh, and drinks a quart of wine: we have many such. And do not those who drink healths upon their knees, sacrifice it to those they drink unto, and make gods of them?

(3.) They abuse the good creatures of God, which they should use for the honour and glory of his name; them they abuse to the maintenance, pleasing, and pampering of their lusts, which are bitter enemies to God and his truths, and ought to be mortified. 1 Cor. x. 31, "Whether ye eat or drink, or whatsoever ye do, do all to the glory of God." What glory hath the Lord, when men make their bellies barrels and pantries; so victual the camp, that they are unfit for motion, and must sleep?

(4.) It is sacrilegious, robbing God of his worship. You know we must honour God with all our hearts, mights, strength; for he is an infinite excellency, worthy of all: but when a man hath crammed himself with meats, is much liquored, how unfit is he to do any acts of worship! his head is heavy, his spirits dull, and God may have his carcass, but as for heart or spirit he hath none for him: Hos. iv. 11, "Wine and new wine take away the heart." Excess in meat and drink causeth defects in the worship of God; he may have bodily worship, lip-labour, sleepy performances; but as for spiritual worship, that is not to be had, though the Lord be a Spirit most holy, great, and glorious, and ought to be worshipped in spirit and truth.

2. As it respects others.

(1.) Those who are given to their bellies, they mind not the condition of the church or state, at least not so much as they should do; so they may have fulness of bread, they care not how it goes with others. Amos vi. 4, 6, "They eat the lambs out of the flock, and the calves out of the midst of the stall; they drink wine in bowls, and anoint themselves with the chief ointments; but they are not grieved for the affliction of Joseph." By Joseph is meant the ten tribes, which were greatly infested and afflicted by the Assyrians: but these men laid it not to heart, did not condole and sympathize with them; they poured not out prayers or tears for them; they minded their own bellies, not their miseries. So Isa. xxii. 12, 13, when God's hand was upon them, and he called to weeping and mourning, what did their gluttonous men? Slay oxen, kill sheep, eat flesh, drink wine; chap. v. 12, "They regard not the work of the Lord, neither consider the operation of his hands."

(2.) They wrong the poorer sort. Gluttons and

drunkards are like caterpillars, locusts, canker, palmer-worms, which devour that which should maintain others. Did not men exceed so much in eating and drinking, there would be more plenty, more cheapness, more relief for the poor; who, had they what is superfluously and sinfully spent in eating and drinking, I believe we should see no beggars in our streets, nor hear any cry at our doors. Prov. xxx. 14, "There is a generation, whose teeth are as swords, and their jaw-teeth as knives, to devour the poor from off the earth, and the needy from among men:" such are the teeth and jaw-teeth of gluttons; they make bread, malt, and grapes dear.

(3.) They wrong the chastity of others. Who make more attempts, or commit fouler acts, than they that feed and drink most liberally? Fulness of bread breeds fulness of lusts: 2 Pet. ii. 13, 14, they rioted, feasted, and had eyes full of adultery, which could not cease from sinning. High diet is the mark of high lusts, and they the parents of heinous actions. Jer. v. 7, 8, "When I had fed them to the full;" God gave them abundance, and thereupon they pampered the flesh, and "then committed adultery, and assembled themselves by troops in the harlots' houses: they were as fed horses in the morning; every one neighed after his neighbour's wife." Intemperance begets incontinency; after rioting and drunkenness follow chambering and wantonness, Rom. xiii. 13. When Lot was filled with wine, then was he fit for incest, Gen. xix. 31—36; and the Sodomites, of whom our text speaks, were guilty of horrible uncleanness, as appears in that chapter, ver. 5, "Where are the men which came in to thee this night? bring them out unto us, that we may know them."

(4.) They give ill example, and draw others to their own practice, to intemperate eating and drinking, which is a great evil. 1 Pet. iv. 4, "They think it strange that ye run not with them to the same excess of riot:" there is a great propensity in men to follow others in eating and drinking excessively; they not only go, but run, to it, a little encouragement that way doth much. Prov. xxviii. 7, "He that is a companion of riotous men shameth his father;" therefore Solomon counselleth his son, chap. xxiii. 20, thus; "Be not among wine-bibbers; amongst riotous eaters of flesh:" he knew that their example, company, and cheer, were strong attractives. Hab. ii. 15, "Woe unto him that giveth his neighbour drink;" the Hebrew is, Woe to him that drinketh to his neighbour. It is not unlawful to drink to another but when it is done with an ill intent, to draw him to excess; and therefore it follows, "that puttest thy bottle to him, and makest him drunken also." The word for bottle is חמתך which Montanus renders, *venenum tuum*, thy poison: it is spoken of Nebuchadnezzar and the Babylonians, who drew in neighbour princes, and others, to eating and drinking, and so poisoned them with gluttony and drunkenness, and spotted themselves with their sin and nakedness; men are poisoned in ill company.

(5.) This sin, fulness of bread, brings down heavy judgments upon places: Eccles. x. 16, "Woe to thee, O land, when thy king is a child, and thy princes eat in the morning!" The surfeiting of great ones brings woes and great judgments to kingdoms: Isa. v. 11, 12, there their intemperance is set down, feasting, drinking, and merry-making; and, ver. 13, behold the judgments, "therefore my people are gone into captivity, because they have no knowledge;" their gluttony and drunkenness made them sensual; "and their honourable men are famished, and their multitude dried up with thirst." So Belshazzar, he feasts and revels with a thousand of his lords, and that night was he slain, and the kingdom was taken by Darius and the Medes, Dan. v.

3. As it respects themselves.

(1.) The soul.

(2.) The body.

(3.) The whole man.

(4.) Their estate.

(5.) Their name.

(1.) The soul: and evils which intemperance causeth, are,

[1.] It clouds the understanding. Such fumes and vapours possess the brain from immoderate eating and drinking, as that men are altogether inept to discourse or judge of things: Prov. xxvii. 7, "The full soul loatheth an honey-comb," it judgeth amiss of it. Fulness of bread infatuates the understanding, blinds the mind, and dams up the spirits with mud: Isa. xxviii. 7, the priests and prophets were given to their appetites; and what then? "they err in vision, they stumble in judgment."

[2.] Disorders the affections; for when, through overmuch eating and drinking, the government of reason is laid aside, or asleep, the affections take their opportunity, and grow disorderly; then wanton lusts, thoughts, desires, and pleasures travel up and down the region of the soul, and peep out at the windows of the house, 2 Pet. ii. 13, 14.

[3.] It hinders the activity of gifts and graces in the soul. When a man is loaded with any burden, he cannot move nimbly; so when one is loaded with meat and drink, his soul cannot act lively, there is so much earth and mud about it, that the operations of it are greatly impeded. Gal. v. 21, the word there for revellings, is κωμοι, eating together, and notes such eating as is a fruit of the flesh, an eating so much as the flesh craves, or can well bear, such eating as strengthens the flesh, the corrupt part in man, which opposes and hinders the spirit and activity of it. How poorly doth grace act in those who are full, and have pampered their bellies! Paul knew this, and therefore was very abstemious, temperate, and much in fasting, 2 Cor. vi. 5.

(2.) The body. Excess causeth sickness, and is destructive of health; the most diseases men have, do come from the abundance of humours which are in their bodies; and whence come these but from intemperance in eating and drinking? take men that are moderate, and sparing in diet, and they are seldom troubled with any diseases. Sobriety is the best nurse to health, and a greater enemy it finds not than intemperance. 1 Cor. xi. 21, 30, the Corinthians were faulty in their feastings and drinking: and what saith Paul? For this cause many are sick and weak. Hos. vii. 5, the princes made the king sick with bottles of wine. It weakens the body; concoction being hindered by fulness, crude humours are gendered, and nourishment of the spirits by pure blood is letted.

(3.) The whole man.

[1.] By intemperance a man is brought into bondage unto the creatures, he is a slave to his appetite, and whatever pleases that: and this is a great evil, for man that hath dominion given him by God over all sublunaries, to become a servant to any of them. Paul was more heroic; 1 Cor. vi. 12, 13, "All things are lawful for me, but I will not be brought under the power of any. Meats for the belly, and the belly for meats;" let the belly crave what meats it will, let meats be never so pleasant or desirable, yet I will not be brought under the power of either of them: but few are so noble-spirited as Paul. The most men are apprentices to their own appetites: the rich man, Luke xvi. 19, "fared sumptuously every day;" no cost must be spared to please his palate.

[2.] Hereby a man is put beneath a brute creature; for those creatures eat and drink only to satisfy nature, and when they have taken so much, you cannot persuade or force them to take more; they observe the law of nature, and follow the instinct thereof; but many men do eat and drink, not only to satisfy nature, but to the surfeiting thereof, and without any persuasion or force overcharge nature with variety of meats and drinks. Yea, sometimes they are so excessive herein, that they become void of sense; Prov. xxiii. 35, when the drunkard was beaten, he felt it not. So void are intemperate persons ofttimes of common sense, as that they neither foresee future danger, to prevent it, nor feel present smart, to profit by it: horse and ass may teach men.

[3.] It hastens death. Many might have lived longer, had they been more sober, more sparing at their tables; many diseases breed in the womb of intemperance, and one or other of them shortens a man's days; many die by the sword, but more by surfeits. Because it is lawful to eat and drink, and what we eat and drink is pleasing, therefore we exceed the due bounds, and so increase humours, quench our natural heat, and precipitate death. The Corinthians' excess sent them to their long sleep: this sin abbreviates or takes away life.

[4.] It makes men very secure and fearless: Isa. lvi. 12, "Come, we will fill ourselves with strong drink; and to-morrow shall be as this day, and much more abundant." A ship loaden much, sinks deep into the water, if overladen, drowns; so man, that is loaden with the creatures, sinks deep into the sea of security, if he be overladen, he drowns himself. Luke xxi. 34, 35, if men's hearts are overcharged, that day will come unawares, as a snare, suddenly.

[5.] Intemperance is such a sin as endangers your eternal estate, yea, and excludes you from coming into heaven. The rich glutton, you know, was cast into hell, that was his portion, Luke xvi. Gal. v. 21, those that "do such things shall not inherit the kingdom of God:" what things? that eat and drink intemperately. Drunkenness and revelling are fruits of the flesh, and suffer not men to enter into the kingdom of heaven.

(4.) Their estates. It brings a consumption upon them: Prov. xxiii. 21, "The drunkard and the glutton shall come to poverty: and drowsiness shall clothe a man with rags." Many who have gluttonized in their youth, have wanted bread in their old age, and instead of feasting, have fasted more than once or twice in a week. The prodigal's excess among the harlots brought him to want among the swine. Prov. xxi. 17, "He that loveth wine and oil shall not be rich."

Diogenes, seeing the house of an intemperate person set to sale, said, I knew the house was so overcharged with meat and wine that it would quickly vomit out the cormorant. He seeing another brought to beggary, and eating olives for his supper, said, If you had so dined, you should not have needed to have so supped.

(5.) Their names and professions suffer by it. Intemperance brings an ill report upon men; Noah's intemperance was a great disgrace to him. Prov. xxviii. 7, "He that is a companion of riotous men shameth his father:" if being only a companion of them be so ill, what is it then to be a riotous person, intemperate in meats and drinks? that doth much more shame the son, and the father too; such a one will men say is a belly-god. Isa. xxviii. 8, "All tables are full of vomit and filthiness, so that there is no place clean." What a disgrace was this to the priests and prophets in those days, and to their profession! Rom. xiii. 13, "Let us walk honestly, as in the day, not in rioting and drunkenness." Let us not be intemperate; intemperance is a night-work, and hath no honesty in it. If it be, therefore, a work of darkness and dishonesty, as the apostle makes it, it must needs disgrace a man. Fabius, who had spent his patrimony, a great estate, was called *Gurges*, a gulf which swallows all; among us such men are called *heluones*, gluttons.

Let us take heed of this sin: why should we pamper our bodies, which must see corruption, and be worm's meat? The apostle's rule is, "Make no provision for the flesh, to fulfil the lusts thereof." He doth not forbid to eat or provide meat, but to make provision for the flesh, their inordinate desires, to satisfy them. Luke vi. 25, "Woe unto you that are full! for you shall hunger."

Christ bids us deny ourselves; and if we will not do it in a little meat and drink, how shall we forsake all, wives, children, friends, lands, life? It was a notable saying of Seneca, *Major sum, et ad majora genitus, quam ut corporis mei mancipium fiam*, I am greater, and born to greater things, than to be servant or slave to my body. He was a heathen, we are christians; let us say, we are greater, and born to greater things, better born, and better taught, than to be slaves to our appetites.

Let us say, as it is Tit. ii. 11, 12, "The grace of God that bringeth salvation hath appeared to all men, teaching us that, denying ungodliness and worldly lusts, we should live soberly, righteously, and godly, in this present world."

"And abundance of idleness was in her and in her daughters." Having spoken of two of the sins of Sodom, we come now to the third, which is, "abundance of idleness."

"Idleness." Hebrew, השקט which is from שקט signifying, to rest, to live in peace, quietly, idly. When people are in peace, they grow secure and idle.

"Abundance." Hebrew, שלות from שלה to be quiet, to rest, to live at ease, and notes tranquillity; so that both words signify the same thing, and may be rendered, rest of rest; the sense whereof is well expressed by our translation, "abundance of idleness," or deep idleness.

I shall show you two things touching idleness:

1. When a man is said to be idle.

2. The evil of idleness.

For the first, a man is said to be idle three ways.

(1.) When he doth nothing, is unemployed. Matt. xx. 3, Christ "saw some standing idle in the market-place." The word for "idle" is, ἀργος, a man without work: so in ver. 6, "Why stand ye here all the day idle?" Many are idle all the day of their life, nothing is done by them; of this sort are many gentlemen and others, that have no calling nor employment for the good of the public: such was Solomon's sluggard, that would not plough by reason of the cold, Prov. xx. 4; but had rather sleep and slumber in his bed, than dig in his vineyard; chap. xxiv. 33, "Yet a little sleep, a little slumber, a little folding of the hands to sleep."

(2.) When they do not what they should do. Some of the learned say, he is idle who does not God's work. There is work of God's appointment for the day, which you ought to take notice of, and do. 2 Thess. iii. 11, There are some among you which work not at all, but are busy-bodies; *μηδέν ἐργαζομένυς, ἀλλα περιεργαζομένυς*, doing no work, yet working about every where. When persons are busy, and do much of that which doth not belong to them to do, it is doing of nothing; therefore Paul, in the first

Epistle, chap. iv. 11, exhorts them to do their "own business."

(3.) When they do not so much as they ought to do, but are lazy in doing little. Rom. xii. 11, "Not slothful in business." Eccl. ix. 10, "Whatsoever thy hand findeth to do, do it with thy might." When men put not forth themselves to do what they ought to do in conscience, and according to right reason, they are justly said to be idle, Prov. xviii. 9.

2. The evil of this sin you may discern in sundry particulars.

(1.) It is against the end of man's creation. God made man for labour; when he was in a state of innocency, he was to dress and keep the garden, Gen. ii. 15; he must not be idle there, taking his pleasure in a paradise, but work he must, though not for a living: so after the fall, Gen. iii. 19, in the sweat of his face he was to eat his bread; he was now to work for bread, and to work hard; if he will have food, he must sweat for it. It is the end of man's creation and birth to be doing: Job v. 7, "Man is born unto trouble," labour, saith the margin, and Montanus, "as the sparks fly upward."

(2.) It is a sin against the light of nature, which puts every thing upon motion. The heavens, with the glorious lights thereof, move, and are constant in their motions: Psal. xix. 5, the sun "rejoiceth as a strong man to run a race." The wind and air fly up and down, the waters run, the earth brings forth, plants and trees grow up; the fishes in the sea, fowls in the air, beasts in the field, have their motions and operations, which is a loud dictate to man that he should not be idle. Prov. vi. 6, "Go to the ant, thou sluggard; consider her ways, and be wise." The ant is a very little creature, but exceeding laborious; nature hath put an instinct into her to be active and working all the summer; she is early and late at it, and will not lose an hour, unless the weather hinder. So the bee is little in bulk, but great in employment, and wonderful busy; and Solomon might have added, Go to the bee, and consider her ways; she flies far, examines the fields, hedges, trees, orchards, gardens, loads herself with honey and wax, and then presently makes return. These creatures, with many others, confute the sluggard daily, preach down idleness, and call for action. Yea, the sluggard's own soul is always in motion and action, and thereby tells him he should not be idle.

(3.) It puts God's family out of order. The world is God's family, and he hath appointed men unto, and fitted them for, some employment; as a wise artist makes no wheel in a clock, or watch, but to move and help on the general work; and if one wheel stand, it is out of order, and hinders all the rest; so here, when men are idle, they stand still, are out of order, and hinder the motion of others. Idle persons are disorderly persons; 1 Thess. v. 14, "Warn them that are unruly," ἀτάκτους, men out of rank, such are idle ones; when others march, they stand still; when others are up, they are down. 2 Thess. iii. 11, "We hear there are some which walk among you disorderly, working not at all:" by "walking" is meant living, and their disorderly living was not working.

(4.) It sets a man among the dead. An idle man is both unsavoury and unactive, as a dead man is, and therefore may well be counted a guest of the grave: 1 Tim. v. 6, the widow that liveth in pleasure, idly, disorderly, neglecting or out of a calling, is dead while she lives. Eccl. ix. 4, "A living dog is better than a dead lion:" the dead lion, saith Paris, is the great man, in wealth and honour, but idle and loose; the living dog is the poor man, but diligent and active. Now the poorest and meanest man of the world that follows a calling, and is laborious in it, is better than the greatest, richest, and most eminent man in the world who lives out of a calling, and doth nothing; one is a living, and the other a dead man: and what the odds is between life and death, such is the difference between idleness and action, sloth and labour.

(5.) Idleness exposes a man to variety of temptations, lays him open to Satan; a man unemployed, is like a city without walls and gates, whither any enemy may easily have entrance: Ezek. xxxviii. 11, "I will go up to the land of unwalled villages; I will go to them that are at rest, that dwell safely, all of them dwelling without walls, and having neither bars nor gates." What God saith here, that Satan saith of idle persons; they are unwalled villages, they have neither bars nor gates, no defensive or offensive weapons, and therefore the devil doth boldly invade, and easily conquer, them with his temptations. Paul knew this, and therefore counselled the Ephesians to make provision against Satan; chap. vi. 11, "Put on the whole armour of God, that ye may be able to stand against the wiles of the devil." An idle man either hath no armour, or if he hath, will not take the pains to put it on. It will require more than ordinary pains to put on the whole armour of God, to be armed completely, and then to stand armed, and withstand all the onsets of principalities and powers; this the sluggard will not do, he must needs therefore become a prey to Satan. A man out of employment, and idle, is like a vessel which is empty, any one that comes to it may put in what he will; so Satan pours into idle persons, which are empty vessels, what liquor he pleases. When men are thoroughly employed, they are incapable of the devil's temptations: you see it daily, that those who are out of God's work are most exercised with the devil's.

(6.) Idleness is the mother and nurse of our most dangerous enemies, viz. lusts. Standing waters corrupt soonest, and more mud, filth, and vermin are to be found in them than in the running waters. To the sink in the ship is the confluence of all filth; idleness is the sink in the ship, and comprehends all noisome lusts in it: silver, gold, iron, out of use, canker and rust. Idleness bringeth much evil, and breeds many evils. Idle and sluggish persons have the foulest bodies, and breed most diseases; and such have the foulest souls, and abound with most noisome lusts. Among the Sodomites was abundance of idleness, and abundance of lusts, which fight and war against the soul; and what madness is it for a man to harbour, feed his enemies that seek his life! idleness, like dung upon the earth, fattens the spoil, makes all rank, especially the weeds, so that the flesh and lusts thereof, even in godly people, they grow headstrong, violent and furious against the Spirit; and in others, they break out into drunkenness, theft, and uncleanness. *Nihil agendo homines discunt male agere,* In doing nothing men learn to do ill. If ever occasion should put as much power into their hands, as idleness hath put villany into their hearts and heads, they will be ready to fire your houses, ravish your daughters, and cut your throats.

(7.) It is against common equity and justice to live upon others, who get their living by the sweat of their brows, and to eat their bread from them. Drones, that eat up the honey of the laborious bee, we condemn; they beat them out, and sting to death; a just punishment for so unjust an act.

Thieves that rob particular persons suffer death, because they do acts of injustice against common equity; and wnat are idle ones but thieves, robbing the public of its maintenance? This made Paul to command the Thessalonians to "work, and eat their own bread," 2 Thess. iii. 12.

(8.) It deprives a man of that privilege which a beast hath. You know a beast may eat, work or work not, but it is not so with man, except he work he may not eat; 2 Thess. iii. 10, "This we commanded you, that if any would not work, neither should he eat." If sickness or weakness hinder not, let man be great or small, rich or poor, what he will, the rule is, if he will not work, he must not eat, neither the state nor the church must maintain such a one.

The Jews say, *Qui non laboraverit in pro sabbato, ne edat in sabbato,* The sabbath was a day of rest, and if any had not so laboured on the day before, as to get wherewithal to maintain him on that day, he must fast.

Matt. x. 10, Christ tells you, "the workman is worthy of his meat," others not: you sin therefore when you relieve such beggars or persons as are able to work, but will not; they are neither worthy of meat, nor should you let them eat. And what if they should perish for want of meat? their destruction is of themselves; the ease of the simple slayeth them, Prov. i. 32. He that will not have a part in daily labour, should not have a part of daily bread.

(9.) Poverty and beggary are the issues of idleness. Prov. vi. 11, Solomon tells the sluggard, that his "poverty shall come as one that travelleth, and his want as an armed man;" he lieth still, but poverty is up, and marching towards him; he is without defence, but that comes armed: the meaning is, poverty will come upon an idle and slothful person suddenly and irresistibly. Prov. xxiii. 21, "Drowsiness shall clothe a man with rags:" by drowsiness understand sloth; and when men go about things as if they were half asleep, lazily, they shall certainly come to a poor condition, which is intimated by rags; the coat that sloth gives is rags. Prov. xviii. 9, A man "slothful in his work is brother to him that is a great waster:" the Hebrew is, A man remiss in his work is brother to a great waster, a much waster; a man that spends profusely must needs come to beggary, he hastens swiftly to it: so doth a sluggard, who is remiss in his work, and so an idle person. Other things may bring some to beggary; sickness, suretiship, fire, robbery, plundering wars; but put them altogether, they beget not so many beggars, so much poverty, as idleness doth; this fills towns and cities with swarms of them.

(10.) Idleness is such a sin as exempts a man from the protection of the angels. A man that hath no calling to walk in, that lives unemployed, he is a vagabond upon the face of the earth. Psal. xci. 11, "He shall give his angels charge over thee, to keep thee in all thy ways:" what ways? those which are according to his will, which his providence leads unto; not in ways of sin. A man that is idle, is in the devil's way, not in God's way; he hath appointed callings for men: 1 Cor. vii. 20, "Let every man abide in the same calling wherein he was called;" ver. 24, "Let every man, wherein he is called, therein abide with God." Some refer the words "called" in both verses, to the spiritual call, viz. to grace and communion with Christ: be that so, yet there is an outward condition of life, a calling that God would have men to be in, and abide in, because it is an abiding with God. God approves it, blesses them in it, if they honour him in a calling according to the rules he hath given in his word, and vouchsafes them a guard of angels to defend them therein; but idle persons that have no calling, go out from God and the guard of his angels: and it is questionable whether those that may work and will not, have any true fear of God, or faith, in them. Did they fear God, they would walk in a calling, and the angels of God would be about them, Psal. xxxiv. 7; and faith is a working grace, witness Heb. xi.; 1 Tim. v. 8.

(11.) Idle persons are burdensome creatures. The fig tree that bare no fruit was a burden to the ground where it stood; Luke xiii. 7, "Why cumbereth it the ground?" it was a burden to the garden, to the gardener, to the other trees, to the lord and master of all. Matt. xx. 6, "Why stand ye here all the day idle?" you do no good o yourselves, none to your neighbours, none to the public, none to posterity, nor bring any glory to God. An idle and fruitless person is good for nothing: Ezek. xv. the vine tree that bare no fruit was not fit to make a pin of, nor for any use but only for the fire.

(12.) It is a wasting of precious time, a hiding of our talent, and so a great provocation of divine Majesty. An idle man trifles away time, which, when men are in straits, they value, and would give thousands for a few days or hours, as it is like the Sodomites would, when their city was on fire; but such persons make no account of time, how precious soever it be, but pass it away in doing nothing, which is a dreadful evil. Time, that is given us to get grace, to work out our salvation in, to glorify God, and do good in, even that doth the idle person squander away, though eternity be in the bowels of it; not minding the apostolical rule, Eph. v. 15, 16, "See that ye walk circumspectly, not as fools, but as wise, redeeming the time." He that sits still and will not walk, he is a fool; and he is the greatest of fools that will not redeem time for the good of his soul, but loiter it away, and lose it daily; though God have given him a talent, yet he will not use it. Matt. xxv. 25, 26, the man who had one talent would not use it, but hid it in the earth; and what followed hereupon? he provoked God greatly, who said, "Thou wicked and slothful servant," (wickedness and sloth go together,) thou oughtest to have improved my talent or money well: seeing it is not done, take it from him, and cast the unprofitable servant into utter darkness, ver. 27, 30.

Having now heard the evil of idleness, let us gird up the loins of our minds, stir up ourselves, and be more diligent in our callings. Sloth brings judgments; the men of Laish were quiet, secure, and had no business with any man, and the Danites came upon them, "smote them with the edge of the sword, and burnt the city with fire," Judg. xviii. 7, 27. Though all idle people meet not with such judgments, yet there is a woe pronounced "to them that are at ease in Zion," Amos vi. 1. Some woe or other will be the portion of those that live idly. We have a multitude of such amongst us, and it were well some course were taken by those in authority to set idle persons on work.

The Athenians did sue idle persons at law; idleness among them did bear an action, and they made inquiry after each man and woman, what trade or course of life they had to live upon. *Rivet. in Gen.* 3.

When Joseph's brethren came into Egypt, and were before Pharaoh, the first question he asked them was, "What is your occupation?" Gen. xlvii. 3. This was a good question of a king, when strangers were to come and dwell in his land, to know whether they had any calling, could get their livings, and not be burdensome to his kingdom and subjects. The Massilians forbade any to come into their city who had no trade or art to live by. And there was a law among the Persians, that every subject, at the year's end, should come to the magistrate and give account of his year's work; it were happy if we had some such laws amongst us. They were great enemies to idleness, and so was Alexander, who, discovering two idle persons in his dominions, made one to flee out of them, and the other to drive him.

In Marcus Aurelius' days, the Romans followed their callings so earnestly, that having occasion to send a letter two or three days' journey from the town, he could not find one idle body in all the city of Rome to carry it. When will it be so with this city? idleness abounds in the streets, and I fear within doors too. But however it be with others, let us hate sin, be diligent in those places and callings God hath set us; for "the hand of the diligent maketh rich," Prov. x. 4; "shall bear rule," chap. xii. 24, and will cause to stand before princes, chap. xxii. 29.

"Neither did she strengthen the hand of the poor and needy." This is the fourth sin of Sodom and her daughters, unmercifulness, inhumanity.

"Did she strengthen." Hebrew is, לא החזיקה she hath not taken them by the hand, and held them up, but let them sink. Jer. xxxi. 32, "In the day that I took them by the hand to bring them out of the land of Egypt;" being there, they were in a low, poor, needy, sinking condition, and God reached out his hand from heaven, took hold of them, and upheld them; he gave them counsel and help. It is the same word there which you have here: these Sodomites did not reach out a hand to support and strengthen their poor and needy. The Septuagint is, they did not succour and help them; the Vulgate, they reached not out a hand to them. She did not make firm and strong the hands of the needy, she did not give them counsel and aid, that they might not despair.

"The poor." Hebrew, עני from ענה to afflict, humble; because poor men are afflicted and humbled under the burden of their poverty. The Hebrew word עני signifies both affliction and poverty; Exod. iii. 7, "I have surely seen the affliction of my people which are in Egypt;" 1 Chron. xxii. 14, "Behold, in my poverty I have prepared for the house of the Lord:" it is the same word in both places; and poor men find their poverty an affliction. Poverty causeth much fear, care, sadness, dejection of spirit, and hath many temptations accompanying it. Montanus reads the word for poor, *egeni*, of the needy, or wanting, which seems to be the true sense of πτωχος in the gospel; for as the word is used there, it notes not absolutely a beggar, but one needy: 2 Cor. viii. 9, it is said of Christ, ἐπτώχευσε, "he became poor," he had not a house to hide his head in, yet he did not go up and down and beg lodging, bread, and other things; and Mark xii. 42, there came χήρα πτωχὴ, a poor widow, yet she had two mites to throw into the treasury: Rom. xv. 26, "Those of Macedonia and Achaia made a contribution for the poor saints at Jerusalem; ἐις τοὺς πτωχοῦστῶν ἁγιὼν, the church did not suffer the poor saints in it to go from house to house begging; this had been a great reproach to the church and way of the gospel. That which hath made men to think πτωχος notes such poor as go from door to door, hath been, that they might distinguish it from πένης, which is a poor man also: 2 Cor. ix. 9, "He hath given to the poor," ἔδωκε τοῖς πένησιν. There is a difference between these words, and so the poor meant by them, but not that difference which by some learned is made. Aristophanes in Pluto saith, πτωχος ἐστιν μηδὲν ἐχων, he is a beggar, or poor man, who hath nothing, and πένης is ὁς ζῇ φειδόμενος καὶ τοῖς ἐργοις προσέχων, who lives sparingly, following his work, that spends all he gets, and hath much ado to live. So Pasor makes πένης to be a man who by his labour gets his living, from πένομαι, to labour; and he is right in this, but out in πτωχὸς, whom he saith to be one *qui ostiatim petit*, who begs an alms at men's doors. It is true Lazarus was such, Luke xvi. 20, but usually in the gospel it notes such poor as have something, though not enough, to live upon, be they aged, sick, weak, lame, or compassed about with any other infirmities.

"Needy." Hebrew is אביון it comes from אבה to will, desire, and notes a man not simply poor and needy, but very poor; so poor, saith Pagnine, *quod omnibus carens, omnia concupiscat*, that wanting all things, he desires all things; rich in desires, but having nothing else, a man of desires. Amos ii. 6, "They sold the poor for a pair of shoes:" the word for poor is the same we have here; and certainly they were very poor that were worth no more than a pair of shoes, and likely old ones too. Montanus interprets the word in our prophet, *mendicus*, a beggar, which notes the extreme poverty that some were in, yet had no help from the rich and full Sodomites. Æcol. hath it *humilis*, of one so needy, that he is humbled to purpose, and lies on the earth, desiring relief. Servius upon Virgil saith, *pejorem esse egestatem paupertate*, that need is worse than poverty. The Vulgate accords with our English, and hath it *egeno*, they reached not out a hand to the poor and needy, which sorts best with the original words. The sum and scope of the words is this; That the Sodomites were unmerciful and hard-hearted; they were not affected with the necessities of the poor; neither their wants, prayers, tears, nor their sad countenance, mournful complaints, nor stretched-out hands, prevailed at all with them.

Men are backward to, if not averse from, giving; 1 Tim. vi. 17, 18, "Charge them that are rich in this world, that they be not highminded, nor trust in uncertain riches; that they do good, that they be rich in good works, ready to distribute." Dives would not give the crumbs and scraps of his table to poor Lazarus, Luke xvi.; so the young man, Matt. xix. 21, 22.

I shall show you what an evil unmercifulness is.

1. It is an argument and evidence of covetousness. When Christ, Luke xvi. 9, bids them make to themselves friends of the mammon of unrighteousness, (which he so calls, because men usually sin in the getting, keeping, or using of them,) and said, they could not serve God and mammon, ver. 13, the Pharisees, who were covetous, derided him; they thought Christ spake like an ignorant man; they could serve God, keep their wealth, and not cast it away upon poor people: this showed their covetousness. And what an evil that is, let Paul tell you: 1 Tim. vi. 10, "The love of money is the root of all evil;" inward and outward evils do spring from it. A covetous man is "an idolater," Eph. v. 5; he hath no inheritance in the kingdom of heaven, 1 Cor. vi. 10; he is abhorred of God, Psal. x. 3. Chrysostom saith, he had rather dwell with a thousand possessed, than with one covetous man; for they hurt their garments and themselves, but a covetous man hurts his neighbours. *Chrysostom on Matt.* x. as cited by *Stella on Luke* xvi.

2. It is argument of unbelief. Men think if they give to the poor, and strengthen the hands of the needy, that themselves shall want and come to poverty. Prov. xxviii. 27, "He that giveth unto the poor shall not lack." Here is the voice of God, who is truth itself, and hath power enough to make good what he hath said, for the earth and fulness of it is his, Psal. xxiv. 1. And yet man's heart distrusts God, and thinks of other ways to provide for itself: I will keep what I have: if this be gone, I know not what I shall have; it is a hard world, and one bird in the hand is worth two in the bush. Thus unbelief discovers itself, and had rather trust in uncertain riches, than in the all-sufficient and omnipotent

God. Saith God, Give to the poor, and thou shalt not lack; saith the hard-hearted man, Give to the poor, and thou shalt lack. Thus doth he cross the will of God, and put the lie upon him: Eccles. xi. 1, "Cast thy bread upon the waters: for thou shalt find it after many days:" No, saith the unmerciful man, I will never cast my bread upon them, for I shall never see it again; and so makes God a liar, and declares himself an unbeliever.

3. It is argument there is no love of God in that man. It is a sad charge to tell any man he doth not love God. John is peremptory in it; 1 John iii. 17, "Whoso hath this world's good, and seeth his brother have need, and shutteth up his bowels of compassion from him, how dwelleth the love of God in him?" he may think he loves God, and others may think and say so, but there is not any dram of God's love in that man. How dwells it in him? this interrogation imports a full negation; for if a man loved God, he would love man, who is the image of God. Christ's command is, that we love one another as he hath loved us, John xv. 12: he testified his love, by giving his blood, his flesh, his life; and we will not give a little bread, an old garment, a little silver: it is a clear demonstration there is no love of God in us.

The primitive christians were distinguished from others by their love, and that made them sell all, bring it and lay it down at the apostles' feet for the relief of the poor christians, Acts iv. 34, 35.

4. It is a sin that hath much cruelty and unnaturalness in it. Isa. lviii. 7, "Deal thy bread to the hungry, cover the naked, and hide not thyself from thine own flesh;" the poor are our own flesh: Mal. ii. 10, "Have we not all one father? hath not one God created us?" Prov. xxii. 2, "The rich and poor meet together; the Lord is the maker of them all:" hence he hath commanded that we should love our neighbours as ourselves, Matt. xxii. 39. Now, if we hide away our eyes from them, if we will not consider their necessities, wants, and relieve them, we are cruel and unnatural. If a man be naked or hungry, a man will seek to clothe and feed himself, he will not hate his own flesh: Eph. v. 29, "No man ever yet hated his own flesh; but nourisheth and cherisheth it." When men, therefore, refuse to strengthen the hands of the poor and needy, they despise, they hate their own flesh, they are unnatural; and to prevent this, God hath laid a command to be merciful, where the strongest reason and plea might be against it; Prov. xxv. 21, "If thine enemy be hungry, give him bread to eat; and if he be thirsty, give him water to drink."

5. It brings a curse, yea many curses, upon men and their estates. Prov. xxviii. 27, "He that hideth his eyes from the poor shall have many a curse:" the poor will curse them; but who bids them curse? When Shimei cursed David wrongfully, saith he, The Lord bid him do it; so, when the poor do curse hard-hearted men that will not pity them, there is something of God in it: this Scripture must be fulfilled though it be their sin, yet it is a just judgment of God upon a merciless man. And not only doth man, but even God himself curseth them. Psalm xli. 1, "Blessed is he that considereth the poor." If a man do it not, shall he have a blessing? Matt. xxv. 41, 42, "Depart, ye cursed, for I was an hungred," &c. The curse of God was upon them before, according to what you find in Prov. iii. 33, "The curse of the Lord is in the house of the wicked." Sometimes they have not a heart to eat, and take the comfort of their estates themselves; sometimes they are perplexed with fears, cares, sorrows about their estates; sometimes they are wasted at law; sometimes by fire, plundering; sometimes in a secret way, that none can give any rational account of, but know the curse of God was there.

6. It makes men altogether unlike God. He is "the Father of mercies, and God of all comfort," 2 Cor. i. 3; "he maketh his sun to rise on the evil and on the good, and sendeth rain on the just and on the unjust," Matt. v. 45; he "giveth food to all flesh," Psal. cxxxvi. 25; he hears the desires of the humble and poor, Psal. x. 17; "he is kind to the unthankful and to the evil. Be ye therefore merciful, as your Father also is merciful," Luke vi. 35, 36. But now a man that is near, pinching, miserable, and regards not the condition of the poor, to comfort their hearts, and strengthen their hands, he is unlike and contrary to God, who is love, bowels, pity, compassion, mercy, and very mindful of the poor. He made a law, Deut. xv. 7, 8, "If there be a poor man in thy land, thou shalt not harden thine heart, nor shut thine hand from thy poor brother; but thou shalt open thine hand wide unto him:" so Lev. xxv. 35. Luke xiv. 13, 14, "When thou makest a feast, call the poor, the maimed, the lame, the blind: and thou shalt be blessed." Luke iv. 18, God anointed Christ "to preach the gospel to the poor;" and, "hath not God chosen the poor to be rich in faith?" Jam. ii. 5. Judas was a hard-hearted wretch that "cared not for the poor," John xii. 6.

7. It puts in a caveat and bar in the court of heaven against their prayers, they must have no entertainment there. Prov. xxi. 13, "Whoso stoppeth his ears at the cry of the poor, he also shall cry himself, but shall not be heard:" this man, before he dies, shall come to some great strait or other, so as to cry either to man or God, and when he cries, he shall not be heard; he would not hear the poor crying, nor God who sent those poor, and cried to him in those poor, therefore when he cries unto man for help, God will stop their ears, turn their hearts from him, yea, stop his own ear, and turn away his own heart. Luke vi. 38, "With the same measure that ye mete withal it shall be measured to you again:" you stop your ears, God will stop his ear; you shut up your bowels, God will shut up his; you withhold your pence, God will withhold his talents. The rich man cried for a drop of water, being in torment, but neither Abraham nor God would hearken to his request; he that would not give one crumb, must not receive one drop: Matt. v. 7, "The merciful shall obtain mercy."

8. It is a shrewd badge of a reprobate condition. A merciless man's name will hardly be found in the book of life. Col. iii. 12, "Put on as "elect of God, bowels of mercies, kindness:" those who are elect of God have had mercy, and being called, they find and feel that mercy, and cannot but put on bowels of mercy, which declares their election. Before, as Paul saith, Tit. iii. 3, men live "in malice and envy, hateful and hating one another;" but when God hath once called them, and manifested their election, then they put on bowels of mercy, and they are as natural to them now, as their lusts were before, as bowels are to a parent; they pity others, as God pitied them: but where there are no bowels of mercy, but churlishness, hardness, unmercifulness, there is the black badge of reprobation rather than of election.

9. It is a degree of murder. Some men hate and curse the poor, and the Scripture blusheth not to call them murderers; 1 John iii. 15, "Whosoever hateth his brother is a murderer:" Job xxiv. 14, "The murderer rising with the light killeth the poor and needy;" he devises ways how to oppress, suck, and squeeze them, and this is killing of them, and he is a murderer for it as well as the other; so, when a

man sees his brother or neighbour poor, sinking, and like to be ruined, and will not relieve him, being able to do it, he falls into a degree of murder. The heathen, Publius Mimus, could see this, who said, *Qui succurrere perituro potest, cum non succurrit, occidit*, He that hath power to succour a man being ready to perish, and succours him not, he kills him. Suppose a man in the water or fire, you pass by, and lend him not your hand, which if you had done, his life had been saved, are not you now guilty of his death? When the priest and Levite passed by the man that, going from Jerusalem to Jericho, fell among thieves, and relieved him not, it was their sin; and had he died in that condition, they had been accessaries to his death. If the poor be our flesh, then our goods are theirs as well as ours; and if we let them perish, we murder them and ourselves to.

10. The end of that man will be very sad who hath been merciless to others; he must have the end of a fruitless, or dead tree, he must be hewn down, and cast into the fire. Jam. ii. 13, "He shall have judgment without mercy, that hath showed no mercy;" all judgment, mere severity, pure wrath, shall be his portion. Matt. xxv. 41, 42, &c. it is the chief, if not the only, sin which Christ mentions at the day of judgment: "I was hungry, and ye gave me no meat, I was thirsty, and ye gave me no drink;" you showed me in my poor members no mercy; "therefore depart from me, ye cursed, into everlasting fire prepared for the devil and his angels."

Seeing, then, uncharitableness is so great an evil, let us put on bowels of mercy, and strengthen the hands of the poor and needy. It is a hard time, things are dear, trading little, poor abound, and therefore now it is seasonable for the rich to open the bowels of their compassion, and to succour those that are in want. Job was "a father to the poor," chap. xxix. 16; he did not eat his morsels alone, the fatherless ate thereof, chap. xxxi. 17; the bellies and loins of the poor blessed him, being filled and warmed with the flesh and fleece of his sheep, ver. 20. Dorcas, Acts ix. 39. It were well if Job's and Dorcas's spirit and compassions were in all rich men, that so the hungry might be fed, the naked clothed, and necessities of the poor supplied. Spare something out of your superfluities for them. Can you adorn your houses with pictures and hangings, your tables with carpets, your shelves with pewter and brass, your closets and cupboards with plate, and have you nothing for the poor, who are the temples of God? can you feed your dogs, parrots, monkeys, pamper your horses, and not mind poor christians which lie at your doors? If it be so, how will the Lord take it at your hands? Remember Dives; he had been better to have given all to Lazarus, than to have met with such an end for his unmercifulness. The Lord Christ hath told you it is a blessed thing to give, Acts xx. 35. You would count it a blessed thing to show kindness to Christ; the paps that gave Christ suck were counted blessed, Luke xi. 27. When you give to the poor, you give to Christ: Matt. xxv. 40, "Inasmuch as ye have done it unto one of the least of these my brethren, ye have done it unto me;" they are Christ's brethren thou dost it unto, and he accounts it done to himself, yea, the least or meanest it is done unto.

Again, is it not a blessed thing to have the Lord of heaven and earth to be indebted to one: Prov. xix. 17, "He that hath pity upon the poor lendeth unto the Lord; and that which he hath given will he pay him again."

1. God is the poor man's Surety.
2. He takes the debt upon himself.
3. Gives thee his word for security; his faithfulness and his honour are engaged for performance. Had you the city's bond, the parliament's security, the public faith, for repayment of what you expend upon the poor, it were nothing to this. O give, give unto the poor, and make God as much as you can indebted to you, he is a good Paymaster: Luke vi. 38, "Give, and it shall be given unto you, good measure, pressed down, and shaken together, and running over." If you will not make God your debtor by giving, he will be your judge for not giving.

We live in dangerous times, and riches are uncertain things: the way to make them safe, is to bestow them upon the poor: Eccles. xi. 1, "Cast thy bread upon the waters: for thou shalt find it after many days;" if you keep it, you lose; if you cast it away, you shall find it again.

One had this epitaph upon his tomb:

Habeo quod dedi, perdidi quod servavi: I possess what I gave; I have lost that which I kept.

If you would keep wine or meal, you put them into empty vessels: Isa. lviii. 10, 11, "If thou draw out thy soul to the hungry, and satisfy the afflicted soul; then shall thy light rise in obscurity, and thy darkness be as the noon day: and the Lord shall guide thee continually, and satisfy thy soul in drought, and make fat thy bones: and thou shalt be like a watered garden, and like a spring of water, whose waters fail not."

Quest. Seeing we are to strengthen the hands of the poor and needy, whether are we to give to all in such case?

Answ. It is the judgment of some, that no beggars should be relieved that go from door to door; they think it an unwarrantable practice for people to do so, and to be relieved upon so doing, it is the nursery of many vagabonds and vile persons: such live in no calling, are under no government, are the shame of the magistrate, a disorder in a commonwealth, and reproach of the laws made for relief of the poor in their several respective places. Certainly those that beg up and down, being able to work, and will not, you ought not to relieve, you sin in doing of it; the apostle's rule is, If any will not work, he must not eat, 2 Thess. iii. 10. And further, when begging is made a trade, I see not how it is justifiable before God, or can be countenanced by man; there are few but can do something towards their living, and if they cannot, they ought to be relieved otherwise than by begging.

Yet, to conclude it unlawful to give to any that beg, I dare not: Christ healed two blind beggars, Luke xviii. 35, 42; John ix. 7, 8, and did not reprove them for their begging. Besides, he hath given out a rule, Luke vi. 30, "Give to every man that asketh of thee;" which would be void and useless, if I might give to no beggars.

1. Then, if you be able, you ought to give to all that are truly poor and needy, justly necessitated to ask, even those that are able to work, and willingly would work, but through the ill disposition of the times cannot get any, or not sufficient to maintain them.

2. If men be not able to relieve all that shall ask, then caution and christian wisdom are to be used. You are to observe the rule of nature, which leads you to give,

(1.) To your kindred according to the degrees thereof.

(2.) To your affinity.

(3.) Your friends.

(4.) Cohabitators of the same village, parish, city, country, kingdom.

(5.) To strangers, whom Providence shall offer unto you.

But more specially, 1. You are to consider whether they be godly poor or not; and if godly, there to place your charity: Gal. vi. 10, "As we have opportunity," &c.

2. Their necessity, and so,

(1.) It may be extreme, they may be in danger of life, ready to starve, as Lazarus did at Dives' door; or in danger of sinning, as captives to turn Turks, and poor amongst us of turning to popery, or to steal: now such are to have help before others.

(2.) It may be great, attended with some grievous inconvenience, as loss of liberty, sinking of a family, scandal to religion; now these are to have a hand reached out to them, when others may not.

(3.) There is a common necessity; when poor want, live not so comfortably as they would: and these, as we have ability and occasion, we may, the other we must relieve.

3. Their impotency: they may be sick, infirm, lame, blind, aged, so that they are not able to do ought for a livelihood.

4. You are to consider their serviceableness formerly. The more useful any have been in church or state, the more good they have done to either or both, the rather should they, in case of want, feel your charity than others; as many now, that have ventured their lives in the wars.

5. The cause of their poverty and want. If men have been brought to it by sickness, by special acts of Providence, fire, losses at sea, plundering, robbery, unfaithfulness of men and their dealings: these are to be pitied, supported before others that have brought themselves to beggary by ill courses.

Ver. 50. *And they were haughty, and committed abomination before me: therefore I took them away as I saw good.*

Here he goeth on in numbering Sodom's sins, and showing Sodom's end; they sinned against God, and he took them away for their sins.

"They were haughty." The Septuagint, they gloried; sin they did grievously, and gloried in their sins. Montanus, they are lifted up. Some expositors read it participially, thus, exalting themselves, they committed abominations.

In the former verse was spoken of pride, and therefore I shall say nothing of haughtiness, it being so near of kin to pride, if not the same.

"Committed abomination." By abomination we may understand that sin which is denominated from that place, viz. "sodomy, unnatural lusts, filthy uncleanness;" for they being proud and haughty, excessive in eating and drinking, abounding in idleness, neglective of the poor and needy, how could it be that they should be chaste? no, they were unclean, and abominably unclean; according to that you read, Rom. i. 27, "The men, leaving the natural use of the woman, burned in their lust one towards another; men with men working that which is unseemly." When the angels came to Lot, Gen. xix. the Sodomites, thinking they were men, both old and young, and all the people from every quarter, compassed his house, and said, Bring out the men that came unto thee, that we may know them, ver. 4, 5.

This lying with the male, an unnatural sin, we first find practised by these Sodomites, who, as Jude saith, gave themselves over to fornication, and went after strange, or other flesh; the women did not content them, but they burned in their lusts men towards men, and committed abomination one with another; it was other flesh than God appointed for generation. Man and wife are one flesh, but man and man, woman and woman, can never be so.

"Before me." That is, publicly, at noon-tide, in the sight of all; suitable to what you find in Isa. iii. 9, "They declare their sin as Sodom, they hide it not." Lawful acts of this nature should be in secret, but they did unlawful acts against the light of nature, and that openly: Zeph. iii. 5, "The unjust knoweth no shame;" such were these Sodomites.

Their sin is set out emphatically, in Gen. xiii. 13, "The men of Sodom were wicked, and sinners before the Lord exceedingly."

1. They were wicked, and intensively wicked, which the words "wicked" and "sinners" import; for the Spirit saith not only they are wicked, but wicked and sinners.

2. Sinners before the Lord; they sinned impudently, openly, and as in the presence of God, himself looking on: and they were sinners against the Lord, as some do read the words, that is, they sinned with a high hand. 1 Sam. ii. 25, "If a man sin against the Lord, who shall entreat for him?" they are heinous sins: and these Sodomites sinned against conscience, common equity, and light of nature.

3. Exceedingly; they were not seldom or little in sinning, but frequent, and much, and their sins of a transcendent nature. As Nimrod was a mighty hunter before God, so these were mighty sinners before him, none equal to them then on the earth.

"I took them away." The Hebrew is, אסיר, I caused them to be removed. What this removing or taking away was, you may see Gen. xix. 24, 25, "The Lord rained upon Sodom and upon Gomorrah, brimstone and fire from the Lord out of heaven; and he overthrew those cities, and all the plain, and all the inhabitants of the cities, and that which grew upon the ground."

Here is one of the most dreadful judgments, if not the dreadfulest, of all that we find in the book of God, executed upon sinners. The Lord, from himself, immediately, miraculously, suddenly sends a rain from heaven, of fire and brimstone, which was dreadful to the sight, to the smell, but worst of all to feel; and they, having been hellish in sinning, are made hellish in suffering; for fire and brimstone is the punishment of hell, Rev. xix. 20; xx. 10. Jude tells us, they suffered the vengeance of eternal fire, ver. 7; they passed through a temporal, or temporary, fire, to an eternal fire: and Peter saith, they were condemned, 2 Epist. ii. 6, God, "turning the cities of Sodom and Gomorrah into ashes, condemned them with an overthrow," he condemned them here, and to eternity. And the prophet Jeremiah, when he was in a cursing vein, curses the man who brought tidings of his birth, thus: "Let that man be as the cities which the Lord overthrew, and repented not," Jer. xx. 16. The prophet judged them accursed, and so separate from God for ever; they repented not of their sin, for Sodom was overthrown in a moment, Lam. iv. 6; neither did God repent of what he had done, and therefore no reconciliation could be between them, but they perished utterly. Not only were the men consumed in this judgment, their houses and buildings turned to ashes, their cattle, corn, and whatever grew upon the ground, but even the ground itself is under a curse still, being *lacus asphaltites*, or *mare mortuum*, nourishing no living creature, and so extremely salt, that it bears up whatever is thrown thereinto; and birds that fly over fall down into it, being suffocated with the poisonous vapours which rise from it: so that now this plain, which was a fruitful valley, and as Paradise, is become, through the people's sins, and just judgment of God, a filthy, and sulphurous, and poisonous lake.

"As I saw good." Some read it, as thou hast

seen. The men of Jerusalem from the turrets of the temple, their prospects in Zion and Jerusalem, could see this lake, and the hand of God upon the Sodomites therein, and therefore saith, as thou hast seen: but the Hebrew is, ראיתי as I have seen. Gen. xviii. 21, the Lord went down to see whether Sodom had done according to the cry of it. The cry of her sins was great and grievous, and the Lord finding it so, he did as he saw good and cause, he dealt with it as you have heard.

Obs. 1. The Lord remembers the iniquities of people long after they are committed, yea, after they are dead and gone. Sodom's sins were not forgotten, though they had sinned them many hundreds of years before; no vestiges left of them or their cities. "Behold, this was the iniquity of thy sister Sodom, pride," &c. God remembered the provocation of him by the Jews at the Red sea, in David's days, which was long before, Psal. cvi. 7, the calf they made at Horeb, ver. 19; their idolatry, fornication, and murmuring, were fresh in God's thoughts in Paul's days, 1 Cor. x. 7, 8, 10. Balaam's, Sodom's, the old world's, the angels', were minded by God, and mentioned by his Spirit, in Peter's days, 2 Pet. ii. 15, 6, 5, 4: the angels had sinned four thousand years before, and above, yet was not their sin forgotten. 1 Sam. xv. 2, "I remember, saith the Lord of hosts, what Amalek did to Israel, how he laid wait for him in the way when he came up from Egypt:" this was four hundred years before. It was twice fourteen generations from David to Christ, and yet there is a gentle touch upon David's sins, Matt. i. 6, 17. God hath a firm and tenacious memory, it lets nothing slip which once it receives: you see sinful acts of men in states are kept upon the file, and on record, and many hundreds of years after are brought forth: God keeps the sins of cities, kingdoms, princes, and people in his book of remembrance, which should lesson us to take heed what we do. Men do not more easily sin, than forget their sins, but God doth not so easily or quickly forget them, Job xiii. 26, "Thou makest me to possess the iniquities of my youth:" Psal. xxv. 7, "Remember not the sins of my youth."

Obs. 2. Plenty is the parent of sin, yea, many sins. Sodom, as hath been shown, was situate in a plain very fruitful and delightful, as appears, Gen. xiii. 10; it had abundance; and what was the effect thereof? pride, fulness of bread, idleness, unmercifulness, haughtiness, and uncleanness. Deut. xxxii. 15, "Jeshurun waxed fat, and kicked: thou art waxen fat, grown thick, thou art covered with fatness: then he forsook God which made him, and lightly esteemed the Rock of his salvation."

When Israel grew rich, had plenty of all things about her, then she became like a fatted ox that kicks at the owner, and cares for none. 1 Sam. ii. 29, "Wherefore kick ye at my sacrifice and at mine offering;" they slighted the sacrifices and offerings of God, and, in so doing, they slighted, they kicked, at God. Nehem. ix. 25, 26, when God had brought them into Canaan, "they took strong cities, and a fat land, and possessed houses full of all goods, wells digged, vineyards, and olive-yards, and fruit trees in abundance: so they did eat and were filled, and became fat, and delighted themselves in thy great goodness. Nevertheless they were disobedient, and rebelled against thee, and cast thy law behind their backs, and slew thy prophets, which testified against them to turn them to thee; and they wrought great provocations."

Solomon, when he abounded most with God's blessings, then he loved strange women, multiplied wives and concubines, and fell to idolatry, as you may see from 1 Kings x. and xi. Jer. v. 27, 28, "They are become great, and waxen rich. They are waxen fat, they shine; they overpass the deeds of the wicked:" they went beyond the very heathen in wickedness, Ezek. v. 6, 7. Jerusalem here, in this chapter, the metaphorical woman, for whom God had done so much, and upon whom he had bestowed broidered work, skins of *tachasch*, fine linen, silk, ornaments, bracelets, chains, jewels, rings, a crown, gold, silver, fine flour, honey, oil, she plays the harlot, abuses those choice blessings and abundance she had to idolatry; she sacrificed her children to idols, and walked in such lewd ways, that the daughters of the Philistines were ashamed of her, ver. 27. Dives was wealthy, and as wicked as wealthy. James v. the rich men, that had plenty of all things, withheld the labourers' hire that reaped down their fields; they lived in pleasure, were wanton, condemned the just.

Plenty is dangerous, yet all men labour to be rich, and have much about them. Men's tables and estates prove snares. The bag caught Judas; and many in prosperity have fallen who stood in the days of adversity.

Obs. 3. The Lord gives outward blessings, not only to saints but to sinners, yea, to great and notorious sinners. Even the Sodomites, that were wicked, and sinners before God exceedingly, had bread, and abundance thereof; that is, of all outward blessings, edible and potable, they had variety, and likewise other things plentifully. Matt. v. 45, "He maketh his sun to rise on the evil and on the good, and sendeth rain on the just and the unjust." Not only Abraham and Lot had the sun and rain, who were righteous persons, but Sodomites, who exceeded all sinners then in the world, had the sun shining upon them, Gen. xix. 23.

Other nations had the dews of heaven, and fatness of the earth, as well as the Jews, God's own people. The Canaanites and others had that pleasant land which flowed with milk and honey before they had it; and they were so wicked that the land could bear them no longer, but even spewed them out, Lev. xviii. 28.

Antiochus, a vile person, had the kingdom, Dan. xi. 21: so Ahab, that sold himself to work wickedness in the sight of the Lord, 1 Kings xxi. 25, he was a king in Israel. The whore of Babylon was arrayed in purple, decked with gold, precious stones, and pearls; and when Jerusalem here was grown worse than the nations round about her, yet then she had the blessings of God in great store: so that "all things come alike to all, and no man knoweth love or hatred by all that is before them," Eccles. ix. 1, 2.

If any man should conclude himself a good man, beloved of God, because he gives him many blessings, much of the creature, then may it be said the Sodomites were good men, for they had plenty. If any should say he is an evil man because he wants these, then Lazarus, the apostles, Christ himself, should be so, because they had little or nothing. God gives his outward blessings promiscuously to good and bad, that men may see he is impartial in his outward dispensations; that good men using them well, and honouring him therewith, might increase their comforts and rewards; that evil men abusing them to the service of their lusts, and dishonour of their Giver, might have the deeper condemnation.

Obs. 4. Cities commonly are guilty of great sins. Sodom was a city; 2 Pet. ii. 6, "the cities of Sodom and Gomorrha;" and there were two more, which you have specified in Deut. xxix. 23, together with the other; "Sodom and Gomorrah, Admah and Zeboim, which the Lord overthrew in his anger and wrath." These four cities perished together, and they were full of crying sins, pride, gluttony, idleness, inhumanity, uncleanness, and the like; these sins run through them all: Jude 7, "Sodom and Gomorrha, and the cities about them, they gave themselves to fornication, and went after strange flesh."

There were high places and idols in the cities of Samaria, 1 Kings xiii. 32; Isa. x. 10; Hos. viii. 5. The woman of one of the cities of Samaria, that talked with Christ, John iv. was very bitter, lived in uncleanness, and worshipped she knew not what. Babylon was full of cruelty and pride, Jer. l.; the bloody city, Ezek. xxiv. 6. Nineveh so abounded with sin in Jonah's days, that had they not repented, destruction had been upon them: see Nahum iii. 13. Jerusalem had violence and strife in it; Psal. lv. 9—11, "Mischief, sorrow, and wickedness are in the midst thereof, deceit and guile depart not from her streets:" Zeph. iii. 1—4, she is called the filthy, polluted, oppressing city; her princes were roaring lions, her judges evening wolves, her prophets light and treacherous persons, her priests polluted the sanctuary, and did violence to the law: Ezek. viii. you may read what horrible abominations were in the temple and city; Lam. iv. 13, her prophets and her priests "shed the blood of the just in the midst of her."

Obs. 5. Sinners in time come to a height and impudency of sinning. "They committed abomination before me;" nothing restrained them, not conscience, light of nature, shame amongst men, fear of punishment, spectacles of death, but they go on and sin in the sight and presence of God: Isa. lxvi. 4, "They did evil before mine eyes;" even in the temple, where God dwelt, they sinned, set up idols, and worshipped them. To what a height of sinning did Manasseh come, and the Jews in his days! they did that which was evil in God's sight, and provoked him to anger, 2 Kings xxi. 15. In tract of time sinners become stout, and will contest: Mal. iii. 13, "Your words have been stout against me. Yet ye say, What have we spoken so much against thee? Ye have said, It is in vain to serve God," &c.

Obs. 6. When God brings terrible judgments upon kingdoms, persons, he seeth cause for it. "Therefore I took them away as I saw good." I saw what sinners they were, I came down from heaven, examined the cry of their sins, and saw sufficient cause to make me stretch out my hand, and rain down fire and brimstone upon them. When God drowned the old world, confounded their language, made the earth to swallow up Korah, Dathan, and Abiram, when he sent fiery serpents amongst them, famines, plagues, wars, captivity, he saw cause for all these.

There is never any public or private judgment befalls states, cities, or persons, but the Lord hath great and just cause to do so; if there were no sin, there would be no punishment: Lam. iii. 39, "Wherefore doth a living man complain, a man for the punishment of his sins?"

Obs. 7. We ought to take notice of God's judgments upon sinful places, and to beware of their sins. God doth therefore tell us in his holy word what he hath done to Sodom and other places for that end: this judgment upon Sodom is oft mentioned, Gen. xiii. 10; Isa. i. 9; Lam. iv. 6; Luke xvii. 29; Rom. ix. 29; 2 Pet. ii. 6; Jude 7. And here also, when God threatens to punish sinful persons and places severely, he tells them they shall be made like Sodom, as in Deut. xxix. 23; Isa. xiii. 19; Jer. xlix. 18; l. 40; Zeph. ii. 9: and in Amos iv. 11, he saith, he had overthrown some of them as he overthrew Sodom. In thirteen places this sore judgment is mentioned, that so we might frequently meet with it, mind it, and abhor the sins which brought it upon them. If the sins of Sodom be found in cities, pride, fulness of bread, abundance of idleness, unmercifulness to the poor, uncleanness, they shall have Sodom's judgment, or some equivalent. It may be, we are free from Sodom's sins, and I would we were; but are we not guilty of worse? I fear we are, if we receive not the gospel in the power of it, as Capernaum did not: Christ tells you it shall be easier for Sodom and Gomorrah in the day, &c. Matt. xi.

Ver. 51, 52. *Neither hath Samaria committed half of thy sins; but thou hast multiplied thine abominations more than they, and hast justified thy sisters in all thine abominations which thou hast done. Thou also, which hast judged thy sisters, bear thine own shame for thy sins that thou hast committed more abominable than they: they are more righteous than thou: yea, be thou confounded also, and bear thy shame, in that thou hast justified thy sisters.*

The scope of these two verses is to convince Jerusalem that she was more wicked than others, than Samaria or Sodom her sisters, and therefore ought proportionably to be confounded and shamed for her abominations.

"Samaria." This was the chief city of the ten tribes, and is here put for the kingdom of Israel, as it is distinct from the kingdom of Judah, and is oft called Israel and Ephraim; and the sins of the Israelites or Ephraimites were exceeding great. Their kingdom was begun in rebellion and idolatry, 1 Kings xii. 19, 28, 29; they rebelled against the house of David, chose Jeroboam to be their king, who set up the golden calves at Dan and Bethel, and drew the people to worship them; he "made priests of the lowest of the people," set up high places, devised feasts and worship of his own, ver. 31—33. And all the kings of Israel were wicked: Ahab so abominably wicked, that none was like unto him, 1 Kings xxi. 25. Jezebel filled the land with wickedness; she caused Naboth to be unjustly accused and stoned to death, chap. xxi. 10; the true prophets were persecuted, eight hundred and fifty false prophets countenanced, chap. xviii.

There was no truth, mercy, or knowledge of God left in the land; swearing, lying, killing, stealing, adultery abounded, Hos. iv. 1, 2; they were profound in slaughtering, chap. v. 2; the priests of Israel were murderers, chap. vi. 9; the pride of Israel was great, chap. vii. 10; they had "deeply corrupted themselves," chap. ix. 9; confederated with the Assyrians and Egyptians, chap. xii. 1; "provoked God to anger most bitterly," ver. 14. They walked in the statutes of the heathen, and of the kings of Israel; they sinned secretly and openly; they set up images and groves on every high hill, under every green tree, burnt incense in all the high places as did the heathen; they rejected the statutes and covenant of God, they left all his commandments; caused their sons and daughters to pass through the fire; they used divination and enchantments, and sold themselves to do evil, 2 Kings xvii. 8—11, 15—17. Now, although the ten tribes, comprised in the word Samaria, were guilty of these and many other sins, yet they were not the half of Jerusalem's sins; "Samaria hath not committed the half of thy sins;" which we are not to account of by arithmetical proportion, as if Jerusalem's sins for number were more than so many more; but the quality and nature thereof were such, so dreadful, so grievous, clothed with such circumstances and aggravations, that, compared together, and all things considered, those of Sodom and Samaria were not half so bad. The Sodomites had only the light of nature to direct them, the Samaritans had a devised worship forced upon them by Jeroboam, and were held to it by succeeding idolatrous kings; they had not the law, the temple, the ark, the prophets, the true priests, sacrifices, solemn feasts, and good kings, as Jerusalem had, therefore Jerusalem's sins were the greater. Samaria had heard and read of God's heavy judgment upon Sodom, for her wickedness; Jerusalem, besides that, had seen God's dealing with Samaria, that the ten tribes were ruined and carried away into captivity, that she alone was preserved and reserved as God's peculiar; and now for Jerusalem to be ungrateful, to fall into, and to continue in, those sins, for which the Israelites suffered so much, notwithstanding the threats of the prophets; yea, to set up the image of jealousy at the gate of the altar, to picture the forms of all creeping things and abominable beasts, and to portray all the idols of the house of Israel upon the walls of the court, and for the elders to offer incense before them; to place Tammuz in the temple, women to weep for that abominable idol, men therein to worship the sun towards the east, and put the branch to their nose, and fill the land with violence, Ezek. viii.; these things make the Lord to say, that "Samaria committed not half of thy sins, but thou hast multiplied thine abominations more than they;" and, as it is Jer. iii. 5, "Behold, thou hast spoken and done evil things as thou couldest." She was become so wicked, had sinned with so high a hand, that she could not do worse, she exceeded all: Ezek. v. 6, 7, "She hath changed my judgments into wickedness more than the nations, and my statutes more than the countries that are round about her; and multiplied more than the nations," more sins, more aggravations.

"And hast justified thy sisters." Hebrew, ותצדקי not, hast made them holy, just, righteous, as the papists do interpret the word when they treat of justification, but by the greatness of thy sins hast declared them to be less sinners than thyself: so Sanctius saith, that *justificare* in this place is the same with *justum ostendere;* and Vatablus, *justiores te esse ostenderis*, thou dost manifest that they are more righteous than thyself; for, set their sins with thine, and the disproportion is so great, that they are not half such sinners as thou art, they seem just in comparison of thee, thy sins are heavy, and theirs are light. This doth not lessen the sins of the Sodomites or Samaritans, or suppose them to be innocent, but only showeth that their sins had not such heinous aggravations as theirs of Jerusalem had.

Ver. 52. "Hast judged thy sisters." Hebrew, פללת hast pronounced judgment. Saith Montanus, פלל signifies, to pray, to appeal, and it is likely the Latin word, *appello*, and English, appeal, do come from it; but frequently, to judge. Avenarius saith it is *verbum juridicum*, and פלילים is, judges, Exod. xxi. 22; Deut. xxxii. 31; Job xxxi. 11. Vatablus saith that *pilalti* signifies *in alios decernere sententiam tanquam merito punitos.* Thus Jerusalem, when she heard of God's severe proceedings with Sodom, she said, their sins were great, and those judgments deserved; when she saw Samaria besieged, taken, and the ten tribes carried away by Shalmaneser into captivity, she did not pity, but censure them, looking at them as rebels, idolaters, apostates, and persecutors, and so adjudged all those punishments due unto them which they underwent, thinking herself more righteous than they of Sodom or Samaria.

"Bear thine own shame." Hebrew, כלמתך שאי the word for shame notes more than ordinary shame; ignominy, reproach, from כלם which signifies, to be calumniated, to have such words and usage as if one were a dog, or esteemed no better than a dog; hence the word *calumnia*, calumny; and it is always used in contemptuous, or in an ill sense, as some critics observe; whereas בוש is not, neither notes so deep a shame, reproach, as כלם doth. Jer. xiv. 3, "They were ashamed and confounded." בשו והכלמו here are both words; one imports, shame, the other, confounding shame, exceeding great shame. Isa. l. 6, "I hid not my face from shame and spitting." When Christ was put to death, you know how ignominiously they used him, scoffing at him, and spitting upon him; they slighted and reproached him to the utmost. The Septuagint renders the word shame in our prophet, *βάσανον*, torment, because such shame is a torment, a burden.

"Bear thine own shame." The meaning of the phrase is this: Seeing thou hast done shameful things, yea so shameful, as the sins of Samaria and Sodom seem little in respect thereof; now look for and submit unto shameful judgments which I shall bring upon thee. I will bring the Assyrians, they shall discover thy wickedness, strip thee of all thy jewels and ornaments, stone thy children, burn thy habitations, carry thee away captive. I will make thee a reproach and hissing in the open view of all the world, as I did the Sodomites and ten tribes, when I punished them for their abominations: I know it will be very heavy for thee, but, however, "bear thine own shame."

This expression of bearing shame you have it not elsewhere than in this prophet, it is peculiar to him, and frequent. It follows here in this verse again, "be thou confounded, and bear thy shame."

The words being opened, and sense given, we should come to the observations; but before we do that, one query is to be made and answered.

The query is, Seeing that Jerusalem's sins were greater than Sodom's and Samaria's, and they righteous in comparison thereof, why had she not greater punishments than they? Sodom was consumed with fire from heaven; the ten tribes so extirpated and captivated, as that they never returned, or became the Lord's people, to this day: God is just, and the greatest sinners should have the greatest punishments.

To this I answer,

1. That as God would have wholly spared Sodom had there been ten righteous in it, Gen. xviii. 32; so there being many righteous in Jerusalem, who cried for mercy, and bewailed the abominations thereof, the Lord lessened the judgment. That there were many righteous in it, who sighed and cried to the Lord, you may see, Ezek. ix. 6; and if the Lord will divert judgments for their sakes, he may also lessen them.

2. God's judgments upon Jerusalem, all laid together, were greater than the fiery hand of God upon Sodom. The famine, which made the pitiful women to eat their children, Lam. iv. 10, the fathers to eat their sons, and the sons their fathers openly, Ezek. v. 10; the pestilence, the sword, and captivity, were, all things considered, sorer strokes of God upon Jerusalem, than the fire from heaven upon Sodom; and you have divine testimony for it, Lam. iv. 6, "The punishment of the iniquity of the daughter of my people is greater than the punishment of the sin of Sodom, that was overthrown as in a moment, and no hand stayed on her." Sodom's punishment was

sharp, but short; Jerusalem's was sharp and long. To kill a man by degrees, by cutting off fingers, toes, ears, arms, legs, is far worse than cutting off the head at once; such was God's dealings with Jerusalem.

3. If the punishment of the ten tribes were greater; for they endured three years' siege, 2 Kings xvii. 5, and were carried away into Assyria, and never returned; I answer, God hath his prerogative to punish sinners with what degree of punishment he please here in this life; he may punish lesser sinners with greater punishments, and greater sinners with lesser punishments, and yet be free from partiality or injustice, because he hath a day to reckon with sinners hereafter, and then will render to them fully according to the merit of their sins: Ezra ix. 13, God punished them less than their iniquities deserved. And if Jerusalem's punishment came short of the ten tribes, the more remained behind, without repentance, and God rendered it in due time; but upon search into the word, it may appear that Jerusalem's punishment was not short, but beyond the ten tribes. Ezek. v. 9—12, God saith there, he will do that in her which he had not done, and whereunto he would not do any more the like. The meaning is, he would punish Jerusalem more and otherwise than he had done Sodom, Samaria, or any other before. God swears there, that he would not spare them, nor have any pity. Samaria was not burned, when taken, and the tribes carried away; but Jerusalem, the temple, and all the holy things in it were burned, and taken away, the people divided into thirds, and each third pursued with judgment.

4. God may show mercy to the greatest sinners, and bring them to a condition of enjoying the greatest privileges, to show the riches of his free grace and mercy; and so he did here those that sinned more than Sodomites or Samaritans; after great sufferings and seventy years' captivity, he brings back to Jerusalem, bestows a new city and temple upon them, with the privileges and ordinances thereof. And besides, we may remember that the promise of return from Babylon was not made to Samaria or the ten tribes after seventy years, but unto Jerusalem, and the two tribes that were left, Jer. xxix. 10. The ten tribes were gone into captivity before Jeremiah's days; about the sixth year of Hezekiah they were carried away, and Jeremiah prophesied not till the thirteenth year of Josiah, Jer. i. 2, and he was then come to the days and reign of Zedekiah, as appears, chap. xxi. 1; and it was above a hundred and twenty years that the tribes had been then carried away, as is evident upon compute of the years, from the sixth of Hezekiah to the times of Zedekiah; therefore it is said, Ezra i. 5, when the time of return came, that the fathers of Judah and Benjamin rose up to go and build the house of the Lord at Jerusalem. God's promise was given out to show mercy to them, and bring them back, which he did, notwithstanding their great sins, to show his faithfulness and fulness of mercy.

Obs. 1. The sins of one people may be greater than the sins of another; all sins are not equal, nor all sinners equally guilty. Jerusalem's sins exceeded Samaria's and Sodom's, they were not half so great sinners as she was.

The more mercies any people enjoy, the greater are their sins if they answer not those mercies.

Jerusalem was taken from a low, bloody, beggarly, perishing condition; God blessed and multiplied her exceedingly, entered into covenant with her, and took her to be his; he bestowed upon her beauty, honour, renown, wealth, all things desirable; he set her in the midst of the nations, Ezek. v. 5, that all might see what he had done for her. She was the "holy city," Matt. iv. 5, and had those privileges, ordinances, and advantages which no city in the world had; he had often delivered her out of the hands of enemies, especially in the days of Hezekiah, when Sennacherib lay before her with one hundred and eighty-five thousand men, 2 Kings xix. 35. Yea, God had wooed her by his prophets, made many gracious promises to her, watered her, and watched her night and day, Isa. xxvii. 3, done what he could for her, chap. v. 4; and yet she sinned notoriously, excessively against God more than the nations. Those who had not half her mercies, did not commit half her sins; such abominations, lewdness, villanies, were not to be found elsewhere. She sinned wilfully, Jer. xliv. 16, 17; she continued in sin, notwithstanding great means used to reclaim her, Neh. ix. 26; she provoked God to his face, Isa. lxv. 3; she was insatiable in wickedness, ver. 28, 29 of this chapter; she caused other nations to sin with her, Ezek. xxiii. 16, 17. These and many other aggravations were in her sins: and as the Jews then sinned greater sins than the Sodomites and Samaritans, so christians now sin greater sins than the Jews did then. Gospel sins are the greatest sins: in the gospel is held out the greatest grace, mercy, and love to sinners; and if these be refused or abused by them, their sins will be exceeding sinful, and it will be more tolerable for Sodomites, Samaritans, Hierosolymites, Ninevites, or any, than for such. Christians' sins will be found the scarlet and unparallelable sins.

Obs. 2. That comparing of sins and sinners together, makes great sins seem little, and great sinners seem righteous.

Sodom's and Samaria's sins were great and grievous; yet compared with Jerusalem's, they seemed little, not half so great or grievous: "Thou hast justified thy sisters, and they are more righteous than thou." Neither of them were little sinners, or had any righteousness; but being laid together, sins and sinners, Jerusalem was transcendently sinful and unrighteous, and they less sinful, less unrighteous. Great things when they are exceeded by greater in view, they seem little; a great house is nothing to a great rock, a great mountain or city; a great river is nothing to the ocean; so a great heap of sins is as nothing to a greater; what is a cartful of dung to a great dunghill? And as it is in quantities, so in qualities: some poisons are so poisonous, so strong, that they kill immediately; others, though more in quantity, yet are longer in producing such an effect, and in comparison they are no poisons; so some sins and sinners compared with others, are as none. Luke xviii. 14, the publican went down to his house justified rather than the Pharisee: this Pharisee compared himself with the publican, and thought himself righteous; but the publican in comparison of him was righteous. There is a righteousness which doth condemn, and there is a sinfulness which doth justify, and both are naught: a pharisaical righteousness damns a man, when a Jerusalem's sinfulness justifies a man. Take heed therefore of comparing yourselves with others who are worse and greater sinners than you, and from thence of framing a righteousness to yourselves notwithstanding. Sodom and Samaria were less sinners, more righteous than Jerusalem, yet you know how God dealt with them, and destruction will be the end of all those who trust to such righteousness.

Obs. 3. Great sinners see not, or forget their own sins, and are apt to censure, judge, and condemn others who are less sinful than themselves, and especially when they are under the hand of God.

Jerusalem, whose iniquities and abominations were incomparable, beyond Sodom's and Samaria's, sees not her own sins, remembers not how she had dealt with her God, her Lord and Husband, but forgets him, Jer. ii. 32; and here judges her sister Samaria, and thought her sins and courses so grievous, so foul, and provoking, that when she was besieged three years, carried into captivity, and suffered sad things, it was well done of the Lord to deal so by her; that she was more wicked than herself or any others. Luke xiii. 1—5, when some out of Galilee were sacrificing, Pilate gave command they should be slain, and so made sacrifices of them; they that saw them brought to such an end, presently judged them to be the greatest sinners of all the Galileans; so those who were slain by the fall of the tower in Siloam: they thought Jerusalem had not greater sins in it; but it was otherwise, Christ told them that they were as great or greater sinners; "Except ye repent, ye shall all likewise perish." It is not warrantable to conclude them to be the greatest sinners who are smitten with some heavy hand of God; then Job and Josiah might have been censured to be the greatest sinners of their times. You may observe in human politics, that oft accessaries and instruments in plots, treasons, rebellions, and murders, do suffer, when principals escape; and so God sometimes executes judgments upon lesser sinners, and lets others who are greater supervive. Let us instead therefore of judging others, judge ourselves, and fear we are reserved for the like or worse judgments, if we repent not. Jerusalem, who judged her sister to be the greatest of sinners, and justified her by the greatness of her own sins, was reserved for greater judgments, and a worse end, because she repented not.

Obs. 4. It is a shame for those who are guilty of the same or greater sins, to judge others. Jerusalem committed the same sins, and did worse, yet she judged Samaria; and this was her sin and shame: in the Hebrew the words run thus, Thou also bear thy shame, who hast judged thy sisters in thy sins, in which thou hast done abominations more than they. It is a shameful thing to reprove, censure, or judge those who are less sinful than ourselves, and especially being under the hand of God for their sins.

(1.) We justify ourselves in so doing, and step into God's throne.

(2.) We give occasion to the censured to say, Thou hypocrite, pull the beam out of thine own eye, before thou meddle with the mote in mine.

(3.) We condemn ourselves in so doing: Rom. ii. 1, he that doth the same thing, or worse, and judges another, he condemns himself.

(4.) We insult over them, and add affliction to affliction, if they be judged by the Lord.

And all these are matters of shame: he that reproves or judges others, should be innocent himself.

When the scribes and Pharisees brought and complained unto Christ of the woman taken in adultery, he said unto them, "He that is without sin among you, let him first cast a stone at her." Christ did not mean simply, he that is without sin, for he knew there were none such living except himself; but he that is without that sin, or sins equivalent, (as they were not, who came to tempt Christ, and get advantage against him, being malicious, and bloodily minded,) let him first throw a stone at her: hereupon being convicted by their own consciences, that they were sinners, and very faulty, they were ashamed, hung down their heads, and went sneaking away, John viii. 9.

Obs. 5. Sin brings shame. "Bear thy shame" for thine iniquities: thou hast sinned, and sinned more than others; thy sins are thy shame, and will bring shame upon thee. What a shame was it to Jerusalem, that she was a greater sinner than Samaria, than Sodom; that she did such things as made the daughters of the Philistines ashamed of her! ver. 27. When Moses was in the mount, this people would have gods to go before them; and the calf being made, what saith the text? Exod. xxxii. 25, "Aaron had made them naked unto their shame amongst their enemies." They were made naked of their ornaments, of God's protection, by this calf, and "changed their glory into the similitude of an ox that eateth grass," Psal. cvi. 20; and this was their shame. When Amnon would have his will upon Tamar, she opposed him with an argument taken from the shame of sin; 2 Sam. xiii. 13, "Whither shall I cause my shame to go? and as for thee, thou shalt be as one of the fools in Israel;" it will be a great reproach unto us both.

The Corinthians' going to law before the unjust, and not taking up the matter among themselves, was their shame, 1 Cor. vi. 1, 5; and chap. xv. 34, "Some have not the knowledge of God; I speak this to their shame." Ignorance is a shame to people, and so is all sin: Rom. vi. 21, the Romans were ashamed of their false worship and sinful lives. Shame is the lackey that waits upon sin, and causeth the conscience to blush as well as the face: Prov. xiv. 34, sin is a reproach to nations.

Obs. 6. Shame in itself, or as it accompanies the judgments of God upon sinners, is a burdensome thing. "Bear thine own shame," reproach, disgrace. Women that are common whores, yet cannot endure to be called so; much less to be used as sometimes they are, carted, pumped, or sent to bridewell. Barrenness in women, because it was a reproach unto them, how burdensome was it of old to them. Rachel was pinched upon this consideration as much as any other, when she said, "Give me children, or else I die," Gen. xxx. 1; for so soon as she had a child, she acknowledged God had taken away her reproach, ver. 23, that was the burden upon her. Psal. lxix. 20, "Reproach hath broken my heart, and I am full of heaviness." His adversaries did unjustly accuse, slander, and disgrace him, and this lay so heavy, like a mountain or millstone upon him, that it broke his heart, and filled him with heaviness. What did the reproach, then, and shame which came upon his defiling Bathsheba, and murdering Uriah, do? they brake and ground his heart to powder. When men are touched in their reputations, it goeth near them; the burden of dishonour and disgrace is so heavy, that sometimes they will venture their lives in duels and quarrels, and rather die than bear the burden of reproach. Shame and reproach have caused many to make away themselves. Saul, fearing the Philistines would abuse and disgrace him, fell upon his own sword, and slew himself. When this city Jerusalem was laid waste, the inhabitants thereof made a curse, reproach, and hissing among all nations, was it not a torment, a burden, and vexation to them? Ezek. v. 14, 15. Jer. xxiii. 40, "I will bring an everlasting reproach upon you, and a perpetual shame, which shall not be forgotten."

Obs. 7. Sinners must bear the judgments of God, and the shame that is due unto them, whoever they be. "Thou also," even thou Jerusalem, "bear thine own shame." Jerusalem had been the faithful city, Isa. i. 21, but was become a harlot; judgment and righteousness did lodge in her, but now murderers. She had sinned, shamed herself before God and man, and she must bear her burden, bear God's judgments, bear shame before heaven and earth.

Ver. 53—56. ***When I shall bring again their captivity, the captivity of Sodom and her daughters, and the captivity of Samaria and her daughters, then will I bring again the captivity of thy captives in the midst of them: that thou mayest bear thine own shame, and mayest be confounded in all that thou hast done, in that thou art a comfort unto them. When thy sisters, Sodom and her daughters, shall return to their former estate, and Samaria and her daughters shall return to their former estate, then thou and thy daughters shall return to your former estate. For thy sister Sodom was not mentioned by thy mouth in the day of thy pride.***

These verses contain more judgment, and the cause thereof. In them you have,

I. Jerusalem's irrecoverableness of her former estate, in ver. 53, 55, laid down under a double comparison, viz. God's dealings with Sodom and Samaria, and their daughters.

II. The scope and end of God in it, ver. 54, that she might bear her own shame, &c.

III. The causes of this judgment; which are,

1. Her being a comfort to them, ver. 54.

2. Her pride and forgetfulness, ver. 56.

Ver. 53. "When I shall bring again their captivity," &c. Hebrew is, ושבתי את־שביתהן Some make this verse, and so the 55th, to be promissory, not minatory; affirming that the Lord here promiseth to show mercy to the captives of Sodom, Samaria, and Jerusalem, and to bring them all back again. But because Sodom and her daughters were utterly destroyed, and they saw not how they could be returned; therefore they labour much to prove, that by Sodom is meant the two tribes and half on the other side Jordan, Reuben, Gad, and half Manasseh; but these are comprehended in Samaria, which was the head city of the ten tribes: and if that should be yielded, the difference between Sodom and her daughters, and Samaria and her daughters, would be great, yet taken away.

Others therefore by Sodom here understand the Moabites and Ammonites, that came from the loins of Lot, who dwelt in Sodom, as appears, Gen. xix. 37, 38. But the Scripture gives no warrant to account these among the Sodomites; rather they should have been called Lothites, or Lottites, seeing they descended from his loins. Besides, the word Sodom is to be taken in its proper and native sense here, as well as Samaria and Jerusalem, and that Sodom to be meant, of which he spake in ver. 49, 50, which was destroyed with her daughters by fire from heaven, and so destroyed that no man can or shall dwell or abide there, Jer. xlix. 18.

Again, if the words do hold out a promise of mercy, it is first to Sodom and her daughters, next to Samaria and hers, and last to Jerusalem and her daughters; so that they must be restored to their former estate before Jerusalem; but neither Sodom nor Samaria were restored before the captivity ended in Babylon. It is clear enough that the words are not a promise of mercy, but a threatening of severity; and it lies thus: When I shall bring again the captivity of Sodom and Samaria, which I will never do, then will I bring again thy captivity. I have destroyed them utterly, and intend not to replant them, but to let them lie in the dark, and abide in captivity; and thy condition shall be like unto theirs.

Some read the words with an interrogation, thus: Shall I bring again their captivity? the captivity of Sodom and her daughters, the captivity of Samaria and her daughters? and shall I bring again the captives? No, I will neither do the one nor the other; thou hast sinned above them, and hast no cause but to expect more rigorous dealings from me than they have had. Piscator, Junius, Polanus read the words conditionally, thus: If I shall return the captivity of Sodom and Samaria, then I will return thine; but it is not in my thoughts, counsels, or purposes to return and restore them, who never provoked me as thou hast done; therefore much less do I intend to do so by thee.

Some take the words ironically: When I restore Sodom and Samaria, then will I restore thee. But they are so destroyed that they are past recovery: I intend never to bring the Sodomites out of the fire, and seat them in Sodom; nor the ten tribes out of captivity, and settle them in Samaria; and no more do I mean to restore thee and thy captives.

Quest. Did not the Lord return the captivity of Jerusalem after seventy years? how is it then true which is said here if this be the sense?

Answ. 1. When God threatens them with utter desolation, it is to be meant of the body of people in general, who had apostatized from God as the ten tribes had done, and there was no help left for them; they were destroyed the most of them in the war, famine, plague, captivity; and so not they, but some of their posterity, were restored, and brought back again. God had promised the Jews who came out of Egypt, that they should enter into Canaan; but observe, Numb. xiv. the people murmured, and God told them, ver. 29—31, their carcasses should fall in this wilderness, and all from twenty years old and upward, that none of them but Caleb and Joshua should come into the land: only their little ones, which they said should be a prey, he would bring into it. So here, it was not the body of the people that returned, but some of their posterity. Those Jews who were at Jerusalem when Ezekiel thus prophesied, it is probable were utterly destroyed, and never had their captivity returned.

2. We may understand it of a full return, which never was; though some Jews came back again, yet multitudes staid behind, and continued in Babylon, as may be gathered from Ezra i. 5.

3. Though the Jews were brought back from Babylon, yet never was Jerusalem in that glory as before; neither was her temple, state, or kingly dignity such as formerly. Ezra iii. 12, many wept when they saw the difference between the latter temple and the former.

Ver. 54. Of bearing shame, and being confounded, was spoken in ver. 52.

"In that thou art a comfort to them." Septuagint reads it thus, ἐν τῷ σε παροργίσαι με, in that thou hast provoked me to anger. Jerusalem's sins exceeding the sins of Sodom and Samaria, this justified them. Some refer it to the punishments and judgments of God upon Jerusalem, which was some ease and comfort to Sodom and Samaria, when they saw her in a suffering condition with themselves.

Ver. 55. "When thy sisters, Sodom and her daughters," &c. This verse is the same for substance with ver. 53.

Ver. 56. "Thy sister Sodom was not mentioned," &c. Hebrew is, לשמועה בפיך there was no hearing of Sodom in thy mouth. Thou didst neither think nor speak of her and my dealings with her for her sins, that so thou mightest have feared, and not fallen into her sins, or greater.

"In the day of thy pride." Hebrew, ביום גאוניך in the day of thy prides or prosperities. When thou hadst honour, wealth, renown, greatness, and abundance of all things, thy heart was lifted up; thou thoughtest thyself happy and innocent, disdaining to mind or mention Sodom, whom thou contemnedst and slightedst; but thy wickedness is come to such a height that Sodom's sin is little in comparison of thine.

Obs. 1. The sins of people may come to such a height, admit of such dreadful aggravations, as to cause God to cut off all hopes of mercy, and cast them into irrecoverable misery. Jerusalem had so sinned here, provoked God so heinously, that he saith he would sooner bring back the captivity of Sodom and Samaria, than hers; they were cut off and cast into such conditions as were irrecoverable, for less sins, and therefore what could she look for? God would not show her any pity, Ezek. v. 11; vii. 4. Read Jer. xv. 1—6, where you shall find God was so provoked by the sins of this people, that though Moses and Samuel should plead for them, his mind could not be towards them; he would cast them out of his sight, and death, sword, famine, captivity should devour them.

Jer. li. 25, 26, "I am against thee, O destroying mountain: I will stretch out mine hand upon thee, and roll thee down from the rocks, and will make thee a burnt mountain. And they shall not take of thee a stone for a corner, nor a stone for foundations; but thou shalt be desolate for ever." It is spoken of Babylon, whose sins had gotten up to such a height, that the Lord threatened her with irrecoverable ruin; he would deal with this Babylonish state as with a thing burnt to ashes, which is unserviceable, irrecoverable; he would so break the power and state of the Babylonish empire, that it should never recover itself more.

Obs. 2. One great end of God's denying hope of mercy, and casting into irrecoverable misery, is to bring sinners to shame and confusion. God saith he will never return her captivity, that she might bear her own shame, and be confounded in all she had done. You have disgraced the holy temple with your idols, the holy city and land with your violence and bloody crimes, my holy name with your inventions and abominations; therefore when once I have sent you into captivity, you shall not return thence at all, but live in disgrace, perish in what you have done, your estate is hopeless and helpless; you have made me to bear shame, but in your captivity you shall bear shame and reproach enough, even to confusion: Jer. xxii. 22, "Thy lovers shall go into captivity; surely then shalt thou be ashamed and confounded for all thy wickedness."

Obs. 3. Great sinners and great sufferers afford comfort, such as it is, to other sinners and sufferers. Jerusalem was a greater sinner, and, all things considered, a greater sufferer, than Sodom or Samaria; and it is here said, "in that thou art a comfort unto them;" her sins justified their sins, her sufferings justified their sufferings. When cities, republics, or persons do see others to exceed them in sins or punishments, they conceive theirs are the less, and so frame a kind of comfort. Those who are miserable, through sin or punishment, do think it some relief to have companions, equals, or those who go beyond them, especially in the same kind. Mark vi. 11, "It shall be more tolerable for Sodom and Gomorrha in the day of judgment, than for that city." This will be a comfort when that day comes, that any have been worse than they in sinning, and suffer more grievously for their sins. When the Jews in Babylon saw those of Jerusalem brought into the same condition with themselves, to be captives, it eased their hearts. When men suffer alone, it stings. In a storm at sea, if one man be shipwrecked, that afflicts more deeply; but if there be fellows, and those suffering more hard things, it eases in some measure. It will be an ease to thousands at the last day, when they shall see the children of the kingdom cast out into utter darkness, that their sins and punishments exceeded theirs.

Obs. 4. God's blessings, and abundance of creature-comforts, through the corruption that is in man, swells them with pride. Jerusalem had variety of mercies, peace and plenty, and she was puffed up. "In the day of thy pride." Prosperity makes proud, and fills with windy conceits of happiness, and continuance in that happiness. Prov. xviii. 11, "The rich man's wealth is his strong city, and as an high wall in his own conceit;" he thinks himself fenced and guarded so strongly, that he is secure, and despises dangers. Ezek. xxviii. 5, speaking of the prince of Tyrus, the prophet saith, "By thy great wisdom and by thy traffic hast thou increased thy riches, and thine heart is lifted up because of thy riches."

It is a hard matter for men of high estates not to have high minds; therefore Paul counsels Timothy to "charge them that are rich in this world, that they be not highminded," 1 Tim. vi. 17. I have lately spoken of this subject; it was Sodom's sin, Jerusalem's sin; and I shall not insist upon it.

Obs. 5. Proud persons mind not God's dealings with others, though like themselves. Sodom's sin was pride, haughtiness, and for these sins she and her daughters were destroyed with fire from heaven; but Jerusalem in her pride forgets Sodom, and never once names her; "thy sister Sodom was not mentioned by thy mouth." She should have considered God's severity against Sodom for her sins, and seen to it that they had not been found in herself; but plenty bred pride, pride blinded, and made her forgetful of that example of divine vengeance. It was near unto them; the place where Sodom stood was a sulphureous lake, a lively monument of Heaven's displeasure against pride and other sins, Lot's wife turned into a pillar of salt, to season them with fear, yet they took no notice of these things; Isa. v. 12, "They regard not the work of the Lord, neither consider the operation of his hands."

Obs. 6. The Lord expects that we should take notice of and improve his judgments upon others. He blames Jerusalem here for not minding Sodom's condition; "thy sister Sodom was not mentioned." God dealt so severely with Sodom, Gomorrah, and the other cities, that all who should hear thereof might be instructed, and fear to offend that God which can at his pleasure rain fire and brimstone. Though judgments were executed long before, yet the Lord would not have men forget them, but keep them fresh in memory, and advantage themselves by them. Jer. vii. 12, "Go to my place which was in Shiloh, where I set my name at the first, and see what I did to it for the wickedness of my people." They had forgotten the judgment of Hophni and Phinehas, and the ark, and therefore he minds them of it. In 1 Sam. iv. 11; Psal. lxxviii. 60; Jer. xxvi. 6, he mentions it unto them.

There are no judgments of God in the world or Scripture, but men ought to mind them, and make use of them. The drowning of the old world, confusion of Babel, seven years' famine in Canaan and Egypt, the ten plagues of Egypt, the fiery serpents in the wilderness, earth opening her mouth and swallowing up Korah, Dathan, and Abiram; the men of Bethshemesh, Sennacherib's army, Jezebel, Ahab and his sons, Baal's priests, Athaliah, Ananias and Sapphira, &c.; these and many others ought to be thought upon to awake our secure spirits, to breed and maintain fear in us, to provoke us to repentance for what is past, and more exact walking for time to come. Luke xvii. 32, "Remember Lot's wife." And 2 Pet. ii. 6, God hath made Sodom and Gomorrah ensamples to "those that after should live ungodly." There is much in the words "that after should live:" what! hath God turned those cities into ashes, set them up as burning beacons, to warn all in the world that they live not ungodly? and shall their very sins be found in cities and families? will any dare to do such things as draw down such judgments? Surely none will; if they do, they must suffer such things for their sins, and hotter fire, yea, more scalding brimstone, because they took not warning by these examples.

Ver. 57, 58. *Before thy wickedness was discovered, as at the time of thy reproach of the daughters of Syria, and all that are round about her, the daughters of the Philistines, which despise thee round about. Thou hast borne thy lewdness and thine abominations, saith the Lord.*

The prophets had told Jerusalem of her wickedness, but she would take no notice of it; much like strumpets, who though they be the common talk of the world for wickedness, yet because they enjoy their lovers, have pleasure and prosperity, mind not their sin or shame; but when some stroke of God is upon them, then their wickedness appears wickedness indeed, however they think of themselves. The 57th verse sets out Jerusalem's pertinacy and stubbornness.

"Of thy reproach of the daughters of Syria." Hebrew is, of the reproach of the daughters of Aram. Aram was one of the sons of Shem, Gen. x. 22, from whom the Aramites descended, who peopled many places, which therefore are mentioned with distinction: Gen. xxviii. 2, "Padan-aram." 2 Sam. x. 6, "The Syrians of Beth-rehob, and the Syrians of Zoba:" the original is, the Aramites of Beth-rehob, and the Aramites of Zoba. "Aram-naharaim," Psal. lx. title; that is, Aram which was between two rivers, called Mesopotamia, Gen. xxiv. 10. So Aram-maachah, 1 Chron. xix. 6, "Syria-maachah;" the original is, Aram-maachah; and 2 Sam. viii. 5, Aram-dammeseck, which in our translation is, "the Syrians of Damascus." The Septuagint renders the word Aram, Syria constantly, as Mizraim, Egypt, and Cush, Ethiopia; and under the name of Syrians were included also the Mesopotamians, Chaldeans, and Assyrians, as Pliny testifies in the fifth book of his Natural History.

Some refer this time to the days of Ahaz, who was exceedingly wicked. In his reign Rezin king of Syria, 2 Kings xvi. 6, the Edomites and Philistines, invaded the land, and brought Judah low; and Tilgath-pilneser, king of Assyria, whom he sent for to help him, distressed him, 2 Chron. xxviii. 17—21, and helped him not, though he gave him the gold and silver of the temple, a portion of his own, and of the princes. This was a great reproach, that they were impoverished, disappointed, and spoiled; and in the time of this distress did Ahaz trespass yet more against the Lord.

This did Jerusalem no good, but she sinned more, and so her wickedness was discovered, both former and present. Or thus you may take the sense: Before thy wickedness was discovered by my sending the Syrians and Philistines upon thee, thou didst never take notice of my proceedings with Sodom and her daughters.

"Which despise thee." Hebrew is, השאטות from שוט or שט a Chaldee word, which signifies to despise, contemn, disgrace, as also to spoil; or from שאט, to prick as with a thorn, and so are either spoilings or despisings, they are as thorns in the sides of those that are spoiled or despised.

Ver. 58. "Thou hast borne thy lewdness." By lewdness here is meant, the punishment of lewdness. In ver. 52, he saith, "bear thy shame;" here, "thou hast borne thy lewdness." She had had a part of her punishment, not all, more was behind than she had received. The Hebrew word for "thou hast borne" is rendered diversely; by some in the future, thou shalt bear; by some in the imperative, bear thou. The context seems to me to call for one of these, either, bear thou thy lewdness; or, thou shalt bear it. The learned do observe, and say, that in the Hebrew tongue oft the preter tense is put for the future, and so it is most suitable here; God was bringing of judgments upon her, and saith in the next verse, "I will deal with thee as thou hast done."

Obs. 1. That wickedness is a close and covert thing, it walks masked, and in the dark. "Before thy wickedness was discovered." Jerusalem's wickedness lay hid: chap. viii. 12, "Son of man, hast thou seen what the ancients of the house of Israel do in the dark, every man in the chambers of his imagery?" Sin loves corners and chambers; they that were the chief men in public, were the chief sinners in secret: Isa. xxix. 15, they "seek deep to hide their counsel from the Lord, and their works are in the dark;" they would neither be seen of men or God: Job xxiv. 15—17, "The eye of the adulterer waiteth for the twilight, saying, No eye shall see me: and disguiseth his face. In the dark they dig through houses, which they had marked for themselves in the day time: they know not the light. For the morning is to them even as the shadow of death," they are afraid of being discovered.

Men whose deeds are evil hate the light, John iii. 20. Wickedness is a night-bird, and loves darkness, veiling, muffling, secrecy: wicked ones take secret counsel, Psal. lxiv. 2; and privily lay snares, ver. 5; and secretly murder the innocent, Psal. x. 8; and slander their neighbours, Psal. ci. 5. Paul tells you it is a shame to speak of those things which are done in secret, Eph. v. 12. The greatest mischiefs, treasons, rebellions, murders are hatched in the dark, and covered over with the fairest pretences: wickedness hath a black and ugly face, which if seen, would affrighten men; she therefore appears covered and disguised.

Obs. 2. Wickedness shall not always be veiled and hid. God will reveal and make known the wickedness of men, cities, states, and kingdoms, he will pluck the vizard from their faces, and discover them to the world, how closely soever their sin was contrived and acted. David sinned closely and cunningly, 2 Sam. ii. 12, but God discovered it. The Israelites did secretly those things that were not right against the Lord their God, 2 Kings xvii. 9, and God made them known. Sinful thoughts, counsels, affections, words, actions, gestures have been discovered, Psal. l. 21; Nahum i. 11; James iv. 4; Mal. iii. 15; 1 Kings xxi. 19; Prov. vi. 13. Christ told you long since, "there is nothing covered that shall not be revealed; and hid that shall not be known," Matt. x. 26; and before Christ's time, Solomon left it upon record, Eccles. xii. 14, that "God shall bring every work into judgment, with every secret thing, whether it be good, or whether it be evil."

Let us judge ourselves thoroughly for wickedness committed, that so it may be hid, and take heed for the future that we do evil no more, lest it be discovered to our shame and confusion. You may remember what discoveries God hath made of treasons, murders, plots, and mischiefs in our days; things have been brought to light that lay in deep darkness, and men have wondered at the discoveries: Job xii. 22, "He discovereth deep things out of darkness."

Obs. 3. Times of trouble are times of discovery; when great afflictions are upon sinners, then their wickedness is made known. When the Syrians and Philistines came against Jerusalem and her territories, spoiled and plundered them sorely, then her wickedness appeared: "Before thy wickedness was discovered, as at the time of thy reproach," &c. Somewhat her wickedness was seen before, but not so fully, so greatly, as then. When cities and states have peace, prosperity, they dissemble and cloak their wickedness, and many that know things, are afraid to speak out; but when God's hand is heavy, by war, plague, or other sad judgments, then men will speak freely, and judge of the sins by the punishments: What grievous punishments! there were grievous sins. When Sodom's judgment was so dreadful, it was a proclamation to the world that her sins were answerable. When winter comes, the birds' nests are seen that were hid before; and so, when the winter of affliction comes, the nests of wickedness do appear. When the leprosy clave to Gehazi, it discovered his covetousness, 2 Kings v. 26, 27. Have not the troubles of England discovered the wickedness of England? I believe England never appeared abroad or at home more ulcerous, black, and loathsome, than now.

Obs. 4. Times of warring, plundering, spoiling, are times of reproach. When the Syrians and Philistines warred against the Jews, took Elath, 2 Kings xvi. 6, Beth-shemesh, Ajalon, Gederoth, Shocho, Timnah, Gimzo, with the villages thereof, 2 Chron. xxviii. 18, this was a time of reproach. "As at the time of thy reproach." It was a reproach to have strangers come armed and invade their land, to beat their men of war, to carry away their wealth, to conquer and keep their towns and cities.

Obs. 5. When people are unfaithful with God, and fall to base ways, and unwarrantable courses, it is just with God to leave them to be contemned and despised of all about them.

Jerusalem was not faithful to her God and Husband, but fell to foul courses, dealt unjustly with God and man; and what then? the daughters of the Philistines despised her round about. Those that honour God he will honour, but those that despise him shall be lightly esteemed, 1 Sam. ii. 30.

Jerusalem despised the holy things of God; Ezek. xxii. 8, "Thou hast despised mine holy things;" therefore the Lord caused her to be despised; and so he will any that turn from him after lying vanities. Job xii. 21, "He poureth contempt upon princes;" Psal. cvii. 40, "And causeth them to wander in the wilderness, where there is no way."

Ver. 59. ***For thus saith the Lord God; I will even deal with thee as thou hast done, which hast despised the oath in breaking the covenant.***

This verse is the conclusion of the fifth part of the chapter, which was a declaration of threatening, and contains the sum of all those judgments fore-mentioned. The parts of it are these:

I. A judicial sentence, "I will even deal," &c.

II. The cause of God's so dealing, which is, "despising the oath, and breaking the covenant."

III. The ratification of this judicial sentence, "Thus saith the Lord."

"I will even deal with thee as thou hast done." Septuagint is, I will do in thee as thou hast done. The Hebrew is, with thee. Thou hast broken the covenant thou madest with me, promising to worship, honour, and obey me, and I will not keep it, who promised to counsel, comfort, and protect thee. Because I entered into covenant with Abraham and your fathers at mount Sinai, you think that whatsoever you do, howsoever you provoke me by your ingratitude, disobedience, idolatries, and apostasies, yet that I am bound by covenant and promise to you, and that there must be performance on my part however things are on your part. But you are deceived; seeing you have first broken with me, I am free, and shall render to you according to your merits; you have sinned excessively, and I will punish you answerably; neither have you cause to blame or censure me as being unfaithful and false, whenas you yourselves are perfidious and covenant-breakers.

"Which hast despised the oath." Hebrew is, בזית which is from בוז or בזה to contemn, despise, disdain: and Avenarius makes it to have affinity with בוס to tread under foot, because we tread upon things despised. The Septuagint is, ὡς ἠτίμωσας, as thou hast dishonoured, disgraced the oath.

"The oath." Hebrew is, אלה which signifies, not simply an oath, but an oath with execration, or cursing: it is such an oath as ties a man to keep promise or covenant, *cum imprecatione mali*, if he do not, and differs from שבועה which is an oath without imprecation of evil, as you have it, Neh. vi. 18; Deut. vii. 8; Psal. cv. 9. But אלה notes swearing with a wishing of evil, as that a man perish, be annihilated, suffer some grievous thing, if he do not perform what he swears: Numb. v. 21, it is called an oath of cursing; and Jer. xliv. 12, "They shall be לאלה for an execration or a curse;" so the verb is used, Judg. xvii. 2; Hos. x. 4; 2 Chron. vi. 22; and when they did swear, it is said, Neh. x. 29, they "entered into a curse," באלה and sometimes the curse was expressed, as 1 Sam. xiv. 44, saith Saul, when Jonathan had tasted the honey, "God do so and more also." His meaning is this; I have cursed the man that shall eat any food this day before evening; and seeing thou hast transgressed, God do so to me and more, let me be accursed, let me die the death, if thou die not. The like to this is that of Jezebel, 1 Kings xix. 2, "So let the gods do to me, and more also, if I make not thy life as the life of one of them by to-morrow about this time;" so chap. xx. 10. Sometimes it was implied, as Gen. xiv. 22, 23, "I have lift up mine hand unto the Lord, that I will not take from a thread even to a shoe-latchet, and that I will not take any thing that is thine." Now it is implied here, if I do, let the Lord do so and so by me. Psal. xcv. 11, "Unto whom I sware in my wrath that they should not enter into my rest;" so it runs in the Hebrew: here is a part of the oath concealed, implied, and not expressed, as thus, If they enter into my rest, let not me live, or let not me be God any longer.

The Septuagint renders אלה by ἀρὰ and κάταρα, malediction and execration: they wished themselves accursed and execrable, if they did not perform what they had sworn. It is the judgment of some, that the curses mentioned in Deut. xxvii. by which the law was established, and unto which they said Amen, are here meant; and doubtless they are, for there curses are pronounced against idolatry, bribery, murder, and other sins; yea, against every man that should not confirm all the words of the law to do them. Now, they did not observe them, but violate them all in a grievous manner, and so despised the oath, that is, the execrations and curses which are called "the curses of the covenant," Deut. xxix. 21.

"In breaking the covenant." God entered into a covenant with his people, ver. 8, and they joined in covenant with him. Exod. xxiv. 7, Moses "took the book of the covenant, and read in the audience of the people: and they said, All that the Lord hath said will we do, and be obedient:" here was a solemn engagement. Deut. xxvi. 17, 18, "Thou hast avouched the Lord this day to be thy God, and to walk in his ways: and the Lord hath avouched thee this day to be his peculiar people:" here was a mutual avouching and owning one another. And Deut. xxix. 12, the people are said to "enter into covenant with the Lord, and into his oath," which he made with them. This covenant they brake.

The Hebrew word is, להפר from פור to break; which in Hiphil. is, to weaken, make void, abrogate. Psal. xxxiii. 10, "The Lord bringeth the counsel of the heathen to nought," הפיר he makes them frustrate; *διασκεδαζει*, Septuagint, He scattered and dashed in pieces their counsels. Here in Ezekiel the Septuagint is, *παραβῆναι*, to violate, or transgress. When any thing material is done contrary to agreement, that is a breaking of covenant.

There are some things set down in the word more particularly, which are violations of the covenant; as not circumcising their males, Gen. xvii. 14; idolatry, Deut. xvii. 2, 3; Josh. xxiii. 16; making a league with the inhabitants of Canaan, Judg. ii. 2, 20; bringing the uncircumcised into the sanctuary, who polluted the worship and ordinances, Ezek. xliv. 7; and the general was, the not observing all things which God had commanded them in the law, Lev. xxvi. 15, 16: if they did not all his commandments, they brake covenant.

This breaking of covenant is set out in the word by several expressions. Sometimes it is called, not continuing in the covenant; as Heb. viii. 9, "They continued not in my covenant:" sometimes unstedfastness in it; Psal. lxxviii. 37, they were "not steadfast in his covenant:" sometimes forgetting of it; Deut. iv. 23, "Take heed, lest ye forget the covenant" sometimes, yea oft, forsaking of it; as Deut. xxix. 25; Jer. xxii. 9; 1 Kings xix. 10, 14; and transgressing it, Hos. vi. 7; Judg. ii. 20; 2 Kings xviii. 12.

Quest. The Scripture saith, that God is a God which keeps covenant, Nehem. ix. 32; yea, faithful in keeping covenant, Deut. vii. 9, and God saith, he will not suffer his faithfulness to fail, nor break his covenant, nor alter the thing gone out of his lips, Psal. lxxxix. 33, 34: how doth the Lord then say here, "I will deal with thee as thou hast done?" Is not he bound up by his faithfulness and promise to do them good though they fail? according to that in 2 Tim. ii. 13, "If we believe not, yet he abideth faithful: he cannot deny himself."

Answ. 1. If the covenant were made upon conditions, and those not observed, no imputation could be laid upon the Lord if he perform not what was his part. The covenant you may see how it runs in several places; Deut. vii. 9, "The Lord thy God, he is God, the faithful God, which keepeth covenant and mercy with them that love him and keep his commandments to a thousand generations; and repayeth them that hate him to their face, to destroy them." All the blessings and cursings, Deut. xxviii. depend upon obedience and disobedience, keeping and breaking covenant, so that the Lord is free to punish if man perform not: Lev. xxvi. 15—17, "If ye will not do all my commandments, but break my covenant, I also will do this unto you; I will even appoint over you terror, consumption, and the burning ague. I will set my face against you, and ye shall be slain before your enemies: they that hate you shall reign over you; and ye shall flee when none pursueth:" so Deut. xxxi. 16, 17, "They will forsake me, and break my covenant. Then my anger shall be kindled against them in that day, and I will forsake them, and I will hide my face from them, and they shall be devoured, and many evils and troubles shall befall them."

2. Though God afflicted them very sorely, and cut off the body of this people by severe judgments, yet he reserved some, continued his faithfulness, kept covenant with them, and manifested his loving-kindness unto them, according to that written, Psal. lxxxix. 28—34. God owned them in Babylon for his people, and dealt like a God in covenant with them there: Ezek. xxxvii. 12, "O my people, I will open your graves, and cause you to come up out of your graves, and bring you into the land of Israel."

Obs. 1. The tie of a covenant between God and man is a strong tie, it hath the nature of an oath, and an oath is the strongest tie of all. "Thou hast despised the oath in breaking the covenant;" that strong tie of an oath wherewith thou wast bound to me thou hast broken.

God promised unto Abraham to give him and his seed the land of Canaan, Gen. xii. 7; xiii. 15. Chap. xv. 18, it is said, God "made a covenant with Abraham, saying, Unto thy seed have I given this land." Now this promise and covenant is called an oath; Gen. xxvi. 3, "I will perform the oath which I swear unto Abraham thy father;" Deut. xxxiv. 4, "This is the land which I sware unto Abraham, unto Isaac, and unto Jacob."

The covenant also which God made with them at mount Sinai is called an oath, Dan. ix. 11. It is so called because of the bindingness of it: a man that enters into covenant with God, is bound as much as if he had taken the most solemn oath. Acts xxiii. 12, they "bound themselves under a curse," or with an oath of execration; as was at the giving out of the law, and making the covenant, Deut. xi. 26—28: they agreed to it, that if they did not do what God commanded, what they covenanted, that the curse should come upon them, Deut. xxvii. when they said "Amen" to the curses; so that there was a strong obligation upon them: hence you have that expression, Ezek. xx. 37, "The bond of the covenant." A wife is not tied more strongly to her husband by the bond of marriage, than a people is unto God by the bond of that covenant they make with him.

God would bring them under the bond of the covenant by those judgments and curses he would pour out upon them, and make them acknowledge him for their God and King, as they did, Dan. ix. 10, 11, We obeyed not the "voice of the Lord our God, to walk in the laws, which he set before us by his servants the prophets. Yea, all Israel have transgressed thy law: therefore the curse is poured upon us, and the oath that is written in the law of Moses."

Obs. 2. Such is the corruption of man, that it violates, frustrates, and makes void the strongest obligations. They brake the covenant, which was a sacred bond, and had the strength of an oath, and bound them under penalty of being cursed. God had set life and death before them, good and evil, Deut. xxx. 15; blessing and cursing, Deut. xi. 26; he had hedged them about with promises, with threats, bound them in a covenant and oath; yet all would not do, such strong bands held them not in, they brake all. God had broken the bands of captivity, Lev. xxvi. 13, and bound them with cords of love, and looked they should have kept close to him; but, Jer. ii. 20, "Of old time I broke thy yoke, burst thy bands; and thou saidst, I will not transgress; when upon every high hill and under every green tree thou wanderest, playing the harlot."

God brake the Egyptian yoke and bonds by a mighty power, and freed them, and they brake his yoke, his bonds, by the mighty power of their corruption, and would rather be in bondage to sin, than in covenant with him; neither was it here and there a man that did so, but it was the body of the people: therefore, Jer. xi. 10, "The house of Israel and the house of Judah have broken my covenant which I made with their fathers;" all Israel and all Judah have done it. Lest God should mistake, he would make trial of those he thought were most likely to have kept his covenant: Jer. v. 5, "I will get me unto the great men, and will speak unto them; for they have known the way of the Lord, and the judgment of their God;" they are in places of authority and honour, and resemble me; they have understanding, knowledge, and time to consider of the covenant, the engagements they are in, the benefits of keeping and evils of breaking it; "but these have altogether broken the yoke, and burst the bonds:" notwithstanding their breeding, the means of knowledge, and many mercies they had above others, and such strong ties to have kept them in bonds; yet they have not regarded me, my commands, threatenings, covenant, or curses. Man's corruption is violent, and will violate all engagements and relations.

Obs. 3. Breaking of the covenant by sinning against God, is a slighting and despising of the threats and curses of God. "Thou hast despised the oath in breaking the covenant."

God hath threatened all sin with woes and curses: see Lev. xxvi. and Deut. xxviii. "Cursed is every one that continueth not in all things which are written in the book of the law to do them," Gal. iii. 10; and, "The wrath of God is revealed from heaven against all ungodliness and unrighteousness of men," Rom. i. 18.

Now if men did not slight and despise threatening, wrath, curses, they would not dare to sin, and break covenant with God: they think words are but wind, that threatenings are but scarecrows, having no great matter in them, or, if they have, they will not suddenly come; as Ezek. xii. when the Lord threatened destruction to the prince, people, cities, and the whole land, they slighted all, and said, "The days are prolonged, and every vision faileth," ver. 22; yea, "the vision is for many days to come," ver. 27; and so went on in their sinful ways, and despised the truths of God.

When a man reproacheth and slanders another privily, he despiseth that branch of the oath, "Cursed be he that smiteth his neighbour secretly."

When children set light by their parents, they despise that part of it, "Cursed be he that setteth light by his father or his mother."

When men take bribes, or reward, to pervert justice, they despise that clause of the oath, "Cursed is he that taketh reward to slay an innocent person;" and so of the rest, Deut. xxvii.

Now what presumption and boldness is it in men to despise the oath, break the covenant, of God, presume they shall do well enough though they sin, and continue in sinful ways: Lev. xxvi. 15, "If ye shall despise my statutes, or if your soul abhor my judgments, so that ye will not do all my commandments, but that ye break my covenant;" I will do so and so by you.

Despising of the law is a despising of God, judging both to be little worth. Shall the infinite, wise, great, and glorious God magnify his law, and make it honourable, Isa. xlii. 1; yea, magnify it above all his name, Psal. cxxxviii. 2; and shall sorry, sinful, foolish man slight, contemn the same? shall he despise the oath, and break the covenant?

Obs. 4. See here the admirable justice of God. "I will deal with thee as thou hast done;" thou shalt be judge thyself; is it not equal to do like for like? "Thou hast despised the oath," I will despise thee; thou hast broken the covenant unjustly to sin against me, I will break it justly to punish thee. Marvel not at that expression of God's breaking the covenant; you have in the word that which is equivalent to it, Numb. xiv. 34, "Ye shall know my breach of promise." God had promised them, sworn to them, that they should enter into Canaan; but they brought up an ill report concerning that land, murmured against God, who thereupon told them they should not come into that land, but wander forty years in the wilderness, till their carcasses were wasted, and so they should know his breach of promise. Had they made good their promise, he would have made good his promise, but because they brake with him in sinning, he brake with them in punishing, and so here was exact justice; as in our prophet's words also, they brake covenant, and despised the oath, and so made God and his ways contemptible; whereupon God breaks with them, and makes them and their ways despicable: Jer. xxii. 28, "Coniah, a despised broken idol." Lam. i. 8, speaking of Jerusalem, he saith, "All that honoured her despise her;" she was a derision, chap. iii. 14; a reproach, Ezek. v. 14; they said, "Sing us one of the songs of Zion," Psal. cxxxvii. 3; a hissing, Jer. xix. 8; "All that pass by clap their hands at her, hiss, and wag their heads," Lam. ii. 15; a curse, Jer. xliv. 12. They despised the curse God made them.

Obs. 5. Breach of covenant is so provoking a sin as God will certainly punish. "Thus saith the Lord God; I will even deal with thee;" thou hast broken the covenant, and I will not put it up at thy hands. The Lord appeared in a judiciary way, and gave out a judicial sentence, ratifying it with "Thus saith the Lord God:" he is a God of truth and power, and will undoubtedly punish the breach of covenant. God is infinitely beyond all creatures: "The nations" to him "are as a drop of a bucket, the small dust of the balance," Isa. xl. 15; yea, "all nations before him are as nothing, less than nothing, and vanity," ver. 17. What was this nation of the Jews, then, for the great God to mind, and so far to mind, affect, as to take to be his people, to enter into covenant withal, to counsel, comfort, protect, prosper, and exalt with privileges above all the nations in the world? It was no better nor bigger than other nations, but it pleased God to bestow himself and his love upon this people, and to join in covenant with them, the highest favour a people could have; but what did they? they brake covenant with God, left him, the fountain of life, love, mercy, and of all good, fell to other gods, other worship, and went a whoring after the sight of their eyes, the inventions of the nations, and imaginations of their own hearts. This provoked God greatly, and made him say, "Be astonished, O ye heavens, at this, and be horribly afraid, be ye very desolate. For my people have committed two evils; they have forsaken me the fountain of living waters, and have hewed them out cisterns, broken cisterns, that can hold no water," Jer. ii. 12, 13. They violated the covenant, and God would visit for it: Josh. xxiii. 16, "When ye have transgressed the covenant of the Lord your God, which he commanded you; then shall the anger of the Lord be kindled against you, and ye shall perish quickly from off the good land which he hath given unto you." God will make quick work with them: Hos. viii. 1, "He shall come as an eagle against the house of the Lord, because they have transgressed my covenant." Eagles fly swiftly; the eagle was the king of Assyria, who hastened to their destruction. Needs must breach of covenant provoke sorely, when it causeth God to pronounce a curse upon the man that shall do it: Jer. xi. 3, "Thus saith the Lord God of Israel; Cursed be the man that obeyeth not the words of this covenant."

A curse is a consuming thing. Persons, towns, cities, nations consume away, because the curse of God is upon them for breaking covenant with him: Isa. xxiv. 5, 6, "The earth is defiled under the inhabitants thereof; because they have transgressed the laws, changed the ordinance, broken the everlasting covenant. Therefore hath the curse devoured the earth, and they that dwell therein are desolate." One place more; Lev. xxvi. 25, "I will bring a sword upon you, that shall avenge the quarrel of my covenant: and when ye are gathered together within your cities, I will send the pestilence among you; and ye shall be delivered into the hand of the enemy." When the covenant is broken, it hath a quarrel with man, pleads against him, calls for vengeance: the original is, נקם ברית the vengeance of the covenant. As there is much mercy in the covenant if it be kept, so there is much vengeance if it be broken; all the woes and curses mentioned in the book of the law are the vengeance of the covenant; therefore, when the Lord told them by Huldah what he would do for the breach of covenant, he said, "Behold, I will bring evil upon this place, and upon the inhabitants thereof, even all the curses that are written in the book which they have read before the king of Judah," 2 Chron. xxxiv. 24.

Ver. 60—63. *Nevertheless I will remember my covenant with thee in the days of thy youth, and I will establish unto thee an everlasting covenant. Then thou shalt remember thy ways, and be ashamed, when thou shalt receive thy sisters, thine elder and thy younger: and I will give them unto thee for daughters, but not by thy covenant. And I will establish my covenant with thee; and thou shalt know that I am the Lord: that thou mayest remember, and be confounded, and never open thy mouth any more because of thy shame, when I am pacified toward thee for all that thou hast done, saith the Lord God.*

We are now come to the sixth and last part of the chapter, which is evangelical, and contains promises of mercy and comfort. Formerly, the prophet had thundered out the threats of God against the multitude and wicked ones; here, he brings forth cordials to refresh the sad hearts and drooping spirits of the saints who were amongst them.

In the words are held out,

I. Mention of a covenant made, and the time of it, "My covenant with thee in the days of thy youth."

II. A double promise.

I. Of remembering that covenant.

2. Of establishing an everlasting covenant, ver. 60, 62.

III. The benefits of the covenant, or effects thereof; which are,

1. Evangelical repentance; ver. 61, "Then thou shalt remember thy ways, and be ashamed;" ver. 63, "That thou mayest remember," &c.

2. Reception of her sisters to mercy, the incorporation of Jews and gentiles into one body, which is done by way of gift and free grace; "I will give them unto thee, but not by thy covenant."

3. Acknowledgment of the Lord; ver. 62, "And thou shalt know that I am the Lord."

4. Patient submission unto the hand of God; ver. 63, "And never open thy mouth any more."

5. Propitiation or pacification; "When I am pacified toward thee."

Ver. 60. "Nevertheless I will remember my covenant with thee." God properly doth neither remember nor forget; they are human acts: remembrance is an act of the understanding, recollecting the species of things forgotten; and forgetfulness is a separation between the understanding and the species of things, not always an abolition: in these senses neither the one nor the other doth befall God. He is said to remember, when he doth that which demonstrates he hath regard to us; and so, to remember his covenant when he deals with us according to the grace and mercy comprehended in it: Psal. cxv. 12, "The Lord hath been mindful of us: he will bless us:" his blessing is evidence of his mindfulness: Psal. cxxxvi. 23, "Who remembered us in our low estate;" God did that which convinced them that he was mindful of them: so Psal. xcviii. 2, 3, "The Lord hath made known his salvation: his righteousness hath he openly showed. He hath remembered his mercy and truth."

God is said to remember in regard of us, not of himself, Chrysostom, Homily 27, in Genesis, because he makes us to know and remember. When he doth such things as are tokens that he is mindful of his covenant; as when God punisheth, lays his hand heavy upon people; he remembers them and their iniquities: and thus Maldonate carries it here, I will remember my covenant; that is, saith he, I will punish you; for punishments are part of the covenant as well as promises. But although he be right in this, that when God punishes, he remembers men, and makes them remember him, yet he is alone with all interpreters I meet with, in putting that sense here upon the words. They all take them to be meant of a gracious remembrance of his covenant; I will remember my covenant; I showed thee much kindness then, and I will again show thee kindness.

"My covenant." I spake largely of the word *berith*, whence it was derived, and of the nature of a covenant, in ver. 8. He saith here, not the covenant, but "my covenant;" he was principal in it, he sware and entered into covenant with them.

"In the days of thy youth." When thou wast in Abraham's family and loins, or when thou wast brought out of Egypt, and wanderedst in the wilderness at mount Sinai, I made a covenant with thee, being newly come out of the house of bondage.

"I will establish." Hebrew is, הקימותי I will confirm. You have the same word, Isa. xxix. 3, and it is translated, "I will raise forts against thee." Septuagint is, ἀναστήσω, you have broken, nulled the covenant what lies in you, but I will raise it up again, and put life and power into it, make it firm and stable.

"An everlasting covenant." Hebrew is, ברית עולם Septuagint, διαθήκην αἰώνιον, an eternal testament. What covenant this was is to be opened. When this people had so grievously sinned, as to be in a great part ruined, and the rest sent into captivity, to outward view God seemed to have no people; the promise made to Abraham, Isaac, and Jacob, that in their seed all the nations of the earth should be blessed, seemed to be void, and the covenant made between God and them at mount Sinai wholly dissolved; but however things appeared, it was otherwise; God minded his covenant, and would establish it with the remnant of them, and make additions of more grace and mercy to it; before, he gave them the law in tables of stone; now, he would write it in their hearts, and give them power to keep it. In Jer. xxxi. 31—34, you have the covenant set down which our prophet here means, and it is called a "new covenant," because of the new addition and new administrations; not that the substance of it is altered; it is the same law which is written in the hearts of those God makes his covenant with as was written in the tables of stone. It is again mentioned in Heb. viii. 10—12. That covenant at mount Sinai some make to be mixed partly of works, and partly of grace; some looked for life and justification by it, but therein it was faulty and weak: see Rom. ix. 31, 32; Gal. iii. 21; Rom. iii. 20; chap. viii. 3: and so far as it comprehended aught of the covenant of works, it was antiquated, and more grace added, Christ and the gospel brought in more clearly and fully.

Obs. 1. Although God's people sin greatly, break covenant with him, meet with sad judgments, yet he will spare some of them, and show mercy to them. Jerusalem had grievously sinned, despised the oath, broken covenant, deserved as ill at God's hands as could be; but what saith God? "Nevertheless I will," &c. However the people of God sin, however he deal with them for a season, yet he will not altogether take mercy from them. Judg. ii. 13, "They forsook the Lord and served Baal and Ashtaroth; whereupon God sold them into the hands of their enemies round about: God was against them for evil, and they were greatly distressed." Ver. 16, "Nevertheless the Lord raised up judges, which dedelivered them out of the hand of their spoilers." Psal. cvi. 7, 8, "They understood not the works of God in Egypt, nor remembered the multitude of his mercies, but provoked him at the sea, even at the Red sea. Nevertheless he saved them for his name's sake." Psal. lxxxix. 31—33, "If they break my statutes, and keep not my commandments; I will visit their transgression with the rod, and their iniquity with stripes. Nevertheless my loving-kindness will I not utterly take from you." Isa. lvii. 17, 18, "For the iniquity of his covetousness was I wroth, and smote him: I hid me, and was wroth, and he went on frowardly in the way of his heart." This was bad enough; and, though God hid himself, yet he saw what he did: "I have seen his ways," cross, perverse, provoking; "nevertheless I will heal him also, and restore comforts unto him."

This sets out the glory and greatness of divine mercy. Are a people rich in sinning? God is rich in mercy; are their sins great? his mercies are greater; are their sins old? his mercies are from everlasting. Let not sour, hard, sinking thoughts lodge in our breasts, whatever our sins have been. Psalm cxlvii. 11, "The Lord hath pleasure in those that hope in his mercy."

Obs. 2. However men forget their promises, covenants, yea, break them; yet God will not forget his promises, his covenant. "I will remember my covenant." Though man had a strict charge not to forget the covenant, Deut. iv. 23, "Take heed unto yourselves, lest ye forget the covenant of the Lord your God," yet he forgot it: yet God doth not so, he is a God who forgets not covenant, ver. 31; he is mindful of it, Psal. cxi. 5; he keeps covenant, 2 Chron. vi. 14; he remembers it for ever, Psal. cv. 8. Men are deceitful, lying, vain things; Psal. lxii. 9, "Surely men of low degree are vanity, and men of high degree are a lie;" but God is real, faithful, and true: hence it is said, Deut. vii. 9, "The faithful God, which keepeth covenant;" Titus i. 2, "God, that cannot lie, promised;" and 2 Tim. ii. 13, "If we believe not, yet he abideth faithful; he cannot deny himself." However the creature prove, God doth things upon the account of his faithfulness: 1 Thess. v. 24, "Faithful is he that calleth you, who also will do it."

Solomon justifies God in this point of his faithfulness observably: 1 Kings viii. 56, "Blessed be the Lord, which hath given rest unto his people Israel, according to all that he promised: there hath not failed one word of all his good promise which he promised by the hand of Moses his servant. So, in Josh. xxiii. 14, saith he, "I am going the way of all the earth: and ye know in all your hearts and in all your souls, that not one thing hath failed of all the good things which the Lord your God spake concerning you; all are come to pass unto you."

Therefore doubting of God's performance is a great sin; to distrust him who cannot fail us or deceive us is intolerable. We apprehend it so through weakness of grace and strength of corruption: Psal. lxxxix. 39, "Thou hast made void the covenant of thy servant;" because things went ill, the church was sorely afflicted, and many suffered hard things, he thought so. God had told David a little before, that he would not suffer his faithfulness to fail. Psal. lxxvii. 8, saith Asaph, "Is his mercy clean gone? doth his promise fail for evermore?"

Let us trust in the Lord for ever, and trust perfectly; he is a God of truth, remembers his covenant: Psal. cxlvi. 5, "Happy is he whose hope is in the Lord," &c.

It should be encouragement to prayer. Psal. lxxxix. 49, "Lord, where are thy former loving-kindnesses, which thou swarest unto David in thy truth?" Psal. lxxiv. 20, "Have respect unto the covenant: for the dark places of the earth are full of the habitations of cruelty:" the covenant with Abraham, Isaac, &c. Abraham is father of all the faithful now; and we may press God with the covenant, as David, "for the dark places of the earth are full of the habitations of cruelty."

Obs. 3. Mercies come from God to a people through the covenant, or for the covenant's sake. Had not the Lord been in covenant with this people, he would have minded them no more than other nations; but because he had made a covenant with them in the days of their youth, therefore he would show mercy, do for them: 2 Kings xiii. 23, "The Lord was gracious unto them, and had respect unto them, and compassion on them, because of his covenant with Abraham, Isaac, and Jacob." Though they were very wicked, murmuring, provoked God many ways, yet, for his covenant sake, he did show them kindness. Psal. cv. 9, he gave them quails, water out of the rock: and why? did they deserve it? no; "for he remembered his holy promise, and Abraham his servant." Moses knew this, and therefore when the people had sinned, so as that God was resolved to destroy them, Exod. xxxii. (the calf, &c.) ver. 13, he sets upon God with this argument: "Remember Abraham, Isaac, and Israel, thy servants, to whom thou swarest by thine ownself." As it is a great condescension in God to make covenant with any, so it is unspeakable mercy to those that are in covenant with him.

Obs. 4. When a covenant is shaken, broken, fallen to the earth, and nulled on man's part, God can raise it up again. "I will establish." Jerusalem had sinned, suffered grievous things, was carried into Babylon, abode there seventy years, and lay buried as in a grave, the Jews were even out of hope; Ezek. xxxvii. 11, "Our bones are dried, and our hope is lost; and we are cut off for our parts." But in the next verse, saith God, "O my people, I will open your graves, and cause you to come up out of them, and bring you into the land of Israel."

Obs. 5. When God doth renew the covenant with his people, he makes some comfortable or gracious additions; as when a house, town, or city are repaired or new built, some enlargements or beautifyings there are, which were not before; so here, "I will establish to thee an everlasting covenant." The covenant before, they brake: but this was a covenant they should not break, Jer. xxxi. 32; therefore this covenant is said, Heb. vii. 6, to be "a better covenant, and established upon better promises." The promises are: "That he will write his law in their hearts;" "That all shall know him from," &c.; "That he will forgive their iniquity, and remember their sin no more." These promises are better:

(1.) More spiritual.

(2.) More free without conditions.

(3.) More extensive.

Second editions have additions. Adam had the promise. Abraham more fully, &c. "with an oath."

Obs. 6. God doth all here upon the account of his own good pleasure; "I will remember," "I will establish."

What saw God now in Jerusalem to cause or incline him to renew the covenant? She had despised the oath, broken the covenant, run out to excessive idolatry; yet, saith God, "I will," &c. Isa. xliii. 25, "I am he that blotteth out thy transgressions for mine own sake," not their sakes. 1 John ii. 12, "I write unto you, little children, because your sins are forgiven you for his name's sake." "A new heart will I give you, a new spirit will I put within you. I will put my spirit within you," &c. Ezek. xxxvi. 26, 27.

Ver. 61. *Then thou shalt remember thy ways, and be ashamed, when thou shalt receive thy sisters, thine elder and thy younger: and I will give them unto thee for daughters, but not by thy covenant.*

God having renewed and established the covenant with Jerusalem, yea, an everlasting covenant, here begin the benefits and fruits thereof; which are,

I. Remembrance of her ways, and shame upon it.

II. Reception of her sisters, "elder, younger," amplified,

1. From the true ground and cause thereof, God's free grace, "I will give," &c.

2. By removal of a supposed and false ground, "not by thy covenant."

"Thou shalt remember thy ways." It imports more than a bare remembrance; for the word זכר as Avenarius observes, signifies *reservare et revolvere in corde*, to keep and roll a thing up and down in the mind, so as thereby to be stirred up to the avoiding of evil, or doing good. Psal. cxix. 55, "I have remembered thy name, O Lord, in the night, and have kept thy law:" Exod. xx. 8, "Remember the sabbath day, to keep it holy;" that is, so muse, meditate on it, as to be stirred up thereby to do those holy duties belonging to it. So here, "Thou shalt remember thy ways;" so think of, consider, and mind them, as to be stirred up thereby to renounce them, and turn from them; suitable to that of David, Psal. cxix. 59, "I thought on my ways, and turned my feet unto thy testimonies." It was an efficacious thinking on them.

"Thy ways." The Hebrew word דרך signifies, a path which leads from place to place, which men do walk in; and metaphorically, it is applied to the customs, manners, actions, religions, and lives of men. Jer. x. 2, "Learn not the ways of the heathen," that is, their customs and manners. Prov. i. 19, "So are the ways of every one that is greedy of gain;" that is, their actions. 2 Chron. xxviii. 2, "Ahaz walked in the ways of the kings of Israel, and made also molten images for Baalim;" that is, he did idolatrously, his religion and worship was as theirs were. Prov. iv. 19, "The way of the wicked is as darkness;" that is, their lives and conversations are as darkness. The ways of sinners in the word are said to be crooked, Psal. cxxv. 5; stubborn, Judg. ii. 19; false, Psal. cxix. 104; grievous, Psal. x. 5; pernicious, 2 Pet. ii. 2. Jerusalem's ways had been crooked, stubborn, false, grievous, pernicious, and these she should remember.

"Be ashamed." The Hebrew is, ונכלמת shalt blush. The word כלם I opened in ver. 52, when I spake of those words, "bear thine own shame." The Septuagint is, ἐξατιμωθήσῃ, which Kircker renders *despicies*, thou shalt despise thy ways; but Stephanus in Thesaur. saith it is, *prorsus et penitus infamia notare*, utterly and thoroughly to brand and infamize; yea, *infami et ignominiosa damnatione plectere*, to sentence and punish in an infamous and reproachful way. So should Jerusalem, upon serious remembrance of her ways, she should utterly renounce them, brand them, yea, shame and condemn herself for them, as not worthy to live.

"When thou shalt receive thy sisters." Hebrew is, in thy receiving; there is no "when." Here the calling and incorporation of the gentiles into the church is presented to consideration, of which much had been said and promised of old. That in Gen. ix. 27, falls in here; "God shall enlarge Japheth, and he shall dwell in the tents of Shem." The posterity of Japheth spread over many parts, and became heathenish; but God in his time did bring them into the tents of Shem, that was, the church; by the sweet voice of the gospel they were wrought upon, and brought in. The promise was to Abraham, that in him and his seed all the families and nations of the earth should be blessed, Gen. xii. 3; xviii. 18; xxii. 18. The heathen were promised Christ for his inheritance, Psal. ii. 8. Isaiah makes frequent mention of the calling and coming in of the gentiles, chap. liv. throughout; xlii. 4: lx. 3—5, &c. "The gentiles shall come to thy light, and kings to the brightness of thy rising. Thy sons shall come from far, and thy daughters shall be nursed at thy side. The abundance of the sea shall be converted unto thee, the forces of the gentiles shall come unto thee," &c. This was made good in Christ's time, and after; when the apostles, who were Jews, preached the gospel, converted some out of several nations, and received them into the christian church.

"Thy sisters." The nations were sisters to the Jews, coming from the posterity of Noah, as the Jews did: or here they may be called sisters, for their likeness in qualities and conditions; Jerusalem was very wicked, and so were the nations. Upon this account you may take that expression, Jer. iii. 7, 8, "Her treacherous sister Judah:" Judah was like Israel in treachery and apostasy from God.

"Thine elder and thy younger." Not Sodom and Samaria, unless taken synecdochically for all the rest. Sodom was not, and Samaria, by which is meant the ten tribes, to this day is not come in to the christian Jerusalem; we must therefore include the nations. The words "elder and younger," in the original are, the greater and lesser, הקטנות הגדלות Those nations that are greater in extent, in people, in honour, in wealth; or less than thyself, that were before thee, or since thee; when thou shalt receive them.

"I will give them unto thee for daughters." Thou shalt by the preaching of the gospel beget them unto thee. In Jerusalem was the first christian church, which consisted most of Jews; and when any were converted in Jerusalem, they were added to that church, Acts ii. 41, 47. Hence Jerusalem had the honour to be called the primitive church. Yea, the christian church is called Jerusalem, and said to be "the mother of us all," Gal. iv. 26. All converted nations or persons are the daughters of the christian Jerusalem.

"But not by thy covenant." Lest thou shouldst think it is for thy faithfulness, holiness, obedience that I do this, I tell thee I will do it, "but not by thy covenant;" which, as thou didst carry it, gendered unto bondage, and made the very sons servants, Gal. iv. 1—3, 24. Thou shalt have daughters, but not *ex vi testamenti veteris*, but *ex vi pacti mei*, by virtue of my covenant made with Abraham; not by the law of works, but by the law of faith; faith in Christ the promised Seed, who is called a Father, Isa. ix. 6, and acknowledges the children which God had given him, Heb. ii. 13, "Behold I and the children which God hath given me." So that thy covenant doth nothing herein, but all this shall be done by the covenant of grace.

Obs. 1. The love, kindness, and mercy of God, is that which causeth a sinful, guilty, unfaithful people to remember their ways, and turn from them. Saith God in the words immediately before, "I will establish unto thee an everlasting covenant," show thee much kindness and mercy; and "then thou shalt remember thy ways;" then thy heart shall melt, break within thee, and renounce the ways thou hast walked in. Ezek. xxxvi. 24—31, God would gather them from the heathen, plant them in their own land, cleanse them from their filthiness and idols, give them new hearts, new spirits, be their God, own them for his people, multiply their corn and fruit: and what upon all this? "Then shall ye remember your own evil ways, and your doings that were not good, and shall loathe yourselves in your own sight for your iniquities and for your abominations." When God did let out love, show kindness, and multiply mercy, then did they remember to purpose their evil ways, how they had profaned his name, his sanctuary, rejected his counsel, his ordinances, his prophets; despised his threatenings, broken covenant, apostatized from him, turned idolaters, became heathenish, yea worse than heathenish, and loathed themselves for such things.

Undeserved or unexpected kindnesses do work upon the hearts of men who have any ingenuity in them; they are coals of fire, and will warm, yea thaw a frozen, icy heart. Prov. xxv. 21, 22, "If thine enemy be hungry, give him bread to eat; and if he be thirsty, give him water to drink: for" in so doing "thou shalt heap coals of fire on his head:" thy kindnesses will work in his head and heart, make him reason thus; Why should I think, speak, or do evil to this man who is so loving, who relieves me in my necessities, and preserves my life? ah, what a wretch was I that had such hard thoughts, spake such bitter words, and did so ill by him! I will never think, speak, or do so more. Here are coals upon his head and heart, that have warmed and melted him to good purpose. If man's kindness prove such coals, how much more will the Lord's! When he heaps kindness upon a people unexpectedly, undeservedly, they will be coals of juniper, causing a flame in their bosoms, making them to say, Ah, what have we done! how have we sinned against a God of love, against mercy, against grace! we will do it no more. Ezek. vi. 9, "They that escape of you shall remember me among the nations whither they shall be carried captives, and they shall loathe themselves for the evils which they have committed." When God did give them their lives for a prey, which was a great mercy, this affected them, caused them to remember how they had sinned against God, and to loathe themselves for what they had done. If common mercies will do this, much more covenant mercies, which was the case here. So when Christ looked upon Peter, how did it affect and break his heart, make him go out and weep bitterly for what he had done, Luke xxii. 61, 62. It was a covenant look, such a look as had influence into his heart, and made him to think. with himself; What! will the Lord Christ vouchsafe to look upon me, who denied him to be my Lord and Master, who denied that I knew him, who forsware him? will he yet mind me? Ah, wretch, that, &c.

Obs. 2. Former ways are matter of shame to true converts and penitents. "Thou shalt remember thy ways, and be ashamed;" not only because she had wounded her honour, her conscience, but especially because she had broken covenant with her God, violated his law, defiled his worship, and stained his glory. That which causeth shame is something evil and naught properly, things forbidden, dishonest, dishonourable. Rom. vi. 21, "What fruit had ye then in those things whereof ye are now ashamed?" When the Romans were converted to the faith, they were ashamed of their former ways, those sins mentioned, chap. i. 29—31. When grace hath got possession of the heart, such a deformity is seen in men's former ways, that their blood appears in their cheeks, and they are greatly ashamed of them. Jer. xxxi. 19, "After that I was turned, I repented; and after that I was instructed, I smote upon my thigh: I was ashamed, yea, even confounded, because I did bear the reproach of my youth." After Ephraim was converted, became truly penitent, then Ephraim's sins were burdensome, shameful, and confounding. When men are changed by grace, then they loathe their sins and themselves: Ezek. xx. 42, 43, they should know God, and remember their ways, and loathe themselves in their own sight for all the evils that they had committed; every sin would be matter of shame and self-abhorrence: they should loathe themselves, not for evil to come upon them, but for evil done by them, for the evil of sin.

Obs. 3. The church under Christ and the gospel, is of larger extent than that under Moses and the law. The church was then shut up under the narrow bounds of Judea or the holy land, but since it is enlarged to other nations: In thy receiving thy sisters, the greater and the lesser.

The gentiles were a long time aliens from the commonwealth of Israel, and strangers from the covenant of promise; they were sisters, but not espoused or married till Christ's time; Jerusalem was taken in to be the Lord's, but not the gentiles. Cant. viii. 8, "We have a little sister, and she hath no breasts; what shall we do for our sister when she shall be spoken for?" Here the church, by a prophetical eye, seeing what should befall the gentiles, that they should be spoken for, and taken in by Christ, or spoken against, when taken in, (for בה will bear both,) calls her sister, and a sister without breasts; she had no means of grace, which are breasts, and breasts of consolation, Isa. lxvi. 11; but, however, a sister she was, and "what shall we do for her?" The Jewish church minded the gentiles, and had it in her thoughts to do for her; why? she was a sister; yet not a daughter: when it pleased God actually to bring in the nations to Christ, then they were Jerusalem's daughters. Some were formerly received in from the gentiles, who were neither called daughters nor brethren, but strangers, Exod. xii. 48, and these were few; but in Christ's time the partition-wall was broken down, and they came flocking in "as doves to their windows," Isa. lx. 8: and they were no longer "strangers and foreigners, but fellow-citizens with the saints, and of the household of God," Eph. ii. 19; and Jerusalem was the mother of them all. So that was made good, Isa. lxvi. 18, "It shall come, that I will gather all nations and tongues; and they shall come, and see my glory;" my glory in Christ, my glory in the gospel. Read Isa. liv. 23.

Obs. 4. The coming in of the gentiles, as it was of special grace and favour, so most certain, infallible. It notes a powerful giving; John vi. 37, "I will give them to thee:" he saith not, they will come to thee, others will bring them; no, but "I will give them." God would work upon them by his word and Spirit, and cause them, being given, to come in. God had given the gentiles to Christ long before, Psal. ii. 8; and though they minded not prophecies, promises, Christ, gospel, Jerusalem, themselves, or their own good; yet God minded them; and as he had freely given them, so freely brought them in, and powerfully. Hence these expressions: Psal. lxxii. 11, "All kings shall fall down before him; all nations shall serve him." Psal. lxxxvi. 9, "All nations whom thou hast made shall come and worship before thee, O Lord, and shall glorify thy name." Isa. xi. 10, "In that day there shall be a root of Jesse, which shall stand for an ensign of the people; to it shall the gentiles seek; and his rest shall be glorious." While Christ lay in the sacrifices and ceremonies, in the prophecies and promises, he was a dark, hidden thing, like a root under ground; but when God sent him into the world, then he was as an ensign lifted up; then he caused the gentiles to see him, and seek to him, and Jerusalem, the place of his rest, was glorious. Isa. xlix. 20, 21, Zion should have so many children come in from the nations, that she should say, "Who hath begotten me these?" It was the Lord begot them by the power of his Spirit, he made them to run unto Christ, Isa. lv. 5. Read the 60th of Isaiah; consider and observe the conclusion, "I the Lord will hasten it in his time." And he did so, pouring out his Spirit upon the apostles, whom he sent abroad into the nations to preach Christ and the gospel, to bring all their brethren for an offering unto the Lord, out of all nations, unto his holy mountain Jerusalem, (that was, the christian church,) Isa. lxvi. 20. So the kingdom was given to the gentiles, Matt. xxi. 43, &c.; they made subjects of Christ, and that fulfilled which you have in Psal. xxii. 30, 31, "A seed shall serve him; it shall be accounted to the Lord for a generation. They shall come, and shall declare his righteousness unto a people that shall be born;" that he hath done this: the Lord did it, and that powerfully; nothing could hinder, neither ignorance, profaneness, nor unbelief.

Obs. 5. When nations or any people receive the gospel of Christ, they have a new relation put upon them, they are daughters of Jerusalem; not Jerusalem in a literal or carnal notion, but of Jerusalem in a spiritual and mystical sense, as it notes out the church, which is the spouse of Christ and God, Hos. ii. 19, 20; 2 Cor. xi. 2. Eph. v. 32, Christ and the church are a great mystery. Rev. xix. 7, the church is called the "Lamb's wife;" so chap. xxi. 9: and she is the mother of the faithful, as Abraham was the father of them; for she brings forth, and with difficulty. Rev. xii. 2, the woman clothed with the sun, viz. the christian church, was with child, fell into labour, and was pained to be delivered: and when any are born of the Spirit, and immortal seed of the word, they are her children, and their privileges are great: I will name two.

(1.) God will be their teacher: Isa. liv. 13, "All thy children shall be taught of the Lord;" and, "who teacheth like him?" Job xxxvi. 22.

(2.) They shall have peace, yea, great peace: "Great shall be the peace of thy children," Isa. liv. 13. Psal. cxix. 165, "Great peace have they which love thy law, and nothing shall offend them:" they are taught of God, and cannot but love the law of God. Therefore let us walk as children of God; 1 Pet. i. 14, 15, as obedient children, not fashioning ourselves according to our former lusts, in our ignorance: but as he which hath called us is holy, so let us be holy in all manner of conversation. It is an honour to be a son or daughter of Zion: Psal. lxxxvii. 5, "Of Zion it shall be said, This and that man was born in her."

Obs. 6. When holy things are abused, many times, God owns them not, but calls them theirs that have abused them; as here, "thy covenant." Jerusalem had broken the oath, and despised the covenant, and God calls it her covenant. Isa. i. 11, 14, "To what purpose is the multitude of your sacrifices. Your new moons and your appointed feasts my soul hateth."

Obs. 7. People are apt to think, who are in relation to God, that for their sakes God doth much. Jerusalem was near unto God, he had taken her to be his; and she thought when the gentiles should be given in to her for daughters, it was for her sake; but the Lord says, No, it is not for thy sake; thou hast not kept covenant with me, nor pleased me; thou couldst not challenge any such thing at my hands, hadst thou walked never so exactly, much less now, having walked contrary unto me; it is not for thy covenant. When God showed mercy to the Jews, Ezek. xxxvi. 32, "Not for your sakes do I this, saith the Lord God, be it known unto you;" you may think it is so, but it is otherwise.

Obs. 8. Not legal, but evangelical dispensations, tenders of free grace and mercy by Jesus Christ, wrought upon the gentiles. It was Christ, not Moses, prevailed with them. The commission was, Mark xvi. 15, "Go ye into all the world, and preach the gospel to every creature." The gospel is the seed of faith; the way in which the Spirit is given, 2 Cor. iii. 8; "word of grace," Acts xx. 32; "grace of God," Titus ii. 11; "word of life," Phil. ii. 16; "power of God to salvation," Rom. i. 16.

Ver. 62, 63. *And I will establish my covenant with thee: and thou shalt know that I am the Lord: that thou mayest remember, and be confounded, and never open thy mouth any more because of thy shame, when I am pacified toward thee for all that thou hast done, saith the Lord God.*

The former verse contained two benefits of the covenant established with Jerusalem after her breach of covenant. These verses tell you of more, which we shall open to you, and finish the chapter.

"I will establish my covenant with thee." Of establishing or raising up the covenant was spoken in ver. 60, and therefore I shall not insist upon that; only note, the repetition of it argues our backwardness to believe it, and God's readiness to assure us of it. Men once sensible of breach with God, are not easily induced to believe that God will bestow great mercies upon them, to make a covenant with them, and to bestow covenant mercies: the Lord therefore, out of his abundant goodness, doubles the promise of making and establishing his covenant with Jerusalem, that so her fears, doubts, and disputes may cease, and she be ascertained thereof.

"Thou shalt know that I am the Lord." The Hebrew word ידע signifies to know, to acknowledge, to understand, to be certain, and properly refers to the mind and understanding: Gen. xlviii. 19, "I know it, I know it;" that is, I certainly know it. The Septuagint, for the word here, saith, ἐπιγνώσῃ, thou shalt acknowledge that I am the Lord.

The knowledge here meant is not common knowledge, but a saving knowledge; not a legal, but an evangelical knowledge; for he speaks not of that knowledge which arises from afflictions and judgments, of which he had oft spoken before. Chap. vi. 7, 13; vii. 4, 9; xi. 10, 12; xii. 20; xiii. 9, 14, 21, 23; xiv. 8; xv. 7; thirteen times the Lord saith, they should know that he was the Lord, that it was by his judgments; but here he speaks of such knowledge as springs from a fountain and foundation of mercy. "I will establish my covenant with thee, and thou shalt know me;" that is, in another manner than thou didst before; thou shalt know me spiritually, with a knowledge of faith and salvation: so much the word know imports in John vii. 17; x. 4. Now this knowledge differs from vulgar, legal, and literal knowledge; for,

1. It is a more distinct knowledge of God; human is more mixed, dark, and confused. Job x. 22, "The light is as darkness:" every ungodly man's light is darkness; but he who hath light from God in covenant, his light is clear. Prov. xiii. 9, "The light of the righteous rejoiceth;" if it were confused and obscure, it would not rejoice. James iii. 17, "The wisdom from above is pure;" and the more pure, the more clear, the more distinct.

2. It is a savoury, relishing knowledge, the soul is affected with it; "Taste and see that the Lord is good." No meat, no wine, no spice tastes more pleasant to the palate of a man, than the goodness of God doth to a man who hath the spiritual knowledge thereof. Tasting notes knowledge and experience: Prov. xxxi. 18, "She perceiveth that her merchandise is good;" the Hebrew word is, she tasteth; the gain of her labour is pleasant and delightful. Exod. xvi. 31, manna had a taste like wafers made of honey. The true knowledge and taste of God is as sweet as any gain, as ever manna was: Cant. ii. 3, "His fruit was sweet to my taste;" and his knowledge hath a savour in it, 2 Cor. ii. 14.

3. It is a deep-rooted and well-settled knowledge. Job xxxviii. 36, "Who hath put wisdom in the inward parts? or who hath given understanding to the heart?" the Lord doth it to those he strikes his covenant with; "Thou shalt know me;" thou shalt have a deeper and more rooted and settled knowledge than others. 2 Cor. iv. 6, "God, who commanded light to shine out of darkness, hath shined in our hearts:" not in our heads only, not on our hearts only, but in our hearts. God seats the knowledge of himself in the hearts of his people; he puts and writes his law in their hearts, Jer. xxxi. 33. Wicked men have knowledge and light in their heads, but darkness in their hearts.

4. It is a knowledge distinguishable from other knowledge by the effects.

(1.) It is peaceable, and causeth men to live peaceably: James iii. 17, "The wisdom from above is pure and peaceable." Isa. xi. 9, "They shall not hurt nor destroy in all my holy mountain; for the earth shall be full of the knowledge of the Lord." When men know God savingly, they love peace, and pursue peace; but when knowledge is literal, they are contentious and bitter.

(2.) It humbleth much; the more men know God in his holiness, glory, and goodness, the more humble they will be. Ezek. xx. 42, 43, "Ye shall know that I am the Lord, and remember your ways and doings: and ye shall loathe yourselves in your own sight for all your evils that ye have done." When Job had a clear and spiritual sight of God, he abhorred himself in dust and ashes, chap. xlii. 5. So Isa. vi. 5, "Woe is me! for I am undone; because I am a man of unclean lips, and I dwell in the midst of a people of unclean lips; for mine eyes have seen the King, the Lord of hosts." See 1 Cor. xv. 8, 9.

(3.) It is working and powerful; like fire, it consumes the lusts of men's hearts, and separates the dross of their spirits. 1 Pet. i. 22, the truth purified their souls. Psal. cxix. 34, "Give me understanding, and I shall keep thy law; yea, I shall observe it with my whole heart." Divine knowledge keeps under what hinders practice, and leads out the soul to action. 1 John ii. 4, "He that saith, I know him, and keepeth not his commandments, is a liar, and the truth is not in him." Men have not the true knowledge of God when their lusts overpower them, and make them disobedient.

4. Trust and confidence in the Lord. The knowledge we speak of hath certainty in it, and causeth venturing: Psal. ix. 10, "They that know thy name will put their trust in thee:" they that know God spiritually, his truths, promises, covenant, faithfulness, will resign up themselves to him, and lean upon him. What is the bottom and ground of the prophet's exhortation? Isa. xxvi. 4, "Trust ye in the Lord for ever; for in the Lord Jehovah is everlasting strength." When a man hath the true, real, and clear knowledge of this, he will trust in God. David had the right knowledge of God, he said of him, "He is my refuge and my fortress; my God; in him will I trust," Psal. xci. 2.

Obs. The true knowledge of God is a covenant mercy; those who are in covenant with God, they have the saving and spiritual knowledge of him. "I will establish my covenant with thee, and thou shalt know that I am the Lord." Jer. xxxi. 33, 34, speaking there of the covenant of grace, saith the Lord, "I will put my law in their inward parts, and write it in their hearts; and will be their God, and they shall be my people. And they shall all know me, from the least of them to the greatest of them:" so Heb. viii. 10, 11. The knowledge here spoken of is not a common, but a choice knowledge, and it is given to those who are in covenant, it is a covenant mercy; none have such knowledge who are out of covenant. They may by their industry get a general, unsavoury, and powerless knowledge of God, but they have not this knowledge we speak of: it is "given," 1 John v. 20, and is called seeing of God. Job xlii. 5; Isa. vi. 5; Mic. vi. 9; "the true light," 1 John ii. 8; "the truth which is after godliness," Tit. i. 1; "the mystery manifest to saints," Col. i. 26; "sound wisdom," Prov. ii. 7; "marvellous light," 1 Pet. ii. 9; "the light of life," John viii. 12; excellent knowledge, Phil. iii. 8; the teaching of God, Psal. xxxii. 8, and his Spirit, John xiv. 26, according to that in Isa. liv. 13, "All thy children shall be taught of the Lord:" he speaks of Jerusalem in covenant: God would give her spiritual children, and they should have spiritual instruction, whereby they should know God to be their God, a Father of mercies, and God of consolations; they should know the riches of his grace, and things freely given them of their God, all the good of the covenant.

Ver. 63. "That thou mayest remember, and be confounded." Of remembering and being ashamed was spoken in ver. 61; and of being confounded in ver. 52, 54.

"And never open thy mouth any more." Hebrew is, פתחון פה the words run thus, and there may not be to thee further opening of thy mouth; that is, that thou mayest be silent, and not open thy mouth any more. In the book of divine things you read of several openings; the opening of the hand, Deut. xv. 11; of the eyes, 2 Kings vi. 17; of the womb, Gen. xxx. 22; of the ear, Job xxxvi. 10; of the lips and mouth, Psal. li. 15; lxxviii. 2: and likewise of answerable shuttings, as the shutting of the hand, Deut. xv. 7; of the eyes, Isa. vi. 10; of the womb, 1 Sam. i. 6; of the ears, Prov. xxi. 13; of the mouth, Isa. lii. 15, "Kings shall shut their mouths at him;" that is, they shall be silent and submit to Christ: so here the not opening of the mouth imports silence, patience, quiet submission; Thou shalt have nothing justly to complain of me, or excuse thyself; thou shalt justify me in all my proceedings with thee, give me glory, and take shame to thyself.

"When I am pacified towards thee." Hebrew is, בכפרי in my being propitious. כפר properly signifieth to cover a thing, with that which cleaveth and sticks to the thing covered; not with dust, grass, earth, wood, for such things may easily be removed; but with pitch, glue, cement, so that the thing covered cannot easily be brought to sight again. Gen. vi. 14, "Pitch it within and without with pitch;" it is the same word: when a thing is pitched over, you cannot suddenly come at the sight of it; and by way of metaphor it is applied to the covering of sin, and wrath caused by sin. Isa. xxii. 14, "This iniquity shall not be purged till ye die:" Hebrew is, covered. So Psal. lxxviii. 38, "He forgave their iniquity:" Hebrew, he covered it. When sin is so covered as not to be seen again, it is purged away, it is forgiven. So for wrath and anger stirred up by sin: Gen. xxxii. 20, Jacob had offended Esau by getting the blessing, and he saith, I will appease his face: Hebrew is, cover his face, or anger that appears in the face. To come to our purpose; Jerusalem had sinned grievously, and God's anger was greatly up, and something there must be to cover her sins, and appease his wrath; and that was, the sacrifice, death, and blood of Christ, who is the only coverer of sin, and appeaser of anger: he is, ἱλασμος, the true propitiation for man's sin, and only pacifier of God's anger, 1 John ii. 2. He is the peacemaker, Eph. ii. 14, the purger of sin, Heb. i. 3, the Mediator, Heb. ix. 15, reconciliation, Eph. ii. 16.

Some read the words thus; When I shall expiate thee from all that thou hast done. Others, When I shall pardon thee, or blot out all thou hast done.

Obs. 1. Godly sorrow and shame for sin arises from the right knowledge of God in the covenant of grace. "I will establish my covenant with thee; and thou shalt know that I am the Lord;" gracious, faithful, merciful; and what then? "that thou mayest remember, and be confounded" and ashamed. Men's sorrow is according to their knowledge; a vulgar knowledge, and a vulgar repentance; a legal knowledge, and a legal repentance: but if the knowledge be spiritual and evangelical, the fruit of the covenant, men's repentance will be suitable; sanctified knowledge will produce sanctified shame, sorrow, and tears. Zech. xii. 10, "I will pour upon the house of David, and upon the inhabitants of Jerusalem, the spirit of grace and of supplications: and they shall look upon me whom they have pierced, and they shall mourn for him, as one mourneth for his only son." When men are in covenant with God, and have the spiritual knowledge of his love and bounty, in giving Christ to take away sin, and look upon him in his piercings and sufferings by and for their sins, then will they mourn with a great, but a spiritual mourning, which is the most kindly and acceptable. When we apprehend God to have taken us into covenant with him, to be our God, to have done great things for us, to have promised great things to us, and to have been very good to us, then the remembrance of our wretched ways causeth a holy shame and a holy sorrow.

Obs. 2. Those who rightly know God in the covenant of grace, will not murmur against or accuse God for any of his dealings with them, but be silent and submissive before him. They know God is infinitely wise, just, and holy; that all their afflictions, chastisements, troubles, temptations, sufferings, are exceeding short of what they deserve; that nothing comes to pass without his providence; that he can wrong none; that he doth use unholy instruments holily, and hath holy ends in all his ways. Till men know the Lord spiritually, in a covenant and gospel manner, they are apt to open their mouths to accuse and blame God; yea, oft they utter unsavoury speeches; but when it is known, it is otherwise. Job i. 22, "In all this Job sinned not, nor charged God foolishly:" he met with very hard things; but knowing God the right way, he opened not his mouth against him, but for him, ver. 21. So David, Psal. xxxix. 9, "I was dumb, I opened not my mouth, because thou didst it." He was silent, and patiently submitted unto the hand of God; he neither accused him, nor excused himself: If I be reproached, persecuted, afflicted any way, I know it is thy doing, and I will be dumb.

When Absalom, that rebellious and unnatural son, had driven David out of all, and sought his life; what said he to it? If God have no delight in me, "behold, here am I, let him do to me as seemeth good unto him." If he will have me cut off and cut down by the hand of mine own wicked son, I am content; if he will have me driven out from the holy city and land, and live in a profane land amongst his enemies, I leave it to him, let him do what he pleases, I know what I have deserved, 2 Sam. xv. 26. When God sent out a fire which consumed Nadab and Abihu for offering strange fire, it was a sad affliction even for a godly parent, and might have made Aaron open his mouth; but saith the text, "he held his peace," Lev. x. 3. It is fit all flesh should be silent before the Lord, as it is Zech. ii. 13; and that every mouth should be stopped, Rom. iii. 19. But most mouths are open against God, more or less; only those who have spiritual knowledge of him, and spiritual sorrow for their sins, are most silent; what condition soever they be cast into, they will say with the church, Micah vii. 9, "We will bear the indignation of the Lord, because we have sinned against him."

Obs. 3. Sin is such an evil as provokes God. "When I am pacified toward thee:" there can be pacification where there is no provocation. Esth. vii. 10, "Then was the king's wrath pacified:" Haman had offended Ahasuerus before, and being hanged for it, his wrath was pacified. Eccles. x. 4, "Yielding pacifieth great offences." If there were not offence, no place would be found for pacification; where this is to be made, provocation hath gone before. Sin is that which provokes a God of patience and long-suffering, it makes him angry and wrathful: Jer. xliv. 8, "Ye provoke me to wrath." Sin provokes him bitterly, Hos. xii. 14, and makes him angry every day, Psal. vii. 11; yea, it provokes him to jealousy, 1 Kings xiv. 22. Let us take heed of sin, and offending God any way; to kindle his anger but a little is a dangerous thing, Psal. ii. 12. Paul knew it when he said, "Do we provoke the Lord to jealousy? are we stronger than he?" 1 Cor. x. 22. We would not provoke a lion, a man of war, such a one as Samson was; and shall we provoke God, who puts all strength into beasts and men, who is a roaring lion and the Lord of hosts?

Obs. 4. Though sin do provoke God greatly and bitterly, yet he is to be pacified. "When I am pacified towards you:" he is not implacable. Jer. iii. 12, he saith, "I will not keep anger for ever." His mercy endures for ever, but not his anger; his wrath is momentary, but his kindness is everlasting, Isa. liv. 8. Aaron made an atonement for the people, Numb. xvi. 46; Phinehas turned away his wrath, Numb. xxv. 11; Moses prevailed with God, and pacified him when he was very angry, Exod. xxxii. 14. The Lord is "a God ready to pardon," Neh. ix. 17; though men have sinned much, long, provoked exceedingly; yet if they sue unto him, he is ready to forgive. When the man who owed ten thousand talents came to the Lord for patience, "Have patience with me, and I will pay thee all;" he did not only forbear him, but forgave him, Matt. xviii. 26, 27. With men it falls out oft, that they will never forgive; but the Lord is forward to it. And when the people were full of sin, had greatly trespassed, "he, being full of compassion, forgave their iniquity, and destroyed them not: yea, many a time turned he his anger away, and did not stir up all his wrath," Psal. lxxviii. 38. When man persists in sin, God ceaseth from his wrath, and reacheth out mercy; Isa. lvii. 17, 18, "I have seen his ways, and will heal him."

Obs. 5. God's being pacified towards a people is a great mercy, which appears here in two things:

(1.) All that hath offended is passed by and forgiven. "When I am pacified towards thee for all that thou hast done:" not for one, two, or three, or a hundred things done, but for all done; the idolatry, oppression, pride, fulness of bread, idleness, neglect of the poor, injustice, profaneness, &c. When God is once pacified, he is fully pacified for all sins. And here is the greatness of divine grace, be sins never so great, old, many, they are all done away.

(2.) He is so pacified, as that he will not be angry again with them for those evil deeds. I told you in the opening the words, that *caphar* notes such covering of them, as they cannot easily be seen again; expiation, blotting out. Isa. xliii. 25, "I am he that blotteth out thy transgressions for mine own sake, and will not remember thy sins:" God so blots out when he is pacified, as not to remember them. Heb. viii. 12, God being in covenant, and so pacified towards his people, he is "merciful to their unrighteousness, and their iniquity will he remember no more." Jer. l. 20, "The iniquity of Israel shall be sought for, and there shall be none; and the sins of Judah, and they shall not be found."

CHAPTER XVII.

Ver. 1—6. *And the word of the Lord came unto me, saying, Son of man, put forth a riddle, and speak a parable unto the house of Israel; and say, Thus saith the Lord God; A great eagle with great wings, long-winged, full of feathers, which had divers colours, came unto Lebanon, and took the highest branch of the cedar: he cropped off the top of his young twigs, and carried it into a land of traffick; he set it in a city of merchants. He took also of the seed of the land, and planted it in a fruitful field; he placed it by great waters, and set it as a willow tree. And it grew, and became a spreading vine of low stature, whose branches turned toward him, and the roots thereof were under him: so it became a vine, and brought forth branches, and shot forth sprigs.*

THIS 17th chapter contains,

I. A preface, in the first two verses.

II. A riddle or parable, from the beginning of the 3rd to the end of the 8th verse.

III. The application of this parable, from the 11th verse to the 22nd.

IV. A promise of mercy, from the 22nd to the end. In the preface you have,

1. The author of what is prophesied in this chapter, who is the Lord; "The word of the Lord."

2. The instrument by which it was conveyed; Ezekiel, it came to him.

3. His appellation or title; "Son of man."

4. A command laid upon him; "Put forth, speak."

5. What; "a riddle, a parable."

6. Unto whom; "to the house of Israel."

I shall pass over all in the preface but these words, "Put forth a riddle, and speak a parable," which I shall open.

"Put forth a riddle." Hebrew is, riddle a riddle, or sharpen a sharpening, whet a whetting. חוד signifies, to propound hard questions, difficult and obscure theses, to sharpen and whet the understanding. Judg. xiv. 12, "I will put forth a riddle." Samson put it forth to try and exercise their wit. Ver. 14, "They could not in three days expound the riddle;" for, saith Avenarius, it is acuteness rather than search which discovers such secrets.

A riddle is a dark and subtle sentence or allegory, containing a sense different from the sound of the words; as that Judg. xiv. 14, "Out of the eater came forth meat, and out of the strong came forth sweetness." The sense and meaning of the riddle is another thing than the words import. The Septuagint here put διήγημα for riddle, which is a narration; but in other places πρόβλημα, a problem or hard question, as Psal. lxxviii. 2; Dan. viii. 23. The Vulgate and others have it *ænigma*, from αἰνίττω, to speak obscurely and perplexedly.

"Speak a parable." Hebrew, ומשל משל of this word was spoken, Ezek. xii. 22, where we insisted largely upon it. There it is called "proverb," here "parable." *Mashal* is a sentence, a speech, axiom, metaphor, allegory, which hath choiceness in it, and is worthy memory. Solomon's wise and excellent sayings are called Proverbs; tried, proved words. Parables are similitudes, much like unto riddles, comprehending the same in them; as Psal. lxxviii. 2, compared with Matt. xiii. 35. *Mashal* and *chidosh* are called parables or similitudes. Heb. xi. 19, Abraham received Isaac from the dead, ἐν παραβολῇ, "in a figure;" figuratively, or representatively, he was dead, and rose. The rabbies say it was in the hand of a parable; here was a lively parable or representation of his death and resurrection. The words are used promiscuously here; and whether riddles or parables, they present one thing in words, another in sense, and require interpretation.

The papists assert the Scriptures are obscure. Barradius the Jesuit saith they are enigmatical, and brings this place for it; "Son of man, put forth a riddle, speak a parable unto the house of Israel:" but he forgot the explication of the riddle and parable afterwards in the chapter. And the father saith, if a thing be spoken obscurely in one place, it is cleared up in another.

We grant there are riddles, parables, hard and deep things in the Scriptures; 1 Cor. xv. 29; Heb. vi. 4, and many places in the Revelation and other books, are difficult, obscure; and the wisdom of God is seen in it; for hereby man's pride is stained and beaten down, his abilities, whatever, moral or spiritual, exercised, and the dignity of Scripture kept up; but in things neccessary to salvation it is plain and easy. Timothy knew the Scriptures when he was a child, 2 Tim. iii. 15. And they are compared unto a light, shining in a dark place, 2 Pet. i. 19. And Christ gives thanks, that the Father hid the things of the gospel from the wise and prudent, and revealed them unto babes, Matt. xi. 25. And Chrysostom saith the Scriptures are so divinely written, that all may read them profitably, both idiots and artists.

The holy Scriptures are frequent in parables; some say they are as many as the weeks in the year, fifty-two. Our prophet and Christ do much parabolize. The use of parables is,

1. To veil divine things, and keep them secret from the knowledge of profane and wicked spirits, as Matt. xiii. 13—15.

2. To help the memory. Parables are taken from things obvious to the senses, and so make a stronger impression upon the memory: as similes are better remembered than naked truths, they take stronger hold of a man's memory; so parables.

3. To stir and quicken the affections and spirits of men. There is a sweetness in truths conveyed by parables, so that they please and provoke to a further inquisition after knowledge. When Christ had spoken in parables, the disciples came to him and said, Declare unto us these parables, Matt. xiii. 36; xv. 15.

4. To convince, and that strongly. When David sinned greatly in slaying Uriah, and defiling Bathsheba, Nathan came with a parable unto him of a rich man having flocks and herds, and a poor man having one lamb, which the rich man took from the poor man, and slew for his friend. David hearing this, gives sentence; "As the Lord liveth, the man who hath done this thing shall surely die." Saith Nathan, "Thou art the man." Now David's mouth was stopped, the conviction strong, he had sentenced himself, 2 Sam. xii. 1—7. So the parable of the householder letting out his vineyard to husbandmen, who beat his servants, and slew his son: When the Lord comes what will he do to those men? They being convinced of this great injustice, pass sentence against themselves, and say, "He will miserably destroy those wicked men," Matt. xxi. 41.

It is the third use our prophet intends here, viz. to quicken their attention, affections, and spirits to those things he was to commend unto them; which had they been in a common and familiar style, they would not have listened unto; but being in a parabolizing way, they caused the greater attention, and made the stronger impression.

Obs. The wisdom of God in giving out Scripture. He ordered it so that all should not be given out in one way, but in several ways, fitting it to the capacities, conditions, and necessities of people; some parts are given out in higher strains, others in lower; some in a plain manner, others in parables and riddles. Isaiah is lofty, Amos is low; sometimes Christ spake plainly, sometimes parabolically; and Ezekiel sometimes is in visions and hieroglyphicals, sometimes in riddles and parables, and sometimes he passes at a lower rate. The manifold wisdom of God shines in it; hereby he invites men to mind his word, to be affected with it so, that, whether great or small, we might repent of our sins, and prevent his judgments.

We come now to the riddle and parable itself.

Ver. 3. *A great eagle with great wings, long-winged, full of feathers, which had divers colours, came unto Lebanon, and took the highest branch of the cedar.*

This parable leads us to the consideration of Nebuchadnezzar king of Babylon, who is likened unto an eagle. This eagle is discovered,

I. From its greatness; "A great eagle," &c.

II. From the extent of its wings; "long-winged."

III. From its featheriness; "full of feathers."

IV. From the variety of these feathers; "which had divers colours."

V. From its actions, two whereof are set down in this verse:

1. He "came to Lebanon."

2. He "took the highest branch of the cedar."

"A great eagle." This eagle is called the king of Babylon, ver. 12, who was Nebuchadnezzar; and now it concerns us to see the correspondency between him and an eagle, and upon what grounds it is that he is so called. Some have told us an eagle was the Babylonian ensign; but that is denied by those who affirm a dove to be their ensign, which they gather from Jer. xxv. 38, where the words, "because of the fierceness of the oppressor," in the original are, because of the fierceness of the dove: and in Jer. xlvi. 16; l. 16, where the words are, "the oppressing sword," in the original they are, the sword of the dove; that is, the sword of Nebuchadnezzar, who bare in his ensign a dove: but the root whence יונה a dove, comes, is ינה which signifies to oppress, and therefore is not amiss rendered by our translators in the places mentioned; and so hath not sufficient strength to prove that the ensign of the Chaldeans or Babylonians was a dove. It might be an eagle, notwithstanding this conjecture; but because both these opinions are uncertain, we shall inquire after truth.

1. Eagles mind high and great things; flies and petty things they look not after. Eagles soar aloft, and are in the clouds; Job xxxix. 27, the eagle mounts up, and makes her nest on high: so Nebuchadnezzar had a high spirit, and minded high, great things, as monarchs and princes do. He made an image of gold, sixty cubits in height, and six in breadth, Dan. iii. 1. He minded kingdoms and nations, Jer. xxvii. 8. His heart was lifted up high when he said, "Is not this great Babylon, that I have built for the house of the kingdom by the might of my power, and for the honour of my majesty?" Dan. iv. 30. He set his nest on high above others.

2. Eagles are swift in their flight and motions. Job xxxix. 30, "Where the slain are, there is she:" she flies swiftly to the prey, and upon all occasions. Deut. xxviii. 49, God threatened if they sinned, to bring "a nation as swift as the eagle flieth." Jer. iv. 13, speaking of Nebuchadnezzar, "He shall come up as clouds, and his chariots as a whirlwind; his horses are swifter than eagles." They found it so; Lam. iv. 19, "Our persecutors are swifter than the eagles of heaven." Alexander was quick in his undertakings; Julius Cæsar expeditious; and Nebuchadnezzar had his excellency: Jer. xlviii. 40, "He shall fly as an eagle, and spread his wings over Moab."

3. Strong and cruel; they are the chief of all which have wings, they are stronger than other fowls: Isa. xl. 31, "They shall mount up with wings as eagles." They have much strength in them, and being strong, do gripe and tear their prey cruelly. Job xxxix. 30, "Her young ones also suck up blood." It is natural to the eagle to be bloody. So Nebuchadnezzar was strong and cruel. Nations served him, Jer. xxvii. 7. He is called an "oppressor," Isa. xiv. 4. "He smote the people in wrath with

a continual stroke, he ruled the nations in anger; persecuted, and none hindered," ver. 6. This Nebuchadnezzar broke the bones of Israel, Jer. l. 17. He heated the fiery furnace seven times hotter than ever, and caused the three children to be thrown in, Dan. iii. 19, 21.

4. Eagles are quick-sighted: Job xxxix. 28, 29, she sits upon the rock, "and her eyes behold afar off." And we use to say of men sagacious and discerning, that they are eagle-eyed. Nebuchadnezzar sat on high in a throne, and so other princes, and they see afar off; they see where prey is to be had; they are greedy of honour, greatness, and wealth, and look every way, far and near, to find out what may satisfy; they have eyes and spies in all parts of their kingdoms, to search and sift out things, and make them known unto them.

"Great." This eagle was no ordinary eagle: Nebuchadnezzar was a great king; Dan. ii. 37, "Thou, O king, art a king of kings; for the God of heaven hath given thee a kingdom, power, strength, and glory." He was great in titles, great in attendants, great in possessions, great in power, and great in name.

"With great wings." This notes his power. Wings are for motion and flight. Nebuchadnezzar had power to move, and move speedily, as you heard before, for his power was great. By wings we may understand his military forces: Jer. xlix. 22, "Behold, he shall come up and fly as the eagle, and spread his wings over Bozrah."

"Long-winged." Hebrew is, long in feather or wing. If you will refer this to the long spears the Babylonians used, you may; but I rather judge it is meant of the vast and extensive greatness of this king; for, Dan. iii. 3, there were many provinces under him, "all the rulers of the provinces were gathered unto him." Chap. iv. 1, "Nebuchadnezzar the king, unto all people, nations, and languages, that dwell in all the earth." His wings were long, that reached to all people: and more than this; ver. 22, "O king, thy greatness is grown, and reacheth unto heaven, and thy dominion to the end of the earth." He had the largest dominions of any prince then living.

"Full of feathers." Hebrew, full of feather, the singular put for the plural. The Septuagint is, full of nails or talons. Others read the words as we do. What is meant by feathers must be seen. Some do understand thereby the great riches and wealth this king had, they were his feathers; and it is a common speech among us, that when men are grown rich, we say they have feathered their nests: and the Germans, when they will punish a man's purse, say, his feathers must be lessened. This eagle had store of these feathers; his empire was oriental, and had exceeding great riches in it: so full of gold, that the king made such an image thereof, as the world never saw before or since, Dan. iii. 1.

But without prejudice to this opinion, I conceive principally by feathers people are understood; they are the feathers of kings. Prov. xiv. 28, "In the multitude of people is the king's honour: but in the want of people is the destruction of the prince." A king may want wealth, and yet be in honour; if the hearts of the people cleave to him, like feathers to the body of an eagle, there is his honour: but though he have treasures of gold and silver, and no people, he is without honour, he is at the border of destruction. That which invites me thus to interpret feathers, is the next words;

"Which had divers colours." Hebrew is, variegation, or variety. We had the word in chap. xvi. 10, where I penned it at large, and therefore shall not criticize upon it at all. Septuagint turns it, τὸ ἥγημα εἰσελθεῖν, tacitly implying the people by feathers; for, not his wealth, but his people, had a will and desire to come to Lebanon, and spoil the Jews.

Besides, as the feathers of the eagle are of divers colours, and carry a kind of embroidery upon them which adorn her much; so these people were of divers colours, being of divers provinces, and of divers customs, manners, habits, ranks, and orders, which served Nebuchadnezzar in his wars with the Jews; and this variety was an embroidering of the army, and a glory to the king.

The next thing is the action of this eagle, which is twofold:

1. He comes to Lebanon. Lebanon is a mountain in Canaan, rising from the back of Sidon, and running fifteen hundred furlongs towards Symira, as Masius observes out of Pliny. It is a hill very high, delightful, and fruitful. It is so called from the whiteness of it; for the height is such, that the snow continues upon it; Jer. xviii. 14, "Will a man leave the snow of Lebanon?" or from the abundance of frankincense there, which is white. It is very delightful by reason of the sweet frankincense trees which grow there, as also the sweet cedars, (Cant. iv. 11, "The smell of thy garments is as the smell of Lebanon,") whereof it is very fruitful, as appears 1 Kings v. 6, and thrived greatly, Psal. xcii. 12, and excelled, Cant. v. 15. Of the cedars which grew upon this mountain Solomon built the temple, which therefore metonymically is called Lebanon: Zech. xi. 1, "Open thy doors, O Lebanon;" that is, O temple, which are built of the goodly cedars which grew upon that mountain, open thy doors. This eagle Nebuchadnezzar came to Lebanon; that is, invaded the holy land which lay contiguous to Lebanon.

"And took the highest branch of the cedar." Hebrew, the top; Septuagint, the choice things; Vulgate is, the marrow of the cedar. The Hebrew is plural, and notes not one, but many branches, the highest branches; but most interpreters render it singularly, and understand by it Jehoiachin king of Judah. There is much written by Pliny of the cedar, which rather hath a show of truth, than reality. It is a tree of goodly stature, and therefore they are called cedars of God; Psal. lxxx. 10, "Like the goodly cedars," Hebrew is, cedars of God. And the wood of it is very durable; therefore the temple was built of it, and Solomon made himself a chariot of it, Cant. iii. 9.

The cedar is in Scripture used to set forth a flourishing condition: Psal. xcii. 12, "The righteous shall grow like a cedar in Lebanon." Numb. xxiv. 5, 6, Jacob's tents and tabernacles were goodly "as cedar trees beside the waters." Here the kingdom of Judah is represented by the cedar, which was very high and flourishing; so you may see the state of the Amorites, Amos ii. 9, "whose height was like the height of the cedars." And as cedars have some branches higher than others, so had this state a top-branch, Jeconiah.

The taking away the highest branch, was the removal of the king from his throne, 2 Kings xxiv.

Ver. 4. ***He cropped off the top of his young twigs, and carried it into a land of traffick; he set it in a city of merchants.***

The prophet here proceeds in setting down the actions of the great eagle he had spoken of before; and here are three actions:

I. Cropping.
II. Carrying.

III. Setting.
He cropped the top of the cedar's young twigs.
He carried it; whither? into a land of traffick.
He set it; where? in a city of merchants.

"He cropped off the top of his young twigs." Hebrew is, he pulled away the head of his tender branches. יניקות is from ינק to suck, because those tender shoots or branches do suck the juice of the tree. Septuagint is, he hath cut off, or taken away, the top of his tenderness.

These twigs or plants were the nobility of Judah, the princes and potentates that were highest in the kingdom, and next unto the king. These did Nebuchadnezzar deprive of their power and greatness, and so spoiled the glory of the land; those who were most eminent he took away. Being young himself, he had such about him.

"And carried it into a land of traffick." Hebrew is, into the land of Canaan; and so the Septuagint. But the word Canaan is not to be taken properly, but appellatively, and notes Chaldea, which is so called, because it is a land of trading and merchandizing; for *Cenaan* in Hebrew is a merchant. Prov. xxxi. 24, "She delivereth girdles unto the merchant," לכנעני so it is used Isa. xxiii. 8; Hos. xii. 7. And some render that in Zech. xiv. 21, "In that day there shall be no more the Canaanite in the house of the Lord," a merchant in the house of the Lord. Chaldea was a land of traffic, as appears by Rev. xviii. 11, "The merchants of the earth shall weep over Babylon, for no man buyeth their merchandise any more." And it follows in our prophet,

"He set it in a city of merchants." The word here for merchant is רכל and noteth especially merchandizing in sweet things, grocery, spicery, perfumes, powders; and therefore in Cant. iii. 6, "With all powders of the merchant," it is the same word, and imports they dealt in myrrh, frankincense, and all powders.

The meaning of this verse is, that Nebuchadnezzar took away the chief men, princes, nobles, counsellors, judges, warriors, and carried them to Babylon, and set them amongst those who were merchants, trading for the chief things the world had. This you may see in ver. 12, and also in 2 Kings xxiv. 12, 14—16.

Ver. 5. *He took also of the seed of the land, and planted it in a fruitful field; he placed it by great waters, and set it as a willow tree.*

"The seed of the land." Jehoiachin, the princes and nobles, being captives in Babylon, he took Mattaniah, who was of the seed of the land of Judah, not of Babylon; of the seed of the cedars, for he was of the blood-royal, uncle unto Jehoiachin, 2 Kings xxiv. 17; him did Nebuchadnezzar set up for king, and changed his name, calling him Zedekiah. His first name was Mattaniah, signifying the gift of God, and according to the Syriac, the expectation of God; this he had from Josiah that godly king, whose son he was. His second name was Zedekiah, given him by Nebuchadnezzar a heathen king, which signifies, the justice of God, whereby he minded him, being set up king by him, and sworn to be subject unto him, 2 Chron. xxxvi. 13, of the justice of God if he should break with him.

"Planted it in a fruitful field." Hebrew, in a field of seed, in a field fit to receive and fertile to bring forth: he did not plant it in Babylon, or any other province of his, but in Judea, which was a fruitful place, Isa. v. 1; it was a land which flowed with milk and honey, and abounded with good things, exceeding all lands, Ezek. xx. 6.

"He placed it by great waters." Husbandmen when they plant trees are observant of the soil, whether dry or moist. So here, Nebuchadnezzar placed this seed and young plant Zedekiah (for he was but twenty-one years old when he began to reign, 2 Chron. xxxvi. 11) near unto or among the waters, that so he might root, grow, and bring forth fruit.

Jehoiachin was planted before, but he took no rooting; he reigned but three months and ten days, 2 Chron. xxxvi. 9, and then was plucked up; but Nebuchadnezzar aimed at the rooting and settling of Zedekiah. The Vulgate reads it, that he might strengthen his roots upon or amongst the great waters. Some by waters understand people: so Rev. xvii. 1, the whore sat "upon many waters;" which, ver. 15, are interpreted people: they are inconstant, movable this way or that way, as waters are. By waters are to be understood the poor.

"And set it as a willow tree." Hebrew, he put it a willow, or as a willow, so interpreters have rendered it, but upon what ground I cannot find; for the word צפצפה is either from a word which is to peep, make a noise like birds, as it is in Isa. viii. 19; x. 14. And so Avenarius deriving the word from hence, interprets our prophet thus, *Stridore et sibilo emisso posuit semen quod ore sustulerat aquila*, He set it with noise and muttering. It is like Nebuchadnezzar was troubled at the doings of former kings, both Jehoiakim and Jehoiachin, and therefore might murmur at the setting up of Zedekiah. Or else it is from a word that signifies to spy, watch, observe, and so signifies circumspection, and here is used adverbially, and may thus be rendered, he set it most circumspectly, or with great circumspection; and so both Junius, Piscator, and Polanus do render it. The Septuagint is, ἐπιβλεπόμενον, he looked into the thing; fearing lest he should fall off, he took an oath of fidelity of him, and he became tributary to him.

Ver. 6. *And it grew, and became a spreading vine of low stature, whose branches turned toward him, and the roots thereof were under him: so it became a vine, and brought forth branches, and shot forth sprigs.*

Here you have the effects of the seed planted; the meaning is this, that Zedekiah being advanced to the throne, he reigned; and while grateful and faithful to Nebuchadnezzar who raised him, he prospered.

"It grew." This plant or seed budded presently, he let the people of Judah see and know that he had power.

"Became a spreading vine." Hebrew is, a luxuriant vine. The vine abounds with leaves and sprigs, and runs out far. Zedekiah increased in riches, friends, power, strength, but never came to any considerable greatness: he was not like the tall cedar, but as a low vine; for it follows,

"Of low stature." Hebrew is, low in stature; the vine is a plant that creeps upon the earth, and grows not high, unless helped by others. Septuagint saith, he became a weak vine, and little in greatness. There was as much difference between his reign and Jehoiachin's, as between a tall cedar and a low shrub: he was under Nebuchadnezzar.

"Whose branches turned toward him." Some doubt there is, whether this "him" be Nebuchadnezzar the eagle, or Zedekiah the vine: to me it is apparent Nebuchadnezzar is pointed at; for both Zedekiah and his branches did depend upon the king of Babylon; and whilst they looked to him, and kept covenant, they flourished, both root and branches grew and spread; but when they failed to perform engagements, the branches were plucked off, and the vine rooted up.

"The roots thereof were under him." Nebuchadnezzar gave rooting to this vine; what power soever Zedekiah had, it was under him; he planted it in Judea, his own country, tied him to conditions, would have defended him from any other invasive power, and had it in his hand to hold him under, or to make him a free prince again at his pleasure. The root hath life, communicates virtue, and bears up the body and branches. But whence hath it all? is it not from the earth, in and under which it is? so Zedekiah had his political or kingly life, all his power and strength, from Nebuchadnezzar, under whom he was.

Obs. 1. That heathen princes may come to much greatness. Nebuchadnezzar, who was a heathen, is called an eagle, who is the chief of all birds; and not simply an eagle, but a great eagle, with great and long wings, full of feathers. He had great power, great territories, multitudes of people, yea, kings and princes under him. Dan. ii. 37, 38, "Thou, O king, art a king of kings: for the God of heaven hath given thee a kingdom, power, strength, and glory. And wheresoever the children of men dwell, the beasts of the field and the fowls of the heaven hath he given into thine hand, and hath made thee ruler over them all." He had vast power over men, fowls, and beasts; he was the greatest eagle of those times.

Profane authors make an eagle an emblem of majesty and greatness. King Pyrrhus would be called an eagle, as Plutarch observes in his Life. Alexander the Great, that day he was born, two eagles were seen to sit upon the top of the house, which presaged his greatness; for he conquered Europe and Asia, two great parts of the world; he was an eagle that had great and long wings, which extended from east to west. Ahasuerus was such an eagle, he "reigned from India even unto Ethiopia, over an hundred and seven and twenty provinces," Esth. i. 1.

Obs. 2. Princes, potentates, who are the eagles of the world, have an ill eye at the church and people of God. This great eagle came to Lebanon, his eye was upon the Jews that dwelt in the holy land, that were the only people of God, and them he made a prey of. Eagles have piercing eyes, strong beaks, terrible talons; and let the doves look to it, if any be in danger, it is they; not puttocks, kites, buzzards do eagles mind, but doves. The church is in holy writ called a dove, Cant. vi. 9; Psal. lxxiv. 19; and it is subject to spoil and prey. The eagles have their eyes upon it, and watch their opportunity to tear and devour it. Did not Sennacherib, that great eagle, who had strong and long wings, come to Judah and take the defenced cities thereof? came he not up to the gates and walls of Jerusalem, with full purpose to spoil and devour? Isa. xxxvi. 1, 2. Did he not say, "I am come to the sides of Lebanon, and I will cut down the tall cedars thereof, and the choice fir trees thereof," chap. xxxvii. 24. It is Zion, Lebanon, Jerusalem, that the monarchs and great ones of the earth have spite at. Did not the great ones of Edom, Ishmael, Moab, Hagaren, Gebal, Ammon, Amalek, of the Philistines, Tyrians, and Assyrians, conspire together against God's people, consult against his hidden ones, and say, "Come, let us cut them off from being a nation, that the name of Israel may be no more in remembrance," Psal. lxxxiii. Mount Seir "had a perpetual hatred against the children of Israel," Ezek. xxxv. 5. Ammon, Moab, and mount Seir, though spared by the Israelites when they came out of Egypt; yet they came against Jehoshaphat and Judah to cast them out of their possessions, 2 Chron. xx. 10, 11. They would not only plunder them, but root them out; they would utterly extirpate them, and the memory of them. Such was the intention and attempt of Haman. Do not the eagles and great ones of the earth seek to lay waste Zion, and root out the generation of the righteous?

Obs. 3. States may rise to a great height, even the height of cedars. The Jewish state is called a cedar, yea, a cedar upon Lebanon, a hill. Cedars are very high: 2 Kings xix. 23, "The tall cedars;" Hebrew is, the tallness of cedars: Amos ii. 9, "Whose height was like the height of cedars." And they were higher than fir trees; Zech. xi. 2, "Howl, fir tree; for the cedar is fallen:" inferiors howl, mourn, when higher than themselves do fall.

The Jewish state being likened to a cedar, was great, high, glorious, powerful, God prospered it so that it flourished greatly; it was like the cedar for tallness, but not for sweetness, for Jehoiachin, who was the top of this cedar, "did evil in the sight of the Lord," 2 Kings xxiv. 9.

Obs. 4. No kings or kingdoms are so high or great, but the Lord can bring them down, and abase them. A great eagle comes and crops the highest branch of the cedar, and the top of his young twigs; Jehoiachin, the princes and nobles, are taken away by him, and deprived of all their greatness and glory. The top of this tall cedar was broken off, and thrown to the ground, and it was done by the counsel, appointment, and providence of God: "Thus saith the Lord, A great eagle came to Lebanon." God sent this eagle to do it: he hath means, ways, times, to un-power kingdoms, to un-king kings, to un-noble nobles; he can at his pleasure remove kings, and take them and others from all rule and government. Dan. ii. 20, 21, "Wisdom and might are his; he changeth the times and the seasons;" the times of all states, empires, governments, are in his hand, and he removes the kings and governors of them at his pleasure. Job tells us, "he looseth the bond of kings," chap. xii. 18; the bond of kings is their authority, the laws and covenants, by which people are bound unto them; the Lord takes away the one, and makes people regardless of the other. "He leadeth princes away spoiled, and overthroweth the mighty," ver. 19; "he poureth contempt upon princes," ver. 21: thus did he deal by Jehoiachin, he loosed his bond, led him away, spoiled, and made him contemptible.

Sometimes God takes them off from the throne by a stroke in war; so Ahab was removed, 1 Kings xxii. Sometimes by the act of their own hand; so Saul, 1 Sam. xxxi. 4. Sometimes by stirring up their own subjects against them; so Nebuchadnezzar, this great eagle, that cropped the cedars of Lebanon, was driven from his nest by the inferior birds: Dan. iv. 32, "They shall drive thee from men, and thy dwelling shall be with the beasts of the field;" and, ver. 33, "he was driven from men." Christian, king of Denmark, was put from the throne by his nobles for his great cruelty, himself, wife, and three children, banished, as Sleid. l. 4. The Roman emperors were sixty-three, and only six died a natural and peaceable death, as Fitzherbert observeth in his treatise concerning Policy and Religion, p. 2. c. 13. They were bloody, tyrannical, and God took them off by unnatural deaths.

Other kingdoms, and this also, can tell you of cedars whose top-branches have been cropped: how it fared with Edward II. is not unknown to you.

If kings would not have God to loose their bonds, let them take heed how they break his bonds, and go beyond the bounds of religion and justice which he sets them.

Obs. 5. Though God do deprive great ones of great mercies, yet not always of all mercies. "The highest branch of the cedar, and the top of his young twigs," are cropped, but they are not thrown away, or thrown into the fire; but they are "carried into a land of traffick, and set in a city of merchants." Jehoiachin, the princes, and glory of the land, are deprived of their power and greatness; that was a sad affliction; but they were provided for in a strange land, suffered to trade and live. God mingles mercy with judgments; yea, when they are great, sharp, proclaim the severity of God, yet even then there is some matter of comfort twisted together with them; if there be severity on the one hand, there is goodness on the other.

It seemed to be the height of rigour to pull Jehoiachin, a young king, from the throne, and to deprive him and the nobles of all the comforts that Canaan, Jerusalem, and the temple could afford; but it was not. Their limbs might have been pulled from them, their eyes put out, their lives taken away; but these are spared, and they are seated, not in a country village, but in a city, and a city of merchants, that so they might have commerce with men of quality, be taken up with merchandizing affairs, and not mind their losses too much.

Obs. 6. God prevents men's expectations, and raises up to that honour and greatness they looked not for. God ordered the spirit of Nebuchadnezzar so, that "he took of the seed of the land, and planted it;" that is, he made Zedekiah king, who looked not for it. He was Jehoiachin's father's brother, 2 Kings xxiv. 17; and, seeing the cedar of Lebanon now cropped, had little cause to think himself, or any of the Jewish race, should be advanced: he might have concluded warrantably that himself should have been carried into Babylon, set in the city of merchants, and not have abode in Canaan, be planted in the fruitful field and city of God; but God's thoughts are not the thoughts of men, he exalts whom he pleases: Psal. lxxv. 6, 7, "Promotion is neither from the east, nor from the west, nor from the south; but God is the Judge; he putteth down one, and setteth up another," and doth it unexpectedly many times. Saul, when looking for asses, had a kingdom, and kingly honour, bestowed on him, 1 Sam. ix. x. When David's thoughts were upon the sheep and sheepfolds, God's thoughts were upon him for higher purposes; he took him from his sheep and sheepfolds to feed Jacob his people, and Israel, &c. Psalm lxxviii. 70, 71. How unexpectedly were Hazael and Jehu raised to kingly dignity, 2 Kings viii. 13; ix. 5, 6. Joseph in Egypt, Daniel, Mordecai, and Esther, in Babylon; did not God prevent their thoughts, and set them higher than their expectations advanced? Hannah saw, and confessed it long since, that the Lord "raiseth up the poor out of the dust, and lifteth up the beggar from the dunghill, to set them among princes, and to make them inherit the throne of glory." Poor and mean men look not for such high things, but the Lord freely bestows it on them: Psal. cxiii. 8, he sets them with princes.

Obs. 7. The disposing of subdued kingdoms is a difficult work, and requires wisdom, care, and caution. Nebuchadnezzar had subdued the land of Canaan, and what doth he? he wisely takes "of the seed of the land," not of the seed of Babylon, not a stranger, which would have bred divisions, contentions, wars, and blood, but one of themselves, and places amongst them, and that with circumspection. He made things sure as he could for himself, and sure for Zedekiah, whom he planted amongst and set over the people; he was very circumspect in this weighty business; so the word *saphsaphah* signifies: men of this world are wise in their generations. This king, when he took away Jehoiachin, "carried away all Jerusalem, and all the princes, and all the mighty men of valour, even ten thousand captives, and all the craftsmen and smiths, the king's wives, and his officers, and all that were apt for war, and none remained save the poorest sort of the land," 2 Kings xxiv. 14—16. He took away all that might be of use to the new king; he would leave him none to give him ill counsel, or assist him in ill enterprises; he planted him "by great waters," among multitudes of poor people, that had little for themselves, and less for their king.

Obs. 8. Tributary princes and kingdoms at first are respectful and grateful to those that they depend upon. Zedekiah was planted by Nebuchadnezzar in Judea, and his branches turned toward him, and the roots were under him: himself, and those who belonged to him, acknowledged their dependence on Nebuchadnezzar. Kindness, favour, is to be owned and confessed, though from strangers and heathens. He sent to Nebuchadnezzar, Jer. xxix. 3, yea, he went to him, Jer. li. 59; so that he was very observable of him. And while he was content with this condition of being under that potent king, and faithful in keeping covenant, and performing articles agreed upon, he and the kingdom thrived; it is said of him, "he grew, and became a spreading vine, which brought forth branches, and shot forth twigs." He grew in estate, in children, in nobles, in offices and officers; he came to the condition of a vine, yea, a spreading vine, that hath leaves and branches.

Obs. 9. When the glory and strength of a kingdom is marred and broken by wars, it doth not easily recover its pristine condition, if ever. The kingdom of Judah, after Nebuchadnezzar's plundering and spoiling of it, in time became a vine, but "of low stature;" in all Zedekiah's days it did not recover itself. When a tree is cropped, it requires time to grow up again, and, it may be, never attains its former height and glory. This kingdom was a tall cedar before, now it was a low shrub; it had not that wealth, power, dignity, greatness it had before. If a family or town be ruined by wars, it may be seven years before they get up again, and seven to that; much more when kingdoms are shaken, battered, wounded.

Obs. 10. See hence the instability of all earthly greatness. Kings and kingdoms that were high and most flourishing, are soon brought low. The kingdom of Judah was glorious, powerful, like the highest cedar upon the hill of Lebanon; but it continued not, it suffered many changes. Ten tribes were rent from it in Rehoboam's days; Sennacherib infested it in Hezekiah's days; Pharaoh-necho in Jehoiakim's, and put it under tax; Nebuchadnezzar, he cropped, cropped the cedar, took off the highest branch, and top of the young twigs, &c. So that the kingdoms of this world cannot be holden long by any. Let us fear that God, who batters and shakes kingdoms in pieces; look after, and labour, for that "kingdom which cannot be moved," Heb. xii. 28. Let us not mind the riches of the world, but labour to be poor in spirit, "for theirs is the kingdom of heaven."

Ver. 7, 8. ***There was also another great eagle with great wings and many feathers: and, behold, this vine did bend her roots toward him, and shot forth her branches toward him, that he might*** *water it by the furrows of her plantation. It was planted in a good soil by great waters, that it might bring forth branches, and that it might bear fruit, that it might be a goodly vine.*

Here you have the second part of the parable, wherein the king of Egypt and Zedekiah's revolting come into consideration.

"Another great eagle." This eagle was the king of Egypt, as the 15th and 17th verses do certify. Kings are called eagles, and upon what account was opened unto you out of the third verse.

This eagle was great in power and dominion, but not so great as the other; for though this eagle had great wings, yet it is not said, he had long wings, as the other had.

"Many feathers." Much wealth, many people and soldiers.

"This vine did bend her roots toward him, and shot forth her branches toward him." Zedekiah looked at the power and greatness of the king of Egypt, and sent ambassadors to him, that they might join forces. The roots of trees do incline that way there is moisture and succour for them; so Zedekiah, apprehending that Pharaoh, king of Egypt, would succour and relieve him, he falls off from Nebuchadnezzar, and seeks to him. He sent his ambassadors, which were as the branches of this vine, into Egypt for horses and people, ver. 15; Jer. ii. 18, "What hast thou to do in the way of Egypt, to drink the waters of Sihor?" Sihor was a little river before Egypt, Josh. xiii. 3, and is put for Nilus, or Egypt, and waters, for the people and forces. Zedekiah sent thither to draw the forces thereof unto his assistance.

"That he might water it by the furrows of her plantation." Hebrew, from, or by, the lines of her plantation. The Hebrew word signifies, a bed; so it is used, Cant. v. 13, and a furrow, which is a line drawn: and Avenarius saith, it is a water line, or furrow through which the waters ran. In Egypt they made furrows and lines through which the waters of Nilus ran and watered the country; so here, Zedekiah endeavoured, by his ambassadors and presents, to join interest with Pharaoh, and so to gain the help of men and horse from him, whereby he might defend himself against Nebuchadnezzar, whom deserting, he provoked against him. Pharaoh entertaining this notion, sends forces, as you may see, Jer. xxxvii. 5, 6: and this was the watering of the Jewish vine in the furrows of her plantation.

Ver. 8. "It was planted in a good soil," &c. This verse sets out the ingratitude of Zedekiah, who might not only have kept his kingdom, but have prospered in it, and come to greatness, for Nebuchadnezzar had planted him "in a good soil," &c.

If a vine be planted in a good and rich soil, it roots, grows, flourishes with branches, leaves, clusters, and becomes useful, delightful unto many; so might this metaphorical vine Zedekiah, for the soil he was planted in was the land of promise, "a fruitful field," as it is expressed in ver. 5; a good field, as the Hebrew hath it here: a good field is a fruitful field, and a fruitful field is a good field.

"By great waters." What was meant by "waters" was shown in ver. 5. When trees are planted by waters, there is no fear of wanting moisture and withering thereupon. Vines do need much moisture, and draw abundantly from the soil; Zedekiah was among the waters, viz. the poor people, who contributed their endeavours to make him great.

"That it might be a goodly vine." The Hebrew word for goodly is, אדרת which signifies, comely, magnificent, strong. Septuagint, εἰς ἄμπελον μεγάλην, that it might be a great vine. Nebuchadnezzar dealt honourably and prince-like by Zedekiah, who being a private man before, and liable to captivity with the rest carried away when Jeconiah was, was not only spared, but advanced to kingly dignity, and set in such a condition that he needed not the help of any, he needed not the waters of Egypt and Nilus: he had Nebuchadnezzar, that great eagle, to be his protector; and had he been faithful in his engagements to him, he might have become a goodly, great, strong, beautiful, excellent, and fruitful vine.

Obs. 1. That the Lord takes special notice of the monarchs and kings of the earth, of their greatness, power, honour, wealth, and glory. In ver. 3, he speaks of Nebuchadnezzar king of Babylon; "A great eagle with great wings, longwinged, full of feathers, which had divers colours;" in this 7th verse, of Pharaoh, king of Egypt, a "great eagle with great wings and many feathers." God's eye is much upon princes and potentates of the earth: Psal. lxxxix. 27, I will make David "higher than the kings of the earth;" he observed them and their height. He sees and notes their rising; Hos. viii. 4, "They have set up kings, but not by me:" their greatness; Dan. iv. 22, "Thy greatness, O king, is grown, and reacheth unto heaven:" their doings; Luke xxii. 25, "The kings of the gentiles exercise lordship over them:" how they set themselves against God, Psal. ii. 2: against him and his people, him and his army; Rev. xix. 19, "I saw the kings of the earth, and their armies, gathered together to make war against him that sat on the horse, and against his army." They are gods upon earth, Psal. lxxxii. 6; they bear his image, have his authority; and if they step aside, and turn their greatness against God, his cause, and people, the Lord will "strike through kings in the day of his wrath," Psal. cx. 5. "He shall cut off the spirit of princes," and be "terrible to the kings of the earth," Psal. lxxvi. 12. Let kings, therefore, be wise, kiss the Son, Psal. ii. 10, 12, and improve all for the interest of Christ.

Obs. 2. The kings and monarchs of the earth are not all alike, they are diverse, and admit of disparity. Nebuchadnezzar and Pharaoh both were eagles, but the Egyptian eagle was not so great and potent as the Babylonian; this was "full of feathers," that had "many feathers;" this had "great and long wings," that only "great;" Pharaoh's power extended not so far as Nebuchadnezzar's. Some princes are little eagles, some are great, and others very great. Those thirty-one kings whom Joshua smote were kings of cities, Josh. xii. 9—24; they were little eagles, and had little nests. Hamor was prince of a country, Gen. xxxiv. 2, he was a greater eagle; so Tidal, king of nations, Gen. xiv. 1, he went beyond Hamor; but others exceeded him. Ahasuerus was an eagle with "great and long wings," his nest was large, a hundred and twenty-seven provinces over which he spread his wings, Esth. i. 1. So Sennacherib, the king of Assyria, is called "the great king, the king of Assyria," Isa. xxxvi. 4. And Nebuchadnezzar, for his greatness, is titled "a king of kings." The Babylon, Assyrian, Grecian, and Roman emperors were great eagles. God gives power, honour, greatness, to whom he pleases, and in what proportion he pleases; some are eagles with greater, longer wings, and more feathers, than others.

Obs. 3. Men's natures are such as that they are seldom content with any condition they are set in. Zedekiah was set in the throne, exalted to kingly honour, but this satisfied him not; "this vine did bend her roots toward" the Egyptian eagle, "and shot forth her branches toward him." Adam and Eve at first were not content with their condition they were set in, but must have and know more than

God allowed them, Gen. iii. 6. "Man being in honour abideth not," Psal. xlix. 12: he abides not satisfied, his brutish desires carry him after forbidden fruit. Habakkuk, speaking of a Chaldean prince, saith, "He keeps not at home, he enlargeth his desire as hell, and is as death, and cannot be satisfied, but gathereth unto him all nations, and heaps unto him all people," Hab. ii. 6. Isaiah tells you the king of Babylon was so unsatisfied with his present condition, that he said he would ascend into heaven, and exalt his throne above the stars of God, be like the Most High; he had made the world a wilderness, and destroyed the cities thereof, and now he would up to heaven, Isa. xiv. 4, 13, 14, 17.

Plutarch in Pyrrho. Pyrrhus, king of Epirus, having enlarged his dominions by the conquest of Macedonia, thirsted after Italy; and demanding the advice of Cineas, his great counsellor, he asked him what he meant to do when he had conquered Italy? Next I mean to get Sicily, which is near, rich, and powerful. When you have gotten Sicily, said Cineas, what then? Africa, saith the king, is not far off, and there be many goodly kingdoms, which, through my fame and valour of my soldiers, I may subdue. Be it so, said Cineas; when you have Africa, and all in it, what will you do then? Said the king, Then thou and I will be merry, and make good cheer. Cineas replied, Sir, if this be the end you aim at, what need you venture your kingdoms, person, life, honour, and all you have, to purchase that you have already; Epirus and Macedonia are sufficient to make you and me merry; had you all the world you could not be more merry, nor have better cheer.

Obs. 4. Discontentedness with the present condition puts men upon unwarrantable practices to relieve and free themselves from what they apprehend burdensome. Zedekiah was discontented that he was tributary to and dependent upon the king of Babylon, he apprehended this a grievous burden; his predecessors most of them free and absolute kings, and he to be under the power of another, and he a heathen! This kindled an ill, fiery, malignant spirit in his breast, and made him sue to Egypt for help to shake off the Babylonish yoke, which was unwarrantable and unlawful for him to do. This is like an ill wife, that finding the yoke of her husband a little pinching, deserts him, and betakes herself to another. Zedekiah should have applied himself to Nebuchadnezzar for relief if any thing were grievous to him, and not to Pharaoh, on whom he had no dependence, from whom he had received no favour; but discontent, and hope of liberty, puts him upon perfidious practices. The Israelites, being discontented with the taxes laid upon them by Solomon, sued to Rehoboam for relief: he unwisely gives them a rough answer, and exasperates their spirits; presently they fall off from him, stone Adoram the tribute-gatherer, make Jeroboam king, and submit to him, 1 Kings xii. 14, 16, 18, 20.

The Jews, hearing the ill report of the land of Canaan, murmur and say, "Would God that we had died in the land of Egypt, or in this wilderness! Wherefore hath the Lord brought us unto this land, to fall by the sword, that our wives and our children should be a prey? were it not better for us to return into Egypt?" And see what their discontent put them upon: "They said one to another, Let us make a captain, and let us return into Egypt," Numb. xiv. 2—4. They were weary of Moses and Aaron, and their government, and now they would make them a captain, a king, say the rabbies, and return to Egypt to the onions and garlic, to their old ways. Such hath been the condition of the people here: Jeroboam thought, by setting up the calves, to secure himself and the kingdom, but that very thing was his ruin.

Obs. 5. The condition Divine Providence sets any in is good, and therein they may prosper if wise and contented. This vine "was planted in a good soil," and to what end? "that it might bring forth branches, bear fruit, and be a goodly vine." Zedekiah, being made king in Israel, was set in a good condition; and had he wisely managed the affairs of the kingdom, and been content with what God gave him in and by the hand of Nebuchadnezzar, he might have prospered greatly, had a glorious kingdom, been a renowned king.

The kingly office is honourable, and when God sets up kings over people, they might be happy, and grow potent. Solomon, who was a wise king, prospered exceedingly in that soil he was planted in, and lived happily; but Rehoboam his son, through his folly and discontentedness with his people, lost ten parts of his kingdom, and made his reign troublesome afterwards, 1 Kings xii. Zedekiah, by his folly and discontent, undid himself; being impatient of the yoke God had put upon him, he foolishly sends to, and relies upon, Egypt, and thinks by Egyptian hands to re-lift himself into a better condition than God had put him in, but this was his ruin: Isa. xxxi. 1, "Woe to them that go down to Egypt for help; and stay on horses, and trust in chariots, because they are many; and in horsemen, because they are very strong; but they look not unto the Holy One of Israel, neither seek the Lord." Had Zedekiah sought to the Lord, he could have watered the furrows of his plantation better than Egypt. It is a common sickness among men, and especially great ones, kings and princes, that they make the good condition God hath set them in unhappy to themselves; would they keep within bounds, be content with what God hath allowed them, and use that wisely, they might do well, and live happily.

The God of Israel and his worship would not content Ahaz, but he must set up the Damascene altar, sacrifice to the gods of Damascus, hoping for help from them; but they proved his ruin, and the ruin of all Israel, 2 Chron. xxviii. 23.

Ver. 9, 10. *Say thou, Thus saith the Lord God; Shall it prosper? shall he not pull up the roots thereof, and cut off the fruit thereof, that it wither? it shall wither in all the leaves of her spring, even without great power or many people to pluck it up by the roots thereof. Yea, behold, being planted, shall it prosper? shall it not utterly wither, when the east wind toucheth it? it shall wither in the furrows where it grew.*

These verses do enigmatically proclaim the event of Zedekiah's revolt; he thought to have mended and made himself by it, but it was his ruin. Being formerly compared to a vine, here the vine is sentenced,

I. Not to prosper; "Shall it prosper?"

II. To be rooted up, so that it shall wither, and neither have fruit nor leaves.

III. How? not by any great power, ver. 9, but by an east wind, ver. 10.

"Shall it prosper?" Hebrew תצלח the word צלח signifies, to divide, cut, pass through; and metaphorically, to pass, break through happily, to prosper. This vine was planted under the wings of the great eagle, who did preserve and protect it while it looked and leaned towards him, and then it prospered, ver. 6. But, seeing the roots and branches of this vine bend and move another way, viz. towards Egypt, "shall it prosper?" no, perfidiousness is not the way to prosper, it will bring the axe to lop and cut it down. This interrogation is a vehement negation: "Shall it prosper?" It is so far from prospering, that its utter ruin is at hand.

"Shall he not pull up the roots thereof?" &c. This metaphorical vine, Zedekiah, should be deprived of kingly power; yea, his children, nobles, counsellors, officers, people, which were the branches and leaves of this vine, should wither and come to nothing; yea, the place it grew in, Jerusalem itself, should be laid waste. The destruction of Zedekiah and his kingdom is likened to the cutting down and plucking up of a flourishing vine. The fulfilling of this you may see in 2 Kings xxv. 7, 18—21. It is said, at Riblah they gave judgment upon Zedekiah, there Nebuchadnezzar called a council of war, told him what he had done for him, in what engagements he stood bound to him, which he expected should have been made good; how he had perfidiously revolted from him, betaken himself for help to the king of Egypt against him, and therefore now he should suffer for it. Whereupon he slew his sons before his eyes, put all the nobles of Judah to death; and when he had seen these sad spectacles, then he also put out Zedekiah's eyes, Jer. xxxix. 6, 7.

"Without great power or many people to pluck it up." Hebrew is, and not in, or with, a great arm; that is, without great power, arm noting power. Some read the words by way of interrogation, thus; Shall he not with great power? insinuating, that Nebuchadnezzar should come with great power and many people, as he did, to cut down and pluck up this vine; but this is rather forced than natural. "Without great power or many people;" Nebuchadnezzar will bring multitudes and great strength, but half, or a third part, will do the business; for Zedekiah hath sinned by his perfidious dealings, provoked me against him, saith God, and therefore I will give him up to the hand of Nebuchadnezzar without much ado; I will be so far from helping him with counsel or protection, that I will facilitate the way for his utter extirpation and ruin.

Ver. 10. "When the east wind toucheth it." Eastern winds are prejudicial, as to other things, so especially to plants, vines, trees; see Hos. xiii. 15; Ezek. xix. 12, an east wind dried up the fruit. It was an east wind made Jonah to faint, chap. iv. 8; an east wind that blasted the ears of corn, Gen. xli. 6.

By east wind here is meant the king of Babylon and his army, who is so called, either because he should be as an eastern wind unto this vine, dry up all the moisture and sap of it, that it should wither in the branches and roots; or else from the situation, Babylon being north-east from Jerusalem.

Hence is it that Nebuchadnezzar and his forces sometimes are called a wind out of the north: chap. i. 4, "A whirlwind came out of the north." And here, a wind of the east, which should no sooner touch this vine, but it should languish. East winds are violent, sudden, and destructive; so should this be to this vine, even a scorching wind.

Obs. 1. When men are perfidious and false in their trust and obligations, though princes, they shall not speed well, they shall not prosper. "Shall it prosper?" shall Zedekiah, his sons, nobles, counsellors, people, that have had a hand in his perfidious doing, "prosper?" No, they shall not prosper, I am resolved upon it. Let them take counsel together, it shall come to nought, as Isa. viii. 10. No counsels, no enterprises, no wars, shall succeed well, I will blow upon and blast all; let them get all their power, their soldiery and strong men, together, go out to war, and see what shall be the issue: Jer. xxxii. 5, "Though you fight with the Chaldeans, ye shall not prosper."

When men are false to God and man, they cannot thrive and prosper in their ways. See what is upon record in 2 Chron. xxiv. 20, "Why transgress ye the commandments of the Lord, that ye cannot prosper?" these words were spoken to a king, and to princes. Joash, his princes, and people, had covenanted, through Jehoiada's means, to be for the Lord, chap. xxiii. 16; but Jehoiada being dead, the princes violated the covenant, and drew the king to idolatry; hereupon saith Zachariah unto them, "Why transgress ye the commandments of the Lord, that ye cannot prosper?" God is not with you, and you cannot prosper in any thing. Have any prospered in the late wars amongst us who were perfidious? Let Wales, Kent, Essex, and the sea itself speak.

Obs. 2. Perfidiousness, treachery in kings, nobles, or any, is so provoking a sin, as oft it moves God to bring severe judgments upon them who are guilty thereof, yea, utter destruction upon them and theirs. Saith God of this metaphorical vine, "Shall he not pull up the roots thereof, and cut off the fruit thereof," &c.? Zedekiah thought by his perfidious ways to advance himself, but his perfidiousness so provoked God, that for it he rooted him and his family up, and ruined the whole kingdom: Zedekiah loses his crown, kingdom, sons, nobles, people, eyes, at once, and afterwards his life. What sad things did that perfidious act bring upon them! *vide* Turkish History, p. 287, battle of Varna, between Uladislaus and Amurath, &c.

Obs. 3. It is no difficult thing for God, being provoked, to pluck up, root out, destroy kings and kingdoms, how strong and well accommodated soever they be. Here was a vine planted in a good soil, by many waters, was likely to prosper, grow, and continue long; but "shall he not pull up the roots thereof, without great power or many people?" A gardener can easily, quickly pluck up a vine, and God did as easily pluck up Zedekiah, who was planted in Jerusalem, compassed about with mountains, assisted with the strength and power of Egypt; it is but sending of a wind, when the east wind toucheth it. I will but call for a wind, saith God, it shall be an east wind, and as soon as that toucheth this vine, it shall wither. A wind seems an unlikely thing to do any great matter, yet it is such as none can prevent, withstand; trees, ships, mountains, &c. have suffered greatly by it.

2 Chron. xxiv. 23, 24, the Syrians came with a small company of men, and the Lord delivered a very great army into their hand; because they had forsaken the Lord God of their fathers, they destroyed all the princes of the people.

Let the power, policy of princes be what it will, if they sin with a high hand against God, he can without a high hand punish them; he hath an east wind, or a north wind, &c.

Obs. 4. God magnifies his justice in punishing wicked men even in the place where they sin, and turning that to their ruin which they thought would have been their raising. "It shall wither in the furrows where it grew." It grew at Jerusalem; there it sinned in bending its roots towards Egypt, and fetching help from thence, and there it shall wither.

Nebuchadnezzar, Dan. iv. 30, 31, where he lifted up himself there it was said, "The kingdom is departed from thee." Those who built Babel, smitten,

&c. Gen. xi.; Sodomites, Gen. xix.; two captains with their fifties, 2 Kings i. If you sin where God hath planted you, even there he can punish you, he can make you wither in the furrows of your plantation.

Ver. 11—15. *Moreover the word of the Lord came unto me, saying, Say now to the rebellious house, Know ye not what these things mean? tell them, Behold, the king of Babylon is come to Jerusalem, and hath taken the king thereof, and the princes thereof, and led them with him to Babylon; and hath taken of the king's seed, and made a covenant with him, and hath taken an oath of him: he hath also taken the mighty of the land: that the kingdom might be base, that it might not lift itself up, but that by keeping of his covenant it might stand. But he rebelled against him in sending his ambassadors into Egypt, that they might give him horses and much people. Shall he prosper? shall he escape that doeth such things? or shall he break the covenant, and be delivered?*

Here begins the explication and application of the former parable concerning the eagle, the cedar, and vine, and it extends unto the 22nd verse.

I. You have a transition in the 11th verse, from the parable itself to the explication of it.

II. An introduction to the explication by way of query in the first part of the 12th verse.

III. The explication itself; "Tell them, Behold the king of Babylon is come," &c.

There is nothing in the transition and introduction needful to open, but these words,

"The rebellious house." Hebrew is, The house of rebellion or bitterness; Septuagint is, πρὸς τὸν οἶκον ἰσραὴλ τὸν παραπικραίνοντα, to the house of Israel that is contentious. And so was this house, which was not the house of Israel strictly taken, but the tribe of Judah; but, in a large sense, it was called the house of Israel, ver. 3.

Obs. 1. The messengers of God must deliver the mind of God, be it pleasing or provoking, be it matter of comfort or terror. Ezekiel must go and tell this rebellious house sad things; that it should not prosper, that it should be rooted up and utterly ruined. They must denounce judgments to the wicked, as well as pardon to the penitent; threats to the stubborn, as well as promises to the fainting; they must not give out what pleases themselves, but what the Lord hints and commands them: "The word of the Lord came unto me, saying, Say now to the rebellious house," &c. It is grievous to the servants of God to be heralds, trumpeters of war, judgments, and death; but they must not decline the service; if they do, it may cost them dear. Jonah, when sent of God to proclaim war against Nineveh, "Yet forty days, and Nineveh," &c. he fled another way; but God pursued him with a tempest, and set the winds and waters in battle against him, and his life was almost gone.

The ambassadors of God and Christ must neither flatter the persons, nor fear the faces, of the greatest among the sons of men. Jeremiah dealt roundly with Jehoiakim and Jehoiachin, and thundered out God's judgments against them, though great kings, chap. xxii. 17—22, 24, &c. So Paul against Elymas, Acts xiii. 10, 11. Neither favour nor fear must strike a prophet dumb; when God hath given in commission, he must give out, let the event be what it will.

Obs. 2. Truths disaffective find cold entertainment; judgments threatened are little minded. "Know ye not what these things mean? do you not understand what is pointed out in this parable and riddle? You may easily attain thereunto, but that you have no heart to it, the things delivered please you not, are cross to your wills, desires, humours, and therefore care not to know the meaning of them: *Quæ nolumus facile et libenter ignoramus*, Men shut their eyes against those things that dislike them, and care not for the knowledge of them. Jeremiah counselled Zedekiah to yield himself to the Babylonians, told him it would be the means to save his life, and the city from fire, Jer. xxxviii. 17, but it suited not with his spirit, and he minded it not. Micaiah prophesied truths distasteful unto Ahab: what followed upon it? he did not only disaffect those truths, but the person also for the truths' sake: 1 Kings xxii. 8, "I hate him," saith Ahab, "for he doth not prophesy good concerning me, but evil." And when he told him that if he went up to Ramoth-gilead he should not prosper, but his men be scattered, and himself not return in peace, he believed it not, but commanded the prophet to prison, for declaring the mind of God. So Luke xvi. 13, 14.

Ver. 12. Tell them, Behold, the king of Babylon is come to Jerusalem," &c. Do you not know what the parable means? The meaning is this: The great eagle, with great and long wings, full of feathers, and of divers colours, is the king of Babylon; Lebanon is Jerusalem; the top of the cedar, and twigs thereof, are Jehoiachin, his princes, and nobles; the land of traffic is Babylon; them hath he taken away, brought thither, and seated there; the seed of the land is Zedekiah, whom he set up to be king in Jerusalem, invested with power, that he might flourish and spread as a vine, &c.

Ver. 13. "And made a covenant with him." The Hebrew is, cut out, or struck, a covenant with him; Septuagint, he ordered, or disposed, a covenant to him. As for the word "covenant," I spake of it largely in chap. xvi. 8. The manner of making a covenant among the Jews you may read of in Jer. xxxiv. 18; but whether the Babylonian king made this covenant with Zedekiah in such a manner is not evident; a covenant he made with him, that he should be tributary to him, and bound it with an oath, as followeth:

"And hath taken an oath of him." Hebrew, hath brought him into an oath; Septuagint, into a curse. The Hebrew word אלה signifies an oath with cursing, or execration; a man ties himself with imprecation of mischief if he perform not his promise, or things agreed upon.

"He hath also taken the mighty of the land." Hebrew is, the rams of the land; Septuagint, the leaders; others, the potentates. Mighty and great men are called rams.

1. They are strong creatures, and have their name from a word which signifies, fortitude, strength, virtue. So great men are strong, they are strengthened with riches, honours, friends, counsel, strong holds, arms, and what the creature can afford, yea, with strong lusts: Dan. viii. 20, "The ram which thou sawest having two horns are the kings of Media and Persia."

2. Rams go before the flock, they have the precedency. Great men, they are the leaders, and go before the people; they carry multitudes after them, people follow the great men as flocks of sheep do the rams. Ezek. xxxi. 11, Nebuchadnezzar is called "the mighty one of the heathen;" the Hebrew is, the ram of the heathen, he went before them and led them.

3. Rams are pushing things. Dan. viii. 4, "I saw the ram pushing eastward, and westward, and

southward; no beast could stand before him:" they oft do fiercely assault one another. So great men are pushing and butting with their power, and who of the people can stand before them? Eccles. iv. 1, on the oppressors' side was power. Ezek. xlvi. 18, princes and great men use to take of the people's inheritance by oppression, and to thrust them out of their possessions.

Many times great ones push and butt at one another till they break each in pieces.

Ver. 14. "That the kingdom might be base," or low. This was Nebuchadnezzar's design, to take away the mighty men, who were the strength of the kingdom, and held it up in greatness and glory, that so it might be base, low, weak; and so the Septuagint renders it, that it might be a weak kingdom, of low stature, as it is, ver. 6. Nebuchadnezzar left none but poor people; 2 Kings xxiv. 14, "None remained, save the poorest sort of the people of the land."

"That it might not lift itself up." Nebuchadnezzar conceived this people, having been free, would hardly submit to his yoke, and depend upon him; he dealt politicly, as princes in such cases use to do when they fear rising and rebellion; they carry away the wise, skilful, strong, and honourable men, disarm them, break down their strong holds, and plant garrisons among them; so he took that course, which he thought should prevent this kingdom's lifting up itself any more. It is like, the great ones were of turbulent, stirring, and active spirits, and he ordered it so as might secure the kingdom to himself, and keep all quiet under Zedekiah.

"That by keeping of his covenant it might stand." Had it kept the covenant Nebuchadnezzar made with it, the kingdom might have continued; but breach of covenant was the breaking of the kingdom: they did lift up themselves, and God threw them down.

Ver. 15. "But he rebelled against him." Zedekiah growing impatient under the Babylonish yoke, shook it off. The Hebrew word for, to rebel, signifies, to cast away the authority of him who hath power over one; Septuagint saith, he receded from him: and so he did, and went, or sent, to Egypt.

"In sending his ambassadors into Egypt." Here was the bending of his roots toward the second eagle, ver. 7. He sent his angels, as the Septuagint hath it, into Egypt, and made a league with Pharaoh, which he had little cause to do, having no such hard conditions put upon him by Nebuchadnezzar as might have been; and besides, the Egyptians had oppressed the Jews of old with bitter and sore bondage, and not long before had put down Jehoahaz, carried him into Egypt, "condemned the land in an hundred talents of silver and a talent of gold," 2 Chron. xxxvi. 2—4.

"That they might give him horses." Egypt had plenty of horses; Solomon had horses from thence, 1 Kings x. 21; and when Shishak, king of Egypt, came up against Jerusalem, he came with twelve hundred chariots, and sixty thousand horsemen; which clearly evidences they abounded in horses, and were notable horsemen. The Jews were apt to look unto the Egyptians and their horse, and placed too much confidence in them, as being mighty and strong, Isa. xxxi. 1, which occasioned the Spirit of God to say, "The Egyptians are men, and not God; and their horses flesh, and not spirit;" you think they are strong, swift, serviceable, as if they were all spirit, but I tell you they are all flesh.

"Shall he break the covenant?" Hebrew, shall he make void the covenant? transgress, violate the covenant? It was no unlawful oath or covenant that Zedekiah took or made: such oaths or covenants bind not. Herod sinned in performing his oath made to Herodias, Matt. xiv. 7, 8.

Quest. What if Zedekiah were forced to this? It may seem it was so; for the Hebrew is, he brought him to an oath, ver. 13. If so, was it binding? are extorted oaths and covenants to be observed?

Answ. If there be nothing simply evil in them, they do bind, and are to be performed. Men, when they make covenants, take oaths, though they do them not with full consent of will, yet they never do them against their wills; for there is something expressed or implied that begets a willingness, if not a complete will. As suppose a thief sets upon a man, robs him, and threatens to kill him if he will not vow, covenant, swear never to discover or pursue him; now rather than lose his life, let the thief spill his blood, add sin to sin, he doth it. So Zedekiah might fear captivity and his life, and upon those considerations enter into covenant; and had it been so, he had been bound in conscience to have made good his engagements. But there were other inducements to bring him into covenant; as advancement to kingly power, enjoyment of the kingdom upon conditions, preservation and protection by Nebuchadnezzar.

Object. It was to his great loss, the prejudice of him and his posterity, to become tributary to a foreign king.

Answ. It is a rule, that in injustice no right is or can be bottomed. If a man will take a kingdom upon such and such terms, it is no injury to him, though abridged of privileges and prerogatives his predecessors had; it is mercy he hath the kingdom, no injury he wants what others had: if he take the kingdom willingly, he takes the terms, conditions of it willingly. Conquerors may put their own terms upon those they do promote. This case of loss and prejudice is resolved by David, Psal. xv. 4; if a man have sworn "to his own hurt," he must not change, break covenant, falsify his oath, if he will be a child of God, or a citizen of heaven.

Obs. 1. God would have people understand his mind and meaning in Scripture, even riddles, parables, dark sayings. "Know ye not what these things mean? tell them, Behold, the king of Babylon is come to Jerusalem," &c. He will have Ezekiel to interpret the whole business unto them: what is given out darkly at one time in one place, at another time in some other place is cleared up, opened, and made more intelligible. The types and sacrifices were expounded and opened in Christ; he oft spake parables, and often opened them; see Matt. xiii. The service of the passover God would have made known to the children that should come after, Exod. xii. 26, 27: it would have been a dark business to them, God therefore provided they should understand it. So for the heaps of stones set in Jordan, and out of it God took care that they and their posterity might know the meaning thereof, Josh. iv. 8, 9, 21—23. The vision that Peter saw was afterwards opened unto him, and he knew the meaning of it, Acts x. Truths, scriptures that are difficult, God causes us to know the meaning of by some other scripture, or by his Spirit, revealing his mind to us in them. An angel was sent to Daniel to make him understand those dark visions he had, chap. viii. ix. x.

Obs. 2. No rank or sort of men are exempt from common and grievous calamities, not kings, not princes, not mighty men. The king of Babylon is come to Jerusalem, and hath taken the king, the princes, and the mighty men of the land, and led them with him into Babylon; they were conquered, plundered, taken, and carried into captivity. Such is the condition of human things, that even kings lose their kingdoms, their glory, greatness, and excellences. Nebuchadnezzar, whose greatness did reach to heaven, and dominion to the ends of the earth, Dan. iv. 22, even "he was driven from men, and did eat grass as oxen," ver. 33.

Dionysius the king, or rather tyrant, was driven out from Syracuse, and glad to teach a school at Corinth. Great men do prey upon, and seek the ruin of one another. Cæsar ruined Pompey; Cassius and Brutus ruined him. Berengarius the emperor, and Albertus his son, being overcome by Otho, were banished. Bajazet, king of the Turks, was brought to that misery as to be a stirrup for Tamerlane to get up upon his horse. Nimrod was a mighty hunter, he hunted men, and afterwards a kingdom, and by ruining of others he raised himself. No sort of men, especially if wicked, can promise any security to themselves long. Roderick, king of Spain, to assure himself against the children and friends of king Vitiza, whom he had deposed, dismantled all the strong holds in Spain, and disarmed the people; whereby, though he strengthened his state in regard of domestic dangers, yet he weakened it in respect of foreign attempts; for the Moors invading him shortly after, and overthrowing him, found so little resistance, that in seven or eight months they conquered almost all Spain. Look abroad, and you may see the kings and mighty men of the earth brought low, if not wholly broken: let China, Turkey, Muscovy, and nearer parts, speak what they feel and find.

Obs. 3. That covenants and oaths are securing and binding things. Nebuchadnezzar makes Zedekiah king, but he will not take his word for dependence on him, and being tributary to him; but he makes a covenant with him, takes an oath of him, and hereupon he thought all was safe.

Oaths are arguments of man's weakness; all human credit is so feeble, that it had need be strengthened with something more firm than itself. Psal. lxii. 9, "Surely men of low degree are vanity, and men of high degree are a lie;" there is no truth, fidelity in them, or their words. Men's hearts and tongues are so deceitful and false, even kings' and princes' as well as others, as that they deserve little or no trust to be given unto them, especially in matters of weight, as government and rule. Oaths therefore being by the great God, who knows the heart, and hears what the tongue utters, came in to strengthen human credit; for had not man sinned, there would have been no need or use of oaths; man's corruption made way for them. An oath therefore is to further man's credit, and it hath been of great authority and weight in all ages, and amongst all people; and Tully saith, antiquity knew no bond stronger than an oath to strengthen men's credit and fidelity. *Juramentum,* saith Aquinas, *a jure dicitur,* An oath was a law, and some used no other law to decide controversies but an oath; and it were well that, according to the apostle, an oath did end our strifes.

Obs. 4. God knows how to embase kingdoms and keep them under. He caused Nebuchadnezzar to take away the mighty men of the land, that the kingdom might be base, and not lift up itself. Men mighty in power, in wisdom, in justice, in wealth, they are the glory and strength of a land, they uphold it; but when a land becomes guilty by sinning grievously, God can bring it low, by foreign forces, as it is in the text, or by civil wars, as it is with us at this day: and not only doth God bring down kingdoms, but keep them so that they cannot get up.

Obs. 5. Faithfulness and justice uphold kingdoms. "That by keeping of his covenant it might stand." Had Zedekiah been faithful in the covenant, just in performing the oath made to Nebuchadnezzar, the kingdom had stood, himself continued reigning, his princes and mighty men abode in honour, and all things flourished.

Fidelity in observing and performing men's words, promises, covenants, oaths, is the foundation of justice, and justice is the strength of the republic. If people be not faithful in their covenants and promises, how can a prince confide in them, that they will be loyal? and if a prince be false in his word, violate protestations, covenants, oaths, what protection, safety, or justice can they expect from him? where is no faithfulness, there can be no justice, and where that is wanting, can be no security to any state. It is justice establisheth a land, "but he who receiveth gifts overthroweth it," Prov. xxix. 4.

Tull. l. 1. de Offic.

Should not a king receive gifts? no, not to pervert justice: if he be covetous, he will be unjust, false, and so overthrow all; but if righteous, he will preserve, uphold all, for "righteousness exalteth a nation," Prov. xiv. 34.

Obs. 6. Violating of covenants, oaths, and perfidious doings, falsifying of trust, is very ill in any, especially in princes, who resemble God; and so ill, that God will not suffer it to go unpunished. Zedekiah rebels, falls off from Nebuchadnezzar, breaks all bonds and engagements made unto him, and sues to Egypt for help. This was a sin of that nature, as made the Lord to say, "Shall he prosper? shall he escape that doeth such things? or shall he break the covenant, and be delivered?" No, he shall not prosper, nor escape, nor be delivered: I appeal to thee, Ezekiel, to all men, whether such a man should find any favour, whether such a man who doth such things, should not be made exemplary to all the world? Yes, he should, and God made him so. When men are perfidious, and violate oaths, they are in credit neither with God or good men, their very names stink, and they live under perpetual infamy. Men's credits are like glasses, which if broken, can never be mended again, especially if stained with perfidiousness, breach of oath and covenant. Other sins may be imputed to frailty and error, and so be more pardonable; but this sin argues a base, vile, and treacherous nature, and is not excusable in any, least of all in princes, who should be noble and ingenuous, and stand more upon their word, covenants, and oaths, than others, because they are public persons, and their actions have great influence into all sorts of persons: they greatly dishonour God, whom they represent, abuse his commission, and shamefully profane his name; God is therefore greatly set against such. Psal. lv. 23, "Bloody and deceitful men shall not live out half their days." Usually men of treacherous spirits are bloody, and God by one judgment or other cuts them off, or their posterity, or both. It fell out so with Zedekiah; and with Saul, who was false and bloody towards David, and towards the priests whom he caused to be slain; he brake the covenant with the Gibeonites, himself fell by the Philistines and his own sword, and seven of his sons were hanged for it, 2 Sam. xxi.

The duke of Bourbon, being made governor of Milan by Charles the Fifth, did so exact of and oppress the people, that they rose up against him; he, to pacify them, bound himself by oath to certain conditions, wishing if he did not faithfully perform them, he might be killed with a bullet in the first occasion of war which should be offered. Notwithstanding his oath and his imprecation, he tyrannized over the people, and shortly after at the siege of Rome, by a soldier of his own negligently discharging a piece of artillery, he was slain.

Henry the Third, king of France, after great differences between him, the cardinal, and duke of Guise, was reconciled unto them, confirmed the reconciliation with many oaths, took the sacrament upon it, and gave himself to the devil, body and soul, in case he meant or should attempt any thing against them. Yet, saith the story, he caused the duke to be killed in his own presence, and the cardinal his brother the next day after. Here was breach of covenant: but did he prosper, escape, do such things, and have deliverance? No; within eight months after he was slain by a friar in the midst of his army.

The ancient Romans were very religious and conscientious in observing their leagues, covenants, and oaths made publicly; and if any violated them, they were held for cursed creatures, and counted unworthy to live in human society.

Ver. 16—21. *As I live, saith the Lord God, surely in the place where the king dwelleth that made him king, whose oath he despised, and whose covenant he brake, even with him in the midst of Babylon he shall die. Neither shall Pharaoh with his mighty army and great company make for him in the war, by casting up mounts, and building forts, to cut off many persons: seeing he despised the oath by breaking the covenant, when, lo, he had given his hand, and hath done all these things, he shall not escape. Therefore thus saith the Lord God; As I live, surely mine oath that he hath despised, and my covenant that he hath broken, even it will I recompense upon his own head. And I will spread my net upon him, and he shall be taken in my snare, and I will bring him to Babylon, and will plead with him there for his trespass that he hath trespassed against me. And all his fugitives with all his bands shall fall by the sword, and they that remain shall be scattered toward all winds: and ye shall know that I the Lord have spoken it.*

These verses comprehend Zedekiah's sin, with some aggravation thereof, and the punishments threatened for the same, and these ratify them.

His sin is, despising the oath, and breaking the covenant, of Nebuchadnezzar, ver. 16, 18, which God calls his "oath" and "covenant," ver. 19, and the trespass trespassed against him, ver. 20.

The aggravations are two:

I. Is from Nebuchadnezzar's kindness and bounty towards him; ver. 16, "That made him king, whose oath he despised."

II. Is from his own act; ver. 18, "When, lo, he had given his hand."

The punishments threatened are,

I. Death; ver. 16, "He shall die," and that in Babylon.

II. Disappointment by the Egyptian army; ver. 17, "Neither shall Pharaoh," &c.

III. Obstructing all ways of escaping; ver. 18, "He shall not escape." Ver. 19, "I will recompense it," viz. his perjury, "upon his own head." Ver. 20, "I will spread my net upon him, and he shall be taken in my snare."

IV. The execution of his fugitives; "They shall fall by the sword," ver. 21.

V. The dispersion of those who should be left; they "shall be scattered toward all winds," ver. 21.

The ratification of them is by an oath; ver. 16, 19, "As I live, saith the Lord."

For the words, they need not much opening.

Ver. 16. "As I live." As sure as I am God, and live, it shall so come to pass, he shall die in Babylon. Of this oath was spoken, chap. v. 11; xiv. 16; and xvi. 48.

"Whose oath he despised." The word in Hebrew for despised notes, despising out of בזה pride and disdain. Zedekiah thought, What should I, that am an Israelite, keep an oath made to a heathen? should I, that am of Zion, be subject to Babylon? No, no, I will be in bondage no longer. It is true, I have made an oath, but that is no great matter, it will be more advantage for me to break with that heathenish king, than to keep the oath: thus did he despise the oath.

"In the midst of Babylon he shall die." Zedekiah had his eyes put out, that he never saw Babylon, and yet he was carried captive thither, and kept in prison there till his death, Jer. lii. 11; Ezek. xii. 13, "He shall not see it, though he shall die there."

Ver. 17. "Neither shall Pharaoh," &c. The first Pharaoh the Scripture mentions was in Abraham's days, Gen. xii. 15; and the last was this here mentioned, who is called Pharaoh-hophra, king of Egypt, and was delivered into the hands of Nebuchadnezzar, king of Babylon, Jer. xliv. 30. From the first to the last was thirteen hundred and thirty-six years, all which time this name was common to all the kings of Egypt, but afterwards ceased. Some have thought this word, "Pharaoh," to be taken from an island so called. Others fetch it from the Hebrew word *pharah*, which signifies, to be free from bondage; whence A Lapide derives the word *baro*, a baron. Kings, saith he, are called *pharaones quasi barones*, free princes. But it is most probable that Pharaoh was an Egyptian name or title, noting sovereignty: Gen. xli. 44, "Pharaoh said unto Joseph, I am Pharaoh, and without thee shall no man lift up his hand or foot in all the land of Egypt." Josephus saith, Pharaoh was a name of honour and principality.

"Make for him." Hebrew, with him. Let Pharaoh come with never so great an army, it will not make with him, he shall never accomplish what he intends thereby; Pharaoh, with all his power, shall not be able to free him from the king of Babylon, and make him great.

"Building forts." The word for "forts" signifies, a wooden tower. In those times they made great engines of wood, like towers, out of which they threw stones or darts into the towns or cities they warred against, and so weakened them. Whether the casting up mounts, and building of forts, were the work of the Babylonish or Egyptian king, is questioned among expositors; but to me it seems evident, by the words, that it was the Egyptian king.

Ver. 18. "When, lo, he had given his hand." To give the hand imports,

1. Society, equality; as Gal. ii. 9, Cephas and John gave Paul and Barnabas the right hand of fellowship.

2. Subjection; as 2 Chron. xxx. 8, "Be ye not stiff-necked, as your fathers were, but yield yourselves unto the Lord." The Hebrew is, give the hand unto the Lord, and serve him. So, 1 Chron. xxix. 24, they "submitted themselves unto Solomon the king." Hebrew is, they gave the hand under him, or to him.

3. Confirmation of a promise, covenant, or oath: Ezra x. 19, "They gave their hands that they would put away their wives;" they promised it, and they confirmed it, by giving their hands to Ezra. Lam. v. 6, "We have given the hand to the Egyptians, and to the Assyrians, to be satisfied with bread;"

we have covenanted to be theirs for bread, and have impawned our fidelity and honesty by giving our hands. So here, Zedekiah had made a covenant with Nebuchadnezzar, and confirmed it, not only with an oath, but also with his hand, that he would be subject unto him. If he forgot his oath, yet how could he look upon his own hand, and not remember how it was engaged.

Ver. 19. "It will I recompense upon his own head." The Lord would bring his perjury upon him. Of recompensing upon the head hath been spoken, chap. ix. 10; xi. 21; xvi. 43.

Ver. 20. "And I will spread my net upon him, and he shall be taken in my snare, and I will bring him to Babylon." These very words you have had opened in chap. xii. ver. 13. The net and snare were the Babylonish army; the Jews, the fishes, &c.

"And will plead with him there." Hebrew is, I will be judged with him; so Montanus reads it. That I may be judged with him; so Vatablus. And the sense is this: I will so clear my justice in punishing this perfidious king, that I will be judged even by heathens, whether he hath not deserved what I shall inflict, and whether I be not righteous in inflicting the same; I know they will justify me, and condemn him. But others render the word actively, I will judge, or plead with, as here; that is, I will punish him. After the city was taken, his sons, princes, and nobles slain, his eyes put out, he was carried into Babylon, where he was put into prison, and imprisoned till his death, Jer. lii. 11.

Ver. 21. "All his fugitives." When Jerusalem was besieged, and began to be broken up, Zedekiah, and many with him, fled, who are threatened here all to fall by the sword; yet presently it is added, "they that remain shall be scattered." How are these words to be taken, so as to make truth out of them?

Answ. Universal notes are not always to be taken universally. All, that is, the greatest part; so it is to be taken, Jer. xiii. 19; xliv. 12; Matt. ii. 3; iii. 5.

Obs. 1. Judgments threatened are not readily and easily believed; if so, there need no swearing to confirm the certainty of them. But man, as he is backward to believe what should do him good, so what is threatened, and tends unto his ruin; therefore God swears, As I live, Zedekiah shall die. Jeremiah had often told Zedekiah that he should be taken and carried to Babylon, chap. xxxii. 4, 5; xxxiv. 2, 3; but he believed it not. 2 Chron. xxxvi. 12, "He humbled not himself before Jeremiah the prophet speaking from the mouth of the Lord;" ver. 16, he and others "mocked the messengers of God, and despised his words, and misused his prophets, until the wrath of the Lord arose against his people, till there was no remedy." Much was given out by the prophets concerning the destruction of Jerusalem, but none would believe that the enemy should ever have entered into the gates of it, Lam. iv. 12. What! God destroy his own city, his own people? how can this be? Judgments are sour things to the spirits of men, very unwelcome, and therefore they shift them off with some pretence or other. God is a merciful God, and will not do such severe things; or if he do, it will not be in our days, as they in Ezek. xii. 22, "The days are prolonged;" or if not, "yet we shall escape."

Obs. 2. Ingratitude to those instruments God hath used to do us good by, he takes special notice of, and will punish. Nebuchadnezzar was the man whom God used to make Zedekiah king; and he, being exalted by him, and having tied himself by the strongest bonds to be grateful and serviceable to him, forgets his benefactor's kindness, and breaks with him; here was hellish ingratitude: hereupon the Lord saith, "In the place where he dwelleth that made him king, even in Babylon, he shall die." His ingratitude so provoked God, that he would punish him exemplarily in that place, where the king of Babylon, and all the Babylonians, might see how greatly the God of Israel abhorred ingratitude.

Jehoiada was the hand of God to set Joash in the throne, 2 Chron. xxii.; and after the death of Jehoiada, Joash slew his son, because he dealt faithfully with him and the princes, in reproving them for falling to idolatry. This the Lord took special notice of, for it is said, "Thus Joash the king remembered not the kindness which Jehoiada his father had done to him, but slew his son," who, dying, said, "The Lord look upon it, and require it," 2 Chron. xxiv. 20—22. And it was not long ere God did require it; for shortly after, an army of the Syrians spoiled him, and his own servants slew him for his ingratitude towards Jehoiada in slaying his sons, ver. 25.

Ahithophel was advanced by David to be his counsellor; he fell in with Absalom's conspiracy against David; the Lord was offended at this wretched ingratitude, and left him to lay hands upon himself, and become a monument and warning-piece to posterity to take heed of the like sin: so Judas. Gideon was a man God used to do Israel much good by; and though the people soon forgot it, yet God did not forget their ingratitude: Judg. viii. 35, "They showed not kindness to the house of Gideon, according to all the goodness which he had showed unto Israel." God expects men should be thankful unto those men he hath employed to do them good; if they be not thankful to men, whom they see, they will not be thankful unto God, whom they see not.

Obs. 3. God is so resolved upon the punishing of perfidiousness, that he swears unto it: As I live, saith the Lord, seeing he hath despised the oath, and broken the covenant, he shall die. And again, As I live, I will recompense it upon his own head. Himself, his princes, false prophets, may think, hope, nay, swear, it will be otherwise; but, as sure as I live, as I am God, he and they shall feel the weight of my displeasure for their perfidiousness and perjury. Kings on the earth take oaths, and little regard them, but the King of heaven doth not so. If the Lord once swear, he will perform, and there is no possibility of escaping. Perjury is a sin which violates the name of God exceedingly, and evidences that men have no fear of God in them, that they make an idol of him to serve their own turns; that such men are neither for God nor man to trust; not only religion, but even common honesty, suffers by them. No marvel, then, that the Lord swears, and swears again, that he will recompense such sins upon men's heads.

Obs. 4. Such is the condition of human affairs, that even kings and great men may fall into the hands, and die in the hands, of foreign enemies. Zedekiah fell into the hands of Nebuchadnezzar, and "even with him in the midst of Babylon he shall die." He made no account of meeting with such a condition, and dying in that place, but his sins brought those evils upon him. Jehoahaz fell into the hands of Pharaoh-necho, and was carried to Egypt, 2 Chron. xxxvi. 4. Jehoiachin, with his princes, officers, and mighty men, was a captive in Babylon, 2 Kings xxiv. 15, 16. God had told them, by Moses, that if they did provoke him by their sins, they should be removed into their enemies' land, Lev. xxvi. 34, 41. And Solomon was jealous of it, 1 Kings viii. 46. As it is a mercy to live and die in one's own land, so it is a judgment to be driven or carried out of it, and to die in a strange land.

On ver. 17, *Obs.* 1. Men look for help from an arm of flesh when in straits. Zedekiah expected that Pharaoh's mighty army, and great company, his chariots and horses, should make for him. It is very incident to us to look unto second causes and creature-help more than God's. Asa, being in distress, did so; "he relied," saith the text, "on the king of Syria, and not on the Lord his God," 2 Chron. xvi. 7; and "in his disease he sought not to the Lord, but to the physicians," ver. 12. Confidence in man is a common practice of the sons of men. Ahaz, he sent to the king of Assyria to help him, 2 Chron. xxviii. 16. So Ephraim, when he saw his sickness, he went to the Assyrian, and sent to Jareb, Hos. v. 13. Men's spirits look any way, turn any whither, for relief rather than unto God; the arm of flesh is more to them than the arm of God. Psal. xx. 7, "Some trust in chariots, and some in horses;" some in riches, Psal. lii. 7; some in falsehood, Jer. xxiii. 25; some in strong holds, Zech. ix. 3; some in men, Isa. ii. 22. But it argues atheism, ignorance, pride, unbelief, that men look not unto God at such times; yea, it proclaims the baseness of our spirits, that we fall upon what is visible, weak, unfaithful, at distance, and neglect God, who is strong, all-sufficient, near; and all because invisible, not seen of us.

Obs. 2. Divine Providence overrules and orders things so, that wicked men are frustrated and disappointed of their hopes and expectations. Zedekiah hoped and expected that Pharaoh, with his great forces, should make much for him; but "neither shall Pharaoh with his mighty army and great company make for him;" it is not kings, armies, counsellors, and counsels, will do it. Pharaoh's army came forth of Egypt, raised the siege when Nebuchadnezzar was before Jerusalem, Jer. xxxvii. 11; yet it did not make for him; the Chaldeans returned again, sat down before the city, took it, Zedekiah, the princes, and others. Ahaz expected help from the king of Assyria; Tilgath-pilneser comes, and what then? he distressed him, but strengthened him not, 2 Chron. xxviii. 20. Absalom expected much from the counsel and advice of Ahithophel, but God turned it into foolishness, 2 Sam. xvii. 14; and all the strength he had made not for him, chap. xviii. Job v. 12, "He disappointeth the devices of the crafty, so that their hands cannot perform their enterprise." Haman could not perform his enterprise. Herod could not accomplish his design to murder Christ, when he slew the infants, Matt. ii. Kings and people imagine vain things, and the Lord laughs them to scorn, Psal. ii. 1, 4. The Lord sees what fools they are to project, plot, expect help from arms of flesh, and makes them to see, find, and feel it in time. He brings "the counsel of the heathen to nought: he maketh the devices of the people," princes, armies, "of none effect," and establisheth his own thoughts and counsels, Psal. xxxiii. 10, 11, and that to all generations. God served his own will upon Pharaoh, and his army. Zedekiah was frustrated, he looked for light, and met with darkness; he leaned upon Pharaoh, a broken reed, that ran into his hand, and pierced him, 2 Kings xviii. 21. The armies and forces raised in this land have not made for the king, nor had the Scots that assistance they looked for, when they so lately came in. God's providence works in all, by all, and overrules all, and he brings to pass his own sacred purposes by kings, armies, by men's wits, wills, policies, and powers.

On ver. 18, *Obs.* The Lord takes notice of the circumstances and aggravations which are in men's sins, especially kings'. "He despised the oath by breaking the covenant, when, lo, he had given his hand." I saw him, saith God, reach out his hand, give it as a pawn and pledge of his fidelity to Nebuchadnezzar; he engaged himself thereby to be subject and tributary unto him. This aggravated his sin much; it was against the light of nature, special mercy; for he had made it a royal hand, the strongest engagement, done upon deliberation. It was against his superior, Nebuchadnezzar, the greatest king then on earth; it was against the good of the whole Jewish state, for it brought war, famine, plague, captivity upon them all: yea, more than all these, it was a high offence against God and his attributes, and therefore the Lord saith, ver. 20, it was a trespass, "he trespassed against me." God minds with what circumstances men's sins are clothed. He noted not only Ahaz' sin, but the time when he sinned: in the time of his distress, when he should have considered his sins, and repented of them, even then did he sin more, 2 Chron. xxviii. 22. So Solomon's sin hath the aggravation nailed to it, 1 Kings xi. 9, "His heart was turned from the Lord God, which had appeared unto him twice."

On ver. 19, *Obs.* Oaths and covenants made with men are divine things, and not to be slighted. "Mine oath that he hath despised, and my covenant that he hath broken:" it was made with Nebuchadnezzar, a heathen king, an idolater, yet God owns it as made with himself, because his sacred and dreadful name was used therein, and judges the breach and violation thereof as bad as if it had been formally made with himself. If Zedekiah had sworn to God, and covenanted with him, and given him his hand that he would have been faithful to him, obedient to any thing propounded by his divine majesty, it had not been worse.

Oaths made between man and man are called in Scripture the "oath of God," Eccles. viii. 2; and the covenant made between Jonathan and David is called "the Lord's oath," 2 Sam. xxi. 7. Let not men, therefore, slight covenants and oaths they have made with men, but remember they have to do with God, who is faithful, performing what he swears, and keeping covenant for ever. It is good to be like unto God, as in other things, so in this. When Joshua had made a league with the Gibeonites, and the princes had sworn unto them, though they were fallaciously brought thereunto by the Gibeonites' craft, yet they durst not violate the league made and sworn, and so put them to the sword as they did others; but said, "We will even let them live, lest wrath be upon us, because of the oath," Josh. ix. 15, 20. You know what great wrath of God hath fallen upon those who invaded us, breaking the covenant and despising the oath.

On ver. 20, *Obs.* The Lord hath nets and snares to catch and take perfidious princes and people in. "I will spread my net upon him, and he shall be taken in my snare." There is no evasion when God seeks after sinners; if he throw the net, it shall encompass the greatest leviathan; if he set the snare, it shall take the stoutest lion.

God had a net for Pharaoh, and caught that great leviathan in the sea. An oak was the net he caught Absalom in, 2 Sam. xviii. 9. The earth was his net to take Korah, Dathan, and Abiram. A heap of stones was his net thrown upon Achan. A cave was the snare he took five kings in, Josh. x. 16—18. The kings of Sodom and Gomorrah were snared in slime pits, Gen. xiv. 10. Herod could not escape the worms, they were God's net and snare to catch him. The Babylonish armies were his nets and snares to take Hoshea, 2 Kings xvii; Manasseh, 2 Chron. xxxiii.; Jehoiakim, Jehoiachin, and Zedekiah, who were all kings, 2 Chron. xxxvi. Zedekiah had thoughts he should escape, but he did not escape besieging, taking, carrying into Babylon. When the city was taken, he fled by night, Jer. xxxix. 4; but God spread his net so, that it fell upon him, and all with him.

Let men take heed of offending the great God of heaven and earth, he hath nets and snares to take them with. If once he throw his net, and set his snare, he will take them; and being taken, you may struggle, but shall never get out. Nets and snares are hidden things, they catch suddenly, and hold certainly.

On ver. 22, *Obs.* Not only princes, but counsellors and co-partners in wickedness, shall be punished. "All his fugitives with all his bands shall fall by the sword." The king was not alone in this defection from Nebuchadnezzar; his princes, nobles, counsellors, joined with him in sending to Egypt, they and the militia in opposing Nebuchadnezzar, who had given them their lives and power, but they all fell by the sword, or were scattered.

Obs. 2. Events declare the truth of threatening, and cause men to see their follies. Zedekiah and others would not believe what was threatened against them and Jerusalem; but when things came to pass, they were convinced, and made to see their errors: they "shall know that I the Lord have spoken it."

Ver. 22—24. *Thus saith the Lord God; I will also take of the highest branch of the high cedar, and will set it; I will crop off from the top of his young twigs a tender one, and will plant it upon an high mountain and eminent: in the mountain of the height of Israel will I plant it: and it shall bring forth boughs, and bear fruit, and be a goodly cedar: and under it shall dwell all fowl of every wing; in the shadow of the branches thereof shall they dwell. And all the trees of the field shall know that I the Lord have brought down the high tree, have exalted the low tree, have dried up the green tree, and have made the dry tree to flourish: I the Lord have spoken and have done it.*

These verses contain a promise of mercy, which is the last general part of the chapter: and it is no mean promise, but an exceeding great and precious promise, namely, of Christ and his kingdom.

The Lord having resolved and sworn, in the former part of the chapter, the rooting up the Jewish vine, namely, the destruction of Zedekiah, his princes, nobles, city, people, and laying all waste, some among them might say, What will now become of his promise to Abraham, to David, and others, that out of their loins and seed should come a blessing to all nations, that the Messiah should spring out of their root? if all Judah be rooted up, and carried out into Babylon, what truth in the promise of God? how will this be made good which hath proceeded out of his sacred lips? What! will the God of truth be unfaithful, and fail now? No, saith the Lord, I am mindful of what I have promised; and though you see not how it shall be accomplished, I do; I have ways not thought of by you: "I will also take of the highest branch of the high cedar, I will set, and plant it," &c.

In the words you have these things considerable:

I. The "high cedar," ver. 22.

II. What God will do to it; "take of the highest branch," &c. ver. 22.

III. What he will do with that branch; "set it, plant it," ver. 22, 23.

IV. Where; "upon an high mountain and eminent," ver. 22; which is specified to be "the mountain of the height of Israel," ver. 23.

V. The effects of this plantation.

1. Growth; "It shall bring forth boughs," ver. 23.

2. Fruitfulness; "and bear fruit," ver. 23.

3. Greatness, or goodliness; "and be a goodly cedar," ver. 23.

4. Security to all fowls; "under it shall dwell all fowl of every wing."

VI. The product of the whole, ver. 24.

I shall open the words, and then give you the observations.

Ver. 22. "I will also take of." The pronoun, "I," seems to be mentioned in opposition to the great eagle, Nebuchadnezzar, who "took the highest branch of the cedar," ver. 3; which he did, to weaken, make tributary, and destroy the kingdom of Israel; though he planted it, yet it prospered not any considerable time. And seeing he did so, saith God, I will also, who am a greater eagle, and more mighty monarch, than he, "take of the highest branch of the high cedar, and plant it," so as it shall grow, prosper, and thereby the kingdom of Israel be raised to a greater height and glory than ever.

"The highest branch of the high cedar." The high cedar was the tribe of Judah, which had the pre-eminence above the rest, the head whereof was the family of David, out of which came the kingly race. The highest branch of it was Jehoiachin, who, though in Babylon, God looked at, and minded not Zedekiah, who was perfidious, his sons were slain, himself laid by, and God would take of Jehoiachin's seed, and from thence raise up the kingdom of Judah. Jehoiachin, who also was called Jeconiah, 1 Chron. iii. 16, in his captivity was said to beget Salathiel, and Salathiel, Zorobabel, Matt. i. 12, who was the tender one cropped off from the young twig, as the Jews expound the place, and make all spoken here to be meant of him and his successors, for he was the chief man that brought them out of Babylon unto Jerusalem again, and reared up the tabernacle of David and the Jewish polity.

Be it granted that he is included in this allegorical promise, yet it cannot be principally understood of him; for something is here spoken that was never verified in him or his successors according to the Jewish account. In ver. 23, it is said, "under it shall dwell all fowl of every wing:" this is of larger extent than the power of Zorobabel or the Jewish estate reached unto. It clearly points at the kingdom of Christ, and all sorts of people coming under his wing and protection; the evidence whereof hath caused some absolutely to interpret all of Christ. But we may look at Zorobabel in it as a type, out of whose root and stock Christ came, as appears, Matt. i.; and safely conclude it had its real fulfilling in him, whom our prophet chiefly aims at in this place, and upon him we shall fasten what is to be said.

"A tender one." The Hebrew word רך from רכך signifies such a tenderness as is opposed to hardness. When a branch of a tree is grown up, it is hard, firm, but when it first shoots forth, it is soft and tender; such a one was Christ. The Septuagint is, καρδία, or, the heart, which is the tenderest part in man; others, a little twig.

"I will plant it upon an high mountain and eminent." This tender one he would not plant in the wilderness, in some obscure place, but upon a mountain, and not any ordinary mountain, but a high and eminent one, which was mount Zion: Psal. ii. 6, "I have set my king upon my holy hill of Zion." Mount Zion was the place he loved, Psal. lxxviii. 68, and where he resolved to dwell, Psal. cxxxii. 14.

It is put oft for the church and people of God, Isa. lx. 14; 1 Pet. ii. 6; Heb. xii. 22. And so the high and eminent mountain here is put for the church, in and over which Christ was to be planted King. God would raise up this "tender one," and make him King. Zion was a little hill in it; but because the law and glory of God was to go out from thence, therefore it was eminent.

Ver. 23. "In the mountain of the height of Israel will I plant it." That is, in the church, which is the height of Israel: Micah iv. 1, "In the last days it shall come to pass that the mountain of the house of the Lord shall be established in the top of the mountains, and it shall be exalted above the hills." Christ's kingdom shall be above all kingdoms: Luke i. 32, "He shall be called the Son of the Highest: and the Lord God shall give unto him the throne of David his father:" ver. 33, "He shall reign over the house of Jacob for ever; and of his kingdom there shall be no end."

"It shall bring forth boughs, and bear fruit." Their tender ones, being planted in the mountain of God, did not wither, but rooted, grew, had boughs and fruit. The boughs you may call Christ's apostles, seventy disciples, his fruit was judgment and justice: Jer. xxiii. 5, "I will raise unto David a righteous Branch, and a King shall reign and prosper, and shall execute judgment and justice." David long before prophesied what his fruit should be: Psal. lxxii. 12—14, "He shall deliver the needy when he crieth; and him that hath no helper. He shall spare the poor and needy, and shall save the souls of the needy. He shall redeem their soul from deceit and violence: and precious shall their blood be in his sight."

The fruit of this Plant is specified by Isaiah, chap. lxi. 1—3, "Preaching good tidings, binding up the broken-hearted, proclaiming liberty to captives, opening the prison to those who are bound, comforting mourners, and making trees of righteousness;" he went up and down "doing good, and healing all that were oppressed of the devil," Acts x. 38. The gospel, with all the ordinances, promises, miracles, and benefits of it, are the fruit of this tree.

"And be a goodly cedar." A great cedar, saith the Septuagint. A stately one, say others. The cedar excels other trees in height, in sweetness, in duration; and hereby the excellency of Christ's kingdom is set out in the spiritualness, fragrancy, and lastingness of it. His "kingdom is not of this world," John xviii. 36; he rules in righteousness, Isa. xi. 4; so that his "name is as ointment poured forth," Cant. i. 3; and of his kingdom there is no end, Isa. ix. 7. This cedar is the most excellent, goodly, odoriferous, and durable, that ever grew in Lebanon. The top of this cedar doth not only reach up to heaven, but is in heaven, Phil. ii. 6—11.

"Under it shall dwell all fowl of every wing." Hebrew, all fowl, all of wing. Septuagint, every beast, and every flying thing. That is, the tribes, and the gentiles, all the elect out of both, they should come flying like birds unto a tree for shelter; all nations should come unto the church for relief. Not all kings, nor angels, but all nations, should come under this cedar, as in Dan. iv. 12, the fowls of the heaven dwelt in the great tree there mentioned. So here, all fowl should come under this goodly cedar. In and under the trees the birds were safe sheltered from the violence of weather, heat of sun, and vermin on the earth; there they bred, there they sung, and there they quietly rested themselves. Such benefit should the faithful find by coming under Christ, the goodly cedar, in Zion. That which is called all "fowl of every wing" here, is called "all nations and tongues," Isa. lxvi. 18; and "all flesh," ver. 23.

Ver. 24. "All the trees of the field." By "trees of the field," some understand all the kings, princes, and potentates of the world; who are so called, because,

1. They are deeply rooted and fastened in the world, as trees are in the earth. You may easily pluck up a flower, a little plant, but not a tree; and so great ones are not easily moved, or plucked up.

2. They are eminent above others, as trees are above bushes, shrubs, little plants, underwood, whose growth they hinder by overshadowing and overdripping them.

3. They are trees in respect of their spreading and extension. The arms, boughs, and branches of trees extend every way, and far; so great men, their power reaches far, and oft too far.

4. In that they succour and harbour others, many shelter themselves under their shadow, as trees do the birds. Oft great men shelter the beasts and vermin of the earth, not the birds of heaven.

5. Trees, in regard of fruitfulness. Great men are very fruitful one way or other, but mostly in wickedness. Zedekiah had his fruit, falseness and perjury. "Every tree that bears not good fruit," &c.

However great ones be trees, yet I conceive not only they, but the people of the nations, are here meant by trees, for he calls them "trees of the field." The Jews were the trees of the orchard and garden of God, but the gentiles were the trees of the field or world; and they should see and know what the Lord's ways were with this Jewish state and people.

"Have brought down the high tree." This high tree was Zedekiah, who would not hear Jeremiah, nor keep covenant with Nebuchadnezzar, but being stubborn and haughty of spirit, would go his own ways, 2 Chron. xxxvi. 12, 13. Some would have it understood of the kingdom of Zedekiah, but that is not congruous with what is in ver. 6, where that is likened to "a vine of low stature;" it is better, therefore, to expound it of the person of Zedekiah; for though the kingdom was low, yet he was haughty and high. Others make this high tree to be the kingdom of Babylon, which was overthrown by the hand of Cyrus, and so way made for the low tree, the Jews in captivity, to return by the hand of Zerubbabel. They, Christ and his kingdom in them, were very low during the captivity, but the Lord brought them forth, exalted them, Christ and his kingdom, in due time.

"Have dried up the green tree." Zedekiah and his kingdom were like a green vine with branches and sprigs, ver. 6; but the Lord rooted up this vine, threw it into Babylon, where it died. "Green" with apprehension they only were the people of God; "green" with conceits of their own righteousness; "green" with hopes of liveliness.

"Have made the dry tree to flourish." By the dry tree Lavater understands the gentiles, who were without promises, covenant. Others, Jeconiah, who was a captive in Babylon, and, after thirty-seven years' imprisonment, exalted by Evil-merodach, and his throne set above the throne of other kings with him; and so the kingdom of David, that had been long a dry tree, began in him, Salathiel, Zerubbabel, and afterward in Christ, to flourish.

Obs. 1. After grievous judgments threatened to come upon a state or church, God propounds matter of comfort to his elect and faithful therein, that so when the execution is, their hearts may be supported and comforted. When God should root out Zedekiah and his people, the kingdom would be laid waste, the faithful should suffer much, lose estates, friends, liberty, country, temple, ordinances, and worship of God. Now for comfort against all these evils, he tells them of the Messiah, whom he would take care should come into the world: " I will take of the highest branch of the high cedar, and will set it." However things went, God would take care that the line of which Christ was to come should be preserved, and that his promise should be made good. So Isa. xi. 1, " There shall come forth a rod out of the stem of Jesse, and a Branch shall grow out of his roots." Now the stem of Jesse seemed to be cut down, and the root of Jesse to be pulled up; but the Lord preserved the root and stem, out of which he brought a rod and a branch for the comfort of the faithful suffering Jews. This promise of the Branch is oft mentioned in holy writ for the comfort of the Jews, Jer. xxiii. 5, 6; xxxiii. 15, 16; Zech. iii. 8; vi. 12, 13.

Obs. 2. The Lord Christ descended from the highest. " I will take of the highest branch of the high cedar." He came from the loins of Jeconiah, who was king of Judah, and from fourteen kings before him, as appears Matt. i.; he was the son of nobles, and born a King; therefore when the wise men came from the east to Jerusalem, they said, " Where is he that is born King of the Jews," Matt. ii. 2. He was the first-born of the kings of Judah, the right heir to, and should have succeeded them in, the kingdom, which Herod at that time usurped. Such a hint being given out by the wise men, it is strange that neither the sanhedrim, the high priests, scribes, nor Pharisees, should search out the truth of it. They were wise and learned in their generation, but blind in all the things of Christ. However they failed, let us take notice of it, that Jesus Christ was the son of nobles, and came of royal blood.

Obs. 3. The beginnings of Christ were mean and low. " I will crop off from the top of his young twigs a tender one." Christ at first was as a little tender shoot of a tree set in the earth; and how weak, mean, low, and inconsiderable is such a thing! If one should take a little twig of a cedar, or an oak, and prick it in the earth in some obscure place, men would not regard it. Christ's beginnings were such: he took flesh of a poor mean virgin, the wife of a carpenter, Matt. i. He was born in a poor village, Mic. v. 2; in a stable, laid in a manger, Luke ii. 7. He was subject to his parents, being poor and low, ver. 51. He lay in the dark till thirty years of age, Luke iii. 23; and then he began with two or three poor fishermen, Matt. iii. 18—22; then some others to the number of twelve; and even now when he seemed to be somebody, he had not a house or bed for himself or them: Luke ix. 58, " Foxes have holes, and birds of the air have nests; but the Son of man hath not where to lay his head." And for his maintenance, it was at the good will of others: Luke viii. 3, " Joanna, Susanna, and many others, ministered unto him of their substance."

Obs. 4. The Lord Christ is planted in the church, and become a fruitful and goodly cedar therein. " I will plant it upon an high mountain and eminent, the mountain of the height of Israel; and it shall bring forth boughs, bear fruit, and be a goodly cedar." Christ was planted in Zion, there he grew, there he brought forth fruit; with the timber of this cedar was the church built, with the fruit of this cedar it is maintained. Isa. iv. 2, " In that day shall the branch of the Lord be beautiful and glorious, and the fruit of the earth be excellent." The branch was Christ, and he should be for beauty and glory to the church, and the fruit that should come from him should be excellent; never tree bare such fruit: the church saith, " His fruit was sweet to my taste." " Wisdom, righteousness, redemption, and sanctification," are the fruits of this cedar, 1 Cor. i. 30; the life of the world, John vi. 33; the ordinances of the gospel, Matt. xxviii. 19; 1 Cor. i. 23; " exceeding great and precious promises," 2 Pet. i. 4; reconciliation, Col. i. 20; the gift of the Spirit or Comforter, John xvi. 7; revelation of the counsels of God, John xv. 15; fellowship with the Father and the Son, John xiv. 9; 1 John i. 3; " eternal life," John x. 28. Such was the fruit this cedar bore. In the midst of the church he was planted, fruitful, and sang praise to God, Heb. ii. 12. And so high is this cedar grown, that it is now in heaven at the right hand of God, " far above all principality, and power, and might, and dominion, and every name that is named, not only in this world, but also in that which is to come," Eph. i. 20, 21. So that the mountain of the Lord is on the top of all mountains, and this cedar on the top of that mountain.

Obs. 5. Unto Christ and his kingdom shall come in all that are elect, both Jews and gentiles. " Under it shall dwell all fowl of every wing:" they shall come, and come flying; let them be in what kingdom they will, in what condition soever, learned, ignorant, rich, poor, weak, strong, sound, sick, young, or old, they shall come to Christ. Isa. lx. 3, " The gentiles shall come to thy light, and kings to the brightness of thy rising." Ver. 4, " Thy sons shall come from far, and thy daughters shall be nursed at thy side." He speaks of the church under Christ: ver. 8, they should come flying " as doves to their windows." Chap. lxvi. 23, " It shall come to pass, that from one new moon to another, and from one sabbath to another, shall all flesh come to worship before me, saith the Lord;" both Jews and gentiles, nothing shall let or hinder, he will bring them, Isa. lvi. 7. And Christ saith, John vi. 37, " All that the Father giveth me shall come unto me;" nothing in Satan, in themselves, in the world, shall keep or let them from coming under this cedar.

Obs. 6. There is safety under Christ, he will protect and defend his people from all harms. " Under it shall they dwell." Men will not dwell where is no safety. Fowls and birds when they get into a great tree, they are secure from any who pursue them, from all harms from above or from beneath; so those who come under Christ's shadow, Christ's power and government, they shall dwell there safely. Ezek. xxxiv. 24, 25, God will set up his servant David a Prince among them, that is, Christ; and what then? " I will cause the evil beasts to cease out of the land;" that is, by the power of Christ: Isa. xi. 4, and they shall dwell safely, there shall be no hurting nor destroying in the mountain of God, ver. 9. And chap. xxv. 10, " In this mountain shall the hand of the Lord rest, and Moab shall be trodden down under him, even as straw is trodden down for the dunghill." Christ will protect his church, and tread down the enemies thereof, whatever their power, policies, and pretences are. He is a cedar in wisdom, Col. ii. 3; a cedar in power, Matt. xxviii. 18; a cedar in his providence and vigilance, Isa. xxvii. 3; hence saith the church, " I sat down under his shadow with great delight," Cant. ii. 3. It is Christ secures from sin, from the wisdom of the flesh, the storms of the world, temptations of hell, and whatever is dangerous: Isa. xxv. 4, " Thou hast been a strength to the poor, a strength to the needy in his distress, a refuge from the storm, a shadow from the heat, when the blast of the terrible ones is as a storm against the wall." If you be under the shadow of this cedar, though the winds blow hard, the floods beat sore, and rain fall with strength, yet you shall be as safe as the house built upon the rock, Matt. vii. 24, 25.

Under other cedars there is no safety. Kings of the earth are cedars, but they prey upon their subjects rather than protect them; they think that all men are made to serve their lusts, and therefore mind themselves, and care not what becomes of the people, so they may grow great and fat on earth: it is otherwise with Christ, he seeks the good, the comfort, the safety, the greatness, and glory of his subjects.

Obs. 7. Princes that are haughty and proud, God will bring them down, though they be in flourishing conditions. "I have brought down the high tree, and dried up the green tree." Zedekiah was a high tree; the king of Judah and his spirit was high, he would not stoop to God or man, he hearkened not to the God of Israel, nor to his prophets; he would not keep covenant and promise with the king of Babylon, but his will was his law; but God laid the axe to the root of this tree, and hewed it down, and great was the fall thereof. No trees are so high, but the Lord, who is higher than they, can lay them low; let them be green with boughs, branches, leaves, let them have many children, many nobles, many soldiers, many counsellors, many kingdoms, all cannot preserve them from ruin. Nebuchadnezzar was a high tree, his top reached to heaven, Dan. iv. 11, he was proud and bloody; and what fell out? "A watcher and an holy one came down from heaven, cried aloud, and said, Hew down the tree, cut off his branches, shake off his leaves, scatter his fruit; let the beasts get away from under it, and the fowls from his branches," ver. 13, 14. There is a watcher observes the spirits, plots, practices of kings, and hews them down at his pleasure; and when they fall, let the beasts and fowls which have harboured under them, and been instruments to accomplish their wicked wills, take heed lest they be crushed in their fall.

Pharaoh was a high tree, the highest in all Egypt; he said, "I will pursue, I will overtake, I will divide the spoil; my lust shall be satisfied upon them; I will draw my sword, my hand shall destroy them:" here was pride and cruelty, which usually go together; and what followed hereupon? "Thou didst blow with thy wind, the sea covered them; they sank as lead in the mighty waters," Exod. xv. 9, 10. Amaziah king of Judah grew proud upon a victory, and provoked Joash to battle; by him God broke him in pieces, brought him low, and afterwards he was slain by his own subjects, 2 Chron. xxv. Saul was a goodly man, a high tree in Israel, he was proud, cruel, false, disobedient to God; and he rejected him, and cut him down by the Philistines and his own sword, 1 Sam. xxxi. So Ahab, 1 Kings xxii.; Herod, Acts xii. 23. Belshazzar lifted up himself against the Lord of heaven, and would not see the hand of God upon his father Nebuchadnezzar, and humble himself; and presently a hand was seen writing his doom, and that night was he slain, Dan. v. 5, 22, 23, 30. Haughty spirits, whoever they are, God will humble and lay low; he beholds them afar off, he resists them, and will scatter them. Isa. x. 33, 34, "Behold, the Lord, the Lord of hosts, shall lop the bough with terror: and the high ones of stature shall be hewn down, and the haughty shall be humbled. He shall cut down the thickets of the forests with iron, and Lebanon shall fall by a mighty one." It is spoken of Sennacherib and his army; this God hewed down by a mighty angel, and himself by his own sons, Isa. xxxvii. 36, 38. The Lord hath days and times to reckon with the high and haughty ones: Isa. ii. 12—17, "The day of the Lord of hosts shall be upon every one that is proud and lofty, and upon every one that is lifted up; and he shall be brought low: upon all the cedars of Lebanon, upon all the oaks of Bashan, upon all the high mountains, and upon all the hills that are lifted up, &c. And the loftiness of man shall be bowed down, and the haughtiness of men shall be made low: and the Lord alone shall be exalted in that day." And then men shall run "into holes and caves for fear of the Lord, and for the glory of his majesty, when he ariseth to shake terribly the earth," ver. 19.

Obs. 8. How low soever the conditions of kingdoms, families, or persons are, God can, and it is his way to raise them. "I have exalted the low tree, and made the dry tree to flourish." The kingdom of Judah, the house of David, the person of Jeconiah, were very low in Babylon, like low shrubs, dry trees; but God's eye was upon them, he wrought for them, he exalted them, and brought a glorious kingdom and church out of those low beginnings. Was not Christ like a low and dry tree, when he lay in the loins of Jeconiah, a prisoner, a captive; when he lay in the womb of the virgin; hewed timber, made houses for his living; especially when he was cut down and laid in the heart of the earth; was he not as a dry tree then? but God exalted him, set him at his right hand, Acts ii. 33, and Peter proclaimed it; "Let all the house of Israel know assuredly, that God hath made that same Jesus, whom ye crucified, both Lord and Christ," ver. 36. Thus did he "grow up before the Lord as a tender plant, and as a root out of a dry ground," Isa. liii. 2. Luke i. 52, "He hath put down the mighty from their seats, and exalted them of low degree."

Obs. 9. God will do these things so eminently, that the world shall take notice, and be filled with the glory thereof. "And all the trees of the field shall know, that I the Lord," &c.; not only the orchard trees, but the field trees, not domestic alone, but wild ones. Isa. ii. 19, men shall fear and hide themselves "for the glory of his majesty, when he ariseth to shake terribly the earth."

CHAPTER XVIII.

Ver. 1—4. *The word of the Lord came unto me again, saying, What mean ye, that ye use this proverb concerning the land of Israel, saying, The fathers have eaten sour grapes, and the children's teeth are set on edge? As I live, saith the Lord God, ye shall not have occasion any more to use this proverb in Israel. Behold, all souls are mine; as the soul of the father, so also the soul of the son is mine: the soul that sinneth, it shall die.*

THE Jews in Babylon meeting with much hardship in their captivity, instead of being humbled for their sins, which brought sad miseries upon them, took up an unjust complaint against God, and charged him to deal unjustly by them; viz. That their fathers had sinned, and they who were their children suffered for their sins; we being innocent, are grievously afflicted for their iniquities. This false charge God clears himself of in this chapter, and shows them that he is most just in punishing and rewarding, that every one shall bear his own sins, and not another's, be rewarded according to what he is, and hath done, be he just or unjust. If the unjust repent of his evil ways, he shall have mercy; if the just turn from his righteousness he shall have judgment. And this is the sum and main argument of this chapter.

In the chapter you have two general parts:

I. God's expostulation with the Jews by the prophet, ver. 1—30.

II. An exhortation to repentance and newness of life, ver. 30 to the end.

Concerning the expostulation, you have,

1. The ground of it, ver. 2, "What mean ye, that," &c.

2. A threatening to take away that evil proverb, ver. 3.

3. God's vindication of himself,

(1.) In general, in ver. 4, "Behold, all souls are mine," &c.

(2.) More particularly, from the beginning of ver. 5 to ver. 19.

4. The Jews' replication in ver. 9, and God's further vindication of himself against their unjust accusation, from the middle of ver. 19 to ver. 25, where,

5. They treble their charge upon God, and tell him his ways are not equal; from which God retorting the accusation upon themselves, doth, as formerly, vindicate himself, to ver. 30.

Ver. 1. "The word of the Lord came unto me, saying." Thus began chap. vi. vii. xii. xiii. xv. xvi. xvii. The Holy Spirit inspired him; as that moved him he spake, and not of his own head, as the false prophets did. Though he were in Babylon, he wanted not divine inspiration, which he often tells them of, that his prophecy might be weighty and authoritative.

Ver. 2. "What mean ye, that," &c. Here is the matter of the expostulation, propounded by way of reprehension: You do use a strange proverb, that tends to my dishonour, and represents me to the world to be an unjust God; but what cause have I given you to speak in this manner? surely I know no cause given you why you should utter such a proverb; if there be, bring it forth, and let me hear it.

"That ye use this proverb." Hebrew is, proverbizing a proverb, as chap. xvii. 2; and it notes the frequent use they made of it, tossing that proverb up and down amongst them; they did not now and then speak it, but it was frequently and constantly in their mouths. Of the nature of a proverb was spoken chap. xii. 22, and xvii. 2.

"Of the land of Israel." That is, of the people of Israel; not the ten tribes, for they were gone into captivity long before, but those of Judea.

"The fathers have eaten sour grapes, and the children's teeth are set on edge." The word for "sour grapes" is בסר which signifies an unripe or wild grape.

"Are set on edge." Hebrew is from קהה which signifies to make blunt and dull, as iron without an edge. Whether the English words, "are set on edge," are so proper, and hold out the sense, I leave to the judgment of the learned; they seem to me to hint a sharpening rather than a dulling. All expositors I meet with make the word to signify obstupescency and hebetation.

Sour grapes, and many other sour things, do disaffect the teeth; sometimes they cause the toothache, sometimes they dull and stupify the teeth, so that those which stand by and see the parties eating them, have their teeth ill affected also; as Aristotle observes in his Problems, and experience teacheth us. Two things are to be considered concerning this proverb: 1. The meaning of it. 2. The occasion.

1. For the meaning. By "sour grapes," the Jews understand sin, not sin simply, but such sins as do bring heavy judgments of God upon a land or people, as idolatry, murder, oppression, trusting in an arm of flesh, unnatural pollutions, illegal mixtures, drunkenness, profaneness, &c. The prophet Isaiah warrants this sense of sour grapes, chap. v. 2, 4, where he calls the sins of Judah, "wild grapes:" God looked that his vineyard should bring forth grapes, good fruit, justice, righteousness, truth, and it brought forth wild grapes, oppression, a cry, covetousness, lasciviousness, drunkenness, pride, of which he speaks in the chapter.

Such sins are called sour or wild grapes, because they wound conscience, are burdensome unto others, are as distasteful unto God as such grapes are to us; they grieve his Spirit, and exasperate him to lay waste the vine that bears such fruit.

By this proverb thus much is signified, that the fathers had sinned, and the children suffered for their sin; the fathers did that which was very offensive unto God, and the children were punished for it; they did eat the sour grapes, brought forth the bitter fruit, and these smarted for it, the children's teeth were set on edge, or stupified, that is, they were punished for what their fathers had done; they thought and said that their fathers were the cause of all the evils which befell them. Like unto this proverb are these: "Kings sin, and the people suffer:" "The child offends, and the servant is beaten."

2. The occasion. The princes and people going on in the idolatrous, oppressing, profane, bloody, and wicked ways of their fathers, the prophets did threaten them with destruction of their temple, city, and estate; hereupon they said, Our fathers did as we do, and they were spared, why should we suffer? And when the prophets pressed the sins of Manasseh, as Jer. xv. 3, 4, "I will appoint over them four kinds, saith the Lord; the sword to slay, the dogs to tear, the fowls of heaven, the beasts of the earth, to devour and destroy: and I will cause them to be removed into all kingdoms of the earth, because of Manasseh the son of Hezekiah king of Judah, for that which he did in Jerusalem." Manasseh's sin struck much upon the heart of God; he made them do more evil than the nations which God destroyed; he filled Jerusalem with innocent blood, 2 Kings xxi. 9, 16; he "made Judah and the inhabitants of Jerusalem to err and do worse than heathen," 2 Chron. xxxiii. 9. When God stirred the prophets to tell them that for his sins he would lay Jerusalem waste, as he had the ten tribes for Jeroboam's sins, they then took up this proverb, and said, "The fathers have eaten sour grapes, and the children's teeth are set on edge;" Ahaz, Manasseh, Amon, and others of our forefathers, have sinned, and we must suffer. Or thus: Zedekiah and his counsellors had perfidiously broken covenant with Nebuchadnezzar, for which the prophets threatened utter ruin to all; hereupon the people said, "Our fathers have eaten sour grapes, and the children's teeth are set on edge;" the kings and nobles have transgressed, and we shall be ruined for it. But the former occasion is the better, because Zedekiah and the nobles did suffer with them, and were punished for their own sins.

This proverb was grown common amongst them, both in Babylon and in Zion, it was tossed up and down and spread. Ezekiel tells them of it in Babylon, and Jeremiah in Zion; chap. xxxi. 29, "They shall say no more, The fathers have eaten a sour grape," &c. The evil of this proverb was great, for besides their charging of God with injustice and partiality, hereby, (1.) they discovered their fathers' sins and nakedness, and that without sorrow or repentance for them. (2.) Made light of any thing the prophets threatened against them. (3.) Obstructed the way against future repentance, or profiting by the judgments of God which should come upon them; for being persuaded and possessed with this opinion, that they suffered unjustly for their fathers' sins, not their own, they would never submit, mourn, condemn, but justify themselves.

Ver. 3. "As I live, saith the Lord God." This oath of the Lord hath several times been spoken of, and therefore I shall now say nothing of it.

"Ye shall not have occasion any more to use this proverb." Hebrew is, If there shall be to you any more to proverbize this proverb. Septuagint, If this parable shall be said any more in Israel; I will take a course that this wicked proverb shall cease. The words may be taken either as a commination, thus; If any of you shall use this proverb any more, as I live, I will punish you; let me be as a dead, dumb, idol god, and not as the living God, if I do it not. Or they may be taken by way of asseveration; I swear that this proverb shall be no more used, I will clear my proceedings with them, so that themselves shall acknowledge, and all the world see and say, they suffer justly; or, I will destroy them for this blasphemous proverb of theirs, and so it shall be heard no more in the land of Israel.

Ver. 4. "Behold, all souls are mine." Here the Lord doth vindicate himself from that unjust crime they laid to his charge, viz. that he punished one for another, the child for the sin of the parent. You mistake, saith God, all souls are mine, I am the common Father of all, I observe the ways of all, and render unto them all according to their works; I do not accept the persons of any in judgment, I neither pronounce nor execute any unjust judgment, but being essentially just, am righteous in all my ways, and holy in all my works, Psal. cxlv. 17. None in heaven or earth hath any sufficient warrant to accuse me, and if I should punish the son for the father's sin, I could give you satisfactory grounds for it.

By "souls," we are to understand persons, a part being put for the whole; and the Scripture doth frequently put the soul for that which is endued with the soul. Lev. vii. 18, 20, 21, "The soul that eateth, the soul that toucheth, any unclean thing, that soul shall be cut off." Josh. xx. 3, "The slayer that killeth any person;" the Hebrew is, any soul. And so here soul is put for the person. Some think that where it is said, the soul of the father, and the soul of the son, it is to be taken properly; but without prejudice to others, I conceive in those expressions the person is meant; the soul of the father is mine, that is, the father is mine; and the soul of the son is mine, that is, the son is mine; the principal part being put for the whole by a synecdoche. Soul, father, son, man, are synonymes here. Ver. 20, it is said, "The son shall not bear the iniquity of the father;" there it is expressed in the person: and Jer. xxxi. 30, "Every one shall die for his own iniquity; every man that eateth the sour grape," &c.; he speaks of the same thing our prophet doth, and puts it upon the person. Hence is no warrant for the death of the soul, though it be said, "The soul that sinneth, it shall die;" that is, the person, whatsoever he be that sins, he shall die for it, he shall be punished for his sins.

There is an opinion among some, that the soul sleeps and dies with the body, and so is mortal for the present, though afterwards both body and it put on immortality; but this opinion is repugnant to divine truth. Eccles. xii. 7, speaking of man's death, saith Solomon, "Then shall the dust return unto the earth, and the spirit shall return unto God who gave it;" the body goes one way, the spirit another; if the spirit or soul were mortal, it should have gone with the body. Matt. x. 28, "Fear not them which kill the body, but are not able to kill the soul." That is such a transcendent and precious thing, as that it is beyond the reach of all mortal power; death, the king of fears, cannot approach it; but if it were of the same constitution or condition the body is, it might fall by the same hand and stroke the body doth. John viii. 51; xi. 26, Christ saith, he that keeps his sayings, and believes in him, he shall never see death, he shall never die. The Greek is, *εἰς τον αἰῶνα*, to eternity, not as if he should see death for a time or times, but he shall ever live; this must be verified of the soul, which sees not the second death, as the souls of the wicked do, nor the first death, as the bodies of all do. 1 Thess. iv. 14, if the soul sleep, it is in Jesus, not in the dust, it is with Christ, not the body; how else will he bring it with him?

"The soul that sinneth, it shall die." These words seem easy, but they are very difficult, and have greatly perplexed interpreters and others. The words import only thus much, that the man which sinneth, whatever he be, he shall suffer, and be cut off for his sin; himself, not any other, shall bear the burden thereof.

The difficulties concerning these words are three.

1. That many sin, and that notoriously, who die not for their sins, but live, adding drunkenness to thirst, and at last go off the stage of the world with as much ease and quiet as other men.

Answ. 1. It is granted that many do not suffer for their sins, though such as deserve suffering; and that,

(1.) To convince men there is a judgment to come. Some suffer here, to show there is a Providence that takes notice of men's ways in the world; and some pass away without any observable judgment upon them, to assure men there is a day of reckoning to come, 2 Pet. ii. 9.

(2.) That the world might not be unpeopled; for if all should be cut off who deserve death, if every soul who sins should die, how few would be left! In the destruction of the old world you know how few were spared.

(3.) That God's long-suffering towards sinners might appear, according to that you have, 2 Pet. iii. 9, "The Lord is long-suffering to us-ward."

2. Sometimes, yea often, it is so, those who are notoriously wicked, they die for it. Prov. x. 27, "The years of the wicked shall be shortened." And Psal. lv. 23, "Bloody and deceitful men shall not live out half their days;" not that all bloody and deceitful men do fall by the stroke of justice, but it is so many times, that by the judge, by their enemies, by themselves, or some hand of God, they perish: therefore the words in the psalmist are not to be taken, *mathematice*, too subtlely, but note out abbreviation of sinners' lives, which is frequently made good; as in Shimei, Joab, Amnon, Ahab, Jezebel, Judas, &c.

3. They die before they can bring to pass fully what they aim at: they break bounds, pervert justice, change times and seasons, think to subject all to their wills, and now while they are in the pursuit of such things, they die, which is a just and heavy judgment of God upon them.

4. By death we may understand a metaphorical death, viz. afflictions, judgments, war, plague, famine, captivity, loss of comforts formerly enjoyed; so it is taken, Exod. x. 17; 2 Cor. xi. 23. And in this sense there is scarce any man who sins beyond the ordinary rule of men's common infirmities, but dies for it, that is, suffers sad afflictions. When David sinned his great sins, the sword was drawn against him, and never departed from his house, 2 Sam. xii. 10. Much more is it so with wicked men; some hand of God or other is upon them.

5. They may humble themselves for their sins, and so they may be spared: Ahab humbled himself,

1 Kings xxi. 29. If they do not suffer themselves for their sins, the judgment follows and falls upon their posterity for their sins, which makes the next difficulty.

2nd difficulty. If the soul that sins shall die, how is it then that the children suffer for their fathers' sins? Where it is said, 1 Kings xxi. 29, "I will not bring the evil in his days," that was Ahab's, "but in his son's days I will bring the evil upon his house." And 2 Kings xxiv. 2, 3, for the sins of Manasseh after he was dead, came sad things upon Judah. 2 Sam. xii. 14, for David's sin the child was stricken with death. Saul's sons were punished for his bloody dealings with the Gibeonites, 2 Sam. xxi.

Answ. 1. We must make an exception here in the point of original sin; for that sin of our first parents, death comes upon all their posterity, Rom. v. 12.

2. For the sin of the father, the child suffers not eternal death, no man is eternally damned for another's sin simply considered; it is a man's own sin which is his everlasting ruin.

3. Temporal and bodily punishments do oft befall the children for their fathers' iniquities, and that justly; for they are parts of them, they come out of their loins, too often inherit their corruptions, imitate and live in their sins; they are part of the family, they make the house: therefore God said he would bring the evil upon Ahab's house, and so he suffered in the suffering of his family. When subjects rebel, fall into treasonable practices, princes deal so with them, that not only they, but their posterity, to divers generations, do suffer; yea, princes themselves have done such acts, as have excluded their posterity from sitting in that throne; and that without imputation of injustice. Besides what is said, children are under the same covenant with their parents; and when magistrates, who are metaphorical parents, or those who are natural parents, do transgress, God may strike the children upon that account, and that to prevent the like evil in them. When fathers are troubled with the gout or stone, physicians prescribe their children to forbear such meats as are dispositive that way.

Whether may the sins of parents being under one covenant, be visited upon the children being under another? as, suppose the parent under the covenant of works, and his children under the covenant of grace, doth it fall out ever that such children suffer for their parents' sins? Yes, they do, as in the case here; Manasseh sinned, and for his sins not only the wicked ones, but Ezekiel and other precious ones, suffered in Babylon: Zedekiah sins, and those that did mourn and sigh, Ezek. ix. 4, for his and others' abominations, suffered greatly. So on the contrary, for the sins of godly parents, who are in one covenant, may their children suffer, that are under another, as in David and Absalom, 2 Sam. xii. 11, "I will raise up evil against thee out of thine own house:" Absalom's rebellion and death, David's sin had the greatest influence into. So Solomon's sin fell heavy upon Rehoboam, 1 Kings xi. 11, 12, and xii. 15, 16, 20. But there is an observable difference in the suffering of the children for the sins of the parents. When the children are gracious, their sufferings upon the account of their parents' sins are chastisements, mercies, and from love; but where they are ungodly, their sufferings are real and true punishments, coming from divine justice and wrath.

3rd difficulty is, The Lord tells them here that for the time to come it should not be so; If the children have suffered for their fathers' sins heretofore, and you have had cause to complain, yet henceforward you shall have no occasion, "the soul that sinneth, it shall die," and no other. Yet shortly after those at Jerusalem suffered; and, Lam. v. 7, took up the complaint here spoken of, "Our fathers have sinned," say they, "and are not; and we have borne their iniquities." Moreover, it is evident to the whole world, that the Jews now do suffer for their fathers' sins: they put the Lord Christ to death, wished his blood to be upon them and their children, and it is upon them in a dreadful manner to this day.

Answ. This is a riddle which I believe will not be fully expounded till the great day of the Lord; only thus much may be said beforehand: Men have extended the sense of those words further than God intended; if we exceed not our limits, but keep to the persons, time, and matter in hand, we may make out the difficulty; as thus, the prophet speaks of the Jews that were already in Babylon, and the others that should suddenly be brought from Jerusalem into the same captivity with them, and principally he hath reference to the sin of Manasseh, as may appear by 2 Kings xxi. 11—14; xxiii. 26, 27; xxiv. 3, 4; Jer. xv. 4, for which they suffered, and made them to complain. Now the Lord intimates, yea assures them, that after their suffering in the Babylonish captivity, he would be satisfied, and they should never suffer more for the sins of Manasseh, but should return again; and if they suffered afterward, it should be for their own sins, not his. In this sense you see the difficulty cleared, but if you enlarge the words to all times and persons, it is beyond the reach of men to answer the difficulty; for we see it daily, that one sins, and others suffer for it; parents sin, and their children suffer; magistrates sin, and cities suffer; princes sin, and people suffer. The Lord did not divest himself here of that power and privilege of visiting the iniquities of parents upon the heads of their children, but takes away that accusation they laid against him for suffering so long and grievous a captivity for the sins of Manasseh. That this is the meaning of the words, and their not using the proverb any more, I am confirmed out of Jeremiah, chap. xxxi. 27—30, "Behold, the days come, saith the Lord, that I will sow the house of Israel and the house of Judah with the seed of man, and with the seed of beast. And it shall come to pass, that like as I have watched over them, to pluck up, and to break down, and to throw down, and to destroy, and to afflict; so will I watch over them, to build, and to plant, saith the Lord." This is meant of their return from Babylon; and what then? "In those days they shall say no more, The fathers have eaten a sour grape, and the children's teeth are set on edge; but every one shall die for his own iniquity." So then after the return this proverb ceased, and to those Jews that suffered upon the account of Manasseh's sins; but it is still of force to other Jews, and among us gentiles.

"The soul that sinneth, it shall die."

Quest. May not God spare a soul that sins? he saith peremptorily here, "The soul that sins shall die;" and if so, it obstructs, bars up mercy, and leaves us all without hope, and ties God's hand, &c.

Answ. 1. I will answer this question by clearing another scripture like unto it; Gen. ii. 17, "In the day that thou eatest thereof thou shalt surely die." This threatening or law was not purely or simply legal, nor from absolute justice, because if we look at the elect, it included the good pleasure of God in the death of Christ for them, and so it had somewhat evangelical in it; but in respect of the reprobate it was merely legal, and from pure justice, whereby God determined to punish sinners: so here, this threatening hath mercy in it, the soul that sins must either die itself, or in Christ; so that in some it is fulfilled evangelically, in others legally.

2. Sin is not against the essence and nature of God, for sin is transgression of a law; had not God made such a law, there had been no sin; "where no law is, there is no transgression," Rom. iv. 15. Therefore sin not being against the nature of God, he might have left all free to man, as well as to beasts, fowls, and fishes: had sin been against his nature, he had been necessitated to punish it, but being against his will, he doth freely punish it, and therefore may not punish it, but spare the sinner. Those rules and laws of justice in the word, are to tie us, and not God; he hath his prerogative above all those laws, and saith, "I will have mercy on whom I will," Rom. ix. 15. And if this do not satisfy, cast your thoughts upon the death of Christ. That Christ died is justice, and so respects the covenant of works; that he died for us is mercy, and so respects the covenant of grace.

Obs. 1. Men are apt to quarrel against God's word, ministrations, and proceedings in the world; they think and say, he deals hardly, if not tyrannically, with them. If he cause wars, send famines, plagues, cast into captivity, and lay his hand heavy upon a nation or family, how apt are the sons of men to murmur and charge God foolishly! But what is flesh and blood unto God? Shall clay dispute with the potter, dust with the balance, the drop with the bucket? He is the Maker of the whole world; let us be silent before him.

Obs. 2. God is just and righteous in his government of the world, and in all his dispensations therein, however things appear, and are accounted of by men. Sometimes the ways of God with the world, kingdoms, families, persons, seem strange, crooked, dark, unequal, not because they are so, but because men are weak, purblind, and cannot penetrate into the depths of them. God's drowning the whole world, shutting up the knowledge of himself so many hundred years in Judea from the rest of the world; his consuming Sodom and Gomorrah with fire and brimstone, slaying so many thousands for looking into the ark; his casting off the Jews from being his people, and letting them go under the curse now sixteen hundred years; his blessing of the wicked, and afflicting of the godly, Jer. xii. 1, 2; his casting off Saul for lesser sins, and sparing David, Solomon, who were guilty of greater; his sending unseasonable weather, to blast, corrupt, and make both corn and cattle unwholesome, unuseful, or less serviceable; his setting tyrants over his people, to impoverish, persecute, and destroy them, without any mercy; his ordering it so, that the young of all brute creatures can shift for themselves presently, and infants, the births of more noble creatures, should be shiftless so long; that so many thousand innocent creatures are cut off, even infants, in public calamities; that the Baptist's head must off, when a Barabbas goes free; "that the race is not to the swift, nor the battle to the strong, nor bread to the wise, nor riches to men of understanding, nor favour to men of skill," &c. Eccles. ix. 11: these and such emergents in the world, prompt occasions unto shallow, silly man, to think that there is no Providence, or that the government of the world is not righteous and just. But as there is a God, so in his wise providence he orders and rules all things, and that righteously: Psal. cxlv. 17, "The Lord is righteous in all his ways;" no ways of his general or special providence have any crookedness in them; whenever thoughts rise in any to that purpose, let them remember what Jeremiah said when his heart was troubled in the same case, "Righteous art thou, O Lord, when I plead with thee;" though I cannot see the ground, cause, reason of thy ways, yet thou art righteous, and that shall suffice me. God is most righteous, he will punish none unjustly, nor neglect to reward any who have done well; see Rom. ii. 6—11.

Obs. 3. God may give and impose what laws he pleases. Isa. xxxiii. 22, "The Lord is our lawgiver;" Hebrew is, our statute-maker; all legislative power is fundamentally in God: James iv. 12, "There is one lawgiver;" he hath given all creatures, as limits for their essence, so laws for their operation: Psal. cxix. 91, "They continue this day according to thine ordinances; for all are thy servants;" they all do the work God appoints, and observe the laws he prescribes. He may command what he pleases: he licensed Adam to eat of some trees, and not of others; he bade Abraham go out of his country, sacrifice his son; the Israelites to rob the Egyptians; he forbade the Jews to eat of several fowls and beasts; he appointed Ezekiel to eat his bread baked in dung, chap. iv.; Saul to slay Amalek, and not to spare man, woman, or child, 1 Sam. xv.; he bade Hosea take a wife of whoredoms, chap. i. 2; he laid circumcision, sacrifices, and all the ceremonials upon the Jews, easier things upon the gentiles: all souls are his, and what laws, statutes, ordinances seem good to him, he may put upon them. The gospel, not the law, faith, not works, he hath made the way to glory. He may prescribe what he list, his will is law unto the creature: he may give us easy or harsh laws, such as tend to our ruin as well as our good; Ezek. xx. 25, "I gave them statutes that were not good, and judgments whereby they should not live." Men may not do so, their laws must be for good, else they are sinful, and not binding.

Obs. 4. Then may the Lord choose whom he will. Rom. ix. 13, 15, 18, "Jacob have I loved, but Esau have I hated. I will have mercy on whom I will have mercy: and whom he will he hardens." May kings choose from among their subjects whom they please to serve them in their courts, and shall not the Lord, whose are all souls, take whom he pleases to serve him in his court of glory? hath every potter power over the clay, to make one vessel to honour, another to dishonour, ver. 21, and shall not the Lord, who is the greatest potter of all, have that prerogative? shall the servant have more than the Master? In this great house of the world, there are vessels to honour and dishonour, 2 Tim. ii. 20; there are some appointed unto disobedience and stumbling, 1 Pet. ii. 8, yea, unto wrath, 1 Thess. v. 9; and who shall question God for so doing? He is not to give account to any man of his actions; he may absolutely do with his own what he list: he made of the same earth man and beast, and shall the beast say to God, Why madest thou me a beast, and not a man? it may as well as man dispute it with God, and say, Why didst thou make me a vessel of dishonour, and not of honour? Should Adam have reasoned it with God, and said, Why didst thou make me the first Adam a natural man, and Christ the second Adam a spiritual man? There is no reasoning with God. Psal. cxxxv. 6, "Whatsoever the Lord pleased, that did he in heaven and in earth;" and whatsoever pleaseth the Lord, that doth he now in heaven and in earth.

Obs. 5. Then may the Lord bestow what gifts he will upon the children of men, excellent or mean, greater or less; he may give one five talents, another two, a third one. A father gives to his children several portions, to one more, to another less, he is not bound to give all alike, but as seems good to himself: men furnish some rooms with richer hangings and materials than others, and that without blame; they plant and beautify some grounds with choice plants and flowers: so deals the Lord with men, some have admirable gifts, others very mean, if you observe God's distributions that way in the world. God hath given the earth to the children of men, Psal. cxv. 16; yet one hath more, another less, one a fat, another a lean portion: so for reason, wisdom, judgment, understanding, memory, utterance, &c. God hath given these to the sons of men; but some have them in a lower, some in a higher degree. David, Solomon, Daniel, were very wise, Samson very strong, Absalom very beautiful; the Corinthians were "enriched with all utterance, and all knowledge," 1 Cor. i. 5; Bezaleel and Aholiab excelled others in skill, Exod. xxxi. And as it is in gifts, so in graces, one hath a little, another a greater portion, one a single, another a double portion; Jonah but little patience, Job much; the disciples of Christ had little faith, the woman of Canaan a great faith: God doth of his own give to his own, what and how much he pleases. By variety of gifts and graces, his manifold wisdom, bounty, and goodness are seen, the world and church are beautified, and each made useful unto the other.

Obs. 6. All being the Lord's, he will take care and provide for them. Nature dictates, yea provokes, every creature to provide for its own; there is no good or wise man who will not do it, much more the Lord. If husbands must provide for their families, 1 Tim. v. 8, God will provide for his. The whole world is God's family, all the living wait upon him, and he feeds them, Psal. civ. 27. Especially man is his, and for him he takes care: 1 Tim. iv. 10, he "is the saviour of all men, specially of those that believe;" it is not meant of eternal salvation; *σωτὴρ* imports a temporal saviour. Matt. viii. 25, *κύριε σῶσον ἡμᾶς, ἀπολλύμεθα*, they were in danger of drowning. Psal. xxxvi. 6, "Thou preservest man and beast:" the word for preserving is ישע whence the name Joshua and Jesus comes; it notes a common, external, temporal salvation. God is good to all souls, his sun shines and rain falls upon good and bad, Matt. v. 45; Acts xiv. 17: chap. xvii. 28, "In him we live," in his providence, power, goodness, blessing, as worms in the earth, fishes in the sea, and birds in the air. And this should be a foundation of comfort, as unto all, so especially unto those who are poor, and mean, and cast upon hard times; and why? because be you never so poor, weak, sickly, destitute, all souls are the Lord's, and he looks after them. Matt. vi. 31, &c. Christ assures you of it; "Take no thought, saying, What shall we eat? or, What shall we drink? or, Wherewithal shall we be clothed? for your heavenly Father knoweth that ye have need of all these things. But seek ye first the kingdom of God, and his righteousness; and all these things shall be added unto you;" not some, but all shall be given unto you.

Obs. 7. He may set up or throw down whom he will. Isa. iii. 4, "I will give children to be their princes, and babes shall rule over them;" children in years, and children in understanding, God sets over people. God set up Solomon, and set by Adonijah, though the elder, 1 Kings i. He took David, the least and unlikeliest of all the sons of Jesse, even from the sheepfold, and set him upon the throne, I Sam. xvi. Gideon was of a poor family, and the least in his father's house, as himself confesses, Judg. vi. 15; yet him did God exalt: so that it is true which Hannah said; "He raiseth up the poor out of the dust, and lifteth up the beggar from the dunghill, to set them among princes, and to make them inherit the throne of glory," 1 Sam. ii. 8. And contrary, as God sets up, so he pulls down whom he pleases. Isa. xlii. 15, "I will make waste mountains and hills, and dry up all their herbs;" be the mountains never so great, the hills never so high, God will lay them waste, and level them with the earth, and whatever their issue, wealth, power, wisdom, relations be, God will dry them all up, and they shall be herbless. Dan. ii. 20, 21, "Wisdom and might are his; he changeth the times and the seasons; he removeth kings, and setteth up kings." Did not the Lord lay by Saul and his family? did he not drown Pharaoh in the bottom of the sea like lead? Herod, Nebuchadnezzar, Belshazzar, and others, did not the Lord lay them low? they were high and green trees, yet the Lord cut them down, and dried them up. You may remember what the Lord said to Ahab; "Hast thou killed? In the place where the dogs licked the blood of Naboth shall dogs lick thy blood, even thine," 1 Kings xxi. 19; and likewise what he saith in Jer. xxii. 24, "As I live, though Coniah the son of Jehoiakim king of Judah were the signet upon my right hand, yet would I pluck him thence;" and Ezek. xvii. 15, of Zedekiah it is said, "Shall he prosper?" no, by the roots shall he be pulled up. God plants and pulls up whom he pleases.

Obs. 8. Then are they in safe custody, and no evil can befall them without the Lord's good pleasure. Men stand for those who are theirs against all opposition, but cannot hinder evil from coming: God stands for his servants, and he can hinder any mischief; none can have any power over or against his people without leave; if God give not commission, nothing can be done by men or devils. John xix. 11, Christ told Pilate he could have no power against him, unless it were given him from above; I am in the hand of my Father, he can defend, deliver me from thine and all adversaries' power; and if he do not, it is by his hand and determinate counsel that thou doest aught against me, and I am content with it. So Luke xxii. 53, "This is your hour, and the power of darkness;" before you could do nothing, now, through divine dispensation, you have leave to seize upon me, to judge me, and take away my life, and I submit thereunto. The devil could do nothing against Job, his sons, camels, sheep, or asses, till he had leave from the Lord, Job i. He is the god of the world, prince of the air, and hath bitter envy, great enmity, against man, but is not able by all his power or policy to take a hair from the head of any man, till the Lord say, Do it, Matt. x. 30. All souls are the Lord's, they are in his hands. It was comfort to David to think his times were in God's hand; Psal. xxxi. 15, "My times are in thy hand;" and so nothing could befall him unseasonably; yea, his person also was in God's hand, and who could touch or harm it without the Lord: Isa. xlv. 7, the good or evil that befalls us is from the Lord.

Obs. 9. Then it belongs to God to hear the pleadings, determine the controversies, that are between those who are his, and to right their wrongs. If all souls be his, he is Judge, and so to hear their suits, decide their differences, and see that one wrong not another. The people Moses was over, are called his people, Exod. xxxii. 7; and he heard their pleadings, ended their controversies, and righted their wrongs, Exod. xviii. 13. All souls being the Lord's, he hath an ear open to hear their suits, and he sits in judgment to do them right that suffer, Psal. cxxv. Hence is it that David appeals to God, Psal. xliii. 1, "Judge me, O God, and plead my cause against an ungodly nation." Others judge unrighteously, but I come to thee, do thou judge me, that art the great Judge; all souls are thine, do thou plead my cause, it belongs to thee to do it, and I wait upon thee for it. So the church in Micah vii. 9, "I will bear the indignation of the Lord, because I have sinned against him, until he plead my cause." The Babylonians oppressed the Jews, Jer. l. 33; 34, and the prophet saith, "The Lord of hosts shall throughly plead their cause, that he may give rest to the land, and disquiet the inhabitants of Babylon." Let Babylonians, others, any molest, oppress, God hears, sees, knows what is done, he will plead and maintain the cause of his people: Psal. ix. 4, "Thou hast maintained my right and my cause; thou satest in the throne judging right." If the cause be a cause of blood, as it was Rev. vi. 10, where the souls cried, "How long, O Lord, holy and true, dost thou not judge and avenge our blood on them that dwell on the earth?" the Lord will not neglect it, for the answer was, ver. 11, that they should rest yet for a little season, and then God would avenge their blood. God hath his times to make inquisition for blood, Psal. ix. 12; and "the earth shall disclose her blood," Isa. xxvi. 20.

Obs. 10. God may employ whom he will, and in what ways and works he thinks good; he is neither tied to any sort of men, nor to the laws or customs of any kingdoms. Nathan thinks David must build the temple, but God employs Solomon, not David, in that work, 2 Sam. vii. He took Amos, who was no prophet, nor son of a prophet, but a herdman, a poor mean man, and would have him to prophesy unto Israel, Amos vii. 14, 15. He took Cyrus, a heathen king, to perform all his pleasure about Jerusalem's rebuilding; he held up and used his right hand to subdue nations, to loose the loins of kings, to break in pieces the gates of brass, and cut in sunder the bars of iron, Isa. xliv. 28; xlv. 1, 2. God employed David, a stripling, despised by his brethren and others, to slay Goliath, and free Israel from the Philistines, 1 Sam. xvii. He took a woman to kill a great prince, even Jael to slay Sisera, Judg. iv. 21. As the Lord may take whom he will, so he may lead them in what ways, and put them upon what designs, himself judges fit and meet, however they seem unwarrantable to us. Isa. xlii. 16, "I will bring the blind by a way that they know not; I will lead them in paths that they have not known; I will make darkness light before them, and crooked things straight;" the blind, that is, men perplexed, in straits and difficulties, not seeing what to do, which way to turn them. Now God, as he is not tied to go in one and the same way, to proceed by the laws, statutes, privileges, customs, usances of kingdoms, cities, or corporations, but hath unknown ways and unwonted paths to tread in himself; so he hath unknown and unwonted paths to lead his servants in upon any occasion. It was no trodden path that Phinehas went in, when he, a priest or a priest's son, no magistrate, thrust a prince and a princess through their bellies with a javelin, and that in the presence of Moses the chief magistrate, Numb. xxv. So Esther's going in to the king was not according to law, chap. iv. 16; she ventured her life upon it: and David's eating the shewbread was an unlawful act, if judged by Exod. xxix. 32, 33; Lev. viii. 31; xxiv. 5; yet justified by Christ, Matt. xii. 3. Samson takes a wife of the daughters of the Philistines, and that against the will of his father and mother, and it was against law for him to marry among the uncircumcised, but he seeth a woman at Timnah, falls in love with her, and must have her, Judg. xiv. 4; this was of the Lord. His burning the Philistines' corn, his slaying a thousand of them with the jaw-bone of an ass, pulling down the house upon his own and others' heads, were irregular ways, yet such ways as God led him in, and he is in the catalogue of believers, Heb. xi. The eunuchs throw Jezebel out at the window upon the command of Jehu, and he trod her to death with his horses, 2 Kings ix. 33. Jehoiada the priest calls forth the soldiers, sets them in ranges, and makes a martial law, that whosoever enters those ranges should be put to death; Athaliah the queen (who had reigned six years) enters, and at his appointment she is put to death, 2 Kings xi. These, and many other, (as Solomon's sacrificing in Gibeon, 1 Kings iii. 4, Paul's shaving of himself, circumcising Timothy,) were irregular and unwonted ways, yet were approved of God, and brought forth unwonted mercies. Let us not be too hasty to condemn persons doing extraordinary things, lest we justle against God, and intrench upon his providence and prerogative; if Peter walk upon the waters, there is somewhat of Christ and God in it, Matt. xiv. 28, 29.

Obs. 11. Let all be faithful in their places. All souls are his, he hath his eye upon all, and upon every one, and there is none but must give account unto him. Whatever talents we have, he will reckon with us for the use or abuse of them: Matt. xxv. 19, the Lord called and reckoned with his servants he had given the talents unto; those who had talents of grace, and used them well, were advanced to heaven to their Master's joy; he who had a talent of nature, for the abuse was thrown into hell. Oh let us be faithful in our places, and use our talents to the honour of that God whose we and our talents are! Belshazzar was set on high, had a talent in his hand, but the charge was heavy upon him, when he that is Lord of all souls called him to an account; Dan. v. 23, "The God in whose hand thy breath is, and whose are all thy ways, hast thou not glorified;" and thereupon he was doomed to death: he did not lay out his power and greatness for the honour of God and good of his people, and better he had been a poor beggar than so great a king. Paul had this consideration in him when he said, "Woe to me if I preach not the gospel!" 1 Cor. ix. 16, 17; and, "if I yet please men, I should not be the servant of Christ," Gal. i. 10. And when he wrote to the Corinthians, "We labour that we may be accepted of him: for we must all appear before the judgment-seat of Christ, that every one may receive the things done in his body, according to that he hath done, whether good or bad," 2 Cor. v. 9, 10. Men must give account of all they have received, and if they be found false and unfaithful, they shall smart for it. Seeing then "every one of us shall give account of himself to God," Rom. xiv. 12, let us all be faithful in the least, in the greatest things committed to us, and so shall we have peace within, praise of God, if not of men, and a sure reward.

Obs. 12. He may take away or continue men here as long or little while as he will; all souls are his, and he may cut off the thread of life, or lengthen it out, at his pleasure. Moses speaking to the Jews as one man saith, "He is thy life, and the length of thy days," Deut. xxx. 20; that is, the shortening or prolonging of thy life and days are in his hand. God therefore told Solomon, that if he would keep his commands, he would lengthen his days, 1 Kings iii. 14. The keys of life and death are in the hand of the Lord, and in a moment he can let out our souls, bring down to and back from the gates of death. Hence is it that some are taken away at the first hour, some at the third, some the sixth, some the ninth, and some lengthened out unto the twelfth, and live more years than others do days or hours: Methuselah lived nine hundred and sixty-nine years, and many children attain not to so many days or hours; from the birth, the womb, and conception,

God takes them away, Hos. ix. 11. He cut off all flesh by the flood, young and old; and long since that he hath threatened to cut off "evil-doers," Psal. xxxvii. 9, and "man from off the land," Zeph. i. 3, and when he pleases he doth it.

"The soul that sinneth, it shall die." Hence

Obs. 1. God may lay what punishment he pleases upon the soul that sins. "All souls are mine," and "the soul that sinneth shall die," it shall suffer whatever I see good, according to the nature of its sin. However the words seem to import an equal punishment for all sins, yet it is otherwise; according to the intrinsical nature, circumstances, and demerit of the sin, shall be the death; God will proportion the one unto the other; as he rewards men according to their works, so he will punish them according to their sins. God hath variety of deaths, and various degrees of those deaths, variety of afflictions, and various degrees of the same; he lays on which, and in what measure, he pleases: how are sinners tortured with colics, stranguries, gouts, stone, plague, and other diseases! If states think good to inflict upon delinquents several punishments, and in a high degree as they find men guilty, how much more may God! He smote Jehoram with incurable and sore diseases, so that his bowels fell out, 2 Chron. xxi. 18, 19. He sent fire and brimstone upon Sodom and Gomorrah, Gen. xix. He did that in Jerusalem which he never did before, nor ever would do the like, he punished them so with famine, that fathers did eat their sons, and sons their fathers, Ezek. v. 9, 10. Neither these nor any that suffer in what kind soever, do suffer unjustly; men may pretend innocency, but if they suffer, and that severely, God is not cruel, they are not guiltless; for "the soul that sinneth shall die."

Obs. 2. Sin is a deadly thing. "The soul that sinneth shall die;" sin is the great murderer, it let death into the world, and keeps death alive; if there were no sin, there would be no death, no punishment, but if men sin, they must suffer. The old world sinned, and died for it; Sodomites sinned, and died for it; the Bethshemites sinned by looking into the ark, and fifty thousand of them died for it; Jerusalem sins, and is burnt for it, and her children buried in a Babylonish grave; Ananias and Sapphira die for their dissimulation: "the wages of sin is death," Rom. vi. 23. Let us then take heed of sin, whereby we offend that God who hath said, "The soul that sinneth, it shall die;" he is a dreadful Majesty, and ought greatly to be feared. Jer. x. 7, "Who would not fear thee, O King of nations? for to thee doth it appertain;" fear is God's due, and your duty; "stand in awe," then, "and sin not," Psal. iv. 4. If you sin, you must die; death is the king of fears, and God is the King of death, he can command it to seize upon you in a moment.

Ver. 5, 6. ***But if a man be just, and do that which is lawful and right, and hath not eaten upon the mountains, neither hath lifted up his eyes to the idols of the house of Israel, neither hath defiled his neighbour's wife, neither hath come near to a menstruous woman.***

The Lord having vindicated himself in general, ver. 4, from that unjust accusation, that their fathers sinned and they who were the children suffered, he comes here in a more particular manner to quit himself from that false imputation. I have told you that the soul which sins shall die, but

I. If a man be just, he shall not die, but live, as appears from ver. 5, to the end of ver. 9.

II. If his son be unjust and wicked, he shall not live, but die, as appears from ver. 10, to the end of ver. 13.

III. If this unjust man beget a son, who lives not in his father's sins, but is just and deals justly, notwithstanding all his father's sins, he shall live, he shall not die, as is evident from the beginning of ver. 14, to the end of ver. 17.

The words in ver. 5—9, contain and specify,

1. A subject, which is, a man just, or a just man.

2. The description of this subject, which is set out,

(1.) In general; ver. 5, "and do that which is lawful and right."

(2.) In particular; and that,

[1.] In duties respecting God, ver. 6, which are set down negatively, and they are two:

First, not eating upon the mountains.

Second, not lifting up the eyes to the idols of the house of Israel.

[2.] In duties respecting man, and they are divers:

First, continency; "neither hath defiled his neighbour's wife."

Second, chastity; "neither hath come near to a menstruous woman." These two are in ver. 6.

Third, innocency; in four things: 1. Not oppressing any. 2. Restoring the pledge. 3. Not spoiling by violence. 4. Withdrawing his hand from iniquity.

Fourth, charity; which is held out in, 1. His feeding the hungry, ver. 7. 2. Clothing the naked, ver. 7. 3. In lending freely, ver. 8, "he that hath not given forth upon usury, nor taken any increase."

Fifth, in righteous judgment between man and man, ver. 8.

Lastly, a general comprehending of these and all other duties, ver. 9, "hath walked in my statutes, and hath kept my judgments, to deal truly."

3. The thing predicated on this subject so described, "he shall live."

I shall open the words, and after come to the observations.

Ver. 5. "If a man be just." Hebrew word, צדיק is a man free from fault, doing things approvable; such a one was Noah, who is called, Gen. vi. 9, איש צדיק such a one was Zacharias, Luke i. 6, δίκαιος, as the Septuagint renders it in this place; and the word for "just" is opposed to רשע a wicked man: Psal. xxxvii. 16, "A little that a righteous man hath, is better than the riches of many wicked." So Psal. i. 6, there is an opposition between the righteous and ungodly, the just and wicked.

"Do that which is lawful and right." Hebrew for lawful and right, is judgment and justice. To do judgment, is not only to do things judiciously and rationally, but here it notes one part of the office of a judge, which is to sentence and condemn the guilty; and so to do justice, is not only to judge without respect of persons, but to absolve and vindicate the innocent. Thus Pradus interprets the words, who thinks these words coming together, not to be exegetical, but signifying distinct things, in a more narrowed sense, than when they are taken absolutely and in their latitude. So Isa. v. 7, "He looked for judgment," that the guilty should be condemned, "but behold oppression," iniquity, a scab, as the word signifies; the delinquents being spared, there was iniquity in the judges, a scab upon the state. I looked "for righteousness" or justice, that the innocent should be vindicated and freed from the accusations, aspersions, oppressions of the wicked, "but behold a cry;" they suffered, were condemned, and this was a crying sin. When men in place do act according to the laws of God, suppressing the wicked, defending and countenancing the good, then they do judgment and justice. Some by these words understand the fulfilling of the law; when a man gives to God and man what is required, then he is a just man, he doth judgment and justice.

Ver. 6. "And hath not eaten upon the mountains." Upon mountains and hills both the Jews and nations used to build high places, images, and altars, 1 Kings xi. 7; 2 Kings xvii. 10; Jer. xvii. 2; Ezek. vi. 13: and there they did sacrifice to their idol-gods; Hos. iv. 13, "They sacrifice upon the tops of the mountains, and burn incense upon the hills:" see Ezek. xx. 28; 2 Chron. xxviii. 4; Isa. lvii. 7. And of those things that were sacrificed to the idols they were wont to eat; Psal. cvi. 28, "They ate the sacrifices of the dead," of those beasts, fowls, or whatsoever things they sacrificed to the dead idols, of those they did eat. Such was the eating, Exod. xxxii. 6; Judg. ix. 27; xvi. 23, 25. This eating of idolothites noted their communion with idols, that they were in near relation, even as near as those that live, sit, feed, and feast together: 1 Cor. x. 20, 21, by their eating and drinking those things which were offered to idols, they had communion with idols and devils.

This eating of such things was a grievous sin; they left God, the Holy One of Israel, and joined themselves to dumb and dead idols, which could do nothing for them but procure the wrath of the true and living God against them.

Not to "eat upon the mountains," then, is to keep oneself free from false worship. They "eat upon the mountains," who worship God any other way than he hath prescribed in his word.

"Neither hath lifted up his eyes to the idols." The lifting up the eye in sacred writ notes,

1. A serious and affective consideration of a thing, as, Isa. xl. 26, "Lift up your eyes on high, and behold who hath created these things;" that is, seriously and affectively consider, contemplate the heavens, and host of them: so here, to lift up the eyes to idols, signifies to affect, mind much, to think upon them, as if they had some special beauty, excellency, or deity in them.

2. To countenance; Psal. iv. 6, "Lift thou up the light of thy face upon us;" the eye is the light of the face, when that is let down, it notes disfavour, discountenancing; but when that is lift up, it imports the contrary; so here, lifting up the eyes to idols, imports a favouring, gracing, countenancing of them.

3. Adoration. Lifting up the eyes is an adoring gesture: Ezek. viii. 16, the five and twenty men there stood with their faces towards the east, their eyes were lift up to the sun, and the sun they worshipped. Job xxxi. 26, "If I beheld the sun when it shined:" did not he see the sun when it shined? yes; but he did not lift up his eyes to adore it, though it were a beautiful and glorious creature, a great benefactor unto the whole world.

4. Invocation and expectation of something the party would have. John xvii. 1, Christ "lifted up his eyes to heaven, and said, Father, glorify thy Son;" he looked up to heaven, prayed, and expected glory. Psal. cxxiii. 1, "Unto thee lift I up mine eyes, O thou that dwellest in the heavens:" here was invocation and expectation of mercy, ver. 2. So lifting up the eyes to idols, argues invoking of and expecting help from them, and the not lifting up the eyes unto them, implies a disaffecting, discountenancing, and detesting them, as lies, vanity, abomination.

"Idols." Hebrew word is, גלולי from גלל dung which is trodden down in the streets. They are stinking, loathsome, defiling things; a man cannot be more annoyed with the dung of man, or any other creature, than he is with idols; they defile the whole man; James iii. 6, an ill tongue defiles the whole body, and an idol defiles the whole soul and body. Septuagint renders the word for idols, ἐνθυμήματα, thoughts, devices; because they are the mere inventions of men's brains, the imaginations of their hearts. God said, "Thou shalt not make to thyself any graven image, or any likeness of any thing," Exod. xx. 4; yet vain, silly, weak, wretched man, will be making to himself likenesses of every thing, and fancy a deity in that which is most unlike, yea, most opposite, to the true Deity.

Stercus quod in platea convolutatum est. *Avenarius.*

"Of the house of Israel." These words are added,

1. To prevent an evasion and excuse of theirs. Had the prophet said, "Neither hath lifted up his eyes to idols," and no more, they would have said, We hate the idols of the nations, and have nothing to do with them, we know such idols are forbidden; to cut off this plea therefore, the words run thus, "idols of the house of Israel."

2. To remind them of God's dealing with the ten tribes for their idolatry, who properly are called the house of Israel, and were carried into captivity, 2 Kings xvii.

3. If by house of Israel be meant those of Judah and Benjamin, which I conceive to be the prophet's mind, it is to take away a false conceit they had of their gods above others: Be it that others have worshipped their idols, given more honour to them than was due, yet we worship the true God, use these idols and images in worship to further our honouring and worshipping God by them; we do not terminate our worship in them, but transmit it by them unto God. Whatever conceits you have of your idols, they are idols, no better than those of the ten tribes and nations, by which they provoked God against them; so do you by these.

"Neither hath defiled his neighbour's wife." From duties respecting God, he comes to duties respecting man, and begins with that which concerns the married estate.

By "neighbour," understand not only him that dwells next you, but any man whatsoever; so "neighbour" is taken, Luke x. 36. The meaning of the words is not that a man may lie with a stranger's, foreigner's, or an enemy's wife, but not with his neighbour's; no, the meaning is, a man must not lie with any man's wife whatsoever; be he single or married, he may not defile the wife of another man, he may not commit adultery with her, which is meant by the word defiling.

לא טמא which the Septuagint renders, hath not contaminated; others, hath not defiled. I shall insist a little upon the evil of this sin.

1. It breaks the order which God in his great wisdom hath set. He hath appointed that two should be one flesh, not three, or more, Gen. ii. 24; and it is oft set down by the Spirit of God, as Matt. xix. 5, 6; Mark x. 7, 8; 1 Cor. vi. 16; Eph. v. 31; that this divine institution may take the deeper impression upon men, and so be kept inviolable: but when adultery is committed, it is against the institution of an infinitely wise God, and dreadful breach of his order, and however it be done in secret, yet the Lord seeth it, Prov. v. 21.

2. It stains the ordinance of God. Marriage is honourable, both in itself, and as it is a resemblance of Christ and his church, Heb. xiii. 4; Eph. v. 31, 32. Now if adultery be committed, the bed is defiled, the honour of the married estate laid in the dust, and the members of Christ made the members of a harlot, 1 Cor. vi. 15. Adulterers therefore sin against Christ, they take away that resemblance which is in marriage between Christ and his church, and prostitute their bodies, what lies in them, to dishonourable acts.

3. It brutifies a man, besots, and makes him who is a rational creature, the chief of God's works here in the world, to be like unto the brute creatures, and to do irrational things. Hos. iv. 11, whoredom is one of the things which take away the heart, that is, a right understanding. Jer. v. 7, 8, like horses, they neighed after their neighbours' wives; they were more like horses than men, and acted like those brutish, unruly creatures; whereupon the Lord saith, chap. xiii. 27, "I have seen thine adulteries, and thy neighings." Adultery makes men so sensual, that they forget reason, it blinds and infatuates them exceedingly. Solomon, who had the greatest portion of wisdom, by his pleasing himself with women, doted and did strange things, he became as blockish as the idols he set up. Men that live in such pollutions of the world, as adultery and other uncleannesses are, the apostle likens them to dogs and swine, 2 Pet. ii. 22.

4. In this sin, man sins against,

(1.) His own body, 1 Cor. vi. 18. Fornication and adultery are sins in a special manner against a man's own body,

[1.] In that he subjects it to another. It is called a bowing down, Job xxxi. 10. To bow down to an adulteress, to bow down to an adulterer, is a subjecting themselves to be one with each other: the thief is not one with the thing he steals, nor the murderer one with him he murders, but the adulterer is one with the adulteress.

[2.] Weakens it, brings diseases, and hastens death; the more prodigal men are in pouring out themselves in filthy practices, the faster they wear out.

[3.] He defiles it; Matt. xv. 19, 20, adulteries, fornications, are among the things that do defile a man; they are unclean persons who fall into those sins. Ceremonial defilements, as touching a leprous person, a dead body, were evil, but this is a moral defilement.

(2.) It is a sin against their names and credit: Prov. vi. 33, "Dishonour shall he get, and his reproach shall not be wiped away;" it sticks fast like the leopard's spots, nothing makes more infamous. Ecclus. xxiii. 26, A shameful report shall she leave, and her reproach shall not be put out; speaking of the whorish woman.

(3.) It is against the peace and comfort of a man, it wounds him sorely: Prov. vi. 33, "A wound shall he get," a wound in his conscience, which is the worst of all wounds. There are some sins that do destroy the conscience, and adultery is one of the chief of them; it devours all the peace, quiet, content, comfort, the soul had, and wounds it so greatly, that sundry times it proves incurable; yea, so fiery, stinging, and tormenting it is, that men make away themselves: Prov. vii. 26, "She hath cast down many wounded."

(4.) It is against a man's own soul: Prov. vi. 32, "He that commits adultery, destroyeth his own soul." The soul is a precious thing, yea most precious, it is better than all the world; what an evil is it then to destroy that which is so excellent! Adultery is the destruction of a soul, therefore it is said, Prov. vii. 27, "Her house is the way to hell, going down to the chambers of death;" Prov. xxiii. 27, "A whore is a deep ditch."

(5.) It is a great offence to the innocent parties; to the wife of the man who commits it, to the husband of the woman who falls into it. Mal. ii. 14, if a man leave his wife, who is his companion, and the wife of his covenant, he deals treacherously and perfidiously with her; he promised, before the Lord, to be for her and none else: so the woman, when she doth so, forsakes the guide of her youth, and forgets the covenant of her God. What greater wrong can a man do to his wife, or a wife to a husband, than to be treacherous the one to the other; they rend themselves each from other, and bestow themselves upon strangers; strangers have their hearts, affections, and company; strangers have power over them, and not their wives or husbands, which they ought to have, 1 Cor. vii. 4.

(6.) It is a sin that prejudiceth the family, and may bring ruin upon it. Bastards, those who are misbegotten, are brought into the family; bitter jarrings, contentions, and jealousies raised therein: Prov. vi. 34, "Jealousy is the rage of a man," and so of a woman. And Job tells you, that this sin is "a fire that consumeth to destruction," it consumes the body, the estate, the family, chap. xxxi. 12, and if I were guilty of it, it "would root out all my increase;" not one or two, but all his increase. This is a sin that hath ruined many families, and is against not only the good of families, but of mankind. Hos. iv. 10, "They shall commit whoredom, and shall not increase;" and what if an adulteress should bring forth, Ecclus. xxiii. 25, "Her children shall not take root, and her branches shall bring forth no fruit."

(7.) It occasioneth, if not causeth, many other sins. Sometimes the adulteress pilfereth from her husband, and wastes his estate, neglects him and her family: sometimes it hath idolatry following it; Solomon's wives, concubines, and whores brought him to idolatry. Jer. xiii. 27, "I have seen thine adulteries, and thy neighings, the lewdness of thy whoredom, and thine abominations on the hills." Corporal and spiritual adultery go together very often; and not only these, but it hath been the cause of untimely deaths and murders: David defiles the wife of Uriah, and he must first be made drunk, and after be murdered, that the fact might be concealed, 2 Sam. xi. Edgar, once king of this nation, falling into adulterous practices with Alfreda, a nobleman's wife, one Ethelwolf, they got him despatched out of the way, that so they might marry. The father saith, that the fruit of adultery is murder and witchery, and that adulteresses do frequently practise murders: Prov. vi. 26, "The adulteress will hunt for the precious life." It is also accompanied with much lying and perjury. Chrysost. in Ps. li. Hom. 1.

Lastly, the evil of this sin is seen, in that it sets Christ and God against a man, and shuts him out of heaven. Mal. iii. 5, "I will be a swift witness against adulterers;" men are backward to meddle in that case, but Christ will be forward to witness against them. It is spoken of him, Heb. xiii. 4, "Whoremongers and adulterers God will judge;" he reserves such to be punished at the day of judgment, 2 Pet. ii. 9, 10; and then he will shut them out of heaven, 1 Cor. vi. 9, 10; Rev. xxii. 15; and they shall have their portion "in the lake which burneth with fire and brimstone," Rev. xxi. 8; and so "shall be punished with everlasting destruction from the presence of the Lord, and the glory of his power," 2 Thess. i. 9.

The punishment appointed by God for this sin here in this world, was no less than death, as you may see, Lev. xx. 10; Deut. xxii. 22; both the adulterer and the adulteress were to be put to death. Job intimates so much, who lived before the law was given, chap. xxxi. 11, "This is an heinous crime; yea, it is an iniquity to be punished by the judges;" he means, it is capital, and deserves death. Boniface, bishop of Mentz, in a letter of his to Theobald king of the Mercians here in England, dissuading him from unclean practices, tells him of the pagans in old Saxony, who knew not the true God, lived chastely with their wives, and if maid or wife were taken in fornication or adultery, they first strangled them and then burnt them. And if the gentiles, who knew not God, had such a zeal and love to chastity, what should you do that are a christian king? If pagans did so hate this sin, how should we christians much more do it! Some would have it punished with death, because the sin is the same it was then, and God the same, hating it as much as ever: be it so, yet the change of punishment maketh the sin neither less hateful or grievous, nor God changeable. Under the law, he that gathered sticks on the sabbath was stoned to death, Numb. xxx.; but Christ excused his disciples when they pulled and rubbed the ears of corn on that day, Matt. xii. The thief was then to restore fourfold; but under the gospel, "Let him that stole, steal no more," only make restitution of the thing stolen, or recompence for it. Neither doth it argue change in God, to change or mitigate the punishment; for then he should be charged with change for changing the ceremonial law, and judicials belonging to it. The law came by Moses, but grace and mercy by Christ; and the times of the gospel abate the rigorous punishments of the law, rather than increase them. Neither do I conceive there should be no punishment for this sin, as some gather from John viii. where Christ did not condemn the woman taken in adultery; he did not thereby abrogate that law, but by his silence showed, that it is not always necessary for states to punish that sin with death, but with punishments of a lower nature. And some of note observe, that it was not single but double adultery when they were put to death for it under Moses' law. "Let every one know how to possess his vessel in sanctification and honour; and not in the lust of concupiscence," 1 Thess. iv. 4, 5.

"Neither hath come near to a menstruous woman." Hebrew is, אשה נדה a woman separate, or put apart, for her monthly courses or terms; for נדה is from נדר or נדה to remove, separate, put away. They were by the law of God, during that time, accounted unclean, that is, unfit for matrimonial acts and use, Lev. xii. 2, and so separate *a loco et sanctuario*, from companying with their husbands, and coming to the sanctuary, Lev. xv. 31.

This practice also was among the heathens, which it is probable they learned from Moses. The Zabians had a law, that such women should dwell apart for a time, and they purged with fire the places where they were. Orpheus gave charge, that women in that condition should not come to the sacred rites of Bacchus; and Diana suffered not a man that had touched a slain person, or a woman in child-bed, or a dead corpse, to come unto her altars, but counted him as unclean.

Willet on Lev. xv. Euripid. Iphig. in Tauris.

"Come near." That is, hath not only not lien with her, but not had any thing to do with her: Lev. xv. 19, "Whosoever toucheth her shall be unclean until the even." If a husband, or any other man, touched the woman in time of her separation, they were unclean for it.

It is that which the wisdom of God hath forbidden, and if there were nothing else in it, that is sufficient. Lev. xviii. 19, "Thou shalt not approach unto a woman to uncover her nakedness, as long as she is put apart for her uncleanness." In this chapter, unlawful marriages and unlawful lusts are forbidden, and it is as unlawful for men to meddle in that case, as to marry their mothers, sisters, aunts, or daughters-in-law; the same authority that hath forbidden one, hath also forbidden the other.

The punishment of this sin is great. Lev. xx. 18, the man and woman are both to be cut off from among their people; the meaning is not, to be separated from the congregation as defiled, but they were to die for their unseasonable lusts, and approaching near to each other. This may seem very severe; but know, if the man did it ignorantly, he was judged unclean seven days, and was to wash and cleanse himself, Lev. xv. 24, 27; but if wittingly and knowingly it were done, they were both to die for it. Answerable to this is what out prophet saith here, If he have not come near to a menstruous woman, he shall live. Solomon understood this, when he said, Eccles. iii. 5, "There is a time to embrace, and a time to refrain from embracing;" or, as the Hebrew hath it, to be far from embracing: and no time hath the Lord so punctually and severely forbidden it as at that time. Though there be not the same punishment in practice amongst us, yet God hates this sin nevertheless, and questionless visits with sharp sickness, yea strange and sudden death, for it.

Let men and women moderate their affections, mortify their lusts, live soberly, and take heed of provoking God by unseasonable embracings, who would have his people to be chaste both in body and soul.

Ver. 7. *And hath not oppressed any, but hath restored to the debtor his pledge, hath spoiled none by violence, hath given his bread to the hungry, and hath covered the naked with a garment.*

"And hath not oppressed any." Hebrew, לא יונה hath not afflicted, molested, oppressed; for so the word יונה signifies, and it is mostly applied to rich and great men, who usually molest and oppress the poor, the fatherless, widows, and strangers: Lev. xix. 33, "If a stranger sojourn with thee in the land, ye shall not vex him," or oppress him; Jer. xxii. 3, "Do no violence to the stranger, the fatherless, nor the widow," do not afflict, molest, oppress either of them; Ezek. xxii. 29, "They have vexed the poor and needy." You have all these together, Zech. vii. 10, "Oppress not the widow, nor the fatherless, the stranger, nor the poor."

Besides these, there were servants also whom they might not oppress: Deut. xxiv. 14, "Thou shalt not oppress an hired servant." These chiefly are subject to oppression; but great and small may vex and oppress one the other: Lev. xxv. 17, "They shall not oppress one another." Sometimes it falls out so, but more frequently the great, rich men in place and power, do oppress those who are inferior to them, and under them.

I. Wherein this oppression consists.

1. In outreaching men in buying or selling: Lev. xxv. 14, "If thou sell aught unto thy neighbour, or buyest aught of thy neighbour's hand, ye shall not oppress one another." Men must neither sell too dear, nor buy too cheap; which is contrary to the practice of the world, for most men, if not all men, will buy as cheap, and sell as dear, as they can.

(1.) It is oppression, when the buyer will wring a commodity out of his neighbour's or brother's hand, which he is unwilling to part withal. Ahab will have Naboth's vineyard, 1 Kings xxi.

(2.) When he makes advantage of the seller's necessity. And so many monied men will furnish sellers and needy men with money, upon condition they may have such wares, such a house, such land, at an easier and under rate: such advantage they made of them, Neh. v. 3, who were necessitated to mortgage their lands, vineyards, and houses, for money to buy corn. So those who sell to the shops, you will have their commodities at, &c.

(3.) When he disparageth the commodities of the seller, who being not so well insighted into the thing to be sold as the subtle buyer, is overreached and defrauded: Prov. xx. 14, "It is naught, it is naught, saith the buyer;" he brings up an ill report upon it, casts a mist before the seller's eyes, that so he may get it at a cheap rate. So in the seller,

[1.] When you sell that for good which is not so: Amos viii. 6, they sold the refuse of the wheat for good wheat. And so for meats, wares, fruits, wines; many help off ill commodities with lies, oaths, false glosses, lights, and pretences that it cost so much, that such would have given them so much, &c.

[2.] When you deceive them in weight and measure: Prov. xx. 10, "Divers weights, and divers measures, are both of them alike abomination to the Lord."

[3.] When you take advantage of the buyer's weakness or necessities. Some, when an ignorant party comes to their shops, they set the dice upon him, and make him pay double, or more than a knowing man should; but this is against the rule; 1 Thess. iv. 6, "Let no man go beyond and defraud his brother in any matter." So for his necessity; many sellers seeing men in straits, and that they must have their commodities, they set them such prices as undoeth them, dealing with them: so that according to Amos viii. 4, "They swallow up the needy, and make the poor of the land to fail."

2. In withholding that which is right and due to others; James v. 4, "Behold, the hire of the labourers who have reaped down your fields, which is of you kept back by fraud, crieth." "The labourer is worthy of his hire," saith Christ, Luke x. 7; and it was quickly to be paid, Lev. xix. 13. Now to deny it, withhold it, to detract from it, or to pay it in money not current, is oppression: Mal. iii. 5, "I will be a swift witness against those that oppress the hireling in his wages, the widow and the fatherless, and turn aside the stranger from his right." If any withhold the portion of orphans, legacies given to the poor, the estates and rights of widows, they will lie under the censure of being oppressors.

3. In laying too heavy burdens and tasks upon others. The Egyptians oppressed the Israelites, Exod. iii. 7; they must make their tale of brick, and gather straw too, which made them cry more than they did before, Exod. v. And so many lay more upon their servants and apprentices than they can well perform; they must be up early, down late, fare hard, lie hard, work hard, and be worn out before their time, if they had not been under such rigid masters and task-masters; and if not so, to break away and run into dissolute and desperate courses: and what is this but oppression in a high degree? whereas the rule is, Col. iv. 1, "Masters, give unto your servants that which is just and equal; knowing that ye also have a Master in heaven."

Likewise the taxing and rating the poorer sort of people beyond their proportion, for the easing of the richer sort, is great oppression: Isa. x. 1, "Woe unto them that decree unrighteous decrees, and that write grievousness which they have prescribed; to turn aside the needy from judgment." Great and rich men usually make the rates and taxes, and what they decree, prescribe, though never so grievous to the poorer sort, must stand; but let them look to it, there is a dreadful woe pronounced against them; and, Amos iv. 1, 2, "Hear this word, ye kine of Bashan, which oppress the poor, which crush the needy. The Lord God hath sworn by his holiness, that the days shall come upon you, that he will take you away with hooks, and your posterity with fish-hooks."

4. In perverting and delaying of justice and judgment, so that the petitions and causes of widows, orphans, and poor people cannot be heard: Isa. i. 23, "Every one loveth gifts, and followeth after rewards; they judge not the fatherless, neither doth the cause of the widow come unto them." The fatherless and widows had no gifts, no bribes, to give them, the rich had, and by that means justice was perverted, and judgment delayed; "yea, judgment was turned into gall, and the fruit of righteousness into hemlock," Amos vi. 12. And this sin is reckoned amongst the mighty ones: Amos v. 12, "I know the mighty sins; they afflict the just, they take a bribe, and they turn aside the poor in the gate from their right." Let the poor man and his cause be never so good and just, rich and great men, by their purses and their friends, have, in all ages, and still do, oppress them in judgment, Jam. ii. 6. When the wolf and sheep were in contention together, the wolf confessed the sheep had a better cause than he, but he had stronger teeth than they; so poor men, widows, orphans, may have a better cause than rich and great men, but they have stronger teeth than they, and therefore Zephaniah is not afraid to call such, evening, yea ravening, wolves, Zeph. iii. 3.

5. In imposing upon men's consciences those things which are doubtful and disputable, whether warrantable or no, yea of unlawful things; this is the greatest oppression of all. When doctrines, worship, disciplines, are imposed upon men's consciences, which cannot clearly be made out to them, it is height of oppression, and the ground-work of persecution. The scribes and Pharisees taught for doctrines the commandments of men, Matt. xv. 9; they laid grievous burdens on men's shoulders and hearts, Matt. xxiii. 4. So did prelacy of late, and oppressed men in their courts for not observing their ceremonies and will-worship; and not only so, but persecuted men, and drove them out of the land. And this is an evil in many families, where husbands, parents, masters, put and press those things upon their wives, children, and servants, which in conscience they cannot yield unto; or, if they do, it is with doubting and scrupulosity: and "whatsoever is not of faith is sin," Rom. xiv. 23: and the rule is, 1 Cor. vii. 23, "Ye are bought with a price; be not ye the servants of men."

II. The evil of oppressing.

1. It is an unnatural evil. No creatures do oppress those of their own kind; take birds of prey, eagles, vultures, hawks, do not prey upon those of their own, but another kind. So lions, tigers, wolves, bears, are favourable to those of their own kind, and prey upon foreigners, those of another kind; but men most unnaturally prey upon one another; one man is a wolf to another: Ezek. xxii. 27, "Her princes are like wolves ravening the prey." And who were the prey? widows and fatherless ones, Isa. x. 2. Lions have spared men, Dan. vi.; ravens fed men, 1 Kings xvii; and yet one man seeks to eat up and devour another.

2. It is argument there is little or no fear of God in their hearts that do oppress others. Lev. xxv. 17, "Ye shall not oppress one another; but thou shalt fear thy God;" whereby is fully intimated, that if they oppress, they do not fear God; if they fear God, they will not oppress; for "by the fear of the Lord men depart from evil," Prov. xvi. 6. When Amalek fell upon the Jews, and smote some of them passing through his country, it is said, "he feared not God," Deut. xxv. 18. The Jews' oppressing one another is attributed to their not fearing of God, Neh. v. 9; Job's eschewing of evil was because he "feared God," Job i. 1.

3. It is against that great and common rule of equity, Matt. vii. 12, "All things whatsoever ye would that men should do to you, do ye even so to them."

The like is in Luke vi. 31. Now, no man that is in his right mind, that hath use of reason, would have another to wrong and oppress himself in estate, name, conscience; he should not do it unto others. Lactantius saith, That is the root and whole foundation of equity, not to do to any what he would not suffer himself; and measure another's spirit or mind by thine own. Hierom calls this sentence of Christ's, "All things whatsoever ye would," &c. the summary of justice, and should always be written upon men's hearts. *Ad Celantiam.*

4. It is a sin which greatly provokes God, hath dreadful woes denounced against it, and brings dreadful judgments upon those who are guilty of it: see Micah ii. 12; Hab. ii. 12; Zeph. iii. 1; Jer. xxii. 13; Isa. x. 1—3. In those places such woes are thundered out against oppressors, as would make even stony hearts to tremble: What will ye do in the day of visitation? to whom will ye flee for help? God will visit for this sin: Prov. xxii. 22, 23, "Rob not the poor, because he is poor; neither oppress the afflicted in the gate: for the Lord will plead their cause, and spoil the soul of those that spoiled them." The Egyptians oppressed the Israelites, and did not God spoil the Egyptians? Exod. xii. 36. Rehoboam would oppress his subjects by laying heavy burdens upon them, and God spoiled him of ten tribes, 1 Kings xii. And he threatens to be a "swift witness against those that oppress the hireling in his wages, the widow, and the fatherless, and that turn aside the stranger from his right," Mal. iii. 5; the meaning is, God will punish them severely. And you may see what God will do, Exod. xxii. 21—24, "If thou afflict, vex, oppress the stranger, the widow, the fatherless in any wise, and they cry at all unto me, I will surely hear their cry; and my wrath shall wax hot, and I will kill you with the sword; and your wives shall be widows, and your children fatherless." Of all people, strangers, widows, fatherless ones, should be pitied, countenanced, counselled, comforted, relieved; for therein lies the fruit and power of true religion, Jam. i. 27. If those, therefore, be afflicted in any wise, and do cry at all, God will hear; his wrath will wax hot, consume you, and bring your wives and children into their condition: therefore, 1 Thess. iv. 6.

"But hath restored to the debtor his pledge," &c. Poor men being in straits, were wont to pawn their garments, their tools, and household stuff, unto their creditors for what they borrowed of them. Men that had money and means were hard-hearted, and would not lend freely; and when they had the poor and needy's pledges, they would keep them. The Lord therefore gave them laws thereabout; as Exod. xxii. 26, "If thou at all take thy neighbour's raiment to pledge, thou shall deliver it unto him by that the sun goeth down:" so Deut. xxiv. 6, 10—13, 17, they might not take the upper millstone, nor a widow's garment, for pledges; and what they did take, they were faithfully and speedily to return. Job complains of the wicked, that they took the widow's ox for a pledge, and the garments of the poor, Job xxiv. 3, 9. It is not unlawful to take a pledge, so it be not of present and necessary use; but to make advantage of the poor, to have pledges double or treble the worth of that men lend, and then to take forfeitures, or withhold the pledges, is cruelty towards man, and iniquity before God, who would have men to be merciful as himself is merciful, to be helps, and not hinderers, to those who are in affliction.

"Hath spoiled none by violence." Hebrew, גזלה לא יגזל hath not taken away by force that which
Nupere spoliare avellere. hath been so gotten by others. The word גזל noteth, a violent taking away, and so it is expressed, Prov. xxii. 22, "Rob not the poor." Robbing is a violent taking from any; and so, Lev. xix. 13, and Amos iii. 10, violence and robbery are joined together. Wicked men are said to "drink the wine of violence," Prov. iv. 17; that is, they spoil others; as ver. 16, "They sleep not, except they cause some to fall:" and what they get that way, they live upon, they make merry therewith, "drink wine in bowls," and that is the wine of violence. So those phrases of, eating violence, Prov. xiii. 2, storing up violence, Amos iii. 10, are to be understood; they feed upon, and furnish themselves with, what they get by violence.

I spake of violence in chap. vii. 11; viii. 17, and therefore shall not insist much on it, but tell you what David saith, Psal. cxl. 11, "Evil shall hunt the violent man to overthrow him." Certain ruin abides the violent man, one judgment of God or other will hunt him like a wild beast, till he be overthrown; yea, his own violent dealings shall come upon him and overwhelm him, Psal. vii. 16.

Samuel could say, "Whose ox have I taken? or whose ass have I taken? or whom have I defrauded? whom have I oppressed?" 1 Sam. xii. 3. It were well such innocency could be found in men; but we have been full of plundering and spoiling one another, yea, many precious ones have been spoiled of all they had, but the Lord will spoil the spoilers, Prov. xxii. 23.

"Hath given his bread to the hungry." The word for "hungry" is from רעב to consume with hunger, and notes such as are pinched with hunger, and have real need of relief: and by "bread" is here meant, not only what in a strict sense we call bread, but whatever is fit for man to eat, as in chap. xvi. 49. Giving bread to the hungry imports not one or two acts, but a constant and free relieving of them, as thou art able, and there is occasion. Isa. lviii. 7, it is to deal the bread to the hungry, to bring the poor who are cast out to thine house, and when thou seest the naked, to cover him.

"Hath covered the naked with a garment." That is, those who have ragged, thin, poor clothing, so that their nakedness is not hid. A man is to mind such, cover their nakedness; as Job saith, chap. xxxi. 19, "If I have seen any perish for want of clothing, or any poor without covering; if his loins have not blessed me, and if he were not warmed with the fleece of my sheep." It is not enough to give food, but there must be clothing too, if need be, James ii. 15, 16. We should be charitable, feed the hungry, and clothe the naked; they are our own flesh: Isa. lviii. 7, "Hide not thyself from thine own flesh." It was the sin of Sodom, not to "strengthen the hand of the poor and needy." It was a damned Dives that would not relieve a poor Lazarus.

God feeds you with the finest of the wheat-flour, clothes you with the choicest clothes, silks, &c. yea, feeds you with manna, flesh of his Son, clothes you with garments of salvation, with the righteousness of Christ.

It is the exercise of faith; Eccles. xi. 1, "Cast thy bread upon the waters, for thou shalt find it after many days."

It makes a man to be of good report; Psal. cxii. 9, "He hath given to the poor; his righteousness endureth for ever:" Mark xii. 42, "And there came a certain poor widow, and she threw in two mites," which were remembered and recorded.

It is argument of a good man; Psal. cxii. 1, 9, "Blessed is the man who fears God: he hath dispersed," &c.

It is feeding of Christ; Matt. xxv. 35, 40, "Inasmuch as ye have done it unto one of the least of these my brethren, ye have done it unto me."

It is an honour to religion; James i. 27, "Pure religion and undefiled before God and the Father is this, To visit the fatherless and widows in their affliction, and to keep himself unspotted from the world."

It procures many a prayer and blessing; 2 Cor. ix. 10, "Now he that ministereth seed to the sower both minister bread for your food, and multiply your seed sown, and increase the fruits of your righteousness:" Job xxix. 13, "The blessing of him that was ready to perish came upon me: and I caused the widow's heart to sing for joy:" 2 Tim. i. 16, "The Lord give mercy unto the house of Onesiphorus; for he oft refreshed me, and was not ashamed of my chain."

It is maintaining and saving of life; Job xxix. 13.

It makes like unto God; Luke vi. 36, "Be ye therefore merciful, as your Father also is merciful:" Psalm cxlvi. 7, he "giveth food to the hungry." It makes like Christ, he fed the multitude, Matt. xiv.

It is lending to the Lord; Prov. xix. 17, "He that hath pity upon the poor lendeth unto the Lord; and that which he hath given will he pay him again."

It is pleasing and acceptable to God; Acts x. Heb. xiii. 16, "To do good and to communicate forget not; for with such sacrifices God is well pleased."

Ver. 8. *He that hath not given forth upon usury, neither hath taken any increase, that hath withdrawn his hand from iniquity, hath executed true judgment between man and man.*

Our prophet is upon declaring who is a righteous man. Sundry characters of such a one he hath laid down before, and here proceeds to add more; and the first is, he meddles not with usury, he increases not his estate that way. It is much in practice among the sons of men, as if Scripture did rather authorize than prohibit it.

"Upon usury," בנשך, from נשך to bite; yea, to bite like a serpent. It is akin to נחש a serpent, saith Avenar. A serpent's biting is little felt at first, but after it inflames and ruins the man; so usury is not much felt at the beginning, but in time eats up and devours a man's whole substance: or, for that it makes a man restless, sleepless, who is bitten with it, as the biting of a serpent doth; or biting, in that, like a hungry dog or wolf, by biting and devouring others, it feeds itself. Chrysostom, *super illud*, Matt. v. *volenti mutuare*, saith, The usurer's money is like the biting of the asp. A man bitten by the asp hath a delightful sleepiness upon him, and dies sleeping, because poison sweetly diffuseth itself through his whole body; so the man that takes money of the usurer, pleases himself, thinking it a kindness and benefit unto him, but it quickly eats up a great part, if not his whole estate. This kind of usury many are against, but other sorts of usury they allow and practise. I shall therefore consider what usury is, and then show you whether the Scripture will warrant any usury.

What usury is.

It is the taking of any thing above the principal, saith Tostat. A receiving more than was lent, Cajet. These are too strict, excluding whatever any return freely by way of thankfulness.

In usury, three things are considerable: lending, gaining, covenanting.

To lend money for gain, *interposita pactione*, that is "usury." When men put out their money to receive more than the principal by virtue of a covenant, contract, or compact, that makes them usurers. It is gain taken merely for the lending of a thing. Herein, it is conceived, lies the formality of it, viz. the covenanting, agreeing, and contracting to have so much for what is lent. This the word points at, Exod. xxii. 25, thou shalt not put usury upon him

Amesius saith, it is gain sought after, aimed at, from what is lent, because it is lent; and he includes in the word *quæsitum*, not only real usury, which is contracted for, but mental usury, which is intended.

Usury thus described I find no warrant for from the word of God, but much against it: look into these places, Exod. xxii. 25; Lev. xxv. 35—37; Deut. xxiii. 19, 20. The great God of heaven and earth commands them not to be usurers, not to lend upon, or take, usury.

The answer and evasion that some have and make here, is this: True, we must not lend upon usury to the poor, who are mentioned in the two first places, and implied in the third, but to the rich we may.

To take away this evasion,

1. Consider, there are other places where no mention of the poor is made. Psal. xv. 5, "He that putteth not out his money to usury." It is spoken indefinitely; they might not put it out to the poor; and who, then, were there to put it out to, but the rich? So in Jer. xv. 10; Ezek. xxii. 12, usury is censured, and yet there is no mention of the poor. Usury seemed a cursed thing.

2. Rich men were their brethren as well as the poor; and, Deut. xxiii. 20, "Unto thy brother thou shalt not lend upon usury." He might not lend to a rich foe, only to a stranger.

3. What countenance, warrant, or encouragement do you find in holy writ for lending moneys to rich and wealthy men, especially with expectation of gain. Luke vi. 34, "If ye lend to them of whom ye hope to receive, what thank have ye? for sinners also lend to sinners, to receive as much again." Wicked men, the worst of all, who have no fear of God in them, will do that; therefore, saith Christ, "Lend, hoping for nothing again." Here is shown who should lend, and to whom. Rich men are to lend, not to borrow; and to those the lending should be who are not able to maintain their charge, drive on their callings, without help; to these rich men should lend freely; and to others that are beggars, truly poor, they should give: Matt. v. 42, "Give to him that asketh thee, and from him that would borrow of thee turn not thou away." It is a duty for rich men to lend, not to borrow; and because they let many families sink these hard times, which would do well enough had they a little support from the rich, it will stand upon their account one day. This is the evil of rich men, because they see such a man decaying, therefore they will not lend him; but because he is upon decaying, therefore they should lend him that he may not utterly decay, Deut. xv. 7, 8.

The second evasion men have is this: Usury, when it is biting, hath the serpent's sting and teeth in it; prejudiceth, and doth not profit, advantage a man, then it is unlawful; but if a man be a gainer by it, it is not unwarrantable; and so they distinguish between biting usury and profiting usury.

Answ. Distinctions and arguments from etymologies are insufficient and weak. Absalom signifies a father of peace, or, the father's peace; but he was a father of war, and his father's trouble. As for "usury," the Scripture knows no such distinction as biting, and profiting, usury; it is a human invention, to make way for the satisfaction of men's covetous and greedy desires. Men think they are safe if they take usury of the rich, not of the poor; but see how the Lord strangles and cuts off this distinction by the next words in the verse.

"Neither hath taken any increase." He must not be a biting usurer, which they grant; neither must he be an increasing usurer; this is forbidden by the same authority that the other is. The word is, תרבית from רבה to multiply and increase, and is rendered by Montanus, *amplius;* so Vatablus and Jerom, He is a just man that takes no more than he lends. Some would have this word to be exegetical, and so think to avoid the force of it: but though the wisdom of man be inventive to promote its own interests, yet it must not null the wisdom of God. Let us grant it exegetical, it is of more force against them; for the latter word must expound the former, and so any increase is the meaning of usury. Upon this account, then, he is a usurer who takes any increase. But this likes not those who plead for it. By increase they would have such increase as burdens, bites, oppresses, and consumes him that gives it.

This is forcing of the word *tarbith*, which notes simply any increase or multiplication; not biting, oppressing, undoing increase. As they therefore stick to the word *nesheck*, to make one sort of usury unlawful, so may we stick to the word *tarbith*, to make that other sort of usury unlawful, because it is said, "he that hath not given forth upon usury, neither hath taken any increase." The word notes increase of victuals, as well as of money: Lev. xxv. 37, "Thou shalt not give him thy money upon usury, nor lend him thy victuals for increase." There must not be increase of money or victuals; it is not meant a burdensome increase of victuals, but no increase at all.

Some plead the lawfulness of it from Deut. xxiii. 20, "Unto a stranger thou mayest lend upon usury; but unto thy brother thou shalt not lend upon usury:" hence they conclude, that usury is not simply unlawful but to a brother.

Answ. God is above the law, and may authorize men to do such things as the letter of the law is against: he bade Abraham sacrifice his son, the Jews to rob the Egyptians. The law, in Lev. xx. 21, is against a man marrying his brother's wife; yet in Deut. xxv. 5, the brother must raise up seed to the brother; and seven brethren had one woman, Matt. xxii. 24—26. And so here, the Lord might give way to the Jews to take usury, he is above the law.

2. Some answer it thus, and say, God permitted it unto them for the hardness of their hearts, who would have taken of their brethren, if they had not had liberty thus to have done. As they were permitted to give a bill of divorce to their wives, and send them away, so it was here. It was a permission, "thou mayest," &c. and permission is of evil, not of good.

3. It was to strangers they might do it; and not to all strangers, but Canaanites only, who were designed of God to destruction; so that those they might destroy with the sword, they might devour with usury. So then, where men are not appointed to death, and to be cut off by war, they may not exercise usury.

4. The distinction of strangers is now taken away; the partition-wall is broken down, and we are all brethren. A stranger that was become a proselyte, and embraced the Jewish religion, they might not take usury of, he was a brother, Lev. xxv. 35, 36; they had all one father, Mal. ii. 10, and so have we, and are brethren. This made Jerom, upon this place, say, In the law, usury was taken off from brethren; in the prophets it is forbid to all; in the gospel is yet more virtue and favour; the Lord saith, "Lend to them from whom ye may expect nothing."

It is the blindness of the Jews, to think they may take usury of christians, when Christ hath made of both one, Eph. ii. 14; and it is our sinful covetousness to take usury one of another when we are brethren. And therefore some affirm that in this place of Deuteronomy, that usury towards strangers is neither commanded nor permitted; but the Scripture would have us acknowledge all our neighbours and brethren; and that if we do exercise usury towards any, we treat them not as brethren or neighbours, but as enemies.

Some ground the lawfulness, and so their practice, of it upon Matt. xxv. the parable of the talents; ver. 27, "Oughtest thou not to have put my money to the exchangers, and then at my coming I should have received mine own with usury." Hence they conclude, that Christ doth not only allow, but justify, usury.

Answ. 1. This is a parable, and solid arguments are seldom drawn from parables.

2. Christ here speaks, not concerning the justice of the matter, as if he approved usurious practices, whereby men of covetous minds do increase their estates; but concerning its mode, the increase that came by such practices, which he propounds to be imitated in spiritual things. You see men of this world improve their moneys, and so should you improve those gifts and graces which are concredited and committed unto you. Christ here justifies usury no more than he justifies the unjust steward, Luke xvi. 8, where it is said, he "commended the unjust steward, because he had done wisely." Why, what had he done? In one account he had defrauded his master of fifty measures of oil; in another account, he cut him short of twenty measures of wheat; yet Christ saith, "he hath done wisely;" that is, wisely for himself, though wickedly for his master. Christ's commendation of him did not legitimate the action. If men's stewards or servants should do so now, and allege his instance, they would not hold them excusable, but have the law against them. Christ saith, that he will come as a thief, Rev. xvi. 15; and that "the day of the Lord so cometh as a thief in the night," 1 Thess. v. 2. Doth this, therefore, countenance or justify theft?

You see, then, no footing for usury in the word of God. It seems to me to make void three great rules which our Lord and Saviour hath given us in the gospel.

The first is that, Matt. vii. 12, "All things whatsoever ye would that men should do to you, do ye even so to them: for this is the law and the prophets." Now, is there any man in straits, in necessities, that would not borrow freely, rather than be tied to pay so much, not knowing whether he shall gain any thing, or preserve the principal: and if any should deny it, I fear their own consciences would condemn them for it. It is true, through the custom and practice of the times, men are willing to borrow upon such rates and terms, because they cannot have moneys otherwise; but if men will lay aside all respects of that kind, and look at the simple nature of the thing, they cannot but confess they had rather have money freely than upon terms; and if so, then they ought to do so to others, and not lay the burden of usury upon them.

2. It is against that great rule and command, Luke vi. 35, "Lend, hoping for nothing again." The Greek is, δανείζετε μηδὲν ἀπελπίζοντες, men should so lend as not to hope for, much less covenant for, any thing again. Any thing for the lending their principal they may; for it is not said, give, but lend, not δῶτε, but δανείζετε; and if you should not have the principal again, it were not δάνεισμα, but δώρημα, not a lending, but a giving: lend, hoping for the principal, but nothing for the loan of it. Such lending is attributed to righteous and good men: Psal. xxxvii. 26, "He is ever merciful, and lendeth;" and, Psal. cxii. 5, "A good man sheweth favour, and lendeth."

3. It is against that great rule and command, Heb. xiii. 5, "Let your conversation be without covetousness." Should poor men be without covetousness who have little, and should not rich men who have much? they usually are the usurers, and so most covetous. Usury is the invention and practice of covetousness, and serves only to feed the appetite thereof. Covetousness is a grievous sin; it is idolatry, as you may see, Col. iii. 5; it makes the times perilous, 2 Tim. iii. 1, 2; it is the root of all evil, 1 Tim. vi. 10; it makes a man unworthy of christian society, 1 Cor. v. 11; to be abhorred of God, Psal. x. 3; and so to be shut out of the kingdom of heaven, 1 Cor. vi. 9, 10; Eph. v. 5: and surely such as the mother is, such is the daughter. Psal. xv. 1, "Lord, who shall abide in thy tabernacle? who shall dwell in thy holy hill?" Ver. 5, "He that putteth not out his money to usury." Of which words Luther, in his Commentary upon that psalm, saith, that place does not need explanation, but obedience. Many councils have condemned it as unlawful. In the first Nicene it was condemned for a mortal sin, can. 17; the first Carthaginian determined it to be base gain, cap. 13; the Lateran saith, Usury is not allowed to redeem captives; Concil. Viennense decrees him to be punished as a heretic who says usury is no sin; the Eliberine council degraded clergymen, and cast the people out of the church, who were usurers, cap. 20. Not only councils, but fathers, have been against it. Augustine upon the 36th Psalm says, *Si plus quam dedisti expectas accipere, fœneratores;* and Bernard calls it, *Venenum patrimonii: inter præcepta famil.* The very heathen have censured and condemned it. Aristotle, in 1 Polit. c. 7, saith, *Usuraria acquisitio est maxime contra naturam,* Because it is barren and not apt to bring forth; and Cato makes usury equal to murder; *Illi fœnerari idem fuit quod hominem occidere, Tul.* 2. *Offic. cited by Aret. in Problem.;* Lycurgus *e tota Sparta usurarios expulit.* Agis burnt all the usurers' tables at Athens; which made Agesilaus to say he never saw a better or brighter light than that fire made, *Alexan. ab Alexand.* lib. 1. *Gen. Dier.* c. 7. Plato would have usurers banished out of the commonwealth, l. 5. *de Legib.*

Let, men, therefore, take heed how they meddle with usury, seeing there is such a cloud of witnesses against it, and not trust to a distinction of man's brain, making biting usury unlawful, and other usury lawful, lest by this distinction they get money in their coffers, and lose their souls at last; for, as Alphonsus saith, such gain is the sepulchre of the soul; and he must not sojourn in the tabernacle of the Lord, that puts his money to usury: and surely it is an ill trade that excludes a man from heaven.

Money at first was invented for exchange of things uneasy to be transported, not, to beget money, or a trade, without labour; for the usurer's trade is most easy and gainful. The ancient Grecians and Romans forbade all usury above one penny for a hundred in the year; and if any took above that rate, he was condemned to restore fourfold, and judged more vile than a thief, who was condemned but in double as much. Afterwards it was brought to a half-penny a year among the Romans, and not long after wholly taken away by the Gemutulian law. And if it were brought to lower rates amongst us, or rather wholly taken away, it were an honour to the gospel, and to our nation.

"That hath withdrawn his hand from iniquity." Hebrew is, hath turned away his hand. The sense of the phrase is, that hath abstained from doing evil, from unjust and sinful acts; not only that keeps his hand from taking bribes, as Polanus; but from wronging any when it is in his power, and occasions are presented. If men be so minded, they shall have variety of occasions to revenge themselves upon their enemies, to crush the poor, to get the wealth and honour of the world, yea, strong temptations to things that are evil; but now when a man will not give way to such temptations and occasions, he is said to withdraw, or turn his hand from iniquity. When Judah said of Joseph, "What profit is it if we slay our brother, and conceal his blood? let not our hand be upon him;" here he kept his own and his brothers' hand from iniquity, Gen. xxxvii. 26, 27. Saul commands his footmen to kill the priests, 1 Sam. xxii. 17, but they would not put forth their hand to fall upon the priests of the Lord; they withdrew their hands from iniquity. Job professes his innocency in this kind; chap. xxxi. 21, "If I have lifted up my hand against the fatherless, when I saw my help in the gate: then let mine arm fall from my shoulder:" he had opportunities and encouragement from others in place, to have wronged the fatherless, but he would not do it; he withdrew his hand from iniquity. Joseph would not hearken unto his mistress; Daniel would not defile himself with the king's portion, chap. i. 8; the three children would not bow to the image, chap. iii.; they withdrew their hands and hearts from iniquity: and so David, he kept himself from his iniquity, Psal. xviii. 23, from that which was most stirring in him. Wicked men withdraw not their hands from iniquity, but, as Mic. vii. 3, they do evil with both hands, and that earnestly: evil is their element, and doing evil is their trade. But a righteous man withdraws his hand from iniquity, yea all iniquity; from all unwarrantable actions, prescriptions, subscriptions.

"Hath executed true judgment between man and man." Hebrew is, the judgment of truth. Whether these words be referred to public magistrates, or private men chosen to end controversies between men at variance, it matters not, both may be included; for whosoever do judge or execute judgment between man and man, they are to judge truly, and execute the judgment of truth: Zech. viii. 16, it is written thus, "Execute the judgment of peace and truth in your gates:" there is a judgment of truth, or, as the Hebrew is, judge truth; see your judgment have nothing in it but truth; see it be according to the word of truth, approved by the God of truth, and then it will be a judgment of peace, else it will breed more contention and heart-burnings. The Scripture speaks of perverting judgment, Prov. xvii. 23; of turning aside judgment, Isa. x. 2; but those who are called to that work should, neither for fear or favour, hatred or love, warp from the rule set of God. No greatness, no relation, no gifts, no respects whatsoever, should draw a man to wrest, pervert, or turn aside judgment of truth, or true judgment. Deut. xvi. 18, 19, "They shall judge the people with just judgment. Thou shalt not wrest judgment; thou shalt not respect persons, neither take a gift: for it blinds the eyes of the wise, and perverts the words of the righteous. That which is altogether just shalt thou follow." God loves true, righteous, and just judgment, and hates what is thereunto contrary. Deut. xxvii. 19, "Cursed be he that perverteth the judgment of the stranger, fatherless, and widow:" his hatred is so great, that he hath laid a curse upon the perverters thereof.

Ver. 9. *Hath walked in my statutes, and hath kept my judgments, to deal truly; he is just, he shall surely live, saith the Lord God.*

We are coming towards an end of the description of a righteous man; one thing or two remains.

"Hath walked in my statutes." There are several expressions in the good word of God consonant unto this: as, walking with God, Gen. vi. 9; walking before God, Gen. xvii. 1; walking after the Lord, 2 Kings xxiii. 3; walking in the Spirit, Gal. v. 25; after the Spirit, Rom. viii. 1; walking in the fear of the Lord, Acts ix. 31; Neh. v. 9.

Several equivalent unto it: as, walking in the truth, Psal. lxxxvi. 11; walking in his ways, Deut. xxviii. 9; walking in the light of the Lord, Isa. ii. 5; walking honestly as in the day, Rom. xiii. 13; walking worthy of the Lord, 1 Thess. ii. 12; walking after his commandments, 2 John v. 6; in the good way, Jer. vi. 16; respecting all his commandments, Psal. cxix. 6; sticking to his testimonies, ver. 2.

It is opposed to other walkings and ways: as, walking in the statutes of the heathen, 2 Kings xvii. 8; in the statutes of Israel, ver. 19; keeping the statutes of Omri, Mic. vi. 16; walking in the ways of the kings of Israel, 2 Kings viii. 18; in the statutes of their father, Ezek. xx. 18; in their own counsels, Psal. lxxxi. 12; the counsels of their evil hearts, Jer. vii. 24; walking after Baalim, Jer. ix. 14; after other gods, chap. xvi. 11; walking according to the flesh, 2 Cor. x. 2; according to the course of this world, Eph. ii. 2; walking after their own lusts, 2 Pet. iii. 3; in the imaginations of their own hearts, Jer. xiii. 10; after our own devices, chap. xviii. 12; walking in pride, Dan. iv. 37; walking in lies, Jer. xxiii. 14; walking in the ways of darkness, Prov. ii. 13; John xi. 10; walking in the vanity of the mind, Eph. iv. 17; in the ways of a man's heart, Eccles. xi. 9; walking after vanity, Jer. ii. 5; after things which do not profit, ver. 8; walking with slander, Jer. vi. 28; walking after customs, Acts xxi. 21; walking with vanity, Job xxxi. 5.

Walking in God's statutes implies several things.

1. Life.
2. Light.
3. Action, motion.
4. Progress.
5. Perseverance.

1. Life. A dead man cannot walk, he lies immovable. Walking is from life; Rom. vi. 4, spiritual walking is from spiritual life, as natural walking is from natural life. Hos. xiv. 9, "The ways of the Lord are right, and the just shall walk in them; but the transgressors shall fall therein." Men justified by faith, they live, and they walk in God's ways, not others; transgressors fall in them, they cannot stand, much less walk in them. If men be not good themselves, they cannot do good.

2. Light. Men must know God's statutes, else how can they walk in them; unknown things are neither desired nor practised. Matt. xxii. 29, "Ye do err, not knowing the Scriptures;" they wandered from God's ways through ignorance; being in the dark, they stumbled. Jer. iv. 22, "To do good they have no knowledge;" an ignorant man cannot walk in God's ways; a servant can never do the will of his master, if he knows it not, nor a son the will of his father, if he understands it not. Prov. xiv. 8, "The wisdom of the prudent is to understand his way;" a prudent man will examine his way, whether it be the way of God he walks in, or the way of the world, flesh, corruption: if it be this last, he will not walk in it, but walk out of it; he will walk into God's way, and walk in his statutes: when he discerns them once to be his, he dares not keep out of them.

3. Action, motion. A man that walks, neither stands nor sits still; he stands not in contemplation, nor sits still in meditation; contents not himself with reading or hearing, but is doing the will of God. Walking and doing are the same: 1 Kings xi. 38, "If thou wilt walk in my ways, and do that is right in my sight, to keep my statutes and commandments:" those that do and keep them, they walk in them. This walking is observing his commandments, Neh. i. 5; obeying the voice of the Lord, Deut. xiii. 4; it is hearkening unto God, Psal. lxxxi. 13; fulfilling the statutes and judgments of the Lord, 1 Chron. xxii. 13; performing his statutes, Psal. cxix. 112.

4. Progress. A man that walks, goes on step by step, and presses on towards that which is before him; he walks in the statutes of the Lord, goes forward, his obedience is more and more. It is said of wicked men, "They proceed from evil to evil," Jer. ix. 3; they walk on in their evil ways. And so do good and just men; they go on from statute to statute, from truth to truth, from grace to grace; Psal. lxxxiv. 7, "They go from strength to strength," and from light to light. Phil. iii. 13, Paul forgot those things which were behind, and reached forth towards those things which were before him; he took long strides towards heaven, and walked fast that way; he forgot how much ground he had walked over, and hastened to his journey's end. In Rom. iv. 12, they are said to walk in the steps of Abraham's faith; Abraham walked in faith, and all believers since have trodden in his steps.

5. Perseverance. That is implied here by walking, as appears by ver. 24, "When the righteous turneth away from his righteousness," &c. Psal. cxix. 112, "I have inclined mine heart to perform thy statutes alway, even unto the end:" a man that walks in God's statutes must never stand still, nor turn back; God hath no pleasure in such, Heb. x. 38. However times prove, whatever troubles arise, however men or Divine Providence acts, those who are in God's ways should proceed and persevere: Psal. xliv. 18, 19, "Our heart is not turned back, neither have our steps declined from thy way. Though thou hast sore broken us in the place of dragons, and covered us with the shadow of death." The word for dragon is תנים and signifies both sea and land dragons, and refers to the gentiles, saith Kimchi, who were as cruel to them as dragons. Now, notwithstanding they met with dragons, were stung with them, and brought unto the point of death, yet they held on in God's ways, neither hand nor foot declined or withdrew at all; they knew it is the end crowns all antecedent acts: Matt. xxiv. 13, "He that shall endure unto the end, the same shall be saved." It is continuance in well doing which arrives at eternal life, Rom. ii. 7.

"Hath kept my judgments." These words express the meaning of the former. Walking in God's statutes, is keeping of his judgments, Judg. ii. 22. Of these words, "statutes" and "judgments," was spoken, chap. v. 6. A word or two of keeping.

To keep, here, is not meant of keeping God's judgments, or laws, from perverting, having corrupt glosses and senses put upon them, as you would keep clothes from moths, which do mar them; neither is it meant of keeping them in memory, as the word is used, Luke ii. 51; but to keep them, is to do and perform them thoroughly, Psal. cxix. 48, 69; Deut. xxiii. 23. Keeping and performing is the same, so observing and keeping, Psal. cv. 45. The Hebrew word שמר signifies to keep, as Pagnine saith, with care and diligence; and, Prov. iv. 23, it is rendered so, "Keep thy heart with all diligence;" מכל-משמר with all care and diligence; and so must the judgments, commands, and ways of God be kept: Deut. vi. 17, "Ye shall diligently keep the commandments of the Lord your God." שמור תשמרון

"To deal truly." Hebrew is, to do truth. There are lies in men's actions as well as in their words. This expression of our prophet, "to deal truly," is consonant to that of Christ, John iii. 21, "He that doeth truth." Men do truth, when their actions are adequate or conformable to the word of God. The Septuagint has it, to do the same things, referring to judgments and statutes. The doing of them is doing of truth: Psal. cxix. 142, "Thy law is the truth." All things in the law of God, all his statutes, judgments, commands, ways, are truth, and the doing of them is doing truth; and when a man deals truly, without fraud, guile, deceit, hypocrisy, which is the thing here intended, he doth truth. You read in holy writ of dealing treacherously, Lam. i. 2; subtly, Acts vii. 19; perversely, Psal. cxix. 78; unfaithfully, Psal. lxxviii. 57; corruptly, Neh. i. 7; deceitfully, Job vi. 15; falsely, Jer. vi. 13. And unto all these is dealing truly opposite; he who doth so, deals neither treacherously, subtly, perversely, nor unfaithfully, corruptly, deceitfully, or falsely.

Dealing truly is hard to find among the sons of men, great or small, prophet or priest, Jer. viii. 10; but where it is to be found, it is a jewel; I say a jewel, enriching the man with peace invaluable, and making him delightful unto God: Prov. xii. 22, "They that deal truly are his delight." Hebrew is, those that do truth; not those that speak truth only, but those whose lives and actions hold out the truth, they are his delight. Men have their delights; one delights in a witty man, another in a learned man, a third in a beautiful man, a fourth in a bountiful man; but God delights in a man that doth truth, or deals truly.

"He is just." Hebrew is צדיק הוא Something I spake of a just man in ver. 5; I shall add something here.

There is a just man in appearance; Matt. xxiii. 28, the Pharisees did outwardly appear righteous. There is a just man in opinion and conceit; Luke xviii. 9, there were those who trusted in themselves that they were righteous. There is a just man in truth, and that either evangelically or legally.

1. Evangelically just. Heb. xii. 23; Luke xiv. 14; Heb. x. 38, they are such as are justified by faith in Christ.

2. Legally just. And such are they who do that which is lawful and right, who live honestly and harmlessly, walking in the ways of God, dealing justly with all men. Such a one was Paul before his conversion, Phil. iii. 6, "Touching the righteousness in the law blameless." Such were Abner and Amasa, 1 Kings ii. 32, who are said to be just or righteous. Of such Solomon speaks, Eccles. vii. 15, "There is a just man that perisheth in his" justice or "righteousness, and there is a wicked man that prolongeth his life in his wickedness." Some are loose, and they are spared in states; others are too strict, and are crushed by states.

Now here is meant by a just man, not one in appearance or opinion, but one in truth; yet not evangelically, but legally: for,

(1.) Here is no mention of Christ, or any reference unto him by faith, both which are requisite unto evangelical justice and righteousness.

(2.) A just man here is put in opposition to the soul that sinneth: ver. 4, "The soul that sinneth, it shall die;" that is, the soul that sinneth, and doth contrary to the duties here mentioned, as appears from the beginning of ver. 10, to the end of ver. 13. He who sinneth such sins shall die, either a metaphorical or violent death, be cast into captivity, or cut off by the sword or some stroke of God; but he who is free from those sins, he is just, he shall not die, but live.

(3.) It is meant of such a just man as may cease to be just: ver. 24, "When the righteous turneth away from his righteousness, and committeth iniquity, and doeth according to all the abominations that the wicked man doeth, shall he live?" &c. This must be the man who is legally just, not evangelically; for the man evangelically just cannot cease to be just; see Ezek. xxxvi. 27; 1 John iii. 9; Heb. x. 14; viii. 12.

"He shall surely live." Hebrew is, he shall live by living. This phrase, he shall live by living, saith Pradus, is to live pleasantly and prosperously, his fathers' and predecessors' sins shall bring no woe, no evils, upon him, he shall reap the fruit of his righteousness. David giveth us some light unto this life, Psal. xxxiv. 12—14, "What man is he that desireth life, and loveth many days, that he may see good?" By "life," and "days," he means such a life and days as have good in them, prosperity, peace, pleasure, comfort; and he shows how to obtain them: "Keep thy tongue from evil, and thy lips from speaking guile. Depart from evil, and do good." This falls in with our prophet; He who doth so shall live a desirable life, and see good days. But if men sin, and their sins be upon them, they pine away in them, they do not live, Ezek. xxxiii. 10; they live not a comfortable life, they see no good days.

Obs. 1. The Lord doth not only, in general, approve of doing good and avoiding evil, but particularly shows them what evils they should not do, and what good things they should do. "If a man be just, and do that which is lawful and right." Here is the general, and then he descends to particulars: "And hath not eaten upon the mountains, lift up his eyes to idols; neither defiled his neighbour's wife, nor oppressed or spoiled any by violence, nor given forth upon usury, nor taken any increase; but hath restored the pledge, given his bread to the hungry, covered the naked with a garment, executed true judgment, and dealt truly."

Here are negative and affirmative particulars. God would have his mind so fully known, all pleas and objections so taken away, that none may have excuse, or say, Had we known what was acceptable to God, we would have done it. Generals we have, but for particulars we are at a loss. God takes away this plea both here and elsewhere, and shows men in special what he approves, and what they should do. See Deut. xxvii. 15—26; there are eleven particulars reckoned up together; and likewise as many in Psal. xv. In Mic. vi. 8; Zech. vii. 9, 10; Rom. xii. 9—12, &c. you have sundry particulars enumerated, and above twenty in the last place. The duties of magistrates, subjects, ministers, people, husbands, wives, parents, children, masters, servants, of all relations, ages, sexes, conditions, are particularly laid down in the word; and all are inexcusable, if they be ignorant or disobedient.

Obs. 2. See here the way to have a good name, esteem with God, and a good report from him. The man who doth the particulars mentioned, "he is just," saith God.

If a man do the duties of the first table, which are implied in not eating upon the mountains, nor lifting up eyes to idols, he is approved of God; and if he do the duties of the second table, which are implied in the other particulars, he is approved of man; and so hath a good report from heaven and earth; God pronounces him just, and man must subscribe unto it. A good name is a great mercy; Solomon tells you it is "better than precious ointment," Eccles. vii. 1, which pleases the senses, and profits the limbs; yea, that it is "to be chosen rather than great riches," Prov. xxii. 1. Make a mountain of silver and gold, a good name is more eligible than that; it is better to fill the world with a good name, than to fill coffers and chambers with rich treasure. The Grecians say it is better to hear well, than to heap up wealth. Many, by caring to grow rich, have wasted their bodies, and drowned their souls in perdition; whereas "a good report maketh the bones fat," Prov. xv. 30.

Take, then, the right way to get a good name; do what is here required, and so shall you be counted just, and have a good report.

Agesilaus, being asked how a man should come to have a good name, his answer was, To speak the best things, and do the most honest. Aristides, by the light of nature, did those things which caused him to be called Aristides the just, an honourable and good name. And shall not we christians, who have, beside the light of nature, divine light, do those things that may cause God to honour us with this title, "he is just?" If we do not this, heathens and others will be witnesses against us at the last day. While we are here, an ill savour will be round about us, and when we are gone, our names will rot; "but the memory of the just shall be blessed."

Obs. 3. Hence note how to come unto it, as to live comfortably. "He shall live," that is, comfortably, sweetly; but who shall do so? the just man, he that doth that which is lawful and right, that walks in God's statutes, that keeps his judgments, and deals truly, he shall surely live; that is, prosperously and pleasantly. So the word life signifieth, Prov. xvi. 15, "In the light of the king's countenance is life;" what life? felicity and prosperity. A man that is morally just shall have much comfort, content, and sweetness in his life; Prov. xii. 21, "There shall no evil happen to the just: but the wicked shall be filled with mischief;" no evil with a sting in it, no evil as shall suck or pluck away the sweet of his life; but a wicked man shall have evils enough, he shall be filled with fears, cares, sorrows, impatience, discontent, and with the guilt of his sins, so as his life will be no life unto him: Deut. xxviii. 66, "Thy life shall hang in doubt before thee; and thou shalt fear day and night, and shalt have none assurance of thy life."

This is spoken of those who do not walk in God's statutes, keep his judgments, and do that which is lawful and right; their lives are continual deaths, they have no assurance of life, which is the most desirable thing, and what comfort or peace can they have in life? But as for the just, who walk in his ways, they live, and live comfortably, no evil befalls them. And no marvel; they are compassed about with favour as with a shield, Psal. v. 12; the Lord upholds them, Psal. xxxvii. 17; they shall not be moved, Psal. lv. 22; they shall flourish as a branch, Prov. xi. 28; their desire shall be granted, chap. x. 24; the wicked shall bow before them, chap. xiv. 19; and the righteous shall see their fall, chap. xxix. 16, enjoy their wealth, chap. xiii. 22, "The wealth of the sinner is laid up for the just:" if the just man fall into trouble, he shall come out of it, chap. xii. 13; blessings are upon his head, chap. x. 6, in his habitation, chap. iii. 33; his house shall stand, chap. xii. 7; thus is he blessed in his life, and "hath hope in his death," chap. xiv. 32. If these blessings be to the just, labour not only to be morally just, but evangelically also, for to such they do especially belong.

Ver. 10—13. *If he beget a son that is a robber, a shedder of blood, and that doeth the like to any one of these things, and that doeth not any of those duties, but even hath eaten upon the mountains, and defiled his neighbour's wife, hath oppressed the poor and needy, hath spoiled by violence, hath not restored the pledge, and hath lifted up his eyes to the idols, hath committed abomination, hath given forth upon usury, and hath taken increase: shall he then live? he shall not live: he hath done all these abominations; he shall surely die; his blood shall be upon him.*

The prophet, having freed the Lord from that aspersion laid upon him, that the fathers did eat sour grapes, and the children's teeth were set on edge; they sinned, and the children suffered for it; and that both in general, ver. 4, and by particular instance of his dealing with a just man, ver. 9; he comes in these verses to another instance, which is the son of this just man. What if he should have a lewd son? will the son's lewdness prejudice the father's righteousness, or the father's righteousness advantage the son's lewdness? Neither the one nor the other; the father shall not be damnified by the son, nor the son benefited by the father, but the one shall live in his righteousness, and the other shall die in his wickedness, and my justice shall appear to all men.

Of the father's righteousness, and his living in it, hath been spoken in the former verses; now we are to come unto his son's wickedness.

Ver. 10. "If he beget a son that is a robber." The Hebrew word for robber is פריץ from פרץ to break, and, to break by violence; to break through, or over, as water doth in a flood, through and over the banks. Montanus renders the word "robber" *effractorem*, a breaker; robbers do break walls, windows, doors, laws, and all bounds of justice, to accomplish their sinful desires. The word is translated "robber," Ezek. vii. 22; (where something was spoken of it;) Dan. xi. 14; Jer. vii. 11. But, in Psal. xvii. 4, it is rendered "destroyer;" "I have kept me from the paths of the destroyer," or robber; because, where robberies are committed, there is great destroying, yea, even of men's lives sometimes. The Septuagint is, υἱὸν λοιμὸν, a pestilent son, one that is a plague to his parents and country.

"A shedder of blood." Hebrew is, שפך דם a man that spills the blood of another; not that only draws blood, but draws and sheds blood, that death follows upon it. So the phrase imports, Deut. xxi. 7; when a man was found slain, the elders of the city next to him must wash their hands, and say, "Our hands have not shed this blood," we have not murdered this man: so it signifies in Gen. ix. 6; Psal. lxxix. 10; 1 Sam. xxv. 31; Prov. i. 16; Gen. xxxvii. 22. This shedder of blood is a murderer, Numb. xxxv. 16, 17; and murder is a crying sin, Gen. iv. 10; it defaces God's image, Gen. ix. 6; it makes a land mourn, Hos. iv. 2, 3; it takes away the life of a man, for which no recompence can be made, Job ii. 4. A man's life is better than all that ever the blood-shedder or all his friends can return, it is a sin for which he must die: Numb. xxxv. 31, they "shall take no satisfaction for the life of a murderer, which is guilty of death, but he shall be surely put to death."

The Jewish doctors say, Though the murderer could give all the riches in the world, and though the avenger of blood were willing to free him, yet he must be put to death, because the soul or life of the party murdered is not the possession of the avenger of blood, but the possession of the most holy God. It is a sin that excludes from the kingdom of heaven, Gal. v. 21; Rev. xxii. 15: such God abhors, Psal. v. 6; if men be bloody, God, who is love, abhors them, and will cut short their days; Psal. lv. 23, "They shall not live out half their days."

Vide Ainsw. Gen. vi. 9.

Of the 11th, 12th, and former part of the 13th verse, was spoken in the 6th, 7th, and 8th verses; the words "poor" and "needy" were opened in chap. xvi. 49; so that there remains nothing to open but a little in ver. 13.

Ver. 13. "Shall he then live? he shall not live." He thinks to live, thrive, prosper in the world; but "shall he live?" what! such a man live? no, "he shall not live." The words are a question and an answer, and discover a vehemency of spirit in the speaker. The son may flatter himself, because his father is just, doth that which is lawful and right, that it shall be well with him notwithstanding all his lewd and villanous practices, that he shall live as happily as ever he did; What! live? saith the Lord; "shall he then live? he shall not live."

This interrogation and answer is like that in chap. xvii. 10, "Shall it prosper? shall it not utterly wither, when the east wind toucheth it? it shall wither."

"He shall surely die." Hebrew is, he shall die in or by dying. This manner of speaking is frequent in the book of God: Gen. xx. 7; xxvi. 11; Exod. xxi. 12, 15, 16, 17, four times in that chapter, and as many in Numb. xxxv. 16, 17, 18, 21. Septuagint is, θανάτῳ θανατωθήσεται, he shall die by death. He shall not escape the jaws, teeth, and sting of death; the famine, plague, sword, or some special hand of God, shall be upon him, cut him off. It is opposed to what we had in the 9th verse, "he is just, he shall surely live:" and this man is unjust, and "he shall surely die;" his comforts, hopes shall cease, his ruin and destruction hastens.

"His blood shall be upon him." Hebrew is, his bloods shall be in him; a substantive plural with a verb singular: דמיו בו יהיה the cause of his death shall be in himself, he shall answer for all the blood he hath shed with his own blood; he hath shed the blood of others, and his blood shall be shed for it. The Chaldee is, he shall be found guilty of his own death, just matter and ground for his death shall be found in himself. Or thus, his blood shall be against him, his bloody and cruel dealings shall come against him. The Hebrew preposition ב or beth, signifies, against, and, upon: against, Gen. xvi. 12, ידו בכל ויד כל בו "his hand will be against every man, and every man's hand against him:" here beth is "against," and so it may be rendered here, His blood shall be against him. It signifies also, upon, Ezek. xxxiii. 4, "His blood shall be" בראשו "upon his own head;" and so it is in this place, "his blood shall be upon him;" he is the cause of his own death, his sinful acts have brought death upon himself.

Obs. 1. That a just man may have a wicked son. "If he beget a son that is a robber, a shedder of blood," &c.: he speaks of the just man who may have such a son. If we search into the bowels of the word, we shall find frequent examples hereof: Jacob had Simeon and Levi, who slew the Shechemites, troubled him, and made him to stink among the inhabitants of the land, Gen. xxxiv. 25, 26, 30; and therefore he called them instruments of cruelty, and laid a curse upon them at his death, Gen. xlix. 5, 7: Abraham had a scoffing Ishmael, Gen. xxi. 9; Isaac a profane Esau, Gen. xxv. 32, 34; old Eli had sons who were sons of Belial, 1 Sam. ii. 12; David had his Absalom, who shed the blood of his brother Amnon, 2 Sam. xiii. 28; Solomon had his Rehoboam, who proved tyrannical, 1 Kings xii.; Hezekiah Manasseh, who filled Jerusalem with innocent blood, 2 Kings xx. 21; xxi. 16; Josiah his Jehoahaz, who did evil in the sight of the Lord, 2 Kings xxiii. 30, 32. It is a great affliction when a good man hath a wicked son: Prov. xvii. 25, "A foolish son is a grief to his father, and bitterness to her that bare him." If a foolish son be so, what is that son that is a robber, a blood-shedder, an idolater, an oppressor? Just men have had such sons, and you must not think it strange if any of yours be such.

Obs. 2. The righteousness of the father neither privilegeth, patronizeth, nor protects a wicked child from the stroke of justice. "If he," viz. the just man, "beget a son that is a robber, a shedder of blood," &c. "shall he live? he shall not live." Though his father be just, his righteousness great, yet it doth not reach to his son, being guilty of such things. The Lord had said, ver. 4, "The soul that sinneth, it shall die," the father's righteousness cannot expiate the son's sin. As the life of the child cannot answer for the sins of the father, nor profit him at all upon that account, Mic. vi. 7, so neither can the righteousness of the father answer for the sin of the child, or advantage it at all in that respect. What Solomon saith of a wise man, Prov. ix. 12, "If thou be wise, thou shalt be wise for thyself," that I may say of a righteous man, If thou be righteous, thou art righteous for thyself, and not for another, no, not for thy own child. David's righteousness did not privilege Absalom; he sinned, and he suffered.

Quest. Is it not said, Prov. xi. 21, "The seed of the righteous shall be delivered?"

Answ. 1. Not for the righteousness of the father, that deserves nothing at God's hands; Job xxii. 3, "Is it any pleasure to the Almighty, that thou art righteous? or is it gain to him, that thou makest thy ways perfect?"

2. It is for the promise and covenant-sake which God hath made: see Gen. xvii. 7; Psal. cxii. 1, 2; lxxxix. 28—34.

3. It supposes continuance in the steps of their fathers, else not; for mark the whole verse, "Though hand join in hand, the wicked shall not be unpunished:" let them plot, act, use all means and ways themselves, their friends, or parties, can make, yet they shall be punished, the just God will bring it about one way or other. Now, if the seed of the righteous prove wicked, they must be punished.

4. Outward calamities and affliction fall alike unto all, but God will deliver the righteous and their seed out of the evil of them, Psal. xxxiv. 19; but wicked men are left to sink in them. Let not children, then, presume upon the righteousness of their parents, and live loosely; if they fall into vicious and lewd courses, they may perish, notwithstanding their righteousness.

Obs. 3. The sins here specified, howsoever they may seem to men, they are abomination unto God. Robbery, blood-shedding, idolatry, adultery, oppression, violence, withholding the pledge, going in to a menstruous woman, which is meant by committing abomination in ver. 12, usury, and taking increase; he hath done all these abominations. The Lord calls them all "abominations," things to be abhorred, loathed, rejected, offensive to all the senses. One sin here among the rest I desire may be taken notice of, and that is, usury and increase; he distinguisheth them here from oppressing the needy and the poor in ver. 12. If it were, therefore, meant of biting usury, as many would have it, that is comprehended in those words, of oppressing the poor and needy, which is abomination. Now, besides that, he adds, giving forth upon usury, and taking increase; and this he calls an "abomination."

Let men take heed how they meddle and please themselves with that which so far displeases, yea provokes, the Lord, that he brands it with the title of an "abomination." If in the judgment of the infinite and only wise God, it be abominable, let not the groundless distinctions and vain pretences of men prevail with thee to judge it warrantable or lawful.

Obs. 4. Great and notorious sinners bring, hasten woes, judgments, deaths upon themselves. "Shall he then live? he shall not live; he hath done all these abominations, he shall surely die;" either metaphorically, or some violent death. God will turn such sinners' prosperity into adversity, their light into darkness, their comforts into crosses and curses. Jer. ix. 13—16, "They have forsaken my law, walked after the imagination of their own heart: therefore saith the Lord of hosts, the God of Israel; Behold, I will feed them, even this people, with wormwood, and give them water of gall to drink." They should have sad and bitter afflictions: and what then? "I will scatter them also among the heathen, whom neither they nor their fathers have known: and I will send a sword after them, till I have consumed them." To be fed with wormwood, and drink gall, is a death; to be scattered among strangers is a death; to have a sword pursuing is a death. Wicked ones have many deaths, they are dying and pining away under threats, fears, strokes, or guilt continually; they may say, as it is Ezek. xxxiii. 10, "Our transgressions and our sins be upon us, and we pine away in them, how should we then live;" the thought of their sins and ways banished all sound comfort from their lives. And oft such sinners are snatched away, cut off by some sudden hand of God; and when it is so, it is most just, their blood is upon their heads, nothing befalls them but what is due and deserved; their sins call for death, and bring the evil upon them. See Lev. xx. 9, 11, 12, 13, 16, 27; 2 Sam. i. 16; where you may find that it was their own sin which brought death upon them.

Ver. 14—18. *Now, lo, if he beget a son, that seeth all his father's sins which he hath done, and considereth, and doeth not such like, that hath not eaten upon the mountains, neither hath lifted up his eyes to the idols of the house of Israel, hath not defiled his neighbour's wife, neither hath oppressed any, hath not withholden the pledge, neither hath spoiled by violence, but hath given his bread to the hungry, and hath covered the naked with a garment, that hath taken off his hand from the poor, that hath not received usury nor increase, hath executed my judgments, hath walked in my statutes; he shall not die for the iniquity of his father, he shall surely live. As for his father, because he cruelly oppressed, spoiled his brother by violence, and did that which is not good among his people, lo, even he shall die in his iniquity.*

The prophet, in these words, presents a third instance to free the Lord from imputation of injustice. You stick not to affirm that he punisheth the children for the sins of the fathers; but behold here the error and wickedness of your assertion. If a wicked father, a robber, a blood-shedder, beget a son that doth not as he hath done, God is so far from punishing him for those sins of his father, that he shall be spared and blessed, he shall not die but live.

Three things are here commended unto us concerning this son of a wicked father.

I. His full observation of his father's evil ways, in these words, "that seeth all his father's sins which he hath done."

II. His effectual consideration of them; "and considereth, and doeth not such like."

III. His doing of the contrary, which is implied in the several particulars mentioned in ver. 15—17.

"That seeth all his father's sins." Sin is not properly visible, it is not the object of the eye; we may see sinful actions, but not the sin of those actions, with the eye of the body; the sight of the sinfulness refers to the eye of the mind. Junius therefore renders the words thus, *qui animadvertat*, he who marks, observes the sins of his father. 1 Sam. xii. 17, "That ye may see that your wickedness is great;" that you may take notice, observe it is so. In this sense it is used, Eccles. v. 8, 13, 18; vi. 1; x. 5; Jer. xiii. 27; xxiii. 13; Job xi. 11. Many children do as their fathers do, and never observe of what nature it is they do, whether good or evil; yea, oft parents possess their children with arguments to justify their ways, which are altogether unlawful.

"All his father's sins." It is impossible any son should see or observe all the sins of his father, many are acted in secret, many abroad; our prophet intends not that every particular sin should be observed by him, but those which are more obvious, and expose to judgments and death, such as he had mentioned before.

"And considereth." The Hebrew word is, ויּרא from ראה which signifies not simply to see, but curiously to look into, to consider and intend a thing. The Septuagint, Vulgate, and some others read it, and feareth, and so derive it from ירא to fear; but Montanus saith, it is from ראה and so our translation hath it. I shall speak to it therefore as it imports consideration, not fearing.

1. Consideration is a serious exercise of the understanding about things to be done, or not to be done, furthering or impeding the execution of them as it sees cause.

(1.) It is an exercise of the understanding, mind, heart; these are at work in consideration: Psal. cxix. 59, "I thought on my ways," or considered them; I turned them over and over, as sempsters do their needle-work; I looked upon all the circumstances and aggravations of them. It is called a speaking or saying, Hos. vii. 2, "They consider not in their hearts;" Hebrew is, they say not to their hearts. It is called a communing with a man's own heart, Psal. lxxvii. 6.

(2.) Serious: it is not a slight general thinking of a thing, but a serious, settled minding of a thing; Heb. x. 24, "Let us consider one another:" it notes the sinking down of a thing into our minds. It is the intention of the mind upon a thing, with great earnestness; Eccles. ix. 1, "I considered in my heart;" Hebrew is, I set to my heart: consideration is a setting the heart to a thing, or upon a thing, as a bee sits upon a flower, and sets her strength to it to draw out the sweet in it.

(3.) It is about things to be done, or not to be done. Contemplation looks upon things as the eye upon the object. Judgment discerneth things whether good or bad, right or wrong, and there leaves them, having pronounced them so. Meditation is a further inquisition into truth, or minding of truth, and comes up nearest to consideration, which is in order to doing or not doing. Men intend this and that, and oft fall upon things rashly to their prejudice, because they consider not; now consideration reflects upon things intended. The two sons in the gospel, one said, I will go, and went not; the other said, I will not go, and went. The one's purpose was to go, the other's not to go; but this last considering of his sinful purpose, intention, and resolution, repented, and went, Matt. xxi. It is taken up about doing, or not doing, as you may see, Prov. xxiii. 1, 2; 1 Sam. xxv. 17; Judg. xviii. 14.

(4.) Furthering or impeding the execution of

them, as it sees cause. Psal. cxix. 59, "I thought on my ways, and turned my feet unto thy testimonies." David considered his ways, and not finding them good, he ceased from walking any longer in them; and seeing God's ways the only good ways, he turned about, stepped into, and walked in them. If upon consideration things be found good, the heart affects them, and so proceeds to the doing of them: the virtuous wife considered a field and bought it, Prov. xxxi. 16. But if things upon consideration be found sinful, the heart disaffects them, and so keeps off: see ver. 28 of this chapter, "He considereth, and turneth away from all his transgressions."

2. Wherein the strength of it lieth.

(1.) In searching out the causes, effects, rising, progress, continuance, and issue of a thing. Judg. xix. 30, the Levite's concubine being cut in twelve pieces, and sent into all the coasts of Israel, they saw it, and said, "Consider of it, take advice, and speak;" let us search out the cause and original of this evil, what damage it hath brought to the Jewish religion, and may bring; what the Levite can say; what will be the issue of this horrible fact.

(2.) In comparing things together, and so drawing up and out that which may be most useful. When all things are laid together, weighed, scanned over again and again, a man takes that which is most necessary, seasonable, suitable, and useful. Eccles. xii. 10, "The preacher sought to find out acceptable words;" he compared one word with another, one truth with another; and then, in ver. 13, "Let us hear the conclusion of the whole matter, Fear God," &c. He had tried books, creatures, all things; and then considering them, sums up, and draws out what was most material.

(3.) In pressing to and assisting the soul in acting. When consideration hath drawn up what is to be done, or not to be done, then it puts it upon the conscience as sinful, if not followed, and directs in the execution. Many things well contrived have miscarried through want of consideration, which looks to the congruency of particulars to the whole: Psal. lxiv. 9, "All men shall fear, and declare the work of God; for they shall wisely consider of his doing." Consideration lays an injunction upon men's wills and consciences to be doing. Did men in these days wisely consider the Lord's doings, they would fear, and declare the work of God.

3. The excellency of it.

(1.) It is that which God himself doth: Prov. xxiv. 12, "Doth not he that pondereth the heart consider?" When God intended to make man, he called a council, Come, let us make man after our image, Gen. i. 26. The Lord considers, ponders, and weighs things, according to the language of Scripture, Exod. xxxiii. 13; Prov. v. 21; Deut. xxxii. 26, 27; Hos. xi. 8, 9.

(2.) It differenceth a man from brutes; they are led by sense, and cannot distinguish whether an action ought to be done or not, this is man's privilege and power. Reason doth distinguish men from beasts, but the generality of men do not use reason; they have souls for salt, their eyes, ears, tastes, their senses are their guides: Jer. x. 14, "Every man is brutish in his knowledge." Men do not reflect upon their actions, and consider them; if they did, they would not be so sensual, so sinful. Isa. i. 3, "The ox knoweth his owner, and the ass his master's crib: but Israel doth not know, my people doth not consider."

(3.) It enables the understanding, completes a man, makes him wise and prudential. Prov. xvii. 27, "He that hath knowledge spareth his words; and a man of understanding is of an excellent spirit." He who considers what advantage may be made of words, and therefore is sparing in speaking, shows the more understanding and excellency of spirit. Prov. vi. 6, "Consider her ways, and be wise." If the considering of an ant's ways will make us wise, much more the consideration of our own ways. Direct acts may enable and perfect others, but reflex acts do enable and perfect a man's self. Consideration looks inward, looks over the same thing again and again, it defecates the understanding of man from those raw and imperfect notions and conceptions which arise at first, and those impertinent ones which interpose afterwards. We say, second thoughts are best, which implies that consideration ripens and perfects the man and his actions; as meat in the pot, if suddenly pulled out, is raw, but if well boiled, is freed from crude humours, and so more wholesome.

(4.) It puts life into those principles and talents God hath given a man; like a drum in an army, when that beats all stir and march; like a spring in a watch, when that goes all the wheels go. Did men consider what graces and gifts God hath given them, they would not let them lie still and fallow, but improve them. Isa. lxiv. 7, "None stirreth up himself to take hold on thee:" they had talents, but did not employ them. Heb. x. 24, "Let us consider one another to provoke unto love and to good works:" consideration will set others' graces on work, and much more a man's own.

A third thing here commended about this son of a wicked father, is his doing the contrary: he worships God in his own way, he eats not upon the mountains, he lifts not up his eyes to idols; but he comes to mount Zion, and lifts up his eyes to the God of heaven whom he serves; he is chaste and charitable, he wrongs none, but doth good to all according to his ability; he executes judgment, and walks in God's ways; and whatever his father's sins have been, though crimson and scarlet abominations, he shall not die for them, but he shall surely live.

Ver. 16. "Hath not withholden the pledge." Hebrew is, hath not pledged the pledge. Hath not taken a pledge, saith Calvin, Lavater, Junius, Montanus; but Piscator saith, the word for pledging doth not signify here to take or receive a pledge, but to detain it being pledged, as appears from ver. 7, where the words are, "hath restored to the debtor his pledge;" and here it must be, not who hath taken, but who hath not withholden being taken: so Vatablus, doth not retain the pledge; and Weems, the repetition of the same word signifies to take away the pledge, and to keep it. Now he who doth not take away, or withhold, but restore the pledge, is just.

Obs. 1. A good son may descend from a wicked parent. A father that is a robber, a blood-shedder, a son of Belial, a plague to city and country, may have a son that is free from his vices, a son that is just; as good parents may have ill children, so ill parents may have good children. God may and doth honour his free grace, when, where, and upon whom he pleases. Manasseh was transcendently wicked, and his son Amon; so 2 Chron. xxxiii. 9, 22, 23; yet out of their loins came Josiah, ver. 25, who hath this testimony; that "he did that which was right in the sight of the Lord, and walked in the ways of David his father, and declined neither to the right hand, nor to the left," chap. xxxiv. 2. Hezekiah was very godly, did much in reformation, restored the passover, walked in the steps of David, and did that which was right in the sight of the Lord, yet he came from as wicked a parent as the world then had, even from Ahaz, 2 Chron. xxviii. 27. Ahaz came from Abijam, who walked in the sins of his father, 1 Kings xv. 3. Abraham descended from idolatrous parents, Josh. xxiv. 2. "Some good thing toward the God of Israel" was found in a son of Jeroboam's, who made Israel to sin, 1 Kings xiv. 13.

Some untoward parents in our days have had good children, and such as have much honoured God. Now this is not from nature, or because they are born under such and such planets, but because they are born of God, and made partakers of the divine nature. If parents have gracious children, let them give the glory thereof to God, whose grace hath made them such. If they have ungracious ones, let them beg hard of God for mercy and grace for them, who hath abundance of the Spirit to bestow on whom he please, and hath promised to those in covenant with him, to pour out his Spirit upon their seed, and his blessing upon their offspring, Isa. xliv. 3.

Obs. 2. It is not always safe, warrantable, to imitate parents, ancestors, predecessors, and to tread in their steps; it may be dangerous, deadly, yea damnable. If the son of the unjust man should follow his father in his ways, he must die for it; but if he see his ways, and doth not such like, he shall live. When the ways of parents are idolatrous, superstitious, profane, oppressive, contrary to, or not grounded upon the word of God, children are not to conform unto them. There is one greater than they, and wiser than they, who is the Father of spirits, and hath more authority over them than their parents after the flesh; him must they hearken unto, his counsels must they embrace, his commands must they obey, his will must they do. The Lord commends the son here that doth contrary to his wicked father. 1 Pet. i. 18, men are redeemed from the vain conversation by tradition from their fathers. Fathers who are vain, have vain conversations, deliver those to their children, but children should not receive their traditions, nor imitate their conversations, they are redeemed from them; but they are apt to do it, Jer. ix. 14; xliv. 17; and it is oft complained of and spoken against in Scripture, 2 Kings xv. 9; xxiii. 32; Neh. xiii. 18; Psal. lxxviii. 57; Ezek. xx. 24, and in other places. There is a full prohibition against it, 2 Chron. xxx. 7, "Be not ye like your fathers, and like your brethren, which trespassed against the Lord God of their fathers, who therefore gave them up to desolation."

Obs. 3. Consideration is a special means to keep men from sinning. If a son see his father's sins, and considereth, and doth not such like. There is a strong inclination in men to sin; example is powerful to draw out that inclination, and especially the example of a father; yet consideration hath virtue in it to stop that inclination, to take off from evil example, and to carry another way. The prodigal, "when he came to himself," that is, considered what he had done, in what case he was, what might be had in his father's house, he comes off from his wicked ways, and returns to his father, Luke xv. 17. It is want of consideration that men sin so as they do; had Noah, Lot, David, Peter, others, well considered, they would not have fallen into such sins as they did; it is rashness, inconsiderateness, that occasions and causeth many sins. Matt. vii. 3, "Why beholdest thou the mote that is in thy brother's eye, but considerest not the beam that is in thine own eye?" Want of consideration makes men censorious and hypocritical, it leads men into a multitude of sinful ways, and keeps them there, Isa. xliv. 19; Hos. vii. 1, 2; Eccles. v. 1; whereas if men would seriously consider, they would neither sin so frequently, nor continue in sin, if overtaken with it. Ezek. xii. 3, "It may be they will consider, though they be a rebellious house." Here the Lord intimates, that if they would consider, they would give over their sinful practices, and not persist in ways to provoke God; they would see so much evil in their own ways, so much equity in God's ways, that they would leave the one and embrace the other.

In ver. 28, of this chapter, you may see the virtue and efficacy of consideration: "Because he considereth, and turneth away from all his transgressions." Nothing more advantages Satan's kingdom than incogitancy and inconsiderateness; and nothing doth prejudice it more than the contrary. Consideration puts a stop to men's sinful ways, and causeth them to turn to God, Psal. cxix. 59. Therefore the Lord calls earnestly for it, Psal. l. 22, "Now consider this, ye that forget God;" and Deut. xxxii. 29, "O that they were wise, that they understood this, that they would consider their latter end!"

Obs. 4. Good children descending from wicked parents, are not to be branded with their vices. If he beget a son who doth not such like; if the son do not tread in the steps of his father, he is just, he shall not suffer for his father's sins; I will not charge the guilt or shame of them upon him, he shall live comfortably, and without infamy. Children choose not their parents, neither could prevent their sin; if they cleave not to their ways, they shall not be spotted with their vices.

The world deals otherwise, it is forward to pick up any thing, yea to seek out matter from parents and predecessors to disgrace their posterity, though they walk not in their sinful paths; this is not to be like unto God, but unto the world, to lay the burden of the guilt upon the innocent.

From ver. 18, observe, that covetous men are oppressors, yea oppressors of those who are near unto them. "Because he cruelly oppressed, spoiled his brother by violence:" the Hebrew is, he oppressed by oppression, and spoiled by spoiling, and that his brother. The word אח notes a brother of the same womb, a kinsman, a brother in friendship, one near and dear to a man. He that is covetous will contend fraudulently, oppress, as עשק signifies, yea spoil, and wrest out of his hand by violence what he hath, as גזל imports. Covetousness is cunning and cruel: Neh. v. 7, "Ye exact usury, every one of his brother." Micah vii. 2, "They hunt every man his brother with a net." Amos v. 11, they take burdens of wheat from the poor; they oppress and crush them, chap. iv. 1. They robbed the fatherless, and made widows their prey, Isa. x. 2. If you would see the cunning and cruelty of covetous men, consult with these texts, Jer. vi. 13; Jam. v. 4; Luke xix. 8; Isa. iii. 14, 15; Micah iii. 2, 3; Ezek. xxii. 7; 1 Kings xxi. 15.

Covetous men little care from whom they pull, so they may get and feed their covetous desires: many have undone their brethren, kindred, friends, fathers, sons, by their cunning, cruel, covetous practices.

Ver. 19, 20. *Yet say ye, Why? doth not the son bear the iniquity of the father? When the son hath done that which is lawful and right, and hath kept all my statutes, and hath done them, he shall surely live. The soul that sinneth, it shall die. The son shall not bear the iniquity of the father, neither shall the father bear the iniquity of the son: the righteousness of the righteous shall be upon him, and the wickedness of the wicked shall be upon him.*

Here begins the Jews' replication, and God's further vindication of himself from what they accused him of, which extends to the end of the 24th verse.

The replication is in these words, "Why? doth not the son bear the iniquity of the father?" Why dost thou deny it, bring arguments against it, attempt to persuade us otherwise? have we not experience of it in ourselves? do not we bear the iniquity of our fathers? The Hebrew word for "why" is מדוע which is used when we desire to know the reason or cause of a thing, as Gen. xxvi. 27, "Wherefore," or why, "come ye to me, seeing ye hate me," said Isaac to Abimelech and his men, let me know the cause of your coming: so here, they would have a reason, know the cause why the Lord spake so, and justified his proceedings with men and government in the world, that he wronged none, but rendered to all according to their ways and works. It is otherwise, we find and feel the contrary, the iniquity of our forefathers is upon us their children; and therefore we wonder how either thyself, or Ezekiel, who pretends to be thy prophet, can assert such things: either that is not true which is said, or our condition is worse than others; if thou dealest justly with others, yet unjustly with us, we suffer for the sins of our parents.

"Bear the iniquity." Iniquity here is put for the punishment due unto it, and so it is frequently used in Scripture: Gen. xix. 15, "Lest thou be consumed in the iniquity of the city;" that is, in the punishment which iniquity hath brought upon it. So Psal. xl. 12; xxxi. 10; Exod. xxviii. 43; Numb. xiv. 34; xviii. 23; Isa. liii. 11; Ezek. xliv. 10: bearing of iniquity in these places is put for bearing of punishment by a metonymy of the efficient.

To this reply and charge God answers,

1. In general, in the rest of this 19th verse, and in the 20th. If a son do that which is lawful and right, if he keep my statutes, he shall live, he shall not suffer (as you reproachfully and blasphemously object against me) for the sins of his father; no, the soul that sins shall die. If the father sin he shall die, if the son sin he shall die, if neither of them sin neither shall die. He who is righteous, his righteousness shall be upon him; he who is wicked, his wickedness shall be upon him.

2. More particularly, in ver. 21—24.

There is nothing more to be opened in the 19th verse. Of doing that which is lawful and right, of keeping statutes, and living, hath been spoken.

Ver. 20. "The soul that sinneth, it shall die." Of these words you heard largely out of the 4th verse. By "soul" is meant person; by dying, suffering of punishment, putting to death: so the words to die do signify, Deut. xvii. 12; xviii. 20; xxiv. 7; 2 Sam. xii. 5; 1 Sam. xiv. 39. The sense of the words then is this; that person who commits sins worthy of death shall die for them, and not another.

"The son shall not bear the iniquity of the father." If he persist not in his father's steps he shall not suffer for his father's sins, that were against the law, Deut. xxiv. 16, "The fathers shall not be put to death for the children, neither shall the children be put to death for the fathers; every man shall be put to death for his own sin." Amaziah remembered this law, and kept it, 2 Chron. xxv. 4; when he slew the fathers, he slew not the children for the fathers' sin. It was otherwise when Joshua put Achan's sons to death for Achan's sins, Josh. vii. 24; and when David delivered Saul's sons to be put to death by the Gibeonites for the sin of their father, 2 Sam. xxi. 9. The law then ties not God, he hath a prerogative above his own laws given out to us: they do and must tie us, and without special warrant, hint, and instinct, we may not do contrary unto them; both Joshua and David had special direction for what they did, or else it was evident to them that they approved and justified their fathers' facts, and so became guilty of the same, and suffered according to law.

"The righteousness of the righteous shall be upon him." Look what the righteous hath done, accordingly shall he have; as iniquity before did note punishment, so righteousness here notes reward, he shall have the fruit of his righteous acts. Isa. xlviii. 18, "Thy righteousness had been as the waves of the sea," that is, the fruit or reward of thy righteousness had been great, and coming in daily: so the word "righteousness" is to be taken, Gen. xxx. 33; James iii. 18; Gal. v. 5.

Some from these words, and those in ver. 19, "Hath kept all my statutes, and done them, he shall surely live," do conclude that a man may keep the law, and so by his own righteousness attain unto, if not merit, life eternal.

But where is that man that ever yet did keep the law exactly? since Adam's fall there is none. If Adam in innocency could not do it, how shall we think men subject to sin and many infirmities can do it? Eccles. vii. 20, "There is not a just man upon earth, that doeth good, and sinneth not." Solomon had observed men, and the best of men; the most just sinned and broke the law: James iii. 2, "In many things we offend all." Paul durst not stick to his legal righteousness, Phil. iii. 9; he knew it was impossible for himself or any other to keep the law. Rom. viii. 3, "What the law could not do in that it was weak through the flesh, God," &c. Gal. iii. 21, "If there had been a law given which could have given life, verily righteousness should have been by the law." The law was weak and unprofitable, it made nothing perfect, Heb. vii. 18, 19: the law neither justifies nor sanctifies, it neither quickens nor comforts. If men think by legal righteousness to attain life eternal, they will fall short of it, as the Jews did, Rom. ix. 31, 32; x. 3, 4. They think to earn eternal life; but that is not earned, it is given, Rom. vi. 23; Eph. ii. 8, 9. The just live by faith, and look for eternal life, not by Moses, but by Christ, Tit. iii. 5—7.

Obs. 1. Erroneous and corrupt opinions being entertained, are not easily got out of the heads and hearts of men. These Jews had drunk in a hard opinion of God, that he dealt unjustly with them, punishing them for their fathers' sins. The Lord by many arguments and instances clears up the justice and equity of his proceedings with the sons of men, that he punished none without just cause, and that it is for their own sin when he doth it: he spends eighteen verses to convince them of the falsehood and evil of their tenet, to remove it out of them; but they, notwithstanding all this, hold their opinion fast, and dispute it with God: "Yet say ye, Why? doth not the son bear the iniquity of the father?" we are of this mind and judgment, and so shall continue for aught thou hast said. Errors quickly root deep, take strong hold, and cannot easily be pulled up.

The Pharisees held corrupt opinions about washings, Matt. xv. 2, dispensing with children's obedience to parents, Mark vii. 11; about swearing, Matt. xxiii. 16, 18, fasting and tithing, Luke xviii. 12. They held many corrupt opinions touching the law, as in Matt. v. appears; and could Christ prevail with them to get those opinions out of them? He brought the clearest light that ever was, yet they loved their own darkness more than his light; yea, they gat him out of the world, before he could get these errors out of them.

The Sadducees denied the resurrection, Matt. xxii. 23; and notwithstanding Christ took pains to convince them, and spake to the astonishment of others, ver. 33, yet their opinion abode with them, and they were of that mind after Christ was gone to glory, even in Paul's days, Acts xxiii. 8. Hymenæus, Alexander, Philetus, had rather be delivered up to Satan, than deliver up their corrupt and damnable opinion, of saying "the resurrection is past already," 2 Tim. ii. 18, with 1 Tim. i. 20. The apostles had taken up an opinion that Christ would be great in the world, and advance them, from which opinion Christ had oft been beating them off, yet it abode with them till his ascension, Acts i. 6. There were those in the church of Pergamos who held corrupt doctrines, and the angel of it could not get them out, Rev. ii. 14, 15. Take heed therefore what opinions you receive. If in John's time there was need to "try the spirits, because many false prophets were gone out into the world," 1 John iv. 1, much more had men now need to try the spirits, because the world is full of false prophets and false spirits; and men are grown so artificial to deceive, that if it were possible the very elect should be deceived, and that finally. Let the apostle's counsel take place, 1 Thess. v. 21, "Prove all things;" take nothing upon trust for the learning, holiness, worth of, or respect you have to any man; but prove all by the word, see it have a sound bottoming there, and then it is good; hold it fast, then it will do you good, let it not go.

Obs. 2. That what punishments soever befall men, they have no just cause to complain of God, though it be punishment unto death; for he hath said, "the soul that sinneth shall die," not another for it, not it for another's sins. If it were so, there were just cause of complaint; if the son should die for the father, or the father for the child, this were injustice; therefore the Lord saith here, "The son shall not bear the iniquity of the father, neither shall the father bear the iniquity of the son," &c. God is most just, and cannot do an act of injustice to any man; and if it be just what he doth, why should man mutter, think, or speak hardly of God? Lam. iii. 39, "Wherefore," saith Jeremiah, "doth a living man complain, a man for the punishment of his sins?" who wrongs him? doth God? he hath wronged God, and God doth but right himself. If a man strike a lion, and the lion bite him, hath he cause to complain of the lion, or his own folly in striking the lion: Prov. xix. 3, "The foolishness of man perverteth his way; and his heart fretteth against the Lord:" but what cause hath he to fret against God, correcting and punishing him for his folly? Men should "accept of the punishment of their iniquity," as it is Lev. xxvi. 41, rather than complain, when it is their own fault that they suffer; yea, men have cause to be thankful to God that he doth punish them less than their iniquities deserve.

Obs. 3. Then God hath authority over souls, to set them what laws he please, and prescribe what punishments he thinks good. "The soul that sinneth shall die:" be persons great or small, honourable or base, wise or foolish, the Lord is above them, hath command over them, hath set them their bounds; which if they transgress, they shall suffer according as his wisdom shall appoint. Have states that power to give laws to the people, and set what punishment they judge fit for the breach of them, as confiscation of estate, imprisonment, mutilation, racking, pressing, decollation? and shall not God much more? Ver. 4, he saith, "All souls are mine; the soul that sinneth shall die:" I have given them all laws, and ordained punishments for the breach of those laws.

Obs. 4. No man's sin shall go unpunished; men shall not sin, and go away without suffering for it. "The soul that sinneth shall die," either a metaphorical death, it shall meet with grievous afflictions, or a violent death, be cut off by some stroke of God, or an eternal death, which is worst of all. Prov. xi. 21, "Though hand join in hand, the wicked shall not be unpunished;" whatever they think or attempt, God will meet with them, whoever they be. Job ix. 4, "Who hath hardened himself against him, and hath prospered?" Did ever any man sin, and enjoy peace, offend God, and have his blessing? No; God hath made men know it is a sad and dreadful thing to sin against him. Adam sinned and God visited him for it; his posterities sin, and they smart for it. In vain do men flatter themselves that they may sin, and not suffer, they may do wickedly, and escape: it cannot be, God who is truth hath said it, "The soul that sinneth shall die." God may defer the stroke, but without repentance it must come. Rom. ii. 9, "Tribulation and anguish shall be upon every soul of man that doeth evil, of the Jew first, and also of the gentile." "The wickedness of the wicked shall be upon him."

Obs. 5. Righteous men shall not lose the fruit of their righteous doings. "The righteousness of the righteous shall be upon him." Psal. xcvii. 11, "Light is sown for the righteous." And Psal. lviii. 11, "Verily there is a reward for the righteous." Prov. xi. 18, "The wicked worketh a deceitful work; but to him that soweth righteousness shall be a sure reward." Isa. xlviii. 18, "O that thou hadst hearkened to my commandments! then had thy peace been as a river, and thy righteousness as the waves of the sea."

Ver. 21—23. *But if the wicked will turn from all his sins that he hath committed, and keep all my statutes, and do that which is lawful and right, he shall surely live, he shall not die. All his transgressions that he hath committed, they shall not be mentioned unto him: in his righteousness that he hath done he shall live. Have I any pleasure at all that the wicked should die? saith the Lord God: and not that he should return from his ways, and live?*

In these verses and the next, you have a more full and particular answer of the Lord's to the unjust replication of the Jews, and charge laid upon him in ver. 19. "Why? doth not the son bear the iniquity of the father?" No, saith God, he that doth right he shall live, and he that sins he shall die. There is the general answer, and here comes the particular.

I. Concerning a wicked man, in ver. 21—23.

II. Concerning a righteous man, in ver. 24.

Concerning the wicked man, here are two things required, and two things promised: the things required are,

1. Turning from all his sins.
2. Keeping all God's statutes.

The things promised are,

1. Life.
2. Not mentioning of his sins.

If the wicked will turn from his evil ways, repent him of what he hath done, and walk in the ways of God for the future, he is so far from suffering or dying for his father's sin, that he shall not suffer or die for his own; he shall live, and his sin not once be mentioned unto him: I am so far from punishing him for another's sin, that upon repentance I punish not a man for his own.

"If the wicked will turn from." The Vulgate is, *si egerit pœnitentiam*, if he shall repent; the Hebrew is, ישוב from שוב and notes turning from ill, and turning to God, which is repentance: so it is used,

Ezek. xiv. 6, "Repent," the word is, שׁובו turn ye, or repent; in repentance there is turning.

This turning from evil is set out by sundry expressions: Isaiah calls it washing, making clean, putting away the evil of men's doings, ceasing to do evil, chap. i. 16. Solomon styles it confessing and forsaking of sin, Prov. xxviii. 13. David terms it departing from evil, Psal. xxxiv. 14; Peter, eschewing of evil, 1 Pet. iii. 11. Daniel's phrase is, breaking off from sin, chap. iv. 27; and Christ's is, "Sin no more," John v. 14.

These words, "if the wicked will turn from all his sins," seem to import power and freedom in man to repent and turn himself. This difficulty was spoken unto chap. xiv. 6, upon those words, "Repent, and turn yourselves." Men may use means, but those means will not produce repentance and turning without God: the Jews used means, Jer. vii. 10, yet could not turn themselves, chap. xiii. 23. Natural instruments have power to work of themselves, there is virtue in them to bring forth such and such effects; but moral instruments, of which sort the word is, do not work so: the word is "mighty through God," 2 Cor. x. 4, 5. Nothing is done towards the conversion of a sinner; therefore repentance is the gift and work of God, Acts xi. 18; v. 31; 2 Tim. ii. 25. Yet when we are called upon to repent, to turn, there is somewhat to be considered: in God's commands, know what you ought to have; in his reproofs, consider it is through your own fault you have it not; in prayer, see where and whence you have it.

Ver. 22. "They shall not be mentioned unto him." Hebrew, לא יזכרו they shall not be remembered. His sins shall not prejudice him, he shall not suffer or be punished for them. To remember sin according to the Scripture sense is, to punish. Psal. cxxxvii. 7, "Remember, O Lord, the children of Edom in the day of Jerusalem; who said, Rase it, rase it;" that is, punish them: in the like sense you have it, Hos. viii. 13, "Now will he remember their iniquity, and visit their sins;" so chap. ix. 9. And not to remember, is to pass by, forget, and not to punish, Isa. lxiv. 9. Psal. xxv. 7, "Remember not the sins of my youth;" let them not move thee to punish or be avenged on me for them; as men, when they remember injuries, seek to be avenged on those who have done them.

"In his righteousness that he hath done he shall live." His righteousness shall preserve him from metaphorical and violent death. The papists from these words pretend that a man is justified before God for his own righteousness; but we know the Scripture runs otherwise: Gal. ii. 16, "A man is not justified by the works of the law;" and, "all our righteousnesses are as filthy rags," Isa. lxiv. 6. See Rom. iii. 24, 28; 1 Cor. iv. 7; Rom. v. 19; 2 Cor. v. 21; which places show that we are justified not by our own works, our own righteousness, but by the righteousness of another. Besides, it is not said here, for his righteousness, but "in his righteousness." Good works do not precede justification, and so merit it; but follow the person justified, and declare his justification; they are the path-way to life and glory.

Again, could a man forsake all sins, keep all God's statutes, yet could he not hereby be justified before God, because there must satisfaction be made to the law, and to God, for those sins now left, and that is not in man's power, Micah vi. 7; Psal. xlix. 7.

Ver. 23. "Have I any pleasure at all that the wicked should die." Hebrew is, החפץ אחפץ the radical word signifies to have pleasure in, to affect, delight, to desire and will; therefore some render it, do I desire or will the death of a sinner? Others, have I pleasure, or any pleasure? You charge me to punish the children for the fathers' sins, and think I take pleasure in the death of sinners, but I neither do the one nor the other; I punish not you for your fathers' sins, but for your own; and when I do punish you for your own, I had rather you should repent and live, than be cut off for them.

This seems contradictory to what is written, Prov. i. 26, "I will laugh at your calamity, I will mock when your fear cometh;" and Ezek. v. 13, "Thus shall mine anger be accomplished, and I will cause my fury to rest upon them, and I will be comforted." If God have no pleasure in the death of sinners, how can these texts be verified? To clear this difficulty, know that it is not absolutely to be taken, that God hath no pleasure in the death of the wicked, unless you mean it of the wicked who do repent; but respectively, thus, if they could turn from their wicked ways, and keep his statutes, he should have more pleasure in this, than in their death; but when they do not repent, he hath pleasure in their punishment and death, as it is an act of justice, and work of God, for God hath pleasure in all his works: the destruction and ruin of Babylon is called "his pleasure," Isa. xlviii. 14, "He will do his pleasure on Babylon, and his arm shall be on the Chaldeans."

Some refer this to the antecedent will of God, and say so he hath no pleasure in the death of a sinner, he wills it not, delights not in it; but in regard of his consequent will he doth.

Obs. 1. Repentance is a turning, and a turning from sin. Ver. 30, "Repent, and turn." Acts iii. 19; xxvi. 20, repenting, and turning to God, are put together. Sin turns men from God; Jer. xxxii. 33, "They have turned unto me the back, and not the face." Repentance is a turning of them again unto God; it turns them from their sinful and wicked ways, 2 Chron. vii. 14; Jer. xxvi. 3; from all sin, and sinful ways, not some few; "if the wicked will turn from all his sins;" so ver. 30, "Turn from all your transgressions;" it turns men from their secret sins, Psal. xix. 12; Isa. lv. 7. If a man turns not from all, he turns from none in truth, because there is the same reason why a man should turn from all, as well as one, viz. the will and command of God. This turning must be with the whole heart, and therefore it is from all sin, Deut. xxx. 10; Joel ii. 12.

Obs. 2. It is not enough to turn from all sin, but we must turn to all good. "If the wicked will turn from all his sins that he hath committed, and keep all my statutes, and do," &c. Negative righteousness is no righteousness, negative holiness is insufficient holiness, 2 Kings xvii. 13. We must turn from the commands of sin, Satan, and the world, unto the commands of God. We must turn from worldliness unto heavenly-mindedness, from pride unto humility, from censuring to loving. It suffices not that the tree bears no ill fruit, but it must bring forth good fruit, else it is a barren tree, and must down. The question will be hereafter, What good have you done? 1 Tim. v. 10, "If she have diligently followed every good work." David fulfilled all the wills of God, Psal. cxix. 6, he had respect unto all his commandments; and christians must observe all things Christ hath commanded, Matt. xxviii. 20.

Obs. 3. The way to live comfortably and prosperously is to be godly. He who turns from all his sins, and keeps all my statutes, and doth that which is lawful and right, he shall surely live; he shall live in living; others are dead in living, they have no comfort in their lives: Prov. iv. 4, "Keep my commandments, and live;" see Isa. lv. 3; Amos v.

4, 6; Psal. xxxiv. 12, 14. It is man's sin which maketh times evil, 2 Tim. iii. 1, 2.

Obs. 4. Note, that to penitent, obedient sinners, mercy is promised. "All his transgressions that he hath committed shall not be mentioned unto him." Those that turn from their wicked ways unto the Lord shall find mercy with him, their sins shall be forgiven; let the sins be what they will for nature, never so many for number, they shall all be blotted out, and not be mentioned, Matt. xii. 31; Isa. lv. 7; Jer. xxxi. 12. It was made good in the prodigal. Remission of sins is promised to repentance, Acts iii. 19; when a sinner hath once repented, God will mention his sins no more, and why should we remember or mention them?

Obs. 5. If the sins of the penitent shall not be mentioned, then there is no purgatory to punish them for the same hereafter. How is it true that God remembereth not, mentioneth not the sins of his friends, of penitents, if he punish them so sharply in purgatory?

Obs. 6. God hath no delight in the death of sinners; if they suffer and perish, it is of and from themselves. "Have I any pleasure at all that the wicked should die?" Ver. 31, "Why will ye die, O house of Israel?" I like it not that men will ruin themselves; I had rather they would consider their ways, turn their feet unto my testimonies, and live. Hos. xiii. 9, "O Israel, thou hast destroyed thyself; but in me is thy help." Destruction is of man, salvation is of the Lord.

Ver. 24. ***But when the righteous turneth away from his righteousness, and committeth iniquity, and doeth according to all the abominations that the wicked man doeth, shall he live? All his righteousness that he hath done shall not be mentioned: in his trespass that he hath trespassed, and in his sin that he hath sinned, in them shall he die.***

Having laid down the case of a wicked man, repenting him of and turning him from his sins, and so cleared the proceedings of God, that such a one finds mercy, and suffers not for his own sin, much less for his father's, he comes here to the use of a righteous man, who if he turn from his righteousness, and fall to wicked courses, his former righteousness shall not advantage him, but he shall be dealt with according to his present sin. The sin of the wicked repenting shall not hinder him from mercy, and eternal life; and the righteousness of the righteous sinning, shall not keep him from justice, and eternal death. Old sins shall not burden a returning sinner, and old righteousness will not help a revolting saint.

Of a righteous man, his turning from his righteousness, and committing iniquity, hath been largely spoken of chap. iii. 20, where the first part of this verse is word for word; yet, because this verse is much controverted, and insisted upon by the patrons of apostasy and falling away, I shall touch upon it.

Who the righteous or just man here spoken of is, may be gathered from the opposition to the wicked man; the one is really wicked, and the other is really righteous, that is, with a legal or moral righteousness. He that hath not eaten upon the mountains, lift up his eyes to idols, defiled his neighbour's wife, oppressed the poor and needy, but given his bread to the hungry, clothed the naked, taken no usury nor increase, that hath executed judgment, and walked in God's statutes, such a one is righteous, and the righteous man in the text.

That here is meant a moral, legal righteousness, appears from those words in the 4th and 20th verses, where it said, "The soul that sinneth, it shall die." If this did refer to the gospel, and righteousness thereof, and not to the law, and legal righteousness, no man could be saved, because all men sin; but notwithstanding their sinning, those who are righteous with the righteousness of the gospel, they shall not die, but be saved: it must therefore be understood of a legal, civil, moral righteousness.

Gerhard brings this verse to prove, that a man by his sins may put away faith and the Holy Spirit, *loco. Theol.* t. 4. *De Bonis Operibus.* Bellarmine brings it, tom. 4. l. 5. *de Grat. et lib. Arb.* c. 29, to prove that a man may lose a new heart; and lib. 3. *de Justif.* c. 14, he makes use of this verse to show that faith may be lost. The Arminians also say, Hence it is so evident that every one may see it, that a righteous man may totally and finally fall away, *Ames. in Antisynod. de perseu. Sanct.* c. 2.

For answer unto these, know,

1. It is said when the righteous man doth turn away, he shall be so dealt with, as if he had never been righteous. It is a caution to prevent a righteous man's falling, rather than an implication that he will or shall turn from his righteousness.

2. The prophet speaks here of a righteous man considered in himself, not in relation to God, or Christ; and so he may turn from his righteousness, as angels and Adam did.

3. The scope of the chapter is, not to prove falling away from grace, but to clear the Lord's justice, and that in two things:

(1.) That he doth not punish one man for the sin of another, if he be not guilty thereof: a guiltless son shall not suffer for the sins of a guilty father, ver. 4, 20.

(2.) That he is not partial in his dealings, either with the wicked or righteous; he punishes wicked men if they sin, he spares them if they repent: and as for righteous men, he blesses, prospers them, because they walk in his statutes, keep his judgments, and deal truly; but if they forsake their righteousness, and fall to sinful courses, he will punish them as he doth wicked men: so that here is not any thing spoken of grace, or faith, whereby men are united to Christ, justified, sanctified, and evidenced to be in covenant with God, through Christ; but what is here said, is spoken in a legal way, namely, to vindicate God from what unjustly they cast upon him, viz. that they suffered for the sins of others. Jer. xxxi. 29—31, "In those days they shall say no more, The fathers have eaten a sour grape, &c. But every one shall die for his own iniquity. Behold, the days come, saith the Lord, that I will make a new covenant with the house of Israel." God is now put upon better terms with the house of Israel, than he was at that time. If they sinned they should die, if they did well they should live, this was the covenant of works; but God promised to make a covenant of grace with them, which they should not break as they had done the former, ver. 32; for he will put his fear into their hearts, that they should not depart from him, chap. xxxii. 40, and his Spirit, which should cause them to walk in his statutes, to keep his judgments, and to do them, Ezek. xxxvi. 27. And Christ tells his disciples, that he would send the Comforter that he might abide with them for ever, that he might dwell with them, and be in them, John xiv. 16, 17. And John saith, "He that is born of God doth not commit sin; for his seed remaineth in him: and he cannot sin, because he is born of God," 1 Epist. iii. 9. If he cannot sin, then surely not so sin as to shake off faith, thrust out the Spirit, totally and finally to fall away. This last place troubleth all those who hold that opinion of falling away. Bellarmine saith, that this place is the hardest of all to answer. Ambrose refers it to the state of glory, in his Commentary upon Isaiah. Bernard, by seed understands *gratiam prædestinationis*, and saith, the predestinate cannot sin so as to harm them, seeing their sins are forgiven, and to work for their good. Others expound it, cannot sin, ought not to sin, Those who are born of God ought not to sin; but that is nothing to purpose, those who are born of God ought not to sin. If sin ought to be, it were not sin, *Aug. Tract.* 5. *in Epist.* Johannis expounds it of deadly sins; and Bellarmine likes this exposition, and acknowledgeth that he who is born of God does not sin nor can sin unto death, while he continues a son of God. The text saith, he neither doth sin, nor can sin, because he is born of God; therefore he shall continue to be the son of God, and so never fall into those sins which will unchild him, disinherit him, unjustify, and unsave him. Some that say, saving faith may be lost, do make three degrees of saving faith.

The first and highest degree is, the attainment of the life and divine nature of Christ into our souls; after which attainment we live still by faith carrying us out after the nourishment of this new life, and nature begotten in us, which are the heavenly satisfactions of God and Christ: from this faith it is acknowledged impossible to fall away.

A second or middle degree of saving faith is, such a belief of Christ's fulness, life, and divine communications, as brings us not only to fall in love with Christ, and those communications in him, of life and divine things, but also causeth us to leave all things in our desires and affections, wholly to depend on God, and to wait with earnestness, longing, and patience, for the giving in of Christ, his life, and divine communications; and though such a degree of faith doth not likely fall away, yet it is possible it may; Heb. x. 35, " Cast not away your confidence," which intimates they might do it.

A third, and the lowest degree of true saving faith, is that which believes the satisfaction and fulness of Christ to be for us, and so affects us therewith, that it carries us out after Christ, for himself, and for the things believed to be in him, causing us to do and forsake much for him, yet brings us not to willing and actual forsaking of all we have for him, Luke xiv. 33. This is true faith, and will make us partakers of Christ, if continued in, Heb. iii. 14: from this faith it is affirmed that we may fall for ever. John viii. 31, 32; Col. i. 23, there is mention of true, saving faith, for it would save them if continued in; and this manner of speech shows, they might not continue, and so lose what they had.

Answ. 1. I find not salvation put upon the strength, but truth of faith, not upon the highest degrees, but any degree of faith, John iii. 16; Mark xvi. 16; 1 Pet. ii. 6; 1 John v. 1; Acts x. 43; xiii. 39; xvi. 31. It is not said in these or other places, if you have such a degree of faith you shall be justified, saved; but simply believing is required, the lowest degree of true faith will do it: Rom. x. 9, " If thou shalt confess with thy mouth the Lord Jesus, and shalt believe in thine heart that God hath raised him from the dead, thou shalt be saved." The thief upon the cross had not attained to such high degrees of faith; he by one act, and that of a weak faith, was justified and saved, Luke xxiii. 42, 43.

2. The power of God is in the weakest faith, as well as in the strongest. 1 Pet. i. 5, " Who are kept by the power of God through faith unto salvation;" it is not, through strong faith, or such a degree of faith, but only, "through faith." The power of God begets faith in the soul, Eph. i. 19; it keeps it alive there, how weak soever it be, and it keeps it unto salvation. That we may be saved by faith, he saves faith in us; he will not let faith perish, that we may not perish. God's power must fail, if true faith in the lowest degree fail. But, John x. 29.

3. If men may fall from true, saving faith, being in its infancy, what hinders but they may fall from it being grown up, and come to man's estate? Death, which seizeth upon infants, seizeth also upon men; water, which extinguisheth a spark, will extinguish also a great fire. The sense and operations of faith men may be without, but the substance of it abides. All the fiery darts of the devil cannot pierce the shield of faith, Eph. vi. 16. All the strength, malice, and opposition of the world, cannot overcome a little true faith; 1 John v. 4, one born of God, though but new born, a very babe, he overcomes the world. He is " born, not of corruptible seed, but incorruptible," 1 Pet. i. 23; he hath an anointing which abides in him, 1 John ii. 27; his faith hath made him a son of God, Gal. iii. 26, and sons abide in the house for ever, John viii. 35. Yea, he that believes " hath everlasting life, and shall not come into condemnation," John v. 24; God puts his fear into his heart, and he shall not depart from him, Jer. xxxii. 40. His Spirit being in the heart of a true believer, causes him to walk in God's statutes, to keep his judgments, and do them; he shall be confirmed to the end, 1 Cor. i. 8. So that by these texts it appears, that where true, saving faith is, it will abide, not be extinct, but will live for ever.

Be it granted, therefore, that in the places mentioned, John viii. 31, 32; Col. i. 23, a true saving faith is meant, then the words, " if ye continue," do not import they should not continue. " If" is not a word of doubt, but of caution and encouragement; so it is taken, 2 Pet. i. 10, " If ye do those things ye shall never fall." This and the like places are encouragements to stir them up unto perseverance, and do show, that none have true saving faith, are intrinsically and really in Christ, but those do continue in the word and faith to the end.

Suppose they do continue and not fall from their faith, yet doth not this word, " if," note a possibility that they may fall from their faith? Conditional suppositions are of things impossible, as well as of possibles. Gal. i. 8, " If we, or an angel from heaven," &c. Matt. xxiv. 24, " If it were possible, they should seduce the very elect:" but they cannot be seduced, and those that have true faith cannot fall away finally. Job xvii. 9, " The righteous shall hold on his way, and he that hath clean hands shall be stronger and stronger." 2 John 2, " The truth dwelleth in us, and shall be with us for ever." And Psal. cxxv. 1, " They that trust in the Lord" are or " shall be as mount Zion, which cannot be removed, but abideth for ever." Mount Zion was a great and firm mountain, which could neither move itself, nor be removed by others; whatever rains, floods, winds, earthquakes there were, yet mount Zion stood immovable; and those who trust in God are, and shall be, like mount Zion for ever. They are not like a ship floating upon the water, a tent pitched upon the earth, a house built upon the sand, which may be sunk, pulled up, or blown down, but like a mighty mountain that stands fast, and is immovable for ever. It is not the freedom of their wills can do it, Psal. xlviii. 14, for " God will be their guide unto death." It is not the strength of corruption can do it, for their faith purifieth their hearts, Acts xv. 9; 1 Pet. i. 22. It is not the world can do it, 1 John

v. 4, nor all the power and policy of Satan, Matt. xvi. 18.

"And committeth iniquity." These words were opened in chap. iii. ver. 20, where they were somewhat largely insisted upon: something is now to be given in about them. This phrase, to commit iniquity, is equivalent to and the same with that in the gospel, viz. to commit sin, 1 John iii. 8; John viii. 34. All men sin, but all do not commit sin; 1 John iii. 9, "Whosoever is born of God doth not commit sin." Sins of infirmity they have; they sin against the inclination and tendency of the divine nature in them occasionally, from some sudden temptation, but they do not commit iniquity. They that do so are under the influence of the love of sin; there is study, counsel, meditation, purpose, resolution in their sinning. John vii. 34, "Whosoever committeth sin is the servant of sin:" and what it is to commit sin, he shows, ver. 40, "Ye seek to kill me," your studies, counsels, meditations, purposes, resolutions, endeavours, are upon that. So Jer. ix. 5, "They weary themselves to commit iniquity." When the bent of the heart and head is that way, studying, plotting, and endeavouring to accomplish some evil thing, then iniquity is committed; as here in our prophet, the man is turned from righteousness, and turned to iniquity, the bent and operations of his heart and head are that way. Such men, by the voice of the Spirit, are said to be given to sinning; as Isa. xlvii. 8, "Thou that art given to pleasures." Jer. vi. 13, "Every one is give to covetousness;" their counsels, thoughts, desires, spirits, are taken up about, and work after their pleasures and covetousness. The Lord Christ calls these "they that work iniquity," Matt. vii. 23; and Luke xiii. 27, "workers of iniquity;" that is the trade they profess, and are skilful in. Samuel calls them, "doers of evil," 2 Sam. iii. 39; Isaiah, evil-doers, chap. ix. 17; Solomon, "wicked doers," Prov. xvii. 4; they do what the wicked man doth, and as he doth.

"According to all the abominations that the wicked man doeth." Of abominations hath been spoken formerly; I pass therefore to the following words.

"All his righteousness that he hath done shall not be mentioned." The Hebrew is, all his righteousnesses, it is plural: whatever good works or righteous acts he hath done, they shall not be mentioned, or remembered.

From these words some gather, that a man pardoned, and justified, may fall into those sins which do cancel his pardon, and reduce him to an unjustified condition, and revive the guilt of his former sins.

This place doth not speak of a man pardoned, and justified by faith in Christ, for such a man, though he may, and sometimes doth fall into foul sins, yet they never prevail so far as to reverse pardon, and reduce to a state of non-justification. Psal. xxxvii. 24, "Though he fall, he shall not be utterly cast down; for the Lord upholdeth him with his hand." He speaks of a good man pardoned, justified; he may fall, but how far? from pardon, from justification? No, then he should utterly fall, be cast down beneath God's hand; but the text saith, "he shall not be utterly cast down; for the Lord upholdeth him with his hand;" or, as Montanus renders the words, the Lord upholdeth his hands, and he will not let him sink into such a condition. If it were so, then sin should have dominion over him, but, Rom. vi. 14, "Sin shall not have dominion over you," and chap. viii. 2, justified ones are freed "from the law of sin and death;" and ver. 30, the predestinated, called, justified, and glorified ones, are so linked together, that there is no breaking their chain; if they do sin, they have "an Advocate with the Father, Jesus Christ the righteous, and he is the propitiation for our sins," 1 John ii. 1, 2.

Further, know that grace and great sins may stand together; though grace consist not with the dominion, strength, and power of sin, yet flesh and Spirit will be together while we live. David's great sins did not destroy and annihilate his grace: Psal. li. 11, "Take not thy Holy Spirit from me." This psalm was made when Nathan came to him, told him of his sins; and then, even then he had the Spirit of God abiding in him, else he could not have made that psalm, nor would have prayed in that manner: so those places in 1 Kings xi. 4, 6; Acts xiii. 22, do testify as much. Peter sinned greatly, yet did not he sin away his faith. His sin, and aggravations of it, you have Matt. xxvi. 70, 72, 74; he denied that he knew Christ, did it with an oath, with swearing and cursing; this was dreadful, yet notwithstanding such sins, his faith abode with him: Luke xxii. 32, "I have prayed for thee that thy faith fail not." Christ's prayer was heard, therefore his faith could not fail; if it failed totally, as men affirm that hold falling away, then Christ's prayer was not heard, which is contrary to John xi. 42, "I knew that thou hearest me always," and he deceived Peter, telling him his faith should not fail. That faith which is in thee shall not fail, not totally; for that which fails totally, fails finally, there is an end of that, and it must be a new faith, not the same, if there be faith given in after a total failing. Peter's faith therefore did neither fail totally nor finally, but did consist with those great sins and shakings of his. Whatever then the sins of the justified, pardoned ones be, though in their own nature such as are destructive to salvation, yet they do not bring them to an unpardoned and unjustified condition; nor do they revive the guilt of former sins with God: with us they may, but not with him; for whom God pardons, he pardons absolutely, not conditionally; he so pardons sin as he will not remember it again: Isa. xliii. 25, "I, even I, am he that blotteth out thy transgressions for mine own sake, and will not remember thy sins." See Jer. xxxi. 34; Mic. vii. 18, 19; Heb. viii. 12.

Aug. Tertull.

"In his trespass." Hebrew is, במעלו in his prevarication. מעל signifies a transgression voluntary and against conscience, with contempt and contumacy, saith Kirker. And it differs from חטא which is, to err, to miss of the mark, to turn aside; and chiefly notes those sins which come from ignorance, and infirmity of the flesh, which are more easily cured; but the trespass here is, of a man turned from his righteousness unto wickedness, and so sins irremediably; for it follows,

"In them shall he die." That is, in the guilt of them shall he die; as Christ told the Jews, John viii. 21, 24, in the guilt of their unbelief they should die; or, for them he shall die: so divers expositors read the words; and by death is not meant only a temporal but an eternal death also.

Obs. 1. There is a righteousness which men may turn from. "When the righteous turneth away from his righteousness." There is an opinionative righteousness, Luke xviii. 9, and Matt. xxiii. 28; many think themselves righteous, and appear so to others: there is also a duty, a moral, or legal righteousness, such as Paul had, Phil. iii. 6: and from these righteousnesses men may and do turn daily. Many attain to a duty righteousness under the gospel, but yet fall off again, as you may see, Matt. xiii. 20—22; 1 Tim. v. 15; John vi. 66; 2 Pet. ii. 2; 1 Tim. iv. 1. Take heed therefore of trusting in or to any righteousness of your own. Matt. v. 20, "Except your righteousness exceed the righteousness of the scribes and Pharisees, ye shall in no case enter into the kingdom of heaven." It is Christ's righteousness only which will let you in thither: lay aside your own righteousness, and labour for that, as Paul did, Phil. iii. 8, 9; and if any fall away, let it not offend and stumble you, knowing it is from their own righteousness, not Christ's. 1 John ii. 19, "They went out from us, but they were not of us, for if they had been of us, they would no doubt have continued with us: but they went out, that they might be made manifest that they were not all of us."

Obs. 2. It is not sufficient to begin well unless we proceed: fair beginnings without progress come to nothing. "If a righteous man turn from his righteousness," if he do not go on with perseverance, it will not advantage him, it is not acceptable with God or men. Joash, while Jehoiada lived, did well, that was his glory; but when he was dead, he fell to commit iniquity, that was his shame. Paul blames the Galatians, chap. iii. 3, 4, who were near the tropics: "Are ye so foolish? having begun in the Spirit, are ye now made perfect by the flesh? Have ye suffered so many things in vain? if it be yet in vain:" it argues great foolishness, and will be accompanied with great loss, if you do go off from your hopeful beginnings. When men withdraw, fall off, it is argument they were never sound. 2 John 9, "Whosoever transgresseth, and abideth not in the doctrine of Christ, hath not God. He that abideth in the doctrine of Christ, he hath both the Father and the Son." If men forsake the ordinances and gospel, whatever they think of themselves, they have neither Father nor Son. Peter thunders against such as fall off from their former professions, 2 Epist. ii. 20—22. Let it not be said of any here, They "did run well," as it is, Gal. v. 7, but let us go on, "run with patience the race that is set before us," Heb. xii. 1; and "so run that we may obtain," 1 Cor. ix. 24. Consider the arguments which lie here in the text, to keep you from falling off, and encourage you to persevere in God.

(1.) If you do turn back you will fall into iniquity; you will commit iniquity, the frame, bent, and set of the heart will be that way; the thoughts, studies, counsels, motions, endeavours, will be towards and in iniquity, you will be an evil-doer, a worker of iniquity.

(2.) He lies obvious to all manner of sin; what will not the man do that turns from his holy profession? He is liable to do according to all the abominations that the wicked man doth: if there be any man more wicked than others, that doth abominable things, such will that man do; and it may be, not some one or two abominations, but all the abominations of the wicked.

(3.) Whatever good he hath formerly done shall be all forgotten: if he have done good to the church and saints, to the state in a military, consultatory, navigatory, or contributary way, if he have done much good to his family, or friends, it shall be all laid aside, buried in the dark, and not once be mentioned unto him. What if he have built an hospital, free-school, redeemed captives, maintained many lectures, relieved thousands of poor, done more good than many others? yet if he turn from his good he was doing, God turns also, and will never mind it more.

(4.) He shall die, and that eternally, in his apostasy, and the guilt, not of one sin, but all his sins, shall be upon him.

Ver. 25—29. *Yet ye say, The way of the Lord is not equal. Hear now, O house of Israel; Is not my way equal? are not your ways unequal? When a righteous man turneth away from his righteousness, and committeth iniquity, and dieth in them; for his iniquity that he hath done shall he die. Again, when the wicked man turneth away from his wickedness that he hath committed, and doeth that which is lawful and right, he shall save his soul alive. Because he considereth, and turneth away from all his transgressions that he hath committed, he shall surely live, he shall not die. Yet saith the house of Israel, The way of the Lord is not equal. O house of Israel, are not my ways equal? are not your ways unequal?*

The Jews had complained of the Lord's hard dealing with them in the 2nd verse, to which unjust complaint he makes a large answer to the 19th verse, where they reply upon God the same thing still; to which reply he returns a sufficient defence, thoroughly satisfactory to any unprejudiced, and that is in the six verses last opened; but they not taking satisfaction from what the Lord gave in by the prophet here, they come again to charge him.

In these verses you have,

I. Their charge; "The way of the Lord is not equal."

II. God's answer to this charge; where,

1. Attention is called for; "Hear now, O house of Israel."

2. An interrogation made; "Is not my way," &c.

3. A retortion of the accusation upon themselves.

4. The probation of the equity of his ways, in ver. 26—28.

5. A repetition of the charge, interrogation, and recrimination, ver. 29.

For the words, something to the opening of them must be spoken.

"The way of the Lord is not equal." The Hebrew word for "not equal" is, לֹא יִתָּכֵן The Septuagint puts it actively, κατορθοῖ, The way of the Lord shall not be direct; we look not upon it as so, but as crooked; or, it doth not direct us, but lead us to think hardly of him; his way is such as would make any sort of men judge that he deals unjustly. The most expositors have it as it is here, "the way of the Lord is not equal." The Hebrew verb, תכן signifies to ponder, weigh, frame artificially; 1 Sam. ii. 3, "By him actions are weighed." The charge here that God's way is not equal, amounts to this; that his way is not well weighed, artificially framed, and exactly done, but irregular, crooked, and sinful: so Munster hath the words, it is not equally carried.

"Way." Hebrew, דרך the work, action, dealing, judgments, and proceedings of God with them: not *ratio*, as Castalio puts it, unless it be taken thus; there is no reason in that which God doth, or he hath no reason for what he doth.

"Is not my way equal?" It is an interrogation, which is more than a plain or naked affirmation; had the Lord said, My way is equal, whatever you think or say, however you carry yourselves, it had not had such weight, efficacy, and strength in it, as now the words contain. "Is not my way equal?" what! not my ways? do you doubt or question the same? If there be not equity in my way, there is none in any way: all ways are rough, crooked, perverse, to my ways; they are weighed exactly, wrought artificially, and done upon such mature, rational, wise, and strong grounds, that neither you nor any have cause to quarrel, and say my ways are not equal; they are equal, yea equity itself.

There are some things which men can catch at to make the ways of God seem unequal, especially these: 1. His punishments. 2. His choices. 3. His distribution of things to men. 4. Disappointments. 5. His rewards.

1. For his punishments. Great was the complaint and charge here in this chapter, that God did punish them for their fathers' sins, to which calumny sufficient hath been spoken. That of Adam's sin, and all his posterity to suffer for it, sticks much with some; that millions should perish upon that account, makes the way of God seem unequal. But upon due consideration it will appear otherwise; for Adam being a public person, represented all mankind; and God covenanted with him, that if he stood and kept that image of God in which he was created, that then his posterity should be like him, and happy with himself; but if he fell, that they should suffer in him, and with him; and what unequalness was here? Adam was the root of all men, had all in his loins; and as all lost the image of God in him falling, Rom. v. 12, 16—19, so all should have had the image of God in him standing.

2. For his choices. God seems to respect persons, because he dealeth unequally with men that are equal. All men are fallen in Adam, equally guilty; yet some of these God chooseth to life, others he leaves and passes by; all are his creatures, and he deals not alike with them. Besides, he chooseth the foolish, the weak, the base and despised, and sets by the wise, mighty, and noble, 1 Cor. i. 26—28; what equity therefore in his ways? yea, ofttimes he takes great, notorious sinners, and those who are less sinful are rejected.

To set all straight here, consider what it is to accept or respect persons. It is to look at men upon external grounds, some outward qualities, and thereupon to do for them, as riches, honour, birth, breeding, power, kindred, family, beauty, strength, condition of life, learning, wisdom, parts, policy, &c. Now the Lord doth not look at any external adjuncts or ornaments in his elections and choices of men; nothing in the creature or from the creature moves him, it is his own good pleasure and will sets him at work to choose any, 2 Tim. i. 9; Eph. i. 5, 11; Rom. ix. 18.

Besides this, know God is not bound to deal equally with men, being equally miserable, for then he must destroy all, or save all, and so have the glory of justice alone, or mercy alone, and not the glory of both; then he should not have made Christ sin for us, 2 Cor. v. 21, but have punished Adam and all those who sinned in him; and what then had become of the world? hell had been full, and heaven empty. And for his choice of any out of those who are equal in sin, or of greater sinners, what doth this show but the freedom of his grace, and his sovereignty over the creatures, to do with them as he pleases? Rom. ix. 21, shall that privilege be denied to God which is given to the potter, and God's way seem more unequal in his dealing with men, than the potter's is with the clay? And whereas God doth take the weak, base, foolish, and despised things of the world, it is argument that he doth not respect persons: he takes those who have nothing in them to move him: should he take the wise, mighty, noble, rich, and learned, then there would be some ground for charging God with acceptation of persons; but examine the Scriptures, and they quit the Lord abundantly from it: Deut. x. 17; 2 Chron. xix. 7; Job xxxiv. 19; 2 Sam. xiv. 14; Acts x. 34; Rom. ii. 11; Gal. ii. 6; Eph. vi. 9; Col. iii. 25; 1 Pet. i. 17; in all these places the Lord is freed from regarding, respecting, or accepting of persons.

3. For his distribution of things, the Lord is accounted to deal unequally. Why, say men of this humour, have many so much, and others so little, or nothing at all? Some have manors, lordships, counties, kingdoms, when others have neither house nor land; some have five talents, others one; some are wise, and others idiots; yea, that which shows the way of the Lord to be unequal, is, wicked men have great estates, high places, they ride, and the righteous go on foot, being poor and low.

For answer to this, know, that the Lord is a free agent, and may give what he pleases, when, where, and in what proportion seems good to himself and to his infinite wisdom. Men blame not Providence, that some trees are stronger, taller, bigger than others: if the vine, olive, and fig tree are lower than cedars and oaks, they are more fruitful, and yield pleasanter fruit. Is the merchant blamable if he fraught one ship with coals, another with corn, one with skins, another with silks, one with boards, another with the richest wines? surely no; and may not the Lord put into these earthen vessels of men what he will, and as much as he will? is he unequal in such dispensations? What if wicked men have much? it is but "thick clay," Hab. ii. 6; "meat that perisheth," John vi. 27; "unrighteous mammon," Luke xvi. 11; "the lust of the flesh, eyes, and pride of life," 1 John ii. 16; "vanity and vexation of spirit," Eccl. i. 14; and that which will not profit in an evil day, Prov. xi. 4. Better things than these are given to the righteous; peace of Christ and God, "which passeth understanding," John xiv. 27; Phil. iv. 7; joy unspeakable and glorious, 1 Pet. i. 8; "precious faith," 2 Pet. 1. 1; "the spirit of power, love, and of a sound mind," 2 Tim. i. 7; the "great and precious promises," yea, "all things pertaining to life and godliness," 2 Pet i. 3, 4. Therefore though they be low in a worldly sense, yet they are lifted up in a spiritual sense, and so highly exalted, that the world is not worthy of them, Heb. xi. 38.

4. His disappointing of men and means which are likeliest to attain unto those ends that are aimed at. Eccl. ix. 11, "The race is not to the swift, nor the battle to the strong, neither bread to the wise, nor riches to men of understanding, nor favour to men of skill." To whom should these be, if not to such? When men use honest means, and with all their might, they are disappointed and discouraged. If the race be to the slow, the battle to the weak, bread to the foolish, riches and favour to the ignorant and unskilful; what equity is there in God's ways, and why should we having talents use them, or using them be disappointed?

This objection seems to strike deep, yet wounds not the honour of the Lord and equity of his ways. For,

(1.) God's ways are not unequal, because we cannot see the reason of them; we are poor purblind creatures, and know little. The Lord's "understanding is infinite," Psal. cxlvii. 5; "there is no searching of it," Isa. xl. 28: his "judgments are a great deep," Psal. xxxvi. 6, there is no fathoming of them; "his ways are past finding out," Rom. xi. 33. It is not safe therefore, because we see not the equity of them, to conclude they are unequal.

(2.) God disappoints men of abilities using lawful and direct means to attain their ends propounded, because they trust in the means, idolize them, looking at God in the second place, or not at all. Acquaint yourselves with these places, and you will find the reality of it, that men are apt to confide in their own abilities, to trust in an arm of flesh, to applaud their own preparations, and expect much from them; Isa. xxxi. 1—3; Jer. ix. 23; Psal. xx. 7; xlix. 6; Jer. vii. 4; Ezek. xvi. 15; Amos vi. 1; Hos. x. 13. If God disappoint them for their own sin of their expectation, what inequality is there in God's ways?

"The wages of sin is death," death of designs and undertakings, as well as of men the undertakers.

(3.) Let it be granted, that men use their abilities and means conducing to their ends propounded, the right way, without confidence in the same, in subordination unto God; yet may the Lord disappoint men's purposes, contrivances, aims, and ends, and that without sin; for the Lord is above all second causes, his providence rules and runs through all, and doth give check when, where, and how it pleases, to all creature motions; and God will have men to see, that, without concurrence of his providence and assistance, nothing can be done. It is not human dispositions, counsels, preparations, operations, use of any medicines, that can produce any effect without God: Lam. iii. 37, "Who is he that saith, and it cometh to pass, when the Lord commandeth it not?" Let princes, potentates, and powers, consult of, attempt, what they will, if the Lord have not commanded the thing, if he do not co-operate with them in doing the thing, it proves abortive: see 1 Kings xii. 21—23; 2 Chron. xxv. 6, 7; Isa. xxxvii. 33, 34, 36; 2 Kings vii. 5—7; Isa. xix. 3; Job v. 12; Isa. viii. 9, 10. The sum of all which is, that in Psal. xxxiii. 10, "He maketh the devices of the people of none effect." If men have that power to stop and frustrate great undertakings at sea and land, shall it be denied to the great God of heaven and earth? God should not be omnipotent, nor reign in the kingdoms of the earth, if men should carry on their designs, and attain their ends, without him.

(4.) Events and successes of things are hidden in the hand of God; men must, therefore, improve their talents, use all lawful means, for accomplishing those things which are good in the sight of God, and wait upon the Lord for discovery of his mind and good pleasure therein. It argues an ill spirit, to say we shall be disappointed, and therefore we will sit still. How know we what shall be the issue of any undertaking? If one enterprise fail, another may take; if one arrow hit not the mark, a second or third may. If we hide our talents in napkins, we shall be found ill servants; and the command is, "Whatsoever thy hand findeth to do, do it with thy might," Eccles. ix. 10. Men must not be idle, but active, and active to the utmost; for, there is a season to every thing, and a time to every purpose, chap. iii. 1. What that season and time will prove, no man knows; you must venture therefore: Eccles. xi. 6, "In the morning sow thy seed; and in the evening withhold not thine hand: for thou knowest not whether shall prosper, either this or that, or whether they both shall be alike good."

(5.) If there be disappointments, God may make them as advantageous to thee as enjoyments, or recompense it in another undertaking. Amaziah hired a hundred thousand mighty men of valour out of Israel for a hundred talents of silver; God sends a prophet, who bids him dismiss them all; this disappointment troubled him; what shall we do for the hundred talents? the prophet answered him, "The Lord is able to give thee much more than this," 2 Chron. xxv. 9. So God is able to make up any disappointment, and more too: what injustice or iniquity then is in his way?

5. The last thing propounded making God's ways to seem unequal, is his rewarding men unproportionably to what they do or suffer. Matt. xx. 12, "These last have wrought but one hour, and thou hast made them equal unto us, which have borne the burden and heat of the day;" we have been eleven or twelve hours in thy vineyard, we have wrought hard, the work hath lien heavy upon our hands; we have endured the heat and scorching of the sun, done ten times as much as those who came in but an hour since; and what justice, what equity is it that they should be equal with us in the pay, that were so unequal in the labour?

To quit the Lord, let us consider only what the parable affords us, and therein is plentiful matter to justify him from wronging those who here did murmur and complain; for,

(1.) Those who were hired earliest in the morning, and so were longest in the vineyard, and at the work, the Lord agreed with them for a penny a day, ver. 2, which he paid them, ver. 10, and therefore did them no wrong, ver. 13.

(2.) Those who were hired at the third, sixth, and ninth hours, ver. 3, and 5, the Lord promised them whatever was right and equal, ver. 9. Whatever they had, then, it was just; and where justice is, there is no ground of complant. So for the eleventh hour men, they had the same promise; ver. 7, "Go ye also into the vineyard; and whatsoever is right, that shall ye receive." How is God's dealing with them unequal and wrong, when he gave them that which was equal and right?

(3.) If the last did not deserve the penny, yet God might give them the penny; and so he did, ver. 14, "I will give unto this last, even as unto thee." God may give what reward he pleases unto those who do him the least and latest service, equalize them with the first, and those who do most, and that without partiality; for it is lawful for him to do what he will with his own, ver. 15.

"Are not your ways unequal?" You observe, complain of my ways, charge them to be unequal; but your ways, if examined, will be found the unequal and unjust ways, the charge you lay upon me will light upon yourselves. The Vulgate reads it, *Non magis viæ vestræ pravæ sunt?* you say my ways are not right, but rather, are not your ways wicked and corrupt? Surely they are, you are blind, prejudiced, and cannot judge aright of me and my ways; but I am God, light and no darkness, I know you and your ways, and do assert them to be unequal: you have forsaken me, Isa. i. 4; even me, "the fountain of living waters, and hewed you out cisterns, broken cisterns, that can hold no water," Jer. ii. 13; you have filled the temple with idols, and the land with violence, Ezek. viii.; you have devised mischief, and given wicked counsel, chap. xi. 2; driven out the brethren, ver. 15; you have scoffed at my prophets and prophecies, chap. xii. 22; you have hearkened to lying prophets and prophetesses who have daubed with untempered mortar; saddened the hearts of the righteous, and strengthened the hands of the wicked, chap. xiii. 10, 22; you have set up idols in your hearts, chap. xiv. 3; you have justified Sodom and Samaria in all their wickedness, and done more abominably than they, chap. xvi. 46, 47; you have broken covenant with Nebuchadnezzar, king of Babylon, and revolted from him, and sent to Egypt for help, chap. xvii. 15. And now, consider, "are not your ways unequal?" yea, most unequal: had you any cause to charge me? have not I just cause to charge you?

Of the 26th, 27th, and 28th verses, hath been spoken before in the 24th, 21st, and 14th verses of this chapter. Only those words in the 27th verse we shall speak a little unto, namely,

"He shall save his soul alive." The Hebrew is, הוא את־נפשו יחיה he shall quicken his own soul. The Septuagint hath it, *τὴν ψυχὴν αὐτοῦ ἐφύλαξε*, he hath preserved, or shall preserve, his own soul. This expression appears contradictory to what is recorded in Psal. xxii. 29, where it is said, "none can keep alive his own soul."

1. We must search out the meaning of the Hebrew word; and,

2. See how to reconcile the places.

1. For the word *vivificare*, or *vivificare animam*, doth not note always bringing to, or begetting, life in the soul, being dead; for how can that which is dead act and produce life in itself: quickening from death, either natural or spiritual, is from the Lord, John v. 21; Eph. ii. 5. Sometimes it notes sparing of a man's life, 1 Kings xx. 31, "Peradventure he will save thy life," it is spoken of Benhadad, being in the hands of Ahab: the Hebrew is, אולי יחיה את־נפשך peradventure he will quicken thy soul. Benhadad was alive, but in danger of death: the meaning therefore is, that, if they tried the king of Israel, he might free him from death, spare his life, and that was the quickening of his soul. In this sense it is used, Gen. xix. 19. Sometimes preserving of life; 2 Kings vii. 4, say the lepers, Let us go to the Syrians, if they save us alive, we shall live; the Hebrew is, if they quicken us; if they will give us to eat and drink, our lives will be preserved; and so the word signifies, Gen. vi. 19; xlvii. 25. Sometimes it notes putting into a former condition, as Neh. iv. 2, "Will they revive the stones out of the heaps of the rubbish which are burned?" that is, Will they restore the stones burnt to ashes, and set them in the wall as formerly. Sometimes to comfort; Ezek. xiii. 18, 19, so the false prophets are said to quicken or save souls that came unto them; they, by their feigned and fair words, did beget hopes in them of good things, and good days. The sense we are to take it in here, is the first and second: "He shall quicken his soul, and make it alive;" that is, save it from death, and destruction, which wicked men are subject unto; they do that wickedness which shortens their days. Job xxxvi. 6, "He preserveth not the life of the wicked:" the original is, he shall not quicken the wicked; he shall not deliver him from the death and judgment he hath brought upon himself, he shall die for his sin. But when a man ceases from wickedness, he shall free his soul from death; and that this is the meaning, is clear from the words in ver. 26, viz. "For his iniquity that he hath done shall he die." A righteous man, turning from his righteousness, and sinning, shall die, shall be cut off; a wicked man, turning from his wickedness, he shall save his life, and preserve it in a comfortable condition, he shall surely live. For the place in the psalmist, you may understand it of a natural death; so, "no man can keep alive his own soul," that is, himself. Or thus, he speaks of Christ in the verse, The rich shall worship him, and the poor shall bow before him; and, as it follows, "none can keep alive his own soul;" that is, without him, without Christ, John xv. 5; without him none can free his soul from wrath, and eternal death. And if any will stretch Ezekiel's words so far, that he shall save his soul alive from wrath to come, and the second death, he must take in Christ; it is not man's own acting will do it.

The 29th verse is a repetition of the 25th, which is not in vain; but,

I. Sets out the impiety and impudence of those who charged God's ways to be unequal.

II. How ill God took it at their hands.

III. It tends to a further clearing of God. And,

IV. A fuller conviction of the chargers, that they were guilty: all which I shall pass by, and come unto some few observations.

Obs. 1. Men are apt to question, quarrel, and carp at God, and the ways of God; they say, "The way of the Lord is not equal." Sometimes men charge his ways to be grievous and burdensome: John vi. 60, "This is an hard saying; who can hear it?" Amos vii. 10, "The land is not able to bear all his words." Sometimes to be dangerous: Prov. xxvi. 13, "The slothful man saith, There is a lion in the streets;" if I walk in God's ways, I shall meet with reproaches, persecutions, temptations, and tempters, and these are all lions. Sometimes to be unprofitable: Mal. iii. 14, "Ye have said, It is vain to serve God: and what profit is it that we have kept his ordinance, and that we have walked mournfully before the Lord of hosts?" so, Isa. lviii. 3, "Wherefore have we fasted, and thou seest not? wherefore have we afflicted our soul, and thou takest no knowledge?" all our labour is in vain, there is no benefit in his ways. Sometimes to be lying, and false: Ezek. xii. 22, "The days are prolonged, and every vision faileth;" 2 Pet. iii. 4, "Where is the promise of his coming?" Sometimes to be heretical, Acts xxiv. 13. And here, they are said to be unequal. And not only do men charge God's ways, but himself also; they blush not to speak it out, that God seeth not, that he hath forsaken the earth, Ezek. viii. 12; ix. 9. Some in these days affirm, that God is the author of sin, that it is injustice in him to punish the souls of the wicked in hell, while their bodies lie at rest in the grave; that God doth as much hurt as good, take one time with another. Oh the corruption, pride, impudency, arrogancy of men, that dare sit in judgment upon God and his ways, charge and sentence him and them so unjustly! And that which is to be lamented, good men sometimes have gone too far this way: see Psal. lxxvii. 7—9; lxxiii. 13, 14; Jer. xx. 12; Job x. 3. Let us take heed of this wretched disposition, humble yourselves for failings this way, and learn not to judge of God and his ways by our fancies and shallow capacities; though we cannot see the reason of his proceedings, let us adore him, and justify them; for,

Obs. 2. God's ways are just and straight, whatever men's thoughts are of them. "Are not my ways equal?" his ways are full of equity. Those which seem grievous are pleasant, Prov. iii. 17; those which are thought dangerous are safe; Prov. i. 33, "Whoso hearkeneth unto me shall dwell safely, and shall be quiet from fear of evil:" those which are said to be unprofitable, are very profitable, Psal. cxix. 56, "This I had, because I kept thy precepts;" Psal. xix. 11, "In keeping of them is great reward:" those which are reckoned false, and heretical, are most true; Psal. cxix. 160, "Thy word is true from the beginning;" Ezek. xii. 23, "The days are at hand, and the effect of every vision;" Rev. xv. 3, "Just and true are thy ways, thou King of saints." God is a God that cannot lie, Tit. i. 2; that cannot deal unjustly, that cannot pervert his ways; and therefore he makes challenge to the sons of men to prove it if they can, to produce one instance of that kind if they can: Mic. vi. 3, "What have I done unto thee? and wherein have I wearied thee? testify against me;" let your kings, nobles, princes, prophets, priests, people, their wise men, and ancient ones, come forth, and testify against me if they can. I have been amongst you ever since I brought you out of Egypt, now almost a thousand years, and if there be any unjust act done by me, if I have walked in any unequal way, let me hear of it, spare me not. So Jer. ii. 5, "What iniquity have your fathers found in me?" God put them to it, to make it out if there were any, but none could be found out. It did stand for a truth in David's days, it doth stand now, and must stand for ever: "The Lord is righteous in all his ways, and holy in all his works," Psal. cxlv. 17.

Obs. 3. When we have a controversy with any, we should not reproach them, be in passion, give them hard language, but gentle, sweet, loving compellations. "Hear now, O house of Israel;" what a loving term was this, what entreaty was here from the great wronged and provoked God! Mic. vi. 2, 3, "The Lord hath a controversy with his people, and he will plead with Israel." But how doth he plead? not in fury, in an upbraiding, reviling way, but in a loving manner, "O my people, what have I done," &c. Men, when they are charged unjustly, and have controversies with others, they forget God, and themselves; they are full of passion, bitterness, reproaching, exasperating, and dangerous expressions; they think they may take liberty to speak and vindicate themselves. True; but not in an unjust way; you must not speak evil of any man: Tit. iii. 2, you must not brawl, you must "be gentle, showing all meekness unto all men." Thus did Christ to a reprobate, Matt. xxii. 12; thus did Michael to the devil, Jude 9.

Obs. 4. When men are once prejudiced against God and his ways, it is hard to unprejudice them. When corrupt opinions are once gotten into the head or heart, they root, take such hold, as it is a great difficulty to get them out again. These Jews said they suffered greatly for the sin of their fathers; that his ways, therefore, were not equal. The Lord spends this chapter upon them, to free them from that prejudice, to extirpate that misconceit they had of him and his ways, and to set himself right in their thoughts; but "yet say ye," ver. 19; "yet ye say," ver. 25; "yet saith the house of Israel, The way of the Lord is not equal," ver. 29. The strong arguments the Lord brought did not prevail with them.

No marvel, then, that ministers cannot prevail; people hold fast errors, lies, delusions, and will not let them go. Many wonder that learned men should not convince those who are unlearned, and weak, and take them off from their opinions; but see here, they stood it out against God. Men are very tenacious of erroneous and false tenets, and being by them prejudiced against God, his truth, and ways, they will not let them go, they will rather die in than depart from them. Ahab is prejudiced against Micaiah, and in him against God: "He prophesies no good, but evil, concerning me;" he is a man I hate, 1 Kings xxii. 8. Jehoshaphat, though a good man, and great king, he could not take him off from this prejudice he had against God and the prophet, but he persisted therein to his death.

One Rabbi Akibba, being imprisoned amongst the gentiles, another rabbi brought him as much water as served to quench his thirst, and wash his hands. The keeper of the prison one day poured out half of it. Akibba, seeing not enough water, said to the other rabbi, Give me that to wash my hands; to which he replied, There is not enough to quench your thirst. Akibba answers, It will be better for me to die for thirst, than to despise the tradition of my elders. *Buxdorf. Synag. Ind.*

The Jews are so strongly possessed with untoward opinions, that no reason, no time will keep them off from them. They still think that neither Elias nor Messiah are come, but look for them daily, and that God deals unkindly with them that he doth not send them. They hold that their Messiah shall not come in such a clandestine way as the christians' Messiah did; he shall have a glorious kingdom here on earth, many wives, and leave children to reign after he is dead and gone. The papists retain their opinions about images, transubstantiation, Christ's descent to hell, purgatory, &c. notwithstanding all the protestants' disputes and writings to the contrary; they will die in their errors, rather than leave them to embrace truth.

Obs. 5. Men faulty themselves, are forward to fault others, even those who are most innocent. These Jews, whose ways were most unequal, they spy faults in God, as they conceive, and say his ways are unequal. Jonah, who ran away from God, yet he was wroth with God for sparing Nineveh, and destroying the gourd; he thought the Lord did ill in both, Jonah iv. And so with men; those who are most guilty and obnoxious, they are usually censuring, accusing, disgracing, condemning. Ahab, who had sold himself to do wickedly, set up idols, and done more abominably than others, yet he sets upon Elijah, and accuses him to be the troubler of Israel, 1 Kings xviii. 17. The scribes and Pharisees, who were very wicked and notorious hypocrites, were most forward to charge Christ.

Ver. 30—32. *Therefore I will judge you, O house of Israel, every one according to his ways, saith the Lord God. Repent, and turn yourselves from all your transgressions; so iniquity shall not be your ruin. Cast away from you all your transgressions, whereby ye have transgressed; and make you a new heart and a new spirit: for why will ye die, O house of Israel? For I have no pleasure in the death of him that dieth, saith the Lord God: wherefore turn yourselves, and live ye.*

In these three verses we have the second general part of the chapter, which is an exhortation to repentance.

The particulars contained in the words are,

I. A conclusion drawn up from the former expostulation; ver. 30, "Therefore I will judge you," &c.

II. The exhortation itself, which is variously set down and under divers expressions.

1. "Repent, and turn yourselves from all your," &c.
2. "Cast away from you all your transgressions."
3. "Make you a new heart and a new spirit."
4. "Turn yourselves."

III. The reasons hereof, which are three.

1. Is, from the benefit of so doing; "so iniquity shall not be your ruin," ver. 30; ye shall live, ver. 32.

2. Is, from the danger, if they do it not; ver. 31, "Why will ye die?"

3. Is, from the disposition of the Lord; he hath no pleasure in the death of a sinner.

Ver. 30. "Therefore I will judge you, O house of Israel, every one according to his ways." You have charged my ways not to be equal, that I have wronged you, and herein you have condemned me, and justified yourselves; but I find mine own ways equal and straight, your ways unequal and crooked. "Therefore I will judge you," even "every one according to his ways;" I will recompense upon you your deserts, and make you experimentally to see and say, that my ways are equal, that you suffer for your own sins, and not the sins of others. The Hebrew is, Therefore every one according to his ways I will judge you; that is, I will so judge you, as I will judge every one of you, not in general, but man by man. Of judging men according to their ways hath formerly been spoken, chap. vii. 3, 8, 27; only take this, That whatever thoughts men have of God's ways and their own, the Lord will judge righteously, and make it appear to the world, and to the consciences of those that misjudged him, that his ways are equal, and himself just in his proceedings with them, and in the government of the world; he will stop the mouth of iniquity itself, and overcome in judgment.

"Repent, and turn yourselves." Of these words was spoken, chap. xiv. 6, where the same words are, "Repent, and turn yourselves."

"Yourselves" is not in the original; some, instead thereof, have, others; Repent, and turn others. So the word *hashivu* is, make to convert, whether themselves or others. When men are once returned from their wicked ways, they will labour to bring others out of them; they will use what means they can to make others partake of their grace and mercy, especially those they have been instruments to draw to sin.

This turning themselves is called, in 1 Kings viii. 47, and 2 Chron. vi. 37, bethinking themselves; if they shall return to their heart, or, bring back to their heart. When men go from God and his ways, they are inconsiderate, without heart and understanding; Prov. xi. 12, he is destitute of heart; but when they repent and turn to him, they come to themselves, Luke xv. 17; then they have hearts, then they understand.

Sometimes repenting and turning is given to man, as here, and in sundry other places; sometimes unto God, as Acts iii. 26; 2 Tim. ii. 25; Jer. xxxi. 18: sometimes to the instrument, or medium, God useth, as Acts xxvi. 18; xix. 26; Luke i. 17; which is done to provoke man to use those talents and abilities God hath given him to further his own good, as also to beget a due esteem of, and respect to, those God employs in such a work; and especially, to cause men to look unto God, who works both the will and the deed, Phil. ii. 13.

"So iniquity shall not be your ruin." The Hebrew for ruin is, מכשול which is, a scandal, an offence, that which causeth a man to stumble, to fall. כשיל is an axe, or hatchet, from כשל to weaken and cause to fall. Scandals are axes, hatchets, which do weaken men, and cause them to fall.

Ver. 31. "Cast away from you all your transgressions." You hug and hold them fast, but cast them away. השליכו cast off, cast out, cast away: ἀπορρίψατε, fling away, rid yourselves of them. This casting away of sin doth import more than cessation from sin, or caution of sin; men may cease from sin, take heed of sin, and yet keep much sin in their bosoms. You may mind such expressions as these in the book of God, as, hiding, and, keeping of sin, Job xx. 12, 13; cleaving unto sin, 2 Kings iii. 3; taking hold of sin, 1 Kings ix. 9; holding it fast, Jer. viii. 5; setting up sin in the heart, Ezek. xiv. 3; gathering iniquity to itself, Psal. xli. 6; regarding of it, Psal. lxvi. 18; setting the heart upon it, Hos. iv. 8; or, lifting up the soul unto it, as the Hebrew sounds. Now casting away of transgressions is contrary to all these; he who doth so, lifts not up his heart to, sets it not upon, sin, regards it not, gathers it not, nor sets it up, he holds it not fast, cleaves not to it, keeps it not, nor takes any hold of it, but to throw it out, to cast it away. Answerable unto which is what you have in Heb. xii. 1, lay aside every burden; "all filthiness, and superfluity of naughtiness," James i. 21; and that in 2 Tim. ii. 21, purging a man's self; likewise what you have, Eph. iv. 22, "Put off the old man;" and Matt. vii. 5, "Cast out the beam out of thine own eye." It is to lay aside, purge out, and put off, and cast forth all sin. There are three things implied in casting away sin.

1. A dissolving of that union which is between sin and the soul. Men and their sins are strongly united together; they love to oppress, Hos. xii. 7; they love flagons of wine, chap. iii. 1; and it is hard to divide between the drunkard and his drunkenness, Prov. xxiii. 35; they love pleasures more than God, 2 Tim. iii. 4. You may sooner pluck men from God than from their sins. Christ tells you, that men's lusts are their eyes, hands, feet, Matt. xviii. 8, 9. Paul calls them "members," Col. iii. 5; as members have union with the body, so men's lust and sins have union with them. Now, when sin comes to be cast away, there must be a breach of this union; until that be, there can be no separation of sin from us. Therefore the Lord calls upon men to rend their hearts, Joel ii. 13; to break up their fallow ground, and not to sow among thorns, Jer. iv. 3: there must be a breach and separation between the earth and thorns, before thorns can be cast away.

2. When the union between sin and a man's heart is broken, he loathes and abhors his sins, and himself for them; Ezek. xxxvi. 31, they loathed themselves for their iniquities; much more, then, did they loathe their iniquities: Psal. cxix. 163, "I hate and abhor lying:" he saw matter of detestation and abhorrency in it.

3. Casting out, and away, that which is loathed and detested. Isa. xxx. 21, 22, when their ears heard the word, "this is the way, walk ye in it," and so were taken off from false ways, then they should cast away the coverings and ornaments of their idols; they should look upon them as loathsome things, and cast them away.

Men cast away things that are either, (1.) Unprofitable and useless; (2.) Hurtful and dangerous; (3.) Loathsome and grievous. Sin is all these.

(1.) It is unprofitable and useless: see Jer. xii. 13; xvi. 19; Prov. v. 10; x. 2. Wickedness hath its treasures, but they are unprofitable; Eph. v. 11, works of darkness are unfruitful: the forbidden tree yields no good fruit; Rom. vi. 21, "What fruit had ye then in those things whereof ye are now ashamed." It is not of God, it hath no good in it, Rom. vii. 18.

(2.) Hurtful and dangerous. Idolatry hurts, Jer. vii. 6; murder hurts, Gen. iv. 23; wantonness and uncleanness wounds, Prov. vii. 26; covetousness hurts, Eccles. v. 13; 1 Tim. vi. 9, 10, it pierces men through, it drowns them in destruction and perdition; lying, fearfulness, unbelief, hurt, Rev. xxi. 8. Nothing harms like unto sin, no poison, no weapon can pain, torment the body, as sin doth the conscience; "A wounded spirit who can bear?" Prov. xviii. 14; it is "more bitter than death," Eccles. vii. 26.

(3.) It is loathsome and grievous. It is likened to mire and dirt, Isa. lvii. 20; to vomit, 2 Pet. ii. 22; is filth, and filthiness, Isa. iv. 4; 2 Cor. vii. 1; it is corruption, pollution, 2 Pet. i. 4; ii. 20; it is abomination, Prov. xv. 26; it is rebellion, and grievous revolting, Prov. xvii. 11; Jer. vi. 28; it is a detestable thing, Ezek. xi. 21. Men's righteousnesses are as filthy rags, Isa. lxiv. 6. What, then, are their sins? they are the quintessence of filthiness, exceeding filthinesses.

"Make you a new heart and a new spirit." These words are made use of by the remonstrants to prove, that the Lord, in conversion of a sinner, doth not use such efficacy of grace as man cannot resist; as also to show, that men not converted have internal grace absolutely sufficient for conversion, or equal to that by which others are converted. Bellarmine brings these words to prove the freedom of will in man. Ames. in Anti. Synodal. de grat. c. 2. lib. 6. c. 10. de gratia et libero Arb.

These words do not favour or countenance such opinions, so far as is thought, if rightly understood. It is a rule in theology, that active verbs are given to those things which do not properly, and by immediate influx, do that which the verbs do signify. And this is fre- Glassius in Philologia, l. 3. p. 290.

quent in the business of man's salvation, where that is attributed to man which is peculiar to God; and he instanceth in this place, "Make you a new heart and a new spirit." This, saith he, is the work of God alone, who by his saving word creates "a new heart and a new spirit" in men; and in other scriptures you shall find it given to the Lord: Psal. li. 10; Jer. xxxi. 33; xxxii. 39; Ezek. xxxvi. 26; xi. 19, where was spoken of "a new spirit," and somewhat about man's liberty and power. God said to Moses, Exod. xiv. 16, "Lift up thy rod, stretch out thine hand over the sea, and divide it:" had Moses power to divide the sea? no, but because there was a certain concurrence of Moses using the rod according to direction, therefore it is attributed to Moses, which was the work of God alone: ver. 21, it is given to God, for when Moses stretched out his hand, it is said, "The Lord caused the sea to go back." So making "a new heart and a new spirit," is given to man, because of that concurrence of man in using the means appointed of the Lord; but when the new heart and spirit are wrought, they are the work of the Lord, as appears, Phil. ii. 13; Eph. ii. 10. Thus we are to understand all those places which put so much upon a man, as to believe, I John iii. 2; to repent, Acts ii. 38; to put off the old man, to be renewed in the spirit of your minds, to put on the new man, Eph. iv. 22—24; to cleanse ourselves from all pollution of flesh and spirit, 2 Cor. vii. 1; to lay hold upon eternal life, 1 Tim. vi. 12; to be filled with the Spirit, Eph. v. 18. In these, and the like places, is nothing given to the power of man, if rightly understood; but man is commanded to apply himself to those means by which God works faith, repentance, holiness, salvation, and conveys the Spirit.

These words, then, do not hinder but that the Lord may, and doth, work efficaciously in the conversion of a sinner. God bids men use means, wait upon him, and he will work powerfully in them by his grace and Spirit; and that the Lord doth work powerfully, see Eph. i. 19; Col. ii. 12, 13; Deut. xxx. 6; John vi. 37.

For man's having internal sufficient grace to conversion, it is strange divinity; it argues a man is converted, and yet unconverted. If a man have grace, he is converted; but you must know that Arminians make reason, understanding, to be grace, and the first grace; but, John iii. 6, "That which is born of the flesh is flesh." And take the excellency of the flesh, even the wisdom of it; Rom. viii. 7, it is "enmity to God; it is not subject to the law of God, neither can be." If men have power and grace sufficient to convert themselves, to make them new hearts and new spirits, why should it be as impossible for men accustomed to do evil to do good, as for an Egyptian to change his skin, or a leopard his spots? Jer. xiii. 23; why is it not easy? what is hard to him who hath power and will? why cannot he be subject to the law of God? why cannot he add a cubit to his stature? Luke xii. 25: surely reason is not grace. The Athenians, who had reason, mocked at Christ and the resurrection, Acts xvii. 18, 32, which if gracious, they would not have done. All men have reason, but all have not grace. "Not many wise men after the flesh are called" or chosen, 1 Cor. i. 26. Had men power in themselves they would boast; that men may not boast, it is of God, ver. 29, 30; it is of grace, not of ourselves, our strength, reason, abilities, Eph. ii. 8, 9.

The ground that papists, Arminians, and others, go upon, is, that commands suppose power in men to do what is commanded. This ground is too weak to build their structure upon. For what man, ever since Adam's fall, had power to keep the law exactly? yet the law consists of commands. Had men been able to have done it, the law would have saved them: Rom. viii. 3, "What the law could not do, in that it was weak through the flesh, God sending," &c.; Gal. iii. 21, "If there had been a law given which could have given life, verily righteousness should have been by the law." Why could not the law give life? because man had not power, strength, to keep it; God may command that which men have not power to do,

1. To break the strength of man's confidence. Men, through apprehension of their abilities, stand much upon doing, and think they can perform much: "What shall I do to be saved?" God may command that now which is beyond man's strength, that so he may know his own weakness.

2. To cause us to sue to him for help to do what is commanded. When Nebuchadnezzar commanded the wise men to tell him his dream, which was impossible, Daniel sought to God for the discovery of the thing, and obtained it: see Dan. ii. 17—19. God commands what we cannot do, that we may know what to ask. If any thing be hard, impossible, let us not stick in ourselves, but run to God.

3. The Lord may do it, because he can give what he commands. Ezek. xi. 4, God bids Ezekiel prophesy; he could not do it unless God gave him the spirit of prophecy; therefore in the next verse it is said, "The Spirit of the Lord fell upon him." Christ saith to Lazarus, "Come forth," John xi. 43; he had no power to do it but he who commanded, accompanied his word with power; and, John v. 25, "The hour is coming, and now is, that the dead shall hear the voice of the Son of God; and they that hear shall live."

The meaning then of these words, "Make you a new heart and a new spirit," is, be not negligent and wanting to yourselves, but use the means appointed of God, give diligence to obtain a change of your hearts and spirits, to get repentance, and bring forth fruit worthy thereof.

"For why will ye die?" Hebrew is, and why will ye die? In the former, these, and the subsequent words, God speaks after the manner of men, as a father doth to his untoward children, or as a minister to a perishing people.

Ver. 32. "For I have no pleasure in the death of him that dieth." Of these words was spoken, ver. 23. I shall give you some few observations, and so end this chapter.

Obs. 1. That repentance is profitable to man, and pleasing to God. "Repent and turn, so iniquity shall not be your ruin: why will ye die?" I have no pleasure in your death, but I have pleasure in your repentance and life. When man hath undone himself, repentance is his setting up again; it is safe landing after shipwreck. The prodigal, repenting and turning, did advantage himself, and please his father, Luke xv. 18—21. "Except ye repent ye shall all perish," saith Christ, Luke xiii. 3, 5: repentance preserves from destruction, and hath that good in it. See Acts ii. 38; iii. 19; Rev. ii. 5, 16; 2 Cor. vii. 9, 10; Acts xi. 18. And that it greatly pleases God, the parable of the lost sheep showeth; Luke xv. 7, there is more joy in heaven for the repentance of one sinner, than for the righteousness of ninety-nine just persons. Sacrifices under the law were pleasing to God; a repentant broken heart is instead of all sacrifices, Psal. li. 17; God will not, he cannot, despise it; he will look to it, Isa. lxvi. 2; he will dwell in it, Isa. lvii. 15.

Obs. 2. Sin is of a ruining nature. "So iniquity shall not be your ruin." Sin, in itself, is destructive. What is said of time, it is *edax rerum*, a consumer of all things, is verified of sin; nay, more than time could do, sin hath done. Time could never have ruined angels; sin did it, sin threw them out of heaven, Adam out of paradise: sin ruined the old world, Gen. vi. 5, 7; it ruined Sodom and Gomorrah, Gen. xix. 13; the cry of their sins was great, and therefore the angels destroyed it. Wars are ruining and desolating things, so is the plague, and famine; but sin brings them all, Ezek. xiv. 13; xvii. 19; and is more ruinating than they all. Sin ruins the name, Prov. vi. 33; it ruins the conscience, and comforts of it, Psal. xxxii. 3; li. 8; it ruins the soul, 1 Pet. ii. 11; 1 Tim. v. 6. These things, the name, conscience, comforts, soul; sword, famine, plague, cannot reach; they may, and do, oft ruin our outward comforts, our flesh, our lives, but further they go not: sin ruins both these and the other. Sin is wonderfully malignant, and proves destructive to them that deal with it. Gideon's ephod was a snare to him and to his house, it ruined him and his, Judg. viii. 27. It was their sin which laid waste the commonwealth of Israel, which brought the slaughtering angels, Ezek. ix. and kindled the fire in the temple and city, and laid all waste.

Obs. 3. That man who in truth comes unto God, must come off from all sin, he must not stick in any. " Repent, and turn from all your transgressions:" cast away all your transgressions; you must not like any, but loathe all, not keep any, but cast out all: if you cast out a thousand, and retain but one, it is no sound coming to God, no true repentance, or turning. Herod turned from many evils, but would not turn from his Herodias, Mark vi. 18—20, and all his turning was nothing. Judas, his life was fair as the other apostles, no visible sin appeared, only he had a covetous heart within; and because that golden devil was not cast out, he was cast into hell; his apostleship, preaching, working of miracles, hearing of Christ, conversing with him, did him no good. Let men go as far as they will in repentance, turning from, and casting off of sin, if it be not from all, it is from none; for if any one sin be kept and lived in, the union between sin and the soul is not dissolved, and so there is no true hatred, no real ejection of sin. If a man did hate sin, and cast it out because it is sin, he would do so by all sin, because there is the same reason for all as for one, and for one as for all. Let us look narrowly to it, that we do not harbour nor spare any sin in our bosoms. Saul spared Agag, and the witch of Endor, whom he should have destroyed, and they were his ruin.

Obs. 4. That for the encouragement of men to use the means, and wait upon God in them, he honours them with the doing of that which is his prerogative and peculiar work. " Make you a new heart and a new spirit, turn yourselves;" these are acts which none but the Lord can do. A new heart, a new spirit, is the work of divine grace. Because there is some effort of man, therefore he is said to do that which the power of divine grace principally effects, *Sanct. in locum.* This is very fair for a Jesuit; but the apostle goeth further, Phil. ii. 13, the will and the deed are of the Lord. Let us be encouraged, therefore, to be diligent in the use of all means, and that constantly. There may be " a new heart and a new spirit" given in from God, his mighty power put forth to work these, and yet be attributed to us, that we have made ourselves new hearts and new spirits.

Obs. 5. The Lord would not have men run on in sinful courses, and die, but turn, and live; he hath not pleasure in their perishing, but in their living. "Why will ye die?" &c. In this question secretly is locked up an answer to all they could object; as,

(1.) We bear the iniquity of our fathers, who sinned greatly, and therefore we must die. No, you shall not die upon that account; ver. 20, " The son shall not bear the iniquity of the father."

(2.) Our sins are great and grievous. What then? " Why will ye die?" " Come, let us reason together: though your sins be as scarlet, they shall be as white as snow; though they be red like crimson, they shall be as wool."

(3.) We have nothing to bring if we come to thee. What then? " Why will ye die?" If you have no money, yet I have mercy, and mercy enough; a sea of mercy, a heaven of mercy, a world of mercy: " Come, buy without money," Isa. lv. 1; I am a God of mercy, delight to show mercy.

(4.) But thou biddest us repent, turn, cast away all our sins, make us new hearts, &c.; we cannot do these things. What then? If you will but look unto me, I can give you what is commanded, it is my way of dealing with sinners; I can give you repentance, power to cast out all your sins; I can give you a new heart, a new spirit; " why will?" &c. Isa. xlv. 22, "Look unto me, and be ye saved, all the ends of the earth."

(5.) Thou hast forsaken us, and left us to our own lusts. But now I sue unto you, call upon you, tender life unto you, hold out my hand, and am desirous to take you in; " why will ye die, O house of Israel?"

(6.) Thou hast threatened our destruction by the prophets, and thy threats must take place; thou wilt make good thy word, take pleasure in fulfilling it, and destroying us. What if my threats be out? so they were against Nineveh; they repented of their sins, I repented of my threats: I do not take pleasure in executing of judgments, nor in your death, and " why will ye die?"

(7.) We are Jews, have apostatized from our profession, from what the prophets taught us; we have lived long in such a way, it is too late now to think of turning. No, not so; turn and live, yet there is mercy.

CHAPTER XIX.

Ver. 1—9. *Moreover take thou up a lamentation for the princes of Israel, and say, What is thy mother? A lioness: she lay down among lions, she nourished her whelps among young lions. And she brought up one of her whelps: it became a young lion, and it learned to catch the prey; it devoured men. The nations also heard of him; he was taken in their pit, and they brought him with chains unto the land of Egypt. Now when she saw that she had waited, and her hope was lost, then she took another of her whelps, and made him a young lion. And he went up and down among the lions, he became a young lion, and learned to catch the prey, and devoured men. And he knew their desolate palaces, and he laid waste their cities; and the land was desolate, and the fulness thereof, by the noise of his roaring. Then the nations set against him on every side from the provinces, and spread their net over him: he was taken in their pit. And they put him in ward in chains, and brought him to the king of Babylon: they brought him into holds, that his voice should no more be heard upon the mountains of Israel.*

THIS chapter is a chapter of lamentation,

I. For the princes of Israel.

II. For Jerusalem, or the kingdom of Judah.

The lamentation for the princes of Israel is set out under the parable, or similitude, of a lion's whelps, from ver. 1 to ver. 10. The lamentation for Jerusalem is, from ver. 10 to the end of the chapter, held out under the resemblance of a vine.

As for the first part, the lamentation for the princes of Israel, we may consider therein,

1. The lamentation, commanded in ver. 1.

2. The mother of the whelps, or the lioness, and what she did, ver. 2, 3.

3. The advance of the whelps, their carriage, ruin, and punishment, in the 3d, 4th, and rest of the verses.

Ver. 1. "Take thou up a lamentation." The Lord here speaks to the prophet to put himself into a mourning posture, and to bewail the conditions of the kings of Israel. The word for lamentation is קִינָה the same that Jeremiah useth in the title of his book called The Lamentations, of which was spoken chap. ii. 10.

"The princes of Israel," These were Jehoahaz, Jehoiakim, Jehoiachin, and Zedekiah, who were kings of Judah, as appears, 2 Kings xxiii. 31, 34; xxiv. 8, 18. They are called the princes of Israel, because that is a comprehensive term, and included Judah in it, which these were kings of, and not of Samaria, for the ten tribes and their kings were captivated before.

Ver. 2. "What is thy mother?" Because it is not said, What is your mother? some think he means the prophet's mother; but it is said "thy mother," in reference to each prince. Jehoahaz, "what is thy mother?" Jehoiakim, "what is thy mother?" and so of Jehoiachin and Zedekiah. By "mother" here is meant Jerusalem, and the kingdom of Judah. Great cities and kingdoms are in a metaphorical sense called mothers, they bring forth kings, they elect, crown, and set them up to rule.

"A lioness." Jerusalem is likened unto a lioness in several respects.

1. A lion or lioness is a noble and kingly creature, and so was Jerusalem a noble and royal city. The ensign of the tribe of Judah was a lion. Old Jacob, Gen. xlix. 9, said, "Judah is a lion's whelp:" that tribe was the royal tribe, and the chief city in it was Jerusalem.

2. A lioness is strong: Judg. xiv. 18, "What is stronger than a lion?" see Prov. xxx. 30. Jerusalem was a strong city, Psal. xxxi. 21; cxxv. 2.

3. A lioness is venturous and bold, Prov. xxviii. 1; 2 Sam. xvii. 10; so Jerusalem was a bold, daring city; the people of it were impudent and provoking, Isa. iii. 8; lxv. 3; Ezek. iii. 7, provoked him to his face.

4. The lioness is cruel and bloody, Psal. vii. 2; Isa. xxxviii. 13; so Jerusalem was an oppressing city, Zeph. iii. 1, 3; a bloody city, Ezek. xxiv. 6.

5. Libidinous, mingles with the leopard and hyæna; so Jerusalem mingled herself with other nations, Ezek. xvi. 26, 28. She was not humane, but lionish in her manners; no piety, justice, humanity were in her; she was brutish.

"She lay down among lions." By lions here, are meant the nations, or kings of the nations, round about, who were profane, barbarous, and cruel; and Jerusalem was like unto them; and therefore it is said to lie down among lions, as one lion doth among others without fear. The gentiles made no conscience of sin, but did whatever they liked or lusted after; and Jerusalem had cast off the worship and ways of God, following their own wills and lusts.

"She nourished her whelps." Hebrew is, she multiplied whelps; in a little time she had many princes, which were to succeed in the kingdom. These whelps were Jehoahaz, Jehoiakim, Jehoiachin, and Zedekiah, whom he calls "whelps,"

1. Because they were young when they began to reign, 2 Kings xxiii. 31, 36; xxiv. 8, 18. One was but eighteen, another twenty-one, a third twenty-three, and the eldest was but twenty-five when he came to the throne.

2. Because they were little, in comparison of former kings. David and Solomon were great lions, in respect of them; the kingdom then flourished, but now it was declining; they reigned long, these but a little while.

3. "Whelps," because of their disposition and propensity to do like lions and lionesses: there is the same nature in the whelps as is in the dams; if the lion be fierce, cruel, the whelps will be so.

"Among young lions." Hebrew, in the midst of young lions. כְּפִיר is a young lion that begins to prey. Whether we take them for the princes of the nations, or the princes and nobles of Jerusalem, (for there were princes who were not of the royal family, 2 Kings xxiv. 12; 2 Chron. xxiv. 17,) they were brought up after their manners and fashions.

Ver. 3. "And she brought up one of her whelps." The Hebrew is, she made one of her whelps to come up; that is, to come up into the throne, and to be king. This was Jehoahaz, whom after the death of Josiah, the people took and made king in his father's stead in Jerusalem, 2 Chron. xxxvi. 1; 2 Kings xxiii. 30; Jerusalem, and the people of the land, joined together to make him king: Jehoahaz was the whelp of this lioness.

"It became a young lion." Being made king, he reigned like a lion, yea, a young lion. He was tyrannical, and tyrants are compared to lions, and you may see a true picture of them in the lion.

1. Their faces are stern, and voices terrible. Amos iii. 8, "The lion hath roared; who will not fear?" It is said of the Gadite soldiers, they had faces like the faces of lions, 1 Chron. xii. 8, terrible. Such are tyrants, their countenances and voices trouble and disturb much. When they send out their edicts, proclamations, commands, which are their voices, and have the effigies of their grim countenances within them, how do they shake cities, kingdoms, nations! When Ahasuerus' decree was given forth for the destruction of the Jews, it is said, "the city Shushan was perplexed," Esth. iii. 15; so all the provinces where the sound of it was. Tyrants roar like lions, they strike terror into all: Prov. xix. 12, "The king's wrath," &c.; xx. 2, "The fear of a king is as the roaring of a lion."

2. As they are roaring, so ravening. They are greedy of their prey; Psal. xvii. 12, "Like as a lion that is greedy of his prey." See Psal. xxii. 13; Lam. iii. 10. Psal. civ. 21, they roar after their prey, and are hardly satisfied; Job xxxviii. 39, "Wilt thou fill the appetite of the young lions?" So wicked rulers and tyrannical princes are ravenous and greedy of the prey. What a strong appetite had Ahab to Naboth's vineyard! he was sick, and refuses to eat, if he have not that morsel to feed upon, 1 Kings xxi. 2, 4. When the Jews would have a king, the Lord told them what a ravenous creature he would be, 1 Sam. viii. 11—17. It is said of Saul, their first king, that he did "fly upon the spoil," chap. xv. 19. What a vast appetite had the king of Babylon, who "enlarged his desire as hell and death, and could not be satisfied, but gathered unto him all nations, and heaped unto him all people," Hab. ii. 5. That princes are greedy of

their prey, see Zeph. iii. 3; Ezek. xxii. 27; Micah iii. 11. Caligula, his impositions, tributes, and new devised exactions, were innumerable, *Herb.* 129.

3. They are vigilant and subtle, lying in wait to get their prey. They sleep little, and when they sleep it is with open eyes; they mind their prey much, and are cunning to catch it. Psal. xvii. 12, "The young lion lurks in secret places;" he hides himself, and when the prey comes near, he suddenly surprises the same. Our prophet saith here of the young whelp, "it learned to catch the prey," it learned the cunning of the old lions.

Basil saith, they use to lie down flat upon their bellies, to counterfeit sleep, not to stir, and to do as cats when they catch birds. Another cunning device the lions have is, when the prey is too swift for them, and so likely to save itself by flight, they roar grievously, which so affrightens the creatures fleeing from them, that their spirits faint, are forced to stand still, and become a prey: he also hides his claws, and covers his steps with dust by his tail, that he may not be discovered.

So tyrannical princes are watchful and cunning to catch their prey. Saul had many stratagems and devices to catch David. What a cunning plot had Jezebel to catch Naboth! The policies of tyrants are infinite to catch the people, and make a prey of them.

4. They are proud and stately. They go alone, they eat not with the lionesses, much less with other creatures; they will not stoop to, or turn away for any, Prov. xxx. 30; they do what they list: such are tyrants. You may see the pride and arrogancy of Nebuchadnezzar, Dan. iv. 30. The prince of Tyre said he was a god, and sat "in the seat of God," Ezek. xxviii. 2. "Who is the Lord, that I should obey his voice?" said Pharaoh, Exod. v. 2.

Alexander would be accounted and worshipped as the son of Jupiter Ammon; Caligula, Domitian, Heliogabalus, would be worshipped as gods.

5. They are cruel, bloody, devouring creatures. Nahum ii. 12, "The lion did tear in pieces, and strangled for his lionesses." They have terrible claws, sharp teeth, and are mighty to crush and break all the bones. The devil is called a devouring lion, 1 Pet. v. 8, because he destroys as lions do: 2 Kings xvii. 26, the lions slew them. Such are tyrannical princes: Prov. xxvii. 15, "As a roaring lion, and a ranging bear; so is a wicked ruler over the poor people." Like as lions and bears in a forest do catch, crush, and devour the sheep, lambs, kids, conies, and whatever they find preyable, so wicked rulers deal with the people: Mic. iii. 1—3, the princes of Israel plucked off the skin and flesh of God's people from their bones, brake and chopped them in pieces as for the pot: when they kill men, they think it lawful, not sinful. Our prophet tells you, that this lion, Jehoahaz, devoured men, he "learned to catch the prey, and devoured men."

History tells us of cannibals, men-eaters; such are tyrannical governors, they feed upon men. Athaliah devoured all the royal seed at a meal, 2 Chron. xxii. Jezebel ate up Naboth at a fast, 1 Kings xxi. What a multitude of children did Herod devour at once in Bethlehem! Matt. ii. 16. What tearing, flesh-eating, bone-breaking was there, when that roaring cruel lion Manasseh filled Jerusalem with innocent blood! 2 Kings xxi. 16. What lions were in the time of the ten persecutions! *Christiani ad leones*, The christians to the lions.

6. It is dangerous to meddle with lions: Numb. xxiv. 9, "He lay down as a lion, and as a great lion: who shall stir him up?" Lions, if offended and provoked, are revengeful. Ælian tells of a bear that came into a lion's den, and bit the whelps she found there. The lion returning, the bear, to shift for herself, got up into a high tree; the lioness watched at the foot of the tree: the lion ranged abroad in the woods, and meets with a man that had an axe, and used to fell trees; this man the lion brings to the den, showed him the wounded whelps, directs him to the tree where the bear was, which he cut down: the bear, being torn in pieces, the man was safely dismissed. In the hunting or taking of lions, the lion observes who wounds him, and on him, if possible, he will be revenged. Such are tyrannical men: it is ill meddling with them; if they be roused, or any of theirs wronged a little, they will remember and revenge.

Ver. 4. "The nations also heard of him." After the death of Josiah by Pharaoh-necho, king of Egypt, Jehoahaz was by the Jews set up king; but the Egyptians thought themselves wronged, that they had no hand in disposing of that kingdom, and placing a king over it; which it is probable the Jews apprehended, in that they passed by Eliakim, who was elder, and set up Jehoahaz, who was younger; as is evident, if you compare 2 Kings xxiii. 31, with ver. 36. They judged this doubtless of a more warlike and lionlike spirit, and so fitter to encounter the Egyptians, if they should assault them; which it is conceived they did, for he reigned but three months and then was taken.

"He was taken in their pit." The word for pit is, *shachath*, which signifies, a net, or, a pit, and is from שחת to corrupt, or kill, because pits and nets are to take creatures, and so tend to their killing and corruption. One way of taking lions was, to observe their haunts, and in that way they used to dig a round pit, leaving a pillar of earth in the midst of it, upon which they tied a lamb, covering the pit with boughs; the hungry lamb, bleating in the evening, invites the lion to supper, who hastening thereunto, falls into the pit, and so is taken. Ezekiel alluding hereunto, saith, Jehoahaz was taken in their pit. Some think he was taken by a wile; that Pharaoh sent for him, under pretence of friendship and kindness, and then when he had him in his power, kept him. Others, that there was a bloody battle between Jehoahaz and Pharaoh, in which though he was taken, yet not without great loss to the Egyptians; therefore the Vulgate renders these words, *Non absque vulneribus sui ceperunt eum*, They took him, but not without wounds.

"They brought him with chains," &c. The Hebrew is, בחחים with hooks. Chains are hooky things linked together; the word "chains" here, in 2 Kings xxiii. 33, is "bands:" Pharaoh-necho put him in bands; he was carried bound to Egypt.

Obs. 1. It is matter to be lamented, when princes are wicked, tyrannical, and ruin themselves and the people they are set over. "Take thou up a lamentation for the princes of Israel;" so Ezek. xxxii. 2, "Take up a lamentation for Pharaoh king of Egypt, and say unto him, Thou art like a young lion of the nations, and thou art as a whale in the seas," &c. When princes, rulers, are roaring and ravening lions, when they are cunning and cruel, and take such courses as tend to the ruin of themselves and others, it is a great and just ground for lamentation. Solomon saith, there is a time to mourn, Eccl. iii. 4; and if any be a fit time to mourn, it is when it goes ill with the church of God, with the state, when rulers are lions, and do like lions. We mourn when some personal or family evil is upon us, but public evils are neglected. Evil rulers, evil princes, evil magistrates are public evils, like so many lions and wild beasts. Where such are, there is a house of mourning, and let the living lay it to heart. I fear we have lions among us, for whom we may justly take up a lamentation.

Obs. 2. That those princes who oppress their people and ruin their kingdoms, are ungrateful and unnatural, for their people and kingdoms are their mothers. "What is thy mother?" Jerusalem, Judea is thy mother. It is the people chooses them, and so brings them forth, sets them up: 2 Kings xxiii. 30, "The people of the land took Jehoahaz the son of Josiah, and anointed him, and made him king in his father's stead." How wickedly did he, therefore, to become a lion to this people, who advanced him! If he were unnatural who ripped up the bowels of his own mother, so likewise is he that rips and rends the bowels of that kingdom which begat him. Princes should entreat them well who have given them their princely being; they have their milk and maintenance from them, and it is height of ingratitude to wrong or ruin them.

Obs. 3. Such as the people are, usually such are the rulers, the princes. If the mother be a lioness, the whelps will be lions; if the lioness be audacious, bloody, libidinous, idolatrous, the lions will be such. Jerusalem was very wicked, and her princes likewise; the princes were like the people. Hos. viii. 4, "They have set up kings, but not by me:" the people set up Jehoahaz, and he was a lion; he did wickedly, 2 Kings xxiii. 32.

Obs. 4. Great is the efficacy of evil example, it prevails more than good example. Jehoahaz had a godly parent, Josiah by name, of whom it is said that there was no king like him before or after him, that turned to the Lord with all his soul, heart, and might, according to all the law of Moses, 2 Kings xxiii. 25. Not the good education nor good example he had from and by his father, did sufficiently antidote him against the poison and power of evil example; he was brought up among lions, and learned of them to catch the prey: they were wicked, covetous, proud, fierce, subtle, cruel, revengeful, and their manners he took up, conformed unto. Wickedness is easily learned; men are so apt to it, that they need no rods to put them on. Parents cannot propagate piety; if that could have been, Josiah would have had sons as eminent for holiness as they were for impiety. Gracious parents have graceless children; let none be troubled thereat as a thing strange, it was so with Josiah. If you be godly, and would have your children so, take heed of being ill examples yourselves, or letting them be amongst those who give ill example; for tinder is not apter to take fire, wax the impression of the seal, paper the ink, than youth is to receive the impressions of wickedness.

Obs. 5. After good princes and great reformers, Divine Providence orders it so, that wretched, wicked kings, enemies to all good, are set up. Josiah was a most godly king, and more thoroughly reforming than ever Judah had any before; yet after him comes a lion, a wicked Jehoahaz. When people are unthankful for good princes and rulers, when they murmur against reformation, have a secret enmity, open bitterness, against godliness, and those who are godly, it is just with God to set lions over them, to be terrible unto them, to eat up their estates and them.

Obs. 6. When wicked men come to places of eminency, they vent their corruptions which lay hid before, they make progress in wickedness, nothing restrains them. When this whelp, Jehoahaz, came to the throne, he became a young lion, a lion rampant, he could catch the prey, and devour men. We oft think that the whelps of great ones are well nurtured, well educated, very hopeful, will prove admirable instruments of God's glory and public good; but we deceive ourselves; when they come to public and high places, their lionish natures do appear, and they grow worse and worse; they perfect wickedness, nothing prevails to keep them in, but they must play the lions, flay the skins, suck the blood, eat the flesh, and crack the bones. There was as great hope of Josiah's sons, as ever of any, yet you see how they proved. Nero at first for five years carried himself well, like a lamb; but he was a lion, and his lionish disposition showed itself to the full. You, who are godly, and have hopeful issue, promise not too much unto yourselves of them; great expectations disappointed cause great vexations.

Obs. 7. That princes pervert the end for which they were ordained of God, and set up by men. God appointed not magistrates, be they princes or others, to lurk for the prey, to devour men, but to preserve men. They should be shepherds, not lions; nursing fathers, not cannibals; they should govern them according to divine rule, Deut. xvii. 18—20, not after prerogative, a devouring beast, which eats up men's estates, honours, lives; they should do justice, not obstruct or pervert it. But where are those princes that answer the end of their institution, that lurk not for prey, that devour not men? In Micah's days, the heads of the house of Jacob, and the princes of the house of Israel, abhorred judgment, and perverted all equity; they built up Zion with blood, and Jerusalem with iniquity: and for their sins and sakes was Zion ploughed as a field, and Jerusalem made heaps. Take heed, you who are governors of families, that you pervert not that institution; be not bitter to your wives, beat not servants for your fantasies, oppress not any who are under you, Ecclus. iv. 30.

Obs. 8. The evil doings of princes fly abroad; if they play the lions, roar, raven, tear, oppress, the nation will hear of it. When Jehoahaz became a lion, caught the prey, devoured men, "the nations also heard of him;" not only his own nation knew it, but the nations round about. Princes, great persons, stand high, their voices are heard and actions seen far: let them whisper in secret, plot mischief in their closets, out they come; cabinet-letters, counsels, designs, treasons, come abroad and spread far. Their projects, how cryptically soever carried, are observed, divulged, and fill the nations with the noise thereof. Princes generally are so wicked, that their evil report is widely spread; chronicles and nations are filled with the reports thereof; if they will do infamous things, they cannot be concealed.

Obs. 9. When princes prove lions, God stirs up some to hunt and take those lions. The nations, hearing that Jehoahaz caught the prey and devoured men, they bethought and bestirred themselves, digged a pit, hunted this lion into it, and took him. When Zimri had gotten the crown, he did rend and tear like a lion; but presently God stirred the people to set up Omri to be king, who hunted that lion into a fiery pit, 1 Kings xvi. Saul played the lion in his reign, and at last he was hunted, slain, and taken by the Philistines, 1 Sam. xxxi. Jehoram became a young lion, preyed upon his brethren, devoured them, 2 Chron. xxi. 4; and the Lord stirred up the spirit of the Philistines and Arabians against him, who came and spoiled him and his, ver. 16, 17. Manasseh was a ramping and roaring lion, he brake the bones of many, and sucked much blood, and he was taken in the pit of the Assyrians, 2 Chron. xxxiii.

When the rulers and potentates of the earth oppress and tyrannize over the people, God, in his wise providence, sets some to work to catch and crush them, Amos iii. 10, 11; one way or other their strength is brought down, and they suffer for their oppressions, and are cut off by violent and untimely deaths. Tiberius was poisoned or smothered by his own nephew; Caligula slain by his own guard; Vitrellius was overthrown in battle, taken prisoner, and drawn with a halter about his neck along the streets, half naked, and after many outrages done unto him, he was killed and cast into Tiber. *Fitzherbert.* Leander, tyrant of Cyrena, was taken alive, and being sewed into a leathern bag, was cast into the sea. Thirty tyrants were slain in one day at Athens by Theramenes, Thrasibulus, and Archippus, who did it with seventy men.

Obs. 10. Princes who, by covetousness and cruelty, spoil others of their estates and liberties, through the just judgment of God come themselves to be deprived of their estates and liberties. Jehoahaz, he caught the prey, and himself was caught and made a prey; he devoured men, and himself was devoured; he fettered, chained others, and himself was put in chains; he lost his kingdom and liberty; Pharaoh took him, bound him, carried him to Egypt. This was he whom Jeremiah calls Shallum, chap. xxii. 11, 12, and saith he should return no more, but die in his captivity. It was a great evil, a sad judgment, to be taken and carried out of his own land, and to die in a profane land amongst Egyptians; therefore it is said, ver. 10, "Weep sore for him that goeth away; for he shall return no more, nor see his native country." Such judgments do princes bring upon themselves; to satisfy some base and bloody lusts, they hazard all, yea oft do lose their kingdoms, liberties, and lives; whereas they might be happy if they would keep within their bounds, yea, live and die comfortably in their own lands; but when they deal injuriously with others, hook, fetter, and spoil them, God meets with them, Amos i. 2. Those who oppressed the poor, and crushed the needy, God would take them with hooks, and their posterity with fish-hooks; he would pull them out of their estates, power, greatness, as fishes out of the water.

Ver. 5. "Now when she saw that she had waited, and her hope was lost." When Jerusalem, the lioness, had expected the return of Jehoahaz from Egypt, and saw it was in vain, that there was no hope of it. The Hebrew runs thus, And she saw, because she hoped, her hope had perished. The Septuagint, for her hope was lost, her substance perished, or was lost. She thought the prince (and so usually do states) was a strong and substantial foundation to build upon; but she was deceived, and her hope failed her.

"Then she took another of her whelps." What whelp this was is controverted amongst expositors. Some make this whelp to be Zedekiah, but there is least reason for that, because hereby both Jehoiakim and Jehoiachin are passed over, who were both kings before Zedekiah; this whelp, therefore, must be one of them. The protestant expositors do make it to be Jehoiakim, called also Eliachim, and Joachim, and so do some others; but the difficulty is, if meant of them, how that is true which is in ver. 9, "They brought him to the king of Babylon: they brought him into holds, that his voice should no more be heard upon the mountains of Israel;" whereas Jehoiakim came back again, if he were in Babylon, and his voice was heard. If it be meant of Jehoiachin, there is also this great difficulty, how he, reigning but three months, could lay waste their cities, and make the land desolate, as it is, ver. 7; being but eight years of age, as it is 2 Chron. xxxvi. 9; or at most but eighteen, as it is 2 Kings xxiv. 8. To let pass Jehoiachin, and to come to Jehoiakim, whom we may take to be the man represented by the whelp here, the difficulty shall be answered when we come to ver. 9.

"She took another of her whelps, and made him a young lion." That is, she set him up to be king. But this seems cross to what you have, 2 Chron. xxxvi. 4; 2 Kings xxiii. 34, where it is said, that Pharaoh "king of Egypt made Eliakim king over Judah and Jerusalem, and turned his name to Jehoiakim." If Pharoah, therefore, made him king, how is it said here, that she, viz. Jerusalem, made him "a young lion," that is, exalted him to kingly dignity? The answer is, that Pharaoh did it not by force, but by the joint consent of the people: Jerusalem's concurrence was in this work; the prophet saith, she "made him a young lion." You may find it frequent in the historical books, that the people did elect and set up their kings. 2 Chron. xxxvi. 1, the people made Jehoahaz king; 1 Kings xxi. 24, the people made Josiah king; they made Omri king, 1 Kings xvi. 16; they made Jeroboam king, 1 Kings xii. 20; they made David king, 1 Chron. xii. 38; they made Saul king, 1 Sam. xi. 15; they made Jephthah head, Judg. xi. 11. God himself, when he commended a king unto them, would have their consent and concurrence in it, Deut. xvii. 14, 15. There is an essential and fundamental right in the people to choose and set up them who are to rule over them; therefore they are called ἀνθρωπίνη κτίσις, 1 Pet. ii. 13, the ordinance of a man, or a human creation.

Ver. 6. "He went up and down among the lions." Being advanced to princely state, here his carriage is set out: he conversed with lions, that is, with wicked men who had lionish dispositions, who were stern, covetous, crafty, and cruel; the king of Egypt, the king of Babylon, the princes about him in the bordering countries; they were lions, and he went up and down amongst them, their counsels he took, their manners, fashions, customs he learned, their steps he trod in, &c.

"Became a young lion." That is, had the nature, properties, and qualities of a young lion; of which you heard before.

"Learned to catch the prey." Hebrew is, to prey the prey. The word טרף is that which wild beasts, hunting, do get and feed upon, from טרף to catch and tear with the teeth, and is applied here unto kings, who are metaphorical lions; and whatever they can get, catch, tear and rend from others, that is their prey, that they feed upon. Psal. lxxvi. 4, there is mention of "mountains of prey," which are the kingdoms of this world. They are like mountains, where wild beasts are, which prey upon what is thereon, or thereabouts; and so kingdoms have wild beasts in them, which prey upon those who are in their kingdoms.

"Devoured men." Septuagint, ἀνθρώπους ἔφαγε, eat men. This young lion fed upon men. The Hebrew is, man, in the singular number, but hath the force of a plural, and so is rendered. This devouring of men was by taking away their estates, liberties, limbs, lives. Jehoiakim was very covetous and very cruel. Jeremiah, chap. xxii. 17, speaking of him, he saith, "Thine eyes and thine heart are not but for thy covetousness, and for to shed innocent blood, and for oppression, and for violence, to do it;" his eyes and heart were set upon nothing else but catching the prey, and devouring of men. 2 Kings xxiii. 35, "He exacted silver and gold of the people of the land;" Pharaoh, that Egyptian lion, commanded him to tax the land: he yields to Pharaoh, taxes and exacts upon the people. It is not improbable that he was perfidious, bloody, and cruel towards the Syrians, Moabites, and Ammonites, who infested him, 2 Kings xxiv. 2, and interpreters say he slew the prophets.

Ver. 7. "And he knew their desolate palaces." Hebrew is, וירע אלמנותיו which Montanus renders, *cognovit viduas ejus*, he knew their widows; the Hebrew, דין אלמנות is so translated, Psal. lxviii. 5, "A father of the fatherless, and a judge of widows, is God:" so it should be; the word is *almanoth*, widows. But in Isa. xiii. 22, it is used for desolate palaces; "And wild beasts of the islands shall cry in their desolate houses." If we take the word for "widows," and so the old translation hath it, the sense is, That Jehoiakim defiled the widows, whose chastity he ought to have preserved; he wronged them greatly, by devouring their husbands and defiling their bodies. Or thus: When their husbands were put to death, and estates unjustly taken away, the widows came petitioning for relief; whereupon he knew them; but was so hard-hearted, as that he was not moved with their tears, cries, requests, or complaints. If we take it for "desolate palaces," as it is here, the interpretation is, That have deprived the palaces of their husbands, their owners and inhabitants, and made them widows; he did confiscate them to his own treasury, he challenged them to be his. Having unjustly devoured the men, he thought he might justly devour their palaces; he knew their palaces, and took possession of them.

"He laid waste their cities." He made their cities to be waste, desolate, or dried up, as the word imports. As the sun dries up ponds, brooks, or some diversion draws away the water, that they are void, empty, so did this king, by his taxes and impositions, draw away their estates, and dry up trading: or, he did those things which caused their cities to be laid waste; he provoked God and men against himself and them, by his tyranny and cruelty; he caused many to fall, many to flee, and forsake their habitation, so that the land was desolate, and the fulness thereof.

"By the noise of his roaring." Hebrew, by the voice of his roaring. שאג is, to roar, as lions do; yea, it is proper to lions, but is metaphorically given to men, as here. The roaring of lions is very terrible: Prov. xix. 12, "The king's wrath is as the roaring of a lion." When the lion roars, it troubles all the beasts of the forest and mountains; and when kings in their wrath roar, and send out their commands, edicts, &c. they trouble and make desolate families, cities, lands.

Ver. 8. "The nations set against him on every side." His wickedness and tyranny was such, as that all the nations were provoked against him, and contributed their help to take this young lion. The original is, the nations gave upon him; they gave their judgments upon him, that he was not fit to range, ramp, and roar any longer. Vulgate reads it, *convenerunt*, they came together, took counsel, resolved to hunt and take this wild beast.

"From the provinces." What provinces these were you may see, 2 Kings xxiv. 2: the Chaldeans, Syrians, Moabites, Ammonites, these all called upon and called out one another, to hunt this lion, and to take him.

"And spread their net over him." Hebrew for net is, רשת which is either from ירש to possess, because a net holds in possession what it catcheth, or from רוש to make poor, because a net deprives of liberty, and oft of life. These hunters prepared a net strong enough to hold this lion, and they spread it out for him.

"He was taken in their pit." Of these words were spoken, ver. 4.

Ver. 9. "And they put him in ward." Hebrew, they put him into safe custody, into some prison; they shut him up, that he might not escape, and be as a lion among the people any more; they put chains upon him, an iron collar, or about his neck a chain, and brought him to the king of Babylon. They did not carry him into Babylon, some think; for, 2 Chron. xxxvi. 6, Nebuchadnezzar king of Babylon came up against him, and bound him in chains or fetters, to carry him to Babylon; but that he did carry him thither, or send him back, having rebelled against him, 2 Kings xxiv. 1, doth not appear, neither is probable. That which makes most for this opinion, is what you have in Jer. xxii. 19, "He shall be buried with the burial of an ass," drawn and cast forth beyond the gates of Jerusalem. These words induce some to believe, that either he went not to Babylon, or, if he did, that he returned, that Jeremiah's prophecy might be made good; and if that were so, how is it true here, "that his voice may be heard no more upon the mountains of Israel?"

To clear this doubt and difficulty, it is most probable that Jehoiakim was carried to Babylon; for that in 2 Chron. xxxvi. 6, of Nebuchadnezzar coming up against him, is to be understood of his forces, rather than his person; and in 2 Kings xxiv. 2, it is said, "bands of the Chaldees," not Nebuchadnezzar himself: our prophet also saith, "they brought him to the king of Babylon." And whereas some affirm he died by the way, (being led in a disgraceful manner, like a wild beast, with an iron collar about his neck, and a chain fastened thereunto,) how suits it with what is recorded, "They brought him to the king of Babylon: they brought him into holds?" That was, saith Piscator, into the city of Babylon, which was full of strong holds; and being there shut up till his death, "his voice was no more heard on the mountains of Israel."

For that in Jeremiah, it is a mistake to conceive the prophet meant that Jehoiakim should die in Jerusalem, be drawn up and down the streets thereof, and be cast out at the gates thereof. The words are, "he shall be cast forth beyond the gates of Jerusalem;" that is, beyond the bounds and limits which belong to Jerusalem. Dying, or being slain, in Babylon, he was cast out, and judged unworthy of burial, his carcass lay like an ass, to be meat for the beasts of the earth and fowls of heaven, to be subject to all wind and weather: Jer. xxxvi. 30, "His dead body shall be cast out in the day to the heat, and in the night to the frost."

Though two whelps only be here spoken of, yet I make no doubt but that the other two also, Jehoiachin and Zedekiah, are intended, who were caught and carried away, "that their voices might no more be heard upon the mountains of Israel."

Obs. 1. The hopes of the wicked are not long-lived, they are soon dashed and disappointed. "When she saw she had waited, and her hope was lost:" she promised much to herself, expected much from Egypt, and from Jehoahaz; but all was in vain, no relief came thence. Prov. xi. 7, "The hope of unjust men perisheth," and that easily and speedily. Job viii. 14, it is likened to a spider's web or house, a little thing; a besom sweeps away the house and inhabitant together, and that in a moment: such is the hope of wicked men, it is suddenly and easily ruined. Had not they great hopes that were before Dublin? did they not think to take it and triumph in it? but I may say of them as Ambrose did of wicked men, They came, they went, they stood still, they vanished. God hath cut down their hopes, and many of them, the spider and her web, are gone together; they may say, the Lord "hath destroyed us on every side, and our hope hath he removed like a tree," Job xix. 10. There is a difference between the hopes of the righteous and those of the wicked: Prov. x. 28, "The hope of the righteous shall be gladness: but the expectation of the wicked shall perish."

Obs. 2. Corrupt states are so affected with and addicted to their princes, that they will set them up, have them rule over them, though it be to their own ruin, and ruin of the state also. Jerusalem, the lioness, sets "up another of her whelps, and makes it a young lion;" she put this whelp into the royal seat, and stirred him up to do lion-like, such things as did undo himself and Jerusalem also. She learned nothing by the loss of her former whelp, but proceeds in her old way, and would have lions, tyrants to be over her; she, being a lioness very corrupt and wicked, couples with that Egyptian lion Pharaoh, and brings forth, advances a lion like themselves.

The over-much love of states, of mothers to their children, is the undoing of them; they set them up who tear out their own bowels. When an astrologer told Agrippina that Nero her son should be emperor, but withal that he should kill his own mother; what said she? even like a fond and foolish woman, So he may reign, I care not, though he be my ruin. The men of Shechem made Abimelech king; but he proved not only a bramble, to scratch them, but a fierce and fiery lion to consume them. Mothers had need consider the temper of their sons, and how they advance them; and states, whom they set over them, lest they become lions unto them.

Obs. 3. Such as men live amongst and converse withal, such they prove. "He went up and down among the lions, and became a lion:" those lions he conversed with, talked of enriching themselves, by laying taxes, rates, and burdens upon the people, by taking them out of the way who should oppose, of making themselves great, of having their wills, and ruling by prerogative; and these things, and such like, were soon learned by this whelp. When Nebuchadnezzar was among beasts, he became brutish, and did as they did. Plutarch reports of a woman brought to a serpentine and poisonous nature by feeding on serpents ordinarily; and those who converse with a generation of vipers, will prove viperous; those who converse with lions will prove lionish. Ill company is the Delilah that bewitches, defiles, undoes many in their estates, names, bodies, and souls. Men that have infectious diseases you will not come near; you love your bodies, your lives. Wicked company have infectious vices; come not near them, neither yourselves nor your children, love your souls and theirs too. If you suffer your children to be among lions, among wicked ones, they will learn their manners; and those who will not leave ill company, it is a thousand to one they will lose their souls. Be choice of your company; it is the making or marring of young ones. Many are choice in their diet, in their apparel, choice in every thing they buy, yet have no care of company. Will you not admit a foul dish to come to your table? and will you admit foul and vicious ones to be your companions? We should touch no unclean thing. Ill company is pitch, it is poison. David knew it, therefore said, "Depart from me, all ye workers of iniquity," Psal. vi. 8; and, "I am a companion of all them that fear thee," Psal. cxix. 63.

Obs. 4. They who converse with wicked ones do not only become wicked, but many times they prove eminently wicked; they are skilful in wickedness, they exceed their teachers. Jehoiakim, by his converse with lions, became not only a lion to catch the prey, but such an one as devoured men, defiled widows, made desolate palaces, laid waste cities, and the land also. He tyrannized so, that he went beyond other tyrants; he was an inventor of wickedness, and profited above others in his way, and came to a perfection of iniquity. It is incident to man's nature to outstrip one the other, if not in good, yet especially in evil. It is said of this Jehoiakim, 2 Kings xxiii. 37, "He did that which was evil in the sight of the Lord, according to all that his fathers had done:" take any, or all his predecessors, he did evil according to all they did.

Obs. 5. Tyranny is hateful unto heathens. "Then the nations set against him on every side." Jehoiakim was such a roaring lion, that the heathens could not endure him; he spoiled their palaces, cities, land, so with his tyrannical proceedings, that he became hateful to all round about him. Doubtless the princes of the nations were tyrannous themselves; yet this man, being a prince of Israel, exceeded so in his tyrannical practices, that he incurred the displeasure and hatred of them all. Tyranny is contrary to humanity. Tyrants cease to be men, and become beasts; therefore here are called lions, and are ranked amongst wild, savage creatures, which none can endure. When there are wild beasts in a land, all are against them, and often there is a mutual agreement and concurrence of all sorts to destroy them, being destructive to the public. So was it here; the nations agreed to hunt and take this lion, which roared, preyed, spoiled, and did so much mischief.

Obs. 6. God hath times, means, ways to catch lions, to deal with covetous, cruel, and bloody men. "Then the nations set against him on every side." When Jehoiakim made desolate the palaces, wasted the cities and land, became a terror to all; then the Lord stirred up the nations; they were his net, his pit, his instruments he used to take this lion withal. When wicked men, tyrannical spirits, are at their height, have filled a land with confusion, oppression, desolation, and bloody doings, through their roarings and tearings, then the Lord appears, roars like a lion against them, and sets his agents on work to catch those roaring and ramping lions; he wants not means to take them, he is richly stored and provided that way; he hath the nations at command, and can call them forth, set them on to hunt lions when he please. Jer. li. 27—29, "Blow the trumpet among the nations, prepare the nations against her," (that is, Babylon and her princes, who were great tyrants,) "call together against her the kingdoms of Ararat, Minni, and Ashchenaz; appoint a captain against her; cause the horses to come up as the rough caterpillars. Prepare against her the nations with the king of the Medes, the captains thereof," &c.

Nebuchadnezzar was a crafty, cruel, and bloody lion, and so were the whelps that came of him and after him, but the Lord had a time and means to catch those lions and whelps. Jer. l. 9, "I will raise and cause to come up against Babylon an assembly of great nations from the north country." Great lions must have great nets, great pits, great doings to take them; God would bring an assembly of great nations.

Obs. 7. Tyrannical princes are not of long continuance; usually they are short-lived; either they lose their power, or their power and lives both. Jehoiakim roared and played the lion eleven years, and then he was taken in the pit of the nations, and lost his power. So Jehoahaz before him, he tyrannized three months, and then was taken. In 2 Kings xv. you may read of four lions which roared, but their roaring quickly hastened their ruin. Zechariah lionized it six months, Shallum one month, Pekahiah two years, and Pekah twenty years, and then they were cut off. When potentates oppress, tyrannize, their ruin is at hand. God hath said, "Bloody men shall not live out half their days," Psal. lv. 23, and he makes it good; "He cuts off the spirit of princes; and is terrible to the kings of the earth," Psal. lxxvi. 12. Stories will tell you what quick despatch hath been made of tyrants.

Obs. 8. Eminent wickedness brings eminent judgments. Both Jehoahaz and Jehoiakim exceeded in wickedness, and their judgments were answerable, they were chained, carried into strange lands, put into strong holds. Abimelech murdered seventy of his brethren, that he might get to the throne; but a woman cast a piece of a millstone upon his head, brake his skull, and manifested the just hand of God upon him, Judg. ix. 5, 53, 56. Jezebel and Ahab were eminently wicked, and God's hand was upon them both in an eminent manner, 1 Kings xxii.; 2 Kings ix.

Richard the third obtained the crown by the murder of his nephews; and having tyrannized two years, two months, and one day, he was slain in a battle at Bosworth Field, his naked body was laid upon a horse like a hog or calf, his head, arms hanging on the one side, and his legs on the other; and being all besprinkled with mire and blood, he was brought into Leicester, where for two days he lay naked and unburied; after, his body was buried, but without solemnity, and the stone chest wherein his body lay is since made a drinking trough for horses at a common inn.

Speed.

Obs. 9. God takes away wicked and tyrannical princes, that it may be well with his people, that Zion may have the benefit of it. Jehoiakim was taken, chained, carried to Babylon, put in strong holds; and why? "that his voice should no more be heard upon the mountains of Israel;" that the people of God might not be terrified with his roarings, nor torn with his teeth, but might enjoy freedom and safety. It is a great mercy when lions are not in a land, nor other hurtful wild beasts; where such are, there is no dwelling or sleeping in safety; but God, for the good of his people, destroys or drives out the wild beasts. Ezek. xxxiv. 25, "I will cause the evil beasts to cease out of the land; and they shall dwell safely in the wilderness, and sleep in the woods." Isa. xxxv. 9, "No lion shall be there."

In the primitive days were many lions, and they roared terribly upon the mountains of Israel; they scattered, tore, and devoured the flocks of the Lord which were feeding upon those mountains; but the Lord hunted those lions into pits, and took them away for his flock's sake.

Sennacherib with a great army comes up to the gates of Jerusalem, roars upon the mountains about it, fills all with fear; but the Lord sends a destroying angel that slew his army, and caused that lion to flee, that "his voice might be heard no more upon the mountains."

Ver. 10—14. *Thy mother is like a vine in thy blood, planted by the waters: she was fruitful and full of branches by reason of many waters. And she had strong rods for the sceptres of them that bare rule, and her stature was exalted among the thick branches, and she appeared in her height with the multitude of her branches. But she was plucked up in fury, she was cast down to the ground, and the east wind dried up her fruit: her strong rods were broken and withered; the fire consumed them. And now she is planted in the wilderness, in a dry and thirsty ground. And fire is gone out of a rod of her branches, which hath devoured her fruit, so that she hath no strong rod to be a sceptre to rule. This is a lamentation, and shall be for a lamentation.*

In these verses is laid down the second general part of the chapter, viz. the lamentation for Jerusalem, or the kingdom of Judah under the parabolical representation of a vine. We may here consider,

I. The state of this vine, as it was in Jehoiachin's, and especially in Zedekiah's days, ver. 10, 11.

II. The misery which befell it, ver. 12, 14.

III. The transplantation of it, ver. 13.

The words must be opened, and then the observations shall be given in.

"Thy mother." That is, Jerusalem, or the kingdom of Judah, which was the mother of princes. "Thy mother," O Jehoiachin: he had spoken before to Jehoahaz and Jehoiakim as whelps of this mother under the notion of a lioness; now he comes to speak of Jehoiachin and Zedekiah, as branches of this mother, under the notion of a vine.

"Is like a vine." Frequently doth the Spirit of God resemble Israel and Judah to a vine, as Isa. xxvii. 2; v. 2; iii. 14; Psal. lxxx. 8, 14, 17. Jerusalem or the kingdom of Judah is likened to a vine,

1. For the excellency or choiceness of it. Vines are noble, choice, and excellent plants; so this kingdom was a noble vine, Jer. ii. 21, a choice vine, Isa. v. 2; and, Psal. lxxviii. 67, 68, "He refused the tabernacle of Joseph, and chose not the tribe of Ephraim; but chose the tribe of Judah."

2. Because the vine spreads and extends itself far. Psal. lxxx. 9—11, the Jewish vine filled the land, and covered the hills, it extended far. This is one thing chiefly intended here; for after Jehoiakim and Jehoahaz, two roaring lions, which laid all waste, were taken and carried to Egypt and Babylon, in the days of Zedekiah this vine did flourish and spread: Ezek. xvii. 6, "It grew and became a spreading vine," &c.; it grew in wealth, in power, in glory.

3. Because vines are fruitful things, no tree, no plant like them: Psal. cxxviii. 3, "Thy wife shall be as a fruitful vine." Vines are fruitful in branches, in leaves, in clusters. This kingdom had princes and nobles, and Zedekiah divers sons, 2 Kings xxv. 7.

"In thy blood." These words are variously rendered by those who touch or treat upon them. The Septuagint is, ὡς ἄνθος ἐν ῥοᾶ or ῥοᾶς, as the flower of a pomegranate or peach; thy mother is ruddy and comely as the flowers of those trees are. But the Hebrew bears not this sense; the word is כדמך if we take the word for quiet and silence, the sense is this; The kingdom flourished and prospered like a vine, while Jehoiachin and Zedekiah were quiet, and did not roar and raven as their predecessors did. Vines torn, cut down in time of war, do grow again and flourish in times of peace. If we read the word, in thy likeness, or, in the likeness of thee, the meaning may be, Thou, O Zedekiah, art a king, but low and mean in comparison of other kings that were before, as Asa and Jehoshaphat, Hezekiah and Josiah; and thy mother is like unto thee: Jerusalem and Judah flourish not as in former days, but are low and little; according to that in Ezek. xvii. 6, "It grew, and became a spreading vine of low stature:" he speaks there of Zedekiah and the kingdom in his days.

But seeing the words are in our translation "in thy blood," and the original bears it so, it is fit to inquire what sense the words so taken may bear. Thou camest of kings, princes, and nobles, they were thy progenitors; and in production of them, Jerusalem, "thy mother, is like a vine in thy blood." It is usual by blood to note the stock, race, and house that men come of. Or, "Thy mother is like a vine in thy blood," that is, in thy seed and issue; thou hast a numerous issue, and this renders thy mother like a vine, a generous vine, bringing forth noble plants. Some think by "blood" is meant *succus, robur;* and then the sense may be this, Thy mother is like a vine upheld by thy influence and strength; thou and thy sons support this feeble kingdom.

"Planted by the waters." In hot countries they were careful to plant their trees and vines where they might not want water. Canaan was a hilly country, yet full of water; Deut. viii. 7, it was "a land of brooks of water," of fountains and depths that spring out of valleys and hills; and their vines planted by the waters could not want moisture, though the heat was great there. Nebuchadnezzar planted Zedekiah among the poor; he carried away with Jehoiachin the princes, nobles, and chief of the land, 2 Kings xxiv. 14, where it is said, "none remained save the poorest sort," and those were the waters this vine was planted amongst and by; chap. xvii. 5, 8, they are called "great waters," and here, "many waters."

"She was fruitful." After the great waste, spoil, made in the palaces, cities, and land by the tyranny of those two lions, Jehoahaz and Jehoiakim, this metaphorical vine did flourish and become fruitful. In chap. xvii. 8, it is said, "it was planted in a good soil by great waters, that it might bring forth branches, and that it might bear fruit;" and here it is said, "she was fruitful and full of branches." She brought forth such as had been carried away; those branches that were plucked off, grew again; smiths, craftsmen, soldiers, mighty men of valour, nobles, princes, counsellors, and such like; the palaces were frequented, the cities rebuilt, the land tilled, the vines dressed.

"By reason of many waters." By waters here we may well understand the mercies and blessings of God upon this kingdom; for as God himself is a "fountain of living waters," Jer. ii. 13, so his blessings, mercies are called waters: Isa. xxvii. 3, speaking of his vineyard, he saith, he "will water it every moment," he will continually bless it, and afford it what may do it good. See Isa. lvii. 18; Hos. xiv. 5. Or if we will understand it of the poor Jews who came "out of the waters of Judah," Isa. xlviii. 1, and are called "waters," Eccles. xi. 1, it was by virtue of God's blessing upon their labours; God watered them, they watered the kingdom, so that it became as a flourishing and fruitful vine.

Ver. 11. "And she had strong rods for the sceptres of them that bare rule." Hebrew is, rods of strength; so the Septuagint, a rod of strength; others, sound, strong rods, boughs, or branches. It is said of this Jewish vine, Psal. lxxx. 10, that "the boughs thereof were like goodly cedars." The meaning is, there were in the kingdom of Israel men of great worth and eminence in David's days. Now it had rods of strength, and such rods as were fit to make sceptres of.

How this suits with what we had in chap. xv. is considerable, where it was said, that the vine tree yields not wood fit for any work, no not to make a pin of it to hang any vessel thereupon; and here it is said, the vine had strong rods for sceptres. There he speaks of the material vine, here of a metaphorical vine; there was shown God's rejection of them, and what the vine was in God's account, here what this vine was fit for in man's account. This kingdom thought every son of Zedekiah, which were the rods of strength, being of royal descent, fit and meet to sway sceptres, rule kingdoms; but the Lord thought not so.

We may by "strong rods" understand not only the royal branches, but also the nobles, judges, counsellors, and men of might, who were of use and great service to those who did bear rule, and fit to be rulers under those who did bear the sceptre.

"Her stature was exalted among the thick branches." Hebrew, her stature was lifted up above among the perplexities, contortions, that is, the thick branches. This kingdom, though greatly battered and broken, yet, like a vine, grew up again to a greatness and height; the people were increased much, and the royal family was exalted high. Zedekiah, though he were a wicked king, yet both he and his were magnified by the people; they were the top branches of the vine. In all states there are some more eminent than others.

"And she appeared in her height with the multitude of her branches." She flourished, spread, multiplied, grew so great and high, that her height and greatness appeared to others. It was evident that God had done much for this kingdom, &c. Thus through the multitude of her branches, and greatness of her power, wealth, and honour, she became proud, despised others, and so appeared in her height. The words thus taken, correspond with what you have in chap. xvi. 15, "Thou didst trust in thine own beauty." He speaks of Jerusalem under the notion of a woman; she being grown into a kingdom, become great, rich, renowned, she waxed proud, and trusted in her own beauty.

Obs. 1. That states and kingdoms broken to pieces, ruined in times of war and trouble, do flourish again in times of quiet and silence. When roaring lions are taken away, and men of peaceable and quiet spirits succeed, then the vine grows, then the land prospers, then breaches are repaired, then wastes are built up, &c. Tyranny, oppression, wars pull down, root up, destroy, 2 Chron. xv. 5, 6; but when there is peace and rest, it is otherwise. Chap. xiv. 7, "They built and prospered;" and why? they had "rest on every side." In storms and fights ships suffer much in their sails, masts, tacklings, often they are greatly broken; but when the storms and fights are over, then all things are mended and made up again. So when state-storms are over, all things begin to grow up again, that were broken or trodden down. Peace after war is like spring after a sharp winter, which revives, causeth growth and greenness; yet know that states ruined by tyranny of princes, by wars, do not suddenly recover themselves, or attain to their former greatness and splendour: though Jerusalem became a vine after the roaring and spoil of Jehoiakim, yet she was a "vine of a low stature." Thy mother is a vine in thy likeness: thou art low, and thy mother is low.

Obs. 2. It is through the mercy, goodness, and blessing of God that wasted kingdoms do become as vines, and flourish again. "Thy mother is like a vine, fruitful and full of branches by reason of many waters." God watered the kingdom with blessings; he gave peace, he gave the poor strength to labour, he rained upon them, and gave sap to the vine, that she was fruitful. When God lays waste his vineyard, then he commands "the clouds that they rain no rain upon it," Isa. v. 6; but when he causes it to flourish, then he calls forth the rain, he moistens the spirits of men of all sorts, to contribute their help, thoughts, counsels for the good of a kingdom; he stirs up the spirits of men to be doing for the public; he gives people planted by him many waters, many blessings. We have been rent, torn, wasted;

God is beginning to make us as a vine fruitful and full of branches; let us take heed we abuse not our mercies, lest God dry up the waters, and so we wither and be utterly laid waste.

3. When mercies are multiplied, men are apt to abuse them, and swell with the enjoyment of them. This metaphorical vine, the kingdom of Judah, had "strong rods, her stature was exalted among the thick branches, and she appeared in her height with the multitude of her branches:" she grew up again to a height, greatness; she had a multitude of branches, variety of mercies, and these swelled her so, that she became proud, insolent, and despised others. Prosperity is a dangerous thing, and hath hazarded many. Isa. xlvii. 5, 7, the Babylonian kingdom was so rich, great, populous, plentiful, that it was called "The lady of kingdoms," and she herself said, "I shall be a lady for ever;" she prided herself in her prosperity: so spiritual Babylon; Rev. xviii. 7, "I sit a queen, and am no widow, and shall see no sorrow." She had abundance of blessings and delicacies, ver. 3, but she glorified herself, not the Lord. When Amaziah had smitten the Edomites, and prospered in his undertakings against them, his heart was lifted up, and that unto boasting, as Joash told him, 2 Chron. xxv. 19. After Hezekiah had received many mercies, "his heart was lifted up," 2 Chron. xxxii. 23—25. Rehoboam, when he was strengthened in the kingdom, "forsook the law of the Lord, and all Israel with him;" here was a sad effect of prosperity, 2 Chron. xii. 1. This people were seldom the better for mercies and blessings bestowed upon them. Jer. xxii. 21, "I spake unto thee in thy prosperity, but thou saidst, I will not hear. This hath been thy manner from thy youth, that thou obeyest not my voice." The Hebrew is, in thy prosperities; for she had many times of prosperity, and in none of them did she hearken, but grew so wicked that the daughters of the Philistines were ashamed of her lewdness, Samaria and Sodom were less sinful, Ezek. xvi. 27, 47. She had forgotten the caution the Lord gave her in the days of her infancy, Deut. viii. 11—14, "Beware that thou forget not the Lord thy God; lest when thou art full, thy herds, flocks, silver, gold, and all thou hast is multiplied, then thine heart be lifted up," &c.

Ver. 12. "But she was plucked up in fury." Here he shows the miserable event of this vine; it was not broken, pruned, cut down, but "plucked up." The Hebrew word signifies to eradicate or pluck up by the roots, as trees and plants are pulled out of the earth, roots and all; and it is metaphorically applied to other things, as Jer. i. 10, "I have set thee over nations and kingdoms, to root out," that is, to prophesy the extirpation of them.

"In fury." Not in mercy, with a gentle hand, as sometimes the owner or vine-dresser doth, but "in fury." When a vine hath been planted in a good soil, watered, and long waited upon, with expectation of fruit, and yields nothing but leaves, suddenly, and in great displeasure, the master of the vineyard comes, lays hands upon it, puts forth all his strength, and pulls it out of the earth, and saith it shall never cumber the ground longer.

"She was cast down to the ground." Vines are weak things, and have props to support and uphold them, and when they are gone they fall to the ground. The Lord would no longer uphold this vine, this kingdom of Judah, he would withdraw all supporting props it had, pull it up, and cast it down; as a man doth a dry or barren plant, when he hath pulled it up, he throws it away in anger. God would bring down the exalted stature of this vine to a low condition.

"The east wind dried up her fruit." Of this east wind was spoken, chap. xvii. 10. East winds are very prejudicial to corn, fruit, and plants, especially to vines; when east winds blow much upon them, they are barren, and often dried up. These winds are scorching and consuming; therefore great afflictions are called east winds, Isa. xxvii. 8. This eastern wind was Nebuchadnezzar with his forces. Habakkuk mentions him and his army under this notion of an eastern wind, chap. i. 9, "They shall come all for violence; their faces shall sup up as the east wind." This wind hath a sucking virtue in it; the water, the moisture of the earth, the juice of trees and plants, are supped up by it, so that it leaves things dry and withered; so should the Chaldeans suck up and devour all the pleasant things of this kingdom, all the fruit of this vine, from the highest branch to the lowest.

"Her strong rods were broken and withered." Montanus reads the words thus, They are broken and withered, and leaves the other words to be joined with what follows, thus, The rod of her strength the fire hath consumed it; and so Lavater. But others read the words as you have them: and which way soever you read them, there is no considerable difference therein. The Hebrew is in the singular number, which frequently in the holy language is put for the plural. The rods of strength on this vine were not only Zedekiah's sons, but all the principal young men, who were full of blood and spirits, as the chief branches in a vine are full of juice. Yea, all that had places of power and trust, and were supporting strength to this vine, did Nebuchadnezzar by his forces pluck away, break in pieces, and make to wither. Break off the strongest part of a vine, the strongest rod upon it, and throw it aside, it quickly dries up; so these being pulled from their places, stripped of their wealth and power, withered.

"The fire consumed them." When the branches, the strong rods of a vine, are plucked off and withered, they are fit for the fire, and that consumes them: these strong rods and branches the fire consumed. This fire was the fire of God's wrath; the coals which the man clothed in linen scattered over the city, chap. x. 2. Jerusalem, with all the precious and pleasant things in it, was burnt with fire, 2 Kings xxv. 9. By the Babylonish army the walls were broken down, the land laid waste, and all considerable things and persons carried away. Thus was this Jewish vine, which had been planted by God's hand in a good ground, plucked up again by him in fury.

Ver. 13. "And now she is planted in the wilderness." This wilderness was Babylon, which was a fruitful, pleasant, and well watered country; the city and land were the "glory of kingdoms," Isa. xiii. 19. It had variety of rivers; Psal. cxxxvii. 1, "By the rivers of Babylon, there we sat down." Some write of it, that it yields two hundred, yea, in the most fertile parts of it, three hundredfold increase; that it abounds with dates, whereof they make honey and wine. Now if this were the nature of the country, how is it here called a wilderness? It is so called not in respect of itself, but in reference to the Jews, who being captives therein, were as in a wilderness.

In a wilderness, 1. A man is destitute of all comforts; 2. Exposed to many dangers. So were the Jews in Babylon.

1. They were destitute of comforts. They came naked into Babylon, where they were amongst a people of a barbarous and unknown tongue, that knew nothing of God; there they had no form of a church or state; they had no life, but were as dry bones, Ezek. xxxvii. 11. There they were captives; Baby-

lon was a prison unto them, and prisons of what kind soever are not pleasing. Prisoners endure much hunger and thirst, and doubtless so did the Jews in Babylon. Though there were plenty, yet they had little enough, and therefore it was " a dry and thirsty land" to them.

2. They were exposed to many dangers, being amongst them that mocked and hated them. The Babylonians were " bitter and hasty, terrible and dreadful," Hab. i. 6, 7. They were like wild beasts in the wilderness, and sought, upon all occasions, to make a prey of the poor captived Jews. They got the three children into the fiery furnace, Daniel into the lions' den, and Haman attempted the total ruin of them.

" She is planted." Before, in ver. 12, it is said, " the fire consumed them :" what is consumed in the fire is burnt to ashes, and how then can that be planted? He doth not say the whole vine was burnt, but her "strong rods" were broken off and burnt; some were burnt and consumed by famine, some by the plague, some by the sword: 2 Chron. xxxvi. 17, "The king of the Chaldees slew their young men with the sword," but "they that escaped the sword he carried away to Babylon, where they were servants to him and his sons," ver. 20.

If it should be granted that the whole vine was dried up, withered, and burnt to ashes, yet these words may bear a good and sound sense, viz. thus, they may be understood of Jehoiachin and those that were with him in Babylon at that time when they were spoken; for the words run in the present tense, " she is planted," not, she shall be planted; for Zedekiah and those that escaped the sword were carried after this prophecy to Babylon.

Ver. 14. " And fire is gone out of a rod of her branches." What this rod was, and the fire that went out of it, is fit to inquire. I will not say that Ishmael was the rod, and the fire that went out of it the destruction of Gedaliah, whom the king of Babylon had left governor over the land, and this Ishmael slew, 2 Kings xxv. 25; Jer. xli. 1—3, with many others: but rather conceive Zedekiah to be this rod, who being of the royal family, was a principal rod of this vine; and the fire which went out of this rod was his rebellion against the king of Babylon, who had set him up upon the throne of Judah; for this act of his stirred up Nebuchadnezzar to come and lay all waste, 2 Kings xxiv. 20; xxv. 1—11; 2 Chron. xxxvi. 13, 17; Jer. lii. 3, 4. So that Zedekiah was a fire and cause of destruction, he did that which brought fire and destruction upon this vine.

" Which hath devoured her fruit." The fire caused by him did devour the young men, maidens, old men, the vessels of the sanctuary, the treasure of the Lord's house, and the treasure of the king and princes, 2 Chron. xxxvi. 17—19.

" So that she hath no strong rod to be a sceptre to rule." The meaning is, that this vine was so ruined, that there was none left to bear rule. Zedekiah's sons were slain, and the princes of Judah, Jer. lii. 10; yet not all, for it is said, 2 Kings xxv. 25, that Ishmael was of the seed royal, or of the kingdom; and Jer. xli. 1, that " the princes of the king, even ten men," that is, those princes or nobles who had escaped, joined with Ishmael in the murdering of Gedaliah; but these and others which had some small power were glad to flee, some to the Ammonites, some to Egypt, for fear, as appears in Jer. xli. and 2 Kings xxv. 26. None of them were able to raise up the kingdom again; now the kingly power was taken from them, and expired in Zedekiah. His daughters were left in the custody of Gedaliah; but it was not for women to sit upon the throne of Judah. The kings and kingdom of Judah were swallowed up in the Babylonish captivity; for afterwards they had no kings, but governors, Haggai ii. 2. And Paul called their state not a kingdom, but " the commonwealth of Israel," Eph. ii. 12. So that in this sense also, she was " planted in a wilderness, in a dry and thirsty land;" she had not virtue, power, strength, to bring forth any rods for kingly government.

The sceptre seemed now to be departed from Judah, there being no strong rod to be a sceptre to rule. Now there was no king in Israel, nor any more to be. True, it seemed so, but it was not so; for though Zedekiah and his seed were cut off, yet the Lord had an eye to his promise, remembered the covenant with David, Psal. lxxxix. 34—36, and showed his faithfulness; for he thought upon Jehoiachin or Jechonias, from whom as a dry root sprouted Salathiel, and Zorobabel, who brought them out of Babylon, and was ruler over this people; and so in him, his, and the high priests after him, was the power of the sceptre continued till Christ came.

The promise was not that there should be kings always of the tribe of Judah, but that ruling power should be in that tribe of one kind or other, which was made good.

" This is a lamentation, and shall be for a lamentation." This prophecy is matter of mourning to me at present; to hear and speak of such sad things coming upon Judah and Jerusalem " is a lamentation," and when they shall be accomplished, they will be " for a lamentation" to posterity; they will lament for the princes of Israel, for Jerusalem, for the temple, and for this vine plucked up by the roots.

Obs. 1. God lays waste, destroys flourishing and potent kingdoms when they provoke him by their sinful and grievous courses. This kingdom of Judah did flourish like a vine, had many branches, strong rods, much wealth and power; but it trespassed grievously, Ezek. xiv. 13, and here God plucks it up in fury, he spares neither branches, body, nor roots. The quiet, happiness, and flourishing condition of earthly kingdoms is not perpetual, God hath ways to weaken them, to ruin and root them up; by the Egyptians he lopped this vine, and by the Babylonians he pulled it up; see 2 Kings xxv. 11; Jer. lii. 15. God had threatened oft before to pluck up and root them out, if they provoked him by their disobedience, Deut. xxviii. 25, 48, 63; 1 Kings xiv. 15: 2 Chron. vii. 20, " I will pluck them up by the roots out of my land which I have given them." " I will pluck up even this whole land," Jer. xlv. 4. God made good his word, he plucked them up; though the house of Israel had been his vineyard, and the men of Judah his pleasant plant, Isa. v. 7. If nations would flourish like vines, and continue in a flourishing condition, they must not provoke the Lord to fury, but bring forth fruit answerable to mercies given in, answerable to the soil they are planted in, the waters they are planted by, the digging, dunging, pruning, hedging, and shining upon they have had; if not, but bring forth sour grapes, injustice, oppression, profaneness, hear what is said, Psal. cvii. 34, " He turneth a fruitful land into barrenness, for the wickedness of them that dwell therein;" yea, he drives out princes for their wickedness, Ezek. xxxi. 11; and men cannot be established thereby, Prov. xii. 4. It is " righteousness exalteth a nation; but sin is a reproach to any people," Prov. xiv. 34; and though they may prosper a while, be like vines, yet God plucks them up at last, and that in fury.

Obs. 2. When God is in his fury, yet he shows some mercy. Although he plucked up this vine, threw her down to the ground, dried up her fruit by an east wind, brake off her strong rods, consumed them in the fire; yet something of this vine he spared and planted in the wilderness, the body and some branches of it were carried to Babylon, and set there, which was mercy. God might have burned them all in his fury and fire of his indignation; but in wrath he remembers mercy; though he let out much wrath, much fury, yet he lets out some mercy. When Pharaoh pillaged this vine, plucked off the principal branch, yet some mercy was shown, Jehoiakim was planted in his room; when Nebuchadnezzar took him away, Jehoiachin was set up, which was mercy; and when both Jehoiachin and Zedekiah were plucked away, yet here was mercy, some were planted in Babylon. The Lord let not out all his wrath at any time against them, but, as Isaiah saith, he left them a remnant, and made them not as Sodom and Gomorrah, chap. i. 9. God's wrath and fury have appeared towards our English vine; and though he hath plucked up many branches and rods of strength, yet hath he not plucked us up in wrath and fury, he hath shown us rich, great, extraordinary mercy. Let us bring forth better fruit henceforward, lest he put forth his hand and pluck us up by the roots.

Obs. 3. Those who are planted amongst wicked and ungodly people, they are in no better condition than men in a wilderness. What though the place be pleasant, well watered, fruitful, and abounding with outward blessings, yet it is no better than a wilderness to them who have lived in Canaan.

When these Jews were planted in Babylon, which was a garden, a land of rivers, of delightful things, it was unto them like a heath and wilderness; things were not suitable to their spirits, they were destitute of true comforts, they had no temple, no sacrifice; they were exposed to great and many dangers, and lived amongst wild beasts. Canaan was the land of the living. There the living God did manifest himself; there were the living oracles, the living waters, and the living people: all lands else were heaths and wildernesses; they had dead and dumb gods, dead worship, dead waters, and were full of dead and dry bones. Such was Babylon, affording no spiritual and living sap to nourish this vine. The Jews could not sing the Lord's song there, Psal. cxxxvii. 4.

When people plant themselves among wicked and profane ones, they plant themselves in Babylon, in a wilderness.

Obs. 4. When men are planted in a good soil, and bring not forth good fruit, it is just with God to remove them from the means they enjoy. This vine was "planted in a good soil," Ezek. xvii. 8, "by many waters," ver. 10 of this chapter; but she brought not forth good fruit, therefore God plucked her up, deprived her of those mercies and means she formerly enjoyed, and "planted her in a dry and thirsty land." Deut. xxviii. 47, 48, "Because thou servedst not the Lord with joyfulness and gladness of heart, for the abundance of all things; therefore shalt thou serve thine enemies which the Lord shall send against thee, in hunger, in thirst, in nakedness, and in want of all things." This it may be they had forgotten, being given out in Moses' days; but Jeremiah oft minded them of it, who lived amongst them, even when they were removed; see chap. xv. 4; xxix. 18; xxxiv. 17. God had brought this vine formerly out of Egypt, and planted it in Canaan, where it took deep root, Psal. lxxx. 8, 9, for it enjoyed many mercies; but because it degenerated, and was like the plant of a strange vine unto God, Jer. ii. 21, therefore he removed it from the pleasant land to the wilderness, he carried it out of his orchard or garden, and set it in the forest.

Obs. 5. The wasting and ruin of kingdoms is from themselves; the cause is intrinsical. "A fire is gone out of a rod of her branches, which hath devoured her fruit." It was not Nebuchadnezzar, but Zedekiah that kindled the fire; he was a rod of this vine's branches, he did the mischief by his rebellion, he brought the eastern wind which dried up the fruit of this vine, broke off her strong rods, and burnt them in the fire. Jehoiakim was a rod of this vine's branches, he likewise rebelled, 2 Kings xxiv. 1; and so fire came out of this rod to destroy the vine; for presently bands of Chaldees, bands of Syrians, bands of Moabites, and bands of the children of Ammon, came against Judah to destroy it, ver. 2. Manasseh was a rod of this vine, and out of him went fire to waste it; he plucked off and consumed many branches of it, 2 Kings xxi. 16; and he caused the Lord to bring in the captains of the host of the king of Assyria to spoil it more, 2 Chron. xxxiii. 11; yea, his sins had the greatest influence into the consumption of this vine, Jer. xv. 4; 2 Kings xxiv. 3.

The desolation of kingdoms usually have been by their own kings and rulers, by those they have brought forth and set up; their follies, cruelties, treacheries, have fired and consumed their kingdoms. It was Hoshea's conspiracy that ruined the kingdom of Israel, 2 Kings xvii. 4—6.

Obs. 6. When a lawful form of government is abused by governors growing tyrannical and unfaithful, God may set by, yea destroy, such governors and their posterity, and change the government. "Fire is gone out of a rod of her branches, which hath devoured her fruit, so that she hath no strong rod to be a sceptre to rule." Zedekiah was tyrannical and perfidious, and here God excludes him and his family from all kingly power and ruling, and changed the government.

The Lord is not tied to any men, any family, any way of government; but whom he please he may pull down, and what form of government he will he may set up. "He bringeth princes to nothing, he maketh judges of the earth as vanity. Yea, they shall not be planted; yea, they shall not be sown; yea, their stock shall not take root in the earth: and he shall also blow upon them, and they shall wither, and the whirlwind shall take them away as stubble," Isa. xl. 23, 24.

CHAPTER XX.

Ver. 1—4. *And it came to pass in the seventh year, in the fifth month, the tenth day of the month, that certain of the elders of Israel came to enquire of the Lord, and sat before me. Then came the word of the Lord unto me, saying, Son of man, speak unto the elders of Israel, and say unto them, Thus saith the Lord God; Are ye come to enquire of me? As I live, saith the Lord God, I will not be enquired of by you. Wilt thou judge them, son of man, wilt thou judge them? cause them to know the abominations of their fathers.*

In this chapter you have,

I. The exordium, in the 1st, 2nd, and part of the 3rd verse.

II. A severe reproof, or refusal, of those that came to the prophet, ver. 3, 4, 31.

III. A relation of God's dealings with them, in Egypt, in the wilderness, and in Canaan, and their sinful carriages towards him, ver. 4—33.

IV. A denunciation of judgment for their hypocrisy, and other sins, mixed with promises of mercy, ver. 33—45.

V. A parabolical declaration of the destruction of Judea and Jerusalem, ver. 45—49.

VI. A doleful conclusion of the prophet, ver. 49.

In the exordium or introduction you have,

1. The time of this prophecy punctually set down, both the year, month, and day, ver. 1.

2. The occasion thereof, which was the coming of the elders to the prophet to inquire of the Lord, ver. 1.

3. The commission the prophet had to give out this prophecy, ver. 2, 3.

Ver. 1. " And it came to pass in the seventh year." That is, of their captivity. Ezekiel began to prophesy in the fifth year thereof, chap. i. 2; and now it was the seventh year of their captivity in Babylon, and of Zedekiah's reign at Jerusalem, and two years and five months before Jerusalem was besieged, as appears, 2 Kings xxv. 1.

" In the fifth month." The Jews, before they came out of Egypt, computed their year from the month Tisri, or Ethanim, which was part of those months we call September and October; but after they came out of Egypt, they began their year from the month Nisan, which comprehends part of March and part of April. Their fifth month was called Ab, which had half of July and half of August in it.

" The tenth day of the month." Often in this prophecy the very day of the month is set down, as chap. i. 2, the fifth day of the fourth month, and chap. viii. 1, the fifth day of the sixth month, and here, the tenth day of the fifth month. The Spirit of God put the prophet upon an exact chronology, both to strengthen the credit of the prophecy, and to mind them of the many years that were yet behind of their captivity, that so they might repent them of their iniquity which had brought them into that condition, and patiently submit to the Babylonish yoke which God had put upon them for seventy years.

" Certain of the elders of Israel came." In chap. viii. 1, the elders of Judah sat before him, and chap. xiv. 1, elders of Israel came unto him, and so it is here. " Certain of the elders of Israel came;" the Hebrew is, men of the elders, that is, some of the ancient that were or had been governors and chief amongst them, they came; from whence? from Jerusalem, say some, but they had Jeremiah there to consult with; and it is not likely that after Zedekiah and the chief men had broken covenant with Nebuchadnezzar, that men of the elders at Jerusalem would take a long journey to Babylon to consult with Ezekiel. Others therefore say, they were of the captives, to whose judgment I should incline, if I could see how that which is said in ver. 34, and so after, might fitly be applied unto them. It seems probable to me, that some of the elders at Jerusalem, upon the revolt of Zedekiah from Nebuchadnezzar, and falling in with the king of Egypt, might send to some of the elders among the captives to make inquiry of Ezekiel touching their affairs.

" To inquire of the Lord." They came to the prophet, that he consulting with God, might make known his mind unto them. They had been now seven years in captivity; the false prophets had possessed them with hopes of returning to Jerusalem, which should abide and not be destroyed, as Jeremiah had said; and therefore some think they came to inquire what should become of them. Others make the ground of their coming to the prophet, and inquiring, to be the rumours of, if not the preparation for, war by Nebuchadnezzar, because the Jews at Jerusalem had rebelled and broken covenant with him. Hereupon they thought it might go ill with themselves, that they might suffer very hard things, if not be cut off by the Babylonians, and therefore came to the prophet to inquire what would be the issue of things. It is probable they were in danger through the perfidiousness of their brethren at Jerusalem, and that the considerations thereof might have some influence into their coming to the prophet; but there was more than so. They now, to secure themselves, thought and resolved of a sinful way; ver. 32, " We will be as the heathen, as the families of the countries, to serve wood and stone;" they conceived, that if they conformed to the Babylonian worship, they should be taken for good subjects, and be safe, whatever befell them at Jerusalem for their provocation of the Babylonish king. This they concealed from the prophet, and come to him to inquire (seeing they were now more odious to the Babylonians than before Zedekiah's breaking covenant) whether it were not better and safer for them to disperse, than to live in bodies, and multitudes together, which caused envy, hatred, and great danger at that time, as they pretended. But they dissembled deeply, for while they lived together, they could not so easily desert the Jewish religion, and embrace the Babylonish idolatry. There would be special observation of it, and bitter reprehension for it. But if they had the prophet's counsel, and consent to scatter themselves, and fix their habitations here and there, they thought they might do it without any noise or check.

" And sat before me." The Hebrew for before me is, before my faces, that is, in my presence, expecting some answer from me.

Ver. 2. " Then came the word of the Lord unto me." The Hebrew is, and the word of the Lord hath been to me.

" Saying." Hebrew is, to say; the Spirit moved him that he might speak to others. There being an opportunity and season for speaking, the Spirit came upon him, and informed him touching the mind of God, and commissioned him to deliver it.

Ver. 3. " Son of man." He saith not, Ezekiel, but, " Son of man," to mind him of his original, that he was his creature, and ought to hearken to and observe the laws of his Creator. Of this appellation hath been spoken heretofore.

" Speak unto the elders of Israel." Here is a command laid upon the prophet. The Lord commands him to speak, and puts into his mouth what he shall speak. False prophets were neither sent of the Lord, nor spake from the Lord, chap. xiii. 3, 6.

" Are ye come to inquire of me?" Or, Do ye come to inquire of me? The words are an interrogation, and this interrogation imports distaste at their coming. Do you come to inquire of me? your hearts are not right in this matter, you play the hypocrites and dissemble egregiously, for you pretend to honour me in asking counsel at my mouth, and that if you knew my mind you would do it, whereas you are resolved beforehand what to do, let my counsels be what they will. O you dissemblers, ye are come to try and tempt me, whether I will give out what suits with your intentions and resolutions; if so you will embrace it, but if not, my counsels must be rejected, and your own established.

" As I live, saith the Lord God, I will not be inquired of by you." This hypocritical carriage of theirs did so displease, yea, provoke the Lord, that he swears he will not be inquired of by them. Had they come in truth and simplicity of heart, intending to hearken to the Lord, and obey his voice, whatever he had advised them, he would have been inquired of by them; but being they had fallacious spirits, and came in a way of mockage unto God, therefore he deals roundly and severely with them, and binds it with an oath, that he will not be inquired of by them.

But they did inquire of God, they came to the prophet to inquire of him, ver. 1; how then is it true that the Lord saith, and swears, he will not be inquired of by them? The meaning of those words is, I will not answer them; let them inquire, ask what they please, I will not answer them, and so it is all one as if I were not inquired of: so the Septuagint, Vulgate, and French have it, though they do ask, they shall not obtain, they shall not prevail, I will not answer; or if I do, it shall not be such an answer as you would have.

Ver. 4. "Wilt thou judge them?" &c. Besides the appellation, this verse consists of an interrogation and an injunction. The interrogation is double, "Wilt thou judge them? wilt thou judge them?" The injunction, "cause them to know the abominations," &c.

In this verse, the Lord doth anticipate and prevent the prophet, who having good thoughts of these elders of Israel, that came to inquire of the Lord, was ready to plead for them, when he saw the Lord so severe and resolute against them, as not to vouchsafe them an answer: Lord, what is the matter? these men are conscientious, they do their duty, they come to consult for the good of the people, they would do nothing, being in a strait and danger, without thee: Lord, be not so peremptory, listen unto them, and give them a gracious answer. God foreseeing that the prophet would be their patron, and plead for them, he takes him off from this, by saying, "Wilt thou judge them?" that is, Wilt thou deem them to be honest, sincere, plain-hearted men, that come with a purpose to know and obey the will of God? thou art deceived, they are deep dissemblers, devilish politicians, pretending one thing and intending another; they come not out of duty or conscience, but to get countenance from me and thee, to cloak their cursed designs; therefore parley not with them, plead not for them, be not troubled about them, pray not to me in behalf of them. So that this interrogation carries the force of a negation and prohibition with it.

The word "judge" is frequently used for pleading, as in Jer. v. 28; Isa. i. 17; Psal. lxxii. 4; Ezek. xxii. 2; xxiii. 36; and so we have interpreted it here. The doubling of the words, "Wilt thou judge them? wilt thou judge them?" sets out the heinousness of their sin, and the severity of the Lord, that would not suffer the prophet to plead for them.

"Cause them to know the abominations of their fathers." Be thou so far from pleading for them, that thou possess them with and present before them the abominations of their fathers which they follow. Of abominations hath been spoken before; by fathers, their predecessors, kings and others, are meant, who were idolaters, oppressors, and profane.

Obs. 1. The Lord keeps an exact account of his people's sufferings; be the time long or short, he observes it. "In the seventh year, fifth month, and tenth day;" that was, of their captivity. The Lord forgot not how long they had been in Babylon, he notes how the time of their trouble passes. In chap. xxiv. 1, the ninth year, tenth month, and tenth day are mentioned; in chap. xxix. 1, the tenth year, tenth month, and twelfth day are set down; in chap. xxvi. 1, the eleventh year and first day of the month are specified; in chap. xl. 1, the twenty-fifth year of the captivity is named. They were captives in Babylon, suffered hard things, but God took notice of the time, and how the years ran out. It is said Israel served Eglon eighteen years, Judg. iii. 14; that Jabin oppressed them twenty years, chap. iv. 3. It is not said only that the woman had a spirit of infirmity, but the time is recorded also, she had it eighteen years, Luke xiii. 11; so in John v. 5, not only the man and his infirmity is mentioned, but the time also how long, thirty-eight years; so Æneas is said not only to have had the palsy, but to have kept his bed eight years, Acts ix. 33. God tells the years, months, and days, that his people endure adversity: seventy years were determined that they should be in Babylon, Jer. xxix. 10, 11, and God gave them to see, he observed as well, yea, better than they, how they passed.

Obs. 2. The time of men's doing some things is specially noted by the Lord. These elders coming to inquire of the Lord, the time of it is recorded, "in the seventh year, fifth month, and tenth day." Though all things be noted by the Lord, yet some things more especially than others. See how the actions of Josiah are observed; 2 Chron. xxxiv. 3, "In the eighth year of his reign, while he was yet young, he began to seek after the God of David his father: and in the twelfth year he began to purge Judah and Jerusalem from the high places." Ver. 8, "In the eighteenth year of his reign" he repaired the house of the Lord his God; and kept the great passover in that year, chap. xxxv. 18, 19. When Jeroboam feasted and sacrificed to the calves he had made, God took notice of the month and day; 1 Kings xii. 32, it was the eighth month and fifteenth day. When Jehoiakim cut the roll, cast it into the fire, and burnt it, God noted the time of it, Jer. xxxvi. 22, 23. When Esther was taken into the royal house by Ahasuerus, the time is eyed by the Lord, and recorded, chap. ii. 16. See Ezra x. 16; 2 Chron. xxix. 17; Esth. ix. 1, 18; Jer. lii. 31; xxxix. 2, where the times of things are specially recorded. Let men take heed what they do, and when they do it. Matt. xxvi. 15, 16, God observed the time when Judas covenanted with the chief priests, to sell Christ for thirty pieces of silver; "from that time forth he sought opportunity to betray him." When the persecution of the church was, God took notice of it; Acts viii. 1, "At that time:" so Herod's slaying of James; "About that time, he stretched forth his hands," Acts xii. 1, 2.

Obs. 3. Hypocrisy is a close sin, and is in those ofttimes we little think. It is found where it was not expected, in "the elders of Israel;" those who here came to Ezekiel, pretended piety, sat before him, as if they would hearken to whatsoever the Lord should say, and do it; yet they intended no such thing, but were resolved to go on in their own ways, and to be as the Babylonians and heathens, as you may see, ver. 32, that so they might enjoy peace and safety. They did here like many that are upon marriage, who will go to two or three to inquire and have counsel, but are resolved to go on, whatever is said unto them; so whatever counsel they should have had given them from the Lord, they meant to go on in their wicked ways; and this was profound hypocrisy, whose wont it is to veil the foulest things with the fairest pretences. In Ananias and Sapphira there was dissimulation, Acts v.; so in those who came to Jeremiah, entreating him to pray for them, and to consult with God for them: it was a time of affliction, and they would do whatever God should say unto them by Jeremiah; but they dealt hypocritically with him, and God; they were resolved to go into Egypt, although they sent Jeremiah to ask of the Lord, whether they should or no. He told them they must not go; if they did, they should perish there; and because they would go, Jer. xlii. 20, he tells them they dissembled in their hearts, when they sent him to the Lord to pray for them: here was damnable hypocrisy in them. So those that came to Christ, Matt. xxii. 16—18, they carried a foul business very smoothly: "Master, we know that thou art true, and teachest the way of God in truth, neither carest thou for any man. Tell us therefore, What thinkest thou? Is it lawful to give tribute unto Cæsar, or not?" Here was villany couched under these words; they thought to entangle Christ, and to have got advantage hereby to have cut him off; and therefore perceiving their wickedness, he saith, "Why tempt ye me, ye hypocrites?" There are many, it is to be feared, who will be found hypocrites at last, who now frequent the assemblies, and come to hear the word of God, but do it not. Are there not many who come to hear and sit before the Lord, and his ministers, as if they would conform to what he should give out by them; but they hold fast their corrupt opinions, vile lusts, wretched practices: and what is this but hypocrisy? Those in Ezek. xxxiii. 31, 32, they came to the prophet, heard him, gave him good words, but nothing they would do; their hearts went after their covetousness, and they were no better than hypocrites. So now, if men come not with honest hearts, intending to do what they hear, they come hypocritically.

Obs. 4. To inquire and ask counsel of the prophets and men of God, is of ancient standing and warrantable. Here the elders of Israel, that had years, experience, they come to a prophet. Their coming was not unlawful or condemnable, but their coming sinfully. It was a frequent practice of old, to consult with the prophets, 1 Sam. ix. 9; 1 Kings xxii. 15; 2 Kings viii. 8; Jer. xxi. 2; xxxvii. 7; and their coming to them was coming to the Lord, as here they came to inquire of the Lord. Then men look the right way upon the prophets, when they look at God in them, and what he saith by them, with resolution to follow the same. What though now there are no prophets nor apostles immediately inspired and infallible to consult withal, yet there are pastors and teachers, with whom Christ hath promised to be to the end of the world, who are given to perfect and edify the body of Christ; and therefore upon consultation with them, you may be helped to that light which of yourselves you cannot attain unto.

Obs. 5. The prophets were to give out the Lord's mind in his name and words, unto those they were sent unto. "Speak unto the elders of Israel, and say, Thus saith the Lord God:" he might not speak his own mind, his own words, in his own name, he must not say, Thus saith Ezekiel, but, "Thus saith the Lord:" this gave weight and authority to the word, and bred the greater reverence in the hearts of the hearers. That which is from the Lord, hath a divine stamp upon it, a divine power in it; but that which is man's is like himself, frail and feeble; you may refuse it without any considerable prejudice, but not so with the word of the Lord.

Obs. 6. How closely soever men carry their wicked devices, with what colours soever they varnish and paint them over, though they may, can, delude and deceive men, even prophets, yet they cannot impose upon God and deceive him. Ezekiel was outreached by these old foxes, these hypocritical elders, because he could not see into their hearts, discern their intentions; but the Lord, whose eye pierceth into the depths, saw what was within, and detected their foul insides, notwithstanding their pious pretences. "Are ye come to inquire of me?" whom do you think I am? what a God do you make of me? am I like unto man, such as yourselves? No, no; I know your hearts, ye hypocrites. How dare you come into my presence to inquire of me, when you are resolved to go on in your own ways? The Lord knew they had idols in their hearts, Ezek. xiv. 1—3; they were elders of Israel likewise. Great men ofttimes are great hypocrites, they think, being crafty, to go beyond God and his prophets; but it cannot be; he knows upon what grounds, with what purpose, intentions, resolutions, men come to hear his word, to ask counsel of his servants. Look to yourselves, spirits, and all your ways; God seeth and knoweth all, and if you be not sincere, upright, without guile and hypocrisy, he will find you out and detect you.

Obs. 7. When men come to God or his ordinances with hypocritical hearts, they get nothing of him; he is so far from accepting and hearing of them, that he rejects them, and resolves not to answer them. "Come ye to inquire of me? as I live, I will not be inquired of by you." Do you think to have my ear, my countenance, my heart, my hand to do for you? No, you shall have nothing at all of me; begone, I will afford you no answer: though ye be elders of Israel, yet you are hypocrites, and they are odious to me, be they of the highest rank, or lowest; it is not your hoary heads will move me, seeing you have hypocritical hearts: you are resolved to go on in your ways, and I am resolved to go on in my way. I will not answer you; come oft, sit long before the prophet, if you will, answer of me you shall have none, none suitable to your desires and expectations. Job, speaking of a hypocrite, saith, "Will God hear his cry when trouble cometh upon him?" chap. xxvii. 9: at such a time he will cry, and cry hard, but will God hear him? No; God hath no pleasure in hypocrites; therefore saith Ezekiel, chap. viii. 18, "Though they cry in mine ears with a loud voice, yet will I not hear them;" the like you have in Micah iii. 4. If men's hearts be not upright, sincere, let them pray, and cry in prayer, let them hear, and hear attentively, let them come to a prophet to ask counsel, and wait, God respects them not, will not answer them: "the upright in their way are his delight," Prov. xi. 20; he delights in their persons, their presence, their prayers, in doing for them. Prov. x. 29, "The way of the Lord is strength to the upright." What is the way of the Lord? Prayer, hearing of the word, asking counsel of his prophets and servants, are the ways of the Lord; in these he appears, is found, lets out strength, but it is when men are upright, not hypocritical. Come not therefore resolved to go on in your own ways, but, as Peter saith, "Lay aside all malice, all guile, and hypocrisies, envies, and evil speaking, and as new born babes," &c.

Obs. 8. Hypocrites and wicked men may carry themselves so, as to deceive the prophets and servants of God. These elders, by their coming, putting the prophet on to inquire of the Lord for them, sitting before him for an answer, bred such good thoughts of them in the prophet's mind, as that when God told him he would not be inquired at by them, he was ready to plead for them, and excuse them from being hypocrites, wondering the Lord should be so hot and resolute against them, as not to vouchsafe them an answer. He thought they were good men, and worthy of better entertainment at the hands of God, than they had, but he was deceived. Simon Magus demeaned himself so, that he begat a good esteem in the heart of Philip, and was admitted to baptism, Acts viii. 13. In John's days many got into the church, who seemed saints, but were hypocrites: 1 John ii. 19, "They went out from us that they might be made manifest." John and others had

had good opinions of them, but were deluded by them. False apostles got into the church of Ephesus, and for a time had gained too much upon the angel thereof, Rev. ii. 2. When the captains and people came to Jeremiah in a smooth way, promising to do whatever the Lord should say by him, they insinuated so far into him, that they prevailed with him to inquire of the Lord for them; but they juggled with him, Jer. xlii. Prophets and ministers may be and are deceived oft with the specious pretences of naughty men; because they would not be uncharitable, they are many times too credulous.

Obs. 9. Hypocrites are not to be pleaded for. "Wilt thou judge them, son of man, wilt thou judge them?" God would not have the prophet to plead for or excuse them. Hypocrites are so odious in God's eye, that he takes it unkindly when his prophets and ministers appear for them; if they have thoughts that way, he dislikes it, and forbids them. This double interrogation is a double negation. These hypocrites would have drawn in God and the prophet to have countenanced their vile intentions, therefore God would neither answer them, nor suffer his prophet to speak for them. Hypocrites are not always the greatest of sinners, but they are ever the worst of sinners, because they pretend to be holy, and under pretence of holiness cover all their wickedness. The devil is never more devil, than when he transforms himself into an angel of light; he seeming light, being darkness, is devilishly hypocritical, hiding all his hellish darkness under pretended light: and so do all hypocrites, who are his eldest sons; under the light of being religious, they do all their deeds of darkness. The Jews were "a hypocritical nation," Isa. x. 6; Jer. vii. 9, 10; and therefore God forbids Jeremiah to pray for them, chap. xiv. 11. And what if they would pray themselves? you have an answer in Job xiii. 16; God tells you that "an hypocrite shall not come before him," that is, to have acceptance of his person, or hear any comfortable answer from him. Christ hath told hypocrites what they must look for, Matt. xxiii. "Woe unto you, scribes and Pharisees, hypocrites!" woes they may look for, and must hear of. Woe to them for imposing upon God, as if he saw not their close wickedness! Woe to them for abusing religion to further their devilish designs! Woe to them for deceiving others by their painted shows and professions! and woe to them for deceiving themselves!

Obs. 10. The prophets and servants of God, when they are inquired of by men, must not proceed according to their desires, or their own apprehensions of them that do so desire, but they must wait for the mind of God, and do answerably thereunto. "Wilt thou judge them, son of man? cause them to know the abominations of their fathers." They would have thee inquire of me for them, but I will not be inquired of, they shall not have their desires: thou apprehendest they are good, and wouldst speak for them, but thou must not do after thy own apprehensions, thou must attend my pleasure, and do what that is; and it is this, "make them to know the abominations of their fathers." They did such things as provoked me to cast these their children into this Babylonish captivity; and will they continue in their ways, or proceed to worse? Go thy ways, lay before them the abominable things their fathers have done, see what effect that will have with them. Mind not their desires, stand not upon thy own apprehensions of them: I have made known my will unto thee, go thou and make it known unto them without dispute or delay. Not the people's desires, nor the prophet's fancies, must be his direction, when he is to make answer to those that inquire; but the will of God made known by his word and Spirit.

Ver. 5. *And say unto them, Thus saith the Lord God; In the day when I chose Israel, and lifted up mine hand unto the seed of the house of Jacob, and made myself known unto them in the land of Egypt, when I lifted up mine hand unto them, saying, I am the Lord your God.*

Here begins the third part of the chapter, which is the relation of God's dealing with them, and theirs towards him;

1. In Egypt, from this verse to the 10th.
2. In the desert, from the 10th to the 27th.
3. In Canaan, from the 27th to the 33rd.

In the first of these you have sundry choice mercies of God set down, with his command, and their notorious wickedness.

The mercies are reckoned up in ver. 5, 6, 7, and 9, and they are these:

(1.) God's election of them.
(2.) His revelation of himself unto them.
(3.) His profession of being their God.
(4.) His promise to bring them out of the land of Egypt into the land of Canaan.
(5.) His confirmation of all these, by lifting up his hand.
(6.) His sparing of them for his name's sake.
(7.) His bringing them forth out of Egypt.

The command is to cease from Egyptian idolatry, ver. 7.

Their sin was rebellion, ver. 8.

I come now to open the words, and so to give you the observations.

"In the day when I chose Israel." The Hebrew is, in the day of my choosing in Israel. Septuagint, from what day I chose the house of Israel.

"Day," here, is not taken in opposition to night, as it is John xi. 9, 10, nor for time indefinitely, as Gen. iii. 5, but for the time wherein some particular thing was evidenced to be done.

By election, here, is not meant the decree or purpose of God, to take the Jews to be his people, that was before all time, from eternity; but the manifestation of that election, In the day that I made it appear that I had elected you. Election or choosing, in the Scripture, sometimes refers to things, as Deut. xxiii. 16; Gen. xiii. 11; 1 Kings xviii. 25; Prov. xxii. 1: sometimes to persons, and then it is either to Christ, as Isa. xlii. 1; or to angels, as 1 Tim. v. 21; or to men, and then it is spoken either of persons who are invisible members of the mystical body of Christ, as 2 Thess. ii. 13, or of a community and visible body, and so it is here. God chose this nation of the Jews to be his nation and church, Deut. vii. 6, to have his oracles, ordinances, and means of grace amongst them.

"In the day when I chose Israel." What time this was, is to be searched out. It was not that time when God manifested himself to Abraham, and bid him get him out of his country, to a land he would show him, and he would make of him a great nation, Gen. xii. 1, 2; nor that time when he appeared to Jacob, and said, "I am God, the God of thy father: fear not to go down into Egypt; for I will there make of thee a great nation: I will go down with thee into Egypt; and I will also surely bring thee up again," Gen. xlvi. 2—4. They were not yet a nation, nor in Egypt, of both which the choice here is meant. The time, then, was, when God took notice of their hard sufferings in Egypt, by the rigorous taskmasters, and appeared to Moses, and bid him say to Pharaoh, "Israel is my son, my firstborn; let my son go, that he may serve me," Exod. iv. 22, 23; and sent Aaron with him upon that message to Pharaoh, chap. v. 1, where they go in to Pharaoh and say, "Thus saith the Lord God of Israel, Let my people go, that they may hold a feast unto me in the wilderness." Thou thinkest these people are thine, and therefore holdest them in servitude and bondage; but the Lord God of heaven is the God of Israel, he challengeth this people to be his, and commands thee to let them go and serve him.

"And lifted up mine hand." Lifting up the hand is a phrase much mentioned in the book of God; it is seven times in this chapter, twice in this verse, once in the 6th, and then it is in ver. 15, 23, 28, and 42. To lift up the hand notes divers things, and was used in divers weighty things.

1. In blessing. Psal. cxxxiv. 2, "Lift up your hands in the sanctuary, and bless the Lord." Lev. ix. 22, "Aaron lifted up his hand toward the people, and blessed them." Luke xxiv. 50, Christ "lifted up his hands, and blessed them."

2. In prayer. Psal. lxiii. 4, "I will lift up my hands in thy name." 1 Tim. ii. 8, "I will that men pray every where, lifting up holy hands." And Psal. lxxxviii. 9, Heman saith, he called upon God daily, and stretched out his hands unto him. Lam. ii. 19, "Lift up thine hands toward him for the life of thy children."

3. It notes open mercy, favour, aid. Isa. xlix. 22, "I will lift up mine hand to the gentiles," that is, I will reach unto them the gospel, and by the power and grace of it, bring them to Zion. In this sense it is to be taken, Psal. x. 12, "O God, lift up thy hand; forget not the humble;" that is, evidence thy power, and help the humble and afflicted against their oppressors.

4. To lift up the hand, imports threatening, hurting, smiting. Psal. cvi. 26, "He lifted up his hand against them, to overthrow them in the wilderness." When men are angry with others, and threaten to do them harm, to ruin them, they oft lift up their hands and fists against them; thus it signifies in Micah v. 9; Ezek. xliv. 12.

5. To lift up the hand, implies swearing. It was a gesture used in that sacred act, Gen. xiv. 22; Deut. xxxii. 40. It is expressed so in Isa. iii. 7, "In that day shall he swear," the Hebrew is, lift up the hand. The first and second sense pertains not to this place; and though some would have it meant of God's lifting up his hand to help the Israelites out of their bondage, by the smiting of Pharaoh and the Egyptians, yet to me the last sense seems most suitable: and lifting up the hand here imports swearing; it refers to what you have Exod. vi. 8, "I will bring you to the land concerning which I did swear," or lift up my hand, "to give it to Abraham, to Isaac, and to Jacob." God had promised and sworn to them, that he would bring their seed out of Egypt, into Canaan, Gen. l. 24; xv. 7, 14, 16.

"Unto the seed of the house of Jacob." Montanus reads the words, for the seed of the house of Jacob. Vatablus, upon, or, on the seed. Here it is, "unto the seed;" God's promise and oath was for them, over them, and unto them. By "seed" is meant, the posterity of Jacob. God had told Jacob that his seed should be as the dust of the earth, Gen. xxviii. 14; and his seed did greatly multiply in Egypt, Exod. i. 7: and his seed is called sometimes "the seed of Israel," Isa. xlv. 25, and "seed of the house of Israel," Jer. xxiii. 8; sometimes "the seed of Jacob," Psal. xxii. 23, and here, "the seed of the house of Jacob," because Jacob or Israel was the root, stock, family out of which the Jews in Egypt sprung.

"And made myself known unto them." Great were the afflictions of the Jews in Egypt; they were like men in a storm at sea, and that in a dark night; when day breaks it is some refreshing, and such was God's making himself known unto them. This making himself known unto them was for their deliverance. God appeared to Moses in the burning bush, and told him who he was, and what he was about to do, Exod. iii. 2, 6—8; he had promised Abraham, Isaac, and Jacob, to give their seed the land of Canaan, and now he was come to give being to that promise, to make himself known by his name Jehovah, which they knew not; in this sense they saw not that promise fulfilled, but Moses, Aaron, and their seed should now see it, chap. vi. 3, 8; God would put forth his mighty power, and by a strong hand bring them forth, ver. 1. God made himself known to them by Moses, who was God's messenger, and instrument to speak, and do what he pleased; Psal. ciii. 7, "He made known his ways unto Moses, his acts unto the children of Israel:" God's pity, faithfulness, and power were abundantly made known.

After the Lord had appeared to Moses, answered all his objections he made against undertaking the difficult work of delivering the people, and joined Aaron with him for his assistant, in chap. iv. they gather all the elders of Israel together, they told them all the words God had spoken, and did the signs by which God had confirmed the words concerning their deliverance; which the people believed, bowed, and worshipped God, ver. 29—31. Here God was made known unto them.

"I am the Lord your God." Hebrew is, I Jehovah your God. The first is absolute, the second relative. Of Jehovah I have spoken heretofore; it notes God's nature and being, which is of itself, within itself, and dependent upon none; all other beings are from him, and depend on him, according to what you have, Rom. xi. 36, "Of him, through him, and to him are all things;" and Acts xvii. 28, "In him we live, move, and have our being."

"Your God." This is a great word, and hath great mercy in it; an engaging word, tying God and all his attributes to them: your God to counsel you, your God to protect you, your God to deliver you, your God to comfort you, your God to plead for you, your God to teach you, your God to set up my name and worship among you, your God to bless you with the dews of heaven and fulness of the earth, your God to hear your prayers and to make you happy.

While they were in Egypt, God professed himself to be their God: Exod. vi. 7, "I will take you to me for a people, and I will be to you a God; and ye shall know that I am the Lord your God." He would not be a titular God unto them, like the heathen's gods; but they should have experience of him and his attributes, he would do by them, and for them, as a God in covenant.

Obs. 1. There are times when the Lord is pleased to show mercy to people in misery and great afflictions. In the day that I chose thee. Israel was in a distressed condition in Egypt, in a very low estate; their lives were imbittered with hard bondage, insomuch that they sighed and cried, Exod. ii. 23; and now at this time, and being in this condition, God heard their groanings, looked upon and had respect unto them, now he chose them, ver. 24, 25; therefore Isaiah saith, chap. xlviii. 10, God chose them "in the furnace of affliction." Times of misery are times of God's showing mercy; when they were in a hot fiery furnace, ready to be consumed to ashes, no likelihood of escaping, yet even then did the Lord appear and manifest his choice of them. Ezek. xvi. when this people were in their blood, filth, nakedness, saith God, "I passed by thee, and looked upon thee, and behold thy time was the time of love; I spread my skirt over thee, and covered thy nakedness," ver. 8: at that time God took this people into favour. God hath his day to bind up the breach of his people, and to heal "the stroke of their wound," Isa. xxx. 26. Hosea tells you, that after two days he will revive his people, and in the third day raise them up; though they be like men dead and buried, yet God hath his time to revive, raise, and to cause to live in his sight. They were as dry bones in Babylon, and served a hard service there; but there was a day wherein God gave them rest from their sorrow, fears, and servitude, Isa. xiv. 3, 4. The gentiles were a long time in the wilderness, in a lost and perishing condition; Eph. ii. 12, there was a time they were without Christ, without hope, without God in the world, but God had a day to manifest his choice of them; ver. 13, "But now in Christ Jesus they who sometimes were afar off, are made nigh;" there was a now, a time, a day for them. So Zeph. iii. 16, 19, 20.

Obs. 2. The taking of a people to be the Lord's, is of mere grace and mercy; it is God's own free act. "In the day when I chose Israel." Israel did not choose him, Israel had nothing to affect him, but out of his good pleasure he chose Israel. The Lord makes open protestation, Deut. vii. 7, 8, that he did not set his love upon them, nor choose them, because they were more in number than other people, but because he loved them. And what made God love them? were they better than other nations? They came of the Amorites and Hittites, they were in their blood, when he said unto them, "Live," Ezek. xvi. 3, 6. Did he foresee they would believe, repent, and persevere in keeping his commands, and honour him above the rest of the world? no, he foresaw that they would be more wicked than the nations and countries round about them, chap. v. 6, 7, and exceed Sodom and Samaria in wickedness, as it is chap. xvi. 47, 51, 52. What was it then caused God to love and choose this people? Nothing without God himself, all was within doors that stirred him up to do it. "I will say to them which were not my people, Thou art my people," Hos. ii. 23. God's will is the cause, and nothing else: Rom. ix. 18, he will have mercy on whom he will: Isa. xli. 9, "I have chosen thee, and not cast thee away."

Obs. 3. When God's people are in troubles, he discovers and reveals himself unto them, one way or other, by one means or other. "I made myself known unto them in the land of Egypt." That was a land and house of bondage to them, they met with reproaches, threats, stripes, rigour, and hard labour there; and when the case was so with them, then God unmasks, and shows himself unto them. When Joseph's brethren were in great trouble, then he made known himself unto them, Gen. xlv.; and so did God unto his people by Moses and Aaron: he made known what promise and oath he had made to Abraham, Isaac, and Jacob; he made known his tender-heartedness to them, that their cries came up to his ears, and that he was affected with their sorrows, and would no longer endure the Egyptians to oppress them; he made known his mighty power unto them, that he was stronger than Pharaoh and all his strength: Deut. iv. 34, 35, "Hath God assayed to go and take him a nation from the midst of another nation, by temptations, by signs, and by wonders, by war, by a mighty hand, by a stretched-out arm, and by great terrors, according to all that the Lord your God did for you in Egypt before your eyes? Unto thee it was showed, that thou mightest know that the Lord he is God." The Lord made himself known by these in an eminent manner unto them. It is God's way to appear to his people in the time of their calamity and darkness: Isa. liv. 11—14, "O thou afflicted, tossed with tempest, and not comforted, behold, I will lay thy stones with fair colours, and lay thy foundations with sapphires. And I will make thy windows of agates, and thy gates of carbuncles, and all thy borders of pleasant stones. And all thy children shall be taught of the Lord; and great shall be the peace of thy children. In righteousness shalt thou be established," &c. What a precious, glorious discovery of God was here unto the church, being in a storm! So when Rachel wept for her children, and refused to be comforted, because they were not, how did the Lord break out of the clouds and shine, when he said to her, "Refrain thy voice from weeping, and thine eyes from tears; for thy work shall be rewarded, saith the Lord; and they shall come again from the land of the enemies," Jer. xxxi. 15, 16. In the time of affliction God's words and works are more observed, take deeper impression, endear more unto him, therefore he loves to manifest himself in them.

Obs. 4. God knowing men's weakness, condescends for to strengthen and establish them in the assurance of his favour towards them. Not only by word and works did God evidence it, that the seed of Abraham, Isaac, and Jacob were his chosen ones, his people, which might have sufficed; but he took his oath upon it; "I lifted up mine hand unto the seed of the house of Jacob;" yea, that it might be the more firm, he doubled it; "When I lifted up mine hand unto them, saying, I am the Lord your God." For God to tell any people he hath chosen them, argues great favour; then, to appear unto them, and make large manifestations of himself and his good will unto them, by words, providential and wonderful working for them, argues more and more favour; and then to swear unto them, or declare he hath sworn unto them, and not only to do some few things for them, but to be their God, this is height of favour, wonderful stooping on God's part; and this he did to confirm their hearts in assurance of his love. God cannot falsify his word, much less his oath. God did swear, that Abraham and his seed might have strong consolation, not stagger, question his love any more; and the apostle applies it to himself, Heb. vi. 17, 18, to all believers, who are heirs of the promise, and under the oath of God, that we might have strong consolation.

Ver. 6. *In the day that I lifted up mine hand unto them, to bring them forth of the land of Egypt into a land that I had espied for them, flowing with milk and honey, which is the glory of all lands.*

God, having chosen the Jews to be his people, made himself known unto them, and professed himself to be their God; here he tells them of the good promise he made unto them, which was, to bring them out of Egypt into Canaan. The praise and encomium whereof is set out more fully in this verse than in any part of holy writ besides. It is threefold:

1. From the Discoverer; it was a land of God's looking out for them.

2. From the commodities it had; that in plenty it flowed "with milk and honey."

3. From the eminency of it above other lands; it "is the glory of all lands."

Of "lifting up the hand," hath been spoken in the former verse.

"The land of Egypt." The Hebrew is, the land of Mizraim. So Egypt is constantly called in the

Old Testament, and thrice, "the land of Ham," Psal. cv. 23, 27, and cvi. 22; and once, "the tabernacle of Ham," Psal. lxxviii. 51. Mizraim was the son of Ham, who possessed that part of Africa, and from him it was called Mizraim, or the land of Mizraim, and sometimes the land of Ham, who was his father. Paræus in Gen. chap. x. Josephus saith, the Egyptians in his time were called Mesræi, by the eastern people. In the Septuagint it is rendered Egypt, so called from one Egyptus, who reigned there some three hundred and ninety years after the Israelites came out of Egypt. This land was very plentiful, Joseph. l. 1. contra Appionem. and in Joseph's days supplied Jacob's family with corn, when the famine was great: for the fruitfulness thereof, it was called the granary of the Roman people; but to the Jews it was a house of bondage.

"Into a land that I had espied for them." This land was Canaan, which God looked out for them amongst all lands in the world. The Hebrew word signifies, to search out by wandering over, and viewing on every side: so did the Lord here; he took special notice of this land; his eyes did run to and fro throughout the earth, to see what land was the chiefest, and Canaan was the land he pitched upon. The Septuagint is, to a land which I had prepared for them: God had long before prepared and provided this land. Israel was his son, his firstborn, and like a loving and provident parent, he provided a land and habitation for him.

"Flowing with milk and honey." This encomium of this land is eighteen several times in the book of God: four times in Exodus, as chap. iii. 8, 17; xiii. 5; xxxiii. 3; once in Leviticus, chap. xx. 24; twice in Numbers, chap. xiii. 27; xiv. 8; six times in Deuteronomy, chap. vi. 3; xi. 9; xxvi. 9, 15; xxvii. 3; xxxi. 20; twice in Jeremiah, chap. xi. 5; xxxii. 22; once in Joshua, chap. v. 6; and twice in this chapter, in this verse and the 15th. Doubtless the land of Canaan abounded with milk and honey, as may appear by Gen. xviii. 8; Prov. xxvii. 27; 1 Sam. xiv. 26; 2 Sam. xvii. 29; but the phrase here, of "flowing with milk and honey," is proverbial, and notes plenty of all good and precious things; as you may see, Joel iii. 18; Amos ix. 13; and in Job, plenty is set out by rivers, floods, and brooks of honey and butter, chap. xx. 17. And it is clear that the fruits of the earth were called "milk and honey;" Numb. xiii. 26, 27, when the spies that searched the land came back and brought of the fruit thereof, they said, "Surely it floweth with milk and honey," and this is the fruit of it; the figs, pomegranates, and grapes, were part of the "milk and honey." So that synecdochically here by "milk and honey," are understood all good things, needful and delightful.

This plenty is set out by "milk and honey," rather than by other things,

1. Because they are most common, serving old and young, all sorts of people. Milk is food for babes, and for those whose age hath so enfeebled their stomachs, as that they cannot bear strong meat.

2. They are always in a readiness. Other meats usually require much time to fit them for our tastes.

3. They are sweet and pleasant. Though other things be so, as oil and wine, yet not comparable to "milk and honey."

That Canaan did abound with all good things, see Deut. viii. 7—9, where it is called, "a good land," in which they should not want any thing. This was partly from the nature of the air and soil, the one being very wholesome, and the other very fat, and partly from the peculiar blessing of God upon the Jews; he gave them the former and the latter rains, he made the land in the sixth year to bring forth fruit for three years, Lev. xxv. 18—21; chap. xxvi. 3—5; Deut. xi. 13—15; which blessing, for their sins, God hath taken away, as he threatened, Lev. xxvi. 20; Deut. xxviii. 38—40; therefore they are deceived that think or say Judea was no fertile place. Rab-shakeh, who was an enemy to the Jews and their God, yet acknowledged their land to be a fertile land, 2 Kings xviii. 31, 32. Whatever men's conceits are of it now, it was a land which flowed with "milk and honey;" which proverbial speech was of use also among others, to set out plenty and fruitfulness by.

"Which is the glory of all lands." The Hebrew is, which is the ornament of all lands, the honour, ornament, or glory of all. The Septuagint hath it, *κηρίον*, the honeycomb; it was so fruitful and pleasant a land, that it was like a honeycomb, wonderful sweet to the inhabitants. Vatablus calls it the land to be desired above all lands. Kircker interprets צבי of that which affects the mind and sense, and invites to the loving of it, affording pleasure and delight. The Spirit of God calls it, the land of desire, thrice, Psal. cvi. 24; Jer. iii. 19; Zech. vii. 14, so the Hebrew is, and so the margin hath it; a "good land," Deut. viii. 7; an "exceeding good land," Numb. xiv. 7. It was not only a "good land," but a land that exceeded in goodness; "that good land," Deut. iv. 22; the words are very emphatical, הארץ הטובה הזאת that land, that good, that. In Dan. xi. it is twice termed the "glorious land," ver. 16, 41. ארץ הצבי the land of ornament, or the land of glory, yea, that glory which no other land attained unto.

The land is thought to be situated in the midst of the world, being very temperate, neither too hot, nor too cold; it is computed to be two hundred miles in length, and not above fifty in breadth. It had thirty-one kings in it when Joshua smote it, when he brought the Jews to possess it, Josh. xii; and in David's days there were found in Israel and Judah (for so it was then divided) thirteen hundred thousand fighting men, besides women, children, and such as were not able to fight, 2 Sam. xxiv. This land was "the glory of all lands," in regard of the fruitfulness and plenty of it, of which see Deut. viii. 7—9; xxxii. 13, 14; Isa. xxxvi. 17; a land beyond Egypt, (though some have affirmed the contrary,) for, Deut. xi. 10—12, "The land thou goest in to possess is not as the land of Egypt, from whence ye came out, where thou sowedst thy seed, and wateredst it with thy foot, as a garden of herbs: but the land whither ye go to possess it, is a land of hills and valleys, and drinketh water of the rain of heaven: a land which the Lord thy God careth for: the eyes of the Lord thy God are always upon it, from the beginning of the year even unto the end of the year." This is a divine testimony, and a high praise of it, and doth justly entitle it to be the "glory of all lands."

What our prophet saith here of Canaan may be suspected, and seems to be contradicted by Isaiah, chap. xiii. 19, where he calls Babylon "the glory of kingdoms;" and if that be the glory of them, how can Canaan be the "glory of all lands?" He speaks of the city Babylon, which was the head of Chaldea, and gave denomination to a great part of Mesopotamia and Assyria, the walls whereof were two hundred feet high, fifty cubits broad, and sixty miles in compass, which the Babylonians counted the glory of kingdoms, and boasted of. If it did exceed Jerusalem in its greatness, richness, strength, and populousness, yet it fell short of it in other things. Jerusalem represented the true church, Gal. iv. 26;

Heb. xii. 22; Babylon, the malignant and false church, Rev. xvii. 5. Glorious things were spoken of Jerusalem; and it was the faithful city, Isa. i. 21; the holy city, Isa. lii. 1; the city of truth, Zech. viii. 3; a city of righteousness, Isa. i. 26; the city of the Lord of hosts: such things were never spoken of Babylon.

Again, if Babylon be the glory of kingdoms, it is not said to be of all kingdoms. It might be the glory of heathenish kingdoms, it was not the glory of Canaan; for there was the idol Bel, other images, and abominable idolatry, Jer. li. 44, 47, which eclipsed the other glory it had.

Again, if it be granted that Babylon was the glory of all kingdoms, and so of Judea or Canaan, yet take Canaan in its latitude, with all its excellences, and so considered, it is the "glory of all lands," and beyond Babylon, taken for the city or the country; for, besides its milk and honey, its fruitfulness and plenty, there was something of a higher nature which made it so. For,

1. It was the land of promise, Heb. xi. 9.
2. A type of heaven, Heb. iii. 11.
3. The land God chose to dwell in, Psal. cxxxii. 13, 14; Exod. xv. 17.
4. In it was the temple, worship, ordinances, and oracles of God, 1 Kings vi. and viii. Whence it was called the holy land, Zech. ii. 12; holy habitation, Exod. xv. 13; the land of the Lord, Isa. xiv. 2; Psal. lxxxv. 2; the land of uprightness, Isa. xxvi. 10; the land of Immanuel, Isa. viii. 8; and upon this account, it was "the glory of all lands;" for no land besides in all the world was so called as this, or had such prerogatives.

Obs. 1. Old mercies should be minded, not only by those they were first bestowed upon, but also by their posterity, who had benefit by them also. In the former verse and this, God minds them of old mercies, his choice of them, his making known himself unto them, his professing himself to be their God, his bringing them out of Egypt, which were some eight or nine hundred years before, and his espying out a land for them, which was four hundred years before that; for it was in Abraham's days that God took notice of that land; Gen. xii. 1, "Get thee to a land that I will show thee;" ver. 7, "Unto thy seed will I give this land." These old mercies God would have them to mind, though they were in Babylon, and deprived of that good land God had given them. Let men be in what condition they will, old mercies should not be forgotten, especially signal, great, emphatical mercies. When God shall publicly own a people, deliver them from great slavery, put them into a state of freedom, safety, and honour, provide all good things for them, such mercies ought not to be forgotten, but to be remembered from generation to generation. This was done in David's days: Psal. xliv. 1, 2, "We have heard with our ears, O God, our fathers have told us, what work thou didst in their days, in the times of old; how thou didst drive out the heathen with thy hand." Judg. vi. 13, fathers told their children of the miracles God had wrought for them, and how he brought them out of Egypt. And because men are apt to forget former mercies, when they grow old they grow out of mind, the Lord laid a charge upon the Jews that they should not forget them, Deut. vi. 10—12; and commanded them to "remember the days of old, and to consider the years of many generations," and to inquire of the ancient what he had done for them, Deut. xxxii. 7. There are no works like unto God's works, and they ought to be had in remembrance. David kept them in mind, for he professes to the Lord himself, "I remember the days of old, I meditate on all thy works, I muse on the work of thy hand:" he looked back to the days of Noah, of Abraham, of Joseph, of the Israelites, and of God's dealing with them; and, because the heart is not quickly affected with old mercies, and works of God, he meditated and mused on them, and that till his heart was warmed, and stirred up to praise; as it is, Psal. cv. 5, "Remember his marvellous works that he hath done; his wonders, and the judgments of his mouth; O ye seed of Abraham his servant."

Obs. 2. That lands, countries, and habitations of people, are appointed, ordered, and disposed of by the Lord. He "brings them forth of the land of Egypt, into a land that he had espied for them." All souls, and all lands, are the Lord's, and whom he will he plants where he pleases; he distributes lands and habitations to whom he thinks meet: "The earth is the Lord's, and the fulness thereof," Psal. xxiv. 1; he is the sole owner thereof, the true Lord of the soil, and all it brings forth, and he hath "given it to the children of men," Psal. cxv. 16; he hath assigned them their several portions. Deut. xxxii. 8, "The Most High divided to the nations their inheritance, when he separated the sons of Adam:" the most high God, being Lord paramount, would not have the sons of Adam to live all in one country, or land, but appointed them several lands and countries to dwell in, and set them their bounds and limits, as you may see in Gen. x. especially ver. 25, where Eber names his son Peleg, (which signifies division,) because the earth was divided in his days. After the flood, at the building of Babel, God confounded the languages, and dispersed the posterity of Noah into divers lands, and set them their bounds, Gen. xi. 9; and so, when he brought the Israelites into the land of Canaan, he gave them their bounds, according to what you find, Psal. lxxviii. 55, "He cast out the heathen also before them, and divided them an inheritance by line, and made the tribes of Israel to dwell in their tents;" he drove out and destroyed the Hittites, the Girgashites, the Amorites, the Canaanites, the Perizzites, the Hivites, and the Jebusites, seven great and mighty nations, Deut. vii. 1, and gave the land unto his people the Jews. If God now will drive out the bloody, perfidious, and idolatrous out of Ireland, and give it unto others, that the seed of his servants may inherit it, and that those which love his name may dwell therein, who shall blame him for it? And that England hath had right thereunto, not only from Henry the Eighth's days, who was proclaimed king thereof, in parliament here, and in an Irish parliament likewise, if Heylin say true, but also from Henry the Second's time, yea, from Edgar's, who was long before, appears by English history.

Obs. 3. The Lord provides and bestows the choicest mercies upon his own people. If there be a land in the world that flows with milk and honey, that exceeds other lands for plenty and pleasantness, his people shall have it; he espies out Canaan for them, that land was too good for heathens, his people must have it. When God carried Jacob and his family into Egypt, he provided the good and fat of that land for them, Gen. xlv. 18; yea, they were placed in the "best of the land," chap. xlvii. 11. God fed and filled his people with the "finest of the wheat," Psal. cxlvii. 14. Moses mentions seven things together in Deut. xxxii. 13—15, as, "honey out of the rock, oil out of the flinty rock, butter of kine, milk of sheep, fat of lambs, and rams of the breed of Bashan, and goats, fat of kidneys of wheat, the pure blood of the grape;" these the Lord provided for his people, and they had all an excellency in them. When God gives honey, oil, butter, milk, fat, flour, wine, he giveth the best and purest. You may read what choice mercies God bestowed upon this people, Ezek. xvi. 10—13; they had "goodly pleasant things," Joel iii. 5; the Hebrew is, goodly desirable things: and David acknowledgeth he had a "goodly heritage." Psal. xvi. 6. God had not measured out to him a mean portion, but a good; yea, a "goodly heritage," that which was so in the eyes of all, even a "wealthy place," Psal. lxvi. 12. God provided the best places in the court for Esther and her maidens, when in Babylon, Esth. ii. 9, 16; so likewise Daniel and the three children were set in eminent places, Dan. ii. and iii. God made his people to ride and tread upon the high places of the earth, and of their enemies, Deut. xxxii. 13; xxxiii. 29.

Obs. 4. Spiritual mercies make a land glorious, yea, more glorious than all lands that want the same, whatever mercies they else enjoy. Canaan was the glory of all lands, not so much for its flowing with milk and honey, its great plenty it had, as for the spiritual mercies it enjoyed; there was the Lord's presence, his prophets, his worship, his oracles, and his ordinances, and these made it glorious, yea, more than all the nations far or near. Psal. lxxvi. 1, 2, "In Judah is God known: his name is great in Israel. In Salem also is his tabernacle, and his dwelling-place in Zion." God was not known in Babylon, in Egypt, in other nations, his tabernacle and dwelling-place was not amongst them, therefore they were not glorious. But see what is in the 4th verse, "Thou art more glorious than the mountains of prey;" thou Judah, thou Israel, thou Salem, thou Zion, that hast spiritual mercies and blessings, art more glorious than they, whatever their glory be. Have the nations abroad goodly towers? thou hast the temple; have they stately cities? thou hast Jerusalem, the city of God; have they wise men? thou hast the prophets; have they gods of gold, silver, and stones? thou hast the true living God, Jehovah, to be thy God; have they human laws that are good? thou hast divine laws that excel; have they temporal excellences? thou hast spiritual; have they the glory of the world? thou hast the glory of heaven. Psal. l. 2, "Out of Zion, the perfection of beauty, God hath shined." What made Zion so glorious and beautiful? it was the presence of God: if he had not been there, Zion had been like other mountains, and Canaan like other nations; but his presence was like the sun, darting out her beams, and making all lightsome, glorious, and beautiful. Spiritual mercies are beams and rays of that God, who is ten thousand times more bright than the sun; by these he shined in Zion, and made it the perfection, or universality, of beauty; by these he shined out of Zion, and darkened all the glory of the nations, what or how great soever it was. Where God and his ordinances are, there is glory; and where these are not, there is no glory, but Egyptian darkness, a land without the sun.

In Canaan was spiritual light and glory. There were glorious appearances of God, glorious praisings of God, glorious conversions of sinners unto God, glorious sabbaths and assemblies; and glorious beauties of holiness, glorious types of Christ, and people who were the glory of God, Isa. iv. 5, and had glorious communion with God. There were glorious truths, ordinances, and dispensations of God.

So then, wise counsellors, good magistrates, stout soldiers, rich merchants, industrious labourers, strong towns, stately houses, high mountains, fertile valleys, pleasant rivers, goodly corn-fields, herds of cattle, flocks of sheep, with plenty of all outward things, do not make a land so glorious as spiritual mercies do: if God, Christ, gospel, and the ordinances of it, be in a land, they make it glorious, and glorious beyond all other things, and above all other nations. Let us learn to know our true glory, even spiritual mercies, and prize them highly, though loathed by some like manna of old, and pray that such glory may ever dwell in our land.

Ver. 7. *Then said I unto them, Cast ye away every man the abominations of his eyes, and defile not yourselves with the idols of Egypt: I am the Lord your God.*

This verse is a command; wherein you have the Commander, the things commanded, and the reason thereof.

I. The Commander; "Then said I unto them."

II. The things commanded; which are,

1. Casting away of abominations; where,

(1.) You have a specification of these abominations, they are the abominations of their eyes.

(2.) The extent of this act, "every man."

2. Non-defilement of themselves with Egypt's idols.

III. The reason; "I am the Lord your God."

"Then said I unto them." For "then," the Hebrew is, and I said to them. Where the Lord said thus to them, we do not find; the words refer to the time of their being in Egypt, and nothing is recorded in Exodus, that the Lord spake thus unto them, before they departed from Egypt. They were a long time in Egypt, and though Moses mentions not this passage, yet our prophet assures us that the Lord said so; whence we may take this observation:

Obs. That many things said and done by the Lord, and his servants, though omitted in those places which seemed most proper for them in penning the Scriptures, yet are occasionally given forth in other places; as this verse, spoken by the Lord when they were in Egypt, omitted by Moses, and now given out to Ezekiel in Babylon, and recorded by him in this place. Enoch's prophecy, being uttered in the infancy of the world, was either unknown to, or passed over, if known by Moses, the prophets, and apostles, till Jude's time, and then it was recorded upon the occasion of the scoffing and profaneness of that time, Jude 14. The names of Jannes and Jambres, who withstood Moses, were not taken into the text till Paul's time, 2 Tim. iii. 8: so Moses his refusing to be called the son of Pharaoh's daughter, his choosing rather to suffer affliction with the people of God, than to enjoy the pleasures of sin for a season, his esteeming the reproach of Christ greater riches than the treasures in Egypt, and his eyeing the recompence of reward, were not mentioned by himself, nor by any other till the apostle set them down, Heb. xi. 24—26: these things they had by the Spirit, not by tradition.

"Cast ye away." Of these words hath been largely spoken in chap. xviii. 31, "Cast away from you all your transgressions;" the word is there the same.

"Every man." In the Hebrew it is איש a man, let man cast away; that is, let every one that hath the name or nature of man do so. It is from a word which signifies, essence, or being, and is often put indefinitely for any man; as Hos. ii. 10, "None shall deliver her out of mine hand;" the Hebrew is, not a man; that is, not any man shall do it: and for "every man;" Psal. lxii. 12, "Thou renderest to every man according to his work;" the word for "every man" is, לאיש to a man, that is, to every man, whoever he be.

"The abominations of his eyes." Of "abominations," formerly. These "abominations" were their idols, things abominable and to be abhorred. They are here called the "abominations of their eyes," because their eyes were lift up unto them, as it is chap. xviii. 6, 12, and went a whoring after them, chap. vi. 9. Their "eyes" were taken with the form, beauty, ornaments of the idols, and so let in that to their hearts which inflamed and provoked them to idolatry.

"And defile not yourselves with the idols of Egypt." Of the word "defile," see chap. v. 11. "With the idols of Egypt;" the Hebrew is, in the idols of Egypt; that is, in the idolatry of the Egyptians, in their defilements, do not you defile yourselves. The Septuagint renders it, in the superstition of Egypt; Junius and Tremellius hath it, with the dirty or dunghill gods of Egypt; and Piscator, with the dung of the Egyptians. They were so addicted to idolatry and superstition, that they made gods of every thing, even of beetles, that live in and feed upon dung; Exod. xii. 12, "Against all the gods of Egypt I will execute judgment." They had many gods and idols, Isa. xix. 1; they had images of the house of the sun, and houses of gods, Jer. xliii. 13. These gods of theirs were all thrown down and broken in the night the Israelites came out of Egypt, say the Jews, which was the judgment executed upon them.

The Jews living in Egypt, fell into their superstitions and idolatries, as appears clearly by that you have in Josh. xxiv. 14, "Now therefore fear the Lord, and serve him in sincerity and in truth: and put away the gods which your fathers served on the other side of the flood, and in Egypt." Their fathers were not only idolaters in Mesopotamia, which was beyond the flood, that is, Euphrates, but also in Egypt; there they were notorious idolaters; and no sooner were they come out of Egypt, but they would have a calf, an Egyptian god, to whom they might attribute the honour of their Egyptian deliverance, Exod. xxxii. 4.

"I am the Lord your God." In the preface to the ten commandments you have these words, "I am the Lord thy God," which is a strong reason why they should have no other gods before him; and so here, they are the reason why they should cast away their idols, and not defile themselves any more with them. The strength of the argument runs thus, I am the Lord of all creatures, it belongs to me to give laws, and command what I please. There is no God besides myself. I allow none in heaven or earth to be set up and acknowledged for God by any, much less by you, whose God I am in a more special manner, whom I have chosen for my people, and made as it were my temple to dwell in; therefore cast ye away all idols, all false gods, defile not yourselves with them, but be a holy people unto me your God, who hate all such things, and delight in holiness.

Obs. 1. That the posterity of good men, by living amongst idolaters, and conversing with them, do in time drink in their opinions and manners, and become like unto them. The Jews, who were the posterity of Abraham, Isaac, and Jacob, the holy seed, by living in Egypt, and conversing with Egyptians, they learned their opinions and practices, they delighted in and served the Egyptian gods. Their fathers' piety, precepts, examples, did not antidote them sufficiently against this contagion. Superstition, idolatry, and profaneness, are prevalent things. Solomon himself, the son of David, was caught in this snare, 1 Kings xi. 4. It is said of the Israelites after they came out of Egypt, that they mingled among the heathen, and learned their works, yea, served their idols, Psal. cvi. 35, 36; by dwelling amongst them, they were transformed into their likeness; what they saw them do, they did, what they saw them worship, they worshipped. The heathens served idols, or griefs, as Montanus hath it, because idols cause grief; and the Hebrews served idols, which brought grief and vexation. There is a secret but strong power in all wickedness to assimilate, and few who dwell near her borders escape subscription to her laws and practices. When Dinah went out to see the daughters of the land, she was caught and defiled, Gen. xxxiv. 1, 2; and when men go not only to see, but to converse with, and live amongst, the daughters of a land, viz. the corrupt inventions and practices thereof, they are in great danger to be caught and corrupted. Grace is not communicable from parents to posterity; corruption is, and that inclines strongly to conform to their ways and worship among whom men live.

Obs. 2. When the Lord shows mercy to a people, doth great things for them, then he requires and expects they should be holy. When the Lord chose Israel, made himself known unto the house of Jacob, promised them to bring them out of Egypt into a land flowing with milk and honey, then he said, "Cast ye away every man the abominations of his eyes, and defile not yourselves with the idols of Egypt;" that is, be ye holy, this I call for, this I look for. Exod. xix. 4, 5, "Ye have seen what I did unto the Egyptians, and how I bare you on eagles' wings, and brought you unto myself. Now therefore, if ye will obey my voice indeed, and keep my covenant, then ye shall be a peculiar treasure unto me above all people: for all the earth is mine." Here the Lord reckons up the great benefits he vouchsafed them: (1.) His dealings with their adversaries; "Ye have seen what I did unto the Egyptians," not, heard, but seen, seen how I plagued them in Egypt, and drowned them in the Red sea for your sakes. (2.) His dealings with them; he "bare them on eagles' wings," that is, carried them out of Egypt, and through the Red sea, with much speed, strength, and tenderness, as an eagle carries her young when in danger, speedily, strongly, tenderly, not in her talons, as other fowls do, but on her back and wings. He took them unto himself; having taken them out of the hands of the Egyptian tyrants and task-masters, he put them not under the power of strangers, but took them to himself, he became their Lord and Sovereign; they took not him, but he took them. Having done such things for them, he expected they should be holy; for he saith, "Now therefore, if ye will obey my voice indeed, and keep my covenant," that is, if you will be holy, and honour me, I will put dignity upon you, such as no people have, "ye shall be a peculiar treasure unto me above all people," as dear, and as much cared for, as any precious things are by princes. God's mercies are engagements unto holiness, Lev. xx. 23, 24; and especially ver. 26, "Ye shall be holy unto me: for I the Lord am holy, and have severed you from other people, that ye should be mine;" distinguishing mercies should breed distinguishing qualities; "I have severed you from other people, that you should" forget their manners, and conform to me, a holy God, even every one of you.

Obs. 3. The eyes are instrumental to, and inlets of, much wickedness. Their eyes behold the idols, and let in that which stirred their hearts and them to do abominably, even to idolatry. Whether more evil enter by the ear, or eye, may be questioned, but most certain it is, that abundance of wickedness is let in to us by the eye. The breach of most, if not of all, the commandments, hath been occasioned by the eye.

Of the first: Hos. iii. 1, they "look to other gods." Of the second: 2 Kings xvi. 10—12, Ahaz saw an altar at Damascus, and makes the like, and sets it in the place of God's altar. Of the third: Mark vi. 22, 23, Herod, being pleased at the sight of Herodias' dancing, swears to give her whatever she would ask, unto the half of his kingdom. Of the fourth: Ezek. xxii. 26, they "have hid their eyes from my sabbaths;" they would not see what holiness that day required, they connived at the pollution and profaning thereof.

Here you see the breach of the first table, and we may find the second violated by means of them.

For the fifth, see Gen. ix. 22, Ham saw the nakedness of his father, and discovered it. For the sixth, see Esth. iii. 5, 6, "When Haman saw that Mordecai bowed not, he was full of wrath. And thought scorn to lay hands on Mordecai alone, but sought to destroy all the Jews." For the seventh, consult Gen. xxxiv. 2; 2 Sam. xi. 2, 4. When Shechem saw Dinah, and David Bathsheba, they were so taken with their beauties, that they committed folly, and brought evil upon themselves and others. For the eighth, that in Psal. l. 18, proves it, "When thou sawest a thief, then thou consentedst with him." For the ninth, consider that in Jer. xxxvii. 13; when Jeremiah was going out at the gate of Benjamin, Irijah, a captain, spies him, and accused him falsely, "saying, Thou fallest away to the Chaldeans." For the tenth, take that place in Josh. vii. 21. "I saw," saith Achan, "among the spoils a goodly Babylonish garment, two hundred shekels of silver, a wedge of gold of fifty shekels weight, then I coveted them, and took them." By these instances you see the eyes have been instruments to further the breach of all the commandments. The sight is a great mercy, a principal sense, yet it had been good for some men if they had been born blind, their eyes occasioned so much sin and wickedness. By the eye the heart sends forth and receives in wickedness; the eye is the pander between both; and what thing created is worse than a wicked eye? Solomon advises you to keep your hearts with all diligence; and you had need keep your eyes with all diligence: both heart and eyes are roving and mischieving things, if not well kept. God calls for both, Prov. xxiii. 26, "My son, give me thy heart, and let thine eyes observe my ways." If this were done, multitudes of sins would be prevented; the eye would let in good to the heart, and the heart send out good by the eye.

Obs. 4. The consideration of God being our God, should take us off from all former engagements, sinful conformities, and false confidences, and cause us to cleave to the Lord, to conform unto and confide in him. The Jews here were engaged to Egyptian gods, conformed to them, and confided too much in them. But, cast them away, defile not yourselves with them; I am the Lord your God, you must engage, conform yourselves to me, and confide in me: I am your God, able to counsel, help, deliver you; so are not, so cannot, the idols of Egypt. I am a holy God, they are abominations; I am for you Israelites, they are for Egyptians. God becoming our God, is a great condescension, a favour beyond comprehension, and should knock us off from all false ways, and cause us to conform to him, Exod. xxiii. 24, 25; Lev. xi. 43—45; xviii. 2—4; xix. 2—4; Numb. xv. 38—41. In all these places God uses this argument why they should conform to him and be holy; because he is the Lord their God, and a holy God. He made them his temple, to dwell in and among, and his temple must not be defiled, admit of any thing unsuitable to his mind; therefore he tells them, Deut. vii. 6, that he hath chosen them to be a special people unto himself, special in their holiness, special in their love, special in their obedience, and special in their confidence in and reliance upon him.

Ver. 8. *But they rebelled against me, and would not hearken unto me: they did not every man cast away the abominations of their eyes, neither did they forsake the idols of Egypt: then I said, I will pour out my fury upon them, to accomplish my anger against them in the midst of the land of Egypt.*

In this verse you have two things to be considered.

I. Their wickedness; which is set out,

1. In general; "they rebelled," they hearkened not.

2. In particular; "they did not cast away the abominations of their eyes," they did not forsake the idols of Egypt.

II. God's purpose hereupon, which was severely to punish them; "then I said, I will pour out my fury," &c.; which is illustrated from the circumstance of the place where he would do it, "in the midst of the land of Egypt." There is little in this verse which hath not been opened and spoken of formerly: the word "rebelled," we had, chap. xvii. 15; ii. 3.

"And would not hearken unto me." The Hebrew is, and have not desired to hearken to me; they had no desire that way, but the contrary. *Non velle* here, is *nolle*, their not willing, was nilling, and Zechariah calls it, refusing, ch. vii. 11; they had not a heart inclinable to hearken unto God.

"Then I said, I will pour out my fury upon them." The Hebrew is, and I said to pour out; that is, I purposed, seeing they dealt thus by me, to make them examples of my fury, and to destroy them. Of pouring out fury, and accomplishing anger, was spoken chap. vi. 12; vii. 8; ix. 8; xiv. 19.

"In the midst of the land of Egypt." We find not in Moses any thing recorded of this nature, but here the prophet delivered what God commanded him; ver. 5, "Say unto them, Thus saith the Lord." He had it not by tradition, that God bid them cast away the abomination of their eyes, and not defile themselves with the idols of Egypt, that they rebelled and would not do so, that God purposed their destruction in Egypt; these things he had not by tradition, but by divine inspiration. They were so corrupted with the idolatry of Egypt, and averse from hearkening to the admonitions, counsels, and exhortations of God, that he thought in his heart to destroy them in the midst of Egypt. Many of their children were drowned, and the oppressions they endured were very great, and long, which, Lavater saith, was for their Egyptian idolatry: Psal. cv. 25, "He turned their heart to hate his people, to deal subtilly with his people."

Obs. 1. Those the Lord hath bestowed great mercies upon, and professed much kindness unto, they, even they, are ungrateful when he calls for reformation at their hands. This people the Lord chose, made himself known to, promised to bring out of Egypt into a land he had looked out for them, even a land flowing with milk and honey, the glory, ornament, desire of all lands; and now, calling upon them to purge themselves from their abominations and idolatries, and to conform to him who professed himself to be their God, what do they? rebel against him; "but they rebelled." Here was ingratitude, and ingratitude at a height. God bids them cast away abominations, and they cast away his counsels; he bids them eye him, his beauty and glory, and they eye the form, beauty, and glory of their idols; he bids them be holy, and they defile themselves with idols; he bids them cleave to him, the God of

Israel, and they cleave to the idols of Egypt; he bids them forsake all their evil ways, and they forsake him. This people were very ungrateful; whatever mercies they had from God, he seldom had any testimony of true thankfulness from them. Neh. ix. see what a multitude of mercies, great, seasonable, wonderful, God bestowed upon them, calling, by his prophets, for turning to him. And did they turn, reform, and testify a thankful frame of heart to be in them? no; they were disobedient, rebelled against him, cast his law behind their backs, and slew his prophets, ver. 26. God did choice things for this people all along, but they forgot him, and provoked him. The 106th Psalm is a psalm of God's mercies, and their ingratitudes; he tells them they had a multitude of mercies, "but they provoked him at the sea, even the Red sea," ver. 7; "but they lusted exceedingly in the wilderness," ver. 14; "but they murmured in their tents," ver. 25; "but they mingled among the heathen," ver. 35. Here are four "buts," testifying their ingratitude.

God hath done great things for us, bestowed Israelitish mercies upon us, he hath made himself known amongst us, brought us out of Egyptian bondage, owned us for his people above any people, and professed himself to be our God, and hereupon called upon us to cast away our abominations, to reform and become a holy people, conformable to his mind; but may not the Lord come in with a reproaching "but," and say, "But ye rebel;" your abominations are not cast away, you do defile yourselves with the idols of England. And notwithstanding all the mercies we have had, God may come in with many buts, and say, "But" you provoke me by your oppressions, divisions, and bitterness; "but" you lust exceedingly after a king, and to be like other nations; "but" you murmur against me, my servants, and dispensations; "but" you mingle with the customs, corruptions, and fashions of the times; "but" you forsake my truths, and run into dangerous and damnable opinions.

Obs. 2. Such is the corruption of men's natures, that frequently the more mercies and means they have, the worse they grow. This people had variety of mercies, and every mercy should have led them to repentance, according to that in Rom. ii. 4, especially such mercies as they had; but, above all, God's speaking to them should have done it. How he spake to them in Egypt we find not, no prophets are mentioned to have been there before Moses. Whether he spake himself unto them, or by angels, or by Joseph, or some others, he did speak, but they rebelled and hearkened not, their corrupt hearts and natures degenerated more and more. The Jews, who had the pleasant land, the prophets, temple, oracles, and ordinances of God, grew worse than any of the nations; see Jer. ii. 10, 11; Ezek. xvi. 47; 2 Chron. xxxvi. 15, 16. It is observable, that men living in the christian world, and where, besides a multitude of other mercies, they have the gospel to do them good, to draw them to God, to direct and enable them to work righteousness, and go beyond heathens in all things, yet in many things they fall short of them, some of them; and divers in many things, are worse than the worst of them. If mercies and means prove not the savour of life, they ripen and perfect men's corruptions, and become the savour of death. Was there heard of amongst the heathens such a wretch as Judas was, who betrayed such a Master as he did? Chorazin, Bethsaida, and Capernaum, were the more unhappy, and exposed to the deeper condemnation, because they had more mercy and means.

Obs. 3. Not doing what God commands, is not hearkening; and not hearkening, is rebellion. They "rebelled," and would not "hearken" unto me, they did not cast away the abominations of their eyes, nor forsake the idols of Egypt. They "rebelled" because they hearkened not, they hearkened not because they "did not;" it is like they heard God commanding, but hearing, and not doing, they did not hearken. Doing, is knowing of God, Jer. xxii. 6; and doing, is hearkening to God, Deut. xxxiv. 9; but not doing, is not hearkening, and not hearkening, is rebellion. Hence not doing is called "rebelling against the command of the Lord," Deut. i. 26; going "backward," Jer. vii. 24; rejecting of the words and law of God, chap. vi. 19; hardening of the neck, Neh. ix. 16, "Our fathers dealt proudly, and hardened their necks, and hearkened not to thy commandments." It is pride, and hardness of heart, not to hearken unto God and his commands.

Obs. 4. Men's not hearkening unto God, puts him upon thoughts and purposes of punishing them, and that severely. "Then I said, I will pour out my fury upon them," and accomplish, consummate, perfect mine anger against them: "then," when they would not do as I bid them, I had thoughts and resolutions to destroy them. When the glorious, great, and only wise God, shall speak to the creature, to do that which tends to its great good, and shall not be heard, but disobeyed and slighted, this provokes God, and procreates thoughts of destruction. When they hearkened not, but sinned so in the business of the calf, it was in the heart of God utterly to destroy them: Exod. xxxii. 10, "Let me alone, that my wrath may wax hot against them, and that I may consume them;" and not only them, but "their name from under heaven," Deut. ix. 14. Had not Moses poured water upon this fire and quenched it, he had done it; they had no longer been a people, nor had any memorial left of them. Of this speaks David, Psal. cvi. 23, "He said that he would destroy them, had not Moses his chosen stood before him in the breach, to turn away his wrath, lest he should destroy them." This is spoken of God, after the manner of men; when they are offended, they purpose and resolve to destroy those who have provoked them, but some friend interposes, prevails with them, and prevents them, as Abigail did David. So Moses here prevented the Lord by his prayers and entreaties from destroying this people. Men's perverse dealings with God do put him upon intentions of their ruin: Deut. xxxii. 26, "I said, I would scatter them into corners, I would make the remembrance of them to cease from among men."

Ver. 9. *But I wrought for my name's sake, that it should not be polluted before the heathen, among whom they were, in whose sight I made myself known unto them, in bringing them forth out of the land of Egypt.*

In this verse are set down God's last kindnesses to this people, being in Egypt; and they are two:

1. His sparing of them for his name's sake.
2. His bringing them out of that condition.

Touching the first, in the latter part of the former verse God had said he would pour out his fury upon them, and accomplish his anger against them in the midst of Egypt; but foreseeing and considering what would be the event thereof, if he should do so, viz. that his name would suffer and be polluted, here he provides for the honour of his own name, and spares them.

"But I wrought." The Hebrew is, I did, or have done, not what I purposed, but what was most convenient for me to do, what was for the honour of my name: when I saw that like to suffer, I did that which prevented it, I took care of my name, had respect unto it.

"For my name's sake." "Name," in the Scripture, as it refers to God, is sometimes put for God himself, as Psal. xxxiii. 21; and Neh. i. 11, "who desire to fear thy name;" that is, God himself, he is the object of fear, Isa. viii. 13; sometimes it is put for God's titles, Psal. lxxxiii. 18; Exod. iii. 13—15; sometimes for the attributes of God, as chap. xxxiii. 19, compared with chap. xxxiv. 6, 7; sometimes for the glory, esteem, and renown of God, Psal. viii. 9, and Psal. lxxvi. 1; here it is put for God's attributes and honour. Three of his attributes had been questioned, if he should have destroyed this people in Egypt.

1. His faithfulness. For God had promised and sworn to bring them out of Egypt, as it is ver. 6; and Gen. xv. 14; xlviii. 4; and had he not done it, Egyptians and others would have charged God with breach of promise, with unfaithfulness.

2. His power and almightiness. For they would have said he was not able to bring them from under the Egyptian gods and Pharaoh, that their power was beyond the power of the Jews' God.

3. His mercy. That he had a people who professed him to be their God, but he was so merciless, that he destroyed and cut them all off; a thing that the heathen gods never did to any which worshipped them.

Now, had the case been thus, how had God's honour been laid in the dust, his glory stained, and renown eclipsed.

"That it should not be polluted." The word, to pollute, in Hebrew, signifies originally, to grieve, to cut; and metonymically, to pollute, to violate, profane, which are grievous and cutting. When God's name is polluted, we are not to conceive any actual defilement to adhere to it, for God's name can no more be defiled than the beams of the sun. It is said to be polluted,

1. When it is not hallowed; that is, not acknowledged, not esteemed to be holy and honourable. As the sabbath, when it was not sanctified, it was polluted; so here, when the glory due to God's name is not acknowledged, it is a polluting of his name.

2. When it is slighted, and not used reverently. God's name is great, glorious, excellent, holy, and dreadful, and ought to be reverenced, Psal. cxi. 9.

3. When occasion is given to the wicked to speak evil of God and his ways. As, 2 Sam. xii. 14, David by his sins gave great occasion to the enemies of the Lord to blaspheme; so, Ezek. xxxvi. 21, the Jews, by their sinful carriage, caused the name of God to be profaned among the heathen.

Had the Lord, then, destroyed this people in Egypt, according as he purposed, the Egyptians and other nations would have slighted him, spoken evil of his doings, blasphemed his name, and wounded his honour. Therefore, though this people deserved to die in the way of justice, yet God spared them in the way of mercy, for the honour of his name.

Quest. Seeing God purposed to destroy them, and did it not, is not his will alterable and inefficacious?

Answ. The counsels, purposes, decrees of God are unalterable, and do take place: see Psal. xxxiii. 11; Isa. xiv. 27; xliii. 13; xlvi. 10; Mal. iii. 6; Heb. vi. 17. For that said and done here, it is after the manner of men. God saw cause sufficient to move him to their destruction, but seeing what evil was like to come from it, he would not destroy them. Had the Lord decreed it before the world, it must have taken place; no change or alteration could have been.

"Before the heathen." The Hebrew is, in the eyes of the heathen. God would not have them to see or behold any thing which might occasion them to dishonour him; he would not slay his people in their sight, but made himself known by his word and mighty works unto the Jews, in the sight of the heathen, so that hereby he was known unto both.

Obs. 1. The Lord spares and saves sinners deserving death, even for his name's sake. "But I wrought for my name's sake." Thou, for thy rebellion, idolatry, and other sins, didst deserve to die, and I could almost have cut thee off, but for my mercy and name's sake, I spared and saved thee: Isa. xlviii. 8, 9, "I knew that thou wouldest deal very treacherously, and wast called a transgressor from the womb;" that is, worthy so to be called, seeing as soon as ever thou camest out of the womb of Egypt, in which thou wast shut up as a child in the womb, thou fellest to idolatry. Here was enough to have caused God to stifle this child; but what follows: "For my name's sake will I defer mine anger, and for my praise will I refrain for thee, that I cut thee not off." Nothing in this metaphorical child, this Jewish people, moved him to show mercy; but his own "name," his own praise, prevailed with him to preserve them from destruction. God's honour and glory are strong arguments to move him to show mercy to his people. This the servants of God have known, and made use of, in their straits. When Jerusalem was in a manner laid desolate, and the jealousy of God burned like fire, what argument did the church use then to move God to show mercy, but his "name," and glory of it? Psalm lxxix. 9, "Help us, O God of our salvation, for the glory of thy name: and deliver us, and purge away our sins, for thy name's sake." The church was low, weak, beset with enemies and sins at once, and now it would have help, deliverance, pardon, and upon the account of God's name; "for thy name's sake" help us, "for thy name's sake" deliver us, "for thy name's sake" purge away our sins. What hurt would it be to God's name if he did it not? It would not be glorious, but dishonoured; for in the next verse it is said, "Wherefore should the heathen say, Where is their God?" they trusted in their God, and he is a non-helping God, a non-delivering God, a non-pardoning God. This was the argument Joshua used when Israel fell before their enemies, "Lord, what wilt thou do unto thy great name?" God's name was precious to Joshua, but more precious to God himself, Josh. vii. 9, and he did great things for his name's sake. When the people forgot the multitude of great mercies they had in Egypt, and provoked him at the sea, even at the Red sea, and deserved to be drowned in it, and that their blood should be mingled with the waters thereof, what saith the text? Psal. cvi. 8, "Nevertheless he saved them for his name's sake." When nothing else induced him to do it, the honour of his name did, that he might appear faithful, merciful, powerful. God did not save them for their prayers, for their faith, for their fathers' sakes, for their righteousness, or for their enemies' sakes, being very malicious and wicked, but for his "own name's sake;" God doth more upon that account alone, than upon the account of all the rest. You may hear the Lord speak graciously to this purpose, Isa. xliii. 25, "I, even I, am he that blotteth out thy transgressions for mine own sake;" here is "I" twice; one "I" referring to them, it is "I" that blot out their transgressions, and none besides; the other refers to God, "I" blot them out "for mine own sake," not your sakes: God doth all freely.

Vide Muscul. in locum.

Obs. 2. God's sparing of his people, and preventing the reproaches, blasphemies, and mischiefs which would come by his destroying of them, is an honouring and sanctifying of his name. I wrought, saith God, that my name might not be polluted before the heathen; that is, that it might be honoured and sanctified in their sight. God doth often spare his people, being ripe for destruction, that the enemy might not blaspheme and profane his name; and when he doth so, he honours his name. Deut. xxxii. 26, 27, God saith there, he would scatter and destroy his people; but why did he it not? he "feared the wrath of the enemy, lest their adversaries should behave themselves strangely, and lest they should say, Our hand is high, and the Lord hath not done all this." God foresaw what they would say and do, if he should have used them as instruments to punish his children; they would have been very outrageous, bloody, and cruel, and when they had vented all their malice against them, and done whatever they would, they would have denied God's hand to have been therein, and arrogated all to themselves, which had been a great dishonour to God; he therefore prevents their blaspheming by sparing of his people, and so provides for the honour of his name. Moses once and twice put God upon it, to take heed he caused not the Egyptians to speak evil of him and his ways, when he was upon the design of destroying his people for their sins: see Exod. xxxii. 10—12; Numb. xiv. 12—16. God deals with his people sometimes, not after the ordinary rule and course of his proceedings, but in a prerogative way; he spares them, though their sins be great, because their enemies would be proud, arrogant, bloody, and blasphemous. And hath he not spared England upon this account?

Obs. 3. That notwithstanding the sins of God's people, he shows them kindness openly, and in the face of their enemies. Though the Jews had rebelled against God, and the Egyptians would have rejoiced in their ruin, yet, in their sight, God made himself known unto them, in bringing them forth out of the land of Egypt. God would have the Egyptians see that he could be kind to his people, though they were disobedient unto him; that he would not break with them, though they broke with him.

When the Jews were in Babylon, under great displeasure of God for their sins, yet God did show them such favour, and do such things for them, that their enemies were convinced, and said, "The Lord hath done great things for them," Psal. cxxvi. 2; he made known his salvation, and openly showed his salvation in the sight of the heathen, Psal. xcviii. 2. This the Lord doth, as to magnify his own name, to rejoice the hearts of his people, and to gain upon them, so to vex and consume the wicked: Psal. cxii. 10, "The wicked shall see it, and be grieved; he shall gnash with his teeth, and melt away." Hath not this been God's method with us? notwithstanding our sins, and ill deserts, hath he not openly made known himself to us, showed us kindness in the sight of our enemies? have they not seen it, grieved, gnashed their teeth, and melted away? they have seen God's kindnesses to us, and we have seen God's vengeance on them.

Ver. 10, 11. *Wherefore I caused them to go forth out of the land of Egypt, and brought them into the wilderness. And I gave them my statutes, and shewed them my judgments, which if a man do, he shall even live in them.*

Having seen and heard of God's dealings with them, and theirs with him, in Egypt, now we are led to consider their mutual dealings each with other in the wilderness, which reacheth to the 27th verse.

Where he shows in general,

I. What benefits he had bestowed upon them.

II. What their sinful deportment was towards him.

III. How worthy they were to perish, if the Lord had not showed them mercy for his name's sake.

In these two verses you have,

1. Their eduction out of Egypt.

2. Their introduction into the wilderness.

3. The donation or promulgation of the law.

"I caused them to go forth." The Vulgate is, I cast them forth, or, drove them forth; which shows their backwardness to leave that land where they were born, had habitations, and other accommodations. It is like many of them neither thought of the promise made to their fathers, nor of the promised land, but thought Egypt a good land, yea, a "land flowing with milk and honey," as they called it, Numb. xvi. 13; only they were troubled at the hard labour the Egyptians held them to. But the word here imports not any violence, but a powerful bringing of them forth. We will inquire,

1. How the Lord brought them forth?

2. When?

1. How? It was not in an ordinary way, but in a way full of extraordinaries. To do it, the Lord came down from heaven, Exod. iii. 8; that was in the vision of the burning bush; he prepared Moses, Aaron, and the people, by signs and miracles, to leave Egypt, and because all the power and wisdom that Pharaoh and Egypt had was employed to retain the Jews there, they being utterly averse from their departure, the Lord sent strange and dreadful plagues, one after another, till their spirits were brought off to let them go, chap. xii. 30—33. Pharaoh was resolved not to let them go, (he had so much profit by their service,) unless it were by a strong hand, chap. iii. 19; and God was resolved to bring them out, and therefore he did arise, put forth his power, and by "strength of hand" brought them out, chap. xiii. 3; by "an high hand," chap. xiv. 8; by "mighty power, and a stretched-out arm," Deut. ix. 29. You have it fully set down in chap. iv. 34, God took them from the midst of another nation by "temptations, by signs, and by wonders, and by war, and by a mighty hand, and by a stretched-out arm, and by great terrors." There was great strife between God and Pharaoh, who should have this people, as there was between Michael and the devil about the body of Moses. Pharaoh pulled hard to hold them in Egypt, but God out-pulled Pharaoh, and pulled them out of Egypt, and so caused them to go forth.

2. When. You have the time punctually set down in Exod. xii. 40, 41, where it is said, "At the end of the four hundred and thirty years, even the self-same day, they went out." Not that they were four hundred and thirty years in Egypt, for they were there but two hundred and ten, or two hundred and fifteen, as chronologies inform upon good account. The four hundred and thirty years are to begin from the time of the promise made to Abraham, which Stephen tells us, Acts vii. 2, was before he dwelt in Charran, even while he was in Ur, and but seventy years old; from which time, to the going out of Egypt, were four hundred and thirty years; two hundred and fifteen, or two hundred and twenty whereof, were run out before Jacob went down into Egypt. From the promise made to Abraham to Isaac's birth, were thirty years, some make it but twenty-five, (they then reckon from his time of departing out of Haran,) for he was a hundred years old when Isaac was born, Gen. xxi. 5; and from thence to the birth of Jacob were

Rivet in Exod.

sixty years, Gen. xxv. 26; and from thence to Jacob's going into Egypt, one hundred and thirty years, chap. xlvii. 9; which, summed up, make two hundred and twenty, at least two hundred and fifteen, and so the rest of the four hundred and thirty they were in Egypt. And at the just time they were accomplished, the Lord brought them out, to show his faithfulness, as it appears, Deut. vii. 8.

"And brought them into the wilderness." There is mention made of one "wilderness" before they passed through the Red sea, Exod. xiv. 11, and of other wildernesses after they had passed the same; as the "wilderness of Sin," chap. xvi. 1; the "wilderness of Paran," Numb. xiii. 3; which doubtless was but one, though diversely called from the several parts it bordered upon. A "wilderness" is a desolate, solitary place, where is no way, where are no comforts, but where are many dangers. Deut. viii. 15, it was "a great and terrible wilderness," wherein were fiery serpents, and scorpions, drought, and no water. It had many wild beasts in it, and therefore was called the "howling wilderness," chap. xxx. 10. Jeremiah tells you, chap. ii. 6, this "wilderness" was a land of deserts, and of pits; but not pits which would hold any water, for he adds, it was a "land of drought," and of the "shadow of death," a land that no "man passed through," and where "no man dwelt;" while they were in this "wilderness," they were in danger of death, or in such straits as that they desired death. The "wilderness" here meant was the "wilderness of Sin," which was not far from Sinai, where the law was given, of which the next verse speaks. Into the wilderness God did bring them, to try them, to humble them, and to do them good at their latter end, Deut. viii. 16.

Obs. 1. That God, for the honour of his name, shows mercy after mercy to his people, deserving no mercy, yea, deserving destruction. In the former verse, to prevent the dishonour of his name, he spared them, made himself known to them, and here he goes on, adding mercy to mercy: "Wherefore I caused them to go forth."

Obs. 2. No length of time, no depth of misery, no power or policy of adversaries whatsoever, can hinder God from delivering his people when his time is come. The Jews had been long in Egypt, suffered very hard things for the space of one hundred and sixteen years, or one hundred and twenty-one, from the time of Joseph's death till their departure out of Egypt, that house of bondage, which was thereabout. They were under heavy pressures and great tyranny; Pharaoh, that great dragon, used all his cunning and power to keep them longer in that condition; but notwithstanding all these, the Lord caused them to go forth, his time was come. The like did God for this people when they had been in Babylon seventy years, were as dry bones, and out of hope, Ezek. xxxvii. 11; he opened their graves, and caused them to come up out of them, and come to the land of Israel, ver. 12. There is nothing too hard for the Lord to do; he can, and will, remove all obstructions, break through all difficulties, and shake the foundations of heaven, earth, and hell, to bring to pass his good pleasure in the time thereof. The state of the Jews in Egypt represents men's condition under sin and Satan; that in Babylon, the condition of God's servants under antichrist. Now, let men be never so long in bondage to either or both of them, suffer never such hard things; let Satan, that red dragon, and antichrist, that man of sin, improve all their craft, skill, and power, to hold men in darkness and ways of false worship; yet when the Lord's day is come, he will cause them to come out of Egyptian bondage, and Babylonian darkness, he will fetch them off from all sinful practices, all invented ways of worship, and bring them into his marvellous and glorious light.

Obs. 3. When God doth show his people special mercy, in freeing them from old and special miseries, he doth not wholly exempt them from new miseries. Though he caused them to go forth of Egypt, yet he brought them into a "wilderness," where they met with hunger, thirst, danger, and death; they were freed from Egyptian miseries, not from wilderness miseries. They thought if once they were freed from their making brick, gathering straw, and rigid task-masters, they should be happy; but they met with new hardships, new miseries; they did ride upon the back of mercy, out of old miseries into new, out of a house of bondage into a wilderness, a howling wilderness, a wilderness that made them howl many a time. It is God's method oft to mingle water with our wine, miseries with our mercies, crosses with our comforts, to lead us out of great straits in much mercy, and to lead us into others for trial. David was delivered oft out of straits, but shortly after he was freed from one he was brought into another, and that by the same hand; which made him say, "Thou hast showed me great and sore troubles," Psal. lxxi. 20. Sometimes he was on the mount of mercies, and sometimes in the valley of miseries, yea, in the valley of the shadow of death. Take it in a spiritual sense, When men are converted, do they not meet with hard things, are they not brought out of Egypt into a wilderness, where are dangers, fiery serpents, scorpions, &c.?

Ver. 11. "And I gave them my statutes, and showed them my judgments." This people being brought out of Egypt, and freed from great bondage, being in a wilderness, might now fancy a total liberty to themselves, and exemption from all obedience. To prevent this, some fifty days after their coming out, the Lord at mount Sinai gives them out his law, by which they might be ordered and regulated.

Of "statutes" and "judgments" hath been spoken formerly; by them, both morals and ceremonials are comprehended.

"Shewed them." The Hebrew is, I made them to know; that is, I caused them to be written in the tables of stone, and proclaimed amongst them; yea, I caused them to be opened and expounded unto them. The Lord made known his mind unto them, though not so efficaciously as in these days.

"Which if a man do, he shall live in them." The doing here is, man's keeping, observing, and obeying these statutes and judgments; and if so, he should not be punished as transgressors are, but live a long and prosperous life, and not only so, but a happy and eternal life; for if the keeping God's statutes and commands should reach but unto a temporal prosperous life, what benefit had the Jews thereby above the gentiles, who by their justice, civility, and moral virtues, obtained great prosperity and length of days. The Lord Christ clears it up unto us, that by life promised upon keeping the law, is meant eternal life: Luke x. 25, saith a lawyer to Christ, "Master, what shall I do to inherit eternal life?" Christ saith, "What is written in the law? how readest thou?" He tells him, ver. 27, what he found there; and Christ upon it tells him, ver. 28, that if he did so, he should live; that is, live eternally. There was a righteousness of the law, which if men came unto, the law conferred life upon them; see Gal. iii. 12; Rom. x. 5; Lev. xviii. 5; there was life in them, life by them, and life from them: but because no man could attain unto the righteousness of the law through the weakness of the flesh, Rom. viii. 3, therefore the law was so far from conferring eternal life upon man, that it excludes him from that life, chap. iii. 20, and takes away the life he hath, chap. vii. 10. The commandment which was ordained to life he found to be unto death; that which in itself held out life, accidentally and eventually proved death unto him.

Paul seems to deny any power to be in the law of giving life; Gal. iii. 21, "If there had been a law given which could have given life, verily righteousness should have been by the law." The impotency is not originally and intrinsically in the law, for that is perfect, and able to give life to any, to all that keep it: Matt. xix. 17, Christ makes the keeping the commandments the entrance into life. The fault is in us, not in the law, which is holy, just, and good; if we could keep the law, it could give us life.

Obs. 1. When God brings his people into straits, he will not leave them destitute, he will show them some mercy in such a condition. He brought them into the wilderness; and what then? he gave them his statutes, and showed them his judgments. When they were in the wilderness, they had the cloud, the pillar of fire, the manna, the tabernacle, the water out of the rock, many great mercies did God bestow on them whilst they were in the wilderness. Jacob, by the hand of God, was brought into straits; he must leave his father's house to secure his life, Gen. xxvii. 42, 43; lie in the open field all night, where the earth was his bed, and the stones his bolsters, where the wild beasts might have found and devoured him; but in this condition the Lord appeared to him, and told him what he would give and do for him. It was a good night to Jacob, he met with sweeter, greater mercies when he lay without doors, than ever he did by lying in his father's house. God brought Jerusalem into a strait by Sennacherib; and did he leave it so, and let him sack and spoil it? no, he prepared an angel that was both σωτήρ and ἀπολλυων, a saviour to the Jews, and a destroyer to the Assyrians. Christ, by the Spirit, was led into the wilderness, where the tempter set upon him very fiercely, and ceased not for forty days together to shoot his fiery darts against him; but did not the Lord mind him in that condition? yes, he sent angels unto him; Matt. iv. 11, "Behold, angels came and ministered unto him."

Obs. 2. God is the Lawgiver to his people. "I gave them my statutes, and showed them my judgments." God gave them laws to govern and direct them, both in their worshipping of him, and carriage one towards another. It was no small mercy that God gave them "statutes and judgments," for no nation had the like mercy: Deut. iv. 8, "What nation is there so great, that hath statutes and judgments so righteous as all this law, which I set before you this day?" said Moses to them. Other nations had their statutes and judgments, but either they were not righteous, or at best not so righteous as theirs were; if some were righteous, others were not. Here all were righteous, Psal. cxix. 128; they are called judgments of righteousness, ver. 7; and commands that are righteousness, ver. 172; they are the judgments and commands of the righteous God, they are full of righteousness, and make men righteous. If the law of the twelve tables among the Romans did exceed all the libraries of philosophers in weight and worth, as Tully said, what then did the "statutes and judgments" God gave to this people? they exceeded all the laws that ever were or shall be. This made David to value them above "thousands of gold and silver," Psal. cxix. 72; and to pray unto the Lord to open his eyes, that he might see the mysteries and depths which were in them, ver. 18, 129; and that he would incline his heart to keep them, ver. 36. God gave them these laws, to show that he would be their Governor, that they ought to obey him: Isa. xxxiii. 22, "The Lord is our lawgiver."

Obs. 3. The great bounty and wisdom of God in making promise of a happy life here, and eternal life hereafter, to the keepers of the law, to those who should observe his statutes and judgments.

First, his great bounty: for, suppose a man could perfectly in all things keep the law, and that perpetually, he deserves nothing thereby; being God's creature, it is his duty to do what he appoints and commands; man's works do not excel, nor carry that intrinsical worth before God, as to merit at his hands: the life therefore attainable hereby is from covenant and promise, not from the nature of man's obedience, but of God's promise; and so is from his bounty and good-will. For God to promise life to man's obedience was great mercy, transcending whatever possibly, or imaginably, could be therein; whereas he might have commanded all man could do without any promise of life at all. Neither let any say, this promise was to no purpose, because man was not able to keep the law; the fault thereof was not in God, nor in the law, but in man himself, who had disabled himself. And here appears,

Secondly, the great wisdom of God, that made this promise of life to the keepers of the law, that so he might draw out their endeavours to the utmost, and that seeing when they were at the height they fell short of that perfection the law required, they might look for life upon another account, viz. the righteousness of faith; see Deut. xxx. 12—15, with Rom. ix. 30—32, and chap. x. 5—8. Therefore the law, finding us incapable of life through our sin, directed us unto Christ, where we might have it through his grace; Gal. iii. 24, "The law was our schoolmaster to bring us unto Christ, that we might be justified by faith."

Ver. 12. *Moreover also I gave them my sabbaths, to be a sign between me and them, that they might know that I am the Lord that sanctify them.*

Here is another mercy which the Lord bestowed upon this people, namely, his "sabbaths," which were,

1. "To be a sign between him and them."
2. To evidence that the Lord was he which sanctified them.

"My sabbaths." The word "sabbath" signifies, rest, and such rest, as work hath gone before; from שבת to cease, to be quiet, and give over working; it imports, not a sitting still, or doing nothing, but a resting from what formerly was a doing. Some by "sabbaths" here understand, not only the sabbath of days, but the sabbatical years also, the seventh and fiftieth years, which were years of rest; but it is more genuine to take "sabbaths" here for sabbatical days, one of which came every week, and those "sabbaths" were the "signs" between God and them. It may be inquired whether they had the sabbath before they came out of Egypt, because it is said, that God brought them out thence into the wilderness, and gave them his sabbaths; and there are some of note, who hold that the sabbath was not given at first, but in Moses' days.

To this inquiry, the answer is, That they had the sabbath before that time of Moses giving the law at mount Sinai, as appears, Exod. xvi. 23, 25, 26, on the sabbath day there was no manna to be found or gathered; and Gen. ii. 3, "God blessed the seventh day, and sanctified it." Surely this blessing and sanctifying of it was for man's use, God needed no day; therefore in that place, Exod. xvi. 29, he saith, "The Lord hath given you the sabbath," alluding to the first institution; and the word "remember," which begins the fourth commandment, imports that the day was given before, though much forgotten and neglected. And what if there be no particular testimony, which mentions the patriarchs' keeping of it before the law? it doth not follow, therefore, it was not kept.

There is no mention of keeping it in Joshua, in Judges, in Samuel; is it therefore a warrantable or good argument, to conclude that it was not kept? yea, if it were granted that they did not keep it, doth this prove that they were not required to keep it? For Justin Martyr, Ireneus, and Tertullian, their scope is to show, that none of the fathers of those times were justified, or obtained salvation, by keeping of the sabbath.

If the "sabbaths" were given before, how are they said to be given when they were in the wilderness? this is answered in the next words.

"To be a sign between me and them." The first giving of the sabbath was to be a memorial of the creation, Gen. ii. 3, and therefore was observed by the primitive fathers, whom the creation of the world did most nearly concern, and was in use before Moses' days, who was above two thousand years after. But when God gave it out again by Moses, it was upon another account, viz. to be a "sign" between him and his people the Jews, whom he brought out of Egypt, and that upon the sabbath day, as Junius observes.

"A sign." The sabbath was a "sign" of the true sabbath, wherein we shall rest from the labour of this world, so Jerom; "a sign" of love and reconciliation, so Vatablus; a "sign" of holiness, that by the time dedicated to God we might know ourselves dedicated to God, so Cajetane; a "sign" of difference between the Jews and all other people, who were profane, and derided the Jews for losing the seventh part of their time, so Tostatus and Sanctius. They were distinguished from other nations by circumcision, and by meats; but these were not so visible, observable, in the eye of the world as their "sabbaths." A "sign" that God had taken this people to himself, separated them from Egyptians, and others, and would have them in a special manner remember their Egyptian deliverance on that day, as formerly the creation. It was a sign between God and them; they glorified him, owning him for their God, and he sanctified them, owning them for his people. So that here was a second edition, and, as it were, a new institution, of the sabbath: because he brought them out of Egypt with a mighty hand, therefore he commanded them to keep the sabbath, Deut. v. 15.

"I am the Lord that sanctify them." Sanctifying, as it refers to God, notes sometimes preparation to some special service; as, Jer. li. 27, 28, "Prepare the nations against her;" the Hebrew is, Sanctify the nations against her; that is, Babylon. Preparing of the nations to the destruction of Babylon, is sanctifying of them. Sometimes it notes separation to a holy use, as Joel i. 14, "Sanctify ye a fast;" that is, separate a time from common employments to religious. So Christ is said to be sanctified, John x. 36. Sometimes it notes making holy, Lev. xxi. 23, "I the Lord do sanctify them;" that is, make them holy; so John xvii. 17; Rom. xv. 16. We are here to take it in the two last senses. I have given them my holy-days, times separated from all common use and worldly employments; times for drawing near to and worshipping of me; times wherein they ought to be holy and to mind holy things; and so know that it is I which separate them from others, and do make them holy, a peculiar people unto myself.

Quest. Whether was not the sabbath a mutable ceremony, seeing he calls it a "sign" here?

Answ. That proves it not to be so; for, Gen. ix. 12, the rainbow is called a "token" or sign between God and man; and that was no mutable ceremony, but continues to the end of the world. Besides, it is not a "sign" or type of future grace, something to come, but a "sign" of their deliverance out of Egypt, or of the creation, which were things past, or a "sign" of God's sanctifying them at the present, when they met before him on those days. And further, "sign" here, by some, is put for proof; it is a note of your distinction from others, of your being my people, and of my sanctifying of you.

Obs. 1. When God is in a way of mercy with a people, he hath his "moreovers." "Moreover I gave them my sabbaths." Neh. ix. he reckons up many mercies; and ver. 22, he saith, "Moreover thou gavest them kingdoms and nations." So in Isa. xxx. he tells them of what mercies they shall have; and ver. 26, "Moreover the light of the moon shall be as the light," &c. God doth always perform his promises, showing his faithfulness; and many times he gives more than he promises, good measure pressed down, and running over, to show his bountifulness.

Obs. 2. That of holy times and days God is the Author. "I gave them my sabbaths." God blessed and sanctified the seventh day, and gave it unto the Jews, Gen. ii. 3. It is his prerogative to make persons, things, or times, holy; it is not in the power of man, or any sort of men, to make days holy. It was no small sin in our forefathers, that took upon them to make Lent and other times holy, and some days more holy than the Lord's day itself. The Jews had no holy days but at the Lord's appointment.

Obs. 3. The Lord gave forth and appointed holy and resting days, upon weighty and considerable grounds, always after some great mercy, some special thing or other which he had done. As here, when he had brought them out of Egypt, drowned Pharaoh and his host in the deeps, then he gave them out the sabbath again. At first it was instituted after that great and glorious work of the creation; God would have great works and mercies to be kept in memory. So the day we keep was appointed in memorial of that great work, man's redemption, by the death and resurrection of Jesus Christ, and therefore is honoured with the title of "Lord's day," Rev. i. 10.

Obs. 4. The sabbath is a day of special concernment to God and his people. "I gave them my sabbaths, to be a sign between me and them." As the rainbow is a sign of special concernment between God and the world, so is the sabbath. It is an argument and evidence that God looks upon them as his people, where his sabbath is, and that they acknowledge God their God, who keep his sabbaths; by it God keeps alive the memory of his glorious, great, and gracious works, and by it the people are brought to glorify and magnify his name for those works; by it he distinguisheth his people from the profane, and by it they distinguish him from the idol gods; in it the Lord sanctifies his people, and they in it do worship him; it is the day wherein they meet, visit, and make each other cheerful and glorious. Let us have more honourable thoughts of the sabbath, and not think it concerns not us; if we be his people, it is still a "sign" between him and them.

If we have no sabbath, or no day answerable to it, we come short of the Jews, who had it given unto them as a great mercy: "I gave unto them my sabbaths," my holy resting days.

Obs. 5. Sanctification is the work of the Lord,

and specially of the Lord when people meet on his day. He gave them his "sabbaths," and they were called holy convocations, because on them the people met, Lev. xxiii. 3. And why did he give them those days? that they might know that he was the Lord, which sanctified them. There is none which can sanctify persons by way of separation or inherent holiness, but the Lord; he assumes this power and privilege to himself; see Lev. xx. 8; Ezek. xxxvii. 28; and his sanctifying is chiefly when people meet on his day. Then the law was read and opened unto them, Acts xv. 21; Neh. viii. 8; then did God appear amongst them, and work by the means he appointed for their sanctification. Psal. lxxxix. 7, "God is greatly to be feared in the assembly of the saints," there he convinces them of their sinfulness and sinful practices; there he beats down their strong holds, and captivates their thoughts to the obedience of his will. What was it made David openly to proclaim it, that "a day in God's courts was better than a thousand?" one sabbath day, wherein he had communion with God, and found him sanctifying his head and heart, was more esteemed of him than a thousand other days: "For the Lord," saith he, "is a sun and shield," he enlightens me, he strengthens me, and so separates my darkness and weakness from me, and makes me more holy. Let us, therefore, look unto God alone for sanctification, and wait upon him on his days in the solemn assemblies, and he will sanctify us; those are days of his special presence, power, and blessing.

Obs. 6. God's people should observe and take notice what God doth in them, on sabbaths, when they appear before him. They had the "sabbaths" given them, that they might know the Lord did sanctify them, that they might have experience in themselves of the powerful operations of God in them; God observed what they did that day, and they were to observe what he did that day. They read the law and the prophets, and expounded them, Acts xiii. 15; Neh. viii. 8; they prayed, Acts xvi. 13; they discoursed, reasoned, and persuaded men out of the Scriptures, Acts xviii. 4; they offered sacrifices, Numb. xxviii. 2, 10; they did sing, Psal. xcii. title. These things they did, and God observed their spirits in the doing of them; he observed how they sanctified the day, and himself in the duties of the day; and they were to observe what he did in the assemblies, and in their bosoms. This David did: Psal. xcvi. 6, "Strength and beauty are in his sanctuary," saith he; and Psal. lxiii. 2, he confesses he had seen God's power and glory there; the "strength" and "beauty" in one place, is the same with "power" in the other. It is a glorious, beautiful work, when God sanctifies a sinner; it is a work of power and strength, when he breaks the snares of our lusts, the chains of unbelief, and enlarges our hearts, quickens, comforts, strengthens, and enlightens us. It is a common sin and sickness amongst christians, that they heed not what the Lord does in his ordinances for them, and in them; they cannot say from experience, We know it is the Lord that sanctifies; most can say this from the tongue, few from the heart. It was not without cause, that Solomon said, "Keep thy foot when thou goest to the house of God, and be more ready to hear, than to give the sacrifice of fools," Eccles. v. 1. Some think he alludes to Exod. iii. 5; xxx. 19; and Josh. v. 15; where is mention of putting off their shoes, and washing their feet, because they were to approach unto the holy God. And surely we had need look to our feet, that is, our affection, (foot is put for feet, the singular for the plural,) for we approach near to God when we go to his house; we go to be sanctified, and therefore should take heed we defile not ourselves.

Ver. 13. *But the house of Israel rebelled against me in the wilderness: they walked not in my statutes, and they despised my judgments, which if a man do, he shall even live in them; and my sabbaths they greatly polluted: then I said, I would pour out my fury upon them in the wilderness, to consume them.*

Having represented unto them the mercies he conferred on them in the wilderness, here he declares what their carriage was towards him therein, and what his purpose was towards them.

I. Their carriage towards him is laid down,

1. In general; "the house of Israel rebelled against me."

2. In special; and that in three particulars:

(1.) "They walked not in my statutes."

(2.) "They despised my judgments."

(3.) They polluted my sabbaths, and that greatly.

Now all these are aggravated,

[1.] From the place where they were done; "in the wilderness," where they had special need of God's protection and provision, where they had and saw his miracles daily.

[2.] From the nature of the statutes and judgments given, which were such, as, if done, they might have lived.

II. The Lord's purpose towards them was, "to pour out his fury upon them," and consume them, and that in the wilderness.

Little shall I speak of this verse, because in the 8th and 11th verses you have already had most things in it.

"The house of Israel rebelled against me." Of their rebellion in the wilderness you may read, Deut. i. 26, 43; Exod. xvii. 7; with Numb. xx. 24, 27; chap. xiv.; Deut. ix. 22.

"They despised my judgments." The Hebrew word for despise, notes, rejecting, hating, vilifying. They looked upon them as contemptible things, and threw them away; they did not only refuse to walk in his law, Psal. lxxviii. 10, but they "despised" his judgments, and abhorred his statutes, Lev. xxvi. 43; it was such despising as had an abhorrency accompanying it.

"My sabbaths they greatly polluted." Of their polluting his "sabbaths," you may read, Exod. xvi. 27, they went to gather manna on the sabbath day; one gathered sticks, Numb. xv. 32; they carried burdens, and did servile work, Jer. xvii. 22, 23; whereas they should have highly praised the "sabbaths," resting from doing their own ways, finding their own pleasure, speaking their own words, and wholly have been taken up in the worship of God, and the duties peculiar to the day.

Obs. 1. Such is the corruption of man's nature, that nothing will keep it within its bounds, but it breaks out against God, neglects and abuses the ordinances and means he hath appointed for man's salvation. "But the house of Israel rebelled against me, they walked not in my statutes, they despised my judgments, and they greatly polluted my sabbaths;" these God gave them for their good, life, salvation, but they slighted, perverted, polluted them. God had done great things for them, he provided for them in the wilderness manna, water, shoes, clothes, all in a miraculous way, so that they could not subsist without him; yet they rebel against him, despise him, Numb. xi. 20; cast off his statutes and judgments, and profane his sabbaths to his face.

Thus they dealt with the Lord when he brought

them out of Babylon, Neh. xiii. 15, 16; they greatly polluted the sabbaths of the Lord; whereupon saith Nehemiah, ver. 18, "Did not your fathers thus," and so bring evil upon us? and will you bring more wrath upon Israel by profaning the sabbaths? Neither the mercies their fathers had, when they were brought out of Egypt, nor the mercies themselves had, when they were brought out of Babylon, kept in their corruptions; but they rose to a great height, and brake out so far as to set at nought all his counsels, Prov. i. 25, to reject the word of the Lord, Jer. viii. 9, to mock and misuse his messengers and prophets, 2 Chron. xxxvi. 16, to speak stoutly against God, Mal. iii. 13; yea, so strong grew their corruptions, that their souls abhorred God, Zech. xi. 8. Is it not thus in our days? neither miraculous mercies, nor wonderful judgments, do keep men within bounds, or chain up their corruptions, but they break out, greatly polluting the Lord's day, despising all or some ordinances. Do they not set at nought and reject the whole counsel of God, the very Scriptures? do they not mock and misuse the messengers and ministers of God? do they not blaspheme, curse, and glory in it? do they not speak stoutly against Christ and God? do not some turn Jews, and others atheists, denying Christ, God? Surely iniquity abounds, and is within little of its perfection; the harvest is near, sinners are almost full ripe for judgment, and ere long God will say, Thrust in the sickle.

Obs. 2. When men do neglect, despise, and abuse the ordinances of God and means of grace, they provoke God even to their destruction. They neglected to walk in God's statutes, they despised his judgments, they polluted his sabbaths; and what then? "Then I said, I would pour out my fury upon them, to consume them." Men think that neglecting and slighting of ordinances, profaning of the Lord's day and holy things, is no such great evil, if it be an evil at all; but there is hardly any thing kindles the wrath of God hotter than the casting off, despising, and abusing the ordinances and mediums appointed of God, for his worship, our good, comfort, and salvation. Their sins here of this nature put God into fury, which is more than anger or wrath; upon pouring out of fury, and such pouring out as to consume them. Heb. x. 25—27, he tells you of some that did forsake the assemblies, cast off the ordinances of God, which was a wilful and provoking sin, excluding mercy, and hastening judgment and fierce indignation, which should destroy. When God in his infinite wisdom and mercy hath condescended to man's weakness, given him ordinances and mediums wherein he will be worshipped, and through which he will do good to the creature, and now the foolish creature to neglect, despise, or profane them, this pierces God's heart, and transforms his patience into fury, and puts him into ways of destruction. Those who despised Moses' law were to die without mercy; and what will be their portion who despise Christ, the gospel, and ordinances thereof? see Heb. xii. 25. Acts iii. 23, "Every soul that will not hear Christ shall be destroyed;" that is, whosoever shall not hearken to Christ's voice in the gospel, submit to the ordinances appointed by him therein, and worship the Father in the way he hath prescribed, he shall be destroyed. The Corinthians abused and profaned the supper of the Lord, and were they not smitten and destroyed for that sin? 1 Cor. xi. 30. Moses had the sword drawn upon him by the Lord himself, because he neglected the circumcision of his son, Exod. iv. 24.

Ver. 14. ***But I wrought for my name's sake, that it should not be polluted before the heathen, in whose sight I brought them out.***

Whilst they were in the wilderness, and Moses in the mount, they made a calf, and fell to idolatry, which exasperated the Lord so, that he thought to destroy them; and had not Moses interposed and pressed God with the honour of his name, he had done it. Exod. xxxii. 12, "Wherefore should the Egyptians speak, and say, For mischief did he bring them out, to slay them in the mountains, and to consume them from the face of the earth? Turn from thy fierce wrath, and repent of this evil against thy people." God did so, and wrought for his name's sake. Of these words was spoken in the ninth verse.

Ver. 15—17. *Yet also I lifted up my hand unto them in the wilderness, that I would not bring them into the land which I had given them, flowing with milk and honey, which is the glory of all lands; because they despised my judgments, and walked not in my statutes, but polluted my sabbaths: for their heart went after their idols. Nevertheless mine eye spared them from destroying them, neither did I make an end of them in the wilderness.*

In the 15th verse you have mention of God's swearing, that he would not bring them into Canaan; in the 16th, the reason thereof; in the 17th, his indulgence and pity towards them.

"I lifted up my hand unto them," &c. This was, when upon the ill report the spies had brought upon the land of Canaan, the Israelites murmured against Moses and Aaron, as you may see, Numb. xiv. 28—30, and chap. xxvi. 65.

But here a difficulty ariseth. In the 6th verse of this chapter, it is said that God had lifted up his hand, and so sworn to bring them not only out of Egypt, but into the land of Canaan; and here it is said, he had lifted up his hand to the contrary, that he would not bring them into the land he had given them: so that it seems here is one oath against another. And in Numb. xiv. 34, God acknowledges his breach of promise, for he saith, "Ye shall know my breach of promise:" I have promised and sworn to bring you into the land of Canaan, but you have so sinned against and provoked me, that I will not do it, yea, have sworn you shall not enter into my rest, Psal. xcv. 11.

This difficulty is removed, by considering, that God did not make promise, or swear, to those individual men that were kept out of Canaan, that they should be brought into it; if it had been so, God had forgot and forsworn himself; but his promise and oath was, that the seed of Abraham, Isaac, and Jacob should be brought into it, Gen. xii. 7; xiii. 15; xv. 18; xxvi. 4; l. 24; Deut. xxxiv. 4; and their seed was brought into the promised land, Josh. i. 2; iv. 1; xiv. 1; xxiv. 13; and so God's promise and oath was kept. Those he swore against, were those that murmured against him, even all from twenty years old and upwards, except Caleb and Joshua, whose carcasses fell in the wilderness, as you may see, Josh. v. 6.

As for that, Numb. xiv. 34, God's breach of promise, the original is, my frustration: You looked certainly to have entered into Canaan, but for your murmuring and unbelief, I have frustrated your expectations: or thus, You think my oath cannot be true, because of a former oath, and that the words I have uttered will prove false, a lie; but you shall know whether my words and oath be false or not. Junius and Piscator read it, *abruptionem meam*, and make the sense this; You have broken off from me, and you shall know what it is to have me break off from you; I will plague you for your murmuring, ingratitude, unfaithfulness, and unbelief, so that you shall never come into the land of promise. The Septuagint hath it, You shall know the wrath of mine anger.

"Flowing with milk and honey, which is the glory of all lands." Of these words hath been spoken largely in the 6th verse. They are repeated here, to show the ingratitude of this people, that were not affected with this land, which was a second Paradise, but despised it, and raised an ill report upon it; as also to show what they lost in being kept out of it, and their folly in preferring Egypt before it.

There is nothing needful to open in the other two verses, because occasion hath been given formerly in this chapter and others to open them.

Obs. 1. Men's sins disappoint them of choice mercies, yea, mercies promised, expected, and near at hand. God had promised them Canaan, they were near unto it, Numb. xiii. expected to go in and possess it; but God would not bring them into the land, because they despised his judgments, walked not in his statutes, but polluted his sabbaths.

In Heb. iii. 19, it is said, "They could not enter in because of unbelief;" and Psal. cvi. 24, "They despised the pleasant land, they believed not his word." It was their sins kept them from so great, so near, so longed-for a mercy. Such is the malignity of sin, that it drives mercies back when they are at the door, and blocks up the passage, that none for the future may issue forth towards us. Isa. lix. 1, 2, "Behold, the Lord's hand is not shortened, that it cannot save; neither his ear heavy, that it cannot hear:" God can hear and help; "but your iniquities have separated between you and your God, and your sins have hid his face from you, that he will not hear:" your sins stand like a brass wall, a mighty mountain, between him and you; they have cramped his will, so that though he can, yet he will neither hear your prayers nor help your persons. It is sin that keeps mercy from us: Jer. v. 25, "Your iniquities have turned away these things;" what things? the former and latter rain, the harvest and fruits of the earth; they were coming to you, but your sins turned them back again, and bid them be gone; Away, rain, away, harvest, away, fruits of the earth! and so the next words import, "your sins have withholden good things from you;" they have forbidden good from you, so Montanus and the Vulgate read the words. Our sins do forbid and withhold good from us; see it, Matt. vi. 15, "If ye forgive not men their trespasses, neither will your Father forgive your trespasses."

John viii. 19, "If ye had known me, ye should have known my Father also." Isa. xlviii. 18, "O that thou hadst hearkened to my commandments! then had thy peace been as a river, and thy righteousness as the waves of the sea: thy seed also had been as the sand," &c. See Luke xiv. 16—20; xiii. 34; John v. 40; Psal. lxxxi. 13, 14: it was their sins which frustrated them of mercies. If the word profit not us, it is sin that hinders the profit, Heb. iv. 2; Jam. i. 21; 1 Pet. ii. 1, 2.

Obs. 2. When the heart is carried out after unlawful things, then the ways and ordinances of God are neglected, slighted, and profaned. This rises from the words of the 16th verse; they despised God's judgments, walked not in his statutes, they polluted his sabbaths; and why did they so? "for their heart went after their idols." These had stolen away their hearts from God; these had their thoughts, desires, affections, and the things of God were of little account with them; his statutes, judgments, sabbaths, were laid aside, and only what their hearts were carried forth unto, that they magnified. Ezek. vi. 9, they had whorish hearts, and whorish eyes, which went after their idols, and made them depart from God, that is, from his judgments, statutes, sabbaths, ordinances: idols had their eyes and hearts, and as to God and the things of God, they were eyeless and heartless. When Solomon's heart was carried out to women and idols, then he did evil in the sight of the Lord, 1 Kings xi. 4—8; then the Lord's ordinances were despised, and his sabbaths polluted. If once the heart go out to unlawful things, it is drawn off from lawful; so much as it adheres to evil, so much it is divided from God and good. Ezek. xxxiii. 31, "Their heart goeth after their covetousness:" so much as it went after riches, so much it was distanced from God, and walking in his ways. David hereupon advised men not to set their hearts upon riches, Psal. lxii. 10; they will then be their idols, and make them forget God and his ways, and do those things which will profane his ordinances. Look well to your hearts, and let not them carry you away, Job xv. 12.

Obs. 3. When sinners provoke God into ways of destruction, he doth not utterly destroy them, but shows some pity and mercy. "Nevertheless mine eye spared them from destroying." God did destroy many of them in the wilderness; three thousand upon their making the calf, Exod. xxxii. 28; twenty-four thousand upon their committing whoredom with the daughters of Moab, Numb. xxv. 9; much people by fiery serpents upon their murmuring, Numb. xxi. 6; Korah, Dathan, and Abiram were swallowed up of the earth, and all theirs, and the two hundred and fifty men that offered incense, were consumed by fire, Numb. xvi. 32, 33, 35; fourteen thousand seven hundred were destroyed by the plague, ver. 49; and many by the Amorites in Seir, Deut. i. 44. Now notwithstanding so many were destroyed, yet all were not; he did not make an end of them in the wilderness, he did not consummate and perfect his wrath upon them, his eye spared them, he was moved to mercy, and had compassion on them.

Though men have sinned much, and God have let out much wrath, yet nevertheless he hath an eye to spare, and a heart to pity. If he should punish, destroy none, he would be thought to be like unto sinners, Psalm l. 21; if he should destroy all, he would be thought to be cruel: to show therefore that he is a just God, he cuts off some; and to show he is a merciful God, he spares some.

In the late powder blow, some were destroyed, some were spared, yea, wonderfully spared and preserved. It was the 4th of Jan. 1649, about eight o'clock at night.

Ver. 18, 19. *But I said unto their children in the wilderness, Walk ye not in the statutes of your fathers, neither observe their judgments, nor defile yourselves with their idols: I am the Lord your God; walk in my statutes, and keep my judgments, and do them.*

In the 18th verse God dehorts them from following their fathers' ways.

In the 19th he exhorts them to follow his ways, and shows them the reason why they should do so, because he is their God.

Where the Lord spake thus unto them in the wilderness, is not recorded by Moses, but that he did speak what is in the 18th verse, our prophet assures us, who spake as he was moved by the Spirit. You have that which is equivalent thereunto, Deut. v. 32, "Ye shall observe to do as the Lord your God hath commanded you: ye shall not turn aside to the right hand or to the left;" not to your fathers on the right hand, nor to the heathen on the left.

The 19th verse you have Lev. xviii. 4, 5, "I am the Lord your God; ye shall therefore keep my statutes and my judgments." Nothing in these verses requires explication. Take these observations.

Obs. 1. Children are prone to follow the corrupt decrees, counsels, and examples of their parents. "I said, Walk not in the statutes of your fathers," that is, in what they decree, appoint; "observe not their judgments," that is, their counsels and advisements; "nor defile yourselves with their idols," that is, follow not their examples. They were addicted much to what their sinful fathers said or did. Of the kings of Israel it is said, they did evil as their fathers had done, 2 Kings xv. 9; xxiii. 32; xxiv. 9: and Jer. xliv. 17, the children would sacrifice to and defile themselves with idols, as their fathers had done. Fathers, laws, customs, traditions, examples, persuasions, counsels, are loadstones, and draw them strongly to that which is evil.

Obs. 2. Posterity are not tied to the statutes and judgments of their fathers or forefathers. "I said, Walk not in the statutes of your fathers, neither observe their judgments," &c. Though there be a strong tie between parents and children, and they are bound by the command of God to obey their parents, yet when they shall command or counsel them any thing unlawful, contrary to the statutes and judgments of God, they are not to hearken, not to observe or obey them. Here is divine authority for it, "I said."

If it be God's command that lead children to obey parents, and people to obey magistrates in lawful things, then God's prohibition must keep them from obeying in unlawful things. When masters or parents are so wicked, as to put their servants or children upon lying or swearing, to put off their commodities, they should remember what God hath said, "Walk not in their statutes," &c.

This holds especially in matters of faith and worship; men's statutes and judgments must not come in there: what is not divine, is no matter for my faith, nor rule for my worship. Men's chaff and bran must not come among God's wheat; their weeds and nettles must not come amongst his flowers: it is not popes' decrees, canons of councils, judgments of fathers, votes of synods, customs of churches, religion of ancestors, that must tie my conscience, or guide my practice in the worship of God. He hath said it, who is above them all, "Walk not in their statutes, neither observe their judgments, nor defile yourselves with their idols." Men have their statutes, their judgments, their inventions and additions to points of faith and matters of worship, which are no other than idols, and will defile.

Obs. 3. That we are only to walk in God's statutes, and to keep his judgments; not men's statutes or judgments. "I am the Lord your God," I have authority over you, I am in covenant with you; I have given you statutes and judgments which are right, Psal. xix. 8, true and good, Neh. ix. 13; therefore "walk in my statutes, keep my judgments." When the Israelites walked in other statutes, the statutes of the heathen, or the statutes that themselves made, the Lord was wroth with them, and afflicted them for it, 2 Kings xvii. 8, 19, 20; and commanded them to observe his statutes and ordinances, and to do them for evermore, ver. 37; see Josh. xxiv. 14, 15.

Ver. 20. *And hallow my sabbaths; and they shall be a sign between me and you, that ye may know that I am the Lord your God.*

In this 20th verse, the Lord proceeds in his exhortation of the children of those rebellious Israelites in the wilderness, and exhorts them to hallow his sabbaths, which their fathers had polluted.

"Hallow my sabbaths." Not make holy, but keep holy; the Hebrew word is the same with that, Exod. xx. 8. The hallowing or sanctifying of the sabbath here, consisteth in two things:

1. In resting from labour and work. "Servile work," Lev. xxiii. 7, 8, that is, such work as men may lawfully do on other days, works for gain and profit, might not be done on sabbath days; they were to rest from their own works, words, and pleasures, Isa. lviii. 13. See Exod. xx. 10; Neh. xiii. 15; Jer. xvii. 22; Exod. xvi. 29; xxxi. 14.

2. In doing those things which God required on that day; as, meditation on the works of creation, for which it was first instituted, Gen. ii. 2, 3; remembrance of their servitude in Egypt, and deliverance thence, Deut. v. 15; meeting in solemn assemblies, Lev. xxiii. 3; in which the word was to be read, opened, and reverently heard, Luke iv. 16; Acts xv. 21; Eccles. v. 1; prayer to be made, Acts xvi. 13; God to be praised, Psal. xcii.; sacrifices to be offered, Numb. xxviii. 9, 10: and they were to exercise works of mercy on that day, Matt. xii. 10—12; John v. 9: and all these duties they were to do with delight, Isa. lviii. 13.

"They shall be a sign between me and you." Of these words you heard in the 12th verse. Besides what was said there, the sabbath was a sign of the covenant God made with them to be their God, and to own them for his people; for it follows,

"That ye may know that I am the Lord your God." The sabbath day was the time wherein God and this people met; God made himself known unto them then, by sanctifying of them, ver. 12, for whom he is a God unto, he blesses and sanctifies, and specially on his sabbaths; then he heard their prayers, accepted their offerings, and let out his loving-kindness unto them.

Obs. 1. Having and hallowing God's sabbaths, is a sign and manifestation that God is the God of that people. The Jews had the Lord's sabbaths, and he bade them hallow them, that so being hallowed, they might signify and certify to them, that God was their God. As circumcision and the passover were signs that the Jews were in covenant with God, so likewise was the sabbath, Exod. xxxi. 13; and because it was a sign of the covenant between them and God, ver. 16, God tells them, they must observe it for a perpetual covenant; and hence it was, that when they violated the sabbath, God accounted it the violation of the covenant between them.

Ver. 21. *Notwithstanding the children rebelled against me: they walked not in my statutes, neither kept my judgments to do them, which if a man do, he shall even live in them; they polluted my sabbaths: then I said, I would pour out my fury upon them, to accomplish my anger against them in the wilderness.*

Here the unsuccessfulness of God's exhortation is evidenced; he pressed them to be obedient, and dutiful to him, being their God, but they rebelled, and would not walk in his statutes, nor keep his judgments; their fathers' statutes and judgments they would walk in and observe; they chose rather to be defiled and die in their fathers' ways, than to be sanctified and live in God's ways: whereupon God had a purpose to destroy them, as he had formerly to destroy their fathers. This verse is the same with the 13th, which hath been opened, and the observations given.

Ver. 22. *Nevertheless I withdrew mine hand, and wrought for my name's sake, that it should not be polluted in the sight of the heathen, in whose sight I brought them forth.*

God having purposed their destruction, saw that if he should proceed thereunto, the heathens would make an ill sense of it, and blaspheme his name; for prevention whereof, he let fall his purpose, and would not destroy them. This verse falls in with the 9th and 14th, only this is in it, which they have not: "I withdrew mine hand." God's hand was stretched out, and he pulled it back again. The Hebrew word notes thus much, I made to return, I made mine arm come back again, when it was going forth to destroy them.

Obs. God's people do oft provoke him, both fathers and children, and so that they are at the door, brink, point of destruction, and yet he is merciful unto them, and that for his name's sake. When he cannot show mercy for their sakes, he will show mercy for his own name's sake. In ver. 8, is set down their "but," "But they rebelled againt me, they would not hearken," they would not forsake their idols, whereupon God purposed to destroy them. In ver. 9, is God's "but," "But I wrought for my name," &c. In ver. 13, again is their "But," "But the house of Israel rebelled," &c.; then God was angry again, and purposed to consume them. In ver. 14, you have God's "but" again, "But I wrought for my name's sake," &c. In ver. 16, you have their "but" the third time, "But they polluted my sabbaths." In ver. 17, you have God's "nevertheless," or but, again, for it is the same in the original, "Nevertheless mine eye spared them," &c. In ver. 21, you have their "notwithstanding," or but, once more, the Hebrew is the same with "but" before; "Notwithstanding," or but, "the children rebelled," &c. And in this 22nd verse you have God's but, or "nevertheless" answering thereunto, "Nevertheless I withdrew mine hand, and wrought for my name's sake." Four times in this chapter you have them provoking God even to their ruin, and as many times his sparing of them: this last time his hand was stretched out, even at the work, and had he strucken one blow, had broken them all; but he recalled his hand, he would not let his power fall upon them to crush them in pieces, but wrought for his name, and their safety. If we have our "buts" and "notwithstandings," importing rebellion, ingratitude, and disobedience, the Lord hath his "buts," and "neverthelesses," importing mercy, patience, and loving-kindness.

Ver. 23, 24. *I lifted up mine hand unto them also in the wilderness, that I would scatter them among the heathen, and disperse them through the countries; because they had not executed my judgments, but had despised my statutes, and had polluted my sabbaths, and their eyes were after their fathers' idols.*

In these two verses you may see,

I. A commination, backed with an oath, in ver. 23.

II. The reason thereof, in ver. 24.

"I lifted up mine hand unto them in the wilderness." Of this gesture used in swearing, you heard before, ver. 5, 6; but where it was done will hardly be found in Moses' writings, that God thus lifted up his hand, and threatened to disperse them. Something like hereunto, see in Deut. iv. 26, 27; xxviii. 25, 36, 37, 64; chap. xxxii. 21—26; Lev. xxvi. 33; in those places the Lord threatens to scatter them; and David tells you, he "lifted up his hand" to do it, Psal. cvi. 26, 27, "He lifted up his hand against them, to overthrow them in the wilderness; to overthrow their seed also among the nations, and to scatter them in the lands." Maldonate makes the lifting up the hand here, to be in way of threatening, not of swearing.

"That I would scatter them among," &c. Of their scattering and dispersion, was spoken in the 5th, 6th, and 12th chapters.

"Because they had not executed my judgments." Some refer these words, and the rest in the verse, to the time after their entrance into Canaan; if then they should not keep God's judgments and do them, he having performed his promise unto them, he would scatter and disperse them among the nations; but because the verse speaks of the time past, we must also look at what was done, as well as what was to do. The children before mentioned had rebelled, and did not keep the judgments of God to do them, they polluted his sabbaths, and defiled themselves with their idols, whereupon God thought to have destroyed them in the wilderness, but spared them for his name's sake, that the Egyptians and nations might not blaspheme and pollute his name; but knowing that when he had possessed them of Canaan, that their children would do as they had done, he lifts up his hand, and threatens their driving out of that land again, and dispersion in the countries, and so makes their sin the cause of their posterity's ruin.

"Their eyes were after their fathers' idols." In the 8th verse, he mentions the idols of Egypt, and they were their "fathers' idols," which the children minded, and were intent upon; for when the eyes go after any thing, there is some affection in the heart unto that thing, ver. 16: and chap. vi. 9, "I am broken with their whorish heart, which hath departed from me, and with their eyes, which go a whoring after their idols:" if the heart did not affect them, the eyes would not. "Fathers' idols" affected both the hearts and eyes of their children; Rachel stole her father's gods, Gen. xxxi. 19, and said, they should be her gods.

Obs. 1. That parents' sins prepare heavy judgments for their posterity many years after. God lifted up his hand in the wilderness, that he would scatter them among the heathen, and disperse them through the countries, because they were statute-breakers, sabbath-polluters, and idol-minders, which fell not upon them, but their posterity many hundred years after; Junius makes it five hundred; and then they were driven out of the land of Canaan, and dispersed into heathenish nations, a judgment that deprives men of all their own comforts, and exposes them to all the injuries of others. One calls this judgment the beginning of new evils, and it may be added, of unknown evils. Let parents therefore take heed how they provoke God by sinful and wicked practices, their posterity may smart soundly for it many years after. Saul's, Jeroboam's, and Manasseh's sins, made their posterity to feel sad strokes long after; and some in our days have suffered for their fathers' sins, and it is just with God they should, when they tread in their fathers' steps, who have rebelled against God.

Ver. 25, 26. *Wherefore I gave them also statutes that were not good, and judgments whereby they should not live; and I polluted them in their own gifts, in that they caused to pass through the fire all that openeth the womb, that I might make them desolate, to the end that they might know that I am the Lord.*

Here is a further progress of God's judiciary dealings with them, which lies,

I. In the statutes and judgments he gave them.

II. In the polluting of them.

Then you have the end of both, which is,

1. To make them desolate.
2. To bring them to the knowledge of himself.

In this verse is first a figure called antanaclasis, which is the reciprocating the same words, in a diverse sense: in the former verse is mention made of statutes and judgments, which God gave them, ver. 11, and were his divine word; here is a mentioning of statutes and judgments, which he gave them as divine punishments, being the commands and devices of men.

Secondly, a figure called meiosis or tapeinosis, which is, when less is expressed, and more intended; as, not good, is a mild expression, but more is intended in it, viz. hurtful, deadly: so these words, "should not live," are moderate, but they include that which is grievous, namely, death, yea, terrible deaths; they should not only have no good by them, but much evil, sore destruction.

"I gave them statutes that were not good." The Hebrew is, statutes not good. These statutes were not the moral law, though it be a killing letter, 2 Cor. iii. 6; for the "law is holy, just, and good," Rom. vii. 12, yea "perfect," Psal. xix. 7: not the ceremonials, viz. sacrifices, and sacraments, as Jerom and Estius calls them; for though these were shadows of things to come, yet they had purifying virtue in them, and led to Christ, Heb. ix. 13; Gal. iii. 24; and in this chapter, God speaking of the statutes and judgments he gave them, which comprehend both morals and ceremonials, he saith, ver. 11, 13, 21, that they were such, as, if they kept them, they might live in them. Neither doth it advantage to say, these are called "not good," because they are less good than those of the gospel; let that be granted, yet those statutes, kept, would afford life, but the statutes here meant, were such as whereby they should not live. Not the tributes and taxes imposed upon them by the nations, when they prevailed against them in war, for they were under none in the wilderness, and these statutes were given when they were there.

Vid. Est. in sent. l. 4. Sect. 27. p. 26. Col. 1. l. 8.

By these statutes are meant,

1. Those punishments that befell them in the wilderness; as, the sword, Exod. xxii. 27, 28, fiery serpents, Numb. xxi. 6, the plague, chap. xvi. 49, the earth swallowing up Korah, Dathan, and Abiram, ver. 31, 32, fire, ver. 35, suspension, chap. xxv. 4: God commanded the hanging up the heads of the people, he appointed the fire, the earth, the plague, the sword, to do execution upon them, these were "statutes not good;" not good for them, but hurtful, yea, very hurtful, for so much "not good" implies, and the next words prove, being a further declaration of these "judgments, whereby they should not live;" these statutes and judgments took away their lives.

2. Those threatenings and curses you find Deut. iv. 26—28; xxvii. 15—26; xxviii. 15—68; Lev. xxvi. 14—40: these were sentences of death.

3. The inventions, laws, rites, decrees, superstitions, of men, which are called statutes, Dan. vi. 7. Micah vi. 16, "The statutes of Omri are kept;" and 2 Kings xvii. 8, "The statutes of the heathen." And God is said to give them, in that he gave them over to these which were not good, but tended to death and destruction: Seeing they would none of mine, I gave them men's.

Obs. When men slight and violate the statutes and judgments of God, he doth not only threaten and punish them with temporal judgments, but also with spiritual. Because they despised God's statutes, and did not keep his judgments, therefore he gave them "statutes not good, and judgments whereby they should not live." God threatened them with cursings, cut off many of them in the wilderness, and gave over others to believe errors, to follow the imaginations of their own hearts, the commandments and statutes of men, which was a more dreadful judgment. When men care not for the ways of God, which have good and life in them, it is just with God to give them over to the ways of men, that have no good, no life in them; nothing but expense, labour, disappointment, vexation, and destruction, Ezek. xxiv. 12; Jer. ii. 36, 37; Prov. xiv. 12. When God's people would not listen to him, he gave them up to their own hearts' lusts, to the perverse intendments and pertinacies of their hearts; they intended the statutes and judgments of men, of heathens and idolaters, those they were set upon, and God gave them up unto them, as you may see, ver. 39 of this chapter, "Go ye, serve ye every one his idols;" seeing you will not submit to me any ways, go to your idols where your eyes and hearts are, and serve them according to the statutes and judgments of the nations whence ye had them; or if they be of your own devising, serve them according to the ways of your own hearts. 2 Thess. ii. 10—12, when men receive not the love of the truth that they might be saved, God sends them strong delusions that they should believe a lie, and be damned; *ἐνέργειαν πλάνης*, the efficacy of error; the truth comes with love, error with efficacy; if truths wooing and love be not entertained, God sends error with efficacy to seize upon men. Because we have been wanton with the truths, ordinances, and things of God, not received the love of them, but busied our wits and parts about them, yea, against them, therefore God hath sent the efficacy of error to take hold of men. Is not the efficacy of error upon them that say, there is no devil but holiness, no heaven nor hell but what is in a man's own conscience, &c.?

"And I polluted them in their own gifts." God being most holy, could not communicate any thing that should defile them; from a holy God comes nothing but that which is holy and good. Some take it in this sense, that God suffered them to do those things which defiled them, to prostitute themselves to all abominations.

Sanctius informs us, that one is said to do a thing, when he declares it to be done: Lev. xiii. 3, "The priest shall look on him," וטמא אתו and shall pollute him, that is, pronounce, declare him polluted; so ver. 6, he shall cleanse him, saith the original, that is, declare him to be clean; and ver. 44, the priest shall by polluting pollute him, that is, declare him altogether polluted; and our Ezekiel is said to destroy the city, whenas he did but declare the destruction of the city, chap. xliii. 3: so here, God is said to pollute them, in that he did declare them polluted; and not only so, but in that he dealt with them as polluted ones, rejecting them and their gifts.

"In their own gifts." The Septuagint reads it, *ἐν τοῖς δόγμασιν αὐτῶν*, in their opinions. When men leave the statutes of God, and take up opinions of their own, or tenets of the world, they pollute themselves, God judges them so, will declare them to be such, and deal with them as such: this by the way.

By "gifts" are not meant all the sacrifices which they brought unto the Lord, but their firstborn, which were to be given to God in remembrance of their coming out of Egypt, when the firstborn of the Egyptians were all slain, and the firstborn of the Israelites all preserved, Exod. xiii. 2, 3, 12.

"In that they caused to pass through the fire all that openeth the womb." The Hebrew is, making to pass all opening of the womb; it is a periphrasis, the opening of the womb, for the firstborn, and that of the male kind, which were to be offered to the Lord; but they offered unto idols, causing them "to pass through the fire," as it is in the 31st verse of this chapter. They were forbidden, and that upon pain of death, to let any of their seed to pass through the fire, or to give them unto Molech, Lev. xviii. 21; xx. 2: God expected they should strictly have observed his ordinance of consecrating their firstborn unto him, and they either sacrificed or consecrated them to idols. David, Psal. cvi. 37, 38, tells you, "they sacrificed their sons and daughters unto devils;" he calls their idols devils, and they sacrificed their sons, not only their firstborn, but others, and not only sons, but daughters, so corrupt were they in their opinions and practice.

If it should be granted here, as some interpreters conceive, that they did not offer their firstborn to idols, but to the true God, that they did not cause them to pass through the fire, as the heathens did, but caused them to pass from themselves, from under their power, and give them to God; yet because they despised his statutes, polluted his sabbaths, minded idols, and kept not his statutes, God polluted them in these gifts, declared them and their gifts to be such.

"That I might make them desolate." The word for "desolate" is, אשמם from שמם to make waste and desolate even to astonishment. Some render it here, that I might destroy them, and then the sense runs thus; I have declared what polluted creatures they are, that I may thence take occasion to destroy them: but this suits not so well with what follows, "that they might know that I am the Lord." To keep then to the word as it is here; God would "make them desolate," by convincing them of the pollution of their offerings, and by afflicting their consciences; making them to see, that though they had offered their sons, their firstborn to him, or to idols, yet they had gained nothing at his hands thereby, but were so far from pleasing him, that they had greatly provoked him, so that they should be amazed at their desolation.

Obs. 1. That if men alienate from God what is due to him, or bring him his due and live in the breach of his commands, he will not respect them, but declare them to be and deal with them as polluted ones. They alienated their firstborn to idols, which God commanded to be consecrated to him; or brought them to God living in the breach of his statutes; and hereupon he saith, "I polluted them in their own gifts." They thought they did me good service, and should obtain much favour at my hands, that I would be a great benefactor unto them, but they were deceived; I look upon them and their gifts as defiled, loathsome things, and pronounced them to be so. Many think their persons, prayers, and other duties are very acceptable to God, but they will find them otherwise, Isa. i. 11—14; Matt. vii. 22, 23.

Obs. 2. The Lord would not have men to confide in their sacrifices and services. He declared them polluted, that he might make them desolate, beat them off from their hopes and confidences they had upon doing these things. We are apt to rest upon duties, and to promise much to ourselves thereupon; but when God shall tell men they are polluted things they offer, yea, that themselves are polluted in those offerings, this will shake their vain foundations and hopes. When God told them, "He that killed an ox was as if he slew a man; he that sacrificed a lamb, as if he cut off a dog's neck; he that offered an oblation, as if he offered swine's blood; he that burned incense, as if he blessed an idol," Isa. lxvi. 3; did he not undermine their strong holds, and make them naked? for he shows that all they did was either lost labour, as the blessing of an idol; or abomination, as swine's blood; or dangerous, as cutting off a dog's neck; or deadly, as killing of a man: thus God "polluted them in their own gifts" and doings, and made them desolate. Thus Christ dealt with the scribes and Pharisees, Matt. xxiii. 13—16, 23, 25, 27, 29; they look for blessings, not for woes; but they were polluted, whatever their confidences were, and Christ declares them to be so, and makes them desolate.

Obs. 3. The Lord strips men of their righteousness, and beats them out of their confidences, that they might come to him, bottom upon him, and find him a sure foundation. God would make them desolate, to the end, that they might know that he was the Lord, that they might not trust in their sacrifices, but in him, the God of them and their sacrifices; in him that could show them their errors, and pardon them being shown. When men are deprived of their supposed comforts, convinced of the falseness of their confidences, surrounded with the guilt and evil of their ways, they begin to look where succour is to be had; to run from the sand to the rock; from themselves, and all that is their own, unto the living God, and look at his promises to believe them, and his statutes to obey them, and so embracing him for the all-sufficient good, abide with and build upon him alone.

Ver. 27—29. *Therefore, son of man, speak unto the house of Israel, and say unto them, Thus saith the Lord God; Yet in this your fathers have blasphemed me, in that they have committed a trespass against me. For when I had brought them into the land, for the which I lifted up mine hand to give it to them, then they saw every high hill, and all the thick trees, and they offered there their sacrifices, and there they presented the provocation of their offering: there also they made their sweet savour, and poured out their drink offerings. Then I said unto them, What is the high place whereunto ye go? And the name thereof is called Bamah unto this day.*

Having spoken of the proceedings between God and this people in Egypt and the wilderness, we are come now to the passages between them in the land of Canaan.

For the Lord's part, he "brought them into the land," ver. 28, which is the only mercy mentioned; but it was such a mercy as included a multitude of mercies in it, for it was a land "flowing with milk and honey, the glory of all lands," as twice you have it in this chapter; and something of the goodness of this land you may see, Deut. viii. 7—9. And, chap. vi. 10, 11, it was the land that God had lifted up his hand, and sware to give them; and he brought them into it, without the help of any other people, even by his own arm, for he destroyed the seven nations in it, Acts xiii. 19; and he "gave them the lands of the heathen; and they inherited the labour of the people," Psal. cv. 44. And why did the Lord bring them into this land? the next verse shows, "That they might observe his statutes, and keep his laws." Which thing they did not; for,

1. They blasphemed him, ver. 27.
2. They fell to idolatry, ver. 28.
3. They persisted in it, ver. 29.

"Yet in this your fathers have blasphemed me." The Hebrew for "yet in this," is, moreover this. Septuagint, even to this; they sinned and dealt ungratefully, not only till they came to Canaan, but in Canaan: they were not content with what they had done in Egypt and the wilderness against me, but they continued in their wickedness, and added sin to sin, doing worse and worse daily. Or, moreover in this, and so it notes some heinous and great offence, viz. what he mentions in the end of the verse.

"Have blasphemed me." The Hebrew word signifies, to revile with words, to reproach, and blaspheme. The Septuagint is, they provoked me, they were contumelious, disgracing me. Our translation has it, blaspheme, which is to hurt the name or fame of any, and is a kind of evil speaking, derogating from the glory of God: God's glory or name in itself is inviolable, but blasphemy doth what it can to violate it.

Aquinas makes it to consist,

1. In attributing to God what is not congruous to him; as to say, He is the author of sin; he sees not, he hath forsaken the earth, Ezek. viii. 12; He is like unto man, Psal. l. 21.

2. In detracting from him what belongs unto him; as to deny his providence, his omniscience, his omnipotence; as, Can he provide a table in the wilderness? Psal. lxxviii. 19; If he should make windows in heaven could this thing be? 2 Kings vii. 2: to which may be added,

3. The doing of such things as cause God's name to be blasphemed; as Rom. ii. 24, "The name of God is blasphemed among the gentiles through you." As there is practical atheism, Tit. i. 16, so practical blasphemy.

"In that they have committed a trespass against me." The Hebrew is, in their prevaricating a prevarication against me. The doubling of the word intends the signification, and notes the greatness of their sin, and progress in their wickedness. The Vulgate is, seeing that despising they have despised me. The word מעל notes such prevarication, and sinning, as hath the will in it: hence Piscator renders the words here, they have perfidiously sinned against me. They sinned not ignorantly, or of common infirmity, but with a high hand. Junius saith, their sin was, speaking against the truth of God's worship, for when people fall to false worship, they will disparage, if not wholly despise, the worship they had before. So then here we may understand, both their speaking against the true worship of God, and practising contrary thereunto.

Obs. Wilful sinning is a reproaching, a blaspheming of God, and provokes him greatly. "In this your fathers have blasphemed me, in that they have committed a trespass against me;" they have spoken against my worship, and run out to other ways which I forbade them; other sins they have committed which I could have winked at, but when they sin wilfully, despising me, my laws, my worship, they reproach, blaspheme, provoke me so, that they shall hear of it. Son of man, go and speak to the house of Israel, go and tell them how they have dealt with me, and how I take it. Such sins deserve death: Numb. xv. 30, "The soul that doeth ought presumptuously, whether he be born in the land, or a stranger, the same reproacheth the Lord." מגדף it is the same word which is here for "blasphemed," and may as well be rendered so as "reproacheth;" (for he that reproacheth the Lord blasphemes him, and he that blasphemes him reproacheth him, they are joined together, 2 Kings xix. 22;) and what then? "That soul shall be cut off from among his people. Because he hath despised the word of the Lord, and hath broken his commandment, that soul shall utterly be cut off." There was no mercy for those who sinned in that manner, Heb. x. 26, 27. Many, I fear, commit such trespasses in these days, by speaking against providence, ordinances, Scriptures, angels, Christ, God himself, and so sin away mercy and their own souls at once. David prayed that God would keep him back from "presumptuous sins," Psal. xix. 13; and we had need do it, for there is that in our natures which carries us on strongly towards them, as much as they did him. Remember what Solomon saith, Prov. xxviii. 14, "Happy is the man that feareth always; but he that hardeneth his heart," that presumeth, that is wilful, pertinacious, "shall fall into mischief;" into mischievous sins, into mischievous judgments. Chap. xiii. 13, "Whoso despiseth the word shall be destroyed; but he that feareth the commandment shall be rewarded;" he that slights the word and ways of God, destruction is his portion; but he that fears to violate the command of God "shall be rewarded," הוא ישלם he shall have peace, safety. A man by despising or fearing the word and command of God, doth neither hurt the one nor advantage the other; but he may, he doth, hurt or advantage himself, and that greatly.

Ver. 28. "Then they saw every high hill," &c. In this verse you have the idolatry they fell into when they came into the land of Canaan, with the degrees thereof.

1. Their leaving of God, and looking unto the hills, yea, "every high hill, and all the thick trees;" they gave liberty to their eyes to spy out places suitable to their idolatrous thoughts; on hills, and places beset with thick trees, the heathens worshipped, and their hearts and eyes were towards such places.

2. Their making altars, and sacrificing there; "they offered there their sacrifices," &c. They should not have sacrificed any where but in the place God appointed, which was first the tabernacle, afterwards the temple; but they spied out hills, groves, thickets, set up altars, and sacrificed on them those offerings which were peculiar unto God.

3. Their continuance and expensefulness therein; "they offered sacrifices, they poured out there their drink-offerings."

4. Their content and delight they took therein; "there also they made their sweet savour."

"The provocation of their offering." The Hebrew is, the indignation and anger of their corban, that is, their approaching gift, or offering. There is a figure in these words called hypallage, which is such a transposing of words, as that is said of one, which should be said of the other, as here, provocation of offerings, for offerings provoking.

"There also they made their sweet savour." The original for "sweet savour" is, literally, the odour of their rests, their acceptable odours; when they had offered these, they thought the Lord smelt a sweet savour, was well pleased with them, and so rested in them; which fancied rest was pleasing to them, though it lasted not, neither had reality in it, for their incense or "sweet savour" was a provocation to God.

Obs. 1. That what the Lord promiseth he makes good, how difficult or impossible soever it seems to man. The Lord had promised them Canaan; and how should they come to it? They were bond-men in Egypt, there is a Red sea, a vast wilderness, between Egypt and Canaan; and besides, Canaan had strong men in it, sons of Anak, cities walled and great, several kings to oppose and keep them out; but notwithstanding all these difficulties, God having promised to bring them in, he did it: "when I had brought them into the land, for the which I lifted up my hand to give it to them." His hand that was lift up to confirm them it should be done, was let out for the doing thereof; that hand that could take away all doubts, could also take away all difficulties. There is nothing too hard for the Lord; he will work, and who shall, who can, let it, Isa. xliii. 13. As he is gracious to promise, so faithful and able to perform, and doth in due time make good whatever he hath promised, though it seem impossible. He said, a virgin should bring forth, Isa. vii. 14; and was it not made good? Matt. i. 18: that Abraham who was aged should have a child, and his seed be as the stars of heaven; and were not both made good? Gen. xxi. 2; Exod. xii. 37; Numb. xi. 21; not one word failed of all that God promised Moses, 1 Kings viii. 56. This should make us believe the promises of God, whatever flesh and blood objects.

Obs. 2. Men's habitations are given and assigned unto them of the Lord. I brought them into the land, I gave it them. If men be removed from place to place, seated here or there, the hand of the Lord is in it; if they have commodious, pleasant, gainful habitations, if they dwell safely under vines and fig trees, as it is 1 Kings iv. 25, it is the Lord's doing, his providence disposed it so; and we should be thankful in and for our habitations, and mind the heavenly Canaan, and those mansions mentioned, John xiv. 2, prepared for those who do believe, and glorify God, out of which, when once we are possessed of them, we shall never be removed.

Obs. 3. Circumstances of time and place do aggravate men's sins, and make them heinous. When I had brought them into the land, then they saw every high hill, *there* they offered sacrifices, *there* they presented the provocation of their offerings, *there* they made their sweet savour, *there* they poured out their drink-offerings; here are four *theres*, every one aggravating and accenting their sins. This was ingratitude with a witness, that the Lord should bring them into such a land as flowed with milk and honey, and they should bestow the milk and honey upon idols; into such a land as was the glory of all lands, and they should defile it, and make it abominable, as it is Jer. ii. 7, "I brought you into a plentiful country, to eat the fruit thereof and the goodness thereof; but when ye entered, ye defiled my land, and made mine heritage an abomination." This, this made their sin exceeding sinful, and the Lord to set the emphasis upon it. *There*, in Canaan, the land I espied out for them, they sinned; *there*, in Canaan, where I fulfilled my promise made to their fathers and them, they sinned; *there*, in Canaan, out of which I drove mighty nations for their sakes, they sinned; *there*, in Canaan, the land I chose to dwell in, they set up altars, and diverted my sacrifices, offerings, and sweet savours unto them; *there*, where I looked they should have become a holy people unto me, they became like the nations, and worse than the nations round about them. Sinning after great mercies bestowed, and where they were bestowed, makes sin sinful above measure.

Obs. 4. When men go out from God's truths, ordinances, and ways of worship, they are restless, and run from opinion to opinion, and from one way to another. "They saw every high hill, and all the thick trees;" they ran from hill to hill, from tree to tree, and were not long satisfied any where; when they had found a hill which pleased them, set up an altar there, and sacrificed awhile, they grow to dislike of that place and that altar; then they must to another hill, have another altar, which had its time, and then that was left; and to the thick trees they go, and there they fall in with the worshippers and ways there in practice; and so from altar to altar, from place to place, and not satisfied, Ezek. xvi. 29. And it is just with God, that those men who go out from him, and off from the ways and forms of worship he hath prescribed, (depriving him of his legislativeness therein,) should be given up unto restlessness of spirit. This is abundantly verified among the papists, where they run from saint to saint, from altar to altar, and from one order of friars and Jesuits to another; yea, this hath been signally fulfilled amongst us, in our days, wherein many having left and cast off God's ways and worship, have run into variety of opinions and practices; they have seen every hill, every tree, every altar, every way; and may it not be said, as of the unclean spirits in the gospel, they have walked in dry places, sought rest and found none? Men's ways, opinions, intentions, are dry things, and have no rest in them. Only God's ways and ordinances have virtue in them, to moisten, quicken, comfort, and satisfy us. Micah ii. 7, "Do not my words do good to him that walketh uprightly?" whatever the sickly fancies of men are, God's words and ways are good, and they only do good to the sons of men that walk uprightly: Prov. x. 29, "The way of the Lord is strength to the upright," not to those who turn aside to the whimsies, fancies, and wills of men.

Obs. 5. That may be offensive and hateful to God, which men judge to be grateful and acceptable. "They presented the provocation of their offering," or provoking offerings. Whom did they provoke? even the Lord, whom they concluded they greatly pleased, for it follows, "there also they made their sweet savour;" they made account their sweet savours would be sweet in the nostrils of God, but they were stinking and loathsome, because not offered where they should have been offered, nor as God had appointed, nor came from hearts believing and obedient. They were at great pains and charges in their sacrifices, offerings, sweet savours; and what was the issue of it? instead of pleasing, they provoked God. Amos v. 21, 22, 24, "I hate, I despise your feast days, and I will not smell in your solemn assemblies. Though ye offer me burnt offerings and your meat offerings, I will not accept them; neither will I regard the peace offerings of your fat beasts. Let judgment run down as waters, and righteousness as a mighty stream." They thought that notwithstanding all their injustice, that their sacrifices and services should be accepted; but God was so far from it, he despised and hated them: the like you have in Jer. vi. 20. Let us take heed lest we provoke God by our sacrifices, while we think we please him. If they be not from gracious hearts, tendered up in faith, according to rule, and for his glory, he will say, as it is Isa. lvii. 6, "Should I receive comfort in these?"

Ver. 29. "Then I said unto them, What is the high place whereunto ye go?" Here the Lord doth reprove them for, and seek to reclaim them from, their idolatry. You know that place I have chosen, where my tabernacle is, the altar I have appointed for sacrifices: what is the high place whither ye go? what is it for? what do you there? why transgress you my statutes, and keep not to them? To this effect and purpose the Lord spake by his prophets unto them.

The word for "high place" is, הבמה that high, or the high place. Some think it a high altar, or a chapel built in a wood, or on a high hill. It was the practice of the gentiles, upon hills, and under green trees, to build altars with steps, or ascensions to go up by, which the Jews imitated contrary to command; for God had bid them to make an altar of earth unto him, and where he should appoint; and if of stone, it must not be of hewn stone, neither might his altar have any steps, Exod. xx. 24—26. Neither was the altar of God ever called "Bamah," a high place, but Mizbeach, the sacrificatory, or the place of slaying and sacrificing. But the Jews falling to heathenish customs and practices, learned their names, and imposed them upon their altars, called them Bamahs or Bamoths. When God therefore saith, "What is the high place," or Bamah? he doth reprove and upbraid them for their idolatry: What madness is this in you, that you have forsaken the temple and altar of God, to go to the Bamahs, the high places, hills and trees of heathens, that you prefer their ways before mine? what is it you find there, that you cannot keep your habitations, and content yourselves with what I have appointed you? Are the gods of the nations, and their high places, better than the God of Israel and his altar?

"And the name thereof is called Bamah unto this day." They desisted not from that idolatrous name and practice they had taken up, but persisted therein; they had called those places Bamah, and would call them so still, they were tenacious of their superstitious opinions, names, and ways; the high places remained till the days of Josiah, 2 Chron. xxxiv. 3.

Obs. 1. Such is the perverseness of men's natures and spirits, that they are not content with what God in his infinite wisdom and goodness hath prescribed them in point of worship. "What is the high place whereunto ye go?" Am not I your God? have not I given you an altar, appointed sacrifices, and told you where and how you must sacrifice? have not I accepted your sacrifices, when brought according to my direction? why do you go out from me, and are not content with what is mine? This is the evil of man's nature, that it oft rejects what is divine, and chooses what is human, it leaves the Creator's, and chooses the creature's: Jer. ii. 13, "My people have committed two evils; they have forsaken me the fountain of living waters, and hewed them out cisterns, broken cisterns, that can hold no water."

Obs. 2. That superstitious names, ways, and practices, once taken up, are not easily laid down again. They had a high place called Bamah, and that high place they would go unto, and keep that name, though the Lord had oft reproved them for it; and not only that, but other high places also: when the altar of Damascus, the image of jealousy, and Tammuz, were once admitted amongst them, they were not suddenly or easily removed again. Ephraim having taken up the names of Baalim, would not lay them aside till God took them out of her mouth, Hos. ii. 17. Are there not names amongst us, kept to this day, which sprung from gross idolatry? Vorstegan tells you, that Sunday was so called from the idol of the sun, unto whose adoration it was dedicated; so Monday from the idol of the moon, Tuesday from the idol Tuisco, Wednesday from the idol Woden, Thursday from the idol Thor, Friday from the idol Friga, or Frea, and Saturday from the idol Seater, not Saturn. These were Saxon idols, and they who gave the days their names, and dedicated them unto such idols, sinned greatly; and it is not excusable that we keep their memory still alive, calling the days by such names, which are dishonourable to God and Scripture. The Rhemists disallow these names of the days; they say Sunday is a heathenish calling, as all other of the week days are; some imposed after the names of planets, as in the Romans' time; some by the name of certain idols that the Saxons did worship, and to which they dedicated their days before they were christians, which names the church used not.

Ver. 30—32. *Wherefore say unto the house of Israel, Thus saith the Lord God; Are ye polluted after the manner of your fathers? and commit ye whoredom after their abominations? For when ye offer your gifts, when ye make your sons to pass through the fire, ye pollute yourselves with all your idols, even unto this day: and shall I be enquired of by you, O house of Israel? As I live, saith the Lord God, I will not be enquired of by you. And that which cometh into your mind shall not be at all, that ye say, We will be as the heathen, as the families of the countries, to serve wood and stone.*

Here you have, besides the prophet's commission in the beginning of the 30th verse,

1. An imputation of their wretched practices unto them; they followed the steps of their fathers, they became idolatrous like them, offering their gifts to idols; they caused their children to pass through the fire; they persisted in their wickedness.

2. God's resolution and oath not to have to do with them; "Shall I be inquired of by you?" &c. ver. 31.

3. His frustration of their counsels and designs; ver. 32, "That which cometh," &c.

"Are ye polluted after the manner of your fathers?" The elders of Israel that were in Babylon came to the prophet to inquire of the Lord, touching the affairs of Jerusalem. The Lord commands the prophet to ask them this question, "Are ye polluted after the manner of your fathers?" intimating that they were, and therefore, their coming to the prophet was but a pretence, and should speed accordingly.

Œcolampadius reads the words thus, Do ye not pollute yourselves in the way of your fathers? Vatablus, Are ye not polluted in the way of your fathers? Castalio hath it without an interrogation, You are polluted with the manners of your ancestors; but it is best with the interrogation. Interrogations in Scripture sometimes serve for admiration, as Luke i. 34, "How shall this be, seeing I know not a man?" sometimes for demonstration, Psal. xv. 1, "Lord, who shall abide in thy tabernacle, who shall dwell in thy holy hill?" Sometimes they are arguments of doubting, as Luke i. 18, saith Zacharias, "Whereby shall I know this? for I am an old man, and my wife well stricken in years." Sometimes they note indignation, as Exod. x. 3, "How long wilt thou refuse to humble thyself before me? let my people go, that they may serve me." Sometimes they hold out accusation, and exprobration, as Mal. iii. 14, "What profit is it that we have kept his ordinance, and that we have walked mournfully before the Lord of hosts?" Here the interrogation notes both indignation and exprobration; "Are ye polluted after the manner of your fathers?" do ye live in their sins, and come to inquire of the prophet, and of me by the prophet? I am angry, and cannot endure such vile pretences and deep dissimulation.

"And commit ye whoredom after their abominations?" By "whoredom" is meant idolatrizing; and wherein idolatry resembles whoredom, hath formerly been hinted unto you, chap. vi. 9. It is a violating the covenant between God and his people, which is called marriage, Jer. iii. 14; Hos. ii. 2; it is to go out from the true God to other gods, Deut. xxxi. 16; it is to sacrifice to devils, Lev. xvii. 7; to mind wizards, chap. xx. 6; to seek after our own hearts, eyes, and inventions, Numb. xv. 39; Psal. cvi. 39.

Ver. 31. "When ye offer your gifts." The Hebrew is, in elevating your gifts. By "gifts," in the 26th verse, were understood their firstborn; but here "gifts" and firstborn are distinct. "When ye offer your gifts," when you make your sons to pass through the fire. These "gifts" were those other oblations appointed in the law, or whatever they voluntarily bestowed upon their idols, as in chap. xvi. 18, 19.

"When ye make your sons to pass through the fire." Of these words something hath been said before in chap. xvi. 20, 21. I shall add a little.

The heathens were wont, in times of public calamity, to sacrifice their children, saith Eusebius; and Lactantius tells of Pescennius Fertus, saying, That the Carthaginians did sacrifice men to Saturn, and being overcome by Agathocles, king of the Sicilians, thinking their god was angry with them, they offered two hundred noblemen's sons to pacify him. Sometimes they killed them, sometimes they drowned them, and sometimes they burnt them.

This practice of sacrificing their children, to pacify their provoked gods, some affirm to be taken up from Abraham's sacrificing of his son, with which God was so well pleased, that he gave forth a large eulogy of him for it. But it is not probable that it proceeded thence, for the Lord suffered not Abraham to do it, and prohibited by a severe law the doing of such a thing, viz. the sacrificing of their children to idols, Lev. xx. 2. It was more likely from the devil in their oracles, for Plutarch tells of the Lacedemonians, who being greatly afflicted with the plague, had an answer from the oracle of Apollo, that the plague should cease, if they sacrificed a virgin chosen out of the chief of the nobility. Doubtless it was Satan put this into the hearts of men, for he "was a murderer from the beginning," and delighteth much in shedding of man's blood, especially in honour to himself, Psal. cvi. 37, for such sacrifices were to him and his. Some sacrificed men to Diana, some to Mercury, some to Saturn, whom divers think and affirm to be Molech, the idol the Jews sacrificed their children unto. They admitted the heathenish idol, and the heathenish practice: 2 Kings xvi. 3, Ahaz made his sons to pass through the fire according to the abominations of the heathen; and it was to Molech that he, and others, made their children pass through the fire unto, chap. xxiii. 10. This Molech was a great brazen idol, having a calf's head and hands to receive whatever was offered; it being hollow, had seven distinct cavities in it. 1. For those who offered fine flower. 2. For those who offered turtles. 3. For those who offered a sheep. 4. For those who offered a ram. 5. For those who offered a calf. 6. For those who offered an ox. 7. For those who offered their children. For the children offered, it is conceived they were burnt alive in that hollow place they were put into, or upon, or else they were put into the arms of the idol, and roasted to death in them; at the doing whereof, they made hideous noises with kettles, or drums, that the screechings and cries of the children might not be heard.

In parallelis, c. 66. cited by Peter Mart. upon the Kings.

Tertul. in Scorpinco.

Vide Petrum Martyr in 2 Kings iii. Ainsworth in Lev. xviii. 21.

Lactantius de Falsa Religio. l. 1.

"And shall I be inquired of by you, O house of Israel?" &c. These words you had in ver. 3, they need not now to be opened, only there is, "elders of Israel," and here it is, "O house of Israel."

Obs. 1. The ways of our forefathers are not always to be trodden in and followed. "Are ye polluted after the manner of your fathers? and commit ye whoredom after their abominations?" Here the Lord is angry with them, accuses and upbraids them, for following their fathers. It is not always unlawful so to do. Josiah walked in all the ways of David his father, and turned not aside to the right hand or to the left, 2 Kings xxii. 2; so Hezekiah did according to all that David his father did, chap. xviii. 3. Men that are good, and walk in the ways of God, they may be followed. Solomon commends them that "walk in the way of good men, and keep the paths of the righteous," Prov. ii. 20: but when men forsake the ways of truth, mercy, and righteousness, fall to false worship, unjust and unwarrantable practices, children ought not to tread in their fathers' steps; if they do, they will pollute themselves, and provoke God against them, as these did here. Forefathers are not to be followed in doctrine, worship, or manners, further than they follow the word and Christ. Paul, that great apostle, would not have any to follow him further than he followed Christ, 1 Cor. xi. 1. The Thessalonians followed Paul, Sylvanus, Timothy, but they followed the Lord also, and these men no otherwise than they followed him. If men will follow their fathers, they must see to it that they were sound in the faith, sound in their worship, and sound in their lives; for the exhortation is, 3 John 11, to "follow not that which is evil, but that which is good. He that doeth good is of God: but he that doeth evil hath not seen God:" and, Heb. vi. 12, Be "followers of them who through faith and patience inherit the promises."

Obs. 2. That children, to uphold the customs and practices of their fathers, will part with things dear, and do unnaturally, especially if pretence of religion come in. The fathers of these in Babylon, they were idolaters, they sacrificed their children to idols, under pretence of the more acceptance; and to uphold such customs and doing of their fathers, the children part with their dear and tender infants, do impious, unjust, and inhuman things, cause their little ones to pass through the fire, to be burnt to ashes, in honour of their feigned and false deities. Superstition and idolatry make men unnatural. Beasts will preserve their young, and venture their lives to save their little ones, when men do willingly destroy theirs under pretence of religion, and put them to such cruel tortures. The papists do uphold the sinful ways of their forefathers at dear rates, and are unnatural in whipping of themselves. If these, and Jews, did part with dear things to maintain the wicked ways of their fathers, and do unnaturally, unjustly, to keep them up, what condemnation will it be to us, if we will not part with things needful, do things christian and just, to uphold true religion, and uphold the lawful and godly practices of our forefathers! If they would part with their children and blood for maintenance of idolatry, what should we think too dear for maintenance of the gospel? People will part with dear things to maintain their opinions, even their modesty, to uphold a conceit of perfection.

Obs. 3. Hypocrisy so displeases God, that he will have nothing to do with hypocrites. These elders, this house of Israel, they polluted themselves in their fathers' sins, they took up ways of false worship, and lived in the same to the day they came to inquire; and what saith God? "Shall I be inquired of by you, O house of Israel?" you dissemble, act the hypocrite's part, and you provoke me not only to refuse to hear you, but to swear against you: "As I live, I will not be inquired of by you." You come not in sincerity, but in subtlety; you pretend to walk in my ways, but you intend to follow your fathers' ways; you make as if you would worship me, but you mean to worship idols. Ah! you old hypocrites, painted sepulchres, why come ye to me? I will not hear, answer, nor have to do with you. Hypocrites seem to do that they do not: 2 Kings xvii. 33, "They feared the Lord, and served their own gods;" that is, they seemed to fear him, but did not, for, ver. 34, it is said, "They fear not the Lord." Hypocrites would join God and their own ways, or fathers' ways, together, but it will not take with him: Matt. vi. 24, "No man can serve two masters." The great Master of truth said this; and when men lean to their fathers' ways, love them and idols, they despise God, and hate his ways. There is no truth in them; no metaphysical truth, their notions agree not with the mind of God; no physical truth, there is no reality in their words or actions; no moral truth, their lives agree not with their professions. John Huss had the devil pictured upon his clothes, but he had Christ within; hypocrites have the picture of Christ without, but the devil within. Satan hath their hearts, or the greatest part of them; Hos. x. 2, "Their heart is divided; now shall they be found faulty: he shall break down their altars:" God will not accept them, nor their sacrifices, he will appear against them and their doings.

Labour, therefore, to be sincere, for the upright are his delight. Those who regard iniquity in their hearts, whoever they be, whatever they inquire and seek for at the hands of God, God will not hear them, but discover them, and give them the reward of hypocrites.

Ver. 32. "And that which cometh into your mind shall not be at all." The Hebrew runs thus, that which ascends upon the spirit by being shall not be; that is, your thoughts, purposes, counsels, determinations, which are risen up in your heads and hearts, and take impression there, have a being in them, they shall lose their being, and come to nothing; you look upon them as having much essence in them, but they shall all vanish. The Vulgate is, the thought of the mind shall not be effected.

"That ye say, We will be as the heathen." Here the thought of their heart is made known. These elders of Israel, considering the condition they were in, thought it best to cast off the God of Israel, and his worship, and to fall to the gods of the nations, and their worship; to cease from their judaism, and to turn to gentilism. They thought the gods of the heathen dealt better with them than the God of the Jews did with them. Or, if their God were the God of all nations, yet he showed more kindness to them, serving wood and stone, than he did to the Jewish people, who were tied up by strict laws, burdened with a multitude of sacrifices and ceremonies, now spoiled, captives, held under hard bondage, in danger of being cut off for Zedekiah's revolt and perfidiousness; whereas the Babylonians and provinces that belonged to them did prosper, were in safety and peace: and let the best be made of it, they knew that they must abide many years under the Babylonish yoke, therefore thought it the wisest course to become like the heathens, to conform to their worship and manners, whereby they should be looked upon as of them, and not of Abraham; as men of Babylon, not of Zion; as gentiles, not Israelites; and so provide for their safety, peace, and prosperity.

"As the families of the countries." They made account to cast off the worship of the God of Israel, which exposed them to reproach, hatred, and hard sufferings, and to give up themselves fully to their gods, their worship, and observance of their rites: they intended to incorporate and become one with the Babylonish race and brood, that so they might have a Babylonish happiness, and be free from the strokes of the God of Israel, under whom they suffered so much.

"To serve wood and stone." That is, gods, or idols, made of wood and stone. See Deut. xxix. 17; chap. iv. 28, "There ye shall serve gods, the work of men's hands, wood and stone."

Obs. 1. How cunningly soever hypocrites do carry their lewd and wicked designs, yet they are known to God, and he will discover them. These elders of Israel were resolved to change their religion, to be like the heathen, and colour it over with coming to the prophet, to inquire how things would proceed with them at Jerusalem; what counsel he would give unto themselves, they would be ready to do it, whereas they never intended it. This the Lord saw, this he discovers, and uncases these dissembling hypocrites. Herod pretended he would go and worship Christ, but his intent was to murder him, Matt. ii. 8, 13, which God discovered.

Obs. 2. There be risings, thoughts in men's hearts which are not of God. What they had in their heads, or hearts, God owned not. Many in these days think every motion they have in their hearts, minds, whatever riseth up there, is of God, and his Spirit, and therefore must be obeyed; hence it comes to pass that darkness is called light, and all vices are practised under the notion of virtue; but corruptions, flesh, old man, Satan, have their operations in the hearts of the wicked always, and too oft in the godly. The earth brings forth weeds of itself, and not corn, unless it be sown.

Obs. 3. Carnal, politic men affect religion as it serves their own interest. These elders, considering what Zedekiah and their brethren had done at Jerusalem, revolted from Nebuchadnezzar; they feared hard measure now would befall them for their Jewish religion, and they resolved not to venture liberty, limbs, or life for that religion, which had been a bondage, and burdensome unto them, and now might hazard all. They would now revolt from God and truth, and be as the heathen, who prospered, were in peace and safety. Politicians think it weakness, foolishness, to suffer for religion. They can change it at pleasure, and fall in with that which hath most pomp and applause in the world. Upon this account many have fallen from protestantism to popery, and from christianity to Turcism: to save their skins, they have parted with their religions. Many men make use of religion as mariners of the winds, merely to serve their own ends; if religion once cross them, they can cast it off, and fall in with those ways of worship which do suit their humours, and further their designs; like children, that, having been held in by their parents, bestow themselves upon any to obtain their own ends. These elders saw their law and worship were differing from the religion of the state where they were, and so exposed them to many inconveniences and dangers; they would therefore be of the state religion, outwardly at least complying with that, serving "wood and stone."

Obs. 4. God sometimes disappoints the designs and expectations of men, who intend and resolve to forsake him, and provide for themselves by sinful and idolatrous ways. "That which cometh into your mind shall not be at all;" you would be as the heathens, but it shall not be; I will not only deny your desires, but dash your designs: you seek heathens' favour, and shall meet with heaven's frowns, and miss of your aims; you would be Babylonians, have the protection and blessing of Babylonish gods, but my thoughts are cross to yours, that which is in my mind shall stand, not what is in yours; that happiness you hope for in the ways and worship of Babylonians you shall not find. Men think, by going out to the world, by conforming to base, vile superstition, and idolatrous practices, to get much; but God, in his infinite wisdom and justice, disappoints them, as Demas and Judas.

Ver. 33. *As I live, saith the Lord God, surely with a mighty hand, and with a stretched-out arm, and with fury poured out, will I rule over you.*

Having showed the ingratitude and untoward carriage of this people in Egypt, in the wilderness, in Canaan, and their resolution to cast off God in Babylon, here begins the fourth general part of the chapter, viz. a denunciation of judgment for their hypocrisy and other sins, together with promises of mercy, extending to the 45th verse. In the verse you have.

I. God asserting his authority and power over this people, who thought to cast him off; "I will rule over you."

II. The manner of his ruling over them, which is,

1. With power.

2. With fury.

III. The ratification of both, and that is by oath, "As I live, saith the Lord."

Touching this oath of God much hath been spoken already, in this and former chapters.

"With a mighty hand." The Hebrew is, in or with a strong hand; with a rigid hand, saith Castalio. By "mighty hand" here is not simply meant God's power, but his power in punishing; so the plagues of Egypt were God's strong and "mighty hand." God would punish them for their dealings, and to that purpose, it should be visibly and openly, and therefore it follows,

"With a stretched-out arm." Sometimes the stretching out of God's arm notes powerful and visible deliverance, Psal. cxxxvi. 12; sometimes powerful and visible punishment, as here. In the inflicting of punishments, men stretch out their hands and arms, which here, after the manner of men, is given to God.

"With fury poured out." Of dealing in "fury," accomplishing, "fury," and pouring out "fury," see before, chap. viii. 18; v. 13; ix. 8.

"Will I rule over you." Ruling imports sovereignty, authority, and power over others. Here the genus, by a synecdoche, is put for the species; the whole work of ruling, for punishing; and the sum of the words is this; You think, by withdrawing from me and my worship, and by Babylonizing, to secure yourselves, to escape danger and all punishment; but know assuredly, you are my subjects, I will not suffer you so to revolt from me, I will put forth mine hand, and mine arm, my fury, punishing you for your rebellions and idolatries, so that, willing or unwilling, me shall you acknowledge to be your Lord and Sovereign.

Obs. 1. It is a vain thing to think of getting from under the dominion of God, and impossible to accomplish. These elders thought to withdraw from under the laws and government of the God of Israel, and put themselves under the Babylonish gods and Babylonian government; but what saith God? "I will rule over you;" take what course you please; transform yourselves into heathenish manners, disperse yourselves into by-corners, villages, towns, cities, plant yourselves in what province soever of the king of Babylon's, use what policy you can to cast off my yoke, yet "I will rule over you," for you cannot go from my presence nor from my power. In the second Psalm, the great ones of the earth thought to exempt themselves from the government of God and Christ; "Let us break their bands asunder, and cast away their cords from us;" but they were laughed to scorn, and vexed for it, ver. 3—5.

Obs. 2. The untoward carriage of God's people causes him to deal more sharply with them. Rebelliousness in them produceth rigidness in him; their treachery bred severity; "With a mighty hand, and fury poured out, will I rule over you." They thought to run from under him, and he held a stricter hand over them; they would not willingly obey as sons, he made them obey as servants. When servants run from their masters, they bestir them, fetch them back with power, punish them severely for their fugitiveness, and hold them harder to it than ever; so did the Lord by these, and made them know that he ruled in Babylon, as well as in Zion, and turned his golden sceptre into an iron rod, and put a yoke of iron upon them. This is that the Lord told them in Moses' days, that if they walked contrary to him, he would walk contrary unto them, and punish them seven times more; that is, rule over them with greater severity, Lev. xxvi. He would make his little finger heavier than his loins had been before.

Obs. 3. God will punish those that shake off his worship to follow false ways, with visible and irresistible punishments. These elders were upon terms of apostatizing from the God of Israel, about to leave his tents, and to betake themselves to the Babylonish temples, therefore the Lord swears he will rule over them with a "stretched-out arm," (he would visibly punish them,) and with "fury poured out;" they should no more be able to withstand it than a man can a great rain or flood. When subjects are upon rebelling, and would fall in with some other, this kindles his fury, causes him to punish them openly and irresistibly. Apostasy is a provoking sin; it is a reproach to God, his truths, and ordinances; it is a violating of all former promises and engagements unto God; it is high ingratitude and rebellion against God; it is a great scandal unto all the godly, especially the weak; it encourages, hardens, and justifies the wicked; it ruins souls; it gratifies Satan; and therefore exposes men to visible and unavoidable judgments. You know how God met with Julian, and other apostates since his time. That men should cast off God, is wonder to heaven and earth; Jer. ii. 12, 13, "Be astonished, O ye heavens, at this; my people have forsaken me;" and because they did so, lions roared upon them, and laid them waste, ver. 15; Egyptians took the crown from their head, ver. 16, 17. It bred astonishment in Paul, that the Galatians were so soon removed from him, that called them into the grace of Christ, to another gospel, Gal. i. 6; they had apostatizing spirits, minding another gospel, another Christ, another way to salvation, than he delivered to them. And may it not be matter of astonishment to us, that many are so shaken, that they have cast off our God, our Christ, our gospel, our ordinances, and have found out another gospel, another Christ, and another way to salvation than ever; but it is to be feared some remarkable and unavoidable judgments are near unto them. God hath no pleasure in those that draw back, Heb. x. 38; they have "cast off the thing that is good: the enemy shall pursue them," Hos. viii. 3. These elders have purposed to become like the heathen, and God sware presently to punish them openly and irresistibly; what will he then do to those who have actually withdrawn from him and his ways? surely his wrath will smoke against them. Let us take heed, in these declining times, of falling away from God and his ways; beware of carnal policy, which was the thing here that put these elders upon it; beware of carnal relations and unmortified lusts, which made Spira and Spalato revolt so foully; beware of promotion and greatness, which made Henry the fourth of France to turn papist; beware of false teachers, corrupt opinions, which have made many among us to go so far from God and his ways. Keep innocency, count all the glory and greatness of the world as nothing; prize truth, and the ways of God, highly; cleave fully to Christ, live by faith, prove all things, and hold fast what is good; so shall there never be an evil heart in you of unbelief, to depart from the living God.

Ver. 34. *And I will bring you out from the people, and will gather you out of the countries wherein ye are scattered, with a mighty hand, and with a stretched out arm, and with fury poured out.*

These words do hold out no good unto them, but declare that what they hoped to be a mercy, should prove a judgment. They thought that if they were scattered up and down among the Babylonians, and quitted the Jewish worship, they should be safe, and live as happily as Babylonians; but God would not lose his right and privilege, he would rule over them; and here he shows the manner of it again, and that more fully, "I will bring you out," &c.

"I will bring you out from the people." Divers expositors, by "people," or nations, understand the Ammonites, Moabites, Tyrians, Egyptians, Idumeans, and Edomites, and cite Jer. xl. 11, 12, and xliii. 7; and so make the prophet to mean it of the Jews dispersed into those places upon the siege, spoiling, and taking of Jerusalem by Nebuchadnezzar in the times of Jehoiachin and Zedekiah; but our prophet and these elders being in Babylon, he speaks of the Babylonians among whom these captive elders and Jews were dispersed, and sought to be like unto them, that so they might be the safer, but God gathered them out from them, and would not suffer them to become Babylonians. Besides, this was in the seventh year of the captivity, as appears, verse 1 of this chapter; and at that time Jerusalem stood, Zedekiah was reigning, and the people were not scattered into those nations mentioned; for Zedekiah reigned eleven years, 2 Chron. xxxvi. 11; and nothing is said of any dispersion when Jehoiachin was taken away, and Zedekiah set up. It is also further added here,

"I will gather you out of the countries wherein ye are scattered." He speaks of those who were scattered at that time. There were many provinces into which they had scattered, or were upon scattering themselves. Vatablus' sense is thus, I will gather you out of the nations among which ye are captives.

Obs. Wherever wicked men hide themselves, or shark for their own safety, God will find them out, and bring them forth to punishment. These elders, and the rest of the captives that were wicked, thought by lurking amongst the Babylonians, and conforming to them in state and religious affairs, they should be safe and well; but saith the Lord, Live where you will, shift for yourselves what you can, be as the heathen, and carry it as close as may be, I will find you out, and bring you forth from them with strength, and punish you to purpose. God's eyes run to and fro throughout the earth, and he quickly spies where sinners lie hid, and brings them forth to justice at his pleasure: Amos ix. 2—4, "Though they dig into hell, thence shall mine hand take them, though they climb up to heaven, thence will I bring them down. Though they hide themselves in the top of Carmel, I will search and take them out thence; and though they be hid from my sight in the bottom of the sea, thence will I command the serpent, and he shall bite them: and though they go into captivity before their enemies, thence will I command the sword, and it shall slay them." The sense of these words is thus much, That whereas other creatures can shift and secure themselves from their enemies; the conies and creeping things by hiding themselves in the holes of the earth, the birds by flying up into the clouds and heavens, the beasts by running to the hills and woods, the fish by sinking down to the bottom of the sea; men that have offended God cannot secure themselves any where, God's eyes are set upon them for evil, and his hand is against them. Isa. xxviii. 15, they were at agreement with death and hell, and thought the overflowing scourge should not come unto them; but, ver. 18, "Your covenant with death shall be disannulled, and your agreement with hell shall not stand; when the overflowing scourge shall pass through, then ye shall be trodden down by it." Babel ascended above the height of the clouds, yet was brought down to hell, Isa. xiv. 14, 15; Jer. li. 53; the high places and hills, whither the Jews oft betook themselves, did not secure them, Jer. xii. 12. Let sinners hide themselves in any place, their sin will find them out, Numb. xxxii. 23; they cannot escape the piercing eye, or punishing hand, of God.

Ver. 35, 36. *And I will bring you into the wilderness of the people, and there will I plead with you face to face. Like as I pleaded with your fathers in the wilderness of the land of Egypt, so will I plead with you, saith the Lord God.*

These verses tell us what God did with them after he had gathered them out of the countries. He did two things:

I. He brought them into a "wilderness."

II. He pleaded with them there; and the manner of his pleading with them is set down,

1. To be "face to face."

2. So as he pleaded "with their fathers in the wilderness of the land of Egypt."

"Into the wilderness of the people." Not into Babylon, which is called a "wilderness," chap. xix. 13, for they were already in Babylon. "Wilderness of the people," doth not signify *desertum inter populos*, but rather *desertum a populis*, as Rom. i. 4, ἐξ ἀναστάσεως νεκρῶν, "by the resurrection of the dead;" that is, by the resurrection from the dead: so "into the wilderness of the people," imports, into a wilderness from the people. Vatablus saith, There was a wilderness between Chaldea and Judea, unto which the Lord alludes; as he brought their fathers out of Egypt into Arabia Deserta, so he would bring them out of Babylon into that wilderness. Junius' sense of this wilderness is, That God would bring them into such a place as all men would fly from on account of its dreadful nature. Others make the meaning of the words to be, That God would bring them into a most miserable estate; they thought they should be best of all if they turned heathens, but this caused God to bring them into a worse condition than they were. I incline to take the words literally, rather than metaphorically, because he speaks of bringing and gathering them out from people and countries, and bringing them "into the wilderness," which notes motion from place to place; and this "wilderness" is paralleled with that of the land of Egypt, which was real, and not metaphorical.

"There will I plead with you." Not only dispute and reason the case with you, but also deal with you according to your sins; I will be revenged on you, I will execute my judgments upon you. As I punished your fathers when they were in the wilderness for their sins, so will I punish you for your sins. They smarted for their murmuring, lusting, whoredom, idolatry, rebellion, ingratitude; and so shall you for doing as your fathers did.

"Face to face." The rabbies, being very propitious to their own nation, interpret these words thus: God alone, having them alone separate from the nations, would punish them, that they might not see what punishment he laid upon them, and rejoice thereat. But the phrase notes God's presence and visible manner of punishing them, so that it should be most evident to be the hand of God.

"As I pleaded with your fathers in the wilderness of the land of Egypt." How God "pleaded" with them in that "wilderness" which belonged to the Egyptians, let us search a little.

1. He pleaded with them speedily. Numb. xxv. 1, "The people began to commit whoredom with the daughters of Moab;" and, ver. 4, the Lord bids Moses "take all the heads of the people and hang them up;" here was quick work. So Exod. xxxii. 7, 10, "Get thee down; the people have corrupted themselves: let me alone, that my wrath may wax hot against them, and that I may consume them:" ver. 28, "There fell of the people that day about three thousand men."

2. He pleaded with them severely. Numb. xxi. 6, "The Lord sent fiery serpents among the people;" these bit them so that many died; their venomous bitings did so inflame them, that they were in a manner burnt to death, which was a dreadful judgment. Before Aaron could take his censer, put in incense, and make an atonement for the people, fourteen thousand and odd were destroyed by the plague, Numb. xvi. 46, 47, 49; which was both sudden and severe pleading with them.

3. Immediately. He caused the earth to open her mouth, and to swallow up Korah, Dathan, and Abiram, them and all theirs; he sent fire and consumed the two hundred and fifty men that offered incense, Numb. xvi. 32, 33, 35; and so were the fiery serpents the immediate hand of God.

4. Openly. Numb. xxv. 4, "Take all the heads of the people, and hang them up before the Lord against the sun." The Septuagint is, make them examples.

5. Strongly. They could not withstand his pleadings, his judgments and strokes were unavoidable. Though Moses and Aaron interposed and pleaded hard with God for them, yet multitudes of them perished by the sword, plague, serpents, fire, and earth. Thus God pleaded with their fathers, and so he would plead with them. Nothing secured their fathers from his judgments, and nothing should secure them; not Babylonians, or Babylonish gods; not their prophets or priests, not prayers or tears: their fathers fell in the wilderness, and so should they; if not by the same judgments, yet by those which were not much unlike, there should be an analogy between them.

Obs. 1. When men seek to avoid straits and dangers by sinful policy, and ways unwarrantable, God meets with them, and brings them into greater straits and troubles. These elders thought, by becoming as the heathens were, that they should free themselves from all the troubles and evils that were like to come upon them for Zedekiah's revolting from Nebuchadnezzar; but the Lord told them that he would bring them into a wilderness, where their condition should be very miserable, and worse than in Babylon, whatever they had suffered there for God and their religion. Jeroboam was in a strait about the people's sacrificing at Jerusalem: if they went up thither, he feared they would be so wrought upon, as to return to Rehoboam, from whom they had fallen, and kill him. To expedite himself out of this strait, he took wicked counsel; set up the calves at Dan and Bethel, telling the people the journey to Jerusalem was too long and tedious for them, they had God nearer to them, and might worship at an easier rate, 1 Kings xii.; but for this sinful policy and subtle design, God brought him into greater straits and difficulties, as you may see, chap. xiii. 4; xiv. 6, 10—12; his hand was withered, heavy tidings denounced against him and his house, and his son died. Saul was in a great strait when the Philistines had invaded him, and God would not answer him; he would not wait in this case, leaving all to God, but runs into an unlawful practice to relieve himself; he consults with the witch of Endor, and is brought into greater and worse straits than before, 1 Sam. xxviii. 17—20. Men in our days have taken wrong courses to extricate themselves out of dangers and troubles, and hath not God brought them into a "wilderness," into greater entanglements and worse perplexities than ever before? It is good to wait upon God, and keep his way; then if dangers and deaths do come, there is comfort, they find you in God's way; but if out of that, they are great evils in themselves, and your being out of God's way is worse than all.

Obs. 2. That God's punishments are his pleadings; when he visits men for their sins he pleads with them. Every rod of his hath a voice, and pleads for God. God's strikings are real pleadings; Isa. lxvi. 16, "By fire and by his sword will the Lord plead with all flesh;" his punishments are arguments he uses to convince or confound sinners; and whatsoever punishments he inflicts upon any, they are just and righteous, for he never pleads an ill cause: they are the judgments of God; he is infinitely wise, and as he judgeth aright, so he executeth judgment righteously.

Obs. 3. Those who are like in sinning, must be like in suffering. "Like as I pleaded with your fathers in the wilderness of the land of Egypt, so will I plead with you." These Jews were their children, and did as their fathers had done. Their fathers shook off the God of Israel, and chose them an Egyptian god, Exod. xxxii. 4; they mingled with the heathen, and learned their works, Psal. cvi. 35; they polluted his sabbaths, caused their children to pass through the fire, ver. 13, and 26, of this chapter; and these their posterity chose Babylonish gods, became as the heathen, made their sons pass through the fire, and trod in their fathers' steps, ver. 30—32.

Ver. 37, 38. *And I will cause you to pass under the rod, and I will bring you into the bond of the covenant: and I will purge out from among you the rebels, and them that transgress against me: I will bring them forth out of the country where they sojourn, and they shall not enter into the land of Israel: and ye shall know that I am the Lord.*

God being in a judiciary way pleading with this people, here he proceeds further in the manner thereof.

1. He would examine and reduce them to their former state, ver. 37.

2. He would make a discrimination between them, ver. 38.

"I will cause them to pass under the rod." The Hebrew word for "rod" is, שבט which in this place may signify either a sceptre, as frequently it doth in Scripture, and is so rendered, chap. xix. 11, 14, or a shepherd's staff, or crook, which he useth among his sheep, so it is used, Psal. xxiii. 4. If it be taken the first way, the sense is this, That though they scattered themselves among the Babylonians, and put themselves under heathenish power, yet the Lord would make them "pass under the rod," that is, come under his kingly power; he would rule over them, they should still be his subjects. But of this he spake in ver. 33, therefore I conceive "rod" here, is to be taken in the latter signification, that God would deal with them like a shepherd or herdsman, who were wont to number their cattle with a wand or rod, which is called "passing under the rod," Lev. xxvii. 32. To this purpose is that of Jer. xxxiii. 13, "In the cities of the mountains, in the cities of the vale, and in the cities of the south, and in the land of Benjamin, and in the places about Jerusalem, and in the cities of Judah, shall the flocks pass again under the hands of him that telleth them:" when the flocks went into the field or fold, and when they went out, their practice was to tell them by a "rod" in their hand, and so they "passed under the rod." Hereunto Christ alludes, John x. 3, when he saith, "He calleth his own sheep by name, and leadeth them out." The meaning, then, of the Lord here is, that he would take an exact account of them, tell them as a shepherd doth his flock, and see which were rotten and which were sound.

God's "rod," are afflictions and judgments, as you may see Psal. lxxxix. 32, "I will visit their transgressions," &c. See Lam. iii. 1.

"I will bring you into the bond of the covenant." You think to break the bond of the covenant made between me and your fathers, by becoming Babylonians, and ceasing to be my people, but it shall not be; I will keep the covenant, and cause you to come under the bond of it, and perform that obedience I look for. The word for "bond" is, במסרת from אסר to bind unto obedience or punishment. When men are in covenant, they are bound to obey, or to suffer if they disobey. Vatablus and others carry it thus, That God would deal with them as he had done with their fathers, that he would make a covenant with these as he had done with them; and so make it another covenant, by which God would bind them up, and refer it to the covenant made in Ezra's days; but rather, I conceive, the Lord intends the former covenant, especially that mentioned, Ezek. xvi. 8, when God, in a solemn manner, took this people to be his in Moses' days, wherein he made good his promise and covenant with Abraham, and bound them unto him by the law; the covenant bound them from other gods and ways of worship.

"And I will purge out from among you the rebels." The Septuagint and Vulgate read the words, I will chase out; the Hebrew ברר signifies both to choose and purge. God would number them, distinguish them one from another, and then "purge out" those who were rebellious; they should no longer be in his flock, but be discovered, and declared to the world what they were. By "rebels," he means those that cast off God and his works, and turned heathens.

"I will bring them forth out of the country where they sojourn, and they shall not enter into the land," &c. The Hebrew is, Out of the country of their sojournings, or peregrinations, I will bring them. Some make these words to point out those who were then in Judea, whom God would bring forth, and not suffer to return any more; and not only them, but many of those who were in Babylon before, God suffered not to return into the land of Israel; for if we understand these words of the return after the seventy years, as they must, long before that time were these Jews with Zedekiah brought out of the "land of their sojourning," and they, with many others, were never suffered to enter into that land more; for here is a comparing of their return from the Babylonish captivity, to that of their coming out of Egypt. Then they were brought into a "wilderness," where their carcasses fell for their rebellions, and so never entered the promised land: so here, likewise, God brought them into a "wilderness," pleaded with, and consumed many of them, who by that means never returned to the land of Israel.

Obs. 1. The Lord doth not only know, but takes special notice of his people, and doth distinguish them from others. "I will cause you to pass under the rod;" I will examine which are sheep, and which are goats, and will sever the one from the other. Christ knew his sheep, his little flock, from all the goats of the mountains, the bulls of Bashan, and wild beasts of the forests: and God knew the "good figs" from the "naughty," Jer. xxiv.; he manifested his love to the good, and displeasure to the bad. When he is in a judiciary way, he knows, owns, preserves his servants, and will not suffer any of them to perish. Ezek. ix. when the men appeared with slaughter weapons in their hands, and execution was to be upon Jerusalem, the Lord made his people to "pass under the rod," he numbered them, and set his mark upon them, that they might not perish in the common calamity; he put a difference between the precious and the vile, as a shepherd doth between sheep and goats, Matt. xxv. 32.

Obs. 2. Though God's people do go out from him, and violate the covenant, yet he will not let them so go, but will look after them, and bring them under his power. These here had transgressed the covenant, broken the bonds, cast off the ways of God, thought to exempt themselves from his rule over them, but, saith the Lord, "I will bring you into the bond of the covenant;" you shall be under my power and law; though I suffer Babylonians, and other nations, to be at their own disposal, to wander where they will, to live as they list, yet it shall not be so with you, who are my people, with whom I am in covenant, and to whom I must be faithful, whatever you are to me, and will be known to be your God and Sovereign; I will have account of you, and make you know you are under my bonds, and not Babylonish ones.

Obs. 3. God's dealings with his people is very different. He brings them "into the bond of the covenant," to see what they are; if they be goats, wicked, he punishes them, and purges them out; if they be sheep, though they have gone astray, he pardons them, keeps them "under the bond of the covenant," and enables them to yield covenant obedience. When God had made them "pass under the rod," and brought them "under the bonds of the covenant," made them know they were his people, though many of them were very wicked, he purged out the rebels, and them that had transgressed against him. He turned the goats out of the fold, and kept the sheep in; he purged out the wicked by judgments and death, and preserved the others: Mal. iii. 17, 18, "In that day when I make up my jewels I will spare them, as a man spareth his own son that serveth him," &c,; so God showed his different dealings between the righteous and the wicked; for, chap. iv. 1—3, the wicked being but "stubble," should be burnt, and be as ashes under the soles of the feet of the righteous. The righteous were jewels, and therefore spared; the wicked were stubble, and therefore destroyed.

Obs. 4. Though the wicked be among the godly,

yet they shall not always be so. "I will purge out from among you the rebels, and them that transgress against me." There were rebels, great sinners, that were among the Israelites in the wilderness of Egypt; Korah, Dathan, and Abiram; others that would have gone back to Egypt; many that murmured, that fell to idolatry, and committed whoredom with the daughters of Moab; but God purged them out from amongst them; and the like he did here. It is God's method, even here in this world, ofttimes, to separate the wicked from the godly, to fan out the chaff from the wheat, to burn the one, and preserve the other. In Sodom God made a separation, preserving Lot, who was wheat, and burning the Sodomites, who were chaff, with unquenchable fire: Isa. i. 25, "I will turn my hand upon thee, and purely purge away thy dross, and take away all thy tin;" the dross and tin were the wicked amongst them, ver. 28, 31, whom the Lord would take away, consume and burn with fire, not to be quenched. Now God's fan is in his hand, and he is purging both the English and Irish floor; yea, he is pulling up the pricking briers, and grieving thorns, that his people may not always be vexed by them, Ezek. xxviii. 24.

Obs. 5. Whatever men's thoughts are of the world, they are but sojourners therein. "I will bring them out of the land of their sojournings," were it Canaan or Babylon: they were no more than "sojourners." Wicked men think they are heirs to, owners and lords of the earth: Psal. xlix. 11, "Their inward thought is, that their houses shall continue for ever, and their dwelling-places to all generations; they call their lands after their own names;" men set their names upon what they conclude is their own. Let lands be good or bad, men are only "sojourners" in them. Godly men, who are said to "inherit the earth," do it but for a season, they are pilgrims and "sojourners" here. David, though king in Israel, yet acknowledgeth himself a sojourner in Canaan, as all his fathers were; they spent a few days therein, and so passed away, and this was his condition. Let us look so upon ourselves, and "pass the time of our sojourning here in fear," 1 Pet. i. 17; and mind that city which hath foundations, out of which, if we be once possessed, we shall never be removed.

Obs. 6. When God brings his people into Canaan, he will shut out the wicked, they shall not enter into the land of Israel. Others shall be brought in, but as for those who would be as the world, as the heathen, as Babylonians, they shall never come into Canaan. Canaan was a type of heaven, and this exclusion of these wicked ones, represented the exclusion of ungodly ones out of heaven. However good and bad are mingled together in this world, and oft in the church, yet when God brings his people to the heavenly Canaan, no unclean thing shall enter there: Rev. xxi. 27, "There shall in nowise enter into it any thing that defileth, neither whatsoever worketh abomination, or maketh a lie." Many may cry, and seek for entrance, as those, Matt. vii. 22; and those foolish virgins, Matt. xxv. 11, 12; but they shall in no wise, by no means, enter; "the unrighteous shall not inherit the kingdom of heaven," 1 Cor. vi. 9; dogs shall be shut out, Rev. xxii. 15.

Obs. 7. Mercies and judgments make God known experimentally. "Ye shall know that I am the Lord." God would purge out the rebels from the obedient, there was mercy; keep them out of the land of Israel, there was judgment; and by these God made them know him to be Jehovah, giving life to his promises, and breath to his threatenings. The rebels should know and acknowledge him to be Jehovah, being convinced with the equity of his judgments, and affected with the severity of them. The godly should do it, being convinced and affected with the nature, greatness, needfulness, and freeness of that mercy. Judgment upon these rebels was mercy to the godly; and mercy to the godly was judgment to the rebels; and both were brought to acknowledge the Lord, but specially the godly. Mercies and judgments work most affectionately and effectually upon them: for it is said, "ye shall know," ye that are purged, ye that shall come to the land of Israel.

Ver. 39. *As for you, O house of Israel, thus saith the Lord God; Go ye, serve ye every one his idols, and hereafter also, if ye will not hearken unto me: but pollute ye my holy name no more with your gifts, and with your idols.*

This verse speaks fully to the elders of Israel, that came to inquire of the Lord, yet were resolved in their hearts to be as the heathen, and to serve wood and stone outwardly at least; seeing it is so, saith God, "Go ye, serve every one his idols, and pollute my name no more."

"Go ye, serve ye every one his idols." These words may be taken for an ironical concession, a yielding that which the Lord would not have done; which is frequent in Scripture, as Amos iv. 4, "Come to Bethel, and transgress; at Gilgal multiply transgression;" Matt. xxiii. 32, "Fill ye up the measure of your fathers." See Eccles. xi. 9; 1 Kings xxii. 15; 1 Cor. xv. 32; Jer. vii. 21; in all these places is an ironical concession, which the Scripture uses to affect men's consciences the more with the wickedness of their ways. So here; "Go, serve your idols." God commands them not to serve idols, then it had been lawful; but by this ironical concession, would affect them more fully with the evil of their idolatry, and so take them off therefrom. This is a good sense of the words, but they are rather a rejection of them; Seeing you are such dissemblers, and have your hearts set upon idols, go your ways, take your fill of them: and so the Lord utterly cast them off, and left them to perish.

"And hereafter also, if ye will not hearken unto me." Sanctius thinks here is a figure called aposiopesis, which is a sudden breaking off the speech, with concealment of some special thing expected: as Luke xiii. 9, "If it bear fruit;" here is somewhat kept in, which any hearing the words expect, as, if it bear fruit, it should be cut down: so 2 Sam. v. 8, "Whosoever getteth up to the gutter, and smiteth the Jebusites, and the lame, and the blind, hated of David's soul:" what then? here is no more, the speech is broken off, and something left to expectation, which is given out, 1 Chron. xi. 6, "He shall be chief and captain." Here seems something to be concealed, "If ye will not hearken unto me," ye shall be scattered, cursed, or slain; but we may read the words thus, referring "and hereafter" to the former words, Go ye, serve ye every one his idols even hereafter; and then read the other words thus, seeing you will not hearken unto me, or, have not hearkened unto me. And thus divers expositors read them, and the sense lieth fair this way; Go, serve your idols hereafter, seeing ye will not hearken unto me.

"But pollute ye my holy name no more with your gifts, and with your idols." The Hebrew is, and pollute ye, which accords with the reading of the former words mentioned. You have pretended, that by your idols set up in my stead, and the gifts you have offered to them, or by them to me, that you have honoured my name, but by joining them and me together, you have polluted my name. I had rather you should be open idolaters, than that, by your hypocritical practices, dividing between me and your idols, you should cause my name to be polluted and disgraced; either be perfect idolaters, or perfectly for me; give not my glory to idols, pretending you worship me.

"My holy name." In the Hebrew it is, the name of my holiness; so in Amos ii. 7; Lev. xx. 3; Ezek. xxxvi. 20, and in most places where mention is made of God's "holy name." By "name" is meant God's worship, attributes, and titles, which are "holy;" or himself, as Sanctius affirms, who is holiness.

Obs. 1. God doth punish hypocrites and idolaters with spiritual judgments. "Go ye, serve ye every one his idols;" the house of Israel, whom these elders represented, were hypocritical and idolatrous, set upon idols, and God gave them over to them. Ephraim was of this humour, thus leavened, and see how God dealt with him; Hos. iv. 17, He "is joined to idols, let him alone;" he likes and loves them, let him live and die with them: and, chap. viii. 11, "Ephraim hath made many altars to sin, altars shall be unto him to sin," he shall have altars enough; he is greedy of them, and his greedy appetite shall be answered: this was a spiritual plague and judgment upon him, to be given up of God to his own heart's lusts.

Obs. 2. Those that will not hear God, shall be rejected of God, which is dreadful. "Go ye, serve every man his idol." I will have no more to do with you, my temple, mine altar, mine ordinances, are no longer for you; none of you shall have my presence, worship, or acceptance. Where men will not be reclaimed, they must be rejected; here they would not hearken unto God, and therefore he bids them be gone. 2 Kings xvii. 15, they rejected his statutes, and his covenant that he made with their fathers, and his testimonies which he testified against them, and they followed vanity, and became vain, and went after the heathen, &c.; "therefore the Lord was very angry with Israel, and removed them out of his sight," ver. 18; only he left Judah; and because Judah would not be reclaimed, the Lord rejected all the seed of Israel, and cast them out of his sight, ver. 20. So, in Jer. xxiii. when they would not hearken to the Lord, who forbid them their mocking of the true prophets, and listening to false ones, what saith the Lord? "Therefore, behold, I, even I, will utterly forget you, and I will forsake you, and the city that I gave you and your fathers, and cast you out of my presence, and I will bring an everlasting reproach upon you." When God rejects, it is grievous; no sorer judgment can befall the sons of men. This David knew, and therefore advised his son Solomon to keep close to God; if he did otherwise, God would cast him off for ever, 1 Chron. xxviii. 9.

Obs. 3. There is no halving, no dividing, between God and idols, God and the creature, in matters of worship and religion. "Pollute ye my holy name no more with your gifts, and with your idols;" you join me and them together, thinking that I am pleased, honoured thereby, but I am provoked, and my holy name is polluted; I abhor such doings. Seeing your idols must have some honour, and I the rest, I will have none, get ye to your idols, let them have all; I like it better that you should be wholly for them, than divide between me and them: I can brook no partner in my worship, I must have the whole heart, the whole soul, the whole body, and strength of all, else I will have none. 1 Kings xviii. 21, when the people stood halting between two opinions,

and were sometimes for God and sometimes for Baal, it pleased neither God nor Elijah; therefore saith the prophet, How long will ye halt between two thoughts, or two branches? how long will ye be like a bird that touches upon one twig, and then upon another, and settles not upon either; so how long will ye be looking one day towards God, another day towards Baal? do ye not yet see the evil of it? while ye stand thus in uncertainty, ye provoke God. If God be God, follow him, and him fully, only, constantly, eternally; and if Baal be god, follow him so; you must follow but one. Christ hath told us, we cannot serve God and mammon, God and the world, God and our bellies, God and our credit, God and our lusts. These are masters who command contrary things, and carry away from God.

Obs. 4. The honour of God's name is dear unto him. "Pollute ye not my holy name." Take God's name for his worship, as it is, Exod. xx. 24; 2 Chron. xx. 8; Mal. i. 6; or for his attributes, as it is, Exod. xxxiii. 19; or for his titles, as it is, Deut. xxviii. 58; his name is very dear unto him; which appears,

(1.) In that he will not endure any mixture with his worship, or tender of any thing to him which hath been in idols' service; the Babylonish gods, wood and stone, and the gifts offered to them, or by them to God, he would not admit.

(2.) He counted it a disparagement to his name, to have half of them, and not all; and therefore would rather have them lay out all upon their idols, than some upon him.

(3.) He shows vehement affection and indignation upon this account; Get ye to your idols, begone! pollute my name no more; out of my sight! I cannot endure it.

(4.) He cares not for the perishing of their souls and bodies, in comparison of his name; Go ye, serve idols.

God's name is exceeding dear unto him: he swears by it, Jer. xliv. 26; he sanctifies it being polluted, and will not suffer any blot or stain to lie upon it, Ezek. xxxvi. 23; he labours and works for the maintenance of it, when it is in danger, as you have it in this chapter, ver. 9, 14, 22; rather than it shall suffer, he will defer his anger and judgments, Isa. xlviii. 9. If false prophets presumed to speak in his name, not sent by him, he cut them off, Deut. xviii. 20; or laid heavy judgments upon them, Ezek. xiii. 9. Whoever takes his name in vain any way, he will not hold him guiltless, Exod. xx. 7; and no marvel, for God's name is his glory, Isa. xlviii. 11; and men must give glory due unto his name, Psal. xxix. 2; not any kind of glory, but that which is proportionable to his glory, even his glorious name, remembering what a magnificent temple Solomon built for the honour of his name, 2 Chron. vi. 34.

Ver. 40, 41. *For in mine holy mountain, in the mountain of the height of Israel, saith the Lord God, there shall all the house of Israel, all of them in the land, serve me: there will I accept them, and there will I require your offerings, and the firstfruits of your oblations, with all your holy things. I will accept you with your sweet savour, when I bring you out from the people, and gather you out of the countries wherein ye have been scattered; and I will be sanctified in you before the heathen.*

Now we are come to the gracious promises of God to this people; and here you have,

I. A promise of reduction, which is implied in ver. 40, and expressed in ver. 41.

II. Acceptation of them, and their services, ver. 40, 41.

III. Sanctification of himself in them, ver. 41.

Antecedent to these promises is a description of the place whither he would bring them, and where he would accept them, and that is in his "mountain," which is described,

1. From its holiness.

2. From its height.

"In mine holy mountain." The Hebrew is, the mountain of my holiness, as ver. 39, the name of my holiness: so, Jonah ii. 4, 7, the temple of thy holiness; Isa. lxii. 12, people of holiness; Psal. lxxxix. 20, oil of my holiness; Psal. li. 11, spirit of thy holiness; Psal. xliii. 3, hill of thy holiness; Psal. lxviii. 5, habitation of thy holiness; in all these places you have the abstract, and it is rendered by the concrete, holy mountain, holy name, holy temple, holy people, holy oil, holy spirit, holy hill, and holy habitation. By "holy mountain," he means mount Zion, which is called the hill of his holiness, Psal. ii. 6; there God recorded his name, set up Christ and his kingdom. By a synecdoche, "holy mountain" is put for Canaan, which prefigured the church of God, in the times of the gospel.

"In the mountain of the height of Israel." Of these words before, chap. xvii. 23. This is spoken, not because Zion was so high a mountain, but because of the honour and glory it had above all other mountains; there was the holy city, the holy temple, the holy ordinances, and the holy God's habitation, Psal. lxxvi. 2.

"There shall all the house of Israel." All that were purged from the rebels and transgressors, ver. 38, all that were true Israelites; for such are described to be the dwellers in God's holy hill, Psal. xv. And not only those of the Jewish race, but even gentiles, that should become christians, and be spiritual Israelites, they should come to the church, which should begin at mount Zion, which represented the true church.

"All of them in the land serve me." That land was Canaan, which being polluted with blood, idols, and other abominations, Psal. cvi. 37—40, God abhorred it, and the people thereof, yea, his sanctuary therein, Lam. ii. 7; which caused him to lay it waste for seventy years, wherein he purged it from its filth and blood, Isa. iv. 4, and them from their iniquities, Ezek. xxxvi. 33, and then brought them in to serve him.

This expression is comprehensive, and imports their worshipping and obeying of God: Exod. x. 7, "Let the men go, that they may serve the Lord their God," that is, worship him: Exod. xx. 5, they must not serve images, that is, worship them, but worship God; the word עבד and so δȣλεύω, which the Septuagint does frequently express it by, signifies, to give up oneself wholly to the service of any; so here, they should serve God wholly, worship him, and not any idols, and his own ways, not their ways, and that in spirit and truth; 1 Sam. xii. 24, "Serve him in truth, with all your heart," and "with all humility of mind," Acts xx. 19.

It notes also to obey, and do what he commands; as Josh xxii. 5, "Take diligent heed to do the commandment and the law, which Moses the servant of the Lord charged you, to love the Lord your God, and to walk in all his ways, and to keep his commandments, and to cleave unto him, and to serve him with all your heart and with all your soul:" serving, here, extends to all outward obedience, as well as worship.

They shall "serve" me, that is, worship me, as the only object of divine worship; they shall obey me as their only King and Lord.

"There will I accept them." The Hebrew is, ארצם Montanus renders it, I will will them. When it refers to God, as here, it imports,

1. Pardoning, and passing by, whatever formerly offended. 2 Sam. xxiv. 23, when David would offer a sacrifice for his sin in numbering the people, and for stopping the plague, saith Araunah, "The Lord thy God accept thee;" that is, pardon thy sin, and remove the judgment. Jer. xiv. 12, "When they offer burnt offering and an oblation, I will not accept them; but I will consume them." Non-accepting, was non-pardoning; and that appears most clearly, Lev. i. 4, "He shall put his hand upon the head of the burnt offering; and it shall be accepted for him to make the atonement:" the laying his hand upon the head of the sacrifice, noted the laying of his sins upon the same; and if God accepted the sacrifice, his sins were forgiven, and peace was made, but when he accepted it not, there was no pardon, no peace. When God therefore saith here, "I will accept them," the sense is, he will pardon them.

2. Approving, receiving with favour and delight. Job xlii. 8, "Him will I accept." God would hear and regard the prayer of Job for his three friends. Eccl. ix. 7, "Eat thy bread with joy, and drink thy wine with a merry heart; for God now accepteth thy works;" רצה he is well pleased with thee, and what thou hast done; so Psal. cxlix. 4, "The Lord taketh pleasure in his people:" and this also is included here, "I will accept them," that is, approve of, favour, and take delight in them. Some render the words, There will I take pleasure in them; when they are come to my holy mountain, to a church state again, being purged from their sins through my grace, I will take pleasure in them, as a husband in a wife, as a father in his children.

"There will I require your offerings." Formerly the Lord had refused their offerings, and manifested his displeasure against them and their offerings; as Mal. i. 10, "I have no pleasure in you, saith the Lord of hosts, neither will I accept an offering at your hand:" see Amos v. 21, 22; Jer. vi. 20; Isa. lxvi. 3; i. 11; but now he would be so far from refusing, hating, and prohibiting of them, that he would call for them, and accept them.

"Offerings." The Hebrew word for "offerings" is, תרומות which notes any offering freely given to the Lord; and frequently it is put for the heave-offering, so called, because it was lifted up unto the Lord. If we take it in this sense, it is, by a synecdoche, put for all their offerings; but we may keep to the words as they are.

"And the first-fruits of your oblations." The Hebrew is, the beginning of your elevations; Septuagint, the first-fruits of your separations; the Vulgate is, the beginning of your tenths. The Jews say, they were to bring the "first-fruits" of seven things only, viz. of wheat, barley, grapes, figs, pomegranates, olives, and dates; but God was to have whatever opened the womb first, of man or beast, Exod. xiii. 2, which may also come in amongst "first-fruits."

"Oblations" and sacrifices do differ thus: that is properly an oblation, which is offered, though nothing be done to it, or about it; a sacrifice is offered, but something is done to it, and about it. The sacrifice was to be killed, flayed, cut in pieces, or the like. By "first-fruits of oblations," we may understand the principal and chief oblations, for ראשית notes, the choicest and most excellent, as well as, the first; and Calvin interprets it, that which was the flower and excellency in your gifts.

"With all your holy things." The Hebrew is, in all your sanctifications. קדש sometimes noted the temple, or sanctuary; sometimes their sacrifices;

sometimes their festivities; and sometimes whatever was dedicated to divine worship: here we may take it in the last sense. Calvin expounds it, in all my worship; and so the sense runs well with that before, I will require your offerings and the first-fruits; i. e. the principal of your oblations, in all your dedications and holy things, and in all my worship. Some read the words, In all the things you shall prepare set a part and conserve for me. If we read it with "all your holy things," the sense is, that the sacrifices, temple, priests, solemnities, and festivals, should be restored.

Ver. 41. "I will accept you with your sweet savour." Of "sweet savour," or savour of rest, as the Hebrew is, you heard in ver. 28 of this chapter, and in chap. xvi. 19. They should be pleasing and delightful unto God, as a sweet savour is unto man. They were wont, when at Jerusalem, to offer incense and sweet things unto God, and he accepted the same; and they should do it again after their return, and be accepted; both they and their sacrifices should be a sweet odour unto God. This, and the like expressions in the Old Testament, the apostle alludes unto, in Phil. iv. 18; 2 Cor. ii. 15; Eph. v. 2.

"When I bring you out from the people, and gather them out of the countries," &c. These words we had before in ver. 34, where they sounded judgment, but here, mercy.

"And I will be sanctified in you before the heathen." The Hebrew is, I will sanctify myself. When sanctification refers to God, it imports,

1. Vindication of his name, being polluted and dishonoured by the sons of men; as Ezek. xxxvi. 23, "I will sanctify my great name, which was profaned among the heathen, which ye have profaned in the midst of them."

2. Making himself known, and acknowledged to be holy, just, and powerful: so it is to be taken, Ezek. xxviii. 22, "They shall know that I am the Lord, when I shall have executed judgments in her, and shall be sanctified in her;" so, Lev. x. 3, by the fury and judgment upon Nadab and Abihu, God sanctified himself, he made himself known to be a holy, just, and dreadful majesty.

3. God's doing of that which redounds to his honour and praise; and thus divers interpreters take it in this place. I will bring you out of Babylon into your own country, unite you into church order, give you another temple, with all the ordinances of it, sanctify you by my word and Spirit, cause you to worship me with pure worship, bringing me the best you have for sacrifices, that so you may praise me for my goodness unto you, and the nations, for the great things done for you. The Lord's bringing them out of the countries where they were scattered, was a great work, and filled the heathens with admiration, making them to say, "The Lord hath done great things for them," Psal. cxxvi. 2; and the Jews also to say, "The Lord hath done great things for us," ver. 3. When the Jews were brought out of Egypt, it is said, Psal. cxiv. 2, "Judah was his sanctuary." God separated them from the Egyptians, as these from the Babylonians, to inhabit their praises, and to be worshipped by them, and so they were his sanctuary, and sanctification.

God doth sanctify himself, when he doth vouchsafe a people manifestations of his goodness, wisdom, mercy, love, and faithfulness, and God is sanctified, when a people doth that which is pleasing and acceptable to God. Numb. xx. 12, "Because ye believed me not, to sanctify me in the eyes of the children of Israel:" unbelief is a non-sanctifying of God, and believing is a sanctifying of him.

Obs. 1. God accounts not apostates and idolaters, but those who are true Israelites, to be his people, his church. "For in mine holy mountain there shall all the house of Israel be:" those who were rebels, and would serve wood and stone, that would not hearken unto him, he purged out, and the house of Israel, purged, must be in his holy mountain. God esteems those who are godly, true believers, Israelites indeed, to be his. There are none but such in the invisible church, Rom. xi. 26; Gal. vi. 16; but in the visible, there are tares and wheat, yet God doth not reckon the tares to be wheat, they are Satan's, not the Lord's, Matt. xiii. 38; there are goats and sheep, yet the Lord reckons not the goats to be sheep, Matt. xxv. 33. Psal. xv. 1, 2, "Lord, who shall dwell in thy holy hill? He that walketh uprightly, and worketh," &c.

Obs. 2. Wherever God's people are scattered, he will bring them, and all of them, into, or unto, Zion, to serve him. "In mine holy mountain, &c. there shall all the house of Israel, all of them in the land, serve me." God would bring them out of Babylon into Canaan, from heathenish mountains to his "holy mountain," from the world and synagogues of Satan into the true church. Wherever God hath any sheep, he will gather them, and all of them, into his fold.

These verses do speak and hold out God's dealing with his people under Christ and the gospel, wherein God would bring them from all nations, to enjoy the great and good things provided for them; of which the evangelical prophet Isaiah speaks at large, chap. lx.; so Zechariah, chap. viii. 20—22; and hereof spoke our Lord Jesus Christ, when he said, John x. 16, "Other sheep I have, which are not of this fold: them also I must bring, and they shall hear my voice." When the prodigal was in a far country, did not the Lord order things so, that he returned to his father's house? when the sheep was strayed and lost, did not the Lord seek it out, and bring it home to the fold? Luke xv.; and did not Christ send out his apostles into all nations, to gather in those who were given him of the Father? Matt. xxviii. 19, 20.

Obs. 3. The Lord is to be worshipped especially in Zion, in his holy mountain, in the solemn assembly. "There shall all the house of Israel serve me." It is not sinful to worship God any where, 1 Tim. ii. 8, or alone, Matt. vi. 6; but chiefly in the congregation it should be, where his worship is publicly held forth, and with the harmoniousness of many spirits held up, where strangers may come in, and see, yea, say, God is here, 1 Cor. xiv. 25; for he is "in the assembly of the saints," Psal. lxxxix. 7. This made the prophet say, Isa. ii. 2, 3, "It shall come to pass in the last days, that the mountain of the Lord's house shall be established in the top of the mountains, and shall be exalted above the hills; and all nations shall flow unto it. And many people shall go and say, Come ye, and let us go up to the mountain of the Lord, to the house of the God of Jacob; and he will teach us of his ways, and we will walk in his paths." But in our days this gracious prophecy hath been greatly crossed; for many have said, Come, let us go from the mountain of the Lord, from the house of the God of Jacob; let us go to our own mountain, follow our own teachings, and walk in our own paths; but God hath made it evident, that their mounts are mounts of corruption, their teachings delusions, their paths crooked and cursed. Let us therefore take the apostle's counsel, Heb. x. 23—25, "Let us hold fast the profession of our faith without wavering; and let us consider one another to provoke unto love and to good works: not forsaking the assembling of ourselves together, as the manner of some is:" nor let us meet as the manner of some is, viz. to wickedness. Let us fulfil the prophecy, call upon one another to go up to the mountain of the Lord, &c. and say, He will teach us his ways, and we will walk in his paths.

Obs. 4. In the Lord's mountain, in the church, God will show favour and mercy to his people. "There will I accept them," that is, pardon, approve of, and receive them. When we come to serve the Lord after his own way, in gospel congregations, meeting in the name of Christ, to know the mind of God, and glorify him, God is the Master of such assemblies, he dispenseth many mercies, and distributes sweetest comforts therein. Isa. lx. 7, "They shall come up with acceptance on mine altar," is spoken of the gospel times; men should come from several quarters to the christian congregations with acceptance; God would meet them there, welcome them thither, there he would bless them: see Jer. xxxi. 12; Isa. lxvi. 18. 2 Cor. vi. 16—18, as every christian, so every congregation, is "the temple of the living God;" therefore he told the church of Corinth, he would dwell in them, be their God and Father, and they should be his people, his sons and daughters; God would accept of them as a father doth of his children, take pleasure in them, and let out choice mercies unto them. When the disciples were met, Jesus came to them, bestowed his peace and Spirit upon them, John xx. 19—22; and see what mercies they met with, who served him in his temple, Rev. vii. 15—17.

Obs. 5. Where the person is accepted of God, there the actions and sacrifices of that person are acceptable also. "There I will accept them, and there will I require their offerings." In Zion God would accept the men, and in Zion he would accept their services. If persons or congregations be not accepted of God themselves, nothing they do or tender is welcome unto him, Gen. iv. 5; but if the parties be under divine favour, their presents and duties are grateful. Isa. lvi. 6, 7, those that joined themselves to the Lord, and took hold of his covenant, "them," saith the Lord, "will I bring to my holy mountain, and make them joyful in my house of prayer: their burnt offerings and their sacrifices shall be accepted upon mine altar." They being in covenant with God, and offering in Zion unto God, he was pleased with them and their offerings. Mal. iii. 1, 3, 4, when Christ, "the messenger of the covenant," should come, refine them, and be delighted in and by them, then should "the offering of Judah and Jerusalem be pleasant unto the Lord." God is desirous of the prayers, praises, and alms of a good man, who is reconciled unto him; they are sweet odours unto him; so they are called in the next verse, "I will accept you with your sweet savour," or savour of rest; when God hath these, his Spirit is at rest, being in a manner troubled when he hath them not. Hence prayers of the godly are likened to "incense," Psal. cxli. 2; their bounty, to the "odour of a sweet smell," Phil. iv. 18; and their praise is preferred before the sacrificing of an ox, Psal. lxix. 31.

Obs. 6. God must have the best tendered up to him in our sacrifices and services; he calls for and expects the best from his people. "I require the first-fruits of your oblations;" the chief, principal, and best you have, in all your holy things. If God have lean, lank, lame, imperfect sacrifices offered to him, it is a dishonour, and offends him: Mal. i. 8, "If ye offer the blind for sacrifice, is it not evil? and if ye offer the lame and sick, is it not evil?" yes, it is very evil, it is extremely evil; the interrogation itself portends so much, and being a double interrogation doubles the evil. What! offer it to me? man would not accept of such offerings; go try, "offer it now unto thy governor," that is brought unto me; go tender it to him, "will he be pleased with thee, or accept thy person?" no, I know he will not; and if man, sorry, sinful man, like thyself, will not accept such things, should I, the great God, do it? God is so far from accepting and showing favour in this kind, that he poureth out a curse upon him that doth so: ver. 14, "Cursed be the deceiver, which hath in his flock a male, and voweth, and sacrificeth unto the Lord a corrupt thing." Men think if they do something in religion, give God a sacrifice, though it be blind, lame, sickly, they shall have a blessing; but see how the Lord brands them, they are deceivers; and whom do they deceive? not God, but themselves; for instead of a blessing they meet with a curse: such dealings with God, cause him, even then when he uses to be most propitious, to throw forth curses. Suitable hereunto, is that in Hos. viii. 13, "They sacrifice flesh for the sacrifices of mine offerings, and eat it; but the Lord accepteth them not; now will he remember their iniquity, and visit their sins;" if they did bring the best they had, yet they had no respect to God, but to their own bellies.

Obs. 7. When the Lord brings his people out of a scattered, captive condition, into church order, he expects they should set up all his ordinances. "I will require your offerings, and the first-fruits of your oblations, with all your holy things;" circumcision, passover, sacrifices, &c. Their being in Babylon was a representation of the church's condition under antichrist; and as then they, being freed from the Babylonish captivity, fell into the ways of worship formerly given out, so now christians, being brought out of spiritual Babylon, should do the like. Neither let any say, those gifts are lost which the churches once had, &c.

Ezra ii. 62, 63, those priests that were put from their places, because their names were not found in the genealogies, the Tirshatha or governor said, "They should not eat of the most holy things, till there stood up a priest with Urim and with Thummim;" that was, never. They lost at the Babylonish captivity, (1.) The ark with the mercy-seat and cherubims; (2.) The fire from heaven; (3.) Sheivah or divine presence; (4.) The Urim and Thummim; (5.) The spirit of prophecy: these all were wanting in the second temple; yet they did not forbear to set up and use the ordinances of God which formerly were appointed.

Obs. 8. The Lord doth those things for his people, which makes him honourable amongst them and others. "I will be sanctified in you before the heathen." The mercy and kindness he showed them in bringing them out of Babylon, and restoring to them their former enjoyments, set them on work to praise the Lord, and made the heathens acknowledge that God was faithful to them in keeping his promise.

Ver. 42—44. *And ye shall know that I am the Lord, when I shall bring you into the land of Israel, into the country for the which I lifted up mine hand to give it to your fathers. And there shall ye remember your ways, and all your doings, wherein ye have been defiled; and ye shall lothe yourselves in your own sight for all your evils that ye have committed. And ye shall know that I am the Lord, when I have wrought with you for my name's sake, not according to your wicked ways, nor according to your corrupt doings, O ye house of Israel, saith the Lord God.*

In these verses you have the event and sequel of the Lord's gracious dealings with this people, in bringing them out of their captivity into their own land again; which is,

I. Experimental acknowledgment of God and his goodness unto them, ver. 42, 44.

II. Consideration of their former ways, ver. 43.

III. Humiliation and repentance for them.

"And ye shall know that I am the Lord." They knew the Lord by the works of creation, by the prophets, by the severe judgments he had executed upon them, but that knowledge had not affected their hearts, and brought them to fear, worship, and serve the Lord answerably; but now upon that great mercy of being delivered out of Babylon, which seemed a thing impossible to them, Ezek. xxxvii. 11, and being brought into Canaan, they should have such knowledge of God as should descend to their hearts, and cause them to hearken to and honour him. They should know him practically, do his will; they should know him to be faithful in performing his promises, powerful and gracious in doing greater things than they looked for, and so should set themselves to serve the Lord. Others knew him by his judgments, ver. 38, which knowledge produced no real effects in their hearts and lives; but these by his mercies and goodness, which knowledge rested not in their heads, but was operative in their hearts, and extant in their lives; so knowing is to be taken, 1 Chron. xxviii. 9.

"When I shall bring you into the land of Israel," &c. Of these words, or not much differing, you heard in the 28th verse. Though the "land of Israel" were a fruitful land, flowing with milk and honey, and so it was a great mercy to be brought in upon that account, yet that was not all; it was the land of promise, the inheritance of their fathers, and their repossession of it evidenced that they were their children, their heirs, the people of God.

Obs. 1. Experimental knowledge of God affects the heart, and makes obedient to his will, to worship and honour God, which other knowledge doth not. Whatever knowledge a man hath of God and his ways, without this, it is a form of knowledge, rather than knowledge itself. 1 John ii. 4, "He that saith, I know him, and keepeth not his commandments, is a liar, and the truth is not in him;" that is, he hath no true knowledge of God in him; for what he saith of love, chap. v. 3, "This is the love of God, that we keep his commandments," that is true of knowledge; there is no right knowledge of God if ye keep not his commandments. Hence saith the Lord, Isa. i. 3, "Israel doth not know;" and Jer. iv. 22: chap. viii. 7, "My people know not the judgment of the Lord;" they had the law, the prophets, yet they did not know; and why? they did not keep his commandments: violation of them is an argument men know not God. Where works of iniquity are committed, there the knowledge of God is wanting: Hos. v. 4, "The spirit of whoredom is in the midst of them, and they have not known the Lord;" and chap. iv. 1, when there was no truth nor mercy in the land, then there was no knowledge of God in it. When men are disobedient to the commands of God, they are ignorant of God in their hearts, deny God in their lives, whatever knowledge they have of him in their heads: you may find it in holy writ, that as those who do evil are said not to know God, Jer. ix. 3, so those that do good, are said to know him, Jer. xxii. 16; and pure religion, which is the right knowledge of God, is put upon doing, James i. 27. Daniel therefore tells us, that turning from iniquity, and so walking in the ways of God, is the way to understand truth, and so to know God, Dan. ix. 13; and Christ hath affirmed it, that doing is the way to knowing, John vii. 17.

Obs. 2. The goodness, mercy, and kindness of God begets experimental knowledge of him in the hearts of men. "Ye shall know that I am the Lord, when I shall bring you into the land of Israel." When God should knock off the Babylonish yoke, and replant them in Canaan, then their hearts should taste and be affected with the dealings of God. Great mercies had great operations upon them, and made deep impressions in them. God teaches men by his works; experimental knowledge comes in that way; when his word is fulfilled in promises or threats, in mercy or judgment, then men come to know God. He is known by executing of judgment, Psal. ix. 16, and known by his mercies, Isa. xix. 20—22. It is one thing to hear of wine, another to find the virtue of it in the stomach; so it is one thing to hear of God and his mercies, another to taste of the loving-kindness of God in his mercies: Psal. xxxiv. 8, "Taste and see that the Lord is good." God's goodness had bred experimental knowledge in David, and he could sensibly speak of it, and provoke others to partake of what he had.

Ver. 43. "And there shall ye remember your ways." These words we had in chap. xvi. 61. The word "remember" notes remembering with affection, so as to do something thereupon.

"And all your doings, wherein ye have been defiled." The Septuagint reads the former words with a part of these, thus, There shall ye remember your ways, wherein ye have defiled yourselves, and leave out these words, "all your doings;" but they are in the Hebrew, and import their idolatries, and other abominations. They corrupted God's worship, fell to Babylonish practices, and greatly defiled themselves.

"And ye shall loathe yourselves in your own sight." In chap. vi. 9, were these words opened, where they are thus, "They shall loathe themselves for the evils which they have committed in all their abominations." The Septuagint is, they shall smite their faces; others, you shall be displeased and wroth with yourselves. The meaning of the verse is, that they should seriously consider their ways, be ashamed of them, truly repent of them; yea, so repent, as to judge themselves worthy to be cut off from being God's people, and to be made a curse.

Obs. 1. Sense of mercies, rather than of judgments, makes sin bitter, and leads unto repentance. Their captivity, and the sad things they suffered therein, did not imbitter their sin unto them, and break their hearts; but God's kindness in bringing them out of Babylon into the land of Israel, that prevailed with them; when they had received marvellous kindness from God, then they were marvellously affected, greatly ashamed of their ways, and loathed themselves. Mercies in Zion produced that which judgments in Babylon did not. Great mercies bestowed upon great sinners, do preach the doctrine of repentance most effectually, convincing them strongly of their unworthy and vile carriages towards the Lord.

1 Sam. xxiv. David's kindness brake the heart of Saul, and made him to weep and say, "Thou art more righteous than I; for thou hast rewarded me good, whereas I have rewarded thee evil." If human favour hath such influence into a sinful heart, what hath divine? Moses by his strokes fetched water out of a rock; David, by his kindness. God sometimes by his judgments humbles men, and brings them to repentance, but mostly by his mercies. The sweet influences of the gospel have pierced deeper into sinners' hearts, than the terrors of the law.

Obs. 2. When the Lord gathers up his people out of the world, and brings them into nearer relation to himself, into Canaan, and church order, he looks they should review their former ways, and be much affected with them, and thoroughly repent for them. "There shall ye remember your ways, and all your doings, wherein," &c. When brought into Canaan, they were not only to eat the milk and honey, to behold the glory thereof, but they were to remember days of old, their sins in Babylon, compliances with Babylonians, how they had polluted themselves and provoked the Lord; and thereupon to mourn kindly for their unkindnesses to him, who had showed such marvellous loving-kindness unto them. When God brings men out of the world now into Zion, gives them the milk and honey of the gospel, shows them the glory thereof, then they look back, wonder at their wickedness, and loathe themselves for it, saying, Who is like unto us in sin and wickedness, and who is like unto our God in grace and goodness, in pardon and forgiveness? Micah vii. 18. When it shall please God to bring the Jews out of that Babylon they are now in, unto the true Canaan, the church of Christ, they will remember their iniquities, their bitter and bloody doings against Christ, mourn and loathe themselves for the same, Zech. xii. 10; Rev. i. 7.

Obs. 3. Where repentance springs from sense of love and kindness, as it is real and deep, so it is secret and universal. They should, being brought into Canaan, not only remember their sins, but they should loathe themselves, be displeased so with themselves, that they should smite and abhor themselves, and that in their own sight, and for all the evils they had committed; when no eye saw them, they would spread all their sins before them, and in the sight and sense of them, be vile in their own eyes.

Ver. 44. "And ye shall know that I am the Lord." These words we had in ver. 42, wherein they were opened and expounded of an experimental knowledge.

"When I have wrought with you for my name's sake." Of these words, see ver. 9, 14, 22. The Vulgate is, when I shall have done good to you. The Hebrew is, when I have done to you, or with you, for my name's sake; that is, when I have dealt graciously and mercifully with you out of my free grace, and for the honour of my name.

"Not according to your wicked ways." Of "wicked abominations" was spoken chap. viii. 9, of "wicked counsel," chap. xi. 2, of "wicked way" and "ways," chap. xiii. 22; xviii. 23. Those are "wicked ways" which lead from God, from truth, from just, honest, and good things. In such they had walked long, but God would not deal with them according to the wickedness of their ways.

"Nor according to your corrupt doings." The word for "corrupt" is from שחת which signifies to corrupt even to the bottom, thoroughly; and such were they: they were not a little corrupt, but totally corrupted, in their judgments, wills, affections, words, and actions; they were like a corrupt spring, that sends forth nothing but corrupt waters; Ezek. xvi. 47, "Thou wast corrupted more than they in all thy ways."

Obs. 1. The Lord is gracious and merciful unto the sons of men, deserving ill at his hands; he deals with them upon the account of his grace, not their deserts. What did their wicked ways and corrupt doings deserve at his hands, but that he should have poured out his fury, and accomplished his anger upon them, as it is chap. vii. 8? but he wrought with them for his name's sake, that is, out of his free grace and favour he spared them, he pardoned them, he delivered them out of Babylon, and brought them into Canaan. When God seeth nothing in the creature to put him on to show mercy, he finds enough in his own name to provoke him thereunto; you have it four times in this chapter, thrice before, and here, that he wrought for his name's sake: whatever mercy this people had, it was from divine favour, not their desert.

If it was free grace brought the Jews out of Babylon into Canaan, what is it but freeness, fulness, and riches of grace to bring men out of the world into the heavenly Canaan? Predestination, calling, justification, and glorification, are acts of mere grace and favour, Eph. i. 5; 2 Tim. i. 9; Rom. iii. 24; viii. 30; 1 Pet. v. 10. All the sons of men enjoy here, or expect hereafter, is from the bounty, favour, and mercy of God, Psal. ciii. 8—12; Luke xii. 32: to attribute aught to our own wills or endeavours, is to derogate from God, and darken the glory of his name and free grace.

Obs. 2. God doth therefore deal graciously with sinners, that they may know him experimentally. "Ye shall know that I am the Lord, when I have wrought with you for my name's sake," &c. God works, and so works, that he makes the hearts of men affected with his works, and to say, Psal. lxxxvi. 8, "Among the gods there is none like unto thee, O Lord; neither are there any works like unto thy works;" none so full of glory, so full of grace and mercy, none so influential and operative upon the heart. It is God's scope and aim in doing good so freely and fully as he doth, to make himself known to the hearts of his people, that so they may be knit to him, provoke them to admire him, and live more fully to him.

Ver. 45—48. *Moreover the word of the Lord came unto me, saying, Son of man, set thy face toward the south, and drop thy word toward the south, and prophesy against the forest of the south field; and say to the forest of the south, Hear the word of the Lord; Thus saith the Lord God; Behold, I will kindle a fire in thee, and it shall devour every green tree in thee, and every dry tree: the flaming flame shall not be quenched, and all faces from the south to the north shall be burned therein. And all flesh shall see that I the Lord have kindled it: it shall not be quenched.*

These verses are the fifth general part of the chapter, viz. a parabolical declaration of the destruction of Judea and Jerusalem.

Some refer these words to the next chapter, and make the beginning of that at the 45th verse of this.

The 45th verse sets before us the divine authority of this prophecy against the Jews that were yet in Canaan; the prophet received it from the Lord, it came from God to him, before it went out from him to men.

In this 45th verse we have,

I. The compellation, "son of man," of which heretofore.

II. A command, to declare and utter the word he had received; "Set thy face," &c.

"Set thy face." Of this expression in chap. iv. 3, 7; vi. 2; xiii. 17. Dispose thyself to, and be undaunted in, what thou art to prophesy, and them thou art to prophesy against; speak then like a man of God, and sent from God, not regarding the frowns or threats of any.

"Toward the south." Babylon was north from Jerusalem, Jer. i. 14, and our prophet being there, and having declared the mind of God against those elders who came subtlely to inquire of him, he is here commanded to set his face "towards the south," that was, towards Jerusalem and Judea.

"Drop thy word toward the south." In the Hebrew is not "thy word," but only thus, drop towards the south. The word נטף properly signifies the dropping of the clouds, or rain, which falls by drops; and metaphorically is put for prophesying and preaching; and Vatablus saith, the Chaldee paraphrase hath it, prophesy; and so it is expressed in the next words of this verse, "prophesy against the forest of the south," which are exegetical of what was before. Preaching or prophesying is likened to rain or the droppings thereof,

1. In respect of the flowing and succession of one drop after another. Judg. v. 4, "The heavens dropped, the clouds also dropped water;" so in prophesying, there is one word, one truth after another; he that prophesieth, poureth out words.

2. In respect of the influence thereof. The drops soak into the earth; so words have influence into men's ears and hearts. Deut. xxxii. 2, "My doctrine shall drop as the rain, my speech shall distil as the dew, as the small rain upon the tender herb, and as the showers upon the grass:" as the rains and dews insinuate themselves into the grass and ground, so do words into the heads and hearts of men; Psal. cxix. 130, "The entrance of thy words giveth light."

3. In respect of the trouble and hurt that oft rains and droppings produce. Prov. xxvii. 15, "A continual dropping in a very rainy day and a contentious woman are alike," alike grievous, troublesome, wasting, and wearying; so prophesying of judgments and destruction is grievous and troubles much, it is like great rains and drops. 2 Chron. xxxiv. 25, "My wrath shall be poured out upon this place;" the original is, shall drop upon this place; there should be a storm, and such great drops of God's wrath, as should consume it.

"Toward the south." The word here for "south" is, דרום a lofty habitation, because the sun goeth high there: and after in the verse you have נגב for the south; the word signifies a dry place, and metonymically it is put for the south, because of the great heat of the sun there; Judg. i. 15, saith Achsah to Caleb her father, "Thou hast given me a south land," that is, a land of drought, "give me also springs of water."

"Prophesy against the forest of the south field." That is, against Jerusalem, and those that dwelt in Judea. The Hebrew for "forest" is, יער a wood; and Judea or Jerusalem is compared to a forest or wood,

1. For the number of those in it. In a wood are a multitude of trees: Jer. xlvi. 23, "They shall cut down her forest, saith the Lord, though it cannot be searched; because they are more than the grasshoppers, and are innumerable;" it is spoken of the people of Egypt: so they of Judea were many.

2. In a wood and forest is no order, the trees stand confusedly; so now there was no order amongst them, all run into confusion: Micah vii. 6, "The son dishonoureth the father, the daughter riseth up against her mother, the daughter-in-law against her mother-in-law; a man's enemies are they of his own house."

3. In a forest, trees are fruitless; or if fruitful, it is wild fruit those trees bear, they are for the axe and fire, Ezek. xv. 6: such were the men in Judea, trees that bare no fruit, or evil fruit; Isa. ix. 17, "Every one is an hypocrite and an evil doer, and every mouth speaketh folly." See Micah vii. 3, 4.

4. Forests and woods are dens of wild beasts, Psal. civ. 20; Jer. v. 6; and Jerusalem was full of wild beasts, Zeph. iii. 3, 4; Ezek. xxii. 25, 27; Micah iii. 10. Ezek. vii. 23, "The land is full of bloody crimes, the city is full of violence." Jer. vii. 9—11, there was robbing, murdering, and all abominations.

Obs. 1. When God calls men to prophesy or preach, they are to prepare for it, and undauntedly to proceed therein. "Son of man, set thy face toward the south, and drop thy word," &c. He must fit himself for that work, and whatever he met with in the work, he must not be discouraged, but go on as one sent out and commissioned by the Lord: thus did Peter and John, Acts iv. 19, 20.

Obs. 2. God's word shall not be in vain, which is given out against hard-hearted sinners. "Drop thy word toward the south, and prophesy against the forest." They would not admit the dews of the word for their good; they must feel the droppings of it for their ruin. Men cannot keep the rain from falling upon the earth and rocks; neither can they keep off the threats of God from falling upon them and theirs; and when they fall they will be terrible unto them. Isa. lv. 10, 11, as the rain hath its end when it falls, so hath the word he sends forth and causeth to be dropped; if he drop a word of wrath, that drop will eat into the most stony heart, and consume it at last. Zech. i. 6, God's words took hold of their fathers; the prophets dropped out such terrible drops of judgment, as consumed them. Let Judea be as a forest full of trees, and mighty ones too, if God once drop his word against it, down must these trees: Hos. vi. 5, God hewed them by his prophets, and slew them by the judgments of his mouth.

Obs. 3. God's threats and judgments are irrespective, and impartial. "Prophesy against the forest;" the whole forest, and highest trees in it, as well as the shrubs and bushes. Wicked cities and countries are no other in God's account, than a forest of wild and fruitless trees, which he lays his axe unto, to cut down for the fire.

Ver. 47. "And say to the forest of the south, Thus saith the Lord," &c. After a command of the prophet to speak, and the forest to hear, you have the parabolical declaration itself, of the destruction of Jerusalem; where you may take notice,

1. Of the judgment, which is fire.
2. The author of it; "I will kindle a fire."
3. The place where; "in thee."
4. The effect of this fire; it should devour every tree, both green and dry.
5. The kind or manner of this fire, inextinguishable; "the flaming flame shall not be quenched."

"I will kindle a fire in thee." By "fire" is meant that warlike invasion by the Babylonians, who by sword, and what accompanied it, laid all waste.

"Every green tree, and every dry tree." Jerom makes these to be saints and sinners; so some others expound the "green tree" of the righteous, and "dry tree" of the wicked; but, Ezek. ix. 4, the righteous mourned for all the abominations that were in Jerusalem, and were marked that they might not be destroyed. It is better therefore to understand by "green tree" the rich and wealthy, the young and lusty, the high and mighty; and by the "dry tree" the old, poor, and such as were underlings and inconsiderable: or by them you may understand all sorts of people, as by green trees and dry trees all sorts of trees in a forest or wood are meant.

"The flaming flame shall not be quenched." The Hebrew is, the flame of flame, the duplication of the word notes the intention of it, a vehement flame, such as should continue, and by no art, power, or policy be extinct; the affliction should be wonderful, sore, and lasting. The war begat famine, famine the plague, plague death; here was a flame of a flame. They strove by the Egyptians to quench that fire, but could not.

"All faces from the south to the north shall be burned therein." Not all destroyed, or be ashamed only, but all through fear, famine, and diseases, should appear as dry, withered, and burnt up, from one end of the land to the other.

Obs. 1. The Lord sends fierce judgments upon his own people for their wickedness, which do consume all sorts of them. "I will kindle a fire in thee," in thee, Jerusalem, in thee, Judea, who gloriest in thy princes, in thy nobles, in thy soldiers, in thy privileges, and churchship, which "shall devour every green tree, and every dry tree." As a fire devours all before it, so do God's judgments. Let houses be strong or weak, great or small, trees be green or dry, fire conquers them, and brings them to ashes; so do God's judgments ruin people, be they high or low, weak or strong, rulers or subjects, and dries up the spirits of those that are living: Lam. iv. 8, "Their visage is blacker than a coal; they are not known in the streets: their skin cleaveth to their bones; it is withered, it is become like a stick." See Isa. xxiv. 4—6.

Obs. 2. God's judgments once begun, cannot be stayed by the skill or power of the creature. "The flaming flame shall not be quenched;" they used all their policy and power to divert the Babylonians from coming, to remove them being come, but nothing prevailed. God's fires are not extinguishable by the arts, counsels, or strengths of men. As we cannot avoid his judgments threatened, so we cannot remove them inflicted: if he send a spirit of division among brethren, who can cast out that spirit? if he commission the sword to walk abroad, who can command it into the scabbard again, and to keep home? if he cause a burning heat in the body, who can quench that heat but himself?

Ver. 48. *And all flesh shall see that I the Lord have kindled it: it shall not be quenched.*

"All flesh." By a synecdoche of the genus for the species, flesh is put for men; and by "all flesh," he intends the people in the regions round about, and Chaldeans themselves.

"Shall see;" that is, shall acknowledge, that this war, this destructive judgment, is not human, but divine. When strange and dreadful things are done, men inquire into the causes. If mountains be set on fire, fire and brimstone come down from heaven, they will see and say this is the hand of the Lord.

"It shall not be quenched." God would continue the burning of this fire, till it had consumed what he had appointed to consumption. Not their prayers, tears, or blood, should extinguish it; he that kindled it, only could quench it; only he that calleth for and causeth war, can cease wars.

Obs. It is one main end of God's severe judgments upon cities, nations, and people, to make them know and acknowledge that he is the causer and continuer of them, yea, that they are unremovable without his hand.

Ver. 49. *Then said I, Ah Lord God! They say of me, Doth he not speak parables?*

Here is the last part of the chapter, viz. a doleful conclusion of the prophet, wherein he complains of the coarse and reproachful usage he had amongst the people; they mocked and scoffed at him and his parables, they told him they were dreams and fancies of his own. What did he tell them of the "south," and "forest of the south field," of "fire," and "flaming flame," of green and dry trees? these were dark things, visions, and divinations of his own head, and as for them, they would not heed what he said; his words savoured more of man than of God, setting forth his wit more than any thing else.

"Doth he not speak parables?" Junius and Tremellius have it, Is not he an artist in parabolizing? Piscator, Is he not a deviser of parables? he vexes us with such things, gives us words we understand not.

Obs. 1. The prophets and messengers of God are subject to scorn and reproach, even from those they are sent unto. See Jer. xviii. 18; 2 Chron. xxxvi. 16; Isa. viii. 18.

Obs. 2. When the messengers of God are burdened with the revilings, scoffs, and reproaches of men, their refuge is to go unto God, and ease themselves in his bosom; as the prophet here doth.

Obs. 3. When prophets and preachings are not pleasing to the people, they are not willing to understand what is delivered. "They say, Doth he not speak parables?" they knew what fire, forest, flame, green and dry trees meant, but because it was a sad prophesy, and struck at their interests, they would not understand, they put off all as mystical and enigmatical.

CHAPTER XXI.

Ver. 1—5. *And the word of the Lord came unto me, saying, Son of man, set thy face toward Jerusalem, and drop thy word toward the holy places, and prophesy against the land of Israel, and say to the land of Israel, Thus saith the Lord; Behold, I am against thee, and will draw forth my sword out of his sheath, and will cut off from thee the righteous and the wicked. Seeing then that I will cut off from thee the righteous and the wicked, therefore shall my sword go forth out of his sheath against all flesh from the south to the north: that all flesh may know that I the Lord have drawn forth my sword out of his sheath: it shall not return any more.*

In this chapter is a double prophecy.

I. One against the land of Israel, and what was therein, from the 1st verse to the 28th.

II. Another against the Ammonites, from the 28th to the end.

Ver. 1. "And the word of the Lord came unto me, saying." The Hebrew for "came unto me," is, was unto me, that is, was put into me by divine inspiration; he spake not of himself, but from God.

Ver. 2. "Son of man, set thy face toward Jerusalem, drop thy word, and prophesy." Of these words see the former chapter, ver. 46, where they were spoken of.

"Toward the holy places." The temple, which is put plurally, because of the several partitions of it, the *sanctum*, and *sanctum sanctorum*, with the buildings contiguous to it, which the Jews esteemed holy.

Here he shows what, in the end of the former chapter, he meant by the "south, forest of the south, and south field," viz. the land of Israel, Judea, and the temple.

Obs. Holiness of places will not privilege unholy people. Sanctuaries are no protections against divine justice. Canaan was the holy land, Jerusalem the holy city, and the temple more holy than both; yet, "Son of man, set thy face toward Jerusalem, and drop thy word toward the holy places, and prophesy against the land of Israel, and say, Thus saith the Lord; Behold, I am against thee," &c.; I will bring the Babylonish army upon thee; which shall utterly destroy thee.

Ver. 3. "Behold, I am against thee." Here was sad tidings to hear, that God was against Jerusalem. See chap. v. 8.

"And will draw forth my sword." By "sword" is meant war, and the grievous evils which accompany it, Lev. xxvi. 33.

"And will cut off from thee the righteous and the wicked." The Septuagint reads the words otherwise, I will destroy out of thee the unjust and lawless; the Chaldee hath it, I will cause thy just ones to go out of thee, that I may destroy the wicked; but the Hebrew is, the righteous and the wicked. How this can be understood of a man truly righteous, I find not, for, Psal. v. 12, the Lord blesseth the righteous, and compasseth him with favour as with a shield; if he cut him off, how doth he compass him with favour, and favour as a shield; how doth he protect him? Gen. xviii. 23, 25, "Wilt thou destroy the righteous with the wicked? far be it from thee: shall not the Judge of the earth do right?" said Abraham to God. He thought it an unjust and grievous evil that God should cut off the righteous and wicked together; and the truly righteous were marked, Ezek. ix. 4, that they might not be slain. Divers expositors, therefore, make the "righteous" here to be such as were reputed so, seemed to be so, but were not in truth so. The holy Scripture speaks often according to the opinions and apprehensions which are had of men, or what they have of themselves, Luke xviii. 9, the Pharisees thought themselves righteous, and were reputed so, but fell short of true righteousness. These were less wicked than others, and so appeared righteous.

Ver. 4. "My sword shall go forth out of his sheath against all flesh from the south to the north." This verse is the same for substance with ver. 47 of the precedent chapter; "fire" there is the same with "sword" here; "green tree" and "dry tree," the same with "righteous" and "wicked;" the burning up of all faces from the north to the south, the same with the words, going out against all flesh.

Ver. 5. "That all flesh may know," &c. "All flesh" was to be cut off in Judea, that "all flesh" in other lands might know the severe judgments of God.

Obs. 1. That wars are the Lord's; they come not without his commission, he sends them, orders them, and ends them at his pleasure. "I will draw forth my sword out of his sheath." Ver. 4, "My sword shall go forth against all flesh from the south to the north;" and, ver. 5, "it shall not return any more," i. e. till it had accomplished the Lord's will. Nebuchadnezzar and his army was the sword, Babylon the sheath; God brought them out of their own country into the land of Israel, which he laid waste from one end to the other; and then, having finished the work of the Lord, they returned.

Obs. 2. Outside righteousness doth not secure men from the judgments of God. "I will cut off from thee the righteous and the wicked." Such righteousness finds not favour with God; it is no better in his account than wickedness. Labour for true righteousness. What if Josiah fell in war, and other righteous ones have been cut off in public calamities, yet know, death is not punishment to them, but glory.

Obs. 3. From the 4th verse, The Lord is severe in his judgments at last. He bare long with the Jews, but now he would unsheath his sword, and "cut off the righteous and the wicked" from the land, yea, "all flesh from the south to the north." None should escape his stroke, he would find them out wherever hid.

Obs. 4. From the 5th verse, That God's end in bringing judgments upon a nation, is to make known his power, justice, and severity against sinners, and their sinful ways. "That all flesh may know that I the Lord have drawn forth my sword out of his sheath." There is a knowledge of God by his works, as well as by his word; and by his judgments, as well as by his mercies. When Nebuchadnezzar and his army, the great sword of God, should come and cut them down, all men should see and say, God is, &c.

Ver. 6, 7. *Sigh therefore, thou son of man, with the breaking of thy loins; and with bitterness sigh before their eyes. And it shall be, when they say unto thee, Wherefore sighest thou? that thou shalt answer, For the tidings; because it cometh: and every heart shall melt, and all hands shall be feeble, and every spirit shall faint, and all knees shall be weak as water: behold, it cometh, and shall be brought to pass, saith the Lord God.*

Here is a command laid upon the prophet, which is, to "sigh." The manner of it is threefold.

I. "With breaking of loins."

II. "With bitterness."

III. "Before their eyes."

"With the breaking of thy loins." Sigh as if thy loins were broken; sigh greatly. It is suitable to that in Isa. xxi. 3, "My loins are filled with pain; pangs have taken hold upon me, as the pangs of a woman that travaileth." A woman in travail thinks her back broken, her loins loosed, and sighs grievously, yea, bitterly, as if herself, child, or both, were losing their lives; so should the prophet sigh here, really, not feignedly, deeply, not superficially, bitterly, not to ease himself.

"Before their eyes." How could this be, whenas Ezekiel was in Babylon, and they at Jerusalem? It is probable there were some of Jerusalem came to see and hear how things would go with them there, seeing they had lately revolted from Nebuchadnezzar; or if it were before the revolt, some might be there to bring the tribute they paid to the Babylonish king yearly.

In the 7th verse is the cause of this great sighing laid down, which is double.

1. "Tidings," that is, of the Babylonish army coming.

2. The effects thereof; which are four:

(1.) Melting of hearts.
(2.) Feebleness of hands.
(3.) Faintness of spirits.
(4.) Weakness of knees.

Such fear should possess them upon the tidings of the Babylonish army's approaching, as should make their rocky hearts melt, as snow before the sun, or fat of lambs before the fire; and the hands, spirits, and knees of their stoutest men to be feeble, faint, and weak; so that they should be inept unto all services, especially military ones.

Obs. 1. The goodness of the Lord towards a stubborn, wilful, perishing people, in that he will have the prophet to see what prophetical signs will do, when prophetical threats did nothing. "Sigh, son of man, with the breaking of thy loins, and with bitterness," &c. These were prophetical sighs, representing unto them the great evils which were coming upon them; that so they might consider, sigh in like manner for their sins, and prevent their destruction, or else certainly expect the same. God laid a heavy burden upon the prophet, to sigh so.

Obs. 2. Ill tidings sink the hearts and spirits of

hypocrites and wicked ones. When they hear of wars and great forces coming against them, not only doth their mirth cease, but their hearts, hands, spirits, knees, fail them. When Nebuchadnezzar came, their hands were upon their loins, they knew not what to do, whither to go, where to hide themselves. Hath it not been so in Ireland? But, Psal. cxii. 7, it is said of a godly man, "He shall not be afraid of evil tidings: his heart is fixed, trusting in the Lord."

Ver. 8—13. *Again the word of the Lord came unto me, saying, Son of man, prophesy, and say, Thus saith the Lord; Say, A sword, a sword is sharpened, and also furbished: it is sharpened to make a sore slaughter; it is furbished that it may glitter: should we then make mirth? it contemneth the rod of my son, as every tree. And he hath given it to be furbished, that it may be handled: this sword is sharpened, and it is furbished, to give it into the hand of the slayer. Cry and howl, son of man: for it shall be upon my people, it shall be upon all the princes of Israel: terrors by reason of the sword shall be upon my people: smite therefore upon thy thigh. Because it is a trial, and what if the sword contemn even the rod? it shall be no more, saith the Lord God.*

The Lord had said before, he would unsheath his sword, and now orders the prophet to cry out, "A sword, a sword;" and shows the approaching of it, for it was sharpened and furbished, he drew it out for service, to slay both people and princes.

Ver. 9. "A sword, a sword." By "sword" you may understand all those judgments which came with Nebuchadnezzar and his army, or more specially, those warlike instruments they prepared and brought with them.

"Is sharpened, and also furbished." If it were blunt before, now it was whetted; if it were rusty, now it is scoured. Now Nebuchadnezzar was ready with all his military preparations, sharp and shining, full of terror, and fit for execution.

Ver. 10. "It is sharpened to make a sore slaughter." Hebrew is, to kill a killing, that is, to make a great slaughter; it was both furbished and sharpened, that it might terrify with its glistering, and cut more sorely with its sharpness.

Obs. When God is bringing judgments upon a people, he will fit instruments for accomplishing of the same, and that to purpose. He will make that which is blunt, sharp; that which is rusty, glittering; and those who are spiritless, full of spirit: he can make one to chase ten, ten a hundred, and a hundred a thousand; his works shall never fail for want of instruments.

"Should we then make mirth?" The Hebrew is, shall we rejoice?

Obs. 1. Times of war and judgments are no times for mirth. The sword is unsheathed, it is whetted, it is furbished, it is approaching; should we then make mirth? that is as unseasonable as snow in summer, and thunder in winter; that is a time for fasting and prayer, for sackcloth and ashes, for judging ourselves and rending our hearts; that is a time to mourn, and not to be merry: Isa. xxii. 12—14, "In that day did the Lord God of hosts call to weeping, and to mourning, and to baldness, and to girding with sackcloth: and behold joy and gladness, slaying oxen, and killing sheep, eating flesh, and drinking wine, &c. And it was revealed in mine ears by the Lord of hosts, Surely this iniquity shall not be purged from you till ye die." It provokes God exceedingly, that man calls for mirth when he call for mourning.

Obs. 2. The godly and faithful, both ministers and people, are affected with judgments coming upon church or state. "Should we then make mirth?" Isa. xxii. 4, 5. "Look away from me; I will weep bitterly, labour not to comfort me, because of the spoiling of the daughter of my people: for it is a day of trouble, and of treading down, and of perplexity." So Jer. ix. 1, "Oh that my head were waters, and mine eyes a fountain of tears," &c. So Christ wept over Jerusalem, Luke xix. 41—44, for the evils he saw coming.

"It contemneth the rod of my son, as every tree." These words are difficult. The Hebrew stands thus, the rod of my son contemning every tree.

The word "rod," שבט some render, tribe, and so make the sense to be, the tribe of Judah, the son of God, which Nebuchadnezzar, the sword of God, despised as every tree; but thus tribe, son, and every tree, do fall in to be the same.

Others make the sense thus, This sword, the rod of my son, viz. my people, I have appointed to punish them with; and however they have been able to endure other rods, yet this is stronger than they, and shall not be broken or frustrated of its end, when I shall use it: this sense is not to be despised; as if by "son," Nebuchadnezzar be meant, who being armed with power, contemned every tree, the green tree and the dry tree, the high and the low tree, all the men of the land of Israel. If Cyrus, who delivered God's people, be styled but his "servant," it were much that Nebuchadnezzar, who destroyed them, should be called his "son."

Others interpret the words of Christ, who is meant by "son," and "rod," to be the sword in Christ's hand; he was resolved now to cut down every tree by his judgment, and to break this nation in pieces by the iron rod and sword he had in his hand: the Father speaks concerning his Son to the prophet. And the 11th verse strengthens this interpretation: "He hath given it to be furbished." Who is that "he," but the Son? and who gave it "into the hand of the slayer," but he? and that was Nebuchadnezzar.

Obs. 1. Christ hath rods and judgments in his hand. "The rod of my Son." Christ is not all mercy, though full of mercy; "the Father hath committed all judgment unto him;" Rev. vi. 16, the Lamb hath wrath in him, as well as meekness; Christ is a Lion to tear in pieces, as well as a Samaritan, &c. See Psal. ii. 12.

Obs. 2. When sinners profit not, but are worse under lesser judgments, this provokes Christ to bring forth more heavy judgments. The rod of my Son, contemning every tree: though they stood it out against other rods, they should not be able to do so against this. When the axe comes to the root of trees, they must down: a knife they may despise, but an axe despises them.

Obs. 3. Some judgments are so grievous, as they sweep away all. This rod despised every tree, the strongest oaks, the tallest cedars, the king, princes, nobles, counsellors, soldiers, artificers, &c.

Obs. 4. From ver. 11, Enemies cannot hurt unless they have power and furniture given them. The sword was fitted for and given into the hand of the slayer; Nebuchadnezzar could not have stirred, destroyed a man in the land of Israel, unless Christ had empowered him. Pilate had no power but what was given him. No man or nation hath power against another, unless they are armed from God or Christ. Had the Jews kept in with them, none should ever have harmed them.

Ver. 12. "Cry and howl, son of man." The word

for "cry" is זעק which signifies to cry out on account of distress of mind. Jer. xxx. 15, "Why criest thou for thine affliction?" afflictions straitened and pressed the spirit of Jacob, so that he cried out. You have the word in Ezek. ix. 8; xi. 13, where it notes, crying from sorrow and pressure of mind.

"Howl." Beasts do howl when pinched with hunger, or suffer some great misery. The Hebrew word, ילל saith Abenacius, hath affinity with אלל and ליל words which signify night, and reduction in a manner to nothing; and when men are encompassed with great calamities, and ready to perish, then they howl. Isa. lxv. 14, "Ye shall cry for sorrow of heart, and howl for vexation of spirit:" the Hebrew is, for breaking of spirit; when their spirits should be broken, and they ready to sink, and be ruined, then they should howl.

"For it shall be upon my people." The Hebrew is, it hath been upon my people: it is usual with the Hebrew to put a preter-tense for the future, to signify the certainty of the thing; and so it is here.

"Upon all the people of Israel." In chap. xi. 1, you have "princes of the people." The word there is, שער whence our English word, sir, which is as much as prince, or lord: here it is "princes of Israel," and the word is, נשיאי *nesiee*, from נשא to prefer, lift up, set on high.

"Terrors by reason of the sword." The word for "terrors" is, מגורי which is variously rendered. The reading we have I like best, and most expositors agree in it; and so the word is rendered, Lam. ii. 22. Jer. vi. 25, "The sword of the enemy and fear is on every side."

"Smite therefore upon thy thigh." In chap. vi. 11, the Lord commanded the prophet to smite with his hand, stamp with his foot, and here to smite upon his thigh; which were gestures to express grief and sorrow in great and sad calamities: *Tundebant fœmora palmis*, They smote upon their thighs with their hands.

Obs. 1. The calamities of wars are matter of great mourning and sad gestures. Cry, howl, smite upon thy thigh. Jer. iv. 6—8, God would bring evil from the north upon them, Nebuchadnezzar the lion was coming; "for this gird you with sackcloth, lament, and howl."

Obs. 2. The sword makes no distinction of persons. "It shall be upon my people, and upon all the princes of Israel;" they should find no more favour than others, not any, not the greatest of them, should be exempted from the evils of the sword. Jer. lii. 10, 11, "The king of Babylon slew the sons of Zedekiah before his eyes; he slew also all the princes of Judah in Riblah. Then he put out the eyes of Zedekiah."

Obs. 3. Times of war are times of fears. "Terrors by reason of the sword shall be upon my people." The sword drawn is a terrible thing, Josh. ii. 9; x. 12; Jer. xv. 8; xlvi. 3—5; xlix. 24, 29. The sword is *magor-missabib*, fear round about; it makes families, towns, cities, nations, to fear and tremble; when the sword is without, there is terror within, and such terror ofttimes as is destructive, Deut. xxxii. 25; men's hearts meditate such terrors, as bereave them of their wits, senses, lives.

Ver. 13. "Because it is a trial." The word for "trial" is, בחן to prove, examine, try. Now they should find and feel the sword more glistering, sharp, and destructive than ever.

"And what if the sword contemn even the rod? it shall be no more." Interpreters are perplexed about these words, as they are in the original, and what to make of them as translated, I know not. Those words, "the sword," and "more," are not in the text, and puzzle the sense. The Hebrew is thus, And what if also the rod despising, hath not been? that is, what if the rod heretofore or hitherto hath not been a despising rod, but rather despised? as Zedekiah and his nobles despised the oath and covenant made with Nebuchadnezzar, chap. xvii. 16; yet now it should be a despising rod: and so it suits with that in ver. 10, The rod of my Son, despising every tree; and that in ver. 12, "It shall be upon all the princes of Israel;" and with that in Hab. i. 10, "They shall scoff at the kings, and the princes shall be a scorn unto them; they shall deride every strong hold." Or thus, There is cause thou shouldst cry, howl, smite upon thy thigh, because the sword shall be a trial; and what also if it shall not be a despising rod? if it be a trying rod, there is cause enough to mourn, but it shall be a despising rod, and so there is more cause to mourn. If this rod make them not try their ways, repent, and turn, it shall be a rod to despise the stoutest of them, and to destroy them.

Obs. 1. That the judgments of God are trials, they discover and make known what people are. The fire tries the metals, and declares what is good silver, good gold, and what is reprobate. Deut. viii. 2, God kept them forty years in the wilderness, to prove them, and know what was in their hearts; the hard things they met with there, discovered some to be murmurers, some idolaters, some fornicators, some backsliders. Isa. viii. 21, "It shall come to pass, that when they shall be hungry, they shall fret themselves, and curse their king and their God:" when evil was upon them, then their wickedness appeared. So Jehoram, 2 Kings vi. 33, belched out his vileness in a time of distress, saying, "This evil is of the Lord; what should I wait for the Lord any longer?" he is a cruel God, destroys the people with famine, and puts them upon eating their own children, therefore I will wait no longer on him. When great winds are abroad, they tell you what trees are sound or rotten.

Obs. 2. God tries before he destroys; rods of trial come before rods of destruction. When the sword is drawn, furbished, and whet, the Lord tries men thereby, whether they will consider their ways, repent, and turn unto him, before he cut and destroy therewith. Tidings and terrors of the sword precede the strokes of it. Amos iv. 6, 9, the Lord sent a famine amongst them, but they returned not unto him; he tried them what they would do, he looked for their return. 2 Chron. vii. 13, 14, "If I shut up heaven that there be no rain, or if I command the locusts to devour the land, or if I send pestilence among my people; if my people which are called by my name, shall humble," &c. God tries his people by threatenings, by bringing judgments near unto them, by inflicting lesser judgments upon them, before he makes an utter destruction of them; that they may learn righteousness, humble themselves, and so either prevent the judgments, or have them turned into mercies.

Obs. 3. When rods of trial do us no good, then follow rods of destruction; when the trying rod hath been dispised, then comes the despising rod, the rod that will not regard young or old, high or low, prince or people. At first God did lightly afflict Zebulun and Naphtali, but that being in vain, afterwards he afflicts them more grievously, Isa. ix. 1. When Dimon profited not by her first strokes, God laid more upon her, Isa. xv. 9. When smiting the lintel of the door, and shaking the posts, did not prevail, then did the Lord cut and slay with the sword, Amos ix. 1. If fear work not, he hath a pit; if that do it not, he hath a snare, Isa. xxiv. 17, 18. When paternal chastisements profit not, God hath destroying judgments; he will deal then with men, not as erring children, but as open enemies.

Ver. 14—17. *Thou therefore, son of man, prophesy, and smite thine hands together, and let the sword be doubled the third time, the sword of the slain: it is the sword of the great men that are slain, which entereth into their privy chambers. I have set the point of the sword against all their gates, that their heart may faint, and their ruins be multiplied: ah! it is made bright, it is wrapped up for the slaughter. Go thee one way or other, either on the right hand, or on the left, whithersoever thy face is set. I will also smite mine hands together, and I will cause my fury to rest: I the Lord have said it.*

The instruments, causes, and end, of the sad judgments coming upon the Jews, being formerly declared, here the manner and circumstances thereof are laid down.

"Smite thine hands together." The Hebrew is, smite hand to hand; כף notes the concavity and hollowness of any thing, and so the hollow and palm of the hand. Whether this smiting of hands imports sorrow or joy is questioned; some make it to signify joy, prefiguring the pleasure of God in executing judgment upon the Jews; but when smiting or clapping of hands is referred to the creature to express joy, other words are used, as *saphack*, Job xxvii. 23; Lam. ii. 15: *macha*, Psal. xcviii. 8; Isa. lv. 12: *takang* or *takah*, Psal. xlvii. 1; Nah. iii. 19. Besides this, the prophet was in a mourning frame; ver. 10, when the sword is coming, "should we then make mirth?" and, chap. vi. 11, smiting with the hand imported sorrow, and so I conceive it doth here: "Smite thine hands together," once, twice, thrice, oft, for the evils that are coming.

"Let the sword be doubled the third time." The word for "doubled" is, כפל which signifies also, to repeat, reply. The sense is, let the sword come the second and third time. Some read the words thus, The sword shall come the third time. Nebuchadnezzar had come twice before, in Jehoiakim's and Jehoiachin's days, and after came in Zedekiah's, carrying him away to Babylon; and this is made the mind of the Lord in these words: but because two of these were past, and the Lord speaks of the time to come, we may understand them of the sword of Nebuchadnezzar upon Zedekiah, 2 Chron. xxxvi.; of the sword of Johanan against Ishmael, and the Jews, for murdering Gedaliah, Jer. xli.; and the sword of Nebuzaradan when he laid all waste, carried all away, leaving only a few to be vine-dressers and husbandmen, Jer. lii.

"The sword of the slain." A sword that is ready to slay, to slay the great ones, and to make great slaughter of them: when many are slain by the sword, that sword is the sword of the slain, or slaying sword.

"It is the sword of the great men that are slain." It is a sword appointed to slay the great men. In the Hebrew it is in the singular number, the sword of the great man slain, or, of great slaying.

"Which entereth into their privy chambers." The Hebrew is, chambering or lodging with them; חדר is a chamber, any secret, close place; it notes the inwards of man's heart, or soul, Prov. xviii. 8: the sword should enter into their chambers, into their bowels and souls, the fear of it should possess them. The Septuagint express it thus, Thou shalt cast them into fear, or amazement; the sword shall first enter into the secret of your souls, and fill you with terrors, and after enter into your bodies, and take away your lives.

Ver. 15. "I have set the point of the sword against all their gates." The word for "point" is אבחת which interpreters render, splendour, clamour, terror, slaughter, and these are all like the point of a sword to those who are besieged: properly it notes the point or edge of the sword, which God set against all their gates, their public gates of the city round about, and the private gates of their several houses; every where should the sword be, both in city and country, where they had gates, any rule or power.

"That their heart may faint." In times of great fears and dangers, men's hearts do often faint and fail them; when they have most need of heart, they are without hearts. God sent and set his sword for to dissolve and melt their hearts, so the word, מוג translated, to faint, signifies; all their spirit, vigour, and courage, should be dissolved, and so they should be faint, feeble, heartless. The Septuagint is, That their heart might be hurt or wounded.

"And their ruins be multiplied." In the Hebrew it is, to multiply offences: the soldiers would offend them, the sword would offend them, their straits would offend them, the slain would offend them, they met with nothing but offences, at which they stumbling fell also. If we take the words passively as they stand, the meaning is, that their destructions might be many, that multitudes of them might fall.

"It is wrapped up for the slaughter." This expression seems unsuitable for a sword, and expositors are put to it to make out the meaning of it. The original word means, to cover, clothe, put on, to hasten, and were better rendered, it is put on, or hastened for slaughter, than clothed or wrapped up for slaughter; it is harsh to say, clothed with the hilt, or wrapped up in the belt. Sanctius makes the clothing for slaughter, to be the fitting of it thereto.

Ver. 16. "Go thee one way or other, either on the right hand, or on the left." Here by an apostrophe the Lord speaks to the sword, and under that to the army of the Chaldeans, commissioning that and them to go through the land of Judea, and to execute his pleasure. The words in the Hebrew run thus, Unite thyself, right-hand thyself, put, or set thyself, left-hand thyself.

"Whithersoever thy faces are prepared." That is, Sword, unite thyself to the soldiers, soldiers, unite yourselves together, go the right-hand or left-hand way, which you have most mind unto, which way your spirits incline you most to, only see to it that you execute my pleasure upon all you meet. Be not afraid at what befell Sennacherib when he went against Jerusalem; I was against him, but I am with you.

Ver. 17. "I will also smite my hands together." In this verse is God's approbation of what the Chaldeans' sword and army should do; they should conquer and destroy the Jewish nation, and he would rejoice in it. Smiting of hands before expressed grief, and here it is an expression of joy; so it is used chap. xxv. 6. It notes not only God's approbation of the Babylonians' undertakings, but his encouragement of them to that work, that so he might execute his vengeance upon them, and be at rest; as it follows:

"I will cause my fury to rest." God's fury was stirred against them, and boiled in him, and when this fury should be poured out upon them by the Chaldeans' army, then should he be at ease, and comforted, as it is Ezek. v. 13, where these words were spoken to.

Obs. 1. It is no new thing for the prophets of the Lord to prophesy in sackcloth. Ezekiel must prophesy and smite his hands together, in token of mourning and heaviness; our prophet was in sackcloth, being a captive in Babylon, seeing the sad judgments which were coming upon Jerusalem. So Jeremiah, Hosea, Joel, Amos, had mournful spirits, and prophesied in sackcloth, they smote their hands together, and dropped out sad things. The times were black in their days, they are not clear now; is not the sword coming the third time? is it not putting on for slaughter? shall not the prophets mourn and smite their hands together?

Obs. 2. Where the word prevails not to reform a people, there the judgments of God will come in, one after another, to the destruction of a people. "Prophesy, and let the sword be doubled the third time." He had oft prophesied, but there appeared no repentance, no returning to God, therefore let the sword come again and again. Had they repented of their sins, God would have repented of the evils intended, Jer. xviii. 7, 8; but when people go on in their sins, God will go on in his judgments, even to destruction. See Lev. xxvi. 21, 22, 31—33; Deut. xxviii. 62.

Obs. 3. When God will punish sinners for their wickedness, there is no hiding-place to secure them from the stroke of God, be they great or mean ones; that is the sword of the great men, which entereth into their privy chambers; whatever holes, recesses, vaults, hiding-places, they had, the sword would find them out. God knows where men are when hid, and his hand can reach them as well as his eye see them. When the Syrians fled to Aphek to secure themselves from the sword of Ahab, a wall fell upon twenty-seven thousand, and slew them, 1 Kings xx. 30. In times of danger men think of shifting for themselves, of hiding here and there; but what are cities, towers, chambers, secret places? there is no safety in any of them, or any other place; see Amos ix. 2, 3. The only safe hiding-place, is in "the secret place of the Most High," Psal. lxxxi. 1, that is, in God himself; Psal. cxix. 114, "Thou art my hiding-place and shield." Be wise then, foresee evil coming, and hide yourselves in this hiding place: Prov. xxii. 3, "A prudent man foreseeth the evil, and hideth himself."

Obs. 4. When the Lord intends the destruction of a people, he will order things accordingly. "I have set the point of the sword against all their gates." Hereby all fleeing was prevented, and if they thought to stand and fight it out with the instruments he used, he made their hearts to faint, he threw stumbling-blocks in their way, he multiplied their ruins. When the Lord is against a nation, he besieges them with evils, stops and shuts up all doors of hope, takes away their hearts, makes those things matter of ruin which they made account would be their refuge. Jer. iv. 9, "At that day the heart of the king shall perish, and the heart of the princes; and the priests shall be astonished, and the prophets shall wonder;" and why? "the sword reacheth unto the soul."

Obs. 5. It is the Lord's commission, encouragement, and providence, which puts life into military undertakings, and makes them successful. "Go thee one way or other, to the right hand or to the left." God bid Nebuchadnezzar, the army, and sword, go; had he not bid them go, been with them in their going, and ordered all their undertakings, they had been vain and fruitless. Armies are but instruments, and if they do execution upon enemies, if they conquer and subdue, it is by the hand and power of God.

Obs. 6. Execution of justice upon sinful persons and nations is pleasing and delightful unto God. He put on Nebuchadnezzar to go and destroy the Jewish nation, and when he went, he smote his hands together at it, he rejoiced; by this means the Lord eased himself of his adversaries, as he speaks, Isa. i. 24, rested from his fury, and comforted himself. They had pleased themselves in their sinnings, but wearied God thereby; now God would please himself in punishing them for their sins, and weary them, yea, waste them with his judgments.

Obs. 7. That which is matter of mourning unto man, is matter of joy unto God. This rises from the various sense of the phrase, smiting of hands; because the sword was come, therefore Ezekiel was to smite his hands together, and manifest mourning, and because it was to come, God would smite his hands together, and manifest joy.

Ver. 18—24. *The word of the Lord came unto me again, saying, Also, thou son of man, appoint thee two ways, that the sword of the king of Babylon may come: both twain shall come forth out of one land: and choose thou a place, choose it at the head of the way to the city. Appoint a way, that the sword may come to Rabbath of the Ammonites, and to Judah in Jerusalem the defenced. For the king of Babylon stood at the parting of the way, at the head of the two ways, to use divination: he made his arrows bright, he consulted with images, he looked in the liver. At his right hand was the divination for Jerusalem, to appoint captains, to open the mouth in the slaughter, to lift up the voice with shouting, to appoint battering rams against the gates, to cast a mount, and to build a fort. And it shall be unto them as a false divination in their sight, to them that have sworn oaths: but he will call to remembrance the iniquity, that they may be taken. Therefore thus saith the Lord God; Because ye have made your iniquity to be remembered, in that your transgressions are discovered, so that in all your doings your sins do appear; because, I say, that ye are come to remembrance, ye shall be taken with the hand.*

These words do treat of Nebuchadnezzar's consultation about his military undertakings, and the way he took to accomplish the same, viz. divination, and the event thereof in respect of the Jews.

"Appoint thee two ways." In the fourth chapter the prophet was to portray out Jerusalem upon a tile, and to lay siege against it; here he is commanded to foretell the coming of the king of Babylon, not verbally, but typically, by way of representation, and he must draw out upon the same tile, or some such thing, two ways; put before thee, or make unto thee, two ways.

"That the sword of the king of Babylon may come." Much was said before of the sword, the drawing, sharpening, furbishing, and slaughtering of it; and here is a plain discovery whose sword it was, the sword of a king, and the king of Babylon.

"Both twain shall come forth out of one land." These two ways must come out of Babylon; he must first draw a line, and then branch it out into two, as a river runs a long tract in one channel, and then divides itself into two.

"Choose thou a place, choose it at the head of the way to the city." Choose you the hand, side, or place, where the king of Babylon, having mustered up his forces, may deliberate and consult what to do, whither to go, which way to take; let it be at the head of the way. Where the beginning of the two ways was, that was the head of the way.

Ver. 20. "Appoint a way that the sword may come to Rabbath." Draw out one way leading to Rabbath, that so Nebuchadnezzar may see work for his sword there. Rabbath was the royal city, and chief city of the Ammonites, 2 Sam. xii. 26, who were the posterity of Ben-ammi, the incestuous son of Lot, Gen. xix. 38.

"And to Judah in Jerusalem the defenced." That the sword may come not only to the Ammonites, but also to the Jews which dwelt in Jerusalem, a city well fortified. Rabbath was strengthened by waters, 2 Sam. xii. 27, and therefore was called "the city of waters;" but Jerusalem was compassed about with hills, Psal. cxxv. 2, had strong towers and bulwarks, Psal. xlviii. 12, 13, and was called a strong city, Psal. xxxi. 21.

Ver. 21. "For the king of Babylon stood at the parting of the way, at the head of the two ways." Here is a preter-tense put for the future; the king of Babylon had not yet stood there, but he shall stand at the parting of the way, at the mother of the way; when a way divides into or begets two ways, the Hebrew calls the first way, the mother of the other, and head of them, as here, "the head of the two ways."

"To use divination." He being doubtful what to do, whither to go, the right-hand or left-hand way, should make a stand, where the way parted, to consult; he thought it not meet to divide his army, and to go both ways at once: to set upon two such great cities as Jerusalem and Rabbath, each of them would require his whole strength, and therefore he would try by divination to which of them he should go.

"He made his arrows bright." This is the first kind, which expositors call, *βελομαντία, seu ῥαβδομαντία*, a divining by weapons, or rods. The Hebrew for "arrows" is, בחצים which signifies an arrow or knife, so called from cutting or dividing, for חץ is from חצה to cut in pieces. Some render it, arrows, as the manner of divining by them, was either by writing the names of Jerusalem upon one, and of Rabbath upon another, and then putting them with other arrows into a quiver. The arrow first drawn out with either of those names upon it, determined the case. If the arrow with Jerusalem upon it was first drawn, they then went thither; if that with Rabbath upon it, then they went to Rabbath. Some affirm they made the arrows to leap out of the quiver by magic art, and that which leaped on the right hand led them to Jerusalem, that on the left hand to Rabbath. So the Septuagint renders the words *τοῦ ἀναβρασάι ῥάβδον*, to make the rod spring forth. Others make the manner of this divining to be, by the king's throwing up an arrow into the air, which if it fell on the right hand, they went the right-hand way; if on the left hand, the left-hand way. Others render the word, knives, and so the sense may run thus; He made bright his knives, to cut open the birds or beasts that were to be sacrificed: or take the word for arrows or knives, he made them bright, he scoured and polished them, that in the brightness of the iron or steel, they might discern something to direct.

"He consulted with images." This is the second kind of divination which he used. שאל בתרפים so is the Hebrew, he asked of or consulted with teraphims. This word teraphim is oft used in the Old Testament, and is divers times translated images, whereas in the Hebrew it is teraphim; so you have it, Gen. xxxi. 19, 34, 35; 1 Sam. xv. 23; xix. 13, 16; Zech. x. 2; 2 Kings xxiii. 24. It is fit to inquire therefore what teraphims were: not instruments of brass to distinguish the minutes or parts of hours, nor astrological images made to speak; but, as Shindler observes, they were images made like men, to this end, that they might in or by them know things to come. So Kircher saith of תרפ they were images of men, made to receive and communicate intelligence from heaven about things to come. The teraphim Michal laid in the room of David, was like unto a man, 1 Sam. xix.; and that it was a divining image, may appear by that you find in Gen. xxx. 27. "I have learned by experience," saith Laban, "that God hath blessed me for thy sake." The Hebrew is, נחשתי I have divined, he had his teraphims by which he could do it; and it is conceived by the learned, that Rachel stole away her father's teraphims upon this ground, that he might not divine by them which way she and Jacob were gone. The Septuagint, Zech. x. 2, calls the teraphim, *ἀποφθεγγομένοι*, speaking; and Hos. iii. 4, *δήλων*, representing, which the Targum renders, *mechoni annuntiantes;* all which do show, that men held a divining virtue to be in their teraphims, and so Nebuchadnezzar conceived, and therefore consulted with his teraphims.

"He looked in the liver." This is the third kind of divination. When they sacrificed, they opened the sacrifice, and observed the inwards and entrails exactly, especially the kidney, the heart, the milt, and the liver, whence they were called *extispices*, and *aruspices*, because they did it at the altar. The liver, as Lavater saith, was *fons vaticinii*, from thence they made their chiefest divinations: if that were sound and good, without blemish, they made successful divinations thereupon; but if vitiated or dislocated, their divinations were untoward and unhappy.

Such divinations as these mentioned were unlawful; Deut. xviii. 10, 11, "There shall not be found among you any one that useth divination, or an observer of times," &c.; they are abomination to the Lord. Divining in such ways was a grievous sin; 1 Sam. xv. 23, "Rebellion is as the sin of divination;" which is not countenanced by that Prov. xvi. 10, "Divination is in the lips of the king," for so the Hebrew is: here the word divining is taken in a good sense, and is spoken of the king sitting in judgment, whom God would guide, so that he should find out the truth; for the next words are, "his mouth transgresseth not in judgment." When the two harlots were before Solomon, pleading each for the live child, and the truth was obscured by their pleading, God endued the king with a divining spirit, so that he found out the truth, and gave a divine sentence; but this makes nothing for the wicked divinations here mentioned.

Ver. 22. "At his right hand was the divination for Jerusalem." Here you have the issue of his divinations, which determined him, being doubtful before, which way he should go, viz. the right-hand way, and that was to Jerusalem; the arrows, images, and livers, did all concur, according to their divinations, that Nebuchadnezzar should go thither.

"To appoint captains." The word for "captains" is, כרים *carim*, from כר *car*, which signifies a pasture, a lamb, and battering-rams, which were military instruments, used in sieges; and so it was rendered, Ezek. iv. 2; and so it is rendered in the latter part of this verse, where it is said, "to appoint battering-rams against the gates;" but because the word is twice in the verse, it is rendered in the first place "captains," for the word signifies the heads and chief men of an army; so you have it, 2 Kings xi. 4, 19. The king having consulted, now fell to action, and appointed captains to lead the army to Jerusalem.

"To open the mouth in the slaughter." It may be read, to open the mouth to slaughter; so Montanus, Lavater, and Vatablus read the words; and the sense is, the captains should exhort and stir them up to kill and slay their enemies. Or if you will, take opening the mouth here, for making a breach in the wall. For "slaughter," *vid.* Junius. The captains should come close, besiege the city, make a breach, enter, and slay, and in their entrance and slaying, should open their mouths, and make shouting; as follows,

"To lift up the voice with shouting." When great exploits are attempted by men against their enemies, oft they shout, and make a great noise, that so they may daunt and terrify them. Doubtless the clamour and shouts of these barbarous Babylonians, did much perplex the Jews, made their hearts faint and hands feeble; to see the mounts, forts, and battering-rams at their gates, could not but trouble them, but when they made breaches in their walls, entered and slew men with shouting, this affrighted them and sunk their spirits. They afflicted Jerusalem with shouting, and the Lord threatened Babylon in the same kind; Jer. li. 14, "I will fill thee with men, as with caterpillers; and they shall lift up a shout against thee."

Obs. 1. The Lord knows things to come most certainly, yea, as certainly as if done already. He knew that Nebuchadnezzar would come out of Babylon, what way he would come, and where he would make a stand and consult, which he shows to the prophet, and speaks of as done already, ver. 21, "The king of Babylon stood at the parting of the way, at the head of the two ways, to use divination." The Lord sees things afar off, and knows what shall be in ages to come. Hereby he confounds all idol gods, and proves himself to be the true God. Isa. xli. 22, 23, "Let them bring forth, and show us what shall happen; declare to us things for to come. Show the things that are to come hereafter, that we may know that ye are gods:" if you cannot discover things that lie in the dark, if you cannot foretell what shall be many years hereafter, you are no gods; I can do it, and therefore am God, the true and only God: Isa. xlvi. 9, 10, "I am God, and there is none like me, declaring the end from the beginning, and from ancient times the things that are not yet done." God had foretold things in Moses' days, that were not accomplished in Isaiah's; and he foretold things in Isaiah's days, that are not yet all fulfilled: see Isa. lx. throughout, chap. lxv. 17; lxvi. 22. In Peter's days, the new heavens and the new earth were expected, 2 Pet. iii. 13, and are not yet given out; so, many things hath the Lord foretold in the Revelation, which we wait still to see fulfilled.

Obs. 2. That even heathens, when they are in straits, doubtful what to do, and how to proceed in their undertakings, will not neglect, but use variety of means for resolution. Nebuchadnezzar uses divination, he makes bright the arrows, consulted his gods, he looked into the liver; these were such means as he conceived conducible to such a purpose, though sinful. Heathens have been forward in their straits and doubts to get resolution, Dan. ii. 1, 2, 5, 6, 9; v. 5—8. It is incident to the nature of man, both heathens and others, to run to unlawful means in their necessities. God's own people did it; Hos. iv. 12, "My people ask counsel at their stocks, and their staff declareth unto them;" they consulted with their images, which in disgrace the Spirit of God calls "stocks," and from their staves or rods they took divinations. Such practices let us abhor, but use those means God approves of, and hath appointed, for our resolution in our doubts and straits. Instead of making bright the arrows, let us purge and make bright our consciences, and they will tell us something; instead of consulting teraphims, stocks, and stones, let us consult with God and his servants; instead of looking into the liver of beasts, let us look into the book of God, there we shall find light to dispel our darkness, and to direct our ways: David made God's testimonies his delight and counsellors, Psal. cxix. 24.

Obs. 3. God overrules the wicked acts of men, and makes them subservient to his will and ends. Nebuchadnezzar uses divinations which God had forbidden; and the divination might have been at his left hand for Rabbath, or Philadelphia, which is the same; but God had a purpose to bring him to Jerusalem, to cast up a mount, to build a fort there, to set battering-rams against the gates thereof, and therefore secretly, by his providence, he ordered the divination, that it should be at his right hand for Jerusalem. Whatever the lot is, wheresoever it be cast, "the whole disposing thereof is of the Lord," Prov. xvi. 33; Providence runs through the evil counsels of men, and makes use of them, their counsels and actions, to accomplish the good pleasure and righteous ends of the blessed God: by the arts, policies, methods, wiles, depths, designs of the devil, and devilish men, God carries on his own work, and nothing puts him or his work out of the way. Divinations of heathens promote the work of Heaven. This is a mystery, but full of truth and admiration, that God makes the worst tools and instruments, all wicked men, and their ways, to serve his providence, further his ends, and advance his glory; the devil did it in tempting Eve, and Judas in betraying Christ.

Ver. 23. "And it shall be unto them as a false divination in their sight." The Jews at Jerusalem would not believe this typical prophecy of Ezekiel, representing the coming of Nebuchadnezzar, and besieging of their city; they looked upon what he said as a false and foolish divination. What! hath Nebuchadnezzar made bright his arrows, consulted his teraphims, looked into the liver? we neither care for nor fear him, or his coming. They saw not God's hand in these things which ordered them so; however superstitious and wicked that Nebuchadnezzar was, he was confirmed in his work and way for their ruin.

"To them that have sworn oaths." The Hebrew is, swearing oaths to them. Rabbi David expresses the words thus, *Propter juramenta juramentorum ipsis*, For the oaths upon oaths made to them. The false prophets had by many oaths confirmed them, that the city should never be taken, whereupon they were secure as men that keep sabbaths, who are at rest. The Septuagint turns those words, ἑβδομαζων τὰς ἑβδομάδας αὐτοῖς, weeking a week, or sabbatizing a sabbath. This variety rises from the Hebrew word שבע which signifies seven, and thereupon a sabbath, and also to swear. In this sense we take it; and the Jews might be secure upon the oaths of their false prophets, but whether they made such oaths is doubtful; rather, because of the oaths between them and the Egyptians, for having violated the oath and covenant with the Babylonians, they entered league with the Egyptians, chap. xvii. 15, who promised them help, horses, and much people, and that against the Babylonians, if ever they should come.

"But he will call to remembrance the iniquity, that they may be taken." The word "he" being הוא in the original, is *hoc*, as well as *hic*, and may make the sense thus, This thing, viz. their slighting the prophecy, as a false divination, and their oathing of it with the Egyptians, shall call to remembrance that iniquity for which they shall be taken: or, This thing, viz. this divination, falling on the right hand of Nebuchadnezzar, and leading him to Jerusalem, will bring to mind the iniquity, that is, the perfidiousness of Zedekiah and the rest, in breaking the oath, that they may be taken. If we read it, "he," that is, Nebuchadnezzar, he will remember the iniquity of Zedekiah, that he and those with him might be taken.

Obs. 1. That the messages and passages of the messengers of God are matter of scorn to profane and wicked men. "It will be unto them as a false divination in their sight." When the prophet portrayed out the way the king of Babylon should come, the things he should do, the siege he should make about Jerusalem, and the effects thereof, all these were reputed by them lying things, false divinations. What he told them in the latter end of the twentieth chapter, they cried out of as parables, dark and obscure things, which they understood not; and here they account his typical threatenings as falsehood and lies. When the false prophets fed them with lying visions and divinations, they were honoured and believed, 1 Kings xxii. 11, 12; Ezek. xiii. 6, but when the true prophets told them the mind of the Lord, they were reproached, as Jeremiah, "Thou speakest falsely," chap. xliii. 2; they were smitten and imprisoned, as Micaiah, 1 Kings xxii; their lives were sought, Jer. xxxviii. 4; yea, they were put to death, 2 Chron. xxiv. 20, 21.

Obs. 2. That those who break and make oaths for their own ends, making no conscience thereof, God leaves them to injudiciousness of spirit, and to stumble at his word and threats. "It shall be unto them as a false divination in their sight, to them that swear oaths." They sware to Nebuchadnezzar, and violated what they had sworn for their own advantages, and then sought for their security to the Egyptians; but what was the fruit hereof? they were given over to injudicious minds and impenitent hearts, so that they discerned not God's proceedings towards them, nor the prophet's language to them. Perfidious and unjust dealings do so blind and harden, that the word and ways of God become snares and stumblingblocks unto them.

Obs. 3. The iniquities of princes and people do not always lie hid, but in time appear for the ruin of those who have committed them. "But he," or, this thing, "will call to remembrance the iniquity, that they may be taken." Zedekiah, his nobles, and people, sinned in breaking with Nebuchadnezzar, and falling in with Egyptians; they thought that time would bring a veil over those passages, that they should be buried in the dark, lie still and never see light more; but those iniquities were brought to mind, when the divination fell on the right hand, and drew Nebuchadnezzar to Jerusalem. He called to mind what cause he had to invade their land, and besiege that city; he remembered how perfidiously they had dealt with him, and thereupon roused up himself and forces, to set upon them with all their might. Princes' and states' iniquities may be couchant and dormant for a season, but at last they will awake, appear, and prove lions rampant. Let not any, great or small, flatter themselves that their sins are forgotten, because they hear not of them; they will be called to mind to their detriment, if not their destruction. Saul's sin in slaying the Gibeonites was unthought of, but by a famine it was called to remembrance, and cost the lives of seven of his sons, 2 Sam. xxi.

Ver. 24. "Because ye have made your iniquity to be remembered," &c. In this verse the Lord gives a definitive sentence concerning the Jews, they "shall be taken with the hand;" and lays down the reasons thereof.

1. They did those things which "made their iniquity to be remembered;" they gloried they had shaken off the Babylonish yoke, which brought their perjury and rebellion to remembrance; God remembered it, Nebuchadnezzar remembered it.

2. They went on in other wicked courses; in all their doings, their sinning appeared, they sinned openly.

You have three words here which seldom meet in one verse, "iniquity," "transgression," and "sin;" the like is in Job xiii. 23, and in Exod. xxxiv. 7.

The word for "iniquity" is עון which signifies, obliquity, crookedness, perverseness, injustice, and is contrary to that which is right and equal; which our English word, iniquity, imports. The word for "transgression" is, פשע which notes rebellion, obstinacy, maliciousness. The third word is, חטאה which is, "sin" in a lower degree; any or every going aside from the rule, any aberration from the way of God, any failing in duty. The first of these the Septuagint terms *ἀδικία*, the second *ἀσέβεια*, the third *αμαρτία*, injustice, impiety, sin, or error.

"You shall be taken with the hand." By "hand" the prophet means the Assyrian army, which should come, take the city, and them in it.

Obs. 1. Open, impudent sinning, brings to mind former iniquities. They had cast off the Babylonish yoke in an unjust and wicked way; they went on glorying in their shame, and their latter sins brought to mind their former; their transgressions were so open, discovered, their sins so apparent in all their doings, that they made their iniquity to be remembered; they provoked God to plague them for their present and former sins. Thieves, when taken in some wicked acts, their former villanies come to light. As one sin begets another, so one sin discovers another. Many, having sinned in prostituting their bodies to those they should not, afterwards make away the children had by them; so their sins breaking out, former iniquities are brought to remembrance, and themselves to punishment; men discover their sins, and their sins discover them. Here they made their iniquities to be remembered, and their iniquities brought them to remembrance.

Obs. 2. Public sins bring public judgments. They had openly broken with Nebuchadnezzar, they gloried in what they had done, and went on in such vile courses as were apparent to heaven and earth; and because it was so, therefore Nebuchadnezzar is sent against them, to take and ruin them. The Lord never lets in public desolations upon a church or state, till their sins are become public and incorrigible. It was so with Jerusalem at first, 2 Chron. xxxvi. 14—17; and it was so with Jerusalem at last, Matt. xxiii. 37, 38; their sins were public, and God most justly brought public evils upon them.

Obs. 3. That God hath hands to apprehend sinners with. "They shall be taken with the hand." The Babylonish army was the hand of God, and with it he apprehended the sinners in Zion, slew many of them, and led the rest captives into Babylon. The instruments God uses to punish his people sinning with, are sometimes called swords, Psal. xvii. 13; sometimes axes, saws, rods, staves, Isa. x. 15; sometimes his battle-axe, and weapons of war, Jer. li. 20; sometimes his net and snare, Ezek. xvii. 20; his pit, chains, chap. xix. 4; all which are the hand of God, Psal. xvii. 14; and in the hand of God he uses them to do that which hands do; by these he takes plagues, and destroys sinners.

Ver. 25—27. *And thou, profane wicked prince of Israel, whose day is come, when iniquity shall have an end, thus saith the Lord God; Remove the diadem, and take off the crown: this shall not be the same: exalt him that is low, and abase him that is high. I will overturn, overturn, overturn, it: and it shall be no more, until he come whose right it is; and I will give it him.*

These words are an apostrophe to the prince of Israel, declaring what should befall him, and the whole kingdom of Israel. He should be deprived of his kingly dignity, the kingdom ruined, and abide so, till the Lord should give it to him it belonged unto.

Concerning the "prince of Israel," he is,

I. Described to be "profane and wicked."

II. The time is intimated of his misery; both which are in ver. 25.

Ver. 25. "And thou, profane wicked prince of Israel." This prince of Israel was Zedekiah, and the titles given him are, not, Your sacred majesty, or, Your excellency's highness, but, "Thou profane wicked prince." His profaneness and wickedness doubtless was great, though much be not specified in the word; yet something is set down therein, 2 Chron. xxxvi. 12, "He did that which was evil in the sight of the Lord his God, and humbled not himself before Jeremiah the prophet speaking from the mouth of the Lord;" he despised the word and prophet of the Lord; and ver. 13, "He rebelled against king Nebuchadnezzar, who had made him swear by God, but he stiffened his neck, and hardened his heart from turning unto the Lord God of Israel;" he profaned the holy name of God. Being perfidious and obstinate, he fell in with Pharaoh king of Egypt, and sought help of him against Nebuchadnezzar, Ezek. xvii. 15; and so trusted in man, and not in God. He was like the other lions, which learned to catch the prey, and devoured men, Ezek. xix.; and so was cruel, bloody. "He did evil according to all that Jehoiakim had done," Jer. lii. 2; and he did abominations, 2 Chron. xxxvi. 8; and in his days was as gross idolatry in Jerusalem, and in the temple, as ever before: Ezek. viii. then was there the image of jealousy; then did the ancients of Israel worship creeping things, abominable beasts and idols; then did they worship the sun towards the east; then was Tammuz in the temple, and women weeping for Tammuz: so that he upheld the vilest idolatry that ever Jerusalem had, he was the cause of their total ruin. It is not without cause, therefore, that the prophet affixes these titles to the crown, "Thou profane wicked prince of Israel:" and profaneness was not peculiar to the prince, but prophets, priests, and people were under that denomination: Jer. xxiii. 15, "From the prophets of Jerusalem is profaneness gone forth into all the land;" the court prophets countenanced and communicated all the court profaneness; and 2 Chron. xxxvi. 14, "The chief of the priests and people transgressed very much, after all the abominations of the heathen."

Vatablus reads the words thus, And thou, O prince, condemned to death: and he cites the Chaldee paraphrast, in which it is to the same purpose, O thou prince of Israel, who art to be cut off by the sword.

The prophet may seem here to forget himself in speaking so opprobriously of the prince, which the law forbad, Exod. xxii. 28. Eccl. x. 20, they might neither think nor speak evil of the ruler, nor wish evil to him; and here Ezekiel calls Zedekiah the prince of Israel, profane, and wicked: and in so doing he sinned not; for being a prophet, he was to give out what the Spirit of God gave in, and moved him unto. So dealt Jeremiah by Coniah, calling him "a despised broken idol, a vessel wherein was no pleasure," chap. xxii. 28. They would not flatter princes, by being false to truth. When it is done from a private and depraved spirit, then it is ill.

"Whose day is come, when iniquity shall have an end." The words in Hebrew are, whose day of his is come, in time or season an end of iniquity. O Zedekiah, the day of thy punishment is at hand, wherein shall be an end of thy wickedness; thou shalt no longer be king, but suffer for what thou hast done.

Some by "iniquity" understand punishment, and so the sense is, thy day is come when punishment, that is, destruction, shall be thy end; thou and thy kingship shall be laid in the dust. The Hebrew for "when" is, עֵת which is of the same signification as καιρὸς is, it notes both time and opportunity of time; and whether by "iniquity," sin, or punishment of sin, be understood, or both, is not much material: God will not suffer thee to go on any longer in thy profane and wicked courses, the time and season is at hand, wherein he will punish thee, and so put an end to thy sinning; as before.

Obs. 1. That princes ofttimes are far from piety and justice. "And thou, profane wicked prince of Israel." Of all princes in the world, the princes of Israel had cause to be holy and just. They were seated where the worship of the true God was; they had the law of Moses, and were commanded to read it continually, and not to depart from it to the right hand or to the left, Deut. xvii. 18—20; they had the sanhedrim, the priests, and prophets to counsel and advise them: yet princes of Israel were profane, they minded not the law of Moses or the worship of God, they despised priests and prophets, they were wicked, they persecuted good men and were perfidious to other princes, both Jehoiakim and Zedekiah were so to Nebuchadnezzar, 2 Kings xxiv. 1, 20. The profaneness and perfidiousness of princes hath been great. Among all the kings of Israel there was none good; they followed Jeroboam and Ahab, who were profane and wicked. Few among the kings of Judah were found good. How profane was Pharaoh, when he said, "Who is the Lord, that I should obey him?" Exod. v. 2. How profane was Belshazzar, when he quaffed in the bowls of the temple! Dan. v. 2—4. How profane was Ahaz, that thrust aside the Lord's altar, and set up the Damascene altar! 2 Kings xvi. How profane was Jehoiakim, that cut the roll of Jeremiah in pieces, and cast it into the fire! Jer. xxxvi. 23. How profane was Herod, who mocked Christ, set him at nought, and arrayed him in a scornful manner! Luke xxiii. 11. They were kings that gave their power and strength to the beast, and made war with the Lamb, Rev. xvii. 12—14. You may read the horrible profaneness of Antiochus in 1 Macc. i. 46—52; he sent letters to Jerusalem to forbid what God had appointed; he commanded them to offer swine's flesh, and unclean beasts; that they should defile their souls, and pollute themselves with uncleanness; that they might forget the law, and change all the ordinances; and if they would not do so, they should die for it. Kings and rulers have been the greatest enemies to the ways of God and Christ; they, above others, have set themselves against them, Psal. ii. 2, 3. Hence they are counselled to "be wise" and to "kiss the Son," ver. 10, 12.

Obs. 2. That the prophets and ministers of God are not to fear the faces or frowns of the greatest, but to reprove them sharply, being evidently guilty. Thus dealt Ezekiel with Zedekiah, "Thou profane wicked prince of Israel:" though he were great, yet he spares him not, but brands him with his wickedness, and sets it upon record for after generations. John Baptist did the like by Herod; when he was upon taking his brother Philip's wife, he told him it was unlawful, and would be an incestuous match, Mark vi. 18; he was faithful in his ministry, and would not flatter Herod himself. Neither magistrates nor ministers should fear or flatter the greatest, because they are agents for and ambassadors of the great God of heaven, in comparison of whom the greatest on earth are as potsherds.

Obs. 3. That as princes have their times for sinning, so there are times for their suffering. Zedekiah's day was come, when iniquity should have an end; he had his times to show his profaneness and wickedness, and God had his time to reckon with him for the same. Princes may abound in wickedness, go long unpunished, but there is a day, a time, coming, wherein they shall smart for their lewdness. David tells you, the day of wicked men is coming, Psal. xxxvii. 13, that is, the time and season set for their destruction; which Peter expresseth thus, 2 Epist. ii. 3, "their judgment lingereth not, and their damnation slumbereth not," it is making towards them, and coming on swiftly, and will be bad to them when it comes. Jer. l. 27, "Woe unto them! for their day is come, the time of their visitation:" that day is a visiting day; God is the visitor, and he will so visit them as shall breed amazement. Job xviii. 20, Bildad, speaking of the calamities which should befall the wicked in his day, saith, "They that come after him shall be astonished at his day, as they that went before were affrighted:" the day of God's visiting those who are eminently wicked, as princes and great ones, is so dreadful, as that it affrights the living which behold it, and astonisheth the generations that come after it. You may see what he doth at such times, Job xii. 17—19, 21; Psal. lxxvi. 12. Psal. cx. 5, he strikes "through kings in the day of his wrath."

Ver. 26. "Thus saith the Lord God; Remove the diadem, and take off the crown." This verse contains a judicial sentence against Zedekiah, and declaration of mercy towards Jehoiachin.

"Remove the diadem." The verb here is infinitive, which may be read, Thus saith the Lord, to remove the diadem, that is, I am now resolved to take the diadem from Zedekiah's head, and to unking him: but it is usual among the Hebrews to put infinitives for indicatives and imperatives, and therefore some read it, I will take it away; others, Take away, remove the diadem. The word for "diadem" is מצנפת the same with צניפ both from צנפ to wrap, or compass about; and sometimes it is expressed by "hoods," which compassed the heads of women about, as Isa. iii. 23; sometimes by "mitres," which compassed the heads of priests about, as Zech. iii. 5; sometimes by "diadem," as Isa. xxviii. 5, which compassed the heads of kings, as here it did Zedekiah's. Some would have the high priest here meant, by the word *mitznepheth*, which they render *hidarim*, and belonged to him, Exod. xxviii. 4; but here is no speech of the high priest, it is spoken of the king, and notes his crown, not the high priest's mitre, and so the next words import.

"Take off the crown." In Hebrew it is, Lift up the crown: it now sits close to his head, and because he hath strengthened himself by making a league with the Egyptians, he thinks it so fast, that it shall not be removed; but lift it up, take it away, it shall no longer rest there. Of the word "crown" was spoken before, chap. xvi. 12; the word is עטרה *gnaterah*, from עטר to surround, to cover on every side. Kings' crowns do compass and cover their heads. So did the king of Rabbath's, which Joab took from the king's head, 2 Sam. xii. 30; the weight of which was a talent of gold, which the Annotations say, was sixty pounds weight; and Ainsworth, on Exod. xxxviii. 24, saith, a talent weighed one hundred and twenty pounds, and Diodate, one hundred and twenty-five. Whatever the natural weight of the crown and diadem was, the metaphorical weight exceeded it, viz. the cares, fears, and troubles of it were exceeding great. Crowns and diadems were *insignia regalia*; and when the Lord saith to the prophet, "Remove the diadem, take off the crown," he intends not that the prophet should do any such thing with his own hand, but that he should declare by his prophesying, that now the time was come, wherein Zedekiah should be stripped of all his regalities, be unkinged, and made as another man.

"This shall not be the same." This, not this, is the original. The Septuagint, *αὕτη οὐ τοιαύτη ἔσται*, This shall not be such. This crown shall not be this man's any longer; or, This crown shall not be thine, O Zedekiah; or, This crown, viz. this kingly government, shall not be this, an end of it is now come, thou art the last that shall be in Judea. Junius reads the words thus, This diadem, the crown shall be no more. Of this land, monarchical government shall down, great confusion shall follow; this shall not be the same. Thou dreamest, through the delusions of the false prophets, that Nebuchadnezzar will not come to invade the land, or if he do come, that thou shalt vanquish him by the help of Egypt, and so that thou and thy posterity shall reign still; but this shall not be, all regal power shall cease from thee and thy posterity.

"Exalt him that is low." The word for "low" is, השפלה from שפל which signifies, to be humbled, oppressed; and so "low" is opposite to proud, haughty, and those who are lifted up; it refers to one who is like a valley, not a mountain, and that was Jehoiachin, who yielding himself, by the counsel of Jeremiah, to Nebuchadnezzar, was carried into captivity, and there imprisoned; God's eye was upon him, and him, being depressed, oppressed, and low, he would have exalted. Some read, I will exalt, some, Exalt; the Hebrew is infinitive, and may be read indicatively or imperatively.

"Abase him that is high." The former words and these may be read thus, Heighten him that is low, and make him low that his high. This high person was Zedekiah, who through his pride and haughtiness of spirit, would not endure the Babylonish yoke; but perfidiously breaking with Nebuchadnezzar, fell in with the king of Egypt, grew confident, and despised the Assyrian power. He had high thoughts, high hopes, high confidences, he was become very mountainous; but this mountain must be levelled. Jeconiah, or Jehoiachin, being a valley, was exalted, Jer. lii. 31; 2 Kings xxv. 27; and Zedekiah being a mountain was abased, 2 Kings xxv. 6, 7; Jer. lii. 8—11.

Obs. 1. The Lord doth strip great ones, even kings and princes, of their glory, depose and abase them for their iniquities. Zedekiah was profane, perfidious, cruel, unjust; and what saith the Lord? "Remove the diadem, take away the crown, abase him that is high." Whoever be the instruments that take wicked kings, that spoil and punish them, it is God that commands and commissions the doing thereof. Nebuchadnezzar and his army were the hand that did the things here; they took Zedekiah, they pulled off his crown, slew his sons, all the princes, put out his eyes, bound him in chains, carried him to Babylon, imprisoned him there; but they could not have done these things, unless they had had commission and power from above: when kings are pulled down and removed, it is the Lord doth it, Dan. ii. 21.

Job xii. 18, "He looseth the bond of kings;" the Vulgate saith, the belt of kings, that is, their authority and power, say some expositors. Vatablus hath it, *disciplinam*, that tyrannical government they use he dissolves, and casts them into reproach, prison, captivity, and so "girdeth their loins with a girdle" of sackcloth and calamity; Vulgate is, he girds their loins with a rope. And ver. 19, "He leadeth princes away spoiled;" the word is, כהנים which though some turn priests, yet it signifies also princes and rulers, 2 Sam. viii. 18; and where our translators, who were much affected to priesthood, have put it priest in the text, as Exod. ii. 16; Gen. xli. 45; xlvii. 22, 26, yet in the margin they have put prince: and such God leads away spoiled; spoiled of their glory, their diadems, crowns, and princely robes; spoiled of their power, their soldiery, and strong holds; spoiled of their stratagems and designs; spoiled of their territories, dominions, and revenues; spoiled of their friends, comforts, and hopes. And whither doth he lead them? *In dementiam*, saith Junius and Tremellius, into madness and brutishness: and so he led Nebuchadnezzar, for his pride and other sins, to bellow and graze amongst the beasts. Into contempt, saith Job, chap. xii. 21, being led out of all desirable and delightful: "He poureth contempt upon them;" that is, he fills them with contempt and scorn, who were wont to be honoured of all, and confer honours upon others: and how grievous this is you may judge by that of Zedekiah, who chose rather to see Jerusalem on fire, than to yield himself into the hands of the Chaldeans, for fear of mocking, Jer. xxxviii. 18, 19; but afterwards he had scorn and misery enough, being roasted in the fire thereof. The Lord throws wicked princes from their height of glory and greatness, into extreme misery. You know how Adoni-bezek was served; and in Isa. xxii. 15—18, you may read of Shebna, who was a great man, "Behold, the Lord will carry thee away with a mighty captivity, and will surely cover thee:" and with what would he cover him? with misery and shame; for it follows, "He will surely violently turn and toss thee like a ball into a large country: there shalt thou die, and there the chariots of thy glory shall be the shame of thy Lord's house." God cast this Shebna, who was proud and high, into extreme misery and disgrace; he was driven out into a foreign land, where he was either torn in pieces by dogs or buried with the burial of an ass.

Obs. 2. The Lord pulls down and puts an end to kings and kingdoms at his pleasure. "This shall not be the same;" this crown shall be no more for thy head, any of thy posterity, or for the kingdom of Israel. Here God pulled down the kingdom of Israel or Judah, when it had stood near five hundred years, and put a period to monarchical government. Josephus, in his tenth book of the Jewish Antiquity, chap. 10, saith, that the kingly government lasted five hundred and fourteen years, six months, and ten days, from the beginning of Saul's reign to the end of Zedekiah's. Kingship began with them in God's wrath, and ended in his fury, 1 Sam. viii.; Ezek. xix. 12. The Assyrian empire lasted some one hundred and twenty years, and then God pulled it down, it was the same no more. The Athenian government by kings was some four hundred and ninety years, and then the Lord said, "This shall not be the same," he changed it into a popular government. The kingdoms of the earth are the Lord's, and he deals with them as he sees good, he breaks them in pieces, and gives them new forms, at his pleasure: Dan. ii. 20, 21, "Wisdom and power are his; he changeth the times and the seasons; he removeth kings, and setteth up kings;" he takes away one form of government, and sets up another; he puts down monarchy, and sets up aristocracy. After the continuation of monarchical government amongst us near six hundred years, the Lord hath said, "Remove the diadem, take off the crown, this shall not be the same;" he hath put a new form upon us, which must have its time, and period also.

What the Lord hath done here, and did long since in Israel, he is about to do in other kingdoms of the earth. The kings generally are so profane and wicked, that the Lord hath a controversy with them, and is speaking to this effect, if not by his prophets, yet by his providences; "Remove the diadem, take off the crown: these shall not be the same."

Seeing it is God which makes such changes, let not us stumble at his providences and dispensations. We are too apt to look at the tools he doth his work by, and to quarrel upon that account, and not to look at his hand which useth those tools. If kings lose their crowns, if their glory be laid in the dust, if posterity be excluded, if great alterations be made, it is the Lord's doing, and should be marvellous in our eyes, and not matter of murmuring.

Obs. 3. That as God brings down the haughty and proud ones, so he raises the humble and dejected. "Abase him that is high, exalt him that is low:" God minds the oppressed. Jehoiachin lay a long time in prison, and that in Babylon, even thirty-seven years, but he was not forgotten; God moved Evil-merodach to bring him out of prison, and lift up his head, Jer. lii. 31; and so made that good, in Job xii. 18, in another sense than you heard before; "He looseth the bond of kings," he brings them out of their disgrace, restraint, and misery, and girds their loins with a girdle of honour, liberty, and comfort. Psal. cxxxviii. 6, "Though the Lord be high, yet hath he respect unto the lowly," he advances and honours them. Job v. 11, he sets "up on high those that be low." Mary was low, and he set her among the highest; which made her to sing and say, Luke i. 52, "He hath put down the mighty from their seats, and exalted them of low degree." Let us take heed of high, aspiring thoughts, and remember what Christ hath given out, Luke xiv. 11, "Whosoever exalteth himself shall be abased; and he that humbleth himself shall be exalted." Self-exaltation makes way for abasement, and self-abasement makes way for exaltation. Psal. cxlvii. 6, "The Lord lifteth up the meek: he casteth the wicked down to the ground." Those who are meekened and sweetened by their afflictions, the Lord lifts up; but the wicked he casts them off, he casts them down, and down to the ground, into extreme misery.

Ver. 27. "I will overturn, overturn, overturn it." This verse is a threatening of the destruction of the kingdom, and the time of its continuance in that condition, which is, till he come, who is the right owner.

The Hebrew word is, עוה *affa*, from עוה which signifies to do crookedly, perversely, untowardly; all which do diminish the glory of what is done; and so here, God would diminish the glory of the crown, yea, the crown itself: "I will overturn it," and bring it to nothing, (for it refers to the crown,) and that should fall to the ground and be no more, the kingdom shall be utterly overthrown and laid waste.

The word is trebled, "I will overturn, overturn, overturn," to show not only the certainty and evidence of the thing, but the gradation and continuance of it; for the kingdom of Judah by certain degrees fell from its height, and was under the dominion of strangers; for after that Zedekiah was deposed by Nebuchadnezzar, there was no crown nor king more in Judah. After the captivity, there were no kings, but governors, captains, rulers, as Zerubbabel, Nehemiah, and others; after them, the high priests had the power, in whose hands it continued, even to Hyrcanus, who usurping kingly authority, saith Pradus, was miserably slain, Herod, a stranger, succeeding.

Sanctius makes this triplication of the word to point out the three great evils Zedekiah suffered. 1. The loss of his kingdom and revenues. 2. The loss of his sons and eyes. 3. His reproachful living in captivity.

A Lapide, and some others, understand by the trebling of the word, the three notable destructions that befell the Jews after this time, the first by Nebuchadnezzar, the second by Antiochus, the third by Titus and the Romans.

Others, by this triplication, judge the time of those three, Assir, Shealtiel, and Pedaiah, to be meant; in whose days the kingdom of Judah was very low, if not quite overthrown, but began to flourish again in the days of Zerubbabel, who was the son of Pedaiah, 1 Chron. iii. 19. But Assir may be read appellatively, and not as a proper name, (it is in the 17th verse of that 1 Chron. iii.) thus, The sons of Jeconiah the bound, for he was then bound, was a prisoner in Babylon; and so the word is used, Isa. xlii. 7, "to bring out the prisoners;" the Hebrew is, אסיר and if it be taken so, this triplication is marred.

Chemnitius hath another exposition of this triplication of the words, which the learned may see in his Harmony upon the Gospel, the first part, third chapter, the latter end.

Men are various in their thoughts about the triplicity of these words, but do generally agree in this, that the overthrow of the kingdom and kingly dignity is designed out thereby.

"It shall be no more." In Hebrew thus, even this hath not been; but here the preter-tense is put for the future, and so the Septuagint reads it, neither shall this be the same. Vatablus hath it, *Etiam hæc non fuit*, which he interprets thus, This alteration shall not be before Nebuchadnezzar come, to whom the judgment belongs, and to him will I deliver Zedekiah: so he. The French is, *et ne sera plus*, it shall be no more, the crown shall be no more, the crown of Judah; no king shall reign therein any more.

All the sons of Zedekiah were slain, Jer. lii. 10; and of Jehoiachin, Jeconiah, or Coniah, it is said, Jer. xxii. 30, "Write ye this man childless, a man that shall not prosper in his days: for no man of his seed shall prosper, sitting upon the throne of David, and ruling any more in Judah;" none of them shall ever come to kingly dignity.

"Until he come whose right it is." The sense is, The crown shall neither fit nor be fastened to any head, till he come that hath the true right to it; and that is neither Nebuchadnezzar nor Zerubbabel; nor Aristobulus, Alexander, or Hyrcanus, who assumed kingly dignity to themselves, in time of the Maccabees; but Christ the Messiah, who is the true Heir and Successor of David: when he comes, he shall raise up the kingdom of Judah, being miserably afflicted, destitute, and lost to the eye of the world; he changing it into a spiritual kingdom, shall restore it to as high, yea, a higher, glory than ever it had. The crown here was reserved and laid up for the Lord Christ, who was born King of the Jews, Matt. ii. 2; to whom the angel told Mary, that the Lord should give the throne of his father David, and that he should reign over the house of Jacob for ever, and have an endless kingdom, Luke i. 32, 33: upon this account it was, that Nathanael called him "the King of Israel," John i. 40; and that Christ said, "The Father hath committed all judgment unto the Son," John v. 22. The Father had appointed Christ to be King and Ruler, Micah v. 2; gave him power, Isa. ix. 6; he was to succeed David, sit upon his throne and kingdom to order the same, ver. 7; and his right thereunto both Matthew, in his first chapter, and Luke, in his third, do clear up, showing how he descended from David.

"And I will give it him." Christ, when he comes, shall not be kept off from his right; "I will give it him;" and he shall have the crown, it will fit his head, and sit fast upon it: though he come in a mean and low way, yet he shall be King, and reign.

Obs. 1. The Lord doth lay the glory of crowns and sceptres in the dust when he pleases. "I will overturn, overturn, overturn it." There is no crown so sure to any mortal's head, no kingdom so stable, but the Lord can pluck away the crown, shake the kingdom to pieces, throw out the possessors, and dispossess their heirs. He pulled the crown from Zedekiah's head, he brake his kingdom in pieces, he threw him out of his throne, deprived him and his sons of ever inheriting more.

Sometimes the Lord doth suddenly overturn empires and kingdoms; as Belshazzar's by Darius the Median, Dan. v. 30, 31; sometimes he proceeds gradually; and so he did with the kingdoms of Israel and Judah, Hos. v. 12, "I will be unto Ephraim as a moth, and to the house of Judah as rottenness." A moth eats up a garment by degrees, now it makes one hole in it, and anon another; so rottenness enters by degrees into a tree, first into one branch, then another, after into the body and root; so God by degrees ate up, wasted, and consumed those kingdoms. But be it suddenly or gradually, he overturns them when he pleases. God overturned the Persian monarchy, by the goat which had the notable horn, Dan. viii. 5, that was Alexander the Great, king of Greece; and when he was grown very great, ruled according to his will, his kingdom was broken, divided to others, and not to his posterity, Dan. xi. 3, 4; the Lord plucked up his kingdom, and quartered it among those who were not his heirs. The Lord made the sceptre depart from Egypt, Zech. x. 11; he cut off him; held the sceptre from the house of Eden, Amos i. 5. He breaks the staves of the wicked, and the sceptres of the rulers, Isa. xiv. 5; crowns, sceptres, kingdoms, he tumbles down, and lays in the dust.

Obs. 2. When God overturns crowns and kingdoms, he keeps them in such a condition while he pleases. "I will overturn, overturn, overturn: and it shall be no more, until he come whose right it is:" this was near five hundred years; for from Zedekiah's deposal to the birth of Christ were four hundred ninety and two years, which was a long season for his crown and kingdom to lie in darkness, and a desolate condition. Hosea told us long since, that the children of Israel should "abide many days without a king, and without a prince," chap. iii. 4. The kingdom of Israel was overturned by the hand of God above a hundred years before the kingdom of Judah, and lies overturned to this day; and so hath been above two thousand years in a sad, dark, distressed condition. When kingdoms, sceptres, and thrones are once overturned, they are not quickly raised up again. Their sins were great which caused the Lord to overturn them, and he lets them lie under the punishment of their iniquity many days and years. When kingdoms are down, many struggle to lift them up again to their former dignity, glory, and greatness; but it must not, it cannot be, till the Lord's time come, till he please to put forth his hand and do it.

Obs. 3. The Lord Christ, the promised Messiah, was the true King of Judah, and Prince of Zion. "Until he come, whose right it is, and I will give it him." The Father had appointed him to be King, given him the kingdom, and made it known long before his coming in the flesh. He was spoken of, Gen. xlix. 10; he was the Shiloh, the Prosperer, unto whom the gathering of the people should be; he gathered Jews and Gentiles together. He was spoken of, Numb. xxiv. 17, "There shall come a Star out of Jacob, and a Sceptre shall rise out of Israel;" so in Psal. xlv. 6, 7, "The sceptre of thy kingdom is a right sceptre, and God hath anointed thee." See Isa. xi. 1, 2; xlii. 1—3; Jer. xxiii. 6; Ezek. xxxiv. 23, 24; Dan. vii. 14, 27; Zech. ix. 9. In these places, and many other, the kingdom of Christ, his right thereunto, and the Father's donation thereof unto him, are spoken of. The people's hearts were towards him, and they would have made him a king, John vi. 15. However he appeared to the world, the apostles beheld glory and majesty in him, John i. 14; 2 Pet. i. 16; and Pilate wrote over his head, "This is Jesus, the King of the Jews," Matt. xxvii. 37. Christ was not a contemptible person, whatever men thought of him; the Father designed him to be a King, gave him a kingdom; the prophet foretold his kingly dignity; he was born a King, died a King, he lives and reigns at this day King of Zion, and of all saints, Rev. xv. 3. We have no cause to be ashamed of our King, but ought to honour him as we honour the Father, seeing all judgment is committed to him, John v. 22, 23.

Obs. 4. The wisdom and goodness of the Lord towards his people, that when he tells them of the severest judgment, he mingles some mercy. "I will overturn, overturn, overturn;" "overturn" the church, "overturn" the state, "overturn" them for a long time; which was very sad and bitter; yet even now, when he is in a full career of overturning, he tells them of the coming of Christ, who should be their King, wear the crown, and raise up the kingdom again. This was great mercy, in the depth of misery; if they lost an earthly kingdom, they should have a spiritual one; if they lost a profane and temporal king, they should have a King of righteousness, an eternal King. It is the method of the Lord, when he is bringing in dreadful judgments upon his people, that have provoked him bitterly, to lay in something that may support and comfort those who have served him faithfully. Amos ix. 8—11, "Behold, the eyes of the Lord God are upon the sinful kingdom, and I will destroy it from off the face of the earth; saving that I will not utterly destroy the house of Jacob, saith the Lord:" there was mercy mingled with judgment. So in the next verse: "For, lo, I will command, and I will sift the house of Israel among all nations, like as corn is sifted in a sieve, yet shall not the least grain fall upon the earth:" here again is mercy in the midst of judgment. So again in the two next verses: "All the sinners of my people shall die by the sword, which say, The evil shall not overtake nor prevent us:" and what then? "In that day will I raise up the tabernacle of David that is fallen, and close up the breaches thereof; and I will raise up his ruins, and I will build it as in the days of old:" here is goodness with severity.

Obs. 5. That how contrary soever God's actings appear, yet he will make good his promises; he is mindful of them, and will be faithful. The Lord had promised to set up his Son Christ to be King in Zion, the hill of his holiness, Psal. ii. 6; that the government should be upon his shoulder, Isa. ix. 6; that he would "cause a Branch of righteousness to grow up unto David, and he shall execute judgment and righteousness in the land," Jer. xxxiii. 15. What likelihood was there that these things should be, when the Lord overturns the land, plucks up all by the roots, and lays all in a dead condition, and that for many days and years? They might have thought and said, Surely, this death of the crown, of church and state, will be the death of all those and other promises; but it was not so. Though a sentence of death was upon the land, upon the Jews, yet the living God kept life in the promises, he minded them, and said, I will give it to him, he shall have this land, the kingdom and the crown, he shall sit upon Zion, reign and execute judgment. The actings of God sometimes are such, that to man's apprehensions they will make void the promises of God. Psal. lxxvii. 7, 8, saith Asaph, "Will the Lord cast off for ever? and will he be favourable no more? is his mercy clean gone for ever? doth his promise fail for evermore?" God's hand was heavy upon him, his proceedings with him such, as his soul was greatly afflicted, questioned the truth of his promises, and was ready to despair. But what saith he in the tenth verse? "This was my infirmity:" there was no infirmity in God; he had not forgotten his promise, it was not out of his sight, though out of Asaph's. Man's faith may fail him sometimes, but God's faithfulness never fails him; Psal. lxxxix. 33, God will not suffer his faithfulness to fail. God's operations may have an aspect that way; the devil's temptations, and our unbelieving hearts, may not only make us think so, but persuade us it is so, whenas it cannot be so, for the Lord will not suffer it, he will not make a lie in his truth or faithfulness; so the Hebrew is: he is a God that cannot lie, he is Truth, speaks truth, and not one of his promises can or shall fail; which may afford strong consolation unto all that are under any promise of God.

Ver. 28, 29. *And thou, son of man, prophesy and say, Thus saith the Lord God concerning the Ammonites, and concerning their reproach; even say thou, The sword, the sword is drawn: for the slaughter it is furbished, to consume because of the glittering. Whiles they see vanity unto thee, whiles they divine a lie unto thee, to bring thee upon the necks of them that are slain, of the wicked, whose day is come, when their iniquity shall have an end.*

In these verses and the rest, to the end, is contained the prophecy against the Ammonites.

Two ways were spoken of in the 19th, 20th, and 21st verse; one leading to the Ammonites, the other to the Jews. Nebuchadnezzar using divinations to discover unto which of these he should go, Divine Providence overruled the divination, so that he was to make his military expedition unto Jerusalem; hence, lest the Ammonites should be secure, and insult over the Jews, whose judgments were now coming upon them, the Lord commands the prophet to denounce judgment, yea, the same judgment unto them.

In his prophecy we have,

I. The judgment, which is the sword, ver. 28.

II. The causes of it:

1. Reproach, ver. 28.

2. Impiety, and inhumanity, ver. 29.

III. The place where it shall be, ver. 30.

IV. The similitudes to which the judgment is likened, ver. 31.

V. The event thereof, ver. 32.

VI. The ratification of the prophecy, ver. 32.

"Concerning the Ammonites." The Hebrew is, to the children of Ammon. These Ammonites came of the Jewish race, for they were from Lot, and his younger daughter, Gen. xix. 38, who being with child by him, named her son Ben-Ammi, who was the father of the Ammonites, and for Lot's sake, who was the root of them, the Lord showed them kindness long after; Deut. ii. 19, when the Jews came into Canaan, they must not distress them, nor meddle with them. The Ammonites' land was given to the children of Lot for a possession; and so the Moabites, ver. 9, had their land upon that account: but the Ammonites, though descended from the Jews, were bitter enemies to them, and made war against them; see Judg. xi. 4; 1 Sam. xi. 1, 2; 2 Chron. xx. 1. They were notorious idolaters; they had Molech and Milcom among them, 1 Kings xi. 7; 2 Kings xxiii. 13; they were cruel and bloody, Amos i. 13.

"Concerning their reproach." Some would have the words taken passively here, for the "reproach" they suffered from the Chaldeans; but they are rather to be taken actively, for the "reproach" which the Ammonites put upon the Jews. So Vatablus understands the words, and other interpreters. A Lapide affirms, that the Ammonites upbraided the Jews and their God as weak and unwarlike, because Nebuchadnezzar was coming to them, and durst not meddle with the Ammonites. It is certain the Ammonites bare the Jews no good will, and were glad of opportunities to vent that ancient hatred they had against them; when, therefore, they saw that Nebuchadnezzar should come, besiege their city, lay all waste, and carry them into captivity, they insulted over the Jews; they said, Where is your God? why doth he not appear for you, defend you against that cruel oppressor Nebuchadnezzar, and deliver you? We see what your God is; our Molech, our Milcom, doth more for us than your God doth for you. Zeph. ii. 8, "I have heard the reproach of Moab, and the revilings of the children of Ammon, whereby they have reproached my people, and magnified themselves against their border." Our prophet is more plain and full, bringing in the Ammonites scoffing at the calamities of the Jews: chap. xxv. 3, 4, "Say to the Ammonites, Hear the word of the Lord; Thus saith the Lord God; Because thou saidst, Aha, against my sanctuary, when it was profaned; and against the land of Israel, when it was desolate: and against the house of Judah, when they went into captivity; behold, therefore, I will deliver thee to the men of the east for a possession," &c.

"The sword, the sword is drawn." By "sword" is meant war, all warlike instruments, and all those evils which attend the same. Here is an epizeuxes, a doubling of the word, "the sword, the sword," which is emphatical, and imports certainty and progress of it to destroy. You Ammonites think the sword is drawn only against the Jews, and that when they are slain it shall be put up, but it is not so; "the sword, the sword is drawn" for slaughter of you Ammonites, as well as the Jews: you have little cause to insult, reproach, or flatter yourselves you shall be secure; your destruction is decreed, it is coming, only the Jews' is first, yours after.

The word for "drawn" is, פתוחה *solutus est;* it was bound up before in the sheath, now it is loosed, unsheathed; now it is at liberty, and in readiness to do execution, even among you Ammonites, at my pleasure.

"For the slaughter it is furbished." Not only was it drawn, but it was "furbished," מרוטה filed, scoured; מרט whence it comes, signifies, to pluck up hairs, or, pull out feathers by the roots, to excoriate, or flay off the skin; and metaphorically, is applied to things which contract rust, and signifies, to remove rust. When swords have been long in their sheaths, undrawn, unused, they become rusty; that rust is like a hairy or feathery skin upon the blades, which must be removed, and that is the furbishing of them. The sword here was not "furbished" for sight, but for use, for slaughter.

"To consume, because of the glittering." The Hebrew is, to sustain by reason of the shining. It is "furbished," that it may suffice for the slaughtering of many, and that it may terrify with its "glittering" those that are to be destroyed. The Syriac, thou art whetted and shining. Lavater, that it may consume, because of the brightness or lightening of it. The sword and military instruments were so glittering, that, like lightning, they should strike sudden terror into them, and quickly consume them.

Obs. 1. When God is bringing, or brings, judgments upon his people for their iniquities, then the wicked, then their enemies take advantage and revile them. The Ammonites, understanding that Nebuchadnezzar was marching with his forces to Jerusalem, they reproached them, being glad that the day of their calamity and suffering was at hand. The Ammonites were their neighbours, they were as brethren, coming from the brother of Abraham, yet they reproached the Jews, and added affliction to affliction; Zeph. ii. 8, both Moab and Ammon reviled and reproached the Israelites, and "magnified themselves against their border."

The rabbies say, that when the Chaldeans carried the Jews captive, through the lands of the Moabites and Ammonites, the Jews wept, and they reproached them, saying, Why do you afflict yourselves? why do you weep? are you not going to your father's house? they meant Chaldea, which was Abraham's country and habitation. These and many other reproachful speeches doubtless they used against the Jews, when they were spoiled and led into captivity, and "magnified themselves against their border." They said, now their border, their land should become theirs; and they did take the advantage, and invaded their possessions. Jer. xlix. 1, "Concerning the Ammonites, thus saith the Lord; Hath Israel no sons? hath he no heir? why then doth their king (that is, the king of the Ammonites) inherit Gad, and his people dwell in his cities?" that is, Seeing Israel hath sons and heirs of his own, and I have given the possessions of Gad, being carried away with the ten tribes, unto Judah and Benjamin, why do the Ammonites usurp, and take possession of that which is none of their own? Thus they reproached and wronged the Jews. So likewise did the Edomites; Psal. cxxxvii. 7, "In the day of Jerusalem," that was, in the day Nebuchadnezzar's forces took and plundered it, they cried, "Rase it, rase it, even to the foundation." In reproach of, and despite to, the Jews, they cried out so, when Jerusalem was destroyed; the adversaries saw her, and did mock at her sabbaths, they scoffed at all her festivals, religion, and worship: Where is your God, whose days you have so religiously observed? why did he not defend you from this day of your sufferings? either he was infirm, and could not, or unfaithful, and would not.

Obs. 2. The Lord takes notice of the enemies' reproaching his people. He tells the prophet of the Ammonites' reproachings. Ezekiel was in Babylon, he knew nothing of it, but God heard and observed it; Zeph. ii. 8, "I have heard the reproach of Moab, and the revilings of the children of Ammon." God's ear is very open in this case, and though his people hear not, yet he heareth; Jer. xlviii. 27, he saith in his indignation unto Moab, "Was not Israel a derision unto thee?" put it off if thou canst, deny it if thou darest. I saw it, I heard it. This is some comfort to the church and people of God, that he observes not only the wrongs wicked men do unto his people, but also the reproaching speeches they utter against them: Lam. iii. 6, Jeremiah comforted himself in this, "Thou hast heard their reproach, O Lord, and all their imaginations against me." When we are reproached, and mischief is imagined against us by wicked ones, let us make use of this Scripture, and comfort ourselves therein, not breaking out into bitterness and passion.

Obs. 3. Reproaching and reviling God's people, when they are in affliction, draws judgment upon the reproachers and revilers. The Ammonites reproached the Jews when the Babylonish sword came upon them, and here the prophet must tell them the sword is drawn, furbished for slaughter and consumption of them. Reproach in this kind is a provoking sin; God's name, truths, ordinances, suffer when his people are reproached for his correcting hand upon them for their iniquities. Jer. xlviii. 26, 27, Make ye Moab drunken; that is, let the cup of God's wrath be given him, let him have judgment after judgment, drink so deep of divine fury, that he shall not be able to stand: and why was this? he magnified himself against the Lord; he derided Israel, ver. 27; he magnified himself against their border, Zeph. ii. 8; and this is called magnifying himself against the Lord, (for what is done against his people, and their borders, is done against him,) and Moab must be made drunk for it; yea, Moab also shall wallow in his vomit, he also shall be in derision, he shall be derided and scorned in his misery, as a drunken man who lies wallowing in his vomit: Moab for reproaching should be reproached; yea, grievously afflicted, yea, utterly destroyed. Zeph. ii. 8, 9, both Moab and Ammon reviled, reproached the Jews, and magnified themselves against their border: "Therefore as I live, saith the Lord of hosts, the God of Israel, Surely Moab shall be as Sodom, and the children of Ammon as Gomorrah, even the breeding of nettles, and saltpits, and a perpetual desolation." The meaning is, not that they should be consumed by fire from heaven, as Sodom and Gomorrah were, but they should suffer extreme and severe judgments at the hands of the Lord, and be perpetually desolate, as they were.

Ver. 29. "Whiles they see vanity unto thee, whiles they divine a lie unto thee." The Hebrew is, In seeing to thyself a vain thing, in divining to thyself a lie. The Septuagint runs to that purpose, In thy vision for vanity, and in thy prophesying a lie to thyself. The Ammonites, like other nations, had their false prophets, diviners, and soothsayers, as you may clearly see from Jer. xxvii. 3, where the prophet, under the type of bonds and yokes put upon his neck, prophesieth the subjection of the nations unto Nebuchadnezzar, and among others, the Ammonites; and, ver. 9, he forbids them to hearken to their prophets, diviners, dreamers, enchanters, sorcerers, which told them they should not serve the king of Babylon. They held them asleep by telling them, either Nebuchadnezzar would not come to them, or if he did, they were a strong people, had strong cities, and needed not to fear any enemy; but they saw vanity, and divined a lie unto them: and this is the sense of the words, both according to the Hebrew and our translation.

"To bring thee upon the necks of them that are slain." Their false prophets and diviners put them on to insult over and trample upon the Jews, when they were slain by the Chaldeans; assuring them of safety. Or thus, to give thee to the necks of them that are slain; so the Hebrew may be rendered; and then the meaning is, Thy false prophets and diviners, by their vanities and lies, do subject thee to the sword of Nebuchadnezzar, and make way for thy destruction, like the Jews.

"Of the wicked, whose day is come." These words, "of the wicked," are joined with the former in the Hebrew, to the necks of the slain of the wicked; and so is the Septuagint. All translations and expositors do join them; and they may refer either to the slain, or slayers, noting their wickedness. Some do refer them to the one, some to the other. Piscator by "wicked" understands the Chaldeans, and reads the words thus, upon the necks of them who are slain by the wicked.

"Whose day is come, when their iniquity shall have an end." The "day" of the Jews, that was "come," wherein God's judgments should cut them off, and put an "end" to their iniquity. Of these words, see ver. 25.

Obs. 1. When the Lord threatens sinful nations with sore judgments, they have those amongst them which divert them from the truth, possess them with delusions, and put them upon destructive practices. The Ammonites were threatened here with the Babylonish sword, but they neither believed Ezekiel nor Jeremiah, who told them the same thing, chap. xxvii. Their false prophets, their diviners, beat them off from it, possessed them with vanities and lies, put them upon insulting over the Jews, when the hand of the Lord was most heavy upon them, and so brought them to suffer by the same sword the Jews did. It is just with God to give men and nations over to believe lies, and lying prophets which shall lead them to destruction, when they have stopped their ears against the true prophets. Ahab would not believe Micaiah, but the false prophets, who spake words according to his mind; but they were vanity, lies, and he smarted for it, 1 Kings xxii.

Obs. 2. Though the Lord forbear sinful nations long, yet he hath his days and times of reckoning with and punishing of them. The Jews' day was come, and their iniquity had an end; the Ammonites' day came, and their iniquity had an end: God punished them severely for their sins, Ezek. xxv. Nebuchadnezzar and the Babylonians were forborne long, but God had his time for them; Jer. xxvii. 7, "All nations shall serve him, and his son, and his son's son, until the very time of his land come: then many nations and great kings shall serve themselves of him." Babylon and its king had a time to sin and a time to suffer. God stayed many days, yet had his day, and came at the day appointed, Jer. l. 31; li. 13, "O thou that dwellest upon many waters, abundant in treasures, thine end is come, and the measure of thy covetousness." Babylon was insatiably covetous, robbing the nations of their riches, but all her wealth could not purchase one day's respite from the wrath of God, nor all her waters preserve her from the fire of his indignation; the fire God sent in his day burnt up their habitations, and licked up the water of Euphrates, whereon Babylon sat. God bare long with us, and the nations about us, but his day is come, he is visiting; we, they, have had our times of sinning, and now must have our times of suffering.

Ver. 30—32. *Shall I cause it to return into his sheath? I will judge thee in the place where thou wast created, in the land of thy nativity. And I will pour out mine indignation upon thee, I will blow against thee in the fire of my wrath, and deliver thee into the hand of brutish men, and skilful to destroy. Thou shalt be for fuel to the fire; thy blood shall be in the midst of the land; thou shalt be no more remembered: for I the Lord have spoken it.*

Some interpret these words of the Babylonians, as if God would deal with them after he had done with the Jews and Ammonites, which he did, according to the prophecies in Isa. xiii. and Jer. xxv. 50, 51; but this prophecy is against the Ammonites, whose land the Babylonish king laid waste some five years after the final destruction of Jerusalem, as Sanctius saith, citing the tenth book of Josephus' Antiquities for it.

"Shall I cause it to return into his sheath?" You Ammonites think that when the sword hath done execution upon the Jews, it will be sheathed, quiet, and proceed no further; but "shall I cause it to return into his sheath?" no, I will not give it any such commission, or if I do, it shall be for a short time, it shall come to you, and slay you as it hath done them. The Hebrew, השב is infinitive put for an imperative, and so is rendered by some expositors, Put the sword, or, thy sword, into the sheath: thou thinkest to draw the sword, to defend thyself against the Chaldeans when I send them upon thee, but it shall be in vain, thou shalt not be able to stand against them; I will make thy strength and weapons useless.

"I will judge thee in the place where thou wast created." That is, I will punish the Ammonites in their own land, where they were born, where my hand created or framed them. They shall not be carried to Babylon, and be preserved there, but they shall be destroyed in their own country, at their own door; yet some were captives, Jer. xlix. Of this expression, "I will judge thee," was spoken, Ezek. xvi. 38.

"In the land of thy nativity." The Hebrew is, in the land of thy mansions, or peregrination. *In terra negotiationum tuarum*, saith Piscator, in the land of thy traffic, where thou hast pleasure and profit.

Ver. 31. "I will pour out mine indignation upon thee," &c. Here you have the resemblances to which God's judgment is likened.

1. It is compared to a flood, or torrent; to a great rain, or water, that runs swiftly, and bears down all; of which before, chap. vii. 8; xiv. 19; xx. 8, 13, 21.

2. To a wind, or storm; I will blow against thee. I will make such a wind, such a storm, as shall throw down all the greatness and glory of the Ammonites.

3. To a fire, which, where it kindles and fastens, consumes all to ashes. Of this before, chap. xv. 7.

"And deliver thee into the hands of brutish men." The word for "brutish" is, בערים from בער to burn, and therefore in the margin it is, burning. God would deliver them into the hands of the Chaldeans, who were burning, that is, choleric, hasty, furious men, Hab. i. 6, "a bitter and hasty nation." The word also signifies, to be brutish, foolish, Psal. lxxiii. 22; I was foolish, brutish, and knew not; so that בער is, a man without knowledge, a barbarian, and so the Septuagint speaks, into the hands of barbarous men.

"Skilful to destroy." In the original, artists of corruption. In killing men they were very expert; they had been sundry times before at Jerusalem, slain many Jews, and knew how to destroy Ammonites.

Ver. 32. "Thou shalt be for fuel to the fire." Thou shalt be meat to the fire, that shall eat up thee, and thy habitations. As fire is fed by wood, coal, straw, turf, and such combustibles, so should the fire of God's wrath be fed with their vineyards, habitations, towns, cities, persons.

"Thy blood shall be in the midst of the land." Thou shalt be slain openly, lie in thy blood, unpitied, unburied.

"Thou shalt be no more remembered." This judgment shall deprive thee of life, and also of thy name; thou shalt have no monument to make mention of thee, but thy memory shall altogether perish, thou shalt be so handled, that not a vestige of thee shall be left.

Obs. 1. The Lord oft doth cross the thoughts and blast the hopes of wicked men. The sword came to the Ammonites when they thought it should not come; they hoped by their swords to beat back the Babylonians, and God bade them put up their swords into the sheaths, they should do them no good, the Babylonians should prevail. Zedekiah and the Jews thought Nebuchadnezzar would not draw his sword against them; if he did, they hoped the Egyptian sword would prove stronger than the Babylonian, but they were deceived in both: see Ezek. xvii. 12, 17. When princes and states trust in their strong men, and look for help, deliverance by them, the Lord disappoints them, and makes the pomp of the strong to cease.

Obs. 2. The Lord punishes sinners in the midst of their conveniences, pleasures, and profits. "I will judge thee in the place where thou wast created, in the land of thy nativity." There they had most conveniences, delights, contents, and thither God brings the sword, there he cuts them off: there they sinned, there they were impious, consulting with false prophets, diviners; there they were barbarous, inhuman, mocking at the calamities of the Jews when God visited them; and there God punished them. Thus hath God dealt with them in Ireland, in the land of their nativity, in the places of their delights and conveniences; where they sinned, there they suffered.

Obs. 3. Suddenly and easily can the Lord destroy sinful nations. "I will pour out mine indignation upon thee, I will blow against thee in the fire of my wrath, and deliver thee," &c. Floods, winds, storms, fires, come suddenly; and blowing is an easy thing: if God do but blow upon a nation in his wrath, it is undone; Isa. xl. 7, "The grass withereth, the flower fadeth; because the Spirit of the Lord bloweth upon it." If the Lord "blow" with a spirit of indignation upon a land or people, they wither away quickly, and come to nothing. Ver. 24, speaking before of princes, judges, and their stock, which seem to be rooted like mighty oaks and tall cedars, it is said, "He shall blow upon them, and they shall wither, and the whirlwind shall take them away as stubble." Let God "blow" upon princes, and their glory fades, their roots dry up. If God let out the fire of his wrath, who, what is not meat, fuel, for that fire? princes, people, cities, nations, are.

Obs. 4. Wicked nations, and persons, God takes away the name and memory of them. "Thou shalt be no more remembered" in way of mercy, or for honour; but if at all, in way of wrath, and for reproach. Many nations since the fall of man, for their sins, are defunct, extinct, and buried in the darkness of oblivion.

Obs. 5. Judgments come not upon nations without the Lord, but because the Lord hath appointed them. The Ammonitish nation must be fuel for the fire, no more remembered; and why? "For I the Lord have spoken;" I, that am faithful, and will not falsify my word; I, that am able, and can inflict what is threatened; I have spoken, decreed, and appointed such things, and they must come to pass.

CHAPTER XXII.

Ver. 1—12. *Moreover the word of the Lord came unto me, saying, Now, thou son of man, wilt thou judge, wilt thou judge the bloody city? yea, thou shalt shew her all her abominations. Then say thou, Thus saith the Lord God; The city sheddeth blood in the midst of it, that her time may come, and maketh idols against herself to defile herself. Thou art become guilty in thy blood that thou hast shed; and hast defiled thyself in thine idols which thou hast made; and thou hast caused thy days to draw near, and art come even unto thy years: therefore have I made thee a reproach unto the heathen, and a mocking to all countries. Those that be near, and those that be far from thee, shall mock thee, which art infamous and much vexed. Behold, the princes of Israel, every one were in thee to their power to shed blood. In thee have they set light by father and mother: in the midst of thee have they dealt by oppression with the stranger: in thee have they vexed the fatherless and the widow. Thou hast despised mine holy things, and hast profaned my sabbaths. In thee are men that carry tales to shed blood: and in thee they eat upon the mountains: in the midst of thee they commit lewdness. In thee have they discovered their fathers' nakedness: in thee have they humbled her that was set apart for pollution. And one hath committed abomination with his neighbour's wife; and another hath lewdly defiled his daughter-in-law; and another in thee hath humbled his sister, his father's daughter. In thee have they taken gifts to shed blood; thou hast taken usury and increase, and thou hast greedily gained of thy neighbours by extortion, and hast forgotten me, saith the Lord God.*

IN this 22nd chapter, you have three messages of the Lord to the prophet. The

I. Is from the beginning to ver. 17, wherein a large catalogue of Jerusalem's sins are set down, with intermixture and addition of some threatenings and judgments.

II. Is from ver. 17—23, wherein is declared what the house of Israel is likened unto, and what the Lord will do with it.

III. Is from ver. 23 to the end, wherein is laid forth the general corruption of all sorts, both prophets, priests, princes, and people, with certainty of their destruction.

Ver. 1. "Moreover, the word of the Lord," &c. Prophets stir not till God stirs them; after God speaks to them, they may speak to others. God hath more still to communicate unto prophets, notwithstanding he hath communicated much: "Moreover the word," &c.; besides all delivered, this I have had from the Lord.

Ver. 2. "Wilt thou judge, wilt thou judge the bloody city?" The Hebrew word שפט signifies to judge; and because in judging two parties are to be dealt with, one wronging, the other wronged, hence the word notes sometimes, to plead for, to defend; sometimes, to sentence and punish: in this place, the former of these is most suitable, Son of man, wilt thou excuse, defend, and plead for this city? I tell thee it is a bloody city, a city that hath wronged me, and must not be pleaded for. Of these words were spoken before, chap. xx. 4.

If we read them as Montanus, Œcolampadius, and some others do, thus, Wilt thou not judge, wilt thou not judge the bloody city? that is, wilt thou not reprove, and tell it thoroughly of its iniquities? what! wilt thou faint, give over, and wink at the wickedness thou seest? is it not a part of thy prophetical office, to lift up thy voice like a trumpet, and to tell my people of their transgressions? Remember thine office, connive not at their sins, but cry out against them. In this sense, it affords this note: That prophetical men are oft discouraged, ready to cease from their work, and need to be roused and quickened thereunto by the Lord.

"The bloody city." The Hebrew is, the city of bloods, Jerusalem, which is so called, because she had shed much innocent blood, and was become very cruel: Jer. xix. 4, Ye "have filled this place with the blood of innocents;" and 2 Kings xxi. 16, Manasseh shed so much innocent blood therein, that he filled Jerusalem from one end to the other therewith: yea, so bloody was Jerusalem, that she filled the land with blood and bloody crimes, Ezek. vii. 23; ix. 9; and how bloody this city was, appears in verses 3, 4, 6, 9, of this chapter.

Obs. The sins of a city and nation may be such, that God will not have his prophets to plead or intercede for them, but to cry out against them. "Son of man, wilt thou judge, wilt thou judge the bloody city?" I know thou art very charitable, and ready to speak for them, but the city is so bloody, and full of abominations, that I will not have thee to appear or move for them, but thou must set their sins in order before them, and thunder out my judgments against them. When there is a fulness of sin, so that it is universal in all sorts, sinners are grown impudent and obstinate, then the Lord stops his ears and the mouths of his prophets, he will have no pleading for such a people. This was the case of Jerusalem, sin had spread itself through all ranks of people, as you shall find in this chapter, and her children were "impudent and hardhearted," Ezek. iii. 7.

Ver. 3. "The city sheddeth blood in the midst of it, that her time may come." Jerusalem shed blood in the midst of herself, so is the Hebrew; that is, publicly, fearlessly, freely, against law and light of nature, without all shame.

"That her time may come." She fills up the measure of her sins, that so the time of her destruction may make haste.

"And maketh idols against herself." In the former words was a violation of the second table, and in these is a violation of the first. Of the word "idols," or, dunghill gods, hath been spoken in former chapters. The Septuagint hath, devices, Jerusalem devised idols, and ways of worship, she fetched in the gods of other nations, and devised some of her own, but they were against herself; she thought they made for her, but they tended to her destruction.

Ver. 4. "Thou art become guilty in thy blood that thou hast shed." The word for "guilty" is, אשמת and the original אשם signifies, to do wickedly, shamefully. Jerusalem, in shedding of blood, had done wickedly, shamefully, and so became guilty with a witness, exceeding guilty; she cut not off the wicked, to take guilt off from herself and the land, but she murdered the innocent, and multiplied guilt thereby upon herself and the nation.

"Thou hast defiled thyself in thine idols which thou hast made." Thou hast made idols, thinking thereby to please God, and pacify his anger, but they have defiled thee, made thee hateful unto God, and increased his wrath much more against thee. God had forbidden them to make to themselves idols or images, Exod. xx. yet they did make them, defiling thereby both the worship of God and their own souls, and so hastened their own destruction.

"Thou hast caused thy days to draw near, and art come even unto thy years." Thou hast, by thy transgressions, broken the thread of my patience, and hastened judgment to come upon thee, I gave thee time to repent, and prevent my wrath from breaking out against thee, but thou, having abused my patience, mispent thy time, art become worse; and now vengeance is at thy gates, and ready to enter. The time is come for the sword to visit thee, and that thou shalt go into captivity.

"Therefore have I made thee a reproach unto the heathen." Jerusalem was the habitation of God, Psal. lxxvi. 2; the city of the great King, Matt. v. 35; which the Lord took leasure to protect and defend, Isa. xxxi. 5; it was the perfection of beauty, Psal. l. 2; the holy city, Matt. xxvii. 53; very honourable: but this city, and the inhabitants thereof, did the Lord make a "reproach" unto heathens. The word for "reproach" is, חרפה which notes, reproach, disgrace in word or action; and doubtless the Jews met with reproachful words and actions from the heathen. They were not yet made a "reproach," but God intended them to be so: the pretertense is put for the future.

"A mocking to all countries." The Hebrew is, קלסה a vilifying and scorning of a man. It is only in this place, and imports the scorning and vilifying of the Jews in all countries. The Septuagint hath it, for a derision and laughing-stock. It is rendered, Heb. xi. 36, "cruel mockings," such mockings as argue cruelty and insulting.

Ver. 5. "Those that be near, and those that be far from thee, shall mock thee." The nations round about thee, the Ammonites, Moabites, Idumeans; and those far off, the Babylonians.

"Which art infamous." In the Hebrew it is, thou art polluted in thy name. Septuagint, who art named impure. Jerusalem, the faithful city, was become an harlot, Isa. i. 21, and like an "imperious whorish woman," Ezek. xvi. 30; Jerusalem's idolatry, blood, uncleanness, and profaneness, had made her infamous, and to be called the filthy, polluted, the oppressing city, Zeph. iii. 1.

"Much vexed." The Hebrew words are, רבת המהומה of much contrition; that is, a city greatly to be broken for thy wickedness. Septuagint, πολλὴ ἐν ταῖς ἀνομίαις, much in wickedness, which brought her much vexation.

From these three verses, thus opened, take these observations.

Obs. 1. That when people become idolatrous, they grow cruel. Jerusalem made idols, and shed blood; bloodiness, cruelty, and idolatry usually go together; she had idols in the midst of her, Ezek. xvi. 24, 25; and she shed blood in the midst of her; she was a public idolatress, and a public murderess. The Babylonians were very idolatrous, Ezek. xx. 32, and they were very bloody, Jer. li. 35. So Rome, which is called Babylon, Rev. xvii. was idolatrous and bloody; those she could not make drunk with the wine of her fornications, those she could not draw to popery and idolatry, she made herself drunk with their blood, ver. 26. How bloody popish idolaters are, the Parisian massacre heretofore, and the Irish of late do witness. When men once make gods, and form ways of worship, to themselves, they are zealous for them, will lavish out gold to maintain them, and be lavish of their blood that oppose them.

Obs. 2. Great sins do accelerate the judgments of God, they put wings unto them, and cause them to make haste. Jerusalem's bloodiness and idolatries made her time to come, and days to draw near. Sinners, by their lewdness, do abbreviate God's patience, and swiften his punishments; Psal. lv. 23, "Bloody and deceitful men shall not live out half their days;" the length and strength of their wickedness shortens their days. In Job xxii. 16, it is said, "wicked men were cut down out of time;" and, chap. xv. 32, "It shall be accomplished before his time;" a wicked man, his life is gone, cut off before the just time; like a green tree, cut down before it come to perfection; and so is out of time, and before his time; he might have lived longer, had he not been so wicked: Eccles. vii. 17, "Be not over-much wicked, neither be thou foolish: why shouldest thou die before thy time?" the Hebrew is, not in thy time. Many men, through drunkenness, thefts, murders, duels, uncleanness, do die, not in their time, not in the time they might have lived unto; they die out of time, and before their time: and what is the cause? their own wickedness, and over-much wickedness precipitates their death. Haman's enmity to Mordecai, and bloodiness against the Jews, brought the halter about his neck before his time. Herod's pride caused the worms to eat him up before his time. The wickedness of many in our days hath brought them to the block, *tempore non suo*, out of time, or before their time.

Obs. 3. The sins of nations, cities, and people, do expose them to the reproachings and scornings of all sorts, both far off and near. Jerusalem and her people were very wicked, therefore saith God, "I have made thee a reproach unto the heathen, and a mocking to all countries. Those that be near, and those that be far from thee, shall mock thee;" Lam. ii. 15, "All that pass by clap their hands at thee; they hiss and wag their head at the daughter of Jerusalem, saying, Is this the city that men call The perfection of beauty, The joy of the whole earth?" All passengers, of what nation soever, when Jerusalem suffered, and was made desolate, clapped their hands, hissed, wagged their heads, gnashed their teeth, ver. 16, which were gestures of scorn and insultation, and uttered this bitter sarcasm, "Is this the city that men call The perfection of beauty, The joy of the whole earth?" see Jer. xviii. 15, 16. It was the Jews' sining against God that made them a perpetual hissing. Lam. i. 8, "Jerusalem hath grievously sinned; therefore she is removed: all that honoured her despise her;" her sin transformed her honour into shame and despite. One of her sins was, that the word of God was a reproach to her and hers, Jer. vi. 10; therefore God made her and hers a reproach, a proverb, a taunt, a curse in all places, whither he should drive them, Jer. xxiv. 9. Not only the Moabites and Ammonites mocked them, when they were leading away captive, Why do you weep? you are going to your father's house; but also the Babylonians: Psal. cxxxvii. 3, "Sing us one of the songs of Zion;" you say Zion is the joy of the whole earth, let us have a song of it, and see how joyful it will make you here in Babylon.

Obs. 4. Sin makes cities and citizens to have an ill name. Jerusalem's wickedness made her infamous; her iniquities were great and many, and they caused her to hear ill. Formerly Jerusalem had been renowned, Ezek. xvi. 14, for beauty; the presence, ordinances, and worship of God, Psal. lxxvi. 1—4; renowned for her faithfulness, Isa. i. 21; for her holiness, Psal. ii. 6; for her justice and righteousness, Isa. i. 21: but now, through her idolatry, cruelty, profaneness, uncleanness, she had lost her beauty, faithfulness, holiness, and righteousness, she was become infamous as any strumpet: and, Ezek. xxiv. 6, 9, hath this infamous motto twice written upon her gates, "Woe to the bloody city!" "Woe to the bloody city!" And what were the citizens? rulers of Sodom and people of Gomorrah. Jerusalem was Sodom, Gomorrah; and what a brand was this to that city! and the people were Sodomites and Gomorrheans; and what an infamy was this unto them! How infamous was Jezebel, Jeroboam, and Judah for their wickedness! The Spirit of God resembles wicked men to things that are vile and infamous; as, the smoke of a chimney, Hos. xiii. 3, which blacks and infects; to sepulchres, which are stinking and loathsome, Matt. xxiii. 27; to despised, broken idols, Jer. xxii. 28; to dogs and swine, 2 Pet. ii. 22; to adders and serpents, Psal. lviii. 4; to dragons, Isa. li. 9; yea, to the devil, John vi. 70. If men would not have an ill name, be likened unto vile things, let them not do such things as will make infamous.

Obs. 5. Sin brings sad afflictions upon the sons of men. "Thou art much vexed." Jerusalem's sins multiplied her sorrows; she "vexed the fatherless and widow," ver. 7; she "vexed the poor and needy," ver. 29; and she had much vexation for it. The Ammonites, Egyptians, Babylonians vexed her; yea, the Lord vexed her with famine, sword, and pestilence. In Deut. xxviii. 20, it was told the Jews that God would send upon them cursing, vexation, and rebuke, till he had destroyed them; and why? because of the wickedness of their doings, because they forsook God; and, Isa. lxiii. 10, "They rebelled, and vexed his holy Spirit: therefore he was turned to be their enemy, and fought against them." When God is an enemy, and fights against a people, they have nothing but vexation. God makes every creature, every condition, vexatious.

Ver. 6. "Behold, the princes of Israel, every one were in thee to their power," &c. The Hebrew stands thus, The princes of Israel, every one according to his arm, were in thee: an arm, is put for power. Vatablus hath it, Every one of the princes, according to his power and place, did put forth himself to do unjust and cruel things. The "princes," who were set up above others, and empowered to have done justice impartially to all, they abused their power and places, to the defiling of Jerusalem with blood; there was no equity amongst them, tyranny prevailed.

Ver. 7. "In thee have they set light by father and mother." The law of God, and light of nature, teaches men to honour their parents, but Jerusalem had those in it, who violated both these laws. Children were come to such a height of wickedness, that they vilified their parents, and reproached them; both their natural and metaphorical parents. Septuagint, ἐκακολόγουν. Isa. iii. 5, "The child shall behave himself proudly against the ancient, and the base against the honourable;" this was now fulfilled in Jerusalem, and that curse pulled upon them, Deut. xxvii. 16, "Cursed be he that setteth light by his father," &c.

"In thee have they dealt by oppression with the stranger." The word for "oppression" is from עשק which signifies, to oppress a man by force or fraud; and though the law was, that they should not vex or oppress a stranger, Exod. xxii. 21, yet now was the wickedness of Jerusalem such, that she by fraud and force did oppress the stranger.

By "stranger" is not meant, any one of other nations that came to Jerusalem, but him who, being
Vid. Rivet in Exod. xxii. 21. adopted into the Jewish nation, became a proselyte. God took special care of such; (and so the Septuagint renders the word, strangers;) that so more might be encouraged to come in to the worship of the true God; but they oppressed them, and so shut the door which God had opened.

"In thee have they vexed the fatherless and the widow." Orphans and widows, being deprived of those who should be their help and strength, God himself hath declared for them, Psal. lxviii. 5, "A father of the fatherless, and a judge of the widows, is God in his holy habitation;" and therefore peremptorily forbids the affliction of any widow or fatherless child, Exod. xxii. 22. And the sense is, not only that they should not harm them, but that they should protect them, plead their causes, and do them good; Isa. i. 17, "Judge the fatherless, plead for the widow;" but they were so far from this, that they afflicted and vexed them. The word here for "vexed" is, הונו from ינה to offer violence, to prey upon; they offered violence to the widows and fatherless, making a prey of them, which was a great vexation to their souls.

Ver. 8. "Thou hast despised mine holy things." The "holy things" were, all those things which were consecrated and dedicated to God, as the priests, the temple, the vessels of it, the sacrifices and sacraments they had, yea, all the ordinances of God, which they despised: the word בזה is, despising, out of pride and disdain. So did the Jews of old, so do many now through pride of heart, despise holy things. Religion was then vilified.

"And hast profaned my sabbaths." Of profaning or polluting the sabbath, you heard, chap. xx. 13, 16. It is the same word for "polluted" there, which you have for "profaned" here. God had commanded them to remember his sabbaths, to sanctify them, and promised great blessings unto them upon the due sanctification of them, Isa. lviii. 13, 14; but Jerusalem "profaned" them, and made them common, or worse than common, days.

Ver. 9. "In thee are men that carry tales to shed blood." The words for "men that carry tales" are, אנשי רכיל for which the Septuagint gives you, ἄνδρες λῃσταὶ, thieves, robbers. *Rachil* is, one that narrowly observes another's words, and perverts them to the prejudice of him whose they were; the word is from רכל *rochel*, a merchant, and so is, one that, by carrying tales, sets to sale the fame, liberty, or life of his neighbour. It signifies also an apothecary, who mingles, blends things together, and sells them for his own advantage; so this carry-tale mingles something of his own with what he heard, and makes his advantage thereby. Montanus renders the words, *viri delationis*, men of carriage, because they seek out, pick up, or invent matter against another, and carry it to those that be in place, which here made way for shedding of blood. This kind of men are very pernicious. Solomon tells you, that the words of tale-bearers are as wounds, "they go down into the innermost parts of the belly," Prov. xviii. 8; they make way for the wounding and spilling the blood of the innocent. There were wicked princes and magistrates at that time in Jerusalem, glad to have occasions against the innocent, and these murderous tale-carriers possess them with falsehoods, to the prejudice of their lives.

"In thee they eat upon the mountains." They did eat there things offered to idols, in honour to the idols, otherwise it was not sinful to "eat upon the mountains." Of these words before, chap. xviii. 6, 11, 15.

"In the midst of thee they commit lewdness." Of "committing lewdness," see chap. xvi. 43. זמה the Septuagint translate, ἀνόσια, unholy things, that is, villanous things; thou that shouldst be holy, doest filthy things. So Lavater; and he saith *zimmah* notes, a villany done not ignorantly, or out of weakness, but on purpose; therefore the translation, which either is Vatablus's, or which he follows, hath it, a plotted wickedness. Chap. xi. 1, 2, Jaazaniah and Pelatiah did devise mischief; and such devised mischiefs are called here, *zimmahs*, lewdnesses. Jerusalem had those in her who made it their practice: Micah ii. 1, "Woe to them that devise iniquity, and work evil upon their beds!" In the night season, when their thoughts and spirits were most retired, fittest and strongest for meditation, then they devised iniquity; how to root out the righteous, to take away the prophets, to pervert the law, to promote idolatry, &c. and these were lewdnesses.

Ver. 10, 11. "In thee have they discovered their fathers' nakedness: in thee have they humbled her that was set apart for pollution. And one" (or, every one) "hath committed abomination with his neighbour's wife; and another hath lewdly defiled his daughter-in-law," &c. In these two verses are set out the incestuous, adulterous, and whorish doings of Jerusalem. In her, sons lay with their mothers, fathers with their daughters-in-law, brothers with their sisters, and every one with his neighbour's wife; and being not satisfied with those times which were fit for embracing, they humbled, they forced those who were set apart for pollution; all which things were forbidden in the law: see Lev. xviii. and xx. So filthy was Jerusalem at this time, that "they were as fed horses, every one neighing after his neighbour's wife," Jer. v. 8.

Ver. 12. "In thee have they taken gifts to shed blood." There are two sorts of gifts: first, such as are bestowed upon friends, and those who deserve well of us: these are lawful, and when given, testify esteem and thankfulness. And secondly, such as are given to retard, pervert, and corrupt justice: such were the gifts here, and they were forbidden, Exod. xxiii. 8; Deut. xvi. 19. This gift-taking was too common in Jerusalem: Isa. i. 23, "Every one loveth gifts, and followeth after rewards: they judge not the fatherless, neither doth the cause of the widow come unto them:" the fatherless and widows had no "gifts" to give them, therefore their causes could not be heard; they petitioned, but petitions without presents would do no good, for they judged for reward, Mic. iii. 11; and said, Give, give, Hos. iv. 18. If there were no "gifts," there was no justice.

"Thou hast taken usury and increase." Of these words, and this sin, was largely spoken in chap. xviii. 8, whither you are referred.

"And thou hast greedily gained of thy neighbours by extortion." Montanus renders the word for "greedily gained," *appetebas, fraudabas*, thou didst covet or deceive thy neighbours. The Hebrew is, בצע which signifies, to wound, to cut in pieces, and, to exercise covetousness. It notes an insatiable desire, which carries a man out to wrest and wring from his neighbour by any means, and so wounds him, squeezes, and cuts him in pieces.

Obs. 1. That great men, the princes and potentates of the earth, lay out themselves to tyrannize over and oppress the people. "Behold, the princes of Israel, every one were in thee to their power to shed blood." They all agreed in these two things, to oppress, and to oppress to the utmost. This doubtless made Jeremiah say, chap. iii. 5, of Jerusalem, "Behold, thou hast said and done evil things as thou couldest:" thy princes, which had arms and power, they have put forth the same, what they could, to do wickedly, to oppress and shed blood; what could they do more than take away the lives of men? This was the way great ones went of old: see Micah iii. 1—3; and Zeph. iii. 3.

Obs. 2. That forgetfulness of God is the cause of all the sins in a city or people. Jerusalem's sins are here reckoned up; cruelty, idolatry, slighting of parents, oppression of strangers, vexing of fatherless and widows, despising of holy things, profaning of sabbaths, tale-carrying to shed blood, eating upon the mountains, devising wickedness, incest, adultery, bribery, usury, extortion. And what is the root of all these? "Thou hast forgotten me, saith the Lord God." When men mind not what God commands, forbids, what he threatens, what he approves, when they acknowledge not his eye, his power, his judgments, the account they must give to him, they fall into all manner of sins, lewdnesses, and transgressions: when men forget God, they do not, they cannot fear him; and where the fear of God is not, they will not stick to shed blood, Gen. xx. 11, or do any wickedness. In Psal. l. 17—20, many sins of the Jews are recited; and what was the ground of those sins? they forgat God; ver. 22, "Consider this, ye that forget God." See Psal. cvi. 19, 20; Jer. xiii. 25; xviii. 15. When men forget God, they forget his law, which should regulate their lives, and so they live without God, and without law; they follow the lusts of their own hearts, and lie exposed to all evils.

Ver. 13—16. *Behold, therefore I have smitten mine hand at thy dishonest gain which thou hast made, and at thy blood which hath been in the midst of thee. Can thine heart endure, or can thine hands be strong, in the days that I shall deal with thee? I the Lord have spoken it, and will do it. And I will scatter thee among the heathen, and disperse thee in the countries, and will consume thy filthiness out of thee. And thou shalt take thine inheritance in thyself in the sight of the heathen, and thou shalt know that I am the Lord.*

Having rehearsed Jerusalem's sins, here the Lord comes to set down his dislike of their ways, the judgments that should come upon them, and the end of those judgments.

I. His dislike, in ver. 13.

II. The judgments, in ver. 14, 15.

III. The end of them, in ver. 15, 16.

Ver. 13. "Behold, therefore I have smitten mine hand at thy dishonest gain which thou hast made." Smiting of hands is sometimes a sign of joy, as chap. xxi. 17, and sometimes of grief and anger, as here. God was so provoked with the heinousness of their sins, that he smites his hands together, both to testify his indignation against them, and readiness to take vengeance on them. When parents smite their hands at the lewd doings of their children, it is an argument of anger and grief, not of joy. God hath no hand, but it is spoken after the manner of men.

The word for "dishonest gain" is, בצע from בצע opened before. Montanus renders it, covetousness. Others, money gotten by fraud and force; such gain is "dishonest gain." The French is, avarice, that gain which comes in by overreaching, by forcing or sinking of others. That is "dishonest gain," when we do not as we would be done unto.

"And at thy blood which hath been in the midst of thee." Here are only two sins mentioned of all that went before, but the other are intended also; God smote his hands against them, though principally against these. Jerusalem had shed much innocent blood, which cried to God for vengeance, and caused him to smite his hands at her.

Obs. Covetousness and cruelty are sins that sorely provoke God. He smote his hands at their dishonest gain, and bloody doings; his spirit boiled up against them, and he was coming to be avenged on them. The Hebrews say there are twenty-four sins reckoned up in this chapter, and that God threatens the destruction of the city only for covetousness. The Jews were a people greedy of gain, given to covetousness, which makes men cruel, and oft bloody: Prov. i. 19, those who are greedy of gain, they take away the life of the owners, they suck their blood; Amos viii. 4, they "swallow up the needy;" Micah iii. 2, 3, they pluck off their skins, break their bones, and eat their flesh. And if covetous men are not cruel and bloody, yet they are abhorred of God for their covetousness: Psal. x. 3, "The wicked blesseth the covetous, whom the Lord abhorreth;" the word for "covetous," and that here for "dishonest gain," are both of the same verb, and differ very little. God abhors the covetous, and smites his hands at covetousness, and so he doth at bloodiness; Psal. v. 6, he "will abhor the bloody and deceitful man;" the Lord abhors them at the present, and he will make it manifest that he doth abhor them: God hath done it in the gospel, 1 Cor. vi. 10. Rev. xxi. 8, there it appears, that neither the covetous nor the bloody shall inherit the kingdom of heaven. Let us learn of God to smite our hands against these sins.

Ver. 14. "Can thine heart endure?" The Hebrew for "endure" is, עָמַד which Montanus and Œcolampadius render, *stabit*, Will thy heart stand, or consist, when I shall deal with thee? The Septuagint is, *ει ὑποςήσεται ἡ καρδία σȣ*, If thine heart shall stand it out; but the interrogation is more emphatical, Can thine heart stand, or endure? and carries the force of a negation. O Jerusalem! thou thinkest that when my judgments come, thou shalt be able to stand under them, but be thine heart never so stout or strong, my judgments will be too heavy for thee to bear them; when they come, thine heart will fail thee, fail thee of counsel, that thou shalt not know what to do, and fail thee of strength, that thou shalt not be able to do what thou knowest; thine heart will be in thine heels, thou wilt be more forward to flee than to consult, or stand it out upon consultation.

"Can thine hands be strong?" Thou thinkest to do some great matters, if Nebuchadnezzar draw near to thy gates; thou wilt call upon thy strong men to appear and make resistance, but their hands will be feeble, and unserviceable, not fit to handle or use weapons of war. Jerusalem, thou art deluded; consider with thyself, can thine hands be strong when I have "smitten mine hands" against thee? canst thou withstand me, or bear my judgments, when I shall thunder and throw them upon thee with a strong hand? Whatever fancies possess thine head, thou art not able to do it.

"In the days that I shall deal with thee." In the days that men have dealt with thee, thy counsel and power have prevailed; but what wilt thou do "in the days that I shall deal with thee?" I, that am "wonderful in counsel, and excellent in working," Isa. xxviii. 29; I, that work and none can hinder, chap. xliii. 13; I, that am "terrible to the kings of the earth," Psal. lxxvi. 12; I, that plead with fire and sword in my hand, Isa. lxvi. 16; I, that make mountains flow, and nations to tremble at my presence, Isa. lxiv. 1, 2; I, that make fruitful places wildernesses, and break down cities, Jer. iv. 26; what wilt thou do then? Those days are coming upon thee, and they will be the saddest days thou ever mettest with.

"I the Lord have spoken it, and will do it." Thou mayest hope it shall not be, that I will deal severely with thee, in whom I have delighted, and upon whom I have bestowed so many mercies; but know, I have resolved, spoken it, and will do it: I am not man, to repent of what I speak or do.

Obs. 1. Sinful cities and creatures are apt to confide in one thing or other, in their wisdom, strength, power, riches, friends. Jerusalem thought she had wherewith to keep off all judgments, or sufficient to enable her to wrestle with them if they came: "Can thine heart endure, or can thine hands be strong?" Jerusalem thought so, had confidence that way, else the Lord would not have put these questions to her. Ezek. xvi. 15, "Thou didst trust in thy beauty;" in thy wealth, in thy walls, in thy soldiers, in thy counsellors, in thy temple, in thy mountains, which were thy beauty. In Jeremiah's days it is evident that the wise, the rich, and strong men of Jerusalem did too much confide and glory in their wisdom, their riches, and strength, chap. ix. 23. Zephaniah saith of Jerusalem, that "she trusted not in the Lord," chap. iii. 2; her confidence was in falsehood, Jer. xiii. 25; that was, in things which proved false and deceitful: one of this kind was the Egyptian strength, Isa. xxx. 2; Ezek. xvii. 17. Not only did Jerusalem confide in falsehoods, but Babylon also, Isa. xlvii. 10; and Rabbah, Jer. xlix. 4; she once trusted in her wickedness, saying, "None seeth me:" the other in her treasures, saying, "Who shall come unto me?" It is not good to lean to our own wisdom, to rest upon our own strength, or strength of others; whoever makes flesh within, or flesh without, his arm, lies under a curse, Jer. xvii. 5; but he that trusts in the Lord, and in him only, he hath the blessing, ver. 7.

Obs. 2. God hath his times to reckon with sinners, to make them smart for their evil doings. "In the days that I shall deal with thee." God had his day to deal with Egypt; Ezek. xxx. 9, "As in the day of Egypt;" he met with Egyptians in the Red sea. He had his day to deal with Midianites; Isa. ix. 4, "As in the day of Midian;" when God smote them by the sword of Gideon, Judg. vii. that was the day God dealt with them. Men have their days to sin, and God hath his days to smite. Ahab had his day to do wickedly, and God had his day to deal with him, 1 Kings xxii. 34, 35. Ahaz had his time to transgress, and God had his time to distress him for his transgressions, 2 Chron. xxviii. 19, 20. Ephraim had his days of sinning, and God had his day of rebuke to lay Ephraim desolate, Hos. v. 9. The Jews had their day to make a calf, and God had his day to cut off three thousand of them, Exod. xxxii. 28. Men sin, and think to hear no more of their sins, but God remembers them, and hath his days to visit for them. He hath a day for every one who is proud and lifted up, Isa. ii. 12; he hath a day for those that decree unrighteous decrees, that write grievousness, that wrong widows and fatherless ones, Isa. x. 1—3; he hath his day to deal with them, and so to deal with them, that they shall not know what to do: "What will ye do in the day of visitation?" to whom will ye flee for help? and where will ye leave your glory? Men will be thinking what to do, whither to flee, how to dispose of themselves and what they have, but the day of the Lord will be darkness and distress unto them. Whoever takes a time to sin against God, must expect a time wherein God will deal with him for so sinning; Rom. ii. 6, 9, God "will render to every man according to his deeds;" he hath his day to render "tribulation and anguish upon every soul of man that doth evil;" he hath his day wherein he will "judge the secrets of men," ver. 16. Would you "see good days, eschew evil, and do good; seek peace, and ensue it," 1 Pet. iii. 10, 11.

Obs. 3. God's judgments discover the vanity and rottenness of human confidences. "Can thine heart endure? can thine hands be strong, in the days that I shall deal with thee?" when I shall bring the sword, plague, and famine? no, thy heart will faint, thy hands will be feeble. If at the tidings of judgments their heart melted, their hands were feeble, every spirit faint, and all knees weak as water, as it is, chap. xxi. 7, what were they at the presence, sight, and sense of those judgments? they were like men without hearts and spirits, without hands and legs. God's judgments are fires which consume men's confidences, and make them see their own weakness. Men think they shall stand in the evil day; but if they cannot stand against the frowns and fury of the creature, how will they stand before the dreadful Creator? if footmen, horsemen, the swellings of Jordan, Jer. xii. 5, weary, sink men, what will the Lord of hosts do? if they cannot bear the lesser judgments, how will they bear the greater? If briers and thorns conceit themselves to be oaks and cedars, can they endure the fire? Isa. xxvii. 4, they will be burnt to ashes. What they said of Jehu, 2 Kings x. 4, Two kings were not able to stand before him, how then shall we stand? he is coming with the sword; may wicked cities more fully say of God, The old world could not stand before him, Sodom and Gomorrah could not stand before him, how then shall we stand? Egypt had men like fatted bullocks, but when the northern storm came upon them, they "turned back, they fled away together, they did not stand, because the day of their calamity was come upon them, and the time of their visitation," Jer. xlvi. 21. You may see what strong, mighty, and courageous men will do, when God deals with them, Joel ii. 14—16; their hearts could not endure, their hands, their feet, were not strong, to act or stand. Let us not sin, provoke the Lord by our vain confidences, for he is stronger than man.

Obs. 4. That the word of the Lord shall take place, whatever men's thoughts are. They thought Nebuchadnezzar would not come, or if he did, that they and the Egyptians should be able to deal with them, and prevent those evils which were threatened by the prophets; but, "I the Lord have spoken it, and will do it." Where he hath a mouth to speak, he hath a hand to do; it is not any power can hinder: "I will work, and who shall let it?" Isa. xliii. 13; not devils or men can do it. Neither will the Lord revoke what he hath said, and so prevent judgments intended; Isa. xxxi. 2, "He is wise, and will bring evil, and will not call back his words." Men often speak, threaten, and then after eat their words, call back their threatenings, saying, they were uttered in passion, inconsiderately, and so show their folly; but God, when he speaks, it is in wisdom, his words shall stand, and not be removed, or called back, Amos vi. 11. Hence is it that, Jer. xliv. 28, the Lord saith, "They shall know whose word shall stand, mine or theirs;" they shall see in a little time that their words are vanity, foolish, and come to nothing, and that my words are the words of wisdom, weighty, and stable. Zech. i. 6, "Did not my words and my statutes take hold of your fathers?" what God said was accomplished, and they could not but acknowledge it; "Like as the Lord of hosts thought to do unto us, so hath he dealt with us."

Ver. 15. "And I will scatter thee among the heathen, and disperse thee in the countries." Of their scattering and dispersing hath formerly been spoken. It was a great comfort to them to have their solemn meetings at Jerusalem, and in the temple; and as great an affliction to be deprived of them, and scattered as dust and chaff among the heathens, whose language they understood not, and whose religion was abomination to the God of Israel.

"And will consume thy filthiness out of thee." The Hebrew is, I will make thy filthiness to fail out of thee: so Montanus, I will make an end of thy filthiness. Thou art now so defiled with idols, blood, and other abominations, that thou art as a heap and bundle of "filthiness," even the filthy city; but I will throw thee into the furnace of affliction, and cause thy "filthiness" to depart from thee. By "filthiness" we may understand, filthy ones, the abstract being put for the concrete. Jerusalem had many filthy persons in it, and God would by his judgments consume them.

Obs. The Lord, by his judgments, doth purge out of cities and nations the wicked, and makes them and their wickedness to cease. "I will consume thy filthiness out of thee;" that is, thy filthy ones, with their "filthiness." God brought the sword, famine, pestilence upon Jerusalem, and by these did cut off and consume the filthy ones there. See Ezek. v. 12; Jer. xiv. 15; xvi. 4; Ezek. xiii. 14. God by his judgments destroyed Jerusalem, and so caused her "filthiness" to be at an end: Ezek. xvi. 40, 41, "They shall stone thee with stones, and thrust thee through with their swords; burn thine houses with fire, and execute judgments upon thee in the sight of many women: and I will cause thee to cease from playing the harlot." The same judgments you have, Ezek. xxiii. 47; and by them he would "cause lewdness to cease out of the land," ver. 48. By his judgments the Lord consumes the filthy out of the city and land, and "filthiness" out of the saints.

Ver. 16. "And thou shalt take thine inheritance in thyself." Hebrew is thus, Thou shalt inherit in thyself; thou shalt be thine own inheritance. Heretofore thou wast mine inheritance, but it shall be so no longer; I will cast thee off, being so filthy as thou art, and thou shalt have no "inheritance" in me, but in "thyself." Some making the word to be from חלל to wound, to profane, do render it in the first person, thus, I will wound thee: so Symmachus, I will defile thee, and profane thee: so Theodotion. The Septuagint, is, I will possess in thee; that is, I will have a people for my possession among you, when you are scattered abroad among the heathens. It is true God had a people among them when they were in Babylon; but the Hebrew is not in the first person. Piscator hath it thus, Thou shalt be made profane in thyself; thou shalt be cast off by me into banishment, and be no other in my account than a common and profane people; I will account of thee so, and deal accordingly with thee. So the words are to be understood, Isa. xliii. 28; xlvii. 6; where the Lord is said to profane the princes, and pollute his inheritance. This sense may well stand with the first, for if God made them a profane and common people, they had no "inheritance" in him, but their "inheritance" was in themselves.

"In the sight of the heathen." Heathens shall see that thou art a people cast off of thy God for thy wickedness, and exposed to reproach, cursing, and as great miseries as ever any people were.

Obs. 1. That the wickedness of God's people doth disinterest them in God; it makes God disown them, and leave them to themselves. They might think and say they were still the people, the "inheritance," of God, that they had interest in him; but "thou shalt take thine inheritance in thyself," I disclaim thee, I cast thee off as profane, and look upon thee no otherwise than I do upon heathens. It was the wickedness of the ten tribes which made the Lord to say, "Lo-ammi, ye are not my people, and I will not be your God," Hos. i. 9; in which prophet you may read largely of their sins. Chapter viii. 3, tells you, that Israel had cast off the thing that was good, viz. the worship of God; and, ver. 5, "Thy calf, O Samaria, hath cast thee off;" that is, thy false worship hath made me to cast thee off, to declare thee to be none of my city, and thy people to be none of mine. In the twelfth chapter of Jeremiah you have that which bears witness fully to this observation; ver. 7—9, "I have forsaken mine house, I have left mine heritage; I have given the dearly beloved of my soul into the hand of her enemies. Mine heritage is to me as a lion in the forest; it crieth out against me: therefore have I hated it. Mine heritage unto me is as a speckled bird, the birds round about are against her; come ye, assemble all the beasts of the field, come to devour." The meaning of these words is this: That the Jews were once very dear to God, even as dear as any wife can be to a husband; but because, like lions, they carried it stoutly against God, and cried out against him and his prophets, therefore he forsook them, hated them, and gave them into the hands of the Babylonians; and because Jerusalem was as a "speckled bird" in the eye of God, through her variety of gods, altars, superstitions, and idolatries, therefore God caused the birds of all the nations to hoot at and hate her, even as birds do a "speckled bird," inviting them, and all the beasts of the field, to come and devour her. And why all this? they dealt treacherously, ver. 1; they were hypocritical, ver. 2; they were wicked, ver. 4. The Jews had been a people precious in the sight of God, and honourable, Isa. xliii. 4; Jerusalem his habitation, and the people of it his inheritance and his glory, whom he protected, Isa. iv. 5; yet by their sins they provoked God, so as that he gave "his strength into captivity, and his glory into the enemy's hand," Psal. lxxviii. 61.

Obs. 2. That God's judgments bring people to the knowledge of God. It rises from the former verse and this laid together. God would scatter them, consume them, cast them off, leave them to themselves, and they should know that he was the Lord: Psal. ix. 16, "The Lord is known by executing judgments;" his power, his justice, and sovereignty are known thereby, and so men are made to fear, and stand in awe of him. When God is silent, and speaks not by his judgments, men think he is like themselves, Psal. l. 21; and are imboldened to sin, Eccles. viii. 11; but when God thunders by his judgments, they have other apprehensions of him, 1 Sam. vi. 19, 20.

Ver. 17—22. *And the word of the Lord came unto me, saying, Son of man, the house of Israel is to me become dross: all they are brass, and tin, and iron, and lead, in the midst of the furnace; they are even the dross of silver. Therefore thus saith the Lord God; Because ye are all become dross, behold, therefore I will gather you into the midst of Jerusalem. As they gather silver, and brass, and iron, and lead, and tin, into the midst of the furnace, to blow the fire upon it, to melt it; so will I gather you in mine anger and in my fury, and I will leave you there, and melt you. Yea, I will gather you, and blow upon you in the fire of my wrath, and ye shall be melted in the midst thereof. As silver is melted in the midst of the furnace, so shall ye be melted in the midst thereof; and ye shall know that I the Lord have poured out my fury upon you.*

In these words is the Lord's second message to Ezekiel, wherein is set forth,

I. The degenerate estate of the Jews, under the similitude of "dross," ver. 18.

II. God's judicial proceeding with them being "dross," ver. 19—22.

1. He would "gather" them together.
2. "Blow" upon them.
3. "Melt" them.

III. The end of his so dealing with them, ver. 22.

Ver. 17. "And the word of the Lord came unto me, saying." These words we have had oft, and in ver. 1 of this chapter. God being upon bringing judgments upon his people, gives them notice thereof by his prophets; he speaks before he strikes.

Ver. 18. "The house of Israel is to me become dross." The house of Israel, viz. the Jews, had been of high account with God, they were once his chosen people above all others, Deut. vii. 6; they were once "a kingdom of priests, and an holy nation," Exod. xix. 6; they were once so honourable and precious, that God gave and destroyed other nations for their sakes, Isa. xliii. 4; they were once his portion, his inheritance, Deut. xxxii. 9; Isa. xix. 25; they were once his vineyard, and pleasant plant, Isa. v. 7; they were once "a people near unto him," Psal. cxlviii. 14; the dearly beloved of his soul, Jer. xii. 7; his peculiar people, Exod. xix. 5: but now they were become "dross," they had degenerated from their former faithfulness, justice, honesty, sincerity, and purity.

The word for "dross" is, סִיג *sig*, which is, whatsoever the fire separates from any metal. Metals have something of an heterogeneal nature to themselves, which being separated by fire or any other way, is that we call "dross." The house of Israel here is not said to be drossy, but to be "dross;" it is fit therefore to see wherein the resemblance lies between them.

1. The "dross" obscures the lustre and glory of the metal, yea, covers it up, so that it appears not; rust and filth compass and hide the gold, so that neither the nature or lustre of it can be seen. So the house of Israel was such at this time, that no gold, no silver appeared: Jer. v. 1, "Run ye to and fro through the streets of Jerusalem, and see now, and know, and seek in the broad places thereof, if ye can find a man, if there be any that executeth judgment, that seeketh the truth;" Jer. ix. 2, "They be all adulterers, an assembly of treacherous men;" Zeph. iii. 7, "They rose early, and corrupted all their doings;" Jer. vi. 28, "They are all grievous revolters, walking with slanders: they are brass and iron; they are all corrupters:" there was no pure metal appeared amongst them, especially gold or silver. If there were some righteous, just, holy, faithful ones amongst them, they lay hid under the "dross."

2. "Dross" is a deceiving thing. It is like metal, but is not metal; the dross of silver is like it, and so the dross of gold is like it, but the dross is neither silver nor gold: so the house of Israel was deceitful, hypocritical, like saints, but not saints; see Isa. x. 6; lviii. 2. Chap. ix. 17, "Every one is an hypocrite, and an evil-doer, and every mouth speaketh folly." They professed themselves to be the people of God, yet were not such as they seemed to be, Jer. vii. 2, 4, 9, 10; they were like potsherds covered with silver dross, Prov. xxvi. 23.

2. "Dross" is not bettered by the fire: put it into the fire time after time, it abides so still. God had oft put the Jews into the furnace of affliction, and heated the furnace sometimes very hot, but they were the same still: they had been in the Egyptian fire, 2 Kings xxiii. 33; in the Syrian and Chaldean fire, chap. xxiv. 2, and other fires; but none of them did them any good: Jer. v. 3, "Thou hast stricken them, but they have not grieved; thou hast consumed them, but they have refused to receive correction;" and not only did the prophet complain thus, but the Lord himself; chap. ii. 30, "In vain have I smitten their children; they received no correction:" they were nothing the better for all God's blows and fires, "dross" they were, and "dross" they continued.

4. "Dross" is a worthless thing. It is of no value, base, vile, contemptible: such was the house of Israel, and chief in it; Jer. xxiv. 8, Zedekiah the king

his princes, and the rest of Jerusalem, were as evil figs which could not be eaten: the kingdom was base, Ezek. xvii. 14; the city a harlot, chap. xvi. 35; she changed the judgments of God into wickedness more than the nations, chap. v. 6; and was more vile than Sodom and Samaria, chap. xvi. 47.

5. It is useless, and to be rejected. The Jews now were so corrupted, so wicked, so unprofitable, that the Lord was casting them off, and out; Jer. vi. 30, "Reprobate silver shall men call them, because the Lord hath rejected them." As the wood of the vine, when fruitless, is not fit for any thing but the fire, Ezek. xv. so the dross of silver is not fit for any thing but rejection. The house of Israel being become "dross," the Lord saith, Jer. vii. 15, "I will cast you out of my sight, as I have cast out all your brethren, even the whole seed of Ephraim:" the ten tribes they proved "dross," and the Lord cast them away, and now he would cast Judah and Benjamin out of his sight; and when he did it, they were the offscouring and refuse in the midst of heathens, Lam. iii. 45.

6. "Dross" is an offensive thing, rust eats into the metal, endangers that, and makes the goldsmith to kindle the fire, to separate it from the gold and silver. So wicked men are offensive to God and good men, and cause the Lord to bring his fiery judgments to separate between the precious and the vile. The wickedness of the house of Israel caused God to bring the sword, famine, plague, captivity, and by these to purge out and consume the filthiness of Jerusalem.

"All they are brass, and tin, and iron, and lead." Before, he had said they were dross; how doth he now call them, brass, iron, tin, lead? these are good metals. True, in themselves they are so, but compare them with silver or gold, they are but as dross, base metals; so tin is reckoned in Scripture account, Isa. i. 25; so brass, iron, and lead are reputed, Jer. vi. 28, 29. When pure religion, judgment, and righteousness were in the house and city of Israel, then she was silver, precious and good metal; but falling to idolatry, oppression, and profaneness, her silver became dross, and her children became brass, that is, "impudent and hardhearted," Ezek. iii. 7; tin, that is, hypocritical, being all in show nothing in substance, chap. xxxiii. 31; iron, that is, cruel, bloody, inflexible, so were the great ones, men in place, chap. xxxiv. 2, 4; Zeph. iii. 3, 4; Jer. v. 5; lead, that is, sottish and stupid, Jer. iv. 22: chap. viii. 9, "They have rejected the word of the Lord; and what wisdom is in them?" that which should have enlightened them, and made them wise, that they rejected, and so were foolish and sottish.

"In the midst of the furnace." In the 11th chapter, 3rd and 7th verses, the city is called a "caldron," and the people the "flesh" to be boiled in it; and here it is called the "furnace," and the people the "brass, tin, iron, lead," to be melted in it. God would make Jerusalem a furnace of affliction, and cast the dross and base metal into it. The Jews had so degenerated from the golden and silvery purity of their fathers, that they had no preciousness in them, nothing left but dross, or that which was base as dross.

"They are even the dross of silver." Their fathers were true believers, sincere worshippers, just dealers, covenant keepers, and so were like unto silver, precious, pure, white, desirable; but these their children were "dross, even the dross of silver," faithless, hypocritical, unjust, perjured. The nations were dross, but not the dross of silver, they were never of higher account than brass, tin, iron, lead; only the Jews were accounted silver, and now they were become the "dross of silver," worse than the nations, 2 Kings xxi. 9.

Ver. 19, 20. "I will gather you into the midst of Jerusalem. As they gather silver, and brass, and iron, and lead, and tin, into the midst of the furnace." The Hebrew is, I will gather you with the gathering of silver, that is, with such a gathering, that like as the founder, silver or goldsmith, when he would prove the metals digged out of the mines, what they are, and separate the dregs and dross from them, he gathers them together, and puts them into the furnace; so would the Lord do by the Jews, he would gather them from all parts of Judea into Jerusalem, which was the furnace, when God brought Nebuchadnezzar with his army to besiege it.

"To blow the fire upon it, and to melt it." When the metals are in the furnace, then the founder causes the fire to be blown, the heat to be heightened, till the metals be melted, that so the scum and dross being taken away, they may be malleable and useful.

"So will I gather you in mine anger and in my fury, and I will leave you there, and melt you." The Lord finding his people to be dross, or mingled with base metals, he was greatly provoked; and so, in his anger and fury, gathered them into the furnace, and there left them to be melted.

The fire God used in the melting of them was famine, plague, and sword, which melted many of them; and then the burning coals scattered over the city, Ezek. x. 2, which melted the furnace, and them that were left in it.

Ver. 21. "I will gather you, and blow upon you in the fire of my wrath." The word for "blow upon you" is, נפחתי the same with that in the 20th verse; that like as the founder blows, and gives not over blowing till the metals are melted, and the dregs separated, so the Lord he would blow upon them, that is, exercise them with severe judgments one after another, till they should be melted and consumed, and the vile separated from the precious. This expression of blowing upon them in the fire of his wrath, is the same with that in the former chapter, ver. 31, "I will blow against thee in the fire of my wrath:" when God blows against any, he blows upon them, and the breath of his nostrils burns as fire.

Ver. 22. "As silver is melted in the midst of the furnace, so shall ye be melted in the midst thereof." Their melting is oft spoken of, ver. 20, 21; and here God was serious in the business, and resolved upon it, nothing should now prevent it, not the intercession of Moses and Samuel, Jer. xv. 1.

"And ye shall know that I the Lord have poured out my fury upon you." Though the greatest part were consumed by those sad and severe judgments God brought upon them, yet some escaped, some were carried into Babylon, another furnace, to melt out their remaining dross; and they were made to know, and acknowledge, that the Lord had poured out his fury upon them.

Of pouring out fury, or fury poured out, see chap. xx. 33.

Obs. 1. That churches or states may degenerate from their preciousness and purity, into vileness and profaneness. "The house of Israel is become dross, even the dross of silver;" it was so degenerated, that it went beyond others in wickedness; which made Isaiah to wonder, chap. i. 21—23, "How is the faithful city become a harlot!" not simply a harlot, but a great and notorious harlot: "it was full of judgment, and righteousness lodged in it," but instead of these, now there was oppression and murder. "Thy silver is become dross, thy wine is mixed with water;" thy money is counterfeit, and thy wine corrupt; or thus, whatever was pure in thee, is now corrupted, the law is corrupted with false expositions, the worship is corrupted with idols and human traditions, justice is corrupted with bribery and bloody oppressions, chastity and sobriety are corrupted with lewd and unclean practices. Jerusalem had lost her excellency, and was become loathsome, as a filthy harlot, doing the work of "an imperious whorish woman," Ezek. xvi. 30: Jer. vii. 9—11, she justified herself in her sinful and shameful practices, and made the house of God a den of thieves. Rome was once a golden city for her faith and holiness, Rom. i. 8; xvi. 19; but now is so corrupt in doctrine, worship, and manners, that she is become "the mother of harlots and abominations," Rev. xvii. 5. The seven churches were once golden candlesticks, but through their corruptions and weaknesses, they soon degenerated into dross.

Obs. 2. That men professing godliness, and living ungodlily, whatever others' thoughts are of them, or whatever they think of themselves, they are not acceptable to God, nor fit materials of a church. "The house of Israel is to me become dross:" they profess my name, and so judge themselves good silver, precious in my sight, and others accord with them therein; but they live wickedly, and to me they are no better than dross, than brass, tin, iron, and lead, too base materials to make a temple for me to dwell in, or a candlestick for me to set a prophetical light in. Such persons, whatever profession they make, whatever parts or privileges they have, they are no silver, but the dross, the excrements of silver, which defile, disgrace the name, the church, the ordinances of God, and must be separated from the gold and silver, 2 Cor. vi. 17. As the prophet saith, "What is the chaff to the wheat?" Jer. xxiii. 28; so, what is the dross to the silver? It is fitter for the dunghill than the temple. Many that appear silver unto men, will be found dross unto God. The best have some dross in them, they are drossy, but not dross. Hypocrites and wicked ones are dross; only hypocrites are the "dross of silver."

Obs. 3. The greatest part of professors, when they come to the trial, will be found corrupt and naught. "All they are brass, and tin, and iron, and lead, in the midst of the furnace." When they came to be tried, what metal they were of, they proved all to be base metal and dross; the furnace discovered them. The prophets told them what they were, Jer. vi. 13; viii. 10; ix. 2—4, viz. covetous, false dealers, treacherous, liars, slanderers, deceivers, &c.; Isa. i. 4, a "sinful nation, a people laden with iniquity, a seed of evil-doers, corrupters," &c. But they believed not the prophets, telling them what they were, and what judgments would come upon them for their sins: but notwithstanding all their wickedness, they cried, "The temple, the temple, the temple," Jer. vii. 4; they worshipped God, and called themselves citizens of the holy city, Isa. xlviii. 1, 2. They leaned upon the Lord, and said, Is not the Lord among us? doth not he own us for his people? are not we his portion, and he our God? none evil can come upon us. Thus they flattered themselves that they were good metal, and precious; but when the Lord gathered them into the furnace, he found them dross; they were no better in the account of God than Sodomites and Gomorrheans, Isa. i. 10; Jer. xxiii. 14; the city, and all the inhabitants of it, were a provocation unto him, Jer. xxxii. 31, 32, and he was destruction unto it and them. In the city was found much dross, but little silver; much brass, tin, iron, lead, but little gold. Since the Lord hath put us into the furnace of affliction, have not many been discovered to be dross, who appeared silver before? Are all those pure metal which make profession now? Most will be found brazen, tinny, irony, and leaden; the number of sincere and silver-like christians will be few. What Paul said to the Corinthians, 2 Epist. xii. 20, that may the Lord say to this city, and professors every where; "I fear, lest, when I come, I shall not find you such as I would, and that I shall be found unto you such as ye would not." Look to it, that you be sincere.

Obs. 4. In the degeneracy of a people, some do degenerate more than others, into a worse condition than the rest. Here some were brass, some tin, some iron, some lead, and some the dross of silver. The house of Israel was degenerated into base metals, which were one worse than another, yea into dross, yea dross (for so the word is in Hebrew) of silver. Some were impudent, some hypocritical, some murderers, some brutish, some idolatrous, some atheistical, some unclean and profane: see Ezek. viii. 10—16. Some did great, and others greater abominations; some did evil with both hands, and that earnestly, Micah vii. 3; the best of them were briers and thorns, ver. 4, and the rest were scorpions, Ezek. ii. 6; and the iniquity of the house of Israel was exceeding great, chap. ix. 9. When once people do degenerate from their honesty, their principles, their profession, some go further than others; Jer. vii. 26, "they did worse than their fathers;" chap. ix. 3, "they proceed from evil to evil;" they stayed not till they became dross, yet one was worse dross than another. In our days hath been great degenerating, and some are degenerated into brass, some into tin, some into iron, some into lead, some into the dross of silver.

Obs. 5. Those who degenerate from God and his ways, from principles of honesty and equity, be it more or less that they degenerate from them, they shall meet with fury and fire from the Lord. "Because ye are all become dross, I will gather you in mine anger and in my fury, into the midst of the furnace, and blow upon you in the fire of my wrath," to melt you, to consume you. When the church of Ephesus decayed in her first love, that of Pergamos turned aside to doctrines of Balaam and the Nicolaitanes, that of Thyatira to the teachings and seductions of Jezebel; when Sardis abated in her zeal, and Laodicea became lukewarm; the Lord threatened them severely; and at last brake the candlesticks, and put out the lights, Rev. ii. and iii. Be they states, churches, families, or persons that degenerate, God hath no pleasure in them, Heb. x. 38; but will cast them "into great tribulation," Rev. ii. 22, and be unto them a consuming fire, Ezek. xxi. 31. And David tells you, Psal. cxix. 119, that God will put away all the wicked of the earth from him like dross, at the last day; this he will do, and be an eternal consuming fire unto them.

Obs. 6. Melting and consuming judgments upon a people are the wrath of God, whoever be the executioners thereof. Nebuchadnezzar should besiege Jerusalem, and make it like a furnace to melt and consume the Jews, and this the Lord owns to be his doing; ver. 22, "And ye shall know that I the Lord have poured out my fury upon you:" it was not Nebuchadnezzar nor the army's fury, but the fury of the Lord; they were only the vials or vessels by which it was poured out. And now if fury have been poured out in Scotland, it is not the army hath done it, but the Lord, who gathered them together, as brass, iron, lead, and tin in a furnace, blew upon them in the fire of his wrath, melted and consumed them as dross; and you must know it was the Lord, not man, that poured out his fury upon them, and those the Lord hath made vessels of mercy unto us, who have been vials of his fury towards them. If you will mourn for God's se-

Sept. 3, 1650, were the Scots routed, four thousand slain, and ten thousand taken.

verity towards them, yet rejoice for his goodness towards us.

Ver. 23, 24. *And the word of the Lord came unto me, saying, Son of man, say unto her, Thou art the land that is not cleansed, nor rained upon in the day of indignation.*

Here begins the third message of the Lord unto the prophet. The 23rd verse is the same with the 17th and 1st, and we pass it by.

Ver. 24. "Thou art the land that is not cleansed." In this verse is laid down the pollution of the land in general; in the verses following it is more particularly expressed.

The word for "cleansed" is from טהר which signifies, to purge from filthiness, and so to purge as to make shining and beautiful. Judea, the land here meant, had been oft cleansing, but was never thoroughly cleansed. Hezekiah and Josiah made the greatest cleansings, but all the sin was not purged out in their days; they took away the objects and mediums of sin, viz. the idols, images, groves, and high places, but the people continued wicked; they did not cleanse their hands, nor hearts, and turn to the Lord, but returned to their former and worse abominations, when those good kings were gone. The Lord had sent them many prophets, who dealt with them several ways to draw them to repentance; sometimes they allured them by sweet promises and invitations, sometimes they threatened them with sharp judgments, sometimes they pressed them with strong arguments, Jer. iv. 1, 3, 4; Ezek. xviii. 31, 32; sometimes they spake plainly to them, sometimes parabolically; sometimes they wept and sighed to the breaking of their loins, doing strange things to affect them, Ezek. xvii. 2; Jer. iv. 19; ix. 1; Ezek. xxi. 6; xii. 5, 6; iv. 1—3, &c. Besides these things, God oft sent sweeping and fierce judgments amongst them, Isa. xxiv.; Amos i. and iv. famine, sword, pestilence; and notwithstanding all these, they returned not to the Lord, but the land, that is, the people of it, did remain uncleansed, they were like a land wherein was nothing but weeds, nettles, briers, and thorns.

Object. Isa. xxvi. 10, it is called a "land of uprightness;" and if so, how is it here said it is a "land not cleansed?"

Answ. The Hebrew is, in the land where men are taught right things; right worshipping of God, right dealing with men, right walking in their several relations: or, "the land of uprightness," for that they ought to have done uprightly; but in that land they dealt unjustly, and filled that land with sin, Jer. li. 5: or, "the land of uprightness," for that it had been so, Isa. i. 21.

"Nor rained upon in the day of indignation." God had oft withheld the former and latter rain from them, and afflicted the land with great drought, Isa. xxiv. 6, 7; Psal. lxviii. 9; 1 Kings xviii. 5; 2 Kings viii. 1; Jer. xiv. 4; Amos iv. 7; and he threatened, Isa. v. 6, to command the clouds to rain no rain upon it: and it was so in Joel's days, chap. i. 9—11, who lived in Manasseh's time, as the rabbies said, and that was a time of indignation, and sorely distressed them, so that man and beast suffered much. In Jeremiah's days also, who lived in the times of Jehoiakim, Jehoiachin, and Zedekiah, were the rains denied unto the land, so that by reason of drought, Judah mourned, the gates thereof languished, Jerusalem cried, the nobles and their little ones were ashamed, confounded, and covered their heads, Jer. xiv. 1—3.

Or thus we may understand these words; Judea, thou art a polluted, filthy land, nothing hath prevailed with thee to cleanse thee, and thou shalt not be rained upon in the day of mine indignation; that is, thou shalt have no mercy when the fire of my wrath is kindled, thou shalt have no rain to quench it, in my wrath I will not remember mercy.

Obs. 1. The Lord takes notice of places, what they are, whether cleansed or not cleansed. "Thou art the land not cleansed:" thou art full of briers and thorns, full of vermin and wild beasts, Ezek. ii. 6; Isa. ix. 18: it was full of wicked and vile men which did defile the land; Ezek. vii. 23, "The land is full of bloody crimes, the city is full of violence." There is not a land, city, town, or family in the whole earth, but the eye of the Lord is upon it, and he sees what it is, whether it be defiled, and how greatly defiled. He knew what Sodom and Gomorrah were, before he sent fire from heaven upon them. He knew how polluted Canaan was by the nations, before he brought the Jews into it, Deut. ix. 4, 5. He took notice of Ammon, Moab, Seir, Edom, Philistia, Tyre, Sidon, and Babylon, he saw what cages of unclean birds they were. Hos. vi. 10, "I have seen an horrible thing in the house of Israel." He saw what the ancients of Israel did, Ezek. viii. 11. He saw folly in the prophets of Samaria, and an horrible thing in the prophets of Jerusalem; they strengthened the hands of evil-doers, Jer. xxiii. 13, 14.

Obs. 2. When lands have had means of cleansing, and are not cleansed, they are matter of indignation and exprobration unto God. Judea had the prophets, sometimes good magistrates, it had great mercies, great judgments, solemn fasts, Isa. lviii. 3; Joel i. 14; but was still uncleansed; therefore saith the Lord, "Thou art the land that is not cleansed." The word "thou" notes God's indignation at them, and his exprobration of them. When a ground is full of thorns, briers, nettles, vermin, and wild beasts, and the husbandman's servants cannot with all their art and pains rid the ground of them, that ground exasperates the husbandman, and makes him say, This is the ground that will not be cleansed, that brings forth nothing which is good: so was it here with Judea; Isa. v. 4, "What could have been done more to my vineyard, that I have not done in it? wherefore, when I looked for grapes, brought it forth wild grapes?" it retained its sourness, notwithstanding all done. Ezek. xxiv. 13, "Because I have purged thee, and thou wast not purged, thou shalt not be purged from thy filthiness any more:" seeing I have used means to purge thee, and thou wilt not be purged, seeing thou art obstinate, and there is lewdness in thy filthiness, there shall no more purgative means be afforded thee, but I will bring my fury, and cause it to rest upon thee. And when it is thus, it is dreadful; Jer. xiii. 27, "Woe unto thee, O Jerusalem! wilt thou not be made clean?"

Obs. 3. The Lord hath his day and time to judge and punish lands uncleansed, people unreformed. "In the day of indignation." Though the Lord bear long with a sinful nation, yet he will not bear always, the time comes at last that his hot anger breaks out and damnifies. This "day of indignation" was when the Lord called the Babylonish army to the walls of Jerusalem, Jer. iv. 6, 7, 9, 13; lii. 4; Zeph. i. 14, 15. The ten tribes not hearkening to the prophets and seers, but proceeding in their wicked ways, 2 Kings xvii. 12—14, found the Lord had a day to send Shalmaneser, who spoiled the land, besieged Samaria three years, and carried them away captive into Assyria; which was the verifying of Isaiah's prophecy against them, chap. xvii. 4, "In that day it shall come to pass, that the glory of Jacob shall be made thin, and the fatness of his flesh shall wax lean." The glory and fat of Jacob, were their princes, counsellors, soldiers, wealth, and strong holds, which the Assyrian deprived them of, and made Jacob thin and lean. God had his day to visit Egypt, by shaking his hand over it, Isa. xix. 16. The Lord had his day to make Tyre "forgotten seventy years, according to the days of one king," Isa. xxiii. 15. About that time which Nebuchadnezzar took Jerusalem, he also took Tyre, and the great merchandizing of it was interrupted seventy years, so long as the Jews were in Babylon, which Isaiah calls "the days of one king." The days of kings, and so other men who lived at ease, were usually counted seventy years. Or thus, according to the days of one kingdom, that is, the days of the Babylonian kingdom; from the time of taking Tyre, for seventy years after, that kingdom ceased, and Darius the Median took it, Dan. v. 31.

Obs. 4. When a land and people retain their filthiness, and rest uncleansed after mercies, judgments, and means used to do them good, God doth not only withhold mercy, but deny hope of mercy. Judea was the land uncleansed, and she should have no rain "in the day of indignation." Her sins kept back the rain in a literal sense, Jer. iii. 2, 3, and cut off the hope of rain in a metaphorical sense. Zeph. i. 17, 18, "I will bring distress upon men, that they shall walk like blind men, because they have sinned against the Lord:" they shall see nothing tending to their comfort, but all working against them; for it follows, "Their blood shall be poured out as dust, and their flesh as the dung. Neither their silver nor their gold shall be able to deliver them in the day of the Lord's wrath; but the whole land shall be devoured by the fire of his jealousy." Gold and silver will do much, but nothing "in the day of wrath," Prov. xi. 4. That place in Isa. viii. 21, 22, is observable; "They shall pass through it, hardly bestead and hungry: and it shall come to pass, when they shall be hungry, they shall fret themselves, and curse their king and their God, and look upward. And they shall look unto the earth; and behold trouble and darkness," &c. When Sennacherib or Nebuchadnezzar should invade the land, the famine should be so great, and the men of Judea so hungry, that they should fret, and curse their king, their God; the one, because he prevented not their misery; the other, because he delivered them not out of it: and they should look up to heaven, down to the church, and find help from neither, nor hope of mercy any where; trouble, darkness, anguish were before them, and they should be driven to them. They disgrace the true prophets, ver. 18; they listened to false prophets and liars, ver. 19; they tried not them and their doctrine by the law and testimonies, ver. 20; therefore God brought evil upon them, yea, such evil as they were helpless and hopeless.

Ver. 25. *There is a conspiracy of her prophets in the midst thereof, like a roaring lion ravening the prey; they have devoured souls; they have taken the treasure and precious things; they have made her many widows in the midst thereof.*

In this verse and the 28th you have the sins of the prophets expressed which defiled the land, and made it to be called, the land uncleansed; and they are,

I. Conspiracy.

II. Cruelty; "like roaring lions," &c.

III. Murder, and that of souls; "they have devoured," &c.

IV. Covetousness; "they have taken the treasure and precious things."

V. Inhumanity or impiety; "they have made her many widows."

VI. Flattery and lying, ver. 28.

"A conspiracy of her prophets." The Hebrew for "conspiracy" is, קֶשֶׁר, which is from a root or word, which signifies to bind, to tie together, as Jer. li. 63; Isa. xlix. 16; and metaphorically is referred to the minds of men combining together, as 1 Sam. xviii. 2, "The soul of Jonathan was knit with the soul of David," was united, bound to, inleagued with the soul of David; and 2 Sam. xv. 31, "Ahithophel is among the conspirators with Absalom," his mind with others were united in a conspiracy against David: so 2 Kings xii. 20, Joash "his servants arose, and made a conspiracy;" the Hebrew is, they conspired a conspiracy, they were all of one heart and mind, and it was to kill their master. Here the prophets had a conspiracy, it is spoken of the evil prophets; they met in Jerusalem, they consulted and consented to prophesy the same thing, that none should prophesy otherwise; if they did, they would cry them down, and those who should follow them: thus they "made a conspiracy" against the true prophets, and those who were truly religious, opposing God and godliness. You may read how they set themselves against Jeremiah, chap. xxvi. 8, and stirred up the princes and people against him, ver. 11; how they prophesied the same things, chap. xxiii. 17; vi. 14.

"Like a roaring lion ravening the prey." Lions are fierce and cruel, especially when hungry; and it is observed of them, that they first roar, whereby they scare men and beasts, and then hunt after the prey: so these prophets did roar against the true prophets and their followers; Jer. xxvi. 11, "This man is worthy to die," not to be silenced, imprisoned, or banished, but "to die;" nothing but death will suffice them; they were greedy of the prey, and said, he should "surely die," ver. 8.

"They have devoured souls." "Souls," that is, men, by a synecdoche of the part for the whole. They preached dreams and visions of their own heads, whereby they seduced and undid multitudes, Ezek. xiii. 10; Jer. xiv. 13; xxiii. 13. When prophets do not tell people of their sins, they destroy them, Ezek. iii. 18; and so when they present their own fancies instead of God's word: Jer. xxiii. 22, with 32, had they delivered the word of God, they should have turned men from their evil ways, but by their lies and dreams they made them to err.

"They have taken the treasure and precious things." The Hebrew word for "treasure" is, חסן which Montanus renders *robur*, strength; and so it is used, Isa. xxxiii. 6; and riches, treasure, are called *cosen*, because men put their confidence in them, and make them their strength, Prov. x. 15. Psal. lii. 7, the word is used for treasure and riches. Prov. xv. 6, "In the house of the righteous is" חסן רב "much treasure," much riches, or much strength: here it is "treasure."

"Precious things." "Precious things," ויקר notes things "much set by," as a good name, 1 Sam. xviii. 30; things beloved, Jer. xxxi. 20, "Ephraim my dear son," בן יקיר υἱός ἀγάπητος, my dearly beloved son, saith the Septuagint: things of great worth, Prov. xx. 15; Isa. xxviii. 16; Jer. xx. 5. Here it notes things of worth, and dear unto them. These prophets were false, and would not prophesy, unless the people gave them, and gave them choice things. Hence Micah saith, the prophets divined for money, chap. iii. 11, and prepared war for them who would not put into their mouths, ver. 5. They did not take by force, or steal away their treasures, but they carried it so, that the people must give, and they had their "treasure and precious things." They were not content with what was their stipends; but, as Lavater speaks, they had ways, arts, devices, to get such things.

The word *jakar* signifies also glory, and honour, Dan. ii. 37; Esth. i. 20; and so it is rendered here by Montanus, Lavater, Œcolampadius, and the French translation. The sense then is this, that these false prophets were ambitious, minding high places and popular glory.

"They have made her many widows." Those men who would not be of their minds, hearken to their prophecies, countenance and maintain them with their treasures and precious things, they prepared war for them, they stirred up the powers and people who were of their own way, to hate them, and deal unkindly with them. Isa. lxvi. 5, "Hear the word of the Lord, ye that tremble at his word; Your brethren that hated you, that cast you out for my name's sake," &c. There were some who trembled at the word of the Lord, the word of the true prophets, and durst not side with the false prophets, their doctrines or practices; these therefore were hated of their brethren, that were their disciples, and cast out. So Ezek. xi. 15, they said, "Get you far from the Lord; unto us is this land given in possession." You have nothing to do here in Judea or Jerusalem, here is no liberty for you; begone, or die for it! Now because many did venture to stay, they prevailed so, that they were put to death, and by this means they made many widows. They also used to encourage the princes to war; as, 1 Kings xxii. the false prophets put on Ahab to go up to Ramoth-gilead, and promised him success in that war, but he fell, and many others with him, and hereby they made many widows.

Obs. 1. In Jerusalem were wicked and false prophets. Jerusalem was the holy city, the city of God, the place where God's name was recorded, a type of the church of God in all ages; yet there, even there, were such prophets: and it holds out clearly to us, that there will be false prophets in the church of God always. In Christ's time there were such; Matt. vii. 15, "Beware of false prophets, which come to you in sheep's clothing." In Paul's time there were such; Acts xiii. 6, there was one Bar-jesus, a Jew, and a false prophet. In John's time there were such; 1 John iv. 1, "Many false prophets are gone out into the world:" so many went out then, that there is a generation of them to this day, and that generation will not cease so long as the Lord hath a church in this world; there will be found false prophets even at doomsday.

Obs. 2. Jerusalem's prophets may be, yea, sometimes are, against Jerusalem. "There is a conspiracy of her prophets in the midst thereof." Those who thought themselves the chief prophets in Jerusalem, met, consulted, and agreed together to preach the same things, to set themselves against the prophets and professors who differed from them, as being unsafe and unsound, and to stir up authority against them. The meetings of prophets are not always for the welfare of Zion: here was a council of them, but it was for mischief: that they thought was very lawful, the Spirit of God calls a "conspiracy." Such was that meeting of the chief priests, scribes, and elders in the palace of the high priest, where they consulted against Christ, Matt. xxvi. 3, 4; and that wherein they agreed, "that if any did confess that he was Christ, he should be put out of the synagogue," John ix. 22. Was not the council of Trent a conspiracy of prophets, who pretended they were for Jerusalem, but were in truth against Jerusalem? Did they not agree together, that whoever preached any thing contrary to their canons and articles, should be anathematized? Did they not stir up princes and powers of the world, to punish those they judged sectaries, schismatics, and heretical? Mr. Fox's "Acts and Monuments" do testify the truth thereof. Have not the prophets of our Jerusalem gone too far this way?

Obs. 3. God takes special notice of the sins of prophets. They are first mentioned in the general corruption that was of all sorts. There were priests', princes', people's sins, but the prophets' are set in the front; they provoked God greatly, they did most hurt. Jer. xxiii. 15, "From the prophets of Jerusalem is profaneness gone forth into all the land." They were corrupt springs, that corrupted the whole Jewish earth with the streams of their false doctrines, and example of their sinful practices. Their sins are very much spoken of in the word, and set upon record: they dealt falsely, Jer. vi. 13; they "belied the Lord," Jer. v. 12; they "taught rebellion against the Lord," Jer. xxviii. 16; xxix. 32; they strengthened "the hands of evil-doers," so that none returned from his wickedness, Jer. xxiii. 14; they were "light and treacherous," Zeph. iii. 4; they deluded the people, and murdered their souls, Jer. viii. 11; Ezek. xiii. 10; they were exceeding covetous, and greedy of gain from every quarter, Isa. lvi. 11; Micah iii. 5; they made the people forget the name of the Lord, Jer. xxiii. 27; they were foxes, and dealt very subtlely, Ezek. xiii. 4. They being defiled with such sins, defiled the land thereby, kindled the indignation of the Lord, and made him to say concerning them, "Behold, I will feed them with wormwood, and make them drink the water of gall," Jer. xxiii. 15; and would consume them by sword and famine, chap. xiv. 15.

Obs. 4. That the men who should openly declare against sin, do openly commit sin. "There is a conspiracy of her prophets in the midst thereof." They roared like lions, not caring who heard or saw them; they made many widows in the midst of Jerusalem. They sinned notorious sins, and were not ashamed of them; Jer. xxiii. 11, "Both prophet and priest are profane; in my house have I found their wickedness, saith the Lord;" in the temple, the most public place of worship, there they set up their idols and detestable things, Ezek. vii. 20. When prophets and men in near relations to God are naught, they proceed from sin to sin, from degree to degree of the same sin, till they become impudent. These prophets conspired against those who were good in Jerusalem; they were cruel, murderous, covetous, inhuman, and that in the midst of Jerusalem; they blushed not at any or all these sins; they proceeded so in their covetousness, that they got the treasure and precious things the people had. Thus was it with the popish clergy; they got the best lands, woods, waters, habitations, they got the treasure and precious things; yea, so covetous were they, that they occasioned that proverb, *a mortuis tributum exigere*, to scrape from the dead; and so openly wicked they were, that in their temples and cathedrals they strove so for place, as they shed blood.

Ver. 26. ***Her priests have violated my law, and have profaned mine holy things: they have put no difference between the holy and profane, neither have they shewed difference between the unclean and the clean, and have hid their eyes from my sabbaths, and I am profaned among them.***

In the former verse you had the prophets' sins, here you have the priests'; and they are three:

I. Violation of the law.

II. Profanation of holy things.

III. Neglect of duty; which is twofold:

1. They did not make difference between the holy and profane, the clean, &c.

2. They minded not the Lord's sabbaths, but hid their eyes from them.

"Her priests have violated my law." The priests were to be men of knowledge, Mal. ii. 7, and to teach the people the true sense of the law, 2 Chron. xv. 3; Deut. xvii. 9—11; (for the priests taught, and not only the Levites, Micah iii. 11;) but now the priests were so blind and ignorant, that they knew not God, Jer. ii. 8, so intemperate, that they erred in the things of God, Isa. xxviii. 7; and rejecting true knowledge, are said to forget the law, Hos. iv. 6, and here, to violate it.

The Septuagint reads it, they have contemned my law, they set light by it. Lavater hath it thus, they have stolen or taken away my law; to which sense Vatablus agrees; for because they were bound to teach the law, and did it not, they are said to have stolen away the law. The Hebrew word חמס signifies, to take away, to offer violence, to handle a thing unjustly. The priests did handle the law, Jer. ii. 8; but they handled it unjustly, they wrested and forced it to speak their sense, to countenance their practices; they cared not for the true sense, nor sought after that, but such senses as would please and suit with the times and men's humours.

The law or word of God is violated,

1. When men do wrong point it, and so mar the sense, and alter it; as those that, to make way for the opinion of the soul's sleeping, do put the point after the word "day," "I say unto thee to-day;" whereas the right pointing is at "thee," not at "day," "I say unto thee, To-day shalt thou be with me in paradise," Luke xxiii. 43; that is, thy soul shall not lie dormant in or with thy body till the day of resurrection, but shall this very day pass into paradise. So, Rev. xiii. 8, the mispointing causes an error in the sense; it is said there, that all shall worship the beast, "whose names are not written in the book of life of the lamb;" there is the comma, and then follows, "slain from the foundation of the world;" whereas the comma, or pointing, should be after "slain," which refers to "lamb," and not to the following words, for those words relate to the names written in the book; and the sense stands thus, "whose names are not written in the book of life, from the foundation of the world."

2. When something of man is added to it, or detracted from it. The scribes and Pharisees joined their traditions with the commandments of God, and thereby offered such wrong unto them, that Christ tells them, they made them of none effect, Matt. xv. 6; they put so much chaff to God's wheat, that it rather choked than nourished the people; they put so much water of their own to his wine, that there were no spirits at all in it. The Jews had joined the statutes of the heathen with the statutes of the Lord, 2 Kings xvii. 8; and the statutes of Omri were observed, Micah vi. 16. The Septuagint, in the 5th of Genesis, have added one hundred years more to the age of the fathers, before they begat children, than is in the original; they have also added much to the end of Job, which the Hebrew hath not. The postscripts after Paul's epistles are not canonical, but additions of those who wrote the epistles, or of some others, and they have little truth in them: see Mr. Perkins upon the 6th chapter of the epistle to the Galatians, on the conclusion.

3. When the translation is erroneous. The Septuagint hath failed in many places; and the Vulgate in most. Lindanus, a popish prelate, saith, it hath monstrous corruptions of all sorts, scarce one copy can be found that hath one book of Scripture undefiled and whole. Many points are translated too intricately and darkly, some improperly and abusively, some not so fully, nor so well and truly; sundry places are thrust out from their plain and natural sense. The translator possibly was no Latinist, but a smattering Grecian. In our Old Translation there were σφάλματα πολλα, many errors, as in
Mal. ii. 16, "If thou hatest her, put her away, saith the Lord God of Israel;" White, in his Way to the Church, p. 29.
whereas he hated putting away; so in 1 Cor. xii. 28, it is "helpers, governors;" whereas it is in the Greek, "helps, governments:" and our last translation, which is the best extant, is faulty in this place, reading those words thus, "helps in government," which was done to countenance all the assistants prelates had in their government. And not only there, but in other places also; as Jer. xxxiii. 16, it is thus translated, "This is the name wherewith she shall be called, The Lord our righteousness;" whereas the Hebrew is, he who shall call her, is the Lord our righteousness; and the contents before the 149th Psalm, insinuate that the church hath power to rule the consciences of men.

4. When the word is constrained to speak that which was never intended of God, when a sense is drawn from it that was never included in it. Tyrabosco, patriarch of Venice, preaching on the miracle of loaves and fishes, made the sense of Philip's words, "Two hundred pennyworth of bread will not suffice," to be this, That all the mysteries of the Old and New Testament are not enough to enlighten the people's blind and ignorant minds, without the seven sacraments; which he made to be the meaning of Andrew's words, "There is a boy here which hath five loaves and two fishes." What forced senses have men put upon White, in his Way to the Church, p. 42.
those scriptures, "Tell the church," and "This is my body!" That is the sense of Scripture which the Spirit intended; if any other sense be imposed on or extracted from the word, it is a violation of it, and so it speaks not the mind of God, but the pleasure and fancies of men.

"And have profaned mine holy things." By "holy things," the Lord means the sacrifices and oblations which they were to order according to the institution and rules given them from God, by Moses; but what was holy upon a legal account, they esteemed common, and slighted, which was a profaning of them. In the 8th verse God told Jerusalem she had despised his holy things; and here he tells the priests they had profaned them, that is, they had ordinary thoughts and esteem of them, and handled them so, as became not "holy things." When the "holy things" were eaten of out of season, or by persons unfit, under legal uncleanness, they were profaned, Lev. xix. 8; xxii. 1—16.

"They have put no difference between the holy and profane." The law tells us what things and persons are said to be holy or profane, clean or unclean, as you may see, Lev. xi. throughout; Numb. xviii. 11—13; Deut. xiv. 3—21; Lev. xix. 7, 8; xxi. and xxii. The priests should have instructed the people, what meats were lawful for them, what not; what sacrifices were fit to be brought to the Lord, and what not; who were worthy, and who not, to eat of the holy things, and to approach unto the holy God. This is acknowledged to have been the duty of the priests, from Lev. x. 10, 11; Ezek. xliv. 23, where mention is made of teaching; and from Haggai ii. 11—13, where they practised it, and told them what was unholy and unclean. But this is not all contained in this text, for the Hebrew word בדל rendered here, to put difference, imports power and authority to separate persons and things one from another, as Gen. i. 4, "God divided" or separated "the light from the darkness;" Deut. iv. 41, "Moses severed three cities on this side Jordan;" 2 Chron. xxv. 10, "Then Amaziah separated them;" and Ainsworth reads those words, Lev. x. 10, That ye may separate between the holy and profane: by that power God had put into their hands, they were to keep the wicked and profane from the holy things, to separate them from the congregation; and so the word is used, Ezra x. 8. The priests sinned in that they did not teach the people what was legally holy, and legally profane, and also in that they did not put forth that power they had, to preserve the holy things of God pure. Those priests therefore that withstood Uzziah the king, attempting to offer incense upon the altar, and thrust him out of the sanctuary, when the leprosy appeared in his forehead, they did their duty, and kept the things of God unpolluted, 2 Chron. xxvi. 20: it was unlawful for him to offer incense, unlawful for him, being leprous, to be in that place where the incense was to be offered; and had not the priests had power, it had been unlawful in them to have thrust him out.

"Neither had they showed difference between the unclean and the clean." The Hebrew word for "showed difference" is, הודיעו they did not make to know, they neglected to teach and instruct them, which was a sin inexcusable; but more than so may be gathered out of this word; they did not make them to know experimentally, by inflicting censures, what the difference was between the clean and the unclean. They had three sorts of excommunication; the lesser, called *niddui*, the middle sort, called *cherem*, and the greatest, called *sammatha*. He who was defiled with leprosy was to be removed out of the camp of Israel, the camp of the priests, and the camp of God. He who was defiled with an issue, was to be removed out of the camp of God, and the camp of the priests, but not out of the camp of Israel. He that was defiled by the touch of a dead body, was only to be removed out of the camp of God. Now it is likely the priests failed in doing their part in some of these, they suffered those who were legally unclean, to come amongst those who were legally clean, and did not, by removal of them, make them to know what a mercy it was to be clean, and what an evil to be unclean. It is said, Judg. viii. 16, that Gideon took briers and thorns, "and with them he taught the men of Succoth," וידע he made them to know, by what they felt and suffered, he made them to know; so the priests should have made them to know, by their removal from the camp and holy things of God, what the great difference was between the clean and unclean. I have met with one author, who reads the words thus, Neither have they broken or divided between the clean and the unclean.

Weemes, in Christian Synagogue.

Vid. Gillespie in his Aaron's Rod blossoming, p. 119.

"And have hid their eyes from my sabbaths." The Hebrew word for "hid" is, עלם *alam*, which properly is spoken of them that have watery, blear, and bloodshot eyes; so that they cannot see well, as Avenarius saith; such eyes had those priests, that they could not see. The ordinary acceptation of the word is, to hide or cover. The Septuagint is, παρεκάλυπτον, they have covered their eyes from my sabbaths. This expression, of hiding their eyes, hath these things in it.

1. They did not mind the holiness and honour of the sabbath. That was a day to be sanctified in a special manner, Exod. xx. 8; Lev. xxiii. 3; Ezek. xx. 20; they should have called the sabbath a delight, holy and honourable, Isa. lviii. 13; for it was a day as for honouring of God, so for God's honouring them with his presence and blessings; but they minded not the holiness or honourableness of the day, and this was hiding their eyes from it.

2. When men by their sinful practices profaned the sabbaths of the Lord, they took no notice thereof, they did not tell them of their sins, convince them of the wickedness of their doings, but connive and wink at their doings. Jer. xvii. 27, there were those who carried in burdens at the gates of Jerusalem on the sabbath day, which God by Jeremiah complained of, and threatened the destruction of Jerusalem for; but the priests, though they knew and saw these things, yet they were silent; and this was hiding their eyes from the sabbaths of the Lord.

3. Themselves did those things on the sabbaths which the law of God did not justify, and they having their pretences and excuses for the same, they did not the duties of the sabbath; they did their own pleasure, walked in their own ways, and spake their own words, contrary to that in Isa. lviii. 13; they did wicked things on that holy day, and profaned the sabbaths of the Lord, ver. 8, of this chapter; Jer. xxiii. 11, "Both prophet and priest are profane," they did profanely, and so they hid their eyes from the sabbath.

"And I am profaned amongst them." The profaning of holy things, the holy day, and holy name of the Lord, are oft mentioned, Lev. xxii. 15; Neh. xiii. 17; Amos ii. 7; Ezek. xx. 9, 14, 22; but here it goes higher, and comes to God himself, who saith, "I am profaned." God in his own nature cannot be profaned, that is incapable of all profanation; but he is said to be profaned, when his commands are despised, his worship corrupted, and evil is spoken of him and his ways. God is sanctified when we fear him in our hearts, Isa. viii. 13, and tremble at his words, Isa. lxvi. 2, worship him according to his own appointments, preserving his worship pure, and so live as to cause others to glorify his name, 1 Pet. ii. 12; Matt. v. 16: when the contrary is done, he is profaned; when men contemn the commands of God, break his laws, defile his sabbaths, they profane the Lord, and by such doings cause his name to be blasphemed by others, and, in that, himself is profaned.

Obs. 1. That holy things are to be kept holy. "They have violated my law, profaned mine holy things, put no difference between the holy and profane," &c. This was the evil, that holy things were profaned. The holy oil, spoken of Exod. xxx. must be kept holy, and none must make or compound any like it, ver. 31, 32; so for the holy perfume, ver. 37. The passover was a holy thing, and the Lord ordered it so, that it might be kept holy; Exod. xii. 43, 44, 48, strangers and uncircumcised might not eat thereof, because that was a defiling of it; those who were legally unclean, were not to keep the passover till they were cleansed, Numb. v. 2, 3: chap. ix. 6, 7, &c. they were put off from the fourteenth day of the first month, unto the fourteenth day of the second month. And so for other of the holy things, see what rules God gives, and how strict he was to prevent the profaning of them; Lev. xxii. 3—7, God threatened to cut off such a soul, that should meddle with the holy things, being unclean. Cut off from children, say some, he should be without posterity; cut off by an untimely death, say others; or cut off from God, and having inheritance with his people in heaven. Hence was it that God committed the holy things to the charge of the priests, Numb. iii. 28, 31, 32, and Levites, chap. xviii. 2—5; and they kept the door of the Lord's house, 2 Kings xii. 9; and when they were defiled, they were not to meddle with the holy things, Ezra ii. 63; Ezek. xliv. 13.

Vide Godwin Antiquit. l. 3. c. 4.

Obs. 2. When those who are near to God are unfaithful, and do not improve their power and interest to preserve the things of God and ordinances holy, it is matter of provocation and complaint. The priests here, who were officers in his house, they dealt unfaithfully, and did not to their interest and power lay out themselves to preserve the things of God from profaning and polluting; and that offended the Lord, and made him to complain of them. Ezek. xliv. 7, 8, God complains of them there, that they brought into his sanctuary uncircumcised in heart and flesh, and polluted it thereby; that they did eat fat and blood, which were prohibited most severely, Lev. vii. 25—27; and so broke his covenant, and kept not the charge of his holy things. When Nadab and Abihu brought strange fire, that is, unholy fire, such as God commanded not, how greatly did it provoke God, even so far as to kindle a fire in his wrath, and to consume them! they were not faithful, they defiled themselves, their censers, and the worship of God, with their unholy fire, Lev. x. 1, 2. You may find the Lord angry with and complaining of some of the angels of the seven churches, for their unfaithfulness and faultiness this way: Rev. ii. 14—16, there God complains of the angel of Pergamos, and tells him that he did not keep out corrupt doctrines, that the doctrine of Balaam and the Nicolaitanes were suffered amongst them: so for the angel of Thyatira, that Jezebel was suffered to teach and seduce the church, and to draw the members thereof to commit fornication, and to eat things sacrificed to idols. Here the Lord was offended with the churches, and complains of them.

Obs. 3. That there is a difference to be made between person and person, when it comes to communion in and participation of holy things. It was the priests' sin here, that they did not put a difference between the holy and profane, the clean and the unclean. This is to be done both doctrinally and practically.

(1.) Doctrinally. The prophets and priests were by their teachings to make a difference. Jer. xv. 19, "If thou take forth the precious from the vile, then thou shalt be as my mouth." The Vulgate reads it, If thou shalt separate the precious from the vile; that is, saith Maldonate, If thou shalt by thy word sever the elect from the reprobate. Piscator likewise interprets the words doctrinally, If thou shalt hold out my gracious promises only for the comfort of the godly, and not of the wicked, then thou shalt be as my mouth; I will own thee for my faithful servant, as having spoken and done what I myself would have spoken and done. Ezek. xiii. 22, God is wroth with the false prophets and prophetesses for saddening the hearts of the righteous, and strengthening the hands of the wicked, that he should not return from his wicked ways, by promising him life: they did not distinguish between the precious and the vile.

(2.) Practically. When any of the people were ceremonially unclean, they were to be kept from the clean, and from communion with them in the holy things. No stranger, no uncircumcised, none that had any running issue, that was leprous, were to eat the passover, or join with the congregation in their holy things, Exod. xii. 48; Lev. xxii. 3. And if ceremonial uncleanness did exclude Israelites from the holy things under the law, moral uncleanness may justly exclude christians under the gospel. 2 Cor. vi. 17, "Come out from among them, and be ye separate, and touch not the unclean thing." Idols and idolaters are unclean things, scandalous and ignorant persons are unclean things, and we must come out from them, if we will have God to receive us; yea, those who are unbelievers, how civil and fair soever their lives be, are unclean things, Tit. i. 15; those that have a form of godliness, and deny the power, are also such, and we must turn from them, 2 Tim. iii. 5, from such, as well as the others before mentioned, you must turn away, and not have communion with. There is a prophecy in the 52nd of Isaiah, ver. 1, that the uncircumcised and unclean should not come into Zion, or the new Jerusalem; and it suits with what you have, Rev. xxi. 27, "There shall in no wise enter into it," viz. the new Jerusalem, "any thing that defileth;" such must be kept out as will defile. There were porters at every gate of Jerusalem when the passover in Josiah's days was kept, and they suffered not unclean or uncircumcised ones to enter; and the Annotations upon this place in the Revelation say, In the last church on earth discipline in likelihood shall be so strictly executed, that no profane persons shall be found there, only elect persons, so far as men can judge; there shall be spiritual porters to keep out defilers. Dead stones must not be laid in a living temple.

Obs. 4. That the profaning of holy things is a profaning of God himself. "They have violated my law, profaned my holy things, &c. and I am profaned amongst them." When holy things are not ordered and regarded as they ought, as becomes them, and him who hath made them holy, it is a profanation of both. There is so near a relation between God and his ordinances, his holy things, that the wrong done to them he accounts done to himself, and the profaning of them, the profaning of himself. When the priests offered polluted bread upon the altar, they polluted God, Mal. i. 7; they brought that which was defective, and not according to the law, and that polluted the altar, which God accounted polluting of himself. And this dealing with God so offends him, that sometimes he breaks out, and smites, yea, destroys persons for the same. When the Bethshemites irreverently meddled with the ark, the Lord did smite fifty thousand and seventy men, 1 Sam. vi. 19; it was a profaning of the Lord, so rudely to touch and peep into the ark. The Corinthians abused, profaned the holy things of God, 1 Cor. xi.; and for that very cause many were made weak and sickly, and others were cut off by death. Look to it then that you be holy, if you will meddle with holy things, and that you handle them holily, lest you profane the Lord: Eccles. v. 1, "Keep thy foot when thou goest to the house of God, and be more ready to hear, than to give the sacrifice of fools."

Ver. 27. *Her princes in the midst thereof are like wolves ravening the prey, to shed blood, and to destroy souls, to get dishonest gain.*

You had the prophets' and the priests' sins in the two precedent verses; in this you have the princes'; which are, violence, cruelty, covetousness.

"Her princes." The Hebrew for "princes" is, שריה from שור to act the part of a prince, to bear rule. The Septuagint hath it, *οἱ ἄρχοντες*, her chief men. Her rulers, her princes, that should have been "such as feared God, men of truth, hating covetousness," Exod. xviii. 21, they were now so degenerated, that they were become like wolves.

"Like wolves." Wolves for their outward shape are like unto dogs, a creature that is strong, swift, fierce, cruel, and crafty, as Franzius observes. Historia Animalium. In them are seen notable resemblances of the devil, heretics, thieves, and tyrants. When princes and rulers oppress the people, they are tyrants, and in Scripture language, "wolves." Now two things in wolves especially they resemble:

1. Their subtlety, or craftiness in getting the prey,

for the wolf comes behind horned beasts, sets upon them unawares, that they may not be able to defend themselves; so tyrants deal craftily with the people, take them suddenly in their stratagems, and spoil them of the benefit of law, and other helps: Exod. i. 10; Acts vii. 19, Pharaoh, that tyrant, dealt subtlely with the Jews; so did Haman, Esth. iii. 8, 9; so did Ishmael, Jer. xli. 5—7.

2. Their cruelty. Wolves are very cruel and bloody, they will kill many lambs, many sheep, and only suck their bloods; nothing do they desire more, than blood, and man's flesh, and when they go out to prey, they do sharpen their teeth with a certain herb they chew. So tyrants are wolvish in this respect. Adoni-bezek, was not he such, when he cut off the thumbs and toes of seventy kings? Judg. i. 7. Was not Herod a ravenous wolf, who sucked the blood of all the children in Bethlehem, and the coasts thereof, under two years old? Matt. ii. 16. What a she-wolf was Athaliah, who murdered all the seed royal! 2 Kings xi. 1. What a cruel, bloody wolf was Menahem, who ripped up all the women with child in Tiphsah! 2 Kings xv. 16. And was not Manasseh a mighty blood-sucking and ravenous wolf, who filled Jerusalem with innocent blood from one end to the other? 2 Kings xxi. 16. Jehoiakim and Jehoiachin were lions and wolves, that caught the prey, and devoured men, Ezek. xix. 3, 6; and in Zedekiah's days the princes and rulers were such, as filled the land with "bloody crimes," Ezek. vii. 23. Not unjustly therefore are they said to be like wolves, yea, to be wolves, Zeph. iii. 3.

"Ravening the prey." These words we had in the 25th verse; the prophets were like lions ravening the prey, and the princes were like wolves ravening the prey: wolves are more ignoble than lions, and the princes were worse than the false prophets, they ravened sorer than they.

"To shed blood." Of this sin mention is made in ver. 4, 6, 9, 12, of this chapter. It is a sin in any, but especially in princes, who should protect their subjects from violence and blood, and rather venture the shedding of their own blood, than suffer the people's to be wrongfully shed; but now the princes were so wicked, that, like wolves, they destroyed and devoured their own sheep, by breaking covenants made with other princes, and so drawing upon them barbarous nations. By receiving bribes, and hearkening to tales, they gave way to the execution of innocent ones, by which sin they destroyed the lives of men, their persons, and the image of God; for which thing no recompence can be made, nor ought to be taken if it could be made. Numb. xxxv. 31, he that shed blood unjustly, was to have his blood shed, whatsoever he were.

"And to destroy souls." Souls are not in the power of princes or other men to destroy or hurt, Matt. x. 28; they are the Lord's, Ezek. xviii. 4, and he only hath power over them. Princes here are said to "destroy souls," because they do what lies in their power to destroy them: or we may take "souls" here synecdochically for the whole man, they shed blood to destroy men; when the blood of men is spilled, they are destroyed.

"To get dishonest gain." The Hebrew is rendered by Montanus, to desire a lust, or to satisfy a lust; and in the margin he hath it thus, that they might covetously or greedily follow covetousness. These princes did covet the wealth of the people, and found out ways to cut them off, that so they might enjoy their estates. These words "dishonest gain," we had in the 13th verse, and therefore shall forbear to add any thing more about them.

Obs. 1. That when prophets and priests are corrupt, the magistrates are not sound. In the 25th verse, the prophets were like lions, they devoured souls; in the 26th, the priests violated the law, and profaned the holy things; and here the princes were like wolves, shedding blood. When the heads in the ecclesiastic estate are evil, those in the civil estate are seldom good; when prophets and priests do wickedly, princes will quickly learn to follow them; they have great influence into the courts and hearts of princes.

Obs. 2. When magistrates and rulers are covetous, they are insatiably covetous, and will be cruel to satisfy their covetous lusts. The princes were greedy of gain; and to get it, they, like wolves, did raven the prey, shed blood, destroy souls. They being princes, had great revenues; but they were not content with what was their own, they cast their eyes and thoughts upon what the people had, and let out their desires after the same; and covetous desires brought forth oppression in taxes, and cruelty, in making away and cutting off many rich ones, under pretence of delinquency, that they might enjoy their lands and livings. When men are "greedy of gain," they will "take away the life of the owners thereof," Prov. i. 19. Ahab and Jezebel took away the life of Naboth for his vineyard, which they greedily coveted, 1 Kings xxi. 19. Solomon tells you that a "wicked ruler is like a roaring lion, and a ranging bear," he is a great oppressor, Prov. xxviii. 15, 16; he threatens them, fills them with fears, and daily is plucking away their estates from them; he rangeth here for a prey one day, and there for a prey another day, and is never satisfied, till he hath devoured them and theirs. Zeph. iii. 3, "Her princes within her are roaring lions; her judges are evening wolves; they gnaw not the bones till the morrow;" they devour the men one day, and their estates the next day; the flesh will not suffice them, but they must eat up bones and all. Covetousness is an insatiable horse-leech, that cries Give, give, and will break all laws, bonds, relations, to enjoy what it desires. There was much in it, when the Lord forbade kings to multiply gold and silver greatly to themselves, Deut. xvii. 17: he foresaw that if their hearts were carried out strongly after such things, that they, having power in their hands, would oppress, shed blood, destroy souls, and all for to get dishonest gain. Isaiah therefore calls such princes "thieves," chap. i. 23; they robbed, they murdered the people to enrich themselves. Vespasian was such a thief to the Roman state, who put in the greatest offices the greatest extortioners, whom he used like spunges, to fill them while dry, and to crush out their liquor when they were full; when they were grown rich then he spoiled them. It is needful to pray for rulers, that they may fear God, hate covetousness, and never prove roaring lions, nor ravening wolves.

Suetonius in Vespasiano.

Ver. 28. *And her prophets have daubed them with untempered morter, seeing vanity, and divining lies unto them, saying, Thus saith the Lord God, when the Lord hath not spoken.*

Here we have the prophets brought in again, where, besides those sins mentioned, ver. 25, you have an addition of their flattery and lying.

"Have daubed them with untempered morter." Of these words see before, chap. xiii. 10, 11. תפל imports, a thing unseasoned, weak, inept to adhere and cleave to a thing, and quickly falling off, having no tenacity in it. When plasterers lay loam or sand upon a wall, and there be nothing binding therein, ere long it falls off again, though for the present it covers deformities, and makes it seem goodly. So these prophets flattered the princes and great ones, and plastered over their vile practices with smooth and fair words, encouraging them in their ways, and promising them safety; which they did, having countenance and maintenance from them, Micah iii. 11, and upon hopes of greater preferment; but it proved otherwise, for when the winds and storms of divine displeasure came, both prophets, princes, and the untempered mortar fell together.

"Seeing vanity, and divining lies unto them, saying, Thus saith," &c. These words were formerly spoken of, chap. xiii. 6, 7. They told the princes and people, that they had visions from God, that he had spoken unto them, and sent them to prophesy such things unto them; whereas they saw nothing, neither heard or had any thing from God, but followed their own spirits, which were vain and lying. Herein they dealt perfidiously with God and man.

Obs. 1. Though princes and rulers be exceedingly wicked, insatiably covetous and cruel, oppressing and destroying the people, yet there are prophets who will flatter, countenance, and encourage them in those ways. The princes were ravening wolves, shed blood, destroyed souls, to get dishonest gain, and Jerusalem's prophets daubed them with untempered mortar: they applauded their practices, justified their doings, and told them that God did approve of their ways. It was not the nobles, citizens, but the prophets of Jerusalem which did this. Princes and great ones want not false and lying prophets to bolster them up, and to bear them out in their vile and detestable courses.

Ahab was a wicked king, and he had a multitude of flattering, daubing prophets: 2 Chron. xviii. 10, 11, "Go, and prosper, for the Lord hath delivered it into the hand of the king;" the enterprise is warrantable, will prove successful; fear not. There were "flattering divinations" among the false prophets, Ezek. xii. 24; and with these they bedaubed the wicked princes, and strengthened the hands of evil-doers, Jer. xxiii. 14. When princes are evil-doers, and encouraged by false or true prophets, they will do mischief with a witness. When the king that lately suffered was upon oppressing designs, to get dishonest gain, did not England's prophets flatter, encourage, and daub with untempered mortar, when they told him, all the people had was his, that he might do what he pleased with his subjects and their estates?

Flattery is evil in any, but worst of all in prophets, and especially when they have to do with wicked princes, whom they harden in their wickedness thereby, and ripen for destruction. Flattery pleases men greatly, it is like tickling; but there is tickling unto death. Reproof is a precious balm, Psal. cxli. 5; but flattery is a destructive net, Prov. xxix. 5. Let the true prophets abhor it; and so speak the truth, that they may appeal to the consciences of great and small, as Paul doth, 1 Thess. ii. 5, "Not at any time used we flattering words, as ye know." It is good to be free from flattery, and also from reviling. Many, that they may not seem to flatter, yet will revile and speak evil of rulers; both which are evil.

Obs. 2. That what false prophets give out is unsavoury, and unsound, weak, and useless. It is untempered mortar: it may stick in men's heads a little, to strengthen them to do wickedly; but it will not stick in their hearts, to strengthen them against the day of evil, and to justify their doings. What is there in vanity and lies to establish? False prophets see vanity and divine lies, which are unsavoury and unprofitable things: it is truth, and divine truth, which establisheth, 2 Pet. i. 19; the vain and lying imaginations of men, do deceive and disappoint. Pashur prophesied lies, the things of his own heart and spirit, which himself and others trusted in; but see how he, and they who believed him, were deceived and disappointed, Jer. xx. 6. The scornful rulers which made lies their refuge, and hid themselves under falsehood, saying, "The over-flowing scourge shall not come unto us," Isa. xxviii. 14, 15; see what the Lord saith in the 17th verse, "The hail shall sweep away the refuge of lies, and the waters shall overflow the hiding-place." False prophecies, false opinions, false confidences, will not advantage in a windy and stormy time; they are all untempered mortar; and what men give out from themselves, and not from God, doth not profit at all, Jer. xxiii. 32.

Obs. 3. The subtlety and impudency of false prophets, to make way for their vanities and lies: they pretend they have messages from God, and say, "Thus saith the Lord God," there is their cunning; and to make God author of their vanities and lies, there is their impudency. They knew their dreams, visions, vanities, lies, would not take with princes or people, if not presented unto them as from God. The true prophets told them, "Thus saith the Lord;" and the false made use of his name and authority, the better to usher in what came from their own spirits; for whatsoever seems to have the authority of men or God to back it, hath the better acceptance, and greater influence. This was the constant practice of false prophets, as you may see, Jer. xxviii. 10, 11; xiv. 14; xxvii. 14, 15; xxiii. 17. Ezek. xiii. 6, 7. They made God the author of all their vanities, lies, dreams, and whatsoever came out of their own heads and hearts, which argued a height of impudency in them. They did not only abuse men, but they greatly abused God; Jer. v. 12, "They have belied the Lord," and made that to be the word of God which was not; they walked in lies, and strengthened the nands of evil-doers; which provoked God so bitterly against them, Jer. xxiii. 14, 15, that he saith, he would "feed them with wormwood, and make them drink the water of gall." And because many prophets amongst us have belied the Lord, in making some scriptures speak that to maintain their opinions and tenets which never was the mind of God in them, therefore he is wroth with them, feeding them with wormwood, and making them to drink the water of gall.

Ver. 29. *The people of the land have used oppression, and exercised robbery, and have vexed the poor and needy: yea, they have oppressed the stranger wrongfully.*

Having spoken of the prophets', princes', and priests' sins, he comes now to the people's; they had no cause to insult over and censure them, for themselves were not free: and their sins were,

I. "Oppression."

II. "Robbery" and covetousness.

Both these aggravated from the persons they oppressed, robbed; and they were,

1. "The poor and needy."

2. "Strangers."

"The people of the land." There were four sorts of men in Canaan; "prophets of Jerusalem," Jer. xxiii. 14; "priests of the Lord," 1 Sam. i. 3, and "of the high places," 2 Kings xxiii. 20; "princes of the people," Ezek. xi. 1; and "people of the land," which were the inferior sort, the vulgar, whom the prophet terms so, not by way of disgrace and opposition to the others, who were in places of eminency, but for distinction only.

"Have used oppression." The Hebrew is thus, did oppress with oppression, that is, did greatly oppress. The word for oppressing, notes oppression by force or fraud, as hath formerly been showed, and is rendered here by Junius, This people deals very deceitfully. Some read the words thus, They did calumniate one another, and so oppress; for calumniation, or slandering, is a great wronging and oppression of a man. Those who are given to oppressing will use slander, fraud, force, any way to accomplish their wills and desires.

"And exercised robbery." These words are the same in the Hebrew with those chap. xviii. 12, "hath spoiled by violence." There the verb is in the singular number, and the substantive in the plural; here the verb is in the plural, and the substantive in the singular number. They did steal and get from one another what they could, secretly or openly, which was violence and robbery, and this they did frequently, they were exercised in it.

"And have vexed the poor and needy." The word for "vexed" here is, עשק the same with oppressed, or used oppression; of which, with the other words, "poor and needy," was spoken chap. xviii. 7, 12; xvi. 49: the poor and needy should have been counselled, comforted, not vexed or oppressed.

"Yea, they have oppressed the stranger wrongfully." Of oppressing the stranger hath already been spoken in the 7th verse of this chapter. The Hebrew for "wrongfully" is, בלא משפט without right. They did unjustly oppress the stranger against all law and right. There was no justice amongst them, in their dealings with natives or strangers; only fraud and force took place.

Obs. 1. That people are usually such as those over them in church and state are. The prophets, the priests, the princes, were wicked, and the people were like unto them. The prophets were covetous, and thereupon oppressed, taking the treasure and precious things, ver. 25; the priests violated the law, and profaned the name of the Lord, ver. 26; the princes, for "dishonest gain," did dishonest and cruel things, ver. 27; and here the people were like them, covetous, using oppression, and exercising robbery. Micah iii. 11, "The heads thereof," that is, of Zion, "judge for reward, and the priests thereof teach for hire, and the prophets thereof divine for money." Here the chief in the state and church had their eyes upon the reward, the hire, the money; and to enjoy the same, they would do, say, any thing. Covetousness is the root of all evil, and causeth all sorts of men in whom it is found, to comply with the humours of others, for its own interest, and to make a prey of those who oppose the same; and were not the people suitable unto these that were over them? Jer. v. 31, "The prophets prophesy falsely, and the priests bear rule by their means; and my people love to have it so:" the false prophets, by their lies and flatteries, did strengthen the wicked priests in their practices; they took into their hands (so the words may be read) more power than they should, and gifts which they should not, and the "people love to have it so;" they love to hear the prophets' lies, and to feed the priests with gifts, to bear them up in their ways. Chap. vi. 13, "From the least of them to the greatest of them every one is given to covetousness; and from the prophet even unto the priest every one dealeth falsely;" and how came it to be so? the people learned it of those in place: Jer. xxiii. 15, "From the prophets of Jerusalem is profaneness gone forth into all the land;" the word may be rendered hypocrisy, dissimulation, deceit; the false prophets were notorious hypocrites, deceivers themselves, and they infected all the land with their leaven. It was the prophets and priests principally that made the "king glad with their wickedness, and the princes with their lies," Hos. vii. 3; and when a prince or "ruler hearkens to lies, all his servants are wicked," Prov. xxix. 12. Wicked prophets and priests make wicked princes; wicked princes make wicked servants and wicked subjects. They tell them tales, lies, accusing unto them those who are contrary to their ways, designs, and interest, or not forwarders thereof; whereupon princes set their servants, creatures, agents on work, to obstruct and pervert justice, to entrap and crush such persons. This was much practised in late days. The prelates possessed the princes with their lies and falsehoods concerning the Book of Sports on the Lord's day, concerning altars and altar-worship, and they quickly infected all their servants, and too many of their subjects therewith; so that if the prophets, priests, and princes be naught, the people are too like unto them.

Obs. 2. Covetous practices in deceiving of, or in getting and griping from others, is plain theft. "The people of the land have used oppression," or deceit, as your margins have it, "and exercised robbery." When covetousness puts men upon deceitful practices, as to use false weights, false lights, false measures, it is robbery; so when corrupt, counterfeit, embased materials be put off for sound and good, be it in moneys, clothing, corn, meal, wines, flesh, fish, any vendible commodity, it is, in the judgment of God, robbery; so exacting of fees, expedition-money, taking advantages of men's necessities, of forfeitures of bonds or lands, withholding of servants' and labourers' wages, altering of wills, forging of deeds, warrants, Luke xix. 8. Lev. xix. 13, "Thou shalt not defraud thy neighbour, neither rob him; the wages of him that is hired shall not abide with thee all night until the morning:" the word for "defraud," notes wresting and plucking from a man, and is the same with the word for oppressing here. So that he who oppresseth, who wrests any thing from another by subtlety, he plays the thief, he robs him; so for the hired man's wages, when the time agreed upon for payment comes, you must not defer one night, one day longer, it is oppression, it is robbery, and cries out against men, James v. 4. When many, for greediness of gain, bought and sold in the temple, Christ called them thieves; "Ye have made it," saith Christ, "a den of thieves," Matt. xxi. 13. The priests, for gain, gave way to others to buy and sell doves and other things which were of use for offerings and sacrifices, and they made them, who bought the same for such purposes, pay dearly for them, and for this they were called thieves, not simply for being in the temple; it was their covetous practices, their deceiving, their griping, that made Christ brand them with that name. When men out of covetousness do grate upon others, defraud and overreach them in bargaining, or otherwise, they are robbers; and such doings is called robbery: Amos iii. 10, "They know not to do right, saith the Lord, who store up violence and robbery in their palaces;" they were so exercised with covetous practices, that "they knew not to do right," only they were acquainted with theft. Nineveh was such a city; Nahum iii. 1, "It is full of lies and robbery," all shops, all places in it, were full of them. I fear London is too like Nineveh, "full of lies and robbery." Are not men's hearts, tongues, hands, exercised with covetous practices? is there not much fraud, griping, and catching advantages in most shops, places, and persons? When will the time come, that this city may be called "a city of righteousness, the faithful city?" If you do find your hearts carried out greedily after gain, and desire to be rich, consider these places of Scripture:

Prov. xxviii. 20, "He that maketh haste to be rich shall not be innocent;" he shall not go without punishment; God will plague him one way or other, send some secret curse into his heart or estate, if not some outward visible judgment.

Prov. xx. 21, "An inheritance may be gotten hastily at the beginning; but the end thereof shall not be blessed." Men may think God blesses them, leaves them, they thrive, they get great estates; but mark the end, the end of an estate so gotten shall not be blessed. How many get great estates in this city, and their children spend it shamefully when they are gone!

Jer. xvii. 11, "He that getteth riches, and not by right, shall leave them in the midst of his days, and at his end shall be a fool." He promises long life to himself, but he shall soon be plucked away, and be declared to be a fool: Luke xii. 19, 20, "Soul, thou hast much goods laid up for many years; eat, drink, and be merry:" he thought he should live long; but what followed? "Thou fool, this night thy soul shall be required of thee; then whose shall those things be which thou hast provided?" It may be you think your children shall have what you get; but it is more than you know, if you will believe David, Psal. xxxix. 6. Suppose your heir do, can you tell what he will prove? it is more than Solomon could tell: Eccl. ii. 19, "Who knoweth whether he shall be a wise man or a fool?"

1 Tim. vi. 9, 10; read, study, mind those verses well, they have much in them.

Obs. 3. Who are a prey and spoil to the rich and great? It is the poor, needy, and strangers: "the people of the land vexed and oppressed them." Those who had estates, purses, and power, they dealt wrongfully with others. The Scripture sets out this evil by various expressions. Men are said to have an evil eye against the poor, Deut. xv. 9; to set their eyes against the poor, Psal. x. 8; to lie in wait to catch the poor, Psal. x. 9; to devise devices to destroy the poor with lying words, when he speaks right, Isa. xxxii. 7; to shame the counsel of the poor, Psal. xiv. 6; to despise the poor, James ii. 6; to mock the poor, Prov. xvii. 5; to hate the poor, chap. xiv. 20; to rule and lord it over the poor, chap. xxii. 7; to bend their bow to cast down the poor, Psal. xxxvii. 14; to grind the faces of the poor, Isa. iii. 15; to turn aside the poor in the gate, Amos v. 12; to take away the right from the poor and needy, Isa. x. 2; to tread upon the poor, Amos v. 11; to sell the poor for shoes, chap. ii. 6; to rob the poor, because he is poor, Prov. xxii. 22; to take away his house violently, Job xx. 19; to devour the poor secretly, Hab. iii. 14; to oppress the poor, crush the needy, Amos iv. 1; to swallow up the needy, chap. viii. 4; to turn aside the stranger from his right, Mal. iii. 5; to oppress him, as here; to slay him, Psal. xciv. 6.

The Lord takes special notice of the poor, and men's carriages towards them. Take heed, then, that the spoil of the poor be not found in your houses, as it is said, Isa. iii. 14; and that their blood be not found on your skirts, Jer. ii. 34; for the Lord will arise "for the oppression of the poor, and sighing of the needy," Psal. xii. 5; he will maintain their right, Psal. cxl. 12. Let your hearts and eyes be towards them, let your hands be stretched out to do them good, for "blessed is he that considereth the poor," Psal. xli. 1; and whoso hath mercy on them is happy, Prov. xiv. 21; be not of that generation, Prov. xxx. 14.

Ver. 30. *And I sought for a man among them, that should make up the hedge, and stand in the gap before me for the land, that I should not destroy it: but I found none.*

The Lord having made a large catalogue of Jerusalem's sins, and shown a universal corruption of all sorts of men, what could be expected but that he should proceed to the destruction of them? But, that he might more fully justify his proceedings towards those that were already in captivity, and likewise towards them that were yet remaining, he tells them what he did; he sought for some one or other to have appeared, interceded, and prevented judgments; he looked some course should have been taken, the land being so guilty, to have kept off destroying judgments; and seeing there was none minded the public good, doing aught that might occasion God to spare them, the fault was in themselves, and not in him, that they were wholly ruined.

"And I sought for a man among them." The Hebrew word ואבקש signifies, to seek with great care; as Kirker observes, an earnest, diligent seeking, a running up and down to find out a thing. So here the Lord made a diligent search, he went up and down from prophet to priest, from priest to prince, from prince to people, to see if he could find out any man. It is spoken of the Lord after the manner of men, and is suitable to that expression, 2 Chron. xvi. 9, "The eyes of the Lord run to and fro throughout the whole earth;" that is, Divine Providence exactly observes all things in the world, especially what men do; and here God looked earnestly upon all sorts of men, to see if any stirred to interpose, and stand in the gap. The French is, I demanded some one among them; I called for a man to come forth, and see if he could prevent those judgments which were coming upon them.

"That should make up the hedge." The Hebrew is, hedging a hedge. The words are metaphorical, and the metaphor is taken from vineyards, gardens, and places enclosed, which use to have fences and hedges about them, to preserve them from every thing that might harm them, both men and beasts. The Jews were God's vineyard, Isa. v. 1; and he had fenced and hedged them, ver. 2, 5; they were God's garden, and he had enclosed them, Cant. iv. 12. The fence, "hedge," or wall, about this people was,

1. God's protection of them. He had a special care of them, being his church and people, above all others; as the city Jerusalem had a wall about it, Neh. i. 3, so God was a wall to the citizens thereof; Zech. ii. 5, "A wall of fire round about them." Isa. xxvii. 3, lest any should hurt his vineyard, he kept it night and day, he watched over it continually, and preserved it.

2. Those things and means God had given them to be a hedge or wall unto them; as,

(1.) Sound doctrine; which was as a "hedge" to keep out all errors, corrupt and heathenish opinions, which they were in danger of, having the nations round about them; but God had given them good doctrine, Prov. iv. 2; right words, Psal. xxxiii. 4; lively oracles, Acts vii. 38; faithful commands, Psal. cxix. 86; sure testimonies, Psal. xciii. 5; such as they were to try all doctrines and opinions by, Isa. viii. 20.

(2.) Pure worship; which was as a "hedge" between them and the heathens. Deut. vi. 13, 14, "Thou shalt fear the Lord thy God, and serve him, and shalt swear by his name. Ye shall not go after other gods, of the gods of the people which are round about you." Ver. 17, 18, "Ye shall diligently keep the command ments of the Lord your God, and his testimonies, and his statutes, which he hath commanded thee. And thou shalt do that which is right and good in the sight of the Lord: that it may be well with thee." 2 Kings xvii. 36, 37, God had appointed them a pure way of worship, which hedged them in from all false ways of worship, from bringing in ought of their own and others'.

(3.) Good laws; Deut. iv. 8, "What nation is there so great, that hath statutes and judgments so righteous?" no nation under heaven had such laws to be governed by as the Jews had, and those laws were "hedges" against all injustice; they might not wrong one another, nor strangers.

(4.) God had given them good prophets, priests, and princes, for their safety, to be a "hedge" unto them. The prophets were to preserve the doctrine sound, the priests to keep the worship pure, and the princes to see justice impartially executed: Elijah, a good prophet, was the horsemen and chariot of Israel, 2 Kings ii. 12; xiii. 14; the priests were mediators between God and the people, Joel ii. 17; the princes were the strength of the land, Prov. xxix. 4: thus you see what the "hedge" was. And if you would have it more briefly, it was the covenant made between God and this people; he had promised to be their God, and to protect them; they had promised to be his people, and to walk in his ways; now when they transgressed the covenant, the "hedge" was broken, and gaps were made.

The Hebrew for gaps is בפרץ in the breach, from פרץ to divide and break through: they had now broke through the "hedge," and made many gaps, which appears thus:

1. The doctrine was corrupted. There was much chaff mingled with the wheat, Jer. xxiii. 28; false prophets gave in that to be divine, which was from their own hearts, spirits, heads, Ezek. xiii. 2, 3; they prophesied lies, Jer. xiv. 14; the providence of God was denied, and his omnipresence, Ezek. viii. 12, "The Lord seeth us not; he hath forsaken the earth;" so his justice, Ezek. xviii. 2, 25, they said his ways were not equal, the fathers had eaten sour grapes and the children's teeth were set on edge; they taught the people to swear by a false god, even by Baal, Jer. xii. 16.

2. For the worship, that was greatly corrupted. The sanctuary was defiled with detestable things, Ezek. v. 11; they had brought images and idols near to the temple, and into the temple, chap. viii.; they had high places and altars in every street, chap. xvi.; they burnt incense to other gods, and worshipped the works of their own hands, Jer. i. 16; the statutes of Omri were kept, and the works of the house of Ahab, Micah vi. 16; and the fear or worship of God was taught by the precepts of men, Isa. xxix. 13.

3. The laws were wrested and perverted, so that there was no justice. Micah iii. 9, "They abhor judgment, and pervert all equity:" all that was right, equal, just, they oppressed or suppressed, and would not let it take place; so that, according to Isaiah, judgment was turned away backward, and justice stood far off; they thrust them out of doors, out of their gates and cities, and when they pressed hard to come in, there was no admission, the doors and gates were locked and bolted upon them, equity could not enter, Isa. lix. 14; only oppression was let in, Isa. v. 7.

4. For the men, who should have been as strong stakes to keep up the "hedge," they were rotten. The prophets were lions, Jer. xxiii. 14; the priests corrupters and wicked, Lam. iv. 13; the princes were rebellious, and companions of thieves, Isa. i. 23; and all of them brake covenant with God, Ezek. xvi. 59; so that it is evident the "hedge" was broken and gaps made.

"To make up the hedge, and stand in the gap." What that is, falls in now to be considered, and it lies in these things:

1. In public opposing those corruptions which were crept in, and practised amongst them. When of old the Jews had broken down the "hedge," by making a calf, Moses appeared for God against this wickedness; he seized upon the calf, Exod. xxxii. burnt it, ground it to powder, made the people drink it, sharply reproved Aaron, and "stood in the gate of the camp, saying, Who is on the Lord's side? let him come unto me;" and when the sons of Levi came to him, he commissioned them to slay the idolaters; and this was the beginning of making up the breach. So when Josiah began to purge Judah and Jerusalem from the high places, the groves, images, and altars, that were therein, then was the "hedge" making up which they had broken down, 2 Chron. xxxiv. 3, 4. In Nehemiah's days, when the "hedge" was new-made about them, there were some began to tread down the "hedge," and make a "gap" therein, by doing unlawful things on the Lord's day; whereupon the zeal of Nehemiah was kindled, so that he contended with the nobles of Judah, who countenanced them, and did violence to the sabbath themselves, saying, "What evil thing is this that ye do, and profane the sabbath?" Neh. xiii. 15—18.

2. In mourning for such breaches, and deprecating the wrath and judgments due for the same. When the calf was made, and the people worshipped it, now the "hedge" was down, God's wrath ready to break in upon them, and to consume them, Exod. xxxii. 10; but Moses, being affected much with what they had done, and with what God was about to do, he falls to praying and interceding for the people; "Lord, why doth thy wrath wax hot against thy people? &c. Wherefore should the Egyptians speak and say, For mischief did he bring them out, to slay them in the mountains, &c. Turn from thy fierce wrath, and repent of this evil against thy people;" and he did so, ver. 14. Now this act of Moses was standing in the breach, and making up the "hedge," Psal. cvi. 23; it kept out the fury of the Lord from breaking in upon them. The intercession of God's servants is a strong "hedge" and wall to prevent judgments; therefore when the Lord was resolved upon the destruction of the Jews, he forbade Jeremiah to pray for them; chap. vii. 16, "Pray not thou for this people, neither lift up cry nor prayer for them, neither make intercession to me: for I will not hear thee." Intercession or deprecation is an obstructing of God in his way. The Vulgate hath it, Do not thou stop or oppose me. When an army is marching to a town to destroy it, if there be a strong wall in their way, that puts them to a stand, and oft causeth them to give over their attempt: so prayers against judgments, when God is marching out to destroy a people, puts him to a stand, and oft causes him to retreat into heaven.

3. In putting things into their primitive condition. When the bushes trod down, and stakes pulled out, are put into their places again, or new in their rooms, then is the "hedge" made up. When Josiah caused the house of the Lord to be repaired, the covenant with God to be renewed, the law to be read, and the passover to be kept according to the institution thereof, and all things were brought to their primitive condition, 2 Chron. xxxiv. xxxv. then was the "hedge" made up, then was there a man stood in the gap before the Lord. So when Jehoshaphat brought back the people from false doctrine, and false worship, to the Lord God of their fathers, that was, to the true religion and worship, and set judges in all the

fenced cities of Judah, and set Levites, priests, and the chief of the fathers in Israel, in Jerusalem, and instructed them to do all things faithfully, with a perfect heart, and for the Lord, 2 Chron. xix. 4, &c. when he brought things to the pattern in Moses' days, then was the "hedge" made up, then God was with them, and protected them against those wild beasts, the Ammonites, Moabites, and those of mount Seir, chap. xx.

"For the land, that I should not destroy it." By "land," is meant the people of the land, the inhabitants, and their habitations, which were all shortly after laid waste by the Chaldean army. The Septuagint renders these words, that I should not destroy it, that I should not leave it for ever. God by degrees left the temple, the city, the land, and none of them entreated him to stay; and when he was gone, destruction came upon them.

"But I found none." Was there not Jeremiah and Ezekiel, who interceded with God for this people? were there not many that mourned for the abominations that were amongst them? Jer. ix. 1; xiv. 11; Ezek. ix. 4, 8.

It is true, Jeremiah did appear for God, he opposed the false prophets, cried out of their false and corrupt ways of worship, the perverting of justice, the iniquities of priests, princes, and people, but they would not hearken to him, Jer. xliv. 16; they devised devices against him, and slandered him, chap. xviii. 18; they sought to put him to death, and cast him into prison, chap. xxxviii. 4, 6; and God had forbid him to pray for them three times, chap. vii. 16; xi. 14; xiv. 11; and he could prevail with none of them towards making up the "hedge."

As for Ezekiel, he was in Babylon, and the Lord looked for a man amongst them in Jerusalem; so the Lord tells Ezekiel here, "I looked for a man among them," not among you.

For the sighers and mourners that were in Jerusalem, they did it in secret, and durst not openly be seen, they had not spirits to contradict the wicked prophets, priests, and princes; or if they had, yet they saw there was no good to be done, the times were exceeding and desperately wicked; a man was made an offender for a word, and a snare was laid for him that reproved in the gate, Isa. xxix. 21; if any appeared openly to speak against them and their ways, they were made a prey. It was an evil time, and the time for the prudent to keep silence, Amos v. 12, 13. So then, there was none among the prophets, the priests, the princes, or people, whom he mentioned in the verses before, that minded or made up the "hedge," or stood in the "gap."

Obs. 1. That sin makes breaches and gaps. In this chapter the Lord, having enumerated the sins of all sorts in Jerusalem, here he tells them the "hedge" was down, and "gaps" were in it. Their sins brake down the hedge, and made those gaps: Isa. xxx. 13, "This iniquity shall be to you as a breach ready to fall, swelling out in a high wall:" as storms, wars, do make breaches in a wall, so doth sin make breaches in a state. Solomon's sins made such a breach therein, that ten tribes were rent therefrom, and given to Jeroboam, 1 Kings xi. 31; whence it came to pass that Ephraim envied Judah, and Judah vexed Ephraim, Isa. xi. 13. Sin made the breach between the tribes, Isa. ix. 21; the breach between them and other nations, (Zedekiah's perfidiousness did it,) Ezek. xvii. 15; the breach between God and them; Isa. lix. 2, their iniquities separated between them and their God, and their sins hid his face from them, that he would not hear; and set God against them, Ezek. v. 8. Sin makes breaches in churches, 1 Cor. i. 11, 12; and breaks churches, Rev. ii. 5; it makes breaches in cities, Luke xix. 14; in families, Ezek. xvi. 38; in men's names, Prov. vi. 33; in men's estates, Deut. xxviii. 15, 16, &c. Mal. ii. 2; in men's consciences, Matt. xxvii. 3, 4; Prov. xviii. 14; xv. 4; and between the chiefest friends, Prov. xvi. 28.

There are some sins which make such breaches as shake the foundations: Psal. lxxxii. 5, "All the foundations of the earth are out of course." The laws were their foundations, but the iniquity of the judges moved those foundations out of place, and the state was like a bowing wall and tottering fence, Psal. lxii. 3. Religion was a foundation unto them, but they had so corrupted the doctrine and the worship, made such breaches therein, that God was departing far from the sanctuary, and so from them, Ezek. viii. 6.

Obs. 2. When breaches and gaps are made by sin, the Lord hath a purpose to let in his judgments thereby, and to destroy for the same. They had trod down the hedge, and God had thoughts to destroy the land, to bring in a flood of wrath. Ezek. xx. 8, 13, 21, you may see how, upon their making breaches upon the worship, statutes, and sabbaths of the Lord, he resolved to pour out his fury upon them, and to consume them. Isa. i. 23, you have the gaps their sins made, and, ver. 24, the resolution of God thereupon, "Ah, I will ease me of mine adversaries, and avenge me of mine enemies;" they had made breaches upon his law, and he would make breaches upon them: therefore, Isa. v. 5, 6, "I will take away the hedge thereof, and it shall be eaten up;" they have trodden down the hedge of justice, made great gaps therein, and I will take away the hedge of my protection, and let in the wild beasts and boars to tread them down, and eat them up: which the Lord did quickly after. When lately the hedge was trodden down here in England, and gaps made in it, did not the Lord let in wild beasts to devour? were not our princes roaring lions, our judges evening wolves? did not the prelates and priests raven the prey, devour souls, take the treasure and precious things? Though now the wild beasts be destroyed, or driven to their dens, yet every gap is not stopped, nor the hedge fully made up.

Obs. 3. When the hedge is down, gaps are made, and judgments ready to come in upon a people, the Lord looks that one or other should appear, put forth himself, to prevent those judgments. "I sought for a man to make up the hedge, to stand in the gap before me for the land, that I should not destroy it;" Jer. viii. 6, "I hearkened and heard, but they spake not aright." God expected they should have repented, and some at least to have said, What have I done? and what have I done? oh, I have trodden down the hedge of Jerusalem, made many gaps therein; I see God's judgments coming in thereat; now, I will labour to make up the hedge, stop the gaps, divert God's wrath, and bring things to their primitive condition: this God looked for, and would have been glad to have heard. So in Isa. lix. 13—15, the hedge was down, gaps were made, God was displeased, and now he looked that one or other should have showed a public spirit, opposed the sinful practices, and deprecated judgments; he looks in all the gaps round about, and, ver. 16, "He saw that there was no man, and wondered that there was no intercessor," none to meet God, to set upon him by prayer and strong arguments to withhold his judgments. The Septuagint is, There was no helper, none to help up the hedge being down, none to help keep out the floods of God's wrath, none to help the state or church in that tottering condition it was, none to settle their foundations, and bring things into a right order.

Obs. 4. Making up the hedge, and standing in the gaps, is the way to save a land from destruction. Let men oppose the sinful practices in a land, deprecate the judgments of God, and reduce things to the primitive condition, to what is required in the word, and then the Lord will spare a sinful nation, a guilty city. Jer. v. 1, "Run to and fro through the streets of Jerusalem, and see now, and know, and seek in the broad places thereof; if ye can find a man, if there be any that executeth judgment, that seeketh the truth; and I will pardon." The hedge of justice was broken down, they had good laws, but they were violated by all sorts; now, if any man would have appeared against injustice and falsehood, and seen justice executed, and so made up the breach, the Lord would not only have withheld judgments, but have pardoned. In such a case one man may do much: Moses stood in the gap, and diverted the wrath of God, Psal. cvi. 23; the hedge of religion and worship was broken down by a golden calf, and he made it up: Numb. xvi. 41, 42, the people murmured, rose up against Moses and Aaron, trod down the hedge of authority, whereupon the plague brake in upon them; presently Aaron steps into the gap, makes up the hedge, and stops the plague, ver. 47, 48. That which they did was honourable; and they were repairers of breaches. We, through infinite mercy, have had some like Moses and Aaron, to make up our hedges, raise up our foundations, to stop some gaps; but all our gaps are not yet stopped. Are there not gaps in the hedge of doctrine? if it were not so, how came in such erroneous, blasphemous, and wild opinions amongst us? Are there not gaps in the hedges of civil and ecclesiastical authority? do not multitudes trample upon magistracy and ministry, all powers, both human and divine? are there not gaps in the worship of God? do not too many tread down all churches, all ordinances, yea, the very Scriptures? are there not gaps in the hedge of justice, through which the bulls of Bashan enter, which oppress the poor, and crush the needy? Amos iv. 1: are there not gaps in the hedge of love; is not that bond of perfection broken? are there not bitter envyings and strife amongst us; do we not bite and devour one another? are there not gaps in the hedge of conscience? is not the peace broken between God and your souls? doth not Satan come in oft at the gap, and disturb you? are there not gaps also in your several relations, whereby he gets advantage? Surely, if our eyes be in our heads, we may see gaps enough. Let us make up the breaches, stop all gaps in the public and private hedges, otherwise God will break in upon us by his judgments: Lev. xxvi. 18, 19, "If ye will not hearken unto me, I will punish you seven times more for your sins, and I will break the pride of your power."

Obs. 5. That in times of general corruption in church and state, it is hard to find a man of a public spirit to oppose those corruptions, to wrestle with God for mercy, and to bring things to their original condition. The Lord "sought for a man amongst them, that should make up the hedge and stand in the gap, but he found none." Isa. lix. 4, "None calleth for justice, nor any pleadeth for truth." The judges and great ones did oppress the people, and none appeared publicly for them, to plead their cause, and reprove the oppressors. Many disliked the carriage of things, but they had no spirit to oppose, they were "not valiant for the truth," as Jeremiah saith, chap. ix. 3; therefore, Isa. lxiii. 5, God saith, "I looked, and there was none to help; and I wondered that there was none to uphold." He doth not say simply, there were "none," but, "none to help, none to uphold;" the state and church were sinking, and not a man stepped out to put to his shoulder to help support them. God looked for and sought for such a man, but could find none; and, to convince them of the truth thereof, he bids them see and seek all Jerusalem over, if there were a man that executeth judgment: neither God nor men could find one. In common corruptions and calamities, few have hearts to appear for the public good, against overspreading evils; sinful prudence, or fear of crushing, makes them silent, and lie hid: Eccles. iv. 1, the oppressions under the sun were great, the tears of the oppressed many, but there was no comforter, none pitied them, none appeared for them, none used any means to relieve them.

Ver. 31. *Therefore have I poured out mine indignation upon them; I have consumed them with the fire of my wrath: their own way have I recompensed upon their heads, saith the Lord God.*

Seeing they were guilty of such sins as are mentioned in the chapter, and so universally corrupt, the Lord, in this last verse, denounces judgments against them. The verbs are in the preter-tense, "I have poured out," "I have consumed," "I have recompensed." So he had done upon those in captivity, but he speaks of those in the chapter who were then at Jerusalem; and it is usual, in the Hebrew, to put a preter-tense for the future, to note the certainty of a thing: and so here God saith, he had done so, because certainly he would do so. The words of this verse we have had before, chap. xxi. 31; xix. 12; ix. 10; xvi. 43.

Obs. 1. When a people is universally corrupt, the hedges of religion and justice trod down, and none appears to make up those hedges, God will certainly visit that people with his judgments. Prophets, priests, princes, and people, were degenerated and greatly corrupted, all hedges down; God looked for some or other to appear against the corruptions which were amongst them, and because there was none, therefore he would pour out his indignation upon them, and consume them with the fire of his wrath; and they found it so shortly after; Lam. ii. 4; iv. 11, they and their foundations were devoured.

Obs. 2. That God, in his severest judgments, is most just. "I have" or will "recompense their own way upon their head." God did not punish them for others' ways, but for their own; it was their own evil doings brought his judgments upon them; he did them no wrong, when sword, famine, plague, fire, consumed them. Whatever dreadful judgments have fallen out in our days, in this or other nations, let us justify the Lord, he hath recompensed men's own ways upon their heads; he is righteous in all his works, and holy in all his ways.

CHAPTER XXIII.

Ver. 1—4. *The word of the Lord came again unto me, saying, Son of man, there were two women, the daughters of one mother: and they committed whoredoms in Egypt; they committed whoredoms in their youth: there were their breasts pressed, and there they bruised the teats of their virginity. And the names of them were Aholah the elder, and Aholibah her sister: and they were mine, and they bare sons and daughters. Thus were their names; Samaria is Aholah, and Jerusalem Aholibah.*

IN this chapter are contained these generals:

I. A complaint of, or prophecy against, the idolatry and wickedness of the whole body of the Jews, under the names of Aholah and Aholibah, showing their several sins, and the greatness of Aholibah's above Aholah's.

II. Denunciation of judgment against them, and their destruction.

Ver. 1. "The word of the Lord came," &c. This verse shows our prophet spake not out of his own heart or spirit, as the false prophets did; it was the Spirit of the Lord brought the "word of the Lord" unto him, and he spake as he was moved by the Spirit, which shows the divine authority of this prophecy.

Ver. 2. "There were two women, the daughters of one mother." The Jews were at first one people, till the days of Rehoboam, and then they were divided. Ten tribes fell off to Jeroboam, which frequently after were called Ephraim, and Israel, or, the children of Israel, the house of Israel. The other two tribes were called Judah, and the house of Judah: one was the kingdom of Israel, the other the kingdom of Judah. These two were the two women here mentioned.

The word for women is, נשים which is from נשה to forget, they are so called, from their forgetfulness; and these metaphorical women, Israel and Judah, forgat their God greatly, and thereupon are called *nashim*, women, or, forgetters.

"The daughters of one mother." In the Scripture language, the whole of things is termed the "mother," and the parts thereof, "daughters." Ezek. xxi. 21, The king of Babylon stood at the mother of the way; so is the Hebrew: while the way was entire and one, it was called the mother, and when it divided into parts, those parts were as the daughters of that mother. The whole body of the Jews was as the one "mother," and when that body divided into two kingdoms, those kingdoms were as the "daughters" of that "mother." When they were in Egypt, and a long time after, they were as one woman, but in Rehoboam's days this woman grew big, brought forth twins, and so became one mother of two daughters, 1 Kings xii.

Ver. 3. "They committed whoredoms in Egypt." They being in the loins of their "mother," forsook the God of Abraham, Isaac, and Jacob, and fell in love with the Egyptian gods: see Josh. xxiv. 14; Ezek. xx. 7, 8.

"They committed whoredoms in their youth." This Jewish nation, at her first beginning, while young and little, played the harlot, and defiled herself with the Egyptian idolatry. What she did is set out by way of aggravation; she sinned in her youth, or these sisters sinned betimes; their spirits were carried out that way early, and that in Egypt, or house of bondage and suffering.

"There were their breasts pressed, and there they bruised the teats of their virginity." The meaning is this, That quickly after the Jews came into Egypt, the Egyptians prevailed with them by flatteries, or threats, to embrace their idolatrous worship, whereby they lost their chastity, and became like the nations.

Ver. 4. "The names of them were Aholah, the elder." Here he comes to the "names" of these women, and shows you who they were. The name of the one was "Aholah," and this Aholah was Samaria, the chief city of the ten tribes, where the kings of Israel had their chief residency. Aholah is from אהל a tent, or tabernacle; and Aholah is, his own, or their own, tabernacle; that is, Samaria, or the ten tribes, have not me, or my worship, amongst them, they have devised a worship of their own, set up golden calves at Dan and Bethel, they have forsaken my temple, and set up their own tabernacle, and dwell by themselves, separate from me.

"The elder." The Hebrew is not "elder," but, the greater. This woman Aholah had ten tribes, the other only two; this we had, chap. xvi. 46, where it is said, "Thine elder sister is Samaria."

"Aholibah her sister." Thus is the name of the other woman. Aholah's sister was "Aholibah," which signifies, my tabernacle, or, dwelling in her; and this was Jerusalem, where the temple and worship of the Lord were; what was done there the Lord himself appointed, and that was the place he chose, Psal. cxxxii. 13, 14.

"They were mine." I tied them unto me by a covenant, Ezek. xvi. 8; I became their God, and they became my people. The Hebrew is, They were for me, that is, for me alone, for no other God, no other way of worship than what I should prescribe them.

"And they bare sons and daughters." God blessed them, so that they multiplied greatly, they had many sons and many daughters; Ezek. xvi. 7, "I caused thee to multiply as the bud of the field."

Obs. 1. That going after false ways of worship is, in God's account, whoredom. "They committed whoredoms." When they bowed to any of the false gods in Egypt, they did as basely and vilely as she that commits filthiness with another.

Obs. 2. The Lord takes notice where and when those who are in relation to him do sin. "They committed whoredoms in Egypt, and in their youth;" they sinned amidst the grand and bitter enemies of God, among Egyptians, and then when they were but growing up to be a people. They should have considered what enemies the Egyptians were to their God and to his worship, how odious their ways and worship were to him, that so they might have kept at a great distance from them; they should have walked circumspectly, that so they might have kept his name from being polluted; and likewise they, being in their youth, under bondage, should have minded God's kindness in preserving them, and making them to prosper; but they did not, "they sinned in Egypt, and in their youth," two great aggravations of their sin. When God is beginning to show kindness to a people in misery, and raising them up to some height and greatness, and then for them to turn aside to lewdness, to superstitious, idolatrous, and heathenish practices, this God observes in a special manner, and it provokes him greatly. See how it affected the Lord, that they sinned presently after he had showed them kindness, in bringing them out of Egypt: Psal. cvi. 7, "They provoked him at the sea, even at the Red sea:" I put forth my mighty power to bring them out to the sea-side, and was ready to divide the sea to carry them through, but even then and there they provoked me. When states, cities, families, degenerate in their youth, it sorely displeases God.

Obs. 3. Wheresoever a devised worship is brought in, there man's tabernacle is set up; where true worship is advanced, there is God's tabernacle. The ten tribes had a worship of Jeroboam's devising, like unto the worship of Jerusalem in many things; but this was Aholah, their own tabernacle, God owned it not, he was not in their assemblies, he accepted not their sacrifices, their incense was a stink in his nostrils; but Jerusalem was Aholibah, there God's own worship was set up, and so long as his worship was there, he acknowledged his tabernacle to be in her. Where his worship is, there he dwells, Psal. lxviii. 16; and is to be seen and inquired of, Psal. xxvii. 4.

Ver. 5—10. *And Aholah played the harlot when she was mine; and she doted on her lovers, on the Assyrians her neighbours, which were clothed with blue, captains and rulers, all of them desirable young men, horsemen riding upon horses. Thus she committed her whoredoms with them, with all them that were the chosen men of Assyria, and with all on whom she doted: with all their idols she defiled herself. Neither left she her whoredoms brought from Egypt: for in her youth they lay with her, and they bruised the breasts of her virginity, and poured their whoredom upon her. Wherefore I have delivered her into the hand of her lovers, into the hand of the Assyrians, upon whom she doted. These discovered her nakedness: they took her sons and her daughters, and slew her with the sword: and she became famous among women; for they had executed judgment upon her.*

In these verses Aholah's sins and judgments are set out.

I. Her sins; which were,

1. Confederating with the Assyrians, ver. 5; see 2 Kings xv. 19; and those Assyrians are described, ver. 6, 7,

(1.) From their garments.

(2.) From their titles.

(3.) From their age.

(4.) From the creatures they used.

2. Entertaining and defiling herself with the Assyrian idols, ver. 7.

3. Retention of her old Egyptian idolatry, ver. 8; there she had a calf, and under Jeroboam and others she had golden calves.

II. Her judgments; which were,

1. Loss of her freedom, ver. 9.

2. Desolation, ver. 10; in which verses we have also,

(1.) The causes of the judgments:

[1.] The principal, God himself, ver. 9.

[2.] The instrumental, viz. the Assyrians.

(2.) The event of those judgments; ver. 10, "She became famous among women."

Ver. 5. "When she was mine." The Hebrew for "mine" is, תחתי when she was under me, under my covenant, under my worship, my power, and authority. Septuagint is, *ἀπ' ἐμοῦ*, she hath gone out from me her husband, and played the harlot; or, instead of me and my worship, she hath taken in other gods and their worship. The Chaldee is, she hath left my pure worship, and fallen to the abominable idolatries of the Assyrians.

"She doted on her lovers." The Hebrew word עגב notes, violent and base love, and is rendered by the Vulgate, *insanivit in amatores suos*, she was mad upon her lovers, the Assyrians and other nations.

Ver. 8. "Neither left she her whoredoms brought from Egypt." That superstitious, idolatrous disposition which she had, being in Egypt, still abode with her; she made leagues with the Egyptians, 2 Kings xvii. 4; she had her calves like the Egyptian calf, 1 Kings xii. 28.

Ver. 10. "These discovered her nakedness." The Assyrians took away her ornaments and clothing, as ver. 26, and used her shamefully and cruelly, as women often are being taken in war, Isa. xlvii. 2, 3.

"She became famous among women." Hebrew is, she was a name to women. Septuagint, *ἐγένετο λάλημα εἰς γυναῖκας*, she was a talk among women. Some talked of her for her whoredoms and filthinesses; others, for her miseries, judgments, and grievous sufferings, and so she was "famous among women."

Obs. 1. That when people go out from God to false ways of worship, and confidences therein, they are violent and strong in their affections thereunto. Aholah doted upon her lovers, her heart was fired with Babylonish gods, and confidences in them.

Obs. 2. What evil persons have practised in their youth, that they affect in their age. Aholah had loved the Egyptian idols in her minority, and after she was grown up, come to her latter days, those idols were not out of her thoughts; her Egyptian lovers were still in her mind, like harlots that mind their former lovers long after they are married. What corruption gets in in youth, grows up and abides; an unclean, idolatrous heart in youth, will be so in age.

Obs. 3. That idolatry may continue long in a nation, but shall at last be severely punished by the Lord. Aholah had been an idolatress from her youth, and when she was grown up to some greatness, then she brake out into gross, notorious idolatry, 1 Kings xii.; in which she continued some two hundred sixty and odd years, and then the Lord plagued, yea, destroyed her, her sons and daughters. It is wisdom to cleave to the Lord and his worship, not to follow or confide in other nations, or their ways.

Obs. 4. God makes places and persons remarkable by the judgments he executeth upon them. Aholah was made famous among women by those judgments he brought upon her. Aholah was Samaria, which Shalmaneser besieged three years, and then took it, 2 Kings xvii. 5, 6; and after burnt it, as Lavater observes.

Ver. 11—21. *And when her sister Aholibah saw this, she was more corrupt in her inordinate love than she, and in her whoredoms more than her sister in her whoredoms. She doted upon the Assyrians her neighbours, captains and rulers clothed most gorgeously, horsemen riding upon horses, all of them desirable young men. Then I saw that she was defiled, that they took both one way, and that she increased her whoredoms: for when she saw men pourtrayed upon the wall, the images of the Chaldeans pourtrayed with vermilion, girded with girdles upon their loins, exceeding in dyed attire upon their heads, all of them princes to look to, after the manner of the Babylonians of Chaldea, the land of their nativity: and as soon as she saw them with her eyes, she doted upon them, and sent messengers unto them into Chaldea. And the Babylonians came to her into the bed of love, and they defiled her with their whoredom, and she was polluted with them, and her mind was alienated from them. So she discovered her whoredoms, and discovered her nakedness: then my mind was alienated from her, like as my mind was alienated from her sister. Yet she multiplied her whoredoms, in calling to remembrance the days of her youth, wherein she had played the harlot in the land of Egypt. For she doted upon their paramours, whose flesh is as the flesh of asses, and whose issue is like the issue of horses. Thus thou calledst to remembrance the lewdness of thy youth, in bruising thy teats by the Egyptians for the paps of thy youth.*

Having set out Aholah's sins in the former verses,

here he comes to Aholibah's sins, and the events of them.

Her sins were,

I. Her not taking warning by her sister to amend, but growing worse, ver. 11.

II. Her confederacy and idolatry with,

1. The Assyrians, ver. 12; who are described,

(1.) From their nearness, "neighbours."

(2.) From their titles or offices, "captains, rulers,"

(3.) From their habit, "clothed most gorgeously."

(4.) From their rank, "horsemen riding upon," &c.

(5.) From their age and comeliness, "all of them desirable young men."

2. The Chaldeans, ver. 14; which idolatry is set out,

(1.) From the occasion of it, viz. pictures, or "images;" which are described, ver. 14,

[1.] From their colouring, "vermilion."

[2.] Their form, "girded, dyed attire," &c.

[3.] Aspect, "princes to look to."

[4.] Pattern and place, ver. 15.

(2.) From the haste she made thereunto, ver. 16, 17.

(3.) The Egyptians, ver. 19; which is aggravated from the violence of her affection, ver. 20.

III. The events were,

1. God's displeasure, ver. 13.

2. Alienation of his mind from her, ver. 18.

Alienation of Aholibah's mind from the Chaldeans, ver. 17.

Ver. 11. "She was more corrupt in her inordinate love than she." The Hebrew is, she corrupted her love more than she. The Septuagint is, *διέφθειρε τῆν ἐπίθεσιν*, she corrupted her desire, she was more filthy and vile in her dotings and violent loves, than her sister. Jerusalem was more addicted unto idols than Samaria.

"And in her whoredoms more than her sister in her whoredoms." In the original it is, her whoredoms were before, or more than, the whoredoms of her sister; she exceeded Samaria and other places in her idolatries, as you may see, Ezek. xvi. 47, "Thou wast corrupted more than they in all thy ways."

Ver. 12. "She doted upon the Assyrians." For "Assyrians," the text saith, the sons of Assur. This you have verified, 2 Kings xvi. 7, 8, when Ahaz hired Tiglath-pileser, king of Assyria, with the gold and silver of the temple, to come and help him.

"Clothed most gorgeously." In the Hebrew it is, clothed with an absolute garment, with every kind of comely clothing. Junius hath it, clothed most perfectly, with every kind of precious garments.

"Desirable young men." The Hebrew is, the elect of desire; such men as desire itself would choose. They were no ordinary men, but such as were comely, amiable, even men of desires, very desirable.

Ver. 14. "Portrayed with vermilion." The Hebrew for "vermilion" is ששר which signifies, red colour, with which any thing is painted. The rabbies say it is red lead. It is but twice used in the holy Scriptures, in Jer. xxii. 14, and here.

Ver. 15. "All of them princes to look to." The word for "princes" is שלישים which Montanus renders, those that were of the third rank or dignity from the king. 2 Kings vii. 2, "Then a lord on whose hand the king leaned answered;" the word is, *hashalish*, one that was a man in place third from the king.

Ver. 17. "The Babylonians came to her into the bed of love, and they defiled her with their whoredom." This is spoken of metaphorical whoredom. The Jews sent to the Babylonians to enter into league with them, and that being done, they brought in their Babylonish idols and worship amongst them, and taught the Jews to sacrifice unto them, and so defiled the temple and ordinances, "the bed of love." Ahaz brought in the altar from Damascus, which did defile, 2 Kings xvi.

"Her mind was alienated from them." In the Hebrew it is, her soul was removed from them. The Septuagint, her soul departed from them. She grew weary of them, and fell in with the Egyptians, 2 Kings xxiv.; those she had doted upon before now she affected no longer, her soul was loosed from them, and as a thing out of joint.

Ver. 19. "In calling to mind the days of her youth." That is, she remembered, and, together with her remembering, exercised her former spiritual whoredom.

Ver. 20. "She doted upon their paramours." The word for "paramours" is, פלגשיהם; פלגש is a concubine. Montanus renders the word here, their harlots. The Egyptians had the neighbouring nations leaguing it with them, and imitating their idolatry; these were Egypt's concubines. Now Aholibah, or Jerusalem, doted upon these also: or rather thus, She doted above their paramours, above their concubines, more than they, she was carried more strongly towards the Egyptians than other nations.

"Whose flesh is as the flesh of asses, and whose issue is as the issue of horses." The strength and wealth of Egypt are here represented, which provoked the Jews to make leagues with them.

Obs. 1. That when God executes severe judgments upon cities, he looks that sister cities should take warning thereby, and reform in those sins which brought such judgments upon them. God destroyed Aholah, or Samaria, for her idolatry, and confederating with heathenish nations. When Aholibah saw this, she reformed not, but was more corrupt. God expected that Jerusalem should hereupon have purged out all idolatry, knocked off her confidences in other nations, and cleaved wholly to him, that so she might have been spared, but she made no good use of his dealings with Samaria.

Obs. 2. That progress in the same sins after judgment executed upon others for the same, and seen, is a fearful aggravation of sin. Aholah's sins were the same that Aholibah's were, and Aholibah saw God's judgments executed upon her for those sins, and yet she continued and proceeded in the same: "When she saw this, she was more corrupt." When God's hand is lift up, judgment executed, men should fear and learn righteousness; but to go on in wickedness is a horrible slighting, yea, despising of God, and his judgments.

Obs. 3. That sinful cities usually grow worse, whatever judgments they see or hear to be executed upon others. Jerusalem was more corrupt than Samaria, and abounded in whoredoms more than she did, and doted more upon the Assyrians, Chaldeans, and Egyptians. So corrupt is the nature of man, that it is not only the worse after mercies, but even after judgments. Are not we in this city and land, worse now after all the judgments and mercies we have seen, felt, and enjoyed?

Obs. 4. The Lord takes notice what ways cities go, and how they do defile themselves. Ver. 13, "I saw that she was defiled" with Assyrians, Chaldeans, Egyptians, by her trusting in them more than in me, by her idols she fetched in from them. God's eye was upon Sodom, Gomorrah, Nineveh, Babylon, Tyre, Rabbath, and all other cities, and so it is now upon Rome, &c.

Obs. 5. From this 13th verse, That sinful cities do

tread in one another's steps. "They took both one way," what one did that the other did; if Aholah was gone to Assyria, Aholibah will follow her; if one run to Egypt, the other will run after her; if one dote upon them both, so will the other; if one prostitute herself to corporal and spiritual whoredom, so will the other: Simeon and Levi were brethren in evil, and went both one way; Samaria and Jerusalem were sisters in wickedness, and went both one way.

Obs. 6. From ver. 14—16, That the eyes are instruments and occasions of great evil. When she saw the images of the Chaldeans in their dresses, with their belts and aspects, she was taken with them. "As soon as she saw them with her eyes;" Hebrew is, at the sight of her eyes she doted upon them; the images affected her eyes, and they conveyed corruption to her heart, or that which stirred the corruption pre-existent in her heart, which set her on work to send into Chaldea for the men themselves. Adultery and idolatry have their chief entrance by the eye, and many other sins likewise: if men and women would have chaste hearts, they must have special care of their eyes: what a sad thing was it, that Jerusalem's eyes should be taken with the painted images of Babylonians! Some confess there is danger by gazing upon living objects, the beauties of men and women, but they fear none from dead objects; but Achan saw a wedge of gold and a Babylonish garment, and they snared him; Aholibah here saw Babylonish pictures, and they insnared her. If you would be safe, keep your eyes from wandering, and beholding wanton pictures; such sights have cost some dear, and brought forth much wickedness.

Obs. 7. From ver. 17, For God's people to confederate with Babylonians, and admit of any part of Babylonish worship, is to defile the bed of love. For a woman to make leagues with other men, and to admit any one into the marriage-bed, is to defile it. God is a jealous God, his worship must be pure, and the heart must be pure; if the worship be mixed, or heart lean upon an arm of flesh, the bed of love is defiled: in the worship and ordinances God lets out his love to the soul; when they are pure, in the heart being pure and confiding in God, God lets out himself and his love. Let us look to our hearts, that they may be disengaged from all creature confidences, and to our worship, that it be according to God, and then the bed of love is undefiled, and we shall have communion with and comfort from our Beloved.

Obs. 8. Wickedness is inconstant. Aholibah doted upon the Assyrians, ver. 12; and again she doted upon the Chaldeans, ver. 16; and here, in ver. 17, her mind was alienated from them. Wickedness is violent and inconstant; she was taken with the very images of the Babylonians; now she cares not for the men themselves, her soul is disjointed from them; but it was to fall in with some others, and they were the Egyptians, ver. 19; but she held not there long; which made the Lord to say, Jer. ii. 36, "Why gaddest thou about so much to change thy way? thou also shalt be ashamed of Egypt, as thou wast ashamed of Assyria."

Obs. 9. Impudence and open sinning cause God to disown and renounce them that do so. Aholibah, ver. 18, discovered her whoredoms and nakedness; she talked openly what she had done with the Babylonians, she set up altars and idols in every street, was openly and impudently wicked, even like a whore that should prostitute herself to any in the streets. Now it being so, saith the Lord, "then my mind was alienated from her;" seeing she is become so audaciously wicked, I can affect her no longer: there is a necessity in it, that I should alineate my heart from her, as I did from her sister Aholah; else I shall be thought not to have dealt justly with her, especially seeing Aholibah's sins exceed Aholah's. Jerusalem's wickedness alienated God's heart from her, that is, made him renounce her for a harlot. It is sad when God renounces. Hos. i. 9, "Lo-ammi; ye are not my people, and I will not be your God;" what more dreadful sound was there ever in the ears of Ephrain, Samaria, or Aholibah, than that? There can be nothing more dreadful, than to have God disclaim and renounce; then is God turned against them; he so renounces; and so he was against Jerusalem, Ezek. v. 8, "Behold, I am against thee, and will execute judments in the midst of thee." If we would not have God's heart alienated from us, and so be disowned, renounced by him, let us take heed of all sins, especially of impudency in any sin; let us give him our hearts, not alienate them from him, and so he will not alienate his heart from us.

Obs. 10. From ver. 19—21, That fresh sins bring to mind former old sins. Aholibah's latter trucking with the Egyptians minded God of her primitive whoredoms and abominations, when she lived in Egypt, which was one thousand years before: there she had her lovers, there she defiled herself "with the idols of Egypt," Ezek. xx. 7; and her affection now to Egypt, and Egypt's paramours, caused God to mind those sins of her youth: he had no pleasure in doing so, but Aholibah called them to remembrance, by acting the same or like things again; she called them out of darkness, and presented them to the view of God.

Ver. 22—35. *Therefore, O Aholibah, thus saith the Lord God; Behold, I will raise up thy lovers against thee, from whom thy mind is alienated, and I will bring them against thee on every side; the Babylonians, and all the Chaldeans, Pekod, and Shoa, and Koa, and all the Assyrians with them: all of them desirable young men, captains and rulers, great lords and renowned, all of them riding upon horses. And they shall come against thee with chariots, wagons, and wheels, and with an assembly of people, which shall set against thee buckler and shield and helmet round about: and I will set judgment before them, and they shall judge thee according to their judgments. And I will set my jealousy against thee, and they shall deal furiously with thee: they shall take away thy nose and thine ears; and thy remnant shall fall by the sword: they shall take thy sons and thy daughters; and thy residue shall be devoured by the fire. They shall also strip thee out of thy clothes, and take away thy fair jewels. Thus will I make thy lewdness to cease from thee, and thy whoredom brought from the land of Egypt: so that thou shalt not lift up thine eyes unto them, nor remember Egypt any more. For thus saith the Lord God; Behold, I will deliver thee into the hand of them whom thou hatest, into the hand of them from whom thy mind is alienated: and they shall deal with thee hatefully, and shall take away all thy labour, and shall leave thee naked and bare: and the nakedness of thy whoredoms shall be discovered, both thy lewdness and thy whoredoms. I will do these things unto thee, because thou hast gone a whoring after the heathen, and because thou art polluted with their idols. Thou hast walked in the way of thy sister; therefore will I give her cup into thine hand. Thus saith the Lord God; Thou shalt drink of thy sister's cup deep and large: thou shalt be laughed to scorn and had in derision; it containeth much. Thou shalt be filled with drunkenness and sorrow, with the cup of astonishment and desolation, with the cup of thy sister Samaria. Thou shalt even drink it and suck it out, and thou shalt break the sherds thereof, and pluck off thine own breasts: for I have spoken it, saith the Lord God. Therefore thus saith the Lord God; Because thou hast forgotten me, and cast me behind thy back, therefore bear thou also thy lewdness and thy whoredoms.*

In these verses you have a declaration of God's dealings with Aholibah, and the grounds thereof: and herein,

I. Whom God would raise up against her, those who had been her lovers; and the cause thereof, her defection from them, ver. 22. Now these are,

1. Nominated and described, ver. 23.

2. The manner of their coming against and judging Aholibah is set down, ver. 24.

3. Specification of the evil they should do unto her, ver. 25, 26, 29.

II. What God would do himself.

1. Like a husband enraged, he would set his jealousy against her, ver. 25.

2. Put her into the hands of those who hated her, ver. 28.

3. Bring her to the condition her sister Samaria was in, she should drink of her cup, and that deeply, ver. 32—34.

III. The grounds moving God thus to deal with her, which are principally two:

1. Her idolatry, ver. 30, 31.

2. Her forgetfulness of God, ver. 35.

IV. The events, which are two:

1. Cessation from her idolatry and confederating with Egypt any more, ver. 27.

2. Scorn and derision, ver. 32.

Ver. 22. "I will raise up thy lovers against thee." The Babylonians were lovers of Aholibah, or Jerusalem, because she had affected their gods, rites, and sacred things, and trusted in them for help against others; but being now fallen off to the Egyptians, God would stir up the Babylonians against her, and so generally, that they should come and compass her round about.

As you may see in Glassius his Philol. Part 3. p. 863.

Ver. 23. "Pekod, Shoa, and Koa." Some make these the names of great men, but they are rather the names of provinces, which were under the Babylonians, the people whereof God stirred up with others to come to the siege of Jerusalem.

Vide Junii Notas in Bibl. et Commentaria in locum.

Ver. 24. "I will set judgment before them," &c. Mariana understands the words thus, I will punish thee, O Jerusalem, the Babylonians beholding it: they were the executioners of God's judgments, and must needs behold them. We may take the words thus, I will make known my mind to the Babylonians concerning thy destruction, and leave thee to them to be punished according to their laws, seeing thou hast been perfidious and treacherous unto them. I will put thee into their hands, give them power to punish thee, and they shall do it according to their laws and judgments.

Ver. 25. "And I will set my jealousy against thee." By "jealousy," Maldonate understands the Chaldeans, because they were the instruments of his wrath: but here the Lord alludes to the practice of jealous husbands, who finding their wives faulty, set themselves against them, and turn them out of doors: so would God deal with this woman whom he had taken to be his; he would drive her out of the land for her spiritual whoredom, he would give her a bill of divorce, and send her away.

"They shall take away thy nose and thine ears." This Aholibah did trust in her beauty, and play the harlot, chap. xvi. 15; and the Lord would have her deformed like a most filthy harlot, whose nose and ears were wont to be mangled or cut off. It was a law or custom in Egypt, that if a man were taken in adultery, he should be beaten with rods, to a thousand stripes, and that a woman found therein, should have her nostrils cut off. And Pradus saith, it was so in many nations, that for the greater disgrace, they used to cut off the nose, lips, ears, tops of the toes and fingers of their enemies, and adulterers, which was shameful to any, specially to women. Hereunto it is conceived our prophet alludes; but because it is doubtful whether any such thing was really done to Aholibah, divers interpret "nose" of the king, and "ears" of the judges, or chief priests: but we need not allegorize; the meaning is, that God would bring Jerusalem to suffer open and extreme shame.

Cælius Rhod. Lect. Antiq. l. 21. c. 45. Diod Siculus. 1, &c.

Ver. 26. "They shall also strip thee out of thy clothes." This metaphorical woman was well clad, she exceeded in her apparel, both for the matter, quantity, and quality, as appeared, chap. xvi.; she took up the fashions of the Babylonians and Egyptians, whom she doted upon, and had confederated with; but whatever she had, when the soldiers came, they stripped her of all. The Hebrew for "strip" is, הפשיטוך they shall make thee to put off; they shall handle thee so roughly, that thou shalt be forced with thy own hands to put off thy garments, and give them to them, those garments thou hast taken much pride and pleasure in. Of these words, and "fair jewels," was spoken, chap. xvi. 39.

Ver. 27. "Thus will I make thy lewdness to cease from thee," &c. By my judgments upon thee, I will make thee give over thine idolatry; thou shalt mind neither Egyptians, nor gods, their idols, thou shalt neither adore nor desire help from them; thou shalt be made to mind other things, as food, raiment, habitations.

Ver. 28. "I will deliver thee into the hand of them whom thou hatest." In chap. xvi. 27, God delivered her into the hand of them that hated her; chap. xxi. 31, he saith, he would deliver her "into the hand of brutish men, and skilful to destroy;" and here, into the hand of those she hated: there was hatred on both sides, she hated her lovers, and her lovers hated her, and into their hands would the Lord put her; she should find it was the Lord's doings.

Ver. 29. "They shall deal with thee hatefully." They shall speak evil of thee, do evil unto thee, they shall show thee no mercy; they shall spare neither thee, nor thy estate, nor thy name, but shall take away all thou hast gotten by thy labour, and make known to the world what a filthy strumpet thou hast been.

Ver. 30. "Because thou hast gone a whoring after the heathen," &c. Thou hast left me thy Husband and Guide, and gone out to the heathenish gods and idols for help; thou hast bestowed thyself and love upon them, and art defiled by taking them into the bed of love: see chap. vi. 9, where you have the same or like words.

Ver. 31. "Thou hast walked in the way of thy sister." Aholah doted upon the Assyrians, made leagues with them, defiled herself with their idols, manifested her idolatrous disposition she had in Egypt to be still living; and thus did Aholibah, ver. 12, 16, 17, 19.

"I will give her cup into thine hand." Ver. 32. "Thou shalt drink of thy sister's cup." Thou shalt be punished with the same punishments Aholah was; she was taken by the Assyrians, shamefully entreated, and her children carried into captivity, and so shalt thou be dealt with; the same cup she drank of, thou shalt also drink of. This metaphor is very frequent in Scripture, Isa. li. 17, 22; Jer. xxv. 15, 17, 28; Psal. lxxv. 8; Lam. iv. 21. Some think this metaphor to be borrowed from physicians giving potions in cups to their patients, which are troublesome to behold and grievous to taste; so God's judgments are cups of that nature. Others think it taken from that practice of giving cups of wine or strong drink to those that were to suffer, Amos ii. 8, which hebetating their senses, should take away the sharpness of their pain. Others fetch it from the practice at feasts, where the master of the feast did temper and proportion a cup for each guest according to his capacity, and for those they purposed to make drunk, they would fill the larger cups. Let the metaphor of "cup" be borrowed from which you will, it notes out here, God's ordering and measuring out of judgments for Aholibah and hers.

"Deep and large." It shall not be a "cup" to drink off at one draught, or in one day, but it shall be a "cup deep and large," containing much, grievous, great, and long afflictions; a "cup" thou shalt be seventy years drinking.

"Thou shalt be laughed to scorn and had in derision." When whores are punished for their whoredoms, they become matter of scorn and derision to all. The like words we had before, chap. xxii. 4, 5.

Ver. 33. "Thou shalt be filled with drunkenness and sorrow." Thy afflictions, thy punishments shall be such, as shall make thee stagger like one that is drunk; thy pains and sorrows shall be great; it shall not be a cup of consolation, but of astonishment to thyself and all about thee, yea, a cup of desolation, and, as the Septuagint hath it, of perdition.

Ver. 34. "Thou shalt even drink it and suck it out." Thou mayest think this "cup" shall pass away from thee, or if not, that thou shalt drink only a little of it, but thou deceivest thyself, it shall not pass from thee, thou shalt drink it, and drink it off all, thou shalt "suck it out," even the lees and dregs of it, how bitter soever they be.

"Thou shalt break the sherds thereof." Not only drink up what is in the "cup," but as drunkards oft break the vessel, and lick the fragments, not suffering the least drop to be lost, so would God make Aholibah to drink every drop of his fury, which he had put in this "cup." The greatness of their punishment is set out hereby.

"And pluck off thine own breasts." In time of great afflictions many do strange things, rend their garments, bite their flesh, tear their hair; and Aholibah should pluck off her breasts. Before she had let Egyptians and Assyrians bruise the breasts of her virginity, and draw her to idolatry, and now she should scratch and rend them; she should express signs of great grief and great misery upon her.

Ver. 35. "Because thou hast forgotten me, and cast me behind thy back." Here is the ground of her wickedness, and God's judgments coming upon her, she forgat God; which words we had, chap. xxii. 12.

"And cast me behind thy back." The Hebrew is, behind thy body: the sense is this, Thou hast turned from me to thy lovers, to the Assyrians and Egyptians, so that thy face and heart are towards them, and thy back is towards me. A like expression we had chap. viii. 16, where it is said, "Their backs were toward the temple of the Lord, and their faces toward the east." Or thus, Thou hast dealt by me as men do by things they throw behind them, they slight them, and mind them no more. Neh. ix. 26. "They cast thy law behind their backs, and slew thy prophets;" that is, they slighted the law, minded it not, it was out of their sight as a thing behind them, as if there were no such thing. When Jeroboam slighted the counsel of the prophet, 1 Kings xi. 38, and set up other gods, then he cast God behind his back, chap. xiv. 9.

Obs. 1. God makes them instruments of our woe and misery, with whom we have sinned. "I will raise up thy lovers against thee," the Babylonians, Chaldeans, Assyrians, "I will bring them against thee on every side." Jerusalem had doted upon and trusted in them, and by them would God plague Jerusalem. She had oft sinned by her confidence in Egypt, Isa. xxx. 2; xxxi. 1; and God by the Egyptians scourged her, 2 Chron. xxxvi. 3. Parents dote upon their children, and oft God makes them rods to whip them, yea, clubs to break their hearts and bones.

Obs. 2. When people go out from God to false ways of worship, and put confidence in arms of flesh, God will deal severely by them. God would put Aholibah into the Babylonian hands, they should do with her as they pleased, judge her according to their judgments. God would set his jealousy against her, thrust her out of doors; and what then? the Babylonians should deal furiously with her, abuse her body, destroy her children, burn her habitation, strip her of her vestments and jewels, take away all she had gotten, lay open her shame, and do hatefully by her; she should be punished with the same punishments Aholah was.

Obs. 3. Judgments and afflictions are cups which the Lord gives sinners to drink of, some more, some less. "Thou shalt drink of thy sister's cup deep and large." Sometimes God's judgments are called a "cup of trembling," as Isa. li. 22; sometimes a "cup of fury," as Jer. xxv. 15; and sometimes a "cup of astonishment," as here; and Aholibah had all these cups given her to drink, they were "deep, large," contained much, and she was made to drink them all off, yea, to drink the very dregs of them: as men fill up the measure of their sins, so God fills up the cups of his judgments; Rev. xviii. 6, "Fill to her double." Babylon's sins were come to the full, and the cup of the Lord's fury was full.

Obs. 4. Neglect and contempt of God, and his word, causes him to execute judgment. "Because thou hast forgotten me, and cast me behind thy back, therefore bear thou also thy lewdness and thy whoredoms;" that is, bear the punishment of thy lewdness and whoredoms; thou hast made me bear thy sins, and thou shalt bear my punishments. As the fear of God is the beginning of wisdom, so the forgetting of God is the beginning of folly and all evil; then God is out of sight, behind the back; and what will not men do when no awe of God or his word is upon them? Then, like Aholibah, they will commit any lewdness; and because they do so, God lets out his wrath, loads them with his judgments, and makes them bear the merit of their wickedness.

God had done much for Aholibah, dealt by her like a loving husband; but she slighted him, went out a whoring from him, did those things which greatly dishonoured him, and so provoked him to mind her, that forgot him, for he fell upon her with his judgments, and destroyed her; and so will the Lord do by all that forget him: Psal. ix. 17, "The wicked shall be turned into hell, and all the nations that forget God:" whatever sins the nations commit, they are comprehended in their forgetting God, that is the root of all evil; and because they did forget God, they should be "turned into hell," and bear the burden of their sins there for ever.

Ver. 36—44. *The Lord said moreover unto me; Son of man, wilt thou judge Aholah and Aholibah? yea, declare unto them their abominations; that they have committed adultery, and blood is in their hands, and with their idols have they committed adultery, and have also caused their sons, whom they bare unto me, to pass for them through the fire, to devour them. Moreover this they have done unto me: they have defiled my sanctuary in the same day, and have profaned my sabbaths. For when they had slain their children to their idols, then they came the same day into my sanctuary to profane it; and, lo, thus have they done in the midst of mine house. And furthermore, that ye have sent for men to come from far, unto whom a messenger was sent; and, lo, they came: for whom thou didst wash thyself, paintedst thy eyes, and deckedst thyself with ornaments, and satest upon a stately bed, and a table prepared before it, whereupon thou hast set mine incense and mine oil. And a voice of a multitude being at ease was with her: and with the men of the common sort were brought Sabeans from the wilderness, which put bracelets upon their hands, and beautiful crowns upon their heads. Then said I unto her that was old in adulteries, Will they now commit whoredoms with her, and she with them? Yet they went in unto her, as they go in unto a woman that playeth the harlot: so went they in unto Aholah and unto Aholibah, the lewd women.*

In these nine verses Aholah's and Aholibah's sins are further declared and amplified.

I. Here is a mandate to the prophet, to declare their abominations, ver. 36.

II. The declaration of those abominations; which are,

1. Idolatry, expressed by the term of "adultery," ver. 37.

2. Cruelty, in sacrificing their children, ver. 37, and slaying of them, ver. 39.

3. Defilement of holy things, "sanctuary, sabbaths," which is set out with aggravation, ver. 38, 39.

4. Invitation, and alluring men of other nations to commit lewdness, ver. 40—42.

5. Incorrigibleness; they were reproved for their wickedness, warned and counselled to desist, but they went on, ver. 43, 44.

Ver. 36. "Wilt thou judge Aholah and Aholibah?" God being very angry with these two women for their lewdness and abominations, turns to the prophet, who being charitable, was ready to excuse them (for so the words may be read, and are by Piscator); See thou do it not, they are inexcusable. But take the words as they are here, "Wilt thou judge Aholah and Aholibah?" thou seest what they have done, what vile strumpets they are, how justly they deserve severely to be punished; what sayest thou, wilt thou judge them, wilt thou reprove and sentence them for their sins? speak, son of man. I see thou art backward to it, thou thinkest there will no good come of it, thou art discouraged; but rouse up thy spirit, it is thy duty to do it, and thou shalt do it.

Ver. 37. "That they have committed adultery, and blood is in their hands, &c. and have also caused their sons, whom they bare unto me, to pass," &c. For this verse see what hath been said, chap. xvi. 16, 20, 21, 32; ix. 9; xxii. 3.

Ver. 38. Moreover this they have done unto me: they have defiled my sanctuary in the same day, and have profaned my sabbaths." Of defiling the sanctuary, see chap. v. 11, where these words, "because thou hast defiled my sanctuary," were handled; and of profaning the sabbaths, was spoken chap. xx. 13, 16; and xxii. 8.

One thing here is to be considered, viz. the time when they did defile the sanctuary, and profane the sabbaths; it is said, "in the same day;" what day that was, the next verse tells more fully.

Ver. 39. "When they had slain their children to their idols, then they came the same day into my sanctuary to profane it." It was unnatural and barbarous for them to slay their children, impious to offer them to idols, to devils; and to do those things upon the sabbath days, wherein they were to rest from ordinary works, how extremely wicked and abominable was it! and then after such evils to come into the temple, and appear before God, as if they had done no wickedness, but well, what height of iniquity was here! The blood of their children was yet hot upon their hands, and fresh upon their skirts, and in that state they came into the temple to have communion with God in his worship.

"Lo, thus have they done in the midst of mine house." They have not only set up idols in hills and groves, offered their children to Molech in the valley of Hinnom, but they have set up idols in the temple, and have sacrificed their children to them there. So I find some interpreters to understand these words. Maldonate saith, Even in the temple itself they have sacrificed their sons; and he grounds it upon Jer. vii. 30; Ezek. viii. 10, 11; which places prove there were idols in the temple, that they sacrificed unto them, but not that they sacrificed their children there; but rather came with the guilt of their children's blood upon them into the temple, and so polluted it, and the worship of it.

Obs. 1. That wicked ones make little or no conscience of horrible sins, or holy duties; they do pass from the one to the other immediately. When Aholah and Aholibah had slain their children to their idols, the same day they came into the sanctuary and joined the duties of the place and day; from shedding of blood and sacrificing to idols, they step into the temple, and worship of God. Had not their consciences been seared, they would have accused them and told them they were unclean, not fit to meddle with holy things, that they might look for vengeance every hour, who had done such things, and that if they come before the Lord, he would be a consuming fire unto them; but they go boldly and impudently into his presence, not being troubled for what they had done, nor considering how they polluted holy things. So in Jer. vii. 9, 10, they did steal, murder, commit adultery, swear falsely, burn incense to Baal, walk after other gods, and then come presently and stand before him in his house, and say, "We are delivered;" they passed from wicked practices unto holy duties, making no conscience of the one or the other.

Obs. 2. The Lord takes notice how men draw near to him on his days, in the duties of his worship. When they slew their children to their idols, then they came to my sanctuary the same day; they defiled themselves with blood and idolatry on my sabbaths, and in those defilements they came to worship me, Jer. vii. 10. God observed them there, how they came in their sins, and stood before him; they were notoriously wicked, and thrust into the temple worship, and into the presence of God, as if they had been innocent, and as acceptable to God as any. Men may deceive others and themselves, but they cannot deceive the Lord; he sees their spirits, knows them fully, whether they come before him with bloody, idolatrous, unclean, profane, covetous, proud, froward, and malicious hearts, or no; whether they come unprepared in the guilt of former or present sins.

Obs. 3. Profaning of holy things is wronging of God, provokes greatly, and causes him to set an emphasis thereon. When they had sinned, and so came into the sanctuary, and profaned that and the sabbath, saith God, "This they have done unto me. Lo, thus have they done in the midst of mine house." God takes the wrong done to his house, worship, and day, as done unto himself; for he dwelt in the temple, instituted the worship and day, had stamped holiness upon them; and therefore the defiling and profaning of them he counted the defiling and profaning of his name, and of himself, and it did so sorely offend him, that he sets a double mark, or brand thereupon: "This have they done to me. Thus have they done in my house."

Three ways especially are holy things defiled, profaned:

(1.) When men come in their sins, without purging themselves, and preparing for them. James iv. 8, if men draw near to God without cleansing their hands, and purifying their hearts, God will not draw near them; he will not touch unclean things, they will defile him.

(2.) When we mingle aught of ours therewith. Additions of human things are pollutions of divine things: when they brought aught into the temple which God appointed not, that was a defiling that, and the worship thereof. When Nadab and Abihu put strange fire into the censers, they defiled them, and the worship, and provoked God to their destruction, Lev. x. And when they set their threshold with God's threshold, they defiled his name and worship, Ezek. xliii. 7, 8.

(3.) When holy things are handled irreverently. The Bethshemites in a rude manner peeped into the ark, and profaned it, which caused the Lord to smite them with sudden death, 1 Sam. vi. 19. Hence it is, that Solomon gives counsel, Eccles. v. 1, that men should keep their feet when they go to the house of God: why then? because they are to be conversant in holy things; and if they look not well to their affections, they will play the fool, and profane those holy things, and procure a curse instead of a blessing.

Ver. 40. "And furthermore, that ye have sent for men to come from far, unto whom a messenger was sent; and, lo, they came." They were not content to do wickedly themselves, but they sent to and invited others, the Chaldeans, Assyrians, and Egyptians. These metaphorical harlots were wanton with those that did provoke them thereto, and also provoked others afar off to wantonize with them, according to what you had, Ezek. xvi. 33; the meaning is, they sent for men of other nations to make leagues with them, and being come, admitted their idols and idolatrous ways of worship, as appeared ver. 17.

"For whom thou didst wash thyself, paintedst thine eyes, and deckedst thyself with ornaments." Here is set forth the practice of whores, they wash, they paint, they deck themselves for their lovers; and so did these city harlots, Aholah and Aholibah, they fitted themselves for the Babylonians and Egyptians, their courtings and loves.

"Paintedst thine eyes." The Hebrew word, כחל is only in this place, and signifies to colour, to paint, with stibium or red. Montanus renders the words, thou hast coloured thine eyes. The Septuagint is, ἐστιβίζου, thou hast stibiumed thine eyes. Stibium was a colouring stuff women used to make themselves black-browed with. "Eyes" here are put synecdochically for the whole face; and by painting their eyes, is meant the painting of their faces: 2 Kings ix. 30, it is said of Jezebel, "she painted her face;" the Hebrew is, she put her eyes in painting, the eyes are put for the face. Painting of faces was long ago in practice. Some out of pride painted them, that none might seem more beautiful than they; some out of lust, that they might please men therewith, and allure them thereby to folly and wickedness: painted faces are like Samson's foxes, which set the corn on fire. This practice is not warrantable. If women may not counterfeit and change their habits, Deut. xxii. 5, why should they counterfeit and change their faces? if the body be more than meat, the face is more than clothes. The apostle forbids us to "take the members of Christ, and make them the members of an harlot," 1 Cor. vi. 15; and may we take the faces which are the Lord's, ver. 19, and make them the faces of harlots by painting them?

Again, all hypocrisy is odious in the sight of God, and there is face hypocrisy as well as heart hypocrisy. This painting is face hypocrisy; women thereby seem that which they are not. Christ calls them hypocrites for disfiguring their faces, that they might appear unto men to fast, Matt. vi. 16; and do not they who paint their faces disfigure the workmanship of God, that they may appear unto men beautiful, which they are not? Matt. xxiii. 27, 28. By this painting you say you are beautiful, but you lie both to God and man, pretending it to be the work of God, when it is not.

"And deckedst thyself with ornaments." Of ornaments, and decking therewith, was spoken in chap. xvi. 11, 13. Aholibah put on her bravery, and trimmed up herself for strangers, as whores do for their lovers.

Ver. 41. "And satest upon a stately bed." The Hebrew is, a bed of honour, or, an honourable bed. Others, in a bed of state. The Scriptures mention two kinds of beds: *lecti cubiculares*, which men sleep in; Psal. vi. 6, "All the night make I my bed to swim:" and *lecti discubitorii*, which they did eat and feast at, Esth. i. 6; Amos vi. 4; and these were called *tricliniares*, tables, or beds, with three feet. Which bed she sat upon is not much material: like the harlot in the Proverbs, chap. vii. 16, 17, she prepared all things to affect and please her lovers; she had a table furnished, and set the incense and oil which were for God's worship, in a readiness for idolatrous worship, or to be spent upon the Chaldeans and Egyptians, when she entertained and feasted them; she was profuse in her expenses upon idolaters.

Ver. 42. "And a voice of a multitude being at ease was with her." When the Chaldeans and Egyptians came to Aholibah and Aholah, they were feasted, leagues made between them, and all were at peace, so that the voice of a multitude at peace was with her; so the word for "ease" signifies, being שלו from שלה to be at peace and quiet. Peace being made they were at "ease," and the voice of music, singing, and rejoicing was amongst them; they walked, they worshipped, they feasted together.

"With the men of the common sort, were brought Sabeans from the wilderness." These harlots were not satisfied with the captains, rulers, lords, and princes of the Assyrians, Chaldeans, and Egyptians; but they invited the baser sort of people, who thought it a great honour that they should be entertained by these famous harlots, Samaria and Jerusalem. Jer. xxvii. 3, there were messengers sent from the kings of Edom, Moab, Ammon, Tyre, and Sidon, which were inconsiderable to the kings of Babylon and Egypt; and as these were drawn in, so men inferior to them, those of the common sort, yea, Sabeans, or drunkards, as some render the word.

"Which put bracelets upon their hands, and beautiful crowns upon their heads." They brought their presents with them, "bracelets and crowns," which they bestowed upon those harlots, who hired and gave gifts to the great ones, to come unto them, chap. vi. 33, 34, but were cunning here, and received gifts of the meaner and under sort. Of "bracelets" and "beautiful crowns," the 16th chapter gave occasion to speak, ver. 11, 12.

Obs. Wicked ones are active and expensive to draw others to themselves and their wicked ways. These harlots, Aholah and Aholibah, sent to Assyria, to Egypt, to others, to come unto them; they trimmed and decked up themselves, made great preparations to entertain them, they spared not for any cost whereby they might please and satisfy them. Thus did the harlot, Prov. vii.; she perfumes her bed, trims up herself, goes forth, and diligently seeks, finds, and brings in a prey. Some, bad enough, compass sea and land to make proselytes: shall wicked ones, and wickedness, be active, expensive to draw and ruin others, and shall not godly ones, and godliness, be as active and expensive, to win and save sinners?

Ver. 43. "Then said I unto her that was old in adulteries, Will they now commit whoredoms with her," &c. What! art not thou yet satisfied? thou art old in wickedness, art like a dry and dead thing; what! can thy lovers have any pleasure in thee, or thou in them? Cease, ye harlots, from your wicked and lewd practices. Here the Lord chides and reproves them, upbraiding them from their long continuance in their sin. Aholah, Samaria, was oldest in her adulteries, she had continued from the time of Jeroboam in her idolatrous worship; and Aholibah had many years lived in that sin. God's reproof, upbraiding, prevailed not, for,

Ver. 44. "Yet they went in unto her, as they go in unto a woman that playeth the harlot," &c.

Obs. 1. Those who are given to corporal or spiritual uncleanness, are seldom recovered, but go on and grow old in those sins. These women had many reproofs and threatenings, but none prevailed. Such sins are bewitching, and hold men captive; Prov. ii. 19, "None that go unto her return again."

Obs. 2. The Lord takes notice of persons' beginning, progress, and continuance in sin. He observed when Aholah began her whoredoms, when the calves were set up at Dan and Bethel, how she grew up and grew old in adulteries. God's eye goes along with sinners, from the beginning to the end.

Ver. 45—49. *And the righteous men, they shall judge them after the manner of adulteresses, and after the manner of women that shed blood; because they are adulteresses, and blood is in their hands. For thus saith the Lord God; I will bring up a company upon them, and will give them to be removed and spoiled. And the company shall stone them with stones, and dispatch them with their swords; they shall slay their sons and their daughters, and burn up their houses with fire. Thus will I cause lewdness to cease out of the land, that all women may be taught not to do after your lewdness. And they shall recompense your lewdness upon you, and ye shall bear the sins of your idols: and ye shall know that I am the Lord God.*

I. In these verses the judgments of God upon those harlots are further set out.

1. They shall be punished like adulteresses and murderesses, ver. 45.

2. They shall be carried into captivity, and spoiled, ver. 46.

3. They, their sons and daughters, shall be stoned and slain, and their houses burned, ver. 47.

II. The events or effects of these judgments are,

1. Cessation of lewdness, ver. 48.

2. Instruction of other women to take heed of doing the like, ver. 48.

3. Conviction of the equity of God's dealings, ver. 49.

Ver. 45. "And the righteous men." The Assyrians and Babylonians who destroyed Samaria and Jerusalem, are called "righteous" or just "men," not that they were so really, but comparatively: they are styled so in respect of the Jews; they were such, Ezek. v. 6, 7; xvi. 27, 47, who exceeded the nations in wickedness; or because they were God's instruments to execute his just judgments upon them, especially for their perfidiousness with those nations.

"They shall judge them after the manner of adulteresses, and after the manner of women that shed blood." Adulteresses were punished with death under the law, Lev. xx. 10; Deut. xxii. 22; and the death was stoning, John viii. 5, 7, else Christ would not have commissioned them to have thrown stones at the woman, if they had been faultless themselves; and as these were to die from their uncleanness, so were those that shed blood. Of these words see chap. xvi. 38.

Ver. 46. "I will bring up a company upon them." I brought up an army against Samaria, and destroyed it; and so I will do with Jerusalem, I will bring the Babylonians upon her, who shall spoil her, by stoning, slaughtering, burning, and removing her into captivity. No enemies can stir out of their country to mischief others, till the Lord call and bring them; and when he doth so, sad effects follow; they lay all waste, making cities heaps, and pleasant lands wildernesses. Of this 46th and the 47th verse, see chap. xvi. 40, 41.

Ver. 48. "Thus will I cause lewdness to cease out of the land." When the Lord should have accomplished his judgments upon these harlots, when Aholah and Aholibah should be destroyed, then idolatry should cease, and be no more in the land; then sacrificing their children to idols, and shedding of blood, should be no more heard of. God's judgments will silence wickedness, and take away evil from the land.

"That all women may be taught not to do after your lewdness." By "women" here understand, cities, provinces, nations, which seeing the just judgments of God upon these whorish women, Aholah and Aholibah, might learn to beware of such sins, and not to go out from God, having once given up themselves to him, lest they draw such severe and shameful punishments upon themselves.

Obs. God's judgments are teaching things. He brought dreadful judgments upon Aholah and Aholibah, that all women might be taught thereby.

Gideon by thorns and briers taught the men of Succoth, Judg. viii. 16; and God by his piercing judgments teaches the nations; he punisheth one city, that others may take warning. There is no judgment of God upon any city, nation, or people, but it speaks and teaches: Micah vi. 9, "Hear ye the rod;" it hath a voice, a teaching voice.

1. It teaches all who are guilty of the same sins, and not visited with the same judgments, to admire the long-suffering and goodness of God towards them.

2. It teaches those presently to consider their ways, turn to the Lord by repentance, who are guilty of such sins, lest the Lord, being now in a way of judgment, should break out also upon them, and make them examples of his justice.

3. It teaches others to fear and flee from such practices, as bring such destructive judgments. When Samaria and Jerusalem shall be destroyed by dreadful judgments for their confidence in arms of flesh, by confederating with other nations, for their idolatry, cruelty, profaneness, and perfidiousness, will not other cities fear to do the like? will not every city learn to see what is the reward of wickedness, in the sufferings of others? This God's judgments teach sinners to do, that so they may consult for their credit and safety.

Ver. 49. "And they shall recompense your lewdness upon you." The Hebrew is, And they shall put your filthiness and lewdness upon you; that is, the nations and cities round about shall concur with the Babylonians to punish you for your wickedness, to bring upon you the merit of your sins; or thus, They shall approve of what the Lord doth in destroying of you, saying, All is the fruit and just recompence of your own doings.

"And ye shall bear the sins of your idols." Their idols did not sin, but they sinned with their idols, and the fruit of those sins they must eat, the punishment due to them they must bear: there is a near connexion between sin and punishment, they have the same names; so ver. 35.

Obs. God's proceeding with sinners in judgment righteously, brings them to acknowledge the equity of his dealing with them. When the just punishment of your lewdness and idolatry shall be upon you, "ye shall know that I am the Lord God," who observed all your ways, who waited long for your repentance, who have dealt justly with you in all the evils I have brought upon you; you cannot but justify me, and condemn yourselves.

CHAPTER XXIV.

Ver. 1—5. *Again in the ninth year, in the tenth month, in the tenth day of the month, the word of the Lord came unto me, saying, Son of man, write thee the name of the day, even of this same day: the king of Babylon set himself against Jerusalem this same day. And utter a parable unto the rebellious house, and say unto them, Thus saith the Lord God; Set on a pot, set it on, and also pour water into it: gather the pieces thereof into it, even every good piece, the thigh, and the shoulder; fill it with choice bones. Take the choice of the flock, and burn also the bones under it, and make it boil well, and let them seethe the bones of it therein.*

THIS chapter is conceived to be the last prophecy against the kingdom of Judah, before the final destruction thereof; which, with the great calamity thereof, is set out under the type of a boiling pot, and the death of the prophet's wife.

In the chapter is contained a double prophecy:

I. That of the boiling pot, and the interpretation thereof, to the 14th verse.

II. That of Ezekiel's wife dying suddenly, his not mourning for her, and the explication thereof, from the 15th verse to the end.

In the verses before us we have,

1. The time of this prophecy, ver. 1.

2. The occasion, ver. 2; which was, the king of Babylon's setting himself against Jerusalem.

3. The prophecy itself, ver. 3—5.

Ver. 1. "In the ninth year, the tenth month, and the tenth day thereof." Our prophet being in Babylon, reckons from the ninth year of the captivity, the time that Jehoiachin, himself, and others, were brought into Babylon, Ezek. i. 2; viii. 1; and not from the time of Zedekiah's reign, though it were the "ninth year, tenth month, and tenth day" thereof, for that day the one was carried away the other was made king. It concerned them in Babylon to keep account of their captivity.

"The word of the Lord came unto me, saying." He had nothing of his own to give out that day, but the "word of the Lord came" to him, the Spirit of the Lord brought it, and with such power, that he must write and speak.

Ver. 2. "Write thee the name of the day, even of this same day." The Hebrew is, Write the name of the day, and the body, or substance, of the same day. It was a day wherein something considerable and substantial was acting. God would have the prophet "write the day," not only to add weight to his prophecy, but to stir them up to be affected, and to see how the providential hand of God ordered things at a great distance.

"The king of Babylon set himself against Jerusalem this same day." Here was the occasion, or cause, of his writing down the day, and so prophesying upon it. Nebuchadnezzar was that "day" sitting down before Jerusalem, as you may clearly see, 2 Kings xxv. 1; Jer. xxxix. 1; lii. 4. When Nebuchadnezzar was upon a warlike expedition, he knew not whether he should go to Rabbath or Jerusalem, chap. xxi. 21; but he was ordered by a divine hand to lay siege to Jerusalem, the tenth day of the tenth month, in the ninth year, which Ezekiel could not possibly know, had not the Lord revealed it. This was a business of high concernment to the Jews in Judea, and those in Babylon.

Obs. 1. The Lord takes notice of what men do, and can make known the same to whom he pleases, at what distance soever. Nebuchadnezzar and his forces were in Judea, sitting down before Jerusalem, and this the Lord revealed to Ezekiel, being in Babylon. It was declared to Elisha, whither the king of Syria would march, and where he would pitch his camp, 2 Kings vi. 9, 10. The death of Herod in Judea was discovered to Joseph, being in Egypt, Matt. ii. 19, 20. And when Moses was in Midian, the Lord told him that all the men were dead in Egypt, which sought his life, Exod. iv. 19.

Obs. 2. There are some things and times the Lord would have his people take special notice of, and keep the chronology thereof. Ezekiel must write the year, the month, and day, of Jerusalem's besieging: "In the ninth year, the tenth month, the tenth day, the king of Babylon set himself against Jerusalem;" that was a sad business and a sad time. When God hath been upon executing great judgments, or showing great mercies, the days and months have been recorded.

The day and month of Noah's entrance into the

ark, and of his coming out again, are mentioned, Gen. vii. 11; viii. 14, 16. The time of the Jews' going out of Egypt you have punctually set down, Exod. xii. 41, 42; so the time of their passing over Jordan, Josh. iv. 19; of Solomon's building the temple, 2 Chron. iii. 2; of Haman's plot to destroy the Jews, Esth. iii. 8, 13; and several other things, the year, month, and day, stand recorded: which shows they were providential, not casual, that the wisdom and power of God were interested in them, whoever were the instruments; and that, being so exactly set down, posterity should not forget them. And questionless the Lord expects, that we should keep a chronology of the great and remarkable things done by him for us: as the fight at Marston-moor, July 2nd, 1644; at Naseby, the 14th of June, 1645; at Maidstone, 2nd June, 1648; Scots routed in England, August 17th, 1648; Ormond beaten from Dublin, August 2nd, 1649, &c.

Ver. 3. "Utter a parable unto the rebellious." The Hebrew is, Speak thou parabolically to the house of rebellion, a parable; that is, Speak thou darkly unto them, that they may the better attend, and make the more diligent inquiry after the meaning of what thou deliverest. Of "parable" and proverbs formerly have been spoken, chap. xvii. 2; and of the "rebellious house," chap. ii. 5.

"Set on a pot, set it on." It is for cooks to set on pots, put in water, then the meat. Ezekiel, he must bid them "set on the pot;" a strange work for a prophet, and because strange, it would make the people mind it the more, and search out the mystery. By this "pot" is meant Jerusalem. Ezek. xi. 3, "This city is the caldron:" הסר it is the same word that is here for "pot," which notes, strength, comprehensiveness, and durableness. So Jerusalem was strong, comprehended much, and was more durable than other places when besieged: not Jerusalem simply, but under judgment, was the "pot."

"And also pour water into it." When pots are set over the fire, they put in and fill them with "water," that so whatever they please may be boiled therein. By this "water" is meant the afflictions and judgments, in which, as in "water," God would boil Jerusalem. Now the king of Babylon was set down round about it, had straitly besieged it, and variety of calamities were upon it, and the waters of affliction began to be hot. So calamities are called, Isa. viii. 7.

Ver. 4. "Gather the pieces thereof into it." When the cook hath set on the pot, filled it with water, then he takes the several pieces of flesh, which are to be boiled, and puts them into the pot; and they are called the "pieces thereof," because they are to be boiled therein.

"Even every good piece, the thigh, and the shoulder." Here the people, or commonwealth of Israel, is likened unto a body dissected; as the Levite's concubine was, Judg. xix. 29: and they must take the good or principal pieces, those that were the strength and support of the body and head, as the thighs and shoulders; that is, the nobles, counsellors, priests, and chief soldiers amongst them.

"Fill it with choice bones." The Hebrew is, Fill it with the choiceness of bones; which Rabbi David interprets, as we do, Fill it with choice bones; that is, with choice pieces; because the pieces, saith he, are cut according to the "bones." This "pot" must not have a "piece" or two, a "bone" or two, put into it, but must be filled with the choicest pieces and bones which were in all the body.

Ver. 5. "Take the choice of the flock." By the "choice" may be understood the king himself, who is the head of the flock; or, the fat and wealthy ones.

"Burn also the bones under it." By "bones" here, divers expositors understand the bones of the innocent prophets, and others, who were slain unjustly. Those the prophet bids them to burn under the pot, and that to manifest the cause of God's great wrath against, and just destruction of, the city. But this interpretation of "bones," suits not with the scope of the place, which is not to disquiet the bones of the innocent, and lay punishment upon them, but to revenge their death. The "bones" here are to suffer as well as the flesh. We may understand these words thus; Let flesh and bones boil together, and when they are so boiled, that all the flesh and fat is taken from the "bones," then burn them; that is, when all the wealth, places, honour are taken from the rich, then let them be destroyed by famine, plague, or sword, and that is the burning of the "bones;" let nothing of them or theirs be spared, but let all be consumed. Or thus, Boil the fat ones in the "pot," and burn the poor under it; they are like "bones" without flesh, make them instrumental to consume the rich; and doubtless, in the famine, they were like a fire devouring the flesh in the "pot."

"And make it boil well." The Hebrew is, רתח רתחיה which Montanus renders, make its boilings to boil, boil it thoroughly. There be old tough pieces in the "pot," which will not easily or suddenly be boiled, they will require a hot and continued fire; therefore Buxtorf interprets the words, see that the boilings be very hot. The Chaldean army were not the "bones" and fire under this metaphorical "pot," but the bellows rather, to blow up and increase the fire.

"And let them seethe the bones of it therein." The Hebrew is, let the bones thereof be sodden in the midst of it; and the stream of interpreters carry the words plurally, and so it suits best with the words going before: Make it boil well, and let the bones thereof be sodden in the midst of it; that is, let them be thoroughly sodden. "Bones" are strong things, they require more than ordinary seething, especially if old; and there be many old bones in the "pot," many hardened sinners, many stout spirits amongst the soldiers, princes, nobles, and others; but let them be soundly boiled in this "pot" of affliction, and that will make them tender. The Vulgate is, the bones are boiled till the flesh and they are sundered, they are thoroughly boiled; and Vatablus makes this the sense of it, let the strongest and stoutest men be slain and consumed in that siege.

Obs. 1. The sinfulness of men hath occasioned God to give out much Scripture. "Speak a parable to the rebellious." God took occasion from their rebelliousness to give forth this "parable," and many others. Much of Jeremiah and our prophet was occasioned to see the world, by the wickedness of the Jews. Sin accidentally occasions good: sin made way for Christ; and as for him, so for much, if not the greatest part, of the holy Scriptures.

Obs. 2. Teaching by parables is warrantable. God sends and commands the prophet to utter a "parable." Isaiah, Jeremiah, Zechariah, were not without parables. Christ was abundant in them. The parables they used were taken from ordinary things, known and familiar, such as were obvious to the senses, as here from a pot, water, pieces of flesh, bones, &c. Hereby the mind and memory are much enlivened, and stronger impression made upon the heart. Chap. xxii. 18, "All they are brass, and tin, and iron, and lead, in the midst of the furnace:" and here they were as flesh, and bones, in the midst of the pot.

Obs. 3. The judgments of God upon places, makes them pots, in which he boils sinners. Now Jerusalem was a "pot" over the fire; the Babylonish forces were round about it, dreadful calamities upon it, multitudes in it who were like pieces of flesh in a boiling pot. What boiling thoughts, fears, cares, distractions, discontents, were amongst them! We may judge what boiling was therein, by the army's lying near this city, and being in readiness to come upon it.

Obs. 4. That God at his pleasure commands judgments upon places. "Set on a pot, pour water into it;" make Jerusalem miserable with plague, famine, and sword. If he speak the word, the thing must be done; whatever he calls for, takes place. Jerusalem, that was a paradise, must now become a boiling pot.

Obs. 5. That when God's judgments are abroad, he meets with all sorts of men, the fat and lean, the strong and weak, the rich and poor. When the "pot" is on the fire, God will have the choice pieces and choice ones into it; the shoulders, the thighs, the choice bones, prince, nobles, men in place, of wealth, as well as the poor and lean ones.

Obs. 6. When God is boiling of sinners in the fire of his judgments, he will boil them to purpose. "Make it boil well, and let the bones thereof be sodden in the midst thereof:" this pot was boiling not a few hours, days, or months, but a year and half, 2 Kings xxv. 1—3. So when God made Samaria a boiling pot, 2 Kings xvii. 5, he boiled the sinners in it three years together. God so boiled them there, and these here, that he made the proudest and stoutest of them to stoop, yea, all of them to become meat to their enemies.

Ver. 6—8. ***Wherefore thus saith the Lord God; Woe to the bloody city, to the pot whose scum is therein, and whose scum is not gone out of it! bring it out piece by piece; let no lot fall upon it. For her blood is in the midst of her; she set it upon the top of a rock; she poured it not upon the ground, to cover it with dust; that it might cause fury to come up to take vengeance; I have set her blood upon the top of a rock, that it should not be covered.***

Here the Lord comes to interpret the parable, denouncing a fearful "woe" to Jerusalem, and giving the grounds thereof; which are,

I. Her bloodiness, with the aggravation thereof, ver. 6, 7.

II. Her unprofitableness under judgments; when she was boiling, her scum abode with her, went not out of her.

Ver. 6. "Woe to the bloody city!" Jerusalem was guilty of much blood, Ezek. xxii. 3, 4, 6, 9, 12, 13, 27; 2 Chron. xxi. 16. Jerusalem was now as bad as Nineveh, which, Nahum iii. 1, is called the "bloody city," and hath the same "woe" denounced against it. By blood, not only murder, but also other notorious wickednesses, which deserved death, are to be understood: Ezek. vii. 23, "The land is full of bloody crimes;" of such sins for which men ought to be cut off. *Vide loc.*

"To the pot whose scum is therein, and whose scum is not gone out of it!" Here it is clear, that by this metaphorical "pot" is meant the city; he calls the city the "pot," which was not without its scum. חלאתה from חלה *ægrotavit*; for the "scum" is *ægritudo ollæ*, the sickness of the "pot." Rabbi Solomon calls it, *excrementum*, the excrement and filth of the pot. The Septuagint is, ἰὸς, the poison of it. The Vulgate is, *rubigo*, the rust of it. Frosterus hath it, *sordes*, those filthinesses, which, through great boiling, do adhere to the "pot," from what is boiled

Avenarius.

therein. By "scum" is meant the sin and wickedness of the city; which is likened thereunto, in respect,

1. Of its loathsomeness. "Scum" and filth are loathsome things; the sins of this city were loathsome, it was full of abominations, blood, idolatry, uncleanness, &c. such evils as made it to be abhorred, Ezek. xvi. 25; as made the Philistines ashamed, ver. 27; such sins as were loathsome afterwards to themselves, chap. xx. 43.

2. Of its visibleness. The "scum" and filth is uppermost, next to view; such were Jerusalem's sins: they were open, she had an eminent and high place in every street, Ezek. xvi. 24; "she opened her feet to every one that passed by," ver. 25; she and her princes shed blood openly, chap. xxii. 6; nothing but sin and wickedness appeared in her.

3. Of its adherency to the "pot." So Jerusalem's sins did cleave close to her; the more she was boiled in the judgments of God, the more fast she held her sins, her scum and filth stuck to every side of her. Jer. viii. 5, "They hold fast deceit:" their sins cleaved to them, as flesh to the bones, as rust to a pot; though they were oft in the fire, or over it, yet their filthiness departed not from them, their scum, their dross, boiled in, and cleaved fast to them, Jer. vi. 29.

"Bring it out piece by piece." He persists in the allegory of the "pot," and orders how they should be dealt with who were in the city. They should be brought out severally, not all at once, but as pieces are taken out of the pot, one after another, till there be no more: so it should be done with this city, one piece of it should be brought out and consumed with famine, another piece of it with the plague, ver. 3, with the sword, ver. 4; should be carried away into captivity, so that it should be emptied of all: so the words are rendered in Vatablus, part by part empty it. This city was emptied somewhat under Jehoiakim, when he was carried to Babylon, 2 Chron. xxxvi. 6, 7; it was emptied more when Jehoiachin was taken, and many with him also carried thither, 2 Kings xxiv. 15; but it was wholly emptied when Zedekiah was taken, and carried away, 2 Kings xxv.

"Let no lot fall upon it." Let it not have that favour or mercy. Among soldiers, in their military discipline, when they take many enemies worthy all to die, they single out some by lots to suffer, and spare the rest; but Jerusalem should not have any spared, they should all, young and old, taste of one judgment or other. We may refer this lotting to the city itself; let it not come to that, as to cast a "lot," whether the city shall be saved or destroyed: such a famous, great, ancient city might fall into consultation, whether it should be ruined or no. Carthage was long in debate in the senate of Rome, saith Lavater, whether it should be utterly destroyed. But the Lord prevents such a consultation, and saith, "Let no lot fall upon it;" I have decreed it to be ruined, and it shall be ruined, utterly ruined.

Ver. 7. "Her blood is in the midst of her, she set it upon the top of a rock," &c. The meaning of this verse is, she shed blood openly, did bloody and notorious things publicly, as if she had done them "upon the top of a rock:" if blood be shed there, it is dry, hard, drinks not in the blood at all, but it lies to be seen of all that come upon the "rock;" whereas, if blood be shed upon the earth, that drinks it in quickly, or it may be covered with dust, that others may not discern it. Jerusalem did not sin closely, and hide her wickedness from the world, but so openly, that all nations took notice of it.

Ver. 8. "That it might cause fury to come up to take vengeance." They did not sin to that end that

God might take "vengeance" on them, but the nature of their sin was such, as it provoked God to "fury," and to hasten vengeance: their sins were open, great, and crying for "vengeance;" their sins ascended, and God's "fury" descended.

"I have set her blood upon the top of a rock." As she did, so did the Lord. She shed blood openly, and was not ashamed of it, and I have shed her blood openly, and am not ashamed of it. She did not cover her sin, but exposed it to the view of all, and God, by his punishments, set it on "the top of a rock," and made it known to the whole world.

Obs. 1. That cities have their filth and scum in them. Jerusalem here is likened to a "pot" with the "scum" in it. The poor are not the "scum" of the city, but the sin and wickedness of poor and rich, that is the "scum;" Jerusalem was full of it. Ezekiel, chapters viii. xvi. and xxii. tells you what "scum," and abundance of it, was in Jerusalem. There was much "scum" in Sodom, much in Samaria, much among the nations, but most in Jerusalem. To great cities there is a confluence of all sorts of people, who bring "scum" and filth with them, and add to what they find there. What scummy doctrine did the false prophets teach in Jerusalem! Jer. xxiii.; what scummy counsel did Jaazaniah and Pelatiah give in that city! Ezek. xi. 1, 2; what dunghill gods did Jerusalem entertain! Jer. ii. 28, "According to the number of thy cities are thy gods, O Judah:" there was no sin against God or man, but it was in Jerusalem. And other cities are not without their "scum," no, not this city.

Obs. 2. Heavy judgments upon sinful places do not work out the wickedness which is in them. Jerusalem was besieged, suffered hard things, and her "scum" went not out of her, it boiled in, she was the worse for all those fiery judgments God brought upon her. Jer. v. 3, "Thou hast stricken them, but they have not grieved; thou hast consumed them, but they have refused to receive correction: they have made their faces harder than a rock; they have refused to return." God did strike them with Egyptian and Babylonish rods, but there were no tears, no relentings, no returnings, but grew harder and harder, even to a rockish hardiness. . Ahaz, the head of this city, in the time of his distress sinned the more against the Lord, 2 Chron. xxviii. 22. When Samaria was besieged by the Syrians, 2 Kings vi. did the "scum" of it boil out? no, Jehoram at that time sent to take off Elisha's head, ver. 31, and said, he would wait no longer for the Lord, ver. 33: his "scum" boiled in, and boiled up to a greater height. Is the "scum" gone out of Ireland, by all the bloody judgments of God which have been upon them? is it gone out of England, or London, by all the sad strokes we have had?

Obs. 3. When judgments prevail not with sinful places to cleanse them from their iniquities, God threatens, and will certainly destroy such places, and that without mercy. Jerusalem was as a pot over the fire, her "scum" went not out of her; and what then? "Woe to the bloody city! bring it out piece by piece; let no lot fall upon it:" because the scum wrought not out, the flesh, the people, must be brought out to destruction, and the pot be broken in pieces. God said of Jerusalem, Jer. xxxii. 31, "This city hath been to me as a provocation of mine anger and of my fury from the day that they built it even unto this day:" sometimes there were good kings, and good people, in it, but generally the people were wicked; and therefore, Jer. xix. 11, "I will break this people and this city, as one breaketh a potter's vessel, that cannot be made whole again." It was bloody, merciless, and now should have bloody judgments without mercy.

Obs. 4. Open, impudent sinning provokes to vengeance, and shall be punished openly. The 7th and 8th verses together yield this observation. Jerusalem shed blood, not in a corner, or some secret place, she had no care to conceal and cover what she did; but openly, as on the top of a rock, she set up scaffolds to execute the innocent; this caused fury to rise in the Lord, and hastened him to take vengeance, and to punish her openly: he called for Nebuchadnezzar to come out of Babylon, he led him to the gates of Jerusalem, caused him to sit down there, and visibly to execute his vengeance upon her, so that her punishment was as open as her sin; she sinned as on the top of a rock, and God set her blood "on the top of a rock." The besieging, taking, and burning of Jerusalem was so known, and famous, as that all the nations took notice thereof, and made themselves sport therewith, Lam. ii. 15, 16; she would not cover her sin and shame, and God would not cover her punishment.

Ver. 9—14. *Therefore thus saith the Lord God; Woe to the bloody city. I will even make the pile for fire great. Heap on wood, kindle the fire, consume the flesh, and spice it well, and let the bones be burned. Then set it empty upon the coals thereof, that the brass of it may be hot, and may burn, and that the filthiness of it may be molten in it, that the scum of it may be consumed. She hath wearied herself with lies, and her great scum went not forth out of her: her scum shall be in the fire. In thy filthiness is lewdness: because I have purged thee, and thou wast not purged, thou shalt not be purged from thy filthiness any more, till I have caused my fury to rest upon thee. I the Lord have spoken it: it shall come to pass, and I will do it; I will not go back, neither will I spare, neither will I repent; according to thy ways, and according to thy doings, shall they judge thee, saith the Lord God.*

In these verses the Lord proceeds,

I. In threatening of judgments, ver. 9, "Woe to the bloody city!" as before, ver. 6.

II. In a parabolical declaration of those judgments, in the end of ver. 9, and in ver. 10, 11.

III. In showing the causes thereof, ver. 12, 13.

IV. In sealing up the certainty and irrevocableness of these judgments, ver. 14.

Ver. 9. "I will even make the pile for fire great." I will bring a multitude of Babylonians, a mighty army, which shall besiege Jerusalem, and be as a great fire unto it; by them I will execute fiery judgments upon the "bloody city." The Hebrew is, I will make a great fire, that is, I will consume the whole city: here are a multitude of houses, stately buildings, and they shall be all as a pile of wood for fire; yea, the inhabitants thereof shall be consumed by the fire of my wrath.

Ver. 10. "Heap on wood, kindle the fire, consume the flesh." The Hebrew verbs in this verse are infinitive, but rendered imperatively. Vatablus reads them in the future, I will heap on wood, I will kindle the fire; that is, saith he, I will add spirit and power to the Babylonish forces, to besiege the Jews, that so by famine, sword, and plague, they may be consumed. According to our reading the words, God calls for, and hastens, the destruction of Jerusalem.

"Spice it well." The Hebrew is, הרקח המרקחה which Montanus renders thus, Season a seasoning with spicery. רקח signifies, to make an ointment, sauce, or seasoning, of divers kinds of grocery or sweets, that so it may be the more pleasing to the nostrils or palate. Cooks "spice" their meats and sauces, that so they may be more acceptable to the taste of those who feed upon them. The spicing here I conceive to be, the various judgments which were to be inflicted upon Jerusalem, which made it as savoury meat both to men and God; when it was salted and spiced with his judgments, God was at rest and comforted, Ezek. v. 13. Their fears, sorrows, distractions, sufferings, famine, were several spices they were spiced withal; and it was meat and drink to the Chaldeans at last, to destroy them, being made faint and feeble with a long siege.

"Let the bones be burned." Let the strongest soldiers, wealthiest citizens, and principal men of the city, be weakened and consumed in this siege, or at the end of it; not only the poor and low ones, but the highest and mightiest ones. The Chaldee hath it, Let her strong men be mad.

Ver. 11. "Then set it empty upon the coals thereof." When the city should be emptied of the inhabitants thereof, it should be as a "pot" set on the fire without any thing in it; when it is so, it quickly melts, consumes, and comes to nothing. This "pot" must be set on,

1. That it may be melted.
2. That the filthiness of it may be separated.
3. That the scum and rust may be consumed.

Obs. 1. That sin and wickedness do defile the places and persons where they are, as filthy liquors, scum, and rust, do the vessels and pots in which they are. This metaphorical "pot" had her filthiness in it; Jerusalem had shed blood, set up altars and idols, oppressed the fatherless, widows, and strangers, and these things defiled her; not only were the citizens, but even the city itself was defiled. The leprosy defiled the garments and the houses, Lev. xiv.; sin is that leprosy which defiles men, garments, houses, towns, cities, and lands: Ezra ix. 11, "The land which ye go to possess, is an unclean land with the filthiness of the people;" filthy people make all like themselves.

Obs. 2. Destructive judgments upon sinful places are pleasing unto God. He encouraged the Chaldeans to "heap on wood," to "kindle the fire, consume the flesh," and to "spice it well." Execution of justice, destruction of sinful cities and persons, is a sacrifice well pleasing to God, delighting him as much as any spiced meats do the palates of men. When Jehu had executed justice upon Ahab's sons and Baal's priests, see what the Lord said; 2 Kings x. 30, "Because thou hast done well in executing that which is right in mine eyes, and hast done unto the house of Ahab all that was in mine heart, thy children of the fourth generation shall sit on the throne of Israel." Was not the destruction of those wicked ones very pleasing unto the Lord, when he rewarded it so well?

Ver. 12. "She hath wearied herself with lies." Montanus renders the Hebrew thus, she hath afflicted or wearied herself with injuries, that is, with wronging others. Vatablus, in his notes, hath it thus, she hath wearied herself, and that in doing injury to others. "Herself" is not in the original; the words may therefore refer to God, and so both Junius and Piscator read them: She hath wearied me with her lies and vexations; I often reproved her for her sins, threatened her by my prophets, visited her with my judgments, but all was to no purpose: if at any time she promised amendment, it was hypocritically, she performed it not; or she took those ways and courses which pleased not me, nor profited herself, and in those she both wearied me and "herself." The word for "lies" signifies, iniquity, vanity.

"Her great scum went not forth out of her." In the sixth verse the words are, "whose scum is not gone out of it;" here, "her great scum went not forth out of her." What course soever she took to advantage herself, her "scum" rather increased than diminished; she pretended oft to part with her "scum," but never did.

"Her scum shall be in the fire." Seeing her "scum" and rust (for so the word may be interpreted) will not be gotten out of her, she shall be served like the unclean vessels, that were to pass through the fire, Numb. xxxi. 22, 23. So this "pot" or city should be burnt with fire, and so her "scum" and rust should be consumed with her.

Obs. 1. Wicked, vain, sinful practices, do weary God, and those that do use them. She hath wearied me, she hath wearied herself with lies; that is, with her wretched doings: I have oft presented mercy to her, she refused it; I have oft called upon her to turn from her idolatry, unjust and bloody doings, but she hath had a deaf ear; I have waited long for her repentance, and she hath dissembled with me, and is grown impenitent; I am weary of waiting any longer. Isa. lxv. 2, 3, "I have spread out my hands all the day to a rebellious people, which walketh in a way that was not good, after their own thoughts; a people that provoketh me to anger continually to my face," &c. How could it be but that God should be weary of such people, and such doings? God tells her, she had wearied him with her iniquities, Isa. xliii. 24. O Jacob, Israel, Jerusalem, thine iniquities are so great, many, oft iterated, that I am weary of beholding, of hearing, of bearing them any longer: others have wearied me with their words, Mal. ii. 17, but you have wearied me with your lying words, and wicked deeds. When my fury hath been kindled in me, so that I have been ready to pour out judgments upon you, I have been stopped by the prayers of some precious ones, and repented me of what I intended against you, but I will do it no more, "I am weary with repenting," Jer. xv. 6: God repented, but they repented not, he would repent no more. And as sinners, by their sinful ways, do weary God, so they weary themselves; Jer. ix. 5, "They have taught their tongue to speak lies, and weary themselves to commit iniquity." Some tire themselves more in the service of sin and Satan, than others do in the service of God and Christ: Isa. v. 18, they draw iniquity, and they toil at it as horses in a cart.

Obs. 2. When the scum will not be got out by the word and lesser judgments, God will destroy both scum and pot together. "Her scum went not forth of her; God's threats by the prophets did no good, his lesser judgments procured it not, the "scum" still boiled in, the rust still cleaved to the pot: what then? "her scum," her rust, "shall be in the fire:" when neither wind nor water will do it, fire shall.

Ver. 13. "In thy filthiness is lewdness." Thou hast defiled thyself with all manner of sin, with idols, blood, profaneness, hypocrisy, covetousness, &c. and to these thou addest "lewdness," that is, obstinacy; thou art settled upon thy lees, and wilt not be reclaimed; no counsel, admonition, reproof, takes with thee, thou standest out against them all. The Vulgate reads it, thy filthiness is execrable. *Zirumah* notes, a resolved wickedness, which is execrable. Œcolampadius makes the "filthiness" to be, evil counsel: Jerusalem had hearkened to the false prophets, taken in their counsel against the true prophets, and was resolved to go on in her ways; Jer. xxiii. 14, "They strengthen the hands of evil-doers, that none doth return from his wickedness."

"Because I have purged thee." The Hebrew is,

tihartich, which Montanus in the margin gives the sense of, I have purged thee; that is, I have commanded that thou shouldest purge thyself. God sent prophets unto Jerusalem, 2 Chron. xxxvi. 15, to tell her of her sins and danger, and to invite and press her to repentance, as Jer. iii. 12—14; who fully declares throughout his prophecy, what sad judgments God would bring upon her, if she did not purge and cleanse herself. See chap. vi. 26; vii. 14; ix. 11; xiii. 17. God affording them means for purging, as prophets, reproofs, admonitions, counsels, exhortations, corrections, is said to have purged them; he did that which in his wisdom he thought meet to do. The purging here meant is from idolatry, injustice, profaneness, &c.

"And thou wast not purged." Hebrew, thou hast not purged thyself; thou didst not entertain and improve the means afforded. When the prophets came to thee, and told thee of thy sins and dangers, thou didst mock at them, 2 Chron. xxxvi. 16, and despise the word they brought. When I smote thee with my correcting hand, thou didst "revolt more and more," Isa. i. 5; and thy children "received no correction," Jer. ii. 30; that is, no benefit by those blows I gave them: thou saidst, "I have loved strangers, and after them will I go," ver. 25; and those in thee said, "We are lords; we will come no more unto the Lord," ver. 31; so Jer. xliv. 16, 17: they did not cease from their wicked ways.

"Thou shalt not be purged from thy filthiness any more." I will cease from using means to purge thee, my prophets shall labour no more in vain about thee; they have spent their lungs and strength to reclaim thee, but they shall not do it again, they shall neither reprove, threaten, counsel, or invite thee any more to turn, but thou shalt be left as desperate and incurable. Hebrew is, thou shalt not purge thyself from thy filthiness any more; if thou wouldest now go about it, it will be in vain, it is too late, I am resolved upon thy destruction.

"Till I have caused my fury to rest upon thee." Anger, indignation, wrath: fury is anger never at rest till vengeance is taken. There is now no purging, but destruction; I shall spend all my judgments upon thee, consume thee and thine, and so my fury shall rest upon thee. These words we had before, chap. v. 13; xxi. 17. "Till" doth not imply a purging afterwards, Psal. cx. 1; Rom. viii. 22; Matt. v. 26, "Till thou hast paid the uttermost," &c.

Obs. 1. Obstinacy in sin provokes God to the destruction of sinners. "Her scum shall be in the fire;" Jerusalem shall be burnt, and why? "In thy filthiness is lewdness;" thou art obstinate, hardened in thy wickedness. All sin offends, some sins provoke to judgments, obstinacy provokes to destruction. Jer. xliv. 15—17, in those verses you have the obstinacy of the Jews in Egypt, (they, and others of them, had been so obstinate in the land of Judea, that God could bear them no longer, but laid the land desolate, and made it a curse, ver. 22,) and see how the Lord threatens them; ver. 27, "I will watch over them for evil, and not for good; and all the men of Judah that are in the land of Egypt shall be consumed by the sword and by the famine, until there be an end of them:" and not only would he destroy them, but Egypt likewise, where they were, ver. 30; even that should fare the worse for their being in it. Obstinacy in sin is worse than the sin itself; many sins are committed against man's will and purpose, but obstinacy in sin hath the will fully in it, and therefore must needs exasperate the Lord. Neh. ix. 30, "Many years didst thou forbear them, and testifiedst against them by thy spirit in thy prophets: yet would they not give ear: therefore gavest thou them into the hand of the people of the lands: ' this stubbornness of theirs made the Lord cast them off, and put them into the hands of heathens. Zechariah tells you, that for this sin "came a great wrath from the Lord of hosts" upon them, chap. vii. 12; not only "wrath," which is destructive in itself, but "great wrath," and that not only from the Lord, but from the "Lord of hosts;" as if the Lord mustered up all his forces, to come against obstinate and rebellious sinners, and pour out great wrath and vengeance upon them. Certainly obstinate sinners are those the Lord will accomplish his wrath upon; 1 Thess. ii. 16, the wrath of God came upon the Jews to the uttermost, even to perfection.

Obs. 2. In Scripture language, that is said to be done, which God or men endeavour to do, though it be not done. "I have purged thee." God using means, and endeavouring, by his prophets, mercies, threats, and judgments, to purge Jerusalem from her sin, is called purging, though Jerusalem were not purged. Psal. lxix. 5, "They that destroy me are mighty:" David's enemies, who sought to destroy him, are said to do it. Rom. ii. 4, "The goodness of God leadeth thee to repentance;" that is, its agency and tendency is that way. Deut. xxvi. 5, "A Syrian ready to perish:" Jacob increased and prospered when he was with Laban, but because Laban did that which tended to his perishing, he changed his wages, he pursued him returning home, therefore he is said to be in a perishing condition. 1 Cor. x. 33, "I please all men in all things:" in the fourth chapter, he tells you he was reviled, persecuted, defamed, made as the filth of the world, and the offscouring of all things, how then did he please all men in all things?" he is said to do it, in that he endeavoured to do it, seeking their good, their salvation. Matt. v. 32, "Whosoever shall put away his wife, saving for the cause of fornication, causeth her to commit adultery;" that is, this action of putting her away exposes her to that sin, whether she fall into it or not. Because, therefore, the man's act in putting away his wife is likely to produce such an effect, he is said to do it, to cause her to commit adultery. Gal. v. 4, "Christ is become of no effect unto you, whosoever of you are justified by the law:" they sought to be justified by the law, and thereupon are said to be so; not that the law justified any, or any could be justified by it. This should teach us how to understand the like scriptures. Things may be said to be done, when only there hath been means used conducing thereunto.

Obs. 3. A people may have the means, and not improve the same for their good. Jerusalem had prophets, ordinances, sabbaths, sacrifices, mercies, judgments, by which God would have purged her, and she was not purged; she did not purge herself, she improved not the same for her good, she did not hearken to the prophets, humble herself for her sins, fear the Lord and his threatenings, observe his sabbaths, worship him only, and execute justice. God called upon her oft to purge herself: Jer. iv. 14, "O Jerusalem, wash thine heart from wickedness, that thou mayest be saved. How long shall thy vain thoughts lodge within thee?" I have given thee water to wash thine heart from all thy vain, base, destructive thoughts, why dost thou not use it? Chap. xiii. 27, "O Jerusalem! wilt thou not be made clean? when shall it once be?" my prophets would cleanse thee, if thou wouldest receive them, and my word by them; mine ordinances would sanctify thee, if thou didst use them according to mine institution of them; my mercies and judgments would cause thee to cleanse thyself, if thou didst well weigh them;

but thou hast means, and dost not improve them. It is not the having of means, but the right use of means, will do good. Jerusalem thought herself clean, not needing to be purged: chap. ii. 23, "How canst thou say, I am not polluted?" Jerusalem, that was more guilty than Sodom or Samaria, justified herself, and so neglected purging; yea, "rejected the word of the Lord," which should have purged her, chap. viii. 9; she gave ear to false prophets and priests, chap. xxiii. 14, who strengthened her in her wickedness, and defamed the true prophets, chap. xviii. 18; she profaned the means, Ezek. xxii. 26; she idolized the means, and rested in the act done, Jer. vii. 4, 9, 10; viii. 8; she went on still in her own ways, whatever God or man said unto her: chap. vii. 28, "This is a nation that obeyeth not the voice of the Lord their God, nor receiveth correction." God had spoken to Jerusalem and Judea oft, yea, corrected them oft, but neither word nor rod did better them.

Obs. 4. People may so slip the time of repenting, and turning to God, as that it may be too late for them to go about the same; they may sin away the time of mercy. Because Jerusalem, having means, took not the opportunity of purging herself, she should never be purged, her filthiness should abide with her. As Judea was the land not cleansed, Ezek. xxii. 24, so was Jerusalem the city not purged; she passed the time of her purging; she lost the season for mercy. The Scripture is clear for it: Psal. lxxxi. 11, 12, "My people would not hearken to my voice; and Israel would none of me. So I gave them up to their own hearts' lust: and they walked in their own counsels." God invited them by means and mercies, which they entertained not so as to profit by them, they stood it out with God, who cast them off, and now it was too late for them to come: "Oh that they had hearkened!" not, Oh that they would hearken! The foolish virgins staid so long before they got oil, that the door of the bridegroom was shut, and no entrance for them, Matt. xxv. they came too late. Matt. xxiii. 37, 38, "O Jerusalem, Jerusalem, how often would I have gathered thy children together, even as a hen gathereth her chickens under her wings, and ye would not!" I used all means, but Jerusalem took not her time to do herself good, therefore her house was left desolate; her temple, her city, should be emptied of all means and mercies, and her children be left in a desolate condition. God would have purged the old world, but it slipped the time of its purging: Gen. vi. 3, "My Spirit shall not always strive with man;" they have been warned, counselled, reproved, convinced by my Spirit, in the patriarchs, and in their bosoms that hath been labouring to bring them to repentance, but they grieve, resist, and vex my Spirit, therefore it shall cease to strive any more with them, to do them any good. Let us not presume upon hereafters, that we will purge, repent, and turn to God hereafter; thy hereafter may be too late: "Seek ye the Lord while he may be found, call ye upon him while he is near," Isa. lv. 6. There is a time when he will not be found, a distance at which he will not hear: Prov. i. 28, "Then shall they call upon me, but I will not answer; they shall seek me early, but they shall not find me." They slighted and improved not the means which God afforded them, thereupon judgments came on them, whereupon they betake themselves to a more serious use of the means; but it was too late, God had no ear to hear them, neither would make any appearance for them. Time present is the acceptable time, 2 Cor. vi. 2. "Let us cleanse ourselves from all filthiness of the flesh and spirit, perfecting holiness in the fear of God," 2 Cor. vii. 1.

Obs. 5. Those who have had means, and not profited thereby, God will deal most severely with, there is no mercy, but altogether judgment, for them. Jerusalem had means, but was not purged, and she should not be purged, but God's fury should rest upon her: "Thou shalt not be purged from thy filthiness any more, till I have caused my fury to rest upon thee;" that is, thou shalt never be purged in mercy, but destroyed in my fury; and so it was quickly after, by the Chaldean army. Capernaum was exalted to heaven in means, but what said Christ? she should "be brought down to hell," Matt. xi.; that is, suffer extreme punishment; and why? she improved not the means; "For if the mighty works which have been done in thee, had been done in Sodom, it would have remained unto this day:" had Sodom had the preaching and miracles thou hast had, it would have made such improvement of them, as to have kept off the fire and brimstone which fell upon it; therefore the punishment of the Sodomites should be less than of the Capernaites, at the day of judgment. God is severe against those who have the means to purge them, and do it not, that have the gospel, and improve it not. The fig-tree in the vineyard had stood there three years, and was not better at last than at first; the influences of heaven, and fatness of the earth, had done it no good; and behold the severity of the owner, "Cut it down; why cumbereth it the ground?" Luke xiii. 7. He saith not, Dig it up, set it elsewhere, but, Cut it down, it is a burden to me, to the earth, and reproach to all the trees in the garden. What made the Lord deal more severely with the Jews than other nations? It was because they had the means to do them that good which others had not: Amos iii. 2, "You only have I known of all the families of the earth;" I have so known you, as to own you for my people, as to give you my prophets, my law, mine ordinances, my covenants, &c.; "therefore I will punish you for all your iniquities," you shall be made as exemplary by my judgments as ever you were by my mercies.

Ver. 14. "I the Lord have spoken it." This verse seals up the certainty of all threatened, and cuts off all evasions which Jerusalem might make whatsoever: as,

1. She might say, Ezekiel hath hard thoughts of me, he speaks these things out of his own head and spirit, they are his devices, and I weigh them not. This is answered in these words, "I the Lord," I, Jehovah, who am of myself, and give being, life, to all my threats, "have spoken." What is said is no vain vision, lying prophecy, like to what the false prophets have given out; what Ezekiel hath said, he had from me, I commissioned him to speak, and it is not he, but I that have spoken it.

"It shall come to pass." 2. Be it so that thou hast spoken it, yet the time may be long ere these threats against me may take place: such thoughts were in the breast of Jerusalem, chap. xii. 27. This is answered here; It comes, באה *venit*, saith Montanus; it is not afar off, for many days, but it is at hand. Others have it, it is ready to come; Nebuchadnezzar is upon his march, hastening to thy gates, and will suddenly sit down before them.

"I will do it." 3. What if Nebuchadnezzar be coming, he and all with him are but men, they may fail of their purposes, sink in their undertakings, and never be able to perform what they enterprise. This shift is here taken off; "I will do it;" I am not man, but Jehovah, I fail not in my purposes, I sink not in my undertaking, I am able to perform whatever I enterprise; the whole work is mine; I have called forth Nebuchadnezzar and his army, I will bring them to thy gates, and enable them to do all my pleasure. I have done it, so is the original, it is as certain as if done.

"I will not go back." 4. Grant it, that the work is thine, and thou hast determined to see it done, yet upon second thoughts thou mayest change thy resolutions, when thou shalt consider that I, Jerusalem, am thy city, and the only city thou hast chosen in all the world; and wilt thou bring a heathenish king and an army to destroy me, and the temple where thou dwellest, and art worshipped? surely it cannot be, Lam. iv. 12. This conceit of hers is blown away by these words, "I will not go back:" thou art a bloody city, thy scum is not gone out of thee, thou art filthy, and in thy filthiness is lewdness, obstinacy, thou goest not back from thy wicked doings; "I will not go back" from doing what I have purposed. The Hebrew is, לא־אפרע I will not retract what I have said and purposed, I will not withdraw myself from it. Avenarius renders the words thus, I will not make holy-day, and cease to prosecute what I have determined.

"Neither will I spare." 5. Jerusalem might yet say, The Lord is merciful; though he be angry, and in his anger bring the enemy to my gates, he will not keep his anger always; when I shall fast, weep, pray, he will be entreated, he will pardon, spare, and not suffer me to be destroyed. This refuge is here made useless; "Neither will I spare," fasting, prayers, and tears, shall do her no good. Jer. xiv. 12, when Jerusalem's children should fast, God would not hear their cry, no, nor Jeremiah for them, chap. xi. 14; nor Ezekiel, chap. ix. 8—10. Though themselves, their prophets, should importune God, he saith, "As for me, mine eye shall not spare, neither will I have pity;" thou hast caused my fury to come up to take vengeance, and I will be avenged on thee; I will not abstain from revenge, so the word signifies.

"Neither will I repent." 6. Thou hast oft repented thee, when thou hast been upon destroying designs; see Jonah iii. 10; Hos. xi. 8; Ezek. xx. 8, 9, 13, 14, 17, 22; and I hope thou wilt repent thee of what thou art about: if thou dost not repent before my destruction, thou wilt repent after it, that thou hast dealt so by me. This strong hold is here battered down; "Neither will I repent;" what though I have oft repented me of the evil I purposed to bring upon thee and thy children, must I always be upon those terms with thee? No, no, Jerusalem, my repentings have not caused thee to repent, my repenting shall now cease: Jer. xv. 6, "I will stretch out my hand against thee, and destroy thee; I am weary with repenting:" I will neither repent when thou art destroying, nor when thou art destroyed; it will be an ease to me to see thee and thy children consumed.

Repentance sometimes in Scripture is attributed to God, and then it is spoken after the manner of men; and it must warily be understood, so as God may not be wronged in men's apprehensions thereby. In men's repentance there is grief, change, something falls out they did not foresee: David repents of murdering Uriah, defiling Bathsheba, because that fell out in it which he did not foresee, as the blaspheming God's name, and the sword it brought upon his house; hereupon he changed his mind, was affected with grief. These things are not in God; he foresees all events, he grieves not, he changes not; therefore in this sense he cannot be said to "repent." Theodoret speaks right, when he saith, Repentance in God is a change in his dispensations: if God had not destroyed Jerusalem, he should have been said to "repent." His repentance is alteration of things and actions, no change of his purpose and will. In human repentance there is the change of the will; in divine repentance there is the willing of a change, and that in the thing, not in the will or counsel of God, which are unchangeable. Here God would not change the thing, "I will not repent."

"According to thy ways, and according to thy doings, shall they judge thee." 7. Jerusalem might yet say, If it be so, that thou wilt not repent, and show mercy unto me, thou wilt show thyself a cruel and merciless God. This imputation is here prevented; "According to thy ways and doings" shalt thou be dealt with: if thy judgments be sharp and dreadful, thou hast deserved them; the equity of my proceedings shall be so conspicuous, that all the world shall clear me, and say, The fault is thine own, that thou sufferest such hard things; thou hast done such wickednesses, lewdnesses, abominations, that God is righteous in consuming of thee, all is suitable to thy "ways."

These words, "they shall judge thee," by the Septuagint are rendered in the first person singular, I will judge thee; and so by the Vulgate. By Junius, in the second person, thou shalt be judged. By others, as here, they shall judge thee, that is, the Babylonians. And these several readings or renderings of the word make up but one and the same sense, thou shalt be judged, that is, by the Lord, and the Babylonians, who are his instruments to execute his pleasure: Ezek. xxiii. 24, "I will set judgment before them, and they shall judge thee;" I will make known to them my purpose of utter destroying thee, and they shall do it.

Obs. 1. Great sinners do not believe judgments threatened, but are apt to shift them off, and flatter themselves with hopes of mercy. Jerusalem had great scum, God threatened to consume her and her scum in the fire, but she believed it not, she shifted off all threatenings, she still expected peace and safety. Jerusalem's prophets had so bewitched and possessed her with thoughts of peace and security from evil coming upon her, Jer. xxiii. 17, that nothing Jeremiah or Ezekiel threatened could be heard; therefore saith God here, "I the Lord have spoken it, it shall come to pass," &c. Thou thinkest I will not do it, that I will recall my threats, spare thee, and repent: such vain thoughts lodged in Jerusalem, Jer. iv. 14, and such vain speeches were uttered by Judah, "Thou sayest, Because I am innocent, surely his anger shall turn from me," Jer. ii. 35. Jerusalem and Judah thought, said, they were innocent, and thereupon shifted off all that was threatened, and flattered themselves with hopes of mercy; but they were guilty, yea, more guilty than all the nations and cities round about them, Ezek. v. 5, 6, and had such judgments coming upon them, as never had any the like, ver. 9, 10; which they would not believe, though the Lord himself told them thereof, for, Jer. v. 12, "They belied the Lord, and said, It is not he; neither shall evil come upon us; neither shall we see sword nor famine:" we shall do well enough in this city; and if they should come, we will appear before him with our sacrifices, and we shall be delivered, Jer. vii. 10. Wicked men do flatter themselves, in their own fancies, shifts, evasions they have, till their iniquity be discovered, and judgment surpriseth them, Psal. xxxvi. 2. That wretched art they have of putting off the evil day, of shifting the threats and judgments of God, undoes them: and many precious souls are too well skilled in this wretched art and work of putting off the promises and mercies of God from themselves, which greatly prejudice their peace and comforts, and gratify the enemy of their souls. Those make conscience of their ways, that desire to be purged and wait on God in the use of means; they lie not under these threats, but are under many gracious promises, especially that, Psal. cxlv. 19, "He will fulfil the desire of them that fear him."

Obs. 2. Those who profess themselves God's people, may be such sinners, as that God resolves their destruction, excluding all hope of mercy. Jerusalem, which was the Lord's city, and the people of it his, had so sinned, that God would irrevocably destroy both it and them. "I the Lord have spoken it; it shall come to pass, and I will do it; I will not go back, neither will I spare," &c. God was fully set upon it, and therefore peremptorily cuts off all hope of mercy. Jer. xvi. 5, "I have taken away my peace from this people, saith the Lord, even loving-kindness and mercies." I have gone up and down and gathered up my peace, my kindnesses and mercies, and carried them away from this people; what hope was then left for them? both the great and the small shall die in this land. God's heart was so against them, that Moses and Samuel could not incline it towards them, if they should entreat for them, chap. xv. 1; and therefore saith God, "Cast them out of my sight," I have no pity, no mercy for them. Ezek. ix. 10, "As for me, mine eye shall not spare, neither will I have pity." If God would not spare them, who would? if he would not have pity on them, who could? they were hopeless, their case was desperate. Chap. v. 8, 11, "Behold, I am against thee; I will not have any pity." Jer. xi. 11, "I will bring evil upon them, which they shall not be able to escape."

Obs. 3. When God cuts off hope of mercy, and brings sinners into a forlorn condition, the fault is in themselves, not in the Lord; it is their own doings, their own ways, which bring irrevocable judgments upon them. "According to thy ways, and according to thy doings, shall they judge thee." Thou hast been irrevocable in thy sins, and I am irrevocable in my judgments; thou hast gone on to commit great iniquities, and I am going on to execute answerable punishments; I could not prevail with thee to desist from sinning, and thou shalt not prevail with me to desist from destroying; thou by thy obstinacy madest me without hope of thy amendment, and now by my threatenings I have made thee hopeless of any mercy. Jerusalem might thank herself, that she was brought to so desperate a condition. Jer. xiii. 22, "If thou say in thine heart, Wherefore come these things upon me?" why must I be besieged? why must plague, famine, and sword devour my children? why must I be burnt to ashes, and have no mercy showed me? the answer is, "For the greatness of thine iniquity:" and what that iniquity is, you have specified, chap. xvi. 11, 12; they forsook God, worshipped other gods, walked after the imaginations of their own hearts, and did worse than their own fathers; they sinned till there was no remedy, 2 Chron. xxxvi. 16. Jerusalem with her children provoked God, so that his glory, his truth, his name, his prophets, must have suffered if they had been spared; therefore the lions roared upon Israel, yelled, and made his land waste: when his cities were burnt, and without inhabitant, what said God? "Hast thou not procured this unto thyself, in that thou hast forsaken God?" Jer. ii. 15, 17.

Ver. 15—18. *Also the word of the Lord came unto me, saying, Son of man, behold, I take away from thee the desire of thine eyes with a stroke: yet neither shalt thou mourn nor weep, neither shall thy tears run down. Forbear to cry, make no mourning for the dead, bind the tire of thine head upon thee, and put on thy shoes upon thy feet, and cover not thy lips, and eat not the bread of men. So I spake unto the people in the morning: and at even my wife died; and I did in the morning as I was commanded.*

The second general part of the chapter begins here, being a prophecy declaring the destruction of the temple and city, represented under the type of the sudden death of Ezekiel's wife. This type is in the words read; the interpretation is in the words following.

The parts of these verses are,

I. The divine authority for this type, and for what is commanded and done thereupon, ver. 15.

II. The narration of the type, ver. 16, "Son of man, behold, I take away from thee the desire," &c.

III. Several commands laid upon the prophet, ver. 16, 17.

IV. The execution of the type, ver. 18.

Ver. 15. "The word of the Lord came unto me." The false prophets ran when they were not sent, and spake when they had no word; but Ezekiel was sent, chap. ii. 3, and he had a word from God when he spake: he durst not be the mouth of God to others, until the Lord had opened his mouth to him; the Spirit of prophecy brought the word to him, and then moved him to utter it to others.

Ver. 16. "Son of man." He saith not, Man of God, or, Son of God, but, Son of Adam, (for so the original is,) that is, son of him who was made of the earth, that had an earthly beginning. Ezekiel, thou art a weak, worthless creature, that ere long must away to the earth from whence thou camest; see thy heart do not swell with the prophetical honour I have put upon thee, the many appearances of my Spirit unto thee, nor be thou refractory, that I put thee upon hard services, or command thee hard things: when thy father Adam disobeyed me, I turned him out of Paradise: obey therefore my voice, and do what I command thee, therein shalt thou show thyself a son of God.

"Behold, I take away from thee the desire of thine eyes." By "desire of thine eyes" is meant, Ezekiel's wife, ver. 18. The Septuagint is, *τὰ ἐπιθυμήματα ὀφθαλμῶν*, the desires of thine eyes. This expression, the desire of the eyes, imports a thing very dear to one; and what is dearer to men than their wives? There are many things to endear a woman to her husband.

1. She was made for man; 1 Cor. xi. 9, "The man was not created for the woman, but the woman for the man." She was made "an help meet" for man, Gen. ii. 18.

2. She is a gift of God, Prov. xix. 14.

3. She is joined to man, by a divine ordinance, and is made one with him thereby, Gen. ii. 24; Matt. xix. 5; 1 Cor. vi. 16; Eph. v. 31.

4. She is "the glory of man," 1 Cor. xi. 7. Man represents God, being his image and glory; and woman represents man, and so is his image and glory.

5. She is "a crown to her husband," a great ornament unto him, Prov. xii. 4.

6. She is the builder of the house; Ruth iv. 11, "Rachel and Leah did build the house of Israel."

7. She is a companion in all conditions, "the wife of thy youth," and the wife of thine age, Prov. v. 18.

8. She is a bosom friend, in whom the heart of her husband may safely trust, Prov. xxxi. 11.

9. She is an heir "of the grace of life," together with her husband, 1 Pet. iii. 7.

These things, besides beauty, amiableness, and sweetness of nature, do endear wives to husbands, and so cause them to eye and mind them the more; for things or persons which are dear to us, our thoughts, our eyes are upon: where love is, there will be the eye. Christ loved his church dearly, and therefore said, Cant. ii. 14, "Let me see thy countenance." The church was black, chap. i. 5, yet the delight of Christ's eyes, because she had inward glory, beauty, excellency; so, many wives, though they be not outwardly so amiable and beautiful as others, yet they may have inward virtues, excellences, and those graces which may make them the desires of husbands' eyes, if gracious themselves. And if such inward attractives be wanting, propriety may do it. Every one affects what is his own; a piece of land, a house, a ship, a child, that is one's own, is more delightful to the owner than what is another's.

Doubtless Ezekiel's wife was amiable, virtuous, gracious, endeared much unto him, upon several grounds, so that she was a delight unto, and the desire of his eyes, else the Lord would not have forbidden him to mourn and weep for her. His love was such to her, that it would have carried him out strongly thereunto, if the Lord had not prohibited it.

"With a stroke." The Hebrew is, במגפה which Montanus renders, *in percussione*, in striking, or, by a stroke; it is from נגף which signifies to beat, to smite, yea, to smite unto death. It hath some affinity with the word נגע which is, to touch or hurt more lightly; but this notes hurting more vehemently, and is applied in Scripture to God's striking with extraordinary judgments: as Exod. viii. 2, "I will smite all thy borders with frogs;" 1 Sam. iv. 2, "Israel was smitten before the Philistines;" 2 Chron. xiii. 15, "God smote Jeroboam and all Israel;" Exod. xii. 29, "At midnight the Lord smote all the firstborn in the land of Egypt." Hence the nouns נגף and מגפה signify, "a stroke," and the heavy strokes of God. Exod. ix. 14, "I will at this time send all my plagues upon thine heart, and upon thy servants, and upon thy people;" the word for "plagues" is the same with that here, the ten plagues of Egypt were ten strokes of God. Sometimes the word is put for that sad stroke of God, viz. the plague: Numb. xvi. 46, החל הנגף "the plague is begun." Some think the "stroke" here was the plague, but whether that, an apoplexy, imposthume, or palsy, is not set down; this only we have for certain, that it was sudden, whatever it was; she did not lie long with a pining disease, but was suddenly snatched away from Ezekiel.

"Yet neither shalt thou mourn." The Jews were wont to honour their dead with great mourning. When Aaron died, "they mourned for him thirty days," Numb. xx. 29; and so many days they mourned for Moses, Deut. xxxiv. 8. Joseph mourned forty days for the death of his father Jacob in Egypt, and seven days after that in the land of Canaan, Gen. l. 3, 10; and seven days' mourning for the dead was the ordinary practice, as Ecclesiasticus observes, chap. xxii. 12; but Ezekiel is here forbid to mourn at all in a public and solemn manner. The Hebrew word for mourning is, ספד which notes mourning by striking the head or breast, and refers most to funeral pomp.

"Nor weep, neither shall thy tears run down." The word for weeping in Hebrew is, בכה which signifies weeping with lifting up of the voice, as Judg. ii. 4; Job ii. 12, "They lifted up their voice, and wept;" and herein it differs from דמע which is to weep also, but silently, without noise. Weeping oft is a great ease to the heart, but Ezekiel must not testify any grief, by voice, tears, or any outward gesture.

Ver. 17. "Forbear to cry." The Hebrew is, Hold thy peace from crying. The Vulgate is, Sigh, holding thy peace, so sigh as none may hear thee. Others allow not so much as sighing, but read the words thus, Let there be no sign of any sigh.

"Make no mourning for the dead." The Jews were wont to bewail their dead: 2 Chron. xxxv. 24, 25, "All Judah and Jerusalem mourned for Josiah; Jeremiah lamented for him, and all the singing men and singing women." Abraham mourned for Sarah, Gen. xxiii. 2. They were wont to cry, "Ah my brother! or, Ah sister!" Jer. xxii. 18; to cut and make themselves bald in their lamentations for their dead, Jer. xvi. 6; which was forbid the priests, Lev. xxi. 5, though they might mourn for their near kindred, ver. 2, 3. But Ezekiel must "make no mourning," he must not put on sackcloth, shave his head, or the corners of his beard, nor cut his flesh at all; he is forbid all funeral pomp and expressions.

"Bind the tire of thine head upon thee." It was in practice among the Jews, sometimes to cover their heads in their mournings, as being unworthy to see the light or any creatures, and sometimes to uncover them, as not being worthy of any ornament. 2 Sam. xv. 32, David and those with him had their heads covered, and went weeping. Lev. x. 6, when Nadab and Abihu were destroyed by fire, and Aaron, with his remaining sons, had great cause to mourn, Moses commands them not to uncover their heads, or rend their clothes, clearly demonstrating that that was their custom in their mournings. They made bare their heads, and laid ashes or earth upon them, as you may see, 1 Sam. iv. 12; Lam. ii. 10. This Ezekiel might not do, he must not throw off his head tire; the word is, פאר *pear*, which signifies, glory, ornament; whatever the prophet did wear upon his head, he must keep it on, and not lay it aside.

"And put on thy shoes upon thy feet." In their mournings and funerals they went barefoot. 2 Sam. xv. 30, David was barefoot when he went up the ascent of mount Olivet. Antonius Margarita, who of a Jew became christian, and wrote of the rites of the Jews, saith, that the kindred at the death of a friend do tear their garments, eat nothing that day in that house, but abroad; that they eat no flesh, drink no wine, unless it be upon the sabbath; and that they follow the hearse with bare feet. To this agrees what Leo Modena hath lately commended to the world. The nearest kindred of the party deceased, when they are returned to their house, they sit down all together upon the ground without shoes upon their feet. This rite of going barefoot was a token of grief and shame, Isa. xx. 2, 4.

"And cover not thy lips." Another ceremony the Jews used in their mournings, was the covering of their chin, mouth, all under the nose, which is understood by the word "lip." Lev. xiii. 45, the leper was to "put a covering upon his upper lip," that so, his mouth being covered, his breath might not infect any. Or we may by "lip" understand the whole face; and so that in Micah iii. 7 may be taken, "They shall all cover their lips;" the Hebrew is, their upper lip; "for there is no answer of God:" the seers and diviners should be ashamed and confounded, having no vision, from being discovered by him to be false prophets, they should cover their faces; so the Vulgate reads it, they shall all cover their faces.

"And eat not the bread of men." Jerom and the Vulgate have it, the bread of mourners; the Hebrew word אנשים signifies men, not simply, but woful, sorrowful, miserable man. *Enosh*, as Pradus observes, is not a word signifying the nature of man, as *Adam;* nor a word to distinguish the sexes, as *Ish;* but it sets out the miserable condition of men, whose days are few, and full of sorrow. It was a custom among the Jews at the death and funeral of friends, to send in meats and drinks to those who were chief mourners, to comfort and refresh them. Jeremiah bears witness to this practice, chap. xvi. 7, 8, "Neither shall men give them the cup of consolation to drink for their father or their mother:" they feasted with them, as the next verse shows, and sought hereby to drive away their sorrows. Not only did the Jews make feasts at the funerals of their dead, but the gentiles also had it much in practice. They had their feasts, called *Parentalia*, and *Silicernia*. Sometimes their feasts were *ad mortuorum memoriam*, for memorials, and honour of the dead; sometimes, *ad hæredum gratiam*, in behalf of their heirs which succeeded them; and mostly, *ad amicorum solatium*, for the comfort of their friends. Prov. xxxi. 6, 7, they that had heavy hearts, were to have wine given them to drink, that being comforted therewith, they might remember their misery no more. Ezekiel must not mourn, neither drink of any thing that belonged to mourners, nor meddle with any of their rites.

Cibot ad te missot a vicinis in solatium. Vatabl. Vide Leo Modena, History of the present Jews, 5 Par. ch. 9.

Ver. 18. "So I spake unto the people in the morning." The next morning Ezekiel makes known unto the people what he had received from the Lord, viz. the parable of the boiling pot, the taking away of his wife by a sudden stroke, and how all mourning and funeral rites were prohibited unto him; which the Lord therefore did, that he might provoke the people to make diligent inquiry into the meaning of the thing, being unusual, yea, contrary to custom.

"And at even my wife died." The Hebrew word for "wife" is, אשה signifying both woman and wife, from *ish*, both man and husband; the woman was of man, and being a wife is for man, for man's help and good, some therefore derive *uxor* from the Hebrew, עזר *auxilium*, help. Others from *αὔξω*, *augeo*, because she increases the family. Here was accomplished what the Lord said, ver. 16.

"I did in the morning as I was commanded." I did forbear all signs of open mourning; I did not weep, sigh, or cry out, I kept my tire upon my head, I walked out with shoes on my feet, with my lip uncovered; I ate not with those that brought the bread of mourners, I drank not with them that brought the cup of consolation.

Obs. 1. Marriage, even in prophets, and men in spiritual functions, is lawful. Ezekiel, a prophet and priest, was in that condition. Jehoiada the high priest was married, and had no meaner person to his wife than a king's daughter, 2 Chron. xxii. 11. Moses was a great prophet, and he had to wife Zipporah, daughter to the prince of Midian, Exod. ii. 16, 21. Isaiah, that evangelical prophet, had his prophetess, which conceived and bare him a son, Isa. viii. 3. Samuel the seer, and man of God, had sons who were judges over Israel, 1 Sam. viii. 1—3. Few of the prophets lived single lives. 2 Kings iv. 1, "There cried a certain woman of the wives of the sons of the prophets," that is, one of the prophets' wives cried "unto Elisha;" which shows that their calling did not exclude them from marriage. God took special care about the priests' marriage, ordering whom they might marry, and whom not, Lev. xxi. 13, 14; Ezek. xliv. 22. Neither was it lawful only for prophets and priests to marry, but for apostles and ministers of the gospel also. Peter himself had a yoke-fellow, Matt. viii. 14. Paul tells you, 1 Cor. ix. 5, that he had "power to lead about a sister, a wife, as well as other apostles, and as the brethren of the Lord, and Cephas;" which evidences, that most of the apostles had their wives, and that Paul had not done ill if he had had is. It is a doctrine therefore of devils, to forbid marriage to any sort of men, 1 Tim. iv. 1, 3, when "marriage is honourable in all" men, Heb. xiii. 4.

Obs. 2. Conjugal affection between man and wife is warrantable and pleasing unto God. Ezekiel's wife was the desire of his eyes, dear and delightful to him, he took pleasure and content in her, as husbands ought to do in their wives. Col. iii. 19, "Husbands, love your wives, and be not bitter against them." God would have no waters of Marah, no bitter passages, to come from husbands against their wives, but altogether and always streams of love; their love to and delight in their wives, should be not only at first, while youth, beauty, and means do last, but all the time they are their wives; no bitter looks, no bitter words, no bitter actions, but their looks, words, carriages, should be full of love and sweetness. God hath therefore not only prohibited bitterness, and commanded love, but given direction for the manner how they should love their wives; Eph. v. 25, "Husbands, love your wives, even as Christ also loved the church, and gave himself for it." Christ loved the church, notwithstanding all its spots, wrinkles, blemishes, sincerely, spiritually, and strongly; and so should men their wives, notwithstanding all infirmities or deformities, they should love them sincerely, spiritually, strongly; yea, ver. 28, "So ought men to love their wives as their own bodies;" men are great self-lovers, and they should be as great wife-lovers; he that loves not, that takes not complacency in his wife, doth not love nor take delight in himself. God would have men so love their wives, as to honour them whatever objection lies in the way; 1 Pet. iii. 7, though the wife be the weaker vessel, yet she must be honoured, her weakness must not hinder her honouring: a Venice glass is a vessel of more honour in the house than a brass pot. The husband is to honour his wife by making known bosom secrets to her, by taking her counsel and advice, by speaking well of her as his glory and crown, by trusting her, by esteeming of her above others, and by taking her part against all others. If God did not approve of love in husbands producing such effects, he would not have said, "Let her breasts satisfy thee at all times; and be thou ravished always with her love," Prov. v. 19. God would have men abound in their love to their wives; and because they fall short therein, he bids them err in their love, for so is the Hebrew, תשגה תמיד *errabis jugiter*, thou shalt love thy wife rather too much than too little. And, did husbands consider, besides God's command, and Christ's example, how it would further their prayers, prevent temptations, and honour a married condition, they would love their wives more conscientiously, sincerely, spiritually, and strongly.

Obs. 3. Our nearest and dearest comforts are in the hand of the Lord, to dispose of as he please. "Behold, I take away from thee the desire of thine eyes:" I have let thee enjoy her thus long, I have continued her with thee many days and years, but now I take her away, she shall abide with thee no longer. A prudent wife is from the Lord, given by him, he brought the woman unto Adam, Gen. ii. 22; and as he gives, he takes at his pleasure. He took away Sarah from Abraham, Gen. xxiii.; Elijah from Elisha, 2 Kings ii. 3; and Rachel from Jacob, Gen. xxxv. Wives, husbands, children, friends, are only lent us of the Lord for a season, and when that season is expired, he takes them to himself; we should therefore in all such cases look unto the hand of God.

Obs. 4. That God can, and sometimes doth, suddenly deprive us of our choicest comforts. "I take away the desire of thine eyes with a stroke." There was no antecedent sickness, no visible symptoms of death, but in a moment was Ezekiel's wife snatched away. How suddenly was the fire kindled that consumed Nadab and Abihu! Lev. x. 2, "There went out fire from the Lord and devoured them" presently. Was not Sodom overthrown in a moment? Lam. iv. 6. Did not the Lord strike fourteen thousand and seven hundred with the plague in a moment? Numb. xvi. 45, 49. Were not all the first-born of the Egyptians smitten and destroyed in an hour at midnight? Exod. xii. 29. Was not Sisera in a minute deprived of his breath, and head? Judg. v. 26. God hath a scourge, yea, many scourges, to slay suddenly, Job ix. 23; he hath arrows to shoot, which wound suddenly, Psal. lxiv. 8; there is no foresight, no preventing of them, nor cure of their wound. How unexpectedly was Rachel made childless, Matt. ii. 16, 18, when Herod slew the children! God hath various strokes, and sudden ones, to take away us, and our comforts; by gunpowder, by fire, &c. Man's calamity comes suddenly, and he is broken suddenly, without remedy, Prov. vi. 15. The consideration hereof should cause us,

(1.) To fear the Lord, that can strike such strokes as to deprive us of our chief comforts in a moment: we should sanctify him in our hearts, and make him our fear, that so he may be a sanctuary unto us, to defend us, and not a hammer or sword to strike or destroy us.

(2.) Not to promise long continuance of any creature comforts unto ourselves; use them for the present, but expect not much, nor long continuance of them. 1 Cor. vii. 29, "The time is short; let them that have wives be as if they had none." Isa. ii. 22, "Cease ye from man, whose breath is in his nostrils."

(3.) To prepare for death. Men put off the evil day, and are snared in an evil time, when the stroke falls suddenly upon them, Eccles. ix. 12. "They spend their days in wealth, and in a moment go down to the grave," Job xxi. 13, which is a sad thing; but if men spent their days in getting grace, labouring to win Christ and be found in him, their end would be happy, though their death be sudden, for "blessed are those that die in the Lord," Rev. xiv. 13. Live every day therefore as your last day.

Obs. 5. Bitter and great afflictions are not always arguments of God's hatred and indignation. Ezekiel was a prophet, a choice servant of the Lord's, yet from him doth God take away the desire of his eyes; which was a very bitter and grievous affliction, if we consider the aggravations which were in it.

(1.) He was now in captivity among Babylonians, where his wife was a sweet companion and comfort unto him, in the midst of all the troubles, reproaches, and difficulties he met with.

(2.) She was taken away, not in the common way of men and women, but by a sudden stroke: such strokes go to the quick, wound deep, and might have sunk our prophet had not the Lord given him a little notice of it.

(3.) That it should be to type out the destruction of the temple and city of Jerusalem: that God should suddenly strike, and take away his wife thereby, to represent the sudden ruin of them, could not but be grievous to him.

(4.) He is forbidden to mourn, weep, or perform any funeral rites for her. Might he have sighed, mourned, wept, that would have eased his heart; might he have used the Jewish rites and customs at her death and burial, that would have testified respect and love unto her; but he might not do either of them.

So then, by these aggravations, you see he had no light affliction upon him, and whatever they were, in them was nothing of divine hatred and indignation. Aaron was "the saint of the Lord," Psal. cvi. 16, and him the Lord gave a bitter cup to drink off; he slew two of his sons at once, both the eldest, Exod. vi. 23, and for offering a little kitchen or strange fire, which was not prohibited, though not commanded, being the first time, and then forbade him and his other sons to mourn for them, Lev. x. 1, 2, 6. Christ was more than a prophet, than a saint, he was a Son, the only begotten, the well-beloved; yet he had a cup given him to drink, which had more gall and wormwood in it than any, yea, than all the cups the prophets and saints had before or since. Afflictions argue not God's hatred; if we say so, we shall condemn the generation of the righteous, and falsify the truth, for it is said, "As many as I love, I rebuke and chasten," Rev. iii. 19. Those therefore that have bitter and heavy afflictions, should take heed how they yield unto the persuasions of Satan and corruption, saying, Surely if God loved you he would never deal so by you.

Obs. 6. That mourning for the dead is not unlawful. Ezekiel would have mourned, wept, and used all funeral rites amongst the Jews, not superstitious, if he had not been forbidden by the Lord. He was not stoical, without affection; neither are the people of God now unnatural, they do and may mourn for their dead, so it be neither excessively nor despairingly. David's mourning for Absalom, and Rachel's for her children, were too excessive, and the Thessalonians' too hopeless; 1 Thess. iv. 13, Paul allowed them to sorrow and mourn for their dead, but not as others which had no hope. Christianity doth not abolish, but moderate and direct affections. Christ himself wept for Lazarus when he was dead; his weeping was with moderation and hope. Many forget themselves in this kind, and give so much scope to their passions, that they offend God, shame their professions, and hazard their own health. But we should remember what Solomon commends unto us, Prov. xvi. 32, "Better is he that ruleth his spirit than he that taketh a city:" the bridling our spirits, and keeping our affections, hath a great excellency in it.

Obs. 7. A gracious spirit will deny itself, and obey God in difficult cases, and that speedily too. No sooner had God made good his word, in taking away Ezekiel's wife, but he did what the Lord commanded. Nature prompted him to mourn, to weep for his wife, but he denies the dictates of nature, and is content to seem unnatural for God. His credit and love to his wife called upon him to show respect unto her dead corpse, as others did in that kind, by funeral rites; but he prefers God's command before his credit, love, and respect to his wife, and is willing to bear the censures and reproachings of the people in this case; his wife dies in the night, and next morning he appears in his wonted habit and tire, he sheds no tears, puts off no shoes, covers not his lip, eats not the bread of men or mourners, shows no sign of sorrow, but was in as sweet and settled a posture as if there had been no stroke in his family; he was the same his wife being dead, as he was she being living; her death that was so dear to him, that was so strange and sudden, that was in such a place, made no alteration in him, and upon this ground only, because God had commanded it should be so. Here is a rare example of obedience, and that in a difficult case. Obedience to God is always commendable, but especially when hard things are commanded. The many difficulties Abraham brake through, to sacrifice his son, made his obedience so acceptable, Gen. xxii. Moses' refusing the honours, dignities, treasures, and temptations of Egypt, and Pharaoh's court, his choosing an afflicted condition, and reproached godliness, endeared him and his obedience unto the Lord, Heb. xi. When servants suffer for well-doing, and go on cheerfully in their work, honouring the gospel, this is acceptable with God, 1 Pet. ii. 19.

Ver. 19—24. *And the people said unto me, Wilt thou not tell us what these things are to us, that thou doest so? Then I answered them, The word of the Lord came unto me, saying, Speak unto the house of Israel, Thus saith the Lord God; Behold, I will profane my sanctuary, the excellency of your strength, the desire of your eyes, and that which your soul pitieth; and your sons and your daughters whom ye have left shall fall by the sword. And ye shall do as I have done: ye shall not cover your lips, nor eat the bread of men. And your tires shall be upon your heads, and your shoes upon your feet: ye shall not mourn nor weep; but ye shall pine away for your iniquities, and mourn one toward another. Thus Ezekiel is unto you a sign: according to all that he hath done shall ye do: and when this cometh, ye shall know that I am the Lord God.*

Having in the former verses spoken typically and darkly, here he comes to open and interpret what he had said; and we have before us,

I. The occasion of his intrepreting these hieroglyphical passages, ver. 19.

II. The interpretation itself, in ver. 21—24.

Ver. 19. "Wilt thou not tell us what these things are?" The people seeing Ezekiel's wife suddenly struck dead, and he not affected with it, which was not only contrary to the Jewish custom, but even to nature itself, they are startled at these things, and set upon the prophet in a heat, and will know what was in these strange things: We know there is some mystery in them, they have relation unto us, and we are unquiet, restless in our spirits, till we know what it is; wilt thou not tell us? Ezekiel, hide it not from us, whatever it be, we must know it. This was the thing God aimed at, in putting Ezekiel upon things unusual and unnatural, to provoke them thereby to consider and make a special inquiry into them. Unwonted things do awaken, breed admiration, and cause examination, men search into the meaning of such things. When Ezekiel sighed to the breaking of his loins, chap. xxi. 7, they said, "Wherefore sighest thou?" When Ezekiel was put upon removing, digging a hole through the wall, and carried his stuff upon his shoulder, as stuff for captivity, God said to him, "Son of man, hath not the house of Israel said to thee, What doest thou?" chap. xii. 9. God expected such strange doings should affect them, and make them consider, ver. 3, and inquire into the matter. Ordinary things are slighted, when extraordinaries have answerable operations.

Ver. 21. "Behold, I will profane my sanctuary." By Ezekiel's wife was typed out the temple, and what was desirable; and by her sudden death, the destruction of the same. The temple was as dear to the Jews as Ezekiel's wife was unto him. God would bring the Chaldeans into it, and they should profane it with the blood of those they found in it, (for many fled thither for refuge,) and then set it on fire. The Jews had profaned it with idols and idolatrous worship, Ezek. viii.; by coming into it with the guilt of notorious sins upon them, Jer. vii. 9, 10; and now heathens should enter into it, defile and destroy it; the thought whereof made the Psalmist long before to complain, saying, "O God, the heathen are come into thine inheritance; thy holy temple have they defiled; they have laid Jerusalem on heaps," Psal. lxxix. 1. The defiling the temple was grievous to prescience, to remote apprehensions; what was it then to those who had the present sight of it! The Septuagint reads the words in Ezekiel thus, I will pollute my holy things, that is, I will cause the heathens to come and profane the temple, the altar, and all the holy things belonging thereunto; yea, so to profane them, as to lay them all waste.

"The excellency of your strength." The Hebrew is, the pride of your strength. גאון signifies majesty, excellency, pride; from גאה to be lifted up, to excel, to grow proud. The translation Vatablus follows hath it, the glory of your strength. The temple was a strong place, in which the Jews put so much confidence, as that they thought it standing they should for ever be safe; they prided themselves in it, and cried, "The temple of the Lord, The temple of the Lord, The temple of the Lord," Jer. vii. 4. They thought none able to harm them, and destroy that temple.

If we read the words, "the excellency of your strength," as Junius, or, your strong excellency, as Piscator, the sense is, that though they had other strong holds and towers, yet none like unto the temple; that excelled all, not only in strength, but in renown. It was for the structure the wonder of the world, fifteen hundred thousand having been employed seven years in the building thereof, 1 Kings v. 15; it bare the name of the Lord, 1 Kings viii. 29; in it God dwelt, Psal. lxxx. 1; of it he had a special care, 1 Kings ix. 3, and it was "the excellency of Jacob," Amos vi. 8.

"The desire of your eyes." Some understand by these words, their wives, but most interpreters expound them of the temple, which seems to me to be the truest interpretation: for Ezekiel's wife typed out the temple; and as she was the desire of his eyes, so was the temple of the Jews' eyes; and the words of this verse do give countenance and life to this sense. "I will profane my sanctuary, the excellency of your strength, the desire of your eyes." What was the excellency of their strength? it was the desire of their eyes, viz. the sanctuary. By "desire of the eyes" is meant, that which is affected and delighted in, and such was the temple or sanctuary: Psal. xcvi. 6, "Strength and beauty are in his sanctuary;" there was material and spiritual beauty; Psal. xxvii. 4, there David desired to dwell all the days of his life, "to behold the beauty of the Lord." The temple was the desire of his eyes; when he was shut out of it, see how he thirsted after it, Psal. lxiii. 1, 2: so of Jonah when he was in the fish's belly, he looked towards the "holy temple," Jonah ii. 4. It was beautiful in itself, and had the beauty of holiness in it, the beautiful ordinances and worship of God; so that hence Zion was called "the perfection of beauty," Psal. l. 2, and "the joy of the whole earth," Psal. xlviii. 2. In Lam. i. 7, it is said, "Jerusalem remembered in the days of her affliction and of her miseries all her pleasant things," the Hebrew is, all her desirable things, that "she had in the days of old;" and the temple was one of them, yea, the most desirable of all her desirables.

"And that which your soul pitieth." *Machmall naphshechem*, that which your souls indulge and favour, viz. the temple, which they dearly affected, and would not by any means that it should be destroyed, or profaned by heathens. The Vulgate hath it, that for which your souls are afraid; men are jealous of that which is dear unto them, lest it should be violated. Isaiah foreseeing by a prophetical eye what would befall the temple, shows how his soul pitied it; Isa. lxiv. 11, "Our holy and our beautiful house, where our fathers praised thee, is burned up with fire; and all our pleasant things are laid waste." The profaning of the temple, which was holy, full of glory and beauty, the place of prayer and praise, went nearer the heart of this great prophet than any thing else. So Jeremiah, Lam. ii. 7, declares what pity he had for the house of the Lord: "The Lord hath cast off his altar, he hath abhorred his sanctuary, he hath given up into the hand of the enemy the walls of her palaces; they have made a noise in the house of the Lord, as in the day of a solemn feast." The temple lay heavy upon Daniel's heart, chap. ix. 17. These words by some are referred to their children, whom their souls pitied, and would have spared, but of them are the words following:

"And your sons and your daughters whom ye have left shall fall by the sword." When the Babylonians should come, profane and destroy the temple, many of their children should suffer and perish, some by famine, some by plague, some by other calamities and casualties; and those that were remaining, he tells them they should fall by the sword. The Lord would take from them, not only the temple, but all things that were dear unto them, their city, their kingdom, their wives, their children.

Ver. 22. "And ye shall do as I have done: ye shall not cover your lips, nor eat the bread of men." You wonder at me that I mourn not for my wife, being taken from me by a sudden stroke, but ere long you will cease to wonder at me, and find the case to be yours: when the enemies shall come, take away the temple, your wives and children, what things soever are dearest to you, then you will be so confounded and amazed, that you will have neither hearts nor opportunity to change your garments, and accompany your dead to the grave, but rather throw them out into the streets, and shift for your lives. Then you will remember me, make no lamentation for your dead; then you will not pull off your tires from your heads, nor the shoes from your feet, nor cover your lips, nor eat the bread of mourners; then you will use no funeral rites or gestures.

Ver. 23. "But ye shall pine away for your iniquities." The word for "pine away," is from מקק to dissolve and melt away, to consume, corrupt, to be filthy, loathsome; because those things which do corrupt, at last become stinking and unsavoury. So these Jews, their spirits, flesh, fat, and strength, should consume, "pine away," till they became even loathsome, and that "for their iniquities," that is, the punishment of their iniquities, for so the word is frequently used, as Isa. liii. 6; and 2 Kings vii. 9, "Some mischief will come upon us," the Hebrew is, iniquity, that is, mischief or punishment.

"And mourn one toward another." In this verse he had said, "ye shall not mourn nor weep," and here, as with the same breath, he affirms, they should "mourn one toward another." Though the words run so, there is no contradiction in them. Though they could not mourn openly, and in a funeral way, yet they should mourn inwardly, and so as to "pine away" themselves. You here in Babylon, when the report comes of taking the city, of burning the temple, and of the spoiling of all the desirable things in them by Nebuchadnezzar's forces, you will be in such a strait, as that you will not dare to mourn for fear of the Babylonians, who will endanger your liberties and lives, if you lament the successes and doings of their king. So that what with God's judgments upon them at Jerusalem, and the fear of the enemies both there and in Babylon, neither Jews in Jerusalem nor in Babylon should dare to mourn, or express any tokens of sorrow, how full soever their hearts were thereof. But when they were in secret, a man with his brother, (for so is the Hebrew,) then they should open their minds "one toward another, and mourn."

Ver. 24. "Thus Ezekiel is unto you a sign." The Hebrew is, למופת *in portentum*, for some prodigious thing. *Mopheth*, it notes a visible sign presaging good or evil, and so accordingly is pleasing to the sight, or horrible; it is that which is unusual, foreshowing somewhat to come. Ezekiel not mourning for the death of his wife, was a sign to them that they should be in such perplexity as not to mourn for their temple, city, and desirable things, which should be pulled from them by a sudden stroke of God. The Hebrew have אות and מופת which coming together are rendered, a sign and a wonder, as Isa. xx. 3; that is *oth*, or "a sign," which is not against nature, as to cure the sick; that is *mopheth*, or a prodigy, which is against nature, as to raise the dead, and do strange things.

"According to all that he hath done shall ye do." You have beheld Ezekiel's doings, and wondered at them; he hath but preached what ye are to do, and the time is at hand wherein he shall see you acting over the same things.

Obs. 1. The resting in holy things, causes God to remove them, how dear soever they be unto us. "I will profane my sanctuary, the excellency of your strength, the desire of your eyes, and that which your soul pitieth:" you confide in the outward means, you are taken with the outward splendour of the ceremonies and pomp of the temple, but the spiritual true worship ye mind not; the temple, city, and state, are dearer unto you than I am, they have your eyes, your hearts, your souls, when I am neglected. I have honoured you with my sanctuary, and all the holy things in it, belonging to it, but you have not honoured me: why is the temple, and not myself, "the excellency of your strength?" why is that "the desire of your eyes," and not myself, who fill the temple with my glory? why is that the pity of your souls? being troubled that it should be laid in the dust, and not my honour, my glory, my name, which are profaned amongst you, and laid in the dust.

Obs. 2. That sometimes men's sins bring them into such straits, that though they have lost their dearest comforts, yet they dare not outwardly manifest any sorrow for them. God would take away the temple, the excellency of their strength, the desire of their eyes, the pity of their souls, their sons and daughters, and they should not dare to "mourn nor weep" openly, but should secretly "pine away," and come to nothing. It was sad to lose their dearest comforts, and more sad that they might not ease their hearts by tears or sighings, and most sad that they must show no respect to their dead friends by any funeral rites. This sad condition had Jeremiah told them of, chap. xvi. 6, 7, "Both the great and the small shall die in the land: they shall not be buried, neither shall men lament for them, nor cut themselves, nor make themselves bald for them: neither shall men tear themselves for them in mourning, to comfort them for the dead; neither shall men give them the cup of consolation to drink for their father or for their mother:" they should be in such straits, through the fury and violence of their enemies, (whom their sins had brought upon them,) that they should not dare to mourn for their dead, and the great evils upon them.

Obs. 3. God may and doth put his own faithful servants upon hard and unwonted things, thereby to declare what shall be the condition of the wicked. "Thus Ezekiel is unto you a sign:" he hath had his dearest comfort taken away by an extraordinary stroke, he hath not been suffered to mourn or weep therefore; and why so? that he may be a sign unto you: you would not be taught by my doctrine, now you must be taught by my example; "according to all that he hath done shall ye do." The things are harsh and unnatural that I have done, but it is for your sakes that I am put upon them; and ye shall do as I have done. Thus Isaiah was put upon it to walk naked and barefoot three years, which was hard and reproachful; and why? that he might be "for a sign and wonder upon Egypt and Ethiopia," Isa. xx. 3. Some may think God deals ill with his servants, in putting them upon harsh, reproachful, unnatural, ridiculous things; but know, all souls are the Lord's, and he may command them what he please: they have comfort in their obedience, whatever men think or say of them; whenas those they are made signs unto have nothing but bitterness and terrors.

Obs. 4. Signs accomplished, convince men of the truth and just proceedings of God. "When this cometh, ye shall know that I am the Lord God;" by the fulfilling what this sign foretold, ye shall be so convinced as to acknowledge Ezekiel was a true sign, made so by me, and that I have dealt justly with you for your iniquities, in bringing you into such straits, as not to dare to mourn openly for your miseries. If Ezekiel have nothing to object against me, from whom, being innocent, I took away the desire of his eyes, and forbade him to mourn for her; what can you object against me, being so guilty as none more, if I rend away your desirable things, and hem you about so with my judgments and enemies, that you shall not dare to mourn?

Ver. 25—27. *Also, thou son of man, shall it not be in the day when I take from them their strength, the joy of their glory, the desire of their eyes, and that whereupon they set their minds, their sons and their daughters, that he that escapeth in that day shall come unto thee, to cause thee to hear it with thine ears? In that day shall thy mouth be opened to him which is escaped, and thou shalt speak, and be no more dumb: and thou shalt be a sign unto them; and they shall know that I am the Lord.*

In these words you may perceive,

I. A repetition of the taking away what was dearest to the Jews, ver. 25.

II. The events thereupon: which are,

1. Tidings thereof brought to the prophet, ver. 26.
2. Freedom of prophesying in Ezekiel, ver. 27.
3. Conviction of the people, ver. 27.

Ver. 25. "When I take from them their strength." What in ver. 21 he called "the excellency of their strength," here he calls "their strength," that was, the temple: it was strong, but should not have been their strength; the God of the temple should have been their hope and confidence.

"The joy of their glory." The word for "joy" is, משוש which is, to have inward delight in the mind, and that without external gesture. The Septuagint is, the lifting up of your glory. The temple was "their glory," and that cheered and lifted up their hearts. Both Junius and Piscator have it, the joy of their ornament. The temple was their ornament, Ezek. vii. 20; nothing did so become and adorn them, as their temple did, and that worship which God appointed to be in it; but they corrupted that worship, stained their glory, and joyed sinfully therein.

"The desire of their eyes." They took pleasure in beholding the temple, which was a stately building, beautified with precious stones, and gold of Parvaim, 2 Chron. iii. 6, 8. The second temple took them much, Matt. xxiv. 1; Luke xxi. 5; yet that was inferior to the first temple. The material temples were very dear unto the Jews.

"And that whereupon they set their minds." In the Hebrew it is, the lifting up of their souls, or minds; that unto which they lift up their soul, so Junius; the Vulgate, that on which their souls do rest: Steph. in Phrasibus Hebraicis, renders the place thus, That their hearts are lifted up unto, or, that which is the burden of their souls, and pressed them most, as the temple, and their children; they were perplexed about the loss of these.

This phrase of setting the mind upon a thing imports,

1. Overprizing of the thing; when the mind is set upon a thing that is valued: every man values what his lust is set upon.

2. Adhering to it. When the mind is set upon a thing, it cleaves to it, and fixes upon it: 1 Sam. ix. 20, "Set not thy mind on them."

3. Taking content and delight in a thing, seeking no further; Col. iii. 2, "Set your affections upon things above."

Ver. 26. "He that escapeth in that day, shall come unto thee to cause," &c. The Lord, in his wise providence, ordered it so, that some three years after this prophecy, there came one who escaped at the delivery up of Jerusalem unto Nebuchadnezzar, and brought tidings that the city was smitten, chap. xxxiii. 21, which was half a year after the smiting of it, if you compare this place in Ezekiel with Jer. lii. 6, and 2 Kings xxv. 3.

"To cause thee to hear it with thine ears." The Hebrew is, to the hearing of the ears; not to tell what he hath heard, as some rabbins would have it, but to tell in the ears of Ezekiel what he had seen, and been an eye-witness thereof. It is not improbable but that they had heard some rumour of it before, it being half a year since the taking of that city, and desolation of all things. This man therefore came to inform Ezekiel of the certainty of all things which had passed.

Ver. 27. "In that day shall thy mouth be opened to him that is escaped, and thou shalt be no more dumb." That Ezekiel was "dumb," and prophesied not at all till the man brought tidings of Jerusalem's destruction, is not the sense of this place; for in the 26th chapter he saith, the word of the Lord came unto him in the eleventh year, in the first day of the month. The meaning then is this; That as to the Jews, he ceased prophesying, and was as a "dumb" man unto them; God gave him not the gift, nor called him to speak any more unto them: they believed not what he had prophesied unto them, but gave ear to false prophets, who seduced them, telling them that they should shortly return, and Jerusalem should not be destroyed; but when the news came to our prophet, that God had fulfilled what he had prophesied against the city and temple, then God put his word into his mouth again, and he spake freely and boldly.

"And thou shalt be a sign unto them." As thou hast oft been "a sign" unto them, sometimes representing an army laying siege against a city, chap. iv.; sometimes a barber shaving the hair, chap. v.; sometimes a man removing his stuff, chap. xii.; sometimes representing a mourner, chap. xxi. 6; sometimes a condition wherein there must not be mourning, as, ver. 16—18 of this chapter; so here he must be a "sign unto them" by his silence. All the time from this chapter to the day that tidings came of the taking and smiting of Jerusalem, he was for "a sign unto them."

"They shall know that I am the Lord." Those that are here in Babylon, those that escape the famine, pestilence, sword, "shall know that I am the Lord," and sent thee to prophesy; "that I am the Lord," and have made good what thou didst prophesy; "that I am the Lord," and have punished them justly for their iniquities.

Obs. 1. That our natures are prone to overprize, adhere to, and rest in external privileges and mercies. The temple they doted upon, they made it their strength, their glory, the joy of their glory, the desire of their eyes; they set their minds upon that, and their sons and daughters; these had their thoughts, affections, and hearts, they ran out strongly unto them, their souls were lift up unto them: they looked at their temple as their strength against all enemies, as their joy at home, and their glory abroad: so for their children, they made idols of them, setting them up in their hearts, and their hearts upon them; Hosea ix. 11, their children were "their glory," they gloried in them, their hearts were set upon them. Because children are parts of their parents, coming out of their loins, because they bear their image, are their hopes, perpetuate their lives, names, and memories, therefore they let out their hearts too far towards them, and set their minds upon them; and not only on these, but on other things also, as riches; Psal. lxii. 10, "If riches increase, set not your heart upon them;" as they increase, usually men's affections and desires increase towards them, so that they come to trust in them: Psal. lii. 7, he "trusted in the abundance of his riches;" they were his security against all dangers, all enemies. There is scarce any thing we have of any moment, but we are apt to set our minds and hearts thereon; hence we are commanded to keep our hearts "with all diligence," Prov. iv. 23; the Hebrew is, above all keeping, keep that. The less we set our minds upon the creatures, the longer we are like to enjoy them; the more we set our minds upon them, the sooner they may be pulled away. God will not endure any thing to deprive him of his interest in the heart.

Obs. 2. God hath his times to take away mercies, privileges, idolized and confided in. "In the day when I take from them their strength, the joy of their glory, the desire of their eyes, and that whereupon they set their minds," &c. God took away the temple, their children, he had his day for them both. 1 Sam. iv. 3, the Jews trusted in the ark, and idolized that; "Let us fetch the ark of the covenant of the Lord out of Shiloh unto us, that when it cometh among us, it may save us out of the hand of our enemies;" but God had a day quickly after that to deprive them of it: ver. 11, "The ark of God was taken;" the Philistines took it, and slew thirty thousand footmen. Ephraim gloried in his children, but God had his time to pluck them away: Hosea ix. 11, 12, "Their glory shall flee away like a bird, from the birth, and from the womb, and from the conception. Though they bring up their children, yet will I bereave them, and there shall not be a man left:" their priding themselves in their children and increase made the Lord to diminish them, he took his times for that purpose. When Jonah idolized the gourd, the Lord had his day to smite it, Jonah iv. 7. Jacob was over-fond of Joseph, and God had his day to send him far from him, Gen. xxxvii.

Obs. 3. That when God is most angry, executing his severest judgments, then, even then, some are spared, some find mercy. When the Lord should take away the temple, city, their sons and daughters, and make good all the dreadful threatenings given out by Jeremiah and Ezekiel against the Jews, by plague, famine, sword, wild beasts, which was as black and sad a time as ever they saw, even then some escaped: "He that escapeth in that day." It was hard for any to escape, when such an army of Babylonians, so cruel and bitter, had lain so long round about Jerusalem, watching as lions for the prey; yet some did escape. Jeremiah saith, Lam. ii. 22, "In the day of the Lord's anger none escaped or remained:" he doth not mean absolutely none, for himself escaped, and divers others; his meaning is, that they were few in comparison of those who suffered. Since the beginning of the world, hath it been heard that God was so severe in any judgment executed upon the sons of men, as to show no tokens of mercy? When he drowned the world, he showed great mercy to Noah and his family; when he consumed Sodom and Gomorrah to ashes, he gave Lot and his daughters their lives for a prey; and when he made Jerusalem here a spectacle of his vengeance, he made an outlet and escape for some. He is a God that "in wrath remembers mercy:" and doubtless, in that great overflowing and drowning made in the Low Countries at this time, as he hath showed much severity, so he hath not forgotten mercy.

Obs. 4. God at his pleasure puts singular honour upon his faithful servants the prophets. He tells Ezekiel that when he shall have accomplished what he had prophesied against Jerusalem, that he should be informed thereof, that he would give some or others their lives for a prey, that they might bring him tidings thereof; and so lift up his head against all his adversaries, who looked upon and counted him a false prophet. Herein was great honour put upon the prophet: "He that escapeth shall come unto thee, to cause thee to hear it," &c. So God honoured Abraham, in telling him what he was about to do unto Sodom; Gen. xviii. 17, "Shall I hide from Abraham that thing which I do?" no; he is a prophet, a friend of mine, my faithful servant; and he would not conceal the matter from him. So, Amos iii. 7, "The Lord revealeth his secret to his servants the prophets;" he sends a messenger unto them, even his Holy Spirit, to acquaint them with what he is doing, and with what he hath done: so he sent an angel to Joseph, to tell him that Herod was dead, who sought the life of the young child, Matt. ii. 20.

Obs. 5. God hath his times of shutting and opening the mouths of his prophets. "Thou shalt speak, and be no more dumb:" after this time the prophet was as a dumb man towards the Jews, because they believed not his prophecies, entertained him not as a prophet, but slighted, mocked, and scorned him for those unusual passages of his, which the Lord put him upon; therefore the Lord took him off from being a prophet unto them, he had no more word for them; the false prophets went on still, but the true prophet is silenced. Men's sins do cause the Lord to stop the mouths of his prophets; their unbelief, unprofitableness, perverse constructions they make of what is said and done by them, their hearkening to lies, errors, and vain visions of false prophets, do discourage them and cause them to be silent. Thus people's untoward carriages made Jeremiah resolve to be silent, and preach no more in the name of the Lord, Jer. xx. 9. The prophets then had, and the prophets now have, great discouragements, and cause enough to be silent; and God may cause them to be as dumb unto them, removing them into corners, or taking them away: the people's sins rob them of spiritual mercies. Ezek. iii. 26, "I will make thy tongue cleave to the roof of thy mouth, that thou shalt be dumb, and shalt not be to them a reprover; for they are a rebellious house:" their sin deprived them of prophecy, and made the prophet "dumb." Let us look to it, that our sins deprive not us thereof, and make our prophets "dumb;" God may in justice make them "dumb to us," and open their mouths to others. If you would still hear the prophets speaking unto you, let the Lord see you practising what they present unto you in his name, yea, let the Lord hear you praying for them: and then see what is written and promised, Isa. xxx. 19—21; then your teachers shall not be removed into corners, but your eyes shall see them, and your ears shall hear them.

Obs. 6. That prophets, when they are discouraged, silenced, and become signs unto the people, they are to be patient, waiting upon the Lord to make good what they have spoken in his name, and for the opening of their mouths again. Ezekiel was a "sign" unto them, being silenced and discouraged; he was patient, expecting that God should accomplish what he had prophesied, and open his mouth again, which he did: "In that day shall thy mouth be opened to him that is escaped."

CHAPTER XXV.

Ver. 1—7. *The word of the Lord came again unto me, saying, Son of man, set thy face against the Ammonites, and prophesy against them; and say unto the Ammonites, Hear the word of the Lord God; Thus saith the Lord God; Because thou saidst, Aha, against my sanctuary, when it was profaned; and against the land of Israel, when it was desolate; and against the house of Judah, when they went into captivity; behold, therefore I will deliver thee to the men of the east for a possession, and they shall set their palaces in thee, and make their dwellings in thee: they shall eat thy fruit, and they shall drink thy milk. And I will make Rabbah a stable for camels, and the Ammonites a couching-place for flocks: and ye shall know that I am the Lord; For thus saith the Lord God, Because thou hast clapped thine hands, and stamped with the feet, and rejoiced in heart with all thy despite against the land of Israel; behold, therefore I will stretch out mine hand upon thee, and will deliver thee for a spoil to the heathen; and I will cut thee off from the people, and I will cause thee to perish out of the countries: I will destroy thee; and thou shalt know that I am the Lord.*

In this prophecy of Ezekiel are four things chiefly considerable: the first is, The destruction of the Jewish state by the Babylonians; which our prophet having declared in the twenty-one chapters preceding, he comes now to the second general head, which is, threatening of judgment to other nations, for their pride, and insulting over the Jews in their misery; and this he doth in the eight next chapters, from the beginning of this to chap. xxxiii.

In this chapter our prophet denounceth the judgments of God against four of those nations, which were enemies to the Jews; as,

I. The Ammonites.
II. The Moabites.
III. The Edomites.
IV. The Philistines.

In these words read, is a prophecy "against the Ammonites," wherein,

1. Their sins are propounded, ver. 3, 6.
2. Their judgments, ver. 4, 5, 7.
3. The end, why God would bring such judgments upon them, ver. 5, 7.

Ver. 1. "The word of the Lord came again unto me, saying." Being taken off from prophesying against the Jews for the present, he receives commission now to prophesy against the gentiles, who accused the God of the Jews either of weakness, that he could not defend his city and temple, or of malice towards his people, whom, if he could deliver, yet he left to the spoil of enemies. The Lord, therefore, would have them know that he is neither weak, nor malicious, but the great God of heaven and earth, who in justice punished his own people for their sins, and would not spare them, being guilty; and therefore commands Ezekiel now to declare his judgments against them.

Ver. 2. "Set thy face against the Ammonites." In chap. vi. 2, God bids him set his "face towards the mountains of Israel;" chap. xiii. 17, "against the daughters of his people;" in chap. xx. 46, God bid him "set his face towards the south;" chap. iv. 3, he bids him set it against the city; and now, to set it "against the Ammonites." This phrase, to set the face against one, imports a full and fixed resolution of doing a thing. Ezekiel must now resolve to look sourly upon the nations, and prophesy as harsh things against them as he had formerly done against the Jews. Jer. xliv. 11, "I will set my face against you for evil, and to cut off all Judah;" God was resolved not to behold them with a countenance promising mercy, but with a countenance threatening judgment and utter destruction: so Ezekiel must "set his face against the Ammonites," and prophesy no pleasing things, but sad, bitter, and destructive. The Ammonites had an incestuous beginning; they came from Lot and his younger daughter, who named her son Ben-Ammi, who was the father of the children of Ammon, Gen. xix. 38; they were bitter and bloody enemies to the Jews, 2 Chron. xx. 1; Amos i. 13; 2 Sam. x. 3, 4, 6; their country was strong, well peopled, and full of cities, Numb. xxi. 24; Judg. xi. 33.

Ver. 3. "Say unto the Ammonites, Hear the word of the Lord God." How the Ammonites should hear Ezekiel being in Babylon, and they far off from him, is inquirable. When he had denounced the judgments of God against them, and left this prophecy upon record, by some Babylonians or Jews it might be conveyed unto them. The words, "hear the word of the Lord," import not, that they should hear it at that instant when he prophesied, but that they should in time know what the mind of the Lord was towards them: and doubtless he was commanded thus to say and prophesy, for the Jews' sake, that they, hearing Ezekiel declare and denounce such judgments against the Ammonites, who had insulted over them, might in some measure be comforted thereby.

"Because thou saidst, Aha, against my sanctuary, when it was profaned." When the "sanctuary" was, by the Babylonians, taken and destroyed, the Ammonites, as one man, or one woman, said, "Aha;" they rejoiced at it, and scoffed at the Jews. The Hebrew word for "Aha" is, האח which is a note of one rejoicing and insulting. Psal. xxxv. 25, it is rendered, "Ah, so would we have it;" and Psal. xl. 15, "Aha, aha;" they rejoiced and insulted in the misery of David. So these Ammonites, that should have grieved at the profaning of the sanctuary, and the holy things thereof, and at the sufferings of God's people, they sported themselves thereat, and said, So would we have it, we are glad to see this day; where now is your God? what are you the better for all your sacrificing and worship? who hath the true religion, you or us? Zeph. ii. 8, they reviled and reproached the people of God, and magnified themselves against their borders, they spake evil of them in the day of their calamity, and added affliction to their affliction. Lam. ii. 16, "All thine enemies have opened their mouth against thee; they hiss and gnash the teeth; they say, We have swallowed her up; this is the day we looked for." The Septuagint for "Aha" is, ye have been glad: the Latin expositors turn it, *Euge, Euge;* they commended the heathen for what they did against the temple and people of the Lord.

"Against the land of Israel, when it was desolate." The ten tribes long before were led into captivity by Shalmaneser, 2 Kings xvii. 5, 6; and when their land was overrun by the heathens, and they carried away, these Ammonites did show hostile minds, then they cried, "Aha;" and not only then, but also,

"Against the house of Judah, when they went into captivity." The "house of Judah went into captivity" by degrees, some with Jehoiakim, some with Jehoiachin, and the residue with Zedekiah; and still when any of them were carried away captive the Ammonites were glad of it, but especially at the last, when all was laid waste, city, temple, land; when Zedekiah and the people were all led into captivity, then they belched out their sarcasms and bitter taunts.

Ver. 4. "I will deliver thee to the men of the east for a possession." The Hebrew is, to the sons of the east. Whom they were, men's thoughts are various. Vatablus makes them the Medes and Persians: some think them to be the Kedarites, who are called "the men of the east," Jer. xlix. 28: others judge them to be the Arabians, which descended from Abraham by Keturah, and were sent eastward, Gen. xxv. 6: but there is no sound reason why we should not conceive them to be the Babylonians, who were not fully north from them, but north-east. And therefore, as they were called sometimes a wind out of the north, Ezek. i. 4, so at other times, a wind out of the east, or an east wind, chap. xvii. 10; xix. 12; and when Nebuchadnezzar began his military expedition, his eye was upon Rabbath of the Ammonites, as well as Jerusalem of the Jews, Ezek. xxi. 21, 22; he used divination to take him off from his indifferency between both, which the Lord by his overruling providence ordered so, as, first, to bring him to Jerusalem, and five years after, unto Rabbath, which he took, subduing the whole country, as Josephus relates. And when the Babylonians had spoiled the Ammonites, and left their country desolate, it is affirmed that the Arabians, who were shepherds, came and possessed the same.

Ant. lib. 10. cap. 10.

"And they shall set their palaces in thee, and make their dwellings in thee." When countries are conquered, the conquerors are careful to keep them in subjection unto them; and therefore place such in them as they may confide in, who build them "palaces," dwelling-places, and strong holds, to secure themselves and the country, and so cut them off from hopes of recovering their liberty. The word for "palaces" is, טירה which is, a castle, or building, having its compass. Palaces, castles, and great houses, are much in compass; or because they are built with squared stones, set equally, and in order: the greater had their "palaces," and the meaner sort their tents, or "dwellings."

"They shall eat thy fruit." Whatever "fruit" thy land bears, they shall have the benefit thereof. Their land was very fruitful, as may appear from 2 Sam. xvii. 27—29; it was near Canaan, the place Lot had chosen, and his children possessed for many years; so pleasant and fruitful, that had not God forbade the Jews to meddle with it, Deut. ii. 19, they would have had it in their possession: now strangers should possess and "eat" the fruit of it.

"They shall drink thy milk." In those eastern and hot countries they were wont to "drink milk." Judg. v. 25, Jael gave Sisera milk to drink. And these Ammonites having much pasturage, and many cattle, abounded in "milk," by which great gain came in unto them; whereupon they are called, milk-eaters, by Lavater; milk-drinkers, by Sanctius. Their land flowed with milk and honey, and now their enemies should "eat" the one, and "drink" the other. The Septuagint renders the word חלב milk, fatness; strangers should eat and drink the fat and sweet, they should possess their land and wealth.

Ver. 5. "And I will make Rabbath a stable for camels." Rabbath was the head city of the Ammonites, so called because of its greatness and populousness. There was another Rabbah, or Rabbath, among the Moabites; for distinction' sake, therefore, this was called "Rabbath of the children of Ammon," Deut. iii. 11; it endured a long siege by Joab, 2 Sam. xii.; in after-times it was named Philadelphia, by Ptolemæus Philadelphus. This great city was taken by Nebuchadnezzar, and made "a stable for camels:" it had been a palace for princes, and was called "the royal city, the city of waters," 2 Sam. xii. 26, 27; and it was made a "stable," and that for "camels," which drank the waters thereof. "Camels" are creatures made to carry burdens, they will carry six hundred, seven hundred, yea, ten hundred weight; they kneel down to take their burdens, and being sufficiently loaded, they will admit no more; they cannot endure the cold, they are content with little meat, and will travel four days without water; they, being weary in journeying, are not put on by blows, but by their keepers going before them and singing. The Hebrew word is, גמל *gamal,* whence our English word camel. This creature is patient of labour, and repays with advantage his master for keeping.

"And the Ammonites a couching-place for flocks." By a metonymy of the adjunct, Ammonites are put for their country; that should be for a bed of the flock, or resting-place of the sheep and goats; for צאן signifies, a flock of sheep and goats. The cities and towns of the Ammonites should be so wasted, that grass should grow there, cattle feed and lie down there.

"And ye shall know that I am the Lord." Now you blaspheme, saying, I was weak, and could not deliver the Jews out of the hands of Nebuchadnezzar, or malicious, and would not; but you shall know that I am a powerful and just God, who dealt so with them, and you also, for your sins.

Ver. 6. "Because thou hast clapped thine hands." He had mentioned their sin before, ver. 3, and here he sets it out more fully, and that in the several degrees of it. 1. They "clapped their hands:" this gesture, chap. vi. 11, noted grief; here it imports gladness, they clapped their hands for joy that the temple was burnt, and the Jews rooted out of their land. Job xxvii. 23, "Men shall clap their hands at him." When God should destroy the wicked man, then others should rejoice at it, and manifest their joy by clapping of hands; and when God did execute his wrath upon Jerusalem, all that passed by did "clap their hands" at her, Lam. ii. 15.

"And stamped with the feet." This is the second

expression of their insulting. This gesture noted grief, chap. vi. 11, but here the contrary. In the Hebrew it is, because thou hast enlarged thyself in foot, that is, stretched out thy foot, and stamped with it. The Septuagint is, hast made a noise with thy feet. Their hands and feet were used in an insulting manner against the Jews in their misery; it is like they skipped and danced for joy, and so made a noise with their feet.

"And rejoiced in heart." Here is a third expression. They were not a little affected, but glad at heart, that Jerusalem was ruined, and the Jews carried away captive: they said, "in heart," Aha! so would we have it. This was as wine unto them, it cheered and enlarged their hearts.

"With all thy despite against the land of Israel." This is a further degree and aggravation of their sin, they insulted, and that with despite: בכל־שאטך in all thy scorn and despite. The word for "despite," is from שאט which is, to thrust a thorn or pointed thing into one to vex. These Ammonites did so contemn, scorn, and despise the Jews in their great sufferings, that they were like thorns and goads in their sides. Avenarius renders the words, in all thy lashing: their scorns and despitings were as so many lashes upon the backs and sides of the Jews; they said, Are these the holy people? is this the holy land? where is your God? why hath he not appeared for you? thus they reproached God's people, "and magnified themselves against their border," Zeph. ii. 8.

Ver. 7. "Behold, therefore I will stretch out my hand upon thee." Thou hast clapped thy hands against me and my people, "therefore I will stretch out my hand upon thee," that is, against thee; it shall be upon thee, to break and destroy thee. I have held in my hand a long time, but now I will stretch it out, and thou shalt feel the power of it. Zeph. i. 4, "I will stretch out mine hand upon Judah, and upon all the inhabitants of Jerusalem; and I will cut off the remnant of Baal from this place, and the name of the Chemarims with the priests:" after stretching, followed cutting off: so Ezek. xiv. 9, "I will stretch out my hand upon him, and will destroy him from the midst of my people Israel."

"I will deliver thee for a spoil to the heathen." In the fourth verse it was said, "I will deliver thee to the men of the east," here, "to the heathen." Those men of the east were heathens, whom the Jews hated as uncircumcised, Judg. xv. 18; as dogs, Matt. xv. 25, 26; Christ speaks according to the esteem the Jews had of the gentiles. To them they should be for "a spoil." The word for "spoil" is, לבג which Montanus renders, for meat; but Piscator thinks it put for לבז for a prey, but that is not needful, because the word *bag* itself signifies meat, a portion; as Dan. i. 5, 8, "the portion of the king's meat," פתבג המלך God would deliver the Ammonites to be meat unto them, they should feed upon them and what they had, as they had done upon the Jews; they should eat their fruit, and drink their milk.

"And I will cut thee off from the people." Thou art now a nation among others, but I will cause thee to cease from being a nation, either by destroying of thee, or sending thee into captivity, scattering thee amongst the heathens. If thou be a people at all, thou shalt be a people without any head, without a name; thou shalt be removed far from the people thou now borderest upon, and they shall know thee no more, thou and thy name shall both perish: so much the next words import.

"I will cause thee to perish out of the countries: I will destroy thee." These last phrases do interpret the former. Causing them to perish out of "the countries," is, cutting them off from the people; and, destroying of them, is both. The Hebrew word for "perish" and "destroy" do signify, an utter and total destruction.

Obs. 1. The Lord having contended with his own family, he contends with others. First, he had a controversy with the Jews, and now he enters into controversy with the nations. "Son of man, set thy face against the Ammonites, and prophesy against them." He had formerly set his face against the Jews, and prophesied sad things against them; which being done, he must set his face against others, and prophesy not only *dura* but *durissima*, the hardest things against them, even utter destruction. When God's people have drunk of the cup, then it shall be given unto others: Jer. xxv. 15—26, God began with Jerusalem, his own people and family, and then caused the cup of his fury to pass unto all nations and kingdoms. So Isaiah, after he had begun with the Jews, and declared what dreadful judgments God would bring upon them, he turns aside to the nations, and lays the burden of the Lord upon them, and that in nine chapters together, from the beginning of chap. xiii. to the end of chap. xxi. Judgment oft begins at God's house, as Amos iii. 2, "You only have I known of all the families of the earth: therefore I will punish you for all your iniquities." God would begin with them; Ezek. ix. 6, "Begin at my sanctuary;" but he ends elsewhere: Psal. lxxv. 8, when God's people have drunk the red wine in the cup, the wicked must drink the dregs; the cup passeth from place to place till all be drunk off. Jer. xxv. 29, "Lo, I begin to bring evil on the city which is called by my name, and should ye be utterly unpunished? Ye shall not be unpunished: for I will call for a sword upon all the inhabitants of the earth." Have I begun with mine own city and people, and do you think to go free? no, the sword is commissioned to come unto you; if that have ate the flesh of my sons, and drunk their blood, much more shall it eat your flesh and bones, and drink your blood. If Jerusalem go down, other cities will not stand; if God spare not his own temple, he will not spare Satan's synagogues: when the green trees are cut down that stood in the garden, the dry trees must expect the axe, which stand in the forest.

Obs. 2. That the Lord takes notice what the ways and carriages of nations are towards him and his. "Thou saidst, Aha, against my sanctuary, when it was profaned; and against the land of Israel, when it was desolate." All the secret consultings, plottings, revilings, attempts that are against the worship, ways, and people of God, among heathens, and heathenish spirits, are minded by the Lord: Psal. lxvi. 7, "His eyes behold the nations," the men of them, their thoughts, words, and ways. When the nations gathered themselves together against Zion, and said, "Let her be defiled, and let our eye look upon Zion," Mic. iv. 11, God then looked upon them, and observed the workings of their hearts, heads, tongues, and hands; yea, their rage and imaginations he animadverts; Psal. ii. 1, "Why do the heathen rage, and the people imagine a vain thing?" He observed how insultingly the Babylonians carried it against his people, Jer. l. 11: Psal. cxxxvii. they rejoiced, they laughed, they said, "Sing us one of the songs of Zion;" they, and the rest of Zion's adversaries, mocked at her and her sabbaths. Whatever the nations now do devise, plot, speak, or enterprise against the people of God, he that sits in heaven beholds the same, and laughs them to scorn.

Obs. 3. To laugh at, and insult over, the calamities

of others, is a grievous and provoking sin. "Because thou saidst, Aha, against my sanctuary, when it was profaned; and against the land of Israel, when it was desolate; and against the house of Judah, when they went into captivity; behold, therefore I will deliver thee to men of the east for a possession," &c. Because the Ammonites insulted, clapped their hands, stamped with their feet, were heartily glad at the sufferings of the Jews, and vented their spite against them, therefore God was exasperated, so as to threaten the Ammonites' ruin, and utter extirpation. They were the neighbours bordering upon them, they were their confederates, in league with the king of Egypt, as the Jews were; they were their half brethren, descending from Lot; and upon these accounts should have sympathized with the Jews, wept with those that wept, Rom. xii. 15; been sensible of their great adversities, Heb. xiii. 3; but they insulted over them, mocked at them, were despiteful against them, and added coals to the fire, weight to their burdens, and more chains to their bonds. It is not only an uncharitable, but also an inhuman, an unnatural, thing to insult, make sport, and domineer at the miseries of others. When there be wars in a land, fires in cities, shipwrecks at sea, robberies of houses, inundations of waters, and many suffer grievous things by such judgments of God, should we rejoice thereat, mock, and make ourselves merry? Surely, if we do so, we offend, we provoke the Lord. Prov. xvii. 5, "He that is glad at calamities shall not be unpunished;" the Hebrew is, shall not be innocent; God will deal with him as a person deeply guilty: he that makes others' calamities the object of his gladness, stirs up God to be the Author of his destruction. Shimei was glad at the expulsion of David by his son Absalom, yea, mocked at, and cursed him, 2 Sam. xvi. 7, 8; he made David's misery the matter of his mirth; but this kindled such a fire in the breast of the Lord, that it made him return his wickedness upon his head, 1 Kings ii. 44, and cut him off from the land of the living. It is an argument of a malicious heart, of an imbittered spirit, to insult over the miseries of others, and mock at their calamities; yea, it is an evidence of a wicked man that doth so; such are Ammonites and Babylonians. Job xxxi. 29, "If I rejoiced at the destruction of him that hated me, or lifted up myself when evil found him." Job professes he did not make the misery of his enemies matter of music, he had a better principle within than to put him on to such a wickedness. So David, though the abjects and base ones rejoiced in his adversity, yet he durst not do so; but when they were sick, he put on sackcloth, he sympathized with them, he humbled his soul with fasting, and prayed for them, Psal. xxxv. 13—15. Of such a spirit was Solomon, who gives wholesome counsel; Prov. xxiv. 17, "Rejoice not when thine enemy falleth, and let not thine heart be glad when he stumbleth:" he that rejoiceth at the misery of his enemy, will be sad at his good; and both are evil. Some, the greater evils befall their enemies, the more they rejoice; if they fall into sin, reproach, or bitter affliction, they are much gladdened at it; but thou that dost so, hast not only stumbled, but art fallen, both into sin, and into the displeasure of God, for ver. 18, is a reason why men should not triumph in the troubles and afflictions of others, lest the Lord see it, and it displease him, and he turn away his wrath from him; thy so doing displeases the Lord, and may cause him to turn away his afflicting hand from thine enemy, and to turn it against thee. In these times this sin is too much in practice, nations and persons rejoicing in the miseries of one another. But we should further consider,

(1.) That if others be under the heavy strokes of God to-day, we may be to-morrow, and therefore should not feast ourselves upon others' calamities. Eccles. ix. 2, "All things come alike to all; there is one event to the righteous and to the wicked:" what befalls thine enemy one day, whom thou thinkest the worst that lives, may befall thee the next day, though thou be the best man that lives; therefore "boast not thyself of to-morrow, for thou knowest not what a day may bring forth;" it may bring forth as much woe and evil to thee, as the former day did to thine enemy or neighbour.

(2.) That we deserve as sad things as any others feel. Are not we sinners, and such sinners as make the times perilous? 2 Tim. iii. 1—5, are not we lovers of ourselves, covetous, boasters, proud, blasphemers, disobedient to parents, unthankful, unholy? &c. If we be so, why should not we fear lest the judgments of God should overtake us, and arrest us, as they have done others. Lam. iii. 22, "It is of the Lord's mercies," saith Jeremiah, "that we are not consumed:" he puts in himself; and it was not single mercy, but mercies, all God's mercies, were at work to keep them alive. We should wonder we are spared, being such sinners as we are, rather than rejoice in the miseries of others, who may be more righteous than ourselves.

(3.) The end of God's laying his hand upon others; it is not that we should rejoice, clap our hands, dance and insult over them that are miserable, but it is to awaken us, and excite us unto repentance. Luke xiii. when God, by his providence, brings sudden and sad strokes upon men, it is that others should consider and repent: the death of the Galileans, and those upon whom the tower of Siloam fell, was for that end; therefore saith Christ, "Except ye repent, ye shall all likewise perish." The miseries of Scotland, Ireland, by the sword, and of the Netherlands by waters, is not that men should rejoice, but sympathize with them, and repent; if others suffer, and we be spared, that is the goodness of God to us, and his goodness therein should lead us to repentance.

(4.) The rule of Christ is otherwise: Matt. v. 44, "I say unto you, Love your enemies, bless them that curse you, do good to them that hate you, and pray for them which despitefully use you and persecute you:" we must not rejoice at their miseries, but love them, and manifest our love by blessing them, doing them good, and praying for them.

Obs. 4. For the sins of the people, God lays nations waste, and disposes of them to whom he please. The sins of the Ammonites caused God to cut them off, to destroy them and their name, and to deliver them for a spoil to the heathen, and their country to the men of the east for a possession: Psal. cvii. 33, 34, "He turneth rivers into a wilderness, and the watersprings into dry ground; a fruitful land into barrenness," or saltness, "for the wickedness of them that dwell therein." He is the Governor among the nations, Psal. xxii. 28, and when they do wickedly, he can break them with his rod of iron, cut them off with his battle-axe, and give their countries to whom he pleases. He set Jeremiah over the nations and kingdoms, to root out, pull down, and destroy, Jer. i. 10; which he did in a prophetical way, chap. xxvii. many lands are reckoned up there; and, ver. 6, saith God, "Now have I given all these lands into the hand of Nebuchadnezzar the king of Babylon." They were wicked, proud, idolatrous, oppressive, and insulted against God's people; and the Lord brake them in pieces, and gave them to the men of the east. God, that made the earth, gives it to whom it seems meet unto him, ver. 5.

Obs. 5. Cities and places which are honourable

among men, for their sins, God pours contempt upon, and puts them into base conditions. Rabbath, that was a royal city, he makes "a stable for camels." Isa. xiii. 19—21, "Babylon, the glory of kingdoms, the beauty of the Chaldees' excellency, shall be as when God overthrew Sodom and Gomorrah. Wild beasts of the desert shall lie there; and their houses shall be full of doleful creatures: owls shall dwell there, and satyrs shall dance there:" for satyrs, the Chaldee saith, dragons; Jerom, devils. So spiritual Babylon, Rev. xviii. 2, "It is fallen, it is fallen, and is become the habitation of devils, and the hold of every foul spirit, and a cage of every unclean and hateful bird." Rome, that was so famous, is, or shall be, a base, contemptible place, a dungeon for devils, a prison for foul spirits, a cage for the worst of birds. Have not the palaces of prelates and their cathedrals been made stables for horses in our days, and prisons for malefactors?

Ver. 8—11. *Thus saith the Lord God; Because that Moab and Seir do say, Behold, the house of Judah is like unto all the heathen; therefore, behold, I will open the side of Moab from the cities, from his cities which are on his frontiers, the glory of the country, Beth-jeshimoth, Baal-meon, and Kiriathaim, unto the men of the east with the Ammonites, and will give them in possession, that the Ammonites may not be remembered among the nations. And I will execute judgments upon Moab; and they shall know that I am the Lord.*

In these verses you have our prophet denouncing judgments against the Moabites. Where comes to be considered,

I. Their sin, ver. 8.

II. The judgments themselves, ver. 9, 10.

III. The end of those judgments, ver. 11.

Ver. 8. "Because that Moab." The Moabites were brethren to the Ammonites, descending from Lot and his eldest daughter, Gen. xix. 37, as the Ammonites did from him and his youngest: they abode not in the ways and worship of the true God long, but fell to idolatry, Judg. x. 8, were bitter enemies unto the Jews. Balak, that hired Balaam to curse them, was king of these Moabites, Numb. xxii. 4; they were men of might, Exod. xv. 15; and had the Jews under eighteen years in the days of Eglon, another of their kings, Judg. iii. 14; whom Ehud slew, and after him ten thousand of the Moabites, all men of valour, ver. 21, 22, 29. They infested the Jews much, and oft were there wars between them and the Jews: see 1 Sam. xiv. 47; 2 Sam. viii. 2; 2 Kings iii. 7; 2 Chron. xx. 10, 11. In their land Moses died and was buried, Deut. xxxiv. 5, 6; from them descended virtuous Ruth, chap. i. 4; of whom also Christ came, Matt. i. 5.

"And Seir." Seir was a part of Edom: Gen. xxxii. 3, "The land of Seir, the country of Edom," or field of Edom. It was a mountainous part of Edom; Gen. xiv. 6, it is called "mount Seir," and that from "Seir" the Horite prince of the country, as Bonfrerius observes, from Gen. xxxvi. 20. The Horites, or Horims, were driven out by Esau, Deut. ii. 22; so that he and his posterity possessed it, having that name before. Esau was "Seir," a hairy rough man, and that place was mountainous and rough where he sat down.

"The house of Judah is like unto all the heathen." The Jews, said they, have stood upon it that their God was the only true God, better and mightier than all the gods of the nations; that they were a people so dear to him that he would defend them and their city, having his temple, his worship, his prophets, Isa. iv. 5; xxxi. 5; but we see their prophets are liars, they are deluded with vain confidences, and their God hath forsaken them; he hath not dealt better by them than our gods have done by us; he hath exposed, yea, delivered them into the hands of their bloody and barbarous enemies: so that Judah is like unto all the heathen, who have not met with worse usage from the Babylonians than the Jews themselves have. Thus Moab blasphemed, and magnified himself against the Lord, deriding Israel, and skipping for joy, Jer. xlviii. 26, 27.

Ver. 9. "I will open the side of Moab from the cities," &c. The word for "side" is, כתף which signifies, a shoulder; and metaphorically, the "side," or strength, of any thing. Here by "side" is meant, the strong cities of Moab, the frontier towns, which were as the shoulders and sides to the country: these God would "open," he would break their ribs and shoulders, and make way into the heart and bowels of their country, Jer. xlviii. 25, "The horn of Moab is cut off, and his arm is broken:" Moab's horns and arms were his frontier towns, castles, and forts, he had to keep out the enemy, but the Lord would break these by the Chaldean, and let him into their land.

"The glory of the country." The Hebrew for "glory" is צבי from צבה to swell, to be lifted up; because those things, which are our glory and ornament, usually do puff us up, and make us to swell. The cities here mentioned were the glory of the Moabites.

"Beth-jeshimoth." This city was near Jordan, in the plain of Moab, between which and Abel-shittim the Israelites pitched their last tents before they entered into Canaan, Numb. xxxii. 49; it was part of Reuben's inheritance at first, Josh. xiii. 20; and signifies, the house of solitariness.

"Baal-meon." This was another city belonging unto them. It is mentioned Numb. xxxii. 38; 1 Chron. v. 8. The Septuagint renders it, upon the fountain: Eusebius saith, it was a great village, nigh a mountain of hot waters.

"Kiriathaim." It was in the tribe of Reuben, Josh. xiii. 19; formerly possessed with giants, Gen. xiv. 5; rebuilt or beautified by the children of Reuben, Numb. xxxii. 37; and after the ten tribes were carried away, who had driven out the Amorites, the Moabites repossessed it, being formerly expelled thence by the Amorites. The word signifies, meetings, or two cities, because two cities met together in it.

Ver. 10. "Unto the men of the east with the Ammonites," &c. God would make way through Moab's chief cities for the Babylonians, who were "men of the east," that they should come in, and take their country in possession. The Hebrew for, "with the Ammonites," is, against the sons of Ammon. God would so deal with the Moabites as he had done with the Ammonites; "the men of the east" should come and take possession of both their countries.

"That the Ammonites may not be remembered among the nations." God would so spoil and waste the nations of the Moabites and Ammonites, that not only themselves should perish, but the memory of them.

Ver. 11. "And I will execute judgments upon Moab." They think I am a God like the gods of the nations, but they shall find my hand so heavy upon them, be so broken and ruined, that they shall know I am far different from all the gods of the heathen.

Obs. 1. Nations are like one another in sin and wickedness. The Ammonites insulted over, and scoffed at, the Jews in the day of their affliction, and so did Moab and Seir. "The house of Judah is like unto all the heathen;" Moab reproacheth, and Ammon reviles them, Zeph. ii. 8. Jerusalem was "great among the nations, and princess among the provinces," Lam. i. 1; but they all were glad of her ruin, and laughed at her suffering, Lam. ii. 15, 16.

Obs. 2. The world, and men of it, judge untowardly of the Lord and his people. What said Moab and Seir? "Behold, the house of Judah is like unto all the heathen;" their God is as our gods, and his people are as we are, they have no more privilege than others. Heathens have heathenish thoughts of God himself, and those who are his. Isa. xxxvi. 18—20, "Beware, lest Hezekiah persuade you, saying, The Lord will deliver us. Hath any of the gods of the nations delivered his land out of the hand of the king of Assyria? Where are the gods of Hamath and Arphad? where are the gods of Sepharvaim? and have they delivered Samaria out of my hand? Who are they among all the gods of these lands, that have delivered their land out of my hand, that the Lord should deliver Jerusalem out of my hand?" Here you see what the thoughts of Rabshakeh, Sennacherib, and his army were, concerning the God of Israel; that he was nothing differing from the gods of the nations; that he was no more able to deliver Jerusalem out of their hands, than the idol gods were to deliver the nations out of them; that the Jews should presently become like other people. You have it more fully in 2 Chron. xxxii. 14, "Who was there among all the gods of those nations that my fathers utterly destroyed, that could deliver his people out of mine hand, that your God should be able to deliver out of mine hand?" No god of any nation, against whom my fathers and myself did ever draw the sword, was able to withstand them or me, and so to protect the people. And what! do you Jews think your God greater and wiser, better, more able to do for you? you deceive yourselves; I am come against you, and you must fall into my hands, and become like the nations.

Obs. 3. Heathens' reproaching God and his people, makes way for sad judgments upon them, ushers in certain destruction. Because Moab and Seir said, "the house of Judah is like unto all the heathen," which was a reproaching of God and his people, "Therefore, behold, I will open the side of Moab;" I will break his ribs, his strong holds, and let in a potent enemy to destroy him and his. When men blaspheme the name of God, and are inhuman towards his people, albeit they be heathens, God is so offended at it, that he will severely deal with them. Zeph. ii. 8—10, "I have heard the reproach of Moab, and the revilings of the children of Ammon, &c. Therefore as I live, saith the Lord of hosts, the God of Israel, Surely Moab shall be as Sodom, and the children of Ammon as Gomorrah, even the breeding of nettles, and salt-pits, and a perpetual desolation: this shall they have for their pride, because they have reproached and magnified themselves against the people of the Lord of hosts." Moab and Ammon were near unto Sodom and Gomorrah, they could not be ignorant of God's dealings with them, and because, in their pride, they reproached God and his people, they should be make like unto them; their judgment should have something extraordinary in it; God's curse should be upon them, they should breed nettles and salt-pits, that is, be fruitless and useless, yea, and that for ever. When Nahash the Ammonite would not make a covenant with the men of Jabesh-gilead, unless he might thrust out their right eyes, and lay it for a reproach upon all Israel, see what the issue was, for intending to reproach God's people, and himself in them: 1 Sam. xi. God stirred up the spirits of Saul and the people, so that they, fighting with the Ammonites, slew them, and scattered them, "so that two of them were not left together," ver. 11. It is ill to have a reproaching desire towards God's people, and far worse to do it. If God do not bring some open judgment upon such, he will secretly consume them. Isa. li. 7, 8, "Fear ye not the reproach of men, neither be ye afraid of their revilings. For the moth shall eat them up like a garment, and the worm shall eat them like wool." Moths and worms are close, hidden things, and do secretly eat into garments and wool, whereby they are altogether marred; so God hath secret and invisible moths and worms, plagues and judgments, to devour those that reproach his people, him, and his ways. If God be severe against heathens doing it, will he spare christians doing such evil?

Obs. 4. When God is wroth with a nation, strong holds and garrisons will not secure and protect them. Moab had frontier towns, and those manned with men of might, but they kept not out the judgments of God; he opened the side of Moab, he brake in upon them, notwithstanding their forts, castles, garrisons, and their great strength. Moab is notable for strong forts and strong men, Jer. xlviii. 17, 18, 25, 41; but how strong soever their cities, their fortifications, their men were, they could not preserve Moab: Isa. xxv. 10, "Moab shall be trodden down under him, even as straw is trodden down for the dunghill:" all Moab's strength was no more unto the Lord than straw. Straw is a weak thing, yea, among the weakest of things, the foot of a child can tread that down; look, then, how easily the foot of a child or man treads down straw, so easily would the foot of God tread down all the strength of Moab. So for Nineveh, the Lord shook down her strong holds as easily as ripe figs are shaken off the fig-tree, Nahum iii. 12. As there is no counsel against the Lord, Prov. xxi. 30, so there is no force or fort can stand out against him: if he give out the command, strong holds are destroyed, Isa. xxiii. 11; if he be angry, they are thrown down, Lam. ii. 2. It is lawful to have strong holds, but sinful and vain to trust in them; that makes what was once profitable to become prejudicial.

Obs. 5. Cities, forts, and strong holds, do adorn and beautify the places where they are. Moab's cities and frontier towns were the glory of the country. Adullam, a city belonging to Judah, Josh. xv. 35, near which was the cave David hid himself in when he fled from Saul, 1 Sam. xxii. 1, is called "the glory of Israel," Micah i. 15. Piscator interprets it of Jerusalem, and makes that "the glory of Israel;" he shall come to Adullam, even to the glory of Israel. Be the words meant of Adullam or Jerusalem, they were the "glory of Israel." Babylon, Isa. xiv. 4, is styled "the golden city;" what an ornament was that unto the province or place where it was! so Tyrus, Isa. xxiii. 8, is named "the crowning city;" it was as great an honour to the country where it was, as a crown to a king's head. In Canaan were "great and goodly cities," Deut. vi. 10; in Midian were cities and goodly castles, Numb. xxxi. 10; and these were the ornaments and glory of those places.

Obs. 6. Strong holds, cities, nations, are the Lord's, and he gives them to whom he will. As he gave the Ammonites', so the Moabites' country unto the men of the east, and that for a possession. Ezek. xxix. 19, "Behold, I will give the land of Egypt unto Nebuchadnezzar king of Babylon." What had the Lord to do with Egypt? was it not Pharaoh's? had he any right to dispose of it to another king? Yes, he had more right to it than Pharaoh himself; Jer. x. 7, he is the "King of nations," and may take from one and give to another at his pleasure. He took the kingdom out of Rehoboam's hands and gave it unto Jeroboam, even ten tribes, 1 Kings xi. 35; he took the land of Canaan from others, and gave it unto Abraham and his seed, Gen. xiii. 12—15; afterward he took it from them, and gave it, with the great city thereof, into the hands of the Babylonians, Jer. xxxii. 3; and with it every strong hold, Hab. i. 10; and after seventy years gave it again unto the Jews.

Ver. 12—14. *Thus saith the Lord God; Because that Edom hath dealt against the house of Judah by taking vengeance, and hath greatly offended, and revenged himself upon them; therefore thus saith the Lord God; I will also stretch out mine hand upon Edom, and will cut off man and beast from it; and I will make it desolate from Teman; and they of Dedan shall fall by the sword. And I will lay my vengeance upon Edom by the hand of my people Israel: and they shall do in Edom according to mine anger and according to my fury; and they shall know my vengeance, saith the Lord God.*

These verses contain a prophecy against the Edomites, who are the third sort of enemies to the Jews mentioned in this chapter. Here likewise, as before, you have,

I. Their sin, ver. 12.

II. Their judgments, ver. 13.

III. The efficient and instrumental causes, ver. 14.

IV. The end of those judgments, ver. 14.

Ver. 12. "Because that Edom hath dealt against the house of Judah." By "Edom" are meant the Edomites or Idumeans, who descended from Esau, who, Gen. xxxvi. 8, 9, is called "Edom," and the "father of the Edomites;" which name he had either from his red skin and hair, Gen. xxv. 25, or rather from his selling his birthright for red pottage; ver. 30, Make me to eat, מן־הארם הארם הזה of that red, that red: he was cruel and profane; not unlike unto him were his posterity, the Edomites, who ever bare ill will to the house of Jacob. When the Jews came out of Egypt, Moses sent to the king of Edom to let them have passage through their country, but he refused, and came out in hostile manner against them, though they were his brethren, Numb. xx. 14, 18, 30: it was Doeg, an Edomite, that fell upon the priests, and slew them, 1 Sam. xxii. 19. That the Edomites' unkindness might not lie upon the spirits of the Jews, and beget ill blood in them, the Lord made a law, that they should "not abhor an Edomite," because they were their brethren, Deut. xxiii. 7; he took care that there might be brotherly love between them, but there was very little.

"Edom hath dealt against the house of Judah by taking vengeance." What cause the Edomites had to deal revengefully with the Jews, we must inquire. They being borderers upon the Jews, Josh. xv. 1, and full of enmity against them, did many times vex and prejudice them; whereupon when Saul was king, he fought against them, as being their common enemies with others, 1 Sam. xiv. 47; and David slew all their males, lying upon them six months with his army, 1 Kings xi. 15, 16, and made them tributary, putting garrisons in all parts of their country, 2 Sam. viii. 14. After this, in Jehoram's days, they revolted, and made themselves a king, and hereupon were smitten by Jehoram and his forces, 2 Kings viii. 20, 21; Amaziah also, in his days, slew ten thousand of them, 2 Kings xiv. 7; and other ten thousand did the children of Judah carry away captive, and threw them off the top of a rock, and broke them in pieces, 2 Chron. xxv. 11, 12. These things, together with that ancient grudge they had against them for Jacob's getting the blessing and birthright from Esau, their father, made them splenetive, and to seek revenge; and therefore, when they had any opportunity, they used violence, and shed innocent blood, Joel iii. 19. And when the Babylonians came against the Jews, carried them away captive, the Edomites rejoiced at it, encouraged them against the Jews, and said of Jerusalem, "Rase it, rase it, even to the foundation thereof," Psal. cxxxvii. 7. They were as the Babylonians, Obad. ver. 11, "Thou wast as one of them:" look what spirit was in a Babylonian, the same was in an Edomite; did they speak proudly? so did the Edomites, ver. 12; did they enter the gates of Jerusalem, and lay hands on the prey? so did the Edomites, ver. 13; did they cut off many? so did the Edomites, they cut off those that did escape, and delivered up those that remained in the day of distress, ver. 14: thus they dealt "against the house of Judah by taking vengeance." The Hebrew for "taking vengeance," is, in revenging a revenge; Edom was greedy of revenge, and set upon it; so much the doubling of the word imports.

"And hath greatly offended, and revenged himself upon them." In the Hebrew it is, they offended in offending; that is, they "greatly offended:" אשם signifies, to do wickedly, shamefully, and also, to make desolate, Ezek. vi. 6, because abominable sins do bring desolation. Junius renders the words thus, and do make themselves guilty for ever; they so offended, as that there was no pardon, no mercy for them. Piscator, they contracted great guilt; their revenging themselves upon the Jews made them exceeding guilty.

1. The Jews were their brethren, Obad. 10; Amos i. 11.

2. They were their neighbours, Idumea and Judea bordered upon one another, Mark iii. 8.

3. They were confederates with the Jews. Jer. xxvii. 3, an Edomitish ambassador was at Jerusalem, who, together with the ambassadors of the other kings there mentioned, were strengthening themselves with Zedekiah against Nebuchadnezzar; see Obad. 7.

They, therefore, to revenge themselves for former wrongs done them upon the Jews, and that in the day of their calamity, this made their sin exceeding sinful.

Ver. 13. "I will also stretch out mine hand upon Edom." In ver. 7, the Lord had said that he would stretch out his hand upon Ammon; that is, he would severely punish it; so now, also, he would "stretch it out upon Edom," and make it exemplary by his judgments; he would "stretch out his hand," not to help, but to destroy "Edom."

"I will cut off man and beast from it." It was a populous country, and abounded much in cattle, but God would cut them all off; Isa. xxxiv. 6, he would make "a great slaughter in the land of Idumea," his sword should eat the fat, and drink the blood, of lambs, goats, and rams.

"And I will make it desolate from Teman." Teman was a principal city in Idumea: Jer. xlix. 7, "Concerning Edom, thus saith the Lord of hosts; Is wisdom no more in Teman? is counsel perished from the prudent? is their wisdom vanished?" Jerom makes it to be in Edom, and intimates to us that the people of "Teman" were wise, learned, and understanding. The inhabitants hereof were called "Temanites," 1 Chron. i. 45, and so all that dwelt thereabouts. In Job you read of "Eliphaz the Temanite," Job xv. 1; xlii. 7, 9; he was of this city, so called from Teman the son of Eliphaz, which Eliphaz was the eldest son of Esau, Gen. xxxvi. 15. Jerom tells us, that the Hebrews call all the south region Theman, and therefore both he and the Septuagint sometimes do render it, the south. From this city, even to Dedan, should all be laid desolate.

"They of Dedan shall fall by the sword." "Dedan" was another city of note in the opposite part of the country to Teman, or a part of Idumea; so called from Dedan that descended from Cush, Gen. x. 6, 7; or that Dedan who was from Jokshan, 1 Chron. i. 32: it was a rich and merchandizing place or city, Ezek. xxvii. 15: the men and merchants of it God threatened to cut off by the sword.

Ver. 14. "And I will lay my vengeance upon Edom." The word for "vengeance" is, נקמה in the Septuagint, ἐκδίκησις, which, in 2 Thess. i. 8, is rendered "vengeance," which is a wrathful retribution of evil, as Leigh saith in his Critica Sacra, or a punishing of sinners unto destruction: it is peculiar to the Lord; see Deut. xxxii. 35; Rom. xii. 19. The meaning here is, that God would punish Edom so as Edom should be destroyed.

"By the hand of my people Israel." The word "hand" is taken by some interpreters for the Babylonians, by whose "hand" and power the Jews were smitten and broken; them God would stir up to be avenged on the Edomites, for their unbrotherly dealings with the Jews. It is true, they were shortly after subdued by the Babylonians, for God had promised to give Edom and other nations unto Nebuchadnezzar, Jer. xxvii. 3, 6: but notwithstanding this were so, that which I find in the prophecy of Obadiah, ver. 18, "The house of Jacob shall be a fire, and the house of Joseph a flame, and the house of Esau for stubble, and they shall kindle in them, and devour them; and there shall not be any remaining of the house of Esau;" this prophecy enforceth me to understand by "hand" here, the "hand" of the Jews, and not of the Babylonians. God would bring back the Jews again from their captivity, and by them plague the Edomites, waste and consume them by their hands, as stubble by a fire; which was done in the time of the Maccabees, 2 Mac. x. 15—23; there you shall find that Judas Maccabæus slew of the Edomites forty thousand. It was prophesied long before, that Edom and Seir should be possessed by the Jews, Numb. xxiv. 18.

Vide Joseph. l. 13. Antiq. c. 17.

"They shall do in Edom according to mine anger and according to my fury." "Mine anger" and "my fury" is great against the Edomites, and whatever thoughts Edomites or Jews have in them, judgments shall be executed upon the one by the other, according to "mine anger," not their anger; according to "my fury," not their fury.

"And they shall know my vengeance." They shall have experience thereof, they shall feel the weight of my "vengeance," and acknowledge it to be very heavy. The Jews had it laid upon them before, and the weight of it brake them in pieces, at which they sported themselves; now by their hand it should be laid upon the Edomites, and they should know and acknowledge that the God of Israel was another kind of God than the gods of the nations.

Obs. 1. That bearing grudges in the mind, and seeking revenge thereupon, doth highly displease the Lord, and put under much guilt. Edom had former unkindnesses in mind, and acted revengefully when opportunity served; by this he contracted great guilt, he greatly offended. Men ought to forgive one another, and not bag up malice in their hearts: Lev. xix. 18, revenge is flatly against the command; ver. 19, it is against the light of nature, which teaches us to do as we would be done unto; it is thrusting God out of his office, and putting ourselves into his place; Heb. x. 30, and these things bring us under dreadful guilt, and make us great offenders. Though revenge be sweet, yet it will be bitterness in the end; therefore let us learn that needful and unpractised lesson, "Owe nothing to any man, but to love one another," Rom. xiii. 8; owe them no hatred, Lev. xix. 18; no grudges, James v. 9; no bitterness, nor evil words, Eph. iv. 31; but owe love, much love, fervent love, constant love, yea fruitful love, one unto another.

Obs. 2. Bitter and malicious practices of brethren against brethren, especially in their misery, cause God to bring in severe and consuming judgments. The Edomites dealt bitterly and maliciously against the house of Judah, and therefore the Lord stretched out his hand upon Edom, cut off man and beast from it, and made it like a wilderness from Teman to Dedan. Their unbrotherly, their enemy-like carriage to the Jews in their distress, was their undoing; see Amos i. 11, 12; and take what Obadiah gives you, ver. 10, "For thy violence against thy brother Jacob shame shall cover thee, and thou shalt be cut off for ever." The papists in Ireland, those Edomites, how bitter, how cruel and bloody, were they against the house of Jacob, all the protestants! and hath not their own doings covered them with shame, and caused them to be cut off for ever? The Edomites in this land, and those in Scotland, how unbrotherly did they deal with us in our low estate! how did they insult over us, speak proudly, and lay their hands upon our substance! and these dealings of theirs have caused the Lord to bring sharp and consumptive judgments upon them.

Obs. 3. When sore judgments and destructive punishments do come upon nations, it is God that doth bring them, whosoever be the executioners of them. In this chapter God takes it off upon himself, "I will lay my vengeance upon Edom;" and ten times before; I will deliver Ammon, ver. 4; "I will make Rabbath a stable for camels," ver. 5; "I will stretch out mine hand, I will cut thee off, I will cause thee to perish, I will destroy thee," ver. 7; "I will open the side of Moab," ver. 9; "I will execute judgments," ver. 11; "I will stretch out my hand, I will make it desolate," ver. 13; and thrice more in the chapter afterwards. Men are backward to eye God; when judgments come, they will not see his hand: the hands of men they see and feel, and thereupon fret, rage, meditate revenge, disquiet themselves, plot mischief, and attempt changes; but did they see God's hand laying vengeance upon them, they would see also how justly he had done it, even for their sins, and so humble themselves, be quiet, submit, and accept the punishment of their iniquities. God hath laid his vengeance upon nations near us, and farther off; they do not, they will not see the Lord, or his hand, but they shall see, and be ashamed for their envy at his people: whatever vengeance is upon any nation, it is the Lord's vengeance, not man's.

Obs. 4. It is God's method to plague and punish the wrongers by the wronged. The Edomites dealt wretchedly, cruelly, against the house of Judah, they were the wrongers, the oppressors; and what saith God? "I will lay my vengeance upon Edom by the hand of my people Israel;" they were the wronged. The Edomites thought the Jews should never be able to get up again, or trouble them, but God had his time to make them instruments to plague and punish those who had entreated them so ill: Obad. 21, the Lord caused "saviours to come up on mount Zion to judge the mount of Esau;" after the Babylonish captivity, the house of Jacob grew strong, became terrible as fire, and burnt the Edomites as stubble and straw: those they had despised and insulted over, at last they suffered by.

Obs. 5. When God employs men to be instruments of executing his judgments, they are carried forth so far as he pleaseth. "They shall do in Edom according to mine anger and according to my fury:" God had conceived great anger against them, had much fury to let out, therefore they should destroy man and beast, make it desolate from one end or side of the country to the other.

Obs. 6. The vengeance of God is an awakening and distinguishing thing. "They shall know my vengeance;" that I am a God of infinite power, most holy and just, differing from all the gods of the nations.

Ver. 15—17. *Thus saith the Lord God; Because the Philistines have dealt by revenge, and have taken vengeance with a despiteful heart, to destroy it for the old hatred; therefore thus saith the Lord God; Behold, I will stretch out mine hand upon the Philistines, and I will cut off the Cherethims, and destroy the remnant of the sea coasts. And I will execute great vengeance upon them with furious rebukes; and they shall know that I am the Lord, when I shall lay my vengeance upon them.*

These verses are a prophecy against the Philistines; where you may take notice of,

I. Their sin; they were revengeful, ver. 15.

II. Their punishment; cutting off, destruction, ver. 16.

III. The manner of God's punishing them; ver. 17, "with furious rebukes."

IV. The end of his punishments; ver. 17, "they shall know that I am the Lord."

Ver. 15. "The Philistines." They came out of the loins of Casluhim, Mizraim, and Ham, Gen. x. 6, 13, 14. Their country was Palestina, which was west of Judea, and bordering upon the sea; it had five great cities in it, Ashdod, Gaza, Askelon, Gath, and Ekron, 1 Sam. vi. 17, each of which had its lord, Josh. xiii. 3. The Septuagint calls them ἀλλόφυλοι, men of another stock, race, nothing allied to the Jews. They owned not the God of Israel, but had other gods, Judg. x. 6. Dagon was a chief god of theirs, Judg. xvi. 23; they had a house of gods, 1 Chron. x. 10; poor and petty gods, that were confined to and comprehended in a house. These Philistines were men of war; they had the Jews under their power eighteen years together, Judg. x. 7, 8; yea, forty years together, Judg. xiii. 1. In Samuel's days, they slew thirty thousand footmen at once, and took the ark of God, 1 Sam. iv. 11; they slew Saul and his three sons in another battle, whereupon they came to possess many cities of the Israelites, 1 Sam. xxxi. They were the greatest enemies the Jews had, and more frequent wars were between them and the Jews than any other.

"Have dealt by revenge." The Hebrew is, for that thou hast had to do in revenge, which is an act of an ulcerous mind, repaying evil for evil. The word נקמה revenge, hath affinity with קום *kam*, to rise up. The revenger riseth up against him who hath wronged him, be the injury real or in imagination, and satisfieth himself for the same. The Philistines, as they had oft conquered and kept under the Jews, so they had oft been conquered and held under by the Jews. Samson in his days plagued and slew many of them, Judg. xiv. xv. xvi. So in Samuel's and Jonathan's times, they suffered much, 1 Sam. vii. 13, and chap. xiv.; but David, 2 Sam. v. viii. xxi. was the great champion that subdued them. Hezekiah also smote them, 2 Kings xviii. 8; and Uzziah brake down the walls of their strong cities, and built cities among the Philistines, 2 Chron. xxvi. 6. These acts of the Jews lodged in their hearts, rankled, begat malicious thoughts in them, and made them from generation to generation to meditate revenge; and having an opportunity, upon the Babylonians coming to besiege Jerusalem, they fell in with them, furnished them with men, ammunition, and what they could, to destroy the Jews.

"And have taken vengeance with a despiteful heart." The words in the original run thus, and have revenged a revenge with contempt in the mind: they contemned and despised them in their hearts, minds, and were glad they had an opportunity to be revenged on them. Piscator reads the words, they did from their heart take vengeance on Jerusalem, by depopulating it: they were very spiteful against them, and used them with the greatest scorn and spitefulness they could. Matt. v. 44, "Pray for them which despitefully use you;" the word for "despitefully use" is, ἐπηρεάζω, from Ἀρης, *Mars*, *bellum*, war, because where there are despiteful actions, there is a hostile and warlike insulting over others, and seeking their harm, yea, oft their ruin.

"To destroy it for the old hatred." Montanus turns the Hebrew thus, to destroy through the enmity of the age; it is like they had great enmity against the Jews at that time; but in the margin he hath it, *inimicitiis perpetuis*, the Philistines had perpetual enmity against them, and upon all occasions manifested it. Œcolampadius, to destroy the eternal hatreds which were between them: the Philistines now made account so to destroy the Jews, as that they should never be troubled or harmed by them more. Our translation is good, which saith, "the old hatred." They hated the Jews from the beginning; Gen. xxvi. 18, the Philistines stopped the wells Abraham had digged, and contended with Isaac when his servants digged new ones; so that he named one Esek, the other Sitnah, that is, Contention and Hatred, ver. 20, 21: and after, the Jews obtaining many victories over them, their hatred increased; and especially for David's slaying their Goliath, 1 Sam. xvii. burning their images, 2 Sam. v. 21, and killing their four giants, 2 Sam. xxi. and making them tributaries. They knew that the Jews and Jerusalem had plagued them many years, and now out of that old hatred they bare to it and them, they would destroy both.

Ver. 16. "I will stretch out mine hand upon the Philistines." Of stretching out the hand, the 7th and 13th verses gave occasion to speak. God had forborne them notwithstanding all their enmity and evil doings against the Jews, but now he would appear and punish them, his hand should bring destruction upon them.

"I will cut off the Cherethims." They were a people dwelling near the sea coast in Palestina, warlike and fierce; they had been subdued by David, and served him, 2 Sam. viii. 18; xv. 18; xx. 7. It is conceived they were David's guard. Some derive their name from כרת *excindere*, because they were men of might, able to cut off and destroy. Symmachus and Theodotion render the word "Cherethims," destroyers. Whatever they were, God here threatens their ruin; and so in Zeph. ii. 5, "Woe unto the inhabitants of the sea coast, the nation of the Cherethites!"

"And destroy the remnant of the sea coast." Those that dwelt upon the coast of the Mediterranean sea. In the Hebrew it is, the remnant of the haven of the sea, that is, the Philistines, whose bounds were the sea.

Ver. 17. "And I will execute great vengeance upon them." In the 11th verse the Lord said he would "execute judgments upon Moab;" in the 14th verse, he would "lay vengeance upon Edom;" and here, he "will execute great vengeance upon" the Philistines and Cherethims. The Hebrew is, great vengeances; they are such as do destroy, and are without mercy.

"With furious rebukes." In the Hebrew it is, with rebukes of fury. God would lay aside all mercy and pity, he would not only be angry, but wrathful, hot, fiery. חמה which is fury, *a calore dicitur;* for both יחם and חמם from one of which it comes, signify to grow hot; and fury is nothing else but *fervor iræ*, the heat and height of anger: and in such a mood would God rebuke them; they should not have verbal rebukes, but real rebukes.

Obs. 1. Enmity once bred between nations, dieth not away, but groweth up, and vents itself upon all occasions. The Philistines took the actions done by the Jews against them so ill, that they hated them, grew in their hatred, and showed their hatefulness of them whenever they had opportunity. In the 15th verse there are several gradations: (1.) They hated the Jews. (2.) Their hatred continued, they would not lay it down, but let it proceed from generation to generation; it was "old hatred," such as had been in their fathers, grandfathers, great grandfathers, and their predecessors many hundred years. (3.) It was not a secret hatred, but such as put them upon "revenge," and brake out in action. (4.) Such as was not content with a few revengeful actions, but carried them on to trade in such actions; they "dealt by revenge," it was their constant practice. (5.) Their heart was in the same, they were given to it, set upon it. (6.) Their hatred was joined with despite, they did insult and domineer over the Jews in their affliction. And, (7.) Their end was the destroying and rooting out of the Jewish nation; they took "vengeance with a despiteful heart, to destroy it for the old hatred." They neighbouring upon the Jews, did oft infest them. In Ahaz's days they invaded the south of Judah, took "Beth-shemesh, and Ajalon, and Gederoth, and Shocho with the villages thereof, and Timnah with the villages thereof, Gimzo also and the villages thereof; and dwelt there," 2 Chron. xxviii. 18. Their hatred to the Jews was implacable and immortal. When enmity began once between Judah and Israel, it lasted from age to age: "There was war between Jeroboam and Rehoboam all their days," 1 Kings xiv. 30: so for Asa and Baasha, there was nothing between them but acts of hatred and hostility, 1 Kings xv. 32.

Obs. 2. Those that hate, oppose, and evil entreat the people of God, he will be revenged on, and that severely. The Philistines dealt despitefully and revengefully with the Jews, and therefore the Lord would cut them off, "execute great vengeance upon them," and that "with furious rebukes." God's people are dear unto him, he that touches them touches the apple of God's eye, Zech. ii. 8: because the Ammonites, Moabites, Edomites, dealt injuriously with the Jews, therefore God laid his vengeance upon them, cut them off, and rooted them out. The Egyptians tyrannized over them in their minority,

and God drowned them in the bottom of the Red sea for it. Sooner or later God met with and plagued all the nations round about the Jews, who dealt unkindly and despitefully with them. The Babylonians were called of God to punish the Jews for their wickedness, but because they carried it bloodily and insultingly against the people of God, Jer. l. 11, therefore the Lord destroyed Babylon and took "vengeance on her," ver. 15, even "vengeance of his temple," ver. 28. God is now at this time revenging the wrongs of his people, done by antichrist and the antichristian party.

CHAPTER XXVI.

Ver. 1—6. *And it came to pass in the eleventh year, in the first day of the month, that the word of the Lord came unto me, saying, Son of man, because that Tyrus hath said against Jerusalem, Aha, she is broken that was the gates of the people: she is turned unto me: I shall be replenished, now she is laid waste: therefore thus saith the Lord God; Behold, I am against thee, O Tyrus, and will cause many nations to come up against thee, as the sea causeth his waves to come up. And they shall destroy the walls of Tyrus, and break down her towers: I will also scrape her dust from her, and make her like the top of a rock. It shall be a place for the spreading of nets in the midst of the sea: for I have spoken it, saith the Lord God: and it shall become a spoil to the nations. And her daughters which are in the field shall be slain by the sword; and they shall know that I am the Lord.*

EZEKIEL having prophesied against the Ammonites, Moabites, Edomites, and Philistines in the former chapter, here he proceeds in prophesying against the Tyrians, foretelling their destruction. In the chapter we have,

I. The time when this prophecy was, ver. 1.

II. The sin of the Tyrians, which caused God here to threaten their destruction, ver. 2.

III. Their destruction, and by whom, with the events thereof, in the rest of the chapter.

IV. The end of God's dealing thus with them, ver. 6.

Ver. 1. "In the eleventh year, the first day of the month." It is evident what year Ezekiel had this prophecy given in, viz. in the eleventh year of Zedekiah's reign, and Jehoiachin's captivity, both which run upon the same account; but for the month it is controverted. Some make it to be the fourth month of the said year, nine days before the city was broken up, Jer. lii. 5—7, which is not mentioned hence by the prophet, because it was such a black and sad month unto the Jews: but if this were a sufficient reason, why did Jeremiah mention it? and why is it expressed 2 Kings xxv. 3? Others make it to be the fifth month, which was the first month after Jerusalem was taken. Between the ninth day of the fourth month and the first day of the fifth month, there being twenty days, the tidings of Jerusalem's ruin came to the Tyrians, who thereupon insulted, and said, "she is broken," ver. 2; which was a great affliction to the superviving Jews, oppressed with miseries, and going into captivity, and would be no less to those who were formerly in Babylon, when they should hear of it.

Note hence, That there are remarkable times when God gives in a word to his servants. When Jerusalem was taken, broken up, and burnt, when heathens insulted over the poor Jews, then "the word of the Lord" came to the prophet, then he must prophesy against their enemies, which was some matter of comfort unto them in their great and extreme sufferings.

Ver. 2. "Because that Tyrus hath said against Jerusalem." The first mention of Tyre in holy writ, is Josh. xix. 29, where it is placed within the lot of Asher, and not in the tribe of Naphtali, as Jerom and Eusebius affirm. And though it were given to Asher, yet that tribe never had possession of it. In Hebrew it is called *Tzur*, or *Tzor*, (which signifies a strait, a rock,) because it was built upon a rock. The Greeks, who could not well pronounce *tzaddi*, turned that into *tau*, whence it was called *Tur*, and so Tyrus. This city was very ancient; Isaiah tells you the antiquity of it; it was "of ancient days," chap. xxiii. 7. Dionysius Alexandrinus called it, The ancient city. And Pliny
Mus. in Josh. xix. calls it, The mother of most ancient cities. It was built above four hundred years before the temple, and more, though Josephus
Lib. 8. Ant. c. 2. saith it was but two hundred and forty years. It was no part of the land of Canaan, but a strong city, in an island seven hundred paces distant from the continent; Junius saith, about one hundred. Hiram, who loved David, and furnished Solomon with cedars for building the temple, was king thereof, 1 Kings v. It was a famous mart town, first taken by Nebuchadnezzar, and after by Alexander, who made it of an island, a peninsula. Tyrus here is put for the Tyrians.

"Aha, she is broken that was the gates of the people." Here was the sin of the Tyrians, they cried, "Aha," when Jerusalem was taken and ruined by the Babylonians, and so insulted over them in their afflicted estate; they said, "she is broken that was the gates of the people." Jerusalem was a city that had many gates, Jer. xvii. 19; whether twelve or more, it matters not: by these gates which it had on every side people of all parts entered into it; so that the confluence of people to Jerusalem, partly for worship, and partly for trading, was very great; she was "full of people, great among the nations, and princess among the provinces," Lam. i. 1. And therefore, because people of all nations had free ingress into her, and egress out of her gates, she is called "the gates of the people;" by "gates" also is noted strength, power, and so Jerusalem was the "gates of the people." The sense is this, Jerusalem hath had all nations flocking thither, crowding in at her gates, but now her strong gates are broken, she is desolate, no foot shall come thither to worship or trade any more.

"She is turned unto me." Now Tyrus shall be Jerusalem, my gates shall be the gates of the people, all that flocked thither will come unto me; I shall now have the great trading and commerce with nations which Jerusalem had. Tyrus was a rich city, had great trading, Isa. xxiii. 3; yet rejoiced in the ruin of Jerusalem, because her merchandizing and wealth would be increased hereby.

"I shall be replenished." My gates, my streets, my shops, my houses, my harbours, my places for worship, shall be filled all of them, and that as much as ever Jerusalem's were; now the people and wealth of all nations will come flowing in to me, so that my greatness, riches, and glory, will equalize, if not exceed, Jerusalem's.

"Now she is laid waste." The Hebrew is, החרבה from חרב to dry up. Now all her streams and springs are dried, now she is like the channel of a river without water or fish, now the pressing in of people at her gates is ceased, now her merchants fail her, now her wealth, strength, and glory are laid in the dust, now she is dry, desolate, and waste.

Ver. 3. "Behold, I am against thee, O Tyrus." This was sad news for Tyrus; to have God declare himself against her, was more than if all nations had done it. The Hebrew is, I am above thee; thou hast lifted up thyself against Jerusalem, and above other cities, but I am above and against thee; I, that am the great God of heaven and earth, that shake the foundations of the world, that have all nations at my command, behold, I am above thee, I am coming against thee.

"And will cause many nations to come up against thee." Nebuchadnezzar had divers nations and provinces under his command. God would order it so, that he should bring an army made up of those nations against Tyrus: what cruelty and violence was wanting in one nation, should be made up in another.

"As the sea causeth his waves to come up." The waves come up thick when the wind blows, they rise, they roar, they rage, they break the ships in pieces; so when God should breathe out a word of command to the nations, they should come like waves of the sea, raging, threatening, and ruining all. Armies and forces are likened to the sea, great waters, and their waves, which roar and destroy. Jer. l. 42; li. 42, there Cyrus his great army is called a sea roaring, and covering Babylon with her waves.

Ver. 4. "And they shall destroy the walls of Tyrus." Cities and towns of note, especially upon the sea coast, use to be well walled; such was Tyrus, being upon a rock in the sea, it had strong walls; but they should be destroyed, and the towers thereof broken down.

"I will also scrape her dust from her, and make her like the top of a rock." God would so destroy Tyrus, that no monument of her shall remain, there shall not be any piece of a house, tower, or wall, not one stone left upon another: I will raze her foundation, and that dust which comes by so doing I will take away, there shall be nothing visible but "the top of a rock;" such as that place and rock was before Tyrus was built, such should it be again. God would exceedingly, yea, utterly deface that city. The word for "scrape" is from סחה *sucha*, to sweep or pare off dirt from the pavement. Septuagint is, λικμήσω, I will fan her dust from her.

Ver. 5. "It shall be a place for the spreading of nets in the midst of the sea." It shall serve for no other use but the nets of fishermen; when they have done their fishing in the sea, they shall come thither, and spread their nets there for drying and mending: where now are pleasant gardens, orchards, walks, stately palaces and buildings, where none but merchants and men of quality come, even there shall poor fishermen come, and spread their nets.

"For I have spoken it, saith the Lord God." You think this impossible, that a city upon a rock in the sea, strongly built, strongly walled and towered, that hath stood many hundred years, should be brought to nothing, and made as a plain or flat for fishermen to spread their nets on; but "I have spoken it, saith the Lord," and I am a God of truth, and able to make good my word.

"It shall become a spoil to the nations." It hath great store of merchants' goods, of ware, and wealth; it is a rich city, and shall be for a prey to the nations; they shall come, take, and carry away all that is in it.

Ver. 6. "And her daughters which are in the

field," &c. Tyrus had many towns and cities upon the land under her command, and these are here called her "daughters in the field:" Solomon gave Hiram, in his days, twenty cities in the land of Galilee, for the gold, cedars, and fir trees he furnished him with, 1 Kings ix. 11; and it is without dispute that he, being king of Tyre, had other towns and cities belonging to him, all which are called "daughters," Tyrus being the metropolis and chief city. Great cities had towns belonging to them, 1 Chron. vii. 28, 29; 2 Chron. xxviii. 18; and these were called "daughters," Jer. xlix. 2, 3; Lam. iii. 51; Ezek. xvi. 46, 48, 49, 53, 55. If we take "daughters" here for the women of Tyre, widows, wives, and maids, who walked out into the fields, Lavater will join issue with us. Understand it of which you will, it is certain both were destroyed by the judgments of God.

Obs. 1. That when God's people are severely dealt with by the Lord for their sins, others do impiously and inhumanly scoff at and insult over them. When Jerusalem was sacked by the Babylonians, the Tyrians cried, "Aha, she is broken:" so the Ammonites, chap. xxv. 3, they had their "Aha" against the sanctuary, and land of Israel: so Ezek. xxxvi. 2, the enemy said, "Aha," against the Jews. Nature teacheth men to sympathize with those who are in misery, not to multiply their miseries by scoffs and mocks; but the nations showed themselves impious and unnatural in dealing so with the Jews. The like may God's people expect now from the world; if they meet with breaking for their sins, the men of the world will say, "Aha," so would we have it; others' mourning is their music, others' tears are their wine.

Obs. 2. That merchandizing cities, through their envy and covetousness, are glad at the ruin of other cities, expecting to enrich themselves thereby. Tyrus was a city of merchants, Isa. xxiii. 11, had great trading, was rich, yet she envied Jerusalem, saying, "she is the gates of the people," she hath the great concourse of all sorts from all nations entering into her, and merchandizing with her; but now "she is broken, she is turned unto me;" all that traded with and enriched her, will come to me, and I shall be replenished: thus she manifested her covetousness, and hope of being enriched by the breaking of Jerusalem. When a city flourishes, and hath great trading, other cities envy them, and if mischief befall them, they are glad, gaping then to be made by their miseries: this is the disposition of merchants and merchandizing places, they look too much at themselves, and so they may gain, it matters not who are losers: let Jerusalem go down, so Tyrus may go up. To rejoice in the ruins of others is wretched, but to rejoice therein that we may be enriched, is accursed. Some are glad when their neighbours' houses are on fire; when they break, they think thereby they shall be made, have the greater trading, be replenished, &c. Let tradesmen and merchants look to it; this was the sin of Tyrus, and did not a little displease the Lord.

Obs. 3. Rejoicing in, and desire to be enriched by, the harms of others, provokes God, so as to bring destruction upon cities and citizens. The Tyrians did so, therefore saith God, "Behold, I am against thee, O Tyrus, and will cause many nations to come up against thee. And they shall destroy thy walls, thy towers, thy daughters, and thou shalt be a spoil unto them." To insult over others in their miseries, and to make a prey of them through covetousness, are dangerous sins; God looks we should pity and help men suffering, by our prayers, counsels, estates; not that we should add to their afflictions, and make their furnace hotter; such doings heat God's fury, and cause it to break out unto destruction: upon this account the Ammonites, Moabites, Edomites, and Philistines, were destroyed. Let us then not sport ourselves at the sufferings of others, nor expect raising from their ruins. "Covetousness is the root of all evil;" it emptied Tyre of its wealth and citizens, yea, helped on its utter desolation.

Obs. 4. The Lord hath the command of nations, and calls them forth when and to what service he pleases. "I will cause many nations to come up against thee." He is "King of nations," Jer. x. 7; "Governor among the nations," Psal. xxii. 28; and if he call, they come; Isa. v. 26, he will "lift up an ensign to the nations," he will "hiss unto them," and "behold, they shall come with speed:" and let the Lord make known his mind by word or sign, by any acts of his providence, and the nations come presently, and are ready to do what he will, to assault cities, even Jerusalem, Rabbah, Tyre, or Babylon itself: Jer. l. 9, "I will raise and cause to come up against Babylon an assembly of great nations from the north country: and they shall set themselves in array against her." God hath the command of great nations, and can cause them to come out of their countries, and do him service, where he please. Let us then fear this God, who hath such command, and say, "Who would not fear thee, O King of nations? for to thee doth it appertain."

Ver. 7—14. *For thus saith the Lord God; Behold, I will bring upon Tyrus Nebuchadrezzar king of Babylon, a king of kings, from the north, with horses, and with chariots, and with horsemen, and companies, and much people. He shall slay with the sword thy daughters in the field: and he shall make a fort against thee, and cast a mount against thee, and lift up the buckler against thee. And he shall set engines of war against thy walls, and with his axes he shall break down thy towers. By reason of the abundance of his horses their dust shall cover thee: thy walls shall shake at the noise of the horsemen, and of the wheels, and of the chariots, when he shall enter into thy gates, as men enter into a city wherein is made a breach. With the hoofs of his horses shall he tread down all thy streets: he shall slay thy people by the sword, and thy strong garrisons shall go down to the ground. And they shall make a spoil of thy riches, and make a prey of thy merchandise: and they shall break down thy walls, and destroy thy pleasant houses: and they shall lay thy stones and thy timber and thy dust in the midst of the water. And I will cause the noise of thy songs to cease; and the sound of thy harps shall be no more heard. And I will make thee like the top of a rock: thou shalt be a place to spread nets upon; thou shalt be built no more: for I the Lord have spoken it, saith the Lord God.*

In these verses is set out,

I. What instrument the Lord will use in this great work of destroying Tyre, and that is, Nebuchadrezzar, with his forces, ver. 7.

II. A narration of his doings, ver. 8—12.

III. The events following thereupon, ver. 13, 14.

Ver. 7. "I will bring upon Tyrus Nebuchadrezzar king of Babylon." This name, "Nebuchadrezzar," we had not in our prophet before; most often it is written, Nebuchadnezzar, yet it is thirty-one times in Jeremiah and Ezekiel "Nebuchadrezzar."

It is a compound name of *Nebo chad* and *netzar* or *retzar*, which are proper and simple Chaldee names, serving to distinguish the Chaldee king from the Assyrian: *Nebo*, according to their account, is one, *chad*, twenty-four, and *netzar*, seven. Nebuchadnezzar some make to signify, the bewailing of that judgment, which is a pressure; Nebuchadrezzar, the mourning of the generation of straitening; he was a man that did oppress and straiten the nations much, and made them to mourn. This man was "king of Babylon," and not only so, but "king of kings," that is, either the chiefest of all kings, or one that had many kings under him; he was a universal monarch, Dan. ii. 37, 38; and, as appears by Jer. lii. 32, left many kings under the power of Evil-merodach, who succeeded him.

Vid. Martin. Lexicon.

Lavater.

Ver. 8. "He shall make a fort against thee, and cast a mount against thee." He shall besiege thee, and use all warlike instruments to batter and break thee. This undertaking of Nebuchadrezzar was very difficult. Tyrus was so situated and fortified, that it was thought impregnable, and had not Nebuchadrezzar been a man exceeding resolute and obstinate in his designs, he had fainted in this business, for the siege lasted thirteen years, as Junius observes out of Josephus, and he out of Berosus, Philostratus, and other Phœnician writers; Ithobalus then reigning there. Hence Ezekiel, chap. xxix. 18, saith, that "Nebuchadrezzar caused his army to serve a great service against Tyre:" for an army to lie thirteen years before a city on a rock in the sea, was a "great service," which he and his army endured, and went through.

Usher's Annals, p. 133.

Ver. 9. "He shall set engines of war against thy walls." The Hebrew is, מחי קבלו the blow of his slings, or battering-rams, shall he give against thy walls; the words properly sound thus, the smiting of her adversary. The walls being over-against these engines, they were their adversaries, and them they did smite and batter.

Ver. 10. "By reason of the abundance of his horses their dust shall cover thee." The "horses" employed in the service were so numerous, that they raised great clouds of "dust," which fell upon their habitations, orchards, and gardens, like snow, and covered them.

"Thy walls shall shake at the noise of the horsemen," &c. Such should be the rattling and "noise" of horses and chariots, that the earth, and things founded upon it, should "shake;" or such fear should the inhabitants be stricken withal, that they should apprehend all to be tottering and shaken.

"As men enter into a city wherein is made a breach." Hebrew, according to the entrance of a city which is broken up. When the walls of a city were broken down, there is great shouting, and men enter with great noise, triumphing, and tumult, which makes the earth to ring, and fills all with trembling.

Ver. 11. "Thy strong garrisons shall go down to the ground." The Hebrew for "strong garrisons" is, מצבות עזך the statues of thy strength. Tyrus being upon a rock in the sea, it is probable had many arches and pillars to support it. The Septuagint is, the subsistence or underpropping of thy strength, or, whatever thou hast gotten to bear thee up. Some by *mazeboth*, statues, lead us to their tutelar gods, Hercules and Apollo, whose statues, saith Pradus, the Tyrians kept bound with chains. The Vulgate hath it, thy noble statues; that is, those statues which were erected for those men who had done great and heroical exploits: their idol gods, their statues, should be thrown down to the earth, and whatever they had considerable in the city. Rabbi David renders the words, the towers of thy strength, or strong towers, which suits with our translation; "thy strong garrisons," even those wherein the Tyrians did much confide, should be levelled with the ground.

Ver. 12. "They shall make a spoil of thy riches," &c. They should take and carry away all that was profitable and portable; and as for other things, they should break them down, and throw them into the sea; their walls, houses of desire, the stones, timber, and dust of the city, should be thrown into the waters. Such should be the ruin of this strong and famous city, that the dust of it should not remain.

Ver. 13. "I will cause the noise of thy songs to cease," &c. "and the sound of thy harps," &c. The Tyrians, being a rich people, were jovial and merry; Ezek. xxviii. 13, they had their tabrets and pipes, their "harps" and "songs;" they so abounded in mirth and music, that their city was called the "joyous city;" Isa. xxiii. 7, "Is this your joyous city?" they were given to delights and sensuality. God would cause their mirth to cease; Jer. xxv. 10, he would take away the "voice of mirth," the "voice of gladness," &c.; God would turn their mirth into mourning, their "songs" into howlings; they should be for a long season in a darksome and suffering condition.

Ver. 14. "Thou shalt be built no more." These words we must not take simply and absolutely, for then they will contradict Isa. xxiii. 15, 16, where it is foretold, that after seventy years Tyre should be again, and sing. The mind, then, of the words is this, "Thou shalt be built no more" to be the metropolis of a kingdom; or, "Thou shalt be built no more" with that strength and glory thou wast before; or, "Thou shalt be built no more" to enjoy the same name, for that city built afterwards in the same place was called Palatyrus; or, "Thou shalt be built no more," that is, for a long time: the word עוד notes a jubilee, or long time.

Obs. 1. Things difficult and impossible in the apprehensions of men, are accomplished by the Lord. Tyrus was a strong city, upon a rock in the sea, had strong walls, towers, garrisons, endured a siege of thirteen years, yet was taken and levelled with the ground, which to men seemed incredible and impossible: therefore let not princes, merchants, citizens, confide in their strong holds, abundance of wealth, or any human foundation.

Obs. 2. The Lord makes places of renown contemptible, and subjects them to vulgar and inconsiderable uses. Tyrus was a famous city, the mart of nations, her merchants were princes, her traffickers the honourable of the earth, Isa. xxiii. 3, 8; and God made her like the top of a rock, a place for fishermen to spread nets upon.

Obs. 3. Wealthy cities are usually given to mirth and sensual delights, which God will make to cease. Tyrus was rich, and she had her songs, music, and sinful delights, which God made in time to cease.

Ver. 15—21. *Thus the Lord God to Tyrus; Shall not the isles shake at the sound of thy fall, when the wounded cry, when the slaughter is made in the midst of thee? Then all the princes of the sea shall come down from their thrones, and lay away their robes, and put off their broidered garments: they shall clothe themselves with trembling; they shall sit upon the ground, and shall tremble at every moment, and be astonished at thee. And they shall take up a lamentation for thee, and say to thee, How art thou destroyed, that wast inhabited of seafaring men, the renowned city, which wast strong in the sea, she and her inhabitants, which cause their terror to be on all that haunt it! Now shall the isles tremble in the day of thy fall; yea, the isles that are in the sea shall be troubled at thy departure. For thus saith the Lord God; When I shall make thee a desolate city, like the cities that are not inhabited; when I shall bring up the deep upon thee, and great waters shall cover thee; when I shall bring thee down with them that descend into the pit, with the people of old time, and shall set thee in the low parts of the earth, in places desolate of old, with them that go down to the pit, that thou be not inhabited; and I shall set glory in the land of the living; I will make thee a terror, and thou shalt be no more: though thou be sought for, yet shalt thou never be found again, saith the Lord God.*

In these verses the prophet proceeds in laying down events and consequences of Tyrus' destruction, As,

I. The shaking and trembling of the islanders, ver. 15, 16, 18, 21.

II. Their mourning and "lamentation" for Tyrus, ver. 17.

III. Desolateness of the place, ver. 19.

IV. Oblivion; she should be forgotten, ver. 20, 21; so destroyed, as not to be found.

"Shall not the isles shake at the sound of thy fall." They look to thee as impregnable, being fortified by art and nature beyond all other cities and places, but when they shall hear of thy fall, they shall tremble, fearing that ruin will be their portion if the enemy shall besiege and assault them. "Shall not the isles shake?" it is an interrogation, which imports they will shake, and shake greatly.

"When the wounded cry, when the slaughter is made in the midst of thee?" When great cities are taken, oft many are slain, and many are sorely wounded; and when the men in the neighbour islands should hear of their sufferings, cries, and fall of the city, they should be troubled, and stand amazed. The Hebrew for "slaughter" is double, בהרג הרג in slaughtering with a slaughter: the "slaughter" was great.

Ver. 16. "Then all the princes of the sea shall come down from their thrones." Tyrus was upon the Mediterranean sea, and that had many islands. Lavater tells us of eight, viz. Rhodes, Cyprus, Crete, Sicily, Melita, Sardinia, Samos, Chius; and others are mentioned, Acts xxvii. In some of these were princes, and they should bewail the fall of Tyrus: or, these were the principal islands of the sea, and had many principal mariners which sailed from port to port, and were as princes and commanders of that sea; both they, and the governors of the islands, shall be straitened and affected with the condition of Tyre; there was wont to be great trading between them and Tyrus, which now should cease.

"And lay away their robes." The Hebrew for "their robes" is, *meileehem,* מעיל by the Septuagint is rendered sometimes, ποδήρης, a coat, Exod. xxviii. 4; sometimes, ὑποδύτης, Exod. xxxix. 22; sometimes, ἐπενδύτης, 2 Sam. xiii. 18; sometimes, διπλοὶς, 1 Sam. xv. 27; sometimes, ϛόλη, Job ii. 12; sometimes, ἱμάτιον, Job i. 20; sometimes, χιτὼν, Isa. lxi. 10; and here, μιτρα: however the Septuagint express it by various words, it signifies such a garment as men of quality did wear.

"And put off their broidered garments." In the Hebrew it is, their garments of broidery. רקמה broidery, was spoken of, Ezek. xvi. 10; these they should "put off;" פשט which is the word for putting off, notes, a forcible putting off: they should. through anger and grief, pull off their rich coats with a violence, and throw them aside, when the news of Tyrus' ruin came unto them.

"They shall clothe themselves with trembling." They shall be greatly afraid, "trembling" shall take hold of them; they shall tremble and tremble; the word is in the plural number, tremblings, from חרד which signifies open and visible "trembling." The downfall and desolation of Tyre, that strong place, should fill them with such astonishment and fear, as they should openly tremble, or be clothed with tremblings, that is, put on such garments as testify grief and fear.

"They shall sit upon the ground." They that sat in the throne a little before, shall sit on the "ground." Sitting on the ground implies, a sad and troubled condition: Job ii. 13, Job and his friends, in the time of their sorrows and trouble, "sat upon the ground:" so Isa. xlvii. 1, Babylon is called to sit on the ground, that is, to a mourning condition, for the judgments which should come upon her: so the evils which came upon Jerusalem made her to "sit upon the ground," Isa. iii. 26, and her elders, Lam. ii. 10.

"And shall tremble every moment." They should have a continual fear upon them, lest Nebuchadrezzar should come, and deal by them as he had done by Tyrus, if that could not resist him; much less could they. The word for "every moment" is, *lir jaim;* a "moment" is a little fragment of time, and it may here note the moment past, as thus, they shall tremble for the moment, the sudden surprise and ruin of Tyrus; or the moment to come, they shall tremble from moment to moment, fearing there will be such a moment for them.

"And be astonished at thee." When they shall hear that thy walls and strong garrisons are broken down, that thy pleasant houses, stones, and timber are laid in the water, that thou art made like the top of a rock, they will be "astonished at thee," at thy desolation.

Ver. 17. "And they shall take up a lamentation for thee." When great judgments and changes fell out, many who were concerned therein did not only grieve, but took up "lamentations," and made a formal business thereof: Jer. xxxi. 15, so Rachel lamented for her children; so Ezekiel for the princes of Israel, Ezek. xix. 1, 14; so the kings of the earth for Babylon, Rev. xviii. 9, 10; and so the princes of the sea took up a "lamentation" for Tyrus.

"How art thou destroyed!" How hast thou perished! so is the original. It is a question full of admiration; they wondered that such a strong city, seated in the sea, that had stood so long inviolable, should now be destroyed. It is a question full of lamentation; "How art thou destroyed?" Oh it grieves us at the heart, and troubles our souls, that thou art thrown down, and laid in the water; we cannot believe it was by an ordinary power that thou art destroyed.

"That wast inhabited by seafaring men." Here is one argument which made the princes of the sea to say, "How art thou destroyed?" we wonder at it, we mourn for it, but cannot tell how it should be, seeing thou hadst a multitude of seamen from all parts, who were able to fetch in provisions upon all occasions to relieve thee, and sufficient to have kept out any enemy from entering into thee. The Hebrew here is, נושבת מימים inhabited by the seas, that is, by merchants and mariners, which dwelt in other sea towns, and came thither by the seas, to sojourn and trade.

"The renowned city." This was a second argument which begat astonishment and grief in them for the destruction of Tyre, she was a "renowned city." In Isa. xxiii. she is called the joyous, the crowning, the merchant city, and here, the "renowned city," העיר ההללה the city most praiseable: being a city of merchants, and these princes, and her traffickers "the honourable of the earth," Isa. xxiii. 8, she must needs be "renowned," and of great fame abroad; which made her friends wonder at her ruin, and mourn that she should be a place for fishermen, and spreading of nets.

"Which wast strong in the sea." Tyrus was a city upon a rock in the sea, the waters compassed it about, and made it an island, so that it was hard to come at; the waters, the rock, the walls, were choice protections to it, so that the "princes of the sea" thought it inaccessible, and if attempted, yet impregnable; and this made them to say, "How art thou destroyed?"

"She and her inhabitants, which cause their terror on all that haunt it!" Tyrus was so seated and fortified, that she was dreadful to all that knew her, to all the islands far and near. She was rich in shipping, furnished with all things needful for a naval expedition, and had the command of the seas, which caused "the princes of the sea" to wonder at, and greatly to lament for, her unexpected ruin.

Ver. 18. "Now shall the isles tremble in the day of thy fall." When some great tower or house is blown up by powder, or falls by an earthquake, it shakes all the houses and parts adjacent. So should the fall of Tyre be, it should make all the islands and islanders to "tremble" openly and visibly; for so חרד is interpreted by Kirker.

"Yea, the isles that are in the sea shall be troubled at thy departure." The word for "troubled" is from בהל which is, to be stricken with sudden fear and trouble: when they hear of thy departure, or going out, that thou art laid waste and become no city, they shall immediately be "troubled" and perplexed, fearing their own desolations and deaths, or captivities.

Ver. 19. "When I shall make thee a desolate city, like the cities that are not inhabited." A city without people is like a field without cattle, corn, or grass, a very wilderness, solitary and dangerous, by reason of serpents and wild beasts which lurk in it. Cities broken down, and uninhabited, are no better: such would the Lord make Tyrus.

"When I shall bring up the deep upon thee, and great waters shall cover thee." In ver. 3 he had said, he would cause "many nations" to come up against Tyrus, that was, a mighty army of Nebuchadrezzar's, which here he calls תהום "the deep," and המים הרבים many or "great waters." Great armies are like waters of the sea, which, breaking into countries, cities, and towns, do multiply their calamities, and lay them desolate.

Ver. 20. "When I shall bring thee down with them that descend into the pit." By "pit" is meant the grave: Psal. xxviii. 1, "Like them that go down into the pit;" that is, like them which die, and go down into the grave. בור signifies a "pit," a prison, a grave. Tyrus should become like one dead and buried.

"With the people of old time." The Hebrew is, אל-עם עולם to the people of old time. God had caused many by the flood, many by the sword, formerly to descend into the grave, and so should the Tyrians. The Vulgate translation is, to the everlasting people, that is, to those that lie from generation to generation in the dust, and must lie there till the day of judgment; to those that "sleep a perpetual sleep," as the phrase is, Jer. li. 57. That place in Lam. iii. 6, "He hath set me in dark places, as they that be dead of old," gives light unto this: those that were dead long ago, lie in the dark, are unseen, unknown, forgotten; and Tyrus, with her people, should be like unto them.

"And shall set thee in the low parts of the earth, in places desolate of old." Thou shalt be made like cities that were ruined long ago, and have no vestiges of them remaining: now thou art high, seen far at sea and land, but thou shalt shortly come down, and be as deep under water and earth as thou art now above them.

"And I shall set glory in the land of the living." "The land of the living" was Canaan, which is frequently so called by David: as, Psal. xxvii. 13; lii. 5; cxvi. 9; cxlii. 5: by Isaiah, chap. xxxviii. 11; liii. 8: by Jeremiah, chap. xi. 19: and by Ezekiel here it was so called, because there "the living God" was known and worshipped, Psal. xlii. 2, with Psal. lxxvi. 1, 2; because there were the living oracles, Acts vii. 38, the living waters, and wells of salvation, Isa. xii. 3; because there were the living saints, and only there. In other lands, though the people had wealth, honour, greatness, natural excellences, yet as to God they were dead, but in Canaan they were quickened and made alive.

For the setting glory therein, understand it of restoring Canaan, or Judea, unto its former condition. Tyrus, thou judgest Canaan now a land desolate, without temple, cities, people, and thinkest it shall for ever be so, but thy glory shall down, descend into the pit; and "I will set glory in the land of the living" again; Jerusalem shall live, and be glorious, but Tyrus shall die, and be ignominious. By "glory," Piscator understands the people, who, being carried into captivity, the Tyrians and heathens thought should never return; but God would bring them back, being his glory, into that land whereby they should enjoy the lively oracles, drink the living waters, and have the special presence and protection of the living God.

"Ver. 21. I will make thee a terror." The Hebrew is, terrors. Thou shalt be matter of terror to every island near or far off; when they shall hear of thy downfall, it shall terrify them. The word for "terror" may be rendered, consumption, being from בלה to wax old, to consume: I will so consume thee as that thy consumption shall be terrible to all others.

"Thou shalt be no more: though thou be sought for, yet shalt thou never be found again." Thou shalt be so demolished, as that a stone upon a stone shall not be left in thee; thou shalt be brought to a nothingness, how bushy and strong soever thou art now; and when thou shalt be sought, and inquired after, thou shalt not be found by this generation. The Hebrew is thus, thou shalt not be found any more for ever, that is, for a long time, so לעולם is oft used; as, Exod. xxi. 6; Psal. lxxxix. 1; Prov. xxix. 14; and so here, for ever, is not absolute, but, for a long time. After seventy years Tyrus was built again, or Palatyrus, near unto that place, but not by the Tyrians, who were either all slain, or carried so away captive, that they perished in their captivity; it was built by strangers.

Obs. 1. God, by his destructive judgments upon strong cities and great states being sinful, makes others to tremble that were secure. "Shall not the isles shake at the sound of thy fall, when the wounded cry, when the slaughter is made in the midst of thee?" God's destroying of Tyrus should awaken and affright all the isles and islanders who were secure, and laughed at the attempt of Nebuchadnezzar against Tyrus; they thought it impossible that ever he should take it, but, being taken and ruined, shaking seized upon them. When the sound of God's judgments come to men's ears, they startle them, and trouble them: Ezek. xxx. 4, "The sword shall come upon Egypt," that is, wars shall lay waste the Egyptians, and "great pain shall be in Ethiopia," their fear shall be such as shall pain and torment them: and, ver. 8, 9, God would set a fire in Egypt, destroy all their helpers, and then messengers should go forth from him in ships, to make the careless Ethiopian afraid. God destroys wicked cities, states, and people, that he may beget fear in others, who were careless. When the Lord drowned the Egyptians in the Red sea, it caused the nations to fear, Exod. xv. 14; when Sihon, king of Heshbon, and Og, king of Bashan, they and their people, were destroyed by Joshua and the Jews, then Balak and the Moabites were sore afraid, Numb. xxii. 2, 3; when God brought destruction upon Babylon, it made all hands faint, all hearts melt, they were as full of fears and pains as a woman in travail, Isa. xiii. 6—8.

Obs. 2. There is that dreadfulness in the judgments of God, as will drive the greatest out of their thrones and glory, make them tremble continually, put on sackcloth, and lie in the dust. "Then all the princes of the sea," be they never so great, so stout, "shall come down from their thrones, lay away their robes, and put off their broidered garments," &c. When Tyrus her streets were trodden down with the hoofs of Nebuchadnezzar's horses, her people slain, her strong garrisons thrown down to the ground, her riches become a prey to the enemy, her stones, timber, and dust laid in the water, then should fear seize upon these princes; the dreadfulness apprehended in that judgment of God should make them forget themselves, their glory, and greatness, and to sit upon the ground trembling, and fearing their own destruction from day to day. God's judgments make great changes; those that sat in the morning like princes in their thrones, commanding at sea and land, in a little time sit on the ground trembling. When the Syrians besieged Samaria, and the famine increased amongst them, it made Jehoram the king to fear, and wear sackcloth next his flesh, 2 Kings vi. 30; and did not Ben-hadad, the king of Syria, and all his men of might, fearing the noise of chariots, horses, and a great host, fear, flee for their lives, and throw away their garments? 2 Kings vii. 6, 7, 15. When the hand of God was stretched out for the Israelites, and against the Egyptians, the dukes of Edom were amazed, and the mighty men of Moab trembled, Exod. xv. 15. When Saul beheld the army of the Philistines, "he was afraid, and his heart greatly trembled," 1 Sam. xxviii. 5. When God brought the destroyer of the gentiles, viz. Nebuchadrezzar, to execute his judgments upon Judea and Jerusalem, then did the heart of king and princes perish, then they laid aside their robes, girded themselves with sackcloth, lamented, and howled, Jer. iv. 7—9.

Obs. 3. That great cities have their periods, they abide not for ever. As they have a time to come into the world, so a time to go out of it; as they have a time to get up on high, so a time to descend low. Tyrus had her day to fall, her day of departure, ver. 18; she descended into the pit with the people of old time, ver. 20. Jerusalem, formerly called Jebus, 1 Chron. xi. 4, and Salem, Gen. xiv. 18; as it had its time for building, so its day for burning, Jer. lii. 12, 13. The like end had Jericho, a walled and strong city, Josh. vi. 24. Babylon had its time to begin, Gen. xi. 8, and its time to cease, Isa. xiv. 4. So Damascus stood long, but at last it became a ruinous heap, Isa. xvii. 1. You may read of Nineveh's raising, Gen. x. 11, and of her desolation, Nah. iii. 7; Zeph. ii. 13. Hence we may see the instability of human things. Learn not to trust in strong holds, neither think it any great privilege to be citizens of such perishing cities, but labour to be citizens of the heavenly Jerusalem, which is the city prepared of God, and hath foundations which shall never be razed, Heb. i. 10, 16.

Obs. 4. God's people are dear unto him, they are glorious, and the glory of a land. That which is the glory of any is dear unto them: God's people are his glory, Isa. iv. 5; Zech. ii. 8; in both those places God's people are called his "glory." They bear his image, 2 Cor. iii. 18; they show forth his praises, 1 Peter ii. 9; they worship him in the spirit, Phil. iii. 3; they are formed for himself, Isa. xliii. 21; they are his vineyard, his pleasant plant, Isa. v. 1, 7; his jewels, Mal. iii. 17; his peculiar treasure, Exod. xix. 5; his pleasant portion, Jer. xii. 10; his spouse, Ezek. xvi. 8; they are near unto God, Psal. cxlviii. 14; anointed ones, Psal. cv. 15; trees of righteousness, Isa. lxi. 3; a congregation of saints, Psal. lxxxix. 5. They have the law of God in their hearts and keep the same, Isa. li. 7, so that they are dear unto him, and his glory; and not only so, but the glory of a land. Joseph and the Jews were the glory of Egypt; Dan. vii. they were the glory of Babylon; and the godly ones were the glory of Zion, Isa. vi. 13, "The holy seed shall be the substance thereof." Saints, a "holy seed," is the substance and glory of any nation. Let men take heed how they wrong them, for in so doing they wrong the glory of God, and the glory of the land.

Obs. 5. There is a difference of lands in the world, all are not alike. There is "the land of the living." Canaan differed from all other lands; there dwelt the living God, there were the living waters, the ordinances and means of grace and salvation, which other lands had not. That land once flowed with spiritual milk and honey, and was the "glory of all lands," chap. xx. 6: Egypt, Chaldea, and the other lands round about, were as dry and dead lands unto that; they had gods in them, but they were idol gods; they had worship, but it was false worship; they had waters, but they were bitter waters, such as God's people could not drink, they killed those that drank of them. Where God's name is recorded, his ordinances set up in purity and power, he worshipped in spirit and truth, there is life, and "the land of the living." David judged himself even among the dead, when he was shut out from the people, presence, worship, and ordinances of God; Psal. lxxxiv. 2, his soul fainted, and he was almost gone. Most lands are lands of darkness, dryness, and death, they have neither the light nor waters of life in them. Let us bless God that we are in the land of the living.

Obs. 6. God's people may be deprived of their privileges and comforts for a season, but he will in due time restore them to the enjoyment of the same. "I shall set glory in the land of the living." God's glory, his people, were in Babylon, but he would not lose nor leave his glory there, he brought them back again, and "set them in the land of the living," he gave them another temple, all those ordinances and privileges they had before: Isa. xlvi. 13, "I will place salvation in Zion for Israel my glory."

CHAPTER XXVII.

Ver. 1—6. *The word of the Lord came again unto me, saying, Now, thou son of man, take up a lamentation for Tyrus; and say unto Tyrus, O thou that art situate at the entry of the sea, which art a merchant of the people for many isles, Thus saith the Lord God; O Tyrus, thou hast said, I am of perfect beauty. Thy borders are in the midst of the seas, thy builders have perfected thy beauty. They have made all thy ship boards of fir trees of Senir: they have taken cedars from Lebanon to make masts for thee. Of the oaks of Bashan have they made thine oars; the company of the Ashurites have made thy benches of ivory, brought out of the isles of Chittim.*

IN this chapter the prophet is commanded to take up a "lamentation for Tyrus;" wherein is set out,

I. The dignity, glory, and excellency of Tyrus, ver. 2—25.

II. The irrecoverable fall and destruction thereof, ver. 26, to the end.

Ver. 1. "The word of the Lord came again unto me." The Hebrew is, and there hath been the word of Jehovah to me, the word of him who is being, hath had being, in me. God is essence, or being unchangeable, and such is his "word," which shows the certainty of the "word." He had twice before received the "word" to prophesy against the nations, and now again he is put on by the same, God commissioning him thereunto.

Ver. 2. "Take up a lamentation for Tyrus." The word נשא to take up, signifies, to take up that which is heavy, burdensome, and lamentations are such things; the Lord would have the prophet sensible of the great misery coming upon Tyrus, and to bewail the same. Jeremiah bewailed the condition of Jerusalem when destruction was coming upon it, Jer. iv. 19; ix. i. God would not have prophets give out judgments and threatenings with bitter spirits, not when they are against heathens, Tyrians; he would have his servants to compassionate others.

Ver. 3. "Say unto Tyrus, O thou that art situate at the entry of the sea." Here he begins to set out the dignity of "Tyrus;" which first he doth, from her situation, she was seated at the "entry of the sea;" she was not only upon a rock, and so eminent for sight, but by the "sea," yea, "the entry of the sea," and so was commodious for trading. The Hebrew for "entry" is, מבואת entries, or ports, from בוא to come in; Tyrus was famous for ports, so that ships might come in, and ride there safely, and go out again at pleasure. It was in an island, and islands have many ports, or harbours.

"Which art a merchant of the people for many isles." Tyrus did merchandize with the isles far and near, she did send out to them, and they brought in to her, what commodities were merchantable. She was a merchant city, Isa. xxiii. 8; the merchants of Zidon traded with her, ver. 2. The Hebrew is, to many isles: the people prepared many vendible commodites, which the isles took off their hands, so that hereby her wealth was greatly increased, and her merchants like princes, Isa. xxiii. 8; and this was another dignity of Tyrus.

"Thou hast said, I am of perfect beauty." כלילת יפי of universal beauty; I am so built that I want nothing to add unto my beauty, it is "perfect." What God said of Zion, Psal. l. 2, that she "was the perfection of beauty," the same said Tyrus of herself, which was her sin. That she was neatly and strongly built was her glory, but that she was proud hereof was her sin and shame; for who can say, "I am of perfect beauty," but the Lord?

Ver. 4. "Thy borders are in the midst of the seas." Some cities border upon hills, valleys, woods, rivers; but Tyrus had no such "borders," her "borders" were in the midst, or, as the Hebrew is, in the heart of the seas. None could come to her by land, being half a mile, or seven hundred paces, from the continent; but Alexander, in his time, made a passage into Tyrus, by filling up the sea. This was the glory of Tyrus, that she was compassed about with the seas, and sat as a virgin city, and queen regent in the deeps.

"Thy builders have perfected thy beauty." Who were the "builders" of Tyrus we find not in Scripture, but Adrichomius, following Berosus and the traditions of the ancients, tells us, that one Tyrus, the seventh of Japheth's sons, built it a little after the flood, and that from him it was called Tyrus. This seems very probable, because it was before Joshua's days, as appears Josh. xix. 29. But whether he or the Sidonians built it, is not clear; but whoever were the "builders," they were masters of architecture, and nothing was left undone which tended to the ornament and strength of the city. The Sidonians were men of skill, artists in hewing and building, 1 Kings v. 6.

Ver. 5. "They have made all thy ship boards of fir trees of Senir." Having showed the dignity of Tyrus from the situation, structure, and trading, now he comes to set it out from the shipping of it. The Tyrians abounded in ships, and are thought to be the first authors of navigation. Pliny saith, the Phœnicians were famous for the invention of the navigatory and military art; and Tibullus saith, that Tyrus first committed a ship to sea, Lib. 1. E. leg. 7, *primo ratem ventis credere docta Tyrus.* Tyrus was the metropolis of Phœnicia.

Lib. 5. c. 12.

Vide Sands' Relat. 3rd Edit. 1627. l. 3. p. 214. Vide Quister. prim. in loc.

"Thy ship boards." לוח is a table, or plank, and כל-לחתים is, all the planks on both sides of the ships: there must be thick and strong planks to make a ship. Some render the word, seats, whereon rowers sit in ships, boats, or galleys.

"Of fir trees of Senir." The word ברשים for "fir trees," some render it, cedars; but, 1 Kings v. 8; Isa. xxxvii. 24, "fir trees" and cedars have distinct names; ארז is, a cedar, and *berosh*, the "fir tree," which is a tree tall and strong, therefore great men are likened unto it; Nahum ii. 3, "The fir trees shall be terribly shaken," that is, the men in place and honour. Planks of fir, it is observed, are smooth, will cleave close together, and so were counted then fittest for shipping. These "fir trees" were taken from Senir, a mount, which had many names; Deut. iii. 9, Moses called it Hermon; the Sidonians, Shirion, or Syrion; the Amorites, Shenir; others, Hor; and some, Sion; Stephanus, in Onomast. interprets it, *dormiens lucerna;* the Chaldee calls it, the snow mount, because the snow used to continue upon it; our prophet here makes it a mount of "fir trees."

"They have taken cedars from Lebanon." This mountain is partly in Canaan, and partly in Syria, or Phœnicia. Solomon sent to Hiram to hew him cedar trees out of Lebanon, that was, from that part of the mount which runs along in Syria and Phœnicia. Some make it a mount in Syria, so high, that in the midst of the summer it preserves the snow on the top of it, which is fetched thence to Tyrus, and made use of to cool their summer cups, and sold to others for the same purpose. It is called "Lebanon," the learned conceive, because of its snowy whiteness; לבן in Hebrew, is white, thence "Lebanon:" Jer. xviii. 14, "Can a man leave the snow of Lebanon?" It abounded with "cedars," which are strong, durable, and tall; Ezek. xvii. 22, they are said to be "high;" and men in high places are compared to high "cedars," exposed to

Mars. Lexic.

winds, storms, shakings, and ruin more than others; by reason of their tallness and strength, they were the fitter for shipping.

"To make masts for thee." The mast is the tree in the ship, which bears up the sails. In Greek, ἱϛος, *ab* ἵϛασθαι, because it stands upright in the ship. Hesychius calls it, τὸ ὀρθὸν ξύλον τῆς νεῶς, the right or straight wood of the ship.

Ver. 6. "Of the oaks of Bashan." "Bashan" was a land beyond Jordan, which bred mighty men, and was called "the land of giants," Deut. iii. 13. Og was king thereof, whose bedstead of iron was nine cubits in length, and four in breadth, ver. 11; this country was large, and fell partly to Manasseh, ver. 14, and partly to Gad, 1 Chron. v. 11, 16; it was a rich soil, and fruitful; the lambs and rams of it are set out in Scripture with an emphasis, Deut. xxxii. 14, "the breed of Bashan," it bred lusty, strong, and fat cattle: hence great ones, and rich men, are likened to the "bulls of Bashan," Psal. xxii. 12; to "kine of Bashan," Amos iv. 1; the mighty ones and princes of the earth are called "fatlings of Bashan," Ezek. xxxix. 18. This land, as it bred men and beasts of strength and stature, so trees likewise, especially oaks, which are set out by way of distinction from others, as, "oaks of Bashan," Isa. ii. 13; by which strong and great men are set out, Zech. xi. 2. The Hebrew for "oaks" is אלונים which some have rendered, pine trees, some, chesnut trees, some, fir trees, but most, "oaks;" for Bashan was a woody country, and did abound with "oaks;" and *allon* signifies, an "oak," Josh. xxiv. 26; Isa. vi. 13, *callonim*, as "oaks."

"Have they made thine oars." The Tyrians made their ships so, that when the wind served not, or not sufficiently, they might row with "oars," and so make more the speed upon occasions. Their "oars" were made of choice oak, which was firm and lasting: משוטים oars, it is from שוט which signifies, to go forward, to impel; the "oars" helped on the motion of the ship, and served to row her in, where winds would not suffer.

"The company of the Ashurites have made thy benches of ivory." In the Hebrew it is אשרים בת the daughter of the Assyrians. Vatablus hath it, the congregation of the Assyrians, which he interprets thus; The best Assyrian artists have made thy "benches of ivory." The Septuagint hath it, dark houses. Others have differing conjectures about the words, which in the original stand thus; They have made thee benches of ivory, the daughter of Ashurim, that is, the daughter of tradings, or goings. To this purpose Junius and Piscator interpret the words; one hath it, *ex ebore tritissimo*, the other, *ex ebore bene attrito*, of ivory well worn, or trodden. And thus doth Buxtorfius render the words שן בת־אשרים *ebur, filius* or *filia gressuum*, i. e. *gressibus tritum*. The word *ashur* signifies, going, treading; and Pliny saith, that ivory which hath
Vid. Buxtor. in verbo Ashur. been long in the earth, and much trodden upon, is the only ivory. The word for "ivory" is, *shen*, a tooth, which by a synecdoche is put for the tooth or teeth of elephants, whereof ivory is made. Some call them the elephant's horns, because they are large and like unto horns. These teeth, or horns, they shed every ten years, and being shed, they hide them, and lay them up.
Martinius in Lexic. Theophrastus and Pliny speak of *ebur fossile*, ivory digged out of the earth, white and black, which may be the teeth, or horns, of the elephant, hid in the earth, and trodden into it.

Of "ivory" the Tyrians made them, "benches." The word for "benches" is, קרש which signifies, a board, a table, or plank, that which may be joined to other things, and may be rendered, the decks or hatches, but because their ships had "oars," it is like there were seats or "benches."

"Brought out of the isles of Chittim." In the word is mention of the land of Chittim, Isa. xxiii. 1; the coast of Chittim, Numb. xxiv. 24; the ships of Chittim, Dan. xi. 30; and here, of the "isles of Chittim." Some make it Italy; the Vulgate hath it, of the isles of Italy. Melancthon thinks it to be Macedonia. Bonfrerius saith, Cyprus was first so called, and after, this name Chittim was given to other islands, as Italy, Greece. A Lapide names Cyprus, Crete, Sicily, the islands of Apulia, and Italy, which he comprehends under the "isles of Chittim." They were so called from Chittim, one of the sons of Javan, who descended from Japheth, the son of Noah, Gen. x. 4, 5, and he, with his brethren, divided the isles of the gentiles, after their tongues and families.

Obs. 1. The men of the world are wise, choosing the fittest places for their own advantage and interest. Tyrus was situate at the entry of the sea, was a merchant of the people for many isles; the Tyrians seated themselves where they might have great trading at sea, and access unto them from all parts, and so grow great and rich. The Canaanites dwelt by the sea, and coast of Jordan, Numb. xiii. 29, places fit for exportation and importation. Babylon was seated upon many waters, Jer. li. 13, the great river Euphrates ran through it, by means whereof it grew rich; for it follows, "abundant in treasures." Those cities or towns that are built upon rivers navigable, and sea coasts, where are ports commodious for shipping, they draw the wealth unto them, and abound in treasure. Let us learn so much of the men of the world, to be wise for our spiritual interest, and seat ourselves near the waters of the sanctuary, that so, trading with God and Christ, we may abound with spiritual treasure.

Obs. 2. Outward excellences lift up men's hearts, beget vain confidences, and cause them to boast. Tyrus was built upon a rock, situate at the entry of the sea, did merchandize with many isles, whereby she got the riches and rarities of other places, and hereupon she swelled, and said, "I am of perfect beauty," I want nothing conducing to essence or ornament, to being or well-being, I and mine are complete every way. Great cities, which have outward advantages of enriching themselves, are full of pride, confidence, and sinful boastings. Babylon was a great and rich city, and, Isa. xlvii. 7, she said, "I shall be a lady," or mighty woman, "for ever:" she took upon her the name of God; ver. 8, "I am, and none else beside me; I shall not sit as a widow;" I am the golden, the beautiful, the strong city, none is comparable unto me, none is able to deal with me, to deprive me of my glory, wealth, greatness, and make me desolate, and sit mourning like a widow: these were the confidences and boastings of Babylon. The like you may read of Rome, which is spiritual Babylon; Rev. xviii. 7, "She said in her heart, I sit a queen, and am no widow, and shall see no sorrow;" I have great command and power, I obey none, nations and kings are under me; I am no widow like other cities, I abound with delicacies and delights; in this condition shall I continue, I shall see no sorrow. This is the great wickedness of cities enriched by God, that they forget him, and glory in external excellences.

Obs. 3. No situation, strength, or outward advantage can secure proud cities. Tyrus' borders were in the heart of the seas, she was compassed about with great waters, judged by all to be impregnable; but God's design was to ruin Tyrus for her pride, and he found out a way and means to do it. Let cities be built where they will, in the deeps, on rocky mountains, wheresoever, if they glory in their strength, beauty, situation, God can bring destruction upon them; nothing shall hinder in nature or art. "He will work, and who shall let it?" Isa. xliii. 13; he will work, and what shall let it? not seas, not rocks, not walls, not strong towers, not multitude of ships. Babylon's many waters could not secure her, when the Lord had a device to destroy her; her pride and insolency caused him to dry up her waters, and make her heaps, Jer. li. 36, 37.

Obs. 4. Artists will put forth themselves to the utmost to show their skill. "Thy builders have perfected thy beauty;" they concealed not their art; what skill soever they had in architecture, they strove to manifest the same.

Ver. 7. ***Fine linen with broidered work from Egypt was that which thou spreadest forth to be thy sail; blue and purple from the isles of Elishah was that which covered thee.***

Having spoken of the substantials, he comes now to the ornament of Tyrus' shipping, viz. their sails.

"Fine linen with broidered work from Egypt." Egypt abounded with flax, which was very "fine," white, and precious, whereof the Egyptians made "fine linen," which, for the excellency and distinction' sake, was called the "fine linen of Egypt," Prov. vii. 16; which was so fine, that divers interpreters have rendered the word שש silk; it was such as, Philostratus saith, was lawful only for noblemen to wear.

Notwithstanding this linen was so fine, they did embroider it, which as it made it more strong, so far more costly. The Hebrew, ברקמה is from רקם to picturize by the needle, and *rochem* is, such an artist as can draw the form and figures of things in divers colours. Linen of Egypt embroidered with the forms and figures of several things had the Tyrians to make sailing for their ships.

"Which thou spreadest forth to be thy sail." The word for "sail" is, נס which some derive from נסה to elevate, for sails are on high. Others, from נסס which is, to set up a banner, to which the soldiers gather; and to the sail, when it is hoisted up, as to the banner of the ship, the winds gather.

"Blue and purple." These might be rich colourings, which they used to beautify and adorn their ships with, or to colour their sails with. In Jer. x. 9, it is said, "blue and purple is their clothing;" their idols were clothed with cloth of those colours; and so here, it is probable they might cover their heads with "blue and purple" cloths to keep off the heat, or deck and cover their ships with cloths so coloured.

"From the isles of Elishah." In Gen. x. 4, 5, Elishah the son of Javan was one of them that divided the isles of the gentiles, and those isles he had were honoured with his name. Theodoret makes them to be the islands of Greece; Jerom, the islands in the Ionian sea. Junius makes Elishah to be author of the Æolians, who were of note for purple. Tyrus had much purple of its own, yet being a mart town, from all places where it was, both that and other rich commodities were brought unto Tyre.

Vid. Jun. Notas in Gen. x. 4.

Obs. 1. The wisdom of God in bestowing several mercies upon several places. No one place hath all his blessings, and hardly any place but hath some distinct blessing. In ver. 5—7, you may see that Senir had fir trees, Lebanon had cedars, Bashan had oaks, the isles of Chittim had ivory, Egypt fine linen, the isles of Elishah blue and purple. All these places had distinct mercies, and Tyrus was beholden to them all. The Scripture speaks of God's assigning distinct mercies to divers places, as balm and myrrh to Gilead, Gen. xxxvii. 25; gold to Ophir, 1 Kings ix. 28; brass to Tibhath and Chun, 1 Chron. xviii. 8; vines to Sibmah, Jer. xlviii. 32; and wines to Lebanon, Hos. xiv. 7: which sets out the manifold wisdom of God, making way thereby for the merchandizing of nations, civilizing of men by commerce, communicating of intelligence, providences, the truth, and gospel of Christ. The Indies have sweet spices, silks, cotton, indigo, cochineal. Constantinople, Smyrna, the Mediterranean islands, and other parts have their commodities. Norway, and those parts, have something peculiar. Our nation hath lead, tin, fullers' earth, wools, and cloths, for which foreigners have been beholden to us.

Obs. 2. Proud spirits spare no cost to satisfy their humours and lusts. The men of Tyrus were rich and proud, they built ships, and beautified them with costly materials; their ship-boards were of fir trees of Senir, their masts were of cedars from Lebanon, their oars were of oaks of Bashan, their benches, holds, or decks, were of ivory, out of the isles of Chittim; their sails were of fine linen from Egypt, and that embroidered; they coloured and covered their ships with blue and purple from the isles of Elishah. Men's lusts are costly things, to gratify them, they will lavish out gold and silver. When sea towns are fatted with the wealth of sea and land, they become proud; and pride, in whomsoever it is, is expensive. Where God gives in great supplies, great means, they are seldom laid out for the honour of that God, but frequently, both among heathens and God's people, are laid out to maintain state, pride, some wretched, some base lust or other. So Jerusalem being enriched with God's blessings, and trading from all parts, Ezek. xxvi. 2, being "the gates of the people," she made of her jewels, gold, and silver, idols, covering them with broidered garments, Ezek. xvi. 17, 18.

Ver. 8, 9. ***The inhabitants of Zidon and Arvad were thy mariners: thy wise men, O Tyrus, that were in thee, were thy pilots. The ancients of Gebal and the wise men thereof were in thee thy calkers: all the ships of the sea with their mariners were in thee to occupy thy merchandise.***

Having spoken of the materials, fabric, and rich ornaments of Tyrus' shipping, in these two verses he treats of the officers and persons employed therein, and multitude of traffickers with Tyrus.

Ver. 8. "The inhabitants of Zidon and Arvad." Zidon was a famous city of Phœnicia, saith Jerom and Eusebius; it was more north than Tyrus, in the north-west of Canaan, at the utmost borders thereof. It was built either by Sidon, the first-born of Canaan, Gen. x. 15, 19, or by the Sidonians, who descending from him, built it in honour to his name. It was a great city, Josh. xix. 28, assigned unto the tribe of Asher; but the inhabitants thereof were not driven out by that tribe, Judg. i. 31. It was more ancient than Tyrus. Strabo makes it two hundred furlongs from Tyre; Bonfrerius, some five or six miles.

Arvad or Arad; the Vulgate reads it, Aradii, the Aradians were thy mariners. It was not Arad, a city in the south, Numb. xxi. 1; for the men thereof were no mariners, it being an inland city. The Hebrew is, Arvad, which Œcolampadius takes to be Damascus. Jerom makes it an island, and so doth Vilalpandus, and that not far from Zidon; but Junius makes it rather, a town in the sea, seven furlongs long, and two hundred paces from the continent. And Pliny tells us, that the Tyrians, Zidonians, and Aradians dwelt near together, and were very skilful in navigation, especially the Zidonians and Arvadites. Of these were their mariners.

Vide Plinii Naturalem Historiam, l. 5. c. 23.

"Thy wise men, O Tyrus, that were in thee, were thy pilots." The Tyrians took mariners from other places, but set men of their own over them, such as were wise and fit for that employment: inferior places they called strangers to; the honourable, and places of trust, they reserved for their own. The Tyrians were wise and skilful in sea affairs; 1 Kings ix. 27, Hiram's shipmen were such as had knowledge of the sea: they knew the several parts, what rocks and sands were in the way to them; they knew how to steer the ship in all winds and weathers, and to order all in the ship for the best advantage: such were their pilots. The word for "pilot" is, חבל *chobel*, which signifies the master, captain, or governor of the ship, which Œcolampadius derives from חבל *funis*, because by them the sails of the ship are extended or contracted at the pleasure of the pilot or governor; but rather it is from חבל *parturire*, like one in travail, who hath many fears and sorrows before she bring forth, so hath the pilot or master of the ship.

Ver. 9. "The ancients of Gebal, and the wise men thereof." Gebal was a province or city in Syria, or Syrophœnicia, near unto Zidon; the men thereof confederated with others against the people of God, Psal. lxxxiii. 7. These Gebalites were men skilful in hewing of stones, 1 Kings v. 18, that is, "stonesquarers." The Hebrew is, גבלים the Giblites, or Gebalites; they, with others, were the hewers of the stones and timber wherewith the temple was built. Among these also were ancient wise and able men for building and calking of ships.

"Were in thee thy calkers." The Hebrew is, מחזיקי בדקך which Montanus renders, strengthening thy clefts, or ruptures; in the margin you have it, stoppers of chinks. Calkers are those that drive in the okum in the clefts, chinks, or distances between the planks of the ship, and then with pitch, rosin, and oil, doth pay the same, that so no water may enter.

"All the ships of the sea with their mariners were in thee to occupy thy merchandise." Ships from all places and parts came to Tyrus, bringing in their commodities thither, and carrying out what Tyrus afforded, glass, purple, and other commodities. The Hebrew word for "ships" is, אניות being the plural number, from אני which sometimes is rendered, a navy, as 1 Kings x. 11, 22; ix. 26, 27; but mostly, a ship, as Prov. xxx. 19; Jonah i. 3, 4, 5; Isa. xxxiii. 21. A ship is a hollow vessel, made to swim or sail upon the waters, and carry burdens. Which Plautus calls a wooden horse; Lucretius, the chariot of the winds; August. a sea waggon. Ships are at sea, what carts, chariots, or waggons, are at land; and as those are drawn by horses, so are they driven on by winds and sails; the word אני being from אנה to impel. It is the wind which causeth the ship to move.

The word for "mariners," in ver. 8, is שטים and in this 9th verse it is מלחים; the first is from שוט to move, go up and down from place to place, and so mariners do, carrying the ship from port to port; the latter word is from מלח salt, *quasi*, salt-men, because they row and sail in the salt sea.

"To occupy thy merchandise." The Hebrew is, to negociate thy negociation, or, to buy thy buying; thou hast played the merchant in buying divers commodities, and merchants come to thee to fetch away those commodities. Vatablus his sense of the words is so, to take off thy wares.

Ver. 10, 11. *They of Persia and of Lud and of Phut were in thine army, thy men of war: they hanged the shield and helmet in thee; they set forth thy comeliness. The men of Arvad with thine army were upon thy walls round about, and the Gammadims were in thy towers: they hanged their shields upon thy walls round about; they have made thy beauty perfect.*

Having spoken of their gallant shipping, their pilots, mariners, calkers, and naval affairs, here he comes to the military; they had considerable forces, from other parts, and of their own, both which are touched in these two verses.

"They of Persia." The Persians were good soldiers; Cyrus the Persian conquered the Chaldeans, and set up the Persian empire. Ammianus saith of the Persians, they are expert in warlike affairs. The Hebrew for "Persia" is, פרס which signifies, to divide; to this Daniel alludes, chap. v. 28, "Peres; Thy kingdom is divided, and given to the Medes and Persians." But the name of Persia was before, and upon another account, from one Perseus a king.

Lib. 31. Martinius in Lexico.

"And of Lud." In the 10th of Genesis there is mention of Ludim the son of Mizraim and Ham, ver. 13, and of Lud the son of Shem, ver. 22. Of the first it is conceived came the Lubims in Africa, who were enemies to the Jews, 2 Chron. xii. 3. Of the second the Lydians, a people in Asia, who were skilful archers, as appears, Jer. xlvi. 9; and Jerom saith, they were counted the strongest among the nations.

"And of Phut." Phut was one of the sons of Ham, Gen. x. 6, from whom both posterity and country were so named. Ezek. xxxviii. 5, Phut is translated Libya, and Jer. xlvi. 9, Libyans; and the Greek Scholiast here turns Phut, Libyas, the Libyans; so the Vulgate; and these were famous warriors, and therefore hired to be defenders of the city of Tyre. Those joined with their own men, made up their army, fighting for them at sea, when occasion was, and constantly guarding their city. The word for "war" is מלחמה from לחם to eat, and to fight, because wars do eat up men, and their estates; hence the sword is said to devour, and that from one end of the land to the other, Jer. xii. 12; and to be drunk with blood, Jer. xlvi. 10. War is bloody, consuming, and devouring.

"They hanged the shield and helmet in thee." The Hebrew for "shield" is, מגן to protect, because it protects and defends him that bears it. The Lord said to Abraham, Gen. xv. 1, אנכי מגן לך I am a shield to thee, that is, I, that am the great God, am thy Protector. Hence great men, who ought to protect the people, the places, and cities they dwell in, are called מגני־ארץ "the shields of the earth," Psal. xlvii. 9.

The word for "helmet" in Hebrew is, כובע Greek, περικεφαλαια, that piece of armour which covers the head. Of old they made helmets of the skins of beasts, afterwards of metals, as brass, iron, silver.

In time of peace, they hanged up their shields and helmets where they might be seen, that so both strangers and others might see they were well provided for wars upon all occasions, or rather, it was to set forth their glory and greatness. It is like they had some public armoury, where their arms were laid up. The Jews stored up theirs in the house of God, 2 Chron. xxiii. 9.

"They set forth thy comeliness." This added much to the beauty and glory of Tyrus, that it had strong men in it, who were expert warriors, and store of arms hung up orderly. Solomon tells you an armoury is very comely, where there hang shields and bucklers of mighty men, Cant. iv. 4; such hangings become an armoury, as well as tapestry or arras do any room.

Ver. 11. "The men of Arvad with thine army were upon thy walls round about." Of the Arvadites was touched before; they, with the Tyrians, and those they had hired for military services, kept watch upon the walls of Tyrus continually. Though it were a strong city, seated upon a rock, in the midst of the seas, yet they thought it wisdom to have a watch on all sides, not knowing but enemies might come by sea, and do them mischief. These Tyrians trusted not only to their walls, a lifeless strength, but had watches of their soldiers, which were living strengths.

"The Gammadims were in thy towers." There is some dispute among interpreters, who these Gammadims were. The Vulgate renders the word, pigmies, and so doth Shindler, whom authors affirm to be a people of three cubits or spans in stature; but it is impossible the Tyrians should employ such, who had sought the strongest and skilfullest of men in other nations, to be an ornament and defence unto them: what glory was it, to have such dwarfs among their valiant men? Some make them to seem pigmies, and little ones, because they were in high towers; this savours more of fancy than of truth; why should not the Tyrians have stout men in their towers, as well as on their walls? The Chaldee reads it, Cappadocians; the Septuagint, φύλακες, keepers; and Jerom, though he renders the word pigmies, yet he adds, *quasi bellatores, ἀπὸ τῆς πυγμῆς, a lucta et certamine*, because they were forward to fight, and were notable fist-fighters. "Gammadim" is from *gomed*, a cubit, which occasioned many to think them to be cubit men; but *gomed* may note the arm, wherein man's strength lies, and hence they are called, *viri brachiales, quod brachio potentes et robusti essent*, because they were men of their arms. And Junius calls them, men of arms and strength, fit to defend what they undertook. Doubtless they were men of stature and strength; otherwise what should they have done with shields, they would have been burdensome to little and weak men. Quistorpius saith, these Gammadims were a warlike people, not inferior to the Persians, Lydians, or Arvadians, so called from a region of that name. A Lapide conceives, "Gammadim" may be from עמד *stare*, and so these Gammadims to be standing soldiers, a standing garrison in the towers of Tyrus.

Buxtor. in verbo Gammadim. Vid. De Dieu, in locum.

"They hanged their shields upon thy walls round about." The word for "shields" differs from that in the former verse, there it is, *magen*, and here it is, שלט *shelet*, whence our English word shield comes; it is from שלט to rule, because those who used shields were like men of power, and enabled to encounter their enemies.

"They have made thy beauty perfect." The Vulgate is, they have filled up thy beauty; the Zidonians, Arvadians, Gebalites, Persians, Lydians, Libyans, Gammadims, every one added something, which made up the beauty of Tyrus. You may confine it to their shipping and arms.

Obs. 1. That even amongst heathens were wise and experienced men. Zidon, Arvad, Tyrus, Gebal, were heathenish, yet had they their wise men, and ancients, חכמים and זקנים All wisdom and experience were not shut up in Judea; the Lord gave gifts unto heathens, so that many of them excelled in wisdom, and had great skill in natural and human things. The word *chacam* imports knowledge and wisdom, in divine and human things. Heathens fell short in the first, but went beyond most in the second. Solomon acknowledged, that there was none among the Jews that had such skill in hewing of timber as the Sidonians, 1 Kings v. 6, and you may read how skilful a Tyrian was, 2 Chron. ii. 14; he was *ish chacam*, ver. 13, it is a "cunning man" in our translation, but rather it should be, a man of wisdom, a man of skill, he was so skilful, as to find out any thing put unto him. There were "wise men" in the nations, Jer. x. 7; Edom had hers, Obad. 8; so Babylon, Dan. v. 7; Egypt had the like, Exod. vii. 11; and Tyre and Zidon had not only wise men, but those who were "very wise," Zech. ix. 2.

Obs. 2. Matters of importance are to be committed to men of wisdom and experience. Tyrus put her naval affairs in the hands of wise men and ancient; she would not trust young, raw, unexpert men to be her mariners, pilots, or calkers; she looked not to kindred, friends, and relations, as states now do; but unto those who were fit and able, wise and experienced in the affairs they were to be employed in. Wisdom directs, Eccles. x. 10; wisdom builds up and establisheth, Prov. xxiv. 3.

Obs. 3. Wise states, as they will make use of foreigners to advance their affairs and secure themselves, so especially they will promote their own unto the principal places. "Thy wise men, O Tyrus, that were in thee, were thy pilots;" Zidonians and Arvadites were her mariners, the Gebalites her calkers, but Tyrians themselves were her pilots. So Persians, Lydians, and Phutians were in the army of Tyrus, but they were not the commanders thereof. Tyrus was careful, and showed her great wisdom in placing men of her own, those who were natives, in the chief places of her navy and of her army.

When strangers are set in chief places, it discontents the natives, causes envy, grudgings, and animosities, so that those under them oft plot against them, and so the work they are in is made unsuccessful. Solomon set his own people over the work, 1 Kings v. 16; and Pharaoh set Egyptians over the Jews and Jewish officers, Exod. i. 11; v. 14.

Obs. 4. The glory of a state and city is made up of and set out by external things. Ships, soldiers, shields, helmets, they made up the beauty of Tyrus, they made it perfect, they became her, and set forth her comeliness. Such comeliness, such beauty, have heathenish states and cities; but there is another beauty, another comeliness, which would far exceed these, and make states and cities very glorious, viz. true doctrine, pure worship, holiness of life, execution of justice, and provision for the poor; these things would make the beauty of a city perfect, and set forth the comeliness thereof unto the life. Zion, that had these things in her, was "the perfection of beauty."

Ver. 12. *Tarshish was thy merchant by reason of the multitude of all kind of riches; with silver, iron, tin, and lead, they traded in thy fairs.*

The glory of Tyrus, being pencilled out from its structure, navy, and militia, now the prophet proceeds to amplify the same from the great merchandizing it had. Isaiah tells you, chap. xxiii. 3, that Tyrus was a "mart of nations;" and Lavater saith, it was as a market or fair for the whole world, which was an exceeding great honour unto Tyrus. This amplification extends unto the 25th verse, and in the several verses are set out the divers sorts of merchants, and their wares.

"Tarshish was thy merchant." This word "Tarshish" hath greatly perplexed interpreters, and their thoughts about it are various. Jerom in most places, and many others that follow him, make it to be the sea, some the Mediterranean, others the ocean; but this Munster likes not, because, as the other sons of Javan divided the isles of the gentiles, and gave their names unto them, so it is probable that Tarshish, being his son, did the like, Gen. x. 4, 5; besides, Psal. lxxii. 10, mention is made of "the kings of Tarshish," which imports it was land, and not sea. In this place the Septuagint hath καρχηδόνιοι; Jerom and the Vulgate, *Carthaginenses*, the Carthaginians, so that they all understand by Tarshish, Carthage. So Mariana likewise, who saith, that Tunis being near Carthage, was called in the Arabic tongue Tharsis, which he hath from Leo Africanus; and in these two places, Isa. xxiii. 1, Ezek. xxxviii. 13, the Septuagint hath Carthage, and the Carthaginians. Pliny makes it a colony of
Lib. 5. c. 19. Tyrus; and Curtius saith, the Tyrians
Q. Curt. l. 4. built Carthage, and were honoured by the Carthaginians, *parentum loco*. Some make Tarshish here to be Tarsus, a city in Cilicia, that which Jonah fled unto, Jonah i. 3; the city whereof Paul the apostle was, Acts xxi. 39; but this Boetius, in his Sacred Animadversions, likes not, because Tarsus
Lib. 4. c. 6. was not a sea, but an inland town; and he cites Pliny for proof of it, saying that the river Cydnus doth divide Tarsus
Lib. 5. c. 2. far from the sea; and moreover, Cilicia had not such metals as here are mentioned. Others therefore make this Tarshish to be Tartessus, a sea town in Spain, which abounded with these metals here mentioned, viz. silver, iron, tin, and lead, which were brought to Tartessus; but whatever probabilities are alleged for this opinion, the prophet Isaiah confounds them all, when he saith, chap. xxiii. 10, that Tyrus was the daughter of Tarshish. Tyrus was very ancient, yet not so ancient as Tarshish, which was some Mediterranean island, with the city thereof, so named from Tarshish the son of Javan, Gen. x. 4, 5. How then can either Carthage or Tartessus be Tarshish, when they were daughters of Tyrus? as Pliny, l. 5. c. 19, and Sanctius, upon Isa. ii. 16, do affirm; and though both of them were ancient, yet must they not compare with Tyrus or Tarshish for antiquity.

The men of Tarshish, what island, city, or place soever it was, they came to Tyrus, and merchandized with her. The word for "merchant" is, סחר *socher*, from *sachar*, to go from place to place, in a trading way, transporting commodities, which is the work of merchants; they themselves, or by their factors, do cause goods to be carried from port to port, and transported beyond sea. Either Tarshish had such mines as yielded the metals spoken of in the verse, or they were brought unto it, and so transported by the merchants thereof to Tyrus.

"With silver, iron, tin, and lead." *Ceseph* is the word for "silver," which comes from כסף to desire; for silver is that which all men covet and desire, yet are not satisfied therewith. So strongly are some carried out in their desires after it, that they venture limbs and life for it, yea, pierce themselves through with many cares, and drown their souls in perdition, 1 Tim. vi. 9, 10.

ברזל is "iron;" *bertz* is a Chaldee word, signifying *transfigere, perforare*, from whence it may be derived, because iron is that which pierceth through, and fastens things together; it is of great use, and could not well be wanted in any state. It is fre-
Scalig. Exerc. 10. 6. 2. quently put in Scripture for that which is made of iron: as 2 Kings vi. 5, 6, that which is called the "axe," in Hebrew is iron; and Psal. cv. 18, "He was laid in iron," that is, in chains made of iron; so Psal. cvii. 10, "Being bound in affliction and iron," that is, in fetters or chains; therefore metaphorically it notes hard things.

"Tin," that is, בדיל from בדל which is, to separate, because it is separated not only from silver in the fire, but other drossy materials; some call it white lead. Our pewter hath much of it mingled with it.

"Lead," the Hebrew is, עופרת *ophereth*, from עפר dust, because it hath much earthiness in it, not because it is fetched out of the dust of the earth, so are other metals which are more noble.

"They traded in thy fairs." The Hebrew runs thus, they have given in these to thy aid: fairs are aids and helps to places where they are kept. Others read for "fairs," in thy leavings they have traded, in the place where all things are left for sale and exchange; the word עזבון or עזבונים notes the place whither wares are brought and left, from עזב *asab*, to leave, and also, to help.

Ver. 13. *Javan, Tubal, and Meshech, they were thy merchants: they traded the persons of men and vessels of brass in thy market.*

Javan was the son of Japheth, Gen. x. 2, from whom came the Ionians, afterwards called the Grecians. Dan. viii. 21, "The rough goat is" מלך יון "the king of Grecia;" and the Septuagint here hath it, ἡ ἑλλὰς, which is Greece: Joel iii. 6, יונים is rendered ἕλληνες, by the Septuagint, and Grecians, by our translators.

"Tubal." Tubal was the son of Japheth also, Gen. x. 2; and as Junius, in his notes upon the place, observes, from him came the Iberians and Albanians. The Iberians were a people in Asia, near the Caspian and Euxine seas, and the Albanians were their neighbours, between Colchis and Armenia. Some expositors do tell us, there were the occidental Iberians, as well as oriental, and by them they understand the Spaniards, who were so called from the river Iber; and they make Tubal the father and founder of Spain, the first Vid. Vilalp. city whereof they affirm to be called Thubal.

"Meshech." Some make him, being the son of Japheth, Gen. x. 2, the father of the Muscovites; others, of the Cappadocians, who formerly were called Meschines, or Meschates. Josephus, in his first book of Antiquities, cap. 7, which is of nations deriving their names from the authors, saith, Meschus was the author of them called Meschates, who were lately named Cappadocians; for they show even at this day a token of their ancient name, to wit, the city of Masaca.

"They were thy merchants." The word for "merchant" here, differs from that in the precedent verse, it is, רכל *rochel*, which properly is a merchant dealing in grocery, spicery, and sweet things; in 1 Kings x. 15, they are called "spice merchants," *harocelim*. There are two words more in the verse for "merchants;" *tor*, תור because they search into the nature of things; and סחר because they send their goods up and down from place to place; but *rochel* is used for those that merchandize in other things, as follows.

"They traded the persons of men." The Hebrew is, בנפש אדם in the soul, or souls of men. So the Septuagint, ἐν ψυχαῖς ἀνθρώπων. The Vulgate is, slaves. Junius and Piscator read it, they traded in men, either they brought men to Tyrus to sell them there, or brought men in to Tyrus to carry elsewhere. This was a frequent practice among heathens, to buy and sell men. If it be thought lawful to sell those who are taken in war, from whom the conqueror might take their lives, what warrant there is to buy and sell other men like beasts in a market, I see not. The Scholiast saith, God here doth accuse their great injustice, who sold men by force. The merchants that dealt with the whore of Babylon, they traded, Rev. xviii. 13, in the bodies, so is the word "slaves" in the original, "and souls of men." They traded in the soul of man, that is, saith Vilalpandus, with the great hazard of their lives; according to that, Lam. v. 9, "We gat our bread" בנפשנו that is, with the hazard of our soul, or life, "because of the sword of the wilderness."

"And vessels of brass in thy market." All kind of brazen vessels were brought thither, and sold into other parts. The word for "market" is, מערב from ערב to mingle, because in markets there are mixtures of all things; in Tyrus were men, brass, lead, tin, iron, silver, and a multitude of other things to be had.

Ver. 14. *They of the house of Togarmah traded in thy fairs with horses and horsemen and mules.*

Togarmah was the son of Gomer, the son of Japheth, Gen. x. 2, 3; and the Chaldee paraphrast makes his country Germany. The Jews understand by the Thogarmæans, the Turks, and by Togarma, Turkey. Others by "the house of Togarmah" mean the Phrygians, who abounded in horses and horsemen, which were skilful in horsemanship. What "house," that is, people, or nation, soever they were, they possessed the northern parts, Ezek. xxxviii. 6.

"Horses, horsemen, and mules." סוסים notes common horses; פרשים *pharasim*, horses for war; פרדים swift horses, such as kings and princes used, saith A Lapide: but *parash* is a horseman, because he urges on the horse with spurs, 2 Chron. i. 14; and *pered* is a mule, from פרד to separate, because the generation of mules is differing from other beasts.

Ver. 15. *The men of Dedan were thy merchants; many isles were the merchandise of thine hand: they brought thee for a present horns of ivory and ebony.*

"Dedan" was a city in Idumea, belonging to the posterity of Esau, Jer. xlix. 8; of it see what was said chap. xxv. 13; those in that city, who were merchants, did merchandize with Tyrus.

"Many isles were the merchandise of thine hand." Isles in the ocean, or Mediterranean sea. Sanctius thinks they could not be the Mediterranean islands, because they yielded not such commodities as are here spoken of. They brought their wares into Tyrus, bargaining with her merchants and inhabitants, which bargains were confirmed by striking hands: or, by the "merchandise of thine hand," may be understood, their bringing wares to her hand, and taking wares off from her hand.

"They brought thee for a present horns of ivory and ebony." Elephants have no horns; but because their teeth grow something like horns, therefore they are called horns, and "horns of ivory," for that the ivory is made of those teeth or horns.

The Hebrew word for "ebony" is, הובנים *hobnim*, which some have interpreted, peacocks; but the word for peacocks is, תכיים 1 Kings x. 22. Ebony is black, solid, and shining wood, so heavy, that it swims not in water, but sinks even like a stone. *Eben* in Hebrew is a stone, and ebony differs not much from it. India is the parent of it.

"For a present," not that they gave the Tyrians their ivory and ebony, but presented them for sale unto them. Therefore Piscator reads the words thus, With horns of ivory and with ebony they have made or rendered thy price; they have given thee these for other commodities.

Ver. 16. *Syria was thy merchant by reason of the multitude of the wares of thy making: they occupied in thy fairs with emeralds, purple, and broidered work, and fine linen, and coral, and agate.*

The word for "Syria" in Hebrew is, ארם Gen. x. 22, Aram was the son of Shem, and from him came the Aramites, or Armenians, who possessed Armenia, so called from Aram, which signifies high, and in Armenia it is conceived was the highest part of the earth; Gen. viii. 4, the ark first rested upon the mountains of Ararat, which were in Armenia. Vilalpandus tells us, that from שור *Sur*, a province therein, it afterward was called Syria. Josephus, Antiq. l. i. c. 7, saith, of Aram came Vid. Martin. in
the Aramæans, whom the Greeks call- verb. Syrus.
ed Syrians. These Syrians were the merchants of Tyrus; but whether the Syrians of Damascus, 2 Sam. viii. 5, or the Syrians of Beth-rehob, or those of Zoba, 2 Sam. x. 6, or the Syrians of Padan-aram, Gen. xxv. 20, or all of them, is uncertain.

"By reason of the multitude of the wares of thy making." In the Hebrew it is, for the multitude of thy works. Tyrus had many artists, which made and multiplied wares for other parts. She employed her people, who filled her with artificial things.

"They occupied in thy fairs with emeralds." The word for "emerald" is, נפך which Rabbi David saith is a kind of precious stone, of black colour. Jerom and Santes make it a carbuncle, and so the French, and Vatablus. Others, the smaragd emerald, or green stone, with which colour the eyes are greatly pleased and delighted.

"Purple, and broidered work, and fine linen." These were rich commodities which the Syrians traded in. Of these before.

"Coral." This grows in the sea; whilst it is under the water it is green, being got above the water, it becomes red: it is called the tree-stone, or stony-tree, because it brancheth out like a tree. The Hebrew, ראמות is from ראם to elevate or raise up, and so doth coral spring up out of the rock or sea.

"Agate." The margin is, chrysoprase, כדכד Jerom professes he knows not what this word means. The Hebrews affirm, that by it are meant all precious wares. It is rendered by interpreters, a carbuncle, a pearl, a crystal, and here, an agate, which is a stone well known. It had its name from Achates, a river in Sicilia, in which, or near to which, it was first found, but afterwards in other places.

Ver. 17. *Judah, and the land of Israel, they were thy merchants: they traded in thy market wheat of Minnith, and Pannag, and honey, and oil, and balm.*

The posterity of Judah, and the inhabitants of Canaan, they abounding with wheat, honey, oil, and balm, exported them to Tyrus; for Tyrus was victualled by Judea, Acts xii. 20; and Hiram king of Tyre had twenty thousand measures of wheat, and twenty measures of oil, yearly from Solomon, for his household, 1 Kings v. 11; what then had all his people from the merchants of the Jews!

"Wheat of Minnith." בחטי מנית. חטה *quasi* חנטה

from חנט to bring forth, to thrust out, because the wheat thrusts itself out of the hose or stalk, and appears above the same. Canaan was *erez chittah*, "a land of wheat and barley, a land of oil-olive and honey," Deut. viii. 8. Minnith was some principal place in it for wheat; it is mentioned only in Judg. xi. 33, and here.

"Pannag." Some translate it, balsam, some, a fig, but Aquilla, Symmachus, and Theodotion do make it a place, as Minnith, which yielded choice wheat. Junius and Piscator call it Phœnicia; and so Buxtorfius.

"Balm." Some render it rosin, which is a humour or juice flowing out of certain trees; but "balm" it is rendered here, and Gen. xxxvii. 35; Jer. viii. 22; xlvi. 11; li. 8; which is the principal of oils, or liquids, that flow out of trees, *quasi* בעל־שמן the lord or king of oils.

Ver. 18. *Damascus was thy merchant in the multitude of the wares of thy making, for the multitude of all riches; in the wine of Helbon, and white wool.*

Damascus was a famous city of Syria, rather than Phœnicia, which Julian called, the eye of the east, between Libanus and mount Hermon. Isaiah tells us it was the "head of Syria," chap. vii. 8, that is, the head or principal city thereof: merchants came from thence to Tyrus, and traded in her wares, and Tyrians went to Damascus, and traded in hers.

"For the multitude of all riches." Tyrus abounded with the riches of sea and land, having commodities fitting for all places.

"In the wine of Helbon." חלבון *chelbon*, signifies milk, or fatness, and metaphorically, it signifies the best of any thing; here it is conceived to
Buxtorf. in verbo Halab. be the name of a place in Syria, where grew choice grapes, of which the best wine was made, wine as pleasant as milk, if not like unto milk in colour.

"And white wool." The Septuagint and Jerom have it, wool from Miletus, a city in the borders of Ionia and Caria, but the Hebrew word is, צחר which is, whiteness, so that the words are, wool of whiteness. In the eastern parts are *arbores laniferæ*, trees that bear wool or cotton, which is very white, and sheep that bear wool of whiteness, or white wool. The word *tzachar* hath affinity with צהר *tzahar*, which signifies light, and all light hath a whiteness and brightness in it.

Ver. 19. *Dan also and Javan going to and fro occupied in thy fairs: bright iron, cassia, and calamus, were in thy market.*

"Dan," the posterity of the patriarch Dan, who inhabited the city Dan near Jordan, both which had their names from him, Josh. xix. 47. That city Dan in Christ's time was called Cæsarea Philippi; and in Jerom's, Paneas: from hence, being some thirty-five miles from Tyrus, came the Danites to trade with the Tyrians.

"Javan going to and fro." Of "Javan" before, ver. 13. The word for "going to and fro," מאוזל *Meuzzal*, some make the name of a place. *Meuzzal*, "from *Uzal*," so Aquila, as if the Danites and Grecians did bring commodities from Uzal to Tyrus; but *meuzel* is a participle from אזל *ezal*, which is, to go, to move. Vatablus turns it, *vagabunda*, for the Greeks, being covetous, did sail and move to all places for gain.

"Bright iron." The Hebrew is, iron made, defecated from all the dross, and made pure, or made into bars or plates.

"Cassia." It is a kind of a sweet cane, or shrub; in Hebrew, קדה from קדד to bow with the head, or top; so this cassia grows with the top inclining or bowing; it is mentioned only here, and in Exod. xxx. 24, where it is reckoned among the "principal spices" for the holy anointing. The word for "cassia" in Psal. xlv. 8, is, קציעות from קצע to shave, unbark; for cassia is an odoriferous shrub, whose bark shaved off is very useful. Vid. Plin. Natur. Hist. l. 12. c. 19.

"Calamus." It is a kind of sweet reed, or cane, full of knots, growing in India. Isa. xliii. 24, it is called "sweet cane," and Jer. vi. 20, "sweet cane from a far country," which was India, saith Jerom. Of it, and other spices, was made the incense. Maldon. in locum.

Ver. 20. *Dedan was thy merchant in precious clothes for chariots.*

The Hebrew for "precious clothes" is, בגדי חפש garments of ingenuity, or liberty; such garments as noble and free men used for their horses and chariots. Men of quality adorn their horses and chariots with rich and precious ornaments, rich saddles, trappings, and coverings.

Ver. 21. *Arabia, and all the princes of Kedar, they occupied with thee in lambs, and rams, and goats: in these were they thy merchants.*

The Arabians dealt much in sheep and goats, they brought thousands of them to Jehoshaphat, 2 Chron. xvii. 11. Arabia Petræa and Deserta bred multitudes of them.

"The princes of Kedar." Kedar, saith Jerom, is a region in the wilderness of the Saracens, so named from Kedar the son of Ishmael, Gen. xxv. 13; in it was a city also of that name, which had divers princes. The Kedarites and Arabians, as they were not far from one another, so not far from Tyrus, because such cattle could not be driven far: in these they traded with the Tyrians.

"In these were they thy merchants." The Hebrew is, the merchants of thy hand, that is, merchants near at hand: they were near, and alway ready to furnish them with lambs, rams, and goats.

Ver. 22. *The merchants of Sheba and Raamah, they were thy merchants: they occupied in thy fairs with chief of all spices, and with all precious stones, and gold.*

In Gen. x. 7, we read of Seba with *samech*, and Seba with *shin*; this Seba with *shin* was the son of Raamah, who inhabited the upper tract, coast, or part of Arabia Felix, and from him that region was named Sheba; the other Seba, with *samech*, was the son of Cush, and nephew of Ham, who possessed that region in Ethiopia, called from him Saba, of which Isaiah speaks, chap. xliii. 3, "I gave Egypt for thy ransom, Ethiopia and Seba," or Saba, "for thee." You have them both Psal. lxxii. 10, "The kings of Sheba and Seba shall offer gifts;" the first is with the letter ש *shin*; the second with ס *samech*. The queen that came to Solomon, was of Sheba, not Seba, or Saba; Sheba, in Arabia the Happy, abounded with those things she presented unto him.

"Raamah." Some make this word an epithet of the former, The merchants of Sheba, even Raamah: or thus, The merchants of Sheba, even thunder, or thunderers; for רעם or רעמה signifies thunder; Job xxxix. 19, "Hast thou clothed his neck with thunder?" speaking of the horse; Hast thou made him terrible? The Sabeans were the disturbers of all things. But I rather conceive, with Junius, it was some place in Arabia the Happy, near unto Sheba; it is more probable the father and the son pitched in those parts which were near one another.

Vid. Jun. in Gen. x. 7.

"With chief of all spices, and with all precious stones, and gold." Arabia Felix did abound with choice spices; Jer. vi. 20, incense came from Sheba; and not only incense, but gold, Isa. lx. 6; the queen of Sheba she brought spices, much gold, and precious stones unto Solomon, 1 Kings x. 2.

Ver. 23. *Haran, and Canneh, and Eden, the merchants of Sheba, Asshur, and Chilmad, were thy merchants.*

Haran, or Charran, was a city in Mesopotamia, where Abraham some time dwelt, Gen. xi. 31; Acts vii. 4. Canneh is no where mentioned but in this place, and it is thought to be some city or region nigh to Haran; Junius makes it the same with Calneh, Gen. x. 10. Eden is spoken of 2 Kings xix. 12, and Isa. xxxvii. 12, where it is said to be in Thelasar. Vilalpandus makes Eden to be a most pleasant region in Syria; others, in Mesopotamia; Junius, in Chaldea.

"Sheba." Some make this Sheba the same with the former. Junius and Piscator difference it from the former, placing it in Arabia Deserta, and think it that Sheba Job speaks of, chap. vi. 19, "The companies of Sheba waited for them."

"Asshur." He was the son of Shem, Gen. x. 22; of him came the Assyrians, who were a scourge and plague to the Jews, Isa. x. 5.

"Chilmad." It is from *lamad*, to teach, and the words may be read thus, The merchants of Sheba and Asshur, being versed and skilled in thy wares and affairs, they were thy merchants; but it is more suitable to look at "Chilmad" as the proper name of a place. It is by the learned made a province of the Medes, between Assyria and Parthia.

Ver. 24. *These were thy merchants in all sorts of things, in blue clothes, and broidered work, and in chests of rich apparel, bound with cords, and made of cedar, among thy merchandise.*

The men of Sheba, Asshur, and Chilmad, they brought the commodities here mentioned unto Tyrus, and sold them in her markets.

"In all sorts of things." The Hebrew is, במכללים Vulgate, *in perfectionibus;* it is from כלל to perfect, and notes variety and multitude of perfect wares, such as were no ways faulty.

"In blue clothes." בגלומי תכלת saith Montanus, in the wrappings of hyacinth; Symmachus, in precious coverings. The word *galom* is a cloak or covering, in which a man doth wrap and cover himself.

"In chests of rich apparel, bound with cords." בגנזי in the cases, or chests; גנז is that in which gold, silver, clothes, and desirable things are laid up in: they put up rich apparel in clothes, and bound them with cords, yea, with cords of silk, saith Vilalpandus.

The word for "rich apparel" is, ברומים only in this place, and it notes precious, desirable garments. The Septuagint turns it, θησαυροὺς ἐκλεκτοὺς, choice treasures.

"Made of cedar." Cedars are well scented, durable, but brittle, of them they made chests for their precious things.

Ver. 25. *The ships of Tarshish did sing of thee in thy market: and thou wast replenished, and made very glorious in the midst of the seas.*

The ships of Tarshish were thy princes, so Montanus; and others, they were the chief of all the ships which came to thee. The Hebrew is, *sharothajick*, which the Hebrews derive from שור to play the prince; but ours, from שור *shur*, to sing; and so, the merchants, or men of Tarshish, that came and traded with thee, they did magnify thee and thy wares, they praised thee above all places, and thy wares above all wares.

"Thou wast replenished, and made very glorious." Thou wast filled with the wares and commodities of all the islands and nations near and far off, so that nothing was wanting in thee, and hereupon thou becamest famous abroad; thou hadst all precious and rare things; whatever was the glory and excellency of other places, was brought to thee, being in the heart of the sea; so it is in the original.

Obs. 1. That merchandizing is ancient and lawful. Tyrus was of great antiquity, Isa. xxiii. 7, and the "mart of nations," ver. 3. In Jacob's days there were Midianitish merchants, Gen. xxxvii. 28; in Abraham's time there were such, Gen. xxiii. 16. Neither is the calling of merchants unlawful, though Chrysostom be against it. He saith, Christ cast the buyers and sellers out of the temple, signifying that a merchant can hardly or never please God, and therefore no christian ought to be a merchant; or if he will, let him be thrown out of the church of God. He cites that in Psal. lxx. 16, according to the Vulgate, Because I have not known merchandizing, I shall enter into the powers of the Lord; (but this is otherwise in the original, in our translation being in Psal. lxxi. 15, 16;) and he gives his reason hereof, because merchandise can hardly be exercised without lying and perjury. This is a hard sentence against them. It is much to be feared that many of them are covetous, deal in bad wares, corrupt those which are good by mixtures of worse with them, set prices too high, do lie, swear, and forswear themselves, in their much dealings; yet all these do not make merchandizing unlawful. Prov. xxxi. 24, the virtuous woman sold her fine linen and girdles unto the merchant; had merchandise been unlawful she would not have done it. Let merchants take heed of covetousness and the evils which are incident to buying and selling, do in all their tradings, with domestics or foreigners, as they would be done unto, and so their calling will not only be warrantable, but of singular advantage unto commonwealths and cities.

Vilalpand. p. 12. col. 2. lit. E.

Obs. 2. Great trading makes places rich and famous. Tyrus had merchants from all parts, and they brought in all sorts of precious commodities, so that she was replenished and glorious; she was full of wealth, and famous in all parts. Babylon had trading with many nations, and she abounded in treasures, Jer. li. 13. When Jerusalem was the gates of the people, when all nations came in to her, then she abounded in wealth and fame.

Obs. 3. True happiness lies not in the abundance of outward things. Tyrus had what the world could afford; men of wisdom, skill, and strength; choice helmets and shields, horses, horsemen, and mules; horns of ivory and ebony, gold, silver, precious stones, emeralds, agates, coral; the choicest wheat, honey, oil, and balm; she had precious clothes, rich apparel, the multitude of all riches in her; yet heathenish, and near unto destruction: Isa. xxiii. 11, "The Lord hath given a commandment against the merchant city, to destroy the strong holds thereof." Outward things make not happy, Psal. cxliv. 15.

Ver. 26—36. *Thy rowers have brought thee into great waters: the east wind hath broken thee in the midst of the seas. Thy riches, and thy fairs, thy merchandise, thy mariners, and thy pilots, thy calkers, and the occupiers of thy merchandise, and all thy men of war, that are in thee, and in all thy company which is in the midst of thee, shall fall into the midst of the seas in the day of thy ruin. The suburbs shall shake at the sound of the cry of thy pilots. And all that handle the oar, the mariners, and all the pilots of the sea, shall come down from their ships, they shall stand upon the land; and shall cause their voice to be heard against thee, and shall cry bitterly, and shall cast up dust upon their heads, they shall wallow themselves in the ashes: and they shall make themselves utterly bald for thee, and gird them with sackcloth, and they shall weep for thee with bitterness of heart and bitter wailing. And in their wailing they shall take up a lamentation for thee, and lament over thee, saying, What city is like Tyrus, like the destroyed in the midst of the sea? When thy wares went forth out of the seas, thou filledst many people; thou didst enrich the kings of the earth with the multitude of thy riches and of thy merchandise. In the time when thou shalt be broken by the seas in the depths of the waters thy merchandise and all thy company in the midst of thee shall fall. All the inhabitants of the isles shall be astonished at thee, and their kings shall be sore afraid, they shall be troubled in their countenance. The merchants among the people shall hiss at thee; thou shalt be a terror, and never shalt be any more.*

Having shown the great wealth and dignity of Tyrus, here the prophet comes to the second general part of the chapter, viz. to show the irrecoverable fall of Tyrus.

In these words we have,

I. The destruction itself of Tyrus.

II. The effects and events that follow.

I. This destruction of Tyrus is set out,

1. By way of metaphor, or similitude, which is implied in ver. 26. Tyrus is likened unto a ship at sea, that suffers by the winds and waters, and so perisheth, being laden with rich commodities.

2. From the moving cause thereof, viz. her "rowers," ver. 26.

3. The instrument or means, "the east wind."

II. The effects.

1. Loss of all, ver. 27, 34.

2. The mourning of pilots and mariners, ver. 28—33, with the manner thereof.

3. The influence it had upon foreigners; astonishment, fear, trouble, it produced in some, ver. 35, and hissing in others, ver. 36.

Ver. 26. "Thy rowers have brought thee," &c. This verse is wholly metaphorical. By "rowers" are meant the great men that ruled and governed Tyrus, who were to the city as rowers to a ship. They by their pride, wicked counsels, and wretched lives, caused God to bring a long siege upon her, and ruin at last, which are called "great waters."

"The east wind hath broken thee." That was Nebuchadnezzar, who came with a great army from the east, besieged, took, and ruined Tyre; he dealt with that metaphorical ship, as a rough east wind doth with a ship at sea, breaks it, and sinks it.

Ver. 27. "Shall all fall into the midst of the sea." &c. The Hebrew is, the heart of the sea; all the wealth, greatness, and glory of Tyrus should be drowned in the sea.

Ver. 28. "The suburbs shall shake." The word for "suburbs" is, מגרשות and *migrash*, saith Pagnine, is a village out of the city. "By suburbs" here, you understand all the villages and colonies belonging unto Tyre. When the pilots, the prince, and governors thereof, should cry for the ruin of it, then should all the towns, villages, colonies, which were under her command, be troubled and shake for fear.

Obs. 1. Nothing human can protect a sinful city and people from the judgments of God. Tyrus was as strong a place as the world had; her walls, towers, ships, wise, strong men, could not do it. Tyrus was as rich a place as any under heaven, she had a multitude of all riches; yet these kept her not from being brought into great waters. What power or art of man can keep off the wind from a ship, when it is at sea? It is not in the power of all the seamen or mariners in the world to do it; neither can any number of men, or all men, keep off a judgment of God when it is coming upon a sinful place. Let us not confide in human things.

Obs. 2. The ruin of cities and states is chiefly from the princes and governors in the same. "Thy rowers," they who sit in the chief places, they "have brought thee into great waters;" they brought war, famine, desolation upon Tyrus. Zedekiah and his nobles breaking with Nebuchadnezzar, brought Judea and Jerusalem into great waters. Pharaoh's sin brought all the plagues upon Egypt. When governors are wilful, covetous, weak, ignorant, careless, given to their lusts and pleasures, they may quickly overthrow all. Rehoboam's folly caused that rent in Israel, which never was made up again. It was Ahaz's sin that brought Judah into deep waters; 2 Chron. xxviii. 19, "The Lord brought Judah low because of Ahaz king of Israel; for he made Judah naked, and transgressed sore against the Lord."

Obs. 3. That cities and states grown rich and renowned, have their periods. Tyrus was replenished with the rarities of the world, she had all excellent things in her, and was very glorious; but what became of her, and all she had? were not her riches, her glory, laid in the seas in the day of her ruin? ver. 27. She had her days for rising, and a day for her ruin. All the glory, bravery, and wealth of this great, strong, and beautiful city, was on a sudden, in a day, buried in the deep sea.

Obs. 4. When the Lord brings his judgments upon sinful cities and states, when he makes great changes in them, or utterly ruins them, then some lament, and some laugh. When Tyrus was besieged, stormed, taken, and ruined, then the rowers, mariners, and pilots, cried, wept, and wailed bitterly, lamenting her destruction; then the merchants laughed and hissed at her. When Jerusalem was taken, burnt, and nothing left but rubbish and ashes, then Jeremiah and many others lamented greatly for the ruin thereof; and then the Ammonites, Moabites, and Edomites, laughed thereat, as you may see, Ezek. xxv. Such is the condition of human affairs, and corruption of human nature, that what is matter of mourning and humiliation to one, becomes matter of rejoicing and insulting to another; but Wisdom hath said, "He that is glad at calamities shall not be unpunished," Prov. xvii. 5.

Obs. 5. The righteous God doth sometimes recompense sinners in the same way they have sinned. Tyrus laughed at the destruction of Jerusalem, Ezek.

xxvi. 2; and here, in this chapter, ver. 36, "The merchants among the people shall hiss at thee." Hissing, as it sometimes notes astonishment, so sometimes gladness and insulting; Lam. ii. 15, 16, "All that pass by clap their hands at thee; they wag their heads, and hiss, and say, This is the day we looked for," &c. At first these merchants might be astonished at the tidings of Tyrus her ruin, and after rejoice, clap their hands, and hiss at her. Agag by his sword had made women childless, and by Samuel's sword his mother was made childless, 1 Sam. xv. 33.

CHAPTER XXVIII.

Ver. 1—10. *The word of the Lord came again unto me, saying, Son of man, say unto the prince of Tyrus, Thus saith the Lord God; Because thine heart is lifted up, and thou hast said, I am a god, I sit in the seat of God, in the midst of the seas; yet thou art a man, and not God, though thou set thine heart as the heart of God: behold, thou art wiser than Daniel; there is no secret that they can hide from thee: with thy wisdom and with thine understanding thou hast gotten thee riches, and hast gotten gold and silver into thy treasures: by thy great wisdom and by thy traffick hast thou increased thy riches, and thine heart is lifted up because of thy riches: therefore thus saith the Lord God; Because thou hast set thine heart as the heart of God; behold, therefore I will bring strangers upon thee, the terrible of the nations: and they shall draw their swords against the beauty of thy wisdom, and they shall defile thy brightness. They shall bring thee down to the pit, and thou shalt die the deaths of them that are slain in the midst of the seas. Wilt thou yet say before him that slayeth thee, I am God? but thou shalt be a man, and no God, in the hand of him that slayeth thee. Thou shalt die the deaths of the uncircumcised by the hand of strangers: for I have spoken it, saith the Lord God.*

IN this chapter you have these general parts.

I. A prophecy against the king of Tyre, in these ten verses.

II. A lamentation for him, and the spoiling of his glory, from the 11th verse to the 19th.

III. A prophecy against Zidon, from the 20th verse to the 23rd.

IV. A prophecy of mercy unto the people of God, from the 24th to the end.

I. In the prophecy against the king of Tyrus, you have,

1. The authority of the prophecy, in ver. 1.

2. The sin that brought destruction upon him, which was his pride, ver. 2, occasioned from his seat, his wisdom, ver. 3, 4, and his wealth, ver. 4, 5.

3. The instruments the Lord would use in his destruction; and they were strangers, ver. 7; the manner of whose dealings with him is set out in ver. 8—10.

Ver. 1. "The word of the Lord came again," &c. Being to speak unto the king of Tyrus, he mentions his commission, that the Lord spake to him, and sent him, one greater than the king himself. Hereby the prophet made way for himself and his message to have the better entertainment; had he come of his own head, delivered things from his own spirit, he had rendered himself contemptible: what he had to declare unto the king, and against him, was not human, but revelation from the Lord.

Ver. 2. "Son of man." The "son of man" must utter the words of God. Heavenly treasure is put in earthen vessels, and makes them honourable. Ezekiel, though he were the "son of man," yet herein he was the servant of God. He sent him, and put his own words in his mouth, full of majesty, and to be believed, notwithstanding his meanness and frailty. This "son of man," is made a son of thunder against a proud and haughty prince.

"Say unto the prince of Tyrus." Some of the fathers do make this prince of Tyrus to be the devil; but they were much mistaken in so conceiting, for here are many things which are incompetent to him, especially what is said in ver. 7, 8. The words are to be taken literally of Ethbahal, or Ithobalus, who was at that time prince of Tyrus, unto whom this prophecy was directed, being in his glory and height; whereas Satan was cast out, and cast down into greater misery than here is mentioned, long before.

"Thus saith the Lord God." Prophets, being subject to the same infirmities and passions as others, are little regarded in the world, especially by princes. Ezekiel therefore must not speak his own words, but say, "Thus saith the Lord God." The Hebrew, *Adonai Jehovah*, are very significant words: Jehovah imports God's being, and giving being unto all things; *Adonai*, his supporting all in their beings, for it is from ארן a pillar, or foundation. Thus saith he, who hath his being of himself, and hath given being to heaven and earth, and all creatures therein, that upholds all by his power, even thee thyself, O prince of Tyrus; thus saith he unto thee.

"Because thine heart is lifted up." By "heart" understand not that little part of flesh in man wherein is the seat of life, but the thoughts, counsels, reasonings, designs, wisdom, workings, and contrivances of the heart: so "heart" is oft to be taken in Scripture; and it is lifted up, when it is carried out after high and great things. Psal. cxxxi. 1, "Lord, my heart is not haughty, nor mine eyes lofty: neither do I exercise myself in great matters, or in things too high for me." Here you may see what it is to have the heart lifted up, or to be haughty; it is גבה in both places, and it is to have aspiring thoughts, to mind high things, to be designing and reaching after them, to have a high conceit of oneself, as this prince of Tyre had, who thought himself above the condition of mortal men; and so the counsels, reasonings, designs, and workings of his heart, were to become a god, and he blushed not to say it.

"Thou hast said, I am a god." Not, thou hast thought so, which had been too much, but, thou hast said it. The word אמר sometimes notes purposing, determining, as in 2 Chron. ii. 1, "Solomon determined to build an house;" he said, that is, he purposed in himself to do it; but here it is more than purposing and determining, the prince of Tyrus "said," he spake it out, what he thought in his heart he uttered with his lips. "I am a god," *El ani*, I am the strong one, I give being to this city and state, I uphold the same, on me they all depend, from me they have counsel, comfort, and protection; I do what I list, my power extends far and near; I open the door and ports for all the isles and nations to trade with thee, O Tyrus, and I can prohibit them at my pleasure: I have filled thee with the riches and rarities of all the nations, I have done great things, I am beyond others, mighty and powerful, a god, and worthy of such honour as becomes the gods.

"I sit in the seat of God, in the midst of the seas." As God is in the heavens, which are inaccessible, none being able to come thither, to wrong or harm him; so am I in Tyrus, seated upon a rock, in the heart or "midst of the seas;" none can come at me to do me prejudice, I am without fear, I am in "the seat of God," not subject to the malice or power of any mortal whatsoever; all the merchants bring presents unto and adore me; I have power, wealth, honour, and all things glorious and delightful, my seat is no other than the "seat of God." Here was the great pride of this prince, who arrogated to himself a deity, and affected divine honour.

"Yet thou art a man, and not God." The Hebrew is, אדם ולא־אל thou art of earth, and not of heaven; thou art a weak, sinful man, that canst do nothing for others or thyself; what! thou *El*, the strong God? no, thou forgettest what thou art; he that is *El* will break thee in pieces like a potter's vessel, and make thee know "thou art man, and not God," that there is no difference between thee and other men; if they be infirm and feeble things, subject to changes, sorrows, sicknesses, and death, so art thou.

"Though thou set thine heart as the heart of God." Thou hast had such thoughts of thy strength, thy glory, thy wisdom, that thou hast persuaded thyself thou art become a god, another god, or as God. The thoughts of God's heart are, that he is strong, glorious, great, and wise, and thou takest up his thoughts: by "heart," the thoughts, imaginations, and devices of it are meant. This prince of Tyrus dreamed, that he was as fit and able to rule in the seas as God was in heaven, and that his wisdom, strength, and government, made him as honourable and glorious as the Lord's made him, that he was invincible, like God himself.

Obs. 1. The Lord takes notice of men's hearts, in what frame they are. "Thine heart is lifted up." Men cannot look into the heart, being shut up in a house of clay; but the eyes of the Lord pierce through our mud walls, and behold our hearts, and the workings of them. 1 Sam. xvi. 7, "The Lord looketh on the heart:" we look upon actions, faces, outward appearances, but God looks inward, and fixes his eye upon the heart; and so, that he knows what is in the heart, and how it works, he understands all the thoughts thereof, and the imaginations of those thoughts, 1 Chron. xxviii. 9, not only the rude draught, but what imaginations are thereupon. He knows men's minds exactly, and can tell you whose hearts are proud and whose are humble, whose are froward and whose are meek, whose are chaste and whose unclean.

Obs. 2. Princes and great ones are prone, not only to be proud, but to deify themselves. The prince of Tyrus his heart was lifted up, and he said, "I am a god." This is the height of pride, to make oneself a god, to arrogate that which is due unto the Lord. God had said it, "I am God, and there is none else; I am God, and there is none like me," Isa. xlvi. 9; now what pride, what blasphemy was it for this prince to say, "I am a god!" There are two things which God challengeth to himself, "vengeance," Deut. xxxii. 35, and godship, Isa. xliv. 8. This prince robbed God of one, making himself God. Sundry of the heathen emperors would either be called or worshipped as gods. Caligula made himself a god, erecting a temple with his image in it, ordaining priests and most costly sacrifices to be offered there to himself. Domitian by a public edict ordained, that in all writings wherein he should be mentioned upon any occasion, he should be called *Dominus Deus*, Lord God. A mad humour of deifying themselves also invaded Alexander the Great and Julius Cæsar. Such is the frame of antichrist's spirit, 2 Thess. ii. 4, "He as God sitteth in the temple of God, showing himself that he is God."

Obs. 3. Haughtiness and pride of spirit, do precede and presage the destruction of men. This prince was near unto utter ruin, and before it his heart was lifted up; he said, "I sit in the seat of God," I punish and I spare whom I please; but quickly after he was thrust out of his seat, and made an example of divine vengeance for his pride and presumption. Edom's heart was proud and high, even before the Lord threw her down, Obad 3, 4. The hearts of Samaria's inhabitants were greatly swollen with pride, and tympanized, when the Lord threatened to bring the adversaries of Rezin against them, Isa. ix. 9—11. Herod's pride bred the worms that did devour him. Prov. xvi. 18, "Pride goeth before destruction, and an haughty spirit before a fall."

Obs. 4. Whatever thoughts and conceits princes or others have of themselves, yet they are but dust and ashes, poor, inconsiderable things in respect of God. "Thou art a man and not God, though thou set thine heart as the heart of God." He was a worthless, despicable thing, notwithstanding he deified himself. Men fancy themselves Elohims, Jehovahs, when they are but Adams, and Enoshes. Jehoiakim made his nest in the cedars, when he was but earth, "a despised broken idol," Jer. xxii. 23, 28, 29. Great men have great thoughts, ranking themselves among the gods of the earth; but, as David expresseth it, "among the gods there is none like unto the Lord," Psal. lxxxvi. 8: they are earthen, proud, foolish, dying gods, Psal. lxxxii. 6, 7; but God is in heaven, holy, wise, ever-living: the greatest and best of the sons of men is no better than a brier or thorn to him, Isa. xxvii. 4; he is "a consuming fire," and what is a brier or thorn to such a fire! In Isa. xxxi. 3, it is said, "the Egyptians are men, and not God:" they had high thoughts of themselves, and the Jews had higher; they looked at them, and not at the Lord; they thought every Egyptian was *El*, a strong God; but the Egyptians were *Adams*, not *El*, men, and not God; the highest of them, their Pharaohs, were men, worms, grasshoppers, nothings, to that God they neglected, and that they should know, when he should stretch out his hand. God's thoughts and men's do differ exceedingly, they think themselves somebodies, as Simon Magus did, Acts viii. 9, gods as the prince of Tyrus here did; but, Psal. lxii. 9, "Men of high degree are a lie," not lying, but a lie; and you know a lie is that which hath no truth in it, no substance, no weight: they think themselves solid, substantial, massy pieces; but they deceive themselves, and others, not God, who tells them they are a lie, false, vain, and empty things. And not only some men, but even all men are so in his eye; Isa. xl. 17, "All nations before him are as nothing; and they are counted to him less than nothing, and vanity." That all are as nothing before him who is infinite, easily will be granted; but that they are less than nothing in his account, this seems strange and questionable. How can all the nations be less than nothing? the sense is, they are extremely inconsiderable. The words in the original are rendered thus by Montanus, They are viewed by him as nothing and vanity; for nothing and emptiness they are reputed or accounted to him, or he reckons them as a thing of nought, and vain.

Ver. 3. "Behold, thou art wiser than Daniel." The Tyrians were wise men, Zech. ix. 2; Ezek. xxvii. 8; 2 Chron. ii. 14; and it is probable their kings were wise, well seen into sea, military, and political affairs; and that the prince of Tyre, here spoken of, was one of the wisest of them, but puffed up with a conceit of more wisdom than he had; therefore here the Lord, in an ironical way, as expositors conceive, gives him a check, saying, "Behold, thou art wiser than Daniel;" thou makest thyself a god, as if thou knewest all things, which Daniel did not. The Septuagint reads the words by way of interrogation, Art thou wiser than Daniel? The words by some are taken by way of concession, Thou sayest thou sittest in the seat of God, and hast a heart as the heart of God; be it so; behold, then, thou art wiser than Daniel; he knew some secrets, thou knowest all. Daniel was very wise, he would not defile himself with the king's meat or wine, Dan. i. 8; he revealed and interpreted the king's dreams, chap. ii. and iv.; he read and interpreted the writings upon the wall, which none of the wise men could do, chap. v.; he had an excellent spirit in him, and was chief president over the one hundred and twenty princes that were set over the whole kingdom; and when the two other presidents, and all the rest of the princes, envied him, and sought occasion against him, he had carried things so wisely and well, that they could find no occasion against him, chap. vi. Daniel had natural, political, and spiritual wisdom, insomuch that it grew into a proverb, "wiser than Daniel." His wisdom was great, dispersed far, and known to the eastern and other parts of the world, and even to Tyrus, which had trading from all parts; and because the prince of it was so wise in his own conceit, the Lord gives him a notable twitch here, "Behold, thou art wiser than Daniel."

Vid. Dan. i. 17, 20.

"There is no secret that they can hide from thee." Thou art so possessed with opinion of thy wisdom, that thou conceivest nothing can be kept secret or hid from thee. The Hebrew word for "secret" is, סתום *sathum*, which signifies a thing shut up; and what is so, is secret and hidden from others: as Dan. viii. 26, "Shut up the vision, for it is for many days." The vision being sealed and "shut up," it was not knowable for a season, men could not tell what was therein, it was hid from them. But this prince of Tyre took upon him to know secrets, and things shut up from the vulgar, and wise also. In the original, the words stand thus, every hidden thing they do not hide from thee; here an active is put for a passive verb, and carries this sense, Every hidden thing is not hid from thee, thou art so wise as that thou piercest into secrets, dark and deep things; thou art a God, and what can men hide, or what can be hidden from thee? The words are spoken ironically, or according to the opinion men had of him.

Obs. 1. Wisdom makes men honourable and famous. Daniel was wise, and his wisdom begat such a high esteem of him, that it became a proverb, "wiser than Daniel." Nebuchadnezzar honoured Daniel much, when he acknowledged Daniel's wisdom to be ten times better than the wisdom of all the astrologers and magicians that were in his realm, Dan. i. 20; but God honoured him more, when he made his wisdom exemplary, and proverbial throughout the world. Wisdom is from God, a "principal thing," Prov. iv. 7; it makes men of an "excellent spirit," Dan. v. 12; Prov. xvii. 27, directing to do like unto God; hence it is, that men endued with it are honourable and renowned. David was wise, and his wisdom is recorded in holy writ for his honour; 1 Sam. xviii. 5, 15, 30, he behaved himself wisely, very wisely, "more wisely than all the servants of Saul;" the widow of Tekoah compared his wisdom to the "wisdom of an angel," 2 Sam. xiv. 20. Solomon was wise, yea, "wiser than all men, than Ethan the Ezrahite, and Heman, and Chalcol, and Darda;" these were wise men, and honoured for their wisdom, but Solomon above them all; his wisdom spread into all courts, and unto all kings of the earth, 1 Kings iv. 31, 34. This made Solomon to say, "The wise shall inherit glory," Prov. iii. 35: a son of wisdom is an heir to glory; he shall not have flitting glory, but fixed, such glory as shall be his inheritance.

Obs. 2. Men know not what themselves are. "Thou art wiser than Daniel." Thou thinkest thyself to be very wise, whereas thou art ignorant, and foolish, and dost manifest it to the full. The irony in the words speaks this out unto us; for an irony is a trope, putting one contrary for another: here wisdom is mentioned, and by it the prince's foolishness is declared; it was so in him, to think himself a God, that he knew every secret; he did not know himself, that is a hard lesson. The apostle tells us, 1 Cor. viii. 2, that "if any man," be he prince, or of what condition soever, "thinketh that he knoweth any thing, he knoweth nothing yet as he ought to know." When men conceit they know something, this puffs them up, makes them despise and neglect others, and they know nothing rightly; for right knowledge of things would make men humble, and direct them to use their talents to the good of others, the glory of the giver, considering they must give account thereof ere long. The doctrine of self-knowledge is out of practice; men study to know other men, other countries, what news, but are strangers to themselves. Hazael knew not himself; when the prophet told him what strange things he should do, he was conceited that such cruelty could not harbour in his nature, 2 Kings viii. 12, 13. The Pharisee knew not himself, when he justified himself so above the publican, Luke xviii. 11. It is the common evil of the world, that men do not know themselves, what in truth they are. Laodicea knew not herself; she said she was rich, increased with goods, and wanted nothing, she knew not that she was wretched, poor, blind, and naked.

Obs. 3. That ironical speeches are not unwarrantable. "Thou art wiser than Daniel;" thou knowest all secrets. They have some tartness in them, yet are frequently used in the word, both by God himself, and his holy servants.

(1.) By God himself. Gen. iii. 22, "Behold, the man is become as one of us, to know good and evil." God had made man after his own image, but he, by believing Satan, telling him he should be as God, knowing good and evil, if he ate of the forbidden fruit, lost that image; and here God upbraids him for it, "Behold, Adam is become as one of us." The meaning is, he is now altogether unlike us, he is deluded by the serpent, and become abominable like the serpent himself: in this expression God laughed him to scorn for his folly. In Judg. x. you have another ironical passage of the Lord's; it is ver. 14, "Go and cry unto the gods which ye have chosen, let them deliver you in the time of your tribulation." Here God cuts them to the quick for their wickedness, idolatry, and blindness: You have been weary of me, better gods have you spied out, chosen, and served, gods that can do great things for you; why come you to me in your straits? go, get you to your new gods; let them, who have had your worship, arise, appear, act for, and deliver you. Such is that of Christ, Mark vii. 9, "Full well ye reject the commandment of God, that ye may keep your own tradition." Did they well to reject God's commands and set up men's traditions? no, they did exceeding ill in it, and that is the mind of Christ; when he saith, "full well," he speaks ironically, and intimates they did extremely evil, most wickedly.

(2.) By men, that were precious in the sight of God. Micaiah being demanded of Ahab, whether he should go up to Ramoth-gilead to battle, said, "Go, and prosper; for the Lord shall deliver it into the hand of the king," 2 Kings xxii. 15. Take the words as they seem to sense, it here is good encouragement, but so they contradict ver. 17, and 28; they are therefore a bitter irony, or sarcasm: All your prophets encourage you to go, and you expect the same from me; well, go, and prosper; his meaning is, go, and perish, that is the spirit and true sense of the words. Job xii. 2, "No doubt but ye are the people, and wisdom shall die with you." Job's friends thought him a silly man compared to them, no better than a beast, chap. xi. 12; but here he hits them home for it: No doubt you are the only people in the world for wit and wisdom, you are the only knowing and all-knowing men, and when you die, there will be a death of all wisdom, the world left in a sad case, having not a wise man in it. Job, by a holy irony, batters the conceit they had of their own wisdom.

Ver. 4. "With thy wisdom and with thine understanding," &c. The king of Tyrus was expert in civil affairs, and by that skill he had therein, he got unto himself much wealth. The Spirit of God calls the cunning and craft he had in worldly affairs, "wisdom and understanding." It cannot be meant of spiritual wisdom, for, Prov. iii. 13, that makes blessed, and this prince was under the curse and judgments of God. He was worldly wise, and set his wisdom on work to get riches.

"Thou hast gotten thee riches." The Hebrew is, thou hast made to thyself riches. The word for "riches" is, חיל which the Septuagint renders, δυνάμιν, power; the Vulgate, strength; and ours, "riches;" for "riches," to rich men's apprehensions, do add strength and power to them. This king made himself rich, and so strong and powerful by his riches. He had all sorts of riches, chap. xxvii.

"And hast gotten gold and silver into thy treasures." The Hebrew for "treasure" is, אוצר *otzar*, from אצר to gather together, to lay up, and it notes both the treasure, and the place where the treasure is laid up; and so it may do here; the king of Tyre had gotten gold and silver into his treasures, that is, among his other treasures he had them, or, they were in his treasury.

Ver. 5. "By thy great wisdom and by thy traffick hast thou," &c. Thou art very wise in thy own opinion, and thou art grown exceeding rich by thy trading and merchandizing with other nations, but thou attributest all to thine own wisdom and industry, nothing is given unto me, no mention is made of me. This king was a great merchant, did mightily increase in wealth, was reputed wise, but was really foolish, as the next words declare.

"Thine heart is lifted up because of thy riches." He had a mountain of wealth, and that made his heart mountainous, his riches puffed him up; he should have been the more humble, having much to answer for, but he was the more haughty, confident, secure, and fearless of danger; he thought, being so rich and great as he was, that he could do any thing, yea, all things.

Obs. 1. That by skill and industry men grow wealthy. The prince of Tyre had insight into trading, which he employed, and so made himself rich. Solomon tells you, Prov. x. 4, that "the hand of the diligent maketh rich:" there is much in diligence to advance a man's estate, especially when diligence and skill go together, when a diligent hand is ordered by a wise head; if there be actings without skill, little will be produced, if skill without acting, nothing comes thereof; where these go together, often they bring in great wealth. Some besides their skill, use craft and cunning, and so suddenly get great estates.

Obs. 2. Great men are prone to covetousness, and lay out themselves to get wealth. "Thou," even the prince of Tyre, "hast gotten thee riches; by thy traffick hast thou increased thy riches." He was covetous, and traded with the isles and nations to feed his covetous humour. Princes are forbidden to multiply gold and silver to themselves, Deut. xvii. 17; they may lose the hearts of their people by it, yea, they may lose themselves also thereby; but this prince made it his work to increase wealth, which is the practice of most princes and people in the world. Men's corrupt natures and carnal wisdom carry them unto it: Prov. xxiii. 4, "Labour not to be rich; cease from thine own wisdom." Men's wisdom puts them on to be rich, it heartens them thereunto, but it is such wisdom as the Scripture condemns. The Arabian proverb is, Justice and covetousness dwell not together: a just man covets not what is another's, but a covetous man will have the prey wherever he finds it, and violate bounds to satisfy his lusts. Ahab's sickness was not cured, till he had eaten Naboth's vineyard and drunk his blood. Hoffing Historia Orientali.

There is a story among the Arabians, of one that had the world presented to him in the shape of an old woman, whom he asked, how many husbands she had? she said, innumerable. The party asked what was become of them? she said, she had killed them all. Then it was replied by the party, I wonder that other men are so foolish, that, seeing how thou hast used thy former husbands, they should still be in love with thee.

Obs. 3. Prosperity makes men proud and insolent. "Thine heart is lifted up because of thy riches:" they begat great thoughts in him, and swelled his heart above his brethren. It is hard to keep the heart low in prosperity. It is a common saying, and too true, As rises my good, so rises my blood. Beggars having gotten estates, account themselves princes; and princes being rich, think themselves gods. When Amaziah prospered in his war against the Edomites, his heart was lifted up, and being but a thistle, he accounted himself a cedar, 2 Chron. xxv.: prosperity begets cedarish spirits. Hos. xiii. 6, "They were filled, and their heart was exalted;" when they had plenty, then they grew proud, and forgat God. There is an aptness in men to dote upon the creature, when they have much, and to magnify themselves. This Agur knew when he prayed that God would not give him riches, lest he should be full and deny God. Men are ready to attribute their riches to their wisdom, industry, favour of their friends, &c.: hereby they exclude and deny God, they allow him no hand, no interest therein; they say, Who is the Lord, that we should be thankful unto him? we are not beholden at all to him, or very little; and thus they deny and belie the Lord too, as the word *cathash* signifies. You that prosper in this world, take heed to your hearts, lest being drunk with this wine, you discover your nakedness.

Ver. 6, 7. "Therefore thus saith the Lord God; Because thou hast set thine heart as the heart of God; behold, therefore I will bring strangers upon thee." Here the Lord tells the prince of Tyrus what he must look for at his hands for his sins, especially his pride; because he magnified himself, and would be as God, therefore he must expect destruction.

"Because thou hast set thine heart as the heart of

God." The Hebrew is, hast given thine heart as the heart of God: Thou hast given liberty to thy heart, to think high and great things; yea, to think thyself equal with God. He thought the infinite, glorious, great God, had not other thoughts in him, or vaster, than himself, and this was setting his heart as the heart of God.

"I will bring strangers upon thee." That is, Nebuchadnezzar, with his forces gathered up out of several provinces, Ezek. xxvi. 7; they were men of a strange language, of strange manners, and out of strange countries, they were strangers to the Tyrians.

"The terrible of the nations." The word for "terrible" is, עריצי *aritze*, which Montanus renders, the strong; the Vulgate, the most mighty; Vatablus, the tyrants of the nations; Septuagint saith, λοιμοὺς, pestilent men, that should be as a plague or pestilence is to a town or country; ours, the "terrible:" ערץ *aratz* signifies, through power to be formidable to others; so should the Chaldeans be to the Tyrians.

"They shall draw their swords against the beauty of thy wisdom." By "beauty of wisdom," understand whatever beautiful things the prince had gotten by his wisdom, as beautiful shipping, beautiful army, beautiful treasure and riches, a beautiful city, a beautiful throne, &c. The Chaldeans should come, and destroy all the beauty of his wisdom, all that by his policy and craft he had gotten. Or thus; Thou thinkest by thy counsels, art, and devices, to prevent the taking of the city, and thyself, which couldst thou do, it would make thy wisdom beautiful and glorious; but they shall draw their swords, and prevail against all thy counsels, machinations, plots, and attempts to secure the city and thyself.

"They shall defile thy brightness." Thou art now in a glorious kingdom, and shinest upon thy seat and throne, all the isles and nations behold thy splendour; but the Chaldeans shall come and cut thee off, and "defile thy brightness" with thine own blood; they shall take away thy kingly dignity and life also.

Ver. 8. "They shall bring thee down to the pit." The word for "pit" is, שחת which signifies corruption, and also a pit, or grave, because that is the place of corruption; men in their graves do see corruption, they turn to dust. It is a proverbial speech, noting death: Prov. xxviii. 17, "A man that doeth violence to the blood of any person shall flee to the pit," that is, be cut off, and thrown into the grave; so here, the strangers should cut off the prince of Tyrus, and cause him to perish.

"Thou shalt die the deaths of them that are slain in the midst of the seas." Thou art in a city upon a rock, well walled, fortified, and manned, thou thinkest thyself secure, invincible; but thou shalt be like those who are slain at sea, and thrown overboard, or sunk into the depths thereof. For kings to be slain by foreigners is dishonourable; when slain, not to be buried as kings, is a greater dishonour; to be cast out, and drowned as common men, is a height of dishonour.

Ver. 9. "Wilt thou yet say before him that slayeth thee, I am God?" Thou hast said that thou art a god; but when the enemy shall be before thy gates, when he shall seize upon thee, and be ready to thrust thee through, what wilt thou then say? wilt thou say thou art a God? no, thou wilt show thyself a man, thou wilt be full of fears, and at thy wit's end.

"Thou shalt be a man, and no God, in the hand of him that slayeth thee." Then shall the vanity of thy thoughts appear, thou shalt see thyself a man, and not God: thou hast thought thyself *El*, the strong, powerful, and stable God, but thou shalt find thyself *Adam*, weakness, misery, instability.

Ver. 10. "Thou shalt die the deaths of the uncircumcised." These words may be taken two ways: either, thou shalt die by the hand of those that are uncircumcised; thou shalt not have the honour to die by the hand of the Jews, who by circumcision are distinguished from all other, thou shalt die by Chaldeans, a profane and barbarous people: or, thou shalt die the death of the uncircumcised, that is, thou shalt so die, as to perish soul and body for ever; thou hast exalted thyself to be a god, and thou shalt be cast into hell. The nations who were uncircumcised were without God, without Christ, Eph. ii. 12, and so perished.

"For I have spoken it, saith the Lord God." Thou mayst contemn this prophecy, and think there is nothing in it; but know, it is not the voice of man, like thyself, but the voice of God, who will fulfil it, and make thee know that thou art man, and not God, that thou hast sinned greatly in comparing thyself with God.

Obs. 1. Haughtiness and pride of spirit provokes God to deal severely with men. "Because thou hast set thine heart as the heart of God, therefore will I bring strangers upon thee, the terrible of the nations." God stirred up, led out, the most terrible of the Babylonians to punish the prince of Tyrus for his pride and insolency. Theudas boasted himself to be somebody, drew followers after him; but he and they were all slain by the just judgment of God, Acts v. 36. Zeba and Zalmunna said, "Let us take to ourselves the houses of God in possession," Psal. lxxxiii. 12; they had aspiring spirits, but the Lord cut them off by the hand of Gideon, Judg. viii. 21. Proud spirits the Lord will meet with, and break in pieces; he hath said it, Isa. ii. 11, "The lofty looks of man shall be humbled, and the haughtiness of men shall be bowed down." Let those that have much, look to it that they be not lifted up, lest they fall, be broken, and rise no more.

Obs. 2. That which is the glory and delight of men, is subject to spoil and profanation. "They shall draw their swords against the beauty of thy wisdom, and they shall defile thy brightness." They laid all the glory of Tyrus, and of the prince thereof, in the dust: there was beauty and brightness in the court, in the city, in the navy, in the armoury, in the treasury; but when the Chaldean came, he spoiled, he stained all: it was not the wisdom of the Tyrian, nor the beauty or brightness of the things, that could keep off the enemies from plundering and profaning; they minded not beauty or brightness, wisdom, real or pretended, but they lay all waste, cut off the prince, and make a beautiful glorious city as a heap of rubbish, or as nothing.

Obs. 3. Approachings of death will make men know themselves. When this prince of Tyrus should be in the hand of his enemies, and at death's door, then he should see that he was no God, but a poor, miserable, mortal man; when death comes, and strikes upon our walls, then we understand ourselves. Psal. ix. 20, "Put them in fear, O Lord; that the nations may know themselves to be but men." When nations prosper, have all things as heart desires, they judge themselves more than men, they are petty gods; but let the Lord send in some sore judgments, that carry death in their foreheads, then the nations will know themselves to be but men; that is, sorry, fading, perishing things: though death shut all men's eyes, yet the approach of death opens them oft to see more of themselves than ever before.

Obs. 4. That wicked princes and others, however they may flourish in the world for a season, yet their ends will be miserable. "Thou shalt die the deaths of the uncircumcised;" a temporal death here, eternal death hereafter, therefore envy not great ones, who flourish here in the world for a season, and after go down to the pit, where they shall suffer sufficiently for their demerit.

Ver. 11—15. *Moreover the word of the Lord came unto me, saying, Son of man, take up a lamentation upon the king of Tyrus, and say unto him, Thus saith the Lord God; Thou sealest up the sum, full of wisdom, and perfect in beauty. Thou hast been in Eden the garden of God; every precious stone was thy covering, the sardius, topaz, and the diamond, the beryl, the onyx, and the jasper, the sapphire, the emerald, and the carbuncle, and gold: the workmanship of thy tabrets and of thy pipes was prepared in thee in the day that thou wast created. Thou art the anointed cherub that covereth; and I have set thee so: thou wast upon the holy mountain of God; thou hast walked up and down in the midst of the stones of fire. Thou wast perfect in thy ways from the day that thou wast created, till iniquity was found in thee.*

Here begins the second general part of the chapter, viz. a lamentation for the prince of Tyrus, and the corrupting of his glory. Besides the lamentation, and authority of it, in ver. 11, 12, you have,

1. The state of this prince, set out from his power, wisdom, wealth, delights, and greatness, ver. 12—15.

2. The cause that his state and glory were destroyed, ver. 15.

Ver. 12. "Take up a lamentation upon the king of Tyrus." In chap. xxvii. 2, the Lord bade him "take up a lamentation for Tyrus;" and here he bids him take up one for "the king of Tyrus," bewail his condition, for he should suffer as well as the city; and though he were a heathen king, yet the Lord would have him to be lamented, the prophet must weep over him.

"Thou sealest up the sum." The Hebrew is, אתה חתם תכנית which Montanus renders, *Tu sigillas dispositionem*: Septuagint, σὺ ἀποσφραγισμα ὁμοιώσεως; the Vulgate, *Tu signaculum similitudinis.* Ours is, "Thou sealest up the sum:" thou having power over all the commodities to be carried out or brought in, sayest how much and how little shall be exported and imported. "Thou sealest up the sum," thou puttest the last hand to the business, and dost complete it; thus some expositors interpret the words. Others, considering *tachnith* is from *tachan*, to weigh, to measure, and notes a thing measured, according to all its dimensions, they make the sense this; Thou art an absolute and complete king, whatever is wanting in others is found in thee; "thou sealest up the sum;" others want wisdom, riches, power, friends, thou hast all that conduceth to the greatness and happiness of a prince. When bags have all the money in them they should have, and writings all things inscribed which should be there, then they are sealed; so this king, in his own conceit, or apprehension of others, had all a king should have, and therefore the seal is set upon him; "thou sealest up the sum," thou art εἰκων βασιλικη, a picture and pattern for all kings.

"Full of wisdom." This prince seemed very wise, having his head filled with cunning, and skill in naval, mercatory, and political affairs. When princes know a little in any thing, they are applauded and magnified for knowing men, but if they have got some deeper insight into things than others, then they are deified.

"Perfect in beauty." This perfection of beauty lay in his buildings, shipping, riches, laws, government, soldiery, court, &c. in all which appeared much beauty and glory. The 27th chapter sets out the beauty and glory of Tyrus, which was also the king's.

Ver. 13. "Thou hast been in Eden the garden of God." Gen. ii. 8, it is said, "God planted a garden eastward in Eden." This Eden was a region in Mesopotamia, or Babylonia, which was a most pleasant place. The word "Eden" signifies delight, and pleasantness. In it God made a garden, which is a place enclosed, separated from what is common; גן a garden, is from גנן to protect, or compass about, because it is fenced in, and so protected from violence and spoil. This garden being planted by God in so pleasant a place as Eden was, exceeded it far, and was such a paradise as never eye saw since. Pleasant and delightful places are likened unto the same, and called Edens, and the gardens of God, Gen. xiii. 18; Joel ii. 3; Ezek. xxxvi. 35. So Tyre, though situate upon a rock, was by the art and industry of man made an Eden, as "the garden of God," very pleasant and delightful: the prince of it was in a paradise, wherein he had all things desirable.

"Every precious stone was thy covering." The merchants of Syria, of Sheba, and Raamah, brought precious stones of all sorts unto Tyrus, chap. xxvii. 16, 22; the chief whereof were set in his crown, canopies, tents, garments, beds, hangings, and other utensils. Princes spare not for cost; if any stone be more precious than others, they will have them, and beautify themselves and theirs with the same.

"The sardius." In Hebrew אדם *odem*, from אדם which signifieth, to be red, for it is of a fleshy or blood colour. It is called "sardius," because the best of them are found in Sardinia. This stone was the first in the breastplate of Aaron, Exod. xxviii. 17. The Chaldee calls it, *samkan*, which Shindler interprets, the ruby, or "sardius." The Romans of old used this stone, being hard and firm, for seals. Much virtue is attributed to this stone, as, to drive away fear, to make confident, to preserve from witchery and poisoning, &c.

"Topaz." The Hebrew word is, פטדה *pitdah*, which the Septuagint renders, τοπάζιον, and so it is called, Rev. xxi. 20. This stone for colour is of a greenish yellow, or yellowish green, such a colour as is in fern, yellow and green together. Some make two sorts of them, one very green and clear, called *prasoides*, another like pure gold, called *chrysopteros.* It is the greatest of all precious stones, saith Pliny, and it is so named a "topaz," from Plin. l. 37. c. 8.
Topazon, an island in the Red sea; yet there were topazes from other places: Job xxviii. 19, "The topaz of Ethiopia shall not equal it:" though those topazes were very precious, yet not comparable to wisdom. The "topaz" Martinius in
is commended for that virtue it hath to Top. Rueus de
stop eruptions of blood, to restrain Gemmis. l. 2. c. 9.
passion and wanton lusts, to help against melancholy, deliriums, phrenzies, falling sickness, and sudden death.

"And the diamond." ויהלם which some render, the jasper; others better, the adamant, or "diamond," for *jahalon* is from הלם *contundere*, to break in pieces: the "adamant" is of that hardness, that it breaks all other precious stones, and continues unbroken itself. In Arabic it is, *diamah*, from דים *dim*, to abide, because of its durableness. It is not so clear as the crystal, but sparkles and sends forth fiery or bright beams, like the sun. Philosophers say the diamond is of great use against poisons and enchantments, that it prevents madness, vain fears, and scarings in the sleep; it pacifies fury and enmity between parties, and maintains love in the nearest relations; at its presence, the loadstone loseth its attractive virtue.

"The beryl." Some have it the hyacinth, some the chrysolite. The Hebrew is, תרשיש which is the sea-beryl, because it resembles the greenness of the sea. Of this stone was spoken, chap. i. ver. 16. Some make it to be of a bluish colour. There are several kinds of them, the best are of a sea-green colour. Watery eyes, sighing, liver-griefs, dulness, are helped by the virtue of this stone; it is beneficial to the brain.

"The onyx." It is a precious stone, like the nail of a man's hand for whiteness. The Hebrew is שהם *shoham*, translated sometimes a sardonyx, sometimes an "onyx," but Rueus makes a difference between them. The Septuagint is very uncertain in the translation of this word *shoham*, the onyx, as you may see in De Dieu, upon Exodus xxviii, p. 76, and in Martinius, on the word "onyx."

"The jasper." The Hebrew being ישפה demonstrates no other stone can be admitted here but only the jasper, which is a stone of much worth and glory: Rev. iv. 3, the glory of God and Christ upon the throne in heaven is likened thereunto; as also the light and glory of the new Jerusalem, Rev. xxi. 11; yea, they were jasper stones which made the first foundation in the walls thereof, ver. 19. Isidore calls it the green gem, or precious stone. There are many kinds of jaspers, green, blue, airy, white, ruddy, purple, spotted. Onkelus turns the word *jaspeh*, in Exod. xxviii. *pantree;* and Jonathan, in this place of Ezekiel, *panterin, a panthera bestia*, because the jasper is spotted like the panther. The green Indian jasper is the chiefest of them all. Pliny affirms he saw a jasper so great, that it weighed eleven ounces. They are preservative against all poisons, dropsies, fevers, restrain blood and sweat, and refresh the eyes with their greenness.

Lib. 37. c. 9.

"The sapphire." Of the sapphire was largely spoken, chap. i. 26. Its colour is like the heavens, azure, or blue, and transparent. There are some sapphires white, others blue, these are the males, the other females, saith Bœtius, in his second book Of Gems. The best of this kind of stones come from the Medes. The virtue of this stone is much; it is a friend to chastity, it is powerful against anger, envy, deceitfulness, sadness; it is good against poisons, ruptures, &c.

"The emerald." נפך in Hebrew. Montanus makes it the carbuncle; Shindler, the smaragd; others, the chrysoprase; and so it is termed here in the margin; and so in chap. xxvii. 16, the margin is, chrysoprase. It is for colour a golden green, like a leek, inclining to yellow green. The best sort of emeralds, or chrysoprases, are those which have golden drops or spots on them. The true beauty and glory of these stones is seen only in the dark. They are comfortable to weak eyes, refresh the heart.

"The carbuncle." It is a precious stone, so called from the shining of it. The name of it in Hebrew is, ברקת from ברק which signifies, lightning, shining. De Dieu saith it is a stone that shines like lightning. Some would have it to be the smaragd, but Mercer and Shindler judge *bareketh* to be the carbuncle; and so Danæus, who saith, the smaragd doth not resemble the brightness of lightning, but the carbuncle, and at midnight, like the sun, it enlightens dark places near unto it. In Chaldee it is called ברקן *barkan*, which by a transposition of letters is קרבן *carban*, whence *carbunculus*. Of all flaming gems, it is counted the chief, and called "carbuncle," being like a burning coal: some call it, *approtus*, because no fire will hurt it. Those who write of it say, it comprehends the virtues of all other precious stones.

De Dieu, in Exod. xxviii. Martin. in Lexi.

"And gold." The Hebrew for "gold" is, זהב *zahab*, or *zahaf*, which hath affinity with צהב *tzahab*, which signifies, yellow; and it is called, *aurum ab aura*, as Isidore observes, because it is shining, or pure, as the air; and *zahaf* metaphorically is put for that which is pure, shining. Job xxxvii. 22, "Fair weather cometh out of the north." The Hebrew is, *zahaf*, gold comes out of the north; the meaning is, clear and pure air, like gold, comes out of that part of the world. So, Zech. iv. 12, the golden pipes are said to empty gold, for so is the original. The meaning is, oil which is pure, and in colour and brightness like gold.

"The workmanship of thy tabrets and of thy pipes was prepared in thee in the day that thou wast created." In the day of his birth, or of his being made king, there was great rejoicing, all instruments of music were used; "tabrets" and "pipes" being put for all the rest by a synecdoche. The Tyrians delighted in music, chap. xxvi. 13, and upon such occasions, as the birth and coronation of princes, they greatly rejoiced, and made use of their choicest instruments.

"The workmanship of thy tabrets." The word for workmanship is מלאכת *melecheth; melachah* signifies, saith Kirker, any thing that is for the service or use of man, whether arts, cattle, or any thing gotten by industry. Here it notes, that artifice was in their "tabrets and pipes;" they were curiously made and wrought, they were not common ones, but the choicest the art of man could produce.

"And of thy pipes." The Vulgate reads the words thus, thy holes, which Maldonate and some others do interpret "pipes," because they are full of holes; for נקבים the Hebrew for "pipes," is from נקב to bore through, and "pipes" are so.

"Was prepared in thee." How they were "prepared" in the king is hard to conceive: Piscator renders it, with thee, or, before thee, at the time of thy creation.

"In the day that thou wast created." Creation is proper to God, and is the production of an entity, or creature, out of nothing, as Gen. i. 1; and sometimes it is called creating, when of pre-existent matter a thing is made new, that it was not before, as man out of the earth; Gen. ii. 7, with Gen. i. 27, he is said to be "created:" and metaphorically it is applied to men, when they are made that which they were not; those who make them so are said to create, and those made so, to be "created:" hence, when men are raised by others, they are called their creatures.

Obs. 1. When men have natural or acquired excellences beyond others, and abuse them, it is matter of mourning. "Take up a lamentation upon the king of Tyrus:" he had more wisdom, beauty, blessing, prosperity, and abundance, than others, but he abused all; his heart was lift up, he honoured not God with what he had, and therefore Ezekiel must lament: so chap. xix. 1, he must lament for the princes of Israel, who abused their power, places, parts, and blessings they had.

Obs. 2. Choice accomplishments, with outward glory and greatness, are no arguments of God's grace, or God's special favour towards men. Heathens, and the worst of men, have had these; the prince of

Tyrus, who blasphemously said he was a god, he sealed up the sum; he was a complete prince, he had choice endowments, he was full of wisdom, perfect in beauty, he had outward glory and greatness as much as any, he was seated in a paradise, he glistered with pearls and precious stones, he had as choice music as was to be had; yet notwithstanding all these, he was a wretched man, under the curse of God, and was to die the death of the uncircumcised. What vanity is it, therefore, to pride ourselves in any human excellences, to set our hearts upon, or confide in, any outward glory or greatness!

Ver. 14. "Thou art the anointed cherub." Here the prince of Tyrus is compared unto an angel. Angels in Scripture are called "cherubims," Gen. iii. 24. The resemblances between him and them take in these particulars:

1. They are full of knowledge and wisdom, 2 Sam. xiv. 20; and it is said of this king, that he was full of wisdom.

2. They are beautiful and glorious creatures; Luke ix. 26, Christ shall come in the "glory of the angels;" so this king was perfect in beauty, and full of glory, being adorned with such precious stones as he was.

3. They are highly exalted above others, having great power and command; see Dan. x. 13, 20; 2 Kings xix. 35; they are called "principalities and powers," Eph. iii. 10: so this king was exalted above others, he had great power and command, so that he was dreadful, as the cherubims that kept the way into Paradise.

"Anointed." The cherubims above the ark, or mercy-seat, were anointed with oil, Exod. xxx. 26; to which here may be an allusion, "thou art the anointed cherub," or, thou thinkest thyself so: or it may be spoken in reference to the kings of Israel and high priest, who were anointed, and so had many prerogatives thereupon; and this man, being made king of Tyrus, had great privileges and prerogatives.

"That covereth." The cherubims had wings which covered the ark, Exod. xxv. 20; and this king had wings of power, stretched out at sea and land, to cover and protect his people.

Kirker. The Hebrew word is, הסוכך from סכך which is, to hide by covering over; a hen hides her chickens by putting her wings over them: it notes also, to protect; when things are covered, they are protected.

"I have set thee so." Thou wast made king, hadst great honour, privileges, and power, thou wast above others; and how camest thou to all this? It was not by any other than myself, "I have set thee so." The Hebrew is, I have given thee, that is, into such dignity and greatness.

"Thou wast upon the holy mountain of God." Some refer this to Hiram furnishing Solomon with materials to build the temple; but this sense of the words is in nowise entertainable, for Hiram was dead long before, and here the prophet speaks of one that was then to be destroyed. Piscator senses the words thus, Thou hast been so gorgeously attired, as if thou wert the high priest of my people, when he is in his robes. Others make this the sense, Thou wast as one upon the holy mountain of God. Tyrus is likened to mount Zion, the king to a cherub in the temple, thereupon it is called the "holy mountain," by way of resemblance; or because Tyre belonged to the tribe of Asher, it was within their lot, Josh. xix. 24, 29, and therefore belonging to God's people; and being on the borders of Canaan, it might be called "holy." If any should question whether Tyrus were on a mountain, know, that in the Scripture, cities, for their high buildings and strong defences, are called "mountains," though they be not on mountains; as, Jer. li. 25, "Behold, I am against thee, O destroying mountain;" it is spoken of Babylon, which was not upon a mountain, but in a plain, upon many waters, ver. 13. So Tyrus, for its high buildings, strong walls, and defences, may be called a "mountain;" but Tyrus was upon a rock, which was high above the waters, if not above the rest of the earth. Some tell us Tyrus was upon a great mountain, and things which are great, and goodly to see unto, are said to be the Lord's.

"Thou hast walked up and down in the midst of the stones of fire." What these "stones of fire" are, hath exercised the heads of men to find out. Some make them the angels, who, Heb. i. 7, are called "a flame of fire;" some will have them to be the two tables of stone given at mount Sinai in fire; some assert them to be the people of the Jews, who for their holiness, zeal, and love, are called "stones of fire;" some tell you they were the precious stones in the temple at Jerusalem, or the common stones gilded over; others by these understand men of excellent parts, spirits, and abilities, with whom the king of Tyre conversed. But these have overlooked the truth lying near at hand, for these "stones of fire" are the precious stones mentioned in the former verse, and are so called for their shining and glistering like fire, especially the carbuncles and diamonds, which sparkle, and seem to cast out fire. Sanctius saith, he walked in the midst of the stones of fire, because his royal palace shined with such stones as might well be called "stones of fire." The Jews at this time were not so holy as to be called or counted "stones of fire," they "committed adultery with stones and stocks," Jer. iii. 9; and were "stones of darkness," Job xxviii. 3, rather than "stones of fire."

Ver. 15. "Thou wast perfect in thy ways." The Septuagint hath the words thus, συ ἄμωμος ἐν ταῖς ἡμέραις σȣ, thou wast faultless, or spotless, in thy days; thou didst keep thyself free from those pollutions which kings usually are defiled with. The Hebrew is, thou wast perfect in thy ways; not in a moral sense, as if he were without sin, but in a political sense; he prospered in what he did, in his naval, military, court, and state affairs; he was successful, he wanted nothing pertaining to kingly greatness, he had all things which might make him complete and glorious.

"From the day that thou wast created." From the time of making thee king. In the day he was "created," all sorts of music were used then, ver. 13; and from that time he had all things conducible to royal greatness.

"Till iniquity was found in thee." There were some sins in this prince which were very provoking.

1. His insulting at the destruction of Jerusalem, which you have, chap. xxvi. 2, "Tyrus hath said, Aha, she is broken that was the gates of the people." Tyrus, that was, the king of Tyrus, and the people, they insulted over the Jews in their misery.

2. His excessive pride in making himself a god, or as God. These were iniquities, and whilst he was free from them, he prospered, his actions were commendable; but when these sprung up, and were discovered, then the Lord threatened him with destruction, and hastened his ruin. The words are spoken of God, after the manner of men; as men search and find out things, so God is here said to do; his finding out is making known things.

Obs. 1. Princes, and men in supreme power, are honourable; they are cherubs, or cherubims, next unto God; in whose word they have many honourable titles given them. They are called "shields,"

Hos. iv. 18, the word for "rulers" is, shields, in the Hebrew; and "shields of the earth," Psal. xlvii. 9; they protect the state where they live. Ezek. xvii. 3, they are named eagles and cedars. Psal. lxxxii. 6, they are termed gods, and children of the Most High; God owns them for his children, and calls them gods, which is a height of honour.

Obs. 2. That kings and potentates have their places, privileges, and power, that they may be protectors of the people. "Thou art the anointed cherub that covereth;" he was on the throne, that he might spread his wings of protection over his subjects, both at sea and land. Magistrates should be as hens to the chickens, as fathers to their children; they are called not only fathers, but "nursing fathers," Isa. xlix. 23; the word in Hebrew is, אמניך thy nursers or nourishers, and notes faithful nursing; they should make it their business to preserve and provide for their people, as nurses do for their nurse child, seeing daily that it be kept from dangers and want nothing. Such a nursing father was David; Psal. lxxviii. 72, "He fed them according to the integrity of his heart, and guided them by the skilfulness of his hands;" David's heart and hands were at work for the good of the people. Such a nursing father was Moses, whom the Lord would have to carry the people in his bosom, as a nursing father beareth the sucking child, Numb. xi. 12. God would have kings, princes, magistrates, to deal tenderly with the people; they should be as cherubs unto them, spreading the wings of protection and justice over them, and when they do otherwise, he is wroth with them. Zeph. iii. 1—3; Micah iii. 1—4, when instead of fathers they are lions, instead of angels they are devils, to the people, God is sorely displeased, and will destroy them.

Obs. 3. That princes are exalted by God, and depend upon him. "I have set thee;" so it is God that raises them, and clothes them with honour and majesty. Prov. viii. 15, 16, "By me kings reign, and princes decree justice. By me princes rule, and nobles, even all the judges of the earth." Here is mention of kings, princes, nobles, judges; what power soever any or all of these have, the highest or subordinate, they have from God, who is the fountain of all power as well as of being; he is Lord of heaven and earth, he is chief Governor among angels and men, Psal. xxii. 28; and he sets up in Tyrus, and in Babylon, in Egypt, and in Jerusalem, whom he pleases. They should consider who sets them up, on whom they depend, and serve him with fear, ruling for the Lord; which, because they do not, they grow proud, insolent, tyrannical; and therefore the same hand that set them up throws them down, Dan. ii. 21.

Obs. 4. God minds the places where princes dwell, and the pomp they live in. "Thou wast upon the holy mountain of God; thou hast walked up and down in the midst of the stones of fire:" thine habitation hath been in a strong, fortified city, thou hast lived in great state and glory, having thy palace glistering with carbuncles and other precious stones. 1 Kings xxii. 39, God took notice of the "ivory house" which Ahab built for his state. Solomon's house, throne, overlaid with the best gold, his pomp and state, God observed, and caused to be recorded, 1 Kings x. 7; and because great ones pride themselves in their seats and palaces, God threatens to smite their winter houses and their summer houses, and tells them that their ivory houses shall perish, and their great houses have an end, Amos iii. 15.

Obs. 5. Princes and states are prosperous and successful in their undertakings, whilst they are free from iniquities. "Thou wast perfect in thy ways from the day thou wast created, till iniquity was found:" so long as thou didst keep thyself from unjust and wicked acts, thou didst speed well in all thy enterprises at sea and land. The Lord blesses heathen kings, while they do just things. It is righteousness exalts a nation, even any nation, Prov. xiv. 3, 4. David told Solomon what was the way for him and his kingdom to prosper; 1 Chron. xxii. 13, he must fulfil the statutes and judgments of the Lord; and then he should prosper in all that he did, and whithersoever he turned himself, 1 Kings ii. 3. Hezekiah was free from iniquities, unjust and cruel acts; and hear what the Spirit of the Lord saith of him, 2 Chron. xxxii. 30, "He prospered in all his works."

Obs. 6. Great and grievous sins may be in princes and states undiscovered, but the Lord will search them out, and make them known. "Till iniquity was found in thee." The prince of Tyrus his sin was secret, and hidden from the world, kept within doors, in his own chamber, palace, city, or territories; but the Lord found it out, and made discovery of it to the prophet, and the prophet to the world. The great ones of Judah thought themselves innocent, yet God found the blood of innocents upon their skirts, and he found it not by secret search, by digging, that is, by taking much pains to find it out, but so soon as he came he spied it upon their skirts, and made it known, Jer. ii. 34. Men plot mischief, do works of darkness, and think they shall not be seen, Isa. xxix. 15; but the Lord sees, will find it out, and bring it into the light. David sinned in secret, but the Lord saw it, and proclaimed it to the world.

Obs. 7. Wickedness blasts prosperous princes and flourishing states. "Thou wast perfect in thy ways, till iniquity was found in thee;" that caused all to wither: his exalting himself to be as God, his insulting over others in their misery, and his unjust actions, caused the Lord to threaten and bring desolation. Iniquity is the canker and plague of prosperity; many princes and states, which were fat and flourishing, have been made lean thereby. Jeroboam's iniquities lost him five hundred thousand men at once, 2 Chron. xiii. 8, 9, 17. When iniquity was found in Zedekiah, breaking with Nebuchadnezzar, and relying upon the king of Egypt, what said the Lord? "Shall he prosper? shall he escape that doth such things?" Ezek. xvii. 15; no, he shall never prosper more. It is said of Jotham that he became mighty, he prospered greatly; and what was the cause? 2 Chron. xxvii. 6, it was because he "prepared his ways before the Lord," or established them before him; he looked to it that he did nothing but what God commanded and approved, he would not defile his heart or hands with iniquity, therefore he grew mighty, and left a flourishing kingdom. But when Ahaz his son came to it, who did wickedly, you may see how the Syrians, Israelites, Edomites, and Tilgath-pilneser, did waste and consume his kingdom, 2 Chron. xxviii. Would princes, rulers, states, cities, families, persons, prosper, let them take heed of wickedness, and remember Malachi iv. 1, "The day cometh that shall burn like an oven; and all the proud, and all that do wickedly, shall be stubble: and the day that cometh shall burn them up, and leave them neither root nor branch."

Ver. 16—19. *By the multitude of thy merchandise they have filled the midst of thee with violence, and thou hast sinned: therefore I will cast thee as profane out of the mountain of God: and I will destroy thee, O covering cherub, from the midst of the stones of fire. Thine heart was lifted up because of thy beauty, thou hast corrupted thy wisdom by reason of thy brightness: I will cast thee to the ground, I will lay thee before kings, that they may behold thee. Thou hast defiled thy sanctuaries by the multitude of thine iniquities, by the iniquity of thy traffick; therefore will I bring forth a fire from the midst of thee, it shall devour thee, and I will bring thee to ashes upon the earth in the sight of all them that behold thee. All they that know thee among the people shall be astonished at thee: thou shalt be a terror, and never shalt thou be any more.*

In these verses you have,

I. The king's sins; which are,

1. Injustice, or violence, ver. 16.
2. Pride, or vain confidence, ver. 17.
3. Profaneness, ver. 18.

II. God's judgments, or punishments of him for his sins; which are,

1. Casting out, and destruction, ver. 16.
2. Casting down, and making exemplary, ver. 17.
3. Burning, and that to ashes, ver. 18.

III. The events of God's so dealing with him; and they are,

1. Astonishment.
2. Terror, ver. 19.

Ver. 16. "By the multitude of thy merchandise." Tyrus was a city of the greatest merchandizing, as appears, chap. xxvii.; and the king of Tyre himself was of the merchants' company, Isa. xxiii. 8, and countenanced their trading greatly. This drew merchants from all places thither; they brought in commodities, and carried out commodities, and there was great trafficking between the Tyrians and them; and what followed thereupon?

"They have filled the midst of thee with violence." The Hebrew word for "violence" is, חמס *chamas*, which notes, that wrong which is a violation of justice. These merchants, seeking themselves, minded not what was just and equal, but made a prey of one another, and so filled the city with injustice, iniquity, and "violence." The Septuagint is, ἀνομίας, that is, with illegality, transgression, unrighteousness.

"And thou hast sinned." Thou, who shouldst have looked to it that no unjust things should have been done in the city, that there should have been no violence, even "thou hast sinned," either by doing as other merchants did, or by being lift up by the abundance of those things thyself and citizens possessed; or rather, thou hast sinned, in suffering those who have done violence to go unpunished, thou hast connived at them, and so given them encouragement to their wickedness. The word *chata* signifies, to err from the way, scope, mark: he should have had justice in his eye, and neither have done unjust things himself, nor have suffered his citizens to have done them.

"Therefore I will cast thee, as profane, out of the mountain of God." The Hebrew is, I will profane thee from the mountain of God. Some understand the words thus, I will blot out the memory of thee from Jerusalem, and from amongst my people; but it is better to understand it of his own city and kingdom, out of which God would cast him. He was an "anointed cherub," set up by God in great honour and dignity, ver. 14; but he not doing answerable to his place, God would pull the crown from his head, take away all his power and greatness, and profane him; that is, make him as a common person, or cast him out as "profane," as one that hath profaned the place of majesty. Of the "mountain of God" you heard in ver. 14, where this king was said to be "upon the holy mountain of God."

"And I will destroy thee, O covering cherub." The word for destroying is, אבד *abad*, which notes an utter destruction, and God would utterly destroy this king for not protecting his people from violence and wrongs. He was an angel for place and power over others, and should have covered them with the wings of protection and justice.

"From the midst of the stones of fire." "The stones of fire" were those precious stones himself and palace were adorned with, all so called because of their glistering and lightening, of which before, ver. 14.

Ver. 17. "Thine heart was lifted up because of thy beauty." In ver. 5, it is said, "Thine heart is lifted up because of thy riches," and here, "because of thy beauty;" he was rich, great, honourable, strong in men, ammunition, shipping, and fortifications, all which had a glory, a "beauty," and that lifted up his heart, made him swell with pride, and think himself more than a man, to imagine that he was a petty god.

"Thou hast corrupted thy wisdom by reason of thy brightness." This king was in repute for "wisdom," ver. 5, 12, by which he attained to great wealth and glory, which here is expressed by "brightness" (for glory is a bright and shining thing). The glory, beauty, and brightness of his condition begat such pride in his spirit, that his wisdom was corrupted, and lost, as the Vulgate reads it; his pride did obscure his understanding, and disfigure his "wisdom." True "wisdom" consists in the knowledge of a man's self, and carrying it humbly when he is highest; but he knew not himself, that would be as God, and make all bow unto him.

"I will cast thee to the ground." Thou art in great glory and honour, eminent and renowned, lifted up above other princes, sitting, as thou fanciest, in the seat of God; but I will strip thee of all thy glory and greatness, bring thee down from thy height, and "cast thee to the ground:" it imports violent and extreme misery.

"I will lay thee before kings, that they may behold thee." I will make thee a public example to the kings of the world; thou shalt be so debased, cast down, and trampled upon, that kings shall mind, and wonder at thy condition, be terrified, and acknowledge the just hand of God upon thee for thy wickedness. The Septuagint is, ἐναντίον βασιλέων ἔδωκά σε παραδειγματισθῆναι, I have given thee, or will give thee, to be an example before kings.

Ver. 18. "Thou hast defiled thy sanctuaries by the multitude of thine iniquities, by the iniquity of thy traffick." By "sanctuaries," or sanctification, some here take to be meant the king's virtues; others, his oaths and covenants: but his royal palace and city, or the palaces where he and his people did worship, and that religion they had, chiefly are intended. Their traffic was great, and the iniquities adhering thereunto were great, as deceit, covetousness, pride, injustice, violence; by which the palace, city, and sacraries, were defiled, and the religion they had, whatever it was. Piscator makes the "sanctuaries" to the king's palaces only, which for their magnificency were answerable to the temple at Jerusalem, and the king, by his iniquities, had given cause to God to bring in the Chaldeans to defile and destroy them. This sense and the former stand well together; for, being formerly defiled with sin, it was just with God to defile them with blood, and utterly to destroy them.

"Therefore will I bring forth a fire from the midst of thee, and it shall devour thee." That Tyre was consumed by fire is probable, if not, it is to be considered what is meant by "fire." Some make it to be the plotting of his own citizens to destroy him; discontented ones should flee to the king of Babylon, besieging the city, and betray him; others make this "fire" to be the judgment of God upon Tyre: she sinned, and the king also, in a special manner, and God from those sins would cause punishment to spring up, which should consume them and him, as a fire kindling in a house eats it up, and consumes it.

"And I will bring thee to ashes upon the earth." These words do hint unto us, that the judgment of God upon Tyrus, after it was taken by Nebuchadnezzar, was "fire." What they could not spoil by their axes, and other warlike instruments, that they set fire unto, and so turned into "ashes" the stately and goodly buildings thereof, the glorious palaces of the king, were made ashes: fire is a consumptive, transforming thing, and so are God's judgments. Of, if we take the words not in a literal, but a metaphorical, sense, "ashes" note a contemptible and base condition: Job xxx. 19, "He hath cast me into the mire, and I am become like dust and ashes;" when Job was stripped of all his honour and glory, set upon the dunghill, then he was as dust and ashes.

"In the sight of all them that behold thee." The word, to "behold," is, ראה which notes not only seeing with the eye, but with the mind also: Jer. ii. 31, "O generation, see ye the word of the Lord;" that is, hear, consider, understand; they could not see it with the eye. And here, not only those that saw with their bodily eyes, but those that heard of it, even the isles which were afar off, are included.

Ver. 19. "All they that know thee among the people shall be astonished at thee." All thy subjects, and all foreigners with whom thou hast traded, and have heard of thy wisdom, beauty, glory, greatness, they shall be astonished at thee; they shall wonder to see thee, the "anointed cherub," brought to so low and despicable a condition. Some conceive, that, as they were astonished at the destruction of Tyrus, and the prince thereof, so they were glad, hissed, and mocked thereat; but, chap. xxvi. 16, 17, they should be astonished, and take up a "lamentation."

"Thou shalt be a terror." In the Hebrew it is, thou hast been terrors, בלהות היית thou, with thy power, greatness, majesty, hast been terrible unto others. The Septuagint is, *ἀπώλεια ἐγενȣ*, thou hast been destruction. Our translation suits well enough with the Hebrew, which oft puts a preter tense for the future; and so the sense is, All those that see to what a desolate condition thou art brought unto, shall be terrified. Chap. xxvi. 21; xxvii. 36, you have this word terror.

"Never shalt thou be any more." Thou shalt never be king more, nor Tyrus ever be built more in such state as formerly it was, nor any king or form of a kingdom be ever seen therein more; for Junius tells us it was upon the re-building of it made a commonwealth. These words we had formerly, chap. xxvi. 21; xxvii. 36.

Obs. 1. That in much trading there is much sin. "By the multitude of thy merchandise they have filled the midst of thee with violence:" the merchants of Tyrus were covetous, fraudulent, unjust, violent, speaking unlawful words, and doing unlawful things, and that so commonly, as that they filled the city and palace with the guilt thereof. Prov. x. 19, "In the multitude of words there wants not sin," that is, there is much sin, many of them are sinful; so in much trading and merchandising there wants not sin, it abounds; sinful thoughts, desires, idle, evil, false, flattering, lying words, adhere to them that are busied therein, and many unjust, yea, oppressing acts are done by them. In heart they have exercised with covetous practices, and many of them do love the wages of iniquity, as Balaam did, 2 Pet. ii. 15; and, like Judas, purchase fields with the reward of iniquity, Acts i. 18. In mart towns, where there is much trading, there is much sinning, much lying, swearing, whoring, drunkenness; merchants bring the vices of their countries, as well as the wares and commodities thereof, and it may be questioned whether the vices brought in do not more harm than all the commodities do good.

Obs. 2. God takes notice of men in place, whether they connive at, or punish, sin. The merchants filled the city and palace of the king with injustice, violence, and all manner of wickedness, and he punished them not, but connived at them; and so, besides his great neglect, which was very evil, he contracted the guilt of their sins upon himself. Governors are sent by God, saith Peter, 1 Epist. ii. 14, "for the punishment of evil-doers, and for the praise of them that do well:" being sent of God, and set up by him, as this prince of Tyre was, ver. 14, God looks after them, observes strictly how they act, whether they encourage men that do well, and punish such as do evil; if they do not, the Lord will charge their sin upon them: "Thou hast sinned, thou hast filled all with violence." Not to punish sin, is to encourage men in sin, and so rulers bring a world of guilt upon themselves; they must answer for the sins of the people, when they prevent not, nor punish, what they might.

Obs. 3. Doing of unjust things, and non-execution of justice, undo the princes and rulers of the earth, they cause God to thrust them out of their thrones and kingdoms, and to lay their glory and greatness in the dust. "Thou hast sinned," that is, done unjustly, and neglected justice, "therefore I will cast thee as profane out of the mountain of God; I will destroy thee, O covering cherub, from the midst of the stones of fire." Nebuchadnezzar and his army were the instruments to do this, but God was the chief agent; "I will cast thee out, I will destroy thee;" and it was for his wicked acts, and want of doing justice. When princes do just things, punish evil-doers, countenance them that do well, then they establish themselves in the mountain of God, in their thrones and greatness; but when they fail therein, they undermine themselves, and hasten their own ruin. The Arabians say, Justice is the sinews and strength of a kingdom; injustice, then, must be the dissolution of it. Psal. lxxxix. 14, justice and judgment are the establishment of God's throne; it is "habitation" in your books, but the margin hath it, establishment; and the word מכון signifies, a basis, or foundation. Justice upholds the very throne of God; should he not execute justice, or do unjust things, his throne would shake, his glory and greatness come down. Would rulers and great ones be established in their places, let them keep justice and judgment, and do wrong to none. Saul spared Agag, when he should have hewed him to pieces, 1 Sam. xv.; he caused to be slain eighty-five priests of the Lord, 1 Sam. xxii.; and shortly after, for his unjust acts, and want of doing justice, he was thrust out of his throne, cast out as a profane prince from the mountain of God, and destroyed from being a covering cherub, and from all his glory and greatness.

Obs. 4. The abundance and glory of outward things occasions men to forget God and themselves. "Thine heart was lifted up because of thy beauty:" he had abundance of all things, and they, with the glory and beauty of them, swelled his heart, made him proud, forget God, the Giver of them, and himself, who was to give account for them. It is hard to keep the heart in a right frame, when we are compassed about with creature plenty, glory, and beauty; pride, disdain, and violence, are the brats and bastards of plenty. It is harder for princes, or any, to regulate their spirits in prosperity than in adversity. A man under pressures is seldom puffed up with pride, overcome with lust, drowned in covetousness, overtaken with surfeiting and drunkenness, or tickled with worldly glory; all which, and many other evils, are incident to them that dwell in the midst of abundance: see Deut. xxxi. 10; viii. 10—14. In their fulness, men forget and forsake God, when, in their adversity, they seek and sue unto him: Hos. v. 15, "In their affliction they will seek me early," or, diligently. Manasseh, in his greatness and fulness, forsook God and his worship, did violent acts; but when he was in fetters in Babylon, and in affliction, then he besought the Lord his God, and humbled himself greatly, 2 Chron. xxxiii. 12; his heart was lifted up before, but now humbled, and that greatly. Affliction pricks the bladders prosperity hath blown up, and filled with pride.

Obs. 5. Men's priding themselves in an outward glory, doth prejudice them in a greater excellency. "Thou hast corrupted thy wisdom, because of thy brightness:" his wisdom was of a higher nature than all his greatness and glory, than his shipping, soldiers, buildings, precious stones, and whatever other external excellences were in Tyrus, but by his pride in these he marred that. Sin is the smoke of the soul; and what smoke is to the eye of the body, that sin is to the understanding, which being darkened, men's wisdom is corrupted. If there be a drop of ink, or poison, in milk or wine, they are corrupted; so if sin, especially pride, be found in a man, his wisdom is corrupted, and he will think, speak, and do corruptly. Prov. xi. 2, "When pride cometh, then cometh shame: but with the lowly is wisdom." When men are puffed up with their parts and enjoyments, then cometh shame; then they will carry themselves so, as others will be ashamed of them, their wisdom is corrupted, and they do foolishly; but when men are low and humble, they are wise, and do things commendable: true, sound, uncorrupted wisdom dwells with the lowly, and is a stranger to the proud.

One saith, upon these words of our prophet, That all proud men are fools, their pride hath darkened their foolish hearts. Let us take heed of priding ourselves in any externals or internals, thereby we shall corrupt our glory; let us be lowly, so shall we have wisdom unspotted, humble, so God will give us more grace, James iv. 6.

Obs. 6. The end of God's dreadful judgments upon sinners is, that they may be examples and warning-pieces unto others. "I will cast thee to the ground, I will lay thee before kings, that they may behold thee," and so take heed of thy ways and practices. God is terrible unto kings, he cuts them off, and makes them exemplary unto others: they are oft blasphemous, proud, unjust, violent, tyrannical; and God, by the thunder of his power, cuts them down, and by their fall sets them up to be lights unto others, that they tread not in their steps, lest they come to their ends. Pharaoh is drowned in the sea; the princes of the people hung up before the sun; Herod is eaten up with vermin; the king of Ai hanged on a tree, Josh. viii. 29; Adoni-zedec and other kings, their necks were made footstools to the Jews, Josh. x. 24; Agag was hewn in pieces, 1 Sam. xv. 33; Joash was slain in his bed, 2 Chron. xxiv. 25; Jehoram was so smitten with sickness, that his bowels fell out, 2 Chron. xxi. 19; Zedekiah had his eyes put out, was bound in fetters, and carried to Babylon Jer. lii. 11, and made a prisoner all his days; the kings of Sodom and Gomorrah were roasted in the fire, and burnt to ashes. And why were these things done to kings? that they might be examples to others, both kings and people: 1 Cor. x. 11, "All these things happened unto them for ensamples: and they are written for our admonition, upon whom the ends of the world are come:" had they not been written, they would have been forgotten; but God in his great wisdom would have them "written," that all that read or hear of them may be admonished by them, and learn to avoid those sins they were guilty of, lest they partake of the same or parallel judgments.

Examples in holy Scripture are used divers ways.

(1.) For arguments in prayer, as Psal. lxxxiii. 9—11.

(2.) As matter to strengthen our faith, Deut. iii. 21, 22; Isa. li. 9, 10.

(3.) As precedents for God to proceed by, Jer. vii. 12, 14; Ezek. xx. 36.

(4.) As motives to repentance, and turning unto God, Luke xiii. 1—5; Amos iv. 11.

(5.) For cautions and admonitions unto us, that we do not commit such things as they did, 2 Pet. ii. 6.

Such an example did God make the king of Tyrus; he was a sea mark to direct kings and others who sit at the stern, that they sail not that way he did, lest they suffer shipwreck. Thus God makes men serviceable after their death, who were sinful and mischievous in their lifetime.

Obs. 7. Sinful practices defile men's chiefest excellences and glories, and expose them to defilement. "Thou hast defiled thy sanctuaries by the iniquity of thy traffic:" covetousness, lying, deceit, violence, pride, luxury, and such like sins, attended their trading, and these sins defiled the city, the court, the crown, their temples, their worship, and whatever was precious unto them. Sin is of a spreading nature, defiling us, and all we have, yea, exposing all to ruin and destruction; see Ezek. v. 11; vii. 24. The Jews defiled God's sanctuary with sin, therefore God would expose them to be defiled by heathens.

Obs. 8. Men's own sins do breed their woes, bring them into contemptible conditions, and to utter destruction. This prince's sins kindled the fire of God's indignation in the midst of his city, palace, and sanctuaries, and such a fire as devoured him, and brought him to ashes. Wood breeds the worms which eat it up, garments the moths which consume them. Men by their follies contract those distempers and diseases which rend them from the land of the living, and enfranchise them among the dead. It is the sin of a nation that tears out the bowels of it, and lays all the pleasant things therein waste. It is princes' sins which shake the crown from their heads; their injustice, tyranny, covetousness, profaneness, throw them out of their thrones, lead them with scorn, and cause the Lord to pour his indignation upon them. There is no nation, city, or family, roasted in the fire of divine, dreadful judgments, but themselves do bring the same upon themselves. Israel destroyed herself, Hos. xiii. 9; that was, by her calves and idolatrous worship. Ireland hath destroyed itself by her treachery and bloody doings; and search into it, you shall find that Scotland hath destroyed itself by its own iniquities: so Worcester, by its own acts, hath brought woes upon itself, &c. Many are brought to ashes at this time, to bondage, base and contemptible conditions, because they fed upon ashes, made lies their refuge, doing dishonourable things: Isa. xxvi. 11, "The fire of their enemies shall devour them;" their sins were the material fire that they brought, &c.

Obs. 9. God's judgments upon wicked princes and places oft are such, as that they become matter of astonishment and terror to others. "All that know thee among the people shall be astonished at thee; thou shalt be a terror:" whosoever should hear what God had done to Tyrus, and the prince thereof, should be amazed thereat, and tremble, chap. xxvi. 15. "He is terrible to the kings of the earth," Psal. lxxvi. 12, and makes them terrors to others.

Ver. 20—23. *Again the word of the Lord came unto me, saying, Son of man, set thy face against Zidon, and prophesy against it, and say, Thus saith the Lord God; Behold, I am against thee, O Zidon; and I will be glorified in the midst of thee: and they shall know that I am the Lord, when I shall have executed judgments in her, and shall be sanctified in her. For I will send into her pestilence, and blood into her streets; and the wounded shall be judged in the midst of her by the sword upon her on every side; and they shall know that I am the Lord.*

In these words you have a prophecy against Zidon, which is the third general part of the chapter: the authority of it is in ver. 20, and the prophet's commission in ver. 21; the prophecy itself in ver. 22, 23, where destruction is threatened to Zidon by "pestilence" and "sword," and the ends of God's judgments declared.

Ver. 21. "Set thy face against Zidon." The word for to "set," notes a setting on purpose, not carelessly, but composedly, intensively. Amos ix. 4, "I will set mine eyes upon them for evil, and not for good;" though formerly I have seriously and purposely set myself to do them good, yet now I will with as much seriousness and resolvedness set mine eyes upon them, or against them, for evil, I will look sourly upon them: so the prophet must fix his face upon Zidon, and look severely, suitable to the judgment he had to threaten against it.

"Zidon." Of "Zidon" was spoken, chap. xxvii. 8. It was seated at the foot of mount Libanus, and terminated the bounds of Canaan in the north-west. Justin saith, it was built by the Phœnicians, and called Zidon, from the multitude of fishes that were thereabouts; for they call a fish, *zidon*. It was a rich and potent city, having its king; for Ethbaal, the father of that wicked woman Jezebel, was king of the Zidonians, 1 Kings xvi. 31; they were idolaters, for Ashtoreth was the goddess of the Zidonians, 1 Kings xi. 5; and Selden judges those four hundred prophets of the groves, which did eat at Jezebel's table, to be the prophets of this goddess. These Zidonians were, for their manners and wickedness, like to the Tyrians, no better than thorns and briers unto the Jews; and hence Ezekiel is commanded to prophesy against them, as Jeremiah was, chap. xxv. 15, 22.

De Diis Syris Syntag. 2. c. 2.

Ver. 22. "Behold, I am against thee." Some read the words thus, Behold, I come to thee; not to show thee kindness, not to protect or comfort thee, but I come to punish, to destroy thee. The words may also be read, Behold, I am above thee, or over thee; thou art strong, wise, wealthy, secure, but I am above thee, and thou canst not escape my hands. But to take the words as here they are, "I am against thee," thou hast me thy enemy; hitherto I have been thy friend, caused thee to grow great and prosper, but now "I am against thee;" it is not men or angels, but I, the Lord of all in heaven and earth, that have the command of all creatures in my hand, that shake the foundations of the earth, and lay waste kingdoms, cities at my pleasure, even "I am against thee."

"And I will be glorified in the midst of thee." Montanus reads the word "glorified" actively, I will glorify myself in the midst of thee; thou hast dishonoured me by thy sins, given mine honour unto idols, but now I will punish thee severely for what thou hast done, and so vindicate my name, make thee know that I am a God differing from thy false gods and goddesses. The Septuagint reads the word passively, ἐνδοξασθήσομαι; so we, and many others, I will be glorified; and the sense is this, I am against Zidon, I will fight her, get the victory over her, by executing my judgments upon her, and so I shall be glorified by all that see my hand upon her. God is glorified when he punisheth evil-doers, and cuts them off: Exod. xiv. 4, "I will be honoured upon Pharaoh, and all his host;" ver. 17, upon his chariots and his horsemen: and how was this done? by drowning them in the midst of the sea, ver. 27, 28: and God is glorified when others take notice of his power, justice, judgments, and praise, and fear him, as it is, Exod. xv. 1, 14. When men do conquer others, all the friends of the conqueror do rejoice, and triumph with him; they go or send to him, as 2 Sam. viii. 10, and give him thanks for what he hath done, which is an honouring of him; and it is no less that his enemies fear him.

"And they shall know that I am the Lord, when I shall have executed judgments in her." The end of God's judgments is, to bring men to a right knowledge of him. When Zidon should receive the punishments due to her sins, then she would know, that is, acknowledge, God to be above all idol gods, that he only was worthy to be feared, adored, praised, and obeyed.

"And shall be sanctified in her." In chap. xx. 41, we had these words, "I will be sanctified in you," where they were opened. They may be taken here actively or passively: I will sanctify myself in her, that is, I will do that in Zidon, execute such judgments in her, as shall declare to all nations that I am a holy God, hating all sin, that my name is holy and reverend; in this sense they are taken actively: passively, thus, Whereas my name hath suffered by the Zidonians, and many have thought me no better than the idol gods, that I take little care of the world, wink at men in their wickedness, and am like unto them; when my judgments are upon Zidon it will be otherwise, then they will have high and honourable thoughts of me, then they will declare me to be a just and righteous God: and so the holy God shall be sanctified in righteousness, as it is Isa. v. 16; that is, made known to be holy for his righteous judgments.

Ver. 23. "For I will send into her pestilence." These are the judgments with which God would visit Zidon. The word for "pestilence" is, דבר which interpreters make to signify, speech, death, and order, as well as the plague, and that to have all these in it; for the plague is a speaking judgment, it speaks out God's severity, it speaks unto us to repent presently. It is a dreadful judgment, few escape that have it, and it hath order in it, for that it goeth from house to house, city to city, and oft sweeps away all.

"And blood into her streets." The Babylonians should besiege Zidon, and after the pestilence had devoured many, they should take the city, slay the citizens, and fill the streets with "blood," dead and wounded bodies.

"And the wounded shall be judged in the midst of her." When towns and cities are besieged, many from within make attempts to raise the siege, or break through, whereupon they come to be wounded, if not slain. So here, many were "wounded" upon such attempts, and after the city was taken, they were judged to death. The Hebrew is, the wounded man shall fall in the midst of her; and so the Septuagint.

"By the sword upon her on every side." There should neither be any articles or terms of peace offered them, nor any way of escape be left them; the soldiers should compass her about "on every side," so that whoever attempted to flee and get away, should fall into their hands.

Obs. 1. That great, flourishing, and strong cities may have God their enemy, and so their enemy, as to declare and proclaim war against them. "Son of man, set thy face against Zidon," tell that great city what the Lord saith, "Behold, I am against thee, O Zidon;" I am coming in a martial way against thee, and will consume thee to ashes.

Obs. 2. God's aim and end in his judgments, is to make himself known, what a dreadful, just, and holy God he is, and that he may be declared by men to be so. God would destroy Zidon by pestilence and war, that he might be glorified and sanctified in her: she would not give glory to God before; the Lord would therefore fetch his glory out of her by his judgments, and cause others should see the same, to confess him to be a God of power, justice, and holiness. Psal. ix. 16, "The Lord is known by the judgment which he executeth;" there are characters of his power, justice, and holiness in them, that men must needs take notice of them, if they be not atheistical. If others will not fear, praise, worship, adore the Lord, whose hand hath lately been lifted up so eminently, yet let us do it; God must be glorified and sanctified one way or other. Let us therefore say, "Great and marvellous are thy works, Lord God Almighty; just and true are thy ways, thou King of saints. Who shall not fear thee, O Lord, and glorify thy name?"

Obs. 3. What judgments soever come into or upon cities and persons, it is the Lord that sends them thither, that brings them upon them. "I will send into her pestilence, and blood into her streets." It is the Lord gives commissions, as to the prophets to prophesy judgments against a city, so to the judgments themselves, to come to and upon them. If in Worcester dead bodies and blood filled the streets, if all houses were plundered, if armies are routed, thousands slain, it is the Lord's doing. Let none stumble by looking at the instruments, they are the sword in God's hand, he causes it to wound and to kill.

Ver. 24—26. *And there shall be no more a pricking brier unto the house of Israel, nor any grieving thorn of all that are round about them, that despised them; and they shall know that I am the Lord God. Thus saith the Lord God; When I shall have gathered the house of Israel from the people among whom they are scattered, and shall be sanctified in them in the sight of the heathen, then shall they dwell in their land that I have given to my servant Jacob. And they shall dwell safely therein, and shall build houses, and plant vineyards; yea, they shall dwell with confidence, when I have executed judgments upon all those that despise them round about them; and they shall know that I am the Lord their God.*

These verses are a prophecy of grace and mercy to the church of God, being the last general part of the chapter; where,

1. You have the things prophesied of; which are,

(1.) Freedom from molestations by enemies, ver. 24.

(2.) Collection of the Jews out of the places they were dispersed into, ver. 25.

(3.) Habitation in the land given to Jacob, ver. 25.

(4.) Safety and prosperity, ver. 26.

2. The time when these things shall be, ver. 26, after judgments executed upon their enemies.

3. The end of this comfortable prophecy, and sweet promises in it, and that is, the knowledge and profession of God, ver. 24, 26.

"There shall be no more a pricking brier." The word for "brier" in the holy language is, *sillon*, a thorn, a sting, a brier; and metaphorically, it is put for a thorny man: hence is σιλλαίνω, saith Avenarius, which signifies, to scratch a man's name with ill words. סלון is no where else used but in Ezekiel, chap. ii. 6, and in this place. The Septuagint turn it, σκόλοψ, which in 2 Cor. xii. 7, is rendered a "thorn," and by the Vulgate, an offence.

"Pricking." ממאיר is from מאר which signifieth, to cause grief, to make the heart ache; so do thorns and briers; when they prick a man, they pain and grieve him.

"Unto the house of Israel." By a synecdoche of the whole for a part, he understands the house of Zidon.

"Nor any grieving thorn." The word for "thorn" here is, קוץ from קוץ to be afflicted, to be in straits, because thorns do afflict and straiten men. Some make it, to differ from others in quantity, and to note, a greater thorn, but it signifies any thorn, thistle, or grieving thing. מכאב grieving, is from כאב to make sad; when a man is pricked with a thorn, it makes him sad.

"Of all that are round about them." These words show who were the briers and thorns, viz. those who dwelt near unto the Jews, on every side, the Tyrians, Sidonians, Philistines, Moabites, Ammonites, Idumeans, and Egyptians. These were subdued by the Chaldeans much about that time Jerusalem was taken, and after their return out of Babylon those nations were brought under by the Maccabees.

"That despised them." In Hebrew השאטים which is from שאט signifying, to provoke one, by contemning and spoiling of them. It is again in ver. 26, rendered in the margin, that spoil them.

Wicked men are likened to thorns and briers.

1. Thorns and briers are of little worth or use; what serve they for but to make a hedge, stop a gap, or burn in the fire: they are inconsiderable things? and such are wicked men; they are vile, Jer. xv. 19; godly men are precious, but wicked ones are little worth, Prov. x. 20. Isa. x. 17, the Assyrians were thorns and briers, and should be burnt up in a day.

2. They change not their nature; wherever you set or plant them, they continue the same, in the wilderness, garden, or orchard; so wicked men, do what you will to them, they change not, neither can thunder, lightning, sunshine, winter or summer, change the one or the other. Pharaoh was a great brier, no miracles altered him. Saul was transplanted, and made a king, yet honour and favour altered not him. Jeroboam, what sweet promises had he from God himself, 1 Kings xi. 37, 38, but they turned not that thorn into a vine.

3. They pester the earth where they are; they suck away the fat, moisture, and sweetness of it, from better plants, corn, and grass; so wicked men, they pester the earth, they get the chief places of power, honour, they get the lordships and manors: Psal. xii. 8, the vilest of the sons of men are exalted. Abimelech, the bramble, is made king by the Shechemites, and slays his seventy brethren, whose right it was to have had the crown before him; and what a plague he was to the Shechemites, see Judg. ix.

4. They are low things, creeping upon the earth, and inclining towards it; they are not like the oaks and cedars, which mount up to heaven; so wicked men are base, low, earthy, minding the things of this world, they incline unto them, they savour the things of the flesh, and what is suitable to their lusts: such a base brier was the fool in the gospel, and Dives also.

5. They are dangerous things to meddle with, they are pricking and grieving. Numb. xxxiii. 55, the inhabitants remaining were "pricks" in their eyes, and "thorns" in their sides, and vexed them. Nabal was very churlish to David, and not over-kind to Abigail; he was a pricking thorn to the one, and a grieving brier to the other.

Quest. Wherein are wicked men pricking briers and grieving thorns?

Answ. 1. In their tongues; they are often full of prickles, their words are pungent.

(1.) They have calumniating and lying words, Neh. vi. 6; Jer. xviii. 18.

(2.) Scoffing words, Neh. iv. 2, 3; the nations scoffed at the Jewish sabbaths, sacrifices, and worship, Lam. i. 7.

(3.) Threatening words, Acts iv. 17; ix. 1.

(4.) Disgracing, undervaluing words. The scribes and Pharisees said of Christ, he was a wine-bibber, a Samaritan, that he had a devil. Tertullus said, Paul was a pestilent fellow, Acts xxiv.

(5.) Provoking words, 2 Chron. xxv. 17; Neh. vi. 2.

2. In their countenances and looks. Wicked men look so big and fiercely ofttimes upon the godly, that they prick and grieve them to the heart. Dan. viii. 23, Antiochus was of a fiery countenance, terrible to look unto. How sourly did Ahab look upon Elijah, when he said, "Art thou he that troubleth Israel?" &c. Wicked men's frowns are sharp thorns in the sides of the godly.

3. In their actions. 2 Pet. ii. 7, 8, Lot's righteous soul was vexed, &c.; Delilah tempted and urged Samson, so that his "soul was vexed unto death," Judg. xvi. 16; see Josh. xxiii. 12, 13; the daughters of Heth were such thorns unto Rebekah, that she was weary of her life, Gen. xxvii. 46; see Psal. xxxvii. 14.

I. Some general observations from hence, that wicked men are thorns.

Obs. 1. Their acquaintance is not desirable. Familiarity with them is dangerous: Prov. xxiv. 1, "Be not envious against evil men, neither desire to be with them;" be they great, honourable, eminent, yet, if wicked, we should neither envy them, nor affect their company: and why? "For their heart studieth destruction, and their lips talk of mischief;" they are the "seed of the serpent," and cannot cordially close with the "seed of the woman;" there is enmity between their seeds. Mic. vii. 4, "The best of them is a brier; the most upright is sharper than a thorn hedge." If the best of them be so, what are the rest? One time or other you will find them so. David chose those for his companions who feared the Lord, Psal. cxix. 63.

Obs. 2. Answerable fruit is to be expected from them. Thorns and briers must bring forth fruit suitable to their natures. Some make no difference between men, but will trust wicked ones as soon as godly ones; but they have been, or may be, deceived; for can good fruit grow upon an ill tree? Christ hath taught us otherwise; Matt. vii. 16, "Do men gather grapes of thorns?" &c. he makes it an impossibility; ver. 18, A corrupt tree cannot bring forth good fruit. Wickedness proceeds from the wicked, it is natural to them to do wickedly, and nothing else: fire comes out of brambles, and devours the cedars of Lebanon, Judg. ix. 15.

Obs. 3. It is rather matter of rejoicing than mourning, when wicked men are cut off, and taken away. They are but thorns and briers, worthless things, cumbering the ground, and bearing ill fruit. Prov. xi. 10, "When it goeth well with the righteous, the city rejoiceth; and when the wicked perish, there is shouting." Unprofitable, hurtful things are taken away. Husbandmen and gardeners are glad when the briers and brambles are pulled up from the corn, flowers, and plants among which they grew. The loss of good men is a great loss, as of Josiah, a good king; but the loss of wicked kings is no loss, it is gain to a state, and matter of rejoicing: they are great brambles, and there is much a do to pull them up, but being up and perishing, multitudes shout for joy, who were scratched and oppressed by them.

Obs. 4. Those who are the Lord's deputies and rulers under him, should see to it, that briers and brambles overrun not all the field and vineyard of God. They do grow high, great, spread, and are like to endanger much if they be not dealt with. There are thorns and briars in all places; there are state brambles, city thorns, and church briers: such were in the church of Galatia, which Paul wisheth were cut off, Gal. v. 12, because they scratched and troubled them; and David's resolution was, to thrust away as thorns all the sons of Belial who troubled the state and city of Jerusalem, 2 Sam. xxiii. 6; and Psal. ci. 8, he saith, "I will early destroy all the wicked of the land; that I may cut off all wicked doers from the city of the Lord." Here was a man after God's own heart, that would not suffer pricking thorns and grieving briers.

II. Some more particular observations from the words of the verse.

Obs. 1. The church and people of God live amongst thorns. They dwell in the midst of wicked men; all that were round about them were pricking briers and grieving thorns. The church is a "lily among thorns," Cant. ii. 2. Jerusalem was amidst heathenish nations; Christ and his apostles were among scribes and Pharisees, whose spirits were thorny. Hence take these inferences:

(1.) Then God's people ought to take heed how they walk. Men who live and walk among briers and thorns, had need have their eyes in their heads; they may otherwise be quickly entangled in the briers, and miserably scratched. Matt. x. 16, "Be wise as serpents," &c.; they live among thorns.

(2.) Then it is not strange if God's people be scratched sometimes by wicked men. They will tear and rend their names, states, comforts, peace, privileges, &c. David, Jeremiah, Paul, were sufficiently scratched by such briers and thorns: whoso toucheth them, had need be fenced with iron, and the staff of a spear.

(3.) Then see a reason why the people of God cannot carry on the work and things of God with more speed. They dwell amongst thorns, and when thorns are in the way things move slowly. When good seed was sown, the thorns hindered the growth of it; when Joshua went about taking Ai, there was Achan, a great thorn, in the way; when Nehemiah was in the work of the temple, Tobias and Sanballat were thorns in the way. The motions of parliament and army were not so speedy, because they met with great thorns and brambles in their ways.

Obs. 2. The church and people of God shall not always be among briers and thorns. They shall have a time of freedom; "There shall be no more a pricking brier and a grieving thorn." Chap. xxxiv. 28, "They shall no more be a prey to the heathen," &c. This was made good to the Jews in the letter after their return; the nations, which had been thorns to them, the Lord destroyed. This promise refers also to the gospel times, the Lord is making way for it now. When enemies have power, strength, counsel, are active and successful, then they are thorny and grievous; but the Lord is disappointing his church's enemies, and consuming them as briers and thorns, Isa. xxvii. 4.

This is matter of comfort to the church, that although she have been long among briers, thorns, and hath been much offended by them, yea, wounded, yet there is a time she shall be freed from them, it is approaching, and makes haste, Luke xviii. 7, 8. The Israelites were freed from the Egyptians, and Lot from the Sodomites, who were thorns, yea, terrible ones, unto them.

This should draw out our spirits in prayer unto the Lord, to hasten the time, and that he would make good what he hath promised: Isa. lv. 13, "Instead of the thorn shall come up the fir tree, and instead of the brier shall come up the myrtle tree." Let us pray earnestly that God would give us fir trees and myrtle trees, in the room of our briers and thorns; good magistrates and good ministers, instead of those who have been no better than thorns and briers unto us.

Obs. 3. Wicked men have ill thoughts of God's people; they slight them. These briers and thorns, the wicked round about the house of Israel, despised them, and scorned them: Psal. lxxix. 4, "We are become a reproach to our neighbours, a scorn and derision to them that are round about us." Wicked men are proud, the ways of God are contrary unto them and their ways; hence they despise his ways, and those who walk in them.

Ver. 25. "Thus saith the Lord God; When I shall have gathered the house of Israel from the people among whom they are scattered," &c. This people of God, the Jews, were scattered into the eastern countries, over several provinces of the king of Babylon, and here the Lord promiseth to gather them out thereof, and to return them to their own land.

"And shall be sanctified in them in the sight of the heathen." Of sanctifying was spoken in ver. 22. The Hebrew is, when I shall sanctify myself, that is, make known myself, by my judgments upon them for their sins, by seventy years' captivity, and cause the heathen to confess that I am a just and righteous God, which will be, when they shall see me gather them up again, and bring them out with a strong hand; then they will say, he hath not utterly cast them off, though he hath severely punished them. The words may be taken passively, as here they are read, when I shall be sanctified in them, or by them; when they shall see me remembering my promises made unto them, and begin to make way for their deliverance, then shall they praise my name, and rejoice in me their God, and tell the heathens, God hath not forgotten them.

Obs. 1. God's people have no fixed, certain habitation in this world, but are subject to scatterings. They were removed out of their land, carried into Babylon; so the church, Acts viii. 1, "was scattered throughout all the regions of Judea and Samaria." Heb. xi. 37, "They wandered about in sheepskins and goatskins, being destitute, afflicted, tormented."

Obs. 2. Whenever God's people are scattered abroad in the world, he hath a care of them, and will sanctify his name in bringing them into a safe and happy condition. They shall be brought into Canaan, that is, into the church, which Canaan represents. As the Jews were gathered out of Babylon, and the provinces thereof, into their own land, so shall all the elect be brought into the church of God, where is peace, safety, and confidence, where they shall find God a habitation, a vineyard. Isa. xi. 10, "The root of Jesse shall stand for an ensign of the people; to it shall the gentiles seek: and his rest shall be glorious;" and ver. 12, "He shall set up an ensign," &c. The Lord Christ was a great gatherer; see Luke xi. 23; xiv. 16, 17, 21, 23.

Obs. 3. The end of God's gathering his people out of their scattered condition is, that they may sanctify him, and that he may be sanctified by them. God's power, faithfulness, and goodness, appear in his gathering and bringing them out of enemies' hands, and so way is made for his praise and honour, and that before their enemies.

Ver. 26. "And they shall dwell safely therein, and shall build houses, and plant vineyards; yea, they shall dwell with confidence, when I have executed judgments upon all those," &c. The word for "safely," and "with confidence," is the same, לבטח it noteth, safety, freedom from danger, fear, and inward confidence, boldness. The Septuagint is, ἐν ἐλπίδι, which is somewhat short of the meaning. Whether this was made good unto them at their return from Babylon is questionable, for they were troubled with Sanballat, Tobias, and Geshem; the workmen had a trowel in one hand, and a sword in the other, Neh. iv. Afterwards Alexander the Great came, and filled all with fears, and they were necessitated to admit him into their city. After this, also, many of them were carried away into Egypt by Ptolemy, the son of Lagus. In the Maccabees' times they had as sharp and miserable wars as ever, and at last were brought under by the Romans. Though sometimes they had quiet rest, as in the days of Ptolemæus Philadelphus, yet they had much trouble, great fears, wars, and ruins. Some, therefore, understand this prophecy of a spiritual restoration by Christ, who, when he came in the flesh, made way for the coming in of all nations, to enjoy perfect peace in himself; according to Gen. xlix. 10, "Unto him shall the gathering of the people be," nations shall flock to him. Hereupon said the Lord Christ, John x. 16, "Other sheep I have, which are not," &c. This restoration began in Christ's days, and shall be perfected at his next coming.

Obs. 1. The Lord will meet with, and cut off, the enemies of his church and people, yea, all of them shall fare alike when I shall have executed my judgments upon those that despise them round about. Those that despise, contemn, and trouble the servants of God, judgments are their portion, they are thorns and briers, and fire shall consume them: see Numb. xxiv. 8; Isa. xli. 11, 12.

Obs. 2. When God separates his people from the wicked, and plagues them for their wronging his people, then shall they have glorious times; they shall dwell safely, build houses, plant vineyards, dwell securely, have confidence, &c.

Obs. 3. The Lord's scope in comforting his people with sweet promises, in delivering them from their enemies, and bestowing choice mercies, is, that they should acknowledge, profess him to be their God, and praise him for his goodness to them: "They shall know that I am the Lord their God."

CHAPTER XXIX.

Ver. 1—7. *In the tenth year, in the tenth month, in the twelfth day of the month, the word of the Lord came unto me, saying, Son of man, set thy face against Pharaoh king of Egypt, and prophesy against him, and against all Egypt: speak, and say, Thus saith the Lord God; Behold, I am against thee, Pharaoh king of Egypt, the great dragon that lieth in the midst of his rivers, which hath said, My river is mine own, and I have made it for myself. But I will put hooks in thy jaws, and I will cause the fish of thy rivers to stick unto thy scales, and I will bring thee up out of the midst of thy rivers, and all the fish of thy rivers shall stick unto thy scales. And I will leave thee thrown into the wilderness, thee and all the fish of thy rivers: thou shalt fall upon the open fields; thou shalt not be brought together, nor gathered: I have given thee for meat to the beasts of the field and to the fowls of the heaven. And all the inhabitants of Egypt shall know that I am the Lord, because they have been a staff of reed to the house of Israel. When they took hold of thee by thy hand, thou didst break, and rend all their shoulder: and when they leaned upon thee, thou brakest, and madest all their loins to be at a stand.*

EZEKIEL having prophesied against the Ammonites, Moabites, Edomites, Philistines, Tyrians, and Sidonians, in the four antecedent chapters, in this, and in the three following, he prophesies against the Egyptians. In this chapter take notice,

I. Of an inscription, or preface, ver. 1, 2.

II. Of a commination against the king of Egypt, the land, and people thereof, ver. 2—12.

III. A promise of restoring Egypt again, ver. 13—16.

IV. A prophecy of giving the land of Egypt unto Nebuchadnezzar, ver. 17—20.

V. A promise of mercy to the Jews, ver. 21.

Ver. 1. "In the tenth year, in the tenth month, in the twelfth day of the month." This prophecy was given to Ezekiel in the tenth year of Jehoiachin's captivity, six months and odd days before the final destruction of Jerusalem, Jer. xxxix. 2. In chap. xxvi. our prophet tells you of a prophecy he had in the eleventh year of Jehoiachin's captivity, for he reckons upon that account, Ezek. i. 1, 2; and here he mentions one he had the year before; so that the order of time is not observed, but inverted. The reasons hereof are made by some to be these: 1. Because Tyrus and Zidon were nearer Jerusalem than Egypt was, and therefore the prophet respected the place rather than the time. 2. Because Tyrus and Zidon were to be destroyed before Egypt. 3. Because the prophet had another prophecy concerning Egypt in the seven and twentieth year of the captivity, ver. 17, and therefore thought meet to join them together.

Ver. 2. "Set thy face against Pharaoh king of Egypt." Of setting the face towards or against places or persons, occasion was given to speak, chap. xxviii. 21; xxv. 2; xx. 46; and vi. 2: by this posture he declared whither his prophecy tended. He was far from Egypt, being in Babylon, but looking towards it fixedly was an argument he had something to say concerning it.

"Pharaoh." This was a name common to the kings of Egypt, as Cæsar was to the Roman emperors, and signifies a king, in the old Egyptian language, as Josephus saith. Some make it to signify denying him, because Pharaoh denied God. Others interpret it, free, because he was absolute of himself; but rather it was a name of honour, given unto them. In the word you have mention of Pharaoh-nechoh, 2 Kings xxiii. 29, that is, Pharaoh the lame; and of Pharaoh-hophra, Jer. xliv. 30, whom Herodotus calls Apries, and is the Pharaoh here meant.

Martinius Leigh.

"Egypt." It is a famous region of Africa, so called either from Ægyptus the son of Belus, or from the blackness of the river Nilus, which formerly was called Sichor, that is, black. The Grecians understanding this, they, in their language, called it αἰγύπτιον, which signifies black, whence in time the land came to be called Egypt. In the Old Testament it is always called the land of Mizraim, from Mizraim the son of Ham; for of this Mizraim came the Egyptians. It is a land very fruitful, the granary of the world. Macrobius gives it this honour, to be the mother of arts: it had famous schools, especially at Alexandria, but abounded with superstition and idolatry. The Egyptians were the first, saith Polydore Virgil, that set up altars, temples, images, and sacrificed to idol gods, and taught strangers to do so.

Lib. 1. de Rerum Inventione, c. 5.

"Prophesy against him, and against all Egypt." These words show the latitude and extent of his prophecy; it was not to be against the king alone, or his nobles, but against them and all the people. He was to prophesy against great and small.

Obs. 1. The Lord would have men mind the time when he sets his prophets on work, and that punctually. The year, month, and day, are here recorded, when he gave out his word to Ezekiel, that the same might be observed by all it concerned. The Jews trusted much to Egypt, and the kings thereof. The Egyptians were haughty and self-confident. Now God records the time of his commissioning Ezekiel to prophesy against the king of Egypt, and the Egyptians, that the Jews, hearing of their ruin, destinated from such a time, they might rely no longer upon them; and that the Egyptians might consider what to do, being in such imminent danger, for their treachery to the Jews, and confidence in what they had.

Obs. 2. That the servants of God must impartially dispense the word committed unto them. "Set thy face against Pharaoh king of Egypt, and prophesy against him, and against all Egypt." He must neither fear nor flatter any, of what condition or rank soever, but declare the mind of God, and denounce his judgments indifferently towards all. When prophets, and the sons of prophets, have to do with great ones, they are apt to be discouraged, and to falter in their work, which they ought not to do, considering God who sends them is greater than the greatest. Jeremiah had something of this nature in him, and therefore see how God rouses him, and steels his spirit; chap. i. 17, 18, "Gird up thy loins, and arise, and speak unto them all that I command thee: be not dismayed at their faces, lest I confound thee before them. For behold, I have made thee this day a defenced city, and an iron pillar, and brazen walls against the whole land, against the kings of Judah, against the princes thereof, against the priests thereof, and against the people of the land. And they shall fight against thee." Jeremiah had high and low, all sorts of men, yea all men, against him; yet he must dispense the truth, and all the truth, impartially, not fearing the faces of any, lest he should be confounded.

Ver. 3. "Behold, I am against thee, Pharaoh king of Egypt." The words may be read, Behold, I am above thee: thou art above others, and thinkest none to be above thyself; but I am above thee, and being above thee in power and greatness, "I am against thee" for thy wickedness. I, that am God, the King of kings, that shake heaven and earth at my pleasure, that tumble down kings from their thrones and seats, "I, even I am against thee."

"The great dragon that lieth in the midst of his rivers." The Hebrew word for "dragon" is, תנין which, Lam. iv. 3, is rendered, a sea monster; in Job vii. 12, a whale; in Isa. li. 9, a dragon; and so here: it notes monstrous and great creatures in the sea or at land, and, according to the subject matter, it is to be understood of the whale, dragon, or crocodile. The Septuagint, Montanus, Vulgate, Vatablus, and our English, have it, dragon. Junius, Piscator, and Lavater, a great whale. Some interpreters make it the crocodile, which is like a dragon or serpent, and lives in the Egyptian fens and waters, chiefly in the river of Nile, and may not unfitly be called the whale or dragon thereof. Pharaoh is likened unto this dragon or crocodile.

1. The crocodile is the chiefest and greatest of all that moved in the Egyptian waters, no fish, no serpent, comparable to it; so Pharaoh was the chiefest and greatest among all the Egyptians.

2. The crocodile is cruel and ravenous, seeking his prey both in the waters and on the land, being armed with sharp claws and teeth; and some of them can swallow an entire heifer, as Sands reports in his Travels: so the Egyptian Pharaohs were cruel and ravenous. Did not Pharaoh command the midwives to kill all the males of the Hebrews at their birth? and when they would not do it, did not he charge his people to drown them? Exod. i.; and did he not seek his prey in the Red sea, when he pursued the Israelites going through it?

3. The crocodile is subtle, and useth cunning ways to get his prey; he will lie as if asleep and dead, with his mouth open, to deceive the birds and passengers. Sometimes also he fills his mouth with water, and spouts it out in the way where beasts and men do pass, that so, it being slippery, they may fall, and become a prey to him. So the Egyptian Pharaohs were subtle, and used much cunning to make a prey of the people, especially the Jews: Exod. i. 10, "Come, let us deal wisely with them;" and how cunning was he in calling forth his magicians, to discredit the miracles of Moses and Aaron! chap. vii. and viii.

"That lieth in the midst of his rivers." The Hebrew for "rivers" is, יארים and notes such as are made by the art and help of man, cut out of some great river for to water the land. In Egypt they had seldom any rain, but cut rivers out of Nilus, by which the land was watered; according to that, Deut. xi. 10, where Canaan is said not to be like Egypt, where they sowed their seed, and watered it with the foot; that is, they digged trenches and little rivers, and so watered Egypt by the help of their feet, but Canaan was watered from heaven. The dragons, or crocodiles, lay lurking in these securely; and so did Pharaoh in his kingdom, which was full of artificial rivers.

"My river is mine own, and I have made it for myself." The words in the Hebrew sound thus, To me is my river, and I have made myself. The Septuagint is, Mine are the rivers, and I have made them; that is, Mine is Nilus, and all the aqueducts, or rivulets, cut out of it: but if we take the words as they are in the original, the sense may be this; To me is my river, it is instead of clouds, rain, heaven, God. I have Nilus, which makes my land as fruitful, comfortable, and beneficial unto me, as all those do the lands of others; if they owe aught to them, I owe as much to Nilus. If we take the words as translated, "My river is mine own," that is, it is so mine that none can take it from me, or hinder me of the benefit of it; here he showed his pride, arrogancy, and vain confidence, for God had in a former Pharaoh's time made Nilus useless unto them in Egypt, Gen. xli. 55, when the seven years' famine was, and he could do it again.

Those words, "I have made it for myself," must not be interpreted as if he made Nilus, for that had its being and flowings many hundred years before, and the spring of it lay unfound-out: but the meaning is, I have by my power, wisdom, and industry, made it advantageous to myself and people; I have enriched them and myself thereby, and so furnished and secured my kingdom by means of it, that I shall neither stand in need of nor fear any. Herodotus saith of this king, whom he calls Apries, that it was his usual saying, no God could move him out of his kingdom, he had so established it.

Obs. 1. God is an open and professed enemy unto wicked kings; he proclaims war against them, be they never so great. "Behold, I am against thee, Pharaoh king of Egypt." Few are the kings which abuse not their authority; they lift up themselves, oppress the people, oppose the interest of God, and therefore he is a declared adversary unto them. Jer. xxv. 18—26, you may see what a multitude of kings the Lord sends the cup of fury unto, and draws out the sword against. There was scarcely one good king at that time upon the face of the earth. God was against them all. It is a dreadful thing for any king to have God denounce war against him, he must needs be conquered, and brought to nothing; for God is the Lord of hosts, armed with such power and majesty as that there is no withstanding him: Isa. xl. 23, "He bringeth princes to nothing;" when they are wicked he will not spare them, though they be as great as whales, as cruel as dragons, and as cunning as crocodiles.

Obs. 2. Wicked kings are resemblances of Satan. Pharaoh is here called "the great dragon," and so is Satan; Rev. xii. 9, "The great dragon was cast out, that old serpent, called the Devil, and Satan." Dragons are dreadful, subtle, and cruel; so are tyrants, so is the devil. The former Pharaohs were dragons, and so called, Psal. lxxiv. 13; Isa. li. 9; they were enemies to the people of God, so are all wicked kings, so is Satan. What were all the persecuting emperors but dragons? they were lively representations of the devil, that great red dragon; and so are all that tread in their steps.

Obs. 3. Princes abounding with outward things, grow secure, arrogant, and confident. Pharaoh lay as a dragon "in the midst of his rivers," he was secure, fed upon the prey, and said, arrogantly enough, and with too much confidence, "My river is mine own." I have water sufficient in Nilus for the watering of Egypt, I need beg no rain of God; let him give his rain to whom he will; and I am so well fortified by my rivers, that I fear no power to dispossess me thereof; I am happy, and who can make me miserable? Here you have the true picture and character of this Egyptian Pharaoh, and in him of all wicked kings, who in their prosperity forget God, promise much safety to themselves, and trust in an arm of flesh.

Ver. 4. "But I will put hooks in thy jaws." Here begin God's judgments upon this confident king. God would deal with him as men do with some great fish; when the hook is in his jaws, they draw him out of the waters to the dry land, where he dies. So God would, by an occasion, draw Pharaoh out of Egypt into another land, and with him a great army of the Egyptians, where they should all perish. The occasion was this, as Junius relates it, out of Herodotus: Adiciam, or Ariciam, king of the Libyans, had put himself under the protection of the king of Egypt, because the Cyreneans had invaded some part of Libya, and had spoiled king Aricranes of his government; hereupon Pharaoh was provoked to lead out an army in Agrum Cyrenaicum, which was the hook God put in his jaws.

The word for "hooks" is, חחיים from חוח a thorn, and metaphorically a hook, such as men bait to catch fish with. Job xli. 1, "Canst thou draw out leviathan with an hook?" the whale was too big to be taken with such a hook, though other fishes were not. God had a hook to take and draw out the Egyptian dragon.

"I will cause the fish of thy rivers to stick unto thy scales." Pharaoh being likened unto the crocodile, or sea-dragon, here his princes, nobles, and people are called fish, and likened unto them for their multitude and dispersion into all parts, and aptness to be devoured one by another. These should adhere unto Pharaoh, as the scales do unto a fish. He had called Nilus his river, and it is said here, "the fish of thy river." The word for "scales" is, קשקשת from קשה which signifies difficult, and the radical letters are doubled, showing that they so tenaciously cleave together, that it is very hard to pierce them. The scales of Pharaoh were the arms that he bare. 1 Sam. xvii. 5, the "coat of mail" which Goliath had on, was a brigandine, or coat of scales, that is, made like the scales of a fish. Such a one it is probable Pharaoh had on; and all his people in their arms suitable followed him.

"I will bring thee up out of the midst of thy rivers." He thought himself so secure in Egypt, as that no danger, no mischief, could befall him. Egypt is so fenced by nature, having the sea on one side, the vast desert on the other, on the right hand such craggy mountains, and on the left such fens, as that it is judged inaccessible; but however it was in itself, yet God saith here, "I will bring thee up out of the midst of thy rivers," I will draw thee out into thine enemy's land, and there thou shalt fall.

Ver. 5. "And I will leave thee, thrown into the wilderness." The Hebrew is, I will leave thee in the wilderness. נטש signifies, to cast off; so to leave, as to have no care of what is left. God would bring this proud, confident king into the Cyrenean wilderness, and there leave him to be a prey unto the enemy; when he and his army were spread over the wilderness, then they should be deserted of God, and left to spoil.

"Thee and all the fish of thy rivers." As a fish drawn out of the water, left upon the land, dies, and becomes a prey, so should the king of Egypt and the Egyptians.

"Thou shalt fall upon the open fields; thou shalt not be brought together, nor gathered." Thine army shall be so beaten, routed, and overthrown, as no one part of it shall be joined to another; there shall be no rallying, no recruiting, no gathering up for burial, but all shall be meat for the beasts of the field and for the fowls of heaven. Some fishes, when they are drawn out of the waters, are taken up, much use is made of them; others are thrown away, Matt. xiii. 48; but here they were so bad, that all should be thrown to the beasts and birds of prey.

Obs. 1. When God is wroth with princes and people, he makes and takes occasions to execute his judgments upon them. Pharaoh and his people had sinned greatly against God, and he stirred up the Cyreneans to invade their neighbour country, the Libyans; whereupon he and his are drawn out to war, and fall thereby. He and his thought to live securely in Egypt, but God had hooks to draw them out, and judgments to inflict upon them being so drawn out. The elder Pharaoh in Moses' days, having greatly provoked God, by detaining the Jews in Egypt, God made an occasion, by dividing the waters of the Red sea, for him to follow them; and then, he and his being in the Red sea, took occasion to be avenged on him, by causing the waters to swallow up him and all his host, Exod. xiv. God drew Zerah, with his huge host of one thousand thousand and three hundred chariots, out of Ethiopia unto Mareshah, which was a city in the tribe of Judah, Josh. xv. 44, and there he smote the Ethiopians, and overthrew them, 2 Chron. xiv. God made Ramoth in Gilead a hook to draw out wicked Ahab to war against the Syrians, and when he was there, he was slain, and his army wholly routed, 1 Kings xxii. God wants not hooks to draw leviathans, dragons, and crocodiles, out of their holes, fens, or rivers, nor swords to pierce them when they are drawn out. He had hooks for Hamilton, and the late king of Scots, to draw them into England, and judgments to inflict upon them being come forth, for their iniquities. Let great and small take heed how they offend the Lord; he hath hooks enough, and can make new if he want them, to drag sinners out of their lurking holes, and vials of wrath to pour out upon them being haled out.

Obs. 2. In those actions men do freely, the wise providence of God acts powerfully, and accomplisheth his designs. Pharaoh and his subjects go out freely to war against their enemies, yet God had a hook in their jaws, and drew them to that work. Rehoboam freely refused the counsel of the wise men, and freely followed the counsel of the young men, yet God's hand was in these actions, his hook was in his jaws; 1 Kings xii. 15, "The cause was from the Lord." Rehoboam carried on freely his own design, and God powerfully carried on his, though Rehoboam discerned it not, neither aimed at it. God sent the Assyrians against the hypocritical Jews, he charged him to take the spoil, and tread them down like mire in the streets. He came freely, though God's hook were in his nostrils; he came to do his own will, not God's, that he aimed not at, for he meant not so, his heart did not think so, Isa. x. 6, 7, yet God's providence overruled so, that he did the work of God. This is a great mystery, all wicked men act freely, drive on their own interests, yet God powerfully moves in these actions, brings to pass his own purposes and counsels, and that without sin.

Obs. 3. The counsels and strength of princes and armies come to nothing, where God doth not assist, but desert. "I will leave thee thrown into the wilderness, thee and all the fish of thy rivers; thou shalt fall." Pharaoh was a great dragon, wise and subtle, he had wise counsellors, strong soldiers, a great army; but neither their counsel nor strength stood them in stead; when God had drawn them into the field, he left them, and they fell. Human wisdom and strength can do nothing without God. Saul had a great army, all Israel were gathered together to fight against the Philistines, but did they prevail? no, they fled, and fell down before their enemies; and what was the reason? Saul tells you, 1 Sam. xxviii. 15, "The Lord is departed from me," he is neither with me nor mine army: all Israel can do nothing against uncircumcised Philistines when God had forsaken them. Jeroboam had an army of eight hundred thousand men, mighty men of valour; Abijah meets him with an army of four hundred thousand, even half so many, and slew of Jeroboam's army five hundred thousand. They were strong men on that side, and two to one, yet more fell by a hundred thousand than Abijah's army consisted of. And what was the cause hereof? 2 Chron. xiii. 3, 12, the cause was, God was with them;

"Behold, God himself is with us for our Captain," he guides us, and girds us with strength, said Abijah: Jeroboam by his golden calves had driven God from him. So then, where God is not, there can be no success. 1 Sam. ii. 9, "By strength shall no man prevail:" let men have strong horses, strong arms, strong bodies, strong counsels, strong armies, strong treasures, if they have not El-shaddai, the strong Almighty God with them, all their strengths will prove weakness: we have seen this made good in our days most eminently.

Obs. 4. God in his just judgments brings princes and armies, who confide in an arm of flesh, to open shame and utter ruin. "Thou shalt fall upon the open fields; thou shalt not be brought together, nor gathered;" thou shalt lie unburied, and be meat for beasts and fowls. This Egyptian great dragon, and all the fish of his rivers, were such as God cast out for naught, and gave to be meat to kites, crows, vultures, dogs, swine, and wild beasts; their shame was open, their end was miserable. Pharaoh that entreated the Israelites so cruelly, did not God bring him to open shame, and his great army? did he not drown this dragon, and all who adhered to him, in the deeps? did he not give their carcasses to be meat to the sea-dragons and sea-leviathans? Absalom and his army met with shame, scorn, and misery enough, 2 Sam. xviii. Jehoiakim was "buried with the burial of an ass," Jer. xxii. 19; that is, he had no burial, but was cast out, to shame, scorn, and feeding of birds and beasts.

Ver. 6. "And all the inhabitants of Egypt shall know that I am the Lord." In this verse the event of the former judgment upon Pharaoh and his army is laid down, together with the cause thereof. The event is this; the Egyptians shall see, that the counsels and confidences of princes are vain, that they are not masters of designs, to carry them on and make them successful according to their minds and wills, but that the great God of heaven and earth overrules all, blasting or prospering the greatest undertakings at his pleasure; and so shall acknowledge him to be the Lord.

"Because they have been a staff of reed to the house of Israel." Here the cause is rendered of God's so dealing with Pharaoh and his army, viz. because they were unfaithful to the house of Israel, and prejudicial. The word for "staff" is, *mishneneth*, from שען to lean upon, because men that are weak do lean and rest upon their staves; and metaphorically it is put for stay, hope, confidence: 2 Sam. xxii. 19, "The Lord was my stay," it is *mishan*, or *mishgnan*, my staff, that is, my stay, my hope, my confidence.

The Jewish state being feeble in its latter days, entered into covenant with the Egyptians, and leaned upon them, as on a staff, for help against its own weakness and others' violence; but Egypt proved "a staff of reed."

The word for "reed" is, קנה whence our English word, a cane. Egypt did abound with reeds and canes, especially the banks of Nilus, where it is probable the little ark which contained Moses was laid, for it is said, Exod. ii. 3, "she laid it in the flags by the river's brink:" flags and reeds did grow there. The Egyptians here, and in other places, are compared unto them.

1. Reeds have nothing solid or substantial in them. They are hollow, empty things, or some slight matter in them; if you trust to them they will deceive you. Such were the kings of Egypt and the Egyptians, they had no solidity in them. Isa. xix. 11, "Surely the princes of Zoan are fools, the counsel of the wise counsellors of Pharaoh is become brutish:" their counsels were not solid, they had no faithfulness in them; they oft promised to help the Jews, but did not, they failed them; Isa. xxx. 2, all the strength of Egypt was but as a shadow, their help was vain, and to no purpose, ver. 7; and it is said, "Pharaoh king of Egypt is but a noise," Jer. xlvi. 17, like a hollow cane without substance. The Jews expected help from Egypt, they leaned upon Pharaoh and his forces as on a staff, but he and they deceived them; so that they complained at last, saying, "Our eyes failed for our vain help; in our watching we have watched for a nation that could not save us," Lam. iv. 17: they earnestly waited for help, they relied wholly upon Egypt, and Egypt did wholly fail them.

2. A reed is a weak thing, and blows this way and that way as the wind blows. Matt. xi. 7, "What went ye out into the wilderness to see? A reed shaken with the wind," an inconstant, weak, flexible thing? John was no such man, but the Egyptians were: Isa. xxxi. 3, "The Egyptians are men, and not God;" they are mutable, uncertain, turning every way for their own advantage; they made leagues with the Jews, held correspondence with them, and at their pleasure violated them again.

3. A reed easily breaks, and when it breaks it endangers those that lean upon it; the splinters and shivers run into the hand and shoulder, ver. 7, and so it not only deceives, but damnifies. Such were the Egyptians, they drew the Jews into sinful leagues with them, and by that means to sinful marriages and sinful worship with them. Lavater tells us that the Egyptians persuaded Zedekiah to break with Nebuchadnezzar, unto whom he was tributary, promising him help to recover former liberty, which Zedekiah attempting, proved ruin to him, and the whole nation; so that the Egyptians were a piercing reed unto them. Rabshakeh knew what the Egyptians were, when he said to Hezekiah, "Behold, thou trustest upon the staff of this bruised reed, even upon Egypt, on which if a man lean, it will go into his hand, and pierce it: so is Pharaoh king of Egypt unto all that trust in him," 2 Kings xviii. 21.

Ver. 7. "When they took hold of thee by thy hand." When the Jews looked towards Egypt, and sent their ambassadors thither for help, Ezek. xvii. 7, 15, they took them by the hand, and the Egyptians promised to do great things for them; and they came with an army out of Egypt, to help them against Nebuchadnezzar, Jer. xxxvii. 5, from whom they had solicited the Jews to revolt; but what was the issue? it follows in the next words:

"Thou didst break, and rend all their shoulder." Nebuchadnezzar being before Jerusalem, raised his siege, and hastened to encounter with the Egyptian army, which returning back into Egypt, caused Nebuchadnezzar to return to the siege, which he continued without any further interruption by the Egyptians, till he took and burnt the city, and carried away the Jews to Babylon, Jer. xxxvii. 5, 7, 8: they leaned upon Pharaoh and his army, to secure them against Nebuchadnezzar, but he failed them, and so brake and rent their shoulder; that is, did them much harm, and grieved them exceedingly; as a man that leans upon a staff, and it breaking runs into his flesh, shatters his shoulder-bone in pieces, he is much damnified and grieved.

"And when they leaned upon thee, thou brakest." The Hebrew word for breaking here is, תשבר the former, תרוץ from רצץ which signifies, to shake, bruise, or break, but not altogether. שבר notes a total breaking, a fragmentation, breaking into pieces. The sense is, the Egyptians did utterly fail and disappoint the Jews, who relied altogether upon them.

"And madest all their loins to be at a stand." The Septuagint translate the words thus, thou hast broken all their loins. The Vulgate is, thou hast loosened all their loins, thou hast filled them with fears and faintings, and caused their strength to fail. But our translation is according to the Hebrew, if we read the words thus, and madest all their loins to stand; thou hast made them to withdraw their confidence in thee, finding thee a broken staff, and to trust unto their own strength, and stand upon their own legs; they gird up their own loins, look to themselves, and trust no more to thee.

Obs. 1. God by his judgments makes himself known to heathens, and to acknowledge him to be another kind of God than their idol gods. "And all the inhabitants of Egypt shall know that I am the Lord;" that I rule and overrule all actions, and do whatever I please in heaven or earth.

Obs. 2. The ruin of princes and their armies is their sins and wickedness. Pharaoh's pride and perfidiousness caused the Lord to leave and overthrow him and his in the wilderness, to give them to be meat to the beasts of the field and fowls of heaven; he thought no power could overpower him, he was unfaithful to the house of Israel, and deceived them, trusting to him for aid, and because of these things, the Lord poured out vials of wrath upon him. Zedekiah's perfidiousness brought sword and fire upon Jerusalem, blindness, captivity, and chains upon himself.

Obs. 3. It is neither pleasing to God, nor safe for God's people, to rely upon heathens and wicked ones for help in their straits and fears. The house of Israel relied upon the Egyptians, and this pleased not the Lord, neither was safe for them. Isa. xxxi. 1, "Woe to them that go down to Egypt for help; and stay on horses, and trust in chariots, because they are many; and in horsemen, because they are very strong; but they look not unto the Holy One of Israel, neither seek the Lord!" The Jews looked to the strength of Egypt, and not to the strength of God, and therefore a woe is denounced against them; God was provoked thereby, and he would bring evil upon them, and saith, that the helped and helpers should both fall and fail together, ver. 3: yea, he tells the Jews, chap. xxx. 3, that the strength of Pharaoh should be their shame, and their trust in the shadow of Egypt their confusion. When Asa relied on the king of Syria, and not on God, Hanani the prophet told him he had done foolishly, and that thenceforward he should have war, 2 Chron. xvi. 7, 9. God's people should trust in God alone, who is all-sufficient for them, and not in an arm of flesh. Idolaters, profane and wicked ones, are seldom cordial to God's people; how can they help the church of God in earnest, which they hate most heartily? The Egyptians loved not the Jews, and therefore they smarted for seeking their help, and trusting to them for help.

Obs. 4. That those mediums men expect comfort and help from, do oft wound them and prove their ruin. The house of Israel leans upon Pharaoh and the Egyptians for relief and aid against the Babylonians, and what did they? break and rend all their shoulder, and dissolve their loins; they failed them, and this proved the rending of the Jewish shoulder, the breaking of them in pieces, and total dissolving of their kingdom: they were to them as a staff to a weak, infirm man; he leans hard upon it, that suddenly breaks, runs into his arm and shoulder, and so falling down wounded, he rises no more; that he trusted to wounded and ruined him. This falls out oft, that men's confidences are their confusions. The things they trust to and lean upon are thorns unto them. Ahaz places his hope in Tilgath-pilneser; when the Edomites invaded Judah, he is sent for, comes, and what then? he "distressed him, but strengthened him not," 2 Chron. xxviii. 20, he was a staff of reed unto him. Benhadad had great confidence in Hazael, but he proved his ruin, 2 Kings viii. 8, 15, he made a prey of him and his kingdom at once. In Obadiah's prophecy, ver. 7, it is said, "The men of thy bread have laid a wound under thee;" that is, those Edom was familiar with, confided in, looked for much comfort from, even they wounded her, they laid snares and traps for her, they became instruments of her ruin.

Obs. 5. Disappointments by and harms from others, do make men wary, and look to themselves. When the Egyptian reed brake and wounded the Jews, then their loins were made to stand, then they recalled their spirits from the Egyptians, and set themselves to secure themselves against the Babylonish forces. While men trust to others, they are usually negligent in their counsels and actions; but when they see others fail them, and feel they have wounded them, then they muster up their spirits, then they consult, watch, and act more vigorously.

Ver. 8—12. *Therefore thus saith the Lord God; Behold, I will bring a sword upon thee, and cut off man and beast out of thee. And the land of Egypt shall be desolate and waste; and they shall know that I am the Lord: because he hath said, The river is mine, and I have made it. Behold, therefore I am against thee, and against thy rivers, and I will make the land of Egypt utterly waste and desolate, from the tower of Syene even unto the border of Ethiopia. No foot of man shall pass through it, nor foot of beast shall pass through it, neither shall it be inhabited forty years. And I will make the land of Egypt desolate in the midst of the countries that are desolate, and her cities among the cities that are laid waste shall be desolate forty years; and I will scatter the Egyptians among the nations, and will disperse them through the countries.*

In these verses you have clearly laid before you these particulars:

I. The judgment God would bring upon Egypt, viz. the sword, ver. 8.

II. The effect or event of this sword; utter devastation, ver. 8, 9, and dispersion, ver. 12.

III. The extent of this devastation, ver. 10.

IV. The duration of the same, ver. 11, 12, which is forty years.

V. One special cause thereof repeated, ver. 9, which is the pride of the king of Egypt.

Ver. 8. "I will bring a sword upon thee." "Sword" in Scripture imports sometimes power, as Exod. xviii. 4, "God delivered me from the sword of Pharaoh," saith Moses, that is, from the power of Pharaoh: sometimes great sorrows, as Luke ii. 35, "A sword shall pierce through thine own soul;" that is, the mockings, reproaches, and evil usages Mary and Christ should meet with in the world, should be as a sword in the heart of Mary, and fill her with sorrows; sometimes it is put for the word of God, as Eph. vi. 17, "The sword of the Spirit, which is the word of God." "Which," in the grammatical construction, may refer to "spirit;" but then the sense is not so clear, for what then shall be the "sword?" It is better therefore to read those words, ὅ ἐστι, which thing is the word of God. Sometimes for division, as Matt. x. 34, "I came not to send peace, but a sword," that is, division; so Christ expresses it in Luke xii. 51: and sometimes war, and the evils which attend it; so it is to be taken here; God would bring the Babylonian army, Nebuchadnezzar, with all instruments of war, upon Pharaoh and his land.

"And cut off man and beast out of thee." God would deal severely with Egypt, not only man should be cut off, but even the beasts also. They had not sinned, and God did not punish the beasts in destroying of them; but he punished their owners, in depriving them of their beasts, who had made them serve their lusts. Egypt abounded with men and cattle, and the Egyptians being wicked, and given to luxury, God brought that judgment upon them, viz. the sword, which spared neither man nor beast.

Ver. 9. "The land of Egypt shall be desolate and waste." Egypt was a fruitful and pleasant land, flowing with milk and honey, Numb. xvi. 13; but here the Lord threatened to make it "desolate and waste." The Hebrew is, it shall be for a desert, and a reproach; the wars should consume all, cities, villages, men, beasts, so that it should be a reproachful wilderness, stripped of all its glory and ornaments.

"And they shall know that I am the Lord." When I shall have brought in a potent enemy upon them, and laid all waste, then they shall know there is one greater than Pharaoh and the Egyptians, to whom belongs the right of lands and rivers.

"Because he hath said, The river is mine, and I have made it." Here the cause is specified, why the Lord would deal so severely with Egypt; because Pharaoh was so proud and arrogated so much to himself, he challengeth Nilus to be his, and that he by his art and industry had made it so beneficial to all Egypt. These words were spoken to in the 3rd verse.

Ver. 10. "I am against thee, and against thy rivers." In the 3rd verse it is said, "Behold, I am against thee, Pharaoh king of Egypt," and here, "I am against thee, and thy rivers." He was proud of and confident in his rivers, that they would fertilize his land, and secure him from enemies; but God was against him and them, and disappointed his confidences.

"I will make the land of Egypt utterly waste." The Hebrew is, the solitudes of solitariness, or the wastings of waste, that is, exceedingly waste, there shall be nothing considerable left therein, it shall be as a dry wilderness.

"From the tower of Syene even unto the border of Ethiopia." Solinus makes Syene to be in the front of Egypt, between Nilus and the Red sea, but others find it to be in the utmost parts of Egypt southward, five thousand furlongs above Alexandria. Pliny reports, under the tropic of Cancer, where, at mid-day of the solstice, bodies have no shadows. Sands also, in his Travels, places it above Thebes, and under the tropic of Cancer, affirming that there was a well of marvellous depth in it, which was filled with light at the summer solstice. It is now called Asna. Bonfrerius saith, it is a city of Egypt, in the utmost part of Thebais, and in the borders of Ethiopia. In Hebrew the word is, סונה in the Septuagint, Συηνη. Therein was a tower, to defend from enemies they bordered upon, or for other uses.

Pliny Natur. Histor. l. 2. c. 73.

Sands' Trav. l. 2. mihi p. 111.

"Even to the border of Ethiopia." These words will not afford good sense so we take Ethiopia as it is commonly taken, for if the desolation were but from Syene to Ethiopia, that was inconsiderable, they being near together, yea, so near that Syene disterminated them. It is improper to say, England shall be destroyed from Berwick to Scotland. The word in Hebrew for Ethiopia is, כוש which in sacred Scripture doth not always note Ethiopia in Africa, though frequently it doth; for, Gen. ii. 13, "The name of the second river is Gihon," which there is said to compass "the whole land of Ethiopia," or Cush, this cannot be the African Ethiopia, for Gihon ran not that way: it was the oriental Ethiopia, of which Moses' wife was, Numb. xii. 1, "Miriam and Aaron spake against Moses because of the Ethiopian woman whom he had married;" the Hebrew is, the Cushite; this woman was Zipporah, the daughter of Jethro, the son of Reuel the Midianite, Exod. ii. 15, 18, 21; iii. 1. So then the Midianites were the oriental Cushites, or Ethiopians of Asia. Of this sort it is probable were those Ethiopians that came against Asa; 2 Chron. xiv. 9, Zerah the Ethiopian came with one thousand thousand; it had been too far a journey for so many to have marched out of the African Ethiopia. Tostatus upon the place saith, the Ethiopians dwelt not only in Africa, but in Asia also. Torncellus and others make this Ethiopia, out of which Zerah came, to be the land of Midian. The word Cush, saith Junius upon the 2nd of Genesis, comprehends the three Arabias, both the Ethiopias, and all the meridian coast. The sense of our prophet is, that all Egypt should be laid waste, even from Syene, in the borders of the African Ethiopia, to Arabia and Midian, which are Cush, viz. the oriental Ethiopia.

Ver. 11. "No foot of man shall pass through it, nor foot of beast shall," &c. By these and such like speeches, great desolation is set forth unto us. We must not take the words so strictly, as if no man or beast should be found or left in Egypt; but it should be so wasted, that trading should cease, there should not be such markets, fairs, and merchandizing in her as was before, men should not mind coming to Egypt, nor have occasion to pass through it, few men or beasts, yet some should be there.

"Neither shall it be inhabited forty years." After the taking of Tyrus by a long siege, Nebuchadnezzar had Egypt given him for that service, which was in the seven and twentieth year of the Jews' captivity, ver. 17; shortly after he made war upon it, spoiled it of man, beast, and all its glory, and so it continued till the Babylonish captivity ceased, which was some forty or three and forty years after. There are different opinions among expositors concerning the beginning of these forty years, and their ending. *Vide* Junium.

Ver. 12. "In the midst of the countries that are desolate." Nebuchadnezzar made many countries desolate, according to the word of Jeremiah, chap. xxv. 9, and among those, Egypt was one; so the words "in the midst" are to be understood.

"And her cities among the cities that are laid waste." As Egypt was fertile, so populous, and abounded in great cities. Lavater informs us, that in the time of king Amasis, it had twenty thousand cities. How many or how great soever, they were laid waste by the Babylonian army, and that forty years.

"I will scatter the Egyptians among the nations." Where wars come, many are consumed by the sword, some are famished, some devoured by the plague and other diseases; and doubtless, though many Egyptians perished by such means, yet some escaped, and those God scattered, and drove into other countries.

Obs. 1. Wars, and the dismal effects of them, are the just judgments of God upon perfidious princes. Pharaoh had deceived the Jews; they leaned upon him for help, but he was a broken reed unto them: "Therefore, behold, I will bring a sword upon thee," and it shall be sharp, I will "cut off man and beast out of thee." Thou occasionedst my people to be cut off through thy unfaithfulness, and I will cause thee and thine to be cut off through my fury. Wars are dreadful, but they are appointed, sent, and ordered by God, wherever they come.

Obs. 2. Such is the efficacy and severity of God's judgments, as that nothing can stand before them, or secure against them. Egypt had strong cities, great rivers, was well peopled, abounded in horses and chariots, Isa. xxxi. 1; yet the land of Egypt shall be desolate and waste. God's judgments would cut off man and beast, destroy her cities, and in effect dry up her rivers, they should be made useless. Egypt struggled to defend and secure herself, but it availed not. Jer. xlvi. 11, "Go up into Gilead, and take balm, O virgin, the daughter of Egypt: in vain shalt thou use many medicines; for thou shalt not be cured." Egypt was yet a virgin, unconquered, and she is bid to go to Gilead, where the most precious and sovereign balm was, and to take thereof; that is, to use the best means she could find out to prevent her ravishing and destruction; and when she had tried one means and another, many medicines, all were vain, her wound was incurable, she had dealt deceitfully with the Jews, and lift up herself against the Lord, robbing him of his glory, whilst she said, The river is mine, I have made it for myself. God's judgments were of that power, and so severe, as Jerusalem, with all her art and means, could not prevent them, or protect herself from them. Jer. ii. 22, "Though thou wash thee with nitre, and take thee much sope," though thou have many excuses, shifts, pretences for what thou doest, though thou send to Egypt for help, though thou fast and pray, these things shall do thee no good; thine iniquity is marked before me, and my judgments must come, and lay thee waste, yea, utterly waste.

Obs. 3. God's judgments are often universal and sweeping. God would lay Egypt universally waste and desolate, and that from one border to another, from the tower of Syene to Arabia, within which bounds all Egypt was comprehended. Jer. xii. 12, "The spoilers are come upon all high places through the wilderness: for the sword of the Lord shall devour from the one end of the land even to the other end of the land: no flesh shall have peace." The Chaldeans were God's instruments, he put the sword in their hand, which did eat and devour from one extreme part of the land to another; no place so strong, so secret, but the sword found it out, and spared neither things nor persons; the judgment was so universal, that no flesh had peace, that is, none of the Jewish nation, the terror of the sword was every where. Zeph. iii. 6, "I have cut off the nations: their towers are desolate; I made their streets waste, that none passeth by: their cities are destroyed, so that there is no man, that there is no inhabitant." God swept away from the heathens their towers, their streets, their cities, their men, expecting his people would have learned to fear him, received instruction, and prevented a universal judgment at least; ver. 7, "but they rose early, and corrupted all their doings;" as God's mercies had not, so his judgments did not do them good. Therefore he complains thus, Jer. xliv. 7, 8, "Wherefore commit ye this great evil against your souls, to cut off from you man and woman, child and suckling, out of Judah, to leave you none to remain; in that ye provoke me unto wrath with the works of your hands:" they put God upon a universal judgment by their universal wickedness.

Obs. 4. That the times of kingdoms' flourishings, and kingdoms' desolations, are in the hand of God; he sets the bounds and periods for their prosperity and their adversity. He said, "The land of Egypt shall be desolate;" he put an end to its glory and greatness; he set the time how long it should prosper, and when that time was come, and it brought to desolation, he determined the time how long it should lie in that desolate condition: It shall not be inhabited forty years; the cities of it shall be desolate forty years. Isa. xxiii. 15, Tyre, as it had its time for reigning, so its seventy years for suffering: the same proportion of years the Lord allotted unto the kingdom of Judah, and to divers nations, Jer. xxv. 11; God put an end to their dominion, and determined the time of their subjection, which was seventy years' service unto the king of Babylon. The life and death of states is in the hand of the Lord, to lengthen and shorten at his pleasure. Some states flourish four hundred, some five hundred, some six hundred years, and then they are made desolate for their forty, their seventy years, or more, as seems good unto the Lord; Dan. ii. 21, "He changeth times and seasons," he removeth kings from their glory and greatness, and throws them into obscurity, what time he hath determined for them.

Obs. 5. In time of wars people are driven from their friends, habitations, and countries. When the sword came upon Egypt, the Egyptians were scattered among the nations, and dispersed through the countries; God made use of them abroad, to declare their own misery, and his justice. It is a sad thing to be amongst strangers, whose language is not understood; to be exposed to the scorns, frowns, and harsh usage of enemies; the smoke of one's own country is better than the fire of another. Many in our late wars have met with this great evil, and can experimentally tell you what it is to be driven out of their own country and habitations into foreign ones.

Ver. 13—16. *Yet thus saith the Lord God; At the end of forty years will I gather the Egyptians from the people whither they were scattered: and I will bring again the captivity of Egypt, and will cause them to return into the land of Pathros, into the land of their habitation; and they shall be there a base kingdom. It shall be the basest of the kingdoms; neither shall it exalt itself any more above the nations: for I will diminish them, that they shall no more rule over the nations. And it shall be no more the confidence of the house of Israel, which bringeth their iniquity to remembrance, when they shall look after them: but they shall know that I am the Lord God.*

These verses are a promise of mercy to the Egyptians; where comes into consideration,

I. The time when this mercy shall be, at the end of the forty years.

II. The mercy itself, which is double:

1. Revocation, ver. 13.

2. Restitution of their kingdom, ver. 14, 15; where the nature of the kingdom is set forth, "it shall be the basest," &c.

III. The end and aim of God in so doing, which is twofold:

1. That Egypt may be no more the confidence of the Jews.

2. Acknowledgment of God, ver. 16.

Ver. 13. "At the end of forty years will I gather the Egyptians." The Egyptians being notorious idolaters, confiding in their own strength, were scattered among the nations, where they wandered, and lived without hope of seeing their own country, and becoming a people or kingdom again; but the Lord out of his abundant goodness, beyond theirs and others' expectation, promiseth, that after forty years expired he would gather them, wherever they were scattered. Forty years he would exercise them with captivity, and those hard things which accompanied the same, but at the end thereof he would show them mercy. This is that which Jeremiah speaks of, chap. xlvi. 25, 26, "The Lord of hosts, the God of Israel, saith; Behold, I will punish the multitude of No," that was a great city in Egypt, afterward called Alexandria, "and Pharaoh, and Egypt, with their gods, and their kings; even Pharaoh, and all them that trust in him;" that was Johanan, and all the Jews who fled into Egypt for safety, contrary to the mind and counsel of Jeremiah, chap. xlii. 19—22; "and I will deliver them into the hand of those that seek their lives, and into the hand of Nebuchadrezzar king of Babylon, and into the hand of his servants." Here you have the judgment of God upon Egypt, Egyptians, and the Jews trusting in them; but now what follows? "And afterwards it shall be inhabited, as in the days of old;" after forty years' suffering, Egypt should receive her scattered ones, and become a kingdom again.

Ver. 14. "And I will bring again the captivity of Egypt." Here the abstract is put for the concrete, "captivity" for captives: so you have it Jer. xlviii. 47, "I will bring again the captivity of Moab;" and Ezek. xxxix. 25, "I will bring again the captivity of Jacob;" that is, the captives of Jacob, the captives of Moab, and the captives of Egypt, or Egyptian captives.

"And will cause them to return into the land of Pathros." Maldonate makes Pathros a city, towards the south borders of Egypt, furthest off from Chaldea. Bonfrerius judges it to be that city in Egypt called Babylon. But here it is called, "the land of Pathros," and Jer. xliv. 1, "the country of Pathros," where the Jews which fled into Egypt dwelt; and though it were distinct from Egypt, Isa. xi. 11, for it is said there, God shall recover his people "from Assyria, from Egypt, and from Pathros," yet it was in the land of Egypt; Jer. xliv. 15, the Jews "dwelt in the land of Egypt, in Pathros." Junius conceives this country to be near unto Arabia Petræa; and by Jerom it was reputed formerly to be *nemus Arabiæ*, a wood of Arabia. Pathros, it is most probable, was so called from Pathrusim, the son of Mizraim, Gen. x. 14: as all Egypt was called Mizraim from the father, so might some part be called Pathros from the son, viz. that part which lay between the Red sea and the Mediterranean sea; and as God had carried them out that way, so he would bring them again the same way.

"Into the land of their habitation." The Hebrew for "habitation" is, מכורתם the land of thy tradings, where they did buy and sell; for the word is from מכר to sell, and deliver wares to others. Piscator hath the words thus, into the land of their commerce. The Egyptians dealt in fine linen, broidered works, flax, silk, and other rich commodities; now God would bring them into the land of their trading again.

Obs. 1. The goodness and mercy of God extends to heathens, he hath a care of them in their captivity, and after they have suffered his appointed time, he will show kindness to them. The Egyptians, after forty years' scattering, shall be gathered. Isa. xix. 23—25, "In that day shall there be an highway out of Egypt to Assyria, and the Assyrian shall come into Egypt, and the Egyptian into Assyria, and the Egyptians shall serve with the Assyrians. In that day shall Israel be the third with Egypt and with Assyria, even a blessing in the midst of the land: whom the Lord of hosts shall bless, saying, Blessed be Egypt my people, and Assyria the work of my hand, and Israel mine inheritance." The Assyrians, Egyptians, and Israelites, had their days and times of suffering, and God had his days and times of showing mercy to those heathen nations, as well as to Israel. It is, Blessed be Egypt my people, and blessed be Assyria the work of my hands, and blessed be Israel mine inheritance.

Obs. 2. The afflictions of nations and persons may be long, yet not without end; they may suffer seven and seven years, yea, twenty, thirty, forty years together, which is a long time, and then see an end of their sufferings. "At the end of forty years will I gather," &c.; the Egyptians were captives forty years to the king of Babylon. The Israelites were in bondage to the Philistines forty years, Judg. xiii. 1, and then there came an end of their slavery; they, and many other nations, were captives to the king of Babylon seventy years, Jer. xxv. 11, which was a long time to sufferers; but when they were run out, their captivities ended. God sometimes lengthens out the afflictions of people very much, for ends best known unto himself; as Gen. xv. 13, God "said unto Abraham, Know of a surety, that thy seed shall be a stranger in a land that is not theirs, and shall serve them; and they shall afflict them four hundred years:" here was a long season to be afflicted, but then it had an end. Jehoiachin was thirty-seven years a prisoner in Babylon, but in the twelfth month of that year he was set at liberty, Jer. lii. 31. The man in the gospel had been afflicted thirty-eight years with an infirmity, John v. 5, and then he was delivered from it. Though wars, famines, plagues, captivities, diseases, and other afflictions, may be long, yet they are not, they shall not be for ever, they must have an end.

Obs. 3. That God sometimes deals more favourably with heathens than with his own people. "At the end of forty years will I gather the Egyptians;" but it was the end of seventy years before he gathered the Jews out of Babylon: his own people were thirty years, or near upon, longer under the Babylonish yoke than the Egyptians. There was just cause for this; God's people had sinned worse than the heathens, and so provoked him above them. Ezek. v. 6, "Jerusalem hath changed my judgments into wickedness more than the nations, and my statutes more than the countries round about her;" there were no people, near or far off, who did like unto the Jews; they forsook God the fountain of living waters, and trusted in Pharaoh that great dragon, and in his rivers of waters.

Obs. 4. Nothing is too hard for God, or can hinder the fulfilling of his will. The Egyptians were scattered among the nations, here a family and there a family, and that forty years together; so mingled with the people of other countries, that they had well-nigh forgotten Egypt, and had so drunk in the manners and customs of the places where they lived, that they were naturalized thereunto; they were so rooted among the nations, that it seemed impossible to pluck them up, and plant them in their own countries; yet notwithstanding these things, saith God, "I will gather the Egyptians from the people whither they were scattered." It is like the Babylonians and other nations that had them, held them under, and made advantage of their labours, made laws against their flight or departure, and struggled hard to detain them, as they of old in Moses' days did to retain the Jews; but whatever opposition was made or difficulty appeared in the way, God said, "I will bring again the captivity of Egypt." Had they bound them all in fetters, laid them in dungeons, set guards of soldiers to have kept them, all these should not have hindered the reduction of them; for, as Jehoshaphat acknowledged in his prayer, God rules over all the kingdoms of the heathen, and in his hand there is power and might, so that none is able to withstand him, 2 Chron. xx. 6; no king, no counsel, no country, no army, no created power is able to withstand him. The Jews had lain longer in Babylon, and were like dry bones in the grave, without hope, Ezek. xxxvii. 11; but God made good his word, he brought them out with a strong hand, breaking in pieces gates of brass, and cutting in sunder bars of iron.

Obs. 5. It is the same hand, the same God, that drives men out of their countries and comforts, into deep and long afflictions abroad, and brings them back out of the same, to enjoy their countries and comforts. God scattered the Egyptians among the nations, he threw them forty years into captivity; and he brought them out again from the nations, and from their captivity, into the land of Pathros, into the land of their commerce. God led them out, and he brought them in; he afflicted them, and he comforted them; God conducted them outward and inward: as the loss of their country was a great affliction unto them, so the repossessing of it was a greater consolation unto them. God threw the Jews into Babylon, those deep and brackish waters they were so long pickled in, and he brought them out again to the sweet waters of the sanctuary. Long afflictions have comfortable ends; the Jews' seventy years' sufferings ended in everlasting kindnesses, Isa. liv. 8.

"They shall be there a base kingdom." The word for "base" is, שפלה which the Septuagint renders, ταπεινὴ, and Montanus, a vile, base, low kingdom. Martinius saith, it should be like a low shrub, that is, little above the earth, such as that kingdom, Ezek. xvii. 6, "of low stature." Some kingdoms are great, high, like cedars of Lebanon and oaks of Bashan. Others are small, like vines and shrubs, that creep upon the earth. Such a kingdom should the Egyptians' be. They were not free, but in subjection to the Babylonians, Persians, Alexander the Great, to Ptolemy, the Romans, who made Egypt a province; after that it was under the Saracens and Turks.

Ver. 15. "It shall be the basest of the kingdoms." Not only shall it be base, as many kingdoms are, especially after wars, but "it shall be the basest of kingdoms;" it should have less power, dignity, and liberty, than other kingdoms.

"Neither shall it exalt itself any more above the nations." It had got power and dominion over other nations, the Pharaohs of Egypt had power over the land of Judea and the kings of Judah, 2 Kings xxiii. 33—35, and other nations; but after this it became an underling, and nothing remarkable is mentioned about it in the word of God. Here God put a band of iron and brass upon this kingdom, to keep it from rising again; it shall not "exalt itself any more above the nations."

"For I will diminish them, that they shall no more rule over the nations." I will make the Egyptians few, and the kingdom little. The Hebrew for "diminish" is, מעט to make little, or few in number. When either or both of these are done, there is a diminishing. Their number might increase, yet they be diminished in power, liberty, and dignity; so that other nations should look upon them as contemptible.

Obs. 1. When kingdoms are ruined, brought to utter desolation, and have lain so a long time, God is able to raise them up again. Egypt was made desolate from one end to the other, man and beast cut off, the Egyptians scattered into remote parts; yet what saith the Lord? "They shall be there a kingdom;" Egypt shall be possessed again, inhabited, become a kingdom, after forty years' desolation. God can raise up great structures out of heaps and ruins. When a kingdom is brought to ashes, the Lord can out of those ashes bring forth another. The Lord causeth kingdoms to cease, Hos. i. 4; he plucks them up, Dan. xi. 4; Jer. i. 10, and he plants and builds them up again, Jer. xviii. 9. Judea and Jerusalem lay waste seventy years, and then God returned the Jews from Babylon, built their city, planted their land, made them a people again.

Obs. 2. The wise providence of God in restoring and ordering of kingdoms, mingles judgment with mercy. They should be a kingdom, but a "base kingdom," they should want that dignity, power, and liberty they had formerly. So the kingdom of Judah after Josiah's days was low and base, Ezek. xvii. 6, 14; Pharaoh and Nebuchadnezzar kept it under. It is from the Lord what condition kingdoms shall be in; they shall be honourable or base, as he pleases.

Obs. 3. Those that lift up themselves above others, shall proportionably be brought down beneath others. Egypt exalted itself above the nations; they were proud, haughty, insolent, but Egypt exceeded them therein; and what came thereof? "It shall be the basest of the kingdoms:" consider what kingdom is basest amongst them all, and Egypt shall be baser than that; as it was the highest in pride, so it should be the lowest through baseness, and most contemptible. The Lord pours out contempt upon kingdoms and kings. Nebuchadnezzar was a son of pride; and did not God drive him out from among men, and make that proud king graze among the beasts? and abase him proportionably to his pride, and cause him to say, "Those that walk in pride he is able to abase?" Dan. iv.: and in his time he will abase all such. He hath abased kingdoms, kings, and potentates in our days, who swelled with pride. The learned Jews tell us what God saith of every man whose spirit is lift up, I and he cannot dwell together in the same world. *Buxtorf. Apoth. Hebr.*

Ver. 16. "And it shall be no more the confidence of the house of Israel." Whilst Egypt flourished, abounding with men, horses, and chariots, the Jews had an eye unto them, and leaned much upon them, Isa. xxx. 2; xxxi. 1; xxxvi. 6, 9; Ezek. xvii. 15; but the Lord laid it waste, brake the pride of its power, made it base, and kept it in that condition, that the Jews might not confide in it; for when they hung so upon the Egyptians for help, that drew them on to their idolatrous practices, and to break the leagues they had made with others.

"Which bringeth their iniquity to remembrance." The Hebrew is, the remembrancer of iniquity. The Vulgate hath it, teaching iniquity, and so refer it to the Egyptians, who being familiar with the Jews, taught them to do evil; but the words refer to confidence, which brought their iniquity to remembrance, viz. that they should forsake God, trust in an arm of flesh, hearken unto idolaters, &c.

"When they shall look after them." Had the Egyptians been restored to their former glory and power, the Jews would have been looking after them, trusted in, and expected help from them; but being low, base, in subjection to others, they would neither look at them nor lean upon them, but leave them, as men do a broken staff.

Obs. 1. God's own people are apt to confide in an arm of flesh. The house of Israel made Egypt its confidence. Asa relied on the king of Syria, 2 Chron. xvi. 7. The Jews were very prone to this sin; sometimes they trusted in their fenced cities, as Jer. v. 17; sometimes in their land of peace, as Jer. xii. 5; sometimes in their multitudes of men, as Hos. x. 13; sometimes in their own glory and greatness, as Ezek. xvi. 15; sometimes in their privileges, as Jer. vii. 4; sometimes in their own wisdom, Jer. viii. 8; and sometimes in others, as the Assyrians, 2 Chron. xxviii. 16, and the Egyptians, as Ezek. xvii. 15. This showed their trust in God was little, and made him say, Jer. xiii. 25, "Thou hast forgotten me, and trusted in falsehood:" בשקר is, a lie; in things that promise help and safety, but cannot make them good, they will deceive you, be a lie and falsehood unto you. This practice of theirs made the Lord to say, Jer. ii. 36, "Why gaddest thou about so much to change thy way? thou also shalt be ashamed of Egypt, as thou wast ashamed of Assyria;" they had formerly trusted to the Assyrians, who, instead of helping, distressed them, 2 Chron. xxviii. 20; and so should the Egyptians, for it follows, "Thou shalt go forth from him, and thine hands upon thine head;" that is, lamenting thy disappointment; "for the Lord hath rejected thy confidences, and thou shalt not prosper in them," that is, thou shalt fail of them, and be undone by them. Let us take heed of bottoming upon any thing beneath the Lord, for, Jer. xvii. 5, a curse is pronounced upon the "man that trusteth in man, and maketh flesh his arm," and whose heart departeth from the Lord: his heart is gone from the Lord who trusteth in any creature.

Obs. 2. Creature confidence brings former sins to remembrance. When the house of Israel looked to Egypt for help, that is, trusted in them, then their former iniquity was brought to mind, that occasioned God to remember other sins. When a wife leaves her husband, or a soldier his commander, this reminds them of former miscarriages; and so when God's people leave him for an arm of flesh, this revives the memory of old iniquities. Ezek. xxi. 24, it is said, they made their iniquity to be remembered; and how came that? by discovery of their transgressions; some new sins appeared, and they caused the former to be remembered. New sins are editions of the old; bankrupts, by some later acts, bring former debts into question, and men, by some new later sin, occasion God to bring their former sins into view.

Obs. 3. That the Lord, for the good of his people, brings down proud nations, and keeps them in servile conditions. Egypt lifted up itself above the nations, but God brake it in pieces, made it base, yea, the basest of kingdoms, decreeing it should not be exalted, but abide so; and why? that the house of Israel might not confide any more in it, that their iniquity might not by so doing be brought to remembrance, that they might know the Lord to be above all nations, princes, and powers whatsoever, and trust in him. Here was wonderful goodness in God towards his church and people, that he would keep under Egypt to prevent their sinning and punishing, and to draw them to trust in himself. Had Egypt been set in its former power, glory, and greatness, the eye and heart of the house of Israel would have been looking that way, iniquity been brought to mind, and their confidence taken off from God; now, rather than such things should be, Egypt shall be made base and contemptible, and kept in that condition. There was a time when we confided too much in Scotland; God hath broken that nation in pieces, and will keep it in a low condition, that we may learn not to depend upon nations, but the God of nations.

Ver. 17—20. *And it came to pass in the seven and twentieth year, in the first month, in the first day of the month, the word of the Lord came unto me, saying, Son of man, Nebuchadrezzar king of Babylon caused his army to serve a great service against Tyrus: every head was made bald, and every shoulder was peeled: yet had he no wages, nor his army, for Tyrus, for the service that he had served against it. Therefore thus saith the Lord God; Behold, I will give the land of Egypt unto Nebuchadrezzar king of Babylon; and he shall take her multitude, and take her spoil, and take her prey; and it shall be the wages for his army. I have given him the land of Egypt for his labour wherewith he served against it, because they wrought for me, saith the Lord God.*

These verses comprehend the fourth general part of the chapter, which is a prophecy of giving Egypt unto Nebuchadrezzar king of Babylon; wherein is set down,

I. The time of this prophecy, when it was, ver. 17.

II. The cause why God gave Egypt to Nebuchadrezzar, ver. 18, 20.

III. The donation itself, ver. 19, 20. Egypt, and the wealth of it, are given him to pay his army.

"In the seven and twentieth year, in the first month, in the first day of the month." This prophecy was sixteen years and upwards after the former, but being of the same nature, is here conjoined with it, though he had many others between them. It was in the twenty-seventh year of Jehoiachin's captivity, sixteen years after the destruction of Jerusalem, and shortly after the taking of Tyrus. The punctual time is here set down, that so the chronology of things done might be known and observed.

Ver. 18. "Nebuchadrezzar king of Babylon caused his army to serve a great service against Tyrus." Tyrus was a strong city upon a rock in the sea, well walled and towered, seven hundred paces from the continent, abounding with ships to supply all things needful, and to secure her by sea, so that in the eye of man it was invincible. Nebuchadrezzar besieged this city with a vast army thirteen years, which Josephus confirms from other historians. Dioclesian, in the second book of his Persian history, and Philostratus, in his Phœnician and Indian history, make mention of this king, saying, that he overcame the city of Tyre at the end of thirteen years, at such time as Ithobald reigned over the Tyrians. In this time he filled up that space of the sea which was between the shore and Tyrus with solid materials, so that the soldiers might foot it even to the walls of Tyre, which cost much sweat and labour, and was a great service, besides all the rest of their labour, watchings, and sufferings of heat and cold. To lie so many winters and summers there, doing ordinary and extraordinary things, was a great service, especially their filling up the sea, which the Tyrians laughed at, and thought impossible.

Joseph. Antiq. l. 10. c. 10, at the end of the chapter.

"Every head was made bald." The Hebrew for "bald" is, מקרח from קרח to pull off the hairs; and it notes natural baldness as well as accidental, the shedding of the hair, and the plucking off the hair: the soldiers, by continual wearing their head-pieces, did shed and wear off their hairs. Some through sickness, and upon other occasions, might become bald.

"And every shoulder was peeled." By the daily carrying of stones, timber, earth, and other things necessary for the siege and taking of Tyrus, their shoulders were peeled. כתף signifies not only the "shoulder," but the side also; and Piscator renders the words, every side was made naked, their garments were worn out, and their sides bare, worn, and peeled.

"Yet had he no wages, nor his army, for Tyrus." This long siege cost Nebuchadrezzar dear, it exhausted the Babylonish treasury greatly, insomuch, that had he taken Tyrus, with all the wealth of it, it would hardly have recompensed his vast expenses; but the Tyrians, when they saw themselves in danger, conveyed away by sea their choicest things to Carthage, and neighbouring islands, as Lavater insinuates, and when they could hold their city no longer, threw their remaining substance into the sea, so that when it was taken, Nebuchadrezzar and his army found little or nothing considerable therein; therefore it is here said, "he had no wages, nor his army."

"For the service he had served against it." The king and soldiers having lain thirteen years before Tyrus, which showed their resoluteness, looked for answerable recompence for so long, difficult, dangerous, and expensive service; but because they were disappointed in Tyrus, therefore the Lord thought upon them, and provided for them elsewhere.

Ver. 19. "Behold, I will give the land of Egypt unto Nebuchadrezzar." Egypt was a rich country, abounding with corn, cattle, and wealth of all sorts; this country did the Lord give unto Nebuchadrezzar and his army, for that they had done him service in executing his judgments upon the Tyrians.

"He shall take her multitude." Multitudes of men were worn out and consumed in the long siege of Tyre, and therefore God would give the king of Babylon Egypt's "multitude;" she was populous, and her "multitude" must serve him forty years. The Hebrew word המנה signifies, multitude of people, and multitude of riches; Nebuchadrezzar should take both.

"And take her spoil." The Hebrew is, he shall spoil her spoil. "Spoil" is, whatsoever may be removed, taken, or driven away, as corn, cattle, household stuff, garments, jewels, plate, plants, ware, &c. The Babylonian should strip Egypt of all her glory.

"And take her prey." In Hebrew it is, he shall prey her prey. The Septuagint is, he shall captivate her captivity. The words being doubled before, and here, import that Nebuchadrezzar should thoroughly spoil and prey upon Egypt.

"It shall be the wages for his army." Seeing his army had so little in Tyre, it shall have enough in Egypt, nothing here shall be conveyed away, embezzled, or kept from him and his army, the whole wealth of Egypt shall be theirs.

Ver. 20. "For his labour." The word פעלה sometimes signifies, the thing produced by work and labour, as Psal. xvii. 4; but here, and in other places, it notes, the very working and efficiency itself: 2 Chron. xv. 7, "Your work shall be rewarded," that is, your labour and pains.

"Because they wrought for me." They looked at their king, who commanded and carried them forth to that work, not unto Jehovah, the Lord of heaven and earth, who set both him and them on work to execute his judgments threatened against Tyre, and in that they did fulfil them, they are said to work for God. Materially they did serve his purpose and providence in the destruction of Tyre, but formally and intentionally they did serve their own wills and lusts. God had a righteous end, and attained it by them; they had an evil end, and obtained it in an ill way; Isa. x. 6, 7, the Assyrian had one meaning, God another, yet he wrought for the Lord.

Vid. Aquin. 1. 2. q. 114.

Obs. 1. That men in misery keep account exactly of their sufferings. Ezekiel was in captivity, and many other Jews, who diligently heeded how the years passed; "In the seven and twentieth year," that was, of the captivity. Ezekiel, and the rest, forgot not how long they had been under the Babylonish yoke: men are best chronologers in adversity.

Obs. 2. When God is upon doing great things, usually he doth make them known unto some of his servants, one way or other. When he was upon destroying Sodom, he made it known unto Abraham, Gen. xviii. 17; when about to destroy Eli's house, he revealed it to Samuel, 1 Sam. iii. 11, 12; the strange things which befell Nebuchadnezzar were revealed to Daniel, chap. iv.; and the Lord showed John things to come, Rev. i. 1; and here, he hides not from Ezekiel that he will give all Egypt to Nebuchadrezzar. This was so frequent of old, that Amos said, "Surely the Lord will do nothing, but he revealeth his secret to his servants the prophets," Amos iii. 7; hardly did God ever any considerable thing, but he gave some hints of it to his servants.

The drowning of the world, the Jews' captivity in Egypt, their coming out of it, their suffering by Nebuchadnezzar, their return out of Babylon, &c. were all hinted and made known to Noah, Abraham, Moses, Isaiah, Jeremiah, and others.

Obs. 3. Princes have power to lead out and employ their subjects against foreigners, when there is cause of warring with them. The king of Babylon caused his army to serve against Tyrus, and before that against Jerusalem; many hundreds of miles did he bring out his army to do him service against the Jews and Tyrians. Had he no particular cause, this was cause enough, that God stirred up his spirit to execute his judgments upon those who had desperately provoked him.

Obs. 4. That heathenish soldiers have undergone very hard things, yea, hazarded their lives to please their heathenish commanders, and all for a temporal reward. Nebuchadrezzar's army served a great service thirteen years together; to lie before a city was hard, their heads were made bald, their shoulders were peeled, they laboured hard, carried heavy burdens, they watched, they suffered heat and cold, and all this for hope of good plunder in Tyrus. If heathens would do and endure so much for their commander, who was an idolater, an enemy to God and his people, how much more should christians do and endure any thing for Christ, their King, and heavenly Commander! If he say, Go, we should go; if, Come, we should come; if, Pluck out your right eye, cut off your right hand, or right foot, we should do so; if he calls us to endure affliction, and suffer hard things, we should not stick at them, no, though it be the jeoparding of our lives, knowing he hath a spiritual and eternal reward for us. Seeing men have done and suffered so much for heathens, how can we do or suffer too much for Christ? Scipio Africanus had three hundred soldiers, who would climb a tower if he bid them, or throw themselves from the top of a tower at his command; what dishonour will it be to Christ, if his soldiers will not do as much at his command as others have done at their lords' commands!

Obs. 5. Armies, with their generals and commanders, may serve long, labour sorely, suffer hard things, and after all these be disappointed of their expectations. Nebuchadrezzar caused his army to serve a great service thirteen years, so that their heads, shoulders, sides, were bald, and peeled; and what then? yet had he no "wages," nor his army; they expected great matters in Tyrus, which was so rich, and full of all sorts of commodities, but found nothing considerable, nothing answering their expectation, or sufficient to recompense their charge and suffering. This undertaking could not be without millions of money; hopes they had, that Tyrus, being now the mart of nations, would repay them with advantage, but Tyrus's wealth was dispersed, and there was no money in cash. Sometimes armies find rich spoil and fat prey in the towns and cities they take, and sometimes they find empty houses.

Obs. 6. Nations, lands, kingdoms, are the Lord's, and he disposes of them to whom he pleases. "Behold, I will give the land of Egypt unto Nebuchadrezzar:" he would take it from Pharaoh, king thereof, and give it to another. Neither did the Lord do any wrong unto Pharaoh, because he was tenant at will, and held upon these terms, to be king while he carried himself well; but he grew proud, insolent, and like a dragon lay in the midst of his rivers, saying, "My river is mine, and I have made it for myself." God therefore took away his kingdom from him, and gave it to the king of Babylon; he looseth the loins of kings, and dismisseth them from their kingdoms. He rejected Saul, 1 Sam. xv. 23, and gave his kingdom to David, chap. xvi. 1, 13; he rent ten tribes from Rehoboam, and gave them to Jeroboam, 1 Kings xi. 31; he cast out many kings, and gave their lands to Nebuchadrezzar, Jer. xxvii. 3, 7; and, ver. 5, you may see upon what ground he doth so: "I have made the earth, the man and the beast that are upon the ground, by my great power and by my out-stretched arm, and have given it unto whom it seemed meet unto me. And now I have given all these lands into the hand of Nebuchadnezzar." He made the earth, he may give it to, and take it from, whom he please; it is his, not ours: no man is owner of the earth, or any part of it, it is the Lord's; therefore if he break in pieces mighty men without number, and sets others in their stead, he wrongs, he oppresses none, Job xxxiv. 24. Let not us be troubled that God hath done such things in our days.

Obs. 7. God, in his holy and wise providence, makes use of heathens, or any instruments, to do his work. Nebuchadrezzar and his army wrought for him, they were his servants, he set them on work, though they knew it not. When armies of heathens do plunder towns, take cities, lay waste kingdoms, they are working for God, they are executing his judgments, though they mind it not; God carries on his work, let instruments be what they will. He can make use of the worst of men, as well as of the best; he can promote his interest by an army of heathens, as well as by an army of christians; and let armies be what they will, good or bad, when they are at work, they work for God. "They wrought for me," saith God. It is good, therefore, not to stick upon the instruments which work, but to look at the hand in which they are, how that directs and regulates them, look at him whose tools, whose servants, they are; this will quiet men's spirits, and keep their tongues within compass.

Obs. 8. The Lord suffers not any, no not heathens and infidels, to labour for him in vain. He gave the land of Egypt, with all the wealth of it, to Nebuchadrezzar and his army, who were the worst of the heathen, Ezek. vii. 24, because they served and wrought for him. God is just, not like those masters, who set men on work and then will give them no wages; whosoever works for God shall have his penny. When the midwives would not destroy the male children of the Jews, but save them alive, because they feared God, he dealt well with them, and gave them houses, Exod. i. 17, 20, 21; he gave them habitations, and blessed their families; they were infidels, yet God rewarded their work. Jehu was wicked, yet because he did the work of the Lord in rooting out Ahab's family, in destroying Baal, with all the priests and temple of Baal, therefore the Lord rewarded him, and that largely: 2 Kings x. 30, "Because thou hast done well in executing that which is right in mine eyes, and hast done unto the house of Ahab according to all that was in mine heart, thy children of the fourth generation shall sit on the throne of Israel;" which was made good in Jehoahaz, Joash, Jeroboam, and Zechariah, who came out of his loins, and reigned after him, 2 Kings xiii. xiv. xv. How should this stir us up to do good, and serve the Lord! if heathens shall not labour for him in vain, much less shall christians, who know how to act from a right principle, in a right manner, and for a right end; if they meet with hardship in his service, he will remember and reward it fully, not with a temporal kingdom, but with an eternal; the land of Egypt shall be given to Babylonians, because the kingdom of heaven shall be given to christians: Luke xii. 32, "Fear not, little flock; it is your Father's pleasure to give you the kingdom." Let us "therefore be stedfast and immovable, always abounding in the work of the Lord, forasmuch as we know our labour shall not be in vain." A cup of cold water, two mites cast into the treasury, a sigh, a tear, laid out for God and his interest, shall not be forgotten: what Paul told the Hebrews, I may tell you, that God is not unrighteous, to forget your work; men may forget, or reward poorly, but God will not forget, because he cannot be unrighteous, nor reward poorly, because he deals bountifully with his servants, Psal. cxvi. 7.

Obs. 9. Execution of judgment upon proud princes, and wicked people, is pleasing unto God. He set Nebuchadrezzar and his army on work to besiege Tyre, to rase it to the ground, he paid them their wages for it, which convinces that the work was pleasing unto him: when men are at great cost and charges in setting many to work, it is argument they take pleasure in such work; so was it here, the work the Babylonish army did was a pleasure unto God, he gave them all Egypt for that service. God delights as well in executing judgment as in exercising mercy; therefore, Jer. xlviii. 10, he curseth those who should be negligent in, or backward to, the slaughter of the Moabites. God sent the Chaldeans to destroy the Moabites, and his heart was so much in this work, that he would have it done thoroughly; and to quicken up the Chaldeans to it, he pronounces a curse upon them if they should forbear to do it, or not do it to purpose. So that, Jer. l. 25, "The Lord hath opened his armoury, and hath brought forth the weapons of his indignation: for this is the work of the Lord God of hosts in the land of the Chaldeans. Come against her from the utmost border:" these words the Lord speaks concerning the destruction of Babylon, which was a work very pleasing to him; he opened his armoury, brought forth his weapons, called men from all parts to come and take these weapons, and employ them against her. Like some mighty prince the Lord doth here, who when he will war against some strong place, opens his armoury and magazine, bringing forth all his warlike instruments, his ammunition and artillery, he calls his soldiers to take them, saying, Come, this is the work I have called thee to, viz. to storm this castle, to destroy this town, this is the work I take pleasure to see done.

Ver. 21. *In that day will I cause the horn of the house of Israel to bud forth, and I will give thee the opening of the mouth in the midst of them; and they shall know that I am the Lord.*

This chapter, according to Junius, ended at the 17th verse, where he begins the thirtieth chapter, but according to our translation, this is the last verse of this chapter, and it is a precious promise of mercy to the house of Israel, and to the prophet. In the words you have,

I. The things promised, which are,

1. Restitution of power to the tribe of Judah, "I will cause the horn," &c.

2. Liberty of prophesying to Ezekiel, "I will give thee the opening of the mouth."

II. The end of his so doing, "They shall know," &c.

III. The time when, "In that day."

Ver. 21. "In that day." When the Egyptians were subdued, and the Babylonish monarchy quieted, and settled in peace, as shortly after Nebuchadrezzar's return from Egypt it was; for he dying, Evil-merodach came to the throne, and then was the "day." "Day" notes not only twelve hours, or, four and twenty, but frequently a short time; as Deut. ix. 1, "Hear, O Israel: Thou art to pass over Jordan this day," that was, shortly, within some few years or months, for they passed not over Jordan till Joshua's days, (when Moses was dead,) and he governed, Josh. iii.; so here, "day" is put for some space of time after the destruction of Egypt.

"Will I cause the horn of the house of Israel to bud forth." "Horn" is proper to a beast, but metaphorically is applied to men, and in holy writ signifies sometimes dignity and glory; as Job xvi. 15, "I defiled my horn in the dust;" whatever made me glorious, honourable, and respected amongst men, that have I laid aside, and counted no more of than the dunghill or dust I sit upon: sometimes kings and kingdoms; as Dan. viii. 21, "The rough goat is the king of Grecia: and the great horn that is between his eyes is the first king," viz. Alexander the Great; and, Psal. cxxxii. 17, "There will I make the horn of David to bud;" the "horn of David" was the kingdom of David: sometimes strength and power; Jer. xlviii. 25, "The horn of Moab is cut off, and his army is broken;" that "horn of Moab" was the strength of Moab; Lam. ii. 3, "He hath cut off in his fierce anger all the horn of Israel," that is, all the strength and power of Israel: sometimes it notes all outward felicity, liberty, and plenty; Psal. cxlviii. 14, "He exalteth the horn of his people," that is, he makes them happy, he gives them freedom, and plenty of all things, and therein exalts their horn: here, all these senses may be taken in, God would make the horn of the house of Israel, that is, the king and kingdom, to rise up again to dignity, strength, and happiness. This was in part made good in the three children, and Daniel, or when Jehoiachin was brought out of prison, and his throne set above the thrones of all the kings who were with him in Babylon, Jer. lii. 31—34; then, doubtless, had the Jews some liberty and privileges granted them, which caused matter of rejoicing: more fully in Zerubbabel, when he brought them out of Babylon: but chiefly in Christ, and the gospel times. This "horn" is budding still, and shall "bud" to the end of the world; the kingdom of Christ shall flourish and grow stronger, as the horns of a beast do yearly.

"I will give thee the opening of the mouth in the midst of them." Ezekiel had been silent and dumb twice before, chap. iii. 24, and xxiv. 27; and here again it is implied; God would give him the "opening of the mouth," or an open mouth. By opening the mouth, we may understand,

1. Freedom of speech. Thou speakest things darkly now, with a trembling voice, but when these prophecies are fulfilled, and the horn of the house of Israel begins to bud, then shalt thou have more freedom of speech, and be troubled no more at the false prophets, which sought to disparage thee.

2. Matter of speaking. When Jeconiah, or Jehoiachin, should have his prison garments changed, and be set above other princes, some freedom granted the Jews, here would be matter for praise and rejoicing.

3. Opportunity of speaking. When an occasion is given unto man to speak, the rabbins call that, the opening of the mouth: thou shalt come openly into the assemblies, having matter, freedom, and opportunity to praise me. Grot. in Eph. c. 6. 19.

"They shall know that I am the Lord." "They" refers not only to the house of Israel, but to the Babylonians also; when they should see the things prophesied of done, then they should acknowledge the Lord. The horn of Israel budded in the midst of the Babylonians, and the prophet's mouth was opened in the midst of them, therefore they should, as well as the Jews, "know that I am the Lord."

Obs. 1. That after the destruction of enemies, God shows mercy to the Jews. Egyptians were no friends to the house of Israel. When Egypt therefore should be spoiled, and brought under the Babylonians, then would he make the horn of Israel to bud; in that day, or after that time, when his justice had fallen upon Egyptians, then his mercy should be extended to Israel. Jer. l. 4, 5, when the Medes and Persians should have laid Babylon waste, and made her land desolate, what then? "In those days, and in that time, saith the Lord, the children of Israel shall come, they and the children of Judah together, going and weeping;" that is, for gladness, for the mercy vouchsafed them; "they shall go, and seek the Lord their God. They shall ask the way to Zion with their faces thitherward." When the Babylonians were brought into bondage, then God gave the Jews their liberty; Isa. x. 26, 27, when the Assyrians should be destroyed, then should the Jews be eased of their burdens.

Obs. 2. How low, weak, afflicted soever the church be, God is able to raise it up, to bring it to glory, strength, and to a flourishing condition. The house of Israel was low, and much afflicted, the horn of it weak, and hardly visible; yet God caused the horn thereof to bud. When we look upon some beasts, they have no horns, but in a short time their heads do bud, and bring forth horns, which are their strength; so God in a little time would cause the glory, strength, happiness of his church and people to appear, though at that time they lay in the dust. The church of God looks ofttimes like a dry and dead tree; but his divine influences make it bud, blossom, and flourish: Isa. xxxv. 1, "The desert shall rejoice and blossom as the rose," it shall blossom abundantly. When Zion was turned into a wilderness, he made it "like Eden, and her desert like the garden of God," Isa. li. 3; when the church was in the most desolate and hopeless condition, he made it glorious, beautiful, and strong. When the tabernacle of David was quite fallen, nothing but ruins and breaches discernible, what said the Lord? "In that day will I raise up the tabernacle of David that is fallen, and close up the breaches thereof; and I will raise up his ruins, and I will build it." This was done literally, after their return out of Babylon, when the second temple was built, and the two tribes of Judah and Benjamin grew up into one body; but spiritual, in Christ's time, not in the resurrection of his body from the grave, but in bringing in the gentiles after his ascension, to make up all the breaches and ruins which were made in the Jewish state; so it is applied, Acts xv. 16. God that gives being to things that are not, can give more glorious and excellent beings to things that are.

Obs. 3. When God shows kindness to his church, he gives his prophets and servants matter, freedom, and opportunity of speaking, and professing the true faith publicly. When the Lord caused the horn of the house of Israel to bud, when he showed favour to his people, then he gave Ezekiel the opening of the mouth. In the times of enemies' prevailing, prophets are silent, or prophesy faintly; if they have matter to utter, they want freedom, they whisper, mutter, and speak as it were with closed mouth, and oft have not opportunity to do so much; Amos v. 13, they are necessitated to be silent: but when times grow better, and God shines upon his people, then the prophets are full of matter, free to speak, and want not seasons to declare the goodness of God, then they are not afraid or ashamed openly to profess the truth, and to praise the Lord. The opening of the mouth is the gift of God: the illness of the people and times may shut the mouths of prophets, but none can open them but God. Since God began to show mercy to his people in this land, hath he not vouchsafed the opening of the mouth to his prophets? their mouths were shut in the prelates' days, but now there is a great opening; blessed be the Lord for it.

Obs. 4. The end of God's showing kindness to his church, and opening the mouths of his prophets, is, that he may have honour and glory thereby from all sorts. "And they shall know that I am the Lord:" they Babylonians, they Jews, shall acknowledge that I have done these things, and that I am the Lord.

CHAPTER XXX.

Ver. 1—5. *The word of the Lord came again unto me, saying, Son of man, prophesy and say, Thus saith the Lord God; Howl ye, Woe worth the day! For the day is near, even the day of the Lord is near, a cloudy day; it shall be the time of the heathen. And the sword shall come upon Egypt, and great pain shall be in Ethiopia, when the slain shall fall in Egypt, and they shall take away her multitude, and her foundations shall be broken down. Ethiopia, and Libya, and Lydia, and all the mingled people, and Chub, and the men of the land that is in league, shall fall with them by the sword.*

THIS chapter is a continuance of the former prophecy, and hath two general parts in it.

The I. is concerning the destruction of Egypt, and those that were confederate with her, to ver. 19.

II. Is concerning Pharaoh king of Egypt, and Nebuchadnezzar king of Babylon, from ver. 20 to the end.

In these verses we have,

1. The authority of the prophecy; it is divine, from the Lord, ver. 1, 2.
2. The thing imposed upon Egypt; howling, ver. 2.
3. The reasons thereof, ver. 3—5.

Ver. 1. "The word of the Lord came again unto me." This preface is to many chapters before; it adds weight to the prophecy, making those concerned to mind it more seriously: when the Lord speaketh, "who can but prophesy?" Amos iii. 8; and who can but mind what is prophesied?

Ver. 2. "Son of man, prophesy." The immortal God speaks to a mortal man, honours him with divine revelations; and, that he might not be exalted therewith, he minds him of his meanness and mortality, saying, "Son of man, prophesy." Prophesying was not at the will of man, but when the Spirit moved them to it, 2 Pet. i. 21.

"Thus saith the Lord God." What the prophets gave forth as prophets, was not from their own hearts and heads, some human thing, but it was altogether divine, from Jehovah, Adonai, whose being is of himself, and hath dominion over all; what they and the apostles wrote, was the word of God, and so ought to be esteemed and received, 1 Thess. ii. 13.

"Howl ye." He speaks to the Egyptians and others, upon whom sad judgments were coming; he calls to them to lay to heart, and lament for, the evils which were at hand. The Hebrew ילל hath agreement with אלל which signifies, to reduce a thing to nothing, because when men do mourn and lament greatly, it wastes and consumes them, so as it well-nigh brings them to nothing.

"Woe worth the day!" The words may be read, Ah the day! "Alas for the day!" as Joel i. 15; or, Oh the woe of the day! an unhappy day, wherein thy cities shall be made heaps, man and beast destroyed, all laid waste and desolate.

Ver. 3. "The day is near, even the day of the Lord is near." "Day" here is put, not for a day in strictness of sense, but for the time wherein those judgments should befall Egypt and other parts; and it is called "the day of the Lord," because of his special manifestation of himself. When God doth, either in mercy or judgment, declare himself emphatically, that is said to be "the day of the Lord:" other days are his days, but such in a special manner. The duplication of the "day" here, is to make the deeper impression both upon the Jews, who rested too much upon Egypt, and also upon the Egyptians, who were secure and feared not: he tells them of the nearness of it, that they may be awakened; and that they might the more fully be awakened, he tells them what kind of day it will be.

"A cloudy day." The Hebrew is, a day of a cloud; there will no sun shine that day, a black, thick, dark cloud will arise that day, and make a terrible tempest. God's judgments are likened unto clouds and rain, for the sadness and terribleness of them: Psal. xi. 6, "He shall rain snares, fire and brimstone, and an horrible tempest."

"It shall be the time of the heathen." "Heathen" may be taken either for the Babylonians, who should come and conquer Egypt, and then do what they pleased therein, and so it should be their day; or for the Egyptians, and the nations adhering to them, and so it should be their day to be spoiled, and suffer grievous things: it was a time of undoing these, and a time of making the other; God had appointed that time for them both.

Ver. 4. "The sword shall come upon Egypt." The Chaldean army shall come and make war upon the Egyptians, and they shall be under all the miseries and mischiefs which attend war, and they are many.

"And great pain shall be in Ethiopia." The word for "pain" in Hebrew is, חלחלה which Montanus renders, shaking: the Septuagint, trouble, or perturbation: the Vulgate, fear: others, great grief, which the word imports; for it is from חול to bring forth, and notes such grief and pain as women have when they are in travail. When the king of Babylon came into Egypt, Ethiopia was in travail.

"When the slain shall fall in Egypt." It were better rendered, when the wounded shall fall. Men slain are fallen, men wounded are ready to fall, or falling. The Hebrew word חלל signifies one wounded.

"And her foundations shall be broken down." By "foundations," cities, towers, forts, castles, any strong holds may be understood. Some make the foundations of Egypt to be their riches, forces, and confederates; but the first sense of the word is more genuine, because he speaks of breaking down, which is proper to the one, and not the other.

Ver. 5. "Ethiopia." In Hebrew, Chus, so called from Chus, the son of Ham, Gen. x. 6, who first inhabited that part of Africa, and from him the people were called Cussites; from the Grecians it received the name of Ethiopia, which is from *αἴθω*, to burn, and *ὄψ*, the countenance, because the heat of the sun there is such, as it scorcheth the faces of the people. This country is judged to be as large as Germany, France, and Italy, but not very populous, because of the extreme heat. They circumcise their males and females, baptizing the males forty days, and the females eighty days, after their circumcision; and they rebaptize themselves in lakes and ponds every year on the day called Epiphany, because they conceive that the Lord Christ was baptized by John in Jordan that very day. But whether this was the Ethiopia Nebuchadnezzar should spoil, some question, because it is said, chap. xxix. 10, that Egypt should be made desolate from the tower of Syene unto the border of Ethiopia, that is, to the Asian Ethiopia. Syene was at the front of the African Ethiopia, and whether Nebuchadnezzar entered that Ethiopia, is doubtful: Quistorpius is peremptory in it, and saith, he never passed beyond Syene into it.

Heylin in his Microcosm.

"Libya." In Hebrew, Phut, from Phut the son of Ham, Gen. x. 6; and the inhabitants thereof were at first called Phuthæi, or Phuttians, and afterward Libyans, the country being named Libya, from Lybs, a king of Mauritania, or from Lybs, the south wind, which gently breatheth there, or from Libya, a queen thereof. It is now called Sorra, which signifies, a desert, because it is a country full of sandy deserts: and Varro will have it called Libya, *quasi λείπουσα τοῦ ὕειν*, because it wants rain. Heretofore all Africa was called Phut, afterwards only the western parts of Africa, as Mauritania and Tingitana, where the kingdom of Fez, or Libya, now is.

Heylin, in Microcos.

"Lydia." The Hebrew is, Lud, from Lud the son of Shem, Gen. x. 22, as some will have it; or from Ludim, the son of Mizraim, as others affirm. This Lydia was a region of Asia the Less, formerly called Mæonia; in it were those famous cities, Philadelphia, Sardis, Pergamus, Thyatira, and Laodicea. A Lapide would not have it to be this Lydia, because those Lydians were too far off to be helpful to the Egyptians; he therefore makes it to be Lydda, Acts ix. 32, where Peter healed Æneas. This city was in the tribe of Ephraim, near unto Joppa; it was therefore taken by Nebuchadnezzar before, when he took Jerusalem, and made the whole land tributary unto him. The distance of Lydia was not such as to hinder the Egyptians from confederating with them; they were on the one side of the Mediterranean sea, and the Lydians on the other.

Heylin, ubi ante.

"And all the mingled people." Montanus saith, all the vulgar. The Hebrew is, all the mixed company, that is, those that came from other parts, to serve the Egyptians for pay. When wars are among nations, strangers will flock out of all parts unto them, to be their auxiliaries. Some make them the Arabians.

"Chub." This word is no where else in holy writ. Symmachus thought it to be Arabia, but interpreters by it understand the Cubæans, and people in the inward Libya, near unto the river Nigris, where Ptolemy, in his Geography, places the city Cuphe.

"The men of the land that is in league." The Hebrew is, the sons of the land of league. Piscator translates the words thus, those who live in a land confederate, that is, these were confederate with the Egyptians: some put these words upon the nations which had engaged themselves to help the Egyptians: others more probably put them upon Judea, which was the land in league with God, for God promised it to Abraham and his posterity, whereupon the Jews were called the children of the covenant, Acts iii. 25: and the Septuagint here hath it, *τῶν υἱων τῆς διαθήκης μου*, the sons of my testament, or covenant. The Jews were in league with the Egyptians, and after the destruction of Jerusalem, Gedaliah being treacherously slain by Ishmael and others, Johanan carrieth the Jews, the sons of the land in league, into Egypt, where they suffered by Nebuchadnezzar what the Egyptians did, Jer. xliii. xliv; some fell by the sword, some were carried captive.

Obs. 1. After days of mirth come days of sorrow. Egypt had seen many days of prosperity and rejoicing, and now, "Howl ye, Woe worth the day!" her summer was over, and winter coming upon her, black, cloudy, stormy, terrible days were at hand. As there is a change in things, so in times: Eccles. iii. 4, "There is a time to weep, and a time to laugh; a time to mourn, and a time to dance;" these succeed each other, and neither keeps possession long; mirth and jollity is thrust out of doors, after a few days, by its contrary. Babylon had her days of delight; she was given to pleasure, Isa. xlvii. 8; but suddenly there was a change; Jer. li. 8, "Babylon is suddenly fallen and destroyed: howl for her."

Obs. 2. The approaching of those days, wherein God will visit and punish sinners, is just cause of mourning. "Howl; for the day of the Lord is near, a cloudy day." The judgments of God were at hand, ready to take hold of the Egyptians, therefore they had sufficient cause to howl. Isa. xiii. 6, "Howl ye; for the day of the Lord is at hand; it shall come as a destruction from the Almighty." It is spoken of the Babylonians, who thought themselves safe, strong, having subdued most nations; but they must howl, for that the day of the Lord drew near: it should be a day for destruction, and not an ordinary destruction, but as a destruction from the Almighty; it should be such a destruction, as should proclaim to the world that the hand of God was eminently in it. Joel ii. 1, "Let all the inhabitants of the land tremble: for the day of the Lord cometh, for it is nigh at hand:" the time of Nebuchadnezzar's coming to execute the judgments of God upon Jerusalem and Judea drew nigh, and thereupon the prophet calls upon all the inhabitants of the land to tremble, to repent and mourn. There is great and just cause so to do at such times, because thereby judgments may be averted, delayed, mitigated, or sanctified unto us.

Obs. 3. God hath his times to visit heathens. "It shall be the time of the heathen." If heathens do God any service, he hath a time to reward them, as he did Nebuchadnezzar, by giving him the spoil of Egypt; if heathens do provoke him by their pride, idolatry, profaneness, oppression of his people, or any other way, he hath his time and day to punish them. Jer. xlvi. 8—10, "Egypt riseth up like a flood, and his waters are moved like the rivers; and he saith, I will go up, and will cover the earth; I will destroy the city" (that was Carchemish, by the river Euphrates) "and the inhabitants thereof. Come up, ye horses; and rage, ye chariots; and let the mighty men come forth; the Ethiopians and the Libyans, that handle the shield; and the Lydians, that handle and bend the bow. For this is the day of the Lord God of hosts, a day of vengeance, that he may avenge him of his adversaries." The Egyptians, Ethiopians, Libyans, and Lydians, were all heathens, and God had his day to visit them: when they went to Euphrates to fight the Babylonians, he made the Babylonish sword drunk with their blood. Not long after, God had a day for the Babylonians: Jer. l. 27, "Slay all her bullocks; let them go down to the slaughter: woe unto them! for their day is come, the time of their visitation;" the princes, nobles, great ones, who were the bullocks of Babylon, had their day of slaughter.

Obs. 4. Where public judgments come, they are troublesome to neighbour nations. "The sword shall come upon Egypt, and great pain shall be in Ethiopia." The evil of the sword was not confined within the Egyptian borders, it reached to the Ethiopians and others, they were filled with fear, they were in pain, as a woman in travail. When evil borders upon us, some evil or mischief is to be feared from thence; if our neighbour's house be on fire, we may fear some sparks of that fire may fall on ours: the wars of England have made the nations about us to be in pain.

Obs. 5. Wars lay all waste, the sword makes no difference between things or persons. "The sword shall come upon Egypt, and her foundations shall be broken down; and the men of the land that is in league shall fall with them by the sword." As the sword spared no city, towers, castles, so no persons, even those Jews that fled to Egypt for safety should not escape; what Jews, what mingled people it found in Egypt, they all suffered alike, the sword pitied, spared none.

Ver. 6—9. ***Thus saith the Lord; They also that uphold Egypt shall fall; and the pride of her power shall come down: from the tower of Syene shall they fall in it by the sword, saith the Lord God. And they shall be desolate in the midst of the countries that are desolate, and her cities shall be in the midst of the cities that are wasted. And they shall know that I am the Lord, when I have set a fire in Egypt, and when all her helpers shall be destroyed. In that day shall messengers go forth from me in ships to make the careless Ethiopians afraid, and great pain shall come upon them, as in the day of Egypt: for, lo, it cometh.***

In these words is further set forth the destruction of Egypt, with those that were her strength and confederates, as also the events following thereupon.

Ver. 6. "They also that uphold Egypt shall fall." The Hebrew word is, סמכי which Montanus renders, upholding; the Septuagint, the foundation of Egypt. These upholders, or foundations, were not the titular gods, but the princes, nobles, rulers, and confederates, who, by their power, policy, persons, and estates, did assist the king of Egypt.

"The pride of her power shall come down." Egypt had strong towns, castles, men, and presumed upon, was proud of them; but these should be destroyed, and taken away, so should her pride come down. The Vulgate is, the pride of her empire shall be destroyed; whatever Egypt confided or gloried in, that should be brought low. Egypt was lifted up with her power, and sat like one on the top of a mountain, and God by his judgments would bring her down.

"From the tower of Syene shall they fall in it by the sword." Of the "tower of Syene," or Sevene, was spoken, chap. xxix. 10. The meaning is, That the sword should pass through all Egypt, from one border to another.

Ver. 7. "And they shall be desolate in the midst of the countries that are desolate." This verse is the same with the 12th verse of chap. xxix. Egypt and her cities should be like other lands and cities, which were extremely wasted.

Ver. 8. "When I have set a fire in Egypt." When God brought the Chaldean army into Egypt, there was a fire in it dreadful and consumptive; the wars were terrible, and devoured all things like fire, and it is probable many strong cities and holds were burnt with fire.

"When all her helpers shall be destroyed." Egypt being rich, powerful, and renowned, had many confederates, which here are called "helpers." They should all be vain "helpers," for they should not secure or save themselves.

Ver. 9. "In that day shall messengers go forth from me in ships." In that day when Egypt was conquered, messengers, not Chaldeans, but Egyptians, or some that escaped the sword, fled into Ethiopia to inform them what the Chaldeans had done, and in what case they left Egypt. They are said to go forth from God, because they went by his counsel and providence, or because they fled from his angry countenance, which appeared in the destruction of Egypt; for the original is, from my face; God sent them to carry tidings of his dreadful judgments to the Ethiopians. They went in ships, בצים in some vessels that were for speed: the Septuagint is, σπευδοντες, hastening.

"To make the careless Ethiopians afraid." Nebuchadnezzar passed through the oriental Ethiopia to come to Egypt, and these "Ethiopians" seem to be the African Ethiopians; and when Egypt was spoiled from one border to another, even to Syene, he was near it, his passage lay fair, open, and easy into it: and it is not said that Nebuchadnezzar should not go beyond Syene, but that Egypt should be made desolate from the tower of Syene to Cush, that was the other Ethiopia. The messengers hasted to this southern Ethiopia, (the inhabitants whereof were a secure, careless people,) and assured them the sword had devoured Egypt, and was come to their gates; this struck fear into them. The Hebrew word, to make afraid, is, חרד which notes outward trembling, from fear of some sudden evil; such tidings put all Ethiopia into trembling.

"And great pain shall come upon them, as in the day of Egypt." When sad and grievous judgments are upon a place, that is called the "day" of that place; as, the day of Jerusalem: Psal. cxxxvii. 7, "In the day of Jerusalem, the Edomites said, Rase it, rase it, even to the foundations thereof." When Nebuchadnezzar besieged, took, spoiled, and burnt Jerusalem, that was the "day" of it: so here, "in the day of Egypt," that was, when the plagues were upon it, especially when their firstborn were slain, then were they in great pain. When the land was in travail, and when they were all drowned in the Red sea, then great pain was upon all the nations round about: so here, Ethiopia should be in travail, filled with fears and shaking fits, as Egypt and the nations then were.

Obs. 1. When God will visit a nation, it is not their great ones in it, or confederates with it, which can secure it. They that uphold Egypt shall fall; the princes, nobles, counsellors, associates, and whosoever were in league with her, should all feel the hand of God, and be crushed with her. When men do storm a city, it is not her outworks, her walls, her gates, her towers, that can preserve her; and when God will destroy a nation, it is not outward nor inward helps can uphold: no policy, no power, no number can stand it out against God.

Obs. 2. States are not to confide in power, but pride and confidence therein hastens their ruin. Egypt had power, was proud thereof, and confided therein, and the Lord said, "The pride of her power shall come down." Isa. xvi. 6, "We have heard of the pride of Moab; he is very proud, even of his haughtiness and his pride: but his lies shall not be so." He thought himself strong, secure, but his pride and confidence did deceive him; for, ver. 7, "Therefore shall Moab howl for Moab, every one shall howl;" the Moabites amongst themselves should howl, one for and with another: "for the foundations of Kir-hareseth shall ye mourn; surely they are stricken." Kir-hareseth was a chief city for strength, in which they placed much confidence, and to which they fled in their straits; but her foundations were stricken, and their hopes disappointed, and the pride of their power brought down. It is the pride of states and princes which levels them with others: Isa. x. 12, "I will punish the fruit of the stout heart of the king of Assyria, and the glory of his high looks." Sennacherib prided himself in his great army, and presumed he should take Jerusalem, and eat up all the prey thereof; but his high looks were abased, and his confidences his ruin, 2 Kings xix. 35—37.

Obs. 3. God sends dreadful and consumptive judgments upon nations, and makes himself known thereby. "They shall know that I am the Lord, when I have set a fire in Egypt, and when all her helpers shall be destroyed." It is God kindles fires in nations and kingdoms, to consume towns and cities; men, and their habitations, they are all his, and he may do to them what he pleases, having transgressed his laws. By fire and sword did the Lord plead with the Egyptians, laying all waste, and by so doing, made himself known to be a powerful, righteous, and dreadful God.

Obs. 4. In the sorest judgments of God upon men, usually some escape. God threatened Egypt, chap. xxix. 8, that he would "cut off man and beast, and make it utterly waste" from one end to the other, ver. 10; yet here in the 9th verse he saith, "Messengers shall go forth;" some should escape to carry tidings of his severe judgments.

Obs. 5. Those things which seem accidental and casual unto us, are ordered by the wise counsel, power, and providence of God. "In that day shall messengers go forth from me in ships." When all Egypt was in a confusion, some running one way and some another to secure themselves, and some hastening unto ships to tell others what the Chaldeans had done, in the midst of these hurries and disorders, God saw, acted, sent out messengers. They went not, however the appearance was to men, without God's ordering hand; themselves thought of no such thing, nor those they went unto; they dreamed not that they were sent forth of God, that they came from him; it was looked upon as a mere contingency, but God's hand was in it. Things may be contingent to us, they are not so to God.

Obs. 6. Such is the efficacy of God's judgments made known, that they do afflict those who are at a distance from them, and fill the most secure with fears and pains. The Ethiopians were absent from the judgments executed upon the Egyptians, they were secure, careless people; but when the messengers told them their cities were burnt, their men slain, their foundations and helpers destroyed, they were afraid, and great pains came upon them, they were in travail for their lives, liberties, and estates. There is a mighty power in the judgments of God to terrify sinners even at a distance. When Tyrus was destroyed, such was the efficacy of that judgment upon those afar off, that it is said, all the princes of the sea clothed themselves with trembling, Ezek. xxvi. 16: so that we may say of God's judgments, as David, Psal. xc. 11, "Who knoweth the power of thine anger?" who knows what efficacy it is of, and how far it extends?

Obs. 7. Former judgments are not to be forgotten. "As in the day of Egypt." God had visited Egypt many hundreds of years before, and now he minds them of that visitation. So, Isa. ix. 4, God mentions the days of the Midianites, minds them of the great destruction of the Midianites by Gideon, Judg. vii. and viii. God minds the days of men's sinning. Hos. ix. 9, "They have deeply corrupted themselves, as in the days of Gibeah;" and therefore he would visit their sins: and when he hath visited for sins, he would have us remember those visitations; Jer. vii. 12, "Go to Shiloh, and see what I did to it for the wickedness of my people Israel." As we should remember ancient and former mercies, to strengthen our faith, so ancient and former judgments, to quicken our fears.

Ver. 10—12. *Thus saith the Lord God; I will also make the multitude of Egypt to cease by the hand of Nebuchadrezzar king of Babylon. He and his people with him, the terrible of the nations, shall be brought to destroy the land: and they shall draw their swords against Egypt, and fill the land with the slain. And I will make the rivers dry, and sell the land into the hand of the wicked: and I will make the land waste, and all that is therein, by the hand of strangers: I the Lord have spoken it.*

These words hold out unto us the efficient and instrumental causes of the forementioned judgments, which are in part repeated.

The efficient cause is God himself, ver. 10, 12.

The instrumental are, Nebuchadrezzar and his people, ver. 10, 11.

The judgments repeated are, the destruction of Egypt and the Egyptians, putting the land into the hands of others, with an addition of drying up the rivers.

Ver. 10. "I will also make the multitude of Egypt to cease." The Hebrew word for "multitude" is, המון which signifies both multitude and noise, or where there is a multitude there will be a noise. Egypt was populous, and God would diminish the people, they should be slain, and carried away captive, so should both the multitude and noise cease. Increase of people is a blessing, the lessening of them a judgment.

"By the hand of Nebuchadrezzar." "Hand" here notes power, as in 2 Chron. xxi. 10; and Job i. 12, "All that he hath is in thy power," the Hebrew is, in thy hand. Nebuchadrezzar, by his mighty, powerful arm, should come and lay all Egypt waste, and make it like a wilderness. Armies are the hands of princes, by which they do great and dreadful things.

Ver. 11. "The terrible of the nations shall be brought to destroy the land." The word for "terrible" is from ערץ to deal violently, to terrify, which Piscator renders, the most cruel; the Septuagint, λοιμοὶ, plagues; and Junius, the most violent: Vatablus calls them, the tyrants of nations; those who were most tyrannical and terrible God brought and set on work to destroy the land. The Chaldeans were a "bitter nation, terrible and dreadful," Hab. i. 6, 7; these words we had chap. xxviii. 7; so terrible they were that they should fill the land with dead bodies. When an army of friends pass through a country no hurt is done; but when an army of tyrants, of strong and terrible enemies, come to spoil, what mischief will they not do!

Ver. 12. "And I will make the rivers dry," Hebrew, drought. Though the Chaldean army was great, yet not so great as to drink up all the waters of Nilus, which is one of the chiefest rivers in the world. Nilus had many rivulets cut out of it, whereby the land was watered; all those might they stop up with earth and other materials, for their better passage, and so the rivers were made dry. Or by rivers we may understand that benefit which came by them; the Chaldeans should take away all the wealth of Egypt which came by the rivers, and so the rivers were as dry things to the Egyptians. So Maldonate and some others interpret the words; but rather thus, God would send great spoil and desolation into Egypt, whereby the rivers might become useless unto them: or, should we take the words literally, as some expositors are of the mind, viz. that for the great wickedness of the Egyptians God dried up Nilus, and punished them with sore famine, as in the days of Joseph it was, when there were seven years of famine, this sense may be safe: or we may take "rivers" for the people and their power.

"And sell the land into the hand of the wicked." The Lord gives, he doth not sell. The word for selling is, מכר which signifies, to give, to deliver, as well as to sell; and the Septuagint saith, *ἀποδωσομαι*, I will give the land. Those who sell do deliver what they sell into the hands of others; and this is attributed to God metaphorically, for that he disposed of the land of Egypt to others, that is, the Chaldeans, who are called wicked: the Vulgate hath it, into the hands of the worst.

"I will make the land waste, and all that is therein." Egypt was a land abounding with men, horses, chariots, wealth, cities, and all desirable things; but God would make it desolate, and all the fulness of it; so the words are in Hebrew, for "all that is therein;" it had a fulness of all things, and by the hand of the Chaldeans it was emptied, who in the next words are called "strangers," because they were such to the Egyptians.

"I the Lord have spoken it." These words are a ratification of what is threatened. Ezekiel hath not spoken a vision of his own, or from his own spirit, but what is said is the word of the eternal God; "I the Lord have spoken it," I have determined it shall be so, and nothing shall let it.

Obs. 1. God hath ways to empty lands of their multitude and fulness. Egypt had her multitude of men, of beasts, of cities, of riches, she had her fulness of all things; and God had an army, a multitude of soldiers, to plunder and spoil her, to empty her of all her multitudes and fulness. Jerusalem had its multitudes and fulness, but Nebuchadnezzar emptied her, and made her like an empty vessel, Jer. li. 34. Babylon had her multitudes and fulness of treasure, Jer. li. 13, and God had fanners to fan her, ver. 2, and empty her land; those fanners were the Medes and Persians, who scattered the Babylonians, and made a prey of their treasures.

Obs. 2. When God will execute severe judgments, he makes use of suitable instruments. He intended utter destruction to Egypt, and "the terrible of the nations" were brought to destroy it. Nebuchadnezzar had men out of many nations, and the terrible ones of those nations, by the secret hand of God, were brought to lay Egypt waste. They roared like lions, Isa. v. 29; they were cruel and without mercy, Jer. vi. 23; they hanged princes by their hands, Lam. v. 12; and here, they filled the land with the slain.

Obs. 3. God's designs shall go on whatever lies in the way to hinder. He was resolved upon the destruction of Egypt, the rivers of it lay in the way, so that an army could not get over Nilus, that great river; if gotten over, it could not march and do the work appointed, for the multitude of little rivers which were in the land: shall these hinder the design of God? no; he will dry up the rivers to make way unto his designs; the Babylonians shall pass over, and pierce through the whole land. When the Israelites were at the Red sea, that lay as an impediment unto God's design, which was to carry them to Canaan; but did it hinder the same? No; "Speak to the children of Israel, that they go forward." What! go forward and be drowned in the sea? No; because they had not faith to go upon the waters, therefore he divides the waters, and makes a dry path for them through the midst of the deeps, Exod. xiv. There were mountains in the way hindering the building of the temple, but one great mountain above all the rest: Zech. iv. 7, "Who art thou, O great mountain?" Whether it were the Persian monarchy, or Satan and all the enemies of the Jews, God made it a plain before Zerubbabel; and notwithstanding all enemies and opposition, he carried on the work of God. Things may be too hard for men, impossible for them, but nothing is too hard for or impossible to the Lord. He enabled Nebuchadnezzar to take Tyrus, to destroy Egypt; all the rivers thereof shall not hinder it, God will dry them up rather than his design shall fail: Psal. lxxiv. 15, "Thou driedst up mighty rivers." God hath divided seas, plained mountains, and dried up rivers in our days, to make way for his designs; and in due time he will dry up the great river Euphrates to make way for the kings of the east, Rev. xvi. 12.

Obs. 4. All lands are the Lord's, and he may dispose of them to whom he will, even to the wicked. He sold, he gave the land of Egypt into the hands of the Babylonians who were wicked, yea, the worst of men, Ezek. vii. 24. Kingdoms are not such excellent things as we imagine; were they so, they would not be given to God's enemies. That kingdom is of great worth which God gives to his children, Luke xii. 32.

Ver. 13—19. *Thus saith the Lord God; I will also destroy the idols, and I will cause their images to cease out of Noph; and there shall be no more a prince of the land of Egypt: and I will put a fear in the land of Egypt. And I will make Pathros desolate, and will set fire in Zoan, and will execute judgments in No. And I will pour my fury upon Sin, the strength of Egypt; and I will cut off the multitude of No. And I will set fire in Egypt: Sin shall have great pain, and No shall be rent asunder, aud Noph shall have distresses daily. The young men of Aven and of Pi-beseth shall fall by the sword: and these cities shall go into captivity. At Tehaphnehes also the day shall be darkened, when I shall break there the yokes of Egypt: and the pomp of her strength shall cease in her: as for her, a cloud shall cover her, and her daughters shall go into captivity. Thus will I execute judgments in Egypt: and they shall know that I am the Lord.*

Having formerly threatened destruction to Egypt and her cities in general, the prophet descends now to particulars, in ver. 13—18; and then, in ver. 19, shows what is the end of God in his exercising judgments, viz. that they may know him to be the Lord.

"I will destroy the idols." Egypt was the most idolatrous land of any, and God would now destroy the idols out of it. The word for idols is, גלולים which Piscator renders, dung, filth, so the word signifies; and their idols were dunghill, filthy gods, fitter to be trodden under foot by man and beast, than to be worshipped.

"I will cause their images to cease." אלילים images, from אליל nothing, for an image or idol is a thing of no account, 1 Cor. viii. 4; it cannot profit: therefore, Isa. ii. 20, they shall cast away their idols as useless things, and God would make them to cease.

"Out of Noph." This "Noph" was a great city in Egypt, very populous, and famous for the pyramids and monuments of kings, who leaving Thebes, made that the royal city: Isa. xix. 13, "The princes of Noph." Thither many of the Jews fled, Jer. xliv. 1. It was seated on the west side of Nilus over-against Cairo. Though it was once the metropolis of Egypt, now nothing remains but the mere ruins. The Vulgate renders it, Memphis, and so it was commonly called by heathen writers; and Hos. ix. 6, "Memphis shall bury them." In this city was that idol Apis, in the form of an ox, worshipped; like unto it was the calf the Jews made when Moses was in the mount, and those calves Jeroboam set up at Dan and Bethel.

"And there shall be no more a prince of the land of Egypt." God would so visit Egypt that he would either cut off all the royal blood, not leaving any of the Egyptian race to reign, or, which is more consonant to truth, he would keep Egypt a long time without any prince. He had threatened in the former chapter, ver. 11, 12, that Egypt should be desolate forty years, and that is the time here meant, "there shall be no more a prince of the land of Egypt." Lavater extends these words no more beyond the forty years, saying, that for a long time they had no kings, for after that time the Macedonians, Romans, and Saracens ruled over them.

"And I will put a fear in the land of Egypt." The Egyptians were like the Ethiopians, a secure, careless people, they trusted in their rivers, their cities, their horse, their foot, their confederates and wealth; therefore God would awaken them, and put a fear into all sorts; they should fear the issue of things, an enemy being at hand, and ready to lay all waste.

Ver. 14. "And I will make Pathros desolate." Of "Pathros" was spoken chap. xxix. 14. There it is joined with "the land of Pathros;" here it is reckoned amongst cities; and Junius saith it is likely to be that city which afterwards men commonly called, the little city of Hercules, because it was strong, and situate in the front of Egypt for defence of it. When Nebuchadnezzar came into Egypt, he made desolate both Pathros the country, and Pathros the city.

"And will set fire in Zoan." "Zoan" was a city in Egypt very ancient, built seven years after Hebron, Numb. xiii. 22; a royal city where the princes resided, Isa. xix. 11, to it came princes from Judea for help, Isa. xxx. 4. The Septuagint calls it Tanis; and because it was not far from Nilus, one of the mouths of Nilus was called Ostium Tanicum, or Taniticum. Among authors there is mention of Tanis in Goshen, and Tanis on the other side Nilus, where Memphis was; and because the Jews dwelt in Goshen, I conceive Tanis in Goshen is sometimes meant in Scripture, and not always the other Tanis, or Zoan; as Psal. lxxviii. 12, 43, God did marvellous things and wonders "in the field of Zoan," or Tanis, that might be that where the Jews inhabited. By "fire" here may be understood fire materially, which consumed Zoan to ashes; or fire metaphorically, God's vengeance upon it by the sword.

"And will execute judgments in No." "No" was another great city in Egypt, of which the prophet Nahum speaks thus, chap. iii. 8, "Art thou better than populous No, that was situate among the rivers, that had the waters round about it, whose rampart was the sea, and her wall was from the sea." The word for "populous" is, אמון which signifies. nourishing. No was the mother and nurse of all Egypt, by reason of her great wealth and traffic, situate amongst the rivers cut out of Nilus. The Septuagint terms it, διοσπολις; the Chaldee paraphrast, rabbies, and most expositors make it to be the city which in after-times was called Alexandria. Junius thinks it that city and tract which Ptolemy calls Neuth. This city God did punish, for it was idolatrous, Jer. xlvi. 25.

Ver. 15. "I will pour my fury upon Sin, the strength of Egypt." Exod. xvi. 1, mention is made of "the wilderness of Sin," which some expositors affirm had its name from this city here called Sin, which afterward obtained the name Pelusium, and was by that mouth of Nilus termed *Ostium Pelusiorum*, over-against Arabia Petræa, and is now called *Damiata Castaldo Zeiglero;* and Suidas names it, *clavis Egypti*, the key of Egypt, and our prophet, "the strength of Egypt:" it was of grand import to hinder the coming in or going out of ships; so strong it was, that God must pour his fury upon it, else it would not be ruined.

"And I will cut off the multitude of No." This city "No" had great trading, and idol gods in it, both which drew multitudes of people; but the Lord would cut them off, some by the sword, some by captivity, and some by other judgments.

Ver. 16. "I will set fire in Egypt." In ver. 14 he said, "I will set fire in Zoan," and here, "in Egypt." The Babylonians were firebrands, whom God brought to consume all Egypt and her glory.

"Sin shall have great pain." The Hebrew is, she shall be in such pain as women in travail are; God would pour his fury upon her, and that would pain her to purpose.

"No shall be rent asunder." Garments we use to rend in pieces, and weak materials. Cities are weak things when God comes to deal with them, he can rend them asunder; the strongest walls, towers, houses, he can in a moment pull in pieces, as easily as the strongest man can paper or clothes.

"And Noph shall have distresses daily." "Noph" shall hear of and meet with those things as should put her into continual straits; provisions should fail her, the spirit of her soldiers and inhabitants should fail her, her hope of help from confederates should fail her; so daily she should have distress, and especially when besieged by the enemy.

Ver. 17. "The young men of Aven." "Aven," the Septuagint has it, Heliopolis, which is, the city of the sun; and Isa. xix. 18, it is called, עיר ההרס the city of the sun, so it is rendered in the margin; and it was so called, because it was the image and temple of the sun. It was sometimes in holy writ called On; Gen. xli. 45, Pharaoh gave Joseph "to wife Asenath, the daughter of Potipherah, priest of On;" of Heliopolis, saith the Septuagint. It was after by the Grecians called Thebe, by the Arabians Bethsemes. The men of this city were accounted the wisest of all the Egyptians; neither their wisdom nor their strength could preserve them from falling by the sword.

"And of Pi-beseth shall fall by the sword." This city is affirmed to be Bubastis or Bubastus, a city in Egypt, where Diana, whom the Egyptians called Bubastis, had a temple; and there was once a year great solemnity had in honour of Diana. By some it is called Pubastum.

"These cities shall go into captivity." The inhabitants of them shall be taken and carried away by Nebuchadnezzar and his forces, viz. the citizens of Aven and Pi-beseth.

Ver. 18. "At Tehaphnehes also the day shall be darkened." Some make this city to be the same with Zoan or Tanis. In Jeremiah it is called "Tahpanhes," chap. xliv. 1; in it dwelt many of the fugitive Jews: it is thought to be so called from Tahpenes the queen wife of Pharaoh, 1 Kings xi. 19. In Isa. xxx. 4, it is named "Hanes" or Chanes; in Jer. xliii. 7, Tahpanhes, so it is in the Hebrew; and it was a royal city, ver. 9, Pharaoh's house was there. It is by some expositors said to be Daphnæ or Daphnis, which was *in ostio Nili Pelusiano*; of this judgment was Junius in his Notes on Jer. xxx. 4; but in this place he makes Tehaphnehes to be in the remotest part of Egypt southward, above Syene, where Nilus makes an island, called Tacompso, or Cacompso, by Herodotus. Now there should the day be darkened, that is, turned into night, by reason of mourning and sadness; all their mirth should be taken away, fears, sorrows, distresses should come as thick clouds upon them, and darken all.

"When I shall break there the yokes of Egypt." The Egyptians held them there in great subjection, ruled over them tyrannically, they made them serve like beasts, with yokes on their necks and burdens on their backs. God would set them at liberty, and put yokes upon the Egyptians' own necks. Junius thinks there were some works or chains in those parts to keep out the Ethiopians from making incursions into Egypt. Lavater reads the words, *vectes Ægypti*, the bars of Egypt. The people thereupon were put to great taxes and hard services, which were yokes. Some read, the sceptres of Egypt, the word מטות is rendered by some, sceptres: where there are sceptres, power, there will be heavy and burdensome things, such laws, decrees, orders, taxes, services imposed upon the people, as that they may well be called yokes, bonds, bars, lets to their liberty and comfort: these yokes would God break and remove from their necks and backs.

"And the pomp of her strength shall cease in her." The Hebrew is, the pride of her strength. Egypt had strong cities, strong garrisons, which made her proud, confident. The Septuagint is, the injury or violence of her power and strength; she abused her strength in oppressing others, and God would put an end unto it, he would destroy it, and she should no more glory in her strong holds, or in her multitudes of men.

"As for her, a cloud shall cover her." Here is a nominative case absolute in the Hebrew, היא which is rendered, "As for her," that is, Tehaphnehes, "a cloud shall cover her;" Nebuchadnezzar's army, which brought a cloud of fears, a cloud of sorrows, a cloud of perplexities, a cloud of reproach. Such a cloud was upon Worcester.

"And her daughters shall go into captivity." By "daughters" we may understand the women of Tehaphnehes, who properly were the daughters thereof; or, the little towns thereabouts, each were under the protection and power of Tehaphnehes, and so were her daughters metaphorically. The inhabitants of them should be carried away into Babylon.

Ver. 19. "Thus will I execute judgments in Egypt." "Egypt" was full of sin, and God filled it with his judgments from one end to the other; he said he would cut off man and beast, break down her foundations, dry up the rivers, lay all waste, fill the land with the slain, send multitudes into captivity; and "thus will I execute judgments in Egypt."

Obs. 1. Idols and idolatrous worship are so far from benefiting a state, as that they provoke God to ruin them, and the state with them. Egypt had many idols, many images, in most cities they were set up and worshipped; this caused God to destroy them, and Egypt with them. "I will destroy the idols, and will cause their images to cease out of Noph; and I will set fire in Egypt." Idolatry is a sin which robs God of his glory, and so provokes him to fury, to take vengeance on idols and idolatrous kingdoms. Jer. xlvi. 25, "I will punish the multitude of No, and Pharaoh, and Egypt, with their gods, and their kings." The kings set up their idol gods, they commanded and countenanced the worshipping of them, therefore they should be punished together. Idolatry is very destructive; it was the destruction of the ten tribes, 2 Kings xvii. 7; and you may see how Judah suffered for this sin: 2 Chron xxviii. 2, Ahaz "made molten images for Baalim," and burnt incense to idols, but what was the issue thereof? ver. 5, 6, the king of Syria "smote him, and carried away a great multitude of them captives. Pekah also the son of Remaliah slew in Judah one hundred and twenty thousand in one day, which were all valiant men, because they had forsaken the Lord God of their fathers;" they fell to idolatry. Besides the loss of those men, two hundred thousand women, sons, and daughters, were carried away captive, ver. 8. Oh what spoil was Judah brought unto for its abominable idolatry!

Obs. 2. God may and can deprive lands of their princes at his pleasure. "There shall be no more a prince of the land of Egypt." Princes have their patents and power from God: Prov. viii. 16, "By me princes rule, and nobles, even all the judges of the earth." It is God sets them up, and he may and doth pull them down as he sees cause: he set up Saul, and he rejected him, 1 Sam. xv. 23; he planted Zedekiah, and pulled him up, Ezek. xvii. 8, 9. "He cuts off the spirit of princes; he is terrible to the kings of the earth," Psal. lxxvi. 12. He cuts them off as suddenly, as easily as the vine-dresser doth branches off the vine; he is terrible unto them, 2 Chron. xxxii. 21, he "sent an angel and cut off all the mighty men of valour, and the leaders and captains in the camp of the king of Assyria:" the angel made terrible work among them in one night. God is King of kings, and in the day of his wrath he strikes through them, and deprives their land of them. He can say to any land, as he did to Egypt, There shall be no more a prince there.

Obs. 3. There is nothing can secure a wicked prince and nation from the judgments of God. Egypt and her king had many cities, strong cities, populous cities, wealthy cities, men of wisdom and might in them, yet these could not keep off the sword and fire: "I will make Pathros desolate, and will set fire in Zoan, and will execute judgments in No, and pour my fury upon Sin; Noph shall have distress, the men of Aven and Pi-beseth shall fall by the sword, and a cloud shall cover Tehaphnehes." Men might run from one city to another, but God's judgments would outrun them; if they escaped one judgment, another would overtake them.

Obs. 4. God hath his times to take off the heavy burdens, tributes, and taxes which are laid upon people by oppressing princes and rulers. "When I shall break there the yokes of Egypt." The rulers of Egypt decreed unrighteous things, oppressed the men of Tehaphnehes, sucked their blood by hard rates and taxes, burdened them with difficult and dangerous services, and made them groan under their yokes: as they did, so do the princes and rulers of most nations in the world; but as they have their times to make and increase such yokes upon the people, so God hath his time to take them off. Lev. xxvi. 13, "I have broken the bands of your yoke, and made you to go upright." The Jews were under the Egyptian yoke a long time; but at last he brake the bands of the yoke, those laws, decrees, that kept them in Egypt, held them to hard labour, causing them to stoop; and made them free, so that they could go upright. Bondage makes men to bow, but liberty, to go upright. Heavy burdens upon people make them sigh, press them down to the earth, and when they are eased they rejoice and look up. It is God breaks the yokes off, whoever puts them on. Isa. x. 27, "It shall come to pass in that day, that his burden shall be taken away from off thy shoulder, and his yoke from off thy neck, and the yoke shall be destroyed because of the anointing." The king of Assyria's burdens and yokes lay heavy and hard upon the Jewish state; but for Hezekiah's sake, or rather Christ's, who is called "the anointing," he would break the yokes, and take off the burdens.

Obs. 5. God makes some nations exemplary with his judgments. "Thus will I execute judgments in Egypt;" thus, as becomes me, a provoked God; thus, as an idolatrous, profane, guilty nation deserves; thus, as themselves and all nations round about shall know that I am the Lord; they shall see that in my judgments which shall convince them that no hand but mine could do such things, take such strong holds, ruin so many cities, and lay waste such a land as Egypt was. Some lands are theatres of God's severe judgments. We have been made monuments of God's choice mercies, wonderful deliverances. Let us fear the Lord and his goodness, lest he turn our mercies into judgments.

Ver. 20—26. *And it came to pass in the eleventh year, in the first month, in the seventh day of the month, that the word of the Lord came unto me, saying, Son of man, I have broken the arm of Pharaoh king of Egypt; and, lo, it shall not be bound up to be healed, to put a roller to bind it, to make it strong to hold the sword. Therefore thus saith the Lord God; Behold, I am against Pharaoh king of Egypt, and will break his arms, the strong, and that which was broken; and I will cause the sword to fall out of his hand. And I will scatter the Egyptians among the nations, and will disperse them through the countries. And I will strengthen the arms of the king of Babylon, and put my sword in his hand: but I will break Pharaoh's arms, and he shall groan before him with the groanings of a deadly wounded man. But I will strengthen the arms of the king of Babylon, and the arms of Pharaoh shall fall down; and they shall know that I am the Lord, when I shall put my sword into the hand of the king of Babylon, and he shall stretch it out upon the land of Egypt. And I will scatter the Egyptians among the nations, and disperse them among the countries; and they shall know that I am the Lord.*

These seven verses are the second general part of the chapter, and treat of two great kings, Pharaoh king of Egypt, and Nebuchadnezzar king of Babylon. Concerning Pharaoh, two things are threatened against him;

I. Diminution of his power, ver. 21, 22, 24.

II. Dispersion of his people, ver. 23, 26.

Concerning Nebuchadnezzar, he is the instrument God will use, and promiseth to strengthen in doing his work, ver. 24, 25. And both these are illustrated from the chronology of this prophecy.

Ver. 20. "In the eleventh year, in the first month, in the seventh day of the month." That was, in the eleventh year of Jehoiachin's captivity, the first month, and the seventh day, Ezekiel had this prophecy given in; it was three months and two days before the taking of Jerusalem, Jer. lii. 5, 6, for it was taken the eleventh year, the fourth month, and the ninth day. This prophecy, though it be set after that in chap. xxix. 17, yet was sixteen years before it. The penmen of the Scriptures do not exactly observe the order where every thing should come in; among the Psalms you have the 3rd Psalm, which was made at that time when David fled from Absalom, set before the 34th, 51st, 56th, 57th, 59th, 60th, and others, which were made before that, as appears by their titles.

Ver. 21. "I have broken the arm of Pharaoh king of Egypt." By "arm" the forces and power Pharaoh had are intended. Vatablus saith the preter tense is here put for the future tense, "I have broken," that is, I will break; but Pharaoh had his arm broken before, when the Babylonian forces beat him and his army by the river Euphrates in Carchemish, which was in the fourth year of Jehoiakim, Jer. xlvi. 2; and at that time he took from him all that he had between Nilus and Euphrates, 2 Kings xxiv. 7; which was the breaking of his arm, and such a breaking as it could not be cured. But notwithstanding this breaking, Pharaoh got up forces again; and when Nebuchadnezzar besieged Jerusalem, he came forth out of Egypt; whereupon Nebuchadnezzar raised his siege, went to meet Pharaoh, and caused him to retreat, Jer. xxxvii. 5, 7, as having a broken arm, and not being able to encounter with him.

"And, lo, it shall not be bound up to be healed," &c. That wound and loss which Pharaoh received by overthrow of his army, he never could cure and recover; neither his own people nor his confederates could set him into his former condition; he is here resembled to a broken arm, which cannot be bound up, or if bound up, not be healed, so as to be useful any more: Pharaoh could never recover his strength and greatness again.

Ver. 22. "Behold, I am against Pharaoh king of Egypt." Here is the cause of Pharaoh's breakings, his not binding up and healing, the Lord was against him; not only the Babylonians and Cyreneans were his enemies, but the Lord himself. When he breaks in pieces, who shall bind up? when he wounds, who shall heal? when he is an enemy, who can stand before him? The Lord makes himself Author of all the judgments which fell upon Pharaoh.

"And will break his arms, the strong, and that which was broken." Pharaoh's arms were, Egypt, and those territories he had from Egypt to Euphrates. His arm was broken already by the Babylonians, as you have it before. One arm yet remained, and that is called a strong one, viz. Egypt with all her strength: this arm God brake by the Cyreneans (against whom

Pharaoh led out an army which they overthrew) and the civil wars amongst them: after that victory they were so consumed and weakened, that they had not hearts nor means to defend themselves against Nebuchadnezzar when he invaded them.

"I will cause the sword to fall out of his hand." When an arm is broken, the hand is disabled from holding any thing; so Pharaoh having his arms broken, Syria and Egypt, the sword shall fall out of his hand, he should not be able any more to make war; he should neither have forces in the one kingdom or the other to do him service: or thus, if he did get up some forces, and engage with the Babylonians, God would so order things that the Egyptians should be overcome, throw down their arms, cry for quarter, or flee for safety.

Ver. 23. "And I will scatter the Egyptians among the nations." The Hebrew word for to "scatter" is, פוץ which signifies to be broken and dispersed: he spake before of the breaking Pharaoh's forces, and now saith they should be scattered, some running one way, some another, some carried into one part of Babylon, some into another.

"And will disperse them." זרה which is the Hebrew word, signifies to disperse by breaking in pieces, and also by fanning. The Septuagint hath it, λικμήσω, I will fan them; and so Lavater, Piscator, and the Vulgate render the word. God would fan them as chaff out of the land of Egypt, and drive them from country to country, as the wind drives chaff from place to place.

Ver. 24. "And I will strengthen the arms of the king of Babylon." חזקתי Montanus renders it, I will comfort; Vatablus, I will make strong; Junius and Piscator, I will confirm; the Septuagint, I will harden. The word חזק saith Kirker, signifies properly, such a taking hold of a man, as thereby to confirm his spirits, and to strengthen him: God would take hold of Nebuchadnezzar and his forces, so as to add spirit, courage, and strength unto them; he would be on their side, and make them victorious. He was against Pharaoh, brake his arms, weakened him; but he would be with Nebuchadnezzar, uphold him, and make his arms strong.

"And put my sword in his hand." I will furnish him with all military instruments, and sufficiency of power to execute my judgments upon Egypt, and upon Pharaoh, king thereof. God would make the sword fall out of his hand, but he would put one into Nebuchadnezzar's hand.

"But I will break Pharaoh's arms." Let them be strong and brawny, I will break them, as wood, bones, earthen vessels are wont to be broken: he is proud, confident, and thinks himself able to withstand the king of Babylon, but by him will I break all his forces, and so break them, that

"He shall groan before him with the groanings of a deadly wounded man." The Hebrew runs thus, he shall cry with cries being deadly wounded before him. Piscator, looking to the former words, "I will break Pharaoh's arms," renders them thus, that he may groan before him, as a man groans being deadly wounded. When a man is חלל thrust through or deadly wounded, he fetcheth deep sighs and groans; and Pharaoh should be so afflicted with the king of Babylon's prevailing against him, that he should greatly mourn and groan. נאק notes such crying, sighing, groaning, as men make when they are wounded unto death.

Ver. 25. "But I will strengthen the arms of the king of Babylon, and the arms of Pharaoh shall fall down," &c. In this verse and the last there is little but what was said before; the prophet repeats the same things, that so he might awaken the Egyptians to consider what dreadful desolations were coming upon them, and beat off the Jews from seeking help at their hands whose destruction was so certainly determined by the Lord.

"And he shall stretch it out upon the land of Egypt." This stretching out may either refer to the stroke, as when men will strike strong and deadly strokes, they stretch out their arms that the stroke may be with more force upon the party to be smitten; or it may note the extent of the sword, it should be stretched out upon the whole land of Egypt, wars should consume the whole nation.

Obs. 1. Men in affliction strictly observe how the time passes away, they mind the years, months, and days. Ezekiel was a captive in Babylon, and he kept account of the time; In the eleventh year, the first month, and seventh day of it, that was, of their captivity; he slipped not a day, but observed it, and what fell out; then the word of the Lord came unto him. Afflictions make good chronologers.

Obs. 2. The Lord makes good his word. He had said by the mouth of David, Psal. xxxvii. 17, "The arms of the wicked shall be broken;" and here he saith, "I have broken the arm of Pharaoh king of Egypt;" he was a wicked king, and God broke his arms. Kings who have great forces, great wealth, numerous cities, and strong navies, if they be wicked, they and all they have are no more to God than one single man, whose arms God can easily break; for he hath "a mighty arm," Psal. lxxxix. 13, and when he makes it bare, then it breaks kings and kingdoms, arms and armies in pieces. It was his arm that brake the Babylonian, Persian, Grecian, and Roman empires, which were all wicked. He brake the arm of Moab, Jer. xlviii. 25. He will break the arm of antichrist, and of all the princes of the earth which help him.

Obs. 3. God sometimes so wounds princes and states, as that their wounds are incurable. "I have broken the arm of Pharaoh, and, lo, it shall not be bound up to be healed;" all the state chirurgeons and physicians could not set the bone again, and heal the wound; much art and industry was used, many plasters applied, but all to no purpose, for God had said, It shall not be healed. Jer. xlvi. 11, "In vain shalt thou use many medicines, for thou shalt not be cured;" it is spoken of this Pharaoh, and the wound he had received. If God deny once to cure the wounds, he makes those wounds prove deadly; not all the balm in Gilead will cure them; not all the wisdom, riches, strength of Egypt, could make Pharaoh whole again. If the Lord himself do not bind up when he breaks, heal where he wounds, nothing but death and dissolution follows.

Obs. 4. It is a dreadful thing to have the Lord declare himself to be an enemy to a king, to a state, to any. "Behold, I am against Pharaoh;" therefore what was broken could not be healed, and what was whole should be broken, he should be more and more disabled: his princes became fools, his wise counsellors brutish, a perverse and seducing spirit was in the midst of them; and Egypt was as women, fearful and weak like women, Isa. xix. 11—16. God being against Pharaoh, all his counsels, enterprises, were blasted, all his forces broken, all his cities made desolate, and all his people consumed or carried into captivity: better he had had all the princes of the world against him than God, for whomsoever he is against must be ruined.

Obs. 5. The flourishing and perishing of kings, kingdoms, and armies, is from the Lord. "I will strengthen the arms of the king of Babylon, and put my sword in his hand: but I will break Pharaoh's arms, and they shall fall down." One of these great kings should prosper, his kingdom flourish, his forces stand and conquer; the other should perish, his kingdom be laid waste, and all his forces broken and scattered. What king, state, or army soever God is with, he will strengthen, uphold; what king, state, or army soever he is against, he will break, ruin, and bring to nothing, whatever their strength, wealth, or counsels are.

Obs. 6. Tyrannical, wicked kings oft come to very sad ends. "He shall groan before him with the groanings of a deadly wounded man." Herodotus saith he was strangled by the Egyptians, which had revolted from him to Amasis. The holy Scripture tells you what ends Adoni-bezek, Athaliah, Jezebel, Ahab, and Sennacherib came unto. Pilate, who put Christ to death, was deposed, banished, and at last slew himself at Lyons in France. Of thirty-two emperors who persecuted the christians, scarce any of them died a natural death; some were poisoned, some killed by the soldiers, some sentenced by the senate, and some slew themselves: Galerius had such a loathsome disease, as that he could not endure the stink of it, but slew himself to avoid it. *Vid. Fox's Acts* and *Mon.* vol. 1. p. 40, 41.

Obs. 7. God is the author of wars, he sets one tyrant against another, and gives commission how far they shall proceed. "I will put my sword into the hand of the king of Babylon, and he shall stretch it out upon the land of Egypt." Nebuchadnezzar was a great tyrant, and God set him upon Pharaoh another great tyrant, and ordered him how far he should go, even over all Egypt. Tyrants cannot stir till God move them: the sword is his; if he will not put it into their hands, they cannot take it up; and when he hath put it into their hands they cannot go one foot further than he hath appointed them.

CHAPTER XXXI.

Ver. 1, 2. *And it came to pass in the eleventh year, in the third month, in the first day of the month, that the word of the Lord came unto me, saying, Son of man, speak unto Pharaoh king of Egypt, and to his multitude; Whom art thou like in thy greatness?*

THIS chapter, as the two former, is a prophecy against the king of Egypt; and in it you have these parts:

I. The chronology of the prophecy, ver. 1.

II. The occasion of it, viz. his pride, and confidence in his greatness, ver. 2.

III. A confirmation of his ruin, set out by an example *a majori ad minus*, ver. 3—18; wherein is notably described the glory of Assyria, her sin, and fall thereupon.

IV. The application of all to Pharaoh, ver. 18.

Ver. 1. "In the eleventh year, in the third month, in the first day of the month." The prophet had not prophecies given in every month, it was a month and twenty-four days from the last prophecy to this, which was one month and eight or nine days before the destruction of Jerusalem, and in the eleventh year of their captivity, the third month, and first day of the month. The Hebrew for "first day of the month," is, one of the month, an hebraism common in the Scripture; as in Gen. i. 5, "The evening and the morning were" one day, so is the Hebrew, that is, "the first day:" Luke xxiv. 1, μια σαββατȣ, upon one of the week, that is, "the first day of the week."

Ver. 2. "Speak unto Pharaoh king of Egypt, and to his multitude." Pharaoh was a great king, and had a great multitude of men, horses, and chariots, and conceited himself greater than he was; but how great soever he were in reality or conceit, God orders a prophet to speak to him, and to demand a question of him. The prophet was in Babylon, Pharaoh in Egypt, and how he could speak to him appears not. It is impossible that he should undertake so long a journey as it is from Babylon to Egypt. It is more consonant to truth, that he penned this prophecy, and sent it unto him by one means or other.

"Whom art thou like in thy greatness?" This was the question Ezekiel must propound to him; and it was an upbraiding question, taxing him for his pride, arrogancy, and vain confidences. He had, like most kings, many flatterers, who flattered him into a conceit that he was greater than other kings, yea, so great in power, that he might encounter God himself. The Lord therefore thought meet to take down his spirit by this question, "Whom art thou like in thy greatness?" what! like unto me? thou art so far from that, as that thou art not comparable to some mortal men. What sayest thou to the king of Assyria? art thou greater, art thou stronger than he? no; he went far beyond thee in power, dignity, and greatness, yet for his pride, arrogancy, and confidences in what he had, he was utterly destroyed; and thinkest thou, who art inferior, to stand and avoid the judgments of God when they come? thou deceivest thyself.

Obs. 1. Kings are prone to be lifted up with and confide in their greatness. Pharaoh swelled with his honour and multitude, putting too much confidence therein; chap. xxix. 3, he is called the "great dragon," and he lay secure "in the midst of his rivers," saying, "My river is mine own, and I have made it for myself;" he was proud and confident, thinking none greater than himself. Nebuchadnezzar was lifted up with his greatness, Dan. iv. 30; so was Sennacherib, Isa. xxxvii. 11—13. And not only wicked kings, but good ones have been overtaken with this evil. David numbers the people, and was too proud of and confident in his multitudes, 1 Chron. xxi. Princes have many things to puff up their spirits, but God knows how to bring them down.

Obs. 2. God will have them told of their sins, and taxed for them. Go, speak unto Pharaoh, and say, "Whom art thou like in thy greatness?" Thou proud tyrant, thou shalt fall: though thou be great, strong, there is a greater than thyself, and one stronger than thou art, who hath sent a prophet to tell thee of thy pride and arrogancy, and to foretell thee of thy destruction. Kings are no more to God than the meanest peasants; if they sin they shall hear of it, and smart for it.

Ver. 3—9. *Behold, the Assyrian was a cedar in Lebanon with fair branches, and with a shadowing shroud, and of an high stature; and his top was among the thick boughs. The waters made him great, the deep set him up on high with her rivers running round about his plants, and sent out her little rivers unto all the trees of the field. Therefore his height was exalted above all the trees of the field, and his boughs were multiplied, and his branches became long because of the multitude of waters, when he shot forth. All the fowls of heaven made their nests in his boughs, and under his branches did all the beasts of the field bring forth their young, and under his shadow dwelt all great nations. Thus was he fair in his greatness, in the length of his branches: for his root was by great waters. The cedars in the garden of God could not hide him: the fir trees were not like his boughs, and the chesnut trees were not like his branches; nor any tree in the garden of God was like unto him in his beauty. I have made him fair by the multitude of his branches: so that all the trees of Eden, that were in the garden of God, envied him.*

In these seven verses is set forth the power of the king of Assyria, who is compared here unto a cedar, which is described,

I. From its place; it was in Lebanon, ver. 3.

II. From its beauty; it had fair branches, ver. 3, and was fair in greatness and length, ver. 7.

III. From the benefit of it; it was a shadowing shroud, fowls, beasts, men were advantaged by it, ver. 3, 6.

IV. From the height of it; it was very high, ver. 3, higher than all the trees of the field, ver. 5.

V. From the thickness; it had thick boughs, ver. 3.

VI. From the cause of all these, viz. the rivers and waters he was planted by, ver. 4, 5, 7.

VII. From his transcendency above all other trees in the field or garden, ver. 5, 8, 9.

Ver. 3. "Behold, the Assyrian." Some would have Pharaoh and the Egyptians to be understood by "the Assyrian," and produce Isa. lii. 4 for it, where it is said, "My people went down aforetime into Egypt to sojourn there; and the Assyrian oppressed them without cause;" that was, Pharaoh and the Egyptians, saith A Lapide; but interpreters generally understand Sennacherib, or Nebuchadnezzar, and their people. By "the Assyrian," therefore, here is meant the king of Assyria, whom divers expositors make to be Esar-haddon, the third son of Sennacherib, of whom see Isa. xxxvii. 38. He was king of Assur, Ezra iv. 2, called also "the great and noble Asnapper," ver. 10. He was king of Assyria and Babylonia, saith Usher in his Chronology, p. 107. Lavater makes him only king of Assyria, for he saith, Ben-Merodach, the governor of Babylon, observing that his two brethren who slew their father, viz. Adrammelech and Sharezer, were lying in wait to dispossess Esar-haddon of the kingdom, he made war upon him, overcame him, and so rejoined the Assyrian kingdom to the Babylonian. Whether him, Sennacherib, or Nebuchadnezzar, it was a king of Assyria, who was great and powerful.

"A cedar in Lebanon." That is, as a cedar in Lebanon. Lebanon was a great and large mountain in Canaan, full of cedars; and this king of Assyria is likened unto the chiefest of them.

"With fair branches." These "branches" were not his sons and nobles, but the several provinces which belonged unto the kingdom of Assyria, over which his princes and nobles did reign. Himself was the cedar, these the branches or arms.

"And with a shadowing shroud." The word for "shroud" is, חרש which Montanus renders, a pruned forest. Buxtorf saith it is, shoots, sprouts, so thick and entangled together, as that they make it shadowy. The Septuagint renders it, thick in the covering; this tree did afford cover and shade to others.

"Of an high stature; his top was among the thick boughs." The king intended Ezek. xvii. 6, was like a vine of low stature; but this king was like a cedar of high stature, glorious, great, and renowned, so high that his top was in the midst of the clouds, like the tree, Dan. iv. 20, "whose height reached unto heaven."

Ver. 4. "The waters made him great." Some trees prosper best in dry places, some by the waterside; the moisture they draw thence makes them to spread and flourish, Psal. i. 3. The tree being here metaphorical, so are the waters. Waters signify sometimes afflictions, Psal. xxxii. 6; sometimes wholesome and good doctrine, Isa. lv. 1; sometimes people, Rev. xvii. 15; here riches, power, victories, and such things by which empires prosper. The Assyrian's wealth, provinces, victories, were as water to his roots, and made him great.

"The deep set him up on high with her rivers running round about his plants." His vast treasure, like a deep not to be drawn dry, raised him to such a height, as waters do a cedar; he did abound with plenty of all things. As plants which have rivers running round about them, do grow and spread, so did the king of Assyria, and his. His riches and greatness were like an ocean, and the provinces, as so many rivers, brought in wealth continually, which supplied them and others.

"And sent out her little rivers unto all the trees of the field." Some commodities, some parts of the Assyrian treasure, were derived to other nations, princes, and people; or, his own subjects had some share with him in his wealth and greatness; all at home, and many abroad, which were the trees of the field, gained by the Assyrian waters.

Ver. 5. "Therefore his height was exalted above all the trees of the field." There were divers trees in the field which were high, many kings and princes who were great, but the Assyrian was the highest, the greatest cedar and monarchy then in the world; his waters exceeded theirs, and they derived moisture from him.

"His boughs were multiplied, and his branches became long." The boughs and branches of this metaphorical tree, were the provinces and countries which belonged to the Assyrian monarchy, which were many, and extended far, even to Media eastward, to Mesopotomia westward, to Armenia Minor northward, and to Susiana southward. "Because of the multitude of waters, when he shot forth." Where there is much water and moisture at the root of a tree, there the branches and boughs do shoot forth faster and further than where it is wanting. The Assyrian having "multitude of waters," viz. treasure, enlarged his empire and borders thereby.

Ver. 6. "All the fowls of heaven made their nests in his boughs." By "fowls of heaven" some understand the nobles and great ones; they built them habitations in his provinces and dominions, which they peaceably enjoyed, as fowls do their nests in the boughs of high trees.

"And under his branches did all the beasts of the field bring forth their young." By "beasts of the field," A Lapide intends the vulgar and more barbarous sort of people. The sense is, that all kinds of people, noble and ignoble, rich or poor, weak or strong, were in safety and multiplied under his protection, as birds and beasts do in and under a great tree.

In this verse and the former are three words which signify boughs and branches. The first, סרעפה *sargnaphah,* signifies a heap or thicket of boughs. The second is, סעף *sagniph,* which notes a top bough. The third is, פארה from פאר to adorn, because boughs are the glory and beautifying of the tree.

"Under his shadow dwelt all great nations." Either they were under his authority or his protection; many great nations were commanded by the Assyrian, and others put themselves under his protection.

Ver. 7. "Thus was he fair in his greatness." The Hebrew is, ויף he was a goodly thing in his greatness. The Septuagint, ἐγένετω κάλλος ἐν τῷ ὕψει, he was beauty in his height and greatness; not only beautiful, but beauty; greatness and height make things goodly and fair.

"In the length of his branches." Here is another word for "branches," דליות which is from דלה to draw, because they draw juice from the roots, or because they move upwards, and so the word *dalah* also signifies. The branches of this tree were the provinces, as before, which extended far, and added to the greatness and glory of the tree.

"For his root was by great waters." These words correspond with those in the fourth verse, "the waters made him great." When a tree is fixed in the earth, where there is no want of moisture, it grows, it spreads, it becomes great and lovely; so this king, being planted among great waters, in the midst of much wealth and power, grew, spread, and became fair in his greatness.

Ver. 8. "The cedars in the garden of God could not hide him." The highest "cedars" that were in any garden, or in Paradise itself, did not exceed this cedar, and so obscure the glory of it; but this kingdom, for the wealth, strength, and greatness of it, went beyond all others, and was for admiration.

"The fir trees were not like his boughs." Fir trees are tall and stately, yet none of the fir trees were comparable to the boughs of this tree. The kingdoms of other princes were not like to the provinces of Assyria.

"And the chesnut trees were not like his branches." The chesnut tree is lower than the fir tree, but more branchy and spreading; yet none of the chesnut trees did equalize any branch of the Assyrian tree.

"Nor any tree in the garden of God was like unto him in his beauty." The Hebrew is, every tree in the garden of God was not like to him in his beauty; that is, no tree therein, no tree in Paradise, no tree in the whole earth, did equalize this metaphorical Assyrian tree in the bulk, arms, branches, or beauty of it.

Ver. 9. "I have made him fair by the multitude of his branches." A tree is much beautified, that hath abundance of boughs shooting out from it; the more boughs, the more beauty. This tree wanted not for boughs; it had many provinces, and every one added to its beauty.

"So that all the trees of Eden, that were in the garden of God, envied him." When other trees, that is, princes, who were seated in pleasant, rich, and fruitful places, saw how much the king of Assyria exceeded them in power, wealth, glory, and greatness, they envied him.

Obs. 1. It is the Lord who makes kingdoms and kings great, and differences them from others. The Assyrian was a cedar in Lebanon, exceeding all others in beauty, branches, height, and thickness; and how came he to be so? ver. 9, "I have made him fair." Whatever virtue, glory, excellency, inward or outward, any trees, any princes, have, it is all from the Lord. All Solomon's greatness and wisdom was from him, 1 Kings iv. 29—31.

Obs. 2. That as trees have need of moisture and waters to make them grow and flourish, so states and princes have need of money to uphold their greatness; they must have revenues come flowing in like rivers, else they will soon wither. The waters made him great, the deep set him up on high, the rivers run round about his plants, he had multitude of waters, his root was by great waters; the Assyrian had great means, which maintained his glory and greatness: so Solomon had great means, otherwise he could not have lived at that height he did; see 1 Kings iv. 22, 23, 26—28; x. 14, 21—23.

Obs. 3. Princes, monarchs, states, ought to protect those who are their subjects, and to communicate good unto them. This cedar in Lebanon was a shadowing shroud, "all the fowls of heaven made their nests in his boughs, under his branches did all the beasts of the field bring forth their young, and under his shadow dwelt all great nations." All sorts had protection from the king of Assyria; and not only so, but those waters which watered him were sent out unto all the trees of the field; he hoarded not up his wealth, but it passed up and down for the good of all. Isa. xlix. 23, it is said of the church, "kings shall be thy nursing fathers," thy nourishers; that is, they shall communicate good things unto thee, as a nurse doth milk unto the child; not only doth she protect the child from harm, but see it wants nothing that is good for it.

Obs. 4. Excellency, greatness, transcendency, beget envy. This Assyrian cedar excelled all the cedars in the garden of God, none of the fir trees, chesnut trees, or any other, did equalize him, he outstripped all the trees in bulk, in height, in branches, in beauty; and what then? "all the trees of Eden, that were in the garden of God, envied him." Envy is against superiors, and contempt is of inferiors. When Daniel was made chief of the presidents and princes, then they envied him, and sought occasion to ruin him, Dan. vi. It is a grief springing up from another man's prosperity; power, honour, strength, riches, greatness, are the causes and occasions of it; there is always a malignancy goes along with it, taking pleasure in hurting, though it gain nothing thereby. Envy is most prejudicial to the party it dwells in, for it is "the rottenness of the bones," Prov. xiv. 30; it eats out the marrow and moisture of them, and makes them putrify. Hence say the Hebrews, an envious eye brings a man to the grave. Buxtorf. Florilegium Heb.

Ver. 10—17. *Therefore thus saith the Lord God; Because thou hast lifted up thyself in height, and he hath shot up his top among the thick boughs, and his heart is lifted up in his height; I have therefore delivered him into the hand of the mighty one of the heathen; he shall surely deal with him: I have driven him out for his wickedness. And strangers, the terrible of the nations, have cut him off, and have left him: upon the mountains and in all the valleys his branches are fallen, and his boughs are broken by all the rivers of the land; and all the people of the earth are gone down from his shadow, and have left him. Upon his ruin shall all the fowls of the heaven remain, and all the beasts of the field shall be upon his branches: to the end that none of all the trees by the waters exalt themselves for their height, neither shoot up their top among the thick boughs, neither their trees stand up in their height, all that drink water: for they are all delivered unto death, to the nether parts of the earth, in the midst of the children of men, with them that go down to the pit. Thus saith the Lord God; In the day when he went down to the grave I caused a mourning: I covered the deep for him, and I restrained the floods thereof, and the great waters were stayed: and I caused Lebanon to mourn for him, and all the trees of the field fainted for him. I made the nations to shake at the sound of his fall, when*

I cast him down to hell with them that descend into the pit: and all the trees of Eden, the choice and best of Lebanon, all that drink water, shall be comforted in the nether parts of the earth. They also went down into hell with him unto them that be slain with the sword; and they that were his arm, that dwelt under his shadow in the midst of the heathen.

Having set forth the greatness and glory of the king of Assyria, in the former verses, under the allegory of a tree, here he comes to show the cutting down and destruction of this tree, with the causes, events, and end thereof.

Ver. 10. "Because thou hast lifted up thyself in height." These words are an apostrophe to the king of Egypt, as Junius and Piscator observe. Here is a sudden interruption and turning of the speech unto Pharaoh, who was proud and haughty like the Assyrian; God by this gives him a hint to look to himself, and so turns again to the Assyrian.

"And he hath shot up his top among the thick boughs." "He," that is, the king of Assyria, he was grown very high, and so high, that his heart was lifted up in his height; saith Piscator, by reason of his height; his height heightened his spirit, he thought himself to have something divine in him, and fit to be worshipped.

Ver. 11. "I have therefore delivered him into the hand of the mighty one of the heathen." The Hebrew is future, I will deliver him, and so Munster reads it. For the better understanding of these words, we must know that the kingdom of Assyria and Chaldea were distinct. The metropolis of Chaldea was Babylon; the metropolis of the Assyrian was Nineveh; the ten tribes were carried away by the Assyrians, the other two tribes by the Chaldeans. Dissensions arising between these two, God delivered the king of Assyria into the hands of the king of Chaldea, who was Nebuchadnezzar, as expositors say, and is here called "the mighty one of the heathen;" he subdued all Assyria, and made that and Chaldea one empire, and afterwards the people were called sometimes Assyrians, sometimes Babylonians, sometimes Chaldeans. Polanus and others interpret these words of Esar-haddon, who, after Sennacherib, was king of Assyria, Isa. xxxvii. 38; whom God delivered into the hand of Berodach-baladan, or Merodach-baladan, being then king of Babylon, Isa. xxxix. 1; 2 Kings xx. 12, who is here called "the mighty one of the heathen." The Hebrew is, into the hand of the god of the nations, so Montanus renders the words: now whether Berodach-baladan were such a god, or "mighty one of the heathen," is doubted, because he was but *præfectus Babyloniæ*.

"He shall surely deal with him." In Hebrew it is, he shall by doing do with him, that is, he shall without difficulty or delay deal with him, he shall deal with him according to his own mind, do what he list unto him, he shall take away his life and kingdom from him. This and the former word is future, put for preter tenses, which is usual among the Hebrews.

"I have driven him out for his wickedness." The word for, to drive out, is גרש which notes not only a simple ejection, a bare driving out, but a disgraceful one, such a casting or driving out as is with disgrace; as when a wife is divorced, she is judged unworthy of bed, board, or cohabitation: Gen. iii. 24, God drove out the man, that was, with disgrace; and so here, "I have driven him out with disgrace for his wickedness."

Ver. 12. "And strangers, the terrible of the nations, have cut him off, and have left him." Here he shows the ruin and downfall of the cedar which was so high, and extended its boughs so far. "Strangers, the terrible of the nations," that is, the Chaldeans, who were cruel and merciless, Jer. vi. 23; they cut him off, the king of Assyria, and left him, not affording the honour due to a dead king.

"Upon the mountains and in all the valleys his branches are fallen, and his boughs are broken by all the rivers of the land." When great trees are cut or blown down, then the branches or arms are broken and pulled off. When the king of Assyria was slain, his princes, nobles, provinces, and people all suffered with him; some were slain upon the mountains, some upon the valleys, and by the rivers, all the land over there were dead and slain persons.

"And all the people of the earth are gone down from his shadow, and have left him." Those which formerly were his confederates, and depended much upon him for counsel and help, seeing him ruined by the Chaldeans, they fell off and would not assist him; or divers of his own, seeing how things went with him, deserted him.

Ver. 13. "Upon his ruin shall all the fowls of the heaven remain, and all the beasts of the field shall be upon his branches." When a tree is pulled up or cut down, the fruit, leaves, and branches gone, there remains the body, or trunk, deformed and spoiled of its beauty and glory, that is the ruin. So here, the king of Assyria being taken and slain, his crown, glory, and greatness laid in the dust, his dead body was the ruin; and now the fowls of heaven, the nobles and great ones of Chaldea, and all the beasts of the field, the meaner sort, made a prey of him and his; him they scorned and vilified, and what was his they seized upon. Lavater saith, his body lay unburied, that crows, ravens, vultures, and such like flesh-fowls fed upon it.

Ver. 14. "To the end that none of all the trees by the waters exalt themselves for their height, neither shoot up their top," &c. This too sets out the end of God's heavy judgments upon the king of Assyria; that other trees, seeing God's dealings with that high cedar for its pride and loftiness, they might take heed of exalting themselves. Men grown great, are apt to grow proud; trees by the waters, that is, men abounding with wealth, honour, greatness, and such things as may puff up; trees by waters grow high, and men in the midst of great means are in great danger to do so.

"Neither their trees stand up in their height, all that drink water." The margin hath it, or stand upon themselves for their height; and so the sense is plain, that none of the trees should exalt themselves, or stand upon themselves, their own strength, wealth, and greatness, they should not rest in themselves, please themselves. If we take the words as they are in the verse, the sense is much the same, "neither their trees stand up in their height, all that drink water;" that is, let none that have means despise others that are inferior, or let them not "stand up in their height;" it will be but for a season, and they must be cut down.

"For they are all delivered unto death, to the nether parts of the earth, in the midst of the children of men, with them that go down to the pit." All the Assyrians were delivered up to the Chaldeans to be slain by them; or all the princes, nobles, and great ones, they shall die, go down into the earth among the meanest, where no difference will be made; therefore rich ones, great ones, should not exalt themselves above others, or stand upon their height.

Obs. 1. Pride and wickedness cause God to bring

dreadful judgments upon kings and their kingdoms. Because the king of Assyria's heart was lifted up in his height, therefore God delivered him into the hand of a mighty enemy, and drove him out for his wickedness. When princes are in the seat of honour, have great means coming in, then they look big, begin to deify themselves, to do what they list, not minding him who exalted them, but confiding in their own strength, power, and greatness, which makes way for their speedy ruin. Solomon tells us that a man shall not be established by wickedness, Prov. xii. 13. Kings, by their wicked policies and practices, cannot establish themselves, their wickedness overthrows them, their pride provokes God against them, Dan. iv. 25. It is good for kings and others to be humble in the midst of their enjoyments, and the greater abundance that they do possess, to carry it still the more humbly; for he that is of an humble mind is worthy of honour, and hath God dwelling with him.

Obs. 2. God hath instruments for the doing of his work, whatever it be, and such instruments as will do it to purpose. He had an Assyrian cedar to cut down, which was very great, whose top was in the clouds, whose boughs extended very far, in whose branches the fowls did make their nests, and under whose shadow dwelt all great nations; and now who shall dare to meddle with this cedar? Yes, the Lord had one that durst attempt and do it, he had a mighty one of the heathens, a god of the nations, into whose hand he delivered the great cedar, and he in doing did unto him all the mind of God, he cut him down and laid him low. Let trees be deeply rooted, grown exceeding great and high, yet God hath hewers to hew down such trees, Dan. iv. 14.

Obs. 3. When great trees are cut down, many other trees suffer with them; when kings fall, they break and undo many. When the king of Assyria was cut off, his nobles and great ones, yea, all sorts, suffered by him. "Upon the mountains and in all the valleys his branches are fallen, his boughs are broken, and all the people of the earth are gone down from his shadow;" all his provinces, princes, people, met with hard things. When Zedekiah was taken and carried away captive, did not the princes, nobles, and people suffer grievous things? see 2 Kings xxv.; Jer. lii. In our days we have seen many suffer by the fall of the king.

Obs. 4. Neither princes, nobles, nor other people, can tell who shall enjoy their wealth. The king of Assyria had great revenues, the Assyrians were well watered, a rich people; but who got all their wealth? the Chaldeans, strangers, the terrible of the nations: "Upon his ruin shall all the fowls of the heaven remain, and all the beasts of the field shall be upon his branches." Little did the Assyrians dream that the Chaldeans should have their jewels, gold, silver, plate, linen, habitations, and lands. Many hoard and heap up for their enemies. Many men are rich, well fraught, like ships at sea, but whose hands their wealth may fall into they know not. David calls it a vanity, and it is a deep, excessive vanity, that men disquiet themselves in heaping up riches, and cannot tell who shall gather them, Psal. xxxix. 6; whether their children or strangers, friends or foes. Solomon was vexed to think he must leave all he had got or done he knew not to whom, whether a wise man or a fool, Eccles. ii. 18, 19.

Obs. 5. God doth therefore destroy kings and kingdoms, that rich ones, great ones, and all sorts, may take heed of their sins, pride, wickedness, and self-confidence. God cuts off the great cedar, the king of Assyria, "to the end that none of all the trees by the waters exalt themselves for their height," nor stand upon themselves for their height; let them not slight other trees which are not by the waters, that are not so bulky, branchy, and leafy, as themselves, nor conceit that their wealth and greatness will always last.

Ver. 15. "In the day when he went down to the grave I caused a mourning." The word for "grave" is, שאל which, among other things, signifies the state of the dead; as, Gen. xxxvii. 35, saith Jacob, "I will go down into the grave unto my son." By "grave" he meant, not hell, nor the grave in a proper sense, for he was persuaded some wild beasts had devoured him, but the state of the dead: and so here, when this high cedar was cut down, when the king of Assyria was slain, and "went down to the grave," that is, the state of the dead, "I caused a mourning;" then there was a sad change, trading ceased, barrenness came upon all the land, the towns and cities were not frequented.

"I covered the deep for him, and I restrained the floods thereof, and the great waters were stayed." If we take the words literally, the sense is, The sea and rivers seemed to mourn the destruction and fall of this cedar; and so, if you take the deep floods and waters for his riches, abundance, and great revenues, they seemed now to put on sackcloth; their lord and master being dead, now there was no more flowing of those waters. The deep, the rivers and waters, had contributed to the greatness of the cedar, and they were affected with his fall.

"I caused Lebanon to mourn for him." In the third verse the Assyrian was called "a cedar in Lebanon," and when this cedar fell, he made the rest of the trees in Lebanon to put on black; the word is, אקדר which signifies, to make dark, obscure, black: all the trees in the Assyrian empire, or in that part of Lebanon which belonged thereunto, I caused to be affected with the fall of this cedar.

"And all the trees of the field fainted for him." All other kings, saith Maldonate: not only kings, but all sorts, were involved in this common calamity; they were so sensible of their sufferings thereby, that they fainted. The word for fainting is, עלף which signifies, to cover for grief, and metaphorically, to faint; when grief is great, then it causeth fainting.

Ver. 16. "I made the nations to shake at the sound of his fall." When high and great trees fall they make a great noise; and so did this king when he fell, his own subjects and other nations were much troubled at his fall.

"When I cast him down to hell with them that descend into the pit." In ver. 15, it is said, "he went down to the grave," or hell; and here, that God "cast him down to hell;" it is the same word: God brought him from his height to the state of the dead, he made him like those that were in the pit.

"And all the trees of Eden, the choice and best of Lebanon, all that drink water, shall be comforted in the nether parts of the earth." Those kings and others which were gone before into the pit he speaks of as living and watered trees; when they should see this great cedar cut down and brought into the same condition with themselves, they should be comforted in that state they were in; that is the common condition of great and small. The Hebrew for "choice and best of Lebanon," is, the election and goodness of Lebanon.

Ver. 17. "They also went down into hell with him unto them that be slain with the sword." Those trees before mentioned, their condition was like theirs who were slain with the sword; and so was this Assyrian, he was cut off from all his glory and greatness, and laid amongst the slain.

"And they that were his arm, that dwelt under his shadow in the midst of the heathen." His princes, nobles, counsellors, soldiers, and confederates, these suffered with him, and had some comfort that they had him with them in the grave, or in hell. The Septuagint for those words, "were his arm," read, *καὶ τὸ σπέρμα αὐτȣ*, and his seed, his posterity and friends, were cut off with him.

Obs. 1. The greatest princes and powers in the world have their day to leave their greatness, and go down to the dust. "In the day when he went down to the grave." The king of Assyria had his day to come down from all his height and glory, and to lie among the slain. Some die natural, some violent, deaths; be they great or small, die they must: "It is appointed unto men once to die," Heb. ix. 27. And as some have their day to grow high and great in the world, so their day to descend into the grave, and be no more in the eye of God than a stinking carcass.

Obs. 2. When great monarchs and princes are cut off, the Lord fills all with mourning, fainting, and shaking. When the Assyrian went down to the grave, the Lord caused a mourning, made changes and alterations at sea and land; he made Lebanon to put on black, the trees of the field to faint, and nations to quake at the sound of his fall. So was it when the king of Tyrus was destroyed, Ezek. xxvi. 15, 16; xxvii. 35. When the gods of the earth are slain, and die like men, the earth and all other creatures have a kind of sense thereof, and are affected at changes.

Obs. 3. When great oppressors and tyrants fall, it affords some kind of comfort to the dead. "All the trees of Eden, the choice and best of Lebanon, all that drink water, shall be comforted in the nether parts of the earth," &c. You have this livelily set forth, Isa. xiv. 9, 10, "Hell from beneath is moved for thee to meet thee at thy coming; it stirreth up the dead for thee, even all the chief ones of the earth; it hath raised up from their thrones all the kings of the nations. All they shall speak and say unto thee, Art thou also become weak as we? art thou become like unto us?" Whether this was Sennacherib, Nebuchadnezzar, or Belshazzar, it matters not; whoever he was, he was a great tyrannical prince, and when he fell, the dead rejoiced at it, and comforted themselves that he was become like unto them.

Ver. 18. *To whom art thou thus like in glory and in greatness among the trees of Eden? yet shalt thou be brought down with the trees of Eden unto the nether parts of the earth: thou shalt lie in the midst of the uncircumcised with them that be slain by the sword. This is Pharaoh and all his multitude, saith the Lord God.*

This verse is the application of the former example unto Pharaoh. The protasis was from the 3rd verse hither, and in this 18th is the apodosis. The same question is put here to Pharaoh which was in the 2nd verse, "To whom art thou like in glory and in greatness among the trees of Eden?" Look about, Pharaoh, thou seest that thou art not like to the Assyrian in Lebanon. Well, who among the trees of Eden art thou like for glory and greatness? it may be thou equallest some of them: be it so, yet thou must be brought down with them to the nether parts of the earth, to the grave, or to hell; thou that art like them in sinning, must be like them in suffering.

"Thou shalt lie in the midst of the uncircumcised." In chap. xxviii. 10, it was said of the prince of Tyrus, "Thou shalt die the death of the uncircumcised;" that was, without any hope of eternal life; and here it is said of Pharaoh, "Thou shalt lie in the midst of those that are uncircumcised;" that is, he should lie in a hopeless and perishing condition of soul and body for ever, as those did who were not in covenant with God.

"This is Pharaoh and all his multitude, saith the Lord God." This is his condition, and the condition of his princes, nobles, and people; whatsoever thoughts he or they may have of themselves, this must be their end.

Obs. God teaches men, by the examples of others, what they must look for. Here, by the Assyrian cedar, the Egyptian Pharaoh is taught what to expect; he being like the Assyrian in his sins, had no cause but to conclude that Assyrian judgments would befall him. What! was he, for his pride and wickedness, driven out, destroyed, brought down to the grave, hell, and an everlasting suffering? so must I, my ways being the same with his; like sins call for like judgments. As the Assyrian was set out for the instruction of Pharaoh, so God sets up Pharaoh for the instruction of all princes and people to the end of the world: "This is Pharaoh and all his multitude."

CHAPTER XXXII.

Ver. 1—10. *And it came to pass in the twelfth year, in the twelfth month, in the first day of the month, that the word of the Lord came unto me, saying, Son of man, take up a lamentation for Pharaoh king of Egypt, and say unto him, Thou art like a young lion of the nations, and thou art as a whale in the seas: and thou camest forth with thy rivers, and troubledst the waters with thy feet, and fouledst their rivers. Thus saith the Lord God; I will therefore spread out my net over thee with a company of many people; and they shall bring thee up in my net. Then will I leave thee upon the land, I will cast thee forth upon the open field, and will cause all the fowls of the heaven to remain upon thee, and I will fill the beasts of the whole earth with thee. And I will lay thy flesh upon the mountains, and fill the valleys with thy height. I will also water with thy blood the land wherein thou swimmest, even to the mountains; and the rivers shall be full of thee. And when I shall put thee out, I will cover the heaven, and make the stars thereof dark; I will cover the sun with a cloud, and the moon shall not give her light. All the bright lights of heaven will I make dark over thee, and set darkness upon thy land, saith the Lord God. I will also vex the hearts of many people, when I shall bring thy destruction among the nations, into the countries which thou hast not known. Yea, I will make many people amazed at thee, and their kings shall be horribly afraid for thee, when I shall brandish my sword before them; and they shall tremble at every moment, every man for his own life, in the day of thy fall.*

This chapter is of the nature of the three former, and contains in it two prophecies, both of them against Pharaoh and the Egyptians.

I. Is, from the beginning to the 17th verse.

II. From the 17th to the end of the chapter.

In the first of these we have,

1. The time of the prophecy, ver. 1.

2. The tyranny and cruelty of Pharaoh, ver. 2, set out by way of lamentation.

3. God's judgments against him, declared in an allegorical way, ver. 3—6.

4. The events thereupon; which are,

(1.) Darkness, ver. 7, 8.

(2.) Vexation, ver. 9.

(3.) Astonishment, fear, and trembling.

Ver. 1. "And it came to pass in the twelfth year, in the twelfth month, in the first day of the month." This was not in the time of Zedekiah, who reigned but eleven years: it was in the twelfth year of Jehoiachin's captivity, the twelfth month, and first day, not long after the taking of Jerusalem, and burning it with fire. The Lord gave out this prophecy then, that the Jews might be taken off from trusting in the Egyptians, having cause sufficient to believe that Ezekiel's prophecies against them should be made good, as well as Jeremiah's against themselves, for it was the same Spirit which breathed in them both; and that they might reap some comfort after their sufferings, in considering God would deal so roundly with the Egyptians, who had deceived them.

Ver. 2. "Take up a lamentation for Pharaoh king of Egypt." Take up a lamentable prophecy, declare what sad things are coming upon Pharaoh. Whether the prophet were to lament for the destruction of Pharaoh and the Egyptians is questionable, for he and they had oppressed others, deceived the Jews, and these judgments of God coming upon them for their wickedness, were just and righteous, and so matter of rejoicing; yet, because he was to utter dreadful and lamentable things, rejoicing became him not, but he was to be affected suitably to the matter delivered.

"Thou art like a young lion of the nations." Wherein tyrannical kings and princes are like unto young lions, hath been showed in chap. xix. The meaning of these words is, that look what a lion is among the beasts of the fields and woods, viz. terrible and cruel, the same was Pharaoh among the nations. Young lions are fierce, and devour their prey with greediness; so are young tyrants.

"And thou art as a whale in the seas." In chap. xxix. 3, Pharaoh is called התנים the dragon, or crocodile; here, כתנים as the whale. It is *tannim* in both places, and signifies a dragon, whale, or sea-monster; and such as a whale is in the seas, viz. troublesome, dreadful, and devouring, such was Pharaoh on the deep; a lion at land, a whale at sea. His dominion was large, and wherever it was, he minded the prey.

"And thou camest forth with thy rivers." The Septuagint has it, ἐκεράτιζες ἐν τοῖς ποταμοῖς σȣ, which the Vulgate following, renders *ventelabas cornu in fluminibas tuis*, thou didst horn it in thy rivers: the whale spouts waters so out at her nostrils, that falling, it makes a kind of horn; and Pharaoh, digging or cutting rivers out of Nilus, they were winding like a horn. Those who are for this sense derive תגח in the text from נגח which is, to strike with the horn; others derive the word *tagach* from גיח which is, to come forth, or, cause to come forth; thou didst invite other nations to revolt from Nebuchadnezzar, or thou didst come forth with thy people, and trouble other nations with invasions and wars.

"And troubledst the waters with thy feet, and fouledst their rivers." He troubled all at home, and all abroad: as the whale, or crocodile, troubles the seas and the rivers, and lets not the fish be quiet any where; they mud the rivers, make the waters boil; so did this Egyptian Pharaoh, he was like Nilus, which had troublesome waters. He troubled the waters when he constrained the people to leave their own land, and to go up to Carchemish by Euphrates, Jer. xlvi. 2; and as they went they must needs foul the rivers, make their comforts as dead and useless.

Obs. 1. That times of public calamities are specially to be noted. Ezekiel sets down the year, month, and day when the Lord told him what dreadful things should befall Pharaoh and the Egyptians: "In the twelfth year, the twelfth month, the first day of the month, he must take up a lamentation." God's judgments sometimes are lasting, and the duration of them cannot be known, unless the beginning of them be taken notice of.

Obs. 2. Lamentations for the sins and destructions of others is from the Lord. "Son of man, take up a lamentation for Pharaoh king of Egypt;" the prophet took it not up of himself, but at the command of the Lord: chap. xix. 1, God bid him take up a lamentation for the princes of Israel; chap. xxvii. 2, he is enjoined to take up a lamentation for Tyrus; chap. xxviii. 12, he must take up one for the king of Tyrus. Lamentations for princes and states are at God's appointment; prophets are to bewail the sins and ruins of princes and their kingdoms when God calls them thereunto.

Obs. 3. The evil qualities and manners of men do make them like unto beasts of the field and fish of the sea. "Thou art like a young lion of the nations;" Pharaoh's roaring and ravening, his terribleness and cruelty, made him like a lion. "And thou art as a whale in the seas;" Pharaoh's tumbling up and down, disquieting the people, and making a prey of them as fishes, transformed him into a whale, or sea-monster. Subtle persons are termed foxes, Luke xiii. 32; lascivious persons are like pampered horses, Jer. v. 8; oppressing princes and judges to lions and evening wolves, Zeph. iii. 3: the wicked qualities of men do make them brutish. Solomon tells you, in favour of this truth, that the wickedness of those in the place of judgment made them beasts, Eccles. iii. 16, 18.

Obs. 4. God hath prophets to tell the worst of princes of their wickedness. Pharaoh was a great king, terrible as a lion, dreadful as a whale, yet God had an Ezekiel to send to him, and to tell him of his tyranny and cruelty: Go, say unto Pharaoh, "Thou art as a young lion of the nations, and as a whale in the seas:" God sent him to deal sharply with him, notwithstanding his greatness. Prophets must not spare princes, when sent of God to reprove them.

Obs. 5. Wicked kings are great troublers of their own and others' waters. They trouble their own people, their own kingdoms, and others also: "Thou camest forth with thy rivers, and troubledst the waters with thy feet, and fouledst their rivers." Pharaoh was neither quiet in Egypt, nor would let others be quiet: he sent out his ambassadors to other nations, which were as his feet, they troubled the waters, the people, in drawing them into league with Pharaoh, in causing them to raise forces to assist him, and so fouled their rivers, unsettled their peace, troubled their spirits and countries. Whales are not more troublesome to the seas, crocodiles to the rivers of Egypt, lions and wild beasts to the land, than tyrants are to their own kingdoms, and those that are near unto them. Ahab was a troubler of Israel, 1 Kings xviii. 18; and of Judah also, in that he drew Jehoshaphat and his people to join with him to go up to Ramoth-gilead, where it had like to have cost him his life, 2 Chron. xviii. Solomon tells us, "He that is cruel will trouble his own flesh," Prov. xi. 17: tyrants are cruel, and they do trouble their own flesh, their own subjects and people; yea, and the flesh of strangers, they make their own rivers and others' to be muddy.

Ver. 3. "I will therefore spread out my net over thee." These words you had, chap. xvii. 20; xii. 13. A "net" is to catch birds or fish: here God represents the person of a fisherman, and would spread out his net to take this whale. The word for "net" is, רשת from ירש to possess, retain, because a net keeps what it catcheth; and *rete* some derive from *retinendo*, from its holding and retaining. This "net" with which God would catch the whale, must be a great net; and so it was, for it was the Chaldean army, which was great, strong, and sufficient to spread over all the rivers of Egypt.

"With a company of many people." When lions or whales are to be taken, multitudes of people get together; and so here, multitudes of Chaldeans came to take this lion and whale.

"They shall bring thee up in my net." Thou liest in thy rivers and deep waters, thinking thyself safe, without the reach of any, but my net shall be so thrown as to encompass and catch thee, and these Chaldeans shall draw thee up out of thy Nilus, yea, out of thine Egypt.

Ver. 4. "Then will I leave thee upon the land," &c. When this great whale shall be drawn out of his waters and country, God will deal by him as fishermen do by the whale; drawn to the shore, they leave him upon the dry ground in open view, exposed to the fowls of heaven and beasts of the earth; they cut him in pieces, whereof some are carried away, others are thrown here and there: so God dealt with Pharaoh, he brought him to open shame and ruin; he made him and his wealth a prey to all sorts of people. Like unto this verse is that you had, chap. xxix. 5.

Ver. 5. "I will lay thy flesh upon the mountains." Thou, or thy soldiers, being overcome, some of you will flee to the mountains for relief; but even there shall they be destitute of help, they shall be slain on the mountains.

"And fill the valleys with thy height." I will make such a slaughter of thy men, as that they shall fill up the valleys, the bodies shall lie so thick one upon another as to make a height. Munster interprets it of the swelling of the bodies; dead bodies do swell much, and increase height. The Vulgate reads the words thus, I will fill thy hills with the corruption which flows from the dead bodies.

Ver. 6. "I will also water with thy blood the land wherein thou swimmest." When Nilus overflowed, then Egypt was full of water, so that this whale might swim up and down in the same. God would cause such a destruction to be among the Egyptians, that there should be a river of blood, which should water the land. Hereby is set out the great abundance of blood that should be shed in Egypt, the land was made drunk with it.

"Even to the mountains; and the rivers shall be full of thee." Not only the lower places should be filled with the blood of the slain, but it should reach to the mountains, and run into the rivers. Sanctius thinks this not to be verified in Egypt, where were no mountains, but in some other place where the Egyptians were drawn out to fight.

Obs. 1. That because kings keep not within their bounds, but are troublesome to their own people and others, therefore the Lord destroys them and their kingdoms. "Thou camest forth with thy rivers, and troubledst the waters with thy feet, and fouledst their rivers; I will therefore spread out my net over thee." The ruin of princes and states are no casual things, they are effected by the counsel, providence, and power of God, punishing them most justly for their sins.

Obs. 2. God hath his nets to catch whales and great fish in. "I will spread out my net over thee." It is not every net will catch whales and great fish, they will break ordinary nets; but God hath nets to take them, he wants not means to bring the mightiest unto punishment. Pharaoh was a lion, a dragon, a crocodile, a whale, and God had a net in the north, the Babylonish army, which he sent for, and caught this Egyptian whale with. God had a net to catch that old whale and sea-monster, who devoured so many of the Israelites' children; he made a net of the waters, and not only caught Pharaoh, but drowned that whale in the Red sea.

Obs. 3. God designs the place of tyrants' suffering, and divides the spoil of them to whom he pleases. "I will leave thee upon the land, I will cast thee forth upon the open field, and will cause all the fowls of the heaven to remain upon thee, and I will fill the beasts of the whole earth with thee." God drew this whale out of his waters, unto the place where he and all the fish which adhered unto him were slain, and made a spoil to all sorts of people.

Obs. 4. When God is in a way of judgment with wicked princes, sometimes he shows exceeding great severity towards them and theirs. "I will lay thy flesh upon the mountains, and fill the valleys with thy height;" thou and thine shall be slain in all places, no safety in the mountains or valleys. "I will also water with thy blood the land wherein thou swimmest;" their blood should be so shed as to make the land drunk with it.

Ver. 7. "And when I shall put thee out, I will cover the heaven, and make the stars thereof dark." Here the prophet comes to show the events of this dreadful and severe judgment of God: "When I shall put thee out," because to show in thine extinction: כבה notes such a putting out, as is of fire or a candle. When God should extinguish Pharaoh's life, then should there be no quiet, peace, joy, safety, but altogether sighing, weeping, complaining, howling, and sad lamentations; so great should be the grief and misery of the Egyptians, that all things should seem dark unto them. In extreme sorrows the sight has failed, and persons think the day to be night, are destitute of counsel, and know not which way to turn them. It is usual in Scripture to set out times of mourning and misery by such expressions as you have here and in the following verse, as Joel iii. 15; Isa. xiii. 10; Mark xiii. 24, 25; Luke xxi. 25; Amos viii. 9.

"I will cover the sun with a cloud, and the moon shall not give her light." God hath the power over the clouds, and he can call them forth at his pleasure to do him what service he please: he would keep the comfortable beams of the sun and moon from them; they had darkness on every side, the very heavens, sun, moon, and stars, hid their faces from them.

Ver. 8. "All the bright lights of heaven will I make dark over thee." The Hebrew is, All the lights of light; they should have no benefit by these bright and shining lights of heaven. Mourners use to cover their heads and faces, and so the lights of heaven are as darkness unto them; or, they shall seem affected with the sore judgments which are upon thee. The Vulgate is, *Omnia luminaria cœli mœrere faciam super te,* I will make all the lights of heaven to mourn over thee.

"And set darkness upon thy land." Darkness is frequently in the word used for affliction and grief, a sad condition; and God would set Egypt, yea, settle it, under darkness, it should be kept in a mourning and miserable condition.

Ver. 9. "I will also vex the hearts of many people." The word for to "vex" is, כעס which signifies not only, to move to anger, but also, to grieve. When the people should hear how Pharaoh, a great king, was conquered, and his kingdom laid utterly waste, this would grieve and vex them; and especially when they consider how great Nebuchadnezzar became hereby, having all Egypt and the adjacent parts under him.

"When I shall bring thy destruction among the nations." The word for "thy destruction" is, שברך thy breaking; for which the Septuagint hath, thy captivity. The nations thought Egypt impossible to be totally broken and ruined, being fortified so with cities, rivers, and the sea. The news of its "destruction" would vex them to the heart.

Ver. 10. "Yea, I will make many people amazed at thee." When God's dealings with Pharaoh, his severe judgments upon him and his, came abroad among the people, they were amazed, not knowing what to think, speak, or do. When strange and dreadful things come suddenly to us, they surprise our judgments, and we are at a stand.

"And their kings shall be horribly afraid for thee." The people should be amazed, and the kings afraid. Chap. xxx. 4, "The sword shall come upon Egypt, and great pain shall be in Ethiopia;" so in Libya, Lydia, and Chub, they and their king should be horribly afraid. The word, to fear, is, שער which notes great fear, even such fear as makes the hair to stand up; and the word is double here, they shall fear with a fear, be exceedingly afraid, for Nebuchadnezzar's prevailing over Pharaoh. When the great whale is taken, the lesser fishes have cause to fear.

"When I shall brandish my sword before them." The Hebrew is, בעופפי הרבי when I shall cause my sword to fly before them; that is, in military language, "when I shall brandish my sword before them." When Nebuchadnezzar came with his forces to Egypt, at the appointment of God, and subdued it, then he brandished his sword before them.

"And they shall tremble at every moment." These words we had in chap. xxvi. 16, where they were opened. They shall be in a continued fear, trembling from day to day lest Nebuchadnezzar should fall upon them, and bring them to Pharaoh's condition.

"Every man for his own life, in the day of thy fall." When the sword is abroad, men's lives are at stake, and when it hath shed so much blood as to water a land, to fill up valleys, and make it reach to mountains, who would not fear lest his life and blood go next? When a great king and kingdom fall by the sword, it is matter sufficient to make neighbouring kings and kingdoms to fear themselves.

Obs. 1. Great ones are lights in the world, and God extinguisheth those lights at his pleasure. "When I shall put thee out." Princes and great ones are examples which most follow, beacons upon a hill, suns in their orbs, which many admire and follow, though they light them downward towards the pit of darkness: these are such great lights, that men dare not snuff, reprove them, but God extinguisheth them; he lighted them up, and he puts them out.

Obs. 2. When God puts out great lights, breaks the candlesticks they stood in, that is, destroys great kings and their kingdoms, then sad events do follow, then the living and senseless creatures are troubled, heaven and earth affected, those near, and those far off, disquieted. Dreadful judgments have dismal consequences. When God destroyed Pharaoh and his army, laid waste Egypt, then darkness was upon the heavens, sun, moon, and stars, then darkness was upon the land, then the hearts of many were vexed, then kings were horribly afraid, and quaked every moment for fear of their kingdoms and lives. When lions and whales are caught and killed, it makes the other beasts and fish to fear; when the high cedars fall, all the other trees tremble.

Ver. 11—16. *For thus saith the Lord God; The sword of the king of Babylon shall come upon thee. By the swords of the mighty will I cause thy multitude to fall, the terrible of the nations, all of them: and they shall spoil the pomp of Egypt, and all the multitude thereof shall be destroyed. I will destroy also all the beasts thereof from beside the great waters; neither shall the foot of man trouble them any more, nor the hoofs of beasts trouble them. Then will I make their waters deep, and cause their rivers to run like oil, saith the Lord God. When I shall make the land of Egypt desolate, and the country shall be destitute of that whereof it was full, when I shall smite all them that dwell therein, then shall they know that I am the Lord. This is the lamentation wherewith they shall lament her: the daughters of the nations shall lament her: they shall lament for her, even for Egypt, and for all her multitude, saith the Lord God.*

These verses belong to the first prophecy in this chapter, and they set out,

I. The instruments God used in executing the judgments threatened against Pharaoh and the Egyptians, ver. 11, 12.

II. The facts of these instruments, the king of Babylon and his army, ver. 12, 13.

III. The events following, ver. 14, 15.

IV. The conclusion of the prophecy, ver. 16.

Ver. 11. "The sword of the king of Babylon shall come upon thee." I will stir up and bring the king of Babylon with a great army, who shall come furnished with all military preparations against thee, and cut thee off.

Ver. 12. "By the swords of the mighty will I cause thy multitude to fall." The word for "mighty" is גבורים and *gibbor* signifies properly, a strong and brave soldier, saith Drusius. The Septuagint has it here, γιγαντων, by the sword of the giants; Egypt had multitudes, but they should fall by the power of these mighty and giant-like men.

"The terrible of the nations, all of them." This expression, "the terrible of the nations," we had thrice before, chap. xxviii. 7; xxx. 11; xxxi. 12. Those men who were most barbarous and bloody, tyrannical and pestilent, should be employed in his work. The Septuagint calls them λοιμοι, such as were the plagues of the country, such as went up and down robbing, stealing, and murdering.

"And they shall spoil the pomp of Egypt." There is pomp in titles, pomp in buildings, pomp in feasting and furniture of houses, pomp in apparel, pomp in funerals, pomp in worships, pomp in multitudes of men, horses, and chariots; whatever the Egyptian pomp were, it should be spoiled. Vatablus interprets their pomp to be their dignity, or beautiful things; Munster makes it, their state and greatness; Junius makes it, the excellency of Egypt, that is, kingly majesty, with all the glory and greatness attending the same.

Ver. 13. "I will destroy also all the beasts thereof from beside the great waters." Egypt abounded with cattle, especially horses, which were serviceable for war and other uses; those fed near to the rivers cut out of Nilus to water the land. What beasts soever they were, God, by the Chaldeans, would destroy them, and they should not be any longer nigh the many waters; so is the Hebrew.

"Neither shall the foot of man trouble them any more, nor the hoofs of beasts trouble them." The destruction should be so great, that man and beast should be cut off, as was said, chap. xxix. 8. These oft troubled the waters with their feet and hoofs, the one with digging, the other by trampling in them.

Ver. 14. "Then will I make their waters deep, and cause their rivers to run like oil." Man and beast being taken away, nothing shall trouble the waters, but they shall be quiet, clear, and smooth as oil. The Hebrew word for, to make deep, is, שקע *shakah*, to be drowned, to sink, I will cause their waters to go to the bottom; which Piscator interprets of the mud, wherewith they had been troubled, that should sink, and the waters become pure. The Septuagint, I will make quiet their waters. When they are clean and quiet, they run without noise, then they are like oil; the waters of Egypt, and of other nations whom the Egyptians troubled.

Ver. 15. "When I shall make the land of Egypt desolate, and the country shall be destitute." He shows when the waters shall be pure and quiet, even when the land is made desolate; Hebrew is, a desolation; and all carried away with which the countries abounded; Hebrew is, shall be destitute of its fulness.

"When I shall smite all them that dwell therein." All were not smitten by the sword, and destroyed, but some were carried away captives, and that was a smiting.

Ver. 16. "This is the lamentation wherewith they shall lament her." This prophecy which I have delivered, is the lamentation wherewith Egypt shall be lamented; not only I, Ezekiel, must lament for her, but all nations shall do it.

"The daughters of the nations shall lament her: they shall lament for her." The cities and people of the nations, hearing of the dreadful judgments of God upon Egypt, that that populous, strong, and flourishing kingdom is brought to utter ruin and desolation, they shall be affected therewith, and lament her condition.

Obs. 1. God makes use of the king and people of one nation to execute his judgments upon the king and people of another nation. "The sword of the king of Babylon shall come upon thee, and by the swords of the mighty will I cause thy multitude to fall." Kings and their people are at the disposal of God, to call out and employ where and in what service he pleases; he serves himself, fulfils his wills and counsels, by kings and great ones, overthrowing one kingdom by another, laying all their pomp and glory in the dust.

Obs. 2. The sins of kings and people cause God to execute his sore judgments, not only upon themselves, but also upon the brute creatures and things inanimate. God would not only destroy Pharaoh and his multitude, but the beasts, the cities, and all the fulness of the land; in the destruction of these, God punished the owners.

Obs. 3. By the destruction of tyrants and their kingdoms, God quiets nations; they by their power, counsels, or agents, trouble their own kingdoms, and others. "Then will I make their waters deep, and cause their rivers to run like oil: when I shall make the land of Egypt desolate." When Pharaoh and his host were cut off, they should trouble the waters no more at home nor abroad, all should be quiet, peaceable.

Obs. 4. God, in his wise providence, so orders his judgments, that they shall affect others, and be had in remembrance. "This is the lamentation wherewith they shall lament her: the daughters of the nations shall lament her." Destruction of great kings and kingdoms have many things considerable in them; there is much of God's power, justice, and severity in the same, which God will have to be observed and remembered in the world. Chap. xix. 14, when God destroyed the princes of Israel, and laid the land of Judah waste, what then? "This is a lamentation, and shall be for a lamentation."

Ver. 17–23. *It came to pass also in the twelfth year, in the fifteenth day of the month, that the word of the Lord came unto me, saying, Son of man, wail for the multitude of Egypt, and cast them down, even her, and the daughters of the famous nations, unto the nether parts of the earth, with them that go down into the pit. Whom dost thou pass in beauty? go down, and be thou laid with the uncircumcised. They shall fall in the midst of them that are slain by the sword: she is delivered to the sword: draw her and all her multitudes. The strong among the mighty shall speak to him out of the midst of hell with them that help him: they are gone down, they lie uncircumcised, slain by the sword. Asshur is there and all her company: his graves are about him: all of them slain, fallen by the sword: whose graves are set in the sides of the pit, and her company is round about her grave: all of them slain, fallen by the sword, which caused terror in the land of the living.*

At this 17th verse begins the second prophecy, and general part of the chapter, in which these things are considerable:

I. The time of this prophecy, ver. 17.

II. The funeral of Egypt, with the solemnity thereof, which is commanded, declared, and confirmed, ver. 18—21, and so on to ver. 31.

III. The conclusion of the prophecy, ver. 31, 32.

Ver. 17. "In the twelfth year, in the fifteenth day of the month." It was in the twelfth year of their captivity, and the fifteenth day of the twelfth month, as it is, ver. 1, fourteen days after the former prophecy, and upon the third sabbath, as Junius observes; then came this prophecy unto Ezekiel.

Ver. 18. "Wail for the multitude of Egypt." The word נהה to lament, signifies internal grief. The prophet is bid not to feign a grief, or a funeral complaint, but to be real, to mourn or to prophesy what mourning should be at the funeral of Egypt.

"Cast them down, even her, and the daughters of the famous nations." The prophet was to do this prophetically, as Jeremiah was to root out, pull down, to destroy and cast down, Jer. i. 10. He prophesied such things, and thereupon was said to do them; and so Ezekiel was to prophesy the casting down of Egypt, her king and people, "and the daughters of famous nations," those that did confederate with her, cities or people; and because of this, he is said to "cast them down." It is God's work to cast down, to throw into the grave and pit, but his prophets declaring what shall be, are said to do the same.

"Unto the nether parts of the earth." The Hebrew is, into the land of hell, or into the lowest part of the earth.

Ver. 19. "Whom dost thou pass in beauty?" Egypt, thou thinkest thyself more beautiful than other nations, that thou hast some excellency beyond them; suppose thou hadst, that must not exempt thee from the common condition of nations: but thou hast not any beauty, excellency beyond them, nay, thou art short of them, therefore lay aside such thoughts; they who were more beautiful and pleasant than thyself, they are gone down into the pit; therefore

"Go down, and be thou laid with the uncircumcised." Thou must not look for any privilege above other nations; thou mayest conceit thy counterfeit circumcision will advantage thee, but thou art deceived; away down to the grave, and lie with the uncircumcised, thy portion must be with the profanest. The word for "be thou laid," signifies, to sleep, also, and may be thus rendered, Sleep with the uncircumcised.

Ver. 20. "They shall fall in the midst of them that are slain by the sword." They that were confederate with thee, and thou with them, shall fall by the Chaldean sword, which hath commission to cut you all off, and to send you to the state of those that formerly were slain by the sword; you think yourself invulnerable, but you shall find the points of the Chaldeans' swords are sharp, and will enter.

"She is delivered to the sword." Egypt, or the multitude of Egypt, is delivered to the sword, appointed to be slain. The Hebrew may be rendered thus, The sword is delivered, or given, viz. into the hand of the Babylonian, to destroy the Egyptian withal.

"Draw her and all her multitudes." "Draw her," Egypt and her people, into the grave: the Babylonians slay her and hers, the sword is in their hand, and then drag them into the pit. But these, and the former words, may be taken otherwise, as, to note out the stately funeral of Egypt. "She is delivered to the sword," or, the sword is laid under her head, or by her side, to show that she was warlike. "Draw her, and all her multitudes;" let her body, being put into a chariot, be drawn in pomp and state, like unto the bodies of great ones.

Vide Junium.

Obs. 1. God made known his mind to his prophets by degrees; something they had in one year given out, somewhat in another year; sometimes in one month, sometimes in another, God spake unto them. Here in the twelfth year, the fifteenth day of the month, the word of the Lord came unto Ezekiel: God had appeared to him the first day, and again the fifteenth day.

Obs. 2. There are seasons to mourn in, as well as to rejoice in. "Son of man, wail for the multitude of Egypt." The providence of God doth not act constantly in one way, but it makes changes and alterations, which afford occasion to mourn and to laugh. When God carried the Jews into Babylon, there they hung up their harps and wept, Psal. cxxxvii.; and when he brought them back again, it was with singing, Isa. xlviii. 20.

Obs. 3. That at the appointment of God we may lament for the sins and judgments of God upon the church's enemies, secret or open. The Egyptians were never real friends to the Jews, but were their secret, if not their open enemies; and now, when God's hand was heavy upon them for their sins, the prophet is commanded to wail for them. When the church's enemies suffer, we are to rejoice; but if God calls to mourning for their sufferings, we must do it.

Obs. 4. The greatest in the greatest kingdoms have no cause to glory and lift up themselves above others, seeing they must come to the common condition of all, even to the pit and grave. The king of Egypt, with his princes, nobles, and confederates of famous nations, must come down to the nether parts of the earth. Egypt was a potent, flourishing kingdom, Pharaoh mighty, but "whom dost thou pass in beauty?" thy beauty, glory, strength, wealth, greatness, are nothing, thou must go down and lie with the uncircumcised. In a moment, at the beck of the Lord, kingdoms are made desolate, kings cast into the grave, and all their pomp buried in the dark: let none despise others, and exalt themselves.

Ver. 21. "The strong among the mighty shall speak to him out of the midst of hell." Here, and so on, the prophet, by a figure called prosopopœia, represents unto us what entertainment Pharaoh should have among the dead. The tyrants, and great men of the world, that were in the grave, or hell, before, shall speak unto him, and congratulate his coming unto them in a taunting way: What Pharaoh! hast thou, who wert so great and glorious, left the earth? art thou come to us weak and wounded, stripped of all, and art become like us? Thou art welcome to hell, and the condition we tyrants are in; be not troubled, here are many great ones before thee, both of the uncircumcised nations, and also of the circumcised.

"With them that help him." They should speak to him and those who were his helpers. Pharaoh had many helpers to carry on his designs on earth, many confederates, and they should be welcomed to hell also.

"They are gone down, they lie uncircumcised, slain by the sword." The Egyptians they are gone down to the grave, they lie or sleep with the uncircumcised, or are in no better condition than uncircumcised ones are in, being slain with the sword. These words may be understood of other nations.

Ver. 22. "Asshur is there and all her company." Here the prophet begins the enumeration of particular nations, whose kings and people were gone to hell beforehand, and would give entertainment to Pharaoh. The first he mentioned is Asshur; the Assyrian monarch was the most ancient, of great power and extent, and the king thereof was in hell, and all the Assyrian company, all his attendants and followers.

"His graves are about him." The king of Assyria is gone down to the grave, and so are his princes, nobles, and people which were slain by the sword; they are in their graves near unto him, round about him, and these will speak to Pharaoh at his coming into the grave or hell.

Ver. 23. "Whose graves are set in the sides of the pit." The Vulgate reads the words thus, whose graves are in the bottom of the lake; importing that they fell from the height of honour into the depth of misery.

"Which caused terror in the land of the living." When the Assyrians were destroyed by the Chaldean or Babylonish sword, it was dreadful to those that were living: or thus; these Assyrians while they were in the land of the living, they caused terror, they were tyrannical, cruel, and filled all with fear. Some restrain "the land of the living" only to Judea, because there the Jews only worshipped the living God, and those who were right amongst them were to enjoy the living God eternally; but we may take "the land of the living" here in opposition to the state of the dead, and so other lands are included, yea, all where are any living.

Ver. 24, 25. *There is Elam and all her multitude round about her grave, all of them slain, fallen by the sword, which are gone down uncircumcised into the nether parts of the earth, which caused their terror in the land of the living; yet have they borne their shame with them that go down to the pit. They have set her a bed in the midst of the slain with all her multitude: her graves are round about him: all of them uncircumcised, slain by the sword: though their terror was caused in the land of the living, yet have they borne their shame with them that go down to the pit: he is put in the midst of them that be slain.*

The Elamites were the Persians and Medes, and what he said of Asshur, that he now saith of Elam. The king of the Medes and Persians, with his multitude, who living were terrible unto many, were now in hell ready to give entertainment to Pharaoh who was coming thither. Of Elam you may read Jer. xlix. 34, to the end of the chapter.

Ver. 24. "Yet have they borne their shame with them that go down to the pit." They were tyrannical, and so a terror to others; but they were cut off by the Scythians, saith Polanus, and carried the shame of their tyranny and wickedness with them, or they died ignominiously.

Ver. 25. "They have set her a bed in the midst of the slain with all her multitude." When great ones remove, preparations are made for them whither they remove; so here, even in the grave and hell a bed was provided for Elam. In the bed is darkness and rest; such was the grave, vault, or sepulchre of Elam. In this verse there is an enallagy of genders and numbers.

Ver. 26—28. *There is Meshech, Tubal, and all her multitude: her graves are round about him: all of them uncircumcised, slain by the sword, though they caused their terror in the land of the living. And they shall not lie with the mighty that are fallen of the uncircumcised, which are gone down to hell with their weapons of war: and they have laid their swords under their heads, but their iniquities shall be upon their bones, though they were the terror of the mighty in the land of the living. Yea, thou shalt be broken in the midst of the uncircumcised, and shalt lie with them that are slain with the sword.*

Here the prophet brings in a third kind of examples, which are Meshech and Tubal.

Ver. 26. "There is Meshech, Tubal, and all her multitude." By "Meshech," some expositors understand the Scythians, others the Cappadocians; and by Tubal, the Iberians and Albanians, which were near together, and both of them in the eastern parts. All these may be understood: for the Scythians passing through Cappadocia, Iberia, and Albania, had many of those countries joining with them, when they brake into Asia, between Pontus and the Caspian sea, and so plagued the Elamites. The kings of these places were not yet slain, and gone down to the pit, though the words import it done, because of the certainty of it; but it was near at hand, and to be effected before the death of Pharaoh, whom they were to speak unto at his coming down to the grave.

"Her graves are round about him," &c. The graves of the men of each country were round about the king of that country; they were people uncircumcised, out of covenant with God, slain by the sword, notwithstanding they were terrible to others.

Ver. 27. "And they shall not lie with the mighty that are fallen of the uncircumcised, which are gone down to hell with their weapons of war." Among the heathens and uncircumcised there were some mighty men which did notable exploits, were famous in their generations, and died honourably in the battle or of their wounds; these had pompous and great funerals, and were buried with their armour; they died honourably, and their honour went with them to the grave, but these should not be reckoned or laid amongst them.

"And they have laid their swords under their heads." When soldiers of note died, the custom was to honour them with laying their swords under their heads, or by their heads; and not only so, but they used to bury them with their arms. Lavater tells us that Giraldus, in a book he hath written of sepulchres and several rites of burying, saith, he saw arms and boots found in old monuments or sepulchres.

"But their iniquities shall be upon their bones." By "iniquities" is meant the punishment of iniquities. Their bones shall be scattered upon the earth for their tyranny and cruelty which they have exercised, and be exposed to the beasts and fowls for a prey; so "their iniquities shall be upon their bones." Or thus; they had their swords and arms go down with them to the grave, instruments of cruelty and blood, signifying that they carried their bloody and tyrannical dispositions with them. "And their iniquities shall be upon their bones." They shall suffer now they are dead and gone a full recompence of reward for all their sins. Or thus; they lived wickedly, and died cowardly, and an ill name shall they leave behind them, cursed shall be their memory.

Ver. 28. "Yea, thou shalt be broken in the midst of the uncircumcised, and shalt lie with them that are slain with the sword." Some interpret this verse of Meshech and Tubal, that they should be broken in pieces, but rather it is the application of the former examples instanced in, viz. Meshech and Tubal, unto Pharaoh. Thou shalt be broken, and become a companion of the uncircumcised, suffering such things as they do; thou shalt be equal to them in punishment, who hast not been behind them in sin.

Ver. 29. *There is Edom, her kings, and all her princes, which with their might are laid by them that were slain by the sword: they shall lie with the uncircumcised, and with them that go down to the pit.*

Esau the son of Isaac was called Edom, who gave that name to the country called Idumea, which had many kings and princes: they were circumcised, being the posterity of Abraham, but notwithstanding their circumcision, being wicked, they obtained nothing thereby; neither that, nor their might and power, stood them in any stead, but they went down to the pit, and had the portion of uncircumcised ones. Here the prophet answers an objection which the Egyptians might make, which was this: We are circumcised, and in that are like the Jews, a holy people, differing from the nations; and therefore we look for some privilege thereby, and cannot be persuaded that our condition shall be like unto the uncircumcised nations. Yes, saith the prophet, your condition will not differ at all from theirs; for the kings and all the princes of Idumea, who came of the Jewish race, and had circumcision upon better grounds than you had it, they are dead, gone to the grave, and laid among the uncircumcised.

Ver. 30. *There be the princes of the north, all of them, and all the Zidonians, which are gone down with the slain; with their terror they are ashamed of their might; and they lie uncircumcised with them that be slain by the sword, and bear their shame with them that go down to the pit.*

The word for "princes" in Hebrew is, נסיכים men anointed with oil; so kings and princes were. These princes of the north were not the Babylonians, whom God used to execute his pleasure upon Pharaoh and the Egyptians; but the Tyrians, those of Damascus and Syria, together with the Zidonians. The princes of those places were north to Egypt, and being men of might, they were a terror unto others; but their might could not preserve them from death; they were therefore ashamed of their might, and are laid with the uncircumcised in the pit.

Obs. 1. That tyrants in hell are glad when other tyrants like themselves come thither. "The strong among the mighty shall speak to him out of the midst of hell." When some great man comes to court, there is rising, complimenting, and welcoming of him thither; so when great tyrants come to the court of hell, there are those who rejoice at it, and congratulate their coming.

Obs. 2. No human power can defend a man against death, or keep him out of the pit. Princes have the greatest power, yet that prevailed not; the strong and mighty who were terrors to others, were no terrors to death, who came and plucked them out of their armies, thrones, castles, greatness, and sent them down to the dead. "Asshur is there and all her company; there is Elam and all her multitude; there is Meshech, Tubal, and all her multitude; there is Edom, her kings, and all her princes; there be the princes of the north all of them, and all the Zidonians;" none of them all could exempt themselves from that condition: it is not policy, power, or greatness, can do it; for the most wise, most powerful, and most great God hath said, Eccles. viii. 8, "There is no man hath power over the spirit to retain the spirit; neither hath he power in the day of death; and there is no discharge in that war, neither shall wickedness deliver those that are given to it." Kings are strong, but death is stronger than they. Kings may make war with men and conquer, or conclude peace; but it is not so with death; if they send out all their forces, death fears them not, but will slay them every one; if they send men to treat and make a peace, it will not be granted, there is no discharge in that war; death will have the bones and carcasses of princes to gnaw upon, as well as the meanest; those that have been terrors, made a great noise in the world, death hath tamed and quieted them.

Obs. 3. The great and most go the wrong way, and have the portion of God's enemies. Kings and princes of countries with their companies and multitudes go to hell, and lie with the uncircumcised. Asshur, Elam, Meshech, Tubal, Edom, with their kings and people, all the princes of the north, with the Zidonians, and those that belonged to them, went thither, and had the reward of the uncircumcised, of such as God owned not for his people, but dealt with as enemies. Some there be that die the death of the righteous, Numb. xxiii. 10, that die in faith, Heb. xi. 13, and in the Lord, Rev. xiv. 13; and these are blessed, their death is precious in the eyes of the Lord, Psal. cxvi. 15; but as for others, they die in their sins, and are accursed.

Obs. 4. Mighty men who have ruffled it in the world, been dreadful unto others, and go down to the grave in pomp, or not, shall afterward bear their shame and sin. The mighty ones of Asshur, of Elam, of Meshech, Tubal, Edom, those of the north, and Zidon, who were a terror in the land of the living, some of them were buried in pomp, they went down to hell with their weapons of war, and they had their swords laid under their heads; others had no funerals, or no pomp at them; but they all did bear their shame, and their iniquities were upon their bones: they lived wickedly, oppressed grievously, played the devils on the earth; they bare their shame, and God punished them for their iniquities. Tyrants are feared and honoured as gods while they live, but being dead, their names do stink, and their torments are terrible, proportioned to the power they have abused, and mischief done by them.

Obs. 5. External privileges profit not princes nor people; unless they be godly, they must perish like those that want those privileges. The Edomites were circumcised, which was a great privilege in Paul's account, Phil. iii. 5, a sign of the covenant between God and his people, Gen. xvii. 11; but because they and their princes were wicked, circumcision profited them not, they were laid with the uncircumcised, they had no more favour from the hand of the Lord than his worst enemies, than those that were out of covenant, and open enemies unto him. Let men take heed how they rest upon their privileges and professions: it is not baptism, being in a church, enjoying of ordinances, having of gifts, high notions, and admirable expressions, will advantage men or women at last; unless they be really godly a thousand such privileges will do them no good: Gal. vi. 15, "In Christ Jesus neither circumcision availeth any thing, nor uncircumcision, but a new creature."

Ver. 31, 32. *Pharaoh shall see them, and shall be comforted over all his multitude, even Pharaoh and all his army slain by the sword, saith the Lord God. For I have caused my terror in the land of the living: and ye shall be laid in the midst of the uncircumcised with them that are slain with the sword, even Pharaoh and all his multitude, saith the Lord God.*

In these two verses is the conclusion of this prophecy, lamentation, or funeral of Pharaoh and the Egyptians; which is the comfort he shall have amongst those mighty men and princes before mentioned; and this is in ver. 31: and then the end of God's judgments upon kings and people, ver. 32.

Ver. 31. "Pharaoh shall see them, and shall be comforted." When Pharaoh shall come to hell or the grave, and see what kings, princes, and multitudes of people are there suffering such things as himself must, this shall comfort him that he hath such companions, and so many. To lose his life, kingdom, and people, were sad things, bitter afflictions; but when he saw others had done so before him, and they as great as himself, this was as a cordial unto him.

"Pharaoh and all his army slain by the sword." Nebuchadnezzar king of Babylon came shortly after this prophecy against him and the Egyptians, and made a great slaughter amongst them, cutting off man and beast from the land, as was said, chap. xxix. 11.

Ver. 32. "For I have caused my terror in the land of the living." Junius reads the words, when I shall put my terror; Montanus, because I have put my breaking in the land of the living, a preter tense for a future. The sense is this; When I shall cut off Pharaoh and his army by the Babylonish sword, this judgment of mine upon them will cause terror in the nations that are living, they will be afraid of my judgments. Pharaoh made them afraid by his wars, and I shall make them afraid by my judgments.

Obs. 1. The comfort that wicked ones have after death in hell is poor comfort, it is imaginary comfort rather than real. What comfort is it to see many in prison, in torment, suffering proportionable punishment for their iniquities? "Pharaoh shall see them, and shall be comforted;" he shall see the kings of several countries there, the great tyrants of the world, and shall be punished like unto them; his comfort was in conceit, but his punishment in reality. Polanus calls it *crudele solatium*, cruel comfort. For a king to be in fire and brimstone with other kings, people to be weeping and gnashing of their teeth with others, is cold and cruel comfort. Many flatter themselves, that if they do go to hell, they shall have companions there, which will be some ease; but it rather will aggravate their misery to hear their dreadful howling and yellings, their cursing one another that ever they knew each other.

Obs. 2. God cuts off kings and nations by his just judgments, that he might strike fear into the living, cause them to cease from sin, and learn righteousness. When Pharaoh and all his army were slain by the sword, then the Lord sent his terror in the land of the living, then the nations far and nigh trembled at the severe judgments of the Lord. Such judgments are awakening things, and call aloud to the inhabitants of the earth to repent and reform their ways.

CHAPTER XXXIII.

Ver. 1—6. *Again the word of the Lord came unto me, saying, Son of man, speak to the children of thy people, and say unto them, When I bring the sword upon a land, if the people of the land take a man of their coasts, and set him for their watchman: if when he seeth the sword come upon the land, he blow the trumpet, and warn the people; then whosoever heareth the sound of the trumpet, and taketh not warning; if the sword come, and take him away, his blood shall be upon his own head. He heard the sound of the trumpet, and took not warning; his blood shall be upon him. But he that taketh warning shall deliver his soul. But if the watchman see the sword come, and blow not the trumpet, and the people be not warned; if the sword come, and take any person from among them, he is taken away in his iniquity; but his blood will I require at the watchman's hand.*

OUR prophet having finished his prophecy against the nations in eight chapters, xxv.—xxxii. which was the second general part of his whole prophecy; comes here again to prophesy unto the Jews, and begins the third general part of his prophecy, which extends to the end of chap. xxxix.

In this chapter are these things laid down:

I. A renovation of the prophet's call to his office, with the description thereof, ver. 1—9.

II. A confirmation of the prophet against the calumnies of the Jews, ver. 10—20.

III. A denunciation of judgment against those that were not smitten at the taking of Jerusalem, ver. 21—29.

IV. A reproof of those that were captives in Babylon for their hypocrisy and covetousness, ver. 30, to the end.

Ver. 1, 2. "Again the word of the Lord came unto me, saying, Son of man, speak to the children of thy people." Ezekiel being taken off by the Lord from prophesying to the Jews, chap. xxiv. 27, he was employed two years and upwards in prophesying to other nations, as appears by comparing chap. xxiv. 1, with chap. xxxii. 1; and having done with them, here he is commissioned again to prophesy to the Jews: "Son of man, speak unto thy people;" cease now to speak any more to the nations which are strangers to thee, and speak to thine own people, to the Jews, which are of the same root, stock, and kindred with thyself. The Hebrew is, to the sons of thy people. It is observable God saith not, to the children of my people, or, to the Jews, but, to thy people; God did disown them, they were so stubborn and disobedient that he would not acknowledge them for his. Oft in this prophecy they are called Ezekiel's people, chap. iii. 11; xiii. 17; and four times in this chapter, in ver. 2, 12, 17, 30; in all these verses it is "the children of thy people." When the Jews sinned that grievous sin in making the calf, God disowned them, and said to Moses, "Go, get thee down, for thy people have corrupted themselves," Exod. xxxii. 7. Sin makes breaches between the nearest relations, and causes God to disown his own people, and his own institutions; Isa. i. 14, "Your new moons and your appointed feasts my soul hateth."

"When I bring the sword upon a land." By "sword" is meant war, and the evils which do attend it, as chap. vi. 3; xiv. 17; xxix. 8; xxx. 4; xxxii. 11. The Hebrew is thus, A land when I shall bring upon it the sword: here is a nominative case, viz. ארץ put absolute; and Sanctius saith, when a pronoun follows, that nominative must be put in the place and case of the pronoun, as our translation hath done, saying, I will bring a sword (not upon it, but) upon the land. "Land" is not put for Judea, but indefinitely for any land.

"If the people of the land take a man of their coasts, and set him for their watchman." When a land is in danger of being invaded, the people's care is to choose out one or other to set him in some eminent place for a watchman. Montanus and the Vulgate render the word מקציהם they take one of the lowest and meanest rank; but קצה notes the border and extreme part of a land, or any other thing. It is better as our translation hath it, "a man of their coasts" or borders, where the enemy was like to make his first approach.

"A watchman." *Tzopheh* is from צפה which is, accurately to observe, to open the eyes, and fixedly to behold an object, and take special notice thereof; so is a watchman to do. 2 Sam. xiii. 34, "The young man that kept the watch, lifted up his eyes, and looked, and, behold, there came much people:" he did not barely look, but lifted up his eyes and looked, he made an accurate observation. So 2 Sam. xviii. 24, "The watchman went up to the roof over the gate unto the wall, and lifted up his eyes, and looked, and behold a man running alone;" he put forth himself to the utmost to make a discovery, his eyes were intent upon it.

Ver. 3. "If when he seeth the sword come upon the land," &c. This verse sets out the office of the watchman; which is,

1. To look diligently about him, whether there be any danger approaching, any enemy near at hand,

coming to invade or make attempts against the land.

2. If so, he is to blow the trumpet presently, and to give warning thereof, stirring up all to procure public safety.

"He blow the trumpet." The Hebrew word to "blow" is, תקע *takah*, which signifies, to fasten; but when it is joined with the word *manus*, it notes to strike the hand or strike hands, when with the word שפר a trumpet, it signifies, to blow; as 2 Sam. ii. 28, "Joab blew a trumpet;" so 1 Sam. xiii. 3, "Saul blew the trumpet;" and Joel ii. 1, "Blow ye the trumpet in Zion." Trumpets of old were made of the horns of beasts, of brass, and silver.

"And warn the people." The blowing of the trumpet was a warning to the people to look to themselves; but this warning was not only by the voice of the trumpet, but also by the voice of the watchman; for having blown the trumpet upon the discovery and approach of an enemy, the watchman was to shift for his life and liberty, by returning to his people, and so to call upon them to provide for public safety. The word in Hebrew for warning is, זהר which signifies, to shine, illuminate; and metaphorically, to warn, because when a man is warned, he is instructed, and hath light given in unto him.

Ver. 4. "Then whosoever heareth the sound of the trumpet, and taketh not warning; if the sword come, and take him away." Many are so taken up with the world, that though they hear of danger at hand, yet they will not hear, but venture so long that they are caught, the sword comes and takes them away. The Hebrew is, he that hearing heareth.

"His blood shall be upon his own head." He hath no cause to blame the watchman, he blew the trumpet and warned him, the fault is in himself, that he took not the warning, that he made not haste to secure his own life; he is guilty of his own death, and hath voluntarily brought it upon himself, the whole fault is his own; that is the meaning of this phrase, "his blood shall be upon him," or, upon his own head, which is frequent in Scripture. Josh. ii. 19, "It shall be, that whosoever goeth out of the doors of thy house into the street, his blood shall be upon his head, and we will be guiltless;" that is, he shall be guilty of his own death, not we. 1 Kings ii. 37, "On the day thou goest out, and passest over the brook Kidron, thou shalt surely die; thy blood shall be upon thine own head;" thou shalt be the cause of thine own death, not I, said Solomon to Shimei.

Ver. 5. "He heard the sound of the trumpet, and took not warning; his blood shall be upon him." Here the reason is given why he is guilty of his own death; because he was within the sound of the trumpet, he heard it, that proclaimed the danger was at hand, but he was secure, minding his profit or pleasure, and took not warning.

"But he that taketh warning shall deliver his soul." He that gives heed to the blowing of the trumpet, and presently hastens into the city, or flees for his life, he shall deliver his soul from the hands of the enemies coming, he shall be safe. The word for, to "deliver," is from מלט which signifies, to provide for oneself by flight, saith Avenarius; he doth so "deliver his soul," that is, himself, for "soul" here is put by a synecdoche for a man's self.

Ver. 6. "But if the watchman see the sword come, and blow not the trumpet, and the people be not warned." All watchmen are not faithful; some are sleepy and careless, they see not the sword coming; some are perfidious, they see it coming, but blow not the trumpet, they warn not the people; and what then?

"If the sword come, and take away any person from among them." That is, if any man being not warned by the watchman shall be surprised, and cut off, as frequently in such cases it is, his blood will lie upon the watchman. The Hebrew for "any person" is, a soul, if the sword come and take a soul from them.

"He is taken away in his iniquity." He is found in his sin, and is cut off for his sin. Most interpreters render the words, for his iniquity; he was wicked, and for his wickedness justly cut off.

"But his blood will I require at the watchman's hand." Here is the punishment laid down of an unfaithful watchman; through his sleepiness, negligence, or treachery, a soul is taken away, a man is slain by the adversary, who, if the watchman had given warning, might have lived; and therefore, because he did not, he is guilty of the man's blood, and must answer for it, at his hands will God require it.

Ver. 7—9. *So thou, O son of man, I have set thee a watchman unto the house of Israel; therefore thou shalt hear the word at my mouth, and warn them from me. When I say unto the wicked, O wicked man, Thou shalt surely die; if thou dost not speak to warn the wicked from his way, that wicked man shall die in his iniquity; but his blood will I require at thine hand. Nevertheless, if thou warn the wicked of his way to turn from it; if he do not turn from his way, he shall die in his iniquity; but thou hast delivered thy soul.*

In these words the Lord applies the former simile of a political watchman unto the prophet; "So thou, O son of man," &c.; and these three verses are the same with the 17th, 18th, and 19th verses of the 3rd chapter of this prophecy.

Ver. 7. "I have set thee a watchman." I have given thee to be a watchman unto the house of Israel, that thou shouldst look about, search the Scriptures, find out what is evil, sinful, and what is the punishment due thereunto, what wrath God hath revealed from heaven against all unrighteousness, and tell the people thereof.

"Therefore thou shalt hear the word at my mouth." Thou must not speak of thine own head, or out of thine own heart, but thou must take all up from me; either what I have given out by Moses and other prophets already, or what I shall give out immediately to thyself. Thus Habakkuk did, chap. ii. 1, "I will stand upon my watch, and set me upon the tower, and will watch to see what he will say unto me:" he would have the word from God's mouth.

"And warn them from me." Thou must not warn them in thine own name, but in my name, whose prophet thou art, whose words thou hast received, and who hath empowered thee to tell men of their sins and dangers.

Ver. 8. "When I say unto the wicked, O wicked man, thou shalt surely die." Where God says so is hard to find in all the book of God. You have not, "O wicked man, thou shalt surely die;" but in generals there is that which is equivalent; as, "The soul that sins shall die—The wicked shall be turned into hell—Upon the wicked he shall rain snares, fire and brimstone, and an horrible tempest—and, The wrath of God is revealed from heaven against all unrighteousness of men." These and such other places are tantamount.

"If thou dost not speak to warn the wicked from his way." When the watchman sees a wicked man in a wicked way, as in a way of drunkenness, whoredom, idolatry, oppression, or any profaneness, he is to warn him, and tell him of the danger of his ways; if he, through fear or favour, incogitancy or carelessness, neglect to do it, the danger is great.

"That wicked man shall die in his iniquity." The wicked man might object and say, Why should I die? I was never warned by the watchman; he saw me daily living in such courses, and had he told me the danger of them, I should have considered my ways and turned from them. This objection is answered: Thou art a wicked man, thou hast lived in iniquity, and now thou shalt die in and for thine iniquity; the light of nature, the dictates of thy conscience, the example of others, might have taught thee to have done otherwise: though the prophet have neglected his duty, thou shalt suffer for thy sins, and he for his.

"His blood will I require at thine hand." I set thee to be a watchman over him, to observe his ways, to tell him of his sins, to invite and provoke him to repentance by promises of mercy and threatening of my judgments, that so he might have been saved; but because thou wast unfaithful, and didst not thy duty, he is lost, and his blood will I require at thy hands, and recompense it upon thy head.

Ver. 9. "Nevertheless, if thou warn the wicked of his way to turn from it." If thou be faithful in thy place, and tell the wicked of his sins, calling upon him to turn from them unto me the living God; if this hath been thy care and practice, thou hast done well.

"He shall die in his iniquity; but thou hast delivered thy soul." Whatever befalls him, death temporal, or death eternal, thou hast freed thyself, and shalt not be responsive for him at all; his blood shall be upon his own head, and not upon thine.

Obs. 1. Wars come not upon any people casually, but by the providence of God. "When I bring the sword upon a land." It is God calls out the sword, and causeth it to come; he is the Lord of hosts, and commissions armies to make invasions where he please.

Obs. 2. In case of common danger, the people have liberty and power to set up a political officer, for their good and safety. When the sword is coming upon the land, "if the people of the land take a man of their coasts, and set him up for their watchman." God expects they should do it, and approves of it when done; they do not their duty, unless they do it; they must not stay till those in authority do it, the land may be invaded, many lose their lives upon that account; but it is their privilege, and in their power, presently to appoint a man who may discover danger, and give them notice of it. Every man is a part of the whole, and when that is endangered, every one is to put forth himself to the utmost for security thereof. The safety of the people is the supreme law.

Obs. 3. That in the ecclesiastic state it is God's prerogative to set up offices and officers. "Son of man, I have set thee a watchman unto the house of Israel." He might not set himself a watchman, nor the people set him to be one. 1 Cor. xii. 28, "God hath set some in the church, first apostles, secondarily prophets, thirdly teachers, after that miracles, then gifts of healings, helps, governments, diversities of tongues." In the political state, men may make what offices and officers they please; but in the ecclesiastic state it is not so. Man must not meddle; God only is the Author of all offices in the church extraordinary or ordinary, and no man ought to come into any of them without commission and direction from God; true ministers are to be called by the church according to God's will, and not by the will of a state. The making of ministers is church work, and not state work.

Obs. 4. Those that are called to office by men or God, in state or church, they are watchmen. They must have eyes in their heads, lift up their eyes and look about them most diligently and conscientiously, lest any mischief come to the one or the other. They are to be men of understanding, especially the spiritual watchman, his lips must preserve knowledge, Mal. ii. 7. He is set to watch; sleepiness and drowsiness do not become him; there is great danger therein: Matt. xiii. 25, "While men slept, the enemy came and sowed tares;" whilst the watchman slept, the devil and his instruments took the opportunity and advantage to sow tares, errors, heresies, and damnable doctrines. Isa. lvi. 10, you may see what watchmen the Lord had in Isaiah's time: "His watchmen are blind; they are all ignorant, they are all dumb dogs, they cannot bark; sleeping, lying down, loving to slumber." The state and church watchmen were such; therefore idolatry, murder, oppression, and profaneness abounded amongst them; they sought themselves and their ease, not the state or church's good. Watchmen should not be for themselves, but for the public good, enduring any hardship rather than the public should be endangered; they must not shrink at wind or weather, but bear the cold of the night and the heat of the day, watching always. Isa. xxi. 11, "Watchman, what of the night? watchman, what of the night?" The watchman was at his work in the night, as well as in the day.

Obs. 5. God hath a special care of his church and people, being exposed to many dangers. "I have set thee a watchman unto the house of Israel." Where watchmen are, dangers are supposed. There are church robbers abroad, that would rob it of the Scriptures, of ordinances, officers, of Christ, and of heaven itself. There are those who would "bring in damnable heresies," as of old, 2 Pet. ii. 1; yea, the church is apt of itself to breed vipers, Acts xx. 30. Thorns, briers, weeds, nettles, do grow up in God's gardens. What errors, heresies, blasphemies, are not revived in our days! Are they not grown up to that height and strength, as to threaten and endanger the foundation? If ever the church is as a lily among thorns, as a lamb among wolves and lions that seek to tear in pieces and devour, it is now. Truth goeth with a scratched face every where, and is so scratched and disfigured that many know her not; she hath many enemies, few friends, and cannot dwell quiet in Zion itself; erroneous opinions are ready to assault her in her own house. There is need therefore of watchmen to discover and prevent dangers; and God hath manifested his care of his church and truth, that he hath given watchmen for the preservation of them, and left it upon record that himself is the watchman of his vineyard; Isa. xxvii. 3, "Lest any hurt it, I will keep it night and day." The fire of contention, the floods of iniquity, and winds of strange doctrine, cannot harm God's vineyard, he is the keeper thereof.

Obs. 6. What gifts or graces soever prophets and men in ecclesiastical places have, they must depend upon God for more, and receive from him before they give out to others. No prophet, no apostle, ever had such a sufficiency of light, knowledge, or grace, as to stand in need of no more. God had set Ezekiel to be a watchman to the house of Israel, he had heard much from God, the Spirit entered into him, he had eaten the roll, and yet he must attend the Lord; "Therefore thou shalt hear the word at my mouth:"

even therefore because he was God's prophet, he was to hear the word at his mouth; not to trust to what he had, not to give out of his own, but constantly to look unto the Lord, to hearken what he would say, and then what he said to make that known unto others. God's prophets, God's ministers, must speak his words, deliver his message. There is a majesty, an efficacy in his words, which are not in the words of men, Heb. iv. 12. The words of false prophets were chaff, without virtue; but the words of true prophets were wheat, full of virtue, for they were the words of God, Jer. xxiii. 28.

Obs. 7. That as it is the duty of watchmen to foresee danger, so to forewarn the people of it. The state watchman ought to do both, and so the church watchman. The one, when he sees the sword to come, is to blow the trumpet and warn the people, that they secure their lives; the other, when he sees men's lives are wicked, tending to the destruction of their souls, when he sees error, heresies, coming to infect and endanger the souls of men, he is to blow the trumpet of the Lord, and to warn them that they take heed of the one, and desist from the other. Isa. lviii. 1, "Cry aloud, spare not, lift up thy voice like a trumpet, and show my people their transgressions, and the house of Jacob their sins." Isaiah was a watchman to the house of Jacob, and he foresaw they were in danger of being ruined and carried into captivity; and what must he do in this case? be silent? no; "Cry aloud," make them to hear, "spare not" thy lungs, thy strength, "lift up thy voice like a trumpet," louder and louder, make all the house of Jacob to hear it; "and show my people their transgressions," present unto them the nature and danger of them, let them not rest or sleep, but tell them of their sins in public, in private, solicit, importune them to cease from their evil ways, and to secure their souls. It is not enough for a spiritual watchman to warn his people once or twice in a year, of the dangerous evils their sins will bring upon them, but he must do it frequently, constantly; this warning must be daily: let the persons be of what rank soever, if they live in ways of wickedness, which may hazard their souls, the watchman must tell them of their sins and danger, admonish them seriously, reprove them sharply, and threaten them with death eternal if they persevere in their ways.

Obs. 8. That prophets, ministers, and watchmen in Zion, are to act in the name and authority of God. "Thou shalt warn them from me." They must let them know that God hath sent them, that they speak from him, not from themselves, not their own words; and this is likeliest to make way for the message they bring, of what kind soever. Here the prophet was to warn them, to tell them of their sins, and the danger of them: and who would not receive an admonition from God, when it comes in his name, backed with his authority; when God in it seeks our good, the freedom of us from death and damnation, the bringing of us unto glory and salvation; and especially when the soul of the watchman lieth at stake for the sinner, if he do not admonish the sinner? Can any sinner be so obstinate as not to consider, relent, and return, when God shall send one in his name unto him, and the prophet shall say, Sir, I come from God unto you, and my life is at stake for you; if I tell you not of your sins, I am a lost man: give me leave therefore to deal plainly with you: you are covetous, unclean, proud, froward, ignorant, unbelieving, having a form of godliness without the power; and unless you take another course, and serve the living God otherwise than you do, you will perish soul and body eternally; but if you will hearken, I will show you the good and right way, the way everlasting, which will make you blessed for ever. When a watchman comes and deals thus with a sinner, hath he cause to be angry? No; he hath cause to fall down, and say, Of a truth God is in you and with you; I thank you for your counsel and seasonable admonitions, and through the grace of God I will improve them, and turn to that God who is so gracious, and would have sinners come to the knowledge of the truth and be saved.

Obs. 9. The Lord knows who are wicked. "When I say to the wicked man." The world calls them wicked who are righteous, and those righteous who are wicked; but it is not so with the Lord, he knows who is a hypocrite, who is covetous, who is a liar, a formalist, an enemy to grace and holiness: "Known unto God are all his works," Acts xv. 18; and he knoweth who are his, 2 Tim. ii. 19, and who are not his. There is not one goat in the world, but the Lord knows him; not a wolf, or lion, but he takes notice of them: he knew the house of Israel better than Ezekiel who dwelt amongst them; whom he said was wicked, was so indeed. It matters not much what the world saith of men: it called Paul a babbler, Acts xvii. 18, a heretic, Acts xxiv. 14, a pestilent fellow, ver. 5; but what said God of him? Acts ix. 15, "He is a chosen vessel unto me, to bear my name before the gentiles, and kings, and the children of Israel." Job's friends and the devil said Job was a hypocrite; but God said he was a perfect man, fearing God, and eschewing evil, Job i. 1. That men are what God, who cannot lie, who cannot be deceived, pronounces them to be; if he in his word do call a man for a hypocrite, an unbeliever, covetous, proud, &c. he is so.

Obs. 10. The power of life and death is in the hand of the Lord. "When I say unto the wicked, O wicked man, thou shalt surely die." God hath authority over the lives of men, and can pronounce a sentence of death upon them at his pleasure. He commissioned Saul to smite Amalek, to "slay man and woman, infant and suckling, ox and sheep, camel and ass," 1 Sam. xv. 3. When Ahab let Benhadad go, a man that God had appointed to destruction, therefore saith he, "Thy life shall go for his life, and thy people for his people," 1 Kings xx. 42. The power of life and death God challengeth to himself; Deut. xxxii. 39, "I kill, and I make alive; I wound, and I heal; neither is there any that can deliver out of mine hand." By this argument he proves himself to be God, and it is none but God that kills, or gives life. Psal. lxviii. 20, "Unto God the Lord belong the issues from death." The Hebrew is, למות תוצאות the goings out to death. It is God that turns the key, and lets out the breath; it is he puts a period to the life of the creature. Would any live? let them fear the Lord, and depart from evil; for "the fear of the Lord prolongeth days," Prov. x. 27. Moses uses this argument to persuade them to love, obey, and cleave to the Lord, "He is thy life, and length of thy days," Deut. xxx. 20. Men have their lives from God, and he draws the thread of them out to what length he please; and therefore men should love, fear, obey, and cleave to that God; if they do not, he will cut the thread of their lives asunder: Prov. x. 27, "The years of the wicked shall be shortened;" by one sickness, judgment, or other, their days and years shall be shortened of what they might have been.

Obs. 11. Those watchmen that are unfaithful in their places, and do not tell the people of their sins and danger, their account will be dreadful. "If thou do not speak to warn the wicked from his way, his blood will I require at thy hand." If a political watchman be unfaithful, so that a man perish by the sword without warning, his blood lieth upon the watchman's head; and if the ecclesiastical watchman be unfaithful, and do not warn the wicked, upon what pretence soever, the blood of that wicked man, dying in his sins, will be required of the watchman, it lies upon his head, and he must answer for it: the case of this latter watchman will be more dangerous than of the former; because the one is to answer for the life of a man, the other for the soul of a man, which is of great price. Let lazy, sleepy, perfidious watchmen look to it; they suffer men to perish through their default, and their blood, lives, souls, stand engaged for the same.

Obs. 12. The failing of the watchman will not excuse or privilege the wicked man. "If thou dost not speak to warn the wicked from his way, that wicked man shall die in his iniquity." Though he be not told that he is in a wrong way, though he pretend ignorance, that will not serve turn, he "shall die in his iniquity," warned or unwarned. The watchman hath not done his duty; what then? must this exempt the wicked man from punishment? No; he hath not done his duty, he should have minded and studied the law of God, walked according to that, and have made it a lamp unto his feet, and a light unto his paths, Psal. cxix. 105. But his neglect of his duty, and ignorance, rather will aggravate than extenuate his fault: the law was near unto him, and he might have known what was forbidden, and so have avoided the same.

Obs. 13. Those that regard not the warning of the watchmen, they bring certain destruction upon themselves. "Whosoever heareth the sound of the trumpet, and taketh not warning, his blood shall be upon his own head;" if the enemy cut off that man, he himself is guilty of his own death, not the political watchman. And so in the church state; if the wicked man be warned of his way, and turn not from it, he shall die in his iniquity, his blood lies at his own door, upon his own head, the watchman is free.

Obs. 14. There is great necessity that the watchmen deal faithfully, and tell the people of their danger and sin. Their souls, their blood lie at stake upon it; if they be not faithful, their lives, their souls go for it. Those watchmen that are silent, are cruel, bloody, and soul-murdering men, they murder the souls of the people, and their own souls also: those that speak, that cry aloud, that tell the people thoroughly of their sins, not fearing their frowns, nor respecting their favours, that so, if it be possible, they may save their souls, these are the most faithful watchmen. Many wonder that the spiritual watchmen are so zealous, particular, that they open the nature of sin so much, threaten such terrible judgments of God against sinners, and preach damnation unto them, that they are so frequent in such ways; but cease to wonder, their souls are in jeopardy if they do it not. If a man's whole estate were in hazard if he did not tell such a man that he were a liar, a drunkard, would he forfeit his estate through silence? No; he would tell him of his sins again and again. The watchman's soul lieth at pawn, and he forfeits that if he should not tell sinners of their sins, and warn them to turn from them. Hence was it that Paul said, "Necessity is laid upon me, and woe unto me, if I preach not the gospel!" 1 Cor. ix. 16: he preached and warned sinners night and day, Acts xx. 31.

Obs. Lastly, That the watchman warning the people, and the people taking warning, they do both secure themselves. If the watchman political or spiritual blow the trumpet, warn the people, he shall deliver his own soul; if the people take warning, they deliver their souls. Safety lies in warning, and in hearkening to warning. Let not the watchmen of God be sleepy or silent, but warn the people constantly, that so they may save themselves and others.

Ver. 10, 11. *Therefore, O thou son of man, speak unto the house of Israel; Thus ye speak, saying, If our transgressions and our sins be upon us, and we pine away in them, how should we then live? Say unto them, As I live, saith the Lord God, I have no pleasure in the death of the wicked; but that the wicked turn from his way and live: turn ye, turn ye from your evil ways; for why will ye die, O house of Israel?*

Here begins the second general part of the chapter, which is a confirmation of the prophet against those calumnies the Jews made against the truth and justice of God.

The first is in the 10th verse.

The second in the 17th and 20th verses.

The calumny they raised against the truth of God was this: in the 5th verse it is said, he that takes warning when the watchmen gives it, shall deliver his soul; this, said the Jews, had not truth in it; for, chap. xxiv. 23, the prophet had told them they should pine away for their iniquities, therefore there was no hope for them, though they took warning at the watchman's mouth; we are appointed to destruction, and it is in vain to mind what the watchman saith. This is answered in the 11th verse. But to open the words:

Ver. 10. "Therefore, O thou son of man, speak unto the house of Israel." God had set Ezekiel to be a watchman unto the house of Israel, to observe their sins and tell them thereof; and here he commands him to do his duty, "Speak unto the house of Israel," thus. The house of Israel was not now the ten tribes, but the two tribes left of the ten.

"If our transgressions and our sins be upon us." Jerusalem being now taken, or upon the taking, the Jews were more sensible of their sins, and so felt the weight of them in that sad judgment which was upon them, or coming upon them. By "transgressions and sins," not only the guilt, but the punishment of them is meant: they had felt much in the time of Jerusalem's siege, and more now in the taking of it. God visited their iniquities upon their heads.

"And we pine away in them." When God's hand is upon persons for their sins, they consume and moulder away; the pain and anguish they are under melts their fat, eats up their strength, and brings them to skin and bone. נמקים from מקק *makak*, which is, to grow lean, to become feeble, to be dissolved into corruption.

"How should we then live?" The Jews seeing Jerusalem now in the enemies' hand, and themselves going into captivity, speak despairingly; saying, We are like never to see good day, but must pine away under the judgments that are upon us; how should we then live? It is in vain to warn us, and tell us of repenting and turning to the Lord, we must die in the condition we are in.

Ver. 11. "Say unto them, As I live, saith the Lord God." This oath of God hath been spoken of, chap. xvi. 48, and v. 11. It is the oath which God most uses. Life is the most precious of all things, and that God swears by: As sure as I live, or am the living God, it is true which I say; or, let me not be the living God, if I speak false: you think I am a hard Master, that you shall pine away in your sins, and find no mercy, though you should repent and return; you are greatly deceived: "As I live, saith the Lord," &c. He swears not by a truth that was questioned, Numb. xiv. 11; nor by his omnipotency, for that was doubted of, Psal. lxxviii. 19; but by his life, which was never in question.

"I have no pleasure in the death of the wicked; but that," &c. The Septuagint reads the words, οὐ βούλομαι, I will not; the Vulgate is, *Nolo mortem impii*, I am unwilling the wicked should die; Junius, If I delight in the death of the wicked; Vatablus, Piscator, I delight not in the death of the wicked, or, I am not delighted therewith. Montanus hath it, If I shall will in the death of the wicked, for so runs the Hebrew. The word חפץ signifies, to desire, love, delight in a thing, as Gen. xxxiv. 19, Shechem delighted in Dinah; he desired her, loved her, and took delight in her. *Chophetz* notes the highest delight and content that can be taken; Psal. xvi. 3, "In whom is" כל-חפצי "all my delight," that is, my greatest delight. Now here it is said, God hath not pleasure in the death of the wicked. This is not an absolute negative, denying God wholly to have delight in death, or in the death of sinful, wicked man, or of any sinful man; for God took delight in the destruction of Pharaoh and his host in the Red sea, which Moses shows, saying, Exod. xv. 1, "He hath triumphed gloriously; the horse and his rider hath he thrown into the sea." God sent Saul to smite Amalek, utterly to destroy him and all his: when Agag was spared, with the best of the sheep and oxen, was he not wroth with him? 1 Sam. xv. 3, 11, 23. When Jehu cut off Ahab's house, what said the Lord? "Because thou hast done well in executing that which is right in mine eyes, and hast done unto the house of Ahab according to all that was in mine heart, thy children of the fourth generation shall sit on the throne of Israel," 2 Kings x. 30. The destruction of Ahab's house was pleasing to God, he commended, he rewarded it. And that God takes no pleasure in the destruction of a sinful, wicked man, is contrary to these texts, Deut. xxviii. 63; Prov. i. 26, 27; Isa. i. 24; Jer. xiv. 12. The words are not to be taken as an absolute negative, but comparatively, thus, I have pleasure in the turning of the wicked from his ways, rather than in his death; or, it is more pleasing to me that a wicked man should turn and live, than that he should continue and die. Such an expression is that in 1 Cor. i. 17, "Christ sent me not to baptize, but to preach the gospel;" not absolutely not to baptize, but rather to preach than to baptize; he had more pleasure in my preaching than in my baptizing: and so here, Let me not live, if I have so much pleasure in the death of a sinner, as in his turning from his sin.

By "death" here some understand eternal death, and it cannot be otherwise, saith Quistorpius; for he speaks of that death, which may be avoided by repentance and turning to God, but temporal death cannot be avoided, either by the penitent or impenitent. But to him that well considers this place, it will appear that here it is spoken of a temporal and violent death, for, ver. 3, he speaks of the sword coming upon a land. They were at this time either straitly besieged, or newly taken by Nebuchadnezzar's forces, and complained that their sins were upon them, provoking God to destroy them; that they pined away, and there was no hope for them of life, though they should repent them of their iniquities: this God answers unto, and tells them, if they turn from their evil ways, there is hope they shall live, for repentance prevents and removes judgments that are destructive. The Ninevites by their repentance prevented the destruction of themselves and their city; at David's repentance the plague was stayed; Ahab's humbling himself prevented God's bringing the evil in his days. So that it is true of natural death, that cannot be avoided by penitency or impenitency, but a violent death may; a death by sword, by famine, by plague, by wild beasts, may. 2 Chron. vii. 14, "If my people, which are called by my name, shall humble themselves, and pray, and seek my face, and turn from their wicked ways; then will I hear from heaven, and will forgive their sin, and will heal their land." Had he spoken of eternal death, it had been no answer to the Jews' objection. Lavater tells us, that by death is meant evil, and by life, good. Men by their sins bring sad calamities and judgments upon themselves, they cause God to punish them with variety of evils, which he hath no pleasure in, nor they cause to complain of, Lam. iii. 33, 39; he had rather they should turn from their sins and live comfortably.

"But that the wicked turn from his way and live." The word for "wicked" is, רשע which the Septuagint renders, ἀσεβής, the irreligious, lewd, ungodly man: here, "wicked," wicked in opinions, wicked in practice, troublesome to God and man, running the wrong way. The word for "way" signifies a path which leads from place to place, and men walk in it: metaphorically it is applied to the customs, manners, actions, religions, and lives of men, Jer. xvi. 2; Prov. i. 19; xxi. 2. Of this before, chap. xvi. 61. The sense lieth thus, As I live, I delight not in the death of the wicked, but if the wicked turn from his way and live, or shall live, that is, according to what I have prescribed in my word, I shall delight in this: or thus, If he turn from his sinful way, that he may live, and live comfortably, I shall delight in it.

"Turn ye, turn ye from your evil ways." Here is an earnest exhortation of them unto repentance, setting out the mercy and goodness of God, who was ready and willing to pardon them, upon their turning from their evil ways. The doubling of the word notes the earnest and real intention of God in it. The sum and substance of the words is to show, that if sinners repent of their former wickedness he will forgive them, and take pleasure in them. "Turn ye, turn ye from your evil ways." If ye pine away under my judgments, the fault is yours; you turn not from your idolatries, oppressions, perjuries, and profanations of my sabbaths and ordinances, these are ways of death; but if ye would hearken to my ways, and turn unto them, they are ways of life. Of turning hath been spoken, chap. xiv. 6. The Septuagint is, Turn you by turning, turn thoroughly from your evil ways.

"For why will ye die, O house of Israel?" Ye are the nation I took and brought out of Egypt by a strong hand, Deut. iv. 34; ye are the people that entered into covenant with me, and avouched me to be your God, Deut. xxvi. 17, and I you to be my peculiar people, ver. 18; ye are they upon whom I have bestowed great privileges, holy ordinances, to whom I have showed mercy and truth, Psal. lxxvi. 1, 2; xcviii. 3; ye are the people I have taken most delight in of all people under heaven, whom I have most honoured, done most for, and made the greatest promises unto, Jer. xxxi. 33, 34; xxxiii. 8, 14. Why therefore have you left me and my ways, and fallen into ways of death? why do you wound and stab yourselves? If you have no regard to me, yet pity yourselves; cease from those ways which will be your death. Why will ye die, O house of Israel? Is it not better to live in my ways, than to die in your own?

Obs. 1. The guilt and punishment of sin are heavy and consuming things. "Our transgressions and our sins are upon us, and we pine away in them." Guilt alone is a great burden. "A stone" (saith Solomon, Prov. xxvii. 3) "is heavy, and the sand weighty; but a fool's wrath is heavier than them both;" and guilt is heavier than them all. "A wounded spirit who can bear?" Prov. xviii. 14. What is guilt then with punishment, but a consuming, a devouring thing? When David had sinned, and God's hand was upon him, what saith he? Psal. xxxviii. 3, 4, 8, "There is no soundness in my flesh because of thine anger; neither is there any rest in my bones because of my sin. Mine iniquities are gone over mine head; as an heavy burden, they are too heavy for me. I am feeble and sore broken: I have roared by reason of the disquietness of my heart." God's hand and his own guilt did eat up his spirit, and bring him to the gates of death: this made him to say, Psal. xxxix. 11, "When thou with rebukes dost correct man for iniquity, thou makest his beauty to consume away like a moth." The word for "beauty" notes that which is desirable in man; whatever is desirable, that melts away when God doth visit man for sin. A little touch of a man's hand crusheth the wings and hazards the life of the moth; a little touch of God's hand, where guilt is, crusheth the beauty and strength of man.

Obs. 2. Sinners under sad judgments are apt to despond, yea, to despair. "If our transgressions and our sins be upon us, and we pine away in them, how should we then live?" They had greatly sinned against God, stood it out against his prophets threatening judgments; and now the judgments were come upon them, their hearts sunk within them, and they conclude there is no mercy for them: Our sins are great, God's judgments heavy upon us, he is resolved now upon our destruction, and what course soever we shall take, all is in vain. What these said in Judea, the like said they in Babylon: Ezek. xxxvii. 11, "Our bones are dried, and our hope is lost: we are cut off for our parts." We are like the bones in a grave, that have all the marrow dried out of them; or like a branch of a tree cut off, and all the sap dried out of it; there is no hope we should ever live, go to Jerusalem, and grow there again into a church or state. Not only the wicked, but even a godly man may be in a desponding, yea, a despairing condition, as David himself; Psal. xxxi. 22, "I said in my haste, I am cut off from before thine eyes;" thou wilt never look upon or favour me more. So Asaph, Psal. lxxvii. 7—9, "Will the Lord cast off for ever? will he be favourable no more? is his mercy clean gone for ever? doth his promise fail for evermore? hath he forgotten to be gracious?" &c. What sad expostulations were these of a good man!

Obs. 3. The cavils, objections, and unbelief of sinners, put God unto his oath. "As I live, saith the Lord," it is not so as you fancy. I have told you that if you turn from your evil ways, you shall live; that I have no pleasure in the death of a sinner, Ezek. xviii. 21—23, 27, 28, 31, 32; but ye believe not my word, ye cavil against it, and say, ye shall pine away in your sins, that what course soever ye take, ye shall not live. Men are backward to believe the word of God, and deal worse with God than with man; they will give credit to an honest man upon his word, but not to God; yea, how many do believe the devil's suggestions and delusions, who is the father of lies, and will not believe the word of God! and what a harsh thing is it, that men will not attribute so much to God as to the devil! Eve took the devil's bare word in Paradise, she put not him to his oath: when he said, "Ye shall not die; your eyes shall be opened, and ye shall be as gods, knowing good and evil;" she believed him presently. But men will not take God's bare word, they put him to his oath, "As I live, saith the Lord." It is a great thing for God to speak, but more for him to swear: he that made the world with a word, is not believed upon his word, he must take his oath upon it; so that it stands God in more to be believed in the world, than it did to make the world; his single word sufficed for the one, his oath was required for the other. And here appears the great goodness of God, that for the good of man will please to take an oath. O happy we, for whose sake God swears! O most unhappy we, if we believe not God swearing! Having therefore God's word and oath, let us believe firmly, and stagger no more.

Obs. 4. Sinners, in what condition soever they be, have no cause to despond or despair of mercy, so that they turn from their evil ways. Let them be great sinners, old sinners, sinners under judgments, ready to be destroyed and cut off by the hands of enemies, as these were, yet if they turn from their sins, there is hope of mercy for them. For,

(1.) God takes pleasure rather in their conversion and salvation, than in their death and destruction: "I have no pleasure in the death of the wicked; but that the wicked turn from his way and live." If a state say to a company of its subjects, who are traitors, and upon traitorous designs, I have no pleasure in your ways which lead unto death, but my pleasure is that you turn from them and live; is not here a large door of hope opened unto them, whatever their treasons be?

(2.) Lest men, being deeply guilty, should suspect the reality of God herein, (for guilt is full of jealousies,) the Lord swears to it, and that by his life, which is the most unquestionable thing of all, for none doubts whether he be the living God; "As I live, saith the Lord, I have no pleasure," &c. So that here is God's word and oath, two sufficient bonds, to secure it.

(3.) Here is God's command and earnest desire of their turning; "Turn ye, turn ye from your evil ways." When a man's servant is abroad on some dangerous design, and his master commands him again and again to leave it off, and come home to him; or if the servant be in a deep water, and the master sees he will be drowned if he come not back again, he calls to him, and commands him to return; is not this an argument that he seeks his good, and would have him safe.

(4.) God sets the strongest arguments before them that can be thought of, life and death. If ye go on, there is no hope of mercy, you must die; if you will turn, here is life, ye shall live: here is great mercy. They are not left unto uncertainties, whether they shall have life or no; but life is propounded and offered unto them, and where that is promised there is a wide door of mercy opened. God is troubled at it, that sinners forsake mercy and embrace it not: Why will ye die? Why will ye not turn from your evil ways unto me the living God? Am I so ill a God? Have I dealt so unkindly with you, as that you will not come unto me? testify against me, tell me wherein. Like that in Micah vi. 3, "O my people, what have I done unto thee? and wherein have I wearied thee? testify against me:" if there be any such thing lie in the way, I am ready to remove it.

Obs. 5. The nature of true repentance lieth in turning. "Turn ye, turn ye." God at first made man upright, with his face towards himself; but he sought out inventions, and turned away from God to the creature, which was a madness, to leave a universal, everlasting, and satisfying good, for a particular fading, and an unsatisfying good; this madness is in the hearts of all men, Eccles. ix. 3, till they come to repenting and turning again unto

God, and setting him in his right posture to behold the Lord. This turning must be from his evil ways; Turn ye from your evil ways, and from all of them, Ezek. xiv. 6; xviii. 21, 31, else it is no turning; if the heart be towards any one sin, lust, creature, or evil way, it is not turned; his back is towards God and not his face; he prefers a creature, a lust, before God.

Obs. 6. Sinners are the authors of their own destruction. "Why will ye die?" They went on in their idolatry, profaneness, oppressions, pollutions of sabbaths, &c. and so brought judgment upon themselves. 2 Chron. xxxvi. 16, 17, "They mocked the messengers of God, despised his word, and misused his prophets, until the wrath of the Lord arose against his people, till there was no remedy. Therefore he brought upon them the king of the Chaldees, who slew their young men with the sword in the house of the sanctuary, and had no compassion upon young man or maiden," &c. So in Christ's days, he would have kept Jerusalem from destruction, but Jerusalem herself would not, she brought it upon herself, Matt. xxiii. 37. The Corinthians' abuse of the supper brought judgment upon them, 1 Cor. xi. 30; and the false teachers brought swift destruction upon themselves, 2 Pet. ii. 1.

Ver. 12—16. *Therefore, thou son of man, say unto the children of thy people, The righteousness of the righteous shall not deliver him in the day of his transgression: as for the wickedness of the wicked, he shall not fall thereby in the day that he turneth from his wickedness; neither shall the righteous be able to live for his righteousness in the day that he sinneth. When I shall say to the righteous, that he shall surely live; if he trust to his own righteousness, and commit iniquity, all his righteousnesses shall not be remembered; but for his iniquity that he hath committed, he shall die for it. Again, when I say unto the wicked, Thou shalt surely die; if he turn from his sin, and do that which is lawful and right; if the wicked restore the pledge, give again that he had robbed, walk in the statutes of life, without committing iniquity; he shall surely live, he shall not die. None of his sins that he hath committed shall be mentioned unto him: he hath done that which is lawful and right; he shall surely live.*

These words do explain and confirm what God had said in the 11th verse, and that by way of contraries.

1. He sets a righteous man before them, and bids the prophet tell them, that if a righteous man turn from his righteousness, and become wicked, his righteousness will not benefit him, but his wickedness will bring judgment upon him.

2. He sets a wicked man before them, and bids the prophet tell them, that if he turn from his wickedness, that shall not prejudice him, he shall not fall thereby, but he shall live.

Here is nothing in these verses of God's decrees of life or death, of salvation or condemnation, and men's being under them. It is said, whilst they are righteous they are under the decree of life and salvation, and when they cease from their righteousness they are under the decree of death and condemnation; and so if a man be righteous one day, and wicked another, and that interchangeably all days of his life, he doth daily pass from under one decree to another, forward and backward. I find no foundation in the words for such a conceit; they hold out God's dealings with men here in this world, according to the conditions he finds them in; if they be just and righteous, he will bless them; if they be unjust and wicked, he will punish them; the one shall live comfortably, the other shall be cut off by some judgment: here is nothing pointing at the decrees of God.

Ver. 12. "The righteousness of the righteous." What "righteous" man is here meant the 15th verse informs us, viz. a man legally righteous, such a man as restores the pledge, gives again what he hath robbed, and walks in the statutes of life without committing iniquity: if a wicked man did these things, he was righteous. It is therefore a righteousness of the covenant of works, not the righteousness of faith, here spoken of; a moral, not a gospel righteousness, which the 13th verse is clear for, calling it his "own righteousness."

"Shall not deliver him in the day of his transgression." The word for "transgression" is, פשע which signifies sin, presumptuous and wilful sin, rebellion, apostasy. Sometimes it is taken for any sin, or failing, as Lam. i. 22, "Do unto them as thou hast done unto me for all my transgressions." Jeremiah had no great sins against light, he did not rebel against God; his transgressions were such as are the ordinary failings of men. So it is used, Job xiii. 23. And the Septuagint hath it, in the day he shall err. Let him have done never so much good, and continued long in so doing, that shall not deliver him in the day of his erring, transgressing, failing. Had Adam stood many days, months, years, and then ate of the forbidden fruit, all his righteousness would not have delivered him; and so here under the covenant of works, there is no deliverance upon any failing. But rather it notes here some grievous sin and way of wickedness, which exposes unto and hastens God's judgments.

"As for the wickedness of the wicked, he shall not fall thereby in the day that he turneth from his wickedness." Let the wickedness of the wicked be great, of what kind soever, against God and man, idolatry, profaneness, oppression, &c. it shall not bring destruction upon him, make him to fall and perish; when he repents of it, turns from it, and walks in those ways that are contrary thereunto, then his former sins shall not be imputed to him, nor the judgments deserved executed upon him. As the righteousness of the righteous shall not deliver him when he sins, so the wickedness of the wicked shall not damnify him when he turns. Here is a nominative case put absolute, "the wickedness of the wicked."

"Neither shall the righteous be able to live for his righteousness in the day that he sinneth." His righteousness shall not uphold him, do him any good, when he falls into sin; his sin will be the death of him, and his righteousness, he cannot live in it, or for it.

Ver. 13. "When I shall say to the righteous, that he shall surely live; if he trust to his own righteousness." Here the case of the righteous man is further amplified and expounded. Let me make him a promise of life, and say, that in living he shall live, (so the Hebrew is,) yet, if he trust to his righteousness and commit sin, he shall not live. When men have a legal righteousness, they are apt to trust in it, to think it makes them acceptable to God, that it will answer justice for their sins, divert wrath, procure favour, and so presume to take liberty, and please the flesh in many things; but their righteousness will not stand them in stead.

"And commit iniquity." Of this, see chap. iii. 20, and xviii. 24, where much hath been said of this expression. The will, affections, and heart are in committing iniquity, it is making a trade of sin; such men are workers of iniquity. Pharisees had a legal righteousness, but they devoured widows' houses, made proselytes, and them twofold more the children of the devil than themselves, Matt. xxiii. 14, 15; these committed iniquity.

"All his righteousness shall not be remembered." That is, none of his righteous deeds shall be so had in remembrance, as to have any acceptance or reward, they shall be laid by and forgotten; instead thereof, he shall have judgment for his wickedness, that shall be remembered and rewarded.

"But for his iniquity that he hath committed, he shall die for it." The reward of his iniquity is death. Either he shall pine away under some stroke of God, which is a lesser kind of death, or he shall be cut off by some judgment, which is a death indeed, a death with a witness.

Ver. 14. "Again, when I say unto the wicked, Thou shalt surely die; if he turn from his sin," &c. In this verse and the two following, the case of the wicked man is further explained. As the promise to the righteous was with condition, so the threatening of the wicked is with exception, He shall surely die, unless he repent and turn, and testify the reality of the same, by doing that which is lawful and right; or, as it is in the Hebrew, by doing judgment and justice, by giving unto God and man what is prescribed. Of these words, see chap. xviii. 5.

Ver. 15. "If the wicked restore the pledge." A "pledge" is something pawned for a thing borrowed, the possession whereof for the present is in the hand of the lender, but the right is belonging to the borrower. *Chabol* is from חבל to bind, because pledges are strong bonds and obligations. Poor people were often necessitated to pawn their garments, beds, cattle, and utensils, which wicked men would keep and make their advantage of, which they ought not to have done, Deut. xxiv. 10—13; therefore it is said here, "If the wicked restore the pledge," if he be merciful to those who are poor and afflicted.

"Give again that he had robbed." Robbers seldom make restitution of what they get by violence. The word גזל signifies, to spoil a man of what is his by open violence, as highway robbers do, and also any violent wresting and forcing men's right out of their hands. Now if the wicked did make restitution of what he had so gotten, and

"Walk in the statutes of life, without committing iniquity." The "statutes of life" are the statutes of God, which being exactly kept, afford life to the keepers of them: chap. xx. 13, "They walked not in my statutes, and they despised my judgments, which if a man do, he shall even live in them," or live by them, as it is Lev. xviii. 5. If a man walk in these from day to day, and keep them perfectly, committing no iniquity, what then?

"He shall surely live, he shall not die." This and the like promises are legal, and made to legal righteousness, and clearly evince that the prophet speaks of a legal righteous man. The gospel saith not, that a just man shall live by doing, but that "the just shall live by faith," and that the law is not of faith. If men could keep the law, do what it requires, they should live by it; but (except Christ) none ever did, and so none was ever justified by the law, Gal. iii. 10—12. If a man could be found that walked in the statutes of life without sinning, he should surely live, and live as comfortably as Adam did in Paradise, and should not die.

Ver. 16. "None of his sins that he hath committed shall be mentioned unto him." The Hebrew is, all his sins which he hath committed shall not be mentioned unto him; that is, none of his sins shall be imputed or charged upon him. See chap. xviii. 22.

"He hath done that which is lawful and right; he shall surely live." The life here spoken of cannot be eternal life, because, 1. A man's turning from his former wicked ways, and making restitution to men for wrongs done, is no satisfaction to the justice of God for the breach of his laws. And, 2. No man can so keep the law or statutes of life, as thereby to obtain life eternal. Here is no mention of Christ, or faith in him, without which eternal life cannot be had. I conceive it is meant of a temporal life: he that ceases from his wicked ways, that lives honestly, doing lawful and right things, he shall not have cause to complain, as the Jews did, that they pined away under their iniquities; but he should live in living, as the Hebrew is, and that is, he should live a very comfortable life.

Obs. 1. There is a righteousness which will not profit a man when he hath most need. When a man sins, then he hath most need of righteousness to cover his sin, to prevent judgment; but then his own righteousness, a legal righteousness, a duty righteousness, will stand him in no stead; "The righteousness of the righteous shall not deliver him in the day of his transgression; he shall not be able to live in the day that he sinneth." Let us, therefore, look after an evangelical righteousness, for Christ hath told us, "that except our righteousness exceed the righteousness of the scribes and Pharisees, we shall in no case enter into the kingdom of heaven," Matt. v. 20. They had a legal, a duty, an own righteousness, but they had not the righteousness of Christ, "the righteousness which is of God by faith;" and that is the only righteousness which will stand in stead against all sin, and let us into heaven.

Obs. 2. It is perseverance will crown men's undertakings, and make them acceptable. It is not enough to begin well, unless we go on; if men be righteous, and give over their righteousness, falling to iniquity, as those that are legally righteous may, they lose their former righteousness, and fall under judgment: "If a righteous man commit iniquity, all his righteousness shall not be remembered, but for his iniquity which he hath committed, he shall die."

Obs. 3. Men are apt to rest upon a legal righteousness. "If he trust in his own righteousness." When men restore the pledge, make restitution for what they have gotten wrongfully, walk in the statutes of life, do that which is lawful and right, they are very prone to trust in this their own righteousness; so did the Pharisees, Luke xviii. 11, 12; so did Paul while he was a Pharisee, Rom. vii. 9; but being become a true christian, and having obtained the righteousness of faith, "he had no confidence in the flesh," Phil. iii. 3, but his whole confidence was in Christ Jesus.

Obs. 4. Let the wickedness of men be what it will, if they turn from the same, it shall not prejudice them, but they shall live a comfortable life. "As for the wickedness of the wicked, he shall not fall thereby in the day that he turneth from his wickedness." If he turn from his sin, and do that which is lawful and right, his sins shall not be mentioned unto him, "he shall surely live," he shall live in living: others, by reason of their iniquities, are dead in living, they have no comfort in their lives, but pine away. It is men's sins which make times evil, and lives uncomfortable: Psal. xxxiv. 12—14, "What man is he that desireth life, and loveth many days, that he may see good? Keep thy tongue from evil, and thy lips from speaking guile. Depart from evil, and do good:" this is the way to live long and comfortably. Righteousness exalts nations, families, and persons.

Obs. 5. God's statutes punctually kept afford life: "He who walks in the statutes of life without committing iniquity, shall surely live." Deut. iv. 1, "Hearken, O Israel, unto the statutes and unto the judgments which I teach you, for to do them, that ye may live, and go in and possess the land." He speaks of a temporal life here; but in Matt. xix. 17, of an eternal life, "If thou wilt enter into life, keep the commandments." The young man spake of eternal life, and Christ bids him "keep the commandments" if he would have that; showing, that if a man could personally and perfectly keep the commands of God, he should have eternal life.

Ver. 17—20. *Yet the children of thy people say, The way of the Lord is not equal: but as for them, their way is not equal. When the righteous turneth from his righteousness, and committeth iniquity, he shall even die thereby. But if the wicked turn from his wickedness, and do that which is lawful and right, he shall live thereby. Yet ye say, The way of the Lord is not equal. O ye house of Israel, I will judge you every one after his ways.*

The prophet having vindicated the truth of God which the Jews calumniated, he comes now to vindicate the justice which they likewise impeached, saying, his proceedings were not equal; and that he doth in these verses.

Ver. 17. "The way of the Lord is not equal." The Septuagint is, the way of the Lord is not right. Others thus, thy people deny that to be equal and just which the Lord doth; they say, He governeth the world unrighteously, and doth not administer justice indifferently to all men, but hath persons in respect, and punisheth one for another: this was that they charged God with.

"But as for them, their way is not equal." Here is answer to that unjust charge they charged God with, and it is by way of recrimination: that they charged upon the Lord is recharged upon themselves; you say, The Lord's ways are not equal; but he saith, Your ways are not equal, just, right, or well ordered: "Your prophets have conspired against me, and devoured souls; your priests have violated my law, and profaned my holy things; your princes have been ravenous wolves to shed blood, and to destroy souls for dishonest gain; the people of the land have used oppression, exercised robbery, have vexed the poor and needy, yea, oppressed the stranger wrongfully, chap. xxii. 25—27, 29; and now whose ways are not equal, yours or mine? Of these words see what hath been said, chap. xviii. 25.

Ver. 18. "When the righteous turneth from his righteousness, and committeth iniquity, he shall even die thereby." You charge me that I respect persons, and punish one for another, the son for the father; but it is not so: and in this verse and the next, the Lord doth clearly free himself from that imputation, hereby showing what his dealings are with a righteous man, whatever he be, father or son, prince or subject: if he "turn from his righteousness," and fall to wicked and vile practices, he shall surely die; God will judge him for his wickedness, and bring some judgment upon him; and there is no injustice in that: if men turn traitors to a state, it is justice in that state to cut them off.

Ver. 19. "But if the wicked turn from his wickedness, and do that which is lawful and right, he shall live thereby." Here also the Lord vindicates himself, by showing what his proceedings are with a man that turns from his wickedness, and doth amend his life, by doing what is lawful and right: that man, whatever he be, shall be spared, he shall live and enjoy blessings from God; it shall go well with the man that turns to God, and ill with him that turns from God, and doth evil. Now if so, what injustice is there in God? what is the evil of his ways? Let them both speak and declare wherein God wrongs either of them, if they can.

Ver. 20. "Yet ye say, The way of the Lord is not equal." Having made it evident, by clear demonstration, that his ways are equal, and that by two instances, viz. one of the righteous, and the other of the wicked; he here upbraids them for their stubbornness and impudency, persisting in their perverse opinion, and saying, "Yet the way of the Lord is not equal;" they might as well have said, the sun was dark, and the night was day.

"O ye house of Israel, I will judge you every one after his ways." Seeing ye are so wicked, perverse in your judgments, as to condemn my ways, and sentence them to be unequal, I will call every one of you to account for this evil way of yours, and the rest of your evil ways, and will judge you accordingly. This is the conclusion the Lord draws up upon the premises.

Obs. 1. Wicked men are apt to complain of, and carp at, the ways of God. They said, "The way of the Lord is not equal." Job xxi. 15, "What is the Almighty, that we should serve him? and what profit should we have, if we pray unto him?" we get nothing by his service, by calling on his name; he is a hard Master, he regards not our labour or prayers. These were of the same spirit with them in Malachi's days, who blushed not to say, "It is vain to serve God; and what profit is it that we have kept his ordinance, and that we have walked mournfully before the Lord of hosts?" Mal. iii. 14. We were told that no service was like unto the Lord's, that those that did mourn for their sins, and walk in his ways, should be blessed, and live comfortably, but we find no such thing; we have tried him, and find that he regards, exalts, and blesses those that never minded him or his ways, ver. 15; therefore, "It is vain to serve him." In the fifth chapter of Jeremiah is a notable instance to this purpose, ver. 11—13, "The house of Israel and the house of Judah have dealt very treacherously against me, saith the Lord. They have belied the Lord, and said, It is not he, neither shall evil come upon us, neither shall we see sword nor famine; and the prophets shall become wind, and the word is not in them." They said God had no reason to threaten them with sword or famine, they deserved no such judgment at his hands, and therefore the prophets that prophesied such things were not sent of God, his word was not in them, they brought windy doctrines of their own, and should, together with their doctrines, become wind; evil shall not come upon us, but upon them. When Christ was on earth, how did the scribes and Pharisees carp at him, his ways, and doctrine! see Matt. xii. 24; John v. 10, 18; viii. 48; x. 32, 33. In our days do not men carp at the Scriptures, ordinances, providences, and dispensations of God? Such is the pride and arrogancy of man, that he dares blame and condemn the ways and things of God.

Obs. 2. Men have no cause to complain of, or cavil against, the ways of God. For,

(1.) His ways are equal, just, righteous, however they appear to men; he is God, and cannot do unjust things; he "is light, and in him is no darkness at all," 1 John i. 5; "Just and true are his ways," Rev. xv. 3; he "is righteous in all his ways, and holy in all his works," Psal. cxlv. 17; "The just Lord is in the midst of the city, he will not do iniquity," Zeph. iii. 5. "Shall not the Judge of all the earth do right?" Gen. xviii. 25: yes, though men do wickedly, God will not. Hab. i. 13, "Thou art of purer eyes than to behold evil, and canst not look on iniquity;" he cannot look on it to approve it, much less to act it.

(2.) Our ways are unequal; and shall the guilty complain of the innocent? Had the Sodomites any cause to complain of God, who were so wicked? had the old world, which was so corrupt, cause to cry out of Heaven, which was pure? No man hath just ground to quarrel against God's dispensations, when himself walks unevenly before God, and his paths are crooked. If just men sin and step aside, Eccles. vii. 20, what do wicked men? they are altogether out of the way, Psal. xiv. 3. They do no good, their lives are a constant sinning, or a continued sin; and should God punish him daily for so doing, he had no just cause to fault the Lord: Lam. iii. 39, "Wherefore doth a living man complain, a man for the punishment of his sins?"

(3.) Upon comparing of his dealings with the righteous falling to commit iniquity, and the wicked turning from iniquity, it appears to all unprejudiced men, who are not blinded with iniquity; the one is punished for his apostasy, the other is pardoned upon his repentance; judgment is the portion of the one, and mercy the portion of the other. If God should punish the repenting wicked man, and spare the apostatized righteous man, then there were cause of complaint; but it is contrary, therefore his ways are equal, and there is no cause to complain of them.

(4.) God hath power over the sons of men, they are his family, and he may exercise discipline in his family, "the house of Israel." The Jews were God's house, he Master of that family, and when any sinned in it, he had power to correct them, or turn them out of doors; and who should fault him? it is not children's duty to complain of their parents, nor for servants to complain of their lord and master.

(5.) Complaints in this kind will do us no good, they will harm us rather, for God is Judge, yea, the highest Judge, and will not only judge us for our other evil ways, but for this very way of charging him to be unjust, and cavilling at his dispensations; he will judge every one after his ways, neither great nor small can avoid his judgment. Let us all, therefore, take heed how we fault the ways of God, how strange or grievous soever they appear or be unto us.

Obs. 3. When men have once taken up prejudice against God and his ways, it is not easy to be removed. The Jews had drunk in this conceit, chap. xviii. that the ways of God were not equal; and much of that chapter is spent in proving the contrary, to extirpate that misconceit: but it took not effect, they let pass God's arguments, whereby he cleared himself, and carried along with them their prejudice against him and his ways, as appears in this chapter, ver. 17, 20, "Yet ye say, The way of the Lord is not equal." When weeds are gotten into the ground, and rooted there, it is not easy to cleanse that ground from them; when errors, delusions, corrupt opinions, and prejudice against the truth, are gotten into the head or heart, it is not an easy thing to get them out. Many wonder that ministers should not convince unlearned and weak men of their errors, and take them off from their opinions and prejudices, but they should consider some men will not be convinced, either by God or man. These here were not convinced by God, nor the Pharisees by Christ, John viii. 6, 7, and chap. x.; nor the Athenians by Paul, Acts xvii.

Ver. 21, 22. *And it came to pass in the twelfth year of our captivity, in the tenth month, in the fifth day of the month, that one that had escaped out of Jerusalem came unto me, saying, The city is smitten. Now the hand of the Lord was upon me in the evening, afore he that was escaped came; and had opened my mouth, until he came to me in the morning; and my mouth was opened, and I was no more dumb.*

Here the third general part of the chapter takes place, and is a denunciation of judgment against those that escaped at the destruction of Jerusalem, ver. 21—30; and this is set out or amplified,

I. From the time and occasion of it, ver. 21.

II. From the efficient cause, ver. 22.

III. From the moving causes, ver. 24—26.

IV. From the final cause, which is in ver. 29.

Ver. 21. "In the twelfth year of our captivity, in the tenth month, in the fifth day of the month." How long this was after the taking and smiting of Jerusalem will appear, by comparing Jer. lii. 5—7, with this verse. "In the eleventh year of Zedekiah, in the fourth month, in the ninth day of the month, the city was broken up." The captivity of the Jews began with Zedekiah's reign, for that time he was made king Jehoiachin was carried away captive into Babylon, 2 Kings xxiv.; now this was in the twelfth year of the captivity, the tenth month, in the fifth day of it, so that it was a year and six months, wanting four days, before these tidings of Jerusalem's being smitten came to Ezekiel.

"One that had escaped out of Jerusalem came unto me, saying." Many perished in Jerusalem by the famine and plague in the time of the siege, many were slain at the taking of it, yet some escaped, and it is probable they hid themselves in holes and woods, among the mountains, or fled to Egypt; one of which, after so long a time as a year, five months, and sixteen days, came to Ezekiel, and told him the city was smitten. It is without question he and others had heard something of Jerusalem's condition before, but no certainty.

"The city is smitten." The word for "smitten" is from נכה which notes so to smite, as not to miss, it was certainly smitten. The Septuagint is, the city is taken; the Vulgate, the city is laid waste, "broken up," as in Jer. lii. 7. This was sad news he brought, that Jerusalem, that famous city, that city of God, was destroyed.

Ver. 22. "Now the hand of the Lord was upon me." This expression we had in chap. i. 3, and iii. 14, "The hand of the Lord was strong upon me." And here, by the "hand of the Lord," is meant, the prophetic influence, prophetical breathings, of God's Spirit were upon the prophet, whereby he was enabled to speak freely and boldly concerning the state of the Jews in Judea that had escaped; God informed the prophet how things were at Jerusalem before the messenger came.

"In the evening, afore he that was escaped came." The "evening" was the beginning of the day among the Jews, and so of much esteem; and God then, by his Spirit, visited the prophet.

"And had opened my mouth, until he came to me in the morning." In chap. xxiv. God had told the prophet that one should escape and bring him tidings of things at Jerusalem, and that in that day his mouth should be opened; and here it is made good. The opening of the mouth implies, 1. Matter of speaking. 2. Freedom of speaking. 3. Opportunity of speaking. All these concurred here. He had matter given in to speak unto those that were escaped, and flattered themselves they should live and recover their losses; he had freedom, Jerusalem being smitten, boldly to maintain what he had formerly prophesied against Jerusalem; and occasion ministered unto him, from the man's coming.

The word עַד for "until" were better rendered, when. There was a sweet harmony and correspondency between what the prophet received from the Spirit of God, and that which this messenger faithfully related unto him.

"My mouth was opened, and I was no more dumb." After this he was so filled with the prophetical spirit, that he was silent no more, but prophesied freely and frequently unto them.

Obs. 1. God's people are sometimes under long afflictions. "In the twelfth year of our captivity." They had endured many miseries in a foreign land, amongst a barbarous people, twelve years. Numb. xx. 15, "We dwelt in Egypt a long time; and the Egyptians vexed us and our fathers." Egypt was a house of bondage and vexation unto them, and when they were brought out God threatened them, that if they would not observe all the words of his law to do them, and fear his glorious name, he would make their plagues great, and of long continuance, Deut. xxviii. 59. And this captivity of theirs was so long, that they thought God had forgotten them; Lam. v. 20, "Wherefore dost thou forget us for ever, and forsake us so long time?" seventy years' time they lay in Babylon, which was no better than an iron furnace. Ezekiel, Daniel, and other godly ones, were in this condition.

Obs. 2. That when utter desolation comes upon places, and God's judgments are severe, yet some have their lives for a prey. "One that had escaped came." Chap. ix. 5, 6, the slaughtermen are commanded to show no pity, but to slay utterly old and young, both maids, little children, and women, only the marked ones they must not touch. It is probable this man that escaped was one of the marked ones, for he had a special care to come and inform Ezekiel what had befallen them and the city, that so he might bear witness both to the truth of Jeremiah's and Ezekiel's prophecies: had he been a wicked man, he would hardly have come to the prophet into Babylon; but whoever he was, he escaped famine, plague, and sword, which cut off thousands of others.

Obs. 3. Ancient, renowned, and privileged cities, have their periods and dissolutions. Jerusalem was very ancient: there is mention of it in Joshua's days, Josh. xv. 8. She was famous throughout the earth, called the gates of the people, for the resort unto her, Ezek. xxvi. 2; she had choice privileges, she was the holy city, Isa. xlviii. 2; the city of the Lord of hosts, Psal. xlviii. 8; the city of solemnities, Isa. xxxiii. 20; the valley of vision, Isa. xxii. 1; the perfection of beauty, Lam. ii. 15; the city judged by all to be impregnable, chap. iv. 12. But whatever Jerusalem was, here is the conclusion, "Jerusalem is smitten, broken in pieces, and laid utterly waste;" kings, princes, nobles, counsellors, judges, prophets, priests, people, all were smitten. In Rev. viii. 12, it is said, the sun, moon, and stars were smitten, a third part of them; but here, the sun, moon, and stars, and orbs they were in, were wholly smitten. Oh what darkness was then upon the face of the Jewish earth! All created and artificial glory is subject to smiting; let not your hearts be taken with sun, moon, or stars, with cities, and the glory of them, &c.

Obs. 4. The faithfulness of God in performing what he foretells and promises. Chap. xxiv. 26, 27, it was hinted to the prophet, that one should escape the fury of the Babylonians, and bring the news of Jerusalem's destruction, and that that day his mouth should be opened, and he should speak; and is it not here fulfilled punctually? That day the party escaped, came with that sad news of Jerusalem's being smitten, was the mouth of the prophet opened: and mark how forward God is to make good what he promises, he opened not his mouth at the end of the day, but the evening before the man came, which was the beginning of their day; he came in the morning, by what time the prophet might be up, but God had been with the prophet before: see Exod. xii. 41. Let us learn to be faithful, and perform to a day what we promise, rather be beforehand with men, than behind with them.

Obs. 5. God is pleased sometimes to confirm the truths delivered by his servants, by witness and signs. Here was a witness came from Jerusalem to assure the prophet and others, that what had been prophesied against Jerusalem was true and made good; here was sign upon sign, he was as dumb before, and now his mouth was opened, which was a confirmation to him and others likewise: Isa. xliv. 26, "He confirmeth the word of his servant, and performeth the counsels of his messengers." Many would not believe Ezekiel, nor Jeremiah, touching the destruction of Jerusalem, but God confirmed their words.

Obs. 6. Liberty to speak the things of God is from the Spirit of God. No man can prophesy or declare the things of the Lord, unless the Spirit of God breathe upon him, and open his mouth: "The hand of the Lord was upon me, and opened my mouth, and I was no more dumb." He had great freedom and boldness of speech when the Spirit of God came upon him, that filled him with sanctuary water, and made the waters flow strongly: before the Spirit waters them prophets are dry, before that speaks they are dumb; but when the hand of the Lord is upon them, then they cannot but speak and distil heavenly dews, or pour out great rains. 2 Cor. vi. 11, "O ye Corinthians, our mouth is open unto you, our heart is enlarged." The Spirit had filled his heart with divine things, and his mouth was open freely and boldly to communicate the same unto them.

Ver. 23—26. *Then the word of the Lord came unto me, saying, Son of man, they that inhabit those wastes of the land of Israel speak, saying, Abraham was one, and he inherited the land: but we are many; the land is given us for inheritance. Wherefore say unto them, Thus saith the Lord God; Ye eat with the blood, and lift up your eyes toward your idols, and shed blood: and shall ye possess the land? Ye stand upon your sword, ye work abomination, and ye defile every one his neighbour's wife: and shall ye possess the land?*

These words contain the causes that occasioned and moved God to denounce judgment against the Jews, who escaped the Babylonish sword when Jerusalem was smitten. The cause occasioning God to threaten them with destruction, was their vain confidence that they should possess the land still, ver. 24; the causes moving God to destroy them, were their sins, which are mentioned, ver. 25, 26.

Ver. 23. "Then the word of the Lord came unto me, saying." When the hand of the Lord was upon him, when the Spirit of prophecy was upon him, then the word of the Lord came unto him. The Spirit brings the word of God unto men; prophets spake as they were inspired by the Spirit of God, not of their own heads; Ezekiel would rather be silent and dumb, than speak from himself.

Ver. 24. "They that inhabit those wastes of the land of Israel." Nebuchadnezzar, having been a year and half (as appears by 2 Kings xxv. 1—3; Jer. lii. 4—6) before Jerusalem with a great army of the worst of men, Ezek. vii. 24, the land of Israel, or Judah, (for Israel here is put for Judah,) could not but be greatly spoiled and laid waste; when once the temple and city were burnt and ruined, then was the land as a wilderness. Zephaniah calls that day "a day of wasteness and desolation," chap. i. 15; and Jeremiah saith, "The land was then a desolate wilderness," chap. xii. 10. Some were left by Nebuzaradan to inhabit the waste and desolate places of the land, Jer. xxxix. 10; he left some poor people, gave them vineyards and fields to labour in, and live upon; and Gedaliah being made governor, many flocked unto him, who had hid themselves in woods, holes, among the mountains, and fled to neighbouring countries for security: see Jer. xl.; 2 Kings xxv. 22, 23.

"Speak, saying, Abraham was one, and he inherited the land." The land of Canaan was promised to Abraham and his seed, Gen. xii. 7; xv. 18; xxvi. 4. Abraham did not inherit it personally, he had not so much as one foot of ground in it, Acts vii. 4, 5; he dwelt in it, Gen. xiii. 12, but had no inheritance in it, therefore they here were mistaken to say, "He was one, and he inherited the land." Abraham was one, yea one that believed, one that feared, loved, and obeyed God, yet for his oneness had he not the land; God gave him the land, having an eye to his faith and obedience, Gen. xv. 6, 7; xxii. 16—18.

"But we are many, the land is given us for inheritance." This was the argument with which they flattered themselves, who were now remaining in Judea, that they should still possess the land, and recover themselves again: The land, said they, was given us for inheritance, who are many, as well as Abraham, who was one; if he enjoyed it, being but one, shall not we much more, being many, and being his seed? What reason hath God to cast us out of that inheritance he gave our father, and us his children? he will not do it, we shall dwell here, grow up quickly, being many, and recover our former liberty and glory. But these men deceived themselves by this foolish reasoning; for God did not give Canaan to Abraham because he was one, and so the beginning of the number of Israel, but because of the covenant which he made with him, Gen. xv. 18; xvii. 7, 8; which covenant Abraham kept, living by faith in God, and bringing forth fruits suitable thereunto, which themselves did not; for had they been the children of Abraham, they would have done the works of Abraham, as Christ said, John viii. 39; but you may see what their works were in the two verses following this we are speaking of. Besides, they had forgotten what God had threatened against those he gave the land unto, if they did forsake and disobey him: Deut. xxviii. 63; xxx. 18, God told them they should not prolong their days, but perish, or be plucked off the land. Little reason had they also to argue that they should be spared and possess the land because they were many, for that, as Junius well observes, a greater number than they who had possessed the land were cut off, or removed out of the land.

Ver. 25. "Wherefore say unto them, Thus saith the Lord God." Their vain confidence provoked the Lord, and therefore here he commissions the prophet to tell them what he judged of them and their sayings. His thoughts were far differing from theirs; and Ezekiel must declare the Lord's, not his own thoughts unto them. And, 1. He charges them with their sinful practices. 2. Denies them the possession of the land.

"Ye eat with the blood." It was commanded, before the law was given, that they should not eat blood, Gen. ix. 4; Lev. xix. 26; that is, neither blood let out from the flesh, nor blood with the flesh. One reason is given, Lev. xvii. 14, "Ye shall eat the blood of no manner of flesh: for the life of all flesh is the blood thereof." The Hebrew is, נפש the soul of all flesh is the blood thereof: *nephesh* is put sometimes for the whole man, as Gen. xlvi. 26, "All the souls of the house of Jacob," that is, all the persons: sometimes for the more noble part of man, viz. the reasonable soul, Matt. x. 28, "Fear not them which kill the body, but are not able to kill the soul:" sometimes for the affections, as Deut. vi. 5, "Thou shalt love the Lord with all thy heart, and with all thy soul: sometimes for the life, as Isa. liii. 12, "He hath poured out his soul unto death," that was, his life, John x. 15; and so it is rendered and to be taken in the place cited. "The life of all flesh is the blood thereof;" blood properly is not the life or soul of flesh, but the life or soul is said to be in the blood. Another reason why they might not eat blood, is in the 11th verse of that chapter, "I have given it to you upon the altar, to make an atonement for your souls; for it is the blood that maketh an atonement for the soul." The blood being to be offered upon the altar, represented the blood of Christ, which was to be shed for the remission of sins, Matt. xxvi. 28, and therefore not to be eaten. A third reason was, that they might not be cruel and bloody-minded, but might in a special manner take heed of shedding man's blood, which is the ground of the prohibition, Gen. ix. 4, 5. But they minded neither the prohibition itself, nor the reasons of it; they did eat with the blood, that is, they did eat the flesh with the blood in it, or they did eat the blood drawn out from the flesh.

Some make question in these days, whether they may eat blood; and the ground of it is from Acts xv. 29, where it is ordered, that christians should abstain from blood and things strangled. But those that scruple eating of blood, do not scruple the eating of things strangled, as fowls and rabbits; and there is as much reason for that as the other. As for the thing itself, I shall only say what Christ saith, Matt. xv. 11, "Not that which goeth into the mouth defileth a man, but that which cometh out of the mouth, this defileth a man;" and Paul, Titus i. 15, "Unto the pure all things are pure;" and 1 Tim. iv. 4, "Every creature of God is good, and nothing to be refused, if it be received with thanksgiving."

"And lift up your eyes towards your idols." Idolatry was forbidden in the law with great severity; see Deut. xvii. 2—5; Exod. xxii. 20; xx. 4, 6; yet these Jews minded idols and affected them. Of lifting up the eyes to idols, see chap. xviii. 5; it notes adoration of them, and expectation of help from them.

"And shed blood." Shedding of blood was a grievous sin; and here it may be understood either of their oppressing innocent ones, taking away their lives illegally, or else of their children which they offered to Molech, which was forbidden unto them, Lev. xviii. 21; of which bloody sacrifices was spoken, Ezek. xvi. 20, 21.

"And shall ye possess the land?" This is a stinging interrogation, intimating, that whoever possessed it, they should not. What! do you look to possess the land, that do such things, that are so impious and profane? Did I not cast heathens for their wickedness out of the land you are in? and do you think to continue in it, that have exceeded them in wickedness? Ezek. v. 6. No, no, the land is not for you; Abraham did not such things, you are not his seed, therefore you shall not inherit the land.

Ver. 26. "Ye stand upon your sword." Not, you are in arms to defend yourselves against Babylonians, but you trust in your strength, are ready for spoil, violence, and shedding of innocent blood. When any offended them in word or deed, they meditated revenge, and laboured by the sword to right themselves, there was no place for justice, "but the land was full of bloody crimes," Ezek. vii. 23.

"Ye work abomination." Of abominations, and what sins are so called, was spoken, chap. v. 9; xviii. 12, 13, in the third observation. Ye do that which is detestable and loathsome to the very senses.

"And ye defile every one his neighbour's wife." Adultery was a grievous sin, and punishable with death, Lev. xx. 10; Deut. xxii. 22; yet this sin was frequent amongst them, Jer. v. 7, 8; vii. 9; ix. 2. That honourable state of marriage was abused, and the bed defiled, and it was a common and universal practice among them, "every one defiled his neighbour's wife."

"And shall ye possess the land?" Do ye trust in your swords, violate all justice, shed innocent blood, do abominable things, defile your neighbours' wives, and yet presume you shall possess the land? O impudent creatures, brazen-faced sinners, what vain persuasions have you taken up! it is madness for you to dream of possessing the land; rather than such as ye shall inherit it, it shall lie desolate without inhabitant. The word here for to "possess" is, ירש which is a word that signifies contrary things, as to possess and dispossess. Josh. xxiii. 5, "The Lord shall drive them from out of your sight, and ye shall possess their land:" here *jarash* signifies, to drive out, and to possess. When the Lord saith, "Shall ye possess the land?" his meaning is, they shall be dispossessed of it, and driven out of it.

Obs. 1. Men in great misery, under grievous afflictions, are apt to flatter and deceive themselves with one vain confidence or other. These Jews were conquered by the Babylonians, had their city, temple, strong holds, and pleasant places, all laid waste; they were a company of poor people that inhabited the wastes of the land, yet they flattered themselves with this conceit, that they should inherit and possess the land; and why? there was a number, a multitude of them: "Abraham was one, and he inherited the land; we are many, and it is given to us." Their afflicted condition might have wrought other apprehensions in them, and made them see and say, All the chief ones of the land are cut off, or carried away captives, the land is fallen into Nebuchadnezzar's hands, we are his servants and slaves, left to till the land and dress the vineyards, that so a revenue may be raised for him; but as for ourselves, we are like to be miserable all our days, yea, and our posterity after us: but their thoughts were otherwise, they looked to inherit the land, and be great ones in it, because of their number. Men in straits, and out of straits, make lies their refuge, which prove their ruin; see Isa. xxviii. 15, 17, 18; Jer. vii. 4; xiv. 15; xxvii. 14—17.

Obs. 2. Expectation of promises to be performed unto us, not performing the conditions required, is foolish and vain. "The land is given us for inheritance;" the Lord hath promised us that we shall inherit the land. They minded the promise, but forgot the condition, which was, That they should keep his judgments, Lev. xxv. 18; walk in his statutes, chap. xxvi. 3—6; then they should be blessed in the land, and dwell safely in it: yea, they were to observe all the statutes and judgments of the Lord, Deut. xi. 31, 32; and if they did not, the Lord threatened to cast them out of his sight, Jer. xvii. 15; and out of the land, Jer. xvi. 13: these things they forgot, catching hold of the promise, saying, "The land is given us for inheritance." It is madness and folly to look that God should perform what he hath promised, when we perform not the condition of the promise. When God promises a thing conditionally, the condition must be performed, else the Lord is not obliged. 2 Chron. vii. 14, "If my people, which are called by my name, shall humble themselves, and pray, and seek my face, and turn from their wicked ways; then will I hear from heaven, and will forgive their sin, and will heal their land." Had they performed the conditions here required, their land had been healed, and not laid waste.

Obs. 3. The way multitudes go is no argument for the rightness and warrantableness of that way. These Jews were absolutely mistaken, yet they were many; the most judged the same thing, and went the same way. The greatest part of people every where mistake, cry, Peace, peace, when war and death are at the doors. The old world could not justify its way, because all walked in it except Noah and two or three more. It is not safe to be of the multitude's mind, and to tread in their steps, "for broad is the way that leads to destruction, and many there be that go in thereat." The prophet counselled the Jews, Ezek. xx. 18, not to walk in the statutes of their fathers, nor to observe their judgments, but to walk in the Lord's statutes and judgments, and to do them: better be alone in God's way, than be with multitudes in a false way.

Obs. 4. The true children of Abraham may be known by their works. These Jews stuck upon this much, that they were Abraham's seed: "Abraham was one, and we are many;" we come from his loins, and the land was given to his seed for an inheritance; and who should inherit it, but we who are his seed, and so the right heirs unto it? If it be true which you assert, you shall inherit the land; if you be the seed and heirs of Abraham, it shall be so. But come, let us try that by your works, saith God; "Ye eat with the blood, and lift up your eyes towards your idols, and shed blood; ye stand upon your sword, work abomination, and defile every one his neighbour's wife." And are these the works of Abraham? he did no such things. Were you the children of Abraham, ye would do the works of Abraham, keep the covenant as he did; ye would fear, honour, love, and obey me, deal justly, live chastely, and do good in your generation: these things you do not, therefore you are not his children, his heirs, have no right to the land.

Ver. 27—29. *Say thou thus unto them, Thus saith the Lord God; As I live, surely they that are in the wastes shall fall by the sword, and him that is in the open field will I give to the beasts to be devoured, and they that be in the forts and in the caves shall die of the pestilence. For I will lay the land most desolate, and the pomp of her strength shall cease; and the mountains of Israel shall be desolate, that none shall pass through. Then shall they know that I am the Lord, when I have laid the land most desolate because of all their abominations which they have committed.*

In the 27th and 28th verses, the judgments threatened are particularly mentioned.

I. The sword for those in the wastes.

II. The devouring beasts for those in the fields.

III. The plague for those in the forts and caves.
IV. Desolation for the land and mountains.
V. Cessation of strength, and the pomp of it.
All these confirmed with an oath.

Ver. 27. "As I live." The vain confidence of these Jews so provoked God, that he swears they shall not inhabit the land, and that by his life; As sure as I am the living God, ye that are so guilty of such great sins, and so unlike unto Abraham, shall be rooted out and destroyed.

"Surely they that are in the wastes shall fall by the sword." After the destruction of Jerusalem, many got into other cities and towns, which had been plundered, fired, and spoiled, thinking that there would be safety for them; but God would cause some to search those places, and sheathe their swords in the bowels of the Jews hid in them. The Hebrew for "by the sword" is, בחרב in the sword, but ב here is "by."

"Him that is in the open field will I give to the beasts to be devoured." Some, in this time of common calamity, kept in the open fields, or in the face of the fields, as the Hebrew is, fearing to venture into any town or city, and so promised to themselves security there; but the fields were no shelter unto them, God had lions, bears, wolves, and such wild beasts, which found them out, tore them in pieces, and devoured them.

"They that be in the forts and in the caves shall die of the pestilence." Some were got into strong forts, others were hid in caves of the earth, where none could find them, or come at them; these seemed to be out of all danger, but the pestilence and famine could reach them there. In that land were forts, rocks, holes to hide men in; see Isa. ii. 19; 1 Sam. xiii. 6; Josh. x. 16; 1 Sam. xxiv. 3; Judg. vi. 2.

Ver. 28. "For I will lay the land most desolate." Canaan was a land which abounded with all good things, it flowed with milk and honey, and was "the glory of all lands," Ezek. xx. 6; yet this land would God lay most desolate. שממה ומשמה desolation, desolation, it should be a wilderness, extremely desolate.

"The pomp of her strength shall cease." In chap. vii. 24, we had these words, "I will also make the pomp of the strong to cease;" and, chap. xxx. 18, "The pomp of her strength shall cease:" the land shall be so battered, wasted, consumed, that she shall no more trust in any strength of hers. Junius refers it to the ark, or sanctuary, called "the excellency of their strength," chap. xxiv. 21.

"The mountains of Israel shall be desolate, that none shall pass through." The land of Israel was full of mountains, which were not barren, but some for pasture, some for vines, some for cedars and other trees, and some for cattle: when they were so, many paths were made to the mountains, and they were frequently visited; but they should be desolate, without cattle, trees, vines, or any to pass by or through them; none should come over the mountains to worship at Jerusalem.

Ver. 29. "Then shall they know that I am the Lord, when I have laid the land most desolate, because of all their abominations which they have committed." Here the final cause of God's destroying them and their land is pointed out, and that is, the glory of God in their acknowledging his just proceedings. Before, they said, "His ways were not equal," but now they should acknowledge the equity of his ways, and that they had deserved such things.

Obs. 1. When God is resolved upon punishing a people, there is no place or refuge to secure them from his strokes and judgments. Here were men got into waste places, into open fields, into forts and caves, yet none of these secured them; the Lord had sworn to destroy them, and the sword finds out those in the waste and ruinous places; the wild beasts finding others in the open fields, devour them; and those who were got into the forts, and hid in caves, the pestilence and famine consumed. They thought to flee and hide themselves from the vengeance of God, but it could not be; had they gone down to the bottom of the sea, yea, down to hell, God would have met with them there, Amos ix. 2—4. No town, no fort, no field, no cave can protect that person whom God pursues; if men and beasts cannot come at him, God hath the arrows of famine and pestilence to shoot into his sides and liver. Let us take heed how we offend God, and provoke him to set upon our destruction; there is no place, person, or privilege, can protect us from his stroke. Let us get into Christ, hide ourselves in him, in the clefts of that Rock; then we shall be safe, whatsoever storms are abroad.

Obs. 2. It is men's sins which lay lands waste, and bring remarkable judgments upon them. Canaan was laid desolate, the pomp of her strength ceased, the mountains had none to pass by or over them; yea, "the land was laid most desolate;" and why? "because of all their abominations." Their sins exceeded the sins of the heathens, and they had answerable judgments; their manifold abominations brought manifold judgments. They had the best land in the world, and should have been the best people; but they degenerated and provoked God so by their abominations, that he made their plagues wonderful great, and of long continuance, Deut. xxviii. 59. Seventy years did they suffer, and the land also, which suffering they brought upon themselves and the land, as the Lord tells them, Zech. vii. 14, "They laid the pleasant land desolate;" they by their abominations did it: they caused the temple to be burnt, the testimonies of divine presence to be removed, the cities, fields, and mountains, to be desolate.

Obs. 3. By severe judgments God convinces men of the equity of his way, and causes them to give glory to his name. "Then shall they know that I am the Lord, when I have laid the land most desolate because of all," &c. Severe judgments awaken conscience, sharpen the understanding, and cause men to search, judge, and condemn themselves, and withal to justify the Lord; they have influence into heathens: Jer. xxii. 8, 9, "Many nations shall pass by this city, and they shall say every man to his neighbour, Wherefore hath the Lord done thus unto this great city? Then they shall answer, Because they have forsaken the covenant of the Lord their God, and worshipped other gods, and served them." Thus they justified God, and gave him glory, when they saw his terrible judgments upon Jerusalem and the land of Canaan.

Ver. 30, 31. *Also, thou son of man, the children of thy people still are talking against thee by the walls and in the doors of the houses, and speak one to another, every one to his brother, saying, Come, I pray you, and hear what is the word that cometh forth from the Lord. And they come unto thee as the people cometh, and they sit before thee as my people, and they hear thy words, but they will not do them: for with their mouth they shew much love, but their heart goeth after their covetousness.*

In these verses, and the rest to the end of the chapter, is contained a reproof or complaint of the captives in Babylon, for their detraction, hypocrisy, and covetousness.

I. Their detraction, in ver. 30.

II. Their hypocrisy in the end of ver. 30, and most of ver. 31.

III. Their covetousness, in the end of ver. 31.

Ver. 30. "The children of thy people." It is not, the children of my people; God would not own them, they were so wicked; but, "the children of thy people." Of these words before, ver. 2.

"Still are talking against thee by the walls, and in the doors of the houses." To speak against God or man is to detract from them, and disparage them. 2 Chron. xxxii. 16, Sennacherib, by his servants, spake against the Lord, and against Hezekiah, and that they said was detracting from the power of God, and truth of what Hezekiah had said. Acts xxviii. 22, "As concerning this sect, we know that it is every where spoken against;" that is, it is disparaged and condemned for a wicked sect. Numb. xii. 1, "Miriam and Aaron spake against Moses because of the Ethiopian woman; and said, Hath the Lord indeed spoken only by Moses? hath he not also spoken by us?" their speaking against Moses was detracting from him. So here, their speaking against Ezekiel was to defame and disparage him; and this they did openly and privately, by the walls where any met, and in their doors where friends met. Some take the words thus, The children of thy people are speaking of thee by the walls, and in their doors; they give thee good words, and consult of coming to thee: but I conceive the former sense best.

"And speak one to another, every one to his brother, saying, Come, I pray you, and hear what is the word that cometh forth from the Lord." Though they vilified the prophet, yet now, one being come to him that had escaped at the destruction of Jerusalem, they excite and stir up one the other to go to the prophet, and hear what he had to say. The smiting of Jerusalem was a great affliction unto them, and they hoped to hear somewhat from him to refresh and comfort them, especially seeing that he had spent three years in speaking against the nations, and said nothing unto them.

Ver. 31. "And they come unto thee as the people cometh." They flocked to the prophet in troops, as people use to do to public places for religion or pleasure; they hasten thither, crowd in, take up all places, and sit in expectation to hear somewhat that may please, or to catch somewhat they may carp at, and make advantage of, which some expositors affirm to be the end of their coming here. The Hebrew for "as the people cometh," is, according to the coming or entrance of the people; some come for to hear notions and novelties, some to scoff, some to censure; few come upon right grounds, or for right ends.

"They sit before thee as my people." They carry it before thee as my people, they hearken to what thou sayest, and make as if they would not lose one truth, but lay up all, and do as my people ought to do, viz. practise what they hear; they seem before thee to be saints, the people of God, as those that would learn righteousness.

"They hear thy words, but they will not do them." They took pains to hear the prophet, they came to his house, as chap. viii. 1; xiv. 1. It was not likely that they had public places of meeting; the Babylonians did not favour them so much as to indulge them with such liberty. Wherever it was they heard the prophet, they did not do what he said, they obeyed not him, nor the Lord who sent him.

"For with their mouth they show much love." From the teeth outwards they professed much kindness to the prophet, they gave him smooth and good words. The Hebrew for "much love" is, עגבים *agavim*, from עגב *agav*, which signifies, to be much in love with one, to be taken with the sight, hearing, or company of one; and they make as if they were deeply in love, much affected with the sight and hearing of thee, when it was not so: here was their hypocrisy. The Septuagint hath these words thus, *ὅτι ψεῦδος ἐν τῷ ϛόματι αὐτῶν*, because there was a lie in their mouth; they dissembled with the prophet. Arias Montanus renders the word *agavim*, *subsannationes*, which is, mockings, with bending the brows, and snuffing the nose. The Vulgate is to that purpose, they turn thy words into a song, they jeer at what thou sayest; so that translation Vatablus follows, they laugh at thy doctrine.

The word for "show" is, עשים *osim*, from עשה *asah*, which usually signifies, to do, to effect, to perfect; but here hath a differing signification, viz. to show, declare, or profess; and so Polanus tells that the word in Matt. xii. 33 is to be taken, "Either make the tree good, and his fruit good; or else make the tree corrupt, and his fruit corrupt: for the tree is known by his fruit." Look upon the works which I have done, and by them profess, declare, what I am; if I have done evil works, declare me and my works to be evil; if I have done good, declare me and my works to be good; for such as the tree is, such is the fruit.

"But their heart goeth after their covetousness." They looked upon the prophet, and listened to his words, but their hearts looked another way. The word for "covetousness" is, *bitzha*, from בצע to wound, break, damnify; and metaphorically, to be covetous, given to get and gain, intimating that covetous men do wound, break, damnify themselves and others. The Septuagint has these words thus, *ὀπίσω τῶν μιασμάτων αυτῶν καρδία αυτῶν πόρευεται*, their heart goeth after their pollutions; "covetousness" is a defiling thing. The Greek word for "covetousness" is, *πλεονεξια*, a desire of having more: not simply of having more, but more than God allows us. When we go beyond the bounds he hath set us, which bounds are in 1 Tim. vi. 8; Heb. xiii. 5, if we be not content with food, raiment, and such things as we have, but let out our desires to more, we are covetous. They being in captivity, having little in respect of what they once had in their own land, they were not contented with what they had, but let out their minds and hearts to more, and so were covetous.

Obs. 1. It is the portion of God's servants to be ill spoken of, and that from time to time, by those they live amongst, and do good unto. "The children of thy people still are talking against thee by the walls, and in the doors of the houses." They had spoken ill of Ezekiel before, they did it still, openly and secretly. David met with such a portion from many; Psal. xli. 7, "All that hate me whisper together against me;" Psal. lxix. 12, "They that sit in the gate speak against me;" Psal. cix. 2, "The mouth of the wicked and the mouth of the deceitful are opened against me; they have spoken against me with a lying tongue;" Psal. cxix. 23, "Princes also did sit and speak against me:" great and small, publicly and privately, did defame David. Jeremiah escaped not the lash of the tongue; chap. xviii. 18, "Come, let us smite him with the tongue." Paul, that precious servant of Christ, how was he spoken against! he saith, he was made as the filth of the world, and the off-scouring of all things, 1 Cor. iv. 13. Look what filth is washed out of, or rust scoured off, from pots, and thrown out of doors, such was Paul and his name made. It is the basest office to set our tongues on work to detract from the worth of any; if there be evil in men, our charity should cover it, if virtue, our wisdom should commend it. It is a devilish sin to speak evil of others; he first brought this sin into the world by speaking evil of God, Gen. iii. 4, 5; and too many are like unto him, in speaking ill of the servants of God, but we must steel ourselves to pass through bad report; see 2 Cor. vi. 8; Rom. iii. 8.

Obs. 2. Whatever wicked men speak against the prophets and servants of God, he knows and takes notice of the same. " Son of man, they speak against thee by the walls and in the doors of the houses." Let them speak openly or secretly, God hears them. When they said, " Come, let us devise devices against Jeremiah; come, let us smite him with the tongue, and let us not give heed to any of his words," chap. xviii. 18, God heard them, and revealed to Jeremiah what they said. There is not a word spoken by any, but the Lord is privy to it; and not only words, but thoughts also; Isa. lix. 7, "Their thoughts are thoughts of iniquity." Let us look narrowly to our hearts and tongues, for God knows the thoughts of the one, and the words of the other.

Obs. 3. How religiously and cunningly soever hypocrites do carry it, their hypocrisy is known to God, and shall be discovered. Hypocrisy is a doing or speaking that to God or men, wherein the heart and spirit of a man is not. Those men pretended religiously, they call upon one another to hear what word the Lord gave out to the prophet, and they come, being excited one by another, and sit before the prophet as God's people; they attended to what he said, as if they meant punctually to observe the same, but they did not do what he said, their hearts were not in the business. What worshipping was this of God, to give him an ear, and the world their heart! So, to speak against the prophet behind his back, and to speak fair, show much love to his face, was not this hypocrisy? did they not carry it religiously towards God, and cunningly towards the prophet? however they carried it, the Lord saw their hypocrisy, and discovered the same. The scribes and Pharisees wore long robes, made long prayers, and under pretence of them devoured widows' houses; but the Lord Christ knew their hypocrisy, and made it known, though religiously and craftily carried, Matt. xxiii.

Obs. 4. Many hearers pretend much love and kindness to the prophets, and yet behind their backs afford them not a good word. When these Jews came to the prophet's house, they showed much love with their mouths; but when they were by the walls, and at their own doors, they showed as much ill will with their mouths, they spake against him, they slandered him, they disgraced him; out of the same mouth came bitter and sweet. The Jews and Herodians pretended much love to Christ, and said, " Master, we know that thou art true, and teachest the way of God in truth, neither carest thou for any man; for thou regardest not the person of men. Tell us therefore, What thinkest thou? is it lawful to give tribute to Cæsar, or not?" Matt. xxii. 16—18. Here they showed much kindness with their mouths, when there was gall and bitterness in their hearts.[1]

Obs. 5. When men draw near to God in any duty of his worship, he principally looks which way the heart stands, whether that be real, and towards him. " Their heart," saith God, " goeth after their covetousness:" it went not after the word, after God himself. Isa. xxix. 13, " This people draw near me with their mouth, and with their lips do honour me, but have removed their heart far from me." When their bodies were in the temple, their hearts were in their shops; when their lips were speaking to God, their hearts were conversing with the creatures: God's eye was upon their hearts. The heart is the principal part in man, and it is the principal thing God aims at: Prov. xxiii. 26, "My son, give me thine heart;" not thy hat, thy hand, thy tongue, thy foot, but " thine heart." Whatever he hath without the heart is nothing, but having the heart, he hath all; whatever is wanting; let the eye be wanting, a man is blind; let the leg be wanting, a man is lame, let the whole body be wanting, a man is sick; yet if God have the heart, he hath all. Delilah had Samson's bodily presence, yet that sufficed her not, because she thought she had not his heart: Judg. xvi. 15, " How canst thou say, I love thee, when thine heart is not with me?" God hath no love from us, nothing of us, when our hearts are not with him.

Obs. 6. Men have carnal hearts in spiritual duties. These men were hearing Ezekiel prophesy, and whilst they were hearing, their hearts went after their covetousness; the word was in their ears, and the world in their hearts; Ezekiel tells them of the things of God, and they mind the things of the earth. To be earthly-minded at any time is blamable, Phil. iii. 19; but to be so in spiritual things is grievous, it is a despising, a debasing of them: when the things of God, of Christ, heaven, salvation, life, grace, and glory, are presented unto us, which should take up our thoughts abundantly, affect our hearts powerfully, for us then to mind the dust, sticks, straws, and pebbles on the earth, to have our hearts upon them, that is a great wickedness, horrible ingratitude. Rom. viii. 6, " To be carnally-minded is death;" it argues a dead soul, it tends unto death, and ends in eternal death.

Obs. 7. Covetousness is a sin which adheres to professors. These that came to hear the prophet, and sat before him as the people of God, their hearts went after their covetousness, they had hearts exercised with covetous practices, as it is in 2 Pet. ii. 14. The Pharisees made profession of religion, they were hearers of Christ, but the text saith, they were covetous, Luke xvi. 14. Judas, an apostle and follower of Christ, had a covetous heart, and sold his Master for thirty pieces of silver, Matt. xxvi. 15. Demas forsook Paul, having loved the present world, 2 Tim. iv. 10; while he was with Paul, his heart was in the world. John, seeing this evil incident to christians, dissuades them from the love of the world by a strong argument; 1 John ii. 15, " Love not the world, neither the things that are in the world. If any man love the world, the love of the Father is not in him:" he doth not know God to be his Father, and love him as a Father, that loves the world; he may think, say, and swear that he loves the Father, but the Spirit of truth saith, "The love of the Father is not in him." Let christians, therefore, take heed of this sin, for besides that it argues the love of God is not in us, it chokes the seed of God's word, which should beget grace in us, Matt. xiii. 22; it makes us idolaters, Eph. v. 5: yea, covetousness unfits us for church communion, 1 Cor. v. 11; it shuts us out of heaven, 1 Cor. vi. 10; it exposes us to wrath, Col. iii. 5, 6, to God's hatred, Psal. x. 3, to a curse, 2 Pet. ii. 14.

Ver. 32, 33. *And, lo, thou art unto them as a very lovely song of one that hath a pleasant voice, and can play well on an instrument: for they hear thy words, but they do them not. And when this cometh to pass, (lo, it will come,) then shall they know that a prophet hath been among them.*

Ver. 32. "Thou art unto them as a very lovely song." The Hebrew is, כשיר עגבים as a song of lovers; so the word is rendered, Jer. iv. 30, "Thy lovers will despise thee," it is the same word. Lovers have delightful songs, to please their ears, and pass away time; so the prophet's preaching was delightful unto them to hear; but as, in music and singing, there is nothing comes of it when done, so, they heard the prophet, but nothing came of their hearing. The Septuagint hath it, ὢς φωνή ψαλτηριυ, as the voice of a psaltery, which was an instrument to sing unto. Some render the words, thou wilt be to them a song of scoffers, that is, however they seem to be greatly pleased and affected with thy prophesying, yet in their hearts they laugh at thee, and deride thee.

"Of one that hath a pleasant voice, and can play well on an instrument." When one both plays well and sings sweetly, that music of all others is most taking, affects the ear, and stirs the spirits; so Ezekiel's voice was pleasing to them, and he handled his matter well, they were, or seemed to be, stirred and affected with what he delivered. The Hebrew for "can play well on an instrument" is, נגן ומטב which Montanus renders, of one that knows well how to play. *Nagan* signifies, to play upon a musical instrument, and also to sing to it.

"For they hear thy words, but they do them not." Some heard not at all; those that heard rested in what they heard, or abused it, jeering and scoffing at the prophet as a pleasant songster; they were not doers of what was taught them, they received not the truth with love, they mingled it not with faith, they yielded not obedience to it, which things do make a doer of the word: see 2 Thess. ii. 10; Heb. iv. 2; Rom. v. 17.

Ver. 33. "When this cometh to pass, (lo, it will come.") When the judgments threatened shall be made good, viz. that those in the wastes shall fall by the sword, and those in the open fields shall be devoured by the beasts, they in the forts and caves shall die of the famine and pestilence, when the land and mountains shall be laid most desolate, which things will certainly come to pass, whatever thoughts they have, or false prophets say to the contrary; for I have determined these things against them, commissioned thee to declare them, and I, being omnipotent, will in due time accomplish them.

"Then shall they know that a prophet hath been among them." The execution of what is threatened shall convince them, and make them say, We were deceived about Ezekiel; he spake not out of ill will to us, or of his own head; but he was sent to denounce the judgments of God against us for our sins, which he faithfully did, and we now feel the weight of them, and find he was a prophet, not a songster, that his matter had dread in it, and was not to be sported with.

Obs. 1. That men may be much affected with hearing the prophets and preachers of God, and yet be vile hypocrites, very wicked. These men that flocked to hear Ezekiel, and unto whom he was "as a very lovely song, as a song of one that hath a pleasant voice, and can play well on an instrument," they were backbiters and covetous. There was none in Babylon pleased them like Ezekiel; they said, Come, come, let us go and hear Ezekiel; they were as much taken with him as any are with music, with pleasant voices, tunes, and songs, which oftentimes ravish the hearers; yet they were unsound at heart, the word did them no good, they amended not their lives, they parted not with their lusts. In Christ's time, the people flocked to hear him, were affected with him; Mark xii. 37, "The common people heard him gladly;" and, chap. xiv. 43, "Judas and a great multitude with him, came to take Christ, and laid hands on him," ver. 46; and, chap. xv. 8, 13, 14, the multitude cried, "Crucify, crucify him." Many of them that heard him gladly before, were much affected with his heavenly doctrine, now cried out, "Crucify him," and so showed what vile hypocrites they were. In our days some preachers are as a pleasant song to some persons, they are affected with their voice, notions, gestures, expressions, matter, arguments, stories; they sigh, they weep sometimes, and are ravished at other times, they never heard such a man, such a sermon, such things; and yet are not changed in their hearts, reformed in their tongues or lives, but are notorious hypocrites.

Obs. 2. When people hear the preacher, and do not practise what is taught, the word is no more to them than a song, or a fit of music, nor the preacher more than a musician or fiddler unto them. "Thou art unto them as a lovely song of one that can play well on an instrument, for they hear thy words, but they do them not." These words are a proof and reason of the former. Should we tell people, You esteem the word preached no more than an idle, amorous, witty, scurrilous song, nor the preacher any more than he that sings such a song, they would think themselves much wronged; but it is so in God's account, when they hear the preacher, and do not practise what they hear. A fit of music affects for the present, but quickly passes away, and both the music and the man are forgotten; so is it here, people are affected somewhat at a sermon, but sermon and preacher are quickly forgotten.

Obs. 3. Hearing of the word is good, but not to be rested in. They are not blamed for hearing, that is a duty which belongs to all, James v. 19; but they rested in their hearing; they made not the "word a lamp unto their feet, and a light unto their paths," as David did, Psal. cxix. 105; they did not meditate on it, digest it, turn it into good nourishment, that so they might express the virtue of it in their lives; they heard the word, and that was all. Of such that is verified, Matt. xiii. 13, "Hearing they hear not;" the word hath no influence into them, impression upon them, expression from them; they are no better than those that never heard; they are like men that observe wind and tide, but never make a voyage. 2 Tim. iii. 7, there were women ever learning, but never attained to the knowledge of the truth; and many are ever hearing, and never come to practice. Luke xiii. 26, "Thou hast taught in our streets;" they had heard Christ, rested in their hearing, and that was their undoing.

Obs. 4. God expects men should be not only hearers, but doers also, of his word. "They hear thy words, but they do them not." Hearing alone pleases not God; he gave not his word to be heard only, but to be heard and practised; they are good hearers who turn words into actions: James i. 22, "Be ye doers of the word, and not hearers only, deceiving your own selves." He tells them they deal fallaciously, they baffle and delude themselves, not others, if they hear the word and do it not; though there be power in the word to save your souls, yet if ye be not doers of it, ye deceive yourselves, and will lose your souls. Matt. vii. 26, 27, "Every one that heareth these sayings of mine, and doeth them not, shall be likened unto a foolish man, which built his house upon the sand: and the rain descended, and the floods came, and the winds blew, and beat upon that house; and it fell, and great was the fall of it."

He that hears Christ's heavenly doctrine and doth not practise it, is not built upon the rock, but upon the sand; and when the trial comes, will be deceived of his expectation, his house will down, his soul will be lost. It is not hearing, it is not crying, "Lord, Lord," that will open a door for a man to enter into heaven by: ver. 21, "Not every one that saith unto me, Lord, Lord, shall enter into the kingdom of heaven;" not any one which goes no further; "but he that doth the will of my Father, which is in heaven." My Father, saith Christ, hath made known his will; he would have men do his will, and then he will open unto them, and let them into heaven. It is not men's hearing or saying, but their doing what they hear, which pleads most strongly for their entrance into heaven. Many men commend the preacher, the word, with their tongues, but disgrace both with their lives: the best commenders of the preachers and their doctrine are men's lives, when they are doers of the word. Matt. xxv. 21, it is "Well done, thou good and faithful servant, enter thou into thy master's joy:" not, well heard, or, well said, but, "well done." Let us see to it, that we be not hearers only, but doers of the word: Rev. xxii. 14, "Blessed are they that do his commandments, that they may have right to the tree of life, and may enter in through the gates into the city."

Obs. 5. The judgments threatened by the prophets of God shall certainly take place. "When this cometh to pass (lo, it will come)." He means the sword, wild beasts, pestilence, utter desolation, which were threatened. It seemed somewhat unlikely, that, after a war, a few poor people left in wastes, holes, caves, forts, woods, and fields, should be cut off; but the Lord had said it, and he did effect it. How improbable or impossible soever things appear to us, what God threatens by his prophets to do (without repentance intervene) he will accomplish.

Obs. 6. Whatever the thoughts of wicked ones are for the present of the prophets, the time will come when they shall have other kind of thoughts of them. "When this cometh to pass, then shall they know," &c. When the sword, wild beasts, pestilence, utter desolation, are upon them and the land, when they are in straits, in the jaws of death, then they will have other apprehensions of Ezekiel than now they have. Ezekiel at present is as a "lovely song, like a man that hath a pleasant voice," some affect him, some scoff at him, others censure him; but when death is before them, then their thoughts will alter, then they will say, Ezekiel told us of these things that are come upon us, and how to avoid them, he called upon us to consider our ways, to turn from all our iniquities, and to provide for our souls; we then slighted him, only gave him the hearing of what he said, but now we see he was a prophet of God, delivered weighty things, and we were fools that we hearkened not unto him, doing what he said. When young men, who despise all the preachers say against whoredom and wanton courses, come to be in years, find their flesh and bodies to be consumed, then will they have other thoughts of them and what they preached, then will they say, "How have we hated instruction, and our hearts despised reproof! we obeyed not the voice of our teachers, nor inclined our ears to them that instructed us," Prov. v. 11—13: there were prophets amongst us, who sought our good, who tendered mercy and many precious truths unto us, but we were so blinded with our lusts, so conceited of our own ways, that we rejected them, and whatever they tendered us.

Obs. 7. The prophets will be witnesses at last against disobedient hearers. "They shall know that a prophet hath been amongst them." They heard Ezekiel, but did not what he said; his person, his doctrine, did at last bear witness against them. Wherever the Lord sets a faithful preacher, who takes pains among the people, declaring the mind of God unto them, and they do not practise what they are taught, that preacher will rise up in judgment against them; his doctrine, his prayers, tears, drops of sweat, his life, his sufferings, reproaches, death, will all be witnesses against them. If the rust of men's silver and gold will be witnesses against them, and eat their flesh like fire, James v. 3, because they let their silver and gold lie by them, and did not improve the same for public good, and in charitable uses; how much more will the truths of God, which the preachers have commended unto them, (being neglected, and not improved to the good of the hearers and others,) bear witness against them, and eat their flesh, yea, their souls, like fire! Thousands who have flocked after ministers to hear them, will find those ministers witnesses against them, because they heard them only, and never did what they heard. What a multitude of witnesses will London and England have against them at the latter day! all the godly, faithful ministers whose doctrine hath been heard, but never obeyed.

CHAPTER XXXIV.

Ver. 1—6. *And the word of the Lord came unto me, saying, Son of man, prophesy against the shepherds of Israel, prophesy, and say unto them, Thus saith the Lord God unto the shepherds; Woe be to the shepherds of Israel that do feed themselves! should not the shepherds feed the flocks? Ye eat the fat, and ye clothe you with the wool, ye kill them that are fed: but ye feed not the flock. The diseased have ye not strengthened, neither have ye healed that which was sick, neither have ye bound up that which was broken, neither have ye brought again that which was driven away, neither have ye sought that which was lost; but with force and with cruelty have ye ruled them. And they were scattered, because there is no shepherd: and they became meat to all the beasts of the field, when they were scattered. My sheep wandered through all the mountains, and upon every high hill: yea, my flock was scattered upon all the face of the earth, and none did search or seek after them.*

Ezekiel having reproved and threatened the judgments of God against the people for their sins, he comes in this chapter to deal with the governors and rulers of them, through whose default they became so wicked, and suffered the Babylonish yoke. In this chapter are these things considerable:

I. A reproof of the shepherds, and judgment threatened against them, in the first ten verses.

II. God's care of, and comfortable provision for, his flock, ver. 11—22.

III. A sweet prophecy of Christ and his kingdom, under the figure of David, ver. 23, to the end.

Ver. 1. "The word of the Lord came unto me, saying." These words we have often had. By them the prophet declares himself to be a true prophet: false ones spake of their own heads, they had no word from God, they deluded the people with lying words; but Ezekiel had a word from God, and that word he commended to the people.

Ver. 2. "Prophesy against the shepherds of Israel." The shepherds of Israel were the chief rulers, both political and ecclesiastical, princes, magistrates, prophets, priests, and Levites. Isa. xliv. 28, Cyrus is called a shepherd; and, Zech. xi. 17, those in the church are called shepherds. Jer. xxv. 34, "Howl, ye shepherds, and cry; wallow yourselves in ashes, ye principal of the flock;" that is, as the flock is considered politically and ecclesiastically, ye are the shepherds, the principal thereof; "howl, ye," &c. They are called shepherds, because they are to govern, protect, provide for, and to feed them.

"Woe be to the shepherds of Israel." Herein general judgment is threatened against these shepherds, "Woe be to them!" This word is a comprehensive word, and includes variety of evils in it; not some one, but divers sad judgments should come upon them. The word for "shepherds" is from רעה to feed, and metaphorically, to govern, teach, and so to feed men.

"That do feed themselves! should not the shepherds feed the flock?" Here was their sin, they fed themselves, not the flock. Those who are shepherds in state or church, are set up for the good of the people, to benefit and advantage them, not to seek themselves, to draw from the people what they can to make themselves great; they should be content with their allowance, and lay out themselves fully and wholly for the good of them that are committed to their trust. This interrogation, "Should not the shepherds feed the flock?" sets out the heinousness of their sin, and the indignation of God against it: What! you shepherds, and not feed the flock? you pervert the course of nature, and violate the order which God hath set, and that is intolerable, he will visit severely for it.

The word for "flock" is, צאן which signifies, a multitude of sheep or goats. The Septuagint renders it, sheep, and in a metaphorical sense it is put for the people: Zech. ix. 16; Micah vii. 14, people are resembled unto sheep.

First, Sheep are foolish, silly creatures, not like foxes, lions, leopards, which are subtle and crafty; so are people for the generality of them. Jer. v. 21, "Hear now this, O foolish people, and without understanding; which have eyes, and see not; which have ears, and hear not:" they had no ears to hearken unto the word of God, no eyes to see the hand of God, no understanding to discern the mind and dealings of God. So Deut. xxxii. 28, "They are a nation void of counsel, neither is there any understanding in them;" they act like foolish, silly people, that know nothing of God.

Secondly, Sheep are apt to go astray; 1 Sam. xvii. 20, David "left the sheep with a keeper," he knew they would wander had they not a keeper; so people are apt to stray from that which is just and equal, to turn aside from the ways of God: Isa. liii. 6, "All we like sheep are gone astray;" and Jer. ii. 13, "My people have forsaken me the fountain of living waters;" that is, they have forsaken me their Shepherd, who provided all good things for them.

Thirdly, When one sheep goes out of the way, many follow, run after that one; so it is with the multitude. 2 Sam. xx. 1, 2, "One Sheba, the son of Bichri, a Benjamite, blew a trumpet, saying, We have no part in David, neither have we inheritance in the son of Jesse; every man to his tents, O Israel. So every man of Israel went up from after David, and followed Sheba the son of Bichri." Here was a ram led all Israel into rebellion. So Theudas stepped out of the way, and presently four hundred others joined themselves unto him; and Judas of Galilee drew much people after him, Acts v. 36, 37.

Fourthly, Sheep are exposed to much danger, they are a prey to dogs, lions, wolves, foxes, bears, and such wild beasts; so are the people exposed to spoil, and to be preyed upon by the great ones: Zeph. iii. 3, Jerusalem's "princes within her are roaring lions, her judges are evening wolves;" they preyed upon the poor people. Jer. l. 17, "Israel is a scattered sheep; the lions have driven him away: first the king of Assyria hath devoured him, and last this Nebuchadrezzar king of Babylon hath broken his bones."

Fifthly, They are subject to many diseases, and apt to infect one another. It is observed, that of all creatures, a man, a horse, and a sheep are subject unto most diseases; and quickly doth one sheep communicate this infection unto another. So people are subject to many distempers, seditions, insurrections, rebellions, errors, heresies, superstition, idolatry, and what not: Ezek. ii. 3, the children of Israel are a rebellious nation; Jer. vi. 28, "They are all grievous revolters, walking with slanders: they are brass and iron; they are all corrupters;" one infected another. Jer. v. 23, "This people hath a revolting and a rebellious heart;" the disease was come to their hearts. Isa. i. 4, "Ah sinful nation, a people laden with iniquity, a seed of evil-doers, children that are corrupters;" they corrupted one another with evil opinions and practices.

Ver. 3. "Ye eat the fat, and ye clothe you with the wool." The Septuagint, Vulgate, and French have it, Ye eat the milk. The Hebrew word is, חלב which signifies fat, because it is made of milk kine fatness; what they feed upon hath a fatty milkiness in it which turns to fat. The word for milk is, חָלָב and that for "fat," חֵלֶב which also notes the principal of every thing. By these expressions of eating the fat, and clothing themselves with the wool, the prophet taxeth the covetousness of the princes, priests, and false prophets, who pretended the public good, but were intent upon their own profit and pleasure: they were not content with what stipends were allowed them, but devised ways and means to draw the wealth of the people into their own coffers, which is here called "the fat and the wool." The word for "wool" is, צמר which notes all sorts of wool, even cotton wool which grows upon trees. Had they any wool upon their backs (as our proverb is) these governors would fleece them of it.

"Ye kill them that are fed: but ye feed not the flock." The Hebrew for the first word is, ye sacrifice the thick; הבריאה is from ברא to create, and בריא *bari*, is, fat, flesh, because a sheep becomes fat and flesh by a kind of creation, there is the power of God put forth in it; and when men grow wealthy it is by the power of God; Deut. viii. 17, 18, it is not men's power, and the might of their hands, that gives them their wealth, but it is the Lord gives power to get wealth. The false prophets kill their souls with lies, with corrupt doctrines; and the magistrates found out ways to cut off them that were rich for their estates: thus they sought themselves, but fed not the flock. The princes and rulers did not maintain justice, preserve the innocent, relieve the oppressed, nor the priests and prophets teach them sound and wholesome doctrine.

Ver. 4. "The diseased have ye not strengthened." Here are five particulars in this verse, concerning the sheep, which the shepherds should have minded, but neglecting them all, are severely taxed for them. 1. They were diseased. Sheep are liable to various diseases, faintings, weaknesses. Montanus renders the word הנחלות those that languish and are feeble; those who languished in their estates or spirits, were not strengthened; those who wanted bread for their bodies and for their souls, were not looked after. The Septuagint is, the weak ye have not strengthened.

"Neither have ye healed that which was sick." 2. A sheep may be diseased, yet not be sick. That is sick, *cui totum corpus dolet*, when the whole body is pained, saith Lavater; the whole body is so distempered that the members of it cannot perform their offices. There were many among the Jews who were sick in their estates and spirits, and could not perform the duties of their general or particular callings, who had none to heal them.

"Neither have ye bound up that which was broken." 3. Brokenness. Some sheep had their flesh torn by dogs or bushes, their legs and other bones about them, broken or put out of joint; divers amongst them had broken estates, broken spirits, and none bound them up. The word חבש signifies binding, as men are bound in prison; binding, as men bind packs to horses; binding, as men are bound by laws to obey or suffer; binding of ornaments to the head, and binding up of wounds to cure and heal them, as here.

"Neither have ye brought again that which was driven away." 4. Some were driven away. Storms, dogs, wolves, and other wild beasts, ofttimes cause the sheep to run this way and that way, to fall into ditches and pits, which, if looked after, might be preserved and reduced. The wars and other evils forced many Jews to flee into other countries, and none in place did think of them, that they might be brought back.

"Neither have ye sought that which was lost." 5. Sheep being wandering creatures are oftentimes lost, Luke xv. 4. Among the Jews there were some who had straggled from the rest, and were lost, lost through corrupt opinions and practices; they left the ways of God, and wandered in by-paths which led to utter destruction; such a losing the word אבד signifies. They were not sought after, they did not make diligent inquiry and search after them.

"But with force and with cruelty have ye ruled them." They dealt not as fathers of their country, but as tyrants, which are the very plagues of the earth; they dealt not as shepherds with their sheep, but as cruel task-masters over servants. The word for ruling is רדה *radah*, which notes such ruling as a master doth exercise over a servant, rigorous ruling; therefore the Jews were forbid to rule over a poor brother, Lev. xxv. 43, "Thou shalt not rule over him with rigour." Here they ruled with rigour, they put forth their power to the breaking and ruin of the people, they were rough and cruel in their government. The Septuagint is, ye weary, wear out, yea, murder the strong with vexation and labour.

Ver. 5. "And they were scattered, because there is no shepherd." The shepherds being either negligent or tyrannical, the sheep were scattered; through default of their political shepherds, they were scattered into waste places, into the open fields, into forts and caves, chap. xxxiii. 27, and into other countries. Had Zedekiah and the nobles been faithful to God, to Nebuchadnezzar, and the people, ruling as he and they should have done, the people had not been so scattered. And through default of their ecclesiastical shepherds, they fell into errors, superstitions, and idolatrous practices; justice, laws, and religion being laid aside, there was nothing remained but confusion, disorder, and dispersion. The Hebrew is, they were scattered without a shepherd; which may be taken thus, being scattered they had no shepherd; or thus, they were scattered because, or for that, they had no shepherd, that is, no faithful shepherd; this is the better sense; and so the Septuagint speaks, for that they had no shepherds, that is, no such shepherds as cared for their good civilly or spiritually.

"And they became meat to all the beasts of the field, when they were scattered." When the sheep are scattered into caves, woods, upon mountains and hills, they become a prey to dogs, swine, wild beasts; so the Jews being scattered into several parts of the world, were exposed to the injuries of strangers, and a prey unto them.

Ver. 6. "My sheep wandered through all the mountains, and upon every high hill." They went from mountain to mountain, and from hill to hill, and set up altars: Jer. ii. 20, "Upon every high hill and under every green tree thou wanderest, playing the harlot;" so Jer. iii. 6. Or they were forced to flee to the mountains and hills, in the time of war and danger which their rulers brought upon them.

"Yea, my flock was scattered upon all the face of the earth, and none did search or seek after them." The Hebrew is, upon all the faces of the earth. Every country hath a several face in a metaphorical sense, as one man hath from another: Egypt had one face, Babylon another, the countries about Judea their distinct faces or superficies; now they were scattered abroad upon them all, and none did search or seek them. Here are two words signifying the same thing, בקש and דרש the first signifies to seek or search with the greatest care, the second, with the most correct judgment.

Obs. 1. Those that are set over the people in church or state are shepherds, and ought to be like unto them towards their flocks. They should govern them gently, protect them constantly, provide for them carefully, and feed them faithfully, and seek their good diligently. God who is the great Shepherd doth so: Isa. xl. 11, "He shall feed his flock like a shepherd: he shall gather the lambs with his arm, and carry them in his bosom, and shall gently lead those that are with young." Isa. xxvii. 3, "Lest any hurt it," (that is, his vineyard, his people,) "I, the Lord, will keep it night and day." Psal. xxiii. 1, 2, "The Lord is my Shepherd, I shall not want:" he provided green pastures and still waters for him, and for all his. Jer. v. 7, he "fed them to the full." He gave them David for a shepherd, "to feed Jacob his people, and Israel his inheritance;" and "he fed them according to the integrity of his heart," Psal. lxxviii. 71, 72; he sought their good, Micah vi. 8; he turned curses into blessings for them, Deut. xxiii. 5: here was a good Shepherd. Magistrates and ministers should be like unto God in all these.

Obs. 2. Few of those that are over God's flock in church or state, do prove such as they ought to be. The political rulers were wicked, and the ecclesiastical rulers were such also. They are called shepherds, but they did not the office or work of shepherds, they were generally naught; the shepherds of Israel did not feed the flock. Ezek. xxii. 25—28, you may see what the prophets, priests, and princes were, not a true shepherd amongst them.

Obs. 3. See here the true characters of wicked shepherds in church or state: and they are three.

(1.) They feed themselves. They were covetous, self-seekers, they did eat the fat, clothe themselves with the wool, and killed them that were fed, full of fat and flesh, they made a prey of the rich and wealthy. The political shepherds were selfish and covetous. Micah iii. 1—3, "Hear, O heads of Jacob, and ye princes of the house of Israel; Is it not for you to know judgment? who hate the good, and love the evil, who pluck off their skin from off them, and their flesh from off their bones; who also eat the flesh of my people, and flay their skin from off them; and they break their bones, and chop them in pieces, as for the pot." Look how butchers deal with oxen and sheep, killing, flaying, chopping in pieces, breaking their bones, selling some, and eating other parts, and whatever they do is for their own interest; so deal these state butchers with the people. The ecclesiastical shepherds were selfish and covetous. Isa. lvi. 11, speaking of the watchmen, he saith, "They are greedy dogs which can never have enough, and they are shepherds that cannot understand; they all look to their own way, every one for his gain, from his quarter:" one's gain comes from one quarter, a second's from another quarter, a third's from a third, and their eyes were upon their gain and nothing else. Micah iii. 11, "The heads of Jerusalem judge for reward, the priests teach for hire, and the prophets thereof divine for money;" thus all sought themselves, and thereby declared what they were.

(2.) They fed not the flock. A good shepherd's care and delight is to feed his flock, and manifest it by strengthening the weak, by healing the sick, by binding up the broken, by bringing back what is gone astray, and by seeking up what is lost. These shepherds did none of these things: the state shepherds neglected the flock, the church shepherds did so, the weak were not strengthened, &c.

(3.) Harsh and cruel usage of the flock: "With force and cruelty have ye ruled them." These shepherds did not distinguish between the weak and strong, the sound and sick, and so rule them wisely, gently, compassionately; but they were rough, rigid, bitter, and cruel unto them. The political shepherds shut up the doors of the temple, and would not let them come in to sacrifice or worship there, 2 Chron. xxviii. 24. They compelled the people to serve idols, 2 Kings xxi. 11. They revolted from under Nebuchadnezzar, and so brought wars and heavy taxes upon the people, Ezek. xvii. 15. "The princes in the midst of Jerusalem were like wolves ravening the prey, to shed blood, and to destroy souls, to get dishonest gain," Ezek. xxii. 27. The ecclesiastical shepherds also ruled after their own wills: the prophets were roaring lions ravening the prey, they devoured souls, they took the treasure and precious things, they made many widows in the midst of Jerusalem; the priests violated the law of God, and so wronged the people, ver. 25, 26. The prophets and priests conspired together to tyrannize over the people, who were so accustomed to it, that they were content to have it so; Jer. v. 31, "The prophets prophesy falsely, and the priests bear rule by their means; and my people love to have it so." The word for bearing rule imports rigorous dealing; they took too much upon them, which you may see, Jer. xxvi. 8, the priests and the prophets took Jeremiah, "saying, Thou shalt surely die." They were bitter enemies to Jeremiah, and those who believed his prophecies. Jer. l. 6, "My people hath been lost sheep; their shepherds have caused them to go astray," &c.

Obs. 4. Such is the condition of God's flock here, that it hath need of shepherds to look after it. There be in it some diseased or infirm, some sick, some broken, some driven away, some straggling and in danger of losing. God's sheep are subject to many evils, distempers, and dangers; to vain customs, Jer. x. 3; to bruising and breaking, Jer. vi. 14; to hunting like wild beasts, Ezek. xiii. 18; to beating and grinding to pieces, Isa. iii. 15; to devouring, Psal. xiv. 4; to errors, heresies, corrupt opinions and practices, Matt. xxiv. 5; 2 Pet. ii. 2; to backsliding, Jer. viii. 5; to mistakes and all sorts of evils, Isa. v. 20. It is mercy, yea great mercy, that God hath appointed shepherds for his flock, civil and spiritual, to provide for the weaknesses, maladies, and dangers of the soul, as well as of the body. Where these are wicked, it goes ill with the flock; if they be selfish, negligent, rigid in ruling, the flock will suffer much. O pray unto God earnestly, that he would give us good shepherds. There is a choice promise or two in Jer. xxiii. 4, "I will set up shepherds over them which shall feed them; and they shall fear no more, nor be dismayed, neither shall they be lacking." And Jer. iii. 15, "I will give you pastors according to mine heart, which shall feed you according to knowledge and understanding." These promises speak of good shepherds for state and church. Let us improve them, and press God for the fulfilling of them.

Obs. 5. That wicked magistrates and ministers, in God's account, are as no magistrates, no ministers. "They were scattered, because there is no shepherd." There were many shepherds in the state, and many in the church, yet all these were as none, because they were wicked, sought themselves, fed not the flock, but ruled with cruelty. When shepherds degenerate so far, as to be contrary to what they should be, then they are as none before God. Such, in Zech. xi. 17, are called "idol shepherds:" idols are nothing, 1 Cor. viii. 4, and so were they as nothing in the sight of God; and when it is so, then the sheep are scattered.

Obs. 6. That as God eyes the great ones in state or church, so he deals impartially with them being wicked. He observed what magistrates and ministers did in their places, and seeing them selfish, negligent, cruel, he threatens them all: "Woe to the shepherds of Israel!" He saw they were all guilty of grievous sins, amended not after his long forbearing them, and therefore without respect denounces judgment against them. God is greater than the greatest, and fears not the faces of princes or prophets; let them have what pretences they will to colour their ways, the Lord discerns them; let them be never so terrible unto men, the Lord will be a terror unto them; let them continue in their wickedness never so long, at last God will be avenged on them.

Ver. 7—10. *Therefore, ye shepherds, hear the word of the Lord; As I live, saith the Lord God, surely because my flock became a prey, and my flock became meat to every beast of the field, because there was no shepherd, neither did my shepherds search for my flock, but the shepherds fed themselves, and fed not my flock; therefore, O ye shepherds, hear the word of the Lord; Thus saith the Lord God; Behold, I am against the shepherds; and I will require my flock at their hand, and cause them to cease from feeding the flock; neither shall the shepherds feed themselves any more; for I will deliver my flock from their mouth, that they may not be meat for them.*

These verses set out the judgments threatened against the shepherds of Israel, for their prementioned sins. In the words take,

I. God's particular application of himself to the shepherds, ver. 7, 9.

II. The certainty of their punishment, ver. 8, "As I live," &c.

III. A repetition of their former sins, ver. 8.

IV. A specification of their judgments or punishments, ver. 10.

Ver. 7. "Therefore, ye shepherds, hear the word of the Lord." These words are again in ver. 9, and show the great indignation which was in the breast of God against these shepherds: O ye princes, priests, and prophets, seeing ye have done such things, and neglected what you should have done, hear the word of the Lord, he is vehemently displeased with you, and can hold no longer.

Ver. 8. "As I live, saith the Lord God, surely." The Hebrew is, I living, if not; the sense whereof is this, Let me not be the living God, but be laid aside as some idol or false god, if I do not punish these shepherds which have dealt so with my flock.

"Because my flock became a prey." The word for "prey" is בז which signifies spoiling, and such spoiling as is with treading down, and despising the thing spoiled; they vilified the flock of God, and spoiled them of what they had.

Kirker.

"And my flock became meat to every beast of the field." Wicked men are here called beasts, and beasts of the field, for that they range up and down to get a prey; and when they have gotten it, tear and rend it in pieces, as a lion or bear doth a lamb or sheep.

"There was no shepherd." Not simply no shepherd, but no shepherd that did his duty, as the next words show, "neither did my shepherds search for the flock;" he saith, my shepherds, because they were in God's stead to look after his flock; but they fed themselves, not the flock; they made laws, imposed burdens, and found out ways to enrich themselves, and impoverish the people.

Ver. 10. "Behold, I am against the shepherds." In this verse the punishments of these shepherds are enumerated, and this is the first, viz. God's enmity against them. They being great princes, priests, and prophets, kept all in such awe that none durst appear in word or action against them; if any did, they were soon crushed: wherefore saith the Lord, "Behold, I am against the shepherds;" I, that am the Governor of nations, the Lord of heaven and earth, and so the dread Sovereign of princes, priests, and prophets; even I, that am Jehovah, that gave being to all creatures, and can take away all again, am against them. The Hebrew is, Behold, I to the shepherds, that is, I come to set myself against them; the Vulgate is, Behold, I am above them; others have the words thus, Behold, I am against these shepherds.

"I will require my flock at their hand." Not only will I have account of them, what is become of my flock, but I will have recompence for every one that is wounded, weak, lost, or slain; I will require at your hand limb for limb, blood for blood, and life for life. This is the second punishment mentioned.

"And cause them to cease from feeding the flock." Here is a third punishment, and it is no less than displacing of them. Some were cut off by the hand of justice, Jer. lii. 10, 11, 24—27; Lam. v. 12. Others were carried away captive, and held in chains and bonds, as Zedekiah, Jeconiah, and many besides.

"Neither shall the shepherds feed themselves any more." Here is a fourth punishment; they should be deprived of those opportunities they had to enrich themselves: they made a prey of the flock, eating the fat, clothing themselves with the wool, and killing those that were fed, they made advantage of the flock, only seeking themselves, not the good of it; but they should not do so any longer.

"For I will deliver my flock from their mouth." They have been feeding upon and devouring my flock a long time; but now I will do by them as a shepherd doth by a lamb in a lion's or bear's mouth, Amos iii. 12. 1 Sam. xvii. 34, 35, David delivered the lamb: so God would pull his flock out of these lions' and bears' mouths, which is a gracious promise of the deliverance of his people.

"That they may not be meat for them." Being once delivered, they shall no more be spoiled and devoured by such tyrants as they were, but shall enjoy liberty and safety.

Obs. 1. When there are no faithful shepherds, the flock is a prey to all sorts of beasts. "My flock became meat to every beast of the field, because there was no shepherd." The princes, nobles, priests, prophets, and all their under officers, made a prey of the flock. The flock was amongst wild beasts of all sorts, and they did eat the milk, shear the fleece, and devour the flesh of the flock. No state officers, no church officers were faithful unto the flock, but all in place and power made a prey of it: it is the nature of dogs, foxes, wolves, bears, lions, and such beasts, to suck the blood, crush the bones, and devour the flesh of the lambs and sheep. Kings, in Dan. vii. 17, are called beasts; and Rev. xiii. 1, 11, there is mention made of a beast which rose up out of the sea, having seven heads and ten horns; and of a beast that rose up out of the earth, which had two horns, like a lamb, but spake like a dragon: these two beasts denote the ecclesiastical and political powers, and how they dealt with the people you may read in that chapter. When God's flock is without faithful shepherds, they are a spoil to sea beasts and land beasts, to all beasts whatsoever.

Obs. 2. That the sins of magistrates and ministers in seeking themselves, neglecting and wronging the flock, do greatly provoke God, bring certain and severe judgments upon themselves. "Behold, I am against the shepherds;" I, that am higher, stronger, greater than them all, even I, and all my attributes, are against them; I will call them to account, and have satisfaction for all the wrong and violence they have done; I will deprive them of their sweet morsels, and throw them with shame out of their places. These are severe judgments, which God swears, by no less than his own life, that he will bring upon them: God commits great trust unto them, and when they are unfaithful God visits severely for it. Jer. xxv. 34—36, "Howl, ye shepherds, cry; and wallow yourselves in the ashes, ye principal of the flock, for the days of your slaughter and of your dispersions are accomplished; and ye shall fall like a pleasant vessel." They should have no way to flee or escape; cry and howl they might, their pastures should be spoiled, and themselves destroyed. The shepherds had been preserved like a pleasant vessel in the hand of God, he esteemed them; but now, being so vile, they should fall, be broken, and not esteemed at all. See Jer. xxiii. 1, 2; Zech. xi. 17. This hath been made good in our days, against the political and ecclesiastical shepherds. Have not our princes, nobles, prelates, and their officers, for their feeding themselves, not feeding the flock, for their ruling them by force and cruelty, have they not had God against them, been deprived of their fat, and sweet morsels? have they not been turned out of their places, and suffered justly for their demerits? The oppressions in state and church were such, that the flock had perished, had not God appeared for it against those lions and wolves: their sins were provoking, and drew the fury of God upon them.

Obs. 3. Those sheep that are under oppressing and devouring shepherds, God will relieve and set at liberty. "I will deliver my flock from their mouth, that they may not be meat for them." Many years had his flock been molested by wicked princes, priests, and prophets; they had eaten up many of his flock, and the rest were in danger of devouring; but the Lord had a care of them, and pulled them out of their jaws. The poor sheep could not withstand their violence; they were like young lions among the flocks, which go through, tread down, and tear them in pieces, and none can deliver, Micah v. 8: but though the sheep had no man able to deliver them from these lion-like shepherds, yet God was able to do it, and did it; he was a lion to these lions, and tore them in pieces, rescuing his flock. It is not long since we were under such shepherds, who made us meat to their teeth, eating up our estates, liberties, and lives; they oppressed and devoured us, and who durst appear for us? if any did, they felt the jaws and claws of these lions: but God at last arose for us, and hath driven away those shepherds, and delivered us from being meat to their mouths.

Ver. 11—16. *For thus saith the Lord God; Behold, I, even I, will both search my sheep, and seek them out. As a shepherd seeketh out his flock in the day that he is among his sheep that are scattered; so will I seek out my sheep, and will deliver them out of all places where they have been scattered in the cloudy and dark day. And I will bring them out from the people, and gather them from the countries, and will bring them to their own land, and feed them upon the mountains of Israel by the rivers, and in all the inhabited places of the country. I will feed them in a good pasture, and upon the high mountains of Israel shall their fold be: there shall they lie in a good fold, and in a fat pasture shall they feed upon the mountains of Israel. I will feed my flock, and I will cause them to lie down, saith the Lord God. I will seek that which was lost, and bring again that which was driven away, and will bind up that which was broken, and will strengthen that which was sick: but I will destroy the fat and the strong; I will feed them with judgment.*

These verses set before us God's care and comfortable provision for his flock, which is the second general part of this chapter; and they have in them,

I. Gracious promises.

1. A promise of seeking out the sheep, ver. 11, 12, 16.

2. A promise of reducing them, ver. 13, 16.

3. A promise of feeding them being reduced, ver. 13—15.

4. A promise of healing the broken and the sick, ver. 16.

II. A declaration how God will deal with the fat and strong ones, ver. 16.

Ver. 11. "Behold, I, even I, will both search my sheep, and seek them out." You think much to look after my sheep, but, behold, I, even I, that am the great Shepherd, the great God, infinitely distanced from you, will both search and seek them out. The word for "search" is, בקר which the Septuagint renders, I will require; it notes searching out what they had done with them, and requiring them at their hand.

Ver. 12. "As a shepherd seeketh out his flock in the day that he is among his sheep that are scattered; so will I seek," &c. When some great storms by wind, rain, thunder, lightning, or wild beasts, have been in the field among the flock, and they are scattered here and there, then the shepherd hastens to them, sees whether any be wanting, and if so, seeks up and down till he finds them, and so brings them together again; which is a great mercy to the scattered sheep, and as great a comfort to the shepherd: so would God seek out his sheep that were scattered into several places, and would deliver them: they had met with storms and wild beasts, which had divided and scattered them, and God, like a choice shepherd, would seek them out, and have a special care of them.

"In the cloudy and dark day." The Hebrew is, ביום ענן וערפל in the day of a cloud and of darkness, thick darkness, so the word signifies. It was a day of a cloud, or a cloudy day, when the Chaldean army besieged Jerusalem; then many were scattered and driven into neighbour nations: and it was a day of thick darkness, when the city was broken up, the temple burnt, Zedekiah's eyes put out, the princes and nobles put to death, many carried captive into Babylon, and the rest dispersed into woods, caves, mountains, and other places.

Ver. 13. "And I will bring them out from the people, and gather them from the countries." God finding his sheep scattered into several nations, where they met with hardships, he graciously promises to bring them out of those nations; they should not always be amongst their enemies, who were no better than wild beasts unto them. This hath an aspect to God's gathering his elect out of the several quarters of the world.

"And will bring them to their own land, and feed them upon the mountains of Israel by the rivers." Being gathered out of foreign lands, God would bring them into their own land, viz. into Canaan, a type of the church; they should both possess their land, and be put into a church condition again, and he would feed them with his word and ordinances, and put them into a better state than ever. This refers to the times of Christ and the gospel; then especially did God gather his sheep out of Babylon and bring them to Zion, then did he feed them upon the mountains of Israel by the rivers. So that in this verse are three grand mercies: 1. Eduction out of a miserable condition. 2. Introduction into a good condition. 3. Preservation in that good condition.

Ver. 14. "I will feed them in a good pasture, and upon the high mountains of Israel shall their fold be." In this verse are two mercies more promised; 1. Good and fat pastures; 2. Rest; both which are very needful for the flock. After their reduction into Canaan, they shall not simply have pasture, but good pasture, fat pasture, viz. the good word of God, the gospel, which is milk, wine, bread, marrow, and fatness; this feeds hungry souls, and makes lean sheep fat: and as their pastures should be fat, so their folds should be good. Sheep have their folds to rest in, and so are safe from heat, cold, and other dangers. The church is the fold for God's sheep, there they have rest and safety; the several churches are the several folds, where the sheep find rest and refreshing.

The Jews from this verse, as Sanctius reports, conclude that the Messiah is not come, because that when Christ was on earth there was no gathering of the Jews, nor feeding of them with such good pastures as were promised to be in the time of the Messiah: Our Messiah, they say, was rather for the dissipating of the Jews, than the congregating of them; he drove them into lean pastures, and gave them no fat pastures, for after his coming they were scattered into all parts of the world.

The gathering here spoken of, was not meant only of the Jews, but of the gentiles also; our Messiah made way for them, and gathered in them, and he would have gathered the Jews to him; Matt. xxiii. 37, "O Jerusalem, Jerusalem, how often would I have gathered thy children together, even as a hen gathereth her chickens under her wings, and ye would not!" The Jews would not be gathered unto Messiah, he would have gathered them, but they would not. They looked for a Messiah in pomp and glory, that should have restored the kingdom to the Jews, and made them great in the world above other nations; great places, riches, and honours were the fat pastures they minded. Christ did not feed his sheep with such pastures; but with spiritual dainties, heavenly manna, divine truths, promises, and ordinances he did. Their refusal of the Messiah, putting him to death, and wishing his blood to be upon their heads, was the cause of those heavy judgments that came upon them, and their dispersion thereupon, 1 Thess. ii. 15, 16.

Ver. 15. "I will feed my flock, and I will cause them to lie down." Other shepherds have neither fed them, nor let them have rest, they have wearied them and preyed upon them; but God would both feed them, and see that they should have rest, he would cause them to lie down as sheep in their folds lie down, and have rest; so God would order it, that his sheep should have rest and refreshing in their folds, in the congregations they are of.

Ver. 16. "I will seek that which was lost, and bring again that which was driven away," &c. In the 4th verse, the neglect of the shepherds of Israel was set out; and here God promises to supply their neglect, and do what they did not.

1. He "will seek that which was lost." They did not so, those that were lost they left them to perish; God is more mindful of his, he seeks them up, and will not lose them: Hos. ii. 23, "I will say to them which were not my people, Thou art my people." Saul was a blasphemer, a persecutor, an injurious person, in a lost condition, and the Lord sought him out, Acts ix.

2. He will "bring again that which was driven away." The Israelitish shepherds did it not, but the God of Israel would do it. David was driven away by Saul and Absalom, but the Lord brought him back again, 1 Sam. xix.; 2 Sam. xv. and xix.

3. He "will bind up that which was broken." They minded not those that were in such a condition, and needed binding up; the Lord did, who is the good Shepherd: Isa. lxi. 1, "He hath sent me to bind up the broken-hearted." When Peter had broken himself by denying the Lord Christ so fearfully as he did, the Lord bound up his wounds, and relieved him.

4. He "will strengthen that which was sick" and weak. They omitted it, but the Lord regarded such and strengthened them. Ezek. ix. there were some sick at heart, lamenting for the abominations done in the midst of Jerusalem, but the Lord sent one to confirm them, and set a mark upon their foreheads.

Obs. 1. God's flock being committed to the vigilancy and care of magistrates and ministers, he will inquire how they have discharged their trust, and require his flock at their hands. "Behold, I will both require my sheep, and seek them out." I committed them to your charge, I expected you should have had a special care of them, kept them so that none should have been wanting or prejudiced any way, like good shepherds; but you have not minded the safety and welfare of my flock: some are wanting; where are they? some are in a languishing and perishing condition; how is it that they are so? give me an account of these things, I will bear it no longer at your hands.

Obs. 2. That God's flock doth sometimes meet with storms, and such foul weather as scatters them here and there. "They have been scattered in the cloudy and dark day." They had not all serene and good days, but many cloudy days and days of darkness. In Manasseh's time they had black and bloody days, which made a great scattering of the sheep, 2 Chron. xxxiii. So in Jehoahaz's, Jehoiakim's, Jehoiachin's, and Zedekiah's reigns, there were clouds, tempests, whirlwinds, from the south, north, and other parts, from Egypt, Babylon, from Moab, Syria, and Ammon, 2 Kings xxiii. xxiv. xxv. which made at last a total dissipation of the flock. Had not we dark and cloudy days, which scattered the flock of God into several countries, in the time of the late princes and prelates? had not Ireland a black day when the massacre was there? And as it is with the flock in general, so with particular sheep and lambs, they have cloudy and dark days wherein they find themselves scattered.

Obs. 3. However others neglect the flock, yet God is a vigilant, faithful, and tender-hearted shepherd over them. God will seek out the sheep, deliver them from enemies, and bring them to Zion; he will give them fat pastures, cause them to enjoy rest in good fields: if any be broken, he will bind them up; if any be weak or sick, he will heal and strengthen them; if any go astray, he will reduce them. David found the Lord to be such a Shepherd unto him: Psal. xxiii. 1—3, "The Lord is my Shepherd, I shall not want." If I be hungry, he hath green pastures for me; if I be thirsty, he hath still waters; if my soul droop, he restores it; if I know not the way, he leads me in the paths of righteousness. O happy man, and happy people, who have the Lord for their Shepherd! and happy are those magistrates and ministers, who are vigilant, faithful, and tender-hearted shepherds over the flock, doing to the same as God himself doth.

"But I will destroy the fat and the strong." Here God declares how he will deal with those that were injurious to others: some amongst them were fat and strong, they were rich and potent. Men in place, and abounding in wealth, are in Scripture language said to be fat, Psal. xxii. 22; Jer. xlvi. 21; and when they are fat they grow wanton. Deut. xxxii. 15, "Jeshurun waxed fat and kicked;" then they kicked at God and his ordinances, and at their fellows which are lean; Amos iv. 1, the kine of Bashan oppressed the poor, and crushed the needy. In Gen. xli. the lean kine did eat up the fat; but here the fat did eat up the lean, and because they did so, the Lord would destroy them. The Hebrew for "destroy" is, שמר which signifies so to destroy a thing as that there shall be no remainders thereof; God would make a total abolition of them. The Septuagint, mistaking the word שמר for שמר renders it, and so the Vulgate, I will keep the fat and the strong; that is, keep them in, and restrain them.

"I will feed them with judgment." Montanus saith, I will feed them in judgment, במשפט which the Septuagint renders, with judgment. The words may import either God's judgments and plagues which he would bring upon the fat and strong, as Jer. xxiii. 15, "Behold, I will feed them with wormwood, and make them drink the water of gall;" or, God's wisdom and judiciousness in feeding of his flock. Foolish shepherds distinguish not between the weak and strong, the sick and sound, they drive, they feed, they govern all alike; but a wise shepherd considers the nature of his flock, what condition every sheep is in, what it is capable of, whether milk or strong meat, oil or wine, and so applies himself accordingly to each. Thus would God do with them, Isa. xl. 11; and so (1 Thess. ii. 7, 8, 11) did Paul with them.

Ver. 17—22. *And as for you, O my flock, thus saith the Lord God; Behold, I judge between cattle and cattle, between the rams and the he goats. Seemeth it a small thing unto you to have eaten up the good pasture, but ye must tread down with your feet the residue of your pastures? and to have drunk of the deep waters, but ye must foul the residue with your feet? And as for my flock, they eat that which ye have trodden with your feet; and they drink that which ye have fouled with your feet. Therefore thus saith the Lord God unto them; Behold, I, even I, will judge between the fat cattle and between the lean cattle. Because ye have thrust with side and with shoulder, and pushed all the diseased with your horns, till ye have scattered them abroad; therefore will I save my flock, and they shall no more be a prey; and I will judge between cattle and cattle.*

These verses exemplify what was said in the latter end of the 16th verse;

I. Declaring how God would deal with the rich who oppressed the poor, ver. 17, 20, 22.

II. Setting out the causes moving God thereunto, ver. 18, 19, 21.

Ver. 17. "As for you, O my flock, thus saith the Lord God." Here is an apostrophe; God turns his speech unto his flock, and shows himself very sensible of their condition, breaking out into a pathetical exclamation: O my flock, thou art oppressed, and sufferest hard things, which I see, am sensible of, and will speedily remedy.

"Behold, I judge between cattle and cattle." I know the cattle are not all of one nature; some are strong, and some are weak; some are clean, and some unclean; and behold I take notice thereof, and put a difference between one and the other. The word for "cattle" is, שה which signifies the small cattle, as lambs and kids; צאן the greater sort of that kind, as sheep and goats; and בקר signifies larger animals, as oxen, asses, and the like.

"Between the rams and the he goats." The word for "rams" is from איל because of their strength, they are very strong creatures. The word for "he goats" is, עתודים which notes the greater goats, those which lead the flock, and metaphorically the rulers and leaders of the people; as Isa. xiv. 9, כל־עתודי ארץ all the great goats of the earth, is the Hebrew; "all the chief ones of the earth," saith our translation. By "rams" some understand the good, gentle, and meek ones; by "he goats," the vile, wicked, and unquiet ones. Diodate interprets "rams" to be the violent, and "goats" the filthy ones. I conceive by "rams and he goats" are meant, the leaders of the flock, the rulers of the people, which differed in dispositions and in actions, as Polanus saith: God would distinguish between the good and bad of these, and so of the people, which are set out by the name of "cattle," and deal with them according to their ways and works; where by "cattle" are meant the meaner and poorer sort of people, by "rams and he goats," the rich and great ones.

Ver. 18. "Seemeth it a small thing unto you to have eaten up the good pasture." Here again by way of apostrophe God speaks to the rams and he goats, which had good pastures, plenty of all things, great blessings, milk, honey, and fat of the land. They had the chief places, lands, and fruits of the earth, they had gotten all considerable in church or state into their own hands, they lived deliciously and oppressed others, which they thought to be nothing; but saith God, Seemeth it a small matter unto you? you deceive yourselves, it is a grievous crime, and that you shall know.

"But ye must tread down with your feet the residue of your pastures?" Wanton sheep, when they are full, run up and down, treading upon the pastures, so that they become uneatable, or less pleasant and nourishing being eaten; so did the rich and great in state and church, they corrupted justice and the word of God with their inventions and traditions, so that the people were not fed, or fed with that which was unsavoury and unprofitable. Or thus; they troubled the poor, and suffered them not quietly to enjoy that little they had; they were cruel to the godly and poorer sort, though they had abundance, serving their pride and lusts therewith; or, having the principal of all things, they slighted and vilified the rest.

"And to have drunk of the deep waters, but ye must foul the residue with your feet?" The word for "deep" is, משקע which properly is whatever settles and goes down to the bottom; so that, by a figure called hypallage, *sedimentum aquarum* is put for *aquas sedimenti*, waters of settling, that is, pure and clear waters; and so divers expositors render the words. Some cattle when they have drunk, stamp and stir the mud in the waters, and so foul them that others cannot drink thereof; so did these rams and goats so mud and foul the waters of the sanctuary, and of the civil state, that the city of God was not made glad with them; there was no true justice nor pure religion.

Ver. 19. "And as for my flock, they eat that which ye have trodden with your feet; and they drink that which ye have fouled with your feet." By "feet" are expressed men's lusts, whereby they do defile things. Mark ix. 45, "If thy foot offend thee, cut it off." "Foot" is not to be taken literally, but for any lust that bears up a man's spirit for the present, and carries it up and down, as the feet do the body. They, out of will, humour, lust, mingled their traditions with the word of God, and corrupted justice, so that the flock had nothing pure in church or state; they laid heavy burdens and taxes upon the people, and the commodities the Lord gave, which troubled their spirits, and soured their comforts unto them. Such interpretations they gave of the law, as made it void and violated it, Ezek. xxii. 26.

Ver. 20. "Therefore," &c. "Behold, I, even I, will judge between the fat cattle and between the lean cattle." Seeing ye deal thus with my flock, saith God, I, even I, that am the great Shepherd, will distinguish and put a difference between cattle and cattle. There be fat ones and lean ones, the one doth wrong and abuse the other; the fat and strong carry it proudly and arrogantly against the lean and weak, which ought not to be. The Septuagint hath it, between the strong sheep and the weak sheep. The Chaldee is, between the rich man and the poor man. The word for "fat" is, *biriah* from *bara*, to create, because there is a creating power put forth in making cattle fat and men rich.

Ver. 21. "Because ye have thrust with side and with shoulder, and pushed all the diseased with your horns," &c. Here he describes the nature and manners of the fat cattle; they being strong were unkind, yea, cruel towards the rest, and thrust them out of the fold, out of the flock, and pastures also. The noble men, the rich, and those in power and place, dealt sometimes cunningly, sometimes openly and violently with the poorer sort, thrusting them out of their possessions, yea out of the land: Ezek. xi. 15, there were those in Jerusalem who said, "Get you far from the LORD; unto us is this land given in possession." Isa. lxvi. 5, their brethren hated them, and cast them out. The word to "push" is, נגח which signifies to push with the horn, as oxen and rams do, Exod. xxi. 29. Now besides this word is added בקרניכם which intends the sense: You have pushed with your horns, you have gored and hurt them greatly, you left not pushing at them till you had slain them, or driven them quite away.

Ver. 22. "Therefore will I save my flock." Seeing men are so unkind and cruel to my flock, using all their art and power to do it mischief, therefore will I take care of it, and deliver it; their sides, shoulders, and horns shall harm it no more; "I will judge between cattle and cattle," I will bring judgment upon those that have entreated my flock so ill, and it shall no longer be a prey unto them.

Obs. 1. All in God's flock are not good, they are not all of one sort; there are some fat, some lean, some strong, some diseased; there are he goats and rams, as well as others. There were in Moses' days them that said, "All the congregation are holy, every one of them," Numb. xvi. 3; but they that said so, were unholy themselves, he goats and strong rams. As it was with Jeremiah's figs, there were good and bad, Jer. xxiv. so was it with the flock of God, there were good and bad in it; there were lions, wolves, goats, and swine mingled with the sheep. Jer. vii. 9, 10, thieves, murderers, adulterers, perjured persons, and idolaters came to the temple with those that were innocent. In the waters are fish and frogs, in the field wheat and tares, and in the flock of God goats and sheep.

Obs. 2. Wicked men may have choice outward blessings, and that in abundance. They had good pastures, and in such abundance as that they trod them down with their feet; the fat and sweet of the land was theirs, the best of all things, places, and preferments were in their hands; honour, power, wealth, they abounded with. Nabal, that stony-hearted man, was very great, he had three thousand sheep, one thousand goats, 1 Sam. xxv. 2. And Job tells you that wicked men "are mighty in power," Job xxi. 7, have houses full of good things, Job xxii. 18. And David saith, they are fat, yea, "enclosed in their own fat," Psal. xvii. 10; they have the choicest of all things round about them. Ahab and Ahaz were both very wicked, yet one was king of Israel and the other king of Judah. Though all things come alike to all, yet usually wicked men have the fattest pastures, for their portion is in this life, Psal. xvii. 14.

Obs. 3. Wicked men being fat and full, in place and power, do abuse the blessings of God, are disquieting and harmful unto others. They are injurious to God, and those they dwell amongst. When their own turns were served, they trod down the residue of the pastures, they fouled the waters, they were unthankful for the best mercies, and made the rest unfit for others; and this was not all, they thrust with their sides and shoulders, and pushed with their horns; their strength, wealth, honour, power, were all abused to the dishonour of God, and prejudice of others. Thus was it of late amongst us, the fat ones in state and church did abuse the blessings God had given them, corrupting justice and religion, disquieting the inhabitants of the land with their inventions, superstitions, oppressions, innovations, &c. And because many would not bow to their wills, they thrust sorely at them with their sides and shoulders, and pushed them so with their horns, that they drove them out of the land. It is hard in prosperity to carry it rightly towards God or man.

Obs. 4. Though men think unthankfulness towards God, and uncharitableness towards men, a small matter, yet it is not so in God's account. "Seemeth it a small thing unto you to have eaten up the good pasture, but ye must tread down?" &c. Must my flock eat and drink that which is trodden down and fouled? and do you think it a small matter? I tell you, my thoughts are far otherwise; it is a provoking sin, calls for a weight of wrath, which when you feel, you will confess your sin was not little. Many deal untowardly with men and God, and when they have so done, make slight of it: Isa. vii. 13, "Is it a small thing for you to weary men, but will ye weary God also?" They refused to hear the prophets, and to hear God, they wearied both with their delays, shifts, and thought it a small matter; but God judged it not so, as ver. 16, 17 show. God blessed Jerusalem with choice and various mercies, and she sacrificed her children unto idols; here she was unthankful to God, unmerciful unto her own flesh, and thought it a matter of nothing: Ezek. xvi. 20, "Is this of thy whoredoms a small matter?" Saith God, Thou thinkest so, but I think they are crying sins, and will visit thee accordingly, ver. 38.

Obs. 5. God will distinguish between the oppressors and the oppressed, between the bad and the good; he will punish the one, and deliver the other. "Behold, I, even I, will judge between the fat cattle and the lean;" and because the fat and strong ones thrust with their sides and shoulders, and pushed with their horns, therefore God would feed them with judgment, (they should have according to their deserts,) and destroy them; but for the weak, diseased, oppressed, he would save them. Rich men, and those that are great in the world, being wicked, do unjust things, thrust hard at the people of God, keep them under, cut them short, deprive them of their rights and liberties, yea, oft push them so with their horns, that they drive them out of all their enjoyments, Jer. xl. 12; xliii. 5. Isa. xvi. 4, "Let mine outcasts dwell with thee, Moab." The goats and rams had driven some of the flock, not only out of the fold, but out of the field; this God beholds, and will recompense upon the oppressors' heads. Psal. xii. 5, "For the oppression of the poor, for the sighing of the needy, now will I arise, saith the Lord; I will set him in safety from him that puffeth at him;" that is, from him that would insnare him. Lot sighed and groaned in Sodom; and when the Sodomites did puff at him, and seek to insnare him, the Lord arose and set him in safety, 2 Pet. ii. 7—9. See Psal. xxxvii. 37—40. Did not the Lord of late make a distinction among us between cattle and cattle? hath he not judged the fat and strong ones, punished the rams and he goats, and provided for his flock? Some there be still, that thrust with the side and shoulder, that push with their horns, with whom ere long God will reckon, and, without repentance, he will destroy them.

Ver. 23, 24. *And I will set up one shepherd over them, and he shall feed them, even my servant David; he shall feed them, and he shall be their shepherd. And I the Lord will be their God, and my servant David a prince among them; I the Lord have spoken it.*

Here begins a sweet prophecy of Christ and his kingdom, with many benefits which the flock of God shall have therein.

I. A happy condition under him and his government, ver. 23.

II. God to be theirs, ver. 24.
III. A covenant of peace, ver. 25.
IV. Protection, ver. 25, 28.
V. Security, ver. 25, 27, 28.
VI. Watering and fruitfulness, ver. 26, 27.
VII. Freedom from enemies, ver. 27, and evils, ver. 29.
VIII. The presence of God, ver. 30.

"And I will set up one shepherd over them." Some make this shepherd to be Zerubbabel, who came of the race of David, and brought the Jews out of Babylon into their old pastures again, viz. into the land of Canaan, where they had their temple, worship, and ordinances, as in former days; but if we consult chap. xxxvii. 24, 25, where he speaks of the same person, you shall find things there incompetent to Zerubbabel, and must refer unto Christ; and the things mentioned here, were not fulfilled in Zerubbabel's days. By "shepherd" is meant the Lord Christ, who is frequently so called in Scripture; as 1 Pet. ii. 25; John x. 16; Zech. xiii. 7; Isa. xl. 11: and not simply a shepherd, but,

1. The true Shepherd; John x. 2, "He that entereth in by the door is the shepherd of the sheep," that is, the true Shepherd, and dischargeth that trust committed unto him most faithfully.

2. "The good Shepherd," John x. 11, 14. Never any like him for goodness; he laid down his life for his sheep; he knew them exactly, and was so conversant with them that they knew his voice; he took not away from, but gave fleeces unto his sheep, and supplied all their wants.

3. The great Shepherd, yea, "that great Shepherd of the sheep," Heb. xiii. 20. He made the sheep, he owns the sheep; he hath more and greater flocks than any other shepherd in the world; he stands and feeds them "in the strength of the Lord, in the majesty of the name of the Lord his God," Micah v. 4.

4. "The chief Shepherd," 1 Pet. v. 4. He sets all others over his flock, and they are under him, 1 Cor. xii. 28; Eph. iv. 11. They are sheep, he is Head of the church, Eph. i. 22, and their Shepherd; Psal. xxiii. 1, "The Lord is my shepherd," saith David, who was a prophet and a king, both an ecclesiastical and a political shepherd.

5. "One Shepherd," as here. One, either in opposition to the multitude they had before, which wronged the flock, Jer. xii. 10, "Many pastors have destroyed my vineyard, they have trodden my portion under foot;" of which sort Christ speaks, John x. 8, "All that ever came before me are thieves and robbers." Or one, that is, the first or only Shepherd, unto whom none is comparable, the only wise Shepherd that gave out living and effectual truth: Eccl. xii. 11, "The words of the wise are as goads, and as nails fastened by the masters of assemblies, which are given from one Shepherd;" that is, from Christ, the only Shepherd; all the masters of assemblies had their words from Christ, which ever did any souls good.

This Shepherd did not intrude himself into the office, but was called and sent of God. "I will set up;" the Chaldee paraphrase is, I will raise up one governor over them, and he shall govern them. This expression of setting up, is in the New Testament set out by giving, John iii. 16, by sending, Gal. iv. 4, by sealing, John vi. 27.

"And he shall feed them." This word "feed" notes the whole office of a shepherd, which is briefly set out, ver. 4; viz. strengthening the diseased or weak, healing the sick, binding up the broken, bringing back that which was driven away, seeking up that which was lost, and ruling gently. Others make these things the complete office of a shepherd, viz. providing good and wholesome pastures for them, bringing back those that go astray, keeping them from wolves and wild beasts, and healing those which are ill affected: all these were found in Christ, Isa. lxi. 1—3; Luke iv. 18, 19; Isa. xl. 11; Jer. iii. 15; Isa. xxvii. 3; Psal. xxiii. 1, 2; Micah v. 4; John x. 4.

Remark the difference between this Shepherd and all others.

1. He is a universal Shepherd, all flocks are his. God saith, Psal. l. 10, "The cattle upon a thousand hills are mine;" and Christ saith, The flocks in a thousand countries are mine. The churches in Judea, Galilee, and Samaria, Acts ix. 31; the churches of Syria, and Cilicia, Acts xv. 41; the churches in Asia, Rev. i. 11; the churches of Macedonia, 2 Cor. viii. 1; the churches of Galatia, 1 Cor. xvi. 1; the churches of the gentiles, Rom. xvi. 4; are all called the churches of Christ, Rom. xvi. 16. They had their particular pastors, teachers, elders, but Christ was the universal Pastor: Paul was the apostle of the gentiles, Peter of the Jews, but Christ was the Apostle and Shepherd of both; therefore saith, John x. 16, that he hath other sheep which he must bring to his fold, meaning the gentiles.

2. Christ is a Shepherd that feeds them with such meat and drink as other shepherds cannot; they may feed them with knowledge and understanding, Jer. iii. 15, but besides this, Christ feeds them with his flesh and blood, John vi. 51, 53—55; Matt. xxvi. 26, 28; he feeds them with his Spirit, John xvi. 7; Acts viii. 15, 17.

3. He enables all other shepherds to discharge the trust committed to them. Those that are over his flocks, he gave them their gifts, their graces, their power, they have nothing but what they received of him; therefore Isaiah, chap. l. 4, saith, "The Lord God hath given me the tongue of the learned, that I should know how to speak a word in season to him that is weary." Isaiah, who was one of the Jewish shepherds, had all his wisdom, skill, and power from the Lord Christ. And when he sent out his twelve apostles, Matt. x. 8, he told them, they had freely received, and must freely give. No shepherds give aught to Christ, he communicates all to them: John xv. 5, "Without me ye can do nothing;" but Christ could do all without them.

4. Christ is an abiding, an everlasting, unchangeable Shepherd. Other shepherds are flitting hither and thither, and at last die and leave the flock; Christ doth not so, he died for the flock, but was brought again from the dead, Heb. xiii. 20, and lives for ever, making intercession for his flock, Heb. vii. 25; he stands on mount Zion, Rev. xiv. 1, beholding and feeding them daily; he walks in the midst of the golden candlesticks, Rev. ii. 1.

5. Christ knows which are sheep, and which are goats, John x. 3, 14, 26, 27; others do not.

"Even my servant David." Christ is here called David, and so in many other places, as Jer. xxx. 9; Hos. iii. 5; Isa. xxxvii. 35; 2 Kings xix. 34; Ezek. xxxvii. 24, 25. In all those places is Christ called David, because he came of "the seed of David according to the flesh," as it is Rom. i. 3, and because David was a type of Christ: he might have said, My servant Abraham, Isaac, Jacob, as Isa. xlix. 3, "Thou art my servant, O Israel;" Christ is called Israel, because he was from the Israelitish nation; but David is named, because he was the first godly king of all Israel and Judah, and so typed out Christ more eminently than his predecessors.

"My servant," so Christ is called, Isa. xlii. 1; lii. 13; Ezek. xxxvii. 24, 25, and in other places. A servant is one who is under another, and who keeps and doth things commended to him by his master. Christ, as man, was under his Father, and kept his commandments, John xv. 10. He served him in taking man's nature upon him, and doing his will in redeeming and saving man, Heb. x. 9; Matt. xx. 28; John xiii. 16; Phil. ii. 7.

"He shall feed them, and he shall be their shepherd." He insists upon and repeats the same thing again, to show the great care, diligence, and intention of Christ in and upon his work of feeding the flock; he shall make it his business to do it: others have made it their work to fleece them, to scatter or devour them, but he shall so mind them, as to make up what was wanting in others, and to do some singular thing for them; he shall go in and out before them, and lay down his life for them.

Ver. 24. "And I the Lord will be their God." The Hebrew is, And I Jehovah will be to them for a God, or a God to them. And I the Lord will be their God; I will set my son, or servant, David over them to feed them, and I the Lord will be their God; they shall find me a merciful and gracious God; they shall find me, in Christ my Son, their Shepherd, reconciling them unto myself, not imputing their trespasses unto them: I will be their God to pardon them, to take special care of them, to deliver them, to comfort and counsel them in all their straits and miseries, and to communicate choice mercies unto them. Of these words before, chap. xi. 20.

"And my servant David a prince among them." The words are to be read thus, My servant David shall be a prince amongst them: if we take the former words with them, it is clear they ought to be read, I will be their God, and my servant David shall be a prince among them.

Whether this prophecy be fulfilled is questionable; there is somewhat in the gospel may make us conceive it is, for Matt. ii. 2, it is said, "Where is he that is born King of the Jews?" and Matt. xxi. 5, "Tell ye the daughter of Zion, Behold, thy King cometh unto thee;" Acts v. 31, "God hath exalted him to be a Prince and a Saviour;" and Rev. i. 5, he is styled "Prince of the kings of the earth:" these scriptures evince that Christ is a King, a Prince, but not that he reigned as a Prince among them; for he professes that he came not to reign but to serve, Matt. xx. 28; Phil. ii. 7; and therefore washed his disciples' feet, John xiii. 12; and when they would make him a king, he would not, John vi. 15. Christ hath appeared fully in his priestly and prophetical office, and hath had the honour of them; but he hath not appeared in his kingly office, nor had the honour of it; therefore it is conceived this prophecy is not yet fulfilled, but that the time is to come wherein he shall reign as a Prince and King in the midst of his people. Luke xxii. 29, 30, "I appoint unto you a kingdom, as my Father hath appointed unto me; that ye may eat and drink at my table in my kingdom." The time is coming that Christ shall reign, and keep a table like a Prince, where his friends shall freely eat and drink. Christ speaks not this of his spiritual kingdom, which is now in the churches and hearts of his people; nor of his kingdom of glory, for there is no eating or drinking; but of his personal, human kingdom, as some term it; for, Rev. iii. 21, Christ hath another throne to sit in than his Father's, in which at the present he doth sit: Christ hath not possession of that throne yet; when he hath, his promise is, that those that overcome shall sit with him therein. I shall have occasion in the 37th chapter of our prophet, to speak to this so controverted a point.

"I the Lord have spoken it." These words are as a seal to and ratification of what went before. If you make question of what is said, if you conceit these promises are too great and good for you, or hard to be accomplished, know, I the Lord, who am Jehovah, and give being to all my promises, I have spoken it.

Obs. 1. The appointing of offices in the church belongs to God, not to man. "I will set up one shepherd over them;" God appointed the office and the officer. 1 Cor. xii. 28, "God hath set some in the church, first apostles, secondarily prophets, thirdly teachers." In the Romish church are many officers which God never appointed; there are popes, cardinals, patriarchs, archbishops, &c. which places were never appointed by God, and therefore have no blessing go along with them, but serve for secular ends, even pomp and tyrannizing over the consciences of men.

Obs. 2. It is a great mercy and happiness to that people, who have Christ for their Shepherd. The Lord doth promise it here as a choice blessing unto them, to give them Christ for their Shepherd. The mercies or blessings are divers.

(1.) They shall be sure to be fed. "He shall feed them;" his heart will be upon them, and take special care that they have wholesome and good food. Ver. 14, "I will feed them in a good pasture," yea, "in a fat pasture shall they feed;" they shall not want, but have the green pastures and still waters, Psal. xxiii. 1, 2; yea, he will feed them with his own flesh, and give them his own blood to drink.

(2.) He will govern them with gentleness, and with skill. Their former shepherds did thrust with the side and shoulder, and push with the horn; Christ would not do so; he is likened to David, who was meek and gentle: 1 Chron. xxviii. 2, "Then David the king stood upon his feet, and said, Hear me, my brethren, and my people;" here he expressed his disposition and affection to his people: so Christ, he was a gentle, mild, and meek Shepherd, Isa. xl. 11. David was wise and skilful, Psal. lxxviii. 72; and Christ orders them by judgment; he judges between sheep and sheep, and deals with them according to their ages, conditions, and capacities.

(3.) He will lead them in the right way. John x. 4, he goes before them, and they follow him. Christ never is out of the way; and where he is the Leader, how can the sheep go astray? Psal. xxiii. 3, "He leadeth me in paths of righteousness." Whoever follows Christ shall be found in a path of righteousness. If we follow others, we may be led into by-ways; therefore saith Paul, 1 Cor. xi. 1, "Be ye followers of me," &c.

(4.) He will keep them so that none shall be lost, or miscarry. He is vigilant and potent, he sees the wolves and lions when they are coming, and suffers them not to destroy his sheep or lambs. John x. 27, 28, "My sheep hear my voice, and I know them, and they follow me: and I give unto them eternal life; and they shall never perish, neither shall any man pluck them out of my hand." All the persecuting emperors could not pluck one sheep out of Christ's hand: out of the hands of other shepherds it is easy to pull them, but impossible to pull them out of Christ's hand: he knows it is his Father's will, that of all he hath given him he should lose nothing, John vi. 39, and Christ will lose nothing.

Ver. 25. *And I will make with them a covenant of peace, and will cause the evil beasts to cease out of the land: and they shall dwell safely in the wilderness, and sleep in the woods.*

The Lord proceeds here in mentioning more benefits which his flock should have in the kingdom and under the government of Christ their Shepherd; and they are three: peace, protection, security.

"I will make with them a covenant of peace." The Hebrew is, I will cut with them a covenant of peace; the reason of which phrase is this: when the Jews made covenants, they used to take a calf and cut it in the midst, laying the two halves at a distance, and so passed between them; this was their manner of covenanting, and hence came the expression of cutting a covenant; see Jer. xxxiv. 18. To this God alludes when he saith, I will cut, or strike, a covenant with them; he did it by making Christ a sacrifice, by shedding his blood, dividing his soul and body, who (Isa. xlii. 6) is said to be the "covenant of the people," that is, the Mediator of the covenant between God and his people.

How the heathens made their covenants, see Piscat in loc. Maldon in Jer. xxxiv. 18.

The word for "covenant" is, ברית of which, and whence it comes, hath largely been spoken, Ezek. xvi. 8. It is not a covenant of works, but a covenant of peace, which some interpret of external peace, plenty, and prosperity which they should have; but the peace here meant reacheth further than to outwards, it is a peace which concerns the soul, a peace procured by the blood of Christ: Col. i. 20, "And, having made peace through the blood of his cross, by him to reconcile all things to himself." Hence as Christ is called the "covenant," so he is called "our peace;" Eph. ii. 14, "He is our peace, who hath made both one:" he is the ground and foundation of peace, between Jew and gentile, between God and man. And the gospel upon this account is called "the gospel of peace," Eph. vi. 15, for Christ preached peace unto them, chap. ii. 17. This peace is not like the peace of the world, John xiv. 27; but it is peace that quiets the conscience, passeth understanding, keeps the heart, and rules in the soul, Rom. v. 1; Phil. iv. 7; Col. iii. 15. Where this peace is neither death nor devil are feared, because sin is remitted, 1 Cor. xv. 55—57; Rom. viii. 33, 34.

"And will cause the evil beasts to cease out of the land." In the seventy years' captivity, when Judea was without inhabitant, wild beasts might multiply therein; these God doth promise to cause to cease, they should be no more. But these evil beasts were rather false teachers, and tyrants, wicked political and ecclesiastical shepherds: God would order it so, that these, who were worse than bears, lions, wolves, and foxes, should be no more; and instead of such, he would give them good magistrates and ministers; Jer. xxiii. 4, "I will set up shepherds over them which shall feed them; and they shall fear no more, nor be dismayed." There is another construction to be made of the words, namely this; that God would cause the wild and beastly dispositions of men to cease, and they should become meek and gentle, according to that in Isa. xi. 6, where it is said, that in the days of Christ, "the wolf shall dwell with the lamb, and the leopard shall lie down with the kid." Wolves and leopards are creatures most fierce and cruel, especially against lambs and kids, yet God would so alter the nature of these, that they should live and lie down together; he would make the most fierce, rugged, cruel men, to become mild and sweet, and to converse with them that were for disposition lambs and kids. Junius' sense of the words is this, That the Lord would take away or restrain every hurtful thing; he would not suffer his people to be infested, or if they were, they should not be damnified by those infestations.

"And they shall dwell safely in the wilderness, and sleep in the woods." These are proverbial speeches, setting out the great security the flock of God should have under Christ. Where there are no wild beasts in the wilderness or the woods, there the sheep feed and rest without all fear, they are most secure; and God's people under the gospel and Christ, have the greatest security. The word for "safely" is, לבטח that is, confidently, they shall be free from the fear of all enemies both corporal and spiritual; Satan shall be cast into the bottomless pit, Rev. xx. 2, 3, and all other enemies brought to such a condition, as that they should not cause fear, Jer. xxiii. 4. The Jews, because they see not such security for themselves any where, do therefore deny that Messiah is come; for when he comes he shall make a covenant of peace, and they shall be in safety, even in wildernesses and woods, because there shall be no enemies, no evil beasts to take away or hinder their peace. Though when the Lord Christ, the true Messiah, came, there was a universal peace through the world, it being at that time when the taxing was in Augustus' days, Luke ii.; and though the wars after were not so much as before; yet I conceive there is a time when this prophecy shall be more fully completed, for every prophecy of Christ was not fulfilled when he came in the flesh, but many were to be fulfilled in after-times, among which this was one. The Jews were mistaken concerning Messiah's coming, but not much concerning this prophecy.

Vid. Sanct. in Isa. ii. 4.

Obs. 1. The infinite goodness, kindness, and condescension of God, who will enter into covenant with sinners, with any of the children of men. Doth not the Scripture say, "Verily, every man at his best estate is altogether vanity," Psal. xxxix. 5; and why should the Lord, who is an infinite excellency, infinitely distanced from all creatures and vanity, enter into covenant with man? what did he see in these Jews, or in the gentiles, to awaken, rouse, and draw out his heart unto such a work? If stubbornness, ignorance, unbelief, idolatry, oppression, and such like, might induce him thereunto, these abounded both in Jew and gentile: there was nothing but God's own goodness, grace, and mercy, to cause him so to condescend, as to make a covenant with man, and such a covenant as a "covenant of peace." This should,

(1.) Raise up our spirits and hearts to admiration, that an infinite, holy, glorious, and great God should mind, converse, and make covenant with dust and ashes. Psal. cxliv. 3, "Lord," (saith David,) "what is man, that thou takest knowledge of him! or the son of man, that thou makest account of him!" David wondered that God should take notice of, especially make account of, so mean a thing as man is, as himself was, though a king and prophet.

(2.) Endear us greatly unto him. When high ones stoop unto those that are low and mean, it gains much upon their hearts, and endears them abundantly unto them. When David condescended to Abigail to take her to wife, it affected her greatly, and endeared her unto him not a little, as you may see 1 Sam. xxv. 41.

(3.) Make us faithful unto God. Is he pleased to make a covenant with man, and shall not man be faithful unto him? A wife should not be unfaithful unto her husband, and break covenant with him, though he be but a little above her; how much less should man break covenant with God, who is so much above him! God complains in Hosea vi. 7, saying, "They like Adam have transgressed the covenant:" I condescended to Adam, and made a covenant with him; yea, I condescended to them, and made a covenant with them; but they both proved unfaithful, father and posterity, they transgressed the covenant.

(4.) Cause us to be free and cheerful in our obedience unto God. When so great a God shall so graciously condescend unto us, as to enter into covenant with us, and that a "covenant of peace," should it not make us run in his ways, and serve him with gladness of heart?

Obs. 2. That men, through sin, are at distance from and enmity with God. "I will make a covenant of peace with them." What needed "a covenant of peace," if there had not been war between God and man? Man being apostatized from God through Adam's fall, lived in enmity to God; Rom. viii. 7, "The carnal mind is enmity against God; for it is not subject to the law of God, neither indeed can be." Men by nature have carnal minds, oppose God, his laws, and ways; and therefore, Rom. i. 30, they are said to be "haters of God;" and in Psal. v. 5, God is said to hate them, "Thou hatest all workers of iniquity." There was such hostility between God and man, as that there was no approach for man to God without a mediator, and such a mediator as could make satisfaction to divine justice, being offended. Col. i. 21, "You, that were sometime alienated and enemies in your mind by wicked works, yet now hath he reconciled." The Colossians, as well as others, were once at a great distance from God, and enemies to God; and wherein lay their enmity? "in their minds;" and how did that appear? "by wicked works:" they plotted, contrived, and did such things as declared them to be enemies to God; and being so, they durst not appear before God. But,

Obs. 3. God by Christ hath been pleased to take away this enmity, and to reconcile sinners unto himself. 2 Cor. v. 18, "All things are of God, who hath reconciled us to himself by Jesus Christ." It is Christ hath paid the price of our redemption, he hath satisfied his justice fully, and delivered us from wrath to come, 1 Thess. i. 10. It is by Christ the Mediator that reconciliation is made; neither angels nor men could do that work; it was a work for one that had more worth in him than all angels or men. Col. i. 19, 20, "It pleased God that in him all fulness should dwell, that so by him he might reconcile all things to himself; by him, whether they be things in earth, or things in heaven." "By him" is twice in the verse, that we may see by whom the enmity was taken away, and from whom the reconciling virtue came, even from the Lord Christ, whose blood made the atonement, Eph. ii. 13—16. How should this teach us to honour and prize the Lord Christ, by whom so difficult, so great, and glorious a work was wrought!

Obs. 4. Those that are received to God by the mediation of Christ, shall be preserved from all hurtful things, receive all good things needful, and enjoy much security. When men are in the "covenant of peace," then God "will cause the evil beasts to cease out of the land," then no creatures, no enemies, no devils shall do them harm, Job v. 23; Prov. xvi. 7; Rom. xvi. 20. Then there will be a communication of all good things needful; "they shall dwell in the wilderness," there they shall have blessings, so as they shall not be put to remove their dwellings for want, Psal. xxxiv. 9, 10; xxiii. 1; lxxxiv. 11. Then shall they "dwell safely in the wilderness, and sleep in the woods;" nothing without or within shall create any fear, or cause any solicitousness in them; they shall have perfect peace, and be as in the suburbs of heaven, Jer. xxiii. 4.

Ver. 26, 27. *And I will make them and the places round about my hill a blessing; and I will cause the shower to come down in his season; there shall be showers of blessing. And the tree of the field shall yield her fruit, and the earth shall yield her increase, and they shall be safe in their land, and shall know that I am the Lord, when I have broken the bands of their yoke, and delivered them out of the hand of those that served themselves of them.*

In these verses, as in the former, the Lord promises sweet mercies unto his people.

I. A blessing in general, ver. 26.

II. Particular blessings; and they are these:

1. Seasonable showers from heaven, ver. 26.

2. Fruitfulness of the earth, and that both of the trees and land, ver. 27.

3. Safety, *ibid.*

4. Acknowledgment of God, *ibid.*

5. Freedom, *ibid.*

III. The time when all these shall be, *ibid.*

Ver. 26. "I will make them and the places round about my hill a blessing." The Jews being in Babylon were for a proverb, a reproach, a taunt, and a curse, Jer. xxiv. 9; xxv. 18; xxix. 18; but God would roll away their reproach, and make them a blessing. The Chaldee is, they shall be blessed. It is usual in Scripture to put the abstract for the concrete; as Gen. xii. 2, "Thou shalt be a blessing;" the Vulgate there is, Thou shalt be blessed. Take the word "blessing" here for the concrete, and the sense is, They shall be blessed with abundance and variety of blessings, they shall be happy and prosperous in all things; but take the word as it is in the abstract, "a blessing," the sense is, they shall be a blessing unto others, they shall be a blessing unto the nations; as they were a curse in the nations, so they should be a blessing unto them: Zech. viii. 13, "It shall come to pass, that as ye were a curse among the heathen, O house of Judah, and house of Israel; so will I save you, and ye shall be a blessing," that is, a blessing unto the nations round about them.

The word "hill" must be interpreted before we can well understand this place. By "hill" is meant mount Zion, where the temple was, and Jerusalem; there God recorded his name, set up his worship, and therefore saith, "my hill." Now these were types of Christ and the church in his time. As the Jews therefore came out of Babylon and other places to mount Zion, to Jerusalem, and the temple when rebuilt; so to Christ and the evangelical church, gentiles flocked out of several nations; and so the church and members of it were a blessing unto them, as mount Zion and the inhabitants of it, together with them who dwelt round about it in Judea or Canaan, were a blessing unto the nations. The "blessing" here, I conceive, principally refers to spiritual blessings: he spake before of a "covenant of peace" wrought by Christ, and now of blessings they should have by him; the church under Christ should be blessed with all spiritual blessings, according to that, Eph. i. 3.

"And I will cause the shower to come down in his season." The word for "shower" is, גשם which notes a great and vehement rain, as Kirker saith, even such as shakes the earth. Most make it signify a strong rain; but Ramban, a gentle rain: be it great or gentle, God would give them rain in season. In Deut. xi. 14, you read of the former rain and the latter rain. The former rain was in October, or September, which was upon the sowing of their corn; and this rain came moderately, Joel ii. 23, that so the corn might swell with moisture, root, and grow. The latter rain was in the first month, as Joel ii. 23, that which we call March, though some others put it in May; and it was to make the ear full: their harvest was sooner than ours, their country being hotter. Under these showers heavenly things are figured unto us; as in Deut. xxxii. 2, "My doctrine shall drop as the rain, my speech shall distil as the dew, as the small rain upon the tender herb, and as the showers upon the grass." Here heavenly doctrine is likened unto rain, dew, showers; and in our prophet is set out by showers, heavenly doctrine, and influences of the Spirit, which do make God's people fruitful in all good works, as the rain doth the earth and trees in all kind of herbs, corn, and fruit. In Christ's time there were many such showers, he rained heavenly ones oft upon the people. In 2 Pet. ii. 17, and Jude 12, false teachers are said to be "wells without water, and clouds without rain;" but Christ's apostles were wells full of water, and clouds full of rain, and by those did Christ water divers persons and places.

"There shall be showers of blessing." The Septuagint is, the rain of blessing, or blessed rain. Piscator renders the words, there shall be plentiful rains. They may be called "showers of blessing," because they are from the blessed God, have a blessing in them, and benefit them they fall upon. Some rains are so great, that they do much harm and little good; these should not be such, they should be seasonable and moderate; they should have heavenly doctrines and blessings seasonable, and as they were capable of them.

Ver. 27. "And the tree of the field shall yield her fruit." After the heavens have sent forth their showers, the trees and earth do send forth their fruit. Not only the tree of the garden, but the tree of the field, being watered, brings forth. The Hebrew for "tree" is, עץ which signifies any wood, and synecdochically a tree, because it is wood.

"And the earth shall yield her increase." When there have been seasonable rains, the earth hath brought forth abundantly, in some places thirty, in some sixty, in some a hundred-fold. The word for "increase" is *jebul*, from יבל to bring, because the earth doth bring profit to the owners thereof. By "tree" and "earth" we may understand the higher and meaner sort of people, who under the gospel and showers of it should become fruitful.

"And they shall be safe in their land." In ver. 25, it is said, "They shall dwell safely in the wilderness," and here, "They shall be safe in their land;" they should have safety every where, and the words are repeated to show the certainty thereof.

"When I have broken the bands of their yoke." This "yoke" was the Babylonish captivity, which is called a "yoke," Jer. xxx. 8; and it lay heavily upon them, Isa. xlvii. 6. The bands of this "yoke" were the Babylonish powers, Nebuchadnezzar, his princes, and officers; but God did break the Babylonish empire in pieces by Cyrus and Darius, and so took the yoke off their necks, setting them at liberty. Yokes are burdensome, restrictive, and reproachful: this breaking yokes and bands, and bringing the Jews out of Babylon, typed out the spiritual liberty of the church in Christ's time, when antichristian bands and yokes should be broken, and people brought out of spiritual Babylon.

"And delivered them out of the hands of those that served themselves of them." The Hebrew is, and shall deliver them out of the hands of them who made them to serve. The Babylonians made the Jews to serve and work for them, being captives among them, they exacted service of them; their dealings with the Jews were like the Egyptians, who were cruel task-masters over them.

Obs. 1. Temporal and spiritual blessings are from God; he makes people blessed, and gives them what blessings he pleases. "I will make them and the places round about my hill a blessing." Gen. ix. 1, "God blessed Noah and his sons, and said unto them, Be fruitful, multiply, and replenish the earth:" here, God is the Author of temporal blessings. Gen. xii. 2, of Abraham God said, "I will bless thee, and make thy name great; and thou shalt be a blessing: and I will bless them that bless thee, and curse him that curseth thee: and in thee shall all families of the earth be blessed:" here God shows himself Author of temporal and spiritual blessings. It is peculiar unto God to bless. Balak was out when he said of Balaam, "I wot that he whom thou blessest is blessed, and he whom thou cursest is cursed," Numb. xxii. 6: no, it is not in the power of any creature to bless or curse; men and devils may utter words of blessing or cursing, but they cannot make blessed or cursed: it is God who turns blessings into curses, Mal. ii. 2; and curses into blessings, Neh. xiii. 2.

Obs. 2. Others fare the better for the church's sake. "I will make the places round about my hill a blessing." On the hill of Zion was the temple, the place where God recorded his name, there were the solemn assemblies, the divine ordinances, God's presence; and all that were near in Judea, yea, the nations round about, had some blessing and benefit thereby. They heard of the God of Israel, that he differed from all idol gods; they heard of his laws, that they were more righteous than the laws of the nations; they saw his sabbaths, how strictly they were kept; they heard of the prophets that were in Jerusalem and Israel: did not Naaman, a Syrian, get a blessing from Elisha? 2 Kings v. The wisdom of Solomon had influence into all the places round about Zion, yea, into all the countries far off; the queen of Sheba heard thereof, and it was a blessing unto her. From any nation they might come to Zion, become proselytes, and enjoy what mercies the Jews themselves enjoyed. Micah iv. 1, 2, "In the last days it shall come to pass, that the mountain of the house of the Lord shall be established in the top of the mountains, and it shall be exalted above the hills; and people shall flow unto it. And many nations shall come, and say, Come, and let us go up to the mountain of the Lord, and to the house of the God of Jacob; and he will teach us of his ways, and we will walk in his paths: for the law shall go forth of Zion, and the word of the Lord from Jerusalem." These things are spoken of Christ's times, when the church should be very eminent and conspicuous, like the highest of hills, when the law of faith and the gospel should go out of Zion and Jerusalem, and be a blessing unto all nations.

Obs. 3. God's blessings are seasonable; both temporal and spiritual are in due time. "I will cause the shower to come down in his season," when it shall be a blessing, do much good; there shall be showers of blessing; Lev. xxvi. 4, "I will give you rain in due season, and the land shall yield her increase, and the trees of the field shall yield their fruit." Those rains are seasonable which cause fruitfulness; those are unseasonable rains which hinder or destroy the fruit of the trees and increase of the earth. The Lord observes times and seasons to do sinners good, both for body and soul: Isa. xxx. 18, "He waits, that he may be gracious;" he waits for fit seasons wherein his mercies may come with advantage and acceptance unto men. Isa. lv. 10, 11, "As the rain cometh down, and the snow from heaven, and returneth not thither, but watereth the earth, and maketh it bring forth and bud," which is an argument it came in season, "so shall my word be that goeth out of my mouth: it shall not return unto me void, but it shall accomplish that which I please, it shall prosper in the thing whereto I sent it." God gives his word seasonably, as he doth the rain: Tit. i. 3, "God hath in due times manifested his word through preaching;" the original is, καιροῖς ἰδίοις, in his own times, and those are the due times, the most seasonable times. Gal. iv. 4, "When the fulness of the time was come, God sent forth his Son, made of a woman;" Christ's birth was at the fulness of time, when it was most seasonable: so his death, Rom. v. 6, "In due time," or according to the season, "Christ died for the ungodly." Psal. lxxii. 6, "He shall come down like rain upon the mown grass: as showers that water the earth:" as Solomon was to the people, by his wisdom and justice, like seasonable rains to the grass and earth, much more is God and Christ so to the church; what seasonable dews, droppings, and influences of the Spirit hath it from them, which make it to grow green and flourish! Let us wait for his showers and influences; none can give them but himself, and when he gives them, it is in season.

Obs. 4. The end of God's blessings is, that we may acknowledge and honour him for them. "I will cause the shower to come in season; I will make the trees fruitful, and the earth increase; I will make them safe in their land, and they shall know that I am the Lord." God's blessings have something of God in them; they are glasses, and show us his power, wisdom, goodness, and loving-kindness, each of which oblige us to acknowledge him the author of them, and to honour him for them.

Obs. 5. God's people are sometimes in subjection and bondage to their enemies, who make them to serve, and serve themselves of them. The Jews were under the Babylonish yoke, they served and suffered hard things under the Babylonians; Jer. l. 33, they were oppressed, held under, and put to do servile things. God had told them by the mouth of Jeremiah, chap. xvii. 4, that they should serve their enemies; and their enemies made them to serve, and advantaged themselves by their service: Lam. v. 4—6, "We have drunk our water for money; our wood is sold unto us;" they could neither have water nor fire unless they bought or earned the same with hard labour: "our necks are under persecution, we labour and have no rest;" this iron yoke of captivity is upon us, we labour and serve these Babylonians, and yet we have no rest; we have not bread to satisfy our hunger: they made the young men grinders in the mill, ver. 13. This was the condition of God's people in Babylon under Nebuchadrezzar and Belshazzar, their grand enemies; and such hath been the condition of God's people since Christ's time; they have been often in subjection and bondage to antichrist, to princes and prelates, who have tyrannized over their souls and bodies.

Obs. 6. God hath his time to set his people at liberty, to break the bands and yokes which they are held in. "When I have broken," or shall break, "the bands of their yoke, and delivered them out of the hand of those that made them to serve." The Jews found their bands and yokes so strong, and fast tied about their necks, that they were without hope of ever having them loosed or removed: Ezek. xxxvii. 11, "Our hope is lost;" this captivity we shall never shake off, nor our posterity. And the Babylonians, they held them fast, and refused to let them go, Jer. l. 33; but when the seventy years were expired, (when God's time was come,) he brake the yokes and bands, he knocked them off, and set them at liberty; for, ver. 34, "Their Redeemer is strong; the Lord of hosts is his name." Let enemies' strength be great, let their yokes be of iron, which they put upon his people's necks, and let them be tied on with the bands of human laws, yet God is stronger than they, he will break empires and emperors in pieces, abrogate their laws, loose the bands, pull off the yokes, and set his people at liberty, he will thoroughly plead their cause, give them and their land rest, and disquiet the inhabitants of Babylon. We were under Romish antichristian yokes a long time, the bands of which were loosened somewhat under Edward the Sixth and queen Elizabeth, but they were tying fast again by their successors, and became so heavy that multitudes of our brethren were glad to flee for the burdensomeness of those yokes; others cried unto God to break them in pieces, and his time being come, he hath done it: our antichristian bands, and Babylonish yokes, are loosened and knocked off our necks; let us take heed lest (through the abuse of our liberty) the Lord cast us into a worse and greater bondage than ever.

Obs. 7. Eminent works of God do cause eminent knowledge of God. "And they shall know me, when I have broken the bands of their yoke, and delivered them out of the hand of those that served themselves of them." This was an eminent work of God to bring them out of Babylon, and this bred eminent knowledge of God in them; then they had large experience of God's power, faithfulness, and goodness unto them, that they said, "The Lord liveth, which brought up and which led the seed of the house of Israel out of the north country, and from all countries whither I had driven them," Jer. xxiii. 8. When their captivity was turned, then they had such apprehensions of God as filled their mouths with laughter, and their tongues with singing; Psal. cxxvi. 1—3, then they said, "The Lord hath done great things for us; whereof we are glad."

Ver. 28. *And they shall no more be a prey to the heathen, neither shall the beast of the land devour them; but they shall dwell safely, and none shall make them afraid.*

The Jews had oft been a prey to the heathen; the Egyptians, Amorites, Moabites, Midianites, Philistines, Babylonians, and others, had oft spoiled and served themselves of them, which the Lord laying to heart, doth here graciously promise, that they shall no more be a prey unto the nations. The Hebrew word for "prey" is, *baz*, from בזז to spoil, to pluck from; and the English word is from *prœda*, which some make to be *corpora rerum captarum*, the bodies of things taken: or thus, "prey" is that which men get and devour for whom it was not prepared or intended; as Heb. x. 34, "They took joyfully the spoiling of their goods;" their goods were not prepared or intended for those that got them. The word for "spoiling" is, ἁρπαγὴ, which signifies a "prey," because it is violently gotten and taken.

"Neither shall the beast of the land devour them." The land of Canaan was the "glory of all lands," chap. xx. 6, yet was it not without wild beasts, which did tear and devour, 2 Kings ii. 24; xvii. 25; but now God would chain up the bears and lions, so that they should do no harm. There is another sense to be made of the words, which is, that God would so order the spirits of wicked magistrates, false prophets, and vile, turbulent spirits, that they should not harm his flock: such men formerly had eaten up many of God's people, Ezek. xxii. 25, 27, 29.

"But they shall dwell safely, and none shall make them afraid." To "dwell safely" is a great mercy, to "dwell" so "safely, that none shall make afraid," is extraordinary mercy. Men are subject unto fears, even the best of men, and that several ways: when fire breaks out in a town, when famine or plague are in a city, when storms and tempests are abroad, when wars begin, persecution, imprisonment, banishment, and death are threatened, then fears seize upon persons, and prevail too far with many; but here the Lord promises that his people shall be free from all fears, none shall make them afraid. The word for making afraid, is from חרד which notes, not a slight fear, but such as is with trembling, outwardly manifested, and it ariseth either from inward solicitousness of mind, or from apprehension of evil impending and at hand.

Obs. God's people are in the safest condition of any; they have promises of protection and security from all their enemies, from those without and those within. "They shall no more be a prey to the heathen," that is, those without, the nations abroad in the world; "neither shall the beast of the land devour them," that is, none within, none of them among whom they dwell, not the magistrates, not the prophets, nor the base and vile ones of the earth, none shall harm them, none shall make them afraid, "but they shall dwell safely." Not to be harmed by the beasts of the land, is mercy; but not so much as to be made afraid by them, is greater mercy. None under heaven are in so good a condition for protection and safety, as God's own people. Job xi. 18, 19, "Thou shalt take thy rest in safety. Also thou shalt lie down, and none shall make thee afraid." Job himself, and all he had, should be in safety, free from fear and danger. Jer. xxxi. 10, "Hear the word of the Lord, O ye nations, and declare it in the isles afar off, and say, He that hath scattered Israel will gather him, and keep him, as a shepherd doth his flock;" here the Lord makes proclamation to the nations, and lays it upon them to make it known to others, that he would have a special care of Israel, that is, his people, "and keep them, as a shepherd doth his flock;" he would not suffer the wolves, lions, bears, and dogs, to hurt them, or make them afraid. Isa. xxvii. 3, lest any hurt the Lord's vineyard, he will keep it night and day; he will not slumber nor sleep, but always watch over it; his care for his is the same in the night when wild beasts are abroad, as in the day when they lie hid in their dens. Psal. xxxi. 20, "Thou shalt hide them in the secret of thy presence from the pride of man; thou shalt keep them secretly in a pavilion from the strife of tongues:" God's people are hidden ones, and so secured from the harm of enemies' hands and tongues.

Ver. 29. *And I will raise up for them a plant of renown, and they shall be no more consumed with hunger in the land, neither bear the shame of the heathen any more.*

This verse speaks out the goodness of God unto his flock abundantly, in positive and negative mercies; he would raise up for it a plant, and that of renown, and he would free it from hunger and shame.

"And I will raise up for them." The words may be read thus, For I will raise up for them, and so be a reason of what went before, viz. They shall no more be a prey to the nations, nor be devoured by the beast of the land, but dwell safely without fear; for I will raise up a plant of renown for them. It is true, the Hebrew particle ו sometimes signifies "for," as Psal. lx. 11, "Give us help from trouble; for vain is the help of man;" ושוא is the word; *ve* is there "for;" so Isa. lxiv. 5, "Behold, thou art wroth; for we have sinned," *ve* is rendered "for." But the prophet here is reckoning up variety of promises, mercies, and benefits, which the Lord makes to, and would bestow upon, his people, and therefore *ve* or *va* is here copulative, continuing the series of mercies and promises, "And I will raise up:" you are like plants plucked up by the roots, scattered here and there like dry branches; but "I will raise up a plant for you," even a

"Plant of renown." The Hebrew is, מטע לשם a plant for name: the Septuagint is, a plant of peace: the Chaldee is, a plantation that they may remain: the Vulgate is, a noble sprig, or plant: Vatablus hath it, a plant of a famous name, that should bring glory and renown unto them: Irenæus saith, a plant for fame: Piscator turns the words thus, a noble plant: Campadius and Lavater are to this purpose, a plant for name or renown; as both the French and our translation is. This "plant of renown" is, by some expositors, interpreted to be the christian church, gathered out of all nations, and planted in Christ, which, Isa. lxi. 3, is called "The planting of the Lord;" and, Isa. lx. 21, "The branch of his planting:" others do expound it of Christ; so do Jerom, Theodoret, and divers later expositors: we may take in both, Christ, and the church which springs up out of him. But chiefly Christ is presented to us by this "plant of renown," which is the same with that in Jer. xxiii. 5, where it is said, "I will raise unto David a righteous Branch, and a King shall reign and prosper:" he shows whom he means by that "righteous Branch," viz. Christ, who was to be King, and to execute judgment and justice in the earth. So here, "the plant of renown" is the "righteous Branch;" God would raise the one and the other: hence, Isa. liii. 2, he is said "to grow up before him as a tender plant, and as a root out of a dry ground." God planted him in Zion, and he came from Joseph and Mary, who were like dry ground; and he is oft called "the Branch," and "Branch of righteousness," and "Branch of the Lord," Zech. iii. 8; Jer. xxxiii. 15: and, Isa. iv. 2, "In that day shall the branch of the Lord be beautiful and glorious," or, beauty and glory, as the Hebrew is. It is evident Christ is the "plant" or "branch," and not simply so, but a "plant of renown." That which makes men renowned, is something extraordinary; what is common extends not far, neither procreates renownedness; but when things are beyond, or above, the common course of things, then they spread and beget fame: now Christ had extraordinaries not a few.

1. His conception and birth were extraordinary, Isa. vii. 14; Matt. i. 18, 20; Luke i. 31, 32, 35.

2. His gifts and graces were extraordinary, Isa. xi. 2, 3; Luke ii. 46, 47; John i. 14; iii. 34; Col. i. 19; ii. 3.

3. He did extraordinary things, and many of that kind. He took away the sin of the world, John i. 29. He brake down the partition wall between Jew and gentile, and reconciled both to God, Eph. ii. 14—16. He laid the foundation, and built the christian church, Zech. vi. 12. He brought in everlasting righteousness, Dan. ix. 24; life and immortality, 2 Tim. i. 10. He did many miracles, John iii. 2; vii. 31; ix. 16, 32; xi. 47; xii. 37. He fulfilled all righteousness, Matt. iii. 15. He authorized and enabled men to cast out devils, to cure all diseases, chap. x. 1. He revealed the Father, chap. xi. 27. He forgave sins, Luke v. 20, 21. He foretold things to come, Matt. xxiv. He sent the Comforter, John xvi. 7. He did such works as never any man did, John xv. 24.

4. He suffered more than other men. His sufferings were extraordinary, Isa. liii. 3—7, &c.; Luke xxii. 44; so Matt. xxvii.; Luke xxiii. He trod the winepress of the fierceness and wrath of Almighty

God, Rev. xix. 15. Paul's sufferings made him famous, Phil. i. 13, much more Christ's.

5. He had extraordinary titles; as Immanuel, Isa. vii. 14. The stone of Israel, Gen. xlix. 24. The Lord our Righteousness, Jer. xxiii. 6. The power and wisdom of God, 1 Cor. i. 24. The heir of all things, Heb. i. 2. King of kings, and Lord of lords, Rev. xix. 16. The light of the world, John viii. 12. The glory of Israel, Luke ii. 32. The Prince of life, Acts iii. 15. Judge of quick and dead, Acts x. 42. The image of the invisible God, Col. i. 15. The Head over all things, Eph. i. 22. The Lamb of God, John i. 29. The Mediator between God and man, 1 Tim. i. 5. The Sun of righteousness, Mal. iv. 2. His name is Wonderful, Counsellor, the mighty God, the everlasting Father, the Prince of Peace, Isa. ix. 6.

6. He had extraordinary honour. When he was brought into the world, God commanded all the angels to worship him, Heb. i. 6. He stirred up the spirits of the wise men of the east, directing them by a star to come and worship him, Matt. ii. 11. When he was baptized, heaven was opened, the Spirit descended like a dove, and a voice from heaven said, "This is my beloved Son, in whom I am well pleased," Matt. iii. 16, 17. When he was transfigured, Moses and Elias appeared unto him; and the same voice of the Father was heard again with some addition, "This is my beloved Son, in whom I am well pleased, hear him:" and he committed all judgment to the Son, that "so all men should honour the Son, even as they honour the Father," John v. 23.

Take this "plant of renown" for the christian church, and it is renowned for that it is planted in Christ, Col. ii. 7; Eph. iv. 15; bears the name of Christ, James ii. 7; is his spouse, Rev. xxi. 9; John iii. 29; under his government, Eph. v. 24; freed from the bondage of the ceremonial law, Gal. iv. 1—5; hath clearer manifestations of God's love in Christ, Eph. ii. 7; extends further than ever the Jewish church did to the gentiles, to all nations, Isa. liv. 1—3; lx. 3; lxii. 2; Rev. xxi. 24, 25; and had such miraculous effusion of the Spirit upon many of the members of it, Acts ii. 3, 4; 1 Cor. xii. 8—10; and is the habitation of God, Eph. ii. 22; visible, and irremovable as mount Zion, Micah iv. 1, 2; Matt. xvi. 18; the ground and pillar of truth, 1 Tim. iii. 15.

"And they shall be no more consumed with hunger in the land." In Jacob's days there was a great famine, and his family had been consumed, if Egypt had not afforded relief. In David's days many suffered by the three years' famine then, 2 Sam. xxi. 1. There was a sore famine in Ahab's days, 1 Kings xviii. 2; and questionless many perished with hunger in the siege of Jerusalem, Lam. iv. 9; and many who were scattered abroad, not having to satisfy their hunger, became a prey to hunger itself. The promise here is, "They shall no more be consumed with hunger;" they shall have plenty of all good things, there shall be no corporal nor spiritual hunger: their teachers had been removed into corners, Isa. xxx. 20; their prophets had been cut off, and were glad to be hid in caves, 1 Kings xviii. 4; but God would set up shepherds over them, which should feed them, and they should not be lacking, Jer. xxiii. 4; "their eyes should see them," Isa. xxx. 20. The word for "consumed" is, *asuppe*, from אסף which signifies, to gather together, to take away, and to consume. In time of famine men get together, consult how to relieve themselves, and when all means fail, the famine consumes them, and takes them away. The Septuagint is, They shall not be few in number, they shall have abundance and multiply.

"Neither bear the shame of the heathen any more." The Hebrew word for "shame" is, כלמה which signifies, reproach. The Babylonians, and others where the Jews were scattered, did reproach them, and said, "Sing us one of the songs of Zion," Psal. cxxxvii. 3; you are the holy people, have holy ordinances, and holy songs, "sing us one of those songs." You thought yourselves safe in your holy city, that your God would protect you from all the nations; but where is your God? what is become of your city, temple, and confidences? are you not in our hands? are you not in bondage and captivity? ye are servants unto us, and shall never be at liberty more. Thus did they "bear the shame of the heathen," they were "a reproach, a proverb, a taunt, and a curse, in all places," Jer. xxiv. 9; but God would set them at liberty, roll away their reproach, and make them honourable: they should be a praise: Zeph. iii. 19, "At that time I will undo all that afflict thee: and I will save her that halteth, and gather her that was driven out; and I will get them praise and fame in every land where they have been put to shame:" and, ver. 20, "I will make you a name and a praise among all people of the earth, when I turn back your captivity."

Obs. 1. The Lord Christ himself, his renown, and that the church hath by him, is from the Lord. "I will raise up a plant of renown." Christ is called "the Word," John i. 1; and God made that Word flesh, ver. 14. He is called a "Rod, a Branch," Isa. xi. 1; and God caused that "Rod" to come out of the stem of Jesse, and that "Branch" to grow out of his roots. God planted Christ at first in the virgin's womb, and from thence he grew up (through God's wise disposing of things) to be "a plant of renown:" and, Luke i. 32, the angel said to Mary, "He shall be great, and shall be called the Son of the Highest: and the Lord shall give him the throne of his father David." This God performed, and so made him a man, a "plant of renown:" he gave Christ to the church, he planted him in Zion, Isa. xxviii. 16; and so all the glory the church had by him (which was, and is, exceeding much) came originally from the Lord: Christ is therefore called "The gift of God," John iv. 10.

Obs. 2. Christ is fruitful, and yields good fruit. He is "a plant of renown:" were this plant barren, or did it bear evil fruit, it could not be "a plant of renown," it would be a plant of contempt. This plant is that "tree of life, which bare twelve manner of fruits, and yielded her fruit every month," Rev. xxii. 2. No barrenness at all was on this tree, it had plenty and variety of fruit summer and winter, and the goodness of this fruit the church will tell you of, Cant. ii. 3, "I sat under his shadow with great delight, and his fruit was sweet to my taste." If the shadow of this tree was very delightsome, certainly the fruit of this tree was exceeding sweet. The man sick of the palsy found the sweet of this fruit, when Christ said unto him, "Son, be of good cheer, thy sins are forgiven thee," Matt. ix. 2. Thousands can tell you how sweet the fruit of this tree hath been to their tastes, to their souls: Acts x. 38, "He went about doing good, and healing all that were oppressed of the devil;" those that laboured and travailed, he said unto them, "Come unto me, and I will give you rest," Matt. xi. 28; you shall rest under my shadow, and be refreshed by eating of my fruit. There must needs be excellency and sweetness in the fruit of this plant, because all desire to have it; Hag. ii. 7, he is "the desire of all nations." Let him be the desire of our souls, and let them feed more upon the fruit this "plant of renown" bears; so shall we live, and live more abundantly.

Obs. 3. That the church under Christ shall be

freed from those evils it hath formerly been subject unto, and shall enjoy the contrary good. "I will raise up a plant of renown, and they shall no more be consumed with hunger." They had been; but now they should have plenty, especially of spiritual food, they should know God from the least to the greatest, out of their bellies should flow rivers of water: "neither should they bear the shame of the heathen any more;" they should not be under their reproach, but should be honourable. God hath promised to take away reproachful terms, Isa. lxii. 4, and to give glorious titles to Zion; "Thou shalt no more be called Forsaken, Desolate; but thou shalt be called Hephzi-bah, Beulah:" yea, he hath said, she shall have abundance of glory, Isa. lxvi. 11. Whether the church hath had such glory is questionable: Christ was reproached himself when on earth, called a Samaritan, a seducer, a devil, and what not? So the christians in the primitive times were said to be factious, infant-killers, &c.: and to this day the church of Christ hath lain under the reproach of heathens and antichrist. But the time is coming, that reproaches shall be wiped away, and the church have abundance of glory, Rev. xxi. 3, 4, 10, 11.

Ver. 30. *Thus shall they know that I the Lord their God am with them, and that they, even the house of Israel, are my people, saith the Lord God.*

Here is a further blessing, viz. conviction of the heathens, that God is the God of that flock that hath suffered so much, and is with them. When God should gather his flock out of the countries where it was scattered, set up one shepherd, even his servant David, to be a prince over it, make a covenant of peace with the same, set it at liberty from all enemies, cause it to be in safety on all sides, take away its reproach, put honour upon it, and satisfy it with blessings temporal and spiritual; when these things were done, then should they, that is, the nations, "know that the Lord their God was with them," and thus should they know. By those gracious acts of God, and great mercies bestowed upon the house of Israel, they should be convinced; as when God begun the work in the type, bringing them out of Babylon, the heathens said, "The Lord hath done great things for them," Psal. cxxvi. 2. The Babylonians and others said, "God had cast off his people," exposed them to reproaches and cursing, that he regarded them not, but had left them to be a prey to all the world; but when they saw God appear so eminently for them, then they understood that God had not left or cast off his people so, but that he was still their God, and they his people.

"The house of Israel." The first mention of the "house of Israel," is in Exod. xvi. 31, and the last is in Heb. viii. 10. It is most mentioned in our prophet Ezekiel, well nigh as often as in all the holy Scriptures besides, if not more often. Gen. xxxii. 28, tells you how Jacob's name was turned into "Israel," whence his sons and posterity were called the "house of Israel;" and in process of time, not only those descended from his loins were so called, but all that believed in the seed promised to Jacob were Israelites, and "the house of Israel." It is not here to be confined to the Jews, but to extend to all believers.

Obs. 1. God hath a people in the world whom he doth own, and afford his presence in a special manner. "I the Lord their God am with them, and the house of Israel are my people." God owned the Jews of old above all the people of the earth; Deut. vii. 6, "The Lord thy God hath chosen thee to be a special people unto himself, above all people that are upon the face of the earth." There were multitudes of nations, all which, or any of which, he might have taken, and left the Jews, but he chose only that nation, Deut. x. 15; and therefore saith, Amos iii. 2, "You only have I known of all the families of the earth;" that is, You only have I known to be your God, to be with you, to be mine; others I have known, but not to be in covenant with them, not to afford them my special presence and favours: Lev. xxvi. 11, 12, God did dwell with and walk amongst them. And as then God had the Jews, so now he hath the christians for his people, whom he owns, and is present with, in a peculiar manner, 2 Cor. vi. 16, 18; Rev. ii. 1; Acts xviii. 9, 10, where you may see how God was with Paul, encouraging him to preach, and upon what ground, "for I have much people in this city;" it was in Corinth. Rev. xxi. 3, "Behold, the tabernacle of God is with men, and he will dwell with them, and they shall be his people, and God himself shall be with them, and be their God." God dwells in the christian church, and is with it to bestow variety of choice blessings upon it, and to protect it.

Obs. 2. Sometimes God's dealings with his people are so distinguishing, that heathens are convinced that they have God on their side, and enjoy special favours from him. "Thus shall they know that I the Lord their God am with them, and that they, even the house of Israel, are my people." "Thus," that is, by my dealings with them, which are different from my dealings with others. Dan. iii. when God preserved the three children in the fiery furnace, and delivered them from that hell, then was Nebuchadnezzar mightily convinced, and said, "Blessed be the God of Shadrach, Meshach, and Abed-nego, who hath sent his angel, and delivered his servants that trusted in him, and have changed the king's word, and yielded their bodies, that they might not serve nor worship any God except their own God. Therefore I make a decree, That every people, nation, and language, which speak any thing amiss against the God of Shadrach, Meshach, and Abednego, shall be cut in pieces, and their houses shall be made a dunghill: because there is no other God that can deliver after this sort," ver. 28, 29. So in Christ's time, and the apostles' times, the miracles done by them in several places convinced unbelievers that God was with them. The great things done in our days have made enemies to say, God hath done great things for them.

Ver. 31. *And ye my flock, the flock of my pasture, are men, and I am your God, saith the Lord God.*

This verse is the key to open what was said before. The Lord had spoken oft of his flock, and lest any should take the same literally, here he unfolds his mind, and tells us plainly, his flock are men, not brute creatures. The Hebrew word for "flock" is twice, "And ye my flock, the flock of my pasture." Some read the words in the future, thus, Ye my flock of my pasture shall be men; hitherto ye have been brutish, ye have savoured the things of the earth, and followed after carnal things, but henceforward ye shall be men cleaving to God and heavenly things. We may take them as they are, and find that sense in them which Sanctius hath: I have told you of great things, that my servant David shall be your shepherd, and a prince among you, that ye shall dwell safely in wildernesses, sleep in woods, and that none shall make you afraid; yea, I have told you, that I will free you from bondage, shame, famine, and that I will make you renowned, blessing you with variety and plenty of temporal and spiritual good things: but you see not how these things can be accomplished; you are men full of infirmities, shallow of understanding, apt to doubt and make objections, but I am God, and your God, I have promised and will perform, saith Adonai, Jehovah; my word is truth, and my power shall give being to whatsoever I have said. There is yet another sense of these words, "Ye, the flock of my pasture, are men;" that is, men called out of the world, men renewed by the transforming of your minds, men walking in the Spirit, not after the flesh, men given up to me and my ways, men dealing justly and honestly, men fearing God and pursuing holiness, men of choice spirits and practices. This sense I should approve of, but that the word for "men" is *Adam*, which rather imports "men" with their frailties, than "men" with their excellences.

"The flock of my pasture." God calls them the "flock of his pasture," because he provided for them food for their bodies and souls, as a shepherd doth provide pasture for his sheep; he gave them manna from heaven in former days, and now he gives them his ordinances, his word, the flesh and blood of his Son. God's flock is different from other flocks, and hath different pastures; they are of the world, and feed upon the acorns and husks of the same; but God's flock is picked out of the world, separate from it, and feeds on heavenly dainties.

"I am your God." This is a great and gracious word. What can the Lord say more than this to any, "I am your God?" what can any desire more than to have God theirs? Psal. lxxiii. 25, "Whom have I in heaven but thee? and there is none upon earth that I desire besides thee," saith Asaph: let others desire what they will in heaven or earth, I desire nothing but God himself. Asaph knew that, in having him for his God, he should have all things. When the Lord saith so, he doth engage himself, all his attributes, and whatsoever he hath, unto the people or person he so saith.

Obs. 1. God hath a peculiar people on earth, which he owns and feeds. "Ye my flock, the flock of my pasture." God hath elect, called, justified, and adopted ones, which make up his flock; see 1 Pet. ii. 9, 10; Titus ii. 14. Zech. xiii. 9, "I will say, It is my people." God hath a people refined and tried in the furnace of affliction, which he is not ashamed of, but owns openly, and this people he provides for: Isa. lxv. 13, "Behold, my servants shall eat, but ye shall be hungry: behold, my servants shall drink, but ye shall be thirsty: behold, my servants shall rejoice, but ye shall be ashamed." God's people shall have meat and drink, and that with gladness, Acts ii. 46; they have hidden manna, Rev. ii. 17; they are fed by the Lamb, and drink of living fountains of waters, Rev. vii. 17. They are a peculiar people, and have peculiar meat and drink.

Obs. 2. That of whomsoever God's flock doth consist, yet they are weak and frail creatures. "The flock of my pasture are men." Noah, Lot, Abraham, Jacob, Job, David, Jeremiah, Peter, Paul, John, who were worthies in Israel, yet had their weaknesses, and showed themselves to be men. "Can God prepare a table in the wilderness?" said the house of Israel: and Mary, whom all generations called blessed, we may call an Adamite, the daughter of Adam, for she showed her weakness when she said, "How can this be, seeing I know not a man?" Luke i. 34.

Obs. 3. The happiness and comfort of God's flock lieth in having God to be their God, and his manifestation of it. Ye are men, feeble, helpless things, but I am your God, saith the Lord. Whatsoever is defective in yourselves is redundant in me; as there is nothing but impotency and misery in you, so there is nothing but power, grace, and happiness in me: I have loved you freely, and taken you to be my flock, I have given myself unto you, and all I have with myself, and this I make known unto you.

CHAPTER XXXV.

Ver. 1—5. *Moreover the word of the Lord came unto me, saying, Son of man, set thy face against mount Seir, and prophesy against it, and say unto it, Thus saith the Lord God; Behold, O mount Seir, I am against thee, and I will stretch out mine hand against thee, and I will make thee most desolate. I will lay thy cities waste, and thou shalt be desolate, and thou shalt know that I am the Lord. Because thou hast had a perpetual hatred, and hast shed the blood of the children of Israel by the force of the sword in the time of their calamity, in the time that their iniquity had an end.*

THE Lord having, in the former chapter, laid down many precious promises for the restoration, freedom, and comfort of his afflicted flock, here he comes to deal with the enemies of his church; and in the chapter are,

I. Threatenings of punishments, ver. 2—4, 6—9.

II. The sins moving God thereunto, ver. 5, 10—13.

III. The end of those threatenings and punishments, ver. 4, 11, 15.

Ver. 1, 2. "Moreover the word of the Lord came unto me, saying, Son of man, set thy face against mount Seir." The prophet received the word from, and was empowered by, God to prophesy against "mount Seir." Of setting the face towards, or against, was spoken before, chap. xx. 46; xxi. 2; xxv. 2; where there is a prophecy against Moab and Seir. He must turn himself another way, and speak boldly against mount Seir; that is, against Idumea, wherein mount Seir was, between the lake Asphaltites and Egypt, where Esau and his posterity dwelt, Gen. xxxii. 3, who were called Edomites, or Idumeans.

Ver. 3. "Behold, O mount Seir, I am against thee." Here is a sad message for "mount Seir," or rather the inhabitants of Idumea, who, by a metonymy, are understood thereby. They had God against them, and this declared, Behold, I am against thee, Idumea, I am against all thine inhabitants; thou hast not Israel against thee, but the God of Israel: I that formed Israel, that formed thee; I that made all the world, and can annihilate it at my pleasure; even I am against thee, to infatuate thy counsels, to weaken thy forces, to frustrate thine enterprises, and to bring thee low.

"I will stretch out mine hand against thee." Stretching out the hand is sometimes in mercy, as Prov. i. 24; and sometimes in judgment, as here, and chap. xxv. 13, "I will stretch out mine hand upon Edom, and will cut off man and beast." This posture of the hand imports vehement displeasure in the party that doth it, and readiness to strike. God was very wroth with these Idumeans, and would set his power on work to smite them with destructive judgments.

"I will make thee most desolate." The Hebrew

is, שממה ומשמה which Montanus renders, desolation, and solitariness. The Septuagint is, I will make thee a wilderness, and thou shalt be a wilderness. When the Hebrew is doubled, that is instead of a superlative; here it is desolation and desolation, which implies most desolateness.

Ver. 4. "I will lay thy cities waste." Idumea had many cities, as Teman, Dedan, Bozra, Maresa, Rhinocorura, Raphia, Gaza, Anthedon, Ascalon, and Azotus, all which God threatens to lay waste, chap. xxv. 14. God said he would lay his vengeance upon Edom, and this was made good in the destruction of her cities and people.

"And thou shalt be desolate." God would, by his judgments, cut off man and beast, chap. xxv. 13, and so made it desolate to purpose. When there are neither men nor cattle in a land, how desolate is it!

"And thou shalt know that I am the Lord." When thy cities are laid waste, when man and beast are cut off, then shalt thou know that I am against thee, and that I am the Lord Jehovah, who hath done such things.

Ver. 5. "Because thou hast had a perpetual hatred." The Hebrew is, for that there is to thee a hatred or enmity of old. This is the first sin mentioned, which provoked God to proceed so severely against them, viz. their ancient hatred to the Israelites. Gen. xxvii. 41, Esau hated Jacob, and purposed in his heart to slay him, because he had got the blessing. This hatred descended to the posterity of Esau, against the posterity of Jacob, and began in the womb of Rebekah, when the children struggled together, Gen. xxv. 22. The Edomites were ever enemies to the Israelites in their hearts; and vented it as they had occasion. When the Babylonians took Jerusalem, they cried, "Rase it, rase it, even to the foundation thereof," Psal. cxxxvii. 7.

"And hast shed the blood of the children of Israel by the force of the sword." In the Hebrew it is thus, and hast poured out the children of Israel by the hand of the sword. The Septuagint, thou hast sat down before the house of Israel by deceit, or thou hast laid wait for the house of Israel by the hand of the enemies' sword. The Tigurine translation is, thou hast terrified them by the sword. The Vulgate is, thou hast shut up the sons of Israel into the hand of the sword; thou stoppedst their flight, and so causedst them to fall by the enemies' sword. Junius, by thy hatred thou effectedst it, that the Israelites were diminished by the sword. Munster differs somewhat from all these; saith he, thou hast forced the Israelites upon the sword, thou camest out against them, and drovedst them back when they thought to escape by thy borders. The word *nagar* signifies, to flow, to pour out, and in Hiphel, to make to flow; the sense is, Thou hast slain the children of Israel, and hast made their blood to flow, or poured out their blood. That in Obadiah gives light to this; ver. 14, "Thou shouldest not have stood in the cross way, to cut off those of his that did escape; neither shouldest thou have delivered up those of his that did remain in the day of distress." When the Babylonians entered Jerusalem, some Jews got away, but the Edomites watched for them at a cross way, and there cut them off, and others they delivered up to be cut off. By the hand of the sword, that is, the power of it.

"In the time of their calamity." Here is the aggravation of their sin, that they were cruel when they should have been compassionate: Job vi. 14, "To him that is afflicted pity should be showed." The Edomites, being brethren, should have pitied the Israelites when they suffered such hard things from the Babylonians; but they were without pity: Amos i. 11, "Edom did pursue his brother with the sword, and did cast off all pity:" he was so far from pitying, that he was cruel, even cruelty itself, he cast off all pity, put on nothing but cruelty; they fled to them for succour, and they destroyed them.

"In the time that their iniquity had an end." Here is another aggravation. "Iniquity" may be taken for sin or punishment: if it be taken for sin, the sense runs thus, That the Edomites shed their blood, when their sins were come to the height, and they put into a condition of sinning so no more; now they should have showed them kindness, not have exasperated them. If we take "iniquity" for punishment, the sense is, In the time that they had their utmost punishment for their sin, when God dealt most severely with them, when city and temple were burnt, laid level with the ground, when church and state were wholly ruined, even thou didst then shed their blood, and dealedst cruelly with them.

Obs. 1. The prophets were ordered by God to prophesy for, or against, whom he pleased. "Son of man, set thy face against mount Seir, and prophesy against it." In the chapter before he had prophesied against the shepherds of Israel, and for God's flock, which he did by divine appointment; and here he is appointed to prophesy against the Edomites, who were as wolves to his flock. The prophets spake as they were moved by the Spirit, and unto whom they were directed by God.

Obs. 2. Those that are enemies to God's people, have God an enemy unto them. The Idumeans were enemies to the Jews, and God declares himself to be an enemy unto them: Behold, O mount Seir, I am against thee, and thou shalt feel the force of mine enmity, as thou hast made my people feel the force of thy sword; thou hast stretched thy hand against them, and I will stretch out my hand against thee; thou hast cut them off, and I will cut thee off; I will lay thy cities waste, and make thee desolate. The effects of God's enmity are dreadful. Woe to that land, those cities and people, whom he is against! see Ezek. xxv. xxvi.; and Isa. lxvi. 14, it is said, "The hand of the Lord shall be known toward his servants, and his indignation toward his enemies." God will put a difference between his people and his enemies; for the one, he will put forth his power for their good, and for the other, he will let out his indignation for their destruction.

Obs. 3. God takes notice how the hearts of men stand towards his people, whether they love them, or hate them. Esau and his posterity hated Jacob and his posterity, and this the Lord noted. Not only doth he observe what they do to his people, but also what spirits they have towards his people. Esth. ix. 1, "The Jews had rule over them that hated them." The Lord regarded the spirits of the Babylonians, how malicious they were toward the Jews.

Obs. 4. The nature of hatred is lasting and destructive. "Thou hast had a perpetual hatred, and hast shed the blood of the children of Israel." This hatred had lasted above twelve hundred years, it was a hatred of ages, it ran through generation after generation, and lasted from Esau's days to the Babylonish captivity; and notwithstanding it was so old, yet it had so much spirit and life in it, as to shed the blood of Israelites. Hatred is implacable, and seeks the utter extirpation of what it hates. Cain hated Abel, and slew him; the Jews hated Christ, and they were restless till they had cut him off from the land of the living. David tells you, Psal. xxv. 19, what is the true nature of hatred; saith he, "They hate me with cruel hatred:" not that any hatred is gentle, ("for the mercies of the wicked are cruel," Prov. xii. 10,) but all hatred is cruel and bloody; it would tear the party hated in pieces, and shred him as herbs for the pot.

Obs. 5. God is much incensed against them who deal harshly with his people, being in a suffering condition. These Edomites were bitter and bloody to the Israelites when they were in great affliction, deprived of all their outward comforts, and fled for their lives: they, being in circumstances of intimate relation, should upon those accounts have had pity on them; or if not on those respects, yet for that they were men, and what befalls one condition of men may befall another; but they showed them no mercy, "they shed their blood in the day of their calamity," and therefore God was wroth, laid waste their cities, and shed their blood: Obad. 10, "For thy violence against thy brother Jacob shame shall cover thee, and thou shalt be cut off for ever." Thus God made good what he gave out by the mouth of Solomon, Prov. xvii. 5, "He that is glad at calamities shall not be unpunished."

Ver. 6—9. *Therefore, as I live, saith the Lord God, I will prepare thee unto blood, and blood shall pursue thee: sith thou hast not hated blood, even blood shall pursue thee. Thus will I make mount Seir most desolate, and cut off from it him that passeth out and him that returneth. And I will fill his mountains with his slain men: in thy hills, and in thy valleys, and in all thy rivers, shall they fall that are slain with the sword. I will make thee perpetual desolations, and thy cities shall not return: and ye shall know that I am the Lord.*

In these verses God's proceeding against the Edomites is more particularly laid down.

I. Here is the destruction of themselves, ver. 6, 8.

II. The desolation and misery of their country, ver. 7, 9.

III. The confirmation of both these by an oath, ver. 6.

Ver. 6. "Therefore, as I live, saith the Lord God." Of this divine oath hath oft been spoken: it is used sometimes to confirm promises, as Isa. xlix. 18, 19, but most frequently to confirm threatenings, which are hardly believed. Seeing thou hast been unbrotherlike, unnatural to the Jews, in shedding of their blood, "therefore, as I live," as sure as I am the living God, "I will prepare thee unto blood:" thou thinkest thyself secure, and that no mischief shall come upon thee, but let not me be the living God, if you escape so.

"I will prepare thee unto blood." The Hebrew is, because I will make thee unto blood; that is, I will fit thee, prepare thee, unto blood, I will order things so, that thy blood shall be shed.

"And blood shall pursue thee." God's oath we may refer to these words, and read the verse thus, As I live, saith the Lord God, because I will prepare thee unto blood, even blood shall pursue thee. By "blood" here we may understand, either the "blood" of the Jews which they had shed, and cried for vengeance like the blood of Abel; or by "blood" may be meant bloody men: those who are thine enemies, they shall pursue thee, and shed thy "blood" without pity.

"Sith thou hast not hated blood." Several ways men render these words, but our translation is most approvable, because, or "sith, thou hast not hated blood;" or, if thou hatest not blood. The Edomites did not hate shedding of blood, but were glad of that opportunity they had to cut off the Jews, that so they might ingratiate themselves with the Babylonians.

Ver. 7. "Thus will I make mount Seir most desolate." "Mount Seir" is put for the land of Idumea, which was a pleasant and fruitful land; but this would God make desolation, even desolation; that is, most desolate, it should be void of inhabitants.

"And cut off from it him that passeth out and him that returneth." God would do by Idumea as men do by a wood, cut down the great trees and the lesser, even every tree and every bush. So not only the great ones in Idumea, but the meaner sort, such as travelled from place to place to get a living, those that carried out commodities, and those that brought them in, they should all be cut off, there should be none left to tread in her paths.

Ver. 8. "And I will fill his mountains with his slain men." Idumea had many mountains, which formerly were filled with sheep and oxen, but now they should be filled with the carcasses of slain men, which shows the greatness of the slaughter that should be made of the Idumeans. Such a general destruction of them there should be, as that in all places the dead should lie in the hills, in the valleys, and in the rivers; they fled to those places to secure themselves from the Chaldean army, and there they slew them, and made them meat for the fowls of heaven and fish in the waters.

Ver. 9. "I will make thee perpetual desolations." There is another scripture speaking thus much, that Edom should not only be desolate, but desolate for ever; as Jer. xlix. 17, 18, it should be made like Sodom and Gomorrah, none should abide or dwell there. Sodom and Gomorrah were never built again, but the cities of Edom were, as appears by Mal. i. 4. Jer. xxvii. 7, "All nations shall serve Nebuchadnezzar, and his son, and his son's son, until the very time of his land come: and then many nations and great kings shall serve themselves of him." Edom was afterwards possessed again, and the Edomites so strong and malicious, that they besieged the Israelites, 1 Macc. v. 3. By "perpetual," therefore, we must not understand eternal, that which had no end, but that which was for a long time; so the word עולם doth usually signify; and it is rendered, by some, age, I will make thee the desolations of an age, thirty, a hundred, or a thousand years; for a long season thou shalt be desolate, without cities and inhabitants.

"And thy cities shall not return." Not till after a long time, and then they shall not return unto that glory, strength, and greatness which formerly they were in. After cities and countries are once wasted, they attain not to their former condition oft in many generations.

Obs. 1. Bloody men frequently have bloody ends. Idumea was cruel and bloody against the Israelites, there God prepared her for blood, and said, "Blood shall pursue thee; sith thou hast not hated blood;" blood calls for blood. The Babylonians were bloody and cruel to the Jews, and hear what the Lord saith, Jer. li. 36, "I will plead thy cause, and take vengeance for thee;" and ver. 40, "I will bring them down like lambs to the slaughter, like rams with he goats." God would deal with them as butchers do with such creatures, they take away their lives, and shed their blood. Hosea i. 4, "I will avenge the blood of Jezreel upon the house of Jehu;" he caused the seventy sons of Ahab to be beheaded by the rulers of Jezreel, 2 Kings x. 1, 7, and this blood did God avenge upon his house. 2 Sam. xxi. 1, Saul's house was bloody, he slew the Gibeonites, and seven sons of his were put to death for it, ver. 6, 9; so God pursued blood with blood. In like manner was Joab dealt withal;

he shed innocent blood, and his blood was shed at the horns of the altar, 1 Kings ii. 29, 31.

Obs. 2. When God doth visit wicked ones for shedding of blood, he doth it fully and thoroughly. God would make mount Seir without inhabitant, those that went out, and those that came in, should be cut off. Such a slaughter would he make amongst them, as that the mountains, hills, valleys, and rivers, should be filled with the slain bodies. Isaiah, speaking of God's visiting the Edomites, chap. xxxiv. 6, 7, saith "The sword of the Lord is filled with blood, it is made fat with fatness, and with the blood of lambs and goats, with the fat of the kidneys of rams: for the Lord hath a sacrifice in Bozrah, and a great slaughter in the land of Idumea. And the unicorns shall come down with them, and the bullocks with the bulls; and their land shall be soaked with blood, and their dust made fat with fatness:" great and small, rich and poor, noble and ignoble, should be cut off.

Obs. 3. That according to the time of men's sinning, God doth lengthen out his judgments. Edom had perpetual hatred, and God saith, "I will make thee perpetual desolations." Edom's anger did tear perpetually, Amos i. 11, and God's judgments upon Edom had a perpetuity, Obad. 10, she was cut off for ever. Those that continue long in a course of sinning, God causes sometimes to lie long under severe judgments: the Jews were seventy years in captivity, they had lived long in idolatry.

Ver. 10. *Because thou hast said, These two nations and these two countries shall be mine, and we will possess it; whereas the Lord was there.*

The Idumeans had a fruitful land of their own, that satisfied them not, covetousness and desire of rule possessed them; they thought and said, the whole land of Judea should become theirs; the Babylonians would root the Jews wholly out, leave the land, and so it would fall to their lot and possession.

"These two nations and these two countries." When God brought the Jews out of Egypt into Canaan, they were one nation, and it one land, and so continued till the rent made by Jeroboam, 1 Kings xii. Then ten tribes falling off from Rehoboam, constituted a new kingdom, and so the people and land were divided into two nations and two countries. The one sort were called Ephraim, the house of Israel, Samaritans, and their country, Samaria. The other sort were called Jews, the house of David, and their country, Judea.

"Shall be mine, and we will possess it." Judea and Samaria, saith Edom, "shall be mine," and we Edomites will possess it, and make it one land again, as it was at first: none have so much right to it as we, who are from the same stock, Isaac, and from the elder brother Esau, whereas they were from Jacob; and seeing the Babylonians are come to cut them off, we will join with them to secure ourselves, and recover our right. When the temple and city were destroyed, the Jews carried into captivity, and the land made desolate, the neighbouring nations gaped for and got what they could of their country; Jer. xlix. 1, "Concerning the Ammonites, thus saith the Lord; Hath Israel no sons? hath he no heir? why then doth their king inherit Gad, and his people dwell in his cities?" Ammonites, Edomites, and others said, "Come, let us cut them off from being a nation, and let us take to ourselves the houses of God in possession," Psal. lxxxiii. 4, 12.

"Whereas the Lord was there." The words may be read thus, though the Lord be there: and so they set out the arrogancy and blasphemy of the Edomites, who said, they would possess the land though the Lord was there; he would not hinder them from coming in, sitting down, and continuing in it. Or the word "there" may relate to the Edomites, the Lord was there amongst them, when they said, "These two nations and these two countries shall be mine, and we will possess it." He heard these words, and was displeased at them, coming from pride and bitterness of spirit. Or, thirdly, the words may be taken as we read them, and afford this sense; The Edomites have presumed much, promised great matters to themselves, to have the whole land of Canaan in possession; whereas the Lord was there, and had that land under his patronage, reserving it for temple worship again, as it had had it formerly. That land was the habitation of God, who would not suffer the bloody Edomites, whatever thoughts they had, or attempts they should make, to inhabit that land, and defile his holy mountain with their idolatrous sacrifices; though he did greatly afflict the land, yet he did not wholly desert it.

Obs. 1. Wicked men, the enemies of Zion, do think and design to raise themselves by the ruins and spoils thereof. Edom said, "These two nations and these two countries shall be mine:" whatever is left of the Jews I will have; if there be nothing but the very land, I will take that for a possession, so shall I enrich myself, enlarge my borders, and become great. Such thoughts and hopes were once in Tyrus, she looked to be made by the sufferings of Jerusalem: Ezek. xxvi. 2, "Tyrus said against Jerusalem, She is broken that was the gates of the people: she is turned unto me: I shall be replenished, now she is laid waste." Tyrus expected that Jerusalem being ruined, all the trading should come to her, that the great concourse of people Jerusalem had, should enter her gates, and tread her streets. Obadiah tells us, that the Edomites laid hands on the Jewish substance "in the day of their calamity," ver. 13. They coveted their wealth, thirsted after their land, and sought to advance themselves by their ruins.

Obs. 2. The desires, hopes, and expectation of the wicked come to nought. The Edomites coveted Canaan, hoped and waited for it, but the Lord was there, and disappointed them; they were shortly after the destruction of Jerusalem destroyed by the Babylonians; Jer. xxvii. 3, 6, God had given them into Nebuchadnezzar's hand. David tells you, Psal. cxii. 10, that "the desire of the wicked shall perish;" and Solomon saith, Prov. x. 28, that "the expectation of the wicked shall perish:" they desire, and expect the fulfilling of their desires, but themselves, their desires, and expectations, come to nought. In Prov. xi. 23, Solomon hath a strange expression; it is this, "The expectation of the wicked is wrath." Do men look for wrath? No, but the event of their expectation is such, they meet with the wrath of God. These Edomites looked for the land of the Jews, and lost their own.

Obs. 3. The Lord keeps and disposes of lands as he pleases. He was in Canaan, "the Lord was there;" he was Patron of it, he kept it out of the Edomites' hands, he reserved it for his people again. Hence Obadiah, ver. 17, saith, "The house of Jacob shall possess their possessions;" they shall come again and inhabit their country which God reserved for them. Jer. xlix. 1, 2, when the ten tribes were carried away, the Ammonites, who dwelt near the tribe of Gad, intruded into it, and the cities of it; but see what God saith in ver. 2, "Behold, the days come, saith the Lord, that I will cause an alarm of war to be heard in Rabbah of the Ammonites; and it shall be a desolate heap, and her daughters," that is, lesser towns, "shall be burned with fire: then shall Israel be heir unto them that were his heirs." Israel shall return out of captivity, and possess his own land, and the Ammonites' also, which for a season got part of his.

Obs. 4. Whatever the fate of a land is, whatever calamities it lies under, yet the Lord is not far from it, he is in it. Judea was laid waste, the temple and cities in it ruined, man and beast cut off, enemies on all sides seeking to get it in whole or in part; and notwithstanding it was in such a case, in such danger, "the Lord was there." God is said to dwell in darkness; Psal. xviii. 11, "He made darkness his secret place:" here was a land of darkness, and God hid himself in it, he was there, though the Edomites saw him not. When Babylonians lay waste Zion, drive out the inhabitants thereof, yet they cannot drive out God; he is in Zion, and will abide in Zion. The bear out of the wood not long since was wasting, and the wild beast of the field devouring, they drove many out of our Zion, but they could not drive God out; he was here when the face of all things was lamentable.

Ver. 11. *Therefore, as I live, saith the Lord God, I will even do according to thine anger, and according to thine envy which thou hast used out of thy hatred against them; and I will make myself known among them, when I have judged thee.*

In this and the two next verses, you have a further discovery of mount Seir's sins, and how God would deal with the inhabitants thereof, and all confirmed by oath.

"I will even do according to thine anger." Thou hast been angry with my people, yea, angry unto death, and I will do accordingly: not that God would be angry, but he would punish them severely for their anger. Anger is not a boiling of the blood and spirits about the heart, as some have made it, for that is rather an effect, than the nature of it; it is an inordinate desire of returning evil to him whom we conceive hath wronged us.

"And according to thine envy." The Edomites envied the Jews, who prospered into a kingdom, and grew renowned, chap. xvi. 13, 14. The nature of envy is to grieve at the good of another man, and to think it an evil to ourselves, that we are exceeded by others in any thing; an envious man is afflicted that any is equal to him, or above him.

"Which thou hast used out of thy hatred against them." Hatred is an enmity of the appetite to things or persons, apprehended contrary to its good and contentment. The Edomites looked at the Jews as enemies, as contrary to their good and content, and so hated them. There is a twofold hatred, or rather two degrees of hatred: the first is, aversion, which only flees from what is hated; we hate toads, serpents, and such venomous creatures, and flee from them: the second is, persecution, which pursues the thing hated to destruction: the one respects the evil simply, the other the thing or person in which the evil is apprehended to be. With this last kind or degree of hatred were the Edomites infected, and so envying them sought their ruin.

"And I will make myself known among them, when I have judged thee." I will execute judgment upon thee, deliver thee and thy wealth into the hands of thine enemies, and my servants shall behold my glory in punishing thee, and my mercy in delivering them; my people shall know what a God I am, when I have visited you for your hatred, envy, and wrath against them; they shall find me a God exercising mercy, as you have found me a God executing judgments; as I have made myself known to you in my power and justice, so I will make myself known to them in mercy and loving-kindness.

Obs. 1. One sinful affection sets others on work. The Edomites' hatred set their anger and envy on work. They used these out of their hatred of the Jews; they hated them, and that hatred stirred up their anger to do them harm, and their envy to persecute them unto death. The apostle saith of love, 1 Cor. xiii. 4, 5, it envies not, it is not easily provoked, it thinks no evil; but hatred envies, is easily provoked, and thinks nothing but evil; it is a root of bitterness, and brings forth bitter fruit, it makes use of other affections to accomplish its ends. Jealousy kindles anger, and casts forth hatred; fear sets grief and despair on work. The affections are seated so near one another in the heart, that if one move sinfully, the rest are ready to stir and accompany the same. Let us look well to our affections, for they are dangerous things; Solomon knew it, and therefore, Prov. iv. 23, counsels us to "keep our hearts with all diligence."

Obs. 2. God will deal with men not only according to their evil actions, but according to their evil affections also. "I will even do according to thine anger, and according to thine envy." Men are convinced they must be responsive for evil actions, but not so for evil affections. The Lord puts it out of doubt here, and swears to it, "As I live, saith the Lord God, I will even do according to thine anger," &c. Matt. v. 22, he that "is angry with his brother without a cause shall be in danger of the judgment." Rev. xxi. 8, "The fearful shall have their part in the lake which burneth with fire and brimstone." Edom's rejoicing is mentioned, Obad. 12, among the sins that caused God to cut her off. John iii. 19, "This is the condemnation, that light is come into the world, and men loved darkness." God will deal with men for their sinful fear, sinful joy, and sinful love; for sinful affections as well as sinful actions. Hence are we counselled to put away all bitterness, wrath, and anger, Eph. iv. 31; to mortify inordinate affection, Col. iii. 5.

Obs. 3. After the insulting enemies of Zion are punished, God will show kindness unto Zion, she shall have expressions of his love. "I will make myself known amongst them," that is, those of Zion, "after I have judged thee," that is, the Edomites. They insulted over the Jews, and added affliction to affliction, which the Lord visited them for, and then comforted his afflicted people. The Babylonians were bitter enemies to the Jews, they insulted over them, and said, "Sing us one of the songs of Zion," Psal. cxxxvii. 3; for which you may see how God would deal with them; Isa. xiii. the Medes should destroy them, and that without pity: and what then? chap. xiv. 1—3, "The Lord will have mercy on Jacob, and will yet choose Israel, and set them in their own land; they shall rule over their oppressors, and have rest from their sorrows." After Sennacherib's army was destroyed by the angel of the Lord, which insulted over the Jews, and spake blasphemous things against God and Hezekiah, did not God express love to Hezekiah, and in him to all the Jews, in granting him fifteen years more unto his days? Isa. xxxvii. and xxxviii. When God had judged the Egyptians, he brought forth the Jews, seated them in Canaan, and showed them not a little kindness there, Acts vii. 7.

Ver. 12, 13. *And thou shalt know that I am the Lord, and that I have heard all thy blasphemies which thou hast spoken against the mountains of Israel, saying, They are laid desolate, they are given us to consume. Thus with your mouth ye have boasted against me, and have multiplied your words against me: I have heard them.*

Their blasphemies against God and Israel are here set down, and the notice God took of them.

Ver. 12. "Thou shalt know that I am the Lord, and that I have heard all thy blasphemies." The Hebrew is thus, Thou shalt know that I the Lord have heard all thy blasphemies. The Edomites spake freely against the Jews, thinking God had cast them off, and cared not for them; but when he should judge and punish them, then they should be convinced that he had heard their blasphemies. The word for blasphemy is, *neatzah*, from נאץ to despise, contemptuously to provoke. Kirker saith, it is to provoke with reproachful and cursed speeches: Junius hath it, all thy provocations: the Septuagint, French, and others, have it "blasphemies."

"Which thou hast spoken against the mountains of Israel." By "mountains of Israel," the land and people of Israel are intended; that land was full of mountains, and among others there was the mountain of the Lord, Psal. xxiv. 3; and they spake against that mountain with the rest.

"Saying, They are laid desolate." Are these words so evil as that they should be judged blasphemy? it is not to be doubted but they said more, though it be not here expressed. Obad. 12, Edom spake proudly in the day of Jerusalem's distress; she insulted and gloried in the sufferings and desolations of the people and land: Where is your temple and city, said they, that stood on mount Zion? where are the cattle that fed upon the mountains, and were for sacrifices? They are laid desolate; now where will you have sacrifices? and whither will ye go to sacrifice? Thus they spake blasphemously.

"They are given us to consume." The Jews are now destroyed and gone into captivity, they shall never return to take possession of these mountains again, they are now given to us to be a prey; but who gave them they declare not. God did not give them unto the Edomites, and no other could, for the land was the Lord's: they took the mountains of Israel, their covetous hearts would have them, ver. 10; and what would they do with them? "Consume them," saith our translation; but the Hebrew is, לאכלה to eat; that is, to bring them under our power, and to make use of for our good.

Ver. 13. "Thus with your mouth ye have boasted against me." Ye have magnified against me, saith the Hebrew; you have spoken great words, your mouth hath been wide open against me, and hath lift you up above me, or against me: Obad. 12, is thus, Thou hast magnified thy mouth, which is rendered, "Thou hast spoken proudly." Jer. xlviii. 26, "Moab magnified against the Lord," that is, magnified his mouth against him by speaking arrogant words: Ezek. xxv. 8, Moab said, "Behold, the house of Judah is like unto all the heathen." When men speak proudly, insolently against God or his people, they do magnify with their mouths, or magnify their mouths.

"And have multiplied your words against me." They spake much more than is expressed. They multiply words; the Hebrew word for multiply here is עתר *athar*, which signifies to abound in words, as in prayer. These Edomites did multiply words, words against the Lord, and their words were stout against him.

"I have heard them." Though you thought me shut up in the heavens, that I could not hear at so great a distance, or that I minded not the affairs of the world, especially what words one nation speaks against another, yet saith God, "I have heard them."

Obs. 1. The Lord takes notice of all the bitter, reproachful, and provoking speeches which wicked ones do utter against the church and people of God. "I have heard all thy blaphemies which thou hast spoken against the mountains of Israel." Whether Edom secretly muttered out or openly vented her blasphemies, the Lord heard them. Ammon said, "Aha, against God's sanctuary, when it was profaned; and against the land of Israel, when it was desolate; and against the house of Judah, when they went into captivity," Ezek. xxv. 3; and Moab said, "The house of Judah is like unto all the heathen." When they said so, was the Lord deaf? Zeph. ii. 8, "I have heard the reproach of Moab, and the revilings of the children of Ammon, whereby they have reproached my people, and magnified themselves against their border." The Lord heard and remembered what they said, and made it known to all ages; so did he hear what Tyrus, the sea-city, said insultingly against Jerusalem, Ezek. xxvi. 2; he took notice of the letter that Rehum the chancellor, and Shimshai the scribe, and the rest of their companions, wrote against Jerusalem, Ezra iv. 8. There is nothing said or thought against the people of God, but he is privy to it: Lam. iii. 61, saith Jeremiah, "Thou hast heard their reproach, O Lord, and all their imaginations against me." God heard not only what their wicked tongues spake, but also what their vile hearts imagined, yea, all that they imagined; he hears imaginations.

Obs. 2. God will convince and make blasphemers know that he heard their blasphemies. "And thou shalt know that I the Lord have heard all thy blasphemies." Men blaspheme heaven and earth, they speak proudly against God, Christ, Scriptures, ordinances, and flatter themselves that they shall never more hear of their blasphemies, they think God minds them not; but God hath times to make such black-mouthed wretches to know that he heard them, even all of them. When God visited Edom with the sword, then they should know it; when death comes, or judgment after death, then shall they know what they have said. If men must give account of every idle word they speak, Matt. xii. 36, much more of reviling and blasphemous words.

Obs. 3. The revilings and blasphemies uttered against the people of God, God accounts as spoken against himself. The Edomites spake against the Jews, and the mountains of Israel; but thus saith the Lord, "With your mouth ye have boasted against me, and have multiplied your words against me;" it is myself you reproach and speak against, when you deal so by my people. What Moab said against the house of Judah, Ezek. xxv. 8, God saith was against himself; Jer. xlviii. 26, 42, "Moab hath magnified himself against the Lord." When the wicked spake against God's servants, truth, and sanctuary, David saith they reproached God: Psal. lxxiv. 22, "Arise, O God, plead thine own cause: remember how the foolish man reproacheth thee daily:" it was God they reproached. As wicked men act against God when they act against his people, (2 Chron. xiv. 11; Numb. xvi. 3; with Numb. xxvii. 3,) so they speak against God, when they speak against his people; all the bitter, reviling, and provoking speeches they utter against them, God hears, reckons as vented against himself, and will recompense into the bosoms of his enemies.

Ver. 14, 15. *Thus saith the Lord God; When the whole earth rejoiceth, I will make thee desolate. As thou didst rejoice at the inheritance of the house of Israel, because it was desolate, so will I do unto thee: thou shalt be desolate, O mount Seir, and all Idumea, even all of it: and they shall know that I am the Lord.*

In this conclusion of the chapter, the Lord further declares his mind concerning Idumea, and tells her she shall suffer when all others shall rejoice: and why? Because she rejoiced at the sufferings of the house of Israel.

Ver. 14. "When the whole earth rejoiceth." If we refer the word "earth" to the land of Judea, the sense may be this, When I shall make that whole land rejoice; or, if we understand by "earth," the other parts of the world, the meaning is, When I shall bring my people out of captivity, and cause the whole earth to rejoice thereat, then will I make thee desolate. But scriptures do hint it to us, that Edom was made desolate before the return of the Jews from Babylon: Jeremiah, chap. xxv. and xxvii. tells us that Edom was given to Nebuchadnezzar, and was to drink the cup of God's wrath like other nations; and sundry expositors agree in this, that shortly after the destruction of Jerusalem, Edom was laid desolate. Some other interpretation therefore of the words is to be looked out: we may refer "earth" to Idumea, and then the sense will be this, As the whole land of Idumea hath rejoiced at the desolation of the Israelites, so will I make it wholly desolate. The Hebrew favours this interpretation, for it is thus, As the whole earth, or land, hath rejoiced in desolation, I will do unto thee. Piscator goeth this way, and saith, As all this land, namely, Idumea, hath rejoiced in desolation, so will I do unto thee, O Idumea.

Ver. 15. "As thou didst rejoice at the inheritance of the house of Israel, because it was desolate." The Edomites, when they saw the temple burnt, Jerusalem made even with the ground, and all the land turned into a wilderness, they rejoiced at it: Obad. 12, they of Edom "rejoiced over the children of Judah in the day of their destruction:" when they saw men and beasts cut off, the goodly cities ruined and the pleasant land laid waste, they laughed at it, and said, "Aha, so would we have it."

"The inheritance of the house of Israel." This "inheritance" was the land of Canaan, which God gave to Abraham, Gen. xv. 7, and to his seed, Exod. xxxii. 13; to Jacob and Israel did God give Canaan, the lot of their inheritance, Psal. cv. 11. And this land was the Lord's inheritance, Exod. xv. 17; he dwelt in it, and owned it for his land; and when the wicked invaded it, the psalmist said, "O God, the heathen are come into thine inheritance," Psal. lxxix. 1; and ver. 10 of this chapter, it is said, "The Lord was there." It was both the Lord's and his people's inheritance, and when it was made desolate, the Edomites were glad thereof.

"So will I do unto thee." Thou hast rejoiced at the calamities of others, and others shall rejoice at thy calamities; thou didst insult and speak proudly when the inheritance of the house of Israel was laid waste, and thou shalt meet with such dealings when thine inheritance shall be laid waste; thy cities shall be destroyed, man and beast shall be cut off, and the nations shall be glad of it.

"Thou shalt be desolate, O mount Seir, and all Idumea, even all of it." When sad judgments are upon lands, some parts are spared, as strong holds, great cities, port towns, and the like; but so severely should the enemy deal with "mount Seir" and "Idumea," that nothing should be left, all, even all should be utterly ruined and made desolate.

Obs. 1. The generality of people are apt to go the wrong way, to rejoice at the evil of God's people. All Idumea rejoiced. The whole earth, the people of it, from one end to another, were glad of the sad things that befell the Jews; not some great ones, not one corner of the land, but all the Edomites throughout the land. Thus did the Ammonites also, they generally concurred in the same sin; Ezek. xxv. 3, they cried, "Aha, against the sanctuary, the land of Israel, and house of Judah, when they were profaned and laid waste." This was the practice of the Tyrians, they all with one consent rejoiced at the sufferings of Jerusalem, Ezek. xxvi. 2. When the two witnesses were slain, the inhabitants of the earth rejoiced over them, made merry, and sent gifts one to another, Rev. xi. 10. The greatest part of men are disaffected towards the people of God, and when evil befalls them, they are glad thereof.

Obs. 2. Men thirsting after what is others', do lose what is their own. The Edomites said, "These two nations, and these two countries, shall be mine, and we will possess it," ver. 10; and not long after, they lost their own country, it was made desolate. Achan was not content with what he had, his heart was upon the Babylonish garment, the two hundred shekels of silver, and the wedge of gold of fifty shekels' weight, and by so doing he lost both estate and life, Josh. vii. Pharaoh-necho was ambitious, he sought to enlarge himself, Jer. xlvi. 2; but his army was beaten, and afterwards he lost his country, Ezek. xxx. Many princes coveting and attempting to enlarge their borders by getting from others, have lost themselves and what they had. The dog catching at the shadow, lost what he had in his mouth; many waste and lose their estates at law, while they seek to get that which is other men's.

Obs. 3. The Lord in due time repays the same, or like things, to wicked ones. Edom rejoiced when the inheritance of the house of Israel was laid waste, and God would lay Edom waste, make her desolate, and others should rejoice at her; "So will I do unto thee, thou shalt be desolate," and meet with those that shall laugh at thy calamity. In Obadiah's prophecy, where the carriage of Edom towards the house of Jacob is fully set out, the Lord saith plainly, "As thou hast done, it shall be done unto thee." Nebuchadnezzar spoiled many nations, and had his pleasure on them, and in due time he was spoiled by the nations: Jer. xxvii. 7, "And all nations shall serve him, and his son, and his son's son, until the very time of his land come; and then many nations and great kings shall serve themselves of him;" then they should do to him as he had done to them, chap. l. 15. Adoni-bezek had his thumbs and toes cut off, as he had served others, Judg. i. 7. Many in our days have met with that measure they measured unto others. Prov. xxvi. 27, "Whoso diggeth a pit shall fall therein; and he that rolleth a stone, it will return upon him:" he that intends or doth mischief to others, that mischief will fall upon himself: Psal. ix. 15, "The heathen are sunk down in the pit that they made, in the net which they hid is their own foot taken." Here is *lex talionis*, the just judgment of God upon evil-doers: all the enemies of Zion God will meet with in due time, and return the same or like things into their bosoms. Vide Quistorpius in Jer. l. 15.

Obs. 4. It is nations' and people's own sins that bring desolation upon them. Edom's rejoicing at Jerusalem's calamities, her anger, envy, and hatred, her boasting and blasphemies, caused God to lay her waste, and utterly waste; "O mount Seir, thou shalt be desolate, and all Idumea, even all of it." Had not these sins preceded, that dreadful judgment had not followed. It was wickedness brought in the flood upon the whole world, and it is wickedness brings desolating judgments upon any part of it. "Who gave Jacob for a spoil, and Israel to the robbers? did not the Lord, he against whom we have sinned? for they would not walk in his ways, neither were they obedient unto his law. Therefore he hath poured upon him the fury of his anger, and the strength of battle." It was Jacob's and Israel's sin that exposed them to spoilers and spoiling, Isa. xlii. 24, 25. God was not forward to this work, but would have had them prevented it: Isa. xlviii. 18, 19, "O that thou hadst hearkened to my commandments! then had thy peace been as a river, and thy righteousness as the waves of the sea: thy seed also had been as the sand, and the offspring of thy bowels like the gravel thereof; his name should not have been cut off nor destroyed from before me."

Obs. 5. God's great design in punishing the enemies of his people, and of showing kindness unto them, is to make known himself experimentally unto them. When the wicked feel the weight of his power, strength of his wrath, severity of his justice, they will acknowledge God, and God to be another kind of God than they imagined; when he shall render to them the same or like things to what they have done, they will be convinced of the equity of his ways. So when God's people taste of his loving-kindnesses, partake of choice deliverances, and find the sweetness of his dispensations towards them, then they say, "Among the gods there is none like unto thee, O Lord; neither are there any works like unto thy works," Psal. lxxxvi. 8.

CHAPTER XXXVI.

Ver. 1—7. *Also, thou son of man, prophesy unto the mountains of Israel, and say, Ye mountains of Israel, hear the word of the Lord: Thus saith the Lord God; Because the enemy had said against you, Aha, even the ancient high places are ours in possession: therefore prophesy and say, Thus saith the Lord God; Because they have made you desolate, and swallowed you up on every side, that ye might be a possession unto the residue of the heathen, and ye are taken up in the lips of talkers, and are an infamy of the people: therefore, ye mountains of Israel, hear the word of the Lord God; Thus saith the Lord God to the mountains, and to the hills, to the rivers, and to the valleys, to the desolate wastes, and to the cities that are forsaken, which became a prey and derision to the residue of the heathen that are round about; therefore thus saith the Lord God; Surely in the fire of my jealousy have I spoken against the residue of the heathen, and against all Idumea, which have appointed my land into their possession with the joy of all their heart, with despiteful minds, to cast it out for a prey. Prophesy therefore concerning the land of Israel, and say unto the mountains, and to the hills, to the rivers, and to the valleys, Thus saith the Lord God; Behold, I have spoken in my jealousy and in my fury, because ye have borne the shame of the heathen: therefore thus saith the Lord God; I have lifted up mine hand, Surely the heathen that are about you, they shall bear their shame.*

The Jews being deprived of their comforts, carried into captivity, they suffered hard things, and lay under great reproach among the nations; whereupon the Lord here in this chapter doth,

I. Denounce judgment against the heathen, setting out the causes moving him thereunto, ver. 1—7.

II. Promise mercy to the land of Israel, which is specified in several particulars, ver. 8—15.

III. Show the causes why the Jews were driven out of their country, ver. 16—20.

IV. Set out the ground of their restoration, ver. 21—24.

V. Multiply promises of spiritual and temporal things upon them and their land, ver. 25, to the end.

Ver. 1. "Thou son of man, prophesy unto the mountains of Israel." In the former chapter he prophesied against mount Seir, in this he is to prophesy to the "mountains of Israel;" against that he prophesied judgment, unto these he prophesieth mercies. These "mountains of Israel," by a synecdoche, are put for the whole land of Judea, and by a metonomy, for the people contained therein, or who had lived therein.

"Hear the word of the Lord." The land mourned because the profane nations had laid it waste, and taken possession of it; the Lord therefore calls to the land, and people that had inhabited it, to let them know that the one should not long lie in so desolate a condition, nor the other always be kept out by enemies from their inheritance.

Ver. 2. "Thus saith the Lord God." These words are in ver. 3, 4, 5, 6, and 7, also. The Jews being cast into so low a condition, might think God had forgotten them, and would leave them to perish in the hands of their enemies; to take off such thoughts, he commands the prophet to say in six verses together, "Thus saith the Lord God:" it is not the voice of Ezekiel, but of Jehovah, who is affected with the insolency of your enemies, and the grievous things you suffer.

"Because the enemy hath said against you, Aha." The Hebrew word for "enemy," is from איב to bear ill will, to hate. This enemy principally was the Edomite, who had a perpetual hatred against the Jews, Ezek. xxxv. 5; and the Ammonite, who cried, "Aha," Ezek. xxv. 3, and entered upon the Jews' inheritance, Jer. xlix. 1; with the Moabite, who reproached the people of God, Zeph. ii. 8, 10. These and others were disaffected to the Jews, and hated them, insulted in the day of their calamity, saying, "Aha." The Hebrew is, האח which is an insulting, provoking, scornful word.

"The ancient high places are ours in possession." במות עולם the ancient mountains, which have kept their station and height in all ages. Septuagint is, the everlasting solitudes; Vulgate, the everlasting height. The land of Israel had many high mountains, which being solitary and desolate, the enemy said, "They are ours in possession," we shall inherit them for ever. The Edomites being from Esau, Jacob's elder brother, the Ammonites and Moabites from Lot, Abraham's brother, they challenged the ancient high places of Israel for their possessions, called *excelsa sæculi*, because God and his worship had been there many years, and the land was promised the Jews for ever.

Ver. 3. "Because they have made you desolate, and swallowed you up on every side." The enemies of the Jews were bitter and bloody, they stripped them of what they had, and devoured them; they did eat them up. שאף signifies, to draw in the air, to suck it up, and metaphorically, to swallow, to devour: they did not, like cannibals, eat the flesh of the Jews, but they dealt cruelly with them, not in one place only, but on all sides; those that were their neighbours cut them off and destroyed them round about.

"That ye might be a possession unto the residue of the heathen." So little did they care for the church of God, his people, and their inheritance, they rule over these few Jews that were left. This made Jeremiah to complain, Lam. v. 2, "Our inheritance is turned to strangers, our houses to aliens."

"Ye are taken up in the lips of talkers." In the Hebrew it is thus, and ye have ascended upon the lip of the tongue, or, ye are made to ascend, ye are the common talk of men, as we use to say, table talk. They were made a reproach, a proverb, a taunt, and a curse amongst the people, according to what is written, Jer. xxiv. 9. Junius and Piscator both have it, You are traduced and slandered through the tongues of the nations, they talk at large of you. The "lip of the tongue" is a hebraism, noting a talkative person, as Job xi. 2, A man of lips, is the Hebrew, that is, a man of talk; and Psal. cxl. 11, "Let not an evil speaker," in Hebrew, a man of tongue; such a one utters much evil, and falls under the denomination of an evil speaker.

"And are an infamy of the people." The word דבה "infamy," is from דבב which signifies, to speak, and to relate the evils of others. The enemies of the Jews related what evils they knew or heard of concerning them, and made them infamous. The Septuagint is, a reproach or scorn to the nations.

Ver. 4. "Thus saith the Lord God to the mountains, and to the hills, to the rivers, and to the valleys, to the desolate wastes, and to the cities that are forsaken." He mentioned the "mountains of Israel" before, and "the ancient high places;" here he adds "hills, rivers, valleys, wastes, cities," to show that he would vindicate the whole land from the possession of the nations, who did so greatly vilify his church and people.

"Which became a prey and derision to the residue of the heathen." The heathen did not only spoil and make a prey of Judea, but also deride the Jews, they scoffed at those that were left, and those that were carried away. The word for "derision" is, לעג which notes deriding with scorn and contempt; and therefore by the Septuagint is rendered, καταπάτημα, a trampling under feet, they derided them as worthy to be trodden under feet.

Ver. 5. "Surely in the fire of my jealousy have I spoken against the residue of the heathen," &c. The Hebrew for "surely" is, אם־לא which implies an oath; Unless I have spoken in the fire of my jealousy, let me not be God, let me never be believed. To speak in the fire of jealousy, is a hebraism; saith Pintus, it notes hot displeasure: Psal. lxxix. 5, "Shall thy jealousy burn like fire?" Here the Lord's jealousy was on fire; he was not only angry with the heathen, but in a fiery jealousy, for jealousy is more than anger, Deut. xxix. 20. Men in their jealousy are extremely moved, and carried out with heat and fury to be revenged on those they apprehend have done them wrong; and so God, after the manner of men, is said to speak in the fire of his jealousy against the heathens, who had wronged him, his people, and the land.

"Which have appointed my land into their possession." Judea, saith God, was my land, I dwelt there, and set up my worship there, I gave it my people for a possession; and though at present they be driven out for their sins, yet I keep it for them, and none ought to meddle with, or challenge that land. How is it then that the Edomites and heathens have consulted and determined to take my land into their possession? they are resolved to rob me and my people of our right, to swallow up our inheritance.

"With the joy of all their heart." Joy is a dilatation of the heart from apprehension of good: these heathens apprehended it good that the Jews were cut off and carried away, that hereupon the land should be theirs; this filled them with joy, and made them attempt with all their hearts the possession of the land.

"With despiteful minds, to cast it out for a prey." The words in the Hebrew are thus, in contempt of mind, for expulsion of it for a prey, so Montanus; שאט signifies depopulation, as well as contempt: they were very earnest and violent in depopulating the land, that the seat of its expelled ones might be for a prey; Piscator saith, that its fields or suburbs might be for spoil. The people being slain or carried away captive, the Edomites and others did with malicious minds expose the land to the spoil of any.

Ver. 6. "Behold, I have spoken in my jealousy and in my fury." Here is an addition of fury to jealousy. Fury is heat of anger, or severe anger; fury is anger with vehemence; when it is given to God, it notes the severe, holy, and just indignation of God.

"Because ye have borne the shame of the heathen." The heathen have reproached you, poured scorn and contempt upon you, made you the filth of the world; Zeph. ii. 8, 10, they so reproached them, that it affected God himself; and Jeremiah, Lam. v. 1, was so pierced with the reproachings of the heathen, that he complains, and cries out, "Remember, O Lord, what is come upon us; consider, and behold our reproach." They jeered and scoffed at them for their temple, worship, city, mountains, songs, yea, for their God. Of bearing the shame of the heathen, see chap. xxxiv. 29.

Ver. 7. "Therefore, thus saith the Lord God; I have lifted up mine hand." Lifting up the hand was a gesture used by men in taking of oaths, as Gen. xiv. 22, Abraham lifted up his hand unto the Lord, that was, in swearing; and this metaphorically is applied unto God, who when he swears is said to lift up his hand, so that swearing and lifting up the hand are equivalent. Numb. xiv. 30, "Doubtless ye shall not come into the land, concerning which I sware to make you dwell therein." The Hebrew for "I sware" is, I lifted up my hand. So then, God's lifting up his hand here is, his swearing, that he would make the nations bear their shame for reproaching his people.

"Surely the heathen that are about you, they shall bear their shame." As sure as I am God, the heathen which have made you a reproach, a proverb, a taunt, and a curse, they shall be a reproach, a proverb, a taunt, and a curse; they have made you infamous, and they shall be infamous; they have covered, loaded you with shame, and they shall be covered and loaded with shame.

Obs. 1. God hath a special care of his church when it is in an afflicted condition. The Jews were dispossessed of their land, carried into captivity, made infamous, and their land usurped by others; hereupon the Lord sends Ezekiel unto them, to prophesy comfort unto them in the destruction of their enemies: "Son of man, prophesy unto the mountains of Israel, and say, Hear the word of the Lord." He hath a terrible word for your enemies, a comfortable word for you; threatenings for them, promises for you. Though men hated his people, yet God himself pitied them; though men swallowed up their habitation, yet God would restore it to them again. Jer. xxx. 6—10, "Wherefore do I see every man with his hands on his loins, as a woman in travail, and all faces are turned into paleness? Alas! for that day is great, so that none is like it: it is even the time of Jacob's trouble; but he shall be saved out of it. For it shall come to pass in that day, saith the Lord of hosts, that I will break his yoke from off thy neck, and will burst thy bonds, and strangers shall no more serve themselves of him: but they shall serve the Lord their God, and David their king, whom I will raise up unto them. Therefore fear thou not, O my servant Jacob, saith the Lord; neither be dismayed, O Israel: for, lo, I will save thee from afar, and thy seed from the land of their captivity; and Jacob shall return, and shall be in rest, and be quiet, and none shall make him afraid." The church was in great affliction, like a woman in travail; and here the Lord showed his goodness towards it, and special care over it; he would break Babylonish yokes and bonds, set it at liberty, restore it to the former, yea, a better condition, viz. such privileges and security it never had.

Obs. 2. When God's people are under affliction, their enemies are glad thereof, and take advantage to disgrace them, and make a prey of what was theirs. The Israelites suffered hard things by the Babylonians; upon this the enemies cried, "Aha," they were glad at the heart, they talked their pleasures of them, and made them the infamy of the people; they swallowed them up on every side, and said, The mountains of Israel are ours, and we will possess the ancient high places. When Zion goes down, Babylon rejoices, the heathens disgrace and devour it, adding affliction to the afflicted; see Zeph. ii. 8; Obad. 10—14. All the enemies which heard of Zion's trouble were glad, Lam. i. 21; they reproached Zion and her children, chap. ii. 15, 16, and said, "They shall no more sojourn there," chap. iv. 15; Judea shall never be repossessed by them, it shall be ours.

Obs. 3. That rejoicing at the sufferings of God's people, disgracing and wronging of them, doth greatly offend the Lord. "Because the enemy cried, Aha," defamed the Jews, arrogated the land for their possession, therefore the Lord spake against them in the fire of his jealousy, and in his fury; he was exceedingly wroth, and would deal severely with them; it went to his heart, and inflamed his spirit, that his people who were so dear unto him, should be derided, despitefully used, what was theirs made a prey of, and that by heathens. Jer. l. 11, 12, "Because ye were glad, because ye rejoiced, O ye destroyers of mine heritage, because ye are grown fat as the heifer at grass, and bellow as bulls; your mother shall be sore confounded;" that is, the city Babylon, or the land of Chaldea, or both; because the Babylonians had dealt so by the people of God and their land, God would not only confound them, but sorely confound them.

Obs. 4. Those that make the people of God infamous, shall themselves be made infamous. The nations made the Jews the infamy of the people, they loaded them with reproaches and shame; and God swears, "Surely the heathen shall bear their shame." Do you mock and hiss at my people? ye shall be mocked and hissed at. In Lam. ii. 15, 16, you have the carriage of all towards Jerusalem; they clapped their hands, they hissed, they wagged their heads, they opened their mouths, and gnashed their teeth, and said, "Is this the city men call The perfection of beauty? we have swallowed her up; this is the day we have looked for." In other places you may observe how God returned their revilings upon their heads: Jer. xlix. 17, "Edom shall be a desolation; every one that goeth by it shall be astonished, and shall hiss at all the plagues thereof." Nineveh was proud and insulted, and God made her infamous; all that passed by hissed and wagged the hand at her, Zeph. ii. 15. Babylon had the same measure; Jer. li. 37, she was made "an hissing, without an inhabitant;" so chap. l. 13; and Isaiah tells us the insulting proverb which was used against the king and city of Babylon when they were destroyed, Isa. xiv. 4, "How hath the oppressor ceased! the golden city ceased!"

Ver. 8—15. *But ye, O mountains of Israel, ye shall shoot forth your branches, and yield your fruit to my people of Israel; for they are at hand to come. For, behold, I am for you, and I will turn unto you, and ye shall be tilled and sown: and I will multiply men upon you, all the house of Israel, even all of it: and the cities shall be inhabited, and the wastes shall be builded: and I will multiply upon you man and beast; and they shall increase and bring fruit: and I will settle you after your old estates, and will do better unto you than at your beginnings: and ye shall know that I am the Lord. Yea, I will cause men to walk upon you, even my people Israel; and they shall possess thee, and thou shalt be their inheritance, and thou shalt no more henceforth bereave them of men. Thus saith the Lord God; Because they say unto you, Thou land devourest up men, and hast bereaved thy nations; therefore thou shalt devour men no more, neither bereave thy nations any more, saith the Lord God. Neither will I cause men to hear in thee the shame of the heathen any more, neither shalt thou bear the reproach of the people any more, neither shalt thou cause thy nations to fall any more, saith the Lord God.*

These eight verses are the second general part of the chapter, containing rich promises of favour and mercy unto the afflicted Jews; and they are,

I. Fruitfulness of their country, ver. 8.
II. Return into it, *ibid.*
III. God's turning unto them, ver. 9.
IV. Multiplication of men and beasts, ver. 10, 11.
V. Rebuilding of their cities, waste places, and reinhabiting of them, ver. 10, 12.
VI. Settling them in a better condition than ever, ver. 11.
VII. Freedom,
1. From destruction, ver. 12—14.
2. From the reproachings of enemies, ver. 15.

Ver. 8. "But ye, O mountains of Israel, ye shall shoot forth your branches." In the time of Jerusalem's siege, the land of Israel was much wasted, the fruitful and useful trees cut down; and during the captivity, it was overrun with briers and thorns, Isa. v. 6; xxxii. 13; yea, all the land was so, chap. vii. 24. But here God's promise is, that the mountains of Israel should be fruitful, they should shoot forth their branches; vines and other trees full of branches should be planted there, and thrive.

"And yield your fruit to my people of Israel." Strangers shall not eat your fruit, as heretofore, but my people shall have the benefit thereof. Israelites shall eat your fruit, not Edomites or Babylonians.

"For they are at hand to come." Here is the reason given why the mountains and land of Canaan should bring forth and yield increase; it was because the time drew near of the Jews returning out of captivity. In the creation God did bid the earth bring forth, prepared a Paradise for man, and then brought man into it; so here he takes care that the mountains and countries should bring forth, for that his people were to come into it. The Chaldee hath it, the day of redemption shall come; and the Septuagint, ὅτι ἐλπίζωσι τοῦ ἐλθεῖν. Seventy years was but a little time unto God, some part of which was expired, and the time hastened for their deliverance.

Ver. 9. "For, behold, I am for you, and I will turn unto you." God had formerly been against them, as appears, Ezek. v. 8; xxi. 3; xv. 7; and they had found it so, being driven out of their own land into Babylon, where God tells them to their comfort, Behold, I am for you, and for the mountains of Israel which have been laid waste; I will turn unto you, and look upon you in mercy.

"Ye shall be tilled and sown." Where bushes, nettles, and briers grew before, there should be ploughing, sowing, and corn in abundance.

Ver. 10. "And I will multiply men upon you," &c. This verse and the next further sets out the effect of God's turning to the mountains; they should abound with men and beasts, the whole land should be possessed, the waste places builded, and the cities inhabited, and both men and beast should be fruitful.

"All the house of Israel, even all of it." When this was fulfilled doth not appear: few of the ten tribes returned, and not all of the other two.

Ver. 11. "I will settle you after your old estates." The Hebrew is, I will make you to dwell according to your antiquities, as you dwelt in Joshua's time, or as you were settled before your captivity; then you had peace, plenty, and many accommodations, which you shall have again, and more; for it follows,

"And will do better unto you than at your beginnings." God had done great things for them formerly; they abounded so in riches, stately buildings, wise, holy, and strong men, in famous victories, and in plenty of all good things, that they exceeded all people; yet God promises here to do better unto them than at the beginning. When this was made good is greatly questioned. Some answer it thus, That when they first came into Canaan, they were low, poor, and not in a capacity to build a temple; but when they returned out of Babylon, they went about and built a temple: but this temple exceeded not the former temple in greatness, richness, ceremony, sanctity, multitude of priests or prophets, Ezra iii. 12. Others say, That after their return from their captivity their bounds were more enlarged than ever before; which they clear from Isa. xlix. 19, 20; Zech. ii. 8, 9; and therein God did better unto them than at the beginning. Others refer this promise to Christ's time, wherein they had choicer mercies than ever, viz. the presence, doctrine, and miracles of Christ, which made the glory of the latter temple greater than the former; according to what Haggai had said, chap. ii. 9. But how if we could not assign a time of God's doing better unto them than at the beginning? that is human weakness; God is faithful, and what he saith he doth accomplish; it was so.

Ver. 12. "And thou shalt no more henceforth bereave them of men." He speaks of the land of Canaan, which the Jews should possess, inherit, and not be deprived of, that is, not for a long time. The words "no more," must not signify for ever, because the Jews were after a long time deprived of their land by the Romans.

Ver. 13. "They say unto you, Thou land devourest up men, and hast bereaved thy nations." This was a charge laid upon Canaan, that she devoured men, that she was destructive to her own children: she was not so called because of her fruitfulness, which caused men to surfeit and so die; but either in regard of the civil wars which were amongst the heathens when they possessed it, which made the spies (Numb. xiii. 32) say, "It is a land that eateth up the inhabitants thereof;" or because that when the Jews possessed it, the nations round about hating them made incursions upon them often, and so destroyed multitudes of the inhabitants; and when they besieged any place of note, as Samaria and Jerusalem, the plague and famine consumed many. The famine was so sore, that women ate their own children, 2 Kings vi. 28, 29; Lam. iv. 10; fathers ate their sons, and sons their fathers, Ezek. v. 10. And as it vomited out the heathens before, (Lev. xviii. 25, 28,) so it served the ten tribes and other two afterwards.

Ver. 14. "Therefore thou shalt devour men no more, neither bereave thy nations any more." Here God promiseth to take away that imputation, and to put them into such a condition as that they should for a long season be free from sword, famine, plague, and such straits as caused consumption of men. The words "bereave thy nations any more," are, in Hebrew, nor cause thy nations to fall any more; they fell by several judgments, but now God being turned unto them, would maintain them in peace, honour, and safety.

Ver. 15. "Neither will I cause men to hear in thee the shame of the heathen any more." They had ofttimes been reproached by the heathen, and borne their shame, ver. 6; but now God in his wise providence would order things so, that heathens should not revile them, but speak honourably of them, as Psal. cxxvi. 2, the heathen said, "The Lord hath done great things for them."

"Neither shall thou bear the reproach of the heathen any more." They reproached one another; the people mocked at the prophets, 2 Chron. xxxvi. 16; Jer. xx. 7, and children behaved themselves proudly and basely against the ancient and the honourable, Isa. iii. 5; but God would take away this evil from them, and cause them to speak well one of another.

"Neither shalt thou cause thy nations to fall any more." The Hebrew is, thy nations; thou shalt not expose thy people to ruin and destruction, by famine, plague, or war. The sense of the whole verse is, that God would turn those evils and curses they endured formerly into blessings.

Obs. 1. When God pours out contempt and shame upon the enemies of his people, he will pour out blessings and mercies upon them. The heathens shall bear their shame, but ye, O mountains of Israel, shall shoot forth your branches; and ye shall have the former and latter rains, and bring forth in abundance. Canaan was God's land, and he had a special eye to that, and would honour it, when he stained the glory of other nations.

Obs. 2. The fruitfulness of mountains and lands depends upon God; he makes them so at his pleasure, by his command and blessing. "O mountains of Israel, ye shall shoot forth your branches, and yield your fruit." Men's wickedness moves God to make lands barren and desolate, Jer. xii. 4; but it is his good pleasure and free grace that moves him to make a land fruitful: Acts xiv. 17, rain and fruitful seasons are the gift of God.

Obs. 3. God is provident for his people when he removes them from place to place, he will not have them to come into empty places. The mountains must shoot forth their branches, and the land yield her fruit; for the Jews were at hand to come. When Jacob went down to Egypt, with his family,

God provided the best of the land for them, Gen. xlvii. When the Jews came first to Canaan, it flowed with milk and honey, it abounded with all good things needful for them.

Obs. 4. When God is reconciled to a people, then he multiplies blessings upon them, then he makes their land bring forth, and themselves and their cattle to increase. "I am for you, and will turn unto you, and ye shall be tilled and sown; I will multiply upon you man and beast, and they shall increase and bring forth fruit." God's favour hath all blessings in the womb of it, and upon what land or people soever that falls, it will make them fruitful; when God is for a people, then he comes unto them as the rain, as the former and latter rain, Hos. vi. 3; he hath various and seasonable blessings for them. Zeph. iii. 20, "At that time will I bring you again, even in the time that I gather you: for I will make you a name and a praise among all people of the earth, when I turn back your captivity before your eyes." When God turned back their captivity he was for them, and turned unto them, they had his favour, and then he would bestow such blessings upon them as would make them renowned among all people: see Jer. xxxi. 10—14.

Obs. 5. God's dealings with his people are best at last; they may have much kindness and mercy in the morning, but they shall have more in the evening. "I will settle you after your old estates, and will do better unto you than at your beginnings." The Jews had the best wine at last; they had milk and honey before, but the feast of fat things full of marrow, and of wines on the lees well refined, were at the latter end of their day given in; they had Christ and the gospel at last. Abraham had much of the world at first, and his Isaac afterward. Job xlii. 12, "God blessed the latter end of Job more than his beginning." Simeon in his latter days saw Christ, and had him in his arms, Luke ii.

Obs. 6. Wicked men do turn the judgments of God upon his land and people into a reproach unto them. Because God for the sins of his people laid the land waste, and cut them off by sore judgments, or removed them into captivity, therefore the heathens reproached Canaan, and said, "Thou land devourest men, and hast bereaved thy nations." They called Emmanuel's land a cursed and bloody land, that did eat up her own children; this was a great reproach to heaven and earth. God's judgments should have caused fear, and taught them to have learned righteousness; for if God spared not the green tree, what will become of the dry trees?

Obs. 7. Such is the goodness of God, that he takes occasion from the wickedness of his people's enemies, to do his people good. Because the heathens said, "Thou land devourest up men, and hast bereaved thy nations," because they reproached the Jews and their land thus, therefore saith God, "Thou shalt devour men no more, neither bereave thy nations any more;" I will bless thee with peace, plenty, and safety; there shall be no wars, no famines, no plagues, nor other judgments to devour the people of the land.

Obs. 8. God in his time takes away the evils that are upon his people, and turns them into blessings. "Neither will I cause men to hear in thee the shame of the heathen any more, neither shalt thou bear the reproach of the people any more, neither shalt thou cause thy nations to fall any more:" these evils will I take away from thee, and not only so, but I will bring in the contrary blessings; instead of shame and reproach, thou shalt have honour, praise, and renown; instead of destroying thy people and nations, thou shalt multiply thy people, and have nations to serve thee, Isa. lx. 12—14.

Ver. 16—20. *Moreover the word of the Lord came unto me, saying, Son of man, when the house of Israel dwelt in their own land, they defiled it by their own way and by their doings: their way was before me as the uncleanness of a removed woman. Wherefore I poured my fury upon them for the blood that they had shed upon the land, and for their idols wherewith they had polluted it: and I scattered them among the heathen, and they were dispersed through the countries: according to their way and according to their doings I judged them. And when they entered unto the heathen, whither they went, they profaned my holy name, when they said to them, These are the people of the Lord, and are gone forth out of his land.*

Men being apt to make perverse constructions of the judgments of God, and to censure his ways to be unequal; here he gives account of his proceedings towards his people, and shows the true grounds and causes why he drove them out of their country; which are set down,

I. In general, ver. 17, amplified by a similitude.

II. In particular, ver. 18, blood and idolatry, which are repeated in general terms, ver. 19.

III. After these he shows what their carriage was in their enemies' land, ver. 20.

Ver. 16. "Moreover the word of the Lord came unto me, saying." The prophet having declared God's jealousy and fury against the enemies of his people, comforted them being in captivity with many choice promises: here he is commissioned by the Lord to speak out the causes which moved God to cast them into that condition.

Ver. 17. "When the house of Israel dwelt in their own land." By "house of Israel," understand not the two or ten tribes, but the whole twelve tribes who possessed Canaan, which is called "their own land," because promised and given unto them by God for their inheritance, Psal. cv. 10, 11.

"They defiled it by their own way and by their doings." The Hebrew is, in their own ways, and in their own doings; they followed their own devices, inventions, desires, customs, manners; they did what was right in their own eyes, and so defiled the land.

"Their way was before me as the uncleanness of a removed woman." Their way was very loathsome before the Lord, he greatly abhorred their manners and practices.

Ver. 18. "Wherefore I poured my fury upon them." They had committed heinous sins, and continued long in them without repentance; this is evident from the Lord's "fury." He is not in fury for small sins, nor presently furious for great sins; but when men go on from day to day in them, his anger grows hotter and hotter, and at last riseth up into fury: and this being increased, the Lord would not let it out in petty judgments, as it were drop by drop, but pour it out in greater judgments, like as the sea pours out water when a breach is in the banks, it pours out water with violence, and drowns up all the adjacent country.

"For the blood that they had shed upon the land." They shed the blood of the prophets, 2 Chron. xxiv. 21; Matt. xxiii. 37; of innocent ones, 2 Kings xxi. 16. They had unjust and unnatural wars, 2 Chron. xxviii. 9; and so shed blood in abundance, Ezek. vii. 23. They poured out blood upon the land, and God poured out fury upon them; it is the same word in the Hebrew for shedding and pouring out.

"And for their idols wherewith they had polluted it." They had many idols, the land was full of them, Isa. ii. 8; which they worshipping defiled the land. The word for "idols" is, גלולים, which Junius renders, dunghill gods; and Piscator, dunghills, for that no dunghill doth so defile a land as idols and idolatry; hence idols are called "abominations," Jer. xxxii. 34; "shames," Hos. ix. 10; "devils," Deut. xxxii. 17.

Ver. 19. "And I scattered them among the heathen." They had learned the manners of the heathen, got their idols, and served them; and for it God "scattered them among the heathen;" they had heathenish spirits, chosen heathenish gods, and so deserved to be driven into heathenish countries.

"And they were dispersed through the countries." The Hebrew word for disperse is, זרה which signifies to disperse by fanning: God had fanned them out of their own land, and dispersed them as chaff before the wind into divers lands; they went from country to country, yea, through whole countries into Chaldea.

"According to their way and according to their doings I judged them." Men might wonder God should deal so with his people, as to pour out his fury upon them, drive them out of their own land, and disperse them amongst heathens, who were his and their enemies; this might carry a face of cruelty; but the Lord clears himself, and shows the equity of his proceedings. "I judged them," that is, I dealt with or punished them according to their ways and doings; had they not deserved such hard things at my hands, I should not have executed them. They drove me out of my sanctuary, and far from it, Ezek. viii. 6; they cast me off, Jer. ii. 13; and is it not equal that I should drive them out of my land, and cast them into foreign lands? Let all the world judge.

Ver. 20. "And when they entered unto the heathen whither they went, they profaned my holy name." When the Jews came amongst the heathen, they profaned his holy name: which is done two ways; either *formaliter*, when men's own words or actions are profane, prostituting the name of God to dishonour; or *occasionaliter*, when occasion is given to others by their words and actions, to profane the holy name of God; as David by his sinful action with Bathsheba, gave occasion to the enemies of God to blaspheme, 2 Sam. xii. 14. And this was the case here; for the Babylonians said,

"These are the people of the Lord, and are gone forth out of his land." The Jews being under sad judgments of God, should have learned righteousness; but they being neither affected with the honour of God, care of their salvation, nor with fear of offending the heathens, persevered in their wicked ways and idolatrous practices, Ezek. xx. 32; whereupon the heathens said, "These are the people of the Lord." They boast of their God to be a holy, omnipotent, and faithful God, but you may know what their God is by their unholy practices: had he been omnipotent, as they say, he would have kept them out of our hands; but he could not, which shows our gods are stronger than he; or if he could, he would not: he was not faithful unto his people, as our gods are unto us, "they are gone forth out of his land," whereas we abide in ours; had their God been such as ours are, he would have protected them, and prevented their casting out of his land.

Obs. 1. The wicked ways of men, especially those of blood and idolatry, are loathsome unto God. "Their way was before me as the uncleanness of a removed woman;" that is, extreme loathsome. All sin is defiling, and so loathsome, abominable unto God, who is holy, yea, holiness itself; but murder and idolatry are most hateful, and most loathsome unto him; Psal. v. 6, the bloody man is abhorred of God: and he lets him not live out half his days, Psal. lv. 23; and, Jer. xliv. 4, the Lord calls idolatry, an abominable thing which he hates; he hates and loathes it infinitely.

Obs. 2. Men by their own sinful doings, do bring evils, mischief, and destruction upon themselves. "When the house of Israel dwelt in their own land, they defiled it by their own way and by their doings; wherefore I poured my fury upon them." Had they not sinned, nor walked in evil ways, they had not met with fury; but because their ways were wicked, bloody, and idolatrous, therefore they had fury, and fury poured out abundantly, their own evil doings brought destruction upon them. Prov. xi. 5, "The wicked shall fall by his own wickedness." Jer. ii. 19, "Thine own wickedness shall correct thee." Jerusalem's own sin was her ruin. And David tells us how God will deal with wicked men, Psal. xciv. 23, "He shall bring upon them their own iniquity, and shall cut them off in their own wickedness." It is ill work wicked ones are about, they make fetters for their own feet, and build houses for to fall upon their own heads; so mischievous is the nature of sin, that it damnifies and destroys the parents of it.

Obs. 3. What judgments soever God brings upon sinners, he is just and righteous in so doing. God poured fury upon them, he drove them out of their own country, he scattered them up and down among heathens, whose language they understood not, who were bitter and harsh towards them; and all this was not more, no, not so much as their sins deserved: "According to their way and their doings, I judged them," saith the Lord; I did them no wrong, they had not any cause to complain of me, the fault was their own. Whatever God's proceedings are with any nation, family, or person, he is righteous; for, Psal. cxlv. 17, "The Lord is righteous in all his ways, and holy in all his works;" there is no spot cleaves to his hand, or any action thereof.

Obs. 4. It is a grievous, provoking thing, when God's people, who profess his truth and worship, give occasion to the enemies thereof to blaspheme and speak reproachfully. The Jews being among the Babylonians spake and did such things as gave occasion to blaspheme; "When they entered unto the heathen, they profaned my holy name." This was a great grief and provocation of God, that his people being afflicted for their sins, yet should carry it so sinfully as to give them advantage of dishonouring God, his truths, worship, and servants. Isa. lii. 5, God complains that his name was blasphemed continually every day. The Babylonians watched the Jews, and caught all advantages to profane the name of the Lord; this was their daily language, "These are the people of the Lord, and are gone forth out of his land;" he could not, or would not, keep them out of our hands; he is a weak, unfaithful, unholy God, and his people are like unto him. When David gave occasion to the enemies of the Lord to blaspheme, it brought forth sad effects, or rather had sad consequences, the death of the child, and sword at his door for ever, 2 Sam. xii. Those therefore who profess the true religion, should be exceeding careful, wherever they be come, that they walk answerable to the religion they profess, that they avoid all sin, and do good, that so the name of God may be glorified, and not profaned or blasphemed.

Obs. 5. Heathens and heathenish spirits are glad of occasions and advantages against the true God, his ways, and people. The Babylonians said, "These are the people of the Lord, and are gone forth out of his land." They were glad they had matter to insult and blaspheme: What is your God better than ours? ye do the things we do; and what is his land better than this land? have not we corn, wine, and oil, milk and honey, as well and as much as you had in that land? Why is Canaan so cried up, and Jerusalem so magnified? our Assyria and our city Babylon are as good, as excellent as they, yea, far beyond them.

Ver. 21—24. *But I had pity for mine holy name, which the house of Israel had profaned among the heathen, whither they went. Therefore say unto the house of Israel, Thus saith the Lord God; I do not this for your sakes, O house of Israel, but for mine holy name's sake, which ye have profaned among the heathen, whither ye went. And I will sanctify my great name, which was profaned among the heathen, which ye have profaned in the midst of them; and the heathen shall know that I am the Lord, saith the Lord God, when I shall be sanctified in you before their eyes. For I will take you from among the heathen, and gather you out of all countries, and will bring you into your own land.*

These verses contain the ground of the Jews' restoration, which is the fourth general part of the chapter: they being in captivity, and sinning there greatly, they caused the name of God to be profaned by the heathens; and so, deserving nothing but confusion, he pitied them, and for his name's sake delivered them; which name of God is set out by two adjuncts, or epithets:

I. Holy.

II. Great.

Ver. 21. "But I had pity for mine holy name." The Hebrew is, And I spared upon the name of my holiness; that is, I spared them upon the account of my holy name; I would not suffer that to be profaned so by the heathen, and therefore did deliver them. The Septuagint is, I spared them for my holy name's sake; I had a tender respect unto my name, which being holy, I would not suffer to lie under heathenish obloquies.

"Which the house of Israel had profaned among the heathen, whither they went." God is styled in Scripture, "The Holy One of Jacob," Isa. xxix. 23; "The Holy One of Israel," Psal. lxxviii. 41; "The Holy One," Isa. xl. 25. And the Jews, above all nations and people in the world, should have had a special care of the name of their God, that the holiness thereof might have been maintained; but they forgat God in Babylon, did wickedly, and so gave occasion to the heathens to blaspheme his holy name.

Ver. 22. "I do not this for your sakes, O house of Israel." They deserved not such a mercy at the hands of God, as reduction out of Babylon into Canaan; they were defiled with blood and idolatry, which moved God to cast them out of their land, and scatter them among the heathen, but they did nothing to incline God to show them the least favour; had they had according to their deserts, they should never have been set at liberty, but have perished utterly in their captivity. They might think, because they were circumcised, came of David, Abraham, Isaac, and Jacob, and were the only people God had in the world, that therefore God would do much for their sakes; but to take them off from such conceits, the Lord makes open profession, that what he was about to do was not for their sakes.

"But for mine holy name's sake." God's name is sometimes put for himself; as Psal. xxxiii. 21, "We have trusted in his holy name," that is, in God himself. Sometimes it is put for his power; Prov. xviii. 10, "The name of the Lord is a strong tower," that is, his omnipotence is such a tower. Sometimes it is put for the attributes and divine perfections of God; Psal. viii. 1, "O Lord, how excellent is thy name in all the earth!" that is, how excellent are thine attributes! Sometimes it is put for the fame and glory of God; as 2 Sam. vii. 23, "To make him a name," that was, to make himself famous and glorious. The two last may be understood here by "name:" the heathens said, God was not wise, not faithful, not omnipotent, that would let his people go into captivity, and become servants unto us; yea, it is evident by his people's doings what a God he is; they are an unholy people, and he is an unholy God; and so his fame and glory were eclipsed: therefore saith God, For mine holy name's sake, which ye have profaned among the heathen, I will vindicate my name, and make heathens know, and you know, that I am a wise, a faithful, an almighty, and holy God.

Ver. 23. "And I will sanctify my great name." I will vindicate my name from all aspersions laid upon it, and make it known to heathens, and to you, O house of Israel, by punishing them for their idolatry and other wickednesses, and by bringing you out of captivity, that I am a God of power, wisdom, faithfulness, and holiness. God sanctifies his name when he clears it from disgrace and reproach cast thereupon, and makes it appear as it is in itself, glorious and holy. God's name hath many epithets given unto it in the word; it is said to be glorious, Psal. lxxii. 19, excellent, Psal. cxlviii. 13, dreadful, Mal. i. 14, holy, ver. 21 of this chapter; and here, great. God hath done great and wonderful things in the world, whereupon he hath a great name, not only in Israel, Psal. lxxvi. 1, but all the world over, Psal. viii. 9. Many men have had great names, yet nothing comparable to the name of the Lord.

"Which was profaned among the heathen, which ye have profaned in the midst of them." The Jews being under the Babylonish yoke for their sins, did not humble themselves before God, repent and turn from their wicked ways, that so God's name might have been sanctified among the heathen; but they persisted in their wicked ways, and were worse than the heathens among whom they were scattered, and so occasioned the heathens to speak evil of their God, their religion, and worship; and not only so, but themselves profaned God's name, they rejected the God of Israel and his ways, saying, "We will be as the heathen, as the families of the countries, to serve wood and stone," Ezek. xx. 32. They made the God of Israel like the heathen gods, and his ways like theirs; which was a great profanation of him and his name.

"And the heathen shall know that I am the Lord, saith the Lord God, when I shall be sanctified in you before their eyes." When the Lord shall manifest his mercy towards them, and put forth his power to bring them out of Babylon, then was he sanctified in the midst of them, then he did vindicate his name from all aspersions, and made the Jews and Babylonians know, that he was a holy, faithful, wise, merciful, and an almighty God; he would make his name honourable before them all, which had been profaned.

Ver. 24. "For I will take you from among the heathen." The heathen make full account you are theirs, that you shall never get out of their borders, or return into your own land; they think that their idol gods are stronger than I, who am the God of Israel; but they shall find it otherwise, for I will by a strong hand take you from among the heathen,

"And gather you out of all countries." They were dispersed into divers countries, into the hundred and twenty-seven provinces that were under Ahasuerus his government, Esth. iii. 8; and it seemed improbable that they should ever be gathered out of so many countries; but the Lord tells them for their comfort, that he would gather them "out of all countries;" no distance of place, or difficulty in any place, should impede his congregating of them.

"And will bring you into your own land." After the seventy years of their captivity were expired, the Lord set them at liberty, and brought them back to the land of Canaan, their own land, because they inherited it from their fathers, unto whom the Lord had given it. This was a glorious and great work, viz. the bringing the Jews out of Babylon, and all the countries where they were scattered, into Canaan; and did prefigure the salvation of the church by Christ, and gathering of those that were his out of all nations unto it, according to what is in John x. 16, and xi. 52.

Obs. 1. The name of the Lord is holy. His essence, his will, his attributes, his works, his word, are his name. All these set out God, make him known, and so are his name, even the name of his holiness, or "his holy name." There is no name under heaven like unto the Lord's; it is a holy name, and so glorious; a great name, and so dreadful. We should sanctify the name of God; which is done by believing: Numb. xx. 12, when Moses and Aaron did not believe God, they did not sanctify his name; but when men believe God's word, then they sanctify his name. It is done also by fearing to displease him, Isa. viii. 13; xxix. 23. It is done also by acknowledging his name to be holy, Matt. vi. 9, when men praise him.

Obs. 2. The profaning of God's holy name, as it is a trouble unto him, so it sticks and abides upon him. Other provocations pass away, but this settles upon his spirit. See here what hold it took; ver. 20, "They profaned mine holy name;" and ver. 21, "The house of Israel profaned mine holy name among the heathen;" ver. 22, "Mine holy name which ye have profaned among the heathen." Thrice the Lord mentions their profaning of his name; yea, in the next verse, as if he could not shake this act of theirs out of his mind, he mentions it twice more, "My name which was profaned, which ye have profaned." God's name being holy is dear unto him, and the profaning of it makes deep impressions in his heart.

Obs. 3. Temporal mercies are not merited at God's hands by men. "I do not this for your sakes, O house of Israel." What was it God did not for their sakes? viz. deliver them from their Babylonish bondage, and bring them into their own country; these were temporal mercies; and though there were godly men amongst them, as Ezekiel, Daniel, Mordecai, Ezra, Nehemiah, and others, yet with all their prayers, fastings, suffering, and holiness, they did not merit these outward mercies: liberty, safety, plenty, possessions, are not the merit or purchase of the creature, but the gift of God; 1 Tim. vi. 17, he "giveth us all things richly to enjoy." Have men more or less of these outward things, they are upon free gift, not any desert; and if we deserve not temporal things, much less do or can we deserve spiritual and eternal things, which are of a transcendent nature: if we do not deserve an outward deliverance, an earthly Canaan, how shall we deserve a spiritual deliverance, a heavenly Canaan? all things of that nature are free gifts, Luke xii. 32; Rom. vi. 23.

Obs. 4. The good which God doth unto his church, be it temporal or spiritual, is for his own sake. What I do, (saith God,) I do it for mine holy name's sake; there is nothing to move me but mine own name; that is holy, great, and glorious, and I will for my name's sake do much for my church and people. That they were preserved in Babylon, was for his holy name's sake; that they were brought out of Babylon, was for his holy name's sake; that they were replanted in Canaan, was for his holy name's sake; that they had a temple, sacrifices, priests, prophets, ordinances again, was for his name's sake; when they were near to destruction often in former days, God wrought for his name's sake, Ezek. xx.; so Isa. xlviii. 8, 9. It is not for the enemies' sake that God doth preserve or deliver his people; nor for their sakes, their prayers, tears, faith, obedience, holiness, that he doth great things for them, bestow great mercies upon them; but it is for his own name's sake. For man's sake God cursed the earth, Gen. viii. 21; but it is for his name's sake that he blesseth it. The choicest mercies God's people have, are for his name's sake: they have pardon of sin for his name's sake, Psal. xxv. 11; 1 John ii. 12; purging of sin for his name's sake, Psal. lxxix. 9; leading in the paths of righteousness for his name's sake, Psal. xxiii. 3; quickening of their dead and dull hearts for his name's sake, Psal. cxliii. 11. Though his people much offend him, yet he forsakes them not for his great name's sake, 1 Sam. xii. 22. The Lord doth all freely and for the honour of his name; let us then say with the prophet, whatever we have, "Not unto us, O Lord, not unto us, but to thy name be the glory:" not unto us, who are thy creatures, not unto us who are tools in thy hand, but to thy name, which is the ground, root, and spring of all our mercies, be the glory, all the glory, and that everlastingly.

Obs. 5. God will not suffer his holy and great name always to lie under aspersions and reproaches of men. "I will sanctify my holy and great name, which was profaned among the heathen, even in the midst of them." He will vindicate his honour and glory. Great men, when their names are blemished, do stand upon it, and will vindicate them with much cost and labour; so God, when wicked ones have profaned his name, and darkened the glory thereof, will stand upon it, and do that which shall clear his name before all his enemies. Goliath for many days defied the God of Israel, and the armies of Israel; but not long after the Lord vindicated his holy and great name, by stirring up and strengthening of David to take off his head, 1 Sam. xvii. 45, 51. When the king of Assyria and Rabshakeh blasphemed the name of God, as they did, Isa. xxxvi. xxxvii. did not the Lord quickly send an angel and destroy their great army of one hundred fourscore and five thousand, and so by this stroke of his made his holy and great name glorious and dreadful? He will scatter the smoke and venomous vapours, that ascend from the tongues and lives of profane persons to hinder the beams of his glorious name from shining, as the wind scatters clouds from before the sun; and as by destruction of his enemies, so by delivering of his servants.

Obs. 6. When God doth great things for his people, and they honour his name for them, then very heathens will be convinced, acknowledge God, and give glory to his name. "The heathen shall know that I am the Lord, when I shall be sanctified in you," that is, in your deliverance, "before their eyes;"

then you will magnify my name, and they will magnify my name, which hath been profaned; then they will see and say that I am another kind of God than their idol gods are, that I am omnipotent, faithful, holy, wise. Psal. cxxvi. 1, 2, when the Lord turned the captivity of his people, as they said, "The Lord hath done great things for us;" so the heathens said, "The Lord hath done great things for them:" so much of God appeared in taking them out of Babylon, that Jewish and Babylonish tongues were constrained to speak out the power, truth, and goodness of God.

Obs. 7. Things difficult, and in the eye of man impossible, are facile to and feasible by the power of God. The Jews were among the heathens, who by their laws, power, and vigilancy kept them in great bondage; they were scattered into one hundred twenty and seven provinces, Esth. viii. 5, with chap. i. 1, and so it seemed impossible that these should be drawn out and carried to Canaan, which was so far off, especially for them who were seated near India; but what saith the Lord to this? "I will take you from among the heathen." He would but put forth his hand and lay hold of them, saying, Come, go with me, and it should be done; he would gather them out of all countries, as a hen gathers her chickens that are dispersed up and down among the bushes, trees, or weeds in an orchard; and as he carried them upon eagles' wings from Egypt to Canaan, so would he bring them upon the same wings from Babylon to Canaan. This work God is upon in these days of Christ, he is bringing out of all nations some unto Christ, and gathering them into spiritual Canaan.

Ver. 25. *Then will I sprinkle clean water upon you, and ye shall be clean: from all your filthiness, and from all your idols, will I cleanse you.*

We are now come to the last general part of this chapter; which consists in the multiplication of promises, both spiritual and temporal, with the ground of them.

I. The spiritual are,
1. Remission of sins, ver. 25, 29, 33.
2. Regeneration, ver. 26.
3. Sanctification, ver. 27.
4. Renovation of the covenant between God and them, ver. 28.
5. Repentance, ver. 31.

II. The temporal are,
1. Repossession of their land, ver. 28.
2. Plentiful maintenance, ver. 29, 30.
3. Re-edifying of their cities and waste places, ver. 33, 35.
4. Increase of men, ver. 37, 38.

The ground of all these sweet and great promises is God's free grace, not man's desert, ver. 32.

"Then will I sprinkle clean water upon you." When they were called and come out of Babylon, then would the Lord sprinkle clean water upon them. The Jews by "water" mean the abundance of outward things. Some others interpret it of the water in baptism; but neither doth abundance of outwards, nor the water of baptism, cleanse from the pollution of idols: for after their return from Babylon, Jason sent money for the sacrifice of Hercules; he, Menelaus, and others, fell to the customs of the gentiles, desired to be like them in all things, they set not by the honour of their fathers, but liked the glory of the gentiles best of all, 2 Macc. iv. And are not many baptized ones amongst the papists and others idolaters? Some other sense of the word therefore must we seek out. By "water," the blood of Christ is intended, say the best expositors. Some make grace the thing; but that is too general, unless we limit it to the blood of Christ, which of grace is given to wash sinners with. These words, "I will sprinkle clean water upon you," have some allusion unto the waters mingled with the ashes of the red cow, which being sprinkled by a branch of hyssop upon the unclean party, he was cleansed; and this water was called the "water of separation," or "purification for sin," Numb. xix. 9. The Septuagint calls it, the water of sprinkling; and so the 18th and 19th verses express it. This red cow figured out Christ in his afflictions and sufferings; and the water mingled with the ashes of it, the blood of Christ, which from hence is called "The blood of sprinkling," Heb. xii. 24.

The water they used in sprinkling was clean water, running or spring water, free from all filth; so the blood of Christ is pure, he was without sin, any blemish, or spot; his blood was precious and pure, 1 Pet. i. 19; and here it is called "clean water."

This sprinkling of clean water upon them, is the application of the blood of Christ, by the Spirit of God: as the priest was to take of the blood of the red heifer with his finger, and to sprinkle it; so God by the hand and finger of his Spirit doth take and sprinkle the blood of Christ, that is, apply the fruit and benefit of it unto the hearts of men, 1 Cor. vi. 11.

"And ye shall be clean." There are three things among others which water serveth for, viz. to cool, to nourish, to cleanse. 1. It quencheth thirst caused by heat, and so cools; the like doth the blood of Christ, being drunk by faith, John vii. 37. 2. It nourisheth and causeth growth; and Christ's blood doth the same, John vi. 55. 3. It cleanseth, which is the use of it here mentioned: water washeth away the filth of garments, vessels, and persons; so the blood of Christ is a cleansing thing. Heb. ix. 13, 14, "If the blood of bulls and of goats, and the ashes of an heifer sprinkling the unclean, sanctifieth to the purifying of the flesh: how much more shall the blood of Christ, who through the eternal Spirit offered himself without spot to God, purge your conscience from dead works to serve the living God?" The argument is *a minori ad majus;* if the blood of typical sacrifices could do that to the flesh for which they were appointed, much more the blood of Christ, the true sacrifice, will do that to the soul and conscience for which it was appointed, viz. purge away the guilt of sin; otherwise the honour and efficacy of the type should be greater than the honour and efficacy of the substance; which the apostle denies, when he tells us types were shadows of good things to come, Heb. x. 1. This cleansing is the remission of their sins through the blood of Christ, or the justifying of their persons, so as they are before God without spot, or fault, Col. i. 14; Rom. v. 9; Rev. xiv. 5. When sins are forgiven, the persons are clean in the sight of God.

"From all your filthiness, and from all your idols, will I cleanse you." They had state defilements and temple defilements, family and personal filthinesses, Zeph. iii. 3, 4; Micah iii. 9—11; Ezek. xxii.; Jer. vi. 13; vii. 9. Whatever their filthinesses were, God would cleanse them; and because idolatry is a sin which exceedingly defiles, and provokes the Lord to jealousy, Exod. xx. 5, to fury, ver. 18 of this chapter, and they might apprehend there was no mercy for them; therefore the Lord mentions the filthiness of idols, and tells them he will cleanse them from that filthiness. It is not material water that washes from the filth of idolatry, but spiritual water.

Obs. 1. When it pleases God to gather his people out of Babylon, and to bring them to Zion, then he will multiply mercies upon them, and do for them great things. I will gather you from among the heathen, out of all countries, and bring you into your own land; and then will I sprinkle you with clean water, then will I give you a new heart, then will I put my Spirit into you, then will I call for the corn, and multiply the fruit of the tree and increase of the field. After great afflictions, God bestows great kindnesses; after sharp sufferings, he gives solid comforts. Isa. liv. 7, " For a small moment have I forsaken thee; but with great mercies will I gather thee:" ברחמים גדולים When God gathers his people out of Babylon, a state of confusion, that is mercy; and when he brings them into Zion, to behold the order, beauty, and glory thereof, that is great mercy; and God will not leave them there, but go on with them, and heap great mercies still upon them: see Isa. xlix. 18—23; Jer. xxxii. 37—41.

Obs. 2. Justification is a gracious act of God upon a sinner. " I will sprinkle clean water upon you." It is God's prerogative to forgive and blot out sins, Mark ii. 7; Isa. xliii. 25; and this he doth freely, it is an act of grace and mercy, Rom. iii. 24, " Being justified freely by his grace." Now in this act nothing is done in a sinner, there is no grace infused, no change made in the heart by it, there are no *χαρισματα* therein, it is upon a sinner: justifying grace is subjectively in God, objectively on man; for it is a judicial act of God, which puts nothing into the creature, Rom. iii. 22, it is " upon all of them that believe."

Obs. 3. The blood of Christ applied by the Spirit of God, is efficacious to free sinners from the guilt of their sins, and of all their sins, of what kind soever they be. " I will sprinkle clean water upon you, and ye shall be clean." Their sins were great, very great; they were guilty of blood, oppressing the widow and fatherless, of idolatry, of despising and profaning holy things, Ezek. xxii. 8, 26. They were under the guilt of all crying and notorious sins, chap. xvi. 47, worse than Sodom or Samaria; than the nations, chap. v. 7; yet the Lord would cleanse them by the blood of Christ; there was virtue in that to cleanse them from their old spots, from their deep guilt, yea, from all their guilt, they should be clean from all their filthinesses. As water washeth all the filth out of a cloth, so doth the blood of Christ all sin out of the soul: 1 John i. 7, " The blood of Jesus Christ cleanseth us from all sin," the guilt of our thoughts, words, acts, neglects; there is no sin defiles the conscience so, but the blood of Christ will purge it away, Heb. ix. 14; i. 3. Christ's blood is of great virtue, it purges away all sin, and procures peace, Col. i. 20; so that " being justified by his blood, we shall be saved from wrath," as it is Rom. v. 9.

Obs. 4. All sin defiles and makes guilty before God, yet some sins defile more than others, and make more deeply guilty. God would cleanse them from all their filthiness, from every sin that had polluted them and made them guilty; and from their idols, which had made them more deeply guilty. Idolatry hath more guilt adhering to it than many other sins; that is a sin breaks covenant with God, deposes God, and sets up an idol in his stead.

Ver. 26. *A new heart also will I give you, and a new spirit will I put within you: and I will take away the stony heart out of your flesh, and I will give you an heart of flesh.*

This is another great promise, even a promise of regeneration; and in it there is considerable,

I. The party promising, " I, I, I, I."

II. The things promised;

1. " A new heart."

2. " A new spirit."

3. Removal of the stony heart.

4. " An heart of flesh."

III. The parties to whom the Lord will do these things, " You, you, you."

IV. The manner of God's doing these things, which is by giving, putting, and taking away.

" A new heart also will I give you." By " heart" in Scripture is signified the judgment and understanding, Eph. iv. 18, the will and affections, Prov. xxiii. 26, and the conscience, 1 John iii. 20; all which are here comprehended in the word " heart." " New " notes sometimes that which is for substance new, totally new; as " new ropes," Judg. xvi. 11, 12; " a new wife," Deut. xxiv. 5; " new gods," Deut. xxxii. 17. And sometimes that which is only for quality new, as the new moon; Isa. lxvi. 23, " From one new moon to another;" the moon is not new for substance, but renewed with light, new in regard of quality: so " new tongues," Mark xvi. 17; they had not their old tongues plucked or cut out of their mouths, and other new ones put in; but those tongues they had before had new languages put into them, new gifts and graces. Here then by " a new heart," is not intended one new for the substance or nature of it, but the same heart altered for the qualities of it, renewed, and endued with other qualities than it had before; such qualities are wrought in the heart, that a man thereupon is said to be regenerate or " born again," John iii. 3, 5—7, and to be " a new creature," Gal. vi. 15.

This " new heart" lieth not in those common gifts which many have, yet without alteration in their hearts. Judas had a covetous, an earthly, an old heart, notwithstanding those great gifts he had; he could cast out devils, and heal all manner of sicknesses, Matt. x. 1, 4. And those, Matt. vii. 22, 23, who had the gift of prophecy, of casting out devils, and working wonders, had no new hearts; for Christ sends them going for workers of iniquity. But it lieth in grace infused, which is a principle of light and life, supernatural and permanent. Man since the fall of Adam is in a state of darkness and death, Eph. v. 8; ii. 5, and when grace is infused, that brings light and life into the heart; John viii. 12, it is called " the light of life:" and when a blind heart sees, a dead heart lives, there is a great and glorious alteration, so that it is become " a new heart;" it hath a new principle which is supernatural and permanent, called " the divine nature," 2 Pet. i. 4; " divine," to show the supernaturalness of it, and " nature," to show the permanency of it.

" And a new spirit will I put within you." These very words we had Ezek. xi. 19, where they were largely opened. " New spirit" there was interpreted to be those excellent qualities and graces God put into the soul, and showed upon what account they were called " spirit " and " new." Here I conceive " a new spirit " is added exegetically, being the same with " a new heart."

This " new heart," or " new spirit," causeth the party in whom it is to look at God as a Father; and so, to honour him, Mal. i. 6; to love him, 1 John v. 1; to fear him, 1 Pet. i. 17; to yield obedience to him, Rom. vi. 17; 1 Pet. i. 14, 15; patiently to bear his chastisements, Heb. xii. 6—9; to eschew sin and work righteousness, 1 John v. 18; iii. 9, 10; to acknowledge how he hath offended him, Luke xv. 18; to pray fervently unto him, Rom. viii. 15; to be like unto him in mercifulness and doing of good, Luke vi. 36; to delight in his ways, and to have communion with him, and his Son Christ, 1 John i. 3; to worship him in spirit and truth, John iv. 23; to be thankful always unto him for all things, Eph. v. 20; to live nobly and spiritually, minding the things of heaven, Rom. viii. 5; 1 Pet. i. 14; John iii. 6; 2 Cor. v. 16; and to love those that are regenerate, 1 John v. 1: and these doing so, God their Father hath a special care of them, and love unto them, Matt. vi. 26, 32; Luke xi. 13; xii. 32.

"Will I give you, will I put within you." The "new heart" and "new spirit" comes from God; he that is the author of "every good and perfect gift," is the author of the same. Now in the working of this "new heart" and "new spirit," observe,

I. Several attributes of God set on work: as,

1. His infinite mercy. That he should mind sinners, who have old, polluted, hard, dead hearts within them, so at enmity with God, that they would pull him out of heaven had they power to do it; for God to mind such hearts and spirits, and make them "new," so as to affect him and his ways, argues unspeakable mercy, loving-kindness superabundant. It was a time of love when God saw Jerusalem in her blood, and said unto her, "Live," Ezek. xvi. 6, 8; it was infinite love, infinite mercy for him to pity Jerusalem in such a case, and to say so unto her: the same it is when God makes of an old heart a new heart, of an old spirit a new spirit.

2. God's infinite power is employed in this work. The making of a dead heart to live, a blind heart to see, an old heart and spirit to become new, requires an omnipotent arm. By the preaching of the word men have great convictions, strong resolutions, and are persuaded almost to be christians; but those convictions and resolutions die away, and they never come altogether to be christians, altogether to be new-hearted and new-spirited, till the Lord put forth his almighty power, and create new hearts and spirits in them: it is a work of creation, Psal. li. 10; 2 Cor. iv. 6; Eph. ii. 10; and such hearts and spirits are called new creatures, Gal. vi. 15; 2 Cor. v. 17.

3. Infinite wisdom. The heart of man "is deceitful above all things, and desperately wicked; who can know it?" Jer. xvii. 9. It is beyond the knowledge of man; it hath so many windings, turnings, pretences, shifts, arguments, wiles, depths, methods, as that none but God knows it; he being infinitely wise, can answer all the objections, arguments, and subtle distinctions of the heart, so that it shall be silent. Man's heart whilst it is old, hath the cunning of the old serpent in it, and pleads hard to keep its old principles, its old ungodly lusts, its old ignorance, its old darkness, its old formal ways of worship, its old fleshly confidences, its old delights and pleasures, its old company, its old customs, its old aims and ends, which were self; it musters up many arguments to defend these; and who can convince the heart of the evil of these, and take it off from them, but God by his infinite wisdom? To make a heart, or spirit, which hath so many oldnesses in it, new, argues more skill and wisdom than dwells in any creature.

4. His infinite holiness and purity. When God takes an old heart, which is as dark as hell, as stinking as any sepulchre, Matt. xxiii. 27; an old spirit, which is as unclean and loathsome as the devils are; when he takes these, and makes them new, he scatters darkness, abolisheth death, separating filthiness; and instead thereof brings in "marvellous light," 1 Pet. ii. 9, a glorious life, Eph. iv. 18, and "true holiness," ver. 24: which import that God is light without darkness, life without possibility of dying, holiness without any spot or imperfection. When the wind cleanseth the air infected, pestilential, and stinking, it argues the wind is pure; when a vessel or house is noisome, and one cleanses and sweetens them, as not enduring them in that condition, it argues their cleanliness, and if they could make them new, it would argue it much more: so here, God makes them new, he puts them into the fire that they may be refined, and partake of his holiness, Heb. xii. 10. It is God's holy arm which makes an unholy heart to become holy, and glorious in holiness.

II. The dignity and excellency of this "new heart" and "new spirit," is worthy the notice.

1. It is that doth discriminate and difference a man from all others. They that have old hearts, old spirits, and new hearts, new spirits, differ as much as light from darkness, life from death, and holiness from filthiness. A man with a new heart, a new spirit, is a living man, whereas others are dead, Eph. ii. 1; he is a seeing man, whereas others are blind, 1 John v. 20; 1 Cor. ii. 14; he is pure, whereas others are filthy, 1 Pet. ii. 9; Tit. i. 15. Hereby a man is differenced from all profane, civil, and moral men; from all gifted men; from all hypocrites, what specious forms of religion and holiness soever they have: whoever hath a new spirit is distinguished from all other spirits, yea, from the devils, who are but unclean spirits.

2. It doth ennoble a man. A new heart and new spirit doth not only distinguish from others, but makes more excellent than others; Prov. xii. 26, "The righteous is more excellent than his neighbour." Righteousness is one of the qualities in the new heart, in the new spirit, Eph. iv. 23, 24; and that nobilitates a man: such a one is "born, not of blood," that is, not of the princes and nobles of the world, who stand upon their blood and greatness; "nor of the will of the flesh," that is, not in the ordinary way; "nor of the will of man," viz. not by education and school principles, "but of God," John i. 13: he is descended from the highest, the King of kings; he is of the most royal blood, even the blood of God, Acts xx. 28. Others are vile, but he is precious, Jer. xv. 19; 2 Pet. i. 1; he is partaker of the divine nature, and lives the life of God, 2 Pet. i. 4; Eph. iv. 18.

3. It fills them where it is with new joys. New things affect much; when the apostles had new tongues given them, they were greatly affected therewith; and when men have new hearts, new spirits, they abound in joy: the greater the mercy, the more full the joy. If when a sinner is converted, there be joy in heaven, what joy is in the sinner's heart then! When Christ came to Zaccheus, and gave him a new heart, a new spirit, he was filled with joy, Luke xix. and new joys. Before his joy was to get money by any means, and treasure it up; now his joy was to disperse, make satisfaction, and to give away, ver. 8. His new heart begat in him new joys, and enabled him to joy in that he could not do nor think of before without sadness. So Paul, when he had a new heart and spirit, he had new joys, fulness of them in those things he could not rejoice in before; 2 Cor. vii. 4, "I am filled with comfort, I am exceeding joyful in all our tribulations;" and, chap. xii. 10, he took "pleasure in infirmities, in reproaches, in necessities, in persecutions, in distresses." Here is the excellency of a new heart and a new spirit, it fills with new joys in God, in Christ, in the promises, in the saints, and enables us to rejoice and "glory in tribulations," Rom. v. 3.

4. It entitles us to divers new and excellent things: as,

(1.) To the new covenant. When a man hath a new heart and a new spirit he hath an interest in the new covenant, Jer. xxxi. 31, 33. The law of sin, and principles of Satan and the world, were written in the old heart, and old spirit, and so the party was under the covenant with death and hell, Isa. xxviii. 15; but in the new heart is written, the law of God, the law of faith, Rom. iii. 27; Heb. viii. 10, and so they are under the new covenant, which is called "grace," Rom. vi. 14.

(2.) To new names. Where there is newness of heart and spirit, there they are sealed in their foreheads with new names; their title is, "new creatures," 2 Cor. v. 17; "the seed of Abraham," Isa. xli. 8; "servants of righteousness," Rom. vi. 18; "children of light," John xii. 36; "conquerors," Rom. viii. 37; God's "workmanship," Eph. ii. 10; "kings and priests," Rev. i. 6; "temples of God," 1 Cor. iii. 16; the "glory" of God, Isa. iv. 5; "newborn babes," 1 Pet. ii. 2; "his saints," Psal. cxlix. 9; "vessels of gold and silver," 2 Tim. ii. 20; "wise virgins," Matt. xxv.; "heirs of salvation," Heb. i. 14.

(3.) To a new Lord and Master. When their hearts were old, Satan was their sovereign, they walked "according to the prince of the air," Eph. ii. 2; see 2 Tim. ii. 26; his lusts they did execute, John viii. 44. But having new hearts, they have a new Lord, a new Master, and that is the Lord Christ; Phil. i. 1, Paul, a servant of Christ. He had a new heart, and now he had a new Master, which was Christ; he would serve Satan no longer, but Christ, who died for sinners, that they might live unto him, 2 Cor. v. 15. When the hearts and spirits of men are new, they are dead to their old masters, and have new, Rom. vii. 4. Christ is the Husband and Head of every one renewed by his grace, he is Lord and Master of all such, 1 Cor. vii. 22; Matt. xxiii. 8.

(4.) To a new guard. Such have a guard of angels about them: before, as they were without God, so without the protection of his angels, exposed to all dangers; but having new hearts and new spirits, being new creatures, they have a multitude of the heavenly host, not only to praise God for their new birth, as they did at Christ's birth, Luke ii. 13, but to attend and protect them: Heb. i. 14, Are not the angels "ministering spirits, sent forth to minister for them who shall be heirs of salvation?" and none shall be such, but those that have new hearts and new spirits, for "flesh and blood cannot inherit the kingdom of God," 1 Cor. xv. 50.

(5.) To new alliance this change is wrought in them. Blasphemers, idolaters, adulterers, drunkards, murderers, liars, unbelievers, hypocrites, and all profane ones, they are very devils themselves, John viii. 44; but when they have new hearts and new spirits, then they have new kindred. As a man that marries a woman, all her kindred become his; so here, all that have new hearts and spirits are his kindred who hath a new heart, he is allied unto them all; Matt. xxiii. 8, "All ye are brethren." All the saints throughout the earth, how great, how learned, how rich, how gifted or gracious soever they be, are all brethren; yea, the angels are brethren unto those that have new hearts, Rev. xix. 10; xxii. 9; and that which is beyond all, Christ himself is their Brother and Father, Matt. xii. 49, 50; Heb. ii. 12, 13.

(6.) To the new mansions in the city made without hands. John xiv. 2, saith Christ, "In my Father's house are many mansions, and I go to prepare a place for you;" you have right and title to them, ye have new hearts, "ye believe in God," ver. 1; and I go to prepare and fit places for you in those mansions.

5. The excellency of a new heart is this, that it sets a high price upon the things of God, and a low price upon the things of the world, how goodly soever they appear; whereas before the things of the world were magnified, and the things of God slighted. When Paul had another heart and another spirit than before, then he had "no confidence in the flesh," then he did not value his great privileges, he counted them and all things but "loss for Christ;" they did damnify him rather than advantage him, and therefore looked upon them as dung, things of no worth, in respect of Christ, his righteousness, and knowledge of him, Phil. iii. 7—9; all which had an excellency, and were so prized by Paul, that he was willing to lay down his life for them, Acts xxi. 13. When Simon Magus offered the apostles money for to have power to give the Holy Spirit, by laying on of hands, Peter, in his own name, and in the name of the rest, said, "Thy money perish with thee;" we value not bags of gold and silver, but the things of God, Acts viii. 19, 20. When the conjurors had the devils cast out of them, and new hearts given them, they brought forth their books which they had highly valued, and burned them before all men, and so many they burned as came to fifty thousand pieces of silver, Acts xix. 19; and instead of these, they prized the books of Moses, the prophets, and apostles. A new heart sees excellency in spiritual things, and saith, it cannot overvalue them, but for other things it puts them under its feet.

6. It is excellent in that it doth really make God its end, and aims at his glory in its operations; before self was all, now God is all. Acts xx. 23, 24, Paul was told by the Spirit of God, that bonds and afflictions did abide him every where, that his life was in danger; now had not Paul been a man of a new heart and spirit, he would have shifted for himself, and let the preaching of the gospel have fallen; but being such an one, what saith he? "None of these things move me, neither count I my life dear unto myself, so that I might finish my course with joy, and the ministry which I have received of the Lord Jesus, to testify the gospel of the grace of God." That was Paul's end, to make known the grace of God in the gospel towards poor sinners, that so they partaking of that grace might give glory to God, and God be glorified by him. God and his glory were so in his eye, that he gave out a rule for all christians to eye and mind God and his glory in all things, 1 Cor. x. 31.

7. It is the principle of eternal life and happiness. When God puts life, light, and grace into the heart, and so makes it new, he hath begun our admission into heaven and happiness; this new heart and spirit are the water which springs up into everlasting life, John iv. 14; they are the eagles' wings which will carry you not only up to heaven, but into heaven.

III. Concerning this new heart and new spirit there are divers mistakes; many think they have the same, when they have it not. There are several things which cause men to judge so.

1. Outward reformation. When men cease from their former lewd courses, when they give over their drunkenness, whoredom, swearing, lying, oppression, and other scandalous practices, they think themselves, and are reputed of others, to be new men, and so to have new hearts; but know, a man may have escaped the pollutions of the world, have changed his manners, yet retain his old heart; a swine may be washed, and yet reserve her swinish nature. Herod reformed in many things, yet had an unreformed heart, Mark vi. 20; Luke iii. 20;

ix. 9. The scribes and Pharisees were whited sepulchres, they had beautiful outsides, they appeared righteous unto men; but what were their hearts? were they not full of hypocrisy and iniquity? Matt. xxiii. 27, 28. Shame among men, fear of punishment, death, hell, terrors of conscience, afflictions, strength of reason, and hope of profits and reward, may make a man reform his life and manners, his heart being still naught; a man formerly wicked may become a new man, and yet not have a new heart.

2. Moral virtues cause many to be deceived about this new heart: because they are temperate, just, prudent, faithful to their friends, true in their speeches, patient under afflictions, seek the public good, not their own interest, are chaste, and courteous unto all, they thereupon conclude that they have the new heart and new spirit here spoken of; but all these are no more than were found in heathens. Scipio, Aristides, Cato, Æmilius, Lepidus, Lucretia, and others, excelled in moral virtues. The Roman faith was in great esteem in all the world, because the Romans kept their word, and made good whatever they promised. Many heathens excelled in moralities, and did virtuous actions for virtue's sake, yet they had no new hearts or spirits; they knew not what regeneration was, they were strangers to the life of God and faith; they attained to what they had by their own industry, and what they did was not done according to the mind of God in his word, and so referring to his glory; they sought their own glory in all.

3. A form of godliness. When men have left their old ways of sin, and taken up a way, or form of godliness, which is new to them, they imagine themselves to be new, and to have new hearts; they read, pray, hear, meditate, and worship God with their hearts, which they never did before, and hence they ground a newness in their hearts. The Jews have a form of godliness at this day, yet are they cast off of God and numbered amongst unbelievers, Rom. xi. 20; such was their godliness, as persecuted true godliness, Acts xiii. 50; 1 Thess. ii. 15. The heathens had forms of godliness: Plato taught men not to sleep without repentance for their sins; Hermes instructed them to pray earnestly unto God, and continually for repentance, to call upon him in the day, and not to forget him in the night; they worshipped by nature those which were no gods, Gal. iv. 8; forms of worship they had, though they worshipped blindly: Socrates saw further than the most of them, who said, God must be worshipped only that way which he hath appointed; yet neither Socrates, nor the rest of the heathens, had new hearts. Christians have forms of godliness, yet all among them have not new hearts; among papists and protestants are many religious, but few pious, they have the form of godliness, but not the power. Painted fire is not true fire, and all that worship God do not worship him in newness of spirit; the most do worship him with old hearts.

4. Some are deceived upon this ground, that they have the law in their hearts, approve of truth, make conscience of their ways, have peace within, and so determine their hearts are new. But here is a great mistake, the law is in men's hearts by nature; Rom. ii. 14, 15, "The gentiles, which had not the law, did by nature the things of the law, and so showed the work of the law written in their hearts;" when they did ill their consciences did accuse them, and when they did well they did excuse them, and so they had peace; here was nothing supernatural: where there is a new heart, a new spirit, there is something supernatural; men have not these by descent from their parents, but they are given, they are put in by God, "I will give you a new heart, and I will put within you a new spirit." The law that all men have in their hearts is by virtue of creation, not of the new covenant; that is another law, Jer. xxxi. 33, which is from grace, not from nature: where this law is written, the heart is new, and so doth not only approve of truth in general, but knows and approves of truth as it is in Christ, Eph. iv. 21, and as it is according to godliness. Truth in a new heart provokes unto godliness, and maketh conscientious towards God and men, Acts xxiv. 16, looking at Christ for peace; Rom. v. 1, "Being justified by faith, we have peace with God," the conscience being purged from dead works by the blood of Christ. Men have sound peace in their new hearts; it is false peace which men of old hearts have, they bribe their consciences with doing something, and that is their peace.

5. New relations make some to fancy they have new hearts and new spirits; they are under church privileges, they are citizens of Zion, inhabitants of Jerusalem, in relation to Christ and his ordinances; this may be, and yet without newness of heart or spirit. Relations made not alterations in men's hearts. Simon Magus was baptized, stood in relation to Christ and the gospel, yet his heart was the same it was before, Acts viii. The Jews gloried they were the seed of Abraham, John viii. 33; yet they were of their father the devil, ver. 44, and had bloody hearts, ver. 40, seeking to kill Christ. Rom. ii. 28, 29, outward privileges may be, as circumcision of the flesh, where there is no circumcision of the heart; and Paul tells us, Gal. vi. 15, that "circumcision nor uncircumcision avail any thing, but a new creature;" they may be where the new creature is not; himself had many privileges, Phil. iii. when he was far from newness of heart.

6. Gifts. They breed mistakes in divers persons: those that have choice and great gifts persuade themselves they have new hearts and spirits, that they are gracious and good; but there is a vast difference between gifts and grace.

(1.) Gifts make not a man a christian. Heathens had great gifts, as Tully, Seneca, Plato, Aristotle, Plutarch. It is grace makes a christian. The gentiles were not christians, and so not acceptable to God, till they were sanctified by the Holy Spirit, Rom. xv. 16. They may make a man a useful man, not a good man; Acts xi. 24, it is faith and the graces of the Spirit make a good man.

(2.) All gifts do seldom or never meet in one man, but graces do, they are the fruits of the Spirit, and grow all in a new heart; John i. 16, "Of his fulness have we all received, and grace for grace." Graces go together, not gifts.

(3.) A man may have gifts and not be saved. Judas had gifts, yet was a son of perdition. The beast which came up out of the earth had miraculous gifts, and the false prophets also, and notwithstanding their gifts, they were both cast into the lake of fire burning with brimstone, Rev. xiii. 11, 13, 14; xix. 20. But he that hath a new heart and new spirit hath grace, and so shall be saved, John iii. 6; 2 Cor. iii. 17; he that is born of the Spirit is a new creature, he hath grace, and shall be saved, Acts xv. 11.

7. Activeness. Some men growing active for God and the public, zealous against corrupt practices in church or state, gather from hence that they have new hearts and spirits; they were not so before, and how can it be that such new operations and activeness should be in them, and from them, and they not be men of new hearts? When men are called

to public employments, they may have other hearts than they had before, yet not such a new heart as is here spoken off. Saul had "another heart," 1 Sam. x. 9, when anointed to be king, yet not a new heart. Credit, profit, and conscience misinformed may make men zealous and active, when they have no other than their old hearts. Paul before his conversion was very active, and exceedingly zealous of the traditions of his fathers, Gal. i. 13, 14. How active are Jesuits! how zealous are papists, and many others! and that from erroneousness of their consciences, not newness of their spirits.

Obs. 1. Men's hearts and spirits, by nature, are old, they are degenerated from that innocency, simplicity, and purity Adam was created in, they are corrupted ever since he ate of the forbidden fruit. Psal. xiv. 1, "Men are corrupt, they have done abominable works, there is none that doeth good:" Psal. liii. 3, "Every one of them is gone back: they are altogether become filthy; there is none that doeth good, no, not one:" such as their hearts are, such are their actions; old hearts have answerable operations: Psal. lviii. 3, "They go astray as soon as they be born;" they brought corrupt hearts and natures with them into the world, and their first actings were against God, truth, justice, and holiness. Men by nature have hearts full of old things: 2 Cor. v. 17, old things are not passed away, but abide. Old principles, old lusts, old desires, old thoughts, old reasonings, old enmities, old confidences, old hardness, old deceitfulness, old frowardness, and old naughtiness, are all found in men's hearts till they are made new: see Gen. vi. 5; Matt. xv. 19.

Obs. 2. A new heart, a new spirit, is not from the power or will of man, but from the grace of God. "A new heart will I give you, a new spirit will I put into you." God bade them, Ezek. xviii. 31, make themselves new hearts and new spirits, but they were not able to do it; he promises therefore to do it for them. It is God's way in his holy word to command and call for that at the hands of men, which he intends to give and work; as Phil. ii. 12, "Work out your own salvation;" and in the next verse it is said, "It is God which worketh in you both to will and to do:" Isa. i. 16, "Wash you, make you clean:" Ezek. xxxvi. 25, "I will sprinkle clean water upon you, and ye shall be clean:" Deut. x. 16, "Circumcise the foreskin of your heart;" they could not do it, therefore, Deut. xxx. 6, "The Lord thy God will circumcise thine heart." These Scriptures evince, that it is the Lord himself who performs what he commands; it is not man's will or power which produceth the new heart, it is the gracious and mighty hand of God which effects it; and when he will work, who shall let it? Shall man's will? Yes, if God did only propound arguments, command, exhort, invite, encourage, threaten, it might; but God doth promise to do the thing, "to give a new heart, put in a new spirit;" and should the liberty of man's will hinder it, how should God be faithful? But, rather than he will be found unfaithful, he will overpower the corrupt wills of men, and make them flexible to his will. The efficacy of grace depends not upon man's will, embracing or refusing what is tendered, but on the good pleasure and power of God, Phil. ii. 13. When it pleases God to put forth his power, the work shall be done, the "new heart and new spirit" shall be wrought in the man, notwithstanding all the oldnesses therein.

"And I will take away the stony heart out of your flesh." In chap. xi. 19, the words are, "I will take the stony heart out of their flesh," and here they are, "I will take away the stony heart out of your flesh." Much was spoken of them there; something I shall speak now.

"The stony heart." The Hebrew is, the heart of stone, that is, the heart which in a spiritual sense is like a stone.

1. A stone is senseless, it feels or perceives nothing; and so is a "stony heart:" Eph. iv. 19, "Who being past feeling;" they were so accustomed to sin, that they felt not any evil in sin. Zech. xiv. 4, we read of a mountain that cleaved in sunder at the presence of Christ; but the hearts of the Jews were so stony, that they were not at all affected at the presence or voice of Christ.

2. A stone is hard and impenetrable, a knife, a sword, a nail, will not enter into it; so a "stony heart" is so hard, that the word of God hath no entrance into it. Psal. cxix. 130, "The entrance of thy words giveth light;" when it enters into the heart it doth so: but though the word be of a sharp and piercing nature, yet it enters not into a "stony heart," it is impenetrable. Zech. vii. 11, "They refused to hearken, and pulled away the shoulder, and stopped their ears, that they should not hear. Yea, they made their hearts as an adamant stone." No truths, no arguments, no invitations, no prayers, no tears, no mercies, no threats, no judgments, do conquer or prevail with it: neither wind, rain, thunder, lightning, sunshine, heat, cold, do change the nature of a rock.

3. A stone is unpolished, and inept for building and other uses, till it be hewn, sawn, and brought into some other form; so a "stony heart" is a heart unpolished, unfit to lie in any part of God's building, or for any service of his, till it be polished, hewn, sawn, hammered, and brought into some other frame. As a stone cannot change itself, no more can a "stony heart." The devil knew that the stones, Matt. iv. 3, could not turn themselves into bread, therefore saith to Christ, "Command that they be made bread." He knew they might be made bread meet to eat: and so "stony hearts," though they cannot make themselves fleshy, yet they may be made fleshy, they may be brought to another form, and so be fit for spiritual employments and uses.

4. A stone doth resist and repel what falls upon it; stones do oft break the instruments which strike them, and force them back, there is a resisting in them; so in "stony hearts" there is much resistance. Luke iv. 28, 29, "All they in the synagogue, when they heard these things, were filled with wrath, and rose up, and thrust him out of the city, and led him unto the brow of the hill that they might cast him down headlong." Their flinty, rocky hearts resisted and rejected all the precious truths Christ had delivered, and made them fall foul upon him, and seek to spill his blood. 2 Tim. iii. 8, "As Jannes and Jambres withstood Moses, so do these also resist the truth: men of corrupt minds, reprobate concerning the faith;" they were men of stony hearts resisting the faith: Acts vii. 51, "Ye stiff-necked, and uncircumcised in heart and ears, ye do always resist," &c.

5. A stone is heavy, Prov. xxvii. 3, and its motion is downwards; it is earth hardened, and its whole tendency is to the earth; so a "stony heart" is heavy, earthy, and tends downwards altogether: Ezek. xx. 16, "Their heart went after their idols:" chap. xxxiii. 31, "Their heart goeth after their covetousness:" and Hosea iv. 8, "They set their heart on their iniquity." Men are born with the stone in their hearts, and naturally they mind earthly things, Phil. iii. 19; their motion is downward: John iii. 31, "He that is of the earth is earthly, and speaketh of the earth;" his thoughts, his words, his motions,

are all that way. The things of heaven are burdensome to a "stony heart," that cannot move upwards.

6. Stones keep their places, and are immovable. Eccles. x. 9, "Whoso removeth stones shall be hurt therewith;" great stones, mountains, rocks, abide fixed, and it is dangerous to meddle with them. So "stony hearts" keep their stoniness, they are immovable; what opinions, principles, conclusions soever they have taken in, though false and corrupt, they are tenacious of, and obstinate in: Judg. ii. 19, "They ceased not from their own doings, nor from their stubborn way." God sold them into the hands of enemies, where they suffered grievous things; God raised them up deliverers, who set them at liberty; yet "they ceased not from their own way," they were immovable from their own opinions, corrupt principles, and dangerous tenets. Men are so self-conceited, self-willed, that they are like rocks, not to be stirred.

7. Stones are dry, and have no moisture in them at all. Take a rock, there is no water in it; take any stone, it is dry; all stones are dry and barren; so stony hearts, they have no moisture of grace in them, they are all dry and barren, the waters of life are not found in them. The woman of Samaria had a "stony heart," and how dry, how barren was it! not a good word came out of it towards Christ, John iv. Whilst the gentiles were without God and Christ in the world, they had "stony hearts," and so were barren and fruitless, Isa. liv. 1. Wheresoever is a "stony heart," there is no melting, no mourning, no tears.

8. Stones are cold. 1 Sam. xxv. 37, it is said, Nabal's "heart died within him, and he became as a stone," that is, cold and senseless. So "stony hearts" are cold, there is no spiritual heat in them; though the word be as fire, yet it heats them not. Men of "stony hearts" are frigid in the things of God, they contend not for the truth, they reprove not wickedness in others, they stand not for the interest of Christ, they are not zealous for God and his glory, they put not their hands to his work, they mind not the conversion of sinners, they are indifferent how things of that nature go. A "stony heart" is a dead heart, and as it hath no life nor motion in it, so no warmth in it; like the Shunammite's son, 2 Kings iv. 34; till Elisha came and stretched forth himself upon it, there was neither life nor warmth in it; and till God's Spirit come and stretch forth its virtue and power upon a "stony heart," it hath neither life nor warmth in it. Thus you see wherein a "stony heart" resembles a stone, or rock.

Quest. What is the evil of a hard heart?

Answ. 1. It is ever unthankful; mercies, kindnesses, do not affect it, and how then can it be thankful? some verbal thankfulness may be in a hard-hearted man, but in his heart, in his life there is nothing. Pour wine, oil, the spirits and quintessence of any thing upon a stone, it is lost, the stone is not at all the better for it, not affected with it; so a "stony heart," let the choicest mercies of heaven or earth be presented to it, they are lost, that heart is unthankful; and whereas we should be thankful in every thing, 1 Thess. v. 18, such a one is thankful in nothing, and makes the times perilous, 2 Tim. iii. 2.

Answ. 2. It grows worse and worse, harder and harder, every day, nothing stops it from proceeding on in its wicked ways. The Jews were a stony-hearted people, and what saith the Lord to them? Isa. i. 5, "Why should ye be stricken any more? ye will revolt more and more:" threatening judgments did not stop or turn them from their wickedness. Pharaoh saw the wonderful judgments of God, ten plagues were upon him and his land, and yet his heart grew harder and harder. They that came to take Christ, went backward and fell to the ground when Christ said, "I am he;" they saw also a miracle wrought by Christ, in restoring to Malchus his ear, which Peter had cut off, yet, being stony-hearted, they proceeded to take Christ, to bind him and carry him to the high priest, John xviii. 6, 10—13.

Answ. 3. It causeth a man to walk contrary to his profession. Those that are christians, profess Christ and the gospel, they have in baptism given up themselves to him, and obliged themselves to walk according to gospel rules: now whence is it that they profess one thing, and practise another, that they profess christianity, and walk as heathens, or worse than heathens? whoredom, drunkenness, covetousness, lying, pride, swearing, theft, murder, witchery, contention, slander, oppression, &c. are they not as frequent among christians as ever they were among heathens? Paul, writing to the Ephesians, exhorted them "not to walk as other gentiles, in the vanity of their minds, having the understanding darkened, being alienated from the life of God, through the ignorance that is in them, because of the blindness of their heart, who being past feeling have given themselves over unto lasciviousness, to work all uncleanness with greediness." It was the hardness of the heathen gentiles' hearts, which made them walk so; and when christian gentiles walk so, it is from the hardness of their hearts. We are of the gentiles, and notwithstanding our christianity, we walk contrary to Christ and the gospel, which is from the stoniness of our hearts, keeping out the power; and this is a grievous evil: we profess Christ and the gospel verbally, and deny both really, and so cause our holy profession, and the Lord Jesus Christ, to be blasphemed, Rom. ii. 24; James ii. 7.

Answ. 4. It is a spiritual judgment, which is worse than all other diseases, than all other judgments. A blind eye, a deaf ear, a dumb tongue, a palsy hand, a gouty leg, a leprous head, the stone in the kidneys or bladder, are nothing to the stone in the heart; no plague is like that plague. Those four sore judgments mentioned chap. xiv. 21, are not so ill as the stone in the heart; men are sensible of those, and tremble at them, but the stoniness of their hearts they neither feel nor fear, by reason of it. Can there be a more dreadful judgment upon a man than to be given up of God to hardness of heart? Psal. lxxxi. 11, 12, "My people would not hearken to my voice; and Israel would none of me. So I gave them up unto their own hearts' lust: and they walked in their own counsels:" they were stubborn, and God punished their stubbornness with stoniness.

Answ. 5. It pleaseth itself in the ways of wickedness: Prov. x. 23, "It is as sport to a fool to do mischief;" and chap. xiv. 9, "Fools make a mock at sin:" fools, that is, wicked men, whose hearts are hardened, who know not the nature of sin, who feel not the weight of sin, they slight sin, they sport themselves with sin, they rejoice to do evil, Prov. ii. 14; "They count it pleasure to riot in the day time," 2 Pet. ii. 13. There is no sin but men of stony hearts take delight in, some in one, some in another, and if they can or cannot commit wickedness themselves, they take pleasure in them that can, Rom. i. 32.

Answ. 6. It is the seat of Satan, he dwells in it. A "stony heart" is the devil's castle: Eph. ii. 2, he is in, and works in the children of disobedience; in their hearts he hath strong holds, keeps possession, and rules them at his pleasure, they are his subjects.

God dwells in a broken heart, Isa. lvii. 15; but the devil in a "stony heart."

Answ. 7. That man that hath a "stony heart" increaseth his own woe daily: Rom. ii. 5, Thou "after thy hardness and impenitent heart treasurest up unto thyself wrath against the day of wrath;" that is, thou causest God to treasure up more severe punishment for thee daily; thou sinnest more and more daily, and God heats the furnace hotter and hotter daily.

"I will take away." The word is in Hiphil, and signifies thus much, I will cause to depart, or, I will make to remove, cause to be gone. Montanus renders it, I will remove it. God doth this,

1. By enlightening the blind heart to see, Acts xxvi. 18; 1 Pet. ii. 9; Eph. iv. 18; v. 8.

2. By enlivening the dead and senseless heart to feel its stoniness. When breath and life entered into the dry bones, they were sensible, Ezek. xxxvii.; and when God breathes upon a stony heart it lives, and is sensible. What an adamantine heart was in Paul, who took pleasure in vexing, imprisoning, and murdering of the saints; but when Christ breathed upon him, and put life into him, he then became sensible of his hard-heartedness, Acts ix.

3. By the warmth of his Spirit, and moisture of his grace, love, and mercy, he melts the "stony heart." Some fire will melt brass and iron, and some waters dissolve any stone; such is the fire of God's Spirit, there is not any iron or brazen heart but that can melt it; such is the water of life, there is not any "stony heart" but that will dissolve it. There is an omnipotent power in the Spirit and grace of God to turn millstones into wax, and rocks into streams; it was verified in Paul, who feeling the mighty power of God's Spirit and grace in his heart, had the millstoniness and rockiness thereof removed, for presently he cried out, "Lord, what wilt thou have me to do?" and fell to weeping and praying.

"Out of your flesh." By "flesh" here is not meant corrupt nature, as Gal. v. 13; but by it is meant man, "I will take away the stony heart out of your flesh," that is, out of you.

Obs. 1. The hearts of men, as they are in themselves, are stony, even stones, senseless of sin, unyieldable to truth, inept for spiritual employments, repelling and rejecting the counsel of God, moving downwards, and minding earthly things, immovable from their tenets, cold, and barren. Such are all men's hearts naturally, and the hardness of them is much increased by actual and customary sins. When men consent to evil thoughts and lusts in their hearts, vent them by actings, and reiterate the same day after day, they make their hearts more and more hard, as the hand is by working, and the foot by walking. Jer. v. 3, "They have made their faces harder than a rock; they have refused to return." If their faces were hardened like rocks, what were their hearts? Zechariah tells you, "They made their hearts as an adamant stone," Zech. vii. 12, which exceeds other stones in hardness; and not some few of them had done so, but even all of them: Ezek. iii. 7, "All the house of Israel are impudent and hard-hearted;" all of them had faces of rock and hearts of adamant.

Obs. 2. It is the prerogative of God, who hath dominion over the heart, to alter the heart. "I will take away the stony heart out of your flesh." They could not change their own hearts, they were not able to get the stone out of them, nor the prophets, who were their spiritual physicians. Kidney-stones, and bladder-stones, men may remove; heart-stones none can remove but God: men cannot remove mountains or rocks, but the Lord can; he hath an arm of strength, his word is a word of power, when he commands, it is done. Though a "stony heart" can stand it out against men, yet it cannot stand it out against God; he fetched water out of a rock, and God can make the hardest rocky heart in the world to melt, repent, and send forth floods of water. Mary Magdalene had an impudent face and a hard heart, but when God dealt with her, he took away the hardness of her heart and impudency of her face, she sat and wept at the feet of Christ, Luke vii. 38: the Lord can turn wildernesses into standing waters, and dry ground into water-springs, Psal. cvii. 35.

Obs. 3. It is a great mercy to have the stoniness of the heart removed. The removal of any evil from the body of man is mercy, as blindness from the eye, deafness from the ear, lameness from the leg, weakness from the stomach; much more, then, the removal of spiritual evil, and that from the heart. Stoniness of heart is the greatest evil which can befall it, and for God to take that away, to cure it, is a rich, a wonderfully great mercy, it is a mercy of the new covenant; it is more than God's delivering Daniel from the lions' den, Jonah from the whale's belly, or the three children from the fiery furnace. They should have been saved had they died in those conditions, but the man that dies with a hard heart perisheth for ever.

"And I will give you an heart of flesh." The "heart of flesh" is opposed to the "stony heart," and it implies several things which are considerable: as,

1. Softness, tenderness. A "stony heart" is hard, but a "heart of flesh" is tender and soft. The Scripture speaks of "a soft tongue," Prov. xxv. 15, and of a "soft heart," Job xxiii. 16; that is, a heart free from stoniness and obduration. Some flesh is brawny and hard, some very tender, as the flesh of those mentioned Deut. xxviii. 56. The "heart of flesh" is a heart like the tenderest flesh, even the flesh of a child new-born.

2. Sensibleness. Some flesh is so hardened, as that it feels nothing, and some is so tender, it is sensible of the least touch. The drunkard's flesh felt not the stripes when he was beaten, Prov. xxiii. 35; but Josiah's heart was sensible of the anger of God, when he heard the law only read, 2 Chron. xxxiv. Christ's heart was tender and sensible of our infirmities, he was touched with the feeling of them, Heb. iv. 15; the least infirmity he was affected with, for he had a "heart of flesh," a heart without any stoniness at all in it; and where a "heart of flesh" is, it is sensible of the least sin, the least dishonour to God; vain thoughts, risings of corruption, extravagancy of affections, all sins are burdensome to it. The man of such a heart hath his senses exercised to discern between good and evil, Heb. v. 14.

3. Meltingness. A "stony heart" never melts, but a "heart of flesh" is of a melting nature. Josiah's heart was not only affected with the law read, but melted also into tears: 2 Kings xxii. 19, his heart was tender, and he humbled himself before the Lord. So David, Psal. xxii. 14, "My heart is like wax; it is melted in the midst of my bowels:" how did it melt after Nathan had told him of his sin! Psal. li.; so after his numbering of the people, 2 Sam. xxiv. 17. Peter's heart was of this nature, for after Christ looked upon him "he went out and wept bitterly," Luke xxii. 62. Such were their hearts, Ezek. ix. 4, who sighed and cried for all "the abominations which were done in the midst of Jerusalem." A heart of flesh melts and mourns that God is dishonoured by others, but most of all that he hath been dishonoured by him in whom it is: that man that hath a "heart of flesh" sheds most tears for

the wrongs himself hath done unto God, Luke xv. 18, 19.

4. Teachableness. A "stony heart" is indocible, inflexible, it repels and keeps out truths, but a "heart of flesh" admits and receives truths, it is yielding and teachable. When Lydia's hard heart was turned into flesh, Acts xvi. 14, she attended unto the things which were spoken by the apostle, she received them, and believed them; she was a good scholar, and constrained her teachers to come and abide at her house, that she might learn more of them, ver. 15. Paul no sooner had his heart of stone made flesh, but he manifested a teachableness in himself: Acts ix. 6, "Lord, what wilt thou have me to do?" I am a blind Pharisee, and have been all my days out of the way; I desire now to learn, and to be taught of thee, whom I ignorantly blasphemed. David shut not his eyes against the light, as many hard-hearted persons do; he prayed that the Lord would open his eyes, that he might behold wondrous things out of the law; he was oft begging of God to teach him, "O teach me the way of thy statutes, and I shall keep it unto the end," Psal. cxix. 18, 33. He was willing to see, to hear, and to do: Psal. cx. 3, "Thy people shall be willing in the day of thy power." When the "stony heart" is removed, and "a heart of flesh" put in the room of it, that is a day of power; and then the people so hearted are willing to hear the Lord speak, to understand his counsels, and to resolve their wills into God's, so that his will is theirs.

5. A disposition to obedience. A "stony heart" is refractory, contradictory, disobedient, but a fleshy heart is yielding and obediential; it is a heart which follows God, as Elisha followed Elijah, virtue went out of the mantle and constrained him to do so; and the virtue gone out from God into "a heart of flesh" prevails with it, and causeth it to follow God, to yield obedience unto him. Caleb had another spirit than the rest of the Jews had, and he followed the Lord fully, Numb. xiv. 24; his spirit was not obstinate, but obediential: and wherever this "heart of flesh" is, it is so far from being contentious against the truth, or withholding the truth in unrighteousness, as that it obeys the truth heartily, Rom. vi. 17.

I. Remark the excellency of a tender heart.

1. It is the mansion of God's Holy Spirit. When the heart is tender and fleshy, God puts his Holy Spirit into it, as in the next verse appears. The Spirit itself is a tender thing, and takes no content in a hard heart: Isa. lvii. 15, it is in the heart of humble and contrite ones that the Spirit dwells. The Corinthians were babes in Christ, very tender, and they were temples of the Spirit, 1 Cor. iii. 1, 16. How excellent is a tender heart, that the "Spirit of grace," Heb. x. 29, "the spirit of glory," 1 Pet. iv. 14, should take it up for its habitation! it was there before as an agent, not as an inhabitant.

2. It cannot endure the dishonour of God; it is much affected, yea afflicted, thereat. When Rabshakeh blasphemed and reviled the God of Israel, how was Hezekiah afflicted at it! "He rent his clothes, covered himself with sackcloth, and went into the house of the Lord;" sends for Isaiah, begs his prayers, spreads the blasphemer's letter he had received before the Lord, and cried unto him for help to vindicate his own name, 2 Kings xix. 1—4, 14—19. Hezekiah had a tender heart, and herein was the excellency of it, he was deeply affected with the dishonour of God. David's heart was touched thoroughly when men violated the law of God, and dishonoured his name: Psal. cxix. 136, "Rivers of waters run down mine eyes, because they keep not thy law." None of his own afflictions, his persecution by Saul, his expulsion by Absalom, did draw so many tears from him as the dishonour of God's name, that made his tender heart like a fountain which sends forth rivers. The heathens, who had hard hearts, said of their heathenish king, "It is not meet for us to see the king's dishonour," Ezra iv. 14. And can christians see the dishonour of the God of heaven? those that have "hearts of flesh" cannot endure to see it; if they cannot help the same, they will mourn, and mourn abundantly for it.

3. It is a strong defence against all sin; it quickly feels the nature of sin, and so flees from it. Touch tender flesh with a needle or pin, it endures not the same, it cries out against, and removes them. Some bodies are so delicate that they feel every wind, every little distemper, and so fortify themselves against them; and some hearts are so tender, that corruption or the devil cannot stir but they discern, feel, and find them, and so set themselves against them. When Joseph's mistress tempted him to folly, his heart startled at it, and caused his tongue to say, "How can I do this, and sin against God?" Gen. xxxix. 9. A tender heart sticks at the appearance of evil, and will not venture there. Abraham would not take any thing of the spoil recovered, but returned all into the hands of the king of Sodom, lest he should say, "I have made Abraham rich," Gen. xiv. 23. This was an excellent frame of spirit, and proceeded from the tenderness of his heart; such tenderness antidotes a man against the poison of sin. Job's heart was flesh, not stone, and not his friends, wife, or devil, could draw him to commit sin; his heart was sensible of his sons' sinning, and on their behalf he offered sacrifice continually, Job i. 5; and that tenderness preserved him from sinning. David's heart smote him when he cut off but the lap of Saul's garment, 1 Sam. xxiv. 5.

4. It is active for God. When Paul's heart was turned into flesh, presently saith he, "Lord, what wilt thou have me to do?" I am now ready to do aught for thee, Acts ix. 6; "and straightway he preached Christ in the synagogues," ver. 20. Josiah was of a tender heart, and he acted notably for God, he destroyed the groves, altars, high-places, images out of Judah and Jerusalem, and other places; he repaired the temple, he caused the law to be read, the people to enter into covenant with God, he kept a most solemn passover, such as had not been from Samuel's days before, 2 Chron. xxxiv. 35. A hard heart is active against God, and a soft heart is active for God. Manasseh, through the hardness of his heart, did more wickedly than any, 2 Chron. xxxiii. And David, through the tenderness of his heart, fulfilled all the will of God, Acts xiii. 22; he durst not neglect any duty the Lord called for, nor do it remissly when he went about it.

II. Inquire what are the mistakes about a tender heart?

1. There is a legal tenderness which arises from apprehension of God's sovereignty and justice, and his wrath due unto men for sin, and their sinful practices, whereupon they humble themselves, mourn, sigh, weep, pray, and so manifest some tenderness of heart. Such, I conceive, was the tenderness of Manasseh's heart, when he was among thorns, bound in fetters, and in affliction, then he besought the Lord, humbled himself greatly, and prayed, 2 Chron. xxxiii. 11—13. Such tenderness had Judas, who repented of what he had done, saying, he had sinned in betraying innocent blood, Matt. xxvii. 3, 4; terrors of conscience put him upon it. This legal tenderness is not that here meant. For,

(1.) Apprehensions of God's power, justice, wrath,

fear of death and hell, do never melt the heart. The law, judgments of God, considerations of death and hell, may break the stony heart into many pieces, yet every piece remain a stone, retain its hardness: when you break a millstone or rock into pieces with a hammer or pick-axe, though broken, yet there is no true softness in them.

(2.) Legal tenderness never loves God, it loves itself, and seeks itself; but evangelical, or spiritual, tenderness carries out the heart to God and Christ. Peter, having hardened his heart by denial of the Lord Jesus once, twice, and thrice, and then being softened again by a look of Christ upon him, Luke xxii. 61, 62, he loved him dearly; and that it might be known, Christ asked him the question, "Simon, lovest thou me more than these?" he saith not, Peter, dost thou love me? but, "dost thou love me more than these?" I know these love me much, how stands thy heart to me? his answer was, Yea, I love thee, and more than these do love thee, and thou knowest it. A tender heart is strongly in love with Christ. Paul, after his heart was regenerate and softened, he was so in love with Christ, that he wisheth Anathema Maran-atha to that man which loves not the Lord Jesus, 1 Cor. xvi. 22.

2. There is a natural fleshiness or tenderness, which is much in women, and sometimes also in men; as when Joseph made himself known unto his brethren, he wept, it was from a natural tenderness in him, Gen. xlv. 1, 2. Some are by nature very tender and pitiful: such tenderness is not what our prophet aims at. For,

(1.) This natural tenderness is born with men, they bring it with them into the world; the other is a gift, "I will give you an heart of flesh;" the one is of nature, the other of grace. Parents procreate the one, God creates the other; the one is from constitution, the other from regeneration.

(2.) Where there is a natural tenderness, it is flexible both ways, to good and evil. Rehoboam, who was a wicked king, having a tender heart, 2 Chron. xiii. 7, he was for evil and for good, he hearkened to the young men's ill counsel at one time, and to Shemaiah's good counsel another time, 1 Kings xii. 14, 24; he was easily drawn this way and that way, like some in the apostle's time, who "were carried about with every wind of doctrine," Eph. iv. 14; they were children, they had a natural tenderness in them, and bowed to sound and corrupt doctrine. But a man that hath the tenderness of heart here intended, is untractable towards evil, and only flexible unto good: 1 John iii. 9, "He cannot sin, because he is born of God;" his heart is obstinate against sin, he keeps himself from the touching of the wicked one, chap. v. 18; but is pliable to the will of the holy one, "prepared unto every good work," 2 Tim. ii. 21.

3. Natural tenderness is faint in the cause of God, it hath no courage, no magnanimity for God, but spiritual tenderness hath. Paul was tender-hearted after his conversion, and see what a spirit he had for God: Acts xvii. 22, 23, "Ye men of Athens, I perceive that in all things ye are too superstitious," &c.: he contested with the whole university of Athens. The Book of Martyrs tells us of Alice Driver, (a tender-hearted woman,) who said, she would set her foot against the foot of any of them all; she meant the bishops and their creatures: she had courage for God and his cause.

4. Natural tenderness is dulled by fasting, prayer, and humiliation, but spiritual tenderness is sharpened and quickened by the same. Esther, after her fasting, praying, and humbling her soul, was more sensible of the state of the Jews, and the great danger they were in, and ventured her life for them, Esth. iv. v.

5. Afflictions, crosses, are very heavy to that heart that is naturally tender, it is restless, unquiet under them; but a heart spiritually tender welcomes afflictions, receives them with joy, Heb. x. 34; and finds sin heavier than afflictions. There are some soft natures which can weep, shed tears in abundance, for loss of relations, estates, favours of great ones, yet never wept for sin; these have a natural tenderness, not a spiritual.

Besides what may be gathered from what is said, I shall,

III. Give some characters of a tender heart.

1. It is sensible of the church's and saints' afflictions, it mourns for and with them; a tender heart bleeds when it goes ill with Zion and the people of God. When the men of Ai smote but thirty-six Israelites, how was Joshua affected with it! "He rent his clothes, and fell to the earth upon his face before the ark of the Lord until the eventide," Josh. vii. 6. You may read, Psal. lxxix. lxxx. how greatly David, or Asaph, were affected with the desolation of Jerusalem, and miseries which befell the church. These were men of tender hearts, and sensible of evils at a distance. Such was Paul, 2 Cor. xiv. 20, and Jeremiah, whose eyes ran down with tears, because the Lord's flock was carried away captive, Jer. xiii. 17.

2. Where a heart hath a gracious and spiritual tenderness, it is affected with the perishing condition of others, it grieves to see men impenitent, unbelieving, going on in the broad way, to be in a state of unregeneracy, and pities them. Rom. ix. 2, 3, Paul had great heaviness, and continual sorrow in his heart, and why? for his brethren, and kinsmen according to the flesh; they rejected Christ and his gospel through unbelief and hardness of heart, they were in the broad way to destruction. Christ, seeing Jerusalem insensible of her own good, he wept over her, Luke xix. 41. And in former times Jeremiah had manifested the tenderness of his heart toward the Jews, when he said unto them thus, "Hear ye, and give ear, be not proud: for the Lord hath spoken. Give glory to the Lord your God, before he cause darkness, and before your feet stumble upon the dark mountains, and while ye look for light, he turn it into the shadow of death, and make it gross darkness. But if ye will not hear it, my soul shall weep in secret places for your pride," Jer. xiii. 15—17.

3. A tender heart dare not go out from God in any case, but commits itself and way to him, it consults with God, and leans upon him for counsel and direction. Josiah, when the law was found, and he understood from it what wrath was due to the breach of it, presently sends men to inquire of the Lord for himself and others what to do; he took counsel of God, and not of man, 2 Chron. xxxiv. 21. So Jehoshaphat, he sought not to Baalim, but to the Lord God of his fathers; and David made God's testimonies his counsellors, Psal. cxix. 24. Hard hearts dare presume and venture to go out from God, and into ways he hath not warranted: so did Gehazi, Judas, and Demas, they followed the imaginations of their own hearts, and declared that their hearts were brass. Those that have hearts of flesh say with them in Isa. ii. 3, "Come, let us go up to the mountain of the Lord, to the house of the God of Jacob; and he will teach us of his ways, and we will walk in his paths," not in our own.

4. It is affected presently at the frowns and chidings of God, at the appearance and shaking of the rod. A child of a tender nature will melt when the

parent begins to manifest displeasure, as to chide, or take the rod into his hand; but it is not so with a stubborn nature, that will hear bitter words, and endure many strokes, before it will melt: Jer. v. 3, "Thou hast stricken them, but they have not grieved; thou hast consumed them, but they have refused to receive correction: they have made their faces harder than a rock; they have refused to return:" these had no tender hearts in them. When Absalom had driven David out of Jerusalem, he went up mount Olivet weeping: he was presently affected with the hand of God, 2 Sam. xv. 30. Moses was presently affected with the wrath that went out from God against the people, Numb. xvi. 46.

5. A tender heart feels much stoniness in itself, and complains of it: Oh what a stony, rocky, adamantine heart have I! saith a tender-hearted man. Its tenderness discovers and feels hardness; Eph. iv. 19, they were hardened in sin, were past feeling. Where hearts are all stone, there is no sensibleness of the stoniness: those have the tenderest hearts, that feel most brass and iron in them. David cried oft to God for quickening; Psal. cxix. 154, 156, 159, "Quicken me according to thy word;" "quicken me according to thy judgments;" "quicken me according to thy loving-kindness." And why did he cry so for quickening? because he felt much deadness and hardness in his heart. A dead heart is a hard heart: a man when dead is cold, stiff, and hard; so a man's heart, if dead within him, is cold, stiff, and stony.

IV. How may the heart be kept tender?

1. By taking heed of every sin, for it is only sin that hardens the heart. As the foot, by treading, hardens the earth, so when sin walks up and down in the heart, it hardens and obdurates the same. Dan. v. 20, Nebuchadnezzar's mind was hardened in pride: and the apostle tells you, Heb. iii. 13, that men's hearts come to be hardened through the deceitfulness of sin. Men think little sins can do them little harm; but they harden their hearts, and is that no harm? is that little harm? it is the greatest harm that can be done you.

2. By searching and examining of your hearts frequently, that is a special means to keep them tender. It is like digging of the garden, and ploughing of the earth, which keeps it from hardening; the more digging and ploughing, the more tender and crumbly is the earth, that is the chiefest way to preserve it so; and they who are ever searching their hearts, examining them daily, have them in a tender frame. David communed oft with his own heart, and his spirit made diligent search, Psal. lxxvii. 6; that kept his heart in a tender frame.

3. By studying the word much, and minding it. There is great virtue in the word, it is like fire, and will not only thaw the iciness of their hearts, but keep them unfrozen: the hardest metals, while they are in the fire, are soft; and whilst men's hearts are in the divine fire of the Scriptures, they will be soft. The word is like water and oil, which moisten and supple the heart, so that the tenderness of it is preserved.

4. By meditating seriously on God's love, the heights, depths, lengths, and breadths of his love. When a soul is taken up with thoughts of the freeness, greatness, strength, sweetness, everlastingness, and fruits of God's love, it will be in a melting frame, that fire works kindly upon the heart; love apprehended makes the heart tender.

5. Look much to Christ crucified, Zech. xii. 10. When we consider what Christ hath suffered for our sakes, it will make and keep our hearts tender. Hence

Obs. 1. A tender heart is a choice mercy. As a "stony heart" is a grievous plague, so a "heart of flesh" is a great blessing; it is sensible of sin, even secret sins, it trembles at thoughts of God, his attributes, and word, it understands divine things, it is teachable and obediential, it is compassionate and full of bowels towards all: such a heart is rare to find, but wherever it is, it is a mercy of mercies, a superlative mercy.

Obs. 2. It is a gift, even the gift of God. "I will give you an heart of flesh." None but he who can fetch water out of a rock, and turn stones into flesh, Matt. iii. 9, can give this tender heart; we can make our hearts stony by sinning, but we cannot soften them again. It is God's prerogative to make and give a "heart of flesh;" he can make the hardest heart exceeding tender. Beg such a heart of him, and press him with his promise; "for faithful is he who hath promised, who also will do it."

Ver. 27. *And I will put my spirit within you, and cause you to walk in my statutes, and ye shall keep my judgments, and do them.*

In the 25th verse remission of sins was promised, in the 26th, regeneration, and in this, infusion of the Spirit is promised. In the words are,

I. The mercy promised, viz. the "spirit."

II. The parties recipient, "you."

III. The effects of this reception, "walking in," &c.

"I will put my spirit within you." By "spirit" here, I understand not the new heart or new spirit mentioned in the verse before, viz. the gifts and graces of the Spirit, but the Spirit itself; so Œcolampadius, Lavater, Junius, and Polonius: and however it be a great dispute among school-men, whether the Spirit itself be given unto men, and dwell in them; some conclude, that the person of the Spirit is not given, but dwells in us only, by his gifts imparted: yet the Scripture is clear, that the Spirit itself is given, and dwells in the sons of men. Rom. v. 5, "The love of God is shed abroad in our hearts by the Holy Spirit, which is given unto us." Here is a distinction made between the grace of the Spirit, and the Spirit itself: the grace of love is shed abroad in the hearts of the saints by the Spirit, and that Spirit which worketh that grace in them, is given unto them. The person of the Spirit is distinguished from the gifts and graces he works in men; 1 Cor. vi. 19, "Know ye not that your body is the temple of the Holy Spirit in you:" a temple is not for gifts or graces, but for a person, a deity, and some special presence of that deity. The world hath God in it, yet it is not called The temple of God, because he is in a general and common manner in the same; but the Spirit is in the bodies of the saints, and that in a special manner: 1 Cor. ii. 12, "We have received, not the spirit of the world, but the spirit which is of God; that we might know the things that are freely given to us of God." By "spirit" here cannot be meant gifts or graces, but the person of the Spirit, "who searcheth the deep things of God," as it is ver. 10, and makes them known by degrees unto those he dwells in, discovering what God hath done for them. Rom. viii. 11, "If the Spirit of him that raised up Jesus from the dead dwell in you:" it is the Spirit of God himself who dwells in believers, and not only the gifts and graces of the Spirit; these are in them as qualities in a subject, but he is in them as an inhabitant in a house.

The Spirit, by reason of its infiniteness, is every where, in trees, worms, flowers, waters, all creatures; is it any otherwise in the saints than in them? True, the Spirit, as to his essence, is in all things; yet,

1. It is not in them by way of union. A fish is in

the water, but not united to the water: the Spirit is in the saints by way of union, therefore is said to "dwell in them" by his own gifts and graces: we are united to the Spirit, and the Spirit to us.

2. It is not in them by way of gracious operation. All he doth in other creatures, is upholding their beings, enabling them to put forth their natural power, vigour, virtue, and ordering their motions to what ends he pleaseth; he worketh nothing in them above their natures: but in those he dwells he worketh gracious effects; in those the Lord gives the Spirit unto, he worketh such operations as are not elsewhere, even such as are above nature; he is in them, by a special title, by an act of grace. A gardener worketh curious knots in the garden, which he doth not elsewhere: God made other works, and set other plants, in Paradise than in the world.

3. As the Deity of Christ is every where, in every creature, yet otherwise in Christ's human nature than in any creature, Col. ii. 9; so the Spirit, though it be every where, yet is otherwise in believers than in other creatures, it is in them as it is in Christ himself, but not in the same measure.

What doth the Spirit, being within us?

1. It unites the Lord Christ and the soul together, it makes a happy union between them two. The Corinthians were espoused to Christ, 2 Cor. xi. 2, not only by the ministry of Paul, but by the Spirit: 1 Cor. xii. 13, "By one Spirit are we all baptized into one body;" that is, the church, the body of Christ. The Spirit is the great Agent in this work.

2. The Spirit gives out divine oracles and truths unto the soul. As in the temple God gave out his mind, made known his will, so doth the Spirit in the heart of man; Matt. x. 20, the Spirit of the Father speaks in believers. 1 John ii. 20, "Ye have an unction from the Holy One, and ye know all things:" that unction is the Spirit, which makes known all needful things unto those it dwells in. It is needful to be instructed, and armed against antichrist and his seducements; it is needful to be directed in the way to heaven: they had the Spirit, which did teach them how to avoid the one, and how to proceed in the other; and so were taught of God: "and who teacheth like him?" Job xxxvi. 22. He teacheth inwardly, infallibly, powerfully.

3. It conquers and drives out the enemies that had possession of and quartered in us. There is no man the Lord puts his Spirit into, but the Spirit finds the devil there; he hath possession of men's hearts, and labours to keep the same. There are also a multitude of base and ungodly lusts which fight for the devil's interest; these the Spirit sets upon, subdues, and casts out. When Christ came into the temple, he whipped out all the money-changers; when Joshua came into Canaan, he drove out the Canaanites and other nations: and when the Spirit comes into a man, it beats down strong holds, drives out Satan and his troops; 1 John iv. 4, "Greater is he that is in you, than he that is in the world." The devil had been in them before, but was now driven out of them into the world by the Spirit which was in them, and their lusts were mortified by the same Spirit, Rom. viii. 13.

4. The Spirit put into man, takes the rule and government of that man into his own hand; he must no longer be under the dominion of sin or Satan, but under the conduct of the Spirit; he, and all in him, must bow to that great Person. When a great man cometh into the country to dwell, he looks for all about him to bow unto him, and to be at his command; hence men that have stout and stubborn spirits which cannot bow use to say, We care not for a great neighbour. The Spirit is greater than all men, and when he is put into men, it is to rule; he is there not to be checked, controlled, opposed, but to bear sway, to have the keys of every room delivered up unto him: he must be, and will be, sovereign in the soul, before him every mountain and hill must be brought low, yea, every creature must swear fealty unto him. Rom. viii. 14, "They are led by the Spirit of God:" the Spirit is the commander and leader of those it dwells in, they follow him and not others; whereas those that are without the Spirit are "led away with divers lusts," 2 Tim. iii. 6; or drawn away with their own lust, James i. 14; and so follow Satan, 1 Tim. v. 15. It is not so with those that have the Spirit; that is called a guide, John xvi. 13; and such a guide, as guides into all truth, and orders them so, as that they shall not miscarry; for it is a Spirit of wisdom, Eph. i. 17; of counsel, Isa. xi. 2; of power, 2 Tim. i. 7: so that he must rule, and where he rules, he doth it wisely.

5. He frames them to his own mind, and transforms them into his own likeness. As a graft put into a stock turns the sap of the stock, and assimilates it and the stock to itself, so doth the Spirit in the parties where it is: 2 Cor. iii. 18, "We are changed into the same image from glory to glory, even as by the Spirit of the Lord," or, by the Lord the Spirit, so the Greek will bear it; we are selfish, sinful, natural, mortal, and the Spirit makes us spiritual. The husband frames the mind of his wife suitable unto his own; when a man comes into an old house, he pulls down and sets up, he takes away and adds what he pleases, and fits the house to his own mind; so doth the Spirit, being in our earthly tabernacles, it abrogates the laws of the flesh, it throws out the principles of Satan and the world, it sets up new laws, and works new principles, Rom. iii. 27; viii. 2.

6. The Spirit being put into man, and man becoming his temple, he doth beautify and adorn that temple, and make it glorious. Solomon overlaid the temple with pure gold, 1 Kings vi. 21; the inside was very glorious: and the Spirit trims up its temple with pure graces, with "love, joy, peace, long-suffering, gentleness, goodness, faith, meekness, temperance," &c. Gal. v. 22, 23; Ephes. v. 9. The Spirit garnished the heavens with those greater and lesser lights, Job xxvi. 13, which fill this lower world with their glory. It is the Spirit which reneweth the face of the earth, Psal. civ. 30, and makes it beautiful; and it is the Spirit reneweth and garnisheth the soul, making it glorious and beautiful with all graces: Psal. xlv. 13, "The king's daughter is all glorious within;" and the Spirit's temple is no less glorious. If Solomon's temple were called "the holy and beautiful house," Isa. lxiv. 11, much more may the temple of the Spirit be so called.

7. It being in man, enables him to do many things, it strengthens him with might to do that which otherwise he could not do, Eph. iii. 16. As,

(1.) To discern between the things of men and the things of God, between the things of Christ and those of antichrist, between true and counterfeit graces. 1 Cor. ii. 15, "He that is spiritual judgeth all things;" he hath the Spirit enabling him to make a difference, and to see the reality, beauty, and excellency of some things above others. The high priests, scribes, and Pharisees, saw no beauty in Christ that they should desire him, but the apostles, who had the Spirit in them, did: John i. 14, "We beheld his glory, the glory as of the only begotten of the Father:" and Paul saw so much in Christ, and the knowledge of him, that he counted all things but loss for the excellency of the knowledge of Christ, Phil. iii. 8.

(2.) It enables them to pray spiritually. Rom. viii. 26, "The Spirit helpeth our infirmities; for we know not what we should pray for as we ought." The Spirit tells us what to pray for, and helps us to bring forth those petitions it hath formed in us: Zech. xii. 10, it is called "the spirit of supplication," because it teaches us what to supplicate God for, and assists us in supplicating. Both Paul and Jude exhorts those they write unto, to pray in the Spirit, Eph. vi. 18; Jude 20; that is, in the strength and help of the Spirit, not in their own strength.

(3.) It enables to stand in time of trouble, persecution, and sufferings. The Spirit prompts answers unto those that are questioned for truth's sake, and helps them against all their opposers: see Mark xiii. 11; Matt. x. 19, 20; Luke xii. 11, 12. When they were led before magistrates and powers, they must take no thought beforehand what to speak, nor premeditate; the Spirit should help them, encourage and uphold them, not an angel, but the Spirit. Acts vi. 10, Stephen was so mightily assisted by the Spirit, that his opposers, viz. the Libertines, Cyrenians, Alexandrians, and others, were not able to withstand him.

(4.) It enables to bring forth good fruit. If there be no sap in a vine, it will bear no fruit: if there be only our own sap, it will yield sour fruit; but if the sap of the Spirit be there, then it will afford good fruit, special fruit. Acts x. 38, "Christ, being anointed with the Holy Spirit, and with power, went about doing good:" so the apostles; Acts i. 8, "Ye shall receive power, after the Holy Spirit is come upon you: and ye shall be witnesses unto me both in Jerusalem, and in all Judea, and in Samaria, and unto the uttermost part of the earth." The Spirit empowered them to walk up and down in the world, to preach the gospel, convert souls, plant churches, and to do them good: so did Paul, Rom. xv. 19. Where the Spirit is, it enables and provokes unto good, John vii. 38, 39.

(5.) The Spirit enables men to keep the word of God, and yield obedience unto it. 2 Tim. i. 14, "That good thing which was committed unto thee keep by the Holy Spirit which dwelleth in us." Timothy, saith Paul, thou hast that which is of great concernment committed to thy keeping, viz. the gospel, the form of sound words, and thou hast a great Helper to enable thee thereunto, even the Spirit of God which dwells in thee; see therefore that thou keep it by the enabling power of the Spirit, which helps not only to remember truth, but also to obey truth: for Peter assures us, that the believing Jews did obey the truth through the Spirit; that is, through the assistance of the Spirit. This is that which follows in the next words to be opened.

"And cause you to walk in my statutes." The Hebrew word for "cause" is, יתישׂע I will make, effect, or bring to pass by the operation of that Spirit I put into you, that you shall walk in my statutes. Vatablus renders it, *efficiam*, which imports, influence of power. David, Psal. cxliii. 10, prays unto the Lord to teach him to do his will; and, Psal. cxix. 35, he saith, "Make me to go in the path of thy commandments:" both these the Spirit, being put into man, performs; it teaches him to do the will of God, and causes him to go in the path of his commandments.

To walk in God's statutes implies several things.

1. The making of godliness and religion our chief work in this life. Other things are to be done as inferior things, this is to be the principal, no work should be so minded as this: saith Joshua, chap. xxiv. 15, "As for me and my house, we will serve the Lord," that shall be our great and chief business in this world. He remembered what God had commended to him and all men: Deut. vi. 6—9, "These words, which I command thee this day, shall be in thine heart: and thou shalt teach them diligently unto thy children, and shalt talk of them when thou sittest in thine house, and when thou walkest by the way, and when thou liest down, and when thou risest up. And thou shalt bind them for a sign upon thine hand, and they shall be as frontlets between thine eyes. And thou shalt write them upon the posts of thy house, and on thy gates." God would have us to be godly inwardly and outwardly, at home and abroad, night and day, and to make our families religious: and they are repeated again, Deut. xi. 18—20, that so they might take the deeper impression upon the hearts of men. David looked at this work above all others: Psal. cxix. 97, "O how I love thy law! it is my meditation all the day." To be godly and religious was his principal care: that is the one thing necessary; and Solomon hath drawn it up into this conclusion, "Fear God, and keep his commandments: for this is the whole duty of man," Eccles. xii. 13.

2. Taking delight in the ways of God. His statutes, commands, and ways are grievous to men, naturally they walk not in them. When men walk in any way, they are delighted with and in that way; so here, walking in God's statutes notes delight: Psal. cxix. 14, "I have rejoiced in the way of thy testimonies, as much as in all riches." Some rejoice in fine houses, some in fertile lands, some in great flocks, some in silver and gold; but David rejoiced in the way of God's testimonies, and as much as any of them, or all of them, in their riches; he found more sweet in them, than they in their wealth: ver. 143, "Thy commandments are my delights;" they were his chief, his satisfying, his sole and soul delights. It was meat and drink to Paul to be doing the will and work of the Lord, Acts xx. 24; as it was unto Christ, John iv. 34.

3. It imports motion and progress. They should not stand still in contemplation, nor sit still in meditation, but they should proceed and go on in the ways of God, they should get nearer their journey's end, be daily more knowing, more holy, more gracious, and godly. The Thessalonians' faith did grow exceedingly, and their charity abounded, 2 Thess. i. 3; they walked from faith to faith, and from love to love. When Paul was converted, and brought into the way of Christ, he increased in spiritual strength, Acts ix. 22; he reached forward, and pressed towards the mark, Phil. iii. 13, 14; he put on mightily for to get the knowledge of Christ, and the power of his resurrection, and the fellowship of his sufferings; he did not only walk, but ran oft, in the way of truth and godliness, 1 Cor. ix. 26.

4. Walking in God's statutes imports perseverance in them; they shall not apostatize and turn back from them, but continue in them. Of a wicked man destitute of God's Spirit, it is said, "He hath left off to be wise, and to do good," Psal. xxxvi. 3; but of a righteous man it is said, he "shall hold on in his way," Job xvii. 9. He knows he is in a safe and good way, a way that will recompense him fully at the end, whatever hardships or storms he meets withal, and therefore will neither sit still nor go back; he may be beside the way sometimes, but never turning back again.

"Ye shall keep my judgments and do them." Statutes and "judgments" are comprehensive words, and sometimes are used promiscuously, as hath formerly been showed in chap. xviii. 9: but here they may be thus differenced; statutes to signify the duties of the first table, the things of God's worship and manner of the same, whether under the law or gospel; and "judgments," the duties of the second table, matters of equity and justice between man and man.

The word for "keep" is, שמר, which imports, keeping with care and diligence; they should not keep them in their houses or memories only, but they should keep them practically, they should "do them."

Obs. 1. God's Spirit differs from all other spirits. Angels are spirits, souls of men are spirits, but these are below God's Spirit. "I will put my Spirit." God's Spirit is a Spirit of holiness, Rom. i. 4; the power of the Highest, Luke i. 35; a Spirit of truth guiding into all truth, John xvi. 13; a spirit of grace, Zech. xii. 10; the oil of gladness, Heb. i. 9; the Comforter, John xiv. 16; a spirit of glory, 1 Pet. iv. 14; a Spirit, that is the Lord, Isa. xi. 2; רוח יהוה The Spirit of Jehovah, shall rest upon him. Whatever excellences may be in souls or angels, they are infinitely short of that that is in the Spirit of God: Psal. cxliii. 10, "Thy Spirit is good;" that is, Thy Spirit, O Lord, is transcendently good. My own spirit is naught, and all other spirits are nothing compared with thy Spirit; that, and that only, is good, good originally, good transcendently, good infinitely.

Obs. 2. The putting in of the Spirit into the sons of men, is a free act of God. He doth it not upon the account of the covenant of works, but by virtue of the covenant of grace. This verse is a branch of the covenant of grace, and agrees with that in Jer. xxxi. 33, "I will put my law in their inward parts, and write it in their hearts;" that God doth, when he puts in his Spirit; 2 Cor. iii. 3, for the Spirit being within, writes divine truths in the heart. Adam had the law written in his heart by the Spirit, but not as it is written by the Spirit in the hearts of believers, who are under the new covenant: the Spirit wrote the law in Adam's heart as concreator with the Father and the Son, not by virtue of any covenant; but believers receive the Spirit, and have the law written in them, by virtue of covenant. God hath covenanted to put his Spirit in them, and they have the Spirit from Christ and the Father. Christ purchased of the Father the mission of the Spirit, therefore saith, he will send the Comforter unto them, John xvi. 7; and that he will pray the Father, and he shall send the Comforter unto them, John xiv. 16; so that believers now have the Spirit from God, as a Father in Christ, from Christ, as Head of the church, and both these by virtue of the new covenant. Adam had not the Spirit so; and for those that had the Spirit under the law, (for some had it, as you may see, Psal. li. 11; Neh. ix 20; Numb. xxvii. 18; Hag. ii. 5,) they had it not by virtue of the covenant of works, "Do this, and live;" for none were able to keep the law, but by virtue of the covenant of grace. There was gospel in the law, yea, the whole ceremonial law was so. The apostle tells us that the Galatians received not the Spirit by the works of the law, but by the hearing of faith, Gal. iii. 2: and look how the gentiles received the blessing of Abraham, viz. the Spirit, which was through faith, and through Christ, ver. 14; so did the Jews likewise.

Neither Jews nor gentiles do bring any preparations or qualifications towards the reception of the Spirit: God gives his Spirit freely where there are no such things. When men are in a state of sin and wickedness, the Spirit is put in; first it is there, and then it works grace; before they have new hearts, new spirits, the stone be taken out of the heart, and there be a "heart of flesh," the Spirit is put in and acts; he finds not qualifications or dispositions, but brings them, works them. The bees, when they come to the hive, find no wax, no honey there, but they bring the wax and honey; so the Spirit, when it comes to men's hearts, it finds no wax, no honey, no graces nor gracious dispositions there, but brings them: when the Spirit comes to regenerate and sanctify, it finds nothing in men but darkness, unbelief, unholiness, and enmity, by which it is no more defiled than an angel by coming into the world, which lies in wickedness, or the sun shining upon a dunghill; but when it comes to be an inhabitant, a Comforter, a Spirit of glory to rest upon a man, then it finds the heart prepared, and made meet for its entertainment and abode.

Obs. 3. The gift of the Spirit is a great and excellent gift. "I will put," or give, "my spirit within you." The greatness and excellency of it appears in these following particulars:

(1.) It is the person of the Spirit which is a fundamental mercy, and more considerable than all his gifts and graces, which flow from him: the tree is better than all the fruit, the sun is of more worth than all his beams.

(2.) It is the procreator of all grace in the soul. Gal. v. 22, "The fruit of the Spirit is love, joy, peace, faith." Take but those four graces, and see how they are exalted: faith is styled precious, 2 Pet. i. 1; peace is said to pass all understanding, Phil. iv. 7; joy to be glorious and unspeakable, 1 Pet. i. 8; and love is magnified by Paul above all gifts and other graces, 1 Cor. xiii. What a gift, then, is the Spirit, which is the parent, not only of these, but of all graces and all gifts! Eph. v. 9, "The fruit of the Spirit is in all goodness."

(3.) It is the conservator of all grace and good things in us. As God conserves the world, which is his creature, so the Spirit conserves grace, which is its creature: the Spirit, as it gives being to all graces, so it preserves them in their beings and operations. It is the Spirit which mortifies lusts, Rom. viii. 13; and it is the Spirit maintains graces. John iii. 6, "That which is born of the flesh is flesh; and that which is born of the Spirit is spirit." As flesh brings forth flesh, so it maintains the same, and as the Spirit brings forth spirit, so it maintains the same; each maintains their own offsprings. The Spirit is the nurse of all those graces it hath brought forth in the heart of any: 2 Cor. iv. 13, it is called "the Spirit of faith," not only because it creates faith in the heart, but keeps it there. So it is called "the spirit of grace," Zech. xii. 10, not only because it works grace in men, but also because it keeps grace in them; hence those who are after the Spirit, are said to mind the things of the Spirit; their graces are maintained by the provision of the Spirit.

(4.) The Spirit is he who actuates and consummates our graces. The Spirit doth not content itself to beget and preserve graces in men's hearts, but improves and perfects them: we and our graces would act very poorly, did not the Spirit assist us. John xv. 5, "Without me, saith Christ, ye can do nothing;" that is, without my Spirit concur with your graces, and actuate them, "ye can do nothing." The mill may have all things fit for motion, the sails may be spread, but if the wind blow not the mill goes not; so a man may, through grace, be prepared and fitted to every good work, but if the Spirit blow not he moves not. John vi. 63, "It is the Spirit that quickens;" it quickens us and our graces also. 2 Cor. iii. 6, "The Spirit giveth life;" life to men's persons, and life to their graces: it is the Spirit makes lively, and sets grace to work. It is the sun and influences of heaven which draw up the sap, and make the tree grow; and it is the Spirit and its influences which draw out our graces into act, they lie still unless fresh blasts of the Spirit come upon us and them. And as the Spirit acts our graces, so it perfects them, it adds supplies unto them, Phil. i. 19; and changes us into further glory day by day, 2 Cor. iii. 18. And what is said of Christ, Heb. xii. 2, that he is "the author and finisher of our faith," the same Christ doth by his Spirit, and so the Spirit is the author and finisher of all our graces.

(5.) The Spirit is a great and excellent gift, in that it doth facilitate, sweeten, and make delightful unto us all the ways of God. They are hard and harsh to flesh and blood, as to deny a man's self, to pass by wrongs, to forgive enemies, to bear the cross cheerfully, &c.; these are things corrupt nature cannot digest; but where the Spirit is given, they become easy: the Spirit is the oil of gladness, and makes the soul cheerfully fall in with whatever is of God. When a child hath the father to go before, and lead it by the hand, though the way be stony, dirty, uphill, it goes willingly; so the soul that hath the Spirit to lead it, let the way be what it will, followeth willingly. Psal. cxix. 32, "I will run the way of thy commandments when thou shalt enlarge my heart." The Spirit doth enlarge the heart; 2 Cor. iii. 17, where that is there is liberty. Let the Lord command things hard, David will run to do them; they are suitable to the Spirit, and the work of the Spirit in the heart.

(6.) The Spirit is an excellent gift, in that it makes them excellent who have it. Dan. v. 10, 11, saith the queen to Belshazzar, "There is a man in thy kingdom, in whom is the spirit of the holy gods," he is an excellent man, none like him in all thy provinces, he hath the spirit of the gods in him, which others have not. Where the Spirit of God is put into a man, that man is an excellent man; he hath an excellent person in him, more excellent than his soul, than all souls, than all angels; he hath excellent graces, and is honourable above others. 1 Sam. ix. 6, "There is in this city a man of God, and he is an honourable man," said Saul's servant; so every one that hath the Spirit, be he in the city or out of it, is a man of God, and an honourable man.

Obs. 4. There is a union between the saints and the Spirit of God. "I will put my spirit within you." It is not said, I will put my Spirit upon you, but "within you;" so that by virtue of those graces it works in you, there shall be a union between you and my Spirit. This union is not such as is between the three John speaks of, 1 John v. 7, for they are one essentially; nor such as is between the Deity and Christ's human nature, Col. ii. 9, for that is personal; but it is a mystical union, a union of persons, not a personal union. It is,

(1.) Real. There is a true oneness between the Spirit and those it is put into: 1 Cor. vi. 17, "He that is joined unto the Lord is one Spirit;" he saith not, is one body, or, one soul, or, hath one spirit with the Lord, but "is one Spirit;" there is as real a union as is between soul and body, he is so one with the Spirit as he is denominated spirit: John iii. 6, "That which is born of the Spirit is spirit."

(2.) It is a wonderful union. The Spirit of God, who is one with the Father and the Son, to be one also with man, and not with one man, but all he is put into, even thousands of men, is wonderful. John tells us, it was a great wonder to see a woman clothed with the sun, Rev. xii. 1; but it is a greater wonder to see a man or woman united to the Spirit of God, which is in our souls and bodies, the faculties and members of them, as the sap is in the root, vine, and branches; and here is the wonder, the same sap to be in every one of these, and in all other vines.

(3.) It is a most glorious union. When the Lord came into the temple, it was filled with glory, 1 Kings viii. 11; and when the Spirit is put into a man, and the union made between them, the man is filled with glory. When the sun shines into a house, it fills it with glory; when the fire is in the iron, how glorious is it! the union between the fire and the iron makes the iron a thick, dark, solid body, as glorious as the fire itself.

(4.) It is a strong and intimate union, which cannot be dissolved: "I will put my spirit within you," that is, into their inward parts. The Spirit is deeply seated, and strongly united unto those it is in. 2 Cor. vi. 16, "I will dwell in them." The Greek is, I will indwell in them; there is such an indwelling of God's Spirit in the hearts of his, that he will neither leave, nor be thrust out of his habitation. John xiv. 16, "I will pray the Father, and he shall give you another Comforter, that he may abide with you for ever." I am leaving you, saith Christ, but when I am gone, I will intercede with the Father for you, and he shall send the Spirit, the great Comforter; and he shall never leave you, he shall abide with you for ever, none shall be able to dispossess or drive him out of you.

Object. But both these seem contrary to Scripture: 1 Sam. xvi. 14, "The spirit of the Lord departed from Saul;" and David did drive away the Spirit, when he committed his great sins of murder and adultery.

Answ. 1. Wicked men have the Spirit from God as a Lord, by virtue of the covenant of works, and so sinning the Spirit departs from them. Thus was it with Saul, he rebelled against God, vexed his Spirit, and so that left him: but David, who was a godly man, had the Spirit from God as a Father in Christ, by virtue of the covenant of grace; and so though the Spirit were grieved by his sins, it did not depart from him; for, Psal. li. 11, he prays unto the Lord, saying, "Take not thy holy spirit from me." Had it been gone, the tenor of his prayer had been for restitution, not against ablation of it.

Answ. 2. The Spirit which departed from Saul was the Spirit of prophecy, and those kingly endowments which he had received, 1 Sam. x. 6; they ceased. The Spirit is oft put for the gifts of the Spirit, and they do ofttimes fail in men.

Answ. 3. All men have the spirit of bondage to fear, but all have not the Spirit of adoption to cry, Abba, Father; whosoever have the same, it abides with them.

Obs. 5. That before the Spirit of God be put into men, they are without life or motion towards God, or spiritual things; they live not to God, they walk not in his statutes; they live to themselves, to the flesh, to the creatures, and wander from God and his ways. Naturally men are destitute of the Spirit, sensual, as Jude tells you, ver. 19, "Sensual, not having the Spirit." Those that have not the Spirit, at the best are but sensual or merely intellectual men; and those who had the best souls, most reason, understanding, knew not God, Acts xvii. 23; 1 Cor. i. 21. David tells us, Psal. xiv. 2, 3, that God looked down from heaven upon the children of men, that is, Jews and gentiles, to see if there were any that did understand, and seek God, that is, whether any did so know God as to set them at work to seek him, as being the highest good, beyond all creature excellency. But what was the issue of God's so looking upon men? "They are all gone aside," that is, from him and his ways; "they are altogether become filthy," their practices are such as make them stink; "there is none that doth good, no not one;" of so many millions of men as are upon the earth, there is not one doth good. There were men of excellent parts then in the world, men of soul, but not one of them did know God, or seek after God; Paul therefore hath laid it down for a universal maxim, That the animal, natural, or intellectual man, receives not the things of the Spirit of God, for they are foolishness unto him; whilst he is without the Spirit of God, they are no better than foolishness unto him, and so are rejected by him.

Obs. 6. The principle of spiritual life and motion is the Spirit of God. "I will put my spirit within you, and cause you to walk." Immediately upon the putting in of the Spirit into the heart of any, there is life and motion; men live and move spiritually. Some make grace the principle of life and motion, but all grace flows from the Spirit, Gal. v. 22, 23; Eph. v. 9; and why should grace have that honour which is due to the Spirit? It was the entrance of the Spirit which quickened the dead bodies of the witnesses, and caused them to move, Rev. xi. 11; and it is the entrance of the Spirit which quickens dead souls, and causes them to move. We must beware of an error here, which hath seized upon divers of late, viz. that because the Spirit is in us, and the principle of life and motion, that therefore the Spirit doth all: Matt. x. 20, "It is not ye that speak, but the Spirit of your Father which speaketh in you;" so it is not you that do, but the Spirit in you; and if the Spirit speak and do all, we must sit still and leave ourselves to the Spirit's motions and actings. This is a dangerous error: know therefore, that though the Spirit be in men, and the principle of life and motion, yet it doth not act or work without us: in the putting in of the Spirit we are passive, John iii. 6; we concur no more to our birth than a child doth to its generation; but when the Spirit is in us and hath quickened us, then there is the co-operation of man with the Spirit: Rom. viii. 16, the Spirit beareth witness to our spirit; ver. 26, it helpeth our infirmities: the Spirit acts us, and we co-act with it. If the Spirit did all, then the Spirit should repent, believe, and not man; but what cause hath the Spirit to repent or believe? it never sinned, it stands not in need of help or mercy. That place, Matt. x. 20, is not absolutely to be taken, that they did not speak, for so it should be false; Luke xii. 12, "The Holy Spirit shall teach you in the same hour what ye ought to say:" they spake, and the Spirit taught them to speak. The place is to be taken comparatively, not you, but the Spirit; that is, it is rather the Spirit than you, the Spirit is the principle which sets you on. For men to sit still, and leave all to the Spirit, is a grieving of the Spirit, and contradicts what the Spirit hath given out: Matt. vii. 7, "Ask, and it shall be given you; seek, and you shall find; knock, and it shall be opened unto you." The Spirit would have us use means, and doth most vigorously assist us when we are most diligent in the use of them, Prov. ii. 3—5; 2 Chron. xv. 2.

Quest. If the Spirit be put into us, dwell in us, and be the principle of life and motion, what need the soul look unto Christ for any fresh or further supply?

Answ. 1. It is granted there is a sufficiency and fulness in the Spirit, yet because it is the will of God that we should look unto Christ, we are bound to do it: Heb. xii. 2, "Looking unto Jesus the author and finisher of our faith;" 2 Tim. ii. 1, "Be strong in the grace that is in Christ Jesus;" and Paul himself, 2 Cor. xii. 8, 9, looked up to Christ for more help, notwithstanding he had a fulness of the Spirit within him, Acts xiii. 9.

Answ. 2. The Spirit is not the head of the body, though it be in the body; that honour is Christ's: Col. i. 18, "He is the Head of the body, the church;" and from it the whole body receiveth influence, Eph. iv. 15, 16; Col. ii. 19. It is requisite, therefore, that every member in the body should look up to the head.

Obs. 7. God first makes men good, and then they do good; first he puts his Spirit into them, and then they walk in his ways. It is said of God himself, he is good, and doth good, Psal. cxix. 68; he is first good, and then good comes from him. So God makes men good by the infusion of his Spirit, and then they bring forth spiritual fruit: Eph. ii. 10, "We are his workmanship, created in Christ Jesus unto good works." Since man's fall, amongst all the sons of men God finds none good: Rom. iii. 10, "There is none righteous, no not one;" if any be so, he is ποίημα τοῦ Θεοῦ, the workmanship of God; God hath made him so by his Spirit, he hath made him a new creature, and so fitted him for good works. The tree must first be good, before the fruit be good: amongst men good actions are first done, and then men are reputed good; but with God it is otherwise, he makes men first good, and then they do good actions: they do not make themselves good by their free will, by frequent acts of good, but God puts in his Spirit, towards which they contribute nothing, and thereby they are made good, and act answerably; then their actions have life in them, worth in them, and are suitable to God, who is a Spirit, and must be worshipped in spirit and truth. Let men look heedfully to themselves, and not stand upon their actions; men may do many actions outwardly glorious, and magnified by men, themselves being corrupt and naught. If men have not the Spirit of God in them, their actions are no better than corrupt fruit of a corrupt tree, they do not please God: "and if any have not the Spirit of Christ, he is none of his;" he is neither good, nor doth good.

Obs. 8. In what heart soever the Spirit dwells, there will be outward and visible manifestations of it. Grace within will appear without. "I will put my spirit within you, and cause you to walk in my statutes, to keep my judgments, and to do them." The Spirit is like the sun in the firmament, which cannot be hid long, though it may be clouded for a season. The cough, and grace, are of such natures as will not be concealed; and the Spirit is of that nature, as it will discover itself in the man it is within, causing him to change his courses, and to walk in other ways than ever he walked in. When the Spirit is put into a swearer, a liar, an unclean person, an extortioner, a bloody persecutor, it makes the swearer fear an oath, the liar speak truth from his heart, the unclean man to possess his vessel in sanctification and honour, the extortioner to make satisfaction, and give half of his goods to the poor, and the bloody persecutor to love and preach the gospel he persecuted, so demonstrating itself to be in them. The Spirit in Scripture is compared to fire, Matt. iii. 11; to a mighty wind, Acts ii. 2; to a fountain or spring, John vii. 38, 39; to an ointment, 1 John ii. 27; to the oil of gladness, Psal. xlv. 7. All which things will be seen, heard, and set out the Spirit's manifestation of itself. The Spirit is an active thing, and makes its inbeing known by men's outward actions, as the inbeing of the soul is by speaking and walking; the sap keeps not always in the root, but ascends, disperseth itself into every branch, and by leaves, blossoms, and fruit, declares the life and nature of the tree. Many whose lives do testify what they are, cheat their own souls with this delusion, they have honest hearts, and are inwardly good, though they be not so gracious and holy outwardly as others; yea, though corruptions do break out sometimes, inwardly they are good. But let such know it is impossible there should be grace,

Christ, or the Spirit within them, and these not appear in their tongues and lives; for out of the abundance of the heart the tongue speaks, and the hand acts: the corruption that breaks out testifies there is a corrupt, graceless, Christless, and spiritless heart within.

Obs. 9. When men have received the Spirit of God, they are assisted and enabled by it to proceed and persevere in the ways of God. "I will put my spirit within you, and cause you to walk in my statutes, and ye shall keep my judgments." As the stoniness of their hearts, and power of their wills, could not hinder God from putting in his Spirit; so the stoniness being removed, the liberty or power of the will cannot hinder the Spirit from carrying on the men in whom it is in the ways of God, it complies and co-operates with the Spirit therein. Man's will, after the Spirit's infusion and work upon it, neither doth, nor can, hinder his proceeding and persevering in the ways of God; for if so, man's will should frustrate the promise of God, and make him in one part of it unfaithful; for he that said, "I will put my Spirit within you," said also, "I will cause you to walk in my statutes, to keep my judgments and do them:" he saith not, If man will it shall be so, but, I will have it so. The Spirit of God is stronger than Satan, 1 John iv. 4; stronger than men's wills and corruptions; and will put forth his strength to maintain the truth and faithfulness of him who put him within men for that end, that he should assist them against whatever should hinder their progress and perseverance in his ways. The Spirit writes the law of God in the hearts of men, 2 Cor. iii. 3; teaches them to understand the same, 1 John ii. 27; and enables them to obey all truth; 1 Pet. i. 22, they obeyed the truth through the Spirit; that caused them to walk in the way of truth, notwithstanding Satan's temptations, the strength of their own corruptions, and liberty of their wills. Those that have the Spirit are led by it, and cannot be under the dominion of sin or Satan, Rom. vi. 14. They are under grace, under the conduct of the Spirit, which will never let them apostatize and perish, 1 John iii. 9. There is a seed in them which will never suffer them so to degenerate, as to become the seed of the serpent.

Obs. 10. Those that have the Spirit in them, do make godliness and the ways of God their business and delight here in this world. They walk in his statutes, that is their work, trade, recreation; no business lies more upon them than to be godly. The world they are dead unto it, Gal. vi. 14, and use it as if they used it not, 1 Cor. vii. 29—31; and sin they are dead unto, they have nothing to do with the unfruitful works of darkness, Eph. v. 11: but they are alive unto God, Rom. vi. 11; they spend their time and strength for him, they live to his praise and glory. So Paul, Phil. i. 21, saith, "To me to live is Christ;" my life is employed and laid out in the service and interest of Christ. Those that have the Spirit in them, live in the Spirit, and walk in the Spirit, according to Gal. v. 25; they show forth the virtues of him that hath put in the Spirit within them, and the virtues of the Spirit being within them.. David had the Spirit of God within him, and he made godliness his principal business, and the statutes of God his delight: Psal. cxix. 164, "Seven times a day do I praise thee;" ver. 62, "At midnight will I rise to give thanks unto thee;" ver. 97, God's law was his "meditation all the day;" Psal. lxxi. 15, "My mouth shall show forth thy righteousness and salvation all the day;" Psal. xxv. 5, "On thee do I wait all the day;" Psal. lxxxiv. 10, "A day in thy courts is better than a thousand. I had rather be a doorkeeper in the house of my God, than dwell in the tents of wickedness;" Psal. xxvii. 4, "One thing have I desired of the Lord, that I will seek after; that I may dwell in the house of the Lord all the days of my life, to behold the beauty of the Lord, and to inquire in his temple." Where is a king, where is a christian, that mindeth godliness as David did, or delights in the ways of God as he did? May it not be taken up for a lamentation, that most christians declare, that neither Christ nor the Spirit is in them, because they neither seek the things of the one, nor savour the things of the other? Phil. ii. 21; Rom. viii. 5.

Obs. 11. A man endowed with the Spirit, must walk in God's statutes, and in his only. "I will put my spirit within you, and cause you to walk in my statutes:" they must not worship God any other way than he hath appointed in his word. Inward and outward worship must be appointed by God; for who knows what will please God but himself? he is a glorious and holy Spirit, infinitely and only wise, and that only must we stick unto as pleasing unto him which himself appoints. Men's inventions and appointments in worship defile men's souls, and provoke Divine Majesty; a godly man therefore is very tender in point of worship, and will practise nothing therein but what he hath found a clear foundation for out of the word of God. He knows that when Nadab and Abihu brought strange fire before God, it brought a strange judgment upon them from God, Lev. x. 1, 2; he knows that all worship after the commandments and traditions of men is in vain, Matt. xv. 9; he knows no coin is current in the court of heaven, but that which hath the image and superscription of God himself upon it; he knows what God hath said, Ezek. xx. 18, 19, "Walk ye not in the statutes of your fathers, neither observe their judgments, nor defile yourselves with their idols: I am the Lord your God; walk in my statutes, and keep my judgments, and do them." He knows that "to fear God, and keep his commandments, is the whole duty of man," Eccles. xii. 13.

Obs. 12. That man that hath the Spirit of God, is for righteousness as well as holiness. He is a second table man, as well as a first table man; he is conscientious towards man, as well as towards God; he keeps the judgments set between man and man, as well as walks in the statutes which are between God and man: as, "Thou shalt love thy neighbour as thyself," Rom. xiii. 9; not to defraud thy brother in any matter, 1 Thess. iv. 6; to do to others as we would be done unto ourselves, Luke vi. 31; to condescend to those of low estate, to recompense to no man evil for evil, but to overcome evil with good, Rom. xii. 16, 17, 21; blessing them that curse you, and praying for them that despitefully use you, Matt. v. 44; to forbear and forgive one another, Col. iii. 13; to bear one another's burdens, Gal. vi. 2; every man to possess his vessel in sanctification and honour, 1 Thess. iv. 4; to speak evil of no man, to be no brawlers, but gentle, showing all meekness unto all men, Tit. iii. 2; to put away all bitterness, wrath, anger, clamour, and evil speaking, with all malice, and to be kind and tender-hearted one to another, Eph. v. 31, 32; not to lie, but speak the truth every man with his neighbour, ver. 25; to distribute to the necessities of saints, Rom. xii. 13; to lend, looking for nothing again, Luke vi. 35, &c. These are judgments God hath set in his infinite wisdom between man and man; and whosoever hath the Spirit of God dwelling in him, keeps these and many other mentioned in sacred writ. David had respect to all the commandments of the Lord, Psal. cxix. 6; those which concerned men, as well as those which concerned God, for they are all of equal authority, being from the same God, and branches of his infinite wisdom; the one tending to man's good, and God's glory, as well as the other, which David knew, and therefore kept. So Paul, his care was not only to mind the duties of holiness towards God, but those of righteousness towards men; Acts xxiv. 16, "Herein," saith he, "do I exercise myself, to have always a conscience void of offence toward God, and toward men." Had he not kept the judgments set of God between man and man, his conscience had not been innocent; but because he did keep them, therefore he could say, Acts xxv. 10, "To the Jews have I done no wrong;" and to the Corinthian gentiles, "We have wronged no man, we have corrupted no man, we have defrauded no man," 2 Cor. vii. 2. He had the Spirit within him, which carried him forth strongly to do just, righteous, and equal things, and to move others thereunto: Phil. iv. 8, "Finally, brethren, whatsoever things are true, whatsoever things are honest, whatsoever things are just, whatsoever things are pure, whatsoever things are lovely, whatsoever things are of good report; if there be any virtue, and if there be any praise, think on these things." He wrote these words unto the Philippians as his last words, that so they might take the deeper impression in them, knowing that if second table duties were not done, first table duties would be in vain. See how the Lord with indignation takes up the Jews for failing in their duties towards men, though they did their duty towards him: Jer. vii. 6, 9, 10, Will ye oppress the stranger, the fatherless, and the widow? will ye steal, murder, and commit adultery, and swear falsely, and come and stand before me in this house? What! do you come hither for to pray, to hear the law, to offer sacrifice, and think I am pleased with these duties? No, no; I will destroy the temple where ye worship, and I will cast ye out of my sight as I have done all your brethren, even the whole seed of Ephraim, ver. 14, 15. It is in vain to be religious, if we be not righteous; such religion is a dreadful provocation of God, as you may read, Isa. i. 10—17. Many are religious in these days, but where is a righteous man? "He that doth righteousness," just and equal things, "is righteous," 1 John iii. 7. Let us learn, as to walk in God's statutes, that is to be religious, so to keep his judgments and do them, that is to be righteous; for of the three great things which God requires of man, this is the first: Micah vi. 8, "What doth the Lord require of thee, O man, but to do justly, to love mercy, and to walk humbly with thy God?"

Ver. 28. *And ye shall dwell in the land that I gave to your fathers; and ye shall be my people, and I will be your God.*

This verse comprehends in it both temporal and spiritual mercy, as repossession of their land, and God's renovation of covenant with them.

"And ye shall dwell in the land which I gave to your fathers." God had long before this time given Canaan unto Abraham and his posterity, who through their sins were driven out of the same, and made captives in Babylon, but he would bring them back again and set them in it, which resembled God's gathering of his people out of all nations, and bringing them into the church of Christ, the city of God, the spiritual Canaan.

"And ye shall be my people, and I will be your God." Like words to these we had, Ezek. xi. 20; xiv. 11; xxxiv. 31; and therefore shall not stand upon them. The sense of them is this: You being in Babylon, think yourselves cast off of God, and that ye shall never again have the honour to be his people, and to have him for your God; but your thoughts are not as mine, for ye shall come again to Canaan, and there I will own you for my people, and ye shall own me for your God: ye shall be my people to worship me, and I will be your God to bless you; ye shall be my people to depend upon me, and I will be your God to protect you; ye shall be my people to obey my commands and do my will, and I will be your God to exalt and honour you; ye shall be my people to love, fear, honour me, and to stand for me and my glory, and I will be your God to counsel, comfort, delight in, and to deliver you, and to plead your cause against all your enemies.

Obs. 1. There is nothing difficult or impossible to God, though it be so in the eye of man. The Jews thought it a hard, if not a thing impossible, for them to get from under the Babylonish yoke into their own country; but God thought not so; saith he, "Ye shall dwell in the land that I gave to your fathers;" I will break off every yoke which hinders, and remove every mountain which lets. And this he did with ease, for he did but stir the heart of Cyrus king of Persia to make a proclamation to this purpose, That whoever among the Jews had a heart to go up to Jerusalem, might do it, 2 Chron. xxxvi. 22, 23, and it was done. The getting Peter out of prison seemed a thing impossible; he was in two chains, between two soldiers, keepers at the door, a first and second ward after these to pass by, and then an iron gate to open: all these things were as nothing to God; he sent an angel, who brought Peter out of prison, notwithstanding all these difficulties, and, as to men, impossibilities, Acts xii. God saith, Jer. xxxii. 27, "I am the Lord, the God of all flesh: is there any thing too hard for me?" Many things are two hard for you, but is there any thing in heaven or earth too hard for me? What! cannot I bring the Jews again to Canaan? ver. 37, "I will gather them out of all countries, whither I have driven them in mine anger, and in my fury, and in great wrath; and I will bring them again unto this place," viz. to Jerusalem.

Obs. 2. Lands are at the disposal of God. "Ye shall dwell in the land that I gave to your fathers." Canaan God first gave to the Canaanites; for their iniquities God took it away, and gave it to the Jews; they provoking God by their idolatries and oppressions, he took it from them and gave it to the Chaldeans; who having possessed it for some years, he took it from them, and restored it again to the Jews. Not only the land of Canaan was disposed of by the Lord, but all lands and nations are his, and given to whom he pleases; Jer. x. 7, he is "King of nations;" he rules in the kingdoms of men, and gives them to whom he will, Dan. iv. 32. All kings are God's copyholders, and he can turn them out of their tenures at pleasure: Jer. xxvii. 5, 6, "I have made the earth and given it unto whom it seemed meet unto me: and now have I given all these lands into the hand of Nebuchadnezzar king of Babylon." He turned out the king of Moab, the king of Edom, the king of the Ammonites, the king of Tyre, the king of Zidon, and gave all their lands into the hands of Nebuchadnezzar.

Obs. 3. No condition of God's people is so grievous, but it shall have a comfortable issue. That the Jews were in captivity, deprived of all those sweet enjoyments they had in the land of Canaan, was grievous; that they were amongst idolaters, blasphemers, in a polluted land, and made to serve the enemies of God, this was exceeding grievous unto them; yet this condition was not to last always, it should have a comfortable end, they should return and dwell in the land of their fathers, and enjoy their ancient, honourable, and comfortable privileges. In the apostles' days the church was under great persecution and many suffered, Acts viii. and ix.; but the persecution and suffering of the saints had an end, yea, a comfortable end; for, chap. ix. 31, it is said, "Then had the churches rest throughout all Judea and Galilee and Samaria, and were edified; and walking in the fear of the Lord, and in the comfort of the Holy Ghost, were multiplied." Here was a blessed conclusion of a sad persecution; this blustering winter had a sweet spring following of it.

Obs. 4. It is an act of grace in God to take any people to be his, and a renewed act of grace to fall in again with those that have revolted from him and he hath cast off. What was in this people of the Jews at first to move him to mind them, to take them for his people? they had that enough in them, and as all other nations have, to make him abhor them, but nothing to incline his heart towards them. Ezek. xvi. 5, 6, 8, When thy person was loathed, and thou wast polluted in thy blood, I said unto thee, Live; I entered into covenant with thee, and thou becamest mine. Here was an act of grace; it was God's pleasure made them his people, 1 Sam. xii. 22, and nothing else; and when they had forsaken God, Jer. ii. 13, and he had cast them out of his sight, Jer. vii. 15, which was done when they were cast into Babylon, to fall in again with these, to own them for his people, and to become their God again, this was a renewed act of grace, height of mercy, strength of love. God might have said, Ye are weary of me, and I am weary of you; I know your thoughts and what comes into your mind, that you would be as the heathen, as the families of the country, to serve wood and stone, Ezek. xx. 32; but God would not suffer it, he would bring them out of Babylon, be their God, and take them to be his people; which sets out the freeness and fulness of divine grace: he would not let his people become heathenish, and worship heathen gods.

Obs. 5. All nations have not an equal interest in God, his favour and grace is not alike dispensed unto all. God said not to the Babylonians, "Ye shall be my people, and I will be your God." This was spoken to the Jews, and to no other nation: therefore saith God of that nation, Amos iii. 2, "You only have I known of all the families of the earth," you have I taken into nearer relation than any other; you have I known by way of covenant, you have I known so as to record my name among you, and to dwell among you; but so I have not dealt with other nations: they were "without God in the world," Eph. ii. 12; they were "far off" (ver. 13) from God, from the means of grace and salvation. The gentiles had not such interest in God as the Jews had; they had common favour as they were his creatures under the covenant of works, these had special favour as they were his people under the covenant of grace. Isa. xliii. 3, "I am the Lord thy God, the Holy One of Israel, thy Saviour; I gave Egypt for thy ransom, Ethiopia and Seba for thee:" God exposed them to destruction for the safety of the Jews.

Obs. 6. That people is honoured and happy, whom the Lord owns to be his, and vouchsafeth to be their God. "Ye shall be my people, and I will be your God." What greater honour could the Jews have in the world, than be taken by the infinite, holy, great, and glorious God, to be his people? It is a great honour when poor beggarly people are taken into great men's and princes' services; much more is it so when a sinful nation is taken in by God to be his people. And not only is it an honour, but a happiness; Psal. cxliv. 15, "Happy is that people whose God is the Lord." Is not that people happy which have peace, and plenty of all good things? Yes, it is a human, a conceited happiness, but it is not a real, a true happiness; that lieth in having God our God, our Lord: propriety in a Deity makes a nation or person happy; Psal. xxxiii. 12, "Blessed is the nation whose God is the Lord; and the people whom he hath chosen for his own inheritance." David, who was a prophet, and a man after God's own heart, fixeth not happiness upon riches, honours, peace, parts, multitudes of soldiers, subjects, or counsellors; but in mutual relation between God and a people, the one owning the other. When God owns a people to be his inheritance, and a people own God to be their God and portion, this is true happiness; such a people may plead with God for great things in prayer, and expect them, as Jehoshaphat did, 2 Chron. xx. 12; and as Asa did, 2 Chron. xiv. 11; and Moses, Exod. xxxii. 11—14.

Ver. 29, 30. *I will also save you from all your uncleannesses: and I will call for the corn, and will increase it, and lay no famine upon you. And I will multiply the fruit of the tree, and the increase of the field, that ye shall receive no more reproach of famine among the heathen.*

These two verses hold out two more great promises unto this people; which are,

I. Ablation of evils, as "uncleannesses, famine, reproach."

II. Collation of good things, "corn, fruit, and increase of the field."

Ver. 29. "I will also save you from all your uncleannesses." This is a special promise, and of great concernment. Some refer it to justification, and make it to be God's free taking away the guilt and punishments deserved by their uncleannesses. Some refer it to sanctification, and make it to be God's cleansing them from the filth and delivering them from the power of sin. They are mistaken who interpret the words of Babylonish uncleannesses, as if God would deliver them out of Babylon, and save them from the pollutions thereof; if that had been the sense, the words should have run thus, I will save you from all their uncleannesses, not, "from all your uncleannesses." To let that exposition pass, we may take in here both their justification and sanctification, and so make the sense full: I will save you from all your uncleannesses by my pardoning grace, that shall acquit you from the guilt and punishment of all your sins; and I will save you from all your uncleannesses by my sanctifying grace, that shall purge out all your defilements and spots. The word for "uncleannesses" is, טמאות which notes not only ceremonial uncleanness, but moral also, as Lev. xviii. 27.

"I will call for the corn, and will increase it." The Hebrew is, I will call to the corn, I will command the corn to grow and bring forth; I will give but a word of power, and as that hath caused all things to be and bring forth, so shall it do with the corn, and not only cause it to grow, but to increase, so that there shall be plenty, and plenty continued; for it follows,

"And lay no famine upon you." The Jews had oft been under grievous famines, as appears, 2 Sam. xxi. 1; 2 Kings vi.; 1 Kings xviii.; Joel i.; Amos iv. 6; 2 Kings xxv. 3. The Lord called for and laid famines upon them; but here he promises not to lay any famine upon them; they should be freed from that judgment, and live in the abundance of good things.

Ver. 30. "And I will multiply the fruit of the

tree." Not only should the corn thrive and bring forth, but the trees also they should be fruitful, yea, very fruitful; God would multiply the fruit of all the trees which used to bear fruit. Some trees are for ornament of the earth, some for timber, some for fire, but most for fruit, and those that were for fruit should bear fruit in abundance.

"The increase of the field." These words are spoken of those things which do grow of themselves without setting, sowing, or planting, they are properly the increase of the field.

"That ye shall receive no more reproach of famine among the heathen." The heathens took occasion from the famines the Jews met with, to reproach them, and say, What! do you want bread? is your God the chiefest and best of gods, and will he see you want? is he hard-hearted, and will not afford you necessaries to live? Surely our gods are better and more merciful than the God of the Jews; they suffer us not to want any thing, we have no such famines as you Jews have; you are hunger-starved wretches, and beholden to us for bread. These were grievous reproaches, which the Lord promised here to take away by giving unto them plenty of all things for their maintenance. They had upbraided the Jews, ver. 13, that their land was a land which devoured men; God therefore now told them, their land should bring forth corn, fruit, and other good things, and so maintain the inhabitants of it.

Obs. 1. When God enters into or renews covenant with a people, he will do much for them. "I will be your God; I will also save you from all your uncleannesses; and I will call for the corn, and increase it, and lay no famine upon you, and I will multiply the fruit of the tree," &c. Here God renewed covenant with them, and promised them spiritual and temporal mercies, which in due time he gave them in. So when he first entered into covenant with them, Ezek. xvi. 8—14, what great things did God do for them! "Then washed I thee with water, yea, I throughly washed away thy blood from thee, and anointed thee with oil: I clothed thee also with broidered work, and shod thee with badgers' skin, and I girded thee about with fine linen, and I covered thee with silk," &c. When God is once engaged to a people, he doth much for them, and great things, he lays out himself and his attributes for their good.

Obs. 2. God is a perfect Saviour. "I will save you from all your uncleannesses." They had many and variety of uncleannesses, ceremonial and moral impurities, inward and outward pollutions; they had much guilt and much filth, but God saved them from them all; he doth perfectly justify, and will perfectly sanctify in due time: there is not one inherent corruption within, cleave it never so fast unto the spirit of man, but God will work it out. He will "take away all iniquity," Hos. xiv. 2, the guilt of sin, the power and pollution of sin, yea, the very being of sin: ver. 25 of this chapter, "I will sprinkle clean water upon you, and ye shall be clean; from all your filthiness, and from all your idols, will I cleanse you." God will do his work of this nature thoroughly and perfectly: David acknowledged it, Psal. ciii. 2, 3, "Bless the Lord, O my soul, and forget not all his benefits; who forgiveth all thine iniquities; who healeth all thy diseases."

Obs. 3. It is no difficulty unto the Lord to make plenty of things, he can easily do it. "I will call for the corn, and will increase it." It is but calling for it, and it comes; if he call for fruitfulness of the field or tree, or both, they come: as servants come at the call of their masters, so any creatures, corn, wine, oil, come at the call of God; if God do but say, Let the earth bring forth, it will bring forth: there is power in his word, it is the word of the greatest King: no earthly king hath fertility or sterility at his command as God hath. Hag. i. 11, he called for a drought upon the land, and it came: 2 Kings viii. 1, he called for a famine, and it came and sojourned seven years with them. If God call for a judgment or a mercy, it comes presently. Let us fear to offend him, lest he call for a famine, the pestilence, or a sword; let us improve mercies for his honour, that he may call for the corn and fruit, and continue the same unto us.

Obs. 4. Whatsoever plenty is in a land, it is from the power, blessing, and bounty of the Lord. "I will call for the corn, and increase it." Though the land have kept her sabbaths, hath not been ploughed or sown in many years, yet I will cause it to bring forth, and that richly; I will multiply the fruit of the tree; the vine, fig tree, and the olive shall be laden with fruit, and that ye take no pains for the tender grass and herbs, the increase of the field. These, even all these, are from the call, benediction, and bounty of God, which we should take notice of, and be thankful for. All the corn we have for bread, all the fruit we have for delight, all the herbs we have for physic, and all the grass and fodder we have for cattle, are all from the Lord; and if we do not use all for his glory, but abuse the same, as Ephraim did, God will deal by us as he did by Ephraim, Hos. ii. 8, 9, even take all from us; "I will take away my corn in the time thereof," &c.

Obs. 5. God takes notice how wicked ones reproach his children being under his judgments, and will cause their reproachings to cease. "Ye shall receive no more reproach of famine among the heathen." It was a vile thing for the Babylonians to cast it in the Jews' teeth, that their land was a land of famine, and so to reproach them for that judgment which God for their sins did oft lay upon them; this was inhuman, barbarous, to add affliction to the afflicted: God observed it, and to comfort them against so sore an affliction, he gives in a promise of a plentiful maintenance, I will call for the corn, and multiply all things, so that there shall be no occasion for an enemy, for any Babylonian, to say so any more; "ye shall receive no more reproach of famine among the heathen."

Ver. 31. ***Then shall ye remember your own evil ways, and your doings that were not good, and shall lothe yourselves in your own sight for your iniquities and for your abominations.***

This verse is the last of the special promises made here unto this people, and it is a promise of repentance. Something like part of this verse we had chap. vi. 9, almost the same words we had chap. xx. 43.

"Then shall ye remember." When I have broken the Babylonish yoke off their necks, brought you into your own land, and done great things for you, then ye shall remember; that is, not simply to call to mind what ye have done, but to roll up and down in your thoughts seriously, to muse upon and ponder, for so much the word זכר signifies, and so to ponder as to do something thereupon.

"Your own evil ways, and your doings that were not good." In chap. xx. 43 it is, "your ways, and all your doings, wherein ye have been defiled;" and here it is "your own evil ways, and your doings that were not good." What their ways and doings were, you may see, Ezek. xxii. throughout the whole chapter. They did speak and do evil as they could, Jer. iii. 5; they were worse than the nations and countries round about them, Ezek. v. 6, than Sodom and Samaria, chap. xvi. 47.

"And shall loathe yourselves in your own sight." Montanus renders the Hebrew thus, ye shall reprobate yourselves in your own sight, ye shall judge yourselves worthy to be cut off, and to be made a curse. The Vulgate is, your iniquities shall displease you: there is more in the word than displeasing; ye shall be for a disdain, a loathing to yourselves. Saith Œcolampadius, ye shall be pricked at the heart, ye shall see yourselves so defiled and deformed through sin, that ye shall loathe and abhor yourselves.

"For your iniquities and for your abominations." "Iniquities" are perverse, crooked, and unrighteous actions; "abominations," things disaffecting and loathsome to the senses.

Obs. 1. God's loving-kindnesses and mercies do work more with sinners than his judgments do. All the time they were in Babylon, their hearts were never so affected for their sins, as after God brought them out, settled them in Canaan, and showed much love unto them; then they should remember their evil ways, before they minded them not; then they should loathe themselves. Mercies in Zion are more efficacious with sinners than judgments in Babylon; God's favour sooner melts hard hearts than the fire of his indignation; his kindness is very penetrative, it gets into the hearts of sinners sooner than his threats and frowns; it is like a small soaking rain which goes to the roots of things, whenas a dashing rain runs away, and does little good. It was David's kindness brake the heart of Saul, 1 Sam. xxiv; and it is God's kindness which breaks the heart of sinners. The milk and honey of the gospel affect the hearts of sinners more than the gall and wormwood of the law; Christ on mount Zion brings more to repentance than Moses on mount Sinai.

Obs. 2. When God brings his people out of Babylon into Canaan, out of the world and antichristian ways, into near relation to himself, and into gospel order, then he will frame their spirits so, that they shall review their former ways, be ashamed of, and loathe themselves for them. Ver. 28, "Ye shall dwell in the land that I gave to your fathers; and ye shall be my people, and I will be your God; and then shall ye remember your doings that were not good, and shall loathe yourselves in your own sight for your iniquities and abominations." When people are delivered from the power of darkness, and translated into the kingdom of Christ, then they come to see what works of darkness they committed, and so to abhor and loathe themselves for the same. When men come out of popish darkness, or the profane courses they have lived in, and are brought near to God, how do they judge, condemn, and loathe themselves for the same! When Paul was translated from his pharisaism into Christ's unity, then God moulded his spirit so, that he saw and confessed what a blasphemer, persecutor, and injurious person he had been, and loathed himself, saying, he was the chief of sinners, 1 Tim. i. 15. And when the Jews shall be brought out of that Babylonish condition they now are in, and become a people near to God, being in the church of Christ, then they will remember their evil doings, their bitterness against christians, and bloodiness against Christ, and loathe themselves for the same, Zech. xii. 10; Rev. i. 7.

Obs. 3. Where repentance comes, it makes a change in men's judgments, affections, and lives. They should loathe themselves in their own sight for their iniquities and for their abominations. What they approved of before, delighted in, and practised, that they should look upon as abominable, loathe, and turn from. Repentance begins in men's minds and judgments, altering them; and when they are altered, the affections and conversation will alter: when the prodigal repented there was a change inward and outward.

Ver. 32. *Not for your sakes do I this, saith the Lord God, be it known unto you: be ashamed and confounded for your own ways, O house of Israel.*

In this verse is comprehended the ground of all the gracious and great promises specified in the words before and following: and,

I. It is expressed negatively, It is "not for your sakes."

II. Implied affirmatively, It is for the Lord's sake.

"Not for your sakes do I this." God saw nothing in them to move him to bring them out of Babylon, or to do aught for them in Babylon; but he beheld that in them, which might have moved him to destroy them; he saw how they profaned his holy name among the Babylonians, ver. 21; he saw how they intended to turn heathens, and worship wood and stone, chap. xx. 32. Being God's people they thought God was bound to do much for their sakes, and that he should not deal justly with them, if he did not mind them, and do for them: see how they expostulated with God, Isa. lviii. 3, "Wherefore have we fasted, and thou seest not? wherefore have we afflicted our soul, and thou takest no knowledge?" They did in effect tell God he dealt not well with them, they deserved better things at his hands than they had; therefore said the Lord here, "Not for your sakes do I this,"

"Be it known unto you." Take notice that what conceits soever ye have of your own worth or deserts, because ye are my people, and of the seed of Abraham my friend, yet I do not bring you out of Babylon for your worth or merit's sake, I do nothing upon that account, and proclaim it openly unto you and all the world.

"Be ashamed and confounded for your own ways." Your ways are so far from meriting at my hands, that they merit not at the hands of men, they are of that nature as you ought to be ashamed and confounded for them. Of the words "ashamed and confounded" was spoken, chap. xvi. 52, 54, 61.

Obs. 1. Men are apt to think they deserve something at God's hands. The house of Israel thought she had suffered a long and sore captivity; and having fasted and mourned every fifth and seventh month throughout the seventy years, Zech. vii. 5, she conceived God now should deal unkindly, yea unjustly, if he should not do some great thing for her; now it was just for him to remember all her tears, sighs, prayers, fastings, and sufferings, to set her at liberty, and give her repossession of her land, rewarding her with old and new privileges. Matt. vii. 22, "Many will say to me in that day, Lord, Lord, have not we prophesied in thy name? and in thy name have cast out devils? and in thy name done many wonderful works?" They thought they had merited heaven by their doings, and looked for some wonderful reward for their wonderful works. The labourers which came into the vineyard at the third and sixth hours, thought they deserved more of the lord of the vineyard than they that went in at the ninth and eleventh hours, Matt. xx. Prone is corrupt nature to conceit it merits somewhat at the hands of God. But,

Obs. 2. Men's ways are such as they ought to be ashamed of themselves, and fear destruction from

God for them. "Be ashamed and confounded for your own ways, O house of Israel;" they are such as you should blush at, and loathe to behold, and make you fear lest my judgments should seize upon you for them. Neh. ix. 30, 31, what saith he of them? Lord, "thou gavest them into the hand of the people of the lands;" that is, thou didst cast them into captivity for their own ways; and what then? "Nevertheless for thy great mercies' sake thou didst not utterly consume them." They had cause to fear consuming; had not mercy, and great mercy, stepped in, they had been utterly consumed. So Jeremiah, Lam. iii. 22, "It is of the Lord's mercies that we are not consumed." If it be mercy that our persons are not destroyed, what do our works or ways deserve from him?

Obs. 3. The promises God makes unto, and the mercies he bestows upon, his people are free, and for his own sake. "Not for your sakes do I this, saith the Lord God, be it known unto you:" I have promised to sprinkle you with clean water, to put a new heart into you, to give you my Spirit, to save you from all your iniquities, to bring you again to Zion, to give you many mercies there, and to do you much good; but these I do not for your sakes, you deserve them not, but for mine own sake, for mine own honour and name; as ver. 22, "I do not this, O house of Israel, for your sakes, but for mine holy name's sake." For man's sake come judgments: the earth was cursed for Adam's sake, Gen. iii. 17; for Achan's sake the Israelites fell and fled, Josh. vii.; for Jonah's sake the sea was tempestuous, Jonah i. 4, 12. But when mercies come at land or sea, it is for the Lord's own sake: he "made all things for himself," Prov. xvi. 4, for his own name's sake; and what good soever he doth to any nations or persons is not for your sakes, but for his own holy name's sake. When the Jews were near destruction, he wrought for his name's sake, Ezek. xx. 9; so when we were near to destruction ofttimes in these nations, the Lord wrought for his own name's sake, not for our sakes. Let us give God the glory of what he hath done for our nation, and for ourselves, and say, "Help us, O God of our salvation, for the glory of thy name, and deliver us, and purge away our sins for thy name's sake."

Ver. 33—35. *Thus saith the Lord God; In the day that I shall have cleansed you from all your iniquities I will also cause you to dwell in the cities, and the wastes shall be builded. And the desolate land shall be tilled, whereas it lay desolate in the sight of all that passed by. And they shall say, This land that was desolate is become like the garden of Eden; and the waste and desolate and ruined cities are become fenced, and are inhabited.*

In these verses the Lord proceeds in temporal promises, and tells them what he will do for them after he hath cleansed them from their sins.

I. Their cities and waste places shall be re-edified.

II. Their cities shall be inhabited.

III. Tillage of the land.

IV. Such a choice blessing upon the land, that it should be thought like Eden.

Ver. 33. "In the day that I shall have cleansed you from all your iniquities." He spake of cleansing them from all their filthiness in ver. 25, and of saving them from all their uncleannesses, in ver. 29. "Iniquities" here imports the same that "filthiness" and "uncleannesses" do there. The sense is this, In the day that I shall forgive your sins, free you from the guilt and punishment of them, by bringing you out of captivity into your own country, then will I do such things for you.

"I will also cause you to dwell in the cities, and the wastes shall be builded." The cities and places which by war and length of time were wasted and decayed, should be built again, repaired and inhabited.

Ver. 34. "And the desolate land shall be tilled." Canaan had lain desolate many years, and kept many sabbaths, there being none to till it; but now God promises it should be ploughed, sown, and yield increase, as it is ver. 29.

"Whereas it lay desolate in the sight of all that passed by it." There being no husbandman to plough the land, to dress the vines, nor others to repair the waste places, all lay desolate, and the desolateness thereof was seen by strangers. Doubtless many travellers turned aside to see the desolations of Jerusalem, the temple, and Canaan, which had been so famous in the world, and when they came they saw all overgrown with thorns, briers, and nettles.

Ver. 35. "This land that was desolate is become like the garden of Eden." God would so bless the land of Canaan, and their labours in it, that it should be like the garden of Eden for order, plenty, and pleasure. They who wondered before at the desolateness of it, should wonder at the great alteration made there; they should see order where was confusion, plenty where was barrenness, and pleasure where was nothing but abhorrence.

"And the waste and desolate and ruined cities are become fenced, and are inhabited." Many cities had been in the land of Canaan, which Nebuchadnezzar's army and forces had laid waste, made desolate, and utterly ruined; but after their return from Babylon, they were not only built, but fortified and fenced with walls.

Obs. 1. When God pardons the sins of his people, then he vouchsafeth them other mercies. "In the day that I shall have cleansed you from all your iniquities I will also cause you to dwell in the cities, and the wastes shall be builded, and the desolate land shall be tilled:" God would bless them with liberty, commodious habitations, and plenty of all things. 2 Chron. vii. 14, "I will forgive their sin, and heal their land." Pardon of sin is a fundamental mercy, and hath many other mercies following of it. Jer. xxxiii. 8, 9, "I will cleanse them from all their iniquity, whereby they have sinned against me; and I will pardon all their iniquities, whereby they have sinned, and whereby they have transgressed against me. And it shall be to me a name of joy, a praise and an honour before all the nations of the earth, which shall hear all the good that I do unto them: and they shall fear and tremble for all the goodness and for all the prosperity that I procure unto it." When God forgives his people their iniquities, he will take delight in doing them good, count it his honour, get himself a name throughout the earth by blessing and prospering them, and Jerusalem, or the church, which is meant by it; so that the enemies shall be afraid of that God and that people.

Obs. 2. The best of lands may be laid desolate. Canaan was a land which flowed with milk and honey, "the glory of all lands," Ezek. xx. 6; and here it is called "the desolate land;" it was deprived of men and beasts, of cities, towns, and houses, it was become a wilderness. For the sins of the people it was brought into that condition: Zech. vii. 11, 12, they were stubborn, hard-hearted, rebellious; and therefore God "scattered them with a whirlwind among all the nations whom they knew not. Thus the land was desolate after them, that no man passed through nor returned: for they laid the pleasant land desolate," ver. 14. It was their sins which made that land of desire a land of desolation.

Obs. 3. Desolate lands shall not always lie in that condition. "The desolate land shall be tilled." If Canaan lie desolate seventy years, at the end thereof she shall be tilled; as she had her time of lying fallow, so should she have her time of ploughing and sowing. "Behold, the days come, saith the Lord, that I will sow the house of Israel and the house of Judah with the seed of man, and with the seed of beast. And it shall come to pass, that like as I have watched over them, to pluck up, and to break down, and to throw down, and to destroy, and to afflict; so will I watch over them to build, and to plant, saith the Lord," Jer. xxxi. 27, 28. As God hath his days and times to lay waste and to pluck up, so to build and plant. He compares men and beasts here to seed, not only because they do multiply themselves, but also because men by the help of beasts should till the land and sow it, whereupon it should bring forth abundantly. And as God deals with desolate lands, so he doth with desolate hearts, he hath his times to till and sow them; as ver. 15—17, Rachel wept and refused to be comforted; but what said God to her? "Refrain thy voice from weeping, and thine eye from tears; for thy work shall be rewarded," &c. God sowed in her heart seeds of hope and comfort.

Obs. 4. What a great and wonderful change God can make in a little time. God can make a desolate land like a garden, and the best of all gardens, viz. "the garden of Eden," which was of God's own planting, Gen. ii. 8. The strangers that saw Canaan in its desolateness, even they should see the change, and wonder at it, saying, "This land that was desolate is become like the garden of Eden;" now there is beauty, plenty, and pleasure in it. God can bring order out of confusion, abundance out of barrenness, and delight out of desolation. When the famine was so sore in Samaria, that women did eat their own children, what a change did God make in a day! "To-morrow about this time shall a measure of fine flour be sold for a shekel, and two measures of barley for a shekel, in the gate of Samaria;" and it proved so, notwithstanding that the nobleman said, viz. "If the Lord would make windows in heaven, might this thing be?" yea, it was, and his eyes saw it, 2 Kings vii. The Syrians fled, left their provisions, which were brought into Samaria, and made such plenty there. When the Israelites wanted flesh to eat in the wilderness, did not God send quails two cubits high upon the face of the earth? Numb. xi. 31. He can make a desert to blossom, and that abundantly, Isa. xxxv. 1, 2.

Ver. 36. ***Then the heathen that are left round about you shall know that I the Lord build the ruined places, and plant that that was desolate: I the Lord have spoken it, and I will do it.***

God having through his grace pardoned his people, brought them to Zion, and bestowed many blessings upon them; here the end of all is set down, and that is, the glorifying of God, not only by the Jews, but also by the very heathens.

"Then the heathen that are left round about you." After Nebuchadnezzar had laid Jerusalem and Judea waste, he fell upon the Ammonites, Moabites, Edomites, Philistines, Tyrians, and Egyptians, and spoiled them; therefore our prophet saith, "the heathen that are left;" some escaped and remained until the Jews' restoration.

"Shall know that I the Lord build the ruined places." They should be so convinced by the return of the Jews, and the mercies they enjoyed, that they should acknowledge it to be the hand of God, that he was faithful in making good his promise to his people, able to save, and bountiful in bestowing such mercies upon them. The word to "build" is, בנה which signifies to build a house, distinguished into its several rooms and parts: the cities, towns, and houses every where had been ruined, and God raised them up again.

"And plant that that was desolate." The word נטע to "plant," signifies the putting of trees, vines, shrubs, or any plants, into the earth, and to cover them so with earth, that they remain fixed therein. The orchards, gardens, vineyards, olive-yards, places of pleasure and profit, were laid desolate; the trees, plants, herbs, and flowers, were all cut down, or pulled up by the roots; those places God did replant, and made as useful and delightful as ever.

"I the Lord have spoken it, and I will do it." I have purposed it in myself, I have spoken it by Ezekiel, and I will do it. The Hebrew is, I have done it, a preter tense for a future, which is frequent; as Isa. xlvi. 11, "I have purposed;" the Hebrew is, *tatzarti*, I have formed, I have created, the preter tense for the future, as the former and following words do show, "I have spoken it, I will also bring it to pass," I will form or create it, "I will also do it."

Obs. 1. That though judgment begin at God's house, yet it ends not there. The Babylonians first fell upon the Jews and destroyed them, and after proceeded to the heathens, they cut off many nations of them. The sword first did eat the flesh of Jews, and then the flesh of Ammonites, Moabites, Edomites, &c. When the green trees are lopped, then the axe cuts down the dry trees. Wicked men and nations are glad when it goes ill with the church and people of God, but usually when God hath corrected his own, he breaks the horns, the back, and bones of their and his enemies. The cup of God's fury began at Jerusalem, but it stayed not there; it passed thence to Egypt, to the mingled people, to Uz, Philistia, Ashkelon, Azzah, Ekron, and Ashdod, &c.; to all the kings of the north, and to all the kingdoms of the world upon the face of the earth, Jer. xxv. 15—26. It were an unrighteous thing if God should judge his friends and spare his enemies; and this he acknowledgeth, ver. 29, "Lo, I begin to bring evil on the city which is called by my name, and should ye" (the heathens) "be utterly unpunished? Ye shall not be unpunished, for I will call for a sword upon all the inhabitants of the earth, saith the Lord of hosts."

Obs. 2. Some works of God are so convincing, that they cause even heathens to see and acknowledge the hand of God in them, and so to glorify him. The bringing the Jews out of Babylon, the replanting them in Canaan, the rebuilding of their waste places, peopling of them rebuilt, and making their country like the garden of Eden, convinced the heathens, so that they said and acknowledged, it was the Lord had done these things, which was a glorifying of his name; Psal. cxxvi. 1, 2, the Babylonians and others said, "The Lord hath done great things for them," when he turned their captivity. There is so much of God's wisdom, power, mercy, bounty, in some of his works, that they constrain all that behold them to acknowledge him in them; see Neh. vi. 16; Psal. xcviii. i. 2; Isa. lii. 9, 10.

Obs. 3. That architecture and husbandry are the work of the Lord. "I build the ruined places, and plant that that was desolate." There is no house, no city built, but the Lord hath the chief hand therein; Psal. cxxvii. 1, "Except the Lord build the house, they labour in vain that build it:" all is nothing without the counsel, assistance, and blessing of God; he teacheth the carpenters and masons their art, he enables them to work, and blesses them working. So for husbandmen, it is God that doth instruct them to discretion, and teach them, Isa. xxviii. 26; they have all their ploughing, sowing, and planting skill from him: "This cometh forth from the Lord of hosts, who is wonderful in counsel, and excellent in working," ver. 29. If a land be well built with houses, cities, castles, it is the Lord that builded them; if it be well tilled and planted with orchards, gardens, vineyards, and nurseries of young trees, it is the Lord that hath tilled and planted them; men's art and industry are nothing without him.

Obs. 4. God's purposes and promises shall take effect, and certainly be fulfilled; God is faithful in what he saith, and will perform the same. "I the Lord have spoken it, and will do it." He will not go back from his word, change his purposes and counsels, or falsify his promises. Isa. xxxi. 2, he "will not call back his words." Chap. xiv. 27, "The Lord of hosts hath purposed, and who shall disannul it?" Chap. xlvi. 10, "My counsel shall stand, and I will do all my pleasure." Jer. xxxii. 42, "I will bring upon them all the good that I have promised them." There is none wiser than God, to advise him so as to alter his purposes or counsels; there is none stronger than God, to hinder him from making good what he hath purposed and promised. Isa. xliii. 13, "I will work, and who shall let it?" All the Babylonians could not hinder God's setting his people at liberty; all the wild beasts, briers, and thorns in Canaan, could not hinder him from bringing them in, and making the land like Eden, plentiful and pleasant; all the policy and power of Tobiah, Sanballat, and others, could not hinder the building of the temple and walls of the city: God had promised Jerusalem should be rebuilt and fenced, that the Jews should have their temple to worship in again, and they had them.

Ver. 37. *Thus saith the Lord God; I will yet for this be enquired of by the house of Israel, to do it for them; I will increase them with men like a flock.*

The word אדרש is from דרש which signifies, to make diligent and careful inquiry. The Vulgate is, Moreover, in this shall the house of Israel find me; when they pray and seek me, I will be found of them, they shall prevail with me to do this for them. Vatablus in his notes hath the words thus, I will be required by the house of Israel, they shall come and mind me, and entreat me to do this for them. Junius is otherwise, I will be exposed to the house of Israel, that I will do this for them. Piscator is more plain, I will show myself to the house of Israel to be found of them, that I may do this for them.

What it is that God will be inquired of for, is next to be spoken of. Maldonate makes it, whatsoever they shall ask. Some refer it to all the promises mentioned before. But both these are too large, and the words would not have been "for this," but, for these things, or these promises, will I be inquired of. Lavater makes "for this" to be, that they may be multiplied and increased again; or, For this, viz. which I have spoken and said, I will do; I have said I will return, rebuild, replant them, and make their desolate land like the garden of Eden, so that the heathens shall wonder at my dealings with them; now for this will I be inquired of by the house of Israel.

"I will increase them with men like a flock." The Hebrew may be read thus, I will increase them like a flock of men. The Septuagint is, I will increase the men themselves, as sheep, I will so multiply them that they shall be like a flock. The Jews greatly desired issue always, and it is probable more strongly after their reduction from Babylon than ever, that so they might plant, build, and fill the land again.

Ver. 38. *As the holy flock, as the flock of Jerusalem in her solemn feasts; so shall the waste cities be filled with flocks of men: and they shall know that I am the Lord.*

In the Hebrew it is, As the flocks of holiness, or holy things. The Jews, besides other feasts, had three great solemn feasts every year at Jerusalem: 1. The passover; 2. Pentecost; 3. The feast of tabernacles; unto which the people came up from all parts of the land; and for their use at those times great flocks of sheep and herds of cattle were brought to Jerusalem. In Josiah's time there were thirty thousand lambs and kids, besides oxen and small cattle, which were for holy services, and therefore here are called, "the holy flock," and "flock of Jerusalem." John v. 2, you read of a sheep market, and by it a pool: great flocks of sheep were brought unto that market, and they were washed in that pool before they were used in holy services. Jerusalem at these feasts was filled with flocks of sheep and men, and God here promiseth, that the waste and desolate places of Judea should be filled with men, and made to abound with inhabitants again, how improbable soever it seemed to the Jews or heathens.

"And they shall know that I am the Lord." They shall acknowledge that my thoughts are not theirs, nor my ways theirs; and that I am faithful, and able to do great things.

Obs. 1. God expects that his people should seek to him for performance of those promises he graciously makes them. "I will for this be inquired of by the house of Israel, to do it for them." It is tender mercy and loving-kindness in God to make promises unto sinners; and it is duty in man to mind them being made, and to sue them out by prayer. David did so: "Remember," saith he, "the word unto thy servant, upon which thou hast caused me to hope," Psal. cxix. 49. And again, "Quicken me, according to thy word," ver. 154. He minded God of his word and promises, and pressed him by hearty prayer to make the same good. So Jacob; Lord, didst not thou bid me return unto my country, and saidst thou wouldst deal well with me; "deliver me, I pray thee, from the hand of my brother, from the hand of Esau, for I fear him," Gen. xxxii. 9, 11. Had not Jacob improved the promise, he might have gone without deliverance. Promises, as they are foundations for faith, so they are incentives unto prayer, and provoke those to whom they are made to sue them out. "O Lord God," said Solomon, "let thy promise unto David my father be established," 2 Chron. i. 9. Thou didst promise him that I should sit upon the throne, Lord, make it good. Jeremiah holds out this truth most clearly, that God expects to be sought unto for the performance of what he promiseth: chap. xxix. 10, 11, "After seventy years be accomplished at Babylon I will visit you, and perform my good word toward you, in causing you to return to this place. For I know the thoughts that I think toward you, saith the Lord, thoughts of peace, and not of evil, to give you an expected end." Here is the promise; what now follows in ver. 12—14? "Then shall ye call upon me, and ye shall go and pray unto me, and I will hearken unto you," &c. See it put in practice, Dan. ix. 2, 3, &c. God tells them, Isa. xliii. 25, that he blots out transgressions for his own sake, and will not remember their sins; but then it is added, "Put me in remembrance," ver. 26.

Obs. 2. That the increase of children is the blessing of God, and he can increase them in a short space to become like a flock. They multiplied and filled the land after their return, and were as the stars of heaven, the sand of the sea-shore, and dust of the earth. The key of the womb is in God's hand, and "he maketh the barren woman to keep house, and to be a joyful mother of children," Psal. cxiii. 9; and he makes the fruitful woman to be more fruitful. He multiplied his people as the bud of the field, Ezek. xvi. 7.

Obs. 3. How desperate soever the conditions of men and things are, the Lord can restore them to their pristine estate, yea, to a better. They were in a low and lost condition in Babylon, all their cities laid waste in their own land, and never like to be built or inhabited; but God delivered them, and restored them to their primitive state, and made all their waste cities populous. Jerusalem formerly was filled with men, now the waste cities should be also filled, abounding with men, now their land should be planted and inhabited: things in that land were often at the point of ruin, and incurable in the eye of men, but God relieved them, raised and restored them. When Sennacherib was there with his great army, and all seemed lost, did not God destroy his army, and relieve them publicly and privately? Though there were now no cities left, God could and did raise them up many cities; though there were no people to inhabit those cities raised, God could raise them up men, and did make them exceeding populous, even as populous as Jerusalem was at her solemn feasts, more populous than ever.

Obs. 4. The end of God's deliverances, works, and mercies, is, that God may be acknowledged and glorified. When I have brought them out of Babylon, planted them in Zion, built their cities, filled them with inhabitants, and blessings of all sorts, then shall they know that I am the Lord; that I am not like the heathenish gods and lords, but that I am faithful, omnipotent, gracious, and merciful, worthy to be honoured and adored by the house of Israel.

CHAPTER XXXVII.

Ver. 1, 2. *The hand of the Lord was upon me, and carried me out in the spirit of the Lord, and set me down in the midst of the valley which was full of bones, and caused me to pass by them round about: and, behold, there were very many in the open valley; and, lo, they were very dry.*

In the former chapter he spake of the Jews' return out of Babylon, and likewise of the kingdom of Christ: in this chapter, also, he proceeds to comfort the Jews, assuring them of their return, who well-nigh despaired thereof, and of the union of the two houses, Judah and Israel.

The parts of this chapter are,

I. A vision of dry bones presented to the prophet, ver. 1—10.

II. The interpretation and application of this vision, ver. 11—14.

III. A type of two sticks, and the uniting of them, ver. 15—19.

IV. The explication of the type, ver. 20, to the end.

Ver. 1. "The hand of the Lord was upon me." By "hand of the Lord," the Chaldee understands, the Spirit of prophecy, which did enlighten and affect the mind of the prophet; so also do divers others. But some take it for the power of God upon him; or a divine instinct, which, like a hand, pulled or moved him to some other thing, as chap. viii. 3. It was the Spirit of God came upon him, as chap. iii. 14; and why it is called the hand of God, see chap. i. 3.

"And carried me out in the spirit of the Lord." The Hebrew may be read thus, and is by Montanus, and the Lord carried me out in the spirit; that is, I was rapt out of myself, and my spirit was carried by the Lord to have a sight or view of bones. If we take the words as they are, the sense is this; The Spirit of God being upon me, carried me out in the Spirit of prophecy, which is the Spirit of the Lord. His body was not carried from place to place; he had a prophetical vision.

"And set me down in the midst of the valley." The prophet seemed to himself to see a hand, and to be led out by that hand into a certain valley; all which was visional, not real. He names no particular valley. A Lapide saith, it was in Campo Sennaar. Mesopotamia and Chaldea were plains; but whether it were in either of them, is not specified. In valleys prophets were wont to have visions. Our prophet's first vision was by the river Chebar, and rivers are always in valleys; and in this valley, it is conceived by some, as Lavater observes, was this vision: but it is safer to judge, that this valley was also visional.

"Which was full of bones." This valley or plain was no burying-place, for then the bones would not have lain upon the face of the earth, and been exposed to view. Some make these bones to be the bones of all mankind being dead, and to respect the general resurrection; but they are out, nothing of that is here intended. Some make them to be the bones of the Babylonians; but the prophet's scope here is not to comfort them; it is the Jews' condition he points at, and therefore by "bones" are meant the Jews, as is clear, ver. 11. These bones were visional also, not real, for then they should not have lain unburied, suffering reproach. Some Jews have an opinion, that these bones were the bones of those Jews that died in Babylon; and one rabbi Jose, a Galilean, saith, that Ezekiel raised those dead Jews, many of which returned into the land of Israel, and had children there: that when this fell into controversy among the Jews, one rabbi Juda the son of Bathira stood up and said, I am of that race which Ezekiel raised; and showed the phylacteries his parent put upon him, and had received from those that were raised.

Ver. 2. "And caused me to pass by them round about." The Lord would have the prophet to take exact notice of them, and therefore made him to pass on every side, that so he might observe the number and quality of them, and where they lay; which he did, for it follows,

"And, behold, there were very many in the open valley." The number of these bones was great, passed number, and they lay in open view, in an open valley, where he had a full sight of them.

"And, lo, they were very dry." These bones were not clothed with flesh, juicy, and full of marrow, which had been more easily raised to life if so: but they were dry, all the moisture was out of them; they had lain long, nigh seventy years, in that condition, and were almost become earth.

Obs. 1. It was the Spirit of God moved the prophets to give out those truths which are now extant in the Scriptures, that directed and enabled them to do what they did. "The hand of the Lord was upon me, and carried me out in the Spirit" to see and give out what you have here. The prophets might not speak or act at their own pleasure, but, as the Spirit of God moved them, 2 Pet. i. 21, so they spake, so they acted. It was the Spirit in the prophets that testified against the Jews, Neh. ix. 30; the words of the Lord of hosts were in the hand and mouth of the Spirit, before they were in the heads and mouths of the prophets. The apostles had the Spirit falling upon and filling them, before they gave out divine truths, Acts ii. 4; which verified what Christ had said of the Spirit, John xvi. 14, "He shall receive of mine, and show it unto you." All the truths Paul hath given forth for the instruction, edification, and consolation of the church of Christ, he received from the Spirit of Christ. Hence he saith, 1 Cor. xi. 23, "I received of the Lord that which I delivered unto you:" and chap. xiv. 37, "The things I write unto you are the commandments of the Lord;" he had them all from his Spirit, chap. ii. 12, 13.

Obs. 2. The true messengers and servants of God come not only with the word of God, but in the Spirit and power of God. Ezekiel had the hand of God with him. So Paul, 1 Cor. ii. 4, 5, his "preaching was not with enticing words of man's wisdom, but in demonstration of the Spirit and of power." False teachers may come with the letter, but only those are the true prophets, the true messengers of Christ, that come in the Spirit, and with the Spirit, are carried out by the Spirit.

Obs. 3. God honours his servants sometimes so as to make them of his council, and copartners with him in his works. God makes known his mind here to Ezekiel, and uses him in the work he was about. Samuel was thus honoured, God made him of his privy-council, and told him what he would do to the house of Eli, 1 Sam. iii. So he dealt by Abraham, not only in the business of Sodom, Gen. xviii. 17, but in that of his posterity, telling him, his seed should be a stranger in a land not theirs four hundred and thirty years, and that afterwards they should come out with great substance, Gen. xv. 13, 14. The prophets and apostles were cabinet men, and knew the secrets of the Lord, and were co-workers with God. The apostle Paul is expressly for it, 2 Cor. vi. 1, they are συνεργοὶ Θεοῦ, men that work together with God in the same work. This is great honour, and such honour as have not all the saints.

Obs. 4. Our God calls and moves his servants, by his Spirit, to do difficult things; he orders them so as to do them safely. It was somewhat averse to nature to go among dead bones, and dangerous to the prophet, being many and scattered up and down the valley; for had he accidentally touched but one of them, he had been unclean, according to the law, Numb. xix.; but God caused him to pass by them, so as he was preserved from pollution: he saw the bones, he touched none of them. It was a sad and dangerous work God called Abraham unto, viz. the sacrificing of his son; but he ordered it so, that Abraham came off, not only without imputation of sin, but with great honour for his obedience.

Ver. 3. ***And he said unto me, Son of man, can these bones live? And I answered, O Lord God, thou knowest.***

This verse is a dialogue between God and the prophet, as Polanus calls it.

I. God propounds a question.

II. The prophet answers it.

The question is this,

"Son of man, can these bones live?" Ezekiel, thou hast had a full view of them, thou seest how dry they are, in what condition they lie; tell me thy thoughts, what thy judgment is of them, I am desirous to know thy mind. Hast thou any art, skill, or power to quicken them? or, knowest thou any creature that hath? To this question the prophet answers in the next words.

"And I answered, O Lord God, thou knowest." The prophet's answer is suitable unto the Lord's question, which was concerning the present life of these bones, not future life at the general resurrection, which he doubted not of, therefore he confesseth his ignorance: I do not know, O Lord, what thy pleasure is; thou art able to put life into these dry bones in a moment, though neither myself nor any other creature can do it; our power is finite, thine is infinite, and thou canst do whatever thou pleasest, but thy pleasure is held from me and others; therefore, "O Lord God, thou knowest."

Obs. 1. Divine interrogations argue not ignorance in God, but are instructory to the interrogated. God knew what these bones could do, before he propounded the question to Ezekiel: it was therefore propounded for his instruction, to acquaint him with the power of God, and his own weakness, that so, knowing the one, and being sensible of the other, he might be the fitter instrument in the hand of God to work by. Christ's question to Peter, John xxi. 15, was of this nature, "Simon, lovest thou me more than these?" It was not so much to prove him, as to instruct and mind him of his former failing, and to fit him for action, viz. the feeding his lambs and sheep.

Obs. 2. God can easily non-plus or silence wise and holy men with a short question. Here he puts Ezekiel to it, "Can these bones live?" The prophet could not tell. When God propounded some questions to Job, was he able to answer him? Job xxxviii. 3, 4, &c. He professes he was not able to do it, but must be silent, chap. xl. 4. Did not Christ by a question put the chief priests, scribes, and elders to silence? He asked them, whether the baptism of John was from heaven or of men? This little question so perplexed them all, that they professed they could not tell, Mark xi. 30, 33.

Obs. 3. It is wisdom and duty in the servants of God to resolve all they cannot reach, or know not how to be effected, into the knowledge and good pleasure of the Lord. "O Lord God, thou knowest." He resolves the question into God's bosom; he had knowledge, power, and will to do whatever seemed good to himself. There are many things in the word mentioned, which man can say nothing unto, but, "Lord, thou knowest:" as, where the sepulchre of Moses was, Deut. xxxiv. 6; the spreadings of the clouds, how they are, Job xxxvi. 29; the wind, whence it comes, or whither it goes, John iii. 8; whether the seed sown in the evening or the morning shall prosper best, or be both alike, Eccles. xi. 6; what is the true interpretation of the number of the beast, "six hundred threescore and six," Rev. xiii. 18; or of the two witnesses, and the time of their prophesying in sackcloth "a thousand two hundred and threescore days," when it began, and when it ended, or shall, Rev. xi. 3. Of these and other things be it said, "Lord, thou knowest."

Ver. 4—10. ***Again he said unto me, Prophesy upon these bones, and say unto them, O ye dry bones, hear the word of the Lord. Thus saith the Lord God unto these bones; Behold, I will cause*** *breath to enter into you, and ye shall live: and I will lay sinews upon you, and will bring up flesh upon you, and cover you with skin, and put breath in you, and ye shall live; and ye shall know that I am the Lord. So I prophesied as I was commanded: and as I prophesied, there was a noise, and behold a shaking, and the bones came together, bone to his bone. And when I beheld, lo, the sinews and the flesh came up upon them, and the skin covered them above: but there was no breath in them. Then he said unto me, Prophesy unto the wind, prophesy, son of man, and say to the wind, Thus saith the Lord God; Come from the four winds, O breath, and breathe upon these slain, that they may live. So I prophesied as he commanded me, and the breath came into them, and they lived, and stood up upon their feet, an exceeding great army.*

The quickening of the dry bones is the great thing considerable in these verses; and it is set out,

From the causes:

I. The efficient.

1. The instrumental, prophesying, ver. 4, 7, 9, 10.

2. The principal, ver. 5.

II. The formal; which is expressed,

1. By coalition of bone to bone, ver. 7.

2. By clothing of the bones with flesh, sinews, and skin, ver. 8.

3. By the entrance of breath, ver. 10.

Ver. 4. "Prophesy upon these bones, and say unto them, O ye dry bones, hear the word of the Lord." This seems an absurd thing, that the prophet should prophesy unto creatures insensible, unintelligible, void of life; it was as if God should bid a man preach unto a heap of stones, or dry chips, which are incapable of hearing. But though these bones were incapable of hearing Ezekiel's voice, yet they were not incapable of hearing God's voice, for all creatures, even the most senseless, hear the Lord when he speaks; the stormy winds fulfil his word, Psal. cxlviii. 8; the heavens and the earth, Isa. i. 2; whales and ravens, Jonah ii. 10; 1 Kings xvii. 4. The Lord intended to bestow life upon these bones, and, that they might have life, they must hear his word, which had enlivening virtue in it. There is an obediential virtue in every creature to yield to the will and command of the Creator, and when it doth so, then it is said to hear the voice of the Lord: then properly men hear God when they do what he requires.

Ver. 5. "Behold, I will cause breath to enter into you, and ye shall live." These words prevent an objection which the prophet might have made, saying, It is in vain for me to prophesy to these dry bones; whatever I shall say over them, or unto them, will come to nothing, and prove ridiculous if any take notice thereof. No, saith the Lord, it shall not be so; for, "behold, I will cause breath to enter into them, and they shall live." The Septuagint saith, Behold, I bring upon you the Spirit of life. Others render the words thus, Behold, I do make the Spirit to enter into you; or, I am about to bring the Spirit into you, and ye shall live: that is, I am ready to breathe life into you; or, I will breathe the breath of life into you. It is life that is here promised; which he mentions, first, to encourage the prophet, though it were performed last; for the bones must first be united, then be clothed with sinews, flesh, and skin, before the breath of life enters.

Ver. 6. "And I will lay sinews upon you." The Hebrew for "sinews" is, גירים which is from גדר to act upon, &c. The nerves in the body do concur unto the duties of sense and motion. Some nerves are soft, some are hard; the soft are specially for sense, and they come from the brain; the hard are chiefly for motion, and they come from the marrow in the backbone. Here God would cause these visional bones to have visional sinews, which might fit them for sense and motion.

"And bring up flesh upon you." The word for "flesh" is, בשר which synecdochically signifies sometimes men, and sometimes other living creatures; but here it notes that part of man's body which is simple, soft, and ruddiest: such flesh would God bring up upon these bones. The Hebrew for "bring up" is, I will make to ascend: God would cause flesh to grow up and ascend out of those dry bones.

"And cover you with skin." When the bones had sinews, and flesh, God would not leave them so; it is unsightly to behold naked, raw flesh: he would give them a garment, viz. cover them with skin. *Incrustabo vos cute,* saith Montanus, I will crust you over with skin. *Superextendam in vobis cutem,* saith the Vulgate, I will stretch over you a skin. The word for "skin" is, עור from ערה to be naked. Though the flesh were covered with skin, yet was not the skin covered with any artificial covering.

"And put breath in you, and ye shall live." These words are the same with those in the fifth verse. Now, when the bones had their sinews, flesh, and skin, and were fitted for the breath of life, they should have it. The Septuagint is thus, *δώσω πνεῦμα μοῦ ἐφ' ὑμᾶς,* I will give my Spirit upon you, that shall beget life in you, and cause you to live.

"And ye shall know that I am the Lord." These dry bones, being so metamorphosed and raised to a living condition, should acknowledge the mighty hand of the Lord, and be convinced that he was able to do whatsoever he pleased.

Ver. 7. "So I prophesied as I was commanded." The prophet stood not disputing the case with God: but he, understanding the mind of God, presently set himself to fulfil it.

"And as I prophesied there was a noise." What Ezekiel prophesied to these bones is not so much to be questioned; he had direction from God what to say unto them, even those words ye have in the 4th, 5th, and 6th verses. And as he was prophesying, before he had uttered all given him in commission, "there was a noise," not of thunder, or of angels, or of an earthquake, but of the bones themselves, which being many, dry, and stirring, could not but make a great noise. This noise was an evident demonstration of divine presence and power, put forth in this miraculous work.

"And behold a shaking." These bones, that were dead and dry, now began to stir and shake, they moved from their places. Maldonate thinks, that the earth was moved, that so the bones which were in the graves, and under the earth, might come forth; but these were bones which lay in an open valley, not under the earth. Their shaking or concussion was with force. It was divine power made them to shake and move. Some refer this shaking to the invasion of the Babylonians by the Medes and Persians, at what time the Jews obtained their liberty.

"And the bones came together, bone to his bone." As timber in a house, so are bones in the body, the strength and support of all. The Hebrew word for a bone is, עצם, *etzem,* from עצם to corroborate and make solid. Bones are the strength and solidity of the body. These bones came together, not promiscuously, the bones of one man or woman to the bones of another man or woman, but bone to his bone, that is, every bone of the same man to its right place, and every bone of the same woman to its right place; the rib-bones, thigh-bones, and ancle-bones came every one to its proper place, and so united together.

Ver. 8. "And when I beheld, lo, the sinews and the flesh came up upon them, and the skin covered them above." Here was a strange sight, to see dry bones come creeping together, every one to coalesce and join in his due place, making up a perfect skeleton; and out of that sinews, flesh, and skin, to ascend: this was such a sight that neither Ezekiel, nor any man, had ever seen before.

"But there was no breath in them." Here were perfect human bodies, as if they had been newly dead, or newly formed out of the earth, as Adam's body was; but there was yet no life in them, they were no other than dead carcasses. The coalition of the bones, the ascension of sinews, flesh, and skin upon them, argued not life in them, but divine power acting and ordering them so.

Ver. 9. "Prophesy unto the wind, prophesy, son of man, and say to the wind." The word רוח *ruach*, signifies several things. Sometimes, the Spirit of God, as 2 Sam. xxiii. 3; sometimes, an angel, as Job iv. 15; sometimes, the soul of a beast, Eccles. iii. 21; sometimes, the wind, as Job i. 19; sometimes, the breath of man, as Job xii. 10; and sometimes, the soul of man, Eccles. xii. 7; Zech. xii. 1. In what sense it is here to be taken, is the question. To let other senses pass, I conceive here it notes the soul or spirit of man, which is called "wind," or "breath;" here it expresses and declares itself by breathing, which is a "wind." When all other signs of life fail, as speech, sight, hearing, motion, &c. yet breath ofttimes remains, and so manifests the soul to be there, which is the breath of life, Gen. vi. 17. These bones being brought into the forms of bodies, lay destitute of souls, and so of life; the prophet, therefore, is commanded to prophesy unto their souls. If any will understand here by "wind," the Spirit of God, which is in Scripture compared to "wind," John iii. 8, and gives life to the dead, Psal. civ. 30, I shall not contend.

"Come from the four winds, O breath, and breathe upon these slain, that they may live." The "four winds" note out here the four chief parts, or quarters, of the world, east, west, north, and south; and the prophet is commanded to call for the souls of these bodies to come from all quarters, wherever they were, to breathe upon them; that is, to enter into them, and to cause them to live. That he called "wind" before, he calls "breath" now. By "slain," are meant, the visional carcasses which lay dead.

Ver. 10. "So I prophesied as he commanded me, and the breath came into them." The prophet doing his duty, the effect followed; he said, "Come, O breath," and the spirit, soul, or breath came into those bodies which lay in his view; they were animated, and thereupon

"They lived, and stood up upon their feet." Immediately upon reception of their souls, they had life and motion. As every bone came to his bone, and made up a body, so every soul came to its own body, and made it to live, and to testify its life by standing up upon its feet.

"An exceeding great army." The bones were many, and they being quickened, and raised, made an army, yea, a great, an exceeding great army. The word for "army" is, חיל which signifies, virtue, courage; and so the words may be rendered, They stood upon their feet, being of very great courage.

Obs. 1. God sometimes puts his servants upon strange employments, even such as seem ridiculous, unseasonable, impossible. He set Ezekiel on work to prophesy over bones, and to say unto them, "O ye dry bones, hear the word of the Lord." This was as if one should water a dry, rotten stick, and say, Grow. God said to Moses, "Lift up thy rod, and stretch out thine hand over the sea, and divide it," Exod. xiv. 16. Here was a strange command, and strange work for Moses to do: could his rod or hand divide the sea? Was it not strange work God put Joshua, the men of war, and the priests unto, when he appointed them to go seven days round about Jericho, six days together once a day, and the seventh day seven times, with trumpets and rams-horns, Josh. vi.? So when God commanded Ezekiel to take a tile, portray Jerusalem upon it, and lay siege against it, with battering-rams, then to set an iron pan between him and the city for a wall; after these things, to lie upon his left side three hundred and ninety days, and after that on his right side forty days; were not these strange kinds of employment which God put the prophet unto? Ezek. iv. So Jeremiah must put bonds and yokes upon his own neck, and then send them to kings by their own ambassadors, which came to Zedekiah at Jerusalem, Jer. xxvii. In all these things there was depth of wisdom, however they seemed unto men.

Obs. 2. Whatsoever means are used, it is God doth all. Here was prophecy used, but that did not the work without God: "Behold, I will cause breath to enter into you, and ye shall live." God could have done this without prophecy, but that was the means he would use and work in or by. We must not neglect means, and leave all to God, that is tempting the Most High; neither must we trust to means when used, that is to idolize a creature: but we must use means, and look unto God to be all in them (for without him nothing is done); and if we make him all in the means, we shall make him all after them,

Obs. 3. How low, deplorable, or desperate soever the creature be, God can alter it, and that easily. These dry bones were almost dust, and come to nothing, their condition was very deplorable and desperate, the prophet himself could not tell what to think of them; and did not God alter their condition quickly and with ease? He bids the prophet prophesy and say, "Hear the word of the Lord, ye dry bones;" and that being done, presently the bones shake, come together, are clothed with sinews, flesh, and skin, receive breath, live, and stand up. Here was a wonderful sudden change wrought with great facility. God can make the dry tree to flourish, Ezek. xvii. 24, Aaron's rod to bud and blossom, Sarah's dead womb to conceive, rivers in high places, and springs of water in dry lands, Isa. xli. 18. If God speak but the word, these things are done; Rom. iv. 17, he quickens the dead, and calls those things which be not, as though they were: let God only give a call, and things without life have life, and things without being have a being, Jer. xxxi. 15—17. Are we in bondage? he can easily set us at liberty, as he did Peter; are we sick unto death? he can easily cure us, as he did Hezekiah; are we poor and despicable? he can easily enrich us, and make us honourable, as he did Job when stripped of all; are we dead in sins and trespasses, that we cannot stir at all towards God? or, are we dead-hearted, that we stir poorly towards him? he can quicken us in a moment, as he did these dry bones, so that we shall live, move, and act vigorously.

Obs. 4. There is a mighty efficacy in God's word, when he is pleased to concur with it, and to be present with it in his own ordinance. Ezekiel prophesies, and as he prophesied there was a noise, a shaking of the bones, a coalition of them, a compassing them about with sinews, flesh, and skin, an entrance of breath, so that they lived, stood up, and were full of vigour. When God accompanies his word, it is a creating word, an enlivening word, yea, and a killing word; Ezek. xi. 14, "It came to pass, when I prophesied, that Pelatiah died." It is said of Elisha, that he should slay those that escaped the sword of Hazael and Jehu, 1 Kings xix. 17; but how should that be? for he was no sword-man: it was to be done by his prophesying, which was sharper than their swords.

Obs. 5. In the resurrection men shall have their own bodies and souls again. This vision of the dry bones is, by the fathers and others, held to be a lively representation of the resurrection. And see here, the bones came together, bone unto his bone, the same bones which were united before were united again in this resurrection; and the sinews, the flesh, the skin, which belonged to them formerly, the same came and covered them again; so the same souls, the same breath, came and entered them, and they lived: the father had not the soul or body of the son, or the daughter the soul or body of the mother, but every one had their own bodies and souls. Job was of this faith, saying, "Though after my skin worms destroy this body, yet in my flesh shall I see God: whom I shall see for myself, and mine eyes shall behold," Job xix. 26, 27.

Obs. 6. The souls of men do not sleep with their bodies in the dust, nor vanish into nothing. The prophet calls for the soul of every body here to come from the "four winds," that is, from those parts where they were. Had they been in the bones or dust of the earth, or vanished into nothing, the Lord would not have directed the prophet to have called for them from all parts of the world.

Ver. 11—14. *Then he said unto me, Son of man, these bones are the whole house of Israel: behold, they say, Our bones are dried, and our hope is lost: we are cut off for our parts. Therefore prophesy and say unto them, Thus saith the Lord God; Behold, O my people, I will open your graves, and cause you to come up out of your graves, and bring you into the land of Israel. And ye shall know that I am the Lord, when I have opened your graves, O my people, and brought you up out of your graves, and shall put my spirit in you, and ye shall live, and I shall place you in your own land: then shall ye know that I the Lord have spoken it, and performed it, saith the Lord.*

The vision being related to the prophet, here application of it is made, by God himself, to the house of Israel.

And here we may consider,

I. The complaint of the house of Israel, ver. 11.

II. God's gracious promises unto the house of Israel, ver. 12, 14.

III. The event or sequel thereof, ver. 13, 14.

Ver. 11. "These bones are the whole house of Israel." The bones themselves were not the "house of Israel," but they signified and represented the condition of the "house of Israel," which being captive in Babylon, were like unto the dry bones in the open valley. To insist a little upon the resemblance between them:

1. The bones were many, very many, the valley was full of bones; when they were quickened, they made a great army. So were the Jews in the valley of Babylon, they were very many. Those that came out with Zerubbabel and Nehemiah were forty-nine thousand eight hundred and ninety-seven, or, fifty thousand wanting one hundred and three, Ezra ii. 64, 65; besides those that came with Ezra afterward, chap. viii.; and many there were which never returned. In those seventy years they were in Babylon, they multiplied into a great number.

2. The bones were without skin, flesh, and sinews, the worms, fowls, or wild beasts, had eaten up them. So the Jews were stripped of wealth and substance, the Babylonians had eaten up that. Lam. i. 10, "The adversary hath spread out his hand upon all her pleasant things;" whatsoever Jerusalem had desirable, the Babylonians laid their hands upon; and, ver. 11, "All her people sigh, they seek bread; they have given their pleasant things for meat to relieve the soul." The Chaldeans dealt hardly with them, in the time of their captivity. Jer. l. 17, 33, they broke their bones, they held them fast, and wearied them with burdens and taxes, they flayed off their skins, ate their flesh, and sucked their blood.

3. The bones were disjointed and separated from their places, one here, another there. So the Jews were rent from their habitations and country, and were scattered all over Babylon: Ezek. xxxiv. 6, "My flock was scattered upon all the face of the earth;" that is, chiefly, the Babylonish earth; they were forced out of Zion, and dispersed into all parts of Babylon. This made Jeremiah to say, chap. l. 17, "Israel is a scattered sheep." The princes, the nobles, the priests, the prophets, and the people, were all scattered one from another; the bones of that commonwealth were pulled all asunder, and thrown into several places.

4. The bones were dry, yea, very dry; they had no moisture or marrow in them. Such was the "house of Israel," being in the furnace of Babylon, their long captivity, with the evils attending it, had dried up their moisture and marrow. They wanted the milk and honey they had in Canaan for their bodies, and the manna they had for their souls; they were without a temple, and the ordinances of it, so that not only their bodies, but their souls also, were as dry bones, for they said they were without hope.

5. The bones being uncovered, lay exposed to the reproach and injury of any foot that passed by them; and the Jews, the time of their being in Babylon, were exposed to scorns and injuries from all sorts: see Ezek. xxxvi. 14, 15, 30; Lam. v. 1; Psal. cxxxvii. 3. The whole house of Israel was a derision and scorn to the Babylonians.

"Behold, they say, Our bones are dried." This speech, "Our bones are dried," is proverbial, and notes a most miserable and forlorn condition, such as those "dry bones" lay in: so far off were they from life, that the prophet could not see a possibility thereof. The Jews in Babylon were in such a condition, they saw no possibility of their returning. Captivity and servitude under enemies is a civil death; such men are like those that are dead, and their bones dried.

"And our hope is lost." "Hope" is the element by which the afflicted live, the anchor of the soul in a storm, the bladder which keeps up a man from sinking when in deep waters, and upholds a man in life when death knocks at the door; but these Jews had lost their "hope," and were at the brink of despair. They said, We hoped a long time to return to our own land, but we were deceived, here we are held fast, Jer. l. 33. Let who will hope to see Canaan again, our hope that way is dead, and in Babylon we must die.

"We are cut off for our parts." This is a proverbial

and metaphorical expression, taken either from the branch of a tree cut off from the body, or from the whole tree cut off from the earth; which no sooner is done, but they wither, become fruitless, and without hope of recovering their pristine condition. So these Jews, who were once God's vine and olive tree, said now, we are cut off from Canaan, the land of the living, where we had such nourishment as made us grow and be fruitful; but here, in our captivity, we have no city, no temple, no sacrifice, and so we are as branches cut off, and trees cut down, never like to be replanted more: see chap. xvii. 9. Like hereunto is that of Job, chap. xix. 10, "He hath destroyed me on every side, and I am gone; and mine hope hath he removed like a tree;" that is, as there is no hope of a tree cut off from the earth, so have I (saith Job) no hope of recovering my former condition.

Ver. 12. "Behold, O my people, I will open your graves." In this verse God promiseth unto them removal of impediments, and reduction of them into their own land. The first is in these words, "I will open your graves." Canaan was so dear unto the Jews, that they counted it death to live out of it; they esteemed it only the land of the living, and had rather have died than left their country: being therefore captives in a strange land, they were as dead men, and that land as a grave unto them. When a man is in his grave, he is cut off from the land of the living, laid in darkness, bound with grave-clothes, and pressed down with earth. So these Jews were cut off from their own land, had long been in Babylonish darkness, were bound up by Babylonish laws and power, and so oppressed and kept down by the tyranny of the Babylonians, that they were without hope of liberty. Hereupon the Lord saith, "I will open your graves;" I will remove all that hinders on the part of the Babylonians; their policy, power, law, oppression shall detain you no longer in captivity; yea, I will remove all that hinders on your part. Your despair and unbelief are like grave-stones, which keep you in a captive and dead condition; but they shall be taken away, and a door opened for your coming forth. It is not irrational to conceive some or many of them might be in prisons, and Babylonish families, whom God would set at liberty.

"And cause you to come up out of your graves," &c. When the graves are opened, the dead cannot rise or come forth, no more than the dry bones could move or stir of themselves. The Jews' deliverance out of captivity is likened to the raising the dead out of their graves. God causeth the dead to rise, Isa. xxvi. 19, and he would cause them to come out of Babylon; and not only bring them out thence, but also bring them into their own land; though they were cut off from their own olive tree, God would ingraft them in again.

Ver. 13. "And ye shall know that I am the Lord, when I have opened your graves," &c. When God should do this wonderful and great work, viz. bring them out of their captivity, raise them from their dead condition in Babylon, and restore them to life in their own country, then they should know and acknowledge God in a special manner.

Ver. 14. "And shall put my spirit in you." By רוח "spirit," here, is not meant breath, or life, as ver. 9, 10; for they were first to be brought up out of their graves, and to have natural life, before the Spirit should be put into them. But by "spirit" here, we understand the Holy Spirit of God; even that Spirit spoken of, chap. xxxvi. 27, where are the same words. Lavater saith, I will put into you another Spirit. Œcolampadius saith, It is the Spirit of adoption, which moderates and acts the sons of God.

"And ye shall live." They lived before a natural life, a sad and melancholy life; but now they should live a spiritual life, a comfortable and heavenly life; they should forget their sorrows, and rejoice in their God. You have been in a dying condition these seventy years of your captivity, but henceforward ye shall live.

"I shall place you in your own land." The Hebrew is, I will make you to rest upon your own land. God would dismiss them from Babylon, carry them upon eagles' wings, and set them down in their own land, where they should be at rest. They had been disquieted and vexed in Babylon many years, and suffered grievous things; but God put an end thereunto, and gave them rest in Canaan; which types out God's dealing with his people under the gospel, viz. the bringing them from under the antichristian state into Zion.

"Then shall ye know that I the Lord have spoken it, and performed it." Ye think it impossible that you should have the Babylonish yoke knocked off, be set at liberty, and planted in your own country; but if I can give life to dry bones, and cause them to stand up and become a great army, which is a more difficult thing, and thou Ezekiel hast seen it; then let the Jews be assured I can deliver them, and return them into their own land, and will do it; and when it is done, they shall know that I am a God of truth and power.

Something we shall observe in general from these words, and something more specially.

Obs. 1. That sense which God gives of visions, types, and parables, is sound and certain, yea, infallible. Ezekiel had a vision of dry bones, and who could tell the meaning of this vision? Many have mistaken about it; but God himself told the prophet, and so all others, what was the sense of that vision; Behold, the bones are the whole house of Israel. God, who is the Author of visions, types, and parables, knoweth best what is the meaning of them. He knew what the golden candlestick, and the two olive trees on the right and left sides thereof, meant, and interpreted them unto Zechariah, chap. iv. Daniel's vision of four beasts, chap. vii. did the Lord open and make known unto him. John's vision of the woman sitting "upon a scarlet coloured beast, full of names of blasphemy, having seven heads and ten horns," the Lord interpreted and made known unto him, Rev. xvii. Christ uttered many parables which were dark, and when he gave the sense of them it was certain and infallible.

Obs. 2. Tropes and types are not in sacred Scripture to be taken literally. "These bones are the house of Israel;" they were not the house of Israel in a literal sense, but they signified the house of Israel. It is frequent, in the word, to give the name of the thing signified to the thing signifying; as 1 Cor. x. 4, "That Rock was Christ;" here the rock is called Christ, whereas the rock did only signify Christ. So Gen. xli. 26, "The seven good kine are seven years, and the seven good ears are seven years;" none of these were years, but all of them signify so many years. So Dan. iv. 22, the tree, which Nebuchadnezzar saw, whose top reached to heaven, and branches to the ends of the earth, is said to be Nebuchadnezzar himself, "It is thou, O king;" that is, it signified him, it was not him himself. The papists trouble the world with their absurd sense of those words, Matt. xxvi. 26, 28, "This is my body, and this is my blood;" they will have them to be taken literally, and make us lose our senses, that we may believe the bread and wine are the very flesh and blood of Christ; but we neither see nor taste any such thing; only we believe, that they represent the same unto us, and are to convey the fruit and benefit of Christ's death unto us.

Obs. 3. God's people are sometimes brought into great straits, they know not what to do, they are heartless and hopeless. "Our bones are dried, our hope is lost: we are cut off for our parts." They saw nothing but destruction before them, they saw no possibility of escaping, they thought their condition desperate. Such was Joseph's condition, when his brethren cast him into a pit, Gen. xxxvii. 24. Such was the Israelites' condition at the Red sea, when the Egyptians were behind them, the sea before them, and no door of hope left unto them, Exod. xiv.; their hope was gone, and nothing but death presented itself unto them, ver. 11. When the anchor of hope is broken, men are in a sea of troubles, tossed up and down, ready to sink every moment. Job himself was some time in this case, chap. vii. 6, "My days are swifter than a weaver's shuttle, and are spent without hope:" he had neither hope of restoration to his former condition, nor of continuance of his life; he looked only to make the grave his house, and darkness his bed, chap. xvii. 13—15; his hope was gone, and he thought he must go to corruption and the worms.

Obs. 4. When men are in great afflictions, they manifest great weakness. These Jews being in such an afflicted condition, they forgot what promises God had made to them of returning after seventy years, Jer. xxv. 12, 13; xxix. 10: they minded not God's power, or faithfulness, but said, "We are cut off for our parts;" God hath cut us off from our land, and cast us into this furnace of Babylon, where we shall be consumed. When Saul hunted David like a partridge upon the mountains, and his life was in jeopardy, did he not say in his heart, "I shall one day perish by the hand of Saul?" 1 Sam. xxvii. 1. Here he manifested his weakness greatly. God had told him he should be king, and sent Samuel to anoint him, chap. xvi.; but he forgot this, and gave way to the reasonings of flesh. Jeremiah being in a suffering condition, scorned and defamed by the people, he resolves to cast aside his commission, and speak no more in the name of the Lord; he curses the day of his nativity, and the man who brought tidings of his birth; wishes he had slain him from the womb, or that the womb had been his grave, &c.; thus did he declare his infirmities, chap. xx. 8, 9, 15—17, not considering what God had promised him, chap. i. 5, 8, 9, 17—19. The like did Job.

Obs. 5. There are states of men in this life which do resemble the dead; and they are two especially, both which are here held forth.

(1.) The state of great and long afflictions. These Jews, in their captivity, are likened unto dry bones, men in their graves. This made Jeremiah say, Lam. iii. 6, "He hath set me in dark places, as they that be dead of old." The state of death is a state of darkness, and so is the state of affliction. Isa. lix. 10, "We grope for the wall like the blind, and we grope as if we had no eyes: we stumble at noon day as in the night; we are in desolate places as dead men." They were in deep affliction, and destitute of all counsel; they saw no way or means how to get out of the same. David being under great calamities, goes further, and shows you, that such a state is not only a state of darkness, but of consumption, of being forgotten, and broken: Psal. xxxi. 9, 12, "I am in trouble; mine eye is consumed with grief, yea, my soul and my belly. I am forgotten as a dead man out of mind: I am like a broken vessel." So Psal. xliv. 19, "Thou hast sore broken us in the place of dragons, and covered us with the shadow of death." He calls great afflictions, the place of dragons, because they sting, bite, and endanger a man's life; and, the shadow of death; death is very near, and overshadows the man who is in them, his grave is designing, and he is ready to be put thereinto. This consideration made Heman say, his soul being full of troubles, "My life draweth nigh unto the grave. I am counted with them that go down into the pit: I am as a man that hath no strength: free among the dead, like the slain that lie in the grave, whom thou rememberest no more: and they are cut off from thy hand. Thou hast laid me in the lowest pit, in darkness, in the deeps," Psal. lxxxviii. 3—6. He shows you clearly, that great afflictions, especially soul-afflictions, are a state of death.

(2.) The state of sin, which these Jews were in; for it is said, "I will put my spirit into you, and ye shall live." At that time they were dead, being in an unregenerate estate. Men being in their sins, are no better than in a state of death. They are in darkness, ignorant of Christ, the gospel, and mysteries thereof, Eph. v. 8. They are in bondage to their lusts, and to Satan, 2 Pet. ii. 19; Rom. vi. 16; 2 Tim. ii. 26; John viii. 44. They are senseless, eyes they have, and see not; ears, and hear not; hearts, and understand not, Matt. xiii. 14, 15. They have hearts of stone, and are past feeling, Eph. iv. 18, 19. They are corrupt and unsavoury, Eph. iv. 22; Rom. iii. 13. This is the condition of sinners, which the gospel accounts and calls, a state of death, Matt. viii. 22; John v. 25; Eph. ii. 5; Col. ii. 13.

Obs. 6. God is afflicted with the afflictions and sufferings of his people. O my people, you are in your graves here in Babylon, you are afflicted, reproached, oppressed; but I am sensible thereof, and do sympathize with you in that condition; not a word is spoken against you, not an unjust act done unto you, but I hear, I feel the same. The words are twice mentioned, "O my people, O my people," in the 12th and 13th verses, to show the Lord was much affected with their calamities and languishing condition. When the Jews were in Egypt, that house of bondage, and in the wilderness, they were like men in their graves, oft covered with the shadow of death; and did not God pity them? Psal. cvi. 44, "He regarded their affliction;" he looked upon them and pitied them; yea, he made their enemies to pity them, ver. 46. In the book of Judges, chap. x. 16, you have a notable expression to this purpose: it is said there, "His soul grieved for the misery of Israel;" his soul was shortened. When things are laid to heart, they dry and shrink up a man's spirits. God laid their misery so to heart, that his soul was, as it were, shrunk up and shortened.

Obs. 7. There is no state of affliction, sin, or death, but God can and will raise his people out of the same. "O my people, I will open your graves, and cause you to come up out of your graves." Though they had lain seventy years in their graves, God would open them. When earth lies long undigged, when graves continue long unopened, it is the harder to remove the earth, and open the graves: what difficulty soever there was in the way, God would step over it, and do the thing. Job lay buried in the grave of affliction a long season, but at length God opened his grave, and led him out; Job xlii. 10, "The Lord turned the captivity of Job." David was in the grave of affliction, but God raised him out of it; Psal. xl. 2, "He brought me up out of an horrible pit, out of the miry clay;" that is, out of the deepest and extremest misery. Mary Magdalene lay in the grave of sin, was in a state of spiritual death, and Christ quickened her, he forgave her sins, Luke vii. 48. The Ephesians did, among other gentiles, lie in their graves of sin, they were shut up under unbelief, that was a weighty grave-stone that kept them under; but God rolled away that stone, opened their graves, and brought them forth; Eph. ii. 1, "You that were dead in sins and trespasses, hath he quickened." Those who are in a literal sense dead, and in their graves, God can open their graves, and bring them forth also. Lazarus had lain four days in his grave, he was corrupted therein and stunk; yet, when Christ said, "Lazarus, come forth," the grave did open, the dead man heard, lived, and came forth, John xi. 43, 44. The keys of life and death are in the hand of Christ; be it a grave of affliction, a grave of sin, or a grave of the body, Christ can turn the key, open the grave, and bring out thereof: at last he will open the graves, and bring forth all the dead bodies.

Obs. 8. Nothing in men moves God to put his Spirit into them. These Jews were in a despairing condition, they said, "Our bones are dried, our hope is lost, we are cut off for our parts." They despaired, dishonoured God highly thereby, and deserved to be cut off and perish for ever; but see how God dealt with them, he promises to put his Spirit in them, ver. 14. The giving of his Spirit is an extraordinary mercy, and he gives it freely. Their goodness did not incline God to give, nor their sin hinder him from giving. God's choicest gifts are freest, as Christ, the Spirit, and gospel; they are the acts of his good pleasure.

Obs. 9. Spiritual life and comfort are from the Spirit's indwelling in men. "I shall put my spirit in you, and ye shall live." Then they shall live, as they had never lived; they should live spiritually, comfortably. Natural life, in its kind, hath an excellency; but it is far beneath a spiritual life, which is called "the life of God," Eph. iv. 18 So the comforts of a natural life may have some sweet and preciousness in them; but they are comfortless comforts to those of the Spirit and spiritual life. Men destitute of the Spirit are dead men, and have but dead comforts; those who have the Spirit are living men, and have living comforts. The Spirit is a Spirit of life and comfort, and wherever it comes, it makes men lively and comfortable.

Obs. 10. When the people of God are gathered into Canaan, they shall have rest there. God would bring these Jews out of Babylon into their own land, which was Canaan, and there they should rest: there is no rest in Babylon. God is gathering his people out of Babylon daily. He saith unto them, as it is in Micah ii. 10, "Arise ye, and depart; for this is not your rest." He is drawing and driving them out of Babylonish and antichristian conditions, and bringing them into Zion, where there is true rest, though not perfect rest; that will be in the heavenly Canaan, whither in due time we shall come.

Ver. 15—19. *The word of the Lord came again unto me, saying, Moreover, thou son of man, take thee one stick, and write upon it, For Judah, and for the children of Israel his companions: then take another stick, and write upon it, For Joseph, the stick of Ephraim, and for all the house of Israel his companions: and join them one to another into one stick; and they shall become one in thine hand. And when the children of thy people shall speak unto thee, saying, Wilt thou not shew us what thou meanest by these? say unto them, Thus saith the Lord God; Behold, I will take the stick of Joseph, which is in the hand of Ephraim, and the tribes of Israel his fellows, and will put them with him, even with the stick of Judah, and make them one stick, and they shall be one in mine hand.*

The vision of the dry bones, and interpretation of them, being ended, here the typical work of two sticks, and the uniting of them, succeeds. In the three first verses you have the author of the type, and the type itself: in the two last, direction what to say, upon inquiry made after the meaning of the type.

Ver. 16. "Moreover, thou son of man, take thee one stick." The prophet before had a vision, here he hath a command. He must take a stick: the Chaldee saith, a table; the Septuagint, a rod: the Hebrew is, wood. Wood, or stick, is, by a metonomy of the matter, put for a table, or tally, whereon something might be written. So it was here; he must write upon it,

"For Judah, and for the children of Israel his companions." These were the words to be written upon the stick. In Numb. xvii. 2, the Lord commanded Moses to take twelve rods, according to the number of the tribes and princes, and to write every man's name upon his rod. To this doth the Lord allude here, commanding the prophet to take a stick, or rod, and write upon it, "For Judah;" that is, Let Judah, the royal and noble tribe, be signified thereby. "And the children of Israel;" by these the tribe of Benjamin is meant, which clave to the house of David, and fell not from Rehoboam to Jeroboam, 1 Kings xii. 23; 2 Chron. xi. 12, as the other tribes did. This tribe did wholly adhere to Judah, and some also out of other tribes did, some out of Levi, and some out of the rest, 2 Chron. xi. 13, 14, 16, 17; xv. 9; and these are called "the children of Israel his companions;" that is, Judah's companions, because they forsook him not, as others did. All these were represented by this first stick.

"Then take another stick, and write upon it, For Joseph, the stick of Ephraim." Having finished the first stick, he is bidden to "take another." The Hebrew is, take one stick; that is, one more, "and write upon it, For Joseph." As the other stick was for Judah, so this for Joseph; viz. to represent the tribe of Joseph, which was the principal of the ten tribes; and his stick was called "the stick of Ephraim." Ephraim was the son of Joseph, and the ten tribes are usually called in Scripture by the name of Ephraim, as Hos. iv. 17; v. 3, 9, 11, 12, 13, 14; but here the tribe of Ephraim is meant. The Chaldee saith, The stick of Ephraim is the tribe of Ephraim. Jeroboam, who made the great rent in the house of David, was of the tribe of Ephraim, and to him did the other tribes adhere.

"And for all the house of Israel his companions." This stick was for the whole ten tribes, which are called "the house of Joseph," Amos v. 6, "The seed of Ephraim," Jer. vii. 15, "Samaria," Hos. viii. 5, and here, "the house of Israel." All these did side with Jeroboam when he revolted, and so were companions with him, with Ephraim and Joseph. Long before this time, the ten tribes were carried into captivity by Shalmaneser king of Assyria; but here the Lord thought upon them, and ordered the prophet to take a stick for them.

Ver. 17. "And join them one to another into one stick." The Hebrew is, and make them come one to one to thee into one stick. Those two sticks he must join together, and make one stick of them. Some do make a miracle here, saying, That as Moses' rod was turned into a serpent, and Aaron's blossomed, Exod. iv. 3; Numb. xvii. 8, by a miraculous work of God; so did Ezekiel's sticks unite together in his hand. It is true, God, by his divine power, could unite them into one; but here he bids the prophet to join them one to another into one stick, which he might do by some artificial means, or else hold them together in his hand, which might suffice for the purpose intended.

"And they shall become one in thine hand." They shall be one in thy hands, so Montanus renders the Hebrew; not, they shall become, but, they shall be, one thing or stick in thine hand; they should no more appear to be two sticks, but one; and the characters written upon them, visible for every man to read. The old translation hath it, they shall be as one in thy hand. While he held them, they were as one, but, had he let them go, they had fallen asunder, and been two sticks as before.

Ver. 18. "And when the children of thy people shall speak nnto thee, saying." In ver. 12, and 13, God had said, "O my people," he owned them for his; here he terms them the prophet's people, "the children of thy people." They were Ezekiel's people, because he was set of God a watchman over them, chap. iii. 17.

"Wilt thou not show us what thou meanest by these?" The Hebrew is, Wilt thou not show us what these things are to thee? So the Septuagint, What is thine intention in taking these sticks, and holding them in thine hand? what is the interpretation thereof? It is a riddle unto us; let us know the sense and meaning thereof.

Ver. 19. "Behold, I will take the stick of Joseph, which is in the hand of Ephraim, and the tribes of Israel his fellows." "The stick of Joseph," that is, the tribe of Ephraim, which was in Jeroboam's hand, who was of that tribe; and not only that, but nine more were under him and his successors a long time, two hundred and sixty years, or thereabout. These ten tribes made up the kingdom of Israel, which was divided from the kingdom of Judah, and therefore are called Ephraim's fellows, not Judah's. All these represented by the stick God would take; and what would he do with them?

"And will put them with him, even with the stick of Judah, and make them one stick, and they shall be one in mine hand." God would make these two sticks one, not one tribe, but one kingdom. They had been two kingdoms, at great enmity, and were at this time scattered abroad among the nations; but the Lord promises to gather them together, and to unite them so, that there shall not be a kingdom of Israel and a kingdom of Judah, but the stick of Ephraim shall be united to the stick of Judah: they should be but one stick, one kingdom, and one king, and that in the hand of the Lord; the Septuagint saith, in the hand of Judah.

Obs. 1. True types have God for the Author of them. God bade the prophet here take one stick and another stick, and write upon them; and thereby to type out the houses of Judah and Israel. Had he taken these of his own head, they had been nothing, bastardly types, not true types. When "Zedekiah the son of Chenaanah made him horns of iron," saying, "Thus saith the Lord, With these shalt thou push the Syrians, until thou have consumed them," 1 Kings xxii. 11; this was a bold presumption of him to make horns typical, without command from God. The event showed him to be a false prophet, and his type to be a lying type. It is peculiar unto God to make divine types.

Obs. 2. God can, and doth, make use of mean things to honourable purposes. Sticks are mean and contemptible things, trodden under foot; yet, God orders sticks here to be taken, written upon, to represent the two principal houses in the world, the house of Judah and the house of Israel, and their uniting together: here was high honour put upon these sticks. God made use of a tile to portray Jerusalem upon, Ezek. iv.; and of hair to type out his judgments, Ezek. v.; which was a great honour unto such despicable things. What honour did God put upon the brazen serpent, to represent Christ thereby! Numb. xxi. 9; John iii. 14. As God puts honour upon mean things, so upon mean persons; 1 Cor. i. 28, "The base things of the world, and things which are despised, hath God chosen; yea, and things which are not, to bring to nought things that are." He exalted Gideon, and did great things by him, Judg. vi. God took Amos "an herdman, a gatherer of sycamore fruit," invested him with the honour of a prophet, Amos vii. 14, 15, and by him confounded Amaziah the priest of Bethel, and Jeroboam's chaplain.

Obs. 3. God hath a care of his people, be they in never so poor, broken, scattered, or despicable a condition. The house of Judah had been now in Babylon upon seventy years, the house of Israel two hundred and four years, if not more; they were despised of men, and seemed forgotten of God: but the Lord had them in remembrance, and bids the prophet write upon one stick, For Judah and his companions; and on another stick, For Joseph, Ephraim, or the house of Israel, and his companions; not one of them were out of God's thoughts. Their forefathers had been four hundred years in Egypt, were tyrannized over by cruel task-masters, looked upon as contemptible; but the Lord had an eye to them, cared and wrought for them. They have now lain sixteen hundred years in darkness, in a desolate and despised condition; yet doubtless they are not forgotten, God's thoughts are upon them to do them good again.

Obs. 4. Typical and obscure things will excite men to inquire after the sense of them. This is intimated in ver. 18, "When the children of thy people shall speak unto thee, saying, Wilt thou not show us what thou meanest by these?" God knew they would inquire. Common things are neglected; but things strange and mysterious are dived into, sought after. When Ezekiel was to dig through the wall, cover his face, and remove his stuff, then the people were stirred and said, "What doest thou?" chap. xii. 9. Those typical actions bred inquisitiveness in their spirits. When the Lord Christ spake parables, they sought to him to know the sense and meaning of them.

Obs. 5. God is pleased to direct his prophets and servants what to say unto the people, when they come to question with them about things. If this people come to Ezekiel to know what he meant by the two sticks, his writing upon them, and holding them in his hand, the Lord tells him what he shall say unto them; "Say, Thus saith the Lord God; Behold, I will take the stick of Joseph, which is in the hand of Ephraim," &c. When God sent Moses unto the people, he was timorous lest he should not know what to say to the people, how to answer their questions; but see how God directs and instructs him. Exod. iii. 13, 14, "Moses said unto God, Behold, when I come unto the children of Israel, and shall say unto them, The God of your fathers hath sent me unto you; and they shall say unto me, What is his name? what shall I say unto them?" I know not how to answer that question. See what now follows; "And God said unto Moses, I AM THAT I AM: and he said, Thus shalt thou say, I AM hath sent me unto you." Thus God taught him what answer to give the people. So, Ezek. xiv. when the elders came to inquire somewhat of Ezekiel, God told him what answer to give them. It was given in of God, by his Spirit, to the apostles, what answer to give governors and rulers, when they were brought before them, Matt. x. 19.

Ver. 20—22. *And the sticks whereon thou writest shall be in thine hand before their eyes. And say unto them, Thus saith the Lord God; Behold, I will take the children of Israel from among the heathen, whither they be gone, and will gather them on every side, and bring them into their own land: and I will make them one nation in the land upon the mountains of Israel; and one king shall be king to them all: and they shall be no more two nations, neither shall they be divided into two kingdoms any more at all.*

The explication of the typical sticks is laid down in these and the subsequent verses.

Ver. 20. "And the sticks whereon thou writest shall be in thine hand before their eyes." The prophet was not to do this privately, but to write upon the sticks, and to hold them in his hand, so that all might see them, and hereby be provoked to inquire what the mystery of them was, and so become partakers of the consolation intended thereby.

Ver. 21. "Behold, I will take the children of Israel from among the heathen, whither they be gone." In this verse is promised the reduction of the twelve tribes, comprehended under these words, "the children of Israel," out of all countries where they were scattered into their own land. Not only Judah and Benjamin should be gathered up, and brought into Canaan again, but the rest of the tribes also. This is a great and gracious promise.

"And will gather them on every side." The ten tribes being carried away by Shalmaneser, were placed "in Halah and Habor by the river Gozan, and in the cities of the Medes," 2 Kings xvii. 6; they were seated in the utmost parts of his dominions, north and east; and the other Jews whom Nebuchadnezzar led away captive, were scattered up and down his manifold provinces, as appears, Esth. iii. 8. Now God would look on every side, and gather them up out of all quarters.

Ver. 22. "And I will make them one nation in the land upon the mountains of Israel." Being brought into their land, here God adds three great promises more. The first is, uniting of them into one nation, who had some hundreds of years been divided, and at bitter enmity one against another.

"And one king shall be king to them all." After the division made by Jeroboam, you read of several kings they had, kings of Judah, and kings of Israel. There were two kingdoms, and divers kings of them both; but the kingdoms being united into one, the Lord promiseth them not a succession of kings over them, but one king to rule over them both; they should be one kingdom, and have one king. This is the second great promise.

"And they shall be no more two nations, neither shall they be divided into two kingdoms any more at all." This is the third promise, and it is a great one also, viz. they shall continue a kingdom, one kingdom, and never be torn or rent in pieces any more; there shall be no Rehoboams or Jeroboams to cause divisions in it.

It will add some light to the words under consideration, if we make inquiry, Whether the type of the two sticks be fulfilled, by the incorporating of the two nations into one, and making of them one kingdom?

It is affirmed by some, that this hieroglyphical prophecy was fulfilled at the return of the two tribes out of Babylon. For then Cyrus king of Persia made a proclamation throughout all his kingdom, to this purpose; "Thus saith Cyrus king of Persia, All the kingdoms of the earth hath the Lord God of heaven given me; and he hath charged me to build him an house in Jerusalem, which is in Judah. Who is there among you of all his people? The Lord his God be with him, and let him go up," 2 Chron. xxxvi. 22, 23. The proclamation excepts no persons, no tribes, but gives full liberty unto all. The ten tribes having been two hundred and four years, or thereabouts, in captivity, it is likely were weary of their condition, and so willing to return into their own country, and so they took the opportunity before them. For it is evident, that some of the ten tribes did return to Jerusalem. Of the Levites there were seventy-four, Ezra ii. 40; Neh. vii. 43; and of the priests, who were of that tribe, as appears, 1 Chron. xxiv. 1, 2, 7; Exod. vi. 16, 18, 20; and Neh. vii. 39, there were nine hundred and seventy-three. Paul was of the tribe of Benjamin, Phil. iii. 5; "Anna, the daughter of Phanuel, of the tribe of Aser," Luke ii. 36. And Paul speaks of the twelve tribes as present in his days at Jerusalem, Acts xxvi. 7. Others think not all this which is said sufficient to prove the union of the two sticks, and so of the two houses of Judah and Ephraim; for of all that returned, there were but forty-two thousand three hundred and sixty, beside servants and maids, whose number amounted to seven thousand three hundred and thirty-seven, as it is, Ezra ii. 64, 65; whereof both Hebrews and other authors observe, there were ten thousand out of the other ten tribes, which is an inconsiderable number for so many tribes, whenas there were thirty-two thousand out of two or three tribes. Besides, it is not clear that those ten thousand were out of the other tribes; for neither Ezra nor Nehemiah do specify so much in the catalogues they make of those returned. Doubtless, had such a number returned out of any, or each of the tribes, as had been considerable, they would have taken notice thereof, and mentioned the tribe, or tribes, and spoken of the uniting of them; for it is said here, "the sticks shall be in thine hand before their eyes:" the union would have been visible and observable by them all, had it then been. Some few of the tribes, it is possible, did return, and of them Paul speaks, Acts xxvi. 7. The bulk and body of them stayed behind, being increased in two hundred years to an innumerable company; and the Jews say, they are shut up in the Caspian mountains, from whence they shall come forth in due time. Manasseh Ben Israel, with Montezinus, say, the ten tribes were the first inhabitants of America, and that they lie hid behind the mountains of Cordillere.

It is the opinion, if not the faith, of many, that the two sticks representing the two houses of Judah and Israel, are yet to be united and made one; and the great reason for it is, because they have not had one king, one shepherd, viz. David, by whom is meant the Messiah, to reign over them. This is that Hosea points at, chap. i. 11, where he saith, "The children of Judah and the children of Israel shall be gathered together, and appoint themselves one head, and they shall come up out of the land." The "head" spoken of by Hosea, is not Zerubbabel, but the same that our prophet speaks of, viz. David, by whom is meant the Messiah; of which mind is Manasseh Ben Israel, who saith, The ten tribes never returned to the second temple, that they there keep the law of Moses and the sacred rites, and at last shall return into their land, with the two tribes Judah and Ben-

In his Epist. to the Hope of Israel. Sect. 25.

jamin, and shall be governed by one prince, who is the Messiah, the Son of David. If it be said, this was made good when Christ was born, and lived at Jerusalem, this will not suffice; for, "He came unto his own, and they received him not," John i. 11. The people of Israel were against Christ, Acts iv. 27; they would not have him to reign over them, Luke xix. 14; they owned no king but Cæsar, and cried, "Crucify him," John xix. And for their crucifying of him, they were scattered, and the wrath of God came upon them to the utmost, 1 Thess. ii. 16. Had the two houses been united, they would themselves have appointed and chosen Christ to have been their Head, continued still undivided and unscattered, submitting to his government, and observing his laws, as it is ver. 24 of this chapter; for, when Christ takes his government upon him, he must rule for ever, Luke i. 33.

There is a place in Zechariah very observable; it is in chap. x. 6—9, "I will strengthen the house of Judah." They of this house were come already to Judea, and Zechariah with them; they were upon building the second temple: now see what follows; "and I will save the house of Joseph, and I will bring them again to place them; for I have mercy upon them: and they shall be as though I had not cast them off: for I am the Lord their God, and will hear them. And they of Ephraim shall be like a mighty man, and their heart shall rejoice as through wine: yea, their children shall see it, and be glad; their heart shall rejoice in the Lord. I will hiss for them, and gather them; for I have redeemed them: and they shall increase as they have increased. And I will sow them among the people: and they shall remember me in far countries; and they shall live with their children, and turn again."

Here you may clearly see two things:

1. That the house of Joseph and Ephraim did not return with the house of Judah.

2. That God hath promised to gather and bring them out of those places where they are scattered; which must be accomplished in its time.

It is no heresy to say, Christ meant the ten tribes when he said, John x. 16, "Other sheep I have, which are not of this fold: them also I must bring, and they shall hear my voice; and there shall be one fold, and one shepherd." Christ here alludes to this 37th of Ezekiel, ver. 22 and 24.

Obs. 1. The conversion of the Jews we may warrantably expect and pray for. God hath promised to gather the children of Israel, and to bring them to David their king, that is, Christ: I will gather them out of every side; I will take the children of Israel from among the heathen whither they be gone; and one king shall rule over them. Seeing God hath promised to do it, we may believe and pray for the same. This conversion of the Jews will be not of some few particulars, but national, though not of every one belonging to the nation. Hos. iii. 5, "The children of Israel shall return, and seek the Lord their God, and David their king; and shall fear the Lord and his goodness in the latter days:" there will be a very general, glorious, and visible return of them; they will prove eminent christians, fearing the Lord and his goodness. Paul hints unto you, that there is a time when the vail shall be taken off the heart of the Jews, and they turn unto the Lord, 2 Cor. iii. 15, 16. And John in his Revelation tells you of a hundred and forty-four thousand which were sealed out of all the tribes of the children of Israel, chap. vii. 4. These were of the Jewish race, who were godly and converted; for, ver. 9, it is said, "A great multitude, which no man could number, of all nations, people, kindreds, and tongues, stood before the throne, and before the Lamb, clothed with white robes, and palms in their hands." These were of the gentiles, as the other of the Jews. If any one doubt this point, let him read and ponder thoroughly what is in Rom. xi. from the beginning of the 11th verse to the 32nd.

Obs. 2. When the Jews are converted they shall repossess the land of Canaan. God "will gather them on every side, and bring them into their own land." Hos. i. 10, "It shall come to pass, that in the place where it was said unto them, Ye are not my people, there it shall be said unto them, Ye are the sons of the living God." This is spoken of the land of Canaan; there he did disown them, and there he would own them again. Testimony to this truth gives Jeremiah, chap. l. 4, 5, "In those days, and in that time, saith the Lord, the children of Israel shall come, they and the children of Judah together, going and weeping: they shall go and seek the Lord their God. They shall ask the way to Zion with their faces thitherward, saying, Come, and let us join ourselves to the Lord in a perpetual covenant." That in Isa. ii. 2, 3, speaks to the same purpose; and most clearly that, Isa. xi. 11, "And it shall come to pass in that day, that the Lord shall set his hand again the second time to recover the remnant of his people, which shall be left, from Assyria, and from Egypt, and from Pathros, and from Cush, and from Elam, and from Shinar, and from Hamath, and from the islands of the sea." And in ver. 12, "And he shall set up an ensign for the nations, and shall assemble the outcasts of Israel, and gather together the dispersed of Judah from the four corners of the earth." Here is mention of a second gathering of them from Assyria, which hath not yet been fulfilled; but shall, when the Lamb will stand upon mount Zion, with his one hundred and forty-four thousand sealed out of all the tribes, Rev. xiv. 1; vii. 4. Consider Isa. lxv. 17—22.

Obs. 3. The Lord knows how to, and can, reconcile divided nations. "I will make them one nation in the land upon the mountains of Israel." The Jews were divided into two nations, or kingdoms; there was the kingdom of Israel and the kingdom of Judah; and they were at great enmity, such enmity that they would have no commerce one with another, John iv. 9. The ten tribes went under the name of Samaritans, the other were called Jews. They were of divers religions, ver. 22. They had their calves at Dan and Bethel; the true worship was at Jerusalem. The enmity grew so great between them, that they were at open wars, and sought the destruction of one another. Those of Israel and Samaria slew in Judah one hundred and twenty thousand valiant men in one day, and carried away captive of their brethren two hundred thousand women, sons and daughters, and those they slew was in a rage which reached up to heaven, 2 Chron. xxviii. 6, 8, 9. Now, notwithstanding all the rage, fury, enmity, bitterness which was in them, one against another, God knows how to reconcile them, and make them one nation, one people; so that "Ephraim shall not envy Judah, and Judah shall not vex Ephraim," Isa. xi. 13, but they shall agree, and cordially love one another. The Jews and gentiles were at a greater distance than the Jews amongst themselves, yet God knew how to reconcile them, and did it, Eph. ii. 12—16.

Ver. 23. *Neither shall they defile themselves any more with their idols, nor with their detestable things, nor with any of their transgressions: but I will save them out of all their dwelling-*

places, wherein they have sinned, and will cleanse them: so shall they be my people, and I will be their God.

In this verse there lieth before us,

I. The renouncing of their idolatrous ways and other evils.

II. Deliverance of them from the places they were captive in.

III. Spiritual cleansing, or sanctification of them.

IV. Renewal of the covenant between them and God.

"Neither shall they defile themselves any more with their idols." The Jews were much addicted to idolatry; no sooner were they out of Egypt, but they parted with their earrings to make a calf, Exod. xxxii. 24. When they were in the wilderness they joined themselves to Baal-peor, Numb. xxv. 3. In time of the Judges, when in the land of Canaan, they served other gods, Judg. x. 13. And after the rent of Jeroboam, the ten tribes did worship the calves at Dan and Bethel, 1 Kings xii. 29, 30. Judah also trod in the same steps, committing adultery with stones and with stocks, Jer. iii. 8, 9. But when they should be united into one nation and kingdom again, Israel should cease from her calves, and Judah from her idols; they should no more go a whoring after them, whereby they defiled themselves and the land.

"Nor with their detestable things, nor with any of their transgressions." Sanctius thinks these three words, "idols, detestable things, transgressions," to signify one and the same thing, to set forth the sinfulness of idols and false religions; they are detestable, and cause the greatest breaches between God and men. The word for "transgression" is, *pesha*, which notes apostasy, rebellion, a proud and malicious violating of a command. We may by "transgressions" here, understand not only their idolatries, but their other capital and crying sins. When God pleases to call and convert the Jews, and form them into one nation, then they shall loathe themselves and their former doings.

"But I will save them out of all their dwelling-places, wherein they have sinned." They were scattered up and down into divers countries, and into several parts in those countries, where they settled themselves, and sinned by conforming to the heathen amongst whom they dwelt, Ezek. xx. 32; Jer. xliv. 8. But in what countries soever they were, the Lord would have an eye to them and deliver them.

"And will cleanse them." The word in Hebrew for cleansing is, טהר which is contrary to טמא signifying to defile, pollute; and, because a thing defiled hath lost its beauty, some make *taher* to import shining or beautiful cleansing; for, when the filth of things is taken away, there is a splendour and beauty. God saith here, he will cleanse them; that is, from their idolatry, and other sins, by the blood of Christ, and by his Holy Spirit.

"So shall they be my people, and I will be their God." Now they lie in a desolate condition, and are looked at as cast off of God; yea, themselves conclude, they are cut off from me, ver. 11. But when they are gathered out of the countries where they are dispersed, and cleansed from their iniquities, then will I manifest to all the world, that they are my people, and that I am their God. They themselves shall see and know it; they shall acknowledge me to be their God, and I will acknowledge them to be my people. The covenant between us shall be renewed and manifested.

Obs. 1. From the two verses before this, and the next, That when God begins to show mercy to his people afflicted, he multiplies mercies upon them. He would take them from among the heathen, bring them into their own land, make them one nation, set one king over them, continue them in the same condition, take their hearts off from idols, cleanse them from their defilements, take them into covenant with himself, give them David to be their king, and keep them in doing of his will. Here is a series of many and great mercies. The like you had, chap. xxxvi. 24—30; so Jer. xxxii. 37—41. When God is in a way of judgments, he adds judgment to judgment, plague unto plague, as you may read, Lev. xxvi. 18, 21, 28. And when he is in a way of mercy, he adds mercy to mercy, as appears in the same chapter, ver. 4—13.

Obs. 2. False religious ways of worship are so far from advantaging men, that they do defile them. The Jews thought to better themselves by conforming to the religion and worship of the heathens; but thereby they defiled themselves. And what is the favour or wealth of heathens, when the conscience is defiled before God? Many, among papists, when they have sinned, run to their golden, silver, brass, stony, and wooden gods, thinking by offering unto them to be purged from their sins, whereas thereby they do more deeply defile themselves.

Obs. 3. When people afflicted receive choice mercies from God, then they will take heed of and renounce former defilements. "Neither shall they defile themselves any more with their idols, nor with their detestable things, nor with any of their transgressions." When I shall show them kindness, and load them with mercies, they will consider what offended me, and cease from it; then they will know me and my ways, and walk in the same, abhorring idols. Hos. xiv. 8, "Ephraim shall say, What have I to do any more with idols?" When mercy comes, it melts the heart, makes a divorce between it and its idols, its beloved sins; then it will have to do no more with heart or house idols, nor with any transgressions.

Obs. 4. God knows the dwellings of men, wherever they dwell, and the sins they commit in their dwellings. These Jews were some in Egypt, some in Babylon, some in Media and Persia, 2 Kings xvii. 6; yet he took notice of all their dwelling-places, wherein they had sinned. There is not a cottage in the wilderness, nor a closet in the city, nor a dungeon in the earth, but the Lord knows the same, and what sins are acted there night and day. Rev. ii. 13, "I know thy works and where thou dwellest:" so saith God of Pergamos, and may say it of every man, family, church, and nation, I know thy sins, and where thou dwellest. Neither we nor our sins are hid from God, dwell we in Canaan or in Babylon. Let us look well to ourselves and to our ways; for, wherever we dwell, whatever we are or do, God's eye is constantly upon us.

Obs. 5. Deliverance out of afflicted and sinful conditions is from the Lord himself. "I will save them out of all their dwelling-places, wherein they have sinned." They were captives in Babylon, and other places; there they sinned, and sinned greatly; and who but God could deliver them either from their sins, or their captivity? Amos ix. 14, "I will bring again the captivity of my people." God could break their bonds, change the laws of the Medes and Persians, alter times and seasons, remove all impediments, and set his people at liberty. Psal. cvii. 19, "He saveth them out of their distresses." When men are distressed at sea, or land, if ever they get out of those distresses, it is by the hand of the Lord, he saveth them. He is the Saviour of Israel in the time of trouble, Jer. xiv. 8. He saveth from uncleanness, Ezek. xxxvi. 29. Salvation from affliction, or from sin, belongs to God, and to him alone, and he challengeth it to himself: Isa. xliii. 11, "I, even I, am the Lord; and beside me there is no Saviour."

Obs. 6. It is the Lord who makes defiled persons clean. They were defiled with idols, detestable things, and transgressions; and what saith the Lord? I will cleanse you. When a house was defiled with leprosy, the priest was to cleanse it with blood and water, Lev. xiv. 52. And when men are defiled, the Lord cleanseth them with blood and water; with the blood of his Son, 1 John i. 7, and with the water of his Spirit, John vii. 38, 39: these are the hyssop with which God cleanseth sinners. Pharisees may cleanse the outside, but it is God that cleanseth inside and outside. Jer. xxxiii. 8, "I will cleanse them from all their iniquity whereby they have sinned against me; and I will pardon all their iniquities, whereby they have sinned." When God justifies and sanctifies a sinner, then is a sinner cleansed indeed, inwardly and outwardly, 1 Cor. vi. 11.

Obs. 7. God takes pleasure in a cleansed people, and owns them for his. "So shall they be my people, and I will be their God;" that is, when they should be cleansed. God hath no delight in polluted ones; he is a holy God, and delights in holy ones. David assures you hereof, when he propounds the question, Psal. xxiv. 3, "Who shall ascend into the hill of the Lord? or who shall stand in his holy place?" and gives answer, ver. 4, "He that hath clean hands, and a pure heart; who hath not lifted up his soul unto vanity, nor sworn deceitfully." Such a man, and such a people, God delights to have in his presence; but the wicked, whatever they be, he puts away like dross, Psal. cxix. 119. The refiner takes pleasure in the pure metal cleansed from the dross; the one he prizeth, the other he rejects.

Ver. 24, 25. ***And David my servant shall be king over them; and they all shall have one shepherd: they shall also walk in my judgments, and observe my statutes, and do them. And they shall dwell in the land that I have given unto Jacob my servant, wherein your fathers have dwelt; and they shall dwell therein, even they, and their children, and their children's children for ever: and my servant David shall be their prince for ever.***

Great promises are made unto the house of Judah and house of Israel, being united.

I. Of a king, called "David," ver. 24.

II. Of holiness, "they shall also walk," &c. *ibid.*

III. Of inheriting the land for ever, ver. 25.

IV. Of having the same king rule over them for ever.

Ver. 24. "And David my servant shall be king over them." By "David" Zerubbabel cannot be meant, for he was not a king; and had he been so, yet he was not their prince for ever, as it is said of this "David." "David" is here put for Christ, which the Holy Scripture doth frequently, as Ezek. xxxiv. 23; Hos. iii. 5; Isa. xxxvii. 35; 2 Kings xix. 34; Jer. xxx. 9. And that you may clearly see it is so, compare Isa. lv. 3, where mention is made of "the sure mercies of David," with Acts xiii. 34, and there it is interpreted of Christ: so that, in Amos ix. 11, "The tabernacle of David," refers to Christ, Acts xv. 16. So then, this "David" is the Lord Christ, who is so called, both because he descended from his loins, Rom. i. 3; whereupon he is oft called "The Son of David," Matt. i. 1; xv. 22; Mark xii. 35; and because David was a type of him in his slaying Goliath, and in his kingly and prophetical office. It is not said here, Abraham my servant, or Jacob my servant, shall be their king, although Christ descended from their loins, as well and really as from David's; but it is said, "David my servant shall be their king;" and the reason is, because David was king over Israel and Judah, which they were not, and the first godly king they had.

"My servant." David did serve the Lord, and fulfilled all his will, Acts xiii. 22; and so Christ was his servant, Isa. lii. 13, "Behold, my servant shall deal prudently," and he did so; for he fulfilled all righteousness, Matt. iii. 15; and did the will of him that sent him, John iv. 34; being in the form of a servant, Phil. ii. 7.

"And shall be king over them." The Jews had many kings: some were very good, as David, Solomon, Jehoshaphat, Hezekiah, Josiah, &c.; but none of them like unto this king, the Lord Christ. The sceptre of his kingdom is a sceptre of righteousness, Heb. i. 8. Other kings had crooked sceptres, and much oppression was in their government; but Christ's sceptre is a righteous sceptre, and none shall be oppressed thereby: "Righteousness shall be the girdle of his loins, and faithfulness the girdle of his reins," Isa. xi. 5; "he will break in pieces the oppressor," Psal. lxxii. 4. The Lord tells you in Jeremiah, what a king this king should be: chap. xxiii. 5, "I will raise unto David a righteous branch, and a King shall reign and prosper, and shall execute justice and judgment in the earth:" so, Psal. xlv. 4, "In thy majesty ride prosperously, because of truth and meekness and righteousness." Most kings of the earth, because they were false, rigid, unrighteous, did not prosper; but Christ, because of truth, should be trusted; because of meekness, should be loved; because of righteousness, should be honoured, and so should prosper.

"And they shall have one shepherd." Of these words hath been spoken, chap. xxxiv. 23. King and shepherd are here equivalent. They should not have mamy shepherds, as formerly, who destroyed them, Jer. xii. 10, but "one shepherd;" that is, one better than them all: one transcendent, and incomparable, a Shepherd after God's own heart, who should "feed them with knowledge and understanding," Jer. iii. 15; who should "gather the lambs with his arm, and carry them in his bosom, and gently lead those which are with young," Isa. xl. 11.

"They shall also walk in my judgments, and observe my statutes, and do them. In chap. xxxvi. 27, you had these words: only here "judgments" are mentioned before "statutes," and there "statutes" are set before "judgments." The meaning is, They shall no more live after the courses of men, or imaginations of their own hearts, but they should consult with the word of God, and frame their lives according to it; they shall trust no longer in their legal performances, but look at David their king, and call him "The Lord our righteousness."

Some look upon this promise of David to be king over the Jews, as accomplished in the reign of Christ the Messiah when here on earth; for he gave out his commands then, and required obedience unto them. Matt. xxviii. 18—20, "All power is given unto me in heaven and in earth. Go ye therefore, and teach all nations; teaching them to observe all things whatsoever I have commanded you." Christ manifests himself here to be King of the Jews, and of all nations.

Others are of a different judgment, and do believe that this great promise made here to the two houses of Judah and Israel, remains yet to be performed:

1. Because the two houses are not yet united into one, as hath formerly been shown, which may further appear from that in Hosea, chap. iii. 4, 5, "The chil-

dren of Israel shall abide many days without a king, and without a prince, and without a sacrifice, and without an image, and without an ephod, and without teraphim. Afterward shall the children of Israel return, and seek the Lord their God, and David their king; and shall fear the Lord and his goodness in the latter days." This prophecy refers to the latter days, which are the days after Christ, not before Christ; and if the two houses were united before Christ's coming in the flesh, and so he King over them, as the promise is here, how did the "sceptre depart from Judah, and a lawgiver from between his feet?" In Gen. xlix. 10, the promise is, it should not be so till Shiloh, that is, the Messiah, should come, and then it should; but if the Messiah were King in Israel, King over both houses united into one, the sceptre did not depart, but was advanced. This knot must be untied, before we can be of their mind who say, this prophecy and promise was at Christ's first coming fulfilled.

2. Because the Jews do not own Christ; neither one house nor the other do it; neither Judah nor Israel acknowledged Christ to be the Messiah. The Jews said, he had a devil, John viii. 52; they sought to kill him, chap. vii. 1; they counsel together to put him to death, chap. xi. 53; when Pilate said, "Behold your king!" they cried, "Away with him, crucify him," chap. xix. 14, 15; they persecuted all them who did adhere unto him, 1 Thess. ii. 15, 16.

3. The Jews have been, and are still, under many kings and shepherds. Some are under heathenish, some under christian kings; but when this scripture is fulfilled, they shall be under none but Christ: "one king shall be king to them all," ver. 22; "David my servant shall be king over them, and they shall have one shepherd."

4. They shall then walk in the ways of Christ, not in the ways of Moses. The Jews every where, to this day, stick unto Moses, and reject the gospel, as in the apostles' days, Acts xiii. 45; xviii. 5, 6; but when this promise is fulfilled, then "they shall walk in my judgments, observe my statutes, and do them, saith the Lord;" that is, those laws and rules which God should give out by Christ for their government: and so the name and worship of God and Christ should be one, Zech. xiv. 9; that is, between Jews and gentiles.

For the scripture, and argument used out of it, Matt. xxviii. 18—20.

1. Take another scripture showing Christ came not to be a king, and reign, at his first coming; it is, Matt. xx. 28, "The Son of man came not to be ministered unto, but to minister;" he came not to sit in a throne, to take upon him the state of a prince, to exercise dominion and authority, to be attended with a life-guard and ministers of state; he came not to assume any thing king-like: but he came in the "form of a servant," Phil. ii. 7, to minister unto, and serve others; yea, to do the meanest office belonging to a servant, as, the washing of his disciples' feet, John xiii. 12.

2. The place in Matthew speaks of that power which was given unto Christ after his death and resurrection, and so was the fruit and purchase of the same. He speaks not of that power which he had as God, nor of that which he had as man; but of that he had as Redeemer of men, and obtained by his sufferings and resurrection, saith Maldonate. (In locum.) It is clear, then, Christ was not King over the Jews before his death, because he had not his power then; and how he was their King afterward, when he quickly left the world and went up into heaven, I desire to learn.

3. The power and laws here mentioned, are spiritual, and refer to the spiritual kingdom of Christ, viz. his church; as, "Teach all nations, and baptize them in the name," &c. These are spiritual laws and ordinances, proceeding from that power Christ had given him, to gather out of all nations those he had redeemed by his death. Here he appoints means for the gathering, preserving, and ruling his church. But this is not the power our prophet speaks of; that is a political power, such as David had, and therefore it is said, He shall sit in the throne of David his father, Luke i. 32; Acts ii. 30. David's throne was an external, visible, political throne: Christ's throne in heaven, his throne in the hearts of believers, his throne in the church, is not the throne of David. You may judge what kind of throne David's was, by Jer. xiii. 13; xvii. 25; xxii. 4, 30; 1 Kings ii. 12, 24. When David, Solomon, and others, sat in that throne, they put men to death, and made wars, which Christ did not when he was here on earth.

Ver. 25. "And they shall dwell in the land that I have given unto Jacob my servant, wherein your fathers have dwelt." This is spoken of the ten tribes, together with Judah and Benjamin, who should return from their captivity, and repossess the land of Canaan. That Judah and Benjamin did, is clear from the Scriptures, and granted on all sides; but that the ten tribes returned is generally denied, and expected to this day to be made good. The promise here is, That the whole body of the Jews, even the house of Judah, and the house of Israel, shall come thither and dwell there: Jer. iii. 18, "In those days the house of Judah shall walk with the house of Israel, and they shall come together out of the land of the north to the land that I have given for an inheritance unto your fathers:" see Jer. l. 45; Ezek. ix. 9; Jer. xxx. 3. Let not man think, because Christ hath said, Matt. xxiii. 38, "Your house is left unto you desolate," that therefore there is no hope of their returning to their land; for this is not spoken of the ten tribes; they were not there at Jerusalem: and, Rev. xiv. 1, "The Lamb stood on mount Zion, with an hundred forty and four thousand," which were gathered out of all the tribes of Israel; and the time is coming when the Jews shall see Christ, and say, "Blessed is he that cometh in the name of the Lord," Matt. xxiii. 39.

"And they shall dwell therein, even they, and their children, and their children's children for ever." Not only will God bring them into their land, but continue them and theirs therein for ever. The house of Judah, after her return from Babylon, continued in the land of promise some six hundred years: for, from the time of Cyrus's proclamation to Christ was five hundred and sixty; and about forty years after the death of Christ, was Jerusalem destroyed, and the Jews wholly scattered. These six hundred years the house of Judah and her children enjoyed, but they fall short of what is promised here unto both houses, viz. inheriting of the land for ever.

"And my servant David shall be their prince for ever." David was dead long before. Messiah, the Lord Christ, is pointed out by "David," who should be their prince, and rule them as David did. David was meek and gentle in his government, 1 Chron. xxviii. 2; faithful and wise, Psal. lxxviii. 72; righteous and just, 2 Sam. viii. 15. Such a king shall Christ be, Psal. xlv. 4; Isa. xi. 4, 5; Jer. xxiii. 5. And whereas David's kingdom was for a time, some forty years, the kingdom of Christ shall have no end, he shall be their Prince for ever. All the kings the Jews ever had reigned not five hundred years, it was about four hundred and ninety-three; but this Prince should exceed them all, Luke i. 33.

Obs. 1. There is a time wherein Christ must reign over the Jews, they must be gathered into one body, and Christ must be their King. "David my servant shall be king over them;" not only in a special way, which hitherto he hath not been, but also in a visible, political way, for he must sit in the throne of David. Hence it is that Christ said, Luke xxii. 29, unto his apostles, "I appoint unto you a kingdom, as my Father hath appointed unto me:" he doth not say he had a kingdom, but that a kingdom was appointed them, and such a kingdom as should be visible; for, ver. 30, it follows, "that ye may eat and drink at my table in my kingdom, and sit on thrones judging the twelve tribes of Israel." There are no tables, no eating, no drinking, no tribes, no judging of them in heaven. In Matt. xix. 28, Christ speaks of twelve thrones, whereon the apostles shall sit and rule the twelve tribes of Israel, together with himself, being in the throne of his glory. And when shall this be? In the regeneration, when the Jews shall be regenerate, when the time of restitution of all things shall be. For the words should be rendered thus, They which have followed me, and there stop: "In the regeneration, when the Son of man shall sit in the throne of his glory," &c. then shall the twelve tribes be there, I be their King, and you judges or rulers under me. Grotius reads the words so, and conceives them to be spoken of the kingdom of Christ, whose kingdom shall not be of Jews only, but of gentiles also; they shall be under this King: Psal. lxxii. 11, "All kings shall fall down before him; all nations shall serve him;" so that "the Lord shall be king over all the earth," Zech. xiv. 9.

Obs. 2. There shall be no changes and alterations in the kingdom of Christ by succession of princes; there they all shall have one Shepherd, one Prince. We see great changes in kingdoms, where they have king after king, be it by election or succession. When Rehoboam succeeded Solomon, what tumults and stirs were then in the house of David! so afterwards in the house of Joseph, when Baasha and Jehu were chosen kings. There shall be no such thing here; one Shepherd shall they have, who shall rule them with righteousness, and feed them with knowledge, Isa. xl. 11; he shall deal like a good shepherd by them, Ezek. xxxiv. 23.

Obs. 3. The subjects of Christ's kingdom shall be holy: "They shall walk in my judgments, and observe my statutes, and do them." They who do the will of God, they who keep his laws, they are innocent, undefiled, Psal. cxix. 1; they are holy ones. The one hundred and forty-four thousand which stood with the Lamb on mount Zion were virgins, without guile, without fault before the throne of God, Rev. xiv. 1, 4, 5. Isa. lx. 21, "Thy people shall be all righteous:" see Zech. xiv. 20, 21, "There shall be no Canaanites then in the house of the Lord of hosts." Then shall be the "new heavens and new earth, wherein shall dwell righteousness," 2 Pet. iii. 14; that is, righteous persons, such as shall do righteous things; for there shall be no exacting, no violence, no destruction, but salvation and praise, Isa. lx. 17, 18; there shall "the righteous flourish," Psal. lxxii. 7.

Obs. 4. We ought to think and speak honourably of the patriarchs, prophets, apostles, and saints of God. God thought and spoke honourably of David, of Jacob; he calls them his "servants;" that is an honourable title which he gives them.

Obs. 5. The Jews and their posterity shall inherit their land again, become a kingdom, and continue so under Christ for ever. "They, and their children, and their children's children, shall dwell in the land, and my servant David shall be their prince for ever." All other kingdoms have been shaken, broken, but this shall abide. Daniel speaks of it in his 2nd chapter, ver. 44, "The God of heaven shall set up a kingdom, which shall never be destroyed; and the kingdom shall not be left to other people, but it shall break in pieces and consume all these kingdoms, and it shall stand for ever." Rev. xi. 15, "The kingdoms of this world are become the kingdoms of our Lord, and of his Christ; and he shall reign for ever and ever."

Ver. 26, 27. *Moreover I will make a covenant of peace with them; it shall be an everlasting covenant with them: and I will place them, and multiply them, and will set my sanctuary in the midst of them for evermore. My tabernacle also shall be with them: yea, I will be their God, and they shall be my people.*

Here are more promises given forth to the houses of Judah and Joseph, being gathered out of the nations, and united into one house. As,

I. Of a "covenant of peace."
II. Of placing or disposing them.
III. Of multiplying of them.
IV. Of God's dwelling amongst them.

Ver. 26. "Moreover I will make a covenant of peace with them." The Hebrew is, I will strike or cut a covenant with them. כרת signifies, to cut, and to cut off by death: 1 Sam. xxxi. 9, the Philistines cut off Saul's head; and, 1 Sam. xxviii. 9, Saul cut off those who had familiar spirits, and the wizards out of the land: also to cut off from place and power, as 1 Sam. ii. 33: but when it is joined with ברית it always signifies, to strike or make a covenant; because it was a custom when they made covenants to kill some beast or other, cut it in the midst, and pass between the parts thereof; manifesting, by so doing, that if they break covenant, they deserved to be cut in pieces, Gen. xv. 9, 10, 17; Jer. xxxiv. 18. This practice was among the heathens, who cut a swine in pieces, passed between them, and so made covenants. The covenant here which God would make with the two houses, was a "covenant of peace."

Stabant et cæsa firmabant fœdera porca. Virg. Æneid, lib. 8.

The word for "peace" is, שלום by which the Hebrews understand not only outward quietness, but all kind of outward happiness. Whatsoever they count in the number of good things, and desirable, that they comprehend under the name of peace; and when they wish all happiness to a man, they wish him peace. Maldonate tells us, that the "covenant of peace" here, is the gospel, wherein we see Christ hath pacified all things by the blood of his cross, Col. i. 20. And Lavater saith it is called a "covenant of peace," because by the merit of Christ peace between God and us was effected; not only outward but inward peace. The Jews had some peace at their return out of Babylon, but, in the time of the Maccabees, they had long, bitter, and bloody wars. When Christ came, there was peace for a time, but, not long after his death, they and their nation were destroyed by the Romans. The "covenant of peace" here is promised to the two houses, who were not then, but still are to be united: and when they shall be united, God will make good his promise, he will strike a "covenant of peace" with them, which shall not be for a few years; but, as it follows,

"It shall be an everlasting covenant with them." God will not make a truce with them for days, months, and years, but a covenant for ever. The Jews opposed Christ when he came first, and had little outward or inward peace; but, when he shall reign over both houses, they shall have everlasting peace.

"And I will place them." In the original it is, I will give them. Piscator confesses he doth not understand the sense of these words. Ghappe saith this is it, I will place them in the holy land. Vatablus is of the same mind, interpreting them thus, I will place them in my land. The Chaldee is, I will bless them. And Mariana, to that purpose, saith, I will give them a blessing. The Vulgate is, *fundabo eos;* which Pinus expounds thus, I will place them in a firm land, where they shall have a solid foundation. Œcolampadius more fully, I will give them to Christ, whom I have promised to be a blessing to the nations; which sense I conceive the best, for he spake in the verse before of dwelling in the land where their fathers dwelt: in that land God would give them to Christ.

"And multiply them." This multiplication is not only in a natural sense to be taken, but in a spiritual also. Their increase will be great, and they shall be believers. Suitable to which is that in Isa. liv. 13, "All thy children shall be taught of the Lord; and great shall be the peace of thy children."

"And will set my sanctuary in the midst of them for evermore." The word for "my sanctuary" is, מקדשי which Montanus renders, my sanctification; the Chaldee, and others, call it, my sanctuary; the Septuagint hath it, my holy things; Mariana saith, my church. After the return of Judah and Benjamin from captivity, they had the temple rebuilt, which in process of time was utterly destroyed; but here the Lord speaks of setting his sanctuary in the midst of the two houses; being united, God will have his church and worship eminently amongst them. Œcolampadius saith, They shall not be without a divine temple, viz. Christ Jesus, he shall be the temple amongst them, Rev. xxi. 22; and as he shall be their prince for ever, so shall he be their temple and sanctuary for ever.

Ver. 27. "My tabernacle also shall be with them." My dwelling shall be with them. משכן signifies, *habitaculum*, a dwelling-place. God assures them here, that though the temple should be destroyed, yet, when Judah and Israel should be united, they should have a temple and tabernacle not subject to destruction. These words receive light from John xxi. 1—3, that when he "saw the new heaven and the new earth, and new Jerusalem coming down from God," then he "heard a voice saying, Behold, the tabernacle of God is with men, and he will dwell with them." What John had in vision lies yet under expectation for fulfilling.

"Yea, I will be their God, and they shall be my people." The Hebrew is, I will be to them for a God, and they shall be to me for a people. Now, I am as no God unto them, and they are as no people unto me; I have no true worship from them, they have no special favour from me: but I will be to them for a God eminently; and they shall be to me for a people eminently; they shall own me for their God in a singular manner, and so will I own them for my people.

From these two verses I shall only give you this observation, That there are great and precious promises, which concern the Jews, yet unperformed. The everlasting covenant of peace, Christ's being their king and temple, with many other, the Jews expect the fulfilling of; and so may we, for God is faithful and will make good his word; and the performance of them may be nearer at hand than is apprehended by most: for one saith understandingly, "God hath, in our days, arrested the Turk's greatness; abated the formidableness of the German-Austrian beast; revealed in a good measure the hypocrisy and lies of the false prophet, who hath his seat at Rome, and hath brought to light the subtleties of Satan, who had shifted himself into several dresses of pretended reformation. He is risen up like a mighty giant against his enemies: amongst us, and elsewhere, he hath pleaded his people's cause so signally, that all those but whose judgment it is to be wilfully blind, will say, 'The Lord is on our side,"' &c.

Mr. Wall, in his Considerations of the Jews' Conversion.

Ver. 28. *And the heathen shall know that I the Lord do sanctify Israel, when my sanctuary shall be in the midst of them for evermore.*

The end of God's dealing so with the Jews, is here laid down, viz. conviction of the heathen.

"I the Lord do sanctify Israel." God is said to sanctify, 1. When he separates things from a common to a holy use, as time, Joel i. 14, and the vessels of the temple itself. 2. When he makes persons really holy, as Lev. xxi. 23, "I the Lord do sanctify them;" that is, I do make them holy. Both these ways of sanctifying may be the sense of this place. God would separate them from the heathens, take them to be his people, give them the means, and make them effectual to their sanctification.

"When my sanctuary shall be in the midst of them for evermore." The Hebrew is, when my sanctification. The Septuagint, when my holy things shall be in the midst of them. When Christ shall be their King, set up his ways and worship amongst them, then they shall be sanctified. So Œcolampadius, When Christ is with his, and gives them his word, there all are sanctified which belong unto him.

Obs. When the two houses are united, and have Christ amongst them with his word and worship, they shall be holy; and so holy, that heathens shall be convinced that God is their Sanctifier, that he doth sanctify Israel: see Zech. xiv. 20, 21; Joel iii. 17; Rev. xxi. 27.

CHAPTER XXXVIII.

Ver. 1—7. *And the word of the Lord came unto me, saying, Son of man, set thy face against Gog, the land of Magog, the chief prince of Meshech and Tubal, and prophesy against him, and say, Thus saith the Lord God; Behold, I am against thee, O Gog, the chief prince of Meshech and Tubal: and I will turn thee back, and put hooks into thy jaws, and I will bring thee forth, and all thine army, horses and horsemen, all of them clothed with all sorts of armour, even a great company with bucklers and shields, all of them handling swords: Persia, Ethiopia, and Libya with them; all of them with shield and helmet: Gomer, and all his bands; the house of Togarmah of the north quarters, and all his bands: and many people with thee. Be thou prepared, and prepare for thyself, thou, and all thy company that are assembled unto thee, and be thou a guard unto them.*

This chapter and the next do treat of "Gog" and "Magog," who were nations against the people of God. This chapter is a prophecy against "Gog;" wherein is set forth,

I. What, and by whom, the people of God were to suffer, to the 18th verse.

II. God's dealings with "Gog," and the event thereof, to the end of the chapter.

Lest the Jews should presently have looked for the fulfilling of those great promises in the former chapter, concerning the uniting the two houses, and Messiah to be their King, and the great privileges they should have thereby, he tells them here of great calamities which they must look for, of sad times, and heavy judgments which should befall their enemies. This in general: now to things more particular.

Ver. 2. "Son of man, set thy face against Gog." There are great variety of opinions concerning Gog and Magog. The Jews affirm them to be the Scythians, which live near Caucasus, and the Caspian mountains: some understand by them the Roman emperors and empire: some, the pope: some, the Turks and Saracens: some, the Goths: some, heretics: some, all the persecutors of the church: others, antichrist: some interpreters understand the affliction of the Jewish nation, by the successors of Alexander, which possessed Asia Minor and Syria. Junius hath laboured to give light here, and tells us, that Gog is the name of a nation, derived from Gyges, or Gog, the servant of Candaules, king of Lydia, whom he killed and married his queen, naming the land Gygæa, or Gog's land, which, saith he, is Asia the Less, and Syria, where was a city called Gog's city: these nations should infest the Jews, which were held by Antiochus, Seleucus, Demetrius, and Nicanor. Bibliander and Bullinger interpret this prophecy literally of Alexander and his successors, especially of Antiochus Epiphanes king of Syria, who, as you find in the Maccabees, did greatly afflict the Jews; and specially of antichrist and his members. A Lapide denies this prophecy to concern Alexander, the kings of Syria and Egypt, because the Jews never conquered them, though they had some notable victories over them; and had they had such a destruction as is spoken of in the end of this chapter, Josephus, who was an exact observer of Jewish affairs, would have mentioned it. Neither did Josephus Gerionides speak any thing thereof, who wrote the history of Gog. Sanctius leans to that opinion which conceives Gog to be Antiochus, in whom antichrist was prefigured, and the great troubles of the church by him; so do many expositors: yet, Maldonate and Vatablus think this prophecy not fulfilled; of which mind are divers who write upon the 20th of the Revelation, where John, in the 8th and 9th verses, alludes to this prophecy. By "Gog" here, understand, the name of a man, not of a province; for he is said to be a "prince," ver. 3; to come "out of the north," ver. 14; and he with his multitude shall be buried in "the valley of Hamon-gog, chap. xxxix. 11: these things cannot be spoken of a province, but of a person. The prophet must set his face against him; that is, he must prophesy constantly and firmly against him.

"The land of Magog." Gog is the name of a king, which rules over Magog; that is, the Scythians, saith Vatablus. "Magog" was one of the sons of Japheth, Gen. x. 2; of whom came the Scythians, or Sarmatians, saith Ainsworth on the place. Josephus saith, Magog dwelt amongst
Antiq. l. 1. c. 7. those who were called Magogins, and by the Greeks, Scythæ, who dwelt in Cœlo-Syria.
Vid. Martin. Lex. in verbo Magog. Marcus Paulus Venetus saith, in Tartary are the regions Gog and Magog, which they call Gug and Mungug.

"The chief prince of Meshech." In Hebrew it is, prince of the head; that is, principal head, or chief prince. This Gog was not only prince of Magog, but of Meshech, that is, Cappadocia; and of Tubal, that is, Iberia, not Spain or Italy, but a country near the Scythians.

"Prophesy against him." Thou hast been prophesying of deliverance and great mercies to my people, now prophesy against Gog, and all his assistants, open or secret. Had Magog, Meshech, and Tubal, been princes with Gog, the Lord would have said, Prophesy against them.

Ver. 3. "Say, Thus saith the Lord God; Behold, I am against thee, O Gog." This is a dreadful message which the prophet must deliver against this great prince. He must declare unto him that there is a greater Prince than himself, even one that is king of nations, that hath all power in his hand, and bringeth princes to nothing, Isa. xl. 23; and that he is against him. Thou thinkest to have thy will upon God's people, to do terrible things unto them; but their God, who is a God of power and wisdom, is against thee. The Hebrew is, Behold, I to thee; that is, I come to thee to destroy thee for thine iniquities and enmity against my people.

Ver. 4. "And I will turn thee back." Lavater and Œcolampadius read these words, I will crush thee: the Vulgate, I will lead thee about: some rabbies, I will deceive thee: others, I will bring or turn thee back. Thou thinkest to have thy pleasure on mine, but I will have my pleasure on thee, and turn thee which way seems good to me. I will bring thee out.

"And put hooks into thy jaws." What the Lord saith here of Gog, he said, chap. xxix. 4, of Pharaoh: "I will put hooks in thy jaws." The Septuagint is, I will put a bridle in thy jaws: thou art like a pampered jade, and thinkest to tread down all, but I will hold thee in. Montanus reads the former words thus, I will bring thee out, and if thou holdest off, I will put my hook in thy jaws, and draw thee out as a fish is drawn out of the waters; which sense is best.

"And I will bring thee forth, and all thine army." I will cause thee to go forth; thou shalt not stay in thine own territories, how little or large soever they be, but shalt muster up thy forces, and lead out all thine armies.

"Horses and horsemen." The word for "horses" is, סוס which notes, any horse of common use. *Sus* signifies both a crane and a horse. The rabbies say he is so called, because a horse is a cheerful creature, and by his mettle and neighing cheers up his rider. פרשים is, horsemen, from פרש which, in Hiphil, signifies, to prick; so that *parash* is, a horseman, because he pricks forward his horse with his spurs.

"All of them clothed with all sorts of armour." They were armed completely from head to foot. The Hebrew is, clothed with all, or with perfection; nothing was wanting requisite to military undertaking.

"Even a great company, with bucklers and shields, all of them handling swords." Gog's army was a great army, and well accommodated. A buckler is a piece of armour to cover and defend the body; and so is a shield: in Hebrew, מגן from גנן to cover. צנה is a buckler, or shield, sharp or piked, which the Latins call *scutum;* the other, *clypeus.* Shields were for footmen, and bucklers for horsemen, saith Servius. These soldiers
of Gog were skilful in military affairs, Vide Martin.
they all were expert at their swords.

Ver. 5. "Persia, Ethiopia, and Libya with them." Here is shown what countries and people should join with Gog, viz. those of the east, Persians; those of the south, the Ethiopians; and those of the west, the Moors, whom Œcolampadius understood by those of "Libya." Of Persia, Ethiopia, and Libya, was spoken, chap. xxvii. 10; xxx. 5.

"All of them with shield and helmet." Whoever joined with Gog were well armed. The Hebrew is, all of them shield and helmet. כובע is, a helmet. Some were made of leather, some of brass, 1 Sam. xvii. 5.

Ver. 6. "Gomer, and all his bands." Under this
Josephus Anti. l. i. c. 7. word "Gomer," are comprehended Galatia, Phrygia, and Bithynia, principal parts of Asia Minor, which were inhabited by Gomer, the son of Japheth, from whom they were called Gomarians, or Gomeriter.

"The house of Togarmah of the north quarters, and all his bands." By "the house of Togarmah," Junius understands Paphlagonia and Cappadocia; others, Armenia the Less. Doubtless by Gomer and Togarmah, all those parts which lay north from Syria, where Antiochus reigned, and so north from Judea, are meant thereby. From these and the forementioned places, had Gog auxiliary forces: for fear, hire, or out of enmity to God's people, they helped him.

"And many people with thee." There were people with him from all quarters, from the east, west, south, and north; which being come together, must make a numerous army.

Ver. 7. "Be thou prepared," &c. Jerom thinks there is an irony in these words; that God exhorts Gog to gather up his forces to strengthen himself, and hasten his design, with what expedition he could; but all his preparations and undertakings should be in vain, he should not escape the vengeance of God, which hung over his head. But here, under a command, is declared what he would certainly do: he would not be wanting to get a great army from all parts, to assault and destroy the people of God; and not knowing what the hazard of war might be, he would prepare for himself, consider, and fit things for himself.

"Thou, and all thy company that are assembled unto thee." Where there is a great army, there had need to be great preparations for their pay, quarters, and protection: they know not what obstructions and enemies they may meet withal.

"And be thou a guard unto them." Princes have great power, and it lies much in them to keep their armies safe. The eye of the general is a special thing to keep an army in order. The Vulgate reads the words thus, *Esto eis in præceptum*, Do thou show thyself an emperor amongst them, command and rule them: or thus, Thou wilt do thy endeavour to preserve them. Junius thinks these words refer to the Jews: that Gog with all his forces compassing about the mountains of Israel, and concluding he had the Jews in his power, as a bird in a cage, to destroy at his pleasure, he should be a guard unto them. God can make those a defence to his people, who seek their destruction. But the other sense is more genuine.

Obs. 1. That after prophecies of grace and mercy, come tidings of affliction and judgments. In the former chapter the Jews heard altogether of mercies from God; here they hear of afflictions from enemies. There, they heard of David their king, and shepherd, who should do great things for them; here, of Gog, a tyrant, their enemy, who should seek to destroy them. God, in his infinite wisdom, orders it so, that his church and people should hear of, and meet with, not only good, but evil; not only comforts, but crosses. Should we only hear of comfortable things, we should presume; and should we only hear of sad things, we should despond. God presents some of both sorts unto us, that so our faith and fear may be exercised, and we kept in a more even frame.

Obs. 2. The great princes of the earth, being no friends to the church of God, have God for their enemy. Gog was prince of Meshech and Tubal, an enemy to the Jews; and, "Behold, I am against thee, O Gog;" how great soever thou art, I, the great God, am against thee; thou wilt oppose my people, and I will oppose thee. Most of the princes of the earth have been against Christ and his kingdom, Psal. ii. 2; and God hath been against them, and vexed them in his sore displeasure. God was against the prince of Tyre, and against Pharaoh king of Egypt, Ezek. xxviii. xxix. Kings generally are proud, profane, tyrannical, false to the trust committed to them, obstructing the way and work of Christ in the world what they can; therefore God is against them: "He is terrible to the kings of the earth," Psal. lxxvi. 12; and their ends have been dreadful. Some have had their bones burnt to lime, Amos ii. 1; some have been eaten with worms, Acts xii. 23; some have been hanged up, Lam. ii. 12; Josh. x. 26; some have died of strange diseases, 2 Chron. xxi. 18.

Obs. 3. The Lord at his pleasure can bring enemies and armies upon his own people. God would bring Gog forth, and all his army, horse and horsemen, a great company; all of them armed with bucklers, shields, and swords. God is the Author of wars, he calls forth what princes and nations he will, to assault and vex the church. The ten tribes, who brought enemies upon them? was it not the Lord? 1 Chron. v. 26, "The God of Israel stirred up the spirit of Pul king of Assyria, and the spirit of Tilgath-pilneser king of Assyria, and he carried them away," &c.: see 2 Kings xv. 19; xvii. 6. It was God stirred up the spirit of the Philistines against Jehoram king of Judah, so that they came and spoiled him of all his substance, of his wives and sons, 2 Chron. xxi. 16, 17. Let God's people take heed how they provoke God, for he is the Lord of hosts, and hath all nations at his command, and can call, yea, bring them forth to trouble Israel itself, and that sorely.

Obs. 4. The Lord can easily bring men to do his work and service, whatever the difficulty or danger be. Here was hard work for Gog, to gather the nations, east, west, south, and northward together, to come out of his country and to invade Judea; a business which required much consultation, admitted many objections and demurs: but God would bring him to it, and make him do it, as easily as a man pulls up a fish out of the water: "I will put my hook in his jaws." Let God put an instinct into a prince or state, once stir their spirits, to make war upon others, the work will go on with facility and expedition. God hath hooks to draw on princes to war, and hooks to draw them off, to draw them back from them, 2 Kings xix. 28.

Obs. 5. From all quarters of the world there are enemies ready to combine and act with Gog and antichrist against the church, truth, and Christ himself. Those of the east comprehended under Persia, those of the south intended under Ethiopia, those of the west included in Libya, and those of the north contained under Gomer and the house of Togarmah, were all at the beck of Gog, to go against Jerusalem, the servants and worship of God therein. The whole world, saith Œcolampadius, contradicts, and observes antichrist. When Christ doth any eminent thing in his church, the nations are quickly misled, and join with some grand enemy to vent their malice: see Rev. xx. 7—9.

Obs. 6. The enemies of the church do make great preparations against the same. "Be thou prepared." This shows and assures that Gog would neglect nothing which might conduce unto the carrying on his designs against the Jews. Isa. viii. 9, 10, those expressions, "Associate yourselves," "Gird yourselves," "Take counsel together," "Speak the word," do hint to us the activity of the church's enemies. Psal. lxxxiii. 2—5, see it there to the life: "Thine enemies make a tumult; they have lift up the head; they have taken crafty counsel against thy people. They said, Come, let us cut them off from being a nation," &c. How did Zerah the Ethiopian, and the commanders of his army, bestir themselves, when they brought an army of a thousand thousand against Judah, and with them three hundred chariots, 2 Chron. xiv. 9.

Obs. 7. Princes, notwithstanding all their preparations, cannot secure themselves, nor those under their command. "Prepare for thyself, be a guard to them." Gog's number, power, policy, preparations, did not advantage himself or his; they went forth to their own ruin and destruction.

Ver. 8. ***After many days thou shalt be visited: in the latter years thou shalt come into the land that is brought back from the sword, and is gathered out of many people, against the mountains of Israel, which have been always waste: but it is brought forth out of the nations, and they shall dwell safely all of them.***

This verse prophesies of Gog's invading the mountains of Israel, the destruction of Gog, and the time of both.

"After many days thou shalt be visited." The Scripture speaks of a double visitation.

1. One in mercy and favour; as Exod. iv. 31, when Moses and Aaron were sent to deliver the Jews out of Egypt; and when Sarah conceived and bare Isaac, Gen. xxi. 1. These were God's merciful visitations of them.

2. One in judgment; as Numb. xvi. 29, "If these men," viz. Korah, Dathan, and Abiram, "be visited after the visitation of all men;" that is, they shall not die a common death, have a common judgment, but some extraordinary punishment: so Psal. lxxxix. 32, "I will visit their transgression with the rod, and their iniquity with stripes," I will punish them. This is the sense here, "After many days thou shalt be visited," that is, punished. The time when it should be is not punctually, but indefinitely, set down, "after many days." If we take Antiochus to be Gog in the type, it was in the Maccabees' days; if we look at the antitype, the time is yet to come.

"In the latter years thou shalt come into the land." From the time of this prophecy unto the death of Antiochus Epiphanes, chronology tells us there were four hundred and twenty or four hundred and thirty years; whereupon expositors do account the years that he came to Judea, and took Jerusalem, and defiled the temple with idols, to be the latter years. Junius saith, In the following years. Piscator hath it, In the after days or times. In the after or latter years, in the time of Christ, saith Vatablus. The Hebrew is, באחרים השנים which Montanus and the Vulgate render, *in novissimo annorum*, in the last of years; which, according to John, is after the one thousand years, Rev. xx. 6—8. And so Mariana, he makes the visitation of Gog to be, in the end of the world, after the thousand years. Then shall Gog come into the land, compass the camp of the saints about, and the "beloved city," ver. 9.

"That is brought back from the sword, and is gathered out of many people." The Jews were driven by the sword into captivity, by it scattered into many provinces, and held under slavery, and so they are at this day; but the time is coming that the two houses, as well as the two tribes, shall be brought back from the sword, and gathered out of many people. "Land" is put for the inhabitants of the land.

"Against the mountains of Israel." The Hebrew word על signifies, to, upon, against. Some, therefore, render these words, to, or upon, the mountains of Israel; and in that sense they refer to the Jews, who were brought back and gathered out of all people to the mountains of Israel, that is, the land of Judea. We read them, "against the mountains of Israel," and so they refer to Gog, who should come against Judea.

"Which have been always waste." The Hebrew word for "always" is, תמיד which signifies, a long time; and so the French translation hath it, deserted, or wasted, for a long time. Seventy years were they desolate, all the time the Jews were in captivity; and shortly after Christ his days were they left desolate, and are so to this day. Some make "the mountains of Israel" to signify, the church; the "sword" and wastings, to be the persecutions which it hath always endured.

"But it is brought forth out of the nations." By "it," the prophet means the "land;" and by "land," the people, who being driven into Egypt, Babylon, Persia, and other places, were to be brought forth to the land of Israel. The words import the thing done, because of the certainty of it.

"And they shall dwell safely; all of them." When the Jews returned out of Babylon, repossessing their own land, they dwelt safely, confidently, without fear or disquietment therein, for four hundred and thirty years, saith Sanctius; after which time Antiochus did sorely vex them, and interrupt their peace, which they thought would be everlasting. So did Demetrius, Nicanor, and others, as in the Maccabees is evident. The time remains for the complete fulfilling of these words.

Obs. 1. God bears sometimes with the worst of men a long time. "After many days." God bears with Gog and antichrist, the grand enemies of his church, worse than whom cannot be found or expected. His patience is large, he is a God long-suffering. He bare with Antiochus, that vile person, Dan. xi. 21, many days. Vessels of wrath are endured by him with much long-suffering, Rom. ix. 22.

Obs. 2. Though wicked men be spared long, yet at last they shall suffer. "After many days thou shalt be visited." God may stay a thousand, yea ten thousand days, and then visit. As there is a time for wicked men to fill up the measure of their iniquities, so there is a time for God to fill up the vials of his wrath; and when they are once full, then they shall be poured out. God sometimes is long before he hears the prayers of his people, but at length he remembers them, Luke xviii. 7, 8; and sometimes he is long before he punisheth the wicked, but at last he visits them, he hath his time for it, Jer. xlix. 8.

Ver. 9. ***Thou shalt ascend and come like a storm, thou shalt be like a cloud to cover the land, thou, and all thy bands, and many people with thee.***

The manner of Gog's proceeding is here set down; and that,

I. Under the similitude of a "storm."

II. Under the similitude of a "cloud."

"Thou shalt ascend and come like a storm." A storm comes suddenly, violently, with noise, and doth much hurt, breaking and bearing down all before it; such should the coming of Gog be. Dan. xi. 40, 41, it is said, "The king of the north shall come against the king of the south like a whirlwind. He shall enter also into the glorious land, and many countries shall be overthrown." This is spoken of Antiochus, whom divers expositors make to be Gog. The word שׁוֹאָה for "a storm," is from שָׁאָה which signifies, to make a noise, to spoil, and to amaze; and so do storms.

"Thou shalt be like a cloud to cover the land, thou, and all," &c. Clouds are vapours drawn up by the heat of the sun into the middle region of the air, where by the cold they are condensated, and so spreading, make the heavens black, and intercept the light. Gog with his forces should be as a cloud spreading over the face of the land, interrupting the peace and comforts of the godly, and by his hostile acts cause fear, sorrow, and mourning. By these two metaphors are set out the tumult, violence, spoil, and multitude of Gog's army; or, by the storm, their threats and cruelty; and by the cloud, false opinions, flatteries, and allurements which they should use to pervert the faith of the saints.

Obs. 1. The church and people of God are subject to calamities. He shall "come like a storm." Winds, clouds, storms, do trouble and terrify men, and so do great armies of heathens, of vile and desperate persons, of Goggites and antichristians; when they come with fury and violence, they plunder, spoil, and fill all with darkness, they cover the land: Jer. iv. 13, "Behold, he shall come up as clouds, and his chariots shall be as a whirlwind; his horses are swifter than eagles. Woe unto us! for we are spoiled:" it is spoken of Nebuchadnezzar and his forces, who were to come up against Jerusalem. The church is oft afflicted and tossed with tempest; but here is some comfort; storms, tempests, and clouds last not long, they cease after a little time, and the sun shines again.

Obs. 2. The goodness of God in foretelling the church what shall come upon it, viz. a storm, and clouds, and perplexity. Gog and all his bands, and many people with him, shall come as a storm, and be as a cloud covering the land. It hath been usual with God to foretell his people what should befall them, as Gen. xv. 13; Jer. xxxii. 28, 29; Dan. x. 14; Matt. xxiv. And in the book of the Revelation, Christ doth tell them what sad things are to come upon his people, how potent, violent, subtle, and destructive their enemies will be: which he doth not to discourage them, but to awaken them unto prayer, holiness of life, and living by faith.

Ver. 10—13. *Thus saith the Lord God; It shall also come to pass, that at the same time shall things come into thy mind, and thou shalt think an evil thought: and thou shalt say, I will go up to the land of unwalled villages; I will go to them that are at rest, that dwell safely, all of them dwelling without walls, and having neither bars nor gates, to take a spoil, and to take a prey; to turn thine hand upon the desolate places that are now inhabited, and upon the people that are gathered out of the nations, which have gotten cattle and goods, that dwell in the midst of the land. Sheba, and Dedan, and the merchants of Tarshish, with all the young lions thereof, shall say unto thee, Art thou come to take a spoil? hast thou gathered thy company to take a prey? to carry away silver and gold, to take away cattle and goods, to take a great spoil?*

In these words we have,

I. The decree and purpose of Gog, ver. 10, 11, which was, to invade.

II. The inviting causes, ver. 11.

III. The end of his invading, ver. 12.

IV. His assistance and confederates in the work, ver. 13.

Ver. 10. "At the same time shall things come into thy mind." In Hebrew it is, words shall ascend, or come upon thy heart, which is an hebraism, and imports a man's thinking and consulting with himself. When men are meditating, various thoughts do rise in their minds, as Luke xxiv. 38, "Why do thoughts arise in your hearts?" דברים signifies, words and things; thoughts are the words and things of the mind.

"And thou shalt think an evil thought." The Hebrew for to "think" is, חשב, *chashab*, which notes such a thinking as takes in the intention of the mind, and exercises a man's head and heart. Gog should bend himself to excogitate something, and it should be an evil thought, or purpose.

Ver. 11. "I will go up to the land of unwalled villages." This was the wicked thought Gog had in his mind, he purposed in his heart to go and invade the land of the Jews; and that which invited and encouraged him so to do was,

1. Their unfortifiedness, they had no walls about their villages. Thought Gog, I shall easily conquer and subdue the Jewish nation, and add it to my territories, for they have no places of strength: some villages they have built, but none of them are walled. The Jews were but lately returned out of Babylon, newly replanted in their land, and could not fortify towns or cities as formerly they were, before Nebuchadnezzar demolished them: being therefore without walls, they lay open to enemies, and obvious to all incursions.

"I will go to them that are at rest, that dwell safely."

2. Their security. The Jews, being wearied with their seventy years' captivity, and come again to their land, had rest and safety, according to what God had promised them, Jer. xxx. 10; xlvi. 27; Ezek. xxxiv. 25, 28; and so manifested their dependence upon God, trusting in him to protect them, though destitute of walls and military defences. Well might they be at rest, and dwell confidently, as the word signifies, to whom God had said, "None should make them afraid." It is to be feared many of them abused his promise, degenerating into a sinful security.

"All of them dwelling without walls, having neither bars nor gates." Where there is fear of enemies and invasions, people do fortify themselves; they wall about their towns and cities, they make strong gates and bars unto them, and set guards to look unto them. The Jews, being fearless, did none of these things: they observed not the counsels and actings of their bordering enemies, which they should have done; and for want thereof, they exposed themselves to imminent dangers.

Ver. 12. "To take a spoil, and to take a prey." The Hebrew is, to spoil a spoil, and to prey a prey. This was the end Gog propounded, viz. to impoverish the Jews, and enrich himself, to deprive them of their land, and add it to his own. Of the words, "spoil," and "prey," hath formerly been spoken.

"To turn thine hand upon the desolate places that are now inhabited, and upon the people that are gathered," &c. Nebuchadnezzar had made the land of Judea desolate for many years, and the Jews being returned from their captivity, inhabited the desolate places of the land, rebuilt them, began to get something about them to live comfortably on; but Gog now intended to come and lay his hand upon them that were spoiled before, and to make another spoiling of them, and to bring them again into bondage: this was the aim of Gog.

"Which have gotten cattle and goods." The Jews dealt much in cattle, and by the increase of them, they got not only necessaries to support them, but also wealth, and became rich, which made them envied.

"That dwell in the midst of the land." For "midst of the land," in Hebrew, it is, the navel of the land: טבור signifies, a navel, also a high place, and the Jews would have the land of Judah called The navel of the earth, because it is the highest of lands; but others, because it is in the midst of the earth, as the navel is in the midst of man's body. It is said of Jerusalem, that she was set in the midst of nations and countries, Ezek. v. 5; hence the salvations God wrought in Judea and Jerusalem are said to be in the midst of the earth, Isa. vi. 12. Whether Jerusalem or Judea be in the middle of the world is doubted. By navel or "midst of the land" here is meant, the higher or more inward parts of the land, where was most security.

Ver. 13. "Sheba, and Dedan, and the merchants of Tarshish." These were auxiliaries unto Gog, and helped forward that damnable design he had to destroy the church of God. By "Sheba" and "Dedan," Polanus understands the Ethiopians and Arabians; Junius, the men of the south and east; and by the merchants of Tarshish, the Tyrians, Zidonians, and maritime coasts, which lay westward. These all confederated with Gog, who lay northward from Judea. In the 27th chapter Sheba, Dedan, and Tarshish, were spoken of.

"With all the young lions thereof." The Septuagint saith, all the villages thereof; the Chaldee, all the kings or princes thereof: but כפיר is, the whelp of a lion, or a "young lion." Junius, Piscator, and Polanus, make these young lions, the merchants, who were as greedy of gain as lions are of their prey: others make them sea-pirates and robbers. But it is not improbable that by "young lions" should be meant the young men of those parts, who are like lions for strength and courage, as greedy of prey as lions are.

"Shall say unto thee, Art thou come to take a spoil? hast thou gathered thy company to take a prey?" Seeing, O Gog, thou gatherest up forces to war against the Jews, to spoil them, and to make a prey of their wealth and land, lo, we are for thee, we will join with thee. Some would have it, that they envied them, and were against them; but 1 Macc. iii. you shall find that the nations joined with Lysias, who was general of Antiochus his army, ver. 24, and how he took away silver, gold, women, children, cattle, and goods, chap. i. 22, 23—35; he robbed the sanctuary, and fired the city. This Antiochus do expositors make to be Ezekiel's Gog.

Obs. 1. God foreknows and determines things to come, even those things which seem most free and contingent, as the thoughts of men's hearts. He saith of Gog, long before his existence in the world, "It shall come to pass, that at the same time shall things come into thy mind, and thou shalt think an evil thought." Some would have God to permit only things to come, not to determine them, and conceive that God's decree of permission supposes a necessity of their futurition and coming to pass; but if God did only permit a thing to come to pass, how could it come to pass without some action, and God's concurrence to that action? for there is no action or cause producing any effect, with which God doth not concur, Lam. iii. 37; Prov. xxi. 1; xvi. 1. Defects are permitted by God, not effects; he concurs to the production of them: be they thoughts, words, or actions, God's wisdom, power, and providence, hath influence into them.

Obs. 2. God doth not only foreknow, but pre-discovers, the purposes, counsels, and plots of his church's enemies, to evidence his care thereof. He made known the design of Gog many years before it came to pass: "Thou shalt think an evil thought; and say, I will go up to the land of unwalled villages." The enemies of Zion are full of evil thoughts and designs to root out and destroy the inhabitants thereof, but God sometimes discovers them beforehand, and oft prevents them. Neh. iv. 11, "Our adversaries said, They shall not know, neither see, till we come in the midst among them, and slay them, and cause the work to cease:" these thoughts and designs of theirs were discovered and prevented by the Lord. Herod thought and purposed to kill the Lord Christ when he was in the cradle, but the all-knowing God revealed it to Joseph, and disappointed it. God is very vigilant over his church, lest any hurt it; he keeps it night and day, Isa. xxvii. 3.

Obs. 3. The enemies of the church do watch, and take advantages against the church; they wait for and seek occasions to ruin the same. "I will go up," saith Gog, "to the land of unwalled villages; I will go to them that are at rest, that dwell without walls, bars, or gates." Because he saw them unarmed and secure, a naked people destitute of human helps, therefore he resolved to invade, plunder, and destroy them. When Saul was pursuing of David, the Philistines invaded the land, 1 Sam. xxiii. 27; and when Elisha was dead, the Moabites did so, 2 Kings xiii. 20: so Haman, because Mordecai would not bow to him, sought advantages to destroy all the Jews, Esth. iii. 6. The wicked are so strong, spiteful, and vigilant to seek and take advantages against God's people, that it were impossible for them to be in safety, had they not a gracious God to take care of them: they are weak, and look not to arms of flesh, but unto "Jehovah, the Rock of ages," who is their shield and safety: they dwell without walls, but God is "a wall of fire round about them," Zech. ii. 5.

Obs. 4. Wicked ones will undertake great matters, and venture their lives to satisfy their lusts. Gog and the rest undertake a war, march many a mile, and put their lives in their hands, and wherefore? "To take a spoil, to get the prey, to carry away silver, gold, cattle, and goods:" all was to satisfy a base, covetous humour. The lust after ruling, and desire of riches, hath stimulated many to attempt great matters, to hazard their lives and souls to all eternity. Wherefore did the children of Ammon, Moab, and mount Seir, undertake a difficult and dangerous war? Jehoshaphat tells you, it was for dominion and wealth, 2 Chron. xx. 11.

Obs. 5. The wicked confederate and combine together to mischief the church of God. Sheba, Dedan, the merchants of Tarshish, with all the young lions thereof, fall in with Gog and his design. The seed of the serpent are unanimous to destroy the seed of the woman. Psal. lxxxiii. Edomites, Ishmaelites, Moabites, Hagarenes, Gebalites, Ammonites, Amalekites, Philistines, Tyrians, and Ashurites, joined all together against God's people, and said, "Come, let us cut them off from being a nation." Ezra iv. 7—10, Bishlam, Mithredath, Tabeel, Rehum the chancellor, Shimshai the scribe, and the rest of their societies, the Dinaites, the Apharsathchites, the Tarpelites, the Apharsites, the Archevites, the Babylonians, the Susanchites, the Dehavites, the Elamites, and the rest of the nations, did all conspire together to hinder the building of Jerusalem, and the walls thereof. Wicked men are thorns, and they cleave together, to scratch and vex the righteous.

Ver. 14—16. *Therefore, son of man, prophesy and say unto Gog, Thus saith the Lord God; In that day when my people of Israel dwelleth safely, shalt thou not know it? And thou shalt come from thy place out of the north parts, thou, and many people with thee, all of them riding upon horses, a great company, and a mighty army: and thou shalt come up against my people of Israel, as a cloud to cover the land; it shall be in the latter days, and I will bring thee against my land, that the heathen may know me, when I shall be sanctified in thee, O Gog, before their eyes.*

In these words we have the place whence Gog should come, the manner of his coming, the persons he should come against, the author, and event of his coming.

Ver. 14. "In that day when my people of Israel dwelleth safely, shalt thou not know it?" When my people are come to their land, dwell safely in towns, without walls, gates, or bars, "shalt thou not know it?" Yes, thou wilt take notice thereof, and be encouraged thereby to come against them. The Septuagint saith, Thou wilt be stirred up; this sense of the words some make: others thus, Thou hast a wicked thought in thy heart, and dost purpose to invade my people, being unarmed, and dwelling safely, and shalt thou not know? that is, Thou shalt know what it is to invade my people, thou shalt feel my judgments, my fury will appear and fall upon thee, to thy destruction, ver. 16, 18. Piscator renders the word thus, Shalt thou not have experience?

Ver. 15. "Thou shalt come from thy place out of the north parts, thou, and many people with thee," &c. Some conceive that Gog, with his great army, came out of Scythia, others, out of Babylon, which lay northwards from Jerusalem. That he came from those parts, is not clear; but most certain, that he came from the northern parts, or sides of the north; and having drawn many to his assistance, they all came riding upon horses: they were all horsemen for speed. The charges of such an army, being all horsemen, must be exceeding great. This army came into the land of Israel, and covered it like a cloud, as we heard, ver. 9.

Ver. 16. "It shall be in the latter days." In the 8th verse it was said, "In the latter years," and here it is said, "In the latter days," or, as Montanus reads them, in the last days. "In the latter days" did Antiochus vex the Jews, and in the last days shall antichrist vex them and the church.

"When I shall be sanctified in thee, O Gog." God is said to be "sanctified," when he manifests himself to be a holy and just God, by inflicting punishment upon evil-doers, whereby others are made to fear and say, Oh what a holy, what a just, what a dreadful God is he who executes such judgments! Ezek. xxviii. 22, we had the same words.

Obs. 1. When God's people are in Canaan, then have they safety. In Babylon they had none, in Egypt they had none, in the wilderness they had little; but when in Canaan, then they had their greatest safety. "In that day when my people Israel dwelleth safely." They had a day, a time of safety, which was when they were settled in Canaan. In Canaan was the church; and where that is in safety, there God is city, walls, gates, and bars himself. He is the Keeper of Israel, Psal. cxxi. 4, 5.

Obs. 2. Those that design and attempt mischief against the people of God, they shall experimentally know that God is their Protector, and the Revenger of their wrongs. Gog thought evil against Israel, and came up against it: and what saith God, "Shalt thou not know it?" This I will make thee to know, that I am Israel's Keeper, and that thou hast done wickedly to invade them. God made Sennacherib know what it was to design and attempt evil against Jerusalem, when he smote one hundred and eighty-five thousand of his soldiers in one night, Isa. xxxvii. 36. When the Ammonites, Moabites, and Seirites thought and attempted mischief against the Jews, viz. to cast them out and possess their land, did not God avenge his people of them, and manifest himself to be their Protector? 2 Chron. xx. 23, 24.

Obs. 3. The secret plots and deep designs of men do at length break out into action. Gog had long thought of invading Israel, and at length he comes from his place out of the north parts, and puts his design into execution. Hidden things of dishonesty sleep not always; they may be dissembled long, but at last they issue into action. The Spanish plot lay in the dark long, but at last it visited our English coasts, where they were made to see that their Armada was not invincible. The massacres of France and Ireland were secret, though plots, at first, but in process of time they came to blood.

Obs. 4. The great enemies of the church have many helpers and adherents, and those fitted to further their wicked designs. Gog had many people with him, and all of them riding upon horses, a great company, and a mighty army: so numerous they were, that like a cloud they covered the land. So antichrist now hath many assistants to promote his wicked and bloody designs against the saints: Rev. xix. 19, "I saw the beast, and the kings of the earth, and their armies, gathered together to make war against him that sat on the horse, and against his army;" that is, against Christ and his church.

Obs. 5. Though all people and lands in the world be the Lord's, yet some people and lands are his in a more peculiar manner. "Thou shalt come up against my people, and against my land." Where God is owned, his ordinances and worship set up, maintained in purity and power, his interest and glory advanced, there is a people God calls his people, and a land God calls his land: there God dwells, peculiarizing both people and land to himself.

Obs. 6. God takes occasion, from the attempts of the wicked, to execute his just judgments upon them, and so to get glory to his name even from heathens. Gog took occasion, from the Jews' weakness, (they were in unwalled villages,) to invade and destroy them; and God takes occasion from his unjust invading the Jews to inflict dreadful judgments upon him and his, that the heathen might know him, when he should be sanctified in Gog. They seeing such just judgments upon Gog, should fear the God of Israel, and learn righteousness: God is known by executing of judgment, Psal. ix. 16; thereby he is known to be the Most High over all the earth.

Ver. 17. *Thus saith the Lord God; Art thou he of whom I have spoken in old time by my servants the prophets of Israel, which prophesied in those days many years that I would bring thee against them?*

The things concerning Gog were neither novelties nor uncertainties, but such as God foreknew would be, and the prophets had prophesied of, and that long before; and not once or twice, but often, even many years. It is of grand importance to inquire what prophets have spoken of Gog and his proceedings. Some would have Moses to speak of him, Numb. xxiv. 7, where it is said, "His king shall be higher than Agag," that is, Jacob's king shall be higher than Gog. The Septuagint reads it, Gog, and so doth Symmachus; his king shall be exalted above Gog; though Gog be great, yet shall he be greater. But in the original it is, Agag, not Gog. Jerom hath it, Gog, and interprets it of antichrist. Some make David to be the prophet prophesying of Gog: Psal. ix. 5, "Thou hast destroyed the wicked one;" that is, thou shalt destroy Gog, that, or the wicked one, called by some antichrist, whom Gog was a type of. To this accords that in Isa. xi. 4, "With the breath of his lips shall he slay the wicked;" Gog in the type, and antichrist in the antitype, 2 Thess. ii. 8. Besides this place in Isaiah, some fix upon Isa. xvii. 12—14, and make that a prophecy of Gog. Some took Psal. lxviii. 14, "When the Almighty scattered kings," i. e. Gog and Magog: Rivet, in [Lat.] *in locum.* Jer. i. 14, "Out of the north an evil shall break forth upon all the inhabitants of the land:" it is granted Gog was to come out of the north quarters, Ezek. xxxviii. 15, and so was Nebuchadnezzar, Jer. x. 22; he speaks rather of Nebuchadnezzar than of Gog. Moreover, his prophesy was but a little before Ezekiel's days, and much of it in his days, whereas here it is said, "Of whom I have spoken in old time by my servants the prophets of Israel." Others therefore refer it to the prophecy of Enoch, mentioned Jude 14, who spake of the Lord's coming with ten thousand of his saints; but nothing of Gog is there specified. That in Joel iii. is more satisfying as to the business in hand, viz. ver. 2, 9, 11, 14, "I will gather all nations, and will bring them down into the valley of Jehoshaphat, and will plead with them there for my people and for my heritage Israel, whom they have scattered among the nations, and spoiled my land," &c. This we may conceive was prophesied of Gog,

1. Because the Jews were to come out of captivity into their own land, before this was done. It is probable that therefore Gog and the nations conspired together to invade and destroy them, because they were settled safely in their land, ver. 1.

2. Because Gog was to fall upon the mountains of Israel, to perish in the land of Judea. Ezek. xxxix. 4, "Thou shalt fall upon the mountains of Israel, thou, and all thy bands, and the people that is with thee." To which agrees that of Joel iii. 12, 13, "Let the heathen be wakened, and come up to the valley of Jehoshaphat; for there will I sit to judge the heathen round about. Put ye in the sickle; for the harvest is ripe," &c.

3. Because of the like effects. Ezekiel saith, when Gog and his army shall be destroyed, there shall be a great shaking in the land of Israel, ver. 19. So Joel iii. 15, 16, at the destruction of the nations and their princes, "The sun and the moon shall be darkened, and the stars shall withdraw their shining. The Lord also shall roar out of Zion, and utter his voice from Jerusalem; and the heavens and the earth shall shake: but the Lord will be the hope of his people, and the strength of the children of Israel."

If it be said, Joel is but one prophet, and the text speaks of prophets, and so of them, as if it were a common thing amongst them to prophesy of or against Gog; to this may be answered, That most of the prophets might speak of Gog, though they wrote not of him; for all which the prophets prophesied did neither themselves nor others always pen; and here it is said, "by whom I have spoken," not, by whom I have written. Moses spake what was not written, Heb. xi. 24—27; so Enoch, Jude, ver. 14, 15; as Christ himself did, John xxi. 25. "By my servants," in Hebrew is, In or by the hand of my servants; and for, "In those days many years," it is, In the days of those years they did prophesy of Gog, that God would bring him upon the Jews.

Obs. 1. The Lord doth infallibly know things to come. He revealed to the prophets of old this Gog here spoken of hundreds of years before he was; neither was God deceived, for in the time appointed he came. He whose understanding is infinite, Psal. cxlvii. 5, must needs know all things, past, present, and to come; should any thing be unknown to God, his understanding could not be infinite. Man's knowledge is borrowed from creatures, to which he gives neither being nor operation; but God's knowledge is from himself; he knows all that is possible in his power, and all that is future in his will. Creatures can neither be, nor operate, without him. He hath such clear vision of all things, that his knowledge must needs be certain. Should he be deceived in any particular, there should be darkness in him; but, "He is light, and in him there is no darkness at all," 1 John i. 5.

Obs. 2. The prophets delivered many things which were not recorded. The prophets of Israel spake of Gog, and yet we cannot find any direct satisfying place in holy writ concerning him. In Matt. xxvii. 9, you have words cited for Jeremiah's which you cannot find in all his prophecies: the words are these, "Then was fulfilled that which was spoken by Jeremiah the prophet, saying, And they took the thirty pieces of silver, the price of him that was valued, whom they of the children of Israel did value:" Matthew saith not, That which was written, but, "That which was spoken." Jeremiah had delivered these words, and many other, doubtless, which are no where to be found. And if any ask, How came Matthew by them? He had them by tradition, say some: others, by revelation, which is safest to say. Solomon, he spake of trees, from the cedar tree that is in Lebanon, even unto the hyssop that springeth out of the wall; he spake also of beasts, and of fowls, and of creeping things, and of fishes, 1 Kings iv. 33; but what he said of these is not to be found or known. Had not Paul helped us to that blessed truth of Christ, "It is more blessed to give than to receive," Acts xx. 35, we had never met with it.

Obs. 3. Those whom God sends to make known his mind to men, he owns, honours, and protects. "My servants the prophets of Israel." Those who had spoken against Gog, and made known his mind, teaching him, God owns for his servants, honours them with this title, "prophets of Israel;" and being his, he hath a special care of them; Psal. cv. 15, "Do my prophets no harm." If the servants and ambassadors of earthly princes be honourable, and have protection from them, much more are the servants and ambassadors of the King of glory honourable and under divine protection. If David would not put up the wrong done to his servants he sent to Hanun, 2 Sam. x. neither will God let the wrongs done to his servants, the "prophets of Israel," go unpunished, 2 Chron. xxxvi. 16.

Obs. 4. It is not an accidental or casual thing that enemies do come against the church. The Lord brought Gog against this people, and the prophets had prophesied many years that God would do so; they made it known to the world what God had decreed to do. Gog could not have stirred or moved one foot towards the land of Israel, unless God had appointed and commanded it to be so. Lam. iii. 37, "Who is he that saith, and it cometh to pass, when the Lord commandeth it not?"

Ver. 18—22. *And it shall come to pass at the same time when Gog shall come against the land of Israel, saith the Lord God, that my fury shall come up in my face. For in my jealousy and in the fire of my wrath have I spoken, Surely in that day there shall be a great shaking in the land of Israel; so that the fishes of the sea, and the fowls of the heaven, and the beasts of the field, and all creeping things that creep upon the earth, and all the men that are upon the face of the earth, shall shake at my presence, and the mountains shall be thrown down, and the steep places shall fall, and every wall shall fall to the ground. And I will call for a sword against him throughout all my mountains, saith the Lord God: every man's sword shall be against his brother. And I will plead against him with pestilence and with blood; and I will rain upon him, and upon his bands, and upon the many people that are with him, an overflowing rain, and great hailstones, fire, and brimstone.*

The time and manner of God's proceedings with Gog is set forth in these five verses.

Ver. 18. "At the same time when Gog shall come against the land of Israel." "Time" is not to be taken strictly for a day, or an hour; as if God should that very day Gog set out, or invaded the land, fall upon him by his judgments, and destroy him; but largely, for the time of that enterprise, whilst he should be upon that design, when he had filled up the measure of his iniquities.

"My fury shall come up in my face." Some read the words thus, My anger shall come up in my face; that is, I will be furious, and manifest hot displeasure; for fury is the heat and height of anger: we read the words, "My fury shall come up in my face." אף signifies, anger, the face, the nose also, because anger appears chiefly in them: God speaking here after the manner of men, saith, "My fury shall come up in my face." Luther, by "fury," or anger, understands Gog himself, who was the vessel of divine anger, by whom God poured out wrath upon the Jews. Maldonate also makes the fury here mentioned to be against the church; but rather it is against Gog; for at the same time that Gog should come against Israel, at that time should God's fury come up in his face, he would be exceedingly displeased with Gog for attempting the destruction of his people; and ver. 21, God will call for a sword against him.

Ver. 19. "For in my jealousy and in the fire of my wrath have I spoken." The Lord being jealous over his people for their good, and seeing what malicious designs Gog and his confederates had against them, was provoked much thereby, and said in his jealousy and fury, that is, promised, or rather threatened the destruction of Gog; and not only so, but confirmed it with an oath in the next words.

"Surely in that day there shall be a great shaking in the land of Israel." These words, אם־לא carry the form of an oath with them, as thus, If not, that is, if there be not a great shaking, let me not be God, let me not be faithful; so sure as I am God and faithful, so sure and certain it is that "there shall be a great shaking in the land of Israel;" רעש signifies, a commotion, an earthquake, and in that day when Antiochus invaded Canaan, there was a great commotion, a great shaking. And so there will be when antichrist, who is Gog mystical, shall invade the church, which Maldonate saith will be in the end of the world.

Ver. 20. "So that the fishes of the sea, and the fowls of the heaven, the beasts of the field, and all creeping things that creep upon the earth, and all the men that are upon the face of the earth, shall shake at my presence." Here is shown the greatness of his shaking, it should be such as should affect and astonish all creatures, even the sensible and senseless. As Gog should come like a storm, so God's judgments should come upon him and his like a storm. When storms are, the winds blow terribly, so that the air, and fowls in it, are troubled, the sea works and rages, so that the fishes in it are disquieted; yea, some storms do so afflict the earth, that beasts, creeping things, and men themselves, are made to quake. When God comes in a way of judgment, it is grievous. All these expressions are to signify the greatness of calamity. God would appear in some dreadful judgment against Gog, and thereby shake all.

"The mountains shall be thrown down, and the steep places shall fall." Sometimes in Scripture by "mountains" are meant men in eminent places, as Dan. ii. 35; Isa. xl. 4; sometimes the church and kingdoms, as Isa. ii. 23; but here some take it literally, and affirm there should be such an earthquake as should shake down "mountains." Lavater by "mountains" understands towers built upon mountains, which then should be demolished. The word for "steep places" is, המדרגות which, Cant. ii. 14, is translated, "stairs;" the Septuagint hath it, valleys; the Vulgate is, the fences; the translation Vatablus follows saith, bulwarks; Piscator and the French say, towers; Œcolampadius and Lavater render it, the steps, stairs, or ascents, whereby they went up. Junius varies from them all, and renders the word, steep places, by which he intends rocks hanging as it were in the air. The sense is, that all places of refuge and safety, seemed they never so strong, should fail.

"And every wall shall fall to the ground." So terrible shall be the shaking, that the walls of cities shall be overthrown; all the towers, forts, and defences whatsoever, shall be levelled with the ground and made useless. Some understand this of Gog's prevailing against the church, laying all waste, so that the people of God shall be in that distress, till God come and execute judgment upon Gog and all his company.

Ver. 21. "And I will call for a sword against him throughout all my mountains, saith the Lord God." "Sword" here is put for swordmen. God would call forth men, and stir up their spirits to oppose Gog and his company, who, filling all with fear, thought to swallow up all; but throughout Judea, that mountainous country, he should meet with those who would give check to his proceedings. Judas Maccabæus, Jonathan, Eleazer, and others, withstood Antiochus and his forces, as you may see in the book of the Maccabees, and therein was this prophecy made good, say interpreters.

"Every man's sword shall be against his brother." Those of Gog's army should, through the just judgment of God upon them, change their thoughts, counsels, intentions; and, instead of killing their enemies, they should sheathe their swords in one another's bowels. God would order it so, that one should destroy another, as the Philistines did; 1 Sam. xiv. 16, "Behold, the multitude melted away, and they went on beating down one another;"

and ver. 20, "Every man's sword was against his fellow." They being full of discontent and perplexity, thought it more honourable to die than to fall into the hands of enemies.

Ver. 22. "And I will plead against him with pestilence and with blood." He shows here what judgments God would bring upon Gog and his armies, judgments from beneath, and judgments from above. The first sort here are "pestilence and blood," by the sword and slaughter. The Hebrew is, I will be judged with him by pestilence and blood; they shall declare that I am a strong and just God.

"And I will rain upon him, and upon his bands," &c. "an overflowing rain, and great hailstones, fire, and brimstone." The second sort of judgments are, rain, hailstones, fire, and brimstone. These words, "overflowing showers" and "great hailstones," we had, chap. xiii. 11, 13. In the tenth chapter of Joshua, we read how God did cast down great stones from heaven upon the Amorites, and slew more with hailstones than the Israelites slew with the sword, ver. 10. To this place it is conceived our prophet alludes, foretelling that the Lord would deal with the Goggites as he did with the Amorites, slay them with extraordinary great hailstones from heaven; and not only so, but with fire and brimstone, which is the punishment of the damned in hell, and was the punishment of Sodom and Gomorrah.

Some, by these expressions, understand manifold and grievous calamities, which befell Gog and his; and will not have them to be understood literally, that so the verification of them may fall upon Antiochus and his forces, who suffered very sad things; for he was smitten by God with an incurable and invisible plague and torment in his bowels, he fell from his chariot, and was bruised with his fall; worms came out of his body in abundance, his rottenness and stink was such as none could bear the same; and while he was alive his flesh fell off for pain, 2 Macc. ix. Let it be granted that these words are not to be taken literally, but metaphorically for heavy judgments befalling Gog and his companions, it will not follow thereupon that Antiochus was the man, though he suffered such grievous things; for it is said of Gog, that he should fall upon the mountains of Israel, he and all his bands, that he and his slain should have graves in Ezekiel, Ezek. xxxix. 4, 11. But as for Antiochus, he died in his bed, and that either in Babylon, as 1 Macc. vi. or at Ecbatane in India, as it is 2 Macc. ix. Neither was there any such vast destruction of Antiochus' forces, which came into Judea under Lysias, as these words hold out, and is more clearly expressed in chap. xxxix. 12, "Seven months shall the house of Israel be burying of them." There must be a wonderful great slaughter, which required so much time for their burial. I conceive, therefore, that these words may be taken in the literal sense, and are yet to be fulfilled; and that which induceth so to judge, is what you have, Rev. xx. 8, 9, where it is said, "Satan shall gather Gog and Magog together to battle, the number of whom is as the sand of the sea. And they went up on the breadth of the earth, and compassed the camp of the saints about, and the beloved city: and fire came down from heaven and devoured them." John saw this in vision, and spake of it as to come, and puts it after the saints' rising and reigning a thousand years with Christ: that time being expired, some grand enemies shall arise against the Jews and people of God, whom he will destroy, not only in an ordinary way, but miraculously also by fire from heaven.

Obs. 1. When wicked men are plotting and attempting the ruin of the church, God's wrath is kindled against them. When Gog comes up against the land of Israel, God's fury comes up in his face. Gog manifests himself to be an enemy to Zion, and God manifests himself to be an enemy to Gog. Wicked men plot, act, proceed far ofttimes, and afflict the servants of God greatly; but, when they think to carry all, God appears, and that in fury. In Nah. i. 2. it is said, "He reserveth wrath for his enemies;" and when they declare their enmity against him and his, he discovers his wrath against them. Zerah had been long plotting against the Jews, at last he comes against them with a thousand thousand, and three hundred chariots, and thought to devour Asa, his army, and land in a day; and whilst he had such apprehensions, the Lord smote him before Asa and Judah, 2 Chron. xiv. 8, 12.

Obs. 2. When mischief is intended against God's people, his love and indignation are manifested then; his love to his people, his indignation towards their enemies. "In my jealousy and in the fire of my wrath have I spoken." When Gog's armies were to harm the Jews, then was he jealous. In jealousy there is ardent love, and vehement indignation; the one is towards his people, the other towards them that wrong his people. Zech. viii. 2, "I was jealous for Zion with great jealousy, and I was jealous for her with great fury." He had strong love to Zion, and great fury against the enemies of Zion; as a man hath ardent love to his wife, and indignation against any that should offer her violence. God is jealous over his church, and therefore will never suffer it to be made a prey of by the wicked. God's love and indignation at such a time are so ardent, that he swears he will be avenged on them that would wrong his people, "Surely in that day there shall be a great shaking in the land of Israel;" Gog and all his forces shall fall.

Obs. 3. The judgments of God are dreadful, they affect all creatures, the fishes of the sea, the fowls of heaven, the beasts of the field, all that creeps upon the earth; all men upon the face of the earth shall shake; mountains, rocks, walls, shall fall. This judgment upon Gog shall be such, as to astonish and trouble all sensible and insensible creatures; so much of God shall be seen in it. When the Lord destroyed Tyrus, it was a dreadful judgment; the isles did shake at the sound of her fall, the princes of the sea did tremble and were astonished, Ezek. xxvi. But at the destruction of Gog, heaven, earth, sea, all men, other creatures, shall shake. There will be more of God seen in that judgment than in most before; his presence, power, and severity will appear eminently in that judgment; it will speak aloud, and fill the world with astonishment.

Obs. 4. God can easily raise forces against his and the church's enemies, he can do it without any trouble. "I will call for a sword against him throughout all my mountains." The mountains of Israel were the Lord's, and all the inhabitants of them, and if he did but call, they came to his standard presently. The princes of the earth find it a hard business to get a great army together, and wait long for it after great consultation how to effect the same; but the Lord only calls, and it is done; he is the Lord of hosts, he hath command of spirits, and can with ease in a little time gather a vast army. The centurion when he said to his servant, Come, he came; and when God shall say to men, Come, they will come, they must come, out of all parts, from all mountains.

Obs. 5. As God can easily gather armies for the good of his church, so he can as easily ruin armies which are against his church: he can mingle a perverse spirit amongst them, so divide them that they shall execute one another. "Every man's sword shall be against his brother." One Goggite should destroy another; they thought to have destroyed God's people, and they fell one upon the other. 2 Chron. xx. 22, 23, the children of Ammon, Moab, and mount Seir, came against Judah, and thought to destroy them, and take their possessions, but God soon ruined their enemies, he set them one against another: "For the children of Ammon and Moab stood up against the inhabitants of mount Seir, utterly to slay and destroy them; and when they had made an end of the inhabitants of Seir, every one helped to destroy another;" the Ammonites destroyed the Moabites, and the Moabites the Ammonites. This "great multitude," for so they are called, ver. 2, did the Lord cause to fall by their own swords. How easily did God scatter the army of the Syrians, which besieged Samaria! He made them to hear a noise of chariots and horses, whereupon they fled for their lives, and left bag and baggage, 2 Kings vii. 6, 7. Did not God at the prayers of a christian legion, in the army of Marcus Aurelius, emperor, scatter and destroy that vast army of the Marcomanni and Quadi, which consisted of nine hundred and seventy-seven thousand? He sent rain at the same time to relieve the emperor's army, which was in danger of perishing by thirst; and also thunder, lightning, and fiery hail, which ruined the enemies. God can with great facility overthrow the greatest armies.

Obs. 6. God hath variety of means and ways whereby to destroy armies and punish enemies. He hath the "pestilence, blood, an overflowing rain, great hailstones, fire and brimstone," to do the same by. He had an angel to destroy Sennacherib's army, Isa. xxxvii. 36; stars to fight against Sisera, Judg. v. 20. The shining of the sun upon the water undid the Moabites, 2 Kings iii. 22—24; the sound in the tops of the mulberry trees did the Philistines no good, 2 Sam. v. 24. God hath natural, casual, and divine means, to plague his enemies with, though they be in great armies.

Obs. 7. Those who join with great ones in wicked enterprises, must look to suffer grievous things with them. "I will rain upon him, and upon his bands, and upon the many people that are with him." They thought themselves safe under Gog, that they should get honour and wealth in that enterprise; but the undertaking was unwarrantable, Gog could not justify his act, nor protect them: they were co-actors in wickedness, and so should be co-sufferers. It is dangerous to adhere to greatness in wicked designs. "Though hand join in hand, the wicked shall not be unpunished," Prov. xi. 21. Let multitudes take Gog and great men by the hand; let them follow their counsels, tread in their steps, do their wills; this cannot secure them, they shall be punished. God is no respecter of persons; in every nation he that doth wickedly, and they that join with him, shall be punished.

Ver. 23. *Thus will I magnify myself, and sanctify myself; and I will be known in the eyes of many nations, and they shall know that I am the Lord.*

This verse shows the end of God's destroying Gog, and in such a manner, viz. that God may be honoured and known.

"Thus will I magnify myself." The Septuagint and some others read the words passively, I will be magnified; but the Hebrew is, I will magnify myself, or, I will make myself great; and that is done, when God doth such things as declare his power, his faithfulness, and his justice. When the Lord should execute his dreadful threatened judgments upon Gog, then his great power would appear, that he had the command of all creatures, that vast armies are nothing to him; so, his faithfulness to his people, who owned him for their God, and his justice in destroying those who would have destroyed his people.

"And sanctify myself." God is not unholy or polluted at any time; but he is said to sanctify himself, when he declares himself to be not impotent, not unfaithful, not unjust, but a powerful, faithful, righteous, and holy God.

Obs. The end of God's judgments upon the wicked is, that he may be known and acknowledged among the nations, and so have a great and holy name. God is known by executing of judgments, Psal. ix. 16: known not to be like unto men, as they conceived, Psal. l. 21; or, a God that sees not, as they said, Ezek. viii. 12; or, a God countenancing and preferring evil-doers, as they affirmed, Mal. iii. 15: but, to be a dreadful God, as when he visited Ananias and Sapphira for their sins, great fear came upon all that heard thereof, Acts v. 11; to be a holy God, as 1 Sam. vi. 20, when he smote the Bethshemites, fifty thousand of them, with sudden death, it was said, "Who is able to stand before this holy Lord God?" By his judgments he hath made his name dreadful among the heathen. What a great and holy name did the Lord make to himself, by the destruction of Pharaoh and his host in the Red sea!

CHAPTER XXXIX.

Ver. 1—7. *Therefore, thou son of man, prophesy against Gog, and say, Thus saith the Lord God; Behold, I am against thee, O Gog, the chief prince of Meshech and Tubal: and I will turn thee back, and leave but the sixth part of thee, and will cause thee to come up from the north parts, and will bring thee upon the mountains of Israel: and I will smite thy bow out of thy left hand, and will cause thine arrows to fall out of thy right hand. Thou shalt fall upon the mountains of Israel, thou, and all thy bands, and the people that is with thee: I will give thee unto the ravenous birds of every sort, and to the beasts of the field to be devoured. Thou shalt fall upon the open field: for I have spoken it, saith the Lord God. And I will send a fire on Magog, and among them that dwell carelessly in the isles: and they shall know that I am the Lord. So will I make my holy name known in the midst of my people Israel; and I will not let them pollute my holy name any more: and the heathen shall know that I am the Lord, the Holy One in Israel.*

EZEKIEL having begun a prophecy concerning Gog and Magog in the former chapter, he proceeds in this also therein; and tells you,

I. Of the severe dealings of God with Gog, ver. 1—24.

II. Of his gracious favour and goodness to his people, ver. 25, to the end.

In these verses we have,

1. The great enemy of Gog, and author of his overthrow, ver. 1.

2. The manner of it, ver. 2, 3, 6.

3. The place where it should be, ver. 4, 5.
4. The greatness of it, ver. 4.
5. The certainty thereof, ver. 5.
6. The end of God in so doing, ver. 7.

Ver. 1. "Behold, I am against thee, O Gog, the chief prince of Meshech and Tubal." These very words we had in the former chapter, ver. 2, 3. He was a great prince, had great command, many confederates to take his part; yet, being wicked and an enemy to God's people, God declares himself to be an enemy to him.

Ver. 2. "I will turn thee back, and leave but the sixth part of thee." These words, "and leave but the sixth part of thee," are variously interpreted. Some say, I will kill five parts of thine army, and leave but a sixth. Some, I will seduce thee. Others, I will judge thee with six judgments, viz. the plague, blood, rain, hailstones, fire, and brimstone, as it is in the former chapter, ver. 22. The Hebrew Montanus renders, I will sixth thee. For the meaning whereof, consider what has been said, chap. xxxviii. 4, "I will turn thee back, and put hooks into thy jaws;" the sense whereof was this, I will not turn thee back, but bring thee out; and because of objections, difficulties, and delays, I will draw thee forth, I will put hooks in thy jaws, and deal by thee as men do by fish in the seas, or things fallen into wells, draw thee out by hooks. The reason it is conceived of this expression is, for that they used irons with six hooks upon them, to catch hold of things fallen into waters, and to draw them out thereby. Hence it is, that the Lord saith, I will sixth thee, as the word signifies, or, draw thee out with hooks, as the sense is.

"And will cause thee to come up from the north parts, and will bring thee upon the mountains of Israel." Of Gog's coming from the north parts we heard, chap. xxxviii. 15. God would cause him to come out of those parts unto the mountains of Israel; which we may take literally, though some do take them metaphorically for the places where the church of God should be.

Ver. 3. "And I will smite thy bow out of thy left hand, and will cause thine arrows to fall out of thy right hand." Bows and arrows were much used in former days, both amongst the Jews and heathens also, as Isa. lxvi. 19; Jer. xlvi. 9; 1 Chron. v. 18; and when they handled them, they held the bows in their left hands and arrows in their right ones. Now when these Goggites should attempt to shoot, and do execution by shooting, God would disappoint them; causing a fear and faintness to fall upon them, so that not only their bows and arrows, but all their military instruments, should be useless; for by these mentioned, are meant all the rest. To smite or break the bow, imports the weakening of forces, or making of warlike instruments inefficacious, as Psal. xxxvii. 15; xlvi. 9; Hos. i. 5; Jer. xlix. 35: in these places, breaking of the bow notes, blasting of their power, and making frustrate all military instruments.

Ver. 4. "Thou shalt fall upon the mountains of Israel, thou, and all thy bands, and the people that is with thee." Not in places conspicuous to the whole church, as some would have it, but in the land and on the mountains of Israel; which Antiochus Epiphanes did not, as I showed formerly. And this verse gives warrant to depart from our translation of those words in the 2nd verse, "And leave but the sixth part of thee;" for Gog, and all his bands and confederates, were to fall upon the mountains of Israel; no sixth part of them were left.

"I will give thee unto the ravenous birds of every sort, and to the beasts of the field to be devoured." When great armies are overthrown, sometimes their carcasses lie unburied, and so are exposed to the fowls of heaven, and beasts of the field, which prey upon them; so should it be with Gog and his for a season: after they had lain a season, they had burial, as appears, ver. 11. The word for "ravenous bird" is, עיט which signifies, a bird of prey, and differs from צפור which is, a small bird.

Ver. 5. "Thou shalt fall upon the open field." The Hebrew saith, Thou shalt fall upon the faces of the field, that is, the superficies, and so lie in open view. We had the same words in chap. xvi. 5, and xxxii. 4.

Ver. 6. "And I will send a fire on Magog." Some by "Magog" understand the land of Gog; when others, a distinct person and prince from Gog. Let "Magog" denote a place or person, God would send a fire, not metaphorical fire only, but material fire, and so it is said, Rev. xx. 9.

"And among them that dwell carelessly in the isles." Pliny saith, there are many islands in the Scythian sea, and it is likely such people as dwell therein are careless, secure, fearing no dangers; yet God would visit them with fire. But there are islands nearer than those upon the Egæan and Mediterranean seas, which dwell confidently, as the word is.

Ver. 7. "So will I make my holy name known in the midst of my people Israel." When great men go forth to war, and obtain some eminent victory, thereby they become famous; so God, by smiting Magog and all his forces, would make his holy name known, that his people should confess him to be a holy God, and his name a name of holiness; for so it is in the original.

"And I will not let them pollute my holy name any more." When men say those things which are derogatory to the name of God, as that he sees not, he hath forsaken the earth, that he is unfaithful, unjust, &c.; or do such things as cause others to blaspheme and speak dishonourably of himself, his word, worship, and providences; then are they said to pollute his holy name. After the destruction of Gog and Magog, God would order things so, that his name should not suffer.

Obs. 1. Those who are enemies unto the church, God is an enemy unto them. Gog's thought and design was to invade the land of Israel; and what saith the Lord? "Behold, I am against thee, O Gog:" hadst thou been a friend to my church, I would have been a friend to thee; but seeing thou art malicious and intendest mischief against the saints, lo, I, even I, the Lord of hosts, that can shake heaven and earth, and destroy the most puissant and politic army in a moment, am against thee. When thou touchest my people, thou touchest the apple of mine eye, and I neither can nor will bear it. Exod. xxiii. 22, "I will be an enemy unto thine enemies, and an adversary unto thine adversaries:" whoever set themselves against Israel, have the God of Israel against them.

Obs. 2. Wicked men may be in great honour and have great power. Gog here, one whom the Lord declared himself against, was a prince, a chief prince of Meshech and Tubal. Ahasuerus, a heathen idolater, had honour and power enough, when he had one hundred and twenty-seven provinces under his command, Esth. i. 1.

Obs. 3. There are seeming contradictions in holy scriptures. In one, God saith, "Behold, I am against thee, O Gog;" in another, "I will cause thee to come up from the north parts," or sides, "and will bring thee upon the mountains of Israel." God was with Gog, and against Gog; with him by his providence, to bring him forth to manifest his spleen and gall against the land of Israel, and against him by his power and justice, to destroy him for his cruelty and bloodiness. Gen. xiv. 14, it is said, Abraham pursued the enemies "unto Dan;" and, Josh. xix. 47, there was no Dan in Abraham's days, for it was so called from Dan the son of Jacob, who was long after him; Moses, who wrote the book of Genesis, speaks of it as it was called in his days, not as it was called in Abraham's days. John i. 21, when John was asked the question, whether he were Elias? he said, "I am not;" but, Matt. xi. 14, Christ saith of John, "This is Elias, which was for to come:" John denies himself to be Elias personally, which was the sense of the questionists, and Christ affirms that he was Elias mystically, that Elias Malachi spake of, chap. iv. 5. There are many scriptures seeming to destroy one another; but if rightly understood, they do sweetly comply and shake hands together.

Obs. 4. God's hand is in the undertakings of enemies against the church. "I will cause thee to come, bring thee upon the mountains of Israel;" and if thou lingerest, I have a sixth-hooked hook to draw thee. Wars are not fortuitous, but by a special hand of God; he brings forth enemies as to correct his church by them, so to destroy them in the presence and view of his church, being corrected. Were not God's hand there, they would ruin the church; and because his hand is in such things, therefore are they ruined. After Pharaoh had afflicted the Jews the time appointed, God drew him on into the Red sea, and there, in the face and view of them, sunk him like lead into the bottom of the deeps.

Obs. 5. It is in the Lord to disable and disappoint warriors when they are ready for battle. When Gog and his soldiers should have the bow in the left hand, and the arrow in the right hand, then I will smite the bow out of the one, and the arrow out of the other hand, saith the Lord. All military strength he can easily blunt, and make all weapons of war inefficacious. He can take off the wheels of chariots, Exod. xiv. 25. He breaks the bow, he blunts the sword, and makes all weapons formed against Israel unprosperous at his pleasure, Isa. liv. 17. God stopped Rehoboam when he was going with a great army to fight Jeroboam, and bring the ten revolted tribes to himself, 1 Kings xii. God hath oft put such fear into the hearts of soldiers, that, when it hath come to a pitched battle, they have presently thrown down their weapons and called for quarter.

Obs. 6. That in the same place where God shows rich mercy to the godly, even there he executes severe judgments upon the enemies. "Thou shalt fall upon the mountains of Israel." Upon those mountains in that land the Lord had showed marvellous kindness to his people, Psal. lxxvi. 1—4, and there should Gog fall. In the Red sea God preserved the Israelites, and destroyed the Egyptians; where the one met with signal mercy, there the other had severe judgment. So Joel iii. 2, "I will gather all nations, and will bring them down into the valley of Jehoshaphat, and will plead with them there for my people;" God would punish them even there where he had done much for his. 2 Chron. xx. 26, the valley where Jehoshaphat blessed God for a victory, it is conceived to be here meant, and called "the valley of Jehoshaphat." The powers of darkness have oft and still do invade the mountains of Israel, the places and persons among whom God doth record his name, and there God overthrows them.

Obs. 7. That armies and others are exposed to public shame and miserable ends, is of God. "Thou shalt fall upon the open field, and I will give thee to the ravenous birds of every sort, and to the beast of the field to be devoured." Want of burial is amongst God's judgments, Jer. viii. 2; xiv. 16. To lie in open view dead, and to be mangled, torn by fowls, beasts, swine, and dogs, is a dishonourable and lamentable thing; but how dishonourable or lamentable soever it be, it is the Lord's doing. He makes wicked armies and persons sometimes as dung upon the face of the earth; they lie unburied.

Obs. 8. What the Lord speaks, that shall certainly take place. "Thou shalt fall upon the open field; for I have spoken it, saith the Lord God." With God is not yea and nay; what he saith is truth, and must infallibly be effected. As nothing can be done unless the Lord speak, so nothing can fail of being done when the Lord hath spoken. Josh. xxi. 45, "There failed not ought of any good thing which the Lord had spoken unto the house of Israel; all came to pass." God promised them to root out the nations, to plant them in Canaan, and to do much for them; and all God had spoken was made good. So, when God threatens evil, whatsoever he speaks in that kind must be fulfilled, because he is faithful, and able to make good his word, whoever opposes.

Obs. 9. When God begins to visit the enemies of his church, he makes progress therein. Not only shall Gog fall, and all his bands and people, but God will send a fire on Magog also, and upon the isles that dwell carelessly: they thought themselves invincible, being fortified by the sea; but when God arises to punish the inhabitants of the earth, who are enemies to his people, he goes from country to country at land, and from isle to isle at sea. When God draws the sword, and gives it commission, it proceeds from place to place, and is restless till all at sea and land be cut off, who are numbered out for destruction. Jer. xlvii. 6, 7, "O thou sword of the Lord, how long will it be ere thou be quiet? put up thyself into thy scabbard, rest, and be still. How can it be quiet, seeing the Lord hath given it a charge against Ashkelon, and against the sea shore? there hath he appointed it." God appoints the sword to visit at land and at sea; when he begins with the enemies of his people, he will make an end with them.

Obs. 10. When God shows mercy to his church, and destroys the enemies of it, then he provides for his own honour, sanctifies his name, and makes himself to be known, distinct from all other gods. When the Jews' church shall be at peace, Gog and Magog be destroyed, then God will be glorious, all speak honourable of him, and acknowledge him to be the Holy One of Israel. When God led the Israelites through the Red sea, and took off the wheels of the Egyptian chariots, the Egyptians said, "Let us flee from the face of Israel, for the Lord fighteth for them against the Egyptians." Here they acknowledged God's power, and that he was a God distinguished from all their idol gods; a God fulfilling his promises and threats, a God able to save and destroy, even the Holy One of Israel.

Ver. 8. *Behold, it is come, and it is done, saith the Lord God; this is the day whereof I have spoken.*

Here the certainty of Gog's overthrow, and the rest, with the time thereof, is pointed out. "It is come, it is done," i. e. this prophecy is so certain, as if it were come and done already. It is usual among the Hebrews to put preter tenses for future, and to speak of things as past which are certainly to come.

"This is the day whereof I have spoken." God

had spoken of Gog and Magog by his prophets formerly, as was showed from the 17th verse of the 38th chapter, that they should come against Israel, and utterly be destroyed in that attempt; which the Lord speaking of here as done, saith, "This is the day," not designing the prefixed day when it should be: it shall be, but when, that is hid.

Obs. 1. There is a certain time determined for the destruction of the church's enemies, which God looks upon as present, and done. "Behold, it is come, it is done;" that is, the day of Gog and Magog's ruin. God foresees things to come as if they were present, not by a presence of existency from eternity, but in his decree, on that his foreknowledge and the certainty of things is founded; we should therefore firmly believe the same, and not give way to dubious opinions thereabout.

Obs. 2. The particular time is hidden from men, and known only unto God. Man cannot say, "This is the day," but the Lord can; he knew the very moment when Gog and his should be destroyed, and the church set at liberty. The thing and time indefinitely were revealed to the prophet, but not the particular, punctual time; the Lord kept that in his own breast, his infinite wisdom saw it not meet to particularize the time. The prophets had spoken of a day that would be for Gog's invading the land of Israel, and of his falling upon the mountains thereof, but the exact time they knew not. John, unto whom the Lord Christ revealed much, tells you, that after one thousand years' reign of the saints with Christ, it shall be, Rev. xx. 7—9.

Ver. 9, 10. *And they that dwell in the cities of Israel shall go forth, and shall set on fire and burn the weapons, both the shields and the bucklers, the bows and the arrows, and the handstaves, and the spears, and they shall burn them with fire seven years: so that they shall take no wood out of the field, neither cut down any out of the forests; for they shall burn the weapons with fire: and they shall spoil those that spoiled them, and rob those that robbed them, saith the Lord God.*

The great victory over Gog and Magog begins in these verses, which is set out by the burning of the weapons, and spoiling them of their goods. Who obtained the victory is not mentioned; it is only said, the Jews shall go out of their cities and gather up the weapons, and burn them, &c. It is conceived the Lord will deal with Gog and his forces in some extraordinary way. Ver. 3, it is said, "I will smite thy bow out of thy hand;" and Rev. xx. 9, "Fire came down from God out of heaven, and devoured them:" but notwithstanding God's extraordinary dealing with them, the Jews were used of the Lord in this victory; for, chap. xxxviii. 21, "I will call for a sword against him throughout all my mountains, saith the Lord God;" so that all Israel shall be in the field against him, and be the conquerors.

Ver. 9. "They that dwell in the cities of Israel shall go forth, and shall set on fire and burn the weapons." After this great and famous victory, the citizens which dwell in the cities of Israel will go forth, to see the slain, and to get spoil; and among other things, they should take of their weapons, and make themselves fire thereof. The word for "weapons" is, נשק, which notes any kind of weapon to oppose the enemy. It is not from נשׂק to burn, but from נשׁק to arm.

"Both the shields and the bucklers, the bows and the arrows, and the handstaves, and the spears." These latter were combustible; but how they should burn the shields and bucklers is not apparent, they being of solid metals; it is like something combustible was annexed unto them.

"And they shall burn them with fire seven years." It must needs be a numerous, or rather numberless army, whose weapons should suffice the Jews seven years for firing. John saith, their number shall be as the sand of the sea, Rev. xx. 8, which exceeds all arithmetic. Some make it a hyperbolical expression, to show the greatness of their overthrow, and multitude of their warlike instruments. Others mind us of a certain time put here for an uncertain, viz. "seven years" put for a long time. The Jewish writers do take the words literally, concluding they shall have such a victory over their enemies, as that for seven years they shall need no other materials to burn than their weapons; and think their Messiah not come, because they have not yet obtained such a victory. Sanctius thinks not that they were seven years in burning the weapons, but that they had such store which might have served them for seven years' fuel; great store, and therefore it is said, they should "burn them with fire seven years." How this was verified in Antiochus, is hard to show. It is nearer to truth, to judge that this scripture remains still to be fulfilled.

Ver. 10. "So that they shall take no wood out of the field, neither cut down any out of the forests." These words taken absolutely, do strengthen the literal acceptation of the former. We may take them comparatively, thus, That in respect of what they did use to take out of the field, and cut out of the forest, they should now cut and take little: and why?

"For they shall burn the weapons with fire." They should so supply them for fuel, that little other wood should serve. This burning of enemies' weapons conduceth much to peace. Where warlike weapons are broken and burned, not reserved, there wars cease and peace follows.

"They shall spoil those that spoiled them, and rob those that robbed them." It is incident to all people and nations to spoil and rob the people of God; and so these Goggites and their confederates, they "compassed the camp of the saints, and the beloved city," saith John, Rev. xx. 9. In all ages, the church hath been made a prey of by one or other; but the time shall be when it shall spoil her spoilers, and rob her robbers.

Obs. 1. God will give victories to his church and people which seem incredible. Here is pointed out such a victory as is full of wonders and matters incredible. Their number is as the sand of the sea, and all of them horsemen, and clothed with all sorts of arms, chap. xxxviii. 4, yet conquered. Their weapons serve for seven years' firing, and their bodies are seven months in burying, as it follows in ver. 12. Will not this be a wonderful victory? Do not these things seem incredible? God of old gave great and strange victories to his people, as the drowning of Pharaoh in the Red sea, the slaying of Sennacherib's vast army in a night by an angel. Great victories since Christ his time have been. The christians have had signal victories against the Turk; and Sanctius tells you of a wonderful victory which the Spaniards had against the Saracens, when at one battle they slew two hundred thousand of them, and lost but twenty-five men; but whenever this overthrow of Gog shall be, it will exceed all former victories.

Obs. 2. The Lord makes that advantageous to his people, which their enemies intended to damnify and ruin them by. The bows, arrows, handstaves, and spears, shall serve the saints for fuel, with which the Goggites thought to destroy them. The sword of Goliath, with which he thought to have slain David and many Israelites, was afterwards given into the hand of David, and serviceable unto him, 1 Sam. xxi. 9. The wise and wonderful providence of God so overrules and orders things, that it makes instruments of death the comforts of life. The chariots of Sisera that came for destruction, were to the Jews for use and recreation.

Obs. 3. After the overthrow of Gog and Magog, antichrist and his adherents, the church of God shall have great peace. All their weapons of war shall be burnt; they shall make head no more against the saints. After the devouring of Gog and Magog by fire from heaven, Rev. xx. 9, the gates of the new Jerusalem were never shut, chap. xxi. 25. They feared no enemies, they had great peace.

Obs. 4. The people of God shall have a day of recompence for the wrongs and injuries they have sustained. They shall spoil those that spoiled them, and rob those that robbed them. The Goggites of the world do fleece the servants of God, eat their flesh, suck their blood, and gnaw their bones; but the day is coming, when the wicked shall be a spoil and prey unto them; which sets out the righteousness of God in his ways and judgments. What can be more equal than that he who spoils should be spoiled? See Isa. xxxiii. 1, "Woe to thee that spoilest, and thou wast not spoiled; and dealest treacherously, and they dealt not treacherously with thee! when thou shalt cease to spoil, thou shalt be spoiled; and when thou shalt make an end to deal treacherously, they shall deal treacherously with thee."

Ver. 11—16. *And it shall come to pass in that day, that I will give unto Gog a place there of graves in Israel, the valley of the passengers on the east of the sea: and it shall stop the noses of the passengers: and there shall they bury Gog and all his multitude: and they shall call it The valley of Hamon-gog. And seven months shall the house of Israel be burying of them, that they may cleanse the land. Yea, all the people of the land shall bury them; and it shall be to them a renown the day that I shall be glorified, saith the Lord God. And they shall sever out men of continual employment, passing through the land to bury with the passengers those that remain upon the face of the earth, to cleanse it: after the end of seven months shall they search. And the passengers that pass through the land, when any seeth a man's bone, then shall he set up a sign by it, till the buriers have buried it in the valley of Hamon-gog. And also the name of the city shall be Hamonah. Thus shall they cleanse the land.*

Having spoken of the great overthrow which Gog and his should have, and the great spoil the Israelites should get thereby; now the burial of the dead carcasses and their bones comes under consideration; where we have, the place of the burial, the time how long they shall be burying, the persons by whom the name of the place.

Ver. 11. "And it shall come to pass at that day, that I will give unto Gog a place there of graves in Israel." When Gog and his forces shall be slain, lie exposed to the fowls of heaven and beasts of the field for a season, then will the Lord give unto them a burying-place; they shall not always lie putrifying above-ground, but they shall be laid in graves; so that they shall neither be a prey to fowls and beasts, nor offensive to man, always. This was favour, that God should give his enemies sepulchres in Israel. The Vulgate and Septuagint have it, A place of name or renown, putting שֵׁם for שָׁם It was honour enough for them to have graves there in Israel. This honour had not Antiochus.

"The valley of the passengers on the east of the sea." What valley this was, is not agreed upon by interpreters. Some affirm it to be a valley near unto the lake of Gennesareth, or sea of Tiberias; others inform us it is about Jordan; some say it is on this side Jordan, some say on that side. It is most probable to be a valley near the Salt or Dead sea, where the five cities, Admah, Zeboim, Segor, Sodom, and Gomorrah, were consumed by fire and brimstone; now called Lacus Asphaltites. There, as Junius notes, men passed from Syria, Mesopotamia, Babylon, and other countries, into Arabia Felix, and Egypt; whereupon it was called "the valley of passengers," and lay eastward from Jerusalem, as the next words show: "on the east of the sea," that is, on the eastern sea. The sea of Tiberias lay northward, but Mare Mortuum lay eastward.

"And it shall stop the noses of the passengers." Such a stink shall be in that valley as shall cause the passengers to stop their noses or mouths, or both. The Spirit of God may have some respect unto the lake Asphaltites, which sent forth poisonous and suffocating vapours; so should the dead bodies of Gog and his send out such a loathsome infecting savour, as travellers should stop their noses as not being able to endure the same.

"There shall they bury Gog and all his multitude." Though Gog had a burial in the land of Israel, yet it was not in the sepulchres of the kings or prophets; it was in "the valley of passengers," near the place of God's remarkable judgment upon the sinful cities.

"And they shall call it The valley of Hamon-gog." In Jeremiah, you read of a "valley of slaughter," Jer. xix. 6; vii. 32; and it was so called from the persons slain there by Nebuchadnezzar's forces, when Jerusalem was besieged and taken. And here is a valley called "the valley of Hamon-gog," that is, of the multitude of Gog; so great a multitude were slain and buried there, as gave denomination to the valley. This valley, Joel in his days was pleased to call "The valley of decision," or threshing, as the word imports, Joel iii. 14.

Ver. 12. "And seven months shall the house of Israel be burying of them." Not some few, but the house of Israel, who were a great number, should be employed seven months in burying of them; which sets out the greatness of the victory; such a number slain as should set many thousands on work so long to bury them; seven years in burning their weapons, and seven months in burying their dead. If a certain number be put here for an uncertain, as some will have it, yet they were a long time about this work.

"That they may cleanse the land." When a multitude are slain, their putrified bodies are apt to corrupt the air and earth, and so to endanger the living. The Israelites therefore, to prevent such a mischief, shall take great pains to bury them, and that without any intention of honouring the dead thereby. When men bury the dead, usually it is for an honour to them, but not so here; the end was, to cleanse the land, which was defiled with the carcasses of these Goggites.

Ver. 13. "Yea, all the people of the land shall bury them." Before he had said, "the house of Israel;" now he adds, "all the men of the land:"

some should give counsel, some should dig the graves or pits, and some should bring and put the dead bodies into them. Some understand by "the house of Israel," and "people of the land," christian people; who shall extinguish the name of antichrist, and bury it, with all his offensive errors, in the grave of oblivion; and that they make the sense of burying Gog and his.

"And it shall be to them a renown." The Hebrew is, for a name. They shall be renowned for this victory, and for their humanity in burying of the dead; their enemies shall speak honourably and well of them.

"The day that I shall be glorified." The Tigurine translation hath it thus, That day, wherein I shall be glorified, shall be famous unto them; they shall have cause to remember that day for ever. What day I shall destroy Gog and Magog with all their forces, and so get glory to myself, that day shall be a day of name, of renown, and of memorial unto them; that day shall be put into their chronicles. The Hebrew stands thus, In the day of me to be glorified; and so may point at their glorifying God for that great destruction of their enemies.

Ver. 14. "And they shall sever out men of continual employment." Gog, and his, being beaten, divers were scattered up and down the land, and by reason of their wounds, fell and lay unburied in many places; whereupon they chose out men of continuance, (so the Hebrew is,) who might go up and down from one part of the land to the other, to find out the dead.

"To bury with the passengers those that remain upon the face of the earth, to cleanse it." As those searchers went up and down, they met with passengers, whom they caused to assist them in the burial of the dead they found. It is probable they made the passengers to take the bodies or bones of the dead, and to bury them; because it was matter of defilement unto the Jews to touch dead bodies; Numb. xix. 11, they that did so, were unclean seven days. These being to cleanse the land, would not defile themselves.

"After the end of seven months, shall they search." Seven months were the people of the land in burying their enemies, they were busied about those that fell by heaps. When these months were at an end, they sent out their searchers to examine woods, hills, caves, valleys, highways, and ditches, where any dead corpse might lie; so careful were they to prevent infection.

Ver. 15. "When any seeth a man's bone, then shall he set up a sign by it." Some bodies lying long, the fowls of the heaven, or beasts of the field, devoured their flesh, ate their bones, and left some fragments of them, which if the passengers and searchers found, they were to set up a sign or mark by them, to give notice thereof. "Man's bone," is a singular number put for a plural, men's bones. The word "a sign" is, ציון which signifies a statue, a title, or sign, setting near to a grave, or a way-mark: as Jer. xxxi. 21, "Set thee up way-marks," the word is, צינים and they were to direct people; so here, they set up signs to direct the buriers what to do concerning those bones.

"Till the buriers have buried it in the valley of Hamon-gog." Those appointed to bury, were to take the bones of men so discovered, and to carry them to the valley of Hamon-gog, and bury them there. There were the multitude of the slain buried, which gave that denomination to the place; and with them must the scattered and collected bones be buried.

Ver. 16. "Also the name of the city shall be Hamonah." What city shall be so called is not set down, and therefore interpreters do vary thereabouts. Some believe there was a city near that valley which had another name, and upon this occasion of slaying Gog and his multitude, lost that, and had this imposed, "Hamonah," her multitude, because a multitude of enemies were slain there. Upon occasions names have been given to places, as appears, Gen. xvi. 14; xxvi. 20—22; Hos. iv. 15; 2 Sam. v. 9; vi. 8. Others judge this city to be Jerusalem, reading the words thus, And her multitude shall be a name (or for a name) to the city; so Junius: or, The name of the city shall be from her multitude; that is, the city Jerusalem: or, The church shall be famous for her inhabitants, which slew such a multitude of Goggites; so Piscator. This sense hath more of truth in it than the other; for we find not any city called Hamonah, since this prophecy: yet those of that opinion say, it was fulfilled in the time of Antiochus.

"Thus shall they cleanse the land." The words are read by some, After they have cleansed the land; by others, When they have cleansed the land, which is the same for sense. God's giving them so great a victory over such a multitude of enemies, and their not abusing, but cleansing the land after it, should be to them for a name, for their great glory and renown.

Obs. 1. God disappoints the expectation of the wicked while living, yet sometimes affords favour when they are dead. Gog, and all his, expected to have had the land of Israel in possession, with all the desirable things thereof; but God disappointed his expectation; slays him and his; and after death, gives him and the rest a place of burial in that land, which was favour. Though they had not what they hoped for, yet they had more than they deserved: for such grand enemies to have a burying-place in that land, which was Emmanuel's land, out of which they would have driven his people, was no small favour; especially, if we add to it, that the place was named after his name, "The valley of Hamon-gog," and this recorded in the book of God, and to remain for ever.

Obs. 2. After great victories, wherein many are slain, people should for public good be careful to bury the dead; though it require time, be troublesome, and chargeable. Here they were seven months in burying the dead carcasses; they appointed men to go throughout the land to search for corpses and bones, which was a chargeable business; and wherever they found any, to bring them unto "the valley of Hamon-gog," which was very troublesome. These things they were to do for public good, that the land might not be infected with those bodies, and so infect the living.

Obs. 3. By great victories over enemies, God honours his own name, and makes his people to have a name. "It shall be to them a renown the day that I shall be glorified." That day my power, my faithfulness, my justice, my mercy, will be seen, acknowledged, and so I shall be praised, made glorious; and in that day my people will be spoken of for their valour, faith, and humanity in burying the dead, and so will be renowned. When God destroyed Sennacherib's army, God did not only make himself a name, but he also made Hezekiah a name; 2 Chron. xxxii. 23, "He was magnified in the sight of all nations from thenceforth;" and that which was his magnification was the magnification of all his people. The honour of the head is the honour of the whole body. How renowned will new Jerusalem be, when God and Magog, antichrist and all that adhere to them, shall be taken away! When the Lord shall destroy them by fire from heaven, and multitudes be cut off by the sword, then shall those multitudes be for a name to the city.

Obs. 4. After conquering, there ought to be cleansing. When Gog and his shall be subdued, then they must cleanse the land; not a dead corpse, not a bone, must be left in it; such things did defile. We have had many victories; but what cleansing hath there been in this land? Dead bodies, limbs, and bones of men have been buried; but what dead works are cleansed out of this land? Do not all sorts of sins abound, yea, superabound? Had we cleansed the land for each victory God hath given us, but of one common sin, by this time we had been spotless, we should not have had any visible iniquities amongst us; but now we are like Golgotha, a place of sculls and dead men; like Sodom and Gomorrah, or the valley of Hamon-gog; we stink so through our blasphemies, errors, and wicked practices, that passengers stop their noses and shake their heads.

Ver. 17—20. *And, thou son of man, thus saith the Lord God; Speak unto every feathered fowl, and to every beast of the field, Assemble yourselves, and come; gather yourselves on every side to my sacrifice that I do sacrifice for you, even a great sacrifice upon the mountains of Israel, that ye may eat flesh, and drink blood. Ye shall eat the flesh of the mighty, and drink the blood of the princes of the earth, of rams, of lambs, and of goats, of bullocks, all of them fatlings of Bashan. And ye shall eat fat till ye be full, and drink blood till ye be drunken, of my sacrifice which I have sacrificed for you. Thus ye shall be filled at my table with horses and chariots, with mighty men, and with all men of war, saith the Lord God.*

These verses speak of a great feast, and the invitation of guests unto the same: strange guests! the fowls of the heaven and the beasts of the field: and they have as strange dishes provided for them, even the flesh of mighty men and princes.

Ver. 17. "Speak unto every feathered fowl, and to every beast of the field." The Hebrew for "every feathered fowl" is, לצפור כל-כנף to the fowl of every wing; that is, to what fowl soever hath wing, let that fowl be invited to come and eat of the feast prepared; and likewise, "every beast of the field," which is a beast of prey.

"Assemble yourselves, and come, gather yourselves on every side." The fowls and beasts being void of reason, could not understand what the prophet said; but God, who had command over them as well as other creatures, would cause them to come, as if they had had reason and understanding. This shows the certainty and greatness of the victory; the fowls and beasts are called to come, and their coming shall not be in vain; they must come "on every side," and therefore great provision shall be made for them.

"To my sacrifice that I do sacrifice for you, even a great sacrifice upon the mountains of Israel." The Hebrew word for "sacrifice" is, זבח *zebach*, which signifies, a sacrifice of a slain beast. When a beast was killed and to be offered up to God, that was a sacrifice properly. Sometimes it notes the killing of men and beasts, as here, which metaphorically is called a sacrifice. Gog with his men and horses were slain, and these God calls his sacrifice, a great sacrifice which he prepared for the fowls and beasts, a great feast or supper; and the place where this should be is, "upon the mountains of Israel."

"That ye may eat flesh, and drink blood." In the former verse he spake of Gog's funeral, and those that were slain with him, even the dead bodies and the bones; how is it now that he speaks of eating their flesh, and drinking their blood, after the seven months were expired, and the searchers had gone through the land? It is not probable, that some were left unburied, and so the fowls and beasts invited to eat their flesh and drink their blood; but having touched a little upon this in the 4th verse, he re-assumes the argument again in this and the three next verses, and speaks more fully to it.

Ver. 18. "Ye shall eat the flesh of the mighty." The Septuagint saith, of giants: by these mighty men, or giants, the chief ones in the army are pointed out, men of power and command.

"And drink the blood of the princes of the earth." In this vast army of Gog, there were the princes of divers countries his confederates, chap. xxxviii. 5, 6. Their blood should the fowls of heaven and beasts of the earth drink, being shed and spilled upon the ground. They should feed upon not the vile and base ones, but the chiefest, and so drink their blood.

"Of rams, of lambs, and of goats, of bullocks, all of them fatlings of Bashan." By these metaphorical expressions are set out the dead carcasses of men, who were of several dispositions and qualities: some were like rams and lambs, others like goats and bullocks; some were sweeter and more tender flesh than others. Rams and goats, or great goats, as the Hebrew word signifies, were leaders; lambs and bullocks were those under the leaders. All of them were well fleshed and fat like the kine of Bashan. Bashan was a high hill, Psal. lxviii. 15, beyond Jordan, which yielded strong oaks, and fat cattle, Ezek. xxvii. 6; Amos iv. 1.

Ver. 19. "And ye shall eat fat till ye be full, and drink," &c. The fowls of heaven and beasts of the field are resembled unto men at a feast, where having meat and drink which likes them, they eat and drink plentifully. The fat, flesh, and blood of men is sweet, and so pleasing to fowls and beasts, which should cram and fill themselves therewith.

Ver. 20. "Thus ye shall be filled at my table." The word for "table" is, שלחן from שלח to send, because it is sent out, or extended at length; so that it may contain many dishes, and guests may sit down thereat to feed upon those dishes. The mountains of Israel were the table here, the carcasses of men were the dishes, the fowls of heaven and beasts of the field the guests. Such plenty and variety of dishes they should have, as had not been seen at any table before; every guest should be filled.

"With horses and chariots, with mighty men, and with all men of war." In the Hebrew it is, with horse, with chariot, with mighty man, and all man of war, all singulars, put for plurals; here it is declared who are meant by rams, lambs, goats, and bullocks in the 18th verse, horsemen, chariot-men, men of might, yea, all men of war.

"Saith the Lord." Lest it should be thought an incredible thing, the Lord ratifies it, saying, Thus saith the Lord God. Jehovah, who is able to make such preparations for the fowls of heaven and beasts of the earth, hath said it, and will do it.

Obs. 1. That all creatures are at the command of God, and ordered to do this or that, according to his wise providence. "Speak to every feathered fowl, and to every beast of the field." Were not these creatures at the beck of the Lord, and subject to his overruling providence, it had been in vain for Ezekiel to have spoken so unto them. In 1 Kings xvii. 4, God commanded the ravens to feed Elijah, and they did come and bring him meat, morning and evening duly, ver. 6. Psal. l. 11, it is said, God knows "all the fowls of the mountains;" and he calls them to what service he pleases. He called for quails to satisfy the lustings of the Israelites, Numb. xi. 31. God asked Job the question, whether the eagle mounted up at his command? Job xxxix. 27; implying, that though man hath no command over the fowls of heaven, yet himself hath. And so over fishes and beasts; Jonah i. 17; ii. 10, the whale came and went at God's command, and did the service he appointed. Lev. xxvi. 22, "I will send wild beasts amongst you, which shall rob you of your children:" and this he did; 2 Kings ii. 24, the Lord caused two she-bears to come out of the wood and destroy forty-two of their children. God is the Lord of hosts, and can command an army of creatures at his pleasure, to benefit his servants, or to plague their enemies.

Obs. 2. God doth execute some great and signal judgment, when he summons the creatures to eat the flesh and drink the blood of the slain. Ofttimes the bodies of Jews and gentiles have been given for meat unto the fowls and beasts, as Jer. vii. 33; xxxiv. 20; Ezek. xxix. 5; but they have not been summoned and called by open proclamation, as here it is. The prophet must "speak to every feathered fowl, and to every beast of the field, and say, Assemble yourselves, and come, gather yourselves on every side." Such a proclamation you have but twice more in all the Scripture: once in Jer. xii. 9, "Come ye, assemble all the beasts of the field, come to devour;" he speaks of that great destruction of the Jews by Nebuchadnezzar. The other place is Rev. xix. 17, 18, "I saw an angel standing in the sun; and he cried with a loud voice, saying to all the fowls that fly in the midst of heaven, Come and gather yourselves together unto the supper of the great God; that ye may eat the flesh of kings, and the flesh of captains, and the flesh of mighty men, and the flesh of horses, and of them that sit on them, and the flesh of all men, both free and bond, both small and great." This place runs parallel with Ezekiel, and sets out the greatness and signalness of God's judgments upon the enemies of the church. And it is conceived by some to be the very same judgment Ezekiel speaks of, viz. that of Gog and Magog.

Obs. 3. It is matter of delight and pleasure unto God, to destroy the enemies of his church and people. "Come to my sacrifice that I do sacrifice for you." The Jews took great pleasure in sacrificing of creatures unto God, 1 Chron. xxix. 21, 22; and God was well pleased with sacrifices, Gen. viii. 20, 21. Here he calls the destroying of Gog and Magog his sacrifice, his feast, or table; he took as much delight in their slaughter as in any sacrifice, or in any feast. Wicked men are briers and thorns, and God hath as much pleasure in the cutting down the one, as the husbandman hath in cutting down the other. God delights in acts of judgment, as well as in acts of mercy. Isa. xlviii. 14, "He will do his pleasure on Babylon, and his arm shall be on the Chaldeans:" the destruction of Babylonians and Chaldeans God calls, "his pleasure;" the Hebrew is, חפצו his will. It is God's will to destroy all the enemies of Zion; and the doing of it pleases him.

Obs. 4. God is impartial in his judicial dispensations, he punisheth the great delinquents as well as the lesser. Mighty men, princes, those that ride in chariots, rams, great goats, are slaughtered and given to the fowls and beasts, as well as the inferior sort, the men of war, lambs, and bullocks: they were all in the same confederacy, in the same war against the land of Israel; and God winked not at the greatest, nor spared the meanest, but made them all a sacrifice. God is a righteous God, and executes his judgments without respect of persons. Let not great men flatter themselves, they will not be exempted when God comes forth to judgment, though they be princes.

Obs. 5. Great men, and vulgar ones also, may be a prey to the creatures, and lie without burial for a season. Princes, mighty men, and others, after their death, lay upon the mountains of Israel, and had their flesh eaten and blood drunk by fowls and beasts, which was another judgment added to the former; and the greater to the heathen, because they thought their souls did wander up and down upon the earth, unless their bodies had been buried, as Tertullian saith. The Athenians had the burial of the dead in such honour, that if a captain neglected to bury the dead which fell in war, they punished him with death for it. It is a great ignominy to lie unburied. Hence the beast, when the witnesses were killed, would not suffer their bodies to be buried, but let them lie in the streets, that so they might be the more ignominious.

Obs. 6. God provides for the brute and dumb creatures, and that abundantly. "Every feathered fowl, and every beast of the field," shall be filled at my table. God doth not only feed the creatures, but sometimes feasts them. This world is God's family wherein are millions of living creatures, and not one of them is neglected of God. Psal. cxlv. 15, 16, "The eyes of all wait upon thee, and thou givest them their meat in due season;" they have their breakfast, dinner, and supper: and lest we should conceit one hath too much, another too little, it follows, "Thou openest thine hand, and satisfiest the desire of every living thing:" he satisfies the fishes of the sea, the beasts of the earth, and fowls of heaven. How should this teach men to depend upon God, not giving way to distrust, or discontent! Matt. vi. 26, "Behold the fowls of the air," saith Christ, "for they sow not, neither do they reap, nor gather into barns; yet your heavenly Father feedeth them. Are ye not much better than they?" He saith not, the fowls of the house, they are cared for; but, "the fowls of the air," that have none to look after them, unless it be fowlers to take away their lives; neither do they know where to get the next meal when they have gotten one, nor what hole or bush to lodge in at night, yet their heavenly Father provides for and feeds them. Does he take care of such creatures, and will he not take care of you? Yes, certainly he will; and why? ye are better than they; ye are rational, they irrational; ye are his sons, they his servants.

Ver. 21, 22. *And I will set my glory among the heathen, and all the heathen shall see my judgment that I have executed, and my hand that I have laid upon them. So the house of Israel shall know that I am the Lord their God from that day and forward.*

The Lord having declared what destructive judgments he would bring upon Gog and Magog, he comes here to make known the end of his so dealing with them, viz. the manifestation of his glory amongst heathens and his own people.

Ver. 21. "I will set my glory among the heathen." I will give my glory, saith the Hebrew, that is, I will cause it to be evident amongst them. By "glory" understand the glory of his justice and power.

"All the heathen shall see my judgment that I have executed." These words give light to the former. The heathen seeing the dreadful judgments of God upon Gog and his, should acknowledge the justice and power of God.

"And my hand that I have laid upon them." They shall not only have a bare sight, but experimental knowledge; they shall find themselves concerned therein, and feel the hand of God heavy upon them; for the strength, wealth, liberty, and glory of the heathen will be much impaired, if not totally ruined, by the overthrow of Gog.

Ver. 22. "So the house of Israel shall know that I am," &c. They did know the Lord to be their God before; but this signal stroke of God upon their enemies, being a signal mercy unto them, should so engage them unto God, that from that time forward they should afresh and eminently acknowledge God to be their God, and none to be like unto him; that he will not desert them in their straits, but be their deliverer.

Obs. 1. The great end of God's judgments upon sinful men is, his glory. "I will set my glory among the heathen, and all the heathen shall see my judgment," &c. God doth therefore execute judgment, that he may be glorified. When sinful people will not give glory to God for his mercies, he will fetch glory out of them by his judgments. They are the work of his hand, and whatever that be, it is "honourable and glorious," Psal. cxi. 3; not only his works of creation, but those of judicial providence. Upon what nation soever, army, or navy, the Lord shall lay his hand, he will work out his glory thereby; that is the end of all his works and judgments.

Obs. 2. Dreadful judgments upon the wicked, are engaging mercies unto the godly. "So the house of Israel shall know that I am the Lord their God from that day and forward." The hand of God upon Gog and his should so affect their hearts, that they should experimentally know, and say, The Lord is our God, he hath laid low our enemies; he hath freed us from their insultings, threats, oppressions: he is our Deliverer, our Saviour, our Redeemer. Isa. xxv. 9, "It shall be said in that day, Lo, this is our God; we have waited for him, and he will save us: this is the Lord; we have waited for him, we will be glad and rejoice in his salvation." When God executed severe judgments upon the enemies of his people, then were their hearts thus affected, and engaged unto the Lord; then they rejoiced in God their Saviour, and said, "He will save," he hath saved us, and he will save us. When the godly see that great judgments upon their enemies are great mercies unto them, their faith is advanced thereby, and they are persuaded God will never leave them; their hearts are warmed, and they cannot but own and praise him.

Ver. 23, 24. *And the heathen shall know that the house of Israel went into captivity for their iniquity: because they trespassed against me, therefore hid I my face from them, and gave them into the hand of their enemies: so fell they all by the sword. According to their uncleanness and according to their transgressions have I done unto them, and hid my face from them.*

The heathen had base and blasphemous thoughts of God, they imagined he was not able to keep his people out of the hands of Nebuchadnezzar and his gods: to vindicate himself, therefore, the Lord tells them the true cause why they were carried into captivity, namely, for their iniquity. It was not impotency in God, but iniquity in them which caused it.

Ver. 23. "The house of Israel went into captivity for their iniquity." The Hebrew is, the house of Israel were led into captivity in their iniquities. God took them in their iniquities, and carried them away into captivity in them, or for them. The Septuagint says, for their sins, their crooked and perverse doings.

"Because they trespassed against me." The word מעל *maal,* signifies, stubbornly and contemptuously to sin; to oppose him one ought to be subject unto: such transgressors were the Jews; they opposed God.

"Therefore hid I my face from them." To hide the face from them imports, 1. The denying of them his favour, his counsel, his help; and, 2. Declaring his anger and severity by sharp judgments. Psal. lxxx. 3, "Cause thy face to shine, and we shall be saved." God's face was clouded, and hid from his church, so that it had neither favour, counsel, nor help from him, but sad afflictions and judgments; for he was angry with the prayers of his people, he fed them with the bread of tears, and gave them tears to drink in great measure: therein he sorely afflicted them.

"And gave them into the hand of their enemies." This followed upon God's hiding his face: they felt acts of his displeasure; he gave or delivered them up into the hands of their enemies; he caused Nebuchadnezzar to come, besiege Jerusalem, and to take it: and then God gives into the hand of others, when his providence acts and orders things so, that men come under their power.

"So fell they all by the sword." Some were carried into captivity, some fled, some were left in the land after Nebuchadnezzar and his forces returned to Babylon; how then is it said, "they all fell by the sword?" The sense is, they were all brought under by the power of the sword, not all killed that were made subject; and some of all sorts killed.

Ver. 24. "According to their uncleanness and according to their transgressions have I done unto them." Here God anticipates what Jews and gentiles might object, viz. that he dealt very harshly, yea, cruelly with them, in breaking them to pieces, in unchurching and unstating of them; but he tells them, what he did was "according to their uncleanness and their transgressions," he did nothing but what they had deserved.

Obs. 1. God doth withhold mercies from his people, and lay sad judgments upon them, for their sins. "The house of Israel went into captivity for their iniquities." Because they trespassed against God, therefore did he hide his face from them, give them into the hand of their enemies; they fell by the sword, and were brought into subjection. If God's own people sin, they shall smart for it; he will not countenance them, hear their prayers, give them counsel, nor put forth his hand to help them. Isa. lix. 1, 2, "Behold, the Lord's hand is not shortened, that it cannot save; neither his ear heavy, that it cannot hear: but your iniquities have separated between you and your God, and your sins have hid his face from you, that he will not hear." Sin is of that nature, that it turns away God's face from his own people, that it stops his ear against their prayers, and shrinks up his arm, so that there is no help for them; and not only doth it keep good things from them, Jer. v. 25, but draw evils upon them, Neh. xiii. 18. It was Israel's sins brought judgment upon them and their city.

Obs. 2. God will convince his enemies of the true cause of his executing dreadful judgments upon his people. "The heathen shall know that the house of Israel went into captivity for their iniquity." They thought there were other grounds for it; that God could not preserve them against such a potent adversary as Nebuchadnezzar was; that his power and wisdom was not such, as was in their gods: but the Lord made them know these were not the grounds why the house of Israel suffered such grievous things, but that it was their iniquities, transgressions, and uncleannesses which brought judgments upon them. When heathens saw what was done to Jerusalem, and being unsatisfied, asked the question, "Wherefore hath the Lord done thus unto this great city?" What! is he unfaithful to his people? Could he preserve it no longer? Are our gods stronger than the God of Israel? No, no; these things are not the cause. Tell them, saith he, what is the true cause; it is, "Because they have forsaken the covenant of the Lord their God, and worshipped other gods, and served them," Jer. xxii. 1, 9.

Obs. 3. None have just ground of complaint, whatsoever judgments are upon them, howsoever God deal by them. "According to their uncleanness and according to their transgressions have I done unto them:" their sins have been great, and I have executed great judgments upon them; they filled up the ephah with wickedness, and I filled up the vial with wrath; they drove me out of my sanctuary, and I drove them out of my land; they turned their hearts from me, and I hid my face from them. God's judgments are righteous; he wrongs no man, no nation; men have cause to complain of their sins, not his judgments: see Lam. iii. 39; Psal. cxlv. 17.

Ver. 25—29. *Therefore thus saith the Lord God; Now will I bring again the captivity of Jacob, and have mercy upon the whole house of Israel, and will be jealous for my holy name; after that they have borne their shame, and all their trespasses whereby they have trespassed against me, when they dwelt safely in their land, and none made them afraid. When I have brought them again from the people, and gathered them out of their enemies' lands, and am sanctified in them in the sight of many nations; then shall they know that I am the Lord their God, which caused them to be led into captivity among the heathen: but I have gathered them unto their own land, and have left none of them any more there. Neither will I hide my face any more from them: for I have poured out my Spirit upon the house of Israel, saith the Lord God.*

The gracious goodness of God towards his people appears in these verses; where we have,

I. The reduction and gathering of them into their own land, ver. 25, 27, 28.

II. The causes moving God to do so; which are, his mercy, and his jealousy, ver. 25.

III. The time when they shall be reduced, ver. 26.

IV. The events following the same; which are,

1. Acknowledgment of God to be their God, ver. 28.
2. The light of God's countenance, ver. 29.
3. Pouring out of the Spirit.

Ver. 25. "Now will I bring again the captivity of Jacob." If we refer these words to the captive Jews in Babylon, the time was drawing nigh of their deliverance, and therefore the Lord saith, "Now will I bring again the captivity of Jacob," that is, the posterity of Jacob being in captivity: but, if we refer these words to what went before in the chapter, the sense is, Gog and Magog being destroyed, and their funeral over, "now will I bring again the captivity of Jacob," the dispersed Jews, or believers, who were the seed of Jacob. A spiritual reduction is here understood by some.

"And have mercy upon the whole house of Israel." Then God will have mercy, not on two tribes, but all the tribes, on "the whole house of Israel;" hitherto it hath not been, but it shall be. God will forgive the sins of the Jews in general, and bring them out of their forlorn condition to glorious enjoyments and liberty. This word רחמתי is from רחם which signifies, to embrace one with a most inward affection of bowels, mercy, or compassion. God would be as merciful to them as a mother to the fruit of her womb.

"And will be jealous for my holy name." In the Hebrew it is, I will be jealous, or zealous, for the name of my holiness, I will not suffer my name to be polluted, as it is ver. 7. The mercies I have promised shall be performed, whatever obstacle is in the way, my holy name is engaged for it, and the jealousy I have for my name will provoke me to do the same. Jealousy is such an ardent affection as will break through all that would retard or frustrate an undertaking. It is given to God after the manner of men, and nothing shall let him from accomplishing what he hath promised.

Ver. 26. "After that they have borne their shame." The Jews being a people distinguished from other nations by their laws and worship, should have so lived, as never to have given God occasion to have cast them off; but they sinning above the nations, were scattered of God into several parts of the world, and there they were reproached by the heathens for their God, their worship, and their laws, and so did bear shame. Or thus, shame may be put for the punishment of their shame, viz. their sin, that was their shame; and sad judgments did they bear for the same, which was also their shame.

"And all their trespasses whereby they have trespassed against me." "Trespasses" here notes punishment; they trespassed against God in Canaan, and he punished them for those trespasses in Babylon, and other places. After they had borne their shame and punishment the appointed time, God would visit them in mercy, bring them back to Zion, and do great things for them.

"When they dwelt safely in their land, and none made them afraid." They had much peace, were secure, feared no enemies nor judgments, and thereupon sinned freely, and multiplied transgressions without number. The word for making afraid is, *charad*, which signifies to be moved in body or mind. Fear doth distemper both; but the Jews had none to disaffect either, by frighting of them.

Ver. 27. "When I am sanctified in them in the sight of many nations." In chap. xxxviii. 23, God saith, he will sanctify himself, that is, declare himself to be a holy God; and here the word is passive, "When I am sanctified," that is, when I am openly acknowledged to be just in punishing of them, and merciful in delivering of them. Piscator carries the words actively thus, I will demonstrate my holiness and majesty, both by afflicting and by freeing of them.

Ver. 28. "Then shall they know that I am the Lord their God, which caused them to be led into captivity among," &c. After their suffering grievous and long afflictions, and receiving choice mercies, they shall know and confess that it was the hand of God which led them into captivity, and not the hand of man; before, their eyes were upon men, Nebuchadnezzar and his forces, they looked not at God; but when they should be thoroughly purged in the furnace of affliction, and be brought out thence to partake of special mercies, then they should see, know, and acknowledge that God did all, that it was his hand did it; that Nebuchadnezzar could not have done aught against them, nor Cyrus aught for them, without his commission. So, when the Jews shall be gathered out of all parts they are now in, they shall know it to be the hand of God. The Hebrew for "which caused them to be led into captivity among the heathen," is, in my transferring them, or causing them to be transferred to the heathen.

"And have left none of them any more there." At the first gathering of the Jews out of Babylon, many were left there; Ezra i. 5, not all the fathers of Judah and Benjamin, but the chief of the fathers, and such whose spirits God had stirred, came thence; not the rest. But here is mention of such a gathering, as that none shall be left. None of those predestinated, saith Maldonate. Not any one willing to return into the country, saith Mariana. But these senses do not come up fully to the words, which are, I will not leave of them any more; formerly, many have been left, but there shall be such a gathering as none shall be left: whole tribes were then left in captivity.

Ver. 29. "Neither will I hide my face any more from them." God hid his face seventy years from them in Babylon; and, since their crucifying of Christ, he hath hid it from them sixteen hundred years. But he hath a time to let them see his face again, and never more to hide it from them; they shall have his favour, his counsel, his help, and protection. They shall not be under severe judgments, but enjoy sweet mercies.

"For I have poured out my spirit upon the house of Israel." Junius hath the words, When I shall pour out my spirit upon them. In the Hebrew it is a preter tense for a future, which is usual therein, to show the certainty of the thing. The Septuagint saith, Because I have poured out my wrath upon them. Their sense is, Seeing I have uttered and accomplished all my displeasure against them, they shall henceforth have my face and favour. The word for "my spirit" is, רוחי the same with that in chap. xxxvi. 27, which the Septuagint renders there, my spirit; and it is so to be taken here. God makes the house of Israel a great promise, he will pour out his Spirit upon the same. It shall have all spiritual blessings in abundance, and the continuation of them.

Obs. 1. The afflictions of God's people may be long and sharp, yet they shall not be always, they shall have an end. There is a time when they shall cease; "Now will I bring again the captivity of Jacob." God brings his people into captivity, and out again in due time. Some vessels must be longer in the fire than others, their dross and rust is so incorporated into them, that they must not only be made hot but melted; and, when they are melted, then they are taken out of the furnace and new moulded. The Jews were long in the wilderness, but at length they were brought into the land of the Amorites, Josh. xxiv. 7, 8. The gentiles must tread down the holy city forty-two months, or twelve hundred and sixty days, and then it shall be freed, Rev. xi. 2, 3. God may be wroth with the sheep of his pasture, his wrath may be hot, may be long, but it shall not be for ever, Psal. ciii. 9. Let us be patient under long afflictions, and wait for deliverance; it is drawing nigh daily, and the set time will come ere long, Heb. x. 37.

Obs. 2. There is a day of mercy to come for the Jews, even all of them. "I will have mercy upon the whole house of Israel;" not one tribe, two, or ten, but "upon the whole house of Israel;" I will pardon their sins, gather them out of the nations, and make them a glorious people. This promise was but in part fulfilled, when Judah, Benjamin, and some of Levi, returned out of Babylon; the complete fulfilling of it remains yet. The Jews do expect the making of it good to this day, saying, they are in a most shameful and distressing captivity; and look for such a gathering as none shall be left. Doubtless there is a time when God will smile upon the Jews, show them mercy, and bring them unto Christ, and make him salvation unto them, Hos. i. 10, 11; Rom. xi. 15—27; Zech. x. 6, 7.

Obs. 3. The great things God doth for his people, are not done for their worth, or merits, but for his holy name's sake. The bringing Jacob out of captivity, and having mercy upon the whole house of Israel, is upon that account; I will be zealous, or jealous for my holy name. God doth all for his name's sake. Ezek. xxxvi. 32, "Not for your sakes do I this, saith the Lord God, be it known unto you:" lest they should think there was something in them deserved at God's hands, and moved him to do for them, he openly declares against it; "Be it known unto you," and to all the world, that it is not for your sakes, for any excellency or good I see in you; but it is for mine own sake, for the honour of mine own holy name, which is so dear and precious unto me, that I am jealous of any thing that tends towards the disparagement of it, and zealous to do whatever I have promised, and may promote the glory thereof. Isa. ix. 7, "The zeal of the Lord of hosts will perform this;" קנאת the zeal, or jealousy, of the Lord will do it: he had made many great promises before, of Christ and his government for ever; and if any thing should rise up to hinder the same, the Lord of hosts would be zealous to see it performed, otherwise his holy name would suffer. God's name is the great motive to him to do for his. This Jeremiah knew full well, and therefore presseth God to do for them upon that account; chap. xiv. 7, "O Lord, though our iniquities testify against us, do thou it for thy name's sake:" there was a great famine, and they deserved not a drop of rain, or bit of bread; but God's name was a strong argument to provoke him to do for them.

Obs. 4. Sin brings men to shame and punishment, which they must undergo one where or other. "After they have borne their shame and trespasses." They sinned in Canaan, and were ashamed and punished in Babylon, and other places. It is only sin which makes men blush and smart.

Obs. 5. In times of peace and safety, usually men forget God, and sin against him. When the Jews dwelt safely, and none made them afraid, then they trespassed against God. At such times, men are scornful and proud, Psal. cxxiii. 4; they trust in mountains, Amos vi. 1; they live sensually, ver. 4—6; they increase the afflictions of the afflicted, Zech. i. 15. When men are in peace, and without danger, they have opportunities for hearing of God's word by his servants; but, Jer. xxii. 21, saith God, "I spake unto thee in thy prosperity; but thou saidst, I will not hear." Jerusalem and her children had deaf ears, and obstinate hearts, in their prosperity. Solomon, who "had peace on all sides round about him," 1 Kings iv. 24, forgat the Lord, married strange wives, and did strange things for them; he built high places for their idol gods, and went himself after other gods, 1 Kings xi. 1, 5, 7, 10. Great is the danger of prosperity, yet all desire it. That caution which God gave his people, when they were to come into Canaan, where they should have peace and plenty, is needful for all in a prosperous condition, Deut. vi. 12, "Beware, lest thou forget the Lord:" men are very apt then to forget him.

Obs. 6. The Lord by open delivering of his people from an afflicted condition, doth sanctify his own, name, and hath it sanctified by others. His gathering them out of enemies' hands, declared his power, his faithfulness, his mercy; and thereby he sanctified his own name; and these attributes being acknowledged by those that are delivered, and by the nations from whom they are delivered, his name is sanctified. God's people are oft under great and long afflictions, and whenever he sets them at liberty, he sanctifies his name, and his name is sanctified; he declares himself, and is declared by others, to be a gracious God. When the Jews were brought out of Babylon, they said, "The Lord hath done great things for us;" and the Babylonians said, "The Lord hath done great things for them," Psal. cxxvi. 2, 3. Thus did God sanctify, and men sanctify; the one, by declaring his omnipotency, faithfulness, and goodness; the other, by acknowledging the same.

Obs. 7. There is a time when the Jews shall not only have mercy, but abundant and lasting mercy. God will gather them, pour out his Spirit upon them, and never hide his face from them any more. This time will be a happy and glorious time. For the house of Israel to be enriched with the gifts and graces of God's Spirit, which are excellent, and to have the light of God's countenance shining upon them, and that always, what can be more desirable? This condition, as Paul saith, will be "life from the dead," Rom. xi. 15. Now they are like dead trees, without any sap in them; but then they will be like trees well-rooted, full of sap, and in their greatest glory; full of branches, leaves, blossoms, fruit, and the sun shining upon them.

CHAPTER XL.

That there be δυσνόητα, things hard to be understood, in the sacred Scriptures, these nine last chapters, as well as the beginning of Ezekiel, do abundantly testify: and such difficult things are in these last, that they have made many men of the greatest parts to tremble at the thought of interpreting them. The rabbins say, that the first of Ezekiel, and these last chapters, are inexplicable secrets, and understood by none; and therefore forbid their disciples to read them, adding, When Elias shall come, he will explain all things. Jerom, that great light in his time, professes his trepidation hereat, that he did knock at a closed door. Gregory the great, when he went about this work, said, We pursue a midnight journey. Maldonate affirms, that this last prophecy of Ezekiel is so difficult and dark that it appears scarcely possible to be understood. Œcolampadius tells us, that in chap. xlii. there is the grand difficulty, which ancient expositors understood not; and he brings in rabbi Solomon, who wrote upon the whole Talmud, saying, that he thinks there is not any thing extant which aids the understanding of it; and professes, that neither by his own study, aid of ministers, or by his own reading, he attained any help in understanding the meaning of this building, but only what he had from Heaven: and of himself he saith, chap. xlv., In this passage, above all others, I feel the weakness of my own understanding, yet silently I adore its mysteries. It is good to tremble at the word of God, both what we understand, and what we understand not, for all is of equal authority; and to him that trembles thereat, the Lord looketh, and will let in light. The vision is dark, but God dwells in darkness; the temple and city are dark, but Jehovah-Shammah, "the Lord is there," whom we most humbly desire to let out some beams of light, whereby we may come to understand something of the incredible sweetness of these dark and deep things.

In Prooemio ad Eustochium.

Prooem. in 2. l. super Ezek. præfat. ad c. 40.

It is not to be expected that I should proceed here, as in the former chapters, by speaking to every verse. Some I shall pass over, and say with Jerom, I know my own ignorance.

Œcol. in c. 42.

Some would have this temple, represented to Ezekiel, to be that built by Zerubbabel and the Jews, after the captivity; but there is much to be said to prove it not to be so.

1. That temple was built in Jerusalem, in the place where Solomon's temple stood; but this temple Ezekiel saw, was to be without the city, as interpreters observe from the 45th and 48th chapters.

2. That temple was for the two tribes of Judah and Benjamin. This of Ezekiel is for the whole body of the Jews, all the tribes are mentioned, chap. xlvii. xlviii.; and strangers had inheritance here amongst the Israelites, chap. xlvii. 22; which was not so in Moses', Solomon's, or Zerubbabel's time.

3. In Zerubbabel's temple there was no such river, nor trees yielding new fruit every month, as is spoken of Ezekiel's, chap. xlvii. 12.

4. God promised, chap. xliii. 7, to dwell among the Israelites of this temple for ever, which cannot be verified of Zerubbabel's temple and city; for the Lord forsook both, and delivered them up to the Romans, who destroyed them.

5. The temple our prophet speaks of, was not to be defiled, nor the holy name of God, by the house of Israel, which should then be, chap. xliii. 7, 8. But Zerubbabel's temple was defiled, as you may read in the Maccabees; and the Jews who returned from Babylon defiled the name of God by their iniquities, as appears, Neh. xiii.

6. The twenty-five thousand reeds, being the length of the holy portion offered to the Lord, and the breadth ten thousand reeds, Ezek. xlv. 1, cannot be understood of any city or temple which the Jews should build after their captivity; for the twenty-five thousand reeds make forty-five miles in length, say some; fifty and upwards, say others; and the ten thousand, sixteen or eighteen miles in breadth: never was any such city built.

There are many other things differing from what was in Moses', Joshua's, and Solomon's days. The measures differ much from those of the tabernacle and temple. The land was not divided in Joshua's time, as here it is to the tribes. The priests and Levites had no portion of land, as here they have. There was no such portion or oblation for the prince. Their sacrifices and oblations are not after the same manner. The altar, chap. xli. 22, differs from the altar of incense, Exod. xxx. 2. The cleansing of the sanctuary, and putting the blood of the young bullock upon the posts and corners of the settle of the altar, chap. xlv. 18, 19, is a new ordinance, not to be found in Moses' law. In Ezekiel's division of the land were no cities of refuge appointed, there would be no need of them, Ezek. xliv. 25.

This vision, therefore, points out the introduction of a better hope, viz. the church of Christ under the gospel. A Lapide tells us, that many rabbins and Jews refer this temple and city to the Messiah, expecting that he should build them; and, because this third temple and new city are not yet built, they think the Messiah is not yet come. This argument was objected by the Jews to Galatinus, who answers it in his 5th book, chap. 10, and concludes thus, The Jerusalem and temple con-

Quod Messias nondum venerit quia tertium templum nondum est ædificatum.

In Apocal. 12. Sect. 33. cerning which Ezekiel speaks, are to be understood mystically. Of that mind is Viega.

It is conceived, therefore, that in this vision is represented the restitution of the Jewish church, their temple, city, and worship, after the captivity, not simply, but as they were types of the church under the gospel; for, as we must not exclude these, so we must know, this is not the principal thing intended. That which the vision doth chiefly hold out unto us is, the building of the christian temple, with the worship thereof, under Jewish expressions, which began to be accomplished in the apostles' days, Acts xv. 16. And that the spiritual temple, consisting of believing Jews and gentiles, is chiefly intended, we may see from that correspondency between Ezekiel and John in his Gospel and Revelation. There are many parallel places in them; as,

Ezek. xxxvii. 22,	compared with	John x. 16.
— xxxvii. 27,	——	Rev. xxi. 3.
— xxxviii. 2, } — xxxix. 1, }	——	— xx. 8.
— xl. 2,	——	— xxi. 10.
— xl. 35,	——	— xi. 1; xxi. 15.
— xliii. 2,	——	— i. 15; xiv. 2.
— xlvii. 1, 2, 12,	——	— xxii. 1, 2.
— xlviii. 1—7,	——	— vii. 4—8.
— xlviii. 31—34,	——	— xxi. 12, 13, 16.

There is one thing more also intended, viz. the restoring of the christian church after its apostasy and suffering in spiritual Babylon under antichrist. Many are the breaches, rents, and ruins of the christian church to this day; and we may see the tabernacle of Christ is fallen. But it is expected that he "whose appearance was like the appearance of brass, with a measuring line in his hand," Ezek. xl. 3, should come and raise it up, and build the ruins thereof, bringing in the fulness of Jew and gentile, that so the state of the church may answer those prophecies made of it, Isa. lx. 17, 18; Ezek. xlv. 8. There shall be no violence, no oppression by princes, or others. Hitherto there hath been little else but oppression in all lands; and the new heaven, and new earth, wherein dwells righteousness, have not yet been created, but are to be expected as things intended in this vision.

Ver. 1—4. *In the five and twentieth year of our captivity, in the beginning of the year, in the tenth day of the month, in the fourteenth year after that the city was smitten, in the selfsame day the hand of the Lord was upon me, and brought me thither. In the visions of God brought he me into the land of Israel, and set me upon a very high mountain, by which was as the frame of a city on the south. And he brought me thither, and, behold, there was a man, whose appearance was like the appearance of brass, with a line of flax in his hand, and a measuring reed; and he stood in the gate. And the man said unto me, Son of man, behold with thine eyes, and hear with thine ears, and set thine heart upon all that I shall shew thee; for to the intent that I might shew them unto thee art thou brought hither: declare all that thou seest to the house of Israel.*

We are come now to the last part of Ezekiel's prophecy, which is a typical prophecy concerning Christ and his church, set forth under the vision of the new temple, city, and kingdom, comprehended in these nine last chapters. In which we have,

I. The building of the new temple, with the several appurtenances thereof, in chapters xl. xli. xlii.

II. The ministry, worship, and ordinances of this new temple, in chapters xliii. xliv.

III. The restitution or reformation of the whole land, the commonwealth, kingdom, and city, with several ordinances for the prince and people, in chapters xlv. xlvi. xlvii. xlviii.

In describing of these, the prophet useth, saith Huffenrefferus, words and phrases suitable to the state of the Jews; he describes, as it were, the temple, worship, and land of the Jews; whereas he aims at no such thing, but intends the spiritual kingdom of Christ and the gospel.

The scope of this vision was to comfort the afflicted Jews, who, being in captivity, lamented the desolation of the temple, city, and commonwealth of Israel. To the prophet, therefore, the Lord shows in a vision the restoration of them again; and not only so, but greater things are held out and promised under them, as the greatness and glory of the church under Christ in time of the gospel, of which John speaks, Rev. xxi. 22. It is not an earthly city, temple, Jerusalem, we are to look at here; but a spiritual city, temple, Jerusalem, viz. the church of Christ, whose name is Jehovah-Shammah.

In this chapter you have,

1. A preface, or introduction to the vision.
2. A narrative of the wall, several courts, gates, the porch, of this new temple, and the measures of them.

In the preface are five things: the time, the manner, the place, the Author, and end of the vision.

Ver. 1. "In the five and twentieth year of our captivity, in the beginning of the year, in the tenth day of the month." Here the time is pointed out when this vision was presented to Ezekiel, which was in the twenty-fifth year of his captivity; so long it was since he, with Jehoiakim, was carried into Babylon, and kept there. His first vision was in the fifth year of his captivity, Ezek. i. 2; and this his last vision was twenty years after, in the beginning of the year, the tenth day of the month; which some make to be in the autumn, others in the spring.

"The fourteenth year after the city was smitten." After Jehoiakim had been eleven years in captivity, the city was smitten and utterly laid waste, which was in the eleventh year of Zedekiah, 2 Kings xxv. 2; Jer. xxxix. 2; lii. 5. From this period, or epocha, is the vision reckoned; fourteen years after the desolation of the city, Ezekiel had it. Some would prove this year to be the year of jubilee, because it was the fiftieth from the eighteenth of Josiah's reign, when the book of the law was found; but that year appears not to be a jubilean year. Mestlinus makes the year of jubilee to be in the tenth of Zedekiah's reign; and if so, this year of the prophet's vision was but sixteen years after the year of jubilee, and thirty-four years before the next jubilee.

"In the selfsame day." The Hebrew is, בעצם היום in the bone, or essence, of the day, in the body of the day, or in the strength of the day, when the heat and light were greatest. The same words are in Gen. vii. 13, where the words are rendered, "the selfsame day," being a Hebrew form of speech.

"The hand of the Lord was upon me," &c. The Chaldee saith, A prophetical Spirit from the face of the Lord resided upon me; others, The strength, or divine virtue of the Lord was upon me. These words we had in chap. i. 3, where they were opened. Here the manner of the vision is set forth; it was by the Spirit of God upon the prophet, enlightening and informing his mind.

"And brought me thither." I was brought in mind, not in body, by the Spirit, thither, that is, to the city that had been smitten, but now seemed to be rebuilt: and so it follows,

Ver. 2. "In the visions of God brought he me into the land of Israel." In those great, glorious, and wonderful visions of God, wrought in the prophet by the Spirit of God, he apprehended that he was in the land of Israel, beholding not only with the eyes of his mind the things presented unto him, but also with the eyes of his body.

"And set me upon a very high mountain." The place where the prophet had this vision was in the land of Israel, and upon mount Zion, or mount Moriah, where the temple was built. Moriah is from ראה to see; this mount is the mount of vision, and on it had Ezekiel this glorious vision. Kimchi saith, This mountain is the mountain of the temple, and this city is Jerusalem on the south, *Lightfoot on the Temple*, chap. iv. ver. 13. The rabbins conceive the land of Israel to be the highest of all lands, and mount Zion, or Moriah, the highest of all the mountains in that land. It was a type of the church of Christ, Heb. xii. 22; and therefore it is represented here to be a very high mountain; and so it was unto John also, Rev. xxi. 10, which words allude to these of Ezekiel. The Hebrew for "set me," is, caused me to rest; when the prophet was brought to this mountain, he had rest: there is no true rest but in the church, in the mount of vision.

"By which was as the frame of a city on the south." The mount itself was south from Babylon, and the city was on the south side of the mount, which was smitten there. Now the prophet sees in vision, as it were, the model or frame of a city; he had seen before the ruin of the city, and now he sees the raising of it.

Ver. 3. "And he brought me thither." That is, the Spirit of God carried him in vision to that mountain, where he saw an idea of a city.

"And, behold, there was a man, whose appearance was like the appearance of brass." Here the author of the vision is specified and described from his appearance, the instruments he had, and the place where he stood. This "man" is made by some an angel, by others, Christ. It was the Son of God appeared in the first vision unto Ezekiel, and so he doth in this last: he was a Master-builder, and appointed of God to build the house: Zech. vi. 12, 13, "Thus speaketh the Lord of hosts, saying, Behold the man whose name is The Branch," that is, Christ, "he shall grow up out of his place, and he shall build the temple of the Lord: even he shall build the temple of the Lord; and he shall bear the glory." And that this man was Christ his appearance declares, for it "was like the appearance of brass;" and so Christ, Rev. i. 15, is said to appear, "his feet were like unto fine brass;" and here his countenance, or whole body, appeared like unto brass, that is, free from spot, beautiful, bright, and shining. Christ was without blemish, or spot, 1 Pet. i. 19; he was holy, harmless, undefiled, Heb. vii. 26; he was "fairer than the children of men," Psal. xlv. 2.

"With a line of flax in his hand, and a measuring reed." These are the instruments which this man had, "a line and a measuring reed." Such instruments are proper to architects and master-builders; and being in the hand of Christ, do demonstrate him to be the chief Builder of the church. The "line of flax" was to measure the great spaces of the ground, viz. the floors, court, and compass of the buildings and walls. The "reed" was to measure the buildings, the thickness, length, and breadth of them. Of such a line and reed is spoken in Zech. ii. 1, 2; Rev. xi. 1; xxi. 15. A reed is smooth, round, and light, and therefore fit for measuring: they were plentiful in those parts.

"And he stood in the gate." The Hebrew is, he standing in the gate; his posture was standing, his place was "in the gate." He stood there to direct the prophet, to show him the measures of the temple, and other things; to manifest he hath command of the temple, and may keep out, and let in, whom he pleased.

Ver. 4. "And the man said unto me, Son of man, behold with thine eyes," &c. In this verse the end of the vision is held forth, which is, that Ezekiel, thoroughly understanding the things comprehended in it, might communicate them to others. Here the Lord Christ is called "man," for that in time he was to be incarnate; and the Son of man speaks to Ezekiel, and commands him two things:

1. To give the most diligent and best attention as possibly might be, and therefore calls for not only the eyes and ears, but the heart also; "Behold with thine eyes, and hear with thine ears, and set thine heart upon all that I shall show thee:" his heart must go with his senses, and seriously ponder what was presented. Some things were to be seen, some things were to be heard, and all to be considered: and why? he was brought thither for that end.

2. To make known what he should see, hear, and observe; "Declare them to the house of Israel." He must not keep things to himself, but publish them to others, to the church and people of Israel.

Obs. 1. The Lord keeps an exact account of the time of his church and people's sufferings. He is the best and most punctual chronologer of all in heaven and earth. Men and angels may mistake, misreckon, but the Lord doth not, cannot. "In the twenty-fifth year of our captivity, in the beginning of the year, in the tenth day of the month, in the fourteenth year after the city was smitten, in the selfsame day;" here the years, the months, and days of the Jews' captivity was observed of the Lord. When we are in misery, and suffering conditions, we think God forgets us, Psal. lxxix. 5; lxxxix. 46; but he takes notice of every hour, day, month, and year.

Obs. 2. When the church is low, in the worst, most desperate, and deplorable condition, even then the Lord hath a care of his church. Now the temple, city, and land of Canaan were utterly laid waste, the people many of them destroyed, the rest in Babylon without hope of ever seeing their own country, chap. xxxvii. 11. In this condition the Lord appears to Ezekiel, and gives him a most singular and excellent vision concerning the restoration of the church, the extent, dignity, and glory of it, whereby he showed both the prophet and the people, whose hearts were filled with sorrow. When the church is in the wilderness, under persecution, in Egypt, or Babylon, the Lord is solicitous for it: Zech. i. 14, "I am jealous for Jerusalem and for Zion, with a great jealousy."

Obs. 3. The church is mount Zion, or mount Zion is the church, wherein God makes known his mind for the comfort of his people. Ezekiel was carried in Spirit into the land of Israel, and set there upon a very high mountain, viz. mount Zion, which typed out the church of God: and there he had this glorious vision, there sweet consolation was given forth for the afflicted. The church is sometimes called a garden, and fountain sealed, as Cant. iv. 12; sometimes a vineyard, Matt. xx. 1; sometimes a house, 1 Tim. iii. 15; sometimes a city, Psal. xlvi. 4; Isa. lx. 14; sometimes a mountain, Psal. ii. 6. And it is so called for the height, the glory, and the strength of it. Mountains are high, conspicuous, and strong, and so is the church; on mountains is good air, so likewise is in the church; hills are nearer heaven than other places; they are below, the church is above the world.

Obs. 4. The church is well seated and well ordered. "Upon which was as the frame of a city." It is seated upon a mountain, the mountain of God's decree, power, and truth; it is well ordered, for it is as the frame of a city, where every thing is in its right place, and all fitly joined together: Psal. cxxii. 3, "Jerusalem is builded as a city that is compact together;" and the church is a body fitly joined together, and compacted, Eph. iv. 16. Hence strength and beauty are to the church, it being so seated and so united. The one made Christ say, "The gates of hell shall not prevail against it," Matt. xvi.; and the other made Solomon to say, "It was beautiful as Tirzah, and comely as Jerusalem," Cant. vi. 4.

Obs. 5. The Man Christ, who is sinless and glorious, is the chief Builder and exact Measurer of the church, and things belonging to it. "Behold, a man, whose appearance was like the appearance of brass, with a line of flax in his hand, and a measuring reed." Christ, without spot, full of glory and wisdom, is the Master-builder: Matt. xvi. 18; xxi. 33; Heb. iii. 3, prophets, apostles, ministers, are his servants, under-officers, instructed, directed, and rewarded by him: he is the Master-builder, the line and reed are in his hand, he measures all the trees and stones used in this building, the outward and inward courts, with all their appurtenances. He was the son of Joseph, a carpenter, and some mystery might lie in that.

Obs. 6. The way into Zion, and unto the Father, is by Christ: he stands in the gate of the temple, ready to receive any that should come and be found fit for entrance: he had his line and reed in his hand to measure them. None unmeasured might enter. Hence it is that Christ saith, John xiv. 6, "I am the way, and no man cometh to the Father, but by me:" and, John x. 9, "I am the door: by me if any man enter in, he shall be saved, and shall go in and out, and find pasture." Christ is the Lord of the fold and field; by him they enter in, by him they are led out to the good pastures, and led in again: he will not suffer any thing that defileth to enter into the fold, the temple, the new Jerusalem, Rev. xxi. 27.

Obs. 7. The Lord Christ, when divine things are presented unto us, would have us attent, intent, and apply the whole heart unto them. Such things as are of weight, slightness and trifling about them are intolerable; therefore it is said here, "Son of man, behold with thine eyes, and hear with thine ears," let thy senses be wholly taken up with these things, "and set thine heart upon all that I shall show thee;" thine heart also must be fixed upon every thing shown thee, thou must let nothing pass without due observation. As Ezekiel was to do thus about the things of his vision, so should all ministers and christians about the things of the gospel, which are revelations of the mind of God by Christ. It is oft said therein, "Who hath ears to hear, let him hear," Matt. xiii. 9, 43; Mark vii. 16; Luke xiv. 35, and in other places, intimating, that if men have either inward or outward ears, they should hearken to the things of God. They are divine, and may infinitely advantage or infinitely prejudice us, if they be not well heeded; if we be not attent unto them, intent upon them, and heartily closing with them, better we had never had them: "it will be easier for Sodom and Gomorrha at the day of judgment, than for such." Let us mind, therefore, and mind to purpose, all things shown us of Christ; let us set our senses and whole hearts upon them.

Obs. 8. What the Lord Christ reveals unto his servants the prophets and ministers, they must not reserve to themselves, but communicate to others for their instruction, edification, and comfort. "Declare all that thou seest to the house of Israel." He must not see, hear, observe for himself, but for "the house of Israel," for the church and people of God. Matt. x. 27, saith Christ to his disciples, "What I tell you in darkness, that speak ye in light: and what ye hear in the ear, that preach ye upon the housetops:" whatever I have imparted unto you that do ye impart unto others, take the best advantages ye can to make the same known. The servants of God and Christ must not only utter what they receive, but utter all they receive: Acts xx. 27, Paul kept back nothing that was profitable for them, but "declared to them all the counsel of God."

Ver. 5. *And behold a wall on the outside of the house round about, and in the man's hand a measuring reed of six cubits long by the cubit and an hand breadth: so he measured the breadth of the building, one reed; and the height, one reed.*

Great houses and cities have walls, 1 Kings iii. 1; vi. 5; so this house had a wall round about it. By this wall we may understand the wall of God's protection, which is round about the church. This wall was in height and thickness alike, six cubits high and six cubits thick; it was strong, securing the house Ezekiel saw. God, who is stronger than all, is the defence of the church, Psal. cxxv. 2. Babylon's wall, which was one hundred cubits high, and thirty feet broad, sufficed not to preserve her from ruins; that wall was battered and levelled with the ground; but Jehovah, the Lord of hosts, is the wall about this building, and such a wall as all the powers of the world and hell cannot shake or batter: Zech. ix. 8, "I will encamp about mine house;" and, chap. ii. 5, "I will be unto Jerusalem a wall of fire round about, saith the Lord." The church of God, having such a wall, is secure and invincible.

The church is called a house, not a tabernacle, because of God's inhabitation of it, and his fixed abiding there: Psal. cxxxii. 13, 14, "The Lord hath chosen Zion; he hath desired it for his habitation. This is my rest for ever: here will I dwell; for I have desired it." Zion notes the church in all ages; there is God's house, there is the desire of his soul, there he rests, he hath no rest in all the world but in Zion.

The measuring reed in the hand of the man is the same with the reed in John's hand, Rev. xi. 1. Those that exercise architecture use lines and reeds to measure things therewith, and so doth Christ here. The line and reed in his hand, is the word, or everlasting gospel, which, Rev. xxi. 15, is called "a golden reed," right, strong, and flexible; with this he measures the church, and all things belonging unto it. By the word he sets out the nature, greatness, power, privileges, and characters of the church; by this he measures out the qualifications, liberty, and power of members and officers therein. Hence the word is called a rule, or canon, Phil. iii. 16.

The Hebrew is, a reed of measure of six cubits in a cubit, and of an hand breadth. Whether these words, "an hand breadth," should be joined to the six cubits taken jointly, or to each cubit distinct by itself, is doubtful: that in chap. xliii. 13, seems to make the hand's breadth to be added to each cubit, for it saith, a "cubit is a cubit and an hand breadth." This we may understand of the legal or sanctuary cubit, not the common one, which was less by a hand's breadth than the other, this being five, the other six hands' breadth. Hence some deny that the hand's breadth must be added to each cubit, for then there will be seven cubits, those six hands' breadth making another cubit. They will have the reed six cubits long, and a hand's breadth over, the sixth part of a cubit more. A cubit is that length between the elbow and top of the middle finger; now this space being longer in some men, and shorter in others, no certainty can be determined, especially, when men differ in their heads more than in their arms; for some make a cubit to be five hand's breadth, some six, some a yard, and some an ell, or ells, some a foot and half.

The line and reed are in Christ's hand, the virtue and benefit of them is from him. This line and reed being the word, hath its efficacy from Christ; out of his hand it is unefficacious, unbeneficial; but being in his hand, his power and Spirit going with it, it measures out and fits materials for this spiritual building. The book written within, and sealed with seven seals, could none open but Christ, Rev. i. 3, 5; and as none could open it but he, so none can make it efficacious besides him. All the efficacy of the word is from Christ by his Spirit: 2 Cor. x. 4, "Our weapons are mighty through God."

All things in the church must be exact, and according to divine order; things must not be jumbled, but fitly framed and joined together, Eph. ii. 21; iv. 16. Nothing is left in this house to the wills, inventions, and humours of men; all things must be measured, and measured by the line and reed of Christ; no men may bring their own reeds or lines to measure aught: Matt. xv. 9, "In vain do they," &c.; this is dangerous. Matt. xvii. 5, "Hear him;" Acts iii. 23, "Every soul that will not," &c. Timothy must not do what he pleased in the house of God, but he must proceed according to rule, according to what Paul, the servant of Christ, had written unto him, 1 Tim. iii. 14, 15.

"The breadth of the building, one reed; and the height, one reed." Here were small beginnings at first; the building was but one reed in breadth and height. This seems to point out the smallness of the christian church at first, it was only in Judea and Jerusalem. Of little breadth, and low in gifts and graces, it knew little of the mysteries of the gospel; and so as little in height, but after it extended in breadth and height.

Ver. 6. ***Then came he unto the gate which looketh toward the east, and went up the stairs thereof, and measured the threshold of the gate, which was one reed broad; and the other threshold of the gate, which was one reed broad.***

There is frequent mention of the gates belonging to this temple, and the courts of it; as the east gate, ver. 6, 32, 44; the north-gate, ver. 20, 35, 40, 44; the south gate, ver. 24, 27, 28. And there were divers east gates, north gates, and south gates, as there were divers walls and courts; so in Solomon's temple, and in that built after the captivity

Christ came from the gate of the outward wall where he first stood, ver. 3, 5, and came to an inward gate, which expositors make to be the gate of the temple. He passed through the first court, which some call the court of the gentiles, and came unto the next gate.

Why Christ came to the east gate rather than to the north gate, this being nearer the gate of the wall which he entered by than the other, is questioned. It is probable it was, because the face of the house looked that way, as it is, chap. xlvii. 1, "The forefront of the house stood towards the east;" and that gate is counted the principal which stands before the face of a house.

The outward wall had but one gate, the other walls of the inward courts had three gates apiece, one eastward, one northward, and one southward, but no gate was westward. The Jews called the east the forepart of heaven, and the west, the backpart of heaven: by the first, they note spiritual things; by the second, temporal and earthly things. Those that come into this temple must mind spiritual things, they must not let out their hearts unto the world and worldly delights, they are western things, and there was no door in the west. They must go upwards, not downwards; keep within, not go out.

The prophet being to measure the gates, was brought first to those of the outward court, and first to the east gate, then to the north gate, and lastly, to the south gate; but when he came to the gates of the inner court, he begins with the south gate, then the east gate, and last of all the north gate. There was a differing order in measuring these gates, ver. 28, 32, 35.

These gates do hint unto us the readiness in Christ and God to receive comers, and the confluence of them from all parts. This temple hath many gates, and those looking to the several quarters of the world. If men come from any of them, there is a gate before them, and admittance for them: Isa. lx. 3—8, "The gentiles shall come to thy light, and kings to the brightness of thy rising. Lift up thine eyes round about, and see: all they gather themselves together, they come to thee: thy sons shall come from far, and thy daughters shall be nursed at thy side," &c. He goes on there, and shows what flowing and flocking shall be to the church, even as doves to a window; and ver. 11, it is said of this Jerusalem, "Her gates shall be open continually; they shall not be shut day nor night:" and that this is meant of new Jerusalem, John satisfies us, Rev. xxi. 25, where he brings in these words, speaking of the new Jerusalem, "The gates of it shall not be shut." It had twelve gates, ver. 13, and not one of them should be shut.

"Went up the stairs thereof." There are stairs and steps spoken of in ver. 6, 22, 26, 31, 34, 37, 49. The temple being upon a mountain, the ascent must needs be by stairs and steps. For the number of them, in the 6th verse, the Septuagint saith they were seven, but the Hebrew mentions not the number in that place. In the 22nd and 26th verses you hear of seven steps, and in the 31st, 34th, and 37th, of eight steps: but these were in several places, and served for several ascents; for that is the use of stairs and steps.

Three things I conceive are hereby held out unto us:

1. That we come to the knowledge of spiritual things by degrees; they are not known at once, but successively. Temple mysteries we come unto by steps. Christ leads his people on from one thing to another, from faith to faith, from strength to strength. Those that come to the temple proceed by degrees, first one step, then another: Ezekiel was carried on in the sight of his vision *gradatim;* he had not the sight of all at once, but one thing after another.

2. The knowledge of divine things is not attained without labour and difficulty. There are steps and stairs in this temple, and those that will behold the glory and understand the mysteries of it, must go upward, first one step, and then another: and it is difficult to go up stairs and steps: it hath cost many hot water who have been going up these steps to find out the secrets comprehended in this vision.

3. In temple work we must make progress. It is

not sufficient to go up a step, a stair, or two, and then stand still, or descend; we must go forward, go up higher, to the top. It is not enough to go up two or three rounds in Jacob's ladder, and look about; but if ever men will get into heaven, they must go to the top of the ladder: Rev. iii. 21, "To him that overcometh will I grant to sit with me in my throne, even as I also overcame, and am set down with my Father in his throne." Christ overcame the difficulties, he went up all the stairs, and, persevering to the end, was crowned.

"And measured the threshold of the gate, which was one reed broad; and the other threshold of the gate, which was one reed broad." Here were two thresholds, the lower and upper, which the Grecians call ὑποθύριον, and ὑπερθύριον; that the foot goeth over, and that the head goeth under; and they were very broad, each a reed, or six cubits, broad, and were to adorn and strengthen the gate. Christ is the gate and door of the church, his human and divine natures are the ornament and strength thereof.

Ver. 7. *Very little chambers.*

In this verse, and ver. 10, 12, 13, 16, 17, 21, 29, 33, 36, 38, 44, 45, 46, of this chapter, you read of chambers. In Middoth, it is said the chambers were one above another, and so it is evident they were, chap. xli. 6. Œcolampadius saith, they were little lodgings, made for the use of those who served in the temple. Their number was great. In some of them, those that either kept the temple, or ministered, dwelt; in others were laid up those things which pertained to the service of the temple.

In the chambers "they laid the meat offerings, the frankincense, and the vessels, and the tithes of the corn, the new wine, and the oil, which was commanded to be given to the Levites, and the singers, and the porters; and the offerings of the priests," Neh. xiii. 5; the tithes were laid up in treasuries and storehouses of the courts, or in the chambers thereof, Mal. iii. 10.

Ezek. xlii. 13, 14, the use of chambers northward and southward is said to be for the priests; "They be holy chambers, where the priests who approach unto the Lord shall eat the most holy things: there shall they lay the most holy things, and the meat offering, and the sin offering, and the trespass offering; for the place is holy. When the priests enter therein, then shall they not go out of the holy place into the outer court, but there they shall lay their garments wherein they minister: for they are holy; and shall put on other garments, and shall approach to those things which are for the people."

These chambers may represent unto us, 1. The mansions which are in heaven: John xiv. 2, "In my Father's house are many mansions," saith Christ: he showed Ezekiel these chambers in this visional temple, and he told his disciples of those celestial mansions which he would prepare for them.

2. That entertainment, rest, and comfort, the saints enjoy, and shall have in the church under Christ. If a man come to his friend's house, and he have never a chamber for his repose, it is poor entertainment, cold comfort, and little ease, if he must lie on the ground; but if he have variety of chambers and beds for him, his entertainment, rest, and comfort will be good; he shall not need to fear wind or weather. When men come to the new Jerusalem, and are citizens thereof, they shall have good accommodation, sweet rest, and sound comfort; there shall be no voice of weeping or crying, Isa. lxv. 19; there shall be no tears, no death, no sorrow, no crying, no pain, Rev. xxi. 4. In the world is tribulation, but in Christ is peace, in Zion is peace; under the new Jerusalem, the devils shall be bound up, and there will be great peace, and spiritual comfort in abundance.

3. These chambers, less and greater, may note out the several congregations, or churches, of the gospel times, be they little or great, all which are in the church of Christ, as these chambers were in this visional temple.

Ver. 8. *He measured also the porch of the gate within, one reed.*

The thresholds, and the porch, were all of one measure, viz. six cubits and a hand's breadth. The word for "porch" here is, אלם and in ver. 10, is rendered "posts;" it signifies both. Porches were for the dignity of the house and accommodation of strangers.

Ver. 9. *Then measured he the porch of the gate, eight cubits; and the posts thereof, two cubits.*

In the verse before it is said, the porch was one reed, that is, six cubits; and here we find the measure of it eight cubits. In the former verse he spake of the breadth, here of the length of it. The posts were the pillars, artificially placed on the one side and on the other.

"The porch of the gate was inward." It was within the wall, looking towards the house itself.

Ver. 10. *And the little chambers of the gate eastward were three on this side, and three on that side; they three were of one measure: and the posts had one measure on this side and on that side.*

The eastern gate, as it had its porch and pillars on each side of it, so it had its three chambers on each side of it, and they were uniform, as the posts or pillars were.

Ver. 11. *And he measured the breadth of the entry of the gate, ten cubits; and the length of the gate, thirteen cubits.*

The Hebrew word for "entry" is, פתח and rendered, a door, ver. 13; and so it is mostly taken in Scripture. If by "entry," be meant the door, how is it said that it is ten cubits in breadth, when the door is never wider than the threshold? which in the 6th and 7th verses is said to be but one reed broad, or six cubits: either it was some other door, or the posts to which the door was fastened and shut to were added to the measure. If we hold to the word "entry," it may be the breadth of the space between the outward gate and the inward.

"The length of the gate thirteen cubits." "Length" here is the height of the gate, it was thirteen cubits high.

Ver. 12. *The space also before the little chambers was one cubit on this side, and the space was one cubit on that side, &c.*

There was גבול a border, or space of a cubit, on each side of the chambers, and yet before them; and the chambers on each side were alike, six cubits apiece.

Ver. 13. *He measured then the gate from the roof of one little chamber to the roof of another: the breadth was five and twenty cubits, door against door.*

These chambers were not continued, nor contiguous, there was the space of five cubits between them; and of twenty-five cubits, in that breadth, was between them, as they stood opposite one to another.

Ver. 14. *He made also posts of threescore cubits, even unto the post of the court round about the gate.*

Posts of this length some think incredible, and therefore divide these cubits between the posts on each side the porch, which reach up unto the posts of the outward court, making them thirty cubits apiece. Some make these posts of sixty cubits to be the cloister, which being supported by posts was sixty cubits long.

Ver. 15. *From the face of the gate of the entrance unto, &c.*

From one gate to the other were fifty cubits, and the porch of the inner gate ten cubits. We are to make progress in the temple, and not to stand still.

Ver. 16. *Of the windows.*

There were several windows in this structure which was presented to our prophet, as appears, ver. 16, 22, 25, 29, 33, 36; and chap. xli. 16, 26. These windows "were narrow windows," that is, narrow without and broad within, that they might receive and let in the light more fully. Such windows were in Solomon's temple, 1 Kings vi. 4; skewed windows.

By these windows is signified the spiritual light which should be in the church of Christ. He is called, Mal. iv. 2, "The Sun;" Isa. ix. 2, "A great light;" John viii. 12, "The light of the world:" and by those windows, the apostles, prophets, evangelists, pastors, and teachers, he hath, and still doth, let in light into the church. The promise was, that "the earth should be full of the knowledge of the Lord," Isa. xi. 9; that he would "pour out his spirit upon all flesh," Joel ii. 28, 29; so that their sons and daughters should prophesy, their old men dream dreams, and their young men see visions; yea, servants and handmaids should have the spirit, and be full of light. This is in part fulfilled, and shall be more and more; for when the "new Jerusalem comes down from God out of heaven," as it is Rev. xxi. 2, then will the light be greater, "and the nations of them which are saved shall walk in the light of it," ver. 24; then will the Lamb be the light thereof.

Also, that spiritual joy which should be in the church: Acts xiii. 52, "The disciples were filled with joy;" chap. ix. 31, "The churches walked in the comfort of the Holy Ghost."

"To the little chambers." The least churches, and least saints, shall not be without windows; they shall have light and joy, teaching and comfort.

In the 17th and 18th verses of this chapter, and 3rd verse of chap. xlii. mention is made of the pavement of the outward court. The Hebrew word for "pavement" is, רצפה which signifieth, a burning coal: Isa. vi. 6, the seraphim had a live coal, רצפה in his hand: the pavement was of stones that seemed like burning coals. If the pavement of this temple were so glorious, what was the temple itself! Solomon's chariot was paved with love; this temple with love and zeal. These stones which made the pavement may show what the meanest and lowest in the christian church should be, viz. shining, living, and lively stones; humbly submitting to the cross, and content to be under, as a pavement.

Of the outward and inward court.

Thirty-five times the terms of court, "outward and inward court," are repeated, in chapters xl. xli. xlii. xliii. xliv. xlv. and xlvi.

The outward court was for the people, the inward court was for priests, and was holy; Ezek. xlii. 14, it is called "the holy place." There was another court, it is observed by some, viz. "the court of the gentiles;" which, it may be, Ezekiel points at, when he distinguisheth the sanctuary from the profane place, chap. xlii. 20. But it is evident from the Scripture, that Solomon's temple had an "outward and inward court," and so had this. The outward court there was great, 2 Chron. iv. 4; and the compass of this temple and city which Ezekiel saw, "was eighteen thousand measures," chap. xlviii. 35.

The courts of Solomon's temple were very large, which comprehended most of the people of Israel, who came thrice a year into them to worship. 2 Chron. xxiii. 5, "All the people shall be in the courts of the house of the Lord." This court, called also "the great court," 2 Chron. iv. 9, was between the court of the gentiles the outward court, and the court of the priests the inward court, and that great court, or court of Israel, was the court of aid; so the word העזרה signifies. Thither they came, there they prayed for aid, and had it from the Lord, 2 Chron. xx. 4.

There seems to be another court belonging to the temple of Solomon; for, 2 Chron. xx. 5, mention is made of a "new court." Some think this the priests' court; so called, because of the altar renewed therein by Asa, 2 Chron. xv. 8; but others make it to be the court of the women, the great court of the people being divided into two, one for the men, and the other for the women. It was not so from the beginning.

In "the outward court" the people stood; and it represented the nations, which are out of the church. In "the inward court," where was the candlestick, the shew-bread, and altar of perfumes, were the Levites and priests; and this court represented the church, where the word of God doth enlighten and nourish us, and Christ is our altar of perfumes. The holy of holies represented heaven, into it the high priest only entered; typifying our High Priest, the Lord Christ, his entrance in there alone by his own power, to bring us thither. So that the first signified the state of nature; the second the state of grace; the third the state of glory.

Hereby the greatness of the church in the time of the gospel, and especially in the time of the new Jerusalem, is pointed out. These courts were of great compass, and had gates looking to the several parts of the world. In Peter's time, many thousands were added to the church; there were Grecians as well as Jews, Acts vi. 1. The extent and largeness of the church is set out fully by Isaiah in his 60th chapter. So Rev. vii. 4—10; and xxi. 24—26, "The nations of them that are saved shall walk in the light of it: and the kings of the earth do bring their glory and honour into it. And the gates of it shall not be shut at all," &c. This church must needs be great, "for from the rising of the sun even unto the going down of the same my name shall be great among the gentiles; and in every place incense shall be offered unto my name, and a pure offering: for my name shall be great among the heathen, saith the Lord of hosts," Mal. i. 11.

In Solomon's time many gentiles came to the Jewish church; a hundred and fifty-three thousand six hundred were found there at once, 2 Chron. ii. 17; which shadowed out the great access which should come to the christian church.

Of the palm-trees.

There were many "palm-trees" seen by Ezekiel in this temple, ver. 16, 22, 26, 31, 34, 47.

Palm trees are trees of great height, and sink not with the weight of burdens; but they are carried upwards, and being cut down, grow up again from the root. The branches are fair, and always green. It was the sign of victory. When Theseus instituted games in Delos, he gave the conquerors palms. The proverb among the Latins, To obtain the palm, was used to mean victory. It notes out a flourishing condition.

These "palm trees" were for ornament of this temple; and the saints in gospel times, being victorious and flourishing, are to be the ornament of the church. Rev. vii. 9, "I beheld, and, lo, a great multitude, which no man could number, of all nations, and kindreds, and people, and tongues, stood before the throne, and before the Lamb, clothed with white robes, and palms in their hands." Psal. xcii. 12, "The righteous shall flourish like the palm tree." Rev. iii. 12, "Him that overcometh, will I make a pillar in the temple of my God, and he shall go no more out."

Ver. 19. *An hundred cubits eastward and northward.*

The floor, or pavement, of the people's court was a hundred cubits square.

Ver. 20. The measures of the north gate, the chambers, windows, and arches thereof, were after the measure of the first gate, ver. 21; that is, after the measure of the gate that looketh toward the east, ver. 22.

Ver. 23. *The gate of the inner court was over against, &c.*

There were gates in the priests' court, and gates in the people's courts; and they were one over against the other, and a hundred cubits distant each from another.

Ver. 24. *After he brought me toward the south.*

When we are in temple work, we must move according to the mind of the Master-builder, and not of our own heads.

"Behold a gate toward the south." The measures of this gate, the posts, windows, and arches, ver. 25, 26, were as the former measures of the gates, they were uniform.

Ver. 26. The south gate had seven steps to go up to it, and so had the north gate, ver. 22; and the east gate had its stairs: see before, ver. 6.

Ver. 27, 28. The prophet from the outward court is brought to the inner court, and first to the south gate; and the measures from gate to gate, as before, were a hundred cubits; and the measures of the little chambers, posts, arches, and windows belonging to the south gate, ver. 19, 30, 31, to the east gate, ver. 32, 33, 34, and to the north gate, ver. 35, 36, were the same, and without difference. There was neither defect nor excess in these measures, but equality.

Ver. 37. *The going up to the north gate of the inner court had eight steps, so had the east gate,* ver. 34, *and the south gate,* ver. 31. *The gates of the outward court had but seven steps.*

The people that came thither were to be holy, but the priests, who came into the inner court, were to be more holy. They who are nearest God should be most holy; they are to be a step, at least, above others.

Ver. 38. *The burnt offering was washed.*

Some, by this washing of the burnt offering, do think baptism to be prefigured; which denotes the washing away the filthiness of sin by the blood of Christ. It may note out to us the purity of that which is to be presented to the Lord; nothing unclean will be acceptable to him.

Ver. 39. *Of the table offerings and sacrifices.*

From the beginning of the 39th verse to the 44th, Ezekiel tells you of the tables seen in this temple; their number, situation, description, and use: their number was eight, some make them twelve: their situation was by the side of the porches and gates, four on one side, and four on another side: for the description of them, they were of hewn stone, a cubit and half long, a cubit and half broad, and one cubit high: the use of them was, to slay the burnt offering, the sin offering, and the trespass offering thereon, and to lay their flesh thereon.

It is not to be imagined, that, under the times of Christ, the Jewish worship should be revived. These expositions of tables, offerings, and sacrifices, import some other thing, viz. the good and plentiful provision which should be in the gospel church. Isaiah speaks of the same, chap. xxv. 6, "The Lord of hosts shall make unto all people a feast of fat things, a feast of wines on the lees, of fat things full of marrow, of wines on the lees well refined:" and, chap. lv. 1, 2, Christ hath water, wine, milk, bread, and fatness in his house. The gospel is called "a great supper," Luke xiv. 16; there was variety of dainties to satisfy the souls of his people. Psal. xxii. 26, "The meek shall eat and be satisfied." Christ hath a table well furnished, Prov. ix. 2; Luke xxii. 29, 30, "I appoint unto you a kingdom, as my Father hath appointed unto me; that ye may eat and drink at my table in my kingdom." It is a "marriage supper" Christ prepares for his people, Rev. xix. 9. In the new Jerusalem is a tree of life, which bears twelve manner of fruits, and yields her fruit every month.

Of the singers.

In the 44th verse, and only there, the singers of this temple are mentioned. There were chambers of singers.

There were singers in Solomon's temple, 1 Kings x. 12; 2 Chron. v. 12; and the number of them was great, 1 Chron. xxv.; and they were to sing praises daily, 1 Chron. xxiii. 30.

Some played on instruments, some sang with voices. Some conceive the Israelites had a part in the instrumental music, but none in the vocal, that was performed by the Levites only. Lightfoot on the Temple. Less then twelve their number was not at any time, but they might be as many as they would above twelve.

These set out the spiritual joy and songs which should be in the church of Christ: Isa. lxv. 14, 17, 18, "Behold, my servants shall sing for joy of heart. For, behold, I create new heavens and a new earth. Be ye glad, and rejoice for ever in that which I create: for, behold, I create Jerusalem a rejoicing, and her people a joy:" her walls shall be Salvation, and her gates Praise, Isa. lx. 18. In this Jerusalem will be an holy priesthood, to offer up spiritual praise, 1 Pet. ii. 5. The Revelation speaks of singers; chap. xiv. 1, 3, there were a hundred and forty-four thousand stood on mount Zion, singing as it were a new song: and, chap. xv. 2, 3, "Those that had gotten the victory over the beast, and over his image, and over his mark, and over the number of his name, sung the song of Moses, and of the Lamb." Conquerors are full of joy, and much in singing praises, especially spiritual conquerors. Such are they, who, the apostle John saith, shall reign with Christ a thousand years, for they shall be priests of God and of Christ, Rev. xx. 6. And wherefore priests? but to offer up spiritual sacrifices, to sing forth the praises of God and Christ, who hath advanced them to a reigning condition.

Ver. 45, 46. *Of the priests.*

This temple had its "priests," who were "the keepers of the charge of the house," ver. 45; "and keepers of the charge of the altar," ver. 46. In time of the tabernacle there were men appointed to take charge of it, and the things pertaining to it, Numb. iii. 25; there were eight thousand six hundred to keep the charge of the sanctuary, ver. 28; and what many of them did you may see 1 Chron. ix. 27—32; xxiii. 27—32. So, in the temple of Solomon, the priests had the charge of the things thereof, 2 Chron. xiii. 10, 11. When Uzziah went into the temple to burn incense, the priests who had the charge of things thrust him out, 2 Chron. xxvi.; these are said to be the sons of Zadok. Zadok was the first high priest who served in the temple of Solomon, 1 Kings ii. 35; and of such worth was he among the priests, and of such esteem with God, that all in this temple are called the sons of Zadok, both priests and Levites, Ezek. xliv. 15.

By these "priests" may be understood the ministers of the gospel, who have the charge of the holy things and persons. 1 Tim. vi. 13, 14, "I give thee charge in the sight of God, that thou keep this commandment without spot:" all the rules he had given him concerning the house of God, the offices, officers, and inhabitants thereof, he calls a "commandment," and lays upon him the charge of keeping of it. So in Acts xx. Paul calls for the elders of the church of Ephesus, ver. 17, and charges them to take heed to all the flock, ver. 28. They are the watchmen, the charge of souls is committed to them, and they must be accountants for them, Heb. xiii. 17.

Or, by these "priests," all the godly (Isa. lxi. 6, "Ye shall be named the priests of the Lord") may be pointed out, who are the sons of Zadok, that is, of the just one. Christ, our High Priest, is Zadok, the Just One, Acts vii. 52; xxii. 14; and he hath not only made us sons, John i. 12, but priests also, Rev. v. 10. So that true christians are priests in this temple, and have some charge of the holy things and persons therein.

Ver. 45, 46. The chambers towards the south and north were for the priests, they were peculiar to them; they had their garments and anointing oil, which others might not meddle with; and so their chambers.

Ver. 46. This coming near of these priests unto the Lord, to minister unto him, points out the priestly office of Christ, who drew near to the Father, to make atonement, and to intercede for us.

Ver. 47. *So he measured the court, &c.*

The Lord Christ lets nothing pass without measuring, he doth all things exactly in his house, and his servants should imitate him.

Ver. 48. ***He brought me to the porch of the house.***

This porch joined to the doors of the temple, into which none might enter but the priests; saith A Lapide, it was covered, that they might be secure from rain and heat. Christ is a porch to his people, Isa. xxxii. 2. It is Jerom's judgment, that whilst we are in this life we are in a porch state. Here we have a body of death, see all things imperfectly; but when we enter into the heavenly temple, we shall be free, and know as we are known.

CHAPTER XLI.

Ver. 1—7. *Afterward he brought me to the temple, and measured the posts, six cubits broad on the one side, and six cubits broad on the other side, which was the breadth of the tabernacle. And the breadth of the door was ten cubits; and the sides of the door were five cubits on the one side, and five cubits on the other side: and he measured the length thereof, forty cubits: and the breadth, twenty cubits. Then went he inward, and measured the post of the door, two cubits; and the door, six cubits; and the breadth of the door, seven cubits. So he measured the length thereof, twenty cubits; and the breadth, twenty cubits, before the temple: and he said unto me, This is the most holy place. After he measured the wall of the house, six cubits; and the breadth of every side chamber, four cubits, round about the house on every side. And the side chambers were three, one over another, and thirty in order; and they entered into the wall which was of the house for the side chambers round about, that they might have hold, but they had not hold in the wall of the house. And there was an enlarging, and a winding about still upward to the side chambers: for the winding about of the house went still upward round about the house: therefore the breadth of the house was still upward, and so increased from the lowest chamber to the highest by the midst.*

The measuring of the outward and inward court being finished, here our prophet is brought to it, and showed the measures of the temple itself, and the things pertaining thereunto.

Ver. 1. "He brought me to the temple." The gates, courts, and porch, hitherto had taken up the prophet, but now he is at the temple; from lower things he is carried to more sublime.

"The posts, six cubits broad." The posts themselves could not be so broad, but the posts, together with the cloisters, which they supported, were so.

The word "temple" is chiefly used in this chapter; once it is mentioned in chap. xlii. 8; here seven times, in ver. 1, 4, 15, 20, 23, 25. It is convenient, therefore, to speak in this place of the temple.

There are three considerable parts of the temple. 1. The porch. 2. The body, or temple itself. 3. The holy of holies.

1. For the porch, of that Ezekiel speaks in the two last verses of the 40th chapter, "And he brought me to the porch of the house," &c. This porch was twenty cubits in length and eleven in breadth; of the same length was the porch of Solomon's temple; and Ezekiel's exceeded it in the breadth thereof one cubit; 1 Kings vi. 3, for the breadth of Solomon's temple was but ten cubits. Nothing is spoken of the height of this porch: Solomon's was one hundred and twenty cubits, 2 Chron. iii. 4; and, doubtless, this was not short of it. The Hebrew calls the porch אולם.

2. The body, house, or temple itself, (it is in the 1st verse,) was that part which stood between the porch and the holy of holies. The length of this was forty cubits, and the breadth twenty cubits.

Solomon's was sixty cubits long, twenty cubits broad, and thirty cubits high, 1 Kings vi. 2; but when it is said, Solomon's was sixty cubits long, the length of the holy of holies is reckoned in, for that was twenty cubits long, and so upon that account Ezekiel's temple was sixty cubits long. They call the temple היכל.

3. The holy of holies. "Then went he inward, and measured the most holy place," ver. 3; so it is called: and it was twenty cubits in length, and ten cubits in breadth; so that the temple being as long again as broad, was quadrangular; and this being as broad as long, was a perfect square. This they call דביר *oraculum.*

As the court before the temple was four-square, one hundred cubits long and one hundred cubits broad, chap. xl. 47; so the temple itself, taken with all the appendices of it, was so. The breadth of the temple courts, and thickness of the walls, &c. make one hundred cubits; and likewise the length of the temple courts, &c. make one hundred cubits, as Haffenrefferus exactly demonstrates.

Of the signification of this temple.

Some make the court belonging to it to represent the world, and the temple to represent heaven. It may be considered, whether the porch do not point out the common professor; the temple, true saints, who are temples of the Spirit; and the holy of holies, the saints in glory, the condition of those made perfect.

The true representation of this temple, I take it, is the body of our Lord Jesus Christ; both his body natural, and his body mystical, viz. the church.

1. It is a representation of his natural body: Solomon's temple, and Zerubbabel's, or the second temple, was so. John ii. 19, saith Christ, "Destroy this temple, and in three days I will raise it up." And why Ezekiel's temple should not type out Christ, I see no cause. There are many things wherein it fitly doth so.

(1.) This temple was holy: ver. 4, "This is the most holy place;" hence it is evident the other part of the temple was holy. The *hecal* was holy, though not so holy as the *devir:* and the body of Christ was holy; Luke i. 35, "That holy thing," &c. Acts xiii. 35, "Thou shalt not suffer thine Holy One," &c. 1 Pet. ii. 22; i. 19; Heb. vii. 26, "He was holy, harmless, undefiled, separate from sinners."

(2.) It was very lightsome and beautiful within. It was adorned "with cherubims and palm trees, ver. 18, 19. So the Lord Christ was full of light; Col. ii. 3, "In him were hid all the treasures of wisdom and knowledge." He was adorned with all the graces of the Spirit; he was full of grace and truth, John i. 14. Cant. v. 10; Psal. xlv. 2, "Thou art fairer than the children of men."

(3.) By the temple, they came to know the mind of God. One part of it was called *devir*, the word, or oracle; there God spake. So by Christ we come to know the mind of God. John i. 1, he is the Word. He brought the mind of God to us, and declared it to the world: Heb. i. 2, God "hath in these last days spoken unto us by his Son." Christ was an Ambassador sent from God, to acquaint us with the mind of the King of nations, and he did it faithfully: John xv. 15, "All things which I have heard of my Father I have made known unto you."

(4.) The temple was God's delight. It is called a house, for God dwelt in it, and manifested his glory there: Ezek. xliii. 4, 5, "The glory of the Lord came into the house;" yea, "the glory of the Lord filled the house." And Psal. xxix. 9, "In the temple doth every one speak of his glory:" there God's glory is seen. Is not Christ such a temple? did not God come into the temple of his body? 1 Tim. iii. 16; Col. ii. 9. There the glory of God was seen fully: John i. 14, "The Word was made flesh, and dwelt among us, (and we beheld his glory, the glory as of the only begotten of the Father,) full of grace and truth." The glory of God never appeared so evidently as in this temple, and God delighted therein: Matt. iii. 17, "This is my beloved Son, in whom I am well pleased." See Rev. iii. 12, "Him that overcometh will I make a pillar in the temple of my God, and he shall go no more out: and I will write upon him the name of my God, and the name of the city of my God, which is new Jerusalem." God is establishing, and will establish, new Jerusalem with pillars daily more and more; and therein is strength to be found; not in the world, or in Babylon, 1 Tim. iii. 15.

(5.) There were cherubims and palm trees in the visional temple, ver. 18, 19, 20, 25, 26; and in the church of Christ there are cherubims and palm trees. These cherubims may note the presence of the angels in the church: 1 Cor. xi. 10, there were angels in the church of Corinth; and so in the temple John speaks of, Rev. xiv. 15, 17. Each cherubim had two faces, one of a man, another of a young lion; to signify the wisdom, strength, and zeal of the angels, which are employed for the good of the church. Or, by cherubims, understand those christians who were wise, stout, and zealous for the truth, and cause of God, such as "loved not their lives unto the death," Rev. xii. 11; "but were beheaded for the witness of Jesus, and for the word of God," Rev. xx. 4. These cherubims looked to the palm trees, they were patient under all crosses, afflictions, in hope of certain victory: Rom. viii. 35—37, "Who shall separate us from the love of Christ? shall tribulation, or distress, or persecution, or famine, or nakedness, or peril, or sword?" &c. "Nay, in all these things we are more than conquerors," &c.: their eyes were upon the palm trees. And, Rev. ix. 7, they had palms in their hands, they were certain of victory, whereof palms and palm trees are emblems.

Remark, there are several things wherein the saints do resemble palm trees.

[1.] They are always green, and growing; so are the saints: Psal. xcii. 12, 14, "The righteous shall flourish like the palm tree: they shall still bring forth fruit in old age."

[2.] Palm trees cannot endure dung. So the saints, they hate superstition, idolatry, and all sin, as dung; they will die rather than worship the beast or his image, rather than receive his mark in their foreheads or their hands, Rev. xx. 4; they watch, and keep their garments undefiled.

[3.] The palm tree bears up against all weight laid upon it; and the saints do the like in all their troubles and afflictions. Paul met with sharp trials, yet he fainted not, but found more strength, 2 Cor. iv. 16. And chap. vii. 4, he saith, "I am filled with comfort, I am exceeding joyful in all our tribulation:" and Rom. v. 3, "We glory in tribulations."

[4.] These cherubims and palm trees were the ornament of the temple: and christians, who are wise, courageous, and patient under all trials, are the ornaments of the church of Christ.

[5.] This temple, with the porch and buildings belonging to it, was great and large; ver. 12—15, one hundred cubits in breadth, one hundred cubits in length; so the church of Christ is great and large. In the apostles' times there were thousands of the Jews believed, Acts xxi. 20. It was prophesied in Isaiah's days, that all nations should flow unto the mountain of the Lord, that is, the church, Isa. ii. 2. And in Daniel's days, chap. vii. 14, "That all people, languages, and nations, should serve Christ." And John, in the vision, saw it made good: Rev. vii. 9, "I beheld a great multitude, which no man could number, of all nations, kindred, people, and tongues, which stood before the throne, and the Lamb."

2. It is the representation of Christ's body mystical, and that in several things.

(1.) All things in this temple were measured, as appears in chapters xl. xli. xlii. xliii. xlvii.; so in the church, the mystical body of Christ. Eph. ii. 21, Paul tells the Ephesians that the saints are a building; and such a building as is fitly framed together; and so framed together as to make a temple: all which could not be done without measuring. Psal. xlv. 10, 11, "Hearken, O daughter, and consider, and incline thine ear; forget also thine own people, and thy father's house. So shall the king greatly desire thy beauty: for he is thy Lord; and worship thou him:" here was measuring of the church and fitting of her for her Beloved. So Rev. xi. 1, John must "measure the temple of God, and the altar, and them that worship therein." All in the church must be measured by the word.

(2.) Christ was in this temple, and did all therein, and showed all to the prophet (as in reading the former, this, and subsequent chapters, is clear). So in the church, Christ is there, and doth all; Col. i. 18, "He is the head of the body, the church," and the head doth all: all influence, all dominion, all direction, is from him. Christ is "in the midst of the golden candlesticks," and walks up and down, doing and declaring what he pleases there, Rev. ii. 1: xxi. 3, "Behold, the tabernacle of God is with men, and he will dwell with them, and they shall be his people, and God himself shall be with them, and be their God."

(3.) In this temple were chambers, galleries, and stories, one above another, as ver. 6 and 16 of this chapter, and ver. 3 and 6 of the 42nd chapter. So in the church, there are several ranks and degrees of officers and members, 1 Cor. xii. 28: Eph. iv. 11, there are apostles, prophets, evangelists, pastors, teachers; elders, 1 Tim. v. 17; deacons, 1 Tim. iii. 8. So for members, some are babes, 1 Cor. iii. 1; some are little children, some young men, some fathers, 1 John ii. 12, 13. In the church of Christ some are higher than others in gifts and graces.

(4.) In this temple were posts and pillars, strong and great, chap. xl. 9, 10, 14, 16, 21, 24, 26, 29, 31, 33, 34, 37, 48, 49; xli. 1, 3, 21; xliii. 8; xlv. 19; xlvi. 2. In Solomon's temple there were pillars, Jachin and Boaz, by which was noted God's establishment of the temple, and the strength that was in it, 1 Kings vii. 21; 2 Chron. iii. 17. And in the church of Christ are posts and pillars. James, Cephas, and John were pillars, Gal. ii. 9. And was not Paul a great and strong pillar, who had "the care of all the churches" upon him? 2 Cor. xii. 28. Are there not many posts and pillars in the church of Christ?

Of the most holy place.

Of it, also, chap. xliv. 13, 45.

In the 4th verse it is described to be twenty cubits long and twenty cubits broad; parallel to the most holy place in Solomon's temple, 2 Chron. iii. 8, which was twenty cubits broad, and twenty cubits long, and twenty cubits high, 1 Kings vi. 20. And though there be no mention of the height of this most holy place, it is probable it was of the same height with Solomon's, as well as of the same breadth and length. This was called the inward, or inward house, or "house within," 1 Kings vi. 15; Ezek. xli. 3; "the oracle," 1 Kings vi. 20; and "the most holy place," 1 Kings vii. 50, "the inner house, the most holy place."

This place leads us to the consideration of heaven, which is the most holy place, Psal. xx. 6. Deut. xxvi. 15, heaven is holy, and God's holy habitation, and our happiness is there. Into this place "the high priest entered once a year, and made intercession for the people," Heb. ix. 7. And Christ is passed into the heavens, and there intercedes for his people, Heb. ix. 24; chap. vii. 25. From the most holy place was the mind of God revealed: Psal. lx. 6, "God hath spoken in his holiness," in his sanctuary, or most holy place. Some render it, There God dwelt, "between the cherubims," and opened himself unto them, Psal. xcix. 1. Numb. vii. 89, Moses "heard the voice of one speaking to him from off the mercy-seat that was upon the ark of testimony, from between the two cherubims." So from heaven, the most holy place, God makes known his mind: Neh. ix. 13, "Thou spakest with them from heaven;" Dan. iv. 31, "There fell a voice from heaven:" so Matt. iii. 17, "Lo a voice from heaven." From thence came both law and gospel, which is called "the word of God," Rev. xx. 4.

In the most holy place the glory of God appeared most, between the cherubims; and in the highest and most holy heavens, there the glory of the Lord is most conspicuous, most eminent, among the angels and glorified saints.

Again, they used to pray, and lift up their hands towards the most holy place: Psal. xxviii. 2, David prayed, and lifted up his hands towards the holy oracle, that was, the most holy place; as is clear from 1 Kings viii. 6. And do not the saints in their worship, especially in prayer, lift up their hands and eyes unto heaven, that holy place? Psal. cxli. 2, "Let my prayer be set forth before thee as incense; and the lifting up of my hands as the evening sacrifice."

Or, this most holy place may prefigure the new Jerusalem, which was to be so holy, that nothing defiled might come there: Rev. xxi. 27, "There shall in no wise enter into it any thing that defileth, neither whatsoever worketh abomination, or maketh a lie; but they which are written in the Lamb's book of life." When Aaron entered into the holy place, he must be washed with water, and be clad with holy garments, Lev. xvi.; and all those that enter into the new Jerusalem must be cleansed from their sin, and clothed with righteousness. Rev. xiv. 4, those that stood with the Lamb were not defiled ones, but such as were "clothed with white robes," Rev. vii. 9.

Ver. 5—7. The side chambers were in three ranks, one above another, and the breadth of the house increased upward; there were winding stairs, and the higher they ascended, the wider was the house. Those in the church are not all of one rank, whether officers, or others; some are of the lower rank, some in the middle, and some uppermost; there are children, young men, and old men; and the higher any get, the more enlargement, and greater breadth, do they see in the things of God and this temple; and notwithstanding this difference among them, there is a sweet harmony between them, and they serve one another.

Ver. 8. *The foundations of the side chambers were a full reed of six great cubits.*

Of the great cubit, see before, chap. xl. 5. Here was good measure: in things belonging to the temple, the Lord should have not common cubit measure, but the great cubit measure.

Ver. 9. *The thickness of the wall was five cubits.*

The breadth or thickness of the wall, say some, was so many cubits from the wall of the house, not so thick in itself. But the Hebrew is, the thickness of the wall was five cubits. It was substantial, and so should temple work be.

"That which was left." Saith Montanus, the empty, or void, place. There will be some void and empty rooms in the church of God.

Ver. 10. *Between the chambers was the wideness of twenty cubits.*

Not between the side chambers themselves, but between them and those over against them. Some had better entertainment than others; some were to be in the chambers, others in the wideness, or empty place.

Ver. 11. *Toward the place that was left.*

See before, ver. 9. It was five cubits round about.

Ver. 12. *The building that was before the separate place.*

Piscator makes the separate place to be, *spatium resectum.* The Hebrew is, *ante faciem segmenti*, before the face of the partition; for it was *particula respecta e suo atrio.*

"Toward the west." Hebrew is, the sea; that is, the Mediterranean sea, which lay westward.

Ver. 13—15. Containing the measures of the house, the building before the separate place, the walks, galleries, and porches of the court, and they were a hundred cubits in length, and a hundred cubits in breadth. Every thing here was measured, and nothing neglected; so exact was the Lord in temple work.

Ver. 16. *The windows were covered.*

Solomon made for the temple windows of narrow lights, but not covered. Sanctius saith they were covered, *Quia in retis modum erant fabricatæ cancellato ordine, aut in pertuso ligno frequentibus perfossæ foraminibus.* They might be covered with lattices, shuttings, or curtains, which might be removed at pleasure.

Ver. 17. *Within and without, by measure.*

Hebrew is, measures. Not only the outside, but inside also is measured, the height, breadth, and length. The Lord Christ will measure christians, of what height, breadth, and depth they are: their actions, affections, and graces, will be measured, Rev. xi. 1.

Ver. 18. *And it was made with cherubims.*

The cherubims import the presence of the angels in the church, 1 Cor. xi. 10; their communion with the saints in worship, 1 Cor. x. 20; Rev. v. 11; vii. 11, 12; their ministration unto, or for them, Heb. i. 14. They are for the Lord of the temple, and those that wait upon him there; they look towards the palm trees, and their wisdom and strength is laid out for their good.

Ver. 19. *So that the face of a man was toward the palm tree on the one side, and the face of a young lion, &c.*

Of the cherubims' faces, see chap. i. 10, what is said there. In ver. 18, 20, 25, 26, the palm trees are mentioned again, which are ever green, growing, tending upwards though pressed down with weight, and signs of victory and great joy, being carried in the hand, or worn on the head; and are ornaments to the place where they are, figuring what the persons in this temple should be, Psal. xcii. 12—14; John xii. 13; Rev. vii. 9. By sufferings and pressures they mount upwards, overcome, are filled with joy, 2 Cor. i. 5; Acts v. 41; and so are great ornaments to the church of God.

Of the altar.

In the 22nd verse it is said, "The altar of wood was three cubits high, and the length thereof two cubits; and the corners thereof, and the length thereof, and the walls thereof, were of wood: and he said unto me, This is the table that is before the Lord." This altar was the altar of incense, and stood before the oracle, or most holy place. Such an altar was in Moses' days made for the tabernacle: Exod. xxxvii. 25, "He made the incense altar." In the temple of Solomon, also, there was an altar of incense: 2 Chron. xxvi. 16, Uzziah "went into the temple of the Lord to burn incense upon the incense altar."

1. This altar was a representation or type of Christ, who is said to be our altar, Heb. xiii. 10; and in many things it did represent him.

(1.) Though it were of wood, yet it was "of shittim wood," Exod. xxx. 1; which the Septuagint renders, of incorruptible wood. So Christ his human nature was incorruptible, it saw no corruption, Acts xiii. 35.

(2.) This altar of incense which Ezekiel saw was larger than that under the law; it was two cubits in length, that but one; it was three cubits in height, that but two; as appears, Exod. xxxvii. 25. This held out that the worship of God in Christ's time should be enlarged; it was among the Jews only before, but then it should be among the gentiles also: Mal. i. 11, "From the rising of the sun unto the going down of the same my name shall be great among the gentiles; and in every place incense shall be offered to my name." 1 Tim. ii. 8, "I will that men pray every where:" under Christ, the incense altar was to be every where.

(3.) Sweet incense was offered up to God, pure incense, Exod. xxxvii. 29, upon this altar, chap. xxx. 7, 8. Where the people prayed, the priest offered incense, Luke i. 9, 10; and when we pray, Christ offers up our prayers, with the incense and perfume of his merits: Rev. viii. 3, 4, "The prayers of the saints ascend up before God out of the angel's hand," who was Christ, the golden altar, for so the altar of incense is called, Numb. iv. 11. Christ perfumes the prayers and services of his saints with his merits, and so presents them unto his Father. It is said, Eph. v. 2, "Christ hath given himself for us an offering and a sacrifice to God for a sweet-smelling savour;" so that whatever he presents to the Father, or is presented in his name from the saints, is pleasing and acceptable to him: all the imperfections and impurities of them are done away by him.

(4.) Upon this altar was incense, morning and evening; it was a perpetual incense, Exod. xxx. 7, 8; so Christ, our Altar, offers up prayers perpetually for us; Heb. vii. 25, "He ever liveth to make intercession for his people."

(5.) This altar of incense had horns, Exod. xxx. 2, 3; at every corner thereof was a horn; which sets out the strength and power of Christ: Rev. ix. 13, "I heard a voice from the four horns of the golden altar," which was Christ, whose power is in all the quarters of the world. Christ's intercession with the Father is powerful to descry the enemies of his people, and to deliver them.

2. This altar is said to be the table that is before

the Lord. There is something in this expression worthy consideration.

(1.) That poor, sinful, weak, unworthy creatures may come to Christ, not only as an altar, to have their prayers presented unto God, but as a table, to have refreshing for their souls. There the hungry may have meat, and the thirsty drink: he is the bread and water of life, his "flesh is meat indeed, his blood is drink indeed," John vi. 35, 55. He hath a kingdom and a table for his, Luke xxii. 30; he "feeds them, and leads them to living fountains of water," Rev. vii. 17. He hath hidden manna for his servants, and a tree of life to refresh them with, Rev. ii. 7, 17.

(2.) That the Lord himself is delighted, and satisfied in, and with, Christ; as we are with a table full of dainties, having the choicest meats and choicest drinks: Matt. iii. 17, "This is my beloved Son, in whom I am well pleased;" with his person, with his graces, with his offices, with his actions, with his sufferings, with his merits, and with the prayers of the saints he presents unto me, "I am well pleased." Christ is the Altar, the Table, the Sacrifice, and the meat and drink upon the same. So is the Lord taken with the intercession and merits of Christ, that his soul delights in him, Isa. xlii. 1. If any of the children of God sin, and thirst for pardon, and peace, we have an Altar, a Table before the Lord: 1 John ii. 1, "If any man sin, we have an Advocate with the Father, Jesus Christ the righteous: and he is the propitiation for our sins:" the Father is so pleased with him, that for his sake presently he grants us pardon and peace.

Of the doors of the temple.

Ver. 23. "The temple and the sanctuary had two doors," which are described in the 24th and 25th verses. These doors were to open and shut at pleasure, and by them the entrance was into the temple, and sanctuary, or most holy place. What else do these suggest unto us, but the means whereby we come to be in, and of, the church of God? The gospel, and its ordinances, faith, repentance, and baptism, are the means to salvation; by them we obtain entrance into the communion of saints, the favour of God, and the kingdom of heaven. Christ is said to be "the way," John xiv. 6; and "the door," John x. 7; because he hath given us the means, which are the way and door to the church, and unto life: these doors are to be open for the sheep, and to be shut against the goats. We may also understand by these doors, the ministers dispensing the gospel and the ordinances thereof; who are to be holy, vigilant, and zealous, as the cherubims; and constantly green, growing, and flourishing, as the palm trees, ver. 25.

Ver. 26. *On the windows, posts, chambers, and thick planks, were palm trees, on the one side, and on the other.*

They had palm trees wrought or engraven on them on both sides; implying, that the materials of Christ's temple must not be common, but curious and carved work. If all the walls of Solomon's house were carved round about with carved figures of cherubims and palm trees, and open flowers, within and without, 1 Kings vi. 9; much more must the house of Christ, and every thing in it, have carved work upon it, viz. the engravings of God's Spirit: see Psal. xlv. 13; Rev. xxi. 18, 19.

CHAPTER XLII.

Ver. 1—7. *Then he brought me forth into the utter court, the way toward the north: and he brought me into the chamber that was over against the separate place, and which was before the building toward the north. Before the length of an hundred cubits was the north door, and the breadth was fifty cubits. Over against the twenty cubits which were for the inner court, and over against the pavement which was for the utter court, was gallery against gallery in three stories. And before the chambers was a walk of ten cubits breadth inward, a way of one cubit; and their doors toward the north. Now the upper chambers were shorter: for the galleries were higher than these, than the lower, and than the middlemost of the building. For they were in three stories, but had not pillars as the pillars of the courts: therefore the building was straitened more than the lowest and the middlemost from the ground. And the wall that was without over against the chambers, toward the outer court on the forepart of the chambers, the length thereof was fifty cubits.*

In this chapter, progress is made in the description of the temple; chambers, walks, ways, galleries, walls, priests, garments, holy things, and the outward courts, are here spoken of.

Ver. 1. "Then he brought me forth into the utter court." Difference there is amongst expositors, what court this was; whether the utmost court of all, which was the court of the people, or the next court to that, which was the priests' court, or the court the temple stood in, where the separate building was; called the outer court, in respect of the temple, into which he was brought out of the temple. Ver. 7, 8, 9, 14, speak of the outer court, and this outward court was that where the temple stood, as Sanctius and others observe.

Formerly hath been spoken of the outward court, representing the amplitude of the church; here it is conceived to hold forth the visibility of the church; that which is outward is visible. The church, whilst it is in this world, is the outward court. It is not the outward court which is the profane place; it is not the world, but the outward court, which is a place separate from the world, yet visible in the world. The church of Christ is prefigured in Scripture, and set out, by visible things. Sometimes by the ark of Noah, as 1 Pet. iii. 20; sometimes by a mountain, as Isa. ii. 2; sometimes by a vineyard, and vine, Isa. v. 1; Psal. lxxx. 8, 9; sometimes by a city, Psal. cxxii. 3; Rev. xxi. 2; sometimes by a ship, Luke v. 3; sometimes by a candlestick, Rev. i. 20; sometimes by a dove-house, Isa. lx. 8; sometimes by a garden, and by a spring, Cant. iv. 12; sometimes by a bird, Hos. xi. 11; sometimes by a flock, and a fold, Psal. lxxviii. 52; John x. 16; sometimes by a temple, 2 Cor. vi. 16. All these are visible things, and set out the visibility of the church eminently.

Ver. 3. "For the inner court." As the church visible is by the outward court represented; so the church invisible, the mystical body of Christ, is by the inner court.

Ver. 4. "Before the chambers was a walk of ten cubits breadth inward, a way of one cubit." There is a broad way, and a narrow way; a ten cubit way, and a one cubit way. The church in this world is under various dispensations: at one time it hath prosperity and freedom; it is in "a walk of ten cubits breadth," it is not straitened at all, as in Solomon's, Hezekiah's, and Josiah's days. So in part of the apostles' days, the church had "rest throughout all Judea, Galilee, and Samaria, and were edified; and walking in the fear of the Lord, and in the comfort of the Holy Spirit, were multiplied," Acts ix. 31. At that time the churches had liberty and prosperity, they had "ten cubits breadth;" and, the time will come, when the church shall have greater latitude, liberty, and prosperity, than ever she yet had.

At another time the church is in straits, afflictions, darkness, temptations, persecutions, &c. It is in "a way of one cubit," ver. 4. Such a way is narrow and strait, and that is the way the church is oft, if not most, in. Was not the church in the way of a cubit, when Elijah could see none but himself in that way?

The Lord Christ told his disciples of such a way, Matt. vii. 14, "Narrow is the way which leadeth unto life," it is a way of one cubit, "and few do find it." There are sharp afflictions, fiery serpents, wild beasts, thorns, briers, pits, stones, rocks, thieves, and robbers, in this way; all which the church of God meets with sooner or later. Rev. vii. 14, "These are they who came out of great tribulation;" these suffered heavy and many things for Christ's sake; they were in the one cubit way.

Ver. 5. "The galleries were higher than these." The Hebrew is, did eat up, or prevail; that is, as Montanus renders the word, they took away some room from the uppermost chambers. There is difference between particular churches; some are higher, some are larger than others.

Ver. 6. "Had not pillars." The strength of this temple was not every where alike, some parts had pillars, some had none, or not equal to others; the chambers had not pillars, as the pillars of the court. So in the church of Christ, some parts of it have strong pillars, eminent teachers, whereas other parts are destitute wholly, or have such as are weak. The church at Jerusalem had strong pillars in it, all the apostles, who were full of the Spirit, and taught infallibly. Other churches had not such pillars. Those in Macedonia wanted help, and therefore Paul had a vision of a Macedonian in the night, begging of him to come thither, and help them, Acts xvi. 9. The primitive churches had able, gracious, and wise officers, such as were pillars of a truth; in them, and sometimes since, have been strong pillars in some parts of the church, pillars of marble, brass, yea, gold; but in others, none, or weak ones.

"The building was straitened more than the lowest and the middlemost from the ground." Some buildings are broadest at the top; this was not so, but more strait upwards. It is harder with some parts of the church than others. Those who are highest in the church, meet with more storms, troubles, temptations, than those who are lower; the upper parts of the house are more obnoxious to winds and weather. Paul was high in the church, and what hardships, what tempests did he meet with! See 1 Cor. iv. 11—13; 2 Cor. iv. 8, 9; chap. xi. 23—27.

These chambers were some greater, some lesser, ver. 5, 6; plainly intimating that in the church of Christ, from what part soever men came, there should be entertainment, and suitable accommodation for them. If the kings of the east come in, Rev. xvi. 12, there shall be chambers for them. Let men come from north, south, or west, there are gates to let them in, and chambers to receive them when they are in. Isa. lx. 8, men shall come flying from all parts, as doves to a dove-house, in which are many holes, or chambers, for all the doves. So in the church of Christ, when men come thither, they shall find chambers, good accommodation.

Ver. 7. "The wall over against the chambers, the length thereof was fifty cubits." This wall was answerable to the chambers, which were fifty cubits in length, ver. 8. The wall of God's protection extends as far as the church doth, or any part thereof.

Ver. 8. *Before the temple were an hundred cubits.*

Fifty cubits in the inner court, and fifty in the outer court, saith Junius.

Ver. 9. *The entry on the east side.*

Some read the words thus, When he that brought me from the east. The prophet was led by a divine hand, from one place to another, chap. xl. 3.

Ver. 10—12. There, chambers towards the east, north, and south are mentioned. These chambers were some greater, &c.

Ver. 13, 14. *Then said he unto me, The north chambers and the south chambers, which are before the separate place, they be holy chambers, where the priests that approach unto the Lord shall eat the most holy things: there shall they lay the most holy things, and the meat offering, and the sin offering, and the trespass offering; for the place is holy. When the priests enter therein, then shall they not go out of the holy place into the outer court, but there they shall lay their garments wherein they minister; for they are holy; and shall put on other garments, and shall approach to those things which are for the people.*

The chambers, and the priests, are the two principal things in these verses.

I. For the chambers, they are described,

1. From their situation; they were north, south, and before the separate place.

2. From their holiness; they were holy chambers.

3. From their use; which was,

(1.) For eating of holy things.

(2.) For custody of holy things.

II. For the priests, here is,

1. Their duty, which is,

(1.) To approach unto God.

(2.) To lay up the holy things.

2. A direction what garments they are to minister in, how to dispose of them, and what they must use at other times.

The building, where these chambers were, was very large, as appeareth from chap. xli. 12; it "was seventy cubits broad, and the wall of the building five cubits thick round about, and the length thereof ninety cubits;" and it "was before the separate place." Some make the separate place the temple, but it is better understood of the space of ground at the west end of the temple; and lay next to the chambers joined to the temple, or between those chambers and the priests' chambers.

In time of the gospel, great numbers in the western parts from Jerusalem, have come in to Christ, and embraced the gospel; which was prefigured by the great building, and the separate place, which were at the west end of Ezekiel's temple: and ever since the gospel came into these western parts, and Christ hath had a church here, there hath been a thick wall of protection about it, so that neither heathenish nor antichristian powers could destroy it.

Here are many things considerable about the ministers of the gospel, who are represented by the priests, what they did, and had.

The priests did approach unto the Lord; it was their office to do so, and to minister unto him, Ezek. xliii. 19. Aaron and his sons ministered unto God in the priest's office, Exod. xxviii. 1, 41, 43. And it is the office of the ministers under the gospel to approach unto the Lord, to offer up prayers unto him for the people, 1 Tim. ii. 1. They are so near unto God, that they are called his stewards, Tit. i. 7, his servants, Acts xvi. 17; they approach unto God as stewards and servants to their lords and masters. The elders were near the Lamb, and had "golden vials full of odours, which are the prayers of the saints," Rev. v. 8; they presented the requests of the saints unto the Lord. In all administrations of the gospel, the ministers approach near unto God; and in all their approaches, he looks to be sanctified by them.

The priests who were in God's service had good accommodations; they had chambers, and were to eat of the most holy things; this signified, the care God would have of the ministers in the days of Christ, and the good provision he would make for them, they should not be without accommodations and means. Gal. vi. 6, "Let him that is taught in the word communicate unto him that teacheth in all good things." Here is large provision made for the gospel ministers; whatever good things people possess, they ought to communicate a part thereof to their teachers; something is due to the teachers, and it is duty in the taught to pay it. The ministers are to have meat, and chambers, accommodations to eat their meat in. 1 Cor. ix. 13, 14, "Do ye not know that they which minister about holy things live of the things of the temple? and they which wait at the altar, are partakers with the altar? Even so hath the Lord ordained, that they which preach the gospel should live of the gospel." Here is a divine ordinance for ministers' maintenance. It is also here hinted to us, that the priests were to eat of the best of the most holy things; that is, the tithes, and offerings, which were to be of the best, Mal. i. 8, 14. And certainly under the gospel, the ministers of it are not to be turned off with the meanest and worst of things: if you have choice spirituals from them, is it not equal they should have answerable temporals from you?

Holy things were to be laid in holy places; holy offerings, and holy garments, were not to be laid any where, but in the holy place. Under the law, some places were holy; but under the gospel, holiness of places is taken away, according to what was prophesied, Mal. i. 11, "From the rising of the sun even unto the going down of the same my name shall be great among the gentiles; and in every place incense shall be offered unto my name, and a pure offering." And according to that Paul gave out, 1 Tim. ii. 8, "I will that men pray every where, lifting up holy hands:" he makes all places alike, for the outward celebration of worship; yet the truths and things of the gospel are to be laid up in holy places, that is, in holy hearts. James iv. 8, "Draw nigh to God, and he will draw nigh to you. Cleanse your hands, ye sinners; and purify your hearts, ye double-minded." Holy hearts are fit places for God, Christ, Spirit, gospel, and all the ordinances of it. James i. 21; 1 Pet. ii. 1, 2; 1 Cor. xi. 28; Heb. x. 22; these places show that holy hearts are requisite for holy things. So, that of Christ, Matt. vii. 6, "Give not that which is holy unto the dogs, neither cast ye your pearls before swine;" their hearts are foul, and so uncapable of holy things; they are not fit repositories for such things.

Here is, in the 13th verse, mention made of three offerings, "the meat offering, the sin offering, and the trespass offering."

1. "The meat-offering," it was of fine flour, oil, and frankincense, or only of fine flour and oil; and then it was to be baked, fried, or sodden: no leaven or honey was to be used therewith; but every meat offering was to be seasoned with salt; see Lev. ii. *per totum.* Or it was of ears of corn, "the first fruits, ears dried by the fire, even corn beaten out of full ears," ver. 14. Part of this meat offering the priests were to "burn upon the altar for a sweet savour," and the rest they were to eat in the holy place, Lev. vi. 15, 16.

2. "The sin offering," whether a bullock, or any other beast, was most holy, yea, whatsoever touched the flesh thereof was holy. Some of the blood of it was to be brought into the tabernacle of the congregation, to reconcile with in the most holy place, which was not to be eaten, but burnt. The priests, and all the males among the priests, were to eat of this sacrifice, &c. Lev. vi. 25—30.

3. "The trespass offering." There was one and the same law for this, and "the sin offering;" it was to be killed where the burnt-offering was, and the blood to be sprinkled round about upon the altar; what was to be burnt, and what to be eaten by the priests, you may see, Lev. vii. 1—7.

These offerings were types of Christ, who is our true meat offering, the bread of life, the nourishment of every hungry and thirsty soul. His flesh, and his blood, are meat and drink indeed; at his table we feed upon him crucified, and so our meat offering. He is our sin offering, and trespass offering; 2 Cor. v. 21, He was made sin for us, that is, a sin offering, "that we might be made the righteousness of God in him." See Heb. x. 12, 14.

In the 14th verse it is said, the priests must "not go out of the holy place into the outward court," which comprehends this mystery in it, viz. that the ministers of the gospel, those who have given up themselves to Christ and the church, ought not to go out from their spiritual employment unto the world, and worldly affairs, but to mind that great work they are called unto; for "who is sufficient for such things?" 2 Cor. ii. 16. Paul instructed Timothy, and, in him, all others in this truth; 2 Tim. ii. 4, "No man that warreth entangleth himself with the affairs of this life, that he may please him who hath chosen him to be a soldier." When men are called to be soldiers, they must mind their soldiery, not other things; it will not please their captains and commanders, they cannot discharge their trust. So ministers, having a great Captain and Commander, the Lord Christ, who hath chosen them to be his soldiers, they must mind their spiritual soldiery, they must not trouble or distract themselves with the cares or affairs of the world; if they do, they can neither be faithful to their interest, nor please their Lord and Master. Rom. xii. 7, those that minister, must wait on their ministering, and those that teach, on their teaching; they must not wait upon or meddle with other things; see Col. iv. 17. Soldiers might not entangle themselves about husbandry, cattle, merchandising, or other affairs, but they were to mind the public.

The priests when they approached to God had other garments on than at other times; they had holy garments on them; they might not come nigh God but in holy garments; afterwards they changed their garments, when they were to deal with the people. Which informs us, that the ministers of the gospel ought to have other frames of spirit in them, when they are nearer unto God in the duties of his worship, than at other times; then they are to put on holy garments, they should be clothed with zeal, fear, and other holy affections. They are to discharge their office with gravity, and authority, that their ministry be not despised. God will be sanctified in them that come near unto him; they must not come in their old garments, with old, ordinary spirits; but with holy garments, holy spirits, sanctifying God in their hearts, making him their fear and dread, and carry themselves as ambassadors of God, standing and pleading for him. But when they are out of public administrations, they may put on other garments; they must be clothed with humility, love, bowels of mercy, meekness, long-suffering, as 2 Tim. ii. 24, 25. In common conversation, and converse with the people, they ought not to be high and haughty, lording it over God's heritage, 1 Pet. v. 3; but to be ensamples to the flock of wisdom, charity, patience, faith, and holiness. They are to become all things to all men, that they may win some to Christ.

Ver. 15—20. *Now when he had made an end of measuring the inner house, he brought me forth toward the gate whose prospect is toward the east, and measured it round about. He measured the east side with the measuring reed, five hundred reeds, with the measuring reed round about. He measured the north side, five hundred reeds, with the measuring reed round about. He measured the south side, five hundred reeds with the measuring reed. He turned about to the west side, and measured five hundred reeds with the measuring reed. He measured it by the four sides: it had a wall round about, five hundred reeds long, and five hundred broad, to make a separation between the sanctuary and the profane place.*

The 15th verse shows us how exact a building the church is, it is a house measured within and without; when Christ had done measuring the inner house, he comes forth and measures the outward parts; nothing is left unmeasured. Solomon's house, or temple, was not so exactly built, and measured, as the church of Christ is; that is God's building, 1 Cor. iii. 9, and he exceeded Solomon in wisdom, and so in building. See what a structure the new Jerusalem is, Rev. xxi. 10, &c.; which makes good that, Psal. cii. 16, "When the Lord shall build up Zion, he shall appear in his glory."

There is difference among interpreters about the reeds, mentioned in ver. 16, 17, 18, 19. Some would have them to be so many cubits only, from that in Ezek. xl. 47, where it is said the court was "an hundred cubits long, and an hundred cubits broad." Others would not have five hundred reeds or cubits to be on any one side, but that all the sides measured made up the sum, be it five hundred cubits, or five hundred reeds. But most interpreters are of the mind that each side was not only of five hundred cubits, but five hundred reeds.

The words for "measuring reed" are, בקנה המדה which was the great reed, saith A Lapide, of six cubits, whereas the vulgar reed was only of five cubits; that this reed was six cubits is clear from chap. xl. 5. So that the five hundred reeds were three thousand cubits, and the four sides came to twelve thousand cubits; which shows how spacious and vast the temple was. From these verses are presented to us,

1. The extent and latitude of the church which should be, in all quarters of the world, under Christ. He measured the gate to the east, and the east side, to make known the eastern people should be of the christian church. He measured the north side, showing thereby that the northern parts should come thither. He measured the south and west sides, assuring us thereby, that the people of those parts should come unto Zion. Christ sent his apostles to all nations, Matt. xxviii. 19. They went east, west, north, and south, enlarging the borders of the gospel, inviting and bringing in the gentiles daily. Mark xvi. 15, "Go ye into all the world, and preach the gospel to every creature." The church of Christ is all the world over; the sound of the apostles "went into all the earth," that is, all parts of the earth, "and their words to the end of the world," Rom. x. 18.

2. The stability and firmness of the church. The temple here measured was a perfect square, five hundred reeds on the east side, five hundred reeds on the west side, five hundred reeds on the north side, and as many on the south side. Buildings which are four-square, are most stable, firm, and lasting. Such is the church, it is stable, and permanent; "the gates of hell cannot prevail against it," Matt. xvi. 18. It is built upon Christ the chief corner stone, Eph. ii. 20; and is established in righteousness, Isa. liv. 14.

3. The lustre and beauty of the church. Great buildings in the form of a square are beautiful and glorious; such was that Ezekiel saw, it was a quadrature, every side proportionable, holding forth beauty and glory. Cant. vi. 4, saith Christ of his church, "Thou art beautiful, O my love, as Tirzah, comely as Jerusalem." Tirzah and Jerusalem were chief cities in Canaan; for at one, kings of Israel kept their courts, 1 Kings xiv. 17; and at the other, kings of Judah dwelt. These cities had much beauty and comeliness in them, and unto them Christ likens his church. Certainly, the church is the most beautiful and glorious thing in the world, to them who have eyes to see it. Many saw no beauty in Christ, Isa. liii. 2; but Christ was beautiful and glorious to them who had eyes to see it, John i. 14. And many see no beauty, no glory in the church of Christ; but where spiritual eyes are, there they are seen. The church is set out by a golden candlestick, Rev. i. 20; and that hath lustre, beauty, and glory. It is set out by "a woman clothed with the sun," Rev. xii. 1; and what lustre, beauty, and glory can there be wanting? It is set out by a bride, the Lamb's wife. When the bride of a great prince hath on her royal apparel, and is decked with all her ornaments and jewels, is she not beautiful, glorious, and shining? Such is the church, "arrayed with fine linen, the righteousness of saints," Rev. xix. 8; such is the new Jerusalem, "having the glory of God," Rev. xxi. 10, 11.

4. The safety of the church. This temple had a wall round about, five hundred reeds long and five hundred reeds broad, sufficient for the defence of it on every side. And the church in the gospel times hath a wall about it, long and broad; a wall that reacheth from east to west, from north to south; a wall higher than the heavens, deeper than hell, and broader than the earth, viz. the power and providence of God. Isa. xxvii. 3, "I the Lord do keep it; lest any hurt it, I will keep it night and day." Here is a wall better than that of wood, Ezek. xli. 22; than that of stone, Prov. xxiv. 31; than that of iron, Ezek. iv. 3; than that of brass, Jer. i. 18. Such walls have been battered, and broken, undermined, or climbed over; but this wall is not subject to any of them. The wall of the new Jerusalem is "great

and high," Rev. xxi. 12, sufficient to secure all that are within.

5. The sanctity of the church. This wall, as it was a wall of security, so of separation; it was to separate between the sanctuary and the profane place, that those in the profane place might not come into the sanctuary, where the holy ones and holy things were. The church of God is a company called out of, and separate from, the world, who have given up themselves unto God and Christ. The Corinthians were called out of the world to be saints, 1 Cor. i. 2; and the Macedonian churches gave up themselves to the Lord, 2 Cor. viii. 5. So that all the churches of God "are a chosen generation, an holy nation," 1 Pet. ii. 9; Cant. iv. 7. Unholy ones, who are without in the profane world, should not enter into the church. God hath set a wall of discipline to keep them out, that the church may not be defiled by them. It is said of the new Jerusalem, that "there shall in no wise enter into it any thing that defileth:" the angels will keep them out; for at the twelve gates thereof will be twelve angels, Rev. xxi. 12, who will let none in but saints, so that "all her people shall be righteous," Isa. lx. 21.

CHAPTER XLIII.

Ver. 1—6. *Afterward he brought me to the gate, even the gate that looketh toward the east: and, behold, the glory of the God of Israel came from the way of the east: and his voice was like a noise of many waters: and the earth shined with his glory. And it was according to the appearance of the vision which I saw, even according to the vision that I saw when I came to destroy the city: and the visions were like the vision that I saw by the river Chebar; and I fell upon my face. And the glory of the Lord came into the house by the way of the gate whose prospect is toward the east. So the Spirit took me up, and brought me into the inner court; and, behold, the glory of the Lord filled the house. And I heard him speaking unto me out of the house; and the man stood by me.*

THIS chapter and the next, in general, speaks of the ministry and sacred worship of the new temple: more particularly in this chapter we have,

1. A new vision, in the first six verses.

2. The speech of the Lord unto the prophet, from ver. 7, to the end of the chapter.

Concerning the new vision, the things considerable are,

I. The time when it was.

II. The place where it was.

III. The object of this vision: where we are to note,

1. The place whence it came.

2. The sign of it.

3. The effects of it.

4. The resemblance of it.

5. The receptacle of it.

IV. The consequents of it; which are,

1. The Spirit's raising up the prophet.

2. His leading him into the inner court.

3. The filling of the temple with glory.

4. The Lord's speaking to the prophet.

V. The presence of Christ with the prophet.

I. When it was that Ezekiel had this vision. Not at his first coming to the temple, but after he had been led from place to place, seen the several gates, courts, chambers, parts, appurtenances, ornaments of the temple, and all exactly measured within and without; after those things he had this vision. Which insinuates thus much, that, after men have waited upon Christ, followed him, and learned the nature and condition of the church invisible and visible, then the Lord affords visions of himself and his glory. When men come first to Zion, enter into church fellowship, they must not think to see the glory of God, till they are acquainted with the inward glory and outward beauty of the church, till they understand the measuring of Christ therein. Those that are in the church, in due time see glory. It is good to be there, and to wait being there.

II. The place was at the east gate. He was brought from the west side of the temple to the east gate, where he had this vision coming out of the east. Christ is the Sun of righteousness; and the sun's motion is from the east, westward: so here, this glorious vision came out of the east, and entered by the east gate, which led directly to the most holy place. It is the Lord Christ brings us out of darkness to light, and shows us the way into the temple and most holy place.

III. The object, glory. "Behold, the glory of the God of Israel." That was, some figure, image, or manifestation, representing the glory of God. In chap. i. 26, 27, Ezekiel saw the likeness of a throne, of a man of fire. And chap. viii. 4; x. 18, there were visions, where he beheld the glory of the God of Israel, and the glory departing; that is, some representation of his glory, which was leaving the temple and them; signifying that God was wroth with them, and departing from them. But here the glory was coming to them, importing that God's wrath was laid down, their sins pardoned, and he graciously reconciled unto them. It was sin caused the glory to depart; man's wickedness draws the glory away, but nothing in or of man caused the glory to return. It is said, "the glory came;" it came freely, undeservedly, unexpectedly; there was cause of great mourning when it departed, and there was as great cause of rejoicing when it returned.

1. Whence came it? "from the way of the east." Christ's star was seen in the east, Matt. ii. 2; his coming was from thence: Zech. iii. 8; vi. 12, Christ is called צמח which the Septuagint renders, ἀνατολή, the Vulgate, *Oriens*, that is, the east; because Christ should come from heaven, and enlighten the dark world, as the sun doth, when it riseth in the east. Luke, in his 1st chapter, ver. 78, calls Christ, ἀνατολή, which we render, "the day-spring," and may be rendered, the east, for the day springs in the east first: be it east, or day-spring, it is from on high. Christ came from heaven to bring light into the blind world. Hence saith Christ, John viii. 12, "I am the light of the world," the great light, the sun of it; which, rising in the east, shines into the utmost parts of the west.

2. The next thing is, the sign of the glory. And that was, a voice, such a voice as "was like the noise of many waters." In chap. i. 24, when the cherubims went, "the noise of their wings was like the noise of great waters." As the voice of the Almighty, waters use to roar, and make a great noise, Jer. xxxi. 35, and li. 55. Such waters are strong, and there is no resistance of them; men cannot row or sail against them. This voice minds us of the voice of Christ in the gospel, the sound whereof "went into all the earth," Rom. x. 18: and, Rev. i. 15, Christ's voice is said to be "as the sound of

many waters;" it was strong, and irresistible. He taught them with majesty and authority, Matt. vii. 29. They were not able to answer him, Matt. xxii. 46; John viii. 9; not to withstand the wisdom and truths he put into his disciples, Luke xxi. 15; Acts vi. 10; Rev. xi. 5. Christ's voice in the gospel is an efficacious voice.

3. The effects of it were two.

(1.) "The earth shined with his glory." Before the coming of Christ, the world was full of heathenish and hellish darkness; and Canaan was full of types, ceremonies, and shadows; there was little light or lustre there. But when Christ came, the oracles of the heathen ceased, and the Jewish shadows vanished, and the earth shined with the glory of the gospel. Matt. iv. 16, "The people which sat in darkness saw great light; and to them which sat in the region and shadow of death light hath sprung up." When the Jews were under clouds and darkness, then Christ came, and brought the glorious gospel to them. When Christ was born, Luke ii. 9, there was glory shone round about the shepherds; signifying, that the glory of the Lord would fill the earth, yea, all the world.

Or, this may refer to the destruction of mystical Babylon, and coming down of the new Jerusalem from heaven: for of the one it is said, Rev. xviii. 1, 2, "An angel came down from heaven, having great power; and the earth was lightened with his glory. And he cried mightily with a strong voice, Babylon is fallen," &c. And, chap. xxi. of new Jerusalem it is said, ver. 23, "The glory of God did lighten it, and the Lamb is the light thereof." When these things be, the earth will be filled and shine with glory.

(2.) Ezekiel fell upon his face. The lustre of divine glory, sense of his own frailty and weakness, caused him to fall upon his face. Here I might enlarge, but of this falling on his face was spoken chap. i. 28, and the observations rising thence are there to be seen.

4. The fourth thing concerning this glory is, the resemblance of it: ver. 3, "And it was according to the appearance of the vision which I saw, even according to the vision that I saw when I came to destroy the city," &c. The prophet being sent of God to prophesy the destruction of Jerusalem, saith here, "when I came to destroy the city." The Chaldee is, when I prophesied. Then had he such a vision as this was, chap. i. That which he declared to be done, he saith he did. The prophet was in Babylon when the city was destroyed, he did not put forth a finger towards destruction of it, he only prophesied against it. So Jeremiah was set over nations and kingdoms, to root out, to pull down, and to destroy; this he did by prophesying against them, not otherwise.

The same vision, which at first appeared to the prophet in a way of judgment, appears now to him in a way of merit; before, it prefigured the destruction, here the restoration of the temple, city, and land. The vision for outward appearance was like what he saw in chap. i. viii. ix. x.; but in the end, and use, totally differing from, yea, contrary unto the same. There he saw God angry, the glory departing from the temple, and going out at the east gate; here he sees God smiling, and the glory returning the same way it went out; here he beholds sweet reconciliation between God and the church, made up by Christ.

5. The fifth thing is the receptacle of this glory; and that was, the temple, or house, which had been measured: ver. 4, "And the glory of the Lord came into the house." This house, or temple, as hath been showed before, signified both the body and church of Christ. For his body natural, that was the receptacle of glory, Col. ii. 9; John i. 14; 1 Tim. iii. 16.

For the church, his mystical body, that is a receptacle of glory also. Isa. lx. 1, "The glory of the Lord is risen upon thee." And ver. 19, "The Lord shall be unto thee an everlasting light, and thy God thy glory." There is an estate of the church to come, wherein it shall be very glorious: in Solomon's temple there was glory, but glory in a cloud, 1 Kings viii. 10, 11; but in Ezekiel's temple there was glory without a cloud, a greater glory, even such a glory as made the earth to shine. This is the glory which the saints look for, and shall see in due time: Rev. xxi. 3, "Behold, the tabernacle of God is with men, and he will dwell with them, and they shall be his people, and God himself shall be with them, and be their God."

What is said of the church, is to be understood also of every believer, who is a receptacle of glory, a temple of the Spirit of Christ and God, 1 Cor. iii. 16; vi. 19; 2 Cor. xiii. 5. Whoever Christ hath measured out to be a temple, shall receive glory. 2 Cor. iv. 6, "God, who commanded the light to shine out of darkness, hath shined in our hearts," saith Paul, "to give the light of the knowledge of the glory of God in the face of Jesus Christ." The gospel is a glass; in it we see the face of Christ, and in his face the glory of the Lord, and "are changed into the same image, from glory to glory," 2 Cor. iii. 18. It is observable here, that when the glory of God departs from a church, or people, it is not for perpetuity, but for a season. The glory went out of the temple, and city, at the beginning of Ezekiel's prophecy; but he saw the same returning, before the end of his prophecy. The ark, when taken by the Philistines, caused Phinehas' wife to name her son Ichabod, saying, "The glory is departed from Israel," 1 Sam. iv. 21; but after seven months, the glory returned again to Israel; chap. vi. the ark was sent home, God caused it to return again. Long have the Jews now been without an ark, and without glory; but in due time the glory of the God of Israel will return unto them; for, Rom. xi. 26, "There shall come out of Zion the Deliverer, and shall turn away ungodliness from Jacob." And when the sealing of the hundred and forty-four thousand out of all the tribes shall be, Rev. vii. then shall they stand on mount Zion with the Lamb, and so the glory will be in the midst of them, Rev. xiv. 1.

IV. The consequents of this vision, or glory returning, come next to be considered: and

The 1st is, the prophet's raising; ver. 5, "So the spirit took me up." He was fallen upon his face, as not able to behold the brightness of that glory which appeared; and being in that posture, the Spirit took him up. In chap. ii. 1, 2, the Spirit spake to Ezekiel, being down upon his face, entered into him, and set him upon his feet; but here he took him up, he dealt with him as a man doth with his friend fallen. Hence springs this consideration, that those that are humbled, and humble, with sense of their own vileness and weakness, through apprehension of glory and greatness, shall soon be raised and comforted. The sight of glory is a humbling thing. Ezekiel, chap. i. 28, and here again, was humbled upon that account; he saw so much lustre in that glory, so much greatness in the Lord, that, convinced of his own vileness and nothingness, he falls down upon his face, as being wholly unworthy to behold such a sight, to partake of such mercy; but presently the Spirit, being full of love, bowels, and compassion, steps to him, and takes him up; he suffers him not to lie affrighted with glory, or affected with misery, but is a speedy comforter unto him. The humble find mercy, and are raised; when the proud meet with judgment, and are thrown down.

The 2nd consequent is, the Spirit leading of him, and that was, "into the inner court." He had led him into several places, and now leads him "into the inner court;" whereby he came to understand the mysteries of, and behold the glory in, the temple, which none are able to do without the leading of the Spirit. None, destitute of the Spirit, can enter into the church, to understand the things thereof, and behold the glory therein, 1 Cor. ii. 14, 15; 2 Cor. iii. 18. It is the Spirit that makes men discern spiritual things; it is the Spirit that leads us from knowledge to knowledge, from mystery to mystery, and from glory to glory; he leads into the temple, and "into the inner court," he reveals the deep and glorious things of God unto the saints.

The 3rd is, the filling of the house, and that with glory: ver. 5, "Behold, the glory of the Lord filled the house." There was abundance of glory in it, the temple and most holy place were full of it. This leads us to consider, not only the temple rebuilt after the Babylonish captivity, which the Lord said by Haggai, chap. ii. 7, that he would fill it with glory, and that the glory of it should be greater than of the former house, ver. 9, which was fulfilled in Christ's bodily presence there; but it leads us also unto Christ, who was filled with the glory of the Spirit, and fulness of the Deity, Col. ii. 9; and unto the church of Christ, which is filled with the glory of the gospel; (for it is glorious, and hath shining light in it, 2 Cor. iv. 4;) but chiefly unto the new Jerusalem, wherein a greater glory is expected to be seen, than hath ever yet been; there will be abundance of grace, and glorious effusions of the Spirit. See how glorious the new Jerusalem is, Rev. xxi.

The 4th thing is, the Lord speaking unto Ezekiel: ver. 6, "And I heard him speaking unto me." The Hebrew is, I heard a saying to me from the house, a saying from the glory, or from the Lord, being in that glory which filled the house: the temple, saith Vatablus; the most holy place, saith Maldonate; but we understand it of both. As the glory was in the temple, so the voice came from the temple. The Lord spake not of the temple, as Lyra would have it; but from, or out of, the temple.

The thing pointed out hereby is this; That God reveals and makes known his mind in his house, in the church; he speaks from the temple unto his people: Isa. lxvi. 6, "A voice from the temple, a voice of the Lord." There God discovered his displeasure towards his enemies, and his good will towards his servants. "In Judah is God known," Psal. lxxvi. There his mind is known; "The law goes forth out of Zion, and the word of the Lord from Jerusalem," Isa. ii. 3. Where his church is, there is his presence, there he utters his voice, there he opens his mind. Why did David desire "to dwell in the house of the Lord all the days of his life," but "to behold the beauty of the Lord," which appeared there eminently; "and to inquire in his temple," because the Lord there spake, and answered the desires of his servants, Psal. xxvii. 4. When he was troubled at the prosperity of the wicked, what did he then but enter "into the sanctuary of God?" and there he was resolved, he "understood their end," Psal. lxxiii. 17. The Spirit, and Christ, spake in the churches, and to the churches, Rev. ii. and iii.; and in chap. xvi. 1, a great voice was heard out of the temple.

"And the man stood by me." The Hebrew is, and a man was standing by me. Some make this man to be an angel; but it was he, mentioned chap. xl. 3, the man "whose appearance was like the appearance of brass, with a line of flax in his hand, and a measuring reed." This was Christ, the Master-builder. Zech. vi. 12, "Behold the man whose name is The Branch, he shall grow up out of his place, and he shall build the temple of the Lord." This Man stood by Ezekiel to assist, encourage, and interpret things unto him.

Whence cometh this observation, That the Lord Christ, who is the chief Architect in temple work, stands by his prophets and servants who are employed therein. When the temple was first built, many were employed therein, but they were not left to their own wisdom and skill. Solomon was principal therein; he was present, counselled, directed, and assisted; therefore it is said, he built the house of the Lord, 1 Kings vi. 2. So in Ezekiel's temple, a type of the gospel temple, Christ was present, he counselled, directed, assisted, he stood by the prophet. He stood by the apostles; Matt. xxviii. 20, "Lo, I am with you alway, even unto the end of the world." He stood by Paul; Acts xviii. 10, "I am with thee;" so chap. xxiii. 11. And Paul doth acknowledge it; 2 Tim. iv. 16, 17, "All men forsook me," they showed their unfaithfulness; "notwithstanding the Lord stood with me, and strengthened me:" he was about temple work, for it follows, "that by me the preaching might be fully known, and that all the gentiles might fully hear." Christ was with him, to instruct, encourage, and bless him and his labours. Christ walks in the midst of the churches, and holds the stars thereof in his right hand, Rev. ii. 1. And, chap. v. 6, it is said, "In the midst of the elders stood a Lamb."

There are two things worthy notice, from the 5th and 6th verses considered together.

The 1st is, the distinction of subsistences in the divine nature and essence. Here are three distinct ones named: (1.) The Spirit, which took up Ezekiel. (2.) The glory of the Lord, whom he heard speaking out of the house, which was the Father. (3.) The Man standing by him, which was Christ. Here is the Spirit, Father, and Son, who as they have distinct personalities, so distinct operations. The Spirit's work is raising up; the Father's, speaking; and the Son's, assisting, or standing by.

The 2nd thing is, the gradual proceedings of God, in carrying on his servants from mercy to mercy. Here are five steps of mercy.

The first is, the Spirit taking up the prophet, being fallen upon his face. Had any one come and raised the prophet, being down, it had been kindness, especially if Daniel, Zerubbabel, or some elder of Israel had done it; but one greater and better than them all did it, viz. the Spirit of God. This was great mercy.

The second is, the Spirit leading of him "into the inner court." He did not raise him, and then leave him, but led him. And whither? not into the outward court, but "into the inner court." This was a further mercy, a choice mercy, to be brought so near the temple.

The third step was, a sight of glory, he saw the glory of the Lord filling the house; this was a grand mercy, which none of the Jews besides himself saw: as when Christ was transfigured, and the mountain shined with the glory of his transfiguration, Peter and John saw it, which was a favour unto them to see such glory, and the greater, because none of the other apostles did see the same.

The fourth step is, the Lord's speaking unto him, being compassed about with glory. To have heard the voice of an angel had been mercy; but to hear the voice of the great and glorious God out of the temple, this was a height of mercy, such as Moses had, Exod. xxxiii. 11.

The fifth and last step is, the presence of Christ; he stood by him. Here was another mercy, and no mean one; Christ, "in whom are hid all treasures of wisdom and knowledge," Col. ii. 3. So then here was the whole Trinity employed at once about Ezekiel; which was transcendent and superlative mercy. Those who are called to be agents in temple work, have need of the whole Trinity; help of the Spirit to raise or lead them; of a sight of glory, to darken all human and mundane glory before their eyes; of hearing God speak, that they may be taught of him; and of having Christ present with them, that they may be enabled to go through their work. John in the Revelation was led from mercy to mercy, from vision to vision, as appears throughout that book, and especially in chap. xxi. 1, 2, &c. The time will come when the Spirit will lead the saints "into the inner court," where they shall see the glory of God, hear his voice, and find Christ standing by them.

Ver. 7—9. *And he said unto me, Son of man, the place of my throne, and the place of the soles of my feet, where I will dwell in the midst of the children of Israel for ever, and my holy name, shall the house of Israel no more defile, neither they, nor their kings, by their whoredom, nor by the carcases of their kings in their high places. In their setting of their threshold by my thresholds, and their post by my posts, and the wall between me and them, they have even defiled my holy name by their abominations that they have committed: wherefore I have consumed them in mine anger. Now let them put away their whoredom, and the carcases of their kings, far from me, and I will dwell in the midst of them for ever.*

The second part of this chapter, being the speech of God to the prophet, begins at the words read: and in them we have,

I. A promise of God's abiding with his people, and the effect thereof, viz. sanctification.

II. A declaration of the cause why God formerly departed from them.

III. A duty, or charge laid upon them, ver. 9.

The promise of divine presence, and continuance, is partly in the 7th verse, viz. in these words, "The place of my throne, and the place of the soles of my feet, where I will dwell in the midst of the children of Israel for ever;" and partly in the 9th verse, the last words of it, viz. "I will dwell in the midst of them for ever."

By the place of God's throne, and of the soles of his feet, is meant the temple, and city of Jerusalem, where God had formerly dwelt. Jer. xvii. 12, "A glorious high throne from the beginning is the place of our sanctuary;" it was God's throne, and it was the footstool of God, 1 Chron. xxviii. 2. It is granted by all, that Jerusalem, having the temple in it, represented the church of God under the gospel, in which the promise here is, that God will dwell for ever. The christian church shall have the presence of God in it, and abiding with it for ever: Matt. xxviii. 20, "I am with you alway, even unto the end of the world." John fixes this presence of God in the new Jerusalem, Rev. xxi. 2, 3. When new Jerusalem came down from heaven, then he heard a voice, "saying, Behold, the tabernacle of God is with men, and he will dwell with them, and they shall be his people, and God himself shall be with them, and be their God." So chap. xxii. 3, "The throne of God and of the Lamb shall be in it:" there both God and Christ will be and dwell.

This sets out the great esteem God had of, and the great complacency he had in, Jerusalem; he esteemed it as his throne, and took delight in it, as in his chiefest dwelling. Isa. lxix. 1, God saith, heaven is his throne, and earth his footstool; this is the honour he puts upon heaven and earth, and the same he puts upon Jerusalem, and now puts upon the christian church; it is his throne, his footstool, the place he esteems above all others, the place he takes more complacency in than all others. Such shall be the presence of the Lord in it, that it shall be called Jehovah-Shammah, that is, "The Lord is there," Ezek. xlviii. 35. And such shall be his content and delight therein, that Jeremiah tells you, it shall be called "the throne of the Lord;" Jer. iii. 17, "At that time they shall call Jerusalem the throne of the Lord; and all the nations shall be gathered unto it."

The effect of God's presence, viz. sanctification, is comprehended in these words, "My holy name shall the house of Israel no more defile, neither they, nor their kings, by their whoredom," &c.

Of profaning and defiling God's holy name was spoken, chap. xxxvi. 20. To let that pass, the sense here is, they shall avoid all things which do defile, and sanctify God's holy name; they should keep the worship of God, keep from idolatry, and all arbitrary inventions of men; which Jerom and Maldonate refer to the heavenly temple, and not to the temple built after the Babylonian captivity, because that was oft defiled, by Antiochus, Pompey, and Titus, and deserted by the Lord. Others refer it, as is here said, to that temple; because the Jews, after their captivity, did for ever hate idolatry, and serve the true God, though not in a right manner. If these words do in part refer to the state of the church after the captivity, yet principally they refer to the state of it after Christ, and that time too when new Jerusalem shall be extant; for antichrist hath greatly defiled the holy name of God with his idols, and will-worship; but then, nothing that defileth shall enter, Rev. xxi. 27; then shall be made good that in Zech. xiv. 21, "In that day there shall be no more the Canaanite in the house of the Lord;" they shall be all true Israelites.

"Nor their kings, by their whoredom." By "whoredom" the prophet understands idolatry, which is spiritual whoredom, of which hath often been spoken. Not only the people, but even kings and princes were given much to idolatry in Israel and in Judah: they caused idols and altars to be set up in most places, and countenanced them; they imitated the very heathens, and became like, yea worse than them, Ezek. v. 6, 7; xvi. 47; 2 Kings xxi. 2—7, 9. It is said of Jehoahaz, Jehoiakim, and Jehoiachin, that they did evil in the sight of the Lord, according to all that their fathers had done, they defiled Jerusalem what lay in them; but of the new Jerusalem it is written, "Kings do bring their glory and honour into it," Rev. xxi. 24.

"Nor by the carcases of their kings in their high places." The word for "carcases" is, פגרים from פגר which signifies to be without strength, slothful; so carcasses are deprived of all strength, and move not; they lie where they are fallen. The rabbies tell us, that the kings of Judah had a house near to the temple, yea, joining to it, and that they were wont to bury their dead in a garden belonging to it. There they say Manasseh and Amon were buried, which they gather from 2 Kings xxi. 18, 26; and that by their carcasses being so nigh the temple, it was defiled. But the places cited do not say, it was in the garden of the house of the Lord; they say, it was "in the garden of Uzza;" neither do they affirm that this garden joined to the temple.

The Vulgate reads the words, in the ruins of the kings; and so some expositors refer it to what we find done by Josiah, 2 Kings xxiii. 12—14, "The altars which were on the top of the upper chamber of Ahaz, which the kings of Judah had made, and the altars which Manasseh had made in the two courts of the house of the Lord, did the king beat down, and brake them down from thence, and cast the dust of them into the brook Kidron. And the high places which were before Jerusalem, which were on the right hand of the mount of corruption, which Solomon the king of Israel had builded for Ashtoreth the abomination of the Zidonians, and for Chemosh the abomination of the Moabites, and for Milcom the abomination of the children of Ammon, did the king defile. And he brake in pieces the images, and cut down the groves, and filled their places with the bones of men." These altars and high places, which Ahaz, Manasseh, and Solomon made, were utterly destroyed by Josiah, and thereupon called, The ruins of kings.

Another exposition of these words is, to understand them of the children which were sacrificed to idols, and passed through the fire: both kings and others did so by their children, 2 Kings xvi. 3; xvii. 17; xxi. 6; Jer. xix. 5; xxxii. 35; Ezek. xvi. 20, 21. This practice of theirs greatly provoked God, and therefore he saith, Jer. xvi. 18, "I will recompense their iniquity and their sin double; because they have defiled my land, they have filled mine inheritance with the carcases of their detestable and abominable things." They are called carcasses of their kings, either from the example of kings, who offered their children; or from their authority, commanding it; or from the names of their idols, which were called Molech, Milcom, and Malcham, 1 Kings xi. 7; 2 Kings xxiii. 13; Zeph. i. 5; which signifies, a king. Moses calls idols carcasses, Lev. xxvi. 30; and such they are, because lifeless, Psal. cxv. 5—7, and loathsome, Ezek. xxii. 3, abominations in the abstract. The carcasses therefore of their kings, it is not amiss to expound of those idols they caused to be set up and countenanced.

The Annotations on this place say, The Jews did deify their dead kings, and kept their bodies for adoration; but, as Sanctius saith, there is no Scriptural evidence that such insane adoration ever existed. That place they cite, Psal. cvi. 28, is impertinent, "They ate the sacrifices of the dead," that is, things offered to Baal-peor, a dead god.

Ver. 8. "In their setting of their threshold by my thresholds, and their post by my posts." The latter part of the former verse, "neither they, nor their kings," &c. together with this verse, declare the cause of God's former departing from them. God did not account the temple defiled because the kings had houses near unto it, in which they did wickedly, whereas they should have been more holy for their proximity to the temple. This sense some fasten upon the words. But that which hath more weight in it is, Manasseh "built altars in the house of the Lord, and set a graven image of the grove there," 2 Kings xxi. 4, 7. In, or near the house of God, there was the image of jealousy, Tammuz, and other abominations, Ezek. viii. 5, 10, 14, 18; so 2 Kings xvi. 11, 12, 14; Ezek. xxiii. 39. These were the threshold by God's thresholds, and the post by God's posts; these things caused God to go far off from his sanctuary, Ezek. viii. 6.

The precepts and traditions of men, with their inventions and additions to the worship of God, are styled posts, and thresholds. The authors of them do lean and stand much upon them, and set them in the way, to hinder others from enjoyment of temple privileges, unless they will own and comply with them; but such posts and thresholds are rotten and faulty. The Lord's institutions and appointments are sound and good; they bear up his name and worship; they are strong, and standing things, and by them we have entrance into his presence.

To make any thing like the institutions and appointments of God is prohibited. Exod. xxx. 32, 33, 37, 38, none might make anointing oil like the holy anointing oil, which God had appointed; if they did, they were to be cut off. And men may not make thresholds and posts like the Lord's thresholds and posts; much less set them up with the Lord's, impose them upon the conscience as the Lord's, giving them equal honour and authority with them. This is defiling the worship and holy name of God, which he will avenge; for he will admit no rival or proprietory in the things of his worship; he saith, "My thresholds, my posts;" he will have no adding to or diminishing from what is his, Deut. xii. 32.

The scope of God in these words is this, that the worshippers in the new temple shall do nothing of their own private spirits, of their own heads; there shall be no superstition, idolatry, or human invention, added to the worship of God; there shall be no heresy, no false doctrines, no traditions or devices of men. Such thresholds and posts shall not be set up by the Lord's; they are defiling things, and such things must not enter into the new Jerusalem, Rev. xxi. 27: neither shall they by their sins cause God to depart from them; but shall do all things according to the line of his word, and apply themselves wholly to do his good pleasure.

"And the wall between me and them." There is but the wall between my sanctuary and their houses, I am but a little distanced from them, and yet they have done these things; they have forgotten me, and defiled my holy name: or, their altars, idols, traditions, inventions are a wall between me and them, so that they neither come at me nor I at them. Isa. lix. 2, "Your iniquities have separated between you and your God;" they are a partition-wall, so thick and high, that there is no seeing or hearing one another.

"Wherefore I have consumed them in mine anger." By their will-worship, and idolatry, they so displeased the Lord, that he departed from them, was wroth with them; and so wroth, that he consumed them by sad and severe judgments: but under the new temple, or gospel church, it should not be so; being reconciled to his people therein by the Lord Jesus, he will not leave them, be wroth with them, or consume them. Sin causes separation, wrath, and consumption.

Ver. 9. "Now let them put away their whoredom, and the carcases of their kings," &c. Junius reads the words in the future tense, Now they shall remove their whoredom far off. The Lord tells Ezekiel what converted Jews and others under the gospel should do, they should put all superstition, idolatry, and will-worship away, and serve the Lord in all purity, and so he would dwell amongst them for ever. Rev. xiv. 1, 4, 5; vii. 14, 15, God is holy, and he will dwell amongst holy ones. 2 Cor. vi. 16—18, God will not leave this temple as he left the former, but be in it, and dwell in it for ever. This is his promise, and it is a great and precious one. The sun's presence in the day is a great mercy, but it is gone in the night, and then all is dark and doleful. In the church of Christ, the new Jerusalem, there will be no night, Rev. xxi. 25. There the sun will always shine, God will be present and perpetually present in it, everlasting light and glory unto it, Isa. lx. 19.

Ver. 10—12. *Thou son of man, shew the house to the house of Israel, that they may be ashamed of their iniquities: and let them measure the pattern. And if they be ashamed of all that they have done, shew them the form of the house, and the fashion thereof, and the goings out thereof, and the comings in thereof, and all the forms thereof, and all the ordinances thereof, and all the forms thereof, and all the laws thereof: and write it in their sight, that they may keep the whole form thereof, and all the ordinances thereof, and do them. This is the law of the house; Upon the top of the mountain the whole limit thereof round about shall be most holy. Behold, this is the law of the house.*

In these verses we have given out,

I. The prophet's duty; which is to show the Israelites the house, with the adjuncts and appurtenances of it.

II. The house of Israel's duties; which are,

1. Humiliation for their sins.

2. Measuring of the pattern.

3. Keeping and observing the forms and ordinances of the house.

III. The law of the house; which is holiness, ver. 12.

Ver. 10. "Thou son of man, show the house to the," &c. The Lord commands Ezekiel to "show the house to the house of Israel:" he had seen the house, with all the forms, ordinances, and adjuncts of it; he had seen the measuring of it, within and without; he well understood both the frame and the house, and the things belonging to it, and so must show it to the Jews. The prophets must first see themselves, before they show to others; they must first be taught of Christ, before they teach others; they must be well acquainted with temple work, know the inside and outside, the forms and laws thereof, first themselves, and then make the same known to others. John first saw new Jerusalem, and the measurings of it, and after that revealed it to others, Rev. xxi. And what they have seen, that they reveal, that they show, and nothing of their own. Ezekiel must show the house he had seen, and only that. Ministers under the gospel should know the form and ordinances of Christ's house, and show them, and them only, to the people.

"That they may be ashamed of their iniquities." This vision was to be shown unto the Jews in captivity, to let them know that there should be a restoration of the temple and church state again; and under it, the state of the church under Christ was typed out; and this was done to bring them to repentance. The word for shame is, כלם which notes, shame for things in themselves shameful, filthy, and loathsome. The words may be read, And they shall be ashamed; or thus, And let them be ashamed.

Obs. When God reveals mercy, and shows kindness to a sinful people, they ought to be ashamed, and repent of all their former iniquities. See Ezek. xvi. 60, 61, 63; xxxvi. 25—31. And here they must be informed of this vision, and the mercy held out in it towards them, that they might consider their idolatries, superstitions, and other iniquities, and so be ashamed, and confounded in themselves. "The house of Israel," all Israel, were to be "ashamed of their iniquities," of all they had done amiss in church and state. And so should the house of England be ashamed of all done amiss in church and state; of all corruptions, abominations, and oppressions, which are in the same: we should be ashamed of them, 1. As acts of filthiness. 2. As acts of folly. 3. As acts of unkindness and ingratitude. 4. As fearing a just reproof. 5. As fearing God's servants, cause, and name will suffer by them. When our shame is of this nature, it is right; if upon other grounds and considerations, it is worthless.

"Let them measure the pattern." Junius reads the words, that they may measure universally. · thers, let them measure. The showing of them the house was that they might measure it; that is, that they might endeavour to understand the measures of it, and so have the knowledge of it, and the christian church, exactly in their minds. It was a spiritual measuring which Ezekiel had; and such a measuring they were to make, to look at the true marks of the church, which are essential and spiritual, not external and accidental.

Obs. Those who have humbled themselves for their former sins, are fit to be spiritual mathematicians. The house of Israel must first be ashamed of her iniquities, and then "measure the pattern." When we reflect upon our sinful ways, and are broken-hearted that we have displeased the Lord; then are we fittest for the knowledge and understanding of spiritual things. Dan. ix. 13, it is clear, that humbling of the soul for sin, and turning from it, makes way for understanding of the truth. The old man is to be put off, that all things may be new, and so we may attain to the knowledge of this temple. Men of corrupt minds and practices are unfit for temple work, and the measurings thereof which must be according to the word.

Ver. 11. "And if they be ashamed of all that they have done, show them the form of the house, and the fashion thereof," &c. These words seem to contradict what is in the former verse, where it is said, "Show them the house, that they may be ashamed of their iniquities;" and here it is, "If they be ashamed of all that they have done, show them the form of the house." In the first, sight of the house is required, as precedaneous to humiliation; and here, humiliation is required as precedaneous to sight of the house. The answer to this seeming contradiction is easy. The sight of the house first, was mercy, and that made way for humiliation; and then their humiliation upon that made way for further mercy. First, they had a general sight of the house, which caused shame; and being thoroughly ashamed, they had a more distinct and particular knowledge of the same.

"The form of the house, and the fashion thereof." In a house there are several parts, as walls, windows, doors, posts, lintels, galleries, stairs, chambers, &c. And these are of several forms and fashions, which he must show to the house of Israel, even "all the forms;" which is twice mentioned, and notes the outward and inward forms of the church.

The outward, lies in profession, in the union and harmony of the parts, in the greatness and extent of the whole, in the discipline and government of it.

The inward forms consist in those gracious principles and qualifications which are in those professors, which make up the house and body of Christ, in the power of godliness, and the cordial closing one with another in the life, spirit, purity, and power of ordinances. There is beauty and glory in the outward forms, but most in the inward. Psal. xlv. 13, "The king's daughter is all glorious within; and her clothing is of wrought gold." The church shines without, but is very glorious within, all glorious. "The kingdom of God is within men," Luke xvii. 21; and that is, in righteousness, peace, and joy. Paul had an eye to both forms, when he told the Colossians, he rejoiced to see their order, and faith, Col. ii. 5.

"And the goings out thereof, and the comings in thereof." There were several gates in this temple, and they were to come in at one and go out at another. Those who came in at the north gate, must go out at the south gate; and they who came in at the south gate, must go out at the north gate, and not at the gates they came in by, Ezek. xlvi. 9. In this temple there was no turning back, but going forward; when the tabernacle was up, there was looking and turning back to Egypt. When Solomon's temple stood, there was of them who went backward, and not forward, Jer. vii. 24; Isa. i. 4; Jer. xv. 6; but in this temple they were to go forward, and not backward. Isaiah prophesied that the people of this temple should "be all righteous," Isa. lx. 21; and the righteous hold on their way, Job xvii. 9.

"All the ordinances and all the laws thereof." The Hebrew word for "ordinances" is, חק from חקק to engrave upon wood or stone; and that for "law" is, תורה from ירה to instruct, or teach; so that this latter imports the instruction of the mind, the former the impression of truth upon the hearts and affections. Suarez saith, that a law, properly so called, is illuminative, reforming and directing the judgment; and impulsive, moving the heart and will to action. Some, by these ordinances and laws, understand the rites and rules they were to observe in relation to the sacrifices; for it is probable, being seventy years in captivity, they had forgotten them in part, if not wholly; but not only these are here intended, for then the scope of the vision would extend no further than Zerubbabel's temple, whereas it refers chiefly to the temple and worship of Christ under the gospel, as hath been showed. The ordinances and laws thereof are here likewise included, and what the worshippers are to do; when, and how, and which belong to the temple.

De Legib. lib. 1. c. 5.

Obs. 1. That to repentant men, ashamed of all their evil doings, the ways of God's house are to be made known by the prophets and ministers. "If they be ashamed, show them the form and fashion of the house," &c. If they were not humbled for and ashamed of their abominations, which caused the destruction of the first temple, they must not be informed in the mysteries of this temple, either by word or writing. Impenitency excludes from temple mercies; but shame, and hearty sorrow for sin, makes way for such mercies. To them so affected, must the forms and fashions, the comings in and goings out of the house, all the outward and inward forms, all the ordinances and laws thereof, be made known, by word, or writing, or both; they are to be admitted to the mysteries and secrets of the temple. As for dogs, holy things are not to be communicated unto them.

Obs. 2. Temple and church work must not be according to men's fancies, but according to the mind of God, and that pattern he gives forth. God set a pattern before Ezekiel, he must set it before the house of Israel, and they must build and order the temple answerably; they must "keep the whole form thereof, and all the ordinances thereof;" they might not add to, nor detract from, what God had prescribed. Moses, in the tabernacle work, must do all after the pattern given him, Exod. xxv. 40; xxxix. 42, 43. Noah, in his ark work, must keep to what God appointed, Gen. vi. 14—16. Solomon, in his temple work, was tied to the pattern given out by the Spirit to David, 1 Chron. xxviii. 11—13. In the gospel church it is so, Matt. xxviii. 20, "Teaching them to observe all things which I have commanded you." Nothing is left to their liberty, God's appointments only must be in his house; neither antiquity, nor custom, nor convenience, nor prudential considerations, nor show of holiness, nor any pretext whatsoever, will warrant any human invention, brought into the church and worship of God.

Obs. 3. That the temple and church of Christ hath distinct and peculiar laws of its own. Ezekiel must show them the laws and ordinances of the house, not those of nature or nations. Cæsar's and Christ's laws do differ; his are civil, and Christ's are sacred, he rules in Zion, and man's laws have no place there.

Obs. 4. The church in due time shall be such a temple as here it is represented by this vision. It shall be one large, strong, and full of glory, as this visional temple was. When God gives forth visions, it is in the thoughts of his heart to make them good. How shall the house of Israel, the true christians, keep the laws and ordinances of his house, if it never be built? God hath not only purposed, but promised to build it, Ezek. xxxvii. 26, 27, "I will set my sanctuary in the midst of them for evermore. My tabernacle also shall be with them; yea, I will be their God, and they shall be my people." And John saw it accomplished in vision, hearing God uttering parallel words, Rev. xxi. 2, 3. And doubtless the time is drawing near for the building of it. Now men see a difference between the stones of Babylon, which must neither be corner, foundation, or wall-stones, Jer. li. 26, and the stones of Zion, which are precious and living; they begin to creep out of the dust of contempt, and to appear like the stars of the morning: now there is a spirit of prayer more than formerly, and more than ordinary, for the accomplishment of this vision, and great expectation raised in many to see such a spiritual temple.

Obs. 5. The end of making known the laws and ways of God's house is, that they may be observed and practised. Ezekiel must show them, and write in their sight, the forms, laws, and ordinances of the house, that they may keep and do them. God propounds not divine things only to be known, but chiefly to be done. It is not enough to know virtue, but men must endeavour to have it, and to do virtuously. Did a man know all the forms, comings in, and goings out of God's house, all the laws and ordinances thereof, and not observe them, it would not advantage him at all, but make his condemnation the greater. The end of human laws and ordinances is observation, else they are no better than ciphers. So the end of God's laws is keeping and doing of them; it is not knowing, nor hearing, nor praising, but practice which commends them. Disobedience is a dishonour to God, to his house, to his laws. Let us hearken to James in this case, chap. i. 22, his counsel is good, "Be ye doers of the word, and not hearers only, deceiving your own selves."

Ver. 12. "This is the law of the house; Upon the top of the mountain the whole limit thereof round about shall be most holy," &c. Sanctius reads the words thus, "This is the law of the house, upon the top of the mountain," and there makes the distinction from the following words. Others make it before, and refer the words "upon the top of the mountain" to the latter words, not the former. There is no considerable difference, whether the note of distinction be in the one or the other place, for the house was upon the top of a mountain, chap. xl. 2.

The law of this house, viz. the fabric, mountain, and whole compass thereof, was holiness; it is here said to "be most holy." The Hebrew is, the holiness of holiness. The Hebrews do double the word when they intend a superlative; as, "a servant of servants," Gen. ix. 25, that is, most servile; "a king of kings," Ezra vii. 12, that is, the most eminent and greatest of kings; and here, the holiness of holiness, that is, the "most holy." Such was this house, and the mountain whereon it stood, and the compass of it round about, which was by a wall of five hundred reeds long, and so many broad; or, thereby was the separation made "between the sanctuary and the profane place," chap. xlii. 20. This house was to be the habitation of God's throne; a representation of new Jerusalem, and heaven itself; therefore it is styled not only holy, but "most holy."

Obs. 1. The church of God hath a good foundation. It is a house upon a mountain, and that is strong; Job xxxix. 28, rocks and mountains are strong places, they stand immovable. The rock, or mountain, on which the church is founded and built, is the Lord Christ himself, 1 Cor. iii. 11; called "a mountain," Dan. ii. 35; "a precious corner stone, a sure foundation," Isa. xxviii. 16; a "rock," 1 Cor. x. 4; "the strength of Israel," 1 Sam. xv. 29; "the root of David," Rev. xxii. 16; and upholder of all things, Heb. i. 3: he upholds the world and the church.

Obs. 2. The church of God is eminent and conspicuous. It is on the top of a mountain, and that mountain was very high, chap. xl. 2, where he saw this temple; which holds forth the visibility and eminency of the church under the gospel. Isa. ii. 2, "It shall come to pass in the last days, that the mountain of the Lord's house shall be established in the top of the mountains, and shall be exalted above the hills; and all nations shall flow unto it." When one mountain is laid upon another, the uppermost must be very eminent. The church here is called "a mountain," and this mountain is seated upon the top of another mountain, even that mountain that fills all the earth, Dan. ii. 35. It must therefore of necessity be high, and be seen of the nations; for it is prophesied that "all nations shall flow unto it." This suits with that, Rev. xxi. 24.

Obs. 3. The whole church of God is to be made up of holy materials. The house upon the top of the mountain, the whole circuit thereof round about shall be most holy. There must not be one part of the house profane, another part holy; but the whole house, and every part thereof, must be holy. Isa. xxxv. 8, there shall be "the way of holiness; the unclean shall not pass over it;" the purity of that way will be such, as wicked ones will not dare to tread in it. Joel iii. 16, 17, "The Lord shall roar out of Zion, and utter his voice from Jerusalem; and the heavens and the earth shall shake:" terrible doings there shall be, "but the Lord will be the hope of his people, and the strength of the children of Israel. So shall ye know that I am the Lord your God dwelling in Zion, my holy mountain: then shall Jerusalem be holy," that is, all Jerusalem shall then be holy, "and there shall no strangers pass through her any more," to pollute and defile her. Then shall "every pot in Jerusalem and Judah be holiness unto the Lord," as Zechariah speaks, chap. xiv. 21. Then shall be shut out all dogs, sorcerers, whoremongers, murderers, idolaters, and lovers with makers of lies, as John saith, Rev. xxii. 15; and whatever defileth, chap. xxi. 27. Peter calls them of this temple "lively stones," 1 Pet. ii. 5. John calls them sealed ones, Rev. vii. 4; such as had the "Father's name written in their foreheads," Rev. xiv. 1; "Precious stones," Rev. xxi. 19; Eph. ii. 19—22.

Obs. 4. The law of this house, which is holiness, is specially to be observed. The verse begins and ends alike: "This is the law of the house. Behold, this is the law of this house." Of this house, so Vatablus. Of that house, so Junius. As the house is emphatical, so is the law of it set out with a Behold! this is the law of it, holiness of holiness; all in this house hath a law of holiness written in it, or upon it. If any thing or person could come in here without holiness, such things and persons would be cast out as unclean, as the man was who came in to the marriage supper without "a wedding garment," Matt. xxii. 12, 13; they violate the law of holiness, and must suffer for it. But such shall not be suffered to enter: Rev. xxi. 27, "There shall in no wise enter into it any thing that defileth;" no false doctrine, no human inventions or will-worship, shall be there; no profane person, no formalist, or hypocrite, shall get in there; "but they who are written in the Lamb's book of life;" ver. 12, there is an angel at every gate to keep out the unworthy. See Isa. lii. 11.

Ver. 13—17. *And these are the measures of the altar after the cubits: The cubit is a cubit and an hand breadth; even the bottom shall be a cubit, and the breadth a cubit, and the border thereof by the edge thereof round about shall be a span: and this shall be the higher place of the altar. And from the bottom upon the ground even to the lower settle shall be two cubits, and the breadth one cubit; and from the lesser settle even to the greater settle shall be four cubits, and the breadth one cubit. So the altar shall be four cubits; and from the altar and upward shall be four horns. And the altar shall be twelve cubits long, twelve broad, square in the four squares thereof. And the settle shall be fourteen cubits long and fourteen broad in the four squares thereof; and the border about it shall be half a cubit; and the bottom thereof shall be a cubit about; and his stairs shall look toward the east.*

In chap. xli. 22, mention was made of an altar, which was of the altar of incense. Here another altar is presented to the prophet, which is the altar of burnt offering; which, with the appurtenances of it, is described, and measured by the cubit; not the common cubit, which consisted of twenty-four fingers' breadth, but the large or royal cubit, which was a hand's breadth more, and is here said to be the cubit, that is, "a cubit and a hand's breadth." This altar was a perfect square, in length and breadth equal, each was twelve cubits; the bottom, breadth, and border, with the lesser and greater settles, have their several measures and distances; it had horns and stairs.

The 15th verse in Hebrew is thus, And the mount of God, four cubits, and from the lion of God and upwards four horns; so it is in the margin, "Harel, the mountain of God." Some understand the space where they put the wood which burned the sacrifice. Others make it the body of the altar, which being between two settles, or benches, was so termed, appearing like a little mountain. האראיל the lion of God, or of the strong God, it is conceived was the grate upon which the holocaust was laid; and this grate was of the form of a lion, as Vilalpandus saith; but rather it was so called, because, as a lion tears and devours the prey, so the fire of this altar did eat up the sacrifices laid upon this grate. Whether the apostle hath not some respect unto this, or Solomon's altar for burnt offerings, when he saith, "Our God is a consuming fire," Heb. xii. 29, is considerable.

This altar had stairs to go up unto it, yet God had forbid steps, or stairs, to be made unto his altar, and gives a reason for it, Exod. xx. 26, which was to be observed of men when they made altars unto God; but when the Lord prescribed the form of an altar for himself, he might, according to his own good pleasure, have it with steps or without. It is probable Solomon's altar had steps, being ten cubits high, as Sanctius and the Annotators observe; the priests also were to wear linen breeches when they were sacrificing.

These stairs looked "toward the east;" that so, when they sacrificed and worshipped God, their backs might be towards the east, and their faces westward; which the wise God ordered so, that he might keep his people from conforming to, and symbolizing with, the idolatrous nations, who with their faces eastward worshipped the sun-rising.

This altar for burnt offerings was a type of Christ, as those of Moses and Solomon were, Exod. xxvii. 1; 2 Chron. iv. 1.

1. This altar was but one; so Christ is our altar, and our only altar, Heb. xiii. 10; the christian church knoweth no other.

2. It had a grate, whereon the sacrifice was laid, and fire put to it, whereby it was burnt; so Christ had a cross, whereto he was fastened; and there the fire of God's anger did fall upon him, which was due to us for our sins, Isa. liii. 5; Matt. xxvii. 46.

3. It had four horns at the four corners thereof, which signified the strength and sufficiency of Christ, for all who should come unto him from the four corners of the earth. When men were in danger of their lives, they fled to the altar, and took hold on the horns thereof, 1 Kings ii. 28; Exod. xxi. 14; and if they were not wilful and presumptuous sinners, they were safe. What sinner soever shall come from any part of the world unto Christ, and take hold of him by the hand of faith, he shall be safe. The four corners of his altar are his "wisdom, righteousness, sanctification, and redemption," 1 Cor. i. 30; and he is able to save them who take hold of him to the uttermost, Heb. vii. 25.

4. This altar was to be seven days cleansed and purified, ver. 26 of this chapter, and Exod. xxix. 37; and so it was holy, and whatsoever touched it was holy. Herein is figured the perfect holiness of Christ, who was "most holy," Dan. ix. 24, and sanctified himself for the service of the church; and whoever toucheth him by faith is made holy; and whatever is offered up to God upon this altar likewise is holy. This altar sanctifieth the gift, Matt. xxiii. 19; Heb. xiii. 15.

5. It was glorious and durable, being of shittim wood and brass, Exod. xxvii. 1, 2; of cedar, and pure gold, 1 Kings vi. 20. And herein it represented the Deity of Christ, which is most glorious and eternal, Heb. i. 3; ix. 14.

6. It was called the mountain of God, being on mount Zion; he did as it were dwell there, and took pleasure in the sacrifices offered on it: and is not Christ *Hariel*, the mountain of God; is not he the altar in the mountain of the Lord's house? Heb. xiii. 10; Isa. ii. 2. Doth not God dwell in him? Col. ii. 9. Was he not a sacrifice well pleasing to God? Eph. v. 2. Are not we "the righteousness of God in him?" 2 Cor. v. 21.

And not only so, but the lion of the strong God: and is not Christ *Haariel*, the Lion of the mighty God? He is "the Lion of the tribe of Judah," Rev. v. 5; the Lion of God, to whom God hath given all power in heaven and earth, Matt. xxviii. 19. This Lion hath rescued us out of the mouth of that "roaring lion," who intended and endeavoured to make a prey of all mankind, 1 Pet. v. 8; Heb. ii. 14. This Lion hath "spoiled principalities and powers," Col. ii. 15; purged away sin, Heb. i. 3; made reconciliation to God, Dan. ix. 24; "abolished death, and brought life and immortality to light," 2 Tim. i. 10.

The exact measuring of this altar dictates this, that ministers should have and hold forth the full knowledge of Christ, and especially of him crucified, as an offering for sin; for therein lieth the benefit of sinners, to know Christ crucified. Hence Paul, 1 Cor. ii. 2, professeth he determined not to know any thing among the Corinthians, (that is, to make known any thing, to preach any thing,) "save Jesus Christ, and him crucified;" that should be his work, to measure out Christ to them. So Philip preached Christ to the Samaritans, Acts viii. 5; and Peter preached Christ unto the Jews, and others, Acts ii. The virtue of Christ crucified is to be made known fully.

Ver. 18—27. *And he said unto me, Son of man, thus saith the Lord God; These are the ordinances of the altar in the day when they shall make it, to offer burnt offerings thereon, and to sprinkle blood thereon. And thou shalt give to the priests the Levites that be of the seed of Zadok, which approach unto me, to minister unto me, saith the Lord God, a young bullock for a sin offering. And thou shalt take of the blood thereof, and put it on the four horns of it, and on the four corners of the settle, and upon the border round about: thus shalt thou cleanse and purge it. Thou shalt take the bullock also of the sin offering, and he shall burn it in the appointed place of the house, without the sanctuary. And on the second day thou shalt offer a kid of the goats without blemish for a sin offering; and they shall cleanse the altar, as they did cleanse it with the bullock. When thou hast made an end of cleansing it, thou shalt offer a young bullock without blemish, and a ram out of the flock without blemish. And thou shalt offer them before the Lord, and the priests shall cast salt upon them, and they shall offer them up for a burnt offering unto the Lord. Seven days shalt thou prepare every day a goat for a sin offering: they shall also prepare a young bullock, and a ram out of the flock, without blemish. Seven days shall they purge the altar and purify it; and they shall consecrate themselves. And when these days are expired, it shall be, that upon the eighth day, and so forward, the priest shall make your burnt offerings upon the altar, and your peace offerings; and I will accept you, saith the Lord God.*

Having prescribed the form of the altar, the Lord gives out to Ezekiel the ordinances thereof, the laws and rites which concerned the sacrifices and priests, showing him what priests he would have employed for the service of this altar, as also what sacrifices, and how the altar is to be purified; which things extend to the 27th verse, and therein the daily work and worship of the altar is appointed.

Although the chief scope of this vision be to set out the glory and greatness of the church under the gospel and among the gentiles; yet, because the

Jews at this time being in Babylon were to return unto Jerusalem, therefore the Lord alludes to ordinances, rites, and ceremonies which were well known among the Jews, holding out under them the spiritual worship of the gospel.

The priests to be in the service of this altar, and to draw near to God, were to be of the seed of Zadok. David being on his death-bed, Abiathar the high priest sided with Adonijah the eldest son, to make him king, but Zadok was for Solomon; whereupon after the death of David, Solomon obtaining the kingdom, Abiathar was put out of his place, and Zadok made high priest, 1 Kings ii. 35. Zadok was constant and faithful, a just and upright man, as his name signifies; and such men were to serve at this altar; such as are constant to Christ, faithful, just, sincere, ought to be in gospel administration, and to draw near to God in these ordinances which belong to the gospel, which differ from the Judaical.

Here are three sorts of sacrifices mentioned, the burnt offering, the sin offering, and the peace offering, ver. 18, 19, 27; of which, and their different rites, you may read, Lev. i. *per totum;* chap. vi. 24, to the end; chap. iii. *per totum,* with chap. vii. 11—22. These sacrifices were not sufficient to expiate sin, but they were means of worship, leading them unto Christ. So baptism and the supper are not of great validity, as to purge away sin; but they are means of worship leading unto Christ, who only is the expiatory sacrifice for sin, Heb. vii. 27; x. 10—12, 14.

Concerning the bullock for the sin offering, two things are proposed.

1. That the blood thereof be taken "and put upon the four horns of the altar, and upon the four corners of the settle, and upon the border round about," ver. 20; and the like was to be done with the "kid of the goats," ver. 22. This presignified the abundant shedding of the blood of Christ, which "cleanseth from all sin," 1 John i. 7; Rev. i. 5; and that Christ crucified should be preached to the four corners of the earth, Matt. xxviii. 19; 1 Cor. i. 23.

2. This bullock was to be burnt in the appointed place of the house without the sanctuary, which shadowed out the place of Christ's suffering, as it is written, Heb. xiii. 11, 12, The sin offering was burnt "without the camp. Wherefore Jesus also, that he might sanctify the people with his own blood, suffered without the gate," even in the place appointed, Luke xxiii. 33.

As for the burnt offering of a young bullock, and a ram out of the flock, both without blemish, the priests were to "cast salt upon them," ver. 23, 24. In Leviticus they were commanded with all their offerings to offer salt, chap. ii. 13. Salt makes all things savoury, and preserveth from corruption, by the heat and sharpness of it; and therefore salt was accounted an emblem of duration and eternity: 2 Chron. xiii. 5; Numb. xviii. 19, we read of "a covenant of salt," which notes an inviolable, incorruptible, and perpetual covenant. Sanctius thinks salt was used in sacrifices, because it notes prudence and wisdom; without which sacrifices are unsavoury. Without question it notes the wholesome doctrine of the gospel, gracious words, and seasonable reproofs, Col. iv. 6; Eph. iv. 29, which are savoury to God and man. This salting the sacrifices by the priests, types out the office of gospel ministers, who are styled by the Lord Christ, "The salt of the earth," Matt. v. 13; and are to season others with wholesome doctrine and sharp reproofs. Titus must rebuke the Cretians "sharply, that they may be sound in the faith," Tit. i. 13; the salt of the gospel will eat out those ill humours which are in men. Christ saith, Mark ix. 49, "Every one shall be salted with fire," that is, with the fire of the Spirit, the fire of afflictions, or the fire of hell; and "every sacrifice shall be salted with salt," that is, with grace, and especially the grace of mortification, which will eat out, and consume, those lusts which are offensive to God, to themselves, and others; and the grace of zeal, which will make the affections mount up to the Lord. True christians are sacrifices well seasoned; uncorrupt doctrines will make uncorrupt souls and bodies, the salt makes both immortal: men soundly salted with gospel truths shall never perish.

Ver. 26. "They shall consecrate themselves." The Hebrew is, they shall fill their hands. Some, by hands, understand the sides of the altar, because יד signifies both a hand and a side: others take hands for the hands of the priests, which should be filled with sacrifices, that is, with sacrificing work, and so prefigured the full employments the gospel ministers should have. But the Hebrew word מלא sometimes signifies, to consecrate, as learned Hebricians observe; Exod. xxviii. 41, "Thou shalt anoint them, and consecrate them;" the Hebrew is, thou shalt fill their hand; so Exod. xxix. 9; Numb. iii. 3; 1 Kings xiii. 33; Judg. xvii. 5. In these places the Hebrew is, filled the hand, which notes consecration, according to the Hebrew dialect, and so it imports the ministers' consecrating and dedicating themselves unto the work of Christ, under the gospel.

The 27th verse speaks of the daily sacrifices, and work of the altar; one sacrifice or other was to be offered daily. Two lambs, one in the morning, another in the evening, were to be offered daily, Exod. xxix. 38, 39; these were for the burnt offering, ver. 42. Besides which, here is mention of a peace offering, of which they were neither to eat the fat nor the blood, Lev. iii. 17; signifying, that those who are at peace with God, through Christ, ought neither to be carnal, nor cruel, but to mortify their carnal lusts, and to be meek as Christ was. The daily sacrificing of the priests' here, showed the daily and constant work of the ministers under the gospel; preaching, administering of sacraments, praying, and praising of God, is to be their daily work; which being done according to rule, and in the name of Christ, makes them and the people accepted.

Ver. 28. *It shall be upon the eighth day.*

Here is foretold, saith Mr. Shepherd, the continuance of the sabbath in gospel days, the eighth day from the creation being the first of our redemption. Noah is called the eighth, 2 Pet. ii. 5; who was the first in regard of his years, and dignity of person, and first entered into the ark, Gen. vii. 7. And so the Lord's day may be the eighth in one sense, and the first in another.

CHAPTER XLIV.

Ver. 1—3. *Then he brought me back the way of the gate of the outward sanctuary, which looketh toward the east; and it was shut. Then said the Lord unto me; This gate shall be shut, it shall not be opened, and no man shall enter in by it; because the Lord, the God of Israel, hath entered in by it, therefore it shall be shut. It is for the prince; the prince, he shall sit in it to eat bread before the Lord; he shall enter by the way of the porch of that gate, and shall go out by the way of the same.*

THIS chapter treats of the priests, and divers ordinances concerning them.

I. Sundry things are presented to Ezekiel touching the priests.

1. The privilege of the high priest, in the three first verses.

2. A reproof of the priests for their profaneness and neglect, from the beginning of the 4th verse to the 8th.

3. The exclusion of some, and deposing of others from the priest's office, ver. 9—14.

4. What priests God will accept of, ver. 15, 16.

II. The ordinances which concern the priests are laid down, from the 17th verse to the end.

Ver. 1. "Then he brought me," &c. The prophet having seen the altar for burnt, sin, and peace offerings, with the ordinances thereof, is brought back to the east gate, or "gate of the outward sanctuary," that which separated the priests' court from the people's, or the outmost gate of all. We must follow Christ, which way soever he leads us, be it backward or forward; he hath something to reveal unto us, which will be for our use.

Ver. 1, 2. "It was shut." What gate soever this was, it was shut; and therefore shut, because the Lord had entered in by it, and no man might, but the prince only.

Some take "prince" literally for the governor of the people, but the best expositors take it for the high priest, who was preferred above, and so prince of, all the rest; for in this chapter he speaks of the orders of the priests. This prince, or high priest, was a type of Christ. The high priest was to be without blemish, anointed with holy oil, to be covered with clean linen, and clothed gloriously; on him was a plate engraven with holiness to the Lord, he had the Urim and Thummim, he bare the names of the twelve tribes of Israel upon his breast and shoulders; as appears, Lev. xxii. 13; Exod. xxix. 7; xxviii. 2; xlii. 36; xxx. 9. So Christ, our High Priest, was without blemish, Heb. vii. 26; anointed with the Spirit, Isa. lxi. 1. He was holy, glorious, yea, holiness altogether, Luke i. 35; Mark i. 24. He had all perfection, Col. i. 19; ii. 3. He bears all Israel in his breast, and on his shoulders, Isa. xl. 11; Heb. vii. 25.

What is meant by the gate shut, is necessary to inquire. It was not the womb of the virgin, which was shut up after the birth of Christ, as popish interpreters expound it. Some of the ancients make it to be heavenly mysteries, which none know but the Father and the Son; some make it the Scripture, or "book sealed with seven seals," Rev. v. 1, which none could open but Christ. This gate shut, rather notes the gate or entrance into heaven, which Adam by his fall had shut, so that no man whatsoever, being sinful, could open it, or enter; only Jesus Christ our High Priest hath opened it, and entered. Heb. iv. 14, "We have a great High Priest, who is passed into the heavens." He hath broken all the bars, locks, and bolts, which kept it shut, and hath opened the same, so that now sinners may have access to God. The high priest once in a year entered into the most holy place, the door opened to none but him; this typified Christ's opening of heaven, and entrance in thither, as is clearly expressed, Heb. ix. 7, 8, 11, 12, 24. The tabernacle and temple were representations of heaven, and so was this vision of Ezekiel; and as the gate here was shut, so was the gate of heaven, till the Lord Christ, the Archbishop of our souls, opened the same, and entered. "No man hath ascended up to heaven, but he that came down from heaven, even the Son of man which is in heaven," John iii. 13; no man ever, by his own virtue or power, ascended up to heaven, but Christ. Enoch and Elijah neither ascended nor entered by their own strength, grace, or goodness. Christ's merits were the key which opened heaven for them and others. Christ is the door, and the way, and no man comes to the Father, but by him, John xiv. 6. It is by Christ alone that we come to the knowledge and fruition of the Father; he reveals him and his mysteries, and brings us unto the enjoyment of him.

Quest. If Christ have entered in by this gate, why is it still shut, why stands it not open? for, ver. 2, it is said, "This gate shall be shut, it shall not be opened, and no man shall enter in by it:" and why? because "the God of Israel hath entered in by it, therefore it shall be shut."

Answ. 1. It is shut for the honour of the prince. Great persons and princes have their gates shut, all must not come at and see them: it was an honour to the spouse, that she was "a garden enclosed, a spring shut up, a fountain sealed," Cant. iv. 12.

2. For the use of the prince, that he might go in and out at his pleasure; that he might let in and keep out whom he pleased. The wise virgins were let in by the bridegroom, but the foolish were kept out, for "the door was shut," Matt. xxv. 10, 11. In the new Jerusalem no unclean thing could enter, though the gates stood open; and out of heaven no clean thing shall be kept, though the gate be shut. Christ hath the key to open it for saints: he opened it for Stephen, Acts vii. 56, "Behold, I see heaven opened, and the Son of man standing at the right hand of God." He opened it for Peter, Acts x. 11.

3. It may be said to be shut, in regard of Christ's long continuance there before his return. It is said, ver. 3, "He shall enter by the way of the porch of the gate, and shall go out by the way of the same." Christ will come again, he is entered into heaven, and there he will, and must, abide, till "the time of restitution of all things," Acts iii. 21: see Acts i. 11; Heb. ix. 28.

Christ, who entered by this gate, was not only man, but God; he was the Lord God of Israel, Jehovah, that he might open heaven for sinners; and man, that he might enter himself.

This gate was "for the prince," that he might "sit in it to eat bread before the Lord." Aaron, the high priest, was to eat sacred flesh, and bread, in the door of the tabernacle, Lev. viii. 31; Exod. xxix. 32. This sitting, and eating bread there, and that "before the Lord," leads us to a double consideration of Christ.

1. His sitting in heaven at the right hand of Majesty, Heb. i. 3. Having finished the work which was given him to do, he ascended on high, and had the greatest glory; he sat at God's "own right hand in heavenly places, far above all principalities, and powers, and might, and dominion, and every name that is named, not only in this world, but also in that which is to come, Eph. i. 20, 21.

2. His communion with, and happiness in, the Lord; which is held forth in his eating "bread before the Lord." The communion and happiness the saints have with and in Christ, is set out by eating and drinking; Luke xxii. 29, 30, "I appoint unto you a kingdom, as my Father hath appointed unto me; that ye may eat and drink at my table, and sit on thrones," &c.; so Matt. xxvi. 29; that is, that ye may have sweet communion with me, and be happy in the fruition of me, as I am in the fruition of my Father, and communion with him.

Ver. 4—8. *Then brought he me the way of the north gate before the house: and I looked, and, behold, the glory of the Lord filled the house of the Lord: and I fell upon my face. And the Lord said unto me, Son of man, mark well, and behold with thine eyes, and hear with thine ears all that I say unto thee concerning all the ordinances of the house of the Lord, and all the laws thereof; and mark well the entering in of the house, with every going forth of the sanctuary. And thou shalt say to the rebellious, even to the house of Israel, Thus saith the Lord God; O ye house of Israel, let it suffice you of all your abominations, in that ye have brought into my sanctuary strangers, uncircumcised in heart, and uncircumcised in flesh, to be in my sanctuary, to pollute it, even my house, when ye offer my bread, the fat and the blood, and they have broken my covenant because of all your abominations. And ye have not kept the charge of mine holy things: but ye have set keepers of my charge in my sanctuary for yourselves.*

Before the reproof of the priests, the second thing considerable in the chapter, here are three things to be minded concerning Ezekiel.

I. His sight of glory.

II. The effects of that sight.

III. The command laid upon him.

For the sight of glory. Being "brought to the north gate," he saw "the glory of the Lord filled the house;" that was, some visible sign of his glorious presence: touching this, was spoken in chap. xliii. 5.

The effect was, he fell upon his face, as before: the sight of glory humbles, and prepares to receive the commands of the Lord. When the glory and majesty of God is seen, and apprehended, the heart is stricken with awe and reverence of God; and the party so affected is humbled before God, and so made fit for impression of divine commands: as here it follows;

Ver. 5. "And the Lord said unto me, Son of man, mark well, and behold," &c. In chap. xl. 4, we had the substance of this verse, and partly the very words. Here, God requires the inward and outward parts, the heart and senses. Those words, "mark well," are, in the Hebrew, set thine heart; so that the heart, the ears, and eyes, are to be attentive, and intentive, on what God commands. The heart must not wander, the ear be heavy, nor the eye rove, when God speaks, and temple work is in hand. The holy God, and holy things, are exactly to be observed and heeded by all; but especially by those who are officers in his house, as Ezekiel was: they must attend to all the ordinances and laws of God's house, for they must make them known to others, and walk by them themselves; they must know how to behave themselves in the house of God, and teach others so to do: especially, they must "mark well the entering in of the house," that is, they must be careful who they admit to be in it, and to partake of the ordinances of it, lest both it and they be defiled; they must mark every going forth of the sanctuary, so that none go out at the same door they entered, that they go forwards, not backwards, that they leave not the house of God, but be looked after.

Ver. 6. "And thou shalt say to the rebellious, even to the house," &c. Ezekiel, being prepared, must go and execute the command of God; which was, to reprove the house of Israel, and chiefly the priests. The sins they are reproved for are, 1. Rebellion. 2. Abominations. 3. Bringing in unworthy persons into the sanctuary, to pollute it. 4. Their sinful sacrificing. 5. Breaking of covenant. 6. Neglecting of their charge, and committing the same to others.

Of the rebellious house of Israel, and their abominations, formerly hath been spoken. It is said here, ver. 6, "Let it suffice you of all your abominations;" that is, they are not few, or light, but many, and grievous; and it is time now that ye should be ashamed of, and humbled for, them, and turn to the Lord from them: him have you provoked bitterly by them, and he hath made you suffer long and sharply for them. O sin no more, cease from idolatries, and unjust practices! let what is past suffice. So Peter, 1 Epist. chap. iv. 3, saith, "The time past of our life may suffice us to have wrought the will of the gentiles."

The third sin was, the introduction of strangers into the sanctuary, and they were men "uncircumcised in heart and in flesh." The gentiles were not circumcised in flesh, they ought not to have entered into the sanctuary, Lam. i. 10. Paul was accused for bringing Greeks into the temple, Acts xxi. 28. The heathen might come into the outward court, or "profane place," as Ezekiel styles it, chap. xlii. 20; but into the temple they might not come, it was a polluting of it. Sanctius thinks the priests received sacrifices and oblations from the hands of the heathen, which they offered to God in the temple, which was contrary to the law, Lev. xxii. 25. The Jews were circumcised in flesh, but many of them were uncircumcised in heart; they were without faith, they followed their own lusts, and imitated the heathens. Such priests were admitted into the sanctuary as were profane. The priests, saith God, "have violated my law, and have profaned mine holy things: they have put no difference between the holy and profane," Ezek. xxii. 26. Eli's sons were wicked, even "sons of Belial," 1 Sam. ii. 12. Urijah the priest made an altar like that of Damascus, and sacrificed on that, according to the command of the king, 2 Kings xvi. 11—16, but contrary to the command of God. Such should not have any place in the house of God, because they were abomination unto him; they polluted the sanctuary and sacrifice, by taking the bread, fat, and blood to themselves, which was against the law, Lev. xxxix. 10, 11, 14, 15—17; xxi. 8, or by offering them with defiled hands and hearts. They also broke the covenant, that is, the laws, which God had given them, concerning the way and manner of sacrificing; they kept not, but violated the same; their own wills were set up, and God's laws laid aside.

The last sin is, their neglect of their charge: ver. 8, "Ye have not kept the charge of my holy things." All things belonging to the tabernacle and temple were holy, and the charge of such things was committed to the priests and Levites, 1 Chron. ix. 27—32, and xxiii. 28—32; and they ought to have had special care of them themselves; but they have suffered strangers, and uncircumcised ones, to be in the sanctuary, to meddle with the holy vessels, and to offer sacrifice: and this they did for their own ease and ends, not for God's glory; for they did the same of their own heads, contrary to the rules and laws of the sanctuary, which, by so doing, they made no better than a den of thieves, or wild beasts; which place was only for whom, and what, God himself appointed, and so for his honour and glory alone.

Observe hence, That those who have the charge of holy things, ought to be exact, observing the order and rules God hath given, and not to deviate from them, doing any thing of their own heads. These men did not keep the charge of the holy things: they should have observed the laws of God's house, which they neglected; themselves should have done all things according to divine order; they set others about the work. God's work must be done by those he appoints, and in the manner he prescribes. Jehoiada observed what was written in the law of Moses, and appointed offices and officers in the house of God accordingly; he durst not vary from what God had given out by Moses, 2 Chron. xxiii. 18, 19. Timothy was charged to keep the command given him by Paul concerning the house of God, and the holy things thereof, "without spot, unrebukeable, until the appearing of our Lord Jesus," 1 Tim. vi. 13, 14: he might not spot the same with his inventions, additions, or detraction. It is great presumption in men to take upon them to alter what the infinite wise God hath prescribed; as if they were wiser than God, and knew what were fitter for his worship and service than himself: men, in so doing, do equalize their will-worship to his divine worship, they set their posts by his, Ezek. xliii. 8; but this provokes, and makes way for judgment. When Nadab and Abihu brought strange fire, such as God commanded not, kitchen fire, not altar fire, their own fire, not God's fire; though it were for nature the same, and would have done what the other did, yet because it was not the appointed fire, God was wroth, and sent out fire which devoured them, Lev. x. 12. When they carted the ark, (which should have been carried upon the Levites' shoulders, Numb. iv. 15,) and Uzzah, without warrant from God, staid it up with his hand, did not the Lord's anger kindle to such a height, that he smote him dead? 2 Sam. vi. 6, 7. David acknowledged this evil, 1 Chron. xv. 23, saying, "The Lord our God made a breach upon us, for that we sought him not after the due order." Men may seek God, and yet if they seek him not in a due order, even that order he hath prescribed, they may be far from mercy, and near unto judgment.

Ver. 9—14. *Thus saith the Lord God; No stranger, uncircumcised in heart, nor uncircumcised in flesh, shall enter into my sanctuary, of any stranger that is among the children of Israel. And the Levites that are gone away far from me, when Israel went astray, which went astray away from me after their idols; they shall even bear their iniquity. Yet they shall be ministers in my sanctuary, having charge at the gates of the house, and ministering to the house: they shall slay the burnt offering and the sacrifice for the people, and they shall stand before them to minister unto them. Because they ministered unto them before their idols, and caused the house of Israel to fall into iniquity; therefore have I lifted up mine hand against them, saith the Lord God, and they shall bear their iniquity. And they shall not come near unto me, to do the office of a priest unto me, nor to come near to any of my holy things, in the most holy place: but they shall bear their shame, and their abominations which they have committed. But I will make them keepers of the charge of the house, for all the service thereof, and for all that shall be done therein.*

In the 9th verse strangers are excluded from the sanctuary, and the service of it. In the rest of the verses those who had abused the priestly office are deposed from it, yet admitted into inferior services.

In Deuteronomy there was a law which prohibited the Ammonites and Moabites from entering into the house of God, which was grounded upon special reasons, Deut. xxiii. 3, 4; but here is a general law, prohibiting all strangers whatsoever to enter into the sanctuary, and bear office there; none ungodly, uncircumcised in heart or flesh, would he have to enter, or minister unto him. And not only so, but the Levites themselves which were corrupted, must be put from their offices. Many of the priests, after the ten tribes revolted, set up calves, and idolatrized; complied much with them, and the sinful practices of the times, and were defiled with the pollutions of them, and so went far from God, and his pure ways, hearkening to the commands of wicked kings, 2 Kings xvi. 11; therefore they must be thrust from the dignity of priesthood into the covert service of the sanctuary, they must "bear their iniquity," the punishment of their sins, viz. loss of their places; they must no longer minister unto God, be priests of God, but ministers of the people; they must be porters of the gates, slayers of the sacrifices, and keepers of the utensils that belonged unto the sanctuary. These were inferior and mean offices. Their departing from God's ways, their drawing the people to sin, and offending the church, made God swear against them, (for so that expression, "I lifted up mine hand against them," is to be understood,) lay shame upon them, and cause them to serve in the basest services; wherein mercy appeared also, in that he did not absolutely reject them. Those who sin through infirmity, and repent, do find mercy.

Ver. 15, 16. *But the priests the Levites, the sons of Zadok, that kept the charge of my sanctuary when the children of Israel went astray from me, they shall come near to me to minister unto me, and they shall stand before me to offer unto me the fat and the blood, saith the Lord God: they shall enter into my sanctuary, and they shall come near to my table, to minister unto me, and they shall keep my charge.*

The other priests being laid aside from all priestly performances, for their apostasy from God, and for their pollutions, here it is declared what priests God would accept of, viz. "the sons of Zadok," who was the first high priest in Solomon's temple, whose posterity was faithful and constant in evil and apostatizing times. When the ten tribes went a whoring from God, and many priests, the sons of Ithamar, were led aside, by the commands of Ahaz and Manasseh, these kept the charge of the sanctuary, and would not, for fear, flattery, or favour, depart from the laws and rites of God's house: these were the men who must come near to God, and minister unto him in the sanctuary.

"Come near to my table." By "table" is meant the altar. Ezek. xli. 22, "The altar of wood" is said to be "the table before the Lord;" and not only the altar for incense was God's table, but that also which was for burnt offerings, Mal. i. 7, 12; that was a table for God's bread and meat.

Obs. 1. The Lord takes notice of those who serve in his house, who are false and who are faithful, in corrupt and apostatizing times. The sons of Zadok, they kept the charge of my sanctuary, when the children of Israel went astray from me. Those who forsook me followed Jeroboam and the calves, but the others would not leave my house, my service, they kept their stations, and were constant. This was their honour, that they were stedfast in the way and work of the Lord; and it was a blot and reproach to them that fell off, for the Lord brands them to be revolters, Hos. v. 1, 2.

Obs. 2. God takes pleasure in and honours those who are faithful and constant in his service. The sons of Zadok were such, and God saith of them, "They shall enter into my sanctuary, they shall come near to me, they shall stand before me, they shall minister to me at my table, they shall keep my charge." By these expressions they are much honoured, and God's pleasure in them much manifested. Those priests, prophets, ministers, who are backsliders, revolters, apostates, are a dishonour to God, and burden to his Spirit. Of such, though they repented, it is said, ver. 13, "They shall not come near unto me, to do the office of a priest unto me, nor to come near to any of my holy things, in the most holy place: but they shall bear their shame, and their abominations which they have committed." God will neither honour them, nor have any pleasure in them; he honours and takes pleasure in those who have been true to him, and faithful.

Ver. 17—22. *And it shall come to pass, that when they enter in at the gates of the inner court, they shall be clothed with linen garments; and no wool shall come upon them, whiles they minister in the gates of the inner court, and within. They shall have linen bonnets upon their heads, and shall have linen breeches upon their loins; they shall not gird themselves with any thing that causeth sweat. And when they go forth into the utter court, even into the utter court to the people, they shall put off their garments wherein they ministered, and lay them in the holy chambers, and they shall put on other garments; and they shall not sanctify the people with their garments. Neither shall they shave their heads, nor suffer their locks to grow long; they shall only poll their heads. Neither shall any priest drink wine, when they enter into the inner court. Neither shall they take for their wives a widow, nor her that is put away: but they shall take maidens of the seed of the house of Israel, or a widow that had a priest before.*

Here, and in the following verses, are certain rules and instructions given forth for the priests: and the first is,

Concerning their vestures and attire. When the sons of Zadok come to minister unto the Lord, they must be clothed all in linen, no woollen garments must be upon them, as it was in Moses' days: Exod. xxviii. 42, 43; xxxix. 27—29; Lev. xvi. 4, they had linen bonnets, linen breeches, linen girdles, and linen coats; woollen was not permitted them, because less pure than linen. And as those linen garments which Aaron and his sons had, noted out the purity and innocency of Christ, so these the sons of Zadok had noted out the purity and innocency of the ministers under Christ and the gospel. The twenty-four elders were clothed in white raiment, Rev. iv. 4; and those who served the Lord in his temple were arrayed with white robes, chap. vii. 13, 15. The ministers of Christ ought to be holy, chaste, unblamable, and patterns of virtue unto others, 1 Tim. iv. 12; 2 Tim. ii. 22; Tit. i. 7, 8. When they savour the things of the flesh, they are brutish, and have on woollen garments, which should not be. They are to avoid all things which may make them infamous, and to hear ill. Sweat is an unsavoury thing, they must not wear any thing which causeth that, signifying they must do nothing which may justly cause an ill savour. Their loins must be girt with sincerity, and their conversations such as may be inoffensive before God and men.

Of putting off their garments, and putting on others, when they go out from their ministration, was spoken, chap. xlii. 14. "And they shall not sanctify the people in their garments." Common things were made holy by the touching of holy things, according to the law, Exod. xxix. 37; the priests therefore put them off, lest going out in them, the people might touch them, and so being sanctified, be necessitated to leave their callings. *Vid.* Diodate. Œcolampadius saith, to sanctify, in this place, is to be willing to be esteemed holy; and so the priests were not to go forth in their garments, that the people might esteem them holy. The Chaldee is, they shall not mingle with the people, being in those holy garments, and so profane them. Pintus hath it to good purpose, thus, they shall not go out in their priestly garments to bless the people, but do it in their common garments; they must be in another frame of spirit in their approaches to God, than in common dealings with the people.

The second rule given them is, concerning their heads, they must not shave them, nor wear long locks, but poll their heads. The heathens used to shave their heads, especially their idolatrous priests; and God would not have those that ministered unto him to conform unto idolaters. His servants must not shave their hair, then it would be too short; nor nourish it, then it would be too long; but "poll" the same, keep a medium between both. The ministers of Christ must not "shave their heads," lest they should symbolize with antichristian monks and friars; nor wear it long, which is the garb of luxurious, barbarous, and military men: they must neither neglect their hair, nor be effeminate in the length, powdering, or curling of the same; but have such a care of that, and their habit, as becomes the gospel, and the servants of Christ.

A third rule is, the prohibition of wine; not simply, but "when they enter into the inner court." This was a law laid upon Aaron and his sons: Lev. x. 9, "Do not drink wine nor strong drink, thou, nor thy sons with thee, when ye go into the tabernacle of the congregation, lest ye die: it shall be a statute for ever throughout your generations." Notwithstanding this law, the priests and prophets were faulty, and complaint is made, Isa. xxviii. 7, "The priest and the prophet have erred through strong drink, they are swallowed up of wine, they are out of the way through strong drink; they err in vision, they stumble in judgment." The Jewish priests were absolutely forbidden wine, it is conceived, lest it should cause them to speak or do indecently in their ministrations. But wine is not wholly prohibited to the ministers of the gospel; Paul bids Timothy drink wine, 1 Tim. v. 23. Here temperance and sobriety are commanded and commended unto the ministers of Christ; they must not be men given to wine, Titus i. 7, but sober, ver. 8.

A fourth rule is, touching their marriage. They are not forbidden to marry, but are cautioned about the same, and showed who they must not marry, not a widow, or one divorced. And Moses mentions two more, Lev. xxi. 14, a profane one, and a harlot, which they might not take; a virgin or a priest's widow they might, and these must "be of the seed of the house of Israel." Strange virgins, or strange widows, they might not join themselves unto. The scope of the words is, that they should marry them who were modest, chaste, pious, sober, and well educated, that so they might be a comfort and an honour to their husbands in that office. The priests were types of Christ, and the ministers of the gospel are in Christ's stead unto the people; and marriage represents the mystical union and marriage between Christ and his church: therefore, of all men, they should see to it what wives they take, even such as will be subject in all things, as the church is unto Christ, Eph. v. 24; and so mind others of their duty.

Ver. 23—27. *And they shall teach my people the difference between the holy and profane, and cause them to discern between the unclean and the clean. And in controversy they shall stand in judgments; and they shall judge it according to my judgments: and they shall keep my laws and my statutes in all mine assemblies; and they shall hallow my sabbaths. And they shall come at no dead person to defile themselves: but for father, or for mother, or for son, or for daughter, for brother, or for sister that hath had no husband, they may defile themselves. And after he is cleansed, they shall reckon unto him seven days. And in the day that he goeth into the sanctuary, unto the inner court, to minister in the sanctuary, he shall offer his sin offering, saith the Lord God.*

More rules are prescribed here for the priests of this new temple.

The first is, that they, putting difference in things and persons, between the holy and profane, the clean and the unclean, should teach the people the same. This was the priests' duty of old, Lev. x. 10, 11; and because it was neglected, God complains of the priests: Ezek. xxii. 26, "They have violated my law, they have profaned my holy things: they have put no difference between the holy and profane, neither have they showed" (that is, to the people) "difference between the unclean and the clean." But now it should be otherwise, the ministers of the gospel should teach the people sound and discriminating doctrine, so that they should know truth from error, men sound in the faith from such as were corrupt and heretical. Paul taught Timothy to discern between men having a form of godliness, and the power of it, 2 Tim. iii. 2—8; and Titus he taught to distinguish of persons, chap. i. 10—16; and John put difference between the clean and the unclean, Rev. xxi. 27; and Christ taught his apostles, and in them all others, that holy things must not be given unto dogs, Matt. vii. 6.

The second rule is, about controversies, and what they are to do therein. When controversies arise, they are to hear, judge, and determine them by the law of God: ver. 24, "In controversy they shall stand in judgment; and shall judge according to my judgments;" not according to their own wills, desires of others, or laws of men, but as God's laws direct and command. Christians should bring their differences to their ministers, and church officers, that they may make and maintain peace between them, judging and determining their controversies according to the word of God. Paul blamed the Corinthians, that brother went to law with brother, and that before unbelievers, and brought not their cases unto the church, 1 Cor. vi. 6. Ecclesiastical differences ought to be decided by ecclesiastical persons, and other differences too, Deut. xvii. 8—11.

The third rule is, about the solemn assemblies and sabbaths: "They shall keep my laws and my statutes in all mine assemblies; and they shall hallow my sabbaths." God would not allow the priests, though never so knowing or holy, to do aught of their own heads in his worship: as they might not prescribe worship itself, so they might not alter it, nor the laws, rites, or manner of performing the same. Religion and worship are such sacred things, that nothing human must be intermingled with them, all things therein must be done according to the mind of God exactly, "they shall keep my laws and statutes." This the ministers of Christ are to do themselves, and to teach others to do the same; they are to sanctify the sabbaths, and to see others do so too.

A fourth rule is, direction about their dead kindred, whom they might bury, and mourn for, viz. "father or mother, son or daughter, brother or sister" a virgin. To these six they were limited, and forbidden to be at the funerals of all others. For those of their consanguinity they might mourn, God would not have them unnatural; yet in their mourning they might not be immoderate, nor disfigure themselves by baldness, shaving their beards, or cutting their flesh, Lev. xxi. 5; they must be patterns of patience unto others, and quietly submit unto the hand of God, in pulling away their near relations: and because it is hard in such cases to keep within bounds, and not transgress, therefore they were to offer a sin offering before they came to public administrations, showing that singular purity is required in the ministers who are to draw near unto God.

Ver. 26. "After he is cleansed," &c. The Lord indulged them so far that they might defile themselves, ver. 25, that is, touch and mourn for their near kindred, but after this they must cleanse themselves according to law, Numb. xix. 11—13, and chap. vi. 9—11. They were to be holy, especially when they came to minister before the Lord.

Ver. 27. "He shall offer his sin offering." When we have indulgence from God in any thing, especially in matter of our affections, we are apt to exceed our bounds, therefore here the Lord provides a remedy.

Ver. 28—31. *And it shall be unto them for an inheritance: I am their inheritance: and ye shall give them no possession in Israel; I am their possession. They shall eat the meat offering, and the sin offering, and the trespass offering; and every dedicated thing in Israel shall be their's. And the first of all the firstfruits of all things, and every oblation of all, of every sort of your oblations, shall be the priest's: ye shall also give unto the priest the first of your dough, that he may cause the blessing to rest in thine house. The priests shall not eat of any thing that is dead of itself, or torn, whether it be fowl or beast.*

The priests and Levites were to have no inheritances in the land of Canaan, Numb. xviii. 20; Deut. x. 9; xviii. 2. God was their inheritance, and provided for them, he gave them the sacrifices which were due to himself: Josh. xiii. 14, "Only unto the tribe of Levi he gave no inheritance; the sacrifices of the Lord God of Israel made by fire are their inheritance." And so here God was the inheritance of the priests of this new temple, and gave them the offerings due unto him, and all the dedicate things; yea, he ordered that the first of all the firstfruits of all things, and all the oblations, should be the priest's, and the first of their very dough; hereby presignifying, that the ministers of the gospel ought to be maintained by the people they preach unto. It is a divine ordinance, that out of their estates and means the ministers should be provided for: see Matt. x. 10, 11; Luke x. 7, 8; Gal. vi. 6; 1 Cor. ix. 13, 14; 2 Cor. xi. 8.

Here is a special reason given why they should

be maintained, and that comfortably: it is in the 30th verse, "That he may cause the blessing to rest in thine house." Junius and Piscator read it, that I may appoint or settle a blessing in their house. Where the faithful ministers of Christ are well provided for by the people, there God singles out blessings for their families, and causes them to rest there: Prov. iii. 9, 10, "Honour the Lord with thy substance and with the firstfruits of all thine increase: so shall thy barns be filled with plenty, and thy presses shall burst with new wine:" so Mal. iii. 10, God had blessings for them under the law, who were forward to uphold his worship, and maintain his servants. And so he hath for those in these gospel-times who do the like: 2 Cor. ix. 6, "He that soweth sparingly shall reap sparingly; and he that soweth bountifully shall reap bountifully."

For the last verse, which forbids the priests to eat fowls or beasts which died of themselves, or were torn by others, the same was prohibited the people also, Exod. xxii. 31; Lev. xvii. 15; Deut. xiv. 21; God would have both priests and people holy, and not defile themselves with such meats. And here it may present unto us the care ministers should have of what they eat. Though all creatures be good, and lawful to eat, yet all are not wholesome, and expedient for them who are employed in sacred things to feed upon. Or thus: They are to be hospitable, and should not provide of the worst to entertain the people of God. Such creatures as died of themselves, are torn by dogs, beasts, or vermin, whatever is unsightly, unwholesome, or unsavoury, should not be at their tables, or distributed at their doors. Or thus: This not eating such things may note sanctification in the priests: they were not to be covetous, or cruel, but to be unblamable, abstaining from evil, and the appearances thereof.

CHAPTER XLV.

Ver. 1—6. *Moreover, when ye shall divide by lot the land for inheritance, ye shall offer an oblation unto the Lord, an holy portion of the land: the length shall be the length of five and twenty thousand reeds, and the breadth shall be ten thousand. This shall be holy in all the borders thereof round about. Of this there shall be for the sanctuary five hundred in length, with five hundred in breadth, square round about; and fifty cubits round about for the suburbs thereof. And of this measure shalt thou measure the length of five and twenty thousand, and the breadth of ten thousand: and in it shall be the sanctuary and the most holy place. The holy portion of the land shall be for the priests the ministers of the sanctuary, which shall come near to minister unto the Lord: and it shall be a place for their houses, and an holy place for the sanctuary. And the five and twenty thousand of length, and the ten thousand of breadth, shall also the Levites, the ministers of the house, have for themselves, for a possession for twenty chambers. And ye shall appoint the possession of the city five thousand broad, and five and twenty thousand long, over against the oblation of the holy portion: it shall be for the whole house of Israel.*

HAVING laid down the platform and measures of the temple, he comes now to the division and measurings of the land: wherein things are dark, difficult, and deep, not to be attempted by human strength, but by the help of Christ's Spirit, which maketh dark things light, difficult things easy, and sounds the greatest depths.

In this chapter are two principal parts:

I. The partition of the land, which is in the first eight verses.

II. Ordinances political and ecclesiastical, from the 9th verse to the end.

For the first. The division of the land is fourfold.

1. A portion for the sanctuary and the priests, in the first four verses.

2. A portion for the Levites, ver. 5.

3. A portion for the city, or people, ver. 6.

4. A portion for the prince, ver. 7, 8.

For the second. The political ordinances, which concern the prince, are from the 9th verse to the 12th.

The ecclesiastical, which concern the people, the prince, and the priests, are from the 13th verse to the end.

There was a distinction of the land of Canaan in Moses' and Joshua's days, Numb. xxxiv. xxxv.; Josh. xiii. xxi. But this division differs much from the same, and when the Jews returned from Babylon, there was no such division made of the land. Had it been, Ezra or Nehemiah would have made mention thereof. This division, therefore, is not to be understood literally, but spiritually; and the completing thereof to be looked for in the church of Christ, not in the Jewish state or temple. Here, then, seems to be a spiritual lotting, and bringing men out of Judaism and heathenism into the kingdom of Christ, and fellowship of the gospel.

These words, "when ye shall divide by lot the land for inheritance," are thus in the Hebrew, when ye shall make the land to fall into inheritance; that is, when ye shall make the lot to fall upon the land, to divide it into inheritances: he alludes herein to the ancient division of the land by lot. That which is by lot, is free; when the lot fell upon Matthias it was free, and declared whom God had chosen, Acts i. 24, 26.

The work of grace, and bringing of men into the church, is free; nothing in man, or from man, procures it: 2 Pet. i. 1, "To them who have obtained like precious faith with us." The word for obtain, is, λαχοῦσι, which notes, that which comes freely to a man, that which, being no debt, nor desert, is lotted out to a man; as, God gives faith to whom he pleases. We have nothing disposes us for grace, or entitles us to any heavenly inheritance: Col. i. 12, it is the Father "who makes us meet to be partakers of the inheritance of the saints in light;" he regenerates, adopts, and sanctifies, and so makes us meet for spiritual enjoyments and privileges, and then lots them out for us, and us for himself; so that true believers are God's lot, portion, and inheritance.

"Ye shall offer an oblation unto the Lord, an holy portion of the land." The Hebrew is, ye shall elevate an elevation unto the Lord; that is, consecrate, or dedicate, a portion of the land unto the Lord, that it may be holy. This portion of land was large, "five and twenty thousand reeds in length;" not so many cubits, as some would have it, for the measuring was by a reed of six cubits, chap. xl. 5; and ten thousand reeds in breadth: and of these, five hundred in length, and five hundred in breadth, were for the sanctuary, with fifty cubits round for the suburbs thereof. This holy portion of land, as it was for the sanctuary, so for the priests, and their houses, the Levites, and their chambers.

Here the first care is for the house-service, and servants of the Lord. It is the duty of christians to promote the worship of God in the first place, and to provide for those who are officers in his house, who are not to be non-resident, but to live in the houses near to their charge.

Some expositors, as Junius and Polanus, inform us, that a new form and state of the church is here represented unto us, viz. the abrogation of the Jewish, and bringing in of the christian; which was done by Christ and his apostles.

By the portion of land, the holiness and amplitude of it, we may understand the church under the gospel, with the holiness and largeness thereof.

1. The church is holy, and a holy offering unto God; "Ye shall offer an oblation unto the Lord." Holiness from the earth, that it separate from the same; or, holiness of earth, that is, holy earth. Such is the church, holiness from the earth, or holy earth, Eph. v. 27. It is the most glorious and pure part of the world, it consists of those who are virgins redeemed from the earth, whose mouths are guileless, and persons faultless, "before the throne of God," Rev. xiv. 4, 5.

2. The largeness of it. Under Christ, the church is greatly enlarged, and extends to all parts. The Thessalonians' faith spread far, 1 Thess. i. 8; and Paul saith, that in every place they called upon the name of Jesus Christ, 1 Cor. i. 2. Peter brings Pontus, Galatia, Cappadocia, Asia, and Bithynia, within the bounds of the church, 1 Pet. i. 1. Not only Asia, Europe, and Africa, but even America, hath some holy ones to be an offering to the Lord: Rev. vii. 9, there were some out of all nations.

We may also here observe, that in the church of Christ there is provision and protection for his people. There is a portion for the priests, possessions for the Levites, and the whole house of Israel; there are portions of land for them, with houses, chambers, and a city. Those who come to Zion shall not be destitute, but meet with maintenance and safety: Jer. xxxi. 12, "They shall come and sing in the height of Zion, and shall flow together to the goodness of the Lord." He will be their Shepherd, and provide for them wheat, wine, and oil, that is, bread and water of life, with the comforts of the Spirit; and make their souls as a watered garden, green and growing, fat and flourishing, fruitful and very fruitful: and being in that condition, he will defend them from wild beasts, and spoil of any. They are his garden enclosed, and fenced about with his power; see Ezek. xxxiv. 26—28.

Again observe, the true church state takes not away propriety, neither consists of levelling principles; it preserves men's rights, and the different degrees and orders that are set amongst men. Here was a portion of land for the priests, a portion for the Levites, and a portion for the citizens, the one might not seize upon the others': here are distinct orders of men, priests, Levites, people, and prince. The order of the gospel is to preserve order, not to bring in confusion, or levelling; see Acts v. 4; xxviii. 30; Philem. i. 8; 1 Cor. xii. 28—30; 1 Tim. ii. 2; 1 Pet. ii. 13, 14.

Ver. 6. "And ye shall appoint the possession of the city." Provision being made for the church, and those who served in it, the next care here is for the people, they must have their portion and possession. The Lord's goodness extends to them, as well as those who are nearest to him in office.

Ver. 7, 8. *And a portion shall be for the prince on the one side and on the other side of the oblation of the holy portion, and of the possession of the city, before the oblation of the holy portion, and before the possession of the city, from the west side westward, and from the east side eastward: and the length shall be over against one of the portions, from the west border unto the east border. In the land shall be his possession in Israel: and my princes shall no more oppress my people; and the rest of the land shall they give to the house of Israel according to their tribes.*

The prince was to have a portion as well as the rest, and it was to be on both sides, on the west side and on the east side; it was to compass in the other portions: intimating to us thereby, that the prince and his estate should be for the preservation of the whole. A prince is to be the defender and bulwark of the commonwealth; himself, and his estate, should rather suffer than it.

Who this prince was is doubted; for, after their return from Babylon, they had neither kings nor princes. Zerubbabel was governor of Judah, not king, or prince, Hag. ii. 21. Some make him to be the high priest, and the 17th verse induceth to believe so, for it saith, "It shall be the prince's part to offer burnt offerings, and meat offerings, and drink offerings, in the feasts, and in the new moons, and in the sabbaths, in all solemnities of the house of Israel: he shall prepare the sin offering, and the meat offering, and the burnt offering, and the peace offerings, to make reconciliation for the house of Israel." To sacrifice was priest-work, not prince-work; civil princes might not sacrifice, had they had them. In the time of the Maccabees, they had high priests, who were over them both in church and state affairs; and these here, it is conceived, are honoured with the title of prince. But it is questionable whether the high priest be the prince here spoken of, because, in chap. xlvi. 2, the prince there is distinguished from the priest. It is better to understand it of Christ, who was "the great high priest," Heb. iv. 14; and "Prince of the kings of the earth," Rev. i. 5. Rabbi David, in his commentary upon this place, saith, that the Hebrews interpret this prince to be the Messiah; so doth Jerom, and some late expositors: and, chap. xxxiv. 24, God had promised the Jews that his "servant David should be a prince among them," that was, Messiah.

This insinuates thus much unto us, that the church is Christ's portion, and Christ the protector of it. His possession lieth in the land of Israel; the saints, the true Israelites, are his portion, his possession; he is "on the one side and on the other" of them, even from west to east: he reigns, and is round about the church, he compasses it with his favour, and his power. New Jerusalem had a wall about it, Rev. xxi. 17: Christ the Prince he is the wall to the whole church, and all the parts of it, to apostles, pastors, and people; not Peter, popes, or priests, are protectors thereof.

"My prince shall no more oppress my people." These princes (whether those who are chief in the church of Christ, or in the civil state) they shall not be covetous, and oppress the people. This was too common before the captivity, as appears, Mic. iii. 1—11; Zeph. iii. 3; Amos iv. 1; Jer. vi. 13; Ezek. i. 22—28; and after the captivity, the nobles and rulers exacted upon their brethren, and oppressed them, Neh. v. 7, 8. But there must be a time for fulfilling this truth, that princes "shall no more oppress the people." Hitherto it can hardly be made out that ever there were such princes, or times, wherein the people were not oppressed. But such are promised as shall be far from oppression, as shall not take away, but give unto the house of Israel according to her tribes. The house of Israel is the whole church of Christ, and the tribes thereof are the particular churches therein; and those princes are the Lord's, (for he saith, "my princes,") shall give unto him their titles, rights, and privileges; they shall acknowledge the Lord Christ to be Prince, and submit unto him, Rev. xxi. 24.

Ver. 9—12. *Thus saith the Lord God; Let it suffice you, O princes of Israel: remove violence and spoil, and execute judgment and justice, take away your exactions from my people, saith the Lord God. Ye shall have just balances, and a just ephah, and a just bath. The ephah and the bath shall be of one measure, that the bath may contain the tenth part of an homer, and the ephah the tenth part of an homer: the measure thereof shall be after the homer. And the shekel shall be twenty gerahs: twenty shekels, five and twenty shekels, fifteen shekels, shall be your maneh.*

These verses contain political ordinances, which are for just and righteous proceedings between prince and people, and people amongst themselves.

Ver. 1. "Let it suffice you, O princes of Israel." Ye have been long given to covetous practices, and thereby increased your revenues to the prejudice of others; but now let what is past suffice you, let there be no more such doings amongst you. The political estate must be reformed, and with you princes the reformation must begin. The princes of Israel were very covetous; Isa. i. 23, "Thy princes are rebellious, and companions of thieves: every one loveth gifts, and followeth after rewards:" they were no better than thieves, robbing the people, perverting all justice through their covetousness. This God complained of them, and minds them of it here, saying, "Let it suffice;" or thus the words may be taken, Be content with the revenues, legal tributes, and customs, thirst after no more, rest satisfied with what you have, and covet no more, let the portion you have please you.

"Remove violence and spoil." When princes use violence to fetch in their revenues, taxes, customs, and to satisfy their desires, spoil follows upon it; men suffer in their estates by those who are employed by them, and oft are undone. Naboth loses his vineyard, and life too, through the violence of Ahab, Jezebel, and the instruments they set on work. But in this new political estate it must be otherwise: Isa. lx. 18, "Violence shall no more be heard in thy land, wasting nor destruction within thy borders."

"Execute judgment and justice." Princes and magistrates are God's deputies, they ought to be like unto him, and to act for him; they should be men of knowledge, able to judge in controversies, to discern where the right lies; Deut i. 16, 17, and men of courage to rule for God, executing judgment and justice impartially. As David did; 2 Sam. viii. 15, he "reigned over all Israel; and executed judgment and justice unto all his people;" and this was one of his last words, "He that ruleth over men must be just, ruling in the fear of God," 2 Sam. xxiii. 3. And when men rule so, there will be no place for injustice and oppression: such we have warrant to expect, for the Lord hath said, "I will make thy officers peace, and thine exactors righteousness," Isa. lx. 17.

"Take away the exactions from my people." The Vulgate reads the words, Separate your confines from my people. When princes and great men have fields and inheritances lying near to their inferiors' grounds, as Ahab's did to Naboth's, they covet the same, and find out ways to get the same, and in time eat up their possessions; therefore, to prevent this, the Lord calls upon them to separate their borders from their neighbours. They force men out of their houses and inheritances; as it is, Mic. ii. 2, "They covet fields, and take them by violence; and houses, and take them away: so they oppress a man and his house, even a man and his heritage:" these were "exactions," as we read it. And of the great ones' "exactions," you may see, 2 Kings xv. 20; xxiii. 35. Sometimes under pretence of law, and necessity, they did exact of the people. But these must cease, and when the new heavens and new earth come, there shall righteousness be in them, no exaction or oppression, 2 Pet. iii. 13.

Ver. 10. "Ye shall have just balances." In this and the other two verses ordinances are given out about weights, measures, and money.

1. Concerning weights, the balances must be just. In former days they did pervert or falsify the balances by deceit, Amos viii. 5; which was "abomination to the Lord," Prov. xx. 10. There was a law in Deuteronomy against the same, chap. xxv. 13—15; it was against diverse weights and diverse measures, tying them to one, and that perfect and just: so here, "just balances" are required; God would have the people just and equal in their dealings, not defrauding one another.

"A just ephah, and a just bath," &c. The measures of the Hebrews were of dry and liquid things, both which are here mentioned. To begin with the homer, which was the greatest measure they had, and signifies, a heap, it held so much; some make the quantity to be what a camel or an ass could bear and carry. The homer is the same with that measure called cor, or corus, as the 14th verse shows; each of them containing ten baths, or ten ephahs. A Lapide makes the bath and ephah to contain three bushels a piece, and so the homer to be thirty bushels. But if we make *modius* to be but half a bushel, then the ephah and bath contain one bushel and a half apiece, and the homer fifteen. But Ainsworth, upon Lev. xxvii. 16, makes the homer to be ten ephahs, that is, ten bushels; so that the ephah and the bath held the measure of a bushel.

The "ephah" was a measure for dry things, wheat, barley, meal, flour, 1 Sam. xvii. 17; Judg. vi. 19; Numb. v. 15; and it was the common measure, and the regulator of all other measures.

There is a seeming contradiction between what you have in Exod. xvi. 36, where it is written, "an omer is the tenth part of an ephah," and what you have here in Ezekiel, who saith, "an ephah is the tenth part of an homer." For answer; know, the words omer and homer in the Hebrew differ: the first is, עמר, omer with ain, which signifies, a handful: Lev. xxiii. 10, "Ye shall bring a sheaf of the firstfruits;" the Hebrew is, a handful, an omer. It is conceived the wheat beaten out of that sheaf did fill the omer, which contained above a pottle, about five pints; and so was "the tenth part of an ephah," which contained of our English measure seven gallons and a half, which makes our bushel.

The second word, חמר is written with ח cheth, and is that great measure containing "ten ephahs," which is spoken of here.

The measure called a "bath," was of liquid things, and contained as much as the ephah, seven gallons and a half, "the tenth part of an homer." Wine and oil were usually measured by it, as 2 Chron. ii.

10; Ezra vii. 22. In Isa. v. 10, we find these words, "Ten acres of vineyard shall yield one bath:" God would so blast their vines, that ten acres planted with vines should not yield ten gallons, they should fill but one "bath;" and the seed of an homer, that is, ten bushels, should yield an ephah, that is, one bushel. Here the "bath" is the measure of wine, and the ephah the measure of corn.

"And the shekel shall be twenty gerahs." Having spoken of the measures, he proceeds to the money, that it might be of a just value. The "shekel" must be "twenty gerahs;" a gerah was to weigh sixteen barley-corns, so that "twenty gerahs" amounted to three hundred and twenty barley-corns, and so much the shekel was to weigh. Of it was spoken, chap. iv. 10. Sixty shekels made the maneh, or pound: some pieces of their money were twenty shekels, some twenty-five, some fifteen, and these together made their maneh.

Obs. 1. Princes and magistrates commonly are covetous and cruel. The princes of Israel used violence and spoil, they exacted upon the people. Zeph. iii. 3, Jerusalem's "princes were roaring lions; her judges evening wolves," they were greedy of the prey. Nero was a lion to the people of God, 2 Tim. iv. 17. Nebuchadnezzar was both a lion, a bear, and a dragon: Jer. li. 34, saith Jerusalem, "He hath devoured me, he hath crushed me, he hath made me an empty vessel, he hath swallowed me up like a dragon, he hath filled his belly with my delicates, he hath cast me out." His belly was so big, his desires so enlarged, that he ate up cities, kingdoms, and nations. As it was said of Pompey, so of most princes in the world may the people say, By our miseries ye are become great.

Obs. 2. Christianity doth not overthrow, but establish, magistracy. The Lord here speaking what reformation should be under the Messiah, doth not take magistrates away, but corrects their exorbitances, saying, "Remove violence and spoil, take away exactions:" he abridges them not of just power, but decries their tyranny. Paul approves of magistrates, Rom. xiii.; 1 Tim. ii. 1, 2; and tells us, "they are the ministers of God for good;" they are appointed for public good, to be a terror to the wicked, a shield to the godly, a husband to the widow, a father to the orphan, a patron to the poor, and a refuge to the oppressed. Such magistrates we expect, and pray for.

Obs. 3. The great thing required of them, is to do justice, execute judgment and justice, do wrong to none, neither suffer wrong to be done. They should see there be no false weights, measures, or moneys, to deceive the people withal. Magistrates are in God's stead, and they should be righteous as God is; he rules so, that he makes appeal to his people, saying, "What have I done to thee? wherein have I wearied thee? testify against me," Mic. vi. 3. So did Samuel; "Behold, here I am: witness against me before the Lord, and before his anointed; whose ox have I taken? or whose ass have I taken? or whom have I defrauded? whom have I oppressed? or of whose hand have I received any bribe to blind mine eyes therewith? and I will restore it," 1 Sam. xii. 4: here was a righteous judge, a man of integrity. Such a one was Nehemiah, chap. v. 14, 15. When magistrates are righteous, and do righteous things, respecting every man's cause, and regard no man's person, they are the glory of heaven, the ornament of the earth, the joy of the just, the desire of all, and blessed themselves, Psal. cvi. 3.

Obs. 4. Princes are not to rule by prerogative in an arbitrary way, but they themselves are tied to the laws of God, and bound up by them. The Lord, who is the great Lawgiver, saith, "Let it suffice you, O princes of Israel, remove violence," &c. He gives them laws here, and his word, which are binding, and ought not to depart from them. If they proceed by their own wills and lusts, they become tyrants, and shall have their reward, Psal. lv. 22; Prov. xxviii. 17; xiv. 11; Job xviii. 15. Therefore kings are commanded to be wise, judges to be instructed, to serve the Lord, kiss the Son, Psal. ii. 10—12; and to keep to the law of God, Deut. xvii. 18.

Ver. 13—17. *This is the oblation that ye shall offer; the sixth part of an ephah of an homer of wheat, and ye shall give the sixth part of an ephah of an homer of barley: concerning the ordinance of oil, the bath of oil, ye shall offer the tenth part of a bath out of the cor, which is an homer of ten baths; for ten baths are an homer: and one lamb out of the flock, out of two hundred, out of the fat pastures of Israel; for a meat offering, and for a burnt offering, and for peace offerings, to make reconciliation for them, saith the Lord God. All the people of the land shall give this oblation for the prince in Israel. And it shall be the prince's part to give burnt offerings, and meat offerings, and drink offerings, in the feasts, and in the new moons, and in the sabbaths, in all solemnities of the house of Israel: he shall prepare the sin offering, and the meat offering, and the burnt offering, and the peace offerings, to make reconciliation for the house of Israel.*

The political ordinances being declared, now he comes to the ecclesiastical, which concern sacrifices and oblations. Of the homer, ephah, and bath, have been spoken in the former verses. The cor is the same measure for quantity with the homer.

1. Here is laid down the things to be offered, wheat, barley, oil, a lamb, and other offerings.

2. The proportion of the dry and liquid things: the sixth part of an ephah of wheat, and barley, and the tenth part of a bath of oil; and so of the lambs, one out of two hundred, and so of other cattle; and these must not be poor, lean ones, but such as came from "the fat pastures of Israel," and might be fit for offering up to God. The sixtieth part of dry things, the hundredth of liquids, and two hundredth of cattle, were to be given.

3. The persons who were to give them, and that is, "all the people," ver. 16. The Hebrew is, all the people in the land shall be in that oblation to the prince in Israel. And then the person who is to offer them, ver. 17, and that is the prince, or high priest.

By the wheat, barley, oil, and lambs, the oblations, offerings to be given to the prince in Israel, are intended the spiritual sacrifices, which the saints under the gospel do give to Christ, 1 Pet. ii. 5; Rev. v. 8—10; vii. 10; xiv. 3; Heb. xiii. 10; viii. 3; Rom. xii. 1; xv. 16. The persons, prayers, and praises of the saints are to be given up to Christ, and by him to the Father.

It is a dispute amongst expositors who is meant by "prince:" some would have it the secular or civil prince; some, the high priest, because of his offering sacrifices. The Jews are here at a stand, not knowing which to determine: but Œcolampadius understands it of the Messiah; he was both a Prince and High Priest; not a common prince, for he would not be made king by men, Job vi. 15; not a levitical high-priest, after the order of Aaron, but an extraordinary one, after the order of Melchizedec, Heb. vii.

11—13; and of another tribe than Aaron was, viz. the tribe of Judah, ver. 14; which imported that Christ should put down Levitical worship, and set up another way of worship in the place thereof, which was prefigured in this vision of Ezekiel.

All the oblations here, and sacrifices, were types of Christ. The wheat, the barley, the oil, the lamb, the sin offering, the meat offering, the burnt offering, and the peace offering, all represented Christ, and were fulfilled in him. He was the expiatory sacrifice, and purged away our sins, Heb. i. 3; he was the propitiatory sacrifice, and made the atonement for us, Rom. iii. 25; v. 11; he was the pacificatory sacrifice, he made peace between us and God, Rom. v. 10; Col. i. 20; he is the eucharistical sacrifice, or thank offering, he gave thanks to God for his favour, mercy, and goodness to us, Matt. xi. 25; John xi. 41: he had the virtue of all the sacrifices in him, and far more. Heb. ix. 23, the words "better sacrifices," are spoken of Christ; he was the one and only sacrifice, and once offered, Heb. x. 12; vii. 27; and yet was sacrifices, because they all signified him, and he had the strength, worth, and benefit of them all in himself; yea, he was better sacrifices than they all; for they were imperfect, for a season, and of little efficacy, but Christ was a perfect sacrifice for ever, and most efficacious, Heb. ix. 11—14; x. 12. He hath made reconciliation for the house of Israel, and maintains it; for he appears in the presence of God for us, Heb. ix. 24; and lives for ever to make intercession for us, Heb. vii. 25. He doth that always, which the priests did in the feasts, new moons, sabbaths, and solemnities; the virtue of this sacrifice is ever useful.

Ver. 18—20. *Thus saith the Lord God; In the first month, in the first day of the month, thou shalt take a young bullock without blemish, and cleanse the sanctuary: and the priest shall take of the blood of the sin offering, and put it upon the posts of the house, and upon the four corners of the settle of the altar, and upon the posts of the gate of the inner court. And so thou shalt do the seventh day of the month for every one that erreth, and for him that is simple: so shall ye reconcile the house.*

Here we have an ordinance for cleansing the sanctuary, much like that ordinance in chap. xliii. for cleansing the altar of burnt offerings. There was no such ordinance among the Mosaicals, as Jerom, Sanctius, and others, observe. This was a new ordinance which the Levitical law knew not, and speaks out the newness of all under the gospel, the cleansing of the church by the blood of Christ, who, in due season, being without sin, was made sin for us, 2 Cor. v. 21; and by his blood washed away the sins of his people, Rev. i. 5; Heb. xiii. 11; and by it made way for entering into the holiest, Heb. x. 19. And whereas "the posts of the house, and posts of the gate, and four corners of the settle of the altar," were all sprinkled with blood; it tells us that all, great or small, whencesoever they come, from east, west, north, or south, cannot be cleansed, or saved, but by blood, even the blood of Christ, Heb. ix. 22, 23. It is nothing in man, or from man himself, not his righteousness, free-will, or sufferings, which doth cleanse him from his sin; that only is from the virtue of Christ's blood, 1 John i. 7.

The 20th verse leads to speak of sins of ignorance. Under the law there was a sacrifice for the man who sinned ignorantly: Lev. v. 17, 18, he was to "bring a ram to the priest," and by the sacrificing of that, his sin "was forgiven him," and peace made. Here the ordinance differs from that. Instead of "a ram" must be "a young bullock" sacrificed; signifying, that the blood of Christ is for the erroneous, simple, ignorant, as well as others. When men sin wilfully, it is dangerous, Heb. x. 26, 27; but for those who are simple, and through ignorance do err, there is a remedy provided: 1 John ii. 1, 2, "My little children, I write unto you that ye sin not." (That is impossible, they might have replied, "for in many things we sin all," James iii. 2.) "And if any man sin," (that is, through weakness, ignorance, simpleness, strength of corruption, or temptation,) "we have an advocate with the Father, Jesus Christ the righteous; and he is the propitiation for our sins." This remedy Christ holds out in the gospel to such sinners, and would have his ministers do the like: Gal. vi. 1, "If a man be overtaken in a fault, ye which are spiritual, restore such an one;" bring him to Christ, cause him to look upon him crucified, and expiating his sin with his own blood, and then he will weep for his error, his simplicity; and so he is restored.

Ver. 21—24. *In the first month, in the fourteenth day of the month, ye shall have the passover, a feast of seven days; unleavened bread shall be eaten. And upon that day shall the prince prepare for himself and for all the people of the land a bullock for a sin offering. And seven days of the feast he shall prepare a burnt offering to the Lord, seven bullocks and seven rams without blemish daily the seven days; and a kid of the goats daily for a sin offering. And he shall prepare a meat offering of an ephah for a bullock, and an ephah for a ram, and an hin of oil for an ephah.*

In these verses are ordinances for keeping the passover, &c. Of the Mosaical, you may see, Exod. xii. and Lev. xxiii.; from which this differs in many things, as Polanus notes, and presents unto us Christ our passover, who was sacrificed for us, 1 Cor. v. 7. The passover was "in the first month, the fourteenth day," when the moon was at the full, and the sun ascending; all things began to revive; which showed that Christ was not to be sacrificed presently after his birth, but when the fulness of ceremonial light was come; and that by his death Jewish shadows being abolished, true light, life, and reviving, came into the world. The feast of unleavened bread showed how we are to keep the feast of the christian passover, viz. not with old leaven, that is, our old corrupt hearts, neither with the leaven of malice and wickedness, but with the unleavened bread of sincerity and truth. Men should not come to his ordinance with old, malicious, or wicked hearts, but with hearts sincere and true; all corruption of nature, doctrine, and manners, should be purged out. And christians should live their whole life (noted by the "seven days" here) free from hypocrisy, lying, malice, and unrighteousness; they should study and endeavour to be holy, as God is holy.

It is said, ver. 22, that the prince must "prepare for himself and for all the people a bullock for a sin offering." This prince, therefore, seems not to be Christ, but the high priest, who was sinful, and offered first for himself, and then for the people, Heb. vii. 27. Christ had no sin, and so could not offer sacrifice for himself.

For answer hereunto, know, that Christ considered in himself was an immaculate Lamb, without blemish, 1 Pet. i. 19; "an High Priest, holy, harmless, undefiled," Heb. vii. 26. But consider him as our Surety, as Head of the body, so he had sin; his own self did bear our sins in his own body, 1 Pet. ii. 24; he was made sin for us, 2 Cor. v. 21; he was offered to bear the sins of many, Heb. ix. 28; the Lord laid upon him the iniquities of us all, Isa. liii. 6; and he was numbered with transgressors, ver. 12. Our sins were imputed to him, so that he stood as a sinner and malefactor in our stead; and offered up himself a sacrifice for himself, that is, for his body the church. Thus nothing hinders but by "prince" here we may understand Christ.

The burnt offering and sin offering, which were to be "daily," set out the virtue of Christ's death and intercession, which is not for a day, or a few years, but for ever; or they may acquaint us with the saints, their total and constant dedication of themselves unto God and his service.

"An hin of oil." Of the ephah, bath, homer, and cor, was spoken in the former part of the chapter. "An hin" was for liquid things, and contained as much as twelve logs, and each log contained six eggs; so that "an hin" held as much wine, or oil, as seventy-two eggs; and, according to some, is three quarts of our English measure.

Ver. 25. *In the seventh month, in the fifteenth day of the month, shall he do the like in the feast of the seven days, according to the sin offering, according to the burnt offering, and according to the meat offering, and according to the oil.*

Passing over the feast of Pentecost, without any mention thereof, he comes to the feast of tabernacles, which was to begin the fifteenth day of the seventh month, Lev. xxiii. 34. And as it was in the feast of the passover, so it must be here; but it was not so in the time of Moses, Lev. xxiii. 39, 40.

This feast of tabernacles, or booths, cannot be understood literally, for there is a prophecy in Zech. xiv. 16, "That those left of the nations which came against Jerusalem should come to worship the King, the Lord of hosts, and to keep the feast of tabernacles;" which in the literal sense was peculiar to the Jews. It figures out, therefore, the gathering of the elect into particular churches in this world, into which they should come, and in which they should have fellowship with the saints, and partake of the grace of God.

By these feasts, and sacrifices also, we are minded of the spiritual joy the saints have in their communion together under the gospel, and spiritual sacrifices they offer up to God by Christ. The primitive christians continued "daily with one accord in the temple, and breaking bread from house to house, did eat their meat with gladness and singleness of heart, praising God," Acts ii. 46, 47.

CHAPTER XLVI.

Ver. 1—8. *Thus saith the Lord God; The gate of the inner court that looketh toward the east shall be shut the six working days; but on the sabbath it shall be opened, and in the day of the new moon it shall be opened. And the prince shall enter by the way of the porch of that gate without, and shall stand by the post of the gate, and the priests shall prepare his burnt offering and his peace offerings, and he shall worship at the threshold of the gate: then he shall go forth; but the gate shall not be shut until the evening. Likewise the people of the land shall worship at the door of this gate before the Lord in the sabbaths and in the new moons. And the burnt offering that the prince shall offer unto the Lord in the sabbath day shall be six lambs without blemish, and a ram without blemish. And the meat offering shall be an ephah for a ram, and the meat offering for the lambs as he shall be able to give, and an hin of oil to an ephah. And in the day of the new moon it shall be a young bullock without blemish, and six lambs, and a ram: they shall be without blemish. And he shall prepare a meat offering, an ephah for a bullock, and an ephah for a ram, and for the lambs according as his hand shall attain unto, and an hin of oil to an ephah. And when the prince shall enter, he shall go in by the way of the porch of that gate, and he shall go forth by the way thereof.*

THIS 46th chapter contains,

I. Ordinances about several gates, the prince and people's going in and out by them, with their oblations and worship, from the beginning to ver. 15.

II. Certain laws are laid down concerning the prince's gifts unto his sons and servants, in the 16th, 17th, and 18th verses.

III. A description of the courts and places where the priests and Levites were to boil and prepare the sacrifices, from the beginning of ver. 19, to the end of the chapter.

The 1st verse speaks of the east gate in the inner court, that was, the gate next to the temple. By this gate the glory of the Lord came into the temple, chap. xliii. 1, 2, 4; and it was to be kept shut all the six working days, and only to be opened on sabbaths and new moons. In chap. xliv. we have the reason why it was to be kept shut: ver. 2, thus saith the Lord, "This gate shall be shut, it shall not be opened, and no man shall enter in by it; because the Lord, the God of Israel, hath entered in by it, therefore it shall be shut;" that is, for the prince, &c.: and here it is, "The prince shall enter by the way," &c.

The things here required are not to be found in the Mosaical law; they represented things under the gospel; that Jewish worship should go down when Christ appeared in the flesh.

The shutting of the gate the six working days tells us, that on those days we are to follow our callings, and earn our daily bread. Christianity doth not open a door to idleness; "We command and exhort," saith Paul, "that with quietness men work, and eat their own bread," 2 Thess. iii. 12. Under Moses God allowed them six days to work, Exod. xx. 9; and the same allowance they have under the gospel, Luke xiii. 14. Some pervert God's order, and make all days alike, either all working days, or all sabbaths, resting days; but God hath distinguished them. As there are working days wherein we must not rest, so there are sabbaths wherein we must not work.

The opening of the gate on sabbath days and new moons, signifies unto us, that the gate of heaven is open unto us, when we have solemn and public meetings on the Lord's day, and other special occasions, to worship God. When all the disciples were assembled together to serve and seek God, then came a sound from heaven, and the Spirit fell upon them like fiery tongues, Acts ii.: so when Peter preached unto the great multitude, the gate of heaven was opened, and power came down from above to convert three thousand, ver. 41: so when there was a solemn meeting in the centurion's house, the word being preached by Peter, the gate of heaven was opened, and the Holy Ghost fell on all that heard the word, Acts x. 44. Such times are times of grace and mercy, God opens heaven, and gives out blessings.

These six days may denote the term of man's life here, which is a time of labour and sorrow, Job v. 7; xiv. 1. He tumbles, or is tumbled, up and down from condition to condition, and hath no rest; but at the end of his life heaven gate is opened, and he hath a sabbath, an eternal rest, where is no labour, sin, nor sorrowing, Heb. iv. 9, 10. Then the gate of the inner court is opened unto him, and then he shall see as he is seen, and know as he is known, 1 John iii. 2. 1 Cor. xiii. 12, here we see and know little, and that little darkly, as in a glass; but then shall we see clearly, and know perfectly, the mysteries of this and other visions and things.

The 2nd verse tells us of the prince, his entering by the way of the porch, and standing by the post of the gate; where he was to worship, but come into the court he might not.

If we understand this of the secular prince, four things are here considerable:

1. That the prince must not enter into the inner court; he must not meddle with the priestly office, or things of God. Princes may not change any thing in the worship of God, abrogate or institute aught by their wills or power. Uzziah was smitten with the leprosy for meddling, 2 Chron. xxvi.; and Ahaz for his adding, 2 Kings xvi. his altering, detracting, and abrogating, 2 Chron. xxviii. was branded for his wickedness. They kept not at the post and threshold of the gate, but entered into the inner court.

2. They are to countenance and maintain the worship of God. The prince must stand at the post of the gate, and see the priests do their office. He found the burnt, peace, and meat offerings, and the priests prepared them, that is, fitted them for sacrifices. The princes and powers of the christian world should countenance, preserve, propagate, and maintain the true worship of God in their territories. When Joash was made king, he had the testimony given unto him, 2 Chron. xxiii. 11; that was, the book of the law: and why was this given him? It was to inform princes, that they should rule according thereunto; that they should countenance, preserve, propagate, and maintain the same, and the worship it held forth.

3. That princes must worship the Lord publicly on sabbath days, and when special occasions are, as well as other people.

" He shall worship at the threshold of the gate." Let princes be never so great, rich, learned, wise, yet they must fall down at God's footstool, serve him with fear, and kiss the Son; they must observe the times of God's worship, bow to him, and not leave all to their inferiors.

4. They must not impede the worship of God. The prince shall go forth, but the gate shall not be shut where he hath worshipped, he must not hinder others. It was a vile practice in those who shut up the doors of the Lord's house, and would not let the people or priests come there to worship, 2 Chron. xxviii. 24. Princes should see to it that the door be open for public worship, not only at the appointed times, but upon special occasions.

If we take the prince here to be Christ, as Œcolampadius and Polanus do, then his coming to, and standing by, the post of the gate, his sacrificing and worshipping, do prefigure his coming in the flesh, and his standing at the gate of heaven for us, offering up prayers and supplications for us, with strong cries and tears, Heb. v. 7; Luke xxii. 44. And whereas it is said, " The priests shall prepare his burnt offering and his peace offerings; this presignified the priests' delivering up Christ to be crucified for us: Luke xxiv. 20, " The chief priests and rulers delivered him to be condemned to death, and crucified him" who was "the Prince of life," Acts iii. 15; yet he " laid down his life freely," John x. 17, 18. And for his " worshipping at the threshold of the gate," it may point out that time when Christ, being on the cross, said, " It is finished: and he bowed his head, and gave up the ghost," John xix. 30. Now was he at the threshold of the gate; for he said to the thief immediately before, " This day shalt thou be with me in paradise," Luke xxiii. 43; then his soul went forth of its earthly tabernacle; and shortly after re-assuming that, he left the world, and went to his Father, John xvi. 28.

The gates standing open until evening, that so the people might come and worship at the door of the gate before the Lord; this some interpret of the door of mercy and reconciliation which Christ hath set open for sinners during this life; and if they come not thither before death and worship God, then it is shut for ever against them. On sabbath days men should draw near to God, seek reconciliation with him, for on such days the gate is widest open for grace and mercy. On the six days it is shut, that is, comparatively shut. Christians do celebrate sabbaths and new moons, when they have inward spiritual rest in their souls, through faith in Christ, and do receive light from him to see what is evil, and so to avoid it, and what is good, and so to practise it.

In ver. 4—7, the offerings, oblations, and sacrifices of the prince for the sabbath days and new moons are mentioned. The olah, or burnt offering for the sabbath, was to be six complete lambs without blemish, and one ram, which differs much from the appointment in Moses' days, Numb. xxviii. 9; then there were but two lambs, here six are appointed. And so the meat offering is larger here than there; but for the offering in the day of the new moon, it was short of that in Moses' time; for then two bullocks, seven lambs, and one ram, were appointed; and here, one bullock, six lambs, and one ram, are nominated for the offering: which shows the Levitical worship was to be changed.

And taking the prince for one of the princes of the earth, it tells us, he ought to provide for the worship of God. But if we take this prince to be Christ, then it imports that Christ hath ordained more spiritual, pure, and efficacious worship on sabbaths under the gospel than was under the law, and more extensive than was before: also, that Jewish shadows are fled away by the coming in of the glorious light of the gospel, " that old things are passed away, and all things become new."

These sacrifices do point out Christ: he was the sum of all: he was the lambs, the rams, the bullock, the meal, the flour, and the oil. This prince sacrificing of himself, did more by that one and once sacrifice, than all the sacrifices from the first to the last, Heb. x. 14.

Ver. 5. " As he shall be able to give." The Hebrew is, the gift of his hand; and so it is in the margin: in ver. 7 it is thus, " as his hand shall attain unto;" and in ver. 11, " as he is able," that is, as God hath blessed him. God in that dispensed with men's disabilities in Moses' law; Lev. v. 11, and xiv. 21, if they were poor, and not able to bring lambs, or two turtle doves, they must bring one lamb, or the tenth part of an ephah of flour; something he would have, and to such a proportion. But here it is left to man's liberty, to give according to his ability, no proportion is prescribed; so men give freely, whatever it be, it shall be accepted. God looks not for much where little is. The grace and favour of God under the gospel, exceed what was under the law.

Ver. 6. "And in the day of the new moon." New-moon days were holy, and had special sacrifices, as in this verse, Numb. xxviii. 11: on those days they might not buy or sell, or do worldly work, Amos viii. 5; but they were to look unto Christ, of whom those days were shadows, Col. ii. 16, 17, and to meditate of that light, grace, and comfort which come by him. The gate of the inner court was to stand open on these days, as well as on sabbaths, ver. 1. And Isaiah prophesied, chap. lxvi. 23, that all flesh should come to worship before the Lord, from one new moon to another, and from one sabbath to another; intimating thereby, that God, in times of the gospel, would accept of true and spiritual worship, performed in the name of Christ, in all places, and at all times, as he did the Jewish worship at Jerusalem, and on the solemn feast days.

Or these new-moon days and sacrifices, may point out the renewing of the church, and the joy thereupon. The church after Christ's time, was oft in the wane, in a suffering and declining condition; but when it hath rest, edification, comfort, and multiplication, Acts ix. 31, then it is new moon with it; and in a short time it becomes "fair as the moon," Cant. vi. 10; and shall be filled with light and joy, as saith Isaiah, chap. lx. 20.

The 8th verse is an ordinance about the prince's going in by the porch of the gate, and going out by the same way. There were divers gates to enter into the inner court, by the north gate, the south gate, as well as the east gate; and this gate was both for the prince and the priests to go in and out at.

Hence two things are observable:

1. That princes are to walk according to divine appointment, especially in matters of worship; they must look unto God, who hath prescribed the way they should walk in; it had been sinful for them to have gone to the north gate, or south gate, and worshipped: their princes must not do aught of their own wills in the things of God. It might seem a bondage to be tied up to the east gate only, and never to have ingress and egress at the other; but, however, princes themselves must be subject to the ordinances of Heaven.

2. That princes and priests, magistrates and ministers, should mutually mind and care for the things of God, countenance and encourage one another therein, and each put to their helping hand to preserve the purity and power of religion. When the powers go one way, and the true ministers of God another way, religion doth not shine: when Josiah and the priests went together hand in hand one way, then there was great reformation in Israel, the worship of God was pure, and religion did flourish.

Supposing this prince to be the Lord Christ, whose ingress and egress was at the same gate, then it notes his coming from heaven, and returning thither again, according to that of John vi. 62; iii. 31; xvi. 28; Acts i. 11.

Ver. 9—15. *But when the people of the land shall come before the Lord in the solemn feasts, he that entereth in by the way of the north gate to worship shall go out by the way of the south gate; and he that entereth by the way of the south gate shall go forth by the way of the north gate: he shall not return by the way of the gate whereby he came in, but shall go forth over against it. And the prince in the midst of them, when they go in, shall go in; and when they go forth, shall go forth. And in the feasts and in the solemnities the meat offering shall be an ephah to a bullock, and an ephah to a ram, and to the lambs as he is able to give, and an hin of oil to an ephah. Now when the prince shall prepare a voluntary burnt offering or peace offerings voluntarily unto the Lord, one shall then open him the gate that looketh toward the east, and he shall prepare his burnt offering and his peace offerings, as he did on the sabbath day: then he shall go forth; and after his going forth one shall shut the gate. Thou shalt daily prepare a burnt offering unto the Lord of a lamb of the first year without blemish: thou shalt prepare it every morning* (or, as the Hebrew, morning by morning). *And thou shalt prepare a meat offering for it every morning, the sixth part of an ephah, and the third part of an hin of oil, to temper with the fine flour; a meat offering continually by a perpetual ordinance unto the Lord. Thus shall they prepare the lamb, and the meat offering, and the oil, every morning for a continual burnt offering.*

The 9th verse contains an ordinance concerning the people's coming to and departing from the public worship: they must not come to the east gate, but to the side gates, the north and south, they might; and this order they were to observe, viz. to go out at that gate which was over against the gate they came in at; he that entered by the north gate must go out by the south gate, and he that entered by the south gate must go out by the north gate. Hence,

Obs. 1. The Lord expects not only prince and priests to worship him in a public way, but the people also. "When the people of the land shall come before the Lord in the solemn feasts." God looks not for great ones, learned ones, rich ones, but all sorts, and all of all sorts, to come before him, to acknowledge him to be their God, Creator, and Lawgiver; he is honoured by the worship of the meaner, if sincere, as well as by the worship of the prince or priest; he is no respecter of persons.

Obs. 2. That the way of God's servants is a straight and right-forth way. There is no crookedness in it: Isa. xxvi. 7, "The way of the just is uprightness;" there is no turning aside to the temptations of Satan, to the beggarly elements of the world, to the enticing delights of the flesh, or any vanity whatsoever. That soul that is in God's way, must not look back to Sodom, as Lot's wife did, and suffer for it, but it must go forward. Matthew being called from the receipt of custom into the way of Christ, Matt. ix. 9, might not return, but follow Christ; for whosoever puts his hand to the plough, and looks back, is not fit for the kingdom of God, Luke ix. 62. Such a one must not look back to his old courses, customs, company, principles, or errors; but leaving them, must go straight on in the way of God, from darkness to light, from imperfection to perfection. Those that come to be the Lord's servants, must continue in his service, and perfect holiness in his fear, 2 Cor. vii. 1; Heb. xii. 1—3; Phil. iii. 13, 14.

Obs. 3. The shortness of man's life is here represented unto us; he enters into the world, goes on a little way, and then goes out of it again. So that man's life is as a passage from one gate to another.

They came in at a north gate, went on a little while, and a little way, and then went out at a south gate, &c. It is no long passage from the doors of the womb to the gates of death, Psal. ciii. 15, 16; Job xiv. 1, 2.

The 10th verse is an ordinance for the prince, showing when he is to come to the public worship, and when he is to depart from it. When the people go in at the gate appointed for them, then must he go in at the gate appointed for him; and so when they go out, he must go out. Those words, "in the midst of them," are not to be taken as if the prince went in the midst of the people to the sanctuary; but they denote, that he went at that time, and when come thither, he was there with them, or among them; or at the east gate, which is between the north and south.

1. Here we may see princes are bound to be present at the public worship of God; and not only to be present, but to be present at the beginning, and to stay till the end thereof. They may not come and go at their own pleasure, but at God's appointment. The presence of great persons at the worship of God is of much concernment, and hath great influence into the people; it encourages them to come to hear, to stay, when greater than themselves do so: people are led much by example of superiors; therefore kings and judges are commanded to serve the Lord with fear, and to kiss the Son, Psal. ii.

2. Here we are informed, taking "the prince" for Christ, that he is in the assemblies of his people; when the saints meet together to worship the Lord, he is in the midst of them. He made a precious promise when he was here on earth, and makes it good daily, though he be in heaven; it is that Matt. xviii. 20, "Where two or three are gathered together in my name, I am there in the midst of them;" to observe, to reward, and punish. The church is called Christ, 1 Cor. xii. 12; and Christ is said to sing praise unto God in the midst of the church, Heb. ii. 12. He being King of saints, loves to be with and among them: he was in the midst of the one hundred and forty-four thousand, Rev. xiv. 1.

The 11th verse treateth of the meat offering, which was to be at feasts and solemnities, directing the particulars and quantities. In Moses' time the tenth part of an ephah of flour, and the fourth part of an hin of oil, was required, Numb. xxviii. 5; Exod. xxix. 40: but here it is otherwise; a whole ephah of meal or flour is appointed to a bullock, a whole ephah to a ram, and a whole hin of oil to each, only the lamb's flour or oil to be offered was left to liberty or ability.

This may teach us, that seeing our light and mercies are greater under the gospel than theirs were under the law, therefore our obedience and service to the Lord should exceed theirs; if they gave him but the tenth part of an ephah, we ought to give him a whole ephah; if they gave him the fourth part of an hin, we must give him a whole hin. The more God communicates to us, the greater returns should be to him.

The 12th verse minds us of the prince's freewill offerings. Besides what was enjoined, he might voluntarily prepare a burnt offering or a peace offering at his pleasure; and at his coming one was to open the east gate unto him, and at his going forth one was to shut the gate. God looks for more from princes and great ones, than what is ordinary, than what is commanded; he looks for voluntary sacrifices, freewill offerings at their hands. It is said of Josiah, that he gave three thousand bullocks, three thousand lambs and kids for passover offerings, and all of the king's substance; and that the princes gave willingly, 2 Chron. xxxv. 7, 8. So free and bountiful they were, that the Lord took notice of it, and hath recorded it in his word, that "there was no passover like to that kept in Israel from the days of Samuel the prophet; neither did all the kings of Israel keep such a passover as Josiah," ver. 18.

We may interpret this verse of Christ, and so it presents to us not only that Christ hath freely and voluntarily offered up himself a sacrifice to God for us, Heb. ix. 14; x. 9, 10; but that he is the substance and quintessence of all sacrifices; and that the Father hath opened the gate of heaven unto him; and that by virtue of his merits and intercession, the door of reconciliation stands open unto us continually; but should he leave heaven, that door should be shut. No patriarch, no prophet, no apostle, no martyr, no saint, no angel, ever had this honour, to have the door of mercy and grace opened and shut at their pleasure: this is an honour peculiar to Christ.

The 13th, 14th, and 15th verses, declare what the daily sacrifices should be every morning, viz. a lamb of the first year without blemish for a burnt offering, and a meat offering with it, the sixth part of an ephah, and the third part of an hin of oil. The daily sacrifice here differs from that in Numb. xxviii. 3—6. Moses requires two lambs, the tenth part of an ephah of flour, and the fourth part of an hin of oil; Ezekiel speaks but of one lamb, the sixth part of an ephah of flour, and the third part of an hin of oil; and here is no mention of the evening: which alterations import that Mosaical rites and sacrifices should expire; and that notwithstanding, God would have a daily sacrifice in the days of Christ; that he would be worshipped, not only on the christian sabbath, but other days also, as was fore-prophesied, Psal. lxxii. 15, "Prayer shall be made unto him continually, and daily shall he be praised."

Ver. 16—18. *Thus saith the Lord God; If the prince give a gift unto any of his sons, the inheritance thereof shall be his sons'; it shall be their possession by inheritance. But if he give a gift of his inheritance to one of his servants, then it shall be his to the year of liberty; after it shall return to the prince: but his inheritance shall be his sons' for them. Moreover the prince shall not take of the people's inheritance by oppression, to thrust them out of their possessions; but he shall give his sons inheritance out of his own possession: that my people be not scattered every man from his possession.*

These verses contain laws to direct the prince's bounty, and to keep him from oppression. 1. Here is a law about giving to his sons, ver. 16. What he gives them, must be their inheritance and possession for ever. 2. Here is a law about giving to his servants, ver. 17. If the prince give a gift to any of his servants or subjects of his inheritance, it must not be theirs for ever, but only to the year of liberty, that was, the year of jubilee; for among the Jews, every fiftieth year was a year of jubilee: Lev. xxv. 10, "Ye shall hallow the fiftieth year, and proclaim liberty throughout all the land unto all the inhabitants thereof; it shall be a jubile unto you; and ye shall return every man unto his possession, and ye shall return every man unto his family." Whatsoever of men's possessions were sold or mortgaged, returned to the owners in the year of jubilee; see ver. 17, and Lev. xxv. 28; and whatever the prince here should give away to any but his own sons, should return to him again at the year of jubilee.

The law to prevent oppression in the prince is in ver. 18. When princes give gifts of inheritance to their sons and servants, and are expensive in their buildings, feastings, and revellings, usually they fetch it out of the people, by squeezing and oppressing them; but the law is, "the prince shall not take of the people's inheritance," lest he should alienate the inheritance which came by parents, from their posterity, unto strangers, and so cause them to desert their country, and to scatter abroad. God would have princes to live upon and give of their own, and by no means to oppress the people. These laws were not amongst the Mosaical ones. And if "the prince" here be taken for the princes of this world, where, when, and by whom hath this prophecy been fulfilled? where dwells the prince, and what is his name, who hath not oppressed the people? We may find the accomplishment of it in Christ, rather than in any of them. But for them we may observe here,

1. That princes should be liberal and bountiful; and not only to their children, but to their servants and subjects; they may deserve well at their hands, and if they be not rewarded and encouraged, men will have no hearts to public, honourable, and difficult employments. When David shall have Saul's daughter, he will venture upon the Philistines, 1 Sam. xviii.

2. That princes being bountiful, must give of what is their own: it is injustice and dishonourable to them, to give away what is another's.

3. They ought to be well content with their own estates, and not to covet and take away from others their goods, houses, or possessions; they should not spoil their subjects of their right, thrust them out of their possessions, take away their privileges, to make themselves great, rich, dreadful. When princes do so, they become tyrants and oppressors, and their ends will be breaking; Psal. lxxii. 4, "He shall break in pieces the oppressor."

To speak somewhat of this prince, as pointing out Christ. He hath sons and servants; to the one he gives graces, to the other common gifts. To his sons he gives a kingdom, Luke xxii. 29; to the wicked who are his servants, he gives a portion in this life, Psal. xvii. 14. And at their death, the time of liberty, and at the time of restitution of all things, the gifts return to the prince again; but the graces and the kingdom are the saints' for ever, they are their inheritance. This Prince gives of his own; for all that the Father hath are his, John xvii. 10; and he is Heir of all things, Heb. i. 2; and he gives bountifully, he pours out his Spirit upon his sons, and fills them with joy glorious and unspeakable.

Ver. 19—24. *After he brought me through the entry, which was at the side of the gate, into the holy chambers of the priests, which looked toward the north: and, behold, there was a place on the two sides westward. Then said he unto me, This is the place where the priests shall boil the trespass offering and the sin offering, where they shall bake the meat offering; that they bear them not out into the utter court, to sanctify the people. Then he brought me forth into the utter court, and caused me to pass by the four corners of the court; and, behold, in every corner of the court there was a court. In the four corners of the court there were courts joined of forty cubits long and thirty broad: these four corners were of one measure. And there was a row of building round about in them, round about them four, and it was made with boiling places under the rows round about. Then said he unto me, These are the places of them that boil, where the ministers of the house shall boil the sacrifice of the people.*

The courts and places where the priests and Levites boiled, baked, and made ready the sacrifices, are here described unto us. On the north side of the priests' court, into which the prince and people were not to enter, were the holy chambers; and westward from them was a place as far from the east gate as might be, where all things were fitted for boiling and baking the sacrifices; in that place were the kitchens for such service. Hither was the prophet brought to see these, and from hence he was carried into the utter court. Some make this utter court the gentiles' or people's court; others, the middle court, called the utter court, because it was so to the inner court.

"In every corner of the court there was a court." According to the Hebrew thus, A court in a corner of a court, a court in a corner of a court; and these little courts were for the Levites, where was a building with boiling places, and there the appointed officers boiled the sacrifices of the people.

"That they bear them not out to sanctify the people." In chap. xliv. 19, "They shall not sanctify the people with their garments," was laid down. What may serve here, unless by sanctifying we understand defiling, as *sanctum* doth? for the Hebrew word קדש signifies sometimes to pollute, as Deut. xxii. 9, "Thou shalt not sow thy vineyard with divers seeds; lest the fruit of thy seed which thou hast sown, and the fruit of thy vineyard, be defiled."

The holy chambers here spoken of, and the four courts in the four corners of the court, do seem to hold out the particular churches which are in all parts of the world; and that these being committed to the ministers of the gospel, they ought to preach Christ unto them, and especially Christ crucified, who is the trespass offering, the sin offering, and meat offering. They must be careful to whom they give holy things; they might not bear out the offerings into the utter court, where all sorts of people were; they would have thought themselves holy by touching holy things, though they had defiled them. As many now by having the supper of the Lord think themselves holy, whenas they have defiled the ordinance and themselves the more by their unworthy receiving. The ministers of the gospel therefore should be very circumspect and careful to whom they give holy things: the profane, ignorant hypocrites should not share in them; those who are true repentants, and true believers, are meet to partake of them. Holy things must be kept within the limits of the church of God, and not extended further than God hath appointed.

Again, it is the ministers who must boil and bake; they are spiritual cooks, and must prepare wholesome food for the people. The people might bring sacrifices, but not prepare those themselves were in part to feed upon, that was the work of the priests and Levites. And now under the gospel, it is the work of pastors and teachers to prepare boiled and baked meat, boiled in the furnace of meditation, and baked in the oven of the heart by spiritual heat. Such meat will nourish and strengthen, make fat and flourishing.

CHAPTER XLVII.

Ver. 1—5. *Afterward he brought me again unto the door of the house; and, behold, waters issued out from under the threshold of the house eastward: for the forefront of the house stood toward the east, and the waters came down from under from the right side of the house, at the south side of the altar. Then brought he me out of the way of the gate northward, and led me about the way without unto the utter gate by the way that looketh eastward; and, behold, there ran out waters on the right side. And when the man that had the line in his hand went forth eastward, he measured a thousand cubits, and he brought me through the waters; the waters were to the ancles;* (or, waters of the ancles.) *Again he measured a thousand, and brought me through the waters; the waters were to the knees. Again he measured a thousand, and brought me through; the waters were to the loins. Afterward he measured a thousand; and it was a river that I could not pass over: for the waters were risen, waters to swim in, a river that could not be passed over.*

IN this chapter are two principal parts:

I. A vision of waters, and the description of them, ver. 1—12.

II. The bordering and dividing the land, ver. 13, to the end.

Concerning the waters, they are described,

1. From their original or place whence they spring and flow, ver. 1, 2.

2. From their increase, ver. 3—5.

The man with the measuring line in his hand, having led our prophet up and down to view the temple, the parts and appurtenances of it, brings him again to the door of the house, that is, to the door of the temple or sanctuary.

"And, behold, waters issued out from under," &c. Vilalpandus makes these waters to be those subterraneal waters which were carried in pipes under ground, and issued forth into the priests' court, to wash the sacrifices, and purge away the blood, excrements, and filth, occasioned by the slaying so many sacrifices; for certainly had there not been aqueducts about Solomon's temple, to have cleansed the places where the sacrifices were slain and prepared, it would have been an unsavoury and unhealthful place. These waters issued forth, some from the threshold, some from the south side of the altar, and so ran away. From these waters, the Lord takes occasion to speak of spiritual waters.

"The waters came down from under from the right side of," &c. The temple was upon a high mountain, Ezek. xl. 2, therefore the waters are said to come down; and they came from the right side of the house, that was, the south side; for the front of the house standing towards the east, when a man stood and looked eastward, his right hand or side was towards the south. The altar for burnt offering was before the porch of the temple, and at the south side thereof did these waters run.

Our prophet having seen the spring and rise of the waters, is led out of the inner court, by the way of the north gate, and brought to the uttermost east gate, where he first entered; and it was to behold how the waters ran out there on the right side also. The words in Hebrew are, מים מפכים; פכה signifies to flow, but gently, he saw the waters run there gently and pleasingly; they ran not fiercely as a torrent, but gently, as oil poured out of a vial.

These waters, though they ran gently, yet increased mightily; for upon Christ's measuring out a thousand cubits, they became waters of the ancles; upon his measuring out the two thousand cubits, they rose to be waters of the knees; upon his measuring out the third thousand of cubits, they ascended to be waters of the loins; and upon measuring the fourth thousand, they became waters for swimming, they could not be waded through, they were so deep, even a great river impassable.

What these waters do signify is worthy inquiry. Some make these waters to signify the prosperity of the church, that great happiness which the Jews had after their return from Babylon. This was an outward mercy, and but for a little season, for they suffered great and grievous things by Antiochus and others, in the Maccabees' times. But here some spiritual mercy is intended by the waters; others therefore understand by them, the waters of baptism, which Christ instituted, and so came from the altar, viz. the side of Christ; but these waters are too shallow to be Ezekiel's waters. A third sort make them to be the Spirit, and gifts of the Spirit. It is true, the Spirit is said to be poured out, Joel ii. 28; but it is not to be understood of the person of the Spirit, which is infinite, indivisible, and immovable, but of the gifts and graces of the Spirit. A fourth sort interpret these waters of the gospel, the glad tidings touching man's salvation by Christ, which is compared to water frequently in Scripture: Isa. xi. 9, "The earth shall be full of the knowledge of the Lord, as the waters cover the sea;" the knowledge of the Lord Jesus shall abound, as the waters of the sea: see Joel iii. 18; Zech. xiv. 8. We may take the gospel, with the gifts and graces of the Spirit, to be these waters; for the gospel is the ministration of the Spirit, as the apostle saith, 2 Cor. iii. 8. And the Spirit, with the graces and gifts, are oft compared to water, as well as the gospel: see Ezek. xxxvi. 25; Isa. xliv. 3; xli. 18; Acts ii. 17; John iv. 14; vii. 37—39. Now it remains to show wherein they are like unto water.

1. Water cleanseth, it purgeth away the filth of the body, and other things. So doth the gospel, with the gifts and graces of the Spirit, cleanse the souls of men, and purge their hearts from sin and filthiness. John xv. 3, "Now ye are clean through the word which I have spoken unto you." Christ spoke unto them the gospel, and that was the word, together with the Spirit, which made them clean from their unbelief, disobedience, and other sins. 1 Pet. i. 22, "Seeing ye have purified your souls in obeying the truth through the Spirit." The Spirit accompanying the gospel, purified their souls, and made them obedient to the truth. See Ezek. xxxvi. 25, 27.

2. Water moistens and softens the earth, which before was dry and hard, so that there was no entrance for the plough; but being well watered with the rain of heaven, it is soft, and fit for the plough. So the gospel, the doctrine of Christ, moistens and mollifies hard and heavy hearts. Those that put Christ to death, were hardhearted sinners; but when they heard Peter preach the gospel, and some of that water fell upon their hearts, they were softened, and became sensible of what they had done; "They were pricked in their hearts, and said, Men and brethren, what shall we do?" Acts ii. 37. So Paul was a stout and stubborn fellow, but the water of the gospel did so supple him, that it made him yield and say, "Lord, what wilt thou have me to do?" Acts ix. 6.

3. Water cools heat; the heat of the earth and air in summer, and the heat of the body in hot weather. Many bathe themselves in the water to cool them. Dives begged a little water to cool his tongue, Luke xvi. 24. The waters of the gospel have a cooling virtue in them; they cool the heat of persecution, Matt. v. 11, 12; they cool the heat of our passions, James iii. 2; Matt. v. 22; they cool the heat of temptations, Rom. xvi. 20; 1 Cor. x. 13; James i. 2, 12; they cool the heat of our lusts, 1 Pet. ii. 11; Rom. viii. 13; 1 Tim. vi. 9, 10; they cool the scorchings of a guilty conscience, and fire of hell, Matt. xii. 31; xi. 28; 1 John i. 7.

4. Water makes the earth fruitful. When they wanted rain, there was barrenness and famine, Jer. xiv.; but when they had the former and latter rain, all things flourished and abounded. Ezek. xxxiv. 26, 27, "I will cause the shower to come down in his season; there shall be showers of blessing; and the tree of the field shall yield her fruit," &c. Literally these words are true, and spiritually also, and set out the fruitfulness of those who were to live under the sweet showers of gospel doctrine. They should be like a watered garden, Jer. xxxi. 12. The doctrine of the Lord is as the rain and dew, which falling upon the tender herbs and grass, cause them to grow, Deut. xxxii. 2. When Zaccheus was watered with this water, he became very fruitful, and gave half of his goods to the poor, Luke xix. 8. Others sold all, and laid the money down at the apostles' feet, Acts iv. 35; they were abundant in love, and in good works.

5. Water quencheth thirst, satisfies and revives the thirsty soul. It was their drink in the infancy of the world, and is still in some hot countries. Samson, when like to perish for thirst, having some water out of the jaw bone of an ass, he revived, and was satisfied, Judg. xv. 18, 19. The waters of the gospel have this property also; when the soul is athirst, there is no water quencheth that thirst, but the water of life, which the gospel showeth and conveyeth unto us. The gospel hath this water of life in it, Christ and the Spirit, which it makes men partakers of. The great and precious promises are satisfying things; the righteousness and Spirit of Christ are satisfying and reviving things. Peter found it so, when he said to Christ, "Lord, to whom should we go? thou hast the words of eternal life:" let others go to what brooks, pits, or cisterns they will, to quench their thirst, we will never go from thee, who hast the words of eternal life; who art the fountain of living waters, and canst satisfy us for ever, John vi. 68. This water quencheth unlawful desires, and satisfieth spiritual desires.

6. Some waters have a curing and healing virtue. The pool of Bethesda healed all manner of diseases, John v. 4. There are waters in our land which have healing virtue in them. Such are the waters here mentioned, for they healed other waters, ver. 8. Gospel waters will heal sick souls and bodies. The centurion said to Christ, "Lord, speak thou but the word only, and my servant shall be healed," and it was so, Matt. viii. 8, 13. Christ cast out devils with his word, and healed all that were sick, ver. 16. The gospel is not only a pattern of wholesome words, but of healing words; also there is no spiritual disease in the soul, but the gospel hath healing virtue to cure it; therefore it is called the "gospel of salvation," Eph. i. 13, and "the power of God unto salvation," Rom. i. 16.

7. Some waters are very cordial, and do greatly comfort the spirits of man. None more than the waters of the gospel, by which the Spirit, the true, solid, and eternal Comforter, flows into the heart. The gospel, and good things of it, are set out by water, milk, and wine, Isa. lv. 1, all which are comforting things. The gospel is glad tidings, and affords strong and everlasting consolation to the soul, 2 Thess. ii. 16; 2 Cor. i. 5. Jeremiah saith, the word of God was the joy and rejoicing of his soul, chap. xv. 16. David professes, he had perished in his affliction, had he not drunk of these cordial waters, Psal. cxix. 92.

To come to those observations which we may pick out of these verses.

Obs. 1. That as it is Christ who makes known the things of the temple; so he doth the same not all at once, but he makes known some at one time, some at another. Formerly Christ had revealed much to the prophet, and here he brings him again to the door of the house, and shows him waters he had not seen before. We are not capable of much at once; like children, we must have line upon line, precept upon precept, here a little, and there a little. Ezekiel is instructed a little in one place, and a little in another place, as he was capable. So Christ, the wise and chief Builder of the temple, deals with him, and revealed one thing after another unto him; and so he dealt with his disciples, John xvi. 12.

Obs. 2. The waters of the gospel, the gifts and graces of the Spirit, do flow from Zion, from Jerusalem, where Ezekiel had his vision, chap. xl. 2. The bitter waters of the law flowed from mount Sinai, but the sweet waters of the gospel flowed from mount Zion. Isaiah long before prophesied whence these waters should come; Isa. ii. 3, "Out of Zion shall go forth the law," that is, the law of faith, not of works, "and the word of the Lord from Jerusalem." So in Zech. xiv. 8, "And it shall be in that day, that living waters shall go out from Jerusalem; half of them toward the former sea," that is, eastward, "and half of them toward the hinder sea," that is, westward: "in summer and in winter shall it be;" there shall be no time wherein these Jerusalem waters shall cease flowing. It is not Rome, or any other city in the world, which hath the honour to send out these waters, but Jerusalem only, where was the true church of God.

Obs. 3. These spiritual waters, although they flowed from Zion and Jerusalem, yet Christ himself was the fountain and original of them; they came from the door and threshold of the house. Christ tells us, he is "the door," John x. 7. All spiritual water is in him, all heavenly doctrine, all gifts and graces. When the Spirit moved holy men to speak, as it is 2 Pet. i. 21, it received of Christ, and showed unto them, John xvi. 14; and all the waters which flowed from the apostles they received from Christ. The Spirit was given them to fill their vessels, and fitted them to carry these living waters from Jerusalem to all parts, Acts ii. 8; and Christ sent them forth to preach the gospel. "All the treasures of wisdom and knowledge" are in him, Col. ii. 3; and he that believes in him, receives living waters from him: all gifts, graces, and divine truths, are from him. The waters of the sanctuary flow from the Lord of the sanctuary.

Obs. 4. God would not have his worshippers to conform to and comply with the world's worshippers. They worshipped with their faces towards the east, that was the nations' practice. The heathen idolaters had their backs to the west; but here the front of the house stood eastward, that when they came to worship the true God, their backs might be towards the east, and their faces towards the most holy place, which was westward. When some Jews, degenerated into heathenish customs, did worship with their faces towards the east, Ezek. viii. 16, and their backs towards the temple, God counted it an abomination, it did greatly provoke him, causing him to deal in fury with them, and to show them no pity, Ezek. viii. 17, 18. God must be worshipped according to his own order, and not after the rites and customs of others.

Obs. 5. The gospel spread first into the eastern and southern parts of the world; it is said, the waters issued out eastward, and came down from the south side; they were dry and hot countries, and God took special care of them, that they should be first watered. In Galilee did Christ first preach the gospel, Matt. iv. 23, and so all Judea over; and after from Jerusalem these gospel waters flowed into all nations: Matt. xxviii. 19, "Go, and teach all nations;" Mark xvi. 15, "Go ye into all the world, and preach the gospel to every creature." The apostles were spiritual clouds, and they were to water, not only Jerusalem and Samaria, but the uttermost parts of the earth, Acts i. 8.

Obs. 6. Those who are preachers of the gospel, must look for hardship, for travail and trouble, for much heat, much cold, for many storms and tempests. They that carry these waters, must travel into all quarters, east, south, north, where are fierce winds, parching heats, terrible storms. Preachers must expect temptations, persecutions, reproaches, accusations, imprisonments, &c.; and notwithstanding these, they must go on and carry sanctuary waters to all places. "Endure hardness," saith Paul to Timothy, "as a good soldier of Jesus Christ." Gospel preachers must not be dismayed at northern or eastern blasts, nor faint at southern heats.

Obs. 7. Sanctuary waters are not common, but choice mercies, they are right-side mercies, south-side blessings. The gospel is a right-hand mercy. Some mercies are left-hand and left-side mercies, they are those of an inferior nature. Others are right-hand mercies, and such are those of the highest nature, amongst which is the gospel. Rev. v. 1, "I saw in the right hand of him who sat upon the throne a book written within and on the back side, sealed with seven seals;" and ver. 7, Christ, who was the Lamb, took this book out of the right hand of God, and so handed it over to us, acquainting us with the mysteries and mercies in it.

Obs. 8. The glorious and blessed truths of the gospel do come from Christ Jesus, as Mediator, and making reconciliation for us with God the Father. These waters are said to flow from the altar, which was a type of Christ. The sacrifices offered upon the altar were for reconciliation; and Christ being both altar and sacrifice, hath reconciled man to God; and as he doth this, so the waters flow from him, so gospel truths are given out by him. The gospel is the purchase of the death of Christ, sealed with his blood, and holds out strong arguments of our being reconciled to God; and therefore it is called "the gospel of peace," Eph. vi. 15.

These are the observations from the two first verses. Now for those that flow from the other three verses.

Obs. 1. The Lord Christ, as he is the Architect of the church, so the Measurer of all things belonging unto it. He is the man in this vision with the line in his hand; nothing is to be done in his spiritual temple, but according to his will and direction. Moses measured out all in the tabernacle, David and Solomon all in the temple, but Christ is the only measurer in this house. Gospel measurings are committed to the Son; Heb. i. 2, "God hath in these last days spoken unto us by his Son;" and he is over his own house, Heb. iii. 6, to order and dispose all things as himself pleaseth.

Obs. 2. The motion of sanctuary waters is not accidental, or human, but according to divine appointment. Christ goeth forth eastward, measures a thousand cubits, and then the waters flow that way; and then he measures a thousand cubits more, and so they flow another way. That way Christ went with his line measuring, the waters still flowed; which imports, that the preaching of the gospel in one place, and not in another, is not casual, or as man will, but the appointment of Christ. He forbade his disciples to go into the way of the gentiles, and into the cities of the Samaritans, but rather go to the lost sheep of the house of Israel, Matt. x. 5, 6. Christ here measured out the cubits, where these gospel waters should flow. Paul and those with him, being forbidden to carry these waters into Asia, and not suffered to go with them into Bithynia, whither their wills were bent, at length by a vision they are directed into Macedonia, assuredly gathering, that the Lord had called them to preach the gospel there, Acts xvi. 6—10. Christ had measured out a thousand cubits there, for these spiritual waters to flow. It is at the appointment of Christ what countries, what cities, what towns, and what families shall have these waters.

Obs. 3. That as it is at Christ's appointment to what places these waters shall flow, so likewise how far therein they shall flow. So many cubits as Christ measures out, so far they shall flow, and not farther. If he measure out a thousand cubits, they shall extend so far; if he measure out but five hundred cubits, or one hundred only, the waters shall run to the borders thereof, and not one cubit beyond, nor one short. So far as Christ's line is stretched over any place, so far the waters of the sanctuary will and must flow.

Obs. 4. The doctrine of the gospel is never rightly understood, unless we be taught it by Christ. He led Ezekiel into the waters of the sanctuary; so is the Hebrew במים and we read it, through them: he instructed him in the nature and qualities of them. Whosoever understands the gospel savingly, is led into that knowledge by the Spirit of Christ. The apostles themselves had not understood the gospel, had not Christ sent them his Spirit: John xvi. 13, "When he, the Spirit of truth, is come, he will guide you into all truth;" that is, he will make you know all truth savingly. The truths of Christ are spiritual, and without the Spirit they are not discerned, 1 Cor. ii. 14, 15. Many wade into these spiritual waters without Christ and his Spirit, and they are of those who are said to be "ever learning, and never able to come to the knowledge of the truth," 2 Tim. iii. 7.

Obs. 5. The doctrine of the gospel, conversion of sinners, and graces of the Spirit, proceed gradually.

(1.) For the doctrine of the gospel, that went out gradually, like water out of a fountain, which may be covered with one's hand, or a dish, but running a little way increases; the waters here, after a little time and motion, were up to the ancles, after to the knees, and then to the loins. The gospel was not given out all at once, but one truth thereof after another. Christ himself first preached one part of the gospel, and then another; he was four years and upwards in letting that sacred water run out of his lips, it came from him by degrees. And so the apostles, who were conduits of this fountain, let out that water little by little; they went up and down preaching here and there, writing an epistle to one place, and an epistle to another place, till they filled the world with these waters. If you read the book of The Acts of the Apostles, you may see how the gospel spread from place to place, and what great progress it had in the world. Paul saith, Rom. x. 18, "Their sound went into all the earth, and their words unto the ends of the world;" and to the Colossians, chap. i. 6, he declares, the gospel was come unto them, and to all the world: from small beginnings here was great increase.

(2.) The conversion of sinners is a gradual work: now one is converted, then another, afterward a third, not all at once. Though the waters of the sanctuary be living waters, yet they do not beget life in all who taste of them. Many scribes and Pharisees, and others, heard Christ preach the glad tidings of the gospel, and speak as never men spake, yet were not converted: some few were wrought upon in Christ's time, in Judea and Jerusalem; some by the apostles in several places where they came, as at Rome, Corinth, Galatia, Ephesus, Philippi, and other places; but the most part remained unconverted, even in Jerusalem itself; which made Christ weep over it, Luke xix. 41, and say, "O Jerusalem, Jerusalem, how often would I have gathered thy children together, even as a hen gathereth her chickens under her wings, and ye would not!" Matt. xxiii. 37. Conversion work went out slowly in Christ's days; it was quicker in Peter's time than ever since, three thousand souls converted at a sermon: now three thousand sermons hardly convert one soul. Paul got at one time a Lydia, at another a jailor, at a third time a fugitive servant; and so by degrees the waters of the sanctuary did good.

(3.) The graces of the Spirit have a gradualness in them. Their knowledge, their faith, their hope, their love, are little at first; but in time they increase, they grow from knowledge to knowledge, from faith to faith, from hope to hope, and from love to love: none are filled with sanctuary waters at first, they come into us little by little, drop by drop. Apollos was more perfectly instructed in the way of God by Aquila and Priscilla, Acts xviii. 26. There are several ages in christianity, babes, children, young men, fathers. Babes are only sprinkled with these waters; in children, they are come to their ancles; in young men, to their knees; and in fathers, they are up to their loins, and drawing near to their chins, they are almost come to perfection: but they and the others must still "grow in grace, and in the knowledge of our Lord and Saviour Jesus Christ," till they all come to "a perfect man, unto the measure of the stature of the fulness of Christ," Eph. iv. 13.

Obs. 6. The gospel hath such depths and mysteries in it, as no human understanding can sound or comprehend. The waters of the sanctuary did rise so high, become so deep, that they could not be passed over; swim in them Ezekiel might, but he could neither find the bottom of them, nor get over them. The gospel is among "the deep things of God," 1 Cor. ii. 10, it is the richest box of the knowledge and wisdom of God; and there is a depth in those riches, Rom. xi. 33: it is "the unsearchable riches of Christ," Eph. iii. 8; it is "wisdom from above," Jam. iii. 17; it is a doctrine of "heavenly things," John iii. 12; Heb. viii. 5; it is not known without "the spirit of wisdom and revelation," Eph. i. 17; neither Christ nor his doctrine are known without revelation, Matt. xvi. 17; Gal. i. 16. The flesh taught the Pharisees to call Christ Samaritan, and to say, he had a devil, John viii. 48; but it is the Spirit which teaches men to own and acknowledge Christ for a Lord, 1 Cor. xii. 3. Are not these mysteries and depths in the gospel; that three should be one? 1 John v. 7; that two should be one, and yet continue two still? that the Maker should be one with the thing made? that he who blesseth all should himself be a curse? that the Prince of life should die? that the debt should be paid and yet pardoned, the fault be punished and yet remitted? that the Head and members of the same body should be in heaven, and on earth, and in the several quarters of the world, at the same time? that God, who is infinite, should dwell in man? These, and such like deeps, are in the gospel. Is not the Revelation alone a great river, which none of our spiritual mariners can sound or sail over? That one place, Rev. xiii. 18, hath put the skilfullest of them to it: "Let him that hath understanding count the number of the beast; for it is the number of a man; and his number is Six hundred threescore and six." In Daniel there are depths; and Peter saith, that in the epistles of Paul there are δυσνόητα, "things hard to be understood," 2 Pet. iii. 16.

Obs. 7. The doctrine of the gospel is pure, and sufficient of itself, it needs no tradition or invention of men. The waters of the sanctuary are holy waters, and a river great and deep, which none can pass over. No waters are like these for purity and perfection; they are not like the muddy waters of Egypt, or puddle waters of Rome; they are pure, without all mixture, and sufficient for all that belong to the sanctuary: so that men need not run to pits or cisterns of their own, or others. The doctrines of men are muddy waters, compared to these, and not sufficient to quench the thirst of any thirsting soul; but these gospel waters are most pure, sufficient, and satisfying.

Obs. 8. From this vision of the waters, That sanctuary waters afford comfort unto the saints in their afflictions, yea, in their deepest distresses. Ezekiel had this vision in the time of his captivity, and it was to comfort him, and the captives in Babylon with him; and so to presignify to us, that the waters of the gospel would yield choice comfort to the saints in their sad, yea, saddest conditions. They are living waters, and do refresh dying souls: the promises are bottles of this water; and when those that are in the greatest afflictions drink the cordial water contained in them, they forget their misery, and are like giants refreshed with wine. The comfort of the Scriptures is choice comfort, Rom. xv. 4. That in Psal. xlvi. 4, is verified in these gospel waters; "There is a river, the streams whereof shall make glad the city of God." Let the city of God be in never so great straits or distresses, the river of the sanctuary, gospel waters, will make it glad.

Ver. 6—12. *And he said unto me, Son of man, hast thou seen this? Then he brought me, and caused me to return to the brink of the river. Now when I had returned, behold, at the bank of the river were very many trees on the one side and on the other. Then said he unto me, These waters issue out toward the east country, and go down into the desert, and go into the sea: which being brought forth into the sea, the waters shall be healed. And it shall come to pass, that every thing that liveth, which moveth, whithersoever the rivers shall come, shall live: and there shall be a very great multitude of fish, because these waters shall come thither: for they shall be healed; and every thing shall live whither the river cometh. And it shall come to pass, that the fishes shall stand upon it from En-gedi even unto En-eglaim; they shall be a place to spread forth nets; their fish shall be according to their kinds, as the fish of the great sea, exceeding many. But the miry places thereof and the marishes thereof shall not be healed; they shall be given to salt. And by the river upon the bank thereof, on this side and on that side, shall grow all trees for meat, whose leaf shall not fade, neither shall the fruit thereof be consumed: it shall bring forth new fruit according to his months, because their waters they issued out of the sanctuary: and the fruit thereof shall be for meat, and the leaf thereof for medicine.*

We have heard whence these visional waters did spring, and of their great increase into a river; and here we have a description of this river,

I. From the trees which were about it, with their leaves and fruit, ver. 7, 12.

II. From the place into which it flows, ver. 8.

III. From the effects, in ver. 8—10.

IV. From the fishers and nets, ver. 10.

V. From the adjunct places, ver. 11.

In ver. 6, the Lord puts a question unto Ezekiel, and it is this, "Son of man, hast thou seen this?" hast thou seen these waters whence they spring? hast thou seen which way they flow? hast thou seen their great increase and unpassableness? If thou hast not, see now fully, and observe them more exactly; that is the intent of the question. There is a corporal sight, and there is an intellectual sight; see with the eye of thy body, and with the eye of thy mind.

Note hence, That the waters of the sanctuary have that in them which is observable to be considered and seriously weighed.

"Hast thou seen this?" how suddenly these waters break forth? how they have followed the measuring line, which way soever it went? how in a little time they have risen up to a river, and such a river as is impermeable? Hast thou seen the mysteries contained in these waters? As the waters abound, so the mysteries thereof abound. The gospel is full of mysteries and depths; the beginnings, increase, and success of it are wonderful things, and ought to be minded; the spreading, converting, and edifying power of the gospel, christians should take special notice of, rejoice at, and bless God for. It is a choice mercy to have the waters of the gospel in a land, or in a town; and what a mercy is it when these waters prove waters of life, to convert and edify those that are there! If Middleton's and Thames' waters are observable, much more mystical waters.

After this question comes action; the Lord brought him, and caused him to return to the brink of the river, or tip of it. Hitherto he had seen the waters; now the Lord would have him to see what was upon the banks or sides of the river, for as there were things considerable in the waters, so on the banks.

Obs. 1. Christ reveals and makes known the mysteries of the sanctuary by degrees, and one after another. Ezekiel sees the waters, and being taught something concerning them, he is brought to the brink of the river, and hath new mysteries presented to him; he is held from seeing the waters of the sanctuary, to behold the trees thereof.

Obs. 2. The scholars of Christ ought to be content with what it pleases the Lord Christ to make known unto them, and to rest satisfied therewith. Ezekiel troubles not himself or Christ about the depth of the river, the multitude of waters, and several measurings; but being set down on the brink of the river, he is content to see and hear what the Lord should show him, and speak unto him. There is an itch in man to know things kept secret and hidden: many, through curiosity, prying into such things, have prejudiced themselves and others; Gen. iii. 6, Eve did so. Let us acquiesce in what Christ reveals, and not thirst after hidden secrets, lest we meet with Satanical delusions, and be given up to believe lies.

In ver. 7, the river is described from the multitude of trees on each side of it. There was very much wood, or very many trees, as Piscator, or very great trees, as Junius and Tremellius have it. As the waters were mystical, so are these trees, and they have a mystical and spiritual signification. They signify the saints under the gospel, those that are true christians; and such are not unfitly compared to trees, for they resemble them in many respects.

(1.) Trees have life in them; so true christians have life in them. When the Romans were become christians, then they were "alive unto God through Jesus Christ," Rom. vi. 11; before they were dry and dead trees, as the Ephesians were, Eph. ii. 1. When men are once true christians, they have life from Christ, John x. 10; xx. 31; 1 John v. 12; Gal. ii. 20.

(2.) Trees are rooted in the firm earth, in rocks and mountains; and true christians are rooted in Christ, who is a firm and solid Rock. The Colossians were rooted in Christ; not in Plato, Aristotle, or human philosophy, but in Christ and his doctrine; they were established in the faith of Christ, so that none could pull them from him, John x. 28.

(3.) Trees draw sap, moisture, and virtue from the earth, and the waters they are near unto, Jer. xvii. 8. Psal. civ. 16, "The trees of the Lord are full of sap," they draw strongly. And so it is with true christians, metaphorical trees, they draw sap from Christ, virtue from his promises, and moisture from his ordinances. Faith and love are like the little fibres which are upon roots; those strings, veins, or sinews draw mightily, and communicate to the whole; so do faith and love abundantly bring in spiritual sap into the soul: John i. 16, "Of his fulness have we all received:" see John xv. 5.

(4.) Trees do grow upwards; Gen. ii. 9, every tree grew: and the saints are of a growing nature; Psal. xcii. 12, "The righteous shall flourish like the palm tree: he shall grow like a cedar in Lebanon." Palm trees and cedars especially grow very high, Amos ii. 9, their tops reached to heaven. And did not the Thessalonians grow exceedingly in faith and charity? 2 Thess. i. 3. Did not Paul grow greatly, when his conversation was in heaven daily? Phil. iii. 20. The saints grow up into Christ in all things, Eph. iv. 15.

(5.) Of trees, some are strong, some are weak, some are high, some are low. So is it with saints, some are strong and high, as the centurion, Matt. viii. 10, the woman of Canaan, chap. xv. 28, James, Cephas, and John, Gal. ii. 9; some are low and weak, as the Corinthians, 1 Cor. iii. 1, and the Hebrews, Heb. v. 12, 13. John hath ranked these spiritual trees into three sorts, 1 John ii. 12—14, little children, young men, and fathers.

(6.) They are fruitful, and bear several kinds of fruit. Hence the tree of the field is said to be man's life, Deut. xx. 19; that is, it brings forth fruit of several kinds, whereby the life of man is preserved; and true christians are not barren trees, or trees which bring forth sour or corrupt fruit; but they are fruitful, and their fruit is good fruit. The Philippians were "filled with fruits of righteousness," Phil. i. 11. Dorcas was "full of good works and alms-deeds which she did," Acts ix. 36. The churches of Macedonia abounded in liberality, 2 Cor. viii. 2; and the church of Corinth in every thing, ver. 7; some had tongues, some interpreted, some wrought miracles, and some prophesied. Those widows which were to be taken into the church had fruit, much and variety of it; they brought up children, they lodged strangers, they washed the saints' feet, they relieved the afflicted, and they diligently followed every good work, 1 Tim. v. 9, 10.

(7.) Some trees are very fragrant, well scented; they perfume the air where they grow. Hos. xiv. 6, "His smell shall be as Lebanon." In Lebanon, which was a great mountain and fruitful forest, were fair trees, cedars, and almug trees, which filled the air with a sweet scent; and like unto Lebanon Israel should be. And Christ saith of his spouse, Cant. iv. 11, "The smell of thy garments is like the smell of Lebanon." The church's garments are the graces and gifts with which the Spirit hath adorned her, as knowledge, faith, love, humility, zeal, wisdom, &c.; these yield a good savour. From the church of Philippi was "an odour of a sweet smell," Phil. iv. 18. The church of Rome in Paul's days had a good scent, her "faith was spoken of throughout the whole world," Rom. i. 8. Gaius was a tree very fragrant, 3 John 2. 5, 6; and Demetrius alone had the smell of Lebanon, of fir trees, cedars, and almugs; for he had good respect of all men, and of the truth itself, ver. 12.

(8.) Trees are exposed to all winds, weathers, storms, to heat and cold; so are saints. Jer. xvii. 8, the man that trusts in God, shall be as a tree planted by the waters; and what though heat and drought come? he shall be prejudiced by neither; his branch is "green before the sun," Job viii. 16. There will be scorching heat and terrible blasts. Christians do meet with Satan's fiery darts, and the dragon's floods; reproaches, afflictions, temptations, troubles of all sorts they are exposed unto; see Psal. xxxiv. 19; 2 Tim. iii. 12.

Ver. 8. "These waters issue out towards the east country, and go down into the desert." These are the places into which the waters of the sanctuary did run. Some render the Hebrew words הגלילה הקדמונה into Galilee of the east; Montanus, to the eastern border. Galilee was eastward from Jerusalem, and in it was Lacus Asphaltites, the lake of Sodom, or Dead sea, so called because no fish could live in it, nor birds fly over it, but died, so deadly were the waters and vapours thereof. Hither the sanctuary waters came, and they went down also into the desert, that is, say some expositors, into the Mediterranean sea, which was in the west; suitable to which interpretation seems that in Zech. xiv. 8, where living waters are said to go out from Jerusalem, "half of them toward the former sea," that is, the Salt or Dead sea, "and half of them toward the hinder sea," that is, the Mediterranean sea. Others conceive these waters of Ezekiel did run only eastward, first into the Dead sea, and then out of that into the deserts or plains of Moab; for here is not mention of several seas, but there is of rivers, ver. 9.

The effects of these waters are,

1. Healing. When they came into the Dead sea, they healed the waters thereof; the sanctuary waters made those deadly waters wholesome and profitable, as the bitter waters of Marah were healed by a tree thrown in, Exod. xv. 25, and the waters of Jericho by a cruse of salt, 2 Kings ii. 20, 21.

2. Production of fishes, and them in abundance. These waters were fruitful waters, ver. 9, they begat life in dead creatures, and caused fish to abound "as the fish of the great sea, exceeding many," as it is in the end of ver. 10. By fish understand those that are wrought upon and brought in by the gospel: and they are so called,

(1.) Because as fish are generated of spawn, or seed, and water; so believers are born of water and the Spirit, John iii. 5.

(2.) Fish it is conceived were not under the curse, that fell upon the earth and things upon it, not on the waters and fish therein; so believers are not under the curse of the law. Unbelievers are under condemnation and wrath, John iii. 18, 36, but believers are free from both.

(3.) They keep fresh in salt and brackish waters; and true converts do so. When there are brackish, corrupt doctrines abroad, hot and fierce persecutions by reason of them, the sound believer is not tainted with them; Arianism, Pelagianism, familism, rantism, and quakerism do not corrupt them; and the greater troubles they meet with, the more lively they are.

(4.) Some fish swim constantly against the stream. Such are true christians, they swim against the stream, they are not led by the multitude. There are several streams, one of profaneness, another of flattery, a third of superstition, a fourth of lukewarmness and formality, a fifth of carnal policy, a sixth of self-seeking: against all these, and many others, doth the sincere christian swim and row daily.

(5.) Fish live in and by the waters, they cannot live on dry land, they presently die without water. And true christians, they live in and by the waters of the sanctuary, they live in and by the Spirit, they drink in the waters of the gospel. These spiritual fish cannot live without them; Rev. xxii. 1, there is "a pure river of water of life," wherein these live and swim.

(6.) Fish of the same kind do sort together. It is so with true converts, they leave their old company, and sort with those that are regenerate and godly. David saith, Psal. cxix. 63, "I am a companion of all them that fear thee." Christ's disciples assembled together, Acts i. 15. Peter and John "went to their own company," Acts iv. 23.

Ver. 10. "The fishers shall stand upon it from En-gedi, even unto En-eglaim." En-gedi was a town near unto the Dead sea, upon the coast of it, having strong holds, 1 Sam. xxiii. 29; called Hazazon-tamar in Jehoshaphat's days, 2 Chron. xx. 2, which A Lapide interprets *urbs palmarum*, a city of palm trees, because they flourished there: it had several vineyards belonging to it, Cant. i. 14. From this place to En-eglaim, should the fishers spread their nets.

En-eglaim was seated at the mouth of the Dead sea, where Jordan emptied itself into it, as Junius and Piscator observe; and it was in the eastern part, as En-gedi was in the western.

Before we proceed further, take some observations from ver. 7—10.

Obs. 1. The waters of the sanctuary, the doctrine of the gospel, doth powerfully and speedily beget and bring men to God. Such was the virtue of the waters Ezekiel saw, that presently they brought forth trees on each side their banks; there were trees of righteousness presently, viz. true christians. When Christ preached, and the apostles, their doctrine was received, and divers believed, John iv. 41; vii. 31; viii. 30; xii. 42; Acts xvii. 11, 12; xviii. 8. The waters of the gospel turn thorns and thistles into vine and fig trees, and make an orchard for God where none was. This was foretold by Isaiah, chap. xli. 18, 19, "I will open rivers in high places, and fountains in the midst of the valleys: I will make the wilderness a pool of water, and the dry land springs of water. I will plant in the wilderness the cedar, the shittah tree, and the myrtle, and the oil tree: I will set in the desert the fir tree, and the pine, and the box tree together." The meaning is, God would cause the gospel to be preached in dry and barren places, and there should some of all sorts come in, believe, and grow up like trees of God. Isa. xliv, 3, 4, "I will pour water upon him that is thirsty, and floods upon the dry ground: I will pour my spirit upon thy seed, and my blessing upon thine offspring: and they shall spring up as among the grass, as willows by the water courses." This water brings forth trees, and makes them good being brought forth.

Obs. 2. The waters of the gospel have, and will have their course; they issue out, who can keep them in? and being out, they go toward the east country, and go down into the desert, and so into the sea; who can stop them? When the gospel began first to be preached, it spread: Mark i. 27, 28, "What new doctrine is this? for with authority commandeth he even the unclean spirits, and they do obey him. And immediately his fame spread abroad throughout all the region round about Galilee." The gospel did run like water, from country to country, and from sea to sea, 2 Thess. iii. 1.

Obs. 3. That people without the gospel, are like unto the Dead sea, that lake of Sodom, into which, by our apostasy from God, we have cast ourselves. The Dead sea in a spiritual sense is the lake of our sins, where all things are loathsome, dead, and deadly; whence nothing but corrupt and pestilent vapours do flow. Men are children of wrath by nature, dead in sins and trespasses, Eph. ii. 1, 3, 5. All men are gone astray, and "all together become filthy," Psal. xiv. 3. "Their throat is an open sepulchre," &c. See Rom. iii. 10—18. They send forth mire and dirt as the sea doth, Isa. lvii. 20; and nothing that is good lives in them: they stifle all good motions, being dead in sin, abominable, and reprobate to every good work.

Obs. 4. The waters of the sanctuary have curing and quickening virtue in them. Where they came, the waters were healed, and every thing lived. When they flowed into the Dead sea, that was healed by them, ver. 8, and every thing lived whither the river came, ver. 9. People in Scripture are compared to waters, Rev. xvii. 1, 15; but they are unsavoury, corrupt waters, like the Dead sea, sending out noisome vapours: but when the doctrine of the gospel comes in power, with the merits of Christ, and graces of the Spirit, it purges the head from infectious errors, the conscience from dead works, the heart from vile lusts, and the life from base practices, and begets life in the dead soul. The Corinthians were a polluted people, given to uncleanness, and all manner of wickedness, 1 Cor. vi.: having reckoned up a catalogue of sinners in ver. 9, 10, he saith in ver. 11, "Such were some of you; but ye are washed, but ye are justified in the name of the Lord Jesus, and by the Spirit of our God." How came they to be so? it was by Paul's preaching the gospel, Acts xviii. 1, 7—11; he brought sanctuary waters unto them, which cured and quickened these Corinthians. In the pool of Bethesda God put forth his power, and healed by those waters all manner of bodily diseases, John v.; and in these sanctuary or gospel waters, he puts forth his power, and heals all spiritual diseases, and quickens those that are spiritually dead, ver. 25. These waters are "living waters," Zech. xiv. 8, and they beget life, and increase life, John iv. 14; x. 10.

Obs. 5. The waters of the sanctuary are fruitful waters, they breed trees on each side, and abundance of fish. The doctrine of the gospel breeds christians and believers in abundance: Acts i. 15, the number of disciples was about a hundred and twenty; chap. ii. 41, three thousand souls were added unto them; chap. iv. 4, the number of believers was about five thousand; chap. v. 14, multitudes both of men and women were added to the Lord; chap. xxi. 20, "Thou seest how many thousands of Jews there are which believe," πόσοι μυριάδες, how many ten thousands; and Rev. vii. 9, "I beheld, and, lo, a great multitude, which no man could number;" the trees and fishes multiplied so much in a little time, that they exceeded man's arithmetic.

Obs. 6. The preachers of the gospel are fishers. Ver. 10, "The fishers shall stand upon it," that is, the river and fish there. Ye know Christ chose fishermen to be his apostles, and told them, that he would make them "fishers of men," Mark i. 17. Men are the fish, and the gospel is the net; the promises are the bait, and preachers are the fishers. Peter threw the net on the right side, when he caught three thousand fishes at once, Acts ii. 41; which was prefigured in the great draught of fishes he took, Luke v. 5, 6. The preaching of the gospel is compared to a net, Matt. xiii. 47: it is good casting this net into the waters where there are store fish, and wise is that man who can catch them; Prov. xi. 30, "He that winneth souls is wise." Some fishers toil all night and catch nothing; but where there is wisdom to handle the net, and bait the hooks well, some fish will be caught.

Obs. 7. These spiritual fishers have large waters to fish in, and are to be frequent in fishing, "from En-gedi even to En-eglaim." "They shall be a place to spread forth nets" from east to west. They are to fish the whole sea; "Go, and teach all nations." The whole world is a sea of fish, and the nets must be spread, not lie still. The fishers may dry and mend their nets, but then they must throw them into the deep, and be fishing for their Lord and Master. Paul charges Timothy to preach the word, to be instant in season and out of season, to take all opportunities to catch fish with the net of the gospel, 2 Tim. iv. 2.

Obs. 8. These gospel fishers do catch some fish of all sorts, some great, some small, some old, some young. When they spread forth their nets, their fish shall be according to their kind; some of every kind shall be caught in their nets: Matt. xiii. 47, saith Christ, "The kingdom of heaven is like unto a net cast into the sea, and gathereth of every kind." The gospel preached gains upon all sorts of people; the priests, Acts vi. 7, and Sergius Paulus, Acts xiii. 12, were great fishes caught in this net; but Lydia and the damsel, Acts xvi. with Onesimus and many others, were little fishes. Nicodemus, John iii. the eunuch, Acts viii. and the elect lady, 2 John, were great fishes; and though "not many wise men after the flesh, not many mighty, not many noble are called," and caught with this net, yet some are; some Jews, some gentiles, some bond-men, &c.

Ver. 11. "But the miry places thereof, and the marishes thereof," &c. Near unto rivers and seas are miry places, and marshes, and they being at a distance from the channel wherein these waters of the sanctuary run, were not healed, made wholesome and useful for fish, but they are left to barrenness; which is the sense of these words, "They shall be given to salt;" for salt causeth barrenness, and is a sign thereof, Deut. xxix. 23; Judg. ix. 45. Psal. cvii. 34, "He turneth a fruitful land into barrenness;" the Hebrew is, saltness. Those that are slothful, impenitent, that go on in filthy practices, trust to their own righteousness, refusing and neglecting these waters, shall never be healed, but be barren, fruitless, and accursed.

Ver. 12. "Upon the bank shall grow all trees for meat." It is a known thing to historians and travellers, that on the banks of the Dead sea, or Lacus

Asphaltites, the place where Sodom and the other cities were destroyed, do grow trees which in show yield goodly fruit, yet not edible; for being touched, it proves ashes and smoke, deceiving the expectation of him that gathers the same; but these waters coming hither, beget better trees, and better fruit, even "trees for meat." Neither tree nor fruit should disappoint them, for the leaves of these trees should not fade, they should always be green and flourishing; neither should the fruit be consumed, they should always have fruit upon them: for as the sap and greenness of those trees continued, so the fruit would continue; no rottenness would cause it to fall, no winds or storms should blow it down.

"It shall bring forth new fruit according to his months." Every month should these trees bring forth new fruit. The word יְבַכֵּר is rendered by some, they shall yield their first-begotten; not only shall they yield fruit monthly, but excellent and choice fruit, ripe fruit, fit for meat. And because this seems strange and impossible, that trees every month should have ripe fruit, he shows in the next words whence it is.

"Because their waters they issued out of the sanctuary." These waters were no ordinary waters, but such as had a fructifying virtue in them, beyond all other waters, and made the trees about it to bear twelve times a year; representing that crystal river that proceeded out of the throne of God and of the Lamb, on either side of which grew "the tree of life, which bare twelve manner of fruits, and yielded fruit every month," Rev. xxii. 2.

"And the fruit thereof shall be for meat, and the leaf thereof for medicine." He shows the excellency of these trees; they shall have nothing useless, their fruit is for meat, and their leaves for medicine. The good works and holy lives of believers are for meat and medicine unto others.

Obs. 1. Wicked men are miry and muddy creatures. Those that are ungodly, are no better than miry places and marshes, which are unsavoury, loathsome, and dangerous, breeding frogs, toads, and other vermin. Such are all wicked men; "their throat is an open sepulchre," Rom. iii. 13, their words are corrupt, deceitful, and poisonous; themselves are loathsome, Prov. xiii. 5; they trust in their own righteousness, which is as filthy rags, Isa. lxiv. 6; they have corrupt minds, as Jannes and Jambres had, 2 Tim. iii. 8; they are full of noisome lusts, subtilty, and all malice, as Elymas was, Acts xiii. 10; they have eyes full of adultery, 2 Pet. ii. 14; they are swine, and love to wallow in the mire, ver. 22; they breed nothing but vermin, base thoughts, vile affections, and produce only what is evil. Paul describes them fully unto us, Rom. i. 29—31, and in 2 Tim. iii. 2—5.

Obs. 2. Those places and persons to which the waters of the sanctuary do not come, or coming do not heal, are designed to barrenness, and so to destruction. Ver. 11, "But the miry places thereof and the marishes thereof shall not be healed." Either the waters came not to them; or if they did, they refused, they neglected them, and so were given to salt, made like Sodom, barren and accursed. Some places have not the waters of the sanctuary, the doctrine of the gospel, and they are barren, and perish for want of the same, as Tyre and Zidon. Some places have them, and because they are impenitent, unbelieving, and will not receive the truth with the love of it, because they will not drink these waters, therefore they are given to salt, they are barren, and must perish. So it was with Capernaum and Jerusalem, Matt. xi. 23, and xxiii. 37, 38; and so is it with many places in this nation, I fear. John iii. 19, "This is the condemnation, that light is come into the world, and men love darkness rather than light, because their deeds are evil." They stick in the mud and filth of their own sins, and will not receive the soul saving truths of the gospel.

Obs. 3. That the saints, true christian believers, are not barren but fruitful trees. Every one of them is a fruitful tree, and yields good fruit. All the trees are for meat, their fruit is for meat. For whom? For Christ; Cant. iv. 16, "Let my beloved come into his garden, and eat his pleasant fruits:" chap. vi. 2, "He is gone to feed in the gardens;" that is, to feed upon the fruit of his churches. And for others, even all men, Gal. vi. 10: their fruit is good, Matt. v. 16, and vii. 17; they are acceptable to God and man, through their fruitfulness, Phil. iv. 18, and an honour to the place where they grow.

Obs. 4. True christians are always fruitful, and nothing can hinder their fruitfulness. They are trees that bring forth fruit according to their months and seasons; neither heat nor cold doth blast their leaves; no wind or weather doth consume their fruit; but they go on, and are fat and flourishing, and still bring forth fruit in old age, Psal. xcii. 14. They are daily adding to their faith virtue; to their virtue knowledge; to their knowledge temperance; to their temperance patience; to their patience godliness; to their godliness brotherly kindness, and to that charity: these things are in true saints, and abound in them, 2 Pet. i. 5—8. The Corinthians abounded in the work of the Lord, 1 Cor. xv. 58. Christians must always profess godliness, and always practise it; their leaf must always be green, and their fruit always ripe; there should not be a day, or an hour, wherein they should not be doing good, or ready to do good, and bear new fruit, Jer. xvii. 8.

Obs. 5. The true cause of fruitfulness, and such fruitfulness in christians, is the doctrine and grace of the gospel. Every tree brought forth fruit according to his month, because the waters issued out of the sanctuary: other waters had not such virtue, such efficacy in them. Those who sit under the heavenly dews and droppings of the gospel, they feel the influences of the Spirit, they are most fruitful.

Obs. 6. The holy profession and gracious language of true saints are medicinable, they heal the sores and bruises of sinners. Their examples, their savoury speeches, do good like a medicine: Prov. xii. 18, "The tongue of the wise is health;" and Prov. xv. 4, "A wholesome tongue is a tree of life," it yields good fruit. And women who are gracious, win their husbands to the faith, 1 Pet. iii. 1, 2, by their examples and good conversations, and so they are healed, and brought to Christ; their leaves are for medicine.

Ver. 13—23. *Thus saith the Lord God; This shall be the border, whereby ye shall inherit the land according to the twelve tribes of Israel: Joseph shall have two portions. And ye shall inherit it, one as well as another: concerning the which I lifted up mine hand to give it unto your fathers: and this land shall fall unto you for inheritance. And this shall be the border of the land toward the north side, from the great sea, the way of Hethlon, as men go to Zedad; Hamath, Berothah, Sibraim, which is between the border of Damascus and the border of Hamath; Hazar-hatticon, which is by the coast of Hauran. And the border from the sea shall be Hazar-enan, the border of Damascus, and the north northward, and the border of Hamath. And this is the north side. And the east side ye shall measure from Hauran, and from Damascus, and from Gilead, and from the land of Israel by Jordan, from the border unto the east sea. And this is the east side. And the south side southward from Tamar even to the waters of strife in Kadesh, the river to the great sea. And this is the south side southward. The west side also shall be the great sea from the border, till a man come over against Hamath. This is the west side. So shall ye divide this land unto you according to the tribes of Israel. And it shall come to pass, that ye shall divide it by lot for an inheritance unto you, and to the strangers that sojourn among you, which shall beget children among you: and they shall be unto you as born in the country among the children of Israel; they shall have inheritance with you among the tribes of Israel. And it shall come to pass, that in what tribe the stranger sojourneth, there shall ye give him his inheritance, saith the Lord God.*

These verses are the second part of the chapter, and contain,

I. The bordering of the land, ver. 13—20.

II. The dividing of it, ver. 21, to the end.

Something was said of the land, chap. xlv. and here that subject is proceeded in. Ver. 13 speaks in the general, and saith, the order whereby they were to inherit the land, must be " according to the twelve tribes of Israel," east, west, north, and south. It is true, that Levi had no border, no possession, Ezek. xliv. 28; yet twelve lots are spoken of, because the sons of Joseph, Ephraim and Manasseh, come in for portions. Josh. xiv. 4, " The children of Joseph were two tribes, Manasseh and Ephraim; therefore they gave no part unto the Levites in the land." See Josh. xvii. 17, 18; 1 Chron. v. 12. They had " two portions," the Hebrew is, lines, because the portions were measured out by lines.

Ver. 14. " And ye shall inherit it, one as well as another." The Hebrew for " one as well as another," is, a man as his brother, which is usual among the Hebrews; for when they speak of two or more in the masculine gender, they say, a man and his brother; and when they speak of two or more in the feminine gender, they say, a woman and her sister. The sense here is, that they should all with equal right possess the land, and each tribe have an equal portion, which differs much from the division made of old; for, Numb. xxxiii. 54, " Ye shall divide the land by lot for an inheritance among your families: and to the more ye shall give the more inheritance, and to the fewer ye shall give the less inheritance:" and if we grant with some, that it was so here, that a greater portion of land was given to the greater tribe, yet it is conceived from these words of Ezekiel, that every one in each tribe had an equal portion, which was not so of old.

" Concerning the which I lifted up mine hand to give it," &c. Of the Lord's lifting up his hand, mention was made, Ezek. xx. 56; xv. 28, 42; xxxvi. 7; and xliv. 12; and it notes God's swearing, that he would give the land of Canaan unto their fathers: as Exod. vi. 6, " I will bring you in unto the land, concerning which I did swear to give it to Abraham, to Isaac, and Jacob;" the Hebrew is, I did lift up my hand.

Ver. 15. " This shall be the border of the land toward the north side, from," &c. He describes first the borders of the whole land, and so makes way to the division of it more particularly. He begins with the north border, which was from that part of the great sea, viz. the Mediterranean sea, which lay northward, and so proceeded to mount Hor, and from thence to Hamath, and so to Zedad, Ziphron, and terminated in Hazar-enan, Numb. xxxiv. 7—9, which was in the north-east. In this description of the northern border, more towns are mentioned than in Numbers, as Hethlon, Berothah, Sibraim, Hazar-hatticon, Hauran, and Damascus, but the extension is the same, from the great sea to Hazar-enan, ver. 15—17.

The east border is laid down ver. 18, and that is, that space which lies between Hauran, Damascus, Gilead, and the land of Israel by Jordan, from the border to the east sea, that is, the lake of Sodom, or Dead sea, as some interpret it. But, Numb. xxxiv. 11, it is extended to " the sea of Chinnereth eastward," which is the sea of Tiberias, or lake of Gennesaret, John vi. 1; Luke v. 1.

The south border is set forth unto us in ver. 19; and it is from Tamar, which Maldonate makes Jericho, others a town near the Dead sea; and from hence to Meribah, or the waters of strife in Kadesh, in the wilderness of Zin, Numb. xx. 13, and xxvii. 14, and so to the river which led to the great sea. That river is called Sihor, Josh. xiii. 3; Jer. ii. 18; and the river of Egypt, Numb. xxxiv. 5; and distinguished the tribes of Simeon and Judah from Egypt, as Sinetius saith, and ran into the Mediterranean sea, which is the great sea; so called, in respect of the sea of Galilee, or Tiberias, and of the Dead sea, which were little ones to that. To this great sea came the south border.

The west border is in ver. 20, from the border of the great sea, that is, from the place where the river of Egypt exonerates itself into the Mediterranean sea, which by geographers is called Rhinocura, and so to Hamath in the north-west towards mount Hor. This tract by the sea was the west border, Numb. xxxiv. 6.

The prophet being shown the borders of the land in the foregoing verses, is brought here to see the division of it in the three last verses. And the division was to be according to the tribes, ver. 21; and this division was to be by lot, the lot was to fall upon it; ver. 22, "Ye shall divide it by lot;" the Hebrew is, ye shall make it fall, that is, under lot. They might not pick and choose what part of the land they had a mind unto, but take their portion where the lot fell; and here it is ordered, that strangers and their children shall not be excluded from inheriting. Not all strangers were to have this privilege, but those that should come and dwell amongst them, and beget children. It was not so in the division of the land by Moses and Joshua, strangers might not inherit amongst them; which clearly intimates there was to be a change of the Mosaical state.

Strangers might come into any of the tribes, which Sanctius understands of proselytes, whose number was great, as he saith; and into what tribe soever they came, there they were to have inheritance; so that now the difference between strangers and natives, Jews and gentiles, was to cease, and they both had the same privilege.

Having given you the literal sense of the words, now let us see what may be the spiritual sense of them; for in the letter they were not fulfilled after the return from Babylon, but mystically under the gospel they were.

1. Then here is held out unto us, the great extent and largeness of the church under Christ and the gospel. The land mentioned, signifies the church's

state; and the bordering of it out, north, east, south, west, the extent of it into all parts. The christian church is larger than the Jewish; that was shut up in one nation, now it reaches to all nations, Matt. xxviii. 19, neither Asia, Africa, Europe, nor America are excluded: see Matt. xxiv. 14; Luke xxiv. 47; Rev. xv. 4. The church under the gospel is universal and invisible.

2. Those that are subjects or members of this church, are not hypocrites, but Israelites. Those that were not Israelites, and true Israelites, were not to be in this church. Hypocrites, scandalous, ignorant, and unregenerate persons, are often in, if not the major part of particular visible churches; but of the universal church of Christ they are not; that consists of true Israelites, such as Nathanael was, John i. 47; of Jews inwardly, such as are circumcised in heart and spirit, Rom. ii. 29; of such as are enrolled in heaven, Heb. xii. 23; of sealed ones, Rev. vii.; and these stood with the Lamb on mount Zion, Rev. xiv. i. These made up the church and body of Christ.

3. The privileges of this church do equally belong to all the members of it; ver. 14, "Ye shall inherit it, one as well as another." None hath pre-eminence above others in the things of Christ and God. As the Jews could not say, This land is more mine than yours, I have the privileges, you have not; so a saint, a christian, a true member of the universal church, cannot say, The church, or privileges of it, are more mine than others who are in the same; "for all are one in Christ Jesus," Gal. iii. 28; and there is but "one body, one Spirit, one hope, one Lord, one faith, one baptism, one God and Father of all," Eph. iv. 4—6: it is one and the same grace of God, one and the same righteousness of Christ, one and the same eternal life, which they are interested in.

4. The state of christians in the church, and all the spiritual blessings they have therein, are of free grace, and mere mercy. "This land shall fall to you for inheritance," ver. 14; and, "ye shall divide it by lot for an inheritance," ver. 22. It was freely given them, and what good soever was there, in all the milk and honey thereof. In like manner, the bringing of men into Zion, to be members of Christ's body, and all the spiritual milk and honey they enjoy in that state, is of mere grace and good pleasure. Saith Christ himself, No man cometh unto me, except the Father draw him, John vi. 44. God hath given unto Christ some men, John xvii. 2; and those God hath given to Christ, he brings them to Christ, from whom they have milk, wine, and honey.

5. The church of God under the gospel, consisted of gentiles as well as of Jews. This appears from this, that strangers might sojourn amongst them. The gentiles were strangers, being neither of the seed of Abraham, nor of the commonwealth of Israel, Eph. ii. 12; but they were under Christ to be in Canaan, that is, in the church. John x. 16, of these Christ spake when he said, "Other sheep I have, which are not of this fold; them also I must bring," that is, into the fold. It was prophesied in Isa. xlix. 22, that the gentiles should come in; "Thus saith the Lord God, Behold, I will lift up mine hand to the gentiles, and set up my standard to the people; and they shall bring thy sons in their arms, and thy daughters shall be carried upon their shoulders," &c.: the gentiles and their children should believe, and come into the church of Christ. And Isa. lvi. 6, 7, "Also the sons of the stranger, that join themselves to the Lord, to serve him, and to love the name of the Lord, to be his servants," &c. "even them will I bring to my holy mountain, and make them joyful in my house of prayer:" see Isa. lxv. 1. Zech. ii. 11, "Many nations shall be joined to the Lord in that day, and shall be my people." These prophecies, and many other to the same purpose, are made good, and the gentiles are in and of the church of God. The gentiles had repentance granted to them unto life, Acts xi. 18.

6. The tenders of mercy, and invitations to Zion, were first to the Jews, and after to the gentiles. The land of Canaan was first for Israelites, and then for sojourners. Christ first tendered himself, and all gospel means, unto the Jews, John i. 11; Matt. xxiii. 37; he sent his disciples first to them, Matt. x. 5—7, afterwards to the gentiles, Matt. xxviii. 19. Hence said Paul and Barnabas, Acts xiii. 46, "It was necessary that the word of God should first be spoken unto you; but seeing ye put it from you, lo, we turn to the gentiles." The Jews were the seed of Abraham, the friend of God, Isa. xli. 8; they were his firstborn, Exod. iv. 22; they were the children of the prophets and of the covenant, and to them God first sent his Son to bless them, Acts iii. 25, 26.

7. That one and the same inheritance belongs to the believing Jew and gentile; the same land was both the Jews' and the strangers' to inherit, which prefigured their being in one and the same church, their having the same privileges, the same interest in Christ; there is one and the same inheritance to both. Col. i. 12, "Giving thanks unto the Father, who hath made us meet to be partakers of the inheritance of the saints in light." All the saints have but one inheritance, and that is reserved in heaven, 1 Pet. i. 4. This inheritance was typified by the land of Canaan. So then the partition-wall is broken down between Jews and gentiles, all former differences are taken away, and they are no more two but one; they are both one, one new man, one body, Eph. ii. 14—16; Jew and gentile are so united as if there had been no distinction between them; Col. iii. 11, "There is neither Greek nor Jew, circumcision nor uncircumcision, barbarian, Scythian, bond nor free; but Christ is all, and in all." The Lord Christ by his death and sufferings hath reconciled those who were at the greatest enmity.

CHAPTER XLVIII.

Ver. 1—7. *Now these are the names of the tribes. From the north end to the coast of the way of Hethlon, as one goeth to Hamath, Hazar-enan, the border of Damascus northward, to the coast of Hamath; for these are his sides east and west; a portion for Dan. And by the border of Dan, from the east side unto the west side, a portion for Asher. And by the border of Asher, from the east side even unto the west side, a portion for Naphtali. And by the border of Naphtali, from the east side unto the west side, a portion for Manasseh. And by the border of Manasseh, from the east side unto the west side, a portion for Ephraim. And by the border of Ephraim, from the east side even unto the west side, a portion for Reuben. And by the border of Reuben, from the east side even unto the west side, a portion for Judah.*

BEING come, through the assistance of God, to open the last chapter of Ezekiel's prophecy, we have in it three parts:

I. An assignation or distribution of particular portions to each tribe, ver. 1—7, 23—29.

II. A description of the offering or holy portion of land, (as it is called, chap. xlv. 1,) with the bounds and parts allotted,

1. To the sanctuary, ver. 8, 9.
2. To the priests, ver. 10—12.
3. To the Levites, ver. 13, 14.
4. To the city and suburbs, ver. 15—19.
5. To the prince, ver. 21, 22.

III. A description of the city.

1. From the dimension of it on each side, ver. 30.
2. From the gates of it, ver. 31—34.
3. From the compass of it, ver. 35.
4. From the name of it, *ibid.*

Concerning the distributions of the land to particular tribes, they differ much from those which were made in Joshua's days. Then the tribe of Benjamin's lot was between Judah and Joseph, as it is Josh. xviii. 11; but in this chapter Benjamin's lot is between Judah and Simeon, ver. 22—24. Then the tribe of Simeon had its lot within Judah, Josh. xix. 19; here, it is out of Judah and next to Benjamin, ver. 24. And so of other tribes; their lot is otherwise in this visional distribution of Ezekiel than it was formerly, and many things he had concerning the temple, sacrifices, the lot of the prince, priests, and Levites, which Solomon never had, and never were had under the second temple, and therefore pointed out the change of Mosaical and Levitical ways, and led to a new state of the church.

Ver. 1. "These are the names of the tribes. From the north end," &c. Of the twelve tribes, seven were in the north and five in the south, as they are set down in this chapter; and the portion of the sanctuary, priests, Levites, cities, and prince, lay between the tribes thus divided.

Dan is the first tribe mentioned in Ezekiel's division. It was not so in Joshua's; then, Dan was the last tribe which had his portion, as is evident, Josh. xix. 40, 49; and because it was too little for them, the men of Dan took Leshem, or Laish, named it Dan, and so enlarged their borders. This tribe first fell from God and embraced idols; for after they had gotten Laish, they set up a graven image, Judg. xviii. 29—31; and therefore this tribe is left out of the catalogue when the other tribes are mentioned, 1 Chron. vii. and Rev. vii. In the prophetical blessings of Jacob, Dan and Issachar were in the midst, Gen. xlix. 14, 16. Here Dan is in the front; which gives us to consider,

1. The truth of what our Lord Christ hath given out, Matt. xix. 30, "The last shall be first:" Dan was the last, and here he is the first; he hath the honour and pre-eminence above the rest. David was the youngest and last of Jesse's sons, and he was made the first, being anointed to be king by Samuel, 1 Sam. xvi. 11—14. Those workers in the vineyard, the Lord ordered that his steward should pay the last first, and the first last, Matt. xx. 8, 16; Mark x. 31. Luke xiii. 30, "There are last which shall be first;" the gentiles were last in the Jews' account, but God made them first: "and there are first which shall be last;" the Jews were first in their own eyes, but they were made last, and of no esteem, in the eyes of God. Luke xviii. 14, the publican, who was last in the account of the Pharisee, was first in the account of God.

2. Those that have deserted God and his ways, gone far and long from him, may find mercy, repent, and be received to favour. These Danites met with mercy from God, repented them of their idolatry, and returned to him again, else they had never been honoured so far as to be set in the first place. When great sinners come unto God, who were looked upon as the last and worst of men, God doth not only pardon them, but ofttimes honours them and makes them the first; as Paul, Acts ix. 15, "He is a chosen vessel unto me, to bear my name before the gentiles, and kings, and the children of Israel." He had been a great persecutor, blasphemous, injurious, but when he embraced the faith of Christ, he was made the chief of the apostles.

3. God, of his good pleasure and free grace, calls and recalls whom he will. These Danites had nothing in them to move God to own them for his people at first, nothing to move him to recall them, being degenerate and fallen into idolatrous passages, unless we make wickedness an argument thereunto; and if so, there is sufficient of that in the devils to move the Lord to show mercy; but wickedness provokes to destroy, not to show mercy. The best thing in man induceth not God to show mercy; that is from his will, Rom. ix. 15. It was God's free grace which took Abraham at first out of an idolatrous country and family, Josh. xxiv. 23: it was free grace that he took Isaac, not Ishmael; Jacob, not Esau: and so that he took Dan at first, and recalled him at last: and so the prodigal.

Dan and the rest of the tribes had their several portions (being all in captivity, both Judah and Benjamin at this time) allotted unto them, which may represent unto us what the condition of the Jews shall be under Christ; however now they be scattered, yet doubtless there is a time when they shall come to Zion, and have their several portions in the church of Christ. John's vision, Rev. vii. adds great weight to this tenet, he "saw twelve thousand sealed out of every tribe," which he distinguishes from those of other nations who are not said to be sealed, hereby strongly intimating they were Jews, whose conversion Paul had spoken of, Rom. xi. 26, "So all Israel shall be saved;" that is, all the twelve tribes shall come in and stand with the Lamb on mount Zion, Rev. xiv. 1.

These tribes had their portions from east to west, all of them, which was the length of this land of Canaan, and their breadth from north to south; which informs us of the large extent of the church of Christ: it reaches to the ends of the earth; for the Father gave him "the heathen for his inheritance, and the uttermost parts of the earth for his possession," Psal. ii. 8; his "dominion was to be from sea to sea, and from the river to the ends of the earth," Psal. lxxii. 8. He was to be "governor among the nations," Psal. xxii. 28; and not only of some few or many of them, but of all them that shall "inherit all nations," Psal. lxxxii. 8; and "be king over all the earth," Zech. xiv. 9. He was from eternity "appointed heir of all things," Heb. i. 2; and he must have possession of all, which John in his vision saw accomplished; Rev. xi. 15, "The kingdoms of this world are become the kingdoms of our Lord, and of his Christ;" so that Christ's church and kingdom is large, and extends to all quarters.

The portion here given to the seven tribes, Dan, Asher, Naphtali, Manasseh, Ephraim, Reuben, Judah, and to the other five tribes, Benjamin, Simeon, Issachar, Zebulun, Gad, in the 23d, 24th, 25th, 26th, 27th, 28th, and 29th verses of this chapter, besides the largeness and unlimitedness of the church, do here inform us,

1. That there is sufficiency of means and mercies for all that have part in the church and kingdom of Christ, Rev. vii. 15—17.

2. That what portion soever any one hath, is by divine appointment. The Lord allots every one his portion, of what kind soever, Rom. xii. 3; Luke xix. 19; xxii. 29.

3. That there ought to be communion between

those who are of Christ's kingdom. The tribes lay near together, and their portions, and were to have communion one with another, Eph. ii. 19.

4. That as there are several portions here for the tribes, so there are several mansions for them in the heavens, John xiv. 2; and not only for believing Jews, but gentiles also, Rev. vii. 9.

Ver. 8—14. *And by the border of Judah, from the east side unto the west side, shall be the offering which ye shall offer of five and twenty thousand reeds in breadth, and in length as one of the other parts, from the east side unto the west side: and the sanctuary shall be in the midst of it. The oblation that ye shall offer unto the Lord shall be of five and twenty thousand in length, and of ten thousand in breadth. And for them, even for the priests, shall be this holy oblation; toward the north five and twenty thousand in length, and toward the west ten thousand in breadth, and toward the east ten thousand in breadth, and toward the south five and twenty thousand in length: and the sanctuary of the Lord shall be in the midst thereof. It shall be for the priests that are sanctified of the sons of Zadok; which have kept my charge, which went not astray when the children of Israel went astray, as the Levites went astray. And this oblation of the land that is offered shall be unto them a thing most holy by the border of the Levites. And over against the border of the priests the Levites shall have five and twenty thousand in length, and ten thousand in breadth: all the length shall be five and twenty thousand, and the breadth ten thousand. And they shall not sell of it, neither exchange, nor alienate the firstfruits of the land: for it is holy unto the Lord.*

The offering of five and twenty thousand reeds of land in length and breadth for the sanctuary, the priests, the Levites, the city, and the prince, we had in the 45th chapter, and therefore shall say little unto these things.

Ver. 8. "The sanctuary shall be in the midst of it." The sanctuary is the habitation of God, and it is in the midst, that all may equally have access unto it.

Ver. 9. The oblation to the Lord was five and twenty thousand reeds in length, and ten thousand in breadth, which was a great compass, and sets out the largeness of the church in the times of the gospel.

The priests had a large portion; ver. 10, five and twenty thousand reeds of land in length, both northward and southward, and ten thousand in breadth, both eastward and westward. This large provision was made for the priests who were holy, from Zadok, which had kept God's charge, and been faithful and constant in apostatizing times. Ver. 11, the Levites also had the same length and breadth of land assigned them, ver. 13. Now neither priests nor Levites might sell, exchange, or alienate the firstfruits of the land, because it was holy, ver. 12, 14; so that holy things, which are the Lord's, and not men's, are not to be bought and sold, and diverted to other uses. Those who sell holy things, sell what is the Lord's, not their own, and there is no justice in that.

By these portions of the priests and Levites, is prefigured the increase and maintenance of the preachers of the gospel; for as maintenance was due to the priests by the Levitical law, so now it is due by the light of nature; 1 Cor. ix. 9, "The mouth of the ox that treadeth out the corn" must not be muzzled; and by the light of the gospel, ver. 14, "the Lord hath ordained that they who preach the gospel should live of the gospel."

Ver. 11. "The priests that are sanctified." The priests were first to be separated, Numb. viii. 14; Deut. x. 8; Heb. v. 1; and their separation was from common persons, things, and ends. They were to be for a holy God, holy services, and for holy ends.

2. They were to be sanctified and consecrated unto God, Exod. xxx. 30; Lev. xxi. 10.

3. They were to approach and come near unto God, Lev. xxi. 17; Numb. iv. 19; Ezek. xliii. 19.

4. They were to offer the sacrifice which the people were to bring unto them, otherwise they were not accepted, Lev. v. 8, 10.

Ver. 15—20. *And the five thousand, that are left in the breadth over against the five and twenty thousand, shall be a profane place for the city, for dwelling, and for suburbs: and the city shall be in the midst thereof. And these shall be the measures thereof; the north side four thousand and five hundred, and the south side four thousand and five hundred, and on the east side four thousand and five hundred, and the west side four thousand and five hundred. And the suburbs of the city shall be toward the north two hundred and fifty, and toward the south two hundred and fifty, and toward the east two hundred and fifty, and toward the west two hundred and fifty. And the residue in length over against the oblation of the holy portion shall be ten thousand eastward, and ten thousand westward: and it shall be over against the oblation of the holy portion; and the increase thereof shall be for food unto them that serve the city. And they that serve the city shall serve it out of all the tribes of Israel. All the oblation shall be five and twenty thousand by five and twenty thousand: ye shall offer the holy oblation foursquare, with the possession of the city.*

The place where the city was to be is called a profane place; not simply and absolutely so, but respectively, as compared with the possessions of the priests and Levites; for in Scripture sense that is counted common, uncircumcised, or profane, which is compared with that which is more holy: see Lev. xix. 23. This place, then, though it were profane in respect of the portion of the priests and Levites, yet was it holy in part, for it was part of the holy portion, chap. xlv. 1; and a type of the heavenly Jerusalem. The city was to be in the midst of it, and was foursquare, having four thousand and five hundred cubits, say some, reeds, say others, and so was of vast extent. The suburbs also on each part of it were alike, of two hundred and fifty measures apiece.

It is said, ver. 18, that the increase of the ten thousand measures eastward and westward shall be for food to them that serve the city. God is careful of, and bountiful to, those who shall serve him; if any shall come to this city, the church of God, and serve him and his people, there they are provided for beforehand; God hath allotted out ten thousand reeds of land, east and west, which he will bless so as it shall increase, and that increase shall be for them. In the apostles' times, when the church was grown numerous, there was not any among them which lacked: God provided for them by stirring up the hearts of owners to sell lands and houses, Acts iv. 34, 35. And not only here are we to look at the temporary provision God makes for the faithful, but that eternal reward also which they shall have in heaven, the city which hath foundations, Heb. xi. 10; where they shall have an "exceeding and eternal weight of glory," 2 Cor. iv. 17.

The 19th verse dictates three things unto us:

1. That the citizens of this city are holy men, not common, profane men; they are Israelites, not Gibeonites; common men do not inhabit the holy city. Rev. xxi. 27, "There shall in no wise enter into it any thing that shall defile;" those that keep the commands of God shall enter into this city. Rev. xxii. 14, 15, dogs, sorcerers, whoremongers, murderers, idolaters, liars, shall be shut out.

2. That they are men chosen, not out of one or two tribes, but out of every tribe; they that serve this city must be out of all the tribes. God did not take some only out of Judah and Ephraim, the great and more honourable tribes, but some out of the other and lesser tribes. God is a free agent, and may take where, when, and whom he pleases; Rev. vii., "some were sealed out of every tribe."

3. Those that are of this city are to be serviceable; they are to improve their talents, whatever they be, for the good of the city: "they that serve the city shall serve it out of all the tribes of Israel." The apostles were servants to this city, and they went up and down into all the tribes of Israel to serve this city. Ministers and christians should now expend themselves for the church of God, and labour to bring some into it out of all parts. God gives gifts and graces to ministers and others for this end, that they should be serviceable to the city of God: 1 Pet. iv. 10, "As every one hath received the gift of God, even so minister the same one to another, as good stewards of the manifold grace of God."

Ver. 20. The whole of the holy oblation made a foursquare, every square being five and twenty thousand reeds. The city which John saw lay foursquare, Rev. xxi. 16; such a figure hath beauty and stability in it, and represented the beautifulness and stableness of the church, Cant. vi. 16; Matt. xvi. 18.

Ver. 21, 22. *And the residue shall be for the prince, on the one side and on the other of the holy oblation, and of the possession of the city, over against the five and twenty thousand of the oblation toward the east border, and westward over against the five and twenty thousand toward the west border, over against the portions for the prince: and it shall be the holy oblation; and the sanctuary of the house shall be in the midst thereof. Moreover from the possession of the Levites, and from the possession of the city, being in the midst of that which is the prince's, between the border of Judah and the border of Benjamin, shall be for the prince.*

The prince here spoken of is the same with him, chap. xlv. 7, 8; interpreted to be neither any civil prince, nor the high priest, but the Lord Christ, who is King of Zion. Whatever of the holy oblation was not for the sanctuary, priests, Levites, and the city, was the prince's; and what was beyond the holy oblation was his. His territories extend far; and such is the dignity of his person, as that the Father hath given him the ends of the earth to possess, Psal. ii. 8. Not only Canaan, which typed out the church, was his dominion, but even the nations and whole earth, Psal. lxxxii. 8: Zech. xiv. 9.

The sanctuary, the city, the priests, and the Levites, were in the midst. The prince's portion was on both sides of them; he was their security and defence. Christ is the defence of his church and people; he is on both sides of them, round about them. He is a wall of fire round about Jerusalem, Zech. ii. 5: he is the watchman thereof, and keeps it night and day, Isa. xxvii. 3: that is his glory, and himself is the defence of his glory, Isa. iv. 5.

Ver. 28. *By the border of Gad, at the south side southward, the border shall be, &c.*

When Jacob did prophetically bless the tribes, Dan and Gad went together, Gen. xlix. 17, 19; but here they are placed opposite; Dan in the utmost part of the north, ver. 1; Gad in the utmost part of the south: for Tamar (which signifies, a palm tree, and after was called Palmyra) was the furthest town southward in Judea, near the lake Asphaltites, or the Dead sea. This portion of Gad reacheth unto Meribah-Kadesh, which was in the wilderness of Zin, Deut. xxxii. 51. There was another Meribah in Rephidim, Exod. xvii. 7, where the Israelites did chide with Moses for want of water, after they came out of the wilderness of Zin, ver. 1, 2. The Lord may dispose of tribes and families, and seat them in north, or south, or wherever he please, in hot or cold countries, in fruitful or barren lands.

Ver. 29. *This is the land which ye shall divide by lot unto the tribes of Israel for inheritance.*

The Hebrew is thus, This is the land which ye shall make or cause to fall from, or for, the inheritance to the tribes of Israel. That is, by lot you shall make the inheritance fall unto every tribe; none were to choose what inheritance they would have, but to take that where the lot fell. This, as Œcolampadius saith, is the conclusion of the whole chapter; and that which follows is the situation and measures, the gates and ministers, of the city, their maintenance and use.

"These are their portions, saith the Lord God." The Hebrew, is, Adonai Jehovah, the Lord Lord, the Lord who is Sovereign of all, the Lord who gives being to all things, and to his word.

Ver. 30—35. *And these are the goings out of the city on the north side, four thousand and five hundred measures. And the gates of the city shall be after the names of the tribes of Israel: three gates northward; one gate of Reuben, one gate of Judah, one gate of Levi. And at the east side four thousand and five hundred: and three gates; and one gate of Joseph, one gate of Benjamin, one gate of Dan. And at the south side four thousand and five hundred measures: and three gates; one gate of Simeon, one gate of Issachar, one gate of Zebulun. At the west side four thousand and five hundred, with their three gates; one gate of Gad, one gate of Asher, one gate of Naphtali. It was round about eighteen thousand measures: and the name of the city from that day shall be, The Lord is there.*

Ver. 30. "These are the goings out of the city." Some understand by the goings out the gates; but Jerom makes them to be the compass of the city, from its four sides; for not the gates, but the sides, had four thousand and five hundred measures; at these goings out was the utmost term and extent of the city.

Ver. 31. "The gates of the city shall be after the names of the tribes of Israel," &c. In the distribution of the portions of land Levi was left out, (he must not be troubled with the things of this world,) but in the assignment of the gates, there is one of Levi, or for Levi; he had right to the city, and all the privileges of it, as much as the other tribes.

In the 45th chapter, and several verses of this 48th, mention is made of the city; but in the sixteenth verse, and these last six verses, is the fullest description of the city: and it is described,

1. From the measures which were on each side; for as the goings out of the city northward were four thousand and five hundred measures, so were the goings out of the south, east, and west: and that we may not question it, the 16th verse asserts it; "These shall be the measures thereof; the north side four thousand and five hundred, and the south side four thousand and five hundred, and on the east side four thousand and five hundred, and the west side four thousand and five hundred;" they were all alike in their measures. What these measures were, is of moment to inquire. We have only two mentioned in this vision, reeds and cubits; by these, the temple, city, and things pertaining unto them, were measured. Chap. xl. 5, the measuring reed in the man's hand was six cubits long, and a hand breadth; and if we take measures here for reeds, viz. four thousand and five hundred reeds, in all they come to eighteen thousand reeds, which make one hundred and eight thousand cubits, and eighteen thousand hands' breadth: and after this account every side of the city is eight miles and one hundred paces; for eighteen thousand reeds make thirty two miles and four hundred paces, as A Lapide observes: so that this city was very large. Others lessen the city greatly, and make the measures to be only cubits, and so each side of the city comes to be a mile and almost a half long, which was no great length nor breadth, being both equal. Haffenrefferus makes the measures to be cubits, and insists upon it much; but others are of a different judgment from him. And seeing the city in the Revelation was measured by the reed, it seems also more than probable that this also was measured by the same measure: Rev. xxi. 15, 16, "He measured the city with a reed, twelve thousand furlongs." As Ezekiel's city exceeded the former city much, so John's city exceeded Ezekiel's far more; for, being square as the other was, it had three thousand furlongs on each side, which make three hundred seventy and five miles, reckoning eight furlongs to a mile. So that this city, being three hundred seventy and five miles in length, and as many in breadth, was the best city that ever was.

2. It is described from the gates of it. This city had twelve gates, three on every side; and these gates were according to the names of the tribes of Israel: Reuben, Judah, Levi, had the north gates; Joseph, Benjamin, Dan, had the east gates; Simeon, Issachar, Zebulun, had the south gates; Gad, Asher, Naphtali, had the west gates: the several names of the tribes were written upon the gates. Herein Ezekiel's and John's city, the new Jerusalem, do fully agree; for John's had twelve gates, three on each quarter, and the names of the twelve tribes written upon them, Rev. xxi. 12.

3. It is described from the compass of it: ver. 35, "It was round about eighteen thousand measures." Take measures for cubits, and then it was not above six miles in compass, but if we take them for reeds, as divers do, then the compass of this city is thirty-two miles and almost a half; but far short of the compass of the new Jerusalem, that great city, which was fifteen hundred miles about, for so many miles do twelve thousand furlongs amount unto. Both the city which John saw measured, and that Ezekiel saw measured, were foursquare, comely, firm, and durable; the court was foursquare, Ezek. xl. 47; the holy oblation was so, chap. xlviii. 20; and so was the city.

4. It is described from the name: ver. 35, "The name of the city from that day shall be Jehovah-shammah, The Lord is there." From the day of its building and inhabitation it shall be called so. Many cities have had glorious and significant names; as Nicopolis, Tit. iii. 12, which signifies, The victorious city: Nazareth, Luke iv. 16, notes, sanctified or separated: Bethsaida, Matt. xi. 21, the house of fruits or meats: Bethlehem, Luke ii. 4, the house of bread: Jerusalem, the vision of peace: but they fall short of this name, "Jehovah-shammah."

Some make the meaning of these words, "the name of the city shall be, The Lord is there," to be this, that God would be in the city; not that the city was, or shall be ever, called so: as it is said of Christ, his name shall be called, "Wonderful, Counsellor, the mighty God, the everlasting Father, the Prince of Peace;" he was so, but not called by those names; and so this city, it shall have God in it there present, yet not be so named. But I see nothing hinders but it may both be so called and have God in it, and because God is there, therefore to be so called.

The name "Jehovah" is a glorious and fearful name, Deut. xxviii. 58. Junius hath the words thus, That name most gloriously and highly to be reverenced. Bernard calls it a majestical name. Some observe that the Jews, after their return from Babylon, had such high and reverential thoughts of the name "Jehovah," that they thought it not fit to be pronounced, but used the name "Adonai" in the stead thereof, lest it should be profaned. This glorious, majestical, and most holy name, is given to this city.

What is meant by "the city," is of concernment to know. Some by it understand Jerusalem literally, as it was rebuilt by the Jews after their return, together with the civil state, in which the prince governed by civil laws, just weights and measures; but such a city as is here described was never built by the Jews after their captivity. To let that opinion pass, some do make this city Ezekiel saw to be a model and platform of that city the Jews (who should be called, converted, and brought to their own land again) should build and inhabit; but because the Jews' return to their own land is denied by some, questioned by many, and doubted by most, whether ever such a city as that which here is held out, viz. of thirty-two miles' compass, shall be built by them, it is safest to interpret this city typically: and in this sense interpreters are not all of a mind; for some make it to be a representative of heaven, and the amplitude or graces thereof; others make it to be a representation of the church under the gospel, in the former times thereof especially, yet short of that city, the heavenly Jerusalem, which John saw, Rev. xxi.; for though this city and that agree in some things, yet they differ in many. I shall show you some difference between them.

1. The gates of Ezekiel's city had no angels to keep it in; but at the twelve gates of John's city there were twelve angels to keep them, Rev. xxi. 12.

2. In Ezekiel's city there was a temple; but in John's there is none, Rev. xxi. 22.

3. The materials of Ezekiel's city were inferior to those of John's, which were gold, pearl, and precious stones, Rev. xxi. 18—22.

4. The waters of this city came from under the threshold of the temple, and from the south side o. the altar; but John's city had a pure river of water of life, clear as crystal, which proceeded from the throne of God and of the Lamb, Rev. xxii. 1.

5. Ezekiel's city had all trees for meat and medi-

cine on both sides of the banks of the river; John's had one by the tree of life, which bears twelve manner of fruits, Rev. xxii. 2.

6. The light and glory of Ezekiel's city fell short of that which John's had, Rev. xxi. 23; for it had no need of the sun nor of the moon to shine in it, for the glory of God did lighten it, and the Lamb is the light thereof.

7. Ezekiel's city was not half so great as John's, the one being only eighteen thousand measures in compass, and the other twelve thousand furlongs in length, breadth, and height, Rev. xxi. 16.

8. John's city had a wall of twelve foundations, and in them the names of the twelve apostles; Ezekiel's city had a wall, chap. xl. 5, but no names in it of prophets or apostles.

Now, notwithstanding this city John saw, the new Jerusalem, exceeded that our prophet saw very much, yet they both represent the church of Christ here on earth, and it will not be denied but that they may in part represent it in heaven.

By this city of Ezekiel I conceive is pointed out unto us the glorious state of the christian church in the latter days; it hath been a long time said to war under antichrist and his instruments; the breaches and ruins of it at this day are great, and the face of such a city hardly visible; but when the times of antichrist's destruction, and the Jews' conversion, do come, then shall this city be built, then shall Zion be in her glory; the christian church shall be then in a greater glory than formerly. If the coming in of the gentiles at first began the foundation of this city, what will the fulness of the gentiles be when that is come, Rom. xi. 25, but a glorious addition to this city? And then when the fulness of the Jews shall be added to the christian church, to this city, what will that be but life from the dead? ver. 15; the perfecting of this city, wherein shall be a temple suitable? which John minds us of, Rev. xi. 1, where the temple, altar, and worshippers are measured; and it is observable where there is mention of measuring, and so building a temple, respect is had unto the Jews: and the one thousand two hundred and sixty days, put for years, are drawing to an end, and God is about some great things to be done in the world, and will ere long break forth.

That by this city is represented the church, some rabbins themselves do acknowledge; for though they deny our Christ to be the Messiah, because he never built them such a temple and city as Ezekiel describes, yet they acknowledge this city and temple to be understood, not corporally or literally, but mystically and spiritually. And the Talmudists affirm, that by Jerusalem we are to understand the gathering of the gentiles to Christ, or the whole body of christians.

There are several things observable concerning this city or church of Christ.

1. That it is well and strongly founded. Usually cities are built upon hills and mountains, which are the strongest parts of the earth; and so was this city. Chap. xl. 2, Ezekiel saw the frame of this city upon a very high mountain, and on such a mountain is the christian church built; on the mountain of God's decree and power, on the mountain of righteousness and truth; it is built upon Christ the Rock of ages, such a Rock as the gates of hell cannot shake or shatter. John tells us of this city, the new Jerusalem, that it had twelve foundations, three on every square, which were sure, firm, and would never fail. The Lord Christ, the holy Scriptures, and the doctrine of the holy prophets and apostles, must fall to the ground before the church shall be ruined, 2 Tim. ii. 19.

2. It is comely and beautiful. Cities which are built foursquare especially are so, and such was this city; it had four thousand and five hundred measures on each quarter; there was nothing unsightly on any of the four quarters, they were all parallel, and had gates alike in them, which presented it very delightful to the eye. The church of Christ is comely and beautiful; it is built not of unhewn stones or timber, but such as are well hewn and orderly laid together. Hence the church of Corinth is called "God's building," 1 Cor. iii. 9; and the church in general the "city of the living God," Heb. xii. 22. The church is such a building, such a city, as is full of comeliness and beauty; it is a "congregation of saints," Psal. cxlix. 1; it is the garden of Christ, Cant. iv. 12; his kingdom, Matt. xiii. 41; his spouse, whom himself saith is fair, yea, the "fairest among women," Cant. i. 8; "pleasant," ver. 16; and "beautiful," chap. vii. 1. The church is Christ's body, Eph. i. 23; the Spirit's temple, 1 Cor. iii. 16; and therefore hath curious work in it, very glorious and beautiful. What David said of Zion, Psal. l. 2, that it was "the perfection of beauty," is most true of the church under Christ and in Christ, it is "the perfection of beauty:" Heb. x. 14, "By one offering he hath perfected for ever them that are sanctified."

3. The greatness and amplitude of this city. It had four thousand and five hundred measures eastward, west, north, and southward; it was eighteen thousand measures in compass; which sets out the greatness and vast extent of the church of Christ. Zech. x. 10, God saith he will bring the Jews from Egypt and Assyria, and so multiply them that place shall not be found for them. Isa. xlix. 20, "The children shall say in thine ears," that is, in the ears of the church, "The place is too strait for me: give place to me that I may dwell." The christian church is spoken of; which should multiply so, that their habitation must be enlarged, as it is, Isa. liv. 1—3. Now the tents and curtains of Zion's habitation are stretched to the ends of the earth, Psal. ii. 8; Mal. i. 11, "From the rising of the sun unto the going down thereof."

4. The city hath access unto it from all parts. Great cities have many gates, east gates, west gates, north gates, and south gates; so had this city twelve gates, in every quarter three, which signifies unto us the great access which should be unto the church of Christ from all parts. Not only Jews should come out of the twelve tribes to enter and dwell in this city, and be under the government of it, but multitudes of gentiles out of all nations and quarters of the world should do so. Rev. vii. John saw not only twelve thousand Jews enter in at each gate, but a great multitude also which no man could number, of all nations, kindreds, peoples, tongues. The Jews were numerable, forty-four thousand, but the gentiles were above so many millions; the number of them which entered by the gates was innumerable.

5. The happiness of this city, which is from the Lord's inhabiting there, and giving it its denomination. The name of it shall be, Jehovah-shammah, "The Lord is there." Alexandria was not so happy in Alexander, nor Constantinople so happy in Constantine, nor Jerusalem in Solomon, as this city shall be in Jehovah. We read in sacred Scripture of a golden city, Isa. xiv. 4; of a royal city, 1 Sam. xxvii. 5; of a renowned city, Ezek. xxvi. 17: but their glory and happiness was a shadow to the glory and happiness of this city; they were cities without God, Jehovah was not there; but here will the Lord himself be.

These words, Jehovah-shammah, import,

1. The presence of God in the church, and that is

a happiness to have his presence. When God left the temple and city of Jerusalem, that was their great misery, Hos. ix. 12. His presence in heaven makes it heaven; and his presence in the church makes it happy: "Thus saith the Lord, I am returned unto Zion, and will dwell in the midst of Jerusalem: and Jerusalem shall be called a city of truth; and the mountain of the Lord of hosts the holy mountain." God's presence makes it a city of truth, and a holy mountain: and that city is happy which hath truth and holiness in it, Zech. viii. 3.

2. His continuance in it. He will not be as a guest in an inn, but as an heir in his inheritance; he will dwell there; he will not leave this city, nor depart from it, as he did from Jerusalem of old, and as he did from the Jews after their captivity: Jer. xxxii. 40, "I will not turn away from them, to do them good:" Ezek. xxxvii. 26, "I will set my sanctuary in the midst of them for evermore:" Rev. vii. 15, "He that sitteth upon the throne shall dwell with them." It is the happiness of a saint to have the Comforter, and his great happiness to have the same abide with him, and that for ever, John xiv. 16; so it is the happiness of the christian to have Christ's presence, and exceeding happiness to have it for ever.

3. His upholding and preserving of it. The church is "God's building," 1 Cor. iii. 9. He said in Isaiah's days, "I will lay thy stones with fair colours, and lay thy foundations with sapphires. I will make thy windows of agates, and thy gates of carbuncles, and all thy border of pleasant stones," Isa. liv. 11, 12: and when the Lord shall do this, he will be Jehovah-shammah, he will uphold and preserve that building: Matt. xvi. 18, "Upon this rock will I build my church; and the gates of hell shall not prevail." He is the Keeper of Israel, Psal. cxxi. 4: I will keep this city from being besieged, stormed, or plundered.

4. His making himself and his mind known in an especial manner, as he did to Moses: Exod. vi. 3, "I appeared to Abraham, unto Isaac, and unto Jacob, by the name of God Almighty, but by my name Jehovah was I not known unto them;" but unto Moses he was known by that name, and imparted his mind unto him above others. So shall it be in this city: Isa. xi. 9, "The earth shall be full of the knowledge of Jehovah:" chap. lii. 6, "My people shall know my name:" chap. lx. 16, "Thou shalt know" (that is, the church) "that the Lord," I Jehovah, "am thy Saviour." They in Judah, Israel, Salem, and Zion, had other knowledge of God and his name than the nations had, and they of this city shall have peculiar knowledge of God: what others had in the ear, they shall have in the eye; what others had in the head, they shall have in the heart. Christ will make great and glorious discoveries of himself and of his mind unto the citizens of this city: Rev. xi. 19, "The temple of God was opened in heaven, and there was seen in his temple the ark of his testament." Christ is the temple of God, and his temple was opened in heaven, that is, the church, frequently called heaven in this book of the Revelation. The ark in the Old Testament temple, which had the table of the law and the pot of manna in it, typed out Christ, the gospel, and mysteries thereof; which held out that Christ, the spiritual Ark, shall not be hid. Jehovah-shammah, God is present in Christ, and Christ will so open himself to this city, that himself, Father, and mysteries of the gospel, will be more plain and manifest than ever.

5. His ruling and governing of this city. And it is a happy city which hath Jehovah, Christ the King of righteousness, to govern it. Zech. xiv. 9, Jehovah "shall be king over all the earth: in that day there shall be one Lord;" not many lords, but one Lord, even the Lord Jesus Christ. Ezek. xxxvii. 22, "One king shall be king to them all," to all the converted Jews and gentiles, which make this city of God. Zech. vi. 13, it is said of Christ there, "That he shall build the temple of the Lord; and he shall bear the glory, and shall sit and rule upon his throne:" Christ shall bear the glory, not only for building the temple and the city, but also for ruling, because he will rule righteously and faithfully to the satisfaction of all: Isa. xi. 5, "Righteousness shall be the girdle of his loins, and faithfulness the girdle of his reins." This girdle he never puts off, but is girt therewith always, showing his readiness to be faithful and righteous in his government.

6. The pouring out of his Spirit. Jehovah is there to pour that out more fully. What men had formerly was only the firstfruits of the Spirit, Rom. viii. 23, a few had it poured out upon them; but then will be a more plentiful effusion, all the citizens of this city shall be filled with the Spirit: Zech. xii. 8, "He that is feeble among them at that day shall be as David; and the house of David shall be as God, and the angel of the Lord before them;" then shall the weakest, by the Spirit of Christ, abound in gifts and graces, and be as David, who excelled all in his days; and his house shall be as God, that is, full of the Spirit; or as the angels, that is, having such grace, qualities, and estimation.

7. The making the city and citizens honourable and glorious. Then shall it be the renowned, royal, and golden city, gilded with the beams of Christ's glorious presence. From the head cometh glory to the body; a wife shineth with her husband's rays, Christ with the glory of the Father, and this city with the glory and beauty of Christ. His presence made the glory of the latter temple and city greater than the glory of the former; and his presence in this temple and city will make the glory of it greater than that of the latter temple and city, for then he was there in a state of humiliation, but he shall not be so in this, he will be in his reigning state, and his citizens will be honourable: Zech. ix. 16, "They shall be as the stones of a crown, lifted up;" not as common stones, but as the stones of a crown; and not as stones of a crown falling to the earth, but as stones of a crown lifted up to be put on the head of a king. How great is the honour of these citizens! They are brought in, Rev. v. 10, speaking of it themselves; Thou "hast made us unto our God kings and priests: and we shall reign on the earth." And this is not all the honour, for besides this, they shall have every one three honourable names; for Christ, Rev. iii. 12, will write upon them the name of his God, and the name of the city of God, and his own new name.

8. The keeping them in unity and love. The citizens shall then be of one mind: Zech. xiv. 9, "In that day there shall be one Lord, and his name one;" the invocation and worship of his name shall be one. Then shall that be fulfilled, Zeph. iii. 9, "Then will I turn to the people a pure language, that they may all call upon the name of the Lord, to serve him with one consent;" the Hebrew is, with one shoulder; a metaphor taken from oxen in the yoke, which draw together, as with one shoulder; so these citizens shall jointly and unanimously knit together and worship the Lord Christ. There shall be no schisms, names of distinction, as now there are; for if, when Christ left the world, the saints were all of one heart, Acts ii. 32, much more so shall it be in this city, when Christ shall be in the midst thereof, and guide them by his Spirit into all truth.

9. These words, Jehovah-shammah, import the great delight the Lord will take in this city, and the citizens thereof, in the church, and members thereof; Isa. lxii. 4, She shall be called Hephzibah, that is, My delight is in her. Then it will appear the church is his pleasant portion, Jer. xii. 10; and the dearly beloved of his soul, ver. 7; his glory, Isa. xlvi. 13; the throne of his glory, Jer. xiv. 21; yea, the crown of his glory, Isa. lxii. 3. He will delight in them, to do them good, to communicate himself unto them: Rev. vii. 15—17, "He that sitteth on the throne shall dwell among them. They shall hunger no more, neither thirst any more; neither shall the sun light on them, nor any heat. For the Lamb which is in the midst of the throne shall feed them, and shall lead them unto living fountains of waters: and God shall wipe away all tears from their eyes." Nothing shall disturb or harm them, they shall have no want, but enjoy all spiritual good, and abound in joy.

To God only be glory, through Jesus Christ.

THE END.

A TABLE

OF THE SCRIPTURES OPENED OR ILLUSTRATED IN THE FOREGOING WORK.

A TABLE

CONTAINING THE PRINCIPAL THINGS IN THE PRECEDENT EXPOSITIONS.

D

E

F

G

H

I & J

N

O

P

Q

R

S

T

U

V

W

Y

Z

Geneva